Reference Guide to

WORLD LITERATURE

SECOND EDITION

VOLUME 1

Reference Guide to

WORLD LITERATURE

SECOND EDITION

Volume 1
A-L

EDITOR
LESLEY HENDERSON

ASSOCIATE EDITOR
SARAH M. HALL

ST. JAMES PRESS

An International Thomson Publishing Company

Changing the Way the World Learns

NEW YORK • LONDON • BONN • BOSTON • DETROIT • MADRID
MELBOURNE • MEXICO CITY • PARIS • SINGAPORE • TOKYO
TORONTO • WASHINGTON • ALBANY NY • BELMONT CA • CINCINNATI OH

I(T)P™   Gale Research Inc., an International Thomson Publishing Company.
         ITP logo is a trademark under license.

10 9 8 7 6 5 4 3 2 1

CONTENTS

EDITOR'S NOTE

The *Reference Guide to World Literature* is the revised and expanded edition of *Great Foreign Language Writers,* first published in 1984. It contains entries on 490 writers, a number of whom are anonymous, and over 500 essays on individual works of literature. This selection is based on the recommendations of the expert advisers listed on page ix. The scope of the *Reference Guide* is historical, ranging from the literature of ancient Greece to that of the present. Selected living writers are included in this *Guide* but readers with a particular interest in contemporary literature should consult our *Contemporary World Writers,* which features full entries on approximately 350 living authors.

The entry for each writer consists of a brief biography; a list of the writer's primary works; a list of bibliographies and critical studies; a signed critical overview of the writer's literary work written by an expert in the field; and, in some cases, additional essays on individual literary works.

Each entry begins with a biographical summary of the subject and includes details (where known) of the author's birth, education and training, military service, and marriage(s), followed by a chronological résumé of the subject's life, and concludes with a list of awards, honours, and honorary degrees. Then follows a list of publications that includes all separately published books, including translations into English. Broadsheets, single sermons and lectures, minor pamphlets, exhibition catalogues, etc., are omitted. Dates refer to the first publication in book form unless indicated otherwise; we have attempted to list the actual year of publication, sometimes different from the date given on the title page. Reprints of works, including facsimile editions, are generally not listed unless they involve a revision of the title. Titles are given in modern spelling and are often in 'short' form. They are always in italic, except for those that are literal (i.e., non-published) translations, which appear in square brackets; these are provided for all non-Romance languages. The publication list contains some or all of the following categories:

Collections: This contains a selection of 'standard' editions, including the most recent collection of the complete works and of the individual genres (verse, plays, fiction). Only those collections that have some editorial authority and were published after the writer's death are cited; collections published during the writer's lifetime are included in the category 'Other.' Ongoing multi-volume editions are indicated by a dash after the date of publication.

Fiction: Where it is not made apparent by the title, collections of short fiction are indicated by the inclusion of 'stories' in parentheses after the title.

Verse: This includes collections and individual poems that were published in book form, listed chronologically by date of publication.

Plays: This includes original plays, adaptations, and other works for the stage (libretti, ballet scenarios, etc.). Dates for both publication and production are given. Titles are arranged chronologically by date of first performance or date of first publication, whichever is earliest. Published English translations are listed, but not those of individual productions.

Screenplays/Television Plays/Radio Plays: These categories include original works and adaptations for these media, listed by date of release or first broadcast.

Other: This includes publications that do not fit readily into the above categories, principally miscellanies and nonfiction writing, such as journalism, essays, theoretical works, travel writing, memoirs, letters, etc.

Bibliography: This includes published works relating to primary and secondary literature. General bibliographies of literary periods, genres, or countries, etc., are rarely listed.

Critical Studies: This includes critical works and biographies of the subject, listed in chronological order of publication. This section concentrates on book-length studies in English published after 1945, although in a few cases selected earlier material is cited. Where there is a noticeable scarcity of critical works in English, publications written in the subject's own language are included. On occasion articles, usually written in English, have also been listed.

The book concludes with a Title Index to the publications lists. This contains titles of all works listed in the fiction, verse, and plays sections of each entry including titles in the writer's original language and English translations, as well as selected important works of nonfiction.

Acknowledgments

We would like to thank all the advisers and contributors for their patience and cooperation. We would also like to thank the following people for their assistance with languages and/or research on the book: Jessica Araha, Barbara Archer, Juliette Bright, Ben Chatterley, Deidrie Clarke, Olive Classe, Michele Cropman, Mark Du Ry, Jackie Griffin, Anders Hansson, Patrick Heenan and Monique Lamontagne, Gary Hill, Susan Mackervoy, Stuart McGregor, John O'Leary, Parvin Pursglove, Tamás Váradi, Libertad West, Brenda Wright, Jackie Wrout and all colleagues at St. James Press, notably John Normansell and Kate Berney. Particular thanks are due to Mark Hawkins-Dady and Tracy Chevalier for shouldering a great deal of the editorial work and whose assistance went far beyond the call of duty, and to Daniel Kirkpatrick, the editor of the first edition, for his invaluable editorial guidance.

ADVISERS

Alison Bailey, University of London
Christopher Cairns, University College, Wales
Marvin Carlson, CUNY, New York
Ruby Cohn, University of California, Davis
James Diggle, Queen's College, Cambridge
David William Foster, Arizona State University
Michael Freeman, University of Leicester
Janet Garton, University of East Anglia, Norwich
Theo Hermans, University College, London
Peter Hutchinson, Trinity Hall, Cambridge

R.S. McGregor, University of Cambridge
A.B. McMillin, University of London
David O'Connell, Georgia State University
P.A. Odber de Baubeta, University of Birmingham
Jerzy Peterkiewicz, London
Christopher R. Pike, University of Keele
Girdar Rathi, New Delhi
G. Singh, formerly of Queen's University, Belfast
Peter Skrine, University of Bristol
Daniel Weissbort, University of Iowa

CONTRIBUTORS

Donald Adamson
Peter F. Ainsworth
Robin Aizlewood
Ali Ahmed
Margareta Alexandroni
Hans Christian Andersen
J.K. Anderson
D.J. Andrews
Alireza Anushiravani
Brigitte Edith Zapp Archibald
A. James Arnold
William Arrowsmith
B. Ashbrook
Keith Aspley
Stuart Atkins
Howard Atkinson
Peter Avery
K.P. Bahadur
Ehrhard Bahr
D.R. Shackleton Bailey
David M. Bain
Barry Baldwin
Alan Bance
Gabrielle Barfoot
John Barsby
Peter I. Barta
Susan Bassnett
Edward M. Batley
Roderick Beaton
David Bell
Ian A. Bell
Thomas G. Bergin
Alan Best
Binghong Lu
Sandra Blane

Elizabeth Bobrick
Joan Booth
Paul W. Borgeson, Jr.
Patrick Brady
Gerard J. Brault
S.H. Braund
Michael Brophy
Catherine Savage Brosman
Gordon Brotherston
Jennifer L. Brown
Penny Brown
Dorothy Bryson
A.W. Bulloch
Alan Bullock
B. Burns
J.M. Buscall
Christopher Cairns
Francisco Carenas
Marvin Carlson
Remo Catani
Philip Cavendish
Mary Ann Caws
Andrea C. Cervi
C. Chadwick
Roland A. Champagne
Tom Cheesman
Mirna Cicioni
John R. Clark
Shirley Clarke
David Coad
Ruby Cohn
Michael Collie
Desmond J. Conacher
David Constantine
Ray Cooke

Thomas L. Cooksey
Neil Cornwell
C.D.N. Costa
Sally McMullen (Croft)
G.P. Cubbin
James M. Curtis
G.F. Cushing
Edmund Cusick
Lóránt Czigány
James N. Davidson
Catherine Davies
Santiago Daydi-Tolson
René de Costa
Alan Deighton
John Dickie
Sheila J. Dickson
C.E.J. Dolamore
Ken Dowden
Sam Driver
John Dunkley
Osman Durrani
Stanislaw Eile
Sarah Ekdawi
Herman Ermolaev
Jo Evans
Michael Falchikov
Nancy Kanach Fehsenfeld
Jane Fenoulhet
Bruno Ferraro
John Fletcher
John L. Flood
David William Foster
A.P. Foulkes
Wallace Fowlie
Michael Freeman
Frank J. Frost
Barbara P. Fulks
Michael A. Fuller
Janet Garton
David Gascoyne
John Gatt-Rutter
Margaret Gibson
Robert Gibson
Mary E. Giles
Donald Gilman
Nahum N. Glatzer
J. Gledson
Gary Godfrey
Ingeborg M. Goessl
Sander M. Goldberg
George Gömöri
D.C.R.A. Goonetilleke
Colin Graham
Peter J. Graves
Roger Green
R.P.H. Green
Claire E. Gruzelier
Albert E. Gurganus
Oscar A. Haac
David T. Haberly
Brigid Haines

Igor Hájek
David M. Halperin
P.T. Harries
Nigel Harris
Patricia Harry
John Hart
Thomas R. Hart
E.C. Hawkesworth
Ronald Hayman
Patrick Heenan
John Hibberd
James Higgins
David Hill
Sabine Hillen
Ian Hilton
Leighton Hodson
Louise Hopkins
Thomas K. Hubbard
Lothar Huber
Peter Hutchinson
Lois Boe Hyslop
Margaret C. Ives
David Jackson
Tony James
Regina Janes
D.E. Jenkinson
Lewis Jillings
D. Mervyn Jones
Roger Jones
W. Glyn Jones
Brian Keith-Smith
Rachel Killick
Jonathan King
Peter King
W.J.S. Kirton
Charles Klopp
A.V. Knowles
Wulf Koepke
Kathleen L. Komar
Linn Bratteteig Konrad
David Konstan
Myrto Konstanatakos
Charles Kwong
F.J. Lamport
Jordan Lancaster
Pierre J. Lapaire
David H.J. Larmour
Rex W. Last
Dan Latimer
Renate Latimer
John Lee
André Lefevere
Harry Levin
Silvano Levy
Virginia L. Lewis
Emanuele Licastro
Maria Manuel Lisboa
Heather Lloyd
Rosemary Lloyd
Ladislaus Löb
Jacqueline Long

Dagmar Lorenz
Andrea Loselle
Gregory L. Lucente
David S. Luft
Torborg Lundell
J.F. Marfany
Gaetana Marrone
David Maskell
Eve Mason
Haydn T. Mason
Gita May
Jane McAdoo
E.A. McCobb
Patrick McCarthy
A. McDermott
David McDuff
Martin L. McLaughlin
Alexander G. McKay
Keith McMahon
Arnold McMillin
Rory McTurk
Gordon McVay
A.J. Meech
Siegfried Mews
Gary B. Miles
Paul Allen Miller
Kristina Milnor
Earl Miner
John Douglas Minyard
Masao Miyoshi
Matthew Mizenko
Nicole Mosher
Anna Lydia Motto
Vanna Motta
Kenneth Muir
Brian Murdoch
S.M. Murk-Jansen
Brian Murphy
Walter Musolino
Susan Napier
Frank J. Nisetich
Bob Oakley
David O'Connell
P.A. Odber de Baubeta
Jeanne A. Ojala
Tom O'Neill
Seija Paddon
Cecil Parrott
Alan K.G. Paterson
Georgina Paul
D. Keith Peacock
Noel A. Peacock
Roger Pearson
Janet Perez
Jerzy Peterkiewicz
Elli Philokyprou
Christopher R. Pike
Donald Peter
Alexander Pirie
David Platton
Gordon Pocock

Valentina Polukhina
Charles A. Porter
Oralia Preble-Niemi
Michael P. Predmore
Nicole Prunster
Joseph Pucci
Judith Purver
Dušan Puvacic
Olga Ragusa
Ana M. Ranero
Judy Rawson
J.H. Reid
Robert Reid
John H. Reilly
Barbara Reynolds
Hugh Ridley
Norma Rinsler
Colin Riordan
Michael Robinson
Philip E.J. Robinson
David Rock
Eamonn Rodgers
Margaret Rogister
Michele Valerie Ronnick
Hugh Rorrison
Wendy Rosslyn
John Rothenberg
Andrew Rothwell
Lisa M. Ruch
R.B. Rutherford
William Merritt Sale, III
Jeffrey L. Sammons
N.K. Sandars
Gerlinde Ulm Sanford
Hélène N. Sanko
Barbara Saunders
Barry P. Scherr
Gerd Schneider
Irene Scobbie
Mary Scott
Edward Seidensticker
Dorothy S. Severin
Sabina Sharkey
Ruth Sharman
Barnett Shaw
David Shaw
Shoichi Saeki
David Sices
John D. Simons
G. Singh
Peter Skrine
Colin Smethurst
C.N. Smith
J. Kelly Sowards
Ronald Speirs
James Russell Stamm
C.C. Stathatos
Susan Isabel Stein
Carl Steiner
R.H. Stephenson
Mary E. Stewart

Alexander Stillmark
Elisabeth C. Stopp
Ian C. Storey
J.R. Stubbs
Arrigo V. Subiotto
Henry W. Sullivan
Helena Szépe
John E. Tailby
Myron Taylor
Anna-Marie Taylor
Philip Thody
David Thomas
Judith Thurman
Robert M. Torrance
Sabine Vanacker
Rolf Venner
Hugo J. Verani
Maïr Verthuy
Robert Vilain
Pascale Voilley
Frank W. Walbank
Albert H. Wallace
George Walsh
J. Michael Walton
Edward Wasiolek
Bruce Watson

Shawncey J. Webb
Daniel Weissbort
David Welsh
A.D. White
Sally A. White-Wallis
Kenneth S. Whitton
Juliet Wigmore
Faith Wigzell
Mark Williams
Rhys Williams
Jason Wilson
Jerry Phillips Winfield
Michael Winkler
A.J. Woodman
M.J. Woods
Tim Woods
James B. Woodward
A. Colin Wright
Barbara Wright
Elizabeth Wright
John D. Yohannan
Howard T. Young
Robin Young
G. Zanker
Jeanne Morgan Zarucchi

ALPHABETICAL LIST OF WRITERS AND WORKS

CHRONOLOGICAL LIST OF WRITERS

fl. 8th century BC(?)	Homer
fl. c.700 BC	Hesiod
c.612 BC- ?	Sappho
c.570 BC-c.475 BC	Anacreon
525/524 BC-456 BC	Aeschylus
518/522 BC-438/446 BC	Pindar
c.496 BC-406 BC	Sophocles
484 BC-420 BC	Herodotus
480/485 BC-c.406 BC	Euripides
c.460 BC-c.399 BC	Thucydides
c.450 BC-c.385 BC	Aristophanes
c.431 BC-c.354 BC	Xenophon
c.429 BC-347 BC	Plato
384 BC-322 BC	Aristotle
384 BC-322 BC	Demosthenes
c.370 BC-c.287 BC	Theophrastus
c.342 BC-c.295 BC	Menander
c.300 BC- ?	Theocritus
c.254 BC-c.184 BC	Plautus
fl. 250 BC	Apollonius
fl. 250 BC	Callimachus
239 BC-169 BC	Ennius
c.200 BC-c.118 BC	Polybius
c.190 BC-159 BC	Terence
106 BC-43 BC	Cicero
c.100 BC-44 BC	Caesar
c.99 BC-c.55 BC	Lucretius
86 BC-35 BC	Sallust
c.84 BC-c.54 BC	Catullus
70 BC-19 BC	Virgil
65 BC-8 BC	Horace
64/59 BC-AD 12/17	Livy
c.57 BC-19/18 BC	Tibullus
57/50 BC-c.16 BC	Propertius
43 BC-AD 17	Ovid
c.4 BC-AD 65	Seneca
c.AD 30-c.AD 104	Martial
AD 34-AD 62	Persius
c.AD 35-c.AD 100	Quintilian
AD 39-AD 65	Lucan
c.AD 46-c.AD 120	Plutarch
AD 50-AD 130	Juvenal
c.AD 56-c.AD 116	Tacitus
d.AD 66	Petronius
c.AD 69-AD 160	Suetonius
c.AD 120-after AD 180	Lucian
AD 121-AD 180	Aurelius
c.AD 123-after 163 AD	Apuleius
2nd/3rd century AD	Longus
c.AD 310-c.AD 395	Ausonius
fl. late 4th century AD	Claudian
c.AD 347-AD 420	St Jerome
AD 348-AD 405	Prudentius

AD 354-AD 430	St Augustine
AD 365-427	Tao Qian
fl. c.AD 400	Kālidāsa
c.AD 480-AD 524	Boethius
701/705-762	Li Bai
712-770	Du Fu
772-846	Bai Juyi
c.935-c.1020	Abu'l Qāsim Ferdowsi
c.978- ?	Murasaki Shikibu
1037-1101	Su Shi
1048-1131	Omar Khayyam
c.1130-1220/1231	Farid al-Din Attār
1160-1210/1220	Hartmann von Aue
fl. c.1170	Chrétien de Troyes
c.1170-c.1230	Walther von der Vogelweide
1179-1241	Snorri Sturluson
fl. late 12th century	Marie de France
fl. 1195-1220	Wolfram von Eschenbach
fl. c.1200	Gottfried von Strassburg
1207-1273	Jalalu'd-Din Rumi
1209-1292	Muslih-al-Din Sa'di
fl. c.1250	Hadewijch
c.1255-1300	Guido Cavalcanti
1265-1321	Dante Alighieri
c.1300(?)-1377	Guillaume de Machaut
1304-1374	Petrarch
1313-1375	Giovanni Boccaccio
1325/26-1389/90	Shams al-Din Muhammad Hafiz
c.1337- ?	Jean Froissart
1363-1443	Zeami
c.1365-c.1430	Christine de Pizan
c.1430- ?	François Villon
1456-1530	Jacopo Sannazaro
1457-1521	Sebastian Brant
c.1465-c.1536	Gil Vicente
1467-1536	Desiderius Erasmus
1469-1527	Niccolò Machiavelli
1470-1520	Bernardo Dovizi da Bibbiena
1470-1547	Pietro Bembo
1474-1533	Ludovico Ariosto
1478/c.1530-1583/1610	Sūrdās
1478-1529	Baldassarre Castiglione
1483-1546	Martin Luther
1483(?)-1553	François Rabelais
1492-1547	Vittoria Colonna
1492-1549	Marguerite de Navarre
1492-1556	Pietro Aretino
1494-1576	Hans Sachs
c.1495-1542	Ruzzante
1498-1546/47	Mīrā Bāī
d.1518	Kabīr
1522-1566	Joachim Du Bellay
c.1524-1554	Gaspara Stampa

1524/25-1580	Luís de Camões
1524-1585	Pierre de Ronsard
1530-1584	Jan Kochanowski
1532-1623	Tulsīdās
1533-1592	Michel de Montaigne
1544-1595	Torquato Tasso
1548-1600	Giordano Bruno
1567(?)-1625	Honoré d'Urfé
1568-1639	Tommaso Campanella
1581-1647	Pieter Corneliszoon Hooft
1585-1618	Gerbrandt Bredero
1587-1679	Joost van den Vondel
1596-1687	Constantijn Huygens
1606-1684	Pierre Corneille
1610-1660	Paul Scarron
1613-1680	François La Rochefoucauld
1616-1664	Andreas Gryphius
1619-1655	Cyrano de Bergerac
1620-1664	Count Miklós Zrínyi
1621-1695	Jean de La Fontaine
1622-1673	Molière
1622-1676	Hans Jakob Christoffel von Grimmelshausen
1623-1662	Blaise Pascal
1628-1703	Charles Perrault
1634-1693	Madame de Lafayette
1636-1711	Nicolas Boileau
1639-1699	Jean Racine
1644-1694	Bashō
1651-1695	Sor Juana Inés de la Cruz
1653-1725	Chikamatsu Monzaemon
1668-1747	Alain-René Lesage
1684-1754	Ludvig Holberg
1688-1763	Marivaux
1694-1778	Voltaire
1697-1763	Abbé Prévost
1698-1782	Pietro Metastasio
1707-1793	Carlo Goldoni
1712-1778	Jean-Jacques Rousseau
1713-1784	Denis Diderot
1724-1803	Friedrich Gottlieb Klopstock
1729-1781	Gotthold Ephraim Lessing
1732-1799	Beaumarchais
1733-1813	Christoph Martin Wieland
1740-1814	Marquis de Sade
1741-1803	Choderlos de Laclos
1745-1792	Denis Fonvizin
1749-1803	Vittorio Alfieri
1749-1832	Johann Wolfgang von Goethe
1751-1792	Jakob Michael Reinhold Lenz
1756-1831	Willem Bilderdijk
1759-1805	Friedrich von Schiller
1766-1817	Madame de Staël
1767-1845	August Wilhelm von Schlegel
1768-1848	Chateaubriand
1770-1843	Friedrich Hölderlin
1772-1801	Novalis
1772-1829	Friedrich von Schlegel
1773-1853	Ludwig Tieck

1775(?)-1831	Caroline de la Motte Fouqué
1776-1822	E.T.A. Hoffmann
1777-1811	Heinrich von Kleist
1777-1843	Friedrich de la Motte Fouqué
1778-1842	Clemens Brentano
1781-1838	Adelbert von Chamisso
1783-1842	Stendhal
1785-1859	Bettina von Arnim
1785-1863	Jacob Grimm
1785-1873	Alessandro Manzoni
1786-1859	Wilhelm Grimm
1788-1857	Joseph von Eichendorff
1790-1869	Alphonse de Larmartine
1791-1861	Eugène Scribe
1791-1872	Franz Grillparzer
1795-1829	Aleksandr Griboedov
1797-1848	Annette von Droste-Hülshoff
1797-1854	Jeremias Gotthelf
1797-1856	Heinrich Heine
1797-1863	Alfred de Vigny
1797-1869	Asadullāh Khān Ghālib
1798-1837	Giacomo Leopardi
1798-1855	Adam Mickiewicz
1799-1837	Aleksandr Pushkin
1799-1850	Honoré de Balzac
1800-1855	Mihály Vörösmarty
1801-1836	Christian Dietrich Grabbe
1801-1862	Johann Nepomuk Nestroy
1802-1870	Alexandre Dumas *père*
1802-1885	Victor Hugo
1803-1870	Prosper Mérimée
1803-1899	Guido Gezelle
1804-1875	Eduard Mörike
1804-1876	George Sand
1805-1868	Adalbert Stifter
1805-1875	Hans Christian Andersen
1808-1855	Gérard de Nerval
1809-1852	Nikolai Gogol'
1810-1857	Alfred de Musset
1811-1872	Théophile Gautier
1812-1859	Zygmunt Krasiński
1812-1891	Ivan Goncharov
1813-1837	Georg Büchner
1813-1863	Friedrich Hebbel
1813-1871	Baron Jószef Eötvös
1814-1841	Mikhail Lermontov
1817-1888	Theodor Storm
1818-1883	Ivan Turgenev
1819-1890	Gottfried Keller
1819-1898	Theodor Fontane
1820-1881	Multatuli
1821-1867	Charles Baudelaire
1821-1880	Gustave Flaubert
1821-1881	Fedor Dostoevskii
1822-1896	Edmond Goncourt
1823-1849	Sándor Petöfi
1824-1895	Alexandre Dumas *fils*
1825-1898	Conrad Ferdinand Meyer
1828-1905	Jules Verne

1828-1906	Henrik Ibsen	1877-1962	Hermann Hesse
1828-1910	Lev Tolstoi	1878-1942	Carl Sternheim
1830-1870	Jules Goncourt	1878-1945	Georg Kaiser
1832-1910	Bjørnstjerne Bjørnson	1878-1952	Ferenc Molnár
1834-1886	José Hernández	1878-1957	Alfred Döblin
1835-1907	Giosuè Carducci	1880-1918	Guillaume Apollinaire
1839-1908	Joaquim Maria Machado de Assis	1880-1921	Aleksandr Blok
1840-1902	Émile Zola	1880-1934	Andrei Belyi
1840-1922	Giovanni Verga	1880-1942	Robert Musil
1842-1898	Stéphane Mallarmé	1881-1936	Lu Xun
1844-1896	Paul Verlaine	1881-1958	Roger Martin du Gard
1844-1900	Friedrich Nietzsche	1882-1949	Sigrid Undset
1844-1924	Anatole France	1883-1923	Jaroslav Hašek
1845-1900	José Maria de Eça de Queirós	1883-1924	Franz Kafka
1846-1870	Comte de Lautréamont	1883-1957	Nikos Kazantzakis
1846-1916	Henryk Sienkiewicz	1883-1957	Umberto Saba
1847-1912	Bolesław Prus	1884-1937	Evgenii Zamiatin
1848-1907	Joris-Karl Huysmans	1884-1951	Angelo Sikelianos
1849-1912	August Strindberg	1885-1922	Velimir Khlebnikov
1850-1893	Guy de Maupassant	1885-1939	Stanisław Witkiewicz
1853-1995	José Martí	1885-1962	Isak Dinesen
1854-1891	Arthur Rimbaud	1885-1970	François Mauriac
1858-1940	Selma Lagerlöf	1886-1914	Alain-Fournier
1859-1943	Kostes Palamas	1886-1951	Hermann Broch
1859-1952	Knut Hamsun	1886-1956	Gottfried Benn
1860-1887	Jules Laforgue	1886-1965	Tanizaki Jun'ichiro
1860-1904	Anton Chekhov	1887-1914	Georg Trakl
1861-1928	Italo Svevo	1887-1961	Blaise Cendrars
1861-1941	Rabindranath Tagore	1887-1975	Saint-John Perse
1862-1921	Georges Feydeau	1888-1935	Fernando Pessoa
1862-1931	Arthur Schnitzler	1888-1948	Georges Bernanos
1862-1944	Jean Giraudoux	1888-1970	S.Y. Agnon
1862-1946	Gerhart Hauptmann	1888-1970	Giuseppe Ungaretti
1862-1949	Maurice Maeterlinck	1889-1957	Gabriela Mistral
1863-1923	Louis Couperus	1889-1963	Jean Cocteau
1863-1933	Constantijn Petrou Cavafy	1889-1966	Anna Akhmatova
1863-1938	Gabriele D'Annunzio	1889-1984	Henri Michaux
1864-1918	Frank Wedekind	1890-1938	Karel Čapek
1866-1944	Romain Rolland	1890-1945	Franz Werfel
1867-1916	Rubén Darío	1890-1960	Boris Pasternak
1867-1916	Natsume Sōseki	1891-1938	Osip Mandel'shtam
1867-1936	Luigi Pirandello	1891-1940	Mikhail Bulgakov
1868-1918	Edmond Rostand	1891-1950	Ivan Goll
1868-1936	Maksim Gor'kii	1891-1970	Nelly Sachs
1868-1955	Paul Claudel	1891-1974	Pär Lagerkvist
1869-1907	Stanisław Wyspiański	1892-1923	Edith Södergran
1869-1951	André Gide	1892-1927	Akutagawa Ryunosuke
1870-1953	Ivan Bunin	1892-1938	César Vallejo
1871-1922	Marcel Proust	1892-1941	Marina Tsvetaeva
1871-1936	Grazia Deledda	1892-1942	Bruno Schulz
1871-1945	Paul Valéry	1892-1953	Ugo Betti
1871-1950	Heinrich Mann	1892-1975	Ivo Andrić
1873-1907	Alfred Jarry	1893-1930	Vladimir Maiakovskii
1873-1935	Henri Barbusse	1893-1939	Ernst Toller
1873-1954	Colette	1893-1945	Mario de Andrade
1874-1929	Hugo von Hofmannsthal	1893-1981	Miroslav Krleža
1875-1926	Rainer Maria Rilke	1894-1938	Boris Pil'niak
1875-1955	Thomas Mann	1894-1939	Joseph Roth
1876-1944	Max Jacob	1894-1941(?)	Isaak Babel

xxv

1894-1961	Louis-Ferdinand Céline	1908-1950	Cesare Pavese
1895-1925	Sergei Esenin	1908-1966	Elio Vittorini
1895-1952	Paul Éluard	1908-1967	João Guimarães Rosa
1895-1960	Iurii Olesha	1908-1970	Arthur Adamov
1895-1970	Jean Giono	1908-1986	Simone de Beauvoir
1895-1974	Marcel Pagnol	1909-1944	Miklós Radnóti
1895-	Ernst Jünger	1909-1945	Robert Brasillach
1896-1928	Paul van Ostaijen	1909-1948	Dazai Osamu
1896-1948	Antonin Artaud	1909-1983	Jerzy Andrzejewski
1896-1953	Martinus Nijhoff	1909-1983	Gabrielle Roy
1896-1957	Giuseppe Tomasi di Lampedusa	1909-1990	Yannis Ritsos
1896-1966	André Breton	1909-1994	Eugène Ionesco
1896-1966	Heimito von Doderer	1910-1976	José Lezama Lima
1896-1977	Carl Zuckmayer	1910-1986	Jean Genet
1896-1981	Eugenio Montale	1910-1987	Jean Anhouilh
1897-1982	Louis Aragon	1910-	Rachel de Queiroz
1898-1956	Bertolt Brecht	1911-1969	José Mariá Arguedas
1898-1970	Erich Maria Remarque	1911-1986	Fritz Hochwälder
1898-1971	Simon Vestdijk	1911-1991	Max Frisch
1898-1987	Tawfiq al-Hakim	1911-	Odysseus Elytis
1899-1972	Kawabata Yasunari	1911-	Naguib Mahfouz
1899-1974	Miguel Ángel Asturias	1911-	Czesław Miłosz
1899-1986	Jorge Luis Borges	1912-1980	Nélson Rodrigues
1899-1988	Francis Ponge	1912-1985	Elsa Morante
1900-1944	Antoine de Saint-Exupéry	1912-	Jorge Amado
1900-1970	Leopoldo Marechal	1913-1960	Albert Camus
1900-1971	George Seferis	1913-1989	Sándor Weöres
1900-1977	Jacques Prévert	1913-1991	Vasco Pratolini
1900-1978	Ignazio Silone	1914-1984	Julio Cortázar
1900-1984	Eduardo De Filippo	1914-	Marguerite Duras
1900-1987	Gilberto Freyre	1914-	Octavio Paz
1900-1991	William Heinesen	1916-1982	Peter Weiss
1900-	Nathalie Sarraute	1916-1991	Natalia Ginzburg
1901-1938	Ödön von Horváth	1916-	Giorgio Bassani
1901-1968	Salvatore Quasimodo	1917-1965	Johannes Bobrowski
1901-1976	André Malraux	1917-1985	Heinrich Böll
1901-1990	Ivar Lo-Johansson	1917-1987	Carlo Cassola
1902-1967	Marcel Aymé	1918-1986	Juan Rulfo
1902-1975	Carlo Levi	1918-	Aleksandr Solzhenitsyn
1902-1983	Gyula Illyés	1919-1987	Primo Levi
1902-1987	Carlos Drummond de Andrade	1920-1959	Boris Vian
1902-1989	Nicolás Guillén	1920-1970	Paul Celan
1902-	Halldór Laxness	1920-1992	Väinö Linna
1903-1923	Raymond Radiguet	1921-1989	Leonardo Sciascia
1903-1976	Raymond Queneau	1921-1990	Friedrich Dürrenmatt
1903-1987	Marguerite Yourcenar	1922-1975	Pier Paolo Pasolini
1903-1989	Georges Simenon	1922-1991	Vasko Popa
1904-1969	Witold Gombrowicz	1922-	Alain Robbe-Grillet
1904-1973	Pablo Neruda	1923-1985	Italo Calvino
1904-1980	Alejo Carpentier	1923-	Endō Shūsaku
1905-1980	Jean-Paul Sartre	1924-1986	Vasil Bykaw
1905-1984	Mikhail Sholokhov	1925-1970	Mishima Yukio
1905-	Elias Canetti	1925-1974	Rosario Castellanos
1906-1972	Dino Buzzati	1925-1977	Clarice Lispector
1906-1989	Samuel Beckett	1925-1981	Iurii Trifonov
1907-1972	Günter Eich	1925-	Ernesto Cardenal
1907-1988	René Char	1926-1973	Ingeborg Bachmann
1907-1990	Alberto Moravia	1926-	Siegfried Lenz
1907-	Miguel Torga	1927-	Günter Grass

ALPHABETICAL LIST OF WORKS

CHRONOLOGICAL LIST OF WORKS

Vedas, anonymous prose and verse, c.3000-c.500 BC

Gilgamesh (Epic of), anonymous poem cycle, early 2nd millennium BC

The Bible, anonymous verse and prose, c.900 BC onwards

Upanishads, anonymous prose and verse, c.800-c.500 BC

The Iliad, poem by Homer, c.750 BC

The Odyssey, poem by Homer, c.720 BC

Fragment 1 ['Address to Aphrodite'], poem by Sappho, 7th century BC

Fragment 31 ['Declaration of Love for a Young Girl'], poem by Sappho, 7th century BC

The City of God, prose by St Augustine, 5th century

Olympian One, poem by Pindar, c.476 BC(?)

The Persians, play by Aeschylus, 472 BC

The Seven Against Thebes, play by Aeschylus, 467 BC

Prometheus Bound, play by Aeschylus, c.466-59 BC

The Suppliant Maidens, play by Aeschylus, c.463 BC

Pythian Odes Four and Five, poems by Pindar, c.462 BC(?)

The Oresteia, play by Aeschylus, 458 BC

Ajax, play by Sophocles, before 441 BC(?)

Antigone, play by Sophocles, c.441 BC(?)

Medea, play by Euripides, 431 BC

Women of Trachis, play by Sophocles, c.430-20 BC

Oedipus the King, play by Sophocles, after 430 BC

Hippolytus, play by Euripides, 428 BC

The Clouds, play by Aristophanes, 423 BC

Electra, play by Euripides, c.422-16 BC

Ion, play by Euripides, c.421-13 BC

Electra, play by Sophocles, c.418-10 BC(?)

The Trojan Women, play by Euripides, 415 BC

The Birds, play by Aristophanes, 414 BC

Lysistrata, play by Aristophanes, 411 BC

Philoctetes, play by Sophocles, 409 BC

Orestes, play by Euripides, 408 BC

The Frogs, play by Aristophanes, 405 BC

Oedipus at Colonus, play by Sophocles, 401 BC

Phaedrus, prose by Plato, 5th/4th century BC

The Republic, prose by Plato, 5th/4th century BC

The Symposium, prose by Plato, 4th century BC

On the Crown, prose by Demosthenes, 330 BC

Characters, prose by Theophrastus, c.319 BC

The Grouch, play by Menander, 316 BC

Aetia, poem by Callimachus, 3rd century BC

Hecale, poem by Callimachus, 3rd century BC

Idyll I, poem by Theocritus, c.270s BC

Idyll IV, poem by Theocritus, c.270s BC

Idyll VII, poem by Theocritus, c.270s BC

Amphitryo, play by Plautus, 2nd century BC

The Brothers Menaechmus, play by Plautus, 2nd century BC

The Pot of Gold, play by Plautus, 2nd century BC

The Eunuch, play by Terence, 161 BC

Phormio, play by Terence, 161 BC

The Brothers, play by Terence, 160 BC

The Aeneid, poem by Virgil, 1st century BC

Epigrams, poems by Martial, 1st century BC

Georgics, poem by Virgil, 1st century BC

Odes Book I, Poem 5, poem by Horace, 1st century BC

Odes Book IV, Poem 7, poem by Horace, 1st century BC

Poem 85, poem by Catullus, 1st century BC

Three Poems: 2, 63, and 76, poems by Catullus, 1st century BC

In Defence of Marcus Caelius Rufus, prose by Cicero, 56 BC

On the Commonwealth, prose by Cicero, c.51 BC

Oedipus, play by Seneca, c.48 BC

Thyestes, play by Seneca, c.48 BC

On Old Age, prose by Cicero, 44 BC

Loves, poem by Ovid, late 1st century BC

The Poetic Art, poem by Horace, late 1st century BC

Mahābhārata, epic poem attributed to Vyāsa, 1st millennium BC/AD

The Art of Love, poem by Ovid, 1st century BC/1st century AD

Metamorphoses, poem by Ovid, 1st century BC/1st century AD

Kalevala, anonymous poem, origins date to early 1st century AD

The Little Clay Cart, anonymous play, 1st century AD(?)

On the Sublime, anonymous poem, late 1st century AD

Rāmāyana, poem attributed to Vālmīki, 1st/2nd century

Lives of Lysander and Sulla, prose by Plutarch, 1st/2nd century AD

Satire 10, poem by Juvenal, 1st/2nd century AD

Annals, prose by Tacitus, early 2nd century AD

Meditations, prose by Aurelius, c.170

Cupid and Psyche, story by Apuleius, c.180

Daphnis and Chloe, poem by Longus, 2nd/3rd century

Confessions, Book I, prose by St Augustine, 4th century

The Mosella, poem by Ausonius, c.371

The Cloud Messenger, poem by Kālidāsa, 5th century

Śakuntalā, poem by Kālidāsa, 5th century

The Rape of Proserpine, poem by Claudian, c.400

The Consolation of Philosophy, prose by Boethius, early 6th century

Táin Bó Cuailnge, anonymous prose, 8th century

'Hard Is the Road to Shu,' poem by Li Bai, c.744

'Invitation to Wine,' poem by Li Bai, 752

The Thousand and One Nights, anonymous stories, 9th century

Journey to the West, anonymous novel, 11/12th century

Ruba'iyat, poems by Omar Khayyam, 11/12th century

Roland, The Song of (Anon), poem, c.1100

Erec and Énide, poem by Chrétien de Troyes, written c.1170

Lancelot, poem by Chrétien de Troyes, written c.1170

The Conference of the Birds, poem by Farid al-Din Attār, c.1177

The Tale of the Campaign of Igor, anonymous poem, c.1185

Guigamor, poem by Marie de France, late 12th century

The Saga of King Óláf the Saint, prose by Snorri Sturluson, 12th/13th century

Aucassin and Nicolette (Anon), romance, 13th century

Egils saga, anonymous prose, 13th century

Hymns to the Night, poems by Novalis, 1800
Mary Stuart, play by Friedrich von Schiller, 1800
René, prose by Chateaubriand, 1802
William Tell, play by Friedrich von Schiller, 1804
'Bread and Wine,' poem by Friedrich Hölderlin, 1806 (written 1800-01)
The Broken Jug, play by Heinrich von Kleist, 1808
Faust, play by Johann Wolfgang von Goethe: part I, 1808; part II, 1832
Elective Affinities, novel by Johann Wolfgang von Goethe, 1809
Michael Kohlhaas, story by Heinrich von Kleist, 1810
'Hansel and Gretel,' story by Jacob and Wilhelm Grimm, 1812
Peter Schlemihl, novella by Adelbert von Chamisso, 1814
The Devil's Elixirs, novel by E.T.A. Hoffmann, 1815-16
The Story of Just Caspar and Fair Annie, novella by Clemens Brentano, 1817
'The Infinite,' poem by Giacomo Leopardi, 1819
The Prince of Homburg, play by Heinrich von Kleist, 1821
'Homecoming,' 20, poem by Heinrich Heine, 1824
Memoirs of a Good-for-Nothing, novella by Joseph von Eichendorff, 1826
'Moses,' poem by Alfred de Vigny, 1826 (written 1822)
The Betrothed, novel by Alessandro Manzoni, 1827
Scarlet and Black, novel by Stendhal, 1830
Eugene Onegin, poem by Aleksandr Pushkin, 1831
The Hunchback of Notre-Dame, novel by Victor Hugo, 1831
The Waves of Sea and Love, play by Franz Grillparzer, 1831
The Bronze Horseman, poem by Aleksandr Pushkin, written 1833
Eugenie Grandet, novel by Honoré de Balzac, 1833
Lorenzaccio, play by Alfred de Musset, 1834
Danton's Death, play by Georg Büchner, 1835 (complete version 1850)
Chatterton, play by Alfred de Vigny, 1835
The Diary of a Madman, story by Nikolai Gogol', 1835
Military Servitude and Grandeur, stories by Alfred de Vigny, 1835
Old Goriot, novel by Honoré de Balzac, 1835
'To Himself,' poem by Giacomo Leopardi, 1835
The Government Inspector, play by Nikolai Gogol', 1836
'The Emperor's New Clothes,' story by Hans Christian Andersen, 1837
Lost Illusions, novel by Honoré de Balzac, 1837-43
The Charterhouse of Parma, novel by Stendhal, 1839
A Hero of Our Times, novel by Mikhail Lermontov, 1840
Dead Souls, novel by Nikolai Gogol', 1842
'Abdias,' story by Adalbert Stifter, 1843
Maria Magdalena, play by Friedrich Hebbel, 1844
The Three Musketeers, novel by Alexandre Dumas *père*, 1844
'The Broom,' poem by Giacomo Leopardi, 1845
'The Snow Queen,' story by Hans Christian Andersen, 1845
The Village Notary, novel by Baron József Eötvös, 1845
Cousin Bette, novel by Honoré de Balzac, 1847
Camille, novel by Alexandre Dumas *fils*, 1848
Memoirs, prose by Chateaubriand, 1849-50
Immensee, novella by Theodor Storm, 1851 (written 1849)
The Jew's Beech Tree, novella by Annette von Droste-Hülshoff, 1851

'Rock Crystal,' story by Adalbert Stifter, 1853
'Art,' poem by Théophile Gautier, 1856
Peasant Tales, stories by Bjørnstjerne Bjørnson, 1856—
Indian Summer, novel by Adalbert Stifter, 1857
Madame Bovary, novel by Gustave Flaubert, 1857
Oblomov, novel by Ivan Goncharov, 1859
First Love, novel by Ivan Turgenev, 1860
'Spleen,' poems by Charles Baudelaire, 1861
'To the Reader,' poem by Charles Baudelaire, 1861
Fathers and Sons, novel by Ivan Turgenev, 1862
Les Misérables, novel by Victor Hugo, 1862
'Windows,' poem by Charles Baudelaire, 1863
Notes from the Underground, prose by Fedor Dostoevskii, 1864
'Hérodiade,' poem by Stéphane Mallarmé, 1864-98
Brand, play by Henrik Ibsen, 1865
'L'Angoisse,' poem by Paul Verlaine, 1866
Crime and Punishment, novel by Fedor Dostoevskii, 1867
Peer Gynt, play by Henrik Ibsen, 1867
The Idiot, novel by Fedor Dostoevskii, 1869
A Month in the Country, play by Ivan Turgenev, 1869
Sentimental Education, novel by Gustave Flaubert, 1869
War and Peace, novel by Lev Tolstoi, 1869
'Le Bateau ivre,' poem by Arthur Rimbaud, 1871
The Birth of Tragedy, prose by Friedrich Nietzsche, 1872
The Devils, novel by Fedor Dostoevskii, 1872
Family Strife in Hapsburg, play by Franz Grillparzer, 1872
'Alchemy of the Word,' poem by Arthur Rimbaud, 1873
Around the World in Eighty Days, novel by Jules Verne, 1873
'Fleurs,' poem by Arthur Rimbaud, 1873
'Art poétique,' poem by Paul Verlaine, 1874
'Il pleure dans mon coeur . . . ,' poem by Paul Verlaine, 1874
Anna Karenina, novel by Lev Tolstoi, 1875-77
'L'Après-midi d'un faune,' poem by Stéphane Mallarmé, 1876
L'Assommoir, novel by Émile Zola, 1877
'A Simple Heart,' story by Gustave Flaubert, 1877
Before the Storm, novel by Theodor Fontane, 1878
A Doll's House, play by Henrik Ibsen, 1879
The Gaucho Martín Fierro, poems by José Hernández, 1879
Woyzeck, play by Georg Büchner, 1879 (written 1835-37)
The Brothers Karamazov, novel by Fedor Dostoevskii, 1880
The Posthumous Memoirs of Braz Cubas, novel by Joaquim Maria Machado de Assis, 1880
Ghosts, play by Henrik Ibsen, 1881
The House by the Medlar Tree, novel by Giovanni Verga, 1881
Thus Spoke Zarathustra, prose by Friedrich Nietzsche, 1883-85
'L'Abandonné,' story by Guy de Maupassant, 1884
'The Necklace,' story by Guy de Maupassant, 1884
The Wild Duck, play by Henrik Ibsen, 1884
Germinal, novel by Émile Zola, 1885
The Death of Ivan Ilyich, novella by Lev Tolstoi, 1886
The Earth, novel by Émile Zola, 1887
'Ses purs ongles trés haut dédiant leur onyx,' poem by Stéphane Mallarmé, 1887
Miss Julie, play by August Strindberg, 1888
Pierre and Jean, novella by Guy de Maupassant, 1888
The White Horseman, novella by Theodor Storm, 1888
Master Don Gesualdo, novel by Giovanni Verga, 1889
Hedda Gabler, play by Henrik Ibsen, 1890

Reference Guide to

WORLD LITERATURE

SECOND EDITION

VOLUME 1

A

ADAMOV, Arthur. Born in Baku, Azerbaijan, 23 August 1908; lived abroad after 1912. Educated at Rosset School, Geneva; lycée, Mainz, Germany, 1922–24; Lycée Lakanal, Paris, 1924–27. Married Jacqueline Trehet in 1961. Translator and writer in Paris; editor of the review, *Discontinuité* in late 1920s and *L'Heure Nouvelle*, 1945–47; increasingly involved in left-wing politics during the 1950s; co-signatory of the 'Manifeste des 121' opposing the war in Algeria, 1960; visiting lecturer, Cornell University, Ithaca, New York, 1964. *Died (suicide) 15 March 1970.*

PUBLICATIONS

Plays

L'Arbitre aux mains vides (produced 1928).
Mains blanches (produced 1928).
La Mort de Danton, from the play by Georg Büchner (produced 1948). 1953.
L'Invasion (produced 1950). With *La Parodie*, 1950; as *The Invasion*, translated by Peter Doan, 1968.
La Parodie (produced 1952). With *L'Invasion*, 1950.
La grande et la petite manoeuvre (produced 1950). 1951.
Tous contre tous (produced 1953). In *Théâtre 1*, 1953.
Le Professeur Taranne (produced 1953). 1953; as *Professor Taranne*, translated by Albert Bermel, in *Four Modern Comedies*, 1960, and by Peter Meyer, in *Two Plays*, 1962.
Le Sens de la marche (produced 1953). In *Théâtre 2*, 1955.
Comme nous avons été (produced 1954). In *La Nouvelle Revue Française*, 1, 1953; as *As We Were*, in *Evergreen Review*, 1(4), 1957.
Théâtre I–4. 1953–68.
La Cruche cassée, from the play by Heinrich von Kleist (produced 1954). In *Théâtre populaire*, 1954.
Edward II, from the play by Christopher Marlowe (produced 1954).
Le Ping-Pong (produced 1955). In *Théâtre 2*, 1955; as *Ping Pong*, translated by Richard Howard, 1959; also translated by Derek Prouse, in *Two Plays*, 1962.
Les Retrouvailles. In *Théâtre 2*, 1955.
Le Pélican, from the play by August Strindberg (produced 1956). In *Théâtre populaire*, 17, 1956.
Les Ennemis, from the play by Maksim Gor'kii (produced 1965). In *Théâtre populaire*, 27, 1957.
Paolo Paoli (produced 1957). 1957; as *Paolo Paoli*, translated by Geoffrey Brereton, 1959.
Le Revizor, from the play by Nikolai Gogol' (produced 1967). 1958.
Vassa Geleznova, from the play by Maksim Gor'kii (produced 1959). 1958.
Le Père, from the play by August Strindberg. 1958.
Les Petits Bourgeois, from the play by Maksim Gor'kii (produced 1959). 1958.
Les Âmes mortes, from the novel by Nikolai Gogol' (produced 1960). 1960.
Le Printemps 71 (produced 1962). 1961.

La Sonate des spectres, with C.G. Björström, from the play by August Strindberg (produced 1962).
La Politique des restes (produced 1963). In *Théâtre 3*, 1966.
Sainte Europe. In *Théâtre 3*. 1966.
M. Le Modéré (produced 1968). In *Théâtre 4*, 1968.
Off Limits (produced 1969). 1969.
La Grande Muraille, from the play by Max Frisch (produced 1969). 1969.
Si l'été revenait (produced 1972). 1970.

Radio Plays: *La Logeuse*, 1950; *Polly*, 1951; *L'Éternel Mari*, 1952; *Le Potier politicien*, 1952; *L'Agence universelle*, 1953; *Lady Macbeth au village*, 1953; *Parallèlement*, 1954; *Les Âmes mortes*, 1955; *Raillerie, satire, ironie et signification plus profonde*, 1957; *L'Autre Rive*, 1959; *Le Temps vivant*, 1963; *En fiacre*, 1963; *Finita la commedia*, 1964; *Du matin à minuit*, 1966.

Television Plays: *La Parole est au prophète*, with Bernard Hecht, 1952; *Tous contre tous*, 1956; *Les Trois Soeurs*, 1958; *Le Manteau*, 1966; *Une femme douce*, 1970; *La Mort de Danton*, 1970; *La Cigale*, 1970; *Vassa Geleznova*, 1971.

Other

L'Aveu (autobiography). 1946; enlarged edition as *Je . . . ils . . .*, 1969; translated in part as *Endless Humiliations*, in *Evergreen Review*, 2(8), 1959.
Auguste Strindberg, dramaturge, with Maurice Gravier. 1955.
Théâtre de société. 1958.
Ici et maintenant (essays). 1964.
L'Homme et l'enfant (autobiography). 1968; as *Man and Child*, translated by Jo Levy. 1992.

Editor, *Le Commune de Paris*. 1959.

Translator, *Le Moi et l'inconscient*, by C.G. Jung. 1938.
Translator, with Marie Geringer, *Le Livre de la pauvreté et de la mort*, by Rainer Maria Rilke. 1941.
Translator, *Crime et châtiment*, by Fedor Dostoevskii. 1956.
Translator, *Les Âmes mortes*, by Nikolai Gogol'. 1956, first part; both parts, 1964.
Translator, *La Mère*, by Maksim Gor'kii. 1958.
Translator, *Théâtre*, by Anton Chekhov. 1958.
Translator, *Oblomov*, by Ivan Goncharov. 1959.
Translator, *Cinq récits*, by Nikolai Gogol'. 1961.
Translator, with Claude Sebisch, *Le Théâtre politique*, by Erwin Piscator. 1962.

*

Bibliography: *Adamov* by David Bradby, 1975.

Critical Studies: *Regards sur le théâtre de Adamov* by Samia Assad Chahine, 1961; *Arthur Adamov* by John H. Reilly, 1974; *The Theatre of Arthur Adamov* by John J. McCann,

1975; *Lectures d'Adamov: Actes du colloque international, Würzburg, 1981*, 1983; *Lecture d'Adamov* by Elizabeth Hervic, 1984; *Langage et corps, fantasme dans le théâtre des années cinquante: Ionesco, Beckett, Adamov* by Marie-Claude Hubert, 1987.

* * *

When Arthur Adamov first began writing for the French stage in the late 1940s and early 1950s, he was considered, along with Samuel Beckett and Eugène Ionesco, one of the most promising dramatists of the burgeoning movement of the theatre of the absurd. Similar to these two playwrights, Adamov wanted to free himself from the normal constraints of dramatic construction, eliminating the traditional concepts of characterization, action, and even time and place, if need be.

He differed from Beckett and Ionesco, however, to the extent that he used the stage as a means of expressing the enormous fears and obsessions that plagued him. For Adamov, the theatre became a personal cry of anguish, a form of catharsis, a way of attempting to liberate himself from his private demons. Essentially, the Russian-born playwright revealed his feelings of injustice and his sense of persecution and victimization in his works. In his early play, *La Parodie* [The Parody], the dramatist communicated the solitude and futility of living. The two central characters are the victims of life's horrors: the one, identified only by the initial 'N', is crushed by a car, his body swept away by the sanitation department; the other, The Employee, ends up in prison, blind, both events spelling out the absurd uselessness of life, which was a reflection of Adamov's state of mind at the time of writing. In one of his most successful works, *Le Professeur Taranne* (*Professor Taranne*), based on a dream Adamov had, Professor Taranne finds himself in a nightmarish situation in which he has been accused by some children of indecent exposure on a beach. By the end of the play, unable to convince anyone of his innocence, he slowly begins to undress, thereby performing the very act with which he had been charged. *Professor Taranne* is a fairly direct translation of the author's most personal fears, dictated by the subconscious. To that extent, it is an honest expression of a soul in torment. This work is probably Adamov's most powerful play, making a highly trenchant statement about humankind at the mercy of fate and expressing more than any other of his dramas the playwright's deep sense of sadness.

At this stage in his writing, Adamov's expression of his personal visions of terror had much in common with the Surrealist movement as well as with the theories of the theatre of cruelty espoused by Antonin Artaud. During the 1950s, however, Adamov took an unusual step—he rejected all of his previous theatre: 'I already saw in the "avant-garde" an easy escape, a diversion from the real problems, the words "absurd theatre" already irritated me. Life was not absurd— only difficult, very difficult'. Having achieved some limited control of his personal obsessions, he was now able to develop his political and social concerns. Much of his drama of that period, like *Paolo Paoli* and *Le Printemps 71* [Spring 71], has strongly Marxist overtones and reflected the alienation effect experienced in the works of Brecht. Another important play of this genre, (and considered by some to be his most successful work) is *Le Ping-Pong* (*Ping Pong*). This is a delicately balanced presentation of the futility of all human action contrasted with the effects on the individual of the capitalist system. Adamov examines two men's obsession

with a simple pinball machine and the disastrous results when they are swept up into the capitalist world of big business. On the one hand, the result is a visual representation of the tragedy of life's wastefulness. Yet the play is also a study of the workings of society, a recognition of its defects, and an exploration of ways of improvement. This new thrust of Adamov's writing stressed that the direction of a person's life was more often dictated by the economic forces surrounding him/her than by the strength of the will.

Yet, finally, while Adamov may have planned to write politically committed theatre, he was basically still dealing with the sense of victimization and injustice that had always pursued him. Probably because of this, his theatre, while often highly acclaimed, never went on to achieve the popularity with the public of the works of Beckett or Ionesco—it was too private, too personal to attain universal appeal. Interestingly enough, Adamov's most successful writing may have been one of his earliest works, *L'Aveu* (*Endless Humiliations*). Written between 1938 and 1943, it is a series of ruthlessly honest journals in which the writer recounted directly the difficulties of existence. In the journals, the most personal form of expression, Adamov may have found his best means of communication.

—John H. Reilly

PROFESSOR TARANNE (Le Professeur Taranne)
Play by Arthur Adamov, 1953.

This short but disturbing play has the bizarre, remorseless logic of a nightmare. It begins abruptly with the eponymous professor in mid-peroration, attempting to rebut a charge of indecent exposure reported to the police by a group of children. In a blustering self-defence he pleads the palpable absurdity of divesting oneself of clothes in such cold weather, the notorious unreliability of juvenile witnesses, and his own international reputation as a scholar; he even alleges persecution at the hands of the children, who, he says, have pointed and jeered at him; but the chief inspector remains sceptically impassive. Taranne is then subjected to humiliation by a succession of unlikely visitors to the police station: a female journalist who denies ever having met him, two men far too engrossed in talking business to recognize him, and an elegant socialite who compliments him on a recent public lecture only to introduce him to the others as Professor Ménard. The scene ends inconclusively with the gradual dispersal of police officers and visitors alike, and the action shifts to the vestibule of a small hotel where Taranne is waiting impatiently for his mail. Two more policemen arrive, accusing him of having deposited litter in some bathing cabins. The policemen are also investigating the ownership of the notebook which Taranne immediately claims as his, although he cannot decipher the handwriting or explain its many blank pages. Again the stage empties as Taranne protests the simple absent-mindedness of a scholar. The hotel manageress brings in a large roll of paper addressed to him, which proves to be the dining-room plan of a luxury ocean-liner with a place mysteriously reserved for him at the captain's table. His sister Jeanne, the only other named character, enters with a letter from the rector of a Belgian university where Taranne has recently lectured: it complains of his general incompetence and, in particular, of his plagiarism of Professor Ménard's work. Indignant initially, Taranne ends by acquiescing to the charges, and on a bare stage, cleared of furniture by the manageress, he hangs up the plan against the rear wall, stares at it long and intently, then slowly begins to remove his clothes.

The oneiric quality of the action is no mere stylistic device: by Adamov's admission, the play is a direct transcription of a dream of his, completed in two days with only minor changes of detail. Given his long history of neurosis—childhood phobias and superstitions, an intense dislike of his commercially prosperous father, subsequently transformed into self-reproach by the latter's suicide, an abiding fear of persecution —which he recounts in his graphically confessional book, *Endless Humiliations*, it is tempting to see the play preeminently in personal terms. In particular, Adamov's sexual impotence and persistent alcoholism could have offered fertile ground for the dream's brooding sense of guilt, while the reiterated cry of the dream professor, 'I am the author of *La Parodie*' (the title of an earlier play by Adamov), would seem to make the identification between playwright and protagonist complete. During his somewhat bohemian adolescence in Paris, when he mixed in Surrealist circles and assimilated their aesthetic, not least their interest in dreams and automatic writing, he had been deeply impressed by a production at Artaud's short-lived Théâtre Alfred Jarry of Strindberg's *A Dream Play* (*Ett Drömspel*), in which there is a similar identification between the personality of the author-dreamer and his dramatic creations. Such was Adamov's preoccupation with dreams and the unconscious that his first published work was a translation from Jung, *Le Moi et l'inconscient* (1938), and *Professor Taranne* itself contains more than a hint of Jungian thinking, enabling it to transcend crude autobiography and situating it on a broader symbolic plane. In his original dream, Adamov, the true author of *La Parodie*, found the legitimacy of his claim to it ignored and subverted by a nightmarish conspiracy of circumstances; in the ensuing dramatic text, however, he cast himself as a more ambiguous character with no external referent, who may be either upright citizen and eminent scholar or pathetic deviant and academic fraud, or indeed someone combining elements of both. It is as if Adamov has reached down into the collective unconscious and produced a powerful image for the essential precariousness of our sense of identity, for the nexus of illusion, veracity, and pretence which holds it together and the link between self-knowledge and self-destruction.

In effect he has given the play some of the properties of an archetypal myth, of the kind advocated by his friend Artaud, whose notion of a theatre of cruelty deeply impressed him and whose contempt for orthodox psychological drama he shared. Atmospherically, too, the play has much in common with the work of other dramatists writing in the two decades following World War II, whose anguished contemplation of the contingency and ultimate meaninglessness of human existence led to its being categorized as 'theatre of the absurd'. In fact, Ionesco's suggestion that burrowing into his own 'darkness' was what allowed him to discover 'the problems and fears of literally everyone' might almost be taken as a recipe for the genesis of *Professor Taranne*. On the other hand, Adamov never loses sight of the objective world altogether: the forces that threaten or oppress his characters come from outside as well as inside the individual—in this case from a somewhat Kafkaesque police force and the academic establishment, in which respects it could be said look forward to his later, so-called 'Brechtian' plays and their overt concern for political and social realities. This may well have been what particularly recommended *Professor Taranne* to the young director Roger Planchon, who staged its first

performance at his Théâtre de la Comédie in Lyon on 18 March 1953, since when it has remained the play by Adamov that commands most attention both in France and abroad.

—Donald Roy

———

AESCHYLUS. Born in Eleusis, Greece, 525 or 524 BC. Fought in the Battle of Marathon, 490 BC, and probably at Artemisium and Salamis, 480 BC. Wrote possibly over 90 plays: won his first playwriting prize in 484 BC, 12 subsequent prizes, and some posthumously; also acted in his plays; visited Sicily to produce plays for Hieron I of Syracuse, soon after the foundation of the city of Aetna, 476 BC, and again in 456 BC. *Died in 456 BC.*

PUBLICATIONS

Collections

[Works], edited by Martin West. 1990; also edited by Ulrich von Wilamowitz-Moellendorff, 1914, Gilbert Murray, 1937, and Denys L. Page, 1972; translated by H.W. Smyth [Loeb Edition; bilingual], 2 vols., 1922–26; also translated by Richmond Lattimore, David Grene, and S.G. Benardete, in *Complete Greek Tragedies* series, edited by Lattimore, 2 vols., 1953–56; Frederic Raphael and Kenneth McLeish, in *Plays 1–2*, 2 vols., 1991.
Fragments, edited by S. Radt. 1985.

Plays

Persae (produced 472 BC). Edited by H.D. Broadhead, 1960; as *The Persians*, translated by S.G. Benardete, in *Complete Greek Tragedies*, 1956; also translated by Anthony J. Podlecki, 1970; Janet Lembke and C.J. Herington, 1981.
Septem contra Thebas (produced 467 BC). Edited by G.O. Hutchinson, 1985; as *The Seven Against Thebes*, translated by David Grene, in *Complete Greek Tragedies*, 1956; also translated by Peter Arnott, 1968; Christopher M. Dawson, 1970; Anthony Hecht and Helen H. Bacon, 1974.
Prometheus Vinctus (attributed) (produced c.466–59 BC). Edited by Mark Griffith, 1983; as *Prometheus Bound*, translated by Rex Warner, 1947; also translated by David Grene, in *Complete Greek Tragedies*, 1956; Warren B. Anderson, 1963; Paul Roche, 1964; Michael Townsend, 1966; Peter Arnott, 1968; James Scully and C.J. Herington, 1975.
Supplices (produced c.463 BC). Edited by H. Johansen and E. W. Whittle, 1980; as *The Suppliant Maidens*, translated by S.G. Benardete, in *Complete Greek Tragedies*, 1956; as *The Suppliants*, translated by Philip Vellacott, 1961; also translated by Janet Lembke, 1975; Peter Burian, 1991.
Oresteia (trilogy; produced 458 BC). Edited by George Thomson, 1966; as *The Oresteia*, translated by Richmond Lattimore, in *Complete Greek Tragedies*, 1953; also translated by Philip Vellacott, 1956; Michael Townsend, 1966; Hugh Lloyd-Jones, 1970; Douglas Young, 1974; Robert Fagles, 1976; Robert Lowell, 1978; Tony Harrison, 1981; David Grene and Wendy Doniger O'Flaherty, 1989; as *The*

Orestes Plays, translated by Paul Roche, 1962; as *The House of Atreus*, translated by John Lewin, 1966.
Agamemnon, edited by Eduard Fraenkel (includes prose translation). 1950; also edited by John Dewar Denniston and Denys L. Page, 1957, and Raymond Postgate, 1969; numerous translations, including by Louis MacNeice, 1936; Anthony Holden, 1969; Hugh Lloyd-Jones, 1970; D.W. Myatt, 1993.
Choephoroi, edited by A.F. Garvie. 1986; also edited by A. Bowen, 1986; as *The Libation Bearers*, translated by Hugh Lloyd-Jones, 1970.
Eumenides, edited by Alan H. Sommerstein. 1989; edited and translated by Anthony J. Podlecki, 1989; as *The Eumenides (The Furies)*, translated by Gilbert Murray, 1925; as *The Eumenides*, translated by Hugh Lloyd-Jones, 1970.

*

Critical Studies: *Aeschylus, The Creator of Tragedy* by Gilbert Murray, 1940; *Aeschylus and Athens: Study in the Social Origins of Drama* by George Thomson, 1941; *Aeschylus in His Style: Study in the Social Origins of Drama* by W.B. Stanford, 1942; *Aeschylus: New Texts and Old Problems* by E. Fraenkel, 1943; *The Style of Aeschylus* by F.R. Earp, 1948; *The Harmony of Aeschylus* by E.T. Owen, 1952; *Pindar and Aeschylus* by J.H. Finley, 1955; *A Commentary on the Surviving Plays of Aeschylus* by H.J. Rose, 2 vols., 1957–58; *Collation and Investigation of the Manuscripts of Aeschylus* by R.D. Dawe, 1964; *Image and Idea of the Agamemnon of Aeschylus*, 1964, and *The Oresteia: A Study in Language and Structure*, 1971, both by Anne Lebeck; *The Political Background of Aeschylean Tragedy* by A.J. Podlecki, 1966; *Aeschylus Supplices: Play and Trilogy* by A.F. Garvie, 1969; *The Author of Prometheus Bound*, 1970, and *Aeschylus*, 1986, both by C.J. Herington; *Studies on the Seven Against Thebes of Aeschylus* by H.D. Cameron, 1971; *Aeschylus: A Collection of Critical Essays* edited by Marsh H. McCall, Jr, 1972; *Aeschylus: Playwright Educator* by R.H. Beck, 1975; *Aeschylean Metaphors for Intellectual Activity* by D. Sansome, 1975; *Aeschylean Drama* by Michael Gagarin, 1976; *The Authenticity of Prometheus Bound* by Mark Griffith, 1977; *The Stagecraft of Aeschylus* by Oliver Taplin, 1977; *Dramatic Art in Aeschylus' Seven Against Thebes* by William G. Thalmann, 1978; *Aeschylus: Prometheus Bound: A Literary Commentary*, 1980, and *Aeschylus: Oresteia: A Literary Commentary*, 1987, both by Desmond J. Conacher; *The Phoenician Presence in The Seven Against Thebes* by Roland F. Perkins, 1980; *Problem and Spectacle: Studies in the Oresteia* by William Whallon, 1980; *The Early Printed Editions (1518–1664) of Aeschylus: A Chapter in the History of Classical Scholarship* by J.A. Gruys, 1981; *Tradition and Dramatic Form in the Persians of Aeschylus* by Ann N. Michelini, 1982; *The Art of Aeschylus* by Thomas G. Rosenmeyer, 1982; *Under the Sign of the Shield: Semiotics and Aeschylus' Seven Against Thebes* by Froma I. Zeillin, 1982; *Studies in Aeschylus* by R.P. Winnington-Ingram, 1983; *Language, Sexuality and Narrative: The Oresteia*, 1984, and *Aeschylus, The Oresteia*, 1992, both by Simon Goldhill; *Apollo and His Oracle in the Oresteia* by Deborah H. Roberts, 1984; *Musical Design in Aeschylean Theater* by William C. Scott, 1984; *The Logic of Tragedy: Moral and Integrity in Aeschylus' Oresteia*, 1984, and *An English Reader's Guide to Aeschylus' Oresteia*, 1991, both by Philip Vellacott; *The Oresteia: Iconographic and Narrative Tradition* by A.J.N.W. Prag, 1985; *Studies in Aeschylus* by Martin West, 1991.

* * *

Aeschylus was the first of the three famous poets (Sophocles and Euripides are the other two) who, from antiquity onwards, have been celebrated as the great tragic dramatists of ancient Greece. In accordance with the conventions of the tragic festivals at Athens, Aeschylus based most of his plays on ancient myths, dating back to the Mycenaean Age at the dawn of Greek civilization; however, like the other Greek tragic poets, he invested this legendary (and, occasionally, historical) material with new, often contemporary, meanings of his own. Whether from choice or because of a convention of early Greek tragedy, Aeschylus composed most of his tragedies in the form of connected trilogies. (Three tragedies, not necessarily related in subject matter, followed by a semi-comic satyr-play, remained the normal requirement for those competing in the tragic festivals throughout the classical period.) A brief survey of his extant plays will illustrate the wide-ranging material of his themes (theological, ethical, and, in the loftiest sense of the term, political), most of which are well suited, by the grandeur of their dramatic conceptions, to the trilogic form of composition.

Persae (*The Persians*), Aeschylus' earliest extant tragedy (and the earliest Greek tragedy which we possess), is exceptional in that it is *not* part of a connected trilogy. It is of particular interest also because it is the only extant Greek tragedy based on historical, not mythological, material. *The Persians* is, however, by no means merely 'dramatized history'. Rather, in his treatment of the recent defeat of the Persian despot Xerxes and his Persian fleet by the Athenians at Salamis, Aeschylus 'mythologizes' history to present a striking illustration of the tragic theme of *koros, hubris, atê*: excessive confidence in wealth and power, leading to an act of outrage (in this case, that of Xerxes overstepping the divinely ordained limits of his rule), which brings down the swift retribution of the gods. To present his material in tragic rather than in 'historical' terms, the poet takes certain bold liberties with the factual material and employs typically Aeschylean touches of symbolism (such as the striking image of 'the yoke of the sea', constraining the great sea-god Poseidon, for Xerxes' bridge of boats across 'the sacred Hellespont') to stress the overreaching ambition of the Persian King.

In *Septem contra Thebas* (*The Seven Against Thebes*) Aeschylus brings to a tragic conclusion (the lost plays *Laius* and *Oedipus* were the preceding plays of this trilogy) the treatment of another of his favourite themes: the working out of a family curse, inevitably fulfilled by the gods through the 'free' decisions of one of its doomed heroic victims.

In the *Oresteia* (*The Oresteia*), Aeschylus' only extant trilogy, the poet combines, in magnificent fashion, both of the above two themes, that of a family curse and that of divine vengeance for a deed of hubristic outrage. In the first play, *Agamemnon*, Agamemnon suffers (by the murderous hand of his queen, Clytemnestra) both for the outrageous deed of his father, Atreus, against the children of his brother Thyestes, and for his own sacrifice ('impious, unholy and polluting', however 'necessitous') of his daughter, Iphigenia, in order to obtain favourable winds for his great assault on Troy. In the trilogy sequel, *Choephoroi* (*The Libation Bearers*), Orestes and Electra, loyal children of King Agamemnon, continue the sequence of 'blood for blood' by murdering, at the god Apollo's command, the usurpers, Clytemnestra (their mother) and her paramour, Aegisthus. Only in the third play, the *Eumenides* (*The Furies*), is the curse on the family, and the attendant blood feud, resolved. In this play, Orestes takes refuge from Clytemnestra's avenging Furies (the chorus in the play), first at Apollo's Oracle at Delphi and then at Athens. Here the goddess Athena institutes a human court of justice (the Areopagus, which was a celebrated Athenian institution of some political importance in Aeschylus' time), in which Orestes (and all homicides thereafter) will be tried. Orestes is acquitted by Athena's casting vote and the Chorus of Furies, exactors of the old 'blood-for-blood justice', are persuaded by Athena, daughter of Olympian Zeus, to become beneficent, though still awe-inspiring, guardians, supporting the new order of justice which Athena has instituted.

This brief review of *The Oresteia* highlights another feature of Aeschylean thought and dramatic structure which some scholars (most notably C.J. Herington in 'The Last Phase', *Arion 4*, 1965) believe was typical of the trilogies (the Danaid and the Prometheus trilogies as well as the *Oresteia*) composed in the final period of the poet's career. Thus, in the Danaid trilogy (only the first play of which, *Supplices* [*The Suppliant Maidens*], survives) a violent sequence of forced marriage and murderous requital appears to have been 'resolved' by the decision of one bride (out of the 50 sworn to slay their violent suitors) who chooses love instead of further bloodshed. As in *The Furies*, a goddess (in this case Aphrodite, as a fragment of the final play reveals) appears as a champion of this fruitful resolution.

Finally, the Prometheus trilogy seems to have presented a comparable sequence of tragic action leading to a positive finale. *Prometheus Vinctus* (*Prometheus Bound*) was probably the first play in the trilogy; we have only fragmentary knowledge of *Prometheus Unbound* and *Pyrphoros* (*Prometheus the Firebearer*), and the Aeschylean authorship of even the extant *Prometheus Bound* has been doubted by some scholars (see especially Mark Griffith, *The Authenticity of Prometheus Bound* and Martin West, *Studies in Aeschylus*). This time the struggle is between Prometheus, divine champion of men, bestower of fire and all the human arts, and Zeus, man's would-be destroyer, here presented as a harsh and tyrannical new god, only recently established as lord of the Universe. That Zeus, the god of power and order, needs Promethean intelligence and foresight is established on the literal level by the fact that only Prometheus has the secret knowledge which can prevent Zeus falling from power. That intelligence and foresight are unavailing when suppressed by power, as demonstrated by the noble martyrdom of the enchained Prometheus, whose heroic defiance ends (in the finale of *Prometheus Bound*) in his further punishment in the lowest depths of Tartaros. Again the fragments of the trilogy (and other external evidence) suffice to indicate its probable denouement. Prometheus and Zeus are ultimately reconciled by their mutual needs. Zeus, saved by Prometheus' foreknowledge, continues to reign supreme over a less troubled universe, and Prometheus, his 'cause' now vindicated, is re-established, under Zeus, as the bestower of the civilizing gift of fire (hence the third title, *Prometheus the Firebearer*) to men. Once again, if this symbolic interpretation of the evidence be sound, we find that the sequence of suffering presented in the trilogy ends in a triumphant resolution.

In this brief survey of the extant themes of Aeschylean tragedy, it has not been possible to do justice to the impressive dramatic structure of his plays and to the grandeur of his choral odes which, particularly in *The Oresteia*, are an integral part of that structure. While it is true, as Aristotle believed, that the plot is the soul of tragedy, in Aeschylus' plays the plots are simple, both 'action' and 'characterization' being kept to the minimum necessary to expound, in compelling dramatic form, the recurrent and meaningful patterns of tragic experience.

—Desmond J. Conacher

THE ORESTEIA
Plays by Aeschylus, 458 BC.

Aeschylus' Orestes trilogy is unique, providing three successive dramas on a single theme, the tragedy of the house of Atreus. Both Homer and Stesichorus, the 6th-century BC Sicilian lyric poet, were acquainted with the story of Agamemnon and Aegisthus. Homer tells the story of Odysseus against the background of the known story of Agamemnon and Orestes; but he does not consider the possibility that Agamemnon deserved his fate, that Clytemnestra may have had good cause to kill Agamemnon, and that Orestes committed a mortal sin in killing his mother. Stesichorus, however, was concerned with an interpretation of the old epic story that would be in keeping with the moral principles held at the time in the Greek world. Agamemnon's guilt in the sacrifice of his daughter Iphigenia, the rape of the priestess Cassandra, and the bringing of the latter home as his concubine, provided Clytemnestra with ample cause for killing her husband. Aegisthus, her paramour and consort, remembered the mistreatment of his brother Thyestes and the slaughter of Thyestes' two sons as a dinner-offering. The throne of Agamemnon rightly belonged to Thyestes, and after him to his son Aegisthus.

Aeschylus' first play of the trilogy, *Agamemnon*, enacts the return of Agamemnon, the confrontation of husband and wife, of the victim and his murderess. Cassandra, never believed, knows what will happen, but the chorus of Argive elders is ignorant and their fear and foreboding become binding elements in the action. Agamemnon's false vanity and modesty and the deceit of Clytemnestra are memorable, and Agamemnon's entry into his palace on a scarlet carpet reserved for divinities is prelude to his slaughter. Cassandra's vision reveals past, present, and future misdeeds of the house of Atreus, and so underscores the link between crime and punishment; she is herself a living symbol of Agamemnon's wickedness. He has defiled a priestess of Apollo and revealed his unfaithfulness to Clytemnestra. The sacrifice of Iphigenia, recalled by the chorus and Clytemnestra, also seals his fate; the Trojan War also resulted in the deaths of many Greeks and in the slaughter of many Trojans. So Aeschylus emphasizes the guilt of Agamemnon without justifying the deed of Clytemnestra. The connection between action and suffering is the theme of the first act of the trilogy. There is evidently a constant imbalance in human nature, either to suffer more than one deserves, or to inflict more evil than one has suffered. The poet also says that what man suffers must be attributed to what man has done in the past. Deeds have consequences, and suffering has a cause.

The action of the second play, *Choephoroi* (*The Libation Bearers*), is based on the action of the first play and parallels it, just as the antistrophe of a lyric poem corresponds to the strophe. The tomb of Agamemnon occupies the position of Agamemnon's chariot in the first play; Orestes and Pylades enter and witness another sacrifice comparable to that in the first play. Both sacrifices are caused by messages from Agamemnon: in the first play, it was the fall of Troy and the return of Agamemnon communicated by beacons from the

Dardanelles to Argos; in the second play, it is a dream announcing the coming of an avenger, Orestes. After the spectacular mutual recognition of Orestes and Electra, the plan is developed to kill the murderers. The murder of Agamemnon, the suffering of Electra, the tyranny of Aegisthus, and Apollo's command to Orestes all justify the deed of retribution. Orestes and Clytemnestra face one another, both deceitful, the one by nature, the other by design. Clytemnestra plays the part that Agamemnon played in the first play. Her vanity and her modesty are both false. She is as blind as Agamemnon was; she alone cannot see what it all means and what is about to happen. The play within the play is a marvellous innovation, the story of Orestes' death invented by Orestes to deceive his mother. Orestes, who reports his own death, witnesses the feigned grief of his mother whom he is set to kill. With the curtain of deceit drawn aside, the play within the play is over; Aegisthus lies dead, and Orestes once more faces his mother, who warns him of the Furies that will pursue the matricide; but Orestes cannot disobey Apollo's command, and expects that her death, inflicted by him and his sister Electra, will end the travails of the house. The noble avenger of the father becomes the killer of his mother; the Furies attack him, and he flees to Delphi.

The third play, *Eumenides* (*The Furies*), presents both the ritual and legal absolution of Orestes. The scene has shifted from Argos to the sanctuary of Apollo at Delphi where Orestes is still pursued by the Furies (*Erinyes*) although he has been purified. Apollo sends him to the sanctuary of Athena in Athens, where the main action takes place. Athena is confronted by the suppliant Orestes and by the Furies, like bloodhounds in pursuit of their prey. She decides to establish a court to resolve the issue of Orestes' guilt or innocence, the court of the Areopagus, the first criminal court in the Western world, and an important institution in the evolution of democratic Athens, particularly during the lifetime of Aeschylus. Before a jury of 12 leading Athenian citizens, presided over by the goddess Athena, Orestes is prosecuted by the Furies and defended by Apollo. The conflict involves the rights and privileges of an older pre-Hellenic dispensation —childish and barbarous, female, chthonic, the prosecutors of Orestes—and those of Apollo who represents a newer Olympian dispensation, youthful and enlightened, civilized, male, and celestial. The votes of the mortal judges are evenly divided, whereupon Athena casts a deciding vote for acquittal. Then, by the exercise of her Zeus-given power, and by the power of persuasion, the Erinyes are pacified and consent to dwell in Athens as 'gracious, kindly goddesses', guarantors of justice in cases of homicide and of Athenian security.

So, with apparent religious (and political) change, the test case of Orestes, embodying the doctrine of 'blood for blood', provides a solution in the principle of legal trial of a killer by a jury of his fellow-men. Such was the will and purpose of Zeus, working in his mysterious way through Apollo his prophet and Athena his daughter. *The Oresteia* is a parable of progress, from butchery and the blood feud to the rule of law.

The trilogy displays prominent themes and motifs: the light that comes out of the darkness; dread compulsion and involvement (evidenced in the images of robe, net, snare, yoke, bit, and goad); animals; medical allusions to recurring sickness; and the ship of state.

By 458 BC, theological drama proper had developed to the point where it was equal in importance to the choral part; the spectacle—in the visions of Cassandra, the pageantry of robes (the Erinyes change from black to crimson cloaks in the final torchlight procession), and horrifying creatures—is prominent and characteristically Aeschylean. Characterization has

also developed greatly: although Agamemnon appears to be little more than *hubris* (arrogance) personified, Clytemnestra ranks with the greatest characters in Greek tragedy.

—Alexander G. McKay

THE PERSIANS (Persae)
Play by Aeschylus, 472 BC.

Aeschylus' *The Persians* is the earliest extant tragedy, unique in the repertoire for its historical subject, the battle of Salamis (480 BC) and the defeat of the Persian fleet under Xerxes. Aeschylus himself was a participant in the action. The political character of the prize-winning trilogy *Phineus*, *The Persians*, and *Glaucus of Potniae* is signalled by the presence of Pericles, the celebrated democratic statesman, as patron (*choregus*) at an early age. The satyr play *Prometheus the Firebearer*, which would have followed the trilogy, no doubt featured a torch race for victory, and perhaps parodied the final play of the trilogy. The plays are linked thematically through subject matter relating to the conflict of east and west, a factor which Herodotus explored in his history of the Persian wars. The religious factor is repeatedly evident in *The Persians*, recalling the religious content of the beginnings of tragic drama. Aeschylus' play unquestionably extols the Athenian victory, not through nationalistic self-eulogy but through Persian eyes. The majesty, nobility, and dignity of the Persians, especially Darius, are noteworthy. Themistocles, the hero of Salamis, and his colleagues are unnamed; the roll-call of Persians is colourful and authentic.

The play is virtually plotless, although the other plays of the trilogy no doubt resonated with livlier librettos if not more exotic costumes, music, and dancing. *The Persians* is limited to two actors and a council of 12 Persian elders who comprise the chorus; the mood shifts, through choral response, from foreboding, through confirmation, to explication and extravagant emotional response at the close. The play opens in a council chamber of the palace at Susa, and later shifts to the tomb of Darius at Persepolis. The chorus plays a major role in the drama; its members' confidence and trust in their own nature, in Atossa, Xerxes' royal mother, and in the deceased Darius, are of major importance to the meaning of the play.

Foreboding and concern dominate the play; specific themes and symbols resonate though the drama, with repeated reference to a moral formula: excess wealth (*koros*), arrogance (*hubris*), persuasion (*peitho*), and ruin (*atê*). Age and antiquity are also pervasive, as embodied in the council of elders, and in the antiquity of the Persian realm. Compulsion, enslavement, and the cruel sea are omnipresent in the symbolic use of language.

Atossa, the queen mother, before whom the chorus lies prostrate, is a vehicle for the omnipresent gold (*koros*) theme, and also of disturbing dreams. In one her son Xerxes yoked two women, Persia and Greece; Persia is docile, but Greece upsets the chariot of Xerxes. The other dream centres on a falcon (embodiment of the sun god) clawing an (imperial) eagle, interpreted as the weaker resisting the stronger bird, which sought refuge at Apollo's hearth at Delphi, a probable allusion to Delphic complicity in the Persian advance into Greece. Atossa's emphasis on Xerxes' autocratic rule over an enslaved people excites the chorus to respond that Athenian soldiers are committed citizens, not slaves. A messenger reports that the Persian forces at Salamis have been totally defeated; Atossa finally learns that Xerxes is a survivor.

The chorus addresses an invocation to Zeus, and contrasts Xerxes with Darius as battle commander. Atossa assembles offerings for Darius' tomb, and the chorus appeals to his ghost to manifest itself. The ghost scene, charged with melodrama and lugubrious music, heightens the expectation of Xerxes' arrival. The ghost also excites reminders of the yoke, fetters, and manacles (and net) used earlier. Concern for Xerxes' clothes leads to Atossa's removal from stage. With the arrival of Xerxes, the play reverts to the original content of tragedy, lamentations exchanged by the actor and the chorus members; the passing parade of Persian names lends an exotic and colourful element to the grand finale. The final lesson is not that Zeus has been the saviour of Athens but that Athenians have been their own champions; Zeus' resistance to arrogance (*hubris*) is perennial and ultimately victorious.

The Persians falls short of being a great play, but attains some distinction for its exotic language, impressive imagery, elaborate spectacle, and dramatic effects.

—Alexander G. McKay

PROMETHEUS BOUND (Prometheus Vinctus)
Play by Aeschylus, c.466–59 BC.

Prometheus Bound depicts the power struggle between the Olympian god Zeus and the Titan Prometheus. The former is presented as a violent and tyrannical divinity who wishes to destroy the human race. Prometheus, by contrast, is the champion of men, who brought them fire and taught them various arts and skills. He also possesses foresight. Zeus is the leader of the new generation of gods and has only recently gained his position of dominance in the universe, after battling with his father and the Titans (all except Themis and Prometheus) with the help of his Olympian brothers and sisters. He is not yet secure, however, and Prometheus alone has knowledge of a secret that will bring about his downfall: Zeus must stay away from the sea-nymph Thetis, who is fated to bear a son greater than his father.

As the play opens, Prometheus is being nailed to a cliff in remotest Scythia by Kratos (Strength) and Bia (Violence), the servants of Zeus. They are accompanied by the god Hephaestus, an Olympian who pities Prometheus. In spite of his torments, Prometheus is defiant, complaining bitterly of his unjust humiliation at the hands of Zeus, who formerly counted him among his allies. He also lists the many gifts he has brought to mankind—architecture, numbers, writing, farming, sailing, medicine, prophecy, mining—for which he is now being punished. In the course of the tragedy, Prometheus is visited by the chorus of Oceanus and his daughters, and also by Io, who herself is a victim of Zeus: she was raped by him and then his wife Hera vengefully turned her into a cow and had her chased all over the world by a gadfly. Prometheus uses his foresight to give Io a detailed account of her future wanderings, and also of her eventual deliverance from suffering by Zeus. In Egypt she will bear him a son, Epaphus. As the play ends, Hermes, the messenger of Zeus, threatens Prometheus with even worse torments: he will be plunged under the earth, and an eagle will gnaw at his liver every day. Prometheus' final words express his continuing defiance: 'O majesty of my mother, O sky revolving the light common to all things: you see me, how I suffer unjust torments'.

Any interpretation of *Prometheus Bound* is complicated by the fact that it was part of a trilogy, the other plays of which survive only in a few fragments. Their titles were *Prometheus Unbound* and *Prometheus the Firebearer*, and a judicious reconstruction of their content has been made by M.L. West ('The Prometheus Trilogy', *Journal of Hellenic Studies*, 1979, 130–48). Additional light is thrown on the matter by the detailed accounts of the Prometheus myth in Hesiod's *Theogony* (*Theogonia*, 507–616) and *Works and Days* (*Opera et dies*, 47–105). The central theme is the need for reconciliation and compromise between Zeus and Prometheus. Zeus must change his ways if he is to survive as the supreme deity of the universe. He must learn compassion and justice. Likewise, Prometheus needs to develop a respect for authority. In all probability, the trilogy ended with a reconciliation of the two gods, and a celebration of moderation on the divine and the human plane. In *Prometheus Bound*, Prometheus appears to foresee an eventual change in Zeus' attitude, and the prophesied end to Io's sufferings parallels the end of his own punishment. It is, in fact, one of the descendants of Epaphus, namely Heracles, who finally releases Prometheus from his bonds. Zeus learns the secret about Thetis, who later bears Peleus a son called Achilles.

The play has a political message relevant to life in the Athens of the mid-5th century: authority must be benevolent in order to be respected, and change and progress must be gradual and orderly. Whether or not the play was actually written by Aeschylus (see Mark Griffith, *The Authenticity of Prometheus Bound*), it contains conflicts which are quintessentially Aeschylean, conflicts which reflect the societal disruption accompanying the birth of Athenian democracy: between old-fashioned authoritarianism and revolutionary reform, between violence and reason, between excess and moderation. The Prometheus trilogy, like the Orestes trilogy of Aeschylus, appears to have been founded on the basic idea that the old ways of violent confrontation will no longer work, and that a new system based on reason and justice is required. This is associated with the patriarchal Olympian religious system which supplanted the earlier matriarchal one, and remnants of this conflict between male- and female-centred orders can be seen in the unhappy union of Io with Zeus, and in the shadowy presence of the Earth goddess (Gaea), who gave birth to the Titans.

The action of *Prometheus Bound* takes place in a mysterious and marginal realm, in the space between the human and divine worlds. Zeus himself does not appear on stage: we see only his representatives. The lengthy geographical descriptions in Prometheus' speeches to Io, however, remind us of the extent of his power. Humankind is also very much in the background, evident mainly in Prometheus' words. The play is unusual in the static nature of the action, which consists almost entirely of various visitors coming to witness Prometheus' sufferings and lament the startling and ignominious spectacle he presents. The most frequent images in the play are those of disease and the yoking of animals, underscoring the web of suffering and domination in which the characters are trapped. The language of the play is also much concerned with sight and seeing: by the end, we realize that 'sight' and 'blindness' are not absolute terms, since all the characters, including Zeus and Prometheus, are in some way blind to certain necessities. Only by recognizing this fact can Prometheus and Zeus come to terms. None the less, Prometheus has proved to be, and remains for many, an inspiring and heroic figure just as he is: to some, he is the creator who stoutly defends his creation, even if it provokes his own terrible suffering; to others, he is the noble rebel who stands alone against oppression, secure in the knowledge that his values will prevail in the end.

—David H.J. Larmour

THE SEVEN AGAINST THEBES (Septem contra Thebas)
Play by Aeschylus, 467 BC.

The Seven Against Thebes is the first known treatment on the Greek stage of the Oedipus story and its aftermath. It formed the last part of Aeschylus' Theban trilogy. Of the first two plays, *Laius* and *Oedipus*, almost nothing survives.

The play is set in time of war and its atmosphere is martial. Aristophanes in *The Frogs* (*Batrachoi*) describes it as 'a drama full of Ares'. Thebes is under siege. Polynices, seeking to oust his brother Eteocles, the king of Thebes, is leading an army of select champions recruited in Argos against his native city. The two brothers are under a curse invoked by their dead father, Oedipus.

For most of the first three-quarters of the play Eteocles occupies and dominates the stage. He is there at the start as commander-in-chief, addressing his people and giving battle orders. A scout arrives and describes the enemy's forces, how they have assembled outside Thebes and how the seven champions have sworn a great oath either to take the city or die in the process. Eteocles chastises and calms the panic-stricken Theban women who form the chorus.

At the play's core is a sequence of seven pairs of speeches delivered by the scout and Eteocles. In his speeches the scout reports the presence of an enemy champion at each of Thebes' seven gates, giving extensive descriptions in epic style of the warrior and of his shield. Eteocles replies and in each instance allocates a Theban to defend the gate. Of the seven attackers, only the seer Amphiaraus is god-fearing and modest. He is there against his will and only with reluctance lifts an embargo on the continuation of the enterprise, reporting Apollo's oracle prophesying its failure. The others are boastful and overbearing in their behaviour. The emblems on their shields reflect their characters and intentions.

The staging of this scene remains a matter of controversy. It is not clear whether the Theban champions are present on stage and despatched at the end of each of the first pairs of speeches, or whether we are to suppose that they have already been assigned to their posts. In his seventh and final speech the scout reveals the identity of the attacker at the seventh gate. It is Eteocles' own brother, Polynices. At this point Eteocles recalls the curse upon the family and sees its fulfilment in the horror that awaits him. He ignores the chorus's pleas not to fight his brother and leaves the stage prepared to face him in mortal combat. There follows a memorable ode in which the chorus reflects on Oedipus' curse and on the troubles of the three generations of the family of Laius, introducing in the second stanza the memorable and characteristically Aeschylean image of Iron, 'the stranger from the Chalybes', as a kind of legal figure, dividing up the legacy of Oedipus and leaving the brothers just enough space to be buried in. A messenger arrives with the news that Thebes is safe and the invaders have been defeated. The good news is tempered with bad. The two brothers have killed each other. Their bodies are brought on and the chorus divides to deliver a song of ritual mourning for each.

At this late stage of the play as we have it a new theme is introduced. A herald announces a ban on the burial of the traitor brother Polynices. An altercation breaks out and the play ends with dissension and a threat of trouble to come. It is generally agreed that the topics of the refusal of burial to Polynices and the threat to defy the ban have been introduced by a later writer or producer anxious to incorporate material from Sophocles' *Antigone* and Euripides' *Phoenissae*. There is room for disagreement about the extent of the interpolator's activity in the last quarter of the play. It is very likely, however, that Aeschylus' play ended at line 961 with the conclusion of the ritual lament of the divided chorus. The manuscripts and some scholars introduce Oedipus' daughters Antigone and Ismene into the last scenes of the play. This was certainly not Aeschylus' intention and probably not the intention of the man who composed the new ending.

The Seven Against Thebes is an impressive and densely poetic play. The interpreter is hampered by the loss of the two opening components of the trilogy to which it belonged: analogy with *The Furies* warns us how many echoes and cross-references we are likely to miss. We would undoubtedly have a clearer understanding of the development and resolution of themes within the trilogy if we possessed even a little of the first two plays. The exact details of Oedipus' curse on his sons cannot be reconstructed from this play alone. One aspect of the play as it stands does emerge clearly enough, although critics have been slow to recognize it: Eteocles is one of the most striking personalities in Greek tragedy, and the manner in which he confronts his fate is truly tragic.

—David M. Bain

THE SUPPLIANT MAIDENS (Supplices)
Play by Aeschylus, c.463 BC.

Aeschylus' *The Suppliant Maidens* is our first extant example of a type of play in which a city is begged to come to the aid of an individual or group often under pressure or constraint from another party: the 'suppliant' play. Later instances are provided by Euripides' own *Suppliant Women* (*Supplices*) and *Children of Heracles* (*Heracleidae*) and Sophocles' *Oedipus at Colonus* (*Oedipus Coloneus*). In this case the suppliants are the Egyptian monarch Danaus and his 50 daughters. The city is their ancestral home, Argos, whose spokesman is the Argive king Pelasgus. Their supplication is for refuge at Argos and protection from their pursuers, the 50 sons of Aegyptus to whom, for reasons not clearly given in the play, they refuse to be given in marriage.

The play starts with the arrival on the Argive coast of the suppliant girls and their father. After a long choral introduction setting the scene, Danaus instructs his daughters on how to conduct their supplication. The arrival (long heralded by Danaus) of the Argive king leads once more to dialogue between actor and chorus in which the Danaids explain their kinship and the reasons for their supplication. In alternating choral lyric and spoken dialogue a great scene of formal supplication develops, culminating in the supreme gesture of the suppliants, the threat to commit suicide by hanging themselves if they are not accepted. The dilemma of the Argive king is great. He can hardly resist such pressure, yet he does not wish to bring about the bloodshed of his subjects in a costly war. He takes Danaus with him to attempt to convince an assembly of Argives to accept the suppliants. This proves successful, and Danaus returns and informs his daughters. Presently Danaus observes the arrival of the Egyptian vessel. The girls flee in terror to altars whence the newly disembarked Egyptian herald seeks to move them. Pelasgus arrives and in a verbal battle drives off the herald, making it clear that Argos will fight to defend its suppliants. The grateful suppliants leave the stage and make for the city, uncertain of the outcome of the impending battle.

Until fairly recently *The Suppliant Maidens* was regarded as our earliest Greek tragedy. However, the publication in 1952 of a scrap of papyrus (P. Oxy. 2256. 3) giving information about one of the tragic competitions at the Dionysia has changed that supposition. In all probability *The Suppliant Maidens* was the first play of a trilogy concerned with the fate of the Danaids (it certainly gives the impression of being the opening of a trilogy). We know also of a play entitled *Aigyptioi*. The papyrus fragment reports a competition in which Aeschylus defeated Sophocles with a trilogy, the final play of which was entitled *Daughters of Danaus*. The titles of the first two plays have yet to be supplied. The most natural assumption is that these were *The Suppliant Maidens* and *Aigyptioi*. If so, *The Suppliant Maidens* is in fact a relatively late play since Sophocles' dramatic career began no earlier than 470 BC. The most likely date for the *Danaid* trilogy is 464–63 BC.

It is not easy to assess critically what is essentially the first act of a drama, the final two acts of which are lost to us. If we had the whole, no doubt much of the thematic material would be seen to have further resonances. Even so, *The Suppliant Maidens* is an impressive and exciting piece, pitching us into a conflict of which it is tantalizing not to know the outcome.

Although the revelation of P. Oxy. 2256. 3 is a salutary warning to those who believe plays can be firmly dated on stylistic grounds, one cannot really blame those who saw in the play an indication of the characteristics of the very earliest tragedy. Certain features have an undoubtedly archaic appearance, most notably the general air of simplicity and grandeur, the role of chorus as actor (in this case the protagonist), and the extreme economy of dramatis personae. Apart from the chorus only three personages appear on stage, namely Danaus, Pelasgus, and the Egyptian herald (it is still a matter of dispute whether a subsidiary chorus of handmaidens features in the conclusion of the play).

The massive choral contributions to the play contain some of Aeschylus' most impressive poetry (some of which is difficult to interpret). The passage on the inscrutability of Zeus' purpose foreshadows the famous Zeus-hymn in *Agamemnon*: 'shaggy and bushy are the devices of his wits and where they stretch is difficult to perceive'.

—David M. Bain

AGNON, S.Y. Born Shmuel Yosef Halesi Czaczkes in Buczacz, Galicia, Austro-Hungarian Empire (now in Poland), 17 July 1888. Educated at private schools; Baron Hirsch School. Married Esther Marx in 1919; one daughter and one son. Lived in Palestine, 1907–13: first secretary of Jewish Court in Jaffa, and secretary of the National Jewish Council; lecturer and tutor in Germany, 1913–24; in Palestine again from 1924. Fellow, Bar Ilan University. Recipient: Bialik prize, 1934, 1954; Hakhnasat Kala, 1937; Ussishkin prize, 1950; Israel prize, 1954, 1958; Nobel prize for literature, 1966. D.H.L.: Jewish Theological Seminary of America, 1936; Ph.D.: Hebrew University, Jerusalem, 1959. President, Mekitzei Nirdamim, 1950. Member, Hebrew Language Academy. *Died 17 February 1970.*

PUBLICATIONS

Fiction

VeHayah he'Akov leMishor. 1919.
Giv'at haChol [The Hill of Sand]. 1920.
Besod Yesharim [Among the Pious]. 1921.
MeChamat haMetsik [From the Wrath of the Oppressor]. 1921.
Al Kapot haMan'ul [Upon the Handles of the Lock]. 1922.
Polin [Poland]. 1925.
Ma'aseh rabi Gadi'el haTinok [The Tale of Little Reb Gadiel]. 1925.
Sipur haShanin haTovot. 1927.
Agadat haSofer [The Tale of the Scribe]. 1929.
Kol Sipurav [Collected Fiction]. 11 vols., 1931–52; revised edition (includes additional volume *Al Kapot HaMan'ul*), 8 vols., 1952–62.
Hakhnasath Kallah. 2 vols., 1931; as *The Bridal Canopy*, translated by I.M. Lask, 1937.
Me'Az ume'Atah [From Then and from Now]. 1931.
Sipurey Ahavim [Love Stories]. 1931.
Sipur Pashut. 1935; as *A Simple Story*, translated by Hillel Halkin, 1985.
BeShuva uveNachat [In Peace and Tranquillity]. 1935.
Kovets sipurim. 1937.
Ore'ah Nata Lalun. 1939; as *A Guest for the Night*, translated by Misha Louvish, 1968.
Elu va'Elu [These and Those]. 1941.
Temol Shilshom [The Day Before Yesterday]. 1945; in part as *Kelev Chutsot*, 1950.
Samuch veNireh [Never and Apparent]. 1950.
Ad Heinah [Until Now]. 1952.
Bilvav Yamim. 1935; as *In the Heart of the Seas*, translated by I.M. Lask, 1948.
Sefer, Sofer veSipur [Book, Scribe, Tale]. 1938.
Shevu'at Emunim. 1943; as *The Betrothed*, translated by Walter Lever, in *Two Tales*, 1966.
Sipurim veAgadot. 1944.
Tehilla (in English). 1956.
Two Tales: The Betrothed, Edo and Enam, translated by Walter Lever. 1966.
Selected Stories (in Hebrew), edited by Samuel Leiter. 1970.
Twenty-One Stories, edited by Nahum N. Glatzer, various translators. 1970; as *Selection*, 1977.
Shirah [Song]. 1971; as *Shira*, translated by Zeva Shapiro, 1989.
Pitchey Dvarim [Opening Remarks]. 1977.
A Dwelling Place of My People: Sixteen Stories of the Chassidim, translated by J. Weinberg and H. Russell. 1983.
Takhrikh shel sipurim (stories), edited by Emunah Yaron. 1984.

Other

Me'Atsmi el Atsmi [From Me to Me]. 1976.
Esterlain yekirati: mikhatavim 684–691 (1924–1931) (letters). 1983.
Kurzweil, Agnon, Greenberg (letters), edited by L. Dabby-Goury. 1987.
Sipure haBest. 1987.

Editor, with Ahron Eliasberg, *Das Buch von den polnischen Juden*. 1916.
Editor, *Yamim Nora'im*. 1937; as *Days of Awe, Being a Treasury of Traditions, Legends, and Learned Commentaries . . .* , translated by I.M. Lask, 1948.

Editor, *Atem re'item.* 1959; as *Present at Sinai: The Giving of the Law*, translated by Michael Swirsky, 1994.
Editor, *Sifrehem shel Tsadikim.* 1961.

*

Bibliography: *S.Y. Agnon: Eine Bibliographie seiner Werke* by Werner Martin, 1980.

Critical Studies: *Nostalgia and Nightmare: A Study in the Fiction of S.Y. Agnon* (includes bibliography) by Arnold J. Band, 1968; *The Fiction of S.Y. Agnon* by Baruch Hochman, 1970; *A Study of the Evolution of S.Y. Agnon's Style* by Joseph Kaspi, 1972; *Agnon* by Harold Fisch, 1975; *Shay Agnon's World of Mystery and Allegory* by Israel Rosenberg, 1978; *At the Handles of the Lock: Themes in the Fiction of S.Y. Agnon* by David Aberbach, 1984; *Character and Context: Studies in the Fiction of Abramovilsh, Brenner and Agnon* by Jeffrey Fleck, 1984; *The Triple Cord: Agnon, Hamsun, Strindberg: Where Scandinavian and Hebrew Literature Meet* by Yair Mazor, 1987; *S.Y. Agnon: Texts and Contexts in English Translation* edited by Leon I. Yudkin, 1988; *S.Y. Agnon: A Revolutionary Traditionalist* by Gershon Shaked, translated by Jeffrey M. Green, 1989; *Between Exile and Return: S.Y. Agnon and the Drama of Writing* by Anne G. Hoffman, 1991; *Agnon's Art of Indirection: Uncovering Latent Content in the Fiction of S.Y. Agnon* by N. Ben-Dov, 1993; *Tradition and Trauma: Studies in the Fiction of S.Y. Agnon* edited by David Patterson and Glenda Abrahamson, 1994.

* * *

S.Y. Agnon was a man of two worlds: the world of his ancestors' Judaic tradition and the realm of modernity. Some literary critics attempt to point to a harmony of the two, while others insist on the radical difference and inconsistency between them.

The province of tradition comprised the daily prayers and the celebration of the Sabbath, the lighting of the candles by the mother with its songs, hymns, special food, and parental blessings; the feasts such as the Passover, celebrating the Exodus from Egypt; Yom Kippur, the most holy Day of Atonement, a fast day and a season of forgiveness; the rabbi's home, the synagogue, and the House of Study; the spirit of neighbourliness and mutual help; the occasions of birth, circumcision, marriage, and death. The learned men were honoured and the youth encouraged to emulate them. The language of everyday was Yiddish, a mixture of Hebrew, German, and Polish (or Russian), while Hebrew was reserved for prayer and the sacred texts; God was exalted for his majesty and goodness and the Messiah expected to redeem Israel and the world.

Agnon grew up in this world. Though the 19-year-old left his native Buczacz, Galicia, in 1907, the memories of the 'old home' were strong and vivid enough to sustain his creative imagination for years to come. He portrays this culture in the novel *Hakhnasath Kallah* (*The Bridal Canopy*) and the short story 'Agadat ha-Sofer' [The Tale of the Scribe]. Agnon was aware of the breakdown of this culture; thus a tragic element enters both the novels and the short stories: in 'The Tale of the Scribe' both the humble and saintly scribe and his pious, chaste wife, as well as the sacred scroll, perish in a conflagration.

Answering some critics' contention that Agnon adheres to

a style patterned after the Jewish folk-tale and the homiletic mode of the ancient Midrash, he wrote a series of pieces in a strictly modern, expressionistic form. Here the laws of cause and effect do not apply; for example, the narrator in one story attends a memorial service for an important person, and returning home he finds that person waiting for him. Agnon made it clear that he was not confined to any one style; moreover, he chose his particular mode because he believed it to be most readily and universally understood by the Hebrew reader. The stories are evidence that the writer was indeed a man of the Western world and that the problems of the Jewish people and those of the world at large meet and cross.

—Nahum N. Glatzer

———

AITAREYA.   See **UPANISHADS**.

———

AKHMATOVA, Anna. Born Anna Andreievna Gorenko in Bolshoi Fontan, near Odessa, Ukraine, 23 June 1889. Educated at girls' gymnasium, Tsarskoe Selo; Smolnyi Institute, St Petersburg; Fundukleevskaia gymnasium, 1906, and law school, 1907, both Kiev. Married 1) Nikolai S. Gumilev in 1910 (divorced 1918), one son, the writer Lev Gumilev; 2) Vladimir Shileiko in 1918 (separated 1920, divorced 1928); 3) Nikolai N. Punin (died 1953). Associated with the Acmeist movement whose members included Gumilev, Mandel'shtam, *q.v.*, Gorodetskii, Narbut, and Zenkevich; worked as a librarian, Institute of Agronomy, Petrograd, 1920; banned from publishing her poetry, 1925–40; lived in Leningrad, evacuated to Moscow, 1941, then to Tashkent; returned to Leningrad, 1945; expelled from Union of Soviet Writers, 1946. Recipient: Taormina prize, 1964. D.Litt.: Oxford University, 1965. *Died 5 March 1966.*

PUBLICATIONS

Collections

Sochineniia [Works], edited by Gleb Struve and Boris Filippov. 2 vols., 1965–68.
Selected Poems, edited by Walter Arndt, translated by Robin Kemball and Carl R. Proffer. 1976.
Stikhi i proza [Poems and Prose] (selections), edited by B.G. Druian. 1977.
Stikhi, perepiska, vospominaniia, ikonografiia [Poems, Correspondence, Reminiscences, Iconography], edited by Ellendea Proffer. 1977.
Sochineniia [Works], edited by V.A. Chernykh. 2 vols., 1986.
The Complete Poems, edited by Roberta Reeder, translated by Judith Hemschemeyer. 2 vols., 1990; revised edition, 1 vol., 1992.

Verse

Vecher [Evening]. 1912.
Chetki [The Rosary]. 1914.
Belaia staia [The White Flock]. 1917.
Skrizhal sbornik [Ecstasy Collection]. 1921.
Podorozhnik [Plantain]. 1921.
Anno Domini MCMXXI. 1922; enlarged edition, 1923.
Forty-Seven Love Poems, translated by Natalie Duddington. 1927.
Stikhi [Poems]. 1940.
Iz shesti knig [From Six Books]. 1940.
Izbrannoe [Selection]. 1943.
Izbrannye stikhi [Selected Poems]. 1946.
Stikhotvoreniia 1909–1945 [Poetry]. 1946.
Stikhotvoreniia 1909–1957 [Poetry], edited by A.A. Surkov. 1958; revised edition, 1965.
Stikhotvoreniia 1909–1960 [Poetry]. 1961.
50 Stikhotvorenii [50 Poems]. 1963.
Rekviem: Tsikl stikhotvorenii. 1963; as *Requiem*, with *Poem Without a Hero*, translated by D.M. Thomas, 1976.
Beg vremeni [The Flight of Time]. 1965.
Selected Poems, translated by Richard McKane. 1969; revised edition 1989.
Poems (bilingual edition), edited and translated by Stanley Kunitz and Max Hayward. 1973.
Tale Without a Hero and Twenty-Two Poems, edited and translated by Jeanne van der Eng-Liedmeier and Kees Verheul. 1973.
Way of All the Earth, translated by D.M. Thomas. 1979.
Poems (selection), translated by Lyn Coffin. 1983.
Three Russian Women Poets (with Bella Akhmadulina and Marina Tsvetaeva), edited and translated by Mary Maddock. 1983.
Twenty Poems, translated by Jane Kenyon and Vera Sandomirsky Dunham. 1985.
You Will Hear Thunder, translated by D.M. Thomas. 1985.
Selected Early Love Lyrics (bilingual edition), translated by Jessie Davies. 1988.
Poem Without a Hero and Selected Poems, translated by Lenore Mayhew and William McNaughton. 1989.
Evening: Poems 1912 (bilingual edition), translated by Jessie Davies. 1990.
A Stranger to Heaven and Earth: Poems, edited and translated by Judith Hemschemeyer. 1993.

Other

Conversations with Akhmatova 1: 1938–1941, edited by Lydia Chukovskaya. 1989.
Anna Akhmatova: My Half Century: Selected Prose, translated by Ronald Meyer. 1992.
The Akhmatova Journals, 1938–1941, by Lydia Chukoskaya, translated by Milena Michalski and Sylva Rubashova. 1993.

Translator, *Koreiskaya klassicheskaya poeziya* [Korean Classical Poetry], edited by A.A. Kholodovich. 1956.
Translator, with Vera Potapova, *Lirika drevnego Egipta* [Ancient Egyptian Lyrics]. 1965.
Translator, *Golosa poetov* [Voices of the Poets]. 1965.
Translator, *Klassicheskaia poeziia vostoka* [Classical Poetry of the East]. 1969.

*

Bibliography: *Anna Akhmatova in English: A Bibliography 1889–1986–1989* by Garth M. Terry, 1989.

Critical Studies: *The Theme of Time in the Poetry of Anna Axmatova* by Kees Verheul, 1971; *Anna Akhmatova* by Sam Driver, 1972; *Anna Akhmatova: A Poetic Pilgrimage* by Amanda Haight, 1976; *Akhmatova's Petersburg* by Sharon Leiter, 1983; *The Prince, the Fool and the Nunnery: The Religious Theme in the Early Poetry of Anna Akhmatova* by Wendy Rosslyn, 1984, *The Speech of Unknown Eyes: Akhmatova's Readers on Her Poetry* edited by Rosslyn, 2 vols., 1990, and *Remembering Anna Akhmatova* by Anatoli Naiman, translated by Rosslyn, 1991; *The Poetry of Anna Akhmatova: A Conquest of Time and Space* by Sonia Ketchian, 1986; *Anna of All the Russias: The Life of Anna Akhmatova* by Jessie Davies, 1988, and *Memoirs of Anna Akhmatova's Years, 1944–1950* by Sophie Kazimirovna Ostrovskaya, translated by Davies, 1988; *Anna Akhmatova and Russian Culture of the Beginning of the Twentieth Century: Papers of the Moscow Conference 1989* by V.N. Toporov, 1989; Anna Akhmatova issue of *Soviet Literature*, 6, 1989; *In a Shattered Mirror: The Later Poetry of Anna Akhmatova* by Susan Amert, 1992.

* * *

Anna Akhmatova occupies a position unique in the history of modern Russian poetry. An established poet before the revolution, she continued her active creative life well into the mid-1960s, and after the death of Pasternak, Akhmatova was the last remaining major link with what had been one of the great ages of Russian poetry.

Her early career was closely associated with Acmeism, a poetic movement which defined itself in opposition to Russian symbolism, stressing craftsmanship in poetry and affirming the significance of this phenomenal world in contradistinction to the abstract 'Other World' of the Symbolists. Akhmatova's early work was perceived as exemplary for the new movement, and achieved a remarkable popular and critical success. The reading public welcomed the clarity, accessibility, and almost conversational style of her brief, fragile love lyrics, especially after the mystifications and abstractions of the Symbolists. The critics recognized and appreciated Akhmatova's innovations, her technical accomplishment, and the extraordinary compactness of her verse. By the publication of her fifth book in 1922, an 'Akhmatova style' in Russian poetry was widely recognized.

As a matter of conscious artistic choice, Akhmatova limited her early themes in large part to love, to poetry, and to her homeland. Settings for the predominant love theme are typically drawn from what has traditionally been thought of as the woman's world: home, interiors, garden, details of decor, and dress. Simple enough in themselves, the images evolve in sum into a complex symbolic system. The otherwise spare and laconic poems are enriched, moreover, by a matrix of images drawn from Russia's cultural history: folk motifs, the old patriarchal life, Orthodoxy, the great cities of Russia. Related to this matrix, and just below the surface of the worldly love lyrics, are the old Orthodox themes of conscience and remorse, sin and retribution, repentance and self-abnegation. It is such themes that developed in the later major works to an extraordinary power and dignity.

Although Akhmatova maintained a remarkable stylistic consistency throughout her career, it was as early as 1924 that her beloved friend and fellow-poet Mandel'shtam noted a 'sharp break' in Akhmatova's work: 'The voice of self-abnegation grows stronger in Akhmatova's poetry, and at present her poetry approaches becoming one of the symbols of the greatness of Russia'. Mandel'shtam's words were prophetic for Akhmatova's longer works like *Rekviem* (*Requiem*), *Poema bez geroia* (*Poem Without a Hero*), and the 'Northern Elegies'.

In the dark years of official disfavour and persecution that followed her former husband's execution, Akhmatova continued to write, but except for a brief respite during World War II she was not permitted to publish any original poetry. Many of her poems were lost in those tragic years; during the worst of them, many were burned by the poet herself. For a long time, Akhmatova did not dare even to set new poems to paper: the more important ones were committed to memory by her friends and thus preserved.

As works from this period began to appear in the 1950s, it was clear that Akhmatova had undergone an amazing growth and development. The poet emerges as a preserver and continuator of a poetic culture older and broader than the one of her current reality. In the longer works, the poet stands also as conscience and judge for a society suffering under the cataclysms of wars and revolution. *Requiem* is an epic lament for a Russia in the grip of the Stalinist Terror. *Poem Without a Hero* is a retrospective of Akhmatova's own world from Petersburg in 1913 to the nightmare of World War II and beyond. It is her judgement on an age and also her retribution for her own suffering. By the time she added the last touches to the poem in 1962, Akhmatova had become for Russian poetry the very symbol of moral rectitude and artistic integrity in the face of intolerable personal hardship and official persecution. Along with some of the shorter poems, these masterworks stand as tribute to one of the great Russian poets of the 20th century.

—Sam Driver

POEM WITHOUT A HERO (Poema bez geroia)
Poem by Anna Akhmatova, 1963 (written 1940–62).

'*Poem Without a Hero* was for Akhmatova as *Onegin* was for Pushkin—a compendium of all the themes, plots, principles, and criteria of her poetry. . . . It is a survey of what she had to struggle against in life, and consequently of what she wrote' (Anatoli Naiman, in Judith Hemschemeyer's translation of *The Complete Poems*, 1990).

This complex and cryptic poem proceeds via an abundance of enigmatic epigraphs, dedications, and prefaces (all containing clues to its deciphering) to its beginning on New Year's Eve 1940, when the poet sets up a magic ritual to summon her beloved (the eponymous but absent hero). However, she rouses instead the shades of her contemporaries from the Petersburg bohemia of 1913, all now dead except herself. The brilliant culture of the period is evoked, but in retrospect seems shameless and frivolous: the year 1913 is perceived as the last flowering of a free but irresponsible culture. The poet's conscience returns to the sins of her youth and at the centre of the 'hellish harlequinade' of 1913 she perceives her own double, an alluring and amoral actress and dancer who pushes a young naive admirer to suicide by her evident preference for his rival. Part Two is set in 1941, when Russia is again on the verge of war. In this intermezzo the poet comments on the poem (hinting in riddles at the way in which it should be read) and reflects on what the 20th century has brought Russia: 'the decades file by,/Tortures, exiles and deaths'. She begins to ask what it was in her own past and that

of her contemporaries that called down this dreadful retribution. By the time of the epilogue Leningrad is under siege and in ruins, punished for its venal past, and the poet is parted from it, but she records her allegiance to her native city and her fellow feeling with all exiles. She has survived to tell of her experience of purgatory.

The poem reflects on the interrelation of Russia's past, present, and future ('My future is in my past'), on the responsibility of individuals for the shaping of history, and on the function of the poet in 20th-century Russia ('to demand the one and only highest Truth'—Akhmatova's description of Pushkin's purpose, and also a self-characterization). On the personal level the poem's theme is the necessity of acknowledging guilt and making atonement for it and the poem is a quasi-religious act of confession and expiation. Akhmatova also shows that the 20th century is 'not unendurable chaotic suffering, but a strange and beautiful and yet cruel and horrible drama in which not to be able to play a role is to be seen as a tragedy' (Amanda Haight, *Anna Akhmatova: A Poetic Pilgrimage*, 1976).

Like most of Akhmatova's writing, the poem is concerned with historical authenticity and has a basis in Akhmatova's own biography. Her actress double is her friend Glebova-Sudeikina whose roles in the cabaret-theatres of the day are accurately recalled; the cigar-smoking Guest from the Future is Isaiah Berlin (with whom Akhmatova had a meeting of mind and spirit in 1946); the young suicide is the minor poet Kniazev, who was in love with Glebova-Sudeikina, and whose fate reminded Akhmatova of a catastrophe in her own life which she would not discuss. But 'the box has a triple bottom'. All the figures are generalized and symbolic, and unravelling the poem's allusions is a matter of collating multiple references so that the young poet is not only based on Kniazev but also associated with Mandel'shtam, whose words he quotes, and must further be seen as an analogy of Lenskii, the shallow romantic whose unnecessary death is enacted in Pushkin's *Eugene Onegin*.

The poem, which the poet calls a 'cryptogram' written in 'mirror writing', is a *tour de force* of periphrasis and quotation which locates the poem firmly as a late flowering of modernism and protected it from the onslaughts of censorship. It claims to be written on the first draft of Kniazev's poems, but quotation is not limited to Kniazev—or Mandel'shtam—and many others of the poetic voices of 1913 are to be heard (Blok, Lozinskii, Kuzmin, Kliuev, Akhmatova herself), alongside T.S. Eliot, Pushkin, and Byron.

Akhmatova listened with interest to interpretations of the poem but refused to explain it. However, commentators, the doughtiest of whom is Roman Timenchik, have elucidated many of the references, generated a vast corpus of exegesis, and offered a variety of hypotheses as to who or what is the missing hero of the poem (Time; Petersburg–Leningrad; Akhmatova's first husband and one of the first poet-martyrs of Bolshevism, Gumilev; etc).

The poem has its roots in the 'Petersburg myth' in Russian literature (tracing its own descent from Pushkin, Dostoevskii, and Blok—as well as from Byron's *Don Juan*). Akhmatova was aware of the perils of imitating Pushkin's *Eugene Onegin* when writing a long poem in Russian, a problem that she solves through a typical paradox by following Pushkin in inventing a stanza form unique to this work.

The poem was begun in 1940, after several arid years. Almost possessed of a life of its own, it continued to haunt Akhmatova through the siege of Leningrad, her evacuation to Tashkent, and the 1946 political campaign against her, into the happier late 1950s, until after several false alarms it was finally declared finished in 1962. Lydia Chukovskaya's diaries of these years lovingly record the minutiae of the poem's difficult creation. In the course of writing, some separate poems were absorbed into it, and some passages evolved into poems which were then separated from it. Attached to the poem are various verse fragments, observations about it in prose, and an uncompleted libretto for its translation into a ballet. There are over 30 variants of parts or the whole: the definitive discussion of editions of the text is E. von Erdmann-Pandžić's '*Poema bez geroja von Anna A. Achmatova*' (1987), which also contains a bibliography of critical material.

—Wendy Rosslyn

REQUIEM (Rekviem)
Poem cycle by Anna Akhmatova, 1963 (written 1939–40).

The *Requiem* cycle describes the suffering of the women of Russia during Stalin's Terror, when it was, as Akhmatova writes here, no longer clear who was an animal and who was still a person. It is 'a map of a journey leading through hell into the light' (Amanda Haight, *Anna Akhmatova: A Poetic Pilgrimage*, 1976).

The kernel of the cycle was a poem written in 1935 when Akhmatova's son Lev Gumilev and her third husband N.N. Punin were arrested. As was usually the case, there was no legal or rational reason for the arrest. Lev's fault, for example, was simply that he was the son of Gumilev, executed for alleged counter-revolutionary activity, and of Akhmatova, also in disfavour (she had been barred from publishing by the Communist Party since the mid-1920s). Both victims were soon released, but Lev Gumilev was arrested again in 1937, exiled, called up to the army, and did not return until 1945. Both Punin and Lev Gumilev were re-arrested in 1949; the former died in a camp and the latter was finally disgorged from the Gulag only in 1956. Most of the cycle (ten poems with preamble and epilogues) was written in 1939–40 but the horrors it describes continued in Akhmatova's life and those of the nation for long after.

'Instead of a Preface' records the urge behind the cycle: to give voice to suffering that turned its victims numb and dumb. Akhmatova's cycle constitutes solidarity which the terror otherwise made impossible. In it she describes the psychological path travelled by Russian women after the arrest of husbands and sons: the immediate pain, the surprise that it can be borne, the urge to block out what has happened, the inability to grasp what is going on, fear for their survival, preparing to hear the sentence of death. When it comes the women are barely sensate but condemned to carry on living. Suffering has brought them to the edge of sanity and their own death would be welcome, but it does not come.

At the harrowing moment when the death sentence is carried out Akhmatova turns to Biblical imagery: Mary stands at the foot of the cross where her son is crucified. The figure of Mary symbolizes the impossibility of running away even from extreme suffering, and the epigraph likewise points to Akhmatova's decision not to emigrate and to go through whatever might befall Russia with her fellow citizens. *Requiem* is one of the many poems in which Akhmatova singles out images of women from history and literature whose fate in some way mirrored her own (Dido, Joan of Arc, Cleopatra, Phaedra, and others).

Critics differ about the significance of religion to the poem. Anatoli Naiman feels that its tragedy is balanced by its basic Christian feeling (in Judith Hemschemeyer's translation of *The Complete Poems*, 1990). Iosif Brodskii writes: 'The degree of compassion with which the various voices of *Requiem* are rendered can be explained only by the author's Orthodox faith; the degree of understanding and forgiveness which account for this work's piercing, almost unbearable lyricism only by the uniqueness of her heart, her self, and this self's sense of time' (*Less than One*, 1986). Others do not conclude that religious language and Biblical quotation imply that Mary's endurance is the result of her faith. Basker finds that her strength is 'built on inconsolable loss and pitilessly searing detachment from the broken and now redundant ordinary self'.

Instead of moving on to resurrection the cycle ends with a defiant and retributive epilogue. Akhmatova declares the cycle an act of remembrance for the hundreds of women who stood for months in queues outside the prisons with her, hoping to find out the whereabouts of their loved ones, or to hand in a parcel. She insists on erecting a (verbal) monument to commemorate what has happened, on making public what the system conspired to conceal.

Foreseeing the possibility that 'they gag my exhausted mouth/Through which a hundred million scream', Akhmatova took precautions: the seditious poems were not written down but memorized by trusted friends. One or two of the poems were published as separate lyrics and the cycle eventually became widely known as a result of *samizdat*. It was published without Akhmatova's permission in Munich in 1963 but had to await *glasnost'* before it could be published in the USSR (1987).

Although the cycle claims to be woven from words overheard in the prison queues and appears to be as simple as *Poem Without a Hero* is complex, it has an elaborate, symmetrical structure (see A.L. Crone, in *The Speech of Unknown Eyes*, 1990) and also uses intertextual allusion to extend its reference to the heroines of Euripides, whose suffering on account of the loss of their children also brings them to the verge of death; the wives of the 17th-century musketeers massacred by Peter the Great for rebellion; and the wives of the Decembrists punished for the 1825 insurrection. The poem thus puts the immediate situation into a long perspective of Russian history.

—Wendy Rosslyn

AKUTAGAWA Ryūnosuke. Born Niihara Ryūnosuke in Tokyo, Japan, 1 March 1892; adopted by uncle and given the family name Akutagawa. Educated at Tokyo Imperial University, 1913–16, degree in English. Married Tsukamoto Fumi in 1918; three sons. Member of literary staff, *Shinshichō* [New Thought Tides], university magazine, 1914, 1916–17; English teacher, Naval Engineering College, Yokosuka, 1916–19; literary staff member, *Osaka Mainichi Shimbun* newspaper, 1919; travelled through China and Korea for *Osaka Mainichi*, March–July 1921. Addicted to opium by 1926. *Died (suicide) 24 July 1927.*

PUBLICATIONS

Collections

Shū [Selected Works], edited by Nakamura Shin'ichirō. 1928; 2 vols., 1953.

Zenshū [Collected Works]. 10 vols., 1934–35; 20 vols., 1954–
57; 8 vols., 1964–65; 11 vols., 1967–69; 9 vols., 1971.
Sakuhin shū [Collection of Pieces], edited by Hori Tatsuo,
Kuzumaki Yoshitoshi, and Akutagawa Hiroshi. 1949.
Bungaku tokuhon [Literary Reader], edited by Yoshida
Seiichi. 1955.
Ōchōmono zenshū. 2 vols., 1960.
Miteikō shū [Unfinished Works], edited by Kuzumaki
Yoshitoshi. 1968.
Jihitsu miteikō zuho [Projects for Unfinished Works in His
Own Hand], edited by Tsunoda Chūzō. 1971.

Fiction

Rōnen [Old Age]. 1914.
Rashōmon. 1915; as *Rashomon*, translated by Takashi
Kojima, in *Rashomon and Other Stories*, 1952; also trans-
lated by Glenn W. Shaw, 1964.
Hana. 1916; as *The Nose*, translated by Glenn W. Shaw,
1930; also translated by Dorothy Britton, 1987.
Imogayu. 1916; as *Yam Gruel*, translated by Takashi Kojima,
1952.
Hankechi. 1916; as *Handkerchief*, translated by Glenn W.
Shaw, 1930.
Gesaku zammai [A Life of Frivolous Writing]. 1917.
Tabako to akuma [Tobacco and the Devil]. 1917.
Jigokuhen. 1918; as *Hell Screen*, translated by W.H.H.
Norman, in *Hell Screen ('Jigokuhen') and Other Stories*,
1948; translated as *Hell Screen*, 1987.
Hōkyōjin no shi. 1918; as *The Martyr*, translated by Takashi
Kojima, 1952.
Kumo no ito. 1918; as *The Spider's Thread*, translated by
Glenn W. Shaw, 1930; also translated by Dorothy Britton,
1987.
Kesa to Moritō. 1918; as *Kesa and Morito*, translated by
Takashi Kojima, 1952.
Kare no shō [Withered Fields]. 1918.
Kairaishi [The Puppeteer]. 1919.
Mikan [Tangerines]. 1919.
Kage dōro [Street of Shadows]. 1920.
Yabu no naka. 1921; as *In a Grove*, translated by Takashi
Kojima, 1952.
Yarai no hana [Flowers from the Night Before]. 1921.
Torokko. 1922; as *Flatcar*, translated by Richard N.
McKinnnon, in *The Heart Is Alone*, 1957.
Ikkai no tsuchi. 1924; as *A Clod of Earth*, translated by
Richard N. McKinnnon, in *The Heart Is Alone*, 1957.
Daidōji shinsuke no Hansei [The Early Life of Daidoji
Shinsuke]. 1924.
Genkaku sanbō [Genkaku's Villa]. 1927.
Kappa. 1927; as *Kappa*, translated by Seuchi Shiojiri, 1947;
also translated by Geoffrey Bownas, 1970.
Tales Grotesque and Curious, translated by Glenn W. Shaw.
1930.
Hell Screen ('Jigokuhen') and Other Stories, translated by
W.H.H. Norman. 1948.
Rashomon and Other Stories, translated by Takashi Kojima.
1952.
Japanese Short Stories, translated by Takashi Kojima. 1961;
revised edition, 1962.
Exotic Japanese Stories, translated by Takashi Kojima and
John McVittie. 1964.
The Spider's Thread and Other Stories, translated by Dorothy
Britton. 1987.

Verse

Kushū [Poems]. 1976.

Other

Toshishun. 1920; as *Tu Tzu-chün*, translated by Sasaki
Takamasa, 1944; revised edition, 1951; as *Tu Tze-chun*,
translated by Dorothy Britton, 1965.
Shina-yuki [Notes on a Chinese Journey]. 1925.
Ume, uma, uguisu [Plum, Horse, Nightingale]. 1926.
Tenkibo [Death Register]. 1926.
Bungeiteki na, amari ni bungeiteki na [Literary, All Too
Literary]. 1927.
Yūwaku [Temptation] and *Asakusa Kōen* [Asakusa Park]
(unproduced film scripts). 1927.
Shinkirō [Mirage]. 1927.
Aru ahō no isshō. 1927; as *A Fool's Life*, translated by Will
Petersen, 1970.
Haguruma. 1930; as *Cogwheels*, translated by Cid Corman,
1987.
The Three Treasures (stories for children), translated by
Sasaki Takamasa. 1944; revised edition, 1951.
Shuju no kotoba (essays). 1968.
Hell Screen, Cogwheels, and A Fool's Life, translated by
Takashi Kojima, Cid Corman, Susumu Kamaike, and Will
Petersen. 1987.

*

Bibliography: in *Akutagawa: An Introduction* by Beongcheon
Yu, 1972; in *The Search for Authenticity in Modern Japanese
Literature* by Hisaaki Yamaouchi, 1978.

Critical Studies: *Akutagawa*, edited and translated by Akio
Inoue, 1961; 'Akutagawa: The Literature of Defeatism' by T.
Arima, in *The Failure of Freedom*, 1969; 'Akutagawa and the
Negative Ideal' by Howard Hibbert, in *Personality in
Japanese History*, edited by Albert Craig and Donald Shively,
1970; *Akutagawa: An Introduction* by Beongcheon Yu, 1972;
in *Modern Japanese Writers* by Makoto Ueda, 1976; 'From
Tale to Short Story: Akutagawa's *Toshishun* and Its Chinese
Origins' and 'The Plot Controversy between Tanizaki and
Akutagawa', in *Reality and Fiction in Modern Japanese
Literature* by Noriko Mizuta Lippit, 1980; 'Akutagawa
Ryunosuke' by Donald Keene, in *Dawn to the West: Japanese
Literature of the Modern Era: Fiction*, 1984.

* * *

Akutagawa's reputation as a purveyor of grotesque and
exotic narratives, suggested by the titles of two collections of
his stories in English, has been reinforced, not only by the
film *Rashōmon,* which Kurosawa Akira based on two of
Akutagawa's stories—*Rashōmon* and *Yabu no naka* (*In a
Grove*)—but also by reference to the facts of his often
unhappy life, ending in a suicide which, committed at the
early age of 35 and leaving three small boys in his wife's care,
was shocking even in a country where suicide is traditionally
regarded with less dismay than in most other cultures.
However, there is more to Akutagawa's work than the
morbidness that all this may suggest. The range of his interests and of the genres he wrote in was unusually broad. His
thoughtful essays on the literature of East and West from
which he drew general inspiration and specific ideas and
images; his stories for children; his reflections on his journey
through China and Korea in 1921—none of these deserves to
be overshadowed, as they often have been, either by the
more popular stories or by *Haguruma* (*Cogwheels*), *Aru ahō*

no isshō (*A Fool's Life*), and the other harrowing autobiographical texts of his final months. Nor are the stories as simple as the conventional labels would indicate. The 'grotesque' stories are vivid explorations of extreme situations and their psychological effects, rather than merely exercises in making the reader shudder. Yoshihide in *Jigokuhen* (*Hell Screen*), continuing painting the fires of Hell even as his daughter burns, is more than just another image of the obsessive artist, though he is that too. He is also a father maddened by grief, whose predicament is so convincingly evoked that the horror of the situation comes to seem understandable. *Rashōmon* stands out among all the many Japanese fictions about Kyoto as a depiction of the ancient capital at its lowest ebb, desolated by war and deserted by most of its population, with a resonance which the course of Japan's history since Akutagawa's death has accidentally enhanced. As for his 'exotic' stories, such as *Kumo no ito* (*The Spider's Thread*), based on Buddhist eschatology, or *Kare no shō* [Withered Fields], depicting the disciples of the 17th-century poet Bashō, these reflect the depth of his knowledge of history and of religion, though it should be stressed that he was neither didactic nor romantic about either of these interests. The best of the many stories which fit neither of these all-too-convenient labels is perhaps *Mikan* [Tangerines], a deft exercise in social observation and psychological insight, in which one simple action transforms the narrator's view of the apparently stupid girl sharing his train compartment.

But the masterpiece among Akutagawa's fictions is the novella *Kappa,* which transcends all labels. There are obvious comparisons to be made between its hero's journey to the land of the *kappa,* the legendary sprites or gnomes that live in Japanese rivers, and the travels of Jonathan Swift's character Lemuel Gulliver. Both are presented in first-person narratives which use imaginary countries to imply critical observations of the authors' own societies; both travellers eventually overcome their initial confusion and mystification about the strange creatures they observe to conclude that human beings are in many ways even stranger. Yet the differences are also telling. Gulliver visits several different societies, takes part in their activities as far as he can, and returns home at last wiser, perhaps more cynical. Akutagawa's hero, a patient in a mental hospital rather than a prosperous sea-captain, is a passive observer of only one society, which turns out to be all too much like his own, and what he learns from the final poem of his dead *kappa* friend Tok supplies a kind of wisdom he would rather not have had. It is as though the misanthropy which marks Gulliver's visit to the land of the Houyhnhnms, the wise and virtuous talking horses, had been extended to a general revulsion from human and non-human creatures alike, since all alike lack wisdom and virtue. For Gulliver, if not perhaps for himself, Swift the Christian was able to find solace and a kind of resolution; Akutagawa, who killed himself some months after finishing *Kappa,* was at the end of his tether. Thus the difficulties that *Kappa* presents, for both Japanese and non-Japanese readers, are not so much stylistic or intellectual—it is a deceptively simple tale, simply told—as emotional. Without any overt use of horrific imagery its cumulative effect is none the less not for the squeamish.

In the end, then, Akutagawa's enduring position as one of the most popular and influential of modern Japanese writers rests on the sheer variety of his subject matter, handled in a lucid and elegant prose style, particularly on his use of Chinese and Japanese themes familiar to generations of his compatriots. But the significance of his work also lies in his efforts to assimilate the impact of Western technology, values, and, not least, literary forms. Before him Natsume Sōseki, of whom Akutagawa considered himself a disciple,

had made his own peace between his heritage as a scholar of Chinese traditions and his career as an English teacher and newspaper contributor (jobs which did not exist for earlier Japanese writers, and which Akutagawa also took). In later years Tanizaki Junichirō, with whom he debated literary principles in *Bungeiteki na, amari ni bungeiteki na* [Literary, All Too Literary], would embrace in turn extreme 'Westernization' and the revival of native tradition, finding means of self-expression within both, at least partly by inheriting and extending Akutagawa's tendencies toward grotesquerie. It is a matter for great regret that Akutagawa's frequently expressed self-disgust should have overwhelmed the intelligence and passion that are the mark of almost all his writings.

—Patrick Heenan

ALAIN-FOURNIER. Born Henri Alban Fournier in La Chapelle d'Angillon, France, 3 October 1886. Educated at the Lycée Voltaire, Paris, 1898–1901, lycée in Brest 1901–03; lycée in Bourges, 1902–03, baccalauréat, 1903; Lycée Lakanal, Paris. Served in the French cavalry and infantry 1907–09, 1911, 1913–14; second lieutenant. Secretary and translator for wallpaper factory, London, 1905; journalist, *Paris Journal,* 1910–12, *L'Intransigeant,* Paris, 1912–14. Tutor of French to T.S. Eliot; secretary to Claude Casimir Périer, 1912. *Died (killed in action) 22 September 1914.*

PUBLICATIONS

Fiction

Le Grand Meaulnes. 1913; as *The Wanderer,* translated by Françoise Delisle, 1928; as *The Lost Domain,* translated by Frank Davison, 1959; also translated by Sandra Morris, 1966; as *The Wanderer; or, the End of Youth,* translated by Lowell Bair, 1971; as *Le Grand Meaulnes: The Land of the Lost Content,* translated by Katherine Vivian, 1979.
Miracles (stories). 1924.
Colombe Blanchet (unfinished), edited by Gabriella Manca. 1990.

Other

Jacques Rivière et Alain-Fournier: Correspondance 1905–1914. 4 vols., 1926–28; revised edition, edited by Isabelle Rivière, 2 vols., 1948; also edited by Alain Rivière and P. de Gaulmun, 1991.
Lettres au Petit B. . . . 1930; revised and enlarged edition, 1986.
Lettres d'Alain-Fournier à sa famille 1905–1914. 1930; enlarged editions 1940, 1949, 1986.
Alain-Fournier–Madame Simone, Correspondance 1912–1914, edited by Claude Sicard, 1992.
Charles Péguy et Alain-Fournier: Correspondance 1910–1914, edited by Yves Rey-Herme. 1973; revised edition, 1990.
Miracles: Poèmes et proses. 1986.
La Peinture, le coeur et l'esprit: Correspondance inédite (1907–1924), with André Lhote and Jacques Rivière, edited by Alain Rivière, Jean-Georges Morgenthaler, and Françoise Garcia. 1986.

Towards the Lost Domain: Letters from London 1905, edited
and translated by W.J. Strachan. 1986.
Chroniques et critiques, edited by André Guyon. 1991.

*

Critical Studies: *Images d'Alain-Fournier*, 1938, and *Vie et
passion d'Alain-Fournier*, 1963, both by Isabelle Rivière; *The
Quest of Alain-Fournier*, 1953, revised edition as *The Land
Without a Name: Alain-Fournier and His World*, 1975, and *Le
Grand Meaulnes*, 1986, both by Robert Gibson; *Portrait of a
Symbolist Hero: An Existential Study Based on the Work of
Alain-Fournier* by Robert Champigny, 1954; *Alain-Fournier
et le Grand Meaulnes* by Jean-Marie Delettrez, 1954; *A
Critical Commentary on Alain-Fournier's 'Le Grand
Meaulnes'* by Marian G. Jones, 1968; *Alain-Fournier: Sa vie
et 'Le Grand Meaulnes'* by Jean Loize, 1968; *Alain-Fournier:
A Brief Life 1886–1914* by David Arkell, 1986; *Le Grand
Meaulnes: Images et documents* edited by Daniel Leuwers,
1986; *Alain-Fournier* by Stephen Gurney, 1987.

* * *

Although Alain-Fournier's fame seems likely to rest on *Le
Grand Meaulnes* (*The Wanderer*), his only completed novel,
he does not deserve to be seen simply as a one-book author.
In his tragically foreshortened life, he produced a number of
poems and short stories as well as an impressive array of
letters and newspaper articles. All this material has now been
published and occupies several hundred closely printed
pages.

None of the 12 poems he completed was published in his
lifetime. The first was written in August 1904 and the last in
August 1906. They are nearly all in free verse form and bear
the clear imprint of the great enthusiasms of his later teens:
Francis Jammes, Jules Laforgue and *Pelléas et Mélisande*.
Their principal interest is that they already include some of
the dominant motifs of his later writing; a pair of sweethearts
in a peaceful country setting, the cooing of doves, the notes of
a distant piano, an elusive girl who is loved in vain. The most
accomplished of these poems, 'A travers les étés . . .', written
in August 1905, was the first attempt to transpose into
polished form his impressions of the brief encounter two
months previously with Yvonne de Quièvrecourt; it was
eventually to become the centrepiece of the fancy dress party
at the lost domain in *The Wanderer*.

The first of his writings ever to appear in print was 'Le
Corps de la Femme', completed in September 1907 just before the author began his two years of compulsory Army
service and published in *La Grande Revue* two months later.
It is a series of vignettes expressing his youthful ideal of
womanhood, composed as a deliberate counter to Pierre
Lous, who sang the praises of the female nude and wrote
captions for pornographic 'art-studies', Alain-Fournier
argued that French women would remain loyal to their gender and to the traditions of their country only if they kept
clothed and remained remote. His next contribution to this
subject, 'La Femme empoisonnée', completed 18 months
later, reveals the effect of Army service on his youthful
ideals: the woman of the title, once the pure girl who sets
schoolboy hearts a-flutter, is now the garrison whore riddled
with the pox.

From 1909 onwards, the consequences of lost innocence
became Alain-Fournier's abiding concern. While he continued to yearn for the inaccessible aristocratic Yvonne, he
embarked on a series of short-lived love-affairs with lower-
class women, the legacy of which was invariably self-disgust.
Loss of purity, he came to believe, squandered his hopes of
happiness and directly threatened the childlike sense of wonderment that he felt was crucial to his art. Variations on this
theme are to be found in the short stories in *Miracles* and in
the earliest attempts he made to write a novel where his
version of the Land of Lost Contentment is simply called *le
pays sans nom* (the land without a name): in *The Wanderer*,
finally completed in 1913 after all manner of false starts, this
becomes the 'Lost Domain' which Meaulnes is convinced he
has no right to re-enter because he is no longer innocent. The
theme was also to have been of central importance to Alain-
Fournier's second novel, *Colombe Blanchet*, only a few fragments of which were ever written. Set like all his fiction
against a rural background, its characters were to have been
young schoolteachers rather than schoolboys in their teens.
The projected epigraph was a quotation from the *Imitation of
Christ*: 'I seek a pure heart and there I will take my rest'.

While Alain-Fournier's poetry and fiction remain deeply
rooted in his rural past, his prolific correspondence and numerous newspaper articles have a spectacularly wider range.
The first of his published letters, written to his parents in
1898, lists his examination successes at the end of his first
term at his Paris lycée; the last, sent to his beloved sister in
September 1914, is from the battlefield of the Marne.
Between these two dates, he wrote scores of letters, many
positively voluminous, to his closest relatives, to schoolfriends, and eventually, as he began to make his way in the
literary world, to such fellow-writers as Gide, Jacques
Copeau, Jammes, and T.S. Eliot, who was, for a brief while
in 1910–11, his private pupil. By some way the most important correspondence is that with Jacques Rivière, his closest
friend and eventually his brother-in-law. Circumstances
separated them for four years and they exchanged long letters
in which they described and analyzed for each other their
evolving thoughts and feelings and their impressions of the
world around them. Alain-Fournier builds up a detailed
picture of the London scene in 1905 and records vivid
impressions of his army service which played so significant a
part in both his sentimental education and his literary
apprenticeship. Especially revealing is the record of their
latest discoveries in the worlds of literature, music, and painting, where they respond with infectious enthusiasm yet ana-
lyze and evaluate with admirable perceptiveness.

Their appetite remained insatiable to the end. While
Rivière went on to become secretary then editor-in-chief of
La Nouvelle Revue Française, Alain-Fournier became a literary critic and gossip-columnist for a variety of newspapers
and journals. By its very nature, much of this work was
ephemeral, but it remains impressive for its wealth of judicious comment and the sheer breadth of its range. Taken
together with his many letters, it constitutes an invaluable
chronicle of that inordinately rich decade in the cultural life of
Paris which preceded World War I.

—Robert Gibson

THE WANDERER (Le Grand Meaulnes)
Novel by Alain-Fournier, 1913.

The Wanderer is a story of youthful idealism and adventure
which grew out of Alain-Fournier's obsession with a young
woman he met briefly at the age of 19 and his subsequent
preoccupation with the search for pure, idealized love associ-

ated with lost childhood. Narrated by François Seurel, the timid son of a schoolmaster, who is both observer and participant in events, the novel reveals a complex web of emotions and relationships. The quest of François's schoolfriend, Augustin Meaulnes, for the unknown, beautiful young woman glimpsed during a fantastical wedding party (the '*fête étrange*') in an old château where he finds himself by chance becomes the great adventure of their adolescence, then François's hero-worship of Meaulnes and identification with his quest gives the quiet, serious boy a vicarious excitement and becomes the focal point of his existence.

The air of mystery that surrounds the 'lost domain' and the young woman (Yvonne de Galais) is sustained by the narrator's use of fairy-tale devices (Meaulnes falls asleep on a cart journey and the horse, wandering from the path, brings him to the old château), dreamlike events (the wedding party run at the whim of children in fancy dress) and initially unexplained happenings (Meaulnes's moodiness; the melodramatic behaviour and reappearances of the flamboyant Frantz de Galais who becomes Meaulnes's hero in turn).

François's eagerness to take over the quest when Meaulnes, discouraged, leaves for Paris, reveals that he shares—even exceeds—Meaulnes's idealism and romanticism. In fact, Meaulnes disappears from the reader's view for large stretches of the book and is then only seen through his letters and diary. François's position as sole narrator privileges his viewpoint, which is deeply subjective, the alluring gloss he puts on people and events seducing the reader into sharing his assumptions and expectations. His presentation of Meaulnes as romantic hero is, however, subtly undermined by Meaulnes's actual behaviour when viewed objectively, though the reader is rarely allowed direct access to his thought-processes. Meaulnes's 'adventure' comes about initially by chance and although he does indeed become a 'wanderer' he seems driven by anguish, indecision, and despair rather than by a dynamic heroism. Similarly, the view of Yvonne as the idealized princess on a pedestal ('la princesse lointaine') is countered by her fragile health and down to earth common-sense when she is allowed to speak in her own voice.

The marriage of Yvonne and Meaulnes, brought about by François in his desire to create a traditional fairy-tale ending to the great adventure, ends in tragedy when Meaulnes, consumed by an obscure and unexplained remorse, adheres to an adolescent pact with Yvonne's self-absorbed and self-dramatizing brother Frantz and leaves Yvonne after their wedding night to search for Frantz's missing fiancée. Although multiple explanations for his behaviour are offered—François's speculations that Meaulnes cannot reconcile his ideal with reality and is driven to destroy his happiness once it has been achieved are characteristically romantic—the real reason, revealed in the rather clumsy device of a diary written by Meaulnes, is more mundane and has significant implications for Alain-Fournier's views on love. Meaulnes's guilt over his relationship in Paris with a young seamstress, Valentine, to whom he turned in despair and whom he rejected when he discovered she was Frantz's lost bride, and his subsequent remorse are the secret burdens which, unknown to François, doom his marriage before it takes place and precipitate his abrupt departure.

Implicit in this tale is the destructive power of obsessive idealism which seeks to impose a false role on other people: both Yvonne and Valentine are victims of this tendency in the men who 'love' them. Valentine tried to evade the stereotype of 'princess' Frantz sought to impose on her by running away, only to find herself cast, by Meaulnes, in another role—that of substitute lover and instrument of his betrayal both of his

friend Frantz and of his own concept of pure, innocent love. The idealization of love relationships is also severely undermined by the tragic fate of Yvonne. Doomed to unhappiness by her loyalty to her brother and to Meaulnes, she is abandoned by her new husband and dies a painful and unromantic death after bearing his child. In effect, both female characters are cast by the author in sexually stereotypical roles—the pure beauty (her sexuality manifested only in her motherhood) and the 'fallen woman'—a division disturbingly exacerbated by social class.

The novel can be seen as a 'rites of passage' narrative, charting the painful transition from adolescence to adulthood. However, there is certainly no fairy-tale happy-ever-after ending and it is debatable whether the characters really do grow up. François, assuming responsibility for Yvonne and her baby, appears to confront and accept reality, and his rejection of the petulant, self-centred behaviour of Frantz suggests that he perceives the pernicious nature of misplaced idealism, but the closing lines, after Meaulnes's return, intimate that François continues to romanticize his friend, for he anticipates Meaulnes's further departure, his little daughter wrapped in a cloak, in search of new adventures. The ending is deeply melancholic. François senses the loss of the only thing left to him of the 'great adventure' in which he has invested all of his energies, emotions, and hope. Even the image of 'the happy couple', Frantz and Valentine, reunited by Meaulnes, is rendered problematic, for their domestic felicity is played out in the context of Frantz's childhood miniature cottage in the woods.

Alain-Fournier wrote of his desire to evoke 'the end of youth' ('la fin de la jeunesse'). The atmosphere of nostalgia and regret and the association of pure, ideal love with the landscape of childhood suggest that the narrative reflects the blighting of youthful ideals by reality. It is equally possible to argue, however, that the tragedy of this novel is that it is real-life happiness that is blighted.

—Penny Brown

ALBERTI (Merello), Rafael. Born in Puerto de Santa María, near Cádiz, Spain, 16 December 1902. Educated at the Jesuit Colegio de San Luis Gonzaga, Puerto de Santa María, 1912–17; studied painting in Madrid, 1917, and lived at the Residencia de Estudiantes. Married María Teresa León c.1930; one daughter. Worked as an impressionist and cubist painter until 1923; suffered from tuberculosis, 1923–24; co-founder, with his wife, *Octubre* magazine, 1934; director, Museo Romántico, Madrid, from 1936; co-founder and co-director, *El Mono Azul*, 1936–38; supported Republican government during Spanish Civil War (1936–39): co-founder, 1936, then secretary, Alliance of Anti-Fascist Intellectuals; subsequently joined the Communist Party; after the War, went into self-imposed exile: in Paris, 1939–40, Buenos Aires, 1940–63, and Rome, 1963–77; returned to Spain, 1977; elected deputy for the province of Cádiz, 1977. Recipient: National literature prize, 1925; Lenin prize, 1965; Etna-Taormina prize, 1975; Strega prize, 1976; Kristo Botev de Bulgaria prize, 1980; National Theatre prize, 1981; Pedro Salinas prize, 1981; Cervantes prize, 1983. Honorary doctorates: University of Toulouse, 1982; University of Cádiz, 1985. Commandeur de l'Ordre des Arts et des Lettres (France), 1982. Lives in Barcelona.

PUBLICATIONS

Verse

Marinero en tierra. 1925; edited by José Luis Tejada, 1987.
La amante: Canciones. 1926.
El alba del alhelí. 1927.
Sobre los ángeles. 1929; as *Concerning the Angels*, translated by Geoffrey Connell, 1967.
Cal y canto. 1929.
Consignas. 1933.
Un fantasma recorre Europa. 1933; as *A Spectre Is Haunting Europe: Poems of Revolutionary Spain*, translated by Ira Jan Wallach and Angel Flores, 1936.
Poesía 1924–1930. 1934.
Verte y no verte. 1934.
13 bandas y 48 estrellas. 1936.
Poesía 1924–1937. 1938.
Poesía 1924–1938. 1940.
Entre el clavel y la espada 1939–1940. 1941.
Vida bilingüe de un refugiado español en Francia. 1942.
Antología poética 1924–1940. 1942.
Pleamar 1942–1944. 1944.
Selected Poems, translated by Lloyd Mallan. 1944.
A la pintura: Cantata de la línea y del color. 1945; revised editions, 1948 and 1953; as *A la pintura*, translated by Ben Belitt, 1972.
Antología poética 1924–1944. 1945; revised edition, 1959.
Poesía 1924–1944. 1946.
El ceñidor de Venus desceñido. 1947.
Coplas de Juan Panadero (Libro I). 1949.
Buenos Aires en tinta china, edited by Attilio Rossi. 1951.
Retornos de lo vivo lejano 1948–1952. 1952; revised edition, 1972.
Ora marítima. 1953.
Baladas y canciones del Paraná. 1954.
Diez liricografías. 1954.
María Carmen Portela. 1956.
Sonríe China, with María Teresa León, illustrated by Alberti. 1958.
Cal y canto; Sobre los ángeles; Sermones y moradas. 1959.
El otoño otra vez. 1960.
Los viejos olivos. 1960.
Poesías completas. 1961.
Diez sonetos romanos. 1964.
Abierto a todas horas 1960–1963. 1964.
El poeta en la calle: Poesía civil 1931–1965. 1966.
Selected Poems, edited and translated by Ben Belitt. 1966.
Poemas de amor. 1967.
Balada de la bicicleta con alas. 1967.
Roma, peligro para caminantes 1964–1967. 1968.
Libro del mar, edited by Aitana Alberti. 1968.
Poesía anteriores a Marinero en tierra 1920–1923. 1969.
Los ocho nombres de Picasso, y No digo más que lo que no digo 1966–1970. 1970; *Los ochos nombres de Picasso* as *The Eight Names of Picasso*, translated by Gabriel Berns and David Shapiro, 1992.
Canciones del alto valle del Aniene, y otros versos y prosas 1967–1972. 1972.
Poesía 1924–1967, edited by Aitana Alberti. 1972.
The Owl's Insomnia: Poems (selection), edited and translated by Mark Strand. 1973.

Poemas del destierro y de la espera, edited by J. Corredor-Matheos. 1976.
Poesía. 1976.
Coplas de Juan Panadero 1949–1977; Vida bilingüe de un refugiado español en Francia 1939–1940. 1977; *Coplas de Juan Panadero* as *Poética de Juan Panadero*, 1987.
Poesía 1924–1977. 1977.
Sobre los ángeles; Sermones y morales; Yo era tonto y lo que he visto ha hecho dos tontos. 1977.
Poemas anteriores a Marinero en tierra; Marinero en tierra; La amante; Dos estampidas reales; El alba del ahelí. 1978.
Los cinco destacagados. 1978.
Signos del día; La primavera de los muebles. 1978.
El matador: Poemas escénicos 1961–1965. 1979.
Fustigada luz (1972–1978). 1980.
Canto de siempre. 1980.
101 sonetos (1924–1975). 1980.
Antología, edited by Jerónimo Pablo González Martín. 1980.
The Other Shore: 100 Poems, edited by Kosrof Chantikian, translated by José A. Elgorriaga and Paul Martin. 1981.
Versos sueltos de cada día: Primer y segundo cuadernos chinos (1979–1982). 1982.
X a X: Una correspondencia en verso (inedita) Roma–Madrid, with José Bergamín. 1982.
Robert Motherwell, el Negro, illustrated by Robert Motherwell. 1983.
Antología poética, edited by Natalia Calamaí. 1983.
Todo el mar. 1986.
Los hijos del drago, y otros poemas. 1986.
Golfo de sombras. 1986.
Retornos de un isla dichosa, y otros poemas. 1987.
Cuatro canciones. 1987.
Accidente: Poemas del hospital. 1987.
Canciones para Altair. 1989.
Antología comentada, edited by María Asunción Mateo. 2 vols., 1990.
Noventa poemas. 1992.

Plays

El hombre deshabitado (produced 1931). 1930; edited by Gregorio Torres Nebrera, with *Noche de guerra en el Museo del Prado*, 1991.
Santa Casilda (produced 1931).
Fermín Galán (produced 1931). 1931.
La pájara pinta (produced 1931?). 1964; in *Lope de Vega y la poesía contemporánea*, 1964.
Bazar de la providencia (produced 1934). In *Dos farsas revolucionarios*, 1934.
Dos farsas revolucionarios: Bazar de la providencia (negocio); Farsa de los Reyes Magos. 1934.
El enamorado y la muerte (produced 1936). In *Revista de Occidente*, 128, 1973.
Los salvadores de España (produced 1936). In *Cuadernos Hispanoamericanos*, 485–486, 1990.
De un momento a otro (produced 1938). 1937; edited by Gregorio Torres Nebrera, with *El adefesio*, 1992.
Radio Sevilla (produced 1937). In *Teatro de urgencia*, 1938.
Numancia, from the play by Cervantes (produced 1937; revised version produced 1943). 1937; as *La destrucción de Numancia*, 1975.
Cantata de los héroes y la fraternidad de los pueblos (produced 1938). 1938.
El ladrón de niños, from a play by Jules Supervielle (produced 1943).
El adefesio (produced 1944). 1944; edited by Gregorio Torres Nebrera, with *De un momento a otro*, 1992.

Farsa del licenciado Pathelin, from an anonymous French play (produced 1944). 1970.
El trébol florido (produced 1966). In *Teatro*, 1950.
Teatro (includes *El hombre deshabitado*; *El trébol florido*; *La gallarda*). 1950; enlarged edition (includes *El adefesio*), 1959.
Noche de guerra en el Museo del Prado (produced 1975). 1956; edited by Gregorio Torres Nebrera, with *El hombre deshabitado*, 1991; as *Night and War in the Prado Museum*, translated by Lemuel Johnson, in *Modern Spanish Theatre*, edited by Michael Benedikt and George E. Wellwarth, 1968.
Las picardías de Scapin, from a play by Molière (produced 1958).
El testamento de la rosa (produced 1962). In *Poemas escénicos*, 1962.
Poemas escénicos (dramatic poems). 1962.
La Lozana andaluza, from a work by Francisco Delicado (produced 1980). In *Teatro 2*, 1964.
Teatro 2 (includes *La Lozana andaluza*; *De un momento a otro*; *Noche de guerra en el Museo del Prado*). 1964.
El despertar a quien duerme, from a play by Lope de Vega (produced 1978). In *Primer Acto*, 178, 1975.

Screenplay: *La dama duende*, with María Teresa León, 1944.

Fiction

Selecciones: Relatos y prosa. 1980.
Prosas. 1980.

Other

La poesía popular en la lírica española contemporánea. 1933.
Nuestra diaria palabra. 1936.
Defensa de Catalunya. 1937.
El poeta en la España de 1931. 1942.
La arboleda perdida, y otras prosas. 1942; revised edition, 1959; as *The Lost Grove: Autobiography of a Spanish Poet in Exile*, edited and translated by Gabriel Berns, 1976.
Eh, los toros!, illustrated by Luis Seoane. 1942.
Imagen primera de Rafael Alberti (1940–1944). 1945.
Suma taurina: Verso, prosa, teatro, illustrated by Alberti, edited by Rafael Montesinos. 1963.
Lope de Vega y la poesía contemporánea (includes the play *La pájara pinta*). 1964.
Prosas encontradas 1924–1942, edited by Robert Marrast. 1970.
A Year of Picasso's Paintings. 1971.
Obras completas. 7 vols., 1972–88.
Picasso, el rayo que no cesa. 1975.
Maravillas con variaciones acrósticas en el jardín de Miró. 1975.
Teatro de agitación política, with others. 1976.
Cuaderno de Rute (1925): Un libro inédito. 1977.
Conversaciones con Rafael Alberti, with José Miguel Velloso. 1977.
Picasso (catologue), with others. 1977.
El poeta en la calle; De un momento a otro; Vida bilingüe de un refugiado español en Francia (poetry and plays). 1978.
Lo que conté y dije de Picasso. 1981.
Aire, que me lleva el aire (for children). 1981.
Federico García Lorca, poeta y amigo. 1984.
Otra Andalucía, with Julio Anguita. 1986.
A una verdad: Luis Cernuda, with others. 1988.
Obra completa, edited by Luis García Montero. 7 vols., 1988– .

La palabra y el signo. 1989.

Editor, *Églogas y fábulas castellanas*. 2 vols., 1944.
Editor, *Romancero general de la guerra española*. 1944.
Editor, with Guillermo de Torre, *Antología poética 1918–1936*, by Federico García Lorca. 1957.
Editor, *Poesías*, by Lope de Vega. 1965.
Editor, *Antología poética: Antonio Machado, Juan Ramón Jiménez, Federico García Lorca*. 1970.
Editor, *Antología poética*, by Pablo Neruda. 1982.

Editor and Translator, *Doinas y baladas populares rumanas*. 1964.

Translator, *Visages*, by Gloria Alcorta. 1951.
Translator, *Homenaje a la pintura*, by Robert Motherwell. 1991.

*

Critical Studies: *Rafael Alberti's Sobre los ángeles: Four Major Themes* by Cyril Brian Morris, 1966; *El mundo poético de Rafael Alberti* by Solita Salinas de Marichal, 1968; *Rafael Alberti* by Ignacio Delogue, 1972; *Rafael Alberti: Prosas encontradas 1924–1942* by Robert Marrast, 1973 (second edition); *Sobre Alberti* by Manuel Bayo, 1975; *Rafael Alberti* edited by Manuel Durán Gili, 1975; *The Theatre of Rafael Alberti* by Louise B. Popkin, 1975; *La poesía de Rafael Alberti* by Ricardo Senabre, 1977; *Rafael Alberti* by Jerónimo Pablo González Martín, 1978; *The Poetry of Rafael Alberti: A Visual Approach* by Robert C. Manteiga, 1978; *El dilema de la nostalgia en la poesía de Rafael Alberti* by Barbara Dale May, 1978; Alberti issue of *Malahat Review*, July 1978; *Revolution and Tradition: The Poetry of Rafael Alberti* by Pieter Wesseling, 1981; *El teatro de Rafael Alberti* by Giorgio Torres Nebrera, 1982; *Rafael Alberti: El escritor y la crítica* by Manuel Durán, 1984; *La poesía de Rafael Alberti* by Antonio Jimenez Millan, 1984; *Dramatists in Perspective: Spanish Theatre in the Twentieth Century* by Gwynne Edwards, 1985; *Multiple Spaces: The Poetry of Rafael Alberti* by Salvador Jiménez Fajardo, 1985; *Rafael Alberti: Poesía del destierro* by Concha Argente del Castillo, 1986; *Rafael Alberti's Poetry of the Thirties: The Poet's Public Voice* by Judith Nantell, 1986; *Antología comentada de Rafael Alberti* edited by María Asunción Mateo, 2 vols., 1990; *Inquietud y nostalgia: La poesía de Rafael Alberti* by Kurt Spang, 1990; *Rafael Alberti: Arte y poesía de vanguardia* by Pedro Guerrero Ruiz, 1991; *Lorca, Alberti, and the Theater of Popular Poetry* by Sandra Robertson, 1992.

*   *   *

Rafael Alberti's theatre and poetry can be separated only with difficulty, for numerous areas of thematic and stylistic similarity exist. Not only does his first attempt at theatre, *La pájara pinta* [The Painted Bird], written in the *guiñolesque* (puppet) tradition, parallel early poetic works, but the surrealism of his poetry collection *Sobre los ángeles* (*Concerning the Angels*), echoes in the imagery of his play of the same period, *El hombre deshabitado* [The Uninhabited Man]. Several of his Civil War plays repeat the titles and themes of poetry collections produced during the conflict (1936–39), while the later play *Noche de guerra en el Museo del Prado* (*Night and War in the Prado Museum*) connects directly to *A la pintura* [To Painting], poetry written in exile and devoted to his cherished avocation.

Alberti is considered primarily a poet, and his fame rests on his lyrics; yet his plays have been performed by numerous troupes since Franco's death: he is not an insignificant dramatist. His plays are largely historical, and their political—even propagandist—intent dominates his 'urgent theatre' (including *Bazar de la providencia* [Bazaar of Providence], *Farsa de los Reyes Magos* [Farce of the Three Kings], *Los salvadores de España* [Saviours of Spain], *Radio Sevilla* [Radio Seville] and *Cantata de los héroes y de la fraternidad de los pueblos* [Song of Heroes and Fraternity Among Peoples]). Because the propagandist content, resulting from war-time urgency, is less overt in *Night and War in the Prado Museum*, this play (influenced by Bertolt Brecht both in its staging conventions —it has a play within the play—and its intent) exemplifies his best political theatre. Recalling the Nationalist bombardment of Madrid, the play depicts efforts of Republican militia and partisans to save national treasures. Characters from Goya's paintings are brought to life to join contemporary patriots in their struggle. Political ideology is essentially absent in earlier plays such as *Fermín Galán*, and is not the major thrust of the plays *De un momento a otro* [From One Moment to the Next], *El trébol florido* [The Flowering Clover], *La gallarda* [The Graceful Woman], or *El adefesio* [The Ridiculous Gentleman]. *La Lozana andaluza* [The Attractive Andalusian Woman] is based on the 1528 picaresque novel by Francisco Delicado.

As one of the more versatile and prolific poets of the Generation of 1927 (which included equally famous contemporaries such as Federico García Lorca, Vicente Aleixandre, and Luis Cernuda), Alberti evolves similarly to those colleagues who survived the Civil War, from early post-romanticism through the baroque, neo-Gongorine mode for which the generation first became known, through subsequent vanguardist experimentation, and then to war-influenced political commitment and engagement. Despite relatively facile initial success with his first three collections, *Marinero en tierra* [Landlocked Sailor], *La amante* [The Lover], and *El alba del alhelí* [Dawn of the Gillyflower], rooted in Spain's popular oral balladry tradition, Alberti consciously incorporated generational innovations in his own verse. Thus a more stylized, baroque poetry appears in *Cal y canto* [Whitewash and Song], whose later poems reflect influences of the Ultraist movement. *Concerning the Angels* (written during a personal crisis) is Alberti's most surrealist work.

The *engagé* ideological nature of his 1930s poetry intensifies from the transitional civil elegy, 'Con los zapatos puestos tengo que morir' [I Must Die with My Shoes On] through *Consignas* [Watchword], *Un fantasma recorre Europe* (*A Spectre Is Haunting Europe*), and *13 bandas y 48 estrellas* [13 Bars and 48 Stripes], culminating in *El poeta en la calle* [The Poet in the Street], 'Romances de la guerra de España' [Spanish War Ballads], and *De un momento a otro* [From One Moment to the Next]. Reflections of exile appear in *Vida bilingüe de un refugiado español en Francia* [The Bilingual Life of a Spanish Refugee in France] and collections written in Argentina: *Entre el clavel y la espada* [Between the Carnation and the Sword]; *Pleamar* [High Tide]; *Retornos de lo vivo lejano* [Songs of a Vivid Past], re-creating some especially significant moments in the poet's life; *Buenos Aires en tinta china* [Buenos Aires in Indian Ink]; and 'Poemas de Punta del Este' [Poems from Punta del Este]. Alberti's leftist political connections motivate a continuing vein of Marxist ideology in much of his exile poetry, notably in *Coplas de Juan Panadero* [Ditties of Juan the Baker] and 'La primavera

de los pueblos' [Springtime of the Peoples]. *Sonríe China* [China Smiles], done in collaboration with his wife, María Teresa León, followed a visit to China.

Alberti's best poetry from Argentina celebrates his paternity and love for his daughter, born in exile, in *Pleamar*, and *Baladas y canciones del Paraná* [Songs and Ballads of the Paraná River]. In Italy, Alberti's political fervour slowly waned, and other emphases appear in *Poemas de amor* [Love Poems], *Roma, peligro para caminantes* [Rome, Danger for Pedestrians], *Los ocho nombres de Picasso* (*The Eight Names of Picasso*), and *Canciones del alto valle del Aniene* [Songs of the Upper Aniene Valley]. *El matador: Poemas escénicos* [The Matador: Scenic Poems] reveals that the bullfight continues to fascinate Alberti just as when he wrote his early elegy on the death of Ignacio Sánchez Mejías, 'Verte y no verte' [To See You and Not See You].

The partisan nature of Alberti's political poetry makes it difficult to read or judge impartially, and certain critics have dismissed it as tendentious and overly propagandist. Some of his verse is excessively allegorical, yet it contains unique rhetorical and metrical innovations and many expressive images, particularly in *Entre el clavel y la espada*, his most creative political expression. The best-known, most frequently studied and anthologized of Alberti's poems are in his first four collections. The childlike perspective and notes of fantasy with which the poet re-creates his native fishing village in *Marinero en tierra* make it a mythical paradise, and here, as in *La amante*, the poet's great love for the sea imbues his lines with lyric passion.

Nevertheless, the darkly serious, subjective poems of *Concerning the Angels* are considered by many his greatest achievement. Through contrasts (of good and evil, light and dark) and antithetical images, Alberti portrays his emotional crisis in an oneiric landscape of air and fire. Another critical favourite, *El alba del alhelí*, recreates popular customs, myths, and beliefs of Andalusia, expressing rural traditions, joys, and sufferings through popular metric forms drawn from oral culture. The unpretentious early works have proven to be the most widely known and enduring aspects of Alberti's work.

—Janet Pérez

ALEIXANDRE (Merlo), Vicente. Born in Seville, Spain, 26 April 1898. Family moved to Malaga, 1900, and to Madrid, 1909. Educated at the Colegio Teresiano, Madrid, 1909–13; entered Central School of Commerce and the University of Madrid (Faculty of Law), 1914, licence in law and diploma in business administration, both 1919. Lecturer in mercantile law, Central School of Commerce, Madrid, 1919–22; worked for Andalusian Railroads, 1921–25: had to retire on grounds of ill health, 1925; staff member, *La Semana Financiera* magazine; full-time writer from 1925; suffered serious illness, 1936–39. Recipient: National literature prize, 1933; Spanish Academy prize, 1934; Critics prize, 1963, 1969, 1975; Nobel prize for literature, 1977. Member, Royal Spanish Academy, 1949, Hispanic Society of America, and Monde Latin Academy, Paris. Corresponding member, Arts Academy, Malaga, and Sciences and Arts Academy, Puerto Rico. Honorary fellow, Professors of Spanish Association (USA).

Grand Cross of Order of Carlos III, 1977. *Died 13 December 1984.*

PUBLICATIONS

Verse

Ámbito. 1928.
Espadas como labios. 1932; edited by José Luis Cano, with *La destrucción o El amor*, 1972.
Pasión de la tierra. 1935; revised edition, 1946; edited by Luis Antonio de Villena, 1976, and by Gabriele Morelli, 1987.
La destrucción o El amor. 1935; edited by José Luis Cano, with *Espadas como labios*, 1972; as *Destruction of Love*, in *Destruction of Love and Other Poems*, translated by S. Kessler, 1977.
Sombra del paraíso. 1944; edited by Leopoldo de Luis, 1976; selection as *Poemas paradisíacos*, 1952, edited by José Luis Cano, 1977; as *Shadow of Paradise*, translated by Hugh A. Harter (bilingual edition), 1987.
Mundo a solas 1934–1936. 1950.
Nacimiento último. 1953.
Historia del corazón. 1954.
Mis poemas mejores. 1956; revised editions, 1966, 1968, 1976.
Poesías completas. 1960.
Poemas amorosos. 1960; revised edition, 1970.
Antigua casa madrileña. 1961.
Picasso, edited by A. Caffarena Such. 1961.
En un vasto dominio. 1962.
Presencias. 1965.
Retratos con nombre. 1965.
Dos vidas. 1967.
Poemas de la consumación. 1968.
Poemas varios. 1968.
Poesía superrealista. 1971.
Antología del mar y la noche, edited by J. Lostale. 1971.
Sonido de la guerra. 1972.
Arguijo: Obra poética. 1972.
Diálogos del conocimiento. 1974.
Antología total, edited by Pere Gimferrer. 1975.
Antología poética, edited by Leopoldo de Luis. 1977.
Twenty Poems (bilingual edition), translated by Robert Bly and Lewis Hyde. 1977.
A Longing for the Light: Selected Poems, edited and translated by Lewis Hyde. 1979.
The Crackling Sun: Selected Poems, translated by Louis M. Bourne. 1981.
A Bird of Paper, translated by Willis Barnstone and David Garrison. 1982.
Primeros poemas. 1985.
Nuevos poemas varios, edited by Irma Emiliozzi and Alejandro Duque Amusco. 1987.
Vicente Aleixandre para niños, edited by Leopoldo de Luis. 1988.
En gran noche: Últimos poemas, edited by Carlos Bousoño and Alejandro Duque Amusco. 1991.

Other

En la vida del poeta: El amor y la poesía. 1950.
El niño ciego de Vázquez Díaz. 1954.
Algunos caracteres de la nueva poesía española. 1955.
Los encuentros. 1958; enlarged edition, edited by José Luis Cano, 1985.
Obras completas. 1968; revised edition, 2 vols., 1977–78.
Epistolario, edited by José Luis Cano. 1986.

Prosas recobradas, edited by Alejandro Duque Amusco. 1987.
Miré los muros: Textos inéditos y olvidados. 1991.
Antología esencial. 1993.

*

Critical Studies: *La poesía de Vicente Aleixandre* by Carlos Bousoño, 1950, revised editions, 1968, 1977; *Vicente Aleixandre* by Leopoldo de Luis, 1970, revised edition as *Vida y obra de Vicente Aleixandre*, 1978; *Vicente Aleixandre* (in English) by Kessel Schwartz, 1970; *La poesía superrealista de Vicente Aleixandre* by Hernán Galilea, 1971; 'The Spiritualization of Matter in the Poetry of Vicente Aleixandre' by Louis M. Bourne, in *Revista de Letras*, 22, 1974; *Tres poetas a la luz de la metáfora: Salinas, Aleixandre y Guillén* by Vicente Cabrera, 1975, and *Critical Views on Vicente Aleixandre's Poetry* (includes translations) edited by Cabrera and Harriet Boyar, 1979; *Vicente Aleixandre* edited by José Luis Cano, 1977; *Conocer: Vicente Aleixandre y su obra* by Antonio Colinas, 1977; *La poesía de Vicente Aleixandre (formacion y evolución)* by Vicente Granados, 1977; *La palabra poética de Vicente Aleixandre* by D. Puccini, 1979; *Vicente Aleixandre: A Critical Appraisal* edited by Santiago Daydí-Tolson, 1981; *Vicente Aleixandre* by J.O. Jiménez, 1981.

* * *

Educated in strict religious private schools, Vicente Aleixandre had no contact with poetry until a chance acquaintance with the future poetry critic Dámaso Alonso, in the summer of 1917, initiated him into it, via the latter's enthusiasm for Rubén Darío. Aleixandre read Antonio Machado and Juan Ramón Jiménez, under whose influence he wrote his first lyrics (never published). The modernist sensibility was foreign to him, but Gustavo Adolfo Bécquer and the Romantics were to be lasting influences, as were the mystic poets, especially St John of the Cross.

Fearing an adverse reception, he kept his poetic activity secret until some poems composed in isolated convalescence in the Guadarrama Mountains were read by friends, who published them in Ortega y Gasset's prestigious *Revista de Occidente* under the title 'Número' [Number], reflecting the 'dehumanized' vogue of poetry of the day. Aleixandre's association with other poets of the Generation of 1927 dates from this time: friendships were initiated with Gerardo Diego, Jorge Guillén, Luis Cernuda, Frederico García Lorca, and Miguel Hernández (and he had met Rafael Alberti at an art exhibition in 1922). Aleixandre participated in the group's homage to the baroque poet Góngora in 1927, and with these colleagues he subsequently moved toward vanguardism.

His first collection, *Ámbito* [Ambit], like 'pure poetry' of that time, sought the geometric ideal of its practitioners whose poems were conceived as polyhedrons. None the less, *Ámbito* was typical of Aleixandre, in its symbols of sea and night (which recur throughout his work) and in its irrational, elusive imagery. Insistent chiaroscuro and visions of cosmic love convey the poet's attempts to fuse with the universe. The surrealistic prose poems of *Pasión de la tierra* [Passion of the Earth] reflect Aleixandre's discovery of Freud (he read the Spanish translation of *The Interpretation of Dreams* in 1928). *Pasión de la tierra* has been considered one of the key works of Spanish surrealism, despite the author's denials of such descriptions. In 1971, Aleixandre published an anthology entitled *Poesía superrealista*, seemingly accepting the label at last. Spanish surrealism is an unorthodox variant, also called 'super-realism', 'hyper-realism', and even 'neo-Romanticism'. While some critics consider it an offshoot of French surrealism, others find its origins in the painters Goya and Solana, and the 'grotesque' plays (*esperpentos*) of Valle-Inclán. Vanguardism in Spain in the late 1920s was not exclusively surrealist, nor were there collective surrealist manifestos, although Aleixandre is reputed to have planned one together with Luis Cernuda and Emilio Prados. Irrationalism and a search for new techniques stand in lieu of common norms, formulated doctrines, and the desire to scandalize.

Like most other Spanish writers classed as surrealist (Lorca, Cernuda, Alberti), Aleixandre is unorthodox, rejecting 'automatic writing', but suppressing logical control via elimination of nexus. He employs normal punctuation in *Pasión de la tierra*, but not in *Espadas como labios* [Swords like Lips] which juxtaposes love and death, offering glimpses of an irrational, erotic pantheism in which Thanatos and Eros are interchangeable.

La destrucción; o, el amor (*Destruction of Love*), won the National literature prize in 1933, and for many represents the zenith of Aleixandre's surrealism. Its exuberant vitalism, directly linked to his illness and successful fight for life, depicts unleashed cosmic forces in a mysterious universe, where nature is simultaneously destroyed and created, and where the inanimate triumphs over the living. Filled with images of light and darkness, the volume has an internal logic resulting from its amorous unity showing love as an all-consuming force.

The pessimistic *Mundo a solas* [World Alone], written shortly after the death of his mother, abounds in telluric beings and powers, expressing a passionate striving towards love, but not exempt from cruelty and morbidity. *Sombra del paraíso* (*Shadow of Paradise*), a book of light and clarity, masterful chiaroscuro, and experimental metaphors, depicts a purified pre-human world of beauty and innocence. The atmosphere is Mediterranean, pantheistic, mythic, with the major theme being the poet's lost paradise of infancy and childhood in Málaga.

Aleixandre describes his works as being illuminated by varicoloured lights—black in *Pasión*, red in *Destruction of Love*, brighter colours in *Mundo a solas*, and, in *Shadow of Paradise*, the white glare of midday. In *Nacimiento último* [Final Birth], a transitional work closing his cosmic cycle, light becomes diaphanous, transparent. Aleixandre's development from the surrealistic prose poems of *Pasión de la tierra* to the stark vision of death in *Nacimiento último* becomes, metaphorically, a drama of progressive enlightenment or illumination. The final stage of this progression is *Historia del corazón* [History of the Heart], with its gamut of light and shade, a turning point emphasizing historical existence, human joys, and sorrows, in a temporal rather than cosmic universe. Considered Aleixandre's masterpiece by most critics, *Historia del corazón* marks man's emergence from the background of the poetry to assume the role of protagonist in the poet's post-war historical and social preoccupations.

En un vasto dominio [In a Vast Domain] unites the human and the cosmic elements through love, its title reflecting the presence of the collectivity. *Poemas de la consumación* [Poems of Consummation] explores the epistemological preoccupations of the ageing poet, who meditates on knowledge, doubt, hope, youth, and old age, as he approaches death. *Diálogos del conocimiento* [Dialogues of Knowledge], Aleixandre's final collection, published when the poet was 76, introduces several speakers whose monologues contrast sensuality and meditation and juxtapose intuitive, existential, idealistic, cynical, and transcendental views.

Social poetry in Spain during the 1950s and 1960s was essentially political, an implied indictment of the ideology perpetuating social injustice—poetry of protest. Aleixandre's treatment of existential material is far removed from sociopolitical criticism and the manner of a sociological casebook to which much poetry of these years descended. His final poetry is less exuberant in its imagery, more restrained and reflective, without being totally purged of surrealistic elements. His last works do not merely repeat the forms of earlier ones, but evolve toward greater sobriety and thoughtfulness—poetry of the intellect and intuition, poetry as epistemology, meditations upon the metaphysical, rendered in a manner somewhere between that of the philosopher and the mystic.

—Janet Pérez

ALF LAILA WA-LAILA. See **THE THOUSAND AND ONE NIGHTS.**

ALL MEN ARE BROTHERS. See **WATER MARGIN.**

ALFIERI, Vittorio. Born in Asti, Italy, 16 January 1749. Educated at Royal Academy, Turin, 1759–66. Served as an ensign, 1766 (resigned commission, 1774). Travelled extensively in Europe, 1767–72; began lifelong relationship with Luisa Stolberg, Countess of Albany, 1777; fled from revolutionary Paris with the Countess, 1792, settled in Florence; left Florence during the French occupation. *Died 8 October 1803.*

PUBLICATIONS

Collections

Opere postume. 13 vols., 1804.
Opere, edited by Francesco Maggini. 1926–33.
Opere, edited by Luigi Fassò and others. 35 vols., 1951– .
Opere I, edited by Mario Fabini and Arnaldo DiBenedetto. 1977.

Plays

Tragedie. 3 vols., 1783–85; enlarged edition, 1789.
Tragedie. 6 vols., 1787–89; edited by U. Brilli, 1961.
The Tragedies, translated by Charles Lloyd. 4 vols., 1815; revised edition, edited by E.A. Bowring, 2 vols., 1876.
Commedie, edited by Simona Costa. 1990.

Verse

L'America libera: Odi. 1784; as *Ode to America's Independence*, translated by Adolph Caso (bilingual edition), 1976.
Parigi sbastigliata. 1789.
Rime. 1789.
L'Etruria vendicata. 1800.

Other

La virtù sconosciuta: Dialogo. 1786.
Della tirannide. 1789; as *Of Tyranny*, translated by Julius A. Molinaro and Beatrice Corrigan, 1960.
Del principe e delle lettere. 1795; edited by Luigi Rosso, 1943; as *The Prince and Letters*, translated by Julius A. Molinaro and Beatrice Corrigan, 1972.
Il misogallo: prose e rime. 1799.
Vita. 1806; as *Memoirs*, translated anonymously, 1810, revised edition, by E.R. Vincent, 1961; as *The Autobiography of Vittorio Alfieri*, translated by C. Edwards Lester, 1845, and by Henry McAnally, 1949; as *Life of Vittorio Alfieri*, 1877.

Translator, *Panegirico a Trajano*, by Pliny. 1787.
Translator, [Works], by Sallust. 1826.

*

Bibliography: *Bibliografia di Vittorio Alfieri* by G. Bustico, 3rd edition, 1927; *La critica alfieriana* by W. Binni, 1951.

Critical Studies: *Vittorio Alfieri: Forerunner of Italian Nationalism* by Gaudens Megaro, 1930; *Alfieri: A Biography* by Charles R.D. Miller, 1936; *Ritratto dell'Alfieri* by Mario Fubini, 1967; *Saggi alfieriani* by Walter Binni, 1969; *Studi e ricerche sulla genesi e le fonti delle commedie alfieriane* by Giuseppe Santarelli, 1971; *Alfieri comico* by V. Placella, 1973; *Studi alfieriani vecchi e nuovi* by Carmine Mensi, 1974; *Gli affetti nella tragedia di Vittorio Alfieri* by Pino Mensi, 1974; *Vittorio Alfieri* by Guido Nicastro, 1974; *Di Vittorio Alfieri e della tragedia* by F. Portinari, 1976; *Il messaggio poetico dell'Alfieri: La natura del limite tragico* by Mario Travato, 1978; *Vittorio Alfieri* (in English) by Franco Betti, 1984; *Vittorio Alfieri e la cultura piemontese fra illuminismo e rivoluzione* edited by Giovanna Ioli, 1985.

* * *

'A truly remarkable individual', Vittorio Alfieri was called by his contemporary Alessandro Verri, a judgement anyone will concur in who reads the *Vita* (*Memoirs*) without being waylaid, as earlier critics were, by doubts as to their reliability. From 1775, after having spent six restless years in intellectually stimulating European travels and three years in frivolous aristocratic pursuits in Turin, Alfieri turned to literature, and henceforth his life was intensely and single-mindedly devoted to his studies and his writing. His major public objective was to give Italy tragedy, the genre it lacked almost completely and which had recently been brought to new splendour in France. To achieve this he had to master a language which, as a French-speaker since birth, was virtually foreign to him. The project came to fruition in 19 tragedies (23, if the first one, rejected by him, and the so-called post-humous ones are added), their range, according to George

Steiner, 'an index to the romantic imagination'. The style he forged for himself was unique, a radical departure from the melodious, often sing-song verses for which Italian lyric poetry, thanks to the *Arcadia* and Metastasio, was famous. 'Mi trovan duro? . . . Taccia ho d'oscuro?' ('They find me difficult/harsh? . . . I have the reputation of being obscure?'), he asked in an epigram dated 30 July 1783, harbinger of his repeated efforts at self-clarification.

Alfieri's tragedies have been classified variously: chronologically by periods, treated as Greek, Roman, and modern; by themes, as tragedies of love, freedom, royal ambition, familial affections, and inner struggle; or again, as those in which fate predominates, those built on the contrast between liberty and servitude, and those in which the tyrant triumphs over his victims. But no doubt the best comprehensive commentary on his work—which he approaches both diachronically and synchronically—is his own self-exegesis: in his answer written to the critic Calsabigi in 1783, in his 'Parere dell'autore su le presenti tragedie' [The Author's Opinions on the Present Tragedies] prepared for the 1789 Paris edition, repeatedly in the *Memoirs*, and indirectly but forcefully in *Del principe e delle lettere* (*The Prince and Letters*). What distinguishes Alfieri's perception of his originality is his self-knowledge: his grounding of the impulse that led him to tragedy in his passionate reaction to great deeds (such as those recorded in Plutarch's *Lives*) and his desire to emulate them in the only arena—art—in which he felt his times gave him freedom to act; and secondly, his intimate understanding of the stubborn determination needed to vanquish the difficulties of a genre which he conceived of as exceptionally concentrated and concise, making no allowances for even such normal procedures in drama as the use of secondary characters and episodic actions. Basing himself on the distinctions of classical theories of rhetoric between *inventio*, *dispositio*, and *elocutio* (the selection of a subject, its distribution into its component parts or acts and scenes, its expression, which in his case meant turning it into verses), he detailed the various stages through which each of his tragedies passed, incidentally leaving an analysis of composition, a blueprint for the construction of a text, which continues to be valid even today. The unity he achieves is not given; it is arrived at. But in a circular movement that goes back to the moment of 'inspiration'—the *impulso naturale*, the *bollore di cuore e di mente* (the natural impulse, the excitement of heart and mind), so eloquently described in *The Prince and Letters*—he ends up by giving its due to the inescapable coherence of content and form in great art.

From the point of view of *inventio* (or originality), Alfieri thought of his tragedies as falling into two groups: the few 'new' ones (on subjects never before treated in tragic form) and the majority, in which he strove to 'make something new out of something old'. Among the first group are two of his recognized masterpieces, *Saul* and *Mirra*, both of which depart from the model most frequently associated with Alfieri, the unmasker of arbitrary power and its trappings as analysed in the treatise *Della tirannide* (*Of Tyranny*). In the dramatization of the struggle between the aged Biblical King and the young David, in which the accent falls on the human rather than regal destiny of the 'tyrant' condemned to fearful solitude, even the usual norms of neo-classical tragedy are broken by the insertion into the text of David's songs (passages that remind us that Alfieri was also a great lyric poet, in the tradition of Petrarch). In his retelling on stage of Ovid's story of the incestuous love of Mirra for her father, Alfieri defies the rules of *bienséance* and creates a work of the utmost dramatic tension as the hapless protagonist—no more than a young girl—is again and again on the verge of revealing a secret (to which the spectator who knows his classics is privy), whose ultimate telling spells self-imposed death.

—Olga Ragusa

SAUL
Play by Vittorio Alfieri, 1785 (written 1782).

Vittorio Alfieri's tragedy, *Saul*, is considered to be one of the dramatist's masterpieces, along with the equally famous work, *Mirra*. Respectful of the Aristotelian three unities of space, time, and action, the play is a testament to the author's concept of liberty. For Alfieri, liberty is more than a political ideal. It is the desire to give value and meaning to his life beyond the confines of death and destiny. Thus the individual affirms the personal dignity of his own spirit. The tragic hero, Saul, is the embodiment of these ideals. *Saul* is the only one of Alfieri's dramas to be drawn from biblical material. Enthusiastic after reading the Old Testament for the first time, the dramatist felt compelled to evoke the figure of the noble hero. Saul was forsaken even by God, but was not content to allow himself to be rendered impotent. His struggle in the face of great adversity rendered him fascinating to the poet. The biblical account on which Alfieri based his plot is contained in the *First Book of Samuel*, 9–31 and the *First Book of the Chronicles*, 10. The details of the story of Saul are made more linear by the poet in order to underscore the psychological study of the protagonist. In a burst of creativity, the frenetic composition of *Saul* took place between April and September of 1782.

Saul, a great warrior of humble origin, has been anointed king by the high priest Samuel, and, as leader of the Israelite army, has achieved numerous victories on the battlefield. As his capacity as a leader increases, Saul gradually detaches himself from his ties of obedience to the priestly caste, revoking the ire of God. Samuel is ordered secretly to anoint as king a humble shepherd, David. The new king becomes the closest friend of Saul's son, Jonathan, and marries Saul's daughter, Michol. Although, initially, Saul loves David as another son, he soon becomes jealous of the young hero and begins to hate him. He persecutes David until the young man is forced into hiding in the enemy camp of the Philistine army. The tragedy takes place at Gelboa where Saul and the Israelite forces are encamped ready to affront an enemy attack. David attempts to reach the Israelite forces in order to help his people in the imminent battle. Alfieri's drama presents an astute psychological study of Saul's final day which ends in a military defeat and the protagonist's suicide. The tragedy takes place entirely in the Israelite camp at Gelboa.

Central to the tragedy is the powerful figure of Saul, who easily overshadows the three supporting characters of his children, Jonathan and Michol, and his enemy, David. Saul, the play's hero, is profoundly alone and, indeed, his only antagonist lies within himself. The spiritual complexity of the protagonist is the key to understanding the drama. The king is torn apart by an intense interior struggle between conflicting passions: his paternal love for Jonathan and Michol, his tyrannical desire for political and military power, the realization of his decadence, and a desperate desire to recover his youthful grandeur. He is overcome by remorse and disgust with the squalid nature of his old age. This explains his ambivalence towards David. Saul's hatred of David is provoked by envy, yet he loves the young hero as a son because he recognizes in David the grandeur of his own lost youth.

Saul is at once a tyrant and a hero: tyrant because he desires total control of every situation and a hero because, in the final scene, he finds the courage to overcome the errors of his past and recuperate once more his own human and royal dignity in death. In the final act of the tragedy, Saul's world disintegrates. Abner announces the enemy's victory and the death of the king's sons before fleeing himself. In choosing suicide, Saul dies a hero. His death represents an act of protest and is a courageous affirmation of his own heroic desire for freedom. Saul's final words: 'Empia Filiste,/ me troverai, ma almen da re, qui . . . morto' V.v. (Vile Philistine, me thou shalt find, but at least a king . . . here . . . dead) show that in his choice of death he becomes master of his own fate. He dies in regal splendour, 'like a king'. The play closes with Saul's moral victory, not only over the tangible, Philistine enemy, but also over the personal demons which torment him: in death, he recovers his dignity. Alfieri is known as a poet of vast emotions ('forte sentire') and the struggles depicted in his portrait of Saul are among the most moving moments of his entire dramatic corpus.

—Jordan Lancaster

AMADO (de Faria), Jorge (Leal). Born in Ferradas, Itabuna, Bahia, Brazil, 10 August 1912. Educated at the Jesuit Colégio Antônio Vieira, Salvador, 1923–26; entered the Ginásio Ipiranga, Salvador, 1926; Faculty of Law, Federal University, Rio de Janeiro, 1931–35, diploma in law 1935. Married 1) Matilde Garcia Roas in 1933 (separated 1944), one daughter; 2) Zélia Gattai in 1945, one son and one daughter. Reporter, *Diário da Bahia*, 1927, and contributor, *A Luva*, *Samba*, *Meridiano*, *A Semana*, *O Momento*, *O Jornal*, *Diário de Notícias*, *A Gazeta de Notícias*, and *O Correiro do Povo*, 1927–30; moved to Rio de Janeiro, 1930; editor, *Revista Rio Magazine*, 1933; worked for José Olímpio, publishers, from 1934; editor, *A Manhã*, the publication of the opposition Aliança Nacional Libertadora [National Freedom Alliance]; co-editor, Centro de Cultura Moderna's *Movimento*, 1934–35; imprisoned for suspected involvement in coup attempt, 1935, and his books banned, 1938–43; travelled to Mexico and the USA, 1937; editor, *Dom Casmurro*, 1938–39, and contributor, *Diretrizes*, 1939; lived mainly in Argentina, 1941–42; returned to Brazil, 1942, and was re-arrested and confined to the Bahia region; contributor, 'Diário da Guerra' column for *O Imparcial*, from 1943; editor, *Hoje*, São Paulo, 1945; after the fall of Getúlio Vargas's regime (1930–45), elected Communist deputy for the São Paulo region, 1945, until the Party again declared illegal in 1947; went into exile: in Paris, 1947–49, Scandinavia and Eastern Europe, 1949–50, and Prague, 1950–51; travelled to China and Mongolia, 1952; returned to Brazil, 1952; founder, *Para Todos*, Rio de Janeiro, and its editor, 1956–58; travelled to Cuba and Mexico, 1962; settled in Salvador, 1963; visited Canada and USA 1971: writer in residence, Pennsylvania State University; lived in London, 1976. Delegate, first Brazilian Writers Congress, 1945; vice-president, Brazilian Union, 1954; co-organizer, first Festival of Brazilian Writing, 1960. Recipient: Graça Aranha Foundation prize; Stalin peace prize, 1951; National literary prize, 1958; Gulbenkian prize (Portugal), 1971; Italian Latin-American Institute prize, 1976; Nonnino literary prize (Italy),

1983; Neruda prize, 1989; Volterra prize (Italy), 1989; Sino del Duca prize (Paris), 1990; Mediterranean prize, 1990. Member, Brazilian Academy, since 1961; corresponding member, East German Academy of Science and Letters. Commander, Légion d'honneur, 1984. Lives in Rio Vermelho, Bahia, Brazil.

PUBLICATIONS

Fiction

Lenita, with Dias da Costa and Edison Carneiro. 1930.
O país do carnaval. 1932.
Cacau. 1933.
Suor. 1934; translated as *Sweat*, 1937.
Jubiabá. 1935; as *Jubiabá*, translated by Margaret A. Neves, 1984.
Mar morto. 1936; as *Sea of Death*, translated by Gregory Rabassa, 1984.
Capitães de areia. 1937; as *Captains of the Sands*, translated by Gregory Rabassa, 1988.
Terras do sem fim. 1942; as *The Violent Land*, translated by Samuel Putnam, 1945; revised editions, 1965 and 1989.
São Jorge dos Ilhéus. 1944.
Seara vermelha. 1946.
Os subterrâneos da liberdade: Os asperos tempos, Agonia da noite, A luz no túnel. 3 vols., 1954.
Gabriela, cravo e canela. 1958; as *Gabriela, Clove and Cinnamon*, translated by William L. Grossman and James L. Taylor, 1962.
Os velhos marinheiros: Duas histórias do cais de Bahia (includes *A morte e a morte de Quincas Berro d'Água*). 1961; *A morte e a morte de Quincas Berro d'Água* published separately, 1978; as *Home Is the Sailor*, translated by Harriet de Onís, 1964; as *The Two Deaths of Quincas Wateryell*, translated by Barbara Shelby, 1965.
Os pastores da noite. 1964; as *Shepherds of the Night*, translated by Harriet de Onís, 1966.
Dona Flor e seus dois maridos. 1966; as *Dona Flor and Her Two Husbands*, translated by Harriet de Onís, 1969.
Tenda dos milagres. 1969; as *Tent of Miracles*, translated by Barbara Shelby, 1971.
Tereza Batista, cansada de guerra. 1972; as *Tereza Batista, Home from the Wars*, translated by Barbara Shelby, 1975.
O gato malhado e a andorinha sinhá (for children). 1976; as *The Swallow and the Tomcat: A Love Story*, translated by Barbara Shelby Merello, 1982.
Tieta do Agreste, pastora de cabras. 1977; as *Tieta the Goat Girl*, translated by Barbara Shelby Merello, 1979.
Farda, fardão, camisola de dormir: Fábula para acender uma esperança. 1979; as *Pen, Sword, Camisole: A Fable to Kindle a Hope*, translated by Helen R. Lane, 1985.
Tocaia grande: a face obscura. 1984; as *Showdown*, translated by Gregory Rabassa, 1988.
O sumiço da santa: Uma história de feitiçaria: Romance baiano. 1988; as *The Golden Harvest*, translated by Clifford E. Landers, 1992.
A descoberta da América pelos turcos ou como do o árabe Jamil Bichara, desbravador de florestas, de visita à cidade de Itabuna para dar abasto ao corpo, ali lhe ofereceram fartura e casamento ou ainda os esponsais de Adma. 1992.

Verse

A estrada do mar. 1938.

Play

O amor de Castro Alves. 1947; as *O amor do soldado*, 1958.

Other

ABC de Castro Alves (biography). 1941.
Vida de Luis Carlos Prestes, o cavaleiro da esperança (biography). 1942; as *O Cavaleiro da Esperança*, 1945.
Obras. 17 vols., 1944–67.
Bahia de todos os santos: Guia das ruas e dos mistérios da cidade do Salvador (travel writing). 1945.
Homens e coisas do partido comunista (political writings). 1946.
O mundo da paz (travel writing). 1951.
Obras ilustradas. 19 vols., 1961–72.
O mistério dos MMM, with others. 1962.
Bahia boa terra Bahia, with Carybé and Flávia Damm. 1967.
Iconografia dos deuses africanos no Candomblé da Bahia, with Pierre Verger and Waldeloir Rego. 1980.
O menino Grapiúna (memoirs). 1982.
A cidade de Bahia, with Carybé, photographs by Mario Cravo Neto. 1984.
Terra mágica da Bahia, with Alain Draeger. 1984.
A bola e o goleiro (for children). 1984.
Navegação de cabotagem. 1992.

*

Bibliography: *Brazilian Literature: A Research Guide* by David William Foster and Walter Rela, 1990.

Critical Studies: *Brazil's New Novel: Four Northeastern Masters* by Fred P. Ellison, 1954; *Escritores Brasileiros Contemporâneos* by Renard Perez, 1960; *Jorge Amado: Vida e obra* (includes bibliography) by Miécio Táti, 1961; 'Poetry and Progress in Jorge Amado's *Gabriela, cravo e canela*' by Richard A. Mazzara, in *Hispania*, 46, 1963; 'The Five Faces of Love in Jorge Amado's Bahian Novels' by Gregory Rabassa, in *Revista de Letras*, 1963; *Gabriela: seu cravo e sua canela*, 1964, *Os mistérios de vida e os mistérios de Dona Flor*, 1972, *O barroco e o maravilhoso no romance de Jorge Amado*, 1973, and *A contraprova de Tereza, Favo-de-Mel*, 1973, all by Juarez da Gama Batista; 'Narrative Focus in Jorge Amado's Story of Vasco Moscoso Aragão' by Judith Bernard, in *Romance Notes*, 8, 1966; 'Afro-Brazilian Cults in the Novels of Jorge Amado' by Russell G. Hamilton, in *Hispania*, 50(2), 1967; 'The "New" Jorge Amado' by Elizabeth Schlomann Lowe, in *Luso-Brazilian Review*, 6, 1969; *Criaturas de Jorge Amado* by Paulo Tavares, 1969; 'Allegory in Two Works of Jorge Amado' and 'Moral Dilemma in Jorge Amado's *Dona Flor e seus dois maridos*' both in *Romance Notes*, 13, 1971, and 'Duality in Jorge Amado's *The Two Deaths of Quincas Wateryell*', in *Studies in Short Fiction*, 15, 1978, all by Malcolm Noel Silverman; 'The Preservation of African Culture in Brazilian Literature: The Novels of Jorge Amado' by Maria Luísa Nunes, in *Luso-Brazilian Review*, 10, 1973; 'Popular Poetry in the Novels of Jorge Amado' by Nancy T. Baden, in *Journal of Latin American Lore*, 2(1), 1976; 'The *Malandro*, or Rogue Figure, in the Fiction of Jorge Amado', in *Mester*, 6, 1976, and 'Double Perspective in Two Works of Jorge Amado', in *Estudios Iberoamericanos*, 4, 1978, both by Bobby J. Chamberlain; 'Jorge Amado, Jorge Desprezado' by Jon S. Vincent, in *Luso-Brazilian Review*, 15 (supplement), 1978; *Jorge Amado: Política e literatura* by Alfredo Wagner Berno de Almeida, 1979; 'The Problem of the Unreliable Narrator in Jorge Amado's *Tenda dos milagres*' in *Romance Quarterly*, 30, 1983, and 'Structural Ambiguity in Jorge Amado's *A morte e a morte de Quincas Berro d'Água*' in *Hispania*, 67, 1984, both by Earl E. Fitz; 'The Guys and Dolls of Jorge Amado' by L. Clark Keating, in *Hispania*, 66, 1983; 'Jorge Amado: Morals and Marvels' by Daphne Patai, in her *Myth and Ideology in Contemporary Brazilian Fiction*, 1983; 'Jorge Amado: Populism and Prejudice' by David Brookshaw, in *Race and Color in Brazilian Literature*, 1986.

* * *

Jorge Amado is described rightly as Brazil's best-known novelist. An exceedingly prolific writer whose work has spanned seven decades, Amado has been writing since 1930 and he published his first novel, *O país do carnaval* [Carnival Country] in 1932; in 1992, the year of his 80th birthday, he published a volume of memoirs, *Navegação de cabotagem* [Coastwise Shipping], and a novella, *A descoberta da América pelos turcos ou de como o árabe Jamil Bichara, desbravador de florestas, de visita à cidade de Itabuna para dar abasto ao corpo, ali lhe ofereceram fartura e casamento ou ainda os esponsais de Adma* [America's Discovery by the Turks, or How the Arab Jamil Bichara, Clearer of Forests, on a Visit to the City of Itabuna to Fortify His Body, was Offered Abundance and Marriage, or Even the Marriage Vows of Adma], destined to mark the quincentenary of Christopher Columbus's discovery of America. His works have been translated into some 40 languages, adapted for film, and serialized for television. There is some disagreement among critics about the 'literariness' of his work, but this has affected neither his popularity nor, indeed, his immense readability. Several controversies surround his literary output, and critical opinion is divided as to whether or not his early novels are little more than crude exposées of sociopolitical conditions driven by left-wing ideology, whether he is sexist in his attitude to women, and whether his works, regardless of how well-intentioned, enshrine and perpetate racist attitudes.

Amado made his literary debut as an exponent of the Northeastern novel, and the greater part of his work has retained this regional bias. Few of his novels do not have as their geographical setting Salvador, capital of Bahia, or the cacao-producing region of Northeastern Brazil.

It is usual to separate Amado's work into two main phases. The first, stemming, from a strong ideological commitment to depict the Northeastern reality as faithfully as possible, begins with *O país do carnaval* and ends with *Capitães da areia* (*Captains of the Sands*). In these novels he chooses as his subject-matter some of the typical motifs of the Northeast: the drought and its effects on the inhabitants of the region; the plight of the hired plantation workers, and the urban poor; the situation of the black man in Brazil. His later works, from *Terras do sem fim* (*The Violent Land*) onwards, are characterized by a greater preoccupation with style and technique, incorporating elements of lyricism, humour, irony, and what some critics have tagged 'magical socialism'.

Any attempt to evaluate Amado's writing must inevitably lead to the conclusion that his major achievement is the group of novels that constitute his 'cacao cycle'. In *Cacau*, the situation in the Northeast is interpreted very much in terms of the class struggle. Although this work is not an aesthetic success, it introduces the themes that find a fuller, more artistic expression years later in *The Violent Land*, a 'tropical western' considered by many to be Amado's best work. It deals with the conquest of the land, when ruthless men cleared the jungle to plant cacao, then fought for political control over their empires. *The Violent Land* focuses on the bloodthirsty struggle between two such planters, Colonel Horácio Silveira and Juca Badaró. The emphasis is on epic deeds rather than denunciation of social evils, and the main protagonist of the novel is the land itself.

São Jorge dos Ilhéus [St George of the Islanders] continues the story told in *The Violent Land*, with more political content than its predecessor. It chronicles the transition from the pioneering days to the emergence of a new ruling class, the exporters, who employ different means to conquer the land. Whereas Amado views the pioneers with mingled affection and respect, it is clear that he feels a profound antipathy for the new order.

Gabriela, cravo e canela (*Gabriela, Clove and Cinnamon*) takes as its subject the city of Ilhéus during the period 1925 to 1926. This is very much a work of Amado's maturity, and romanticism and humour take precedence over social and political comment. The background of the novel is one of social change, with an ongoing conflict between defenders of the *status quo* and those who desire progress. Against the backdrop is narrated the love story of Nacib, the son of immigrants, and Gabriela, the picaresque *mulata* who comes out of the backlands to fuel male fantasies.

In 1984 Amado returned to the early days of the cacao region in *Tocaia grande: a face obscura* (*Showdown*), whose tone is predominantly nostalgic.

In his later works, Amado becomes increasingly interested in the art of story-telling, introducing elements of fantasy and popular culture into his novels. He is particularly interested in presenting strong female protagonists who symbolize for him the struggle against exploitation—the most notable being Tereza Batista in *Tereza Batista, cansada de guerra* (*Tereza Batista, Home from the Wars*) and Tieta in *Tieta do Agreste* (*Tieta the Goat Girl*)—and showing how they overcome adversity by using their sexuality as a weapon. However, as feminist critics have pointed out, the author is not advocating a radical change in the situation of women; rather he tends to emphasize the traditional stereotype of women as dependent on men for emotional and financial security.

The importance of Afro-Brazilian elements in Amado's work should not be overlooked—for instance, in *Jubiabá*, *Gabriela, Clove and Cinnamon*, and *Tenda dos milagres* (*Tent of Miracles*). In the numerous interviews he has given over the years, Amado has always insisted that Brazilian society, just as Brazilian Portuguese, must be understood as the product of the intermingling of various cultures, religions, and traditions. Thus he makes much of the religious syncretism to be found in the Northeast. It has, however, been suggested that his novels also reinforce white myths about the Afro-Brazilian containing what might be perceived as elements of prejudice.

Amado selects very specific aspects of the Brazilian social reality, focusing on the poor and disadvantaged, on blacks and women, as well as the rich and powerful. He might almost be described as the Master of the Brazilian picaresque, concentrating on the marginal elements of society and recounting their adventures with evident gusto, for instance, the escapades of Vadinho in *Dona Flor e seus dois maridos* (*Dona Flor and Her Two Husbands*), or the eponymous Quincas Berro d'Água (*The Two Deaths of Quincas Wateryell*).

Amado's writing derives much of its vigour from oral narrative tradition and his subject-matter is unashamedly popular and picturesque. His overall achievement has been to write with exuberance and affection about the region and society he knows best. He will be remembered above all for his rich and creative use of the Brazilian idiom and for the essentially Brazilian characters he has created.

—P.A. Odber de Baubeta

———

ANACREON. Born in Teos, Ionia, Asia Minor, c.570 BC. When the Persians invaded in about 540 BC, left for Thrace, where he helped compatriots found the Greek colony of Abdera; tutor to the son of the tyrant Polycrates at Samos; after Polycrates' fall, invited to Athens by Hipparchus, son of the tyrant Pisistratus; may have gone to Thessaly after the assassination of Hipparchus in 514 BC. Honoured by statue on Acropolis. *Died c.475 BC.*

PUBLICATIONS

Verse

[Works], edited by T. Bergk, in *Poetae lyrici Graeci*, vol. 3, 1843, and in *Anthologia lyrica*, 1854; also edited by Valentino Rose, 1868, B. Gentile, 1948, and M.L. West, 1984; selections in *Poetae Melici Graeci* (with commentary), edited by Denys Page, 1962, *Supplementum Lyricis Graecis*, 1974, and in *Greek Lyric Poetry* (with commentary), edited by David A. Campbell, 1982.
Anacreon Done into English, translated by Francis Willis, Thomas Wood, Abraham Cowley, and John Oldham. 1683, reprinted 1923.
The Odes, translated by Thomas Moore. 1800; also translated by Erastus Richardson, 1928.
The Anacreonta, translated by P.M. Pope. 1955.

*

Critical Studies: *Anacréon et les poèmes anacréontiques*, edited by A. Delbaille, 1891, reprinted 1970; *Sappho und Simonides* by U. von Wilamowitz-Moellendorff, 1913; *Anacreon* (in Italian) by B. Gentili, 1958; *Greek Lyric Poetry* by C.M. Bowra, 1961; *The Poetics of Imitation: Anacreon and the Anacreontic Tradition* (with Greek and Latin texts) by Patricia A. Rosenmeyer, 1992.

* * *

Anacreon composed various kinds of poetry, including iambics, elegies, epigrams, and choral maiden-songs, but he is most celebrated for his short lyric pieces. The setting for many poems is the aristocratic symposium, where wine and witty conversation flowed freely. Anacreon wrote mainly in the metre known as the 'anacreontic' (anaclastic ionic dimeter) or in a mixture of glyconic and pherecratean rhythms; his poetry represents the peak of technical skill in the Greek monodic tradition. The careful choice and deft positioning of words create a concise and symmetrical perfection of expression, as exemplified by poem 395:

My temples are already grey and my head white;
Graceful youth is no longer with me, my teeth are old,

And of sweet life no long time is now left:
So often I weep, terrified of Tartarus,
For the chasm of Hades is dreadful, and the road down
    is
Painful; and, for certain, he who goes down does not
    return.

Epithets and colours are judiciously chosen: the spear is 'tearful' and Eros is 'melting', while nymphs are 'blue-eyed', Eros is 'golden-haired' throwing a 'purple' ball, and Persuasion shines 'silver'. Effective metaphors are found, such as the 'crown' of the city, referring to its walls, and also images, such as the leap from the Leucadian rock, 'into the grey wave, drunk with love'.

The subject matter of Anacreon's lyrics is typical of the genre: love, wine, the onset of old age, and death. He generally eschews certain other topics, such as politics and warfare, which were so popular with poets like Alcaeus. In eleg. fragment 1, he makes clear his preference:

I do not like the man who, while drinking wine near a
    full mixing-bowl,
Speaks of strife and tearful war,
But whoever, by combining the shining gifts of the
    Muses and Aphrodite,
Recalls the lovely good cheer.

Personal invective in the tradition of Archilochus is represented by poem 388, which ridicules a certain Artemon, who used to go about in filthy clothes and hang around with whores: now he travels in a lady's carriage, holding an ivory parasol. This piece indicates that Anacreon was well able to compose in the barbed style.

In the poems and fragments which survive, the poet is particularly concerned with the bittersweet experience of love with both boys and girls, as in poem 360:

O boy with the girlish look,
I am after you, but you do not notice,
Unaware that you hold
The reins of my soul.

Several poems are addressed to Eros, the god of love, who is variously depicted as a boxer, a smith, and a dice-player (with dice called Madness and Confusion). In Anacreon's verses, Eros is often a violent and disruptive force, envisaged as a personal opponent, who toys with and abuses his victims. Yet at the same time there is a general lightness of tone in the description of these little love affairs, befitting their sophisticated symposiastic context. Thus, even though the poet often names the objects of his passion, such as Cleoboulus, there is a sense that the romance is inevitably fleeting, and all part of the delightful intoxication induced by the 'honey-sweet wine'. After Eros, the deity most frequently mentioned is, appropriately enough, Dionysus.

Fragment 347 comes from a poem which appears to have been a not entirely serious lament for the lost locks of Smerdis, who has come back from the barber looking less beautiful than before:

Now you are bald and your hair,
Having fallen into rough hands,
Has flown down all at once
Into the black dust,

Having miserably fallen upon
the cut of the iron;
and I am worn away with anguish. . . .

Anacreon's verses, then, are not simply frivolous, but lack the personal intensity of, say, Sappho. Their tone is usually ironic, which creates a distancing effect. Here, the cutting of a youth's hair provokes an exaggerated and amusing reaction in his lover. The almost tragic tone of the lament sits incongruously with such a trivial event. Yet the falling of the severed hair into the black dust is symbolic of death, and the 'iron' suggests not only the barber's blade, but also the sword of war. The cutting of the young man's hair represents a rite of passage, and momentarily takes us away from the carefree atmosphere of the banquet to the harsh world of daily life and its conflicts. For the young Greek male, warfare was almost as inevitable as death itself. It is this co-existence of the light and the dark, of the comic and the serious, which gives Anacreon's poetry its peculiar charm and which led to numerous imitations. Sixty of these are collected in a 10th-century manuscript of the Palatine Anthology and are known as the *Anacreonta*. None of the imitations is likely to be earlier than the Hellenistic period; while falling short of the original in linguistic virtuosity and versification, they are not without charm, and testify to the distinctive contribution of Anacreon to the Greek poetic tradition.

—David H.J. Larmour

ANDERSEN, Hans Christian. Born in Odense, Denmark, 2 April 1805. Educated at schools in Odense to age 14; alone in Copenhagen, 1819–22, and patronized by various benefactors: loosely associated with the singing and dancing schools at Royal Theatre, 1819–22; attended Slagelse Latin school, 1822–26, and Elsinore grammar school, 1826–27; tutored in Copenhagen by L.C. Müller, 1827–28; completed *examen artium*, 1828. Freelance writer from 1828: royal grant for travel, 1833, 1834, and pension from Frederik VI, 1838; granted title of professor, 1851; privy councillor, 1874. Knight of Red Eagle (Prussia), 1845; Order of the Dannebrog, 1846; Knight of the Northern Star (Sweden), 1848; Order of the White Falcon (Weimar), 1848. *Died 4 August 1875.*

PUBLICATIONS

Collections

Samlede skrifter [Collected Writings]. 33 vols., 1853–79; 2nd edition, 15 vols., 1876–80.
Romaner og rejseskildringer [Novels and Travel Notes], edited by H. Topsøe-Jensen. 7 vols., 1941–44.
Fairy Tales, edited by Svend Larsen, translated by R.P. Keigwin. 4 vols., 1951–60.
Complete Fairy Tales and Stories, translated by Erik Haugaard. 1974.
Samlede eventyr og historier [Collected Tales and Stories], edited by Erik Dal. 5 vols., 1975.

Fiction

Improvisatoren. 1835; as *The Improvisatore; or, Life in Italy*, translated by Mary Howitt, 1845.
Eventyr: Fortalt for børn [Fairy Tales for Children]. 6 vols., 1835–42; *Nye Eventyr* [New Fairy Tales], 4 vols., 1843–47; edited by Erik Dal and Erling Nielsen, 1963–; numerous subsequent translations.

O.T. 1836; as *O.T.; or, Life in Denmark*, translated by Mary Howitt, with *Only a Fiddler*, 1845.
Kun en Spillemand. 1837; as *Only a Fiddler*, translated by Mary Howitt, with *O.T.*, 1845.
Billedbog uden billeder. 2 vols., 1838–40; as *Picture Book Without Pictures*, translated by Hanby Crump, 1856; as *Tales the Moon Can Tell*, translated by R.P. Keigwin, 1955.
Eventyr og historier [Tales and Stories]. 1839; *Nye Eventyr og Historier*, 6 vols., 1858–67; edited by Hans Brix and Anker Jensen, 5 vols., 1918–20.
De to baronesser. 1848; as *The Two Baronesses*, translated by Charles Beckwith Lohmeyer, 1848.
A Poet's Day Dreams (selected tales). 1853.
At være eller ikke være. 1857; as *To Be, or Not to Be?* translated by Mrs Bushby, 1857.
Later Tales, translated by Caroline Peachey. 1869.
Lykke-Peer. 1870; as *Lucky Peer*, translated by Horace E. Scudder, 1871.

Verse

Digte [Poems]. 1830.
Samlede digte [Collected Poems]. 1833.
Seven Poems, translated by R.P. Keigwin. 1955.
Udvalgte digte [Selected Poems]. 1975.

Plays

Kjærlighed paa Nicolai Taarn [Love on St Nicholas Tower] (produced 1829). 1829.
Skibet, from a play by Scribe. 1831.
Bruden fra Lammermoor, music by Ivar Bredal, from the novel *The Bride of Lammermoor* by Scott (produced 1832). 1832.
Ravnen [The Raven], music by J.P.E. Hartmann, from a play by Gozzi (produced 1832). 1832.
Agnete og Havmanden [Agnete and the Merman], music by Nils V. Gade, from Andersen's poem (produced 1833). 1834.
Festen paa Kenilworth [The Festival at Kenilworth], music by C.E.F. Weyse, from the novel *Kenilworth* by Scott (produced 1836).
Skilles og mødes [Parting and Meeting] (produced 1836). In *Det Kongelige Theaters Repertoire*, n.d.
Den Usynlige paa Sprogø [The Invisible Man on Sprogø] (produced 1839).
Mulatten [The Mulatto], from a story by Fanny Reybaud (produced 1840). 1840.
Mikkels Kjærligheds historier i Paris [Mikkel's Parisian Love Stories] (produced 1840).
Maurerpigen [The Moorish Girl] (produced 1840). 1840.
En comedie i det grønne [Country Comedy], from a play by Dorvigny (produced 1840).
Fuglen i pæretræet [The Bird in the Pear Tree] (produced 1842).
Kongen drømmer [Dreams of the King] (produced 1844). 1844.
Dronningen paa 16 aar [The 16-Year-Old Queen], from a play by Bayard. 1844.
Lykkens blomst [The Blossom of Happiness] (produced 1845). 1847.
Den nye barselstue [The New Maternity Ward] (produced 1845). 1850.
Herr Rasmussen (produced 1846). Edited by E. Agerholm, 1913.
Liden Kirsten [Little Kirsten], music by J.P.E. Hartmann, from the story by Andersen (produced 1846). 1847.

Kunstens dannevirke [The Bulwark of Art] (produced 1848). 1848.

En nat i Roskilde [A Night in Roskilde], from a play by C. Warin and C.E. Lefevre (produced 1848). 1850.

Brylluppet ved Como-Søen [The Wedding at Lake Como], music by Franz Gläser, from a novel by Manzoni (produced 1849). 1849.

Meer end perler og guld [More Than Pearls and Gold], from a play by Ferdinand Raimund (produced 1849). 1849.

Ole Lukøie [Old Shuteye] (produced 1850). 1850.

Hyldemoer [Mother Elder] (produced 1851). 1851.

Nøkken [The Nix], music by Franz Gläser (produced 1853). 1853.

Paa Langebro [On the Bridge] (produced 1864).

Han er ikke født [He Is Not Well-Born] (produced 1864). 1864.

Da Spanierne var her [When the Spaniards Were Here] (produced 1865). 1865.

Other

Ungdoms-forsøg [Youthful Attempts]. 1822.

Fodreise fra Holmens Canal til Østpynten af Amager i 1828 og 1829 [A Walking Trip from Holmen's Canal to Amager]. 1829.

Skyggebilleder af en Reise til Harzen. 1831; as *Rambles in the Romantic Regions of the Harz Mountains*, translated by Charles Beckwith Lohmeyer, 1848.

En digters bazar. 1842; as *A Poet's Bazaar*, translated by Charles Beckwith Lohmeyer, 1846; as *A Visit to Germany, Italy and Malta*, translated by Grace Thornton, 1987.

Das Märchen meines Lebens ohne Dichtung (in collected German edition). 1847; as *The True Story of My Life*, translated by Mary Howitt, 1847; as *Mit eget eventyr uden digtning*, edited by H. Topsøe-Jensen, 1942.

I Sverrig. 1851; as *Pictures of Sweden*, translated by Charles Beckwith Lohmeyer, 1851; as *In Sweden*, translated by K.R.K. MacKenzie, 1852.

Mit livs eventyr. 1855; revised editions, 1859, 1877; edited by H. Topsøe-Jensen, 1951; as *The Story of My Life*, translated by D. Spillan, 1871; as *The Fairy Tale of My Life*, translated by W. Glyn Jones, 1954; in part as *The Mermaid Man*, translated by Maurice Michael, 1955.

I Spanien. 1863; as *In Spain, and A Visit to Portugal*, translated by Mrs Bushby, 1864; as *A Visit to Spain*, edited and translated by Grace Thornton. 1975.

Collected Writings. 10 vols., 1870–71.

Breve, edited by C.S.A. Bille and N. Bøgh. 2 vols., 1878.

Briefwechsel mit dem Grossherzog Carl Alexander von Sachsen-Weimar-Eisenach, edited by Emil Jonas. 1887.

Correspondence with the Late Grand-Duke of Saxe-Weimar, Charles Dickens, etc., edited by Frederick Crawford. 1891.

Optegnelsesbog, edited by Julius Clausen. 1926.

Breve til Therese og Martin R. Henriques 1860–75 (correspondence), edited by H. Topsøe-Jensen. 1932.

Brevveksling med Edvard og Henriette Collin (correspondence), edited by H. Topsøe-Jensen. 6 vols., 1933–37.

Brevveksling med Jonas Collin den Ældre og andre Medlemmer af det Collinske Hus (correspondence), edited by H. Topsøe-Jensen. 3 vols., 1945–48.

Romerske Dagbøger [Roman Diaries], edited by Paul V. Rubow and H. Topsøe-Jensen. 1947.

Brevveksling (correspondence), with Horace E. Scudder, edited by Jean Hersholt. 1948; as *The Andersen–Scudder Letters*, translated by Waldemar Westergaard, 1949.

Reise fra Kjøbenhavn til Rhinen [Travels from Copenhagen to the Rhine], edited by H. Topsøe-Jensen. 1955.

Brevveksling (correspondence), with Henriette Wulff, edited by H. Topsøe-Jensen. 3 vols., 1959–60.

Breve til Mathias Weber (correspondence), edited by Arne Portman. 1961.

Levnedsbog 1805–1831 [The Book of Life], edited by H. Topsøe-Jensen. 1962.

Et besøg i Portugal 1866, edited by Poul Høybye. 1968; as *A Visit to Portugal 1866*, translated by Grace Thornton, 1972.

Skuggebilleder, edited by H. Topsøe-Jensen. 1968.

Breve til Carl B. Lorck (correspondence), edited by H. Tøpsoe-Jensen. 1969.

Dagbøger 1825–75, edited by Kåre Olsen and H. Topsøe-Jensen. 12 vols., 1971–76; as *Diaries*, edited and translated by Patricia Conroy and Sven H. Rossel, 1989.

Tegninger til Otto Zinck [Drawings for Otto Zinck], edited by Kjeld Heltoft. 2 vols., 1972.

Rom dagbogsnotater og tegninger [Diary and Drawings from Rome], edited by H. Topsøe-Jensen. 1980.

Album, edited by Kåre Olsen and others. 3 vols., 1980.

*

Bibliography: *Andersen bibliografi 1822–1875* by B.F. Nielsen, 1942; *Andersen litteraturen 1875–1968* by Aage Jørgensen, 1970, supplement, 1973.

Critical Studies: *Hans Christian Andersen: His Life and Work* edited by Svend Dahl and H. Topsøe-Jensen, 1955; *Hans Christian Andersen: A Biography* by Fredrick Böök, 1962; *Hans Christian Andersen and the Romantic Theatre* by Frederick J. Marker, 1971; *Hans Christian Andersen and His World* by Reginald Spink, 1972; *Hans Christian Andersen: The Story of His Life and Work, 1805–75* by Elias Bredsdorff, 1975; *Hans Christian Andersen* by Bo Grønbech, 1980; 'Andersen's Love' by Peter Brask and Turid Sverre, in *The Nordic Mind: Current Trends in Scandinavian Literary Criticism* edited by Frank E. Andersen and John Weinstock, 1986; *H.C. Andersen og Thalia* by Hans Christian Andersen, 1992.

* * *

The fame of Hans Christian Andersen—H.C. Andersen to his fellow countrymen and Hans Andersen to countless readers outside Denmark—is founded on paradox. Although he was—and is—a very distinctly Danish author, he was anything but parochial. Well-read, well-informed about the cultural and scientific developments of his time, and well-travelled—some of Andersen's travel-books still deserve attention, e.g., *En digters bazar* (*A Poet's Bazaar*)—he made a name for himself both in his own country and internationally as a novelist during his own lifetime. And yet, as the physicist H.C. Ørsted told a sceptical Andersen, if his novels made him famous, his fairy-tales would make him immortal.

Andersen's first love was the theatre, but in spite of his many works for the stage—of which *Mulatten* [The Mulatto] was the most significant—he was more at home in the free form of the novel than in the conventionally more disciplined forms of lyric and drama. His first novel, *Improvisatoren* (*The Improvisatore*), soon became popular abroad because of its perceptive descriptions of the colourful Italian life and landscapes. Like much of Andersen's work, including the fairy-tales, it had its roots in his own experience, and aspects of his own childhood among the lower classes formed part of the next two novels, *O.T.* and *Kun en Spillemand* (*Only a Fiddler*). He described his life directly in his autobiography, *Mit livs eventyr* (*The Fairy Tale of My Life*).

If the novel had given him greater freedom, it was only in the shorter form of the fairy-tale, which did not demand control of long plots or complex characterization, that he found his true medium. Andersen's first tales were published in 1835. That they gave him a reputation as a children's writer is no coincidence: the earliest among his 156 tales were written for children, and until 1843 his published collections carried the subtitle 'Told for Children'. As he gained confidence and increasingly wrote original stories—in fact only a minority, e.g., 'Fyrtøjet' ('The Tinder Box'), 1835, derive from traditional folk-tales—he abandoned that subtitle and increasingly addressed himself to a grown-up audience. Stories like 'Historien om en Moder' ('Story of a Mother', 1848) can be understood but not fully appreciated by children. Andersen's great achievement was to develop the form of the folk-tale into original, mature art in a way which has not been surpassed, and he did so partly by creating a new literary language which was essentially that of spoken narration, free of abstractions, concrete and deceptively simple. His best tales reveal his keen sense of observation of human behaviour and his deep understanding of the major issues of human existence, told with humour and sympathy.

—Hans Christian Andersen

THE EMPEROR'S NEW CLOTHES
Story by Hans Christian Andersen, 1837.

Hans Christian Andersen wrote this story, about a vain emperor who would rather spend his time in his dressing room than in the Council Chamber, in 1837, borrowing the plot from a Spanish tale. It is one of his most popular stories and has been translated into at least 25 languages. The story tells how one day two rascals come to the emperor, claiming to be the best of weavers. Not only was their cloth unusually beautiful, but clothes made from it were invisible to everyone who was either incompetent or exceedingly stupid.

The emperor thought this was an excellent opportunity to learn who was stupid and incompetent and who was not, so he employed the two impostors. They immediately began work, asking for the finest silk and gold, which they put in their bags, while they pretended to work on the empty loom. After a while, the emperor wanted to know how much they had done but, as he was a little hesitant about going himself, he sent his old and trusted Prime Minister. The old man looked at the loom and saw nothing. He was not, however, about to admit to this, because he did not believe himself to be either incompetent or stupid. Thus he praised the invisible cloth and memorized the weaver's description of it. A little later the emperor sent another trusted statesman who also pretended to see the fabric in the empty loom. Everyone was talking about the marvellous cloth. Finally, the emperor himself, together with a select group of trusted advisers, went to see the weavers who demonstrated the 'fantastic fabric'. Everyone, including the emperor, pretended to see the beautiful cloth and it was decided that the emperor was to wear the clothes made from it at the next great parade.

Soon the rascals set out to make the clothes and, when the day for the parade arrived, the emperor stepped out on the street stark naked, under the banner heading the parade. Everybody admired his new clothes and commented on how magnificent they looked, until a little child said: 'But he has no clothes at all'. Soon people began to whisper to each other what the innocent child had said. The whispers grew louder until all the people shouted the truth. The emperor himself believed them to be right but nevertheless finished the parade in style.

This ending was an afterthought, as Andersen initially ended the story with everyone admiring the new clothes. Not until he had sent the manuscript to the printer did he come upon the present ending. A major change from the original Moorish version was the quality of the cloth itself. In the original it was invisible to any man not a son of his presumed father, which makes it a tale about men's fear and suspicions about women's fidelity and trustworthiness and their power over men's honour. Andersen, however, made it a tale about human weakness in a more general sense. To borrow some phrases from Bo Grønbech, he made it a tale about how people are afraid of other people's opinion, how people are afraid to see things as they are, and how people do not dare to be honest to themselves. Interestingly, in Andersen's tale it is the adults who believe in magic, and the child who sees reality.

'The Emperor's New Clothes' has posed a special challenge to illustrators, despite being a popular subject. How, after all, do you draw an emperor without clothes? A popular solution, particularly with the earlier illustrators such as Vilhelm Pedersen, was to picture him in his undershirt, decently covering his body down to his knees. Some early illustrators did show the emperor naked, but placed members of the crowd so that decency was maintained. Arthur Rackham drew him in silhouette, somewhat ridiculous with a fat stomach. The tale's potential for political satire was used by a Czech artist in 1956 who pictured the emperor as a fat pig. A 1923 woodcut from Germany displays mean and power-hungry faces on the emperor and his retinue.

As time has progressed and the rules about decency have become more relaxed, the emperor has become gradually more naked. In a number of children's books from the 1980s he is a fat, jovial ruler with bare buttocks. It should be remembered, however, that Andersen's emperor kept his dignity even as the whisperings around him grew stronger, and continued the parade carrying himself more proudly than ever. Thus, while he did not set out to be a good role model for emperors and others, he ended up as such.

—Torborg Lundell

THE SNOW QUEEN
Story by Hans Christian Andersen, 1845.

'The Snow Queen' is one of the most striking and original, and the longest, of Andersen's fairy-tales. It is though, in some ways, atypical. This is most obvious in its peculiar structure, consisting of one long story formed by seven shorter tales. As the individual stories would make little sense on their own, these divisions seem at first to be entirely arbitrary. Closer study reveals that they serve to divide the action, like a dream (and like many traditional fairy-tales), into a series of 'moves'. Each move offers a new narrative and a new scene to deal with previously established themes and symbols.

In terms of plot, 'The Snow Queen' is the story of the search by a little girl, Gerda, for her friend Kay, who has been seduced from his home by the Snow Queen. Through this outward task Gerda is launched on what becomes an inner quest to strength and maturity. At the climax of her journey, her kiss redeems little Kay from the Snow Queen's physical and spiritual imprisonment, symbolized by a lump of ice in his heart. Both may then return to the known world they have left behind, whereon they find they have reached adulthood.

In thematic terms, 'The Snow Queen' is generated by the opposition of two principles. The story plays continually with the interaction of these two principles, and of the symbols that represent them. The first is the summer principle of joy and sacrificial love, symbolized by the rose, by tears, and by the colour red. The second is the winter principle of evil, cold calculation, and spiritual death. It is symbolized by the Snow Queen, by snow and ice, and by the colour white. The polarization between these two forces, and the moral values they carry, is made apparent early on in the tale when we are told that in summer the rose bushes formed a bridge between the children, but in the winter the snow divided them. Shortly after, Kay issues a challenge to the Snow Queen: 'Only let her come . . . I'll set her on the stove and then she'll melt'. The Snow Queen does come but, far from conquering her, Kay is drawn captive into her queendom, first inwardly, then outwardly.

Searching to find Kay again, Gerda is at first drawn away from him into the heart of the opposing queendom, symbolized by the colour red. Throughout the tale, the clothing and nakedness of Gerda's hands and feet take on unusual prominence: on her departure from the Princess's bedchamber she has acquired 'not only boots but also a muff', and it is her red shoes which lead her to the red house. There she falls under the benign spell of a good witch, is fed with cherries, and sleeps in a bed 'with red silk pillows embroidered with coloured violets, and she dreamed as pleasantly as a Queen on her wedding day'.

The witch's garden is stocked with beautiful flowers. Gerda converses with seven of the flowers, and subtle symbolism threads through their apparent nonsense. While Gerda learns nothing about little Kay from them, each flower's tale contains a hint or glimpse of her own destiny. The narcissus tells of a girl half undressed, discovering herself; the convolvulus of a maiden waiting for her knight; the hyacinth of three sisters, the last clad in white, who, while beautiful, are dead; the tiger-lily of a Hindu woman, clad in red, burning herself for love; the buttercup of a holy kiss which turns everything to gold; and the snowdrop, of a burst bubble. The flowers themselves, and their tales, each reflect an aspect of the climactic scene of Kay's redemption. When Gerda has listened to each of their tales she is inwardly prepared. At once she finds the summer has gone and she must seek Kay in the winter world of the Snow Queen.

The world she enters is a bare, fantastic landscape of castles and wastes of snow. Like a dream the tale shows an almost infinite capacity for creativity within its established symbols. Rose and snow undergo the magical transformation of their form into another substance, creating strange and beautiful harmonies. Beneath Kay's magnifying glass snowflakes appear as roses of ice; in the Princess's Palace the flowers appear inwrought into the furnishings: 'Over the centre of the floor two beds, each resembling a lily, hung from a step of gold. One, in which the princess lay, was white, the other was red'.

That Andersen is interested in the unconscious mind is demonstrated even within the story. In the palace Gerda finds herself mysteriously transposed in 'inner', psychic, space where the shadowy forms of the sleepers' dreams throng around her.

This magical world that at once represents the worlds 'within and without' has a profoundly different atmosphere from the enchanted but familiar feel of most of Andersen's other tales. It is a truly fantastic realm, embodying elements of psychic experience in symbolic form. It is a spiritual landscape, conveyed at times in ecstatic prose: 'Over them flew the black screaming crows and above all shone the moon, clear and bright—and so Kay passed through the long winter's night, and by day he slept at the feet of the Snow Queen'.

Gerda's journey has the same unearthly quality, lit by the quivering red fires of the Aurora Borealis. The apocalyptic landscape has a mythic quality far exceeding the normal writ of fairy-tale. Like the confused letters of ice which at last spell the word 'eternity', and like the glittering immensity of the Ice Palace itself, it seems to stem from a visionary realm. In this realm, the things of the spirit, like the Princess's dreams, take on a visible form. As Gerda prays, her breath freezes in the cold air, and her words take on living shapes, turning into angels.

The harmony between the worlds within and without is maintained, unbroken, to the tale's ending. As they make their escape from the domain of the Snow Queen it becomes summer and Kay and Gerda, having been tried, tested, and saved, can take on adulthood.

—Edmund Cusick

ANDRADE, Carlos Drummond de. Born in Itabira do Mato Dentro, Minas Gerais, Brazil, 31 October 1902. Educated at Arnaldo College, Belo Horizonte, 1910–13; forced to return home because of poor health, where he was educated privately; Jesuit Anchieta College, Novo Friburgo, 1916–18 (expelled); studied pharmacy 1923–24, qualified 1925, but never practised. Married Dolores Dutra de Morais in 1925; one daughter. Journalist, Belo Horizonte and Rio de Janeiro, 1920–22; co-founding editor of the magazine, *A Revista*, 1925: closed after three issues; teacher of geography and Portuguese, Itabira, 1926; worked on newspapers *Diário de Minas*, 1926–29, and *Minas Gerais*, 1929, both Belo Horizonte; civil servant from 1928: chief secretary to minister of education, Rio de Janeiro, 1934–45 (resigned); briefly co-editor, *Tribuna Popular*, 1945; worked for Office of the National Historical and Artistic Heritage, 1945–62. Visited Buenos Aires, 1950 and 1953. Contributor to several newspapers and journals, including *Correio de Manhã* and *Jornal de Brasil*, 1963–84. Recipient: Brasília prize for literature (refused), 1975; National Walmap prize for literature, 1975. *Died 17 August 1987.*

PUBLICATIONS

Collection

Obra poética. 8 vols., 1989.

Verse

Alguma poesia. 1930.
Brejo das almas. 1934.
Sentimento do mundo. 1940.
José. 1942.
Poesias. 1942.

A rosa do povo. 1945.
Novos poemas. 1948.
Poesia até agora (includes *Novos poemas*). 1948.
Claro enigma. 1951.
Viola de bolso. 1952.
Fazendeiro do ar e Poesia até agora. 1954.
A vida passada a limpo. 1959.
Antologia poetica. 1962.
Lição de coisas. 1962.
In the Middle of the Road (selected poems), translated by John Nist. 1965.
José e outros. 1967.
Boitempo; A falta que ama. 1968.
Reunião (includes all collections published 1930–62, except *Viola de Bolso*). 1969.
As impurezas do branco. 1973.
Menino antigo—Boitempo II. 1973.
Poesia completa e prosa. 1973.
Souvenir of the Ancient World, translated by Mark Strand. 1976.
Discurso de primavera. 1977; enlarged edition, 1978.
O marginal Clorindo gato e a visita. 1978.
Esquecer para lembrar—Boitempo III. 1979.
A paixão medida. 1980.
The Minus Sign: A Selection from the Poetic Anthology, translated by Virginia de Araújo. 1981.
Nova reunião. 2 vols., 1983.
Corpo. 1984.
Amar ds aprende amando. 1985.
Travelling in the Family, edited by Thomas Colchie and Mark Strand, translated by Colchie, Strand, Elizabeth Bishop, and Gregory Rabassa. 1987.
Poesia errante, derrames líricos. 1988.

Fiction

O gerente (stories). 1945.
Contos de aprendiz (stories). 1951.

Other

Confissões de Minas. 1944.
Passeios na Ilha (articles and essays). 1952.
Fala, Amendoeira. 1957.
A bolsa e a vida (includes verse). 1962.
Rio de Janeiro em prosa e verso, with Manuel Bandeira. 1965.
Cadeiro de balanço (articles). 1966.
Obra completa. 1967.
Caminhos de João Brandão (includes verse). 1970.
O poder ultrajovem (includes verse). 1972.
De notícias o não notícias farz-se a crônica, histórias, diálogos, diragações. 1974.
Os dias lindos: crônicas. 1977.
Contos plausíveis. 1981.
Boca de Luar. 1984.
História de dois amores (for children). 1985.
O observador no escritório (diary). 1985.
Moça deitada na grama (chronicles). 1987.
Auto-retrato e outras crônicas (articles), edited by Fernando Py. 1989.
O avesso das coisas: aforismos. 1989.

Translator, *Uma gota de veneno,* by François Mauriac. 1943.
Translator, *As relações perigosas,* by Choderlos de Laclos. 1947.
Translator, *A fugitiva,* by Proust. 1956.
Translator, *Artimanhas de Scapino* by Molière. 1962.

*

Bibliography: *Bibliografia comentader de Carlos Drummond de Andrade (1918–1930)* by Fernando Py, 1980.

Critical Studies: 'Conscience of Brazil: Carlos Drummond de Andrade', in *Américas,* 15(1), 1963, and *The Modernist Movement in Brazil,* 1967, both by John Nist; *Lira e antilira: Mário, Drummond, Cabral* by Luiz Costa Lima, 1968; *A rima na poesia de Carlos Drummond de Andrade* by Hélcio Martins, 1968; 'Inquietudes na Poesia de Drummond' by Antônio Cândido, in his *Vários Escritos,* 1970; *Drummond: A Estilística da Repetição* by Gilberto Mendonça Teles, 1970; *Carlos Drummond de Andrade* (biography) by Assis Brasil, 1971; *A Astúcia da Mímese: Ensaios sobre lírica,* 1975, and *Verso universo em Drummond,* 1975, both by José Guilherme Merquior; *Terra e família na poesia de Carlos Drummond de Andrade* by Joaquim Francisco Coelho, 1973; *Poetas modernos de Brasil, 4. Carlos Drummond de Andrade* by Silviano Santiago, 1976; *Coleção fortuna crítica, 1. Carlos Drummond de Andrade* edited by Sônia Brayner, 1977; *Drummond: Uma poética do risco* by Iumna Maria Simon, 1978; *A dramaticidade na poesia de Drummond* by Donaldo Schuler, 1979; *Drummond o 'Gauche' no tempo,* 1972, and *Carlos Drummond de Andrade: análise da obra,* 1980, both by Affonso Romano de Sant'Anna; *Poesia e poética de Carlos Drummond de Andrade* by John Gledson, 1981; 'The Precarious Self: Carlos Drummond de Andrade's *Brejo das Almas',* in *Hispania,* 65, 1, 1982, and *The Unquiet Self: Self and Society in the Poetry of Carlos Drummond de Andrade,* 1984, both by Ricardo da Silveira Lobo Sternberg.

* * *

In the middle of the road there was a stone
there was a stone in the middle of the road
there was a stone
in the middle of the road there was a stone.
I shall never forget this event
in the life of my tired eyes.
I shall never forget that in the middle of the road
there was a stone
there was a stone in the middle of the road
in the middle of the road there was a stone
(translated by John Nist)

If Carlos Drummond de Andrade were still alive he might well feel irritated at being reminded that the above poem, 'No meio do caminho' ('In the Middle of the Road'), remains his best known, and in a sense, most celebrated, poem. It was certainly, along with 'Ode ao burguês' [Ode to the Bourgeois] by Mário de Andrade, the greatest *succès de scandale* created by the Brazilian Modernist Movement in the 1920s. It is but one of the 56 poems that comprise Drummond's (he liked to be know by his mother's family name) first collection that he did not publish until the age of 28. At first sight it looks like yet another of those *poemas-piadas* (joke-poems) with which the cheerfully irreverent Modernists either delighted or scandalized their public. Less charitably, one critic described this poem as the work of a man who had turned into a parrot.

The poem, like many more in *Alguma poesia* and the collections that followed it, *Brejo das almas* [Marsh of the Souls], *Sentimento do mundo* [Sentiment of the World], *José,* and *A rosa do povo* [The People's Rose], is the *reductio ad absurdam* of the peculiarly drummondian poetic process whereby poetry is distilled from the banal. Contemplation of the stone is a metaphor for life that is senselessly circular, returning one ceaselessly to the blank contingency of matter. Repetition, in the poem, as in life, reigns supreme. In another early poem Drummond writes: 'Planet, planet, vast planet/if I had been christened Janet/it'd be a rhyme, much less a start./ Planet, planet, vast planet/But so much vaster is my heart.' In the same poem, Drummond creates the concept of the *gauche*: 'Go, Carlos! Be *gauche* in life'. The poet's fallible subjectivity will always torment him. He, the subject, confronts the ineffability of the object. His mission is to achieve an equilibrium between these two. The timid poet from the exterior of Minas Gerais would confront and interpret existence. Poetry is provoked out of a desperate search for this equilibrium over some 60 years of poetic creation.

The poetic stance of the *gauche*, the awkward, left-handed, marginalized outsider *avant la lettre*, was Drummond's response to the riddle of existence. In one of his rare prose poems, entitled 'O enigma', composed some 20 years later, he confronts again the image of an irreducible and incomprehensible object in the road, but it is not a stone; it is an 'enigma', an 'enormous thing'. There are stones, but these are, presumably, human beings on the road of life. The mysterious form stands in their path; it paralyses them forever. Of course, as the poet observes, if the enigma could be interpreted it would no longer be an enigma. It is a projection of man's own imagination and his contradictions. The stones bewail their lot:

Oh! what good is intelligence . . . We were intelligent, and yet, to ponder on the threat is not to remove it; that only creates it. Oh! what good is sensitivity—sob the stones. We were sensitive, and the gift of compassion rebounds upon us, when we thought to show it to less favoured species.

'O enigma' is the final poem in *Novos poemas*, and like his most celebrated volume, *A rosa do povo*, was a product of the 1940s in which Drummond did attain some kind of equilibrium between the utterly unreliable self, or subject, and the equally unknowable world of things. In 'A flor e a náusea' he portrays himself as defeated prisoner of society and oppressed by tedium; and yet in the 'river of steel' that is the busy street, a flower is born: 'It is ugly. But it is a flower. It has made its way through the asphalt, the tedium, the loathing and the hate'. The flower, traditional symbol of life and hope, joins with the very visual image of the *gauche* in the figure of Charlie Chaplin, another obscure marginal—but with the power, as Drummond portrays him in the final poem of *A rosa do povo*, entitled 'Canto ao homem ao povo Charlie Chaplin' [Song of the Man of the People Charlie Chaplin], to bring a form of redemption to the oppressed: 'and they speak as well, the flowers that you love so dearly when they are trodden underfoot'.

This is a humane poetry of love; but despite the strong vein of eroticism in the early volumes—Drummond's very last collection was an entire set of erotic poems—and the strong theme of human solidarity that informs the poetry of the 1940s, love is seen, in the present tense, as a sad game, and in retrospect, as an aching nostalgia for the passing of all that, with hindsight, one might still hold dear. Like the Modernist Movement which in his youth inspired him, Drummond seeks to forge an identity for Brazil, but in doing so creates a tragic vision of his destiny in the historical continuum that is Brazil. If the *modernistas* reached out into the four corners of their vast country to seize, spatially, the totality of their nation, Drummond's mission turned out to be more temporal. He chose to plunge into the past, the past he knew, that of rural Minas Gerais, in order to articulate his own destiny as well as that of Brazil. In the process, he universalized his poetic

drama: by evoking the past, he hoped to explain the present. It is a painful process that may be doomed to failure. His supreme myth plucked out of past time is his birthplace, Itabira: 'Itabira is just a photograph on the wall./But how it makes me suffer!' It is above all the poet's lucidity, honesty, and struggle for truth that makes him suffer in the course of his odyssey through the past and present of Minas Gerais. The great church clock in the poem 'O relógio' [The Clock] in the collection *Boitempo* [Ox-time] symbolizes Drummond's fate as the poet from Minas whose function is to bear witness, record and interpret Brazil, past, present, and future. But the poet in his old age has travelled far not only in terms of longevity but also in terms of ontological and poetic investigation. The poetry of *Boitempo* and beyond seeks profound acceptance and disengagement, yet always within the unspoken pact forged with the phenomenological and spiritual world in his most overtly philosophical collection, *Claro enigma* [Clear Enigma]. Minas Gerais means 'General Mines', seen as a landscape of untold mineral wealth since the discovery in the 18th century of silver, gold, diamonds, and later, iron ore in vast quantities. This wealth built the now decaying baroque cities of Minas. Drummond meditates in 'Os bens e o sangue' [The Gods and the Blood] on the wealth of which he has been disinherited and the blood he has inherited.

As he contemplates the family archive, his ancestors seem to address him across the decades and acknowledge his role in the continuum: 'You are our natural seed and we fructify you,/we are your explanation, your simplest virtue . . . /For it was only right that one of us should deny us the better to serve us'. Thus does Drummond fulfil a destiny, tragic in its resignation. In another poem from *Claro enigma*, 'Morte das casas de Ouro Preto' [Death of the Houses of Ouro Preto], the rain falls endlessly on the decaying mansions of the once fabulous city. Water in Drummond is flux, passing time, destruction, and eternity. Now it is no longer a matter of change but of the absorption of man-made structures into the timeless pathos of Minas, back into the soil of Minas in order to complete the cycle: 'May the beams of today body forth into trees!/May the dust on them be again the dust of the highways!'.

For all his intermittent engagement with the theme of love, with the problems of urban society and with politics, Drummond is, ultimately, a great existential poet; perhaps the greatest that America has produced.

—R.J. Oakley

ANDRADE, Mário (Raul) de. Born in São Paulo, Brazil, 9 October 1893. Educated at Escola de Nossa Senhora do Carmo, São Paulo, 1905–09; Álvares Penteado Commerical School, São Paulo, 1910; studied piano at the Musical and Dramatic Conservatory, São Paulo, 1911, degree 1917. Involved in avant-garde artistic circles in the 1920s: co-organizer, the Modern Art Week at the Teatro Municipal, São Paulo, 1922; professor of the history of music and aesthetics, São Paulo Conservatory, 1925; contributor, 'Taxi' column for *Diário Nacional*, from 1928; worked for the Ministry of Education's schools' music reform programme, 1930; co-founder, with Paulo Duarte, and director, Municipal Department of Culture, São Paulo, 1934–37: founded the

Municipal Library, the Department of National Heritage, the journal *Revista do Arquivo Municipal de São Paulo*, and São Paulo's Ethnography and Folklore Society (and its first president); moved to Rio de Janeiro, 1937; director, Federal University Institute of Arts, Rio de Janeiro, 1938–40, and held the chair of philosophy and history of art; headed the *Enciclopédia Brasileira* project for the National Book Institute, 1939; made anthropological research trips to northern Brazil, under commission from the Department of National Heritage, 1941. Organizer, first National Language Congress, 1937; co-founder, Brazilian Society of Writers, 1942. Member, São Paulo Academy of Letters. *Died 25 February 1945.*

PUBLICATIONS

Collections

Obras completas. 24 vols., 1960–91.
1. *Obra imatura.*
2. *Poesias completas.*
3. *Amar, verbo intransitivo.*
4. *Macunaíma.*
5. *Os contos de Belazarte.*
6. *Ensaio sobre a musica brasileira.*
7. *Música doce música.*
8. *Pequena história da música.*
9. *Namoros com a medicina.*
10. *Aspectos da literatura brasileira.*
11. *Aspectos da música brasileira.*
12. *Aspectos das artes plásticas no Brasil.*
13. *Música de feitiçaria no Brasil.*
14. *O baile das quatro artes.*
15. *Os filhos da Candinha.*
16. *O padre Jesuíno de Monte Carmelo*
17. *Contos novos.*
18. *Danças dramáticas do Brasil.*
19. *Modinhas imperiais.*
20. *O empalhador de Passarinho.*
21. *Quatro Pessoas.*
22. *Dicionário musical brasileiro.*
23. *Vida de cantador.*
24. *Cartas de Mário de Andrade a Luís da Câmara Cascudo.*
Obras [50th Anniversary of Modern Art Week Edition]. 15 vols., 1972.
Poesias completas, edited by Diléa Zanotto Manfio. 1987.

Verse

Há uma gota de sangue em cada poema (as Mário Sobral). 1917.
Paulicéia desvairada. 1926; as *Hallucinated City* (bilingual edition), edited and translated by Jack E. Tomlins, 1968.
Clã do Jabuti. 1927.
Remate de Males. 1930.
Lira paulistana. 1946.

Fiction

Primeiro andar (stories). 1926.
Amar, verbo intransitivo. 1927; edited by Telê Porto Ancona Lopez, 1982; as *Fräulein*, translated by Margaret Richardson Hollingsworth, 1933.
Macunaíma. 1928; edited by Telê Porto Ancona Lopez, 1978; as *Macunaíma*, translated by Edward Arthur Goodland, 1984.
Belazarte. 1934.
Contos novos. 1947.

Other

A escrava que não é isaura. 1925.
Compêndio de história da música. 1929; revised edition, as *Pequena história da música*, 1942.
Modinhas imperiais. 1930.
Música, doce música. 1933.
O Aleijadinho e Álvares de Azevedo. 1935.
A música e a canção populares no Brasil. 1936.
Namoros com a medicina. 1939.
A expressão musical dos Estados Unidos. 1940.
Música do Brasil. 1941.
O movimento modernista. 1942.
Aspectos de literatura brasileira. 1943.
O baile das quatro artes. 1943.
Os filhos da Candinha. 1943.
O Empalhador de Passarinho. 1944(?).
Cartas de Mário Andrade a Manuel Bandeira. 1958.
Danças dramáticas do Brasil. 3 vols., 1959.
Música de feitiçaria do Brasil. 1963.
Setenta e uma cartas de Mário de Andrade. 1963.
Aspectos das artes plásticas no Brasil. 1965.
Mário de Andrade escreve a Alceu, Meyer e outros, edited by Lygia Fernandes. 1968.
Itinerário: cartas a Alphonsus de Guimaraens filho. 1974.
Táxi e crônicas no Diário Nacional. 1976.
O turista aprendiz (diaries), edited by Telê Porto Ancona Lopez. 1976.
O banquete. 1977.
A lição do Amigo: cartas de Mário de Andrade a Carlos Drummond de Andrade. 1982.
Correspondente contumaz 1925–1944 (letters to Pedro Naval), edited by Fernando da Rocha Peres. 1982.
Cartas: Mário de Andrade, Oneyda Alvarenga. 1983.
Entrevistas e depoimentos, edited by Telê Porto Ancona Lopez, 1983.
Cartas de Mário de Andrade a Álvaro Lins. 1983.
Os cocos, edited by Oneyda Alvarenga. 1984.
Cartas de Mário de Andrade a Prudente de Moraes, edited by Georgina Koifman. 1985.
Miguel de Andrade por el mismo, edited by Paulo Duarte. 1985.
Dicionário musical brasileiro, edited by Oneyda Alvarenga and Flávia Camargo Toni. 1989.
Cartas de Trabalho: Correspondência com Rodrigo Mello Franco de Andrade (1936–1945). 1989.
A lição do guru: cartas a Guilherme Figueiredo, 1937–1945. 1989.
Querida Henriqueta: cartas de Mário de Andrade a Henriqueta Lisboa, edited by Lauro Palú. 1991.
Será o benedito! Artigos publicados no suplemento em rotogravura de O Estado de S. Paulo, edited by Telê Porto Ancona Lopez. 1992.

*

Bibliography: *Mário de Andrade: Bibliografia sobre a sua obra* (*Revista do Libro* supplement) by António Simões dos Reis, 1960; *Brazilian Literature: A Research Guide* by David William Foster and Walter Rela, 1990.

Critical Studies: *Lição de Mário de Andrade* by Lêdo Ivo, 1952; *Mário de Andrade* by Fernando Mendes de Almeida, 1962; 'Some Formal Types in the Poetry of Mário de Andrade' by David William Foster, in *Luso-Brazilian Review*, December 1965; *The Modernist Movement in Brazil: A Literary Study* by John Nist, 1967; 'The Literary Criticism of Mário de Andrade' by Thomas R. Hart, in *Disciplines of Criticism: Essays in Literary Theory, Interpretation, and History* edited by Peter Demetz and others, 1968; *Roteiro de Macunaíma* by M. Cavalcanti Proença, 1969; *Poesia e prosa de Mário de Andrade* by João Pacheco, 1970; *Morfología de Macunaíma* by Haroldo de Campos, 1973; *Roteiro de Macunaíma* by M. Cavalcanti Proença, 1977; *Política e poesia em Mário de Andrade* by Joan Dassin, 1978; 'Macunaíma as Brazilian Hero', in *Latin American Literary Review*, 1978, and *Literatura e Cinema: Macunaíma: do modernismo na literatura ao cinema novo*, 1982, both by Randal Johnson; *Mário de Andrade e a revolução da linguagem* by José Maria Barbosa Gomes, 1979; 'Preguiça and Power: Mário de Andrade's *Macunaíma*' by Renata R. Mautner, in *Luso-Brazilian Review*, Summer 1984; *Mário de Andrade: Hoje* edited by Carlos E.O. Berriel, 1990; *A presença do povo na cultura brasileira: ensaio sobre o pensamento de Mário de Andrade e Paulo Friere* by Vivian Schelling, 1991.

* * *

To call Mário de Andrade the creator of Brazilian modernism is an oversimplification, but if Oswald de Andrade, fellow poet and novelist, was its catalyst and presiding genius, Mário was surely the doyen, supreme symbol, and principal ideologue of that iconoclastic and brilliant artistic movement that burst upon the Brazilian cultural scene in 1922, changing forever the aesthetic landscape of Brazil. Andrade also distinguished himself in more, and disparate, fields than any other single individual among the talented generation of writers and artists that included the sculptor Brecheret, the composer Villa Lobos and the important poets Oswald de Andrade, Manuel Bandeira, and Carlos Drummond de Andrade.

Born in São Paulo in 1893, Andrade first studied sciences, but entered the São Paulo Conservatory of Musical and Dramatic Art in 1911, graduating in 1917 with the piano as his special subject. His musical background and a lifelong passion for folklore and the plastic arts caused him to make a mark early in his writing career as journalist, critic, and essayist. His writings on music, painting and folklore, especially that of his native Brazil, run to many volumes; but he was to make his mark most spectacularly as writer of lyric poetry and prose fiction. At the time of World War I, the predominant fashion in Brazilian poetry was that of a polite symbolism and Parnassianism. Andrade's first volume, *Há uma gota de sangue em cada poema* [There is a Drop of Blood in Every Poem] betrays the Parnassian influence but it contains, too, the unmistakeable rebelliousness and innovatory drive of all his imaginative *oeuvre*. He was destined to spearhead the artistic revolution of *modernismo* that was inspired by the Symbolist and Expressionist currents abroad in Europe in the last decades of the 19th century and the first two decades of the 20th. In formal terms, this meant experimentation with free verse, a broadening of terms of reference with regard to the possible thematics of poetry, and an impulse to embrace, artistically, the whole of lived experience—all the phenomena of early 20th-century life; hence the inordinate impact on Andrade and his artistic comrades-in-arms of Marinetti's Futurist Manifesto published in Paris in 1909. The age of

speed and of the machine would fuel the imagination of the Brazilian Modernist movement in its heroic phase. Indeed, Andrade and his friends were called 'futurists' in the months leading up to the São Paulo Modern Art Week they organized in February 1922. Andrade had written most of his second and most famous book of poetry, *Paulicéia desvairada* (*Hallucinated City*)—referring to São Paulo—in 1920, but it had been quoted extensively in the press and widely disseminated by members of the group, so that the poetry of the man whom Oswald de Andrade had hailed in a famous article as 'my Futurist poet' was predictably greeted with boos and catcalls of the massed opponents of *modernismo* who crowded the hall in February of that year to hear it recited. The impact of this aggressive, anti-bourgeois poetry has a very rough English parallel in the reception accorded to the poetry of T.S. Eliot up to and including *The Waste Land*, although *Hallucinated City* and the febrile urban poetry that was to follow it was far more uneven in quality; but just as Eliot found himself the poet of London, so Andrade became in the 1920s the quintessential urban poet of São Paulo.

The collections of poetry that Andrade published later in the 1920s and in the 1930s add to the iconoclasm, the humour and the irreverence a wealth of allusion to Brazilian myth and folklore. At its worst, this poetry is undisciplined and structured in a wayward fashion. This ill-discipline is redeemed by the humour, the by now typically Modernist incorporation into lyric poetry of the rhythms and lexis of colloquial speech —the language of the street—and by the pervasive, gentle lyricism. In 'Momento' (1937) he writes:

> The wind cuts people in two
> Only a desire for clarity buoys up the world . . .
> The sun shines. The rain rains. And the gale
> Scatters in the blue the trombones of the clouds.
> Nobody gets to be one in this city.
> The doves cling to the skyscrapers, comes the rain.
> Comes the cold. And comes the anguish . . . It is this
>   violent wind
> That bursts out of the gorges of the human soil
> Demanding sky, peace and a little spring.

Andrade was to earn considerable critical acclaim within Brazil for his prose fiction. Few Brazilians have written better short stories, but it is his novel, *Macunaíma*, that has brought him most enduring, and international, celebrity as a storyteller. *Macunaíma* ('The Hero Without Character' is a translation of its subtitle) is a surrealistic fantasy in which Andrade draws on his compendious folkloric research in order to weave a coherent fiction that is, at the same time, also a compendium of Brazil itself. Here, he demonstrates his lifelong contention that popular forms of expression are legitimate material for the elaboration of high art—a cornerstone of Brazilian Modernist ideology. Thus are Brazil and its culture rescued from its European and colonialist past. Yet, the protagonist has no character because of his colonial status. The 20-year-old, magical Amazonian chief whose hilarious passage along with his brothers Jiguê and Maanape through the society and the streets of São Paulo is wide-eyed and innocent. Macunaíma, the hero, exhibits all of the vices and virtues Andrade saw in his countryman together with an unformed character: only when Brazil comes of age, Andrade declared, will she emancipate herself from Europe and acquire a character. The setting of the opening chapters is Amazonian, but the novel is by no means regionalist. Macunaíma's magical journeys quarter the length and breadth of Brazil from the island of Marajó in the mouth of the Amazon to Rio Grande in the far south. In the course of these peregrinations Macunaíma experiences extreme suffering and extreme joy. At the close of his journeying he is in a state of profound disenchantment. The Brazilian gods take pity and transform him into a new constellation of stars—the Great Bear, in the midst of which 'he broods along in the vast expanse of heaven'.

Andrade succeeded, as perhaps only Lima Barreto among Brazilian writers before his time did, in viewing Brazil and its people through entirely Brazilian eyes. This capacity, he felt, was the true legacy of Brazilian modernism. Barreto had opined that in Brazil 'the desert encircles the city'. Andrade, urban poet, expressed eloquently his awareness of the difficulty of this pan-Brazilian enterprise, the dilemma of the mutually alienated Brazils, in his 'Dois poemas Acreanos' [Two Poems Concerning Acre]:

> Brazilian rubber-tapper,
> In the gloom of the forest
> Rubber-tapper, sleep.
> Striking the chord of love I sleep.
> How incredibly hard this is!
> I want to sing but cannot,
> I want to feel and I don't feel
> The Brazilian word
> That will make you sleep . . .
> Rubber-tapper, sleep . . .

—R.J. Oakley

ANDRIĆ, Ivo. Born in Trávnik, Bosnia (then in the Austro-Hungarian Empire), 9 October 1892. Educated at schools in Višegrad and Sarajevo, 1898–1912; University of Zagreb, 1912; Vienna University, 1913; Jagiellonian University, Cracow, 1914; Graz University, Ph.D. 1923. Married Milica Babić in 1959 (died 1968). Member of Mlada Bosna [Young Bosnia] and interned for three years during World War I; served in the army, 1917; in the Yugoslav diplomatic service, 1920–41, in the Vatican (Rome), Geneva, Madrid, Bucharest, Trieste, Graz, Belgrade, Marseilles, Paris, Brussels, and, as Ambassador to Germany, Berlin; full-time writer, 1941–49; representative of Bosnia, Yugoslav parliament, 1949–55. Co-founder and member of the editorial board, *Književni jug* [The Literary South], 1918–19. President, Federation of Writers of Yugoslavia, 1946–51. Recipient: Yugoslav Government prize, 1956; Nobel prize for literature, 1961; Vuk prize (Serbia), 1972. Red Cross medal, 1936; Légion d'honneur (France), 1937; Order of the Supreme Commander of Resurgent Poland, 1937; Order of St Sava, first class (Yugoslavia), 1938. Honorary doctorate: University of Cracow, 1964. Member, Serbian Academy; honorary member, Bosnian Academy, 1970. *Died 13 March 1975.*

PUBLICATIONS

Collection

Sabrana djela [Collected Works], edited by Risto Trifković and others. 17 vols., 1984.

Fiction

Pripovetke [Stories]. 3 vols., 1924–36.
Gospodjica. 1945; as *The Woman from Sarajevo*, translated by Joseph Hitrec, 1965.
Travnička hronika. 1945; as *Bosnian Story*, translated by Kenneth Johnstone, 1958; as *Bosnian Chronicle*, translated by Joseph Hitrec, 1963; as *The Days of the Consuls*, translated by Celia Hawkesworth and Bogdan Rakić, 1992.
Na Drini ćuprija. 1945; as *The Bridge on the Drina*, translated by Lovett Edwards, 1959.
Priča o vezirovom slonu. 1948; as *The Vizier's Elephant: Three Novellas*, translated by Drenka Willen, 1962.
Nove pripovetke [New Stories]. 1949.
Priča o kmetu Simanu [The Tale of the Peasant Simon]. 1950.
Novele [Short Stories]. 1951.
Pod Grabićem: Pripovetke o životu bosanskog sela [Under the Elm: Stories of Life in a Bosnian Village]. 1952.
Prokleta avlija. 1954; as *Devil's Yard*, translated by Kenneth Johnstone, 1962; as *The Damned Yard*, translated by Celia Hawkesworth, in *The Damned Yard and Other Stories*, 1992.
Panorama: Pripovetke [Panorama: Stories] (for children). 1958.
Izbor [Selection]. 1961.
Ljubav u kasabi [Love in a Market Town]. 1963.
Anikina vremena [Anika's Times] (stories). 1967.
The Pasha's Concubine and Other Tales, translated by Joseph Hitrec. 1968.
Kula i druge pripovetke (for children). 1970.
The Damned Yard and Other Stories, translated by Celia Hawkesworth. 1992.

Verse

Ex ponto. 1918.
Nemiri [Anxieties]. 1919.

Other

Lica [Faces]. 1960.
Goya. 1972.
Letters, edited and translated by Želimir Juričić. 1984.
The Development of Spiritual Life under the Turks, edited by Želimir B. Juričić and J.F. Loud. 1990.
Conversation with Goya, Signs, Bridges, translated by Celia Hawkesworth and Andrew Harvey. 1992.
Diplomatski spisi [Diplomatic Papers]. 1992.

*

Bibliography: *Andrić: Bibliografija dela, prevoda, i literature 1911–1970*, 1974; in *A Comprehensive Bibliography of Yugoslav Literature in English, 1953–1980* by Vasa D. Mihailovich and Mateja Matejić, 1984, supplements, 1988, 1992.

Critical Studies: 'The French in *The Chronicle of Travnik*' by Ante Kadić, in *California Slavic Studies*, 1, 1960; 'The Work of Ivo Andrić' by E.D. Goy, in *Slavonic and East European Review*, 41, 1963; 'The Later Stories of Ivo Andrić' by Thomas Eekman, in *Slavonic and East European Review*, 48, 1970; 'Ivo Andrić and the Quintessence of Time' by Nicholas Moracevich, in *Slavic and East European Journal*, 16(3), 1972; *Ivo Andrić: Bridge Between East and West* by Celia Hawkesworth, 1984; *Ivo Andrić: Proceeedings of a Sympos-*

ium Held at the School of Slavonic and East European Studies 10–12 July 1984, 1985; 'Ivo Andrić and World Literature' by Milan V. Dimić, in *Canadian Slavonic Papers*, 27(3), 1985; *The Man and the Artist: Essays on Ivo Andrić*, 1986, and 'Andrić's Berlin Writings: Between the Two Sirens', in *Russian, Croatian and Serbian, Czech and Slovak, Polish Literature*, 30(1), 1991, both by Želimir B. Juričić; 'Ivo Andrić and the Swing to Infinity', in *Scottish Slavonic Review*, 6, 1986, and 'The Short Stories of Ivo Andrić: Autobiography and the Chain of Proof', in *Slavonic and East European Review*, 67(1), 1989, both by Felicity Rosslyn; 'Narrator and Narrative in Andrić's *Prokleta avlija*' by Anita Lekić-Trbojević, in *Serbian Studies*, 4(3), 1987; 'Some Rhetorical Aspects of the Novel *The Bridge on the Drina*' by Vladimir Miličić, in *Serbian Studies* 4(3), 1987; 'Ivo Andrić's Historical Thought' by Predrag Palavestra, in *Reflets d'histoire européenne dans l'oeuvre d'Ivo Andrič* edited by Dragan Nedeljković, 1987; *Ivo Andrić: A Writer's Life* by Radovan Popović, 1988; 'The Echoes of the Second World War' by Dušan Puvačić, in *Serbian Studies*, 4(4), 1988; *Ivo Andrić: A Critical Biography* by Vanita Singh Mukerji, 1991; 'Ivo Andrić: A Yugoslav Career' by Hans-Peter Stoffel, in *New Zealand Slavonic Journal*, 1992.

*   *   *

The work for which Ivo Andrić is probably best known outside Bosnia is *Na Drini ćuprija* (*The Bridge on the Drina*), a chronicle of the life of the small Bosnian town of Višegrad over several centuries. This rich fusion of legend and history is given shape by the central symbol of the bridge, linking East and West, past and future, and instilling in the townspeople a sense of harmony and the endurance of life despite individual transience.

The major part of Andrić's fiction—five novels and six volumes of short stories—is set in his native Bosnia and informed by a detailed knowledge of this region of the Balkans under Ottoman and, later, Habsburg rule. This precise setting in time and space is an essential feature of Andrić's work, but it has proved an obstacle to his reception in some countries, despite the fact that he has been extensively translated. There has been a tendency not to look beyond the 'exotic' setting in this 'remote' corner of Europe. Andrić focuses his attention on Bosnia because it represents a particularly varied concentration of cultures: an indigenous population of both Catholic and Orthodox Christians, a large Muslim community, Jews, and gypsies. Bosnia also represents a crossroads between East and West, visited by Ottoman dignitaries and European merchants, diplomats, and administrators. It serves consequently as a microcosm of both the variety of human life and the arbitrary divisions and antagonisms between men.

A detailed exploration of this clash of cultures is offered by *Travnička hronika* (*Bosnian Story* or *The Days of the Consuls*) in which the French and Austrian consuls and the Turkish vizier confront and, when international politics permit, console each other in this harsh and hostile land. Andrić exploits this setting to reveal universal patterns of behaviour and experience, drawing on legend, myth, archetype, and symbol. The complement of the symbol of the bridge in Andrić's work is that of its opposite, the prison, suggesting all the constraints which compel an individual to seek some way out of the fundamental laws of human existence. The image is most fully developed in the short novel, or novella, *Prokleta avlija* (*Devil's Yard* or *The Damned Yard*), in which the prison inmates 'escape' by telling stories. It is perhaps in the shorter prose forms that Andrić excels and the best of his stories offer a vivid, intensely suggestive and often disturbing image or anecdote, rich in meanings and associations.

Andrić also wrote verse intermittently throughout his life. More characteristic, however, are his prose reflections, jottings prompted by experiences of all kinds. Selections of these were published posthumously in his collected works as *Znakovi pored puta* [Signs by the Roadside] and *Sveske* [Notebooks], providing insight into the fine and subtle mind of this otherwise very private man. Parallels may be drawn between Andrić's work and that of Thomas Mann, Joseph Conrad, and Henry James. He was an avid reader and himself spoke of a sense of affinity with a wide variety of writers from Camus and Goethe to Marcus Aurelius.

—E.C. Hawkesworth

THE BRIDGE ON THE DRINA (Na Drini ćuprija)
Novel by Ivo Andrić, 1945.

The Bridge on the Drina consists of a 400-year chronicle, covering the period from the moment in 1516 when the future bridge is first imagined by the ten-year-old child ultimately responsible for building it, up to the partial destruction of the bridge during World War I. In between the narrator tells of the bridge's construction, of the human dramas that it witnesses, of the historical events that affect the nearby regions most directly, and of the manner in which the bridge itself comes to influence the lives of those who live near it.

Like most of Andrić's fiction, *The Bridge on the Drina* deals with Bosnia's past. His 'protagonist' is an actual stone bridge in the city of Višegrad. Much of what is described in the novel follows historical fact closely: there really was a Bosnian peasant's son who was pressed into the service of the Ottoman court; having risen to become grand vizier, he then ordered the building of this bridge in the land of his origin. Bosnia itself remained under Turkish rule until the late 19th century, though the empire's decline—indirectly but effectively portrayed throughout the novel—caused shifts in power toward the nearby Christian countries. Of central concern to the novel is the religious and ethnic mix of Višegrad—primarily Moslem and Orthodox Christian, but also with a few Jews and, particularly after Austrian influence grew, Roman Catholics as well. Decades of peaceful if at times uneasy co-existence are regularly swept away by the passions arising from distant events. In this sense, the novel turned out to be tragically prescient of the events that would follow the break-up of modern Yugoslavia and the civil war that once again wreaked havoc on this region.

The book therefore reminds its modern readers that the death and suffering of most recent times have their origins in the past. During the bridge's construction Christian peasants are forced to work to the point of exhaustion, and the impalement of one of them, who has tried to sabotage the Moslem-led effort, is described in clinical detail. Later, in the 19th century, the bridge is regularly adorned with the heads of those accused of being involved with a Serbian revolt against the Turks. Much of what the bridge witnesses involves the cruelty and harshness of people toward others.

While wars and natural disasters bring suffering to the inhabitants of Višegrad, the bridge stands seemingly aloof, above and apart from the tragedies of individual lives. It outlasts the humans that come and go, and appears to stand for continuity, for an almost reassuring sameness and durability. These qualities are emphasized again and again by the narrator, who seems more concerned with the course of history than with the lives of the fragile and often undeserving mortals who live near the bridge.

Andrić's achievement is to undercut the outlook of his own third-person narrator and to offer a much more sensitive and profound view of human nature. One of the negative figures is a schoolmaster who himself keeps a chronicle of life in the town, but it remains only a few pages long, since to him virtually no event is of sufficient importance to be included. To Andrić, though, any event, whether small or large, that distinguishes good from evil, or inner strength from moral weakness, is significant. Humans can be and often are cruel, but evil exists in this book as the backdrop against which more noble deeds occur.

Some of the grandest actions are, in keeping with the narrator's view, carried out by historically notable people: the novel judges the decision of Mehmed Pasha to build the bridge positively, despite the hardship that he unwittingly inflicts on many. However, much attention is paid to those more ordinary people who show a capability for change, who turn out to be either better or worse than their past actions would lead others to expect. Of all the young Serbian men who meet on the bridge shortly before World War I it is the least prepossessing of these, a person whose own grandfather (another figure in the novel) had died in a lunatic asylum, who goes off to fight the Austrians. History itself seems to recognize and record good or brave actions and to punish evil. Thus Radisav, the person who had been sabotaging the construction of the bridge, lives on in legend. Meanwhile the man responsible for capturing and executing him goes insane, and the narrator, for all his meticulousness, is able to identify him only as the 'Plevljak', the man from Plevlje. His name has been obliterated by history, while Radisav's survives.

The Bridge on the Drina is, then, ultimately concerned with individual lives and individual fates; the story of the bridge provides an opportunity not just for a meditation on historical events but even more for an examination of the moral issues illustrated by the characters who come and go throughout the novel. Not by chance, Andrić devotes the final two-thirds of his novel to the last 35 or so years that it covers. In this way he is able to develop a few characters in greater depth and to draw careful parallels between some of the earlier figures and those with whom he deals toward the end.

The lessons that he thereby presents are perhaps best illustrated by Alihodja Mutevelić, who gradually comes to the fore. A member of the family that for centuries had served as guardians of the bridge, he is nailed to the bridge by his ear for refusing to support the resistance to the Austrian takeover in chapter 9, and in the last chapter, 24, he dies just after a pier of the bridge is blown up in the war. It turns out, despite the narrator's belief in immutability, that nothing is forever. Alihodja, a person who seems to have lived in harmony with life's flow and to have accepted the inevitable changes, views the bridge's missing span. His last thought is that, despite everything, people of exalted soul who would make the world a better place cannot have vanished from the earth, for if they were to do so then the love of God would not exist either. This faith—that good people and the memory of goodness will endure—runs throughout the novel and constitutes perhaps the most salient moral to be drawn from the story of the bridge on the Drina.

—Barry P. Scherr

ANDRZEJEWSKI, Jerzy. Born in Warsaw, Poland, 19 August 1909. Educated at a gymnasium in Warsaw 1919–27; University in Warsaw, 1927–31. Married Maria Abgarowicz. Took part in underground cultural work in Warsaw during World War II. Writer from 1932; editor of literature section of weekly *Prosto z mostu*, 1935–37; after the war moved to Cracow: chair of the Cracow Division of Polish Writers Union, 1946–47; involved in social work in Szczecin, 1948–52; joined Polish Communist Party, 1949; editor-in-chief of weekly *Przegld kulturalny* [Cultural Review], 1952–54; member of the Polish parliament, 1952–56: resigned his Party membership in protest when the government banned a new literary magazine, 1957. His book *Apelacja* (*The Appeal*) was banned in Poland, 1968. Recipient: Polish Academy of Literature Young Writers prize, 1939; Cracow prize, 1946; Odrodzenie award, 1948; Order of the Banner of Labour (1st Class), 1949; Polish Readers prize, 1959, 1964, and 1965; Złoty Kłos award, 1965. *Died 19 April 1983.*

PUBLICATIONS

Fiction

Drogi nieuniknione [Inescapable Ways] (stories). 1936.
Ład Serca [Peace of Mind]. 1938.
Wielki tydzień [Holy Week] (novella). 1943.
Noc [Night] (stories). 1945.
Popiół i diament. 1948; as *Ashes and Diamonds*, translated by D.F. Welsh, 1962.
Wojna skuteczna [An Effective War]. 1953.
Złoty lis [The Golden Fox] (story). 1955.
Ciemności kryją ziemię [Darkness Covers the Earth]. 1957; as *The Inquisitors*, also translated by Konrad Syrop, 1960.
Bramy Raju. 1958; as *The Gates of Paradise*, translated by James Kirkup, 1962.
Niby gaj: Opowiadania 1939–58 [As if the Grove] (stories). 1959.
Idzie skacze po górach. 1963; as *A Sitter for a Satyr*, translated by Celina Wieniewska, 1964; as *He Cometh Leaping upon the Mountains*, translated by Wieniewska, 1965.
Apelacja. 1968; as *The Appeal*, translated by Celina Wieniewska, 1971.
Teraz na ciebie zagłada [Now Annihilation Is Coming upon You]. 1976.
Już prawnie nic [Already Next to Nothing]. 1979.
Miazga [Pulp]. 1979.
Nowe opowiadania [New Tales]. 1980.
Nikt [Nobody] (novella). 1983.
Intermezzo, i inne opowiadania. 1986.

Plays

Święto Winkelrida [Winkelreid's Day], with J. Zagorski. 1957.
Prometheus. 1972.

Screenplays: *Popiół i diament*, with Andrzej Wajda, 1958; *Niewinni Czarodzieje* (collaborator), 1959.

Other

Aby pokój zwyciężył [May Peace Win]. 1950.
Wyznania i rozmyślania pisarza [Confessions and Thoughts of a Writer]. 1950.
O człowieku radzieckim [About the Russian Man]. 1951.
Ludzie i zdarzenia [People and Events]. 1952.

Partia i twórczość pisarza [The Party and Writer's Works].
1952.
Książka dla Marcina [The Book for Martin: Reminiscences].
1954.
Gra z cieniem (diary). 1987.
Z dnia na dzień: Dziennik literacki 1972–1979 (newspaper
articles). 2 vols., 1988.
Listy [Letters], with Andrzej Fiett. 1991.

*

Critical Studies: *Andrzejewski* by Wacław Sadkowski, trans-
lated by Krystyna Cękalska, 1975; *Jerzy Andrzejewskis
Roman 'Ciemności kryj ziemię' und die Darstellung der
Spanischen Inquisition in Werken der fiktionalen Literatur* by
Jürgen Schreiber, 1981.

* * *

Jerzy Andrzejewski is one of the best Polish novelists of the
20th century. It would be difficult, however, to pin down his
literary masterwork. He has left a number of novels and short
stories of challenging content and skilful narration. Following
various narrative styles of modern times that reflect the
meanders of his intellectual search and formal experiments,
and being, in turn, a Catholic, a Communist, and an outspoken dissident, Andrzejewski defies easy classifications. It
appears, however, that the impact of Conradian solipsism,
apart from his Marxist phase, influenced him until the last
days.

Joseph Conrad's principle that there is no escape from the
prison of the self and that, consequently, one is unable to
communicate with others, thus living in solitude and despon-
dency, forms the basis for Andrzejewski's first collection of
short stories *Drogi nieuniknione* [Inescapable Ways]. The
best account of anxieties caused by such a situation was the
novel *Ład Serca* [Peace of Mind], in the mould of Georges
Bernanos's Catholic fiction. Its extraordinary setting in a
secluded Belarusian village, surrounded by forests, exudes
the atmosphere of symbolic darkness and unavoidable fate.
The story of a parish priest, tormented by a guilty conscience,
and the misfortunes of his forlorn flock, represents a world of
feeble mortals, where God seems far away, His grace scarce,
while evil is on the rampage. Christian ideas of love and
repentance are eventually engulfed by despair over the
absence of justice and moral order. This kind of pessimism
dominates the war fiction, the short stories published in
Andrzejewski's first post-war volume *Noc* [Night], and in
later collections. The symbolic 'night' reveals a similar distress, magnified only by a much more ruthless background,
where fighting intensifies inborn human wickedness and increases hatred and isolation. The portrayed events polarize
between unrestricted killing and preposterous patriotic gestures of sham conspirators.

At the end of World War II Conradian solitude was suspended in favour of a growing belief in the power of collective
efforts. In the final, reworked version of the novella *Wielki
tydzień* [Holy Week], one of the underground soldiers advocates a united front of all freedom fighters. According to the
writer's own confession, he was looking for a 'magic circle of
a well-ordered world' and eventually found it in Marxism. As
a result, he published his controversial novel about the first
days of the Polish People's Republic, *Popiół i diament* (*Ashes
and Diamonds*), subsequently filmed by Andrzej Wajda.
The biased picture of the non-Communist Home Army

and staunch support for the Party line secured official recognition, and over 25 editions were printed. Nevertheless
Andrzejewski's traditional categories of human loneliness in
the world of conflict between good and evil have simply been
adjusted to new, Marxist-inspired views on history and progress. The unequivocal condemnation of the recent past and
those hostile to communism resulted from that approach.

Andrzejewski's fairly brief links with communism were
reflected in political articles and in the unsuccessful satirical
novel *Wojna skuteczna* [An Effective War]. The publication
of *Ciemności kryją ziemię* (*The Inquisitors*) marked a fundamental rejection of any political system that upholds the
supremacy of ideology over personal freedom. Accordingly,
the portrayal of the Inquisition in medieval Spain can be
understood as an allegory, referring above all to Stalinism. In
this account, absolute power destroys individual conscience
and human loyalty, transforming even committed idealists
into the blind instruments of terror. Similar scepticism about
the human values of any dogma guided Andrzejewski's
experimental short narrative, *Bramy Raju* (*The Gates of
Paradise*), where several confessions follow each other without any full stops. In this story the authentic pilgrimage to
Jerusalem by French youngsters is described as a mundane
affair, whose participants are motivated not by divine love
but by adolescent sensuality and carnal desires. The worst,
however, is their leader, an idealist, whose erroneous belief
in Jerusalem's golden gates to paradise makes him unwittingly a false prophet, deluding others.

Idzie skaczc po górach (*He Cometh Leaping upon the
Mountains*), set in contemporary France, can be regarded as a
pastiche of various narrative styles, including the stream of
consciousness, still fashionable at that time. Its portrayal of
French writers and artists contains satirical undertones, condemning what amounts to the commercially oriented and
relatively decadent western civilization. The author's irony
embraces his own narrative commentaries, where various
intellectual trends such as psychoanalysis and anthropology
are taunted.

Apelacja (*The Appeal*), published in the West and subsequently banned in Poland, aims at the simplicity of confession, articulated by a 'little man' whose obvious mediocrity
accounts for the impression of documentary truth. A former
officer of the 'people's militia' and a party *apparatchik*, he
eventually finds himself in a mental hospital, persecuted by
the Kafkaesque nightmare of being constantly spied upon by
secret agents. Once an autocratic and suspicious administrator himself, he can be regarded as a victim of his own
standards, but his naive faith in the party, which has survived
all ups and downs, shifts responsibility mostly upon the system and its destructive potential.

Andrzejewski's last novel, *Miazga* [Pulp], planned first as a
portrayal of the Polish cultural and political élite, eventually
turned into an experimental attempt to lay open the author's
growing doubts about story-telling and moral commitment.
Its crumbled form questions the reliability of fiction by giving
two parallel accounts of the same event; blends invented
stories with documents (the author's diary) and quasi-
documents (the 'biographies' of Poles); and includes short
stories written by the main character, which were published a
year later under Andrzejewski's own name, in *Nowe opowiadania* [New Tales]. The Conradian prison of the self eventually inhibits all attempts to say anything more than personal
truth: 'the writer narrates and asks questions. Nothing more'.

The novella *Nikt* [Nobody] is Andrzejewski's final expression of disillusionment and bitterness. This openly personal retelling of the story of ageing Odysseus contains
nothing but scepticism about the power of love and the

human search for truth. The fear of death, distressing the Homeric hero, is superseded only by his own legend, that is, by his fictitious *alter ego*.

—Stanislaw Eile

ASHES AND DIAMONDS (Popiół i diament)
Novel by Jerzy Andrzejewski, 1948.

Ashes and Diamonds, first published in the literary magazine *Odrodzenie* in 1947 under the title *Zaraz po wojnie* [Just after the War], is one of the most controversial Polish novels written in the post-war period. Set in a provincial capital, Ostrowiec, between 6 and 9 May 1945—that is, during the first days of Polish People's Republic—it portrays circumstances related to the Communist takeover. Its manifold story-line centres upon the assassination of Stefan Szczuka, the local secretary of the Polish Worker's Party, by Maciek Chełmicki, a soldier of the anti-Communist Home Army. The main conflict between the underground forces and those who support the new order is shown in the broader context of post-war society, which embraces not only heroes and villains, but also the confused victims of declined moral standards. Vengeful officers of the Home Army, youthful delinquents turned into criminals, a judge who attempts to get over his disgraceful conduct in a concentration camp and make a fresh start, a mixture of spineless people and cynical careerists—these represent the damage inflicted by the war upon the Polish population.

Andrzejewski's resolute support for the new political system and his corresponding condemnation of those who oppose it failed initially to satisfy the most orthodox Marxists. *Ashes and Diamonds*, however, eventually became a classic of the Polish People's Republic, where more than 25 editions of the novel were printed and where it remained on the school syllabus. The international success of Andrzej Wajda's film also contributed to the novel's high reputation. With the emergence of political opposition and post-Communist Poland, however, the novel's seriously biased message has been challenged subsequently.

Ashes and Diamonds, despite its pro-Communist dedication, can hardly be regarded as a typical example of Socialist Realism. Andrzejewski, once a Catholic writer, attempted to adjust his old dichotomy of good and evil to the Marxist understanding of class struggle and progress. Within this frame, he simply related evil to the 'forces of the past' and good to those who fought for 'the future' and were thus reshaping the existing social order. Following the novel's epigraph, taken from Cyprian Norwid's poem, he asks whether ashes will eventually bring to light a 'starlike diamond', hidden under the post-war rubble. The apocalyptic power of physical and moral devastation, caused by recent events, has been distributed, though, according to the political criteria, where those who do not belong to 'the forces of history' and their march forwards are sentenced to be astray also in a moral sense. The ethical decadence of Judge Kossecki, who attempted to survive a concentration camp at any cost, is branded as 'the bankruptcy of a petit bourgeois' by an upright Party member, Podgórski. By contrast, Maria Szczuka, a Communist, sacrificed herself in support of her fellow prisoners and died with dignity in Ravensbrück. A party in the Monopol Hotel, which has assembled former aristocrats as well as members of the intelligentsia and the political élite, exudes an apocalyptic atmosphere, while a polonaise danced in the reception room apparently symbolizes an ill-matched alliance between the old and the new.

In a similar way Andrzejewski approaches the political struggle between the Home Army and the Communists, where—despite endeavours to avoid black-and-white simplifications—the latter are ultimately represented as wholly in the right. They are portrayed as deserted heroes, in the middle of an unresponsive, immature society, who fight against the odds for a brilliant future. The Home Army, by contrast, represents only hatred and death, as a force that has placed itself on the wrong side of the barricade. By espousing a cause hostile to progress the Home Army is represented as having reduced to absurdity a sense of duty and often authentic patriotism. As a result, the most conscientious soldiers of the Home Army, such as Andrzej Kossecki and Maciek Chełmicki, are afflicted by an internal struggle between the innate human inclination towards love and friendship and the politically motivated inclination towards hatred and murder. Since the idealized Communists do not share such dilemmas, only the members of the Home Army are tormented by half-conscious longings for peace and normal life. Scenes portraying Andrzej Kossecki's streak of sympathy with a Russian soldier as just another human being, or Chełmicki's instinctive solidarity with his prospective victim, Szczuka, a stranger 'unknown but cherished', subordinate humanitarian principles to the writer's political end. Maciek and Andrzej, in Andrzejewski's view, belong to the 'lost generation' degraded by the war and the wrong cause. Hence, their tragedy is authentic but inevitable. Maciek's death, despite its appearance of accidental killing, represents the logical outcome of his life. It is a form of punishment not only for the assassination of Szczuka, but for the wrongly chosen political code as well. In other words, the author tries to demonstrate that Maciek has been trampled upon by the victorious forces of history, as an individual who has tragically forfeited his rights to love (represented by his affair with Krystyna Rozbicka) and family life in a new society.

Ashes and Diamonds is a novel with an unequivocal message. Sympathy for some 'misguided' soldiers of the anti-Communist underground does not undermine convictions, articulated by Szczuka, that only the Party represents the right path, even if on its way it makes mistakes. Consequently, the narrative form is very traditional, to accommodate this ideological commitment. Andrzejewski leaves no doubt as to who is right and who is wrong. Every dispute seems to envisage its unavoidable conclusion. Well-argued doubts, voiced by a devoted socialist, Kalicki, Szczuka's old friend, are flatly rejected by Szczuka as the pure misunderstanding of historical inevitability. Still, with all its faults, *Ashes and Diamonds* is skilfully narrated and this accounts for its popularity.

—Stanislaw Eile

ANNUNZIO, Gabriele d'. See **D'ANNUNZIO, Gabriele**.

ANOUILH, Jean (Marie Lucien Pierre). Born in Cérisole, Bordeaux, France, 23 June 1910. Educated at École Colbert, Bordeaux; Collège Chaptal; studied law at the Sorbonne, Paris, 1928–29. Military service during the 1930s. Married 1) the actress Monelle Valentin in 1931 (divorced 1953), one daughter; 2) Nicole Lançon in 1953, two daughters and one son. Publicity and gag writer for films, and advertising copywriter for Publicité Damour, Paris, 2 years; secretary, Louis Jouvet's Comédie des Champs-Élysées, Paris, 1931–32; assistant to the director Georges Pitoëff; full-time writer; also a film director. Recipient: Grand prize of the French Cinema, 1949; Tony award (USA), 1955; New York Drama Critics Circle award, 1957; Cino del Duca prize, 1970; French Drama Critics award, 1970; Paris Critics prize, 1971. *Died 3 October 1987.*

PUBLICATIONS

Plays

L'Hermine (produced 1932). 1934; as *The Ermine*, translated by Miriam John, in *Plays of the Year*, 13, 1956; also translated by John, in *Five Plays* (I), 1958.
La Mandarine (produced 1933).
Y'avait un prisonnier (produced 1935). In *La Petite Illustration*, 1935.
Le Voyageur sans bagage (produced 1937). In *Pièces noires*, 1942; edited by Diane W. Birckbichler, 1973; as *Traveller Without Luggage*, translated by John Whiting, 1959; also translated by Whiting, in *Seven Plays*, 1967; Lucienne Hill, 1959.
La Sauvage (produced 1938). 1938; as *The Restless Heart*, translated by Lucienne Hill, 1957; also translated by Hill, in *Five Plays* (II), 1959.
Le Bal des voleurs (produced 1938). 1938; as *Thieves' Carnival*, translated by Lucienne Hill, 1952; also translated by Hill, in *Seven Plays*, 1967.
Léocadia (produced 1940). In *Pièces roses*, 1942; edited by Bettina L. Knapp and Alba Della Fazia, 1965; as *Time Remembered*, translated by Patricia Moyes, 1955; also in *Five Plays* (II), 1959; as *Léocadia*, translated by Timberlake Wertenbaker, in *Five Plays*, 1987.
Marie-Jeanne; ou, La Fille du peuple, from a play by Dennery and Mallain (produced 1940).
Le Rendez-vous de Senlis (produced 1941). In *Pièces roses*, 1942; as *Dinner with the Family*, translated by Edward O. Marsh, 1958.
Eurydice (produced 1942). In *Pièces noires*, 1942; edited by E. Freeman, with *Médée*, 1984; as *Point of Departure*, translated by Kitty Black, 1951; as *Legend of Lovers*, translated by Black, 1952; as *Eurydice*, translated by Black, in *Five Plays* (I), 1958.
Pièces roses (includes *Le Bal des voleurs*; *Le Rendez-vous de Senlis*; *Léocadia*). 1942; enlarged edition (includes *Humulus le muet*). 1958.
Pièces noires (includes *L'Hermine*; *La Sauvage*; *Le Voyageur sans bagage*; *Eurydice*). 1942.
Antigone, from the play by Sophocles (produced 1944). 1946; edited by W.M. Landers, 1954; also edited by R. Laubreaux, 1965, and J. Monférier, 1968; as *Antigone*, translated and adapted by Lewis Galantière, 1946; also translated by Lothian Small, with *Eurydice*, 1951; in *Five Plays* (I), 1958; Barbara Bray, in *Five Plays*, 1987.
Roméo et Jeannette (produced 1946). In *Nouvelles pièces noires*, 1946; as *Romeo and Jeannette*, translated by Miriam John, in *Five Plays* (I), 1958.

Nouvelles pièces noires (includes *Jézabel*; *Antigone*; *Roméo et Jeannette*; *Médée*). 1946.
Médée (produced 1953). In *Nouvelles pièces noires*, 1946; as *Medea*, translated by Lothian Small, in *Plays of the Year*, 15, 1956; as *Medea: A 'Black' Play*, translated by Luce and Arthur Klein, 1957; also translated by Klein and Klein, in *Seven Plays*, 1967.
L'Invitation au château (produced 1947). 1948; as *Ring Round the Moon*, translated by Christopher Fry, 1950.
Ardèle; ou, La Marguerite (produced 1948). 1949; as *Ardele*, translated by Lucienne Hill, 1951; also translated by Hill, in *Five Plays* (II), 1959.
Les Demoiselles de la nuit (ballet scenario; produced 1948).
Épisode de la vie d'un auteur (produced 1948). With *La Belle Vie*, 1980; as *Episode in the Life of an Author*, translated by Miriam John, in *Seven Plays*, 1967.
Humulus le muet, with Jean Aurenche (produced 1948). N.d; as *Humulus the Mute*, translated by Michael Benedikt, in *Modern French Theatre*, 1964.
La Répétition; ou, L'Amour puni (produced 1950). 1950; as *The Rehearsal*, translated by Pamela Hansford Johnson and Kitty Black, in *Five Plays* (I), 1958; also translated by Jeremy Sams, 1991.
Colombe (produced 1951). In *Pièces brillantes*, 1951; as *Colombe*, translated by Denis Cannan, 1952; as *Mademoiselle Colombe*, in *Five Plays* (II), 1959.
Monsieur Vincent (screenplay), with Jean Bernard Luc. 1951.
Pièces brillantes (includes *L'Invitation au château*; *Colombe*; *La Répétition*; *Cécile*). 1951.
Cécile; ou, L'École des pères (produced 1954). In *Pièces brillantes*, 1951; as *Cecile; or, The School for Fathers*, translated by Luce and Arthur Klein, in *From the Modern Repertoire*, 3, edited by Eric Bentley, 1956; also translated by Klein and Klein, in *Seven Plays*, 1967.
La Valse des toréadors (produced 1952). 1952; as *Waltz of the Toreadors*, translated by Lucienne Hill, in *Plays of the Year*, 8, 1953; revised translation by Hill, in *Five Plays*, 1987.
La Nuit des rois, from the play by Shakespeare (produced 1961). In *Trois comédies*, 1952.
Le Loup (ballet scenario), with Georges Neveux. 1953.
L'Alouette (produced 1953). 1953; edited by Merlin Thomas and Simon Lee, 1956; as *The Lark*, translated by Christopher Fry, 1955; in *Five Plays* (II), 1959; translated by Fry, in *Five Plays*, 1987.
Ornifle; ou, Le Courant d'air (produced 1955). 1956; as *Ornifle*, translated by Lucienne Hill, 1970; as *It's Later Than You Think*, translated by Hill, 1970.
Il est important d'être aimé, with Claude Vincent, from the play by Oscar Wilde (produced 1964). In *L'Avant-scène*, 101, 1955.
Pauvre Bitos; ou, Le Dîner de têtes (produced 1956). In *Pièces grinçantes*, 1956; as *Poor Bitos*, translated by Lucienne Hill, 1964; revised translation by Hill, in *Five Plays*, 1987.
Pièces grinçantes (includes *Ardèle*; *La Valse des toréadors*; *Ornifle*; *Pauvre Bitos*). 1956.
Five Plays (I) (includes *Antigone*; *Eurydice*; *The Ermine*; *The Rehearsal*; *Romeo and Jeannette*), translated by Miriam John, Lucienne Hill, Lewis Galantière, and Kitty Black. 1958.
Five Plays (II) (includes *The Restless Heart*; *Time Remembered*; *Ardele*; *Mademoiselle Colombe*; *The Lark*), translated by Lucienne Hill, Patricia Moyes, Louis Kronenberger, and Lilian Hellman. 1959.
L'Hurluberlu; ou, Le Réactionnaire amoureux (produced 1959). 1959; as *The Fighting Cock*, translated and adapted by Lucienne Hill, 1960.

Becket; ou, L'Honneur de Dieu (produced 1959). 1959; as *Becket; or, The Honor of God*, translated by Lucienne Hill, 1961.

Madame de . . . (in English, produced 1959). 1959.

La Petite Molière, with Roland Laudenback (produced 1959). In *L'Avant-scène*, 1959.

Le Songe du critique (produced 1960). In *L'Avant-scène*, 143, 1959.

Pièces costumées (includes *L'Alouette*; *Becket*; *La Foire d'empoigne*). 1960.

La Foire d'empoigne (produced 1962). In *Pièces costumées*, 1960; as *Catch as Catch Can*, translated by Lucienne Hill, in *Seven Plays*, 1967.

Tartuffe, from the play by Molière (produced 1960). In *L'Avant-scène*, 1961.

La Grotte (produced 1961). 1961; as *The Cavern*, translated by Lucienne Hill, 1966.

Victor; ou, Les Enfants au pouvoir, from the play by Roger Vitrac (produced 1962). In *L'Avant-scène*, 1962.

L'Amant complaisant, with Nicole Anouilh, from the play by Graham Greene (produced 1962). 1962.

L'Orchestre (produced 1962). 1970; as *The Orchestra*, translated by Miriam John, in *Seven Plays*, 1967; published separately, 1975.

Richard III, from the play by Shakespeare (produced 1964). N.d.

L'Ordalie; ou, La Petite Catherine de Heilbronn, from a story by Heinrich von Kleist (produced 1966). In *L'Avant-scène*, 1967.

Collected Plays. 2 vols., 1966–67.

Seven Plays (includes *Thieves' Carnival*; *Medea*; *Cecile; or, The School for Fathers*; *Traveller Without Luggage*; *The Orchestra*; *Episode in the Life of an Author*; *Catch as Catch Can*), translated by John Whiting, Luce and Arthur Klein, Miriam John, and Lucienne Hill. 1967.

Le Boulanger, la boulangère, et le petit mitron (produced 1968). 1969.

Théâtre complet. 9 vols., 1968.

Cher Antoine; ou, L'Amour raté (produced 1969). 1969; as *Dear Antoine; or, The Love That Failed*, translated by Lucienne Hill, 1971.

Le Théâtre; ou, La Vie comme elle est (produced 1970).

Ne Réveillez pas Madame (produced 1970). 1970.

Les Poissons rouges; ou, Mon père, ce héros (produced 1970). 1970.

Nouvelles pièces grinçantes (includes *L'Hurluberlu*; *La Grotte*; *L'Orchestre*; *Le Boulanger, la boulangère, et le petit mitron*; *Les Poissons rouges*). 1970.

Tu étais si gentil quand tu étais petit (produced 1971). 1972.

Le Directeur de l'Opéra (produced 1973). 1972; as *The Director of the Opera*, translated by Lucienne Hill, 1973.

Pièces baroques (includes *Cher Antoine*; *Ne Réveillez pas Madame*; *Le Directeur de l'Opéra*). 1974.

Monsieur Barnett (produced 1974). In *L'Avant-scène*, 559, 1975.

L'Arrestation (produced 1975). 1975; as *The Arrest*, translated by Lucienne Hill, 1978.

Le Scénario (produced 1976). 1976.

Chers Zoizeaux (produced 1976). 1977.

Pièces secrètes (includes *Tu étais si gentil quand tu étais petit*; *L'Arrestation*; *Le Scénario*). 1977.

Vive Henri IV. 1977.

La Culotte (produced 1978). 1978.

La Belle Vie (television play), with *Épisode de la vie d'un auteur*. 1980.

Le Nombril (produced 1981). 1981; as *Number One*, translated by Michael Frayn, 1984.

Pièces farceuses (includes *Chers Zoiseaux*; *La Culotte*; *Épisode de la vie d'un auteur*; *Le Nombril*). 1984.

Oedipe; ou, Le Roi boiteux, from the play by Sophocles. 1986.

Thomas More; ou, L'Homme libre (screenplay). 1987.

Five Plays (includes *Antigone*; *Léocadia*; *The Lark*; *Poor Bitos*; *The Waltz of the Toreadors*), translated by Barbara Bray, Timberlake Wertenbaker, Christopher Fry, and Lucienne Hill. 1987.

Plays 2 (includes *The Rehearsal*; *Becket*; *Eurydice*; *The Orchestra*). 1992.

Screenplays: *Les Dégourdis de la onzième*, with Jean Aurenche, 1936; *Vous n'avez rien à déclarer*, with Jean Aurenche, 1937; *Les Otages*, with Jean Aurenche, 1939; *Cavalcade d'amour*, 1939; *Le Voyageur sans bagage (Identity Unknown)*, with Jean Aurenche, 1944; *Monsieur Vincent*, with Jean Bernard Luc, 1947; *Anna Karenina*, with Julien Duvivier and Guy Morgan, 1948; *Pattes blanches*, with Jean Bernard Luc, 1949; *Caroline chérie*, 1951; *Deux sous de violettes*, with Monelle Valentin, 1951; *Le Rideau rouge*, 1952; *Le Chevalier de la nuit*, 1953; *La Mort de belle (The Passion of Slow Fire)*, 1961; *La Ronde*, 1964; *A Time for Loving*, 1972.

Television Plays: *Le Jeune Homme et le lion*, 1976; *La Belle Vie*, 1979.

Other

Michel-Marie Poulain, with Pierre Imbourg and André Warnod. 1953.

Fables. 1962.

Robert Brasillach et la génération perdue, with others. 1987.

La Vicomtesse d'Eristal n'a pas reçu son balai mécanique: souvenirs d'un jeune homme (autobiography). 1987.

*

Bibliography: *Jean Anouilh: An Annotated Bibliography* by Kathleen White Kelley, 1973.

Critical Studies: *Anouilh* by Marguerite Archer, 1951; *Jean Anouilh: Poet of Pierrot and Pantaloon* by Edward O. Marsh, 1953; *The World of Jean Anouilh* by Leonard C. Pronko, 1961; *Anouilh: A Study of Theatrics* by John Harvey, 1964; *Anouilh: La Peine de vivre* by Clément Borgal, 1966; *Jean Anouilh* by Philip Thody, 1968; *Anouilh* by Alba della Fazia Amoia, 1969; *Jean Anouilh: Textes d'Anouilh, points de vue critiques, témoignages, chronologie, bibliographie, illustrations* by Paul Ginestier, 1969; *'Antigone': Analyse critique* by Etienne Frois, 1972; *Théâtre d'Anouilh* by Bernard Beugnot, 1973; *Jean Anouilh: Stages in Rebellion* by Branko Lenski, 1975; *La Pureté dans le théâtre de Jean Anouilh* by André F. Rombout, 1975; *Le Théâtre de Jean Anouilh* by Jacques Vier, 1976; *Anouilh, littérature et politique* by Élie de Comminges, 1977; *Jean Anouilh* by Lewis W. Falb, 1977; *Lecture d'Anouilh: Textes et réflexions critiques* by Benito d'Ajetti, 1978; *Jean Anouilh: Les Problèmes de l'existence dans un théâtre de marionettes* by Thérèse Malachy, 1978; *The Theatre of Jean Anouilh* by H.G. McIntyre, 1981; *Anouilh: Antigone* by W.D. Howarth, 1983; *Jean Anouilh: Life, Work, and Criticism* by Christopher Smith, 1985.

*   *   *

After two early plays, *L'Hermine* (*The Ermine*) and *Y'avait un prisonnier*, considered promising but not extremely successful, Jean Anouilh achieved his real breakthrough, artistically and financially, with *Le Voyageur sans bagage* (*Traveller Without Luggage*), and later seasons in Paris almost always included a new Anouilh work, many subsequently revived in England and America. These three works, along with the contemporary *Jézabel*, and *La Sauvage* (*The Restless Heart*), were characterized by their author as *pièces noires* ('black plays'), in contrast to three other works of the same period, *Le Bal des voleurs* (*Thieves' Carnival*), *Le Rendez-vous de Senlis* (*Dinner with the Family*) and *Léocadia* (*Time Remembered*), which he designated *pièces roses* ('rose plays'). A common theme of these plays is shared by Anouilh with the pioneers of modern realistic drama, especially Ibsen—the burden of the environment and especially of the past on a protagonist seeking a happier, freer existence. Although neither type of play takes an ultimately optimistic position, the 'black plays' generally demonstrate the hopelessness of this dream, while the 'rose plays' allow their protagonists at least a temporary happiness, often through an escape into a world of make-believe.

During the 1940s Anouilh, while maintaining his complex tonality and deft dramatic technique, turned from contemporary to mythical, classic, and historic subjects and to themes more closely related to the concerns of such writers as Sartre and Camus. Now the past was regarded as only part of the contingent circumstances of existence against which the independent spirit of the protagonist must define itself. The best-known play of this group is *Antigone*, which established Anouilh as a leading dramatist, not only because of the power with which he drew the classic confrontation between the uncompromising Antigone and the politically expedient Creon, but because French theatre-goers under the occupation read the play as a contemporary political parable. The immediate post-war plays *Roméo et Jeannette* (*Romeo and Jeannette*) and *Médée* (*Medea*) similarly focused upon protagonists who refused to strike a bargain with the world of compromise. Much the same spirit infuses Anouilh's Joan of Arc story *L'Alouette* (*The Lark*), the success of which rivalled that of *Antigone*.

With the exception of *The Lark*, Anouilh's plays of the late 1940s and the 1950s depict a darker and crueller universe, where his heroic protagonists give way to more common souls who have in one way or another accepted life as it is—simply and unquestioningly, as victims, or calculatedly and manipulatively. Anouilh divided his plays of this period into *Pièces brillantes* ('brilliant plays') and *Pièces grinçantes* ('grating plays'). The 'brilliance' of the first group, *L'Invitation au château* (*Ring Round the Moon*), *Cécile*, *La Répétition; ou, L'Amour puni* (*The Rehearsal*), and *Colombe*, comes from their elegant, aristocratic settings and from their polished, witty language, often reminiscent of the sparkle of Marivaux (indeed it is a Marivaux play that is being rehearsed in *The Rehearsal*). The pain and cruelty of life and the inevitability of death are still present, but these can be put aside at least temporarily by the pleasures of living for the moment, often developed in specifically theatrical metaphors. A darker tone and a more bitter humour mark the 'grating plays', *Ardèle*, *La Valse des toréadors* (*Waltz of the Toreadors*), *Ornifle*, *Pauvre Bitos; ou, Le Dîner de têtes* (*Poor Bitos*), and *L'Hurluberlu; ou, Le Réactionnaire amoureux* (*The Fighting Cock*). Here, as in the 'brilliant plays', the idealistic young lovers of Anouilh's early works have been replaced by middle-aged characters, all too aware of the disillusion of passing time.

Becket, a major international success, depicts another his-

torical martyr, Thomas à Becket, and *La Foire d'empoigne* (*Catch as Catch Can*) pits a cynical and gross Napoleon against a noble but ineffective Louis XVIII. These, along with *The Lark*, were characterized by Anouilh as his *Pièces costumées* ('costume plays'), although they share not only historical 'costumed' settings, but also an idealistic protagonist seeking a moral path in a world of corruption and manipulation. In each case the quest ends in death and apparent defeat, but the hero leaves the history of his struggle as an example and inspiration for others, and so the forces of nobility achieve at least a qualified affirmation.

Anouilh's final period begins with *La Grotte* (*The Cavern*). It is a Pirandellian work, whose central character is a frustrated author and whose action concerns the tensions of a play he has been unable to write. Anouilh felt his subsequent plays took a new direction, but this is more a matter of emphasis than of actual new concerns. The interrelationship of theatre and life is a theme recurrent throughout his *oeuvre*, but it takes on a special prominence in these late works, whose central figures are most often dramatists or theatre directors. Family relationships and the tensions of private life, another long-time concern, are also central in the late plays. In a number of them a special relationship exists between theatre and family, suggesting, as Maeterlinck argued in 'The Tragedy in Everyday Life', that the inner drama of everyday interpersonal relationships is more profound and more important than the traditional heightened action of 'theatre'. Antoine, the playwright-protagonist of *Cher Antoine; ou, L'Amour raté* (*Dear Antoine; or, The Love That Failed*), advocates an attention to such *pièces secrètes* ('secret dramas')—the title of an Anouilh collection.

In the last plays, concluding with *Le Nombril* (*Number One*), the author, however successful and honoured, becomes ever more isolated from friends and family, who simultaneously blame him for all their misfortunes and feed upon his success. Anouilh's dark view of the human condition here reaches its final expression. His young heroes are constrained by the past and by social circumstances; the more mature protagonists of the 'grating plays' suffered more personal unhappiness from their own ageing and in their human relationships. The artists of the final plays, with death close upon them, find that even the closest relationships are tainted by selfishness and greed, and offer as consolation only whatever appreciation artist and audience may derive from a sensitive awareness of life's 'secret drama'.

—Marvin Carlson

ANTIGONE
Play by Jean Anouilh, 1944.

In Greek mythology Antigone, Oedipus' daughter, is put to death because she acts against an edict, made by her uncle Creon, forbidding the burial of her brother Polynices. Sophocles' play *Antigone* dramatizes the story, and it is this on which Anouilh's version is based.

The original play begins after Oedipus' two sons, Eteocles and Polynices, have killed each other over the crown of Thebes, and Creon, the new king of the city and brother of Oedipus' mother and wife, has just given Eteocles an honourable funeral while decreeing that Polynices should suffer the dishonour of remaining unburied on account of his treachery. In spite of this prohibition and the death penalty attached to its violation, Antigone, Polynices' sister, dares to perform the ritualistic burial. When she is caught and brought before the king, she defiantly expresses her fidelity to her brother and her resolution to adhere to the laws of the gods rather than those of her uncle. Creon declares that he will not permit her to act against his authority and condemns her to death. At this point Haemon, Creon's son and Antigone's fiancé, begs his father to moderate his severity but succeeds only in angering him. Tiresias, the blind high priest, warns the king that his excessive use of power will be punished by the gods. Creon's eventual decision to release Antigone comes too late: his niece has hanged herself, his son accidentally kills himself in a struggle with him, and his wife, Eurydice, commits suicide.

In rewriting the story, Anouilh omits the character Tiresias and adds that of the nurse to stress the fact that, as opposed to Sophocles' Amazon-like heroine, Antigone is a young girl who needs reassurance and affection. However, in a scene invented by Anouilh in which Antigone renounces her love for Haemon, she is also shown to be courageous. Creon too is changed. Although, like Sophocles' character, he is angry and indignant when he learns that his orders have been disobeyed, he is less of a tyrant and more of a diplomatic statesman. When he discovers who the culprit is, he quickly becomes concerned with avoiding scandal. In a section that owes little to Sophocles, he tries to persuade his niece to give up her stand and offers to hush up the affair. To convince her, he points out that Polynices and Eteocles were both equally villainous and even admits that her brothers were so unrecognizable after their battle that there was no way of knowing which body had been retrieved and given state honours. It is clear that he does not want Antigone to die, and when he does condemn her it is a political decision aimed at reestablishing his authority and preventing anarchy rather than a punishment for the violation of his law. As in the Greek tragedy, Antigone hangs herself and Haemon and Erydice commit suicide.

Anouilh's play is about the revolt of disillusioned but heroic youth against oppression. Antigone would rather die than live without freedom and ideals. Her confrontation with Creon represents the ageless response of adolescence to the adult world of pragmatism and resignation. She is intractably stubborn and refuses any concession or compromise: if she cannot be free to live according to her moral principles and so retain her self-respect, she prefers to die. What makes this point valid is that her loyalty to her brother comes before her duty to the state. However, the tragic nature of the play lies in the fact that Creon's attitude is equally justifiable. Although he is shown to be wrong in assuming that there are no limits to his power, his primary duty as ruler is the assurance of state security and his decision to let Polynices' body rot in the sun is forced upon him by political necessity. Antigone's heroic stance can therefore also be regarded as unrealistic and immature.

Antigone was first produced in occupied Paris in February 1944 and was, at the time, interpreted as symbolizing the struggle between the resistance and the collaborators. Anouilh was criticized for writing an apparently Nazi play in which Creon, taken to represent Laval and Pétain, is treated sympathetically.

—Silvano Levy

APOLLINAIRE, Guillaume. Born Guillaume Apollinaris de Kostrowitzky in Rome, Italy, 26 August 1880. Educated in Monte Carlo, Cannes, and Nice, until 1897. Married Jacqueline Kolb in 1918. Served in World War I, 1914–16: invalided out. Moved to the Ardennes, 1899; began using name Apollinaire, 1901; tutor in Germany, 1901–02; freelance writer and critic in Paris; editor, *Le Festin d'Ésope*, 1903, and *La Revue Immoraliste*; helped organize cubist room at Salon des Indépendants, 1911, and wrote manifesto on Futurism; imprisoned briefly on suspicion of art theft, 1911; art critic, *Le Petit Bleu*, 1912; editor, *Les Soirées de Paris*, 1912–14. *Died 9 November 1918.*

PUBLICATIONS

Collections

Selected Writings, edited and translated by Roger Shattuck. 1950.
Oeuvres poétiques, edited by Michel Décaudin and Marcel Adéma. 1956.
Oeuvres complètes, edited by Michel Décaudin. 4 vols., 1965–66.
Oeuvres en prose, edited by Michel Décaudin. 1977.
Oeuvres. 5 vols., 1983–84.
Oeuvres en prose complètes, edited by Pierre Caizergues and Michel Décaudin. 1993.

Verse

Le Bestiaire; ou, Cortège d'Orphée. 1911; translated as *Le Bestiaire*, 1977; as *Bestiary; or, the Parade of Orpheus*, translated by Pepe Karmel and Lauren Shakley, 1980.
Alcools: Poèmes 1898–1913. 1913; edited by Tristan Tzara, 1953, and Garnet Rees, 1975; as *Alcools*, translated by William Meredith, 1964, also translated by Anne Hyde Greet, 1965.
Case d'armons. 1915.
Vitam impendere amori. 1917.
Calligrammes: Poèmes de la paix et de la guerre 1913–1916. 1918; as *Calligrammes: Poems of Peace and War (1913–1916)*, translated by Anne Hyde Greet (bilingual edition), 1980.
Le Cortège priapique. 1925.
Julie; ou, La Rose. 1927.
Le Condor et le morpion. 1931.
Ombre de mon amour. 1947; revised edition, as *Poèmes à Lou*, 1955.
Le Guetteur mélancolique. 1952.
Tendre comme le souvenir. 1952.
Selected Poems (bilingual edition), edited and translated by Oliver Bernard. 1965, enlarged edition, 1986.

Plays

Les Mamelles de Tirésias (produced 1917). 1918.
Couleur du temps (produced 1918). 1949.
Casanova. 1952.
La Température, with André Salmon (produced 1975). In *Oeuvres en prose*, 1977.
A Quelle Heure un train partira-t-il pour Paris?. 1982.

Fiction

Les Exploits d'un jeune Don Juan. 1907; as *The Exploits of a Young Don Juan*, translated by Alex Lykiard, 1986.
Les Onze Mille Verges. 1907; as *The Debauched Hospodar*, translated by Arcan Mole, 1953; as *Les Onze Mille Verges;*

or, the Amorous Adventures of Prince Mony Vibescu, translated by Nina Rootes, 1976.
L'Enchanteur pourrissant. 1909.
L'Hérésiarque et cie. 1910; selection, as *Contes choisis*, 1922; as *The Heresiarch and Company*, translated by Rémy Inglis Hall, 1965; as *The Wandering Jew and Other Stories*, 1965.
La Fin de Babylone. 1914.
Les Trois Don Juan. 1915.
Le Poète assassiné. 1916; edited by Michel Décaudin, 1959; as *The Poet Assassinated*, translated by Matthew Josephson, 1923; also translated by Ron Padgett, 1968.
La Femme assise: Chronique de France et d'Amérique. 1920.
Les Épingles: Contes. 1928.
Que faire?. 1950.

Other

Méditations esthétiques: Les Peintres cubistes. 1913; edited by Leroy C. Breunig and J.-Cl. Chevalier, 1965; as *The Cubist Painters: Aesthetic Meditations 1913*, translated by Lionel Abel, 1944; revised editions, 1949, 1962.
Le Flâneur des deux rives. 1918.
Il y a. 1925.
Anecdotiques. 1926.
Contemporains pittoresques. 1929.
Oeuvres érotiques complètes (verse and prose). 3 vols., 1934.
L'Esprit nouveau et les poètes. 1946.
Lettres à sa marraine. 1948.
Chroniques d'art, 1902–1918, edited by Leroy C. Breunig. 1961; as *Apollinaire On Art: Essays and Reviews*, translated by Susan Suliman. 1972.
Correspondance, with André Level, edited by Brigitte Level. 1976.
Petites flâneries d'art, edited by Pierre Caizergues. 1980.
Correspondance avec son frère et sa mère, edited by Gilbert Boudar and Michel Décaudin, 1987.
Correspondance, with Jean Cocteau, edited by Pierre Caizergues and Michel Décaudin. 1991.
Journal intime: 1898–1918, edited by Michel Décaudin. 1991.

Editor, *Chronique des grands siècles de la France*. 1912.

*

Critical Studies: *Apollinaire* by Marcel Adéma, 1954; *The Evolution of Apollinaire's Poetics, 1901–1914* by Francis J. Carmody, 1963; *Apollinaire, Poet among Painters* by Francis Steegmuller, 1963, reprinted 1985; *Apollinaire* by Margaret Davies, 1964; *Apollinaire* by Scott Bates, 1967, revised edition, 1989; *Apollinaire* by Leroy C. Breunig, 1969; *The Drama of Self in Apollinaire's Alcools* by Richard Howard Stamelman, 1975; *Guillaume Apollinaire* by Roger Little, 1976; *Guillaume Apollinaire as an Art Critic* by Harry E. Buckley, 1981; *The Creative Vision of Apollinaire: A Study of Imagination* by David Berry, 1982; *Apollinaire: Catalyst for Primitivism, Picabia and Duchamps* by Katia Samaltanos, 1984; *Alfred Jarry and Guillaume Apollinaire* by Claude Schumacher, 1984; *Reading Apollinaire: Theories of Poetic Language* by Timothy Mathews, 1987.

* * *

Guillaume Apollinaire's culture was eclectic. He preferred the Latin of the mystics to that of Virgil, heretical theologians to St Thomas, Italian story tellers of the Renaissance to Dante, The Kabbala to the Bible. In contrast to his learning, his heart was simple and limpid. At the publication of *Alcools* in 1913, Georges Duhamel called Apollinaire a pedlar with the mingled characteristics of a Levantine Jew, a South American, a Polish gentleman, and an Italian porter. To these roles might be added that of the innocent hero, part braggart, part simpleton, who discovered in war the brotherhood of man, and revealed to his many friends one of the truly noble, truly good souls of his age.

His poetry is composed of influences, readings, memories, echoes of many poets, from Villon to Verlaine and Jarry. But his voice is also bare and personal. The story of his life was the effort he made to guard secrets and mysteries, and to create for his friends and his public a character whom they would love and yet not know too intimately. The buffoonery of his character, his endless anecdotes and pranks, permitted him to conceal or disguise the nostalgia and sadness and even perhaps the tragedy of his life. But the poetry of Apollinaire is not mask and deceit. It is fantasy in the deepest sense of the word. It is lawful fantasy: its images rightfully conceal and communicate at the same time the emotions he had experienced.

His poetic fantasy was, first, that of revolt, by which he always remained precious and close to the Surrealists. He broke with the familiar patterns of thought, with the poetic clichés and literariness of the Parnassians and Symbolists, and with the familiar units and rules of syntax. His poetry comes together in a great freedom of composition, as if he allowed the images and emotions to compose themselves. In his poetry, phantoms, wanderers, mythic characters bearing sonorous names, appear and disappear as do the laws of syntax and prosody.

It was appropriate that Apollinaire, coming after the highly self-conscious and studied literary school of Symbolism, would, in rebellion against such artifice, seek to return to the most primitive sources of lyricism. His adventure, if we were to extract such a subject from his work, would closely resemble Gide's adventure: the lessons on freedom and gratuitousness and individual morality, which were being formulated at the same time. Apollinaire thus prolongs the lesson of Rimbaud and Mallarmé, in considering poetic activity as a secret means of knowledge, self-knowledge and world-knowledge.

All the opposites are joined and harmonized in his poetry: fire and water, day and night, the bookish and the popular, the libertine and the sorrowing lover. All the myths are in his verses, in close company with pure inventions. He called upon his immediate knowledge of cities and ports, of unscrupulous *voyous* and popular songs, in order to speak in his tone of prophet and discoverer. His universe is one of chance and naivety, of a certain childlike candour which the Surrealists would later try to reconstruct. He was the first to use a facile exoticism and eroticism which today is found in American films and jazz music. But in his most facile songs, as in 'Le Musicien de Saint-Merry', he is able to generate a delicate irony from the shifts in tone.

There is a record of Apollinaire's voice reciting 'Le Pont Mirabeau', which contains his most persistent theme—the passing and change of sentiments, and the poet's own stability:

> Vienne la nuit sonne l'heure
> Les jours s'en vont je demeure

The chance meetings in the world and their dissolutions bear relationship with the chance meetings of words in a poem. Apollinaire is first a poet of regret, of delicate nostalgia, and then, in a very mysterious way, he is the poet of resurrection and exaltation. His memory of the dead makes them into constant presences. 'Vendémiaire', the long poem that ends *Alcools*, is a striking evocation of Paris and of all the myths of poetic preservation, of Orpheus and of Icarus who tried to possess the world. The wine of the universe brought contentment to 'oceans animals plants cities destinies and singing stars'. The poem also contains accents of sorrow and Apollinaire's familiar reference to the sadness of children with their salt tears that taste of the ocean. But it is at the same time a poem on hope and one of the most stirring of the century.

The contrast between Apollinaire's erudition, nourished on pornography, magic, popular literature, encyclopedias, and his total simplicity as a song writer, explains to some degree the profound irony pervading all of his poetry. His appearance, at the beginning of the 20th century, coincided with many new aesthetic preoccupations to which he brought his own inventiveness and speculative inquiry. His work joined with that of Max Jacob, Picasso, Braque, Derain, and Matisse in a series of fantasies and works of art that have gone far in shaping modern sensitivity. A farcical festive air presided over many of the modes of art that were given the names of cubism, fauvism, Negro art, cosmopolitanism, erotology. Apollinaire himself was responsible for the term 'surrealism'. He literally became a prophet in his support of aesthetic innovations that were to become the accepted forms of the future. His articles on painting place him second to Baudelaire among the aestheticians of modern France.

The lesson Apollinaire teaches about poetry is the most important in France since Rimbaud's. ('La Chanson du mal-aimé' has become for our age what 'Le Lac' and 'Tristesse d'Olympio' were for the 19th century.) His poetry does not try to fathom the supernatural, but simply to state the incomprehensibility of the ordinary and the commonplace. Every human expression he saw became sphinx-like for him, and every word he overheard resembled a sibyl's utterance. Nascent language it would seem to be, as the poet, performing his earliest role of demiurge, calls the world to be born again by naming it.

—Wallace Fowlie

LA CHANSON DU MAL-AIMÉ (Song of the Ill-Beloved)
Poem by Guillaume Apollinaire, 1913.

Apollinaire's 'La Chanson du mal-aimé' is from his first collection, *Alcools*, in which poems from his early years embrace a variety of emotional upheavals and random events in the poet's psyche, presenting what Roger Little has called the 'protean life of the imagination' (*Guillaume Apollinaire*, 1976). *Alcools* generally presents the loss of the labours of love, or an elegy to lost love, and this poem was written at the end of Apollinaire's romance with Annie Playden. Through a combination of a number of disparate sources and fragments, 'La Chanson du mal-aimé' mixes this sense of sad loss with self-pity, frustration, excitement, and retrospective and proleptic views of the narrator's life, all of which add up to a veiled celebration of rhetorical and linguistic power.

'La Chanson du mal-aimé' is carefully structured around a main narrative divided into four sections by three interpolated episodes. Walks across two cities, London and Paris, provide the narrative framework for the poem and act as the prompting for an exploration of the narrator's mind and memory. Thus, the chronology of 'real' time is played off against the pressures of emotional time. Written in a series of five-line octosyllabic stanzas (or quintils), the poem maintains

a tight rhyme scheme (ababa) that provides a strict formality within which the poem runs the gamut of emotions—hope, despair, madness, jealousy, hatred—all caused by the demise of love. The poem works through a series of metamorphoses of the narrator, as he merges his personal emotions with analogous narratives and images.

The poem opens with the narrator wandering through the foggy London streets. His beloved appears in various forms (a ruffian, or a drunk staggering from a pub), which he chases as vainly as Pharaoh pursuing the Israelites. Clutching at these apparitions in the London streets, he realizes that he is not Ulysses with a patient Penelope, or King Dushyanta with a loyal Sakuntala. Evoking paradigms for testing the qualities, commitments, and fidelity of his past love, he is someone who, having lost love, now needs to seek a new identity and to rebuild his life. The predominant imagery of powerful kings in the poem, 'rois heureux', 'rois maudits', 'rois persécuteurs', and 'rois fous', and 'les rois du monde'—only serves to stress the impotence and emptiness of the narrator's actions.

After the refrain about the former beauties of love, the mood switches to the fresh albeit clichéd joys of pastoral love in the 'Aubade chantée à Laetare un an passé' ('Aubade sung at Laetare a year ago'). Here 'L'aube au ciel fait de roses plis' ('The dawn makes pink folds in the sky') and gods dance in accompaniment to Pan's music. Yet this apparent state of happiness takes an ironic twist, since 'Beaucoup de ces dieux ont péri' ('Many of these gods have died') and the narrator returns to his previous despair.

The narrative then breaks to a comparison of his former love with the fidelity of the Zaporogian Cossacks to their habitat of the Steppes and Christianity. The poem exemplifies fierce loyalty and fidelity, by narrating the Cossack's mocking refusal to obey the Sultan's demand for their allegiance to Islam. In the 'Answer of the Zaporogian Cossacks to the Sultan of Constantinople', the poem presents a series of calculated insults delivered to the Sultan in defiance of his command.

The refrain of the poem concerning the issue of lost love in the image of the Milky Way returns, before the poem finally introduces the third interlude, a section on the symbolism of 'Les Sept Épées' ('The Seven Swords'). This section oscillates between the eroticism of the phallic swords and the Christian religious symbolism of the seven swords piercing the heart of Our Lady of Sorrows, and is a good example of how Apollinaire attempts to turn legends into psychological truths. Linked to his earlier sorrow as 'Sept épées de mélancolie/Sans morfil' ('Seven swords of melancholy/with no blunt edge'), each sword is carefully described with its attributes. The refrain returns, before a final meditation on destiny occurs, in which the narrator's madness finds an analogue in the story of the mad King Ludwig of Bavaria, and exemplifies the results of power being brought low by fate. The poet finds himself back in sparkling Paris, although with his sorrow unalleviated, musing over the demise of his love and of his power to articulate his emotions.

The principal focus of the poem is on a return to clear comprehension after illusion and hallucination. In making such a progression, the narrator seeks to define what constitutes true and false love. As the epigraph to the poem suggests in the image of love as a phoenix rising from the fire, the poem charts a movement from despair to a reconciliation with loss and a new optimism for the future born out of the trials of the past misfortune. Yet it also suggests the ways in which private sorrow is inextricably linked to public expression. In gesturing to various forms like the ballad, the epic, and the pastoral lyric, and demonstrating a debt to the aesthetic preoccupations and penchants of Symbolist and Parnassian art, the poem establishes the self as the site of narrative construction, and the individual psyche as an amalgamation of social myths.

—Tim Woods

ZONE
Poem by Guillaume Apollinaire, 1913.

'Zone' is the threshold poem that leads the reader into *Alcools*. The term 'alcools' suggests both 'intoxication' and 'distillation', and the volume encompasses all the passions of a volatile man, while each poem tries to express the quintessence of a moment. Every such moment speaks true, engaging the poet's whole being until it evaporates, and is replaced by another equally true and equally transient. Apollinaire remarked in 1913 that each of his poems commemorates an event in his life 'and generally with sadness'. Certainly the dominant mood in 'Zone' is melancholy, and the joyous moments are all irretrievably past. There is also little of the wry humour that can be found elsewhere in *Alcools*. But 'Zone' is rich in something that Apollinaire considered to be both the source and the most effective expression of creativity: surprise. Surprise is generated by unexpected juxtapositions; it forces us to look at the world with new eyes. Like the Surrealists, Apollinaire dislocates the everyday world, offering us dreamlike images, sometimes sinister, sometimes comic, always moving and mysterious. He is at his most resonant when he is melancholy, but he had an appetite for life and a deep curiosity that show themselves in his use of rare or invented words, his delight in obscure legends, his experiments with form and metre, his interest in modern art, and his love of both the natural world and the city. He is an eminently receptive creature. Particularly clear in 'Zone' is his compassion for the lost souls on the margins of society. His own experience of hopeless love and of stateless and rootless wandering taught him sympathy for the city's outcasts, and for all those displaced persons who trailed across the map of Europe in the years before World War I, bearing with them, as he says in 'Zone', their faith, their hopes, and their 'unreal' crimson eiderdowns, as he carries with him his own burden, which seems equally unreal: his heart, his dreams, and his words.

'Zone' is written in free verse, rhythmical rather than metrical, but modulating occasionally into regular metre: lines 60–70, which describe the formal procession of the birds of the air, are appropriately written in classical alexandrines. The poem is organized by its rhyming couplets, rather than by stanzas, with the rhyme sometimes replaced by assonance. The method is apt: the poem is a long meditation which follows the poet's wanderings in Paris, from early morning to the following dawn. The sections are irregular, their length and shape determined by the shifts in the poet's attention, the movement of his thought, and the strength of his feeling. There is no punctuation in *Alcools*. Apollinaire believed that the rhythm and the lay-out of the text should shape our reading. If at times we hesitate over the placing of a pause, that is part of the poet's intention, for it opens up possibilities, where punctuation would fix and limit meaning, and it encourages us to read with closer attention.

'Zone' begins tentatively with a sequence of three single lines. In the first and third of these, the poet speaks of himself in the familiar second person: 'tu es las de ce monde ancien . . .', 'Tu en as assez . . .' ('you are tired of this ancient

world', 'You have had enough'), while the second line conjures up a familiar landmark in a startling image: 'Shepherdess, O Eiffel Tower, the flocks on the bridges are bleating this morning'. The power of that line depends on a paradox: it brings the modernity of the city into the poem, but does so with an image drawn from the pastoral tradition, turning the stream of traffic into a flock of sheep; later, the poet's solitude is emphasized by the 'herds of lowing buses' driving past him. A group of three lines next introduces the theme of religion, which seems to the poet more modern than the city, because it is timeless. Yet all the poet's love of Paris appears in his picture of a sunlit street, and all his feelings for people whose lives are ruled by the factory siren that groans and the 'rabid clock' that 'barks'. Apollinaire here transmutes the everyday—shop-signs, posters, newspaper headlines—into a world that hovers between vision and nightmare. The movement gathers pace as he recalls his childhood and the role of religion in his life. A lyrical passage links the modern and the ancient, imagining the risen Christ as an aviator, flying high, followed by an aeroplane, escorted by figures from Greek legend and Jewish and Christian tradition who ascended the heavens, greeted by all the birds of nature and of poetry, real or imaginary, the larks and the phoenix. Back on earth, the poet is alone in the crowd, grieving for lost love, regretting the innocent faith of former centuries which was also the faith of his childhood, and mocking his inability to seek consolation in religion. He is a child of his century, doomed to ironic self-awareness and inhibition. The poem begins to fragment as the poet, again addressing himself in the second person, recalls images from his past ('You're in the garden', 'Here you are in Rome'), moving restlessly from the south of France to Prague, from Rome to Amsterdam. Summing up his life, he links past and present, second person and first, in six anguished lines:

> Tu as fait de douloureux et de joyeux voyages
> Avant de t'apercevoir du mensonge et de l'âge
> Tu as souffert de l'amour à vingt et à trente ans
> J'ai vécu comme un fou et j'ai perdu mon temps
> Tu n'oses plus regarder tes mains et à tous moments je
> voudrais sangloter
> Sur toi sur celle que j'aime sur tout ce qui t'a
> épouvanté.

> (You made both painful and happy journeys
> Till you learned of the existence of lies and of age
> You suffered in love at twenty and at thirty
> I have lived like a madman and wasted my time
> You no longer dare to look at your hands and at every
> moment I want to weep
> For you for the woman I love for everything that has
> appalled you.)

But at this point the poet's eye turns outwards again, and he speaks 'with tears in your eyes' of the emigrants in transit whom he has seen in the Gare Saint-Lazare, exhausted Jews on their way across the Atlantic; and of those who decide to stay in Paris, where they live like exiles in dark hovels. The image recalls the description, a few lines earlier, of the poet himself in the Jewish quarter of Prague, 'like Lazarus terrified of the daylight': resurrection and rescue are painful, profoundly disturbing experiences. Sitting in the garden of an inn near Prague, he observes 'instead of writing your story in prose/The beetle that sleeps in the heart of the rose'. Prague is the setting of his tale of the Wandering Jew, 'Le Passant de Prague' ('The Passer-by of Prague', in *L'Hérésiarque et Cie*). Images of alienation and exile, of being doomed to wander and unable to die, come together in 'Zone' and make of the poet a modern Wandering Jew.

Now the poem becomes increasingly fragmented, a sequence of single lines offering snapshots, in the present tense, of bars, cafés, and brothels where the poet has felt both his own humiliation and the pitiable humanity of the poor and the degraded. As dawn approaches he is still alone, listening to the milk-churns clanking in the street, gulping down a last raw drink ('Cet alcool brûlant') as he has swallowed the painful events of his life, which like alcohol both stimulate and destroy. The poem ends as he turns towards home, to sleep among his collection of native fetishes and masks (like his friend Picasso, he was fascinated by African artefacts). They are, he says, the Christs of another, lesser religion, but powerful symbols of hope none the less. They take us back to the poem's beginning, yearning again for religion's power to console. But the poet is no longer a child, and he is lost in a relativist limbo: the word 'zone' once denoted the area around the walls of Paris that was neither city nor country-side. He desperately needs to believe in what his intellect cannot accept; love eludes him, memory mocks him, and he is afraid of the very renewal that he desires. In the final lines of the poem, the sun rises in a blood-red sky, evoking a dead body with its throat cut: 'Soleil cou coupé'. It would be an unbearable desolation were it not that the poem makes a persuasive harmony out of its discords. Free verse alternates with traditional metre to mirror the problematical coexistence of past and present, and the poem achieves a balance that softens its final despair.

The last poem in *Alcools*, 'Vendémiaire' (the name of the harvest month in the Revolutionary calendar), describes another walk through Paris, from evening to dawn; it lacks the magic of 'Zone' because it explicitly claims a victory that in 'Zone' is slowly and painfully achieved, so that the reader lives through it: the dawning awareness that the poem's creation is the one consolation that endures.

—Norma Rinsler

APOLLONIUS of Rhodes. Born Apollonius Rhodius in Alexandria, Egypt, possibly c.295 BC. Active during first half of 3rd century BC, and possibly later. Studied under Callimachus, *q.v.*: said to have quarrelled with Callimachus and retired to Rhodes, but evidence for this is unreliable. Held post of director (*prostates*) of the Museum Library at Alexandria, possibly c.260–247 BC; tutor to Ptolemy III Euergetes. In addition to various poems, of which only the *Argonautica* survives, wrote scholarly works on Homer, Hesiod, and Archilochus, now lost. *Died c.215 BC.*

PUBLICATIONS

Verse

Argonautica, edited by H. Fränkel. 1961; also edited by F. Vian (includes French translation), 3 vols., 1974–81; Book III edited by R.L. Hunter, 1989; as *The Tale of the Argonauts*, translated by A.S. Way, 1901; as *Argonautica*, translated by R.C. Seaton (prose), 1912; also translated by Charles E. MacBean, 1976; as *The Voyage of the Argo*, translated by E.V. Rieu (prose), 1959; as *Jason and the Golden Fleece (The Argonautica)*, translated by Richard Hunter, 1993.

*

Critical Studies: *Hellenistic Poetry* by A. Körte, 1929; *Echoes and Imitations of Early Epic in Apollonius Rhodius*, 1981, *Index verborum in Apollonium Rhodius*, 1983, and *Studies in the Third Book of Apollonius Rhodius' Argonautica*, 1983, all by Malcolm Campbell; *Epic and Romance in the Argonautica of Apollonius* by C.R. Beye, 1982; *Landscape in the Argonautica of Apollonius Rhodius* by Mary Frances Williams, 1991; *The Best of the Argonauts: The Redefinition of the Epic Hero in Book 1 of Apollonius's Argonautica* by James J. Clauss, 1993; *The Argonautica of Apollonius* by Richard Hunter, 1993.

*   *   *

The only work of Apollonius which survives is the epic *Argonautica*, written in hexameters, the traditional epic metre, with the high archaic language and style of the Homeric poems. After the *Iliad* and *Odyssey* the *Argonautica* is the most important epic from the ancient Greek world, and it was soon recognized as such; Virgil's *Aeneid* was profoundly influenced by it (behind Virgil's Dido, for instance, stand Apollonius' Hypsipyle and Medea). Early history of the work is uncertain. The Greek biographical tradition (which usually contains much palpably fictitious material) reports that the *Argonautica* was at first badly received in Alexandria and suggests that Apollonius was at odds with his 'teacher' Callimachus, the most important scholar and poet of the Hellenistic period, who radically changed the course of Greek poetry, but only amid great controversy; to what extent the *Argonautica* was considered by Apollonius' contemporaries more traditional than avant-garde is no longer known, but there are many cross-references between the poems of Callimachus and the *Argonautica*, and Apollonius' poem is thoroughly modernistic in tone and style.

Superficially the *Argonautica* would seem to be an orthodox work aiming for a place in the mainstream tradition of heroic epic (though of literate, not oral, composition), and it has often been so regarded; modern critics who view it in this way generally contrast the *Argonautica* with what they see as the straightforward heroic world of the Homeric poems and conclude that Apollonius' work is an interesting failure. However, the *Iliad* and *Odyssey* are far from simplistic in outlook, and recent scholarship on Hellenistic poetry suggests that the *Argonautica* is a complex and original poem which successfully reworked the old epic form and reflects the troubled and introspective mentality of 3rd-century BC Alexandria.

The *Argonautica* can appear to be an episodic, disjointed work with many characteristically Hellenistic 'travelogue' features (it touches often on matters of ethnography, geography, anthropology, etc.); but in fact the poem is remarkably whole. The work's perspective is established not through narrative directness, or through imagery or symbolism, but by a process of reversal often thought of as 'irony' in the 20th century: the familiar is taken for granted and suppressed in favour of the less familiar, and what is important is most often expressed indirectly and at a secondary level. The result can be enigmatic but genuinely disturbing, and an effective way of conveying a pessimistic vision of a fragile and fragmented world. First, the story of the voyage of Jason and the Argonauts to Colchis in the distant parts of the Black Sea to capture the Golden Fleece, and of the difficult but crucial passion of the local princess Medea for Jason, was an ancient one, and Apollonius assumes that his audience do not need to have it retold in all its details; Jason's subsequent abandonment of Medea, for example, is nowhere recounted openly (the poem even ends just before the Argonauts reach home), but the whole poem broods on the issues of commitment, trust, and deception. Secondly, Apollonius takes for granted a familiarity with the two monumental epics preceding his own, and, by using the *Iliad* and *Odyssey* as 'archetypal' reference points against which the Argonauts and their various encounters are juxtaposed and interpreted, he creates a multiplicity of dimensions and a kind of commentary to his *Argonautica*; thus Medea does not appear until Book III (the poem consists of four long 'books'), but the most substantial episode of Book I, the Argonauts' visit to the strange island of Lemnos with its all-female population, turns out to be diagnostic for Colchis. Although Jason's affair with the Lemnian queen Hypsipyle seems idle and inconsequential on the surface of the narrative, once Apollonius' references to Homer are recognized and Hypsipyle is considered as a figure reminiscent of Nausicaa and Circe, and Jason as an Odysseus or even Agamemnon, the real issues of ambivalence, pressure of circumstance, and expedient compromise begin to emerge. These are the issues underlying the whole poem, whether in the exotic account of the outward journey of Books I and II, the pathology of Medea's awful passion and conflict in Book III, or the alienated return home through the strange, semi-mythical half-real world of the Adriatic and north Africa in Book IV.

—A.W. Bulloch

APULEIUS, Lucius. Born in Madaura, province of Africa (now M'Daourouch, Algeria), c.AD 123–25. Educated in Carthage, Athens, and Rome. Married Aemilia Pudentilla; possibly had a son called Faustinus. Lived in Oea (now Tripoli) where he married; acquitted of a charge of magic at nearby Sabratha; later lived in Carthage, where his success in public speaking led to various honours, including a statue and the important priesthood of Asclepius. *Died later than AD 163* (probably much later).

PUBLICATIONS

Collection

[Works], edited by Rudolph Helm and P. Thomas. 3 vols., 1907–31.

Fiction

Metamorphoses, edited by D.S. Robertson. 3 vols., 1940–45; also edited by Rudolph Helm, 1955, and C. Giarratano, revised by P. Frassinetti, 1960; edited and translated by J. Arthur Hanson [Loeb Edition], 2 vols., 1989; as *The Golden Ass*, translated by William Adlington, 1566, reprinted 1967, revised by Stephen Gaselee [Loeb

Edition], 1915, also revised by Harry C. Schnur, 1962; also translated by Thomas Taylor, 1822; H.E. Butler, 2 vols., 1910; Jack Lindsay, 1932; Robert Graves, 1950; P.G. Walsh, 1994; as *The Isis-Book*, translated by J. Gwyn Griffiths, 1975; in part as *Cupid and Psyche*, edited and translated by E.J. Kenny, 1990; commentaries by A. Scobie (Book I), 1975, R.T. van der Paardt (Book III), 1971, B.L. Hijmans, Jr and others (Book IV), 1977, (Book VI and VII), 1981, (Book VIII), 1985, and J.G. Griffiths (Book XI), 1975.

Other

Apologia, Florida, edited (with French translation) by P. Vallette. 2nd edition, 1960; as *The Apologia and Florida*, translated by H.E. Butler, 1909.
Philosophica (includes *De deo Socratis*; *De dogmate Platonis*; *De Mundo*), edited (with French translation) by J. Beaujeu. 1973.

*

Bibliography: *Ad Apulei Madaurensis Metamorphoseon librum primum commentarius Exegeticus* by Margaretha Molt (dissertation, Groningen), 1938; 'The Scholarship on Apuleius since 1938' by Carl C. Schlam, in *Classical World*, 64, 1971.

Critical Studies: *Apuleius and His Influence* by E.H. Haight, 1927; *The Ancient Romances* by B.E. Perry, 1967; *Aspects of the Ancient Romance and Its Heritage: Essays on Apuleius, Petronius, and the Greek Romances* by Alexander Scobie, 1969; *The Roman Novel: The 'Satyricon' of Petronius and the 'Metamorphoses' of Apuleius* by P.G. Walsh, 1970; *Cupid and Psyche: Apuleius and the Monuments*, 1972, and *The Metamorphoses of Apuleius: On Making an Ass of Oneself*, 1992, both by Carl C. Schlam; *Amor and Psyche: The Psychic Development of the Feminine: A Commentary on the Tale by Apuleius* by Erich Neuman, 1973; *Aspects of the Golden Ass* edited by B.L. Hijmans, Jr and R. Th. van der Paardt, 1978; *Apuleius and the Golden Ass* by James Tatum, 1979; *Shakespeare's Favourite Novel: A Study of the Golden Ass as a Prime Source* by J.J.M. Tobin, 1984; *Auctor and Actor: A Narratological Reading of Apuleius' Golden Ass* by John J. Winkler, 1985; *Unity in Diversity: A Study of Apuleius' Metamorphoses* by Paula James, 1987; *The Metamorphoses of Apuleius* by Judith K. Krabbe, 1989; *The Golden Ass of Apuleius: The Liberation of the Feminine in Man* by Marie-Louise von Franz, revised edition, 1992.

* * *

Apuleius is best understood as a performer. He regularly gave public speeches before the large crowds they attracted in his age, and his written work too reflects a concern to use style and knowledge to capture and maintain an audience's attention.

The *Florida*, a collection of the most 'florid' parts of his public speeches, displays a man supremely confident before his admiring audience. He speaks with authority on a multitude of subjects, from Alexander the Great to parrots, though usually in a philosophical or cultural key. His style is as luxuriant as his subjects: in defiance of the careful, if at times precious, styles of the Golden and Silver Ages of Latin literature before him, his own style overflows with archaism, colloquialism, neologism, particularly if it will add to the rhythm, balance, music, or patterning. His style not only exemplifies the new tendencies of the age, but pushes them to an extreme.

Public speakers such as Apuleius considered they had a duty to educate, and some fulfilled this duty through a sort of popularizing philosophy. Apuleius had pretensions to being a Platonist philosopher, and there survive works ascribed to him which expound the philosophy of Plato as understood in his time. Most Apuleian is the energetic showpiece *De deo Socratis* [On the God of Socrates], which analyses the way in which an intermediary spirit connects us with God and which, for instance, memorably depicts the human condition in 19 successive epithets! Otherwise, these philosophical works are more disappointing and sometimes simply translate minor Greek works, although the translations seem to have proved useful to Greekless readers, if one may judge by the example of St Augustine.

Once, Apuleius *needed* to deliver a speech, to defend himself against the charge of winning the rich widow Pudentilla's affections by magic. The *Apologia* (or *On Magic*) is the only surviving classical Latin law-court speech not by Cicero, and, at least in its published form, displays the style of the *Florida* and a wicked sense of humour that we meet again in his novel.

The *Metamorphoses*, or *The Golden Ass* as it is generally known, is Apuleius' sole surviving novel (novels were in any case rare, late, and unprestigious in Greek and Roman literature), and is what Apuleius is best known for today. He takes a Greek short story and lengthens it to five times its original size by inserting stories (unlikely to be his own invention), thus making a Latin novel of some 250 modern pages. The Greek tale told how Lucius, dabbling in magic, was accidentally turned into an ass and underwent various adventures before being restored. Apuleius enriches the simple style of the original, producing something not easily translated into modern English. The inserted stories—of magic, brigands, and adultery—are related with verve and humour. Apuleius is interested too in psychological portrayal, though not in psychological development current in the modern novel; rather, the mind is as promising a subject for a description as is a brigands' camp or a god's garden.

The longest inserted tale, the celebrated story of *Cupid and Psyche*, is different. Its magical tone stands in stark contrast to the rumbustiousness of most of the novel. It adds, too, problems of interpretation: it is like a folk-tale, and thought by many to *be* a folk-tale; but it is difficult to deny some connection with the Platonic doctrine that Soul (*Psyche*) reaches its divine target through an intermediary spirit, Love (*Cupid*). The ending of the novel too, where Apuleius' hero is saved by initiation in the rites of the Egyptian goddess Isis, is thought by some to be a mere show of seriousness to finish, but by others to be the climax of a novel all along about the dangers of worldly vices.

We know nothing of the initial reception of the novel; and something of our assessment must depend on the precise interpretation adopted. But the extraordinary energy of the work is undeniable, as is the success of the frame-and-insertion structure in maintaining an unflagging interest. It displays many contrasts, from the flippant to the gruesome, from realism to make-believe, from bawdiness to extravagant piety. In character development it has the limitations of all ancient novels and most ancient thought. Its style has offended purists, but may be more validly criticized for unrelievedly trying too hard. Apuleius seems self-indulgent, but,

more accurately, is preoccupied with dazzling his audience, an aim in which, as a professional, he generally succeeds.

—Ken Dowden

CUPID AND PSYCHE
Story by Lucius Apuleius, c. AD 180.

Cupid and Psyche appears as a long tale embedded in the *Metamorphoses*, also known as *The Golden Ass*, by Lucius Apuleius. *The Golden Ass* closely resembles the shorter *Lucius the Ass* of the satirist Lucian, leading some scholars to posit the possibility of some lost common source, although Lucian's satire does not include a version of the Cupid and Psyche story. Conventionally dated to around AD 180, *The Golden Ass* represents the only extant example of a complete novel in Roman literature. It presents the first-person account of the misadventures of Lucius, a naive young man who supposes himself sophisticated in the ways of the world. Driven by an unhealthy curiosity about black magic and witchcraft, as well as by lust for Fotis, the Venus-like slave girl of his host, young Lucius finds himself accidentally transformed into an ass. This begins a physical and spiritual pilgrimage that leads poor Lucius through a series of hardships that are only finally resolved through the intervention of the great mother goddess Isis. Here Apuleius is an advocate of the Alexandrian mystery cult of Isis and Serapis, which posited Isis as the universal Mother, the true godhead of all the goddesses of the world.

Like Boccaccio's *Decameron* or Chaucer's *Canterbury Tales*, both of which draw on Apuleius, *The Golden Ass* is a narrative containing many shorter narratives recounted during the course of the novel. *Cupid and Psyche* is presented in the form of a story told by an old woman to comfort a young girl named Charity, who has been kidnapped by bandits. This in turn is overheard by Lucius, the ass. The story parallels the fate of Charity and serves as an allegorical gloss of the larger narrative of Lucius, although it may stand on its own as a masterpiece of Silver Age Latin prose fiction.

The story of *Cupid and Psyche*, like that of Lucius, revolves around the pattern of fall, trial, and salvation. Because of her great beauty, a young woman named Psyche has received the attention of many men, thereby earning the jealous enmity of the goddess Venus. Venus orders her son Cupid (Eros) to make Psyche fall in love with some outcast. Cupid, however, having himself fallen for the beauty of Psyche, disobeys his mother and arranges to marry Psyche secretly. Hiding his true identity, Cupid establishes his bride in a luxurious palace, attended by magical servants. Psyche may enjoy everything in this earthly paradise with the one stipulation that she never look at her husband, who remains invisible except at night. All goes well until Psyche, driven by a combination of curiosity and uncertainty about the identity of her mysterious husband, looks on his sleeping form one night. Seized by lust, she spills hot oil from her lamp on his leg. Enraged, Cupid flies off, and Psyche finds herself cast out, abandoned to the wrath of Venus.

In the hands of Venus, Psyche is compelled to perform a series of progressively more dangerous and difficult tasks in order to expiate her guilt. First she must sort seeds from a great heap, then she must get a piece of wool from ravenous golden sheep, then water from the middle of a waterfall on the River Styx guarded by dragons, and finally a box of beauty from Proserpina, goddess of the dead, a journey that involves resisting many dangers and temptations. Because of her beauty and goodness, in each case she is secretly helped by various creatures, and in the last test by her husband. Thus reconciled with both Cupid and Venus, Psyche is made immortal, and in due time bears her husband a daughter named Pleasure [Voluptas].

The old woman's tale comforts Charity with the prospect that she may be rescued from misfortune and indeed she is, through the courage of her fiancé. At the same time, Psyche's misadventures, caused as they are by her lust and curiosity as well as her trials at the hands of Venus, echo the trials and misfortunes of Lucius. On a deeper level, the allegorical relationships suggested by the characters' names point to the philosophical themes at the heart of both the tale of *Cupid and Psyche* and the larger narrative of *The Golden Ass*. Influenced by the philosophical school of Middle Platonism, and especially the Platonic doctrine of love found in Plato's *Symposium* and *Phaedrus*, Apuleius uses his narrative to dramatize and describe the transformation of the soul (Psyche), as she is driven by love (Eros/Cupid) towards salvation and enlightenment. Psyche's development follows that described by the stairway of love in the *Symposium,* which begins in the love of bodies and culminates in the love of the form of beauty. Thus Psyche begins with the physical love represented by Venus, and ends with a pure love represented by that of a mother for her child (Pleasure). Psyche's salvation, through the redirection of erotic passion towards pure beauty and enlightenment, anticipates that of Lucius through the actions of the mother goddess Isis. Both stories point to the importance and power of erotic passion and beauty as the driving forces in the life of the soul. The problem, as Plato noted, is the direction, whether the soul be guided by an empty desire for trivial matters and idle curiosity, or by the desire for true beauty and enlightenment. Both Psyche and Lucius must triumph over their physical passions if they are to enjoy spiritual metamorphosis.

Apuleius' allegory of the eros and the soul presents a masterful synthesis of Plato's philosophical doctrine with religion and the nature of religious experience. Self-contained, and yet commenting both on the immediate narrative of Charity and the larger story of Lucius, the tale of *Cupid and Psyche* is an exquisitely carved gem set into an intricately wrought work of art.

—Thomas L. Cooksey

THE ARABIAN NIGHTS. See **THE THOUSAND AND ONE NIGHTS.**

ARAGON, Louis. Born in Paris, France, 3 October 1897. Educated at the Lycée Saint-Pierre, Neuilly, 1908–14; studied medicine, University of Paris, 1916–17. Served in the French army, medical auxiliary, 1918; medical corps, 1939–40, captured by the Nazis, escaped; active with the French Resistance, 1940–45: Croix de Guerre, 1918. Married the writer Elsa Kagan Triolet in 1939 (died 1970). Co-founding editor, with André Breton and Philippe Soupault, *Littérature,* 1919–24; active advocate of Dada, 1921–24, moved towards Surrealism from late 1920s; joined the Communist Party, 1927; attempted suicide, 1928; travelled to the Soviet Union, with his wife, November 1930; attended Revolutionary Writers Congress, Kharkov, publicly rejected Surrealism, 1931; lived in the Soviet Union, 1932–33; reporter and columnist, *L'Humanité,* 1933–34; member of the editorial board, *Commune,* 1933–36, both Paris; representative, 1st Congress of Soviet Writers, Moscow, 1934; organizer, 1st Congress of Writers in Defense of Culture, Paris, 1935; returned to the Soviet Union, June–December 1936; founding editor, *Ce Soir,* Paris, 1937–39 (publication banned 1939) and 1944–46; editor, *Les Lettres françaises,* 1953–72. Recipient: Renaudot prize, 1936; Lenin Peace prize, USSR, 1957. Order of October Revolution, USSR, 1972; Order of People's Friendship, USSR, 1977; Chevalier, Légion d'honneur, 1981. *Died 24 December 1982.*

PUBLICATIONS

Collections

Oeuvres romanesques croisées d'Elsa Triolet et Aragon, edited by Robert Laffont. 42 vols., 1964–74.
Oeuvre poétique. 15 vols., 1974–81.
Poésie. 1980.

Fiction

Anicet; ou, Le Panorama. 1921.
Les Aventures de Télémaque. 1922.
Le Con d'Irène (as Albert de Routisie). 1928; as *Irène,* 1968; as *Irene,* translated by Lowell Bair, 1970.
Les Plaisirs de la capitale. 1923.
Le Monde réel:
  Les Cloches de Bâle. 1934; as *The Bells of Basel,* translated by Haakon M. Chevalier, 1936.
  Les Beaux Quartiers. 1936; as *Residential Quarter,* translated by Haakon M. Chevalier, 1938.
  Les Voyageurs de l'impériale. 1942; as *The Century Was Young,* translated by Hannah Josephson, 1941; as *Passengers of Destiny,* translated by Josephson, 1947.
  Aurélien. 1944; as *Aurélien,* translated by Eithne Wilkins, 1946.
Servitude et grandeur des Français: Scènes des années terribles (stories). 1945.
Trois contes (stories). 1945.
Les Communistes. 1949–51; revised edition, 4 vols., 1966.
La Semaine sainte. 1958; as *Holy Week,* translated by Haakon M. Chevalier, 1961.
La Mise à mort. 1965.
Shakespeare (stories), illustrated by Picasso. 1965; as *Shakespeare,* translated by Bernard Frechtman, 1965.
Blanche ou l'oubli. 1967.
Henri Matisse. 2 vols., 1971; as *Henri Matisse,* translated by Jean Stewart, 1972.
Théâtre/Roman. 1974.
Le Mentir vrai (stories). 1980.
La Défense de l'infini (includes *Les Aventures de Jean-Foutre La Bite*). 1986.

Verse

Feu de joie. 1920.
Le Mouvement perpétual. 1926.

La Grande gaîté. 1929.
Persécuté persécuteur. 1931.
Front Rouge. 1931; as *The Red Front*, translated by E.E. Cummings, 1933.
Hourra l'Oural. 1934.
Le Crève-coeur. 1941; part translated in *Aragon: Poet of the French Resistance*, edited by Malcolm Cowley and Hannah Josephson, 1945.
Cantique à Elsa. 1941.
Brocéliande. 1942.
Les Yeux d'Elsa. 1942.
En français dans le texte. 1943.
Le Musée Grévin (as François La Colère). 1943.
Poèmes français. 1943.
France, écoute. 1944.
Le Crève-coeur et Les Yeux d'Elsa. 1944.
Neuf chansons interdites, 1942–1944. 1945.
En étrange pays dans mon pays lui-même (includes *En français dans le texte*; *Brocéliande*; *De l'exactitude historique en poésie*). 1945.
La Diane française. 1945.
Le Nouveau Crève-coeur. 1948.
Les Yeux et la mémoire. 1954.
Mes caravanes et autres poèmes. 1954.
Le Roman inachevé. 1956; as *The Unfinished Romance*, 1956.
Elsa. 1959.
Choix de poèmes. 1959.
Poésies: Anthologie, 1917–1960. 1960.
Les Poètes. 1960; revised edition, 1968 and 1976.
Le Fou d'Elsa. 1963.
Il ne m'est Paris que d'Elsa (anthology). 1964; revised edition, 1975.
Le Voyage de Hollande. 1964.
Élégie à Pablo Neruda. 1966.
Les Chambres. 1969.
Élégie à Romano, with Hamid Foulâdvind. 1980.
Les Adieux: poèmes. 1981.
Les Adieux et autres poèmes. 1982.

Plays

L'Armoire à glace un beau soir. 1924; as *The Mirror-Wardrobe One Fine Evening*, translated by Michael Benedikt, in *Modern French Theater*, edited by Benedikt and George E. Wellwarth, 1964.
Au pied du mur. 1924.
Le trésor des Jésuites. 1929.

Other

Le Libertinage (essays; includes play). 1924. as *The Libertine*, translated by Jo Levy, 1987.
Le Paysan de Paris (essays). 1926; as *Nightwalker*, translated by Frederick Brown, 1970; as *Paris Peasant*, translated by Simon Taylor Watson, 1971.
Traité du style. 1928.
La Peinture au défi. 1930.
Pour un réalisme socialiste. 1935.
Le Crime contre l'esprit, par le témoin des martyrs. 1942.
Les Bons Voisins (as Arnaud de saint Roman). 1943.
En français dans le texte. 1943.
'Matisse-en-France'. 1943.
Je vous salue ma France. 1944.
Saint-Pol-Roux, ou l'espoir. 1945.
Servitude et grandeur des Français. 1945
L'Homme communiste. 2 vols., 1946–53.
Apologie du luxe. 1946.

Chroniques du bel canto. 1947.
La Culture et les hommes. 1947.
La Lumière et la Paix. 1950.
Hugo, poète réaliste. 1952.
L'Exemple de Courbet. 1952.
La Vrai Liberté de la culture, réduire notre train de mort pour accroître notre train de vie. 1952.
Les Egmont d'aujourd'hui s'appellent André Stil. 1952.
Le Neveu de Monsieur Duval. 1953.
Journal d'une poésie nationale. 1954.
La Lumière de Stendhal. 1954.
Les Yeux et la mémoire. 1954.
Littératures soviétiques. 1955.
Entretiens sur le Musée de Dresde, with Jean Cocteau. 1957; as *Conversations on the Dresden Gallery*, 1982.
J'abats mon jeu (essays). 1959.
Histoire parallèle des États-Unis et de l'URSS, with André Maurois. 4 vols., 1962; revised edition as *Les Deux Géants: Histoire des États-Unis et de l'URSS de 1917 à nos jours*, 5 vols., 1962–64; translated in part as *A History of the USSR: From Lenin to Krushchev*, by Patrick O'Brian, 1964.
Entretiens avec Francis Crémieux. 1964.
Les Collages. 1965.
Aragon parle avec Dominique Arban. 1968.
Fernand Séguin rencontre Louis Aragon. 1969.
Je n'ai jamais appris à écrire; ou, Les Incipits. 1969.
Comme je vous en donne l'exemple. 1974.
Vie de Charlot: Charles Spencer Chaplin, ses films et son temps, with Georges Sadoul. 1978.
Écrits sur l'art moderne (essays), edited by Jean Ristat. 1981.
Réflexions sur Rimbaud. 1983.
Pour expliquer ce que j'étais (journal). 1989.
Une vague de rêves. 1990.

Editor, *Avez-vous lu Victor Hugo?*. 1952.
Editor, *Introduction aux littératures soviétiques: Contes et nouvelles*. 1956.
Editor, *Elsa Triolet choisie par Aragon*. 1960.

Translator, *La Chasse au snark*, by Lewis Carroll. 1928.
Translator, *Fraternity*, by Stephen Spender. 1939.
Translator, *Cinq Sonnets de Pétrarque*. 1947.
Translator, with A. Dimitriev, *Djamilia*, by Tchinghiz Aitmatov. 1959.

*

Bibliography: *Louis Aragon: Essai de bibliographie* by Crispin Geoghegan, 1979–80; *Louis Aragon: Bibliographie analytique* by Marie Lemaître, 1983.

Critical Studies: *Aragon: Poet of the French Resistance* (includes translations from *Le Crève-coeur*) edited by Malcolm Cowley and Hannah Josephson, 1945, as *Aragon: Poet of the Resurgent France*, 1946; *Aragon* by Hubert Juin, 1960; *Aragon: Romancier* by Pierre Lescure, 1960; *L'Itinéraire d'Aragon* by Roger Garaudy, 1961; *Aragon* by Georges Raillard, 1964; *Malraux, Sartre and Aragon as Political Novelists* by Catherine H. Savage, 1964; *Aragon, prosateur surréaliste* by Yvette Gendine, 1966; *Aragon: Le Réalisme de l'amour*, 1966; *The Poetry of Dada and Surrealism: Aragon, Breton, Tzara, Éluard and Desnos* by Mary Ann Caws, 1970; *Louis Aragon* by Lucille F. Becker, 1971; *Aragon* by Bernard Lecherbonnier, 1971; *La Résistance et ses poètes* by Pierre Seghers, 1974; *Aragon: Une vie à changer* by Pierre Daix, 1975; *Un nouveau cadavre: Aragon* by Paul Morelle, 1984;

Aragon: The Resistance Poems by M. Adereth, 1985; *Aragon romancier: d'Anicet à Aurélien* by Jacqueline Lévi-Valensi, 1989.

* * *

One of the most considerable French writers of the mid-20th century, Louis Aragon produced a large and varied body of work that is representative of the political aspirations and artistic orientations of the intellectuals of his age. From an early age he was a committed Marxist, although he did not always toe the Moscow line, and, like Jean-Paul Sartre, to quote another very notable instance, he was always ready to turn to journalism as well as to literature in order to express and communicate his ideas.

On return from service in the army medical corps during World War I, Aragon joined with André Breton and Philippe Soupault to found the magazine *Littérature* for avant-garde poetry. Its original tendency was Dadaist, in accord with the negative spirit born of the despair of the war years and disgust with bourgeois aesthetic values. Before long, however, Aragon and Breton, who had both studied medicine and had an interest in psychiatry, abandoned Dadaism in favour of surrealism, which combined an abiding concern with the operation of the unconscious with marked left-wing political concerns.

In 1921, a year after publishing *Feu de joie* [Bonfire], his first collection of verse, Aragon brought out the first of his major prose works, *Anicet; ou, Le Panorama* [Anicet; or, The Panorama Novel]. Though the very title challenges the surrealist tenet that the traditional novel was a spent force, Aragon uses his narrative very freely, borrowing some distancing techniques developed in the 18th century by Voltaire and Diderot to depict a poet, the eponymous Anicet. Anicet's education has left him emotionally parched, and the novel is essentially an account of his discovery of the significance of love that culminates in admission to a clandestine cult devoted to a female symbol of modern beauty. This was followed by *Les Adventures de Télémaque* [The Adventures of Telemachus]. The title is taken from the classic 17th-century educational novel by Fénelon, Archbishop of Cambrai, and in a radical re-interpretation of the original, Aragon explores the theme of personal freedom. Published in 1926, *Le Paysan de Paris* (*Paris Peasant*), with a striking oxymoronic title that points to a relationship with the artificially constructed environment as close and intimate as the one that peasants are traditionally supposed to have with the soil they till, is generally regarded as Aragon's most important single contribution to surrealism because of the way in which it displays how the quotidian can be transformed magically by the free imagination of the passer-by. The most famous section is the presentation of the arcade called 'The Passage de l'Opéra'. Though Aragon attacked established classics and orthodox contemporary writers such as Mauriac and Gide in his *Traité du style* [Treatise on Style], he also revealed that he was beginning to lose sympathy with surrealism in what was for him a time of personal crisis that he resolved partially by taking up a firmer political stance, especially after a visit to Russia.

As well as becoming a journalist, working for the French Communist newspaper *L'Humanité*, founding *Ce Soir*, and visiting Spain in 1937 to support Spanish intellectuals, Aragon wrote *Les Cloches de Bâle* (*The Bells of Basel*), which was followed by *Les Beaux Quartiers* (*Residential Quarter*), *Les Voyageurs de l'impériale* (*The Century Was Young*) and *Aurélien*. They form a series of novels under the global title of *Le Monde réel* [The Real World] that present, from a Marxist perspective, a historically-based and at times autobiographical picture of the struggles of the French bourgeoisie to maintain its position in the face of working-class challenges. In the course of World War II, during which he was associated with the Resistance, and in the turbulent post-war period, Aragon turned increasingly towards journalism and political writing. *Les Communistes* is devoted primarily to extolling the role played by women in the evolution of communism in France. The style owes a great deal to documentary techniques, and the characterization is shallow, being determined largely by class and circumstance.

If *Les Communistes* appeared to support the view that the novel was not a form that really appealed to Aragon, *La Semaine sainte* (*Holy Week*) seemed to rebut it. Set against a familiar background of stirring historical events as Napoleon returns from exile in Elba to eject the restored monarchy of Louis XVIII, and reclaim the imperial crown, the novel centres on the painter Théodore Géricault and what might be called his political education as he witnesses people's responses to the crisis.

In addition to his prose, Aragon wrote a great deal of verse, and the poetry he wrote in later life is particularly admired. The poetry inspired by his love for his companion, Elsa Triolet, a Russian-born novelist and journalist whom he had first met in 1928, struck a particular responsive chord. As well as choosing themes with a wide appeal, Aragon was able to mix tradition forms and innovatory techniques in his versification that found a receptive audience.

—Christopher Smith

LE CRÈVE-COEUR
Poems by Louis Aragon, 1941.

Le Crève-coeur consists of 22 poems and a brief theoretical essay, 'Rhyme in 1940' ('La rime en 1940'). Thirteen of the poems were written between September 1939 (when Aragon, aged 42, was enlisted into the army) and May 1940 (when his unit went into action). The last of these, 'The Interrupted Poem' ('Le Poème interrompu'), was literally and dramatically interrupted when Aragon's regiment was ordered into Belgium in advance of the Allied armies. Aragon escaped via Dunkirk, returned immediately to France, and was involved in action right up to the ceasefire in June. He was demobbed in July, and began to compose the nine remaining poems of *Le Crève-coeur*, which appeared in book form in 1941.

The first 13 poems are Aragon's response to the *drôle de guerre* (phoney war) and the final nine his memories of combat and defeat. Several of the poems are also inspired by Aragon's separation from his beloved wife, Elsa Triolet.

Aragon had not in fact published any poetry since 1934, preoccupied instead with journalism, fiction, and politics. It was the traumatic nature of the events of 1939–40, together with the enforced inactivity of eight months of 'phoney war', which caused his return to the genre in which he had begun his literary career. In many of the poems the historical is intertwined with the personal. Indeed, it is part of Aragon's purpose to convince us that these two levels of experience are inseparable. In 'The Time of Crossword Puzzles' ('Le temps des mots croisés'), looking back regretfully and self-critically on the pre-war years, Aragon writes:

Too little have we prized those double hours
Too little asked if our dreams were counterparts
Too lightly probed the look in troubled eyes
Too seldom talked of our concurrent hearts

The 'we' is the poet and Elsa; but it is also 'we' the French people and even 'we' the human race. Sometimes Aragon's love for Elsa serves as a counterpoint to humanity's inability to love. This is the case in 'Printemps' ('Spring'):

But we were eyeless, loveless, brainless, phantoms,
Ghosts parted from ourselves . . .

Throughout the poems written before the defeat Aragon's love for Elsa acts as a kind of foil to the collapse of human values, to the sense of impending disaster. Underlying a number of these poems is the anxiety that poetry may not be sufficient to the tasks Aragon has assigned to it, to convey love in a context that denies love:

My love we have only words
Our lipstick
Only frozen words . . .
('Les Amants séparés' [The Parted Lovers])

or to reach out with words to the ordinary people caught up on the apocalypse:

But the sergeant
I show these verses to
Gets lost in my analogies . . .
('Romance du temps qu'il fait'
[Romance of the Present Time])

The central, dominant image of the poems looking back on defeat comes in 'The Lilacs and the Roses' ('Les Lilas et les roses'): 'June with a dagger in its heart'. This poem uses its central flower imagery to explore the many different realities and emotions experienced by the poet as he witnesses defeat. The imagery is paradoxically delicate, in sharp contrast to 'Tapestry of the Great Fear' ('Tapisserie de la grande peur'), where it has a nightmarish and grotesque quality, reminiscent of Aragon's Surrealist youth:

This landscape, masterpiece of modern terror
Has sharks and sirens, flying fish and swordfish . . .
A tame bear. A shawl. A dead man dropped like
An old shoe. Hands climbing the torn belly . . .
Evening soars down with silent wingbeats, joining
A velvet Breughel to this Breughel of hell.

But at the same time as allowing his imagination full scope, Aragon is also concerned to point to historical continuities. The poems overflow with references to France's past: Richard II, Joan of Arc, the Crusades. He sees himself as a *national* poet, creating together with personal, idiosyncratic imagery references recognizable to the national community.

In *Le Crève-coeur* Aragon confronts implicitly some of the central dilemmas of modern poetry. He confronts these same problems explicitly in the appended essay 'Rhyme in 1940'. Aragon believes that poetry, because of its flexibility and inherent adventurousness, is the medium best equipped to respond creatively to the unprecedented nature of contemporary historical events. But poetry has become remote from ordinary people. According to Aragon, *rhyme* is at the centre of this problem, and also its potential solution. Rhyme, poetry's surviving link with popular song, is indispensable to a popular poetry. But rhyme has fallen into disrepute in modern poetry. Through renovating rhyme, Aragon believes, both the energy and popularity of poetry can be renewed. In *Le Crève-coeur* he experiments extensively with rhyme. For example, he employs what he calls 'rime enjambée' (rhyme astride the line) in 'Little Suite for Loudspeaker' ('Petite Suite san fil'):

Ne parlez pas d'amour J'écoute mon coeur *battre*
Ne parlez plus d'amour Que fait-elle là-*bas*
*Tr*op proche . . .

(Don't speak of love I listen to my heart-beat
Don't speak any more of love What is she doing there
Too near . . .)

where 'battre' rhymes with 'bas' + 'Tr'; or, in 'The Unoccupied Zone' ('La Zone des étapes'), he uses a *rime complexe* (complex rhyme):

Nous ne comprenons rien à ce que nos *fils aiment*
Aux fleurs que la jeunesse ainsi qu'un *défi sème*
Les roses de jadis vont à nos *emphysèmes*

(We don't understand what our sons love
The flowers youth throws down like a challenge
The roses of long ago go to our emphysemas)

where 'fils aiment' is rhymed first with 'défi sème' and then with part of the single word 'emphysèmes'.

Le Crève-coeur is not simply a spontaneous response to events. It is highly ambitious, artistically and culturally. Interweaving intimate and collective experience, it appeals to a common patrimony and seeks a poetry both innovative and popular.

—J.H. King

PARIS PEASANT (Le Paysan de Paris)
Poem by Louis Aragon, 1926.

Paris Peasant is commonly considered the most exhilarating and enduring of Aragon's surrealist prose works. It appeared in instalments in *La Revue européenne* before being published as a single text in 1926. It comprises four sections: 'Preface to a Modern Mythology' ('Préface à une mythologie moderne'), 'The Passage de l'Opéra' ('Le Passage de l'opéra'), 'A Feeling for Nature at the Buttes-Chaumont' ('Le Sentiment de la nature aux Buttes-Chaumont'), and 'The Peasant's Dream' ('Le Songe du paysan')—the last was added for the 1926 publication.

The first section is a quasi-philosophical diatribe against rational mental habits and the pursuit of truth. In keeping with ideas being circulated by the Surrealist group of which Aragon was a key member, the narrator sets out his intention to apprehend the sense of the marvellous suffusing everyday existence. 'The Passage de l'Opéra' and 'A Feeling for Nature' constitute the core of the text and are literary reconstructions or meditative strolls in two places in Paris, the first a 19th-century arcade in the Opéra *quartier*, and the second a park in the north-east of the city. The fourth section is a further pseudo-epistemological debate and a series of pronouncements echoing one of the Surrealists' elected predecessor's texts: Lautréamont's *Poésies*.

Breton chided Aragon for betraying surrealism in *Paris Peasant*. An essential aim of the movement was to undermine rational thought in order to reveal the hidden part of the mind. They derided narrative since it relies on logic and on coherent, commonsense temporality. Aragon creates a kind of narrative out of those fragments which were generally considered by the Surrealists to be outside narrative structure. Thus a collage of shop signs, newspaper cuttings and municipal inscriptions are incorporated verbatim into the text in what is teasingly a disruption of the narrative and at the same time a revitalizing of it. These signs are made to glow strangely by appearing in a literary text, just as in the real world they are imbued, for all their ordinariness, with the spirit of the marvellous. Aragon has described *Paris Peasant* as a work of 'surrealist realism', and this (collage) procedure is a textual imitation of how the marvellous erupts in reality. The implied dialectic here is that just as societal language can become poetic, so poetic language ought to be useful to society. Surrealist procedures imitate and parody both the serious philosophical debate about objective reality in which the Surrealists were then engaged, and the lyrical excesses inherent in automatism. *Paris Peasant* is full of extraordinary and ingenious arbitrary imagery, and there is a genuine parody of automatic writing in part V of 'A Feeling for Nature'.

The 'Passage de l'Opera' section is in part a vociferous defence of the arcade's small traders against its proposed demolition by the Boulevard Hausmann Building Society in collusion with the City of Paris administrators. This defence includes collage material, and also involutes into the text the tradesmen who have read the early part of 'Passage de l'Opéra', a literary trick possibly borrowed from Gide. The ironical pamphleteering embedded in the text hints perhaps at the revolutionary political position that Aragon was to adopt from 1930.

The walk in the arcade provides a pretext for abstruse musings and poetic observations on the following locales, trades and services: lodging-house (for liaisons), bookshop, the Certa café, restaurant, stamp-dealer, hairdresser, wine-merchant, tailor, shoeblack, lavatory, gunsmith, orthopaedist, massage-room, and (erotic) theatre. As the narrator on his stroll pauses (in his narrative) before each window, a series of panegyrics is delivered. In *Aragon romancier* Lévi-Valensi has drawn attention to the textuality of the arcade that can be seen as a metaphor for future novels. The arcade is also a microcosm of the city and of modern mental life. With its display of desired objects it is also a paradigm for the unconscious.

The Buttes-Chaumont park is as ambiguous an environment in which to take a stroll as the Opéra arcade. Where the arcade, as Benjamin has shown, is at the same time public street and private interior, so the park is a condensation of the countryside, both town and country, a public space for private thoughts 'the town's collective unconscious'. Reflection on how mythologies are created in cultures leads the narrator to the discovery that his own mind follows the same procedure when it contemplates objects. The charm of 'A Feeling for Nature' relies chiefly on the collision of different discourses to humorous effect. In part VI Aragon meets Noll and Breton, who propose a stroll in the Buttes-Chaumont. They arrive by taxi, 'drunk with open-mindedness', and part VII then consists entirely of a physical geography of the park, complete with details of its roads and contours, followed in part VIII by a delirious monologue addressed to Night. Another collision follows with the inscriptions of municipal worthies, when Noll perceives a white spectre on the Suicides' Bridge. After a passage of Hegel-inspired thought ('the concrete notion emerging from the pure reedless waters'), Woman, the eternal female, is suddenly invoked as the cohesive force behind the world's appearances. In contrast, in the last pages the narrator tears his head from his body and it undergoes exaggerated metamorphoses into, for example, a blackberry picked and discarded by a schoolboy, until the man finally becomes 'a sign among the constellations'.

'The Peasant's Dream' relaunches the inquiry into the purpose of metaphysics, concluding that it is 'notion or knowledge of the concrete'. The philosophical utterances are best read in the same way as the vertiginous imagery. The narrator proceeds to describe how the 'general law' is accessible through a specific woman and falling in love. Among many bizarre and some unfathomable statements, the narrator-poet makes an impassioned plea for a poetry of the concrete.

Paris Peasant is a grand surrealist work, in its imagery, its obsession with identity and chance, its dream-evocations of 'real' Paris, its discrediting of reality. It celebrates the ordinary, glories in anti-elitism, eulogizing waiters and hairdressers and spelling out a utopia in which everyone is an artist. It is a memorable experiment in constructing narrative from the raw material of the external world and in baring the process of its attempt.

—Rolf Venner

ARETINO, Pietro. Born in Arezzo, Florentine Republic (now in Italy), 20 April 1492. Moved to Perugia, 1508. Studied poetry and painting in Perugia. Had two daughters, the first by Caterina Sandella. First poetry published, 1512; moved to Rome, 1517, under protection of Agostino Chigi, and entered political and artistic circles; under protection of Pope Leo X and the Medici, wrote lampoons and 'pasquinades' against influential and powerful contemporaries, often gaining their enmity; fled Rome on the election of Pope Adrian VI, 1522, whom he had satirized; returned to Rome on election of Giulio de' Medici as Pope Clement VII, 1523; following assault by servants of a Curia official, left Rome again, and finally settled in Venice, 1527. *Died 21 October 1556.*

PUBLICATIONS

Collections

Teatro, edited by Nunzio Macarrone. 2 vols., 1914.
Works, translated by Samuel Putnam. 2 vols., 1926.
Poesie, edited by Gaetano Sborselli. 2 vols., 1930–34.
Tutte le comedie, edited by G.B. Sanctis. 1968.
Teatro, edited by Giorgio Petrocchi. 1971.

Fiction

Ragionamenti, edited by Dario Carraroli. 2 vols., 1914; edited by Giovanni Aquilecchia, 1980; as *The Ragionamenti: The Lives of Nuns; The Lives of Married Women; The Lives of Courtesans*, edited and translated by Peter Stafford, 1971.
Ragionamento della Nanna e della Antonia. 1534; as *The Lives of Nuns*, in *Works*, 1926; also translated in *The Ragionamenti*, 1971.
Dialogo nel quale la Nanna insegna a la Pippa. 1536; as *The Lives of Married Women*, in *Works*, 1926; also translated in *The Ragionamenti*, 1971.
Ragionamento de le corti. 1538; edited by Guido Batteli, 1914; as *The Lives of Courtesans*, in *Works*, 1926; also translated in *The Ragionamenti*, 1971.

Le carte parlanti. 1543; edited by F. Campi, 1926.
A Dialogue of Dying Well, translated by Richard Verstagen. 1603.
Sei giornate: Ragionamento della Nanna e della Antonia; Dialogo nel quale la Nanna insegna a la Pippa, edited by Giovanni Aquilecchia. 1969.
Aretino's Dialogues, translated by Raymond Rosenthal. 1972.
Sei giornate, edited by Guide Davico Bonino. 1975.
Il romanzo della ruffiana, edited by G.B. De Sanctis. 1977.

Verse

Opera nova del fecundissimo Giovane Pietro Pictore Arentino zoe strambotti sonetti capitoli epistole barzellette ed una desperata. 1512.
Marfisa. 1532.
Stanze in lode di Madonna Angela Sirena. 1537.
Sonetti lussuriosi e pasquinate (selection), edited by M.B. Sirolesi. 1980.
Sonnets, translated by Oscar Wilde. N.d.

Plays

Il marescalco (produced 1526/27). 1533; as *The Stablemaster*, translated by George Bull, in *Five Italian Renaissance Comedies*, edited by Bruce Penman, 1978; as *The Marescalco*, translated by Leonard G. Sbrocchi and J. Douglas Campbell, 1986.
La cortigiana (produced 1537). 1534 (edited version); in full, edited by Giuliano Innamorati, 1970.
La Talanta (produced 1542). 1542; as *Talanta*, translated by Christopher Cairns, in *Three Renaissance Comedies*, edited by Cairns, 1991.
Lo ipocrito (produced 1545). 1542.
L'Orazia. 1546.
Il filosofo. 1546.

Other

La Passione di Giesu. 1534.
I Sette Salmi della penitenzia di David. 1535; as *A Paraphrase upon the Seven Penitential Psalms*, translated by Robert Persons, 1635.
Tre libri de la Humanità di Cristo. 1535.
Lettere. 6 vols., 1537–57; edited by Fausto Nicolini, 2 vols., 1913–16, and by Francesco Flora and A. Del Vito, 1960; selections as *Lettere scelte*, edited by Guido Battelli, 1913, and as *Lettere sull'arte*, edited by E. Camesasca, 3 vols., 1957–60; selections translated by Thomas Caldecot Chubb, as *The Letters*, 1967, and by George Bull, as *Selected Letters*, 1976.
Il Genesi. 3 vols., 1538.
Vita di Maria Vergine. 1539.
Vita di Caterina vergine e martire. 1540; edited by Flavia Santin, 1978.
Orlandino. 1540.
Vita di san Tommaso signor D'Aquino. 1543; edited by Flavia Santin, 1978.
Prose sacre, edited by Ettore Allodoli. 1926.

*

Critical Studies: *Pietro Aretino e le sue opere* by C. Bertani, 1901; *Le commedie di Pietro Aretino* by U. Fresco, 1901; *Pietro Aretino: The Scourge of Princes* by Edward Hutton, 1922; *L'Aretino: Le cause della sua potenza e della sua fortuna* by A. Del Vito, 1939; *Pietro Aretino* by Giorgio Petrocchi, 1948; *Pietro Aretino: Studio e note critiche* by Giuliano Innamorati, 1957; *Progetto corporativo e autonomia dell'arte in Pietro Aretino* by Giovanni Falaschi, 1977; *Le voci dell' istrione: Pietro Arentino e la dissoluzione del teatro* by Giulio Ferroni, 1977; *L'Aretino* by Cesare Marchi, 1980; *Pietro Aretino and the Republic of Venice: Researches on Aretino and His Circle in Venice, 1527–1556*, 1985, 'Aretino's Comedies and the Italian "Erasmian" Connection in Shakespeare and Jonson', in *Theatre of the English and Italian Renaissance* edited by J.R. Mulryne and M. Shrewsbury, 1991, and 'Aretino's *Talanta* (1542) and the Influence of Vasari', in *Italian Renaissance Festivals and Their European Influence* edited by Mulryne and Shrewsbury, 1992, all by Christopher Cairns; 'Rhetoric and Drama: Monologues and Set Speeches in Aretino's Comedies' by Richard Adams, in *The Languages of Literature in Renaissance Italy* edited by Peter Hainsworth and others, 1988; *Periegesi aretiniane, testi, schede e note biografiche intorno a Pietro Aretino* (includes texts) by Angelo Romano, 1991; *Aretino Dead or Alive: A 500th Birthday Tribute* by W.A. Caswell, 1992.

* * *

Pietro Aretino is known chiefly for his plays (five comedies, one tragedy), dialogues, including the *Dialogues on Courts and Cards*, and the publication of his letters to the rich and famous. From 1538 he was the first to publish his own letters in the vulgar tongue (i.e. not in Latin). Six letter books were to follow until 1557 (one posthumously) constituting a rich vein of information on the customs of the times, as well as a valuable register of the current movements of artists and the creation of artworks. Aretino was on friendly terms with many of the greatest artists working in Venice, including Titian and Tintoretto. Representing the glitter and the license of the Renaissance, he also experienced the Catholic Reformation, and its censure of his sonnets written to accompany the *Sedici modi* (a book of sexual postures) by Marcantonio Raimondi, after designs by Giulio Romano, and his *Ragionamenti* or *Sei giornate* (dialogues between whores). For these activities, Aretino was classified by figures of the English Renaissance, such as Thomas Nashe and Ben Jonson, as the representative of Italian private or domestic vice, to parallel Machiavelli as the representative of Italian public vice (in politics).

Aretino was born in Arezzo in 1492 and of humble stock. He seems to have had early experience as a painter: he was described as Pietro *pictore* Aretino in his first anthology of youthful poems, the *Opera nova*. An aspiring courtier at the papal court of Pope Leo X and in the household of Agostino Chigi, the papal banker who was also the patron of Raphael, Aretino's first comedy, written in 1525, was *La cortigiana* [The Courtesan], a satirical exposé of conditions for the courtier in Rome (it was later revised for publication in Venice to include references to his new Venetian patrons). Aretino was also notorious for the *pasquinate* (libellous satirical poems lampooning both prominent members of the papal court and candidates for the papal conclave), which were traditionally affixed to the statue of Pasquino in Rome.

When the election of Pope Adrian VI and the repercussions from the *Sedici modi* made Rome too dangerous for him, Aretino moved to the camp of the condottiere Captain Giovanni dalle Bande Nere, and thence to the Gonzaga Court of Mantua, where the second comedy, *Il marescalco* (*The Stablemaster*) was composed. This satirized (while implicitly accepting) the subservient status of a courtier obliged to marry at his master's bidding in spite of his clearly homosexual proclivities. In Venice, in 1527, Aretino had at last found a permanently safe haven. Protected by the Doge Andrea Gritti, and fêted by artists and writers alike, he began a life of writing and self-publicity, using the nascent Venetian printing press. A wide variety of works flowed from his pen in the following years, including: revised versions of the first two comedies in 1533–34; works of religious orientation in deference to the growing influence of Catholic reformist currents; and the above-mentioned *Sei giornate* in 1534–36. With the arrival of Nicolò Franco—colleague, later enemy, and sometime secretary—in Venice and with Venetian bookshops full of the fashion for Erasmus's Latin letters, the idea was born to publish his own letters in Italian. Part literature, part journalism, the first collection of these saw the light of day in 1537, going through some ten editions within the year. Quite apart from any literary merit, this success was due partly to the novelty of the enterprise. Profits for the author consisted of both rewards from the published letters' recipients (both fictional and actual) and payments for his silence. Further religious works followed, with the lives of three saints in 1540, encouraging the author's hopes for possible church preferment, and two more comedies, *Lo ipocrito* [The Hypocrite] and *La Talanta* (*Talanta*) in 1542. The latter was produced in Venice that year in a celebrated performance against a perspective set of Roman monuments by Giorgio Vasari, author of the *Lives of the Artists*. *Talanta* marked a return to the traditional unities for Aretino's comedy and contained what can be interpreted as early examples of *commedia dell'arte* stereotypes. Aretino himself complained in a letter that his actors had exceeded their brief in using plebeian accents. This play highlighted the Venice-versus-Rome polemic, as well as featuring a tour of the set in the script. *Lo ipocrito* was written in the same year, and launched a literary character, the religious pedant, possibly derived from Aretino's own society, but which has had a long history culminating in Molière's *Tartuffe*.

The last comedy, *Il filosofo* [The Philosopher], satirizing the pretensions to authority of philosophers, was published in 1546. Aretino's only tragedy, *L'Orazia*, of the same year, is now highly regarded as a distinguished example of this 16th-century genre. By 1545, his prestige and notoriety was such that he enjoyed the friendship, or respect, of most of the crowned heads of Europe, and made a celebrated ride to Peschiera in the company of the Emperor Charles V. Predictably within a year of his death, in 1556, the whole of Aretino's literary production was on the Catholic Index, although the publication of his comedies and dialogues in London in the 1580s, in Italian, must doubtless have done as much to propagate his reputation in Europe as the earlier *succès de scandale* of the *Sei giornate* and the *Sedici modi*. The subject of vituperation and prejudice on moral and religious grounds for centuries, Aretino's works are only now being treated as subjects for serious literary study.

—Christopher Cairns

LA CORTIGIANA
Play by Pietro Aretino, 1534 (written 1525).

La cortigiana [The Courtesan], written while Aretino was still living in Rome, but first published in modified form in 1534 after the author's transferral to Venice, is constructed on two distinct yet interconnected planes. The first of the two intertwined plots involves the Sienese Maco, who arrives in Rome determined to become firstly a courtier and then a cardinal with the help of Andrea (a character derived from a friend of the dramatist's, a Venetian painter celebrated in Rome rather more for his witticism and jesting than for his art). The second involves the Neapolitan Parabolano, a courtier duped by his servant Rosso who learns of his master's infatuation for a noblewoman, Livia, and ridicules him by arranging a tryst not with Livia, but with Togna, the baker's wife. It is these two plots that provide the basis for the comic action, and from which the anti-court satire emerges.

There are no less than 24 characters appearing in the comedy, who use a variety of linguistic registers as they move through the streets of Rome, including the colloquial Italian, at times mixed with Spanish, of servants, the Latin of pedants and religious hypocrites, and exaggerated Petrarchisms. An essential innovation of *La cortigiana* is its break with the fixed setting characteristic of erudite comedy. Here, the streets of Rome are the physical, material link between tavern and palace, just as such characters as Rosso and Andrea are the social and psychological link. The street endows all characters with full theatrical citizenship, be they nobles, servants, priests, procuresses, doctors, fishermen, and so on, while simultaneously providing a reason for their interrelationships.

Developed upon the dual plot of *La cortigiana* is a discussion of the nature and function of comedy itself. The drama is the theatrical 'fixing' on stage of one of the 'one hundred comedies' being enacted daily on the natural stage of the Roman streets and within its palaces. It was inspired by a real, everyday spirit of buffoonery, transformed from life into theatre. Various characters had also been transplanted from 'real' life onto the stage; all are aware of their comic role and strive to maintain it, together with the abstraction 'Monna Commedia' herself. It is in the final scenes of the comedy that this discussion reaches its climax. From being participants in their own comedies, the characters emerge, regarding themselves objectively as instruments of a comic form. Thus the servant Valerio indicates to Parabolano (Act V, scene 18) the face-saving device of taking his own misadventures in good spirit so as to minimize his ridiculousness in the eyes of the others. Parabolano emerges from the comic plot when he urges the baker to refrain from violence because 'it would be a shame if such a fine comedy were to finish in tragedy' (Act V, scene 21). Thus, his role in the play changes: from being simply a comic type he develops into a complex figure aware of his own theatrical function. His final role in the play is that of guardian of the comic form which, up to that point, had protected him from harm: 'Step back! Don't do it! Don't do it! Don't kill our comedy!' (Act V, scene 24). *La cortigiana* thus illustrates the process of life becoming theatre, with Parabolano fully aware of the transition.

Society, as it is represented in *La cortigiana*, is divided into two principal levels: the courts, in which a man is powerful due to his inherited title or acquired wealth—as is the case with Parabolano—and the world of the lower classes, consisting of servants, tradesmen, and so on, in which the powerful are those who use their wits to exploit others less wily than themselves. It is a social hierarchy in which the balance of power is continually shifting: the servant dupes his master who, in turn, dupes his employees and punishes unjustly his few faithful servants. Moreover, true social position and character may be easily misrepresented: the Giudeo is mistaken for a friar: the fisherman is thought to be possessed by devils; Valerio is wrongly believed to be disloyal; Rosso is mistaken for a nobleman twice because of the clothes, stolen or borrowed, he wears. It seems, then, that little is required for one to become a member of the court beyond possessing adequate amounts of money and maintaining appearances. What Aretino laments, in this comedy, is the loss of the society of ancient Rome, with its well-defined aristocracy and impeccable values: the Livias, Camillas, and so on.

While Maco's criticism of Rome—the city in which he intends ascending to the ultimate heights of courtier—is unintentional, direct criticism is levelled frequently at it by representatives of the lower classes. As the deterioration of social and political conditions is directly attributable to the machinations of the court institution, and only indirectly to the presence of the Spaniards in Italy, the blame lies squarely with the hegemonic class. Taverns are described as everything the courts should be but are not, while the happy reflection on them gives rise naturally to references to the Rome of Julius Caesar's time. Thus, while the court lords are perennially occupied in ridiculous amorous escapades, their servants prefer the multiple pleasures of the taverns.

Two of the principal characters of *La cortigiana* are Rosso and Parabolano: the former creates the comic situations that others then enact; the latter has created his own comedy (as the *innamorato*) and lives it out from within the play. The other main source of comic interest is the Sienese Maco, a character that had traditionally enjoyed fame as a fool. Aretino's contribution to the development of this character-type is in Maco's language, childish and usually lacking in logic. His answers are random and irrelevant, and his every comment lacks consequence. He exists through his unpredictable language, oblivious to his own shortcomings, wholly temporal.

Despite the fact that much of the play's action depends upon women, only three female characters actually appear on stage: the procuress Alvigia, Togna, and, briefly, Biagina, a servant of the courtesan Camilla. This is due, in part, to Aretino's desire not to sully the virtue of such characters as Camilla and Livia who contribute to the idealized representation of ancient Rome. Those female characters who do appear on stage are portrayed favourably: Alvigia ranks equally with Rosso in guile, and Togna is to be admired for disregarding social edicts in seeking to satisfy her instincts. If the court is so markedly devoid of women it is because, according to Rosso, they are no longer needed there. Men, in their emasculated state, seek husbands. Yet Rosso's own position in court, like his relationship with Parabolano, is highly ambiguous. It seems that the servant, in his cynicism, obtains what he wants by whatever means are available to him.

Parabolano, at the end of *La cortigiana*, comments on the comedy, laughing at himself as one of its protagonists, suspended momentarily between life and pure theatre. His return to sanity has come too late to be of any benefit to the court. He has made the transition from life into art as a result of his own character, formed and nurtured by a society and an institution which, in ironic similarity to ancient Rome, is bringing about its own demise.

—Nicole Prunster

ARGUEDAS (Altamirano), José María. Born in Andahuaylas, Apurímac region, Peru, 18 January 1911. Lived in San Juan de Lucanas, 1917–24. Educated at Colegio Miguel Grau de los Padres Mercedarios, Abancay, 1924–25; Colegio San Luis Gonzaga, Ica, 1926–27; Colegio Santa Isabel, Huancayo, 1928–30; Colegio de Mercedarios, Lima, 1929–30; studied literature and anthropology at San Marcos University, Lima, 1931–32 (university closed by authorities, 1932), 1935–37, 1947–50, degree 1957, doctorate 1963. Married 1) Celia Bustamante in 1939 (divorced 1966); 2) Sybila Arredondo in 1967. Worked for the Peruvian postal service, Lima, 1932–37; co-founder and co-editor, *Palabra*, 1936; imprisoned for involvement in demonstrations against the insurrection in Spain, 1937–38; teacher of Spanish and geography, Colegio Nacional Mateo Pumacahua, Sicuani, 1939, and continued as secondary school teacher until 1946; lived in Mexico, 1940–42; returned to Lima, 1942, and worked with government commission for education reforms; teacher, 1942–47, Colegio Alfonso Ugarte and Colegio Guadalupe, both Lima, and the Instituto Pedagógico, Varones, 1950–53; suffered nervous breakdown, 1943; curator-general, 1947–50, then director, 1950–53, Ministry of Education Department of Folklore and Fine Art, Lima; travelled to Chile, 1951; director, Museum of Peruvian Culture Institute of Ethnological Studies, 1953; travelled to Spain, 1957–58; professor of Quechua and ethnic studies, San Marcos University, 1958–63, and later lectured at the Agrarian University, 1962–66; director, Institute of Contemporary Arts, Lima, 1961; director, Casa de la Cultura, 1963–64; director, Museum of the Republic (Museum of National History), Lima, 1964–66; founder, *Cultura y Pueblo*, 1964; visited the USA, 1965; attempted suicide by overdose of barbiturates, 1966; visited Cuba, 1968. Recipient: Javier Prado prize, 1958; Ricardo Palma prize, 1959, 1962; William Faulkner Foundation certificate of merit, 1963; Inca Garcilaso de la Vega prize, 1968. *Died (suicide) 2 December 1969.*

PUBLICATIONS

Collection

Obras completas. 5 vols., 1983.

Fiction

Agua (stories). 1935.
Runa yu pay. 1939.
Yawar fiesta. 1941; revised and corrected edition, 1958; as *Yawar Fiesta*, translated by Frances Horning Barraclough, 1985.
Diamantes y pedernales (includes 'Diamantes y pedernales', 'Orovilca', and the stories of *Agua*). 1954.
Todas las sangres. 1954.
Los ríos profundos. 1958; edited by William Rowe, 1973; as *Deep Rivers*, translated by Frances Horning Barraclough, 1978.
El sexto. 1961.
La agonía de Rasu-Ñiti. 1962.
Amor mundo y otros cuentos (includes 'La agonía de Rasu-Ñiti' and the stories of *Agua*). 1967; enlarged edition, 1972.
Amor mundo y todos los cuentos. 1967.
El zorro de arriba y el zorro de abajo (unfinished), edited by Eve Marie Fell. 1971; enlarged edition, 1990.
El forastero y otros cuentos (includes 'El barranco', 'Orovilca', 'Hijo solo'). 1972.
Cuentos olvidados, edited by José Luis Rouillon. 1973.
Relatos completos, edited by Jorge Lafforgue. 1975; revised edition, 1977.
Breve antología didáctica (stories). 1986.

Diamantes y pedernales; La agonía de Rasu-Ñiti; El sueño del pongo; Cuentos olvidados; Taller. 1986.
Relatos completos. 1987.

Other (including Quechua works)

Canto Kechwa (songs in Spanish and Quechua). 1938; translated in *The Singing Mountaineers*, 1957.
Cuzco. 1947.
Canciones y cuentos del pueblo quechua, with Jorge A. Lira. 1949; translated in *The Singing Mountaineers*, 1957.
Cuentos mágico-realistas y canciones de fiestas tradicionales en el valle del Mantaro. 1953.
Apu Inca Atawallpaman: Elegía quechua anónima (Spanish and Quechua), edited by José M.B. Farfán. 1955.
The Singing Mountaineers: Songs and Tales of the Quechua People, edited and translated by Ruth Stephen. 1957.
Estudio etnográfico de la Feria de Huancayo. 1957.
Ollantay: Cantos y narraciones quechuas, with César Miró and Salazar Bondy. 1957.
El arte popular religioso y la cultura mestiza. 1958.
Kunturpa munaskkan sipasmanta/De la amante del Cóndor (Quechua and Spanish), with Jorge A. Lira. 1961.
Tupac Amaru Kamaq taytanchisman: Haylli-taki/A nuestro padre creador Tupac Amaru: Himno-canción (Quechua and Spanish). 1962.
El sueño del pongo: Cuento quechua; Pongo mosqoynin: Qatqa runapa willaskusqan (Spanish and Quechua). 1965.
Dioses y hombres de Huarochirí (Spanish and Quechua). 1966.
Notas sobre la cultura latinoamericana y su destino, with Francisco Miró Quesada and Fernando de Szyszlo. 1966.
Las comunidades de España y del Perú. 1968.
El sueño del pongo; Canciones quechuas tradicionales, with recording. 1969.
Temblar/Katatay (Spanish and Quechua). 1972; edited by Sybila de Arguedas, 1984.
Páginas escogidas, edited by E.A. Westphalen. 1972.
Formación de una cultura nacional indoamericana. 1975; edited by Ángel Rama, 1981.
Señores e indios: Acerca de la cultura quechua (journalism), edited by Ángel Rama. 1976.
Temblar; El sueño del pongo; Katatay; Pongo mosqoynin (Spanish and Quechua). 1976.
Evolución de las comunidades indígenas: Dos estudios sobre Huancayo. 1977.
Nosotros los maestros (selection), edited by Wilfredo Kapsoli. 1986.
Indios, mestizos y señores (journalism), edited by Sybila de Arguedas. 1989.

Editor, with Francisco Izquierdo Ríos, *Mitos, leyendas y cuentos peruanos* (Quechua miscellany). 1947.
Editor, *Poesía quechua.* 1966.

*

Bibliography: 'Bibliografía de José María Arguedas' by William Rowe, in *Revista Peruana de Cultura*, 13–14, 1970; 'José María Arguedas' in *Peruvian Literature: A Bibliography of Secondary Sources* by David William Foster, 1981.

Critical Studies: *La multitud y el paisaje peruanos en los relatos de José María Arguedas*, 1939, and *José María Arguedas: Etapas de su vida*, 1972, both by Moises Arroyo Posadas; 'The Quechua World of José María Arguedas', in *Hispania*, 45, 1962, and *The Modern Short Story in Peru*, 1966, both by Earl M. Aldrich; *Arguedas: Un sentimiento trágico de la vida* by César Levano, 1969; *El tema de la violencia en Yawar fiesta* by François Borricaud, 1970; *José María Arguedas y la nueva novela indígena del Perú* edited by Julio V. Flores, 1970; 'The Literary Progression of José María Arguedas' by Phyllis Rodríguez-Peralta, in *Hispania*, 55(2), 1972; *Los universos narrativos de José María Arguedas* by Antonio Cornejo Polar, 1973; *La experiencia americana de José María Arguedas* by Gladys C. Marín, 1973; *José María Arguedas: El nuevo rostro del indio, una estructura mítico-poética* by Antonio Urello, 1974; *Recopilación de textos sobre José María Arguedas*, 1976; 'The Foxes in José María Arguedas's Last Novel' by F. Mitchell, Jr, in *Hispania*, 61, 1978; *José María Arguedas: Entre sapos y halcones* by Mario Vargas Llosa, 1978; *Mito e ideología en la obra de José María Arguedas* by William Rowe, 1979; *Cultura popular andina y forma novelesca: Zorros y danzantes en la última novela de Arguedas* by Martin Lienhard, 1982, enlarged edition, 1990; *Arguedas: Mito, historia y religión; Entre las calandrias* by Pedro Trigo and Gustavo Gutierrez, 1982; *Arguedas; o, La utopía de la lengua* by Alberto Escobar, 1984; 'Arguedas the Innovator: Yawar fiesta and Tupac Amaru' by T.K. Lewis, in *Discurso Literario*, 3(1), 1985; *Mythological Consciousness and the Future: José María Arguedas* by Claudette Kemper Columbus, 1986; *El modo épico en José María Arguedas* by Vincent Spina, 1986; *José María Arguedas y el mito de la salvación por la cultura* by Silverio Muñoz, 1987; *Estudios sobre José María Arguedas y Vargas Llosa* by F.J. Carranza Romero, 1989; *De Yawar fiesta a El zorro de arriba y el zorro de abajo* by C. Vildoso Chirinos, 1989; *José María Arguedas, del pensamiento dialéctico al pensamiento trágico, Historia de una utopía* by Roland Forgues, 1989.

* * *

José María Arguedas ranks as one of Peru's two leading novelists, the other being Mario Vargas Llosa. However, while Vargas Llosa belongs to the Western mainstream, Arguedas wrote as a spokesman of the indigenous Quechua-speaking Andean world, setting out to correct the distorted, stereotyped image of the Indian presented by earlier fiction. While his own portrayal of the Indian is still the view of an outsider, being the work of a non-Indian writing for a non-Indian public, it offers a deeper insight into the Indian mentality than anything published hitherto. The basis of Indian culture, we are shown, is a magical-religious view of the world that regards the earth not merely as something to be conquered and exploited, but as a single cosmic order animated by supernatural forces and linked in a universal harmony.

In his early fiction Arguedas's success in communicating that world view was restricted by his continuing reliance on a conventional realist manner, but from *Los ríos profundos* (*Deep Rivers*) onwards he evolved a more effective lyrical style akin to that of the Mexican, Juan Rulfo. Artistically, too, he was faced with the problem of translating into the alien medium of Spanish the sensibility of a people who express themselves in Quechua. His initial solution was to modify Spanish in such a way as to incorporate the basic features of Quechua syntax and thus reproduce something of the special character of Indian speech; but these experiments were only partially successful and subsequently he opted for a correct Spanish skilfully manipulated to convey Andean thought-patterns.

The context of Arguedas's fiction is the semi-feudal socio-economic order that prevailed in the Andean highlands from the Spanish Conquest until recent times. However, while earlier writers had simplistically depicted a black-and-white confrontation between oppressive white landowners and a downtrodden Indian peasantry, Arguedas presents a much more complex picture of Andean society. *Yawar fiesta* highlights the social tensions within the various racial groups. It also challenges the conventional image of abject, defeated natives by emphasizing the resilience that has enabled the Indians to survive centuries of oppression. Indeed, oppression is seen to have actually strengthened their culture, for it is by clinging to their traditional ways and refusing to be absorbed into the Western order that they have retained their pride and sense of identity. Furthermore, Arguedas demonstrates that centuries of co-existence have brought about a process of transculturation and that, if the whites dominate socially and economically, it is the Indian influence that predominates culturally, pervading the outlook of the whites despite their assumptions of cultural superiority. This paradoxical situation is encapsulated in the festival around which the novel revolves, an Indianized bullfight which simultaneously re-enacts racial hostilities and binds the whole community together in a common enthusiasm.

Most of Arguedas's novels are very much social in character in that they attempt to convey an overview of Andean society. However, another important strand in his work draws on his personal experience to depict the clash of Peru's two main cultures at an individual level, by focusing on the predicament of a young boy torn between the two. Thus, the child protagonist of the stories of *Agua* [Water] rejects the cruelty and injustice of the white landowning society into which he was born, and identifies emotionally with the Indians among whom he was brought up and whose culture affords him the comfort denied him by his own kind, but he can never escape the fact that he is different. Likewise, the protagonist of *Deep Rivers* is cut off from the beloved Indian world of his childhood when he is sent to a Church-run school to receive the education that will equip him to take his place in white society. In the oppressive atmosphere of the school he finds himself completely alienated and his faith in Indian culture is undermined by its seeming ineffectiveness in the world of the whites; but, in a triumphal climax, that faith is restored as the downtrodden Indians assert the validity of their culture by challenging the dominant social order and forcing it to accede to their demands. This autobiographical element was to resurface more directly in Arguedas's last, uncompleted novel *El zorro de arriba y el zorro de abajo* [The Fox of Above and the Fox of Below], where the narrative is interspersed with sections of diary recording the crisis that led him to commit suicide.

Arguedas's work also explores the impact of change on traditional Andean society. In *Yawar fiesta* we see the region emerge from its centuries-old isolation, progress being symbolized by a government decree banning non-professional bullfights; but the novel highlights the paradox that the very modernity that promises to liberate the Indians also threatens to destroy their culture and thereby their existence as a separate people. *Todas las sangres* [All Bloods] reflects the political and economic changes that had been taking place in Peru since the mid-1950s. The most optimistic of Arguedas's novels, it portrays the break-up of the traditional semi-feudal order and the emergence of the newly mobilized Indian peasantry as a political force, and expresses confidence in the ability of Quechua culture to adapt to a modern industrial society without losing its distinctive identity. Subsequently, Arguedas was to become disillusioned as the country embarked on an uncontrolled process of capitalist develop-

ment that brought with it a depopulation of the countryside and the erosion of traditional ways of life. *El zorro de arriba y el zorro de abajo* paints a horrific picture of this new reality, epitomized by the coastal boom-town of Chimbote. None the less, a positive note is maintained by the pervasive presence of the Quechua culture of the Andean migrants, and it is implied that out of the melting-pot that is present-day coastal Peru there will emerge a new Indianized national culture.

—James Higgins

DEEP RIVERS (Los ríos profundos)
Novel by José María Arguedas, 1958.

Generally regarded as Arguedas's best novel, *Deep Rivers* marks a break with his earlier work in that he abandons conventional realism in favour of a lyrical manner more appropriate to the Andean magical-religious worldview he seeks to communicate. Another significant evolution in his style relates to the problem of translating into the medium of Spanish the sensibility of a people who express themselves in Quechua. Whereas previously he had sought to modify Spanish so as to incorporate basic Quechua syntax, here he chose to write in correct Spanish adroitly managed so as to communicate Andean thought.

This book also differs from his other novels in that while the latter are social in essence, being concerned to present a totalizing overview of Andean society, here he draws on his own experience for his portrayal of the conflict between the indigenous and the Western at an individual level, and concentrates on the situation of a young boy pulled in both directions. The poor relation of a powerful landowning family, his protagonist, Ernesto, rejects the 'white' world to which he belongs by birth and identifies emotionally with the Indians among whom he spent the happiest period of his childhood. However, in the early chapters he is uprooted and sent to boarding-school to receive the education that will enable him to assume his role in 'white' society.

The Church-run school, whose value system is that of the landowning class it serves, stands as a microcosm of Andean society at large, and in its oppressive atmosphere Ernesto finds himself alienated. However, he is able to recharge himself emotionally by listening to Indian music in the native quarter of the town and by making trips into the countryside to renew his bonds with nature. These excursions become a vehicle for insights into Andean culture, for not only does the novel abound in observations on Quechua music, language, and folklore, but it conveys the functioning of magical-religious thought by showing it at work at the level of Ernesto's subjective experiences.

For most of the novel Ernesto's perspective is an ambivalent one as he confusedly adapts to his new circumstances. He is partially absorbed into white society, for though he feels himself to be different, he has inherited many of the attitudes of his class, and his teachers and comrades embrace him as one of their own. Furthermore, his experiences conspire to undermine his faith in Indian values by calling into question their effectiveness in the world of the whites, for not only does he see the Indian people downtrodden and humiliated at every turn, but even the magical forces of nature seem to lose their power when they come into confrontation with Western culture.

In the latter part of the novel, however, a series of events occurs that further estrange Ernesto from the 'white' world and consolidate his allegiance with the Indians. First the *chicheras* (female vendors of maize beer) challenge the established order by breaking into the government salt warehouses and distributing the contents among the poor. Then, following an outbreak of plague, the *colonos* (hacienda tenant labourers) shake off their servility and mobilize themselves. Believing the plague to be a supernatural being which can be destroyed only by religious means, they march on the town to demand that a special mass be said for them, and force the authorities to accede.

The novel thus ends with a victory of the Indians over the social order, a triumph that is paralleled on the internal plane by Ernesto's unreserved adherence to the Quechua ethos. His identification with the *chicheras* and *colonos* against his own kind is more than solidarity with the downtrodden, for his faith in the Quechua values he has grown to live by depend on the outcome of the conflict between the two ways of life. In a very real sense his personal salvation hinges on the ability of the Indians to assert the validity of their culture by asserting themselves socially. With the victory of the *colonos*, his faith is vindicated.

None the less, the ending is somewhat problematic. On one level, if Ernesto appears to have resolved his inner conflict by embracing Quechua culture with complete faith in its effectiveness, he clearly faces a future fraught with tensions, since he must live by its values in the alien world of the whites. On another level, there is a pathetic disproportion between the strength the *colonos* acquire and the tragically limited purpose to which it is put. Here the Indians' magical-religious outlook reveals itself to be both a strength and a weakness, for if it gives them the capacity to challenge the dominant order and win, it also substitutes a mythical enemy for the real enemy (the society that condemns them to live in subhuman conditions) and diverts them from practical political struggle. However, it would seem that Arguedas was concerned to demonstrate that the strength they display in pursuing religious objectives is capable of being harnessed to a social and political consciousness. Likewise, Ernesto's faith in Quechua culture would seem to reflect Arguedas's own newfound confidence in the ability of that culture not only to survive, but, with increasing migration to the cities of the coast, to spread beyond its traditional geographical boundaries to permeate and change the character of Peruvian society as a whole.

—James Higgins

ARNIM, Bettina von. Born Catharina Elisabetha Ludovica Magdalena Brentano in Frankfurt, Germany, 4 April 1785. Granddaughter of the writer Sophie von La Roche, sister of the writer Clemens Brentano, *q.v.* Educated at a convent in Fritzlar, 1794–97, then in Offenbach, Frankfurt, and Marburg. Married Ludwig Achim von Arnim in 1811 (died 1831); seven children. Became a friend of Goethe, whom she met in 1807; lived in Berlin from 1817; associated with Ludwig Tieck, the Grimm brothers, the Humboldt brothers, F.H. Jacobi, and F. Schleiermacher; acquainted also with Beethoven, Franz Liszt, and Hans Christian Andersen; began her literary career in the 1830s, after her husband's death. *Died 20 January 1859.*

PUBLICATIONS

Collections

Geschichten der Bettina von Arnim (selection), edited by Karl Hans Strobl and Karl Wilhelm Fritsch. 1908.
Sämtliche Werke, edited by Waldemar Oehlke. 7 vols., 1920–22.
Werke und Briefe, edited by Gustav Konrad and Joachim Müller. 5 vols., 1959–63.
'*Die Sehnsucht hat allemal Recht*': *Gedichte, Prosa, Briefe*, edited by Gerhard Wolf. 1984.
Werke, edited by Heinz Härtl. 1986—.
Werke und Briefe, edited by Walter Schmitz and Sibylle von Steinsdorff. 1986—.
Bettina von Arnim: Ein Lesebuch, edited by Christa Bürger and Birgitt Diefenbach. 1987.

Fiction

Goethes Briefwechsel mit einem Kinde. Seinem Denkmal. 1835; as *Goethe's Correspondence with a Child: For His Monument*, translated in part by the author, 1837, Book 3 translated as *The Diary of a Child*, 1838; translated by Wallace Smith Murray, in *German Classics of the Nineteenth and Twentieth Centuries*, vol. 7, 1913.
Die Günderode. 1840; as *Miss Günderode*, translated (incomplete) by Margaret Fuller, 1842; as *Correspondence of Fräulein Günderode and Bettine von Arnim*, complete translation by Minna Wesselhöft and Margaret Fuller, 1861.
Clemens Brentanos Frühlingskranz aus Jugendbriefen ihm geflochten, wie er selbst schriftlich verlangte. 1844.
Ilius Pamphilius und die Ambrosia. 1847–48.
Drei Märchen. 1853.
Das Leben der Hochgräfin Gritta von Rattenzuhausebeiuns, with Gisela von Arnim, edited by Otto Mallon. 1926.

Other

Dédié à Spontini. 1843.
Dies Buch gehört dem König. 2 vols., 1843.
An die aufgelöste Preussische National-Versammlung. Stimmen aus Paris (political pamphlet). 1848; as *Polenbroschüre*, edited by Ursula Püschel, 1954.
Gespräche mit Daemonen. Des Königsbuches zweiter Band. 1852.
Sämtliche Schriften. 11 vols., 1853.
Bettine von Arnim und Friedrich Wilhelm IV (correspondence), edited by Ludwig Geiger. 1902.
Achim von Arnim und Bettina Brentano (correspondence), edited by Reinhold Steig. 1913.
Goethes Mutter in ihren Briefen und in den Erzählungen der Bettina Brentano, edited by Kate Tischendorf. 1914.
Bettinas Briefwechsel mit Goethe: auf Grund ihres handschriftlichen Nachlasses nebst zeitgenössischen Dokumenten über ihr persönliches Verhältnis zu Goethe, edited by Reinhold Steig, 1922; revised edition edited by Fritz Bergemann. 1927.
Bettina in ihren Briefen, edited by Hartmann Goertz. 1935.
Bettina von Arnim und Rudolf Baier (correspondence), edited by Kurt Gassen. 1937.
Die Andacht zum Menschenbild. Unbekannte Briefe von Bettine Brentano, (correspondence with Carl von Savigny), edited by Wilhelm Schellberg and Friedrich Fuchs. 1942.
Clemens und Bettina: Geschwisterbriefe, edited by Ina Seidel. 1948.

Du wunderliches Kind . . . Bettine und Goethe. Aus dem Briefwechsel zwischen Goethe und Bettine von Arnim, edited by Alfred Kantorowicz. 1950.

Goethes Briefwechsel mit einem Kinde: aus dem Briefwechsel zwischen Goethe und Bettine von Arnim, edited by Gustav Konrad. 1960.

Achim und Bettina in ihren Briefen: Briefwechsel Achim von Arnim und Bettina Brentano, edited by Werner Vordtriede. 2 vols., 1961.

Das Armenbuch, edited by Werner Vordtriede. 1969.

Der Briefwechsel zwischen Bettine Brentano und Max Prokop von Freyberg, edited by Sybille von Steinsdorff. 1972.

Der Briefwechsel Bettine von Arnims mit dem Brüdern Grimm 1838–1841, edited by Hartwig Schultz. 1985.

Bettine und Arnim, Briefe der Freundschaft und der Liebe, edited by Otto Betz and Veronika Straub. 2 vols., 1986–87.

'. . . und mehr als einmal nachts im Thiergarten'. Bettina von Arnim und Heinrich Bernhard Oppenheim. Briefe 1841–1849, edited by Ursula Püschel. 1990.

Editor, with Wilhelm Grimm and Karl August Varnhagen von Ense, *Sämmtliche Werke*, by Ludwig Achim von Arnim. 2 vols., 1853–56; revised edition, 21 vols., 1857; reprinted 1982.

*

Critical Studies: *Bettina: A Portrait* by Arthur Helps and Elizabeth Jane Howard, 1957; 'The Reception in England and America of Bettina von Arnim's *Goethe's Correspondence with a Child*' by Hildegard Platzer Collins and Philip Allison Shelley, in *Anglo-German and American-German Crosscurrents*, (2), 1962; *Bettina von Arnim* by Hans von Arnim, 1963; *Bettina von Arnim. Romantik-Revolution-Utopie* by Ingeborg Drewitz, 1969; *Bettina von Arnim: Eine weibliche Sozialbibliographie aus dem 19. Jahrhundert* by Gisela Dischner, 1977; *An der Grenze einer neuen Welt: Bettina von Arnims Botschaft vom freien Geist* by Frieda Margarete Reuschle, 1977; *Steuerromantik: Rund um Bettina von Arnims Hundesteuerprozess* by Alfons Pausch, 1978; *Bettina von Arnim* by Gertrud Mander, 1982; *Bettina von Arnim: Eine Chronik: Daten und Zitate zu Leben und Werk*, edited by Heinz Härtl, 1984; *Bettina von Arnim: Ein Leben zwischen Tag und Traum* by Fritz Böttger, 1986; *Bettine von Arnim: Romantik und Sozialismus (1831–1859)* by Hartwig Schultz, Heinz Härtl, and Marie-Claire Hoock-Demarle, 1987; *Bettina von Arnim und Goethe: Topographie einer Beziehung als Beispiel weiblicher Emanzipation zu Beginn des 19. Jahrhunderts* by Birgit Weissenborn, 1987; *Bettine von Arnim and the Politics of Romantic Conversation* by Edith Waldstein, 1988; *Ordnung im Chaos: Studien zur Poetik der Bettine Brentano-von Arnim* by Ursula Liebertz-Grün, 1989.

*   *   *

One of the most remarkable and controversial figures of her generation, distinguished both by her striking personality and her multiple artistic gifts, Bettina von Arnim played a unique role in the political and intellectual life of her age. No German woman of letters has had a more profound effect on other artists: Beethoven esteemed her; Schumann and Brahms dedicated compositions to her; authors as diverse as Balzac, Immermann, and Rilke commemorated her in their novels; she gathered material for Goethe's autobiography and for the important collection of poetry by her husband and brother, *Des Knaben Wunderhorn* (*The Boy's Magic Horn*); she influenced Turgenev; and in recent times she has held a particular fascination for German women writers such as Sarah Kirsch, Ingeborg Drewitz, and Christa Wolf. While she is still most widely known for her cult of Goethe and her part in the reception of his work, her practical political concerns and her advocacy of disadvantaged social groups—Jews, the poor, victims of political persecution—are equally noteworthy.

Goethes Briefwechsel mit einem Kinde (*Goethe's Correspondence with a Child*), her first publication apart from minor items of verse and song settings, catapulted her on to the literary scene and became her most famous work both in Germany and abroad. Like three of her subsequent books—*Die Günderode* (*Miss Günderode*), *Clemens Brentanos Frühlingskranz* [Clemens Brentano's Spring Garland], and *Ilius Pamphilius und die Ambrosia*—it is an epistolary novel based on actual but heavily edited, altered, and supplemented letters, and hence occupies an ambivalent position between fact and fiction. Conceived as a literary monument to Goethe, it celebrates him as the quasi-divine incarnation of the spirit of poetry. The rapturous tone, cult of genius, and secularized religious vocabulary which characterize the novel were inspired in part by her reading of Goethe's works, notably *The Sufferings of Young Werther*, which reflects his attraction to her mother, Maximiliane, and letters that he had written to her grandmother, Sophie von La Roche, in the early 1770s. To these influences from Goethe's *Sturm und Drang* period must be added Arnim's personal acquaintance with his mother, whose reminiscences she had noted down and made available to Goethe as well as using them herself; the androgynous child-woman, Mignon, from his novel, *Wilhelm Meister's Apprenticeship* (1795–96), with whom Arnim identified; and the decisive significance for her of Romantic thought, in which the child embodies the original, innocent, paradisal relationship of humanity with the divine before the Fall. By casting herself in the role of the child-muse, Arnim evokes these associations and symbolizes her own spiritual rebirth through contact with the creative genius of Goethe.

On its appearance the *Correspondence* provoked a heated public debate, which had as much to do with the polarized political, religious, and cultural climate of contemporary Germany as with the merits of the book itself. Reactions ranged from moral outrage on the part of both Catholics and Protestants to the unqualified praise of Jacob Grimm, who declared that the book had no equal in the power of either its language or its thought, and the enthusiasm of the young German writers, who saw it as an emancipatory tract and elevated Arnim to mythical status as an embodiment of the progressive *Zeitgeist*. By combining Romantic qualities with the apotheosis of Goethe—regarded in Germany as the embodiment of classicism—and patriotism with liberal attitudes, Arnim challenged the antithetical view of late 18th and early 19th-century German culture which was current in the mid-1830s and still colours perceptions of the period today. Although her translation of the *Correspondence* into English, which was intended to finance the Goethe memorial that she designed, proved a financial disaster, the book was well received in intellectual and artistic circles abroad, particularly in Russia, in France, and among the Transcendentalists in the USA. A partial Russian translation by Mikhail Bakunin appeared in 1838, an American edition in 1841, and a complete French translation in 1843.

Arnim's other major epistolary works, *Miss Günderode* and *Clemens Brentanos Frühlingskranz*, commemorate, respectively, her friend Karoline von Günderode, a writer who had taken her own life in 1806 at the age of 26, and her favourite brother, who died in 1842. Both the dedication of *Miss Günderode* to 'the students' and the title of the 'Spring Garland' have political connotations, reflecting Arnim's concern with the younger generation and with the projection of a forward-looking image of Romanticism in contrast to contemporary criticism of the movement as reactionary and narrowly denominational. Thus in the *Frühlingskranz* she stresses her brother's unorthodox youth rather than the conservative Catholicism of his later years, while in *Miss Günderode*, drawing upon the traditions of the Enlightenment, Goethe, and early Romanticism, in particular the thought of Schleiermacher, she undertakes a radical critique of orthodox Christianity and proposes a new religion based on the Romantic conception of divine love as the principle of creation.

Like the *Correspondence, Dies Buch gehört dem König* [This Book Belongs to the King] caused a sensation. A fictitious dialogue dedicated to King Frederick William IV of Prussia, it advocates, through the figure of Goethe's mother, a constitutional monarchy, social reforms, a free press, and extensive civil liberties. Crime is attributed to social deprivation; consequently, Arnim opposes the death penalty and pleads for prison reform and education for offenders. An appendix documents conditions in a Berlin slum. In 1844, Arnim planned a comprehensive documentary study of poverty, *Das Armenbuch* [Book of the Poor]. She collected 'pauper lists' from all over Germany, especially Silesia, but was dissuaded from publication by the uprising of the Silesian weavers in June of that year (the extant documents were first published by Werner Vortriede in 1962). The appearance of her correspondence with her young friend Philipp Nathusius (*Ilius Pamphilius*), and the sequel to the 'King's Book', *Gespräche mit Daemonen* [Conversations with Spirits], met with little response, though the latter provoked accusations of communism. She spent her final years editing and publishing her husband's collected works.

—Judith Purver

ARIOSTO, Ludovico. Born in Reggio Emilia, Ferrara territory (now in Italy), 8 September 1474. Studied in the law faculty, University of Ferrara, 1489–94. Married Alessandra Benucci Strozzi in late 1520s; two earlier illegitimate children, whom he recognized. Took a court post during the political unrest of the 1490s; captain of the garrison, Canossa, 1502–03; courtier, diplomat, and writer in service of Cardinal Ippolito d'Este until 1517; in service of Alfonso d'Este, Duke of Ferrara, 1518–33; commissario of the Garfagnana, 1522–25. *Died 6 July 1533.*

PUBLICATIONS

Collections

Le commedie, edited by Michele Catalano. 2 vols., 1933.
Opere minori, edited by Cesare Segre. 1954.
Commedie, edited by Cesare Segre. 1974.
The Comedies (includes *The Coffer* [prose and verse versions]; *The Pretenders*; *The Necromancer*; *Lena*; *The Students*), edited and translated by Edmond M. Beame and Leonard G. Sbrocchi. 1975.
Satire e lettere, edited by Cesare Segre. 1976.
Opere, edited by Adriano Seroni. 1981.

Verse

Orlando furioso. 1515 (40 cantos); revised version, 1521; 3rd edition, 1532 (46 cantos); additional *Cinque Canti* published in 1545 edition; edited by S. De Benedetti and Cesare Segre, 1960, edited by Segre, 1976, and by Emilio Bigi, 1982; as *Orlando Furioso*, translated by John Harington, 1591, and by William Stewart Rose, 2 vols., 1823–31; as *The Frenzy of Orlando*, translated by Barbara Reynolds, 2 vols., 1975–77; several prose translations including by A. Gilbert, 1954, and by Guido Waldman, 1974.
Satire. 1534; edited by Cesare Segre, 1976; as *Seven Planets Governing Italy*, 1611; as *The Satires*, translated by Peter DeSa Wiggins, 1976.
The Satires, edited by R.B. Gottfried. 1977.

Plays

La cassaria (produced 1508). 1509; revised version, in verse (produced 1531), 1546; as *The Coffer*, in *The Comedies*, 1975.
I suppositi (produced 1509). 1509 or 1510; revised version, in verse, 1525; as *Supposers*, translated by George Gascoigne, 1566; as *The Pretenders*, in *The Comedies*, 1975.
La Lena (produced 1528). 1533 or 1536; edited by Guido Davico Bonino, 1976; as *Lena*, in *The Comedies*, 1975; as *La Lena*, in *Five Italian Renaissance Comedies*, edited by Bruce Penman, 1978.
Il negromante (produced 1529). 1535; as *The Necromancer*, in *The Comedies*, 1975.
La scolastica, completed by Gabriele Ariosto. 1547; as *The Students*, in *The Comedies*, 1975.

Other

Lettere, edited by A. Stella. 1965.
Lettera della Garfagnana, edited by Gianna Scalia. 1977.

*

Bibliography: *Ludovico Ariosto: An Annotated Bibliography of Criticism 1956–1980* by Robert J. Rodini and Salvatore Di Maria, 1984; 'Selected Bibliography of Ariosto Criticism 1980–87', by Robert J. Rodini, in *Modern Language Notes*, 1988.

Critical Studies: *The King of the Court Poets: A Study of the Work, Life, and Times of Ludovico Ariosto* by Edmund G. Gardner, 1906, reprinted 1969; *The Figure of the Poet in the Renaissance Epic* by R.M. Durling, 1965; *Ariosto: A Preface to the Orlando Furioso* by C.P. Brand, 1974; *Ludovico Ariosto* by Robert Griffin, 1974; *Names on the Trees: Ariosto into Art* by Rennsselaer W. Lee, 1977; *Ariosto and the Classical Simile* by Kristen Olson Murtaugh, 1980; *Figures in Ariosto's Tapestry: Character and Design in the Orlando Furioso* by Peter DeSa Wiggins, 1986; *Ariosto's Bitter Harmony: Crisis and Evasion in the Italian Renaissance* by Albert Russell Ascoli, 1987; *The Poetics of Ariosto* by Marianne Shapiro, 1988; *Cervantes and Ariosto* by Thomas R. Hart, 1989; *Proclaiming a Classic: The Canonization of Orlando Furioso* by Daniel Javitch, 1991.

* * *

Ariosto's masterpiece, *Orlando furioso* (*Orlando Furioso*), is the culmination of a long tradition. Beginning in the 11th century with the Old French epic, *La Chanson de Roland* (*The Song of Roland*), it continued in Italy (as elsewhere) in a series of extravagant romances, both oral and written. The legends, relating to Charlemagne and his paladins in their defence of Christendom against the Muslims, became part of folklore, as may be seen in Sicily where puppet masters in Palermo still perform the stories and where the sides of donkey carts are painted with colourful scenes of the combats.

In the 15th century Luigi Pulci of Florence wrote an elaborate version of Roland's (Orlando's) adventures. This was *Il Morgante*, a poem in rhymed octaves, much admired by Byron, who translated the first canto. Pulci was followed by Matteo Boiardo of Ferrara, who complicated the story still further with oriental elements and combined it with episodes and characters drawn from the Arthurian cycle. Boiardo's poem, also in rhymed octaves, was entitled *Orlando innamorato* [Roland in Love]. In 1494, when the French invaded Italy, he felt unable to continue and laid down his pen. Violent events had irrupted into his world of fantasy and destroyed it.

A generation later Ariosto undertook to complete Boiardo's poem. The result was his *Orlando Furioso* [Roland Driven Mad by Love]. In Ariosto's hands chivalrous romance becomes romantic epic. To the themes of war, chivalry, and love, already in Boiardo, Ariosto added history, from mythological antiquity down to contemporary times, from the Fall of Troy to the Sack of Rome. The factual is rendered poetic; the poetic acquires the solemnity of historical fact. It is this which converts romance into epic. Epic also is the intensity with which Ariosto visualizes and communicates his world. His descriptions of beauty, chivalry, noble achievement, violence, and evil are on a scale that exceeds life. Yet the work is far from solemn throughout. The legacy of exuberant exaggeration, rollicking humour, suspense and wilful complexity, inherited from the conventions of the *cantastorie* (narrators who recited the tales in public), as well as from Pulci and Boiardo, enriches and varies the 46 cantos. Ariosto's octaves justly deserve the epithet of 'golden'.

To 16th-century critics *Orlando Furioso* appeared to lack unity, and the stories it contained were dismissed as unworthy of the attention of serious-minded men of letters. Ariosto has also been condemned for his adulation of the House of Este, the rulers of Ferrara and his patrons. Such criticisms, still voiced in modern times, can be answered. On the charge of adulation it can be said that Ariosto's praise of Ferrara and of the Estense dynasty was in the tradition of works of praise (encomia), which had the warrant of Aristotle and also of Erasmus, who held that the most efficacious way of correcting a prince was to present him, in the guise of flattery, with an ideal picture of himself. This may have been Ariosto's intention in those octaves in praise of Duke Alfonso and his brother, Cardinal Ippolito, to whom he dedicated the poem. But the praise was not all flattery. There was much to admire in the achievements of the Dukes of Ferrara and in the world of beauty they created. Furthermore, what Ariosto thought worthy of condemnation he condemned: the use of gunfire in battle, for instance (in which Duke Alfonso was a pioneer), and the neglect of poets by their patrons.

The charge of disunity in the *Orlando Furioso* is based on assumptions which are not relevant to the nature of Ariosto's art. The poem is composed not of homogeneous elements arranged with predictable symmetry, but of vastly disparate material, controlled and balanced with apparent nonchalance but, in reality, with subtle skill. Thematic unity resides in the concept of Europe as the civilizing force both of antiquity and of the newly extended Christian world. The contemporary danger of Turkish power is imaged in the menace of the Muslims in the time of Charlemagne; and Charles V, on his election as Emperor, may have been seen by Ariosto, as his poem progressed, to be a natural symbol of that other Charles, the 8th-century head of Christendom.

Ariosto takes up the story at the point where Agramante, king of the Moors, and Marsilio, the Saracen King of Spain, have invaded France. Orlando has escorted the Princess Angelica from the Far East to the Pyrenees and is at once caught up in the war. Angelica was introduced into the story by Boiardo to serve, with her dazzling beauty, as a distraction to Christian and Muslim knights alike. Orlando and his cousin, Rinaldo, both love her and their rivalry is a danger to the Christian side. Angelica, unmoved by the adoration she inspires, eventually falls in love with a wounded Moorish soldier, whom she nurses back to health and marries. The discovery of this causes Orlando to lose his wits and supernatural aid is required before he can be brought back to sanity.

In constructing this sequel to Boiardo's poem Ariosto had three main tasks: to bring the war to a close, to disentangle both Orlando and Rinaldo from their infatuation for Angelica, and to enable Rinaldo's sister, Bradamante, to marry a noble warrior, Ruggiero, who, though fighting for the Infidel, is, as he discovers, of Christian origin. From their union is destined to descend the illustrious line of the House of Este. All three tasks are accomplished and all the minor stories left unfinished by Boiardo are likewise brought to a conclusion. The *Orlando Furioso* is, however, far more than an appendix to the *Innamorato*. It is an original work in its own right, dazzling in the *bravura* of its execution.

Ariosto's other works include *capitoli* (burlesques), satires, and five comedies on the models of Plautus and Terence, whose plays were then fashionable in Ferrara. Ariosto had acted in the court theatre in his youth and during his last years he was director of theatrical entertainments. His *Orlando Furioso* is itself rather like a huge theatrical production, of which the author is also the stage-manager and property-man.

—Barbara Reynolds

ORLANDO FURIOSO
Poem by Ludovico Ariosto, 1515–32.

Orlando Furioso is the culmination of the Italian tradition of chivalric literature. The Renaissance saw a decline in the chivalric tradition, with Pulci's *Morgante*, a parody in the Florentine comic-realistic vein, and, in France, the satirical tales of Gargantua and of Pantagruel by Rabelais. Ariosto was to remedy this situation. A courtier to the Este family, rulers of Ferrara, the poet wrote for a public of noblemen, knights, and ladies who were knowledgeable enthusiasts of the chivalric genre. It was the explicit intention of Ariosto to continue the unfinished poem written by a poet of the preceding generation at the court of Ferrara, Matteo Maria Boiardo. In *Orlando innamorato*, Boiardo tells of Orlando's unrequited love for the beautiful oriental princess, Angelica, and Ariosto goes on to complete the saga, by narrating how Orlando becomes mad ('furioso' in Italian) for love.

Ariosto continued the narrative with the same characters

used by his predecessor, with a few orthographic changes to names: Ranaldo becomes Rinaldo, Ferraguto becomes Ferrau. Like Boiardo before him, the poet also follows the model of the united traditions of the Breton and Carolingian cycles. The genre of chivalric poetry had originated in France in the Middle Ages and came to Italy by way of the Franco-Venetian poets of the 13th century. The Carolingian cycle told of the feats of Charlemagne's courtiers whereas the Breton cycle relates the romantic tales of the knights of King Arthur's Round Table. Another element used by Boiardo and continued by Ariosto is the stylistic choice of the narrative octave, verses of eight endecasyllables, the first six with an alternating rhyme, followed by a concluding couplet (ABABABCC). Although the octave had been used often in chivalric and other forms of literature, it is Ariosto who is credited with ennobling the verse to the point that his are often referred to as 'golden octaves'. It is the ideal form for his conversational and yet elegant narrative style.

The chivalric tradition was also an oral tradition, and the stories of Roland (Orlando) and his knights were often related at court by wandering troubadours. Thus Ariosto's narrative follows tradition in that the narrator is omnipresent in the poem, providing the reader with occasional ironic commentary on the events related. In the first lines of the poem, the narrator declares: 'Le donne, i cavallier, l'arme, gli amori,/le cortesie, l'audaci imprese io canto' ('Of women, knights, weapons, loves, courtly life and audacious feats I sing'). Thus the reader is given a ready catalogue of the multiple subjects of the work, a panorama of courtly life and wars rather than a straightforward narrative of the life of Orlando.

In the first verse of the poem quoted above, the poet promises to narrate not only tales of war, but also tales of love. Against the background of the Holy War between Charlemagne's knights and the Saracen army of Agramante, Ariosto tells two love stories. Orlando's love for Angelica is unrequited and, when he discovers that she loves the simple soldier Medoro, the knight in love becomes crazy with despair ('furioso'). He turns into a brute, and Astolfo must undertake a voyage to the moon in order to recover Orlando's brain. After recovering his reasoning faculties, Orlando is again a fearless knight and brings victory to Charlemagne's army. Boiardo had invented the character of Ruggiero in tribute to his patrons, the Este family. The second major love story of the poem is that of Ruggiero and the female warrior, Bradamante, destined one day to marry. Their descendants would then become the mythical ancestors of the Este family. Of course, because the marriage of Bradamante and Ruggiero must constitute the conclusion of the poem, both Boiardo and Ariosto place many obstacles in the path of their happy union in order to continue the other narratives of Orlando and Angelica, and the war.

The narrative skips between these tales, often leaving a dramatically crucial moment of the plot to pick up another interrupted adventure in midstream. In this way, dramatic tension is increased for the reader, using a technique common in serialized novels and today's television soap operas.

The definitive work is divided into 46 cantos and, despite the interweaving of story lines, does have a definite beginning, middle, and end. Boiardo's poem was left unfinished in the middle of a great battle between Christians and infidels. Before this battle, Charlemagne had asked old Namo to look after Princess Angelica, the object of the desires of the two feuding cousins, Orlando and Rinaldo. Namo was to give Angelica as the victor's prize at the end of the battle, but she escapes and Ariosto's poem begins with Orlando and others on the heels of the fleeing princess. The central canto of the work is dedicated to a description of Orlando's love sickness and ensuing madness. Finally, the work concludes, just as Boiardo had planned, with the wedding between Bradamante and Ruggiero.

The harmony of the poem makes it a symbol of its age. The theories of Castiglione's ideal courtier and Bembo's ideal Italian vernacular are exemplified in Ariosto's art. The *Orlando Furioso* is one of the great masterpieces of the Italian Renaissance.

—Jordan Lancaster

ARISTOPHANES. Born in Athens, possibly c. 450 BC, possibly as late as 444 BC. May have lived or owned property on Aigina. His first plays directed by others; *Hippeis* (*The Knights*, 424 BC) was his first production in his own name. Won at least four prizes at the City Dionysia and Lenaia festivals. Besides the 11 surviving comedies, 32 other titles are known (some possibly alternative titles; four probably spurious), and nearly 1,000 fragments survive. His son, Araros, produced his last two plays; all three of his sons are known to have written plays of their own. Served on the *boule* (the Athenian Senate) in the early 4th century BC. *Died c.385 BC*.

PUBLICATIONS

Collections

[Comedies], edited by F.W. Hall and W.M. Geldart. 2 vols., 1901–02; also edited by Johannes van Leeuwen, 11 vols., 1893–1906, and Victor Coulon (includes French translations), 5 vols., 1923–30; edited and translated by B.B. Rogers, 11 vols., 1902–15, and Alan H. Sommerstein (bilingual editions; with commentary), 8 vols., 1980–94; as *The Complete Plays*, edited by Moses Hadas, translated by Hadas, B.B. Rogers, R.H. Webb, and Jack Lindsay, 1962; also translated by David Barrett and Alan H. Sommerstein, 3 vols., 1964–77; Patric Dickinson, 2 vols., 1970; Kenneth McLeish, 3 vols., 1993–94.
Poetae comici graeci (includes the fragments of lost comedies), edited by R. Kassel and Colin Austin. 1983.

Plays

Acharnes (produced 425 BC). Edited by William W. Merry, 1880; also edited by W. Rennie, 1909; edited and translated by W.J.M. Starkie, 1909; as *The Acharnians*, translated by Douglass Parker, 1961; also translated by B.B. Rogers, in *The Complete Plays*, 1962; Jeffrey Henderson, 1991.
Hippeis (produced 424 BC). Edited by William W. Merry, 1887; as *The Knights*, edited by Robert A. Neil, 1901; translated by R.H. Webb, in *The Complete Plays*, 1962; also translated by David Barrett and Alan H. Sommerstein, 1978; Kenneth McLeish, 1979.
Nephelai (produced 423 BC, partially revised 419–17 BC; only the revision has survived). Edited by William W. Merry, 1879; also edited by K.J. Dover, 1968; as *The Clouds*, edited and translated by W.J.M. Starkie, 1911; translated by Patric Dickinson, 1957; also translated by William

Arrowsmith, 1962; Moses Hadas, in *The Complete Plays*, 1962; Alan H. Sommerstein, 1973; Kenneth McLeish, 1979; James H. Mantinband, in *Four Plays*, 1983; commentary by Raymond K. Fisher, 1984.

Sphekes (produced 422 BC). Edited by William W. Merry, 1893; also edited by Douglas M. MacDowell, 1970; as *The Wasps*, edited and translated by W.J.M. Starkie, 1897; translated by Douglass Parker, 1962; also translated by Moses Hadas, in *The Complete Plays*, 1962.

Eirene (produced 421 BC). Edited by William W. Merry, 1900; also edited by H. Sharpley, 1905, and Maurice Platnauer, 1964; as *The Peace*, translated by Doros Alastos, 1953; also translated by B.B. Rogers, in *The Complete Plays*, 1962.

Ornithes (produced 414 BC). Edited by William W. Merry, 1889; also edited by T. Kock, revised by O. Schröder, 1927, and N.V. Dunbar, 1994; as *The Birds*, translated by William Arrowsmith, 1961; also translated by Dudley Fitts, in *Four Comedies*, 1962; R.H. Webb, in *The Complete Plays*, 1962; Patric Dickinson, 1970; Kenneth McLeish, 1970; Alan H. Sommerstein, 1977; James H. Mantinband, in *Four Plays*, 1983.

Lysistrate (produced 411 BC). Edited by U. von Wilamowitz-Möllendorff, 1927; also edited by Jeffrey Henderson, 1987; as *Lysistrata*, translated by Jack Lindsay, 1925, and in *The Complete Plays*, 1962; also translated by Charles T. Murphy, 1944; Donald Sutherland, 1961; Dudley Fitts, in *Four Comedies*, 1962; Douglass Parker, 1964; James H. Mantinband, in *Four Plays*, 1983; Jeffrey Henderson, 1988.

Thesmophoriazousai (produced 411 BC). As *Ladies' Day*, translated by Dudley Fitts, in *Four Comedies*, 1962; also translated by B.B. Rogers, in *The Complete Plays*, 1962; as *The Poet and the Women*, translated by David Barrett, 1964.

Batrachoi (produced 405 BC). Edited by William W. Merry, 1884; also edited by T.G. Tucker, 1906, L. Radermacher, 1954, W.B. Stanford, 1963, and Kenneth Dover, 1993; as *The Frogs*, translated by Gilbert Murray, 1908; also translated by Dudley Fitts, in *Four Comedies*, 1962; Richmond Lattimore, 1962; R.H. Webb, in *The Complete Plays*, 1962; Patric Dickinson, 1970; Kenneth McLeish, 1970; James H. Mantinband, in *Four Plays*, 1983.

Ekklesiazousai (produced c.392 BC). Edited by R.G. Ussher, 1973; as *Women in Parliament*, translated by Jack Lindsay, 1929, and in *The Complete Plays*, 1962; as *The Congresswomen*, translated by Douglass Parker, 1967; as *Women in Power*, translated by Kenneth McLeish, 1979.

Ploutos (produced 388 BC). As *Plutus*, translated by William Rann Kennedy, 1912; also translated by B.B. Rogers, in *The Complete Plays*, 1962; as *Wealth*, translated by Alan H. Sommerstein, 1978.

Four Comedies (includes *Lysistrata*; *The Frogs*; *The Birds*; *Ladies' Day*), translated by Dudley Fitts. 1962.

Four Plays (includes *The Birds*; *The Clouds*; *The Frogs*; *Lysistrata*), translated by James H. Mantinband. 1983.

*

Critical Studies: *Aristophanes: A Study* by Gilbert Murray, 1933; 'Aristophanes and Politics' by A.W. Gomme, in *Classical Review*, 1938; *Incongruity in Aristophanes* by C.C. Jernigan, 1939; *The Art of Greek Comedy* by K. Lever, 1956; *The People of Aristophanes: A Sociology of Old Attic Comedy* by Victor Ehrenberg, 1962, revised edition, 1974; *Aristophanes: His Plays and His Influence* by L.E. Lord, 1963; *Aristophanes and the Comic Hero* by C.H. Whitman,

1964; *The Origin of Old Attic Comedy* by F.M. Cornford, 1968; *Twentieth Century Interpretations of the Frogs* edited by D.J. Littlefield, 1968; *Aristophanic Comedy* by K.J. Dover, 1972; 'The Political Opinions of Aristophanes', Appendix XXIX of *The Origins of the Peloponnesian War* by G.E.M. de Ste Croix, 1972; *The Living Aristophanes* by A. Solomos, 1974; *The Stage of Aristophanes* by C.W. Dearden, 1976; *Aristophanes* by R.G. Ussher, 1979; *Studies in the Manuscript Tradition of the Ranae of Aristophanes* by Charles N. Eberline, 1980; *The Theatre of Aristophanes* by Kenneth McLeish, 1980; *Aristophanes: Essays in Interpretation* edited by Jeffrey Henderson, 1981; *Aristophanic Poetry* by Carroll Moulton, 1981; *Aristophanes and Athenian Society of the Early Fourth Century BC* by E. David, 1984; 'Comedy' by E. Handley, in *Cambridge History of Classical Literature*, vol. 1 edited by P. Easterling and B.M.W. Knox, 1985; *Aristophanes: Poet and Dramatist* by Rosemary M. Harriott, 1986; *Political Comedy in Aristophanes* by Malcolm Heath, 1987; *Aristophanes' Old-and-New Comedy* by Kenneth J. Reckford, 1987; *Cleon, Knights and Aristophanes' Politics* by Lowell Edmunds, 1988; *Aristophanes and His Theatre of the Absurd* by Paul Cartledge, 1990; *Politics and Persuasion in Aristophanes' Ecclesiazusae* by Kenneth S. Rothwell, 1990; *The Mask of Comedy: Aristophanes and the Intertextual Parabasis* by T.K. Hubbard, 1991; *Ancient Comedy, the War of the Generations* by D.F. Sutton, 1993; *Aristophanes and Women* by Laura K. Taaffe, 1993; *Comic Angels* by O. Taplin, 1993; *Aristophanes: Myth, Ritual and Comedy* by A.M. Bowie, 1994; *Aristophanes, an Author for the Stage* by C.F. Russo, 1994.

* * *

Aristophanes is the best-known (and only surviving) exponent of Old Comedy, an art form which, like its older sister Tragedy, was performed as part of the artistic competitions at the civic festivals at Athens in honour of Dionysus, god of drama. Old Comedy reached its highest point during the last third of the 5th century BC, the years of the age of Pericles and of the vigorous Athenian democracy. Old Comedy was very much a child of that democracy. In the very best sense of the word, Aristophanes' comedy was 'political' (*polis* = city-state), as his plays are concerned essentially with the Athens of his day, supplying him with his inspiration, his themes and issues, his jokes, characters, and personalities. Firmly anchored in the social milieu of 5th-century Athens, his work exhibits a unique mixture of humours, ranging from political satire to obscenity and toilet humour, from sophisticated parody to slapstick, from utopian fantasy to personal abuse. His comedy is without parallel or successors in Western literature.

Aristophanes is neither a master of comic plot (the 'comedy of errors' on which so much Western comedy depends) nor a creator of subtle interaction between characters. Rather the kernel of his comedy is the establishment of a fantastic idea, a grand scheme, the more outrageous the better, whose implementation and consequences form the action; 'plot' is not a term useful in Aristophanic criticism. Examples include *Acharnes* (*The Acharnians*) where the hero (whose name means 'Just City') makes his own personal peace treaty with the Spartan enemy, or *Lysistrate* (*Lysistrata*) in which the wives of Greece occupy the Athenian acropolis and embark on a 'sex-strike' to force the men (successfully) to end the war. The *grande idée* is developed in a series of more or less formal structural features, e.g. *parodos*, the visually splendid entry of the chorus who provided either an on-stage audience or the opposition; *agon*, a formally constructed debate in which the great idea was contested or explained; *parabasis*, in which the chorus spoke directly to the audience, often for the comedian himself; and the *episodes*, a series of loosely connected scenes in which the consequences of the great idea are worked out. In his later plays Aristophanes begins to employ a freer use of the traditional forms; *Thesmophoriazousai* (*The Poet and the Women*), in particular, most resembles a later Western comedy.

Space does not allow for individual discussion of the comedies. In the 11 extant comedies we can see that all aspects of Athenian life were fair game for the comic poet. There are the so-called 'peace plays', *The Acharnians*, *Eirene* (*The Peace*), and *Lysistrata*, from which it is clear that Aristophanes was not himself a pacifist, but an ardent opponent of the Peloponnesian War (431–04 BC). *The Acharnians*, with its unparalleled identification of the protagonist with the comic poet and its open hostility to Athens' war policy and its proponents, is worthy of special attention. *Hippeis* (*The Knights*) and *Sphekes* (*The Wasps*) are both largely concerned with politics and the demagogues, especially Kleon whose distinctive political style is subjected to a sweeping and at times coarse caricature in *The Knights*. *The Wasps*, a humorous satire on the jury system and Kleon's manipulation of it, features Philokleon, perhaps the most appealing rogue in ancient literature. Philosophy and drama form the themes of *Nephelai* (*The Clouds*) and *The Poet and the Women*, the former containing the infamous depiction of Socrates as a sophistic charlatan, which Plato tells us contributed to his condemnation in 399 BC. *Lysistrata*, *The Poet and the Women*, and *Ekklesiazousai* (*Women in Power*) make up the 'women's plays'; the last portrays the seizure by women of the government at Athens and the institution of a communistic regime very much like Plato's ideal Republic. *Lysistrata*, with its themes of 'Women's Liberation' and 'Make love, not war!', has become the favourite of modern audiences.

Two plays, *Ornithes* (*The Birds*) and *Batrachoi* (*The Frogs*), stand out as Aristophanes' masterpieces. *The Birds* features two Athenians who flee the problems of life in Athens to take refuge among the birds. They join with them in founding the now famous city, Cloudcuckooland, and in the end displace the Olympian gods as the rulers of the universe. *The Frogs* shows Dionysus, god of drama, descending to the underworld to bring back Euripides, the recently deceased and controversial tragic poet. After some amusing adventures, Dionysus ends up judging a witty contest between Euripides and Aeschylus, the old master, in which Dionysus eventually judges Aeschylus the victor and brings him back to Athens 'to save the city'. Produced in the months preceding Athens' defeat, this comedy with its mingling of political, literary, and religious themes provides an elegant farewell to Athens' greatness.

Critical discussion has focused on the motives of the comedian. In a landmark article A.W. Gomme argued that no serious political or satirical purpose was to be found in Aristophanes; his *forte* was a brilliant, revolutionary comedy. De Ste. Croix argued in return that although creation of comedy was his first concern, a consistent and intentional political stance may be ascertained, that of a 'conservative', but neither oligarchic nor radical democrat. His opposition to Kleon and the demagogues is clear, as is his hostility to the war with Sparta. Aristophanes is essentially a regressive; the final scenes of *The Knights* and *Lysistrata* make clear his affection for the glorious days of Athens of previous generations, the triumphs of the Persian Wars. Similarly, despite his obvious fondness for the modern and avant-garde

Euripides, he chooses Aeschylus in the end. Technical ability yields to the moral purpose of art. Yet Aristophanes is no anti-intellectual; his caricature of Socrates is more humorous than satirical, and his appreciation of and affinity with Euripides are evident. He, like Socrates and Euripides, was *sophos* (smart) and *dexios* (clever). Likewise in the treatment of the real people made fun of in his plays (*to onomasti komodein*—to make fun of by name), commentators have been quick to detect a moral purpose behind the jokes, but here too comedy should take precedence over satire. Only with Kleon and the demagogues can we detect any real malice. For the most part we should regard Aristophanes as what he himself claimed to be, a superb creator of imaginative and fantastic comedy.

—Ian C. Storey

THE BIRDS (Ornithes)
Play by Aristophanes, 414 BC.

Aristophanes' *The Birds* ranks as one of the greatest sustained comic fantasies, but the play took only second prize at the Dionysia of 414 BC. It features two Athenians, Peithetairos ('Persuasive Companion') and Euelpides ('Son of Good Hope'), who abandon Athens for a life among the birds. In 5th-century Greek, 'to go to the birds' was a way of saying 'go to hell'. They seek out Tereus, a mythical character with Athenian associations now become a hoopoe, who agrees to introduce them to the birds and to convince the latter to overcome their fear of men.

It is here that the *grande idée* is conceived by Peithetairos, and in place of the usual *agon* (contest) a two-part exposition ensues, in which Peithetairos persuades the birds that birds used to rule the universe can do so again by building a city in the air to intercept the sacrifices of men to the gods and thus to starve the gods into submission. This city is, of course, the now famous Cloudcuckooland.

The parabasis differs from those in the comedies of the 420s BC in that the chorus does not speak directly for the comedian, but remains in character, outlining a marvellous cosmogony in which birds are the eldest children of Love, creator of the universe, and benefactors of mankind. In the second half the newly created Cloudcuckooland is besieged by intruders (lawseller, priest, poet, town planner). All are driven off by Peithetairos. In a second series of intruders he dismisses first potential undesirables of city life (a parent beater, an informer, the airy-fairy poet Kinesias) and then Iris (Rainbow), the messenger of the gods, who is roughly treated and even sexually threatened. Finally Prometheus, the great friend of humanity, enters under cover to warn Peithetairos that the gods are in deep trouble and that an embassy is on its way to Cloudcuckooland. Peithetairos is to hold out for the hand of Basileia ('Sovereignty') in any terms of treaty. Peithetairos easily outmanoeuvres the ambassadors and wins Basileia. In a glorious finale this man–bird–god takes his new bride and becomes ruler of the universe.

What are we to make of this incredible and unflagging comedy? Critics usually fall into one of two camps, thinking either that the play is just a brilliant piece of comic escapism, or that in his creation of a city in the clouds Aristophanes has in mind certain contemporary events, with more than a hint of ironic criticism. Those of the latter opinion cite the Athenian atrocity at Melos (416–15 BC), the aggressive expedition launched against Sicily (415 BC), or the religious and political scandals of 415 BC that had driven many prominent

Athenians into exile and had caused the downfall of the charismatic leader Alcibiades. Most assume an ironic tone for the comedy, but the overall impression is one not of irony or satire, but of boundless exuberance and high spirits. Aristophanes does attack some of his usual targets, the law courts, demagogues, and charlatans (e.g. Socrates), but on the whole the play is a glorification of the Athenian spirit. Alan Sommerstein makes the excellent point that if the comedy does reflect the atmosphere of 415–14 BC, it does so with optimism and bellicosity. This play harmonizes well with the public mood, as described by Thucydides.

Other critics adopt an approach that generally eschews any serious political relevance, and find in *The Birds* deep and serious levels of meaning, often involving an extended and almost metaphysical symbolism. Thus for Whitman the comedy is an elaborate metaphor of 'the anatomy of Nothingness' —the universe is absurdly created by Love from a wind-egg. Kenneth J. Reckford views *The Birds* as an expression of the creative power of Love: comedy, like Love, creates a splendid fantasy out of original chaos. T.K. Hubbard adds a satirical theme, by stressing the confusion between men and gods—Athens' problems in 415 BC are 'rooted in the sophistic delusion that Man himself can somehow become God'.

Yet one must always be careful in attributing such depths to Aristophanic comedy. His plays were intended to be popular and imaginative fantasies, creations of the moment, often trivial and frivolous. Such art is by nature not receptive to the grandiose and metaphysical interpretations that modern critics have constructed. It is probably safer to read the play as an excellent fantasy based on the absurd concept of men 'going to the birds'. Political and social ironies as well as grand critical readings are not the natural interpretations one should draw from such a play.

The Birds is a conspicuous example of the utopian theme in Greek literature. Such ideal creations range from the lost Golden Age of Hesiod, to the Islands of the Blest at the end of the world (Homer, *Odyssey* IV; Pindar; Lucian), to the regions of the next world reserved for the virtuous (as in *The Frogs*). Comedy too had its paradises, usually places where work is unknown and food and drink and sex are found in abundance. Thus in the prologue the Athenians come in search of 'a soft and woolly place', where the 'problems' of life are attending a wedding feast and realizing a homoerotic fantasy with an attractive boy. There is nothing radically new in Aristophanes' utopia, but he has explored brilliantly the concept of such a paradise among the birds, and to that end the lines between bird and man are deliberately and persistently blurred (e.g. the costuming of Tereus, Euelpides, and Peithetairos; the choral description of the advantages for men of having wings; the identification of a dozen contemporary Athenians as birds). That he can maintain this creation for over 1,750 lines (*The Birds* is longer than any extant Greek tragedy or comedy, save only Euripides' *The Phoenician Women* (*Phoenissae*)), is testimony to a comedian at the height of his powers.

—Ian C. Storey

THE CLOUDS (Nephelai)
Play by Aristophanes, 423 BC.

The Clouds, as it exists today, is not the play of 423 BC performed in the city Dionysia. That play, much to Aristophanes' chagrin, failed, only obtaining third prize. What we have is an unperformable revision whose date is not certain. How much of the original has been left intact is still a matter of controversy. The play takes its title from its chorus, whose members are introduced as the only divinities accepted by the new enlightenment, but in a volte-face at the end of the play reveal themselves as guardians of the old morality. In this, perhaps his most ambitious play, Aristophanes confronted one of the great issues of his day, the moral effect of the Greek 5th-century intellectual revolution. The so-called sophistic movement, which, among other things, sought to explain the workings of the universe in terms of scientific necessity rather than divine causation, undermined traditional worship and traditional morality. In *The Clouds* we are shown what happens when the man in the street becomes involved with representatives of the movement. An old farmer Strepsiades, beset by debts incurred by his son Pheidippides in his manic pursuit of equestrianism, decides to enlist the help of new thinkers. One of their specialities is training in public speaking, and Strepsiades has heard that in their college (*phrontisterion*, literally 'think-shop') there are to be found two 'arguments', 'the better' and 'the worse', and that the worse argument is capable of defeating the better. If Pheidippides can master this argument, Strepsiades will be able to dismiss his creditors without having to pay up. Pheidippides, however, refuses to have anything to do with this suggestion and Strepsiades himself attempts without success to acquire a sophistic education. After his failure he coerces his son into following him to the college, where the young man is confronted by the physical embodiments of the two arguments. In a formal contest (the *agon*) they debate the merits of traditional and modern education. The worse argument (in other words 'Wrong') wins hands down and Pheidippides is taken into the school. He proves an apt pupil and with his advice Strepsiades deals confidently with his creditors.

The new training, however, has a less pleasant outcome for Strepsiades. Taught to reject traditional morality, Pheidippides now sees no reason why he should not beat his father if he so wishes. A second debate takes place in which Strepsiades takes on the defence of older morality and Pheidippides shows off his new sophistic powers. Naturally he wins the argument, ending by saying that he is also perfectly entitled to beat his mother. Realizing that he has a monster on his hands, Strepsiades turns on the chorus and blames it for leading him on. The chorus reveals that it has been dissembling and that in reality it is part of a divine plan to teach respect for the gods. With the help of his slave, Strepsiades attacks the college, demolishing and setting fire to it. The play ends as the inmates rush out in terror, fleeing for their lives.

One issue dominates critical reaction to *The Clouds*. The avaricious proprietor of the college and arch-sophist who is a professed expert on every subject under the sun—language, astronomy, biology, etc.—is none other than the famous Socrates. His portrayal in the play is a stark contrast to what we are told about him by his admirers Plato and Xenophon. Their Socrates does not teach for money, is vehemently opposed to the great practising sophists like Protagoras and Hippias, and disowns any claim to expertise in the field of learning, science, or the arts. The contradiction between the two portraits becomes explicable if one bears in mind that to the laymen the historical Socrates may not have appeared to be different in kind to his opponents, the sophists. Both parties were, after all, talking about the same things and Socrates' association with Athenian aristocrats might well have suggested that he accepted some kind of subsidy from the rich. Moreover, Aristophanes is dealing not so much with an individual as with a comic type, the bumptious intellectual.

He has collected a multitude of traits associated with contemporary intellectuals (some of them contradictory) and foisted them on the character of Socrates.

How serious the intent behind this assault on the new learning may have been is debatable. It must be borne in mind that the normal stance of Old Comedy is backward-looking and philistine. As elsewhere in Aristophanes, however, the old does not escape penetrating satire any more than does the new. The better argument is represented as a spluttering incompetent who cannot conceal his own sexual obsession with boys' genitals.

The ending of the play with its stark portrayal of the conflict between generations and the violent assault on the college and its inmates leaves a slightly sour taste, paralleled only in Aristophanes perhaps by the ending of *The Wasps*. If this was how the play ended in its production at the Dionysia, we may have an explanation for its lack of success.

—David M. Bain

THE FROGS (Batrachoi)
Play by Aristophanes, 405 BC.

Along with *The Birds*, *The Frogs* may fairly claim to be Aristophanes' masterpiece. A brilliant mix of fantastic humour and serious matters, it brings together contemporary politics, literary criticism, gods, and religion into a comedy that won not only the first prize at the festival but also the unusual honour of a repeat production (though exactly when is debated).

Like all of Aristophanes' extant comedies, *The Frogs* is a flight of comic imagination based on the contemporary city of Athens. The 'plot' depends on the recent deaths of Sophocles and Euripides, two of the three 'Masters' of tragedy; Dionysus, the patron god of drama, struck by the loss of good poets, descends to Hades to bring back Euripides ('a creative genius who can utter a good phrase'). *The Frogs* reverses the normal comic structure, in that the episodes and adventures precede the resolution of the great idea. In the first half the cowardly Dionysus encounters a corpse, is forced by Charon to row across the lake of death, defeats an invisible chorus of frogs (for whom the play is named), and falls in with a group of initiates who form the real chorus. Four door-scenes follow, full of slapstick, changes of identity, and general discomfort for Dionysus and his faithful servant Xanthias.

After the parabasis, the play re-opens with Dionysus invited to judge a contest between Aeschylus, the grand old master of tragedy, and Euripides, the clever modern iconoclast; the winner is to hold the throne of tragedy and to return with Dionysus to Athens. The change in the plot from Dionysus' original intention to retrieve Euripides has bothered some scholars unnecessarily; consistency is not an Aristophanic hallmark. The second half features a formal *agon* (contest), in which Euripides claims for his drama realism, relevance, and common sense, and Aeschylus grandeur, nobility, and moral excellence. There follow investigations of Aeschylean and Euripidean prologues—the latter's ruined by a little oil-flask—parodies of Aeschylus' lyrics and Euripides' monodies, and a weighing scene where Aeschylus' ponderous grandeur overwhelms the scales. Finally Dionysus asks each 'how to save the city', and despite clever and revealing answers, decides finally for 'the one in whom my soul delights', Aeschylus. The play ends with a rousing send-off for Aeschylus and a general disparagement of current politicians.

The Frogs mixes three recurrent themes: religion (comedy was part of Dionysus' worship and the chorus a 'sacred band'), politics (and not just in the parabasis where the comic poet advises the people to re-instate disenfranchised oligarchs and compares present political leaders to debased coinage), and poetry ('For what does one admire a poet?—For cleverness and for his teaching because we make people better citizens'). These strands are interwoven with consummate skill and come together forcefully in the parabasis ('it is right for the sacred chorus to advise and teach what is good for the city'), but especially in one telling moment near the end ('I came down for a poet.—Why?—So that the city might be saved'). Although the play is ostensibly about tragedy's role in the state, it is a short step to that of comedy, for which Aristophanes seems to claim a role like that of Aeschylus.

Critics have discussed endlessly the significance of the contest and Aeschylus' eventual victory. Elsewhere Aristophanes is a devotee of Euripides, and the words he uses of that tragedian (*sophos*—smart; *dexios*—clever) are words he uses of himself. Is Aeschylus' victory assured from the outset, or is it a close match with points scored on both sides? And what does it say about Aristophanes' own attitudes to these poets? The attentive reader will notice that Aeschylus has the second role in the *agon* (the traditional place of the victor), but also that neither the *agon* nor the parodies is actually resolved. Aristophanes is a traditionalist, and the victory of Aeschylus accords well with his other appeals to 'the good old days' (e.g. in *The Knights* and *Lysistrata*). As much as he appreciates brilliant art, the poet as teacher is serious business for Aristophanes. The exchange at 1052–56 not only sums up most of subsequent Western literary criticism (freedom of artistic expression versus the moral responsibility of the artist), but seems also to reflect the comedian's own thoughts:

Did I make up the story of Phaedra?—No, but a poet must hide what is bad, not put it on the stage. Little boys have a teacher to instruct them; grown-ups have the poets. What we say must be good and proper.

Some critics have found in *The Frogs* far more sophisticated and even metaphysical levels of meaning. For C.H. Whitman, Dionysus is Athens in search of its identity; for Charles Segal the theme of descent and rebirth 'concern the regeneration of the *polis*' through this general attempt to unify religion and art. Kenneth Reckford views the heavy presence of death as a sign of the death of 'the old tragedy, the old Athens, and even the old comedy'. For T.K. Hubbard, *The Frogs* was Aristophanes' final attempt to reconcile his 'Euripidean side' (realism and modernism) with his 'Aeschylean side' (imagination and moral purpose). One does wonder, however, if the essentially transitory and frivolous nature of comedy can really bear the weight of such sophisticated interpretations. Aristophanic humour is brief and to the point. There is much to commend in W.B. Stanford's assessment:

In planning *Frogs*, he seems to have thought of something like this: 'Let's send Dionysos off to Hades in search of a poet, give him plenty of adventures, have a contest between Euripides and Aeschylus, decide it quite whimsically, and end up with the usual victory-scene'. The more variety and absurdity he can insert into this loose framework, the better.

Set in the shadows of the last year of the War, *The Frogs* is a marvellous comic fantasy revolving around the city and its cults, the city and its politics, the city and its poets. A legitimate classic, it bids an elegant farewell to Athens' greatness.

—Ian C. Storey

LYSISTRATA (Lysistrate)
Play by Aristophanes, 411 BC.

Lysistrata is doubtless Aristophanes' boldest and bawdiest drama. Composed at the height of the devastating Peloponnesian War (431–404 BC), when Athens and Sparta were locked in a protracted battle for dominance in Greece—a war that rendered all of the Greek mainland a battleground, and a war that Athens would eventually lose—*Lysistrata* dramatizes the tale of rebellious women imposing an end to the hostilities. Tired of all the bellicosity and loss of life, an heroic Athenian housewife, Lysistrata, convenes a secret congress of Greek women. They agree to withhold all sexual favours from the men until peace is restored. The males soon grow half-crazed with frustration, deprivation, and desire. (Old Comedy is usually raucous and bawdy; choruses frequently wore large leather phalluses on stage—props especially appropriate for this drama.) Although the women, sexually agitated themselves, would just as well surrender their advantage, Lysistrata repeatedly and tirelessly shames them into upholding the sex embargo. Indeed, the Athenian girls seize the Acropolis, the sacred ground reserved for temples and shrines, and lock up the treasury—thereby establishing a first-rate blockade, which isolates the men from their gods, their money, and their women. The chorus of Athenian elders is ignominiously defeated, and all the so-called warriors of Greece are overcome and sexually disarmed.

Soon, male sentinels and ambassadors from every part of Greece converge on Athens, eager to surrender, rabid to restore sexual relations, and, as it were, win the peace. The women drive a hard bargain and carry the day. All the men are utterly defeated by the women's stratagems, are brought to the bargaining table, and are forced to yield to the women's terms and to a cessation of hostilities. The women, as the saying goes, come out on top; they conclude the play with a grand victory and a celebration party.

Clearly there is here a plenitude of controversial material: patriots would be upset by the women's consorting with the enemy; members of the war party would be shocked by the suggestion that there ought to be 'peace at any price', especially a 'peace without honour'; pious Athenians would be offended at the sacrilegious seizure of the holy shrines; and politicos would be nonplussed by the trivialization of government and of law and order. Furthermore, the play constitutes a direct blow to Athens' intellectual pride—for Athenians presented their society as a city-state founded upon principles of 'wisdom', and perceived themselves as being engaged in a century of philosophical and cultural growth and sophistication. Instead, Aristophanes dramatizes irrationality and decline. Epic heroism is humbled in the dust, for the psychological implications of this dramatic fiction are that male aggressiveness, realized in its penchant for swordsmanship, is nothing more than the sexual urge run wild. Men are accordingly depicted as mechanical warrior-studs, helplessly gripped by carnal and disruptive instincts and drives. However, women hardly fare any better; throughout, they are portrayed as wavering and fickle, with tendencies toward nymphomania and alcoholism. No one is spared.

But hardest hit by the play's satiric ploys is self-satisfied male chauvinism. Athenian society was complacently and intransigently male-dominated, its women not even granted citizens' rights. A woman's place was in the home. It is in this area that Aristophanic satire is brought most heavily to bear, turning custom and convention upside-down. What would have outraged much of the audience is precisely this 'women's issue': quite simply put, in Aristophanes' satiric plot, women take over. It was clearly a humorous—but galling—thesis, annoying enough to the audience, doubtless, to earn his play low grades in the annual dramatic competition.

In fact, however, Aristophanes liked this ploy well enough to utilize the theme of women coming into power in two more of his extant plays—*Thesmophoriazousai* (*The Poet and the Women*) and *Ekklesiaszousai* (*Women in Power*). Such a dramatic theme also allowed Aristophanes to mock Platonic ideas of an ideal utopian republic. Victorious feminism was a topic that disturbed his audience and captured their attention while doubtless making them uneasy.

—Anna Lydia Motto & John R. Clark

ARISTOTLE. Born in Stagira, Macedonia, in 384 BC. Pupil, then teacher, in Plato's (*q.v.*) Academy, Athens, 367–47 BC; on Plato's death he left the city to live with other philosophers from the Academy, at Assos, in the Troad. Married Pythias, niece of the tyrant Hermeias; after Pythias' death, had a son by Herpyllis. After the murder of Hermeias he went to live and teach at Mytilene on Lesbos; tutor to the son of Philip II of Macedon, the future Alexander the Great, from c.342 BC; returned to Athens in 335 BC and founded his own school of literature, science, and philosophy, the Lyceum, whose students were known as 'peripatetics'; after death of Alexander the Great in 323 BC Aristotle was accused of impiety and retreated, leaving his school to Theophrastus, *q.v.*, in Chalcis, Euboea. *Died 322 BC.*

PUBLICATIONS

Collections

[Works], edited by J.A. Smith and W.D. Ross. 12 vols., 1908–52; also edited by John L. Ackrill, 1962–, revised edition edited by Jonathan Barnes, 2 vols., 1984; translated by Thomas Taylor, 1812.

Works

De anima [On the Soul], edited by W.D. Ross. 1956; translated by Kenelm Foster and Silvester Humphries, 1951; Books II and III translated by D.W. Hamlyn, revised edition, 1993.

De arte poetica, edited by R. Kassel. 1965; as *Aristotle on the Art of Poetry*, translated by Ingram Bywater, 1920; as *Poetics*, translated by John Warrington, with *On Style* and *On the Sublime* by Demetrius, 1963; also translated by D.W. Lucas (with commentary), 1968; M.E. Hubbard, in *Ancient Literary Criticism*, 1972; L. Golden and O.B. Hardison, 2nd edition, 1981; James Hutton, 1982; Stephen Halliwell (with commentary), 1987; as *Aristotle on the Art of Fiction*, translated by L.J. Potts, 1968.

De coelo, as *On the Heavens* (bilingual edition), translated by W.K.C. Guthrie. 1939.

De generatione et corruptione, translated by C.J.F. Williams. 1982.

De generatione animalium, selections as *Generation of Animals*, translated by D.M. Balme, 1972, revised edition, 1992.

De incessu animalium, with *De motu animalium*, as *On the*

Movement and Progression of Animals, translated by Anthony Preus. 1981.

De motu animalium, edited and translated by Martha C. Nussbaum. 1978; with *De incessu animalium*, as *On the Movement and Progression of Animals*, translated by Anthony Preus, 1981.

De partibus animalium, as *On the Parts of Animals*, translated by W. Ogle. 1882, reprinted 1987; as *Parts of Animals*, translated by D.M. Balme, 1972, revised edition, 1992.

De republica Atheniensium, as *The Constitution of Athens*, in *Aristotle and Xenophon on Democracy and Oligarchy*, edited and translated by John M. Moore. 1975; as *The Athenian Constitution*, translated by H. Rackham, 1935; also translated by P.J. Rhodes, 1984.

Ethica, as *Ethics*, translated by David Ross, 1925, revised by John L. Ackrill and J.O. Urmson, 1980; also translated by Hippocrates G. Apostle, 1975.

    Nichomachean Ethics, edited by G. Ramsauer (with commentary). 1878, reprinted 1987; translated by J.A.K. Thomson, 1953, revised edition, 1976.

    Ethica Eudemia, edited by R.R. Walzer and J.M. Mingay. 1991; as *Eudemian Ethics*, edited and translated by M. Woods (with commentary), 1982; translated by H. Rackham, 1935.

Historia animalium, edited and translated by D.M. Balme. 1991; translated by A.L. Peck, 1965.

Metaphysica, edited by W.D. Ross (with commentary). 2 vols., 1928; also edited by Werner Jaeger, 1957; as *Metaphysics*, translated by Hippocrates G. Apostle (with commentary), 1966; part as *Oeconomica and Magna moralia*, translated by G.C. Armstrong, 1935; part as *Metaphysics, Books Gamma, Delta and Epsilon*, translated by Christopher Kirwan, 1971; Books VII and VIII translated by David Bostock, 1994.

On Fallacies, translated by Edward Poste. 1866, reprinted 1987.

Organon, edited by W.D. Ross. 1958; part as *Analytica priora et posteriora*, edited by W.D. Ross, 1964; part as *The Categories* and *On Interpretation*, translated by H.P. Cooke, 1938; part as *Prior Analytics*, translated by Hugh Tredennick, 1938; part as *Prior and Posterior Analytics*, translated by John Warrington, 1964; part as *Posterior Analytics*, translated by J. Barnes, revised edition, 1993.

Parva naturalia, as *Aristotle on Memory*, edited and translated by Richard Sorabji. 1972.

Physica, as *Physics*, translated by P. Wicksteed and F. M. Cornford. 2 vols., 1929–34; Books I and II translated by William Charlton, 1970.

Politica, edited by Johann Gottlob Schneider. 2 vols., 1809; also edited and translated by Stephen Everson, 1988; as *The Politics of Aristotle*, translated by Benjamin Jowett, 1895; as *The Politics*, translated by T.A. Sinclair, 1962, revised by Trevor J. Saunders, 1981; also translated by Carnes Lord, 1984.

Rhetorica, as *The Rhetoric of Aristotle*, translated by Lane Cooper. 1932; as *On Rhetoric*, translated by George A. Kelly, 1991; as *The Art of Rhetoric*, translated by H.C. Lawson-Tancred, 1991.

*

Bibliography: *Aristotle: A Select Bibliography*, by Jonathan Barnes, Malcolm Schofield, and Richard Sorabji, 1977.

Critical Studies: *The Poetics of Aristotle* by Lane Cooper, 1924; *The Psychology of Aristotle* by Clarence Shute, 1941;

Aristotle's Theory of Poetry and Fine Art by S.H. Butcher, 1951; *The Philosophy of Aristotle* by D.J. Allan, 1952; *Aristotle* by A.E. Taylor, 1955; *Aristotle's Poetics* by A. House, 1956; *Tragedy: Serious Drama in Relation to Aristotle's Poetics* by F.L. Lucas, 1957; *The Development of Aristotle's Thought* by W.D. Ross, 1957; *Aristotle's Theory of Poetry and Drama, with Chapters on Plato and Longinus* by P.S. Shastri, 1963; *New Essays on Plato and Aristotle* by Renford Bambrough, 1965; *Aristotle's Ethical Theory* by William F. Hardie, 1968; *Prelude to Aesthetics* by E. Schaper, 1968; *On Aristotle and Greek Tragedy* by J. Jones, 1971; *The Eudemian and Nichomachean Ethics: A Study in the Development of Aristotle's Thought* by C.J. Rowe, 1971; *Towards Greek Tragedy* by B. Vickers, 1973; *Aristotle on Emotion* by Will Fortenbaugh, 1975; *Aristotle* by John B. Morrall, 1977; *Word and Action* by B. Knox, 1979; *Essays on Aristotle's Ethics* edited by Amélie Oksenberg Rorty, 1980; *Aristotle the Philosopher* by John L. Ackrill, 1981; *Poetic and Legal Fiction in the Aristotelian Tradition* by Kathy Eden, 1986; *Plato and Aristotle on Poetry* by Gerald F. Else, 1986; *Aristotle's Poetics* by Stephen Halliwell, 1986; *The Fragility of Goodness* by Martha C. Nussbaum, 1986; *Aristotle's Two Systems* by Daniel W. Graham, 1987; *Substance, Form and Psyche: An Aristotelian Metaphysics* by Montgomery Furth, 1988; *Aristotle's First Principles* by Terence Irwin, 1988; *Ethics with Aristotle* by Sarah Broadie, 1991; *Aristotle and the Later Tradition* edited by Henry Blumenthal and Howard Robinson, 1991; *Aristotle on the Perfect Life* by Anthony Kenny, 1992.

* * *

Written by a philosopher and scientist who was not born until 20 years after the death of Sophocles and Euripides, *De arte poetica* (the *Poetics*) is an unlikely candidate for founder document of European dramatic theory. In fact it has no rival, offering the earliest view of the origins and form of Greek tragedy as well as a theoretical and structural base for all subsequent serious drama.

This is unlikely to be what Aristotle had in mind when he first committed his comparison of epic and dramatic poetry to paper. The *Poetics* appears to be unfinished or, at least, unrevised, and is widely believed to be no more than lecture notes. A companion volume on comedy has failed to survive. In early life Aristotle had studied under Plato who, in the *Republic* and elsewhere, had rejected the claims of drama and theatre to a place in his ideal state. This world, according to Plato, is no more than a pale reflection of reality, which is itself a reflection of the pure Idea. Drama, by being an imitation of an imitation, is doubly suspect. The capacity of actors to transform themselves is equally dangerous, as is the tendency of an audience to become engaged by fiction or 'lies'.

Aristotle sets out in the *Poetics* to compare the forms of epic and dramatic poetry and justify both. The information he provides, intriguing as it is, about the history of the theatre in Athens, is incidental to the main argument. In the light of subsequent scholarship, theatrical, historical, and anthropological, there is no reason to accept all of Aristotle's beliefs as necessarily historically accurate. When he talks of tragedy and comedy as 'at first improvised' (or 'in an experimental stage'), or of tragedy 'moving from trivial plots and comic diction, exchanging satiric method for solemnity only late', he offers little more than hearsay evidence of the first form of 'tragedy' in Athens. On the other hand, his assertion that Aeschylus introduced a second actor and relegated the chorus in favour of dialogue appears to be borne out by the surviving plays of Aeschylus. Sophocles, according to Aristotle, 'increased the number of actors to three and introduced *skenographia*' (scenic decoration). Tantalizingly, Aristotle offers no further indication of the physical conditions in the Athenian theatre.

Though his remarks on the early form of theatre in Athens are incomplete, it is as a theorist on tragic structure that Aristotle was most influential, and most misinterpreted. The three unities, of time, place, and action, were treated as rules for the proper writing of tragedy as late as the 19th century in France. Extant Greek tragedies by Aeschylus, Sophocles, and Euripides pay no more than incidental attention to the notion that a play should take place within a single day and in a fixed location. Whatever later critics chose to believe, Aristotle himself treats such things as no more than passing recommendations. The unity of action has more substance but seems to be a by-product of a dramatic form whose rhythm derives from a chorus which dances and sings an interlude between the dramatic scenes.

The most stimulating and widely known section of the *Poetics* includes the famous definition of tragedy which is at the heart of Aristotle's argument in favour of a therapeutic purpose to dramatic performance:

> Tragedy is the representation (*mimesis*) of an action which is worthy of concern (*spoudaios*), complete in itself and of some substance. Heightened in language, different aspects of which are in the various parts, it takes the form of action (*praxis*), not narrative, by creating pity and fear causing the purgation (*katharsis*) of such emotions.

The precise meaning has been argued over for centuries, but a further reference to the cathartic effect of music in his *Politica* (*Politics*) implies that Aristotle considers emotions, of which 'pity' and 'fear' are examples rather than the gamut, to be unhealthy if denied an outlet. Music and theatre allow for a *katharsis*, a purgation or exorcizing of these emotions, and thereby help to create emotional balance. That the main function of tragedy was to induce emotional response was to remain virtually unchallenged as a principle until Brecht in the 20th century asserted the need for a detachment of response on the part of the spectator if theatre was to show how the world could be changed.

Much of the rest of the *Poetics* is taken up with the comparison between epic and dramatic poetry. Aristotle divides tragedy into six elements, 'plot, character, speech, thought, the visual and song', these in order of importance, and uses examples from a number of plays to identify the better and less satisfactory elements of plays with which he is familiar. In this he shows himself to be more familiar with Sophocles and Euripides than with Aeschylus, whose plays were less often revived in the 4th century BC. Sophocles' *Oedipus Tyrannus* proves to be his example of all that is best in drama.

For all the fascinating insights that the *Poetics* supplies, it serves better as a discussion document than as a playwriting manual it was never intended to be. Aristotle does not write as a theatre goer but as a theorist. His final conclusion that dramatic poetry is more satisfactory than epic may appear to allow for a performance dimension. His corresponding belief that tragedy may well be better enjoyed on the page than on the stage is a comment both on Aristotle and on the theatre of his period.

—J. Michael Walton

ARTAUD, Antonin (Marie Joseph). Born in Marseilles, France, 4 September 1896. Served in the French military: medical discharge, 1916. Suffered from meningitis, hospitalized frequently, 1915–20; moved to Paris, 1920; co-editor, *Demain*, 1920–21, and *Le Bilboquet*, 1923; actor and designer for Lugné-Poe, Charles Dullin, and Georges Pitoeff theatre companies, Paris, 1921–24; actor in films by Abel Gance, Carl Dreyer, and others, 1924–35; director, Bureau of Surrealist Research, 1925, and editor of 3rd issue of *La Révolution Surréaliste*, 1925; founder, with Roger Vitrac and Robert Aron, Théâtre Alfred Jarry, Paris, 1926, and Théâtre de la Cruauté, 1933; lecturer on theatre, the Sorbonne, Paris, 1928, 1931, 1933; confined in various asylums, primarily in Rodez, 1937–46. Drawings exhibited: Loeb Gallery, 1947. Recipient: Sainte-Beuve prize, 1948. *Died 4 March 1948.*

PUBLICATIONS

Collections

Oeuvres complètes. 24 vols., 1956–81; revised edition, 1970– .
Artaud Anthology, edited by Jack Hirschman. 1965.
Collected Works, translated by Victor Corti. 4 vols., 1968–5.
Selected Writings, edited by Susan Sontag, translated by Helen Weaver. 1976.

Plays

Les Cenci (produced 1935). In *Oeuvres complètes*, 4, 1967; as *The Cenci*, translated by Simon Watson Taylor, 1969.
Pour en finir avec le jugement de Dieu. 1948; as *To Have Done with the Judgment of God*, translated by Helen Weaver, in *Selected Writings*, 1976.

Verse

Tric-trac du ciel. 1923.
Artaud le mômo. 1947; as *Artaud the Momo*, translated by Clayton Eshlemen and Norman Glass, 1976.
Ci-gît, précédé de la culture indienne. 1947.

Other

Le Pèse-nerfs. 1925; with *Fragments d'un journal d'enfer*, 1927.
L'Ombilic des limbes. 1927.
Correspondance, with Jacques Rivière. 1927.
L'Art et la mort. 1929.
Le Théâtre Alfred Jarry et l'hostilité public, with Roger Vitrac. 1930.
Le Théâtre de la cruauté. 1933.
Héliogabale; ou, L'Anarchiste couronné. 1934.
Le Théâtre de Séraphin. 1936.
Les Nouvelles Révélations de l'être. 1937.
Le Théâtre et son double. 1938; as *The Theatre and Its Double*, translated by Mary Caroline Richards, 1958; also translated by Victor Corti, 1981.
D'un voyage au pays de Tarahumaras (essays and letters). 1945.
Lettres de Rodez. 1946.
Van Gogh, Le Suicidé de la société. 1947.
Supplément aux Lettres de Rodez suivi de Coleridge le traître. 1949.
Lettres contre la Cabbale. 1949.
Lettres à Jean-Louis Barrault. 1952.

La Vie et mort de Satan le feu. 1953; as *The Death of Satan and Other Mystical Writings*, translated by Alastair Hamilton and Victor Corti, 1974.

Les Tarahumaras (letters and essays). 1955; as *The Peyote Dance*, translated by Helen Weaver, 1976.

Galapagos, Les Îles du bout du monde (travel). 1955.

Autre chose que l'enfant beau. 1957.

Voici un endroit. 1958.

Mexico. 1962.

Lettres à Anaïs Nin. 1965.

Poète noir et autres textes/Black Poet and Other Texts, edited by Paul Zweig. 1966.

Lettres à Génica Athanasiou. 1969.

Nouveaux écrits de Rodez. 1977.

Lettres à Anie Besnard. 1977.

Artaud on Theatre, edited by Claude Schumacher. 1989.

Translator, *Le Moine*, by Matthew Gregory Lewis. 1931.

Translator, with Bernard Steele, *Crime passionnel*, by Ludwig Lewisohn. 1932.

*

Bibliography: in *Artaud et le théâtre* by Alan Virmaux, 1970.

Critical Studies: *The Dramatic Concept of Artaua* by Eric Sellin, 1968; *Antonin Artaud: Man of Vision* by Bettina L. Knapp, 1969; *Antonin Artaud: Poet Without Words* by Naomi Greene, 1970; *Antonin Artaud* by Jean-Louis Brau, 1971; *Antonin Artaud* by Martin Esslin, 1976; *Artaud's Theatre of Cruelty* by Alfred Bermel, 1977; *Artaud and After* by Ronald Hayman, 1977; *Antonin Artaud* by Julia F. Costich, 1978; *Antonin Artaud: Blows and Bombs* by Stephen Barber, 1993.

* * *

Paradox envelops Antonin Artaud. The man who wished to de-emphasize words in theatre—'No more masterpieces!' —has written 24 volumes of words. A theatre prophet who valued performance far above theory, Artaud's productions were limited to a few sporadic efforts of his Alfred Jarry Theatre and 17 performances of *Les Cenci* (*The Cenci*) as an example of theatre of cruelty; in contrast, Gallimard publishers printed 100,000 copies of *Le Théâtre et son double* (*The Theatre and Its Double*), his 1938 collection of manifestos and letters which has had wide influence. A strikingly handsome film actor, Artaud drew self-portraits when he was ill and haggard. Plagued with illness all his life, Artaud undertook to cure what he saw as a sick civilization. After nine years of neglect in asylums, he became a cult figure in post-World War II Paris, during the last two years of his life. After his death, Artaud inspired two divergent movements: 1) the experimental theatre groups of the 1960s, particularly in the USA; 2) the 'human science' intellectuals of that same decade, particularly in France.

Artaud's writing takes many forms—fiction, drama, essays, diatribes, production plans, poems, and letters that sometimes read like soliloquies to be declaimed. All his writing is seared by his flaming self-consciousness; he flaunted his suffering with inimitable intensity. Up until the time of his incarceration in 1937, Artaud espoused theatre as an instrument of civilizational catharsis, and he equates theatre with plague, alchemy, metaphysics, and cruelty—doubles all. At Rodez Asylum and later, however, his long poems and essays lacerate in order to scourge. With sound play, obscenity,

neologisms, occult and fantastic reference, Artaud inveighs against Western materialism; as *poète maudit* he curses the familiar scenes of modern life. His passion—utterance and suffering—has inspired theatre practitioners like Jean-Louis Barrault, Roger Blin, Peter Brook; and thinkers like Gilles Deleuze, Jacques Derrida, and Susan Sontag. Less read than read about, Artaud is only recently being studied as a writer rather than as a martyr.

—Ruby Cohn

THE THEATRE AND ITS DOUBLE (Le Théâtre et son double)
Prose by Antonin Artaud, 1938.

In February 1938 Artaud's revolutionary ideas on the theatre, and in particular theatrical production, were grouped together in one volume entitled *The Theatre and Its Double*. This collection of miscellaneous essays and letters comprises a statement on the dramatic arts, equalled only in its influence over the development of 20th-century theatre in the west by the vision of Brecht. Seminal extracts, including his essay on Balinese theatre (first published in the *Nouvelle Revue Française* issue of October 1931), the lectures at the Sorbonne—'La Mise en scène et la métaphysique' ('The Metaphysics of Theatre Production') in December 1931 and 'Le Théâtre et la peste' ('The Theatre and the Plague') in April 1933, and the Duchamp-inspired 'Le Théâtre alchimique' ('The Alchemical Theatre') initially conceived in 1932, convey the essence of a concept which has since become synonymous with the name of Artaud, the theatre of cruelty.

Artaud's original manifesto for the theatre of cruelty heralded the inception of a new metaphysics, to be fashioned out of words, experiences, and gestures, but based on cosmic notions involving Creation, Becoming, and Chaos, which would save contemporary theatre from the moribund psychologizing to which it had fallen prey. The word 'cruelty' is mentioned only perfunctorily. From the second and even the third manifestos it is still unclear what this new 'theatre' actually is. Quite what Artaud envisaged is only tangible when *The Theatre and Its Double* is considered as a whole.

The cruelty is that which is inflicted through the medium of an Artaudian theatrical production on the haplessly passive spectator, whose emotional and physical turmoil will first replicate (double) and then rejoin the spectacle, thereby authenticating what should be, as Artaud saw it, the unitary experience of theatre. His aim was to involve the audience deeply in the performance, and in a direct way that would be entirely beyond the scope of other artistic media. In a sense this involves the reorientation—back to its classical roots—of theatre, which should concentrate all its forces on its own unique status, as a live (and therefore perishable) form of communication. However, *The Theatre and Its Double* proposes radical manoeuvres by which this goal may be attained. Artaud wrote:

We abolish the stage and the auditorium and replace them by a single site, without partition or barrier of any kind, which will become the theatre of the action. A direct communication will be re-established between the spectator and the spectacle.

He conceived a kind of frontal assault on the spectator, a total theatre in which all available means of expression would be brought to bear. Thus, *The Theatre and Its Double* redefines the language of theatre as consisting:

of everything that occupies the stage, everything that can be manifested and expressed materially on a stage and that is addressed first of all to the senses instead of being addressed primarily to the mind as in the language of words . . . such as music, dance, plastic art, pantomime, mimicry, gesticulation, intonation, architecture, lighting, and scenery . . .

Artaudian theatre is, then, anti-bourgeois and intensely visceral. But it need not necessarily be a temporary hell of blood and fear; the theatre of cruelty, as is made clear in *The Theatre and Its Double*, stakes claim to a fundamental truth of human existence, it is, above all, an 'ontological cruelty', linked to the suffering of existence, and to the 'poverty of the human body'.

In 'Le Théâtre alchimique' Artaud wrote that the theatre:

must be considered as the Double not of everyday, ubiquitous reality, of which it has gradually become the inert copy, as vain as it is watered down, but of another, dangerous type of reality, in which the Principles like dolphins poke their heads out of the water before returning in haste to the darkest depths of the ocean.

What impressed him about the Balinese troupe he saw in action (in July 1931 at the Colonial Exhibition in the Bois de Vincennes) was the extent to which their performance expressed these mysterious Principles. Their stylized movement, syncopated vocal delivery, elaborate costume, pantomimist gestures, and attention to rhythm in music and dance were a revelation. These 'animated hieroglyphs' realized a new physical language, based on the sign rather than the word. In bypassing the intervention of the verbal, the textual, the Balinese captured, with the utmost rigour, Artaud's idea of 'pure theatre'. He interpreted their 'symbolic sketch' as a triumphant valorization of the role of the theatre producer, whose creative power 'eliminates the words'.

Like Artaud, Brecht capitalized on the immediacy and intimacy of the theatrical performance, but he moved in the opposite direction. Employing a technique he labelled *Verfremdungseffekt* ('alienation effect') Brecht sought to break the implicit social tie between actor and audience, so as to recreate their relationship in terms of a dialectic. In Artaud's case, technical innovation in the theatre stemmed from absolute need. Throughout his life, consciousness usually involved some form of physical or mental pain. A dreadful stammer prevented him from ever producing a conventional acting performance, though everything he did on stage (and on film) was virtuoso. Drugs, especially opium, provided anaesthesia and the possibility of creation (rarely achieved) through the perception of a Rimbaldian *dérèglement*, disturbance or unjumbling (depending on one's point of view), of the senses. But, even in a drug-induced state, Artaud was acutely conscious of the limits alternately prescribed and transgressed by his own physical condition. The image is that of a tormented physical presence, stacked with creative energy waiting to be released. It is perhaps ironic that the theories of someone who is primarily considered an abstract theorist, who so rarely put his theories into practice, should be so corporeally centred.

But this fact is crucial to the appreciation of Artaud's work. As Jacques Derrida puts it, he 'knew that each word, once it falls from the body, offering to be understood or received, exhibiting itself, becomes a stolen word'. The Double in Artaud's theatre is thus an illusion. The plague is not the image of the theatre; it *is* the theatre. Similarly, the theatre *is* metaphysical, just as it *is* alchemical. The relation between the theatre and its double (the spectacle and the spectator) is, therefore, one of the exact identity, born of a dynamic interaction of the senses in which all traces of convention have been systematically effaced.

—David Platten

ARTHAVA-VEDA. See **THE VEDAS**.

ASSIS, Joaquim Maria Machado de. See **MACHADO de Assis, Joaquim Maria**.

ASTURIAS, Miguel Ángel. Born in Guatemala City, Guatemala, 19 October 1899. Family moved to Salamá fearing government persecution, 1903; returned to the capital, 1908. Educated at schools in Guatemala City; abandoned studies in medicine, 1917; studied law at San Carlos University, Guatemala City, 1917–23, degree 1923; also helped found the People's University [Universidad Popular] of Guatemala, 1922, and the Association of University Students; studied anthropology under Georges Raymond, the Sorbonne, Paris, 1923–28. Married 1) Clemencia Amado (separated 1946–47), two sons; 2) Blanca de Mora y Araujo in 1950, two sons. Founder, *Tiempos Nuevos*, 1923; travelled to England, 1923; based in Paris, 1923–32, mixing study and journalism; travelled through Europe and the Middle East in the 1920s; returned to Guatemala, 1933, and worked as radio broadcaster (co-creator, 'Diario del aire' series, 1937) and journalist, 1933–42; a deputy, Guatemalan National Congress, 1942; undertook diplomatic posts, 1945–54: cultural attaché, Mexico City, 1945–47, and Buenos Aires, 1947–53, minister-counsellor, Buenos Aires, 1951–52, Guatemalan ambassador, Paris, 1952–53, and San Salvador (El Salvador), 1953–54; exiled for his support of the left-wing leader Jacobo Árbenz Guzmán, 1954, and moved to Argentina; journalist, *El Nacional* (Venezuela), 1954–62; cultural exchange programme member, Columanum, Italy, 1962; Guatemalan ambassador, Paris, 1966–70; spent last years in Madrid. Recipient: Sylla Monsegur prize for translation, 1932; William Faulkner Foundation Latin American award, 1962; International Lenin Peace prize, 1966; Nobel prize for literature, 1967. *Died 9 June 1974.*

PUBLICATIONS

Collection

Edición crítica de las obras completas, various editors. 24 vols., 1977—.

Fiction

El Señor Presidente. 1946; edited by Ricardo Navas Ruiz and Jean-Marie Saint-Lu, 1978; as *The President,* translated by Frances Partridge, 1963; as *El Señor Presidente,* translated by Partridge, 1964.
Hombres de maíz. 1949; edited by Gerald Martín, 1981 and 1992; as *Men of Maize,* translated by Martín, 1974.
Viento fuerte. 1949; as *The Cyclone,* translated by Darwin Flakoll and Claribel Alegría, 1967; as *Strong Wind,* translated by Gregory Rabassa, 1968.
El Papa verde. 1954; as *The Green Pope,* translated by Gregory Rabassa, 1971.
Week-end en Guatemala (stories). 1956.
Los ojos de los enterrados. 1960; as *The Eyes of the Interred,* translated by Gregory Rabassa, 1973.
El alhajadito (novella). 1961; as *The Bejeweled Boy,* translated by Martin Shuttleworth, 1971.
Mulata de tal. 1963; as *Mulatta,* translated by Gregory Rabassa, 1967; as *The Mulatta and Mr Fly,* translated by Rabassa, 1967.
El espejo de Lida Sal (stories). 1967.
Maladrón: Epopeya de los Andes verdes. 1969.
Novelas y cuentos de juventud, edited by Claude Couffon. 1971.
Viernes de Dolores. 1972; edited by Marcel Brion and others, 1978.
Tres obras (includes *Leyendas de Guatemala; El Alhajadito; El Señor Presidente*), edited by Giuseppe Bellini. 1977.

Verse

Émulo Lipolidón. 1935.
Sonetos. 1937.
Anoche, 10 de marzo de 1543. 1943.
Poesía: Sien de alondra. 1949; complete edition, 1954.
Ejercicios poéticos en forma de soneto sobre temas de Horacio. 1951.
Alto es el sur. 1952.
Bolívar. 1955.
Obras escogidas. 3 vols., 1955.
Nombre custodio, e Imagen pasajera. 1959.
Clarivigilia primaveral. 1965.
Sonetos de Italia. 1965.
Sonetos venecianos. 1973.
Tres de cuatro soles (prose poem), edited by Dorita Nouhaud. 1977.

Plays

Rayito de estrella (in verse). 1925.
Alclasán: famtomina (in verse). 1939.
Soluna: Comedia prodigiosa en dos jornadas y un final. 1955.
La audiencia de los confines: Crónica en tres andanzas. 1957.

Teatro: Chantaje; Dique seco; Soluna; La audiencia de los confines. 1964.
Juárez. 1972.

Other

Sociología guatemalteca: El problema social del indio. 1923; as *Guatemalan Sociology: The Social Problem of the Indian,* translated by Maureen Ahern, 1977.
La arquitectura de la vida nueva (essays and lectures). 1928.
Carta aérea a mis amigos de América. 1952.
Rumania, su nueva imagen. 1964.
Juan Girador. 1964.
Obras escogidas. 2 vols., 1964.
Torotumbo; La audiencia de los confines; Mensajes indios (selection). 1967.
Coloquio con Asturias, with Hugo Cerezo Dardón and others. 1968.
Latinoamérica y otros ensayos (essays). 1968.
Antología, edited by Pablo Palomina. 1968.
Asturias: Semblanza para el estudio de su vida y obra, con una selección de poemas y prosas. 1968.
Obras completas, introduced by José María Souviron. 3 vols., 1968.
Comiendo en Hungría (verse and illustrations), with Pablo Neruda. 1969; as *Sentimental Journey around the Hungarian Cuisine,* translated by Barna Balogh, 1969.
The Talking Machine (for children), translated by Beverly Koch. 1971.
El problema social del indio y otros textos, edited by Claude Couffon, 1971.
El novelista en la universidad. 1971.
América, fábula de fábulas y otros ensayos (essays). 1972.
Novela y novelista: reunión de Málaga, with others. 1972.
Mi mejor obra. 1973; as *Lo mejor de mi obra,* 1974.
Conversaciones con Asturias, with Luis López Álvarez. 1974.
Sinceridades (essays), edited by Epaminondas Quintana. 1980.
Actos de fe en Guatemala, photographs by Sara Facio and María Cristina Orive. 1980.
El hombre que lo tenía todo, todo, todo, illustrated by Jacqueline Duheme. 1981.
Viajes, ensayos y fantasías. 1981.
París 1922–1923: Periodismo y creación literaria (articles), edited by Amos Segala. 1988.
Cartas de amor, with Blanca de Mora y Araujo, edited by Felipe Mellizo. 1989.

Editor, *Leyendas de Guatemala* (stories). 1930; enlarged edition, 1948; as *Leyendas,* 1960.
Editor, *Poesía precolombina.* 1960.
Editor, *Páginas de Rubén Darío,* 1963.

Translator, with J. Manuel González de Mendoza, *Los dioses, los héroes y los hombres de Guatemala antigua; o, El libro del consejo, Popol vuh de los indios quichés.* 1927; revised edition as *Popol vuh, o, el libro del consejo de los indios quichés,* 1969.
Translator, with J. Manuel González de Mendoza, *Anales de los xahil de los indios cakchiqueles* by Georges Raynaud. 1928.
Translator, *Antología de la prosa rumana.* 1967.

*

Bibliography: *Miguel Ángel Asturias: Anticipo bibliografíco* by Pedro F. de Andrea, 1969; *Asturias: A Checklist of Works and Criticism* by R.E. Moore, 1979.

Critical Studies: *Miguel Ángel Asturias* by Atilio Jorge Castelpoggi, 1961; *Asturias* by Earl and Beverly Jones, 1967; *Miguel Ángel Asturias* by G.W. Lorenz, 1968; *Miguel Ángel Asturias: Semblanza para el estudio de su vida y obra* by Marta Pilón, 1968; *El carácter de la literatura y la novelística de Miguel Ángel Asturias* by Iber Verdugo, 1968; *La narrativa de Miguel Ángel Asturias*, 1969, *Il laberinto magico*, 1973, *Il mondo allucinante: Da Asturias a García Márquez*, 1976, and *De tiranos, héroes y brujos: Estudios sobre la obra de Miguel Ángel Asturias*, 1982, all by Giuseppe Bellini; *Artists and Writers in the Evolution of Latin America* edited by Edward D. Terry, 1969; *Asturias* by Richard Callan, 1970; *Homenaje a Miguel Ángel Asturias* edited by Helmy F. Giacoman, 1971; *Miguel Ángel Asturias: La función de lo ancestral en la obra literaria* by Eladia L. Hill, 1972; *Miguel Ángel Asturias* by J. Sáenz, 1973; *El Miguel Ángel Asturias que yo conocí* by J. Olivero, 1980; *Asturias y Neruda* by G. Tavani, 1985; 'Tall Tales Made to Order: The Making of Myth in *Men of Maize* by Miguel Ángel Asturias', in *Modern Language Notes*, 101, 1986, 'The Unifying Principle of *Men of Maize*', in *Modern Language Studies*, 16(2), 1986, and 'The New American Idiom of Miguel Ángel Asturias', in *Hispanic Review*, 56(2), 1988, all by R. Prieto; *La problemática de la identidad en El Señor Presidente de Miguel Ángel Asturias* by T. Rodríguez, 1989.

* * *

The poetry, drama, essays, and articles for which Miguel Ángel Asturias received the 1967 Nobel prize for literature demonstrate his preoccupation with social and political conditions in Latin America (especially Guatemala) and with the region's mythic past. Critical attention has generally focused on his fiction (novels and 'legends'), unfortunately eclipsing his achievements in other genres. In an essay about his aesthetic principles, Asturias characterized his fiction as 'realismo mágico' (magic realism), a term he coined to define writing which, while closely related to surrealism, depicts a uniquely Latin American, fictional ambience that bridges two realities—one being the everyday lives of characters who speak the language of the Guatemalan people and are involved with their social and political concerns, the other an imaginary realm immersed in dreams and hallucinations. The oneiric quality of his fictional worlds is achieved by juxtaposing Guatemalan folk traditions and myths from the Mayan sacred book (the *Popol vuh*) with everyday reality.

Asturias came to the attention of international literary circles with the publication of *Leyendas de Guatemala* [Legends of Guatemala], a collection of short fictional pieces described in Paul Valéry's preface as 'poems-dreams-fantasies'. He continued writing 'legends' in this 'magical' vein throughout his career, and they appear in two later collections, *Week-end en Guatemala* [Weekend in Guatemala] and *El espejo de Lida Sal* [Lida Sal's Mirror].

From his first novel, *El Señor Presidente* (*The President*), to his last, *Viernes de Dolores* [Good Friday], Asturias's novels are social and political, reflecting the reality of Guatemala's people, on the one hand, and oneiric, magical, and mythical on the other. *The President* combines these two qualities very effectively. The most immediate quality of this novel is its unvarnished realism in which torture, graft, and injustice are seen as part of everyday life in a military dictatorship and are depicted in ghastly detail. A surreal atmosphere is discernible from the novel's opening passage, a diabolical, jabberwocky-like incantation: 'Boom, bloom, alum-bright, Lucifer of alunite!'. The 'magical' ambience is achieved by the use of mythical motifs and poetic or incantational language. These provide a mesmerizing experience for the reader. Asturias's last novel is based on the student strike that occasioned his first exile. Its narrative is tinged with the humour and idealism of the young Asturias and the irony and disillusion of the man close to the end of his life.

Other novels with significant socio-political content include *Viento fuerte* (*Strong Wind*), *El Papa verde* (*The Green Pope*), and *Los ojos de los enterrados* (*The Eyes of the Interred*), a trio often referred to as the 'Banana Trilogy'. They enunciate a protest against the exploitation of Guatemala's agricultural resources by foreign interests. Asturias resists a temptation to tar all his fictional United States citizens with the same brush. In *Strong Wind*, for example, the American Lester Mead makes common cause with the plantation labourers against Tropical Banana Inc., a fictionalized United Fruit Company.

Other Asturias novels are less political and more mythical. His characters move in a magic-realist world, with one foot in the prosaic reality of Guatemala, the other in the magic of the *Popol vuh* and traditional folk beliefs. This group includes *Hombres de maíz* (*Men of Maize*), *Mulata de tal* (*The Mulatta and Mr Fly*), *El alhajadito* (*The Bejeweled Boy*), and *Maladrón* [Evil Thief]. The duality of Asturias's novelistic reality may be identified most readily in *Men of Maize*, where he depicts the cultivation of corn for profit as a practice that leads to abuse of the land and disrespect for nature. Simultaneously, he creates a 'magical' context that alludes to ancient myths, for his characters descend from the first Mayans whose flesh was created from corn by the gods of the *Popol vuh*. Guatemalan folk tradition is present in the form of his characters' *nahuales* (animal counterparts believed to protect individuals, and whose form may be assumed by their protégées in times of need).

Asturias's poetry, most of which is gathered in *Poesía: Sien de alondra* [The Lark's Brow], has received undeserved short shrift from critics. The early poems are completely traditional —with the sonnet his favourite form—and are subjective and personal in content; but, by the mid-1940s, his poetic themes are universal, and, to re-create Guatemala's ancient Mayan atmosphere and re-mythologize its reality, he uses the parallel constructions, repetitions, and onomatopoeia characteristic of pre-Columbian Indian poetry. This trend culminates in *Clarivigilia primaveral* [Springtime Bright-Vigil], a book-length poem in which Asturias creates a new 'myth' about Latin American artist gods. In this poem as elsewhere, while not actually alluding to characters from ancient Mayan myth, he creates characters and events with a mythic quality of relevance to modern Guatemala.

Asturias's theatrical works explore the essence of Guatemalan reality in the same way that his works of fiction and poetry do. *La audiencia de los confines* [The Royal Tribunal of the Frontier] is a historical play dealing with the duplicity of Church and State at the time of Fray Bartolomé de las Casas's defence of the Indians. *Chantaje* [Blackmail] and *Dique seco* [Dry Dock] are plays of social criticism with touches of the absurd. *Soluna* [Sun-Moon], perhaps the best known of his plays, uses the magic-realism characteristic of his fiction. In it, a myth (when the sun and moon merge during an eclipse, time accelerates, compressing years into moments) provides the solution to the protagonist's dilemma. Asturias's language in his plays is, as it is in other genres, essentially poetic. In fact, he inserts poetic passages in several of his plays. His three 'fantomimas' (fantasy-mimes), however, are dramas entirely in verse. He returns to the poetic theatre tradition of the Spanish Golden Age, using traditional Spanish versification. Ironically, these characteristics accentuate a very 20th-century quality of his theatre: the aesthetic distance created by the use of neologisms, repetitions, onomatopoeia, and jabberwocky-like passages.

Asturias's writings in every genre captivate his readers, pulling them into the ancient, mythical ambience of Guatemala, thereby forcing them to reconsider everyday reality.

—Oralia Preble-Niemi

THE PRESIDENT (El Señor Presidente)
Novel by Miguel Ángel Asturias, 1946 (written 1922–1932).

The President, Asturias's first novel, although not published until 1946, following the fall of the Guatemalan dictator Jorge Ubico, was written in Guatemala and Paris during the 1920s and early 1930s. Asturias wrote it as an attack against the dictatorship of Manuel Estrada Cabrera, but the novel comes to represent the horror of all Latin American dictatorships. The grotesque, violent, and nightmarish vision of despotism depicted in this novel is presented within a complex narrative structure punctuated by stream-of-consciousness subjectivity, multiple perspectives, punning onomatopoeia, and free association. The beauty of Asturias's literary language serves as a powerfully ironic means of highlighting the horror and violence of dictatorship. While the President himself rarely appears in the novel, he acts as the malevolent, invisible motivator of most of the action, his power and knowledge are a continual threat to everyone, and his command over their mental states is complete. Asturias created a gripping portrait of a nation controlled by fear.

One of the central motifs of the novel involves the forces of light against those of darkness, of angels pitted against Lucifer. In this infernal world, plots are continually hatched and assassinations planned against those who were previously allies, and individuals are thrown into the dungeon for no apparent reason, or tortured to death for telling the truth. At any moment, the President can turn against his allies for the most trivial infraction, real or imagined. It is useless to try to determine whether one should tell the truth or not: the system for torture and punishment is so arbitrary that some characters never know why they are in the dungeon—or why a lucky few are released.

The story begins with the murder of Colonel Parrales Sonriente by an idiot he has taunted, and the President decides to blame the colonel's death on two men he wants to get rid of: one of them, a lawyer, is arrested and shot; the other, General Canales, escapes to the mountains after being warned by Don Miguel Cara de Ángel, the President's favourite. The narrator characterizes Cara de Ángel, whose name means 'angel-face', as a fallen angel, one who is as beautiful and evil as Satan. A handsome and debonair young man, Cara de Ángel has never questioned his duties and obligations as the President's favourite, nor does he realize that his commission to warn Canales is actually part of the President's plan to assassinate the general. Canales, however, is successful in his escape thanks to Cara de Ángel's aid, and the young man is left to escort the general's daughter, Camila, to the home of one of her uncles. However, none of her relatives is willing to take her in as they are afraid of being compromised politically, and she falls gravely ill with pneumonia. It is while Cara de Ángel is taking care of the sick girl

that he falls in love with and marries her. In so doing, he is transformed from a selfish and self-centred puppet of the President into a man who puts another person's welfare before his own for the first time in his life. This act of falling in love, of making Camila's life dearer to him than his own, constitutes Cara de Ángel's betrayal of the President, whose law is to control and destroy with hatred, violence, and fear. Although Cara de Ángel never has any intention of harming the President, he ultimately becomes the victim of the tyrant's most vicious and sadistic punishment. One character maintains that only love can oppose death; the President, who realizes that Cara de Ángel has committed no overt act of disloyalty, can none the less only respond to the discovery of this love as if it were an act of treason punishable by death.

Cara de Ángel plans to escape with Camila to Washington, but he is captured and tortured by the President's henchmen, and thrown into the deepest and darkest cell in the dungeon to die. And he does die, after many years in the dungeon, when a fellow prisoner, planted by the President, falsely insinuates to him that Camila has become the President's favoured mistress.

Asturias's novel, deeply poetic as it is, may be characterized as a metaphysical as much as a political treatment of dictatorship; Cara de Ángel's personal spiritual transformation and triumph over his previous existence would otherwise be seen as an empty victory, especially in light of the horrible and painfully slow death he meets, disillusioned and broken-hearted in the dungeon, defeated were it not for the conscious desire to do good that has freed him from the clutches of the President's dark forces and redeemed him. The President must eliminate him precisely because, as the embodiment of the force of evil, he senses, on an instinctual level, the threat of such goodness to his powers. Camila is left with a baby son at the end of the novel, a symbol of the couple's triumph over the forces of annihilation, which separated them, but which could not destroy the fruit of their love.

—Susan Isabel Stein

ATTĀR, Farid al-Din Abu Hamid Mohammad. Born in Nishāpūr, Persia (now Iran), c.1116–41. Trained and practised as a pharmacist (*attār*) and as a physician; reputedly, travelled throughout the Muslim Middle East, India, and Turkestan; after retirement became a member of the Sufi sect, writing numerous poems and compiling biographies of Sufi saints (*Tazkerāt al-'Awliā*). Around 20 of the works attributed to him in the past are now thought to be spurious. According to tradition, killed during the Mongol invasion of Persia. *Died c.1220–31*.

PUBLICATIONS

Verse

Ilāhi-nāma, edited by H. Ritter. 1940; as *Book of God*, translated by John Andrew Boyle, 1976.
Manteq al-Tayr, edited by S. Gowharin. 1964; as *The Conference of the Birds*, translated by C.S. Nott (from French), 1954; also translated by Afkam Darbandi and

Dick Davis, 1984; abridged version, as *The Bird Parliament*, translated by Edward Fitzgerald, 1899; as *Persian Mysticism*, translated by R.P. Masani, 1981.

Other

Tazkerāt al-'Awliā [The Memoirs of the Saints] (biographies), edited by R.A. Nicholson. 2 vols., 1905–07; part as *Muslim Saints and Mystics*, translated by A.R. Arberry, 1965.

*

Bibliography: in *Persian Literature* by C.A. Storey, 1953.

Critical Studies: *The Persian Mystics: Attar* (includes translations) by Margaret Smith, 1932; *Attar: Concordance and Lexical Repertories of 1000 Lines* by Daniela Meneghini Correale, 1993.

* * *

Farid al-Din Abu Hamid Mohammad Attār of Nishāpūr, known as Farid al-Din Attār, was an eminent Islamic mystic (Sufi) and Persian poet who was born during the 12th century in Nishāpūr, in what is now north-east Iran. The word *attār* in Persian is derived from the word *atr* which literally means perfume; an *attār* is a perfume seller, and the word also refers to a pharmacist. Attār says that he composed some of his works in *dāru khāneh*, which in modern Persian means a pharmacy, and he was also familiar with the practice of medicine. There are references in his early works to the many patients he received every day in his pharmacy. Later in his life he gave up his job, became a Sufi, and lived in seclusion. It is during this later period that he produced his most significant works.

Attār travelled extensively and visited Egypt, Damascus, Turkistan, Mecca, and India in pursuit of knowledge. During these travels he met great Sufis of his time, and learned the stories he used in his later works. He was a prolific poet and writer who composed, according to his biographers, as many as 114 works. Although this figure seems exaggerated, Attār's contribution to Islamic mysticism is undeniable. To appreciate his works one has to be familiar with the basic doctrines of Islamic mysticism (Sufism), including the Unity of Being (*wahdat al-wujūd*) which, briefly, means that the created universe is a manifestation of the Divine Reality. This must not be confused with pantheism, because the Oneness of God is at the heart of this doctrine. The created, which is an image of the Creator, will not rest until it achieves the esoteric knowledge (*ma'refat*) necessary for experiencing mystical union with the Divine. The unique relationship between the spiritual master (*morād* or *shaikh*) and the disciple (*morid* or *sālek*) is another cornerstone of Sufism. During the spiritual journey, the disciple constantly seeks his master's clarification on the subtleties of the path and depends on him to resolve his problems.

Attār delineated the doctrines of Sufism delicately and in a simple language in books that are among his best works of poetry and prose. In *Asrār-nāma* [The Book of Secrets] the narrator admonished the reader to leave his worldly desires behind and start looking for the Divine Reality. It is similar to another of his books, *Manteq al-Tayr* (*The Conference of the Birds*) in urging man to embark upon the spiritual journey. However, unlike his other major poetical works which have one general frame story with several embedded stories, this poem has no frame. *Ilāhi-nāma* (*Book of God*) is a poetical dialogue between a king and his six sons who are in pursuit of worldly happiness. The king tries to prove to them the absurdity and vanity of their pursuit through anecdotes and examples.

The Conference of the Birds, completed in 1177, is considered Attār's greatest poetical work. This poem is an allegorical account of Islamic mysticism. The story is about the birds of the world who are looking for a king. The hoopoe, Solomon's special messenger to Belqays, the Queen of Sheba, assumes the role of the spiritual master and leads them to the royal court of the Simurgh, the king of the birds. Once the birds are confronted with the insurmountable difficulties of the journey, they come up with various excuses as to why it is impossible for them to undertake the journey. Their excuses express typical weaknesses of human beings on the path of spirituality but in bondage to material things. Through a series of questions and answers, the hoopoe finally succeeds in encouraging them to embark on the trip, narrating admonishing stories and thus expounding the doctrines of Sufism. The hoopoe explains the seven valleys that lead to the Simurgh's court: quest (*talab*), love (*ishq*), esoteric knowledge (*ma'refat*), independence (*isteghnā*), unity (*towhid*), bewilderment (*hayrat*), poverty (*faqr*), and annihilation (*fanā*). These are the seven stages on the path of the seeker's spiritual journey which have to be completed before reaching the royal court. The path of spirituality is dangerous and difficult and not everyone can make it to the end. Only 30 birds reach the court of His Majesty. Finally, when they are admitted to His Presence, they see themselves in His Majesty's mirror. The 30 birds are the Simurgh (*si*: 30, *murgh*: bird), and their journey is a conceptualization of man's spiritual journey to the Divine Reality.

Tazkerāt al-'Awliā [The Memoirs of the Saints], Attār's most important prose work, is the hagiography of 96 Islamic saints and mystics. In this book Attār shows his high opinion of the Islamic saints and mystics whose sayings he considers next to the Qur'ān and hadith (the sayings of the Prophet) in their authoritative voice. Two mystics in whom Attār shows a great deal of interest are Mansur Hallāj (d. 922) and Bāyazid Bastāmi (d. 874), both of whom were executed for their heretical views by the orthodox theologians. In compiling this book, Attār used several sources on the life of Sufis available to him. His achievement is, however, in using these stories for expounding Sufi principles.

Attār chooses his characters from common people and animals. In his works we see people from all layers of society including dervishes, beggars, craftsmen, and merchants. He has no interest in the aristocratic class, and whenever he mentions the word 'king', he refers to the Divine Being. As a mystic, Attār was never concerned with material gain and never sold his poetic genius to earthly rulers to make a living. As a true Sufi he believed only in the Celestial King whose love was the only moving force in the poet's life. Attār has a talent for putting the most complicated ideas into simple language, masterfully using allegories to express the inexpressible experience and to describe the indescribable.

—Alireza Anushiravani

THE CONFERENCE OF THE BIRDS (Manteq al-Tayr)
Poem by Farid al-Din Attār, c.1177.

The Conference of the Birds is the most important narrative poem of Farid al-Din Attār, the 12th/13th-century Persian poet. It is a long narrative poem of 4,600 rhyming couplets (*masnavi*), consisting of 45 discourses, each containing several embedded stories. The poem, which is a collection of Sufi tales, is an allegorical account of Sufism (Islamic mysticism). The art of story-telling enables Attār to communicate his subtle and complicated mystical ideas in a simple language which would otherwise be difficult for the reader to understand.

The book begins with the praise of God, the Prophet, and the Four Caliphs (Abu Bakr, Omar, Osmān, and Ali). The story then starts with the quest of the birds of the world for a king who can protect them from the perils of life. The hoopoe (*hud-hud*), known as Solomon's messenger to Belqays, the Queen of Sheba, is spiritually the best qualified bird to lead them to their king. Their king, who is called the Simurgh, abides behind the far-away Mount of *Qāf* (a legendary mountain imagined to surround the world).

The hoopoe explains that the journey to the Simurgh is long and difficult and that it requires dedication and effort to find one's way to his court. As soon as the birds find out about the difficulties of the journey, their eagerness disappears and they try to excuse themselves from undertaking the journey. Their apologies illustrate the typical characteristics of each species of bird. The first bird to withdraw from this journey is the nightingale, who cannot renounce his passionate love for the rose. The other birds, including the parrot, the peacock, the duck, the partridge, the *homa* (royal eagle, also a bird of happy omen), the falcon, the heron, the owl, and the goldfinch, follow the nightingale, each giving a reason why it is impossible to make the journey. The hoopoe resorts to story-telling in answering their excuses and other subsequent questions. The stories, which are thematically linked to each other, are meant to awaken the soul of the birds to the Divine Reality, and thus to encourage them to embark on the journey to the royal court.

Inspired by the hoopoe's stories, the birds set out to meet their king. The path to the Simurgh's court, however, is filled with obstacles, and the birds need further encouragement and clarification of their goal and path. The hoopoe explains the seven valleys (spiritual stages) that they have to cross before reaching their goal, the Absolute Being. First is the valley of quest (*talab*) in which the seeker has to go through thousands of tests in order to be purged from any impurities. At this stage the seeker of the path has to leave the material world behind and prepare himself to receive divine grace. Second is the valley of love (*ishq*) which will set the seeker's soul and body on fire. The ardent lover who is consumed in the fire of love is beyond good and evil. Third is the valley of esoteric knowledge (*ma'refat*). Esoteric knowledge transcends rational and logical knowledge; it is not to be learned from books but acquired by meditation and intuition. Fourth is the valley of independence (*isteghnā*) in which the seeker becomes completely independent of the outside world and detaches himself from the material world. He becomes so rich spiritually that the outside world is worth nothing to him. Fifth is the valley of unity (*towhid*) in which the seeker achieves a unitary vision. Duality disappears and everything becomes a part of the whole. There is no more talk of 'I' and 'Thou'. There is no being except the Absolute Being. Sixth is the valley of bewilderment (*hayrat*). This is the valley of lamentation and confusion. The seeker does not know himself any longer; he does not know to which religion or nation he belongs. In fact, he has gone far beyond these artificial boundaries; he has achieved a cosmic consciousness by which he transcends the binary definitions of the material world. The last is the valley of poverty and annihilation (*faqr* and *fanā*). This is the last stage on the path of the Sufi where his individual self is annihilated and he becomes one with the Absolute Being. Finally the seeker who has constantly been looking for his Beloved becomes one with Him, like a drop of water joining the ocean. In other words, the lover is totally absorbed in the Beloved, and thus achieves the highest stage of spiritual growth.

Many of the birds die on their way to the royal court from the insurmountable hardships they encounter. From hundreds of thousands of birds who had initially started the trip, only 30 birds complete the journey. When these 30 birds finally reach His Majesty's court, they are exhausted, but they soon find out that the whole universe is nothing but dust in comparison with His Majesty. They wonder if a bunch of miserable creatures like themselves are worthy of meeting him. In fact, His Majesty's chamberlain receives them very coldly and sends them back. But the birds have no intention of going back now that they have had a glimpse of His Majesty. First they must be purified from all their previous sins. When they are finally admitted to his presence, they discover that His Majesty, the Simurgh, is only a mirror in which they see their own image. They are the Simurgh.

Actually the whole story is based on a pun. The word *simurgh* in Persian can be the name of a mythical bird, referred to also as *anqā* (the phoenix), and is usually associated with the Divine; it also means '30 birds' (*si* = '30', *murgh* = 'bird').

The 30 birds in *The Conference of the Birds* represent 30 mystics on their path to perfection, to God, the Absolute Being. The dedicated pilgrims blessed by His grace depend on a spiritual master (*pīr* or *morād*) for direction and guidance. The real search is within and the ultimate goal is annihilation in God (*fanā fel-lāh*), and the discovery of everlasting life in God (*baqā bel-lāh*). The 30 birds eventually find eternal life through mystical union with the Simurgh.

In the conclusion Attār recounts the hardships he has gone through while composing *The Conference of the Birds* and hopes that his readers will find his book a source of guidance and inspiration on their path to the Divine Reality.

—Alireza Anushiravani

AUCASSIN AND NICOLETTE (Aucassin et Nicolette). Anonymous 13th-century romance. Written c.1200 in the form of a *chante-fable* (narrative comprised of alternate prose and verse passages), probably in the dialect of Picardy; single manuscript found in 1752.

PUBLICATIONS

Aucassin et Nicolette, edited by Hermann Suchier. 1878; also edited by Francis William Bourdillon, 1887, revised 1897, 1919; Mario Roques, 1925, revised 1929; Jean Dufournet, 1973; Modern French translations by La Curne de Sainte-Palaye, 1752, as *Les Amours du bon vieux temps*, 1756; Legrand d'Aussy, in *Fabliaux et contes du XIIe et du XIIIe siècle*, vol. 2, 1779; Claude Fauriel, in *Histoire de la poésie provençale*, vol. 3, 1846; Alfred Delvau, in *Bibliothèque bleue: Collection des romans de chevalerie*, vol. 1, 1859, and in separate volume, 1866; Alexandre Bida, 1878; Gustave Michaut, 1901, revised 1905; Albert Pauphilet, 1932; Marcel

Coulon, 1933; Gustave Cohen, 1954; Maurice Pons, 1960; Jean Dufournet, 1973; translated as *Aucassin and Nicolette*, in *Tales of the 12th and 13th Centuries*, vol. 2, 1786; also translated by A. Rodney Macdonough, 1880; Francis William Bourdillon, 1887; Andrew Lang, 1887; Elias John Wilkinson Gibb, 1887; M.S. Henry and Edward W. Thomson, 1896; Edward Everett Hale, 1899; Laurence Housman, 1903; Eugene Mason, 1910; Harold Child, 1911; Dulcie Lawrence Smith, 1914; Michael West, 1917; Edward Francis Moyer and Carey DeWitt Eldridge, 1937; Norma Lorre Goodrich, 1964; Pauline Matarasso, 1971; Glyn S. Burgess, 1988.

*

Bibliography: *Aucassin et Nicolette: A Critical Bibliography* by Barbara Nelson Sargent-Baur and Robert Francis Cook, 1981.

Critical Studies: *Studies in the History of the Renaissance* by Walter Pater, 1873; *Le Legs du moyen âge* by Albert Pauphilet, 1950; *Étude stylo-statistique du vocabulaire des vers et de la prose dans la chantefable 'Aucassin et Nicolette'* by Simone Monsonégo, 1966; *Love's Fools: Aucassin, Troilus, Calisto, and the Parody of the Courtly Lover* by June Hall Martin, 1972; *Les Temps du passé dans 'Aucassin et Nicolette'* by Lene Schøsler, 1973.

*   *   *

Aucassin and Nicolette is an anonymous French romance composed during the first half of the 13th century. Termed a *chante-fable*, the form of the narrative comprises alternating prose and heptasyllabic verse passages, thereby recalling the structure of Boethius' *De Consolatione philosophiae* (*On the Consolation of Philosophy*). An engaging story with witty dialogue, unexpected events, and fortunate conclusion, the work resembles a *fabliau* or *conte*. However, it is generally agreed that it was a dramatic recitation presented by one actor for the prose passages and possibly sung by minstrels for the lyrics. The narrative tells of an adventure of two lovers that suggests parallels with Greek Byzantine romances, but extensive undercutting argues for classifying the work as a parody or satire. The difficulties in determining genre extend to language. In employing the dialect of Picardy, the author appears to be northern French. However, references to Beaucaire and Valance situate the story in the south of France, thereby justifying claims that the original but inextant version was written in Provençal.

The narrative of the romance moves from contention to reconciliation and from separation to reunion. Aucassin loves Nicolette, a Saracen slave converted to Christianity. Aucassin's father, Garin de Beaucaire, forbids marriage, imprisons Nicolette, and insists that his son marry a lady of equal station, and that he fight against Bougars de Valence who has ravaged Garin's country. Aucassin refuses. However, his father consents that, in exchange for waging war, Aucassin can see and embrace Nicolette. Aucassin delivers Bougars to his father, but Garin does not honour his pledge. Aucassin is imprisoned. Nicolette escapes, informs Aucassin of her plans, flees to the forest, and requests shepherds to advise Aucassin of her location. Aucassin learns of the shepherds' encounter with Nicolette and, after meeting a herdsman who has lost one of his oxen, he rejoins Nicolette.

Because of Garin's threat to execute Nicolette, the lovers seek refuge in Torelore where Aucassin supports the king in war. The Saracens, though, take the country and abduct the lovers in separate ships. Aucassin's vessel is wrecked near Beaucaire where he hears of his father's death and his subsequent succession as ruler. Nicolette, arriving in Carthage, learns that she is the king's daughter. She leaves for Beaucaire and, disguised as a minstrel, sings her story to Aucassin and discovers the constancy of his love. Returning to her godparents' house, she is restored to her beauty and reveals her identity to Aucassin. The reunited lovers live happily in marriage.

The adventures and eventual consummation of love recall the narratives of 12th-century romances. Arthurian romances as popularized by Chrétien de Troyes recount the superhuman feats of the legendary king and his knights, and were continued into the 13th century by works such as the *Queste del Sainte Graal* (*Quest of the Holy Grail*) and *La Morte le Roi Artu* (*King Arthur's Death*). Whereas Arthurian romance evokes a mysticism that encourages allegorical interpretation, non-Arthurian romance conveys a realism that often avoids direct moral didacticism. Through courage and perseverance, Aucassin and Nicolette display qualities of Arthurian heroes and heroines, and conform to codes of courtly love. However, irony undercuts the seriousness of circumstances and tone, and allusions to the significance of money and law add a realism that argues for the classification of the work as a non-Arthurian romance. Any direct borrowing from Greek Byzantine romances is unlikely. Nevertheless, tales and themes from this tradition were disseminated by returning crusaders and by Latin and Latinized Greek works, and did inform the plots and character portrayals in Gautier d'Arras's *Eracle* (1174), Aimon de Varenne's *Florimont* (1188), and the widely enjoyed anonymous romance, *Floire and Blancheflor* (c.1175).

A sharp delineation and a subtle development of character complement the themes of unrequited love, war, and familial disputes. Nicolette, despite the precariousness of imprisonment and risks of escape, remains faithful. Aucassin, like Chrétien's courtly-love heroes, matures in depth and breadth. Initially, he thinks only of his passion for Nicolette; but, after fighting against Bougars, he expands his vision, replacing an ox lost by the herdsman, waging war against the Saracens, and becoming a wise ruler of Beaucaire. Realism penetrates illusion and affords unexpected turns in plot and psychological portrayal. Nicolette assumes her rightful noble standing and, at the end, exchanges the mask of darkened face for her own beautiful complexion. Aucassin recognizes the realities of contentions and, although shunning any training in combat, evolves into a fearless warrior and just lord. A resolution to the romantic entanglements, moreover, requires the use of money, an understanding of circumstances, an insight into emotions, and the recognition of legal ramifications (e.g., the shepherds' refusal to betray Garin) that must be respected but overcome.

Irony and inversion create illusions of simplicity and the fantastic. Aucassin, obsessed by love, notes naively that the sole consequence of decapitation is the incapacity to speak with Nicolette. Compared to a fleur-de-lis 'sweeter than the grape', Nicolette lives in a hut built with fragrant flowers and fern leaves. The Queen of Torelore replaces her husband in leading a burlesque campaign against the Saracens, waged with apples, eggs, and cheese.

An artistic eclecticism explains, in part, the originality of this work. By reworking plots and images associated with Arthurian and Greek Byzantine romances, the author shapes an engaging, intricate narrative to established structures and themes. Allusions to contemporary concerns, moreover, enhance relevance, but the extensive employment of lyric verse foreshadows the singing and dancing in Adam de la Halle's dramatic *pastourelle, Jeu de Robin et Marion* (*Play of Robin and Marion*). Finally, the use of irony in characterization, language, and imagery provides a verve and vibrance characteristic of the parodies in later *fabliaux* and *farces*. In deflating the seriousness of Arthurian romances, ambiguity, exaggeration, and wit heighten the charm and entertainment of a narrative conventional in themes but complex in tone and genre.

—Donald Gilman

———

AUGUSTINE, St. Born Aurelius Augustinus in Tagaste (now Souk Ahras, Algeria), 13 November AD 354. Reared as a Christian; educated in Tagaste and Carthage. Had a son by his concubine. Taught rhetoric in Tagaste, one year, Carthage, eight years, in Rome, 383–84, and Milan, 384–86, where he met the bishop Ambrose; after a period of Manichaeism, turned to Neoplatonism; converted to Christianity, 386: baptized by Ambrose, 387; returned to Tagaste, 388; ordained as a priest in Hippo Regius (now Annada, Algeria), 391, and became its bishop, 396–430, where contended with Donatist schism, Pelagian heresy, and Vandal invasions. *Died 28 August AD 430.*

PUBLICATIONS

Collections

[Works], in *Patrologia Latina*, edited by Jacques Paul Migne, vols. 32–47. 1844–64; translations in *A Library of Fathers of the Holy Catholic Church*, edited by E.B. Pusey, 12 vols., 1840–57; *Library of Nicene and Post-Nicene Fathers*, edited by Marcus Dods, 15 vols., 1871–76, revised edition, as *A Select Library of the Nicene and Post-Nicene Fathers*, edited by Philip Schaff, vols. 1–8, 1886–88; *Ancient Christian Writers*, edited by Johannes Quasten and Joseph C. Plumpe, 9 vols., 1946–61; *The Fathers of the Church*, edited by Ludwig Schopp, R.J. Defervari, and others, 10 vols., 1947–63; *Library of Christian Classics*, edited by John Baillie, John T. McNeill, and Henry P. Van Dusen, vols. 6–8, 1953–55; and *The Works of St Augustine*, edited by John E. Rotelle, 7 vols., to 1994.
Basic Writings, edited by Whitney J. Oates. 2 vols., 1948.
Selected Sermons, edited and translated by Quincy Howe. 1966.
An Augustine Reader, edited by John J. O'Meara. 1973.
Selected Writings, translated by Mary T. Clark. 1984.
Sermons, translated by Edmund Hill. 2 vols., 1990.

Works

Confessiones, edited by P. Knöll. 1909; also edited by M. Skutella, revised by H. Juergens and W. Schaub, 1969, also revised by James J. O'Donnell, 1992; as *The Confessions*, translated by Sir Tobie Matthew, 1624; also translated by William Watts, 1631; E.B. Pusey, 2 vols., 1838; Charles

Bigg, 1898; F.J. Sheed, 1943; J.M. Lelen, 1952; R.S. Pine-Coffin, 1961; Rex Warner, 1963; E.M. Blaiklock, 1983; Henry Chadwick, 1991; James J. O'Donnell, 1992.
Contra litteras Petiliani, as *Answers to Letters of Petilian*, translated by J.R. King, in *A Select Library of Nicene and Post-Nicene Fathers of the Christian Church*, vol. 4. 1887.
De baptismo, contra Donatistas, as *On Baptism, Against the Donatists*, translated by J.R. King, in *A Select Library of Nicene and Post-Nicene Fathers of the Christian Church*, vol. 4. 1887.
De beata vita, edited by Michael Schmaus. 1931; as *The Happy Life*, edited and translated by Ludwig Schopp, 1939.
De civitate Dei, edited by B. Dombart. 1853, revised by A. Kalb, 1928–29; also edited by J.E.C. Welldon, 1924; edited and translated by George E. McCracken and William C. Greene [Loeb Edition], 7 vols., 1957–72; as *The City of God*, translated by John Healey, 1610, revised by R.V.G. Trasker, 2 vols., 1945; also translated by Marcus Dods and George Wilson, in *Library of Nicene and Post-Nicene Fathers*, 1872, reprinted 1950; translated in *The Fathers of the Church*, vols. 6–8, 1950–54.
De doctrina Christiana, edited by H.J. Vogels. 1930; as *On Christian Doctrine*, translated by F.J. Shaw, in *A Select Library of Nicene and Post-Nicene Fathers of the Christian Church*, vol. 2, 1886.
De dialectica, edited by Jan Pinborg, translated by B. Darrell Jackson. 1975.
De Genesi ad literam [Literal Commentary on Genesis], edited and translated by John Hammond Taylor. 1948.
De gratia Christi et de peccato originali, as *On the Grace of Christ and on Original Sin*, translated by Peter Holmes, in *A Select Library of Nicene and Post-Nicene Fathers of the Christian Church*, vol. 5. 1888.
De libero arbitrio, as *On Free Will*, edited and translated by Francis E. Tourscher. 1937; also translated by Carroll Mason Sparrow, 1947; Anna S. Benjamin and L.H. Hackstaff, 1964; as *The Problem of Free Choice*, translated by Mark Pontifex, in *Ancient Christian Writers*, 1955.
De natura et gratia, as *On Nature and Grace*, translated by Peter Holmes, in *A Selected Library of Nicene and Post-Nicene Fathers of the Christian Church*, vol. 5. 1888.
De sermone Domini in monte, as *Commentary on the Lord's Sermon on the Mount*, translated by Denis J. Kavanagh, in *The Fathers of the Church*, vol. 5. 1948.
De spiritu et littera, as *On Spirit and the Letter*, translated by Peter Holmes, in *Basic Writings*. 1948.
De trinitate, edited by M.F. Sciacca. 1973; as *On the Trinity*, translated by Arthur W. Haddan, in *A Select Library of Nicene and Post-Nicene Fathers of the Christian Church*, vol. 3, 1887; also translated by Stephen McKenna, in *The Fathers of the Church*, vol. 45, 1963.
De vera religione, as *Of True Religion*, translated by J.H.S. Burleigh. 1953.
Enarrationes in Psalmos, translated as *On the Psalms*, in *Ancient Christian Writers*. 1960.
Epistolae, edited by L. Carrozzi. 1974; translated as *Letters*, in *The Fathers of the Church*, 1947–63; as *Select Letters* [Loeb Edition], 1930.
Soliloquia, as *The Soliloquies*, translated by Rose E. Cleveland. 1910; also translated by Thomas F. Gilligan, in *The Fathers of the Church*, vol. 5, 1948.
Tractatus in Epistolam Joannis ad Parthos, translated as *Ten Homilies on St John's Epistle*, in *Library of Christian Classics*, vol. 8. 1955.
Tractatus in Joannis Evangelium, as *Homilies on the Gospel of John*, translated by H. Browne, in *A Select Library of*

Nicene and Post-Nicene Fathers of the Christian Church, vol. 7. 1888.

Regula, translated as *The Rule of St Augustine*. 1942; also translated by Raymond Canning, 1984.

*

Bibliography: *Revue des études augustiniennes*, 1956–; *Répertoire bibliographique de saint Augustin 1950–1960* by T.J. van Bavel, 1963; *Fichier augustinien*, 4 vols., 1972; *Bibliographia Augustiniana* by Carl Andresen, 1973; *Augustinian Bibliography 1970–1980* by Terry L. Miethe, 1982.

Critical Studies: *St Augustine's Philosophy of Beauty* by Emmanuel Chapman, 1939; *The City of God* by J.H.S. Burleigh, 1949; *A Companion to the Study of St Augustine* edited by R.W. Battenhouse, 1955; *St Augustine and His Influence Through the Ages* by H.I. Marrou, 1957; *The Christian Philosophy of St Augustine* by Etienne Gilson, 1960; *St Augustine the Bishop* by F. van der Meer, 1961; *St Augustine of Hippo: Life and Controversies*, 1963, and *God's Decree and Man's Destiny: Studies on the Thought of Augustine of Hippo*, 1987, both by Gerald Bonner; *Augustine of Hippo*, 1967, and *Religion and Society in the Age of St Augustine*, 1972, both by P.R.L. Brown; *St Augustine's Confessions: The Odyssey of a Soul*, 1969, *Art and the Christian Intelligence in St Augustine*, 1978, and *Imagination and Metaphysics in St Augustine*, 1986, all by R.J. O'Connell; *Augustine: A Collection of Critical Essays* edited by R.A. Markus, 1972; *Augustine's De moribus ecclesiae catholicae: A Study of the Work, Its Composition and Its Sources* by John Kevin Coyle, 1978; *Augustine: A Wayward Genius* by David Bentley-Taylor, 1980; *The Problem of Self-Love in St Augustine* by Oliver O'Donovan, 1980; *The Young Augustine: An Introduction to the 'Confessions' of St Augustine* by John J. O'Meara, 1980; *Augustine: His Life and Thought* by Warren Thomas Smith, 1980; *Political Theory as Public Confession: The Social and Political Thought of Augustine of Hippo* by Peter Dennis Bathory, 1981; *St Augustine of Hippo* by Gabriel McDonagh, 1982; *Augustine* by Henry Chadwick, 1986; *The Reality of the Mind: Augustine's Philosophical Arguments for the Human Soul as a Spiritual Substance* by Ludger Hölscher, 1986; *Augustine of Hippo and His Monastic Rule* by George Lawless, 1987; *Augustine's Philosophy of Mind* by Gerald J.P. O'Daly, 1987; *Original Sin in Augustine's Confessions* by Paul Rigby, 1987; *Christian Love and Just War: Moral Paradox and Political Life in St Augustine and His Modern Interpreters* by William R. Stevenson, 1987; *Augustine* by Christopher Kirwan, 1989; *Augustine's Prayerful Ascent: An Essay on the Literary Form of the Confessions* by Robert McMahon, 1989; *Jerusalem and Babylon: A Study into Augustine's City of God and the Sources of His Doctrine of the Two Cities* by Johannes van Oort, 1991.

* * *

St Augustine's works are characterized by their number and their variety. When he came to edit them at the end of his life he had 93 on his library shelves, not including vast numbers of letters and sermons as well as the numerous abandoned projects that littered his life. His writings chart the stages of his personal development, from ambitious young career-maker to international religious thinker and controversialist: he described himself as one who writes because he has made progress and who makes progress—by writing.

Augustine received the traditional late classical education in rhetoric, the influence of which is apparent in his love of sophisticated wordplay, paradox and contrast, vivid similes and verbal fireworks. His works show a precision in choice of words, a phenomenal memory for, and telling use of, both classical and scriptural quotations, and a mastery of dry irony and sarcasm. The abstract quality of his mind prevented him from dwelling on landscape or nature but he was attracted by light, faces, music, and above all by the rhythms of speech. Augustine addressed in different capacities a diverse range of audiences, and varied his style accordingly. Thus he composed the monumental and learned *De civitate Dei* (*The City of God*), with its expansive, orderly argumentation and sweeping periodic style; powerful, demagogic sermons with lapses into common parlance, the better to communicate with his congregation; letters to personal friends, officials of church and state, and a correspondence with St Jerome notable for its tone of courteously veiled rancour; and outright ecclesiastical propaganda such as *De agone Christiano* (*On the Christian's Conflict*), written in deliberately simple Latin, and the literature attacking the Donatists, full of colloquialisms and popular jingles. Augustine was the only major Latin philosopher who never properly learned Greek, but he turned this seeming deficiency to advantage and ended by replacing the largely Greek culture of the contemporary church with his own works of scholarship, such as *De trinitate* (*On the Trinity*) and his commentary *De Genesi ad literam* [On Genesis]. Much of his philosophy was merely garnered from Cicero and translations of the Neo-Platonists, but with it Augustine transformed the shape of Latin Christianity.

Augustine's talents lie chiefly in self-justification and dialectic, and this is nowhere clearer than in *Confessiones* (*The Confessions*). This work, and the *Soliloquia* (*Soliloquies*) preceding it, were startling innovations with their welding of classical and religious language and ideas and their ferocious self-analysis. *The Confessions* is not autobiography in the usual sense—Augustine wholly ignores such details as the number of his family, the name of the friend whose death caused him to flee to Carthage or of his faithful concubine who bore his son—rather it is an account of the emotional evolution of a relentless seeker after Truth and Perfection, an anatomy of the most well-documented conversion of antiquity. It is also the therapeutic self-reassessment of a man entering middle age and seeking to interpret his past from the viewpoint of a bishop of a provincial town on the frontiers of a collapsing empire. The public aspect of these preoccupations emerges in his polemical works against ecclesiastical opponents—Donatists, Pelagius, and Bishop Julian.

The climax of Augustine's career was the move outwards from himself and his community to address no less a task than the transformation of the secular pagan state. In *De doctrina Christiana* (*On Christian Doctrine*) he sought to strip the pagan gods and the empire itself of centuries of mystique. Finally, in *The City of God*, an outline for a theology of history depicting two cities—earthly and divine, of unbelief and of faith—Augustine exploited the resources given him by his education in the old tradition to transform it into a vehicle for the new.

—Claire E. Gruzelier

AUGUSTINE: CONFESSIONS, BOOK I　83

THE CITY OF GOD (De civitate Dei)
Prose work by St Augustine, c.AD 413–26.

Although St Augustine was, by training, a rhetorician, which allowed him to speak movingly about matters he himself did not necessarily feel strongly about (as he confessed), his greatest works were deeply felt and emerged from profound crises. The autobiographical *Confessions* derived from his own tormented conversion to Christianity. By contrast, *The City of God* responded to a spiritual crisis of national proportion.

On 24 August AD 410, Alaric and Goth and his army entered the city of Rome, initiating three days of looting and burning that sent shock waves through the Empire. Although the Empire, divided into East and West, had been officially Christian for almost a century, and the imperial residence and administrative centre of the Western Empire had moved to Ravenna, Rome remained the spiritual and symbolic centre for both pagans and Christians. To the pagans, the sack of Rome by the (Christian) Goths signified divine retribution for the abandonment of the old gods. For the Christians it raised doubts about the relationship between religion and the secular state. Augustine, Bishop of Hippo from AD 396, took up both issues, working sporadically from AD 413 to 426, drawing on his vast command of history, philosophy, and classical literature, as well as theology and the Bible, to produce the monumental work, *The City of God*. The work represents both an articulate and sophisticated defence of Christianity against its pagan critics and, more fundamentally, an attempt to elaborate a comprehensive philosophical explanation of Christian doctrine in order to create a Christian vision of history and universal society.

In a letter to the priest Firmus, Augustine suggested that the 22 books (*quateriones*) of *The City of God* should be subdivided into five sections. The first (Books I to V) was explicitly polemical, defending Christianity against the charges related specifically to the sack of Rome. The second (Books VI to X) shifted to an examination of Christian ethics in relation to the classical schools of philosophy. The third (Books XI to XIV) explained the creation of the two cities as it related to philosophy and religion. The fourth (Books XV to XVIII) traced the parallel historical development of the two cities. Finally, the fifth (Books XIX to XXII) envisioned the ends of the two cities, the goal of God's plan, and man's place in history.

The Donatist philosopher Ticonius had earlier distinguished between the cities of God and the Devil, using imagery from the Psalms. Augustine appropriated this distinction, transforming it according to his own philosophical and theological conception. Throughout his later writings he described the secular city, embodied in the City of Babylon and manifest historically in the Assyrian and Roman empires. This he contrasted with the City of God, embodied in Jerusalem and manifest in the Christian community, especially the Catholic Church. Looking specifically at the sack of Rome, Augustine sought to defend Christianity by pointing out that the sack was not the first disaster to assail the city. Indeed, what was unique to this disaster was the willingness of the Goths to spare those Christians and pagans who took refuge in churches. More to the point, however, the city of the Christian is not a physical place in space and time, but the otherworldly city of God. Thus, lamentably, while many may have suffered, if they were true to Christianity their true substance remained unviolated. Pointing to a parallel with the ancient story of the rape of Lucretia, he cited approvingly the statement that only Lucretia's assailant was guilty of adultery.

The fundamental philosophical problem for Augustine was how to account for the apparent dualism between matter and spirit, and to reconcile the presence of evil in the world with the notion that everything derived from a single omnibeneficent creator of the universe. Both problems looked back to his early obsession with Manichaean doctrine. Revealing a great debt to Plato and Platonism, Augustine argued that all reality emanated from God, positing a qualitative hierarchy that stretched from pure reality or absolute order (God) to nothingness or absolute disorder (chaos); from pure spirit to pure matter and inertia. In effect, the world is perfect, but incomplete. Humankind stands midway in this qualitative hierarchy, less real than God, more real than chaos, a mixture of spirit and matter. In this way Augustine accounted for the apparent dualism of spirit and body as a mixture of one substance in varying degrees of creation, thus preserving the notion of one reality created by God.

Accepting the classical philosophical model, Augustine equated the ethical good with the pursuit of happiness, linking this with the exercise of free will. When the ethical model is correlated to Augustine's conception of reality, human beings fall into one of two camps, according to the disposition of their wills. Either they are oriented toward absolute order and by extension God, or they are oriented toward disorder. The former is the basis of an ethical and moral good, the latter, the basis of evil. The community of those oriented toward the good form the City of God, the other the secular city. Here, Augustine argued, was the uniqueness of the Christian message. Classical philosophy and even Platonism had focused on a physical happiness, pointing ultimately toward chaos. Only Christianity (embodied in Christ) seeks true happiness, which is found only in an orientation toward God. Thus in its ultimate sense, the whole problem of the sack of Rome is irrelevant. Such a concern informs a will directed towards illusory happiness and, in reality, evil. The history of the two cities traces in time the unfolding and fulfilment of God's plan in a movement toward absolute order. This, Augustine suggested, is the eighth and final day of God's creative labour. 'On that day we shall rest and see, see and love, love and praise—for this is to be the end without the end of all our living, that Kingdom without end, the real goal of our present life.' Only in this City of God will true happiness be possible.

The City of God stands as Augustine's attempt to defend Christianity. In so doing, he transcends polemics to articulate a comprehensive ethical and metaphysical vision of Christianity that makes it an integral contribution to the western philosophical tradition, inspiring philosophers and theologians from the Middle Ages to the present. If *The Confessions* are perhaps Augustine's literary masterpiece, *The City of God* is his philosophical *magnum opus*.

—Thomas L. Cooksey

CONFESSIONS, BOOK I
Prose by St Augustine, late 4th century.

No ancient book begins in a more disconcerting way for the modern reader than Augustine's *Confessions*. Knowing only that he desires to praise God, and so find rest in him, Augustine begins by raising a series of acute theological problems: should one know God before invoking him; how can God come to a human being; in what sense does God fill somebody or something; who or what, indeed, is God?

As well as a confession of sin and a confession of praise

in the sense of the Psalms (as ever, a strong influence on Augustine's thinking), his work is the dialogue between a highly intelligent and relentlessly inquiring mind and its creator. No sooner has he begun his life story than he raises the vexed question, which he does not resolve even in the more exclusively philosophical later books of the *Confessions*, of whether the soul has an existence before entering the body. A discussion of the nature of time (developed in a later book) arises out of an apparent quibble about where his infancy went when it left him and was replaced by adulthood. It is not surprising that many of his ideas appear modern, for example his observation that an infant, far from being 'innocent' (witness the jealousy of a twin), is resolutely manipulative and intent only on making others conform to its wishes, or his stress on the educational importance of giving free rein to the curiosity of children. These are, however, related to theological concerns such as original sin and the chastisement of God, whose law restrains curiosity, whether in the classroom or in the wider world. The classroom is a microcosm of the world; it is a 'stony path' that adds to 'the toil and sorrow of the sons of Adam'. Augustine takes all his early recollections very seriously, even though he realizes that other adults, and even God himself, might smile indulgently at such foibles.

Augustine's account of the upbringing and education that he received—Book I takes him up to the age of 15—is another major source of the book's appeal, but it must always be borne in mind that the memories of the child are strongly overlaid by the comments of the bishop that Augustine, in the last years of the 4th century, had now become. It is clear that as a child he disliked Homer (too many Greek words to learn), but loved Virgil's *Aeneid*, written as it was in the language that he had learnt instinctively and by imitation from an early age, and was touched by the tragic story of Dido for much the same reasons as its modern readers, although they would express their reasons very differently. He seems, however, to have lived for his games and for playtime, and found the three Rs pure drudgery. His judgements on the fictions of Virgil, or rather his own stupidity in preferring them to subjects of greater utility, are clearly a later construct, as is his unrelenting criticism of the hypocrisy, inertia, and commercialism of the whole system and its inverted values. Teachers beat children for enjoying games, but they have their own adult games to play, and parents side with the tormentors in spite of the fact that they want their children to grow into adults who can win status and prestige by pandering to the universal desire for entertainment. (Augustine does give credit at least to his mother Monica, who was very concerned for his spiritual and physical health, especially on one occasion when he was dangerously ill.) The Latin language is learnt through texts which are not only fictive, but immoral and obscene, and the system produces people who take more pride in following the rules of grammar than in avoiding the spiritual dangers of envy or dishonesty.

Augustine writes as one not immune from such faults himself—indeed he calls himself the lowest of the low and an outstanding liar—but he is not so lost in his sins and the sins of the world that envelop them that he cannot see some good in his upsetting experiences. He says that as well as a dislike of pain and depression he has acquired an aversion to ignorance, a respect for the evidence of his senses, a high regard for friendship and truth, and a good memory and command of words. The style of the *Confessions*, as of his other works, illustrates that these intellectual qualities remained with him. A mind trained to observe and memorize every detail in a classical text was put to fruitful use in building up an astonishingly thorough knowledge of scripture from which he constantly drew new insights by his learned juxtaposition of diverse passages. Notwithstanding his strictures about the uselessness and perversity of the system that had developed them, his verbal skills—especially his expertise in rhetoric, of which he later became a professor—were consciously turned to the new task of articulating theological insight and divine praise. The power of its style contributes to the impact of this book no less than the intensity of its feeling and the profundity of its ideas.

—R.P.H. Green

AURELIUS (Antoninus), Marcus. Born Marcus Annius Verus in Rome, 26 April AD 121. Married Annia Galeria Faustina in 145 (died 176); one daughter and one son. Gained favour of Emperor Hadrian, who made him a Salian priest at age of 8, supervised his education, and arranged his marriage; adopted (as Marcus Aelius Aurelius Verus Caesar) by emperor designate Antoninus Pius in 138: quaestor in 139, consul with Antoninus Pius in 140, and also in 145 and 161; tribunicia potestas and proconsular imperium, the main formal powers of emperorship, conferred on him in 147; abandoned study of rhetoric about this time, and began study of philosophy; succeeded Antoninus Pius as emperor in 161, and elevated his fellow-consul for that year, Lucius Verus, to joint authority with himself (Verus died in 169); negotiated with German tribes in Aquileia, 168; fought the Marcomanni and Quadi, two Danube tribes, 170–74; visited Syria and Egypt to settle revolts, 175–76; raised his son Commodus to rank of Augustus, 177; fought the Marcomanni, 177–78. *Died 17 March AD 180.*

PUBLICATIONS

Works

Meditations, edited by A.S.L. Farquharson. 2 vols., 1944 (includes translation); numerous subsequent translations including by C.R. Haines [Loeb Edition], 1930, G.M.A. Grube and Maxwell Staniforth, 1964, Roy Alan Lawes, 1984.
Letters, edited by L. Pepe. 1957.
The Meditations and a Selection from the Letters of Marcus and Fronto, translated by A.S.L. Farquharson and R.B. Rutherford. 1989.

*

Critical Studies: *Marcus Aurelius: His Life and His World* by A.S.L. Farquharson, edited by D.A. Rees, 1951; *Marcus Aurelius: A Biography* by Anthony Birley, 1966, revised edition, 1987; *The Meditations of Marcus Aurelius: A Study* by R.B. Rutherford, 1989.

* * *

Marcus Aurelius' writings are unusual in the extant literature of the ancient world in being almost wholly personal documents, not intended for publication. He was a prolific letter writer, sometimes dispatching three notes to a friend in a single day, and there are about 200 letters still surviving. Many of these are preserved in the correspondence of Fronto, his tutor, for whom he shows great affection and concern. They date from between 139 and 166, when Fronto died, and shed passing illumination upon Marcus Aurelius' youthful enthusiasms, family concerns, and personal habits.

But his major work is that 'breviary for contemplatives' which we call the *Meditations*, but should more correctly be translated (from the Greek) as *To Himself*. It consists of 12 books of unsystematic private reflections, addressed to himself in the second person like a dialogue, which lends itself to being sipped from time to time rather than drunk off in a draught. Historians concerned with facts are disappointed in their perusal of the *Meditations* since Marcus Aurelius makes little reference, except incidentally, to external events, and the books are consequently hard to date, beyond saying that they were largely written on campaign in the last ten years of his life. The present arrangement of the books is possibly not his own and certainly not chronological, since the first book, a summing up of all he owes to his family, friends, and associates, appears to have been written last. The manner of transmission is also uncertain—whether his notebooks were entrusted to his secretary's care or found among his papers after his death is not known—but there is little trace of organized editing since the work often progresses in a disconnected fashion from one topic to another and is full of repetitions and loose ends.

It is written in Greek, the language of upper-class, educated men. However, Marcus Aurelius abandoned rhetoric early in life, and his style, while being slightly old-fashioned and awkward, is plain and unadorned—an index of its private nature, but also of the character of the writer. He has a talent for epigrammatic brevity, and often resorts to quick enumeration of points as they occur to him, or even preserves straight lists of quotations from his reading of philosophers and poets. He has a quick eye for natural detail, such as the cracks in a loaf of baked bread or the way a sunbeam streams into a dark room, and his writing is full of brief, vivid similes showing an acute observation of the everyday scene like army surgeons' instruments, a fire burning a pile of rubbish, lotions and poultices for the sick, scuffling puppies, or fights in the arena. His comparisons are all drawn from war, dancing, wrestling, eating—the common occupations of life within his personal experience—and he employs certain predictable, recurring images: life as a road, time as a river, reason as a helmsman, the sphere as perfection.

Marcus Aurelius is not notable as an original thinker; he modestly considered scholarship and philosophy far above him. His attitude is mainly Stoic: a belief in calm acceptance of one's lot, a view of the world as a unified organism constantly changing and of the life spirit returning after death to the universal fire. But he read widely among different schools of philosophy and made his own choice influenced by his personal experience, transmuting pure Stoicism into an individual code for living, a code that in many ways prefigures Christianity.

The *Meditations* is a kind of spiritual last will and testament —the thoughts of an ill and ageing man aware of the increasing nearness of death and taking stock of what life has taught him: to accept himself, making a conscious effort to improve his failings, striving to assimilate the bad things that happen to good people as part of a universal plan of nature; to bear pain gracefully in the belief that there is a reason for suffering; to face the world with fortitude and his fellow man with understanding; to see man in his correct perspective in re-

lation to the great universe as a transient piece of nothingness, so as to be able to accept approaching death as a small change and another of the processes of nature which is the universal lot of mankind.

Marcus Aurelius has often been accused of being a moral prig and a humbug, but it is obvious from his writings that he was a genuinely good man of sincere and sensitive character, conscious of his duties as emperor and military leader, who endured many personal griefs and public misfortunes and ended with a realistic, if melancholy, view of life—that one may not be rewarded for service or affection to others, but one does not cease to act according to personal canons of rightness because of this.

—Claire E. Gruzelier

MEDITATIONS
Prose by Marcus Aurelius, c.170.

Although remembered as a virtuous and honourable ruler, Marcus Aurelius is most famous for his *Meditations*, a work his subjects never saw, the intimate notebook in which he recorded his own reflections on human life and the ways of the gods. Internal evidence suggests that he was past his prime when he wrote, and that parts, at least, were composed during his lengthy campaigns against the German tribes. The work seems to have survived almost by accident; it was unknown to the writers of his time and for long afterwards, but seems to have surfaced in the 4th century AD. It was written in Greek, the language of philosophy, and its content is largely philosophic in nature, especially reflections on morality and social virtue.

Although divided by modern editors into 12 'books', the work seems not to have a clear structure (except for 'Book I'); rather, it represents the emperor's notes and self-admonitions as recorded in his leisure moments, perhaps before retiring at night. Brief epigrammatic remarks are juxtaposed with quotations (usually of moral tags) and with more developed arguments on, for example, divine providence, the brevity of human life, the necessity for moral effort, and tolerance of his fellow human beings. Frustratingly for the historian, these *pensées* are almost invariably generalized: we do not learn Marcus Aurelius' secret thoughts about his family, his position, members of the court, or military policy. We do, however, get some idea of his personality and preoccupations, and also of the influence which philosophic doctrine (in his case, the teachings of Stoicism, particularly absorbed through study of the Stoic teacher Epictetus) might have upon an educated and thoughtful Roman statesman.

The first book of the *Meditations* is a different matter, and may have been composed independently. It forms a more coherent whole than the others. Here Marcus Aurelius goes through a list of his closer relatives and several teachers, recording what he owes to each: in some cases a specific lesson, but more often a general moral example. This list culminates in two long passages on what he owes to his predecessor Antoninus Pius, and to the gods. These passages, though often allusive and obscure, give us unique access to the mind of an ancient ruler.

Turning back to the main body of the work, certain recurrent themes stand out: the need to avoid distractions and concentrate on making the correct moral choice; the obligation of individuals to work for the common good (for example, 'What does not benefit the hive does not benefit the bee'); and insistence on the providence of the gods, often combined with vigorous rejection of the alternative view, espoused by the Epicureans, that all is random movement of atoms. Duty and social responsibility are strongly emphasized; and the emperor is also keenly aware of the temptations of power ('it is also possible to live well in a palace'; 'do not be Caesarified'). Thoughts of providence lead him to contemplate the vastness of time and space, and the guiding pattern that according to the Stoics gives order to the universe ('Whatever befalls you was prepared for you beforehand from eternity and the thread of causes was spinning from everlasting both your existence and this which befalls you'). There is also a more melancholy note, of resignation and pessimism, which sometimes seems in conflict with the positive strain of Stoicism. Though determined to persevere in his moral efforts, the author is often resigned to their futility ('Even if you break your heart, none the less they will do just the same'; 'who will change men's convictions?'). Hymns to the grandeur and order of the universe can give way to revulsion and disgust ('As your bath appears to your senses—soap, sweat, dirt, greasy water, all disgusting—so is every piece of life and every object'). Above all, Marcus Aurelius is fascinated by life's transience and the way in which all great men, even philosophers and emperors, pass on and are forgotten. Although it is presumably accidental that this passage ends the *Meditations* as we have them, xii. 36 provides a splendid coda, capturing the near-poetic quality of the emperor's sombre self-reproach:

> Mortal man, you have been a citizen in this great city; what does it matter to you whether for five or fifty years? For what is according to its laws is equal for every man. Why is it hard, then, if Nature who brought you in, and no despot nor unjust judge, sends you out of the city—as though the master of the show, who engaged an actor, were to dismiss him from the stage? 'But I have not spoken my five acts, only three.' 'What you say is true, but in life three acts are the whole play.' For he determines the perfect whole, the cause yesterday of your composition, today of your dissolution; you are the cause of neither. Leave the stage then, and be content, for he who releases you is content.

—R.B. Rutherford

AUSONIUS, Decimus Magnus. Born in Burdigala (now Bordeaux, France) c.AD 310. Educated in Burdigala and Tolosa (now Toulouse). Married Lucana Sabina (died in childbirth); three children. Taught grammar and rhetoric in Burdigala for 30 years; appointed tutor to Gratian, son of the Roman emperor Valentinian I: fought with both against the Alamanni, AD 368–69; on Gratian's accession, made prefect of Gaul and other provinces; consul by 379; retired to his Bordeaux estates after the murder of Gratian in 383. *Died c.AD 395.*

PUBLICATIONS

Collections

[Works], edited by K. Schenkl. 2 vols., 1883, reprinted 1961; also edited by Rudolph S. Peiper, 1886, reprinted 1976, A.

Pastorino, 1971, Sesto Prete, 1978, and R.P.H. Green, 1991; translated by Hugh G. Evelyn White [Loeb Edition], 2 vols., 1919–21.

Verse

Mosella, as *Die Mosella*, edited by Carl Hosius. 1894, 3rd edition, 1926; as *The Mosella*, translated by F.S. Flint, 1915; also translated by E.H. Blakeney, 1933.

*

Critical Studies: *Ausonius* by Evelyn Gurney, 1989; *Ausonius of Bordeaux: Genesis of a Gallic Aristocracy* by Hagith Sivan, 1993.

* * *

Ausonius of Bordeaux, a teacher of the Greek and Latin classics for some 40 years and after Gratian (his most famous pupil) became emperor, a powerful courtier for a further ten, is one of the most versatile and prolific writers of the 4th century AD. In his meticulous knowledge of the Latin classics, or the measured rhetoric of the speech that is his only surviving work in prose, the evidence of the schoolroom is seldom far away. However, his multifarious writings contain much that is refreshingly new. The range is very wide and is informed by a conviction that a wide variety of subjects were worthy of expression in verse. Most striking and appealing is his variety of intimately personal poetry: the poem on the birth of his new child, the *epicedion* (obituary) of his father, the poem of encouragement (*protrepticum*) to his grandson, and the poem about his inherited villa. Ausonius is not a profound thinker, nor does he probe deeply into his own feelings and experiences, least of all his experiences in political life. His 30 or so letters, for example, reveal little of substance. Where we see him faced with a real problem, such as the withdrawal of his favourite pupil Paulinus into monastic life, he adopts a distant style and takes refuge in the opacity of rhetoric, although it is clear that he saw no need to conceal his Christian beliefs. He wrote both Christian and pagan prayers, and unusually for a man of this period seems to have felt no tension between the old and the new.

His superficial experiences, whether as teacher, traveller, or family man, form the core of his poetry. He loves to record, to describe, and to enumerate. There is a poem on the leading cities of the Roman Empire, past and present—'Ordo Urbium Nobilium'; one on the emperors—'Caesares'—perhaps designed to extend into his own times; and there are fragments of one on the Roman consuls—'Fasti'. A painting of Cupid in hell, which he saw in someone's dining room in Trier, was elaborated into the short poem 'Cupido Cruciatus'; his masterpiece on the Moselle was also inspired by a prolonged stay in the area. His *Parentalia* is a series of recollections of departed relatives while his *Professores* commemorates deceased teachers and colleagues from the schools of Bordeaux and nearby towns. He appended to them a series of epitaphs of heroes and heroines from the Trojan War. Some of his more humble topics seem to derive if not from schoolroom diversions then from a schoolmaster's idea of fun. In the *Technopaegnion* all the lines end with a different monosyllable; the *Ludus Septem Sapientium* is a playlet in Plauto–Terentian form about the sayings of the Seven Sages; and the *Nuptial Cento* describes a wedding and the wedding-night by means of assorted lines and half-lines filched from

Virgil. Ausonius is one of few poets to put mathematics into verse, and his miscellany of *Eclogues* is based to a large extent on pseudo-scientific material.

A lifelong student of the classics, Ausonius is adept at imitating and representing their forms and styles, and does so with taste and discrimination. After his *Epigrams*, perhaps his earliest work, and based on Greek models more than Roman ones, he tends to go his own way, weaving into his various poems passages in the style of epic, lyric, didactic, or satirical poetry, but seldom descending to pastiche. Particularly distinctive are his versified letters; part of a real correspondence, or two sequences in polymetric format, the *Daily Round*, an account of a typical day in his life, and *Bissula*, on a captive German girl who enthralled him. Both of these, though sadly curtailed in transmission, offer a succession of lively tableaux in changing metres. Even without them he would be one of ancient Rome's most metrically creative craftsmen.

Ausonius was a small-scale poet, with an outlook of limited depth, but one whose novelty of theme and originality of treatment combine to create a collection of surprises. His favoured register, certainly a constantly recurrent one, is a *humilitas* of style and tone which he sometimes exploits as a foil to his actual achievement but which is no doubt the way in which, for all his eminence, he wanted to be remembered. Nowhere is this clearer than in his preface to the general reader, a typical mix of modesty and pride. Just as the image of devoted family man and teacher, content with what he portrays as an average portion of worldly goods, makes a striking contrast with the external grandeur of his public career, so the unassuming tenor of much of Ausonius' verse is in marked antithesis to the love of the formal and spectacular which dominated the taste of his age.

—R.P.H. Green

THE MOSELLA
Poem by Ausonius, written c. AD 371.

River poems are not unusual in modern European literature, but Ausonius' poem in praise of the Moselle is a unique example of the genre from antiquity. It is also unsurpassed in any genre for its elaborate attention to visual detail. There is a series of intensely realized descriptions—of waving grasses on the river bed, of the dark spots on a trout's back, of the lengthening reflections of green foliage in the river at dusk—punctuated with a remarkably fresh set of similes in which, for example, he likens the reactions of sailors as they gaze into the clear water to a young girl's first experience of a mirror, or the struggles of an expiring fish to a pair of bellows hard at work. Similes are a traditional part of epic, but with his gift being for description rather than narrative, Ausonius seems to draw more from the didactic tradition than the epic. The main classical influences on this original poem are Virgil's *Georgics* and Statius' *Silvae*, with which the poem conducts a complex dialogue.

The presentation of the theme is systematic rather than impressionistic, but the snapshots, as they have been called, are not organized spatially, as a guided tour of the river, or chronologically, as the ordered experiences of a single day. If anything, the principle of organization is rhetorical, as the description moves upwards from the river bed to the overhanging crags and houses. In structuring his introduction as a journey from the Rhine frontier to Neumagen (on the Moselle, a little below Trier) Ausonius prepares a series of contrasts which are fully realized as he and his readers burst out of the wooded wastes east of the river into the dazzling air of the Moseltal. The river is as clear as the air is pure, and within it, upon it, and on its banks are life, peace, and beauty. The area is benign to its inhabitants, and the river convenient to its various users.

The first description is of the river's limpid depths; the second a portrayal of no fewer than 15 species of fish with an accuracy that suggests a close experience beyond the gastronomic. This *tour de force*, although obviously based on a common theme of mosaic pavements, excited the incredulous admiration of at least one contemporary. From a new vantage point, the river's gorge is compared to a theatre, though the only noise to disturb the almost pastoral stillness is the crude catcalling of a wayfarer. In a rare piece of mythological fantasy the poet pretends that in the heat of midday, an intrusive touch of the traditional Italian environment of Latin poetry, such pleasances are exploited by satyrs and naiads. Later, by contrast, the appearance of the river at twilight is rendered in exquisite chiaroscuro. At other times there is great bustle, much of it concerned with fishing. One of the poem's most elaborate vignettes presents a young angler who jumps in after an escaping fish and gets the soaking that he deserves. The final scene offers a composite view of the river snaking between banks crowned with villas of various shapes and sizes, likened with characteristic hyperbole to some of the seven wonders of the world.

By conscious choice little is said of the inhabitants. Although Ausonius claims in part of his long conclusion that he will one day write a poem to give them their due, this is just polite convention. Such individuals as do enter his verses are conspicuously placed in rather demeaning contrast to the world they invade. Particularly noteworthy, given the political conditions of the late Roman Empire and the importance of panegyric, is the scarcity of allusion to the emperor or the royal house, especially as they were his employers and had been responsible for bringing Ausonius to the region. Strangely but symptomatically, the Roman capital city of Trier, the centre of the area and the support of its prosperity, is never named and barely referred to. Apart from a reference to an important recent victory over a German tribe in AD 368 (the poem was written in about AD 371), there is little recognition of the imperial peace and those who preserved it by force of arms. All this serves a clear purpose, one of privileging the world of nature—a nature organized into neat fields and vineyards—and belittling the activities of man. When Ausonius breaks off his enthusiastic description of individual scenes, he appeals to the tributaries of the Moselle to add their own tribute of praise; and when, at the end, he considers what the reception of his poem will be, he thinks of the fellow rivers of Gaul rather than human readers. This world, 'where every prospect pleases, and only man is vile', does not issue from a political stance. Ausonius was not a 'green' *avant la lettre*, let alone a misanthrope or anti-imperialist, and goes beyond the limits of traditional rhetoric. The poem is in all probability an essentially personal construct and, like most of his work, directly founded upon personal experience.

—R.P.H. Green

AYALA, Ramón Pérez de. See **PÉREZ DE AYALA, Ramón.**

AYMÉ, Marcel. Born in Joigny, France, 29 March 1902. Educated at school in Dôle, 1910–19; Lycée Besançon, baccalauréat, 1919. Married Marie-Antoinette Arnaud in 1927. Served in the French army, 1922–23. Lived in Germany, 1921–22; worked at a variety of jobs including reporter, clerk, translator, and film extra in Paris; wrote for various pro-German reviews during the Occupation, including *La Nouvelle Revue française*; visited the USA; contributed to *Collier's* magazine, New York, 1950. Recipient: Prix de la Société des Gens de Lettres, 1926; Théophraste Renaudot prize, 1933. *Died 14 October 1967.*

PUBLICATIONS

Collections

Oeuvres romanesques. 6 vols., 1977.
Oeuvres romanesques complètes, edited by Yves-Alain Favre. 1989.
[Novels and Stories]. 1991–.

Fiction

Brûlebois. 1926.
Aller retour. 1927.
Les Jumeaux du diable. 1928.
La Table-aux-crevés. 1929; as *The Hollow Field*, translated by Helen Waddell, 1933.
La Rue sans nom. 1930.
Le Vaurien. 1931.
Le Puits aux images (stories). 1932.
La Jument verte. 1933; as *The Green Mare*, translated by Norman Denny, 1955.
Les Contes du chat perché (stories; for children). 1934; as *The Wonderful Farm*, translated by Norman Denny, 1951.
Le Nain (stories). 1934.
Maison basse. 1935; as *The House of Men*, translated by Norman Denny, 1952.
Le Moulin de la Sourdine. 1936; as *The Secret Stream*, translated by Norman Denny, 1953.
Gustalin. 1937.
Derrière chez Martin (stories). 1938.
Le Boeuf clandestin. 1939.
La Belle Image. 1941; as *The Second Face*, translated by Norman Denny, 1951; as *The Grand Seduction*, translated by Denny, 1958.
Travelingue. 1941; as *The Miraculous Barber*, translated by Eric Sutton, 1950.
La Vouivre. 1943; as *The Fable and the Flesh*, translated by Eric Sutton, 1949.
Le Passe-muraille (stories). 1943; as *Across Paris and Other Stories*, translated by Norman Denny, 1950; as *The Walker-Through-Walls and Other Stories*, translated by Denny, 1950.
Traversée de Paris (stories). 1945.
Le Chemin des écoliers. 1946; as *The Transient Hour*, translated by Eric Sutton, 1948.
Le Vin de Paris (stories). 1947.
Uranus. 1948; as *The Barkeep of Blémont*, translated by Norman Denny, 1950; as *Fanfare in Blémont*, translated by Denny, 1950.
En arrière (stories). 1950.
Autres contes du chat perché (stories). 1950; as *Return to the Wonderful Farm*, translated by Norman Denny, 1954; as *The Magic Pictures: More About the Wonderful Farm*, translated by Denny, 1954.

Derniers contes du chat perché (stories). 1958.
Sorties de la ville et des champs. 1958.
Les Tiroirs de l'inconnu. 1960; as *The Conscience of Love*, translated by Norman Denny, 1962.
The Proverb and Other Stories, translated by Norman Denny. 1961.
Enjambées (stories). 1967.
L'Étrange, le merveilleux et le fantastique. 2 vols., 1983–84.
La Fille du shérif (stories), edited by Michel Lecureur. 1987.

Plays

Les Grandes Étapes, L'Image (produced 1933).
Vogue la galère (produced 1948). 1944.
Lucienne et le boucher. 1947.
Clérambard (produced 1950). 1950; as *Clérambard*, translated by Norman Denny, 1952.
La Tête des autres (produced 1952). 1952.
Les Quatre Vérités (produced 1954). 1954.
Les Sorcières de Salem, from a play by Arthur Miller. 1955.
Les Oiseaux de lune (produced 1955). 1956; as *Moonbirds*, translated by John Pauker, 1959.
La Mouche bleue (produced 1957). 1957.
Vu du pont, from a play by Arthur Miller. 1958.
Louisiane (produced 1961). 1961.
La Nuit de l'iguane, from a play by Tennessee Williams. 1962.
Les Maxibules (produced 1961). 1962.
Le Minotaure (produced 1966). With *Consommation* and *La Convention Belzébir*, 1967.
La Convention Belzébir (produced 1966). With *Le Minotaure* and *Consommation*, 1967.

Screenplays: *Le Club des soupirants*, 1936; *Madame et le mort* (adaptation by Aymé), 1942; *Désert vivant*, with others, 1954; *Papa, maman, la bonne et moi*, with others, 1954; *Papa, maman, ma femme et moi*, with others, 1955.

Other

Silhouette du scandale (essay). 1938.
Le Trou de la serrure (essays). 1946.
Le Confort intellectuel (essays). 1949.
Attente, Almanach du théâtre et du cinéma (autobiography). 1949.
Paris que j'aime, with Antoine Blondin, and Jean-Paul Clébert. 1956; as *The Paris I Love*, translated by Jean-Paul Clébert, 1963.
Images de l'amour. 1957.
L'Épuration et le délit d'opinion. 1968.
Marcel Aymé journaliste (articles), edited by M. Lecureur and Y.-A. Favre. 1988.
Du côté de chez Marianne: Chroniques 1933–1937, edited by Michel Lecureur. 1989.

*

Critical Studies: *Marcel Aymé; ou, Le Paysan de Paris* by Jean Cathelin, 1958; *Marcel Aymé insolite* by Georges Robert and André Lioret, 1958; *Introduction à Aymé* by Pol Vandromme, 1960; *The Comic World of Marcel Aymé* by Dorothy Brodin, 1964; *Marcel Aymé et le merveilleux* by Jean-Louis Dumont, 1970; *The Short Stories of Marcel Aymé*, 1980, and *Marcel Aymé*, 1987, both by Graham Lord; *Écriture et dérision: Le Comique dans l'oeuvre littéraire de Marcel Aymé* by Claude Dufresnoy, 1982; *L'Oeuvre de*

Marcel Aymé, de la quête du père au triomphe de l'écrivain by Jean-Claude Veniel, 1990.

* * *

Marcel Aymé was born in 1902, in Joigny in the remote Jura region of France, the youngest of six children. Aymé's mother died when he was only two years old. His father placed the oldest children in boarding school and sent Marcel and his sister Suzanne to live with their maternal grandparents in the village of Villers-Robert near Dôle. He stayed there for six years and was then taken in by an aunt in Dôle. In later years he was always reluctant to talk much about his youth and childhood, but his philosophical attitudes in life (mainly characterized by sympathy for the underdog and a thirst for the truth underlying outward appearances) were shaped and formed during these early years. This experience of living in small towns and remote villages in close proximity to craftsmen and peasants would later have a strong influence on his work. What the sociologists call today 'la France profonde' (the daily routine and belief system of provincial France which changes little over the decades as opposed to the instability and glitter of the Parisian spectacle), would become the stuff of much of his best work.

His first novel, *Brûlebois*, was followed by *La Table-aux-crevés* (*The Hollow Field*) and *La Jument verte* (*The Green Mare*). The action of each of these novels, set in his native Franche-Comté, portrays simple peasants and townspeople, republicans and clerics, humans and animals to convey his bittersweet view of life. These books use local linguistic terms and exploit regional folklore, including the marvellous and fantastic, to put across Aymé's essentially moderate conservative, commonsense view of life. *La Vouivre* (*The Fable and the Flesh*) is perhaps his best novel in this mode.

Aymé excelled in a number of different genres. Between 1926 and 1967, he wrote numerous novels and plays, three polemical essays and 83 short stories. He was also very active as a journalist throughout his career. Until 1944, the novel and short story were his preferred means of expression. But with the play *Vogue la galère*, written in the mid-1930s and published in 1944, his theatre career began. Astonishingly, Aymé never repeated himself. All of his works, especially the novels and plays, are quite different from each other.

In his novels, which dealt at first with rural people and then later with urban proletarians and sensitive political questions involving the politically potent Parisian bourgeoisie, Aymé sought to unmask hypocrisy, scandal, and the suppression of the truth. But when his novels showed how the Left could be as hypocritical as the Right, he began to find himself in trouble. His three novels of the 1930s and 1940s are unique in French literature and offer a revealing glimpse of what France was really like at this time. *Travelingue* (*The Miraculous Barber*), dealing with the era of the Popular Front, *Le Chemin des écoliers* (*The Transient Hour*), chronicling the early years of the Occupation, and *Uranus* (*The Barkeep of Blémont*), covering the end of the Occupation and Liberation, offer a view of these periods that is rich in complexity. Aymé's vision is a far cry from the simple-minded version presented in the press or, for that matter, by many academics. In the first of the three works Aymé sympathizes with the Left, but since he also applies the same moral

yardstick in *The Barkeep of Blémont*, where he shows how the Communists and their Resistance friends simply replaced the Gestapo and the Wehrmacht after they came to power in 1944, he incurred the wrath of the politically powerful (*The Barkeep of Blémont* later became an internationally acclaimed film directed by Claude Béri in 1991). His essay *Silhouette du scandale*, published just before the war and generally overlooked at the time, can be read as an introduction to these novels. It lays bare the hypocrisy of successive governments of both Left and Right for the first 40 years of the century and is a masterpiece of understatement.

Since Aymé wrote and published in collaborationist newspapers during the war, the Comité National des Écrivains, largely dominated by Communists, resolved to settle accounts with him. Although he was not imprisoned, he was blacklisted. His fidelity to friends and personal courage were remarkable. He stood up for his friend Louis-Ferdinand Céline, as well as for the collaborationist writer Robert Brasillach, who was executed in February 1945 for having had incorrect political opinions during the war. Two years later, when Brasillach's brother-in-law, Maurice Bardèche, was censured for questioning the legality and fairness of the Nuremberg trials (*Nuremberg; ou, La Terre promise*, 1947), Aymé continued to support the principle that no writer should be punished for merely expressing an opinion. His voice was a lonely and courageous one at the time and, with the passage of time, we must admit largely a correct one. Aymé's courage in speaking out about the hypocrisy of the Left branded him as a voice of the Right. The tag has stuck with him ever since.

Aymé was unusually productive and successful as a short story writer. His 83 stories were published in seven main collections between 1932 and 1958, and he is widely recognized as one of the most important and versatile French short story writer of the 20th century. Like the novels, the stories treat rural and urban characters as well as the hypocrisy of the ruling classes. The style and tone of these pieces also vary widely, and include the use of dialectic terms and slang. Most successful of all are his children's stories built around the interaction of two little girls, Delphine and Marinette, with various representatives of the animal world.

After the war, a trip to the USA sponsored by *Collier's* magazine resulted in several stories that have never been studied seriously, but which reflect his reactions to American life and what Aymé took to be its materialism and hypocrisy ('Le Mendiant', 'Louisiane', 'La Mouche bleue').

The first volume of the critical edition of Aymé's novels and stories appeared in the prestigious Éditions de la Pléiade in 1991. Three more are in preparation at time of writing. Inclusion in the Pléiade series is the highest practical form of recognition that a writer can receive in France. Serious research on his work will be possible in the years ahead. Certain stories, like 'Le Nouveau Passe-Muraille' and the war-time trilogy, are truly masterpieces. He is one of the outstanding French fiction writers of the 20th century.

—David O'Connell

B

BABEL, Isaak (Emmanuilovich). Born in Odessa, Ukraine, 13 July 1894. Educated in Nikolaev; Nicholas I Commercial School, Odessa, 1905–11; Institute of Financial and Business Studies, Kiev, later in Saratov, 1911–15, graduated 1915. Served in the army, 1917–18. Married Evgeniia Gronfein in 1919, one daughter; also one daughter by Antonina Pirozhkova. In St Petersburg from 1918: worked on Gor'kii's, *q.v.*, magazine *Novaya Zhizn'* [New Life], 1918; editor, Ukrainian State Publishing House, 1919–20; news service correspondent with First Cavalry on the Polish campaign, 1920, and correspondent for *Tiflis* newspaper in Caucasus; in Moscow from 1923; secretary of the village soviet at Molodenovo, 1930; out of favour in the 1930s, and arrested, 1939; manuscripts confiscated, 1939. His exact fate remains unknown; probably shot soon after arrest. Posthumously cleared of charges against him, 1956. *Died (allegedly) 17 March 1941.*

PUBLICATIONS

Collections

Collected Stories, edited and translated by Walter Morison. 1955.
Izbrannoe [Selected Works]. 1957; another edition, 1966.
Detstvo i drugie rasskazy [Childhood and Other Stories], edited by Efraim Sicher. 1979.
Izbrannye proizvedeniia [Selected Works]. 2 vols., 1988.
Sochineniia [Works], edited by A.N. Pirozhkova. 2 vols., 1990.

Fiction

Rasskazy [Stories]. 1925.
Konarmiia (stories). 1926; revised edition, 1931; edited by C.D. Luck, 1994; as *Red Cavalry*, translated by N. Helstein, 1929; also translated by John Harland, 1929.
Bluzhdaiushchie zvezdy: Rasskaz dlia kino [Wandering Stars: A Cine-Story]. 1926.
Istoriia moei golubiatni [The Story of My Dovecote]. 1926.
Benia Krik: Kinopovest. 1926; as *Benia Krik: A Film-Novel*, translated by Ivor Montague and S. S. Nolbandov, 1935.
Korol' [The King]. 1926.
Odesskie rasskazy [Odessa Stories]. 1931.
Benya Krik, The Gangster, and Other Stories, edited by Avrahm Yarmolinsky. 1948.
Lyubka the Cossack and Other Stories, edited and translated by Andrew R. MacAndrew. 1963.
The Lonely Years 1925–29: Unpublished Stories and Private Correspondence, edited by Nathalie Babel, translated by Max Hayward and Andrew R. MacAndrew. 1964.
You Must Know Everything: Stories 1915–1937, edited by Nathalie Babel, translated by Max Hayward. 1969.
The Forgotten Prose, edited and translated by Nicholas Stroud. 1978; as *Zabytyi Babel*, 1979.

Plays

Zakat (produced 1927). 1928; as *Sunset*, translated by Raymond Rosenthal and Mirra Ginsburg, in *Noonday 3*, 1960.
Mariia (produced 1964). 1935; as *Marya*, translated by Michael Glenny and Harold Shukman, in *Three Soviet Plays*, edited by Glenny, 1966.

*

Critical Studies: *The Art of Isaac Babel* by Patricia Carden, 1972; *Isaak Babel* by Richard W. Hallett, 1972; *Isaac Babel, Russian Master of the Short Story* by James E. Falen, 1974; *An Investigation of Composition and Theme in Babel's Literary Cycle 'Konarmija'* by Ragna Grøngaard, 1979; *Isaac Babel's Red Cavalry* by Carol Luplow, 1982; *Metaphor in Babel's Short Stories* by Danuta Mendelsohn, 1982; 'Art as Metaphor, Epiphany, and Aesthetic Statement: The Short Stories of Babel', in *Modern Language Review*, 1982, 'The Road to a Red Cavalry: Myth and Mythology in the Works of Babel', in *Slavonic and East European Review*, 1982, and *Style and Structure in the Prose of Isaak Babel*, 1986, all by Efraim Sicher; *The Place of Space in Narration: A Semiotic Approach to the Problem of Literary Space, with an Analysis of the Role of Space in Isaak Babel's Konarmija* by J.J. von Baak, 1983; *Isaac Babel* by Milton Ehre, 1986; *Isaac Babel* edited by Harold Bloom, 1987; *The Field of Honour* by C.D. Luck, 1987; *Procedures of Montage in Isaak Babel's Red Cavalry* by Marc Schreurs, 1989; *Isaak Babel and His Film Work* by Jerry Heil, 1990; 'A Poetic Inversion: The Non-Dialogic Aspect in Isaac Babel's *Red Cavalry*' by David K. Danow, in *Modern Language Review*, 86(4), 1991.

* * *

Isaak Babel is, along with Zamiatin and Olesha, an outstanding exponent of short prose of the decade or so in which, following 1917, modernist experimentation flourished in Soviet Russian fiction.

Babel's work is notable for its treatment of Jewish and revolutionary themes and for its cultivation of the 'cycle' form: an open-ended series of short stories, linked by theme, character, setting, and imagery, with additions being made at will—e.g., that of 'Argamak' (1931) to *Konarmiia* (*Red Cavalry*), 1926, with 'The Kiss' (1937) and further (unwritten) stories possibly being intended for the same sequence.

Red Cavalry, Babel's best known work, deals by unusual techniques of snapshot and montage (Babel enjoyed close associations with the film industry) with the fortunes of Budenny's First Cavalry in the Polish campaign of 1920. A series of 35 'miniatures' examines the nature and ethics of personal and revolutionary violence, portraying a Jewish intellectual's quest for true fraternity amid Cossack fellow soldiers and assorted Jews, Poles, and peasants. Violence, sex, art, and nature are treated in rhythmic prose and striking images. Ambiguity, paradox and polarity, and the use of subsidiary narrators are key devices. Actions and perceptions are presented subjectively in an interplay of varied points of view underlined by use of metaphor; interpretations and judgements are left to the reader.

Other, less complete, main cycles ('definitively' ordered by Sicher in his 1979 edition) are set in the Jewish 'Moldavanka' of Odessa. *Odesskie rasskazy* [Odessa Stories] features the exploits of Benia Krik (modelled on the real Mishka-Iaponchik), while the 'early childhood' series, collected under the title *Istoriia moei golubiatni* [The Story of My Dovecote], concentrate on Jewish upbringing amid the pogroms of 1905.

The degree of overall unity varies, as much for biographical as for artistic reasons. *Red Cavalry*, with its clear time span and largely sequential plot development, can be viewed as an episodic modernist novel (Mendelson, 1982) or as 'a 20th-century version of a Renaissance novella cycle' (Lowe, 1982). Important 'independent' stories are 'Line and Colour' (1923) and 'Guy de Maupassant' (1932). However, the all-pervading presence of a purportedly autobiographical or obviously Babelian narrator suggests the possibility of considering Babel's short fictional *oeuvre* as a unit—a single collective 'super-cycle'.

Compression, to achieve a close organic unity of form and content, is the essence of Babel's compositional method. Plays and film scenarios apart, few of Babel's stories exceed ten pages. 'A truly cautious master' (Mendelson), Babel re-worked his stories tirelessly, pruning every spare word, tightening paragraphing and punctuation. The resulting language is frequently called 'a collision of styles'; words and their associations are foregrounded rather than the ideas behind them, while Babel's constant switches in modes of narrative discourse create a calculated role for the reader.

Babel was again neglected in the Soviet Union during the Brezhnev period, no edition of his works appearing after 1966. However, recent western studies (notably by Mendelson and Sicher) have advanced Babel criticism onto promising new ground, while the Gorbachev era supplied a two-volume 'Selected Works' in 1988.

—Neil Cornwell

RED CAVALRY (Konarmiia)
Story cycle by Isaak Babel, 1926.

In the acute clarity of its descriptive detail and in its psychological realism, Babel's story cycle *Red Cavalry* bears many similarities to other works by Soviet writers about the Russian Civil War of 1918–21, including Dmitri Furmanov's *Chapaev*, Aleksandr Fadeev's *Razgrom* (The Rout), and the short stories of Vsevolod Ivanov. Its experimentalism is in some ways related to that of the Serapionovii brat'ia (Serapion Brothers) and its pictorial vividness has a counterpart in Sholokhov's *Quiet Flows the Don* (*Tikhii Don*). The principal differences between Babel's cycle and those other novels is that Babel's work is that of a Russian-Jewish writer, not a Russian one.

Red Cavalry marks the pinnacle of Babel's literary achievement—it is the work that demonstrates the duality of his nature most forcefully and vividly, and in it his personality splits in two. Without it being immediately obvious, the stories have two narrators: one is the Jewish war correspondent, Kirill Vasil'ievich Liutov, bespectacled, bookish, and sensitive, and the other is the person whom Liutov would like

to become, and constantly strives to be—a true revolutionary and Bolshevik soldier with no fear of blood and killing. This dichotomy accounts for the extreme physical violence that is manifested in many of the stories; it is as though Babel were trying to overcome his own horror at what he has seen and witnessed, and to turn it into a kind of violent, surreal poetry. At the opposite end of the spectrum is the character of the Jew Gedali, who believes in 'the International of good men' and with whom Liutov vainly remonstrates, more than half-convinced that the old man is right:

'. . . The International, *panie* comrade, one does not know what to eat it with . . .'
'One eats it with gunpowder', I replied to the old man.
'And seasons it with the finest blood . . .'

The conflict is also sharply delineated in the character of the Red army soldier Bratslavskii, the son of the Zhitomir Rebbe Motale Bratslavskii, in the story 'The Rebbe's Son'. The chaos of Bratslavskii's life as he dies of typhoid on the floor of the train is reflected in the contents of his trunk:

Here everything had been dumped together—the warrants of the agitator and the commemorative booklets of the Jewish poet. Portraits of Lenin and Maimonides lay side by side. Lenin's nodulous skull and the tarnished silk of the portraits of Maimonides. A strand of female hair had been placed in a book of the resolutions of the Sixth Party Congress, and in the margins of communist leaflets swarmed crooked lines of Ancient Hebrew verse. In a sad and meagre rain they fell on me—pages of the Song of Songs, and revolver cartridges.

Bratslavskii is in a sense Liutov's double, manifesting in an extreme form the latter's uncertainty about his personal, social, and historical identity. To the theme, common enough in 'revolutionary' literature, of the wavering intellectual, detached from the 'masses', Babel adds the new theme of the intellectual Jew, unable to reconcile himself to the brutality and slaughter involved in the creation of the 'radiant future'. The story 'My First Goose' is the most famous example of this dilemma, with its attendant sense of helplessness and despair, in Babel's writings. But there are others, such as the scene depicted in 'Beresteczko', of a group of Bolshevik-led Cossacks executing an aged Jew:

Directly under my window several Cossacks were shooting an old Jew with a silvery beard for espionage. The old man was screaming and trying to tear himself free. Then Kudria from the machine-gun detachment took the old man's head and put it under his arm. The Jew calmed down and stood with his legs apart. With his right hand Kudrya pulled out his dagger and carefully cut the old man's throat, without splashing any blood on himself. Then he knocked on the closed-up window-frame.
'If anyone's interested,' he said, 'they can come and get him. He's all yours . . .'

These scenes, with their intense concrete and sensuous actuality, suggest nothing so much as scenes from a motion picture, and indeed this cinematic aspect of Babel's story-telling art is strongly pronounced in the cycle. It is as though Babel conveys Liutov's fear and squeamishness to the reader by putting him in Liutov's place, by making him see things through Liutov's eyes. From the depiction of the ravaged beehives of Volhynia ('The Way to Brody'), of Dolgushov's slow and agonizing death, his stomach torn out and exposed ('The Death of Dolgushov'), and of Matvei Pavlichenko's sadistic murder of his 'master' ('The Life-Story of Pavlichenko, Matvei Rodionych'), to the unnervingly lifelike descriptions of fighting (in 'Chesniki' and 'After the Battle'), Babel seems intent on making us *see*—and this is reinforced by his use of colour imagery, which recurs throughout the stories. Seldom, however, does the author attempt to interpose himself between the reader and the events described. Indeed, the suspension of moral judgement is perhaps the feature of the cycle that a new reader will find most shocking and disturbing; for it is as if the author were reliving an experience in which no morality exists, and in which human life is no longer of any more account than the life of an animal.

—David McDuff

BACHMANN, Ingeborg. Born in Klagenfurt, Austria, 25 June 1926. Spent her childhood in Carinthia. Educated at coeducational high school until 1938, girls' school, 1938–44; studied philosophy at Graz, Innsbruck, and Vienna universities, Ph.D. in philosophy 1950. Lived with the composer, Hans Werner Henze, 1953–56; the writer, Max Frisch, *q.v.*, 1958–62. Script writer and editor, Rot-Weiss-Rot radio station, Vienna, 1951–53; freelance writer in Ischia, Naples, Rome, and Munich, 1953–57, visited the United States in 1955; lived in Rome and Zurich, 1958–62, West Berlin, 1963–65, Rome, from 1965; visiting lecturer on poetics, Frankfurt University, 1959–60. Recipient: Gruppe 47 prize, 1953; Culture Circle of German Industry literature award, 1955; Bremen prize, 1957; Association of German Critics literary award, 1961; Büchner prize, 1964; Great Austrian State prize, 1968; Wildgans prize, 1971. *Died 17 October 1973.*

PUBLICATIONS

Collections

Werke, edited by Christine Koschel, Inge von Weidenbaum, and Clemens Münster. 4 vols., 1978.
Sämtliche Erzählungen. 1980.
Sämtliche Gedichte. 1983.
In the Storm of Roses: Selected Poems, edited and translated by Mark Anderson. 1986.

Verse

Die gestundete Zeit. 1953.
Anrufung des grossen Bären. 1956.
Gedichte: Eine Auswahl. 1966.
Die Gedichte. 1980.

Fiction

Das dreissigste Jahr (stories). 1961; revised edition 1966; as *The Thirtieth Year*, translated by Michael Bullock, 1964.
Malina. 1971; as *Malina*, translated by Philip Boehm, 1989.
Simultan (stories). 1972; as *Three Paths to the Lake*, translated by Mary Fran Gilbert, 1972.
Undine geht: Erzählungen. 1973; as 'Undine Departs', translated by Cedric Hentschel, in *German Short Stories*, 1975.
Meistererzählungen. 1974.
Der Tag des Friedens. 1976.

Der Fall Franza. Requiem für Fanny Goldmann. 1979.
Die Fähre. 1982.

Plays

Der Idiot, music by Hans Werner Henze (produced 1952). 1955.
Der gute Gott von Manhattan. 1958.
Der Prinz von Homburg (opera libretto), music by Hans Werner Henze, from the play by Heinrich von Kleist (produced 1960). 1960.
Der junge Lord (opera libretto), music by Hans Werner Henze (produced 1965). 1965; as *The Young Milord*, translated by Eugene Walter, 1967.
Die Hörspiele (radio plays; includes *Ein Geschäft mit Träumen*; *Die Zikaden*; *Der gute Gott von Manhattan*). 1976.

Radio Plays: *Ein Geschäft mit Träumen*, 1952; *Das Herrschaftshaus*, 1952; *Herrenhaus*, 1954; *Die Zikaden*, 1955; *Der gute Gott von Manhattan*, 1958.

Other

Jugend in einer österreichischen Stadt (memoir). 1961.
Gedichte, Erzählungen, Hörspiele, Essays. 1964.
Ein Ort für Zufälle. 1965.
Frankfurter Vorlesungen: Probleme zeitgenössischer Dichtung. 1980.
Die Wahrheit ist dem Menschen zumutbar: Essays, Reden, kleinere Schriften. 1981.
Das Honditschkreuz. 1983.
Wir müssen wahre Sätze finden: Gespräche und Interviews, edited by Christine Koschel and Inge von Weidenbaum. 1983.
Liebe: Dunkler Erdteil. Gedichte aus den Jahren 1942–1967. 1984.
Anrufung der grossen Dichterin (essays). 1984.

Translator, *Gedichte: italienisch und deutsch*, by Giuseppe Ungaretti. 1961.
Translator, with others, *Italienische Lyrik des 20. Jahrhunderts*, edited by Christine Wolter. 1971.
Translator, with others, *Freude der Schiffbrüche*, edited by Christine Wolter. 1977.

*

Bibliography: *Ingeborg Bachmann: Eine Bibliographie* by Otto Bareiss and Frauke Ohloff, 1978.

Critical Studies: *Ingeborg Bachmann: Die Auflösung der Figur in ihrem Roman Malina* by Ellen Summerfield, 1976; *Malina. Versuch einer Interpretation des Romans von Ingeborg Bachmann* by Robert Steiger, 1978; *Women Writers —The Divided Self: Analysis of Novels by Christa Wolf, Ingeborg Bachmann, Doris Lessing and Others* by Inta Ezergailis, 1982; *Der dunkle Schatten, dem ich schon seit Anfang folge. Ingeborg Bachmann. Vorschläge zu einer neuen Lektüre des Werks* edited by Hans Höller, 1982; *Ingeborg Bachmann* by Kurt Bartsch, 1988; *Ingeborg Bachmann* by Peter Beicken, 1988; *The Voice of History: An Exegesis of Selected Short Stories from Ingeborg Bachmann's Das dreissigste Jahr and Simultan from the Perspective of Austrian History* by Lisa de Serbine Bahrway, 1989.

* * *

Ingeborg Bachmann first made her name as a poet with the collections *Die gestundete Zeit* [The Respite] and *Anrufung des grossen Bären* [Invocation of the Great Bear]. Her poems reveal discontent with present time and a utopian vision of a different world, often conveyed through metaphor or paradox; an awareness of the limitations imposed by language; and a sense of the precariousness of human existence, reflecting the influence of existentialism on her writing in the 1950s, as in the poem 'The Respite':

> Do not look round
> Tie your shoelace
> Drive back the dogs.
> Throw the fishes into the sea.
> Put out the lupins!
> A harder time is coming.
> (translated by Michael Hamburger)

In later years, Bachmann expounded her ideas mainly in prose fiction. Important themes are individual identity, possibilities for change, and the role of language. In the title story of the collection *Das dreissigste Jahr* (The Thirtieth Year), a man, in the year preceding his 30th birthday, decides it is time for a new departure. He relinquishes his home and his job and sets out to see the world and to find himself, realizing that this may be his last chance to make substantial changes to the pattern of his life. Eventually he returns, having realized, in Bachmann's famous formulation, that there can be 'no new world without a new language'. The insight that substantive change is not possible, together with a near escape from death, results in increased awareness of his own existence and in acceptance of life as it is. Reluctance to admit human imperfection, and the final acknowledgement of it, is also a theme of the story 'Everything'. A father attempts to prevent his son from acquiring a corrupt colloquial language, on the assumption that if the child developed his own language instead he would retain his original purity, innocence, and natural creativity. However, far from being innocent, his son contains the seeds of moral rottenness, as is conveyed metaphorically by his death caused by a brain tumour.

In most of these early stories the narrative centres on a male character, but there are two significant exceptions which address themselves specifically to women's predicament. 'Undine geht' ('Undine Departs') reworks the myth of the water spirit Undine, who was permitted to join her male lover on land only if she accepted great physical suffering. Bachmann treats Undine's torment as a metaphor for women's suffering at the hands of men. In 'A Step Towards Gomorrah', the problem of women's relations with men is made more explicit, when Charlotte, an artist, is presented with the possibility of experiencing new and different types of relationships. When a younger woman, Mara, attempts to lure her into a sexual relationship, Charlotte momentarily glimpses an alternative to her present problems and constraints. However, this possibility remains merely theoretical and the story ends, like other stories in the collection, in resignation.

In the novel *Malina*, the question of the identity of a woman artist becomes central and is presented in a narrative of great structural complexity. From a first-person perspective, the novel depicts a woman writer's struggle with various dimensions of patriarchal society. Her emotional life is elucidated through her relationship with her elusive lover, Ivan; her intellectual struggle is represented by the mysterious figure of Malina, her alter ego, with whom she shares her flat.

The conflicting aspects represented by these two men are necessary to her survival as an artist. In the central section of the novel, entitled 'The Third Man', another dimension is invoked, as the narrator experiences nightmares about her father—he appears in the guise of a Nazi doctor and mistreats her as one of his victims. The problem of the woman artist is thereby associated with the idea of oppression in a historical and social context. Finally, in a metaphorically suggestive ending, the narrator, abandoned by Ivan and maltreated by Malina and her 'father', disappears 'into the wall', as if transcending natural boundaries, but with little suggestion that this process leads in a more positive direction.

The later collection of stories *Simultan* (*Three Paths to the Lake*) depicts female figures from different facets of Viennese society. In the title story, Bachmann again takes up the problem of language and identity, now placed in a professional context. The central figure, Nadja, an interpreter, is estranged from her Viennese roots and her native language by her profession, which involves her constantly using other people's words and foreign languages, but rarely her own. This predicament acts as a metaphor for her crisis about her own identity, something which she partially succeeds in resolving when she takes a holiday with a fellow Viennese and is enabled to confront emotional issues in her own language. Her new insight is however achieved at considerable cost, as she is compelled to accept her professional and personal limitations. The wider perspective given by this analysis of professional life is also apparent in 'The Barking', in which a psychiatrist, Leo Jordan, appears to use professional authority and jargon as a means of refusing to face his own complicity regarding the Nazi past. This attitude towards society at large is reflected in Jordan's lack of responsibility towards his own family. Bachmann's critique emerges through the relationship which develops between his mother and his wife, who, though victims of his behaviour, also connive with it.

Apart from these major works, Bachmann left an unfinished novel, *Der Fall Franza* [Franza's Case], in which she attempts to relate the oppression of women by men to the processes underlying imperialism and fascism. The wide range of her writing also includes some successful radio plays broadcast in the 1950s. In partnership with the composer Hans Werner Henze, she wrote opera libretti, including *Der Prinz von Homburg*, from the play by Heinrich von Kleist. Her essays on literary and philosophical topics, collected after her death under the title *Die Wahrheit ist dem Menschen zumutbar* [Truth Can Be Expected], both shed light on her own writing and have been influential to other writers, notably the East German Christa Wolf.

—Juliet Wigmore

———

BAI JUYI [Po Chü-i]. Pen name, Xiangshan. Born in Xinzheng, Henan province, China, in 772. Passed provincial examinations in 799 and imperial examinations in 800; also received instruction at a Buddhist monastery. Married. Began career as an imperial official in Chang'an (the capital city), 801; moved to a minor county post, 806; passed State exams, and returned to Chang'an as official censor, 808; resided at Xiagui, in mourning for his mother, 811–14; exiled from Chang'an, after his criticism of official corruption, 815, but soon rehabilitated; recalled to Chang'an, 820, and was then appointed to various offical portfolios: Supervisor of Royal Documents, 820, Prefect of Hanzhou, 822, Prefect of Suzhou, 825, Chief Magistrate, Henan province, 831, and Minister of Justice, 842; retired from official posts, 842. Member of the Hanlin Literary Academy, 807. *Died in 846.*

PUBLICATIONS

Verse

Baishi Changqing ji [Collected Works]. Edited by Wang Liming (includes 2,900 poems), 1702; modern edition, 4 vols., 1979; as *Translations from Po Chü-i's Collected Works*, translated by Howard S. Levy, 4 vols., 1971–75; selections in: *170 Chinese Poems*, 1918, and *More Translations from the Chinese*, 1919, both translated by Arthur Waley (reissued together as *Chinese Poems*, 1946); *In the Jade Mountain*, translated by W. Bynner and Kiang Kang-hu, 1929; *The Everlasting Woe*, translated by Tai Jen, 1939; *The White Pony*, translated by R. Payne, 1949; *Gems of Chinese Literature*, translated by A. Giles, 1965.

Other

Po Chü-i as a Censor: His Memorials Presented to Emperor Hsien-tsung During the Years 808–810, translated by Eugene Feifel. 1961.

*

Critical Study: *The Life and Times of Po Chü-i* by Arthur Waley, 1949.

* * *

Poetry flourished during the Chinese Tang dynasty, and among 2,000 or so Tang poets, Bau Juyi enjoys world renown and ranks next to Du Fu and Li Bai.

Bai Juyi was born into a minor official's family and was a precocious boy. As he explained in a letter to his friend Yuan Zhen, he understood some written characters at the age of six or seven months and had mastered Chinese phonology when he was only nine years old. As a teenager he took to writing, and his poem 'The Grass on Ancient Plain', written around the age of 15, won him considerable fame. In his early days he moved from place to place with his father, who was transferred at the order of the Emperor. Bai Juyi's life spanned the reign of six emperors, and from childhood he witnessed the political upheaval and decline of the once strong and unified Tang Empire. At 12 he had to leave Central China for South China to seek refuge from the war. Here he tried unsuccessfully to win an official post through the civil examination but instead won fourth place in the highest imperial court examination at the age of 29 and was given a minor post in a county in 806. Disappointed as he was, it gave him opportunity to see the corruption of the Tang bureaucrats and the sufferings of the common people. During that short period he wrote well-known poems such as *Chang hen ge* (*The Everlasting Woe*) and 'Watching the Wheat-Reapers'. He was summoned to Chang'an, the capital, in 807 and appointed, after further examinations, to various posts in the court. This gave him access to the Emperor and enabled him to experience at close quarters the political schemes and extravagant life at the palace. His duty was to give advice and present memorials to the Emperor, and he wrote into his memorials could not express in explicit terms. Most of these poems are included in what he called 'satires': his satirical poems are exposés of the corruption and decadence of government officials. In his letter to Yuan Zhen he claimed, 'When the influential nobles and Emperor's favourites at court heard my *Songs of Qin*, they changed their countenance, looking at one another; when the persons holding office heard my poem "Delightful Garden", they sighed; when the chiefs of the army heard my poem "Lodged in Purple Tower Mountain Village", they gnashed their teeth in hatred'. His suggestion for redressing malpractice and corruption offended court officials and even the Emperor; consequently he lost favour and was banished from the capital on charges made up by his opponents. This was the turning point in his life and he asked to leave to avoid the conflicts among the bureaucrats, and he took up the governorship first in Hangzhou, and later in Suzhou. In later years he pursued a reclusive lifestyle until his death.

Bai Juyi was a prolific poet. His extant poems, about 3,000, outnumber the works of any other Tang poet. He classified his works as poems of satire, leisure, sentiment, and miscellaneous *lüshi* ('standard' poems with eight lines, each having five or seven characters, and with a strict tonal and rhyme pattern). However, this classification was not strictly observed. He attached great importance to content in poetry. His 'New Yuefu Ballads' and 'Songs of Qin' are representative of satirical poems which, as he put it, 'aim at remedying social faults and prevailing wrongs'. 'The Charcoal-seller' describes the bitter life of a charcoal burner and exposes with fury the extortion of court officials: 'A whole wagon of charcoal,/ more than a thousand catties! If the officials choose to take it away,/ the wood-man may not complain' (translated by Arthur Waley). 'The Old Man with the Broken Arm' condemns the war imposed by Prime Minister Yang through the heartbreaking narrative of an old man who, at the age of 24, broke his arm with a huge stone in order to escape being conscripted. Among his poems of sentiment, 'Chang hen ge' and 'Piba xing' [Lute Song], the best-known of all his works, are facile in style and appealing in narrative. His leisure poems are lyric poetry written in his own style and tinged, sometimes, with Buddhism and Daoism. His miscellaneous *lüshi* account for about two-thirds of his poems, 'The Grass on Ancient Plain' mentioned above being one of the representative works of this kind.

Bai was a poet of genius who inherited the legacy of classical Chinese literature and also learned from folk literature. On the other hand, he was creative and formed a distinctive style of his own. His language was plain, which helps to contribute much to his popularity. As he said in the aforementioned letter to Yuan Zhen, his poems were 'inscribed on the walls of country schools, temples, inns, and travelling ships'. And Yuan Zhen confirmed in the 'Preface to Bai Juyi's Works' that Bai's poems were widely read and frequently on the lips of kings, princes, concubines, ladies, and grooms. His poems were circulated in Japan and Korea during his lifetime and are said to have been copied and read by the then Japanese king. Indeed, he has enjoyed high national as well as international renown to this day.

—Binghong Lu

BALZAC, Honoré de. Born in Tours, France, 20 May 1799. Educated at pension Le Guay-Pinel, Tours, 1804–07; Collège de Vendome, 1807–13; L'Institution Lepître, Paris, 1815; L'Institution Ganzer et Beuzelin, Paris, 1815–16; attended law lectures, the Sorbonne, Paris, baccalauréat of law 1819. Married Mme Hanska (Eve Rzewuska) in 1850. Clerk for M. Guillonnet de Merville, 1816–18, and M. Passez, 1818–19; then writer, editor, magazine writer: obtained printer's license, 1826–28; owner, *La Chronique de Paris*, 1835–36; editor, *La Revue Parisienne*, 1840. President, Société des Gens de Lettres, 1839. Chevalier, Légion d'honneur, 1845. *Died 18 August 1850.*

PUBLICATIONS

Collections

Oeuvres complètes, edited by Marcel Bouteron and Henri Longnon. 40 vols., 1912–40.
La Comédie humaine, edited by Marcel Bouteron. 11 vols., 1951–58; revised edition, edited by Pierre-George Castex and Pierre Citron, 1976– .
The Human Comedy, edited by George Saintsbury. 40 vols., 1895–98.
Works. 1901.

Fiction

L'Héritage de Birague, with Le Poitevin de Saint-Alme and Etienne Arago. 1822.
Jean-Louis; ou, La Fille trouvée, with Le Poitevin de Saint-Alme. 1822.
Clotilde de Lusignan; ou, Le beau juif. 1822.
Le Centenaire; ou, Les Deux Beringheld. 1822; as *Le Sorcier*, in *Oeuvres complètes de Horace de Saint-Aubin*, 1837.
Le Vicaire des Ardennes. 1822.
La Dernière Fée; ou, La Nouvelle Lampe merveilleuse. 1823.
Annette et le criminel. 1824.
Wann-Chlore. 1825; as *Jane la pâle*, in *Oeuvres complètes*, 1836.
Le Dernier Chouan; ou, Le Bretagne au 1800. 1829; revised edition, as *Les Chouans; ou, Le Bretagne en 1799*, 1834; as *Le Chouan*, 1838; as *The Chouans*, translated by George Saintsbury, 1890.
Mémoires pour servir à l'histoire de la révolution française, with Lheritier de l'Ain. 1829.
La Physiologie du mariage; ou, Méditations de philosophie éclectique. 1829; as *The Physiology of Marriage*, 1904.
Scènes de la vie privée. 1830; enlarged edition, 1832.
Le Peau de chagrin. 1831; edited by S. de Sasy, 1974; as *The Magic Skin*, 1888; as *The Wild Ass's Skin*, translated by Ellen Marriage, in *The Human Comedy*, 1895–98; as *The Heartless Woman*, translated by Owen Snell, 1945; as *The Fatal Skin*, translated by Cedar Paul, 1946.
Romans et contes philosophiques. 1831.
Contes bruns, with Philarète Chasles and Charles Rabou. 1832.
Les Salmigondis: Contes de toutes les couleurs. 1832; as *La Comtesse à deux maris*, in *Scènes de la vie privée*, 1835; as *Le Colonel Chabert*, in *Comédie humaine*, 1844.
Les Cent Contes drôlatiques. 3 (of an intended 10) vols., 1832–37; *Quatrième dixain* (fragments), 1925; as *Contes drôlatiques*, translated by George R. Sims, 1874; as *Droll Stories*, translated anonymously, 1948; Alec Brown, 1958.
Nouveaux contes philosophiques. 1832.
Le Médecin de campagne. 1833; excerpt, as *Histoire de Napoléon*, 1833; edited by Patrick Barthier, 1974.

Études de moeurs au XIXe siècle. 12 vols., 1833–37; includes reprints and the following new works:
  La Fleur des pois. 1834.
  La Recherche de l'absolu. 1834; as *Balthazar; or, Science and Love*, translated by William Robson, 1859; as *The Alchemist*, 1861; as *The Quest of the Absolute*, translated by Ellen Marriage, in *The Human Comedy*, 1895–98; as *The Tragedy of a Genius*, translated by Henry Blanchamp, 1912.
  Eugénie Grandet. 1833; as *Eugenie Grandet*, translated anonymously, 1859; several subsequent translations including by E.K. Brown, with *Père Goriot*, 1950; Marion Ayton Crawford, 1955; Henry Reed, 1964; as *Eugénie Grandet*, translated by Sylvia Raphael, 1990.
  La Femme abandonnée. 1833.
  La Grenadière. 1833.
  L'Illustre Gaudissart. 1833.
  Les Marana. 1834.
  Histoire des treize. 1834–35; as *History of the Thirteen*, translated by Herbert J. Hunt, 1974; translated in part by Lady Knutsford, as *The Mystery of the Rue Soly*, 1894; *The Girl with the Golden Eyes*, translated by Ernest Dowson, 1896; *The Duchess of Langeais*, translated by D. Mitford, 1946.
  La Vieille Fille. 1837.
  Illusions perdues (part I: *Les Deux Poètes*). 1837.
  Le Père Goriot. 1835; as *Daddy Goriot*, translated anonymously, 1860; as *Père Goriot*, translated 1886, and by E.K. Brown, with *Eugenie Grandet*, 1950; as *Old Goriot*, translated by Ellen Marriage, in *The Human Comedy*, 1895–98, and by Marion Ayton Crawford, 1951; as *Old Man Goriot*, translated by Joan Charles, 1949, and by Minot Sedgwick, 1950; as *Le Père Goriot*, translated by A.J. Krailsheimer, 1991.
  Le Livre mystique (includes *Louis Lambert* and *Séraphita*). 1835; translated as *Louis Lambert* and *Seraphita*, 2 vols., 1889.
Études philosophiques. 20 vols., 1835–40; includes reprints and the following new works:
  Un drame au bord de la mer. 1835.
  Melmoth réconcilié. 1836.
  L'Interdiction. 1836.
  La Messe de l'Athée. 1837.
  Facino cane. 1837.
  Les Martyrs ignorés. 1837.
  Le Secret des Ruggieri. 1837.
  L'Enfant maudit. 1837.
  Une passion dans le désert. 1837.
Le Lys dans la vallée. 1836; as *The Lily of the Valley*, translated by Lucienne Hill, 1891.
L'Excommunié, with Auguste de Belloy, in *Oeuvres complètes de Horace de Saint-Aubin*. 1837.
La Femme supérieure. 1837; as *Les Employés*, 1865; as *Bureaucracy*, 1889.
Histoire de César Birotteau. 1838; as *History of the Grandeur and Downfall of Cesar Birotteau*, 1860; as *The Bankrupt*, translated by Frances Frenaye, 1959; as *Cesar Birotteau*, translated by Robin Buss, 1993; also translated by Graham Robb, 1994.
Le Femme supérieure, La Maison Nucingen, La Torpille. 1838.
Les Rivalités en province. 1838; as *Le Cabinet des antiques* (includes *Gamara*), 1839; as *The Jealousies of a Country Town*, in *The Human Comedy*, 1895–98.
Gambara; Adieu. 1839; translated as *Gambara*, in *The Human Comedy*, 1895–98.
Une fille d'Eve (includes *Massimilla Doni*). 1839; as *A*

Daughter of Eve and *Massimilla Doni*, in *The Human Comedy*, 1895–98.

Un grand homme de province à Paris (Illusions perdues II). 1839; as *A Great Man of the Provinces in Paris*, 1893.

Béatrix; ou, Les Amours forcées. 1839; edited by Madeleine Fergeaud, 1979; as *Beatrix*, translated by Rosamund and Simon Harcourt-Smith, 1895.

Pierrette. 1840; translated as *Pierrette*, 1892.

Physiologie de l'employé. 1841.

Physiologie du rentier de Paris et de province, with Arnould Frémy. 1841.

Le Curé de village. 1841; as *The Country Parson*, translated anonymously, in *The Human Comedy*, 1895–98.

Oeuvres complètes: La Comédie humaine. 20 vols., 1842–53; includes reprints and the following new works:

  Albert Savarus. 1842; as *Albert Savarus*, translated by Ellen Marriage, 1892, and by Kathleen Raine, 1951.

  Autre étude de femme. 1842.

  Illusions perdues (part III). 1843; parts I and III translated as *Lost Illusions*, 1893.

  Esquisse d'homme d'affaires; Gaudissart II; Les Comédiens sans le savoir. 1846.

  Un épisode sous la terreur; L'Envers de l'histoire contemporain; Z; Marcas. 1846; *L'Envers . . .* translated as *Love*, 1893.

Ursule Mirouët. 1842; as *Ursula*, translated by Clara Bell, 1891; also translated by Donald Adamson, 1976.

Scènes de la vie privée et publique des animaux. 1842.

Mémoires de deux jeunes mariées. 1842; as *Memoirs of Two Young Married Women*, 1894; as *Two Young Birds*, translated anonymously, 1902.

Une ténébreuse affaire. 1842; edited by René Guise, 1973; as *The Gondreville Mystery*, 1898, also translated by Gerard Hopkins, 1958; as *A Murky Business*, translated by Herbert J. Hunt, 1972.

Les Deux Frères. 1842; as *Un ménage de garçon en province*, in *Comédie humaine*, 1843; as *La Rabouilleuse*, in *Oeuvres complètes*, 1912; edited by René Guise, 1972; as *The Two Brothers*, 1887; as *A Bachelor's Establishment*, in *The Human Comedy*, 1895–98; as *The Bachelor's House*, translated by Francis Frenaye, 1956; as *The Black Sheep*, translated by Donald Adamson, 1970.

Un début dans la vie (includes *La Fausse Maîtresse*). 1844.

Catherine de Médicis expliquée; Le Martyr calviniste. 1845; translated as *Catherine de' Medici*, 1894.

Honorine (includes *Un prince de la Bohème*). 1845.

Splendeurs et misères des courtisanes: Esther. 1845; as *A Harlot's Progress*, in *The Human Comedy*, 1895–98; as *A Harlot High and Low*, translated by Rayner Heppenstall, 1970.

La Lune de miel. 1845.

Petites misères de la vie conjugale. 1845–46; as *The Petty Annoyances of Married Life*, 1861.

Un drame dans les prisons. 1847.

Le Provincial à Paris (includes *Gillette, Le Rentier, El Verdugo*). 1847.

Les Parents pauvres (includes *La Cousine Bette* and *Le Cousin Pons*). 1847–48; as *Poor Relations*, translated by Philip Kent, 1880; as *Les Parents pauvres*, translated by James Waring, 1991; as *Cousin Pons*, 1886; as *Cousin Betty*, 1888; as *Cousin Bette*, translated by Kathleen Raine, 1948, and by Marion Ayton Crawford, 1965.

La Dernière Incarnation de Vautrin. 1848.

Le Député d'Arcis, completed by Charles Rabou. 1854; as *The Deputy of Arcis*, 1896.

Les Paysans, completed by Mme Balzac. 1855; as *Sons of the Soil*, 1890; as *The Peasantry*, in *The Human Comedy*, 1895–98.

Les Petits Bourgeois, completed by Charles Rabou. 1856; as *The Lesser Bourgeoisie*, 1896; as *The Middle Classes*, 1898.

Sténie; ou, Les Erreurs philosophiques, edited by A. Prioult. 1936.

La Femme auteur et autres fragments inédits, edited by le Vicomte de Lovenjoul. 1950.

Mademoiselle du Vissard, edited by Pierre-George Castex. 1950.

Selected Short Stories. 1977.

Gillette; or, the Unknown Masterpiece, translated by Anthony Rudolf. 1988.

Plays

Vautrin (produced 1840). 1840; translated as *Vautrin*, in *Works*, 1901.

Les Ressources de Quinola (produced 1842). 1842; as *The Resources of Quinola*, in *Works*, 1901.

Paméla Giraud (produced 1843). 1843; translated as *Pamela Giraud*, in *Works*, 1901.

La Marâtre (produced 1848). 1848; as *The Stepmother*, in *Works*, 1901, also translated by Edith Saunders, 1951.

Le Faiseur (produced 1849). 1851; translated as *Mercadet*, in *Works*, 1901.

L'École des ménages, edited by le Vicomte de Lovenjoul (produced 1910). 1907.

Other

Du droit d'aînesse. 1824.

Histoire impartiale des Jésuites. 1824.

Code des gens honnêtes; ou, L'Art de ne pas être dupe des fripons. 1825.

Mémoires de Mme la Duchesse d'Abrantes, with the duchess. vol. 1 only, 1831.

Maximes et pensées de Napoléon. 1838.

Traité de la vie élégante. 1853.

Lettres à l'étrangère (to Mme Hanska). 4 vols., 1899–1950.

Cahiers balzaciens, edited by Marcel Bouteron. 8 vols., 1927–28.

Le Catéchisme social, edited by Bernard Guyon. 1933.

Traité de la prière, edited by Philippe Bertault. 1942.

Journaux à la mer, edited by Louis Jaffard. 1949.

Correspondance, edited by Roger Pierrot. 5 vols., 1960–68.

Editor, *Oeuvres complètes*, by La Fontaine. 1826.
Editor, *Oeuvres complètes*, by Molière. 1826.

*

Bibliography: *A Balzac Bibliography* and *Index* by W. Hobart Royce, 1929–30; *Bibliography of Balzac Criticism* by Mark W. Waggoner, 1990.

Critical Studies: *Balzac and the Novel* by Samuel G.A. Rogers, 1953; *Balzac: A Biography*, 1957, and *Balzac's Comédie Humaine*, 1959, both by Herbert J. Hunt; *Balzac the European* by Edward J. Oliver, 1959; *Balzac and the Human Comedie* by Philippe Bertault, translated by Richard Monges, 1963; *Prometheus: The Life of Balzac* by André Maurois, 1965; *Balzac: An Interpretation of the Comédie Humaine* by F.W.J. Hemmings, 1967; *The Hero as Failure: Balzac and the Rubempré Cycle* by Bernard N. Schilling, 1968; *Balzac* by V.S. Pritchett, 1973; *Balzac's Comedy of Words* by Martin Kanes, 1975; *Balzac's Recurring Characters* by Anthony

Pugh, 1975; *Balzac Criticism in France (1850–1900): The Making of a Reputation*, 1976, *Balzac: La Cousine Bette*, 1980, and *Balzac: Old Goriot*, 1987, all by David Bellos; *Balzac: Fiction and Melodrama*, 1978, and *Order of Mimesis: Balzac, Hugo, Baudelaire, Flaubert*, 1988, both by Christopher Prendergast; *Honoré de Balzac* by Diana Festa-McCormack, 1979; *Unwrapping Balzac: A Reading of 'La Peau de chagrin'* by Samuel Weber, 1979; *Balzac: Illusions Perdues* by Donald Adamson, 1981; *Balzac and His Reader* by Mary Susan McCarthy, 1982; *Balzac and the French Revolution* by Ronnie Butler, 1983; *Balzac, James and Realist Novel* by William W. Stone, 1983; *Balzac and the Drama of Perspective: The Narrator in Selected Works of La Comédie humaine* by Joan Dargan, 1985; *Family Plots: Balzac's Narrative Generations* by Janet L. Beizer, 1986; *Honoré de Balzac: Eugénie Grandet* by Arnold Saxton, 1987; *Realism and the Drama of Reference: Strategies of Representation in Balzac, Flaubert and James* by H. Meili Steele, 1988; *The Golden Scapegoat: Portrait of the Jews in the Novels of Balzac* by Frances Grodzinsky, 1989; *Evolution, Sacrifice and Narrative: Balzac, Zola and Faulkner* by Carol Colatrella, 1990; *Balzacian Montage: Configuring La Comédie humaine* by Allan H. Pasco, 1991; *Paratextuality in Balzac's La Peau de chagrin/The Wild Ass's Skin* by Jeri DeBois King, 1992; *Honoré de Balzac* (in French) by Roger Pierrot, 1994; *Balzac* by Graham Robb, 1994.

* * *

Honoré de Balzac's first sustained piece of writing was *Cromwell*, a stillborn historical tragedy in verse. Towards the end of his career he turned to drama once again, and it was probably not solely the need to raise some cash in a hurry that impelled him to do so. *La Marâtre (The Stepmother)*, for instance, was well received by the critics in 1848, and after initial difficulties when first produced, the five-act melodrama *Vautrin* was a popular success at the Théâtre Porte-Saint-Martin. Yet though Balzac remained fascinated throughout his life by the drama of his age whose emphatic acting styles and tempestuous emotionality left their distinctive stamp on his style and imagination, it was not in the theatre that he was destined to make his mark. Instead we must look to his three sets of quasi-Rabelaisian *Contes drôlatiques (Droll Stories)*, published between 1832 and 1837, and to his towering achievement, the teeming fictional world of *La Comédie humaine (The Human Comedy)*, the creation of a lifetime devoted to writing, a work which though never carried through to completion encompasses upwards of 80 novels and tales.

The sheer scope of the enterprise is deeply impressive, even within the context of the enormous output of vast novels in the 19th century, and the audacity of transmuting the title of Dante's epic has been allowed to pass unchallenged, even though there are few obvious connections. A reliable census of Balzac's fictional world has established that it is peopled by over two thousand named characters. Nearly all are sharply individualized, by sex and, equally strongly, by social class, by temperament, appearance, mannerism, and speech habits. Many appear only fleetingly, but others are developed very fully, dominating the scene on occasion or else present as more or less shadowy background figures to events in which they do not play the primary role. A number of these characters, like some in Dickens and Dostoevskii, have made such an impact on the general consciousness that they have come to be regarded as having a status similar to that of historical personages, possessing individuality that seemingly transcends fiction. For a setting Balzac usually, though not exclusively, chose the period in French history just before the time at which he was writing. His characters stand before the backdrop of the French Revolution and the Empire, of the Restoration and the July Monarchy, an era of political turmoil and social upheaval that placed ordinary people under exceptional pressure and allowed unusual opportunities for outstanding individuals to develop their personalities to the full.

Balzac had a considerable number of major novels to his name before the grand concept of *The Human Comedy* dawned on him. *Les Chouans (The Chouans)* of 1829 reflected the current fashion for historical romance. That same year *La Physiologie du mariage (The Physiology of Marriage)* though not important in itself, marked the crucial decision to use the novel for the study of social conditions in relation to the individual. *Eugénie Grandet* and *Le Père Goriot*, two of Balzac's most popular novels, are evidence that he had indeed struck a rich vein, with observation and imagination combined in good proportion. But in the early 1830s he also began to perceive the possibility, indeed the necessity, of thinking not in terms of single novels but of sets of what he liked to think of as fictionalized studies of 19th-century French society. Slowly the idea crystallized, and in 1842 Balzac was ready to present his views, in somewhat oracular tones, in his famous Preface to *The Human Comedy*. In it he acknowledged his debt to Walter Scott who had raised the status of the novel by using it for the serious investigation of society in former times. The influences bearing on Balzac are not, however, just literary. He invokes the name of famous naturalists such as G.-L. Leclerc de Buffon and Geoffrey de Saint-Hilaire, and of mystical thinkers like Charles Bonnet, Emanuel Swedenborg, and L.-C. de Saint-Martin. What Balzac sought and found in their writings was some sort of corroboration of his intuitions of the unity of observed creation. In the rich variety of human life as he witnessed it there could, he believed, be perceived the working out of a single vital principle. His object became to present individual human beings as the products of the social forces bearing in on them just as biology was attempting to relate specialization and variation to environmental factors.

The pretension to using fiction as a tool for scientific analysis or even just demonstration is, of course, inadmissible, and despite Balzac's efforts to make his examination of society as comprehensive as possible and his mapping out *The Human Comedy* as 'studies' of various aspects, the procedure inevitably lacks compelling experimental rigour. Though Balzac felt obliged to return to some of his earlier novels and make some changes, critics have, however, been ready to accept that the unifying vision emerged from the fiction, as a scientific observation might, and was not something deliberately imposed after the event. As early as 1834 Balzac had begun to employ the device of making the same character reappear in different novels, and the tendency to bring out patterns of continuity becomes more and more marked from then on. *The Human Comedy* is not a serial novel nor the chronicle of a family, but something more complex; it is a fictional world in which individual destinies may be best appreciated in wider perspectives. In his descriptions Balzac revealed himself as an observer of exceptional acumen. Yet to hail him primarily as a recorder of the life of his times is to diminish his achievement. Though *The Human Comedy* represented a major step in the direction of Realism, Balzac is too much of a visionary to be thought of as a Realist. His prose style sometimes lacks elegance, and credibility is occasionally taxed by emotionality and improbability. These excesses are, it seems, inseparable from the vigour and vitality of his vision of human nature and the inescapable conflicts between the demonic forces that spur on mankind and the constraints of religion and the monarchy that alone may hold them in check.

Balzac's rank as a novelist was in question throughout his life. Only towards the end of the 19th century was it generally recognized that his importance, both as an observer and as an imaginative visionary, decisively outweighed a degree of clumsiness in execution and of coarseness in sensibility.

—Christopher Smith

COUSIN BETTE (La Cousine Bette)
Novel by Honoré de Balzac, 1847.

Cousin Bette is one half of a diptych that includes *Cousin Pons*, Balzac's last major achievement. Its action takes place entirely in Paris between 1838 and 1946. Never elsewhere in *The Human Comedy*, and seldom elsewhere in literature as a whole, has the explosive force of love been so vividly presented. This love takes numerous forms, all of them responding to, or exploiting, physical attraction rather than the cash nexus of the marriage market.

Adeline Hulot loves her husband; with wifely modesty she practically worships him, forgiving him any number of marital indiscretions precisely because of the force of her sexual love. In the relationship between her daughter Hortense and Wenceslas Steinbock we see the 'normal' love of a young couple. Adeline's cousin Lisbeth (or Bette) Fisher loves Steinbock with a semi-maternal affection that he does not reciprocate in the same possessive sense, and which perhaps does not include any element of physical fulfilment. Crevel loves the courtesan Josépha Mirah with physical passion; he finally marries Valérie Marneffe, with whom Montès de Montéjanos has also had a strong physical bond. Valérie (if we exclude her husband!) has two other admirers: Steinbock loves her with carnal and adulterous passion; so too does the latter's father-in-law, Hector Hulot, who takes his place in *The Human Comedy* as one of Balzac's eight great monomaniacs; for, besides the four incidental affairs mentioned in *Cousin Bette*, Hulot also loves Josépha Mirah, stealing her from Crevel. There have been many such women throughout Hulot's life and, it seems, things will continue in this way.

Another of Balzac's eight great monomaniacs is Bette, whose jealous love for Steinbock prompts insatiable yearnings for revenge when she loses him to Hortense. *Cousin Bette* is the only fiction in *The Human Comedy* in which two monomaniacs are presented side by side with virtually equal prominence. Balzac shows his eponymous heroine shaking and trembling from head to foot, glaring like a tigress and burning like a volcano: Bette is destroyed by her monomania, whereas Hulot's, like Vautrin's, does not destroy him physically.

But although *Cousin Bette* focuses on sexual love, that is by no means its only concern. Other important themes are chastity, artistic creativity, the decline of the notion of honour, and the imperfections of the modern world. By means of direct speech, the symbolic event, and also some authorial intervention, the narrator voices his own attitude towards this aftermath of the Napoleonic era. It is a time, says Hulot's son Victorin, when children ought to, but cannot, teach their parents how to behave; a time when all ethical integrity appears to be dead. After the discovery of Hector Hulot's embezzlement of public funds, his brother, Marshal Hulot hands him pistols with which to do the honourable thing: but to no avail! Even amid the mass warfare of the Napoleonic era, when normal moral codes were partially suspended, there was, it seemed, a sense of honour and moral responsibility that has ceased to exist under the July Monarchy.

The five-franc piece is the only god worshipped in Louis-Philippe's reign, a fact proclaimed by Crevel, the retired perfumer who (in the tradition of César Birotteau) is the ultimate embodiment of philistine bourgeois values in *The Human Comedy*. In Crevel's sexual rival Hulot Balzac goes even further than this. Detesting the July Monarchy for its double standards, he shows corruption in the higher administrative echelons of government. A key symbol of these double standards is Valérie Marneffe, who conveys the impression of being a respectably married woman. The very outrage unleashed by the publication of this novel was a further sign of the public two-facedness to which Balzac took strong exception.

Cousin Bette does not adopt a moralizing attitude with regard to private virtue, even though its narrator explicitly—and its author personally—deplored what appears (from *Les Deux Frères* [*The Black Sheep*] and elsewhere) to have been a general contemporary decline in moral standards. Adeline Hulot may well turn the other cheek, yet it is impossible to say whether the narrator of *Cousin Bette* considers her a 'virtuous' woman. Like her husband, and like Bette, she is a force of nature, endlessly predetermined by her own nature: endlessly forgiving, just as Bette is endlessly vindictive, and just as Hulot's lechery seems as ardent as ever—though, by the time when *Cousin Bette* ends, he is already 74 years old. It is through melodrama that Balzac can provide some sort of moral commentary, as when Montès infects both Valérie and Crevel, thereby causing the deaths of both. Not only melodrama but drama itself is the stuff of this novel: in his later years Balzac took an increasing interest in the writing of plays. Drama juxtaposes viewpoints without the need for authorial commentary; and this narrative ambiguity is essential to the presentation of issues of private morality in *Cousin Bette*.

There is, on the other hand, plentiful and unambiguous authorial commentary concerning the dramas of artistic creation. For, even at the very end of his own creative life, Balzac still upheld the Romantic view (previously expressed in *Illusions perdues* [*Lost Illusions*] and *The Black Sheep*) that art is a sacred calling and that, as also in religion, the sacerdotal function—that of Execution rather than Conception—is essentially male. Hence Steinbock's importance, and the varying nature of Bette's, Hortense's, and Valérie's influence upon him, while the statues of Samson and Delilah, a subject also memorably treated by Vigny, aptly symbolize the downfall of Steinbock's artistic talent. Hence too the early idea of beginning *Cousin Bette* with a description of the young sculptor. But, as the novel's actual first pages show, Balzac (building upon the examples of *Histoire de César Birotteau* [*Cesar Birotteau*] and *Ursule Mirouët* [*Ursula*]) had become to prefer the vivid opening *in medias res*—partly because of the influence of the theatre, and partly because of newspaper serialization.

—Donald Adamson

EUGENIE GRANDET
Novel by Honoré de Balzac, 1833.

Eugenie Grandet is one of Balzac's earlier works, and one of the very earliest of his writings for which it is possible to claim the status of a novel rather than a short story. In common with about half of his fiction, it is set in the provinces: in this case in Saumur, in the Touraine where Balzac was born and which he knew well. It is sometimes considered to be the first of his four inheritance novels. More importantly, it is the first of his major works to deal with the theme of monomania: in this instance, Félix Grandet's miserliness.

Grandet, a self-made multimillionaire, has an only child, the eponymous heroine. Her cousin Charles comes from Paris in 1819 to stay with his uncle and cousin after the bankruptcy and suicide of his father Guillaume. Charles is the epitome of the Parisian dandy, fashionable and ultimately calculating and self-seeking but because of the cultural divide separating Paris from the provinces he does not realize his uncle's immense wealth. Charles and Eugenie fall in love; the young man goes off to Java to seek his fortune; but before he leaves Saumur, he and Eugenie exchange tokens: they promise to marry on his return home.

A sub-plot is the rivalry of two unattractive suitors, pillars of the Saumur community, for Eugenie's hand in marriage. (The Saumur families have only a limited awareness of Grandet's wealth.) Charles meanwhile has engaged in the slave trade in the Dutch East Indies. Failing to appreciate that his cousin is one of the richest of French heiresses, he marries a young aristocratic woman on his return home, a comparatively rich man, in 1827. Heartbroken, Eugenie bestows her hand upon one of her Saumur suitors. The marriage is never consummated and Eugenie, soon widowed and ever mindful of the betrayal of her early and only romantic love, austerely devotes her life and fortune to the doing of good works: not least the repayment in full of Guillaume Grandet's still remaining debts.

Money, rather than the subject of an inheritance as such, is central to *Eugenie Grandet*, a novel which is the first of Balzac's full-length works to be acutely concerned with this theme. It provides a detailed and artistically convincing description of financial and economic activity in a provincial setting. *Eugenie Grandet* is also one of the first novels—indeed, one of the first works of literature—ever to ascribe such huge importance to financial matters. More than at any other time in human history, Balzac writes, money 'dominates the law, politics and social morality' and, in so doing, it also undermines religious belief: this is the spirit of bourgeois capitalism, and he dreads the time when the working classes will adopt the same outlook. Thus Grandet is not only a monomaniac but a larger-than-life symbol: not, however, a symbol of the industrialism that was gaining ground in England at this same period. Although concerned with enhancing agricultural productivity, he still lives in, and does nothing to change, an agrarian economy. His non-agricultural wealth arises exclusively from speculation in Government stock. At his death he leaves a fortune of 17 million francs. When a friend expressed her reservations about the likelihood of his amassing such a huge sum, Balzac was little moved by such criticism—evidently viewing Grandet as a mythical representation of emergent capitalism: not, however, a fully convincing one at the level of historical accuracy.

Written, broadly speaking, before his invention of the system of recurring characters, *Eugenie Grandet* is one of the few of Balzac's works to have a strong flavour of self-containment which comes from being set apart from the rest. The description of the Grandet household has many of the characteristics of a Dutch genre-painting: stillness, reserve, and mystery. The character of Félix Grandet is one of the most memorable in French fiction; he is a counterpart to Molière's Harpagon. Mme Grandet and Nanon the maidservant are also sharply individualized. A still finer creation is Eugenie herself; her love-story—the blossoming and blight-

ing of her love—is the finest thing of its kind ever achieved in *The Human Comedy*. Balzac's use of tricks of speech surpasses even Molière's. Whereas Harpagon has his 'without a dowry', Félix Grandet has his 'we'll see about that'. But something never achieved by Molière is the transmission of the trick of speech from one generation to the next, as Eugenie herself uses the same trick of speech towards the end of the novel. Balzac skilfully describes the daughter's rebellion against her father while at the same time showing how she gradually grows to resemble him. Eugenie's rebellion is quite unlike that of Harpagon's children: it represents the coming to full strength and maturity of a person who is as strong-minded as her father but who was prepared, within limits, to submit to his paternal authority for as long as he was alive.

Such is one aspect of Balzac's 'realism': recognizing both the transmission of genetic characteristics and also the determinism that implies. Another aspect is the vastly intriguing portrait of Saumur. No novel gives a more 'realistic' picture of what it must have been like to live in French provincial society around the years 1819–33. Yet beneath this solid 'realism' Balzac delights, as so often in *The Human Comedy*, in revealing all the strange and unexpected realities that lie close to the surface. These realities are as mystifying to us, his readers, as were the outer appearances of Grandet's house to Charles. Balzac, therefore, is as ludic towards his readers as (on the novelist's own admission) Grandet is towards his wife and daughter and indeed towards the whole of Saumur.

This 'realism' is well contrasted with the 'romantic' yearnings of unselfish love, a love shared by Eugenie and Charles (and symbolized by her store of gold coins, his mother's sewing-box, and Grandet's walnut tree) in the earlier part of the novel.

—Donald Adamson

LOST ILLUSIONS (Illusions perdues)
Novels by Honoré de Balzac, 1837–43.

Lost Illusions resembles another of Balzac's novels, *The Black Sheep*, in that it is set partly in Paris and partly in the provinces. It is unique, however, among the novels and short stories of *The Human Comedy* in the even-handedness with which it treats both Paris and the provinces.

Lucien Chardon de Rubempré is the pivotal figure of the entire work. Even as Part I, *Les Deux Poètes* (*The Two Poets*) begins, he has already written a historical novel and a sonnet-sequence; his friend David Séchard is a scientist. But both, according to Balzac, are 'poets' in that they creatively seek truth. Theirs is a fraternity of poetic aspiration, whether as writer or as scientist: thus, even before David marries Lucien's sister, the two young men are spiritual brothers. At the very end of *The Two Poets* Lucien is carried off to Paris by the provincial bluestocking Mme de Bargeton.

In Part II, *Un grand homme de province à Paris* (*A Great Man of the Provinces in Paris*), Lucien is contrasted both with the journalist Lousteau and with the high-minded writer Daniel d'Arthez. Jilted by Mme de Bargeton for the adventurer Sixte du Châtelet, Lucien moves in a social circle of high-class actress-prostitutes and their journalist lovers; soon he is the lover of Coralie. He becomes a reviewer, thus prostituting his literary talent. But he still nurtures the ambition of belonging to high society and longs to assume by royal warrant the surname and coat of arms of his mother's family (now sadly fallen in the world). In the furtherance of this social ambition, and urged on by Coralie's well-meaning advice, he switches his allegiance from the liberal opposition press to the one or two royalist newspapers that support the government. This act of betrayal earns him the implacable hatred of his erstwhile journalist colleagues, who destroy Coralie's theatrical reputation. In the depths of his despair he forges his brother-in-law's name on three promissory notes: this is his ultimate betrayal of his identity. After Coralie's death he returns in disgrace to Angoulême, stowed away behind the Châtelets' carriage: Mme de Bargeton has just married du Châtelet, who has been appointed prefect of that region.

Part III of the novel begins as a long flashback. At Angoulême David Séchard is betrayed on all sides but is supported by his loving wife Ève. He invents a new and cheaper method of paper production (the commercialization of paper-manufacturing processes is closely interwoven, at a thematic level, with the commercialization of literature). Lucien's forgery of his signature almost bankrupts him, and he has to sell out the secret of his invention to business rivals. The whole of Lucien's world has collapsed around him too. He is contemplating suicide when he is approached by a sham Jesuit priest, the Abbé Carlos Herrera, alias the escaped convict Vautrin whom Balzac had already presented in *Le Père Goriot*. Herrera takes Lucien under his protection; and off they drive to the capital, there to begin the assault on Paris anew.

Balzac revels in strong contrasts: Lucien and David, art and science, Lousteau and d'Arthez, journalism and literature, Lucien and Ève, Coralie and Ève, Paris and the provinces. Metaphorical hyperbole intensifies these contrasts: thus, Daniel d'Arthez and his followers in the upper room are like Jesus and his disciples (and Lucien/Judas betrays him), while Lucien's crucially testing week in Paris is compared to Napoleon's retreat from Moscow. Lucien's return to Angoulême behind the Châtelets' carriage stands in stark contrast to his departure from Angoulême in a carriage with Mme de Bargeton: no other symbol—and a symbol of such simplicity—could so powerfully have conveyed the extent of his downfall.

Such contrasts, at a less superficial level, are features of technique rather than of substance. Characters and viewpoints are polarized, usually for structural and therefore narrative reasons. This polarization reaches the point of melodrama as Balzac appears to draw moral distinctions between 'vice' and 'virtue'. Coralie is the Fallen Woman, Ève an Angel of strength and purity; yet Balzac also describes Coralie's love for Lucien as an 'absolution' and a benediction'. Thus he underlines what he considers to be the fundamental resemblance of opposites: a philosophy of hypostatic monism. (The same point is made by Blondet, in discussion with Lucien, Lousteau, and Vernou. This theme is present almost everywhere in *The Human Comedy*, except notably in *The Black Sheep*.)

Like all the major works of *The Human Comedy*, *Lost Illusions* pre-eminently focuses upon the social nexus. Within the nexus of love, in her relationship with Lucien, Coralie is life-giving; her love has a sacramental quality. In an environment of worldly manoeuvring her influence upon him is fatal. She is, in other words, both a Fallen and a Risen Woman; all depends upon the nexus within which she is viewed. In the unfavourable environment of Angoulême Mme de Bargeton is an absurd bluestocking; transplanted to Paris, she undergoes an immediate 'metamorphosis', becoming a true denizen of high society—and rightfully, in Part III, the occupant of the *préfecture* at Angoulême.

Even the change of tempo from Part II to Part III is but a superficial point of contrast between life as it is lived in the capital and life in the provinces. Everywhere the same laws of human behaviour apply. A man's downfall may come from the rapier thrust of the journalist or from the slowly-strangling machinations of the law. But duplicity is omnipresent in the world: that two-facedness of human life in all its aspects, from the universal to the specific, both in Paris and Angoulême.

In so many ways Lucien has two 'faces'; he even has two surnames! But is he endowed with real talent? Is he, despite the title of Part I, a true poet? Is his downfall brought about by a philistine commercial world, or does it result from a multiplicity of accidental factors? Does it arise from some deep-rooted shortcoming within himself? Balzac, criticized by Zola (among others) for his authorial commentaries and interventions, offers no real clue to this enigma.

—Donald Adamson

LE PÈRE GORIOT
Novel by Honoré de Balzac, 1835.

In Balzac's enormous literary production *Le Père Goriot* occupies a pivotal position. For the first time, Balzac wrote with the idea of using recurring characters to paint all of the French society of his period. Consequently, *Le Père Goriot* is as much about the education of the young and naive Rastignac as it is the story of old Goriot, a 'Christ of fatherhood', a martyr of unworthy daughters. Rastignac and Paris —a Paris corrupted by money—are as important as the title character, and will survive him with a life of their own in other works of *The Human Comedy*.

In 1819, at Madame Vauquer's sordid and mysterious boarding-house, which is described in great detail, rumours abound about Monsieur Goriot, a retired vermicelli manufacturer. Every year he moves to a cheaper room on a higher floor; two rich young women visit him, although less and less frequently. Some say they are his mistresses; he protests they are his daughters. Among the other boarders are Eugène de Rastignac, a poor, provincial law student, and Vautrin, a rather menacing figure with an unusual knowledge of the ways of the world.

Little by little, Rastignac discovers Goriot's story: his two daughters, Anastasie and Delphine, now known respectively as Countess de Restaud and Baroness de Nucingen, thanks to successful marriages and solid dowries, are ruining him with their frivolous ways. Meanwhile, Rastignac's cousin, Viscountess de Beauséant, educates the ambitious student about Paris and opens the doors of society to him.

Rastignac discovers that Paris is 'a heap of filth', 'an ocean of mud'. He himself is not cynical enough to accept Vautrin's invitation to court Victorine Taillefer, a boarder in the Vauquer house and prospective heiress to a large fortune. But he does follow Madame de Beauséant's advice to seduce Delphine de Nucingen in order to advance in the world; in so doing, he befriends Goriot, who relishes talking about his daughter. The old man expresses his fear of not keeping his daughters happy, since his financial resources are getting so meagre. As he becomes involved with rich people, Rastignac too is pressed for money; he requests and gets funds from his family, and finally agrees to court Victorine.

Two of the Vauquer boarders, Poiret and Mademoiselle Michonneau, motivated by greed, report Vautrin to the police who arrest him. Vautrin's true identity is discovered:

he is the famous criminal Jacques Collin, also known as 'cheat-death'.

Goriot, Delphine, and Rastignac share some happy moments together. The young couple are to move into an apartment of their own, with Goriot occupying a room above. But Delphine is too financially dependent upon Nucingen to gain her freedom, and the prospect of happiness for all of them is soon shattered. At the same time, Anastasie is involved in a costly love affair, and both daughters beg their father with tears and cries for more money. Rastignac saves Anastasie by forging a draft made out to Vautrin.

His daughters' demands and misadventures prove too much for Goriot, who becomes ill and is cared for by Bianchon, a medical student and boarder in the Vauquer house. Despite Rastignac's pleas to the daughters to visit their dying father, the two women can think only of Madame de Beauséant's final ball. Goriot's condition worsens. During his agony (which is probably the most emotional scene in the novel), he realizes that his daughters will not come to see him on his deathbed and curses them.

Goriot is buried in a pauper's grave at Rastignac's and Bianchon's expense. The daughters, too preoccupied with their own lives, send their empty carriages to follow the hearse. From the highest point of the Père-Lachaise cemetery, Rastignac defies Paris and, 'as a first act in his challenge of Society', he goes to dine with the Baroness de Nucingen.

Balzac's characters are dominated by their passions. Goriot's single-minded devotion to his daughters is tainted by his absolute and selfish disregard for anything else: he will stop at nothing on their behalf, declaring himself ready to 'kill a man' or 'go to the penitentiary' for them. Vautrin and Rastignac prove equally extreme and corrupt in the pursuit of their goals.

Vautrin sees corruption as the law of all men: 'Man is the same at the top, in the middle, at the bottom of the social ladder.' Indeed, all of the characters in *Le Père Goriot* are partners in crime: Goriot made his fortune during the Revolution by selling flour for ten times what it had cost him; Gobseck, the money lender, a recurring character in *The Human Comedy*, attends to the needs of rich and poor alike; Madame Vauquer, Mademoiselle Michonneau, Nucingen, Madame de Beauséant's lover, and Goriot's daughters all fall victim to greed.

Vautrin's vision of society ('*Succeed!* Succeed at any cost!') is no different from Madame de Beauséant's, who foresees Rastignac's revelations: 'the world is ignoble and nasty. You will discover how deeply corrupt women are, and you'll measure the enormous and wretched vanity of men. Treat this world as it deserves. The more coldly you calculate, the farther you'll climb'. By the end of the novel, Rastignac himself has become one of the people he first despised, one of those described by Vautrin for whom 'there are no such things as principles, there are only events: there are no such things as laws, there are only circumstances'.

Le Père Goriot is the unveiling of the modern world by a lucid conscience: 'Law and morality [are] impotent among the rich. In wealth [Rastignac] saw the *ultima ratio mundi*'. Morality is foreign to both poles of society, as much to the Vauquer boarding-house as to the Beauséant mansion. In this respect, *Le Père Goriot* is a testimony to the beginnings of the modern age in France.

Balzac's stated aim in the novel is not to reason about right and wrong, but to show what simply is:

This drama is no work of fiction, no mere novel! It is all true, so true that everyone may recognize its elements within himself, perhaps in his very heart.

Indeed, it is for Balzac's remarkable attention to realistic detail, the breadth of his creative imagination, and the sense of inescapable fatality which pervades it that *Le Père Goriot* has been acclaimed as one of the major novels of modern literature.

—Pierre J. Lapaire

BARBUSSE, Henri. Born in Asnières, France, 17 May 1873. Educated at Collège Rollin, Paris; graduated 1895. Military service, 1893–94; served in the French army infantry during World War I, invalided out, 1917: Croix de Guerre, 1915. Worked in the civil service, Paris; contributor, *Petit Parisien* and *Echo de Paris*; founding editor, *Clarté*, 1917, and *Monde*, 1928; journalist and reviewer, *L'Humanité*, 1920s. Involved in pacifist groups, Revue de la Paix and Paix par le Droit, 1903; founder member, Republican Association of War Veterans, 1917, and Clarté, 1919; member, Communist Party, 1923; president, Comité Mondial contre la Guerre et le Fascisme, 1933. Recipient: Goncourt prize, 1917. *Died 30 August 1935.*

PUBLICATIONS

Fiction

Les Suppliants. 1903.
L'Enfer. 1908; as *The Inferno*, translated by Edward O'Brien, 1913; as *Inferno*, translated by John Rodker, 1932; as *Hell*, translated by Robert Baldick, 1966.
Meissonier. 1911; as *Meissonier*, translated by Frederic Taber Cooper, 1912.
Nous autres. 1914; as *We Others: Stories of Fate, Love and Pity*, translated by Fitzwater Wray, 1918.
Le Feu: Journal d'une escouade. 1916; edited by Pierre Paraf, 1965; as *Under Fire: The Story of a Squad*, translated by Fitzwater Wray, 1917.
Clarté. 1919; as *Light*, translated by Fitzwater Wray, 1919.
L'Illusion. 1919.
Les Enchaînements. 2 vols., 1925; as *Chains*, translated by Stephen Haden Guest, 2 vols., 1925.

Verse

Pleureuses. 1895.

Other

La Lueur dans l'abîme. 1920.
Paroles d'un combattant: articles et discours. 1920.
Le Couteau entre les dents. 1921.
Quelques coins du coeur, illustrated by Frans Masereel. 1921.
Lettre aux intellectuels. 1921.
L'Étrangère. 1922.
Trois films: Force; L'Au-delà; Le Crieur. 1926.
Les Bourreaux. 1926.
Jésus. 1927; as *Jesus*, edited by Malcolm Cowley, translated by Solon Librescot, 1927.
Les Judas de Jésus. 1927.
Manifeste aux intellectuels. 1927.

Faits divers. 1928; as *And I Saw It Myself*, translated by Brian Rhys, 1928; as *Thus and Thus*, translated by Rhys, 1929.
Voici ce qu'on fait de la Géorgie. 1929.
Ce qui fut sera. 1930.
Élévation. 1930.
Russie. 1930; as *One Looks at Russia*, translated by Warre B. Wells, 1931.
J'accuse. 1932.
Zola. 1932; as *Zola*, translated by Mary Balairdie Green and Frederick C. Green, 1932.
Staline: Un monde nouveau vu à travers un homme. 1935; as *Stalin: A New World as Seen Through One Man*, translated by Vyvyan Holland, 1935.
Lettres de Henri Barbusse à sa femme 1914–1917. 1937.

*

Critical Studies: *Henri Barbusse, soldat de la paix* by A. Vidal, 1953; *Henri Barbusse: Sa marche vers la Clarté, son mouvement Clarté* by Vladimir Brett, 1963; *Communism and the French Intellectuals 1914–1960* by David Caute, 1964; *Three French Writers and the Great War: Studies in the Rise of Communism and Fascism* by Frank Field, 1975.

* * *

Henri Barbusse was a writer and political activist at the centre of the preoccupation with Russian communism which characterized so many French intellectuals and artists in the early part of the 20th century. He began his career as a poet in the symbolist vein, wrote a naturalist novel *L'Enfer* (*The Inferno*), and then came the key novel *Le Feu: Journal d'une escouade* (*Under Fire: The Story of a Squad*), which won him the prestigious Goncourt prize. A further novel *Clarté* (*Light*), also the name of a political organization he co-founded, marked a movement on his part towards a strong political commitment to Marxism which culminated in the adulatory biography of Stalin.

When he first made the change from poetry to the novel in *The Inferno*, the move was fuelled by his sense of the helpless suffering of human beings in the face of the passions and ambitions that dominate them. In the novel, a man comes to Paris in order to work in a bank. Through a hole in the wall, he witnesses the actions of his neighbours and recognizes that there is no possibility that they can escape the futile suffering of existence. This bleak pessimism is both underpinned and, to some extent, transcended by his experiences of the war and the writing of *Under Fire*. As in Remarque's *All Quiet on the Western Front*, it is in the comradeship of the front line soldier that Barbusse sees some sense of meaning holding existence together, despite all the terrors of war.

The path which took him towards socialism, atheism, and humanism was greatly influenced by his experience of the horrors of World War I. Although he had symbolist beginnings, it was clear that, unlike the majority of those in that movement, he was not able to detach himself from awareness of and fellow feeling for the pain of others. *Under Fire* conveys not just a direct and uncompromising picture of the sufferings of the common soldiers in World War I, but also their political aspirations towards a world of equality and international brotherhood. As in much of his writing, political conviction rubbed shoulders uncomfortably with emotional commitment and narrative power. *Under Fire* in particular expresses this duality between creative writing and propaganda.

Barbusse was a genuine patriot, who saw in World War I a horror so great that it would purge humanity for ever of the lust for battle. He began to turn his attention more towards political activism in the movement Clarté, founded in 1919 and conceived as an international intellectual organization dedicated to peace. The committee that was to run Clarté contained a prestigious roll-call of names, among them Thomas Hardy, Georges Duhamel, Upton Sinclair, H.G. Wells, and Stefan Zweig. This left-wing movement had strong links with the French Communist Party (PCF), and it is typical of the contemporary relationships between the left-wing in France and intellectuals that so many writers and thinkers joined its ranks. Despite his political views, though, Barbusse held off from joining the PCF until 1923, at the time when France occupied the Ruhr, an act opposed by the PCF. He then resolved to become an activist on behalf of socialism and internationalism. The concept of the nation state should be overcome by the brotherhood of man, by joining hands across political frontiers. He became convinced that Lenin was right in stating that imperialism and capitalism were responsible for military aggression. To overcome these twin evils, even the use of force was (ironically) justified.

In 1929, the worldwide financial collapse coupled with the rise of fascism underpinned even further Barbusse's communist convictions. He became increasingly pro-Soviet, and for a man who was not an unquestioning supporter of the party line, it was somewhat paradoxical to see in his biography of Stalin writing in unquestioningly glowing tones about the Soviet leader. His defence of Soviet communism was not so much an act of simple faith as a recognition on his part that it alone could act as a defence against fascism and the threat of yet another European war. In sum, Barbusse was a man of great conviction so convinced of the evils of capitalist society and the horrors of world war that it had spawned that it had failed to see the even greater dangers of world communism.

—Rex Last

UNDER FIRE: THE STORY OF A SQUAD (Le Feu: Journal d'une escouade)
Novel by Henri Barbusse, 1916.

Under Fire: The Story of a Squad was actually written partly in the front-line trenches of World War I, partly in hospital after Barbusse had been wounded. His works have always tended to be a less than easy compromise between narrative and message, in which the propaganda element tends to stand constantly in the way of the relating of a tale. Add to this a strong measure of fiery emotionalism and it is not surprising that much of his writings could be encompassed in Brian Rhys's description of one of Barbusse's non-fiction works as 'inspiring and exasperating by turns'.

Under Fire is not immune from these deficiencies, even though it is drawn from direct experience of war-time fighting in the trenches. It begins with a strange section marked 'Vision', in which those remote beings at the seat of power determine that war shall break out, while the millions who fight and suffer as a result of that edict are depicted as slaves who are driven by the horrors of the military conflict to experience the will to rise up, like some military proletariat, and create a new internationalist world.

Like its frankly far superior German counterpart, *All Quiet on the Western Front*, the novel is written in the first person and the historic present, which clearly lend it immediacy and directness of impact, although it is drawn from such close quarters that there is little sense of a positively structured literary whole. It is more a collection of episodes than a coherent narrative strand.

The common soldiers who are depicted in *Under Fire* are largely working class in origin, very diverse in their backgrounds yet very much on common ground in that they have been forced by the brutal and brutalizing conditions of war to revert to a primeval, semi-animalistic state. Life is reduced to the basics of eating, drinking, sleeping, and fighting. They become very much creatures who are close to the earth. They share a sense of class solidarity and of contempt for their social superiors, as one incident illustrates. A couple of journalists dressed up to the nines appear on a visit of inspection, to be condemned by one of the *poilus* as 'trench tourists'. These visitors speak of the common soldiery as if they were an alien race. It is almost as if the journalists were enjoying a trip to the zoo, observing the animals and their antics behind bars.

As in *All Quiet on the Western Front*, the events in the life of the ordinary private soldier are seen in terms of setting off, joining battle, and returning—but unlike the Crusades, these episodes are seen as fundamentally meaningless: chance, not fate, determines who lives and who dies. In depicting this constant struggle against the odds to survive, dialogue, for the most part taut and well-written, predominates. But there are also telling moments of descriptive writing, notably when the soldiers go with one of their number to visit his native village, which has been retaken, only to find that the village has been totally obliterated in the fighting. There is a powerful evocation of the senselessness of a victory that destroys what it purports to be defending.

In the end, though, the descriptions of battle, all uniformly harrowing, tend to desensitize the reader with their routine awfulness:

I recall that I strode over a smouldering corpse, quite black, with a rivulet of red blood shrivelling on him . . .
In the ground there are several layers of the dead . . .
There are no bodies. But worse than that, a solitary arm protrudes bare and white as stone, from a hole which shows faintly on the other side of the water . . .

It is almost as if language itself is giving up the unequal struggle to express that which cannot adequately be conveyed by mere words.

During one advance, an officer leads the soldiers under his command astray, and in order to proceed further they are faced with the choice of exposing themselves to the withering fire in the open or picking their way through a latrine trench. The debasement that they are forced to confront if they are to stand a chance of survival epitomizes both the way in which war has crushed every last drop of civilized humanity out of them and also the total inability of those who have been set in authority above them to rise to the challenges of leadership.

At the end of the novel, the soldiers discuss the meaninglessness of the conflict. As one of them puts it: 'Two armies fighting each other—it's just like one huge army committing suicide!' The only possible meaning to come out of the war would be that its sheer awfulness would ensure there would be no more war, and that the common people should be instrumental in bringing reality to this resolve: 'All the masses should agree together. . . . All men should be equal.'

The political message then emerges fully into the light of day. Of the triumvirate of abstractions on which the French revolution was founded, only one has any validity: 'Equality is for ever unchanging. Liberty and fraternity are just words, whilst equality is a fact.' The novel ends on a note of half-optimism: 'Between two masses of gloomy cloud a tranquil gleam emerges, and that sliver of light, so edged in black, proves none the less that the sun is there.'

—Rex Last

BARCA, Pedro Calderón de la. See **CALDERÓN de la Barca, Pedro.**

BASHŌ. Born Matsuo Munefusa at Ueno, near Kyoto, Japan, in 1644. In service to a local lord of samurai status, and studied poetry with him until the lord's death in 1666; then led an unsettled life: in Edo (now Tokyo) after 1672; lived in a recluse's hut near Edo from 1680, and took his name from banana (*bashō*) tree growing there, which he admired for its lack of practical utility: in Japan it produces no fruit and its leaves give no shade; his travels were described in verse and prose in journals and diaries; collections of his works appeared from 1684. *Died early Autumn 1694.*

PUBLICATIONS

Collection

Zenshū [Complete Works], general editor Komiya Toyotaka. 10 vols., 1959–69.

Works

Oku no hosomichi. 1702; as *The Narrow Road to the Deep North*, translated by Nobuyuki Yuasa, in *The Narrow Road to the Deep North and Other Travel Sketches*, 1966; also translated by Earl Miner, in *Japanese Poetic Diaries*, 1969; as *The Narrow Road to the Deep North*, translated by Dorothy Britton, 1974; as *Narrow Road to the Interior*, translated by Sam Hamill, 1991; selections translated by Donald Keene, in *Anthology of Japanese Literature*, 1955; selections as *Back Roads to Far Towns*, translated by Cid Corman and Kamaike Susumu, 1968.
Haiku (includes about 250 verses by Bashō), translated by R.H. Blyth. 4 vols., 1949–52.
'Basho's Journey to Sarashina', translated by Donald Keene, in *Transactions of the Asiatic Society of Japan*. December 1957.
'Basho's Journey of 1684', translated by Donald Keene, in *Asia Major*. December 1959.
The Narrow Road to the Deep North and Other Travel Sketches, translated by Nobuyuki Yuasa. 1966.
A Darkening Sea: Poems of Basho, translated by David Aylward. 1975.
The Monkey's Straw Raincoat and Other Poetry of the Basho School, translated by Earl Miner and Hiroko Odagiri. 1981.
One Hundred Frogs, edited by Hiroaki Sato, various translators. 1983.

Traveler My Name, translated by Lucien Stryk. 1984.
On Love and Barley: Haiku of Basho, translated by Lucien Stryk. 1985.

*

Critical Studies: *An Introduction to Haiku*, by H.G. Henderson, 1958; *Zeami, Basho, Yeats, Pound: A Study in Japanese and English Poetics*, 1965, *Basho*, 1970, and *Basho and His Interpreters: Selected Hokku with Commentary*, 1992, all by Makoto Ueda; 'Basho' by Earl Miner, in *Textual Analysis: Some Readers Reading* edited by Mary Ann Caws, 1986; 'The Meaning of Basho's *shigure*' by Ock Hee You, in *Transactions of the International Conference of Orientalists in Japan*, 33, 1988.

*   *   *

Bashō is recognized as one of Japan's greatest literary figures. He transformed haiku from a somewhat frivolous pastime into a serious art form and he remains to this day its greatest exponent. He was in addition a seminal critic and teacher. Though he himself produced only a few works of criticism, many of his critical opinions and comments are preserved in the voluminous notes and accounts of his pupils, particularly Mukai Kyorai and Hattori Doho. Such is the importance of his critical precepts and the example of his poetry that no writer of haiku from his time to the present has been able to escape his influence.

In Bashō's own day the haiku was regarded not as a form in itself but as the first stanza (the *hokku*) of a longer poem consisting of up to a hundred linked stanzas written by two or more poets taking turns. Much of Bashō's effort was given to this type of composition, known as *renku* or *haikai no renga*, and it was in this field that he showed his greatest superiority, for he was an unrivalled master at the subtleties of linking stanzas and controlling the changes of pace, mood, and theme, which are the essence of this extremely demanding form.

Bashō was also a skilled prose writer. He was as meticulous in his prose as in his verse and virtually forged a new style, in which he integrated prose and poetry to an extent never before achieved. In addition to his few critical commentaries, he produced *haibun*, which are short occasional essays written in the haiku spirit, and travel journals. His *Genjuan no ki* [Essay on the Unreal Dwelling] is a moving apologia for his life and is generally considered the finest *haibun* ever written. His travel journal *Oku no hosomichi (The Narrow Road to the Deep North)* is his most famous work and one of the masterpieces of Japanese literature, in which he displays his mastery of prose style together with a sure command of form and the highest skill at reshaping events into art.

Bashō's greatness lies not only in his technique but in the depth of his probing of life. To him art was a way of life, a search for religious truth, which was to be found in nature: and this search led to continuous development, giving his work a variety that can appeal to all types of reader. Following his move to Edo, his style changed from refined and often artificial wit to genuine humour in more mundane subjects; and on settling at his Bashō hermitage he continued this trend towards greater simplicity, objectivity, and description, creating a style of his own. The years of his wanderings saw his creative peak in the style of *sabi* ('loneliness'), in which nature, usually in its most insignificant forms, is shown quietly fulfilling its often bleak destiny. In his final years he turned to *karumi* ('lightness'), an obscure term that seems to imply a more contented attitude of acceptance and less tension within a poem. To some, this step was retrograde, but however it is judged, it shows Bashō developing and striving to the end to perfect his art in the light of his philosophy of life.

—P.T. Harries

———

BASSANI, Giorgio. Born in Bologna, Italy, 4 April 1916. Educated at Liceo Ludovico Ariosto, Bologna; University of Bologna, from 1934, degree in literature. Began anti-fascist activity in 1942: imprisoned briefly, 1943, and after release took part in the Resistance; used pseudonym Giacomo Marchi for several years to avoid Nazi and Fascist persecution. Married Valeria Sinigallia in 1943, one son and one daughter. Lived in Ferrara until 1943, then in Rome; after World War II worked as scriptwriter and film dubbing editor; editor, *Botteghe Oscure*, Rome, 1948–60; co-editor, *Paragone*, Milan, 1953–55; editor, Feltrinelli, publishers, Milan, 1958–64; instructor in history of the theatre, Academy of Dramatic Art, Rome, 1957–68; vice-president, Radio Televisione Italiana, Rome, 1964–65. President, from 1966, and currently honorary president, Italia Nostra. Recipient: Veillon prize, 1955; Strega prize, 1956; Viareggio prize, 1962; Campiello prize, 1969; Nelly Sachs prize, 1969; Bagutta prize, 1983. Lives in Rome.

PUBLICATIONS

Fiction

Una città di pianura (as Giacomo Marchi). 1940.
La passeggiata prima di cena. 1953.
Gli ultimi anni di Clelia Trotti. 1955.
Il romanzo di Ferrara. 1974; revised edition, 1980.
  Cinque storie ferraresi. 1956; revised edition, as *Dentro le mura*, 1974; as *A Prospect of Ferrara*, translated by Isabel Quigly, 1962; as *Five Stories of Ferrara*, translated by William Weaver, 1971.
  Gli occhiali d'oro. 1958; with variants, 1970; as *The Gold-Rimmed Spectacles*, translated by Isabel Quigly, 1960; as *The Gold-Rimmed Eyeglasses*, translated by William Weaver, in *The Smell of Hay*, 1975.
  Il giardino dei Finzi-Contini. 1962; as *The Garden of the Finzi-Continis*, translated by Isabel Quigly, 1965; also translated by William Weaver, 1977.
  Dietro la porta. 1964; as *Behind the Door*, translated by William Weaver, 1973.
  L'airone. 1968; as *The Heron*, translated by William Weaver, 1970.
  L'odore del fieno (stories). 1972; as *The Smell of Hay* (includes *The Gold-Rimmed Eyeglasses*), translated by William Weaver, 1975.
Una notte del '43. 1960.
Le storie ferraresi (includes the five stories of *Cinque storie ferraresi*, *Gli occhiali d'oro*, and the stories 'Il muro di cinta' and 'In esilio'). 1960.
Due novelle. 1965.
Di là dal cuore. 1984.

Verse

Storie di poveri amanti e altri versi. 1945; enlarged edition, 1946.

Te lucis ante. 1947.

Un' altra libertà. 1952.

L'alba ai vetri: Poesie 1947–1950. 1963.

Epitaffio. 1974; parts translated in *Rolls Royce and Other Poems*, 1982.

In gran segreto. 1978; parts translated in *Rolls Royce and Other Poems*, 1982.

In rima e senza. 1982.

Rolls Royce and Other Poems (bilingual edition), edited and translated by Francesca Valente and others. 1982.

Play

The Stranger's Hand (screenplay), with Guy Elmes and Graham Greene. 1954.

Screenplay: *The Stranger's Hand*, with Guy Elmes and Graham Greene, 1954.

Other

Le parole preparate e altri scritti di letteratura (essays). 1966.

*

Critical Studies: *Bassani* by Giorgio Varanini, 1970; 'The *Storie ferraresi* of Giorgio Bassani', in *Italica*, 49, 1972, and 'Bassani's Ironic Mode', in *Canadian Journal of Italian Studies*, 1, 1978, both by Marianne Shapiro; '*The Garden of the Finzi-Continis*' by Stanley G. Eskin, in *Literature/Film Quarterly*, 1, 1973; 'Mythical Dimensions of Micòl Finzi-Contini', in *Italica*, 51, 1974, 'A Conversion to Death: Giorgio Bassani's *L'airone*', in *Canadian Journal of Italian Studies*, 1, 1978, and *Vengeance of the Victim: History and Symbol in Giorgio Bassani's Fiction*, 1986, all by Marilyn Schneider; 'Transformation in Bassani's Garden', in *Modern Fiction Studies*, 21, 1975, 'The Closed World of Giorgio Bassani', in *Italian Culture*, 3, 1981, 'Exile in the Narrative Writings of Giorgio Bassani', in *Italian Culture*, 5, 1984, 'Bassani: The Motivation of Language', in *Italica*, 62(2), 1985, *The Exile into Eternity: A Study of the Narrative Writings of Giorgio Bassani*, 1987, and 'Bassani: The Guilt Beyond the Door', in *Gradiva*, 4(2[6]), 1988, all by Douglas Radcliff-Umstead; 'Art and Death in Bassani's Poetry' by Stelio Cro, in *Canadian Journal of Italian Studies*, 1, 1978; *Invito all lettura di Bassani* by Massimo Grillandi, 1980; 'Giorgio Bassani: The Record of a Confession' by Diego L. Bastianutti, in *Queen's Quarterly*, 88(4), 1981; *Le forme del sentimento: Prosa e poesie in Giorgio Bassani* by Anna Dolfi, 1981; 'Insiders and Outsiders: Discourses of Oppression in Giorgio Bassani's *Gli occhiali d'oro*' by Mirna Cicioni, in *Italian Studies*, 41, 1986; 'Visual Memory and the Nature of the Epitaph: Bassani's *Epitaffio*' by Linda Nemerow-Ulman, in *Italian Quarterly*, 27(106), 1986; 'Narrated and Narrating I' in *Il giardino dei Finzi-Contini* by Harry Davis, in *Italian Studies*, 43, 1988; 'The Structures of Silence: Re-reading Giorgio Bassani's *Gli occhiali d'oro*' by Lucienne Kroha, in *The Italianist*, 10, 1990.

* * *

All Giorgio Bassani's fiction is set in the Northern Italian town of Ferrara in the years from the beginning of the 20th century to the late 1940s. He painstakingly revised his fictional writings twice, and finally published them as a whole under the comprehensive title *Il romanzo di Ferrara*. The town is a microcosm of Italian society, revisited in the light of memory by the first-person narrator of *Gli occhiali d'oro* (*The Gold-Rimmed Eyeglasses*), *Il giardino dei Finzi-Contini* (*The Garden of the Finzi-Continis*), and *Dietro la porta* (*Behind the Door*): a young middle-class Jew, who observes and judges the effects of history on social life and relationships between people divided by politics, sex, class, and, above all, race. Bassani's main focus is on the small Jewish community of Ferrara, which is represented as at first fully integrated with, and almost completely assimilated into, Gentile bourgeois—and later Fascist—society, only to face the shock, isolation, and despair of being labelled 'other' and 'undesirable' by the 1938 anti-semitic laws. In a 1964 interview Bassani defined himself as 'the historian of the past', and 20 years later stated that he had been the first Italian writer to have written about Italian Jews within their historical and political context. The emphasis in all his writings on meticulous reconstruction of details—such as street names, trade names of watches, bicycles, and typewriters, and contemporary cultural references such as journal articles, popular films, and names of well-known public figures—can thus be interpreted as a desire to commit the past to memory as accurately as possible, because that past was irreparably lost with the Holocaust. This desire is fully consistent with the basic notion in Jewish culture that remembering the past is a religious duty for each Jew, and that temporal history is indissolubly connected with sacred history.

This historical perspective has a linguistic correlative in Bassani's writings in its 'social indirect speech', where the narrator voices the collective opinions and judgements of the Ferrara bourgeoisie in its own vocabulary and phraseology. This 'social indirect speech', however, like the community itself, is never fully homogenous: the narrator distances himself from it by expressing his own historical and moral judgements, and within the community individual characters attempt to formulate alternative political and social discourses.

The protagonists of the *Cinque storie ferraresi* (*Five Stories of Ferrara*) are individuals who are, at the same time, both part of the Ferrara community and isolated from it, physically and socially: they are enclosed behind windows and within cell-like rooms, locked within their historical and personal failures. A Jewish doctor marries outside his faith and his class; an old Socialist schoolteacher under house arrest fruitlessly attempts to convey her historical insights to a young middle-class Jew; an invalid refuses to give evidence against the Fascist murderers of 11 anti-Fascist and Jewish prisoners; and, most compelling of all, a Jew returns to Ferrara from Buchenwald and disappears again after trying unsuccessfully to make the town confront its historical responsibilities.

The Gold-Rimmed Eyeglasses, set in 1937, depicts conflicting discourses about integration and 'outsiders'. The heterosexual Jewish narrator tells the story of the gradual ostracism and destruction by the heterosexual bourgeoisie of a Gentile homosexual doctor who is driven to suicide, while his former Jewish friends, unable or unwilling to support him, begin to experience the alienation of the anti-semitic laws and to feel the shadow of their own destruction.

The title of *The Garden of the Finzi-Continis* displays both the self-imposed exile of the aristocratic Jewish family that lives within the garden's walls, and a temporary illusion of solidarity when its gates are opened up to the ostracized

Jewish youth after the advent of the anti-semitic laws. Some of the characters (the 20-year-old narrator; his integrated, Fascist father; his friends Micòl and Alberto Finzi-Contini, and their elderly, scholarly father) do endeavour to define their identity in a multiplicity of Jewish discourses. However, none of these discourses is presented as strong enough to oppose the dominant Fascist ideology. Significantly, the novel is pervaded by images of death, from the opening scene which links an Etruscan necropolis to the Jewish cemetery of Ferrara, to recurring references to cemeteries and literary references to silence and mourning.

In *Behind the Door*, set during 1929–30, the first-person narrator recounts his loss of innocence and trust at the age of 15, as a consequence of being ruthlessly betrayed by a Gentile classmate, and emphasizes the covert intolerance present in Ferrara long before the anti-semitic laws.

With *L'airone* (*The Heron*)—his last novel, set in 1947—Bassani returned to third-person narration. The protagonist, a wealthy Jew who has survived the war relatively unscathed, resolves to take his own life because of his hopeless disillusionment with the new social order, and his own lack of a cultural and personal identity. His spiritual emptiness is heightened by his isolation and alienation from what is left of the Jewish community, irreparably shattered by the war. Symbols of death also abound in this work: the protagonist identifies his pain and despair with those of a heron wounded by a hunting party, and his longing for peace away from life with a display of stuffed animals in a taxidermist's window.

The Ferrara Cycle also includes *L'odore del fieno* (*The Smell of Hay*), a series of separate stories which further develop characters or situations mentioned in the longer fiction works. Bassani's poetry—most of which has not been translated into English—moves from early reflections on his own Jewishness to later sarcastic observations on the cultural trends of the Italy of the 1970s. Significantly, many poems have an hourglass shape: although Bassani's major 'historiography' project is now complete, all his writings share its historical dimension.

—Mirna Cicioni

BAUDELAIRE, Charles (Pierre). Born in Paris, France, 9 April 1821. Educated at Collège de Lyon, 1832–36; École Louis-le-Grand, Paris, 1836; expelled 1839; completed studies at Pension Levêque et Bailly, Paris, baccalauréat, 1839; law student, University of Paris, 1839–41. Contracted syphilis and fell into debt; sent on a voyage to India by his parents, 1841, left the ship in Mauritius and returned to Paris; after 1842, was able to live on an inheritance from his father; art critic and translator; publication of *Les Fleurs du mal*, 1861, led to a trial for indecency, fined for offences against public morals and six poems were suppressed; moved to Brussels, 1864; returned to Paris, 1866; spent rest of his life in a sanatorium. *Died 31 August 1867.*

PUBLICATIONS

Collections

Oeuvres complètes: Les Fleurs du mal; Curiosités esthétiques; L'Art romantique; Petits poèmes en prose, Les Paradis artificiels, La Fanfarlo, Le Jeune Enchanteur, foreword by Théophile Gautier. 4 vols., 1868–69.
Oeuvres complètes, edited by Jacques Crépet and Claude Pichois. 19 vols., 1922–53.
Oeuvres complètes, edited by Claude Pichois. 2 vols., 1975–76.
Complete Verse (bilingual edition), edited and translated by Francis Scarfe. 2 vols., 1986–89.

Verse

Les Fleurs du mal. 1861; revised editions, 1861, 1868 (in *Oeuvres complètes*); as *The Flowers of Evil,* 1909; numerous subsequent translations including by George Dillon and Edna St Vincent Millay, 1936; Geoffrey Wagner, 1946; Roy Campbell, 1952; W. Aggeler, 1954; Francis Scarfe (in prose), 1961; Florence Louie Friedman, 1966; Richard Howard, 1982.
Les Épaves. 1866.
Le Parnasse contemporain (includes 'Les Nouvelles Fleurs du mal'). 1866.
Petits Poèmes en prose. 1869; as *Paris Spleen,* translated by Louise Varèse, 1869; as *Poems in Prose,* translated by Arthur Symons, 1905; as *Little Poems in Prose,* translated by Aleister Crowley, 1928; as *The Parisian Prowler,* translated by Edward K. Kaplan, 1989.
Vers retrouvés. 1929.
Selected Verse, translated by Francis Scarfe. 1961.
Flowers of Evil and Other Works, edited and translated by Wallace Fowlie. 1964.
Selected Poems, edited and translated by Joanna Richardson. 1975.
City Blues, translated by F.W.J. Hemmings. 1977.
Selected Poems, translated by John Goudge. 1979.
Spleen, translated by Elliot Ross. 1984.
The Prose Poems and La Fanfarlo, translated by Rosemary Lloyd. 1991.

Fiction

La Fanfarlo. In *Oeuvres complètes,* 1868–69; as *La Fanfarlo,* translated by Greg Boyd, 1986; also translated by Rosemary Lloyd, 1991.

Other

Salon de 1845. 1845; edited by André Ferran, 1933.
Salon de 1846. 1846; edited by David Kelley, 1975.
Théophile Gautier. 1859; edited by Philippe Terrier, 1985.
Les Paradis artificiels: Opium et haschisch. 1860.
Richard Wagner et Tannhäuser à Paris. 1861.
Le Peintre de la vie moderne. 1863.
L'Oeuvre et la vie d'Eugène Delacroix. 1863; as *Eugene Delacroix: His Life and Work,* translated by Joseph Bernstein, 1948.
Journaux intimes. 1920; as *Intimate Journals,* translated by Christopher Isherwood, 1930.
Selected Writings on Art and Artists, translated by P.E. Charvet. 1932.
Selected Critical Studies, edited by Douglas Parmée. 1949.
The Mirror of Art: Critical Studies, edited and translated by Jonathan Mayne. 1955.
Baudelaire: A Self-Portrait (selected letters), edited by Lois Boe and F.E. Hyslop. 1957.
Baudelaire as a Literary Critic (essays), edited and translated by Lois Boe and F.E. Hyslop. 1964.

The Painter of Modern Life and Other Essays, edited and translated by Jonathan Mayne. 1964.

Art in Paris 1845–1862: Salons and Other Exhibitions, edited and translated by Jonathan Mayne. 1965.

Edgar Allan Poe, sa vie et ses ouvrages, edited by W.T. Bandy. 1973.

Correspondance, edited by Claude Pichois and Jean Ziegler. 2 vols., 1973.

Selected Letters, edited by Rosemary Lloyd, 1986.

My Heart Laid Bare and Other Prose Writings, edited by Peter Quennell, translated by Norman Cameron. 1986.

Critique d'art; suivi de, Critique musicale (essays), edited by Claude Pichois. 1992.

Translator, *Histoires extraordinaires, Nouvelles histoires extraordinaires, Aventures d'Arthur Gordon Pym, Euréka, Histoires grotesques et sérieuses*, by Edgar Allan Poe. 5 vols., 1856–65.

*

Bibliography: *Baudelaire et la critique française 1868–1917* by A.E. Carter, 1936, supplemented by W.T. Bandy, 1953, and P.M. Trotman, 1971; *Baudelaire Criticism 1950–1967* by R.T. Cargo, 1968.

Critical Studies: *Baudelaire the Critic* by Margaret Gilman, 1943; *Baudelaire* by P. Mansell Jones, 1952; *Baudelaire: A Study of His Poetry* by Martin Turnell, 1953; *Baudelaire: Les Fleurs du Mal* by Alison Fairlie, 1960; *Baudelaire's Tragic Hero* by D.J. Mossop, 1961; *Baudelaire: A Collection of Critical Essays* edited by Henri Peyre, 1962; *Baudelaire* by M.A. Ruff, 1966; *Baudelaire and Nature*, 1969, *Collected Essays, 1953–1988*, 1990, and *Charles Pierre Baudelaire: Les Fleurs du mal*, 1992, all by F.W. Leakey; *Baudelaire as a Love Poet and Other Essays* edited by Lois Boe Hyslop, 1969, and *Baudelaire, Man of His Time* by Hyslop, 1980; *Baudelaire* (in English) by Enid Starkie, 1971; *Baudelaire: A Lyric Poet in the Era of High Capitalism* by Walter Benjamin, translated by Harry Zohn, 1973; *Baudelaire, Prince of Clouds* by Alex de Jonge, 1976; *Baudelaire and Freud* by Leo Bersani, 1977; *Charles Baudelaire* by A.E. Carter, 1977; *Baudelaire: A Fire to Conquer Darkness* by Nicole Ward Jouve, 1980; *Baudelaire's Literary Criticism* by Rosemary Lloyd, 1981; *Baudelaire the Damned: A Biography* by F.W.J. Hemmings, 1982; *Baudelaire, Mallarmé, Valéry: New Essays in Honour of Lloyd Austin* edited by Malcolm Bowie, Alison Fairlie, and Alison Finch, 1982; *Exploding Poetry: Baudelaire/Rimbaud* by Georges Poulet, 1984; *Baudelaire: La Fanfarlo and Le Spleen de Paris* by Barbara Wright and David H.T. Scott, 1984; *Baudelaire and Le Spleen de Paris* by J.A. Hiddleston, 1987; *Baudelaire in 1859: A Study of the Sources of Poetic Creativity*, 1988, and *Baudelaire and the Second Republic: Writing and Revolution*, 1991, both by Richard D.E. Burton; *Baudelaire and the Poetics of Craft* by Graham Chesters, 1988; *The Comical as Textual Practice in Les Fleurs du mal* by John W. MacInnes, 1988; *Narrative as Performance: The Baudelairean Experience* by Marie Maclean, 1988; *Baudelaire* by Claude Pichois, translated by Graham Robb, 1989; *A Poetics of Art Criticism: The Case of Baudelaire* by Timothy Raser, 1989; *Baudelaire's Prose Poems* by E. Kaplan, 1990; *Baudelaire's Argot plastique: Poetic Caricature and Modernism* by Ainslie Armstrong McLees, 1990; *Baudelaire and Intertextuality* by Margery A. Evans, 1992; *Baudelaire and Caricature: From the Comic to an Art of Modernity* by Michele Hannoosh, 1992; *Baudelaire* by Joanna Richardson, 1994.

* * *

Poet, critic, translator, Charles Baudelaire, though largely ignored in his own time, is today considered one of the literary giants of the 19th century. His translations of five volumes of Edgar Allan Poe's tales, in addition to his three essays on the American writer, are mainly responsible for Poe's fame in France and throughout Europe. His essays on art and literature and his article on Wagner make him one of the greatest critics of the 19th century. And finally his volume of verse *Les Fleurs du mal* (*The Flowers of Evil*) and his *Petits Poèmes en prose* (*Little Poems in Prose*) have earned him the title of our first modern poet as well as one of the finest of city poets.

Baudelaire is often called 'the father of modern criticism' and 'the first aesthetician of his age', not so much because of his value judgements of individual artists and writers as because of the ideas and principles he articulated. If his essays on art are usually considered superior to those on literature, it is mainly because demands of publishers often made it necessary for him to discuss a number of minor writers, while laws of censorship forced him to resort to irony, parody, and pastiche in order to express unpopular opinions.

Except during the Revolutionary period, when for a short time he adopted a more utilitarian conception of art, Baudelaire, like Flaubert, believed that the goal of art was beauty—beauty which, when 'purified by art', could be derived from even ugliness, evil, and horror. That is why, in an unfinished epilogue intended for the second edition of *The Flowers of Evil*, he could say to the city of Paris: 'You have given me your mud and I have turned it into gold.'

Baudelaire's personal conception of beauty, as noted in his *Journaux intimes* (*Intimate Journals*), was much like that of Poe. Though he was obviously influenced by the American writer, even to the point of extensively plagiarizing him in his three Poe essays, recent investigation has proved that what he found in Poe's literary doctrine was a confirmation of his own poetic practice as well as an affirmation of aesthetic principles he had already espoused.

Like Poe, Baudelaire prefers a beauty tinged with melancholy, regret, and sadness. Like Poe also, he insists on the importance of the bizarre or strange—'an artless, unpremeditated, unconscious strangeness', as he wrote in his *Exposition universelle*. In his 1857 essay on Poe, he even agrees that 'the principle of poetry is . . . human aspiration toward a superior beauty'—a definition less characteristic of his poetry than his observation that 'every lyric poet by virtue of his nature inevitably effects a return to the lost Eden'. In his verse, Baudelaire himself often made that return, whether to the Eden of his childhood or to that of tropical seas and skies and of happiness he had known with his dark-skinned mistress.

With Delacroix, whose art he never ceased to glorify and whose opinions he frequently cited, Baudelaire believed that every age and every nation possesses its own particular beauty. In addition to its eternal or absolute element, all beauty, he maintained, must necessarily contain this particular or transitory element which, for him, was really synonymous with modernity. It was his emphasis on modernity—his call for 'the heroism of modern life' and his belief that Parisian life was 'rich in poetic and marvellous subjects'—that did much to change the course of both literature and painting and is often reflected in his own best verse.

Baudelaire was violently opposed to the servile imitation of nature as practised by the Realists. For him, as for Delacroix, nature was a dictionary whose hieroglyphics he sought to interpret. Imagination, the 'queen of all faculties', alone permits the poet to discover in the vast storehouse of nature the symbols, analogies, and correspondences that can transform reality into the poet's own vision of reality.

Baudelaire's chief claim to fame is his volume of verse *The Flowers of Evil* in which can be seen a strange amalgam of old and new. Classic in its clarity, discipline, and reliance on traditional forms, Romantic in its subjectivity, its spirit of revolt, and its macabre elements, *The Flowers of Evil* is also considered a distant forerunner of Surrealism in its use of dreams, myths, and fantasies. Far more important, however, is the fact that, by its use of suggestion as opposed to description and narration, it anticipates Symbolism and opens the door to modern poetry.

The unifying theme running throughout the six sections of *The Flowers of Evil* is that of the human condition, of the conflict between good and evil, spleen and ideal, dream and reality. Obsessed with a belief in original sin and in the duality of man and using his own personal experiences as raw material, Baudelaire examined the spiritual problems of his age with a probing, almost brutal self-analysis. Unlike the Romantics, however, he saw himself not as unique but closely akin to the reader, whom he addresses in his introductory poem as 'hypocritical reader, my counter-part, my brother'.

One of Baudelaire's most important innovations is his use of correspondences. Although in his essays he speaks of the transcendental correspondences between the visible and invisible worlds, it is the synesthetic correspondences between colours, sounds, and perfumes that he employs in both his poetry and prose. Even more characteristic is his use of the correspondences between exterior nature and his own inner world. By finding symbols in outer reality that correspond to and suggest his inner thoughts and feelings, he often succeeds in creating what he himself called 'a suggestive magic . . . containing the world exterior to the artist and the artist himself'—a suggestive magic leaving a 'lacuna' to be filled by the reader. Such use of the symbol not only allowed him to exteriorize his idea or mood, by giving concrete form to the abstract, but also helped him achieve what he termed an 'indispensable obscurity' that stops short of being hermetic.

Almost as important as his use of suggestion is Baudelaire's use of the cityscape to replace the nature description of the Romantics. Although the city is never described, its sounds are heard almost everywhere, and its presence everywhere felt. Both *The Flowers of Evil* and the *Little Poems in Prose* are permeated with the omnipresence of the city, if only through choice of imagery or through implication.

In style, Baudelaire introduced a number of innovations that have since been adopted by most modern poets. As a result of his emphasis on suggestion, the image, no longer merely peripheral, often becomes the very essence of the poem. His tendency to introduce a prosaic or even crude image in the midst of an otherwise highly poetic style as well as his remarkable ability to treat sordid reality without losing poetic elevation have been widely imitated. Equally characteristic are his musical sonorities, his subtle and suggestive rhythms, his frequent use of monologue or dialogue to achieve dramatic effect, and his mingling of the grand manner with a quiet, subdued, and conversational tone.

—Lois Boe Hyslop

SPLEEN
Poems by Charles Baudelaire, 1861 (written 1845–51).

'Spleen' is the title of four poems in *The Flowers of Evil* that are usually grouped together. It would not have been a wholly inappropriate heading for some of the neighbouring pieces, but Baudelaire also employed this anglicism as one of the two opposed elements in the most substantial section, 'Spleen and Ideal', of that volume. Moreover, *Le Spleen de Paris* is the alternative title for his *Little Poems in Prose*.

The first 'Spleen' poem is a sonnet beginning with a personification of 'Pluviôse', the rainy fifth month of the Republican calendar, corresponding more or less in time to Aquarius, from the latter part of January to the latter part of February. Its opening quatrain is very atmospheric and could be seen equally in terms of a 'tableau parisien' (Parisian scene), but the introduction of the poet's cat in the second quatrain establishes a *correspondance* between it and Baudelaire himself:

> Mon chat sur le carreau cherchant une litière
> Agite sans repos son corps maigre et galeux;
> L'âme d'un vieux poète erre dans la gouttière
> Avec la triste voix d'un fantôme frileux.

> (The tiles afford no comfort to my cat
> that cannot keep its mangy body still;
> the soul of some old poet haunts the drains
> and howls as if a ghost could hate the cold.)

The poem loses some of its intensity, however, as the spotlight switches to 'the dapper Knave of Hearts and the Queen of Spades', figures from a pack of cards rather than real people, despite their symbolism.

The second poem, of 24 lines, beginning 'J'ai plus de souvenirs que si j'avais mille ans' ('Souvenirs?/More than if I had lived a thousand years!'), evokes very well the poet's host of memories, but they are recollections redolent of death and decay rather than sweet souvenirs. Some of the images, however, are very striking: 'Je suis un cimetière abhorré de la lune' ('I am a graveyard that the moon abhors'), 'Je suis un vieux boudoir plein de roses fanées' ('I am an old boudoir where a rack of gowns,/perfumed by withered roses, rots to dust'); and in the final section of the poem the portrait of the artist as an old Sphinx forgotten and ignored. Here Baudelaire spells out the slow pace of time and makes explicit mention of 'ennui' (boredom), the synonym of 'spleen', 'fruit de la morne incuriosité/Prend les proportions de l'immortalité' ('the fruit of glum indifference which gains the dimension of eternity').

The third poem, one dense block of 18 alexandrines, depicts the poet as the king of a rainy realm, rich but impotent, young and yet very old. Most of all he is *bored*. Nothing can distract him, his hounds, his hawk, his fool, the ladies of the court. His appetites are dulled, sex has lost its appeal, 'the bed of state becomes a stately tomb'. His malady has transformed him into a paradoxical young skeleton or a dazed corpse in whose veins the green waters of Lethe have taken the place of blood. If the identity of the king remains unclear, the message of the poem is plain for all to see.

The last of the quartet commences—'Quand le ciel bas et lourd pèse comme un couvercle' ('When skies are low and heavy as a lid'). The first three of the five quatrains are subordinate clauses beginning with an anaphoric 'when'. They create a claustrophobic feeling of darkness, depression, and confinement. In the eyes of the poet, the whole planet has become a damp dungeon and the falling rain resembles prison-bars. In this context the best image that Baudelaire can find for hope is a bat beating the walls of the cell with its wings and banging its head against the rotting ceiling.

In the main clause, held back until stanza 4, the 'action' is in the form of a sudden peal of bells, whose din is interpreted by the poet as a frightful howl of fury. After this unexpected outburst of noisy protest, the imagery of the last stanza is more reminiscent in its tonality of that of lines 1–12: in a nightmarish vision of silence in his soul a line of hearses files slowly by, hope now defeated can but weep, and the earlier 'ennuis' are replaced by a more acute despotic *Angst*, dramatically planting its black flag (historically the emblem of all-out war, or popular fury, and of anarchy) on the poet's bowed skull.

Yet there is an incantatory musicality in the lines, created in part by repetition, alliteration, and onomatopoeia, in part by rhythm and rhyme, as is exemplified by the third quatrain:

> Quand la pluie étalant ses immenses traînées
> D'un vaste prison imite les barreaux,
> Et qu'un peuple muet d'infâmes araignées
> Vient tendre ses filets au fond de nos cerveaux

> (When rain falls straight from unrelenting clouds,
> forging the bars of some enormous jail,
> and silent hordes of obscene spiders spin
> their webs across the basements of our brains)

The word 'spleen' was perhaps first used in French in 1745. For Chateaubriand, it was already a 'physical sadness', a 'veritable malady'. In Baudelaire's case, it would probably be futile to speculate at length on the extent to which it may have had its source in a innate melancholic disposition, physical or psychological in its nature, or in the 'atony' to which he sometimes referred, or in hashish, or in the syphilis he contracted at the age of 19. What is really important is the fact that he was able to transmute the negative experience into positive expression: viewed in this way, the 'spleen' may stand for all the forms of evil that Baudelaire transformed into the flowers of his poems.

—Keith Aspley

TO THE READER (Au Lecteur)
Poem by Charles Baudelaire, 1855.

This poem, the opening text of *The Flowers of Evil*, appeared in print for the first time in June 1855 in the *Revue des Deux Mondes* in a selection of 18 Baudelaire poems. In both contexts it operates as an introduction or prologue. In *The Flowers of Evil* it also constitutes a second dedicatory text, to the reader, after the first one, 'to the impeccable poet/to the perfect magician of French letters/to my beloved and revered master and friend/Théophile Gautier/with a sense of the deepest humility/I dedicate these sickly flowers'. As the famous final line of 'To the Reader' destined to be incorporated by T.S. Eliot into *The Waste Land*, reveals, Baudelaire associates himself with his reader, the 'hypocrite lecteur,—mon semblable,—mon frère!' ('hypocrite reader, my alias,—my twin!').

In the ten quatrains of alexandrines Baudelaire paints a sorry portrait of the human condition, as the opening four lines amply demonstrate:

> La sottise, l'erreur, le péché, la lésine,
> Occupent nos esprits et travaillent nos corps,
> Et nous alimentons nos aimables remords,
> Comme les mendiants nourissent leur vermine.

> (Stupidity, delusion, selfishness and lust
> torment our bodies and possess our minds,
> and we sustain our affable remorse
> the way a beggar nourishes his lice.)

The poet and his reader are shown to be weak, cowardly, and sinful.

Right from this liminal text Baudelaire issues a series of reminders of the evil he chose to couple with the flowers in the title of the collection. The devil and demons are living forces at work in his universe and present in this poem, but in the third stanza Satan is rendered more God-like by the epithet Trismegistus that Baudelaire transfers to him from Hermes. As is the case elsewhere in *The Flowers of Evil*, Satan, for Baudelaire, is an ambiguous figure, not lacking in attraction, and in 'To the Reader' God is conspicuous by his absence.

Baudelaire was very aware, from bitter-sweet experience, of a whole series of dualities—God and the devil, good and evil, heaven and hell, 'Spleen and Ideal', man and woman. Aspects of the battle between body and soul are suggested in lines 7 and 8: 'Et nous rentrons gaiement dans le chemin bourbeux,/Croyant par de vils pleurs laver toutes nos taches' ('How cheerfully we crawl back to the mire:/a few cheap tears will wash our stains away!'). The full carnality of the weakness of the flesh is conveyed by the fifth stanza:

> Ainsi qu'un débauché pauvre qui baise et mange
> Le sein martyrisé d'une antique catin,
> Nous volons au passage un plaisir clandestin
> Que nous pressons bien fort comme une vieille orange.

> (Like a poor profligate who sucks and bites
> the withered breast of some well-seasoned trull,
> we snatch in passing at clandestine joys
> and squeeze the oldest orange harder yet.)

The feeling that animal passions are rampant is reinforced by references to jackals, panthers, female hounds, monkeys, scorpions, vultures, and snakes, and by the enumeration of adjectival present participles to describe the monsters—yapping, howling, grunting, crawling.

Baudelaire wallows in self-pity to some extent, giving the impression that his will is weak, but in the poem he writes of 'the precious metal of *our* will': indeed the first person plural is employed throughout, at least until the direct address in the last two lines to the reader.

There is a baroque quality in some of Baudelaire's images, in the band of demons revelling in our brains, in the play of antithesis, in the general fascination with death. At the same time he seems very original, whether it be in the inventiveness of the rhyming of 'helminthes' (helminths, intestinal worms) with 'plaintes' (complaints or moans)', or of 'houka' (hookah) with 'délicat' (delicate), or in the concentration on 'l'Ennui' which comes across as an updated version of the Romantics' *mal du siècle*.

The poem builds to a climax as Baudelaire holds back until the start of the tenth stanza that noun, the key-word probably of the whole volume, presented as a monster whose introduction occupies the whole of the previous stanza:

> Il en est un plus laid, plus méchant, plus immonde!
> Quoiqu'il ne pousse ni grands gestes ni grands cris,
> Il ferait volontiers de la terre un débris
> Et dans un bâillement avalerait le monde;
> C'est l'Ennui!—l'oeil chargé d'un pleur involontaire,
> Il rêve d'échafauds en fumant son houka.

(He is even uglier and fouler than the rest
although the least flamboyant of the lot;
this beast would gladly undermine the earth
and swallow all creation in a yawn;
I speak of Boredom which with ready tears
dreams of hangings as it puffs its pipe.)

Boredom, or 'spleen' or 'ennui', is depicted as an insidious vice and a squeamish monster, not manifesting itself in grand gestures or loud cries, but none the less laying waste to the earth and engulfing its inhabitants with a yawn.

It has been claimed that 'To the Reader' changes the emphasis from physical to moral evil. Man sins through insecurity, and insecurity, unfulfilment, is the very condition of life. (A.E. Carter, *Charles Baudelaire*, 1977). Moreover, there is a ruthlessness and a realism about Baudelaire's dissection of mankind: he observes our delight in stolen pleasures, he lays bare our all too human frailties, he is aware of our inability to resist sin and temptation. The poem becomes a panorama of life and, as such, a microcosm of a significant part of *The Flowers of Evil*. The address to, and identification with, the reader at the end, act perhaps as a warning as well as a reminder, before the reader proceeds to the remainder of the volume, where at least in the texts that are illustrations of the 'ideal', the other side of the coin, some of man's more noble, more positive aspirations, could be revealed.

—Keith Aspley

WINDOWS (Les Fenêtres)
Poem by Charles Baudelaire, 1863.

Baudelaire's problematic collection, *Le Spleen de Paris* (*Paris Spleen* or *The Parisian Prowler*), is also known as *Little Poems in Prose*. The author died before its publication and never settled on a definitive title for the collection. Indeed, although the poems' published order was set according to a plan that Baudelaire had drawn up, there is no certainty as to the author's ultimate intentions concerning them. Since they were written for the most part during the final period of his life, after the publication of *The Flowers of Evil*—Claude Pichois calls the prose poems Baudelaire's '*Fleurs du banal*' ('Flowers of Banality')—at a time when the poet's illness and general deterioration precluded careful editorial attention, there is no saying whether he would ultimately even have published them as a volume. Although Baudelaire oversaw the printing of 20 of them as *Little Poems in Prose* in three issues of *La Presse* (August–September 1862), and publication of six more was planned in a fourth issue (they were rejected, apparently on moral grounds), he himself pointed out in his dedication the fragmentary, unstructured nature of the volume, comparing it to the severed vertebrae of a snake, which can be reassembled in any order desired. Even more than his other works, the poems in *Paris Spleen* can be judged as 'provocative' in every sense of the term, perhaps the extreme example of that transmutation of 'muck' into 'gold' he claimed as the goal of his poetry in the unpublished epilogue to the 1861 edition of *The Flowers of Evil*. In a letter to Sainte-Beuve, Baudelaire spoke of a 'disagreeable moral' that typically characterized or defined his prose poems. They can also, however, be seen as a valid response to Rimbaud's later accusation that Baudelaire's 'vaunted form [in the verse poems] is shoddy (*mesquin*)': as his quintessential poetic vision freed from the shackles of French classical prosody. As such they were very influential on subsequent French poets,

starting with Rimbaud himself in his *Illuminations* and *Une saison en enfer* (*A Season in Hell*).

'Vision' is indeed what 'Windows' is primarily about, as the poem's title suggests. Typically, in a collection of works that generally eschew narration, rhythm, and rhyme, though not 'music' (as the poet points out in his dedication), this poem is a brief text, almost an essay, in five unequal paragraphs describing a characteristic Parisian situation reminiscent of the one in the poem 'Parisian Landscape' ('Paysage') of *The Flowers of Evil*. The speaker looks out of his window, across a 'wave of roofs', at another, dark window through which he sees an old woman, and he 'remakes [her] story', which he 'sometimes recounts to himself, weeping'. It could just as well be an old man, the poet says. What matters is not the reality he is looking at, but how he perceives it: the most important thing is that it 'helps [him] to live, to feel that [he] is, and what [he] is.'

The poem's longest paragraph is the first: a disquisition on windows. To the poet, the darker they are the better; candle illumination from the inside is even more satisfactory: 'There is no object more profound, more mysterious, more fruitful, more shadowy, more dazzling than a window illuminated by a candle.' Like many of Baudelaire's most important poems, this one is both visionary and *about* poetic vision, both creative and critical. His poet is a 'voyant' a seer, as in Rimbaud's celebrated formulation, but he is also, like many residents of the city, a 'voyeur'. What he is looking at is at the same time matter for penetration and food for creative imagination. As such is both essential, on the one hand, and dispensable or interchangeable, on the other. It is this dichotomy that permitted Baudelaire to write 'traditional' poetry on what he considered new—read urban—subjects, as epitomized in the 'Parisian scenes' of *The Flowers of Evil*, and helped him to become what he called in his well-known essay on Constantin Guys 'the painter of modern life'.

Dichotomy, polarity, and paradox, so characteristic of this poem, are the true stuff of Baudelaire's poetics. The 'two simultaneous postulations, one toward God, the other toward Satan', of which he speaks in his private diary, 'Mon coeur mis à nu' ('My Heart Laid Bare'), inform his thinking and his creation. It is thus we find the hyperbolic series of contradictory adjectives cited above, applied to the windows that compose the poem's subject, contradictorily described somewhat later as a 'black or shining hole,' as well as the polarity between the poet and the old woman at whom he is looking (and not looking, and who could as well be an old man), whose 'history, or rather her legend', he has recast. Liberated from the constraints of traditional form in his final creative period, Baudelaire was enabled here, even more than in his verse poems, to discover and to sing the mystery of the modern city, the poetry of the everyday, the transcendence of the commonplace.

—David Sices

BAZÁN, Emilia Pardo.   See PARDO BAZÁN, Emilia.

BEAUMARCHAIS. Born Pierre-Augustin Caron, in Paris, France, 24 January 1732. Educated at École des Métiers d'Alfort, for three years, to age 13, then apprenticed to his clockmaker father. Married 1) Madeleine-Catherine Franquet in 1756 (died 1757); 2) Geneviève-Madeleine Warebled in 1768 (died 1770), one son (died in infancy); 3) Marie-Thérèse Willermawlas in 1786 (divorced 1794; remarried 1797), one daughter. Clockmaker: his work recognized by Academy of Sciences, 1754, and popular at court; bought title of Clerk Controller in Royal Household, 1755; took name Beaumarchais from first wife's estate, 1757; also a harpist (improved the pedal system): gave lessons and organized concerts at court; bought title of Secrétaire du Roi, 1761 (and consequently ennobled, 1761), and Lt.-General of hunting in the Varenne du Louvre, 1761; visited Spain, 1764–66; involved in several spectacular court cases in 1770s; government agent, 1774–75, and responsible for aid to American insurgents, 1775; involved in founding the Bureau de Législation Dramatique (later Société des Auteurs et Compositeurs Dramatiques), 1777; arrested on suspicion of profiteering from arms, 1792, took refuge in London, but imprisoned for debt, 1792; released on payment of ransom, returned to France, 1793; left for Holland, on mission to buy arms; family imprisoned, 1794; exiled in Holland and Germany until 1796. *Died 17/18 May 1799.*

PUBLICATIONS

Collections

Oeuvres complètes, edited by Édouard Fournier. 1876.
Théâtres, Lettres relatives à son théâtre, edited by Maurice Allem and Paul Courant. 1957.
Oeuvres complètes, edited by Albert Demazière. 1973.
Théâtre, edited by Jean-Pierre de Beaumarchais. 1980.
Oeuvres, edited by Pierre Lathomas. 1988.

Plays

Colin et Colette; Les Bottes de sept lieues; Les Députés de la Halle; Léandre Marchand d'Agnus; Jean Bête à la foire (farces: probably produced c.1760–63). In *Théâtre*, 1957.
Eugénie (produced 1767). 1767; as *The School for Rakes*, translated by Elizabeth Griffith, 1769.
Les Deux Amis; ou, Le Négociant de Lyon (produced 1770). 1770; as *The Two Friends; or, the Liverpool Merchant*, translated by C.H. London, 1800.
Le Barbier de Séville; ou, La Précaution inutile (produced 1775). 1775; as *The Barber of Seville*, translated by Elizabeth Griffith, 1776; also translated by Arthur B. Myrick, 1905; W.R. Taylor, 1922; Stewart Robb, 1939; Wallace Fowlie, in *Classical French Drama*, 1962; Vincent Luciani, 1964; John Wood, 1966.
La Folle Journée; ou, Le Mariage de Figaro (produced 1784). 1785; as *The Follies of a Day; or, The Marriage of Figaro*, translated by Thomas Holcroft, 1785; as *A Mad Day's Work; or, The Marriage of Figaro*, translated by Brodbury P. Ellis, 1961; as *The Marriage of Figaro*, edited by Malcolm Cook, 1992; translated by Vincent Luciani, 1964; also translated by John Wood, 1966; William Gaskill, in *Landmarks of French Classical Drama*, edited by David Bradby, 1991.
Tarare, music by Antonio Salieri (produced 1787; revised version, produced 1790). 1790; translated as *Axur, King of Ormus*, 1813.
L'Autre Tartuffe; ou, La Mère coupable (produced 1792).

1794; as *Frailty and Hypocrisy*, translated by James Wild, 1804; as *A Mother's Guilt*, in *The Complete Figaro Plays*, 1983.

Other

Mémoires contre M. Goëzman. 1775.
Mémoires, edited by J. Ravenal. 4 vols., 1830.
Lettres inédites, edited by Gilbert Chinard. 1929.
Correspondance, edited by Brian N. Morton. 1969—.
For the Good of Mankind: Political Correspondence Relative to the American Revolution, edited and translated by Antoinette Shewmake. 1987.

*

Bibliography: *Bibliographie des oeuvres de Beaumarchais* by H. Cordier, 1883; *Beaumarchais: A Bibliography* by Brian N. Morton and Donald C. Spinelli, 1988.

Critical Studies: *Beaumarchais* by G. Lemaître, 1949; *The Comic Style of Beaumarchais* by J.B. Ratermanis and W.R. Irwin, 1961; *The Real Figaro: The Extraordinary Career of Caron de Beaumarchais* by Cynthia Cox, 1962; *Beaumarchais: Le Barbier de Séville* by Robert Niklaus, 1968; *A Critical Commentary on Beaumarchais's 'Le Mariage de Figaro'* by Anthony Pugh, 1968; *Beaumarchais* by Joseph Sungolowski, 1974; *Beaumarchais: The Man Who Was Figaro* by Frédéric Grendel, translated by Roger Greaves, 1977; 'Beaumarchais's Transformations' by Jack Undank, in *Modern Language Notes*, 100(4), 1985; *Beaumarchais: The Barber of Seville* by John Dunkley, 1991.

* * *

The creator of Figaro, perhaps the best known of all French fictional characters, was a highly successful businessman who smuggled arms to the American rebels of 1776, published a complete edition of the works of Voltaire between 1783 and 1790, and founded one of the first organizations to protect authors' rights, the *Société des Auteurs Dramatiques* (Society of Dramatic Authors), in 1777. The readiness of Figaro to defy his master Almaviva verbally in *Le Barbier de Séville* (The Barber of Seville) and to intrigue against him in *La Folle Journée; ou, Le Mariage de Figaro* (The Marriage of Figaro) was thus not the expression of any personal resentment on Beaumarchais's part towards a society which had not allowed him to prosper. It was much more the statement of a general need for the hierarchical, unjust, and inefficient society of the late 18th century to change so that other men of talent could more easily rise, as Beaumarchais himself had done, from being sons of clockmakers to becoming successful businessmen and even purchasing patents of nobility.

Both Beaumarchais's plays about Figaro have been turned into operas, the first by Rossini and the second by Mozart, and the musical genius of *Le Nozze de Figaro* inevitably makes a straight performance of the original play seem a little tame. Both plays are saved less by the plot, which is unoriginal in *The Barber of Seville* and not always easy to follow in *The Marriage of Figaro*, than by the character of Figaro himself, with his ready wit, verbal dexterity, and indomitable ingenuity. In this respect, he represents the archetypal Frenchman as the French would like to see themselves, mercifully free from the tendency to sentimental moralizing that makes its way into *The Marriage of Figaro* with the character of Marcelline, and which inspired other unperformable plays, such as *L'Autre Tartuffe; ou, La Mère coupable* (*A Mother's Guilt*). For Beaumarchais was also a man of his time in that he shared the opinion of Diderot about the need for serious plays that dealt in a serious manner with the sexual and other problems of the middle class. It is this rather than any Oedipal impulses that explains the presence of Marcelline as Figaro's mother in *The Marriage of Figaro*, and there is an interesting contrast with the lack of conviction which she carries for modern audiences and the much more genuine affection which links Figaro to Suzanne. In the history of the theatre, Beaumarchais stands as the first successful practitioner of a comic style deriving its appeal from rapidity of action, vivacity of dialogue, and complexity of intrigue. Sociologically, he provides a comment on his society by exploiting the paradox that it is the social inferior, Figaro, who far exceeds his official master, Almaviva, in wit and intelligence, and can thus be seen as an ancestor to the Jeeves/Bertie Wooster relationship in P.G. Wodehouse.

—Philip Thody

THE BARBER OF SEVILLE (Le Barbier de Séville)
Play by Beaumarchais, 1775.

This was the first comedy Beaumarchais wrote for the public stage and the first play in the Figaro trilogy—the second and third being *The Marriage of Figaro*, likewise a comedy, and *A Mother's Guilt*, a drama. Its evolution was unusually protracted. It grew initially out of a short farce (an *intermède*), *Le Sacristain* [The Sacristan] written for the private theatre of Le Normand d'Étoiles and derived from the Spanish *entremeses* (short farcical plays, often with music, performed between the acts of a longer work) with which Beaumarchais had become familiar during his stay in Spain in the mid 1760s. *Le Sacristain* also resembles the indigenous French *parades* in its scabrous tone and its conventional plot whereby Lindor, the young lover, tries to seduce Pauline, wife of the aged and impotent Bartholo.

From the incomplete manuscript of *Le Sacristain* we can see that Beaumarchais revised his text, first changing Pauline to Rosine and Lindor to Le Comte, who, from being a student, was transformed into a philandering husband who neglects his wife. Beaumarchais also introduced yet more indecent allusions into his text. Such material was clearly not intended for public performance. The text's next transformation was into an *opéra comique*, entitled *Le Barbier de Séville* and no longer extant. It was here that the character of Figaro was first introduced, in order that the 'ennobled' Lindor should not demean himself by having to cope with all the material paraphernalia involved in the multiple disguises he needed to use in order to gain access to Rosine. But leaving the physical problems to Figaro had the effect, perceptible in *The Barber of Seville* as we know it today, of marginalizing the Count (now turned into a bachelor again) and profiling the factotum. The choice of a barber character was determined by the figure's traditional use, along with the (young and attractive) sacristan, in the *entremeses*.

When this *opéra comique* was offered to the Comédie-Italienne in Paris, it was refused. Beaumarchais then expunged the obscenities and most of the songs from his text and, early in 1773, offered it to the Comédie-Française, where it was accepted for performance and passed by the censor, Marin. It was due to be performed in February 1773, but the opening was postponed when Beaumarchais was

imprisoned as a result of the Chaulnes affair. The Goezman affair followed and, having incorporated into his text allusions to his personal difficulties and those responsible for them, Beaumarchais submitted it to a second censor, Arthaud, who reported favourably. The premiere, announced for February 1774, was again postponed, frustrated in part by Madame Du Barry and in part by the author's loss of his civil rights at the close of the Goezman affair. When the play, in five acts and carrying the approval of a third censor, Crébillon *fils*, was finally staged on 23 February 1775, it was a failure. The reasons appear to have been partly that the actress who sang Rosine's songs was nervous and inaudible, partly that the plot is inadequate to fill five acts, but more importantly that the five-act text to which Beaumarchais had gradually added an excess of dubious jokes and uninteresting allusions to his personal life, was not the one which the actors were familiar with (the play had been in rehearsal for two years), and they performed badly. Beaumarchais promptly stripped away the 'accretions', so accelerating the action and emphasizing the elliptical wit of the dialogues. Three days later, the four-act version (a very unusual length) was a resounding success.

Beaumarchais's stated aim with this play was to restore to the theatre something of the fun and verve it had lost during the century, especially in the heyday of the moralizing *drame*. Though the *précaution inutile* (fruitless precaution) theme, whereby the old man tries in vain to isolate his young wife or intended wife from other potential lovers, was a hackneyed one in French literature by the 1770s, Beaumarchais infuses it with new life through memorable characters and a brilliantly honed dialogue in which he exploits fully the resources of ellipsis, assonance, pun, etc. The setting is not an accurate portrayal, but a fantasized Spain, evoked by costume (for which Beaumarchais made exact stipulations), and small details, such as guitar-playing, *alguazils*, and Spanish forms of address. Traces of the earliest heroine, Pauline, are still visible in the role of Rosine (it is impossible to categorize her as solely either an innocent or a coquette), and Figaro, though he appears in relatively few scenes, is memorable for his (more apparent than real) air of energetic omnicompetence. Bartholo, more astute than the *barbons* (aged guardians or tutors) who were his dramatic forbears, in a well-developed character whom Beaumarchais makes at times surprisingly penetrating, while at other times he intervenes artificially to thwart his villain's intentions, which are at base odiously self-indulgent. It is only in the 20th century that Bazile, Bartholo's venal accomplice (who is involved both with the Church and the fringes of the underworld) has assumed a high-profile role, thanks to the interpretation of Édouard de Max at the Comédie-Française (1916–24). His satanic pre-eminence rests largely on two particularly memorable scenes, and especially the 'hymn to calumny' of Act II, scene 8. Though Figaro has sometimes been identified with Revolutionary sentiments, this is a forced interpretation, and his remarks about the advantages conferred by the mere fact of being born noble are no more than commonplaces of the period.

—John Dunkley

BEAUVOIR, Simone (Lucie Ernestine Marie) de. Born in Paris, France, 9 January 1908. Educated at Institut Normal

Catholique Adeline-Désir, Paris, 1913–25; studied philosophy and literature at the Sorbonne, Paris, 1926; Institut Sainte-Marie, Neuilly-sur-Seine; École Normale Supérieure, Paris, agrégation in philosophy 1929. Began lifelong relationship with the writer Jean-Paul Sartre, q.v., in 1929. Part-time teacher, Lycée Victor Duruy, Paris, 1929–31; philosophy teacher, Lycée Montgrand, Marseilles, 1931–32, Lycée Jeanne d'Arc, Rouen, 1932–36, Lycée Molière, Paris, 1936–39, and Lycée Camille-Sée and Lycée Henri IV, both Paris, 1939–43. Founding editor, with Sartre, Les Temps Modernes, Paris, from 1945. Member of the Consultative Committee, Bibliothèque Nationale, 1969; president, Choisir, 1972; president, Ligue des Droits des Femmes, from 1974. Recipient: Goncourt prize, 1954; Jerusalem prize, 1975; Austrian State prize for European literature, 1978. Honorary LL.D.: Cambridge University. *Died 14 April 1986.*

PUBLICATIONS

Fiction

L'Invitée. 1943; as *She Came to Stay,* translated by Yvonne Moyse and Roger Senhouse, 1949.
Le Sang des autres. 1945; edited by John F. Davis, 1973; as *The Blood of Others,* translated by Yvonne Moyse and Roger Senhouse, 1948.
Tous les hommes sont mortels. 1946; as *All Men Are Mortal,* translated by Leonard M. Friedman, 1956.
Les Mandarins. 1954; as *The Mandarins,* translated by Leonard M. Friedman, 1957.
Les Belles Images. 1966; as *Les Belles Images,* translated by Patrick O'Brian, 1968.
La Femme rompue (includes *L'Âge de discrétion* and *Monologue*). 1968; as *The Woman Destroyed* (includes *The Age of Discretion* and *The Monologue*), translated by Patrick O'Brian, 1969.
Quand prime le spirituel (stories). 1979; as *When Things of the Spirit Come First: Five Early Tales,* translated by Patrick O'Brian, 1982.

Play

Les Bouches inutiles (produced 1945). 1945; as *Who Shall Die?,* translated by Claude Francis and Fernande Gontier, 1983.

Other

Pyrrhus et Cinéas. 1944.
Pour une morale de l'ambiguïté. 1947; as *The Ethics of Ambiguity,* translated by Bernard Frechtman, 1948.
L'Amérique au jour le jour. 1948; as *America Day by Day,* translated by Patrick Dudley, 1952.
L'Existentialisme et la sagesse des nations. 1948.
Le Deuxième Sexe: Les Faits et les mythes and L'Expérience vécue. 2 vols., 1949; as *The Second Sex,* edited and translated by H.M. Parshley, 1953; vol. 1 as *A History of Sex,* 1961, and as *Nature of the Second Sex,* 1963.
Must We Burn de Sade?, translated by Annette Michelson, 1953, and in *The Marquis de Sade,* edited by Paul Dinnage, 1953.
Privilèges (includes *Faut-il brûler Sade?*; *La Pensée de droite aujourd'hui*; *Merleau-Ponty ou le pseudo-sartrism*). 1955.
La Longue Marche: Essai sur la Chine. 1957; as *The Long March,* translated by Austryn Wainhouse, 1958.

Mémoires d'une jeune fille rangée. 1958; as *Memoirs of a Dutiful Daughter,* translated by James Kirkup, 1959.
Brigitte Bardot and the Lolita Syndrome, translated by Bernard Frechtman, 1960.
La Force de l'âge. 1960; as *The Prime of Life,* translated by Peter Green, 1962.
Djamila Boupacha, with Gisèle Halimi. 1962; as *Djamila Boupacha,* translated by Peter Green, 1962.
La Force des choses. 1963; as *Force of Circumstance,* translated by Richard Howard, 1965.
Une Mort très douce. 1964; as *A Very Easy Death,* translated by Patrick O'Brian, 1966.
La Vieillesse. 1970; as *Old Age,* translated by Patrick O'Brian, 1972; as *The Coming of Age,* translated by O'Brian, 1972.
Toute compte fait. 1972; as *All Said and Done,* translated by Patrick O'Brian, 1974.
La Cérémonie des adieux. 1981; as *Adieux: A Farewell to Sartre,* translated by Patrick O'Brian, 1984.
Lettres à Sartre, edited by Sylvie Le Bon de Beauvoir. 2 vols., 1990; as *Letters to Sartre,* edited and translated by Quintin Hoare, 1991.
Journal de guerre: septembre 1939–janvier 1941, edited by Sylvie Le Bon de Beauvoir. 1990.

Editor, *Lettres au Castor et à quelques autres 1926–1939* and *1940–1963,* by Sartre, 2 vols., 1983; as *Witness to My Life: The Letters of Jean-Paul Sartre to Simone de Beauvoir 1926–1939* and *Quiet Moments in a War: The Letters of Jean-Paul Sartre to Simone de Beauvoir 1943–63,* translated by Lee Fahnestock and Norman MacAfee, 1993–94.

*

Bibliography: *Les Écrits de Simone de Beauvoir* by Claude Francis and Fernande Gontier, 1979; *Simone de Beauvoir: An Annotated Bibliography* by Jay Bennett and Gabriella Hochmann, 1989.

Critical Studies: *Simone de Beauvoir: Encounters with Death* by Elaine Marks, 1973, and *Critical Essays on Simone de Beauvoir* edited by Marks, 1987; *Simone de Beauvoir* by Robert D. Cottrell, 1975; *Simone de Beauvoir on Woman* by Jean Leighton, 1975; *Hearts and Minds: The Common Journey of Simone de Beauvoir and Jean-Paul Sartre* by Axel Madsen, 1977; *Simone de Beauvoir* by Konrad Bieber, 1979; *Simone de Beauvoir: A Life of Freedom* by Carol Ascher, 1981; *Simone de Beauvoir and the Limits of Commitment* by Anne Whitmarsh, 1981; *Simone de Beauvoir: A Study of Her Writings* by Terry Keefe, 1983; *Understanding 'The Second Sex'* by Donald L. Hatcher, 1984; *After 'The Second Sex': Conversations with Simone de Beauvoir* by Alice Schwarzer, translated by Marianne Howarth, 1984; *Simone de Beauvoir: A Feminist Mandarin* by Mary Evans, 1985; *Simone de Beauvoir* by Judith Okely, 1986; *The Novels of Simone de Beauvoir* by Elizabeth Fallaize, 1987; *Simone de Beauvoir: A Critical View* by Renee Winegarten, 1987; *Simone de Beauvoir: A Life, A Love Story* by Claude Francis and Fernande Gontier, translated by Lisa Nesselson, 1987; *Simone de Beauvoir* by Lisa Appignanesi, 1988; *Simone de Beauvoir* by Jane Heath, 1989; *Feminist Theory and Simone de Beauvoir* by Toril Moi, 1990; *Simone de Beauvoir: A Biography* by Deirdre Bair, 1990; *Simone de Beauvoir: The Woman and Her Work* by Margaret Crosland, 1992.

* * *

Biographical criticism may be regarded in some quarters as an outmoded literary tool. However, exceptions seem to be made when discussing the work of French novelist, essayist, and thinker Simone de Beauvoir. As Toril Moi points out in *Feminist Theory and Simone de Beauvoir*, critical accounts of de Beauvoir's work regularly reduce her literary output to questions of personality, in a way that is not apparent (and would be regarded as unacceptable) in accounts of the work of contemporaries. More than almost any other woman writer, de Beauvoir has been subjected to accusations of bad faith, inauthentic experience, and compliance with masculine domination. This adverse reception has been particularly pronounced in her native France, among the second wave of feminist thinkers who emerged in the late 1960s, with more favourable appraisals coming from Britain and the United States.

Why this situation has developed with such a courageous writer can be difficult to understand. Moi locates the dismissal of de Beauvoir to the supplanting in France of her humanist and existentialist beliefs by other intellectual interests such as structuralism and post-structuralism, and to the dominant media image of the writer as a blue-stockinged, masculinized woman, an *ersatz* Sartre. This negative response, however, denies the achievement of de Beauvoir, whose literary output deserves continued interest and covers a lifetime of scrupulous thought. Although educated as a philosopher, de Beauvoir wrote only one full-length philosophical study, *Le Deuxième Sexe* (*The Second Sex*), her study of female identity, preferring to employ the literary forms of the novel, play, and autobiography to act as practical examples of her philosophical creed. In her fiction, she works through, and refines upon, ideas from Sartrian Existentialism, with problems relating to liberty, action, choice, responsibility, and the certainty of death prominent throughout. Although to some extent didactic, her work is no abstract demonstration, and her writing is further characterized by considerable incorporation of personal experience. However, such is the clarity and crispness of her expression, coupled with the continuing pertinence of many of her ideas, that it is possible to read her work without any knowledge of her philosophical tenets and biographical details.

De Beauvoir's first literary work to be published was *L'Invitée* (*She Came to Stay*), an account of how a couple's life is placed under scrutiny by the advent of a young girl from Rouen. This work investigates a theme prominent in de Beauvoir's work, that of jealousy. Françoise Miquel has had a happy relationship with the actor Pierre Labrousse for eight years. However, the pairing is threatened when Xavière Pagès comes into their life. To Françoise, Xavière represents a most unsuitable match for Pierre, and the novel ends in tragedy with Françoise murdering her rival. This tale of a *crime passionnel*, told from different viewpoints, goes beyond a realistic study of excessive jealousy, infidelity, and desire, though, as de Beauvoir also attempts to provide a concrete example of Sartre's concept of the Other (as outlined in *L'Être et le néant* [*Being and Nothingness*]), with Xavière's presence providing an extreme example of how an understanding between two people is tested by the intervention of a third.

On the whole, de Beauvoir's writings alternate between those that are locked into depicting personal relationships as such, and those that portray people's interaction within the context of historical and political events. Her only play, the overlooked *Les Bouches inutiles* (*Who Shall Die?*), adapts the Italian chronicles of Sismondi to examine the issues of political power and choice. The inhabitants of Vaucelles in Flanders have freed themselves from the tyranny of the Duke of Burgundy and have set up a representative government. But food is scarce, and the town's council must decide who is to die and who can live. The 'useless mouths' of the title represent the weaker members of the community—women, the infirm, and children—who, in a reversal of humanitarian practice, are chosen to die.

With its vivid picture of French political life on the Left in the 1930s and during the early years of the war, *Le Sang des autres* (*The Blood of Others*) also has a firmly realized political context. The head of a resistance group is waiting beside his lover who has been wounded in a rescue attempt sanctioned by him. As he waits for Hélène to die, Blomart has to decide whether to carry out political action on the following day. He muses upon his bourgeois upbringing, upon his rejection of his family's values, and upon his relationship with Hélène. In recalling his past, de Beauvoir's narrative moves from personal memories to a more objective evaluation of how Blomart was viewed by others. As in her other novels, the narrative structure of *The Blood of Others* is divided up between characters; here between the once self-centred but now politically-committed Hélène and the serious, guilt-obsessed Blomart. As in *She Came to Stay*, the issues raised here are those of interdependence, personal liberty, and responsibility, to which de Beauvoir adds questions of moral choice and commitment in times of personal and political crisis.

Tous les hommes sont mortels (*All Men Are Mortal*) stands out, rather as Sartre's *Les Jeux sont faits* (*The Chips Are Down*), does in his *oeuvre*, as a departure from the consistent realism of her works. Here de Beauvoir explores the omnipotence of death by creating a love affair between a mortal woman, Régine, an actress who is terrified of death, and Fosca, who is immortal. Régine wishes to challenge Fosca's immortality by loving him more than any previous woman. Fosca recounts his life, and rather in the way that *The Second Sex* provided a broad historical sweep of a single issue (woman's identity as Other), she leads us through a questioning of justifiable political measures from the 13th century onwards.

Régine is death-haunted, self-centred, and ambitious, while Fosca is unable to die, altruistic, and in his immortality deprived of personal goals. The pairing of individuals with very different personae is a strategy used throughout de Beauvoir's work, and appears again in her longest and most accomplished novel, *Les Mandarins* (*The Mandarins*). In this expansive work, de Beauvoir returns to a contemporary setting, and drawing extensively upon her acquaintances and experience, she outlines the manners and mores of the Paris-based Left just after the Liberation. The debate begun in *The Blood of Others*, on commitment, responsibility to self and others, and the difficult ethical choices posed by political action, is continued in this stimulating and densely textured account of de Beauvoir's circle. Centred on the threat to the autonomy of a political magazine (not that remote from *Les Temps Modernes*, to which she contributed), this novelization of lived events contrasts the political behaviour of an enthusiastic and vital writer, Perron, with that of an older, more pragmatic and experienced political activist, Dubreuilh. A further perspective is provided by Anne Dubreuilh, who is a watchful and contained figure compared to the impulsive and active Henri.

De Beauvoir's next novel, *Les Belles Images*, recreates the codes and types of behaviour of a certain social group as acutely as *The Mandarins* does. This is much less of a *roman à clef* than previous works, as the milieu that de Beauvoir has chosen is that of the well-heeled elite who work in the media (*la grosse bourgeoisie technocratique*). Surrounded by expensive possessions, entertained by fashionable chatter, and preoccupied by getting on, the characters in *Les Belles Images* have affairs, take expensive holidays, and suffer under the stresses of late 20th-century affluence. *Les Belles Images* deals with the question of personal development, above all that of children. The book's main character Laurence, whose own mother is successful and domineering, is challenged by her daughter Catherine's awareness of poverty and misery outside their comfortable world. Forced to recall her own childhood and to reappraise her relations with her ambitious mother and her surprisingly self-centred father, Laurence undergoes a personal crisis.

Despite the fact that de Beauvoir elected not to be a mother, family life, in particular the effect of ageing on existing relationships, dominates this phase of her writing career, as is evident from her collection of short stories *La Femme rompue* (*The Woman Destroyed*), and her studies of old age, *Une Mort très douce* (*A Very Easy Death*), which deals with her mother's final illness, and *La Vieillesse* (*The Coming of Age*). In her three stories, de Beauvoir dissects the fears, failings, and personal stagnation of women who have reached a certain age. *L'Âge de discrétion* (*The Age of Discretion*) investigates how an elderly teacher has to come to terms with her son becoming another person from the one that she has nurtured and idealized. Unable to change or compromise, she rejects him and finds herself at odds with her husband's more phlegmatic attitude. *Monologue* is a powerful, first-person account of a woman consumed by self-destructive spleen and antagonism towards her family. Alone on New Year's Eve, Murielle, who has been rejected by two husbands, on account of her being held responsible for her daughter's suicide, rages madly against her lot. *The Woman Destroyed* is the strongest piece in the collection, and is a diary account of a middle-aged woman discovering her husband's infidelities. Monique has deceived herself into thinking she has the perfect marriage. Her husband's infatuation with what Monique considers to be a totally unsuitable woman, a glamorous and striving lawyer, leaves the distraught wife trapped within what remains of her marriage, unable to break free and create a life for herself.

The desire to seize what choices are possible, and to subject your own life to constant scrutiny, are the central impressions of de Beauvoir's four-part autobiography that runs alongside her fictional work. As with Anaïs Nin's journals, these volumes provide a fascinating account of intellectual and artistic life in Paris, here from 1914 to the 1960s. The first volume, *Mémoires d'une jeune fille rangée* (*Memoirs of a Dutiful Daughter*), investigates her own upbringing as a child of a Parisian middle-class family and her rejection of her family's religious and moral views. *La Force de l'âge* (*The Prime of Life*) evaluates her intellectual and personal development after leaving university and during the war years. *La Force des choses* (*Force of Circumstance*), the most pessimistic of her memoirs, delineates her life in the context of political events such as the liberation, the revelation of Nazi atrocities and the Algerian war of independence. *Toute compte fait* (*All Said and Done*), set in the 1960s, reveals de Beauvoir as more confident about her political involvement and socialist beliefs.

—Anna-Marie Taylor

THE MANDARINS (Les Mandarins)
Novel by Simone de Beauvoir, 1954.

Although de Beauvoir was awarded the 1954 Goncourt prize for *The Mandarins* and the novel enjoyed great critical success at the time of publication, de Beauvoir's challenging account of post-Occupation manners and morality has suffered a degree of critical neglect in recent years.

There are several reasons for this oversight. Its reputation as a *roman à clef* may not endear the work to a readership no longer eager (or able) to identify the members of de Beauvoir's 'family' described in fictional terms. Furthermore, just as the characters may seem locked into a particular period, the book's concern with political action and morality on the Left, and its discussion of the independent Left's relationship to the Communist Party, may seem less relevant in today's changed political climate. Similarly, the central Existentialist debate in *The Mandarins* about individual freedom and its curtailment by personal involvement and political practice may also seem to belong to a particular epoch and social group.

The Mandarins, though, is by no means a dull and worthy period-piece, and its depiction of life among a group of Paris-based intellectuals (the mandarin caste of the title) from Christmas 1944 to 1948 is still of consequence, thought-provoking and interesting 50 years on. De Beauvoir's longest novel provides us with a closely observed portrait of the hopes and endeavours of the French Left immediately after the Liberation, a picture that is multi-dimensional and finely drawn. To stress the complex nature of historical change, and the difficult ethical questions raised by involvement in political action, de Beauvoir constructs her novel around several different stories and viewpoints. The way her narrative is textured emphasizes the consequences of individual actions, with de Beauvoir threading in the various personal histories, each of which poses different questions about the nature of personal freedom and public action. As the novel consists mainly of satellite stories, it is hard to identify and summarize any central plot in the work, and perhaps easier to analyse the manner in which the structure of *The Mandarins* is organized. Each individual tale concerns one of a group of writers, journalists, friends, and political activists associated with the journal *L'Espoir* ['Hope']. Foremost in these stories is the relationship between Henri Perron, the editor of the journal began during the Resistance, and the much older Robert Dubreuilh, a formidable political activist and writer. Dubreuilh is much more of a pragmatist and more accustomed to *Realpolitik* than Perron, and attempts to persuade the younger man to align *L'Espoir* to the independent socialist group that he is founding. The complex relations of these two men are set against a troubled background of political events and decisions that include the bombing of Hiroshima, revenge killings of collaborators by Leftist acquaintances, and the disclosure of the realities of Stalin's regime. Their friendship (and shared political ideals) eventually founder over Henri's decision to publish accounts of Soviet labour camps.

Although we are given a sure sense of what motivates Dubreuilh, *The Mandarins* is more concerned with the progress of Perron. Parallel to his post-war fate is the story of Anne Dubreuilh, Robert's wife. She is the same age as Henri (late thirties) and is a psychiatrist. Unlike Henri, who embraces experience and partakes actively in whatever befalls him, Anne is characterized as controlled and watchful, a witness to events rather than a participant. Her public and private lives are tested throughout the novel. Questions are raised about the basis of her work and about the validity of fostering individual happiness in a world of mass poverty and misery. In the personal sphere, she longs for some kind of re-awakening before she moves towards old age and death, and finds her identity as wife and mother tested through her affair with an American writer, Lewis Brogan. Although Henri emerges as the more vital character, it is Anne who is accorded the first-person voice in a novel that is for the main part related in the third person. This directness of address, coupled with the descriptions of de Beauvoir's own visits to the US (with Brogan resembling her former lover, Nelson Algren), and the echoing of her fears of ageing, may lead us to think that Anne's voice is that of the author. However, it does not seem likely that this is the case, rather that de Beauvoir's own arguments, emotions, and experiences are dispersed throughout the various private histories so convincingly related in the novel.

The Mandarins was de Beauvoir's first novel after her analysis of women's place in society, *The Second Sex*, and it is interesting to look at the personal and political choices available for women here. De Beauvoir could be criticized for the novel's lack of adequate role models, as the female characters do not appear to share the confidence and vigour of her male creations. However, de Beauvoir's commitment to revealing true relations and circumstances, rather than idealized notions of action and behaviour, is seen in her positioning the women in the novel as caught between personal and public life. Their inability to seize authentic freedom, tied as they are to relationships with men, disempowers them from full and active involvement in the political and public sphere. The most extreme example is the passive and beautiful Paule, who has given up a career as a singer to devote herself to Henri, feeling that her love is sufficient. When Henri no longer loves her, Paule loses her reason for living and has a breakdown, rather like the betrayed wife in *The Woman Destroyed*. Paule's rival, the rich Josette, who wishes to make a career as an actress, is portrayed as equally vulnerable to male attention, her beauty even sold off during the occupation to German soldiers by her ruthless and *arriviste* mother.

Anne herself is seen as unable to change herself, haunted as she is by the certainty of death, and, although she rejects suicide at the end of the work, she resigns herself to life and to staying with Robert. Her relationship with her daughter, Nadine, is far from easy, with Anne often offering control and responsibility in the absence of love. The gawky Nadine herself is the most active woman in the work, but it is a restless activity born out of unpredictability and irresponsibility rather than conscious intervention and willed choice. And again and again, it is the question of choice, and how it is possible to act ethically when asked to choose particular courses of behaviour, that occurs in *The Mandarins*. What is fascinating in this work, and what marks it out as a novel that has contemporary resonance, is de Beauvoir's insistence that it is the political that is personal; that political action and public behaviour have their basis in personal relations and commitments.

—Anna-Marie Taylor

THE SECOND SEX (Le Deuxième Sexe)
Prose by Simone de Beauvoir, 1949.

First published in 1949, de Beauvoir's path-finding study of women's position in society has played a significant role in the founding of modern feminist studies. Attacked in its day by the Right (and blacklisted by the Pope) for its attacks on marriage and motherhood, her study has also attracted criticism for its unwitting sexism, as well as its underrating of the unconscious, from later feminist writers. *The Second Sex*, completed in less than three years and covering over 1,000 pages, is divided into two volumes, and synthesizes its author's extensive, interdisciplinary reading. As Elias Canetti does in an equally eclectic and expansive study *Crowds and Power*, de Beauvoir incorporates historical, social, anthropological, psychoanalytic, and literary studies.

The first volume, *A History of Sex* (*Les Faits et les mythes*), deals with the ways that women have been prevented from seizing independent identities and destinies for themselves distinct from men's. In the same way that Canetti orders his diverse material around a central unifying argument, de Beauvoir argues throughout her work that woman's oppression lies with the apprehension of herself as Other to men. Her experience is not authentic in its own right, always measured as it is against male achievements. In existentialist terminology, woman is constantly in a state of immanence (or, worse still, stagnation), as long as social organizations privilege man's experience, allowing him to find transcendence (positive vindication of being) in his actions. Throughout the work, de Beauvoir's arguments allow for a two-fold appraisal of women's consciousness, as they explain woman's position as inferior yet also look to possibilities of her liberating herself from such a fixed identity.

De Beauvoir sees this unequal state of affairs as not being predetermined. Sex may be fixed, but the manufacture of gender is fluid, for as she states in what became a rallying slogan—'One is not born, but rather becomes, a woman'. To prove this point, de Beauvoir looks at three explanations of sexual difference, finding in them evidence for her contentions but also seeing each theory as not providing a complete answer. Looking at physiological views of women's behaviour, de Beauvoir shows that, although the female species is more tied to her biological functions than the male, this dependence on the body does not account for her secondary status throughout history. It was when hunting cultures developed and when male prowess in war and hunting was valorized that the child-bearing, home-based female began to be denied transcendence.

De Beauvoir then examines psychoanalytic ideas, and, although discovering much to explain how gender is perceived and formed, she is wary of adopting Freud's theories on female motivation, as they seem to be a modified version of male psychology. She further rejects the notion that sexuality is the main determining factor in behaviour. The last part of this section is devoted to historical materialism, with de Beauvoir arguing that people inhabit a historical reality in which a metaphysical idea of transcendence becomes material. While espousing this Marxist Existentialism (and supporting self-determination in a Marxist sense), de Beauvoir finds Engels' unwillingness to speculate upon how communal ownership changed to private property a serious failing. Having analysed these positions, de Beauvoir embarks on a succinct historical survey, providing a history of woman's Otherness (and her complicity in her subjection) from the Nomads to contemporary France, and showing how economic and legal institutions have fixed female aspirations.

With its weight of evidence, the final part of this first volume, that deals with how men have enshrined and vilified women in their myth-making, is much more impressionistic. De Beauvoir's evaluation of the images of women in five male authors (Breton, Claudel, Lawrence, Montherlant, and Stendhal) anticipates much work in literary studies almost a quarter of a century later, of which Kate Millett's *Sexual Politics* is one of the best known examples.

Nature of the Second Sex (*L'Expérience vécue*), which

forms part two of *The Second Sex*, is a more personal appraisal of the social institutions that shape and limit female experience. De Beauvoir provides a very sensitive account of girls' development through childhood and adolescence, that looks forward to her own testament of youth, *Memoirs of a Dutiful Daughter*. She adds to her picture of female maturation by sketching in the various roles that women are coerced to adopt in adulthood. In particular, the so-called 'natural' identities of mother and wife are sharply attacked for thwarting female liberation. In contrast, de Beauvoir reinstates lesbianism as 'natural', arguing that women in their original attachment to their mothers are homosexual. De Beauvoir's account of female development moves finally to a typology of fixed identities, such as The Woman in Love, The Narcissist, and The Independent Woman. In her description of the last type, de Beauvoir speculates on women's liberation and challenges existing notions of 'natural' behaviour, arguing forcefully that women must have control over production and reproduction, and that men and women must one day recognize each other as subjects, 'yet remain for the other an *other*'. To reiterate her plea for self-fulfilment, de Beauvoir includes in the French edition a description (missing from Parshley's English translation) of 50 remarkable French women, reclaiming them for history. Such an excavation of female achievement can also be seen in later feminist works such as Elaine Showalter's critical survey, *A Literature of Their Own* and Caryl Churchill's play, *Top Girls*.

While de Beauvoir's novels are characterized by an elegant, precise, and detached style, such as might be expected from a trained philosopher, it is a surprise that her major philosophical work is composed in a rather turgid and overembellished way. Many of the points that she makes in *The Second Sex* are further illustrated in her fiction, where she provides a practical demonstration of her philosophical conclusions, and shows how women's personalities and capabilities are diminished by the circumstances of their lives.

—Anna-Marie Taylor

BECKETT, Samuel (Barclay). Born in Foxrock, near Dublin, Ireland, 13 April 1906. Educated at Ida Elsner's Academy, Stillorgan; Earlsfort House preparatory school; Portora Royal School, County Fermanagh; Trinity College, Dublin (foundation scholar), B.A. in French and Italian 1927, M.A. 1931. Married Suzanne Deschevaux-Dumesnil in 1961 (died 1989). French teacher, Campbell College, Belfast, 1928; lecturer in English, École Normale Supérieure, Paris, 1928–30; lecturer in French, Trinity College, Dublin, 1930–31; translator and writer in Paris in the 1920s and 1930s, and closely associated with James Joyce's circle; in Dublin and London, 1933–37; returned to Paris, 1937; joined French Resistance, 1940; fled to Roussillon in unoccupied France, where he remained 1942–45; worked at the Irish Red Cross Hospital, St Lô, France, 1945; resumed literary activity in Paris after World War II; after 1945, published the majority of his work in both French and English versions. Recipient: *Evening Standard* award, 1955; Obie award, 1958, 1960, 1962, 1964; Italia prize, 1959, International Publishers prize, 1961; Prix Filmcritice, 1965; Tours film prize, 1966; Nobel prize for literature, 1969; National Grand prize for theatre (France), 1975; New York Drama Critics Circle citation,

1984. D.Litt.: Dublin University, 1959. Member of the German Academy of Art; Companion of Literature, Royal Society of Literature, 1984; member, Aosdána, 1986. *Died 22 December 1989.*

PUBLICATIONS

Collection

The Complete Dramatic Works. 1986.

Plays

Le Kid, with Georges Pelorson (produced 1931).
En attendant Godot (produced 1953). 1952; as *Waiting for Godot: Tragicomedy*, translated by Beckett, 1954.
Fin de partie: suivi de Acte sans paroles, music by John Beckett (produced 1957). 1957; as *Endgame*, edited by John Fletcher and Beryl S. Fletcher, 1970; as *Endgame: A Play in One Act; Followed by Act Without Words: A Mime for One Player*, translated by Beckett, 1958.
All That Fall (broadcast 1957; produced 1965). 1957; as *Tous ceux qui tombent*, translated by Beckett and Robert Pinget, 1957.
Krapp's Last Tape (produced 1958). With *Embers*, 1959; as *La Dernière Bande*, translated by Beckett and Pierre Leyris, 1960.
Embers (broadcast 1959). With *Krapp's Last Tape*, 1959; as *Cendres*, translated by Beckett and Robert Pinget, 1960.
Act Without Words II (produced 1960). In *Krapp's Last Tape and Other Dramatic Pieces*, 1960; as *Acte sans paroles II*, translated by Beckett, 1966.
La Manivelle/The Old Tune (bilingual edition), from the play by Robert Pinget. 1960; Beckett's text only (broadcast 1960), in *Plays 1*, by Pinget, 1963.
Krapp's Last Tape and Other Dramatic Pieces (includes *All That Fall*; *Embers*; *Act Without Words I* and *II*). 1960.
Happy Days (produced 1961). 1961; as *Oh, Les Beaux Jours*, translated by Beckett, 1963; bilingual edition, edited by James Knowlson, 1978.
Words and Music, music by John Beckett (broadcast 1962). In *Play and Two Short Pieces for Radio*, 1964; as *Paroles et Musique*, translated by Samuel Beckett, 1966.
Cascando, music by Marcel Milhalovici (broadcast in French 1963). In *Dramatische Dichtungen 1*, 1963; as *Cascando: A Radio Piece for Music and Voice*, translated by Beckett, in *Play and Two Short Pieces for Radio*, 1964.
Play (in German, as *Spiel*, produced 1963; as *Play*, produced 1964). In *Play and Two Short Pieces for Radio*, 1964; as *Comédie*, translated by Beckett, 1966.
Play and Two Short Pieces for Radio. 1964.
Eh Joe (televised 1966; produced 1978). In *Eh Joe and Other Writings*, 1967.
Va et vient: Dramaticule (in German as *Kommen und Gehen*, produced 1966; as *Va et vient*, produced 1966). 1966; as *Come and Go: Dramaticule*, translated by Beckett, 1967.
Eh Joe and Other Writings (includes *Acts Without Words II* and *Film*). 1967.
Cascando and Other Short Dramatic Pieces (includes *Words and Music*; *Eh Joe*; *Play*; *Come and Go*; *Film*). 1968.
Film (screenplay). 1969.
Breath (part of *Oh! Calcutta!* produced 1969). In *Breath and Other Shorts*, 1971.
Breath and Other Shorts (includes *Come and Go*; *Act Without Words I* and *II*; and the prose piece *From an Abandoned Work*). 1971.

Not I (produced 1972). 1973; as *Pas moi*, translated by Beckett, 1975.

Fragment de théâtre. 1974; as *Theatre I* and *II*, translated by Beckett, in *Ends and Odds*, 1976.

Ghost Trio (as *Tryst*, televised 1976). In *Ends and Odds*, 1976.

That Time (produced 1976). 1976; as *Cette fois*, translated by Beckett, 1978.

Footfalls (produced 1976). 1976; as *Pas*, translated by Beckett, 1977.

Ends and Odds: Eight New Dramatic Pieces (includes *Not I*; *That Time*; *Footfalls*; *Ghost Trio*; *Theatre I* and *II*; *Radio I* and *II*). 1976; as *Ends and Odds: Plays and Sketches* (includes *Not I*; *That Time*; *Footfalls*; *Ghost Trio*; . . . *but the clouds* . . . ; *Theatre I* and *II*; *Radio I* and *II*), 1977.

Rough for Radio (broadcast 1976). As *Radio II*, in *Ends and Odds*, 1976.

Theatre I and *II* (produced 1985). In *Ends and Odds*, 1976.

A Piece of Monologue (produced 1980). In *Rockaby and Other Short Pieces*, 1981.

Rockaby (produced 1981). In *Rockaby and Other Short Pieces*, 1981; as *Berceuse*, translated by Beckett, 1982.

Rockaby and Other Short Pieces. 1981.

Ohio Impromptu (produced 1981). In *Rockaby and Other Short Pieces*, 1981; as *Impromptu d'Ohio*, 1982.

Catastrophe (produced 1982). 1982; in *Collected Shorter Plays*, 1984.

Catastrophe et autres dramaticules: Cette fois, Solo, Berceuse, Impromptu d'Ohio (produced 1982). 1982; in *Collected Shorter Plays*, 1984.

Three Occasional Pieces (includes *A Piece of Monologue*; *Rockaby*; *Ohio Impromptu*). 1982.

Quad (as *Quadrat 1+2*, televised in German 1982; as *Quad*, televised 1982). In *Collected Shorter Plays*, 1984.

Nacht und Träume (televised 1983). In *Collected Shorter Plays*, 1984.

What Where (in German, as *Was Wo*, produced 1983; in English, produced 1983). In *Collected Shorter Plays*, 1984.

Collected Shorter Plays. 1984.

Ohio Impromptu, Catastrophe, and What Where. 1984.

The Shorter Plays, edited by S.E. Gontarski. 1992.

Screenplay: *Film*, 1965.

Radio Plays: *All That Fall*, 1957; *Embers*, 1959, *The Old Tune*, from a play by Robert Pinget, 1960; *Words and Music*, 1962; *Cascando*, 1963; *Rough for Radio*, 1976.

Television Plays: *Eh Joe*, 1966; *Tryst*, 1976; *Shades* (*Ghost Trio*, *Not I*, . . . *but the clouds* . . .), 1977; *Quadrat 1+2*, 1982 (Germany); *Quad*, 1982; *Nacht und Träume*, 1983.

Fiction

More Pricks Than Kicks. 1934.

Murphy (in English). 1938; translated by Beckett and Alfred Péron, 1947.

Molloy (in French). 1951; translated by Beckett and Patrick Bowles, 1955.

Malone meurt. 1951; as *Malone Dies*, translated by Beckett, 1956.

L'Innommable. 1953; as *The Unnamable*, translated by Beckett, 1958.

Watt (in English). 1953; translated into French by Ludovic and Agnès Janvier in collaboration with Beckett, 1968.

Nouvelles et textes pour rien. 1955; as *Stories and Texts for Nothing*, translated by Beckett and Richard Seaver, 1967.

From an Abandoned Work, 1958; as *D'un ouvrage abandonné*, translated by Ludovic and Agnès Janvier in collaboration with Beckett, 1967.

Three Novels. 1959.

Molloy, Malone Dies, The Unnamable. 1960.

Comment c'est. 1961; as *How It Is*, translated by Beckett, 1964.

Imagination morte imaginez. 1965; as *Imagination Dead Imagine*, translated by Beckett, 1965.

Assez. 1966; as *Enough*, translated by Beckett, in *No's Knife*, 1967.

Bing (in French), 1966; as *Ping*, translated by Beckett, in *No's Knife*, 1967.

Têtes-Mortes (includes *D'Un Ouvrage Adandonné*; *Assez*; *Bing*; *Imagination morte imaginez*). 1967; translated by Beckett, in *No's Knife*, 1967.

No's Knife: Collected Shorter Prose 1945–66 (includes *Stories and Texts for Nothing*; *From an Abandoned Work*; *Enough*; *Imagination Dead Imagine*; *Ping*). 1967.

Dans le cylindre. 1967.

L'Issue. 1968.

Sans. 1969; as *Lessness*, translated by Beckett, 1970.

Mercier et Camier. 1970; as *Mercier and Camier*, translated by Beckett, 1974.

Séjour. 1970.

Premier Amour. 1970; as *First Love*, translated by Beckett, 1973.

Le Dépeupleur. 1971; as *The Lost Ones*, translated by Beckett, 1972.

The North. 1972.

Abandonné. 1972.

Au loin un oiseau. 1973.

First Love and Other Shorts. 1974.

Fizzles. 1976.

Pour finir encore et autres foirades. 1976; as *For to End Yet Again and Other Fizzles*, translated by Beckett, 1976.

All Strange Away. 1976.

Four Novellas (*First Love*; *The Expelled*; *The Calmative*; *The End*). 1977; as *The Expelled and Other Novellas*, 1980.

Six Residua. 1978.

Company. 1980.

Mal vu mal dit. 1981; as *Ill Seen Ill Said*, translated by Beckett, 1982.

Worstward Ho. 1983.

Stirrings Still. 1988.

Nohow On (includes *Company*; *Ill Seen Ill Said*; *Worstword Ho*). 1989.

Soubresauts. 1989.

Dream of Fair to Middling Women, edited by Eoin O'Brien and Edith Fournier. 1992.

Verse

Whoroscope. 1930.

Echo's Bones and Other Precipitates. 1935.

Gedichte (collected poems in English and French, with German translations). 1959.

Poems in English. 1961.

Poèmes. 1968.

Collected Poems in English and French. 1977; revised edition, as *Collected Poems 1930–1978*, 1984.

Mirlitonnades. 1978.

Other

'*Dante* . . . *Bruno. Vico* . . . *Joyce*,' in *Our Exagmination Round His Factification for Incamination of Work in Progress*. 1929.

Proust. 1931; with *Three Dialogues with Georges Duthuit*, 1965.

Bram van Velde (in French), with Georges Duthuit and Jacques Putman. 1958; translated by Beckett and Olive Classe, 1960.

A Beckett Reader. 1967.

The Collected Works. 1970.

I Can't Go On: A Selection from the Work of Beckett, edited by Richard Seaver. 1976.

Disjecta: Miscellaneous Writings and a Dramatic Fragment, edited by Ruby Cohn. 1983.

Collected Shorter Prose 1945–1980. 1984.

Happy Days: The Production Notebook, edited by James Knowlson. 1985.

As the Story Was Told: Uncollected and Late Prose. 1990.

Krapp's Last Tape: Beckett's Theatrical Notebook, edited by James Knowlson. 1991.

The Theatrical Notebooks of Samuel Beckett, edited by Dougald McMillan, James Knowlson, and S.E. Gontarski. 4 vols., 1992.

Translator, *Negro: An Anthology.* 1934.

Translator, *Anthology of Mexican Poetry*, edited by Octavio Paz. 1958.

Translator, *The Old Tune*, by Robert Pinget. 1960.

Translator, with others, *Selected Poems*, by Alain Bosquet. 1963.

Translator, *Zone*, by Guillaume Apollinaire. 1972.

Translator, *Drunken Boat*, by Arthur Rimbaud, edited by James Knowlson and Felix Leakey. 1977.

Translator, with others, *No Matter No Fact.* 1988.

*

Bibliography: *Samuel Beckett: His Works and His Critics: An Essay in Bibliography* by Raymond Federman and John Fletcher, 1970 (works to 1966); *Samuel Beckett: Checklist and Index of His Published Works 1967–76* by Robin John Davis, 1979; *Samuel Beckett: A Reference Guide* by Cathleen Culotta Andonian, 1988.

Critical Studies: *Samuel Beckett; A Critical Study*, 1961, revised edition, 1968, and *A Reader's Guide to Samuel Beckett*, 1973, both by Hugh Kenner; *Samuel Beckett: The Comic Gamut*, 1962, *Back to Beckett*, 1974, and *Just Play: Beckett's Theater*, 1980, all by Ruby Cohn, and *Samuel Beckett: A Collection of Criticism*, 1975, and *Waiting for Godot: A Casebook*, 1987, both edited by Cohn; *Samuel Beckett: The Language of Self* by Frederick J. Hoffman, 1962; *Beckett* by Richard N. Coe, 1964, retitled as *Samuel Beckett*, 1964; *The Novels of Samuel Beckett*, 1964, and *Samuel Beckett's Art*, 1967, both by John Fletcher, and *Beckett: A Study of His Plays* by Fletcher and John Spurling, 1972, revised edition as *Beckett the Playwright*, 1985; *Samuel Beckett* by William York Tindall, 1964; *Samuel Beckett: A Collection of Critical Essays* edited by Martin Esslin, 1965; *Journey to Chaos: Samuel Beckett's Early Fiction* by Raymond Federman, 1965; *Beckett at 60: A Festschrift* edited by John Calder, 1967; *Samuel Beckett's 'Murphy': A Critical Excursion* by Robert Harrison, 1968; *Samuel Beckett* by Ronald Hayman, 1968, revised edition, 1980; *All I Can Manage More Than I Could: An Approach to the Plays of Samuel Beckett* by Alec Reid, 1968; *Twentieth Century Interpretations of 'Endgame'* edited by Bell Gale Chevigny, 1969; *The Long Sonata of the Dead: A Study of Samuel Beckett* by Michael Robinson, 1969; *Samuel Beckett: A New Approach* by Guy C. Barnard, 1970; *Samuel*

Beckett Now: Critical Approaches to His Novels, Poetry, and Plays edited by Melvin J. Friedman, 1970; *Samuel Beckett: Poet and Critic* by Lawrence E. Harvey, 1970; *Beckett: A Study of His Novels*, 1970, and *The Plays of Samuel Beckett*, 1972, both by Eugene Webb; *Samuel Beckett* by Francis Doherty, 1971; *The Shape of Chaos: An Interpretation of the Art of Samuel Beckett* by David Hesla, 1971; *Angels of Darkness: Dramatic Effect in Samuel Beckett* by Colin Duckworth, 1972; *The Fiction of Beckett: Form and Effect* by H. Porter Abbott, 1973; *Samuel Beckett* by A. Alvarez, 1973, revised edition, 1992; *Art and the Artist in the Works of Samuel Beckett* by Hannah Case Copeland, 1975; *Samuel Beckett's Dramatic Language* by James Eliopulos, 1975; *Beckett the Shape Changer* edited by Katharine J. Worth, 1975, and *Waiting for Godot and Happy Days* by Worth, 1990; *Condemned to Life: The World of Samuel Beckett* by Kenneth and Alice Hamilton, 1976; *Samuel Beckett* by John Pilling, 1976, and *The Cambridge Companion to Beckett* edited by Pilling, 1994; *Forme et signification dans le théâtre de Samuel Beckett* by Betty Rojtman, 1976; *Beckett and Broadcasting: A Study of the Works of Samuel Beckett for and in Radio and Television* by Clas Zilliacus, 1976; *Beckett's Happy Days: A Manuscript Study*, 1977, and *The Intent of Undoing in Samuel Beckett's Dramatic Texts*, 1985, both by S.E. Gontarski, and *On Beckett: Essays and Criticism*, 1986, and *The Beckett Studies Reader*, 1993, both edited by Gontarski, 1993; *Beckett/Beckett* by Vivian Mercier, 1977; *Samuel Beckett: A Biography* by Deirdre Bair, 1978; *A Student's Guide to the Plays of Samuel Beckett* by Beryl S. Fletcher, 1978, revised edition, with John Fletcher, 1985; *The Shape of Paradox: An Essay on Waiting for Godot* by Bert O. Slates, 1978; *The Samuel Beckett Manuscripts: A Critical Study* by Richard L. Admussen, 1979; *Samuel Beckett: The Critical Heritage* edited by Raymond Federmand and Lawrence Graver, 1979; *Beckett and Joyce: Friendship and Fiction* by Barbara Reich Gluck, 1979; *Frescoes of the Skull: The Later Prose and Drama of Samuel Beckett* edited by James Knowlson and John Pilling, 1979; *The Transformations of Godot* by Frederick Busi, 1980; *Waiting for Death: The Philosophical Significance of Beckett's En attendant Godot* by Ramona Cormier, 1980; *Samuel Beckett and the Voice of Species: A Study of the Prose Fiction* by Eric P. Levy, 1980; *Accommodating the Chaos: Samuel Beckett's Nonrelational Art* by J.E. Dearlove, 1982; *Abysmal Games in the Novels of Samuel Beckett* by Angela B. Moorjani, 1982; *Beckett's Real Silence* by Hélène L. Baldwin, 1983; *Samuel Beckett: Humanistic Perspectives* edited by Morris Beja, S.E. Gontarski, and Pierre Astier, 1983; *Samuel Beckett* by Charles Lyons, 1983; *Canters and Chronicles: The Use of Narrative in the Plays of Samuel Beckett and Harold Pinter* by Kristin Morrison, 1983; *Beckett's Theaters: Interpretations for Performance* by Sidney Homan, 1984; *The Development of Samuel Beckett's Fiction*, 1984, and *Innovation in Samuel Beckett's Fiction*, 1993, both by Rubin Rabinovitz; *Samuel Beckett and the Meaning of Being: A Study in Ontological Parable* by Lance St John Butler, 1984, *Rethinking Beckett: A Collection of Critical Essays* edited by St John Butler and Robin J. Davies, 1990, and *Critical Essays on Samuel Beckett* edited by St John Butler, 1993; *Samuel Beckett: Modern Critical Views* edited by Harold Bloom, 1985; *Beckett on File* edited by Virginia Cooke, 1985; *Beckett at 80/Beckett in Context* edited by Enoch Brater, 1986, and *Beyond Minimalism: Beckett's Late Style in the Theater*, 1987, and *Why Beckett*, 1989, both by Brater; *Samuel Beckett* by Linda Ben-Zvi, 1986, and *Women in Beckett: Performance and Critical Perspectives* edited by Ben-Zvi, 1990; *Understanding Beckett: A Study of Monologue and Gesture in the Works of*

Samuel Beckett by Peter Gidal, 1986; *As No Other Dare Fail: For Samuel Beckett on His 80th Birthday*, 1986; *Beckett's New Worlds: Style in Metafiction* by Susan D. Brienza, 1987; *Beckett Translating/Translating Beckett* edited by Alan Warren Friedman, Charles Rossman, and Dina Sherzer, 1987; *The Broken Window: Beckett's Dramatic Perspective* by Jane Alison Hale, 1987; *Myth and Ritual in the Plays of Beckett* by Katherine H. Burkman, 1988; *Beckett: Repetition, Theory, and Text* by Stephen Connor, 1988; *Beckett and Babel: An Investigation into the Status of the Bilingual Work* by Brian T. Fitch, 1988; *Beckett's Critical Complicity: Carnival, Contestation and Tradition* by Sylvia Debevec Henning, 1988; *Beckett in the Theatre: The Author as Practical Playwright and Director 1: From Waiting for Godot to Krapp's Last Tape* by Douglas McMillan and Martha Fehsenfeld, 1988; *Theatre of Shadows: Beckett's Drama 1956–1976* by Rosemary Poutney, 1988; *The Humour of Beckett* by Valerie Topsfield, 1988; *Beckett and Zen: A Study of Dilemma in the Novels of Samuel Beckett* by Paul Foster, 1989; *Beckett: Waiting for Godot* by Lawrence Graver, 1989; *Beckett in Performance* by Jonathan Kalb, 1989; *Beckett* by Andrew K. Kennedy, 1989; *The World of Beckett* by Alan Astro, 1990; *Waiting for Godot: Form in Movement* by Thomas Couisneau, 1990; *Beckett's Fiction: In Different Words* by Leslie Hill, 1990; *Beckett's Self-Referential Drama* by Shimon Levy, 1990; *Unwording the World: Beckett's Prose Works after the Nobel Prize* by Carla Locatelli, 1990; *Paradox and Desire in Beckett's Fiction* by David Watson, 1990; *Early Beckett: Art and Allusion in More Pricks Than Kicks and Murphy* by Anthony Farrow, 1991; *Wandering and Home: Beckett's Metaphysical Narrative* by Eyal Amiran, 1993; *Beckett's Dying Words: The Clarendon Lecture 1990* by Christopher Ricks, 1993.

* * *

Samuel Beckett has achieved recognition as a powerful creative writer working in both English and French. His prose fiction and drama are often startlingly innovative in form, and this break with tradition links him to the French new novelists, and to the theatre of the absurd. Like other writers of the 1950s and 1960s he moved away not only from realism and psychological presentation of character, but also from the limitations of rational sequence and plot. Beckett cannot be labelled however. He has a distinctive voice that places him outside all schools and categories. His best work combines a fiercely uncompromising struggle with essential questions and an awareness that there are no answers: the key word in his work is 'perhaps'. This awareness that his is 'an art of failure' could lead to despair, and most of his characters are certainly living in a grimly purgatorial world, condemned to talk or write, in the forlorn hope of finding the words which will give them the right to silence, or simply to help pass the time of waiting, as in *En attendant Godot* (*Waiting for Godot*). What makes the works life-enhancing is the fact that the black vision of characters struggling to make sense of a cruel universe is coupled with a superb poetic feeling for language, and a brilliant, self-mocking sense of humour.

Beckett wrote *Watt*, his last major novel in English, in 1953, and the change to French clearly marks a change of direction, and the discovery of his mature style. During the earlier period he published some poetry, and his first successful novel, *Murphy*. This has a serious theme, as Murphy, a 'seedy solipsist', seeks to escape the outer world, and spend more time in his mind, 'in the dark, in the will-lessness', but his way of achieving this, by tying himself up naked in a rocking chair, typically undermines the seriousness. The novel works best as a brilliantly comic account of Murphy's battles with the everyday world he wishes to escape. *Murphy* is an odd novel, but it has characters, a plot, and a recognizable setting in London. Such traditional elements have been dropped in *Watt*, and the fiction in French confirms this new form.

The first major work in French is the trilogy: *Molloy*, *Malone meurt* (*Malone Dies*), and *L'Innommable* (*The Unnamable*). *Molloy* tells us at the beginning of his narrative that he is now in his mother's room, compelled to write stories, and aware of an inner voice which speaks 'of a world collapsing endlessly, a frozen world, under a faint untroubled sky'. He tells the story of his journey, through a hostile world, towards his mother. His progress is marked by a steady physical deterioration, until he is finally crawling through a forest, with the aid of his crutches. This grim quest is constantly interrupted by comic digressions that Molloy uses to escape from his 'calvary with no hope of crucifixion'. For the reader these episodes, such as the detailed account of how Molloy organizes his 'sucking stones', give the novel a defiantly comic vigour, in the face of suffering. There is also a black irony about the society through which the tramp-like Molloy journeys: 'Day is the time for lynching, for sleep is sacred'. The second part of *Molloy* is narrated by Moran, who seems the opposite of Molloy, comfortably settled in a regular social and domestic routine, until he is sent on a mission to find Molloy. He is vaguely aware at the outset that the Molloy he has to find is within himself, and by the time he returns he has come to resemble his quarry. The novel can be interpreted, John Fletcher suggests, as 'an epic of the search for one's real self' (*The Novels of Samuel Beckett*, 1964), and this is a central theme of the whole trilogy. *Malone Dies* focuses on the writer in his room, waiting to die, but hoping to tell the right story meanwhile. 'Words and images run riot in my head', he writes, but his stories are interrupted by comments on the decrepit, suffering body, whose pain is so bearable compared with that of the questing mind.

Malone wonders at times if he has not already died. The narrator of *The Unnamable* is simply a voice, not knowing whether he has died, or is waiting to be born. He is in a 'hell of stories', forced to go on speaking, but hoping to attain silence and peace. If he ever reaches that silence, however, he will not know it: 'in the silence you don't know'. The final words of the desperate voice are: 'I can't go on, I'll go on'. Beckett himself did go on, and in the best of his later works found completely new ways of pursuing the same concerns, often starting from the images of suffering and guilt in the trilogy. *Comment c'est* (*How It Is*) for instance, develops around the image of a muddy hell, in which torturer and victim endlessly exchange roles.

Beckett's plays explore the same themes as the novels, but in *Waiting for Godot* the two old tramps, waiting day after day for the mysterious Mr Godot to come, are given a comical human warmth towards each other that counterpoints the bleak hopelessness of their waiting. The only people who do pass by the stretch of country road, with its solitary tree, are the brutal whip-cracking Pozzo and his slave, Lucky. Perhaps, it is hinted, Pozzo is Godot, and they have not recognized him. They hope that Godot will 'save' them—he is the only reason for their suffering existence; but when the second act shows the same situation, with Pozzo now blind, and Lucky dumb, this hope seems futile, and Pozzo sums up the feeling of the play in the image 'they give birth astride of a grave'. The best productions keep a balance between the comic games the tramps play, and the blackness they are trying to forget. *Fin de partie* (*Endgame*) is more inhuman.

Hamm, blind and crippled, spends his days in a cell-like room with Clov, perhaps his son, and his parents, confined to dustbins. They are waiting, but only for the end, which may never come. They pass the time with wearisome routines, aware that what keeps them there is the dialogue. The later plays take the process of compression even further, using powerful theatrical images, which work despite the absence of action or plot. In *Happy Days* (*Oh, Les Beaux Jours*) Winnie is buried to the waist in the earth, and by Act II she has sunk to her neck. The contrast between her situation and her determinedly optimistic chatter is the basis for the play. In *Not I* (*Pas moi*) the character is physically reduced to a mouth, pouring out a stream of words in the hope that one day she will be allowed to fall silent.

Beckett's mastery of form, the 'power of the text to claw', is an important element in his success, but so too is the fact that he struggles painfully, humorously, with questions which have always been central for the human spirit.

—John Rothenberg

ENDGAME (Fin de partie)
Play by Samuel Beckett, 1957.

Over four years elapsed between the premiere of *Waiting for Godot* and that of Beckett's next play, *Endgame*, in April 1957. The plays share some similar features particularly in the ratio of three clown-like characters to one 'serious' character. In *Endgame* the paralyzed blind man, Hamm, is central, and dictates the overall tone of the play.

Of the four characters, Hamm's servant, Clov, is the only one who can walk. Confined to an armchair, which is on castors, Hamm orders him about, depending on him to push the armchair into different positions, while Hamm's ancient parents, Nagg and Nell, are confined to bobbing up and down in their dustbins. The interdependence of master and servant is reminiscent of that between Pozzo and Luck in *Godot*; Hamm and Clov are similarly interdependent—Hamm can't stand, while Clov can't sit. But the restrictions on movement limit possibilities for the kind of knockabout comedy that was so important in the earlier play. Clov, like Lucky, rushes frantically about, mostly in obedience to orders from his master, fetching whatever Hamm wants, appearing whenever he's whistled for, fetching, carrying, climbing up and down ladders. Beckett is inventive within the limits he sets for himself, but these are so narrow that the play seems to contain much less physical action than *Godot*.

Blind from the beginning of the play—Pozzo goes blind halfway through *Godot*—Hamm is in some ways like a god who has abdicated control of a world that is rapidly approaching its end. All he can do is wait, with the few other survivors, for non-entity to supervene. The powerful central image is derived from chess, and we have to watch the game from the viewpoint of the players, understanding why neither Hamm nor Clov can merely walk away from the chess-board, though both wish the stalemate could be checkmate. Allusions to *Oedipus* and *King Lear* suggest that art is part of the game which is ending, but the text is mined with self-deflating devices that discourage us from regarding it as art.

> HAMM: We're not beginning to . . . to . . . mean something?
> CLOV: Mean something! You and I, mean something! (*Brief laugh*) Ah that's a good one!

The action is less circular than that of *Godot*. Both plays move in the direction of an indeterminate viewpoint situated somewhere outside space and time, but the set of *Endgame* presents an outsized visual pun that admits the possibility of equating the action with life inside the brain. Two windows can be taken to represent eyes and Clov's opening the curtains and removing the dust-sheet that has been covering Hamm parallels the process of waking up in the morning. The two dustbins that house Hamm's parents are like receptacles for useless memories of the past.

There are many built-in contradictions, and the evidence that supports an equation between Hamm and God is counterweighted by indications that he represents the void:

> HAMM: I was never there.
> CLOV: Lucky for you. (*He looks out of the window*)
> HAMM: Absent, always. It all happened without me. I don't know what's happened.

Underneath his dark glasses, his eyes have gone all white, and seeing nothing, he can see nothingness.

The play progresses by cancelling itself out; there are sequences that appear to have no function except to discredit the vision which has already been presented. Hamm talks about a madman who thought the end of the world had come:

> I'd take him by the hand and drag him to the window. Look! There! All that rising corn! And there! Look! The sails of the herring fleet! All that loveliness! (*Pause*) He'd snatch away his hand and go back into his corner, Appalled! All he had seen was ashes.

When Clov looks out of the window, he reports 'nothing' and 'zero', but if Hamm is mad to think the world is ending, Clov may be no more than a function of his madness.

At the end of the play, the appearance of a small boy contradicts all the indications we have been given that nothing has survived outside. Not that we have to choose between these mutually exclusive versions of the overall situation. Beckett maroons us between them. The play fights abrasively against our habit of assuming that information contained in dialogue and action should be self-consistent, that a situation should be coherent, that a character must seem to exist as a whole personality, that the total work of art represents 'reality'.

Occasionally it is the words that contradict each other, as when Hamm says: 'The bigger a man is the fuller he is . . . And the emptier'. More often it is the indications about situation and action that cancel each other out. What's going on in the world outside the space we're watching? The contradictions have the effect of making the words more like objects in their own right and less like component elements in a theatrical reproduction of reality. In an article about painting, Beckett wrote 'each time that one wishes to make words do a true work of transference, each time one wishes to make them express something other than words, they align themselves in such a way as to cancel each other out'. In *Endgame* he encouraged them in this tendency.

—Ronald Hayman

MOLLOY, MALONE DIES, THE UNNAMABLE (Molloy, Malone meurt, L'Innommable)
Novels by Samuel Beckett, 1951–53.

The three novels *Molloy*, *Malone Dies* and *The Unnamable* come together to form what is otherwise known as 'The Beckett Trilogy' (all originally written in French). While each can be read as a separate piece there is some attempt at progression and coherence across these three 'novels'.

Indeed to say there is an attempt at progression through the works is to point to one of the major obsessions of the interior monologues of which these three works consist; each character is in search of something, on the way to somewhere, or wondering where it may be he is going. In *Molloy*, Molloy, incapacitated, sometimes on crutches, on his bicycle, or crawling, is going to meet his mother. Moran is in search of Molloy, though is reluctant to find him, having forgotten what it is he is meant to do with Molloy once he has found him. Malone, bedridden, is moving towards death. And the voice that speaks *The Unnamable* moves towards its objective, silence. Beckett, though, continually shies away from absolutes. The shift throughout the trilogy from physical movement (however sad, farcical, and restricted, as with Molloy) to Malone controlling his surroundings from his bed using a stick, to 'the unnamable', seemingly egg-shaped and in a jar, is not pushed to its 'logical' conclusion. There is not the final paralysis and silence which at times *The Unnamable* tends towards but instead *The Unnamable* ends, not in the ultimate static nothingness, but at 'the threshold of my story' saying 'you can't go on, I can't go on, I'll go on'. And this, given the sense of decay, hopelessness, and loss of fixed identity which precedes it, is in many ways a final affirmation of hope.

These three novels together form a sharp questioning of accepted concepts of the 'self', of the relation of character to action, and of the usefulness of language in conveying any sense of reality. Beckett's characters carry the full weight of these questions around with them, and at times their monologues are frantic with the panic which comes from worrying over these considerations. Molloy and his mother exemplify the inability of humans to communicate with each other. Molloy is able to make his mother understand him only by tapping her skull with his knuckles; since he decides that three raps means 'money' and his mother seems to have the ability only to count to two, he then makes one thump on the skull equal 'money'. To counter the utter bleakness, Molloy at one point resorts to an intense experiment in order and the random. To pass the time more than anything, he sucks pebbles. His obsession is to ensure that he never sucks the same one of his pebbles twice in a row and this leads to a need to suck the pebbles randomly while ensuring that order is introduced to maintain the random nature of the sucking. Molloy speculates intensely on the different ways in which he could group the pebbles and the number of pockets he could use or would need. The effect of this is, above all, comic (an aspect of Beckett's writing that is often ignored). But while there is a futility in all of Molloy's calculations, there is in this futility the seed of the drive that persuades the voice of *The Unnamable* to end the trilogy by saying 'I'll go on'. Earlier the voice of *The Unnamable* has said 'They taught me to count, and even to reason. Some of this rubbish has come in handy on occasions . . . I still use it to scratch my arse with'. But even 'the unnamable' gets 'little attacks of hope' from an attempt to understand, in a way similar to Molloy's calculations with the pebbles, how to keep a constant water level in a series of jars. While they are undermined in Beckett's fiction until they almost no longer exist, the vestiges of a more solid sense of human character and knowledge are the shaky props to a fading but still existent hope in these characters.

Beckett's method of interiorizing the thoughts of his characters is obviously influenced by the modernist writers of the earlier 20th century and in particular Joyce (with whom Beckett was acquainted, and part of whose early work-in-progress on *Finnegans Wake* Beckett helped translate into French). In these three texts it is the questioning of the very ideas of self and character that makes the sustaining of the interior monologues so remarkable and important for 20th-century literature. The awareness that the 'self' is a slippery entity intrudes further into the texts as they progress, until in *The Unnamable* it is apparent that the voice itself is primarily engaged in either proving to itself the concreteness of its existence or, having failed to prove it, lapsing into the relief of silence. It is difficult, especially *The Unnamable*, not to see Beckett rehearsing the questions which he, as a novelist, felt faced him in the creation of characters and texts. He does this partly through a self-referentiality in the three texts, which confuses the boundaries between author (as creator) and text: both Malone and 'the unnamable' are the creators of fictive characters and scenarios (which are often indistinguishable from 'reality'), and all three of the main protagonists in the trilogy show an awareness of characters from Beckett's other prose works, such as Murphy, Watt, and Mercier. It sounds like the voice of the writer when Malone says 'with practice I might produce a groan, before I die' (a groan is better than silence?). Or, even less hopefully, when 'the unnamable' says 'When I think of the time I've wasted with these bran-dips, beginning with Murphy'. The pronounless voice of *The Unnamable* is the ultimate acknowledgement of the unsustainability of the notion of the writer's only material ('blank words, but I use them', 'the unnamable' says).

Yet given all these questions and uncertainties, the hopelessness of knowing anything, the desire to 'go silent', there is among the despair still that which enables 'the unnamable' to say 'I'll go on'. If it is as much Beckett as 'the unnamable' speaking when he says 'Ah, if only I could find a voice of my own, in all this babble', then one can only reply by saying that *Molloy*, *Malone Dies*, and *The Unnamable* contain a very distinctive 'babble', out of which, against all expectation, emerges the will to continue, to 'go on'.

—Colin Graham

WAITING FOR GODOT (En attendant Godot)
Play by Samuel Beckett, 1952.

Waiting for Godot is now a classic of the modern theatre. When it was first performed in Paris in January 1953 and in its subsequent productions around the world, however, the situation was entirely different. Most spectators were confused and many left before the performance had ended. Those who stayed had difficulty understanding what this new type of theatre was about. The normal dramatic structure had totally changed. The language very often did not have a sequential rational pattern; communication among the characters was difficult and they frequently resorted to incomplete, childish sentences in order to make themselves understood. At times, the visual actions spoke more directly than words. The set was composed only of a mound of dirt and a bare tree. Finally, there seemed to be no plot, nothing appeared to be happening.

In the first act, we are introduced to two elderly men, Vladimir and Estragon, who could be tramps. They are awaiting the arrival of a Mr Godot, who is going to save them. Pozzo and Lucky pass by and, eventually, a young boy appears and says that Mr Godot will not arrive today, but will surely come tomorrow. Following this broad outline, the second act is a duplication of the first.

The play contains no progression of plot, no development of characterization, no climax. This complete reversal of the traditional theatre techniques announced a major change in modern drama. Beckett happened to be writing at the same time as a number of other dramatists, all independently transforming the shape of theatre, writing plays that would later be classified under the rubric of the theatre of the absurd, the new theatre or the anti-theatre. All of these new playwrights were expressing the absurdity and the hopelessness of the human condition and they were to have a lasting effect on the direction of drama, perhaps none more so than Beckett and *Waiting for Godot*.

In the play, Vladimir mentions that one of the two thieves crucified with Christ was saved and the other was damned. He is preoccupied, however, with the fact that only one of the four Evangelists provides this account, thus making the odds for salvation even less promising. This concern with salvation —at best one out of two will be saved—is the kernel of the play and all of the characters are presented in pairs: Vladimir and Estragon, Pozzo and Lucky, the boy in the first act and the boy in the second.

The two main couples of the play (Vladimir and Estragon, Pozzo and Lucky) are different but, at the same time, they complement each other. Vladimir, called Didi, is the more philosophical of his pairing, while Estragon, called Gogo, is the more active. Didi is the one who remembers that they are waiting for Godot, while Gogo is uncertain as to what he has seen or heard or why he is there. Pozzo and Lucky represent master and slave, since Lucky is tied to Pozzo and is often whipped by him. When Pozzo orders Lucky to speak, Lucky appears to utter gibberish, although he is really expressing his sense of the absurdity of the human condition. In the final analysis, all four of the characters are caught in the void of existence.

Their only hope for salvation from this nothingness is the arrival of Godot, who will provide the sense of coherence and purpose that they lack. While waiting for Godot, the characters are forced to go through their lives suffering but hoping for salvation. One of the ways that Didi and Gogo get through their suffering is by following a series of habitual routines that allow them to 'pass the time' without thinking too much.

Yet, in spite of their many activities, nothing really changes and they have moments when they are agonizingly aware of this. All they can do is to wait for the salvation that they hope Godot will bring. At the same time, their lives sometimes assume an arbitrary brutality. Gogo goes off-stage at one point and says that he was beaten by unknown people. Although Godot is supposed to represent salvation, Gogo is afraid of him and he thinks that the vicious Pozzo, who beats Lucky, may be Godot. In addition, there is the fear that the two tramps may be 'tied' to Godot in the same way that Lucky is tied to Pozzo.

At one point, Didi recites a piece of doggerel about a dog who stole a crust of bread in which the story repeats itself endlessly, exactly like the life the two tramps are leading. Beckett once said that he did not need to write a third act to the play, since he had already pointed out the stagnant repetitiveness of life by the end of the second act. The two men are still waiting and they are still uncertain about the past or the future. This sense of uncertainty leads to the feeling of hopelessness and the frequent repetition of the phrase, 'I can't go on'.

The one element that does seem certain is the passage of time and its fleeting quality. Didi sums up the state in which he and Gogo find themselves:

Was I sleeping while the others suffered? Am I sleeping now? To-morrow, when I wake, or think I do, what shall I say of to-day? That with Estragon my friend, at this place, until the fall of night, I waited for Godot? That Pozzo passed, with his carrier, and that he spoke to us? Probably. But in all that what truth will there be? . . . He [Estragon]'ll know nothing. He'll tell me about the blows he received, and I'll give him a carrot. (Pause.) Astride of a grave and a difficult birth. Down in the hole, lingeringly, the grave-digger puts on the forceps. We have time to grow old. The air is full of our cries.

The main image of the hopelessness and despair of the situation is brought forth compellingly at the end of each act. At the end of Act I, Estragon says, 'Well? Shall we go?' Vladimir replies, 'Yes, let's go'. The stage direction says: 'They do not move'. The end of Act II is exactly the same, with the exception that the two characters exchange their parts in the dialogue. At the final point of each act, the actions of the two men speak more directly than their words. It is clear that they cannot go, they must wait for Godot. It is also clear that Godot will not arrive.

—John H. Reilly

BELYI, Andrei. Born Boris Nikolaevich Bugaev in Moscow, Russia, 26 October 1880. Educated at gymnasium, Polivanov, 1891–99; studied science, then philology, then philosophy, University of Moscow, 1899–1906. Married 1) Asia Turgeneva, c.1910 (separated 1914); 2) Klavdiia Vasil'eva in 1924; 3rd marriage in 1931. Associate editor, *Scales*, 1907–09; associated with the publishers Musaget, 1909; travelled abroad, studying with Rudolf Steiner, 1910–16; lecturer in Moscow and St Petersburg; in Berlin, 1921–23; editor, *Epopeia*, 1922–23. *Died 7/8 January 1934.*

PUBLICATIONS

Collections

Stikhotvoreniia i poemy [Poetry and Narrative Verse], edited by T. Iu. Khmel'nitskaya. 1966.
Complete Short Stories, edited and translated by Ronald E. Peterson. 1979.
Stikhotvoreniia [Poetry], edited by John E. Malmstad. 3 vols., 1982–84.
Selected Essays, edited and translated by Steven Cassedy. 1985.
Sochineniia [Works], edited by V. Piskarev. 1990.

Verse

Zoloto v lazuri [Gold in Azure]. 1904.
Pepel [Ashes]. 1909; revised edition, 1929.
Urna [The Urn]. 1909.
Christos voskres [Christ Is Arisen]. 1918.
Pervoe svidanie. 1921; as *The First Encounter*, translated by Gerald Janeček, 1979.
Posle razluki: Berlinskii pesennik [After the Parting: A Berlin Songbook]. 1922.
Stikhi o Rossii [Poems about Russia]. 1922.
Vozvrashchen'e na rodinu [Returning Home]. 1922.

Stikhotvoreniia [Selected Poetry]. 1923.
Stikhotvoreniia [Selected Poetry]. 1940.

Fiction

Serebrianii golub'. 1909–10; as *The Silver Dove*, translated by
George Reavey, 1974.
Peterburg. 1916; revised edition, 1922; as *St Petersburg*, trans-
lated by John Cournos, 1959; complete version, as
Petersburg, translated by R.A. Maguire and John E.
Malmstad, 1978; as *Petersburg Nineteen Eighteen*, edited
by Efraim Sicher, 1989.
Kotik Letaev. 1922; as *Kotik Letaev*, translated by Gerald
Janeček, 1971.
Moskva. 1926.
Kreshchenyi kitaets. 1927; as *The Christened Chinaman*,
translated by Thomas R. Beyer, 1991.
Maski [Masks]. 1932.

Other

Simfoniia (2-aia, dramaticheskaia). 1902; as *The Dramatic
Symphony*, translated by Roger and Angela Keys, with *The
Forms of Art*, 1986.
Severnaia simfoniia (1-aia, geroicheskaia) [Northern
Symphony (First, Heroic)]. 1904.
Vozvrat: III-ia simfoniia. 1905; as *The Forms of Art*, trans-
lated by John Elsworth, with *The Dramatic Symphony*,
1986.
Kubok metelei: Chetvertaia simfoniia [A Golet of Blizzards:
Fourth Symphony]. 1908.
Lug zelonyi [The Green Meadow]. 1910.
Simvolizm [Symbolism]. 1910.
Arabeski [Arabesques]. 1911.
Tragediia tvorchestva: Dostoevskii i Tolstoi [The Tragedy of
an Oeuvre]. 1911.
Revoliutsiia i kul'tura [Revolution and Culture]. 1917.
Rudol'f Shteiner i Gete v mirovozzrenii sovremenosti [Rudolf
Steiner and Goethe from a Contemporary Viewpoint].
1917.
Na perevale [At the Divide]. 3 vols., 1918–20.
Korolevna i rytsari [The Princess and the Knights]. 1919.
Zapiski chudaka [Notes of an Eccentric]. 2 vols., 1922.
Glossolaliia: Poema o zvuke [Glossolalia: Poem about
Sound]. 1922.
Putevye zametki: Sitsiliia i Tunis [Travel Notes: Sicily and
Tunis]. 1922.
*Poeziia slova: Pushkin, Tiutchev, Baratynskii, V. Ivanov, A.
Blok* [Poetry of the Word]. 1922.
Vospominaniia o Bloke [Reminiscences of A.A. Blok]. 1922–
23.
Odna iz obiteley tsarstva tenei [In the Kingdom of the
Shades]. 1924.
Veter s Kavkaza [A Wind from the Caucasus]. 1928.
Ritm kak dialektika i 'Mednyi vsadnik' [Rhythm as Dialectic
and 'The Bronze Horseman']. 1929.
Na rubezhe dvukh stoletii [On the Brink of Two Centuries].
1930.
Nachalo veka [The Turn of the Century]. 1933.
Masterstvo Gogolia [The Art of Gogol']. 1934.
Mezhdu dvukh revoliutsii [Between Two Revolutions]. 1934.

*

Critical Studies: *The Frenzied Poets: Andrey Bely and the
Russian Symbolists* by Oleg Maslennikov, 1952; *Andrey Bely*
by Konstantin Mochulsky, 1955, reprinted as *Andrei Bely:
His Life and Works*, translated by N. Szalavitz, 1977; *Andrey
Bely*, 1972, and *Andrey Bely: A Critical Study of the Novels*,
1983, both by J.D. Elsworth; *The Apocalyptic Symbolism of
Andrej Belyj* by Samuel D. Cioran, 1973; *Andrej Belyj: The
'Symphonies'* by Anton Kovač, 1976; *The Poetic World of
Andrey Bely*, by Boris Christa, 1977, and *Andrey Bely:
Centenary Papers* edited by Christa, 1980; *Andrey Bely: A
Critical Review* edited by Gerald Janeček, 1978; *Andrei Bely's
Short Prose* by Ronald E. Peterson, 1980; *Word and Music in
the Novels of Andrey Bely* by Ada Steinberg, 1982; *The
Dream of Rebirth: A Study of Andrej Belyj's Novel 'Peter-
burg'* by Magnus Ljunggren, 1982; *Andrei Bely: The Major
Symbolist Fiction* by Vladimir E. Alexandrov, 1985; 'From
Fact to Fiction: The Role of the Red Domino in Belyi's
Peterburg' by Milicz Banjanin, in *Russian Language Journal*,
40(135), 1986; *Andrey Bely: Spirit of Symbolism* edited by
John E. Malmstad, 1987; *Body of Words: A Reading of Bely's
'Kotik Letaev'* by M. Molnar, 1987; 'The Grotesque Style of
Belyi's *Moscow* Novels' by Olga Muller Cook, in *Slavic and
East European Journal*, 32(3), 1988; 'Andrej Belyi's *Dramatic
Symphony*' by Willem G. Weststeijn, in *Avant-Garde:
Interdisciplinary and International Review*, edited by
Weststeijn and Jan van der Eng, 1991.

* * *

Andrei Belyi, Russia's greatest modernist writer and a
leading poet of that most remarkable period of Russian intellectual history which is called the Silver Age, was also a
theorist of symbolism, a pioneer in the structural method of
literary analysis, and, according to Briusov and later
Pasternak, 'the most interesting man in Russia'. Before he
became A. Belyi (in 1901), he considered himself a philosopher, a follower of the mystical philosopher Solovev, a
scientist, and a composer, regarding himself as 'simply a
person who is searching'.

In his search to find new forms of art, he wanted to fuse art
with music and religion, 'to escape into a primitive phase of
culture, into rhythm and gesture . . .' ('About Myself as a
Writer'). He maintained that life reveals itself only through
creative activity which is 'unanalysible, integral, and omnipotent'. It is only expressible in symbolic images which
envelop the idea. In the process of cognitive symbolization
the symbol becomes reality, it can run ahead, depicting the
future. He claimed that he had foreseen in his novels people
and historical events, such as Rasputin in *Serebrianii golub'*
(*The Silver Dove*), the downfall of tsarist Petersburg in
Peterburg (*Petersburg*), and the fascist conspiracy in his projected novel *Germany*. Symbolism for Belyi was a way of
thinking, writing, and living. The Belyi-Briusov-Petrovskaia
triangle, and Belyi's dramatic affair with Blok's wife, con-
formed to the Symbolist doctrine that life and art should be
unitary. The principal hero of his novels is a philosophizing
eccentric, a madman-artist 'whose only art is the creation of
himself'. Even the choice of the colour white (belyi) for his
pseudonym was to be significant. White is a recurrent symbol
in his poetry: it stands for the snowstorm, that vast elemental
force, and for life itself. Sounds and colours always had for
Belyi a mystical significance. As Belyi himself tells us, the
subjects of his first four books 'were drawn from musical
leitmotifs, and I called them not stories or novels but
Symphonies'.

Belyi believed that, in moving towards music, a work of art
becomes more profound. All his prose has distinct rhythmical
qualities. The story *Kreshchenyi kitaets* (*The Christened*

Chinaman), for example, was composed from the sounds of Schumann's *Kreisleriana*. The regular beat, the pause for breath are supposed to express a deep secret rhythm of the spirit. In poetry, too, phonetic structure is often more important than meaning. Words with similar consonants clutch at one another, cling to each other, echoing his favourite images of wind and storm. He deliberately obliterated all discourse from his poetry. There are hardly any developments of thought; instead Belyi repeats certain images pointing to a central theme. His poetry is, however, inferior to his prose. He saw rhythm as a 'principle which unites poetry with prose'. He called his last novel, *Maski* [Masks], a 'lyrical epic poem'. He often thought of himself more as a theoretician than as a poet. He devoted many years (from 1902 to 1910, and again from 1918 to 1921) to the development of the theory of symbolism. He gave many public lectures, wrote hundreds of essays, which were collected in the most complex book, *Simvolizm* [Symbolism]; he also conducted seminars and research work in the field of prosody. Only in 1924 did he return to literature completely, and he then began to fall into obscurity.

Like Blok, he saw the October Revolution as the birth of a new cosmical world. But Russia, risen anew, failed to appreciate him. In 1921, after Blok's death, he left Russia for Berlin only to find out that 'the Russian émigré is as alien to me as the Bolsheviks'. The two people he wanted to be with most, Asia Turgeneva and Rudolf Steiner, didn't need him. Bitterly disenchanted, exhausted and sick, he came back to Moscow: 'I returned to my grave . . . all journals, all publishing houses are closed to me'. After Trotskii's merciless attack, stating that Belyi's novels 'poison your very existence', he appealed to Stalin (1931), and compromised with his conscience by becoming a Marxist. In Soviet Russia he remained a controversial writer, too modernist for the literary officials, too incomprehensible for the reading public. In the West his works have always been praised 'without being understood or read', as the translators of *Petersburg* put it. Although Nabokov included *Petersburg* among the four 'greatest masterpieces of 20th-century prose', Belyi never achieved such enormous popularity as Joyce, Kafka, and Proust. Like them he did his best to destroy the simplicity of forms, but it was precisely his linguistic experiments that cut him off from the foreign reader.

—Valentina Polukhina

PETERSBURG (Peterburg)
Novel by Andrei Belyi, 1916.

Although compared by some critics to Joyce's *Ulysses* with its broad scope and challenging formal innovations, *Petersburg* has none the less remained a relatively obscure and little-known work. It appeared in 1916 to immediate acclaim and after Belyi's 1922 revisions, although suffering from the Soviet censors intent on establishing Socialist Realism, it nevertheless went through several reprints. Originally conceived as part of a projected trilogy about western versus eastern cultures and their conflicting representations of life, Belyi radically changed his conception of this novel during the process of its composition.

The novel is set in the autumn of 1905, a turbulent period of political instability with a series of mutinies, strikes, and assassinations, which create an air of being on the brink of cataclysmic change. This atmosphere of conspiracy, political anxiety, and fear propels the narrative. Nikolai Apollonovich

Ableukhov, a student of neo-Kantian philosophy, who was once incautiously involved with a revolutionary group and their plot to assassinate a prominent government official, is now asked to plant the bomb. In a cruel twist, the eminent politician turns out to be his father, senator Apollon Apollonovich. Although the assassination plot ultimately fails, this main narrative thread weaves together a wide variety of subplots that involve linguistic and philosophical concerns, with a number of characters and ideological perspectives of Russian society. From the powerful and influential Ableukhovs and their circle, to the antagonistic and poverty-stricken Dudkin and the peasant Stepka, the multiplicity of characters in the text presents one with a cross-section of a society locked in struggle.

The novel's careful detail establishes a 'realism' which is nevertheless constantly subverted by the question of 'unreality'. A dichotomous tension between appearance and illusion is always evident, especially in the subplot of the elusive Red Domino, and the other frequent allusions to masks, disguises, and hidden activities. Even 'shadowy consciousness' itself is regarded as a site of fantastic and duplicitous activity: 'Cerebral play is only a mask. Under way beneath this mask is the invasion of the brain by forces unknown to us'.

Thus, the novel makes the interrogation and exploration of the nature of reality a central concern. Various philosophies of consciousness are considered, including those of Kant, Comte, Nietzsche, Bruno, and Bergson. A tension emerges as subjects oscillate between desiring consciousness to be a stable centre for the self and finding that consciousness is constantly upset, distorted, and de-centred, as it verges on a chasm of darkness and emptiness: 'Consciousness struggled in vain to give illumination. . . . And there was no centre of consciousness'. The certainty of subjectivity falls away into a morass of indescribable blankness: 'And the "I" proved to be merely a black receptacle, if not a small cramped storeroom'. Indeed, far from proving to be the manageable instrument of an autonomy that threatens to subvert the "I"'s power, '. . . there were swarms of thoughts thinking themselves; and it was not he thinking, but thoughts thinking themselves— something was being thought, was being sketched, was arising'.

Belyi utilizes various mythologies concerning St Petersburg in the layered construction of this novel, alluding to the works of Pushkin, Dostoevskii, Chekhov, Tolstoi, and others. Belyi's principal text is Pushkin's poem *Mednyi vsadnik* (*The Bronze Horseman*), which focuses on the statue that is one of the principal landmarks of the city. In Belyi's personification of the city—the whirlwind, the caryatid, the buildings—this statue haunts the characters, as it hovers ominously and apocalyptically over both the city and the novel. As with many modernist texts, temporality and spatiality are important foci of the novel's interrogation. St Petersburg's geography is always minutely detailed throughout the novel, as the narrative constantly relates the characters' imaginative relationship with the physical urban space of the city. The city is often the locus of delusion, almost indeed the limit of perception: 'There is an infinity of rushing prospects with an infinity of rushing, intersecting shadows. All of Petersburg is an infinity of the prospect raised to the nth degree'. This boundlessness equally extends to the temporal dimension, since although the novel's final chapters are structured around the elapse of the 24 hours of the bomb, time nevertheless expands in the characters' consciousnesses. They frequently find themselves adrift in a timelessness which is profoundly disturbing. In order to preserve some sense of subjective integrity in the face of this temporal disorientation, characters construct various systems around them, like Apollon Apollonovich's fascination with 'proportionality and symmetry'.

The novel's philosophical explorations into the nature of reality are intricately linked to its formal experimentation, much of which derives from Belyi's interest in Symbolist aesthetics. A central feature of Belyi's aesthetic innovation lies in his conception and treatment of language. In a society where human subjectivity is splintered and uncertain, communication appears to be similarly fragmented: 'all the words jumbled and again wove in to a sentence; and the sentence seemed meaningless'. Dialogues are often abruptly wrenched through unexpected interruptions and gaps; the text itself is fractured and dispersed into smaller units by a series of dashes and dots. Belyi recognizes that language can reinforce and create social abstractions and illusions if its partiality is ignored or forgotten. Therefore, he highlights the materiality of language, and emphasizes the production of words as sounds and contingent human ideas. To aid this aesthetic principle, the text utilizes clusters of certain sounds, as for example in Belyi's description of his use of the sounds 'll', 'pp', 'kk', and 'rr' (see Penguin translator's introduction, p. xvii). The text also makes extensive use of neologisms, puns, and letter games, such as Dudkin's confusion over Shishnarfne and Enfranshish. The recurrence of specific symbolic motifs, like the swirls of dust with their apocalyptic associations, reinforces the patterned structure of the novel.

Petersburg demonstrates an ingenuity, diversity, and intensity equal to that of the most significant 20th-century texts, while its formal and aesthetic experimentations broaden the boundaries and understanding of European modernism.

—Tim Woods

BEMBO, Pietro. Born in Venice, Venetian Republic, 20 May 1470. Lived in Florence, where his father was ambassador, 1478–79. Educated by the humanists Giovanni Alessandro Urticio and Giovanni Aurelio Augurello; studied Greek at the school of Costantino Lascaris, Messina, c.1491–93. Lived with Morosina (died 1535) in the 1520s, one daughter and two sons. Accompanied his father on his ambassadorial mission in Rome, 1487–88; lived in Bergamo, where his father was podesta [governor], 1489–91, and subsequently returned to Venice; collaborated with the publisher Aldus Manutius: published his first work, *De Aetna*, at Manutius' press, 1496; lived in Ferrara, where his father was Vicedomino [co-ruler], 1497–99; studied philosophy under Niccolò Leoniceno; returned to Venice, 1499, and attempted to enter politics, with little success; lived at the court of Duke and Duchess of Urbino, 1506–12; lived in Rome, 1512–21; papal secretary to Leo X, 1513–21; settled in Padua, 1522; took up an ecclesiastical career, by virtue of his membership of the Order of Jerusalem; became historiographer and librarian of the Republic of Venice, 1530; elected to College of Cardinals, 1539, and moved to Rome; Bishop of Gubbio, 1541–44; lived in Rome, 1544–47. *Died 18 January 1547.*

PUBLICATIONS

Collections

Opere, edited by A.F. Seghezzi. 4 vols., 1729.
Prose e rime, edited by Carlo Dionisotti. 1960.
Opere in volgare, edited by Mario Marti. 1961.

Verse

Rime. 1530; revised and enlarged editions, 1535, 1548.
Sonetti inediti, edited by Rinaldo Sperati. 1899.

Other

De Aetna (dialogue). 1496; as *On Etna*, translated by Betty Radice, in *De Aetna/On Etna* (bilingual edition), 1969.
Gli Asolani (treatise). 1505; revised edition, 1530; as *Gli Asolani*, translated by Rudolf Gottfried, 1954.
De imitatione Libellus. 1514 (unauthorized edition); 1530 (authorized edition).
Le prose della volgar lingua (treatise). 1525; revised edition, 1538; edited by Mario Marti, 1955, and by Carlo Dionisotti, 1955.
De Virgilii Culice et Terentii Fabulis. 1530.
De Guido Ubaldo Feretrio deque Elisabetha Gonzaga Urbini Ducibus. 1530.
Imitatione libri tres. 1541.
Carmina quinque illustrium poetarum. 1548; as *Carminum libellus*, 1552.
Lettere. 2 vols., 1548–50.
Rerum venetarum historiae libri XII. 1551; as *Della historia vinitiana*, 1552.
Epistulae familiares (letters). 3 vols., 1552; as *Lettere*, 4 vols., 1562; edited by Ernesto Travi, 2 vols., 1987–90.
Lettere giovanili. 1554.
Nuove lettere famigliari (letters to his nephew G.M. Bembo). 1564.
Carteggio d'amore, with Maria Savorgnan (letters), edited by Carlo Dionisotti. 1950.
The Prettiest Love Letters in the World: Letters Between Lucrezia Borgia and Pietro Bembo, translated by Hugh Shankland. 1987.

Editor, *Le cose volgari*, by Petrarch. 1501.
Editor, *Commedia*, by Dante. 1502.
Editor, *Opera*, by Virgil. 1535.

*

Critical Studies: *Un decennio della vita di M. Pietro Bembo (1521–1531)*, 1885, and *Un medaglione del Rinascimento: Cola Bruno messinese e le sue relazioni con Pietro Bembo*, 1901, both by Vittorio Cian; *La gioventù di M.P. Bembo e il suo dialogo Gli Asolani* by M. Tamburini, 1914; *Pietro Bembo e le sorti della lingua nazionale nel Veneto* by N. Schileo, 1923; *Pietro Bembo* by M. Santoro, 1937; *Il Bembo critico e il principio d'imitazione* by G. Santangelo, 1950; *La vita avventurosa di Pietro Bembo, umanista–poeta–cortigiano* by G. Meneghetti, 1961; *Il petrarchismo del Bembo e di altri poeti del '500* by Giorgio Santangelo, 1967; 'Pietro Bembo's Gli Asolani of 1505' by C.H. Clough, in *Modern Language Notes*, 84(1), 1969; 'Imitatio: Theory and Practice—The Example of Bembo the Poet' by Dante Della Terza, in *Yearbook of Italian Studies*, 1, 1971; *Pietro Bembo ed il suo epistolario* by Ernesto Travi, 1972; 'Bembo's Maneuvers from Virtue to Virtuosity in Gli Asolani' by Susan Delaney, in *Italian Quarterly*, 27(106), 1986; 'Pietro Bembo and the Vat. Lat. 3226' by John N. Grant, in *Humanistica Lovaniensa*, 37, 1988; 'Bembo and the Dialogic Path of Love' by Olga Zorzi Pugliese, in *Italiana 1988* edited by Albert N. Mancini and others, 1990.

* * *

Pietro Bembo is remembered chiefly as the foremost pioneering theoretician of the Italian language and the architect of its use as a vehicle for serious literature fit to stand beside the Latin of humanistic culture, based on the example of the great medieval writers: Dante, Petrarch, and Boccaccio. In particular for poetry, Bembo proposed imitation of the model of Petrarch, and in *Gli Asolani*, a discussion of the issues of love between three men and three women, set in Asolo at the court of Caterina Cornaro, Queen of Cyprus, he established Petrarch as the model for Italian love poetry, just as in his *Prose della volgar lingua* he was to establish Florentine as the vernacular language, and rules for the correct use of the Italian language in prose that have been widely influential since.

A Venetian patrician, expert in the courtier arts, Bembo had travelled widely, including to the court of Urbino that had produced Castiglione's *Il libro del cortegiano* (*The Book of the Courtier*)—in which he appears as a fictional protagonist. He rose to eminent positions, firstly as papal secretary, and later as cardinal. Bembo was among the first Renaissance figures to study Greek; he wrote fluently in Latin, and acquired a unique position in the Italian Renaissance as an arbiter of literary taste. The now famous exchange of letters between Bembo and Giovan Francesco (nephew of the famous Pico) della Mirandola in 1512, in which the latter upheld the independence of style of the individual writer, became a classic text on the principle of literary imitation in Latin proposing Cicero as a model for prose and Virgil for poetry. Thus was reached an ideal of classical literary imitation, which would be elaborated for the Italian language using the models of Petrarch for poetry and Boccaccio for prose in Bembo's *Le prose della volgar lingua*. The Italian language would henceforth acquire the dignity and reverence previously accorded only to the classics.

In *Gli Asolani*, Bembo discusses the relative merits of erotic and platonic love, describing the different kinds of love whose parameters are clearly Petrarchan, although there is no explicit reference to Petrarch: a schematization of the love of Petrarch's Laura, with her counterpart (a less literary and more sensual ideal), which is contrasted, in the work's third book, in the discussion of earthly and platonic love, with the conclusion that platonic love is the more elevated spiritual kind and brings the lover closer to God. The exposition of platonic love in the third book of *Gli Asolani* has been called 'love in a cold climate', but it looks forward to the concluding section of Castiglione's *The Book of the Courtier* where, quite deliberately, the defence of Platonic love is voiced by the character of Pietro Bembo himself.

Bembo's own lyric poetry is the first chapter in the long history of Petrarchism. The poems were published first in a collection in 1530 as *Rime* (although many were well known to contemporaries long before then), and they put into practice the theories established in *Gli Asolani*. The slavish imitation of Petrarch's *Canzoniere* is apparent everywhere, and even whole lines are quoted from the poetry of the master, as in the celebrated example of 'Solingo augello, se piangendo vai', where critics have identified quotations from five different Petrarchan poems. The whole is refined, elevated, literary—an intellectual elaboration of the imitation principle—but without the passion or individuality of a basis in real life or love, in the eyes of both modern commentators and contemporary satirists and parodists such as Berni and Aretino. None the less, in spite of his detractors, Bembo's

position as a figure of literary transition in the tradition of the love lyric was to be decisive.

Le prose della volgar lingua is Bembo's monumental contribution to the 'questione della lingua' debate in the Italian Renaissance. It imagines a debate in Venice in 1502 between such celebrated contemporary authorities on the matter of the appropriate language for literature as Giuliano de'Medici, Federigo Fregoso, Ercole Strozzi, and Carlo Bembo (brother of the author, and so his spokesman), who vigorously advance the theory of the supremacy of Florentine as the only language for literature, on the models of Petrarch and Boccaccio. Bembo's standpoint is that of the maintenance of literary and artistic validity—not factors to do with the spoken language—in his strict adherence to the Ciceronian principle of imitation of one model. So, the questions of everyday usage, accessibility to speakers, and a widening of the circle of readers are scarcely parts of this thesis. Bembo is concerned above all with formal elegance and literary precedent, convinced that the fullest intellectual expression of a language is in the work of its writers. Writers will be writing for posterity as much as for contemporaries. The novelty for readers of his works in the early 16th century would have been that Italian—in the examples of its great literary masters from the past—was now to take its place alongside Latin and Greek as one of the languages for great literature.

Among Bembo's minor works (apart from the recently discovered letters to Maria Savorgnan, datable to Bembo's youth in 1500–01) only his letters, written while he was Pope Leo X's secretary, and his history of Venice are worthy of mention here. The first establishing his literary credentials as a humanist (Latin) writer, and the second the recognition of his cultural and literary pre-eminence in his own time by his native Republic of Venice. A symbol and incarnation of all his efforts in a long career is his own translation of the history from Latin into Italian.

—Christopher Cairns

———

BENN, Gottfried. Born in Mansfeld, Germany, 2 May 1886. Educated at the Gymnasium, Frankfurt, 1896–1903; studied philosophy and theology, University of Marburg, 1903–04; studied medicine, University of Berlin, 1904–05; Kaiser Wilhelm Academy, 1905–12, Ph.D. 1912. Married 1) Edith Brosin in 1914 (died 1922), one son (from Brosin's previous marriage) and one daughter; 2) Herta von Wedemeyer in 1938 (committed suicide 1945); 3) Ilse Kaul in 1946. Served in the army, discharged because of health problems 1912; served in the army medical corps, 1914–18, and 1935–45: awarded Iron Cross, second class, 1914. Assistant, Pathological Institute Westend Hospital, 1912–13; ship's physician, 1913; after 1918, specialist in skin disease and sexually transmitted infection, Berlin; embraced National Socialism, 1932–34, renounced National Socialist Party, 1934; acting chairman, literary section of the Prussian Academy of Art, 1933; after World War II, forbidden to publish anything he had written since 1937; private medical practice, West Berlin, from 1945. Member: Prussian Academy of Art, 1932. Recipient: Büchner prize, 1951; Order of Merit, first class, Federal Republic of Germany, 1952. *Died 7 July 1956.*

PUBLICATIONS

Collections

Gesammelte Werke, edited by Dieter Wellershoff. 4 vols., 1958–61.
Primäre Tage: Gedichte und Fragmente aus dem Nachlass, edited by Dieter Wellershoff. 1958; as *Primal Vision: Selected Writings*, edited by E. B. Ashton, 1960.
Medizinische Schriften, edited by Werner Rübe. 1965.
Späte Gedichte: Fragmente, Destillationen, Aprèslude. 1965.
Poems, translated by Michael Lebeck. 1967.
Selected Poems, edited by Friedrich Wilhelm Wodtke. 1970.
Sämtliche Erzählungen. 1970.
Gesammelte Werke in der Fassung der Erstdrucke, edited by B. Hillebrand. 1982–.
Sämtliche Werke, edited by Gerhard Schuster. 4 vols., 1986–89.
Prose, Essays, Poems, edited by Volkmar Sandor. 1987.
Poems 1937–1947, translated by Simona Dradhici. 1991.

Verse

Morgue und andere Gedichte. 1912.
Söhne. 1913.
Fleisch. 1917.
Schutt. 1924.
Betäubung. 1925.
Spaltung. 1925.
Die Dänin. 1925.
Gesammelte Gedichte. 1927.
Ausgewählte Gedichte: 1911–1936. 1936.
Zweiundzwanzig Gedichte: 1936–1943. 1943.
Statische Gedichte. 1948.
Trunkene Flut: Ausgewählte Gedichte. 1949.
Fragmente. 1951.
Destillationen. 1953.
Aprèslude. 1955.
Gesammelte Gedichte 1912–1956. 1956.
Lyrik: Auswahl letzter Hand. 1956.

Plays

Ithaka. 1919.
Etappe. 1919.
Der Vermessungsdirigent. 1919.
Das Unaufhörliche (oratorio), music by Paul Hindemith (produced 1931). 1931.

Radio Play: *Die Stimme hinter dem Vorhang*, 1952.

Fiction

Gehirne. 1916.
Diesterweg. 1918.
Die gesammelten Schriften. 1922.

Other

Das moderne Ich. 1920.
Gesammelte Prosa. 1928.
Fazit der Perspektiven. 1930.
Nach dem Nihilismus (essays). 1932.
Der neue Staat und die Intellektuellen (essays). 1933.
Kunst und Macht (essays). 1934.
Ausdruckswelt: Essays und Aphorismen. 1949.
Drei alte Männer. 1949.

Goethe und die Naturwissenschaften. 1949.
Der Ptolemäer. 1949.
Doppelleben: Zwei Selbstdarstellungen (autobiography). 1950.
Frühe Prosa und Reden. 1950.
Essays. 1951.
Probleme der Lyrik (speech). 1951.
Frühe Lyrik und Dramen. 1952.
Monologische Kunst: Ein Briefwechsel zwischen Alexander Lernet-Holenia und Gottfried Benn. 1953.
Altern als Problem für Künstler. 1954.
Provoziertes Leben: Eine Auswahl aus den Prosaschriften. 1955.
Reden. 1955.
Soll die Dichtung das Leben bessern?, with Reinhold Schneider. 1956.
Über mich selbst: 1886–1956. 1956.
Dr. Rönne: Frühe Prosa, edited by Ernst Neff. 1957.
Ausgewählte Briefe. 1957.
Briefe an Carl Werckshagen. 1958.
Roman des Phänotyp: Landsberger Fragment, 1944. 1961.
Das gezeichnete Ich: Briefe aus den Jahren 1900–1956. 1962.
Weinhaus Wolf und andere Prosa. 1967.
Briefe an F.W. Oelze, edited by Harald Steinhagen and Jürgen Schröder. 3 vols., 1977–80.
Briefwechsel mit Paul Hindemith, edited by Ann Clark Fehn. 1978.
Gottfried Benn, Max Rychner: Briefwechsel 1930–1956, edited by Gerhard Schuster. 1986.
Briefe an Tilly Wedekind 1939–1955. 1986.

Editor, *Lyrik des expressionistischen Jahrzehnts*. 1955.

*

Critical Studies: *Gottfried Benn, Phänotyp dieser Stunde: Eine Studie über den Problemgehalt seines Werkes* by Dieter Wellershoff, 1958; *Gottfried Benn's Critique of Substance* by Marion L. Adams, 1969; *Die Statischen Gedichte von Gottfried Benn* by Harald Steinhagen, 1969; *Gottfried Benn: The Unreconstructed Expressionist* by J.M Ritchie, 1972; *Gottfried Benn: The Artist and Politics 1910–1934* by Reinhard Alter, 1976; *Change and Permanence: Gottfried Benn's Text for Paul Hindemith's Oratorio Das Unaufhörliche* by Ann Clark Fehn, 1977; *Consistency of Phenotype: A Study of Gottfried Benn's Views on Lyric Poetry* by Angelika Manyoni, 1983.

*   *   *

Gottfried Benn was one of the most important German poets of the 20th century. His early work—notably the poems of *Morgue* (1912) and the innovative prose works of the years 1915–21 (the so-called 'Rönne stories')—forms a significant but not always typical part of the German Expressionist movement. The poems of *Morgue* take up themes and topics not unknown in European poetry since Baudelaire, but approach them with a sense of the grotesque which is quite removed from all sentimentality, and with a metonymic technique which strongly alienates and shocks the reader. After this collection, a landmark in German literature, Benn's development in poetry was towards a Dionysian, ecstatic voice and—after a deep crisis in his life and work in 1921—subsequently towards a more and more absolutist cult of formal art.

During the 1920s, when Benn was working as a doctor in Berlin, the city to which he remained loyal throughout his life, his cult of art was based on a growing rejection of civilization and reason and on the withdrawal of the poetic into a hermetic world of dream, trance, and hallucination. His essays of this period—on history, technology, alternative medicine, and the psychopathology of the artist—have a provocative and critical tone that at the time caused Benn to be considered a radical critic of bourgeois society. Increasingly, however, public disputes with representatives of the political left, who were unwilling to accept the party-political independence of his aesthetic position, caused Benn to indentify with the right. In 1933 he was one of the most prominent (and certainly one of the most surprising) writers to remain in Germany after the fascist take-over. He identified with Hitler's Germany not just in acquiescence but through active support for the state: a support that led to the celebrated controversy with Klaus Mann, who had appealed to Benn to recognize the barbarity of the National Socialist state (Benn's reply was the infamous speech 'To the Literary Emigrés: A Reply', 1933). Benn went so far as to express naive yet disquieting support for aspects of the new state's eugenic measures ('Züchtung 1' [Breeding I], 1933) and finally completely compromised his own cherished principles of the self-referential nature of formal poetry (on whose distance from reality and social life he had insisted), as he identified aesthetic form with the brutal order of National Socialist Germany. Of Stefan George's poetry he wrote perhaps the most extraordinary sentence to be found in the unappetizing debris of cultural fascism: in one of George's most sensitive autumnal poems Benn claims to identify the spirit of the storm-troopers, for, he writes, discipline moves 'in George's art and in the march-step of the brown batallions as *one* imperative'.

Disillusionment set in after the Röhm putsch in 1934, and Benn took refuge in the German army—in an insensitive phrase he referred to his move as 'the aristocratic form of emigration'—and continued to publish until 1938, when (as part of the general hostility of the state to artistic modernism) his works were banned. The lyrical products of these years are collected in *Statische Gedichte*, which, after initial problems with allied censorship, appeared in 1948. In the following year the volume *Der Ptolemäer* [The Ptolemean] appeared. It contains the prose works that he had written in 1944, most notably the remarkable *Roman des Phänotyp* [Novel of the Phenotype], in which the pursuit of a world of pure expression and form—what Benn calls the *Ausdruckswelt*—leads to prose of a rare and formal innovation and intensity. Benn referred to these works as 'absolute prose'. The controversial autobiography *Doppelleben*—the title refers to the double life of the artist in society—made clear that Benn's involvement with fascism was a topic for neither personal analysis nor regret.

The poems of the 1950s, by common critical consent, seldom attain the quality of *Statische Gedichte*. The speech *Probleme der Lyrik* [Problems of Lyric Poetry] became one of the most influential poetological works of the 1950s in West Germany. In this speech Benn tried to bring developments in modern poetry to the attention of a post-war German public whom—it has been argued—the Third Reich had cut off from international developments. Benn's judgements, like the language and themes of his own poetry at the time, were highly influential in the succeeding generation. The rehabilitation of Expressionism in West Germany (following its abrupt fall from grace in the 1930s) owes much to Benn's essays and anthologies in the years immediately before his death.

Voices critical of Benn had not been silent in the 1950s, but his influence waned sharply with the student revolt of the 1960s. The increasing interest in the socio-political function of literature and the subsequent (but by no means co-extensive) interest in the poetry of Bertolt Brecht contributed further to this decline. It was felt by young poets that aspects of Benn's language and poetic technique had exhausted themselves and that new models were called for. Benn's work came to be strongly identified with the restorative nature of the Adenauer years. The subsequent eclipse of Marxist positions and the establishment of post-modernism cleared a way for Benn's re-emergence. It is to be feared that present opinion is open more to the tired, sophisticated resignation of the later Benn than to the magnificent modernist experiments of the early poetry and prose.

—Hugh Ridley

PALAU
Poem by Gottfried Benn, 1922.

This poem first appeared in *Der Neuë Merkur*, 5(1), April 1922. Its original title 'Rot' was changed to 'Palau' in a subsequent publishing of the poem in the collection *Spaltung* and has since retained that title. The island in question is situated in the south west Pacific, north of New Guinea. Ever since Gauguin's trip to Tahiti, interest in the South Seas had been stimulated among German expressionists, not least the painters Max Pechstein and Emil Nolde. In literature too, that lure—as a means of flight into the exotic—was manifested. Here Benn distances himself from the perceived tired and outworn civilization of northern Europe (it was the time of Oswald Spengler's major philosophical work *Der Untergang des Abendlandes* (*The Decline of the West*) to an island, redolent of the exotic, that serves as the goal of his escape.

The impression of exotic tropicality is deftly suggested with the briefest of images: heat, reefs, the smell of eucalyptus, palm trees (II. 9–10); Sepia, coral (II. 41–42). It is eventide ('The evening is red on the island of Palau') and the approach of darkness ('and the shadows sink' I. 2), ('soon it will be night and lemurs' II. 7–8) induces the poet to reflect on the vegetative and also the biological processes in the natural order. The richness of sexual experience ('it is good to drink from the cup of woman' II. 3–4) is then linked in the second stanza with the very primal biological processes of nature ('in the depths of the womb of the darkening seas' II. 15–16).

But the concomitant factor with life is death. This idea has been introduced at the outset of the poem with the mention in the opening stanza, as the red of the evening sky changes to black with the approach of night, of 'Totenvögel' and 'Totenuhren'. In the third stanza—where the 'refrain' in the poem's opening couplet is now incorporated into the text itself—death is further mentioned directly ('all the deaths in the world/are ferries and fords' II. 21–22). Indeed the poet allows himself then in the fourth and fifth stanzas the opportunity to call to mind some examples of the comparative nature of death rites, as he considers the functional similarities of such rites in Nordic and classical mythology (the hammer of Thor, the ferryman Charon on the river Styx) in relation to the practices of the Micronesians.

The conjuring-up of the natural scene and the pursuant homing-in on the processes of life and death permit the poet to distance himself not only spatially, but also temporally, as he moves from consciousness of the transience of time to that of 'static' timelessness. By means of a series of pairings of words and images, Benn seeks a poetic balancing of these polarities: 'what still remains standing/also craves disembodiment down to a limbless state,/ down to the void' (II. 11–14) —which in turn leads here of course to the very positive value of 'the depths of the womb of the darkening seas' (II. 15–16); and in a repeated form, 'what still holds and rises,/ will also crumble' (II. 43–44); 'never and always' (I. 20, I. 48).

In short, this poem does not belong to the early aggressive poems of Benn, where he often seeks to *èpater les bourgeois* in his first verse collection, *Morgue* (1912) (e.g. the poem 'Man and Woman Go Through the Cancer Ward'). Here in this poem of regression, a calmer, more contemplative note is observable. Little more than half a year earlier, Benn had been writing in a mood of creative crisis: 'I am now 35 years of age . . . I can't write anything anymore. I can't read anything any longer. I can't think any thought through to its conclusion'. In 'Palau', the contextual balance is further matched by its structural form—from the very composition of the poem with its six eight-line stanzas, coupled with the regularity of an alternating masculine and feminine rhyme scheme, down to the deliberate and careful repetition, or slight variation, of phrase and line interwoven into the different stanzas, to create musical and colourful patterns of imagery that help to persuade the reader, as Benn moves beyond the level of man and nature to embrace religious/ mythical and cultural dimensions. Dissolution of consciousness, regression is what Benn seeks and effectively finds in 'Palau'.

—Ian Hilton

———

BEOLCO, Angelo.   See **RUZZANTE**.

———

BERGERAC, Cyrano de.   See **CYRANO DE BERGERAC**.

———

BERNANOS, Georges. Born in Paris, France, 20 February 1888. Educated at Jesuit school, Paris, 1897–1900; Notre-Dame-des-Champs, Paris, 1901–03; Collège Saint-Célestin, Bourges, 1903–04; Collège Sainte-Marie, Aire-sur-la-Lys, baccalauréat, 1905 and 1906; studied law and literature, University of Paris, 1906–09. Military service, 1909–10, served in the French army, 1914–19. Married Jehanne Pauline Marie Talbert d'Arc in 1917; three sons and three daughters. Travelling salesman for an insurance company, 1922–26; editor, *L'Avant-garde de Normandie*, 1913– 14; columnist, *Le Figaro*, 1930–32; evicted from family home due to financial difficulties; moved to Majorca, Spain, 1934–

37; returned to France, 1937; travelled to Buenos Aires, via Rio de Janeiro, en route to Paraguay, in an attempt to establish a French colony, stayed in Paraguay for five days only and returned to Rio de Janeiro. Settled in Brazil, involved in the resistance movement, 1938–44; returned to France, 1945; contributor to numerous journals including *Combat*, *La Bataille*, and *Le Figaro*; travelled to North Africa, Switzerland, and Belgium giving lectures. Recipient: prix Fémina, 1929; Grand prize for fiction, Académie française, 1936. *Died 5 July 1948.*

PUBLICATIONS

Collections

Dialogue d'ombres (collected stories). 1955.
Oeuvres complètes, edited by Maurice Bardèche. 12 vols., 1955–65.
Oeuvres romanesques, edited by Michel Estève. 1961.
Essais et écrits de combat, edited by Yves Bridel, Jacques Charbot, and Joseph Jart. 1971.

Fiction

Sous le Soleil de Satan. 1926; edited by William Bush, 1982; as *The Star of Satan*, translated by Veronica Lucas, 1927; also translated by Pamela Morris, 1940; as *Under the Sun of Satan*, translated by Harry L. Binsee, 1949.
L'Imposture. 1927.
Dialogue d'ombres (stories). 1928.
La Joie. 1929; revised edition, edited by Albert Béguin, 1954; as *Joy*, translated by Louise Varèse, 1946.
Un crime. 1935; as *The Crime*, translated by Anne Green, 1936, as *A Crime*, translated by Green, 1946.
Journal d'un curé de campagne. 1936; edited by Eithne M. O'Sharkey, 1969; as *The Diary of a Country Priest*, translated by Pamela Morris, 1937.
Nouvelle histoire de Mouchette. 1937; as *Mouchette*, translated by J.C. Whitehouse, 1966.
Monsieur Ouine. 1943; revised edition, edited by Albert Béguin, 1955; as *The Open Mind*, translated by Geoffrey Dunlop, 1945.
Un mauvais rêve, edited by Albert Béguin. 1951; as *Night Is Darkest*, translated by Walter J. Strachan, 1953.

Play

Dialogue des Carmélites (produced 1949). 1949; as *The Fearless Heart*, translated by Michael Legat, 1952; as *The Carmelites*, translated by Gerard Hopkins, 1961.

Other

Saint Dominique. 1927.
Noël à la maison de France. 1928.
La Grande Peur des bien-pensants. 1931.
Jeanne, relapse et sainte. 1934; as *Sanctity Will Out: An Essay on St Joan*, translated by R. Batchelor, 1947.
Les Grands Cimetières sous la lune. 1938; as *A Diary of My Times*, translated by Pamela Morris, 1938.
Scandale de la vérité. 1939.
Nous autres, Français. 1939.
Lettres aux Anglais. 1942; as *A Plea for Liberty*, translated by Harry Lorin Binsse, 1944; also translated by Binsse and Ruth Bethell, 1970.
Écrits de combat. 1943–44.

Le Chemin de la Croix-des-Ames (articles). 4 vols., 1943–45; 1 vol, 1948; revised edition, 1987.

La France contre les robots. 1944; edited by Albert Béguin, 1955; also edited by Jean Loup Bernanos, 1970; as *Tradition of Freedom*, translated by Helen Beau Clark, 1950.

Réflexions sur le cas de conscience français. 1945.

Oeuvres. 6 vols., 1947.

Les Enfants humiliés: journal 1939–1940, edited by Albert Béguin, 1949; as *The Tradition of Freedom*, 1950.

La Liberté pour quoi faire?, edited by Albert Béguin, 1953; as *Last Essays*, translated by Joan and Barry Ulanov, 1955; as *The Last Essays of Georges Bernanos*, translated by Green, 1968.

Bernanos par lui-même, edited by Albert Béguin. 1954.

Le Crépuscule des vieux (articles), edited by Albert Béguin. 1956.

Français, si vous saviez, 1945–1948 (articles). 1961.

Le Lendemain c'est vous!, edited by Jean-Loup Bernanos. 1969.

Correspondance inédite, edited by Albert Béguin and Jean Murray. 2 vols., 1971.

La Vocation spirituelle de la France, edited by Jean-Loup Bernanos. 1975.

Les Prédestinés (essays), edited by Jean-Loup Bernanos. 1983.

Lettres retrouvées 1904–1948, edited by Jean-Loup Bernanos. 1983.

Georges Bernanos à la merci des passants (selection), edited by Jean-Loup Bernanos. 1986.

Bernanos (autobiography), edited by Jean-Loup Bernanos. 1988.

*

Critical Studies: *The Double Image: Mutations of Christian Mythology in the Work of Four French Catholic Writers* by Rayner Heppenstall, 1947; *The Poetic Imagination of Georges Bernanos* by Gerda Blumenthal, 1956; *Bernanos: His Political Thought and Prophecy* by Thomas Molnar, 1960; *Georges Bernanos*, 1965, and *Georges Bernanos: Un triple itinéraire*, 1981, both by Michel Estève; *Bernanos: An Introduction* by Peter Hebblethwaite, 1965; *Georges Bernanos* by Max Milner, 1967; *Bernanos* by Roger Pons, 1967; *Georges Bernanos* by William Bush, 1969; *Georges Bernanos: Journal d'un curé de campagne* by John Flower, 1970; *Georges Bernanos: A Study of the Man and the Writer* by Robert Speaight, 1973; *Bernanos et la politique: La Société et la droite françaises de 1900 à 1950* by Serge Albouy, 1980; *Georges Bernanos: A Study of Christian Commitment* by John E. Cooke, 1981; *La France dans l'histoire selon Bernanos* by Alan R. Clark, 1983; *Bernanos et l'angoisse* by Pierre Gille, 1984; *Bernanos aujourd'hui* by Jean-Loup Bernanos and Luc Balbont, 1987; *Temps et récit dans l'oeuvre romanesque de Georges Bernanos* by Elisabeth Lagadec-Sadoulet, 1988; *Bernanos et le monde moderne* (essays) edited by Monique Gosselin and Max Milner, 1989; *From Heaven to Hell: Imagery of Earth, Air, Water and Fire in the Novels of Georges Bernanos* by Daniel R. Morris, 1989; *Les Dialogues dans l'oeuvre de Bernanos* by André Not, 1990.

*   *   *

Today the fame of Georges Bernanos rests largely on three works that have been successfully translated for the stage and/or the screen. *Dialogue des Carmélites* (*The Fearless Heart*) was turned into an opera in 1957 by Francis Poulenc. *Journal d'un curé de campagne* (*The Diary of a Country Priest*), first adapted by Robert Bresson in a characteristically austere style, attracted a new generation of Bernanos enthusiasts when it was revived in the 1980s as a stage monologue starring Thierry Fortineau. Finally *Sous le Soleil de Satan* (*The Star of Satan*), made into a film starring Gérard Depardieu and Sandrine Bonnaire by Maurice Pialat, fuelled controversies at the Cannes Film Festival in 1987. However, for his contemporaries Bernanos was as much of a polemicist as he was a novelist. But breadth and variety of inspiration were never his trademark: both his essays and his fiction deal with a small number of themes: on a mundane level, the mediocrity or even corruption of secular and ecclesiastical authorities; on a metaphysical level, the inner tragedy brought about by pride, self-hatred, despair, or lack of faith.

Born in Paris in 1988, Bernanos owed his happiest and most vivid memories to his holidays in the north of France where hunting became one of his favourite pastimes at an early age (which would explain why firearms feature in most of his novels). A pupil of the Jesuits, he was soon noticed for his independent, passionate personality. The pantheon he selected for himself, composed of Barbey d'Aurevilly, Chateaubriand, Balzac, Maurras, Barrès, and Leon Daudet among others, helped shape the course of his religious and political development. Just before World War I he was offered the editorship of a provincial monarchist weekly. The masterpiece of his later years, *The Fearless Heart*, presents a vision of the French Revolution predicated on his monarchist convictions. After the war, however, he had to give up journalism for a more lucrative job with an insurance company. He was nearly 40 when he published his first novel, *The Star of Satan*, to considerable critical acclaim. Bernanos had the idea of *The Star of Satan* as early as 1918, and the novel, published eventually in 1926, owes its coherence to certain thematic concerns rather than to its discontinuous structure. Donissan, who gives his name to the third part of the book, 'The saint of Lumbres', is the first in the long series of priests who people Bernanos's fiction. After his encounter with the young murderess and suicide-victim Germaine (nicknamed Mouchette), Donissan's spiritual crisis, which had culminated in a violent inner struggle with Satan, resolves itself. The novel follows Donissan's troubled spiritual itinerary. It is Donissan's fate to be first beset by doubts about his calling, and then to have to fight the temptation of desire at every step of the way.

Bernanos's decision to support himself and his family entirely through his writing from then on shows that he had come to trust in his creative gift. Yet, with six children born between 1918 and 1933, he was permanently under severe material pressure, a fact which obviously affected his career, though money was already a pervasive theme in his early stories. Thus, pressed for money, he abandoned his ambitious plan for a novel which was to be called *Les Ténèbres* (*Darkness*) in favour of an, in his eyes, unsatisfactory diptych, *L'Imposture* [The Imposture], ready for publication in book form at the end of 1927, and *La Joie* (*Joy*), published in 1929. In 1933 a motor-bike accident crippled him for life. Ever more financially desperate, he then took two important steps: the first was to try and earn some easy money by writing thrillers, the second was to move to Majorca where the cost of living was lower than in France. History caught up with him in Spain. Moved by the Spanish Civil War, which he witnessed *de facto* at closer range than most European intellectuals, he felt called upon to give up fiction for committed writings. Admittedly, this change in focus probably coincided with a major crisis that revealed to him that his inspiration was running out. Such at least can be assumed from the most poignant passages about the exhausted novelist Ganse in *Un mauvais rêve* (*Night Is Darkest*). From 1938 to 1945 Bernanos lived in Brazil, where he carried on his work as a polemicist while trying his hand at farming. After the war he returned to France, but found it impossible to settle back into his own country after so many years abroad. His last residence was in Tunisia, but he died in Neuilly in 1948.

The Diary of a Country Priest is an important document because of the serious discussion it contains of Christian values in an indifferent society. But once again it is the outstanding portrayal of the priest that has grabbed the attention of generations of readers and spectators. This priest is a Christ-like figure but retains throughout the book his credibility as a human being. In *The Diary* Bernanos explores another type of saintliness—the country priest, unlike Donissan, attains sainthood through his humility and naive self-sacrifice.

Equally unique is Bernanos's skill at suggesting the power of evil. In *Un crime* (*The Crime*), the Simenon-inspired detective novel he always unjustly despised, he gives an hallucinatingly ambiguous portrayal of a young sapphic murderess who for a few days impersonates the priest she has killed before taking her own life. The choice of a lesbian dressed as a man of God for his heroine allows him to weave a brilliant web of images suggesting the Fallen Angel. Another study of a possessed soul is that of the priest and historian Cénabre who does not leave the Church even though he suddenly realizes that he has lost his faith. Cénabre is one of Bernanos's most interesting characters because of the writer's ability to make us empathize with Cénabre's excruciating terror in front of the void opened in his intellectual life by the loss of his faith. Bernanos is at his most oneiric when probing such dark areas of the mind and of the soul, a tendency still accentuated in his uncompleted novel *Monsieur Ouine* (*The Open Mind*), which accomplishes much more than a satire of the sterile introspective writer epitomized in his view by André Gide. At his best, Bernanos is indeed closest to Dostoevskii.

—Pascale Voilley

BERNHARD, Thomas. Born in Heerlen, near Maastricht, The Netherlands, 10 February 1931. Lived in Austria from 1932. Educated at Salzburg Gymnasium, 1943–47, studied singing, directing, and theatrical technique, 1952–55, and at the Salzburg Mozarteum, 1955–57. Commercial apprenticeship, Viennese Academy of Music and Drama, Salzburg, 1947–51; contracted tuberculosis and spent two years in convalescence, 1951–52; journalist for the socialist *Demokratisches Volksblatt*, from 1952, and contributor to the newspaper *Die Furche*, 1953–55; intermittent travel to Italy and Yugoslavia, 1953–57, to London, 1960, and to Poland, 1962–63; settled on a farm in Ohlsdorf an Herzversagen, Upper Austria, 1965. Recipient: Bremen prize, 1965; Austrian State prize, 1967; Wildgans prize, 1968; Büchner prize, 1970; Grillparzer prize, 1971; Séguier prize, 1974; Premio prato, 1982; Premio Mondello, 1983; Prix Médicis, 1988. *Died 12 February 1989.*

PUBLICATIONS

Collection

Gesammelte Gedichte, edited by Volker Bohn. 1991.

Fiction

Frost. 1963.
Amras. 1964.
Verstörung. 1967; as *Gargoyles*, translated by Richard and Clara Winston, 1970.
Prosa. 1967.
Ungenach (stories). 1968.
Watten: Ein Nachlass. 1969.
Ereignisse (stories). 1969.
An der Baumgrenze. 1969.
Das Kalkwerk. 1970; as *The Lime Works*, translated by Sophie Wilkins, 1973.
Gehen. 1971.
Midland in Stilfs: Drei Erzählungen. 1971.
Der Kulterer. 1974.
Korrektur. 1975; as *Correction*, translated by Sophie Wilkins, 1979.
Der Wetterfleck. 1976.
Der Stimmenimitator. 1978.
Ja. 1978; as *Yes*, translated by Ewald Osers, 1991.
Die Erzählungen, edited by Ulrich Greiner. 1979.
Die Billigesser. 1980; as *The Cheap-Eaters*, translated by Ewald Osers, 1990.
Beton. 1982; as *Concrete*, translated by David McLintock, 1984.
Der Untergeher. 1983; as *The Loser*, translated by Jack Dawson, 1991.
Holzfällen: Eine Erregung. 1984; as *Woodcutters*, translated by David McLintock, 1987; as *Cutting Timber: An Imitation*, translated by Ewald Osers, 1988.
Alte Meister: Komödie. 1985; as *Old Masters*, translated by Ewald Osers, 1989.
Auslöschung: Ein Zerfall. 1986.
In der Höhe: Rettungsversuch. 1989; as *On the Mountain: Rescue Attempt, Nonsense*, translated by Sophie Wilkins, 1991.

Plays

Die Rosen der Einöde: Fünf Sätze für Ballet, Stimmen und Orchester (opera libretti; includes *Die Rose*; *Der Kartenspieler*; *Unter den Pflaumenbäumen*; *Der Kalbskopf*; *Phantasie*). 1959.
Köpfe (libretto; produced 1960). 1960.
Ein Fest für Boris (produced 1970). 1970; as *A Party for Boris*, translated by Peter Jansen and Kenneth Northcott, in *Histrionics: Three Plays*, 1990.
Der Berg, in *Literatur und Kritik 5*. 1970.
Der Ignorant und der Wahnsinnige (produced 1972). 1972.
Die Jagdgesellschaft (produced 1974). 1974.
Die Macht der Gewohnheit (produced 1974). 1974; as *The Force of Habit* (produced 1976), translated by Neville and Stephen Plaice, 1976.
Die Salzburger Stücke (includes *Der Ignorant und der Wahnsinnige* and *Die Macht der Gewohnheit*). 1974.
Der Präsident (produced 1975). 1975; as *The President*, translated by Gitta Honegger, with *Eve of Retirement*, 1982.
Die Berühmten (produced 1976). 1976.
Minetti: Ein Porträt des Künstlers als alter Mann (produced 1976). 1977.

Immanuel Kant (produced 1978). 1978.
Der Weltverbesserer (produced 1980). 1979.
Vor dem Ruhestand (produced 1980). 1979; as *Eve of Retirement*, translated by Gitta Honegger, with *The President*, 1982.
Über allen Gipfeln ist Ruh: Ein deutscher Dichertag um 1980. 1981.
Am Ziel (produced 1981). 1981.
Der Schein trügt (produced 1984). 1983; as *Appearances Are Deceiving*, translated by Gitta Honegger, 1983.
Die Stücke 1969–1981. 1983.
Der Theatermacher (produced 1986). 1984; as *Histrionics*, translated by Peter Jansen and Kenneth Northcott, in *Histrionics: Three Plays*, 1990.
Ritter, Dene, Voss (produced 1986). 1984; as *Ritter, Dene, Voss*, translated by Peter Jansen and Kenneth Northcott, in *Histrionics: Three Plays*, 1990.
Einfach kompliziert (produced 1986). 1986.
Elisabeth II (produced 1989). 1987.
Heldenplatz (produced 1988). 1988.
Der deutsche Mittagstisch: Dramolette. 1988.
Stücke. 4 vols., 1988.
Claus Peymann kauft sich eine Hose und geht mit mir essen: Drei Dramolette, 1990.
Histrionics: Three Plays (includes *A Party for Boris*; *Histrionics*; *Ritter, Dene, Voss*), translated by Peter Jansen and Kenneth Northcott. 1990.

Screenplay: *Der Italiener*, 1971.

Verse

Auf der Erde und in der Hölle. 1957.
Unter dem Eisen des Mondes. 1958.
In hora mortis. 1958.
Psalm. 1960.
Die Irren—Die Häftlinge. 1962.
Ave Vergil. 1981.

Other

Die Ursache: Eine Andeutung. 1975.
Der Keller: Eine Entziehung. 1976.
Der Atem: Eine Entscheidung. 1978.
Die Kälte: Eine Isolation. 1981.
Ein Kind. 1982.
Wittgensteins Neffe: Eine Freundschaft. 1982; as *Wittgenstein's Nephew: A Friendship*, translated by Eward Osers, 1986.
Gathering Evidence: A Memoir (includes *Die Ursache*; *Der Keller*; *Der Atem*; *Die Kälte*; *Ein Kind*), translated by David McLintock. 1987.

*

Bibliography: *Bernhard Werkgeschichte* by Jens Dittmar, 1981.

Critical Studies: *Über Thomas Bernhard* edited by Anneliese Botond, 1970; *Thomas Bernhard* edited by Heinz Ludwig Arnold, 1974; *Thomas Bernhard* by Herbert Gamper, 1977; *Thomas Bernhard* by Bernard Sorg, 1977; 'The Plays of Thomas Bernhard: A Report' by Alfred Barthoder, in *Modern Austrian Literature*, (11), 1978; 'Bernhard's Austria: Neurosis, Symbol, or Expedient?' by A.P. Dierick, in *Modern Austrian Literature*, (12), 1979; *New German Dramatists* by Denis Calandra, 1983; 'The Works of Thomas Bernhard: Austrian Literature?' in *Modern Austrian Literature*, (17), 1984, and 'Life (and Death) after Life: The Portrayal of Old Age in the Works of Thomas Bernhard' in *University of Dayton Review*, (20), 1990, both by Gerald A. Fetz; *Leiden an der 'Natur': Thomas Bernhards metaphysische Weltdeutung im Spiegel der Philosophie Schopenhauers* by Gerald Jurdzinski, 1984; *Sprache, Handlung, Wirklichkeit im deutschen Gegenwartsdrama: Studien zu Thomas Berhard, Botho Strauss und Bobo Kirchoff* by Siegfried Steinmann, 1985; 'Theatertheater/Theaterspiele: The Plays of Thomas Bernhard' by Nicholas Eisner, in *Modern Drama*, (30), 1987; 'Thomas Bernhard Issue' of *Modern Austrian Literature*, (20), 1988.

*   *   *

Praised for his radical exposure of a disintegrating world and for his calculating and uncompromising prose style, Thomas Bernhard developed in his writing a singlemindedly pessimistic view of life, in which cruelty, disease, and injustice dominate the world. The pointlessness and bleakness of human existence pervade his vast output, which ranges through poetry, plays, novels, and autobiographical works. With its intricate black humour and satirical portraits of the Austrian culture, society, and authorities, Bernhard's literary *oeuvre* has often evoked comparison with Kafka's labyrinthine irony, Beckett's theatre of the absurd, and Artaud's theatre of cruelty.

The element of melancholy and despair permeated his writing from the outset. Three early volumes of poetry deal with suffering and depression, *Auf der Erde und in der Hölle* [On Earth and in Hell], *In hora mortis* [In the Hour of Death], and *Unter dem Eisen des Mondes* [Under the Iron of the Moon]. The imagery of death and mourning in these early poems reveals what Bernhard described as the 'uncertainty of the dim Gods'. 'Death is my theme because life is my theme', said Bernhard, and the early novel *Frost* pursues this idea through the narration of the report of a medical student about a doomed painter, while *Amras* intensified this theme. *Verstörung* (*Gargoyles*) continued the macabre tone, with a doctor visiting a succession of grotesque figures and deformed consciousnesses: a diabetic industrialist in an incestuous relationship with his half-sister; three brothers who delight in strangling exotic birds; and a crippled musical prodigy whose sister keeps him locked in a cage. These stories of illness, brutality, and malice are characteristic of the preoccupations of Bernhard's fiction. Often dealing with the mentally ill or physically disabled, Bernhard asserts that all life is motivated by madness and disease. In *Das Kalkwerk* (*The Lime Works*), the story begins with Konrad having just blown off his wife's head, after imprisoning himself and her in a disused lime works so that he may experiment with sounds, in preparation for his masterwork, 'A Sense of Hearing'. The story is narrated by a life-insurance salesman, and tells of the events leading up to this dramatic opening. Again, in *Ein Fest für Boris* (*A Party for Boris*), legless guests attend a party hosted by a wealthy woman who is herself legless. Indeed, physical disability, mental disturbance, and obsessively cruel behaviour are not considered as extraordinary characteristics in humans, but exemplary of the overall pattern of things. People's activities are merely pathetic distractions from this basic and fundamental truth.

The five volumes of Bernhard's autobiography, *Die Ursache* [The Cause], *Der Keller* [The Cellar], *Der Atem* [The Breath], *Die Kälte* [The Cold], and *Ein Kind* [A Child], recount a disturbed and unhappy childhood: unsettled by illegitimate birth, the oppressive regimes of Nazi and Catholic boarding-schools, a debilitating illness which developed into tuberculosis, and years of poverty as a student. Attempting to exorcise the misery of his past, he explodes the myth of Salzburg as a centre of cultural value in familiar terms in *Der Keller*: 'My home city is in reality a deadly disease'. He vents his criticism of Austrian society and its cultural community further in *Holzfällen* (*Cutting Timber* or *Woodcutters*).

Individual freedom and development are often curtailed by circumstances beyond one's control. Family relationships are frequently the locus of social imprisonment and repression, wherein a master-slave dialectic operates (as for example in *A Party for Boris* and *Am Zeil*). Elsewhere, subjects find themselves engaged in artistic projects which are fated to fail— Konrad's study of hearing in *The Lime Works*, or Rudolf's work on Mendelssohn in *Beton* (*Concrete*). Alternatively, the exigencies of creative practice placed upon artists transform them into performing automatons indistinguishable from circus creatures—as in the plays *Der Ignorant und der Wahnsinnige* and *Die Macht der Gewohnheit* (*The Force of Habit*).

It is noted frequently how Bernhard's prose, utilizing a variety of unusual techniques, embodies a musical structure, with its counterpoint and fugal patterns, its leitmotif and harmony. The repetition and variation evident in the overall formal structure of the novels are complemented by an intricate, interlaced structure at the level of the sentence. His circular sentences and syntactical experimentation often set up the framework of traditional fictional expectations, only to undermine it. Describing the novel *Korrektur* (*Correction*), which recounts the self-corrective and self-refining actions which prompt Roithamer's suicide, George Steiner has described Bernhard's style as a 'recursive and tidal motion', and commented on the 'clipped understatement' and 'the bone-bleached economy' of the language. A characteristic sense of life appears in *Correction*. 'Peace is not life, Roithamer wrote, perfect peace is death, as Pascal said, wrote Roithamer, I shouldn't waste my time on truisms already demonstrated by history'. Bernhard deliberately models some of his subjects on real people, as when in this novel the character Roithamer is a reflective allusion to Ludwig Wittgenstein; while Paul Wittgenstein appears in *Wittgensteins Neffe* (*Wittgenstein's Nephew*), the pianist Glenn Gould in *Der Untergeher* (*The Loser*), the philosopher in *Immanuel Kant*, and the actor in *Minetti*.

Bernhard's plays tend to be long monologues with a scarcity of action and satirical of human foibles, especially intellectual and artistic pretensions, as in *Der Weltverbesserer*, *Über allen Gipfeln ist Ruh*, and *Der Theatermacher* (*Histrionics*). With dark and forbidding subjects like the Third Reich in *Vor dem Ruhestand* (*Eve of Retirement*) and his assertion that anti-semitism is rife in Austria in *Heldenplatz* or the more general political satire in *Der Präsident* (*The President*), his plays are usually made palatable by a lighter, ironic streak.

Nothing in Bernhard's world is left sacred, including his own status as a writer, which he constantly calls into question. He considers, like Nietzsche, that truths are illusions, only just not recognized as such. Bernhard's despair over the impersonality, the dreariness, of a manic world devoid of God, and his representations of lonely individuals trying to cast aside their isolation through the temporary use of language, are nevertheless offset by his unerring dedication and commitment to a quest for truth.

—Tim Woods

THE LIME WORKS (Das Kalkwerk)
Novel by Thomas Bernhard, 1970.

The Lime Works, which, together with *Gargoyles* (*Verstörung*), marks the culmination of Bernhard's early fiction, is characterized by a narrative structure which is at once both complex and lucid. The main narrator, an insurance agent, collects, sifts, and compiles an objective sounding account of the events which ended in the murder of a crippled woman, Mrs Konrad, by her husband in the isolated lime works where they had lived for the previous five years. The narrator himself remains in the background. He reports information given by the few men of the village, such as Fro and Wieser, with whom Konrad had social contact and to whom he had spoken about his daily life. Much of the narrative takes the form of reported speech, as the narrator records details of what his informants in turn have been told by Konrad. The narrator thereby attempts to formulate a precise and objective account of what occurred.

Think of it, my dear Fro, everything I am telling you, intimating to you, Konrad is supposed to have told Fro, basically goes on here every day, over and over again! Everything that goes on here goes on day after day, it's the height of absurdity, and by dint of being the height of absurdity it is the height of terribleness, day after day. It's true, Fro's testimony agrees in every respect with Wieser's testimony, the works inspector confirms everything Fro and Wieser have said, and conversely, both Wieser and Fro confirm what the works inspector says, basically one confirms the other, they all confirm each other's testimony.

The sense of detachment and objectivity, created by the apparent presence of multiple narrators, is simultaneously undermined by the fact that the narrative is largely a monologue based on Konrad's words, the man at the centre of the story. The relentlessness of the style reflects his own obsessive pursuit of the scientific study of 'hearing'. He believes that his investigation, which he is attempting to put in writing, will be enhanced by living in the remote lime works, where he anticipates few external distractions. However, the harder he tries, the less he succeeds in writing up his ideas: often he blames the difficulty he experiences on intrusions from outside. Yet the distractions are largely internal: the more obsessional Konrad's ideas become, the less he is able to communicate them in written form.

Konrad's tendency to extremes is graphically conveyed through superlatives and spatial extremities of height and depth. Through practice, he has succeeded in hearing sounds not normally accessible to human hearing, such as those which occur at the bottom of the lake on which the lime works is situated. His 'hearing things' becomes a metaphor for his incipient madness. His inclination to pursue everything to its ultimate point also characterizes his relationship with his wife, whom he subjects to the rigours of the 'Urbanchich method'. This series of hearing exercises, named after the scientist Victor Urbanchich, was intended to provide a means of re-integrating deaf people into society. By contrast, Konrad's obsessive practice of the method is self-indulgent and self-delusory, and it merely intensifies his wife's, and his own, isolation from the villagers.

The novel depicts the sterile inner world of Konrad, the scientist and intellectual. His wife, who is also his half-sister, offers a mirror image of his obsessiveness. While Konrad is engaged in his 'study', she pursues an equally futile activity, knitting mittens which he would never wear: she constantly unpicks her work and starts again with wool of a different colour as if never satisfied with her work. The complementary nature of the relationship between Konrad and his wife is also apparent in their intellectual preferences: while his favourite reading matter is the anarchist scientist Kropotkin, his wife is occasionally rewarded by his reading Novalis to her, a Romantic poet who combined scientific leanings with a mystical approach to life. Both these writers had utopian visions which caused them to reject modern society. The incongruity of their idealism in the Konrads' life shows up the author's attack on Konrad's misuse of scientific endeavour. It is also science, in the form of incorrect medication, which is to blame for Mrs Konrad's physical incapacitation and general decline. Konrad's debility, on the other hand, is largely psychological: his concentration on the sense of hearing, to the exclusion of all else, suggests the alienation of the scientist, and perhaps of modern man in general, from the wholeness of the healthy human being, an approach ironically at variance with that of his own humanistic heroes, Kropotkin and Urbanchich.

The abandoned lime works, which had long since ceased production, itself offers an external representation of Konrad's mindset. First obsessed with acquiring it from his nephew Hörhager (the name suggests 'poor hearing'), his desire to withdraw to it from the world, and his paranoia, are represented by the heavy bolts which he has had fitted to all entrances. The layout of the building, too, epitomizes the conflicting, but complementary, patterns displayed by the Konrads: while Mrs Konrad occupies the smallest room, near the top of the house, he is more concerned with plumbing the depths of the lake and cellar. As a result of a series of expensive lawsuits, Konrad has been forced to sell most of the furniture, so that, although inhabited, it has a desolate atmosphere. External space reflects the emptiness and sterility of Konrad and his enterprise, and the lime works offers a powerful metaphor for human decline, alienation, and madness.

—Juliet Wigmore

BETTI, Ugo. Born in Camerino, Italy, 4 February 1892. Educated at Parma University, law degree 1914. Married Andreina Frosini in 1930. Artillery officer during World War I: captured by the Germans after the Italian defeat at Caporetto, 1917: prisoner-of-war October 1917–December 1918; magistrate, 1919–23, then judge, 1923–26, in Parma; judge in Rome, 1930–43; contributor to *Oggi*, from 1933; retired to Camerino, 1943, later officially cleared of charges of supporting Mussolini; librarian, Ministry of Justice, 1944; spent last years as legal adviser for the Coordinamento Spettacolo, a national association for writers and publishers. Recipient: Mondadori Academy prize, 1932; Italian Institute of Drama prize, 1949. *Died 9 June 1953.*

PUBLICATIONS

Collections

Teatro. 1955.
Teatro postumo. 1955.
Teatro completo. 1957.

Scritti inediti, edited by Antonio di Pietro. 1964.
Teatro completo. 1971.

Plays

La padrona (produced 1926). 1929.
La donna sullo scudo, with Osvaldo Gibertini (produced 1927). 1957.
La casa sull'acqua (produced 1929). 1935.
L'isola meravigliosa (produced 1929). In *Teatro*, 1955.
Un albergo sul porto (produced 1933). In *Teatro*, 1955.
Frana allo scalo nord (produced 1936). 1939; as *Landslide*, translated by G.H. McWilliam, in *Three Plays on Justice*, 1964.
Una bella domenica di settembre (produced 1937). In *Teatro*, 1955.
I nostri sogni (produced 1937). In *Teatro*, 1955.
Il cacciatore d'anitre (produced 1940). In *Teatro*, 1955.
Il paese delle vacanze (produced 1942). 1942; as *Summertime*, translated by Henry Reed, in *Three Plays*, 1956.
Notte in casa del ricco (produced 1942). In *Teatro*, 1955.
Il diluvio (produced 1943). In *Teatro*, 1955.
Il vento notturno (produced 1945). In *Teatro*, 1955.
Ispezione (produced 1947). In *Teatro*, 1955; as *The Inquiry*, translated by D. Gullette and Gino Rizzo, in *Ugo Betti: Three Plays*, 1966.
Marito e moglie (produced 1947). In *Teatro*, 1955.
Favola di Natale (produced 1948). In *Teatro*, 1955.
Corruzione al palazzo di giustizia (produced 1949). In *Teatro*, 1955; as *Corruption in the Palace of Justice*, translated by Henry Reed, in *The New Theatre of Europe 1*, edited by Robert Corrigan, 1962.
Lotta fino all'alba (produced 1949). In *Teatro*, 1955; as *Struggle Till Dawn*, translated by G.H. McWilliam, in *Three Plays on Justice*, 1964.
Irene innocente (produced 1950). In *Teatro*, 1955.
Spiritismo nell'antica casa (produced 1950). In *Teatro*, 1955.
Delitto all'isola delle capre (produced 1950). In *Teatro*, 1955; as *Goat Island*, translated by Henry Reed, 1960; as *Crime on Goat Island*, translated by D. Gullette and Gino Rizzo, in *Ugo Betti: Three Plays*, 1966.
La Regina e gli insorti (produced 1951). In *Teatro*, 1955; as *The Queen and the Rebels*, translated by Henry Reed, in *Three Plays*, 1956.
Il giocatore (produced 1951). In *Teatro*, 1955; as *The Gambler*, translated by B. Kennedy, in *Ugo Betti: Three Plays*, 1966.
L'aiuola bruciata (produced 1953). 1953; as *The Burnt Flower-Bed*, translated by Henry Reed, in *Three Plays*, 1956.
La fuggitiva (produced 1953). 1953; as *The Fugitive*, translated by G.H. McWilliam, in *Three Plays on Justice*, 1964.
Acque turbate; o, Il fratello protegge e ama (produced 1962). In *Teatro postumo*, 1955.
Three Plays (includes *Summertime*; *The Queen and the Rebels*; *The Burnt Flower-Bed*), translated by Henry Reed. 1956.
Three Plays on Justice (includes *Landslide*; *Struggle Till Dawn*; *The Fugitive*), translated by G.H. McWilliam. 1964.
I tre del pra' di sopra (screenplay). In *Scritti inediti*, 1964.
Ugo Betti: Three Plays (includes *The Inquiry*; *Crime on Goat Island*; *The Gambler*), translated by D. Gullette, B. Kennedy, and Gino Rizzo, edited by Rizzo. 1966.

Fiction

Caino (stories). 1928.
Le case (stories). 1933.

Una strana serata (stories). 1948.
La piera alta, from his screenplay *I tre del pra' di sopra*. 1948.
Raccolta di novelle, edited by Lia Fava. 1963.
Novelle (stories), edited by Mario Ortolani. 1968.

Verse

Il re pensieroso. 1922.
Canzonette—La morte. 1932.
Uomo e donna. 1937.
Poesie (includes poems written 1938–53). 1957.
Il filo verde, poesie, edited by L. Fontanella. 1993.

Other

Considerazioni sulla forza maggiore come limite di responsabilità del vettore ferroviario (essay). 1920.
Religione e teatro. 1957; as 'Religion and Theatre', translated by Gino Rizzo, in *Tulane Drama Review*, 8, 1964.

Translator, *Le nozze di Teti e di Peleo*, from poems by Catullus. 1910.

*

Critical Studies: *La poesia di Ugo Betti* by E. de Michelis, 1937; *Il teatro di Ugo Betti* by E. Barbetti, 1943; *Ugo Betti* by N.D. Aloisio, 1952; *Ugo Betti* by A. Fiocco, 1954; *La fortuna del Teatro di Ugo Betti*, 1959, and *Ugo Betti*, 1960, both by F. Cologni; 'Interpreting Betti' by G.H. McWilliam, in *Tulane Drama Review*, 5, 1960; *Ugo Betti* by A. Alessio, 1963; 'Regression-Progression in Ugo Betti's Drama' by G. Rizzo, in *Tulane Drama Review*, 8(1), 1963; *L'opera di Ugo Betti* by Antonio di Pietro, 2 vols., 1966–68; 'Ugo Betti: The Theater of Shame' by Harold Watts, in *Modern Drama*, 12, 1969; 'The Purgatorial Theatre of Ugo Betti' by Robert Corrigan, in his *The Theatre in Search of a Fix*, 1973; *Il teatro di Ugo Betti* by Gildo Moro, 1973; *Impegno e astrazione nell'opera di Ugo Betti* by F. Musarra, 1974; 'Ugo Betti's Last Plays' by Antonio Illiano, in *Perspectives on Contemporary Literature*, 1(1), 1975; *Coscienza e responsabilità nell'opera di Ugo Betti: Da La padrona a Corruzione al palazzo di giustizia* by Gianni Spera, 1977; *Atti del congresso internazionale Betti drammaturgo* edited by F. Doglio and W. Raspolini, 1984; *Il teatro di Ugo Betti* by Giorgio Fontanelli, 1985; *Ugo Betti: An Introduction* by Emanuele Licastro, 1985; *La drammatica di Ugo Betti. Tematiche e archetipi* by Gaetana Marrone, 1988; 'Tragedy in a Postmodern Vein: Ugo Betti, Our Contemporary?' by Lloyd A. Arnett, in *Modern Drama*, 33, 1990.

* * *

Of all the Italian dramatists, Ugo Betti is undoubtedly one of the best known and yet still little understood. Such critics as Pandolfi, Quasimodo, and Momigliano have addressed his thematic texts in a variety of ways, but have failed to grasp the core of Betti's artistic world, its 'vibrant poetic truth' as philosopher Gabriel Marcel has called it. After World War I, during the years of disillusionment and despair which brought to power Benito Mussolini, Betti, a socialist, emerged with poems, short stories, and plays that debated modern man's metaphysical predicament and moral anguish. Betti's work is often compared to that of his illustrious contemporary Luigi Pirandello. Like the Sicilian playwright, the basic terms of

Betti's existentialist discourse are alienation and authenticity, but their conclusions ostensibly differ. With modern notions of absurdity and nihilism, Pirandello dissects man's soul and traditional values. A passionate reader of Tolstoi and Dostoevskii, Betti revitalizes formal techniques for the projection of haunting images of death and loneliness. He is concerned with the immediate realities of the human experience and refuses to abide on nothingness, whereas Pirandello's appeal is toward the appropriation of the absurd in order to discover man's ambivalent nature. Anyone who attempts to acquire a comprehensive view of Betti discovers that, beyond the familiar paradigms of guilt, justice, and redemption, his is a disconcertingly complex road to follow.

Chronologically, any fundamental approach to Betti ought to begin with *La padrona* [The Mistress], which became an instant success in 1926. Simple in plot and naturalistic in style, *La padrona* is remembered mostly for its 'Preface', an ideal introduction to Betti's theatre. From the beginning, the playwright promotes a plane of existence that is ethical. He explores the power of determining one's choice, the freedom of will that displaced Adam's progeny into a liminal stage of suffering. To Betti, 'we are all poor, restless creatures, who try to understand the incongruity between our actual existence and the potential nature given to us'. Guilt is a *felix culpa* motif. Angelo says in *Delitto all'isola delle capre* (*Crime on Goat Island*): 'Our salvation is in sin; it's only our wretched pride that doesn't want to accept it'. The ontological basis of Betti's tragic vision rests upon the myth of the Fall, which supports the heroic dimension of life, an idea of disorder which initiates the character's revolt and search for self-knowledge.

Betti's theatre evolves from realism into myth. The earlier plays evoke the dark settings of French naturalism. For example, in *Un albergo sul porto* [An Inn on the Harbour], the emblems of estrangement are foreshadowed by sailors, unscrupulous merchants, and prostitutes: in *Il cacciatore d'anitre* [The Duck Hunter], the symbolic inquiry into the unconscious is personified by the diabolic Michial, a wealthy merchant, and by Marco, an idealistic young man who uses logos and intuition to comprehend the most obscure part of himself, and chooses death over psychological chaos. The archetype of the unconscious is fully explored in *La fuggitiva* (*The Fugitive*), a posthumous play. The fugitive of the title is Nina, a neurotic character in whom Betti portrays the dialectic of the ascent from the abyss (a demonic parody of the Lost Eden) to the top of the mountain—the sacred space that defines microcosm and macrocosm. For Betti, man's test starts at the bottom: 'What I would like to do, in my writings, is to place certain characters and certain feelings, naked and alone, almost at the bottom of a big ladder. And to watch if there is in them, without any help, the capacity and the need to climb'. This premise is implied in the dramas of Eros. *Crime on Goat Island*, *La padrona*, and *Acque turbate* [Troubled Waters] examine a theology of sin embodied in devouring female figures; they represent an epitome of desire and transgression, and yet are instrumental in any aspiration to a superior level of being. In *Crime on Goat Island*, Agata debates the causality of good and evil before letting Angelo die in the well; in *Acque turbate*, Alda's incestuous love for her brother, revealed by anamnesis, promotes cosmic awareness. Betti's plays on justice implement this investigation into man's existential stance by representing the legal responsibilities of guilt through an inquiry that is both judicial and metaphysical. To Betti, we are all part of 'a machine that moves us'. Consequently, a crime triggers reactions that invalidate any individual punishment and call for collective responsibility. In *Ispezione* (*The Inquiry*), *Frana allo scalo* nord (Landslide), and Corruzione al palazzo di giustizia (Corruption in the Palace of Justice), Betti's Kafkaesque inspectors search for individual guilt, but they ultimately formulate a broader definition that transforms the verdict into a crisis of conscience. In existentialist terms, guilt is an essential liminal situation.

Betti's minor works are also worthy of consideration— poems, short stories, screenplays, essays, and a novel—most of which are an orchestration of his dramatic themes. Excluding a translation of Catullus' Epithalamion, Betti's first literary endeavour was a collection of poems, Il re pensieroso [The Pensive King], written in German prison camps between 1917 and 1918. This overture—like the subsequent Canzonette—La morte [Little Songs—Death] and Uomo e donna [Man and Woman]—seems designed to serve as a meditation on human suffering. The adult's cosmic terror, often symbolized by the myth of the child, remains a vital motif in the short story collections, Caino, Le case [Houses], Una strana serata [A Strange Evening], and the novel La piera alta [The High Stone], all of which are an elaboration on loneliness and authenticity. In the dramatic ballet L'isola meravigliosa [The Marvellous Island], the solitary King Nadir and his elusive quest for happiness symbolize the alienation of 20th-century guilt-ridden man. During the 1930s, Betti's escapist mood was translated into fables and farcical comedies. Il diluvio [The Flood], Una bella domenica di settembre [A Beautiful September Sunday], Il paese delle vacanze (Summertime), I nostri sogni [Our Dreams], and Favola di Natale [Christmas Story] engage in a critique of bourgeois values. Through the analysis of mediocre characters, obsessed by the urge to hide their defeats and weaknesses, Betti exposes the inauthenticity of conventional living.

Betti was not a formalist. In emphasizing his thought, as well as his theatrical achievements, we must remember, however, that Betti considered himself primarily a poet whose interest was ethical, and whose ultimate goal was artistic. Betti sought to restore to mankind a meaningful contact with transcendence. As in Il giocatore (The Gambler), should the protagonist dare to pass the threshold, there is the promise of an unprecedented encounter with the mystery of man himself. Ennio's leap of faith will be rewarded: 'He is a bad gambler who cannot risk all at the last moment'. Compelled at every step to realize himself freely, but without the support of any established certainties, modern man must risk it all. Betti's theatre affirms faith not as a theological speculation but as a norm, bound to the moral life of the individual in society.

—Gaetana Marrone

BHAGAVADGĪTĀ. Poem of 18 songs and 700 verses, from Book 6 of the Sanskrit epic Mahābhārata, q.v., dating from c.400–c.200 BC, and traditionally attributed to Vyāsa (the supposed compiler of the Vedas, q.v.).

PUBLICATIONS

Bhagavadgītā. 1808; edited by F.O Schrader (Kashmiri rescension), 1930; also edited by R.N. Narayanaswami (with translation and commentary), 1936, Franklin Edgerton (bilingual edition, including Edward Arnold's translation), 2 vols., 1944, S.K. Belvalker, 1945, revised 1968, H.M. Lamber (with translation by V.G. Pradhān), 1967–69, R.C. Zaehner, 1969, bilingual edition, 1973, K.K. Bhattacharya, 1972, Tulsīrāmaswami, 1977, J.A.B. van Buitenen (bilingual edition), 1981, G.S. Sadhale, 3 vols., 1985, and R. Iyer (with the Utarragita), 1985; as Bhăgvăt-Gēētā, translated by Charles Wilkins, 1785, reprinted 1972; as either Bhagavadgītā or Bhagavad Gītā (sometimes without accents) translated by John Davies, 1882; K.T. Telang, 1882; Mohini M. Chatterji, 1887; Annie Besant, 1895, revised, 5th edition, 1918; Lionel D. Barnett, 1905; Charles Johnston, 1908; Arthur Ryder, 1929; Franklin Edgerton (bilingual edition), 1952, English only, 1972; Swami Nikhilananda, 1944; Swami Prabhavananda and Christopher Isherwood, 1944; Sarvepalli Radhakrishnan, 1948, bilingual edition, 1970; Nataraja Guru (bilingual edition), 1962; Juan Mascaró, 1962; P. Lal, 1965; Eliot Deutsch, 1968; Kees W. Bolle (bilingual edition), 1979; A.C. Bhaktivedanta, 1981; Nikunja Vihari Banerjee, 1984; Eknath Easwaran, 1986; Hasmukh M. Raval with John L. Safford, 1990; D. Prithipaul (bilingual edition), 1993; as The Song Celestial, translated by Edwin Arnold, 1885; as The Song of the Lord translated by Edward J. Thomas (bilingual edition), 1931; selections translated in Hindu Scriptures, translated by R.C. Zaehner, 1966; The Song of a Thousand Names, 1976; Selections, translated by Francis G. Hutchins, 1980.

*

Critical Studies: Age and Origins of the Gita by J.N. Farquhar, 1904; Notes and Index to the Bhagavad Gītā by K. Browning, 1916; Essays on the Gita by Sri Aurobindo, 1928; The Bhagavad Gita by Douglas P. Hill, 1928; The Gita: A Critique by P. Narasimham, 1939; The Bhagavad-Gītā and Modern Scholarship by Satis Chandra Roy, 1941; A Christian Approach to the Bahagavadgita by P.S. Mathai, 1956; Talks on the Gita by A.V. Bhave, 1960; The Ethics of the Gītā by G.W. Kaveeshwar, 1971; Early Buddhism and the Bhagavadgītā by K.N. Upadhyaya, 1971; Introduction to the Bhagavad-gītā by G.A. Feuerstein, 1974; Bhagavad-Gītā: An Exegetical Commentary by R.N. Minor, 1982; Gītā: The Science of Living by Jayantil S. Jarivalla, 1984; Bhagavad Gita Reference Guide by R.D. Singh, 1984; The Bhagavadgītā and Jīvana Yoga by R.N. Vyas, 1985; Modern Indian Interpreters of the Bhagavadgita edited by Robert N. Minor, 1986; The Hindu Gītā: Ancient and Classical Interpretations of the Bhagavadgītā by Arvind Sharma, 1986; The Universal Gītā: Western Images of the Bhagavadgītā: A Bicentenary Survey by Eric J. Sharpe, 1986; Influence of Bhagavadgita on Literature Written in English edited by T.R. Sharma, 1987; 20th-Century Interpretations of Bhagavadgita: Tilak, Gandhi and Aurobindo by P.M. Thomas, 1987.

* * *

The Bhagavadgītā (Gītā for short) is just an episode in Vyāsa's Mahābhārata, but it has achieved even more fame than the larger work. Most devout Hindus recite a few lines of it daily in their homes. The Gītā is really a dialogue between Arjuna, the Pandava hero, and Krsna, his divine charioteer, to dispel his hesitation and gloom in having to kill his own kinsmen in order to procure an empire.

Krsna tells Arjuna that death is really of no consequence

for it means only rebirth in another form. The immortal soul never dies. Even if you do not believe in the soul's immortality and reincarnation, Kṛṣṇa tells him, 'you should still not grieve. For it is certain that death is inevitable and controlled by destiny. So why worry about what *has* to happen, and of which you are merely the instrument?'. Kṛṣṇa goes on to explain how one can achieve emancipation. It can be either by knowledge, by perfect devotion to god, or by altruistic works. Thus the *Gītā* is a kind of philosophical synthesis. It is also a practical guide to human conduct, and favours renunciation. A man should do his own work and not bother about that of another. Work should be done to perfection, for it is a kind of yoga. It is the man at the top who should set the standard in conduct, for the others lower down follow his example. The wise man makes no distinction between a learned person, a cow, an elephant, a pariah, and even a dog: he is kind to them all. All works should be unselfish, and one should act according to conscience without expecting any reward or fearing any punishment. 'Your right is to actions alone', Kṛṣṇa tells Arjuna, 'not to their fruit. Nor should you be enamoured of inaction'.

Apart from its unrivalled philosophy, the *Gītā* is also a literary work. The Sanskrit of its verses is simpler in structure than that of other Hindu works on philsophy. It has greater fluidity and smoothness. It has a mixed metre, the *upajati*, some lines being in the *indravajra* and others in the *upendravajra* form. Both of these have 11 syllables each. The poet uses language to suit the occasion, as for example in the musical stanzas of Arjuna's prayer to the Lord when he has disclosed his cosmic form. Death is a mere 'change of clothes'. Enjoyments come to a calm man yet leave him undisturbed, as rivers entering the sea. The mind of the yogi is like 'a light in a sheltered place'. Passion, anger, and greed are 'the triple gates of hell'. Creation is like the huge spreading Indian fig tree; its roots are the Preimal Being, its stems the creator, its leaves the scriptures, and its branches the living creatures with all their frailties. One is tempted to fell this tree with the formidable axe of dispassion.

The keynote of the *Gītā* is renunciation, and it strongly advocates self-control and the relinquishment of all sensual pleasures—even the thought of them. But it is against ascetics who torture their bodies, calling them 'fiends'. It considers the *Vedas* merely as aids to emancipation, and 'like a tank flooded with water' when the goal is achieved. The universality of the *Gītā* lies in its complete freedom from all dogma. After propounding his doctrine, Kṛṣṇa tells Arjuna, 'Don't take my word for it. Reflect on what I have told you and do as you like'. In fact Kṛṣṇa goes to the extent of saying, 'They are also my devotees, who with faith worship other gods'. The *Gītā* is undiluted philosophy expressed in layman's language, and effectively holds a high place in the spiritual literature of the world.

—K.P. Bahadur

THE BIBLE. Compilation of Hebrew and Greek texts. Old Testament collects Hebrew prose and verse works dating from c.900–100 BC: Pentateuch (Genesis, Exodus, Leviticus, Numbers, Deuteronomy) canonized c.400 BC; the Former Prophets, principally historical works, canonized c.200 BC; miscellaneous Writings (e.g. Books of Psalms, Proverbs, Job)

gradually canonized individually to c.AD 90, when selection for and authorization of the Old Testament was completed. The first Greek translation, known as the Septuagint (containing some additional writings), was made in the 3rd century BC, revised by Aquila c.AD 135. New Testament collects Greek prose writings from c.AD 50–100: letters of Paul, other letters, the three synoptic gospels (Matthew, Mark, Luke), and the Johannine writings; 39th Easter Letter of Athanasius suggests canonical list completed by AD 367. Non-canonical works of both periods are collected into Old and New Testament Apocrypha. First Latin translation of Old and New Testaments, the Vulgate, made by St Jerome, *q.v.*, c.AD 383–405.

PUBLICATIONS

Bible, translated by Wyclif and others. c.1380; first printed edition of St Jerome's Vulgate (Gutenberg), 1452–55; Marietti edition (with variants), 1459; first Hebrew edition of Old Testament, 1488; New Testament (Greek and Latin), edited by Erasmus, 1516; Tyndale, 1525–26 (New Testament), 1530 (Pentateuch); Coverdale, 1535; Rheims-Douai version (Roman Catholic): 1582 (New Testament), 1609 (Old Testament); King James Version, 1611; Revised Standard Version, 1946–52; New English Bible, 1961–70; and many others; annotated editions include *The Interpreter's Bible*, edited by George Buttrick and others, 1952–57, *The Oxford Annotated Bible*, edited by Herbert C. May and Bruce M. Metzger, 1962, *The Jerusalem Bible*, 1966, revised edition, as *The New Jerusalem Bible*, edited by Henry Wansborough, 1986, and *Tyndale's New Testament*, 1989, and *Tyndale's Old Testament*, 1992, both edited by David Daniell.

*

Critical Studies: *The Old Testament in Modern Research* by Herbert F. Hahn, 1954, revised bibliographical essay by Horace D. Hummel, 1970; *The New Testament Background: Selected Documents* edited by C.K. Barrett, 1956; *History of the Bible in English* by F.C. Bruce, 1961, revised editions, 1970, 1979; *The Interpreter's Dictionary of the Bible* edited by George Buttrick, 4 vols., 1962, supplementary volume edited by Keith Crim, 1976; *The Cambridge History of the Bible* edited by P.R. Ackroyd, C.F. Evans, G.W.H. Lampe, and S.L. Greenslade, 3 vols., 1963–70, and *Cambridge Bible Commentary* edited by Ackroyd, A.R.C. Leaney, and J.W. Parker, n.d.; *The Old Testament: An Introduction* by Otto Eissfeldt, revised edition, 1965; *Irony in the Old Testament* by Edwin M. Good, 1965; *The Art of the Biblical Story*, 1979, and *Narrative Art in the Bible*, 1989, both by Shimon Bar-Efrat; *The Art of Biblical Narrative* by Robert Alter, 1981; *The Great Code: The Bible and Literature*, 1982, and *Words with Power, Being a Second Study of 'the Bible and Literature'*, 1990, both by Northrop Frye; *Poetics and Interpretation of Biblical Narrative* by Adele Berlin, 1983; *The Poet and the Historian: Essays in Literary and Historical Biblical Criticism* edited by Richard E. Friedman, 1983; *The Bible: Story and Plot* by Frank Kermode, 1984, and *The Literary Guide to the Bible*, edited by Alter and Kermode, 1987; *The Bible as Literature* by John B. Gabel and Charles B. Wheeler, 1986; *Literary Approaches to Biblical Interpretation* by Tremper Longman, 1987; *The Book and the Text: The Bible and Literary Theory* edited by Regina M. Schwartz, 1990; *The Bible: God's Word or Man's?* by Stephen

Prickett and Robert Barnes, 1991, and *Reading the Text: Biblical Criticism and Literary Theory* edited by Prickett, 1991; *The Passion of Interpretation* by W. Dow Edgerton, 1992; *A History of the Bible as Literature: From Antiquity to 1700* and *From 1700 to the Present Day* by David Norton, 2 vols., 1993; *Dialogues of the Word: The Bible as Literature According to Bakhtin* by Walter L. Reed, 1993; *The Oxford Companion to the Bible* edited by Bruce M. Metzger and Michael D. Coogan, 1994.

* * *

The sacred book of Christianity, the Bible, is divided into two parts. The Old Testament is a religious history of the Jews beginning at the creation of the world; the New Testament is a record of the life and teachings of Jesus and his followers. The Old Testament comprises many of the sacred texts of Judaism. In Christianity, Jesus's life is regarded as the ultimate fulfilment of a destiny long promised, and gradually revealed, to the Jewish people.

The gradual process of divine revelation is reflected in the Bible's structure: it is not one book, but a collection of over 60 books, written over centuries. Within these different books are widely different varieties of writing: heroic prose sagas such as those of Samson and David, the explicit sexual love poetry in the Song of Songs, the prophetic visions of Ezekiel and Isaiah. Through all these different kinds of writing moves the idea of God, an idea that undergoes its own gradual evolution. In Genesis, the earliest book, God has physical, anthropomorphic form, walking in the Garden of Eden and wrestling with Jacob. His sons mate with the most beautiful of mortal women, producing a race of mighty heroes. In the final book, Revelations, God is a terrifying cosmic force surrounded by spirits of Death, Famine, War, and Plague, promising the scourging and cleansing of the earth. The tension this suggests between God as a loving and as a threatening force is writ large throughout the Bible. In Judges, God demands the genocide of women and children in the land of Canaan to provide room for the newly arrived Israelite settlers. In the Psalms, God is seen to lavish his love on the individual soul.

Despite its apparent catholicity, however, the scope of the Bible is far from universal. The New Testament is only a selection of the texts available to those who compiled it. To elevate it to its canonical status some Christian texts had to be preserved, while others were excluded and suppressed. Surviving or recently discovered extracanonical texts such as the Gospel of Thomas offer glimpses of the richness of the Christian scriptures (and the theological concepts) excluded from the religion the Bible has served to define.

In examining the Bible as literature or as a religious text, one must consider its peculiar relationship to language. How can the divine, which is by definition infinite and, ultimately, unknowable, mediate something of its nature through the limited resources of language? At some of its most mystic and allusive moments, the Bible suggests that language is intimately entwined with God's own nature. Christ is 'the Word' made flesh. Which word, or the nature of that word, is never revealed. We can only approach this unspoken, unwritten Word through its incarnation in human form. Christ claims the alphabet was one of the symbols of his being, 'I am alpha and Omega' (Revelations 22:13). By implication, language itself, all that is or can be written, is an expression of God.

The Bible privileges language as a divine and perfect gift—it is in his perfect state in Paradise that Adam gives the first names to living things. After the Fall, the perfect and universal language is shattered by God at the tower of Babel, to prevent man prying too deeply into His domain. Writing within post-lapsarian language, the Bible is by necessity driven to indirect means of expression, conveying God through riddle, song, and symbol. God manifests Himself not in words but in visual images: a pillar or fire, or a burning tree. Those who attempt to capture God in words fail. Jacob wrestles all night with God, and at dawn asks Him for His name. God's only reply is: 'Wherefore is it that thou dost ask after my name?' (Genesis 33:29). When Moses sees God in a fiery tree and asks a similar question, God replies 'I AM THAT I AM' (Exodus 4:12). Christ too resists any definition of the divine nature, offering instead symbolic utterances which demand an understanding beyond the literal: 'I am the vine' (John 15:1), 'I am the sheepfold' (John 10:19), 'I am the bright and morning star' (Revelations 22:16).

The tension between the Holy Book and the failings of the written word is demonstrated in the structure of the New Testament. It offers not one account of Jesus's life, but four different, and at time contradictory, accounts side by side. The Gospels give accounts of God in the external world, through quasi-historical records. Revelations shows the manifestation of God in the inner world of the psyche, through the spiritual world of esoteric visionary experience. Here God makes Himself known through a stream of images both awesome and fascinating: a man who holds in his hand the constellation of the Great Bear; a city built of gems; a woman crowned with stars; a whore clad, evocatively, in a scarlet robe and holding a chalice.

Jesus's own teaching is in the form of narrative—parables, or stories, which teach about God by casting Him in simple domestic or agrarian roles. Jesus's moral teachings are most concisely expressed in Matthew, chapters 5, 6, and 7. They urge compassion, generosity, tolerance, and trust in God.

The most important and influential English translation of the Bible has been the 'Authorised' or 'King James' version of 1611. Its stark, largely monosyllabic Saxon vocabulary in strongly metred, paratactic prose renders the text with directness, simplicity, and strength. The Bible has contributed to Western culture a stock of symbols: the mountain, the garden, the heavenly city, which have echoed through the art and literature of every age. Its central narrative, that of innocence and temptation, fall and redemption, has impressed its pattern on narrative art from Chaucer to the contemporary novel. Its consistent use of literary symbolism to present divine truth has arguably been instrumental in the development of Western symbolism.

—Edmund Cusick

BIBBIENA, Bernardo Dovizi da. See **DOVIZI da Bibbiena, Bernardo**.

BILDERDIJK, Willem. Born in Amsterdam, The Netherlands, 7 September 1756. Studied law at Leiden, 1780–82.

Married 1) Catharina Rebecca Woesthoven in 1785 (marriage not dissolved), one daughter; 2) Katharina Wilhelmina Schweikhardt. Lawyer in The Hague; because of his loyalty to the House of Orange he was forced to leave the Netherlands after French troops proclaimed it a republic in 1795; lived in exile in London, then in Germany; returned to the Netherlands in 1806; King Louis Napoleon's court poet and private tutor in Dutch; nominated member of Royal Dutch Institute, 1808; sheltered from financial difficulties by the King; promised university post in 1813 by Regent William I but blocked by other academics. *Died 18 December 1831.*

PUBLICATIONS

Collections

Geschiedenis des Vaderlands [History of the Fatherland], edited by H.W. Tydeman. 13 vols., 1832–53.
Brieven [Letters], edited by W. Meeschert. 5 vols., 1836.
Dichtwerken [Poetical Works], edited by I. da Costa. 16 vols., 1856–59.

Verse

Prijsvaerzen [Prize Verses]. 2 vols., 1776–77.
Op het afsterven van den dichter Lucas Pater [On the Death of the Poet Lucas Pater]. 1781.
De Leydsche Weezen aan de burgery. 1781.
Myn verlustiging [My Delight]. 1781.
Ellius. 1788.
Vertoogen van Salomo [Sayings of Solomon]. 1788.
De alleenheersching [Sole Rule]. 1793.
Treurzang van Ibn Doreid [Lament of Ibn Doreid]. 1795.
Urzijn en Valentijn [Urzijn and Valentijn]. 1795.
Mengelpoezy [Miscellaneous Verse]. 1799.
Raad van een Hollander aan Engeland [Advice from a Dutchman to England]. 1799.
Losse stukken in verzen [Loose Pieces in Verse]. 1803.
Mengelingen [Miscellaneous]. 1804.
Vaderlandsche oranjezucht [Patriotic Longings for the House of Orange]. 1805.
Ode aan Napoleon [Ode to Napoleon]. 1806.
Nieuwe mengelingen [New Miscellany]. 1806.
Aan den Koning [To the King]. 1807.
De ziekte der geleerden [The Disease of the Learned]. 1807.
Najaarsbladen [Autumn Leaves]. 1808.
Odilde. 1808.
Vreugdezang [Song of Joy]. 1808.
Konings komst tot den throon [Accession of the King]. 1809.
Pestel. 1809.
Verspreide gedichten [Scattered Poems]. 1809.
Wapenkreet [Call to Arms]. 1809.
Hulde aan Zijne Koninklijke en Keizerlijke Majesteit [Homage to His Royal and Imperial Majesty]. 1810.
De geestenwereld [The Spirit World]. 1811.
Winterbloemen [Winter Flowers]. 1811.
De echt. 1812.
Geologie. 1813.
Krijgsdans [War Dance]. 1813.
Affodillen [Asphodels]. 1814.
Nieuwe uitspruitsels [New Shoots]. 1817.
Wit en rood [White and Red]. 2 vols., 1818.
De ondergang der eerste waereld [The Ruin of the First World] (unfinished). 1820; edited by J. Bosch, 1959.
Zedelijke gispingen [Moral Strictures]. 1820.

Taal en dichtkundige verscheidenheden [Linguistic and Poetical Varieties]. 4 vols., 1820–22.
De muis en kikvorschkrijg [The Battle of Mice and Frogs], from Homer. 1821.
Sprokkelingen [Gleanings]. 1821.
Ter uitvaart van Nicolaas Schotsman [On the Passing of Nicholas Scotsman]. 1822.
Krekelzangen [Cricket Songs]. 3 vols., 1822–23.
De derde october [The Third of October]. 1823.
Aan de Roomsch-Katholieken dezer dagen [To Present-Day Catholics]. 1823.
Spreuken [Sayings]. 1823.
Rotsgalmen [Rock Echoes]. 2 vols., 1824.
Navonkeling [Afterglow]. 1826.
Oprakeling [Raking Up]. 1826.
Afscheid aan Leyden [Farewell to Leiden]. 1827.
Nieuwe oprakeling [New Raking Up]. 1827.
De voet in 't graf [A Foot in the Grave]. 1827.
Avondschemering [Twilight]. 1828.
Naklank [Echo]. 1828.
Vermaking [Amusement]. 1828.
Nieuwe vermaking [New Amusement]. 1829.
Schemerschijn [Twilight]. 1829.
Proeve eener navolging van Ovidius' gedaanterverwisselingen [Result of an Adaptation of Ovid's Metamorphoses]. 1829.
Nasprokkeling [Late Gleaning]. 1830.
Rondedans [Round Dance]. 1832.
Nederland hersteld [The Netherlands Reinstated]. 1836.

Plays

Floris de Vijfde [Floris V]. 1808.
Treurspelen [Tragedies], with K.W. Bilderdijk. 3 vols., 1808–09.

Fiction

Kort verhaal van eene aanmerkelijke luchtreis (story). 1813; as *A Remarkable Aerial Voyage and Discovery of a New Planet*, translated by Paul Vincent, 1986.

Other

Brief van den navolger van Sofokles' Edipus [Letter from the Adaptor of Sophocles' Oedipus]. 1780.
Redevoering over de voortreffelijkheid der schilderkunst [Discourse on the Excellence of Poetry]. 1794.
Verhandeling over de geslachten der naamwoorden [Treatise on the Gender of Nouns]. 1805.
De kunst der poezy [The Art of Poetry]. 1808.
Het treurspel [Tragedy]. 1808.
Van het letterschrift. 1820.
Geslachtslijst der Nederduitsche naamwoorden [List of Gender of Low-German Nouns]. 1821.
Korte ontwikkeling der gronden van het natuurrecht [Short Essay on the Fundamentals of Natural Law]. 1821.
Verhandelingen de zede en rechtsleer betreffende [Discourse on Morality and Law]. 1821.
De bezwaren tegen den geest der eeuw van Mr I. da Costa toegelicht [Objections to the Spirit of the Age Elucidated by Mr I. da Costa]. 1823.
Bijdragen tot de toneelpoezy [Contributions to Dramatic Poetry]. 1823.
Nieuwe taal- en dichtkundige verscheidenheden [New Linguistic and Poetical Varieties] (collected works on philology). 4 vols., 1824–25.
Nederlandsche spraakleer [Dutch Grammar]. 1826.

Korte aanmerkingen op Huydecopers Proeve van taal en dicht-kunde [Brief Remarks on Huydecoper's Essay on Language and Poetry]. 1827.
Grondregelen der perspectief of doorzichtkunde [Ground Rules of Perspective]. 1828.
Uitzicht op mijn dood [Prospect of My Death]. 1829.
Beginschels der woordvorsching [Principles of Linguistic Research]. 1831.

Translator, *Edipus, Koning van Thebe*, by Sophocles. 1780.
Translator, *De Dood Van Edipus*, by Sophocles. 1789.
Translator, *Het Buitenleven*, by J. Delille. 1803.
Translator, *Fingal, in zes gezangen*, by 'Ossian' [James Macpherson]. 1805.
Translator, *Lofzangen*, by Callimachus. 1808.
Translator, *De Mensch*, by Pope. 1808.
Translator, *Hekeldichten*, by Persius. 1820.
Translator, *Cinna*, by Corneille. 1824.
Translator, *De Cycloop*, by Euripides. 1828.
Translator, *Redevoeringen*, by St John Chrysostom. 1832.
Translator, *Kerkredenen*, by Merle d'Aubigné. 1833.
Translator, *Het Bewijs en gezag der Christelijke openbaring*, by T. Chalmers. 1833.

*

Critical Studies: *De mensch en de dichter Willem Bilderdijk* by I. da Costa, 1859; *Bilderdijk, zijn leven en zijn werken* by R.A. Kollewijn, 1891; *Bilderdijk als denker en dichter* by H. Bavinck, 1906; *Gedenkboek voor Mr W. Bilderdijk* by R.A. Kollewijn, 1906; *Willem Bilderdijk als dichter* by A. Heyting, 2 vols., 1931–40; *Een Eeuw strijd om Bilderdijk* by P. Geyl, 1958; *Folia Bilderdijkiana* edited by M. van Hattum and others, 1985.

* * *

Willem Bilderdijk is without a doubt the most prolific Dutch writer but probably the least read, both by his country-men and by the world at large. Virtually none of his huge output has been translated into English. His large output was caused mainly by the fact that he had to live off his pen, but also because he found writing easy. Bilderdijk was probably one of the last Dutch writers to be seen as a major figure on the cultural, social, and political scene of his time, but his influence scarcely survived his death. Although his many works had been brought out by different publishers, when one of them tried to launch a collected edition a few years after Bilderdijk's death, the project had to be abandoned for lack of interest.

Bilderdijk made his most lasting mark as one of the leading figures of what Dutch historians have called the 'Réveil', or national awakening, under the leadership of the still largely autocratic first king of the Netherlands, William I. Bilderdijk's anti-republican, ultra-patriotic, and exceedingly conservative ideas proliferate in his lectures on the history of the Netherlands which he gave in his own living room in Leyden (at no point in his life did he become linked to any Dutch university) to a select group of people who were to become the leaders of the new Dutch state after 1815. Not only did Bilderdijk write an *oeuvre* of almost unbelievable volume, he did so in different languages and on a variety of topics. He wrote about law in Latin and in Dutch, about philology and literature in French and in Dutch, about botany in French, and about philosophy, theology, and history in Dutch. Three years before his death he published a theoreti-cal book on perspective.

Bilderdijk probably learned to write with such ease in the *dichtgenootschappen* (poetry clubs) that existed throughout the Netherlands until the French occupation and beyond. His father belonged to one, and that is probably where the young Bilderdijk acquired what was then known as 'Parnassian lan-guage', the polished, ornamental, somewhat obscure, sonor-ous, and mostly bombastic diction, replete with classical and mythological references, which he used both in his verse and in his prose. He supplemented it however, with strict metrical schemes in his verse, the only part of his *oeuvre* ever to be republished in anything resembling a collected edition.

The diction that greatly facilitated Bilderdijk's enormous production also proved an insurmountable barrier between his work and those who tried to read it in later generations. One has the feeling of a machine running on, endlessly and effortlessly, and only very few readers ever catch a glimpse of the sensitive, honest, sometimes even witty ghost imprisoned within it. Bilderdijk wrote in all the genres expected of a true man of letters at the time: prose, mainly polemical, political, and scientific, with his greatest output in verse. His tragedies were inspired by Dutch history and more exotic tales; an epic, *De ondergang der eerste waereld* [The Ruin of the First World], published unfinished during his lifetime, became his most popular work, and is perhaps the best example of his stature in the Dutch world of letters during his lifetime. Perhaps the truest measure of the reversal of fate Bilderdijk has suffered since his death is the fact that his only complete work that is readily available in Dutch bookstores today is *Kort verhaal van eene aanmerkelijke luchtreis* (*A Remarkable Aerial Voyage and Discovery of a New Planet*), published in 1813, the first work of science fiction to be written in Dutch. Science fiction was the only genre in which Bilderdijk was an innovator in Dutch literature, albeit not consciously so. He probably believed that he was continuing 18th-century travel writing, but with other means: after the discovery of Australia, strange lands had to be looked for, and found, on other planets.

In his other works Bilderdijk never progressed beyond the 'Parnassian speech' he found so easy. What is still published on Bilderdijk today is published in the form of articles on certain manageable aspects of his work, not on the work as a whole. Those few literary historians tempted to tackle Bilderdijk find his translations easier and more rewarding to read than his original work. Bilderdijk translated Ossian, Delille, and Alexander Pope, but also Sophocles, Persius, and Ovid. His Ossian translation was highly influential in the development of Dutch pre-Romanticism. One gets the im-pression that only in his translations does his work become less self-referential. Here Bilderdijk was relieved to be the craftsman and nothing more. In his other writings, whatever the subject, the reader is extremely likely to meet Bilderdijk. Many of the tragedies and the narrative poems contain thinly veiled autobiographical passages, and Bilderdijk unasha-medly pushes his own views in his more 'scientific' writings as well. His literary craftsmanship allowed him to cut a wide path for himself through the contemporary world of letters, so wide that none attempted to follow. Similarly, his unself-conscious egocentrism served as a protective armour. He was in his world but not really of it, like the sickly child not expected to take too great a part in everyday life.

In many ways Bilderdijk occupies a position in Dutch literature and culture not unlike that of Goethe in German literature and culture. Goethe, however, was a genius, whereas Bilderdijk was, in the words of the Dutch historians Annie and Jan Romein, a 'genius crippled', a prophet with a club foot.

—André Lefevere

BJØRNSON, Bjørnstjerne (Martinius). Born in Kvikne, Norway (then united with Sweden), 8 December 1832. Educated at Molde grammar school, 1844–49; Christiania University, Christiania (now Oslo), 1852–54. Married the actress Karoline Reimers in 1858. Contributed articles to newspapers while at university; theatre reviewer, *Morgenbladet*, 1854–56; editor and contributor, *Illustreret Folkeblad*, from 1856; director (succeeding Ibsen, *q.v.*), Det Norske Theater [Norwegian Theatre], Bergen, 1857–59; editor, *Bergensposten*, Bergen; returned to Christiania to edit the newspaper *Aftenbladet*, 1859, but subsequently had to resign because of his political views; founder, Norwegian Cultural Society; lived in Rome, 1860–62; director, Christiania Theatre, 1865–67; editor, *Norsk Folkeblad*, 1866–71; returned to Rome, 1873; became increasingly involved in political and social debate in the late 1870s; travelled and lectured in the USA, 1880–81; lived in Paris, 1882–87; promoter of world peace and minority rights during the 1890s. Recipient: Nobel prize for literature, 1903. *Died 26 April 1910.*

PUBLICATIONS

Collections

Works, edited and translated by Rasmus B. Anderson. 6 vols., 1882.
Novels, edited by Edmund Gosse. 13 vols., 1895–1909.
Samlede værker, edited Carl Nærup. 11 vols., 1900–02.
Samlede digter-verker, edited by Francis Bull. 9 vols., 1919–20.
Samlede digte, edited by Francis Bull. 2 vols., 1926.
Samlede verker. 5 vols., 1960.

Plays

Mellem slagene (produced 1857). 1857; translated as *Between the Battles*, in *The Nobel Prize Treasury*, 1948.
Halte-Hulda [Limping Hulda] (produced 1858). 1858.
Kong Sverre [King Sverre] (produced 1861). 1861.
Sigurd Slembe (produced 1863). 1862; as *Sigurd Slembe*, translated by William Morton Payne, 1888.
Maria Stuart i Skotland (produced 1864). 1864; as *Mary Stuart in Scotland*, translated by August Sahlberg, 1912; as *Mary, Queen of Scots*, translated by Sahlberg, 1912.
De nygifte (produced 1865). 1865; as *The Newly-Married Couple*, translated by Sivert and Elizabeth Hjerleid, 1870; also translated by R. Farquharson Sharp, in *Three Comedies*, 1912; as *The Newly Married*, translated by John Volk, 1885; as *A Lesson in Marriage*, translated by Grace Isabel Colbron, 1910.
Sigurd Jorsalfar [Sigurd the Crusader]. 1872; in *Kongebrødrene*, edited by Francis Bull, 1932.

Redaktøren (produced 1875). 1874; as *The Editor*, translated by R. Farquharson Sharp, in *Three Dramas*, 1914.
En fallit (produced 1875). 1874; as *The Bankrupt*, translated by R. Farquharson Sharp, in *Three Dramas*, 1914.
Kongen (produced 1902). 1877; as *The King*, translated by R. Farquharson Sharp, in *Three Dramas*, 1914.
Det ny system (produced 1878). 1879; as *The New System*, translated by Edwin Björkman, in *Plays 1*, 1913.
Leonarda (produced 1879). 1879; as *Leonarda*, translated by Daniel L. Hanson, in *The Drama*, 3, 1911; also translated by R. Farquharson Sharp, in *Three Comedies*, 1912.
En hanske (produced 1883). 1883; as *A Gauntlet*, translated by H.L. Brækstad, 1880; also translated by Osman Edwards, 1894; R. Farquharson Sharp, in *Three Comedies*, 1912; as *The Gauntlet*, translated by Edwin Björkman, in *Plays 1*, 1913.
Over ævne I (produced 1886). 1883; as *Pastor Sang*, translated by William Wilson, 1893; as *Beyond Our Power*, translated by Edwin Björkman, in *Plays 1*, 1913; as *Beyond Human Power*, translated by Lee M. Hollander, in *Chief Contemporary Dramatists*, edited by T.H. Dickinson, 1915.
Geografi og kjærlighed (produced 1885). 1885; as *Love and Geography*, translated by Edwin Björkman, in *Plays 2*, 1914.
Over ævne II (produced 1895). 1895; as *Beyond Human Might*, translated by Edwin Björkman, in *Plays 2*, 1914.
Lyset (libretto). 1895.
Paul Lange og Tora Parsberg (produced 1901). 1898; as *Paul Lange and Tora Parsberg*, translated by H.L. Brækstad, 1899.
Laboremus (produced 1901). 1901; translated as *Laboremus*, 1901; also translated by Edwin Björkman, in *Plays 2*, 1914.
På Storhove [At Storhove] (produced 1902). 1902.
Daglannet [Dag's Farm] (produced 1905). 1904.
Når den ny vin blomstrer (produced 1909). 1909; as *When the New Wine Blooms*, translated by Lee M. Hollander, 1911.
Three Comedies (includes *The Newly-Married Couple*; *Leonarda*; *A Gauntlet*), translated by R. Farquharson Sharp. 1912.
Plays (vol. 1 includes *The Gauntlet*; *Beyond Our Power*; *The New System*; vol. 2 includes *Love and Geography*; *Beyond Human Might*; *Laboremus*), translated by Edwin Björkman. 2 vols., 1913–14.
Three Dramas (includes *The Bankrupt*; *The Editor*; *The King*), translated by R. Farquharson Sharp. 1914.
Kongebrødrene (includes *Sigurd Jorsalfar* and *Kong Eystejn*), edited by Francis Bull. 1932.

Fiction

Synnøve Solbakken. 1857; as *Trust and Trial*, translated by Mary Howitt, 1858; as *Love and Life in Norway*, translated by Augusta Bethell and Augusta Plesner, 1870; as *Betrothal*, translated in *Half Hours with Foreign Novelists*, 1880; as *Synnove Solbakken*, translated by Julie Sutter, 1881; also translated by Rasmus B. Anderson, 1881; part translated as *Sunny Hill*, 1932.
Arne. 1858; translated as *Arne*, 1861; also translated by Augusta Plesner and S. Rugeley-Powers, 1866; Rasmus B. Anderson, 1881; Walter Low, with *The Fisher Lassie*, 1890.
En glad gut. 1859; as *Ovind*, translated by Sivert and Elizabeth Hjerleid, 1869; as *The Happy Boy*, translated by Helen R.A. Gade, 1870; as *A Happy Boy*, translated by Rasmus B. Anderson, 1881; also translated by W. Archer, 1896; translated as *The Happy Lad*, in *'The Happy Lad' and Other Tales*, 1882.
Smaastykker [Sketches]. 1860.

Fiskerjenten. 1868; as *The Fisher-Maiden*, translated by M.E. Niles, 1869; as *The Fishing Girl*, translated by Augusta Plesner and Frederika Richardson, 1870; as *The Fisher Girl*, translated by Sivert and Elizabeth Hjerleid, 1871; as *The Fisher Maiden*, translated by Rasmus B. Anderson, 1882; as *The Fisher Lassie*, translated by Walter Low, with *Arne*, 1890; translated as *The Fisher Lass*, 1896.
Fortællinger [Tales]. 2 vols., 1872.
Brudeslåtten. 1872; as *The Bridal March*, in *Life by the Fells and Fjords*, translated by Augusta Plesner and S. Rugeley-Powers, 1879; also translated by Rasmus B. Anderson, in *'The Bridal March' and Other Stories*, 1882; J. Evan Williams, 1893.
Magnhild. 1877; as *Magnhild*, translated by Rasmus B. Anderson, 1883.
Life by the Fells and Fjords. 1879.
Kaptejn Mansana. 1879; as *Captain Mansana*, in *'Captain Mansana' and Other Stories*, translated by Rasmus B. Anderson, 1882; also translated by Marian Ford, 1883.
Frygten for flertallet. 1881.
'The Bridal March' and Other Stories, translated by Rasmus B. Anderson. 1882.
'Captain Mansana' and Other Stories, translated by Rasmus B. Anderson. 1882.
Det flager i byen og på havnen. 1884; as *The Heritage of the Kurts*, translated by Cecil Fairfax, 1890.
Støv. 1887.
På guds veje. 1889; as *In God's Way*, translated by Elizabeth Carmichael, 1890.
Nye fortællinger [New Tales]. 3 vols., 1893–94.
Mary. 1906; as *Mary*, translated by Mary Morison, 1909.

Verse

Digte og sange [Poems and Songs]. 1870.
Arnljot Gelline. 1870; as *Arnljot Gelline*, translated by William Morton Payne, 1917.
Poems and Songs (collection), translated by Arthur Hubbell Palmer. 1915.

Other

Mine brev til Petersburgskija Vjedomosti m.m. (letters). 1898.
Udvalgte artikler og taler (articles and speeches). 4 vols., 1902–04.
Aulestad-breve til Bergliot Ibsen, edited by Bergliot Ibsen. 1911.
Gro-tid: Breve fra årene 1857–1870, edited by Halvdan Koht. 2 vols., 1912.
Udvalgte artikler og taler (articles and speeches), edited by Christen Collin and H. Eitrem. 2 vols., 1912–13.
Brytnings-år: Breve fra årene 1871–1878, edited by Halvdan Koht. 2 vols., 1921.
Breve til Alexander L. Kielland, edited by Francis Bull. 1930.
Kamp-liv: Breve fra årene 1879–1884, edited by Halvdan Koht. 2 vols., 1932.
Bjørnstjerne Bjørnsons og Christen Collins brevveksling, 1889–1909, edited by Dagny Bjørnson Sautreau. 1937.
Brevveksling med danske 1875–1910, edited by Øyvind Anker, Francis Bull, and Torben Nielsen. 3 vols., 1953.
Din venn far, edited by Dagny Bjørnson Sautreau. 1956.
Breve til Karoline 1858–1907, edited by Dagny Bjørnson Sautreau. 1957.
Brevveksling med svenske 1858–1909, edited by Øyvind Anker, Francis Bull, and Örjan Lindberger. 3 vols., 1960–61.

Brevveksling med danske 1854–1874, edited by Øyvind Anker, Francis Bull, and Torben Nielsen. 3 vols., 1970–74.
Selvstændighedens Æresfølelse: artikler og taler i utvalg 1879–1905, edited by Knut Johansen. 1974.
Land of the Free: Bjørnson's American Letters, 1880–1881, edited and translated by Eva Lund Haugen and Einar Haugen. 1978.
'Og nu vil jeg tale ut'—'men nu vil jeg også tale ud', brevvekslingen mellom Bjørnstjerne Bjørnson og Amalie Skram 1878–1904, edited by Øyvind Anker and Edvard Beyer. 1982.
Briefwechsel mit Deutschen, edited by Aldo Keel. 1986.
God morgen, Rosalinde! brev til Rosalinde Thomsen, Bjørnstjerne Bjørnson, edited by Bodil Nævdal. 1990.

*

Bibliography: *Bjørnson-bibliografi* by Arthur Thuesen, 5 vols., 1948–57.

Critical Studies: *Critical Studies of Ibsen and Bjørnson* by Georg Brandes, 1899; *Bjørnstjerne Bjørnson: Hans barndom og ungdom* [Bjørnstjerne Bjørnson: His Childhood and Youth] by Christen Collen, 1907, revised edition, 2 vols., 1923; *Bjørnstjerne Bjørnson 1832–1910* by William Morton Payne, 1910; *The Norwegian-American Reaction to Ibsen and Bjørnson, 1850–1900* by Arthur Paulson, 1937; *Bjørnstjerne Bjørnson: A Study in Norwegian Nationalism* by Harold Larson, 1944; *Bjørnstjerne Bjørnson, the Man and His Work* by Øyvind Anker, 1955; 'Bjørnson and Tragedy', in *Scandinavica*, 1(1), 1962, and 'Bjørnson', in his *Modern Norwegian Literature, 1860–1918*, 1966, both by Brian Downs; 'Bjørnson Research: A Survey' by Harald Noreng, in *Scandinavica*, 4(1), 1965; 'Bjørnson's "Trond" and Popular Tradition', in *Scandinavian Studies*, 41(1), 1969, *Bjørnson's Bondefortellinger and Norwegian Folk Literature*, 1970, and 'The Self in Isolation: A New Reading of Bjørnson's *Arne*', in *Scandinavian Studies*, 45(4), 1973, all by Henning K. Sehmsdorf; 'The Multifarious Bjørnson' by Øystein Rottem, in *Scandinavica*, 24(1), 1985.

* * *

Bjørnstjerne Bjørnson, along with Henrik Ibsen and August Strindberg, focused the attention of the world upon Scandinavian theatre during the late 19th century. Each of these authors began his career by drawing upon the stories and myths of the Nordic tradition. Bjørnson, a Norwegian, was a prolific and distinguished writer in a number of fields, leaving 21 plays, eight novels, many short stories and poems, several epic-lyric works, critical articles, and nearly 20 volumes of letters. The variety of his literary interest was clear early in his career. In 1857 he published *Synnøve Solbakken*, the first of the Norwegian peasant tales that gained him renown throughout Scandinavia, as well as his first play, *Mellem slagene* (*Between the Battles*), a one-act work set in the 12th century. The following year saw the play *Halte-Hulda* [Limping Hulda] and the story *Arne*. The eponymous Synnøve and Arne, placed in poetically rendered northern landscapes, can be taken as two aspects of the Norwegian peasant, the one rough and swaggering, the other gifted with fancy and imagination, both seen (in a somewhat less sympathetic treatment) in Ibsen's more famous *Peer Gynt*. *Kong Sverre* [King Sverre] continued to work the popular vein of Romantic interest in national history and folklore, and was staged by Ibsen at the nationalist Norwegian Theatre in Christiania (now Oslo). The first of several epic poems on Nordic themes, 'Bergliot', appeared the following year.

The play that first gained Bjørnson a major following was the brilliant historical trilogy *Sigurd Slembe*, much admired by Ibsen, and echoed to some extent in Ibsen's great success in historical drama, *Kongs-Emnerne* (*The Pretenders*). This was followed by *Maria Stuart i Skotland* (*Mary Stuart in Scotland*) in 1864. Having achieved success in national historical dramas, Bjørnson, like Ibsen, but over a decade earlier, then turned to a realistic study of contemporary domestic life. His popular problem play, *De nygifte* (*The Newly-Married Couple*), looks backward to Augier and Dumas *fils* and forward to Ibsen's *Et dukkehjem* (*A Doll's House*). Indeed, Ibsen's play may be seen in part as a corrective to Bjørnson's, which focuses upon the adjustment of the husband to married life: a husband who, in Bjørnson's own phrase, is treated 'like a doll'. Ibsen, once embarked upon his studies of contemporary life, continued to work that vein consistently for a series of brilliant dramas, but Bjørnson, after *The Newly-Married Couple*, returned to the themes and subjects of his earlier years, producing some of his most popular works, beginning with the short story *Fiskerjenten* (*The Fisher Maiden*) in 1868. Two years later appeared both the short but tremendously influential and popular collection of lyric and patriotic verse *Digte og sange* [Poems and Songs] and the lengthy poem *Arnljot Gelline*, with an epic imagination and lyric beauty as powerful as anything in this artist's extensive canon. Another Romantic historical work, *Sigurd Jorsalfar* [Sigurd the Crusader], was completed in 1872.

In 1875, encouraged perhaps by Georg Brandes's call in 1871 for a Nordic literature engaged with the problems of the present, Bjørnson returned to the territory opened by *The Newly-Married Couple* with two new problem dramas: *Redaktøren* (*The Editor*), showing how an unscrupulous journalist destroys the reputation of a leading citizen, and *En fallit* (*The Bankrupt*), his best-known work internationally and Norway's first drama on a financial theme. The latter is a naturalistic study of a wealthy family achieving a happier, if more modest, domestic life after the loss of its ill-gotten riches. Despite its rather dry and untheatrical discussions, *Kongen* (*The King*), which questioned the significance of royalty in a democratic era, aroused strong protest from those who considered it an attack not only on the monarchy, but on the Church and other traditional institutions. *Det ny system* (*The New System*) responded, like Ibsen's later *En folke-fiende* (*An Enemy of the People*), to such attacks with an allegory depicting the social martyrdom of a protagonist who dares to express an unpopular truth. Bjørnson's Kampe, however, is a closer relative to Holberg's Erasmus Montanus than to Ibsen's Dr Stockmann, giving up at last to the superior social force of his opponents.

Bjørnson's two 'women's' plays, *Leonarda* and *En hanske* (*A Gauntlet*), continued to bring their author under attack as unsocial and immoral, since the first sympathetically portrays the efforts of a divorced woman to make her way in society and the second attacks a social system that has different laws of morality for men and for women. Both plays, however, were overshadowed at the time and subsequently by the much more radical and more richly textured contemporary social dramas of Ibsen, beginning with *A Doll's House* in 1879.

Like many European authors of his generation, Bjørnson experienced the tension between traditional religious beliefs and the new scientism represented by such authors as Hippolyte Taine, J. Ernest Renan, and Charles Darwin. This tension forms the basis for what has often been considered his greatest play, *Over ævne I* (*Beyond Human Power*), depicting the agony of the Nordic Pastor Sang, whose miraculous powers of healing cannot save his dying and unbelieving wife. The faith and power of God are shown at last beyond human control or comprehension, even by so inspired a figure as Sang. In a much weaker sequel, *Over ævne II* (*Beyond Human Might*), Sang's two sons carry on his quest, seeking salvation on the social level through the new religion of revolution. This dynamic is also proven to be beyond their control, and the ever pragmatic Bjørnson seems to advocate a kind of Fabian gradualism to the solving of human problems.

The suicide of a former friend, in whose political downfall Bjørnson may have played a role, inspired the scathing *Paul Lange og Tora Parsberg* (*Paul Lange and Tora Parsberg*), which returns to the condemnation of political intolerance previously dealt with in *The Editor*. Of Bjørnson's final plays, including *Laboremus*, *På Storhove* [At Storhove], and *Daglannet* [Dag's Farm], only the last, *Når den ny vin blomstrer* (*When the New Wine Blooms*), a gently ironic study of a somewhat eccentric family disturbed by the stresses of the new feminism, achieved a continuing success.

—Marvin Carlson

PEASANT TALES (Bondefortelling)
Stories by Bjørnstjerne Bjørnson, 1856—.

The first of Bjørnson's peasant tales appeared in 1856 in the periodical *Illustreret Folkeblad* which he was editing to assist an impoverished printer. The tales are contemporary portraits of Norwegian peasant life and although the place names and descriptions of nature are characteristically Norwegian they were sufficiently ambiguous to appeal to peasants of the entire nation.

According to Bjørnson himself, in an essay entitled 'Hvorledes jeg blev digter' [How I Became a Poet] (1872), his poetic mission became clear to him on a trip to a student gathering in Uppsala (Sweden) in 1856 when he was gripped by 'historical envy' at the Swedish security of national identity. Norwegians had been denied this by 400 years of Danish rule.

With a firm belief in the great heroic past of the Vikings and the view that the peasant was the key figure of national self-awareness—the custodian of the traditional Viking values of spiritual and moral existence—Bjørnson strove through his tales to stimulate national self-assertion against the superior foreign culture of Denmark. For Bjørnson, the peasant was the living embodiment of an exemplary way of life linking the people of contemporary Norway with the 'Golden Age' before the throne had passed to the Danes. The peasant, like the Viking, was powerful but undemonstrative in feeling, with a strength of will and purpose, self-disciplined, and supremely loyal to kinsman and friend. Bjørnson believed that upon these virtues a glorious national future could be built, and this is a predominant theme to which he returns throughout his peasant tales.

Unlike the overt national Romanticism of writers like J.S. Welhaven, Bjørnson's tales are not idyllically Romantic portraits of Norwegian life. The tales also address the social and political issues of the day, as in *Arne* where Nils Skredder represents the irresponsible, heavy-drinking peasant who terrorizes his family. However, the majority of the tales reflect Bjørnson's intention to present an alternative to the negative view of peasants being promoted by the sociologist Eilert Sundt around this time. Sundt's research revealed the high rate of unmarried mothers, illegitimate children, and alcoholism in the farming communities of Norway.

From the outset, Bjørnson's tales introduced the public to a stylistically fresher and more direct narrative technique, simultaneously inaugurating what was to become virtually a national campaign: a literary programme in national pride. The most important peasant tales are *Synnøve Solbakken*, *Arne*, *The Fisher Maiden*, *En glad gut* (*A Happy Boy*), *Brudeslåtten* (*The Bridal March*), and 'Fadren' ('The Father'). In a letter to Paul Botten Hansen, Bjørnson characterizes his own narrative style, declaring 'Jeg respekterer intet Grammatik-Norsk: jeg bruger Bryst-Norsk!' [I have no respect for Norwegian grammar: I use Norwegian from the heart!]. The tales have a spoken quality about them, characteristic of the oral story-telling, and invoke comparison with the earlier sagas and folk literature of his day, such as the works of Asbjørnson and Hans Christian Andersen.

There are primarily two themes that dominate the peasant tales, the first being the stifling of talent, brought about by poverty or the misunderstanding of others. In the very first tale 'Aanun', a gifted child whose family does not understand him is corrupted by an evil schoolteacher and an ignorant priest. The second theme concerns marriage between the social classes—for example, the lowly farm hand who either works hard or displays great feats of physical prowess and is rewarded with the hand of the farmer's daughter, like Thore in 'Et farligt Frieri' [A Dangerous Courtship].

Like Thorbjørn in *Synnøve Solbakken*, who must overcome the savagery in his own nature, and Øyvind in *A Happy Boy*, who is hampered by his personal ambition and narcissism, all of Bjørnson's heroes must pass through a period of suffering before reaching a greater insight into their own nature.

Bjørnson's female heroes almost exclusively represent the male hero's 'prize' and the majority of the tales end happily with the marriage ceremony, reminiscent of folk-tales and reflecting Bjørnson's belief in the church during this period of his authorship. Religion was expected to teach people to turn from self-love to neighbourly love and was part of his overall view that the nation required a national identity of which it could be proud.

The central stylistic achievement in these tales, although varying in quality and reminiscent of other literary genres, is found in Bjørnson's ability to give psychological insight to his characters by 'showing' rather than 'telling' the reader about their feelings. This is best seen in 'The Father', where a conceited, demanding farmer, who has always pressured the local pastor to get the very best for his son, loses the son in a freak boating accident. When he visits the pastor to make amends for his arrogant life and to donate half the money he has received for the sale of his farm to the church, he appears as a broken man. The emotion of deep shame and newly acquired humility is implied by action and dialogue rather than the omniscient voice of the author.

Of all the tales the short story 'The Father' and the novel *Synnøve Solbakken* illustrate the best qualities of Bjørnson's writing. They are well-constructed narratives, devoid of all unnecessary embellishment, and allow characters to come into direct contact with the reader through action and direct speech. This evokes psychological insight and pre-empts the work of the later Scandinavian writers of the 1880s and 1890s—the period of the 'Modern Breakthrough'. Between them these works convey the dominant themes found repeatedly throughout the first 15 years of Bjørnson's prose writing, collectively known as the 'peasant tales'.

—J.M. Buscall

BLIND MAN'S BOY. See **LAZARILLO DE TORMES**.

BLIXEN, Karen. See **DINESEN, Isak**.

BLOK, Aleksandr (Alexandrovich). Born in St Petersburg, Russia, 28 November 1880. Educated at Vvedenskii School, St Petersburg, 1891–99; studied law, 1899–1901, and philology, 1901–06, University of St Petersburg. Married Liubov Dmitrievna Mendeleeva in 1903. Professional writer from 1906; served behind the lines in 1916; later had government jobs: verbatim reporter, Extraordinary Investigating Commission, 1917–18; on various cultural committees after 1918: in theatrical department of People's Commissariat for Education (and chairman of Repertory Section), 1918–19, and involved with Gor'kii's publishing house Vsemirnaia Literatura [World Literature], 1918–21; adviser, Union of Practitioners of Literature as an Art, 1919; chairman of Directorate of Bolshoi Theatre, 1919–21. *Died 7 August 1921.*

PUBLICATIONS

Collections

Sobranie stikhotvorenii [Collected Poetry]. 3 vols., 1911–12.
Sobranie sochinenii [Collected Works]. 7 vols. (of 9 planned), 1922–23; edited by Vladimir N. Orlov and others, 8 vols., 1960–63 (includes diaries and letters), in 6 vols., 1971 (includes notebooks).
Selected Poems, edited by James B. Woodward. 1968.
Selected Poems, edited by Avril Pyman. 1972.
Selected Poems, translated by Jon Stallworthy and Peter France. 1974.
Collected Poems, translated by Sidney Guthrie-Smith. 1975.
Teatr, edited by P.P. Gromova. 1981.
Selected Poems, translated by Alex Miller. 1981.

Verse

Stikhi o prekrasnoi dame [Verses on a Most Beautiful Lady]. 1905.
Nechaiannaya radost' [Unexpected Joy]. 1907.
Snezhnaia maska [The Snow Mask]. 1907.
Zemlia v snegu [The Earth in Snow]. 1908.
Nochnye chasy [The Night Watches]. 1911.
Skazki: Stikhi dlia detei [Fairy Tales: Poems for Children]. 1913.
Kruglyi god: Stikhotvoreniia dlia detei [All the Year Round: Poetry for Children]. 1913.
Stikhi o Rossii [Poems about Russia]. 1915.
Solov'inyi sad [The Nightingale Garden]. 1918.
Dvenadtsat', with *Skify*. 1918; *Dvenadtsat'* (bilingual edition), edited by Avril Pyman, 1989; as *The Twelve*, translated by C.E. Bechhofer, 1920; also translated by B. Deutsch and Avrahm Yarmolinsky, 1931; Robin Fulton, 1968; as *The Twelve and the Scythians*, translated by Jack Lindsay, 1982.
Iamby: Sovremennye stikhi (1907–1914) [Iambs: Contemporary Poems]. 1919.
Za gran'iu proshlykh dnei [Beyond the Bounds of Days Gone By]. 1920.
Sedoe utro [The Grey Morning]. 1920.
Stikhotvoreniia [Poetry]. 1921.
The Twelve and Other Poems, translated by Peter France and Jon Stallworthy. 1970.

Plays

Balaganchik (produced 1906). In *Liricheskie dramy*, 1908; as *The Puppet Show*, translated by M. Kriger and Gleb Struve, in *Slavonic Review*, 28 (71), 1949–50.
Korol' na ploshchadi [The King in the Square]. 1907.
O lyubvi, poezii i gosudarstvennoi sluzhbe; as *Love, Poetry and the Civil Service*, translated by F. O'Dempsey, 1953. 1907.
Pesnia sud'by [The Song of Fate]. 1907; revised edition, 1919.
Liricheskie dramy [Lyrical Dramas]. 1908.
Neznakomka [The Stranger] (produced 1914). In *Liricheskie dramy*, 1908.
Primater' [The Ancestress], from a play by Grillparzer (produced 1908).
Roza i krest (produced 1921). 1913; translated as *The Rose and the Cross*, in *The Russian Symbolist Theatre*, edited and translated by Michael Green, 1986.
Ramzes [Ramses]. 1921(?).

Other

Molnii iskusstva [Lightning Flashes of Art] (travel sketches; unfinished). 1909–20(?).
Sobranie stikhotvorenii i teatr [Collected Poetry and Plays]. 4 vols., 1916.
Rossiia i intelligentsiia (1907–1918) [Russia and the Intelligentsia] (essays). 1918; revised edition, 1919; translated in part in *The Spirit of Music*, 1943.
Katilina. 1919.
Otrocheskie stikhi; Avtobiografiia [Adolescent Poems; Autobiography]. 1922.
The Spirit of Music, translated by I. Freiman. 1943.
An Anthology of Essays and Memoirs, edited by Lucy E. Vogel. 1982.

Editor, *Poslednye dni imperatorskoi vlasti* [The Last Days of the Imperial Regime]. 1921.

*

Bibliography: *Blok* by N. Ashukin, 1923; in *O Bloke* by E. Blium and V. Goltsev, 1929; by E. Kolpakova and others, in *Vilniusskii gosudarstvennyi pedagogicheskii Institut 6*, 1959; by Avril Pyman, in *Blokovskii Sbornik 1*, 1964, and in *Selected Poems*, 1972; by P.E. Pomirchiy, in *Blokovskii Sbornik 2*, 1972.

Critical Studies: *Blok, Prophet of Revolution* by C.H. Kisch, 1960; *Aleksandr Blok: Between Image and Idea* by F.D. Reeve, 1962; *Alexander Blok: A Study in Rhythm and Metre* by Robin Kemball, 1965; *Aleksandr Blok: The Journey to Italy* (includes translations) by Lucy Vogel, 1973; *The Poet and the Revolution: Aleksandr Blok's 'The Twelve'* by Sergei Hackel (includes translation), 1975; *Listening to the Wind: An Introduction to Alexander Blok* by James Forsyth, 1977; *The Life of Aleksandr Blok* by Avril Pyman, 2 vols., 1979–80; *Hamayun: The Life of Aleksandr Blok* by Vladimir N. Orlov, translated by Olga Shartse, 1981; *Alexander Blok as Man and Poet* by Kornei Chukovsky, translated and edited by Diana Burgin and Katherine O'Connor, 1982; *Aleksandr Blok* by Konstantin Mochulsky, 1983; *Aleksandr Blok's Ital'yanskie stikhi: Confrontation and Disillusionment* by Gerald Pirog, 1983; *Aleksandr Blok Centennial Conference* edited by Walter N. Vickery, 1984; 'The Structure and Theme of Blok's Cycle *Jamby*' by James B. Woodward, in *Scando-Slavica*, 31, 1985; *Aleksandr Blok and the Dynamics of the Lyric Cycle* by David A. Sloane, 1987; *Between Time and Eternity: Nine Essays* by P. Kirschner, 1992; *Aspects of Dramatic Communication: Action, Non-action, Interaction* by J. Stelleman, 1992.

*   *   *

Aleksandr Blok is Russia's last great Romantic poet and one of her most charismatic personalities. Blok's legend began when he discovered his great theme of the Eternal Feminine—this myth-making Symbolists' ideal, which they saw as the link between the earthly and the divine. His first book of poems, *Stikhi o prekrasnoi dame* [Verses on a Most Beautiful Lady], comprised 800 'romantic hymns to one woman', his future wife Liubov Mendeleeva. These, the most immaterial, rarified lyrics in Russian literature, are 'poems of praise', 'heavenly songs' to idealistic Beauty. Blok believed that the world was created according to absolute Beauty. The ecstatic vision of the Beautiful Lady appeared in Blok's poetry in various incarnations representing the spirit of harmony. It became the Symbolists' symbol of symbols and 'passions' game'. B. Eikhenbaum called Blok a 'dictator of feelings', saying that Blok always lived in the 'aura of those emotions which he himself aroused'. Blok, indeed, 'went from cult to cult' (Mandel'shtam), from the Beautiful Lady and 'The Unknown Lady' through 'The Snow Mask' and 'Carmen' to Russia and the Revolution. He tried to find 'the truth' through intensely lived emotional experiences, and his poetry mirrored his inner life which was essentially dualistic. 'I am afraid of my two-faced soul', he confessed, 'and carefully bury its demonic and fierce visage in shining armour'. He was torn between his apocalyptical predictions and hope for future harmony, between the music of the spheres and the tumult-rhythms of the coming social upheavals.

Russia, as the theme of his life, also troubled him with her two faces—beautiful and hungry, great and drunken. The dissonance between vision and reality constitutes Blok's tragedy: 'The love and hate I have within me—no one could endure'. He found irony as the best weapon to deal with discontent and despair. He ridiculed mysticism in his dramatic trilogy *Balaganchik* (*The Puppet Show*), *Korol' na ploshchadi* [The King in the Square], and *Neznakomka* [The Stranger]. Blok shed his mysticism by 1906 but wanted to stay in touch with the infinite, having the capacity to hear the music of the 'world's orchestra'.

Music was the 'essence of the world' for Blok. He built his metaphysical system on the conception of the 'spirit of music': 'There are . . . two times, two dimensions', he wrote in his essay 'The Downfall of Humanism', 'one historical, chronological, the other immeasurable and musical'. Unlike Belyi, Blok was never a theorist or a thinker. He possessed enormous sensitivity and an impeccable ear, but not a great intellect. Blok's strictly poetic achievement has usually been exaggerated. As Mandel'shtam said: 'In literary matters Blok was an enlightened conservative. He was exceedingly cautious with everything concerning style, metrics or imagery: not one overt break with the past'. Harmony between the ear and the eye led him to use symbols of an auditory nature, elemental sounds, the wild howl of violins, the tune of the wind, the harps and strings of a blizzard. He incorporated the lilting rhythms of gypsy songs, their uneven beat and abrupt alternations of fire and melancholy. Many of his best lyrics are a curious transposition of gypsy tunes into the moods, forms, and vocabularies of modern symbolism. The predominance of the musical over the discursive and the logical was a feature of his poetry as much as of his character.

Blok dreamt all his life about creating a musical poem that would reflect this antimusical world. He realized his dream in the poem *Dvenadtsat'* (*The Twelve*), which he wrote in two days. Here chaos and music almost fuse. The imagery of snow-storms formed the background of the birth of the new world. Twelve Red soldiers, spreading terror and death, become 12 apostles with Christ as their invisible leader. In the Revolution Blok saw a new manifestation of 'the Spirit of Music'. But it was too loud for Blok's hypersensitive ear: soon after *The Twelve* and *Skify* (*The Scythians*), 1918, he ceased to 'hear'. 'I have not heard any new sounds for a long time; they have all vanished for me and probably for all of us . . . it would be blasphemous and deceitful to try deliberately to call them back into our soundless space', he told Chukovsky, and he ceased writing poetry. Not all Blok's friends shared his belief that the time had come for the intellectuals to sacrifice themselves under the wheels of the 'troika'. Hostility toward Blok was inevitable. He was told to his face that 'he had outlived his time and was inwardly dead'—a fact with which, Pasternak told us, he calmly agreed. Russia's last poet-nobleman with Decembrist blood in his veins was out of time. It was unfortunate for Blok that greater poets followed him so quickly. For them, however, Blok, as a man and a poet, became a symbol, a 'monument of the beginning of the century' and the 'tragic tenor of the epoch' (Akhmatova).

—Valentina Polukhina

THE TWELVE (Dvenadtsat')
Poem by Aleksandr Blok, 1918.

Written in January 1918, *The Twelve* is Blok's poetic response to the Bolshevik Revolution and is acknowledged as the greatest poetic work inspired by this climactic event in Russian history. It is at once a celebration and a highly personal interpretation of the Revolution, and it marks the culmination of Blok's development as a poet.

For all its ostensible realism and sustained sense of immediacy, *The Twelve* is a work of Symbolist art inseparably related by its imagery and by the ideas which underlie it to the three volumes of Blok's lyric poetry. It is not, therefore, primarily a political poem. It is an immensely complex work conceived in a very real sense as a parallel to the revolution that it depicts, for the Revolution was seen by Blok as an explosion of the same creative energy that is experienced by the artist in the act of poetic creation. His term for this creative force was 'the Spirit of Music', and from 1908 onwards it became increasingly associated in his thought with the Russian masses. 'Art is born', he wrote, 'of the eternal interaction between two kinds of music—the music of the creative individual and the music which sounds in the depths of the popular soul, the soul of the masses'. The 12 sections, therefore, into which the poem is divided may be characterized as the movements of an essentially musical composition designed to evoke a process of cultural transformation that was itself conceived in musical terms, as a process in which destruction and creation were apprehended as dissonance and harmony. This 'musical' conception is reflected in the use of metre, rhyme, assonance, and alliteration, in the repetition of images (especially colour symbols), in the snatches of folk songs, revolutionary songs, and romances that interrupt the narrative, and in the stylistic discords produced by the juxta-

positions of obscenities, slang, and contemporary political slogans with literary allusions and religious imagery.

The central figures of the poem embody 'the music which sounds in the depths of the popular soul'. They are the 12 Red guards patrolling the streets of revolutionary Petrograd to whom the title refers and who are transformed in the course of the work from an undisciplined, vengeful, and destructive rabble into a cohesive force capable of building the future and led by Christ. Together with the number 12, the appearance of Christ in the last line of the work has been taken to suggest that a parallel to the 12 apostles was intended. The hypothesis is strengthened by the names given to the two named members of the Twelve—Pet'ka/Petrukha and Andriukha (diminutives of Petr [Peter] and Andrei [Andrew])—and by statements in Blok's diary and notebooks of the period. The portrayal of the Twelve, however, cannot easily be reconciled with this view, and sceptics have pointed also in this connection to Blok's professed discontent with his Christ image. The reasons for his dissatisfaction and the meaning of the image are among the major subjects of debate provoked by the poem. As a symbol of salvation, of Russia's rebirth and redemption through blood and torment, it was clearly an appropriate image. In addition, it may have been intended to express the belief, bequeathed by Gogol' and, most notably, Dostoevskii, that the Russian people were destined to restore Christ to a world which had lost Him. Yet the Revolution was seen by Blok as giving birth to a new era unlike any that had been known in human experience. To the extent that it failed to express this idea, the Christ image may be said to have fallen short of his requirements, and herein, perhaps, lies the main reason for his reservations about it.

Less contentiously the Twelve have also been interpreted as embodying one of the pivotal 'pagan' concepts in Blok's thought and poetry—the concept of 'the elemental' (*stikhiia*) which ultimately merged in his thinking with that of 'the Spirit of Music' and which developed under the influence of the Platonic ideas that he absorbed at the beginning of his career. It was his term for the concept of matter derived from Plato as a chaotic, inert force which forms the raw material of life and art and is ever resistant to the Good that would change it. Such inertia and resistance to change are indeed the dominant features of the Twelve in the first ten sections, and the plot of the poem, modelled on the *commedia dell'arte* plot that Blok had employed previously in his play *The Puppet Show*, is a dramatization of their release from these restraining attributes. Its symbolic expression is the accidental shooting by Petrukha of their seductive embodiment, his former girlfriend Kat'ka, the eventual effect of which is the new sense of purpose reflected towards the end in the 'sovereign tread' of their march and in the increasingly disciplined verse that evokes it. In section 12 the tortuous transition is finally completed from the mixed metres, variable line-lengths, and changing rhyme-schemes of section one to regular quatrains of trochaic tetrameters culminating in a nine-line stanza in the same metre in which the conflicting elements of the poem are integrated in a final harmonious chord.

Pointing to the future, this sense of harmony produced by the poem's conclusion implies also a comment on Russia's past. It expresses Blok's hopes for the restoration of a harmonious, unified Russian nation, for a nation no longer split by the religious reforms of the 17th century which had alienated the Old Believers or by the legacy of Peter the Great's westernizing policies which had antagonized both the Old Believers and much of the peasantry. As Blok's notebooks confirm, the Revolution was closely associated in his thought and imagination with the great peasant rebellions of the 17th and 18th centuries. He saw it as an expression of the same anger, as a reawakening of the same alienated masses, and with his Old Believer spelling of the name 'Jesus' in the poem's last line he reaffirmed his faith in their historical destiny as at once the creators of a new civilization and the healers of ancient national wounds.

—James B. Woodward

BOBROWSKI, Johannes. Born in Tilsit, East Prussia (now Sovetsk, CIS) 9 April 1917. Educated at high school in Königsberg (now Kaliningrad); studied art history, University of Berlin, 1937–41. Married Johanna Buddrus in 1943; four children. Served in the army 1939–45; prisoner of war in Russia, captured 1945, released 1949. Editor, Lucie Groszer, children's book publishers, Berlin, 1950–59, and with Union Verlag, East Berlin, 1959. Recipient: Gruppe 47 prize, 1962; Alma König prize, 1962; Heinrich Mann prize 1965; Veillon prize (Switzerland), 1965; Weiskopf prize, 1967 (posthumously). *Died 2 September 1965.*

PUBLICATIONS

Collections

Gesammelte Werke, edited by Eberhard Haufe. 3 vols., 1987.
Shadow Lands: Selected Poems (includes the collections *Shadow Land* and *From the Rivers* and other poems), translated by Ruth and Matthew Mead. 1984.

Verse

Sarmatische Zeit. 1961.
Schattenland Ströme. 1962.
Wetterzeichen. 1966.
Shadow Land, translated by Ruth and Matthew Mead. 1966.
Im Windgesträuch, edited by Eberhard Haufe. 1970.
Selected Poems: Johannes Bobrowski, Horst Bienek, translated by Ruth and Matthew Mead. 1971.
Gedichte 1952–1965. 1974.
From the Rivers, translated by Ruth and Matthew Mead. 1975.
Literarisches Klima: Ganz neue Xenien, doppelte Ausführung. 1978.
Yesterday I Was Leaving, translated by Rich Ives. 1986.

Fiction

Levins Mühle. 1964; as *Levin's Mill*, translated by Janet Cropper, 1970.
Böhlendorff und andere: Erzählungen. 1965.
Mäusefest und andere Erzählungen. 1965.
Litauische Claviere. 1966.
Der Mahner: Erzählungen und andere Prosa. 1968.
Erzählungen. 1969.
Drei Erzählungen. 1970.
I Taste Bitterness (stories), translated by Marc Linder. 1970.
Die Erzählungen. 1979.
Böhlendorff: A Short Story and Seven Poems, translated by Francis Golffing. 1989.

Other

Nachbarschaft: Neun Gedichte; Drei Erzählungen; Zwei Interviews; Zwei Grabreden; Zwei Schallplatten; Lebensdaten. 1967.

Editor, *Die schönsten Sagen des klassichen Altertums*, by Gustav Schwab. 1954.
Editor, *Die Sagen von Troja und von der Irrfahrt und Heimkehr des Odysseus*, by Gustav Schwab. 1955.
Editor, *Der märkische Eulenspiegel*, by Hans Clauert. 1956.
Editor, *Leben Fibels*, by Jean Paul. 1963.
Editor, *Wer mich und Ilse sieht im Grase: Deutsche Poeten des 18. Jahrhunderts über die Liebe und das Frauenzimmer*. 1964.

Translator, with Günther Deicke, *Initialen der Leidenschaft*, by Boris Pasternak. 1969.

*

Bibliography: *Das Werk von Johannes Bobrowski* by Curt Grützmacher, 1974; bibliography by Adolf Sckerl, in *Schattenfabel von den Versuchungen. Johannes Bobrowski. Zur 20. Wiederkehr seines Todestages*, 1985.

Critical Studies: *West-Östliches in der Lyrik Johannes Bobrowski* by Sigrid Höfert, 1966; *Johannes Bobrowski: Selbstzeugnisse und Beiträge über sein Werk*, 1967, expanded edition, 1982; *Bobrowski und andere. Die Chronik des Peter Jokostra*, 1967; *Johannes Bobrowski. Leben und Werk*, 1967, and *Beschreibung eines Zimmers. 15 Kapitel über Johannes Bobrowski*, 1971, both by Gerhard Wolf; *Johannes Bobrowski. Versuch einer Interpretation* by Rudolf Bohren, 1968; *Johannes Bobrowski* by Brian Keith-Smith, 1970; *Beschwörung und Reflexion. Bobrowskis sarmatische Gedichte* by Wolfram Mauser, 1970; *Johannes Bobrowksi. Prosa. Interpretationen* by Mechthild and Wilhelm Dehn, 1972; *Johannes Bobrowski. Chronik, Einführung, Bibliographie* by Bernhard Gajek and Eberhard Haufe, 1977; *Facetten. Untersuchungen zum Werk Johannes Bobrowskis* by Alfred Behrmann, 1977; *Erinnerung Johannes Bobrowski* by Christoph Meckel, 1978; *Ahornallee 26; oder, Epitaph für Johannes Bobrowski* edited by Gerhard Rostin, 1978; *Johannes Bobrowski. Studien und Interpretationen* by Bernd Leistner, 1981; *Johannes Bobrowskis Lyrik und die Tradition* by Fritz Minde, 1981; *Die aufgehobene Zeit. Zeitstruktur und Zeitelemente in der Lyrik Johannes Bobrowksis* by Werner Schulz, 1983; *Schattenfabel von den Versuchungen. Johannes Bobrowski. Zur 20. Wiederkehr seines Todestages*, 1985.

* * *

Johannes Bobrowski, who died from peritonitis in 1965 at the age of 45, was one of the most humane German writers of the 20th century, and the concept of 'humanitas' to bind communities together informs his works. This implies a willingness to learn from past mistakes and an openness to the needs of others. His declared central theme of atonement for German crimes against Eastern neighbours implies an awareness both of hidden, half-forgotten forces in the landscape and of a variety of ethnic characteristics among the villages and small towns along the river Memel. His combination of locally-based prejudices and events—the novel *Levins Mühle* (*Levin's Mill*) and a sophisticated application of culture from the classical world (the sapphic form of 'Ode to Thomas Chatterton'), 18th-century writers and musicians (the story 'Epitaph for Pinnau' and his unpublished anthology 'Lieder von Heinrich Albert') produced a highly personal style. Essential was the relationship of the individual to his environment and to language (the poem 'Dead Language'). This led him to search for the lifestyle and history of his ancestors (as can be seen from documents in his posthumous papers), and also to speak out against the inhumanity of his time, especially the Nazi period (the poem 'Report'). The border atmosphere and village life as a world theatre in miniature form the background to his landscape poetry (the poems 'Das Holzhaus über der Wilna', 'Village', and 'The Sarmatian Plain', also the stories 'Lipmann's Leib' [Lipmann's Body] and 'In Pursuance of City Planning Considerations'). Equally important to him were the river landscapes (the poems 'In the Stream', By the River', 'The Don') that he presents as coordinates of both time and place. School in Königsberg—the town of Hamann and Kant—opened up to him a rich literary and musical heritage, and he developed a taste for Baroque music, for Bach, Buxtehude, and Mozart. He also learnt to appreciate the form and discipline of classical Greek and Latin writers. War service, especially in the army invading Poland, made him realize how fragile common humanity can be. This influenced much of his early, sometimes unpublished poetry and some of his short prose texts (the poems on Russia and texts such as 'Mouse Banquet' and 'The Dancer Malige').

The link between his poetry and prose, which was written mainly during the last few years of his life, lies in the use of signs, on which Minde and Behrmann among others have written. Yet he was constantly aware of the foreshortening, deadening, and dehumanizing potentials of language—hence the search in his second novel *Litauische Claviere* for an operatic form where reconciliation of political views and fusion of modes of expression might be fully explored. His works, set in a frontier land of German and Lithuanian districts (e.g. the novels *Levin's Mill* and *Litauische Claviere*) include examples of a level of consciousness between dream and wide-awake reality (the poem 'Eichendorff' and the short story 'Das Käuzchen' [The Little Owl]) where memories bring an awakening to a further dimension of reality. Through an unexpected event the everyday is revealed as only one level of experience (the poem 'Elder Blossom').

Literature can function as a breaker of time barriers and create a sense of mythic existence as in the poem 'Die Günderrode' [Gunderrode]. A *Weg nach innen* (way inwards) à la Novalis is based on the magic power of the word, yet Bobrowski used myth not to expand into the elemental, endless, or universal as with the Romantics, but to refer with his metaphors to a more intense understanding on the local human level. His works were thus a deliberate quest for cultural, historical, and natural roots. The use of open form bringing heterogenous elements together in an apparently often unresolved manner was designed to shock the reader, assist him sometimes to laugh, and help him to comprehend more fully the nature of the reasons behind his existence (the poem 'Village Music' and the short story 'De homine publico tractatus'). In both prose and poetry he paid strict attention to metric as opposed to strophic or linear structure as basic building blocks, thus emphasizing his sense of control, of *Bebauung* over his material.

The more 'naive' evocation of the past in his poems of the 1950s—'Der litauische Brunnen' [The Lithuanian Well], 'Der Singschwan' [Singing Swan], 'Die alte Heerstrasse [The Old Army Road]—contained a definite epic quality. This gave way to a tone of lament for the loss of a previous world, and the poetic images began to assume the qualities of a cipher

('Always to Be Named', 'Nänie'). He became a master of finding objective correlatives and set them with great verbal economy and rich variety of poetic device. Most of his poems are short, but they are full of nuances and hidden allusions. His prose works also developed from evocation and direct assimilation of the past towards emphatic statements of a new sense of community service ('Contemplation of a Picture'). Basic to poems and prose is often a structure that includes a negative warning that registers the past, followed by a call for closer involvement with nature, and finally an act of naming or finding the fitting poetic language to resuscitate a lost dimension of human awareness.

By including the perspective of a narrator, Bobrowski often ensured that sentimentality is cut out and the reader becomes aware of a directed form of detailed portrayal highlighting the co-existence of different worlds (especially in the longest of his short prose works 'Böhlendorff'). A form of score with variants and counterpoint emerged in his prose works, just as with a work for an organ, an instrument that Bobrowski particularly cherished.

Since his early death Bobrowski has become known throughout the world because he developed a poetic language with a mastery of imagery, rhythm, and musicality. He understood the everyday world and political theories to be sterile and non-creative—the interplay of history and landscape seemed to him healthier and closer to the secret wishes of man in general. He combined a serious-minded, peace-loving message with an almost therapeutically ironic distancing from all human foibles. It is not surprising that half of his posthumous papers consist of letters from friends from many countries, for he sought above everything dialogue between all human beings (the poem 'The Word Man'). The freshness of his works depends on his success in keeping them free from nostalgia and sentimentality, his rare mastery of technical detail, knowledge of several historical atmospheres, a light touch, and an eye for positive humanity.

—Brian Keith-Smith

BOCCACCIO, Giovanni. Born in Florence or Certaldo, between June and July in 1313. Apprentice in his father's banking business, Naples, 1327–31; studied canon law, 1331–36. Worked in banking in Naples until 1341; returned to Florence in 1341 and was there during the Black Death, 1348; met Petrarch, *q.v.*, in 1350 and thereafter devoted himself to humanistic scholarship; took minor clerical orders, 1357; active in Florentine public life, and went on several diplomatic missions in the 1350s and 1360s; lectured on Dante, *q.v.*, in Florence, 1373–74. *Died 21 December 1375.*

PUBLICATIONS

Collections

Opere latine minori, edited by A.F. Massèra. 1928.
Opere, edited by Vittore Branca and others. 12 vols., 1964.
Opere minori in volgare, edited by Mario Marti. 4 vols., 1969–72.
Opere, edited by Cesare Segre. 1980.

Fiction

Elegia di Madonna Fiammetta, edited by Cesare Segre, 1966, and by Mario Marti, in *Opere minori*, 3. 1971; as *Amorous Fiammetta*, translated by Bartholomew Young, 1587, reprinted 1926; as *The Elegy of Lady Fiammetta*, edited and translated by Mariangela Causa-Steindler and Thomas Hauch, 1990.

Decameron, edited by Vittore Branca. 1976; as *The Decameron*, translated anonymously, 1620; numerous subsequent translations including by John Payne, 1866 (revised edition by Charles Singleton, 1984); Richard Aldington, 1930; Frances Winwar, 1930; G.H. McWilliam, 1972; Mark Musa and Peter E. Bondanella, 1977; J.M. Rigg, 1978.

Il filocolo, edited by Antonio Enzo Quaglio. 1967; translated in part as *Thirteen Questions of Love*, edited by Harry Carter, 1974.

Boccaccio's First Fiction, edited and translated by Anthony K. Cassel and Victoria Kirkham. 1991.

Play

L'ameto, edited by Antonio Enzo Quaglio, in *Opere*, 2. 1964; as *L'ameto*, translated by Judith Powers Serafini-Sauli. 1985.

Verse

Il filostrato, edited by Vittore Branca, in *Opere*, 2. 1964; as *The Filostrato*, translated by N.E. Griffin and A.B. Myrick, 1929; as *Il Filostrato: The Story of the Love of Troilo*, translated by Hubertis Cummings, 1934.

Rime, edited by Vittore Branca. 1958.

Il ninfale fiesolano, edited by Armando Balduino. 1974; as *The Nymph of Fiesole*, translated by Daniel J. Donno, 1960; as *Nymphs of Fiesole*, translated by Joseph Tusiani, 1971.

La caccia di Diana, edited by Vittore Branca, in *Opere*, 1. 1964.

Il Teseida, edited by Alberto Limentani, in *Opere*, 2. 1964; as *The Book of Theseus*, translated by Bernadette Marie McCoy, 1974.

L'amorosa visione, edited by Vittore Branca, in *Opere*, 3. 1964; translated by Robert Hollander, Timothy Hampton, and Margherita Frankel, 1986.

Eclogues, translated by Janet Levarie Smarr. 1987.

Other

Le lettere, edited by Francesco Corazzini. 1877.

Trattatello in laude di Dante, edited by Pier Giorgio Ricci. 1974; translated in *The Early Lives of Dante*, 1904; as *The Life of Dante*, translated by Vincenzo Zin Bollettino, 1990.

Il commento alla Divina Commedia e altri scritti intorno a Dante, edited by Domenico Guerri. 4 vols., 1918–26.

De genealogia deorum gentilium [The Genealogies of the Gentile Gods], edited by Vincenzo Romano. 1951; section as *Boccaccio on Poetry*, translated by Charles Osgood, 1930; as *Boccaccio: In Defense of Poetry*, edited by Jeremiah Reedy, 1978.

De claris mulieribus, edited by Vittorio Zaccaria. 1967; as *Concerning Famous Women*, translated by Guido A. Guarino. 1963.

De casibus virorum illustrium, abridged as *The Fates of Illustrious Men*, translated by Louis Hall. 1965.

Il corbaccio, edited by Tauno Nurmela. 1968; as *The Corbaccio*, edited and translated by Anthony K. Cassell, 1975.

*

Bibliography: *Linee di una storia della critica al Decameron. Con bibliografia boccaccesca completemente e aggiornata* by Vittore Branca, 1939; *Boccacciana: Bibliografia delle edizioni e degli scritti critici 1939–1974* by Enzo Esposito, 1976; *Giovanni Boccaccio: An Annotated Bibliography* by Joseph P. Consoli, 1992.

Critical Studies: *Boccaccio: A Biographical Study* by E. Hutton, 1910; *The Life of Giovanni Boccaccio* by Thomas C. Chubb, 1930; *The Tranquil Heart: Portrait of Giovanni Boccaccio* by Catherine Carswell, 1937; *Boccaccio* by Francis MacManus, 1947; *Boccaccio in England from Chaucer to Tennyson* by Herbert G. Wright, 1957; *Nature and Love in the Middle Ages: An Essay on the Cultural Context of the Decameron* by Aldo D. Scaglione, 1963; *An Anatomy of Boccaccio's Style*, 1968, and *Order from Chaos: Social and Aesthetic Harmonies in Boccaccio's Decameron*, 1982, both by Marga Cottino-Jones; *The Writer as Liar: Narrative Technique in the 'Decameron'* by Guido Almansi, 1975; *Nature and Reason in the Decameron* by Robert Hastings, 1975; *Critical Perspectives on the Decameron* edited by Robert S. Dombrowski, 1976; *Boccaccio: The Man and His Works* by Vittore Branca, translated by Richard Monges, 1976, and *Boccaccio medievale e nuovi studi sul Decameron* by Branca, 1986; *Boccaccio's Two Venuses*, 1977, and *Boccaccio's Last Fiction: Il Corbaccio*, 1989, both by Robert Hollander; *Studies on Petrarch and Boccaccio* by Ernest H. Wilkins, 1978; *An Allegory of Form: Literary Self-Consciousness in the Decameron* by Millicent Joy Marcus, 1979; *Boccaccio* by Thomas G. Bergin, 1981; *Five Frames for the Decameron: Communication and Social Systems in the Cornice* by Joy Hambuechen Potter, 1982; *Giovanni Boccaccio* by Judith Powers Serafini-Sauli, 1982; *Religion and the Clergy in Boccaccio's Decameron* by Cormac O'Cuilleanáin, 1984; *Chaucer and the Early Writings of Boccaccio* by David Wallace, 1985; *Boccaccio and Fiammetta: The Narrator as Lover* by Janet Levarie Smarr, 1986; *The World at Play in Boccaccio's Decameron* by Giuseppe Mazzotta, 1986; *Before the Knight's Tale: Imitation of Classical Epic in Boccaccio's Teseida* by David Anderson, 1988; *The Shades of Aeneas: The Imitation of Vergil and the History of Paganism in Boccaccio's Filostrato, Filocolo and Teseida* by James H. MacGregor, 1991; *Ambiguity and Illusion in Boccaccio's Filocolo* by Steven Grossvogel, 1992.

* * *

Boccaccio's literary production is characterized by an unusual versatility; his work, both in prose and verse, contains a variety of genres, many of which were pioneer ventures, destined to exercise a powerful influence on succeeding generations. His essay in the field of narrative in verse was *La caccia di Diana* [Diana's Hunt], an allegory of love, designed, it would seem, to memorialize the glamorous ladies of the Neapolitan court. It is a very 'Dantean' composition, written in *terza rima* and with numerous echoes of *Commedia* (*The Divine Comedy*); it is a trifle but a well-constructed trifle. Of the same period is *Il filocolo* (*Thirteen Questions of Love*), a prose romance of Byzantine stamp composed, the author tells us, in honour of his 'Fiammetta', the Neapolitan siren who charmed and betrayed him. Called by some critics 'the first prose romance in European literature', *Thirteen Questions of Love* is long and digressive; although the central characters are of royal blood, the peripatetic plot anticipates the picaresque. For all its rhetoric and prolixity the narrative is well told and the characters in the main believable. This cumbrous initiative was followed by *Il filostrato* (*The Filostrato*), telling in *ottava rima* of the ill-starred love of the Trojan prince Troiolo for the faithless Criseida. It is a skilfully planned composition, set forth with economy, and successful in its depiction of characters; the romantic prince is artfully paired with the worldly Pandaro, his friend and counsellor. *Il Teseida* (*The Book of Theseus*), which followed a few years later, is, in spite of its Greek title and background, essentially a medieval work; the 'epic' is actually a love story. All of these early productions reflect the feudal tastes of the Neapolitan court.

A change of inspiration becomes evident in the works written after Boccaccio's return to Tuscany in 1341. *L'ameto* is a moralizing allegory, combining prose and verse (as had Dante's *La vita nuova*) yet the use of 'frame' to serve as a background for moralizing tales (paradoxically erotic in tone) points to *The Decameron*. In *L'amorosa visione* [Vision of Love] (a somewhat confused allegory) the presence of Dante is even more patent. *Elegia di Madonna Fiammetta* (*The Elegy of Lady Fiammetta*), which follows, is by contrast, original and strikingly 'modern'—one might say timeless. The abandoned Fiammetta, who tells in her own words (in prose) of her misplaced obsession for a false lover, though somewhat prolix, wins our sympathy. In one sense the *Fiammetta* is a reversion, for the background is Naples. Truly Tuscan, on the other hand, is the charming idyll *Il ninfale fiesolano* (*The Nymph of Fiesole*). With winning simplicity in *ottava rima* of unpretentious construction, the story is told of a simple shepherd and his beloved 'nymph of Diana' who is in effect a simple *contadina*.

The Decameron, Boccaccio's masterpiece, marks a new departure in the author's trajectory. We deal no more with Trojan princes or even woodland nymphs—we have left Naples for good, and allegory has no part in the author's intention (though it must be conceded that in the flight of the narrators of the 'frame' from the plague-stricken city one can argue some implications regarding the relation of art to its subject matter). The essential feature of *The Decameron* is realism; the world of the tales is the world of here and now. The demographic range is wide: it includes not only lords and princes but merchants, bankers, doctors, scholars, peasants, priests, monks—and a surprising number of women. A token of the feminist thrust of the work may be seen in the fact that seven of the ten 'frame characters' or narrators are women. All of the actors in this extensive comedy are presented deftly, with sympathetic tolerance for their motivation and participant relish in their adventures, vicissitudes, and resourceful stratagems. If the work is without didactic intent— 'Boccaccio doesn't want to teach us anything', the Italian critic Umberto Bosco has justly observed—yet the nature of its substance carries its own implications. *The Decameron* is democratic, feminist, and *au fond* optimistic. No doubt heaven is our destination but life can be joyous too, given a certain amount of wit and adaptability. Only in the last day does a kind of medievalism creep in, as the author sets before us a series of *exempla*, signifying sundry abstract virtues. Yet the narratives told even on that day are set forth with skill and verve and without undue lingering on their moralizing purpose; Griselda, for example, may seem an absurdly morbid creature (as in fact she does to some of the frame characters), but her story is told with a *brio* that compels the reader's attention. As entertaining today as when it was written, Boccaccio's great work both reflects and inspires a new appreciation of the human pilgrimage.

Save for *Il corbaccio*, a violent misogynistic satire, *The Decameron* is the last work of a creative nature to issue from Boccaccio's pen—and the last work in the vernacular as well. Moved by the example of Petrarch, he put aside fiction and turned to exercises in erudition, notably the massive compilation of the *De genealogia deorum gentilium* [The Genealogies of the Gentile Gods], an encyclopedia that would serve scholars for generations to come, and the catalogue of rivers, lakes, and mountains, both composed in Latin, as were his *Eclogues* (*Buccolicum Carmen*), patently in imitation of his revered master. After *The Decameron*, too, a certain inner spiritual change is apparent in the hitherto worldly Boccaccio; he took holy orders, and although the instinct for story-telling was still strong—witness *La vita di Dante* (*The Life of Dante*) and *De claris mulieribus* (*Concerning Famous Women*)—it was clearly affected by his new outlook on life. A letter suggests even a repudiation of *The Decameron*. His last work, and one of importance to Dantists, was his exposition of *The Divine Comedy*, a series of lectures given in Florence.

Many of Boccaccio's creative works are seminal: *The Book of Theseus* foreshadows the Renaissance epic, *The Filostrato* has left a trail of progeny ranging from Chaucer through Shakespeare to many contemporary writers. *The Nymph of Fiesole* has 15th-century echoes. And *The Decameron* has had many imitators. Boccaccio's contribution to the literature of the Western world is of impressive and all but unique dimensions.

—Thomas G. Bergin

THE NINTH TALE OF THE FIFTH DAY OF THE DECAMERON
Story by Giovanni Boccaccio, 1470 (written 1349–1351).

The Ninth Tale of the Fifth Day of *The Decameron* combines two of the leading strands of Boccaccio's masterpiece: love and fortune. Fortune, however, is not conceived as the medieval ancilla of God's providence but as the erratically pagan force, and love is not presented in a familiar, fleshy, and saucy manner but rather on the courtly or *stilnovistic* conception on which the story is based: a conception, of course, which belongs not to the time of the writing but to the preceding age, where nine-tenths of the events and characters of all the tales come from.

Boccaccio succeeds in distancing the events of this tale even further from the present by placing them in an atmosphere of legend: in fact, Federigo, the protagonist, is a descendant of the Alberighi, one of the most ancient Florentine families, a family which Dante Alighieri's great-great-grandfather Cacciaguida mentions as noble in *Paradise* (XVI, 89). The name itself evoked for Boccaccio's contemporaries, more than for us, perhaps, a life where courtly love was possible. This chronological and imaginative distance is paralleled by a formal, aesthetic detachment: Filomena, the narrator, declares she will recount one 'among the beautiful things' told by Coppo di Borghese Domenichi, who not only was an 'excellent person . . . revered more for his manners and virtues than for his nobility of blood' but could also speak 'better and in a more orderly way . . . and with more ornate speech than anyone else'.

The stage is set for a romance, beautifully told. Federigo, the most accomplished young man in all of Tuscany, falls in love with Monna Giovanna, one of the most beautiful and graceful ladies in Florence. Boccaccio describes both of them as *gentile* (noble) which cannot fail to remind the reader of Guinizelli's and Dante's theories of love, and especially of Guinizelli's famous line, 'Al cor gentil repara sempre Amore', the first verse of the *canzone*-manifesto of the *Stilnovo*. We are told that Federigo falls in love, 'as often *avviene* (happens)' to a noble heart: there is a sense of fairy-tale inevitability, of enchantment or curse; only in choosing Monna Giovanna instead of someone else does his choice appear an act of will. In fact, the verb *avvenire* (to happen) will be a refrain in the story. All the main events are introduced by it or by a circumlocution. Fortune dominates the will of man, though a happy love story requires that 'voluntary element' by which medieval courtly ladies distinguish marriage from love. Monna Giovanna, 'not less chaste than beautiful', cannot be conquered by Federigo's jousts, tourneys, and feasts.

The defining characteristic of the medieval lord with a noble heart is his liberality: largesse implied a disregard for the material and a preference for the lofty. Federigo squanders all his riches for Monna Giovanna save his falcon, 'among the best in the world'. No longer able to afford city life, he goes to live on his small farm near Florence, where he spends his days hawking, 'patiently endur[ing] his poverty'. The falcon, a well-known symbol of victory over passion, is a metaphor of Federigo's contemplative life.

From this point in the story, however, Fortune rules. Immediately after learning of Federigo's poverty, we are told '[n]ow it happened' (*[o]ra* avvenne) that Monna Giovanna's husband, near death, left his patrimony to his wife 'if it happened' (*se avvenisse*) that their only child died without heir. After his death, Giovanna passes the summer in the Florentine countryside in one of her farms 'very close' to Federigo's. So 'it happened' (*avvenne*) that her son grew friendly with Federigo and much admired his falcon. When later 'it happened' (*avvenne*) that the boy got very sick, he asked his mother for the falcon. After some hesitation, Monna Giovanna decides to go to Federigo, but instead of behaving as a mother whose only child is near death, she presents herself with 'womanly charm' (*donnesca piacevolezza*). She says she has come to dine with him to 'make amends for the damage he suffered' because of her. Still devoted to her beauty, Federigo's noble answer is in content and style that of a *stilnovistic* poet: she has done him 'no damage but so much good that if he was ever worth anything it was owing to her worth and the love she bore it'. His speech is so lofty that it includes three hendecasyllables. His lordly largesse induces him to sacrifice his falcon, the only 'food worthy such a lady'. When their reciprocal misunderstanding is discovered, Federigo sighs that he 'shall never know peace of mind again', whereas Mona Giovanna scolds him 'for having killed such a falcon to make a meal for a woman', however inwardly she commends his magnanimity.

After her son's death, her brothers push her, since she is 'very rich and still young', to remarry. 'Remembering Federigo's worthiness and generosity', Monna Giovanna agrees to marry only the very poor Federigo. *Amor vincit omnia*, including Fortune; determinism seems to have been broken by will. In the beginning Federigo chooses Monna Giovanna for her beauty; in the end Monna Giovanna chooses Federigo for his magnanimity. Exceptionally, marriage and love are united in a tale appropriate to the Fifth Day on which 'tales are told of those lovers who won happiness after grief and misfortune'.

The tale's rich texture is not limited to the enveloping literary tradition of courtly love. As in all of *The Decameron*, one can perceive what critics call Boccaccio's 'narrative contemporanization': he imbues his pages with the cultural myths and social structures of his time. In the tale of Federigo and his falcon, contemporaneity is suggested by the name of a Florentine family and more specifically by such routine details as the expense of living in Florence, the particulars of a last will, and the summer customs of Florentine ladies. Nevertheless, one must invoke 'realism' cautiously in a tale where the combined lines required to kill off a father and his child are far fewer than those used to kill off a falcon.

At tale's end Federigo has become a *miglior massaio* (a more prudent administrator). Such routine information would be unimaginable in a love story of old. Only in a society of merchants, bankers, and incipient capitalism can it make any sense, although the detail can be read as a parody of courtly love: magnanimous, open-handed, and carefree Federigo becomes just another burgher. This detail also mocks the new ideals of Boccaccio's society. It is an ironic thrust aimed at those of his contemporaries much too interested in materiality, as if to say that the chivalrous ideal and the poetic ideal are no longer possible, just as liberality is no longer possible, and that all that remains is the prudent administration of property.

—Emanuele Licastro

BOETHIUS. Born Anicius Manlius Severinus Boethius, probably in Rome, c.AD 480. Married to Rusticiana; two sons. Consul under the Ostrogothic King Theodoric, 510; head of government and court services (*magister officiorum*), 520; accused of treason, practising magic, and sacrilege: sentence ratified by the Senate, and he was imprisoned near Pavia, 522. Also a Hellenist: translator (with commentary) of works of Aristotle, Plato, and Porphyry. *Died (executed) in AD 524.*

PUBLICATIONS

Collections

[Works], edited by J.P. Migne, in *Patrologia Latina.*, vols. 63–64. 2 vols., 1847.
The Theological Tractates and The Consolation of Philosophy [Loeb Edition], translated by S.J. Tester, H.F. Stewart, and E.K. Rand. 1918, revised edition, 1973.

Works

De arithmetica, De musica, edited by G. Friedlein. 1867.
De consolatione philosophiae (prose and verse), edited by Rudolph Peiper. 1871; also edited by A. Fortescue and G.D. Smith, 1925, G. Weinburger, 1934, and Ludwig Bieler, 1957; as *The Consolation of Philosophy*, translated by 'I.T.', 1609, revised by H.F. Stewart [Loeb Edition], with *Tractates*, 1918; also translated by Richard Green, 1963; V.E. Watts, 1969; R.W. Sharples, 1992; commentaries by H. Scheible, 1972, J. Gruber, 1978, and J.J. O'Donnell, 1984.
De divisione, edited by Paulus Maria de Loe. 1913.

De institutione musica, as *Fundamentals of Music*, translated by Calvin H. Bower. 1989.

De syllogismo hypothetico, edited by Luca Obertello. 1969.

De topicis differentiis, translated by Eleanore Stump. 1978.

In Ciceronis topica, edited by J.C. Orelli and G. Baiterus, in *Ciceronis opera*, vol. 5, pt 1. 1833; translated by Eleanore Stump, 1988.

In Isagogen, edited by Samuel Brandt. 1906.

In Perihermeneias, edited by Carl Meiser. 1880.

Tractates, edited and translated by E. Rapisarda. 1960; as *Tractates* [Loeb Edition], translated by H.F. Stewart and E.K. Rand, with *The Consolation of Philosophy*, 1918.

[Commentaries on *De interpretatione* by Aristotle], edited by Carl Meiser. 2 vols., 1877–80.

[Commentaries on Porphyry], edited by G. Schepss and Samuel Brandt. 1906; translated by E.W. Warren, 1975.

Translator, *Categoriae, De interpretatione, Analytica priora, Topica, Elenchi sophistici*, by Aristotle, edited by Lorenzo Minio-Paluello, in *Aristoteles Latinus*. 1961– .

*

Critical Studies: *The Tradition of Boethius: A Study of His Importance in Mediaeval Culture* by Howard R. Patch, 1935; *Boethius: Some Aspects of His Times and Works* by Helen M. Barrett, 1940; *Poetic Diction in the Old English Meters of Boethius* by Allan A. Metcalf, 1973; *Boethian Fictions: Narratives in the Medieval French* by Richard A. Dwyer, 1976; *Boethius and the Liberal Arts: A Collection of Essays* edited by Michael Masi, 1981; *Boethius: His Life, Thought, and Influence* edited by Margaret Gibson, 1981; *Boethius: The Consolations of Music, Logic, Theology, and Philosophy* by Henry Chadwick, 1981; *The Tradition of the Topics in the Middle Ages: The Commentaries on Aristotle's and Boethius' Topics* by Niels Jørgen Green-Pedersen, 1984; *Boethius and Dialogue: Literary Method in The Consolation of Philosophy* by Seth Lerer, 1985; *The Fate of Fortune in the Early Middle Ages: The Boethian Tradition* by Jerold C. Frakes, 1988; *Boethius on Signification and Mind* by John C. Magee, 1989; *The Poetry of Boethius* by Gerard O'Daly, 1991; *The Consolation of Boethius: An Analytical Inquiry into His Intellectual Processes and Goals* by Stephen Varvis, 1991; *Chaucer's 'Boece' and the Medieval Tradition of Boethius* edited by A.J. Minnis, 1993.

* * *

As a member of the Roman senatorial class, which still kept its identity in the barbarian Italy of c.AD 500, Boethius expected to hold political and ceremonial office: he was consul and (fatally) *magister officiorum*, the dispenser of patronage at Theodoric's court in Ravenna. But most of his time was his own. He lived in his town house and his country estates immersed in his books, and also entertaining his friends: see Sidonius Apollinaris' letters and poems on the life of 'senatorial ease' in Roman Gaul in the later 5th century. It was for these friends and protegés of his own family and class that Boethius wrote his literary and scholarly works. He was no schoolmaster, no compiler of encyclopedias, dependent on an unknown popular audience.

Boethius' interest in language and the structure of argument is seen in his many studies of logic and rhetoric. He translated some key texts from the Greek, and much of his analysis derived from Greek writers and teachers in the universities of Athens and Alexandria. These translations gave readers who knew only Latin access to mainstream philosophical discussion. In the same way Boethius' highly technical writing on mathematics and musical theory made Greek thought available to a Roman audience. That is the context for his 'papers'—they are too brief to be called books —on Christian doctrine: Boethius' careful definitions have a solid basis in Greek philosophy.

His masterpiece, *De consolatione philosophiae* (*The Consolation of Philosophy*), is his most readable and literary work. He had been informed on by his enemies and faced almost certain death. Could he face it? He argues through issue after conflicting issue, still the practised logician: but now he himself is a term in the problem. Why me? Why do the wicked prosper? Doesn't God care? Can God care? His partner in the argument is the Lady Philosophy, who is the traditional literary, mathematical, and philosophical learning to which he has devoted most of his life. Later readers thought of her as the Wisdom of the Old Testament: 'Wisdom hath builded her house, she hath hewn out her seven pillars'. But Boethius is not so easily brought into line. His argument with himself in *The Consolation of Philosophy* reaches the point of an omniscient God, who is fully in control of the universe. Because it is an argument—rather than, for example, a vision or a confession—it *can* go no further. *The Consolation of Philosophy* stops short of the Christianity in which Boethius, judging by his theological papers (above), was an informed believer.

Boethius was executed in 524. His books seem to have lain undisturbed until about the time of Charlemagne (c.800), when Alcuin and succeeding medieval scholars with little or no Greek read and transcribed and discussed this treasury of material on argument and on mathematics. Above all they welcomed *The Consolation*, in which the great questions of justice, chance, and freedom were analysed by the man who, in a changed intellectual climate, was now regarded as 'Boethius, the Christian philosopher'.

—Margaret Gibson

THE CONSOLATION OF PHILOSOPHY (De consolatione philosophiae)
Prose and verse by Boethius, early 6th century.

The Consolation of Philosophy is the spiritual and psychological autobiography of Boethius, written while its author was in prison awaiting execution for treason. Composed in the form of the so-called Menippean satire, with alternating sections of prose and poetry, the work also conforms to the generic dictates of the classical consolation and the dialogue style made famous by Plato. Generically a composite, *The Consolation* takes shape most substantially as a dialogue, however, for in the ongoing debate bruited between Boethius and Lady Philosophy much of *The Consolation*'s wisdom emerges. Appearing to him at the work's opening as the guide Boethius seeks in his time of sorrow, the task of Lady Philosophy is to lead Boethius to heart-wholeness, to freedom, and to the mental and spiritual consonances that proffer happiness.

To achieve this end, several preliminary tasks are required. First Lady Philosophy asks Boethius to consider the distinctive activities Fortune pursues. That consideration serves as the foil for much of *The Consolation*'s subsequent arguments about true, as against chance, happiness. Then, although Boethius has suffered a grievous blow to his social and physical well-being, Lady Philosophy shifts the burden of her argument for happiness entirely to the mental realm, ratifying the focus of her task under the rubrics of spirituality and psychology. Owing to the initial questions raised by Boethius, Lady Philosophy then finds it necessary to affirm the implicit order of all creation, an order, it seems, not easily discerned by humanity's imperfect vision, and an order condensed at the work's opening in the dilemma now facing Boethius whose very life hangs in the balance.

While the present dilemma of Boethius forms the backdrop against which *The Consolation* takes shape, the work develops along its own internal logic, and turns increasingly to consider the problems it raises from more abstract and formally philosophical angles. The necessity to articulate the nature and qualities of human happiness, for example, are presently considered from the wiser purview of Lady Philosophy herself, at a distance from Boethius' sorrowful plight. In the event, as Lady Philosophy makes clear, only a level-headed, logical approach of the kind she is about to offer can proffer to Boethius the sort of mental hygiene he seeks. Wallowing in his problems will only serve to make matters worse.

It is hard to be happy because happiness is not an obvious quality of human existence. Indeed, there are two kinds of happiness, chance happiness and true happiness, the former governed by those things that are subject to change, the latter by those things such as emotions and ideas that abide in and out of time. True happiness, in the event, is governed by a larger principle, divine love, articulated poetically in Book II as the acme of divine order. That order, written on the heart of humanity, is all that humans require, for happy would be 'the race of men/if the love [*amor*] by which heaven is ruled/ruled your hearts'.

Love is good and, in its third book, *The Consolation* articulates the central place that love holds in the attainment of true happiness. Humankind holds a variety of mistaken notions of happiness, Lady Philosophy repeats. Neither wealth, nor high office, nor power, nor fame, nor bodily pleasure, are paths by which true happiness is attained, ' . . . because they can neither produce the good they promise nor come to perfection by the combination of all good'. The essential ingredient in the attainment of happiness is the comprehension of one's own self-sufficiency, grounded in the cosmic notion of unity, articulated poetically near the mid-point of Book III. The superb and timeless coherence of God's creation symbolizes the potential for humans to participate with God. The unity obtained through participation with divinity forms the key ingredient in the therapy by which true happiness is achieved.

If love is good, then evil is not, and the problems presented by evil require attention. The good are always strong, Lady Philosophy tells Boethius, and the evil always lack power. Moreover, the good seek what is good in the proper way, for which reason they are happy, while the evil seek what is good in a perverse and, therefore, ineffective way, which explains their depravity. More than being unable to achieve the happiness they seek but do not know how to find, those who are evil do not exist, according to Lady Philosophy, because 'a thing exists when it keeps its proper place and preserves its own nature. Anything which departs from this ceases to exist, because its existence depends on the preservation of its nature'.

However, a fundamental difficulty remains in Lady Philosophy's presentation. Having staked so much of her argument on the consonance and implicit order of God's creation, Lady Philosophy must now explain how order can be defended in the face of the patent disorder of human affairs. She addresses herself to this problem by positing the nurturing oversight of God's thought, which she calls Providence, and the unfolding of those thoughts in time and space, which she calls Fate. Fate, which proceeds in the cosmic order from Providence, appears to those who experience it to be disjointed, disconnected, now chaotic, now inchoate. But it is, Lady Philosophy asserts, part of the divine and abiding order of God. 'Whenever, therefore, you see something happen here different from your expectation, due order is preserved by events, but there is confusion and error in your thinking.'

This affirmation of cosmic unity brings Lady Philosophy around full-circle at the conclusion of Book IV, for Fortune is recalled by her there as a means to enjoin Boethius to 'the middle way', a way depicted by negation in Poem Seven, where the immoderate histories of Agamemnon, Odysseus, and Hercules are recounted as a means to embolden the truly strong to be on their way. This injunction is squarely a function of self-knowledge, the focus of *The Consolation* from its opening lines. It is fitting, therefore, for Book V to deal with the problems of divine knowledge and for it to conclude with an explanation of God's perfect ability to know. However, human self-knowledge is no less glorious, even if it is imperfect by comparison to God's providential consciousness. Because it is itself a reflection of God's intimate and all-expansive intellect, it is a profound and beautiful thing in its own right, offering a wisdom which eventually supercedes the bounds of its own language, the surest measure of its success:

> Go now, ye strong, where the exalted way
> Of great examples leads. Why hang you back?
> Why turn away? Once earth has been surpassed
> It gives the stars.

—Joseph Pucci

BOILEAU (-Despréaux), Nicolas. Born in Paris, France, 1 November 1636. Educated at Collège d'Harcourt, Paris, 1643–48; Collège de Beauvais, Paris, 1648–52; studied law, University of Paris, 1652–56; admitted to the bar 1656. Writer from 1657: slowly achieved a reputation; friend of Molière, Racine, La Fontaine; favoured by the court from 1674; historiographer to Louis XIV (with Racine), 1677. Member, Académie française, 1684. *Died 13 March 1711.*

PUBLICATIONS

Collections

Works, translated by Nicholas Rowe. 3 vols., 1711–13.
Oeuvres complètes, edited by Charles-H. Boudhors. 7 vols., 1932–43.
Oeuvres complètes, edited by Françoise Escal. 1966.

Verse

Satires (12). 1666–1711; edited by A. Adam, 1941; translated as *Satires*, 1904.

Épîtres (12). 1670–98; edited by A. Cahen, 1937.
Oeuvres diverses. 1674; enlarged edition, 1683.
L'Art poétique, in *Oeuvres diverses.* 1674; edited by V. Delaporte, 3 vols., 1888; as *The Art of Poetry,* translated by William Soames (in verse), 1683; revised edition by John Dryden, 1710.
Le Lutrin. 1674–83; translated by Nicholas Rowe, 1708.

Other

L'Arrêt burlesque. 1671.
Réflexions sur Longin. 1694; as *On Longinus,* edited by John Ozell. 1972.
Selected Criticism, translated by Ernest Dilworth. 1965.

Translator, *Traité du sublime,* by Longinus, in *Oeuvres diverses.* 1674.

*

Critical Studies: *Boileau and the Classical Critics in England* by Alexander F.B. Clark, 1925; *Racine and the 'Art Poétique' of Boileau* by Sister M. Haley, 1938; *Boileau and Longinus* by Jules Brody, 1958; *Pour le commentaire linguistique de l'Art poétique* by John Orr, 1963; *Boileau* by Julian Eugene White, Jr, 1969; *Boileau and the Nature of Neo-Classicism* by Gordon Pocock, 1980.

* * *

Although Nicolas Boileau's fame has rested as much on his reputation as high-priest of French classicism as on his poetry, it is doubtful whether he added much to the critical ideas of his day, or significantly influenced his contemporaries.

His literary personality is complex. His iconoclasm comes out strongly in his early satires, and remains in his later work, even when he was in favour at Court. His early series of *Satires* (I–IX) is concerned with literary and social themes. In his social satires (I, III, IV, V, VI, and VIII), he often paints with representational detail, but his comic exuberance lifts them well beyond realism. In the literary satires, he is less a critic of specific authors than a creator of startling images of poetry at war with dunces. The best of his satires (especially VII and IX) are dramatic in method. They bring together with kaleidoscopic brilliance wit, word-play, eloquence, and straight-speaking, leading the reader to heightened awareness of his responses which transcends the often banal content. The first series of *Epistles* (I–IX) is frequently plainer and more didactic, but even those addressed to Louis XIV (the *Discourse to the King,* Epistles I, *IV,* and *VIII*) mix humour with seriousness. *Epistles VII* and *IX,* on literary themes, express poignantly Boileau's sense of the high role of poetry, and its vulnerability in the face of ignorance and barbarism.

His verse *L'Art poétique (The Art of Poetry)* is on the surface an assertion of the Classical demand for rationalism and craftsmanship, with summaries of the neo-Aristotelian rules for different kinds of poem. More fundamentally, however, it demonstrates again Boileau's use of verbal dexterity (it is full of puns) to dramatize the effect of good and bad poetry on the reader. The mock-heroic *Le Lutrin* [The Lectern] is in lighter vein, but dazzles by its mixture of comedy with genuine grandeur.

His later works show a slackening of verve. The best are the long *Satire X* [On Women] in which some of the portraits recapture his earlier mordant vigour, and *Epistles X* and *XI,*

in which he skilfully represents himself as a man of honest but endearing simplicity. The last works, much concerned with theological disputes, are clumsily written and hectoring in tone.

Boileau's lyrics have little merit. His ambitious *Ode on the Capture of Namur* fails to accommodate in lyric form his mixture of grandiloquence and satire. Of his prose, the early *L'Arrêt burlesque* [Mock Edict] is the liveliest, with its exuberant satire on official hostility to new ideas. His translation of Longinus with his *Remarks* and *Reflections* on it and his 1701 preface to his works, gave him the opportunity to reassert the moral and aesthetic dignity of poetry, against what he saw as the triviality and decadence of his contemporaries. Of his work as historiographer to Louis XIV (a post he shared with Racine) only a few occasional pieces remain. His surviving letters, mainly from his old age, display his passionate and quirky temperament.

—Gordon Pocock

THE ART OF POETRY (L'Art poétique)
Poem by Nicolas Boileau, 1674.

Boileau's long four-part poem, *The Art of Poetry,* was first published in France in 1674, and in its trenchant style and vigorous argument it laid out the terms of neo-classical criticism in the most accessible and influential way. Along with Rapin's *Réflexions sur la Poétique et les Poètes* [Reflections on Poetics and Poets] from the same year, and Le Bossu's *Traité du Poème épique* [Treatise on the Epic] (1675), Boileau's poem disseminated and consolidated a set of aesthetic principles that dominated European writing and critical thinking for at least 50 years. As the name 'neo-classical' suggests, Boileau looks back to the writers of Greece and Rome for critical guidance and authority, but he does so in a less deferential and systematic form than Rapin, and his views overall seem less doctrinaire than pragmatic.

In the earlier part of the poem, Boileau reviews the history of French writing up to the present day, wittily cataloguing the continually difficult task of being a poet, and gently pointing out the failings and limitations of his French predecessors, including Malherbe and Villon. The problem, as he formulates it at the beginning, lies in the relationship between form and content, in the conflicts that arise between meaning and technique:

> Quelque sujet qu'on traite, ou plaisant, ou sublime
> Que toujours le bon sens s'accorde avec la rime:
> L'un l'autre vainement ils semblent se hair
> La Rime est une esclave, et ne doit qu'obéir
>
> (Whatever one's subject, be it light or sublime
> Let good sense and rhyme be in accord:
> Although they seem to be at odds,
> Rhyme is but a slave, and must obey.)

The guiding light for any poet must always be 'la raison' for reason alone can arbitrate between the competing claims of an over-ornate and an excessively prosaic style. Throughout the opening canto, Boileau offers a number of bits of equally pragmatic advice, hoping to encourage and advise fledgling writers, after the fashion of his eminent predecessor Horace.

The critique of contemporary writing is developed in Canto II through an elaborate and stylized discussion of the various poetic genres. In pastoral, Boileau claims, too many poets err regularly on the side of bombast or mundanity, and lack the requisite knowledge of Virgil and Theocritus that would show them the middle path. In the elegy, Boileau expresses his distaste for those poets whose emotions, over-calculated, come over as frigid. For them, he recommends the study of Tibullus and Ovid, masters of the correct statement. In the ode, the epigram, and the satire (of which Boileau himself was an influential writer), similar failings can be found, and the cure is always the same: study the classics, particularly those recognized as having excelled in particular genres, and learn from them.

Canto III gives more developed consideration of tragedy and the epic, offering the same advice and providing an extended critique of contemporary acting styles. The conclusion remains the same: read Sophocles and Homer, and admire their workmanship as much as their genius:

> Un poème excellent, où tout marche et se suit
> N'est pas de ces travaux gu'un caprice produit:
> Il veut du temps, des soins, et ce pénible ouvrage
> Jamais d'un écolier ne fut l'apprentissage.

> (A fine poem, whose every part functions and fits in
> Is not the product of a whim:
> It demands time and careful effort:
> Such a difficult task is not for a tyro.)

The argument thus sees poetry as a craft, reliant not wholly on inspiration, but on skills and learning. Yet Boileau is neither dismissive of 'genius' nor wholly deferential to the classical masters. It is most important to see that he recommends imitation of their work not for its own sake, but because they are demonstrably better-equipped to deal with nature, the goal of all writing. And only the contemporary writer of genius knows how to imitate properly.

In the fourth and final canto of the poem, the negotiation between genius and learning continues, and Boileau seeks to enhance the status of poetry by comparing it with other activities. In poetry, there cannot be, as there may in all other arts and crafts, degrees of competence, only absolute success or failure in any of the specialized genres. There follows, as in Alexander Pope's An Essay on Criticism (1711), which was influenced heavily by Boileau, a ringing catalogue of maxims, designed to encourage the poet's high-mindedness and the pursuit of excellence. So alongside the recommendation to learn the tools of the poetic trade, Boileau's poem also defends the genius of the great writer. The poem ends with a patriotic call to Boileau's fellow writers to live up to the models of the classical authors, and a reminder that good writers need equally good critics.

The poem quickly became influential, and its less rigorous defence of the classics gave it strong currency. As it advises and recommends rather than commands, it falls into the more relaxed end of neo-classical thinking. It was known throughout Europe within a few years of publication, being first translated into English by Sir William Soames in 1683. Soames's translation was adapted by John Dryden, who described Boileau as 'a living Horace and a Juvenal' and Boileau's influence on English writers of the early 18th-century was considerable.

—Ian A. Bell

BÖLL, Heinrich (Theodor). Born in Cologne, Germany, 21 December 1917. Educated at Gymnasium, Cologne; University of Cologne. Served in the German army, 1939–45; prisoner of war, 1945. Married Annemarie Cech in 1942; three sons. Joiner in his father's shop, then apprentice in the book trade before the war; full-time writer from 1947; co-editor, Labyrinth, 1960–61, and L, from 1976; president, PEN International, 1971–74. Recipient: Bundesverband der Deutschen Industrie grant; Gruppe 47 prize, 1951; Rene Schickele prize, 1952; Tribune de Paris prize, 1953; Prix du Meilleur Roman Étranger, 1955; Heydt prize, 1958; Bavarian Academy of Fine Arts award, 1958; Nordrhein-Westfalen prize, 1959; Veillon prize, 1960; Cologne prize, 1961; Elba prize, 1965; Büchner prize, 1967; Nobel prize for literature, 1972; Scottish Arts Council fellowship, 1973. Honorary degrees: D.Sc.: Aston University, Birmingham, 1973; O.Tech.: Brunel University, Uxbridge, Middlesex, 1973; Litt.D.: Trinity College, Dublin, 1973. Died 16 July 1985.

PUBLICATIONS

Fiction

Der Zug war pünktlich. 1949; as The Train Was on Time, translated by Richard Graves, 1956; also translated by Leila Vennewitz, 1973.
Wanderer, kommst du nach Spa. . . . 1950; as Traveller, If You Come to Spa, translated by Mervyn Savill, 1956.
Die schwarzen Schafe. 1951.
Wo warst du, Adam? 1951; as Adam, Where Art Thou?, translated by Mervyn Savill, 1955; as And Where Were You Adam?, translated by Leila Vennewitz, 1973.
Nicht nur zur Weihnachtszeit. 1952.
Und sagte kein einziges Wort. 1953; as Acquainted with the Night, translated by Richard Graves, 1954; as And Never Said a Word, translated by Leila Vennewitz, 1978.
Haus ohne Hüter. 1954; as Tomorrow and Yesterday, translated by Mervyn Savill, 1957; as The Unguarded House, translated by Savill, 1957.
Das Brot der frühen Jahre. 1955; as The Bread of Our Early Years, translated by Mervyn Savill, 1957; as The Bread of Those Early Years, translated by Leila Vennewitz, 1976.
So ward Abend und Morgen. 1955.
Unberechenbare Gäste: Heitere Erzählungen. 1956.
Im Tal der donnernden Hufe. 1957.
Doktor Murkes gesammelte Schweigen und andere Satiren. 1958.
Der Mann mit den Messern. 1958.
Die Waage der Baleks und andere Erzählungen. 1958.
Der Bahnhof von Zimpren. 1959.
Billard um halb zehn. 1959; as Billiards at Half-Past Nine, translated by Patrick Bowles, 1961.
Als der Krieg ausbrach, Als der Krieg zu Ende war. 1962; as Absent Without Leave (2 novellas), translated by Leila Vennewitz, 1965.
Ansichten eines Clowns. 1963; as The Clown, translated by Leila Vennewitz, 1965.
Entfernung von der Truppe. 1964.
Ende einer Dienstfahrt. 1966; as The End of a Mission, translated by Leila Vennewitz, 1967.
Eighteen Stories, translated by Leila Vennewitz. 1966.
Absent Without Leave and Other Stories, translated by Leila Vennewitz. 1967.
Geschichten aus zwölf Jahren. 1969.
Children Are Civilians Too (stories), translated by Leila Vennewitz. 1970.
Gruppenbild mit Dame. 1971; as Group Portrait with Lady, translated by Leila Vennewitz, 1973.

Der Mann mit den Messern: Erzählungen (selection). 1972.
Die verlorene Ehre der Katharina Blum. 1974; as *The Lost Honor of Katharina Blum*, translated by Leila Vennewitz, 1975.
Berichte zur Gesinnungslage der Nation. 1975.
Fürsorgliche Belagerung. 1979; as *The Safety Net*, translated by Leila Vennewitz, 1982.
Du fährst zu oft nach Heidelberg und andere Erzählungen. 1979.
Gesammelte Erzählungen. 2 vols., 1981.
Das Vermächtnis. 1982; as *A Soldier's Legacy*, translated by Leila Vennewitz, 1985.
Die Verwundung und andere frühe Erzählungen. 1983; as *The Casualty*, translated by Leila Vennewitz, 1986.
Der Angriff: Erzählungen 1947–1949. 1983.
Veränderungen in Staeck: Erzählungen 1962–1980. 1984.
Mein trauriges Gesicht: Erzählungen. 1984.
Frauen vor Flusslandschaft: Roman in Dialogen und Selbstgesprächen. 1985; as *Women in a River Landscape: A Novel in Dialogues and Soliloquies*, translated by David McLintock, 1988.
Stories, translated by Leila Vennewitz. 1986.
Der Engel schwieg. 1992.

Plays

Die Brücke von Berczaba (broadcast 1952). In *Zauberei auf dem Sender und andere Hörspiele*, 1962.
Der Heilige und der Räuber (broadcast 1953). In *Hörspielbuch des Nordwestdeutschen und Süddeutschen Rundfunks*, 4, 1953; as *Mönch und Räuber*, in *Erzählungen, Hörspiele, Aufsätze*, 1961.
Ein Tag wie sonst (broadcast 1953). 1980.
Zum Tee bei Dr. Borsig (broadcast 1955). In *Erzählungen, Hörspiele, Aufsätze*, 1961.
Eine Stunde Aufenthalt (broadcast 1957). In *Erzählungen, Hörspiele, Aufsätze*, 1961.
Die Spurlosen (broadcast 1957). 1957.
Bilanz (broadcast 1957). With *Klopfzeichen*, 1961.
Klopfzeichen (broadcast 1960). With *Bilanz*, 1961.
Ein Schluck Erde (produced 1961). 1962.
Zum Tee bei Dr. Borsig (includes *Mönch und Räuber*; *Eine Stunde Aufenthalt*; *Bilanz*; *Die Spurlosen*; *Klopfzeichen*; *Sprechanlage*; *Konzert für vier Stimmen*). 1964.
Hausfriedensbruch (broadcast 1969). 1969.
Aussatz (produced 1970). With *Hausfriedensbruch*, 1969.

Radio Plays: *Die Brücke von Berczaba*, 1952; *Ein Tag wie sonst*, 1953; *Der Heilige und der Räuber*, 1953; *Zum Tee bei Dr. Borsig*, 1955; *Anita und das Existenzminimum*, 1955, revised version, as *Ich habe nichts gegen Tiere*, 1958; *Die Spurlosen*, 1957; *Bilanz*, 1957; *Eine Stunde Aufenthalt*, 1957; *Die Stunde der Wahrheit*, 1958; *Klopfzeichen*, 1960; *Hausfriedensbruch*, 1969.

Verse

Gedichte. 1972.

Other

Irisches Tagebuch. 1957; as *Irish Journal*, translated by Leila Vennewitz, 1967.
Im Ruhrgebiet, photographs by Karl Hargesheimer. 1958.
Unter Krahnenbäumen, photographs by Karl Hargesheimer. 1958.

Menschen am Rhein, photographs by Karl Hargesheimer. 1960.
Brief an einen jungen Katholiken. 1961.
Erzählungen, Hörspiele, Aufsätze. 1961.
Assisi. 1962.
Hierzulande. 1963.
Frankfurter Vorlesungen. 1966.
Aufsätze, Kritiken, Reden. 1967.
Leben im Zustand des Frevels. 1969.
Neue politische und literarische Schriften. 1973.
Politische Meditationen zu Glück und Vergeblichkeit, with Dorothee Sölle. 1973.
Der Lorbeer ist immer noch bitter: Literarische Schriften. 1974.
Drei Tage in März, with Christian Linder. 1975.
Der Fall Staeck; oder, Wie politisch darf die Kunst sein?, with others. 1975.
Briefe zur Verteidigung der Republik, with Freimut Duve and Klaus Staeck. 1977.
Einmischung erwünscht: Schriften zur Zeit. 1977.
Missing Persons and Other Essays, translated by Leila Vennewitz. 1977.
Querschnitte: Aus Interviews, Aufsätzen, und Reden, edited by Viktor Böll and Renate Matthaei. 1977.
Werke, edited by Bernd Balzer. 10 vols., 1977–78.
Gefahren von falschen Brüdern: Politische Schriften. 1980.
Warum haben wir aufeinander geschossen?, with Lew Kopelew. 1981.
Rendezvous mit Margaret. Liebesgeschichten. 1981.
Was soll aus dem Jungen bloss werden?; oder, Irgendwas mit Büchern. 1981; as *What's to Become of the Boy?; or, Something to Do with Books* (memoir), translated by Leila Vennewitz, 1984.
Der Autor ist immer noch versteckt. 1981.
Vermintes Gelände: Essayistische Schriften 1977–1981. 1982.
Antikommunismus in Ost und West. 1982.
Ich hau dem Mädche nix jedonn, ich han et bloss ens kräje. Texte, Bilder, Dokumente zur Verteilung des Ehrenbürgerrechts der Stadt Köln, 29 April 1983. 1983.
Ein- und Zusprüche: Schriften, Reden und Prosa 1981–83. 1984.
Weil die Stadt so fremd geworden ist. 1985.
Bild-Bonn-Boenish. 1985.
Die Fähigkeit zu trauern: Schriften und Reden 1983–1985. 1986.
Denken mit Heinrich Böll. 1986.
Rom auf den ersten Blick. Landschaften, Städte, Reisen. 1987.

Editor, with Erich Kock, *Unfertig ist der Mensch*. 1967.
Editor, with Freimut Duve and Klaus Staeck, *Verantwortlich für Polen?*. 1982.

Translator, with Annemarie Böll:

Kein Name bei den Leuten [No Name in the Street], by Kay Cicellis. 1953.
Ein unordentlicher Mensch, by Adriaan Morriën. 1955.
Tod einer Stadt [Death of a Town], by Kay Cicellis. 1956.
Weihnachtsabend in San Cristobal [The Saintmaker's Christmas Eve], by Paul Horgan. 1956.
Zur Ruhe kam der Baum des Menschen nie [The Tree of Man], by Patrick White. 1957.
Der Teufel in der Wüste [The Devil in the Desert], by Paul Horgan. 1958.
Die Geisel [The Hostage], by Brendan Behan. 1958.
Der Mann von morgen früh [The Quare Fellow], by Brendan Behan. 1958.

Ein wahrer Held [The Playboy of the Western World], by J.M. Synge. 1960.

Die Boote fahren nicht mehr aus [The Islandman], by Tomás O'Crohan. 1960.

Eine Rose zur Weihnachtszeit [One Red Rose for Christmas], by Paul Horgan. 1960.

Der Gehilfe [The Assistant], by Bernard Malamud. 1960.

Kurz vor dem Krieg gegen die Eskimos, by J.D. Salinger. 1961.

Das Zauberfass [The Magic Barrel], by Bernard Malamud. 1962.

Der Fänger im Roggen [The Catcher in the Rye], by J.D. Salinger. 1962.

Ein Gutshaus in Irland [The Big House], by Brendan Behan, in *Stücke*. 1962.

Franny and Zooey, by J.D. Salinger. 1963.

Die Insel der Pferde [The Island of Horses], by Eilís Dillon. 1964.

Hebt den Dachbalken hoch, Zimmerleute; Seymour wird vorgestellt [Raise High the Roof Beam, Carpenters; Seymour: An Introduction], by J.D. Salinger. 1965.

Caesar und Cleopatra, by G.B. Shaw. 1965.

Der Spanner [The Scarperer], by Brendan Behan. 1966.

Die Insel des grossen John [The Coriander], by Eilís Dillon. 1966.

Das harte Leben [The Hard Life], by Flann O'Brien. 1966.

Neun Erzählungen [Nine Stories], by J.D. Salinger. 1966.

Die schwarzen Füchse [A Family of Foxes], by Eilís Dillon. 1967.

Die Irrfahrt der Santa Maria [The Cruise of the Santa Maria], by Eilís Dillon. 1968.

Die Springflut [The Sea Wall], by Eilís Dillon. 1969.

Seehunde SOS [The Seals], by Eilís Dillon. 1970.

Erwachen in Mississippi [Coming of Age in Mississippi], by Anne Moody. 1970.

Candida, Der Kaiser von Amerika, Mensch und Übermensch [Candida, The King of America, Man and Superman], by G.B. Shaw. 1970.

Handbuch des Revolutionärs, by G.B. Shaw. 1972.

*

Bibliography: *Heinrich Böll: Eine Bibliographie seiner Werke* by Werner Martin, 1975; *Der Schriftsteller Böll: Ein biographisch-bibliographischer Abriss* edited by Werner Lenging, 5th edition, 1977; *Heinrich Böll in America 1954–1970* by Ray Lewis White, 1979; *Heinrich Böll Auswahlbibliographie zur Primär- und Sekundärliteratur* edited by Gerhard Redemacher, 1989.

Critical Studies: *Böll, Teller of Tales: A Study of His Works and Characters* by Wilhelm Johannes Schwartz, 1969; *A Student's Guide to Böll* by Enid Macpherson, 1972; *Böll: Withdrawal and Re-Emergence*, 1973, and *Heinrich Böll: A German for His Time*, 1986, both by J.H. Reid; *The Major Works of Böll: A Critical Commentary* by Erhard Friedrichsmeyer, 1974; *The Writer and Society: Studies in the Fiction of Günter Grass and Heinrich Böll* by Charlotte W. Ghurye, 1976; *The Imagery in Böll's Novels* by Thor Prodaniuk, 1979; *Heinrich Böll* by Robert C. Conard, 1981; *Heinrich Böll* by Klaus Schröter, 1982; *Heinrich Böll and the Challenge of Literature* by Michael Butler, 1988.

*   *   *

More consistently than any of his contemporaries Heinrich Böll documented the development of the Federal Republic from its inception. In doing so he achieved the remarkable feat of becoming a best-selling author who was under constant attack from the popular press. His works are invariably provocative and the subject of critical disagreement in both academic and non-academic circles. Abroad he had a solid reputation as 'the good German' who unambiguously condemned fascism and the less appealing features of the land of the Economic Miracle. Sales of his books in Eastern Europe are still considerable and in the former Soviet Union he is one of the best-known Western writers.

Implicit in all his works is the theme of the individual under threat from impersonal forces of all kinds. In *Wo warst du, Adam?* (*And Where Were You Adam?*) and *Ende einer Dienstfahrt* (*The End of a Mission*) it is the war machine; in *Und sagte kein einziges Wort* (*And Never Said a Word*) and *Ansichten eines Clowns* (*The Clown*) it is the Roman Catholic church; in *Gruppenbild mit Dame* (*Group Portrait with Lady*) it is big business; in *Die verlorene Ehre der Katharina Blum* (*The Lost Honor of Katharina Blum*) and *Fürsorgliche Belagerung* (*The Safety Net*) it is the unholy empire of press and industry working hand in hand with the police. His standpoint is that of left-wing humanism tinged with a strong element of non-conformist, anti-clerical Catholicism. He was publicly involved in all the important issues of his day. Böll's particular literary strength lies in satire, the medium most suited to his conception of a literature which must in content be socially committed and in technique 'exaggerate' ('Second Wuppertal Speech', 1960), test the limits to artistic freedom by 'going too far' ('The Freedom of Art', 1966); it also relates to his notable sense of humour allied to his eye for the significant, absurd detail. His most memorable writings include those on the broadcaster who collects 'silences', the family which celebrates Christmas all the year round, and the man who is employed to defeat the packaging industry by *unpacking* goods for the customer.

Böll was essentially a writer of prose fiction—his few excursions into other genres were unsuccessful. He experimented in a moderate way with narrative techniques. In the 1950s his favourite form was the short story, that genre peculiarly suited to existentialist statement. His novels of these years are marked by a preoccupation with the phenomenon of time and make extensive play with fluctuating narrative perspectives. *Billard um halb zehn* (*Billiards at Half-Past Nine*) comes closest to the *nouveau roman* of the day. In the more politically charged atmosphere of the 1960s and later, his writing became deliberately more casual and direct, although the ironic play with the convention of a first-person biographer-narrator in *Group Portrait with Lady* betrays a continued concern for questions of form. It is interesting therefore that *The Safety Net* reverts to the peculiar narrative economy of the earlier works with its condensation of narrated time and its use of multiple limited points of view.

—J.H. Reid

GROUP PORTRAIT WITH LADY (Gruppenbild mit Dame)
Novel by Heinrich Böll, 1971.

Group Portrait with Lady, published in 1971, was Böll's most commercially successful novel, selling 150,000 copies within six months.

Böll develops the rather ironic, pseudo-objective narration

of his previous novel, *The End of a Mission* (*Ende einer Dienstfahrt*), a device that was to be developed further—and most successfully—in *The Lost Honor of Katharina Blum*. In *Group Portrait with Lady*, the narrator is a researcher, whose attempt to construct an objective study of the central character demands almost as much attention as the completed study itself (even generating a plot of its own: the narrator falls in love with a nun whom he interviews about the case in hand, and she leaves her order to become his collaborator). This structure effects to allay doubts about the uses of fiction by reducing the novelist to a finder of facts (and the rather sloppy, non-literary style reinforces this impression and disguises the narrator's real depth of emotion, as in Max Frisch's *Homo Faber*); but in reality it allows him even greater freedom than the traditional narrator, since he can envisage two or more interpretations of the same 'facts' without having to commit himself.

At first cogitations about the business of collecting evidence prevail, but gradually these are brought to a conclusion and the main plot gains in prominence, only to issue forth suddenly in a description of the present-day state of affairs. The central character, Leni Gruyten, is the daughter of a builder whose business enjoys a meteoric success during the Nazi period until he is caught defrauding the government (his main customer). After the death of her fiancé and soulmate Erhard and a short marriage to the less congenial Alois Pfeiffer, killed in the war, Leni has to cope with her father's imprisonment, the death of her mother, and the death of her childhood mentor Rahel in distressing circumstances. (A nun in the convent where Leni is educated, a qualified doctor of Jewish birth, Rahel falls foul first of Catholic orthodoxy which demotes her to menial tasks because of her outspokenness, then of Nazi anti-semitism which makes her an 'unperson' with no food allowance.) Leni, falling on hard times, works through the war and post-war years making wreaths for the florist Pelzer; the great passion of her life is for a Russian prisoner-of-war, Boris Lvović Koltowski, who is allocated to Pelzer's workshop as a labourer. Boris, victim of a confusion of identities in the chaos of the ending of the war, dies as a German prisoner-of-war working in a French mine. Their son, Lev, a difficult child, eventually becomes a refuse collector. Living in straitened circumstances (and quite impractical with money), Leni sells the house containing her flat cheaply to the Hoyser family, with whom she was thrown together during the war. In the flat, the last remnant of the one-time riches of the Gruytens, filled with her inherited furniture, well-read books, and an ambitious painting she is working on (of the surface of a retina with its millions of rods and cones), she collects sub-tenants from the lower reaches of society, notably Lev's Turkish colleagues. The Hoysers, objecting to this diminution of the value of their house, determine to evict Leni, whose rent is in arrears, but her admirers prevent this, by organizing 'accidents' with dustcarts which block the streets against the bailiffs and by taking up a collection to pay her back rent.

The novel rambles, and has puzzling features. The period from 1945 to about 1970 is almost entirely neglected in the narration. The narrator spends much time (and fictitious money, carefully accounted for to a fictitious tax-office) collecting a confusingly long series of informants from all walks of life, and commenting on their various degrees of reliability; but the perspective Böll wishes to give on Leni's life is clear enough, so the invitation to the reader to make up his or her own mind on the basis of the evidence is an empty one. The content is sometimes fantastic (the roses which stubbornly grow in winter on the grave of Sister Rahel, much to the embarrassment of the determinedly modern-minded

ecclesiastical powers-that-be), and sometimes needlessly embarrassing (Rahel's views on the training of girls to defecate without needing any toilet paper, and on the diagnostic value of inspecting the results). And could a Russian really have recommended Kafka to a German woman during the war—with the result that she has to be told not only that Kafka was a Jew, but also that Jews' writings and Jews themselves are frowned upon in Germany.

Böll returns to some of the themes of his earlier works: anti-militarism, anti-clericalism, and the defence of the social outsider. Another related attitude, manifesting Böll's rejection of the Cold War, is an emphatic sympathy for Russians. But he is perhaps overemphatic. Boris becomes a quite improbable paragon of tenderness and culture. The episode of Rahel's roses is created mainly in order to satirize the Catholic hierarchy, and diverts attention from the plot. Another mystical incident, the appearance of the Blessed Virgin Mary to the non-church-going Leni on the television screen after close-down, is self-parodying—especially when interpreted at the end of the novel as an optical illusion that produces an image of Leni herself! Böll's coquettish heresies about the sacramental value of erotic fulfilment are equally *de trop*. Rhineland separatism and anti-Prussianism is another sub-theme that lacks weight and relevance here.

Leni herself is a dunce at school who somehow gains enough intellectual awareness to read Trakl and Kafka; she plays a limited piano repertoire of Schubert to a good professional standard; once nominated as a member of the board of her father's company, she is, however, unable to look after even the small amount of domestic property left to her. On the dustjacket of the first edition, we see the negative of a photo of a group of people, the face of the woman in the centre being a blank: an all too true representation of the novel.

Group Portrait with Lady does have its high points. The narrator's interview with the distasteful Hoyser family (in their ultra-modern skyscraper where nobody dares open a window for fear of confusing the air-conditioning) shows that Böll's satire is not blunted; the way the press distorts its reporting of the dustcart blockage foreshadows *The Lost Honor of Katharina Blum*. The scene in which Leni offers some of her own coffee, the best available, to the despised prisoner-of-war in her workplace, cutting through the whole ideology of race and all the war-time propaganda with a few pointed gestures, is an object-lesson in how to make a moral point in literature without preaching.

—Alfred D. White

THE LOST HONOR OF KATHARINA BLUM (Die verlorene Ehre der Katharina Blum)
Novel by Heinrich Böll, 1974.

Böll exemplifies the post-war German tradition of socially engaged literature, but while all his works betray concern for the political and moral health of the Federal Republic, the social antecedent is most specific in *The Lost Honor of Katharina Blum*. On 22 December 1971 a bank in Kaiserslautern was robbed and a policeman murdered. Assuming that this had to be the work of West Germany's then most notorious terrorists, *Bild*, the sensationalist newspaper owned by the press magnate Axel Springer, ran a front-page headline the next morning: 'Baader-Meinhof gang kills again'. Two weeks later Böll wrote an essay in the news magazine, *Der Spiegel*, in which he launched a virulent attack upon *Bild*, accusing the paper of stirring up lynch justice, of condemning without evidence, and of creating an atmosphere in which Ulrike Meinhof could never give herself up for fear of 'landing in a cauldron of demagogy like some medieval witch'. He finished by pleading that the terrorists be offered the prospect of fair trial rather than death in a hail of bullets. *Bild* responded with a campaign of character-assassination against Böll, calling him a terrorist sympathizer and likening him to Goebbels. Asked the following month by a Swiss newspaper whether he might one day turn the whole experience into a novel, Böll replied: 'No, though it may be that one or two elements will be adapted and used for revenge. Even a writer sometimes wants to avenge himself'. That vengeance came, two and a half years later, with the publication of *Katharina Blum*.

From the outset Böll makes no bones about his primary target. Having declared, in the traditional author's disclaimer, that characters and plot are fictitious, he continues (in an addition curiously omitted from the English translation): 'Should the depiction of certain journalistic practices suggest similarities with the practices of *Bild*, such similarities are neither intentional nor coincidental but unavoidable'. Katharina Blum, the victim in this case, is an unexceptional woman, 27 years of age, housekeeper to a professional couple, working hard to pay off her mortgage and rebuild her life after a broken marriage. At a fancy-dress party during Carnival in February 1974 she encounters a young man called Götten and spends the night with him, unaware that he is under observation as a suspected terrorist. Next morning he slips through the police net, and she is interrogated as an accomplice. Despite the rough handling she receives from the police, her real ordeal begins when the press becomes involved, specifically a newspaper called simply '*News*' (the capitalized German original, *ZEITUNG*, conveys better than the English the paper's meretricious tone). With no more than circumstantial evidence their screaming headlines and histrionic reporting present Katharina as a criminal and a slut. Her private life is publicly dissected, her friends are harassed, and facts are shamelessly twisted to fit the preconceived picture. Finally one of the journalists, in search of a quote, invades the hospital where Katharina's mother is seriously ill, and the old lady subsequently dies. Katharina arranges a meeting with the reporter concerned and, as he is making a crude sexual advance to her, she shoots him dead.

Böll's works are generally constructed on a dualistic pattern, one in which individual values such as integrity, love, and faith, are set against, and frequently overcome by, a social environment with different priorities, whether these are the war aims of the Third Reich or the materialistic preoccupations of the Federal Republic. *Katharina Blum* shows a similar configuration: a fundamentally decent citizen (whose name, to put the point beyond any doubt, means 'pure flower') is crushed by agencies allegedly existing for her benefit. Throughout the text there is a sense of powerful forces behind the scenes, not just the press but also the police, politicians, and the business community, working together to protect their own interests above everything else. The story's subtitle, 'How violence develops and where it can lead', makes plain that the source of the violence should be seen, not with the woman who shot the journalist, but with those who perpetrated the character assassination that brought her to that point. The revelation at the end that Götten was, after all, not a terrorist but simply an army deserter who had absconded with some cash serves further to put the authorities in the wrong and emphasize Katharina's role as victim, albeit one who, unusually for a Böll heroine, strikes back.

The story is presented by an unnamed narrator who affects the viewpoint of a detached observer trying to piece events together, but his protestations of impartiality are constantly undercut by irony. He cannot disguise his sympathy for Katharina nor his dislike of her persecutors, who show themselves in a persistently negative light and are also made the butt of several satirical digressions (rather heavy-footed ones, it must be said). Böll himself called *Katharina Blum* a 'pamphlet disguised as a narrative', and the anger beneath the surface composure is very apparent. But it is also here, in the priority of polemical intent over aesthetic quality, that the text's main failings lie. The narrative structure, for instance, is at times self-consciously arch, and touches of sentimentality, never far from Böll's writing, creep into his portrait of Katharina. There is, in addition, for all the passion of the message, a distinctly contrived aspect to the plot, with the boundaries between vice and virtue too tightly drawn. The story created a considerable impact when it was first published, and Volker Schlöndorff turned it into a highly successful film, but it seems likely to survive more as an interesting social document than as a work of great literature.

—Peter J. Graves

THE BOOK OF THE THOUSAND NIGHTS AND ONE NIGHT. See THE THOUSAND AND ONE NIGHTS.

BORGES, Jorge Luis. Born in Buenos Aires, Argentina, 24 August 1899. Educated at Collège de Genève, Switzerland; Cambridge University. Married 1) Elsa Millan in 1967 (separated 1970); 2) María Kodama in 1986. Lived in Europe with his family, 1914–21; co-founding editor, *Proa*, 1924–26, and *Sur*, 1931; also associated with *Prisma*; literary adviser, Emecé Editores, Buenos Aires; columnist *El Hogár* weekly, Buenos Aires, 1936–39; municipal librarian, Buenos Aires, (fired from his post by the Péron regime) 1939–46; poultry inspector, 1946–54; went blind, 1955; director, National Library (after Péron's deposition), 1955–73; professor of English literature, University of Buenos Aires, 1955–70; Norton professor of poetry, Harvard University, Cambridge, Massachusetts; visiting lecturer, University of Oklahoma, Norman, 1969. President, Argentine Writers Society, 1950–53. Recipient: Buenos Aires Municipal prize, 1928; Argentine Writers Society prize, 1945; National prize for literature, 1957; Prix Formentor, 1961; Ingram Merrill award, 1966; Bienal Foundation Inter-American prize, 1970; Jerusalem prize, 1971; Alfonso Reyes prize, 1973; Cervantes prize, 1979; Yoliztli prize, 1981. Honorary Degrees: D.Litt.: University of Cuyo, Argentina, 1956; Oxford University, 1971; Columbia University, New York, 1971; University of Michigan, East Lansing, 1972; University of Chile, 1976; University of Cincinnati, 1976; Ph.D.: University of Jerusalem, 1971. Member, Argentine National Academy; Uruguayan Academy of Letters. Honorary fellow, Modern

Language Association (USA), 1961. Member, Légion d'honneur. Order of Merit (Italy), 1968; Order of Merit (German Federal Republic), 1979. Honorary KBE (Knight Commander, Order of the British Empire). *Died 14 June 1986.*

PUBLICATIONS

Fiction

Historia universal de la infamia. 1935; as *A Universal History of Infamy*, translated by Norman Thomas di Giovanni, 1971.
El jardín de senderos que se bifurcan. 1942.
Seis problemas para don Isidro Parido, with Adolfo Bioy Casares (as H. Bustos Domecq). 1942; as *Six Problems for Don Isidro Parodi*, translated by Norman Thomas di Giovanni, 1981.
Ficciones (1935–1944). 1944; enlarged edition, 1956; as *Ficciones*, edited and translated by Anthony Kerrigan, 1962; as *Fictions*, translated by Kerrigan, 1965.
Dos fantasías memorables, with Adolfo Bioy Casares. 1946.
Un modelo para la muerte, with Adolfo Bioy Casares (as B. Suárez Lynch). 1946.
El Aleph. 1949; as *The Aleph and Other Stories 1933–1969*, edited and translated by Norman Thomas di Giovanni, 1970.
La muerte y la brújula. 1951.
La hermana de Elosía, with Luisa Mercedes Levinson. 1955.
Crónicas de Bustos Domecq, with Adolfo Bioy Casares. 1967; as *Chronicles of Bustos Domecq*, translated by Norman Thomas di Giovanni, 1976.
El informe de Brodie. 1970; as *Dr Brodie's Report*, translated by Norman Thomas di Giovanni, 1972.
El congreso. 1970; as *The Congress*, translated by Norman Thomas di Giovanni, 1974.
El libro de arena. 1975; as *The Book of Sand*, translated by Norman Thomas di Giovanni (includes *The Gold of the Tigers*), 1977.

Verse

Fervor de Buenos Aires. 1923.
Luna de enfrente. 1925.
Cuaderno San Martín. 1929.
Poemas 1922–1943. 1943.
Poemas 1923–1958. 1958.
El hacedor (includes prose). 1960; as *Dreamtigers*, translated by Mildred Boyer and Harold Morland, 1964.
Obra poética. 6 vols., 1964–78.
Para las seis cuerdas. 1965; revised edition, 1970.
Nueva antología personal. 1968.
Elogio de la sombra. 1969; as *In Praise of Darkness*, translated by Norman Thomas di Giovanni (bilingual edition), 1974.
El otro, el mismo. 1969.
El oro de los tigres. 1972.
Selected Poems 1923–1967, edited by Norman Thomas di Giovanni. 1972.
La rosa profunda. 1975.
La moneda de hierro. 1976.
Historia de la noche. 1976.
The Gold of the Tigers: Selected Later Poems, translated by Alastair Reid, in *The Book of Sand*, 1977.
Adrogué (includes prose). 1977.

La cifra. 1981.
Antología poética, 1923–1977. 1981.

Screenplay: *Los orilleros; El paraíso de los creyentes*, with Adolfo Bioy Casares. 1955.

Other

Inquisiciones (essays). 1925.
El tamaño de mi esperanza (essays). 1926.
El idioma de los Argentinos (essays). 1928; enlarged edition, as *El lenguaje de Buenos Aires*, with José Edmundo Clemente, 1963.
Evaristo Carriego (essays). 1930; as *Evaristo Carriego: A Book about Old-Time Buenos Aires*, translated by Norman Thomas di Giovanni, 1983.
Discusión. 1932.
Las Kennigar. 1933.
Historia de la eternidad. 1936; enlarged edition, 1953.
Nueva refutación del tiempo. 1947.
Aspectos de la literatura gauchesca. 1950.
Antiguas literaturas germánicas, with Delia Ingenieros. 1951.
Otras inquisiciones 1937–1952. 1952; as *Other Inquisitions 1937–1952*, translated by Ruth L.C. Simms, 1964.
El 'Martín Fierro', with Margarita Guerrero. 1953.
Obras completas, edited by José Edmundo Clemente. 9 vols., 1953–60.
Leopoldo Lugones, with Betina Edelberg. 1955.
Manual de zoología fantástica, with Margarita Guerrero. 1957; revised edition, as *El libro de los seres imaginarios*, 1967; as *The Imaginary Zoo*, translated by Tim Reynolds, 1969; revised edition, as *The Book of Imaginary Beings*, translated by Norman Thomas de Giovanni, 1969.
Antología personal. 1961; as *A Personal Anthology*, edited and translated by Anthony Kerrigan, 1967.
Labyrinths: Selected Stories and Other Writings, edited and translated by Donald A. Yates and James E. Irby, 1962; enlarged edition, 1964.
The Spanish Language in South America: A Literary Problem; El Gaucho Martin Fierro (lectures). 1964.
Introducción a la literatura inglesa, with María Esther Vázquez. 1965; as *An Introduction to English Literature*, edited and translated by L. Clark Keating and Robert O. Evans, 1974.
Literaturas germánicas medievales, with María Esther Vázquez. 1966.
Introducción a la literatura norteamericana, with Esther Zemborain de Torres. 1967; as *An Introduction to American Literature*, translated by L. Clark Keating and Robert O. Evans, 1973.
Nueva antología personal. 1968.
Conversations with Borges, by Richard Burgin. 1968.
Borges on Writing, edited by Norman Thomas di Giovanni, Daniel Halpern, and Frank MacShane. 1973.
Obras completas, edited by Carlos V. Frías. 1974.
Tongues of Fallen Angels: Conversations with Borges, edited by Selden Roman, 1974.
Prólogos. 1975.
Qué es el budismo?, with Alicia Jurado. 1976.
Libros de sueños. 1976.
Borges oral (lectures). 1979.
Siete noches (essays). 1980; as *Seven Nights*, translated by Eliot Weinberger, 1984.
Prosa completa. 2 vols., 1980.
Borges, A Reader: Selections from the Writings, edited by Emir Rodríguez Monegal and Alastair Reid. 1981.
Nueve ensayos dantescos. 1982.

Borges at Eighty: Conversations, edited by Willis Barnstone. 1982.
Atlas, with María Kodama. 1985; as *Atlas*, translated by Anthony Kerrigan, 1985.
Conversaciones, with Alicia Moreau de Justo. 1985.
Borges en dialogo, with Osvaldo Ferrari. 1985.
Los conjurados. 1985.
Conversaciones, with Roberto Alifano. 1986.
Conversaciones, with Francisco Tokos. 1986.
Textos Cautivos: Ensayos y reseñas en El Hogar (1936–1939), edited by Enrique Socerio-Gari and Emir Rodríguez Monegal. 1987.
Paginas escogidas, edited by Roberto Fernandez Retamar. 1988.
Biblioteca personal: Prólogos. 1988.
Ultimas conversaciones con Borges, with Roberto Alifano. 1988.

Editor, with Pedro Henriques Ureña, *Antología clásica de la literatura argentina*. 1937.
Editor, with Silvana Ocampo and Adolfo Bioy Casares, *Antología de la literatura fantástica*. 1940; as *The Book of Fantasy*, 1988.
Editor, with Silvana Ocampo and Adolfo Bioy Casares, *Antología poética argentina*. 1941.
Editor, with Adolfo Bioy Casares, *Los mejores cuentos policiales*. 2 vols., 1943–51.
Editor, with Silvina Bullrich Palenque, *El Campadrito: Su destino, sus barrios, su música*. 1945.
Editor, with Adolfo Bioy Casares, *Prosa y verso*, by Francisco de Quevedo. 1948.
Editor, with Adolfo Bioy Casares, *Cuentos breves y extraordinarios*. 1955; as *Extraordinary Tales*, edited and translated by Anthony Kerrigan, 1971.
Editor, with Adolfo Bioy Casares, *Libro del cielo y del infierno*. 1960.
Editor, *Paulino Lucero, Aniceto y gallo, Santos Vega*, by Hilario Ascasubi. 1960.
Editor, *Macedonia Fernández* (selection). 1961.
Editor, *Páginas de historia y de autobiografía*, by Edward Gibbon. 1961.
Editor, *Prosa y poesía*, by Almafuerte. 1962.
Editor, *Versos*, by Evaristo Carriego. 1963.
Editor, with María Komada, *Breve antología anglosajona*. 1978.
Editor, *Micromegas*, by Voltaire. 1979.
Editor, *Cuentistas y pintores argentinos*. 1985.
Editor and translator, with Adolfo Bioy Casares, *Poesía gauchesca*. 2 vols., 1955.

Translator, *La metamorfosis*, by Kafka. 1938.
Translator, *Bartleby*, by Herman Melville. 1944.
Translator, *De los héroes; Hombres representativos*, by Carlyle and Emerson. 1949.

*

Bibliography: *Borges: Bibliografía total 1923–1973* by Horacio Jorge Becco, 1973; *Jorge Luis Borges: An Annotated Primary and Secondary Bibliography* by David William Foster, 1984.

Critical Studies: *Borges, The Labyrinth Maker* by Ana María Barrenchea edited and translated by Robert Lima, 1965; *The Narrow Act: Borges's Art of Illusion* by Ronald J. Christ, 1969; *The Mythmaker: A Study of Motif and Symbol in the Short Stories of Borges* by Carter Wheelock, 1969; *Jorge Luis Borges*, 1971, and *Borges and the Kabbalah and Other Essays on His Fiction and Poetry*, 1988, both by Jaime Alazraki, and *Critical Essays on Jorge Luis Borges* edited by Alazraki, 1987; *Borges*, 1971, and *Borges Revisited*, 1991, both by Martin S. Stabb; *The Cardinal Points of Borges* edited by Lowell Dunham and Ivor Ivask, 1971; *Jorge Luis Borges* by John M. Cohen, 1973; *Prose for Borges* edited by Charles Newman and Mary Kinzie, 1974; *Borges: Ficciones* by Donald Leslie Shaw, 1976; *Paper Tigers: The Ideal Fictions of Borges* by John Sturrock, 1977; *Borges: Sources and Illumination* by Giovanna De Garayalde, 1978; *Jorge Luis Borges: A Literary Biography* by Emír Rodríguez Monegal, 1978; *Jorge Luis Borges* by George R. McMurray, 1980; *Borges and His Fiction: A Guide to His Mind and Art* by Gene H. Bell-Villada, 1981; *The German Response to Latin American Literature and the Reception of Jorge Luis Borges and Pablo Neruda* by Yolanda Julia Broyles, 1981; *The Aleph Weaver: Biblical, Kabbalistic and Judaic Elements in Borges* by Edna Aizenberg, 1984, and *Borges and His Successors: The Borges Impact on Literature and the Arts* edited by Aizenberg, 1990; *The Prose of Jorge Luis Borges: Existentialism and the Dynamics of Surprise*, 1984, and *The Meaning of Experience in the Prose of Jorge Luis Borges*, 1988, both by Ion Tudro Agheana; *Jorge Luis Borges: Life, Work and Criticism* by Donald Yates, 1985; *Jorge Luis Borges* edited by Harold Bloom, 1986; *The Literary Universe of Jorge Luis Borges: An Index to References and Allusions to Persons, Titles and Places in His Writings*, 1986, and *Out of Context: Historical Reference and the Representation of Reality in Borges*, 1993, both by Daniel Balderston; *The Poetry and Poetics of Jorge Luis Borges* by Paul Cheselka, 1987; *The Emperor's Kites: A Morphology of Borges's Tales* by Mary Lusky Friedman, 1987; *In Memory of Borges* edited by Norman Thomas Di Giovanni, 1988; *A Dictionary of Borges* by Evelyn Fishburn, 1990; *Jorge Luis Borges: A Study of the Short Fiction* by Naomi Lindstrom, 1990; *Orientalism in the Hispanic Literary Tradition: In Dialogue with Borges, Paz and Sarduy* by Julia A. Kushigian, 1991; *Borges and Artificial Intelligence: An Analysis in the Style of Pierre Menard* by Ema Lapidot, 1991; *The Contemporary Praxis of the Fantastic: Borges and Cortázar* by Julio Rodríguez-Luis, 1991; *Jorge Luis Borges: A Writer at the Edge* by Beatriz Sarlo, 1992.

*   *   *

Jorge Luis Borges was one of the most influential writers of the 20th century. His lasting contribution to world literature is to be found in his short stories. *Ficciones (Fictions)* and *El Aleph (The Aleph and Other Stories)* collect his classic tales, the ones that secured his place among the masters of world literature and became the cornerstone of the new Spanish-American narrative. It is in these two books, along with the essays of *Inquisiciones* and the texts (prose, poetry, fragments) of *El hacedor (Dreamtigers)* that the synthesis of his literary art can be found. In later books of short stories, such as *El informe de Brodie (Dr Brodie's Report)*, he turned to simplicity, to straightforward storytelling. *El libro de arena (The Book of Sand)*, however, his last collection of short stories, returned to the creative lines developed early. The recurrent aesthetic and philosophical concerns of his writing (time, the identity of the self, human destiny, eternity, infinite multiplicity, the double, the mirages of reality) remained predominant themes, but the rigorous verbal precision of his celebrated stories becomes a freer, simpler, and more direct prose.

His narrative develops within a tradition that has been called fantastic literature. Borges himself highlights the four basic procedures of fantastic fiction: the work of art within the work of art, the contamination of reality by dream, travels through time, and the use of the double. These procedures, along with his favourite devices and symbols (the labyrinth, mirrors, symmetry, plurality and multiplicity, infinite bifurcations, the cyclical nature of reality), contribute to reveal the essential unreality of all human constructions. His stories focus on man's relation with the world and convey a deep and disquieting uneasiness. Borges's fictions are a lengthy interrogation (philosophical, theological, metaphysical) without a possible answer, a terrifying questioning of the problematic and illusory nature of reality, of the existence itself of the universe. The anguish caused by the implacable destiny of humanity haunted by the passing of time and by the dissolution of the image of the self is a basic motif of all his writing.

Borges founded an imaginary universe based on intellectual premises (idealism is a guiding principle of his fiction), and discovered in literature a coherent order in contrast with the chaos of the world, but his fictions always ended up by being a terrifying duplication of our chaotic universe. Incapable of comprehending reality, he wrote self-reflective, involuted, ironic, or *ludic* stories, that become continuous dialogues with nothingness, where reality and dream are indistinguishable.

Borges's technical control, the evocative and allusive strength of his prose, the verbal rigour, the subtle conceptual irony, the lucid exercise of intelligence, and the power to create a world of his own, distinguishable from any other, are lasting contributions of his prose. He proposed that literature be, above all, literature, and that fiction accept, in the words of Rodríguez Monegal, 'deliberately and explicitly its character of fiction, of verbal artifice'.

Borges's writing can be seen, in short, as an elaborate way to justify life through art. His inexhaustible imagination justified, aesthetically, his reason for being. Borges found in the creative act and in the invention of ideal worlds a provisory salvation. He created his own reality in order to erase the inscrutable chaos of the world. 'Unreality is the condition of art', he wrote in 'The Secret Miracle', and in 'Examination of the Work of Herbert Quain' he affirmed that 'of the many joys that literature can provide, the highest is invention'. Borges's scepticism with regard to the elusive and inexplicable universe becomes elaborately constructed fictions, games that mirror life but undermine all facile assumptions.

—Hugo J. Verani

DEATH AND THE COMPASS (La muerte y la brújula) Story by Jorge Luis Borges, 1942.

'Death and the Compass', now part of his *Ficciones*, definitive edition 1956, reveals Borges at his best: densely labyrinthine, ironic, and multilayered.

The image of the labyrinth is one of Borges's favourites. In their repeated appearances in varied guises Borges's labyrinths all point to the same general idea: the near-impossibility of achieving full understanding and control of our own fate. Some of his characters cannot solve the puzzle of the labyrinth; those who do, through miraculous interventions, find destruction and even humiliation awaiting them. The labyrinth, then, symbolizes that which remains permanently out of reach of human abilities and aspirations,

that which we could reach only through the loss of our humanity: it represents the frustration of the universal desire for transcendence.

The labyrinth also serves as an apt symbol of Borges's tales themselves, whose 'architecture' is filled with tricks and false paths, and whose true way is complex and sometimes obscure. In 'Death and the Compass', Borges takes his reader along his own literary labyrinth, just as Red Scharlach leads Lönnrot on the path he has built for him.

Lönnrot's immediate problem, as a detective, is to solve a murder (and also to avoid being murdered by his arch-enemy Scharlach). Ironically, the solution is presented immediately by Commissioner Treviranus, but rejected by Lönnrot on the grounds that this explanation lacks 'interest'; for the death of a rabbi he prefers a 'rabbinical' explanation, whether Treviranus is right or wrong. (While he never actually rejects his colleague's hypothesis, he simply is compelled, for reasons we understand only later, to find a more aesthetic solution.) 'Truth', for Lönnrot, matters less than the appropriateness of things and the elegance of reason.

Unfortunately for Lönnrot, Scharlach knows him very well indeed, and flawlessly anticipates his reactions. Planting a series of 'clues', he leads his evidently unwitting victim, just erudite enough to interpret them, through a labyrinth constructed just for him. Following Scharlach's path, Lönnrot reasons that there will be a fourth crime after the series of three he attributes to his rival, and in this he is correct; what he learns in the last paragraphs is that this last crime consists of his own murder.

We now enter the multiple ironies of this story. Firstly, Lönnrot is led to humiliation and destruction by the very values Borges (and his presumed reader) hold: intelligence, diligence, and learning. Hence the first real theme of the tale is the limitations of these same qualities, for they are never enough to solve all the mysteries we face. Lönnrot makes the fatal mistake of assuming causality in things that turn out to be unrelated: the first crime was unintended, the second (the murder of an accomplice of Scharlach) merely a matter of mob justice; the third is a simulated kidnapping. The second theme is that life continues to resist our desires and needs for things to make sense, and that in seeking meanings where there may well be none we may in a sense be 'noble', but we are mistaking a pleasant illusion for reality.

Scharlach, then, traps Lönnrot in a multilayered labyrinth: geographical (following the layout of a city, possibly Paris), intellectual, aesthetic, and numerical (numerical symbols lead his enemy to his denouement at Triste-le-Roy). And of course, we readers are also trapped, led to follow the same clues to the same finality—our 'death' as readers as we finish the tale.

This last irony (Borges is to the reader as Scharlach is to Lönnrot) is developed fully in the startling final pages. We have seen how the two main characters of this 'fiction' exist as each other's counterpart, in terms of their rivalry only; we now also see how our identity as readers, and the artist's as writer, are another dependent duality wherein both exist only during the act of reading (a common sub-theme of Borges). So, firstly, both dualities form a single identity. This is why Scharlach detests duplicated images and speaks so bitterly of the two-faced—but single-headed—god Janus: duality reminds him that he, although nearly omnipotent, is still bound to his Other. (They even share the same single name, since both mean 'red'.) Therefore, his murder of the detective is also a form of suicide.

There is yet another twist to these matters. The text tells us that Scharlach fires his gun at his rival; it does not actually tell us Lönnrot dies. In fact, we are led to assume he does not, for in the obligatory 'explanation scene' (where the criminal tells how he pulled off his deed) we learn of an extraordinary aspect of the Janus-like pair of rivals: they fully expect to live again, to re-enact their pursuit and vengeance and for the outcome to be the same. They are, then, in a circular existence, entering into new *avatars* (the word is used by Lönnrot) at the close of each 'chapter' of their ongoing series of fatalistic incarnations. It seems that Lönnrot's only hope of 'escape' is to make the next pursuit a more 'interesting' one, in a different sort of labyrinth, one made of a straight line instead of the geometric patterns of this sequence. Now at last we understand his obsession with the subjective adequacy of explanations, why he rejected Treviranus's interpretation: the individual who knows he or she is trapped can do little but try to make the paths leading to destruction aesthetically and intellectually interesting. The truth, in such a situation, is pitiful, melancholy, and, so to speak, must be transcended.

What, then, of Lönnrot's fate the next time? It is possible he hopes that Scharlach will be unable to overtake him in their new labyrinth. Sadly, however, the manner in which he asks for this more 'interesting' labyrinth suggests little or no real hope: 'when, in some other incarnation, you hunt me'. His feeling of inevitability is echoed when his enemy indeed promises to murder him again.

Clearly, this is a complex narrative. It is at once a detective story, a reflection on the limitations of the intellect, an exposition of the conflict between materiality and the ideal (or, to put it another way, between reality and what could be), and an allegory on the nature of reading and writing. Like those of many of Borges's 'fictions' (a blend of the essay and the short story), the underlying themes of 'Death and the Compass' are in the end melancholy, but there is a compensation to this basic fatalism. The labyrinth to which literature is assigned is, in fact, lineal (as Lönnrot wished his own to be), for literature cannot escape linearity because it can only be read according to the flow of time. Borges, our 'Scharlach', in fact gives us the aesthetic satisfaction that his Lönnrot seeks. It may not solve the mysteries or the traps of life, but readers the world over enjoy Borges's (and their own) walks through the labyrinth of his art, and are, each in their own way, reborn with each new reading.

—Paul W. Borgeson, Jr

BRANT, Sebastian. Born in Strasbourg, Germany, 1457. Educated privately; studied law, Basle University, 1475–77, baccalauréat, 1477. Married Elisabeth Burg in 1485. Licentiate in Canon law, 1484; doctor of Roman and Canon law, 1492, dean of the faculty of law, 1496, Basle University; editor for numerous publishing houses in Basle; set up as legal adviser to city council, Strasbourg, 1501; summoned to Innsbruck by Emperor Maximilian as a consultant, 1502 and 1509; town clerk, 1503, and municipal secretary, 1504, Strasbourg. *Died 10 May 1521.*

PUBLICATIONS

Verse

Rosarium ex floribus vitae passionisque domini nostri Jesu Christi consertum. 1492.

Das Narrenschiff. 1494; edited by Friedrich Zarncke, 1854; reprinted 1964, also edited by H.A. Junghans (modern German translation and commentary), 1966, and by Manfred Lemmer, 1968; as *The Ship of Fools of the World*, translated from the Latin version by J. Locher and adapted by Alexander Barclay, 1509, reprinted 1874 and 1970; as *The Great Ship of Fools of the World*, translated by Henry Watson, 1517; as *The Ship of Fools*, translated by Edwin H. Zeydel, 1944, reprinted 1966; also translated by William Gillis, 1971.
Carmina in Laudem B. Mariae Virginis multorumque sanctorum. 1494.
Varia carmina. 1498.

Other (selection)

Von der wunderbaren geburd des kinds bey wurmbs. 1495.
Von der wunderlichen zamefügung der öbersten Planeten. 1504.
Von dem anfang und Wesen der statt Jerusalem. 1518.
In Laudem divi Maximiliani Caesaris invict. 1520.

Editor, *De civitate Dei* by Saint Augustine. 1489.
Editor, *De moribus et facetijs mense Thesmophagia*, by Reinerus. 1490.
Editor, *Opera Sancti Ambrosii.* 1492.
Editor, *De conceptu et triplici Mariae Virginis gloriosissimae candore.* 1494.
Editor, *Vita beati Brunonis.* 1495.
Editor, *Concordantiae maiores Bibli.* 1496.
Editor, *Theologica emphasis*, by Jacob Locher. 1496.
Editor, *Passio St Meynrhadi martyris et heremite.* 1496.
Editor, *Librorum Francisci Petrarchae Annotatio.* 1496.
Editor, *Joannis Reuchlin Phorcensis Scenica Progymnasmata.* 1498.
Editor, *Aesopus appologi sive Mythologi cum quibusdam carminum et fabularum.* 1501.
Editor, *De philosophico consolatu sive de consolatione philosophie*, by Boethius. 1501.
Editor, *Hortulus animae.* 1501.
Editor, *Der heilgen leben nüw mit vil Heilgen, und clarz der Passion und die Grossen fest, das lessen, mit figuren zierlich und nutzlich den menschen.* 1502.
Editor, *Opera*, by Virgil. 1502.
Editor, *De laudibus crucis*, by Hrabanus. 1503.
Editor, *Bescheidenheit*, by Freidank. 1508.
Editor, with Jacob Locher, *Layen Spiegel*, by Ulrich Tengler. 1509.
Editor, *In mortem Johannis Keiserspergii.* 1510.
Editor, *Der richterlich Clagspiegel.* 1516.
Editor, *Von der Artzney beyder Glück, der guten und widerwertigen.* 1532.

Translator, *Phagifacetus seu de moribus et facetiis mensae.* 1490.
Translator, *Liber faceti.* 1496.
Translator, *Liber moreti.* 1496.
Translator, *Disticha Catonis.* 1498.

*

Bibliography: *Sebastian Brant Bibliographie* by Thomas Wilhelmi, 1990; *Sebastian-Brant-Bibliographie. Forschungsliteratur von 1800 bis 1985* by Joachim Knape and Dieter Wuttke, 1990.

Critical Studies: *The English Versions of the Ship of Fools* by A. Pompen, 1925; *Sebastian Brant: Studies in Religious Aspects of His Life and Works with Special Reference to the Varia Carmina* by Mary A. Rajewski, 1944; *Studien zu Sebastian Brants Narrenschiff* by Ulrich Gaier, 1966; *Sebastian Brant, Das Narrenschiff* by Barbara Könneker, 1966; *Sebastian Brant* by Edwin H. Zeydel, 1967; *Das Narrenschiff* by Klaus Manger, 1983; *Dichtung, Recht und Freiheit. Studien zu Leben und Werk Sebastian Brants 1457–1521* by Joachim Knape, 1992; *Sebastian Brant's The Ship of Fools in Critical Perspective, 1800–1991* by John Van Cleve, 1993.

* * *

After graduating from the University of Basle in 1477 Sebastian Brandt studied and subsequently taught and practised law there, receiving his doctorate in 1489. From 1486–96 he also lectured on poetics. During this period he wrote occasional verse, some of it published as broadsides illustrated with woodcuts, on such topics as floods on the Rhine in 1480, an eclipse in 1485, or a hailstorm in 1487. A collection of his religious verse appeared in 1494, followed in 1498 by his *Varia carmina*, containing many panegyrics on Maximilian I and poems on various historical and contemporary personalities. Most of this early verse was in Latin and pedantic in style, but he soon started experimenting with translation into German, publishing versions of medieval didactic works: *Thesmophagia*, *Disticha Catonis*, *Facetus*, and *Moretus* in 1490. His interest in such writings points forward to the work for which he is chiefly remembered today, *Das Narrenschiff* (*The Ship of Fools*).

The Ship of Fools was an instant success. The first edition (Basle 1494) was followed in the same year by unauthorized reprints from Nuremberg, Reutlingen, and Augsburg, as well as by a Strasbourg edition with interpolations. New editions and adaptations continued to appear right down to 1625. The learned abbot Johannes Trithemius declared *The Ship of Fools* to be a 'Divine Satire', the equal of Dante's *Commedia* (*Divine Comedy*), and the Strasbourg humanist Jacob Wimpheling likewise compared Brant to Dante and Petrarch and considered that even Homer could not have produced a poem to match it; he proposed to introduce *The Ship of Fools* as a school textbook. The renowned Strasbourg preacher Johann Geiler von Kaisersberg delivered more than a hundred sermons based on it in Strasbourg Minster in 1498, as though it were a canonical book of the church. Its success was not confined to southern Germany. Low German versions were published at Lübeck in 1497 and Rostock in 1519. The year 1497 also saw the publication of a Latin translation, made by Jacob Locher and supervised by Brant, and printed at Basle under the title *Stultifera navis*. Through this translation the book came to the attention not only of a humanist public but of an international readership too; indeed it was the only work of German literature to achieve international acclaim before Goethe's *The Sufferings of Young Werther* (1774). The Latin text was soon translated into French, English (by Alexander Barclay and Henry Watson), and Dutch, these versions becoming popular in their turn. The work had a major role in establishing 'folly literature' as a genre which was cultivated by writers like Thomas Murner, Hans Sachs, and Johann Fischart and would remain popular down to the 17th century. To the modern reader, the book's extraordinary success is something of a mystery. Even specialists in the field have been baffled. Thus Zarncke, who edited the work in 1854, felt that it was only 'the intellectual impoverishment' of Brant's age which could explain the success of this 'compilation' which bore the marks of 'laboured industry and countless sleepless nights!'

One reason for its success is the appeal of the figure of the fool, though Brant cannot be credited with creating it—it has both medieval and classical antecedents, and of course the distinction between fools and wise men is as old as the Bible. Brant parades before us 112 fools, each of them standing for a different kind of breach of moral or social convention. In its way, the book is an illuminating document on the intellectual and moral history of the period. Brant is a stern moralist, conservative in his religious convictions, who does not share the humanists' sneaking belief in the innate goodness of man. For him it is foolish to sacrifice eternal salvation for passing pleasures. The 'follies' that he castigates—whether blasphemy, adultery, or slavery to fashion, gluttony, sloth, or gossiping in church, bibliomania, failing to follow doctor's orders, or selling forged relics—seem to him to be equally reprehensible. The fool is not seen as a social outcast but rather as a person who fails to heed a warning about the folly of his ways, Brant's criticism being aimed at people who, despite warnings, persist in their sinful folly. The satire is rarely relieved with flashes of humour.

Each chapter can be read independently of the whole. Some scholars have believed that the individual chapters may originally have been published as separate poems. While this cannot be substantiated, it is certainly the case that approximately two-thirds of the chapters, especially in the first half of the work, were designed to fill neatly a two-page opening of the book, with the left-hand page having a three-line motto and a woodcut; the main text, usually 34 lines of rhyming couplets, then fills the rest of the page and the whole of the recto. The later chapters vary considerably in length. Another indication of Brant's changing approach to the work is that the allegory of the ship voyaging with a full complement of fools is treated in a sustained manner only in the second half of the work and in the prologue (which was probably written last). The concept of the ship of fools is not Brant's invention; the most likely source, albeit perhaps indirect, was a sermon, apparently preached in Strasbourg in the 1460s or 1470s, in which the anonymous preacher describes a ship laden with 21 fools who are invited by Christ to board his own St Ursula's ship. What Brant did invent is the pun on German *Narr* 'fool' when he says that the starting point of the voyage is Narbonne and the destination is the land of Narragonia.

The Ship of Fools can be said to have 'grown' rather than to have been planned. In another sense, too, the work is a compilation. Brant is always at pains to buttress his arguments by citing recognized authorities, principally the Bible (notably Proverbs and Ecclesiastes), then canon law, the Church Fathers, and ancient writers (particularly Plutarch, Xenophon, Homer, Ovid, Juvenal, and Seneca). Gaier (1966) has also revealed the classical rhetorical structures underpinning the chapters, so that we are again able to understand more readily some of the subtleties appreciated by Brant's contemporaries.

But one feature that appeals to us as much as it did to them is the woodcuts which are an indispensable, integral part of the work. Brant himself says that he wanted to ensure that even fools unable to read might recognize themselves in the pictures. The woodcuts, which are remarkable for their vitality, are clearly the work of several artists; some have been attributed to the young Albrecht Dürer. Though Brant claims in the preface (line 25) to have designed the pictures, this doubtless means no more than that he suggested motifs and collaborated closely with the artists.

—John L. Flood

THE SHIP OF FOOLS (Das Narrenschiff)
Poem by Sebastian Brant, 1494.

Brant's *The Ship of Fools* is a didactic-satirical work, originally written in German verse and was first published in Basle in 1494. It consists of a prologue and 112 short chapters, almost all of which deal with a particular kind of fool or manifestation of folly considered by Brant to be prevalent in the society of his day. His gallery of fools is extraordinarily varied: some merely display a tendency towards unwise or immoderate conduct (such as those who follow ostentatious fashions in dress [chapter 4], or who devote themselves to unprofitable study [chapter 27]); whereas others are unequivocally sinners (each of the medieval Seven Deadly Sins is for example cast by Brant as a form of folly). What all of Brant's fools have in common, however, is a lack of accurate self-knowledge, combined with a failure to take account of the fact that they will die and be judged. For him, folly is at root a misguided attitude, but one which must inevitably lead to improper and ultimately sinful behaviour. Nevertheless, except in the case of certain irredeemable fools (such as heathen, heretics, and suicides, discussed in chapter 98), it can be overcome: if a fool attains self-knowledge and begins to live in the light of his own immortality, he can in time become wise and, eventually, inherit eternal life. It is precisely this process that *The Ship of Fools* seeks to initiate. As Brant states in both his prologue and his last chapter, he intends that his work should act as a mirror, into which a fool may look and, in so doing, recognize his folly and reform his behaviour accordingly.

Such a concept of folly owes much to medieval perceptions, most notably in the close parallel Brant draws between a fool and a sinner; but his proposed solution, with its implication that an individual can redeem himself without the intervention of the Church, or indeed even of Christ, is strikingly unmedieval. Like several other aspects of the work, it reveals the unmistakable influence of Renaissance humanism.

Brant does not present his fools to the reader in any obvious order; and this, along with his failure to exploit the narrative and structural possibilities of the notion of a ship of fools, has led certain critics to charge his work with lacking an overall plan. Nevertheless it is given a degree of unity not only by the all-embracing theme of folly, but also by the fact that, as a general rule, the layout of the individual chapters is consistent. In the original edition (and in some subsequent reprintings), the first page of each chapter, generally a verso, contains its title along with three or four-line motto and a substantial woodcut; and the remaining text of the chapter is printed on the facing recto. Furthermore the argument within chapters is often developed along similar lines: the initial motto tends to be followed by a brief definition or discussion of the folly involved, and then by a series of quotations or exempla, drawn primarily from Biblical or classical sources.

The woodcuts, which are reproduced in the English translations of both Edwin H. Zeydel and William Gillis, are of great interest. Their quality is for the most part remarkably high (it is generally accepted that as many as two-thirds of them were executed by no less a figure than Albrecht Dürer), and they are clearly viewed by Brant as an integral part of the work. Indeed, his prologue expresses the wish that those who are unable or unwilling to read his text might none the less be able to recognize and amend their folly simply by looking at the pictures. Given that numerous woodcuts do not obviously depict the folly that forms the subject of the accompanying chapter (several for example illustrate proverbs or exempla referred to in passing in the text), and indeed that some six woodcuts are used twice to illustrate quite different follies, this is surely an unrealistic hope; nevertheless the woodcuts do in most cases confirm, and in some cases indeed add to, Brant's didactic message. Moreover, the arrestingly humorous touches many of them display form a welcome complement to the somewhat relentless moralizing of much of the text.

Although it has been regarded by several modern critics as a work of only mediocre quality, *The Ship of Fools* enjoyed quite extraordinary popularity among Brant's contemporaries, and throughout the 16th century. It was not only enthusiastically lauded by his fellow humanists, but was clearly also read by an exceptionally wide range of people: no fewer than 16 German editions were published between 1494 and 1519, and already by 1500 it had been translated into Latin, French, and Dutch. Furthermore it was referred to, quoted from, and preached on by an enormous number of late 15th- and 16th-century authors.

There were no doubt many reasons for its success. Intellectual humanists were presumably attracted to its extensive use of quotations from classical literature and of Ciceronian rhetorical techniques, as well as to features such as Brant's comments on contemporary politics (notably in chapter 99) and his consistent, if often only implicit anticlericalism. At the same time, the work's generally simple language, its widespread use of well-known proverbs, its largely traditional (medieval) rhyme scheme and metre, and above all its woodcuts, plainly made it palatable to a wider audience. Above all, however, Brant's concept of folly must have struck a chord with many who, perhaps like the author himself, felt confused or threatened by the complexity and instability of an age in which the medieval and early modern worlds converged. An approachable vernacular work that described countless contemporary follies, but reduced these to a readily comprehensible common denominator and prescribed for them an apparently straightforward remedy, must have seemed like the answer to many prayers.

—Nigel Harris

BRASILLACH, Robert. Born in Perpignan, France, 31 March 1909. Educated at Lycée Louis-le-Grand, Paris, 1925–28; École Normale Supérieure, Paris. Served in the French army during World War II, taken prisoner, released 1941. Associated with the fascist press during the 1930s; literary critic, *L'Action française*, 1929; contributor, *Le Coq Catalan*, Perpignan, *L'Intransigeant*, and *Candide*, both Paris, during 1930s; staff writer, *La Revue Universelle*, 1930s; member of the editorial board, with Marcel Aymé, q.v., and Jean Anouilh, q.v., *Je Suis Partout*, 1936–44 (resigned). Gave himself up to the Resistance, imprisoned and tried. *Died (executed) 6 February 1945.*

PUBLICATIONS

Collection

Oeuvres complètes, edited by Maurice Bardèche. 12 vols., 1963–66.

Fiction

Le Voleur d'étincelles. 1932.
L'Enfant de la nuit. 1934.
Le Marchand d'oiseaux. 1936.
Comme le temps passe. 1937; as *Youth Goes Over*, translated by Warre Bradley Wells, 1938.
Les Sept Couleurs. 1939.
La Conquérante. 1943.
Six heures à perdre. 1953.
Les Captifs (unfinished). 1974.

Plays

Bérénice. 1954; as *La Reine de Césarée* (produced 1957). 1957.
Domrémy. 1961.

Verse

Poèmes. 1944.
Poèmes de Fresnes. 1949.

Other

Présence de Virgile. 1931.
Portraits. 1935.
L'Histoire du cinéma, with Maurice Bardèche. 1935; as *History of the Film*, translated by Iris Barry, 1938; as *History of Motion Pictures*, translated by Barry, 1970.
Animateurs de théâtre. 1936.
Léon Degrelle et l'avenir de Rex. 1936.
Les Cadets de l'Alcazar, with Henri Massis. 1936; as *The Cadets of the Alcazar*, translated anonymously, 1937.
Le Siège de l'Alcazar, with Henri Massis. 1936.
Pierre Corneille. 1938.
Histoire de la guerre d'Espagne, with Maurice Bardèche. 1939.
Notre avant-guerre. 1941; as *Une génération dans l'orage*, 1941.
Le Procès de Jeanne d'Arc. 1941.
Les Quatre Jeudis. 1944.
Chénier. 1947.
Morceaux choisis, edited by Marie Madeleine Martin. 1949.
Lettres écrites en prison (correspondence). 1952.
Journal d'un homme occupé. 1955.
Lettre à un soldat de la classe 60, suivie de textes écrits en prison. 1960.
Poètes oubliés. 1961.
Ecrit à Fresnes (correspondence). 1967.
Vingt lettres de Robert Brasillach. 1970.

Editor and translator, *Anthologie de la poésie grecque*. 1950.

*

Critical Studies: *Robert Brasillach* (in French) by Bernard George, 1968; *The Fascist Ego: A Political Biography of Robert Brasillach* by William Rayburn Tucker, 1975; *The*

Mystique of Fascism: Ideological and Artistic Function in the Works of Brasillach by Peter Tame, 1980; *Robert Brasillach; ou, Encore un instant de bonheur* by Anne Brassié, 1987; *Brasillach; ou, La célébration du mépris* by Jacqueline Baldran and Claude Bochurberg, 1988; *Robert Brasillach maître de l'évasion* by Marie-Luce Parton Monferron, 1988; *Brasillach: L'Illusion fasciste* by Pascal Louvrier, 1989; *Littérature et fascisme: les romans de Robert Brasillach* by Luc Rasson, 1991.

*   *   *

Robert Brasillach's short life had to it many aspects of that of a 19th-century Romantic struck with a severe case of the *mal du siècle*. That boredom, or *ennui*, which was essentially a rejection of traditional bourgeois values, had no real political dimension to it, but its 20th-century counterpart, fascism, had a strong attraction for young men like Brasillach. Somewhat anarchistic by nature (but not without a great deal of ambition), he left the provinces as a boy to attend the Lycée Louis-le-Grand in Paris at the age of 16. From there he passed the difficult competitive entrance examination for the École Normale Supérieure, yet he seems to have frittered away his time there, spending all too much energy as an extreme right activist in rebellion against the status quo.

He began his career as a right-wing journalist in 1931, working on the literary staff of the *L'Action française*, Maurras's royalist newspaper. He embarked on a parallel career as a critic and novelist at the same time. Having excelled in his studies of Greek and Latin, his first book, *Présence de Virgile*, established one of the underpinnings of his life's work: his admiration for classicism and Mediterranean culture. His later admiration for Mussolini would be partly attributable to this, as were later books on Corneille and the *Anthologie de la poésie grecque*, which he prepared in prison shortly before his death in 1945.

Brasillach continued to spread himself very thin throughout this decade, using his vast energies to study and elucidate widely divergent fields. Thus, in collaboration with his brother-in-law Maurice Bardèche, he published the *Histoire du cinéma* (*History of the Film*) and the *Histoire de la guerre d'Espagne* [History of the Spanish War]. From 1937 to 1943 he was a key member of the right wing and later collaborationist daily newspaper *Je Suis Partout* [I Am Everywhere], which in its heyday boasted a circulation of 300,000. Brasillach had an enormous audience before he resigned from the paper in 1943 because it had gone too far in its pro-German commitment. In the European civil war of the day, Brasillach was surely a 'national' who bitterly opposed the Allied 'cosmopolitans', but at the same time he refused to allow his identity as a Frenchman to be lost in the alliance with Germany. After the Liberation of Paris, he deliberately did not listen to the advice of friends who counselled emigration to Switzerland. Instead, he chose to face up to what he seems to have known would be his fate. He was arrested in September 1944; his trial in January of the following year was delayed while the authorities looked for a judge who would be willing to decree the death sentence for the crime of having an unpopular opinion. When that judge was found, the trial was conducted quickly and Brasillach was predictably sentenced to death, like so many other victims of the *épuration* (purge). Despite a petition signed by many intellectuals of both Left and Right, including a direct appeal to General de Gaulle by François Mauriac (who had so often been on the receiving end of Brasillach's barbs during the war), he was executed on 6 February 1945. In the last half century he has taken on the status of a martyr among French nationalists, who liken him to Joan of Arc in his honesty and courage in standing up to the English-led cosmopolitan coalition of the 1940s.

Interest in recent years has turned to Brasillach the novelist. The blacklisting of his work by intellectuals was far more effective than the one used on Céline, for example, and it remained in effect well into the 1970s. If Brasillach is to be truly rehabilitated, as his admirers seek to do, he must be shown to have been more than a mere journalist, albeit a courageous one. His first novel, *Le Voleur d'étincelles*, appeared in 1932. The hero, Lazare, like Brasillach, is about 23 years old. In his desire to escape from the dreaded landscape of bourgeois conformity, he discovers a mythological world of dreams. Brasillach's classical background and his own personal debt to the author of *Le Grand Meaulnes* (*The Wanderer*) are evident influences here. This theme of escape was continued in the next novel, *L'Enfant de la nuit* [Child of the Night], but with an important modification. Brasillach, still young and looking for something to say, links the notion of escape to that of discovery. Thus his young hero, Robert breaks out from his rather self-centred bourgeois universe to discover the everyday world of ordinary Parisians. Literary populism was in the air and the novel of social concern was thriving. In addition, a film like René Clair's *Sous les toits de Paris* [Beneath the Roofs of Paris], which brought out whatever poetic elements were to be found in working class existence of the day, had been an enormous success. Brasillach's novel tries to exploit, but unconvincingly, this formula. *Le Marchand d'oiseaux* [The Bird Seller] continues in the same vein. *Comme le temps passe* (*Youth Goes Over*) utilizes once again Robert, the narrator of *L'Enfant de la nuit*, but here his escape takes place not so much in space as in time—back to the days before World War I. Like many people who could see a new war coming, Brasillach seemed to be trying to stop the passage of time in this novel, as if to somehow stave off World War I. Some critics have seen this as his best fictional effort, but it has the same self-referential and somewhat decadent limitation as the earlier ones. Brasillach's hero never really overcomes his obsession with himself.

Les Sept Couleurs [The Seven Colours] signalled a new and welcome departure. It is a political novel whose action is set in the late 1930s. It was widely read and commented upon at the time, and nominated for the Goncourt prize. The seven colours of the title represent as many different fictional techniques, which are used in the various sections of the novel. Brasillach exhibits impressive control over each form while depicting the lure of escape for his young hero, Patrice, who discovers fascism in Italy and who attends the Nazi Party Congress in Nuremburg in 1938. This is Brasillach's major literary achievement, although to date it has not been studied seriously. It combines in potent form his interest in ancient Mediterranean culture (rekindled in Italian fascism) with the desire to escape into a world of dreams (as represented in the disciplined and anti-bourgeois *mise en scène* at Nuremburg). Patrice's fantasy is skilfully played off against the lucidity of his friend and classmate Catherine, who is able to accept bourgeois reality. This lucidity sets the work apart from the earlier novels as well as from *La Conquérante* [The Conquering Woman], an escapist work set in Morocco at the turn of the century, and *Six heures à perdre*, a pseudo-detective novel written in the spring of 1944 before Brasillach's arrest and execution.

Brasillach has emerged from literary and civil purgatory in the last ten years and a large amount of research is now being done, mostly biographical. An objective assessment of the quality of his aesthetic achievement as a novelist has not yet

begun, but this will be a critical stage in the process of rehabilitation if he is to be remembered as more than a mere journalist. In the meantime, the arbitrary and unjust death sentence that was imposed upon him for political reasons will continue to exert a powerful attraction for many.

—David O'Connell

BRECHT, Bertolt. Born Eugen Berthold Friedrich Brecht in Augsburg, Germany, 10 February 1898. Educated at elementary school, 1904–08, and Gymnasium, Augsburg, 1908–17; University of Munich, 1917–18, 1919. Served as medical orderly during World War I. Married 1) Marianne Zoff in 1922 (divorced 1927), one daughter; 2) the actress Helene Weigel in 1929, one son and one daughter; also had one son by Paula Banholzer. Drama critic, *Der Volkswille*, Augsburg, 1919–21; dramaturg, Munich Kammerspiele, 1923–24; in Berlin, 1924–33; dramaturg, Deutsches Theater; following Hitler's assumption of power, left Germany, 1933; based in Denmark, 1933–39; stripped of German citizenship, 1935; editor, with Lion Feuchtwanger and Willi Bredel, *Das Wort*, 1936–39; moved to Sweden, 1939; fled Sweden, 1941, arrived in the United States via Moscow and Vladivostock; based in California, 1941–47, called before the House Un-American Activities Committee, 1947; flew to Europe immediately after testifying; based in Switzerland, 1947–49; became Austrian citizen, 1950; moved to East Berlin after 1949: artistic adviser, Berliner Ensemble (directed by his wife), 1949–56. Recipient: Kleist prize, 1922; Stalin Peace prize, 1954. *Died 14 August 1956.*

PUBLICATIONS

Collections

Gesammelte Werke (*Stücke, Gedichte, Prosa*, and *Schriften*). 20 vols., 1967; supplemented with: *Texte für Filme*, 2 vols., 1969; *Arbeitsjournal*, 2 vols., 1974; *Gedichte aus dem Nachlass*, 2 vols., 1982.
Collected Plays, edited by John Willett and Ralph Manheim. 1970– ; the UK and US versions of this collection have a slightly different arrangement; some translations reprinted as *Plays*.
Poems 1913–1956, edited and translated by John Willett and Ralph Manheim. 3 vols., 1976; revised edition, 1979.
Collected Short Stories: 1921–1946, edited by John Willett and Ralph Manheim, translated by Yvonne Kapp, Hugh Rorrison, and Anthony Tatlow. 1983.
Werke: Grosse kommentierte Berliner und Frankfurter Ausgabe, edited by Werner Hecht and others. 1989– .

Plays

Baal (produced 1922; revised version 1926). 1922; revised version, in *Stücke*, 1, 1955; edited by Dieter Schmidt, 1968; as *Baal*, translated by Eric Bentley, in *Baal; A Man's A Man; The Elephant Calf*, 1964; also translated by Peter Tegel, in *Collected Plays*, 1970.
Trommeln in der Nacht (produced 1922). 1922; as *Drums in*

the Night, translated by Frank Jones, in *Jungle of Cities and Other Plays*, 1966; also translated by John Willett, in *Collected Plays*, 1, 1970.

Im Dickicht der Städte (as *Im Dickicht*, produced 1923; revised version 1927). 1927; edited by Gisela E. Bahr, 1968; as *In the Jungle of Cities*, translated by Gerhard Nellhaus, 1957; as *Jungle of Cities*, translated by Anselm Hollo, in *Jungle of Cities and Other Plays*, 1966.

Pastor Ephraim Magnus, with Arnolt Bronnen, from the work by Hans Henry Jahn (produced 1923).

Leben Eduards des Zweiten von England, with Lion Feuchtwanger, from the play by Christopher Marlowe (produced 1924). 1924; edited by Reinhold Grimm, 1968; as *Edward II*, translated by Eric Bentley, 1966; as *The Life of Edward II of England*, translated by Jean Benedetti, in *Collected Plays*, 1, 1970.

Die Kleinbürgerhochzeit (as *Die Hochzeit*, produced 1926). 1966; as *A Respectable Wedding*, translated by Jean Benedetti, in *Collected Plays*, 1, 1970.

Mann ist Mann, with others (produced 1926). 1927; as *Man Equals Man*, translated by Eric Bentley, in *Seven Plays*, 1961, also translated by Gerhard Nellhaus, in *Collected Plays*, 2, 1979; as *A Man's a Man*, also translated by Bentley, in *Baal; A Man's a Man; The Elephant Calf*, 1964.

Das Elefantenkalb. With *Mann ist Mann*, 1927; as *The Elephant Calf*, translated by Eric Bentley, in *Baal; A Man's a Man; The Elephant Calf*, 1964; also translated by Gerhard Nellhaus, in *Collected Plays*, 2, 1979.

Kalkutta 4 Mai, with Lion Feuchtwanger, from a play by Feuchtwanger, in *Drei Angelsächsische Stücke*. 1927; translated as *Warren Hastings*, in *Two Anglo-Saxon Plays*, 1928.

Die Dreigroschenoper, music by Kurt Weill, from the play *The Beggar's Opera* by John Gay (produced 1928). 1929; as *The Threepenny Opera*, translated by Desmond I. Vesey and Eric Bentley, in *From the Modern Repertoire*, edited by Bentley, 1958; also translated by Hugh McDiarmid, 1973; Ralph Manheim and John Willett, in *Collected Plays*, 2, 1979.

Happy End, with Elisabeth Hauptmann, music by Kurt Weill (produced 1929). *Happy End*, translated and adapted by Michael Feingold, 1982.

Lindberghflug, music by Kurt Weill and Paul Hindemith (produced 1929). 1929; retitled *Der Ozeanflug*.

Aufstieg und Fall der Stadt Mahagonny, music by Kurt Weill (produced 1930). 1929; as *The Rise and Fall of the City of Mahagonny*, translated by W.H. Auden and Chester Kallman, 1976.

Das Badener Lehrstück vom Einverständnis, music by Paul Hindemith (produced 1929). In *Versuche*, 2, 1930; as *The Didactic Play of Baden-Baden on Consent*, in *Tulane Drama Review*, May 1960.

Der Jasager/Der Neinsager, music by Kurt Weill (produced 1930). In *Versuche*, 4, 1931; edited by Peter Szondi, 1966; as *He Who Said Yes; He Who Said No*, translated by Wolfgang Sauerlander, in *The Measures Taken and Other Lehrstücke*, 1977.

Die Massnahme, music by Hanns Eisler (produced 1930). In *Versuche*, 4, 1931; edited by Reiner Steinweg, 1972; as *The Measures Taken*, translated by Eric Bentley, in *The Modern Theatre*, 6, edited by Bentley, 1960; in *The Jewish Wife and Other Short Plays*, 1965; also translated by Carl R. Müller, in *The Measures Taken and Other Lehrstücke*, 1977.

Versuche, 1–7, 9–15. 14 vols., 1930–57.

Die heilige Johanna der Schlachthöfe (broadcast 1932; produced 1959). In *Versuche*, 5, 1932; edited by Gisela E. Bahr, 1971; as *Saint Joan of the Stockyards*, translated by

Frank Jones, in *From the Modern Repertoire*, series 3, edited by Eric Bentley, 1956; also translated by Ralph Manheim, in *Collected Plays*, 3, 1991.

Die Mutter, music by Hanns Eisler, from the novel by Gor'kii (produced 1932). In *Versuche*, 7, 1932; edited by W. Hecht, 1969; as *The Mother*, translated by Lee Baxandall, 1965; also translated by Steve Gooch, 1978.

Die Sieben Todsünden der Kleinbürger, music by Kurt Weill (produced 1933). 1959; as *The Seven Deadly Sins of the Petty Bourgeoisie*, in *Plays*, 1979.

Die Rundköpfe und die Spitzköpfe, music by Hanns Eisler (produced 1936). In *Gesammelte Werke*, 2, 1938; as *Roundheads and Peakheads*, translated by N. Goold-Verschoyle, in *Jungle of Cities and Other Plays*, 1966.

Die Gewehre der Frau Carrar (produced 1937). 1938; as *The Guns of Carrar*, 1971; as *Señora Carrar's Rifles*, in *Collected Plays*, 4, 1983.

Furcht und Elend des Dritten Reiches (produced as *99%*, 1938). 1945; as *The Private Life of the Master Race*, translated by Eric Bentley, 1944; as *Fear and Misery in the Third Reich*, in *Collected Plays*, 4, 1983.

Die Ausnahme und die Regel, music by Paul Dessau (produced 1938). In *Gesammelte Werke*, 2, 1938; as *The Exception and the Rule*, translated by Eric Bentley, in *The Jewish Wife and Other Short Plays*, 1965; also translated by Ralph Manheim, 1977.

Die Horatier und die Kuriatier, music by Kurt Schwän (produced 1958). In *Gesammelte Werke*, 2, 1938; as *The Horatians and the Curatians*, in *Accent*, 1947.

Das Verhör des Lukullus (broadcast 1940; revised version, music by Paul Dessau, produced 1951). 1951; as *The Trial of Lucullus*, translated by H.R. Hays, 1943; as *Lucullus*, in *Plays*, 1, 1960.

Mutter Courage und ihre Kinder (produced 1941). 1949; In *Versuche*, 9, 1949; revised edition, 1950; edited by W. Hecht, 1964; as *Mother Courage and Her Children*, translated by H.R. Hays, 1941; also translated by Eric Bentley, in *Seven Plays*, 1961, and *Collected Plays*, 2, 1962; John Willett, in *Collected Plays*, 5, 1980.

Der gute Mensch von Sezuan (produced 1943). In *Versuche*, 12, 1953; revised edition, 1958; edited by W. Hecht, 1968; as *The Good Woman of Setzuan*, translated by Eric Bentley, in *Parables for the Theatre*, 1948; as *The Good Person of Szechwan*, translated by John Willett, in *Plays*, 2, 1962; as *The Good Person of Sichuan*, translated by Michael Hofmann, 1989.

Galileo (produced 1943; revised version, with Charles Laughton, produced 1947; revised version, as *Leben des Galilei*, produced 1955). 1955; edited by W. Hecht, 1963; as *Galileo*, translated by Brecht and Charles Laughton, in *From the Modern Repertoire*, series 2, edited by Eric Bentley, 1953; as *The Life of Galileo*, translated by Desmond I. Vesey, 1960; also translated by John Willett, in *Collected Plays*, 5, 1980.

Der kaukasische Kreidekreis (produced 1948). In *Sinn und Form—Sonderheft*, 1949; as *The Caucasian Chalk Circle*, translated by Eric Bentley, in *Parables for the Theatre*, 1948; also translated by James and Tania Stern, with W.H. Auden, in *Collected Plays*, 7, 1960.

Herr Puntila und sein Knecht Matti (produced 1948). In *Versuche*, 10, 1950; as *Mr Puntila and His Man Matti*, translated by John Willett, in *Collected Plays*, 6, 1977.

Die Antigone des Sophokles, from Hölderlin's translation of Sophokles' play (produced 1948). 1955; translated as *Antigone*, 1989.

Der Hofmeister, from the play by J.M.R. Lenz (produced 1950). In *Versuche*, 11, 1951; as *The Tutor*, in *Collected*

Plays, 9, 1973 (US edition only); also translated and adapted by Pip Broughton, 1988.
Herrnburger Bericht, music by Paul Dessau (produced 1951). 1951.
Der Prozess der Jeanne d'Arc zu Rouen 1431, from his radio play (produced 1952). In *Stücke*, 12, 1959; as *The Trial of Joan of Arc*, in *Collected Plays*, 9, 1973 (US edition only).
Don Juan, from the play by Molière (produced 1953). In *Stücke*, 12, 1959; as *Don Juan*, in *Collected Plays*, 9, 1973 (US edition only).
Die Gesichte der Simone Machard, with Lion Feuchtwanger (produced 1957). In *Sinn und Form*, 5–6, 1956; as *The Visions of Simone Machard*, translated by Hugh and Ellen Rank, in *Collected Plays*, 7, 1976.
Die Tage der Kommune, music by Hanns Eisler (produced 1956). In *Versuche*, 15, and *Stücke*, 10, both 1957; as *The Days of the Commune*, in *Dunster Drama Review*, 1971; also translated by Clive Barker and Arno Reinfrank, 1978.
Pauken und Trompeten, with Elisabeth Hauptmann and Benno Besson, music by Rudolf Wagner-Regeny, from a play by George Farquhar (produced 1956). In *Stücke*, 12, 1959; as *Trumpets and Drums*, in *Collected Plays*, 9, 1973 (US edition only).
Der aufhaltsame Aufstieg des Arturo Ui (produced 1958). In *Stücke*, 9, 1957; as *The Resistible Rise of Arturo Ui*, translated by Ralph Manheim, in *Collected Plays*, 6, 1976.
Schweik im zweiten Weltkrieg, music by Hanns Eisler (produced 1957). In *Stücke*, 10, 1957; edited by Herbert Knust, 1974; as *Schweik in the Second World War*, translated by William Rowlinson, in *Collected Plays*, 7, 1976.
Coriolan, from the play by Shakespeare (produced 1962). In *Stücke*, 11, 1959; as *Coriolanus*, in *Collected Plays*, 9, 1973 (US edition only).
Seven Plays (includes *Jungle of Cities*; *Man Equals Man*; *St Joan of the Stockyards*; *Mother Courage and Her Children*; *Galileo*; *The Good Woman of Setzuan*; *The Caucasian Chalk Circle*), edited and translated by Eric Bentley. 1961.
Der Bettler; oder, Der tote Hund. In *Stücke*, 13, 1966; as *The Beggar; or, the Dead Dog*, translated by Michael Hamburger, in *Collected Plays*, 1, 1970.
Er treibt den Teufel aus. In *Stücke*, 13, 1966; as *Driving Out a Devil*, translated by Richard Greenburger, in *Collected Plays*, 1, 1970.
Lux in Tenebris. In *Stücke*, 13, 1966; as *Lux in Tenebris*, translated by Eva Geisel and Ernest Borneman, in *Collected Plays*, 1, 1970.
Der Fischzug. In *Stücke*, 13, 1966; as *The Catch*, translated by John Willett, in *Collected Plays*, 1, 1970.
Jungle of Cities and Other Plays (includes *Jungle of Cities*; *Drums in the Night*; *Roundheads and Peakheads*), translated by Anselm Hollo and others. 1966.
Turandot; oder, Der Kongress der Weisswäscher, music by Hanns Eisler (produced 1969). In *Gesammelte Werke*, 1967.
Der Brotladen (produced 1967). 1969.
Kühle Wampe: Protokoll des Films und Materialien, edited by W. Gersch and W. Hecht. 1969.

Screenplays: *Kühle Wampe*, with others, 1932; *Hangmen Also Die*, with John Wexley and Fritz Lang, 1943.

Radio Plays: *Macbeth*, from the play by Shakespeare, 1927; *Hamlet*, from the play by Shakespeare, 1931; *Die heilige Johanna der Schlachthöfe*, 1932.

Fiction

Der Dreigroschenroman. 1934; as *A Penny for the Poor*, translated by Desmond I. Vesey and Christopher Isherwood, 1937; as *Threepenny Novel*, translated by Vesey and Isherwood, 1956.
Kalendergeschichten. 1948; as *Tales from the Calendar*, translated by Yvonne Kapp and Michael Hamburger, 1961.
Die Geschäfte des Herrn Julius Cäsar. 1957.

Verse

Taschenpostille. 1926.
Hauspostille. 1927; as *Manual of Piety*, translated by Eric Bentley, 1966.
Lieder Gedichte Chöre, with Hanns Eisler. 1934.
Svendborger Gedichte. 1939.
Selected Poems. 1947.
Die Erziehung der Hirse. 1951.
Hundert Gedichte. 1951.
Gedichte, edited by S. Streller. 1955.
Gedichte und Lieder, edited by P. Suhrkamp. 1956.
Selected Poems, translated by H.R. Hays. 1959.
Poems on the Theatre, translated by John Berger and Anna Bostock. 1961.
Gedichte aus dem Nachlass, edited by Herta Ramthun. 2 vols., 1982.
Poems and Songs from the Plays, translated by John Willett. 1990.

Other

Gesammelte Werke. 2 vols., 1938.
Theaterarbeit, with others. 1952.
Gesammelte Werke. 40 vols., 1953— .
Kriegsfibel. 1955.
Schriften zum Theater. 1957; as *Brecht on Theater*, edited and translated by John Willett, 1964.
Flüchtlingsgespräche. 1961.
Dialoge aus dem Messingkauf. 1964; as *The Messingkauf Dialogues*, translated by John Willett, 1965.
Arbeitsjournal, edited by Werner Hecht. 2 vols., 1973; as *Journals, 1934–1955*, edited by John Willett, translated by Hugh Rorrison, 1993.
Autobiographische Aufzeichungen 1920–1954, Tagebücher 1920–22, edited by Herta Ramthun. 1975; *Tagebücher* as *Diaries 1920–22*, translated by John Willett, 1979.
Briefe, edited by Günter Gläser. 2 vols., 1981.
Über die bildenden Künste, edited by Jost Hermand. 1983.
Letters 1913–1956, edited by John Willett, translated by Ralph Manheim. 1990.

Translator, with Margarete Steffin, *Die Kindheit*, by Martin Andersen-Nexö. 1945.

*

Bibliography: in *Sinn und Form*, 1957; *Brecht-Bibliographie* by Gerhard Seidel, 1975— .

Critical Studies: *Die dramatischen Versuche Bertolt Brechts 1918–1933*, 1955, and *Drama und Geschichte. Bertolt Brechts 'Leben des Galilei' und andere Stücke*, 1965, both by Ernst Schumacher; *Brecht: A Choice of Evils: A Critical Study of the Man, His Work, and His Opinions* by Martin Esslin, 1959, 4th revised edition, 1984; *The Theatre of Bertolt Brecht*, 1959, revised edition, 1977, and *Brecht in Context: Comparative Approaches*, 1984, both by John Willett; *Brecht: A Collection of Critical Essays* edited by Peter Demetz, 1962; *Bertolt Brecht: The Despair and the Polemic* by C.R. Lyons, 1968; *Bertolt Brecht: His Life, His Art, and His Times* by Frederic Ewen, 1970; *The Essential Brecht*, 1972, and *Bertolt Brecht: Chaos, According to Plan*, 1987, both by John Fuegi; *Understanding Brecht* by Walter Benjamin, 1973; *Essays on Brecht: Theater and Politics* edited by Siegfried Mews and Herbert Knust, 1974; *Brecht Chronicle*, 1975, and *Brecht: A Biography*, translated by John Nowell, 1979, both by Klaus Völker; *The Dialectic and the Early Brecht: An Interpretative Study of 'Trommeln in der Nacht'* by David Bathnick, 1975; *Bertolt Brecht's Adaptations for the Berliner Ensemble* by Arrigo Subiotto, 1975; *Brecht the Dramatist* by Ronald Gray, 1976; *Der Hofmeister: A Critical Analysis of Bertolt Brecht's Adaptation of Lenz's Drama* by Laurence P.A. Kitching, 1976; *The Mask of Evil: Brecht's Response to the Poetry, Theatre and Thought of China and Japan* by Anthony Tatlow, 1977; *Brecht: A Study* by Michael Morley, 1977; *Towards Utopia: A Study of Brecht* by Keith Dickson, 1978; *Bertolt Brecht and Post-War French Drama* by Victoria Williams Hill, 1978; *Bertolt Brecht* by Karl H. Schoeps, 1978; *Bertolt Brecht's Great Plays* by Alfred D. White, 1978; *Brecht's Misgivings* by Roy Pascal, 1978; *Approaching 'Mother Courage', or, 'Who's Afraid of Bertolt Brecht?* by Christopher Michael Sperberg, 1979; *Brecht as Thinker: Studies in Literary Marxism and Existentialism* by Ralph J. Ley, 1979; *Bertolt Brecht in America* by James K. Lyon, 1980; *Bertolt Brecht: Political Theory and Literary Practice* edited by Betty N. Weber and Hubert Heinen, 1980; *The Morality of Doubt: Brecht and the German Dramatic Tradition* by Edward McInnes, 1980; *Brecht* by Jan Needle, 1981; *Brecht's America* by Patty Lee Parmalee, 1981; *The Brecht Commentaries 1943–1980*, 1981, and *The Brecht Memoir*, 1985, both by Eric Bentley; *Brecht in Perspective* edited by Graham Bartram and Anthony Waine, 1982; *Characterisation of Women in the Plays of Bertolt Brecht* by Bernard Fenn, 1982; *Brecht's Early Plays*, 1982, and *Bertolt Brecht*, 1987, both by Ronald Speirs; *Brecht in Exile* by Bruce Cook, 1983; *Brecht: A Biography*, 1983, and *Bertolt Brecht: The Plays*, 1984, both by Ronald Hayman; *Brecht's Poetry: A Critical Study* by Peter Whitaker, 1985; *Lukács and Brecht* by David Pike, 1985; *Exception and Rules: Brecht, Planchon and 'The Good Person of Szechwan'* by Pia Kleber, 1987, and *Re-interpreting Brecht: His Influence on Contemporary Drama and Film*, edited by Kleber and Colin Visser, 1990; *Bertolt Brecht: Dialectics, Poetry and Politics* by Peter Brooker, 1988; *Critical Essays on Bertolt Brecht* edited by Siegfried Mews, 1989; *Brecht and the West German Theatre: The Practice and Politics of Interpretation* by John Rouse, 1989; *The Poetry of Brecht* by Philip J. Thomson, 1989; *Postmodern Brecht: A Re-presentation* by Elizabeth Wright, 1989; *Brecht and the Theory of the Media* by Roswitha Müller, 1990; *Leitmotif and Drama: Wagner, Brecht and the Limits of 'Epic' Theatre* by H.M. Brown, 1991; *Received Truths: Bertolt Brecht and the Problem of Gestus and Musical Meaning* by Kenneth Fowler, 1991; *The Young Brecht* by Hanns Otto Münsterer, translated by Tom Kuhn and Karen Leeder, 1992.

* * *

Bertolt Brecht is the single most innovative and influential force in 20th-century theatre. He wrote some three dozen plays, and these, together with his theories and productions, prose and verse, are all of a unity, generated by and contributing to a coherent and rational philosophy of man and society. This philosophy is essentially political in the widest sense, defining theatre as the depiction in artistic terms of the interaction of individuals in social situations, affecting each other's lives. Brecht was not satisfied with illusory depiction—the mimetic reproduction of the world, he was a realist who aimed at illuminating his audience's perception of society. He sought to articulate the underlying, objective 'truth' of a situation, to explain how 'what is' comes about. Such a view rested on the conviction that all human actions are explicable in terms of the workings of society, that 'the fate of a man is determined by other men'.

For most of his life Brecht was a Marxist. He endeavoured to assimilate into drama the investigative methods and findings of the 'new' sciences of sociological, political, and economic analysis, and tried to evolve for the theatre a strategy of writing, acting, and production that would render it adequate to its role in the contemporary world. This he called 'epic' theatre because of its fundamental rejection of the primacy of illusion and emotion, and its emphasis on the 'narrative', reflective stance of the historian.

In his early plays after World War I Brecht showed a predilection for the rejects of society, victims of the grinding capitalism of the bourgeois world. The 'beaten hero', as Walter Benjamin called him, reflected the imbalance of overwhelming economic forces and individual powerlessness. *Baal* showed an asocial hero in an asocial world; *Im Dickicht der Städte* (*Jungle of Cities*) provided a model of the isolated individual's struggle for survival in a capitalist structure; and the dismantling and reassembly of the hero in *Mann ist Mann* (*Man Equals Man*) thematized the manipulation of human beings by exploitative powers. During the period of his systematic study of Marxism after 1926 Brecht evolved from a rebellious to a disciplined supporter of the working-class struggle. The idiosyncratic 'learning plays' like *Die Massnahme* (*The Measures Taken*) and *Die Ausnahme und die Regel* (*The Exception and the Rule*) are milestones in Brecht's developing conception of the function of theatre in a social context, offering openly didactic Marxist studies in models of (political) action. Even the apparently innocuous entertainment of *Die Dreigroschenoper* (*The Threepenny Opera*)—audiences have long been captivated by Kurt Weill's catchy tunes—masked a virulent attack on the bandit morality of bourgeois capitalism.

On the accession to power of the Nazi regime in 1933 Brecht immediately went into exile. This caesura paradoxically signalled the start of his most productive period, an astounding output of major plays, theoretical essays, prose writing, and a stream of poetry from 1933 to 1945. It is symptomatic of Brecht's single-mindedness, perseverance, and vision that at this time, driven as he was from one country to another and almost entirely deprived of a German-speaking public—Denmark, Finland, and the USA were his major staging-posts—he created a handful of plays that were to establish his truly international reputation: *Mutter Courage und ihre Kinder* (*Mother Courage and Her Children*), *Galileo* (*The Life of Galileo*), *Der gute Mensch von Sezuan* (*The Good Person of Szechwan*), *Herr Puntila und sein Knecht Matti* (*Mr Puntila and His Man Matti*), *Der kaukasische Kreidekreis* (*The Caucasian Chalk Circle*). To some extent these plays compromise with the traditional Aristotelian drama from which Brecht had earlier dissociated himself so vehemently. They rely partly for their effect—and certainly for their popularity—on full-bodied characters caught in the classical dilemmas of dramatic heroes. Yet Brecht does ascribe the emotionally absorbing contradictions of human behaviour to the dialectics of society and its distorting, brutalizing effects on human personality.

The Nazis provided Brecht with a precise and concrete target in place of the formless, anonymous capitalism of Marxist theory and rhetoric, for he saw the actual fascist regime in Germany as a manifestation of 'the most naked, shameless, oppressive and deceitful form of capitalism'. His literary attacks on this virulent menace range from the sober documented realism of *Furcht und Elend des Dritten Reiches* (*The Private Life of the Master Race*), culled from newspaper items and information leaking from inside Germany, to the gangster satire of *Der aufhaltsame Aufstieg des Arturo Ui* (*The Resistible Rise of Arturo Ui*), and a range of vitriolic, elegiac, admonishing, hopeful poems.

After World War II Brecht eventually made his way back to Europe, settling in East Berlin in 1949. Here he was afforded every facility as the most prized cultural figure in the German Democratic Republic; supported by generous subsidies, he founded the world-renowned Berliner Ensemble with his wife, the actress Helene Weigel. Under Brecht's direction this theatre company established a wide-ranging repertoire, including Brecht's own plays as well as his free adaptations of many classics, such as Shakespeare's *Coriolanus* and Molière's *Don Juan*. Brecht also had the freedom and complete control of theatrical resources to try out, alter, and refine his ideas on epic writing, acting, and production. It was largely in these years until his death in 1956 that Brecht's dramatic style and theories were disseminated throughout the world to establish him as the focal point of 20th-century theatre.

The most important element in Brecht's theories was the celebrated 'alienation effect' (*Verfremdungseffekt*), a term he used to describe the technique of 'distancing' the audience from the play. The purpose of this was to enable the spectator to retain a detached, dispassionate, critical view of the events being enacted on stage, and not to be totally absorbed emotionally with a consequent loss of rational judgement. Brecht demanded that an alienating depiction should be 'one that allows the object to be recognized but at the same time makes it appear unfamiliar'; it requires 'a technique of taking the human social incidents to be portrayed and labelling them as something striking, something that calls for explanation, and is not to be taken for granted, not just natural. The object of this "effect" is to allow the spectator to criticize constructively from a social point of view'. Alienation, Brecht found, could be induced in many ways. Hence his free borrowing and parodying of other writers, his liberal use of music and songs (along with all the other 'sister arts' of theatre), his exploitation of full lighting, placards, masks, 'montage' and cinematic techniques—all to break the 'atmosphere' of the stage and prevent the mystification of the spectator. By these means Brecht tried to reflect in the dialogue, structure, and production of individual scenes and whole plays the inconsistencies, ironical illogicalities, and dialectical contradictions of history and of individuals. His purpose was to foster insight into the workings of society and open the way to progress by emancipating man's thinking from the rigidities of tradition.

—Arrigo V. Subiotto

BAAL
Play by Bertolt Brecht, 1922.

Although written from an ideological position very different from the Marxist one on which his later, better-known plays were based, Brecht's first full-length play set a pattern to be followed by the playwright throughout the rest of his career inasmuch as it was subject to a process of repeated revision. The first version, written in 1918, was strongly stamped by Brecht's aversion to another play, *The Lonely One*, by the Expressionist (and later National Socialist) dramatist Hanns Johst. Johst's play had depicted, sympathetically, the downfall of the poet, playwright, and misunderstood 'genius' Christian Dietrich Grabbe, as a process of self-destruction prompted by spiritual anguish. Brecht's hero, too, is a poet, but one whose self-destruction buys him a life of great intensity, every passing moment of which is savoured to the full. By 1919 Brecht had already revised the play once, by 1920 for a second time and by 1922 it had undergone a third revision. By now it was acceptable to a publisher, although Brecht felt that it had lost much of its vitality in the process of revision. Certainly, the 1919 version provides the fullest exposition of Baal's subjectivity, but it is still influenced excessively by the polemic against Johst, whereas the first published version is more clearly structured and has been cut to a more performable length. In 1922 the play was given a brief and rather unsuccessful first run after the very considerable theatrical success of Brecht's second play, *Drums in the Night* (*Trommeln in der Nacht*).

The year 1926 saw the completion of yet another version of the play, now with a new title, *Biography of the Man Baal*. The curious mention of 'man' in the title reflects the fact that the mythical qualities in the original figure (implicit in his name, which is that of a Canaanite fertility god, and highlighted in his own 'Chorale of the Great Baal') have been largely eliminated in favour of a sardonic account, in the manner of the modish 'Neue Sachlichkeit' or 'New Realism' of the mid-1920s, of the increasingly desolate life of a poet-cum-motor-mechanic. When this Baal runs away from civilization, he finds precious little nature to return to, since it is being engulfed by the relentless spread of the great cities. From the beginning of the 1930s onwards, after Brecht had begun to devote his writing to the cause of a Communist revolution, he experimented with yet another approach to his egocentric first creation. The result was just a few, fragmentary scenes for a work to be entitled 'Wicked Baal, the Asocial One'. Brecht's unrealized intention was to build a *Lehrstück* (teaching play) around this anarchic figure, so that those performing the play could discover for themselves both the destructive and the creative potential inherent in Baal's self-centred quest for pleasure. Although Brecht failed to carry out the project of a *Lehrstück*, this approach to the character bore fruit elsewhere, in that the 'Baal type' re-appeared in numerous guises in other plays (Mauler in *Saint Joan of the Stockyards*, Galileo in *The Life of Galileo*, Puntila in *Mr Puntila and His Man Matti*), where the function of the figure is to illustrate the conflicts of interest between the individual and society that any social revolution must address.

Baal was originally conceived not simply as the life of a poet but as a poetic drama or 'scenic ballad', as it is sometimes called. The play unfolds in a loose sequence of scenes that show Baal moving even further away from social existence until he is left to die alone, crawling out of a woodcutter's hut to gain a last glimpse of the stars.

The nearest approach to a plot is provided by Baal's relationship with Ekart, a musician who challenges Baal to cut his ties to society, becomes one of his lovers, and is eventually killed by Baal for flirting with a tart in an inn. The play's unity is created on the level of image and symbol rather than through plot. Baal's most important relationship is not with any individual but with Death, who is present wherever Baal looks, goading him with reminders of transience and thus prompting him to live each moment with the utmost intensity. Death is both Baal's enemy and his ally. Thus Baal's poems are all, indirectly, hymns to Death, sensuous, pathetic, funny, and macabre celebrations of that process of decay which is life-in-death. If one follows Brecht's later injunction to look for the specific historical features of cultural products, the concerns and style of the play point to the background of World War I against which it was conceived. Brecht himself contrived to avoid active military service, but many of his schoolfriends were sent to the front and many did not return. One who did survive, Caspar Neher (a gifted artist who was later to design many sets for Brecht), responded to the play in a manner probably typical of that generation: 'Your Baal is as good as ten litres of schnapps.'

—Ronald Speirs

THE CAUCASIAN CHALK CIRCLE (Der kaukasische Kreidekreis)
Play by Bertolt Brecht, 1948.

The notion of a play based on the Chinese parable dramatized by Li Hsing Tao probably occurred to Brecht in the early 1920s. He suggested the theme to Klabund (1890–1928), whose *Chalk Circle* (*Der Kreidekreis*) was produced in Berlin in 1925 by Max Reinhardt, under whom Brecht studied stage craft. In Danish exile Brecht returned to the motif and framed a story that he completed in Finland in 1940, setting the action in his hometown at the end of the Thirty Years War. The protagonist of 'The Augsburg Chalk Circle' is Anna, servant to a wealthy Protestant named Zingli. When the household is sacked by Catholic troops, Frau Zingli abandons her young son and flees. Anna spirits the boy out of the city, enters into an unhappy marriage of convenience, and raises him as her own, only to see him reclaimed by Frau Zingli after the peace in an attempt to regain her, by then, late husband's property. Anna appeals to the earthy Judge Dollinger, who awards her custody after subjecting both 'mothers' to the chalk circle test reminiscent of King Solomon's sword.

In 1943 in Los Angeles Brecht began recasting the story for a Broadway debut and enlisted Ruth Berlau as collaborator. A draft of *The Caucasian Chalk Circle* was finished in June 1944 with a revision in September, but the Broadway production never materialized before Brecht was subpoenaed to testify in the congressional hearing on 'communist infiltration of the motion picture industry'. He left the United States the day after his testimony. The play was first produced in English by the Carleton College Players on 4 May 1948 at the Nourse Little Theatre in Northfield, Minnesota. The German premiere, with music by Paul Dessau, was staged by Brecht's own Berliner Ensemble on 7 October 1954 at the Theater am Schiffbauerdamm. Of the three dozen or so plays Brecht wrote, *The Caucasian Chalk Circle* is considered—together with *The Life of Galileo*, *Mother Courage and Her Children*,

The Good Person of Szechwan, and *Mr Puntila and His Man Matti*—as one of his five great works.

Between story and play the setting of the main action shifted from Augsburg to Grusinia during one of the myriad Persian wars. This 'parable-like play', as Brecht styled it, is in six acts, the first serving as a prologue. A tribute to Soviet Marxism, the prologue opens in Georgia, after Hitler's defeat. Members of two communes, the Rosa Luxemburg fruit growers and the Galinsk goat breeders, convene to resolve their dispute over a valley. The goat breeders, who were relocated during the war, want to use the valley as pasture, but the fruit growers' plan to irrigate it for orchards and vineyards. The fruit growers' project is by common agreement the more productive. To conclude the meeting, the fruit growers present a play directed by the singer Arkadi Cheidze for the entertainment of their comrades. The singer functions as chorus, both narrating and interpreting the action.

'In olden times, in bloody times' Grusinian governor Georgi Abashvili is deposed and executed by order of Prince Kazbeki, one of a clique of disaffected princelings. While escaping from the palace the governor's wife leaves behind her infant son Michael. The child is saved by Grusha, an unmarried kitchen maid. Pursued by hostile soldiers in search of the heir, Grusha makes her way over the mountains to her brother's farm. In transit she once abandons the child herself —exemplary of Brecht's *Verfremdungseffekt* (alienation effect), calculated here to prevent the audience from sympathizing too strongly with the heroine and thus relinquishing critical judgement—but retrieves him. Before her pious sister-in-law, Grusha is compelled to pass the child off as her own and play along with her pusillanimous brother's fabrication that she awaits her husband's return from the front. Through autumn and winter she rears Michael on the farm, teaching him how to speak and to play the games that prepare him for a life of farmwork. For the sake of a marriage certificate Grusha's brother arranges for her to wed Yussup, a dying peasant. Although Grusha is already engaged to Simon, a soldier in Persia, she agrees reluctantly with the plan, convinced that Yussup hasn't long to live. Yussup, however, recovers when news breaks that the war has ended—and with it conscription. In a poignant scene Simon arrives to claim his bride, only to find her married. Even as Grusha tries to explain how she acquired a husband and child while remaining faithful, soldiers appear and seize Michael. Here the plot takes a twist. Prince Kazbeki has been beheaded, and the governor's wife, Natella Abashvili, seeks to establish maternity in court in a bid to claim the Abashvili estates as Michael's regent.

The focus in act five is on Azdak, poacher and intellectual turned judge. In staging notes Brecht describes Azdak as a 'disappointed revolutionary posing as a human wreck'. For having unwittingly sheltered the grand duke, deposed on the same day as his vassal Georgi Abashvili, Azdak denounces himself to the martial authorities. He becomes judge by chance, chosen as a joke by soldiers called upon by Prince Kazbeki to appoint a successor to a lynched judge. Azdak travels the district trying cases, taking bribes from the rich, and dispensing his singular justice. 'It's men with nothing in their pockets who alone are able to corrupt Azdak.' To save time he occasionally hears two cases at once. When the grand duke is returned to power, he confirms Azdak's authority, who by now is about to be lynched.

The stories of Grusha and Azdak converge in the final act. It is Azdak who hears Lady Abashvili's appeal and Grusha's contesting of it. Natella's counsels bribe Azdak accordingly, whereas Grusha brings friends who perjure themselves on her behalf. Azdak elects to hear an elderly couple's divorce case simultaneously. He curtails testimony over Michael and has the bailiff draw a circle on the floor and place the boy in it. Natella and Grusha are each then charged to seize a hand and attempt to pull Michael out of the circle on Azdak's signal. Twice Lady Abashvili jerks him to her side, twice Grusha lets go to prevent his injury.

Azdak awards Michael to Grusha, confiscates the estates for a public park, and pronounces an errant verdict in the divorce case—divorcing Grusha from Yussup that she may marry Simon. The singer intones the moral: 'Things should belong to those who do well by them / Children to motherly women that they may thrive / . . . And the valley to those who water it, that it may bear fruit.'

— Albert E. Gurganus

THE GOOD PERSON OF SZECHWAN (Der gute Mensch von Sezuan)
Play by Bertolt Brecht, 1943.

Like Brecht's other three most celebrated plays (*Mother Courage*, *The Life of Galileo*, and *The Caucasian Chalk Circle*) *The Good Person of Szechwan* was written during the author's period of exile from Germany. It remains one of Brecht's most frequently staged plays. Its popularity may be ascribed to the almost folksy simplicity of the action, perhaps also to the fact that it may be interpreted—like so much of Brecht's work—both at a harmless, superficial level and in a more radical way: what some spectators will see as a slightly sentimental story of a tart with a heart of gold is in fact a striking condemnation of capitalism. The action consists of ten scenes, a prologue, short 'interludes' that serve as commentary to the main action, and a verse epilogue.

The play begins with three gods, who are in search of a good person, looking for a night's shelter in Szechwan province. They are doing this in response to the complaint which has been heard for 'almost two thousand years', that the commandments of the gods are too strict, and economic reality too harsh, to enable men both to be good and to survive. The gods finally find shelter with Shen Te, a young woman who is spontaneously kind and who 'cannot say no', an ironic description given the fact that she has been forced into prostitution through poverty. Divine gratitude takes the form of a substantial sum of money, with which Shen Te buys a small tobacco shop which she hopes will enable her to do good deeds. Her unquestioning generosity soon leads her into both financial and emotional trouble. At the suggestion of one of the people she is trying to help, she 'invents' a stern male cousin, Shui Ta, by assuming a male disguise. Shui Ta is as callous as Shen Te is generous, motivated totally by self-interest and cold calculation. Shen Te finds recourse to this bizarre 'helper' increasingly necessary, particularly when she discovers she is pregnant by her lover, Yang Sun, who exploits her goodness like all the others. Shen Te spends so much time in the guise of Shui Ta that she is accused of Shen Te's murder. At the trial the gods arrange to take the place of the normal judges and try Shui Ta. When the court is cleared Shen Te reveals her secret and admits to the gods both her desperate plight and her equally desperate attempt to remedy it. The gods withdraw on a pink cloud, benignly smiling and waving, leaving Shen Te in despair.

The epilogue follows. By now it is clear that the gods are nothing but convenient dramatic fictions. From the outset they lack substance: although we are assured that they exhibit an excellent likeness to their images in the temple (which temple? which religion?), they are both ineffectual—they are forbidden to 'interfere in the economic sphere'—and all-too-human. Whereas the first god tends to deny anything is ever amiss, ('Shall the world be changed? How? By whom? No, everything is in order!'), the second seeks rational explanations—flooding is caused by poorly maintained dykes, it is not a punishment for ungodly behaviour—while the third god always has a kind word at hand. The gods are mere ciphers, they motivate the action but are totally incapable of useful intervention. Their elevation to the role of judges at the end is merely authorial sleight of hand (a parallel to Azdak's service on the bench in *The Caucasian Chalk Circle*), and in no way confers authority. Their abandonment of Shen Te at the end of the play does indeed cry to heaven—but even the gods admit that the heavens are a void. If a solution is to be found, it must be found on earth. The gods are in fact the *reverse* of the *deus ex machina* of ancient tragedy. As they drift upwards, smiling and waving like superannuated royalty, we realize that their function is merely to pose the problem; they cannot even conceive of a solution.

On one level the transformation of Shen Te into Shui Ta is simply a comic device, effected by a mask, a change of clothing, a lowering of the voice, and a replacing of female body-language by its male equivalent—a stage fiction which is abundantly clear to the audience. More importantly, however, it is a powerful symbol for the way in which a world based on ruthless exploitation literally tears apart a person who seeks to behave with that decent, kindly, humane generosity that Brecht always sought, so infrequently found, and so convincingly invented. Although there is a sentimental streak in Shen Te, which emerges most clearly in the early days of her infatuation with Yang Sun, her 'goodness' is never seriously called into question, merely its potentially destructive nature in the exploitative society in which she lives. It is most convincingly demonstrated in her stubborn resolve to provide for her as yet unborn child, linking her positively with Brecht's other great mother figure, Grusha in *The Caucasian Chalk Circle* (which might equally well have been entitled 'The Good Person of the Caucasus'). The counter example is, of course, Mother Courage who, ostensibly dedicated to the preservation of her three children, loses them all because of her blind addiction to business.

Shen Te's creation of Shui Ta does not in any sense 'save' the situation into which she is forced by her generosity. Shui Ta merely substitutes kindness for brutality. A proponent of 'Victorian values' of the least savoury kind, he sets up a tobacco factory with illegal working conditions in complicity with the corrupt authorities. Behind a façade of 'entrepreneurial' efficiency, he creates an industrial jungle where dog eats dog for minimal wages, turning Yang Sun, ever the cynical opportunist, into a willing slave-driver who seriously contemplates supplanting his master. In an earlier prose version of the story, Brecht speaks of a 'sweatshop of the worst kind', and the stage directions describe the workers as 'horribly huddled together'; like animals. In fact their conditions are illegal, and Shui Ta has to allow them more space. The authorities agree to turn a blind eye, if he employs no more than *twice* the legal number of workers per unit space. Shui Ta's 'solution' is merely a desperate, brutal—and illegal—response to a world based on exploitation. It compounds the evil. (In an alternative version of the play, Brecht turns the tobacco factory into an opium factory, to demonstrate the true nature of Shui Ta's beneficial activity.)

Like the gods, Shui Ta is part of the problem, not part of its solution. The dilemma is presented with dramatic mastery. But is there a solution? The epilogue, which Brecht added in the final version of the play, is both clear yet characteristically hesitant. The mock apology is not out of place: indeed 'the curtain is closed and all the questions open'. But are the questions so open now? That the solution cannot be brought by 'merely' another set of gods, or no gods at all, needs no further demonstration. Should it be a different set of people, or a different world? We do not get a clear call to a Marxist revolution at any price, as in Brecht's earlier play, *The Measures Taken*, which is also set in China. Yet it remains undeniable that the agonizing questions raised in this challenging theatrical parable could be answered by a society that puts people before profit.

—Bruce Watson

THE LIFE OF GALILEO (Galileo)
Play by Bertolt Brecht, 1943.

The Life of Galileo follows Galileo from his 'invention' of the telescope through his confrontation with the reactionary power of the Church to his writing of the Discorsi in old age under virtual house arrest. It is unique among Brecht's plays in taking as its central character a major figure from history. Many of the other characters with whom he interacts are also powerful historical figures, and many of the events portrayed in the play are based in reality, although Brecht does attribute to Galileo an entirely unhistorical sense of being at the dawn of a 'new age' of science for the people. Brecht holds Galileo responsible both for the frustration of the hopes of the people for social change and the subsequent development of 'pure' science. When Galileo confirms the validity of the Copernican system by observation with his telescope, he places science at the barricades for progress towards the possibility of a new social order and the rejection of blindly accepted authority, represented by the Church's adherence to the Ptolemaic system. With his recantation, Brecht's Galileo allows that authority to reassert itself, to stifle legitimate research, and to appropriate for its own benefit the results of scientific enquiry.

With its concentration on the fate of its central character and its indoor locations, *The Life of Galileo* lacks the epic breadth of his other major plays. It does, however, contain some of Brecht's most theatrically effective scenes demonstrating on stage the concrete nature of the truth Brecht was seeking to represent. In the robing scene Brecht develops a stunningly telling image. The mathematician Pope Barbarini starts the scene with rational acceptance of the truth of Galileo's discoveries. As the scene progresses and he puts on the vestments, he physically becomes the image of the head of the Church, and his rationality is progressively overwhelmed until he accepts the authority vested in him. As the scene ends he is ready to deny Galileo's discoveries, rejecting what he knows to be the truth to preserve the power of the Church. Equally effective is the play's first scene in which, after visibly enjoying his bath, Galileo demonstrates the movement of the earth around the sun to Andrea by physically picking him up on his stool and moving him.

With this concrete demonstration of a complex scientific concept Brecht's Galileo shows his intensely physical nature. The excitement he shows in his explanation of the movement of the earth is as sensual as the pleasure he takes from a bath. His scientific research derives from the same motivation as his eating and drinking. He is a glutton. His appetite is as keen for a goose dinner as it is for discoveries in astronomy. As with many self-indulgent people, however, he is a physical

coward, and recants on sight of the instruments of torture. While not a consciously cruel man, his self-absorption in his work, which amounts to monomania, loses his daughter her husband, and might have cost his landlady her life in the plague.

The first version of *The Life of Galileo* was written in Denmark in three weeks during 1938 as the first major play of Brecht's exile from Germany, and performed in Zurich in 1943. In it the cunning Galileo is presented in a positive light, recanting in public only to continue his ground-breaking work in private. This stratagem is adopted by a number of Brecht's characters in the face of overwhelming opposition. It was indeed not unfamiliar to Brecht himself, and he might be seen as propounding it as a way for dissenting thinkers to survive under the Nazis. However, in 1945, after revelations of the Nazi abuse of science and the dropping of the first atom bomb on Japan, Brecht in his second version of the play gives the aged Galileo a moving speech in which he accuses himself of releasing scientific research from legitimate responsibility. Brecht no longer believed in the primacy of free scientific enquiry which he saw during World War II as being subjected to immoral exploitation by the scientists' political masters. His Galileo rejects this stratagem of deceit, calling instead for a version of the Hippocratic oath for scientists, to force them to face the consequences of their research and for them to assume a proper responsibility for it.

For the stage premiere of the 'American' version of the play at the Coronet Theatre, Beverly Hills in 1947, Brecht himself produced an English translation with the actor Charles Laughton. As Brecht spoke poor English and Laughton no German the translation was the result of a search for English equivalents by Laughton for Brecht's 'gestic' performances of the German. This version was later translated into German for staging in Cologne in 1955, and, altered further by Brecht, was performed at the Berliner Ensemble in 1957 in a production started by Brecht and continued after his death by Erich Engel.

The character of Galileo, with its dynamism, confidence, and energy so quickly collapsing at his recantation into self-loathing and recrimination, is one of Brecht's most impressive inventions and a marvellous opportunity for character actors of the calibre of Ernst Busch in 1957 and Ekkehard Schall in 1978 at the Berliner Ensemble, and Michael Gambon at the National Theatre, London, in 1980. But the split in the characterization between the essentially sympathetic and positive portrayal of the first part of the play and the judgemental picture of the traitor to science presented in the penultimate scene has for some actors proved unbridgeable, despite Brecht's insertion of more negative elements in the third version.

Galileo's moral and physical weakness may lead him to recant, but his character embodies for Brecht the essence of scientific enquiry—an insatiable thirst for experimentation arising out of a conviction that one should doubt everything, only accepting an idea when, despite one's best endeavours, it cannot be disproved. It is this questioning attitude when applied to society and human interaction that is at the heart of Brecht's concept of a 'Theatre for a Scientific Age'.

—A.J. Meech

MOTHER COURAGE AND HER CHILDREN (Mutter Courage und ihre Kinder)
Play by Bertolt Brecht, 1941.

Brecht wrote the first version of *Mother Courage and Her Children*, probably his best-known play, in the autumn of

1939, although it is likely that he had been developing the idea for some years. At that time he was in exile in Scandinavia where he was deeply disturbed by the readiness of Scandinavian countries, especially Denmark, to trade with Germany despite what he regarded as the very obvious signs that Germany was planning an expansionist war of which the Scandinavians were likely to be early victims. The play sought to teach some timely lessons, namely that war is nothing but business conducted with other means and in other commodities ('instead of cheese it's now with lead'), that only those with a large 'pair of scissors' can make their cut out of the business of war, and that, for the little man at least, there are no winners since 'war makes all human virtues deadly, even for those who possess them'. His method of teaching these lessons was one he used in most of his 'classic' later plays. It involved the techniques of 'estrangement' or de-familiarization (presenting something all too familiar in a new light, so as to challenge common assumptions), and 'historicization', stepping back from the immediate present in order to gain a distanced, larger, and fundamental grasp of the issues. Hence he set *Mother Courage* in the period of the Thirty Years War (1618–48) which swept across most of the Continent, causing great loss of life not only among fighting men but also among civilians because of the famines and pestilence that followed in its wake.

Brecht's dramatic chronicle centres on the family of Anna Fierling, known as 'Mother Courage' because of her willingness to risk her life for the sake of her business, an opportunistic camp-follower who sets out to make a living for herself and her children by selling wares to whichever army is willing to buy them. The play opens in the spring of 1624. Mother Courage's wagon, pulled by her two sons, is stopped by two recruiting officers on the look-out for new men. While Mother Courage is distracted by the chance of selling a belt-buckle, her 'bold' son Eilif is lured away to join the soldiers. The scene ends with an explicit lesson which will be repeated and varied throughout the play: 'If from the war you would live, to the war you must give'. Mother Courage is shown constantly in a double perspective, as an object both of criticism and of sympathy. She is criticized for her entrepreneurial approach to war as an opportunity for gain; as such she shares the guilt of all war-profiteers and thus only gets what she deserves when she loses her children one by one to the war. In each case where a child is taken away (Eilif), killed (Swiss Cheese), or mutilated (Kattrin), Mother Courage's business dealings are directly implicated. On the other hand she pursues her business not out of mere greed, but in order to provide for herself and her family. She is a 'great living contradiction', a mother who loses her children by trying to provide for them, the embodiment of a human virtue rendered deadly by war. She could also have lost them if, like other 'little people' (e.g. peasants) in the play, she had simply worked the land peacefully, for war destroys bystanders as well as those who go out to meet it. Brecht constructed such situations of coerced culpability and inescapable self-injury because, as a Marxist, he wanted the audience to recognize that there is no simple and, above all, no piecemeal-reformist solution to the dilemma. The contradictions which tear the family and Mother Courage apart are endemic to class society, the result of a competitive, self-centred form of social and economic organization. The play displays half-guilt and suffering in order to challenge the audience to reflect on the changes that would be necessary to make human virtues productive rather than destructive.

The play is an example of Brecht's epic theatre, a form of play in which events are mediated to the audience via a narrative voice in various guises, in the form of banners strung across the stage summarizing the content of the scene that follows, in the form of rhyming couplets or songs addressed directly to the audience (thus stressing the theatricality rather than the illusory reality of the performance), and in the manner of acting, whereby the actor is required to 'show' the behaviour of his or her character critically rather than simply impersonate that character. However, Brecht's theatre did not eschew emotion entirely. No one can watch Mother Courage as she hears her son being executed off-stage, unable to scream lest she betray herself, without identifying with her pain. But for Brecht empathy was not an end in itself; it was only useful if it promoted critical reflection and the will to remove the causes of suffering. As a piece of epic theatre *Mother Courage* has no truck with the unities of action, time, and place typical of classical drama. The play is unified not by plot but by argument, each episode contributing to the 'dialectical' demonstration of the lessons the playwright wishes the audience to learn. In many instances the lesson is left implicit, so that the spectator has to draw conclusions from the juxtaposition of contradictions, as when one scene ends with Mother Courage cursing the war while the very next shows her singing its praises again, seemingly mindless now of her bandaged daughter. When orthodox communist critics complained that the play seemed to lack a positive message and in particular that Mother Courage fails to learn from experience, Brecht's reply was characteristic: what mattered was not whether Mother Courage learned anything but that the audience should learn to see things differently.

—Ronald Speirs

THE THREEPENNY OPERA (Die Dreigroschenoper)
Play by Bertolt Brecht, 1928.

Brecht's reworking of John Gay's *The Beggar's Opera*—translations by Elisabeth Hauptmann and music by Kurt Weill—opened on 31 August 1928 at the Schiffsbauerdamm Theatre in Berlin. Its enormous popular success provided one of the theatrical sensations of the decade. Brecht retained considerable elements of Gay's original story unchanged. In particular he preserved the 'alienating' equation between the bourgeoisie and a gang of criminals on which Gay's work was based, as well as the element of the parody of conventional art-forms. In Gay's play the forms and attitudes of Handelian opera are the target, in Brecht's case various aspects of bourgeois theatre (the happy end, identification with the hero/ine) and (reinforced by Weill's score) the sentimentality general within bourgeois culture. Brecht transposed the action into early Victorian London and enriched the story with songs in cabaret style, using a number of disparate sources, among them François Villon and Rudyard Kipling—so much so that he was rather unfairly (and not for the last time) accused of plagiarism. Of the songs, 'Mack the Knife' has become a popular standard.

Macheath, leader of a violent London gang, marries Polly, the daughter of Peachum, 'the beggars' king', leader of a rival gang devoted to exploiting the poor and monopolizing the crime of the city. Peachum's intrigues to bring Macheath to justice eventually succeed—despite Macheath's close friendship with chief police Brown—but the play finishes with a happy end, a mock-heroic liberation scene parodying Beethoven's *Fidelio* in which Macheath receives a royal pardon and is elevated to the ranks of the hereditary peerage.

In the combination of popular and classical musical traditions, its unique evocation of a seedy yet glitzy underworld, its brilliant dialogue and humour, Brecht's *Threepenny Opera* is a typically ambiguous product of the 'Golden Twenties': socially critical and radical in its attitudes, but by no means unenjoyable to its supposed target, the bourgeoisie. Like all Brecht's early work it illustrates certain of his theories of the epic theatre, which Brecht began to formulate systematically in his *Notes on 'Mahagonny'* in 1930. His use of the 18th-century source shows clearly Brecht's fascination with those traditional forms of theatre that do not conform to the conventions of the 'theatre of illusion' perfected by the late 19th-century dramatists and producers. The play is neatly poised between the anarchy and cynicism of the early plays (*Baal*, *Drums in the Night*, and *In the Jungle of Cities*) and the more didactic tone of the works of the early 1930s.

The success of the stage show led to a film version, in the course of which Brecht was involved in (unsuccessful) litigation when he tried to have the story-line changed for greater political effect, among other things expanding Macheath's business into the world of banking. His own *Threepenny Novel* (1934) is an attempt to rework elements of the material into a more hard-hitting political statement. But the dispute with the film company enabled Brecht to explore the particular theory of culture distinctive to the film, and to reflect on the consequences for his own subsequent writing of the *Threepenny Opera*'s extraordinary mixture of glamorous and popular success with political satire and social criticism. While the play remains—with *Happy End* and *The Rise and Fall of the City of Mahagonny*—a work highly evocative of the 1920s, it has a significant place in the evolution of Brecht's mature style.

—Hugh Ridley

BREDERO, Gerbrand Adriaensz. Born in Amsterdam, The Netherlands, in 1585. Studied painting with Francesco Badens: only one painting survives. Associated with the Amsterdam Rederijkerskamer (Rhetoricians' Club, established by Burgundians in 15th century for staging of plays and pageants) and d'Eglantier; broke to join the Nederduytsche Academie; ensign in Schutterij (local militia). Lived in Amsterdam all his life; friend of Pieter Hooft, *q.v.*, and Hugo Grotius. *Died 23 August 1618.*

PUBLICATIONS

Collections

Alle de spelen [Complete Plays], edited by P. van Waesberge. 1622.
Werken [Works], edited by J. ten Brink, H.E. Moltzer, G. Kalff, and others. 3 vols., 1890.
Werken [Works], edited by J.A.N. Knuttel. 3 vols., 1918–29.
Verspreid werk [Extended Work], edited by G.A. Stuiveling and B.C. Damsteegt. 1986.

Plays

Treur-spel van Rodd'rick ende Alphonsus [Tragedy of Roderick and Alphonse] (produced 1611). 1616.

Griane (produced 1612). 1616.
Klucht van de koe [Farce of the Cow] (produced 1612). 1619, reprinted 1971.
Klucht van den molenaer [Farce of the Miller] (produced 1613). 1618, reprinted 1971.
Het Moortje [The Little Moor], adaptation of *Eunuchus* by Terence (produced 1615). 1617.
Lucelle. 1616.
De Spaanschen Brabander Ierolimo. 1618; as *The Spanish Brabanter*, translated by H. Dixon Brumble, 1982.
De stomme ridder [The Mute Knight] (produced 1618). 1619.
De Klucht van Symen sonder soeticheyt [The Farce of Simon Without Sweetness]. 1619, reprinted 1971.
Klucht van den hoochduytschen quacksalver [Farce of the German Quack], from Terence. 1619.
Van een huys-man en een barbier [Of a Householder and a Barber]. 1622.
Claes Cloet met een roumantel [Claes Cloet in Penitential Garb]. 1622.
Angeniet, completed by Jan Starter (produced 1628). 1623.
Schijn-heylich [Hypocrite]. 1624.

Verse

Apollo of Ghesangh der Musen [Apollo or Song of the Muses]. 1615.
Geestigh Liedt-Boecxken [Spiritual Verse Book]. 1616; corrected posthumous edition, 1621.
Boertigh, amoreus, en aendachtig groot Lied-Boek [Comic, Amorous, and Religious Verse Book]. 1622, reprinted 1974; two poems and two songs translated by Paul Vincent, in *Dutch Crossing*, 25 and 27, 1985.

*

Bibliography: *G.A. Bredero: Eene bibliographie* by J.H.W. Unger, 1884.

Critical Studies: *Bredero* by J.A.N. Knuttel, 1949; *De Waardering van Gerbr. Adr. Bredero* by J.P. Naeff, 1960; *Memoriaal van Bredero* and *Rondom Bredero, een viertal verkenningen*, both by Garmt Stuiveling, 1970; *'t Kan verkeren, Leven en werk van Gerbrandt Bredero* by H. Cartens, 1972; *Bredero* edited by M.A. Schenkeveld van der Dussen and others, 1985.

* * *

Like his contemporaries Pieter Hooft and Joost van den Vondel, Gerbrand Adriaensz Bredero belongs to the generation of Dutch writers that made the transition between the Middle Ages and the Renaissance. He learned to write in the medieval genres and traditions established and propagated by the Rederijkerskamers (Rhetoricians' Club), but celebrated his greatest successes with works that adhered more closely to the emerging Renaissance poetics.

Bredero's first works for the stage were *kluchten*, or farces, often realistic and sometimes more than a trifle scatological, in the medieval tradition that confronted the audience with its failings in order to cure it of them. Bredero succeeded admirably in the former, as he was to prove again in his farces *Klucht van de koe* [Farce of the Cow], *Klucht van den molenaer* [Farce of the Miller], and *Klucht van den hoochduytschen quacksalver* [Farce of the German Quack]. Like his contemporaries, he wrote for a double audience. The farces and, generally speaking, the works more attributable to the Middle Ages, were aimed at the less educated, whereas the Renaissance comedies were addressed to the educated but written in a way that appealed to every spectator and reader. Of all the Dutch writers of the 'Golden 17th Century', Bredero had perhaps the closest personal experience of this dichotomy. Unlike his contemporaries, he did not receive a classical education, although he knew French. As a result, even though he could read the Classics in translation, he did not—with the exception of *Het Moortje* [The Little Moor], a transposition to Amsterdam of Terence's *Eunuchus*—write any of his works on a Classical theme, as other writers of his time did as a matter of course.

Bredero's tragicomedies and poems may be said to occupy a middle position between medieval and Renaissance poetics. The tragicomedies continue the Dutch medieval tradition of the *abele spelen* by dramatizing epic/novelistic sources, while the title of Bredero's final collection of poems very obviously reflects the traditional division of poetry (humorous, amorous, and religious) established by the Rhetoricians. This mid-way position may well have made Bredero's poems popular with the readers of his day; they were given the highest accolade readers could bestow on them at the time—three pirated editions (of which not a single copy survives, suggesting that they were literally 'read to pieces') appeared before Bredero himself prepared a more or less authorized fourth one, published posthumously.

Romantic critics, in particular, have tried to reveal Bredero, the man behind the poet, but to little avail. The myth of the *poète maudit*, driven to drink because he could not marry any of the better-educated women he wooed, and who repented on his death bed, has been shattered by the discovery that the very poem often quoted as 'proof' of the man's heartfelt repentance was, in fact, a translation of a French original made by the poet interested in a fellow poet's work. Today Bredero the poet is generally considered a consummate craftsman, trying his hand at various genres, not only with a view to emulating them in the Renaissance tradition, but also with a sound instinct for what would go down well with the audiences of his time.

He first established himself as a writer for the theatre which, in his time, led a somewhat precarious existence in Amsterdam under the stern gaze of orthodox Calvinist preachers. While continuing to produce farces, he began to write tragicomedies, modelled not on Aristotle, but rather on contemporary English and Spanish drama. This 'modern' theatre was much more popular than the 'classical' comedies and tragedies written for the élite. Bredero found the material for his tragicomedies in the immensely popular Spanish romances of chivalry published, in his time, as frequently in Antwerp (the richest city in the Spanish Empire, a day's journey south of Amsterdam) as in Madrid, and translated into Dutch. They are constructed around the age-old 'boy meets, loses, weds girl' sequence. Bredero's own hand can be seen in the transposition of the material to the Netherlands, in particular Amsterdam, the city whose speech he incorporated into many of his works, giving it literary respectability at a time when his contemporaries tried to write a less regionally marked Dutch, more closely modelled on Greek and Latin.

Bredero's most celebrated play is the comedy *De Spaanschen Brabander Ierolimo* (*The Spanish Brabanter*). Its protagonist, Ierolimo, is one of the many immigrants from what is now Flanders, in the north of Belgium, who flocked to Amsterdam after the Spanish armies reconquered Antwerp. These immigrants, usually much richer and better educated than the Amsterdammers themselves, were to no small extent responsible for the phenomenal growth of their adopted city.

They also caused enormous resentment, thematized in the play by the exchanges between the would-be rich and educated, foppish and Hispanicized Ierolimo, and his down-to-earth Amsterdam servant Robbeknol, who confirms the native Amsterdammers in the audience in their self-esteem. Even though Bredero used as his source *Lazarillo de Tormes*, recently published in Antwerp, Ierolimo and Robbeknol are to some extent reminiscent of Don Quixote and Sancho Panza. The archetypal nature of both the characters and their situation has allowed them to transcend the context of 17th-century Amsterdam.

Because of the 'uncouth' nature of his material, Bredero was held in low esteem by subsequent writers and critics who propagated the ideals of French neo-classicism. By casting him in the role of a *poète maudit*, Romantic critics managed to credit him with a certain acceptability. In recent years, Bredero has regained his popularity—his works are taught in literature courses and, more importantly, staged in theatres. These historical metamorphoses seem fitting for a writer who signed most of his works with the motto 'Things change'.

—André Lefevere

BRENNU-NJÁLS SAGA. See **NJÁLS SAGA**.

BRENTANO, Clemens (Maria Wenzeslaus). Born in Ehrenbreitstein, Germany, 9 September 1778. Grandson of the writer Sophie von La Roche and brother of the writer Bettina von Arnim, *q.v.* Spent his youth in Frankfurt and Koblenz. Educated at the University of Bonn, 1794; Halle University, 1794; studied medicine at the University of Jena, 1798–1800. Married 1) Sophie Mereau in 1803 (died in childbirth 1806); three children (all deceased in infancy); 2) Auguste Busmann in 1807 (dissolved 1810, divorced 1812). Met Achim von Arnim in Göttingen, 1801 and travelled the Rhine with him, 1802; associated with the Heidelberg group of Romantics; founding editor, with von Arnim, of the journal *Zeitung für Einsiedler*, 1808; lived in Bohemia, 1811–13 and Vienna, 1813–14. Amanuensis for the nun Anna Katharina Emmerich, 1817–24. *Died 28 July 1842.*

PUBLICATIONS

Collections

Die Märchen, edited by Guido Görres. 2 vols., 1847.
Gesammelte Schriften, edited by Christian Brentano. 9 vols., 1851–55.
Ausgewählte Schriften, edited by J. Diel. 2 vols., 1873.
Die Märchen von Clemens Brentano, edited by Hans E. Giehrl. 1955.
Gedichte, Erzählungen, Briefe, edited by Hans Magnus Enzensberger. 1958.
Werke, edited by Friedhelm Kemp. 4 vols., 1963–68.

Gedichte, edited by Wolfgang Frühwald. 1968.
Werke, edited by Max Preitz. 3 vols., 1974.
Sämtliche Werke und Briefe, edited by Jürgen Behrens, Wolfgang Frühwald, and Detlev Lüders. 6 vols., 1975–85.
Gedichte und Erzählungen, edited by Hans-Georg Werner. 1986.

Plays

Satiren und poetische Spiele. Gustav Wasa. 1800.
Die lustigen Musikanten (opera libretto), music by E.T.A. Hoffmann (produced 1805). 1803.
Ponce de Leon. 1804; as *Valeria; oder, Vaterlist* (produced 1804), 1901.
Die Gründung Prags. 1815.
Viktoria und ihre Geschwister mit fliegenden Fahnen und brennender Lunte. 1817.
Aloys und Imelde, edited by Agnes Harnack. 1912.

Fiction

Godwi; oder, Das steinerne Bild der Mutter. 1801.
Entweder wunderbare Geschichte von Bogs dem Uhrmacher, wie er zwar das menschliche Leben längst verlassen, nun aber doch, nach vielen musikalischen Leiden zu Wasser und zu Lande, in die bürgerliche Schützengesellschaft aufgenommen zu werden Hoffnung hat; oder, die über die Ufer der badischen Wochenschrift als Beilage ausgetretene Konzert-Anzeige, with Joseph von Görres. 1807.
Geschichte vom braven Kasperl und dem schönen Annerl. 1817; published separately, 1838; as *Honor; or, The Story of Brave Caspar and the Fair Annerl*, translated by T.W. Appell, 1847; as *The Story of Just Caspar and Fair Annie*, translated by Helene Scher, in *Four Romantic Tales*, 1975.
Die drei Nüsse. 1834.
Gockel, Hinkel, und Gackeleia (stories). 1838; as *The Wondrous Tale of Cocky, Clucky, and Cackle*, translated by C.W. Heckethorn, 1889; as *The Tale of Gockel, Hinkel and Gackeliah*, translated by Doris Orgel, 1961.
Die mehreren Wehmüller und ungarischen Nationalgesichter. 1843.
Fairy Tales from Brentano, translated by Kate Freiligrath Kroeker. 1885.
New Fairy Tales from Brentano, translated by Kate Freiligrath Kroeker. 1888.
Das Märchen von dem Baron von Hüpfenstich (stories). 1918.
Die Schachtel mit der Friedenspuppe, edited by Josef Körner. 1922.
Chronika eines fahrenden Schülers (stories). 1923.

Verse

Legende von der heiligen Marina. 1841.
Romanzen vom Rosenkranz. 1852.
Gedichte. 1854.

Other

Universitati Litterariae Kantate auf den 15 October 1810. 1810.
Der Philister vor, in und nach der Geschichte. 1811.
Rheinübergang; Kriegsrundgesang. 1814.
Das Lied vom Korporal. 1815.
Das Mosel-Eisgangs-Lied von einer wunderbar erhaltenen Familie und einem traurig untergegangenen Mägdlein in dem Dorf Lay bei Koblenz. 1830.

Die Barmherzigen Schwestern in Bezug auf Armen-und Krankenpflege; Nebst einem Bericht über das Bürgerhospital in Koblenz und erläuternden Beilagen. 1831.
Das bittere Leiden unseres Herrn Jesu Christi. Nach den Betrachtungen der gottseligen Klosterfrau Anna Katharina Emmerich. 1833; as *The Passion of Our Lord Jesus Christ According to the Revelations of Anna Catharina Emmerich*, 1914.
Rothkehlchens, Liebseelchens, Ermordung und Begräbnis. 1843.
Der unglückliche Franzose, oder der deutschen Freiheit Himmelfahrt, ein Schattenspiel mit Bildern, edited by Christian Brentano. 1850.
Leben der heil. Jungfrau Maria. Nach den Betrachtungen der gottseligen Anna Katharina Emmerich. 1852; as *Das Marienleben nach Betrachtungen der Anna Katharina Emmerich*, edited by Claire Brauflacht, 1952; as *The Life of the Blessed Virgin Mary from the Visions of Anne Catherine Emmerich*, translated by Michael Palairet, 1954.
Das Leben unseres Herrn und Heilandes Jesu Christi, edited by Karl E. Schmöger. 3 vols., 1858–60; as *The Life of Our Lord and Saviour Jesus Christ, combined with the Bitter Passion of the Life of Mary from the Revelations of Anne Catherine Emerrich as Recorded in the Journals of Clemens Brentano*, 1954.
Lied von eines Studenten Ankunft in Heidelberg. 1882.
Briefe an Johann Georg. 1888.
Briefwechsel zwischen Clemens Brentano und Sophie Mereau, edited by Heinz Amelung. 1908.
Clemens Brentano and Edward von Steinle, edited by Alexander von Bernus and Alfons M. von Steinel. 1909.
Clemens Brentano und Minna Reichenbach. Ungedruckte Briefe des Dichters, edited by W. Limburger. 1921.
Rheinmärchen: für die romantische Gemeinde neu bearbeitet, edited by Vereger Werneck. 1926.
Satiren und Parodien, edited by Andreas Müller. 1935.
Das unsterbliche Leben. Unbekannte Briefe von Clemens Brentano, edited by Wilhelm Schellberg and Friedrich Fuchs. 1939.
Clemens und Bettina: Geschwisterbriefe, edited by Ina Seidel. 1948.
Briefe, edited by Friedrich Seebass. 2 vols., 1951.
Briefwechsel mit Heinrich Remigius Sauerländer, edited by Anton Krättli. 1962.
Briefe an Emile Linder, edited by Wolfgang Frühwald. 1969.
Clemens Brentano (correspondence), edited by Werner Vordtriede and Gabriele Bartenschläger. 1970.
Clemens Brentano, Philipp Otto Runge: Briefwechsel, edited by Konrad Feilchenfeldt. 1974.
Visionen und Leben: Anna Katharina Emmerich aufgezeichnet, edited by Anton Brieger. 1974.
Lebe der Liebe und liebe das Leben: der Briefwechsel von Clemens Brentano und Sophie Mereau. 1981.

Editor, with Sophie Brentano, *Spanische und italienische Novellen.* 2 vols., 1804–06.
Editor, with Ludwig Achim von Arnim, *Des Knaben Wunderhorn: Alte deutsche Lieder.* 3 vols., 1806–08; translated in part by Margarete Münsterberg as 'The Boy's Magic Horn', in *The German Classics of the Nineteenth and Twentieth Centuries*, edited by Kuno Francke and W.G. Howard, vol. 5, 1913.
Editor, *Der Goldfaden: Eine Schöne alte Geschichte*, by Jörg Wickram. 1809.
Editor, *Trutz Nachtigall, ein geistlich poetisches Lustwäldlein*, by Friedrich Spee. 1817.

Editor, *Goldnes Tugendbuch*, by Friedrich Spee. 2 vols., 1829.

*

Bibliography: *Clemens Brentano: Ein Lebensbild nach gedruckten und ungedruckten Quellen* by Johannes B. Diel and Wilhelm Kreiten, 2 vols., 1877–78.

Critical Studies: *Romantic Orpheus: Profiles of Clemens Brentano*, 1974, and *Clemens Brentano*, 1981, both by John F. Fetzer; 'Anxiety of the Spirit: Brentano and Arnim' by Eric A. Blackall, in *The Novels of the German Romantics*, 1983; *Negative Spring: Crisis Imagery in the Works of Brentano, Lenau, Rilke, and T.S. Eliot* by David B. Dickens, 1989; *Poetic Wreaths: Art, Death and Narration in the Märchen of Clemens Brentano* by Lawrence O. Frye, 1989.

* * *

Clemens Brentano's work is both intensely personal and extensively reflective. The contemporary satire in early works such as *Gustav Wasa* and *Entweder wunderbare Geschichte von Bogs dem Uhrmacher* [Bogs, The Watchmaker] made them effective only within the age they depicted. In spite of their linguistic virtuosity they are now considered merely as literary-historical documents.

If the same fate has been shared by Brentano's first novel *Godwi*, it is due mainly to the overly complex plot and the often slight characterization, both typical failings of the 18th-century novel. There is much in this work that demonstrates the influence of the Romantic school. The construction of the narrative in the form of letters, with each character presenting their own view of events, is reminiscent of Ludwig Tieck's *William Lovell* and reflects a modern, Romantic awareness of reality as a purely subjective category. The epistolary framework breaks down in the second part of the work, and in discussions between the main character and the fictional author on the writing of the novel the fiction reflects on itself as fiction: an illustration of Friedrich Schlegel's theory of 'poetry of poetry'. *Godwi* also confirms to Schlegel's concept of the novel as a mixed form, incorporating prose, lyric, and drama: a principle which was to characterize all Brentano's work.

Brentano's receptiveness to outside influence explains the importance he placed on joint literary ventures. He worked with Achim von Arnim on the collection of folk-tales *Des Knaben Wunderhorn* (*The Boy's Magic Horn*) and with Joseph von Görres on 'Bogs, The Watchmaker'. His *Romanzen vom Rosenkranz* [Romances of the Rosary] was conceived in conjunction with illustrations by the artist Philipp Otto Runge, and Brentano's interest in the project faded after Runge's death. More significantly, Brentano's own work is 'contaminated' by outside influences. Rather than merely copying or quoting, this procedure involves the reworking of sources into a new and personal construct. In the editing of *The Boy's Magic Horn* this entailed both contributors adapting their sources and even inserting examples of their own work, while in the publication of the poetry of Brentano's wife Sophie Mereau and later of Luise Hensel, and finally in the recording of the visions of the ecstatic nun Anna Katharina Emmerick, Brentano interwove his own ideas inextricably with those of his subject.

Subjective adaptation also informs Brentano's creative writing. Much is inspired by old material, but all is imbued with the poet's own personality and style. Wherever Brentano turns to sources he blends report with interpretation, fact with opinion. This results in a complex mix of history and mythology in its widest sense in the prose fragment 'Poor Raymond', the drama *Die Gründung Prags* [The Foundation of Prague], the revised version of the fairy-tale *Gockel, Hinkel and Gackeliah*, and the ambitious cycle of poetry *Romanzen vom Rosenkranz*, which was to unite Biblical themes (the flight into Egypt; original sin and redemption) with legend (Tannhäuser), history (the arrival of the gypsies in Europe; the Crusades), and mythology (the origin of the Rosary).

Brentano's Italian fairy-tales are based on Giovanni Battista Basile's *Il Pentamerone* (*The Pentamerone*), but Brentano devises his own tales, which become tales for their own sake, told and enjoyed for the linguistic exuberance of the plays on words, sounds, and meanings, and the verbal leitmotifs which culminate in the endless variations of the egg theme in 'Gockel and Hinkel'. His Rhine fairy-tales are inspired by the traditional folk-tales of this area, but again Brentano allows his fertile imagination full rein, and these stories, with their digressive, oral style, are a further testimony to his talent as a storyteller and to his linguistic inventiveness. Brentano's true virtuosity in these tales, however, lies in his amalgamation of simplicity and subtlety in both structure and content. These are sophisticated revisions of children's stories, which do not lose the freshness and vigour of the original.

Brentano's poetry likewise combines old and new, spontaneity and self-awareness. In 'The Song of the Spinning-Woman' and 'On the Rhine' the simple language and tone of the folk-song is enriched by subtle imagery and intricate construction. In the poem 'Spring Song' Brentano takes a medieval love lyric as the basis for a complex personal statement. His sensitivity to language is evident in the exploitation of sound, rhythm, and rhyme, for example, in 'Nightingale' or in Radlauf's song in 'The Story of Miller Radlauf'.

It is perhaps in his poetry that Brentano expresses his most personal feelings. Erotic and religious sentiments are repeatedly interlinked, for example, in 'Love's Despair at Love' and 'The Evening Breezes Blow', reflecting his unceasing attempt to reconcile these two kinds of love and achieve sanctuary from isolation. The poem 'A Servant's Spring Cry from the Depths' is the anguished cry of a sinner for redemption.

Brentano's work on *The Boy's Magic Horn* and the folk-tale orientation of his own poetic creations indicate his profound interest in the common people and his genuine belief in the aesthetic stature of their art. 'The Rose', 'The Minstrel', and 'The Chronicle of the Travelling Scholar' turn to the idealized simplicity of the middle ages to depict young and innocent men in harmony with God and nature. The naivety is, however, studied. These works express the longing for innocence by the sinner, for simplicity by the sophisticate. In such works the self-conscious author adopts the mask of spontaneity, aware that this is a game. In the poem 'On the Rhine' the mask is of a fisherman, dreaming of his dead lover. In the final stanza the third-person narrative voice reveals itself as a first-person lyrical self, expressing personal experience in the guise of objective report. In the poem 'Lore Lay' the same device is employed in triplicate.

It is in this sense that art becomes understood as artificiality in Brentano's work, reflected, for example, in the melancholy Johannes feels when comparing his mother's song to that of the nightingale (representing nature and naturalness) in the poem 'The Song of the Spinning-Woman', in 'The Chronicle of the Travelling Scholar', and in the despair of the siren in the poem 'Lore Lay', whose evil magic is poetry itself.

The poet's alienation and his tragic yearning for lost innocence and harmony are articulated in the poems 'Echoes of Beethoven's Music' and 'When the Crippled Weaver Dreams' which, like *Godwi*, exemplify modern aesthetic self-reflection.

In the novella *Geschichte vom braven Kasperl und dem schönen Annerl* (*The Story of Just Caspar and Fair Annie*), the contrast of naive and self-aware is presented through the confrontation of a poet, torn by religious and poetic self-doubt, with an old woman, a genuine folk figure secure in her beliefs, who weaves her personal experience quite unconsciously into an artistic tale. The poet as scribe to the natural folk-poet was the role Brentano wished for himself, but he never succeeded in eliminating subjectivity and self-consciousness from his work.

—Sheila J. Dickson

THE STORY OF JUST CASPAR AND FAIR ANNIE
(Geschichte vom braven Kasperl und dem schönen Annerl)
Novella by Clemens Brentano, 1817.

The Story of Just Caspar and Fair Annie had an interesting genesis. Written at a time when Brentano was seeking to return to the Roman Catholic faith in which he had been brought up, it is basically an amalgam of two stories, supposedly derived from real-life incidents narrated by him to a friend. The first story, that of Caspar, is based on an account of the suicide of a young soldier, who feels he has been dishonoured; the second, which centres on the fate of the fair Annie, relates to a case of infanticide said to have happened in Silesia and which may also contain elements taken from a well-known German folk-song. Another source is thought to be the memoirs of the public executioner of Nuremberg, which had appeared in 1801, and which would undoubtedly have appealed to Brentano's enthusiasm for popular traditions.

The English title as it stands is somewhat misleading. 'Just' suggests someone concerned with equity in the administration of the law, whereas in the German original Caspar is 'brav'— that is, honest, upright, decent, law-abiding. Anxious above all about his 'honour', his reputation in the eyes of the world, he has the misfortune to discover that his father and step-brother are horse thieves and, unable to bear the disgrace, shoots himself over his mother's grave in the cemetery. Meanwhile, his fiancée Annie has left their native village to take up a better position as a maidservant in an aristocratic household. Here she is seduced, and in a sequence reminiscent of the Gretchen tragedy in Goethe's *Faust* murders her illegitimate child and is herself executed.

Although the story is usually regarded as an important example of the German novella, the narrative techniques adopted by Brentano are by no means straightforward. There are two main narrators. The first of these, thought by some critics to reflect Brentano's own personality, is a man of some education and leisure who is nevertheless plagued by doubts and insecurity as to his purpose and mission in life. The second, Caspar's grandmother Anna Magaret, is a formidable old lady, a woman of the people, firm in her religious faith and confident that God knows what is best for us. After hearing her version of the events that have befallen Caspar and Annie, the first narrator intervenes in the action and is able to restore their lost honour by ensuring that both will have a decent Christian burial. Interspersed throughout the text, however, are several much shorter narratives. There is a story about a French lieutenant who shoots himself after being ordered to do something dishonourable; there is the story of the huntsman Jürge, whom Anna Margaret persuades to ask for forgiveness on the eve of his execution; and there is the story of Annie's childhood where an encounter with the public executioner seems to foreshadow her destiny. Although these different strands are woven together with consummate mastery, it is undoubtedly the case that there are several separate foci. The German literary historian Benno von Weise thus considers the work to have a seminal character. It is the starting-point, he claims, for the development in 19th-century German literature of both the detective story and the novella of village life, while at the same time— through the commentary of the first narrator—it explores the late Romantic interest in the psychology of the creative personality.

There is certainly general agreement that *The Story of Just Caspar and Fair Annie* is an outstanding achievement of German Romanticism. The most obvious Romantic element is the supernatural fate-motif; the executioner's sword rattles in its case when Annie passes it as a child and she is subsequently bitten by the severed head of the huntsman. Beyond this, however, is Brentano's conscious adoption of the language of the people in Anna Margaret's narration. The tone is colloquial, and at times ungrammatical; the syntax is simple, and often illogical, the main events being recounted in a series of 'leaps and bounds' that Brentano—and Herder before him—held to be typical of the genuine folk-song and ballad. Above all, the characterization of Anna Margaret herself represents Brentano's tribute to the wisdom and simple piety of unspoilt ordinary people. Believing as he did that such people have much to teach the so-called better and more sophisticated classes, she becomes his medium for a religious outlook on life to which he aspired but which he himself felt unable to attain. For her, striving for honour in the eyes of the world, as both Caspar and Annie try to do, is presumption. God alone is the judge of honourable conduct, and what is dishonourable in terms of worldly reputation may yet be honourable in His sight. If Caspar had hurried home and not been so attentive to what people were saying about his treatment of his horse, he would have forestalled his father and step-brother and prevented them from committing their crime; if Annie had borne her illegitimate child, her village would have tried to help and support her.

Brentano is sometimes accused of inconsistency, but his message is perfectly clear. Wherever worldly honour comes first, there is disaster; when worldly honour is thrown to the winds, the outcome is propitious. This is demonstrated when the first narrator refuses to be intimidated by ceremonial etiquette and audaciously demands an interview with the Duke which leads to the posthumous pardon for both Caspar and Annie. In addition, the Duke's mistress, on discovering that her brother, Annie's seducer, is being attacked by an angry crowd, casts off her disguise and thus invites public scandal. The Duke, however, is shamed into marrying her, and the story ends with the unveiling of an allegorical statue depicting both justice and mercy. Felt by many critics to be a little too contrived for modern tastes, this represents Brentano's conviction that, beyond all the incongruities and cruelties of this transient life, there is an eternal order in which all paradoxes are reconciled.

—Margaret C. Ives

BRETON, André (Robert). Born in Tinchebray, France, 19 February 1896. Educated at Collège Chaptal, Paris, 1906–12; Faculté de Médecine, Paris, 1913–15. Served as medical assistant in army psychiatric centres, 1915–19, and medical director of École de Pilotage, Poitiers, 1939–40. Married 1) Simone Kahn in 1921 (divorced); 2) Jacqueline Lamba in 1934 (divorced), one daughter; 3) Elisa Bindhoff in 1945. Co-founding editor, with Louis Aragon and Philippe Soupault, *Littérature*, 1919–24; founded Bureau of Surrealist Research, 1924; editor, *La Révolution Surréaliste*, 1925–29, *Le Surréalisme au Service de la Révolution*, 1930–33, and *Minotaure*, 1933–39; joined the Communist Party, 1927; broadcaster, Voice of America, 1942–45; editor, *VVV*, 1942–44; director, Galerie à l'Étoile Scellée, 1952–54; editor, *Le Surréalisme Même*, 1956–57. Organized exhibitions of Surrealist art from 1936. *Died 28 September 1966.*

PUBLICATIONS

Collection

Oeuvres complètes [Pléiade Edition], edited by Marguerite Bonnet. 1988– .

Verse

Mont de piété. 1919.
Les Champs magnétiques, with Philippe Soupault. 1920; as *The Magnetic Fields*, translated by David Gascoyne, 1985.
Clair de terre. 1923.
Ralentir travaux, with René Char and Paul Éluard. 1930.
L'Union libre. 1931.
Le Revolver à cheveux blancs. 1932.
L'Air de l'eau. 1934.
Le Château étoilé. 1937.
Fata morgana. 1941; as *Fata Morgana*, translated by Clark Mills, 1969.
Les États-Généraux. 1943.
Pleine marge. 1943.
Young Cherry Trees Secured Against Hares, translated by Edouard Roditi. 1946.
Ode à Charles Fourier. 1947; as *Ode to Charles Fourier*, translated by Kenneth White, 1969.
Martinique charmeuse de serpents. 1948.
Poèmes. 1948.
Au regard des divinités. 1949.
Constellations. 1959.
Le là. 1961.
Selected Poems, translated by Kenneth White. 1969.
Poems (bilingual edition), translated by Jean-Pierre Cauvin and Mary Ann Caws. 1982.
Earthlight, translated by Bill Zavatsky and Zack Rogow. 1993.

Other

Manifeste du surréalisme; Poisson soluble. 1924, enlarged edition, 1929.
Les Pas perdus (essays). 1924.
Légitime défense. 1926.
Introduction au discours sur le peu de réalité. 1927.
Le Surréalisme et la peinture. 1928, enlarged edition, 1965; as *Surrealism and Painting*, translated by Simon Watson Taylor, 1972.
Nadja. 1928, revised edition, 1963; as *Nadja*, translated by Richard Howard, 1960.

Second manifeste du surréalisme. 1930.
L'Immaculée Conception, with Paul Éluard. 1930.
Misère de la poésie: 'L'Affaire Aragon' devant l'opinion publique. 1932.
Les Vases communicants. 1932; as *Communicating Vessels*, translated by Mary Ann Caws and Geoffrey T. Harris, 1990.
Point du jour (essays). 1934, revised editions, 1970, 1992.
Qu'est-ce que le surréalisme? 1934; as *What Is Surrealism?*, translated by David Gascoyne, 1936.
Position politique du surréalisme. 1935.
Notes sur la poésie, with Paul Éluard. 1936.
L'Amour fou. 1937; as *Mad Love*, translated by Mary Ann Caws, 1987.
Arcane 17. 1944, enlarged edition, 1947.
Situation du surréalisme entre les deux guerres. 1945.
Yves Tanguy (bilingual edition). 1946.
Les Manifestes du surréalisme. 1947, revised editions, 1955, 1962; complete edition, 1972; as *Manifestations of Surrealism*, translated by Richard Seaver and Helen R. Lane, 1969.
La Lampe dans l'horloge. 1948.
Flagrant délit: Rimbaud devant la conjuration de l'imposture et du truquage. 1949.
Entretiens 1913–1952. 1952, revised edition, 1973.
La Clé des champs (essays). 1953.
Toyen, with Jindrich Heisler and Benjamin Péret. 1953.
Adieu ne plaise. 1954.
Farouche à quatre feuilles, with others. 1954.
L'Art magique, with Gérard Legrand. 1957.
Pierre Moliner: Un film de Raymond Borde. 1964.
Perspective cavalière (essays), edited by Marguerite Bonnet. 1970.

Editor, *Trajectoire du rêve.* 1938.
Editor, with Paul Éluard, *Dictionnaire abrégé du surréalisme.* 1938.
Editor, *Anthologie de l'humour noir.* 1940(?), enlarged edition, 1950.

*

Bibliography: *André Breton: A Bibliography* by Michael Sheringham, 1972; *André Breton: A Bibliography (1972–1989)* by Elza Adamowicz, 1992.

Critical Studies: *Surrealism and the Literary Imagination: A Study of Breton and Bachelard*, 1966, *The Poetry of Dada and Surrealism*, 1970, and *Breton*, 1971, all by Mary Ann Caws; *Breton, Arbiter of Surrealism* by Clifford Browder, 1967; *André Breton, Magus of Surrealism* by Anna E. Balakian, 1971, and *André Breton Today* edited by Balakian and Rudolf E. Kuenzli, 1989; *André Breton and the Basic Concepts of Surrealism* by Michael Carrouges, translated by Maura Prendergast, 1974; *Breton and the First Principles of Surrealism* by Franklin Rosemont, 1978; *Breton: 'Nadja'* by Roger Cardinal, 1986; *André Breton: Sketch for an Early Portrait* by J.H. Matthews, 1986; *André Breton the Poet* by Keith Aspley, 1989.

* * *

Founder of the Surrealist movement, André Breton was one of the 20th century's great writers; his highly poetic prose, even more than his poems, bears witness to a magnetic power of language as the equivalent of thought.

Believing that we can remake the world by our imagination as it is activated by and through our words, Breton was able to persuade, by those words, a whole generation of thinkers and artists to pay attention to their inner gifts and intuitions as they could be seen not only to respond to the world outside but even to discover in that world 'an answer to a question we were not conscious of having'. By what he called the law of objective chance, it comes about that the inner and the outer experiences mingle in an ongoing constant communion he compared to the scientific experiment of *Les Vases communicants* (*Communicating Vessels*). Like the mingling of day and night, life and death, up and down, the two contraries are held in balance and provide the dynamism of the activated images which make over, for us, what we live by, 'the unacceptable human condition'.

Surrealism is, then, by the vision of Breton, turned towards a positive future possibility; surrealist sight insists—with the Zen master Basho—that, instead of, for example, removing the wings from a dragonfly and calling it a red pepper, we add wings to the pepper to have it become that dragonfly. The attitude is characteristic of the entire movement, whose comportment Breton repeatedly defined as 'lyric'.

In his own works, Breton stressed the overwhelming power and frightening effect of love *L'Amour fou* (*Mad Love*) as it participates in the a-rational mystery of complete surprise. Walking amid the garbage peelings on the streets of the marketplace at midnight, wondering whether it is not too late to turn back, the narrator and the poet are one with the observer of that love itself, always to be kept as marvellous, safe from the 'null and void moments' that go to make up an ordinary life.

Nadja, Breton's quite unordinary heroine, herself mad, is no more adapted to 'real' life than were the alchemists, with whom Breton feels such a bond—they aimed at transmuting our own base metal into our highest or golden selves. The impulse towards the arcane (*Arcane 17*) in no way rules out an openness to the simple everyday things; nor does madness invalidate the love of the marvellous, that child-like expectation of the next moment, this 'disponibilité' or openness to chance that infuses surrealist writing and thinking at its best.

Nor was Breton separated from dailiness: against the worst of it, he insisted that art had to maintain its own urgency, 'for the problem is no longer, as it used to be, whether a canvas can hold its own in a wheat field, but whether it can stand up against the daily paper, open or closed, which is a jungle'. Art has to hold good against famine, against reality, and against what people have done and thought.

Surrealism, as Breton conceived it, was directed against habit and against the predictable: the famous experiments in automatic writing, made to unleash the dams of imagination as the Surrealist manifestos point out, provocatively, worked towards this end, as did the images in the poems, upsetting to 'normal' ways of seeing. But always the style and the vision of Breton went far past the limits of any experiment, and worked together to—as he put it—'prevent the paths of desire from being overgrown'.

In a time of despair and uncaring, Breton may be read as resolutely turned towards what he perceived as just, with an ardour we know as genuine, and with a poetic temperament that is all too rare.

—Mary Ann Caws

FREE UNION (L'Union libre)
Poem by André Breton, 1931.

First published anonymously in 1931, 'Free Union', a blazon of the female body, is widely regarded as one of Breton's finest poems. It has been claimed that the inspiration was Suzanne Musard, but Breton is alleged to have told both his second and his third wives that 'the poem could refer to the essence of woman, in a universalized sense', as Anna E. Balakian explains in *André Breton, Magus of Surrealism*.

The title could imply that the poet had in mind the alchemists' concept of the free union of two autonomous principles, in addition to the free union of man and woman.

Although its 60 lines of free verse are not divided into stanzas or obvious sections, the poem is structured in terms of little blocks of images, most of which are devoted to one part of the body, but there are gradual shifts, for instance from the shoulders to the wrists to the fingers.

At first glance the portrait of woman in this poem is composed of a quick-fire succession of images, the vast majority of which are Surrealist in their apparent gratuitousness, but a few come as less of a surprise. The 'hour-glass waist' in line 3 is virtually a cliché, but the 'champagne shoulders' (line 15) and the 'armpits of marten and beech-nuts/Of Midsummer night/Of privet and wentletrap nests' (lines 20–22) are novel and bring the imagination of the reader fully into play.

In fact, the poem is not really a portrait of the beloved or of woman but rather an amorous or erotic litany in which the verbal is arguably more important than the visual, though the reader inevitably and immediately visualizes some of the images; the reader 'sees' the matchstick wrists, the fingers of new-mown hay, the tongue of rubbed amber and glass, the tongue of a stabbed host, the tongue of a doll whose eyes open and close, the tongue of incredible stone.

At the same time, however, the reader's ears are stimulated by the bonds that the words themselves seem to seek out and generate. In places these links are semantic ones: the image of the woman's back 'of a bird in vertical flight' (line 39) prefigures the reference to a swan's back in the evocation of the buttocks ten lines later; in the presentation of the hips the thought of the feathers of an arrow in line 45 leads instantly to that of the scapes of white peacock feathers.

Elsewhere the links are more phonic. Because they are easily lost in translation, it is better to cite some of them in the original, for instance the transition from 'Ma femme au cou d'orge imperlé' ('My wife with her neck of pearl[ed] barley') to 'Ma femme à la gorge de Val d'or' ('My wife with her throat [or bosom] a Golden Valley'), or the syllabic repetition in the line 'Ma femme au *ventre* de dépliement d'*éventail des jours*' ('My wife with her stomach like the spreading fan of days'). Words appear to attract or conjure up other words, there seems to be an accumulation of subtle shifts, modifications, metamorphoses.

At times the links are simultaneously semantic and phonic. Some of these are inherent in the French language: the juxtaposition in lines 11 and 12 of the evocation of the 'cils' (eyelashes) and 'sourcils' (eyebrows). Others, like the coupling of the first half of the word 'hasard' and 'as' in the presentation of the fingers, 'Ma femme aux doigts de hasard et d'as de coeur' ('My wife with fingers of chance and ace of hearts') are illustrations of what the concept of verbal alchemy may mean in practice.

The poem moves to an apparent climax in the evocation of the sex in terms of successively a gladiolus, a placer (deposit where precious metals such as gold or platinum may be found), a duck-billed platypus, seaweed, old sweets, and a mirror. The surprise and the erotic excitement are engendered most of all by the diversity of the imagery discovered or devised to evoke this particular part of the female anatomy.

The real and ultimate climax is constituted by the last six lines devoted, quite characteristically for Breton, to the eyes. He proceeds from utterly simple statement (eyes full of tears), via the imagery of eyes of purple panoply and a magnetic needle, of savannah eyes, eyes of water to drink in prison, eyes of wood ever under the axe, to an amazing fusion of the elements in the final line (eyes of water-level, air, earth and fire-level). It is as if woman opens the eyes of her lover to the whole universe, as if she is indeed the microcosm and it the macrocosm.

Yet it has been claimed, not wholly implausibly, by Christine Martineau-Genieys 'Autour des images et de l'éro-tique surréalistes: "L'Union libre". Étude et synthèse', in *Réflexions et recherches de nouvelle critique*, 8, 1969) that there are two persons present in the poem: in this scenario Breton is undoubtedly the lover as well as the spinner of words or the creator of images. As its title implies, this poem was meant to be a celebration of free union, and its cascading words are the expression of this celebration of an extra-marital passion to be savoured to the full.

—Keith Aspley

MAD LOVE (L'Amour fou)
Prose by André Breton, 1937.

Published in 1937, *Mad Love* follows on from *Nadja* and *Communicating Vessels* to form the third element of a prose quartet completed by *Arcane 17* in which Breton presents and examines various aspects of his affective life and his artistic preoccupations. All four works constitute a particular kind of autobiographical writing in which reflection and analysis complement and at times replace chronological narrative in the elaboration of the discourse. As in the two earlier works, Breton makes use of photographs, not just to eliminate the need for verbal descriptions but to accompany and illustrate certain phrases or references in the text.

Mad Love continues the account of the quest for a new love commenced in *Communicating Vessels*, but the fourth of the seven chapters contains an evocation of Breton's encounter with the woman, Jacqueline Lamba, who was to become his second wife.

In Chapter I Breton is more ostensibly concerned with the definition and illustration of the Surrealist concept of 'convul-sive beauty': indeed its final paragraph consists of the dramatic proclamation, 'Convulsive beauty will be'. Among the examples of the concept that he cites are Prince Rupert's drops, crystals, alcyonarians, madrepores, corals—and poetic images, of the kind produced by automatic writing.

The value of the opening chapter as a prefiguration of what is to come later in the book is provided more obviously, however, by the pretty waitress in a little restaurant and the word-play on 'l'Ondine' and 'l'on dîne' ('the Udine' and 'One dines'): she could be seen as a modern water-sprite, since she was a performer in an aquatic show.

Chapter II begins with the repetition of a pair of questions with which Breton and Éluard had launched an inquiry in the review *Minotaure*: 'Can you say what has been the most important encounter in your life? To what extent has this encounter given you the impression of being fortuitous? Or necessary?' Breton goes on to consider various definitions of chance, including the one by Souriau 'the meeting of an external causality and an internal finality', and concluding

with that of the modern materialists, according to which 'chance would be the form of manifestation of external neces-sity working its way into the human subconscious'; and the chapter closes with a recognition of the manoeuvrings of desire in search of its object.

In Chapter III this abstract theme is made concrete in the account of a visit made by Breton and Giacometti to the Flea Market in Paris in the spring of 1934. The sculptor at that time was endeavouring to solve a problem posed by the face of a female statue: the discovery there of a mask-cum-helmet was to prove the decisive key. For his part Breton picked up a wooden spoon with a shoe at the end of the handle which satisfied his previous wish, inspired by a curious phrase 'le cendrier Cendrillon'; ('the Cinderella ashtray'), that Giacometti should make for him a glass slipper, Cinderella's lost slipper, to be used as an ashtray. In the postscript to the chapter the sexual connotations of the spoon and the slipper reminded Breton of Freud's theories ('Concerning Eros and the struggle against Eros') and of Freud's proposition that 'the two instincts, both the sexual instinct and the death-instinct, behave like self-preservative instincts'.

Chapter IV gravitates around the account of Breton's en-counter with the beautiful young woman who was soon to become his new bride, and subsequently by his commentary on his 1923 poem, 'Tournesol', a commentary which seeks to demonstrate its prophetic nature in relation to this meeting with Jacqueline.

The fifth chapter is essentially a lyrical presentation of the couple's reactions to the Canary Islands. Here the themes of love and desire are accompanied by suggestions of paradise regained. Breton refers to the title of the Buñuel and Dali film *L'Âge d'or* [The Golden Age] in contrast with the 'age of mud' that contemporary Europe called to mind, before clos-ing this part of the book with a passionate invocation to Mount Teide, the volcano that dominates Tenerife.

The study is pursued from a different angle in Chapter VI, where the author discovers that the mirror of love between two people can be clouded by circumstances totally foreign to their love, but the final chapter, in the form of a letter to their daughter Aube, intended to be read by her when she was 16, dispels the impression that life and love are full of vicissi-tudes. Breton expresses the hopes that Aube will embody the eternal power of Woman and that the idea of 'mad love' will be her guiding principle, before closing with the words 'I wish you to be madly loved'.

The publication of *Mad Love* was an indication of the importance of the title-theme for members of the Surrealist movement. The precise significance of the word 'amour' for Breton is revealed in a couple of sentences slipped into Chapter V:

Love, the only love there is, carnal love, I adore, I have never ceased to adore your pernicious shadow, your mortal shadow. A day will come when man will know how to recognize you for his sole master and honour you even in the mysterious perversions with which you sur-round him.

—Keith Aspley

ODE TO CHARLES FOURIER (Ode à Charles Fourier)
Poem by André Breton, 1947.

While in exile in the United States during World War II Breton came across the complete works of Charles Fourier, the French social theorist, in a New York bookshop. They were his reading during a journey to Arizona, Nevada, and New Mexico in the summer of 1945. This *Ode* is his response to this particular conjunction of circumstances.

The poem is divided into three movements after the basic manner of the Greek ode, but here two lyrical sections in free verse surround a seemingly more prosaic central part.

The first movement, the first address to Fourier, seeks to relate the state of mankind at the end of World War II to Fourier's early 19th-century philosophy. In the central section, consisting of 12 paragraphs, the balance sheet is drawn up between the Utopian dream and contemporary reality. The final part, the renewed invocation to Fourier, is inspired by Breton's contact with native American civilization and the beauty of the American countryside: the new Eden seems a little less distant.

References to the prospectors in the desert and images from classical mythology (especially Jason's voyage in search of the Golden Fleece) introduce the theme of the quest for gold: this helps to reinforce the dream of a Golden Age, which stems implicitly from the poem's overt invocation and tribute to Fourier.

Breton was fascinated by Fourier's law of 'passionate attraction'. He could not fail to sympathize with Fourier's condemnation of the ills produced by the system of free economic competition, his disgust for war and armies, his conviction that the human condition in general could not improve before the condition of women was changed for the better. Breton shared Fourier's dislike of the domination of the family unit in modern civilization; he would have been impressed by Fourier's reasoning that the workings of society should be based on a scheme of natural association in which the gratification of individual desires and passions should serve the general good. Breton no doubt admired the absolute quality of Fourier's attack on 'civilization'.

Allusions to Fourier's thought constitute an important element of Breton's poem: Breton employs certain phrases or ideas of Fourier as springboards for his own imagination, or else some aspect of contemporary reality calls to mind observations made by Fourier. Concepts such as the 'gastrosophic régime' and 'phanerogamous morals' are incorporated into Breton's scornful survey of a world at war.

The central section, written in prose, rigidly follows Fourier's tableau of the 12 radical passions, divided into three branches of the tree of 'Unityism'. In the first of these subsections Breton composes five analyses of the passion corresponding to the five senses. In the second subsection Breton evokes friendship, love, ambition and the family (for Fourier the dominant drives of the four ages of man: childhood, youth, maturity, and old age). The third subsection of the central movement is devoted to the three distributive or mechanizing passions: the Cabalist or intriguing passion, the Butterfly or alternative passion (the penchant for variety and contrast), and the Composite, the most beautiful of the passions for Fourier.

In the poem's third and final movement the style of the allusions to Fourier's thought reverts to that of section I, save for a long extract near the end from the third volume of Fourier's *Theory of Universal Unity*, evoking life in a Fourierist *phalanstère* (or community).

The contrast between the harsh contemporary reality and the Utopian dream runs through most of the poem. On the one hand there are references to shortages and the black market, the unscrupulousness and the scandal of the commercial world, the violence and the butchery of war. On the other hand there is the affirmation, near the end of the poem, of Breton's basic optimism:

Filtering the thirst for greater well-being and maintaining it against all that could make it less pure even if and it is so I considered it proven that the betterment of human fate can be effected only very slowly and fitfully by means of down-to-earth demands and cold calculations the real lever remains nonetheless the unreasoned belief in the movement towards an edenic future and after all that is also the only leaver of the generations your youth.

(translated by Kenneth White)

This contrast is symbolized to a degree by the change of setting from the Old World of the first movement to the New World of the third. Paris is the focal point of the imagery of the first part. The poem opens with the recollection of the sight one morning in 1937 of Fourier's statue on the Boulevard de Clichy. On its plinth Breton noticed a bunch of violets, placed there, he assumes, by a woman, to commemorate the centenary of the visionary's death. By the final movement there is a step forward in both time and place, as Breton is inspired by the environment in which the *Ode* was written. He employs the gallicized name of The Petrified Forest, a national park in Arizona, as a symbol of the state or culture at that time, and writes other stanzas from the Grand Canyon and Nevada. He realizes that the place where he was writing had once been the Eden of the Indian peoples: it is from a Hopi *kiva* (or underground chamber) that he draws the inspiration for the final stanzas of the poem, alluding at one stage to the celebrated Snake-Dance.

The poem acquires an epic grandeur partly because Breton resists the temptation to dwell on his personal reasons for the trip to Reno, a quick divorce and remarriage. Thanks to such features as the anaphoric leitmotif 'Parce que' in the final movement, he is able to compose a persuasive and lyrical demonstration of his conviction that the end of the war could signal the dawn of a new era for mankind and the final word is, significantly, 'liberté' (freedom).

—Keith Aspley

BRUHADĀRANUYAKA.   See **UPANISHADS**.

BROCH, Hermann. Born in Vienna, Austria, 1 November 1886. Educated privately, 1892–96; Imperial and Royal State Secondary School, Vienna, 1897–1904; Technical College for Textile Manufacture, Vienna, 1904–06; Spinning and Weaving College, Mülhausen, 1906–07. Administrator for Austrian Red Cross during World War I. Married 1) Franziska von Rothermann in 1909 (divorced 1923), one son; 2) AnneMarie Meier-Gräfe in 1949. Managed family's factory in Teesdorf, 1907–27; reviewer, *Moderne Welt*, Vienna, 1919; studied mathematics, philosophy, and pyschology, Vienna University, 1926–30; then writer; arrested by the Nazis and detained briefly, 1938; moved to London, 1938; then settled in the United States; involved in refugee work, from 1940; became American citizen, 1944; fellow, Saybrook College,

Yale University, New Haven, Connecticut, 1949. Recipient: Guggenheim fellowship, 1941. Member, American Academy, 1942. *Died 30 May 1951.*

PUBLICATIONS

Collections

Gesammelte Werke, edited by Felix Stössinger and others. 10 vols., 1953–61.
Kommentierte Werkausgabe, edited by Paul Michael Lützeler. 13 vols., 1976–86.

Fiction

Die Schlafwandler: Ein Romantrilogie. 1952; as *The Sleepwalkers: A Trilogy*, translated by Edwin and Willa Muir, 1932.
    Pasenow; oder, Die Romantik—1888. 1931.
    Esch; oder, Die Anarchie—1903. 1931.
    Hugenau; oder, Die Sachlichkeit—1918. 1932.
Die unbekannte Grösse. 1933; as *The Unknown Quantity*, translated by Edwin and Willa Muir, 1935.
Der Tod des Vergil. 1945; as *The Death of Virgil*, translated by Jean Starr Untermeyer, 1945.
Die Schuldlosen. 1950; as *The Guiltless*, translated by Ralph Manheim, 1974.
Der Versucher, edited by Felix Stössinger. In *Gesammelte Werke*, 4. 1953.
Der Bergroman, edited by Frank Kress and Hans Albert Maier. 4 vols., 1969.
Barbara und andere Novellen, edited by Paul Michael Lützeler. 1973.
Die Verzauberung, edited by Paul Michael Lützeler, 1976; as *The Spell*, translated by H.F. Broch de Rothermann. 1987.

Plays

Die Entsühnung (produced 1934).
Aus der Luft gegriffen; oder, die Geschäfte des Baron Laborde (produced 1981).

Other

Zur Universitätsreform, edited by Götz Wienold. 1969.
Gedanken zur Politik, edited by Dieter Hildebrand. 1970.
Briefwechsel 1930–1951, with Daniel Brody, edited by Bertold Hack and Marietta Kleiss. 1971.
Völkerbund-Resolution, edited by Paul Michael Lützeler. 1973.
Hofmannsthal und seine Zeit: Eine Studie. 1974; as *Hugo von Hofmannsthal and His Time: The European Imagination 1860–1920*, edited and translated by Michael P. Steinberg, 1984.
Menschenrecht und Demokratie: Politische Schriften, edited by Paul Michael Lützeler. 1978.
Briefe über Deutschland, 1945–1949: Die Korrespondenz mit Volkmar von Zühlsdorff, edited by Paul Michael Lützeler. 1986.

*

Critical Studies: *Broch* by Theodore Ziolkowski, 1964; *The Sleepwalkers: Elucidations of Broch's Trilogy* by Dorrit C. Cohn, 1966; *The Novels of Hermann Broch* by Malcolm R. Simpson, 1977; *Hermann Broch* by Ernestine Schlant, 1978; *Hermann Broch: Eine Biographie* by Paul Michael Lützeler, 1985, translated by Janice Furness, 1987; *Sprache und Metaphorik in Hermann Broch's Roman Der Tod des Vergil* by Barbara Lube, 1986; *Sympathy for the Abyss: A Study in the Novel of German Modernism: Kafka, Broch, Musil and Thomas Mann* by Stephen D. Dowden, 1986, and *Broch: Literature, Philosophy, Politics* edited by Dowden, 1988; *Hermann Broch* by Rudolf Koester, 1987.

* * *

At the age of 42, Hermann Broch gave up a distinguished career in industry to devote himself to writing. His first major work, the trilogy *Die Schlafwandler* (*The Sleepwalkers*), is set in Germany between 1880 and 1918. It depicts a society in crisis: the old social and political order is breaking up, traditional ethical and religious tenets are being challenged. People, left without moral guidance, seem like sleepwalkers, only dimly aware of their course of action.

The first novel of the trilogy, *Pasenow; oder, Die Romantik —1888* [The Romantic], portrays the symptoms of decline among the aristocracy; in the second part, *Esch; oder, Die Anarchie—1903* [The Anarchist], a bookkeeper, failing in his search for justice, turns against society. The last novel, *Hugenau; oder, Die Sachlichkeit* [The Realist], set during the revolution of 1918, shows how the total disregard for moral values leads to betrayal and murder.

In the course of writing, Broch began to experiment with new modes of narration. His essay 'James Joyce und die Gegenwart' ['James Joyce and the Present'] (1936) is a tribute to Joyce and to the modern novel in general. It also reveals much about Broch's own thoughts about art. He rejects the purely aesthetic point of view as 'Kitsch', arguing that as science promotes man's material well-being, art should set standards for his ethical conduct. The main theme of Broch's works is a plea for a re-evaluation of moral values without which he thought the political and social decay of modern society could not be prevented.

Besides being a prolific essayist, Broch wrote plays and poems which, however, do not seem to measure up to his accomplishments as a novelist.

In the light of Broch's earlier dedication to modern narrative techniques, his next major work, *Der Bergroman* (which went through three versions), marked a surprise return to the traditional form of the novel. The narrator is an old country doctor who witnesses with horror and some fascination how a charlatan is able to gain, at least for a short time, control over the minds of his villagers.

Der Tod des Vergil (*The Death of Virgil*), considered by many critics to be Broch's greatest achievement, depicts in the form of inner monologue Virgil's visions and dreams during the last 18 hours before his death.

Broch's last work, the short story cycle *Die Schuldlosen* (*The Guiltless*), is essentially a reworking of earlier published material. *The Death of Virgil*, therefore, remains, as Broch had wished it to be, his true farewell as a writer.

—Helena Szépe

THE DEATH OF VIRGIL (Der Tod des Vergil)
Novel by Hermann Broch, 1945.

Broch's meditative and essayistic novel about the death of the Roman poet Publius Vergilius Maro (70–19 BC) started inconspicuously as a short story, 'Die Heimkehr des Vergil' [The Return of Virgil]. It had been commissioned by RAVAG radio in Vienna (which broadcast the first half of it on 17 March 1937) as a fictional contribution to a topic that was much discussed at the time: the role of art at the end of a cultural era. Broch's major source of information was Theodor Haecker's book *Vergil—Vater des Abendlands* (1931), which interprets Virgil as a prophetic precursor of a Christian Europe. An expanded fragmentary version titled 'Erzählung vom Tode' [Tale of Death], written during winter 1937–38, suddenly assumed an immediate personal relevance for its author when he was jailed in March 1938 in Altaussee, Styria, on suspicion of 'cultural bolshevism'. Broch feared for his own life and continued to expand his manuscript 'as a private confrontation with the experience and reality of death' (letter to H. Zand of 12 February 1947). After his flight to London and then to St Andrews in Scotland and directly upon his arrival to New York City on 9 October 1938, he resumed work on a story that by then had grown to the dimensions of a novel. He made good progress during his stay at the artists' colony Yaddo in Saratoga Springs, New York in summer 1939, where he met the poet Jean Starr Untermeyer who became his translator. But the precarious circumstances of his life in exile and his preoccupation with studies of mass psychology impeded the completion of the *Virgil*-book. It underwent several revisions and was not published until June 1945 (by the exile publisher Kurt Wolff's Pantheon Books), its concurrent editions in German and English receiving considerable critical attention. The translation was often praised as more accessible because it has reduced the excesses of Broch's at times overly abstract and hymnically 'mystic' style.

The Death of Virgil recounts the dying poet's last day in four sections of uneven length that, in tracing the course of his (and all) life back to its earliest beginnings, evoke the four elements of ancient philosophy. In the first section, 'Water—the Arrival', after landing in Brundisium with the imperial fleet on his return from Greece, Virgil slowly advances through the destitute urban masses of the harbour as he is being carried to his apartment in the palace. His encounters with human misery, especially as personified by throngs of howling women, the 'mass animal', make him despair of his poetic ideals so that he curses the dignified aloofness of his privileged life as an aesthete. His disenchantment turns into disorientation when a boy, Lysanias, appears as his psychopomp, the guide of his soul into the underworld. The second section is 'Fire—the Descent', in which, in imitation of Orpheus and Aeneas, Virgil's mind, feverish at night, leads him into the abyss of self-castigation. He vows to destroy the unfinished *Aeneid* in sacrificial atonement for his irresponsible life of aesthetic self-sufficiency. Disturbed by nightmarish visions he listens to three drunkards outside his window whose quarrels almost end in murder. Terrified by his helplessness he condemns all creation of beauty as a frivolous game, cruel for its lack of ethical values. In the third section, 'Earth—the Expectation', on the next day Virgil's literary friends Lucius Varius and Plotius Tucca and the court physician Charondas visit and express their utter disbelief over his decision to burn his poetic *chef d'oeuvre*. A long conversation with Augustus convinces him, however, that his act of contrition also demands humility and love and understanding of the needs of others, and it is as a sign of his appreciation for the emperor's practical purposes that he leaves the *Aeneid* to posterity. Hallucinations begin to haunt him as he relives episodes from his earlier life: his beloved Plotia whom he had left appears to him in an arcadian landscape; Lysanias turns into his *alter ego* and evokes further reminiscences of his life as a youthful poet; a slave persuades him to relinquish any

pretence that salvation may be obtained through art, and admonishes him, in an allusion to the 'Christ-prophecy' of the *Fourth Eclogue*, to place his trust in a child-saviour. As Virgil dictates his last will, his visions take him back to the harbour and out onto the infinite sea. In the last section, 'Ether—the Homecoming', as his consciousness gradually returns to its origins, Virgil's mind traverses creation in reverse order. All material manifestations dissolve and are transformed ultimately into an Orphic 'dark radiation'. The metamorphosis of his self as he submerges into cosmic totality progresses until a new 'reversal' takes place: he apprehends the (Christian) figure of a mother and child, the last in a sequence of archetypal images. It may signify both the promise of his salvation and his rebirth, as his soul, at last, experiences God's presence as a gust of wind in a primal realm that lies 'beyond language'.

The novel is a lyrical exploration of the limits of art and life. It balances precise and imaginative descriptions of a distant physical world with extensive dialogues and various forms of inner monologue. Its distinct feature is the use of a great variety of mythical images, archetypal symbols, and mathematical signs together with a hymnic, mystically paradoxical, and ecstatically abstract language that seeks to evoke a supernatural reality. In the final analysis, *The Death of Virgil* conveys a contradictory message, though. For Virgil's abjuration of aesthetic autarchy and his moral awareness that most people must contend with a very ugly life does not preclude the 'beautiful' process of his euphoric dying. The vindication of the poet as a mediator of knowledge about a transcendent world and about the fundamental verities of life conflicts with the historical reality of mass extermination and the millions of anonymous dead. This is a dichotomy Broch was unable to solve artistically but which he sought to alleviate through complementary activities: his charitable work, his political programmes, and his studies of mass psychology.

—Michael Winkler

THE SLEEPWALKERS (Die Schlafwandler)
Novels by Hermann Broch, 1931–32.

Broch wrote his trilogy, *The Sleepwalkers*, between 1928 and 1932. It is an experimental work of extraordinary intensity both in its thematic concerns and in its stylistic complexity. Its central metaphor refers to an essential state of profound disarray: traditional values prove ever more ineffective in the search for individual orientation and in sustaining the established institutions, and no values have yet been found to satisfy the different needs of a new social order. Man's quest for self-assurance within communal bonds is therefore guided by spurious precept and deceptive promise, his irrational mind incapable of genuine experiences and thus groping to find spiritual security in various compensatory obsessions. Broch, in essence, sees the cause of all modern catastrophes in the disintegration of a premodern hierarchy of religious verities. His trilogy portrays what he considers to be the final phase of an accelerating decline into chaos, which he seeks to illustrate through a variety of emblematic situations.

Three years (1888, 1903, and 1918), which occur during the reign of the last German emperor (Wilhelm II), are exemplified in the life stories of three main characters (the Junker Joachim von Pasenow, the petty bourgeois accountant August Esch, and the upstart businessman Wilhelm Huguenau), who represent three distinct patterns of psychosocial behaviour with its value system and sense of existential identity (romanticism, anarchy, realism). These concepts, somewhat at variance with their accepted definitions, signify attempts to control the perplexities of life in three different ways: through recourse to anachronistic conventions, in aggressive outbursts of sexual and religious sensuality, and with unscrupulous egotism.

Broch's fictional programme includes an astounding variety of narrative devices. They range from the speculative abstractness of a ten-part excursus on historical cognition and the disintegration of values to a form of Platonic dialogue, from parabolic tales to hymnic poetry, and from realistic descriptions to phantasmagoric inventions. This stylistic diversity supports an ever-expanding constellation of symbols and motifs, of carefully orchestrated variations, cross-references, reprises, and allusions. Especially in the second half of book III, this fictional technique reveals a compulsive tendency to construct systematic order, if not harmonious closure. The novel's structure thus anticipates, surely not inadvertently, that 'mystery of unity' toward which its principal characters can only grope with unfulfilled longing.

Broch's narrational attitude, while often opting for the immediacy of homiletic appeals and a rhetoric of ecstatic enchantment, alternates between didactic satire, resigned irony, and analytical naturalism. What epistemological persuasiveness it loses through its fixation on a monocausal theory of history, it regains in the subtle elaboration of psychological insights. This suggests that the figure of Eduard von Bertrand, a successful cotton broker and entrepreneur with a lucidly critical mind, refined sensibilities, and a profound aversion to any social doctrine, is the pivotal character of the trilogy, even though he does not directly appear in its third part. His self-conscious nihilism with its graceful rejection of all intellectual and emotional illusions can only end in suicide after Esch, the fanatical agitator for social justice, had inveighed, in a scene of surrealistic intensity, against his effete withdrawal from the responsibilities of life. But his death also exemplifies the novel's implicit argument that such a reduction to nothingness must precede the spiritual renascence to come, which makes Bertrand also a precursor of the next historical era.

None of the other characters share his freedom from obsessions. Joachim von Pasenow, after a clumsy though liberating affair with a bar dancer, clings to the strictures of feudal convention when his brother's death in a duel 'for their family's honour' necessitates his return to the ancestral estate. He must now marry a woman of his own class, Elisabeth Baddensen, who loves Bertrand, while he is still emotionally attached to the 'exotic' foreigner Ruzena. As he turns his wife into an icon of purity, he himself becomes an ever more rigid paragon of patriotic provincialism. By contrast, the unemployed accountant Esch, a person of 'impetuous attitudes', tries to bring order into a life of erratic upheavals and to rectify the universal 'bookkeeping error' created by industrial capitalism. His milieu is the workers' quarters along the Rhine between Mannheim and Cologne with their stolid propriety and with their tawdry amusements. He carries his outrage at the many small injustices perpetrated against the underclass (e.g. the shabby treatment accorded the vaudeville artist Ilona and the harassment of the union organizer Martin Geyring) with missionary zeal but he succumbs more and more to the irrational conviction that all the world's ills result from the irresponsible practices of industrialists like Bertrand. Inevitably, his various efforts to promote freedom from abuse fail, and his goal of spiritual redemption recedes into a haze of hallucinations. Both his plan to emigrate to America and his hope of experiencing a mystical transformation through marriage (to a middle-aged

tavern keeper, Mother Hentjen) are disappointed. As Esch slides back into obscurity, the deserter Huguenau assumes paradigmatic relevance. He imposes his control over a small town in the Mosel valley where a senile Pasenow serves as garrison commander and Esch owns the local newspaper. Driven by egocentric compulsions and free of moral restraints, the footloose Huguenau is a ruthless opportunist, a rapist and murderer, and the only one to profit from the impending revolutionary destruction of the old order. But the story of his career is only one section within a kaleidoscopic sequence of similarly parabolic tales, e.g. that of the young lieutenant Jaretzki, an alcoholic amputee, or that of Hannah Wendling, the case study of a genteel woman with social ambitions who ends in suicidal loneliness, or that of the bricklayer Gödicke who rebuilds his life after having been buried alive in a trench, and, perhaps most significantly, the improbable love story of the Salvation Army girl Marie in Berlin and the Talmudic scholar Nuchem.

The Sleepwalkers is a work of high intellectual ambition. Its complex fictional structure, the rigour of its moral concerns, and its psychological acuity make it one of the last outstanding examples of expressionist prose. It is also a major document of that cultural pessimism that was prevalent among liberal-conservative intellectuals during the 1920s. Exacting and of emphatic precision as Broch's philosophical temperament was in chronicling the decline of German (and Austrian) bourgeois culture and society, he had at best an uncertain vision of the future. In response to the competing ideological programmes that had gained currency after 1900, the conclusion of his trilogy projects no more than the utopian potential of Platonic idealism and of Paulinian spirituality. This reveals a deeply ambivalent disposition that is both driven by the dynamic of progressive modernism and tempered by the need for retrospective assurances.

—Michael Winkler

BRODSKII, Iosif (Aleksandrovich) [Joseph Brodsky]. Born in Leningrad, Soviet Union, 24 May 1940; emigrated to the United States in 1972, naturalized 1977. Educated at schools in Leningrad to age 15. Married; one son and one daughter. Convicted as a 'social parasite' in 1964 and served 20 months of a five-year sentence of hard labour in the far north; later exiled by the Soviet government; poet-in-residence and special lecturer, University of Michigan, Ann Arbor, 1972–73, 1974–80; has taught at Queen's College, City University of New York, Columbia University, New York, New York University, Smith College, Northampton, Massachusetts, Amherst College, Massachusetts, and Hampshire College. Currently professor of literature, Mount Holyoke College, South Hadley, Massachusetts. Recipient: Guggenheim fellowship; MacArthur fellowship; Mondello prize (Italy), 1979; National Book Critics' Circle award, 1987; Nobel prize for literature, 1987. D.Litt.: Yale University, New Haven, Connecticut, 1978; D.Litt.: Oxford University, 1991; Légion d'honneur (France), 1991. Member, American Academy of Arts and Letters: resigned in 1987 to protest against Evgenii Evtushenko, *q.v.*, being made an honorary member; corresponding member, Bavarian Academy of Sciences. US Poet Laureate, 1991–92. Lives in the United States.

PUBLICATIONS

Verse

Stikhotvoreniia i poemy [Poems and Narrative Verse]. 1965.

Elegy to John Donne and Other Poems, edited and translated by Nicholas Bethell. 1967.

Ostanovka v pustyne [A Halt in the Wilderness]. 1970; corrected edition, 1988.

Selected Poems, translated by George L. Kline. 1973.

Debut, translated by Carl R. Proffer. 1973.

The Funeral of Bobo, translated by Richard Wilbur. 1974.

Three Slavic Poets, with Tymoteusz Karpowicz and Djordje Nikolic, edited by John Rezek. 1975.

Konets prekrasnoi epokhi: Stikhotvoreniia 1964–1971 [The End of the Belle Epoque: Poetry]. 1977.

Chast' rechi: Stikhotvoreniia 1972–1976 [A Part of Speech: Poetry]. 1977.

V Anglii [In England]. 1977.

A Part of Speech, translated by Anthony Hecht and others. 1980.

Verses on the Winter Campaign 1980, translated by Alan Meyers. 1981.

Rimskie elegii [Roman Elegies]. 1982.

Novye stansy k Avguste: Stikhi k M.B. 1962–1982 [New Stanzas to Augusta: Poems to M.B.]. 1983.

Uraniia [Urania]. 1987.

To Urania: Selected Poems 1965–1985, translated by Brodskii and others. 1988.

Primechaniia paporotnika [A Fern's Commentary]. 1990.

Osennii krik iastreba [The Hawk's Cry in Autumn]. 1990.

Stikhotvoreniia [Poetry]. 1990.

Chast' rechi: Izbrannye stikhi 1962–1989 [A Part of Speech: Selected Poems]. 1990.

Nazidanie [Edification]. 1990.

Pis'ma rimskomu drugu [Letters to a Roman Friend]. 1991.

Kholmy: bol'shie stikhotvoreniia i poemy [Hills: Poetry and Narrative Verse]. 1991.

Rozhdestvenskie stikhi [Christmas Poems]. 1992.

Forma vremeni [The Form of Time] (vol. 2 includes essays and plays). 2 vols., 1992.

Kappadokia: stikhi [Cappadocia: Poems]. 1993.

Izbrannoe [Selected Poems]. 1993.

Izbrannye stikhotvoreniia [Selected Poetry]. 1994.

Plays

Mramor. 1984; as *Marbles: A Play in Three Acts*, translated by Alan Myers, 1989.

Demokratiia!/Démocratie!, translated by Véronique Schiltz (bilingual edition in Russian and French). 1990; translated as *Democracy*, 1990.

Other

Less than One: Selected Essays (in English). 1986.

The Nobel Lecture. 1988.

Razmerom podlinnika [In the Metre of the Original] (essays; includes essays by others about Brodskii's work). 1990.

Ballada o malen'kom buksire: detskie stikhi [Ballad about a Small Tugboat: Children's Poems]. 1991.

Bog sokhraniaet vse: stikhi i perevody [God Preserves All: Poems and Translations]. 1992.

Watermark. 1992.

Vspominaia Akhmatovu [Remembering Akhmatova] (interview), with Solomon Volkov. 1992.

Sochineniia [Works]. 4 vols., 1992–95.

Editor, with Carl R. Proffer, *Modern Russian Poets on Poetry: Blok, Mandelstam, Pasternak, Mayakovsky, Gumilev, Tsvetaeva*. 1982.

Editor, *An Age Ago: A Selection of Nineteenth-Century Russian Poetry*. 1988.

*

Bibliography: by George L. Kline, in *Ten Bibliographies of Twentieth Century Russian Literature*, 1977; in *Joseph Brodsky: A Poet for Our Time* by Valentina Polukhina, 1989.

Critical Studies: 'A Struggle against Suffocation' by Czesław Miłosz, in *New York Review of Books*, 14 August 1980; *Joseph Brodsky: A Poet for Our Time*, 1989, and *Brodsky Through the Eyes of His Contemporaries*, 1992, both by Valentina Polukhina, and *Joseph Brodsky's Poetics and Aesthetics* edited by Polukhina and Lev Loseff, 1990; *Joseph Brodsky and the Creation of Exile* by David M. Bethea, 1994.

* * *

Iosif Brodskii seems to be condemned to success not only by his enormous talent and his desire 'to go always for a greater thought', but also by the attention of the state. On the latter, Anna Akhmatova commented: 'What a biography they're fashioning for our red-haired friend! It's as if he'd hired them to do it on purpose'. On the basis of the former she declared him a genius after he read his 'Bol'shaia elegiia. Dzhonu Donnu' ('Great Elegy to John Donne') to her in 1963 and endorsed him as the heir of Mandel'shtam. It looks as if he justified her judgement by becoming, in 1987, the youngest ever poet to receive the Nobel prize for literature. His unique position in Russian literature is underlined by the fact that as a poet, essayist, and playwright he is widely known and read in the English-speaking world: in May 1991 he was appointed as Poet Laureate of the United States. His complex cultural inheritance includes the Latin and English Metaphysical poets, Derzhavin and Tsvetaeva, Frost and Auden. He also learned a great deal from classical music.

Right from the start he struck a searingly tragic note in his poetry that set him apart from the work of his contemporaries. His first collection of poetry, *Stikhotvoreniia i poemy* [Poetry and Narrative Verse], was published in the USA while he was still in his Northern exile. It reveals him as a lyrical and melancholic ironist brimming with understatement. It was followed by his second book, *Ostanovka v pustyne* [A Halt in the Wilderness]. The vulgarity of the human heart is his greatest enemy and a target for his art: 'I'm trying to see how inhuman you can become and still remain a human being'. His superiority lies, however, not so much in the subject matter as in its treatment. His main concern has always been to write better. He experiments with various poetic genres—descriptive poems, odes, elegies, and sonnets—by introducing new and provocative elements in their structure, prosody, and syntax. It is on the level of syntax, of this 'circulatory system of poetry' (Mandel'shtam) which can so easily be struck by sclerosis, that Brodskii's innovations are especially significant. He uses ellipses, short nominative phrases alternating with cumbersome periods, which occupy an entire stanza. In his extensive use of enjambment, which allows the renovation of Russian rhymes, he takes after Tsvetaeva, another metaphysical maximalist. If he is not aiming to surpass her, he is moving in that direction: like Tsvetaeva he is a poet of ultimate truth, and as with

Tsvetaeva all his devices display the unity of ethics and aesthetics, craftsmanship and humility. Unlike her, he is always restrained both in his grief and in his joy. His is the style of coolness, of irony with an air of reserve.

With the physical journey away from his native city, Brodskii began his anti-lyrical journey. In the poetry he has published since he was forced into exile, the stylistic vector is clearly directed towards abstraction, rationalism, and even greater tonal neutrality. To use Coleridge's expression, Brodskii does not operate under the 'despotism of the eye', but under that of reason. What makes his poetry so semantically saturated is his intense thought. Trying to re-examine traditional conceptions of good and evil, he has forced his poetry to discuss the 'accursed' questions in the context of the post-Christian situation. In changing his angle of vision, intensifying his focus, Brodskii carries on from where Dostoevskii, Berdiaev, and Shestov left off. Like these predecessors, he is not afraid to admit aloud: 'Here is one more/combination of numbers/that hasn't opened the door'. Brodskii has done for Russian poetry what Dostoevskii did for Russian prose: he has stripped it of naivety and innocence.

The greatest compensation for all the losses of 1972 was the meeting with W.H. Auden. Their meeting is commemorated in the poem 'York' in the cycle of poems dedicated to England (in his collection *Uraniia* [Urania]). Here Brodskii clearly orientates himself towards the Auden text, in which landscape is used for meditating on death, love, and poetry. The elegy's deliberate prosaic quality is supported by excess of enjambments that are motivated by one of the themes of the elegy, the theme of death. He learned from Auden the poetic qualities he admired most: intellectual wit, unpredictability of plot, dry tone, and the sense of perspective. He was captivated by English poetry from youth, and this lasting love affair has brought something qualitatively new to Russian poetry: he has adjusted some aspects of Russian prosody, has introduced an unusually restrained tone to his poems, and to a quite incredible extent has widened harmonic range in Russian poetic tradition.

For the English reader Brodskii's greatness is made clear by his prose more than by his poetry. His collection of essays, *Less than One*, won the USA National Book Critics' award for criticism in 1987. It is the best introduction to Brodskii's poetry because most of his essays have 'borrowed the clothes of poetry itself' or, to use Brodskii's own words, they are 'nothing but continuation of poetry by other means'. This book includes his historical and culturological musings, homages to his favourite poets (Cavafy, Montale, Auden, Walcott, Akhmatova, Mandel'shtam, Tsvetaeva) and writers (Dostoevskii, Platonov, Nadezhda Mandel'shtam), and a personal memoir. Broad in scope, they stress the unity of European culture.

Critics are more ambiguous about Brodskii the playwright. His first play, *Mramor* (*Marbles*), is a philosophical dialogue between two prisoners in a luxury cell in Rome which is part ancient and part futuristic. This ironic journey to antiquity is a variation on some of Brodskii's main themes: empire, time, and the fate of culture in the post-Christian civilization. Here Brodskii also deals with the 'after end' theme which he touches upon in many of his poems—after the end of love, after the end of life in Russia, after the end of Christianity. Furthermore, the play echoes his two masterpieces: a long poem dialogue, 'Gorbunov i Gorchakov' (1965–68), a reflection on his own experience in the Soviet prison, and *Rimskie elegii* [Roman Elegies], a brilliant succession of snapshots of the city in August where one 'runs the risk of being turned to stone' (George Nivat). Brodskii's second play, *Demokratiia!*

(*Democracy*), is a humorous musing on the collapse of communism in the Soviet Union. In both plays, with a certain dose of puns, paradox, and irony, Brodskii doesn't quite succeed in creating effective stage characters.

But, whatever Brodskii writes, his readers are aware of his relentless thinking on the grand scale. Finding himself outside his own culture, Brodskii continues to serve it by introducing to Russian culture an entirely different sensibility. Trying to get rid of its sentimentality, Brodskii has encountered all kinds of fierce resistance and criticism. At the same time his universality has earned him comparison with Pushkin himself. No Russian poet could ask for more.

—Valentina Polukhina

A PART OF SPEECH (Chast' rechi)
Poems by Iosif Brodskii, 1977.

A Part of Speech is the title of Brodskii's second English collection and of his fourth Russian collection. The contents of these two collections are, however, different: while the Russian collection includes poems written after his exile from Russia (1972–76), the poems in the English book stretch from 1965 to 1978. Brodskii has been fortunate with his translators (who include Richard Wilbur, Anthony Hecht, and Derek Walcott): 'every poem in the book reads as if English had been its first home' (Henry Gifford). It is no wonder that this book has established Brodskii as one of the major figures in the Western literary landscape. Apart from diversity of style and theme, this collection has immense breadth and cultural resonance: Greek mythology ('Odysseus to Telemachus'); the Old and New Testament ('Nunc Dimittis'); and the classical world of the Latin poets ('Letters to a Roman Friend'). One can also hear the voices of Samuel Beckett, T.S. Eliot, W.H. Auden, and Robert Lowell. Beckett had a very specific impact on Brodskii's poetics and *Weltanschauung*. The ninth part of 'Nature Morte' opens with the simplest and most terrifying description of death in Russian poetry, a description which is reminiscent of Beckett: 'A thing. Its brown colour. Its/blurry outline. Twilight./Now there is nothing left./Only a *nature morte*'. In one of the most perfect poems in the collection, 'The Butterfly', Brodskii exhibits an amplitude that no other Russian poet among his contemporaries can claim. His range is such that he combines the incompatible: a Pushkinian lightness and elegance of style and thought with Beckett's way of looking at the world, which demands a dotting of all the 'i's and then leaves only the dots: the butterfly is seen as merely a 'frail and shifting buffer', dividing nothingness and man.

Three or four themes dominate this book: exile, empire, language, and time. Finding himself 'in a strange place', he wrote the poem '1972', his 'first cry of speechlessness', in which, amidst irony, wit, sarcasm, and philosophical digressions, we find the first serious reproach against Russia. But thanks to his poetic skill, the acute feeling of orphanhood and fear of silence are conveyed only indirectly, through his triple dactylic rhymes: '*otchaian'ia/odichaysn'ia/molchaniia*' ('despair/isolation/silence'). Other structural and semantic resources fulfil the almost Calvinistic function of the dismissal of pain and loss, so that 'each poem becomes an exercise in stamina' (Czesław Miłosz). The poet has succeeded in placing the very tragedy of exile under the control of his art. The exile poet has become a unique tool of his native language: 'A man gets reduced to pen's rustle on paper, to/wedges, ringlets of letters, and, due/to the slippery surface, to commas and full stops'. Talking of linguistic isolation, he said: 'It helps you to win a notion of yourself unimpeded. It's not pleasant, but it is a more clinical notion of yourself. The relationship with your own language becomes more private and intricate'. He put language at the centre of his poetic world and created a solid ground for himself in exile. The supremacy of language is underlined by the very title of the book. For Brodskii, poetry is 'an instrument of self-betterment', 'a form of sentimental education', as well as 'the highest form of linguistic activity'. A poet is merely an embodiment of language: 'I'm a mumbling heap/of words'.

Empire is one of Brodskii's conceptual metaphors. It runs through several poems in the collection and stands for forced harmonization, for the state in general. Brodskii's witty elaboration on the imperial theme attains its full glory in 'Lullaby of Cape Cod' (named after the jazz classic 'Lullaby of Birdland'), where he achieves a baroque sense of wonder and displays his formal and linguistic virtuosity. But perhaps the most technically accomplished poems are those from the cycle 'A Part of Speech', where the mastery of rhyme, enjambment, and trope is especially striking. This cycle can be seen as poetry of the psyche. His lyrical persona is influenced by the principal oppositions within the major themes: individual versus empire; man versus time; time versus faith, love, memory, and creativity. Among some excellent translations by Brodskii himself, the splendid 'Elegy: For Robert Lowell' was composed in English. In both languages Brodskii is seeking to preserve 'words against the time of cold'. By his own admission, Brodskii writes 'exclusively about one thing: about time and what time does to man, how it transforms him'. It is identified now with cold, now with dust; things, too, can be regarded as masks for time. In the face of time, the generally accepted hierarchy of things appears to be defective and is replaced by the principle of relativity, and this is stated in many of Brodskii's poems: 'What remains of a man is a part/of speech'; 'From great things, the words of language remain'. The tragic pathos of Brodskii's poetry can be felt in his attempt to overcome time and alienation by faith and creativity, and in his awareness of the illusory nature of this attempt. For Brodskii, an almost stoic resistance to all life's calamities forms the structure of the human soul.

—Valentina Polukhina

BRODSKY, Joseph. See **BRODSKII, Iosif.**

BRUNO, Giordano. Born Filippo Bruno, in Nola, Kingdom of Naples, in January or February 1548. Admitted as a novice to the Dominican monastery of San Domenico Maggiore, 1565, assumed the monastic name Giordano; studied theology, 1572–75; lived in various priories in the Kingdom of Naples, 1565–76; left Naples after charges of heresy were levelled against him by the Inquisition, 1576, and spent 15 years travelling in Europe: travelled through the northern Italian states, Savoy and Lyon, 1577–79, before arriving in Geneva, where he was briefly a follower of Calvinism; taught and studied (degree in theology), University of Toulouse, 1579–81; reached Paris, 1581, found favour with Henri III, who awarded him a lectureship, and first published his writings, 1582; accompanied French ambassador to England, lectured briefly at Oxford University, and lived in London, 1583–85, published prolifically and frequented the court of Elizabeth I (and was associated with Sir Philip Sidney and Robert Dudley); returned to Paris, 1586; moved to Marburg, 1586; lectured at the University of Wittenberg, 1586–88, and converted to Lutheranism; visited Prague, 1589, and Helmstädt; lectured in Frankfurt, 1590–91; returned to Venice, 1591, and lived in the household of Giovanni Mocenigo; denounced to the Inquisition by Mocenigo, 1592: on trial in Venice, 1593, and in Rome, 1593–1600, found guilty of heresy. *Died (burned at the stake) 17 February 1600.*

PUBLICATIONS

Collections

Opere italiane. 2 vols., 1830; edited by P. de Lagarde, 2 vols., 1888; edited by Giovanni Gentile and Vincenzo Spampanato, 3 vols., 1925–1927.
Opera latine conscripta publicis sumptis edita, edited by F. Fiorentino, Felice Tocco, and G. Vitelli. 3 vols., 1879–91; reprinted 1962.
Le opere latine esposte e confrontate con le italiane, edited by Felice Tocco. 1889.
Scritti scelti, edited by Luigi Firpo. 1950.
Opere, edited by A. Guzzo and Romano Amerio. 1953.
Opera Latine, edited by Carlo Monti. 1980.

Prose

De umbris idearum (includes *Ars memoriae*). 1582.
Cantus Circaeus. 1582.
De compendiosa architectura et complemento artis Lullii. 1582.
Ars reminiscendi; Explicatio triginta sigillorum; Sigillus sigillorum. 1583.
La cena delle ceneri. 1584; edited by Giovanni Aquilecchia, 1955; as *The Ash Wednesday Supper*, translated by Stanley L. Jaki, 1965; also translated by E.A. Gosselin and L.S. Lerner, 1977.
De la Causa, Principio et Uno. 1584; edited by A. Guzzo, 1933, and by Giovanni Aquilecchia, 1973; as *Concerning the Cause, Principle and One*, translated by D.W. Singer, in *The Infinite in Giordano Bruno*, by Sidney T. Greenberg, 1950; as *Five Dialogues by Giordano Bruno: Cause, Principle and Unity*, translated by Jack Lindsay, 1962; second dialogue translated by I. and K. Royce, in *Rand's Modern Classical Philosophies*, 1908.
De l'Infinito Universo et Mondi. 1584; as *On the Infinite Universe and Worlds*, translated by D.W. Singer, in *Giordano Bruno: His Life and Thought*, 1950.
Lo spaccio de la bestia trionfante. 1584; as *The Expulsion of the Triumphant Beast*, translated by W. Morehead, 1713; also translated by Arthur D. Imerti, 1964.
La cabala del cavallo pegaseo. 1584.
L'asino cillenico del Nolano. 1584.
De gli eroici furori. 1585; as *The Heroic Enthusiasts*, translated (first part only) by L. Williams, 2 vols., 1887–89; as *The Heroic Frenzies*, translated by Paul E. Memmo, 1964.
Dialogi duo de Fabricii Mordentis Salernitani. 1586.

Idiota triumphans; De somnii interpretatione; Dialogi duo de Fabricii Mordentis Salernitani. 1586.

Centum et viginti articuli de natura et mundo adversus peripateticos. 1586.

De lampade combinatoria Lulliana. 1587; translated in part by J. Lewis McIntyre, in *Giordano Bruno*, 1903.

De progressu et lampade venatoria logicorum. 1587.

De specierum scrutinio et lampade combinatoria Raymondi Lullii Doctoris. 1588.

Camoeracensis acrotismus. 1588.

Articuli centum et sexaginta adversus huius tempestatis mathematicos atque philosophos. 1588.

Summa terminorum metaphysicorum ad capessendum logicae et philosophiae studium. 1595; edited by Eugenio Canone, 1979.

In tristitia hilaris, in hilaritate tristis, edited by E. Troilo. 1922.

Documenti della vita di Giordano Bruno, edited by Vincenzo Spampanato. 1933.

Due dialoghi sconosciuti e due dialoghi noti: Idiota triumphans; De somnii interpretatione; Mordentius; De Mordentii Circino, edited by Giovanni Aquilecchia. 1957.

Dialoghi italiani: Dialoghi metafisici e Dialoghi morali, edited by Giovanni Aquilecchia and Giovanni Gentile. 1958.

Praelectiones geometricae e ars deformationum: Testi inediti, edited by Giovanni Aquilecchia. 1964.

Verse

De monade, numero et figura libea consequens quinque de minimo magno. Menura. 1591.

De innumerabilibus, immenso et infigurabilii seu de universo et mundis. 1591.

De triplici minimo et mensura ad trium speculativarum scientiarum et multarum activarum artium principia. 1591.

De imaginum, signorum, et idearum compositione. 1591; as *On the Composition of Images, Signs and Ideas,* translated by Dick Higgins, 1991.

Play

Il Candelaio. 1582; edited by Vincenzo Spampanato, 1923, and by G. Barbieri Squarotti, 1964; as *The Candle Bearer,* translated by J.R. Hale, in *The Genius of the Italian Theater,* edited by Eric Bentley, 1964.

*

Bibliography: *Bibliografia delle opere di Giordano Bruno e degli scritti a esso attinenti* by Virgilio Salvestrini, 1926; revised edition, as *Bibliografia di Giordano Bruno (1582–1950),* by Luigi Firpo, 1958.

Critical Studies: *Life of Giordano Bruno* by J. Frith, 1887; *Giordano Bruno* by J. Lewis McIntyre, 1903; *La filosofia di Giordano Bruno* by E. Troilo, 1907; *Giordano Bruno, His Life, Thought and Martyrdom* by W. Boulting, 1914; *Giordano Bruno e il pensiero del Rinascimento* by Giovanni Gentile, 1920, revised edition, 1925; *Vita di Giordano Bruno con documenti editi ed inediti* by Vincenzo Spampanato, 1921; *Giordano Bruno* by L. Olschki, 1927; *Il pensiero di Giordano Bruno nel suo svolgimento* by A. Corsano, 1940; *Il processo di Giordano Bruno* by Luigi Firpo, 1949; *The Infinite in Giordano Bruno* by Sidney T. Greenberg, 1950; *Giordano Bruno: His Life and Thought* by D.W. Singer, 1950; *The Renaissance Philosophy of Giordano Bruno* by I.L. Horowitz, 1952; *La filosofia di Giordano Bruno* by N.

Badolini, 1955; *From the Closed World to the Infinite Universe* by A. Koyré, 1957; *The Individual and the Cosmos in Renaissance Philosophy* by E. Cassirer, 1963; *Eight Philosophers of the Italian Renaissance* by O. Kristeller, 1964; *Giordano Bruno and the Hermetic Tradition,* 1964, *The Art of Memory,* 1966, and *Lull and Bruno,* 1982, all by Frances A. Yates; *Giordano Bruno* by E. Garin, 1966; *The Infinite Worlds of Giordano Bruno* by A. Mann Paterson, 1970; *Giordano Bruno* by Giovanni Aquilecchia, 1971; *La ruota del tempo: interpretazione di Giordano Bruno,* 1986, and *Giordano Bruno* (includes critical bibliography) both by M. Ciliberto, 1990; *The Renaissance Drama of Knowledge: Giordano Bruno in England* by Hilary Gatti, 1989; *Giordano Bruno and the Embassy Affair* by John Bossy, 1991.

* * *

The number of Giordano Bruno's writings exceeds 60 works, the majority written in Latin. These include works concerning philosophy, astronomy, mathematics, mnemonics (which was not 'a mere set of mechanical rules for aiding memory, but was freighted with a very large content of mysticism and magic', as Gosselin and Lerner point out in the introduction to *The Ash Wednesday Supper,* 1977), and the various controversies in which Bruno was engaged. Bruno was asked on several occasions to give lectures on a variety of subjects; he became famous especially for his interest in mnemonics and the works of the 14th-century Catalan monk Ramón Lull.

By the time he left Naples, Bruno had embraced the system of belief called hermetic Neoplatonism or Hermeticism. In the Renaissance the prestige of this system was fostered by the belief that it was based on the writings of Hermes Trismegistus, an Egyptian sage who foretold the advent of Christianity, and whose wisdom had inspired Plato and the Platonists. Bruno held the belief that the Hermetic religion (with its magical component) was the only true religion, and felt a need to return to the beliefs of the Egyptians. He also believed in metempsychosis (the transmigration of souls at the time of death) and that the living earth moved around the divine sun; this latter belief brought him to embrace Copernicus' ideas and to formulate his most notable theories on the infinite universe and the multiplicity of worlds. Bruno's religion cannot be separated from his philosophy, and while he was conciliatory towards religious practices, he was intolerant of pedants and those who would not, or could not, accept occult truths: hence his anti-Aristotelianism. A brief survey of his major works will illustrate the broad spectrum of Bruno's ideas.

The *De umbris idearum* [The Shadows of Ideas], with the *Ars memoriae* [The Art of Memory] in appendix, was published in Paris during Bruno's first visit to that city. These two works consolidated his fame as an expert in mnemonics, and earned him the privilege of entering the group of *lecteurs royaux* (royal lecturers) whose attitudes, in contrast with their Sorbonne counterparts, were anti-Aristotelian. In the first part of the *De umbris,* Bruno re-elaborates material dealing with Lull and mnemonics with a didactic purpose: he intends proving, from a platonic point of view, the correspondence between the physical and the ideal world. The Neoplatonists relied on the directness of intuition concerning high matters since man is incapable of achieving the essence of truth; hence our ideas are only shadows of truth and, in mnemonics, are shadows (signs) of these shadows. The second and third parts of the *De umbris* are a mnemotechnic manual purporting to instruct the reader, as Bruno does in the *Ars memoriae,* by drawing upon elements from the astrological and Hermetic traditions. The art of memory in its incantational perception —since the nature of memory is occult, the recall of ideas may be regarded as a magical exercise—forms the basis for the *Cantus Circaeus* [The Incantation of Circe]. By far the most successful and enjoyable publication of Bruno's first visit to Paris is *Il Candelaio* (*The Candle Bearer*), a play in five acts with 18 characters, written in popular Italian, but with many plebeian expressions derived from Neapolitan dialect. The play mainly satirizes three aspects of human behaviour and belief in Bonifacio's love, Bartolomeo's alchemy, and Manfurio's pedantry.

In 1583, while a guest of the French ambassador in London, Michel de Casteineau, Bruno lectured at Oxford on the Copernican theory of the movement of the earth, thus anticipating by one year what he says in *La cena delle ceneri* (*The Ash Wednesday Supper*). It is in the five dialogues making up this work that Bruno recaptures the ill-fated evening of 14 February 1584, when he walked out of a dinner party at Sir Fulke Greville's house because of the intolerance shown by two Oxonian doctors towards his explanation of heliocentric theories. From Copernicus, Bruno moves on to other theories of astronomy (plurality of worlds in an infinite universe), language (repudiation of Latin and adoption of vulgar Italian in scientific treatises), and politics (support for Robert Dudley's puritanical faction). Besides its philosophical and theological content (God is defined along the lines of the Hermetic tradition as an infinite sphere, the centre of which is everywhere and the circumference of which is nowhere), *The Ash Wednesday Supper* lashes out at the English society of the times and, particularly, at the pedantry of the Oxonian doctors who had prevented Bruno, the year before, from completing his course of lectures on the grounds that he had been plagiarizing Marsilio Ficino's *De vita Coelitus Comparanda*. Bruno's publication of *De la Causa, Principio et Uno* (*Cause, Principle and Unity*) was intended to fend off the criticism aroused by his previous work. Bruno failed to do this, but produced a most brilliant and original treatise on metaphysics, dealing with the concepts of 'causa' and 'principio' which, according to his physical theory, are to be considered the equivalents of 'forma' [form] and 'materia' [matter]: together they form an inextricable unity ['l'uno']. In elaborating this theory, Bruno rejects the traditional dualism inherent in Aristotelian physics, and moves instead towards a monistic conception of the world. These ideas are also reaffirmed in the *De l'Infinito Universo et Mondi* (*On the Infinite Universe and Worlds*).

The first dialogue of *Lo spaccio de la bestia trionfante* (*The Expulsion of the Triumphant Beast*) is a satire on contemporary superstitions and vices, embodied in the 'triumphant beast', which, Bruno implies, have distorted man's reason in all ages and cultures. In *The Expulsion* Bruno reaffirms that the search for truth is the very foundation of the ethical system, and he equates truth with Divinity itself. Bruno leans heavily upon the Pythagorean belief in metempsychosis, a teaching considered heretical by the Catholic Church since it does not uphold the ultimate return of the soul to its resurrected body. The relationship between the individual and universal soul is taken up in the *Cabala*. In *De gli eroici furori* (*The Heroic Frenzies*), dedicated to Sir Philip Sidney, Bruno establishes the premise that intellectual love is superior to physical love, and declares that the soul, in its pursuit of truth, progressively strives for an intellectual understanding of the Being, Truth itself. Couched in Ficinian terminology the ten dialogues also become testimony to Bruno's criticism of Aristotelian poetics and imitation of Petrarch in the 16th century.

The remainder of Bruno's works that were published in his lifetime are all in Latin, and are, to a large extent, a re-elaboration of the theories expounded in the Italian dialogues. Worthy of mention however, are the three verse dialogues published in Frankfurt in 1591. In the *De minimo* [Concerning the Least], the argument is concerned with three units: God (the unit of units), the soul (the eternal minimum) and the atom (the physical minimum). *De monade* is filled chiefly with mystical, philosophical and geometrical constructions, founded upon the theory of mathematical *minima* invested with metaphysical significance: one is the perfect number, the source of infinite series. The *De immenso* [Concerning the Immeasurable] amplifies Bruno's philosophy of the infinite universe and the innumerable worlds, which Bruno had derived from Lucretius, 'animating it with the universal animation of the magical philosophy and using it in the Hermetic manner, to reflect in the *mens* the universe in this immensely extended form and so to absorb the infinite divinity' (Frances A. Yates, *Giordano Bruno and the Hermetic Tradition*).

Bruno's originality and legacy appear to be ambiguous: on the one hand he transformed the art of memory from a fairly rational technique into a magical and religious instrument for reaching towards the divine, and, he thought, obtaining divine powers. Even the concepts of an infinite universe, of planetary life derived from the sun, and of the cosmic insights (which anticipate the findings of Galileo, Kepler, and Newton) are connected to his attempts to picture the intangible, the unknown, the arcane: this approach is in line with the Hermetic aim of becoming one with the universe through imaginative effort (as Yates explains). On the other hand, Bruno, in his endeavour to establish truth, defied the ecclesiastical authorities, most blatantly when he embraced the Copernican theories of heliocentricity; on account of this, Bruno is regarded as a precursor of modern scientific thought. At his trial Bruno made several attempts to demonstrate that his views were not incompatible with the Catholic conception of God and creation. He first retracted some of the contentious theological points on which he was to be found guilty, but, at the end, he refused to do so because he did not know any longer (after eight years' imprisonment) what he was expected to retract. It is his final stance at the trial (well documented in Luigi Firpo's *Il processo di Giordano Bruno*) and his horrific death that have made him a symbol of freedom and humanistic activism, while his emphasis on the magical and the occult dimmed his image as scientific investigator. The fact remains, however, that Bruno stands as one of the most thought-provoking and complex figures in the history of western thought.

—Bruno Ferraro

BÜCHNER, Georg. Born in Goddelau, Duchy of Hesse Darmstadt, Germany, 17 October 1813. Educated at Carl Weitershausen's school, 1822–25; Gymnasium, Darmstadt, 1825–31; studied medicine at University of Strasbourg, 1831–33, and University of Giessen, 1833–34; studied biology: arned membership of the Strasbourg Société d'Histoire Naturelle and a doctorate from University of Zurich, 1836. Politically active as a student in Darmstadt, founded the society, Gesellschaft der Menschenrechte, 1834, and wrote

the political pamphlet *Der hessische Landbote*, 1834; fled
Germany to escape impending arrest for sedition, 1835, and
sought refuge in Strasbourg. Lecturer in comparative anatomy, University of Zurich, 1836–37. *Died 19 February 1837.*

PUBLICATIONS

Collections

Nachgelassene Schriften, edited by Ludwig Büchner. 1850.
Sämtliche Werke, edited by K. Franzos. 1879.
Gesammelte Werke und Briefe, edited by Fritz Bergemann.
   1922.
Complete Plays and Prose, translated by Carl Richard
   Mueller. 1963.
Sämtliche Werke und Briefe, edited by Werner R. Lehmann.
   2 vols., 1967–71.
Plays, translated by Victor Price. 1971; also translated by
   Michael Hamburger, 1972.
Complete Works and Letters, edited by Walter Hinderer,
   translated by Henry J. Schmidt. 1986.
Complete Plays, edited by Michael Patterson, translated by
   John MacKendrick. 1987.
Werke und Briefe, edited by Karl Pörnbacher. 1988.
Complete Plays, Lenz and Other Writings, edited and trans-
   lated by John Reddick. 1993.

Plays

Dantons Tod (produced 1902). 1835 (incomplete version);
   complete version in *Nachgelassene Schriften*, 1850; as
   Danton's Death, translated by Stephen Spender and
   Goronwy Rees, 1939; also translated by T.H. Lustig, in
   Classical German Drama, edited by Lustig, 1963; James
   Maxwell, 1968; Victor Price, 1971; Jane Fry and Howard
   Brenton, 1982; John MacKendrick, 1987.
Leonce und Lena (produced 1895). In *Mosaik, Novellen, und
   Skizzen*, edited by K. Gutzkow, 1842; as *Leonce and Lena*,
   translated by Eric Bentley, in *From the Modern Repertoire*,
   3, 1956; also translated by Victor Price, 1971.
Woyzeck (produced 1913). As *Wozzeck*, in *Sämtliche Werke*,
   1879; as *Woyzeck*, translated by Theodore Hoffmann, in
   The Modern Theatre, 1, edited by Eric Bentley, 1955; also
   translated by Carl Richard Mueller, in *Complete Plays and
   Prose*, 1963; Henry J. Schmidt, 1969; Victor Price, 1971;
   Michael Hamburger, 1972; John MacKendrick, 1979.

Fiction

Lenz. In *Telegraph für Deutschland*, January 1839; as *Lenz*,
   translated by Carl Richard Mueller, in *Complete Plays and
   Prose*, 1963; also translated by Michael Hamburger, in
   Three German Classics, edited by Ronald Taylor, 1966;
   F.J. Lamport, in *The Penguin Book of Short Stories*, 1974;
   John MacKendrick, in *Complete Plays*, 1987.

Other

Der hessische Landbote, with Pastor Weidig (pamphlet). 1834
   (privately printed); as *The Hessian Courier*, translated by
   John MacKendrick, in *Complete Plays*, 1987; as *The
   Hessian Messenger*, translated by Henry J. Schmidt, in
   Complete Works and Letters, 1987.

*

Bibliography: *Das Büchner Schrifttum bis 1965* by Werner
Schlick, 1968; 'Kommentierte Bibliographie zu Büchner' by
Gerhard P. Knapp, in *Text und Kritik Sonderband Büchner*,
1979; revised edition, 1984; *Georg Büchner* by Marianne
Beese, 1983.

Critical Studies: *Georg Büchner* by Arthur Knight, 1951;
Georg Büchner by Herbert Lindenberger, 1964; *Satire,
Caricature, and Perspectivism in the Works of Büchner* by
Henry J. Schmidt, 1970; *Georg Büchner* by Ronald Hauser,
1974; *The Drama of Revolt: A Critical Study of Georg
Büchner* by Maurice B. Benn, 1976; *Georg Büchner and the
Birth of Modern Drama* by David G. Richards, 1977; *Georg
Büchner* by William C. Reeve, 1979; *Georg Büchner* by
Julian Hilton, 1982; *Georg Büchner's 'Dantons Tod': A
Reappraisal* by Dorothy James, 1982; *Lenz and Büchner:
Studies in Dramatic Form* by John Guthrie, 1984; *Love, Lust,
and Rebellion: New Approaches to Georg Büchner* by
Reinhold Grimm, 1985; *Büchner in Britain: A Passport to
Georg Büchner* edited by Brian Keith-Smith and Ken Mills,
1987; *Georg Büchner's Woyzeck* by Michael Ewans, 1989;
George Büchner: Tradition and Innovation: Fourteen Essays,
1990; *Büchner, Woyzeck* by Edward McInnes, 1991.

*   *   *

Georg Büchner died in 1837 at the age of 23 with only one
play, *Dantons Tod* (*Danton's Death*), in print and that in a
bowdlerized version. His *Woyzeck* was not performed until
the centenary of his birth. Yet he is now acknowledged to be
a crucial link in the chain of innovative German drama which
stretches from J.M.R. Lenz through Büchner, Frank
Wedekind, the Expressionists, and Bertolt Brecht to the
present day. In a wider context he is recognized as a seminal
figure in the history of modern drama.

At Giessen University Büchner was a republican activist
and co-editor of *Der hessische Landbote*, an inflammatory
pamphlet exposing the exploitative taxation which kept the
aristocracy in Hesse in luxury. This led to a warrant being
issued for his arrest, and he had to flee the country and
complete his studies in Strasbourg. It was while he was in
hiding on the way that he wrote *Danton's Death*, which broke
with the idealist drama of Schiller and tried to present history
'as it really happened'. He revealed the bloody and bawdy
side of revolution, showing the clash between Robespierre's
ideological asceticism ('Virtue is the strength . . . terror the
weapon of the Republic') and Danton's liberal hedonism as a
mere phase in the inexorable, inscrutable cycle of history. It is
a powerful but bleak piece of writing, in which the masses
feature mainly as rabble, and it is so poised that left and right
wing interpreters have struggled in vain for half a century to
make it their own. *Leonce und Lena* (*Leonce and Lena*) is an
ironic, satirical variant of the romantic comedy, set among
the blasé and inane aristocrats of the lands of Pipi and Popo.

Büchner left his most important work, *Woyzeck*, unfinished, with only vague indications of possible endings. It is
a study of social victimization. The passive, plebeian hero,
Woyzeck, is a common soldier who acts as barber to his
Captain and as dietetic guinea-pig to a demented physician in
order to support his mistress and child. She succumbs haplessly to the crude blandishments of the virile Drum-major,
and Woyzeck, hounded by imaginary voices, stabs her to
death. The fragment, of which there are several drafts, ends
with Woyzeck wading into a pond to recover the murder
weapon he has thrown away, but the play would not have
ended there. Büchner based it on the controversial case

of a murderer who was executed in Leipzig in 1824 after two years of medical examinations to determine whether he was responsible for his actions, and here, as in *Danton's Death*, historically authentic speeches are woven seamlessly into the dialogue. Büchner presents a *crime passionnel* in which degradation, debility, sexuality, love, and Christian conscience weave an intricate, compelling pattern which, one is tempted to say, positively benefits from being incomplete. Its 24–29 brief scenes (depending on the edition), which add up to a longish one-act play, are the model for the *montages* of short scenes that are characteristic of Expressionism and epic theatre. Like Danton and Robespierre, Woyzeck is a puppet with an inscrutable controller. Inside themselves, Büchner's more positive characters see an abyss. Büchner was a humane pessimist to whom human life seemed locked in the grip of events. He has the unblinking vision of the moderns, and he provides his suffering characters, no matter what their station, with a voice that is natural and authentic, and at the same time universal and poetic.

—Hugh Rorrison

DANTON'S DEATH (Dantons Tod)
Play by Georg Büchner, 1835 (complete version 1850).

Danton's Death was written in five weeks during January and February of 1835 while the 21-year-old revolutionary author was hiding from the police in his parents' house in Darmstadt. Büchner claimed that he wrote the play simply to make money, much to the amusement of the militant liberal Karl Gutzkow, who published the play, first in a periodical in March and April 1835, then in book form later that year. The text was severely edited in order to manoeuvre it past the pervasive censorship. The play's public premiere did not occur until 1902, in Berlin, although there had been a private performance in Zurich about ten years earlier.

The action of the play takes place in the spring of 1794, near the climax of the Reign of Terror and of the French Revolution itself. Robespierre has disposed of the egalitarian Hébertists on his left and is heading for a showdown with the newly moderate Dantonists, who are pressing for a conclusion to the Revolution. Danton, a revolutionary leader with an energetic, even brutal past, is strangely passive at this crisis; he and his friends spend their time dallying with women and exchanging cynical or obscene *bons mots*. Danton claims to believe that the Jacobins will not dare to harm him, but in fact a sense of futility has overcome him. He defends himself too late to avoid the guillotine, a fate that Robespierre will later share. The external form of *Danton's Death*, unlike that of *Woyzeck*, appears relatively conventional: it is divided into acts and scenes, has an exposition, and a rising and falling action. In the background lies the model of Goethe's *Egmont*, especially in the interspersed folk scenes and the fatal indecisiveness of the protagonist, and there are echoes of Shakespeare too—Danton's wife, Julie (her name changed from the historical Louise), recalls Juliet; Camille Desmoulin's wife, Lucile, recalls Ophelia. In other respects, however, the play is astonishingly original.

It is, first of all, a pioneering example of what came to be called documentary theatre. Approximately one-sixth of the text is taken verbatim from historical sources. These are, primarily, the histories of the French Revolution by Adolphe Thiers and François Mignet, a memoir of Louis-Sébastien Mercier, and a German-language compendium of documents of contemporary history. There has been a great hunt for Büchner's exact sources; more have been adduced than he could possibly have had time to read in the circumstances. Judging from his own comments, he had an austerely realistic intention of putting history itself on the stage as objectively as possible. But a comparison with the sources does not strictly bear this out. For Danton and his friends evince a preoccupation with sexual libertinage and luxuriant sensuality for which there is practically no warrant in the sources. This, in turn, generates the most original dimension of the text: a slangy, vulgar, colourfully obscene language never before seen in a German literary work and not soon to appear again.

Danton's Death has been the object of endless critical disputes. The main problem has been to locate Büchner in his play. As a revolutionary activist in his time he ought to be a partisan of the French Revolution. But the Revolution is imaged with grim ambiguity. The Dantonists are certainly to some degree attractive. But in their cynicism and self-indulgence they seem to have become irrelevant to the Revolution and its social issues, while Danton is haunted by the memory of past atrocities committed in the name of political necessity. Robespierre, on the other hand, is pinched and puritanical; an imagined soliloquy shows him no less at odds with himself than Danton, and his vaunted virtue in its savage ruthlessness has the appearance of a neurotic symptom. St Just, whose terrifying speech to the Convention Büchner invented, sounds like a fascist. As for the common people, they complain justly that the Revolution is giving them heads instead of bread, but they are crudely comic, easily duped, and fickle. Some critics have tried to identify Büchner with the engaging Camille and his sensualism. While working on the play, Büchner read Heinrich Heine's just-published essay 'On the History of Religion and Philosophy in Germany' and attributed to Camille its doctrine of sensual emancipation as the true revolutionary issue. But others see Camille as a self-indulgent adolescent. Marion's laudation of totally amoral sensualism, the most lyrical moment in the play, is qualified by the Dantonists' mocking insolence toward the diseased prostitutes Rosalie and Adelaide.

Few critics have been able to avoid the impression of contradictoriness in the play and in the characters themselves, especially Danton. Not only is it difficult to reconcile his lethargic present self with his activist past; his whole tone becomes abruptly more resolute when he at last defends himself before the Convention. But here Büchner, returning to his sources, may be showing something about the autonomy of revolutionary rhetoric, as verbal machinery running by itself, detached from the realities of those who employ it. The play is relentlessly anti-heroic; the condemned can no longer even devise dignified last words that are not scoffed at as trite by the public and their own comrades. It is in any case important to remember that Büchner was a very young man with intense but by no means settled ideas: the scientist's materialistic determinism collides with a sympathetic awareness of the suffering of real human beings; his revolutionary ardour becomes entangled with scepticism born of the failures of 1789 and 1830; the youthful excitement of sexual liberation clashes with the insight that neither it nor anything else the revolutionary leaders say or do is relevant to the plight of the people, and the people know it. The play is best understood, not as an ideological manual, but as the fervent engagement of an uncommonly powerful creative spirit with the dilemmas of his age.

—Jeffrey L. Sammons

WOYZECK
Play by Georg Büchner, 1879 (written 1835–37).

Büchner was one of Germany's leading avant-garde dramatists of the 19th century and his reputation is based largely on the strength of the drama *Woyzeck*. His other avant-garde drama is *Danton's Death* of 1835, dealing with the French Revolution. Büchner himself was involved in German revolutionary events, caused by the July revolution of 1830 in Paris. Because of his authorship of the politically radical pamphlet *Der Hessische Landbote* (*The Hessian Courier*) of July 1834, Büchner was forced to flee to Strasbourg in March 1835. He finally settled as a political refugee in Switzerland. After completion of his medical studies, Büchner was appointed lecturer of comparative anatomy at the University of Zurich, where he died of typhoid in 1837.

The problem with the text of *Woyzeck* is the fact that there is no authorized version. Written between 1835 and 1837, the collection of manuscripts was first deciphered by Karl Emil Franzos and published in 1878 and 1879 under the title *Wozzek*. All subsequent versions in print are reconstructions on the basis of this manuscript, which comprises some 27 scenes (some editions are divided into 24 or 29 scenes) with no act divisions, and whose sequence cannot be clearly established. For all practical purposes, however, there is a commonly adopted sequence of scenes which serves as both a reading and an acting text. The reader or audience, however, must be aware that there is no final version, authorized by Büchner. Even the ending of the play is not fully ascertained. The work was first performed on 8 November 1913 at the Residenztheater in Munich and had a great influence on German naturalist and expressionist drama and a particular influence on Bertolt Brecht and Antonin Artaud. Alban Berg based his opera *Wozzeck* (1921) on the text edited by Karl Emil Franzos in 1878 and 1879. His opera ends with Marie's son being told of his mother's death and continuing to ride his hobbyhorse, uncomprehending. A film version was directed and produced by Werner Herzog in 1979.

Based on an actual murder, committed by a Johann Christian Woyzeck, and the subsequent discussion of his presumed insanity in the forensic medical literature of the 1820s, Büchner's play deals with the murderer as a victim of political and social conditions rather than as a criminal. Franz Woyzeck is a common soldier, barely making a living to support his common-law wife Marie and his son born out of wedlock. Although criticized for his immoral life by his captain and used for medical experiments by a doctor, Woyzeck manages to survive in his working-class environment. His world collapses, however, when he begins to suspect Marie of betraying him with the drum major. Marie and the child have been the centre of Woyzeck's life and the loss of both lover, and child drives him to murder and suicide (unless one of the final scenes is read to suggest a trial and perhaps execution). Woyzeck kills Marie in a fit of jealousy, but this jealousy is based on an ontological tragedy which he understands, even though he cannot articulate it. Woyzeck's world has become uncentred, and he asserts his identity through this violent act, before he is destroyed himself. Superficially a 'working-class tragedy', in the words of Victor Price, *Woyzeck* is a drama of metaphysical nihilism. There is no hope of divine intervention or justice, only the awareness of tremendous forces driving man to his self-destruction. Woyzeck cannot control these forces, only grasp their enormity.

—Ehrhard Bahr

BULGAKOV, Mikhail (Afanas'evich). Born in Kiev, Ukraine, 3 May 1891. Educated at First Kiev High School, 1900–09; Medical Faculty, Kiev University, 1909–16, doctor's degree 1916. Served as doctor in front-line and district hospitals, 1916–18. Married 1) Tatiana Nikolaevna Lappa in 1913; 2) Liubov' Evgenievna Belozerskaia in 1924; 3) Elena Sergeevna Shilovskaia in 1932. Doctor in Kiev, 1918–19, but abandoned medicine in 1920; organized a 'sub-department of the arts', Vladikavkaz, 1920–21; in Moscow from 1921: journalist for various groups and papers; associated with the Moscow Art Theatre from 1925: assistant producer, 1930–36; librettist and consultant, Bolshoi Theatre, Moscow, 1936–40. Much of his writing was published posthumously. *Died 10 March 1940.*

PUBLICATIONS

Collections

P'esy [Plays]. 1962.
Dramy i komedii [Dramas and Comedies]. 1965.
Izbrannaia proza [Selected Prose]. 1966.
The Early Plays, edited by Ellendea Proffer, translated by Ellendea and Carl R. Proffer. 1972.
Sobranie sochinenii [Collected Works], edited by Ellendea Proffer. 1982–90.
Romany [Novels]. 1988.
P'esy 1920-kh godov [Plays of the 1920s]. 1989.
Sobranie sochinenii v piati tomakh [Collected Works]. 5 vols., 1989–91.
Izbrannye proizvedeniia [Selected Works]. 1990.

Fiction

Zapiski na manzhetakh [Notes on the Cuff]. 1923.
Diavoliada: Rasskazy. 1925; as *Diaboliad and Other Stories*, edited by Ellendea and Carl R. Proffer, translated by Carl R. Proffer, 1972.
Rasskazy [Stories]. 1926.
Dni Turbinykh (Belaia gvardiia). 2 vols., 1927–29; as *The White Guard*, translated by Michael Glenny, 1971.
Rokovye iaitsa [The Fatal Eggs] (stories). 1928.
Zapiski iunogo vracha. 1963; enlarged edition as *A Country Doctor's Notebook*, translated by Michael Glenny, 1975.
Zapiski pokoinika (Teatralnyi roman), in *Izbrannaia proza.* 1966; as *Black Snow: A Theatrical Novel*, translated by Michael Glenny, 1967.
Master i Margarita. 1965–66; uncut version, 1969; complete version, 1973; as *The Master and Margarita*, translated by Mirra Ginsburg, 1967; uncut version, translated by Michael Glenny, 1967.
Sobach'e serdtse. 1969; as *The Heart of a Dog*, translated by Michael Glenny, 1968; also translated by Mirra Ginsburg, 1990.
Notes on the Cuff and Other Stories, edited by Ellendea Proffer, translated by Alison Rice. 1992.

Plays

Dni Turbinykh, from his novel (produced 1926). With *Poslednie dni (Pushkin)*, 1955; as *The Days of the Turbins*, in *Six Soviet Plays*, translated by Eugene Lyons, 1935; also in *The Early Plays*, edited by Ellendea Proffer, 1972; as *The White Guard*, translated by Michael Glenny, 1979.
Zoikina kvartira (produced 1926). Edited by Ellendea Proffer, 1971; as *Zoya's Apartment*, in *The Early Plays*,

edited by Proffer, 1972; as *Madame Zoya*, translated by Michael Glenny, in *Six Plays*, 1991.

Bagrovyi ostrov (produced 1928). In *P'esy*, 1971; as *The Crimson Island*, in *The Early Plays*, edited by Ellendea Proffer, 1972.

Mertvye dushi [Dead Souls], from the novel by Gogol' (produced 1932). With *Ivan Vasil'evich*, 1964.

Kabala sviatosh (as *Mol'er*, produced 1936). In *P'esy*, 1962; as *A Cabal of Hypocrites*, in *The Early Plays*, edited by Ellendea Proffer, 1972; as *Molière*, translated by Michael Glenny, in *Six Plays*, 1991.

Skupoi [The Miser], from the play by Molière, in *Polnoe sobranie sochinenii*, 4, by Molière. 1939.

Don Kikhot [Don Quixote], from the novel by Cervantes (produced 1940). In *P'esy*, 1962.

Poslednie dni (Pushkin) (produced 1943). With *Dni Turbinykh*, 1955; as *The Last Days (Pushkin)*, in *Russian Literature Triquarterly*, 15, 1976; also translated by William Powell and Michael Earley, in *Six Plays*, 1991.

Rashel', edited by Margarita Aliger, music by R.M. Glière (broadcast 1943; produced 1947). Edited by A. Colin Wright, in *Novyi zhurnal*, 108, September 1972; Bulgakov's original text, 1988.

Beg (produced 1957). In *P'esy*, 1962; as *Flight*, translated by Mirra Ginsburg, 1969, and with *Bliss*, 1985, also translated by Michael Glenny, in *Six Plays*, 1991; as *On the Run*, translated by Avril Pyman, 1972.

Ivan Vasil'evich (produced 1966). With *Mertvye dushi*, 1964; as *Ivan Vasilievich*, in *Modern International Drama*, 7(2), 1974.

Poloumnyi Zhurden, from *Le Bourgeois Gentilhomme* by Molière (produced 1972). In *Dramy i komedii*, 1965.

Blazhenstvo (Son inzhenera Reina v 4-kh deistviakh), in *Zvezda vostoka*, 7. 1966; as *Bliss*, translated by Mirra Ginsburg, with *Flight*, 1985.

P'esy: Adam i Eva; Bagrovyi ostrov; Zoikina kvartira. 1971.

Adam i Eva, in *P'esy*. 1971; as *Adam and Eve*, in *Russian Literature Triquarterly*, 1, Fall 1971; also translated by Michael Glenny, in *Six Plays*, 1991.

Minin i Pozharskii, music by Boris Asafiev, edited by A. Colin Wright, in *Russian Literature Triquarterly*, 15. 1976.

Voina i mir [War and Peace], from the novel by Tolstoi, edited by A. Colin Wright, in *Canadian-American Slavic Studies*, 15, Summer–Fall. 1981.

Batum. 1988.

Chernoye more [The Black Sea]. 1988.

Petr Veliky [Peter the Great]. 1988.

Six Plays (includes *The White Guard*; *Madame Zoya*; *Flight*; *Molière*; *Adam and Eve*; *The Last Days*), edited by Lesley Milne, translated by Michael Glenny, William Powell, and Michael Earley. 1991.

Other

Zhizn' gospodina de Mol'era. 1962; as *The Life of Monsieur de Molière*, translated by Mirra Ginsburg, 1970.

Rannjaja neizdannaja proza [Early Unpublished Prose] (German edition). 1976.

Rannjaja nesobrannaja proza [Early Uncollected Prose] (German edition). 1978.

Rannjaja neizvestnaja proza [Early Unknown Prose] (German edition). 1981.

Pod piatoi. Moi dnevnik (early diary entries). 1990.

Manuscripts Don't Burn: A Life in Letters and Diaries, edited by J.A.E. Curtis. 1991.

*

Bibliography: *An International Bibliography of Works by and about Bulgakov* by Ellendea Proffer, 1976; *A Bibliography of Works by and about Mikhail Bulgakov* by Nadine Natov, in *Canadian-American Slavic Studies*, XV, 1981; *Mikhail Bulgakov in English: A Bibliography 1891–1991* by Garth M. Terry, 1991.

Critical Studies: *Bulgakov's 'The Master and Margarita': The Text as a Cipher* by Elena N. Mahlow, 1975; *The Master and Margarita: A Comedy of Victory*, 1977, and *Mikhail Bulgakov: A Critical Biography*, 1990, both by Lesley Milne; *Mikhail Bulgakov: Life and Interpretations* by A. Colin Wright, 1978; *My Life with Mikhail Bulgakov* by L.E. Belozerskaia-Bulgakova, 1983; *Bulgakov: Life and Work* by Ellendea Proffer, 1984; *A Mind in Ferment: Mikhail Bulgakov's Prose* by Kalpana Sahni, 1984; *Mikhail Bulgakov* by Nadine Natov, 1985; *Mikhail Bulgakov v Khudozhestvennom teatre* by Anatolii Smel'ianskii, 1986; *Between Two Worlds: A Critical Introduction to the Master and Margarita* by Andrew Barratt, 1987; *Bulgakov's Last Decade: The Writer as Hero* by J.A.E. Curtis, 1987; *Vospominaniia o Mikhaile Bulgakove*, 1988; *Zhizn' i smert' Mikhaila Bulgakova* by Anatolii Shvartz, 1988; *Zhizneopisanie Mikhaila Bulgakova* by M. Chudakova, 1988; Mikhail Bulgakov issue, *Soviet Literature*, 7(484), 1988; *Pis'ma. Zhizneopisanie v dokumentakh* edited by V.I. Losev and V.V. Petelin, 1989; *Biografiia M.A. Bulgakova. Pis'ma. Zhizneopisanie v dokumentakh* by P.S. Popov, 1989; *The Apocalyptic Vision of Mikhail Bulgakov's The Master and Margarita* by Edwin Mellen, 1991; *The Writer's Divided Self in Bulgakov's The Master and Margarita* by Riitta H. Pittman, 1991.

* * *

Mikhail Bulgakov is today one of the best-loved writers in the former Soviet Union, seen by many as reflecting the absurdities of that society under Stalinism and—although he died in 1940—of a later period as well. Although he was generally acclaimed following the publication of his masterpiece *Master i Margarita* (*The Master and Margarita*) in 1965–66, official attitudes towards him remained tolerant rather than acclamatory (with many works remaining unpublished) until the advent of *glasnost'* in the late 1980s. The first Soviet edition of his *Sobranie sochinenii* [Collected Works] was published just in time for the centenary of his birth in 1991, and his plays are now widely performed throughout Russia and other former republics of the USSR, as well as in Eastern Europe.

Bulgakov began his career as a doctor, and his experiences in a country hospital during World War I became the basis for a number of humorous stories which may be seen as self-satire (later collected under the title *Zapiski iunogo vracha* (*A Country Doctor's Notebook*)). After leaving his native Kiev in 1919 for Vladikavkaz in the Caucasus—the result of being forcibly mobilized into various different armies during the Civil War and then attempting to find his younger brother—he abandoned medicine for literature, becoming 'literary manager' for a 'sub-department of the arts' and writing five plays (which have not survived) for the local population. Returning to Moscow in 1921, he supported himself and his wife by journalism, writing feuilletons which, although of minor literary value, provide an interesting and amusing picture of Russian life in the 1920s. He also published a number of satirical stories, of which *Sobach'e serdtse* (*The Heart of a Dog*) is best known. With its bitter criticism of

Communist society, this story long remained unprintable—and indeed unmentionable—in the Soviet Union, but, with *glasnost'*, not only has it been widely published but dramatizations of it have been performed in most major cities (Bulgakov himself had intended to adapt it for the stage in 1926). Bulgakov's first major work was his novel, *Belaia gvardiia* (*The White Guard*), based on his own experiences in Kiev during the Civil War. After its publication in 1925—although only in part, since the journal in which it appeared was closed down—Bulgakov was invited to re-write it as a play for the Moscow Art Theatre. Its performance in 1926 as *Dni Turbinykh* (*The Days of the Turbins*) was a major theatrical event in that, despite the necessary changes to make it more politically acceptable, it was a sensitive portrayal of the problems of a 'White' family during the upheavals that followed the revolution. (It has now been performed in an earlier version, without the politically motivated changes.) Withdrawn in 1929, along with two further plays *Zoikina kvartira* (*Madame Zoya*), a surrealistic tragi-farce, and *Bagrovyi ostrov* (*The Crimson Island*), an allegory on the revolution and a satire on censorship, *The Days of the Turbins* was restaged in 1932 with Stalin's approval. Indeed, in the later, oppressive post-war years of Stalinism, when Bulgakov's name could not even be mentioned publicly, he would be remembered, if at all, only as the author of this play. Another play *Beg* (*Flight*), with its psychological study of a White general in the Civil War, was banned while still at the rehearsal stage.

In 1930, after an unsuccessful appeal to Stalin to be allowed to leave the country, Bulgakov was found employment with the Moscow Art Theatre, which led ultimately to his (uncompleted) satire *Teatralnyi roman* (*Black Snow: A Theatrical Novel*) including a humorous portrait of Stanislavskii in his later years. Bulgakov's stage version of Gogol's *Mertvye dushi* (*Dead Souls*) enjoyed a modest success, as did too, posthumously, an adaptation of Cervante's *Don Quixote* and a play about Pushkin, *Poslednie dni* (*The Last Days*). The failure of his major play *Mol'er* (*Molière*), in which he treated the French dramatist as a fallible human being instead of the 'great man' Stanislavskii demanded, led to his resignation from the Art Theatre in 1936, when he became a librettist for the Bolshoi. Further works include an imaginative biography, *Zhizn' gospodina de Mol'era* (*The Life of Monsieur de Molière*); a pacifist and anti-Communist play, *Adam i Eva* (*Adam and Eve*); two comedies, *Blazhenstvo* (*Bliss*) and *Ivan Vasil'evich*; an adaptation of Tolstoi's *Voina i mir* (*War and Peace*); various film scenarios and opera librettos; and a play based on the young Stalin, *Batum*, none of which appeared during Bulgakov's lifetime.

Aware that he was suffering from nephrosclerosis and had little time remaining to him, Bulgakov devoted his last years to a major effort to complete *The Master and Margarita*, dictating the final changes to his wife (his third, on whom the figure of Margarita was based) on his deathbed after he had become blind. His principal claim to fame in the West rests on this novel, arguably one of the major works of world literature of the 20th century. Published 25 years after his death, it combines an account of the devil's visit to Moscow in the 1930s with an unorthodox interpretation of Christ before Pilate in ancient Jerusalem: this presented through a 'novel' written by the book's hero. As well as being fantasy, satire, comedy, mystery, and romance, it is a work of considerable philosophical depth, drawing equally on biblical and apocryphal sources and on the Faust tradition. Its basic postulates are that 'Jesus existed', that 'manuscripts don't burn'—a belief in the enduring nature of art—and that 'everything will turn out right. That's what the world is built on': an extraordinary metaphysical optimism for a man whose life was characterized by recurring disappointment.

—A. Colin Wright

THE MASTER AND MARGARITA (Master i Margarita)
Novel by Mikhail Bulgakov, 1965–66 (written 1934–40).

The Master and Margarita was essentially completed in 1940 but its origin goes back to 1928, when Bulgakov wrote a satirical tale about the devil visiting Moscow. Like his literary hero, Gogol' (as well as the Master in his own novel), Bulgakov destroyed this manuscript in 1930 but returned to the idea in 1934, adding his heroine, Margarita, based on the figure of his third wife, Elena Sergeevna Shilovskaia. The novel went through a number of different versions until, aware that he had only a short time to live, he put other works aside in order to complete it, dictating the final changes on his deathbed after he had become blind. It remained unpublished until 1965–66, when it appeared in a censored version in the literary journal *Moskva*, immediately creating a sensation. It has since been published in its entirety, although the restored passages, while numerous, add comparatively little to the overall impact of the novel. It has been translated into many other languages. (In English, the Glenny translation is the more complete, while the Ginsburg translation is taken from the original *Moskva* version.)

The novel's form is unusual, with the hero, the Master, appearing only towards the end of the first part, and Margarita not until Part Two. It combines three different if carefully related stories: the arrival of the devil (Woland) and his companions in contemporary Moscow, where they create havoc; Margarita's attempt, with Woland's assistance, to be reunited with her love after his imprisonment and confinement in a psychiatric hospital; and an imaginative account of the passion of Christ (given the Hebrew name of Yeshua-Ha-Nozri) from his interrogation by Pontius Pilate to his crucifixion. Differing considerably from the gospels, the latter consists of four chapters which may be regarded as a novel within a novel: written by the Master, related by Woland, and dreamed of by a young poet (Ivan Bezdomnyi, or 'Homeless') on the basis of 'true' events. Correspondingly, the action takes place on three different levels, each with a distinct narrative voice: that of Ancient Jerusalem, of Moscow of the 1930s (during the same four days in Holy Week), and of the 'fantastic' realm beyond time. The book is usually considered to be closest in genre to Menippean satire.

Despite its complexity, the novel is highly entertaining, very funny in places, and with the mystery appeal of a detective story. In the former Soviet Union, as well as in the countries of Eastern Europe, it was appreciated first of all for its satire on the absurdities of everyday life: involving Communist ideology, the bureaucracy, the police, consumer goods, the housing crisis, various forms of illegal activities and, above all, the literary and artistic community. At the same time it is obviously a very serious work, by the end of which one feels a need for more detailed interpretation: what, in short, is it all about? The problem is compounded by the fact that it is full of pure fantasy and traditional symbols (features associated with devil-lore, for example), so that the reader is uncertain what is important to elucidate the meaning. Leitmotifs (such as sun and moon, light and darkness, and many others) connect the three levels, implying the ultimate unity of all existence.

Soviet critics tended to dwell initially on the relatively

innocuous theme of justice: enforced by Woland during his sojourn in Moscow, while Margarita tempers this with mercy in her plea to release a sinner from torment. Human greed, cowardice, and the redemptive power of love are other readily distinguishable themes. More fundamental ones are summed up in three key statements: 'Jesus existed' (the importance of a spiritual understanding of life, as opposed to practical considerations in a materialistic world that denied Christ's very existence); 'Manuscripts don't burn' (a belief in the enduring nature of art); and 'Everything will turn out right. That's what the world is built on': an extraordinary metaphysical optimism for a writer whose life was characterized by recurring disappointment. There is indeed a strong element of wish-fulfilment in the book, where characters are punished or rewarded according to what they are seen to have deserved.

Thus the novel's heroes, the Master and Margarita, are ultimately rescued, through the agency of Woland, in the world beyond time. They are, however, granted 'peace' rather than 'light', from which they are specifically excluded: a puzzle to many critics. Here, on a deeper philosophical level, there is an undoubted influence of gnosticism with its contrasting polarities of good and evil—which, as I have argued elsewhere, are reconciled in eternity, where 'peace' represents a higher state than the corresponding polarities of light and darkness. Another influence is the Faust story, with Margarita (a far more dynamic figure than either the Master or Goethe's Gretchen) partly taking over Faust's traditional role, in that she is the one to make the pact with Woland, rejoicing in her role as witch. A major scene is 'Satan's Great Ball', a fictional representation of the *Walpurgisnacht* or Black Mass.

Bulgakov, however, reinterprets his sources—*Faust*, traditional demonology, the Bible, and many others—in his own way, creating an original and entertaining story which is not exhausted by interpretation. His devil is helpful to those who deserve it and is shown as necessary to God's purposes, to which he is not opposed. Bulgakov's Christ figure, a lonely 'philosopher', has only one disciple (Matthu Levi)—although eventually Pontius Pilate, 'released' by Margarita from his torments after 2,000 years, is allowed to follow him as well. Woland too has his disciples: Azazello, Koroviev, and a huge, comical tomcat called Behemoth. So has the Master, with Ivan Bezdomnyi. Like Faust, the Master is the creative artist, 'rivalling' God with the devil's help; like Yeshua he is profoundly aware of the spiritual plane, but is afraid, cowed by life's circumstances.

Endlessly fascinating, the novel indeed deserves to be considered one of the major works of 20th-century world literature.

—A. Colin Wright

THE WHITE GUARD (Belaia gvardiia)
Novel by Mikhail Bulgakov, 1927–29 (written 1924–29).

The White Guard is Bulgakov's first novel, dating from 1922, although he had been working on related themes since at least a year earlier. The initial manuscript was completed in 1924, and two of the book's three parts were published the following year in the literary journal *Rossiia*, which, however, was closed down before the final part could appear. Publication details are complicated by the fact that Bulgakov was then invited by the Moscow Art Theatre to turn the book into a play, which for many years was far better known in the

Soviet Union than the novel. The premiere of *The Days of the Turbins*, as it was called, was a major theatrical event of the decade: a *succès de scandale*, in that it was seen as an apologia for the old regime—a criticism which was also applied to the book. (Banned in March 1929, it was restaged in February 1932 with Stalin's approval, remaining in the repertoire until 1941.) The play differed considerably from the original novel, however, both for valid theatrical reasons and for political ones. With an increased interest in the book, the first two parts were republished in Riga (Latvia) in 1927, but with the addition of a fraudulent third part based not on Bulgakov's manuscript but on an early version of the play. The novel was first published in its entirety in Paris (1927–29), in a version authorized by Bulgakov after he had rewritten its final part. (See for this Lesley Milne's account in her *Mikhail Bulgakov: A Critical Biography*, 1990.) The complete version did not appear in the Soviet Union until 1966, 26 years after the author's death, in a volume of his selected prose.

Essentially, *The White Guard* is a historical novel based on Bulgakov's own experiences in his native Kiev during 1918–19. With the end of World War I, the German occupying armies are forced to leave the Ukraine, taking with them the 'Hetman' Skoropadskii, the leader of the puppet government set up by them. Kiev is then occupied temporarily by the Ukrainian nationalists under Semen Petliura, until they are driven out by the Red army. (The later reoccupation of the city by the Whites is outside the scope of the novel.) Seen as a historical account the book may not be objective, but as a novel it gives a vivid depiction of events from the perspective of the Russian intelligentsia in the city, isolated from 'the real Ukraine, a country of tens of millions of people'. Emotionally attached to the old regime, the 'White Guard' consider themselves duty-bound to defend the Hetman, who for all his government's inadequacies comes closest to representing their own values. Preparing to go into battle, however, they learn that he has fled and there is no one left to defend. To them Petliura's forces seem little more than barbarians, and there is thus no choice but to welcome the Bolsheviks when they defeat Petliura 47 days later.

There is perhaps something of a Tolstoian flavour in Bulgakov's portrayal of a clash of peoples, represented by numerous characters, from the commanding officers to the ordinary people in the street—whether they support the Hetman, Petliura, or the 'third force' of the Bolsheviks. The main protagonists, however, are based on members of the author's own family. Alexei Turbin (like Bulgakov at that time) is the conscientious doctor, enlisting with the forces to defend the city; Nikolka, his brother, the young, enthusiastic cadet. Their sister Elena takes over the role of their recently deceased mother, but is herself abandoned by her husband, Talberg, a White officer who leaves with the Hetman for Berlin. Surrounding them are their friends (also army officers) and their young, lovingly clumsy cousin, Lariosik. With their traditions of order, decency, and honour, they stand in sharp contrast to the many who act out of cowardice or their own self-interest, including their landlord, the comical Vasilisa, who lives in the downstairs apartment with his avaricious wife Wanda.

The house, in fact, is recognizably the one actually occupied by the Bulgakovs in Kiev (opened in 1991 as the Bulgakov Museum), symbolized by its stove with tiles showing scenes from the life of Peter I, by its clocks, its chocolate-coloured books and cream-coloured blinds. The importance of family is a major theme: 'For this . . . [man] goes to war, which, if the truth be known, is the only cause for which anyone ought to fight'. But the family members cannot escape outside events, as symbolized in the conflict between Mars and Venus, in the 'snowstorm from the north' and apocalyptic visions from the Book of Revelations.

There are many scenes of brutality, but also of tenderness and humour, and an awareness of life's continuity, against the background of the eternal and rather mysterious city of Kiev. Alexei, trying to return home, is wounded and pursued, but is rescued by a mysterious woman who visits him after he has miraculously recovered from near-death. A major theme throughout is that of a deep but undogmatic religious belief, and of death and resurrection—for Alexei is said actually to have died and is saved only as a result of Elena's prayers to the Virgin Mary. (Previously he had dreamt of Paradise, into which all are admitted regardless of their beliefs: a passage inadvertently omitted from Glenny's English translation, but included as an appendix in Milne's book referred to above.) The final paragraph, one of the most beautiful in Russian literature, uses the symbol of the stars to conjure up a vision of eternity:

But the sword is not fearful. Everything passes away— suffering, pain, blood, hunger and pestilence. The sword will pass away too, but the stars will still remain when the shadows of our presence and our deeds have vanished from the earth. There is no man who does not know that. Why, then, will we not turn our eyes toward the stars? Why?

—A. Colin Wright

BUNIN, Ivan Alekseevich. Born in Voronezh, Russia, 10 October 1870. Educated at the Gymnasium, Elets, 1881–85, and then at home in Ozerki; University of Moscow. Married 1) Anna Nikolaevna Tsakni in 1898 (separated 1900), one son; 2) Vera Muromtseva, with whom he had lived since 1907, in 1921. Editorial assistant, *Orlovskii vestnik* [Orel Courier], 1889–91; secretary, department of statistics, Poltava district administration, 1892–94; opened bookstore, 1894, and distributed publications of Tolstoi's, *q.v.*, publishing house, Posrednik: arrested for selling books without a licence, but escaped prison sentence; entered literary circles in St Petersburg and Moscow, 1895: in early years associated with the Symbolist publishing house Skorpion, and, after 1901, with Gor'kii's, *q.v.*, Znanie publishing house until 1909; travelled to Switzerland and Germany, 1900, Constantinople (now Istanbul), 1903, Egypt, Ceylon (now Sri Lanka) and Singapore, 1911, and three times to Capri, visiting Gor'kii, 1911–14; lived in Moscow, Kiev, and Odessa during Revolutionary turmoil, 1918–20; moved to Constantinople, 1920, and eventually arrived in Paris, 1923, via Serbia and Bulgaria: settled in Grasse, southern France. Elected to the Russian Academy of Sciences, 1909. Recipient: Pushkin prize, 1903, 1909; Nobel prize for literature, 1933. *Died 8 November 1953.*

PUBLICATIONS

Collections

Sobranie sochinenii [Collected Works]. 5 vols., 1956.
Sobranie sochinenii [Collected Works]. 9 vols., 1965–67.

Sochineniia [Works]. 3 vols., 1982–84.
Sobranie sochinenii [Collected Works], edited by A.K. Baboreko. 6 vols., 1987.
Sobranie sochinenii [Collected Works]. 4 vols., 1988.

Fiction

Derevnia. 1910; as *The Village*, translated by Isabel F. Hapgood, 1923.
Sukhodol [Dry Valley]. 1911.
Grammatika liubvi. 1915; as *The Grammar of Love*, translated by John Cournos, 1977.
Gospodin iz San-Frantsisko. 1915; as *The Gentleman from San Francisco and Other Stories*, translated by Bernard Guilbert Guerney, 1934.
Fifteen Tales, translated by Bernard Guilbert Guerney. 1924.
Zhizn' Arsen'eva [The Life of Arsen'ev]. 1933; complete edition, 1952; translated in part as *The Well of Days*, by Gleb Struve and Hamish Miles, 1934.
The Dreams of Chang and Other Stories, translated by Gleb Struve and Hamish Miles. 1935.
The Elaghin Affair and Other Stories, translated by Bernard Guilbert Guerney. 1935.
Temnye allei [Dark Avenues] (stories). 1943.
Dark Avenues and Other Stories, translated by Richard Hare. 1949.
Vesnoi, v Iudee [Spring, in Judea]. 1953.
Petlistye ushi i drugie rasskazy [Loop Ears and Other Stories]. 1954.
Rasskazy [Stories]. 1955.
Lika. 1958.
Shadowed Paths, translated by Olga Shartse. 1958.
Povesti. Rasskazy. Vospominaniia [Short Stories. Stories. Reminiscences]. 1961.
Rasskazy [Stories]. 1962.
Rasskazy [Stories]. 1971.
Povesti. Rasskazy [Short Stories]. 1973.
Sueta suet [The Fuss of Vanities]. 1973.
Povesti i rasskazy [Short Stories]. 1977.
Poslednee svidanie [The Last Meeting]. 1978.
Stories and Poems, translated by Olga Shartse and Irina Zheleznova. 1979.
Rasskazy [Stories]. 1980.
Chasha zhizni [The Cup of Life]. 1983.
In a Far Distant Land: Selected Stories, translated by Robert Bowie. 1983.
Long Ago: Fourteen Stories, translated by David Richards and Sophie Lund. 1984.
Kholodnaia vesna [Cold Spring]. 1986.
Poeziia i proza [Poetry and Prose]. 1986.
Light Breathing and Other Stories, translated by Olga Shartse. 1988.
Velga (for children), translated by Guy Daniels. 1989.
Wolves and Other Love Stories, translated by Mark C. Scott. 1989.
Povesti i rasskazy [Short Stories and Stories]. 1990.

Verse

Stikhotvoreniia [Poetry]. 1956.
Listopad [Autumn]. 1982.
Stikhotvoreniia. Rasskazy [Poetry. Stories]. 1986.

Other

Sobranie sochinenii [Collected Works]. 1934–35.
Osvobozhdenie Tolstogo [The Emancipation of Tolstoi] (biography). 1937.

O Chekhove [About Chekhov] (unfinished manuscript). 1955.

Okaiannye dni: k dvadtsatiletiiu so dnia smerti I.A. Bunina [The Last Days: Twenty Years after the Death of I.A. Bunin]. 1973.

Buninskii sbornik [Bunin's Notebook]. 1974.

Pis'ma Buninykh k khudozhnitse T. Loginovoi-Murav'evoi (1936–1961) [Letters from the Bunins to the Artist T. Loginova-Murav'eva]. 1982.

Ivan Bunin i literaturnyi protsess nachala XX veka [Ivan Bunin and the Literary Process at the Beginning of the 20th Century]. 1985.

Stikhotvoreniia i perevody [Poetry and Translations]. 1985.

I sled moi v mire est'. . . = j'ai laissé une trace dans ce monde . . . [I Have Left My Mark on the World]. 1989.

Lish' slovu zhizn' dana . . . [Life is Given Only to the Word . . .]. 1990.

Ivan Bunin (collections). 1991.

Solnechnii udar [Sunstroke]. 1992.

Russian Requiem 1885–1920: A Portrait from Letters, Diaries and Fictions, edited by Thomas Gaiton Marullo. 1993.

Translator, *Pesn' o Gaivate*, by G.V. Longfellow. 1941.
Translator, *Zolotoi disk* (poems). 1975.

*

Critical Studies: 'The Art of Ivan Bunin' by Gleb Struve, in *Slavonic and East European Review*, 11, 1932–33; 'The Art of Ivan Bunin' by Renato Poggioli, in *The Phoenix and the Spider*, 1957; *The Works of Ivan Bunin* by Serge Kryzytski, 1971; *Ivan Bunin: A Study of His Fiction* by James B. Woodward, 1980; *Ivan Bunin* by Julian W. Connolly, 1982.

* * *

Ivan Bunin was the last major Russian writer to emerge from the ranks of the landed gentry and the first Russian writer to win the Nobel prize for literature. His most notable early successes were achieved as a poet and translator of poetry, and he continued to write poetry throughout his career. His reputation rests chiefly, however, on his two short novels *Derevnia* (*The Village*) and *Sukhodol* ('Dry Valley'), the autobiographical novel *Zhizn' Arsen'eva* [The Life of Arsen'ev], and, above all, his collections of short stories. All his work reflects the loyalty to the 19th-century realistic tradition which he advocated passionately in the literary polemics of the pre-revolutionary years. But the mark of the 'Silver Age' is nevertheless visible in his outlook as a writer, in the poetic qualities of his prose and meticulous attention to matters of style and craftsmanship, and in the general character of an art that eschews ideas and attaches greater importance to tone than to incident.

One of the most frequently noted features of Bunin's art is the impression of coldness that it conveys, and his fastidiousness as a stylist is commonly adduced in this connection as a contributory factor. The explanation lies mainly, however, in the conception of life that informs almost all his work and in its implications for the status of the individual in his fiction. It is a view of man's life as governed by irrational forces that perpetually defy and subvert all his efforts to control it. In his early stories, such as 'Antonovskie iabloki' ('Antonov Apples') and 'Epitafiia' ('The Epitaph'), these forces are social. Reflecting the experience of his own family, they evoke lyrically and nostalgically the passing of the traditional rural way of life in which the landed gentry and peasantry, in Bunin's somewhat idealistic portrayal, lived in harmony with each other and in contented communion with nature. But in the transition from these stories to *The Village* and *Sukhodol* nostalgia and sorrow give way not only to anger and embitterment, but also to a broader philosophical understanding, according to which this process of social change is seen as the expression of an impersonal law of nature, of the natural law of decay to which societies, he had come to believe, like individuals, are unalterably subject and which begins ineluctably to operate as soon as the communion with nature is broken. In the two short novels, as in the stories 'Veselyi dvor' ('A Happy Farmhouse'), 1911, 'Ermil' (1912), and 'Vesennii vecher' ('An Evening in Spring'), 1914, the behaviour and attitudes of individual landowners and peasants are examined as reflections of the moral and psychological effects of this law which Bunin interprets as inducing a kind of mental paralysis, a compulsion to maim and destroy, and a crippling insensitivity to the irrational aspects of life. By 1914, drawing on the experience of his travels in Europe and his journeys to Turkey and the Middle East described in 'Ten' ptitsy' [The Shadow of the Bird] (1907–11), he was already intent on demonstrating the universal implications of this judgement. Hence 'Brat'ia' ('The Brothers') and his most famous tale, *Gospodin iz San-Frantsisko* (*The Gentleman from San Francisco*), in which the same symptoms of moral decay, attributed to essentially the same basic cause, are explored in the portraits of an English traveller in Ceylon and an American capitalist on a voyage to Europe.

The most striking feature of all these works is the switch of emphasis from character to setting that results from the impersonality of Bunin's thought. Here action results not from rational decisions or free moral choices but from psychological conditions represented as reflecting the relation of the characters to the world about them. Thus the murder committed by the brutal Sokolovich in 'Petlistye ushi' ('Loop Ears'), in which Bunin directly challenges Dostoevskii's faith in conscience and free will, is implicitly explained by nature's exclusion, by the transposition of the action to the dehumanizing urban setting of Petrograd. The result in each case is that descriptions of the setting acquire an unusual prominence. Often describing the structure and style of these works in musical terms, Bunin regarded them as performing an essentially musical function, as evoking a sense of the 'rhythms' of life that determine the conduct of men and societies. He conceived of motivation as deriving less from events than from 'harmonies' or 'discords' between these 'rhythms' and the human psyche.

The philosophical impersonality that gave birth to this distinctive kind of short story explains the profound interest, documented in 'The Brothers' and later in 'Noch'' ('Night') and *Osvobozhdenie Tolstogo* [The Emancipation of Tolstoy] (1937), that Bunin had in Buddhism and the Buddhist conception of personality. It also determined his treatment of the theme that developed ultimately into the principal expression of his view of life—the theme of love. The most notable pre-revolutionary stories devoted to this theme are 'Ignat', 'Pri doroge' ('By the Road'), 'Legkoe dykhanie' ('Light Breathing'), and 'Syn' ('The Son'), and after his emigration to France it became almost his only theme, inspiring such well known works as 'Mitina liubov'' ('Mitia's Love'), 'Delo Korneta Elagina' ('The Elaghin Affair'), *Solnechnii udar* ('Sunstroke'), and the stories that comprise his final volume *Temnye allei* [Dark Avenues]. As depicted by Bunin, love is always a pre-eminently sensual experience, a blinding flash of light that briefly illuminates the ultimate realities of life: the impotence of human reason, the impermanence of everything on earth, and man's inescapable thraldom to remorseless impersonal forces. With few exceptions, therefore, the love stories are tragic tales, the characters of which are torn by passion from the normal routines of their lives and repeatedly impelled, like automata, to embark on self-destructive courses of action. Here love is almost invariably experienced in the shadow of death. Yet the tragic conclusions of these tales are to be taken as expressing a judgement less on love than on life. For, as 'Sunstroke' and the stories of *Temnye allei* make abundantly clear, love was also for Bunin the source of the greatest happiness that life affords man, offering an intensity of experience that transforms all preconceived notions of life and its meaning. Like *Zhizn' Arsen'eva*, the love stories convey the supreme value attached to sensory experience by a writer who thanked God for every moment that he spent on earth, yet was able to conceive of Him only as the creator of the laws of nature. For this reason Bunin continued to wrestle to the end with the mystery of man's ephemeral existence, for the representation of which he developed his highly personal and expressive medium.

—James B. Woodward

THE GENTLEMAN FROM SAN FRANCISCO (Gospodin iz San-Frantsisko)
Novella by Ivan Bunin, 1915.

The gentleman from San Francisco is a 58-year-old American who had made his fortune through hard work but also as a result of the hard work of others. To reward himself for his efforts he plans an extended trip abroad with his wife and daughter. He makes the journey across the Atlantic in the steamer *Atlantida*, which is outfitted with every amenity guests may desire. During the trip—on the island of Capri—he dies suddenly while waiting for dinner, and his body is unceremoniously hidden from the other guests. It is carried back to America ignominiously in a soda box, in the hold of the same ship that carried him to Europe. The structure of the story is an ironic commentary on the materialism of the New World and its insignificance in the face of nature and death.

The gentleman from San Francisco (he does not have a name) is crude, self-satisfied, commanding, and insensitive to others and especially to man's place in the cosmos. He has lived so long for pleasure and power that he has come to expect them as his just due. Bunin is at pains to show that such power is really powerless before the eternal truths of the world. Bunin was convinced that 20th-century man was progressively insulating himself from his place in nature, and confining himself to a world of his own making. This is revealed through Bunin's depiction of life aboard the *Atlantida*. It is described in exquisite detail as a vessel catering to human needs and pleasures—defiant of the storms that rage outside. In the thoroughly 'civilized' and artificial world of the ship, the gentleman from San Francisco, and others like him, can command the satisfaction of every whim. Life is a continual round of eating, drinking, bathing, relaxing, and untaxing conversation. While the gentleman from San Francisco, 'his face cleaned and rubbed to a high lustre', sits in his white dinner-jacket in the comfort of the brightly lit salon, sipping cognac and other liqueurs and discussing the latest stock-market news with other gentlemen, sailors on watch freeze on deck in a raging storm and a 'great host of servants work below in the kitchens and wine cellars'. In the very bowels of the ship, workers, half-naked and red from the furnaces, labour to carry him to the old continent, and when the *Atlantida* reaches Naples, crowds of Italian porters rush to help him. All these people, he believes, serve him willingly and in good faith. Bunin, it will be noticed, is at pains to show the injustice of the class system that has arisen in the New World of power and money. The gentleman from San Francisco and his like assume in their arrogance that they have the right to command, and they take for granted the ministrations of the obsequious help that caters to their desires.

But the social structure of the 'haves' and the 'have-nots' is not, in Bunin's view, natural and real. The gentleman from San Francisco lives in the thoroughly artificial and unreal world of modern civilization. He does not have the power he assumes he has; those who serve him do so in pretence and hypocrisy, and the pleasures he seeks and 'enjoys' are unsatisfying and short-lived. What is real for Bunin is the world of nature, of both the physical world and the human heart. In the world of men the gentleman's will meets no obstacles, but in the world of nature his will is constantly thwarted. He had planned to enjoy the sun of Italy, but the sun that appears for a short time like some deceptive allurement at Gibraltar disappears as the *Atlantida* draws close to Naples. Once the gentleman from San Francisco and his family have landed, the weather behaves capriciously, deceiving him with its momentary rays of sunshine, fog, and unpromising skies. The family departs for Capri hoping to find it sunnier, warmer, and more comfortable there. The sun does not break out in its full splendour until the morning after his death.

Bunin is a superb craftsman and stylist and constructs the story on a series of delicately-wrought contrasts: power and powerlessness, nature and civilization, the natural and the artificial, light and dark, and upper and lower classes. Each of these contrasts is qualified paradoxically. The gentleman from San Francisco goes abroad in the splendidly-lit *Atlantida* and returns in the bottom of the ship and in the dark. He commands the lower classes, but after his death they mock him. He seeks light and warmth and ends in darkness and cold. Bunin's 'message' is thoroughly objectified in his style and craft. There is little commentary from the author himself; he lets the events and the details speak for themselves. What they have to say is portentous and ominous for the new man and the new world of pleasure and power.

—Edward Wasiolek

BUZZATI, Dino. Born Dino Buzzati-Traverso in San Pellegrino, near Belluno, Italy, 16 October 1906. Educated at the Ginnasio Parini, Milan, 1916–24; University of Milan, 1924–26, 1927–28, degree in law 1928. Military service, 1926–27: 2nd lieutenant. Married Almerina Antoniazzi in 1966. Correspondent, *Il Corriere della Sera*, Milan, 1928–72, which first published much of his writing; contributor, *Il Popolo di Lombardia*, from 1931; war correspondent for various newspapers, 1940–43; reporter in Tokyo, 1963, Jerusalem, New York, Washington, DC, and Bombay, 1964, Prague and New York, 1965. Also a painter (first exhibition, 1958, and subsequent exhibitions in Milan and Paris, 1966, Rome, 1971, Milan 1972) and occasional director of plays, operas, and ballets. Recipient: Gargano prize, 1951; Naples prize, 1954; Strega prize, 1958; Paese Sera prize, 1969; Mario Massai prize (for journalism), 1970. *Died 28 January 1972.*

PUBLICATIONS

Collection

Teatro, edited by Guido Davico Bonino. 1980; selections as *Un caso clinico e altre commedie in un atto*, 1985.

Fiction

Barnabò delle montagne. 1933.
Il segreto del Bosco Vecchio. 1935.
Il deserto dei Tartari. 1940; as *The Tartar Steppe*, translated by Stuart C. Hood, 1952.
I sette messaggeri (stories). 1942.
La famosa invasione degli orsi in Sicilia (for children), illustrations by Buzzati. 1945; as *The Bears' Famous Invasion of Sicily*, translated by Frances Lobb, 1947.
Paura alla Scala (stories). 1949.
Il crollo della Baliverna (stories). 1954.
Esperimento di magia. 1958.
Sessanta racconti (includes *I sette messaggeri*; *Paura alla Scala*; *Il crollo della Baliverna*). 1958.
Il grande ritratto. 1960; as *Larger Than Life*, translated by Henry Reed, 1962.
Egregio signore, siamo spiacenti di . . . (stories). 1960.
Un amore. 1963; as *A Love Affair*, translated by Joseph Green, 1964.
Il colombre e altri cinquanta racconti (stories). 1966.
Catastrophe: The Strange Stories of Dino Buzzati, translated by Judith Landry and Cynthia Jolly. 1966; as *Catastrophe and Other Stories*, translated by Landry and Jolly, 1982.
La boutique del mistero. 1968.
Poema a fumetti. 1969.
Le notti difficili (stories). 1971.
Romanzi e racconti, edited by Giuliano Gramigna. 1975.
180 racconti, edited by Carlo Della Corte. 1982.
Restless Nights: Selected Stories, translated by Lawrence Venuti. 1984.

Verse

Il capitano Pic e altre poesie. 1965.
Due poemetti. 1967.
Poesie. 1982.

Plays

Piccola passeggiata (produced 1942). 1942.
La rivolta dei poveri (produced 1946). In *Teatro*, 1980.
Un caso clinico, from his story 'Sette piani' (produced 1953). 1953.
Ferrovia soprelevata, music by Luciano Chailly (produced 1955). 1960.
Drammatica fine di un noto musicista (produced 1955). In *Teatro*, 1980.
Sola in casa (produced 1958). In *Teatro*, 1980.
Una ragazza arrivò (radio play; broadcast 1959). 1958.
Le finestre (produced 1959). In *Teatro*, 1980.
L'orologio (produced 1959). In *Teatro*, 1980.
Procedura penale, music by Luciano Chailly (produced 1959). 1959.
Il mantello (produced 1960). In *Teatro*, 1980; revised version, music by Luciano Chailly (produced 1960), 1960.
Un verme al ministero (produced 1960). In *Teatro*, 1980.
I suggeritori (produced 1960). In *Teatro*, 1980.
L'uomo che andrà in America (produced 1962). 1968.
La colonna infame (produced 1962). In *Teatro*, 1980.

Battono alla porta, music by Riccardo Malipiero (television opera; broadcast 1962; produced 1963). 1963.
Era proibito (produced 1962). 1963.
La fine del borghese (produced 1966). 1968.

Radio Play: *Una ragazza arrivò*, 1959.

Television Writing: *Battono alla porta*, music by Riccardo Malipiero, 1962.

Other

Il capitano delle pipe, with Eppe Ramazzotti. 1945.
In quel preciso momento (miscellany). 1950; enlarged edition, 1955.
Miracoli di Val Morel (sketches). 1971.
Cronache terrestri (essays), edited by Domenico Porzio. 1972.
Il pianeta Buzzati (biographical documents, photographs), edited by Almerina Buzzati. 1974.
I misteri d'Italia. 1978.
Dino Buzzati al Giro d'Italia. 1981.
Cronache nere (essays), edited by Oreste Del Buono. 1984.
Il reggimento parte all'alba. 1985.
Lettere a Brambilla, edited by Luciano Simonelli. 1987.
Le montagne di vetro (stories and articles). 1989.

*

Critical Studies: *Dino Buzzati* by Fausto Gianfranceschi, 1967; *Il racconto fantastico da Tarchetti a Buzzati* by Neuro Bonifazi, 1971; *Dino Buzzati: Un autoritratto* by Yves Panafieu, 1971; *Invito alla lettura di Dino Buzzati*, by Antonia Arslan Veronese, 1974; *Come leggere Il deserto dei Tartari* by Marcello Carlino, 1976; 'Spatial Structures in the Narrative of Dino Buzzati' by Elaine D. Cancalon, in *Forum Italicum*, 11(36–46), 1977; *Dino Buzzati* by Ilaria Crotti, 1977; *Anormalità e angoscia nella narrativa di Dino Buzzati* by Mario B. Mignone, 1981; *Guida all lettura di Dino Buzzati* by Claudio Toscani, 1987; *Dino Buzzati* by Giovanna Ioli, 1988; *Il coraggio della fantasia. Studi e ricerche intorno a Dino Buzzati* by Nella Giannetto, 1989.

* * *

The critical fortunes of Dino Buzzati have fluctuated with the times. In the 1950s and 1960s he was extremely highly regarded as a writer, but after his death in 1972 his international popularity declined in the face of more fashionable Italian writers, such as Italo Calvino, Umberto Eco, and Primo Levi. Nevertheless, as the less ephemeral aspects of his output are being reassessed he is once again recognized as a major writer, both within and outside Italy.

A journalist for most of his life on Italy's leading daily newspaper, *Il Corriere della Sera*, Buzzati was convinced in theory, and proved in practice, that the best journalism could also be good literature. His first novel, *Barnabò delle montagne* [Barnabò of the Mountains], concerns a young woodsman who waits years for revenge, but when he finally has his enemy in his sights he refuses to shoot him. The two themes of waiting and abnegation, as well as a passion for mountain landscapes, recur in all Buzzati's works. His second novel, *Il segreto del Bosco Vecchio* [The Secret of the Old Wood], is, in its woodland setting, reminiscent of Tolkien; but it was his third and most ambitious novel that established the authentic Buzzati style.

Buzzati wrote *Il deserto dei Tartari* (*The Tartar Steppe*) in the first year of World War II, typing it in the mornings after he finished night shift at the *Corriere*. Perhaps these circumstances account for some of the pessimistic *ennui* of the novel, but there was also a considerable streak of innate melancholy in Buzzati himself. The novel's hero, Giovanni Drogo, sets out for military duty in a fortress that guards the steppe across which the Tartars may invade at any moment. Drogo spends the whole of his life there, waiting for the attack which only materializes when he is too old and too ill to fight. At the end, Drogo's true moment of glory arrives when he learns to face his own death, in an anonymous hotel room, with a stoicism that would have befitted the battlefield. The novel, later translated into French by Camus, was a resounding success. Its Kafkaesque pessimism suited the dark days of its composition; but there are many memorable passages which still appeal. Particularly powerful are his exploration of the passing of time, his visual descriptions of the mountains and the desert, his attention to sonorous detail in describing military routine, and his celebration of the mediocre existence of an everyman.

After this work, Buzzati was to write only two more novels, and both were flawed affairs, inspired by external contingencies rather than by an inner compulsion to write: *Il grande ritratto* (*Larger Than Life*) was submitted anonymously to a competition run by the magazine *Oggi*, while *Un amore* (*A Love Affair*) was written only after the death of Buzzati's mother, with whom he had lived until he was 55, and after he himself had fallen seriously in love for the first time.

In the meantime, Buzzati had found his true vein as a writer of short stories. His first collection, *I sette messaggeri* [The Seven Messengers] was enlarged to become *Sessanta racconti* [Sixty Stories], which included the best of his output to date, and which won him Italy's major literary prize, the Strega prize, in 1958. This latter volume includes some of the masterpieces in the genre. 'Il mantello' ('The Cloak'), for example, which is like *The Tartar Steppe*, in miniature, has a haunting opening passage reminiscent of Poe at his best; it contains dialogue full of pathos in the exchanges between a mother and her son who, unknown to her, has died in battle but has been allowed to visit her; and it concludes with an evocative finale, as the black figure waiting outside the garden gate accompanies the son to his final destination. 'Qualcosa era successo' ('Something Had Happened') is in the same dark vein: the passengers in the northbound express realize some unknown disaster must have occurred in the north, since from the window they can see the inhabitants fleeing southwards in cars and trains. As they arrive in the deserted northern station a woman's scream concludes the tale in a verbal equivalent of Edvard Munch's famous painting 'The Scream'. There are also sunnier stories in the collection. 'Il disco si posò' ('The Saucer Landed'), for instance, opens with a village priest noticing a flying saucer landing on the church roof and two Martians coming out to investigate its cross. When Don Pietro launches into the story from the Bible in order to convert them, he learns, to his chagrin, that the Tree of Good and Evil is still blooming on Mars, since the ancestors of these superior intelligences obeyed God's command. Yet, underneath this more humorous style, Buzzati remains melancholic about the imperfection of humanity. He published other volumes of short stories, including *Egregio signore, siamo spacienti di . . .* [We Are Sorry To . . .], *Il colombre*, the title story being about a mythical sea monster, and *Le notti difficili* [Difficult Nights]. However, none of them has attained the impressive consistency of *Sessanta racconti*.

Buzzati's abilities as a visual artist not only inform some of the stories and adorn most of his own book covers, but also led to his publication of picture books, including a children's book, *La famosa invasione degli orsi in Sicilia* (*The Bears' Famous Invasion of Sicily*), a book about curious ex-votos in Northern Italy, and *Miracoli di Val Morel* [Miracles of Val Morel], as well as a reworking of the Orpheus myth, in which Orpheus is a rock singer in 1960s Milan.

The themes of Buzzati's work are co-terminous with some of the key themes of 20th-century literature: man's solitude, the ineluctability of time and destiny, and the frisson of pleasure and terror inspired by landscapes of mountains, deserts, and cities. Though many critics have written of Kafka's influence, Buzzati evolved, in his best short stories and in his major novel, a compelling and distinctive style with which to elaborate these motifs.

—Martin L. McLaughlin

BYKAW, Vasil (Vladimirovich). Born in Chernovshchina, Vitebsk region, Belorussia, Soviet Union (now independent as Belarus), 19 June 1924. Educated at art academy, Vitebsk. Served in the army during World War II: officer; remained in the army for ten more years; journalist for newspaper in Grodno; deputy of the Supreme Soviet of Belorussia. Member of the Bureau of the secretariat of the Writers Union of the USSR, 1986. Recipient: Belorussian Republic Yakub Kolas prize; State prize, 1974; Lenin prize, 1986. Lives in Minsk.

PUBLICATIONS

Fiction

U toy dzien' [That Day]. 1949.
U pershym bai [In the First Battle]. 1949.
Abaznik [The Transport Driver] (story). 1956.
Žhurawliny kryk [The Cry of the Crane] (stories). 1956.
Zdrada [Treachery]. 1961.
Tretstsya raketa (stories). 1962; as *The Third Flare*, translated by Robert Daglish, 1966.
Al'piyskaya balada. 1964; as *Alpine Ballad*, translated by George Hanna, 1966.
Mertvym ne balits' [The Dead Feel No Pain]. 1965.
Praklyataya vyshynya [The Accursed Hill]. 1968.
Kruhlyansky most [The Bridge at Kruhlyany]. 1969.
Sotnikaw. 1970; as *The Ordeal*, translated by Gordon Clough, 1972; as *Sotnikov*, translated by Brian Bean, in *Soviet War Stories*, 1990.
Abelisk [The Obelisk] (story). 1971.
Dažhyts' da svitannya (story). 1973; as *His Battalion and Live until Dawn*, translated by Jennifer and Robert Woodhouse, 1981.
Vowčhaya zhraya (story). 1974; translated as 'The Wolf Pack', in *Soviet Literature*, 5, 1975; as *A Pack of Wolves*, 1981.
Paystsi i ne viarnutstsa [To Go and Not Return]. 1978.
Znak byady. 1982; as *Sign of Misfortune*, translated by Alan Myers, 1990.
Kar'er [The Pit]. 1987.

V tumane [In the Mist]. 1987.
Ablava [The Swoop]. 1989.

Plays

Rashenne [The Decision]. 1972.
Aposhni shants [The Last Chance]. 1974.

Other

Reč' na s'ezde Soiza pisatelei Belorussii [Speech to the Union of Belarusian Writers], in *Grani*, 61. 1966.

*

Critical Studies: *Vasil Bykaw: Narys tvorchastsi* by Vasil Buran, 1976; 'Vasil' Bykov and the Soviet Byelorussian Novel', in *The Languages and Literatures of the Non-Russian Peoples of the Soviet Union*, 1977, 'War and Peace in the Prose of Vasil Bykau', in *Die Welt der Slaven*, 8(1), 1983, and 'Recovery of the Past and Struggle for the Future: Vasil' Bykaw's Recent War Fiction', in *World War II and the Soviet People*, edited by John and Carol Garrard, 1993, all by Arnold B. McMillin; *Vasil' Bykov: Ocherk tvorchestva*, 1979, and *Vasil Bykov* (in English; includes interviews with Bykaw), 1987, both by L. Lazarev; 'The Growth of Crystal: Vasil' Bykov, Characters and Circumstances' by Igor' Shtokman, in *Soviet Studies in Literature*, 15(2), 1979; *Vasil' Bykov: Ocherk tvorchestva* by I. Dedkov, 1980; *Vasil' Bykov: Povesti o voine* by A. Shagalov, 1989; 'The Art of Vasil' Bykov' by Deming Brown, in *Zapisy Belaruskaha Instytuta Navuki i Mastatstva*, 20, 1992.

* * *

Vasil Bykaw, an outstanding figure in present-day Belarusian prose, has chosen to write almost exclusively about World War II, raising the genre of war literature from one beset by cliché and hollow heroics to a level of sophistication marked by unvarnished realistic description of small-scale events, and a psychological truthfulness matched by few, if any, of his contemporaries. The consistent and unflinching moral focus of Bykaw's prose fiction brought him great popularity in the post-Stalin era, and, particularly in the last years of the Soviet Union, he has played a major role in the struggle for Belarus's true independence. He has more than once been described by his fellow-countrymen as 'the conscience of the Belarusian people'.

Bykaw's writing came to prominence in the atmosphere of comparative freedom associated with the Thaw. Only 17 when the war broke out, he characteristically makes very young men the central figures in his stories and novellas, seeing events, actions and moral decisions through their eyes, and often contrasting them with the demagogy, self-seeking, bullying, and, at times, treachery and cowardice of their superiors, whose actions in the fight against a cruel enemy can sometimes be hardly less ruthless. Bykaw depicts the war on a human rather than epic scale, using tight spatial and temporal contexts, often at moments of life-and-death crisis for a small group of soldiers or partisans. Stark moral choices are to the fore, and it is Bykaw's highlighting of uncomfortable questions, often with a strong contemporary resonance that, with his avoidance of cant and stereotyping, helps to account for his works' great popularity and also for the fierce attacks he sustained from Communist critics in the 1960s and 1980s.

The narrow compass of Bykaw's works is often extended by means of memory, flashback, and dreams. Alluding to such features of Stalinism as sudden arrests and collectivization, Bykaw shows how their consequences affected the conduct of Soviet citizens during the war. For example, an episode in *Zdrada* [Treachery] tells the story of how a popular Komsomol secretary had been declared an 'enemy of the people' in the 1930s before reappearing as a regular frontline soldier; in a later work, *Znak byady* (*Sign of Misfortune*), the behaviour of some Nazi collaborators is implicitly traced back to the bitter injustices suffered by their parents during the enforced collectivization of agriculture a decade earlier.

Often, too, Bykaw relates his war fiction to the present day, underlining the lessons of Stalinist immorality for Belarus and, indeed, the whole Soviet Union in the 1960s and 1970s. In his most expansive, autobiographical, and controversial novel, *Mertvym ne balits'* [The Dead Feel No Pain], a work long banned by the authorities, cruel and immoral Stalinist attitudes are graphically shown as being no less strong in Belarus of the 1960s than in the war; in *Abelisk* [The Obelisk] wartime injustices are hard to put right, even in the conditions of peace, and at the end of the novella Bykaw, never a dogmatist, seems to leave the ultimate decision to the reader: 'And now let the reader decide. Let him sort it out. Each according to his outlook on the world, his view of the war, of heroism, of his obligation to conscience and to history . . .'. The linking of past and present is continued in Bykaw's latest works, such as *Kar'er* [The Pit].

Bykaw's thematic consistency has led to hostile critics accusing him of repetition, but there is a world of difference between his first major novella, *Žhurawliny kryk* [The Cry of the Crane], the outstanding story, *Kruhlyansky most* [The Bridge at Kruhlyany], the novel *Mertvym ne balits'*, his gripping first partisan novella, *Sotnikaw* (*The Ordeal*), and *Sign of Misfortune*. Not only does the last centre on old people rather than young heroes, it is set not in an area of conflict but in a run-down and deserted farm which has been taken over by the Germans and is being plagued by their henchmen. Again moral choices are prominent, but Bykaw shows a sensitive understanding of the various shades of grey, at the same time creating two memorable and contrasting peasant characters, and throwing much light on the misery of their lot in Soviet peacetime as well as war.

The moral imperative found throughout Bykaw's writing does not in any way impair his works' literary quality. His prose is always muscular and often lapidary, capable of vivid description and concise characterization, with sparing but effective imagery. The crises around which nearly all his works revolve make them both exciting and thought-provoking to read, both at a universal level and for a specifically Soviet readership, all too well aware that Khruschchev's denunciation of Stalin in 1956 did not mean abolition of Stalinist attitudes.

Translated into many languages (usually from Russian versions, no longer subjected to political bowdlerization in the process), Bykaw's works have set new moral and artistic standards for Soviet and Belarusian literature. Topicality and universality combine in what is amongst the most powerful war prose in any language.

—Arnold McMillin

THE ORDEAL (Sotnikaw)
Novel by Vasil Bykaw, 1970.

The Ordeal is the second of Bykaw's works on the theme of partisans in World War II, and one of the finest examples of all his prose fiction, displaying many of the features that have made him perhaps the leading Belarusian prose writer today.

The story concerns a particularly difficult mission by two partisans in occupied Belarus, and the different reactions of the two, both highly committed and competent fighters, to the disaster of failure and capture. Bykaw is a realistic writer with a strong gift for portraying physical experiences, and the reader shares the partisans' discomfort, despair, and acute pain as they struggle against the harsh and punishing forces of the bleak Belarusian terrain in winter, despite the fact that one of the two, Sotnikaw (whose name forms the title of the original version of this work), is sick even before they set out and only volunteers through pride. For this reason, apart from its inherent hazards, the successful outcome of the mission is in doubt from the start. As things get worse Sotnikaw only fights to stay alive out of loyalty to his comrade, Rybak; for his part, Rybak begins to blame their fearsome predicament on his sick partner. Briefly sheltered by some peasants, one of whom turns out to be the village headman, they are put to the supreme test by the ruthless Belarusian puppet police (*Polizei*) into whose hands they soon fall; Sotnikaw passes the test—and dies; his comrade, Rybak, under similar interrogation and torture, makes first one (clearly rational) compromise and then another, ending as a collaborator and witness, indeed, helper, at the public hanging not only of his comrade, but also of two peasants and a 13-year-old Jewish girl. The test of courage in the face of adversity which Bykaw gives his characters in many stories has led some critics to compare him to Jack London (a well-known writer to all Soviet readers), but there is nothing gratuitous in Bykaw's unflinching portrayal of suffering, for example, as a result of torture inflicted by the *Polizei*: the Belarusian is more interested in motive than in results, and his works have a great deal more psychological substance than London's.

The story is told from two different points of view, those of Sotnikaw and Rybak, which lends the work not only objectivity but also exceptional psychological depth, bringing the reader to the heart of the partisans' appalling situation. Bykaw makes far from a blanket condemnation of Rybak's weakness; rather, by following his thought processes, he shows how thin a line there can be between bravery and cowardice; how a game of cat-and-mouse with ruthless captors, albeit inspired by the entirely reasonable motive of trying to win time, could lead in this instance to moral degradation. Bykaw's message is not so much one of no compromise, but of the ease with which things can go wrong

in a maximally tense wartime situation: each case, each individual fate, the author is stressing (in the face, of course, of inflexible dogmatism and maximalism in Soviet attitudes to World War II) should be considered separately, not in terms of doctrine but of understanding. The reader is made not only to experience the physical fear and hardship of the partisans, but also to think what he or she would do in comparable circumstances. Throughout his writing Bykaw has consistently resisted dogmas that ignore real circumstances: like Alexander Solzhenitsyn, at much the same time, he has defended those who, merely for the misfortune of having been surrounded by the enemy, have been classified as traitors, the victims of collectivization, the fates of simple German as well as Russian and Belarusian soldiers, even those who (sometimes for excellent and selfless reasons) accepted official posts, such as that of village headman, under German occupation. It is, incidentally, noticeable in *The Ordeal* that Rybak, the future quisling, adopts a far more intransigent attitude to the village headman than his morally sturdier companion Sotnikaw. It is Bykaw's very strength as a realistic and psychologically acute writer that makes his constant moral witness against 'paper truth', the rigidity and cruelty associated with Stalin, and the simplification and trivialization of war, so moving for readers and so important in the whole context of Soviet morality.

The Ordeal is a powerful example of Soviet war literature, reflecting many of the strengths of Bykaw as a writer. Broadly referential (for example, to the notorious Finnish campaign) and unflinchingly realistic, this novel, written at a time of Soviet stagnation in literature, has become a classic example of psychological war-writing at its best.

—Arnold McMillin

BYKOV, Vasil. See **BYKAW, Vasil**.

C

CAESAR, (Gaius) Julius. Born in Rome in 100 or 102 BC. Married 1) Cornelia in 83 BC (died); 2) Pompeia in 67 BC (divorced 62 BC); 3) Calpurnia in 59 BC. Exiled in Asia because of opposition to Sulla, 82–78 BC; fought his first military campaign in Asia, 81 BC; on return to Rome entered politics and may have assisted in Catiline's conspiracy against Cicero, *q.v.*, and other senators; after a successful military campaign and governorship in Spain (61 BC), returned to Rome in 60 BC and formed a triumvirate with Pompey and Lucinius Crassus; consul, 59 and 56 BC; won support by his conquest of the province of Gaul, of which he was made governor, 58–50 BC; invaded Britain in 55 and 54 BC, subduing part of the country; crossed the river Rubicon without the authorization of the Senate, in effect declaring war on Pompey, his rival for power, but was victorious in the three months of civil war that followed; appointed dictator for one year; after Pompey's death, appointed for another year, and consul for five years; subdued Egypt and placed Cleopatra on the throne; made consul for ten years, and, in February 44 BC, dictator for life. *Died (assassinated) 15 March 44 BC.*

PUBLICATIONS

Collections

[Commentaries], edited by Bernard Hübler. 3 vols., 1893–97; also edited by Alfred Klotz, 3 vols., 1920–27, and by Klotz, Otto Seel, and Winifried Trillitzsch, 1961– ; as *War Commentaries,* edited and translated by John Warrington, 1953; as *The Commentaries*, translated by William Duncan, 1753; also translated by Somerset de Chair, 1951; as *The Gallic War and Other Writings*, translated by Moses Hadas, 1957; as *War Commentaries of Caesar*, translated by Rex Warner, 1960.

Works

De bello civili, edited by Charles E. Moberly, 1872; also edited by F. Kraner and F. Hofmann, revised by H. Meusel, 1906; Books I and II edited and translated by J.M. Carter, 1991; as *Civil War with Pompeius*, translated by F.P. Long, 1906; as *The Civil Wars* [Loeb Edition], translated by A.G. Peskett, 1914; as *The Civil War*, translated by Jane F. Mitchell (now Gardner), 1967.
De bello Gallico, edited by Charles E. Moberly. 2 vols., 1871; also edited by John Brown, 7 vols., 1900–03, T. Rice Holmes, 1914, and E.C. Kennedy, 1959– ; as *Commentaries on the Gallic War*, translated by F.P. Long, 1906; also translated by T. Rice Holmes, 1908; as *The Gallic War*, translated by H.J. Edwards, 1917; as *The Conquest of Gaul*, translated by S.A. Handford, 1951; also translated by Anne and Peter Wiseman, 1980; as *The Gallic Wars*, translated by John Warrington, 1954.

*

Critical Studies: *Julius Caesar* by Alfred Duggan, 1955; *Caesar as Man of Letters* by Franz E. Adcock, 1956; *Julius Caesar* by Michael Grant, 1969; *Caesar and Roman Politics 60–50 BC* by James S. Clare, 1971; *Caesar and Contemporary Roman Society* by Erik Wistrand, 1979; *End of the Ancient Republic: Essays on Julius Caesar* by Jan H. Blits, 1983; *Julius Caesar and His Public Image* by Zwi Yaetz, 1983; *Julius Caesar, the Pursuit of Power* by Ernle Bradford, 1984.

* * *

'In eloquence and in military skill Julius Caesar equalled or even surpassed the most famous'. This was the judgement of Suetonius, a biographer not given to excessive praise, and what is particularly noteworthy is that Caesar is praised as much for his excellence in the arts of language as for his prowess as a soldier. This tireless man of action, one of history's most accomplished captains, a politician whose burning ambition was matched by his consummate skill, and a lover whose passions have beguiled the imaginations of later generations, was also an orator whose reputation in Rome in the first century BC was second only to Cicero's and a writer whose excellence won the admiration of all around him.

Such was Caesar's personality that it might be supposed his was an untutored talent. However, nothing could be further from the truth. In his early years he received a basic training in oratory from the freed slave Antonius Gnipho and put his newly acquired skills to use when, in a speech which he is reported to have delivered in a somewhat high pitched voice with great fluency and vehement gestures, he accused the provincial governor Dolabella of extortion. He did not secure a conviction but he succeeded in his primary aim of drawing attention to himself. Shortly afterwards, on his way to the island of Rhodes, Caesar was taken prisoner by pirates, released on ransom, and then returned to punish his captors with condign severity. That characteristic and colourful episode becomes even more interesting when it is recalled that his motive for this journey was, in fact, the desire to study under Apollonius Molon, one of the great teachers of rhetoric of the time. Whether or not the politically clever speech attacking Catiline, which is cited by Sallust, is in fact an accurate reproduction of the words Caesar actually spoke, we certainly have further evidence here of his importance as an orator. Cicero himself draws particular attention in his *Brutus* to the purity of Caesar's Latin style.

Caesar's speeches are, however, no more the most important part of his literary output than is a work he wrote on philological concerns, though that too shows his concern for language. What really counts, of course, are the seven books of his *De bello Gallico* (*The Gallic War*) and the three of his *De bellum civile* (*The Civil War*). As an account of major events related by the principal actor in the unfolding drama, this is a work without parallel in ancient historical writing. The literary aspect, however, is hardly less remarkable. *The Gallic War* and *The Civil War* are categorized technically as 'commentaries'. They are not what the Greeks and Romans of the days would have classed as 'histories'. What commentaries were supposed to provide was only a bald, factual narrative of events. This was thought to be only the bare bones of history, considered a high literary form, replete with graphic battle scenes, for instance, and stirring speeches allegedly delivered to the troops by eloquent generals at suitable moments in the campaign. Nowadays we set the highest premium on the truthfulness of any historical narrative, but for antiquity some embellishment of fact was deemed legitimate in turning commentaries into the distinctly superior literary form of history.

Although Caesar purported to be writing only commentaries, it seems likely that he saw in their plain style an ideal way of presenting himself favourably to the public as an energetic man of deeds. 'Gaul is all divided into three parts', the famous opening of *The Gallic War*, reveals something of his manner, especially when it is recalled that the sequence of Latin words permitted Caesar to place the word 'three' emphatically after the noun 'parts'. It was notorious that Gaul was a vast, inchoate mish-mash of warring tribes, but the businesslike commander Caesar cut the problem down to size. He likewise rejected the contemporary fashion of seeking to impress both by complexity in syntax and by inexhaustible variety in vocabulary, opting for something far more straightforward. His contemporaries, with their expertise in rhetoric, recognized that Caesar was, in fact, turning away from the so-called Asiatic style and using instead the Attic. Whether Caesar consciously adopted it may perhaps be debated, but that his choice was educated is undeniable. Successive generations have lauded Caesar's language as the reflection of a soldier's mind. The point that has not always been properly understood is that Caesar composed his commentaries precisely in order to create that impression.

The Gallic War, with its accounts of vast conquests north of the Alps and including, at the end of Book IV and the beginning of Book V, fascinating information about the Romans' first two raids on Britain, and *The Civil War*, describing the complex operations after 50 BC, were most likely written year by year after campaigning stopped. They succeeded admirably in ensuring that heed is paid above all to Caesar's role in events and to an interpretation that is most flattering to himself. What is more, it was recognized from the outset that there was in fact no way in which some man of letters could improve these particular commentaries by giving them literary polish and transforming them into history. Typically enough, Caesar had triumphed in yet another field of human endeavour.

—Christopher Smith

CALDERÓN de la Barca, Pedro. Born in Madrid, Spain, 17 January 1600. Educated at the Jesuit Colegio Imperial; studied canon law at the University of Alcalá, 1614–15, and University of Salamanca, 1615–c.21, no degree. Entered the household of the Constable of Castille, Don Bernardino Fernández de Velasco, 1621; began writing plays for the court from 1623; entered order of St James, 1637; served in the campaign against the Catalans, 1640–42; served in the household of the Duke of Alba from 1645; became a priest in 1651,

but continued to write plays as court dramatist for Philip IV; chaplain of the Chapel of Reyes Nuevos, Toledo, from 1653, but lived in Madrid after 1657: Honorary Chaplain to the King, 1663. *Died 25 May 1681.*

PUBLICATIONS

Collections

Obras, edited by Joseph Calderón. 5 vols., 1636–77.
Autos sacramentales. 1677.
Obras, edited by J. de Vera Tassis. 9 vols., 1682–91.
Poesías, edited by Adolfo de Castro Cádiz. 1845.
Dramas of Calderón: Tragic, Comic and Legendary (includes *Love after Death*; *The Scarf and the Flower*; *The Physician of His Own Honour*; *The Constant Prince*; *The Purgatory of St Patrick*), translated by Denis F. McCarthy. 2 vols., 1853.
Six Dramas of Calderón (includes *The Mayor of Zalamea*; *Beware of Smooth Water*; *Gil Perez the Gallician*; *Keep Your Own Secret*; *The Painter of His Own Dishonour*; *Three Judgements at a Blow*), translated by Edward Fitzgerald. 1853; revised and enlarged edition as *Eight Dramas* (including additionally the adaptations *Such Stuff as Dreams Are Made Of* and *The Mighty Magician*), 1906.
Mysteries of Corpus Christi (includes *The Divine Philothea*; *Belshazzar's Feast*; *The Poison and the Antidote*), translated by Denis F. McCarthy. 1867.
Three Dramas of Calderón (includes *The Devotion of the Cross*; *The Sorceries of Sin*; *Love Is the Greatest Enchantment*), translated by Denis F. McCarthy. 1870.
Calderón's Dramas, translated by Denis F. McCarthy. 1873.
Obras escogidas. 1940.
Obra lírica, edited by M. de Montoliu. 1943.
Obras completas, edited by Luis Astrana Marín and Ángel Valbuena Briones. 3 vols., 1956–59:
  1. *Dramas*, edited by Luis Astrana Marín. 1959.
  2. *Comedias*, edited by Ángel Valbuena Briones. 1956.
  3. *Autos sacramentales*, edited by Ángel Valbuena Prat. 1959.
Four Plays (includes *Secret Vengeance for Secret Insult*; *The Devotion of the Cross*; *The Mayor of Zalamea*; *The Phantom Lady*), translated by Edwin Honig. 1961.
Tragedias, edited by Francisco Ruiz Ramón. 3 vols., 1967–69.
Four Comedies (includes *From Bad to Worse*; *The Secret Spoken Aloud*; *The Worst Is Not Always Spoken*; *The Advantages and Disadvantages of a Name*), translated by Kenneth Muir. 1980.
Three Comedies (includes *A House with Two Doors Is Difficult to Guard*; *Mornings of April and May*; *No Trifling with Love*), translated by Kenneth Muir and Ann L. Mackenzie. 1985.
Teatro cómico breve, edited by María Luisa Lobato. 1989.
Plays 1 (*The Surgeon of Honour*; *Three Judgements in One*; *Life Is a Dream*), translated by Gwynne Edwards. 1990.

Plays (selection: modern editions or plays translated into English)

A María el corazón, edited by Giacomo Vaifro Sabatelli (with *La hidalga del valle*). 1962.
A secreto agravio, secreta venganza, edited by Edward Nagy. 1966; in *Tragedias*, 2, 1968; as *Secret Vengeance for Secret Insult*, translated by Edwin Honig, in *Four Plays*, 1961.

El alcalde de Zalamea, edited by Peter N. Dunn. 1966; also edited by Alberto Porqueras Mayo, 1977; as *The Mayor of Zalamea*, translated by Edward Fitzgerald, in *Six Dramas*, 1853, and *Eight Dramas*, 1906; also translated by William E. Colford, 1959; Edwin Honig, in *Four Plays*, 1961; Walter Starkie, in *Eight Spanish Plays of the Golden Age*, 1964; adapted by Adrian Mitchell, 1981.

Amar después de la muerte, as *Love after Death*, translated by Denis F. McCarthy, in *Dramas of Calderón*. 1853; also translated by Roy Campbell, in *Classic Theatre*, 3, edited by Eric Bentley, 1960.

Amar y ser amado; divina Filotea, as *The Divine Philothea*, translated by Denis F. McCarthy, in *Mysteries of Corpus Christi*. 1867.

La aurora en Copacabana, edited by Antonio Pages Larraya. 1956.

La banda y la flor, as *The Scarf and the Flower*, translated by Denis F. McCarthy, in *Dramas of Calderón*. 1853.

Los cabellos de Absalón, edited by Helmy F. Giacoman. 1968, also edited by Evangelina Rodríguez Cuadros, 1989.

Cada uno para sí, edited by José M. Ruano de la Haza. 1982.

Casa con dos puertas mala es de guardar, edited by G.T. Northrup, in *Three Plays*. 1926; as *A House with Two Doors Is Difficult to Guard*, translated by Kenneth Muir and Ann L. Mackenzie, in *Three Comedies*, 1985.

El castillo de Lindabridis, edited by Victoria B. Torres. 1987.

Celos aun del aire matan, edited by J. Subirá. 1933; as *Even Baseless Jealousy Can Kill*, translated by M. Stroud, 1981.

La cena de Baltazar, in *Tragedias*, 3. 1969; as *Belshazzar's Feast*, translated by Denis F. McCarthy, in *Mysteries of Corpus Christi*, 1867.

La cisma de Inglaterra, as *The Schism in England*, edited and translated by Ann L. Mackenzie and Kenneth Muir. 1990.

La dama duende, edited by José Luis Alonso. 1966; as *The Phantom Lady*, translated by Edwin Honig, in *Four Plays*, 1961.

La desdicha de la voz, edited by Gwynne Edwards. 1970.

La devoción de la Cruz, edited by Sidney F. Wexler. 1966; in *Tragedias*, 3, 1969; as *The Devotion of the Cross*, translated by Denis F. McCarthy, in *Three Dramas of Calderón*, 1870; also translated by Edwin Honig, in *Four Plays*, 1961.

Dicha y desdicha del nombre, as *The Advantages and Disadvantages of a Name*, translated by Kenneth Muir, in *Four Comedies*. 1980.

La divina Filotea, edited by José Carlos de Torres Martínez, in *Segismundo 3*. 1967.

El divino Jasón, edited by Ignacio Arellano and Ángel L. Cilveti. 1992.

Eco y Narciso, edited by Charles V. Aubrun. 1961.

En esta vida todo es verdad y todo mentira, edited by D.W. Cruickshank. 1971.

Los encantos de la culpa, as *The Sorceries of Sin*, translated by Denis F. McCarthy, in *Three Dramas of Calderón*. 1870.

La estatua de Prometeo, edited by Charles V. Aubrun. 1961; also edited by Margaret Rich Greer, 1986.

Fieras afemina amor, edited by Edward M. Wilson. 1984.

El golfo de las sirenas, edited by Sandra L. Nielson. 1989.

El gran duque de Gandía, edited by Václav Cerný. 1963.

El gran teatro del mundo, edited by Eugenio Frutos Cortés. 1958; also edited by Domingo Ynduráin, 1973; as *The Great Theatre of the World and Genius of Calderón*, translated by Richard C. Trench, 1856; as *The Great World Theatre*, translated by Francis E. Sipman, 1955; as *The Great Stage of the World*, translated by George W. Brandt, 1976.

Guárdate del agua mansa, edited by Ignacio Arellano and Víctor García Ruiz. 1989; as *Beware of Smooth Water*, translated by Edward Fitzgerald, in *Six Dramas*, 1853, and *Eight Dramas*, 1906.

Gustos y disgustos son no más que imaginación, edited by Claudio Y. Silva. 1974.

La hidalga del valle, edited by Giacomo Vaifro Sabatelli (with *A María el corazón*). 1962.

La hija del aire, edited by Gwynne Edwards. 1970; also edited by Francisco Ruiz Ramón, 1987.

Luis Pérez el gallego, as *Gil Perez the Gallician*, translated by Edward Fitzgerald, in *Six Dramas*, 1853, and *Eight Dramas*, 1906.

El mágico prodigioso, edited by Alexander A. Parker and Malveena McKendrick. 1972; as *The Wonderworking Magician*, translated by Denis F. McCarthy, in *Calderón's Dramas*, 1873; also translated by Bruce W. Wardropper, 1982; as *The Mighty Magician*, translated by Edward Fitzgerald, in *Eight Dramas*, 1906; as *The Prodigious Magician*, translated by Wardropper, 1982.

Mañanas de abril y mayo, as *Mornings of April and May*, translated by Kenneth Muir and Ann L. Mackenzie, in *Three Comedies*. 1985.

El mayor encanto amor, as *Love Is the Greatest Enchantment*, translated by Denis F. McCarthy, in *Three Dramas of Calderón*. 1870.

El mayor monstruo los celos, edited by Everett W. Hess. 1965; in *Tragedias*, 1, 1967.

El médico de su honra, edited by C.A. Jones. 1961; in *Tragedias*, 2, 1968; also edited by D. W. Cruickshank, 1981; as *The Physician of His Own Honour*, translated by Denis F. McCarthy, in *Dramas of Calderón*, 1853; as *The Surgeon of His Honour*, translated by Roy Campbell, 1960; as *The Surgeon of Honour*, translated by Gwynne Edwards, in *Plays 1*, 1990.

Mejor está que estaba, as *Fortune Mends*, in *The Theatrical Recorder*, 2. 1806.

Nadie fie su secreto, as *Keep Your Own Secret*, translated by Edward Fitzgerald, in *Six Dramas*. 1853, and *Eight Dramas*, 1906.

No hay burlas con el amor, edited by I. Arellano. 1981; as *No Trifling with Love*, translated by Kenneth Muir and Ann L. Mackenzie, in *Three Comedies*, 1985.

No hay cosa como callar, edited by Ángel Valbuena Briones, in *Comedias de capa y espada*, 2. 1954.

No hay más fortuna que Dios, edited by Alexander A. Parker. 1949.

No hay que creer ni en la verdad, edited by Václav Cerný. 1968.

No siempre lo peor es cierto, edited by Luis G. Villaverde and Lucile Fariñas. 1977; as *The Worst Is Not Always Certain*, translated by Kenneth Muir, in *Four Comedies*, 1980.

Peor está que estaba, as *From Bad to Worse*, translated by Kenneth Muir, in *Four Comedies*. 1980.

El pintor de su deshonra, edited by Manuel Ruiz Lagos. 1969; as *The Painter of His Own Dishonour*, translated by Edward Fitzgerald, in *Six Dramas*, 1853, and *Eight Dramas*, 1906; as *The Painter of His Dishonour*, edited and translated by A.K.G. Paterson, 1991.

El pleito matrimonial del cuerpo y el alma, edited by Manfred Engelbert. 1969.

El postrer duelo de España, edited by Guy Rossetti. 1977.

El príncipe constante, edited by Alexander A. Parker. 1975; as *The Constant Prince*, translated by Denis F. McCarthy, in *Dramas of Calderón*, 1853.

Tu prójimo como a ti, edited by Mary Lorene Thomas. 1989.

El purgatorio de san Patricio, as *The Purgatory of St Patrick*, translated by Denis F. McCarthy, in *Dramas of Calderón*. 1853.

El secreto a voces, edited by José M. de Osma. 1938; as *The Secret Spoken Aloud*, translated by Kenneth Muir, in *Four Comedies*, 1980.

El sitio de Bredá, edited by Johanna R. Schrek. 1957.

Las tres justicias en una, as *Three Judgements at a Blow*, translated by Edward Fitzgerald, in *Six Dramas*. 1853, and *Eight Dramas*, 1906; as *Three Judgements in One*, translated by Gwynne Edwards, in *Plays 1*, 1990.

El veneno y la triaca, translated in part as *The Poison and the Antidote* by Denis F. McCarthy, in *Mysteries of Corpus Christi*. 1867.

El verdadero dios Pan, edited by José M. de Osma. 1949.

La vida es sueño, edited by Augusto Cortina. 1955; also edited by A.E. Sloman, 1961, Everett W. Hesse, 1978, José María García Martín, 1983, J.M. Ruano de la Haza, 1992, and by Ann L. Mackenzie, 1992; as *Such Stuff as Dreams Are Made Of*, translated by Edward Fitzgerald, in *Eight Dramas*, 1906; several subsequent translations as *Life Is a Dream*, including by William E. Colford, 1958, Roy Campbell, in *The Classic Theatre 3*, edited by Eric Bentley, 1960, Kathleen Raine and R.M. Nadal, 1968, and by Gwynne Edwards, in *Plays 1*, 1990.

Verse

Psalle et sile, edited by Leopoldo Trenor. 1936.

Other

Obras menores, edited by A. Pérez Gómez. 1969.

*

Bibliography: *A Chronology of the Plays of Calderón de la Barca* by H.W. Bilborn, 1928; *Bibliografía temática de estudios sobre el teatro español antiguo* by Warren T. McCready, 1966; *Calderón de la Barca Studies 1951–69* by Jack H. Parker and Arthur M. Fox, 1971.

Critical Studies: *The Allegorical and Metaphorical Language in the Autos Sacramentales of Calderón* by Frances de Sales MacGarry, 1937; *The Allegorical Drama of Calderón*, 1943, and *The Mind and Art of Calderón: Essays on the 'Comedies'*, 1988, both by Alexander A. Parker; *The Dramatic Craftsmanship of Calderón: His Use of Earlier Plays* by Albert E. Sloman, 1958; *Pedro Calderón de la Barca: A Biography* by Harry Lund, 1964; *Critical Essays on the Theatre of Calderón* edited by Bruce W. Wardropper, 1965; *A Literary History of Spain: The Golden Age: Drama* by Edward M. Wilson and Duncan Moir, 1971; *Calderón and the Seizures of Honor* by Edwin Honig, 1972; *The Textual Criticism of Calderón's Comedias* by E.M. Wilson and D.W. Cruikshank, 1973; *Calderón de la Barca: Imagery, Rhetoric, and Drama* by John V. Bryans, 1977; *The Prison and the Labyrinth: Studies in Calderonian Tragedy* by Gwynne Edwards, 1978; *On Calderón* by James E. Maraniss, 1978; *Calderón's Characters: An Existential Point of View* by Barbara Louise Mujica, 1980; *Critical Perspectives on Calderón de la Barca* edited by Frederick A. De Armas and others, 1981, and *The Return of Astrea: An Astral–Imperial Myth in Calderón* by De Armas, 1986; *The Characters, Plots and Settings of Calderón's Comedias* by W. Richard Tyler and Sergio D. Elizondo, 1981; *Calderón de la Barca at the Tercentenary: Comparative Views* edited by P. Sydney Cravens, 1982; *Reason and the Passions in the 'Comedias' of*

Calderón by David Jonathan Hildner, 1982; *Calderón: The Secular Plays* by Robert Ter Horst, 1982; *Approaches to the Theater of Calderón* edited by Michael McGaha, 1982; *The Development of Imagery in Calderón's Comedias* by William R. Blue, 1983; *Calderón in the German Lands and the Low Countries: His Reception and Influence 1654–1780* by Henry W. Sullivan, 1983; *The Limits of Illusion: A Critical Study of Calderón* by Anthony J. Cascardi, 1984; *Calderón and the Baroque Tradition* edited by Kurt Levy, Jesús Ava, and Gethin Hughes, 1985; *Kings in Calderón: A Study in Characterization and Political Theory* by Dian Fox, 1986; *Myth and Mythology in the Theater of Pedro Calderón de la Barca* by Thomas Austin O'Connor, 1988; *The Mind and Art of Calderón: Essays on the Comedias* by Alexander A. Parker, 1989; *On the Boards and in the Press: Calderón's 'Las tres justicias en una'* by Isaac Benazbu, 1991; *The Play of Power: Mythological Court Dramas of Calderón de la Barca* by Margaret Rich Greer, 1991; *Calderón: The Imagery of Tragedy* by Charlene E. Suscavage, 1991.

*   *   *

Don Pedro Calderón de la Barca, one of the two greatest dramatists of the Spanish Golden Age, was extremely prolific, and his work was of many different kinds. Although he was not ordained until he was over 50, his plays are frequently religious in spirit, and many of them are directly doctrinal. In particular he wrote more than 70 one-act allegorical dramas which Shelley, although an atheist, called 'incomparable autos'. They resemble, but are greatly superior to, English Morality plays; and, like the Mystery cycles, they were performed on wagons in the open air. The best known of the autos, outside Spain, is *El gran teatro del mundo* (*The Great Stage of the World*) in which representative human beings are put into the world to perform their allotted parts on the stage of life. Calderón sometimes rewrote his secular plays as allegories: there is, for example, an *auto* of *La vida es sueño* (*Life Is a Dream*) and another based on *El mayor encanto amor* (*Love Is the Greatest Enchantment*), dramatizing the story of Ulysses and Circe.

Several of Calderón's full-length plays, written for performance in the public theatres of Madrid, have religious themes. It is arguable that *El mágico prodigioso* (*The Wonderworking Magician*) is the finest religious play in any language; and *El príncipe constante* (*The Constant Prince*), in which the phantom of the martyred prince leads the Portuguese army to victory, and *La devoción de la Cruz* (*The Devotion of the Cross*), which ends in the miraculous resurrection and repentance of a scoundrel, are among Calderón's most admired plays. When he wrote about Henry VIII in *La cisma de Inglaterra* (*The Schism in England*), he concentrated, in a way Shakespeare did not, on the religious issue. His most famous play, *Life is a Dream*, is directly didactic, demonstrating that the pursuit of fame or wealth is foolish, that we ought to overcome our passions, and set our hearts on eternal things. Segismundo, returned to prison, is made to believe that he has only dreamed that he was a prince with absolute power; but when he is released again he decides to behave morally instead of selfishly.

Several of Calderón's important plays are marriage tragedies, demonstrating the disastrous effects of the code of honour under which husbands were expected to kill their wives on the mere suspicion of infidelity. In two of these plays the wives are innocent and in a third the imprudent wife has been compelled to marry a man she does not love. In *El médico de su honra* (*The Surgeon of Honour*) a husband has his wife bled to death; in *A secreto agravio, secreta venganza* (*Secret Vengeance for Secret Insult*) another deluded husband murders both his wife and her lover; and in *El pintor de su deshonra* (*The Painter of His Own Dishonour*) Juan Roca kills the innocent wife whom he still loves. Calderón contrasts the honour code with Christian ethics, most obviously in the first of these plays, but the husbands are regarded as mistaken rather than evil: one is provided by the King with another wife, another, tortured with remorse, is allowed to go free, and the third seeks to die in battle. Othello, who commits suicide when he discovers that Desdemona was innocent, provides an illuminating contrast. A modern reader has to make an effort of imagination to put himself in the place of the original audience; but it is important to note that the cruelty of the code is criticized by a number of sympathetic characters, even by those who conform to it in practice.

One of the most popular of Calderón's dramas, *El alcalde de Zalamea* (*The Mayor of Zalamea*), contrasts two conceptions of honour: that of the aristocratic rapist who prefers to die rather than marry the woman he has wronged, and that of her father, the Mayor, who believes that his own honour can be redeemed by the marriage of the rapist to his daughter or, failing that, by his execution. The King, who arrives opportunely, commends the justice of the execution, although the man should properly have been given a court-martial.

Calderón also wrote a large number of love comedies—cloak and sword plays, as they are often called. These have ingenious plots, witty dialogue, charming poetry, comic jealousy, sword fights, confusion over identity, humorous servants, and romantic lovemaking. The heroes, fashionable gallants, are, as Goethe complained, often indistinguishable; but the heroines, whether unjustly suspected of unchastity or gay flouters of convention, are expertly characterized. In a male-dominated society, with rigid notions of female propriety, they can obtain the husbands of their choice only by refusing to conform. One of the two heroines of *Mañanas de abril y mayo* (*Mornings of April and May*) finally persuades her jealous lover to trust her, and not to insist on a proof of her innocence; the other one exposes, and refuses to marry, a conceited philanderer. Marcela, in *Casa con dos puertas malas es de guardar* (*A House with Two Doors Is Difficult to Guard*), secures a husband by meeting her brother's guest clandestinely; Angela in *La dama duende* (*The Phantom Lady*) uses a concealed door to obtain access to a guest's room; and the lovers in *El secreto a voces* (*The Secret Spoken Aloud*) communicate with each other in public by use of an ingenious code.

These comedies often have an element of satire, as of the affected Beatriz in *No hay burlas con el amor* (*No Trifling with Love*). Other plays in this genre raise more serious issues: *Dicha y desdicha del nombre* (*The Advantages and Disadvantages of a Name*) contains an attempted murder and an attempted rape; and *No hay cosa como callar* begins with a rape and ends, years later, with the marriage of the rapist to his victim.

In his later years Calderón wrote mainly for the Court theatres, and here he made use of elaborate scenery, spectacle, and music. The plays were often on classical and mythological subjects, and usually didactic.

There were adaptations of some of Calderón's plays in France and England during the second half of the 17th century; but if one compares, for example, Wycherley's *Love in a Wood* with *Mornings of April and May*, Calderón's plots are submerged in several others; the tone is vulgarized; the rake

is rewarded with a bride; and undistinguished prose is substituted for the delicate verse of the original.

—Kenneth Muir

THE GREAT STAGE OF THE WORLD (El gran teatro del mundo)
Play by Pedro Calderón de la Barca, c.1649 (written c.1633–35).

The Great Stage of the World is one of Calderón's many *autos sacramentales*. These are one-act dramatic compositions in verse, generally allegorical in nature, which always refer to some aspect of the Christian Eucharist and often incorporate a Eucharistic celebration. Many *autos*, including this one, were written specifically for the celebration of the feast of Corpus Christi. The *autos* have a liturgical and didactic function, and dramatize fundamental theological or doctrinal issues in a forthrightly allegorical manner.

The *Great Stage of the World* begins with the appearance of the Author, who creates the stage setting and the characters who will figure in the work and summons the World to appear on stage. World explains the history of man on earth according to a salvationist narrative. The first epoch of human history contains the story of existence from creation to the time of the great flood, and goes on to include man's salvation from the flood, and the covenant of peace, to the institution of natural law. The second epoch of human life corresponds to the period of the written law (i.e. to the Old Testament), and the third to the law of grace or of Christian salvation.

After the scene has been made ready, the characters themselves appear on stage. Author once again speaks, and creates the allegorical characters of Rich Man, Worker, Poor Man, King, Beauty, and Discretion. Before these characters are fashioned they lack free will and so are unable to choose their roles in life; but afterwards it is up to them to choose to do good or evil according to their free will. They will be rewarded according to the way in which they exercise their capacity for choice. Calderón affirms that the social and material differences among men may be radically contingent; the distinctions of social status are not arbitrary creations of men but correspond to the needs of social life. But it is essential to do good works regardless of one's station in life: 'Obrar bien, que Dios es Dios' ('Do good, for God is God'). Each man who plays one of the assigned parts thus also has an individual purpose—to gain his own salvation.

As the play proceeds, Author watches the theatre-like actions or 'representation' of the various characters he has created. He himself intervenes on only two occasions: at the beginning, in order to indicate his transcendent position with respect to his characters and to warn them that what they do will be seen from on high; and later in order to remind them that they can mend their ways but must always act in accordance with their freedom of will. In the representation itself the characters are associated in terms of contrasting groups: Discretion and Beauty, Poor Man/Worker, and Rich Man. When World declares the representation concluded, and when the celestial globe is closed, he asks each one what they have done. All are required to return the gifts with which they were endowed at the opening of the representation, except Child and Poor Man, who had nothing to begin with. The characters seek out the banquet of rewards promised by the Author to all those who played their roles well. This is the Eucharistic moment of the *auto*, when the celestial orb is once again revealed, along with the chalice and host, and the Author is seated on his throne. Discretion and Poor Man are called directly to share in the glory of the Eucharist, while King and Worker are sent to Purgatory. But since King assisted Religion in its time of need, he is pardoned and allowed to share directly in the Eucharistic reward.

The Great Stage of the World must first be understood as a theological and allegorical work, one that is fully informed by Calderón's knowledge of theology through his Jesuit education. Its teachings are those of post-Tridentine Spain, and are influenced heavily by Calderón's Christian neo-scolasticism. At the same time, the play cannot be isolated from its social and political content and represents an alliance of three important spheres of culture in Golden Age Spain: religion, theatre, and state power. The work is representative of Spanish culture in the declining years of the Golden Age, when the influence of the Council of Trent was still indirectly felt, yet when the theocratic State had gained ideological control of the means of representation.

The Great Stage of the World stands out among Calderón's *autos* as the one that is simplest in its diction and most straightforward in its execution. And yet the play is not without its internal complexities. *The Great Stage of the World* is one of the most important examples of Calderonian metatheatre. Theatre and the allied, moral concept of role serve as the vehicles of a theological allegory, which teaches a Christianized version of the moral lesson to be drawn from the awareness that the world is a stage and that men are but actors on it. Yet Calderón's representation of the play within a play also displays a high degree of artistic self-consciousness, and the *auto* must be appreciated for the sheer brilliance of its language and the elegance of its allegorical construction as well as for its doctrinal lessons.

—Anthony J. Cascardi

LIFE IS A DREAM (La vida es sueño)
Play by Pedro Calderón de la Barca, 1636.

Life Is a Dream is the story of Segismundo, a Polish prince, imprisoned from birth by his father, King Basilio, as a result of omens and prophecies predicting disaster for the kingdom. Act I reveals that, despite Segismundo's violent behaviour, Basilio has decided, 20 years later, to give his son an opportunity to rule, and in order to do so he has him transported secretly to the palace under the influence of a powerful drug. Act II sees Segismundo awakening in the palace and, informed of his new power, proceeding to take revenge on those who have wronged him in the past or displease him in the present: his jailer, Clotaldo; his father, Basilio; a prince, Astolfo; a young woman, Rosaura; and an upstart servant. Convinced that the omens were true, Basilio imprisons his son again and instructs Clotaldo to inform him that the palace experience was merely a dream. When in Act III Segismundo is released by soldiers supporting his claims to the throne, he is unable to decide if he is dreaming or not, but feels he should behave more prudently. Confronting those people he saw previously in his 'dream', he resists the impulse of the moment and, having defeated his father in battle, forgives him. The prophecy that he would see his father at his feet is fulfilled, but in a way that rejects vengeance in favour of forgiveness.

The sources of Calderón's play are many. The story of the awakened sleeper occurs in the *Thousand and One Nights*, as well as in the work of Spanish writers from the 14th century. The theme of the individual seeking to avoid, but merely confirming, what is foretold was also common, as in the collection of stories, *Barlaam and Josaphat*. And the idea of life as fleeting and dream-like was central to both oriental and Christian religions. But the direct source of *Life Is a Dream* was Calderón's earlier play written in collaboration with Antonio Coello, *Yerros de naturaleza y aciertos de la fortuna*, in which, despite differences of detail, the basic ideas are the same: a prince who recovers his throne; a young man who, apparently unfit to rule, learns to do so, suggesting in the process that men can shape their destiny.

Life Is a Dream is, however, a much more complex play. The idea that men can shape their destiny is linked now both to the process of self-discovery and to the realization that the objects of human ambition—power, wealth and pleasure—are insubstantial in comparison with true spiritual values. Moreover, these are themes that are embodied in all the characters and incidents of the play. The affairs of Segismundo and Basilio are paralleled by the efforts of Rosaura, abandoned by Prince Astolfo, to recover her honour, which she achieves through Segismundo's recovery of his throne and his appreciation of the worth and rights of others. Basilio's initial irresponsibility towards his son has its counterpart in the self-interested behaviour of many other characters, all of whom grow wiser through disillusionment, achieving knowledge of themselves and of the world. In terms of the complex interlocking of incident and character in a meaningful and illuminating way, *Life Is a Dream* is one of Calderón's most accomplished plays.

Like Don Juan, Segismundo is one of the truly memorable characters of 17th-century Spanish theatre: a man-beast initially at the mercy of his volatile emotions, subsequently bewildered by his inexplicable changes of fortune, and finally groping his way towards a greater understanding of himself and his fellow-men. But the play has other interesting characters too: Basilio, tortured by his son's predicament; Rosaura, passionate in her pursuit of honour, confused by her loss of it; Clotaldo, her father, confounded by the arrival of a child he has never seen; Astolfo, as powerful as he is insincere; and Clarion, Rosaura's servant, the self-interested seeker responsible for his own death. The gallery of brilliantly drawn characters answers the charge that Calderón was much more interested in plot than characterization.

The characters have their counterpart in highly evocative settings, suggested, of course, by the dialogue itself. The opening scenes take place as darkness descends and they conjure up a gloomy tower, a flickering light, and a chained man dressed in skins. In total contrast the subsequent palace-scenes shimmer with silks, brocades, jewels, music, and beautiful women. The effect is truly of *chiaroscuro*, splendidly dramatic, but while the changing landscapes of the play are effective backdrops, they are also reflections of the characters' emotional and mental conflicts, evoking the movements from darkness to light that in one way or another affect all the characters of the play.

Calderón's language, here as elsewhere, is highly stylized, even 'operatic'. Segismundo's opening soliloquy, for example, is not unlike an aria, as are other long speeches in the play. They reveal Calderón's liking for repetition, symmetry, and pattern in the structure of his verse, as well as an overall sense of musicality. The effect of such stylization is not, however, to mute or straightjacket the emotional charge of the lines but, by channelling it into a disciplined form—lines of eight syllables in a variety of stanza forms—to intensify it further. In emotional terms the language has enormous range, from the violence of Segismundo's outbursts to his lyrical praise of female beauty.

Life Is a Dream, written in a strongly Catholic climate, is not a religious play, though it does, in a more general way, expound the theme of the triumph of free will, at the heart of Calderón's particular brand of catholicism. Rather it is a play about man at any time and in any place, at the mercy of deficiencies within and without himself, and struggling to overcome them. It is this more general relevance that accounts for its lasting appeal and allows for varying interpretations that may embrace existentialism on the one hand or the efforts of post-war Poland to resist Soviet authoritarianism on the other.

—Gwynne Edwards

CALLIMACHUS. Born in Cyrene, North Africa (now Libya), c.310–305 BC; active during first half of 3rd century BC and until at least 246 BC. Said to have been a schoolteacher in the Alexandrian suburb of Eleusis before working at the royal library and museum at Alexandria; once believed to have been librarian, but apparently never held that post, though he was responsible for compiling the main bio-bibliographical reference catalogue (*Pinaces*) from which is derived much of the information we have today about ancient Greek writers and their works. Traditionally supposed to have quarrelled with Apollonius of Rhodes, *q.v.*, but evidence for this is poor, though he does seem to have been involved in numerous literary enmities. The scholars Eratosthenes and Aristophanes of Byzantium were among his pupils. *Died c.240 BC.*

PUBLICATIONS

Collections

[Works], edited by R. Pfeiffer. 2 vols., 1949–53; supplemented by P. Parsons and H. Lloyd-Jones, in *Supplementum Hellenisticum (Texte und Kommentare 11)*, 1983; translated by A.W. and G.R. Mari [Loeb Edition], 1921, and C.A. Trypanis [Loeb Edition], 1958; selection translated by Robert A. Furness, 1931.

Verse

Hymn to Zeus, edited by G.R. McLennan (with commentary). 1977.
Hymn to Apollo, edited by F. Williams (with commentary). 1978.
Hymn to Delos, edited by W.H. Mineur (with commentary). 1984.
Hymn to Demeter, edited by N. Hopkinson (with commentary). 1984.
The Fifth Hymn, edited by A.W. Bulloch. 1985.
Hymns, Epigrams, Select Fragments, translated by Stanley Lombardo and Diane Rayor. 1988.
Hecale, edited by A.S. Hollis (with commentary). 1990.

*

Critical Studies: *The Discovery of the Mind* by Bruno Snell, 1953; *History of Classical Scholarship from the Beginnings to the End of the Hellenistic Age* by R. Pfeiffer, 1968; *Callimachus' Iambi* by D.L. Clayman, 1980; *Callimachus* by John Ferguson, 1980; *Cambridge History of Classical Literature I: Greek Literature* edited by P.E. Easterling and B.M.W. Knox, 1984; *The Well-Read Muse: Present and Past in Callimachus and the Hellenistic Poets* by Peter Bing, 1988; *Callimachus: Hecale* by A.S. Hollis, 1990.

*　*　*

Callimachus was the most brilliant intellectual and poet of his time, and, although an extremely controversial figure, had a more radical influence on the course of Greek (and Roman) poetry than almost any other writer except Homer. He wrote prolifically, but few of his works now survive (or they are known only in fragmentary form), and we have to gauge Callimachus' importance from his effect on other writers. Yet his vivacious, penetrating, and rather quixotic intelligence shows through in almost every line that we have. He was said to have written more than 800 works altogether, and was one of the few writers who was equally scholar and poet, in both activity and achievement.

His research involved compilation and classification of data rather than speculative thinking; he wrote scarcely anything of a philosophical or historical nature, and although some of his works have titles such as *On Birds*, or *On Winds*, these were surveys rather than scientific enquiries based on independent observation. However, his work was of fundamental importance in another way: he lived at a point in history when modern scholarship was just beginning to evolve, and in a place where the resources to conduct that scholarship were being assembled for the first time; the principles of philosophical and scientific enquiry were laid down in Athens by Plato and Aristotle and their pupils, but the idea of a body of *knowledge*, and its collection and transmission, came to maturity in 3rd-century BC Alexandria. Callimachus played a key part in the evolution of the principles and standards of true, energetic scholarship, and was one of its most important practitioners; many of the great intellectuals of the next generation were his pupils. His most important work, the *Pinaces*, the reference catalogue to the library, consisted of 120 books, and was the first of its kind and exemplary: it classified the works of all Greek writers of any importance and attempted to provide all the basic information that a reader might need (biography, contents, authenticity, etc.). In effect the *Pinaces* was the first encyclopedia in Western culture.

As a poet Callimachus was equally vigorous and idiosyncratic. He thought that he diagnosed muddle and mediocrity in the mainstream of contemporary Greek poetry, and set a premium in his own work on originality and refreshment of the language. Late in his career Callimachus produced a collection of his own poetry, and wrote a preface for it, in verse, expounding the critical principles that had guided him as a writer ('The Prologue' to the *Aetia*). He claimed to have avoided the trite, uninspired, hackneyed, 'high' manner which was popular at the time and to have been uncompromisingly unorthodox and original, even if that took him 'along a narrower path'. Concision and clarity were of the utmost importance in his work; he was fascinated by language and words, and set out, almost ideologically, to transform the linguistic material of poetry. Like any Greek poet he was thoroughly imbued with Homer, but was too great a writer to think that Homer needed to be overthrown: he advocated passionately the creation of a 'fine', spare, even elegant style, with none of the inflation of unthinking traditionality. Poetry had to be wrought, and writing was the result of work. Despite being a court poet, dependent on, and gratefully acknowledging, the support of royal patronage, he was a nonconformist, an experimenter, at times an iconoclast, and seems always to have been controversial and involved in fierce argument and criticism. He had a perpetual sense of the odd or bizarre. Thus it was the mundane dimensions of what were supposed to be the ideal realms that intrigued him: what are the practicalities of being a hero, and what are the day-to-day effects when man encounters god? His gods are often children and his men involved in pursuing their own odd rituals, and although he represents religious passion with sympathetic insight, he suggests that the only real meaning comes from the limited warmth of human friendship, not from the spiritual or the sublime.

His most important work was the *Aetia* [Origins or Causes], an eccentrically learned work in 4,000–6,000 lines, which mixed strange and wonderful stories into an episodic, almost picaresque narrative of religious rituals and practices: the length was epic, but the style and concerns crankily different, with off-beat accounts, bizarre humour, unpredictable climaxes, and intricate but razor-sharp language. Narrative poetry was never the same again. The *Hecale* was an inverted epic, nominally 'about' Theseus' defeat of the bull of Marathon, but mostly comprising an account of his stay overnight, during a rainstorm, in the hut of a solitary peasant woman. His 13 *Iambi* were mostly social satire, with some personal invective, directed at the foibles of human ambition. None of these works survives in full, but we do possess the complete text of six 'hymns'. All are complex but fine texts, superficially dealing with the myths and rituals connected with some of the principal Olympian deities, with some recognition of the semi-divine power of his royal patrons; but their overall effect is to convey, behind a brilliant, edgy, and often entertaining manner, that traditional religion is puzzling and disturbing. All is not, in fact, right with the world. Callimachus also wrote epigrams which are taut, wry, witty, and pungent, and among the very best in the long history of the genre.

Callimachus changed the course of Greek poetry: writers who saw themselves as 'mainstream' thereafter were deeply influenced by both his style and outlook, and for poets rebelling against their own traditions he was the archetypal avant-garde nonconformist.

—A.W. Bulloch

AETIA
Poem by Callimachus, 3rd century BC.

The *Aetia*, which in antiquity was Callimachus' most famous poem, dealt with the mythological origins of customs, cult rites, and names from throughout the Greek world. It has come down to us in a very fragmentary state. We can for the most part, therefore, reconstruct the poem only in broad outline. It was written in elegiacs and consisted of four books, possibly totalling between 4,000 and 6,000 lines, thus attaining epic length.

As we have it, the *Aetia* begins with a defence of Callimachus' literary principles, then depicts the poet's transportation in a dream from his native Cyrene to Mount Helicon, where he meets the Muses, just as his model for the encounter, Hesiod, claimed to have done at the beginning of his *Theogonia* (*Theogony*). Books I and II of the poem are thereafter cast in the form of a dialogue, the Heliconian Muses answering in a learned fashion the poet's antiquarian questions. In Books III and IV the dialogue form is dropped, a unity being imposed by two framing references to Queen Berenice, whose husband Ptolemy III Euergetes was crowned King of Egypt in 247 BC. Book III begins with an elegiac celebration of a victory by Berenice's chariot at the Nemean Games, and then proceeds to describe the origin of the games, which Callimachus ascribes to a command of Athene to Heracles after his victory over the Nemean lion. Book IV closes with the famous 'Lock of Berenice' (translated by Catullus), which discovers the origin of the constellation Coma Berenices (Lock of Berenice) in the disappearance from a temple of the strand of hair which the queen had dedicated to secure her husband's safety as he went off to war; its translation to heaven was 'identified' by the court astronomer, Conon. Our version of the *Aetia* concludes with an epilogue in which the poet announces that he will now pass on to the 'pedestrian pasture of the Muses', evidently referring to his more prosaic *Iambi*.

It is generally agreed that the *Aetia* was originally composed quite early in Callimachus' career and was published only as Books I and II. At some point after 247 BC, Books III and IV were added, together with the Berenice pieces, of which the 'Lock' seems at first to have been circulated independently. Given the epilogue's reference to the *Iambi*, it may be that Callimachus brought the two works together in a collected edition at the same time. It seems certain that the polemical prologue, the 'Reply to the Telchines' was placed at the head of the *Aetia* at this juncture too, as an attack on Callimachus' detractors and as a defence not only of the *Aetia* itself but of the poet's entire output, now in its final edition.

In the 'Reply', Callimachus represents his critics, whom he calls the Telchines (fabled metal-working sorcerers of notorious maliciousness), as protagonists of 'one continuous song in many thousands of lines . . . on kings or . . . heroes of old'. This makes them traditionalists in poetic taste, and squares with what we know of, in particular, the epic written at this period. Callimachus claims a preference for poetry of shorter compass and expresses an abhorrence of bombast. He says that Apollo told him early in his career as a poet to 'keep the sacrificial victim as fat as possible, but keep the Muse slender', and to strike out on untrodden poetic paths. As we have seen, the *Aetia* was of epic length, but it featured a deliberate discontinuity, which Callimachus may well have felt had a forebear in the disjointed poems of Hesiod, whom he allusively 'cites' as a model in his story of his dream encounter with the Muses. Moreover, though he did write poetry in praise of 'kings' and traditional 'heroes', his treatment of them is sharply at variance with the bombastic poetry, especially epic, written on such themes during the period.

His practice is illustrated by his poem on the victory of Berenice. This is, of course, in elegiacs, which in itself must have seemed innovatory, since victory odes were traditionally written in lyric metres. The poem leads into the *aition* describing the origin of the Nemean Games. This devotes considerable space to the story of how Heracles spent the night with the poor but generous Molorchus before he set out against the Nemean lion. In fact, the heroic feat is set in juxtaposition with something rather less elevated, Molorchus' struggle with household mice, and the *aition* on the Nemean Games is set in ironic contrast with another, on the origin of the mousetrap! This is hardly the grand traditional style.

Another fascinating index of the poet's approach is the story of Acontius and Cydippe, again from Book III. The ostensible point of this poem is to give the history of the famous Acontiad family on the island of Ceos, for which Callimachus draws on the writings of the 5th-century chronicler Xenomedes, actually naming him as his source. But the impression of dry erudition is offset by the love interest in the narrative of the young lovers' difficult path to eventual happiness, and, though the romance is set in the heroic past, the accent is on more everyday human experience, and this is clearly the real point of the poem. Literary self-consciousness, learnedness, a preoccupation with vividness in the depiction of everyday and low motifs, and a love of irony and contrast are thus some of the main hallmarks of the *Aetia*.

As a collection of 'origins', the *Aetia* may be a response to the feeling that Greek culture was to some extent under threat after the expansion of the Greek world by Alexander the Great and in view of the levelling of the local dialects of the Greek language itself. In this case, the famed learnedness of the *Aetia* need not in every instance be considered a display of erudition for its own sake.

—G. Zanker

HECALE
Poem by Callimachus, 3rd century BC.

The *Hecale* has come down to us in a highly fragmentary state, but this century has seen some remarkable papyrological discoveries and feats of reconstruction which have greatly enhanced our knowledge of the poem and are now conveniently assembled by A.S. Hollis in his 1990 edition, *Hecale*. We can now tell the poem, in heroic hexameters, must have been about 1,000 lines in length, though possibly somewhat more, and we are in a position to understand the peculiar genius which made it so influential in subsequent classical poetry (Ovid's debt in the Philemon and Baucis story in *Metamorphoses* being only a more familiar example).

The beginning of the epic refers to its titular heroine and her generous hospitality. From there we pass to the arrival of the young Theseus at Athens from Troezen, where his father, Aegeus, king of Athens, had sent him to be reared. Theseus' stepmother, Medea, tries to poison him, but he is saved in the nick of time by Aegeus, who places him under strict surveillance for his safety. We next find Theseus longing for adventure and pleading with Aegeus to let him slay the Marathonian bull, but he is forced to escape against his father's will. In the evening of his journey to Marathon a storm bursts upon him, and he takes refuge in Hecale's hut. Her reception of him was evidently described in some detail, from the moment he shakes the rain off his cloak to the moment she sits him down, washes his feet, and gives him a meal. Theseus explains his mission, and asks Hecale to tell him why she lives in such an isolated place in her old age. She reveals that her present poverty is not ancestral, and goes on to narrate how her husband was killed at sea, sent to fetch horses from Laconia by Peteos, who was in fact an enemy of Theseus' father. She describes how she lost her elder son and then her sole support, her younger son; he was killed when forced to wrestle with the murderer Cercyon, whom she curses, wishing she could stick thorns in his eyes and eat his flesh raw. Theseus tells her that he himself has killed the bandit, so that another link is forged between the two. They go to sleep, Hecale having improvised bedding for the young hero. Theseus rises early the next day, and we are possibly given a final picture of the old woman as she comes out to bid Theseus farewell.

The actual fight between the Marathonian bull and Theseus seems to have been narrated quite briefly, and we next take up the story as the hero drags the animal along, with one horn smashed off by Theseus' club, and is greeted on his way back to Athens by countryfolk who cannot even look at the huge man and the monstrous bull until Theseus asks someone to go ahead to Athens to tell Aegeus that he is alive and victorious, whereupon the bystanders sing a paean to Theseus and honour him with a ritual shower of leaves.

During a gap of some 22 lines in the text, the scene has changed to a conversation between a crow and another bird (an owl?), perched on a tree in the night. The crow tells the story of how she once brought the news to Athene that her child Ericthonius, whom the goddess wanted to be reared in secret, had been discovered, for which reason Athene forbade crows from entering the Acropolis. The crow also prophesies how Apollo will punish the raven for bringing him news that his human beloved, Coronis, had made love, while pregnant to Apollo, with the mortal Ischys; the raven will be changed from white to black. The connection between these digressions and the narrative frame seems to be the motif of relaying bad news; the crow is advising the other bird not to tell Theseus that Hecale has died in the interim. The two birds fall asleep, and we are given a graphic picture of the dawn that follows soon after as humans light their lamps, fetch water, are woken up by the creaking of wagon axles, and are tormented by the noise of the blacksmith.

Theseus returns from Athens to Hecale's cottage to thank her, but finds the neighbours preparing her funeral. Her neighbours celebrate her hospitality, Theseus laments her, and institutes in her memory a deme named Hecale, an annual banquet, and a sanctuary of Zeus Hecaleius.

Even in its fragmentary state, the *Hecale* amply demonstrates the broad tonal range, allusiveness, and innovative literary approach of Callimachus. On the level of diction, we find words taken from the different dialects of Greece, though of course Attic is highlighted in the interests of local colour, and lowly words for couches and the like contrast with words on a higher stylistic register, in Hecale's autobiography and in the mythological sections, for example. An analogous contrast exists between the recondite nature of Callimachus' deployment of myth and the lowly and the visually vivid images of human life and likewise with the allusions to earlier Greek literature: Hecale's impassioned curse of Cercyon for killing her son reminds us of Hecuba in the *Iliad* (44.212f) cursing Achilles for killing her own Hector, while the whole hospitality motif draws self-consciously on the reception of Odysseus by Eumaeus and Eurycleia in the *Odyssey*. Callimachus' foregrounding of a poor woman is innovative: she may indeed be of noble blood, like her literary forebears in the *Odyssey* or the farmer in Euripides' *Electra*, but she is the first figure of reduced circumstances and low social standing to play a leading part in epic, displacing Theseus' traditional heroism from centre stage, and her generosity is the theme of the beginning and the close of the whole epic. Callimachus seems to be deliberately subverting the grander traditional expectations of the epic hero.

—G. Zanker

CALVINO, Italo. Born in Santiago de las Vegas, Cuba, 15 October 1923. Family moved to San Remo, Italy, 1925. Educated at Ginnasio-liceo Cassini, San Remo; University of Turin, 1941–47; Royal University, Florence, 1943. Conscripted into the Young Fascists, 1940: left, sought refuge in the Alps with his brother, and joined the Communist Resistance, 1943–45. Married Esther Judith Singer ('Chichita') in 1964, one daughter. Contributor, *La Nostra Lotta*, *Il Garibaldino*, *Voce Della Democrazia*, and other periodicals, from 1945; first contributed to *L'Unità*, 1945; member of the editorial staff, Einaudi, publishers, Turin, 1948–84; contributor, *Contemporaneo* and *Città Aperta*, from 1954; co-editor, with Elio Vittorini, *Il Menabò*, Milan, 1959–67; travelled to the USSR, 1952, and the USA, 1959–60; settled in Paris, 1967, while continuing to work for Einaudi; contributor, *La Repubblica*, from 1979; moved to Rome, 1980; member, editorial board, Garzanti, publishers, 1984. Recipient: *L'Unità* prize, 1945; Viareggio prize, 1957; Bagutta prize, 1959; Veillon prize, 1963; Feltrinelli prize, 1972; Austrian State prize for European literature, 1976; Nice Festival prize, 1982. Honorary member, American Academy, 1975. *Died 19 September 1985.*

Publications

Collection

Romanzi e racconti, edited by Claudio Milanini, Mario Barenghi, and Bruno Falcetto. 1991—.

Fiction

Il sentiero dei nidi di ragno. 1947; as *The Path to the Nest of Spiders*, translated by Archibald Colquhoun, 1956.
Ultimo viene il corvo. 1949; as *Adam, One Afternoon, and Other Stories*, translated by Archibald Colquhoun and Peggy Wright, 1957.
I nostri antenati. 1960; as *Our Ancestors*, translated by Archibald Colquhoun, 1980.
  Il visconte dimezzato. 1952; as *The Cloven Viscount*, translated by Archibald Colquhoun, with *The Non-Existent Knight*, 1962.
  Il barone rampante. 1957; edited by J.M. Woodhouse, 1988; as *The Baron in the Trees*, translated by Archibald Colquhoun, 1959.
  Il cavaliere inesistente. 1959; as *The Non-Existent Knight*, translated by Archibald Colquhoun, with *The Cloven Viscount*, 1962.
L'entrata in guerra (trilogy of stories). 1954.
I racconti (stories). 1958.
Marcovaldo; ovvero, Le stagioni in città, illustrations by Sergio Tofano. 1963; as *Marcovaldo; or, The Seasons in the City*, translated by William Weaver, 1983.
La giornata d'uno scrutatore. 1963.
La nuvola di smog e La formica argentina. 1965; *La nuvola di smog* as *Smog*, in *Difficult Loves; Smog; A Plunge Into Real Estate*, 1983.
Le cosmicomiche (stories). 1965; enlarged edition, as *Cosmicomiche, vecchie e nuove*, 1984; as *Cosmicomics*, translated by William Weaver, 1969 .
Ti con zero (stories). 1967; as *T Zero*, translated by William Weaver, 1969; as *Time and the Hunter*, translated by Weaver, 1969.
La memoria del mondo e altre storie cosmicomiche. 1968.

Gli amori difficili. 1970; as *Difficult Loves*, in *Difficult Loves; Smog; A Plunge Into Real Estate*, 1983.
The Watcher and Other Stories, translated by William Weaver and Archibald Colquhoun. 1971.
Le città invisibili. 1972; as *Invisible Cities*, translated by William Weaver, 1974.
Il castello dei destini incrociati. 1973; as *The Castle of Crossed Destinies*, translated by William Weaver, 1976.
Il gigante orripilante. 1975.
Se una notte d'inverno un viaggiatore. 1979; as *If on a Winter's Night a Traveller*, translated by William Weaver, 1981.
Palomar. 1983; as *Mr Palomar*, translated by William Weaver, 1985.
Difficult Loves; Smog; A Plunge Into Real Estate, translated by William Weaver, Archibald Colquhoun, and Peggy Wright. 1983.
Sotto il sole giaguaro (unfinished). 1986; as *Under the Jaguar Sun*, translated by William Weaver, 1988.
Prima che tu dica 'Pronto'. 1993.

Plays

La panchina (libretto), music by Sergio Liberovici (produced 1956).
La vera storia (libretto), music by Luciano Berio (produced 1982).
Un re in ascolto (libretto), music by Luciano Berio (produced 1984).

Other

Italo Calvino racconta l'Orlando furioso di Ludovico Ariosto, edited by Carlo Minoia. 1970.
Una pietra sopra: Discorsi di letteratura e società (essays). 1980; as *The Uses of Literature*, translated by Patrick Creagh, 1986; as *The Literature Machine*, translated by Creagh, 1987.
Collezione di sabbia: Emblemi bizzarri e inquietanti del nostro passato e del nostro futuro gli oggetti raccontano il mondo. 1984.
Lezioni americane: Sei proposte per il prossimo millennio (texts for Charles Eliot Norton lectures). 1988; as *Six Memos for the Next Millenium*, translated by Patrick Creagh, 1988.
Sulla fiaba, edited by Mario Lavagetto. 1988.
La strada di San Giovanni. 1990; as *The Road to San Giovanni*, translated by Tim Parks, 1993.
Perchè leggere i classici (essays). 1992.

Editor, *Fiabe italiane: Raccolte della tradizione popolare durante gli ultimi cento anni e trascritte in lingua dai vari dialetti*. 1956, re-edited by Ersilia Zamponi, 3 vols., 1986–89; selections as *Italian Fables*, translated by Louis Brigante, 1959; as *Italian Folk Tales*, translated by Sylvia Mulcahey, 1975; as *Italian Folktales* (complete), translated by George Martin, 1980.
Editor, *Poesie edite e inedite*, by Cesare Pavese. 1962.
Editor, *Lettere 1945–1950*, by Cesare Pavese. 1966.
Editor, with Lorenzo Mondo, *Lettere 1924–1950*, by Cesare Pavese. 1966.
Editor, *Vittorini: Progettazione e letteratura*. 1968.
Editor, *Teoria dei quattro movimenti: Il nuovo mondo amoroso e altri scritti*, by Charles Fourier. 1971.
Editor, *Porfira*, by Silvina Ocampo. 1973.
Editor, *Il Principe Granchio e altre fiabe italiane*. 1974.
Editor, *Le più belle pagine*, by Tommaso Landolfi. 1982.

Editor, *Racconti fantastici dell'Ottocento*. 2 vols., 1983.

Translator, *I fiori blu*, by Raymond Queneau. 1967.
Translator, *La canzone di polistirene*, by Raymond Queneau. 1985.

*

Critical Studies: *Italo Calvino* by Germana Pescio Bottino, 1967; *Italo Calvino: A Reappraisal and an Appreciation of the Trilogy* by J.R. Woodhouse, 1968; *Invito alla lettura di Calvino* by Giuseppe Bonura, 1972, revised edition, 1987; *Italo Calvino* by Contardo Calligaris, 1973, augmented by G.P. Bernasconi, 1985; *I segni nuovi di Italo Calvino* by Francesca Bernardini Napoletano, 1977; *Italo Calvino: Writer and Critic* by Jo Ann Cannon, 1981; *With Pleated Eye and Garnet Wing: Symmetries of Italo Calvino* by I.T. Olken, 1984; Calvino issue of *Review of Contemporary Fiction*, 6(2), 1986; *Italo Calvino: Metamorphoses of Fantasy* by Albert Howard Carter III, 1987; *Italo Calvino: Tra realtà e favola* by Giovanna Finocchiaro Chimirri, 1987; *Italo Calvino: Introduzione e guida allo studio dell'opera calviniana: Storia e antologia della critica* by Giorgio Baroni, 1988; *Introduzione a Calvino* by Cristina Benussi, 1989; *Le capre di Bikini: Calvino giornalista e Saggista 1945–1985* by Gian Carlo Ferretti, 1989; *Calvino Revisited* edited by Franco Ricci, 1989; *L'Utopia discontinua. Saggio su Italo Calvino* by Claudio Milanini, 1990; *Calvino and the Age of Neorealism: Fables of Estrangement* by Lucia Re, 1990; *Difficult Games: A Reading of I racconti* by Franci Ricci, 1990; *Italo Calvino: a San Remo* by Piero Ferrua, 1991; *Calvino's Fictions: Cogito and Cosmos* by Kathryn Hume, 1992.

* * *

Italo Calvino was perhaps the greatest, and certainly the most versatile, Italian novelist in the second half of the 20th century. This versatility is apparent not only in the sophisticated content of his prolific output, but also in the complex structuring devices and the range of styles he deployed in his many fictions.

He began as a 'neorealist', one of the post-World War II generation of Italians who sought to depict, in a new, explicit style influenced by American novelists, the new realism of Italy which had been ignored in the 20 years of Fascist rule. His first novel, *Il sentiero dei nidi di ragno* (*The Path to the Nest of Spiders*), examined the partisan movement not in hagiographic terms, but as seen through the naive eye of an engaging urchin, Pin. This technique allowed Calvino to mix a serious message with irony, and blend realism with elements borrowed from fairy-tales and Robert Louis Stevenson's *Treasure Island*.

At the beginning of the 1950s, disillusioned with trying to deliver a serious socialist message in tales that could no longer narrate the heroics of the Resistance, Calvino turned to writing the kind of story he himself would have liked to read. *I nostri antenati* (*Our Ancestors*) is a trilogy which, in its three separate parts, owes much, respectively, to the fairy-tale, the adventure story, and the chivalric romance. In *Il visconte dimezzato* (*The Cloven Viscount*), a viscount is torn in two by a cannon-ball, and the two halves, the Good Half and the Bad Half, return to torment his kingdom with both excessive goodness and excessive cruelty. *Il barone rampante* (*The Baron in the Trees*) also has an allegorical dimension, but is a fuller story; indeed it is the longest novel Calvino ever wrote.

It recounts the life of a rebel aristocrat who rejects the outmoded values of his eccentric family to embrace the ideals of the French Enlightenment and Revolution. Although the cause (refusing to eat a plate of snails) and nature (climbing into the trees and staying there) of his rebellion seem trivial, the book argues a profound view about the place of the intellectual in society during times of ideological upheaval. *Il cavaliere inesistente* (*The Non-Existent Knight*) narrates a young knight's search for identity between the extremes offered by Agilulf, who is a perfect being devoid of body but inhabiting a suit of armour, and Gurdulù, who is all body and no intellect. Yet the novel is also about narratology, most of the characters opening with the thoughts of Suor Teodora, who is the narrator and who speculates about the limits of realism and other authorial problems. The final volte-face, in which the nun Teodora is revealed to be the female warrior Bradamante, typifies Calvino's anxieties in this period about his own role as contemplative intellectual, as opposed to active political partisan.

The rest of Calvino's output up to 1963 was in the form of short stories or novellas, either in a fantasy vein, as in the humorous cycle of Marcovaldo stories, or in ironic attempts at realism, as in *Gli amori difficili* (*Difficult Loves*), 'La speculazione edilizia' (*A Plunge Into Real Estate*), and *La nuvola di smog* (*Smog*). The year 1963 was a turning-point in the author's career, neatly encapsulated by the publication of *La giornata d'uno scrutatore* [The Watcher], the last 'full-length' novel he published (though even it is under 100 pages long) and of *Marcovaldo*, the first work of Calvino's new 'serial' manner, based on a sequence of modular units combined to form a single, composite macrotext. In a prophetic passage in *La giornata d'uno scrutatore* the protagonist rejects novels about people and turns instead to scientific works.

Le cosmicomiche (*Cosmicomics*) inaugurated fully this new anti-novelistic and 'scientific' period. The stories which comprise the volume are each introduced by an epigraph from a scientific text (about the Big Bang, the appearance of the first mammals, etc.), which is then illustrated in a comical manner by the protagonist with the unpronounceable name, Qfwfq. Calvino here is consciously challenging some of the assumptions of realism—about human protagonists, with human lifespans and recognizable names. *Ti con zero* (*Time and the Hunter*) contains more Qfwfq tales, but also includes others that showed Calvino's new interest in deductive logic and mathematical constraints on narrative, as practised then by Calvino's friends Queneau and other members of the 'Ouvroir de littérature potentielle'. Further experiments with combinatorial narrative technique followed: in *Il castello dei destini incrociati* (*The Castle of Crossed Destinies*), in which storytelling is carried out by means of tarot cards, since the knights in the enchanted castle have all been struck dumb; and in *Le città invisibili* (*Invisible Cities*), in which Marco Polo describes to the Great Khan, in 55 sections of poetic prose, the cities of his empire. These last two books, broadly based on works by Ariosto and Marco Polo, testify to Calvino's interest in rewriting texts. This fascination is also evident in his masterpiece, *Se una notte d'inverno un viaggiatore* (*If on a Winter's Night a Traveller*), which in structure is a reworking of *The Thousand and One Nights*. This 'hypernovel' consists of a frame of 12 chapters, in which 'you', the reader (a male subject) and a female reader try to read Calvino's *If on a Winter's Night*, but instead are given an apocryphal first chapter from ten different novels. This approach allows Calvino to parade his virtuosity in reproducing widely differing styles of contemporary fiction, and at the same time to play off the events in the frame-story against the episodes read by the readers. The whole book is informed by Calvino's narrative verve, as well as his sense of humour and his interest in contemporary literary theory.

The final work published in his lifetime, *Palomar* (*Mr Palomar*), represents a complete change of style, since it consists of the meditations of Mr Palomar, an elderly man living in 1980s Italy, but it is divided into 27 sections, each of which is subdivided into three units. The protagonist takes his name from the huge astronomical telescope in California, thus linking Calvino's twin fascinations—observation and scientific exploration of the universe. *Sotto il sole giaguaro* (*Under the Jaguar Sun*), published posthumously, continues Calvino's predilection for narrative patternings. An unfinished work, it was to have consisted of five stories about the five senses; but in the end only those concerning smell, taste, and hearing were written.

A provocative essayist as well as occasional librettist, Calvino holds an important place in world literature because of his constant awareness of the limits of realism and the written word in general, and his brilliant and humorous attempts to expand those limits, to innovate constantly, and to inscribe history, science, and philosophy within literature.

—Martin L. McLaughlin

IF ON A WINTER'S NIGHT A TRAVELLER (Se una notte d'inverno un viaggiatore)
Novel by Italo Calvino, 1979.

Metafiction—a fiction about the reading and writing of fiction—is the business of this book, which can barely be defined as a novel. It opens with the words: 'You are about to begin reading Italo Calvino's new novel, *If on a Winter's Night a Traveller*', and ends correspondingly. Calvino cunningly contrives a story out of the semiotic, structuralist, and post-structuralist insights of the 1960s and 1970s, and out of the material processes of writing, producing, distributing, and consuming the literary artefact. 'You', the Reader, a male subject, are the central character, and the Reader finds, on coming to the second chapter of *If on a Winter's Night* that, thanks to a binding error, it, and all the succeeding chapters are repetitions of the first. Thus begins the potentially endless quest for the text, which takes the Reader back to his bookseller, then to the publisher, then into academe, the library, and so on. On each occasion the Reader lights upon the beginning of another novel, whose reading in turn is similarly interrupted.

The series of false starts (and false ends) produces ten foreshortened narratives that are actually virtuoso short stories, alternating with the chapters that relate the story of the Reader's quest for the complete authentic story. This brings the Reader into contact with the female Other Reader, who is on the same trail. Two trails now intertwine. The pursuit of the text leads to ever more exotic adventures involving revolutionary aircraft hijackers (for whom the authentic text is powerfully subversive), samizdat circles, the elusive Ermes Marana, a counterfeiter of texts, and the burnt-out best-selling novelist Silas Flannery. Extreme ways of producing or consuming texts are encountered: computers may replace either readers or writers; a sculptor sculpts books instead of reading them. The book itself, as commodity or contraband, is the protagonist of this trail.

The other trail is the love story, which leads the two Readers to an erotic reading of each other's bodies and to marriage as the end of reading. The female Reader acquires a name—Ludmilla—and a distinctive character—femaleness. She is a Reader with a difference.

While these intertwined trails pursue never-ending narrative as a metaphor of (male-centred) desire, conjugality, and continuity, it is the eternal ending of death that dominates the ten inset narratives, ten short versions of different sub-genres. Their consecutive titles spell out a long question that ends 'Around an empty grave what story down there awaits its end?'. Each deadly tale is itself a meta-narrative, brilliantly telling itself by displaying the technique of its own composition. The very first one, for instance, opens: 'The novel begins in a railway station, a locomotive huffs, steam from a piston covers the opening of the chapter, a cloud of smoke hides part of the first paragraph'. The ten tales progress from the pole of detached impersonal narration to the opposite pole of solipsistic notation, taking in along the way a dazzling variety of formal techniques. The book as a whole is Calvino's celebration of story-telling as mankind's profound game-playing analogue to its game of love and death, and the 11th chapter contains a fitting tribute to the narrative archetype of *The Thousand and One Nights*.

If on a Winter's Night a Traveller may be viewed as a fruitfully delayed product of the debate over the relationship between literature and industry, which took place in Italy in the late 1950s and early 1960s, and in which Calvino himself, and his friend Vittorini, figured prominently, particularly in their journal significantly entitled *Il Menabò* [The Printer's Dummy]. The argument focused on the impact of the second industrial revolution and on the need for writing itself to match the new techniques of mass reproduction, with their seemingly inexhaustible capacity to transform anything into something else. The post-modern writer's interest thus appears to be displaced from substance (themes, referential content) to process.

Yet this novel, far from negating the specifics of place, time, ethnicity, and individuality, realizes a multiplicity of these specifics with remarkable intensity—the epic of a small Baltic nation, the fate of a Paris hoodlum, a Mexican vendetta, and seven other equally diverse situations. They are more than pastiches, but they produce a paradoxical effect. On the one hand, the disdainful virtuosity of the story-telling makes all story-telling appear obsolete. On the other hand, the intense impression produced of authenticity and seriousness in the manner in which the diverse experiences are rendered is a triumphant vindication of the power of story-telling to negotiate 'reality'. Likewise, in the frame-story of the Readers, many problematic aspects of the role of textuality in the tendentially homogenized order characteristic of the westernized world are captured with diagnostic precision in their up-to-the-minute historicity. Calvino is no apostle of the inability of language to refer to anything but itself: his is a transitive semiotic, in which communication concerns something of moment to both sender and receiver, though there can never be any last word. We produce meanings, not truths.

—John Gatt-Rutter

CARLET DE CHAMBLAIN DE MARIVAUX, Pierre.
See **MARIVAUX**.

CAMÕES, Luís (Vaz) de. Born in Portugal, possibly in 1524 or 1525. May have attended the University of Coimbra. Served as a soldier in North Africa, and may have lost an eye, perhaps in combat; went to India as a soldier, 1553; stayed for a year or two in East Africa, and possibly went to Macao and Goa; returned to Lisbon, 1569; received a small pension from the king. *Died in 1580.*

PUBLICATIONS

Collections

Obras completas, edited by Hernâni Cidade. 5 vols., 1946–47.
Obra completa, edited by Antônio Salgado, Jr. 1963.

Verse

Os Lusíadas. 1572; edited by Frank Pierce, 1973; as *The Lusiads*, translated by Richard Fanshawe, 1655; also translated by Leonard Bacon, 1950; William C. Atkinson, 1952.
Rhythmas. 1595, as *The Lyricks*, translated by Richard Burton, 2 vols., 1884.
Lírica completa, edited by Maria de Lurdes Saraiva. 3 vols., 1980–81.

Plays

Auto dos Enfatriões, from a play by Plautus, in *Autos e comedias portuguesas*. 1587.
Auto de Filodemo, in *Autos e comedias portuguesas*. 1587.
El Rei-Seleuco, in *Rimas*. 1645.

*

Critical Studies: *The Lusiads*, in *From Virgil to Milton* by C.M. Bowra, 1945; *Forms of Nationhood: The Elizabethan Writing of England* by Richard Helgerson, 1992; *Epic and Empire: Politics and Epic Form from Virgil to Milton* by David Quint, 1993.

* * *

Luís de Camões's most important work is his epic poem, *Os Lusíadas* (*The Lusiads*), which deals with Vasco da Gama's successful attempt to discover a sea route to India. Camões's poem owes a great deal to classical epic, and especially to Virgil's *Aeneid*. Gama is not, however, the protagonist of Camões's poem, as Aeneas is of Virgil's. For much of the poem he is not an actor at all but a narrator, and the story he tells is not just that of his own voyage, like the account of his adventures that Aeneas gives Dido, but embraces the whole history of Portugal from its legendary beginnings right down to Camões's own day.

The Lusiads offers abundant evidence of Camões's mastery of the sublime style that he inherited from Virgil. Like Virgil, Camões is fond of complex sentences, full of subordinate clauses, but, again like Virgil, his predilection for elaborate patterns of subordination does not keep him from being a superb story-teller. On the contrary, it can be said, as C.S. Lewis said of Milton, that he 'avoids discontinuity by avoidance of what grammarians call the simple sentence' and that he 'compensates for the complexity of his syntax by the simplicity of the broad imaginative effects beneath it and the perfect rightness of their sequence'.

The Lusiads is not merely a faithful imitation of an admired model. Perhaps the most striking feature of the poem is the way it combines repeated reminders that it belongs to the noblest of the established literary kinds, the epic, with daring innovations. Camões repeatedly acknowledges Homer and Virgil as his models but he insists just as firmly on the differences that separate his work from theirs. The most important difference is that the story he tells is true. Many passages of the poem follow closely the accounts given by the great Portuguese historians of Asia who were Camões's contemporaries, most notably João de Barros. Camões repeatedly asserts that the real achievements of the Portuguese rival can even outdo the fictional ones attributed to Odysseus and Aeneas. It is because he has a greater subject than the ancient epic poets that his poem may hope to surpass theirs. Camões stresses not only the truthfulness of his account but also its exemplary character. He believes, like Dryden, that 'the design of [the heroic poem] is to form the mind to heroic virtue by example'. Camões's conception of heroic virtue is, however, one that many modern readers find hard to accept; *The Lusiads* can serve as a magnificent example of Wallace Stevens's assertion that 'poetry is a cemetery of nobilities'. Another obstacle for many modern readers is Camões's readiness to evoke the hand of God to explain the course of historical events, a readiness he shares with many 16th-century historians.

Much of the poem is, of course, invention, not historical reporting. Sixteenth-century poets saw the marvellous as an indispensable element in poetry, and Camões supplies it in his mythological frame-story which pits Venus against Bacchus, one aiding Gama and the other opposing him. For many readers the most memorable episodes in the poem are those that spring from Camões's imagination, often sparked, of course, by his memories of classical poetry: the giant Adamastor, for example, a personification of the Cape of Good Hope, who represents the hostile forces of nature that the Portuguese must confront on their voyages of discovery, on the Isle of Love, where Venus and her nymphs offer Gama and his men an erotic romp on their return voyage to Portugal.

The Lusiads is an extremely personal poem. Just how personal is difficult to appreciate without some familiarity with Camões's lyrics, which elaborate many of the motifs touched on in the epic, most notably a note of melancholy which has much in common with the Virgilian *lacrimae rerum*. The lyrics are not autobiographical poetry; they do not deal directly with the experiences of the poet's life but rather with their emotional effect on him. For this reason, and because so little is known with certainty about Camões's life, they have often served as points of departure for arbitrary and incompatible biographical interpretations. Like *The Lusiads*, Camões's lyrics offer an astonishing fusion of tradition and innovation. He is a master of both the principal currents that flow into 16th-century Portuguese poetry, one deriving from the 15th-century *cancioneiros* (songbooks, though the poems in them were not always intended to be sung) and the other from the love-poetry of Petrarch and his 16th-century Spanish followers, notably Garcilaso de la Vega. Camões sometimes combines elements of both traditions in a single poem, just as he sometimes combines traditional materials with an intensely individual development presumably drawn from his own lived experience. An outstanding example is the long poem 'Sôbolos rios', which begins as a paraphrase of Psalm 137 ('By the waters of Babylon . . .') and turns into a moving meditation on the poet's own life, expressed with incomparable grace in an inimitably personal style that nevertheless is firmly rooted in the tradition of the songbooks.

Camões's three plays turn away from the classical comedies and tragedies of Francisco de Sá de Miranda and António Ferreira and return to the tradition established by Gil Vicente, though with important differences, most notably Camões's choice, in two of the three, of subjects drawn from classical antiquity. The apparent amorality of Camões's theatre also sets it apart from that of Vicente. The prose passages in the *Auto de Filodemo*, like Camões's letters, show a mastery of language comparable to that of his lyrics or of *The Lusiads*, though both style and subject matter are entirely different. In the plays and letters we often encounter a playful and mocking Camões quite unlike the despairing lover of some of the lyrics or the inspired bard of *The Lusiads*.

—Thomas R. Hart

THE LUSIADS (Os Lusíadas)
Poem by Luís de Camões, 1572.

Camões is the greatest poet in the Portuguese language, and *The Lusiads* is his finest achievement. Although a master of the Petrarchist lyric and the author of exquisite sonnets in this vein, he has always been best known for this epic poem, which is perhaps the best example of the genre in post-classical European literature. The 16th century believed firmly in the hierarchy of literary forms and placed the epic at the very summit of poetic creation. Camões responded by marrying the noblest style to the greatest heroic exploits of his time. *The Lusiads* is thus a poem fit for heroes.

The word takes its name from the mythical father of the Portuguese nation, Lusus, and is clearly meant to rival the great epics of antiquity. The author says as much in his opening stanzas, declaring—in an obvious reference to the first line of Virgil's *Aeneid*: 'Arma virumque cano' ('I sing of arms and the man')—that he will praise the deeds of those famous Portuguese heroes who left their Lusitanian shore to sail previously uncharted seas and discover new worlds, carrying to the very heart of the Infidel's territory the message of the Christian faith and the Portuguese empire. He calls upon the *tágides*, or nymphs of the river Tagus, to inspire him to write a work worthy of these intrepid adventurers whose exploits far outshine those of Ulysses or Aeneas, Alexander or Trajan. This is, then, a truly national epic and one which has truly great events to celebrate. In a poem of close on 9,000 lines, divided into ten cantos and just over 1,100 stanzas, Camões provides his public with a pageant of Portuguese history. Published for the first time in 1572, in the somewhat febrile atmosphere of the reign of King Sebastião (to whom it is dedicated), who dreamed of feats of arms and a Portuguese empire that would rival that of ancient Rome in glory, it exalts and exemplifies what many felt to be the country's special mission. The result is, in the words of Frank Pierce in his 1973 edition of the work, 'a remarkable poetic record of the rise of Portugal and its emergence as a power of European importance and the creator of the first modern overseas empire'.

Little is known about Camões's life, and this has allowed critics to embroider and fantasize. What is clear, however, is that he was a man of deep learning and justifiably patriotic sentiments. Taking his reader through Portugal's history, he selects the high points of its past to suggest that it has a unique place in the scheme of things. Very much a Renaissance man (he was probably born in 1525 and may have attended the University of Coimbra before embarking on a life of adventurous wanderings in Portugal's overseas possessions), he does not hesitate to call on the gods and goddesses of pagan mythology to help illustrate his heroic tale. Thus, in Canto I, the gods assemble on Olympus to debate whether or not to support the Portuguese as they watch Vasco da Gama's ships set sail on their voyage of discovery. Venus and Mars (representing the idealized Portuguese attributes of sensuality and valour) wish them well, but Bacchus comes out against them. By Canto II we see the ships, despite Bacchus' continued attempts to hinder them, rounding the coast of Africa and reaching Malindi (in what is now Kenya) and a warm welcome. In Canto III, for the benefit of his foreign hosts (and, of course, for Camões's public and potential patrons) Vasco da Gama surveys his nation's history. The most famous section deals with the tragic love-affair of Inês de Castro, which leads on to reflections on the power of love and, especially, the trouble it can cause. A typical litany of sinful lovers from King David and Bathsheba to Mark Antony and Cleopatra brings the canto to an end on a moralistic and melancholy note, although the real purpose of this apparent digression may well be elsewhere. As we know from his other poetry, Camões is sensitive to love's hurts. But there may also be a political consideration here: it is surely not without significance that the poet alludes to examples from Portugal's recent past (to Inês, and to the adulterous love-affair between the weak King Ferdinand and Leonor Teles) and concludes that 'um baxo amor os fortes enfraquece' ('base love weakens the strong'). A message here perhaps for King Sebastião?

Cantos IV and V take us through the great age of Portuguese history, with the revolution of 1383 and the rise to power of King João I, naturally stressing the battle of Aljubarrota which sealed Portugal's independence, and the first overseas voyages. Here too, though, there are some discordant notes as Camões introduces the Old Man of Restelo, who watches the departing ships from the banks of the Tagus, warning against ambition and the vanity of restless endeavour. These Cassandra-like sentiments no doubt reflect Camões's humanist awareness of the limits of fame and of the active life in the search for human happiness. Similarly, in Canto V, which includes the famous episode of the giant Adamastor, there is a gentle reminder of the status of the writer (a typically humanist theme) and a plea for greater recognition. The following cantos continue the narrative of Vasco da Gama's adventures, interspersed with moralistic and philosophical comments (on life's injustices, the dangers of ambition, etc.) before finishing with an extraordinary episode—and one which has shocked some readers—in which the Portuguese are guided to the Isle of Love by amorous nymphs who delight in being ravished by the lustful mariners. The final and very lengthy canto (156 stanzas) is by turns descriptive and philosophical: it serves, above all, to extol heroic values and ends with an appeal for fortitude and high enterprise.

Camões's great epic is firmly rooted in the moral and political atmosphere of its time. Beneath the surface optimism and pride in Portuguese achievements there is an unmistakable note of doubt and criticism. But *The Lusiads* is beautifully written, eminently quotable and, to the Portuguese, the equivalent of the Bible and Shakespeare. It is, and deservedly so, the touchstone of Portuguese culture. Camões's is the voice of that 'Portuguese sea' of which Fernando Pessoa speaks, perpetuating the memory of those discoverers whose birthplace was a small country but who chose the wide world as their grave.

—Michael Freeman

CAMPANELLA, Tommaso. Born Giovan Domenico Campanella in Stilo, Calabria, Spanish Viceroyalty of Naples, 5 September 1568. Studied law in Naples. Entered Dominican Order, 1582, took the monastic name Tommaso, and studied logic, physics, and Aristotelian metaphysics at the Convent of San Giorgio Morgeto, 1583–85. Lived in Nicastro, 1586–87, Cosenza, 1588, Altomonte, 1588–89; returned to Naples, 1589, and moved into the palazzo of Mario del Tufo, 1590; his views and writings brought him into increasing conflict with the Order, from 1592; travelled throughout Italy, 1592–93; first arrest by the Inquisition, 1594: imprisoned and tortured, 1595–96, and forbidden to publish; rearrested, 1597, on accusations of heresy, released and returned to Calabria, settled in Stilo, 1598; forced to flee to Franciscan monastery in Stignano, 1599, subsequently captured and imprisoned in Naples for involvement with (and possible organization of) an abortive anti-Spanish rebellion; sentenced by the Holy Office in Rome to life imprisonment for heresy, 1602, remained in confinement in the castles of Uovo, Sant'Elmo, and Nuovo, 1602–26, where he continued writing; released in May, 1626, but rearrested in June and taken to Rome; allowed by the Inquisition to live under house arrest, and settled in the Dominican Convent of Santa Maria sopra Minerva; pardoned completely by Pope Urban VIII, 1629, and his name and works deleted from the Inquisition's Index; named a Master of Theology by the Dominican Order, 1629; lived under papal patronage, 1629–34; fled to Paris, via Marseilles, because of the repercussions of a pupil's involvement in an anti-Spanish plot, 1634; received a pension from Louis XIII, 1635, and spent final years publishing many of his works. *Died 21 May 1639.*

PUBLICATIONS

Collections

Opere, edited by Alessandro d'Ancona. 2 vols., 1854.
Tutte le opere, edited by Luigi Firpo. 1954.
Opera Latina Francofurti Impressa Annis 1617–1630, edited by Luigi Firpo. 1975.
Opere letterarie, edited by Lina Bolzoni. 1977.

Works

Philosophia sensibus demonstrata. 1591; as *La filosofia che i sensi ci additano*, edited by Luigi De Franco, 1974.
Prodromus philosophia instaurandae (Compendium de rerum natura). 1617.
De belgio sub hispani potestatem redigendo. 1617.
Monarchia di Spagna. In German, as *Von der spanischen Monarchie*, 1620; as *De monarchia hispanica*, 1640; as *Monarchia di Spagna*, 1854; as *A Discourse Touching the Spanish Monarchy*, translated by Edmund Chilmead, 1654; as *Tommaso Campanella . . . His Advice to the King of Spain*, 1659.
De sensu rerum et magia, edited by Tobias Adami. 1620; as *Del senso delle cose e della magia*, edited by Antonio Bruers, 1925.
Apologia pro Galileo. 1620; edited by R. Carebba, 1911, also edited by Salvatore Femiano, 1971; as *Apologia di Galileo*, edited by Luigi Firpo, 1969; as *The Defense of Galileo*, translated by Grant McColley, 1937.
Civitatis solis. In *Realis philosophae epilogisticae partes quatuor*, 1623; single edition, 1643; in Italian, as *La città del sole*, 1840; edited by Edmondo Solmi, 1904, also edited by Norberto Bobbio (Italian and Latin), 1941, Adriano Seroni, 1977, F. Bartoletta, 1985, and by G. Berrettoni, 1991; as *The City of the Sun*, translated by Thomas W. Halliday, in *Ideal Commonwealths*, edited by Henry Morley, 1885, revised edition, 1901; reprinted in *Ideal Empires and Republics*, 1901, *Famous New Deals of History*, 1935, and *Famous Utopias of the Renaissance*, 1948; also translated by William J. Gilstrap, in *The Quest for Utopias*, edited by Glenn Negley and J. Max Patrick, 1952; Daniel J. Donno (bilingual edition), 1981; R. Millner and A.M Elliott, 1981.
Realis philosophae epilogisticae partes quatuor. 1623; revised and enlarged edition, as *Disputationum in quatuor partes suae philosophiae realis*, 4 vols., 1637.
Astrologicorum. 7 vols., 1629; 8 vols., 1630.
Atheismus triumphatus. 1631.
Monarchia messiae (political treatise). 1633; edited by Luigi Firpo, 1960.
Medicinalium iuxta propria principia. 7 vols., 1635.
Philosophiae rationalis. 5 vols., 1638.
Universalis philosophiae, seu metaphysicarum rerum iuxta propria dogmata partes tres. 18 vols., 1638; as *Metafisica*, edited by Giovanni Di Napoli, 3 vols., 1967.
De libris propriis et de recta ratione studendi syntagma. 1642; edited by Vincenzo Spampanato, 1927.
Discorsi politici ai principi d'Italia, edited by Pietro Garzilli. 1848; also edited by Luigi Firpo, 1945.
Opere scelte, edited by Alessandro d'Ancona. 2 vols., 1854.
Theologicorum, edited by Romano Amerio. 1936–88; of the 30 books in Campanella's manuscript, the following have been edited:
Teologia (Book I). 1936; as *Dio e la predestinazione*, 2 vols., 1949–51.
La prima e la seconda resurrezione (Books XXVII–XXVIII). 1955.
Magia e grazia (Book XIV). 1957.
De sancta monotriade (Book II). 1958.
Cristologia (Book XVIII). 2 vols., 1958.
Della grazia gratificante (Book XIII). 1959.
Il peccato originale (Book XVI). 1960.
De homine (Book IV, part II). 1961.
Vita Christi (Book XXI). 1962.
Cosmologia (Book III). 1964.
I sacri segni (Book XXIV). 5 vols., 1965–68.
De Antichristo (Book XXVI). 1965.
De dictis Christi (Book XXIII). 1969.
E scatalogia (Books XXIX–XXX). 1969.
Le creature sovrannaturali (Book V). 1970.
Della beatitudine (Book VII). 1971.
Origine temporale di Cristo (Book XIX). 1972.
Le profezie di Cristo (Book XXV). 1973.
De remediis malorum (Book XVII). 1975.
Delle virtú e dei vizi in particolare (Book X). 1976; as *De virtutibus et vitiis Speciatum*, 1984.

De virtutibus supernaturalibus quibus ad beatitudinem homo regitur (Books XI–XII). 1988.
Epilogo magno, edited by Carmelo Ottaviano. 1939.
Aforismi politici, edited by Luigi Firpo. 1941.
Poetica, edited by Luigi Firpo. 1944.
Antiveneti, edited by Luigi Firpo. 1945.
Opuscoli inediti, edited by Luigi Firpo. 1951.
Articuli prophetales, edited by Germana Ernst. 1977.
Parole universali della dottrina politica, edited by Giuseppe Campanella. 1980.
Mathematica, edited by Armando Brissoni. 1989.

Verse

Scelta d'alcune poesie filosofiche. 1622; edited by Vincenzo Paladino, 1977, enlarged edition, 1983; as *Poesie filosofiche*, edited by Giovanni Gaspare Orelli, 1834, and by Marziano Guglielminetti, 1982; as *Le poesie*, edited by Giovanni Papini, 2 vols., 1913, by Giovanni Gentile, 1915, and by Mario Vinciguerra, 1938; parts translated by J.A. Symonds, in *The Sonnets of Michael Angelo Buonarroti and Tommaso Campanella*, 1878.
Ecloga Christianissimus regi et reginae in portentosam delphini. 1639.

Other

Lettere, edited by Vincenzo Spampanato. 1927.

*

Bibliography: *Bibliografia degli scritti di Tommaso Campanella* by Luigi Firpo, 1940; *Tommaso Campanella in America: A Critical Bibliography and a Profile*, 1954, and *A Supplement to the Critical Bibliography*, 1957, by Francesco Grillo.

Critical Studies: *Campanella* by Léon Blanchet, 1920; *Tommaso Campanella*, by C. Dentice D'Accadia, 1921; *Tommaso Campanella and His Poetry* by Edmund Gardner, 1923; *Tommaso Campanella, metafisico* by Maria M. Rossi, 1923; *La filosofia politica di Tommaso Campanella* by Paolo Treves, 1930; *Campanella* by Nino Valeri, 1931; *Studi campanelliani* by Romano Amerio, 1934; *Famous Utopias* edited by Charles Andrews, 1937; *Tommaso Campanella* by Aldo Testa, 1941; *Studi campanelliani* by R. De Mattei, 1943; *Tommaso Campanella* by A. Corsano, 1944, revised edition, 1961; *Ricerche campanelliane* by Luigi Firpo, 1947; *Tommaso Campanella filosofo della restaurazione cattolica* by G. Di Napoli, 1947; *Tommaso Campanella* by Alfio and Antonietta Nicotra, 1948; *Tommaso Campanella: La crisi della coscienza in sè* by A. Maria Jacobelli Isoldi, 1953; *Tommaso Campanella* by Nicola Badaloni, 1965; *Lo spiritualismo di Tommaso Campanella* by Salvatore Femiano, 2 vols., 1965; *Renaissance Philosophers: The Italian Philosophers* edited by Arturo B. Fallico and Herman Schapiro, 1967; *Il sistema teologico di Tommaso Campanella* by R. Amerio, 1972; *L'eresia cattolica e riformatrice di T. Campanella e il Concilio Vaticano II* by F. Grillo, 1975; 'Tommaso Campanella's *La città del sole*: Topography and Astrology' by Ilona Klein, in *Italiana 1987* edited by Albert N. Mancini and others, 1989; 'Tommaso Campanella and the End of the Renaissance', in *Journal of Medieval and Renaissance Studies*, 20(2), 1990, and 'Tommaso Campanella and Jean de Launoy: The Controversy over Aristotle and His Reception in the West', in *Renaissance Quarterly*, 43(3), 1990, both by John M. Headley.

*   *   *

Born in Calabria amid the harsh realities of Southern Italy and of an illiterate family sunk in the most extreme poverty, Campanella was educated in the only way possible for the poor—by taking priestly vows as a Dominican monk. He lived a life of incredible hardship, torture, persecution, and rejection by his contemporaries. However, upheld by an insatiable thirst for knowledge, an irrepressible intellectual curiosity, and a highly developed memory, he rose above the most extreme misfortune and the cruelty of the Inquisition to compose works on every subject imaginable—from philosophy to science and literature (over 100 works)—publicly championed Galileo at both his trials, yet he received only abuse in return, and lived in exile in Paris, at last recognized by educated society as a phenomenal intellectual, and able to oversee publication of many of his works. In a sense, the last Italian 'Renaissance' man and a champion of the inexhaustibility of human knowledge, Campanella also preserved enough faith in human destiny to compose his own utopia (in the wake of Plato's *Republic* and More's *Utopia*), *La città del sole* (*The City of the Sun*), and composed moving poems and letters to contemporaries.

After initially devouring the knowledge available in his first monastery library, his first attempt to broaden his knowledge by moving to another monastery was harshly suppressed by his superiors, obliging him to flee to Northern Italy. By the age of 27 he had already been forced to adjure heresy by the Roman Inquisition, and by 1598 was obliged by the church to return to Calabria, where he became involved in an idealistic attempt to found an independent utopian state in the mountains, one governed by egalitarian principles and freed from the yoke of foreign domination. The harsh repression by the vice-regal government, with its mass arrests and executions, brought a swift end to this conspiracy, and Campanella, an acknowledged ringleader, was dragged in chains to Rome, only escaping execution by his resistance to torture and by feigning madness, to languish in prison almost forgotten, for 27 years.

Nevertheless, the creation of an enduring work of the literary imagination from first-hand experience of utopian idealism gave posterity *The City of the Sun*, the only work by Campanella to survive the test of time. In it, he described an utopian civilization located on a remote island in the Indian Ocean, founded on egalitarian principles and the rule of reason, where the Christian religion has not arrived to favour the life to come over earthly happiness, and where greed and corruption are not society's prime movers. Nature becomes the universal law, and a communistic sharing of property and duties characterizes this society, while children are brought up not by families, but by society, generated by principles of selection that smack (perhaps uncomfortably) of far more modern times. The city is laid out according to principles of the greatest benefit to all, while eating, sleeping, and working are all controlled by rigid rules, as are the clothes worn by the citizens—reminiscent to us of the uniforms of the science-fiction imagination. Work is for all—of both sexes—and absolute equality between men and women extends even to military service.

The only hierarchy permitted is that of merit—an archetypal meritocracy—but defined in the terms of Campanella's time as the search for knowledge of all things: he who can understand more of nature's knowledge has the whip-hand in guiding those who know less, in working together for the common good. Thus we have a portrait of a society of happiness and peaceful concord, where private ambitions and clan affinities have been abandoned and family affection and concern for the future have been swept aside in favour of zealous dedication to the common good, leaving time for the cultivation of genial pursuits and learning.

It is clear that this utopian vision is the fruit of wide reading and not only of Campanella's experience of the failed Calabrian insurrection (and we have mentioned Plato and More in this connection). But there is also an autobiographical element stemming from Campanella's memories of his native Calabria—of the discipline of the monastic regime with its rigid rules, of the hardships of poverty, ignorance, and superstition that characterized Southern Italy. These were elevated here by one of the region's most distinguished sons —against impossible odds and through incredible hardships— to the dignity of great literature, almost constituting a cry for a better society, founded on saner principles and guided by the light of reason, that resounds down the centuries to the present, where, however dated and naive it is in certain respects, it none the less seems to have an enduring vitality.

—Christopher Cairns

CAMUS, Albert. Born in Mondovi, Algeria, 7 November 1913. Educated at the University of Algiers, graduated 1936. Married 1) Simone Hié in 1934 (divorced); 2) Francine Faure in 1940 (died 1979), twin son and daughter. Worked as meteorologist, shipbroker's clerk, automobile parts salesman, clerk in the automobile registry division of the prefecture, actor and amateur theatre producer, Algiers, 1935–39; member of the Communist Party, 1935–39; staff member, *Alger-Républicain*, 1938–39, and editor, *Soir-Républicain*, 1939–40, both Algiers; sub-editor for layout, *Paris-Soir*, 1940; teacher, Oran, Algeria, 1940–42; convalescent in central France, 1942–43; joined Resistance in Lyon region, 1943; journalist, Paris, 1943–45; reader, and editor of Espoir series, Gallimard, publishers, Paris, 1943–60; co-founding editor, *Combat*, 1945–47. Recipient: Critics prize (France), 1947; Nobel prize for literature, 1957. *Died 4 January 1960.*

PUBLICATIONS

Collections

Complete Fiction, translated by Stuart Gilbert and Justin O'Brien. 1960.
Théâtre, récits, nouvelles; Essais, edited by Roger Quilliot. 2 vols., 1962–65.
Collected Plays, translated by Stuart Gilbert and Justin O'Brien. 1965.
Oeuvres complètes. 5 vols., 1983.

Fiction

L'Étranger. 1942; as *The Stranger*, translated by Stuart Gilbert, 1946; as *The Outsider*, translated by Gilbert, 1946; also translated by K. Griffith, 1982; Joseph Laredo, 1984.
La Peste. 1947; as *The Plague*, translated by Stuart Gilbert, 1948.
La Chute. 1956; as *The Fall*, translated by Justin O'Brien, 1957.
L'Exil et le royaume (stories). 1957; as *Exile and the Kingdom*, translated by Justin O'Brien, 1958.
La Mort heureuse. 1971; as *A Happy Death*, translated by Richard Howard, 1972.
Le Premier Homme (unfinished). 1994.

Plays

Le Malentendu (produced 1944). With *Caligula*, 1944; as *Cross Purpose*, translated by Stuart Gilbert, with *Caligula*, 1948.
Caligula (produced 1945). With *Le Malentendu*, 1944; 1941 version (produced 1983), 1984; as *Caligula*, translated by Stuart Gilbert, with *Cross Purpose*, 1948.
L'État de siège (produced 1948). 1948; as *State of Siege*, translated by Stuart Gilbert, in *Caligula and Three Other Plays*, 1958.
Les Justes (produced 1949). 1950; as *The Just Assassins*, translated by Stuart Gilbert, in *Caligula and Three Other Plays*, 1958; as *The Just*, translated by Henry Jones, 1965.
La Dévotion à la croix, from the play by Calderón (produced 1953). 1953.
Les Esprits, from a work by Pierre de Larivey (produced 1953). 1953.
Un cas intéressant, from a work by Dino Buzzati (produced 1955). 1955.
Requiem pour une nonne, from the novel by William Faulkner (produced 1956). 1956.
Le Chevalier d'Olmedo, from the play by Lope de Vega (produced 1957). 1957.
Caligula and Three Other Plays (incudes *Cross Purpose*; *State of Seige*; *The Just Assassins*), translated by Stuart Gilbert. 1958.
Les Possédés, from the novel by Dostoevskii (produced 1959). 1959; as *The Possessed*, translated by Justin O'Brien, 1960.

Other

L'Envers et l'endroit. 1937.
Noces. 1939.
Le Mythe de Sisyphe. 1942; as *The Myth of Sisyphus and Other Essays*, translated by Justin O'Brien, 1955.
Lettres à un ami allemand. 1945.
L'Existence. 1945.
Le Minotaure; ou, La Halte d'Oran. 1950.
Actuelles [1]-3: Chroniques 1944–1948, Chroniques 1948–1953, Chronique algérienne 1939–1958. 3 vols., 1950–58.
L'Homme révolté. 1951; as *The Rebel: An Essay on Man in Revolt*, translated by Anthony Bower, 1953.
L'Été. 1954.
Réflexions sur la guillotine, in *Réflexions sur la peine capitale*, with Arthur Koestler. 1957; as *Reflections on the Guillotine*, translated by Richard Howard, 1960.
Discours de Suède. 1958; as *Speech of Acceptance upon the Award of the Nobel Prize for Literature*, translated by Justin O'Brien, 1958.

Resistance, Rebellion, and Death (selection), translated by Justin O'Brien. 1960.

Méditation sur le théâtre et la vie. 1961.

Carnets: Mai 1935–fevrier 1942. 1962; as *Carnets 1935–1942*, translated by Philip Thody, 1963; as *Notebooks 1935–1942*, 1963.

Lettre à Bernanos. 1963.

Carnets: Janvier 1942–mars 1951. 1964; as *Notebooks 1942–1951*, edited and translated by Justin O'Brien, 1965.

Lyrical and Critical (essays), edited and translated by Philip Thody. 1967.

Le Combat d'Albert Camus, edited by Norman Stokle. 1970.

Selected Essays and Notebooks, edited and translated by Philip Thody. 1970.

Le Premier Camus. 1973; as *Youthful Writings*, translated by Ellen Conroy Kennedy, 1977.

Journaux de voyage, edited by Roger Quilliot. 1978; as *American Journals*, translated by Hugh Levick, 1987.

Fragments d'un combat 1938–1940: Alger-Républicain, Le Soir-Républicain, edited by Jacqueline Lévi-Valensi and André Abbou. 1978.

Correspondance 1932–1960, with Jean Grenier, edited by Marguerite Dobrenn. 1981.

Selected Political Writings, edited by Jonathan King. 1981.

Oeuvre fermée, oeuvre ouverte, edited by Raymond Gay-Croisier and Jacqueline Lévi-Valensi. 1985.

Carnets: Mars 1951–décembre 1959. 1989.

Translator, *La Dernière Fleur*, by James Thurber. 1952.

*

Bibliography: *Camus: A Bibliography* by Robert F. Roeming, 1968; and subsequent editions by R. Gay-Crosier, in *A Critical Bibliography of French Literature*, 6, 1980; *Camus in English: An Annotated Bibliography of Albert Camus's Contributions to English and American Periodicals and Newspapers* by Peter C. Hoy, 2nd edition, 1971.

Critical Studies: *Albert Camus: A Study of His Work*, 1957, *Albert Camus, 1913–1960: A Biographical Study*, 1961, and *Albert Camus*, 1989, all by Philip Thody, 1961; *Camus* by Germaine Brée, 1959, revised edition, 1972, and *Camus: A Collection of Critical Essays* edited by Brée, 1962; *Albert Camus: The Artist in the Arena* by Emmett Parker, 1965; *Camus* by Phillip H. Rhein, 1969, revised edition, 1989; *Albert Camus* by Conor Cruise O'Brien, 1970; *The Theatre of Albert Camus* by Edward Freeman, 1971; *Camus: The Invincible Summer* by Albert Maquet, 1972; *The Unique Creation of Albert Camus* by Donald Lazere, 1973; *Witness of Decline: Albert Camus: Moralist of the Absurd* by Lev Braun, 1974; *Albert Camus: A Biography* by Herbert R. Lottman, 1979; *The Descent of the Doves: Camus's Journey to the Spirit* by Alfred Cordes, 1980; *Camus's Imperial Vision* by Anthony Rizzuto, 1981; *The Narcissistic Text: A Reading of Camus's Fiction* by Brian T. Fitch, 1982; *Camus: A Critical Study of His Life and Work*, 1982, and *Camus: The Stranger*, 1988, both by Patrick McCarthy; *Exiles and Strangers: A Reading of Camus's Exile and the Kingdom* by Elaine Showalter, Jr, 1984; *Exile and Kingdom: A Political Rereading of Albert Camus* by Susan Tarrow, 1985; *The Ethical Pragmatism of Albert Camus: Two Studies in the History of Ideas* by Dean Vasil, 1985; *Beyond Absurdity: The Philosophy of Albert Camus* by Robert C. Trundle, 1987; *Camus: A Critical Examination* by David Sprintzen, 1988; *Albert Camus and Indian Thought* by Sharad Chaedra, 1989; *Understand-ing Albert Camus* by David R. Ellison, 1990; *Camus's L'Étranger: Fifty Years On* edited by Adele King, 1992.

*   *   *

Although French critics on the Right and the Left have proclaimed Albert Camus *passé* for every imaginable reason, he has remained the bestselling author of France's largest and most prestigious literary publisher, Gallimard. In 1971, eleven years after his death at the age of 46, the publication of an early novel that Camus had had the good sense to abandon stimulated sales that pushed the French edition of *La Mort heureuse* (*A Happy Death*) to the top of the bestseller list within a few weeks. This is but one belated aspect of the paradox of Camus's career and reputation as a writer. When he was selected in 1957 to receive the Nobel prize for literature, he was, at 44, the youngest literary laureate but one, Rudyard Kipling having received the prize at 42. He himself stated publicly at the time that he would have voted for Malraux.

Camus is exceptional among French writers, the majority of whom have come from comfortable middle-class origins even in recent times. He was reared in Algiers by his mother, an illiterate charwoman. His first writings published in Paris catapulted him to a literary celebrity for which he was ill prepared. The climate of the immediate post-war period, combined with his position as a popular editorial writer for the Resistance newspaper *Combat*, rapidly created an aura about Camus that he had not sought and that was to cause him considerable difficulty a decade later.

In the first important review of *L'Étranger* (*The Outsider* or *The Stranger*), Jean-Paul Sartre was struck by the contemporaneity of this objective, apparently dispassionate, non-novel. An essay on the notion of the Absurd, entitled *Le Mythe de Sisyphe* (*The Myth of Sisyphus*), has been taken by many readers since Sartre to be the theory of which *The Outsider* is the illustration. Camus's Absurd is a description of a state more familiar to some English-speaking readers as a variety of contemporary thought posited on the death of God. It owes a great deal to such thinkers as Pascal, Kierkegaard, Dostoevskii, and Nietzsche. Camus was at pains to point out that there were, in his view, few points of contact between the Absurd and Sartrean existentialism, a distinction that readers, critics, and historians have tended to honour in the breach. The third piece in this cycle is *Caligula*, which remains the most important and the most popular of his plays.

Camus's view of his own career involved cycles of trilogies. The cycle of the Absurd antedates his experience of the war in the Resistance. It was essentially complete by 1941, and in 1942 he began work on the cycle of Revolt which owed a great deal more to the war than did its predecessor. Once again the trilogy included a novel, *La Peste* (*The Plague*), an essay, *L'Homme révolté* (*The Rebel*), and a play, *Les Justes* (*The Just Assassins*). *The Rebel* was attacked in *Les Temps Modernes*, a pro-communist magazine edited by Sartre. The subsequent polemic caused Camus to break with Sartre and to become disgusted with left-wing intellectuals. Several works written after this experience testify to a deepened awareness of human motivation, resulting in a more complex and satisfying style. The most substantial of these is *La Chute* (*The Fall*). During the 1950s Camus turned progressively to the theatre for both solace and stimulation. At the time of his death he was preparing a third cycle, to be called Nemesis, and had begun a novel entitled *Le Premier Homme* [The First

Man], which was published in 1994. He left interesting *Carnets* (*Notebooks*), in three volumes, and an important collection of journalistic writings, *Actuelles*.

—A. James Arnold

THE FALL (La Chute)
Novel by Albert Camus, 1956.

The Fall is a confession of a moral decline. In an unbroken monologue, Jean-Baptiste Clamence recounts to a stranger how, far from being the model citizen he once believed himself to be, he has come to realize that he is no more than an egocentric hypocrite who treats others with disdain. He cannot bear to be judged, however, and sets about finding a means of averting this seemingly inevitable consequence.

The confession begins in an Amsterdam bar, where Clamence introduces himself to a chance acquaintance as a *juge-pénitent* (judge-penitent). To begin his explanation of this 'profession' he recounts how several years earlier he had been leading a successful life as a well-known, charitable Parisian lawyer always ready to defend worthy causes. His virtues extended to the social sphere, where he was also highly regarded. One evening, however, his self-satisfaction and good conscience were suddenly dispelled when he heard a mysterious and apparently judgemental laugh. This triggered a sequence of memories that jolted him into becoming conscious of the fact that what lay behind his virtue was, in fact, vanity and egotism. Gradually he recalls various proofs of this duplicity (vices within virtues). He realizes that when, during a confrontational traffic incident, he had been humiliated and embarrassed in public, his primary concern was revenge and that, therefore, although outwardly philanthropic, on a deeper level he was motivated by a desire to dominate. This, in reality, was his reason for championing the weak and for making women suffer in relationships. But his sense of shame centres on a more specific incident: he had ignored the cries of a woman drowning in the Seine. This made him guilty of not having helped someone who was dying. Later, he was to remember an even worse crime: while imprisoned in a war camp, he had stolen the water of a dying comrade and had thus precipitated his death. Clamence became aware that he was not as 'admirable' as he had previously thought, that, in fact, he had enemies and was the subject of derision. He began to examine himself and soon discovered that his duplicity was central to his nature: each of his virtues had another side. Realizing that people are quick to judge to avoid being judged themselves, he sought to ward off ridicule in various ways. He became cynical and mocked all human and social values. Incapable of either falling in love or of maintaining chastity, he adopted a life of debauchery, which he found equally 'liberating'. But, when he subsequently mistook a piece of floating debris for a corpse, it was brought home to him that he was unable fully to escape his deep sense of guilt. The only way of averting this demise of his self-esteem and of recapturing his former sensations of superiority, Clamence explains, was by adopting the role of 'judge-penitent'. By being a penitent and accusing himself of the blackest deeds he would gain the right, he maintains, to judge others (and so dilute his own guilt feelings in the general guilt extended to all) without the risk of being accused in return. What is more, this venture is facilitated by the fact that his confession is, as he sees it, simultaneous with an accusation of others: the self-portrait which he creates 'becomes a mirror', which reminds his interlocutors of *their* culpability. It is through self-accusation then that Clamence finds a long-sought comfort, being in a position to 'judge the whole world' while escaping the repercussions, without *being* judged. This release can only occur, clearly, at the expense of others, as a result of their concomitant fall. To achieve his objective, so save himself from falling, Clamence is ready to condemn the rest of humanity.

Guilt is the central theme in *The Fall*. Clamence presents his personal guilt as being indicative of the true nature of all humans: he regards everyone as being guilty of shameful acts, as having fallen. He proclaims universal corruption. Even Christ is seen as guilty in that he is indirectly responsible for the murder of the innocents and, consequently, the ideals of purity and innocence based on his model themselves become hollow and dishonest. The fact that Clamence is bent on the downfall of Christianity has led critics to identify him with Lucifer, an anti-Christ. Indeed, his various allusions to religious imagery are consistently blasphemous. It is with derision that he adopts the name 'Jean-Baptiste' for, while the biblical precursor used water to baptize *out* of sin, in Clamence's case water (the Seine in which the woman drowned) is the instrument of his fall *into* culpability. Equally, in his role of 'pope' in the war camp he increased suffering. Clamence says that people's most deeply-rooted belief is that they are innocent. In attacking this conviction and precipitating their 'fall' into guilt, he becomes the enemy of humanity. His fundamental rationale is to secure innocence for himself by depriving everyone else of it. At the end of his monologue he invites his interlocutor (and presumably the reader) to examine his conscience and to confess *his* sins.

—Silvano Levy

THE OUTSIDER (L'Étranger)
Novel by Albert Camus, 1942.

The principal character in *The Outsider*, Meursault, is a French Algerian clerk who kills an Arab, is imprisoned, tried, and sentenced to death. The novel begins with Meursault's unemotional announcement that his mother has just died. He goes to the funeral and when he returns he carries on with his daily routine as if nothing had happened: he goes swimming, meets a woman called Marie, takes her to the cinema, and begins an affair. For some weeks he works as usual and sees Marie on Saturdays. During that time he refuses an offer of promotion from his employer and also agrees to marry Marie even though he does not love her. One day Meursault's friend, Raymond, brawls with his Arab girlfriend whom he suspects of infidelity and, as a result of his efforts to help, Meursault becomes involved in the antagonism between Raymond and his mistress's brother and friends. These Arabs, on a subsequent occasion, wound Raymond in a fight on the beach. Later that day, Meursault, who has Raymond's revolver with him, encounters one of the Arabs, who is armed with a knife. Being suddenly confused by the blinding sun, Meursault mistakes flashes of light for a blade and shoots and kills the Arab. After the man falls, Meursault fires four more shots into the body.

The primary concern throughout the ensuing investigation and trial is not so much the killing of the Arab, which would not have been punishable by death, as Meursault's nonconformity with social norms. A large part of the case against him focuses on his relationship with his mother, his reactions at her wake and funeral and his involvement with Marie. By pointing out that he had not wanted to see his mother's body and that shortly after her burial he had gone to see a comic film with Marie and had then spent the night with her, the prosecution argues that Meursault is a moral misfit devoid of filial grief and that, consequently, he deserves punishment. To that extent Camus engages in a critique of a self-righteous society that assumes the right to judge and condemn a man for not sharing its moral and religious values.

Meursault's whole way of life represents a defiance of those values. Far from considering himself to exist within a rational, justifiable, and comprehensible social order, he rejects even the idea that there can be a meaningful pattern of life. To him the notion of striving for social and economic progression is devoid of meaning and for this reason he rejects the offer of promotion from his employer. To have done otherwise would have meant believing in a coherent world based on logical principles and within which ambitions and hopes for a better future can exist. Meursault simply refuses to become involved in the mechanisms of a world, which, to him, does not make sense. He cannot see the point of having aims or of wanting to change his existence in a world impervious to human aspirations to determinism. To the extent that he consciously considers life as a sequence of inconsistent events that have neither reason nor purpose, his view of the world can be termed Absurdist.

This concept is based on the premise that the world is devoid of divine intention and that human existence arises from chance and arbitrary contingencies. Man can neither understand nor control the world, which unfolds in a haphazard manner regardless of human volition. According to Camus, the Absurd is a confrontation between man's determination to make sense of reality and a world which is essentially unmotivated and meaningless.

Meursault's attitudes acknowledge this 'divorce', to use Camus's term. Free from a belief in a system of values, Meursault lives in a way that is spontaneous and amoral. All that matters to him is the present, which he dissociates from the past and the future. He regards his relationship with Marie, for example, as momentary pleasure and he never places it within the more far-reaching permanence of love. His agreement to marry her is, to say the least, unenthusiastic. Equally, he does not see the purpose of connecting his mother's death with a subsequent feeling of grief or, indeed, with his desire to enjoy Marie's company. In fact, when he is asked by the *juge d'instruction* (examining magistrate) whether he loved his mother, a sentiment which would have implied a lifelong attachment, his reply is noncommittal. Above all, he refuses to attribute a cause or justification to his crime. When questioned, he simply repeats the non-explanation 'because of the sun'. Meursault admits that, in general, he has got out of the habit of asking himself for explanations. For him there are no meanings which either account for existence or formulate it into a continuum.

Once any notion of long-term or overall coherence in life has been discounted, what remains is a belief in the here and now. Throughout the first half of *The Outsider* Meursault is seen to base his existence on the present instant and on the impulsive, spontaneous sensations that it offers. His response to the world is dominated by a heightened sensitivity to physical phenomena; colour, smells, fatigue, pain, the heat of the sun. What is more, these are evoked within the transitory context of an immediate present, the word 'today' appearing in the first sentence of the first three chapters. When the freedom to live in this 'instinctive' way is taken away from Meursault by his incarceration and pressure is put on him to identify with the alternative values of religion and social

responsibility, he accepts death rather than compromise his nihilistic stand. To the last Meursault remains at odds with the society which condemns him. He remains an outsider.

—Silvano Levy

THE PLAGUE (La Peste)
Novel by Albert Camus, 1947.

The Plague is Camus's longest and most elaborate work of fiction. To this day, the novel has enjoyed unfaltering success and has been read by several million readers worldwide. *The Plague* is an allegory on the subject of evil, a reflection on the lessons that World War II taught, or should have taught, mankind. One of the main characters, Tarrou, claims that 'each of us has the plague within him; no one, no one on earth is free from it'. *The Plague* is a search for the meaning of life and an eloquent recognition of collective existence and solidarity.

An unidentified narrator sets out to relate the 'unusual events' which take place in Oran, Algeria, in 194–. In April, rats come out to die by the thousands in the streets, houses, and buildings. Soon the people themselves start dying in increasing numbers, and Dr Rieux must fight an epidemic of plague that compels the authorities to seal off the city. All must now learn to live in isolation, 'exiled' from the rest of the world, and from this point the narrator uses 'we' rather than 'I' in his narration. Rieux rejects all metaphysical interpretations of that evil, unlike Father Paneloux, a learned and militant Jesuit, who sees in the plague a divine punishment for human sins. Little by little, all the characters are introduced: Rambert, the Parisian journalist, whose only concern is to escape back to the woman he loves; Cottard, a shady character, who rejoices at the relaxed enforcement of laws during the epidemic; Tarrou, whose notebooks will be another source of information to the reader; judge Othon, who represents the established social order, in the same way as Paneloux embodies religion; Grand, a clerk at the Municipal Office; old Dr Castel, who first encountered the plague in China; an old asthmatic Spaniard, and others.

During the summer, the epidemic is at its worst. Burials are expedited as mere administrative formalities; disposing of the corpses is a major problem; isolation camps are created for relatives of the dead; riots at the city gates are commonplace. All must now come to terms with the plague. Tarrou best represents the new attitude: although a non-believer, he sets up sanitation teams of volunteers, thereby illustrating his moral 'comprehension'. There is now 'only a collective destiny, made of plague and the emotions shared by all', a life confined to the present with no values attached to anything.

In the autumn, while all still work feverishly and wearily without any improvement in the situation, Rambert, who had the opportunity to leave the city, decides to stay because 'it may be shameful to be happy by oneself'; the plague is now 'everybody's business'. Judge Othon's young son dies in horrible agony while doctors try unsuccessfully to save him by means of an anti-plague serum created by Castel. This death shakes Father Paneloux's beliefs, since the child was obviously an innocent creature: after a confused sermon, Paneloux dies, probably from the plague, but is listed as a 'doubtful case'. During an evening together (followed by a temporary and illegal escape to the beach), Tarrou explains to Rieux that even before the plague struck he knew he would always take the victim's side as the only way to be 'a saint without God'; Rieux replies that he just wants to be 'a man'.

By December, the new serum begins to work. Grand recovers from the fever; however, Othon and Tarrou die. At the same time, Rieux receives notification that his wife, who was away for unrelated medical reasons, has also died. Finally, the plague recedes. The gates of the city are reopened a few weeks later, allowing all those who had been separated for so long to be reunited. Alone, Rieux then reveals that he is the narrator and that he decided to write his 'chronicle' because 'it was up to him to speak for all', so that other men would know 'what had to be done and what assuredly would have to be done again in the never ending fight against terror and its relentless onslaughts'.

The epidemic of plague brings into shocking relief the mortality of men; it makes daily life more perceptible. The style of Camus's writing serves the same purpose: by writing a 'chronicle', Rieux displays objectivity and emphasizes factual narration. There are moments of passion, such as the exchange between Rieux and Paneloux at the time of young Othon's death, and the evening conversation between Rieux and Tarrou, but Camus always restrains his lyricism in favour of the logical and the impersonal.

The Plague came under attack from some for avoiding the human side of evil. Rachel Bespaloff, echoing later critics (most notably Barthes and Sartre), noted in 1950 that *The Plague* 'has no symbolic equivalent for the humiliation of the suffering inflicted upon man by man'. She concluded that a moral based upon solidarity means that all 'stubborn heroes of *The Plague* remain subjected to the precariousness which binds them to the *we*'. In this respect, the allegory falls short of offering an absolute answer to the absurd divorce of man from his environment. More recently, the absence of both female and Arab characters has also attracted critical attention. Nevertheless, Camus's lesson in modesty and pragmatism has not been lost, as the warm reception of the novel attests to this day.

Camus called *The Plague* his 'most anti-Christian' writing: in a world devoid of hope, it seeks to reaffirm human dignity amid the destruction wrought by World War II and its tangible illustrations of the Absurd. Coming after the revelation of the absurd and the need for man to rebel against his estrangement from his world, *The Plague* stands out among Camus's works as a balanced, yet optimistic, answer. Rieux states this moderately positive view in these terms: 'there are more things to admire in men than to despise'. The real hero of *The Plague* is Grand, the clerk who just does 'what has to be done' while refusing to allow the 'unusual events' to change his life. Despite the plague, Grand never gives up the quest for the perfect opening sentence to the novel he wants to write. He continues to compile statistics for the sanitary groups. But 'this insignificant and obscure hero who ha[s] to his credit only a little goodness of heart and a seemingly absurd ideal' offers man's obstinate yet moderate answer to the absurd.

—Pierre J. Lapaire

CANETTI, Elias. Born in Ruse (Ruschuk), Bulgaria, 25 July 1905. Educated at schools in England, Austria, Switzerland,

and Germany; University of Vienna, Ph.D. in chemistry, 1929. Married 1) Venetia Taubner-Calderón in 1934 (died 1963); 2) Hera Buschor in 1971 (died 1988), one daughter. Full-time writer; resident of England from 1939. Recipient: Foreign Book prize (France), 1949; Vienna prize, 1966; Critics prize (Germany), 1967; Great Austrian State prize, 1967; Büchner prize, 1972; Nelly Sachs prize, 1975; Franz Nabl prize (Graz), 1975; Keller prize, 1977; Order of Merit (Bonn), 1979; Europa Prato prize (Italy), 1980; Order of Merit (Germany), 1980(?); Hebbel prize, 1980; Nobel prize for literature, 1981; Kafka prize, 1981; Great Service Cross (Germany), 1983. D.Litt.: University of Manchester. Honorary Ph.D.: University of Munich. *Died 14 August 1994.*

PUBLICATIONS

Fiction

Die Blendung. 1936; as *Auto-da-Fé*, translated by C.V. Wedgwood, 1946; as *The Tower of Babel*, translated by Wedgwood, 1947.

Plays

Hochzeit (produced 1965). 1932; as *The Wedding*, 1986.
Komödie der Eitelkeit (produced 1965). 1950; as *Comedy of Vanity*, translated by Gitta Honegger, with *Life-Terms*, 1982.
Die Befristeten (produced 1967). In *Dramen*, 1964; as *Life-Terms*, translated by Gitta Honegger, with *Comedy of Vanity*, 1982; as *The Numbered*, translated by Carol Stewart, 1984.
Dramen (includes *Hochzeit*; *Komödie der Eitelkeit*; *Die Befristeten*). 1964.
Comedy of Vanity and Life-Terms, translated by Gitta Honegger. 1982.

Other

Fritz Wotruba. 1955.
Masse und Macht. 1960; as *Crowds and Power*, translated by Carol Stewart, 1962.
Welt im Kopf (selection), edited by Erich Fried. 1962.
Aufzeichnungen 1942–1948. 1965.
Die Stimmen von Marrakesch: Aufzeichnungen nach einer Reise. 1967; as *The Voices of Marrakesh*, translated by J.A. Underwood, 1978.
Der andere Prozess: Kafkas Briefe an Felice. 1969; as *Kafka's Other Trial: The Letters to Felice*, translated by Christopher Middleton, 1974.
Alle vergeudete Verehrung: Aufzeichnungen 1949–1960. 1970.
Die gespaltene Zukunft: Aufsätze und Gespräche. 1972.
Macht und Überleben: Drei Essays. 1972.
Die Provinz des Menschen: Aufzeichnungen 1942–1972. 1973; as *The Human Province*, translated by Joachim Neugroschel, 1978.
Der Ohrenzeuge: 50 Charaktere. 1974; as *Earwitness: Fifty Characters*, translated by Joachim Neugroschel, 1979.
Das Gewissen der Worte: Essays. 1975; as *The Conscience of Words*, translated by Joachim Neugroschel, 1979.
Der Überlebende. 1975.
Der Beruf des Dichters. 1976.
Die gerettete Zunge: Geschichte einer Jugend. 1977; as *The Tongue Set Free: Remembrance of a European Childhood*, translated by Joachim Neugroschel, 1979.

Die Fackel im Ohr: Lebensgeschichte 1921–1931. 1980; as *The Torch in My Ear*, translated by Joachim Neugroschel, 1982.

Das Augenspiel: Lebensgeschichte 1931–1937. 1985; as *The Play of the Eyes*, translated by Ralph Manheim, 1986.

Das Geheimherz der Uhr: Aufzeichnungen 1973–1985. 1987; as *The Secret Heart of the Clock: Notes, Aphorisms, Fragments 1973–1985*, translated by Joel Agee, 1989.

Translator, *Leidweg der Liebe*, by Upton Sinclair. 1930.
Translator, *Das Geld schreibt: Eine Studie über die amerikanische Literatur*, by Upton Sinclair. 1930.
Translator, *Alkohol*, by Upton Sinclair. 1932.

*

Critical Studies: *Canetti: Stationen zum Werk* by Alfons-M. Bischoff, 1973; *Kopf und Welt: Canettis Roman 'Die Blendung'* by D.G.J. Roberts, 1975; *Canetti* by Dagmar Barnouw, 1979; *Essays in Honor of Elias Canetti*, translated by Michael Hulse, 1987.

*   *   *

Elias Canetti has never been widely known in Britain, although he lived in England from 1939. From 1981, when he won the Nobel prize for literature, the contemporary relevance of his work once again attracted attention. A reticent man, Canetti dedicated his life to the study of a single theme: the behaviour of the individual within the mass and the power struggle associated with this conflict.

His best known works are the novel, *Die Blendung* (*Auto-da-Fé*), and a study of the behaviour of the mass, *Masse und Macht* (*Crowds and Power*). His autobiographies of more recent years, *Die gerettete Zunge* (*The Tongue Set Free*), *Die Fackel im Ohr* (*The Torch in My Ear*), and *Das Augenspiel* (*The Play of the Eyes*) have underlined the origins of and inspiration for his lifetime's work. His dramas and essays, too, reflect a pre-occupation with hallucination, political pressure, linguistic ambiguity, and the destructive power of the masses.

The events of most outstanding significance for Canetti in the formation of his interest in crowd psychology and the hypnotic power of the masses were the awaited arrival of a comet in Ruse, the sinking of the Titanic, the fire at the Law Courts in Vienna in 1927, and an experience in Vienna's Alserstrasse in the winter of 1924–25. These powerful emotional experiences are linked in Canetti's mind and work by images of great energy, of blood, of a rushing sound, and of fire. Fire is frequently seen as a magnetic driving force and is associated with the uncontrolled rhythm of the masses. These symbols recur in Canetti's work. Sight and blindness, insight and illusion are related themes. In *Auto-da-Fé* the central character, Kien, who becomes increasingly deluded by his world of books, eventually perishes in a fire with them. Canetti is always at pains to point out the contrasts and similarities between a character's external appearance, his environment, and his use of language. Each character, e.g., the man of books, the collector, the spend-thrift, has 'fixed ideas' which stand out because reality is portrayed as fragmented, communication as very partial. Canetti distanced himself from the suggestiveness of his characters, and yet he had clearly been closely involved with the experience of each of them. Attempts at communication between these different kinds of people are often portrayed as grotesque, leading only to an intensification of individual isolation.

Despite themes which are characteristic of a period of social and political upheaval, Canetti's style is serene, controlled, and lucid, almost part of another era and tradition. His work reflects self-assurance and composure. Its stylistic poise and balance based on an authoritative use of language, rich in imagery, set him apart from many younger contemporary writers.

Nevertheless, his subject matter is complex and his vision powerful—a confidence in one's own destiny, a respect for the experience of others, and a resistance to illusion, manipulation, and death.

—Barbara Saunders

AUTO-DA-FÉ (Die Blendung)
Novel by Elias Canetti, 1936.

Canetti wrote his only novel between autumn 1929 and October 1931 in Vienna but it was four years until he found a publisher, with help from Stefan Zweig. Provisionally titled *Kant fängt Feuer* [Kant Catches Fire], it was planned as a first in a series of eight novels. Each protagonist was to represent a specific social type whose dedication to a single ideal or concept had become an all-consuming obsession. This 'Human Comedy of Madmen' was to include the man of truth, the visionary who wants to live in outer space, the religious fanatic, the compulsive collector, the spendthrift, the enemy of death, the actor, and the man of books. Their pathologies comprise the spectrum of existential defects and perversions that are endemic to intellectuals in technological mass society. Since many of these personae were included in *Auto-da-Fé*, Canetti abandoned the larger project in favour of a satirical play, *Komödie der Eitelkeit* (*Comedy of Vanity*, completed in January 1934), an (unfinished) novel about the 'Tod-Feind' (literally, the enemy of and unto death), and, ultimately, work leading to his monumental study *Masse und Macht* (*Crowds and Power*). In January 1939, shortly after Canetti's escape to London, he resolved to abstain from all fictional and dramatic writing so long as Hitler was in power, a decision that included the stipulation that new translations of his novel should not be published until the end of World War II.

The three parts of *Auto-da-Fé* (A Head Without a World, Headless World, The World in the Head) portray different ways in which intellectualism encounters social reality. The protagonist through whom these confrontations are acted out is a reclusive private scholar, Dr Peter Kien, aged 40 and the world's foremost sinologist. He lives entirely for and in his library of 25,000 volumes, a misanthropist hermit with a pathological devotion to his learned pursuits. He treats his books as if they are human, even adding them as imaginary acquaintances in his four-room flat on the top floor of 24 Ehrlichstrasse (literally, honest street), whereas 'real people', rather than profit from a noble mind, only meet with his derisive scorn and harsh commands. But in the long run he is bested by his primitive housekeeper Therese Krumbholz whom he marries after she wins his confidence by feigning admiration for a particular book. She systematically mistreats him in order to gain control of his bank account and then drives him from his last room where he had barricaded himself behind a wall of books. Helplessly drifting through the city's underworld, Kien befriends a variety of shady characters who conspire to swindle him out of his money. A Jewish midget, the hunch-backed Fischerle, who claims to be the world's greatest chess player, devises the most successful stratagem to fleece his victim: knowing that Kien will redeem, even at inflated prices, all books pawned at the Theresianum and return them to their owners, he organizes a gang of thieves, involving also Therese and a brutally abusive retired policeman, Benedikt Pfaff, from whom Kien buys back his own library. When Kien discovers their scheme, a row ensues that lands him into police custody where, hallucinating that he has locked his wife in the apartment to die of starvation, he accuses himself of her murder. But Pfaff secures his release by having him declared mentally unfit and keeps him in a completely dark basement room, physically debilitated and close to insanity even though his mind is still lucid. At this stage Kien's brother Georges, a prominent psychiatrist from Paris with 'the world in his head', comes to straighten out his affairs but, deceived by Peter's mental acuity, fails to diagnose his incurable madness correctly. The demented scholar, fearing another scheme to take from him the treasures of his library and in his final delusion ever more ravingly the 'head without a world', sets his books ablaze and with them burns to death, laughing maniacally.

Canetti's plot, while coherent and credible even in its grotesque episodes and in other excesses of the imagination, appears to be secondary to the novel's extraordinary characters. They lack virtually all the elements that usually define the contradictory but coherent diversity of the human psyche, and they have created for themselves a social environment of stunning depravity. The absence of any redeeming features such as are traditionally accorded to even the most despicable villains lays bare a system of elementary impulses and instinctual drives that serve a very limited number of primitive goals. Most prominent among them are the ruthless, even sadistic enjoyment of power and the greedy satisfaction of basic physical pleasures. *Auto-da-Fé* is thus peopled with a set of monstrous cripples whose single-mindedness forestalls the development of narrative tension through moral complications and subtle psychological contrasts. The resultant intense monotony is highlighted by episodes of an ever more bizarre surreality that, while unpredictable, is none the less fully consistent in its own insane logic. A carefully sustained attitude both of intimate familiarity with and satirical remove from his figures allows the narrator to depict a world blinded by its ferocious obsessions in a style that combines precise observation with grim humour. His own penetrating intellectualism, while loath to provide explanatory comments, has an edge of critical sharpness that shuns the illusions of comforting sentiment and that is never flushed with streaks of warmth or whimsy. Canetti claimed Kafka and Gogol' as his stylistic models; like these congenial spirits and no less radically than Beckett among his contemporaries, his fictional seismogram of the fascist mentality forces his readers to change their habits of aesthetic perception and to re-examine their own social experiences.

—Michael Winkler

ČAPEK, Karel. Born in Malé Svatoňovice, Bohemia (now in the Czech Republic), 9 January 1890; brother of the writer Josef Čapek. Educated at Charles University, Prague, 1909–15, Ph.D. in philosophy 1915; universities of Paris and Berlin, 1909–10. Married the actress Olga Scheinpflugová in 1935. Journalist, *Lidové noviny*; co-founder, with Josef Čapek, František-Langer, and with Edmond Konrad, of the avant-garde circle 'The Pragmatists'; stage director and dramaturg, Vinohrady Theatre, Prague, 1921–23. *Died 25 December 1938.*

PUBLICATIONS

Collections

Spisy bratří [Collected Works]. 51 vols., 1928–47.
Spisy [Works]. 1981.
Toward the Radical Center: A Karel Čapek Reader, edited by Peter Kussi. 1990.

Fiction

Zářivé hlubiny a jiné prózy [The Luminous Depths and Other Prose Works], with Josef Čapek. 1916.
Boží muka [Stations of the Cross]. 1917.
Krakonošova zahrada [The Garden of Krakonos], with Josef Čapek. 1918.
Trapné povídky. 1921; as *Money and Other Stories*, translated by Francis P. Marchant, Dora Round, F.P. Casey, and O. Vočadlo, 1929.
Továrna na absolutno. 1922; as *The Absolute at Large*, translated by M. and R. Weatherall, 1927.
Krakatit. 1924; as *Krakatit*, translated by Lawrence Hyde, 1925; as *An Atomic Fantasy*, translated by Hyde, 1948.
Povídky z jedné kapsy [Tales from One Pocket], *Povídky z druhé kapsy* [Tales from the Other Pocket]. 2 vols., 1929; in part as *Tales from Two Pockets*, translated by Paul Selver, 1932.
Apokryfy; Kniha apokryfů. 2 vols., 1932–45; as *Apocryphal Stories*, translated by Dora Round, 1949.
Devatero pohádek a ještě jedna od Josefa Čapka jako přívažek. 1932; as *Fairy Tales with One Extra as a Makeweight*, translated by M. and R. Weatherall, 1933.
Hordubal. 1933; as *Hordubal*, translated by M. and R. Weatherall, 1934.
Povětroň. 1934; as *Meteor*, translated by M. and R. Weatherall, 1935.
Obyčejný život. 1934; as *An Ordinary Life*, translated by M. and R. Weatherall, 1936.
Válka s mloky. 1936; as *War with the Newts*, translated by M. and R. Weatherall, 1937; also translated by Ewald Osers, 1985.
První parta. 1937; as *The First Rescue Party*, translated by M. and R. Weatherall, 1939.
Život a dílo skladatele Foltýna. 1939; as *The Cheat*, translated by M. and R. Weatherall, 1941.
Nine Fairy Tales and One More, translated by Dagmar Hermann. 1990.

Plays

Lásky hra osudná [The Fateful Game of Love], with Josef Čapek (produced 1922). 1910.
R.U.R. (produced 1920). 1920; as *R.U.R. (Rossum's Universal Robots)*, translated by Paul Selver, 1923.
Loupežník (produced 1921). 1920; as *The Robber*, translated by Rudolph C. Bednar, 1931.

Ze života hmyzu, with Josef Čapek (produced 1922). 1921; as
  *And So Ad Infinitum (The Life of the Insect): An
  Entomological Review*, translated by Paul Selver, 1923; as
  The Insect Play, translated by Selver, 1923; as *The World
  We Live In (The Insect Comedy)*, adapted by Owen Davis,
  1933.
Věc Makropulos (produced 1922). 1922; as *The Macropoulos
  Secret*, translated by Paul Selver, 1927.
Adam Stvořitel, with Josef Čapek (produced 1927). 1927; as
  Adam the Creator, translated by Dora Round, 1929.
Bílá nemoc (produced 1937). 1937; as *Power and Glory*,
  translated by Paul Selver and Ralph Neale, 1938.
Matka (produced 1938). 1938; as *The Mother*, translated by
  Paul Selver, 1939.

Other

Pragmatismus; čili, Filosofie praktického života [Pragmatism;
  or, a Philosophy of Practical Life]. 1918.
Kritika slov [A Critique of Words]. 1920.
Italské listy. 1923; as *Letters from Italy*, translated by Francis
  P. Marchant, 1929.
Anglické listy. 1924; as *Letters from England*, translated by
  Paul Selver, 1925.
O nejbližších věcech. 1925; as *Intimate Things*, translated by
  Dora Round, 1935.
Jak vzniká divadelní hra a průvodce po zákulisí. 1925; as
  How a Play Is Produced, translated by P. Beaumont
  Wadsworth, 1928.
Skandální aféra Josefa Holouška [The Scandalous Affair of
  Josef Holoušek]. 1927.
Hovory s T.G. Masarykem. 3 vols., 1928–35; as *President
  Masaryk Tells His Story*, 1934, and *Masaryk on Thought
  and Life*, 1938, both translated by M. and R. Weatherall.
Zahradníkův rok. 1929; as *The Gardener's Year*, translated
  by M. and R. Weatherall, 1931.
Výlet do Španěl. 1930; as *Letters from Spain*, translated by
  Paul Selver, 1932.
Minda; čili, Ochova psu. 1930; translated as *Minda; or, On
  Breeding Dogs*, 1940.
Obrázky z Holandska. 1932; as *Letters from Holland*, trans-
  lated by Paul Selver, 1933.
O věcech obecných; čili, Zoon politikos [Ordinary Things; or,
  Zoon Politikon]. 1932.
Dášeňka čili Život štěněte. 1933; as *Dashenka; or, the Life of a
  Puppy*, translated by M. and R. Weatherall, 1940.
Legenda o člověku zahradníkovi [Legend of a Gardening
  Man]. 1935.
Cesta na sever. 1936; as *Travels in the North*, translated by M.
  and R. Weatherall, 1939.
Jak se co dělá. 1938; as *How They Do It*, translated by M. and
  R. Weatherall, 1945.
Kalendář [Calendar]. 1940.
O lidech [About People]. 1940.
Vzrušené tance [Wild Dances]. 1946.
Bajky a podpovídky [Fables and Would-Be Tales]. 1946.
Sedm rozhlásku [Seven Notes for the Wireless]. 1946.
Ratolest a vavřín [The Sprig and the Laurel]. 1947.
*In Praise of Newspapers and Other Essays on the Margin of
  Literature*, translated by M. and R. Weatherall. 1951.
Obrázky z domova [Letters from Home]. 1953.
Sloupkový ambit [The Pillared Cloister]. 1957.
Poznámky o tvorbě [Comments on Creation]. 1959.
Na břehu dnů [On the Boundaries of Days]. 1966.
Divadelníkem proti své vuli [A Drama Expert Against My
  Will]. 1968.

V zajetí slov [In the Bondage of Words]. 1969.
Ctení o T.G. Masarykovi [Readings about T.G. Masaryk].
  1969.
Místo pro Janathana! [Make Way for Jonathan]. 1970.
Listy Olze 1920–38 [Letters to Olga]. 1971.
Drobty pod stolem doby [Crumbs under the Table of the
  Age]. 1975.
Listy Anielce [Letter to Anielce]. 1978.
Neuskutečněný dialog [Selected Essays], edited by Gustav
  Földi. 1978.
Dopisy ze zásuvky [Letters Out of a Drawer] (letters to Vera
  Hruzová), edited by Jiří Opelik. 1980.
Cesty k přátelství [Selected Correspondence]. 1987.
Od člověka k člověku [From Person to Person]. 1988.
Filmová libreta [Film Libretto]. 1989.

*

Bibliography: *Bibliografie Karla Čapka: soupis jeho díla*,
1990; *Karel Čapek, bibliogrofie díla a literatury o životě a díle,
publikace v Československu a v Sovětském svazu* by Margita
Křepinská, 4 vols., 1991.

Critical Studies: *Karel Čapek* by William E. Harkins, 1962;
Karel Čapek: An Essay by Alexander Matuška, 1964; *Karel
Čapek* (in German) by Eckehard Thiele, 1988.

* * *

Karel Čapek sprang into world fame with his play *R.U.R.*
about the production and commercial exploitation of semi-
human automata. It gave the English language a new word—
'robot'. He and his brother Josef followed this up with *Ze
života hmyzu* (*The Insect Play*), where the jungle law of the
insect world was portrayed as a reflection of the amorality of
human society. Later plays included *Věc Makropulos* (*The
Macropoulos Secret*) (best known today in Janáček's operatic
version) about a woman who was the victim of an experiment
to prolong life, in which Čapek, unlike Shaw, reached the
comforting conclusion that our existing life span is about
right.

Although Čapek was a gifted playwright, his best work did
not lie in the theatre. The world publicity he received for his
plays with their sensational themes obscured the merit of his
more philosophical works like his 'Trilogy'—*Hordubal,
Povětroň* (*Meteor*), and *Obyčejný život* (*An Ordinary Life*)—
his series of short stories *Povídky z jedné kapsy* and *Povídky z
druhé kapsy* (*Tales from Two Pockets*), and his *feuilletons*,
which were admirably suited to his particular genius. His
delightful travel books, some of which he illustrated himself,
achieved popularity in the countries he was describing.

In his 'Trilogy' Čapek expresses his relativist view of life by
showing that human personality comprises many disparate
elements, some completely hidden and others only rarely
coming to the surface. The Ukrainian peasant Hordubal is
murdered by his wife and her paramour, but at the trial it is
clear that the facts and motives are impossible for outsiders to
determine. In *Meteor* three people make conflicting but plausible conjectures about the past history of an unknown airman
who has been brought into a hospital unconscious, while in
An Ordinary Life a man discovers, in retrospect, that he has
had not one personality but several. Čapek adopts the same
approach in his last, unfinished novel, *Život a dílo skladatele
Foltýna* (*The Cheat*).

In his brilliant 'Pocket' tales Čapek shows himself to be a

master of short-story writing, following the example of G.K. Chesterton, just as his 'utopian' plays and novels show the influence of H.G. Wells.

Less successful was his satirical fantasy *Tovàrna na absolutno* (*The Absolute at Large*), which tells how the discovery of the power of electrons and their application in a factory lead to over-production and unemployment (including not 'butter mountains' but all other 'mountains' from tacks to rolls of paper) and release 'fall-out' in the form of widespread religious hysteria; *Krakatit*, a half-mystical and strongly erotic story of the struggle of foreign powers to obtain the secret of an atomic bomb; and *První parta* (*The First Rescue Party*), a social realist novel about working-class heroism during an accident in a coal mine. His novel *Válka s mloky* (*War with the Newts*)—an extension of the theme in *R.U.R.*—was particularly topical at the time as it reflected the alarm felt at the power of the Nazi system and the threat of Hitler's aggression.

Čapek's writings are the product of his highly original imagination and deep philosophical thought. They are strongly influenced by his preoccupation with epistemology. His novels and plays are full of thought-provoking ideas and intriguing situations but lack fully rounded characters. He has continued to maintain his hold over the Czech reading public in spite of (or perhaps because of) his close identification with the officially rejected Masaryk Republic, but his work is today less well-known abroad, perhaps because many of the problems he dealt with so imaginatively have been overtaken or are seen today in a more modern light. The failure of existing English translations to match his highly individual literary style has proved an additional handicap to full appreciation of his talents. He had great faith in the West, and the Munich 'betrayal' robbed him of his will to live. 'It's not so bad. They haven't sold us out, only given us away' (*Bajky* [*Fables*]).

—Cecil Parrott

THE INSECT PLAY (Ze života hmyzu)
Play by Karel Čapek, 1921.

The Insect Play (subtitled *And So Ad Infinitum*) was written in 1921 by the Czechoslovakian playwright Karel Čapek in collaboration with his brother Josef, a cubist painter and writer. The play, which exhibits the influence of German expressionism, is divided into a prologue, three acts, and an epilogue, and is a combination of dream allegory, in which a narrator is transported in sleep to another world, and animal allegory, in which animals are used to represent human qualities. The 'dreamer' is, in this case, the lowest common denominator of mankind, a tramp. It is he who in the prologue transports the audience into the world of the insects, is at hand to underline the moral embodied in each act, and conveys humanity's mortality by dying during the epilogue having learned from his observation of the insects to live and let live. Throughout the play runs the theme of the continuity of the life force of which humans and insects are merely a part.

Humanity is divided in the play into four broad types—hedonists, materialists, parasites, and workers. In Act I the hedonists are butterflies whose romantic dalliance and quest for superficial enjoyment evokes the world of the carefree 'gay young things' of the 1920s. Towards the end of the act

the Tramp makes clear in verse the moral to be drawn from their selfish devotion to the pursuit of pleasure:

> Ho! 'Igh Society, what? Powder yer nose,
> Strip to yer waist—and let the *rest* show through!
> Put it blunt-like—Lord Alf and Lady Rose
> Be'ave exactly like them insec's do.

While the first act satirizes those who simply live for pleasure, the second represents more harshly the selfishness generated by humanity's desire for material possessions. Those who hoard their wealth are represented by two beetles whose 'capital', in the form of a huge dung-ball, is stolen by another beetle while they are away looking for a place to hide it. The aggression generated by the competitiveness of human society is represented by an Ichneumon Fly who kills other insects in order to feed his spoiled child. The amorality generated by this struggle is seen in the behaviour of the Parasite who, masquerading as a 'working man', steals what he can from those around him. In the second act we are introduced to the figure of the Chrysalis who, here and in the third act, is poised to be reborn. Its speeches are poetic and idealistic and serve to counterpoint the much less idealistic behaviour of the other insects. Again, at the close of the scene, the Tramp draws explicit parallels in verse between the insect and human worlds.

In the third act the Tramp is introduced to a society whose members work to a 'general scheme' and are prepared to fight and perish for the State. This socialist state is represented by an Ant Heap in which the individual ants work as an efficient industrial unit for the general good. The capacity for industrial efficiency is however turned to the production of a weapon of mass destruction, while the sense of common purpose that inspires the Ant society is employed by a Dictator to create a disciplined army. Although initially the Tramp finds this form of society attractive, he soon learns that state control may easily be employed in a struggle for world domination which, in totalitarian double-speak, is justified as a means of ensuring world peace. The ensuing lengthy battle with the Yellow Ants offers opportunities for vivid stage action which culminates in the victory of the Yellows whose triumphant leader is destroyed by the Tramp in disgust at the madness of war.

As in other dream-allegories, the play's Epilogue returns the focus to the dreamer. The Tramp wakes to a reprise of voices from the earlier scenes and to a ballet of moths who, joined by the moth that has now liberated itself from its chrysalis, celebrate the continuity of the life-force and expire. Their death is followed by that of Tramp himself. Thus is represented once more the eternal round of life and death already conveyed throughout the play. The audience is brought back to present reality by the arrival of a woodcutter and a woman carrying a new-born baby who discover the Tramp's corpse. 'One's born and another dies', remarks the Woodcutter, 'No great matter, missus', and the play ends with the arrival of children, the next generation, singing and dancing with the carefree spirit of youth.

The play was extremely popular during the inter-war years and was performed in translation in both Britain and America. The satire of the modern industrialized state and of the stupidity of war must have appeared particularly pertinent to contemporary audiences recently faced with the foundation of the Soviet State and the mechanized killing of World War I. Although it must be admitted that the play's philosophy is hardly profound, its revue-like combination of satire, verse, song, dance, and comedy and the opportunities it offers for imaginative, non-realistic staging, extravagant costume, bold lighting, and evocative sound effects, make it a play still worthy of production.

—D. Keith Peacock

R.U.R.
Play by Karel Čapek, 1920.

The enigmatic title of the Czechoslovakian writer Karel Čapek's play refers to its setting and subject matter, the factory and products of 'Rossum's Universal Robots'. Written in 1920, during his country's brief period of independence between the two World Wars, *R.U.R.* brought its dramatist international recognition and introduced the word 'robot' (from Czech *robotit*, to drudge) into the English language.

The play is set sometime in the future. Its plot concerns the construction, in a factory located on a remote island, of what we would now describe as androids—machines outwardly resembling human beings—which are intended, in the factory manager Domain's idealistic words, to free humanity 'from the degradation of labour'. In order to achieve maximum occupational efficiency the robots have been constructed as simplified versions of the human worker, so that 'mechanically they are more perfect than we are, they have enormously developed intelligence, but they have no soul'.

Into this situation is introduced the figure of Helena, a representative of the Humanity League, whose aim is to bring civil rights to the robots. It is through her that we are gradually introduced to the ethical conflicts which the ability to create a worker population has produced. The project itself, we learn, was the outcome, not of idealism but of megalomania. Old Rossum, a physiologist who initiated the experimental programme aimed at reproducing human beings that culminated in the production of the robots was, according to Domain, was a madman who 'wanted to become a sort of scientific substitute for God'. Rossum's work has been simplified and perfected by his son, an engineer. It was he who, while continuing to construct machines with the outward appearance of human beings, in the cause of greater labour efficiency created them devoid of human sensations and emotions. Dr Gall, the head of the factory's physiological department, has however modified the robots by installing a limited nervous system in order to introduce suffering and thereby avoid the corporeally damaging results of industrial accidents arising from the robot's inability to feel pain. It is these two elements, established in a traditionally discursive manner in an exposition involving Domain and Helena, that generate the action of the play and produce its climax. The human appearance of the robots causes Helena, and to some extent the audience, to view the machines as repressed human beings. This appears to be further supported by the fact that they occasionally experience 'Robot's Cramp' during which they cease to operate and gnash their teeth.

Thus, by the end of Act I, in the manner of the well-made play, the audience is introduced to the issues and complications of the play. Also following the pattern of the well-made play the second act brings a further complication in the form of a rebellion of the world's robots. It is five years later and Helena is married to Domain. The robots have been used by many nations as soldiers but have turned their guns against those who employ them. Humanity now feels superfluous and is losing the will to reproduce itself. By the end of the second act the island's robots have become aggressive and appear poised to attack their human creators.

The final act brings the play to its climax. Under pressure from Helen, Dr Gall has given the robots various human responses which amount to a kind of 'soul'. This has caused them to view humanity as redundant and to hate their own subjection. They rise in rebellion, destroying all human beings except one, Alquist, who, as the Clerk of Works of the factory and a builder, they consider to be subservient like themselves. The third act closes with the victory of the robots.

While illustrating humanity's failings, its violence, and its lust for power, Čapek is unwilling to conclude the play on a note of pessimism and so introduces a typical dénouement in the form of an Epilogue. Using a traditional, melodramatic plot-device, he reveals here that, unfortunately for the robots, old Rossum's manuscript containing the formula crucial to their construction has earlier been burnt by Helena. Alquist does not possess the knowledge to rediscover the formula, the human race has died out, and the robots, with their limited working life and inability to reproduce, will likewise be extinct in 20 years' time. The end of the world is indeed nigh, but is averted by the sexual awakening of two recently constructed robots, one named Helena after Domain's wife and the other aptly called Primus. Tested by Alquist, they reveal that they care for each other, indeed are willing to die for each other, and are sent out into the world by Alquist as the second Adam and Eve who will 'be fruitful and multiply and replenish the earth . . .'.

Although the plot itself follows the pattern of the well-made play, *R.U.R.* also reflects the influence of German expressionism. The apocalyptic vision of a future society in which industry appears to have become the master rather than the servant of mankind bears similarities to such plays as Georg Kaiser's *The Coral* (*Die Koralle*, 1917) and *Gas, I* and *II* (1918 and 1920). The groupings of characters in terms of their social roles—the scientists and engineers who run the factory and speak almost chorally, the robot-workers and the idealistic, enquiring young intruder, Helena—are all reminiscent of the generic characterization of expressionism. Finally, the optimism of the play's Epilogue, in which the new Adam and Eve are about to re-establish humanity after the apocalypse, can be seen as a clear parallel to the mood of early German expressionism.

—D. Keith Peacock

CARDENAL, Ernesto. Born in Granada, Nicaragua, 20 January 1925. Family moved to León, 1930. Educated at the Colegio Centro América, Granada; National Autonomous University, Mexico City, 1944–48, degree 1948; Columbia University, New York, 1948–49. Travelled through France, Italy, Spain, and Switzerland, 1949; co-founder, Hilo Azul publishers, 1951; member, National Union for Popular Action, and contributor of political articles to *La Prensa*, 1950s; Trappist novice, Gethsemani, Kentucky, 1957–59; member of Benedictine monastery of Santa María de la Resurrección, Cuernavaca, Mexico, 1959–65, and a seminary in Colombia, 1961; ordained Roman Catholic priest, 1965; founder and leader, religious community 'Nuestra Señora de Solentiname', Solentiname Archipelago, Nicaragua, during the 1960s and 1970s; visited Cuba to serve on poetry jury, 1970; chaplain, anti-government Sandinista Front, and subsequently appointed Minister of Culture in the Sandinista government in 1979. Recipient: Managua Centenary prize, 1952; Christopher Book award, 1972; La Paz prize grant, 1980. Lives in Managua.

PUBLICATIONS

Verse

La ciudad deshabitada. 1946.
Proclama del conquistador. 1947.
Gethsemani, Ky. 1960.
La hora 0. 1960.
Epigramas: Poemas. 1961.
Oración por Marilyn Monroe, y otros poemas. 1965; as *Marilyn Monroe and Other Poems*, edited and translated by Robert Pring-Mill, 1975.
El estrecho dudoso. 1966.
Antología. 1967.
Poemas. 1967.
Salmos. 1967; as *Psalms of Struggle and Liberation*, translated by Emile G. McAnany, 1971; as *Psalms*, translated by Thomas Blackburn, 1981.
Mayapán. 1968.
Poemas reunidos 1949–1969. 1969.
Homenaje a los indios americanos. 1969; as *Homage to the American Indians*, translated by Carlos and Monique Altschul, 1973.
La hora 0 y otros poemas. 1971; as *Zero Hour and Other Documentary Poems*, edited by Donald D. Walsh, translated by Paul W. Borgeson, Jr and Jonathan Cohen, 1980.
Antología, edited by Pablo Antonio Cuadro. 1971.
Poemas. 1971.
Antología. 1972.
Canto nacional. 1973.
Oráculo sobre Managua. 1973.
Poesía escogida. 1975.
Apocalypse and Other Poems, edited and translated by Robert Pring-Mill and Donald D. Walsh. 1977.
Antología. 1978.
Canto a un país que nace. 1978.
Poesía de uso: Antología, 1949–1978. 1979.
Poesía. 1979.
Nueva antología poética. 1979.
Tocar el cielo. 1981.
Waslala, translated by Fidel López-Criado and R.A. Kerr. 1983.
Antología: Ernesto Cardenal. 1983.
Poesía de la nueva Nicaragua. 1983.
Vuelos de victoria. 1984; as *Flights of Victory: Songs of Celebration of the Nicaraguan Revolution*, translated by Marc Zimmerman (bilingual edition), 1985.
Quetzalcóatl. 1985.
With Walker in Nicaragua and Other Early Poems, 1949–1954, translated by Jonathan Cohen. 1985.
From Nicaragua with Love: Poems, 1976–1986, translated by Jonathan Cohen. 1987.
Cántico cósmico. 1989; as *The Music of the Spheres* (bilingual edition), translated by Dinah Livingstone, 1990; as *Cosmic Canticle*, translated by John Lyons, 1993.
Los ovnis de oro: Poemas indios. 1991; as *Golden UFOs: The Indian Poems*, edited by Russell O. Salmon, translated by Carlos and Monique Altschul. 1992.

Other

Vida en el amor. 1970; as *To Live Is to Love*, translated by Kurt Reinhardt, 1972; as *Vida en el amor/Love*, translated by Dinah Livingstone, 1974.
En Cuba. 1972; as *In Cuba*, translated by Donald D. Walsh, 1974.
Cristianismo y revolución, with Fidel Castro. 1974.
Cardenal en Valencia (interviews). 1974.
El Evangelio en Solentiname. 1975; as *The Gospel in Solentiname*, translated by Donald D. Walsh, 1976; as *Love in Practice: The Gospel in Solentiname*, 1977; selections as *Evangelio, pueblo, y arte*, 1983; selections as *The Gospel in Art by the Peasants of Solentiname*, edited by Philip and Sally Sharper, 1984.
La santidad de la revolución. 1976.
La paz mundial y la revolución de Nicaragua. 1981.
Nostalgia del futuro: Pintura y buena noticia en Solentiname. 1982.
La democratización de la cultura. 1982.
Nicaragua: La guerra de liberación—der Befreiungskrieg, with Richard Cross. 1982(?).
Nuevo cielo y tierra nueva. 1985.

Editor, with José Coronel Urtecho, *Antología de la poesía norteamericana*. 1963.
Editor, with Jorge Montoya Toro, *Literatura indígena americana: Antología*. 1964.
Editor, *Poesía nicaragüense*. 1973.
Editor, *Poesía nueva de Nicaragua*. 1974.
Editor, *Poesía cubana de la revolución*. 1976.
Editor, *Antología de poesía primitiva*. 1979.
Editor, *Poemas de un joven*, by Joaquín Pasos. 1983.
Editor, *Antología: Azarias H. Pallais*. 1986.

Translator, *Catulo-Marcial en versión de Ernesto Cardenal*. 1978.
Translator, *Ezra Pound: Antología*, with José Coronel Urtecho. 1979.
Translator, *Tu paz es mi paz*, by Ursula Schulz. 1982.

*

Bibliography: *An Annotated Bibliography of and about Ernesto Cardenal* by Janet Lynne Smith, 1979.

Critical Studies: *Poetas de América en España: Cardenal, político* by M.R. Barnatán, 1973; *Emblems of a Season of Fury* by T. Merton, 1973; *Homenaje a Ernesto Cardenal*, edited by P.R. Gutierrez, 1975; 'Daniel Boone, Moses and the Indians: Ernesto Cardenal's Evolution from Alienation to Social Commitment', in *Chasqui*, 11(1), 1981, and 'The Image of the United States in the Poetry of René Depestre and Ernesto Cardenal', in *Revista/Review Interamericana*, 11(2), 1981, both by Henry Cohen; 'A Search for Utopia on Earth: Toward an Understanding of the Literary Production of Ernesto Cardenal' by C. Schaefer, in *Crítica Hispánica*, 4(2), 1982; *Ernesto Cardenal en Solentiname* by H. Torres, 1982; 'The Evolution of Ernesto Cardenal's Prophetic Poetry', in *Latin American Literary Review*, 12(23), 1983, 'Cardenal's Poetic Style: Cinematic Parallels', in *Revista Canadiense de Estudios Hispánicos*, 11(1), 1986, and 'Cardenal's Exteriorismo: The Ideology Underlying the Esthetic', in *Mid Hudson Languages Studies*, 10, 1987, all by Jorge H. Valdés; 'Prophecy of Liberation: The Poetry of Ernesto Cardenal' by Edward Elias, in *Poetic Prophecy in Western*

Literature edited by Jan Wojcik and Raymond-Jean Frontain, 1984; *La poesía de Ernesto Cardenal: Cristianismo y revolución* by E. Urdanivia Bertarelli, 1984; 'Poetry in the Central American Revolution: Ernesto Cardenal and Roque Dalton' by John Beverley, in *Literature and Contemporary Revolutionary Culture*, 1, 1984–85; 'Peace, Poetry and Popular Culture: Ernesto Cardenal and the Nicaraguan Revolution' by Claudia Scharfer-Rodríguez, in *Latin American Literary Review*, 13(26), 1985; 'Tradition and Originality in the *Denunciator y Salmos* of Ernesto Cardenal' by G.B. Barrow, in *Chispa*, 1987; 'Political Poetry and the Example of Ernesto Cardenal' by Reginald Gibbons, in *Critical Inquiry*, 13(3), 1987; 'Ernesto Cardenal and North American Literature: Intertextuality and Reality and the Formulation of an Ethical Identity', in *Inti*, 31, 1990, and 'Ernesto Cardenal's *El estrecho dudoso*: Reading/Re-Writing History', in *Revista Canadiense de Estudios Hispánicos*, 15(1), 1990, both by Steven F. White.

*   *   *

In reading Ernesto Cardenal's poetry one must separate the charismatic personality of the ex-Sandinista Minister of Culture, and once Trappist priest, from the actual poems. Cardenal's crucial position in the Nicaraguan hierarchy, and his public image, have lead to him being heavily criticized in Mario Vargas Llosa's novel about a failed revolutionary in Peru, *Historia de Mayta* (*The Real Life of Alejandro Mayta*), and positively celebrated in Julio Cortázar's short story 'Apocalypse in Solentiname'.

When Cardenal began publishing his poems in the 1940s it was under two crucial influences, one literary, the other political. Literary surrealism had an enormous liberating impact on Latin American poetry, for it seemed to combine personal freedom of expression with a revolutionary context. Cardenal first published poems in the magazine *Letras de México* in 1946 in free verse, and he has acknowledged his debt to the 'mad' Nicaraguan poet Alfonso Cortés. However, the ferocious political situation under the successive dictatorships of the Somozas made Cardenal reconsider the ambition of a merely personal liberation in a written text. From this questioning emerged one of the constants of Cardenal's developing poetics. The position of the poet's 'ego' is made secondary to the need to write a poem that urges action. By taking the *effect* of the poem on the reader as central to the poem's area of action, the poet relegates the more Romantic notion of the poem as the sincere expression of his own inner world.

Cardenal discovered the means to carry out his new perception of the role of the poet in an illiterate country like Nicaragua through reading Ezra Pound while studying at Columbia University in New York. He began translating Pound, William Carlos Williams, and others, aware that most of the Latin American poets of his generation were still, like Rubén Darío before him, looking towards French culture, and especially French surrealism, for their examples. To Cardenal, Pound's *Cantos*, with their incorporation of quotations, with the collage technique of confronting documentary texts with Chinese poems, and with their ambitious attempt to go beyond the limitations of an individual's private world, suggested a new sound to poetry. Cardenal called this technique 'exteriorismo' (exteriorism), the term denoting an attitude that pays more attention to the outer world than to the inner one. It must be emphasized that Cardenal sounded strange and new to most of his contemporaries because he had turned to another literary tradition. Over time Cardenal

published his translations in *Antología de la poesía norteamericana* [Anthology of North American Poetry], and *Ezra Pound: Antología*.

The briefly mentioned political context to Cardenal's poetry further drives the ego-obsessed Romantic out of the poems. In 1961, in Mexico, Cardenal published his *Epigramas*, based, through Pound, on his reading of Latin and Greek poets. Cardenal develops a counterpointing technique of opposing the past (Caesar and others) with the present (Somoza), and by pretending to write love poems avoids direct political denunciation. His little poem 'Imitation of Propertius' ends, 'And she prefers me, poor, to all Somoza's millions'. Through Pound, Cardenal also learnt that a poem must be clear and understood immediately. The epigrams remain fresh and provocative.

For protest poetry to work on its audience it must be direct, immediately comprehensible, and, in Latin America, readable aloud. The Chilean poet Pablo Neruda had led the way in the early 1950s with his realization that a poem must be read aloud to spread beyond the confines of the printed word and the few who can afford to buy books. Surrealism, with its twisted dark metaphors, its forays into the unconscious, would not do. All Cardenal's post-1960s poetry is narrative. It avoids the condensation of meaning in metaphors and uses the syntax of prose.

In some ways Cardenal, by expanding what can be included in a lyrical poem, has become the unofficial historian of Nicaragua, then Central America, and finally for the whole Latin American sub-continent. In *La hora 0* ('Zero Hour') there are poems with specific references to local Nicaraguan revolutionaries like Adolfo Báez Bone or Sandino; Cardenal names places, dictators, characters from the past and the present that have no universal poetic appeal as such, but who represent his version of evil. It is this moral vision that allows Cardenal to blend his Christian messianism (he was ordained as a priest in 1965) with his reading of Karl Marx. *Salmos* (*Psalms of Struggle and Liberation*) combines a rewriting of the Biblical psalms with a critique of Somoza. This political-religious vein continues through the poems of *Oración por Marilyn Monroe, y otros poemas* (*Marilyn Monroe and Other Poems*) where, in the title poem, Cardenal mentions Monroe's last unanswered phone call and ends 'Lord answer that phone'. The title of that poem shows how Cardenal has moved beyond Pound to the pop-culture of 1960s America; but he gives Warhol's icon a moral value. His criticism of the United States' consumer culture flows from this stance.

In the collections *El estrecho dudoso* [The Doubtful Strait] and *Homenaje a los indios americanos* (*Homage to the American Indians*) Cardenal expands his poems by re-creating the history of the conquest of Central America and catalogues the pre-Columbian Indian heritage, basing his work on archival studies, and incorporating voices and historical documents into the poems so that a reader actually learns about the forgotten past. A good example is 'Economy of Tahuantinsuyu', where Cardenal contrasts capitalist North American uses of money with pre-Columbian ones, where political truth and religious truth 'were but the one truth for the people'. The poem that best conveys Cardenal's radical moral vision is his lament on the death of his mentor, the Trappist poet Thomas Merton (whose poems Cardenal has translated into Spanish), which ends, 'We only love and only are on dying/The final deed the gift of all one's being/okay.' On reading this poem in conjunction with the notes he was allowed to write during his stay at the Trappist monastery (see his *Gethsemani, Ky*) few would doubt Cardenal's deserved position as a much-admired poet.

Cardenal has written, *Vida en el amor* (*To Live Is to Love*), a book on love, which is close in form to a sermon, *En Cuba* (*In Cuba*) on his crucial stay in Cuba, *El Evangelio en Solentiname* (*The Gospel in Solentiname*) on his religious beliefs, as well as poems celebrating the Sandinista victory of 1979, *Vuelos de victoria* (*Flights of Victory*). His poem *Cántico cósmico* (*Cosmic Canticle*) is a celebration of the energy of the cosmos, based on his reading of science and cosmology in pursuit of an interest that derives from his earlier reading of the theologian Teilhard de Chardin. However, in this later poetry the fertile juxtaposition of his moral stance with his readings of Pound and his opposition to Somoza has given way to a lax prose syntax that carries few poetic surprises.

—Jason Wilson

CARDUCCI, Giosuè [or Giosue] (Alessandro Giuseppe).
Born in Valdicastello, near Pisa, territory of Tuscany, 27 July 1835. Lived in Maremma, 1838–49. Educated at home; studied the humanities, rhetoric, and philosophy in Florence, from 1849; Scuola Normale, Pisa, 1853–56, degree in philology and philosophy 1856. Married Elvira Menicucci in 1859, two sons and three daughters; had affair with Carolina Cristofori Piva ('Lina') in the 1870s. Co-founder, Amici Pedanti society; teacher of rhetoric, Ginnasio di San Miniato al Tedesco, 1856–57; returned to live with his family in Florence, 1857; private tutor, and edited and wrote prefaces to the Diamante series of classics produced by Barbèra, publishers, Florence, from 1858; professor of Greek, then Italian and Latin, Liceo Forteguerri, Pistoia, 1860; professor of Italian, University of Bologna, 1861–1904 (retired). Elected as republican deputy to parliament, 1876; later a monarchist candidate, but failed to get elected; named a senator, 1890. Recipient: Nobel prize for literature, 1906. *Died 16 February 1907.*

PUBLICATIONS

Collections

Opere. 20 vols., 1889–1909.
Edizione nazionale delle opere. 30 vols., 1935–42; supplemented with *Lettere* (21 vols.), 1938–60, and *Aggiunte* (1 vol.), 1968.
Poesie, edited by Albano Sorbelli. 1950.
Poesie scelte, edited by P. Treves. 1968.
Poesie scelte, edited by Luigi Baldacci. 1974.
Poesie e prose scelte, edited by Aulo Greco. 1974.
Poesie, edited by Giorgio Barberi Squarotti. 1978.
Poesie, edited by Guido Davico Bonino. 1980.

Verse

Rime. 1857; as *Juvenilia* (definitive edition), 1880.
Levia gravia. 1868; definitive edition, 1881.
Poesie: Decennalia, Levia Gravia, Juvenilia. 1871; revised edition, 1875.
Primavere elleniche. 1872.

Nuove poesie. 1873.
Odi barbare. 3 vols., 1877–89; in 2 vols., 1893; edited by M. Valgimigli, 1959, and Gianni A. Papini, 1988; parts translated in *Poems*, 1907, and by J.E. Watson as *To the Sources of the Clitumnus*, 1912; as *The Barbarian Odes*, translated by William Fletcher Smith, 1939, revised (bilingual edition), 1950.
Il canto dell'amore. 1878.
Satana e polemiche sataniche. 1879.
Giambi ed Epodi. 1882; edited by E. Palmieri, 1959.
Ça ira. 1883.
Rime nuove. 1887; edited by P.P. Trompeo and G.B. Salinari, 1961; parts translated in *Poems*, 1907; as *Rime nuove*, translated by Laura Fullerton Gilbert, 1916; as *The New Lyrics*, translated by William Fletcher Smith, 1942.
Poems, translated by Frank Sewall. 1892.
La chiesa di Polenta. 1897.
Rime e ritmi. 1899; edited by M. Valgimigli and G.B. Salinari, 1964; parts translated in *Poems*, 1907; as *The Lyrics and Rhythms*, translated by William Fletcher Smith, 1942.
Poesie, edited by Carducci. 1901.
Poems of Italy, translated by M.W. Arms. 1906.
Poems (selections), translated by Maud Holland. 1907.
Carducci: A Selection of His Poems, translated by G.L. Bickersteth. 1913.
A Selection from the Poems, translated by Emily A. Tribe. 1921.
From the Poems of Giosuè Carducci, translated by Romilda Rendel. 1929.
Political and Satirical Verse, translated by William Fletcher Smith. 1942.
24 Sonnets, translated by Arthur Burkhard (bilingual edition). 1947.

Other

Studi letterari. 1874.
Delle poesie latine edite ed inedite di L. Ariosto. 1875; as *La gioventù di L. Ariosto e le sue poesie latine*, 1881.
Ai parentali di Giovanni Boccaccio in Certaldo. 1876.
Bozzetti critici e discorsi letterari. 1876.
Confessioni e battaglie. 3 vols., 1882–84.
Eterno femminino regale: Dalle mie memorie. 1882.
Conversazioni critiche. 1884.
Petrarca e Boccaccio. 1884.
Il libro delle prefazioni. 1888.
L'opera di Dante: Discorso. 1888; as *Dante's Work*, translated by Gina Dogliotti, 1923.
Lo studio bolognese: Discorso. 1888.
La libertà perpetua di San Marino. 1894.
Degli spiriti e delle forme nella poesia di Giacomo Leopardi: Considerazioni. 1898.
Discorsi letterari e storici. 1899.
Da un carteggio inedito (letters to Countess Silvia Pasolini-Zanelli). 1907.
Antologia carducciana: Poesie e prose, edited by Guido Mazzoni and Giuseppe Picciola. 1908; several subsequent editions.
Lettere, edited by Alberto Dallolio and Guido Mazzoni. 2 vols., 1911–13.
Pagine di storia letteraria (selection), edited by G. Lipparini. 1913.
Pagine autobiografiche, edited by G. Lipparini. 1914.
Prose scelte, edited by L. Bianchi and P. Nediani. 1935.
Lettere (supplement to *Opere*). 21 vols., 1938–60.

Il Carducci (selection), edited by F. Selmi. 1965.

Prose e poesie, edited by G. Getto and Guido Davico Bonino. 1965.

Poesie e prose scelte, edited by M. Fubini and R. Ceserani. 1968.

Lettere scelte, edited by G. Ponte and F. De Nicola. 1985.

Prose critiche, edited by Giovanni Falaschi. 1987.

Editor, *Satire e poesie minori*, by V. Alfieri. 1858.

Editor, *La secchia rapita e l'Oceano*, by A. Tassoni. 1858.

Editor, *Poesie minori*, by G. Parini. 1858.

Editor, *Poesie liriche*, by V. Monti. 1858.

Editor, *Del Principe e delle lettere con altre prose*, by V. Alfieri. 1859.

Editor, *Poesie di Lorenzo de' Medici*. 1859.

Editor, *Poesie di G. Giusti*. 1859.

Editor, *Satire odi e lettere di S. Rosa*. 1860.

Editor, *Poesie di Gabriele Rossetti*. 1861.

Editor, *Rime di M. Cino da Pistoia e d'altri del Secolo XIV*. 1862.

Editor, *Canti e poemi di V. Monti*. 1862.

Editor, *Le Stanze l'Orfeo e le Rime di Messer A. Ambrogini Poliziano*. 1863.

Editor, *Di T. Lucrezio Caro Della natura delle cose Libri VI volgarizzati da A. Marchetti*. 1864.

Editor, *Tragedie drammi e cantate di V. Monti*. 1865.

Editor, *Rime di Matteo e di Dino Frescobaldi*. 1866.

Editor, *Poeti erotici del Sec. XVIII*. 1868.

Editor, *Versioni poetiche di V. Monti*. 1869.

Editor, *Lirica del Sec. XVII*. 1871.

Editor, *Cantilene e ballate, strambotti e madrigali nei secoli XIII e XIV*. 1871.

Editor, *Satire, rime e lettere scelte*, by B. Menzini. 1874.

Editor, *Rime di F. Petrarca sopra argomenti storici morali e diversi*. 1876.

Editor, *Strambotti e rispetti dei secoli XIV, XV e XVI*. 1877.

Editor, *Lettere*, by F.D. Guerrazzi. 2 vols., 1880–82.

Editor, *La poesia barbara nei secoli XV e XVI*. 1881.

Editor, *G. Garibaldi: Versi e prose*. 1882.

Editor, with U. Brilli, *Letture italiane*. 1883.

Editor, *Lettere disperse e inedite di Pietro Metastasio*. 1883.

Editor, *Scelte poesie di V. Monti, con le varie lezioni*. 1885.

Editor, *Cacce in rima dei secoli XIV, XV*. 1896.

Editor, *Letture del Risorgimento italiano*. 2 vols., 1896–97.

Editor, with S. Ferrari, *Le rime di Francesco Petrarca di su gli originali*. 1899.

Editor, with others, *Raccolta degli storici italiani dal 500 al 1500 ordinata da L.A. Muratori*. 1900.

Editor, *Scritti politici*, by A. Mario. 1901.

Editor, *Scritti letterari e artistici*, by A. Mario. 1901.

Editor, *Primavera e fiore della lirica italiana*. 1903.

Editor, *Carlo Goldoni: Sonetti*. 1903.

Editor, *Giuseppe Monti: Epodo . . .: Documenti storici*. 1904.

Illustrator, *Della Scelta di curiosità letterarie inedite o rare illustrazione*. 1863.

*

Bibliography: *A Bibliography of Critical Material (1859–1940) on Giosue Carducci* by William Fletcher Smith, 1942.

Critical Studies: *Giosuè Carducci* (in English) by Orlo Williams, 1914; *L'uomo Carducci* by G. Papini, 1918; *Giosuè Carducci: Studio intorno alla critica e alla lirica carducciana* by E. Palmieri, 1926; *Giosuè Carducci: L'uomo e il poeta* by G. Petronio, 1930; *L'opera critica di Giosuè Carducci* by D. Mattalia, 1934; *I giorni e le opere di Giosuè Carducci* by Giulio Natali, 1935, reprinted as *Giosuè Carducci*, 1950; *Giosuè Carducci: Studio critico* by Benedetto Croce, 1937; *Carducci: His Critics and Translators in England and America 1881–1932* by S.E. Scalia, 1937; *La prosa di Giosuè Carducci* by A. Cerea, 1957; *Carducci senza retorica* by L. Russo, 1957; *Giosuè Carducci: L'uomo, il poeta, il critico e il prosatore* by N. Busetto, 1958; *Il grande Carducci* by F. Giannessi, 1958; *La poesie e la prosa di Giosuè Carducci* by Francesco Flora, 1959; *Discorsi nel cinqantenario della morte di Giosuè Carducci* by various authors, 1959; *Il poeta della Terza Italia: Vita di Giosuè Carducci* by M. Biagini, 1961; *Carducci nelle lettere* by R. Bruscagli, 1973; *Carducci* (survey of criticism) by Giorgio Santangelo, 1973; *Per una lettura storica di Carducci* by F. Mattesini, 1975; *Carducci poeta barbaro* by Franco Robecchi, 1981; 'The Mixed Blessings of Tradition: An Examination of Carducci's "Idillio maremmano"' by Remo Catani, in *The Italian Lyric Tradition*, 1993.

*   *   *

Giosuè Carducci's critical fortune has swung sharply from inordinate veneration to out-and-out rejection. With the passing of the historical and political circumstances of a recently united Italy, which had assured the fame of Carducci's patriotic compositions, he came to be regarded as rhetorical, outdated, and of doubtful creative ability. This view has, however, been moderately redressed in recent decades through a quiet appreciation of more intimate aspects of his writings.

His reputation owes much to a vast output of critical, occasional, and epistolary prose, but his contribution to creative literature is his verse. The collections, as definitively established by Carducci himself, are the result of a meticulous lifelong process of reordering and reworking. These give the mistaken impression that, after youthful experimentation, a period in which his work had a socio-political orientation was succeeded by a calmer phase, imbued with classical myth, whereas the two aspects in fact co-existed throughout his productive life. The reordering process responds to the desire for a classical ideal of harmony and represents the attempt to transcend a dialectic that sees the poetry of commitment vying with that of aesthetic purity.

The imitative early poems of *Rime* (*Juvenilia*) draw heavily on the classical tradition, but often herald the mature Carducci, both in their robust tone and in the combination of personal sadness (memories of his brother Dante's tragic suicide) and patriotic feeling (support of the house of Savoy in its quest to unify Italy). A similar amalgam can be found in *Levia gravia*, where Carducci finds something of his own voice in the forceful expression of socio-political sentiment and a new-found republicanism, and in the introduction of elegiac and idyllic notes. Important, too, in the evolution of his style, is the controversial 'Inno a Satana' ('Hymn to Satan') of 1863 where, in a vigorous outburst of anti-clerical materialism, he exalts the forces of science, progress, and freedom of thought. His satire and political invective culminate in *Giambi ed Epodi* [Iambs and Epodes], which are classical in form, as the title indicates, but are concerned with contemporary issues and, in part, influenced by Hugo. It can be argued that here Carducci gives vent to his indignation and anti-papal feeling in too strident a voice; yet the collection has been admired by Natalino Sapegno who sees it as the most vital part of the poet's opus.

Carducci's creative peak, however, is generally perceived in the poems of *Rime nuove* (*The New Lyrics*) and parts of *Odi barbare* (*The Barbarian Odes*). While maintaining a thematic mixture, these collections introduce a restrained intimacy, the hallmark of his maturity, in the intense poems of longing, suffering, nostalgia and melancholy, as well as in the more imaginative of the historico-literary compositions. The expression of these feelings is not dissipated in sentimental effusion but translated into rapid movements and sharp visions that have found the approval of even the harshest critics.

Although some poems in *The New Lyrics* are inspired by history (like the 'Ça ira' cycle on the French Revolution), the majority are personal, recalling Carducci's childhood in the Maremma—'Davanti a San Guido' ('In Front of San Guido') —and the death of his son Dante—'Pianto antico' ('Ancient Lament')—or animated by his love for Lina Piva. Many depict the simple attractions of rustic life—'Il bove' ('The Ox') or 'Idillio maremmano' ('Maremman Idyll'). The collection also amply illustrates Carducci's mastery of the sonnet form.

The Barbarian Odes reproduce the rhythm of quantitative classical metre through the 'barbarian' use of the tonic accents of modern Italian. Although this erudite experiment, with its origins in the Renaissance, had little following and now seems idiosyncratic, it was a bold and partially successful attempt to renew Italian verse. But too many odes seem outmoded in their rhetorical exaltation of the values of ancient Rome—'Alle fonti del Clitumno' ('At the Source of the Clitumnus')—in their scholastic idealization of epic and dramatic literature—'Presso l'urna di P.B. Shelley' ('Near P.B. Shelley's Urn')—or in their pedantic examination of the workings of historical Nemesis—'Per la morte di Napoleone Eugenio' ('On the Death of Napoleon Eugene'). Yet the collection is largely redeemed, and the potential of Carducci's innovations revealed, in a few simple odes that present the ancient world as an ideal source of solace, as in 'Fantasia' ('Fantasy'), or which express a universal feeling of melancholy and transience that communicates the *ennui* of the modern psyche, as in 'Alla stazione in una mattina d'autunno' ('At the Station on an Autumn Morning') and 'Nevicata' ('Snowfall').

The later poems collected in *Rime e ritmi* (*The Lyrics and Rhythms*) show a tired Carducci flagging in inspiration, producing commemorative verses that accentuate his academic shortcomings, and they are only occasionally relieved by more felicitous, impressionistic moments.

Although it is often claimed that Carducci's classicism and rhetorical nationalism, which dominated the second half of the 19th century, exerted a regressive influence on Italian culture, isolating it from avant-garde Europe, a total repudiation of Benedetto Croce's fundamental approbation would be extreme. It has nevertheless been argued convincingly that Carducci marks the end of an era, and that the moral basis of his poetry separates him from Giovanni Pascoli and Gabriele D'Annunzio with whom he is traditionally linked. Conversely, one should not disregard the merits of his rigorously traditional aesthetics in the crisis and confusion of post-unification culture. His classicism is polemical: it militates against the excesses of both the late Romantics and the bohemian Scapigliati, and strives for a return to ancient naturalism in the name of lay values and scientific progress. What is more, his poetry was enriched by an assimilation of writers such as Hugo, Heine, and Shelley; and recent critical examination of unpretentious moments of everyday realism and inner feeling has brought out a modern affinity: Carducci emerges, at least in part, not as the national poet of yester-year, but as an elegiac poet of wider appeal, who, while remaining undaunted in his classicism, reveals a Romantic need for the illusion of beauty in the ephemerality of the past.

—Remo Catani

———

CARPENTIER (y Valmont), Alejo. Born in Havana, Cuba, 26 December 1904. Educated at the University of Havana. Married Andrea Esteban. Journalist, Havana, 1921–24; editor, *Carteles* magazine, Havana, 1924–28; director, Foniric Studios, Paris, 1928–39; writer and producer, CMZ radio station, Havana, 1939–41; professor of history of music, Conservatorio Nacional, Havana, 1941–43; lived in Haiti, Europe, the United States, and South America, 1943–59; director, Cuban Publishing House, Havana, 1960–67; cultural attaché, Cuban Embassy, Paris, from 1967. Columnist, *El Nacional*, Caracas; editor, *Imam*, Paris. *Died 24 April 1980.*

PUBLICATIONS

Collection

Obras completas. 9 vols., 1983–86.

Fiction

¡Écue-yamba-Ó!. 1933.
Viaje a la semilla (story). 1944.
El reino de este mundo. 1949; as *The Kingdom of This World*, translated by Harriet de Onís, 1957.
Los pasos perdidos. 1953; as *The Lost Steps*, translated by Harriet de Onís, 1956.
El acoso. 1956; as *The Chase*, translated by Alfred MacAdam, 1989.
Guerra del tiempo: Tres relatos y una novela: El Camino de Santiago, Viaje a la semilla, Semejante a la noche, y El acoso. 1958; as *War of Time* (includes *The Highroad of Saint James*; *Right of Sanctuary*; *Journey Back to the Source*; *Like the Night*; *The Chosen*), translated by Frances Partridge, 1970.
El siglo de las luces. 1962; as *Explosion in a Cathedral*, translated by John Sturrock, 1963.
El derecho de asilo, Dibujos de Marcel Berges (stories). 1972.
Los convidados de plata. 1972.
Concierto barroco. 1974; as *Baroque Concerto*, translated by Asa Zatz, 1991.
El recurso del método. 1974; as *Reasons of State*, translated by Frances Partridge, 1976.
Cuentos (stories). 1976.
La consagración de la primavera. 1978.
El arpa y la sombra. 1979; as *The Harp and the Shadow*, translated by Thomas and Carol Christensen, 1990.

Plays

Yamba-Ó, music by M.F. Gaillard (produced 1928).
La passion noire, music by M.F. Gaillard (produced 1932).

Verse

Dos poemas afrocubanos, music by A. García Caturla. 1929.
Poèmes des Antilles, music by M.F. Gaillard. 1929.

Other

La música en Cuba. 1946.
Tientos y diferencias: Ensayos. 1964.
Literatura y consciencia política en América Latina. 1969.
La ciudad de las columnas (on Havana architecture), photographs by Paolo Gasparini. 1970.
Letra y solfa (articles), edited by Alexis Márquez Rodríguez. 1975.
Crónicas (articles). 1975.
Críticas de arte: 1922–39. 1975.
Razón de ser (lectures). 1976.
Bajo el Signo de la Cibeles: Crónicas sobre España y los españoles, 1925–1937, edited by Julio Rodríguez Puértolas. 1979.
El adjectivo y sus arrugas. 1980.
Ese músico que llevo dentro (selection), edited by Zolla Gómez. 1980.
La novela latinoamericana en vísperas de un nuevo siglo y otros ensayos. 1981.
Ensayos (essays). 1984.
Entrevistas, edited by Virgilio López Lemus. 1985.
Conferencias, edited by Virgilio López Lemus. 1987.

*

Bibliography: *Carpentier: 45 años de trabajo intelectual*, 1966; *Bibliografía de Alejo Carpentier* by Araceli García-Garranza, 1984.

Critical Studies: *Three Authors of Alienation: Bombal, Onetti, Carpentier* by M. Ian Adams, 1975; *Major Cuban Novelists: Innovation and Tradition* by Raymond D. Souza, 1976; *Alejo Carpentier: The Pilgrim at Home* by Roberto González Echevarría, 1977, revised edition, 1990; *Alejo Carpentier and His Early Works* by Frank Janney, 1981; *Carpentier: Los pasos perdidos* (in English) by Verity Smith, 1983; *Alchemy of a Hero: A Comparative Study of the Works of Alejo Carpentier and Mario Vargas Llosa* by Bob M. Tusa, 1983; *Alejo Carpentier* by Donald L. Shaw, 1985; *Myth and History in Caribbean Fiction: Alejo Carpentier, Wilson Harris and Édouard Glissant* by Barbara J. Webb, 1992.

*   *   *

Musicologist, journalist, critic, leader in the Afro-Cuban and vanguardia movements in Cuba in the 1920s, associate of the surrealists in Paris in the 1930s, Alejo Carpentier gave to 20th-century Latin American letters an important critical concept and a distinctive vision of American identity through history. In the prologue to *El reino de este mundo* (*The Kingdom of This World*), Carpentier proposed that there exists 'lo real maravilloso americano' ('marvellous American reality'). A conflation of the vocabulary of surrealism ('marvellous') and the primitivism of the Afro-Cuban movement, the term has, along with 'magic realism', been used to justify and to describe the element of the fantastic so promi-

nent in much Latin American writing of the 20th century. (Among the authors significantly influenced by Carpentier's precept and practice is the Colombian Gabriel García Márquez.) Almost as soon as he had elaborated the concept, however, Carpentier turned in his own work from the marvellous as the impossible and folkloric to the marvellous as the real, perceived by a modern, alienated eye, struck by the incongruity and irreality of what it really sees.

His early works include the first history of Cuban music, a scenario for an Afro-Cuban ballet, poems on Afro-Cuban themes, and a novel, *¡Écue-yamba-Ó!*, which follows a contemporary rural black into the city and through the rites of the santería and ñañigo cults. His second novel was a product of his middle age, and in it he began to redefine the essentially American less as the primitive than as a paradoxical synthesis of times, peoples, cultures, and styles, simultaneously primitive and sophisticated, European, African, and Indian. While his fictions remained conventional in structure, over time he elaborated an allusive, witty, ornately encrusted style, heterogeneous and baroque, itself both original and a synthesis.

Set in Haiti during the period of the French Revolution, *The Kingdom of This World* juxtaposes the effete high culture of Europeans with the primitive powers of their black slaves. Such folkloric impossibilities as taking animal shapes parallel cyclic political metamorphoses in which a black revolution re-enacts and intensifies the white oppression violently thrown off and is in its turn violently replaced by the oppressive rule of mulattoes. In *Los pasos perdidos* (*The Lost Steps*) a modern protagonist is on a search for primitive musical instruments from inauthentic, synthetic Paris through a Latin American city in the grip of a civil war that appears to be a quarrel 'between the Guelphs and the Ghibellines' to the upper reaches of the Orinoco, a journey still further back in time, to 'the roots of life'. In part a parable of Carpentier's own efforts to discover the essential America, the project of modern man's finding himself by losing himself in the primitive is doomed: the journey cannot be made twice.

Thereafter, Carpentier embraced his distinctive vision of Latin America as a place and a history split between its American realities and its European origins and consciousness. A volume of short stories, obsessed with origins, returns, and time, four novels and a fragment, all of the first order, complete an *oeuvre* distinguished by a paradoxical habit of seeing things twice, as past and as present, a multiplication of illusions with artifice as the nature of man, fallen into history, committed to 'Adam's task of naming things'. *El siglo de las luces* (*Explosion in a Cathedral*) returned to the Caribbean to chart once again the betrayals of the French Revolution, but this time from the perspective of the creole bourgeoisie. *El recurso del método* (*Reasons of State*) set an exemplary dictator amid real and fictive personages in Paris in 1913, and followed him back and forth across the Atlantic, never fully at home on either side, until his death in homesick Parisian exile, sometime in the 1940s, with a brief epilogue dated 1972. *Concierto barroco* (*Baroque Concerto*) reached an apotheosis of heterogeneous synthesis as a Mexican and his black servant give Vivaldi a topic for an opera, *Motezuma*, and as the trumpet in Handel's *Messiah* becomes the trumpet of Louis Armstrong, a glorious concert of incongruities in which all is transformed, but nothing is lost. It is a final, fitting paradox that Carpentier, still writing at the age of 76, should have died while at work on a novel celebrating a triumph of the Cuban revolution—in Paris.

—Regina Janes

THE KINGDOM OF THIS WORLD (El reino de este mundo)
Novel by Alejo Carpentier, 1949.

In the now famous prologue to this novel, Carpentier introduced his term, 'lo real maravilloso' ('marvellous reality') as a concept that gives access to a deeper, more authentic understanding of Latin American reality. He criticizes the utterly trivialized images of European surrealism and turns to Latin America in search of a genuinely marvellous essence in its racial, geographical, and historical realities. Carpentier affirms that what is truly magical and mystical can be observed in the primitive vestiges of the New World: the opposition between civilization and barbarism is inverted by him to elevate the authentic power and innocence of nature in opposition to alienated and degraded (European) culture. For Carpentier, surrealism exists in Latin America as a commonplace, everyday aspect of reality; the magical beliefs of primitive religions keep the real marvellous aspect of reality alive. In *The Kingdom of This World*, the author embodies this opposition between magical nature and decadent culture in the virility and vitality of the black slaves who, through their collective faith, always retain their essential links to nature, in contrast to the effeminate and impotent French landowners for whom ritual is an empty gesture.

The novel is set in Haiti during the period of the French Revolution. While it is based faithfully on a series of real historical incidents and figures, the plot is developed in a seemingly chaotic manner and appears to lack unity. In effect, the free flow of the fictionalized events corresponds to the image of history Carpentier wishes to project in this novel, a history whose order comes from a non-linear source. History can be understood as a series of cyclical repetitions: the fall of the French ruling élite in Haiti, the rise and fall of the black dictator Henri Christophe, and the rise at the end of the novel of a new mulatto ruling class (all these narrated from the perspective of a slave named Ti Noel) make it impossible for the reader to conclude that this tale ingenuously pits evil whites against virtuous blacks.

A runaway slave named Mackandal escapes to the mountains, where he builds up his magic powers and begins to send poisonous mushrooms back to the other slaves, who kill livestock and Frenchmen in order to prepare the way for a slave uprising. Mackandal acquires the power to metamorphose into an insect, an animal, or a bird, and his faithful followers believe him to be invulnerable. When he does return finally in human form, he is captured by the French and burned at the stake; the slaves are not at all agitated by the execution, as it is their belief that the African gods have saved him. A second rebellion 20 years later is crushed and followed by fierce repression. Eventually a former cook named Henri Christophe seizes power at the moment of the French Revolution. Christophe's tyrannical and grotesquely Europeanized dynasty, however, comes to resemble the one recently overthrown in France, and the new black dictator ruthlessly exploits his subjects even more harshly than the white settlers ever did, forcing them into an abominable and violent continuation of slavery.

The collapse of Christophe's dynasty occurs and Ti Noel, now an old man, observes the rise of the new mulatto ruling class, as anxious to dominate and exploit forced black labour as all of the leaders, both black and white, who preceded them. Ti Noel transforms himself into a series of creatures in an attempt to understand history and mankind: an ant, toiling endlessly and anonymously; a powerful stallion subject to enslavement at the hands of mankind; a goose, who attempts to enter the aristocratic order of the clan only to be shut out.

The principle of society, Ti Noel discovers, appears to revolve around the eternal recurrence of oppression and exclusion; history repeats itself endlessly, mankind exploits mankind (even those from its own clan), but the old man continues to affirm that human greatness can be discovered in the agonistic and conflictive kingdom of this world. Ti Noel proclaims once more his declaration of war against the new ruling class, in the never-ending cycle of revolution and renovation. He dies at the end of the narrative *or* he is transformed into an old vulture: the final ambiguity reinforces Ti Noel's magical and mystical links to nature as well as his acceptance of the eternal cycle of birth, death, and transmutation.

—Susan Isabel Stein

THE LOST STEPS (Los pasos perdidos)
Novel by Alejo Carpentier, 1953.

Regarded by many critics as Carpentier's most important novel and the one that cemented his fame at the international level, *The Lost Steps* contains autobiographical elements (it parallels the author's experiences in Venezuela in 1947) and depicts as well in its nameless protagonists the general malaise of the post-war intellectual whose struggle against an alienated and inauthentic existence leads him to search for his own lost identity in the jungles of Latin America. It is a tale of the return through time to the lost origins of nature; by the same token, the narrative insists upon the impossibility of such a return to original innocence: the civilized man—the artist-intellectual—can never reclaim such innocence.

The narrator is a composer living in a large, cosmopolitan North American city with his wife Ruth, an actress whom he hardly ever sees. He feels himself to be lost in a dissolute and meaningless existence in which his artistic talents are commercially exploited and all of his friends are pseudo-intellectuals. He bitterly counts himself among them, and seeks escape through alcohol, sex, and self-recrimination. He portrays himself as a man without a country, a culture, or a profession; he resents the alienating, lonely life of the city and longs to be a different man with a different destiny. Nevertheless, his idealized yearning for an authentic existence and homeland is continually undermined by the facility with which he indulges in the behaviour he portrays as dissolute: he has no respect whatsoever for his French mistress, Mouche, but he cannot leave her bed. He sees himself as Sisyphus, condemned to a futility against which he cannot rebel.

The narrator accepts a commission from an old friend, the Curator, to go on an expedition into the jungles of Orinoco in search of primitive musical instruments, a trip that will offer him the opportunity to escape from his meaningless life and thereby rid himself of the guilt he suffers for having prostituted his talents. He is accompanied by Mouche, a vulgar woman who cannot withstand the harsh environment of the tropics and falls ill; the narrator has meanwhile fallen in love with a native woman named Rosario and abandons Mouche in order to join with his new lover and a band of travellers seeking to found their own city in the virgin interior. He is transformed once he leaves Mouche, the last vestige of his previous life, behind, and commits himself to Rosario; a striking contrast is established between his appetites and desires in the city as apposed to his basic needs in the jungle, where he grows lean, contented, and healthy on hard work, simple food, and Rosario's love.

When the travellers reach Santa Mónica de los Venados, the new city, the narrator perceives it as situated in the world of Genesis: he has travelled back to the origins of time. He decides never to return to the city, but he also discovers the urge to compose a threnody in the jungle, which makes the irony of his situation complete: he must return to civilization in order to obtain paper on which to compose his masterpiece, inspired by his escape from his previous existence! When a two-man search party arrives at Santa Mónica de los Venados, the narrator accompanies them back to the city, assuring Rosario he will return; she, however, turns away from him coldly, knowing he will not return. In the city, he becomes embroiled in a nasty divorce from his wife, and when, many months later, he does attempt to return to Rosario, he cannot find the secret opening in the jungle leading back to Santa Mónica de los Venados. The artist-intellectual is left, at the end of the narrative, to face a destiny and responsibility he cannot escape. He admits to himself that the creative act achieves nothing in a vacuum, and that he must affirm his legitimate place within the artistic community.

The narrative elements retrace the steps to a paradise lost and a reality regained. The contrasts between culture and nature, alienation and authentic existence, lust and love, the narrator's digressions on Romantic art, the horror and alienation of the 20th century, and his perception of the voyage he makes as a journey back through time to lost origins, are all woven together to form a reflection of the cosmopolitan artist's dilemma. His attempts to synthesize the reality of the culture he must be a part of with his longing for a lost innocence or lack of consciousness reinforce the fact that the artistic endeavour itself is as close as he will ever come to this lost utopian existence.

—Susan Isabel Stein

CASSOLA, Carlo. Born in Rome, Italy, 17 March 1917. Educated at the University of Rome, 1935–39, degree in law 1939. Military service in Spoleto, 1937. Married Giuseppina Rabage, one daughter. Journalist after World War II; lived in Grosseto, Tuscany, from 1950, where he was a teacher of history and philosophy; contributor, *Il Contemporaneo*, *Il Mondo*, *Nuovi Argomenti*, and other publications. Recipient: Prato prize, 1955; Salento prize, 1958; Marzotto prize, 1959; Strega prize, 1960; Naples prize, 1970; Bancarella prize, 1976; Bagutta prize, 1978. *Died 29 January 1987.*

PUBLICATIONS

Fiction

Alla periferia (stories). 1942.
La visita (stories). 1942; enlarged edition (includes *Alla periferia*), 1962.
Fausto e Anna. 1952; revised edition, 1958; as *Fausto and Anna*, translated by Isabel Quigly, 1960.
I vecchi compagni. 1953.
Il taglio del bosco (stories). 1954; edited by Tom O'Neill, 1970; as *The Cutting of the Woods*, translated by Raymond

Rosenthal, in *Six Modern Italian Novellas*, edited by William Arrowsmith, 1964.
La casa di via Valadier. 1956.
Un matrimonio del dopoguerra. 1957.
Il soldato. 1958.
La ragazza di Bube. 1960; as *Bebo's Girl*, translated by Marguerite Waldman, 1962.
Un cuore arido. 1961; as *An Arid Heart*, translated by William Weaver, 1964.
Il cacciatore. 1964.
Tempi memorabili. 1966.
Storia di Ada (includes *La maestra*). 1967.
Il soldato e Rosa Gagliardi. 1967.
Ferrovia locale. 1968.
Una relazione. 1969.
Paura e tristezza. 1970; as *Fear and Sadness*, translated by Peter N. Petroni, in *Portland Review*, Fall–Winter 1981.
Monte Mario. 1973; as *Portrait of Helena*, translated by Sebastian Roberts, 1975.
Gisella. 1974.
Troppo tardi. 1975.
L'antagonista. 1976.
La disavventura. 1977.
L'uomo e il cane. 1977.
Un uomo solo. 1978.
Il superstite. 1978.
Il paradiso degli animali. 1979.
La morale del branco. 1980.
Vita d'artista. 1980.
Ferragosto di morte. 1980.
Il ribelle. 1980.
L'amore tanto per fare. 1981.
La zampa d'oca. 1981.
Gli anni passano. 1982.
Colloquio con le ombre. 1982.
Mio padre. 1983.

Other

Viaggio in Cina. 1956.
I minatori della Maremma, with Luciano Biancardi. 1956.
Poesia e romanzo, with Mario Luzi. 1973.
Fogli di diario. 1974.
Ultima frontiera. 1976.
Il gigante cieco. 1976.
Conversazione su una cultura compromessa, edited by Antonio Cardella. 1977.
La lezione della storia. 1978.
Letteratura e disarmo: Intervista e testi, edited by Domenico Tarizzo. 1978.
Il mondo senza nessuno. 1980.
Il romanzo moderno. 1981.
Cassola racconta (interview), edited by Pietro Poiana. 1981.
La rivoluzione disarmista. 1983.

*

Critical Studies: *Letteratura e ideologia: Bassani, Cassola, Pasolini* by Gian Carlo Ferretti, 1964; *Carlo Cassola* by Rodolfo Macchioni Jodi, 1967, revised edition, 1975; *Carlo Cassola* by Renato Bertacchini, 1977; *Invito all lettura di Cassola* by G. Manacorda, 1981; *Existence as Theme in Carlo Cassola's Fiction* by Peter N. Pedroni, 1985.

* * *

Although born in Rome in 1917, Carlo Cassola chose Tuscany and the Maremma as the background against which he placed much of his early work, including the autobiographical novel *Fausto e Anna* (*Fausto and Anna*), based on his experiences as a partisan in 1944. This choice of a topographical setting that is neither city nor countryside but a twilight zone between the two—it is significant that one of his early works was in fact called *Alla periferia*—provided Cassola with the possibility of exploiting to the full his predilection for an understated, almost colourless style of writing such as that used by Joyce in *Dubliners*, a book that Cassola admitted influenced him profoundly. More significantly, however, the peripheral setting of much of Cassola's early—and best—work underlines his attitude to life and the transformation of life into art. In other words it gives him the possibility of expressing his fascination with a life lived on the margins of society, a life that does not have any precise or easily defined characteristics or outlines. Hence Cassola's adoption, at the beginning of his career, of the word *sublimare* to describe his poetics, which he saw as the translation of the subconscious emotions of the artist into a language that was divested of all overt ideological, ethical, or psychological attributes. This early understated style adopted by Cassola reached its highest point artistically in the short novel *Il taglio del bosco* (*The Cutting of the Woods*), written shortly after the death of his wife.

In the novels published after *The Cutting of the Woods*, and in particular in *Fausto and Anna*, *I vecchi compagni* [The Old Companions], *La casa di via Valadier* [The House in the Via Valadier], and *Un matrimonio del dopoguerra* [A Post-War Marriage], there emerges a rather polemical tone, as the author seeks to investigate the disappointed hopes and aspirations of the partisans. His often ambiguous attitude to the achievements of the Resistance movement as expressed through the dialogue and through the protagonists' attitudes characterizes this second phase of Cassola's writing, and has been criticized by the Italian Left, including such writers as Pier Paolo Pasolini and Giorgio Bassani: when, for instance, the prizewinning *La ragazza di Bube* (Bebo's Girl) was published in 1960.

From 1961 onwards, with the publication of *Un cuore arido* (*An Arid Heart*), Cassola may be said to have returned, more or less, to his early style in which the rhythm of the narration seems to coincide with the rhythm of life itself—the humble, usually uneventful life of unsophisticated characters who nevertheless impart dignity to that life by virtue of their calm and stoical acceptance of the odds against them, mostly of an economic kind. It must be added, however, that it is only in such works as *Ferrovia locale* [Local Railway] that Cassola manages to recapture the high artistic tone of his best work. For the most part, unfortunately, in this last phase, the reader is made increasingly uneasy by a sense of aridity in the lives of Cassola's protagonists—a sense of lost opportunities and in the last analysis, of an inability to live life in any full or meaningful human sense of the term.

—Gabrielle Barfoot

CASTELLANOS, Rosario. Born in Mexico City, Mexico, 25 May 1925. Grew up in Comitán; family moved to Mexico City, 1941, after losing its estate in land reforms. Educated at the National Autonomous University, Mexico City, 1944–50, M.A. in philosophy 1950; University of Madrid, 1950–51. Married Ricardo Guerra in 1958 (divorced); one son. Visited Spain, France, Austria, Italy, the Netherlands, and Germany, 1951; director, Chiapas cultural programmes, 1951–53, and staff member, Institute of Arts and Sciences, both in Tuxtla Gutiérrez; director, El Teatro Guiñol (puppet theatre) for the National Indigenist Institute, San Cristóbal, 1956–59, and toured Chiapas, 1956–58; journalist for various Mexico City newspapers and periodicals, from 1960; press and information director, 1960–66, and professor of comparative literature, 1967–71, National Autonomous University, Mexico City, 1960–66; visiting professor of Latin American literature at the United States universities of Wisconsin, Indiana, and Colorado, all 1967; Mexican ambassador to Israel, Tel Aviv, and lecturer in Mexican literature, Hebrew University, Jerusalem, 1971–74. Recipient: Mexican Critics' award, 1957; Chiapas prize, 1958; Xavier Villaurrutia prize, 1961; Woman of the Year award, Mexico, 1967. *Died 7 August 1974.*

PUBLICATIONS

Collections

A Rosario Castellanos Reader, edited and translated by Maureen Ahern, with others. 1988.
Obras, edited by Eduardo Mejía. 1989.
Another Way To Be: Selected Works (poetry, essays, stories), edited and translated by Myralyn F. Allgood. 1990.

Fiction

Balún Canán. 1957; as *The Nine Guardians*, translated by Irene Nicholson, 1959.
Ciudad Real: Cuentos (stories). 1960; as *The City of Kings*, edited by Yvette E. Miller, translated by Gloria Chacon de Arjona and Robert S. Rudder, 1993.
Oficio de tinieblas. 1962; fragment as *Office of Tenebrae*, translated by Anne and Christopher Fremantle, in *Latin American Literature Today*, 1977.
Los convidados de agosto (stories). 1964.
Álbum de familia (stories). 1971.

Verse

Trayectoria del polvo. 1948.
Apuntes para una declaración de fe. 1948.
De la vigilia estéril. 1950.
Dos poemas. 1950.
Presentación al templo: Poemas (Madrid, 1951), with *El rescate del mundo*. 1952.
Poemas 1953–1955. 1957.
Al pie de la letra. 1959.
Salomé y Judith: Poemas dramáticos. 1959.
Lívida luz. 1960.
Materia memorable (verse and essays). 1969.
Poesía no eres tú: Obra poética 1948–1971. 1972.
Looking at the Mona Lisa, translated by Maureen Ahern. 1981.
Bella dama sin piedad y otros poemas. 1984.
Meditación en el umbral: Antología poética, edited by Julian Palley. 1985; as *Meditation on the Threshold* (bilingual edition), translated by Palley, 1988.

Selected Poems (bilingual edition), edited by Cecilia Vicuña and Magda Bogin, translated by Bogin. 1988.

Plays

Tablero de damas: Pieza en un acto. In *América: Revista Antológica*, 68, 1952.
El eterno femenino. 1975; as *Just Like a Woman*, translated by V.M. Bouvier, 1984; as *The Eternal Feminine*, in *A Rosario Castellanos Reader*, 1988.

Other

Sobre cultura femenina (essays). 1950.
La novela mexicana contemporánea y su valor testimonial. 1965.
Rostros de México, photographs by Bernice Kolko. 1966.
Juicios sumarios: Ensayos. 1966; revised edition, as *Juicios sumarios: Ensayos sobre literatura*, 2 vols., 1984.
Mujer que sabe latín (criticism). 1973.
El uso de la palabra (essays), edited by J.E. Pacheco. 1974.
El mar y sus pescaditos (criticism). 1975.

*

Bibliography: 'Rosario Castellanos (1925–1974) by Maureen Aherne, in *Spanish American Women Writers*, edited by Diane E. Marting, 1990; 'Rosario Castellanos' in *Mexican Literature: A Bibliography of Secondary Sources* by William David Foster, 1992 (2nd edition).

Critical Studies: *Rosario Castellanos: Biografía y novelística* by Rhoda Dybvig, 1965; *La obra poética de Rosario Castellanos* by Víctor N. Baptiste, 1972; *Rosario Castellanos* by Beatriz Reyes Nevares, 1976; 'Images of Women in Castellanos' Prose' by Phyllis Rodríguez-Peralta, in *Latin American Literary Review*, 6, 1977; 'Women and Feminism in the Works of Rosario Castellanos' by Beth Miller, in *Feminist Criticism: Essays on Theory, Poetry, and Prose*, edited by Cheryl L. Brown and Karen Olson, 1978; *El universo poético de Rosario Castellanos* by Germaine Calderón, 1979; *Homenaje a Rosario Castellanos* edited by Maureen Ahern and Mary Seale Vásquez, 1980; 'Point of View in Selected Poems by Rosario Castellanos' by Esther W. Nelson, in *Revista/Review Interamericana*, 12(1), 1982; 'Women in the Work of Rosario Castellanos' by Claire Tron de Bouchony, in *Cultures*, 8(3), 1982; 'Rosario Castellanos and the Structures of Power' by Helene M. Anderson, in *Contemporary Women Authors of Latin America: Introductory Essays*, 1983; *Rosario* by Oscar Bonifaz Caballero, 1984, as *Remembering Rosario: A Personal Glimpse into the Life and Works*, translated by Myralyn F. Allgood, 1990; '*Balún-Canán*: A Model Demonstration of Discourse as Power', in *Revista de Estudios Hispánicos*, 19(3), 1985, and 'Onomastics and Thematics in *Balún-Canán*', in *Literary Onomastic Studies*, 13, 1986, both by Sandra Messinger Cypress; 'The Function of Interiorization in *Oficio de tinieblas*' by Frank R. Dorward, in *Neophilologus*, 69, 1985; *The Double Strand: Five Contemporary Mexican Poets* by Frank N. Dauster, 1987; 'Toward the Ransom of Eve: Myth and History in the Poetry of Rosario Castellanos' by N. Mandlove, in *Retrospect: Essays on Latin American Literature* edited by E.S. and T.J. Rogers, 1987; *Lives on the Line: The Testimony of Contemporary Latin American Authors* edited by Doris Meyer, 1988; *Women's Voice* by Naomi Lindstrom, 1989; 'Rosario Castellanos:

Demythification through Laughter' by Nina M. Scott, in *Humor*, 2(1), 1989; 'Confronting Myths of Oppression: The Short Stories of Castellanos' by Chloe Funival, in *Knives and Angels* edited by Susan Bassnett, 1990.

* * *

In 'If Not Poetry, Then What?' Rosario Castellanos identifies three points she considers cardinal in her writing: 'humour, solemn meditation, and contact with my carnal and historical roots'. Her complete works give evidence that she kept these points in mind. Her historical and carnal roots are most evident in 'El hombre del destino' ('Man of Destiny'), an essay about Lázaro Cárdenas (post-revolutionary Mexican president), and in 'Tres nudos en la red' ('Three Knots in the Net') and *Balún Canán* (*The Nine Guardians*), works that chronicle fictionally her family's adjustment to the loss of their properties when Cárdenas's administration implemented agrarian reform. In fact, most of her writing is intimately bound to her biography, reflecting from her personal perspective events and conditions around her. A preferred mode of approach to 'solemn meditation' in her writing is through a domestic vignette which then yields to thoughtful reflection. Humour in her writing takes the form of irony.

In Castellanos's works, significant thematic unity exists across genres. Themes in her essays (weekly newspaper columns written for several Mexico City newspapers) such as social inequality, injustice, and feminist thought, along with a sense of personal isolation and an almost obsessive concern with death, are echoed in her novels, short stories, theatre, and, especially, poetry.

Her early fiction portrays the lives of contemporary Indians in her native state of Chiapas, defining the people's existence in terms of their history and mythology and the relation to, and contrast with, the history and mythology of Creole society. Castellanos's Indians are neither Romanticism's 'noble savages' nor the positive pole of the Manichean opposition (good Indian victim/evil Creole oppressor) of the Indigenist movement. Her Indian characters seem authentic because they emerge from her first-hand observation of, and personal contact with, the Tzotzil-Tzeltal Indians of Chiapas. Her recognition of the unequal status of Indians in relation to Creoles is evident in 'La suerte de Teodoro Méndez Acubal' ('The Luck of Teodoro Méndez Acubal'). Inequality of status and the tragedy to which it often leads are explored in her essays such as 'Discriminación en Estados Unidos y en Chiapas' ('Discrimination in the United States and in Chiapas'), her novels (*The Nine Guardians* and *Oficio de tinieblas*—a fragment of which has been translated as *Office of Tenebrae*), and many of her short stories.

Oficio de tinieblas provides a bridge between her advocacy of the Indian and her focus on women from a feminist perspective. The protagonist is deemed inferior by both Indians and Creoles because she is a woman, an Indian, and barren. However, by mastering the healing arts, she becomes a leader in her community and catalyses actions that lead to an Indian boy's expiatory crucifixion. Castellanos's concern for the Indians oppressed by Chiapas's feudal society yields to probing examinations of the subordinate status of all women in that society. The questions of the subjugation of women—who are expected to be 'under a man's hand', 'be it her father's, her brother's, her husband's, or her priest's'—and of masculine honour, which depends upon the behaviour of women, are given fictional form in many of her short stories, notably 'El viudo Román' ('The Widower Román'), 'El advenimiento del águila' ('The Eagle'), and 'Las amistades efímeras' ('Fleeting Friendships'). An evolution from Rosario's concepts of woman's inherent intellectual inferiority expressed in *Sobre cultura femenina* [On Feminine Culture], to feminist conviction is easily discernible. She labours to raise the consciousness of her contemporaries, pointing out inequalities between the sexes in Mexico, yet insisting (as in 'Self-Sacrifice Is a Mad Virtue') that Mexican women have no right to complain about their subordinate status because they remain subjugated by choice in their failure to avail themselves of 'what the constitution gives them: the category of human being'.

Castellanos's theatrical works include two long dramatic poems and a play. *El eterno femenino (The Eternal Feminine)*, despite its ironic humour, is a serious work, which deserves to be regarded as the pinnacle of her feminist writings. Using a double stage, Castellanos criticizes the reality of contemporary Mexican women as they play the roles dictated by the present-day myths of innocent bride, self-sacrificing wife, fulfilled mother, emancipated woman, mistress, and prostitute, while simultaneously re-creating more authentic portraits of historical women long ago rendered into myths in Mexico: Eve, Sor Juana Inés de la Cruz, the Empress Carlotta, Malinche (Cortés's Indian mistress/translator), and so on.

Women's alienation and their oppression in contemporary urban life is the thread that runs through the short stories of *Los convidados de agosto* [The Guests of August] and *Álbum de familia* [Family Album]. The best known of these is 'Lección de cocina' ('Cookery Lesson') a story that alternates the preparation of a meat recipe with acerbic comments on the life of a new bride.

A consummate poet, Castellanos once acknowledged that she 'came to poetry after discovering that other roads were not viable for survival'; that for her, 'the words of poetry constituted the only way to achieve permanence in this world'. Still, in 'An Attempt at Self-Criticism', she admits that it was not until 1950 that she 'was beginning to discover [her] individuality and validity which, in poetry, has to express the moods of the soul'. But discover it she did: her poems have unequivocally a woman's poetic voice. She speaks directly and intimately to her women readers about their isolation and the constraints that have limited their lives. By defamiliarizing the feminine context, she makes it, and its inequalities, visible, and leads her readers in the search for another way of being female, as she says in 'Meditación en el umbral' ('Meditation on the Brink'), one 'que no se llame Safo/ni Mesalina ni María Egipciaca/ni Magdalena ni Clemencia Isaura' ('that's not named Sappho/or Messalina or Mary of Egypt/or Magdalene or Clémence Isaure').

Both in her early works expressing concern for the Indian's unjust existence in Chiapas and in her later writings about woman's inequitable situation in the world, Castellanos acknowledged 'the other' and attempted to span the space of alienation with her poetic words.

—Oralia Preble-Niemi

CASTIGLIONE, Baldassarre [or Baldesar]. Born in Casatico, territory of Mantua, 6 December 1478. Studied Latin and Greek at the school of Giorgio Merula and Demetrio Calcondila, Milan, early 1490s. Married Ippolita Torelli in 1516 (died 1520); one son and two daughters. Attended the Court of Ludovico Sforza ('il Moro') in Milan, c.1494–99; returned to Mantua, 1499, and entered service of the French-sponsored Francesco Gonzaga, ruler of Mantua, as diplomat and military commissioner: participated in the Battle of Garigliano against the Spanish-controlled Viceroyalty of Naples, 1503; entered the service of Guidobaldo di Montefeltro, Duke of Urbino, and his wife Elisabetta, 1504: commanded 50 men-at-arms to recapture lost territory for Urbino, 1504; travelled to England to receive the Order of the Garter from Henry VII, 1506; ambassador in Milan, 1507; on death of Guidobaldo, 1508, continued service with his successor, Francesco Maria, nephew of Pope Julius II; participated with papal forces in the Romagna campaign against Venice, 1509, the siege of Mirandola, 1511, and the reconquest of Romagna and Emilia after the Battle of Ravenna, 1512; wrote the prologue for *La calandria* by Dovizi da Bibbiena, *q.v.*, 1513; ambassador in Rome on the death of Julius II and election of Leo X, 1513; received the castle of Novilara for his diplomatic and literary services, 1513, but settled in Rome as ambassador, 1514–16; followed Francesco Maria into exile in Mantua after the conquest of Urbino by papal forces, 1516; re-established stable relations between Rome and Mantua, 1519; resettled in Rome, 1520, and remained in the service of Rome and Mantua, 1520–24; neutral broker between Milan, France, and Spain to decide the fate of Lombardy, 1524; nuncio for Pope Clement VII at the Court of Emperor Charles V, Madrid, 1525–29. *Died in 1529.*

PUBLICATIONS

Collections

Opere volgari e latine, edited by G.A. and G. Volpi. 1733.
Opere di Baldassarre Castiglione e Giovanni Della Casa, edited by G. Prezzolini. 1937.
Il libro del cortegiano con una scelta delle opere minori, edited by Bruno Maier. 1955; second edition, 1964; third, supplemented edition, 1981.
Opere di Baldassarre Castiglione, Giovanni della Casa, Benvenuto Cellini, edited by Carlo Cordié. 1960.

Prose

Il libro del cortegiano. 1528; edited by Vittorio Cian, 1894, revised editions, 1910, 1929, and 1947, also edited by G. Preti, 1960, Ettore Bonora, 1972, Salvator Battaglia, 1988, and Carlo Cordié, 1991; as *The Book of the Courtier*, translated by Sir Thomas Hoby, 1561, reprinted 1974; also translated by Robert Samber, 1724; Leonard Eckstein, 1901; Charles Singleton, 1959; George Bull, 1967.

Plays

Il tirsi, with Cesare Gonzaga (produced 1506). 1553; edited by F. Torraca, in *Teatro italiano dei seccoli XII–XV*, 1885.

Other

L'epistola ad regem Henricum de Guidubaldo Urbini duce. 1513.

Lettere (includes the Latin poetry and vernacular works). 2 vols., 1769–71.

Lettere inedite o rari, edited by G. Gorini. 1969.

Tutte le opere: Lettere, edited by Guido La Rocca. 1978.

*

Bibliography: 'Studi sul Castiglione' by G.G. Ferrero, in *Rivista di Sintesi Letterari*, II, 1935.

Critical Studies: *Baldassarre Castiglione, the Perfect Courtier: His Life and Letters* by Julia Cartwright, 2 vols., 1908; *Baldassarre Castiglione* by G. Bongiovanni, 1929; *Baldassarre Castiglione: Il cortegiano, il letterato, il politico* by A. Vicinelli, 1931; *La lingua di Baldassarre Castiglione*, 1942, and *Un illustre nunzio pontificio del Rinascimento: Baldassarre Castiglione*, 1951, both by Vittorio Cian; *Baldassarre Castiglione: La sua personalità; la sua prosa* by Mario Rossi, 1946; *Il Cortegiano nella trattatistica del Rinascimento* by G. Toffanin, 1962; *La seconda redazione del Cortegiano di Baldassare Castiglione* edited by Ghino Ghinassi, 1968; *Courtly Performances: Masking and Festivity in Castiglione's Book of the Courtier* by Wayne A. Rebhorn, 1978; *La misura e la grazia sul Libro del cortegiano* by Antonio Gagliardi, 1989; *The Economy of Human Relations: Castiglione's Libro del Cortegiano* by Joseph D. Falvo, 1992.

*   *   *

Combining a noble upbringing with a humanistic education, Baldassare Castiglione's life—as a soldier, diplomat, courtier, and papal legate—never gave him the freedom to develop a literary career in the generation of Bembo, Ariosto, and Machiavelli, and gave rise to his *Il libro del cortegiano* (*The Book of the Courtier*) for which he is best remembered, as well as an eclogue, *Il tirsi*, and Latin and Italian verses. He is also remembered for a production at Urbino in 1513 of Bibbiena's comedy, *La Calandria* (*The Follies of Calandro*), for which it was long held that he had written a prologue.

The genesis of *The Book of the Courtier* took place at, and the work was modelled on, the court of Urbino under Francesco Gonzaga, where Castiglione resided between 1504 and 1513, though it is really more of a nostalgic memoir of the rule of Frederico da Montefeltro some years before. This exposition of the qualities of the ideal courtier, the archetype and model for many treatises on behaviour and books of manners that were to follow, was circulated among scholars for suggestions, debate, and corrections from the time of its inception in 1507–08 until publication in 1528, and translated the Ciceronian idea of the perfect orator (*De Oratore*) into the Renaissance concept of a manual and formula for the perfectibility of the gentleman (and lady) at court. Others had written treatises for the perfect cardinal (Cortese) and the perfect prince (Machiavelli). Yet the realism of Machiavelli's *Il principe* (*The Prince*) contrasted starkly with the idealism of Castiglione's *The Book of the Courtier*: like the theoretical writings on language by Bembo, the latter was a refined and cultivated literary ideal, based as much on cultural antecedents and tradition as on observed experience at the court of Urbino. Castiglione's treatise provided a model for the educated and cultivated gentleman at court (the basic social structure for the power base and government of many European states, and most, though not all, of the Italian states in the Renaissance period) and projected into the arena of politics and government the idea of the polymath, an educated ideal of the multi-talented humanist, an ideal that has had a measurable impact on subsequent educational systems. All this was articulated as the ideal in spite of the traditional clash of interests between the form of the principality as an absolutist state and the freedom of an artist's creativity, enshrined in the complaints of writers from Ariosto to Tasso (and projected by the iconoclasm or anti-classicism of satirists like Aretino), which began in Castiglione's own generation and continued long after him. By 1525, Castiglione's refined ideal courtier had its antidote in the satire of the papal court in Aretino's courtesan (*La cortigiana*), since, as noted, the book had been widely read long before its official publication.

The Book of the Courtier identifies the qualities a successful courtier should possess, from the martial arts to artistic flair in poetry and music, from *sprezzatura* (an effortless gracefulness in accomplishments that eschews the boastful and arrogant) to a finely developed aesthetic sense. Already we have the formula for a gentleman which was to be widely influential. But the gentleman must have his mate, and the *donna di palazzo* is given similar arts and graces (and similar artfulness and gracefulness) in the work, and a notable equality with man that is in tune with the prominence of women (as warriors, as poetesses, as governors) in the society of Ariosto and Castiglione. On the appropriate language for discourse (as opposed to writing) Castiglione is more pragmatic than Bembo is in *Le prose della volgar lingua*, since usage is admitted as arbiter, though in the conclusion to *The Book of the Courtier* the supremacy of the Platonic ideals of Ficino is given to Bembo to expound. In broadest outline then, *The Book of the Courtier* is a discussion between Castiglione's authoritative contemporaries, and roughly approximates to the three ages of man: youth, maturity, and old age. The first part, from Ludoviso di Canossa and Federico Fregoso, represents the earthly and humanistic courtier; the second, from Ottaviano Fregoso, projects the ideal courtier as wise counsellor to the prince; whereas the third proposes the sublimation of love into the metaphysical Neoplatonic philosophy of Ficino, through the mouth of Pietro Bembo.

Politically, of course, *The Book of the Courtier* had to favour the form of a principality, for this is its explicit frame of reference; but the work does not blind itself to other possibilities, and contemporary 'mixed' forms of government (from Machiavelli in the most recent exposition) find their way in with election of councils of nobles and the people, even if, with the image of Duke Federico da Montefeltro in the background as memory and inspiration, the figure of the prince is benignly paternalistic, caring, civilizing, and morally upright—at some remove, therefore, from the opportunism and pragmatism of the Machiavellian idea. As a window on the world of the Italian Renaissance—whether escapist fantasy fossilized in an already outdated cultural ideal, or a manual for courtly deportment and a survival package in an age of rapidly changing values—*The Book of the Courtier* has had an enduring influence on educational and political thinking ever since it was written, and seems resolutely contemporary in several of its themes—in man's sense of cultural identity and the function of the arts in his make-up and personal ambitions, in the notion of *mens sana in corpore sano*, and, not least, in the long debate between service (servility) and freedom in politics.

—Christopher Cairns

THE CATTLE RAID OF COOLEY (Táin Bó Cuailnge). Irish prose epic, based on oral tales of the 6th century AD and later, and first written down during the 8th century. The principal surviving manuscript versions are those in the *Lebor na h-Uidre* (*Book of the Dun Cow*) of the late 11th- or early 12th-century (also in the 14th-century *Yellow Book of Lecan*) and the *Lebor na Nuachongbála* (*The Book of Leinster*) of c.1150.

PUBLICATIONS

The Táin Bó Cuailnge. As *Die altirischen Heldensage Tain Bo Cuailnge nach dem Buch von Leinster* (after the *Book of Leinster*), edited by Ernst Windisch (Irish text, with German commentary and translation), 1905; as The *Táin Bó Cuailnge from the Yellow Book of Lecan, with Variant Readings from the Lebor na h-Uidre*, edited by J. Strachan and J.G. O'Keefe, 1912; as *The Stow Version of the Táin Bó Cuailnge*, edited by Cecile O'Rahilly, 1961; as *Táin Bó Cúailnge from the Book of Leinster* (bilingual edition), edited by Cecile O'Rahilly, 1967; as *Táin Bó Cuailnge: Recension I* (after the *Yellow Book of Lecan*), edited by Cecile O'Rahilly, 1976; as *Táin Bó Cúailnge from the Book of the Dun Cow* (bilingual edition), edited by Cecile O'Rahilly, 1978; as *The Cattle Raid of Cuailgne*, translated by Lucy Winifred Faraday, 1904; as *The Ancient Irish Epic Tale Tain Bo Cuailnge*, translated by Joseph Dunn, 1914; as *The Táin*, translated by Thomas Kinsella, 1969.

*

Critical Studies: *The Cuchullin Saga in Irish Literature*, 1898, and *A Text Book of Irish Literature*, Part I, 1923, both by Eleanor Hull; *Die Irische Helden- und Komigsae* by Rudolf Thurneysen, 1921; *The Historical Geography of Early Ireland* by Walter Fitzgerald, 1925; *Early Irish History and Mythology* by T.F. O'Rahilly, 1946; *Early Irish Literature* by Myles Dillon, 1948, and *Irish Sagas* edited by Dillon, 1959; *The Irish Tradition* by Robin Flower, 1948; *Gods and Heroes of the Celts* by Marie Louise Sjoestedt, 1949; *Studies in Irish Literature and History*, 1955, and 'Early Irish Literature: The State of Research', 1979 both by James Carney; *Celtic Heritage* by Alwyn and Brinley Rees, 1961; *The Backward Look—A Survey of Irish Literature* by Frank O'Connor, 1967; *Proceedings of the Sixth International Congress of Celtic Studies* edited by Gearoid Mac Eoin, Anders Alqvist, and Donncha O hAodha, 1983; *Tense and Time in Early Irish Narrative*, by J.L.C. Tristram, 1983; 'Shamanism in the Old Irish Tradition' by P.R. Lonigan, in *Eire*, 20, 1985; 'The Masks of Medb in Celtic Scholarship: A Survey of the Literature Stemming from the Iana' by Arthur Gribben, in *Folklore and Mythology Studies*, 10, 1986; 'The World, The Text and the Critic of Early Irish Heroic Narrative' by Marie Herbert, in *Text & Context: A Journal of Interdisciplinary Studies*, 8, 1988.

* * *

The Cattle Raid of Cooley (*Táin Bó Cuailnge*) is the oldest vernacular epic in Western literature with a lengthy oral existence preceding its first written form in the 8th century. It underwent further elaboration and development until recorded in manuscript forms in the 12th century. From the monastery at Clonmacnoise, *Lebor na h-Uidre* (*Book of the Dun Cow*) provided a fragmentary version of the text, as did the 12th-century *Book of Leinster* and the 14th-century *Yellow Book of Lecan*, and these first two manuscripts are the main extant recensions for contemporary editions and translations.

The Cattle Raid of Cooley, like most narratives of the early Irish period is predominantly prose, but with verse selections. The prose sections drive forward the action, while the verse, called *rosc* and *retoiric*, is reserved for intense moments of emotional or symbolic significance. The language of the poetry, at once classical and archaic, suggests that sections of the work date as far back as the 6th century.

In subject matter, it is thought that the text reflects the culture of a period from the 1st to the 5th centuries AD when a warrior tribe called the Ulaidh controlled the whole of the Northern Kingdom of Ireland, before having to relinquish power. Generically, *The Cattle Raid* belongs to a branch of thematically linked early Irish narratives. Contemporary Celtic scholars have re-classified these thematic categories into broader cycles (Ulster, Fenian, etc) and they identify *The Cattle Raid* as the single most important text within the Ulster cycle. The Ulster cycle reflects a golden, heroic (pre-historic) age where the Ulaidh, led by King Conchobhar Mac Nessa, won fame and advancement through their combative skills and unfailing chivalry.

The plot of *The Cattle Raid of Cooley* involves an attempted foray into the kingdom of Ulster, to steal the magnificent Brown Bull (Donn Cuailnge). Medhbh, the warrior queen of Connacht, incites her army to this act, for she and her husband Ailill have found that they are equal in all other respects but for the white-horned bull (Finnbennach) in Ailill's possession.

Medhbh's depiction in the text suggests that she is a personification of the goddess of sovereignty and of war, and she is undoubtedly first in the list of vividly realized Irish heroines, such as Deirdre, Macha, and Aife. Medhbh's name means literally 'the intoxicating one'. By the end of *The Cattle Raid* her war-drunk followers have been overwhelmed by the Ulaidh, and the white-horned bull of Connacht dismembered by the brown bull of Cooley. This ending has been interpreted mythically as an Irish version of the Indo-European myth of cosmic creation and the overthrow of feminine sovereignty by a patriarchal order. The latter is best expressed by Fergus, a principal warrior in Medhbh's army, who, at the conclusion of text, notes that 'we followed the rump of a misguiding woman . . . it is the usual thing for a herd led by a mare to be strayed and destroyed'.

The cattle raid itself is predominantly the vehicle for a series of heroic episodes. A mysterious sickness afflicts the men of Ulaidh who are incapacitated and thus unable to defend themselves against the Connacht invasion, until the last moment. Meanwhile only one youth, Cu Chulainn, is exempt from this fate, a fact which in itself authorizes his singular status as hero. The body of the text relates his adventures as he succeeds singlehandedly in defending the borders of the kingdom, intercepting and reversing the Connacht army's approach.

The work is without any unifying narrative tone: Cu Chulainn as central hero is the link between loosely knit events and tonal registers ranging from the ribald to the solemnly prophetic. Another major unifying feature of the text, however, is its concern with the topographic. As the invasion into Ulster is successfully resisted by Cu Chulainn, much of the action focuses on the Connacht men's journeying across the land. During this itinerary the etymology of place-names is recounted, to the degree that this activity sometimes seems directive of, rather than incidental to, the plot: Cu Chulainn, ill after battle, is healed by the waters of myriad rivers, the Sas (for ease), the Buan (for steadfastness), and so on; Cethern, his ally, lies wounded, stricken by Medhbh herself—Cu Chulainn provides the remedy, a 'mash' of bone-marrow from slain animals in which the wounded warrior sleeps and is healed, and we are told that from this episode the area known as Smironmair, or 'Bath of Marrow' takes its name; finally, after the triumph of the brown bull over the white, the wounded victor traverses the landscape for the last time, and at each point at which the animal stops to drink or rest retains a name relating to the episode. Thus, *The Cattle Raid* ends with this climax of place-naming and with a peace struck between the forces of Medhbh and the triumphant Ulaidh.

—Sabina Sharkey

CATULLUS. Born Gaius Valerius Catullus, c.84 BC. Father a citizen of Verona; lived in Rome, and probably had a villa near Tivoli; also owned property at Sirmio (now Sirmione); friend of Cicero and other important men; accompanied C. Memmius Gemellus on visit to Bithynia, Asia Minor, 57–56 BC. *Died c.54 BC.*

PUBLICATIONS

Verse

[Verse], edited by R.A.B. Mynors. 1958, revised edition, 1972; also edited by Henry Bardon, 2nd edition, 1973, D.F.S. Thomson, 1978; edited and translated by G.P. Goold, 1983; translated by Frederick A. Wright, 1926; also translated by Jack Lindsay, 1929; Horace Gregory, 1956; Frank Copley, 1957; R.A. Swanson, 1959; C.H. Sisson, 1966; Peter Whigham, 1966; Reney Myers and Robert J. Ormsby, 1972; James Michie, 1972; Frederic Raphael and Kenneth McLeish, 1978; Charles Martin, 1979; Guy Lee, 1990; commentaries by Robinson Ellis, 1876; Elmer T. Merrill, 1893, reprinted 1951; C.J. Fordyce (in part), 1961; Kenneth Quinn, 1970, revised edition, 1973; and J. Ferguson, 1985.

*

Bibliography: *A Bibliography to Catullus* by Hermann Harrauer, 1979; *Gaius Valerius Catullus: A Systematic Bibliography* by James P. Holoka, 1985.

Critical Studies: *Catullus and His Influence* by Karl P. Harrington, 1923; *Catullus in English Poetry* by E.S. Duckett, 1925; *Catullus and Horace: Two Poets in Their Environment* by Frank Tenney, 1928; *Catullus and the Traditions of Ancient Poetry* by A.L. Wheeler, 1934; *Catullus and the Traditions of Ancient Poetry* by E.A. Havelock, 1939, revised edition, 1967; *Catullus in Strange and Distant Britain* by J.A.S. McPeek, 1939; *The Catullan Revolution*, 1959, revised edition, 1969, and *Catullus: An Interpretation*, 1973, both by Kenneth Quinn, and *Approaches to Catullus* edited by Quinn, 1972; *Enarratio Catulliana* by C. Witke, 1968; *Style and Tradition in Catullus* by David O. Ross, Jr, 1969; *Catullan Questions*, 1969, and *Catullus and His World*, 1985, both by T.P. Wiseman; *Studies in Catullan Verse* by Julia W. Loomis, 1972; *Interpreting Catullus* by G.P. Goold, 1974; *Catullus' Indictment of Rome: The Meaning of Catullus 64* by David Konstan, 1977; *Catullan Self-Revelation* by E. Adler, 1981; *Catullus' 'Passer': The Arrangement of the Book of Polymetric Poems* by M.B. Skinner, 1981; *Sexuality in Catullus* by Brian Arkins, 1982; *Three Classical Poets: Sappho, Catullus, and Juvenal* by Richard Jenkyns, 1982; *Catullus 68: An Interpretation* by John Sarkissian, 1983; *Catullus: A Reader's Guide to the Poems* by Stuart P. Small, 1983; *Catullus* by John Ferguson, 1988; *The Student's Catullus* by David H. Garrison, 1989; *The Abhorrence of Love: Studies in Rituals and Mystic Aspects in Catullus' Poem of Attis* by Britt-Mari Näsström, 1989; *Roman Catullus and the Modification of the Alexandrian Sensibility* by J.K. Newman, 1990; *Catullus* by Charles Martin, 1992; *Catullus and His Renaissance Readers* by Julia Haig Gaisser, 1993; *'When the Lamp Is Shattered': Desire and Narrative in Catullus* by Micaela Janan, 1994.

* * *

Catullus' poems are traditionally divided into three distinct groups: the short polymetric poems (1–60), the long poems (61–68), and the epigrams (69–116). Whether this arrangement, and that of the poems within each group, were Catullus' own work is much disputed; some, for example, believe that he intended 65–116 as a group, since they are all written in elegiacs. At present, the weight of scholarly opinion favours the view that at least the majority of the polymetrics were arranged in their present order by the poet, though some interference by a later editor is generally accepted to be evident.

Two types of poem, by virtue of their frequency, dominate the polymetrics and epigrams. First, there are roughly three dozen poems of invective (e.g., 28–29, 39, 69, 71, 94), which very often employ obscene language (incest is a recurrent theme) and of which several are directed at a single target (thus 74, 88–91, 116 against one Gellius). Second, and most famously, there are between two dozen and 30 poems which relate to Catullus' love affair with Lesbia (the exact number is uncertain because she is named explicitly in only 13). This woman ('Lesbia' is a pseudonym) is usually identified with Clodia, the wife of Q. Metellus Celer who was consul in 60 BC and died the following year.

These two main types of poem are interspersed with a refreshing variety of others: e.g., poems on homecoming (4, 9, 31, 46), homosexual love (e.g., 15, 48, 81, 99), his dead brother (101) and the death of a friend's wife (96), and literature (e.g., 35, 50, 95); there are mock hymns (36, 44) and a real hymn (34); and there is *vers de société* (e.g., 10, 12–13, 25, 55, 84, 103), sometimes of a risqué nature (e.g., 6, 32, 56, 110). As for the group of long poems, there are two on weddings (61–62); one (63) on the fanatical cult of the goddess Cybele, depicting the self-castration of her devotee Attis; an epyllion (miniature epic) on the marriage of Peleus and Thetis (64); a translation into Latin of Callimachus' 'Lock of Berenice' (66), together with its epistolary introduction in verse (65); a dialogue with a door (67); another verse letter, on the death of his brother (68A); and an elegy which combines the themes of his brother's death and his love for Lesbia with a complicated series of mythological illustrations (68B) (these last two are written as a single poem in the MSS and are still so regarded by many scholars). Of these long poems, 63 is one of the most remarkable poems in Latin on account of its theme; 64 is the only epyllion which survives from the literature of the late republic and early empire; and 68B is the forerunner of the poetry of Propertius, Tibullus, and Ovid. On these grounds alone, Catullus' work would be significant; but his principal achievement lies elsewhere.

Such long poems as 64, 68, and 68B are characterized above all by the *doctrina* (learning, scholarship) which was dear to the other *novi poetae* (new poets) of Catullus' generation and which was inspired by the work of the Greek librarian-poet Callimachus (fl. 250 BC). Until fairly recently it was often thought that there were, so to speak, 'two Catulluses': the scholar-poet of the long poems, whose obscure and allusive verse was very much an acquired taste; and the simple poet of the polymetrics and epigrams, whose direct and passionate language had impressed centuries of readers. Yet this myth has been exploded by more recent scholarship, which has shown that learning, allusiveness, and technical refinement are not restricted to the long poems but permeate much of the other poetry too. Indeed it is precisely in the area where *doctrina* interacts with the portrayal of emotion that Catullus holds most fascination for the reader who knows Latin and Greek and is prepared to put his knowledge to good use. For it is by no means easy fully to appreciate the poetry written by Callimachus and his followers, and many of Catullus' polymetrics and epigrams require considerable effort for their understanding. Six examples, which appear to reflect his love affair from its beginning to its end, will make this clear.

Poem 51 is an expression of Catullus' love for Lesbia, yet the poem is a translation and adaptation of a famous poem by Sappho (31); and the fact that Catullus has troubled to clarify the meaning of his exemplar suggests that he expected his readers, including Lesbia, to be aware of the problems raised by Sappho's poem and to notice his own view of their solution. Poems 7 and 70 both have a 'twin' (5 and 72 respectively), which suggests that all four poems reflect episodes in the poet's affair and are thus heavily biographical; yet 7 is full of learned allusion to the life and works of Callimachus, quite apart from treating us to a virtuoso display of oral imagery, while 70 is actually an adaptation of an epigram by Callimachus (25), which Catullus has completely transformed. Poem 85 is a two-line epigram of deceptive simplicity; yet its first three words (*Odi et amo*, 'I hate and love') recall a theme which echoes back to the beginnings of Greek personal poetry, and the remainder of the couplet is a superb example of the arrangement and suggestiveness of apparently simple words. Poems 8 and 11 reflect the end of the affair, with all its bitterness; yet the former seems inspired by a soliloquy from the comic playwright Menander's *Samia* (*The Girl from Samos*), and in the latter Catullus finds time to demonstrate his knowledge of the vernacular name for Egypt,

of the original name for the Nile, and of the etymology of the word 'Alps' (we must remember that Callimachus' most famous work was entitled *Origins* and that another work dealt with the foundations of islands and cities and their changes of name).

To the modern reader, these and countless other instances of *doctrina* may seem strange; but it is vital to appreciate that they in no way detract from, but rather enhance, the conviction with which Catullus expresses himself. He achieved that fusion of form and emotion which many believe to be the quintessence of poetry and which has made his work everlastingly memorable.

—A.J. Woodman

POEM 85
Poem by Catullus, mid-1st century BC.

Odi et amo. quare id faciam fortasse requiris?
nescio, sed fieri sentio et excrucior.

(I hate and I love. Why I do that you perhaps are
   asking?
I don't know, but I feel it happening and I'm tortured.)

This is the most famous distich in Latin, to whose unique combination of intense emotion and verbal simplicity no translation does justice. The one given here has deliberately been kept strictly literal and follows the Latin word order almost exactly. An interesting collection of freer and more creative versions, however, with perceptive criticism, is available in *Lines of Enquiry* by Niall Rudd (1976).

The elegiac epigram, a very brief poem, rarely amounting to more than ten lines and often to less, in elegiac couplets (a longer and a shorter line alternating, each basically conforming to a set rhythmic pattern), had a long history before Catullus. Love, and frequently what purports to be the author's own love, was a favourite subject of it in the Hellenistic Greek period (3rd to 1st centuries BC). Ambivalent and conflicting feelings, too, were expressed at times, as in the following poem by Philodemus of Gadara (c.110–c.40/35 BC):

My soul warns me to stop yearning for Heliodora,
acquainted as it is with tears and jealousies past.
It tells me, but I haven't the strength to stop; for she,
   the shameless creature,
warns me herself, and even as she warns is giving me a
   kiss.

For all his profession of mental conflict, Philodemus, in the typical way of the Hellenistic epigrammatists, is amused and amusing, wittily playing with words for intellectual and aesthetic pleasure, as in the artistic repetition of 'warn' and 'stop', and the tension between 'warn' and 'kiss'—neater still in the original Greek, with its greater conciseness and more manipulatable word order. Catullus, on the other hand, turns to traditional epigrammatic brevity and antithesis to convey emotional pain of searing intensity.

The ultimate cause of this pain must be assumed to be his obsession with the woman he calls Lesbia (probably she was the aristocratic Clodia Metelli, whose freewheeling behaviour Cicero famously attacked in *Pro M. Caelio* [*In Defence of Marcus Caelius Rufus*]). Catullus makes this the explicit subject of many other poems; the affair went sour for him, he claims, because she failed to recognize or return the selfless spiritual affection he felt for her as well as physical desire. He pinpoints the difference between the two in Poem 72, where he attempts an objective analysis of his situation, and sees the persistence of desire without affection as the root of his anguished conflict:

You said one day you only knew Catullus, Lesbia,
And you'd refuse to embrace even Jove instead of me.
I loved you then, not only as common men their girl-
    friend
But as a father loves his sons and sons-in-law.
I know you now. So though my passion's more intense,
Yet for me you're much cheaper and lighter-weight.
'How can that be?' you ask. It's because such hurt
    compels
A lover to love more but to like less.

                              (translated by Guy Lee)

No such analysis is attempted in 85; indeed Catullus sets up his addressee as an imaginary interrogator precisely to reject the very possibility of a rational explanation for his suffering. The phraseology of the question suggests that his mental conflict is of his own making ('Why *I do* that . . .'), while that of his answer makes clear his utter helplessness ('I feel it *happening* . . .'). Arguably his anguish seems all the more real and immediate because of the prose-like plainness of his vocabulary and syntax: seven verbs, six of them in the first-person singular, with present significance, and no nouns or adjectives at all. The nearest thing to a metaphor is tellingly kept for the very last word, *excrucior* ('I'm tortured'). The root meaning of this verb is 'suffer on the cross', and crucifixion's agonizing pinioning of both upper and lower extremities vividly conveys Catullus' mental torture by two conflicting emotions, from neither of which he can escape. The concept of the love-hate relationship is one which most modern readers will instinctively understand; in Poem 72 Catullus himself attempts to understand it as hatred of Lesbia for her treatment of him and love of her for her sex appeal, though he does not use the terms 'hate' and 'love' antithetically in that poem. Here, however, by simply saying 'I hate' and 'I love', without specifying what or whom, and professing not to understand at all how such conflicting emotions can simultaneously co-exist, he contrives to invest a potentially banal observation with a peculiar menace. Nowhere else in surviving Latin love poetry is anything quite like it to be encountered.

                              —Joan Booth

THREE POEMS: 2, 63, and 76
Poems by Catullus, mid-1st century BC.

Catullus' poems are normally divided into three groups: the polymetricals (Poems 1–60), the long poems (61–68), and the elegies (69–116). Each group is sometimes considered a collection unto itself, with its own principles of order and thematic coherency. The issue of the collection aside, there can be no denying that Catullus' poems divide themselves as to metre and topic. The polymetricals deal centrally with the affair Catullus apparently carried on with his lover, whom he calls Lesbia and who is usually identified historically as Clodia Metelli. They also give shape to a variety of circumstances quite apart from the affair with Lesbia, evoking the full range of human emotion. The long poems deal mostly with topics that centre around nature, convention, or myth. They dem-

onstrate that this superbly accomplished lyricist was also able to write on larger topics with equal authority. The elegies, on the other hand, while also treating the affair with Lesbia, give shape to a panoply of encounters, emotions, and thoughts, now complementing, now expanding on the topics raised in the polymetricals. The elegies are perhaps noteworthy also for the tremendous emotional swings depicted in them (particularly poems 76 and 85) and for their obscenity.

Many of the polymetricals are exemplary of their group, but none perhaps more than poem 2, which introduces Catullus' readers to his 'girl' (*puella*) and her sparrow (*passer*). As there is no critical consensus about the symbolical value of the sparrow, readers make of the bird what they will. It is perhaps most useful to see the bird in its Greek context, where it takes pride of place in the fragments of Sappho as Aphrodite's special bird. More specifically, the sparrow is depicted in Sappho's fragments (and elsewhere) as the bird that conveys Aphrodite physically from her home with the other gods to earth. The sparrow can be understood to mediate, in this way, the movement from ideal to real space.

Given this, we might see the sparrow of Poem 2 as symbolic of Lesbia's love psychology. This poem bemoans the fact that Lesbia is somehow assuaged by the bird's activity, while Catullus can only pine away at the poem's end, wishing he might feel the better for its devotion. Since the sparrow mediates, in its Greek context, the gulf between ideal and real space, we might see its symbolical resonance in Poem 2 as portending Lesbia's own flight from a more idealized repose, in which she contemplates love from afar, to a more active response on her part toward Catullus' advances. The death of the sparrow in Poem 3 announces just such a movement on her part in its celebration of Lesbia's submission to Catullus. Poems 5 and 7, in quick succession, give fuller shape to the ways in which the affair proceeds, before it suddenly ends, for whatever reasons, in Poem 8. It is a strategic reminiscence in Poem 8 when Catullus asks Lesbia rhetorically 'whose lips will you now bite'. Initially, the sparrow danced about Lesbia's body, erotically nibbling her fingertips and flittering about her breast and lap. In recalling those nibbles at the end of the affair, Catullus brings the opening poems of the Lesbia cycle, of which Poem 2 is the crux, full circle, confirming the importance of this sparrow, possibly the most famous bird in all of Western writing.

If the polymetricals are laden with the emotions of love won and love lost, the long poems are no less emotionally charged, but in the less personal manner befitting their subject matter. These poems abound in stunning moments of raw emotion and pure vision, but there is nothing in Western writing quite like Poem 63. The poem's story, given here somewhat roughly for the sake of brevity, considers the figure of Attis, who was conceived from the castrated genitals of the androgynous Cybele and the daughter of the river Sangarios. Attis grew into a beautiful man, and Cybele later fell in love with him. In order to prevent him from marrying and belonging to someone else, Cybele made Attis go mad, and in his rage, castrate himself.

Poem 63 commences *in medias res*, on the night in which Attis disfigures himself. Central to the poem's drama is Attis' transformation from male to female, for it renders to the poem's situation a tension that is broken only at its conclusion, when Attis realizes the permanence and the dimension of what he/she has wrought. A night of frenzied celebration precedes that moment of truth, however, and Catullus articulates the full force of the ritual dancing, drum beating, and singing, played in honour of Cybele. Eventually, having worked him/herself into a fever pitch of devotion,

Attis sleeps a drunken sleep. When he/she is awakened the next morning by the bright light of the sun and recognizes what has transpired he/she pines for a restoration of who he/she was and a return to Attica, whence he/she came to Phrygia, the setting for the poem's drama. There can be no escape, however, from the devotion demanded by Cybele, a fact not lost on Catullus, who prays at the poem's end for the goddess to avert his house from the grip exerted on her worshippers.

Part of the virtuosity of the poem lies outside of the story it tells in the skills of prosody that Catullus brings to bear in its construction. Always in Catullus, but especially in the long poems, sound, in Alexander Pope's phrase, is equal to sense. Repetition is one strategy deployed to ensure this equilibrium, as in vv. 63–71, where the personal pronoun 'I' (ego) is repeated ten times by Attis, almost as a mantra to reclaim his/her lost sense of identity. Consistent alliteration also helps to stress certain points, as, for example, at the poem's conclusion, where the determination of the poet's prayer to avert the fury of Cybele is confirmed in the repetition of labial and dental sounds (b and d). Catullus' poem also excites its reader's attention on the grounds of its individuality, for there is much that is original in Catullus' treatment of Attis. Also unique, though in a different way, is the prayer at the poem's end, which renders to what had been seemingly a detached version of an old story a personal resonance. Nor is the force of that prayer wasted in the context of the larger collection of poems. It helps to link this bizarre story of sexual extremism, shifting identities, and blurred genders, to the other poems of Catullus' collection, where love is often conceived (especially where Lesbia is concerned) as both madness and slavery.

The themes of madness and slavery also converge in the elegiac Poem 76 where the affair with Lesbia has gone sour many times over and the poet is reduced to pleading to the gods, in whom he never seemed to believe, to cure him of his illness. Now Catullus can no longer bear the emotional or spiritual dependencies and can no longer muster the mental energy required to forbear. He does the only thing left for him to do, which is to look to a higher power for relief. The pure energy of love's emotion, captured with such acumen in preceding poems, confirms the seriousness of Catullus' situation in this poem and the difficulty of his task in the absence of divine intervention. One wonders if Catullus did, in fact, recover the wholeness of his heart. If the collection as we have it is any indication of the chronology of the affair and the emotional life of its author, then the vague musings, the soft pornography, the sometimes harsh obscenities of some of the later elegies, may be a witness to the faltering emotions of a heart that is not whole.

—Joseph Pucci

CAVAFY, C(onstantine) P(etrou). Born in Alexandria, Egypt, 29 April 1863. Lived in England as a child, 1872–79, and in Constantinople, 1882–85; otherwise lived in Alexandria. Educated at Hermis Lyceum, 1879. Worked at Egyptian Stock Exchange, 1888; clerk, Irrigation Service, Ministry of Public Works, 1892–1922. Issued one private pamphlet of his verse in 1904, and thereafter compiled notebooks of verse for distributing to friends. *Died 29 April 1933.*

PUBLICATIONS

Collections

Poiemata, edited by Alexander Singopoulos. 1935.
Poems, translated by John Mavrogordato. 1951.
Complete Poems, translated by Rae Dalven. 1961; enlarged edition, 1976.
Collected Poems, edited by G.P. Savidis, translated by Edmund Keeley and Philip Sherrard. 1975.
The Greek Poems, translated by Memas Kolaitis. 2 vols., 1989.

Verse

Fourteen Poems, translated by Nikos Stangos and Stephen Spender. 1966.
Anecdota poiemata 1882–1923 [Unpublished Poems], edited by G.P. Savidis. 1968.
Passions and Ancient Days: Twenty One New Poems, translated by Edmund Keeley and G.P. Savidis. 1972.
Ta Apokirigmena: Poiemata kai Metafrasis [The Rejected Works: Poems and Translation]. 1983.

Other

Peza [Prose], edited by G. Papoutsakis. 1963.
Anecdota Peza [Unpublished Prose], edited by M. Peridis. 1963.
Epistoles ston Mario Valano [Letters to Mario Valano], edited by E.N. Moschou. 1979.

*

Critical Studies: *Constantine Cavafy*, 1964, and *Three Generations of Greek Writers: Introductions to Cavafy, Kazantzakis, Ritsos*, 1983, both by Peter Bien; *Cavafy: A Critical Biography* by Robert Liddell, 1974; *Cavafy's Alexandria: Study of a Myth in Progress* by Edmund Keeley, 1976; 'A Concise Introduction to Cavafy' by Marguerite Yourcenar, in *Shenandoah*, 32(1), 1980; 'Cavafy Issue' of *Journal of the Hellenic Diaspora*, 10, 1983; *The Mind and Art of C.P. Cavafy: Essays on His Life and Work* by Denise Harvey, 1983; *The Poetics of Cavafy: Textuality, Eroticism, History* by Gregory Jusdanis, 1987; *C.P. Cavafy* by Christopher Robinson, 1988.

* * *

Solemnly asked his opinion of his own work, C.P. Cavafy towards the end of his life is said to have replied, 'Cavafy in my opinion is an ultra-modern poet, a poet of future generations'. History has proved him right, but the tone of the reply also reveals an important ingredient of the unique poetic voice that is Cavafy's: a gentle mockery of all pretension, even that of the poet interviewed about his own work, and a light-hearted concealment of his true self at the very moment when he appears about to lay his cards on the table. 'Cavafy', he says, not 'I', as if 'Cavafy' were someone different.

Cavafy's poetry is distinguished by many subtle forms of irony, and also by an intriguing self-effacement in poems that purport to tell of personal experience and feeling. The subject matter of his poems is equally unusual. Approximately half of what that he published in his lifetime (consisting of 154 fairly short poems) and a similar proportion of those published posthumously, are devoted to subjects taken from Greek history, chiefly between 340 BC and AD 1453, while the remainder deal more or less explicitly with homosexual encounters against a backdrop of contemporary Alexandria.

Cavafy's uniqueness has posed a problem for critics, for whom he continues to exercise a profound fascination. To many his erotic poetry is a disreputable appendage to more 'sublime' poetry dedicated to the Greek past, but Cavafy's uncompromisingly 'historical' treatment of that past has also disconcerted many. And those critics who have not chosen to ignore the erotic poems have been hard put to identify the source of powerful emotion, felt by many readers, in response to poems from which all reference to love is lacking, and the sordidness and triviality of the sexual encounters evoked are freely confessed.

The common denominator between Cavafy's two principal preoccupations, the distant Greek past and contemporary homosexual experiences, is time, which plays a major role in both types of poem. Often it appears that the true subject of the erotic poems is not the experience described so much as its loss to the passage of time. Time takes away and alienates all real experience, but through art the poet can sometimes regain it in the creation of a poem, though what is regained is both more and less than the original. More, because, as the poet frankly says in several of these poems, he is free to touch up reality in the imaginative act of writing; less, because, no matter how 'perfect' an experience can become thus imaginatively recreated, it is only imaginary, the real thing remaining lost to the past. This sense of 'lost to the past' is central, too, to Cavafy's historical poems, in which he juxtaposes vivid pictures of flesh-and-blood, fallible human beings with a chillingly historical sense of how remote they are, and how futile are these people's preoccupations now.

In their treatment of time, *all* Cavafy's poems can be said to belong to his third type, into which he once said his work could be divided, namely 'philosophical' poetry.

—Roderick Beaton

WAITING FOR THE BARBARIANS (Perimenontas tous Barbarous)
Poem by C.P. Cavafy, 1904 (written 1898).

'Waiting for the Barbarians' was written in 1898 and printed in 1904, as a self-contained pamphlet for private distribution, in accordance with Cavafy's idiosyncratic publishing practices. Although it is not among the poems the poet disowned (in the year he regarded as a watershed in his artistic development, 1911), 'Waiting for the Barbarians' was not included by the poet in later collections of his work. It does, however, form the subject of a lengthy self-commentary note found among Cavafy's papers and thus it would appear that the poet acknowledged its position among the works of his maturity. It is generally regarded by critics as an example of his best work.

Cavafy distinguished three broad categories into which his poetic *oeuvre* could be divided: historical, erotic, and philosophical. Critics have sometimes relabelled the third category 'didactic', but this term sits uneasily with what Cavafy himself called the 'light irony' characteristic of his work. Boundaries between the three categories remain, in any case, highly unstable, since eroticism and history frequently coincide in

the poems and the term 'philosophical' could be loosely applied to almost all of them. Most of the poems are in some sense historical, since there is a marked tendency to return to the past, and it is, perhaps, this category that the poet regarded as his most characteristic, in view of his own designation of himself as a 'historian-poet'.

'Waiting for the Barbarians' is ostensibly a historical poem set in Rome: it refers to an emperor, praetors, consuls, and senators. The scenario is, however, imaginary and the poem takes the form of a pseudo-historical dialogue. It is not clear whether there is actually more than one speaker or whether a single voice is both posing and answering questions. Further, in spite of period detail (such as the embroidered togas worn by the consuls and praetors), the poem presents not facts, but speculation about what will happen when the barbarians arrive—barbarians who turn out, in the end, to be non-existent.

The poem falls into two unequal parts: the dialogue of lines 1–33 and the closing couplet (lines 34–5). It is metrically stricter than the Cavafian norm, which is unrhymed iambic lines of varying lengths. Here, Cavafy elects to use 15-syllable lines (the standard line of Modern Greek poetry, deriving from the folk tradition) for questions, and 12- or 13-syllable lines (a non-standard line-length) for answers. The final couplet is in 13-syllable lines, and the poem does not make use of rhyme. One reason for the use of the 15-syllable line may be to subvert the reader's expectations by expressing doubt in what is normally the discourse of authority. Cavafy may also be consciously alluding to a common device of Greek folk poetry known as 'questions that miss their target'.

The main body of the poem consists of a series of questions, beginning in the opening line: 'What are we waiting for, assembled in the forum?'. The questioner goes on to ask why the senators have stopped legislating, the emperor and dignitaries are in ceremonial garb, and the orators are conspicuous by their absence. The invariable response is: 'Because the barbarians are coming today'. The last of these questions is:

Why this sudden bewilderment, this confusion?
(How serious people's faces have become)
Why are the streets and squares emptying so rapidly,
everyone going home lost in thought?

The answer is that the barbarians have not come and are not coming: 'There are no barbarians any longer'. The couplet that closes the poem also takes the form of a question and a response; this time, the response explains the question without answering it: 'Now what's going to happen to us without barbarians?/Those people were a kind of solution'.

'Waiting for the Barbarians' is open to a variety of conflicting readings and thus exemplifies the obliqueness and understated irony characteristic of the mature Cavafy. Some critics have read it as an allegory of Cavafy's own time and place (Alexandria at the turn of the century), identifying the Romans as the Egyptians and the barbarians as the English forces of occupation. Others have suggested that the poem refers to a predicament in the poet's personal life. Others again have seen the poem as a timeless and universal symbol of the human condition. It has also been read as an allegory of writing.

Cavafy's own note on the poem remains, in many ways, the most instructive reading available, although it shares some of the elusiveness of the poem itself. The poet hints at a parallel with modern history, but says that both Romans and barbarians are symbolic and do not represent anyone in particular. He suggests that the poem concerns people who wish they did not have knowledge and long to lead the simple life of the uneducated for whom nothing is jaded. In other words, at one level, 'Waiting for the Barbarians' is about the desire to abdicate responsibility and set aside the trappings of civilization. The barbarians are the noble savages of civilized man's imagination.

'Waiting for the Barbarians' defies reduction to any single reading, since its implied terms of reference encompass Roman history, modern Egyptian politics, the poet's personal circumstances, and mankind's dilemma. Its teasing ambiguity and multiplicity of levels are characteristic of Cavafy's mature work.

—Sarah Ekdawi

————

CAVALCANTI, Guido. Born in Florence, c.1255; member of a Guelph merchant family. Engaged to Bice, a member of the Ghibelline family, in 1267. Guelph guarantor for a peace settlement, 1280; member of the general council of the commune, 1284 and 1290; an ardent supporter of the white Guelph faction, he was banished on 24 June 1300 by order of the council on which Dante, *q.v.*, served as a prior (from June to August) and confined to Sarzana. Contracted malaria and was recalled to Florence in August but died soon after. Friend of Dante, whose *La vita nuova* was dedicated to him but who no longer spoke of him after his death. *Buried 29 August 1300.*

PUBLICATIONS

Collections

The Poetry, edited and translated by Lowry Nelson, Jr. 1986.
The Complete Poems, translated by Marc Cirigliano (bilingual edition). 1992.

Verse

Rime, edited by Guido Favati. 1957; also edited by Marcello Ciccuto, 1978; translated by Dante Gabriel Rossetti, in *The Early Italian Poets*, 1861, revised edition, as *Dante and His Circle*, 1874; as *The Sonnets and Ballate*, translated by Ezra Pound, 1912.

*

Critical Studies: *Guido Cavalcanti's Theory of Love: The 'Canzone d'Amore' and Other Related Problems* by J.E. Shaw, 1949; 'Cavalcanti' by Ezra Pound, in *Literary Essays*, 1954; *Medieval Latin and the Rise of the European Love Lyric* by Peter Dronke, 2 vols., 1968; 'Pound and Cavalcanti' by G. Singh, in *Essays in Honour of J.H. Whitfield*, 1975.

*   *   *

Guido Cavalcanti's merit as a lyricist has never been overshadowed by the genius of his close friend Dante. A *dolce stil nuovo* poet, he imposed on the conventions of that school his own particular individuality and moulded them to suit his own taste and poetic exigency. Ezra Pound, the creator of modern poetry, singled him out as an inspiration in his own poetry, and as an embodiment of something authentically modern. He put Cavalcanti in the same category as Sappho and Theocritus—poets who have sung, 'not all the modes of life, but some of them, unsurpassedly; those who in their chosen or fated field have bowed to no one'. What characterizes Cavalcanti's lyricism as such is the dramatic intensity of his passions as well as the stark individuality of diction in which it is couched, together with the conceptual richness and subtlety of his content. If, as Pound said, 'no psychologist of emotions is more keen in his understanding, more precise in his expression' than Cavalcanti, it is because he conveys the feelings, intuitions, and convictions of a highly gifted mind and because of his use of a singularly concrete and poetically charged language with no trace of conventionality.

Cavalcanti's concept of love—and love is the leitmotif of the *dolce stil nuovo* school of poetry—is significantly different from that of a contemporary like Guido Guinizzelli, in that it is conceived more in earthly and sensuous terms than in mystical and transcendental ones, and the language Cavalcanti uses to characterize it is direct and graphic rather than symbolic or abstract. And this in spite of the fact that he brought to bear on his treatment of love all his philosophic learning and intellectual curiosity, a large share of it derived from Averroès, so that his similes, metaphors, and descriptions, even though they might at times appear to be arid and prosaic, always embody a definite concept or meaning as well as a fineness of perception. Apropos of this, Pound's evaluative comparison between Cavalcanti and Petrarch, or between Cavalcanti and Dante, is worth quoting. After noting how Cavalcanti 'thought in accurate terms' and how his phrases 'correspond to definite sensations undergone', Pound goes on to argue that 'the "figure", the strong metaphoric or "picturesque" expression in him is there to convey or to interpret a definite meaning. In Petrarch, on the other hand, it is ornament, the prettiest ornament he could find, but not an irreplaceable ornament, or one that he couldn't have used just about as well somewhere else'. Pound's comparison between Cavalcanti and Dante is equally illuminating—Dante 'qui était diablement dans les idées reçues', Cavalcanti more independent and unconventional; Dante willing 'to take on any sort of holy and orthodox furniture', Cavalcanti 'eclectic', swallowing 'none of his authors whole', and lastly, 'Dante himself never wrote more poignantly, or with greater intensity than Cavalcanti . . . a spirit more imperious, more passionate, less likely to give ear to sophistries; his literary relation to Dante is not unlike Marlowe's to Shakespeare' (though, Pound adds, 'such comparisons are always unsafe').

—G. Singh

————

CELA (Trulock), Camilo José. Born in Iria Flavia, La Coruña, Galicia, Spain, 11 May 1916. Educated at the University of Madrid, 1933–36, 1939–43. Served in General Franco's forces during the Spanish Civil War, 1936–39: corporal. Married 1) Maria del Rosario Conde Picavea in 1944 (divorced 1990), one son; 2) Marina Castaño in 1991. Freelance writer in Madrid until 1954, then in Palma de Mallorca; travelled to Chile, 1952, and Venezuela, 1953; founder, *Papeles de Son Armadans*, 1956–79; travelled to Italy, France, and USA, 1990. Recipient: Critics prize, 1956; National literature prize, 1984; Prince of Asturias prize for literature, 1987; Nobel prize for literature, 1989; Santiago de Compostela gold medal, 1990. Honorary doctorates: Syracuse University, USA, 1965; University of Santiago (Chile), 1974 (refused); University of Birmingham (England), 1976; John F. Kennedy University, Buenos Aires, 1978; Interamericana University, Puerto Rico, 1980; University of Palma, Mallorca, 1980; Hebrew University, Jerusalem, 1986; University of Miami, University of Tel Aviv, University of San Marcos, Peru, Dowling College, New York, Millersville University, Pennsylvania, and University of Murcia, all 1990; Universidad Complutense, Madrid, and La Trobe University, Australia, 1991. Honorary professor, University of Santo Domingo, 1990. Member, Spanish Royal Academy, since 1957. Created Royal Senator, 1977. Lives in Guadalajara, Spain.

PUBLICATIONS

Fiction

La familia de Pascual Duarte. 1942; edited by Jorge Urrutia, 1977, and by Harold L. Boudreau and John W. Kronik, 1989; as *Pascual Duarte's Family*, translated by John Marks, 1946; as *The Family of Pascual Duarte*, translated by Anthony Kerrigan, 1964.
Pabellón de reposo. 1943; as *Rest Home*, translated by Herma Briffault, 1961.
Nuevas andanzas y desventuras de Lazarillo de Tormes. 1944.
Esas nubes que pasan . . . 1945.
El bonito crimen del carabinero y otras invenciones. 1947.
El gallego y su cuadrilla y otros apuntes carpetovetónicos. 1949; enlarged edition (includes 'En el lomo de la cubierta dice'), 1951.
La colmena. 1951; edited by Jorge Urrutia, 1988; as *The Hive*, translated by J.M. Cohen, 1953.
Santa Balbina 37, gas en cada piso. 1952.
Timoteo, el incomprendido. 1952.
Café de artistas. 1953.
Mrs Caldwell habla con su hijo. 1953; as *Mrs Caldwell Speaks to Her Son*, translated by J.S. Bernstein, 1968.
Baraja de invenciones. 1953.
Historias de Venezuela: La catira. 1955.
El molino de viento y otras novelas cortas. 1956.
Nuevo retablo de Don Cristobita: Invenciones, figuraciones y alucinaciones. 1957.
Cajón de sastre. 1957.
Historias de España: Los ciegos, Los tontos. 1958.
Los viejos amigos. 2 vols., 1960–61.
Gavilla de fábulas sin amor. 1962.
Tobogán de hambrientos. 1962.
Once cuentos de fútbol. 1963.
Las compañías convenientes y otros fingimientos y cegueras. 1963.
El solitario; Los sueños de Quesada. 1963.
Garito de hospicianos o Guirigay de imposturas y bambollas. 1963.
Cuentos 1941–1953; Nuevo retablo de Don Cristobita. 1964.
Apuntes carpetovetónicos: Novelas cortas 1949–56. 1965.
A la pata de palo: Historias de España; La familia del héroe; El ciudadano Iscariote Reclús; Viaje a USA. 4 vols., 1965–

67; selection as *El tacatá oxidado: Florilegio de carpetovetonismos, y otras lindezas*, 1973.
Nuevas escenas matritenses. 7 vols., 1965–66; as *Fotografías al minuto*, 1972.
San Camilo, 1936: Vísperas, festividad y octava de San Camilo del año 1936 en Madrid. 1969; as *San Camilo, 1936: The Eve, Feast and Octave of St Camillus of the Year 1936 in Madrid*, translated by J.H.R. Holt, 1992.
Café de artistas y otros cuentos. 1969.
Timoteo el incomprendido y otros papeles ibéricos. 1970.
Obras selectas. 1971.
Oficio de tinieblas 5 o Novela de tesis escrita para ser cantada por un coro de enfermos. 1973.
Cuentos para leer despues del baño. 1974.
Prosa, edited by Jacinto-Luis Guerña. 1974.
Café de artistas y otros papeles volanderos. 1978.
El espejo y otros cuentos. 1981.
Mazurca para dos muertos. 1983; as *Mazurka for Two Dead Men*, translated by Patricia Haugaard, 1993.
Cristo versus Arizona. 1988.
Las orejas del niño Raúl (for children). 1989.
Cachondeos, escareos y otros meneos. 1991.
O Camaleón solteiro. 1991.

Plays

Maria Sabina, music by Balada (produced 1970). 1967.
Homenaje al Bosco I: El carro de heno o El inventor de la guillotina. 1969.

Verse

Poemas de una adolescencia cruel. 1945; as *Pisando la dudosa luz del día*, 1945.
Cancionero de la Alcarria. 1987.

Other

Mesa revuelta. 1945; enlarged edition (includes *Ensueños y figuraciones*), 1957.
San Juan de la Cruz (as Matilde Verdú). 1948.
Las botas de siete leguas: Viaje a la Alcarria. 1948; as *Journey to the Alcarria*, translated by Frances M. Lopez Morillas, 1964.
Ávila. 1952; revised edition, 1968.
Del Miño al Bidasoa: Notas de un vagabundaje. 1952.
Ensueños y figuraciones. 1954.
Vagabundo por Castilla. 1955.
Mis páginas preferidas (selection). 1956.
Judíos, moros y cristianos: Notas de un vagabundaje por Ávila, Segovia y sus tierras. 1956.
La rueda de los ocios. 1957.
La obra literaria del pintor Solana. 1957.
Recuerdo de don Pío Baroja. 1958.
La cucaña: Memorias. 1958.
Primer viaje andaluz: Notas de un vagabundaje por Jaén, Córdoba, Sevilla, Huelva y sus tierras. 1959.
Cuaderno del Guadarrama. 1959.
Cuatro figuras del '98: Unamuno, Valle-Inclán, Baroja, Azorín y otros retratos y ensayos españoles. 1961.
Obra completa. 17 vols., 1962–86.
Toreo de salón. 1963.
Izas, rabizas y colipoterras. 1964.
Páginas de geografía errabunda. 1965.
Viaje al Pirineo de Lérida: Notas de un paseo a pie por el

Pallars Sobira, el Valle de Aran y el Condado de Ribagorza. 1965.
Viajes por España. 3 vols., 1965–68.
Madrid. 1966.
El solitario, illustrated by Rafael Zabaleta. 1966.
Calidoscopio callejero, marítimo y campestre de Camilo José Cela para el reino y ultramar. 1966.
Xam, with Cesáreo Rodríguez Aguilera. 1966.
Viaje a USA. 1967.
Diccionario secreto. 2 vols., 1968–71.
Al servicio de algo. 1969.
La bandada de palomas (for children). 1969.
Barcelona, illustrated by Federico Lloveras. 1970.
La Mancha en el corazón y en los ojos. 1971.
La bola del mundo: Escenas cotidianas. 1972.
Fotografías al minuto. 1972.
A vueltas con España. 1973.
Cristina Mallo (monograph). 1973.
Balada del vagabundo sin suerte y otros papeles volanderos. 1973.
Diccionario manual castellá-catalá, catalá-castellá. 1974.
Danza de las gigantas amorosas. 1975.
Rol de cornudos. 1976.
Crónica del cipote de Archidona. 1977.
La rosa. 1979.
Los sueños vanos, los ángeles curiosos. 1980.
Lectura de Quijote. 4 vols., 1981.
Vuelta de hoja. 1981.
Los vasos comunicantes. 1981.
Album de taller (art commentary). 1981.
Enciclopedia de erotismo. 4 vols., 1982–86; revised edition, as Diccionario del erotismo, 2 vols., 1988.
El juego de los tres madroños. 1983.
Madrid, color y siluta. 1985.
Nuevo viaje a la Alcarria. 1986.
El asno de Buridán (articles). 1986.
Of Genes, Gods, and Tyrants: The Biological Causation of Reality. 1987.
Conversaciones españolas. 1987.
Los caprichos de Francisco de Goya y Lucientes. 1989.
Vocación de repartidor. 1989.
Toda la vida a una carta. 1989.
Obras completas. 37 vols., 1989–90.
Cela, lo que dijo en TVE. 1989.
Galicia. 1990.
Blanquito, peón de Brega. 1991.
Páginas escogidas (anthology). 1991.
Desde el palomar de Hita. 1991.
Torerías: El gallego y su cuadrilla; Madrid toreo de salón. 1991.
El camaleón. 1992.
El huevo del juicio. 1993.
Memorias, entendimientos y voluntades. 1993.

Editor, Homenaje y recuerdo a Gregorio Marañón (1887–1960). 1961.

Translator, La Celestina, by Fernando de Rojas. 1979.
Translator, La resistible ascensión de Arturo Ui, by Bertolt Brecht. 1986.

*

Critical Studies: El sistema estético de Camilo José Cela by Olga Prjevalinsky, 1960; Camilo José Cela: Acercamiento a un escritor by Alonso Zamora Vicente, 1962; The Novels and Travels of Camilo José Cela, 1963, and 'Camilo José Cela's Quest for a Tragic Sense of Life', in Romance Quarterly, 17, 1970, both by Robert Kirsner; 'Social Criticism, Existentialism and Tremendismo in Camilo José Cela's La familia de Pascual Duarte', in Romance Quarterly, 13 (supplement), 1967, and Forms of the Novel in the Work of Camilo José Cela, 1967, both by David William Foster; El léxico de Camilo José Cela by Sara Suárez Solís, 1969; Camilo José Cela by D.W. McPheeters, 1969; Cela by Mariano Tudela, 1970; La novelística de Camilo José Cela, 1971, and 'The Politics of Obscenity in San Camilo, 1936', in Anales de la Novela de Posguerra, 1, 1976, both by Paul Ilie; Cela issue of Contemporary Fiction, 4(3), 1984; Cela: Masculino singular: Biografía by Francisco García Marquina, 1991; La familia de Pascual Duarte by Alan Hoyle, 1994.

*   *   *

Camilo José Cela's first novel, La familia de Pascual Duarte (Pascual Duarte's Family), is a strange hybrid, reading in parts like a picaresque novel (though managing, unlike the later Nuevas andanzas y desventuras de Lazarillo de Tormes [Further Adventures of Lazarillo de Tormes], to keep away from pastiche), and in parts like a Lorca 'rural tragedy'. These sources of inspiration reveal the combined ideological intentions that underlie the book: nationalism, vitalism, and aestheticism. The nationalism is most evident in the choice of the picaresque as a model, while it is in the passages inspired by 'rural tragedy' that can best be seen the vitalistic philosophy that pervades the whole story and provides its main message: Pascual is a primitive man who has not learned to interpose between his actions and the mysterious natural forces that rule them—as they rule all other men's—the distorting screen of civilization. In return, however, Pascual keeps in close contact with those same forces and, unlike the rest of us, is able to understand them intuitively, which is the only way in which they can be understood. Pascual is a nationalistic Spanish version of a Nietzschean hero, and the novel, rather then the isolated exception it is usually made out to be, is arguably the best example of the Spanish brand of fascist literature that flourished briefly during the very early Franco years.

The aestheticist dimension of Pascual Duarte's Family is developed more fully in some of Cela's early stories and in his second novel, Pabellón de reposo (Rest Home), in which the flimsy story line is entirely subservient to the elegant narrative orchestration and the poetic prose. This purely aestheticist strain remains a constant, if secondary, aspect of Cela's work, re-emerging in occasional short stories, in the never completed pseudo-memoirs 'La cucaña' [The Greasepole] and, in tediously extreme form, in Mrs Caldwell habla con su hijo (Mrs Caldwell Speaks to Her Son). But, above all, aestheticism is inseparable from the other two essential dimensions of Cela's literature, and the full measure of it is given precisely by the marriage of the crudeness of the subject matter to the lyricism of the prose, as illustrated by his best short stories, like 'Marelo Brito', 'La naranja es una fruta de invierno' [Oranges Are Winter Fruit], or the significantly entitled 'El bonito crimen del carabinero' [The Carabinero's Lovely Murder]. With Viaje a la Alcarria (Journey to the Alcarria), Cela's nationalism too gets partly shunted off into a special genre, though description is not Cela's forte and his travelogues tend to become a series of vignettes of (largely imaginary) encounters with odd characters. Yet nationalism is also an essential component of Cela's work as a whole, embedded in the stories themselves: the sickening brutality of their world is to be seen as a vital national Spanish characteristic, not to be decried, but to be upheld as such.

Cela's best work is undoubtedly *La colmena* (*The Hive*), which, however, is neither the technically sophisticated nor the social-realist novel it is often made out to be. It was, in the Spain of its day, innovative, but it is most emphatically not objectivist: its supposedly lifelike randomness is largely an illusion. It does reflect very accurately the reality of 1940s Spain, not so much on the surface, where it leans often to the atypical, but at a deeper level, conveying the essential truth about that society—its sharp division between winners and losers, and the uninhibited exploitation and constant humiliation of the latter by the former. This it does, however, almost entirely by accident, for Cela believed that Spanish society was like that not because of its recent history, but because any human society must always be like that. The specific circumstances of Franco's Spain simply fitted his social and Darwinistic preconceptions. Still, *The Hive* remains an accurate portrayal of post-war Spain, and is also the best expression of Cela's artistic powers. It manages to keep a balance between being moving and being outrageously funny, and to retain its coherence in spite of its very fragmented structure, and, though many of its characters are on the fringes of normality or even beyond it, it gives, somehow, an overall impression of social realism. Here also, Cela's distinctive style reaches its perfection. The style is very simple, based almost entirely on one single technique, the delaying of the conclusion of his sentences by a series of triple repetitions at every syntactical level. It works, however, to great effect, thanks above all to Cela's extremely rich lexical resources.

After *The Hive*, Cela's work declined sharply. His travelogues became collections of improbable anecdotes involving freakish characters and having little to do with any actual place, and his stories degenerated into hackneyed portraits of misfits with ludicrous names and ludicrous lives, generously spiced for titillation with vulgarity and gratuitous violence. In fact, Cela simply parodied himself endlessly, in a descent into the pits of shallow commercialism which reached its bottom with *Enciclopedia del erotismo* [Encyclopedia of Eroticism]. He eventually tried his hand again at some real writing with *San Camilo, 1936*, a version of *The Hive* translated to the days of the outbreak of the Spanish Civil War. Unfortunately, the vision had not changed. At the very time when their collective destiny is being decided, the characters of *San Camilo* are all shown scurrying about purposelessly, obsessed only with the urge to satisfy their most basic needs. This is demonstrably false: there is abundant evidence that, at that fateful moment, many Spaniards were only too conscious of what was happening to them and were determined to shape history one way or another. But the worst thing about *San Camilo* is that Cela, having neglected his artistic powers for so long, failed to recapture them. The precarious but real balance between outrageous humour, lyricism, and social observation that he had achieved in *The Hive* eluded him this time, and his characters were too much the hacked versions of *Los viejos amigos* [Old Friends] and *Tobogán de hambrientos* [Tramps Down the Chute] rather than their original selves.

—J.F. Marfany

PASCUAL DUARTE'S FAMILY (La familia de Pascual Duarte)
Novel by Camilo José Cela, 1942.

Essentially, the text of *Pascual Duarte's Family* is the autobiography of a man, Pascual Duarte, who, seemingly driven by circumstances to a series of senseless killings of people and animals, is garrotted in prison for the murder of a local wealthy landowner.

Pascual writes his own memoirs during the few months between the trial and his execution. Preceding the autobiographical tale there are three brief texts: a preliminary note by the transcriber, Pascual's letter to the recipient of his manuscript, and an extract from the last will and testament of Don Joaquín relating to this manuscript. The main text is followed also by a note by the transcriber, an affidavit by the jail's chaplain, and another affidavit by the prison guard who witnessed Pascual's execution: but these provoke suspicion and doubt about the story instead of convincing the reader of its veracity. From reading the texts one draws the conclusion that little can be trusted. There is nothing like an objective account here; there are only apparent truths, authorized ones, manipulated and mutilated ones, which preclude a naive and passive reading. These implications highlight the role of the narrator in the elaboration of the text, destroying the myth of a transparent correspondence of the text to an exterior reality. One infers the need for a critical reading, capable of deciphering that which is implicit, and which censorship does not permit to be exposed more openly. For all these reasons, the novel imposes its own method of reading. It tells us that in immediately post-war Spain, a critical reading was considered subversive, since against the passivity and the position of inferiority demanded by dictatorial discourse it requires the active participation of the reader in the creative process.

The autobiographical mode of *Pascual Duarte's Family* implies that the name of Pascual has two different functions—that of protagonist and that of narrator of his own story. A comparative analysis of both would allow us to determine the nature of the relationship between these functions.

Pascual has two inner characteristics—tenderness and a strong sense of justice—but he is uncultured. Such lack of education means not only a lack of knowledge about the world, but also ignorance about himself and an inability to reflect on his own behaviour. The narrator points out that the character fails to recognize the motivations of his acts. From this lack of knowledge come the inability to control himself and a tendency to be carried away by impulses. Another consequence of such a lack of culture is the reduced capacity for symbolic activity, which limits the possibilities of self-expression, and prevents social communication. The only way of communicating is through violent actions. In the semantic organization of the novel, silence and violence are opposed to words and communication.

Pascual's first social experience is of violence in the family, which teaches him resignation in the face of the unavoidable. The key to the code of social values here is manhood, the defence of one's honour through physical aggression. This social law means reduction of the individual to the level of his physical power, and the regarding of others as aggressors and potential enemies, implying the institutionalization of violence as moral duty. According to the code of manhood, the innate qualities of Pascual—his affection and sense of justice —become feminine weaknesses; the assertion of manly strength is more important than expression of feelings: 'You know that a real man does not cry like a woman'. The code of violence transforms society into a battlefield.

Pascual draws another lesson from his social experience: the impossibility of choosing one's own destiny, amply illustrated by the metaphor of the pre-ordained path. But even though the stereotyped language of the uncultivated peasant attributes to God the responsibility for his destiny, the organization of the text makes it clear that the determinant of destiny is not divine but social. The habit of violence is a social inevitability. Its generalization in the community, and the lack of a reflective capacity which, in turn, generates routine and immobility, are symbolized by the dried fountain and the stopped clock in the square.

The inability to innovate implies denial of freedom. No choice is possible for him who plays an active role only in appearance. For the judicial system Pascual is the one who commits the crimes, but a thorough analysis reveals that he is rather the victim, dominated by circumstances instead of controlling them. What he does is merely the fulfilment of another's will. He merely responds to a previous aggression. The active and passive roles are superimposed on him. The distribution of roles assigned by the narrator and by the judicial system are radically different. The active–passive, aggressor–victim duality is reversed and, instead of opposing Pascual to society, it identifies him with the collective subject, thus rendering illegitimate the trial and the death penalty. The logic of the action is a war logic, in which the only alternatives are either to kill or to be killed, physically or symbolically (by loss of honour, of social consideration, and so on). These alternatives enclose the protagonist, and with him the collective subject, in an infernal spiral of violence from which it is impossible to escape. The memoirs are thus highly subversive, since they reverse the relationship between judge and criminal. They ascribe to the convicted man a natural goodness. The narrator accuses society of having institutionalized hate and violence, of not leaving the individual any alternative but to kill or be killed. In the light of this analysis, the final rebellion of Pascual acquires a new meaning, totally different from the one given by the guard and the priest. It is not a matter of cowardice but of legitimate rebellion, on the part of one who realizes that he is going to be executed for having applied in his life the laws that the collectivity taught him. We can understand now why in his letter to Don Joaquín he refuses to ask society for forgiveness.

The transformation of the character into narrator constitutes an authentic conversion. The passing on of his memoirs to Don Joaquín and their later publication shows the desire to communicate this process of individual conversion, making it a proposal for collective therapy. This transformation is made possible by Pascual's insertion into a new space, the jail. A place of confinement becomes a space of freedom. Rather than a denial of freedom, prison really represents the impossibility of acting. Pascual sees himself deprived of his usual mode of expression and immediate physical reaction. Jail interposes between him and his acts a distance that substitutes mental activity for physical action. He ceases reproducing, mechanically, a behaviour dictated by society and begins a personal and original consideration of such behaviour. The writing of his memoirs implies an effort of reflection, a process of learning about himself, which compensates for his deficiencies. The methodical exploration of the past allows him to acquire the abilities given to others by education. Whereas the protagonist let himself be controlled by circumstances and abdicated responsibility for his actions, the narrator is transformed into a subject in control of the story of his life. The roles, therefore, are reversed. His experience as a writer gives him the chance to learn symbolic behaviour and oral communication and thus to escape from the inevitability of violence. The memoirs, being a written artefact, require a reader.

So, the progression of this peasant transformed into a writer shows a progression from the denial of education to an affirmation of its necessity. *Pascual Duarte's Family* is thus a critique of the climate of the Spanish Civil War, still persisting in 1942, whose practices were in direct contradiction to the ideological principles upon which it based its legitimacy, those of Christianity.

Sending his memoirs to Don Joaquín, the narrator is advocating a social reconciliation, in the name of Christianity, among all Spaniards. If the reality of censorship at the time hindered an explicit presentation of the message, the real winner is literature itself: this masterpiece transcends its historical circumstances and continues to offer us the renewed pleasure of deciphering the enigma proposed in its own dedication: back in the 1940s, Cela had already brought the Spanish novel into 'the age of the reader'.

—Francisco Carenas

CELAN, Paul. Born Paul Antschel in Czernowitz, Bukovina, Romania, 23 November 1920. Educated at the Czernowitz Gymnasium; École de Médecine, Tours, France, 1938–39; University of Czernowitz, 1939–41; studied for a Licence-ès-Lettres in Paris, 1950. Married Gisèle Lestrange in 1952. In a forced labour camp during World War II; emigrated to Vienna, 1947; settled in Paris in 1948: language teacher and translator. Recipient: Bremen literary prize, 1958; Büchner prize, 1960; Nordrhein-Westfalen prize, 1964. *Died (suicide) 20 April 1970.*

PUBLICATIONS

Collections

Gedichte. 2 vols., 1975.
Gesammelte Werke, edited by Beda Allemann and S. Reichert. 5 vols., 1983; volume 3 as *Collected Prose,* translated by Rosemarie Waldrop, 1986.
Gedichte 1938–1944. 1985.

Verse

Der Sand aus den Urnen. 1948.
Mohn und Gedächtnis. 1952.
Von Schwelle zu Schwelle. 1955.
Sprachgitter. 1959.
Die Niemandsrose. 1963.
Atemwende. 1967.
Totnauberg. 1968.
Fadensonnen. 1968.
Lichtzwang. 1970.
Speech-Grille and Selected Poems, translated by Joachim Neugroschel. 1971.
Schneepart. 1971.
Selected Poems, translated by Michael Hamburger and Christopher Middleton. 1972.
Nineteen Poems, translated by Michael Hamburger. 1972.
Zeitgehoft: Späte Gedichte aus dem Nachlass. 1976.
Poems (bilingual edition), translated by Michael Hamburger. 1980.
65 Poems, translated by Brian Lynch and Peter Jankowsky. 1985.

Thirty-Two Poems, translated by Michael Hamburger. 1985.
Last Poems (bilingual edition), translated by Katharine Washburn and Margaret Guillemin. 1986.

Other

Edgar Jené und der Traum vom Traume. 1948.
Der Meridian. 1961.
Übertragungen aus dem Russischen. 1986.

Translator (into Romanian), *Taranii*, by Chekhov. 1946.
Translator (into Romanian), *Un eroual timpalu*, by Mikhail Lermontov. 1946.
Translator (into Romanian), *Chestinnea Rusa*, by Konstantin Simonov. 1947.
Translator, *Lehre vom Zerfall*, by E.M. Cioran. 1953.
Translator, *Die Zwölf*, by Aleksandr Blok. 1958.
Translator, *Das trunkene Schiff*, by Arthur Rimbaud. 1958.
Translator, *Gedichte*, by Osip Mandel'shtam. 1959.
Translator, *Die junge Parze*, by Paul Valéry. 1960.
Translator, *Gedichte*, by Sergei Esenin. 1961.
Translator, *Im Bereich einer Nacht*, by Jean Cayrol. 1961.
Translator, *Maigret und die schrecklichen Kinder; Hier irrt Maigret*, by Georges Simenon. 1963.
Translator, *Dichtungen*, by Henri Michaux. 1966.
Translator, *Einundzwanzig Sonette*, by Shakespeare. 1967.
Translator, *Gedichte*, by Jules Supervielle. 1968.
Translator, *Vakante Glut: Gedichte*, by André du Bouchet. 1968.
Translator, *Das verheissene Land*, by Giuseppe Ungaretti. 1968.

*

Critical Studies: *Zur Lyrik Celans* by P.H. Neumann, 1968; *Über Celan* edited by Dietlind Meinecke, 1970, revised edition, 1973; *Celan* by Jerry Glenn, 1973; *Celans Poetik* by Gerhard Buhr, 1976; 'Celan Issue' of *Text + Kritik* (53–54), edited by H.L. Arnold, 1977; *Paul Celan* by Holger A. Pausch, 1987; 'Celan Issue' of *Acts: A Journal of New Writing*, (8–9), 1989; *Paul Celan: Holograms of Darkness* by Amy Colin, 1990; *Paul Celan: A Biography of His Youth* by Israel Chalfen, translated by Maximilian Bleyleben, 1991; *Word Traces: Readings of Paul Celan* edited by Floretas Aris, 1994; *Holocaust Visions: Surrealism and Existentialism in the Poetry of Paul Celan* by Clarise Samuels, 1994.

*   *   *

Paul Celan is arguably the most important poet who wrote in German in the period after 1945. His poetry met with early and widespread recognition, although critics have always found difficulty in reconciling its manifestly superior stature —it has an immediate and haunting appeal—with its considerable resistance to interpretation.

Celan's complex poetic idiom is rooted in the Jewish-Hasidic mystical tradition of his ancestors, and also in the heritage of European symbolism. The uncompromisingly reflexive nature of his language—as elusive as it is allusive—has, however, less in common with the hermeticism of Mallarmé's art, than with the extreme tendency towards internalization that characterized the work of Hölderlin, Trakl, and Rilke.

Celan's poetry is a profoundly serious response to the darkest period of modern history, and a statement, too, of its own invalidity in such an age of crisis. One cannot afford to overlook the significance of Celan's position as a Jew writing in German after the Holocaust; the poet's parents were among the millions who are mourned in countless of his poems. The most famous of these—'Todesfuge' ('Death Fugue'), in *Mohn und Gedächtnis* [Poppy and Memory]— superbly illustrates his ability to fuse the historically specific with the universal; to term his poetry political is indeed to underestimate its power and relevance, for, above all, the fate of the Jew in the Diaspora is for Celan a metaphor for the existential condition of humanity as a whole.

Acutely aware of the chasm dividing individual perception from the generalities of speech, which can convey but a 'darkling splinterecho' of a distorted, fragmented reality, Celan's poetic voice withdraws into extreme semantic privacy. The metaphor of the 'Sprachgitter' (*Speech-Grille*)—the title of one poem and the collection in which it stands—is applicable to his poetry as a whole. Representing language as a complex framework which obstructs man's relation to reality, it is also a metaphor for the net of words and associations with which we attempt to capture that reality. Such paradox is central to Celan's art. As the bars of the grille delimit and connect empty spaces, so Celan used language to circumscribe the silent interstices between words. He was constantly preoccupied with the poem's precarious, marginal existence 'on the verge of falling silent'. However, his poetry remains essentially dialogic (between man and woman, man and God, life and death—the situation is rarely fully defined), and this communicative quality constitutes a dimension of hope.

Celan's work does not allow for easy division into 'phases': from the flowing rhythms and surrealistic imagery of *Mohn und Gedächtnis* it developed steadily towards increasing concentration and fragmentation, while continuing to draw and elaborate on a wide range of recurring metaphors and highly expressive neologisms, and making intricate use of repetition, allusion, antithesis, and paradox. The same features mark Celan's prose poem 'Gespräch im Gebirg' [Conversation in the Mountains] (in *Neue Rundschau*, 71(2), 1960), which directly complements his theoretical discussion of his art in *Der Meridian* [Meridian].

—Andrea C. Cervi

DEATH FUGUE (Todesfuge)
Poem by Paul Celan, 1952 (written 1948).

Theodor Adorno's famous statement, made in 1949, that 'to write poetry after Auschwitz is barbaric' reflects not only the cultural dislocation in Germany at the end of World War II but above all a sense that, since the enormity of Nazi crimes seems to place them beyond aesthetic treatment, the only fitting artistic response must be silence. Celan's 'Death Fugue', however, written in 1948 (although it was not widely published until 1952) by a Romanian German of Jewish extraction who lost both parents in the death camps, illustrates that the language of poetry, with its compressed metaphors, its suggestive allusions, and its emotional intensity, is capable of confronting even such horrors and indeed can articulate them with a force and immediacy that prose, let alone bare statistics, would struggle to match.

In just 36 lines 'Death Fugue' seeks to convey the Jewish experience of Auschwitz. From the opening oxymoron of the 'black milk' which the inmates must drink, to the closing juxtaposition of the golden-haired German girl and the ashen-haired Jewess, the poem is built upon contrast. Murder is carried out to the background of music performed by the prisoners themselves, the victims are promised death as if through the generosity of the perpetrators, while the officer in charge of the carnage, having killed Jews by day, writes love-letters home at night. And the whole deranged world is evoked by the poet within the structure and discipline of a fugue. It is this last contradiction which is probably the most shocking, as the beauty of a form normally associated with praise of the divine clashes with the vileness of the material it sustains.

Like its musical counterpart this verbal fugue establishes a theme, repeats, develops, and modifies it, at the same time introducing contrasting matter which is interwoven with, and played off against, the original. So the Jews drink their 'Black milk of daybreak' at evening, at noon, at morning, at night, in varied and anachronic sequence. This sinister image, running throughout the poem, may well carry associations of the gas with which the Jews were killed, or the smoke from the crematoria that filled the air, but it is a mistake to pin it down to a single static meaning, for it signifies the depravity of a whole system, one which violated the order of nature and compelled the victims to become agents in their own destruction. The only other action in which the Jews here are seen engaging, apart from playing violins to accompany the slaughter (in Auschwitz there was indeed an 'orchestra' of inmates), is the digging of their own graves.

In counterpoint to this helplessness there appears in line five the man who gives the orders. With the enigmatic statement, made on four occasions, that he 'plays with the serpents' he is aligned with the archetypal emblems of evil, and he shows his malign power by whistling up 'his Jews' as he would whistle out his dogs, commanding the musicians to play 'more sweetly' while deriding his victims for their imminent fate. Menacingly he reaches for the gun in his belt, then closes one of his blue eyes to take careful aim and fire: 'he strikes you with leaden bullet his aim is true'. In the last third of the poem Celan introduces what has become one of the best-known phrases from the literature of this period, a sombre incantation which is repeated at intervals three more times, like a dark chord drowning out the other instruments: 'death is a master from Germany'.

His day's work done, the man retires to his house to indulge in romantic thoughts and write to Margarete in Germany. This symbol of Aryan womanhood is contrasted throughout the poem with the figure of Shulamith, her Jewish counterpart. In the Old Testament Song of Solomon the beautiful Shulammite woman had possessed hair 'like purple' (7:5), but now it is ashen, consumed by fire. Resonances of the Old Testament recall the timelessness of Jewish persecution. In Babylonian exile too the Jews had been forced by their captors to make music against their will (Psalm 137), and the Book of Lamentations recalls a time when the servants of God had been 'whiter than milk', as against their present condition with faces 'blacker than a coal' (Lamentations 4:7–8). Such Old Testament experiences, however, are usually in the context of Israel departing from the Lord and receiving just retribution, and there always remains the hope of restoration. In Celan's poem there is no such underlying moral order: the Jews, so it seems, have been deserted by both God and man, left to suffer for no reason other than their race, in a world devoid of logic or compassion.

One critic, L.L. Duroche, has suggested that in the poem's final couplet, 'your golden hair Margarete / your ashen hair Shulamith', there is a hint of reconciliation, even of redemp-

tion through the power of love, but this is a grotesque misreading. 'Death Fugue' offers no explanation and holds out no comfort; its conclusion is not harmony or resolution but an obscene discord. Celan later repudiated the poem as too explicit, and it is certainly more accessible than his later work. Yet with its haunting imagery and its incongruous marriage of form and meaning, it expresses something of a reality whose full terror must, in truth, remain beyond words. It is a chilling and deeply memorable poem.

—Peter J. Graves

CÉLINE, Louis-Ferdinand. Born Louis-Ferdinand Destouches in Courbevoie, France 27 May 1894. Adopted the pseudonym Céline. Educated at a school in Paris; Diepholz Volksschule in Germany, 1908; a school in Rochester, Kent, 1909; worked as a clerk in a silk shop, an errand boy in Paris and Nice, and for a goldsmith while studying for his baccalauréat; Rennes Medical School, 1919–24, qualified as doctor 1924. Married 1) Suzanne Nebout in 1915 (marriage never registered); 2) Edith Follet in 1919 (divorced 1926), one daughter; 3) Lucette Almanzoe in 1943. Served in the French cavalry, 1912–15: sergeant; military medal; worked in French passport office, London, 1915; worked as ship's doctor, 1939–40. Trader for a French forestry company, West Africa, 1917; practising doctor: in Rennes, then with League of Nations, 1925–28; in Clichy, 1928–38; in Bezons 1940–44, Germany, 1944–45, and Denmark, 1945; imprisoned in Denmark, 1945–47; returned to France in 1950: found guilty of collaboration with Germany during World War II, and sentenced to one year in prison: pardoned in 1951; then lived in Meudon, near Paris. Recipient: Prix Renaudot, 1933. *Died 1 July 1961.*

PUBLICATIONS

Collections

Oeuvres complètes, edited by Henri Godard. 2 vols., 1962–74.
Oeuvres, edited by Jean Ducourneau. 5 vols., 1966–69.
Oeuvres, edited by Frédéric Vitoux. 1981– .

Fiction

Voyage au bout de la nuit. 1932; revised edition, 1952; as *Journey to the End of the Night*, translated by John H.P. Marks, 1934, revised edition, 1983; also translated by Ralph Manheim, 1988.
Mort à crédit. 1936; as *Death on the Installment Plan*, translated by John H.P. Marks, 1938; also translated by Ralph Manheim, 1966; as *Death on Credit*, translated by Manheim, 1989.
Guignol's Band. 1944; translated as *Guignol's Band*, translated by Bernard Frechtman and Jack T. Nile, 1954.
Féerie pour une autre fois. 1952; edited by Henri Godard, 1985.
Normance. 1954.
D'un château à l'autre. 1957; as *Castle to Castle*, translated by Ralph Manheim, 1968.

Nord. 1960; as *North*, translated by Ralph Manheim, 1972.
Le Pont de Londres. 1964.
Rigodon. 1969; as *Rigodon*, translated by Ralph Manheim, 1974.
Maudits soupirs pour une autre fois, edited by Henri Godard. 1986.
Cannon Fodder, translated by K. De Coninck and B. Childish. 1988.

Plays

L'Église. 1933.
Ballets, sans musique, sans personne, sans rien (includes *La Naissance d'une fée* and *Voyou Paul, Pauvre Virginie*). 1959.
Progrès. 1978.

Other

La Quinine en therapeutique. 1925.
Mea Culpa, suivi de La Vie et l'oeuvre de Semmelweis. 1936; as *Mea Culpa and the Life and Work of Semmelweis*, translated by Robert A. Parker, 1937.
Bagatelles pour un massacre. 1937.
L'École des cadavres. 1938.
Les Beaux Draps. 1941.
A l'agité du bocal. 1948.
Foudres et flèches. 1948.
Casse-pipe: suivi du Carnet du Cuirassier Detouches. 1949.
Scandale aux abysses. 1950.
Entretiens avec le Professor Y. 1955; as *Conversations with Professor Y* (bilingual edition), translated by Stanford Luce, 1986.
Céline et l'actualité littéraire 1932–1957 and *1957–1961*, edited by Jean-Pierre Dauphin and Henri Godard. 2 vols., 1976.
Cahiers. 1976– .
Semmelweis et autres écrits médicaux, edited by Jean-Pierre Dauphin and Henri Godard. 1977.
Lettres et premier écrits d'Afrique (1916–1917), edited by Jean-Pierre Dauphin. 1978.
Lettres à des amies, edited by Colin W. Nettelbeck. 1979.
Lettres à Albert Paraz, 1947–1957, edited by Jean-Paul Louis. 1980.
Chansons, edited by Frédéric Monnier. 1981.
Lettres à son avocat: 118 lettres inédites à maître Albert Naud, edited by Frédéric Monnier. 1984.
Lettres à Tixier: 44 lettres inédites à maître Tixier-Vignancourt, edited by Frédéric Monnier. 1985.
Lettres à Joseph Garcin (1929–1938), edited by Pierre Lainé. 1987.
Lettres à N.R.F: 1931–1961, edited by Pascal Fouché. 1991.
Lettres à Marie Bell Céline, edited by Jean Paul Louis. 1991.
Céline et les éditions Denoël 1932–48: Correspondances et documents, edited by Pierre-Edmond Robert. 1991.

*

Bibliography: *Essai de bibliographie des études en langue française consacrées à Louis-Ferdinand Céline*, 1977; *A Half-Century of Céline: An Annotated Bibliography, 1932–1982* by Stanford Luce, 1983.

Critical Studies: *The Crippled Giant: A Literary Relationship with Louis-Ferdinand Céline* by Milton Hindus, 1950, revised edition, 1986; *Céline* by David Hayman, 1965; *Céline and His Vision*, 1967, and *Voyeur Voyant: A Portrait of L.-F.Céline*, 1971, both by Erika Ostrovsky; *Céline: The Novel as Delirium* by Allen Thiher, 1972; *Céline, Man of Hate* by Bettina L. Knapp, 1974; *Céline* by Patrick McCarthy, 1975; *Louis-Ferdinand Céline* by David O'Connell, 1976; *Louis-Ferdinand Céline* by Merlin Thomas, 1979; *Understanding Céline* by James Flynn and C.K. Mertz, 1984; *Céline and His Critics* edited by Stanford Luce, 1986; *Céline's Imaginative Space* by Jane Carson, 1987; *The Golden Age of Louis-Ferdinand Céline* by Nicholas Hewitt, 1987; *Language and Narration in Céline's Writings: The Challenge of Disorder* by Ian Noble, 1987; *Enfin Céline vint: A Contextualist Reading of Journey to the End of the Night and Death on the Installment Plan* by Wayne Burns, 1988; *Louis-Ferdinand Céline: Journey to the End of the Night* by John Sturrock, 1990; *Louis-Ferdinand Céline: The I of the Storm* by Charles Krance, 1992; *Understanding Céline* by Philip Solomon, 1992.

*   *   *

Louis-Ferdinand Céline emerged as a great writer in 1932 with his first novel, *Voyage au bout de la nuit* (*Journey to the End of the Night*). Although the early pages, which depict the carnage of World War I and hallucinatory journeys to Africa and America, are more brilliant and were responsible for the book's immediate success, the second half of the book may be of greater significance. The doctor-hero, Bardamu, undertakes a quest to understand and absorb the suffering of modern life, which allows Céline to demonstrate not merely the collapse of traditional values but the inadequacy of traditional fiction with its reliance on plot, rounded characters, and familiar language.

So in *Mort à crédit* (*Death on Credit*) he dismembers his sentences and introduces a tide of Parisian slang that is meant more as a lyrical than as a realistic device. This novel reverses the conventional view of childhood in order to depict the pain the child undergoes as he awakens to his surroundings, and the broken rhythms, the slang, and the obscenity permit Céline to render the child's world with great immediacy.

Obsessed with his own nightmares and convinced that another world war was imminent, Céline then wrote his pamphlets *Bagatelles pour un massacre* [Bagatelles for a Massacre] and *L'École des cadavres* [School for Corpses]. Although their message is appalling, they are an integral part of his work and cannot be ignored. The solution to Hitler's threat is, Céline maintains, appeasement and the author of all the world's evil is the Jew. Whereas evil in Céline's novels is not so easily explained away for it is inherent in the human condition, here it is personified in the figure of the Jew. During the Occupation Céline remained in France and continued to publish and, while in no sense a leading collaborator, he certainly helped the cause of anti-semitism.

For this reason his work was banned at the Liberation, was afterwards long neglected and has only in the last 20 years been widely read. His later novels are generally considered to be less good than the early ones, but one of them, *Féerie pour une autre fois* [Fairy-Tale for Another Time], is a fascinating work that is an investigation both of World War II and of artistic creation itself. Céline attempts to incorporate into the novel other arts like painting and film while giving pride of place to the ballet. Art is depicted as making and unmaking the universe, and its demonic, destructive quality is emphasized, although the role of the ballet-dancer is to restore harmony. In this novel Céline created a multiple work of art that is not governed by a single point of view and invites many different readings.

The only one of his later novels to be appreciated in his lifetime was *D'un château à l'autre* (*Castle to Castle*), a satire of the collaborators and a good example of Céline's black humour. In general Céline was the voice of the 1930s and 1940s who sought to express with a novel intensity the violence of his age. But he was also a consummate artist whose experiments with the language and structure of novels have influenced contemporary writers, both French and foreign.

—Patrick McCarthy

JOURNEY TO THE END OF THE NIGHT (Voyage au bout de la nuit)
Novel by Louis-Ferdinand Céline, 1932.

The appearance of *Journey to the End of the Night* provoked scandal and controversy in French literary circles. It was included in the 1933 list of candidates for the coveted Goncourt prize with Léon Daudet vigorously campaigning in its favour, but it narrowly missed, receiving shortly thereafter the Renaudot prize. Whereas that year's Goncourt nomination has passed into oblivion, Céline's novel ranks among the great novels of the 20th century. As Leon Trotskii remarked in 'Céline et Poincaré' (1933), 'Céline walked into great literature the way others walk into their own homes'.

Belonging to that category of novels with famous opening sentences, the *Journey*'s first sentence defied accepted literary and grammatical conventions with its colloquial use of the contraction ça (that, it) instead of the correct form of *cela*: 'Ça a débuté comme ça' ('Here's how it started'). Such double emphasis announced, as Céline called it, his modest invention of a prose style patterned on popular, spoken French. Céline thus broke away from the naturalist tradition that generally confined popular speech to phonetic transcription and passages of dialogue. The *Journey*'s originality lay in its implicit rejection of the popular *roman à thèse*; it was not a safely contained slice of life so much as a way of life that aesthetically revolutionized the French novel with the rhythmic flow of its slang and its linguistic post-positions and prepositions (unfortunately, these do not translate well in to English), which are so common to French speech patterns but innovative to prose. Céline's conception of language as a living entity in opposition to writing's arrested state would have much to do with the *Journey*'s major themes. In one famous passage, speech is considered a physical calamity:

When you stop to examine the way in which words are formed and uttered, our sentences are hard put to it to survive the disaster of their slobbery origin. The mechanical effort of conversation is nastier and more complicated than defecation. That corolla of bloated flesh, the mouth, which screws itself up to whistle, which sucks its breath, contorts itself, discharges all manner of viscous sounds across a fetid barrier of decaying teeth—how revolting! Yet that it what we are abjured to sublimate into an ideal. It's not easy. Since we are nothing but packages of tepid, half-rotted viscera, we shall always have trouble with sentiment. Being in love is nothing, it's sticking together that's difficult. Faeces on the other hand make no attempt to endure or to grow. On this score we are far more unfortunate than shit: our frenzy to persist in our present state—that's the unconscionable torture.

The connection between speech's 'viscous sounds' and bodies as 'packages of tepid, half-rotted viscera' forecloses aesthetic idealization (i.e., writing) and triggers other considerations on the human condition as decay and the frenzy of exacerbated psyches on the verge of mass destruction and biological breakdown.

Lauded nevertheless by many critics and writers at the time as a left-wing novel, the *Journey* explores through the eyes of its hapless first-person protagonist, Bardamu (pushed on through life by his burden; *barda* = knapsack, *mu* = driven, propelled), the profound cruelty of the powerful and the deep despair of the ragged, rationalized 'minions of King Misery'. But Céline's aim is not to idealize their social condition. From a psychological and biological perspective, he examines man's egoism and vanity in collusion with his self-destructive biological cells. The famous Freudian hypothesis of the death drive lies just below the surface of Bardamu's explorations and reflections on the human condition.

If Céline's language was ground-breaking, the *Journey*'s narrative development, as is evident from its title, is organized around the cliché often found in the novel, 'life is a voyage'. Céline begins his second epigraph by stating: 'Travel is useful, it exercises the imagination, all the rest is disappointment and fatigue. Our journey is entirely imaginary. That is its strength.' The epigraph concludes with the affirmation that the *Journey* is a work of the imagination, but this first sentence interestingly establishes the link between travel and work ('exercises' translates *travailler*) through the etymological root that *travel and travail* have in common. This equation both popularizes the novel and aestheticizes the popular.

Although its episodic sections (not chapters) loosely imitate picaresque, narrative structure, the *Journey* can be broken down into two basic parts. The first half contains Bardamu's experiences as a brigadier in World War II, his wound, mental trauma, and breakdown, and his passages to Africa and America. The second half contains his return to Paris to finish his medical degree, his routine life as a doctor for the poor, and his continued encounters with Robinson, Bardamu's double, who, first encountered by Bardamu in the dark during the war, in the first half is the object of the protagonist's wanderings in Africa and America and later, in the second half, becomes the protagonist's dependent. Bardamu's role shifts from follower to followed, a reversal predicated on the decline of Robinson's self-esteem and health and on Bardamu's change in social position from poor itinerant worker to established doctor for the poor.

Céline's account of the war counts among some of the most critical and irreverent pages on the experience of modern war: 'Horses are lucky, they're stuck with the war same as us, but nobody expects them to be in favour of it, to pretend to believe in it. Unfortunate, yes, but free! Enthusiasm, the stinker, was reserved for us!' Bardamu suffers a mental breakdown, which he attributes to his great fear of death. Refusing the unimaginative vocation of death, he opts for cowardice, a survival tactic, bringing him down in the eyes of his zealous American girlfriend, Lola, a nurse of the American Expeditionary Force stationed in Paris; but, for Bardamu, survival means placing imagination (i.e., fear) above suicidal patriotism (i.e., courage). Discharged from the army, Bardamu embarks for the French Congo.

As in Gide's scandalous exposure of colonialism in his *Voyage au Congo* (1927), Bardamu encounters depraved colonials intent on making their fortunes by robbing the native population of their dignity and the fruits of their hard labour. These colonials are, however, victims too, being ill-equipped for the heat, moisture, and malaria, which only accelerate their physical and moral decay. In a malarial delirium,

Bardamu sets fire to his isolated encampment and escapes the jungle only to find himself a purchased galley slave aboard a boat headed for America. He lands at Ellis Island where he finds employment as a flea statistician. He manages to escape to Manhattan, a concrete jungle of money temples and distant people: 'The bigger and taller the city, the less they care.' Penniless, he eventually tracks down his old girlfriend, Lola, who bribes him to leave town. From here he travels to Detroit, where he will find employment at the Ford factory. Rationalization and Fordism convert the poor and the handicapped into machines, while the factory's deafening noise is reminiscent of war: 'It's not shame that makes them bow their heads. You give into noise as you give in to war.' Life at the factory is only made bearable by Bardamu's love affair with the magnanimous prostitute, Molly, whom he leaves behind with regret in order to pursue a new identity in Paris.

Among his responsibilities as doctor, Bardamu finds himself mixed up with Robinson, who has accepted payment from the Henrouilles to murder Grandma Henrouille, one of Bardamu's patients. Robinson, however, temporarily loses his sight in a botched attempt to rig a rabbit hutch with explosives destined for Grandma Henrouille. With the help of Bardamu and the Abbé Protiste (whose mouth it was that led to the description above of grotesque speech), the Henrouilles manage to rid themselves of Robinson and Grandma Henrouille by sending them to Toulouse to work in a catacomb run by a convent. Robinson becomes engaged to a young dressmaker, Madelon, who also works part-time at the vault. Realizing that his solitary nature goes against married life, Robinson tries to extricate himself from his commitment to Madelon, who becomes increasingly possessive and paranoid. Matters between them go from bad to worse and Bardamu is unsuccessful in his attempts to help his friend. During a violent dispute in a taxi cab, Madelon shoots Robinson in front of Bardamu and his companion, Sophie. The novel ends with Robinson's death.

A mixture of slang and lyricism, black humour and aphorisms, verging at times on the sentimental, *Journey to the End of the Night* was not only a turning point in Céline's career but also a turning point in the French novel.

—Andrea Loselle

CENDRARS, Blaise. Born Frédéric Sauser Hall in La Chaux-de-Fonds, Switzerland, 1 September 1887. Naturalized French citizen, 1916. Educated at International School, Naples; Basle Gymnasium; L'École de commerce, Neuchâtel, 1903–04; studied medicine and philosophy, University of Berne, 1908–09. Served with the French Foreign Legion during World War I; injured in Navarin, right arm amputated, 1916: Order of the Army, Croix de Guerre, and Médaille Militaire, all 1915. Married 1) Fela Poznanska in 1914 (divorced), one daughter and two sons; 2) Raymone Duchâteau in 1949. Assistant to the film director, Abel Gance, Rome, 1918–20. Worked at a variety of jobs including juggling, prospecting, journalism; producer and director of films in France, Italy, and Hollywood; travelled extensively throughout Africa and South America. Editor, *Les Hommes Nouveaux* and *Paris-Soir*; reporter for several provincial newspapers, including *Le Jour* and *Paris-Soir*, 1934–40.

Associated with the early Cubist movement. Recipient: Grand prix littéraire de la ville de Paris, 1961. *Died 21 January 1961.*

PUBLICATIONS

Collections

Oeuvres complètes [Denoël Edition]. 8 vols., 1960–65.
Selected Writings, edited by Walter Albert, translated by Albert, John Dos Passos, and Scott Bates. 1962.
Poésies complètes 1912–1924. 1967.
Oeuvres complètes. 16 vols., 1968–71.
Selected Poems, translated by Peter Hoida, 1979.

Fiction

La Fin du monde. 1919.
L'Anthologie nègre (folklore). 1921; as *The African Saga*, translated by Margery Bianco, 1927.
La Perle fiévreuse. 1921–22.
L'Or, la merveilleuse histoire du Général Johann August Sutter. 1925; as *Sutter's Gold*, translated by Henry Longan Stuart, 1926; as *Gold: The Marvellous History of General John Augustus Sutter*, translated by Nina Rootes, 1982.
Moravagine. 1926; revised edition, 1956; as *Moravagine*, translated by Alan Brown, 1968.
L'Eubage: Aux antipodes de l'unité. 1926; as *At the Antipodes of Unity*, 1922.
Petits contes nègres pour les enfants des Blancs. 1928; as *Little Black Stories for Little White Children*, translated by Margery Bianco, 1929.
Le Plan de l'aiguille. 1929; as *Antarctic Fugue*, translated anonymously, 1948; as *Dan Yack*, translated by Nina Rootes, 1987.
Les Confessions de Dan Yack. 1929; as *Confessions of Dan Yack*, translated by Nina Rootes, 1990.
Rhum, ou l'aventure de Jean Galmot. 1930.
Comment les Blancs sont d'anciens Noirs (stories). 1930.
Carolina (story). 1931.
Vol à voile. 1932.
Histoires vraies (stories). 1937.
La Vie dangereuse (stories). 1938.
D'Oultremer à Indigo (stories). 1940.
Emmène-moi au bout du monde! . . . 1956; as *To the End of the World*, translated by Alan Brown, 1967.

Verse

Les Pâques. 1912; as *Les Pâques à New York*, 1918; as *Easter in New York*, translated by Scott Bates, 1918.
La Prose du Transsibérien et de la petite Jehanne de France. 1913; as *The Trans-Siberian*, translated by John Dos Passos, in *Panama; or, the Adventures of My Seven Uncles*, 1931.
Séquences. 1913.
La Guerre au Luxembourg. 1916.
Le Panama; ou, les Aventures de mes sept oncles. 1918; as *Panama; or the Adventures of My Seven Uncles*, translated by John Dos Passos, 1931.
Dix-neuf poèmes élastiques. 1919; edited by Jean-Pierre Goldenstein, 1986.
Sonnets dénaturés. 1923.
Feuilles de route I: Le Formose. 1924; with parts I and II, in

Poésies complètes, 1944; in *Complete Postcards from the Americas*, translated by Monique Chefdor, 1976.
Kodak. 1924; as *Kodak*, translated by Ron Padgett, 1976; in *Complete Postcards from the Americas*, translated by Monique Chefdor, 1976.
Poésies complètes. 1944; as *Complete Poems*, translated by Ron Padgett, 1992.
Du monde entier au coeur du monde (complete poems). 1957.
Amours. 1961.

Plays

Danse macabre de l'amour. 1912.
La Création du monde (ballet, with Darius Milhaud and Fernand Léger; produced 1923). 1931.
Films sans images (radio plays). 1959.

Screenplays: *La Roue*, 1922; *La Fin du monde*, 1931.

Other

Le Cahier noir, le cahier rouge (lectures). 1906.
Novogorod, la légende de l'or gris et du silence. 1909.
Le Dernier des masques: Rémy de Gourmont. 1910.
Moganni Nameh. 1912.
Profond aujourd'hui. 1917; as *Profound Today*, translated by Harold Loeb, 1922.
J'ai tué. 1918; as *I Have Killed*, translated by Harold Ward, 1919.
Peintres. 1919.
L'A B C du cinéma. 1926.
L'Éloge de la vie dangereuse. 1926.
La Métaphysique du café. 1927.
Une nuit dans la forêt. 1929; as *Night in the Forest*, translated by Margaret Ewing, 1985.
Aujourd'hui. 1931.
Cassandra. 1933.
Panorama de la pègre (articles). 3 vols., 1935.
Hollywood, la Mecque du cinéma. 1936.
Chez l'armée anglaise (articles). 1940.
L'Homme foudroyé (autobiography). 1945; as *The Astonished Man*, translated by Nina Rootes, 1970.
La Main coupée (autobiography). 1946; as *Lice*, translated by Nina Rootes, 1973.
Bourlinguer (autobiography). 1948; as *Planus*, translated by Nina Rootes, 1972.
La Banlieue de Paris (on Robert Doisneau's photographs). 1949.
Le Lotissement du ciel, photographs by Robert Doisneau. 1949.
Blaise Cendrars vous parle (interviews with Michel Manoll). 1952.
Le Brésil—Des hommes sont venus, photographs by Jean Manzon. 1952.
Noël aux quatre coins du monde (radio broadcasts). 1953.
Trop c'est trop (articles and stories). 1957.
A l'aventure (selection). 1958.
Films sans images: Sarajevo, Gilles de Rais, Le Divin Arétin (radio broadcasts). 1959.
Dites-nous, Monsieur Blaise Cendrars, edited by Hughes Richard. 1969.
Inédits secrets (journals, correspondence, plays), edited by Miriam Cendrars. 1969.
Paris ma ville. 1987.
John Paul Jones; ou, L'Ambition. 1989.
J'écris. Écrivez-moi: Correspondance Blaise Cendrars–

Jacques-Henry Lévesque: 1924–1959, edited by Monique Chefdor. 1991.
Modernities and Other Writings (essays), edited by Monique Chefdor, translated by Esther Allen. 1992.

Translator, *Hors la loi!*, by Alphonso J. Jennings. 1936.
Translator, *Forêt vierge*, by Ferreira de Castro. 1938.

*

Bibliography: *Bibliographie générale de l'oeuvre de Blaise Cendrars* by Hughes Richard, 1965.

Critical Studies: *Blaise Cendrars* by Henry Miller, 1951; *Blaise Cendrars* by Jean Buhler, 1960; *Situation de Blaise Cendrars* by Jean-Claude Lovey, 1965; *Blaise Cendrars; ou, La Passion de l'écriture* by Yvette Bozon-Scalzitti, 1977; *Cendrars aujourd'hui; présence d'un romancier* edited by Michel Décaudin, 1977; *Au coeur du texte: essai sur Blaise Cendrars* by John Carlo Flückiger, 1977; *Blaise Cendrars: Bilans nègres* by Martin Steins, 1977; *Blaise Cendrars: Discovery and Re-Creation* by Jay Bochner, 1978; *Blaise Cendrars* by Monique Chefdor, 1980; *Blaise Cendrars* by Miriam Cendrars, 1984; *Le Premier Siècle de Cendrars 1887–1987*, 1987, and *Cendrars et l'Homme Foudroyé*, 1989, both edited by Claude LeRoy; *Genèse et dossier d'une polémique: 'La Prose du Transsibérien et de la petite Jehanne de France'* by Antoine Sidoti, 1987; *Le Texte cendrarsien* edited by Jacqueline Bernard, 1988; *Blaise Cendrars* by Anne-Marie Jaton, 1991.

* * *

A fast-moving, exciting novel whose graphic events come gradually to take on a mythic character, *L'Or* (*Sutter's Gold*) is a work that reflects in fiction many of the factors making up Blaise Cendrars's complex personality, including a tendency to mingle fact and fantasy in an inextricable web. General John Augustus Sutter, based on a historical figure, is Swiss, like Cendrars, and around his life story the novelist weaves a tale of travel, violence, and adventure. This man, 'bankrupt, vagabond, thief and swindler', as he is uncompromisingly described, sets out from his village, makes his way through France to Le Havre, whence, on a square-rigged paddle-steamer, he crosses the Atlantic to New York where in 1834 'all the shipwrecked souls from the Old World disembark'. Before long Sutter is making his way west, farming in Missouri and then moving eventually on to California where he acquires land and becomes master of a vast domain. All might seem set fair. In 1848, however, gold is discovered on his land, and in the rough and tumble of the gold rush, Sutter finds, not prosperity, but personal ruination. At the end we see the figure of a pathetic old man in his second childhood. Told in short chapters and laconic prose, *Sutter's Gold* captures all the excitement of an epic life that rises from the depths only to fall again, and the novel, which has been translated into many languages, remains Cendrars's most popular work.

Before writing it, Cendrars had had an exciting life which included journeys from his native Switzerland to Russia and to the United States. His period of service in the French Foreign Legion ended with the amputation of his right arm after he had been wounded in the Battle of the Marne in September 1915. Though his education hasd been cut short, he had, from his childhood on, always been a voracious reader, especially of the French Romantic authors, and he had soon also begun to find expression of his restless and enquiring spirit in the more advanced forms of literature and the other arts. He wrote experimental poetry, and he became particularly involved in the emergence of Cubism. The cinema was another medium that seemed to him to have great potential, and a collection of his film reviews was published in his *L'A B C du cinéma* in 1926. Another interest was jazz, at a time when its lively rhythms and vivid instrumental colour struck European ears as the sort of music that had genuine elemental vigour. A product of this interest was Cendrars's collaboration with Darius Milhaud, one of the group of French avant-garde composers known as 'Les Six', on the jazz ballet *La Création du monde*. It was first performed by the Ballets Suédois in Paris in 1923, with its 'African' idiom inevitably provoking something of an outcry. Work of this sort appealed, however, only to a relatively restricted coterie, and Cendrars owes his wider reputation to his prose works.

Sutter's Gold was published in 1925, and *Moravagine*, of which excerpts had been printed half a decade earlier, followed the year after. In it is reflected the Surrealists' passionate curiosity about the nature of insanity. This topic is explored through the investigations carried out by a young psychiatrist on Moravagine, a particularly fascinating patient. Moravagine is an old man who turns out to be the heir to the Hungarian throne. Having been brought up in isolation, he has become excessively inward-looking and consequently developed a morbid sensitivity. Doctor and patient flee from the Swiss sanatorium. Moravagine subsequently becomes a serial killer of women before getting involved in terrorist activity in Moscow at the time of the 1905 uprising then escaping to the New World. *Les Confessions de Dan Yack* (*Confessions of Dan Yack*) also has adventurous journeying as one of its major structures, this time by a playboy from St Petersburg who goes to the Antarctic, but the second volume of the two in which it was originally published is an exploration of the hero's relationship with his wife who had died some time earlier.

Rhum, l'aventure de Jean Galmot [Rum, Jean Galmot's Adventure] owes something to the style and to the inspiration of *Sutter's Gold*. It is based on a real-life event that Cendrars was invited to report on for the Paris newspaper, *Vu*—the trial of the murderer of Jean Galmot, a *député* for Guiana in the French National Assembly whose rise and fall in exotic surroundings had been as spectacular as that of Sutter.

Cendrars continued to write throughout his life, producing film criticism and a book on Hollywood as well as novels and verse. In the first year of World War II he was attached as a war correspondent to the British Headquarters in France, publishing a collection of his newspaper articles in *Chez l'armée anglaise* [With the British Army] in 1940. Cendrars also wrote a number of autobiographical books, the exact veracity of which has been increasingly questioned by critics who are now more inclined to see them either as exercises in mystification or as quasi-fictional works.

—Christopher Smith

CERNUDA (y Bidón), Luis. Born in Seville, Spain, 21 September 1902. Educated at school in Seville, 1914–18;

University of Seville, 1919–25, degree in law 1925. Military service, 1923. Lecturer in Spanish literature, École Normale, Toulouse, 1928–29; worked in bookshop, Madrid, 1929; contributor to *Heraldo de Madrid*, 1933–34; worked for the government Misiones Pedagógicas, 1934; secretary to Spanish ambassador in Paris, 1936; returned to Madrid, 1936, and wrote for several newspapers; Spanish assistant, Cranleigh School, Surrey, England, and gave pro-Republican lectures, 1938; reader in Spanish, Glasgow University, 1939–43; Cambridge University, 1943–45; lecturer, Instituto Español, London, 1945; professor of Spanish, Mount Holyoke College, Massachusetts, 1947–52; moved to Mexico, 1952; professor of Spanish, Autonomous University of Mexico, Mexico City, 1954–60; visiting professor, University of California, Los Angeles, and San Francisco State College, 1960–62. *Died 5 November 1963.*

PUBLICATIONS

Collections

Poesía, edited by A.E. Kins and D. Morris. 1971.
Poesía completa, edited by Derek Harris and Luis Maristany. 1974; revised edition, 1977.
Prosa completa, edited by Derek Harris and Luis Maristany. 1975.

Verse

Perfil del aire. 1927.
La invitación a la poesía. 1933.
Donde habite el olvido. 1934.
El joven marino. 1936.
La realidad y el deseo. 1936; revised editions, 1940, 1958, 1964; edited by Miguel Flys, 1982.
Ocnos (prose poems). 1942; revised and enlarged editions, 1949, 1963; edited by D. Musacchio, 1977.
Las nubes. 1943; edited by Luis Antonio de Villena, with *Desolación de la quimera*, 1984.
Como quien espera el alba. 1947.
Poemas para un cuerpo. 1957.
Díptico español (1960–1961). 1961.
Desolación de la quimera. 1962; edited by Luis Antonio de Villena, with *Las nubes*, 1984.
Antología poética, edited by P.L. Ávila. 1966.
Antología poética, edited by Rafael Santos Torroella. 1970.
Eglogà, edited by Gregorio Prieto. 1970.
Perfil del aire; Con otras obras olvidadas e inéditas, edited by Derek Harris. 1971.
The Poetry of Luis Cernuda, edited by Anthony Edkins and Derek Harris. 1971.
Invitación a la poesía de Luis Cernuda, edited by Carlos Peregrin Otero. 1975.
Antología poética, edited by Philip W. Silver. 1975.
Selected Poems, translated by Reginald Gibbons. 1977.
El exilio en la poesía de Luis Cernuda (selection), edited by Douglas Barnette. 1984.
Sonetos clásicos sevillanos. 1986.
The Young Sailor and Other Poems, translated by Rick Lipinski. 1987.
Luis Cernuda para niños. 1992.

Fiction

Tres narraciones. 1948.

Other

Variaciones sobre tema mexicano. 1952.
Estudios sobre poesía española contemporánea. 1957.
El pensamiento poético en la lírica inglesa (siglo XIX). 1958.
Poesía y literatura. 2 vols., 1960–64; in one volume, 1971.
Crítica, ensayos y evocaciones, edited by Luis Maristany. 1970.
Cartas a Eugenio de Andrade, edited by Ángel Crespo. 1979.
Epistolario inédito. 1981.
La familia interrumpida; Juegos de memoria y olvido por Octavio Paz. 1988.

Translator, *Poemas*, by Friedrich Hölderlin. 1942; revised edition, 1974.
Translator, *Troilo y Cresida*, by Shakespeare. 1953.

*

Critical Studies: *Cuadrivio* (on Darío, López Velarde, Pessoa, Cernuda) by Octavio Paz, 1965; *Et in Arcadia Ego: A Study of the Poetry of Luis Cernuda*, 1966, and *De la mano de Cernuda*, 1989, both by Philip W. Silver; *Other Voices: A Study of the Late Poetry of Luis Cernuda* by J. Alexander Coleman, 1969; *A Generation of Spanish Poets 1920–1936* by Cyril Brian Morris, 1969; *El periodo sevillano de Luis Cernuda*, 1971, and *El surrealismo en la poesía de Luis Cernuda*, 1976, both by J.E. Capote Benot; *La poesía de Luis Cernuda: Estudio cuantitativo del léxico de La realidad y el deseo* by J.A. Bellón Cazabán, 1973; *Luis Cernuda: A Study of the Poetry* by Derek Harris, 1973, and *Luis Cernuda* (in Spanish) edited by Harris, 1977; *La poética de Luis Cernuda* by Agustín Delgado, 1975; *Luis Cernuda y su obra poética*, 1975, and *Luis Cernuda y la generación del 27*, 1983, both by C. Real Ramos; *El espacio y las máscaras: Introducción a la lectura de Luis Cernuda* by Jenaro Talens, 1975; *Luis Cernuda* edited by Gil de Biedma and others, 1977; *Luis Cernuda* (in English) by Salvador Jiménez-Fajardo, 1978, and *The Word as Mirror: Critical Essays on the Poetry of Luis Cernuda* edited by Jiménez-Fajardo, 1989; *Arte, amor y otras soledades en Luis Cernuda* by Carlos Ruiz Silva, 1979; *Españoles en la Gran Bretaña: Luis Cernuda: El hombre y sus temas* by Rafael Martínez Nadal, 1983; *Cernuda y el poema en prosa*, 1984, and *La prosa narrativa de Luis Cernuda*, both by James Valender, 1984; *En torno a la poesía de Luis Cernuda* by Richard K. Curry, 1985; *Luis Cernuda: Escritura cuerpo y deseo* by Manuel Ulacia, 1986; *Luis Cernuda and the Modern English Poets* by Brian Hughes, 1988; *Los finales poemáticos en la obra de Luis Cernuda* by Hilda Pato, 1988.

* * *

Luis Cernuda was a member of that brilliant group of Spanish poets known as the Generation of 1927, which included such major poets as Federico García Lorca, Jorge Guillén, Pedro Salinas, Gerardo Diego, and Rafael Alberti. Not until the decade of the 1960s did Cernuda achieve his just recognition as one of the most original and profound poets of 20th-century Spain. With exemplary versatility, depth, and poetic skill he explored a number of poetic techniques from the romantic to the surrealistic. Thematically, Cernuda's is a poetry of continuous tension, grounded in his desperate attempt to escape the conflicts between reality and desire, appearances and truth. He sought to escape an alienating and hostile world in the dream of some transcendent existence which would unify self and world. *La realidad y el deseo* [Reality and Desire] became the title of his collected work, and has continued to influence the generations of Spanish poets that followed him.

The first book of poetry by Cernuda was entitled *Perfil del aire* [Profile of the Air]. In an impressionistic and melancholy work, the young poet seeks to fuse his personal experience and the surrounding environment. Re-creating the memories of his childhood, he retreats to a hidden garden symbolic of Paradise and escapes the threatening world of objective reality. This first collection is reminiscent of the impressionistic techniques of Juan Ramón Jiménez and the refined Romantic verse of Gustavo Adolfo Bécquer, and the classical forms and elegance recall the poetry of Jorge Guillén. The theme of the artist isolated in a lost Paradise continues in 'Égloga, elegía, oda' [Eclogue, Elegy, Ode], with its extended verse and classical form.

Cernuda himself later repudiated what he felt to be the artificiality and imitative beauty of these early volumes, and with 'Un río, un amor' [A River, a Love] embraced the techniques of surrealism, which offered a new freedom in its use of free association to explore the subconscious. This collection initiates the perception of the vital conflict between reality and desire, an opposition which evolves into the dominant force in the poetry of Cernuda. The persona of the poems is hurled into a fractured and alien world of tearless sorrow, pits of snakes, thorns, and ashes—pain upon pain. The poem 'As the Wind' portrays the weary speaker abandoned, as the reality of love becomes the threat of death:

> As the wind throughout the night
> Love in torment or lonely body,
> Knocks in rain against the glass,
> Abandons corners, sobbing.
> (translated by Anthony Edkins)

'Los placeres prohibidos' [Forbidden Pleasures] continues the theme of rejection and, in a number of poems, the surrealistic technique. The defence of erotic desire as a part of the self implies an increasingly apparent ethical concern on the part of the poet. As the eroticism of the verse intensifies, so does the indictment of a blind and repressive society paralysed in the false dichotomy of good versus evil. Surrealism not only liberated Cernuda's poetics; it also encouraged a more intellectualized response to his feelings. Because the poet finds the knowledge of self in memory, a bond is created between image and memory.

Donde habite el olvido [Where Oblivion Dwells], whose title is taken from Bécquer, moves from surrealism to the dark images of romanticism and its idea of an Edenic private world created by the dual attraction of love and death. While the verse is calmer and more measured, the reader encounters a cold scepticism and disillusionment as Cernuda reflects on the adolescent years. The private dream has become a spiritual wasteland, and desire becomes suffering. With this collection, Cernuda enters a more meditative phase. Seeking knowledge of himself by confronting reality, he discovers solitude and alienation as the truth of the human condition. If love can lead only to destruction and pain, then the only exit leads to oblivion and insensibility:

> Where oblivion dwells
> In vast gardens without a dawn;
> Where I shall only be
> The memory of a stone . . .
> (translated by Anthony Edkins)

Acute consciousness of the vocation of the poet is apparent in the poems of 'Invocaciones' which Cernuda began in 1935 and which were later included in *La realidad y el deseo*. While it is somewhat more hopeful than the verse of *Donde habite el olvido*, the themes of evasion, isolation, and solitude dominate the work.

The title of Cernuda's masterpiece, *La realidad y el deseo*, is an encapsulation of his experience, poetry, and philosophy of life. The work ultimately was to include 11 separate editions under the same title. From its inception, the verse of Cernuda merged an erotic awareness with the essence of poetry. The struggle to acknowledge his homosexuality and to identify its relationship with his poetry was arduous and painful. In the later poetry this becomes the defence of his own identity and an attempt to unify self and world. Yet, as Derek Harris observes in *Luis Cernuda: A Study of the Poetry* (1973), this vital existential question of Cernuda's homosexuality creates a metaphor for the alienation of the human condition, for 'he was not a homosexual poet, but a homosexual *and* a poet'.

The tone of the elegiac form of *Las nubes* [The Clouds] is distant and aloof. This verse represents the mature poetry of Cernuda, with the appearance of autodialogue and monologue. Poems like 'Elegía española' [Spanish Elegy] and 'A un poeta muerto' [To a Poet Dead]—dedicated to the assassinated poet Federico García Lorca—lament the destruction of the values, vitality, and spirit of Mother Spain by her sons. Spain as a social and political entity is a new theme, although Cernuda does not address the horrible reality of the Civil War directly. In one of the most acclaimed of the poems, 'La adoración de los Magos' [The Adoration of the Magi], the Wise Men find the God for whom they are sent, but cannot recognize him. 'They sought a new god, and some say they found him/I rarely saw men. I have never seen any gods'. Man is estranged from any idea of God or gods. Some of Cernuda's finest poetry appears in this collection, which reveals a compelling artistry in the complexity of its images, metaphors, and symbols.

In another work of this period *Como quien espera el alba* [Like Someone Waiting for the Dawn], Cernuda continues to seek both engagement with the world and the discovery of his identity in the essence of his poetry. Such poems as 'La familia' [The Family] and 'Las ruinas' [The Ruins] give voice to his alienation and defiance. 'Noche del hombre y su demonio' [A Man's Night with His Demons] finds the poet alone in tormented dialectic with the demonic, as the demon tempts him with the idea of social acceptance and attacks the illusion that there is immortality in art. The commitment of the poet to the meaning and authenticity of his verse holds firm as the poem ends in sad resignation. Death itself is viewed as offering dimensions and a sense to life, as well as providing energy to create and even to love. In the mature verse, Cernuda finds beauty, however transitory, superior to reality, and several of the poems are devoted to the creation of pure lyric.

The next two collections of exile poetry, 'Vivir sin estar viviendo' [Living Without Being Alive] and 'Con las horas contadas' [With Time Running Out], became part of the 1958 edition of *La realidad y el deseo*. The perception of time as fleeting and escaping becomes more intense, as the preoccupation with self-analysis is reflected in only slightly disguised self-portraits. There is a new acceptance of alienation and suffering as real and inseparable from the eminent calling of the poet. In 'Sombra de mí' [Shadow of Myself]' the poet suffers, weeps, and desires, but possesses '. . . the shadow/of love which exists in me/While my time is still not run out'.

The final work of Cernuda, *Desolación de la quimera* [The Disconsolate Chimera], takes its title from *The Four Quartets* by T.S. Eliot, whom Cernuda greatly admired. It is clearly intended as a final testament of his poetic creed, and his attitudes regarding Spain, art, and beauty—in sum, his life philosophy. A good number of the verses reveal a dark cynicism and anger regarding what he denounces as a spiteful misunderstanding of his personality and work. It is a work of incredible honesty, however, without apology or false humility. Cernuda fuses art and the self, and, in the process of re-creating and restructuring reality, art creates its own vision and ultimate reality. With complex imagery and multiple metaphors, Cernuda offers changing and increasing planes of meaning which evoke the universal from personal experience in such celebrated poems as 'Luis de Baviera escucha *Lohengrin*' [Ludwig of Bavaria listens to *Lohengrin*].

Cernuda's poetry is the chronicle of a proud and sensitive man's search for individual truth. He sought to flee an alienating and hostile world in a dream of Paradise inspired by his Andalusian youth. The dream of unity somewhere between reality and desire was never fully realized; the existential pain of the confrontation between the poet's experience and his personal desires endured. Finally, he learned to accept the tension of an imperfect reality in the understanding that the poetic and vital struggle itself was the instrument of self-realization. His work reflects a singular dimension of passion, integrity, and ethical dignity in the pursuit of truth and beauty.

—Jerry Phillips Winfield

CERVANTES (Saavedra), Miguel de. Born in Alcalá de Henares, Spain, October 1547. Grew up in Córdoba, Cabra, and Seville. Attended the Estudio de la Villa, Madrid, 1567–68, and studied under the Erasmian humanist, López de Hoyos. Married Catalina de Salazar y Palacios in 1584; had one daughter by Ana Franca de Rojas. Went to Rome in 1569, possibly after a brawl in Madrid; chamberlain to Cardinal Giulio Acquaviva, 1570; enlisted as soldier by 1571; fought with the Spanish fleet at the battle of Lepanto, 1571, sustaining an injury; later, expeditions to Corfu and Navarino, 1572, and to Tunis, 1573, then in garrisons at Palermo, Sardinia, and Naples; was captured by pirates and imprisoned by Turks in Algiers, 1575–80: ransomed, 1580; went on diplomatic mission to Oran, North Africa, 1581; returned to Spain, tax inspector and purchasing agent (excommunicated briefly in 1587 for financial zeal); suffered bankruptcy and two short prison terms (1597 and 1602) for financial irregularities; application for administrative post in America denied; lived mainly in Seville, 1596–1600, and Madrid after c.1606. *Died 23 April 1616.*

PUBLICATIONS

Collections

Obras, edited by B.C. Aribau and Francisco Ynduráin. 2 vols., 1846.
Obras completas, edited by J.E. Hartzenbusch and C. Rosell. 1863.
Complete Works, edited by James Fitzmaurice-Kelly. 1901–03.

Obras completas, edited by R. Schevill and A. Benilla y San Martín. 16 vols., 1914–41.
The Portable Cervantes, edited and translated by Samuel Putnam. 1947.
Obras completas, edited by Ángel Valbuena Prat. 10th edition, 1956.
Obras completas, edited by Germán de Argumosa. 2 vols., 1964–65.

Fiction

La Galatea. 1585; edited by Juan Bautista Avalle-Arce, 1987; as *La Galatea*, translated by Gordon W.J. Gyll, 1867.
El ingenioso hidalgo Don Quijote de la Mancha. 2 vols., 1605–15; edited by Francisco Rodríguez Marín, 8 vols., 1911, and by Vicente Gaos, 3 vols., 1987; as *The History of Don Quixote of the Mancha*, translated by Thomas Shelton, 1612; numerous subsequent translations including by Tobias Smollett, 1755, Charles Jarvis, 1883, Samuel Putnam, 1949, J.M. Cohen, 1950, Walter Starkie, 1957, and P.A. Motteux, 1991.
Novelas ejemplares. 1613; edited by F. Rodríguez Marín, 2 vols., 1969, also edited by Juan Bautista Avalle-Arce, 3 vols., 1987; as *Exemplary Novels*, translated in part by James Mabbe, 1640; B.W. Ife and others, 4 vols., 1992; as *Six Exemplary Novels*, translated by Harriet de Onís, 1961; as *Exemplary Stories*, translated by C.A. Jones, 1972.
Los trabajos de Persiles y Sigismunda. 1617; as *The Travels of Persiles and Sigismunda*, translated by 'M.L.', 1619; also translated by Louisa Dorothea Stanley, 1854; as *The Trials of Persiles and Sigismunda*, translated by Celia Richmond Weller and Clark A. Colahan, 1989.
A Dialogue Between Scipio and Berganza; The Comical History of Rincon and Corlado (in English). 1767.

Plays

Ocho comedias y ocho entremeses nuevos. 1615.
La Numancia, El trato de Argel (with *Viage del Parnaso*). 1784; as *El cerco de Numancia*, edited by Robert Marrast, 1984; as *Numantia; The Commerce of Algiers*, translated by Gordon W.J. Gyll, 1870.
Entremeses, edited by Miguel Herrero García. 1945; also edited by Alonso Zamora Vicente, 1979, and by Nicholas Spadaccini, 1985; as *The Interludes*, translated by S. Griswold Morley, 1948, also translated by Edwin Honig, 1964; as *Interludes/Entremeses*, translated by Randall W. Listerman, 1991.

Verse

Viaje del Parnaso. 1614; edited by Miguel Herrero García, 1983; as *Journey to Parnassus*, translated by J.Y. Gibson, 1883.
Viaje del Parnaso y poesías varias, edited by Elias L. Rivers. 1991.

*

Bibliography: *Cervantes: A Bibliography* by R.L. Grismer, 1946; *An Analytical and Bibliographical Guide to Criticism on Don Quixote (1790–1893)* by Dana B. Drake and Dominick L. Finello, 1987.

Critical Studies: *Cervantes* by Aubrey F.G. Bell, 1947; *Cervantes in Arcadia* by J.B Trend, 1954; *Don Quixote's Profession* by Mark Van Doren, 1958; *Don Quixote: An Introductory Essay in Psychology* by Salvador de Madariaga, 1961; *Cervantes's Theory of the Novel* by Edward C. Riley, 1962; *Cervantes and the Art of Fiction* by George D. Trotter, 1965; *Cervantes: A Collection of Critical Essays* edited by L. Nelson, Jr, 1969; *Cervantes: His Life, His Times, His Works* edited by Arnaldo Mondadori, 1970; *Cervantes, The Man and the Genius* by Francisco Navarro y Ledesma, 1973; *Cervantes* by Manuel Durán, 1974; *The Golden Dial: Temporal Configuration in Don Quixote*, 1975, and *A Critical Introduction to Don Quixote*, 1988, both by L.A. Murillo; *Cervantes: A Biography* by William Byron, 1978; *The Romantic Approach to 'Don Quixote': A Critical History of the Romantic Tradition in 'Quixote' Criticism*, 1978, and *Miguel de Cervantes: Don Quixote*, 1990 both by Anthony Close; *The Individuated Self: Cervantes and the Emergence of the Individual*, 1979, *The Substance of Cervantes*, 1985, and *In the Margins of Cervantes*, 1988, all by John G. Weiger; *Don Quixote in World Literature* by Dana B. Drake, 1980; *Cervantes* by Melveena McKendrick, 1980; *The Unifying Concept: Approaches to the Structure of Cervantes's Comedias* by Edward H. Friedman, 1981; *Cervantes: Pioneer and Plagiarist* by E.T. Aylward, 1982; *Cervantes and the Humanist Vision: A Study of Four Exemplary Novels*, 1982, and *Cervantes and the Mystery of Lawlessness: A Study of El casamiento engañoso y El coloquio de los perros*, 1984, both by Alban K. Forcione; *Don Quixote and the Shelton Translation: A Stylistic Analysis* by Sandra Forbes Gerhard, 1982; *Skeptisism in Cervantes* by Maureen Ihrie, 1982; *The Chivalric World of Don Quixote: Style, Structure and Narrative Technique* by Howard Mancing, 1982; *Madness and Lust: A Psychoanalytical Approach to Don Quixote* by Carroll B. Johnson, 1983; *Beyond Fiction: The Recovery of the Feminine in the Novels of Cervantes* by Ruth El Saffar, 1984; *The Half-Way House of Fiction: Don Quixote and Arthurian Romance* by Edwin Williamson, 1984; *Cervantes* by P.E. Russell, 1985; *Don Quixote* by E.C. Riley, 1986; *Cervantes: Modern Critical Views* edited by Harold Bloom, 1987; *Don Quixote: An Anatomy of Subversive Discourse* by James A. Parr, 1988; *Cervantes the Writer and Painter of Don Quixote* by Helena Percas de Ponseti, 1988; *The Novel According to Cervantes* by Stephen Gilman, 1989; *Cervantes and Ariosto* by Thomas R. Hart, 1989; *Cervantes* by Jean Canavaggio, translated by J.R. Jones, 1990; *The Solitary Journey: Cervantes' Voyage to Parnassus* by Ellen D. Lokos, 1991; *Cervantes and the Burlesque Sonnet* by Adrienne Laskier Martin, 1991; *Allegories of Love: Cervantes's Persiles and Sigismunda* by Diana de Armas Wilson, 1991, and *Quixotic Desire: Psychoanalytic Perspectives on Cervantes*, edited by de Armas Wilson and Ruth Anthony El Soffar, 1993; *Through the Shattering Glass: Cervantes and the Self-Made World* by Nicholas Spadaccini and Jenaro Talens, 1992.

* * *

Biographers and critics of Miguel de Cervantes have been no less fascinated by his remarkable life and personality than by the quality of his literary work. Few of our great geniuses have been more stringently treated by luck or fortune, and fewer still have borne life's ill will with greater magnanimity and creative resignation. Cervantes suffered, precisely in the period which for most men offers the opportunity to build a foundation for their future lives, the most arduous fate that might befall a Spaniard of his times: five years of imprisonment and slavery under the Moors in Algeria, from the age of 28 to 33. His heroism as a soldier in the battle of Lepanto and other encounters with the Turks had been rewarded with highly laudatory letters of recommendation. On the basis of these commendations, his captors set a correspondingly high price for his ransom.

When this was finally achieved, and he returned to Spain, he found that his exploits were not to be rewarded with favouritism in the Court. He was a valiant but minor hero of battles now forgotten. The wounded veteran, now well into the fourth decade of his life, decided to pursue a literary career and very consciously modelled his early works on currently popular genres. The pastoral novel was enjoying vogue, and his first novel, *La Galatea*, was cast in that mode. Few read the work today, but it was certainly among the best of the Spanish mannerist style and represented fertile possibilities to this new author, who prided himself on his elegant prose style, his gift for dialogue and plot, and his ability as a poet. *La Galatea* was an ample showcase for these talents, and to the end of his life the author promised a continuation of the novel, but it was never written.

Cervantes proved to be an untalented literary businessman. He was never able to make his living by the pen, although most of his works had moderate success for the period, and translations and pirated editions, while they brought him no income, established his name quite firmly in the literary world. He was forced to seek his livelihood with commissions as a tax collector and purchasing agent for the Spanish government. Through bad management or actual misappropriation, he was twice imprisoned—a popular conjecture is that he wrote the early chapters of *El ingenioso hidalgo Don Quijote de la Mancha* (*Don Quixote*) in the infamous dungeons of Seville—and he was briefly excommunicated for expropriating grain from Church stores.

While pursuing such minor bureaucratic and commercial occupations, Cervantes seems never to have stopped writing —poetry, plays, short comedies, some works of prose. Much of his early work is lost, but it is doubtful that it would have added much of value to the Cervantine corpus we have. The writer did not prize very highly the forgotten plays and poetry to which he refers in passing, and he had little success even with those works that were produced. Better dramatic writers than he—especially Lope de Vega—had 'run off with the monarchy of the theatre', and his poetry, he admitted ruefully, was never of the highest quality.

Cervantes's talent lay above all in narration, in the novel, a genre which was just achieving solidity and definition at the beginning of the 17th century. He claims in the prologue to his *Novelas ejemplares* (*Exemplary Novels*) that he is the first to 'novelize' in Castilian, a boast that is only partly true. The novella was well established in Italy and had been introduced to Spain at least half a century earlier in the form of very short narrative pieces taken from a variety of sources, and Mateo Alemán, his contemporary, had intercalated *novelas* in his picaresque work *Guzmán de Alfarache* (1599). But it is true that Cervantes brought wholly new dimensions to the form in terms of giving each of the 12 tales autonomy and a much broader development of plot and character.

Don Quixote, which began as a parody of the popular books of chivalry, was his superb creation. The immense body of critical examination and eulogy stresses his perspectivism, his ability to create character, contrast, and believable dialogue; his comprehensive knowledge of his own time and of the currents of the age, and the tone of optimistic good humour and moral clarity that characterizes his treatment of the society of his time. *Don Quixote* is referred to frequently as the first modern novel, and very rightly so. It is the first

extensive work of narrative fiction conceived on a grand scale which engages the reader with basic human questions of integrity, folly, social honesty, moralistic delusion, idealism, practical interest, basic concepts of justice, and the strengths and weaknesses of our best resolve. It is certainly the first work of western literature to offer the reader a world view and, as well as telling him an involved and entertaining story, it invites him to think about life and experience in very broad terms.

The first part of *Don Quixote* (1605) had very wide success, but Cervantes had sold his rights to the book for a ridiculously small sum of money. He had begun the promised second part of the novel when a plagiarist published a spurious continuation (1614), probably based on an incomplete manuscript which Cervantes had allowed to circulate in the literary court of Madrid. The real identity of the plagiarist is still unknown, but the apocryphal work, not entirely without merit, is decidedly inferior to the first part of *Don Quixote* or to Cervantes's own continuation (1615). The authentic second part abandons much of the parodic quality with which the novel had begun, to enquire more deeply into the nature of human consciousness, faith in ourselves and beyond ourselves, and the moral perspectives by which we live. Most critics have seen more conceptual depth in the second part, but it is the first which continues to be more widely read and which forms the basis for our English adaptation of the word 'quixotic'.

Cervantes was a writer totally, perhaps obsessively, committed to his craft, and it is with the urgency of impending death that he completed his last novel, *Los trabajos de Persiles y Sigismunda* (*The Trials of Persiles and Sigismunda*), a rambling account of adventures, separations, reunions, and recognitions, a form rare in Spanish Golden Age literature: the Byzantine novel. He had long planned the work, and had extravagant hopes for its success. Aware that his time was mercilessly short, Cervantes was forced to write the last chapters hurriedly. Perhaps the last strokes of his pen were the lines of the dedicatory prologue to the Count of Lemos, which quote an ancient poem which begins, 'puesto ya el pie en el estribo'—'with one foot already placed in death's stirrup'. This last book was not a success either in popular or critical terms, although many later Cervantists have sought to find value in the work.

Cervantes must be read and re-read in his masterpieces, not sought in his minor works, where so many flaws are overwhelmingly evident to the most ingenuous and tolerant eye. These great works are half a dozen of the *Exemplary Novels* and, above all in western literature of the 17th century, the two parts of *Don Quixote*, where the incredible mind of Cervantes lays bare the human soul in all of its possibilities for good, for hope, and for imaginative moral creation.

—James Russell Stamm

DON QUIXOTE (El ingenioso hidalgo Don Quixote de la Mancha)
Novel by Miguel de Cervantes, 1605–15.

Cervantes was 58 when Part One of *Don Quixote* was first published in Madrid in 1605, and 68 by the time Part Two was brought out. By then he had had a varied life that might have provided him with all the inspiration needed for his masterpiece. It is, however, more fruitful to suggest that his experiences brought into particularly sharp focus a set of issues that plainly were major preoccupations of his contemporaries all over western Europe and especially in Spain. Cervantes's father was an impoverished gentleman who had been obliged to train as a surgeon, which was hardly the sort of career a person of his status would have sought, yet the fact that it was understood he had no real choice but to earn a living is revealed by the readiness of another impecunious member of his class to allow his daughter to marry him. Equally significant, however, was Miguel's refusal to follow in his father's footsteps. Instead, after acquiring what education he could, he proposed to put it to good use by turning to writing. It was a way of attracting attention. Another way of coming to the fore was accepting the risks of warfare: he fought heroically at the Battle of Lepanto in 1571 when the Turks were heavily defeated. Cervantes was, however, taken prisoner by the Turks some four years later and spent half a decade in captivity. On his return to Spain, Cervantes again divided his time between literature, with scant success, and attempts to earn a living in the public service. It was the era of the Spanish Armada, and its defeat is a symbol of the decline of the once great state in whose decayed nobility Cervantes aspired to play a minor role. Literature could offer an escape into idealism, and in 1584 he brought out a pastoral romance called *La Galatea*. Finally he found a more satisfactory outlet for his frustrations in the irony and humour of *Don Quixote*. It struck a chord, as is shown by the fact that it was soon translated into all the European languages, with Thomas Shelton's English version appearing in 1612.

Cervantes's story of the adventures of a knight of shreds and patches who embarks on a long series of adventures with his steed Rosinante and his squire, Sancho Panza, has counterparts in a long series of works of fiction that reflect Europe's long fascination with the ideal of chivalry. This led first to romances, then to their reversal in spoofs that are often all the funnier for being addressed to a lower-class readership. At the origins of the tradition stand, if not Alexander and the Greek heroes, then King Arthur and Charlemagne, and the Middle Ages developed the genre, presenting in the mounted knight's quest a figure of all that was noblest in human aspiration. At the start of the 16th century *Amadis de Gaule* swept Europe, appearing to reinvigorate the tradition, but reaction soon set in, in response both to excessive idealization and to the evident decline of nobility as monarchs became absolute and the bourgeoisie claimed a status to match its increasing material prosperity. In France, Rabelais invented *Gargantua*, adding an attack on scolasticism to a satire on chivalric romance as handed down by the chapbooks, and in Italy Ariosto wrote *Orlando furioso*. Meanwhile in Spain the anonymous *Lazarillo de Tormes* gave a worm's eye view of the shams of Spanish society in the mid-16th century, and after that the rich picaresque tradition developed to provide an ironic reflection of the endeavour of knightly romance in an inconsequential rogue's progress. It was from these literary origins and with personal experience to reinforce the impression that Spain was a great civilization in decline that Cervantes derived his comic masterpiece, finding in laughter a release from disgust.

The narrative, a true one, as we are assured tongue-in-cheek, is long and digressive, but it is held together by the characters who have become almost proverbial. Chapter headings lead the reader on, often undercutting the events described by lauding them in extravagant terms that cannot be taken seriously. Sancho too sets up perspectives that ensure we are not tempted to take his master more seriously than he does. Above all we have the figure of Don Quixote, thinking yet not truly reasoning, going on his way from one setback to the next with a self-assurance that would be heroic if it were not crazy. Don Quixote is an unexpectedly upbeat epitaph to a grand tradition that had to die at the start of the early modern period.

—Christopher Smith

CHAMISSO, Adelbert von. Born Louis Charles Adelaide de Chamisso de Boncourt in Champagne region, France, 3 January 1781. Emigrated with his parents to Prussia to escape the French Revolution in 1790. Lived in the Hague, Düsseldorf, Würzburg, and Bayreuth, settled in Berlin from 1796. Educated at Berlin University, studied medicine, 1812–13. Married Antonie Piaste in 1819 (died 1837); several children. Attendant to Queen Friederike Luise, 1796. Commissioned as ensign in the Prussian army, 1798, lieutenant, 1801, engaged in active service in Hameln 1806; discharged 1808. Co-founding member of the liberal literary club Nordsternbund [North Star Alliance], 1803; travelled throughout France and Switzerland, 1806–12; naturalist on Otto von Kotzebue's expedition to the South Seas and to the Northern Pacific, 1815–18; curator, Berlin Museum Botanical Gardens, Berlin 1819; co-editor, with Gustav Schwab, *Deutscher Musenalmanach*, Berlin, 1833–38. Member, Berlin Academy of Sciences, 1835. Hononary doctorate: University of Berlin, 1819. *Died 21 August 1838.*

PUBLICATIONS

Collections

Poetische Werke. 1868.
Aus Chamissos Frühzeit: Ungedruckte Briefe nebst Studien, edited by Ludwig Geiger. 1905.
Sämtliche Werke, edited by Ludwig Geiger. 4 vols., 1907.
Werke, edited by Hermann Tardel. 8 vols., 1907–08.
Werke, edited by Peter Wersig. 1967.
Sämtliche Werke, edited by Jost Perfahl. 2 vols., 1975.

Fiction

Peter Schlemihls wundersame Geschichte, edited by Friedrich de la Motte Fouqué. 1814; revised edition 1827; as 'Zauberposse', 1817; as *Peter Schlemihl*, translated by John Bowring, 1823; also translated by Leopold von Löwenstein-Wertheim, 1957; as *The Wonderful History of Peter Schlemihl*, translated by William Howitt, 1843; also translated by Frederic Henry Hedge, 1899, Theodore Bolton, 1923, and Peter Rudland, 1954; as *The Shadowless Man; or, the Wonderful History of Peter Schlemihl*, 1845.
Erzählungen. 1947.

Verse

Gedichte. 1831.
Zwei Gedichte (ein altes und ein neues): Zum Besten der alten Waschfrau. 1838.
Frauen-Liebe und Leben: Ein Lieder-Cyklus. 1879; as

Women's Love and Life: A Cycle of Song, translated by Frank V. Macdonald, 1881.

The Castle of Boncourt and Other Poems, translated by Alfred Baskerville, in *German Classics of the Nineteenth and Twentieth Centuries*, vol. 5, 1913.

Plays

Faust. 1803; in *Musenalmanach auf das Jahr 1804*, edited by Chamisso and Karl August Varnhagen von Ense, 1804; as *Faust: A Dramatic Sketch*, translated by Henry Phillips, Jr, 1881.

Die Wunderkur (produced 1825).

Der Wunder-Doktor, from a play by Molière. 1828.

Fortunati Glückseckel und Wunschhütlein, edited by E.F. Kossmann. 1895.

Other

De animalibus quibusdam e classe Vermium Linnaeana in circumnavigatione terræ auspicate comite N. Romannzoff, duce Ottone de Kotzebue annis 1815. ad 1818. 1819.

Bemerkungen und Ansichten auf einer Entdeckungs-Reise, unternommen in den Jahren 1815–1818 . . ., in *Entdeckungsreise in die Südsee und nach der Berrings-Strasse zur Erforschung einer nordöstlichen Durchfahrt unternommen in den Jahren 1815–1818*, by Otto von Kotzebue, vol. 3, 1821; as *Remarks and Opinions of the Naturalist of the Expedition*, translated by H.E. Lloyd, in *A Voyage of Discovery into the South Sea and Beering's Straits, for the Purpose of Exploring a North-east Passage, Undertaken under the Command of the Lieutenant in the Russian Imperial Navy, Otto von Kotzebue*, 1821.

Cetaceorum maris Kamtschatici imagines, ab Aleutis e ligno fictas. 1825.

Übersicht der nutzbarsten und der schädlichsten Gewächse, welche wild oder angebaut in Norddeutschland vorkommen: Nebst Ansichten von der Pflanzenkunde und dem Pflanzenreiche. 1827.

Plantae Ecklonianæ Gentianearum et rosacearum novearum descriptiones fusiorea. 1833.

Werke. 6 vols., 1836–39; vols. 5–6 edited by Julius Eduard Hitzig.

Reise um die Welt mit der Romanzoffischen Entdeckungs Expedition in den Jahren 1815–1818. 1836; as *A Voyage Around the World with the Romanzov Exploring Expedition in the Years 1815–1818 in the Brig Rurik*, edited and translated by Henry Katz, 1986; translated in part by Robert Fortuine as *The Alaska Diary of Adelbert von Chamisso Naturalist on the Kotzebue Voyage 1815–1818*, 1986.

Über die Hawaiische Sprache: Versuch einer Grammatik der Sprache der Sanwich-Inseln. 1837.

Leben und Briefe, edited by Julius Eduard Hitzig. 1839; revised edition, 1842.

Adelbert von Chamisso und Helmina von Chézy: Bruchstücke ihres Briefwechsels, edited by Julius Petersen and Helmuth Rogge. 1923.

Editor, with Karl August Varnhagen von Ense, *Musenalmanach auf das Jahr 1804* [*1805, 1806*]. 3 vols., 1804–06.

Editor, with Gustav Schwab, *Deutscher Musenalmanach für das Jahr 1833* [*1834, 1835, 1836, 1837, 1838*]. 6 vols, 1833–38.

Editor, with Franz Gaudy, *Deutscher Musenalmanach für das Jahr 1839*. 1839.

Editor and translator, with Franz Gaudy, *Bérangers Lieder*, by Pierre Jean de Béranger. 1838.

*

Bibliography: *Bibliotheca Schlemihliana: Ein Verzeichnis der Ausgaben und Übersetzungen des Peter Schlemihl* by Philipp Rath, 1919; *Chamisso als Naturforscher: Eine Bibliographie* by Günther Schmid, 1942.

Critical Studies: *Chamisso: A Sketch of His Life and Work* by Karl August Lentzner, 1893; *A Poet Among Explorers: Chamisso in the South Seas* by Niklaus R. Schweizer, 1973.

* * *

Forced into exile from France by the Revolution, Adelbert von Chamisso learned German in his teenage years, and fell under the spell of German Romanticism when he settled in Berlin in the early years of the 19th century. His verse reflects in various ways the burden of his cosmopolitan inheritance. Poems set in France include the 'Das Schloss Boncourt' [Boncourt Castle], in which Chamisso accepts the ruin of his ancestral home and blesses the farmer who now tills the soil where the family residence once stood; its calm, conciliatory tone is in marked contrast to the impassioned idealism of earlier Romantics. Many of his poems retell legends that had recently been collected and anthologized by the Grimm brothers; in these 'German sagas', Chamisso seems more intent on evoking situations with precision than on creating a nostalgic atmosphere. The emphasis is often on the pragmatic need to deal honestly and tolerantly with one's subordinates. Thus the giant's daughter in 'Das Riesenspielzeug' [The Giant's Plaything] is rebuked by her father for treating the farmer she comes across as a mere toy; here the poet reinterprets the ancient saga in order to comment on some of the factors that brought down the aristocracy in France. In 'Die Weiber von Winsperg' [The Wives of Winsperg], Emperor Conrad's advisers try in vain to make their masters retract his generous promise to the women of Winsperg, and the poem ends with a dark hint that future rulers may turn out to be less honourable in dealing with their subjects. Sympathy with the poor and sick is vividly documented in many other works, such as 'Die alte Waschfrau' [The Old Washerwoman] and 'Der Invalid im Irrenhaus' [The Invalid Soldier in the Madhouse].

It was partly Chamisso's lightness of touch that made him more popular with the reading public of his time than many of his more literary contemporaries. A wry sense of humour comes through in many sketches of odd individuals and curious scenes from modern life. His poem 'Das Dampfross' [The Steam Horse] is one of the earliest to deal with the potential of the railway. But he was especially interested in psychology, as is evidenced by his sensitive exploration of feminine aspirations in the cycle *Frauen-Liebe und Leben* (*Women's Love and Life*). His most harrowing investigation of the inner recesses of the human mind is found in the narrative poem 'Salas y Gomez'. Comparable in some ways to Coleridge's 'Rime of the Ancient Mariner', it relates the experiences, visions, and hallucinations of a shipwrecked sailor who survives in complete solitude for nearly a century on a small island in the Pacific. This poem is again no ideal

Romantic vision, but is firmly based on experiences which Chamisso gained on his journey around the world and constitutes a far from idyllic counterblast to the myth of Robinson Crusoe.

Chamisso's most celebrated prose narrative is the story *Peter Schlemihls wundersame Geschichte* (*Peter Schlemihl*), an account of a man who is persuaded to sell his shadow to a diabolical stranger. In some ways reminiscent of the *Faust* tradition, this story has been read both as an allegory of the artist as a social outcast and as an autobiographical statement by the deracinated poet. Eventually, the hero finds solace in travel and in the contemplation of Nature. Like Schlemihl, but unlike many Romantics whose tormented fantasies expressed frustrated longings for freedom, Chamisso was able to live out a vision of himself as a restless wanderer during his voyage around the world between 1815 and 1818. He showed a particular interest in the negative consequences of European colonization and was fascinated by the uncontacted tribes of the remote Marshall Islands. This journey provided Chamisso with unique insights into the biology, botany, and culture of the Pacific, many of which are recorded in the autobiographical *Reise um die Welt* (*A Voyage Around the World*). Back in Germany, he became increasingly active as a botanist, collecting and classifying more than 2,500 plant species, and eventually obtaining a research post in the Berlin botanical gardens.

Chamisso stands at the threshold between the dreamy world of Romanticism and the empirically determined attitudes that were to gain ground during the 19th century. All poetry, he once remarked, should be based on events that can be retold in the manner of a short story, and his own neatly constructed and clearly focused poems have little in common with the often formless outpourings of his predecessors. He was undoubtedly a victim of prejudice in a society where Germans saw him as French while the French treated him as a German. Protestants and Catholics, democrats and aristocrats viewed him with misgivings, but he survived the petty antagonisms of his contemporaries and gave his name to the Chamisso prize, which is reserved for distinguished non-German authors writing in German.

—Osman Durrani

PETER SCHLEMIHL (Peter Schlemihls wundersame Geschichte)
Novella by Adelbert von Chamisso, 1814.

Peter Schlemihl is the work by which the poet and scientist Chamisso is now best known. It was first published in 1814, at the end of the High Romantic period in German literature, and over 20 years after its French-born author and his parents had settled in Prussia after fleeing France during the Revolution. Chamisso served as a page at the Prussian court and in 1798 became an ensign in the Prussian army, but his parents had returned to France in 1801. The year after its publication he set off on a voyage around the world as the scientist attached to a Russian expedition commanded by Captain Otto von Kotzebue, the son of the internationally popular dramatist August von Kotzebue. His record of this expedition, published in 1836, is a classic of German travel literature.

Chamisso's story reflects his innate restlessness and his search for an identity. As it opens, Peter Schlemihl, its first-person narrator, returns from a perilous sea voyage. His return to familiar, safe surroundings is deceptive, however. He looks up a certain Herr Thomas John, to whom he has a letter of introduction. This innocuous action proves to be his introduction to a bewildering sequence of adventures in a world which does not operate according to the laws of normal, conventional reality. At Herr John's opulent home he encounters a mysterious, withdrawn, gaunt, and elderly man, dressed in grey, whose extraordinary actions the other members of the company take in their stride. Before long, the gentleman makes Schlemihl an offer he cannot resist: in return for the shadow he is casting that fine sunny day, he is offered the magic purse of Fortunatus which, as the old chapbook story has it, never runs out of money. Before Schlemihl realizes what is happening, he has parted with his shadow.

Until that moment, Schlemihl, like all human beings, had taken his shadow for granted. But Chamisso's tale brings home the terrifying enormity of its loss. A shadow is the visual proof of the physical existence of a solid body: from now on Schlemihl finds himself living his life without this vital proof of his existence. Wherever his adventures take him, someone sooner or later notices that he has no shadow; repeatedly and inevitably this leads to his rejection by his fellow men and to his social ostracism, for without a shadow he is 'different'. In fact his name is taken from the Old Testament Book of Numbers and means, 'The unlucky one' or, literally, 'The Beloved of God', a paradox which Chamisso was keen to explore, though not in religious or racial terms.

The central metaphor so tangibly presented by the story is open to a number of interpretations, which makes it fascinating without in any way diminishing its readability as a good yarn: not surprisingly, it has always enjoyed great popularity as a children's classic. In a discerning essay written in 1911, Thomas Mann argues that it is no fanciful allegory, but the penetrating portrayal of the romantic sensibility and the price that has to be paid for it. Schlemihl's shadow, Mann suggests, is a symbol of middle-class solidity and of 'belonging': its loss is therefore a metaphor for the loss of social status. The ensuing story of Schlemihl's wanderings can be seen as an expression of Chamisso's search for stability which should be viewed in direct though ironic connection with his own apparently successful attempts to settle down to the demands of professional and domestic life both as an admired writer and as the keeper of the botanical garden and herbarium in Berlin.

Chamisso's story is a remarkably original and largely successful amalgam of disparate motifs given cohesion and credibility by its subjective truth and its close reflection of the economic facts of early 19th-century middle-class life. The result is a tale which, for all its superficial naiveté, subtly reveals the relationship between self and world. This is also apparent in its presentation, which is in the form of letters addressed by the fictitious narrator to Chamisso himself. Written towards the end of the German Romantic period, it succeeds in combining the mysterious and fantastic elements of the Romantic fairy tale, such as the wager between a human being and an emissary from the supernatural world, with the new preoccupations of 19th-century realism, such as the relationship of money to social identity and social acceptance. Schlemihl's ultimate rejection of the grey man and the bottomless purse brings about a change in his fortunes. As the story draws to its conclusion, he ceases to be the haunted outsider at the mercy of the world and of his own baser instincts. Released from the twin burdens of conformity and rejection, he finds a freer and more forward-looking fulfilment as his wanderings turn into travels in pursuit of the objectives of the scientific observer. Thus the story bridges the gap between necromancy and empirical science in a way which met with the approval of a wide spectrum of readers.

—Peter Skrine

————

CHANDOGYA. See **UPANISHADS**.

————

LA CHANSON DE ROLAND. See **ROLAND, The Song of**.

————

CHAR, René (-Émile). Born in L'Isle-sur-Sorgue, Vaucluse, France, 14 June 1907. Educated at Lycée d'Avignon, baccalauréat; École-de-Commerce, Marseilles, 1925. Served in the French artillery, Nîmes, 1927–28, and Alsace, 1939–40; served during the Resistance in France and North Africa: Médaille de la Résistance; Croix de Guerre. Married 1) Georgette Goldstein in 1933 (divorced 1949); 2) Marie-Claude de Saint-Seine in 1987. Moved to Paris in 1929 and met Aragon, Éluard, and Breton: associated with the Surrealists during the second period of the movement, 1930–34. Contributor to *Le Surréalisme au service de la Révolution*, 1930. Recipient: Critics prize (France), 1966. Member, Bavarian Academy; honorary member, Modern Language Association (USA). Chevalier, Légion d'honneur. *Died 19 February 1988.*

PUBLICATIONS

Collection

Selected Poems, edited and translated by Mary Ann Caws and Tina Jolas. 1992.

Verse

Les Cloches sur le coeur, illustrated by Louis Serrière-Renoux. 1928.
Arsenal. 1929; as *De la main à la main*, 1930.
Artine. 1930; enlarged edition, as *Artine et autres poèmes*, 1967.
Ralentir travaux, with André Breton and Paul Éluard. 1930; revised edition, 1989.
Le Tombeau des secrets. 1930.
L'Action de la justice est éteinte. 1931.

Le Marteau sans maître, etchings by Miró. 1934; revised edition with *Moulin premier*, 1945.
Dépendance de l'adieu. 1936.
Placard pour un chemin des écoliers. 1937.
Dehors la nuit est gouvernée. 1938.
Seuls demeurent. 1945.
Premières alluvions. 1946.
Le Poème pulvérisé, illustrated by Braque. 1947.
Fureur et mystère. 1948; revised edition, 1962.
Fête des arbres et du chasseur. 1948.
Les Matinaux. 1950; revised edition, 1964; as *The Dawn Breakers*, edited and translated by Michael Worton, 1990.
Art bref, suivi de Premières alluvions. 1950.
Amitié cachetée. 1951.
La Lettre I du dictionnaire. 1951.
Pourquoi le ciel se voûte-t-il?. 1951.
Quatre fascinants: La Minutieuse. 1951.
D'une sérénité crispée. 1951.
Poèmes. 1951.
La Paroi et la prairie. 1952.
Le Rempart de brindilles. 1952.
Homo poeticus. 1953.
Lettera amorosa. 1953.
Choix de poèmes. 1953.
A la santé du serpent. 1954.
Le Deuil des Nevons. 1954.
Poèmes des deux années 1953–1954, illustrated by Giacometti. 1955.
Chanson des étages. 1955.
La Bibliothèque est en feu, etchings by Braque. 1956.
Les Compagnons dans le jardin. 1956.
Hypnos Waking: Poems and Prose, edited by Jackson Mathews, translated by Mathews, William Carlos Williams, and others. 1956.
Jeanne qu'on brûla verte. 1956.
Pour nous, Rimbaud. 1956.
En trente-trois morceaux. 1956.
L'Abominable Homme des neiges. 1957.
La Bibliothèque est en feu et autres poèmes. 1957.
L'Une et l'autre. 1957.
Épitaphe. 1957.
De moment en moment, engravings by Miró. 1957.
Poèmes et prose choisis. 1957.
Le Poète au sortir des demeures. 1957.
Rengain d'Odin le Roc. 1957.
Élizabeth, petite fille. 1958.
Cinq poésies en hommage à Georges Braque. 1958.
L'Escalier de Flore, illustrated by Braque. 1958.
La Faux relevée. 1959.
Nous avons (prose poem), illustrated by Miró. 1959.
L'Allégresse. 1960.
Anthologie. 1960; revised edition as *Anthologie 1934–1969*, 1970.
Les Dentelles de Montmirail. 1960.
Deux poèmes, with Paul Éluard. 1960.
Éros suspendu. 1960.
Pourquoi la journée vole. 1960.
Le Rebanque. 1960.
L'Inclémence lointaine (selection). 1961.
L'Issue. 1961.
La Montée de la nuit. 1961.
La Parole en archipel. 1962.
Deux poèmes. 1963.
Impressions anciennes. 1964.
Commune présence (anthology). 1964; revised edition, 1978.
L'An 1964. 1964.
L'Âge cassant. 1965.

La Provence, point Oméga. 1965.
Retour amont, illustrated by Giacometti. 1966.
Le Terme épars. 1966.
Les Transparents. 1967.
Dans la pluie giboyeuse. 1968.
Le Chien de coeur. 1969; as The Dog of Hearts, translated by
    Paul Mann, 1973.
Dent prompte, illustrated by Max Ernst. 1969.
L'Effroi la joie. 1971.
Le Nu perdu. 1971.
La Nuit talismanique. 1972; revised edition, 1983.
Le Monde de l'art n'est pas le monde du pardon. 1974.
Contre une maison sèche. 1975.
Aromates chasseurs. 1975.
Faire du chemin avec . . . 1976.
Poems, edited and translated by Mary Ann Caws and
    Jonathan Griffin. 1976.
Chants de la Balandrame 1975–1977. 1977.
Tous partis!. 1978.
Fenêtres dormantes et porte sur le toit. 1979.
D'Ailleurs. 1981.
Joyeuse. 1981.
La Condamnée. 1982.
Loin de nos cendres. 1982.
Les Voisinages de Van Gogh. 1985.
Le Gisant mis en lumière. 1987.
Éloge d'une soupçonnée. 1988.

Plays

La Conjuration (ballet). 1947.
Claire. 1949.
Le Soleil des eaux. 1951.
Trois coups sous les arbres: Théâtre saisonnier (includes Sur
    les hauteurs, L'Abominable Homme des neiges; Claire; Le
    Soleil des eaux; L'Homme qui marchait dans un rayon de
    soleil; La Conjuration). 1967.

Other

Moulin premier. 1936.
Feuillets d'Hypnos (war journal). 1946; as Leaves of Hypnos,
    translated by Cid Corman, 1973.
Arrière-histoire de 'Poème pulvérisé'. 1953.
Recherche de la base et du sommet; Pauvreté et privilège
    (essays). 1955; revised edition, 1965.
Arthur Rimbaud. 1957.
Le Dernier Couac. 1958.
Sur la poésie. 1958.
Aux riverains de la Sorgue. 1959.
Flux de l'aimant. 1964.
La Postérité du soleil, with Camus. 1965.
L'Endurance de la pensée, with Martin Heidegger. 1968.
L'Egalité des jours heureux. 1970.
Boyan sculpteur. 1971.
Picasso sous les vents étésiens. 1973.
Le Monde de l'art n'est pas le monde du pardon. 1974.
Sur la poésie 1936–1974. 1974.
Oeuvres complètes. 1983.

Translator, Le Bleu de l'aile, by Tiggie Ghika. 1948.
Translator (into English), Le Réveil et les orchidées, by
    Théodore Roethke. In Preuves, 1959.
Translator, with Tina Jolas, La Planche de vivre: Poésies.
    1981.

*

Bibliography: Bibliographie des oeuvres de Char de 1928 à
1963 by Pierre André Benoit, 1964.

Critical Studies: René Char by Pierre Guerre, 1961; René
Char issue of L'Arc, 1963; The Poetry and Poetics of René
Char by Virginia La Charité, 1968; René Char issue of
Liberté, 1968; René Char issue of L'Herne, 1971; The
Presence of René Char, 1976, and Char, 1977, both by Mary
Ann Caws; Worlds Apart: Structural Parallels in the Poetry of
Paul Valéry, Saint-John Perse, Benjamin Péret, and René
Char by Elizabeth Jackson, 1976; René Char issue of World
Literature Today, 1977; Char: The Myth and the Poem by
James R. Lawler, 1978; Orien Resurgent. René Char: Poet of
Presence by Mechthild Cranston, 1979; Lightning: The Poetry
of Char by Nancy Kline Piore, 1981; René Char issue of Sud,
1984; La Poésie de René Char by Jean-Claude Mathieu, 2
vols., 1984–85; René Char (includes bibliography) by
Christine Dupouy, 1987; René Char issue of Europe, 1988;
René Char: Traces by Philippe Castellin, 1989; René Char:
faire du chemin avec by Marie-Claude Billet, 1990; René
Char: Les Dernières Années by Michael Bishop, 1990; René
Char by Eric Marty, 1990; Lectures de René Char edited by
Paul Smith and Tineke Kingma, 1990; René Char et ses
poèmes by Paul Veyne, 1991.

*   *   *

If being is indeed a storehouse of insurgent impulse, as the title of one of René Char's earliest works, Arsenal, would seem to imply, the poet's ceaseless task is to stir, channel, and articulate such impulse as unflinching and passionate response to the surrounding world and to one's condition in it. Char's is, from the beginning, a metaphysical vision of 'man massacred and yet victorious', of defeat breeding new aspiration, of suffering mysteriously shaping unexpected affirmation. So Char remains the protector of being's 'infinite faces', of being at once exultant and weak, ferocious and muted, emphatic and evasive, and the poem, set against the abundant forces of nature, becomes the very birthplace of an ungleaned and myriad truth by which, once again, we may begin to know ourselves and, consequently, gather strength.

The Surrealist movement provided Char with initial models of expression and disclosure, but it was his experience of war, accompanied by a purposeful self-distancing from Surrealism, that determined the more evaluative and succinct nature of his writing. From a self willed event, the poet is forced to turn to the immediate import of external event. From the teeming images upheld in Le Marteau sans maître [The Hammer Without a Master] that bespeak a linguistic unfettering of the unconscious, he progresses, through Dehors la nuit est gouvernée [Outside the Night Is Governed], to a broader, more universal summoning that embraces the real as a source not only of present oppression and limitation, but also of undying breadth and possibility. 'We oppose consciousness of the event to the gratuitous', he declares in his wartime journal included in Fureur et mystère [Fury and Mystery], a stunning volume containing some of Char's most powerful and poignant writings. Playful outpouring yields to urgent response; oneiric indulgence is indeed obliterated by the impact of many brutish and unpardonable acts. The expansive majesty of the poem is replaced by dense aphorisms, clustered shards of reflection that express, in the very face of death and destruction, the enduring desire for a dignified and resistant whole. Through brevity, the poet avoids useless obsession. Through and with his other, wedded at the same time to an earthy locality of place in his native Provence, he comes to a true knowledge of his condition as man and his function as poet.

It is his tremendous regard for the other that allows Char a writing ever practised and diversified beyond the narrow constraints of self. While such figures as Heraclitus and Georges de La Tour, Nietzsche and Heidegger, remain central to his development as a poet and thinker, many are those who touch him and spawn in his work an arterial complexity of connection shunning all boundaries. 'Moving, horrible, exquisite earth and heterogeneous human condition seize upon each other and qualify each other mutually', he declares. The poem is the attempted sum of these (inter) relations mingling being and nature, for though the latter, divided within, also prove infinitely warring in their differences without, they remain wondrously bound together as an inexhaustible whole. Thus Char draws, from a language at once shared and intensely private, the revelation of a unity fraught with contradiction, but a unity nevertheless— endlessly emergent, furiously willed. Enlightened by the will of others, dependent in many ways on past and present models of ardent literary and artistic endeavour, he shapes his writing as a coercive act that seeks, not least through violence, ever increased measures of inclusion. So, onwards, from *Les Matinaux* (*The Dawn Breakers*) through, for example, *Le Nu perdu* [The Lost Nude] and *Aromates chasseurs* [Hunting Aromatics] to *Les Voisinages de Van Gogh* [The Vicinities of Van Gogh] and *Éloge d'une soupçonnée* [Praise for a Suspected One], Char imperatively restakes and redefines the shifting ground of our existence, as others have previously viewed it and as many to come, through furious toil, will continue to transform and secure it.

There can be no end to such an effort, no final (re)solution, for living, as Char teaches us, is a constant becoming. From the prehistoric visions of the Lascaux paintings to the fierce fragility of Vincent Van Gogh, from the timeless myth of Orion resurgent to the particular predicament of those caught in war, a vast array of references bear witness to a shared condition that escapes single definition but lies ever-changing around and within us, demanding constant reacquaintance. Thus Char's work encourages less familiarization than pursuit; it does not flatter immediate comprehension but, rather, a searching poised on the threshold of things dawning and passing; it rejects mastery in the hope of ample and passionate exchange. The hunter, a recurrent figure in this poetry, does not seek a mere victim in the hunted but a joining that will fuel new desire. His embrace of the other, as apparent to Char in a Lascaux painting, is also the accepted dissolution of an old self. Each meeting is never one of simple possession but enacts simultaneous degrees of communion and erosion, of tolerance and severance, of triumph and loss. Indeed, from and beyond such an active and indisputable erotic grappling, new appetite and vigour are born.

Chaos and dislocation, though ineradicable, are countered for Char by the promise of an eternal remaking that is ever the gift of being and nature, of being with nature, and it is the exploration of this gift that he obstinately and durably charts for us. His poetry thus remains an opening for desire and hope, its message never simple since it pleads not only for what we have lost and forgotten but for what, through combined and renewed effort, we must yet come to welcome, celebrate, and magnanimously release.

—Michael Brophy

CHATEAUBRIAND, (François-René August), Vicomte de. Born in Saint-Malo, France, 4 September 1768. Educated at schools in Saint-Malo and Dol, 1777–81; Collège de Rennes, 1781–83; Collège de Dinan, 1783–84. Married Céleste Buisson de la Vigne in 1792. Entered the army, 1786; visited America, 1791; served in the Prussian army briefly, 1792; taught French in Beccles and Bungay, Suffolk, 1792–1800; returned to France and joined state service: secretary to Embassy in Rome, 1803; appointed Chargé d'Affaires to Swiss canton of Valais, 1804, but resigned, 1804; appointed Minister of Interior of Government in exile, 1815, and Ambassador to Sweden (not taken up); honorary Minister of State, 1815–16; made Peer of France, 1815, and President of Electoral College of Orleans, 1815; envoy extraordinary to Berlin, 1821; ambassador to London, 1822; attended Congress of Verona, 1822; minister of Foreign Affairs, 1823; ambassador to Rome, 1828. Editor, *Le Mercure*, 1800s. Many women friends, especially Mme Récamier. Member, Academie-française, 1815. *Died 4 July 1848.*

PUBLICATIONS

Collections

Oeuvres complètes. 31 vols., 1826–31, and later revised editions.
Oeuvres romanesques et voyages, edited by Maurice Regard. 2 vols., 1969.

Fiction

Atala; ou, Les Amours de deux sauvages dans le désert. 1801; edited by J.M. Gautier, 1973; as *Atala*, translated anonymously, 1825; also translated by James Spence Harry, 1867; Irving Putter, 1952; Walter J. Cobb, 1962; Rayner Heppenstall, 1965.
René; ou, Les Effets des passions. 1802; edited by Armand Weil, 1947, also edited by J.M. Gautier, 1970; as *René: A Tale*, translated anonymously, 1813; also translated by Irving Putter, 1952; Rayner Heppenstall, 1965.
Les Martyrs; ou, Le Triomphe de la religion chrétienne. 1809; original version edited by B. d'Andlau, 1951; as *The Martyrs*, translated by W. Joseph Walter, 1812, revised translation by O.W. Wight, 1859; *The Two Martyrs*, translated by Walter, 1819.
Les Aventures du dernier Abencérage, in *Oeuvres complètes*. 1826; as *Aben-Hamet, the Last of the Abencérages*, translated, 1826; as *The Adventures of the Last of the Abencérages*, translated by H.W. Carter, 1870; as *The Last Abencerage*, translated by Edith M. Nuttall, 1922.
Les Natchez. 1827; edited by G. Chinard, 1932; as *The Natchez*, translated anonymously, 1827.

Other

Essai historique, politique, et moral sur les révolutions anciennes et modernes. 1797; edited by Maurice Regard, 1978.
Le Génie du christianisme; ou, Beautés de la religion chrétienne. 5 vols., 1802; edited by Maurice Regard, 1978; as *The Genius of Christianity*, translated by Charles I. White, 1802; also translated by Rev E. O'Donnell, 1854; as *The Beauties of Christianity*, 3 vols., translated by Frederic Shoberl, 1813.
Itinéraire de Paris à Jérusalem et de Jérusalem à Paris. 3 vols.,

1811; as *Travels in Greece, Palestine, Egypt, and Barbary*, translated by Frederic Shoberl, 2 vols., 1812.

De Buonaparte et des Bourbons. 1814.

Réflexions politiques. 1814; as *Political Reflections*, translated anonymously, 1814.

Mélanges de politique. 2 vols., 1816.

De la monarchie selon la charte. 1816; as *The Monarchy According to the Charter*, translated anonymously, 1816.

Mémoires, lettres, et pièces authentiques touchant la vie et la mort du duc de Berry. 1820.

Maison de France; ou, Recueil de pièces relatives à la légitimité et à la famille royale. 2 vols., 1825.

Voyage en Amerique, Voyage en Italie. 2 vols., 1827; as *Travels in America and Italy*, translated anonymously, 2 vols., 1828.

Mélanges et poésies. 1828.

Études ou discours historiques sur la chute de l'empire romain, la naissance et les progrès du christianisme, et l'invasion des barbares. 4 vols., 1831.

Mémoires sur la captivité de Mme la duchesse de Berry. 1833.

La Vie de Rancé. 1844; edited by Fernand Letessier, 1955.

Les Mémoires d'outre-tombe. 12 vols., 1849–50; edited by Maurice Levaillant and Georges Moulinier, 2 vols., 1951; as *Memoirs*, translated anonymously, 3 vols., 1848; complete version, 1902; selections edited and translated by Robert Baldick, 1961.

Souvenirs d'enfance et de jeunesse. 1874.

Correspondance générale, edited by Louis Thomas. 5 vols., 1912–24.

Le Roman de l'occitanienne et de Chateaubriand (letters). 1925.

Lettres à la comtesse de Castellane. 1927.

Lettres à Mme Récamier pendant son ambassade à Rome, edited by Emmanuel Beau de Loménie. 1929.

Lettres à Mme Récamier, edited by Maurice Levaillant. 1951.

Mémoires de ma vie: Manuscrit de 1826, edited by J.M. Gautier. 1976.

Correspondance générale, edited by Pierre Riberette. 1977– .

Translator, *Le Paradis perdu*, by Milton. 2 vols., 1836.

*

Bibliography: *Bibliographie de la critique sur François-René de Chateaubriand: 1801–1986* by Pierre H. and Ann Dubé, 1988.

Critical Studies: Société Chateaubriand *Bulletin*, 1930– ; *Chateaubriand, Poet, Statesman, and Lover* by André Maurois, 1938; *Chateaubriand: A Biography* by Joan Evans, 1939; *Chateaubriand* by Friedrich Sieburg, translated by Violet M. Macdonald, 1961; *Chateaubriand* by Richard Switzer, 1971; *Chateaubriand: A Biography* by George D. Painter, vol. 1, 1977; *Chateaubriand: Composition, Imagination, and Poetry* by Charles A. Porter, 1978; *Back to the Garden: Chateaubriand, Senancour and Constant* by Michael J. Call, 1988.

*   *   *

Chateaubriand's dozen and a half major works and copious tracts, discourses, and parliamentary opinions appeared during that most political half-century beginning with the Revolution and ending with the fall of the July Monarchy. His most original narratives portray the emotions and yearnings of the Romantic self amid historical European landscapes or against the background of the North American wilderness. In his vigorous and wide-ranging polemical writings he argues the Christian and royalist cause with sarcasm and an idealistic vision. His major literary distinction has been as a stylist.

Not all Chateaubriand's narrative writings are frankly autobiographical. The figure of the brooding, proud, aristocratic European in the post-Revolutionary world, partially discernable in the American Indian brave, Chactas of *Atala* and *Les Natchez* (*The Natchez*), appears more clearly as the protagonist of Chateaubriand's best-known story, *René*, confession of a self-exiled Frenchman in the American forest in the early 18th century. The life of the 17th-century Trappist serves in the late *La Vie de Rancé* as the locus of curious digressions about both Chateaubriand and 17th-century France. *Itinéraire de Paris à Jérusalem et de Jérusalem à Paris* (*Travels in Greece, Palestine, Egypt, and Barbary*) is Chateaubriand's first autobiographical book. His most important work, composed and often refashioned over 30 years into the 1840s, is his autobiography, *Les Mémoires d'outre-tombe* (*Memoirs*).

Much of the charm of Chateaubriand's narratives comes from evocative descriptions and the metaphors and complex rhythms of his prose. His descriptions of America in the 'Indian' works, and of his childhood Brittany, Rome, the Near East in the autobiographical writings, present a nearly seamless web of memories of earlier travel accounts, his own personal observation, and, no doubt, brilliant invention: scholars will continue to differ over how much of the America he described he ever actually saw. His descriptive prose, characterized by visual detail and suggestive, often exotic names, is arranged in rhythmically ordered sentences and chapters. His polemical writings scan more like oratory; there too nouns and figures of speech focus the meaning. The Château de Chambord, with all its chimneys, is personified in the *La Vie de Rancé* as 'une femme dont le vent aurait soufflé en l'air la chevelure' ('a woman with wind-blown hair'); in 1815 in Louis XVIII's antechamber he sees a 'vision infernale': Talleyrand supported by Fouché, 'le vice appuyé sur le bras du crime' ('vice leaning on the arm of crime').

The force of his narratives stems from their subtle analysis of the difficulties of modern life: how to be both an aristocrat and a leader in the new democratic world, appreciate the beauties of religion in the age of science, live true to one's own sensibilities without shirking one's duties toward others. Unfortunately the autobiography—though not the autobiographical fictions—is weakened by Chateaubriand's determination to hide almost everything intimate, including his many passionate liaisons. The strength of the polemical writings lies in their juxtaposition of noble themes—fidelity, honour, national pride—with a quick, savage denunciation of posturing and opportunism.

Abundance characterizes his rhetoric; his writing displays ease and vigour in invention, high colour, passion and sentiment. Admiration, anger, scorn, enthusiasm animate sometimes flowing, sometimes cadenced and elaborate prose. The criticism though often harsh is never mean, the praise though sentimental is grand, and the ever-present portrait of the self is pompous, often insincere, indiscreetly long—and lucid, probing, subtle, and finally very moving.

—Charles A. Porter

MEMOIRS (Les Mémoires d'outre-tombe)
Prose by Chateaubriand, 1849–50 (written 1809–41).

Chateaubriand's original intention, as his title indicates, was that the *Memoirs* would not be published until after his death. He was writing them, as he said, as a man would write sitting on his coffin. This would avoid the scandal which had accompanied the publication between 1765 and 1770 of Rousseau's *The Confessions*, the first great autobiography of French romantic literature and would also, be hoped, give a kind of objectivity to the account of a life which had involved exile, war, literary fame, prison, politics, and, finally, poverty. For it was the need for money that made Chateaubriand sell the rights of certain sections of the *Memoirs* to a financial company composed mainly of supporters of the exiled French king, Charles X. The first extract thus appeared in 1836, 12 years before Chateaubriand died. When the first complete edition did appear, in 1850, it had less success than Chateaubriand had hoped. George Sand commented that a ghost in ten volumes was rather long, and the book had none of the provocative honesty about his own failings which makes Rousseau's *The Confessions* still worth reading. The discovery, in 1930, of a complete manuscript revised in 1847 by Chateaubriand himself provided the basis for a completely new edition in 1948, exactly 100 years after the author's death on 4 July 1848, two months short of his 80th birthday.

Chateaubriand was a Breton aristocrat, the tenth child of Count René-Auguste de Chateaubriand, and his account of his eccentric and terrifying father dominates the opening volumes. The terror inspired by René-Auguste made François-René draw particularly close to his sister, Lucille, four years his elder but presented in the *Memoirs* as having been born in 1766, two years before his own birth on 4 September 1768. This attachment provided the emotional force behind Chateaubriand's first bestseller, the short story *René*, published in 1802. René is the archetypal romantic hero, of the same type as Goethe's Werther, Byron's Manfred, or the doomed heroes of Victor Hugo's later dramas, but one whose misery offers the additional interest of incest. It is his fatal love for his sister, Amélie, which is the root cause of his troubles, in addition to the world-weariness, loneliness, and pre-existential *angst* which made him so popular with the European reading public of the 1800s that Chateaubriand wished he had never created him.

René, like the companion story *Atala*, was taken from the work which Chateaubriand published in its entirety in 1802, *The Genius of Christianity* (*Le Génie du christianisme*). This put forward the argument that Christianity is better than other religions because of its moral superiority over paganism (Christ teaches a higher ethic than Socrates) and because works of art inspired by Christianity are better than those coming down to us from classical antiquity (Gothic cathedrals are better than the Parthenon, Dante a better poet than Homer, Shakespeare a better playwright than Sophocles). As the *Memoirs* insist, there was nothing deliberate about the fact that this attempt to restore to Christianity the artistic and intellectual validity taken from it during the 18th-century enlightenment was published within a year of Napoleon's signature of the *Concordat* with the Catholic church on 16 July 1801. In May 1798, while in exile in England, Chateaubriand had learnt of the death of his mother, had wept, and had believed. The total self-centredness which characterizes the *Memoirs*, Chateaubriand's insistence on having always been right (Louis XVIII agrees with him that the monarchy is finished; there is nothing to be said in favour of the greatest politician of his age, Talleyrand, other than the fact that when he appears in company with the regicide, Fouché, it is 'vice leaning on the arm of crime'), his obsessive preoccupation with the double nature of his own personality are, nevertheless, redeemed by the way in which he writes. With him, French prose breathes a more rhythmic, colourful,

and exotic air. He was one of the first Europeans to write poetically about North America, when it was still a land of virgin forests. His account of the changes which, in his lifetime, included the fall of the monarchy, the triumph and defeat of Napoleon I, two attempts at monarchical restoration, and the beginnings of the industrial revolution in France, is still worth reading. At one point, in the closing pages, he even anticipated the disappearance of frontiers between the European states. Chateaubriand's influence on the writers of his generation was considerable and he marks the beginning of a new mood in French literature as well as a new set of moral and intellectual attitudes. For the writers of the classical period, form mattered as much as, if not more than, content, and technique more than sincerity. It would never have occurred to Boileau to ask whether Racine or Corneille 'really meant' what they wrote. For Chateaubriand, sincerity was everything, and there is no reason to disbelieve the portrait which he gives of himself in the *Memoirs*. He was highly emotional, he did lead a varied life, he did meet the people he claimed to know, he was very fond of his sister, he did believe in Christianity, he was convinced of his own genius. It is, nevertheless, unlikely that as he claimed in *The Natchez*, the epic from which the short stories *René* (1802) and *Atala* (1801) were extracted, he saw crocodiles in the Mississippi.

—Philip Thody

RENÉ
Prose by Chateaubriand, 1802.

René was first published, together with a companion piece, *Atala*, as a fictional episode or literary illustration contained within a much longer non-fictional work of Christian apologetics, *The Genius of Christianity*. Following the huge success of the two narratives, Chateaubriand excerpted them from the larger work and published them on their own. It is in this form that they have normally appeared since then. *René*, in particular, has come to be seen as embodying many of the aspects of French Romantic sensibility, with the eponymous hero-narrator suffering from storms of passion that he can never define fully ('le vague des passions') and carrying a contemporary moral and psychological sickness ('le mal du siècle'), whose roots are hinted at but never made explicit.

The work is short, barely 30 to 40 pages long in most editions, and takes the form of a brief prologue and epilogue framing a narrative by René of episodes of his life. The prologue offers a stylized, picturesque evocation of the banks of the Mississippi and the Louisiana countryside. Within this exotic landscape, two companions, Chactas, an aged, blind Indian who is the adoptive father of René, together with *père* Souël, a French missionary, press René to explain how an aristocratic young Frenchman came to bury himself in exile in the 'deserts' of Louisiana and why he is so melancholic.

René's narrative, effectively a sort of confession, begins hesitantly and with a sense of shame to speak of self-inflicted grief and torment. He evokes a sad childhood and adolescence, dominated by the deaths of his parents and a sense of solitude. His only consolation lies in the tender love of his elder sister Amélie, with whom he shares the mournful pleasures of wandering the autumn countryside. As a result of his meditations on nature, death, and eternity, he is tempted by the idea of seeking in monastic retreat a refuge from the world, but then, typically, decides instead to travel. Neither the poetic ruins of the ancient world of Greece and Rome, nor modern London, nor even the Ossian-inspired songs of the last bard in Caledonia succeed in comforting his unquiet soul. His state of mind is symbolized by the image René offers of himself seated weeping on the summit of Mount Etna, contemplating the distant dwellings of the plain and the volcanic abyss at his side. René's narrative repeatedly proposes this mix of seething passion combined with a sense of alienation from other human beings.

After this unusual variant on the Grand Tour, René returns to Paris where he experiences a renewed feeling of isolation. Paris for him as a vast human desert. His restlessness draws him back to the country, where the absolute sense of solitude and the spectacle of nature give rise to lyrical evocations of ecstatic torment. Late-adolescent idealized erotic reveries are deflated by a sense of the purposelessness of existence. He writes to his sister to announce his intention to commit suicide. Amélie rushes to him and falls into his arms. The drama of incest which follows is only hinted at. René gives the impression he does not understand why his sister appears to be keeping a secret from him, in spite of the fact that at the time of narrating the events he knows the reason for the secret. This narratorial complication raises for the reader the question of whether René's narrative is a full confession of his emotions or an obscure attempt to disculpate himself from a shared forbidden passion. Amélie attempts to resolve the situation by withdrawing to a convent, committing herself to God and good works. René, after a final visit to the now abandoned family château, arrives at the convent for a last exchange with Amélie only to be asked to assist at her taking the veil. In a climactic scene of religious emotion, combined with images of death, sexual excitement, and scandal, the brother and sister are separated, and René takes the decision to go into what he sees as exile. René's last days before departing are given over to extracting some satisfaction from his excess of grief and from meditations on the peace within the convent walls and the storms and uncertainties outside.

The epilogue offers two contrasting comments on René's story. Chactas expresses pity and sympathy for those who suffer such emotional trials and, in an echo of the prologue, conjures up an image of the proud Mississippi regretting the natural simplicity of its source. Père Souël, however, severely catechizes René for self-indulgent morbidity and calls on him to think of his duties towards fellow human beings and of the harm he has caused. The cast of the tale are rapidly extinguished: Amélie dies of a disease caught from fellow nuns she was nursing; Chactas, père Souël, and René are killed in the wars between the French and the Natchez Indians.

In René, the convention of the 18th-century novel of sensibility and a vocabulary of emotional religiosity are aimed by Chateaubriand at offering a demonstration of the superiority of Christian-inspired literature over that of pagan antiquity or what he saw as the godless literature of the 18th century. No simple moral conclusions are offered, however. René does not turn to religion to solve his mysterious dilemmas. In practice, attention has focused on the hero as the tragic, modern figure of the young, isolated individual alienated from society. His lyrical rêveries and melancholic wanderings charmed all the French Romantics at the same stage. A more specifically socio-political reading sees René as an aristocrat caught in the upheavals following the French revolution. Psychologically, the text offers meditations on the links between desire, death, and the family, with the breaking of the incest taboo as a pathological attempt to return to paradise

lost. Put in more abstract terms, René explores the contradictions between human aspirations and an intimate conviction of the pointlessness of everything.

—C. Smethurst

CHEKHOV, Anton (Pavlovich). Born in Taganrog, Russia, 17 January 1860. Educated at a school for Greek boys, Taganrog, 1867–68; Taganrog grammar school, 1868–79; Moscow University Medical School, 1879–84, graduated as doctor, 1884. Married the actress Olga Knipper in 1901. Practising doctor in Moscow, 1884–92, Melikhovo, 1892–99, and in Yalta after 1899. Freelance writer while still in medical school, especially for humorous magazines, and later for serious ones; travelled to Sakhalin Island, 1890; suffered severe haemorrhage of the lungs, 1897. Recipient: Pushkin prize, 1888. Member, Imperial Academy of Sciences, 1900 (resigned 1902). *Died 2 July 1904.*

PUBLICATIONS

Collections

Plays, translated by Marian Fell. 1912.
Plays, translated by Julius West. 1916.
The Cherry Orchard and Other Plays, translated by Constance Garnett. 1923.
Plays, translated by Constance Garnett. 1929; retitled *Nine Plays*, 1946.
Polnoe sobranie sochinenii i pisem [Complete Works and Letters], edited by S.D. Balukhatyi and others. 20 vols., 1944–51; new edition in 30 vols., 1974–83.
The Brute and Other Farces, translated by Eric Bentley and Theodore Hoffman. 1958.
Plays, translated by Elisaveta Fen. 1959.
Six Plays, translated by Robert Corrigan. 1962.
The Oxford Chekhov, edited and translated by Ronald Hingley. 9 vols., 1964–80; excerpts as *Seven Stories*, 1974; *Eleven Stories*, 1975; *Five Major Plays*, 1977; *The Russian Master and Other Stories*, 1984; *Ward Number Six and Other Stories*, 1988; *A Woman's Kingdom and Other Stories*, 1989, *The Princess and Other Stories*, 1990; *The Steppe and Other Stories*, 1991.
The Major Plays, translated by Ann Dunnigan. 1964.
Ten Early Plays, translated by Alex Szogyi. 1965.
Four Plays, translated by David Magarshack. 1969.
Plays, edited and translated by Eugene K. Bristow. 1977.
The Early Stories 1883–1888, edited and translated by Patrick Miles and Harvey Pitcher. 1982.
Plays, translated by Michael Frayn. 1988.
The Sneeze: Plays and Stories, translated by Michael Frayn. 1989.

Plays

O vrede tabaka, in *Peterburgskaia gazeta* [Petersburg Gazette]. 1886; several revisions: final version in *Sobranie sochinenii*, 1903; as *On the Harmfulness of Tobacco*, translated by Constance Garnett, in *Plays*, 1935; as *The Harmfulness of Tobacco*, translated by Eric Bentley and Theodore Hoffman, in *The Brute and Other Farces*, 1958; as *Smoking Is Bad for You*, translated by Ronald Hingley, in *The Oxford Chekhov*, 1968; as *On the Injurious Effects of Tobacco*, translated by Eugene K. Bristow, in *Plays*, 1977.

Ivanov (produced 1887; revised version, produced 1889). In *P'esy*, 1897; as *Ivanov*, translated by Marian Fell, in *Plays*, 1912; numerous subsequent translations including by Elisaveta Fen, in *Three Plays*, 1951; Robert Corrigan, in *Six Plays of Chekhov*, 1962; Alex Szogyi, in *Ten Early Plays*, 1965; David Magarshack, 1966; Ariadne Nicolaeff, 1966; Ronald Hingley, in *The Oxford Chekhov*, 1967.

Lebedinaia pesnia (produced 1888). In *P'esy*, 1897; as *Swan Song*, translated by Marian Fell, in *Plays*, 1912; also translated by Theodore Hoffman, in *The Brute and Other Farces*, 1958; Ronald Hingley, in *The Oxford Chekhov*, 1968; Alex Szogyi, in *Ten Early Plays*, 1965.

Medved' (produced 1888). In *Novoe vremia* [New Time], 1888; as *The Bear*, translated by Julius West, in *Plays*, 1916; also translated by Constance Garnett, in *The Cherry Orchard and Other Plays*, 1923; Elisaveta Fen, in *Plays*, 1959; Ronald Hingley, in *The Oxford Chekhov*, 1968; as *The Boor*, 1915; as *The Brute*, translated by Theodore Hoffman, in *The Brute and Other Farces*, 1958.

Leshii (produced 1889). 1890; as *The Wood Demon*, in *Calender of Modern Letters*, 2, 1925–26; also translated by Robert Corrigan, in *Six Plays of Chekhov*, 1962; Ronald Hingley, in *The Oxford Chekhov*, 1964; Alex Szogyi, in *Ten Early Plays*, 1965.

Predlozhenie (produced 1889). 1889; as *A Marriage Proposal*, 1914; also translated by Theodore Hoffman, in *The Brute and Other Farces*, 1958; as *The Proposal*, translated by Julius West, in *Plays*, 1916; also translated by Constance Garnett, in *The Cherry Orchard and Other Plays*, 1923; Elisaveta Fen, in *Plays*, 1959; Ronald Hingley, in *The Oxford Chekhov*, 1968; Alex Szogyi, in *Ten Early Plays*, 1965.

Tragik ponevole (produced 1889). 1890; as *A Tragedian in Spite of Himself*, translated by Julius West, in *Plays*, 1916; as *The Reluctant Tragedian*, translated by Alex Szogyi, in *Ten Early Plays*, 1965; as *A Tragic Role*, translated by Ronald Hingley, in *The Oxford Chekhov*, 1968.

Svad'ba (produced 1900). 1889; as *The Wedding*, translated by Julius West, in *Plays*, 1916; also translated by Constance Garnett, in *Plays*, 1929; Ronald Hingley, in *The Oxford Chekhov*, 1968; Alex Szogyi, in *Ten Early Plays*, 1965; as *A Wedding*, translated by Theodore Hoffman, in *The Brute and Other Farces*, 1958.

Iubilei (produced 1900). 1892; as *The Anniversary*, translated by Julius West, in *Plays*, 1916; also translated by Constance Garnett, in *Plays*, 1929; Ronald Hingley, in *The Oxford Chekhov*, 1968; Alex Szogyi, in *Ten Early Plays*, 1965; as *A Jubilee*, translated by Elisaveta Fen, in *The Seagull and Other Plays*, 1953; as *The Celebration*, translated by Theodore Hoffman, in *The Brute and Other Farces*, 1958.

Chaika (produced 1896). In *P'esy*, 1897; revised version (produced 1898), 1901; as *The Sea Gull*, translated by Marian Fell, in *Plays*, 1912; numerous subsequent translations including by Constance Garnett, in *The Cherry Orchard and Other Plays*, 1923; Stark Young, 1939; Robert Corrigan, in *Six Plays of Chekhov*, 1962; Fred Eisemann, 1965; David Magarshack, in *Four Plays*, 1969; Lawrence Senelick, 1977; Milton Ehre, in *Chekhov for the Stage*, 1992; as *The Seagull*, translated by Elisaveta Fen, in *Plays*, 1959; also translated by Ronald Hingley, in *The Oxford*

Chekhov, 1967; Eugene K. Bristow, in *Plays*, 1977; John-Claude von Italie, 1977; David French, 1978; Tania Alexander and Charles Sturridge, 1986; Michael Frayn, 1986.

Diadia Vania (produced 1897). In *P'esy*, 1897; as *Uncle Vanya*, translated by Marian Fell, in *Plays*, 1912; numerous subsequent translations including by Jennie Covan, 1922; Constance Garnett, in *The Cherry Orchard and Other Plays*, 1923; Rose Caylor, 1930; Elisaveta Fen, in *The Seagull and Other Plays*, 1953; Stark Young, 1956; David Magarshack, in *The Storm and Other Russian Plays*, 1960; Robert Corrigan, in *Six Plays of Chekhov*, 1962; Ronald Hingley, in *The Oxford Chekhov*, 1964; Eugene K. Bristow, in *Plays*, 1977; Michael Frayn, 1987; Milton Ehre, in *Chekhov for the Stage*, 1992.

Tri sestry (produced 1901). 1901; as *The Three Sisters*, translated by Julius West, in *Plays*, 1916; numerous subsequent translations including by Robert Corrigan, in *Six Plays of Chekhov*, 1962; David Magarshack, in *Four Plays*, 1969; Eugene K. Bristow, in *Plays*, 1977; Milton Ehre, in *Chekhov for the Stage*, 1992; as *Three Sisters*, translated by Constance Garnett, in *Plays*, 1929; Elisaveta Fen, in *Three Plays*, 1951; Ronald Hingley, in *The Oxford Chekhov*, 1964; Randall Jarrell, 1969; Michael Frayn, 1983.

Vishnevyi sad (produced 1904). 1904; as *The Cherry Orchard*, translated by M. Mandell, 1908; numerous subsequent translations including by Julius West, in *Plays*, 1916; Constance Garnett, 1923; Jenny Covan, 1923; C.C. Daniels, and G.R. Noyes, in *Masterpieces of the Russian Drama*, edited by Noyes, 1933; Hubert Butler, 1934; S.S. Kotelianskii, 1940; Stark Young, 1947; Elisaveta Fen, in *Three Plays*, 1951; Ronald Hingley, in *The Oxford Chekhov*, 1964; Tyrone Guthrie and Leonis Kipnis, 1965; David Magarshack, in *Four Plays*, 1969; Eugene K. Bristow, in *Plays*, 1977; Laurence Senelick, 1977; Michael Frayn, 1978; Jean-Claude von Italie, 1979; Milton Ehre, in *Chekhov for the Stage*, 1992.

Neizdannaia p'esa, edited by N.F. Belchikov. 1923; as *That Worthless Fellow Platonov*, 1930; as *Don Juan (in the Russian Manner)*, translated by Basil Ashmore, 1952; as *Platonov*, translated by David Magarshack, 1964, also translated by Ronald Hingley, in *The Oxford Chekhov*, 1967; as *Wild Honey*, translated by Michael Frayn, 1984.

Tatiana Repina, in *Polnoe sobranie sochinenii i pisem*. 1944–51; as *Tatyana Repin*, translated by S.S. Kotelianskii, in *Literary and Theatrical Reminiscences*, 1927; also translated by Ronald Hingley, in *The Oxford Chekhov*, 1968.

Na bolshoi doroge, in *Polnoe sobranie sochinenii i pisem*. 1944–51; as *On the Highway*, in *Drama*, 22, 1916; as *On the High Road*, translated by Julius West, in *Plays*, 1916; also translated by Constance Garnett, in *Plays*, 1929; Ronald Hingley, in *The Oxford Chekhov*, 1968; Alex Szogyi, in *Ten Early Plays*, 1965.

Fiction

Pestrye rasskazy [Motley Tales]. 1886; revised edition, 1891.
V sumerkakh [In the Twilight]. 1887.
Nevinnye rechi [Innocent Tales]. 1887.
Rasskazy [Tales]. 1889.
Khmurye liudi [Gloomy People]. 1890.
Duel [The Duel]. 1892.
Palata No. 6 [Ward No. 6]. 1893.
Tales, translated by Constance Garnett. 13 vols., 1916–22.
The Unknown Chekhov: Stories and Other Writings Hitherto Untranslated, edited by Avrahm Yarmolinsky. 1954.

Early Stories, translated by Nora Gottlieb. 1960.
The Image of Chekhov (selected stories), translated by Robert Payne. 1963.
The Lady with Lapdog and Other Stories, translated by David Magarshack. 1964.
Chuckle with Chekhov: A Selection of Comic Stories, translated by Harvey Pitcher. 1975.
The Kiss and Other Stories, translated by Ronald Wilks. 1982.
The Duel and Other Stories, translated by Ronald Wilks. 1984.
The Party and Other Stories, translated by Ronald Wilks. 1985.
The Black Monk and Other Stories, translated by Alan Sutton. 1985.
The Fiancée and Other Stories, translated by Ronald Wilks. 1986.
Longer Stories from the Last Decade, translated by Constance Garnett. 1994.

Other

Ostrov Sakhalin [Sakhalin Island]. 1895; as *The Island: A Journey to Sakhalin*, translated by Luba and Michael Terpak, 1967; as *A Journey to Sakhalin*, translated by Brian Reeve, 1993.
Sobranie sochinenii [Collected Works]. 11 vols., 1899–1906.
Pis'ma [Letters]. 1909; *Sobranie pis'ma*, 1910; *Pis'ma*, 1912–16, and later editions.
Zapisnye knizhki. 1914; as *The Note-Books*, translated by S.S. Kotelianksii and Leonard Woolf, 1921.
Letters to Olga Knipper. 1925.
Literary and Theatrical Reminiscences, edited by S.S. Kotelianskii. 1927.
Personal Papers. 1948.
Selected Letters, edited by Lillian Hellman. 1955.
Anton Chekhov's Life and Thought: Selected Letters and Commentary, edited by Simon Karlinsky, translated by Michael Henry Heim. 1973.
A Life in Letters, edited and translated by Gordon McVay. 1994.

*

Bibliography: *Chekhov in English: A List of Works by and about Him* edited by Anna Heifetz and Avrahm Yarmolinsky, 1949; *The Chekhov Centennial: Chekhov in English: A Selective List of Works by and about Him 1949–60* by Rissa Yachnin, 1960; *Anton Chekhov: A Reference Guide to Literature* by K.A. Lantz, 1985; *Chekhov Bibliography: Works in English by and about Anton Chekhov*, 1985, and *Chekhov Criticism: 1880 Through 1986*, 1989, both by Charles W. Meister; *Anton Chekhov Rediscovered: A Collection of New Studies with a Comprehensive Bibliography* edited by Savely Senderovich and Munir Sendich, 1987.

Critical Studies: *Anton Chehov: A Critical Study* by William Gerhardie, 1923, revised edition, 1972; *Chekhov: A Biographical and Critical Study*, 1950, revised edition, 1966, and *A New Life of Anton Chekhov*, 1976, both by Ronald Hingley; *Chekhov: A Life*, 1953, *Chekhov the Dramatist*, 1960, and *The Real Chekhov: An Introduction to Chekhov's Last Plays*, 1972, all by David Magarshack; *Anton Chekhov* by Walter Horace Bruford, 1957; *Tchekov, the Man* by Beatrice Saunders, 1960; *Chekhov: A Biography* by Ernest J. Simmons, 1962; *The Breaking String: The Plays of Anton Chekhov* by Maurice Valency, 1966; *Chekhov and His Prose* by Thomas Winner, 1966; *Chekhov: A Collection of Critical Essays* edited by Robert Louis Jackson, 1967; *Anton Chekhov* by J.B. Priestley, 1970; *Chekhov in Performance: A Commentary on the Major Plays* by J.L. Styan, 1971; *The Chekhov Play: A New Interpretation* by Harvey Pitcher, 1973; *Chekhov: The Evolution of His Art* by Donald Rayfield, 1975; *Chekhov: A Study of the Major Stories and Plays* by Beverly Hahn, 1977; *On the Theory of Descriptive Poetics: Anton Chekhov as Storyteller and Playwright* by Jan van der Eng, 1978; *Chekhov as Viewed by His Russian Literary Contemporaries* by Henry Urbanski, 1979; *Chekhov: A Structuralist Study* by John Tulloch, 1980; *Chekhov's Great Plays: A Critical Anthology* edited by Jean P. Barricelli, 1981; *Chekhov: The Critical Heritage* edited by Victor Emeljanow, 1981; *Anton Chekhov* by Irina Kirk, 1981; *Chekhov and the Vaudeville: A Study of Chekhov's One-Act Plays*, 1982, and *Chekhov in Performance in Russia and Soviet Russia*, 1984, both by Vera Gottlieb; *Chekhov's Art: A Stylistic Analysis* by Peter M. Bitsilli, 1983; *Chekhov's Poetics* by Aleksandr Pavlovich Chudakov, 1983; *Chekhov: A Study of the Four Major Plays* by Richard Peace, 1983; *Chekhov: New Perspectives* edited by René and Nonna D. Wellek, 1984; *A Chekhov Companion* edited by Toby W. Clyman, 1985; *Anton Chekhov* by Laurence Senelick, 1985; *Chekhov* (biography) by Henri Troyat, translated by Michael Henry Heim, 1986; *File on Chekhov* by Nick Worrall, 1986; *Chekhov and Women: Women in the Life and Work of Chekhov* by Carolina de Maegd-Soëp, 1987; *Chekhov on the British Stage, 1909–1987: An Essay in Cultural Exchange* by Patrick Miles, 1987; *Chekhov: The Silent Voice of Freedom* by Valentine Tschebotarioff Bill, 1987; *Chekhov: A Spirit Set Free* by V.S. Pritchett, 1988; *Critical Essays on Anton Chekhov* edited by Thomas A. Eekman, 1989; *Chekhov on the British Stage* edited by Patrick Miles, 1993.

*   *   *

The leading exponent of the short story and the drama in modern Russian literature, which is otherwise dominated by poetry and the novel, Anton Chekhov began to write for money while he was a medical student. The majority of his early comic stories are characterized by the muddles and confusions of life. They portray overweening Russian respect for authority and hilarious conflicts between the sexes and the generations, in which the expected 'triggers' of social occasions, chance meetings, love entanglements and relatives, children and animals rarely fail to appear. Nevertheless, the best of these stories already illustrate the serious aspects of Chekhov's vision. 'The Death of a Clerk' is a reworking of Gogolian menace. 'Daughter of Albion', 'The Upheaval', and 'Spat' khochetsia' ('Sleepy') all explore the relationship between master and servant. None of these is actually funny: the first two reveal the humiliation of servants, while the third is an early demonstration of Chekhov's ability to conjure horror out of commonplace situations, as the exhausted girl servant unemotionally smothers her masters' crying baby. Chekhov's medical training, to be evident later in the illnesses that afflict many of his characters, influences his study of adolescence, 'Volodia', with its themes of corruption, sexuality, and suicide. In stories such as 'The Huntsman', 'Happiness', and 'The Steppe' Chekhov showed his ability to describe the natural settings and atmosphere of rural Russia, featuring within them episodic moments of communication between man and his world or between men themselves against a background of silence, emptiness, and timelessness.

Later, the comic element in Chekhov ceases to be the framework of an attitude to life and becomes instead the sometimes relieving, always revealing observation, a perception of the continuity of life and of man's remarkable ability to endure it. In the stories of 1888–96 the still young Chekhov captures the loss of momentum in middle age ('A Dreary Story'). The grim *Palata No. 6* (*Ward No. 6*) and 'The Black Monk' study psychological alienation, while other stories explore sexual relations. A wife's abuse of a weak, loving husband in 'The Butterfly' is counterbalanced by the wife's triumph over her husband in 'The Order of St Anne'. In 'The Artist's Story' romance itself is shown to be imbued with misunderstanding, potential disaster, and the loss of opportunity. The most positive story of this period is undoubtedly 'The Student', in which myth and beauty inspire a moment of communication against the background of an atmospherically evoked rural evening and the passage of centuries.

In Chekhov's last years stories of loneliness and isolation reveal fear of life ('A Hard Case'), the sadness of missed opportunities for happiness ('Concerning Love'), and estrangement ('The Bishop'). Chekhov also exposes the suffocating power of bourgeois self-satisfaction, materialism, and philistinism that is contained in the one Russian word *poshlost'*: this is what overcomes the vitality of Startsev in 'Ionych' and what permeates the life of Olga Semenovna in 'The Darling'. In 'A Case History' the gentry shelter helplessly from the world of peasant-workers and alien factories, while 'The Peasants' and 'In the Hollow' take us to the primitive world of the peasant and the kulak. Here materialism and greed emerge as violent weapons by which the strong abuse the weak. One of Chekhov's last stories is perhaps his best creation, 'Dama s sobachkoi' ('The Lady with a Dog'): for once, a story of mature love, of genuine communication and self-sacrifice, in which the characters respect each other enough to face their uncertain future consciously and courageously.

Chekhov's 'vaudevilles', his comic one-act plays—such as *Medved'* (*The Bear*) and *Predlozhenie* (*A Marriage Proposal*)—are mainly dramatized encounters, in which human feelings and follies undermine the solemnity of social occasions and rituals. Here, as in the major plays, dialogue and the revelation of character and atmosphere predominate over event. The major plays themselves, the foundation of Chekhov's reputation in the West, give dramatic form to the themes of the later stories. The way in which history overtakes the gentry is illustrated in Chekhov's bewildered central characters as they confront their own failure, the success of others, and the new strangeness of the world beyond their estates. Characters 'in mourning for their lives' immerse themselves in nostalgia, petty rivalries, games, and hopeless dreaming or planning, while the forces of *poshlost'* and social change threaten their way of life and their future. The pathos and bathos of the unloved pervade *Chaika* (*The Seagull*), while *Diadia Vania* (*Uncle Vanya*) traces the erosion of hopes and dreams by age and failure. The despair of provincial life is all too evident in *Tri sestry* (*The Three Sisters*), but this play also shows how the characters' own self-indulgences and self-delusions frustrate their yearning for 'Moscow'. Finally, in *Vishnevyi sad* (*The Cherry Orchard*), the axes are being sharpened not just for trees, but for the softer material of a self-obsessed gentry that has lost the will to resist.

Chekhov does not abandon plot altogether, but he creates a startling division between the extreme events of his plays, whether on or off stage (suicide, duel, attempted murder, fire, and death), and the spelling-out through stage direction, dialogue, and sub-text of the ironies of man's hopes and fears. The atmosphere created by the chartacters' inertia, the sounds of their surroundings, and their own silences resonates at one moment with amusement, affectation, and confusion and at the next with bitterness, recrimination, and loss. Chekhov's integration of these resonances into frameworks of 'everyday life' was a major dramatic innovation, one which was not accomplished without difficulty or with complete success. The balance between laughter and tears is sometimes too precarious in these plays, the relationship between exposition and natural discourse too artificial. Nevertheless, they are dramatic masterpieces, which have had the most significant influence on 20th-century Western drama.

Throughout, Chekhov preserved his humanity and his practical activity. Continuing to practise frequently as a doctor, he made a remarkable journey in 1890 across Siberia to visit the penal colony on Sakhalin Island, later producing an extensive account of conditions there, and in 1892 he helped in famine relief (as did Tolstoi). Although he was not devoid of the prejudices and shortcomings of his age, the simplicity, modesty, and gentle but firm truthfulness of Chekhov's vision mark him out among modern Russian writers.

—Christopher R. Pike

THE CHERRY ORCHARD (Vishnevyi sad)
Play by Anton Chekhov, 1904.

The Cherry Orchard is Chekhov's swan song. The Moscow Art Theatre first performed the play on 17 January 1904, and Chekhov died on 2 July of the same year. As a physician, Chekhov knew that he had only a short time to live, and this would be his last major work. Thus, he went beyond the themes of his earlier plays to include the decline of the nobility and the rise of an entrepreneurial class in Russia. In so doing, he was giving his own distinctive treatment to themes that had previously appeared in such important works of Russian literature as Tolstoi's novel *Anna Karenina* (1875–77) and Aleksandr Ostrovskii's play *The Forest* (*Les*), 1871. The opposition between Liubov Ranevskaia, the elegant but hopelessly impractical aristocrat, and Ermolai Lopakhin, the hard-working entrepreneur whose father and grandfather had been serfs on her family's estate, also owes something to the somewhat similar opposition between Julie and Jean in Strindberg's *Miss Julie* (1888). Yet Chekhov made that opposition more subtle and complicated than Strindberg did. At first Lopakhin genuinely wants to help the aristocrats resolve their financial difficulties, but when they cannot understand the need to act, he buys the estate himself.

Only by understanding the delicate balance between all the sets of oppositions in *The Cherry Orchard* can we remain true to the vision that informed Chekhov's art. Thus, a balance exists between the charm of the aristocrats' way of life and the immorality of serfdom that made it possible; and between the aristocrats' ready empathy with others in personal relationships and their indifference to their own fates and those of others who depend on them.

The play itself remains balanced between the characters, who cannot quite say what they mean, or do what they want to do, and their symbolic environment. The cherry orchard itself, which symbolizes the old ways, is thus connected with the billiard cue that Epikhodov, the clown-like clerk, breaks during the ball scene in Act III. This incidental action, which occurs offstage, suggests that by playing billiards Epikhodov is encroaching on gentry prerogatives. It forms a subtle analogy for Lopakhin's far more disruptive encroachment on gentry prerogatives in buying the estate and chopping down the cherry orchard. Billiards links Epikhodov to Leonid Gaev, Ranevskaia's feckless brother, who hides his incompetence by pretending to play billiards. He can neither work nor play, so he plays at playing.

Arrivals and departures frame the drama, as they do for each of Chekhov's four major plays. The play begins in the manor house, as Lopakhin impatiently awaits the arrival of Madame Ranevskaia and her entourage from Paris, and ends —almost—as they leave. In a typically anti-climactic touch, Chekhov has old Firs, the senile butler, wander on stage after everyone else has left. They have forgotten about him, and locked him in. Serfdom has so deprived Firs of a sense of self that he cannot think of himself; he can only wonder whether Gaev has worn the right coat. He lies down to take a nap and presumably to die, and a way of life will die with him.

The principle of balance holds for the relationship between the past and the present, too. The continuity in Russian life appears in the similarities between Gaev and Petr Trofimov, a university student from the proletariat and a former tutor of Madama Ranevskaia's son who drowned several years previously. Despite their differences in class origin and attitudes, both of them engage in the very Russian tendency to make speeches for the sake of making speeches. Gaev makes a speech to the bookcase in Act I, and his sister later rebukes him for making a speech to the peasants. Similarly, Trofimov makes speeches welcoming the new life that will come after the passing of the gentry. Both resort to speechifying in an unconscious attempt to mask their inability to cope with life's challenges. In a way then, to understand the balance of the play is to understand that the French saying 'Plus ça change, plus c'est la même chose' applies fully to *The Cherry Orchard*. The theme of the passing of the gentry way of life has served as the subject for a number of major 20th-century works, such as George Bernard Shaw's play *Heartbreak House*, Jean Renoir's film *The Rules of the Game*, and Bernard Bertolucci's film *1990*. All three of these works derive to a greater or lesser extent from *The Cherry Orchard*. The play also marks the end of an era in Russian culture. After Chekhov's death, Russian theatre became known more for its innovative stage sets and great directors than for its plays. No Russian play written since 1904 has enjoyed more than occasional performances in other countries.

—Jim Curtis

THE LADY WITH A DOG (Dama s sobachkoi)
Story by Anton Chekhov, 1899.

Vladimir Nabokov considered 'The Lady with a Dog', which Chekhov wrote in 1899, 'one of the greatest stories ever written'. Throughout the 20th century, critics have hailed it as a masterpiece, and it has influenced several generations of writers, particularly in England and America. Moreover, Joyce Carol Oates has even reworked the story and given it an American setting in her version, 'The Lady with a Toy Dog'.

Chekhov began work on 'The Lady with a Dog' in August or September of 1899, and published it in the December 1899 issue of a major journal of the day, *Russkaia mysl'* [Russian Thought]. He later made some revisions to the story for the edition of his collected works that appeared in 1903.

Like most of Chekhov's works, the story has a simple plot. Dmitrii Dmitrich Gurov, who is vacationing in the resort town of Yalta on the Black Sea, meets a woman, Anna Sergeevna von Dideritz. They have a love affair, after which he returns to his wife and children in Moscow, believing that they have had only a brief encounter. However, he finds that he cannot forget Anna, and seeks her out in the provincial town of S. (usually considered to be Saratov), where she lives. He astonishes her by appearing without warning in a theatre, and she promises to come to Moscow to see him. When they renew their affair in Moscow, they realize that they truly love each other. 'And it was clear to both that it was a long way to the end, and that the most complicated and difficult part was only beginning'.

'The Lady with a Dog' provides a good example of the way Chekhov often acknowledged the masterpieces of the past, while simultaneously reacting against them. In 'The Lady with a Dog' he is reacting against the treatments of the theme of adultery in Flaubert's *Madame Bovary* and Tolstoi's *Anna Karenina*. In both novels, the heroine is a married woman who has an affair, and commits suicide as a result. In Chekhov's story, however, the married woman who has an affair finds true love. Chekhov was also reacting against the portrayals of love in popular fiction which, in his day as in ours, tended to equate love with happiness. Thus, Anna neither commits suicide nor finds lasting happiness.

The story has a similar relationship to Impressionist painting. The story begins in the summer, at a resort, which was a setting that the Impressionists often depicted. In fact, the artist Konstantin Korovin, a good friend of Chekhov's, painted an Impressionist work, *Cafe in Yalta* (1905), which the story probably inspired. Just as the Impressionists often used arbitrary, asymmetrical framing in their pictures, Chekhov used open endings in his stories and plays, which rarely come to a clear resolution. However, Chekhov reacted against Impressionist painting by emphasizing psychological development, as Monet and Renoir rarely did.

The principal psychological interest in 'The Lady with a Dog' lies in Gurov's development. At the beginning of the story, he has a cynical attitude towards women, to whom he refers as a 'lower race'. After he and Anna go to bed together for the first time, she wants reassurance that he still respects her. He cannot respond to her need, however, and merely eats a slice of watermelon. But when he returns to Moscow, and finds that he cannot forget her, he attempts to tell a dinner companion about her. 'If you knew what an enchanting woman I met in Yalta', he says. But his friend can only reply, 'You were right: the turbot was a bit off'. When his friend cannot respond to him, as he could not respond to Anna, he begins to understand what she experienced. As his capacity for empathy increases, his capacity for love and self-awareness increase as well. Chekhov signals this change when he and Anna are in a hotel room in Moscow at the end of the story, and he looks in the mirror. He notices that his hair has turned grey; 'And only now, when his head had turned grey, did he fall in love, as one ought to, really—for the first time in his life'. It is one of the great moments in modern literature.

'The Lady with a Dog' shows Chekhov at the height of his powers. The story's subtlety, its masterful understatement, and interplay of character and environment place it among the masterpieces of modern short fiction.

—Jim Curtis

THE SEAGULL (Chaika)
Play by Anton Chekhov, 1896.

The Seagull provided the occasion for the greatest trauma of Chekhov's life, and for his greatest triumph. The premiere of the play, in St Petersburg on 17 October 1896, caused his greatest trauma because the audience did not understand his dramatic innovations, and booed. Although subsequent performances went well, Chekhov withdrew the play and swore that he would never write for the theatre again. Fortunately for us, however, Vladimir Nemirovich-Danchenko, an experienced drama coach, persuaded him to let a new theatrical venture in Moscow stage the play. Nemirovich-Danchenko collaborated with Konstantin Stanislavskii to form the Moscow Art Theatre. Its production of Chekhov's play, which opened on 17 December 1898, proved a great success, and has become legendary. Its meticulous attention to detail, naturalistic acting, and ensemble work created an extremely influential theatrical style that continues to affect the performing arts today.

The series of interrelationships between and among two pairs of characters provides a key to understanding *The Seagull*. One of these pairs consists of a well-known actress, Irina Arkadina, and her lover, Boris Trigorin, an established writer. The other consists of two young people: Konstantin Treplev, Arkadina's son, an aspiring writer, and Nina Zarechnaia, an aspiring actress. A subtle interplay of tensions soon develops that involves all four characters. When Treplev hopes to gain some recognition from his mother by putting on an avant-garde play in which Zarechnaia has the only role, his mother feels threatened, and makes fun of the attempt. Treplev brings down the curtain, and stomps off in disgust. He later shoots a gull, and lays it at Zarechnaia's feet, stating that he will shoot himself in the same way. Zarechnaia, however, has attracted Trigorin's attention. He says that he wishes to get to know her, since he believes that he depicts young girls poorly in his stories. Arkadina quickly senses the attraction between the two of them.

Thus, emotions swirl among these characters in what Stanislavskii called 'underground currents'. They all seek fulfilment through love and art. Yet Chekhov has created the situation so cleverly that these professional and personal concerns merge for each of them. Thus Arkadina's vanity as an actress prevents her from giving her son the recognition (and money) that he needs. Trigorin's professional success and his role as Arkadina's lover make Treplev jealous. Trigorin's status as a celebrity initially attracts Zarechnaia to him, but then she falls in love with him.

Characteristically, Chekhov leaves these tensions unresolved. Between Acts III and IV, Trigorin and Zarechnaia have a love affair. He abandons her when she becomes pregnant. She has the child, who dies soon afterward. She then succeeds in finding work as an actress in a provincial theatre. These events, which Treplev summarizes at the beginning of Act IV, prepare us for he crucial final scene between Treplev and Zarechnaia. She returns briefly, just to be near Trigorin, whom she still loves. She advises Treplev, 'Believe, and bear your cross'. But this is just what he cannot do. Convinced that he has no talent (although he has started to publish short stories), unloved by his mother, and abandoned by the woman he loves, he shoots himself offstage. While Treplev has experienced actual death, Zarechnaia has experienced a metaphorical death. The giddy, naive part of her has died, and has been resurrected as a mature woman. In Zarechnaia, Chekhov thus presents a secular version of one of the great themes in Russian culture: death and resurrection.

An awareness of the relationship between *The Seagull* and *Hamlet* deepens our understanding of Chekhov's play. (Both works feature a play within the play; the characters in *The Seagull* also quote from *Hamlet* on several occasions.) Thus, Treplev corresponds to Hamlet, Zarechnaia to Ophelia, Trigorin to Claudius, and Arkadina to Gertrude. In each case, however, the outcomes are reversed. Hamlet does not commit suicide, but Treplev does; Ophelia commits suicide, but Zarechnaia does not. Claudius is a usurper and a murderer, but Trigorin is an authentic creator. Gertrude is implicated in Claudius' crime, but Arkadina is guilty of nothing more than vanity. Such intertextuality, or a relationship between texts that the audience needs to understand as part of the meaning of the work, appears very frequently in modern art, but no major playwright had ever used it before to create characters. In its blend of psychological subtleties and sophisticated intertextuality, *The Seagull* is that rare work—a play whose greatness was recognized in its time and that continues to hold the stage today.

—Jim Curtis

THE THREE SISTERS (Tri sestry)
Play by Anton Chekhov, 1901.

The third of Chekhov's great plays, *The Three Sisters* was written specifically for the Moscow Art Theatre, where it was first produced on 31 January 1901 with Stanislavskii in the role of Vershinin and Chekhov's wife Olga Knipper as Masha. The play received a lukewarm reception from the critics, but soon became a favourite of audiences, turning into the longest running play in Russia. Knowing that he was writing for a particular company sympathetic to his dramatic innovations, Chekhov was able to create this play as more of an ensemble piece than had been possible with either *The Seagull* or *Uncle Vanya*. It is not so much individual characters as a provincial world of hopeless dreams and nostalgia that is evoked by the three educated Muscovite sisters, Olga, Masha, and Irina, who with their brother Andrei have been stranded in a provincial backwater by the death of their father a year before the action opens. The plot is minimal, depicting merely the changes in this environment over three and a half years during which Andrei marries the vulgar, self-seeking Natasha and the sisters lose the opportunity and the hope of leaving the town as their friends the artillery officers do in the end. In this respect it is a supreme example of Chekhov's ability to strip away the artificial elements of traditional dramatic plotting, focusing the audience's attention instead on the human situations presented. As Beverley Hahn remarks, 'the drama conveys both the provisional, chaotic, and unpredictable nature of each moment of life and yet the peculiar consistency with which these moments add up to a given fate'.

In essence the characters and situation are comic: the three sisters, passive and hampered by cultural pretensions and dreams of the metropolis, see their goal receding. Natasha in her bourgeois vulgarity is obviously a butt while Masha's husband Kulygin is simply a joke of a Latin teacher, and yet this play is not a comedy. Whereas Chekhov deliberately entitled *The Seagull* and *The Cherry Orchard* comedies, this one he called a drama. Following his views that drama should imitate real life albeit with elements of poetry, Chekhov weaves into his play elements of lyricism and of everyday banality. The manner in which the predatory Natasha, all demure smiles when she is being courted by Andrei, proceeds to turn her husband from a potential scholar into a fat drunken slob and make herself the mistress of the house is far too sinister to be simply funny.

The lyricism and elegiac mood of *The Three Sisters* are a

more complex matter, created partly through technical devices such as disjointed conversations where characters pursue their own thoughts behind a mask of conventional exchanges, or silences which indicate the importance of what is not being said, or else auditory devices like Masha's endless singing of a snatch of song emphasizing the dull repetitiveness of life. The sisters themselves, with their poetic search for meaning expressed in images of snow or birds, lift their predicament out of either the comic or the merely depressing. Most effective of all in creating a lyrical mood, however, is the use of different time planes: all three sisters live partly in the future which is represented by the idea of a return to Moscow, city of opportunity and real life. With masterly effectiveness Chekhov uses the opening moments of Act I not only in traditional manner to present to us information about Olga, Masha, and Irina's background but also to reveal the depth of their nostalgic attachment to the past and hence to the dream of the future. As the play progresses Olga becomes a headmistress—clearly she is destined to remain there for ever. Masha is forced by the departure of her lover to return to her boring provincial husband and Irina's attempts to escape through marriage are also doomed when her fiancé Tuzenbakh is shot by the malicious Solenyi in a futile duel. Dreams fade and the sisters are forced into the present, where, unlike Natasha, Kulygin, and Natasha's lover Protopov, they have never made any attempt to belong. In the other great Chekhov plays there is always one character at least who, albeit absurdly, expresses an unbounded optimism in the future, however remote, but in *The Three Sisters* it seems at best half-hearted. As the regiment that had brought colour and hope into their lives moves away to the rousing strains of a military march, Olga feels that maybe if we wait a little longer, we shall find out why we live and suffer, and only Masha, following the now dead Tuzenbakh, can be more optimistic. '. . . we must just go on working . . . It's autumn now, winter will soon be here, and the snow will cover everything . . . but I'll go on working and working! . . .', while Olga, who has the concluding line, underscores the frustration and desperation of that optimism with her sigh: 'if only we knew, if only we knew!'.

It is not only the lyricism of the play but also the tension between values, spiritual versus practical, and the themes of betrayal and disillusion versus hope and a search for a meaning in life that give the play its depth. Comic elements there certainly are (one need only think of Natasha boring everyone by talking about her baby while Solenyi has the courage to suggest the child should be boiled in oil) but these merely serve to keep the play from sliding too much into gloom. While it is conventional to remark that Chekhov's characters belong to the dying era of tsarism, it is also true that the evocation of lost chances and frustrated ideals is one with an almost universal relevance.

—Faith Wigzell

UNCLE VANYA (Diadia Vania)
Play by Anton Chekhov, 1897.

'*Uncle Vanya* is an unforgettably good play . . . It is a real tragedy. It has in it the flatness and poignancy of life itself. There is no depth of reflection upon humanity at which it were inappropriate to discuss this play if one were master of obedient words'. Desmond MacCarthy's thoughts (in *The New Statesman*, 16 May 1914), prompted by the London premiere at the Aldwych Theatre, remain equally valid today.

To the superficial eye, Chekhov's 'scenes from country life' may appear singularly unexciting, a tedious demonstration of the dramatist's advice (quoted by I.Y. Gurliand in *Teatr i iskusstvo* [*Theatre and Art*], 11 July 1904) that 'everything on stage should be just as complex and also just as simple as in life . . . . People eat their dinner, just eat their dinner, yet at the same time their happiness is taking shape and their lives are being smashed . . .'. Against a background of rural torpor, one high summer in the 1890s, a tightly knit group of characters dream and yearn, rage and pine, as happiness eludes them.

There are eight leading roles—an old, retired professor (Serebriakov) and his young second wife Elena); the doting mother of his first wife (Mme Voinitskaia) and his estate-manager, brother of his late first wife (Ivan Voinitskii, known as Uncle Vanya); the Professor's unmarried daughter by his first wife (Sonia); a doctor (Astrov); an old nurse (Marina); and an impoverished landowner (Telegin). Tensions mount during the disruptive visit of Serebriakov and Elena to the provincial estate that once was owned by the Professor's first wife.

On one level, *Uncle Vanya* illustrates a typically Chekhovian theme, the inexorable passage of time. For six years, unnoticed, Sonia has loved Astrov; for 25 years, unvalued, Vanya has slaved for his idol, Serebriakov. Ten years ago, Vanya might have proposed to Elena, but did not; during those ten years, Doctor Astrov has become overworked, cynical, unloving.

For the past 50 years, Vanya's mother has scribbled pointless notes in pointless pamphlets; if we are to believe Vanya, for 25 years Professor Serebriakov has delivered worthless lectures and concocted worthless books. Astrov's maps chronicle the degeneration of the flora and fauna over the past half- or quarter-century.

Time's corrosiveness eats also into the future. Elena, aged 27, declares that she too will be old five or six years hence, and she wonders how they will live through the long Russian winter; Vanya, aged 47, ponders how to fill the next 13 years, should he survive till 60.

More than any other Chekhov play, *Uncle Vanya* is weighted towards old age and autumn. Its first act has no equivalent of Nina (*The Seagull*), Irina (*Three Sisters*), or Anya (*The Cherry Orchard*), young women greeting the springtime of life with innocent hopes and dreams. Of its principal characters, four are old and emotionally sterile—Serebriakov (unloved by his young wife), Voinitskaia (unloving towards her son), Telegin (abandoned the day after his wedding), and Marina (preoccupied with noodles and knitting). The 'younger' quartet, caught in a web of emotional–sexual non-fulfilment, lacks all youthful buoyancy. Vanya and Astrov hurtle towards loveless middle-age; Elena drifts lethargically, purposeless and beautiful; Sonia works unceasingly, stoical and plain.

Uncle Vanya is perhaps Chekhov's saddest play. Like Astrov's maps, it seems to chart man's foolish flight from happiness and harmony. The 'demon of destruction' to which Elena refers lies deep in everyone, despoiling the planet and producing endless human waste. Caught in the isolation of unrequited love or idiotic self-love, the leading characters are frozen in frustration.

Confronted by this spectacle of loneliness, lethargy, and non-achievement, a deflated audience might easily echo Vanya's bitter remark: 'Lovely day to hang yourself . . . .'. One of the first Russian reviewers of the play described it as 'mood (*nastroenie*) in four acts' (N. Rok [N.O. Rakshanin], in *Novosti i Birzhevaia gazeta*, 6 November 1899). But this 'mood' is not one of sorrow unconfined. Like all Chekhov's major plays, *Uncle Vanya* abounds in comic touches. Characters laugh at themselves and at each other, while sensitive audiences respond with a smile or shiver of self-recognition.

After the London premiere in May 1914, Desmond MacCarthy wisely observed that 'we have no right to label this atmosphere "Russian", and regard it with complacent curiosity . . . If Tchekov's intellectuals are half dead, the other half of them is very much, painfully much, alive. They suffer more consciously; there is intensity in their lassitude . . .'. MacCarthy subsequently added (in *The New Statesman and Nation*, 13 February 1937): 'If you regard *Uncle Vanya* as a study in Russian character you will miss its point, and worse, you will not be touched . . . Though the atmosphere of it is Russian, the human nature in it is universal. That is what makes it moving'.

Chekhov's play also offers an element of muted optimism and faith. No one dies, and life continues (as in Beckett). Numerous characters complain of their 'unbearable' sufferings (Serebriakov, Elena, Astrov, Vanya), yet suffering must be borne, as Sonia advocates. Hope and hopelessness are held in fine balance; endurance may be the closest we can come to happiness.

A successful production of *Uncle Vanya* should be poignant but never ponderous, comic but never cold. The Act III map-scene between Astrov and Elena fuses serio-comic eroticism with ecological earnestness, while Vanya's bungled attempt to shoot Serebriakov combines tragic desperation and absurd farce. Chekhov's depiction of stunted lives contains a tantalizing dream of life as it could or should be.

Significantly, Chekhov himself detested an earlier version of *Uncle Vanya*, a rudimentary farce-melodrama known as *The Wood Demon* (*Leshii*), 1889. Although the two works have many characters, speeches, and situations in common, their essence is radically different. *Uncle Vanya* (written at some unknown point between 1890 and 1896, probably in 1896 itself) represents a condensation and distillation of its ungainly predecessor. Whereas *The Wood Demon* resolves life's problems much too neatly (a bullet for Voinitskii, a husband for Sonia, reconciliation for Elena with Serebriakov), *Uncle Vanya* displays wondrous insight into perpetual frustration, waste, and grief.

When the curtain finally falls, with Sonia seeking to console her inconsolable uncle, wry smiles and kindly laughter cannot conceal the aching desolation.

—Gordon McVay

CHIKAMATSU Monzaemon. Born Suigimori Jirokichi (adult name Nobumori) into a samurai family, in Echizen Province (now in Fukui district), Japan, in 1653. Family moved to Kyoto, c.1667. Married (wife died 1734); two sons. In the service of the nobleman Ichijo Zenkakuekan until c.1671–72; began writing plays, at first for Uji Kadayū [Kaga-no-jō] and other chanters of the *jōruri* (puppet) theatre; wrote for the chanter Takemoto Gidayū's theatre, Takemoto-za, Osaka, from 1686; also wrote kabuki plays, from 1684; house writer for Sakata Tōjūrō I's theatre, Miyako-za, Kyoto,

1695–1703; following Tōjūrō's retirement, c.1703, resumed collaboration with Gidayū in Osaka; wrote solely for the puppet theatre, chiefly in the genres of the domestic drama (*sewamono*) and historical play (*jidaimono*), after c.1705; moved back to Osaka, and became staff writer for the Takemoto-za, 1706. *Died in 1725.*

PUBLICATIONS

Collections

[Works], edited by Takam Tatsuyuki and Kuroki Kanzo. 10 vols., 1924.
[Works], edited by Kitano Hogi. 16 vols., 1925.
Masterpieces of Chikamatsu (includes *The Courier for Hades*; *The Love Suicide at Amijima*; *The Adventures of the Hakata Damsel*; *The Tethered Steed*; *Fair Ladies at a Game of Poem-Cards*; *The Almanac of Love*), translated by Asatoro Miyamori. 1926.
Chikamatsu zenshū [Complete Works], edited by Fujii Otoo. 12 vols., 1927.
Major Plays of Chikamatsu (includes *The Love Suicides at Sonezaki*; *The Drum of the Waves of Horikawa*; *Yosaku from Tamba*; *The Love Suicides in the Women's Temple*; *The Courier for Hell*; *The Battles of Coxinga*; *Gonza the Lancer*; *The Uprooted Pine*; *The Girl from Hakata*; *The Love Suicides at Amijima*; *The Woman-Killer and the Hell of Oil*), translated by Donald Keene. 1961.

Plays (selected *jōruri* plays)

Yotsugi Soga [The Soga Heir] (produced 1683).
Shusse Kagekiyo [Kagekiyo Victorious] (produced 1686).
Semimaru (produced 1686). As *Semimaru*, in *The Legend of Semimaru*, translated by S. Matisoff, 1978.
Sonezaki shinjū (produced 1703). As *The Love Suicides at Sonezaki*, translated by Donald Keene, in *Major Plays of Chikamatsu*, 1961.
Yomei tenno shokunin kagami (produced 1705).
Horikawa Nami no tsuzami (produced 1706). As *The Drum of the Waves of Horikawa*, translated by Donald Keene, in *Major Plays of Chikamatsu*, 1961.
Shinjū nimai ezōshi [Love Suicide and the Double-Folded Picture Books] (produced 1706).
Shinjū kasaneizutsu [Love Suicide at the Sunken Well] (produced 1707).
Tamba Yosaku (produced 1708). As *Yosaku from Tamba*, translated by Donald Keene, in *Major Plays of Chikamatsu*, 1961.
Shinjū mannenso (produced 1708). As *The Love Suicides in the Women's Temple*, translated by Donald Keene, in *Major Plays of Chikamatsu*, 1961.
Keisei hangoko (produced 1708).
Imamiya shinjū [Love Suicide at Imamiya] (produced 1711).
Meido no Hikyaku (produced 1711). As *The Courier for Hades*, translated by Asatoro Miyamori, in *Masterpieces of Chikamatsu*, 1926; as *The Courier for Hell*, translated by Donald Keene, in *Major Plays of Chikamatsu*, 1961.
Yugiri awa no naruto (produced 1712). Part translated as *Love Letter from the Licensed Quarter*, in *Kabuki*, by James R. Brandon, 1975.
Kokusenyā Kassen (produced 1715). As *The Battles of Coxinga*, edited and translated by Donald Keene, 1951, and in *Major Plays of Chikamatsu*, 1961.
Ikudama shinjū [Love Suicide at Ikudama] (produced 1715).

Yari no Gonza (produced 1717). As *Gonza the Lancer*, translated by Donald Keene, in *Major Plays of Chikamatsu*, 1961.

Nebiki no kadomatsu (produced 1718). As *The Uprooted Pine*, translated by Donald Keene, in *Major Plays of Chikamatsu*, 1961.

Soga kaikeizan (produced 1718). As *The Soga Revenge*, translated by Frank A. Lombard, in *Outline History of the Japanese Drama*, 1928.

Heike Nyogo no shima (produced 1719). Part translated by Samuel L. Leiter, in *The Art of Kabuki: Famous Plays in Performance*, 1979.

Hakata kojorō namimakura (produced 1719). As *The Adventures of the Hakata Damsel*, translated by Asatoro Miyamori, in *Masterpieces of Chikamatsu*, 1926; as *The Girl from Hakata*, translated by Donald Keene, in *Major Plays of Chikamatsu*, 1961.

Shinjū ten no Amijima (produced 1721). As *The Love Suicide at Amijima*, translated by Asatoro Miyamori, in *Masterpieces of Chikamatsu*, 1926; as *The Love Suicides at Amijima*, translated by Donald Keene, in *Major Plays of Chikamatsu*, 1961.

Onnagoroshi abura jigoku (produced 1721). As *The Woman Killer and the Hell of Oil*, translated by Donald Keene, in *Major Plays of Chikamatsu*, 1961.

Kwan-hasshu tsunagi, as *The Tethered Steed*, translated by Asatoro Miyamori, in *Masterpieces of Chikamatsu*. 1926.

Kaoyo utragaruta, as *Fair Ladies at a Game of Poem-Cards*, translated by Asatoro Miyamori, in *Masterpieces of Chikamatsu*. 1926.

Koi hakkée hashiragoyomi, as *The Almanac of Love*, translated by Asatoro Miyamori, in *Masterpieces of Chikamatsu*. 1926.

*

Critical Studies: *Studien zu Chikamatsu Monzaemon* by Detlef Schauwacker, 1975; *World Within Walls* by Donald Keene, 1976; *Circles of Fantasy: Convention in the Plays of Chikamatsu* by Andrew C. Gerstle, 1986.

* * *

Chikamatsu, sometimes referred to as the 'Japanese Shakespeare', is widely considered Japan's most notable dramatist. Born in 1653, he became a major writer of the end of the 17th century and beginning of the 18th, producing plays for the puppet theatre (*ningyo jōruri*) and, in the middle period of his career, for the kabuki stage.

In Chikamatsu's day, the puppet theatre consisted of relatively simple puppets, operated from beneath the stage, with music provided by a *shamisen* player, and the dialogue, scenic evocations, and commentary delivered by a chanter. The plots drew largely on traditional forms and subject matter, including semi-historical stories of war and scenes of allegorical journeys (*michiyuki* scenes) but, as with any great dramatist, Chikamatsu is notable for his distinctive use of, and modifications to, existing conventions. Thus, the first play to which Chikamatsu's name is attached, *Yotsugi Soga* [The Soga Heir], based its plot on a traditional revenge tale concerning the Soga brothers, but introduces two courtesans who imbue the play with a level of pathos through their discussions of the pitfalls of love with the mother of the dead Soga brothers. Though this play is often considered crude and clumsy in many respects, already evident in it is the increased sophistication of emotional content brought about through the use of the mistress/courtesan figure—a figure that was to become characteristic of Chikamatsu. In his next important play, *Shusse Kagekiyo* [Kagekiyo Victorious], the mistress of Kagekiyo is, according to one critic, 'a believable woman with the contradictions and complexities that distinguish human beings from puppets', and possesses a 'genuine tragic intensity'.

Shusse Kagekiyo was written for the famous chanter Takemoto Gidayū, with whom Chikamatsu was collaborating from 1686. But (and perhaps logically, considering his increasing 'humanization' of character-types) Chikamatsu turned increasingly towards the kabuki theatre of live actors, and wrote almost exclusively for the kabuki stage from 1693 to 1703, becoming a contracted writer for the actor Sakata Tōjūrō I in Kyoto. He probably wrote about 30 kabuki plays, but those that have survived (rarely in complete form) are not regarded as highly as the puppet plays by most commentators. Above all, and perhaps to Chikamatsu's disappointment, kabuki theatre was one in which the actor was pre-eminent, and the writer's scripts, often produced in collaboration, were more bases for histrionic improvisation than structured, literary products.

Whether because of artistic limitations of the kabuki stage, the retirement of Tōjūrō, the resurgence in popularity of Gidayū's puppet theatre, or other reasons (an open biographical question which has intrigued scholars and theatre historians), Chikamatsu returned to writing puppet plays in the early 1790s, and wrote almost wholly in this form after 1795. It is from this period that those works generally considered his masterpieces derive. The later puppet plays fall into two categories—the *sewamono* form (domestic tragedies, also described as 'dramas of contemporary life') and the *jidaimono* form (historical plays).

In the *sewamono* category are the 'love suicide' plays, notably *Sonezaki Shinjū* (*The Love Suicides at Sonezaki*) and *Shinjū Ten no Amijima* (*The Love Suicides at Amijima*). The former of these drew on actual reports of the suicide of a pair of lovers, a shop assistant and a prostitute, and formed the basis for this entire genre of puppet plays. Chikamatsu wrote more than 11 'love suicide' plays, whose plots were usually based on the efforts of the male lover to buy his beloved from the brothel where she has been sent by her father, with the tragic element often involving the destitution brought about thereby. The characters' heroism does not derive from any innate 'superhuman' qualities or attributes, but emerges through their struggles, sacrifices, and the depth of their love—elements brought out particularly in the *michiyuki* scenes. Chikamatsu was able to make extensive use of irony, tragic pathos, and social and economic realism to produce an extremely popular dramatic concoction—indeed one so popular that the plays increased the rate of such suicides in real life, causing consternation for the authorities and new legislation criminalizing such suicide attempts.

Most of the plays of the *jidaimono* category, the historical plays, have faded into relative obscurity, although Chikamatsu composed around 50 of them, and they were given higher priority in the theatre of his time. Nevertheless, the category does contain the play sometimes cited as his greatest achievement—*Kokusenyā Kassen* (*The Battles of Coxinga*). It was certainly his greatest popular success, achieving an extraordinary run of around 17 months. Its treatment of history is highly fantastic—it presents the story of the almost single-handed rescue of the Ming dynasty in China from the Tartar tyranny by a half-Chinese, half-Japanese fisherman—and its contrasts are stark in tone, including broad humour, heroic and sensational feats, vivid exploitation of the audience's unfamiliarity with a foreign setting, and, by virtue of the hero's semi-Japanese lineage, patriotic appeal. Such a play as *The Battles of Coxinga* is a world away from the concerns of the *sewamomo* works, and it is the latter which tend to be the better known today, particularly in the West.

—Noel Stanley

CHIN P'ING MEI. See **GOLDEN LOTUS.**

CHRÉTIEN de Troyes. Almost nothing is known of his life; because of dedications of his works, it is commonly assumed that he knew or served Countess Marie de Champagne at her court in Troyes and Philip of Alsace, Count of Flanders; works were probably written in the 1170s and 1180s.

PUBLICATIONS

Collections

Sämtliche Werke, edited by Wendelin Foerster. 4 vols., 1884–99; reprinted 1965.
Arthurian Romances (includes translations of *Erec and Énide*; *Cligès*; *Yvain*; *Lancelot*), edited by D.D.R. Owen, translated by W.W. Comfort. 1914; reprinted 1975.
Arthurian Romances (includes translations of *Erec and Énide*; *Cligès*; *Lancelot*; *Yvain*; *Perceval*), translated by D.D.R. Owen. 1987.
The Complete Romances, translated by Donald Staines. 1990.
Arthurian Romances (includes translations of *Eric and Énide*; *Cligès*; *The Knight of the Cart* [*Lancelot*]; *The Knight with the Lion* [*Yvain*]; *The Story of the Grail* [*Perceval*]), translated by William W. Kilber and Carleton W. Carroll. 1991.

Verse

Philomena, edited by C. de Boer. 1909.
Erec et Énide, edited by Mario Roques. 1952; as *Erec and Enid*, edited and translated by Carleton W. Carroll, 1987; also translated by Dorothy Gilbert, 1992.
Cligès, edited by Alexandre Micha. 1957; also edited by Claude Luttrell and Stewart Gregory, 1993.
Yvain (Le Chevalier au Lion), edited by Mario Roques. 1960; also edited by T.B.W. Reid, 1967; as *Yvain*, translated by Robert W. Ackerman and Frederick W. Locke, 1957; also translated by Ruth Harwood Cline, 1975; edited and translated by William W. Kibler, 1985; Burton Raffel, 1987.
Lancelot (Le Chevalier de la charrette), edited by Mario Roques. 1958; as *Lancelot; or, The Knight of the Cart*, edited and translated by William W. Kibler, 1981; also

translated by Deborah Webster Rogers, 1984; Ruth Harwood Cline, 1990.
Le Conte du Graal (Perceval), edited by William Roach. 1959; also edited by Félix Lecoy, 2 vols., 1972–75; as *Perceval: The Story of the Grail*, translated by Nigel Bryant, 1982; also translated by Ruth Harwood Cline, 1985; William W. Kibler, edited by Rupert T. Pickens, 1990; as *The Story of the Grail*, translated by Robert White Linker, 1952.

*

Bibliography: *Chrétien de Troyes: An Analytic Bibliography* by Douglas Kelly, 1976.

Critical Studies: *Arthurian Tradition and Chrétien de Troyes* by Roger Sherman Loomis, 1949; *Romance in the Making: Chrétien de Troyes and the Earliest French Romance*, 1954, and *Chrétien de Troyes: Inventor of the Modern Novel*, 1957, both by Foster E. Guyer; *The Portrait in Twelfth-Century French Literature: An Example of the Stylistic Originality of Chrétien de Troyes* by Alice M. Colby, 1965; *Aesthetic Distance in Chrétien de Troyes: Irony and Comedy in Cligès and Perceval* by Peter Haidu, 1968; *Chrétien de Troyes* by Urban T. Holmes, 1970; *Chrétien Studies* by Z.P. Zaddy, 1972; *The Allegory of Adventure: Reading Chrétien's Erec and Yvain* by Tom Artin, 1974; *The Creation of the First Arthurian Romance: A Quest* by Claude A. Luttrell, 1974; *Chrétien's Jewish Grail: A New Investigation of the Imagery and Significance of Chrétien de Troyes's Grail Episode Based Upon Medieval Hebraic Sources* by Eugene J. Weinraub, 1976; *Structure and Sacring: The Systematic Kingdom in Chrétien's Erec et Énide*, 1978, and *The Arthurian Romances of Chrétien de Troyes: Once and Future Fictions*, 1991, both by Donald Maddox; *The Craft of Chrétien de Troyes: An Essay on Narrative Art* by Norris J. Lacy, 1980, and *The Legacy of Chrétien de Troyes* edited by Lacy, Douglas Kelly, and Keith Busby, 2 vols., 1987–88; *Chrétien de Troyes: A Study of the Arthurian Romances* by Leslie T. Topsfield, 1981; *Chrétien de Troyes: The Man and His Work* by Jean Frappier, translated by Raymond J. Cormier, 1982; *The Dream of Chivalry: A Study of Chrétien de Troyes's Yvain and Hartmann von Aue's Iwein* by Ojars Kratins, 1982; *Love and Marriage in Chrétien de Troyes* by Peter S. Noble, 1982, and *Chrétien de Troyes and the Troubadours* edited by Noble and Linda M. Paterson, 1984; *Chrétien de Troyes* by Lucie Polak, 1982; *The Sower and His Seed: Essays on Chrétien de Troyes* edited by Rupert T. Pickens, 1983; *The Portrayal of the Heroine in Chrétien de Troyes's Erec et Énide; Gottfried von Strassburg's Tristan and Flamenca* by Nancy C. Zak, 1983; *Chrétien de Troyes: Erec et Énide* by Glynn S. Burgess, 1984; *The Romances of Chrétien de Troyes: A Symposium* edited by Douglas Kelly, 1985; *Chrétien de Troyes: Yvain (Le Chevalier au Lion)* by Tony Hunt, 1986; *From Topic to Tale: Logic and Narrativity in the Middle Ages* by Eugene Vance, 1987.

* * *

Chrétien de Troyes brought the nascent romance form to one of its highest points and gave Arthurian characters and situations their courtly cast. Some of his early works—adaptations of Ovid and a version of the Tristan story—have not survived; others are of doubtful attribution or of marginal interest (the *Philomena*, the *Guillaume d'Angleterre*, and two short lyrical poems); on the other hand, his five major romances have earned him great critical acclaim. A product of the revival of interest in the classics, notably Ovid, and of the vogue of Celtic tales and of courtly love, these compositions written in octosyllabic rhymed couplets are among the most sophisticated literary creations of the 12th-century Renaissance. Chrétien was encouraged and probably supported for a while by Countess Marie of Champagne, daughter of King Louis VII of France and Eleanor of Aquitaine.

Erec et Énide (*Erec and Énide*) is the first full-blown account of King Arthur and the knights of the Round Table. After Erec weds the fair Énide, he becomes so enamoured of her that he loses interest in chivalry. Prodded into taking up arms again by his bride's hasty words, the hero forces her to accompany him on a series of perilous adventures in the course of which he proves his valour and Énide her loyalty and devotion to him.

Cligès (c.1176) appears to have been modelled in part on Thomas's *Tristan* whose heroine Chrétien criticized. Unlike Isolt, Fenice refuses to become involved with two lovers simultaneously. With the aid of magic potions, she prevents her husband from consummating their marriage, then, after feigning death, flees with Cligès to an idyllic hideaway. When the husband succumbs, the lovers are finally free to marry. In this romance, Chrétien developed the soliloquy as a means of analysing love's torments.

There is some evidence that Chrétien worked alternately on his next two romances in the late 1170s. *Lancelot (Le Chevalier de la charrette)* (*Lancelot; or, The Knight of the Cart*) is perhaps the author's best-known story. Held hostage by the evil Meleagant, Queen Guinevere is rescued by her secret lover Lancelot who must first overcome several obstacles and, above all, suffer the humiliation of mounting a cart driven by a dwarf. Guinevere is a haughty and demanding mistress who makes her lover give in to all her caprices; Lancelot is a model of chivalry and courtesy for whom love-service has many of the characteristics of religious devotion and even mysticism.

Yvain (Le Chevalier au Lion) (*Yvain; or, The Knight of the Lion*) recounts the adventures of a hero who weds the widow of a man he has slain. Though passionately in love with his bride, Yvain becomes so preoccupied with tourneying that she is soon out of his mind. The two are eventually reconciled after Yvain expiates his fault.

Le Conte du Graal (Perceval) (*Perceval: The Story of the Grail*), of 1181 or later, is about a naive young man who, after receiving training in chivalry and courtesy at King Arthur's court, happens upon a mysterious castle whose host is the Fisher King. There he witnesses a curious procession that includes a bleeding lance and a grail. Perceval fails to inquire about the significance of these objects and must then face the consequences. Medieval continuators gave a Christian interpretation to this story and some scholars believe Chrétien intended to provide this kind of explanation. However, the poem was left unfinished and constitutes one of the most fascinating literary conundrums of all time.

—Gerard J. Brault

EREC AND ÉNIDE (Erec et Énide)
Poem by Chrétien de Troyes, written c.1160–70.

Erec and Énide is the first of Chrétien's romances, and one of the earliest Arthurian romances. Like most works of this type, it focuses not on King Arthur, but on one of the knights of the Round Table: in this case, Erec, son of Lac, a Breton king. Chrétien claims to be writing this story in order to do away with mistakes made by previous story-tellers, who 'usually mutilate and spoil' tales. His version, he claims, 'will be remembered as long as Christianity endures'.

The poem, comprising 6,878 lines of rhymed couplets, can be divided into three sections: Arthur's and Erec's parallel hunts, which culminate in the marriage of Erec and Énide; the series of tests which Erec and Énide must endure to prove their love; and the Joy of the Court episode, which establishes their love firmly within their social setting. Integrated into these episodes are folkloric elements which were extremely popular in the oral tradition of the time.

The initial episode, that of the hunts, is, in itself, a unified tale. Arthur hunts the white stag in the hope of winning the traditional reward, a kiss from the fairest maiden in the court. Erec jousts for the beautiful sparrowhawk, for the reward of a lovely maiden of his own choosing. In doing so, he revenges himself on Yder, son of Nut, who has insulted him through his disrespect for the queen. Erec falls in love with and betroths himself to Énide, whom he takes back to Arthur's court, where she is admired by one and all.

Their wedding feast is sumptuous and is followed by a month's celebration. Marital bliss, however, causes Erec to forget his chivalric duties. Énide blames herself for this and begs her husband to prove himself once again by seeking further adventures. The two ride out together and soon are obliged to affirm their love for one another: Erec, through battles with knights, a dwarf king, and others: and Énide, through various tests of wifely devotion.

The concluding episode, that of the Joy of the Court, features Erec's test in a fantastic garden, inhabited by a fair lady and a strong knight who is defending her, and decorated with a row of heads impaled on stakes and one horn. Erec and the knight, Mabonagrain, engage in battle. Finally yielding, Mabonagrain tells Erec the story of his imprisonment by the fair lady and asks him to blow the horn. Once Erec has done this, Mabonagrain is released from the garden, leaving only the lady, who is somewhat comforted when she learns that she is Énide's cousin. The poem ends with the crowning of Erec and Énide on Christmas Day.

While the three episodes can stand separately, they do flow easily from one to the other. The opening section characterizes Erec as a valorous knight by paralleling him structurally with Arthur. Énide, while appearing to be poor, displays noble attributes of beauty, modesty, and faithfulness. In the next section, the two display their worthiness and love through their tests. While they seem to be estranged for a while by their trials, their eventual reconciliation serves to strengthen the bond between them. The final episode allows them to prove their love even further, not just to each other, but to all the court as well. The earlier opposition of love and knightly duties fades as the two are joyfully accepted by their people as king and queen.

Chrétien's first romance proved to be extremely popular. Shortly after its composition it was adapted into German by Hartmann von Aue, the traces of it can be seen in many other medieval works. It appears in Old Norse as the *Erex Saga*, and similarities to it can be seen in 'Gerain Son of Erbin', one of the tales in the Welsh *Mabinogion*. It was adapted by Alfred, Lord Tennyson in his *Idylls of the King* as 'Geraint and Enid'.

Not simply an adventure or a love story, *Erec and Énide* teaches that a balance must be reached between love and duty, and that both the man and the woman must share in seeking this equilibrium. Chrétien weaves this lesson masterfully into a tale that is replete with both physical and psychological adventures, ably realizing his intention that 'it is right that all always aspire and endeavour to speak eloquently and to teach well'.

—Lisa M. Ruch

LANCELOT
Poem by Chrétien de Troyes, written c.1170–80.

Lancelot, also known as *The Knight of the Cart*, is the Chrétien's third Arthurian romance. Its inspiration can be found in the Celtic abduction tale, in which a maid or maiden is captured, a knight sets out to rescue her and must undergo many trials, and they are brought together through his prowess. In this case, the maid is Guinevere, wife of King Arthur, and the brave knight is Lancelot, champion of the Round Table.

The poem—7,112 lines of rhymed couplets—follows the structure of its Celtic model, but elaborates on it with its multiple adventures and tales of knightly prowess and chivalric acts. Through this elaboration, we see Lancelot compared to Gawain, another favourite of Arthur's court. Lancelot consistently appears as the better of the two, and thus proves his worthiness as Guinevere's lover.

Chrétien dedicates the poem to his patroness, Marie de Champagne, declaring that she provided him with the *matière* and the *sen*: the subject matter and the meaning. Chrétien states simply that 'he undertakes to shape the work, adding little except his effort and his careful attention'. Curiously enough, he did not finish the tale himself, but left it to his clerk, Godefroi de Lagny, to conclude. Godefroi states unequivocally that he followed Chrétien's directions in doing so, and added nothing of his own.

As the poem opens, an unknown knight rides into Arthur's court and informs those gathered there that he is holding many of its subjects captive in his own land. He then challenges Arthur to release Guinevere to him as the prize for a tournament. Kay insists on being her escort, but is swiftly defeated by the stranger once they are outside Camelot. Gawain, who is in pursuit, meets with Lancelot, who, travelling incognito, is also after Guinevere and her captor. Both knights continue on, Lancelot always surpassing Gawain in his deeds. He commits his one error when he hesitates before boarding a cart, which is a test of his humility and love. He successfully copes with other tests, such as a flaming lance and a perilous bed. As the knights travel along, they meet a number of maidens, one of whom informs them that Guinevere's kidnapper is Meleagant, son of Bademagu, the king of Goirre. In another adventure, Lancelot visits a cemetery in which the gravestones are reserved for the future dead. He lifts the heavy stone on a tomb reserved for himself, which proves his role as the messiah-figure who will free the imprisoned subjects in Meleagant's land. This land is bounded by water, which can be crossed by means of a Sword Bridge or an Underwater Bridge. Gawain opts for the Underwater Bridge, the easier of the two, leaving the Sword Bridge for Lancelot. Lancelot's love for Guinevere helps him to forget the pain as he crosses the bridge with bare feet and hands. Later he is obliged to rescue Gawain, who is having difficulties with his crossing. Lancelot fights with Meleagant and betters him, although Meleagant will not admit defeat and imprisons Lancelot after catching him in bed with Guinevere. Lancelot is eventually released from his prison by

Meleagant's sister, and battles with Meleagant once again, this time killing him. Thus, the freedom of the captives is ensured.

One of the most striking additions to this abduction tale is Chrétien's concern with the psychology of his characters. Lancelot's love for Guinevere is displayed by his complete absorption in thoughts of her. By concentrating on her, he can overcome the pain of his injuries, and the mere sight of her renews his energy in his first tournament with Meleagant. However, she tests his psyche even more completely when she spurns him at her rescue because of his hesitation at the cart. The following scene, in which both of them react to rumours of the other's death, allows us to glimpse into both of their minds. By portraying both the external and the internal trials of his protagonist, Chrétien creates a fully-rounded character who is both active and contemplative.

This poem, the earliest surviving tale of Lancelot, portrays the love affair that supplanted that of Mordred and Guinevere as the factor that brings about the fall of the Round Table in Arthurian legend. It was incorporated into the French Vulgate cycle of the 13th century, and developed further in the *Queste del Saint Graal* (*Quest for the Holy Grail*). Malory drew from this tradition when he wrote the *Morte d'Arthur*, and the love of Lancelot and Guinevere is still the focus of many writers of Arthurian works in the 20th century.

—Lisa M. Ruch

CHRISTINE DE PIZAN (or PISAN). Born in Venice, Italy c.1365. Moved to Paris at an early age. Father was medical adviser and astrologer to Charles V. Married Étienne de Castel in 1380 (died 1390); two sons (one died in infancy) and one daughter. Started writing career shortly after the death of her husband; attracted the attention of members of the French Royal Court and became society poet; worked as a copyist in the book trade; fled to a Dominican Abbey in Poissy to escape the civil war. *Died c.1430.*

PUBLICATIONS

Collections

Oeuvres poétiques, edited by Maurice Roy. 3 vols., 1886–96; reprinted 1965.
Ballades, Rondeaux and Virelais, edited by Kenneth Varty. 1965.

Works

L'Avision-Christine, edited by Sister Mary Louise Towner. 1932.
Les Cent Ballades d'amant et de dame, edited by Jacqueline Cerquiglini. 1982.
Le Débat sur le Roman de la Rose, edited by Eric Hicks. 1977.
Le Ditié de Jehanne d'Arc, edited and translated by Angus J. Kennedy and Kenneth Varty. 1977.

L'Epistre de la prison de vie humaine, edited by Angus J. Kennedy. 1984.

L'Epitre d'Othéa, as *The Epistle of Othea to Hector*, edited by George F. Warner, 1904; also edited by James D. Gordon and translated by Anthony Babington, 1942; as *The Epistle of Othéa*, edited by C.F. Bühler and translated by Stephen Scrope, 1970.

Le Livre de la cité des dames, edited by M.C. Curnow. 2 vols., 1975; as *The Book of the City of Ladies*, translated by Earl J. Richards, 1982; also translated by Thérèse Moreau and Eric Hicks, 1986.

Le Livre de la mutacion de Fortune, edited by Suzanne Solente. 4 vols., 1959–66.

Le Livre de la paix, edited by Charity Cannon Willard. 1958.

Le Livre des faits et bonnes meurs du sage roy Charles V, edited by Suzanne Solente. 2 vols, 1936–40.

Le Livre des faits d'armes et de la chevalerie, as *The Book of Feats of Arms and of Chivalry*, translated by William Caxton, 1498, reprinted and edited by A.T.P. Byles, 1932; revised edition, 1937.

Le Livre des trois vertus; ou, le Trésor de la citié des dames, edited by Eric Hicks. 1989; as *Le Livre des III vertus a l'enseignement des dames*, edited by Charity Cannon Willard, 1989; as *The Treasures of the City of Ladies; or, The Book of the Three Virtues*, translated by Sarah Lawson, 1985; *A Medieval Woman's Mirror of Honor*, translated by Willard, 1989.

Le Livre du chemin de long estude, edited by Robert Püschell. 1881; revised edition, 1887, reprinted 1974.

Le Livre du corps de policie, edited by Robert H. Lucas. 1967.

L'Oroyson nostre dame: Prayer to Our Lady (bilingual edition), translated by Jean Misrahi and Margaret Marks. 1953.

Les Sept Psaumes allégorisés, edited by Ruth Ringland Rains. 1965.

The Book of the Duke of True Lovers, translated by Alice Kemp-Welch. 1966.

The Epistle of the Prison of Human Life with An Epistle to the Queen of France and Lament of the Evils of the Civil War, edited by Josette A. Wisman. 1984.

Poems of Cupid, God of Love (includes *Epistre au dieu d'amours* and *Le Dit de la rose*), edited and translated by Thelma S. Fenster and Mary Carpenter Erler. 1990.

*

Bibliography: *Christine de Pisan: A Bibliography of Writings by Her and About Her*, 1982, and *Christine de Pisan: A Bibliography*, 2nd edition, 1989, both by Edith Yenal; *Christine de Pisan: A Bibliographical Guide* by Angus J. Kennedy, 1984.

Critical Studies: *Christine de Pizan: Ballades, Rondeaux and Virelais*, 1965, and *Epistre de la prison de vie humaine*, 1984, both by Angus J. Kennedy; *The Order of the Rose: The Life and Ideas of Christine de Pizan* by Enid McLeod, 1976; *Ideals for Women in the Works of Christine de Pizan* edited by Diane Bornstein, 1981; *Christine de Pisan* by Régine Pernond, 1982; *Christine de Pizan: Her Life and Works* by Charity Cannon Willard, 1984; *Politics, Gender and Genre: The Political Thought of Christine de Pizan* edited by Margaret Brabant, 1992; *Reinterpreting Christine de Pizan* edited by Earl Jeffrey Richards, 1992.

* * *

Christine de Pizan, the early 14th-century writer, composed a voluminous body of works. Writing both poetry and prose, she produced autobiographical texts, love lyrics, religious works, and treatises on education, warfare, peace-making, and proper behaviour, as well as polemics on the 'woman question'. She was also the official biographer of Charles V of France.

Christine began her literary career from necessity, after her husband died leaving her virtually impoverished with three small children and considerable debts. Since she earned her living solely by her pen, she is often referred to as the first professional writer. Her first endeavours were poems lamenting her husband's death and depicting her grief. She wrote about 20 such ballads. Soon she began to produce more traditional love lyrics and to experiment with both themes and lyrical forms.

Two of her longer poems, *Epistre au dieu d'amours* [Epistle to the God of Love], written in 1399, and *Le Dit de la rose* [The Story of the Rose], written in 1402, were composed as part of Christine's challenge to Jean de Meung's slanderous depiction of women in the second half of the *Roman de la rose* (*The Romance of the Rose*). Christine was in fact the main correspondent in the Quarrel of the Rose in which she and others such as Jean de Gerson, chancellor of the University of Paris, attacked the immorality and misogyny of Jean de Meung's poem.

The *Epistre au dieu d'amours* presents ladies from all social classes who complain to Cupid about those who slander them, Ovid and Jean de Meung in particular. It concludes with the banishment of all defamers of women from the court. In *Le Dit de la rose* she founds the Order of the Rose which rewards those knights who defend the honour of woman. The Quarrel of the Rose extended Christine's fame throughout Europe.

With the exception of two poems treating common courtly love themes, 'Le Dit de deux amans' [The Story of Two Lovers] and 'Le Livre des trois jugements' [Story of the Three Judgements], dedicated to the Seneschal de Hainaut, the only other major poem not connected to Christine's personal life is *Le Ditié de Jehanne D'Arc* [Joan of Arc's Story]. Christine had been in retirement at Poissy and had not written for years, when she heard about Joan of Arc and wrote this poem celebrating Joan as the saviour of France. For Christine, she was proof of the value of women and of their worth in God. The poem was the only work written in Joan of Arc's honour during her lifetime.

Among the personal or autobiographical poems, we find a poem written for Christine de Pizan's son, Jean de Castel. This work, 'Enseignements et proverbes moraux' [Moral Proverbs], became very popular in England. 'Le Livre du dit de Poissy' describes an elaborate party given for guests at the convent where her daughter lived. *Le Livre de la Mutacion de Fortune* [Mutation of Fortune] composed between 1400 and 1403, is the longest of her works in verse. It includes an allegorical sea voyage in which Christine depicts her transformation from wife to writer. She is adrift and helpless; Fortune takes pity upon her and by touching her renders her stronger in every sense. Her wedding band falls symbolically from her finger, for, as Christine tells us, she has become a man (lines 1,359–61). She is no longer a wife, but a person alone. The second part contains a description of Fortune's castle. In the *Le Livre du chemin de long estude* [The Long Study], Christine, in a dream vision, visits the Court of Reason and then returns to earth with the knowledge necessary to correct the Earth's faults by founding a world empire. Christine's prose works explore the same topics as her poems. There are a number of letters that she wrote as part of her polemic against Jean de Meung. She addresses the subject of world reform in *L'Avision-Christine* and the problem of strife and the necessity for peace in *Le Livre du corps de policie* [Book of the Body Politic], written 1406–07 and based on John of Salisbury's *Policraticus*, and in *Le Livre de la paix* [Book of Peace], 1412–14, which was actually a book of instruction written for the dauphin. Her interest in politics, society, and history is also evidenced in her manual on military ethics, *Le Livre des faits d'armes et de chevalerie* (*The Book of Feats of Arms and of Chivalry*) and in her commissioned work on the reign of Charles V, *Le Livre des faits et bonnes meurs du sage roy Charles V* [Deeds and Manners of Charles V], which was intended as a manual of good government for the dauphin. In addition, Christine wrote two religious works: *Les Sept Psaumes allégorisés* [Seven Allegorical Psalms] with a prose meditation for Charles le Noble, and the consolation, *L'Epistre de la prison de vie humaine* [Prison of Human Life], dedicated to Mary of Berry, who had lost so many of her family in the civil strife.

Her two major prose works, *Le Livre de la cité des dames* (*The Book of the City of Ladies*) and *Le Livre des trois vertus; ou, le Trésor de la citié des dames* (*The Treasures of the City of Ladies; or, The Book of the Three Virtues*), develop further the subject of greatest concern to her, the rehabilitation of the image of women. In these two works, we find a detailed presentation of her basic beliefs and her own view of woman's place in society. In the *City of Ladies*, using once again an allegorical setting and a subtle method of attack, she refutes the many accusations against women. Drawing examples from various sources, Christine compiles a gallery of heroic, intelligent, virtuous women. Using an allegory of three ladies sent by God to help her build in the City, she enhances her work with divine approval and strengthens her refutation of the then popular belief that women were less holy, less valuable. This motif of Christine as an intermediary between the misguided world and the elements of right-thinking, justice, and holiness appears in several of her works (*L'Avision-Christine, Le Livre du chemin de long estude*).

Having established the value and talents of women, she continued her work on women by writing a manual of proper conduct in the companion text, *The Treasures of the City of Ladies*. In spite of her own unorthodox life as a professional writer and her decision to remain a widow, Christine saw woman's role as primarily that of a wife. Some feminists have tended to shy away from her because of this aspect of her work; however, given the world in which she was living, her stand against the accepted devaluation of women, supported by the Church as well as the majority of male intellectuals was a bold move. To have believed that women's situation could have been totally transformed would have been impractical, even foolish. Moreover, Christine had enjoyed a happy marriage. Her goal was to gain respect for women in their established role in society, not to revolutionize her world. Nevertheless, for her period, Christine was a strong advocate of women and deserves to be considered one of the first feminists. During her time, she was recognized as both an accomplished lyric poet and a respected authority on the status of women.

—Shawncey J. Webb

THE BOOK OF THE CITY OF LADIES (Le Livre de la cité des dames)
Prose by Christine de Pizan, written 1405.

The Book of the City of Ladies was written as a defence of women and is one of several works that Christine wrote on this subject. Christine states clearly her position on the worth of women and refutes the unfavourable portrayal of women prevalent at the time.

By writing the work and drawing upon many literary sources, Christine became, herself, an example of the abilities and worth of her female contemporaries. However, as scholars have attested, she was not interested merely in composing a defence of these women but also in creating a universal history of women, past, present, and future which would evidence the innate talents and qualities of woman.

The work is written in the form of an allegory depicting three ladies, Reason, Justice, and Rectitude (this third lady, called Droiture in French, translated as either Rectitude or Right-thinking, was added by Christine to the usual list of allegorical figures) who visit Christine in her study. She introduces her subject matter by describing her despair upon reading in text after text of the little value and many vices attributed to women and of their inferiority of body and mind. She humbly laments her disappointment at discovering that she is such a vile, worthless creature and apologizes to God for being a woman. She next asks God why he created her such rather than making her a man. (The underlying irony is scarcely concealed here, for how could she have read and understood the texts if she were as worthless as they tell her?) Suddenly a light appears and she sees three ladies who have been sent by God to help her see her error in believing the falsehoods she has been reading. These ladies, Reason, Justice, and Rectitude, also have come to assist her in the construction of a city of ladies. By using this motif, Christine immediately connects her work to the *City of God* of St Augustine and to Christianity. Her refutation of misogyny is surrounded by holy approval; woman is to be vindicated of the role in which she has, unjustly, been cast.

Drawing upon a number of sources, especially Boccaccio's *Concerning Famous Women*, Christine recounts many examples of brave, virtuous women from both ancient and contemporary times, from pagan and Christian societies. She divides the book into three parts: Part I, The Foundation and the Walls, Part II, The Buildings and Their Dwellers, and Part III, The Towers and the Noble Ladies Chosen to Dwell There. In Part I, Reason answers Christine's questions and guides her to the truth. In this section, Christine speaks of the intentions and motivations of the slanders of women and cites examples contrary to the accusations made. She also includes examples of women's ability in politics, in science, and in war. In Part II, Christine questions Rectitude about the accusations against women, such as lack of loyalty, infidelity, unchasteness, and weakness of character. She also discusses the value of women to society, the benefits of good marriages (based on the Christian concept of perfect union, viewing husband and wife in the same relationship as Christ the Bridegroom and his Bride the Church) and the usefulness of study for women. In this section, the 'High Women of France' are welcomed into the city. Part III contains Justice's defence of women. More illustrious women, mostly martyrs, are welcomed into the city. This is perhaps the weakest section of the work because of the very long and repetitious accounts of the martyrdom of these women. Christine concludes her book by exhorting all women to be virtuous and earn a place in the City of Ladies.

Throughout the text, Christine uses the device of appearing

to be convinced, although with enormous sadness, of the contrary side of the argument that she is intent upon proving. Her immediate stimulus to writing is her reading of the *Lamentations of Mathéole*, a text that supposedly extols the value of women but in reality slanders them. Puzzled by what she has read in the light of her own experience as a woman, she senses that the texts, Mathéole's as well as others she has read, are wrong, but accepts them, since so many learned men are in agreement. Here, Christine attacks blind obedience to majority opinion. The three ladies condemn her acceptance of these ideas and say they have been sent to enlighten her; by enlightening Christine they also enlighten the reader.

Within the work, Marina Warner has identified five recurring themes that treat the five areas in which Christine feels her society needs enlightenment and in which she hopes to achieve improvement by leading people to right-thinking. They are as follows: lack of access to education for women; the disappointment evidenced by the birth of a girl; the accusation that women encourage and welcome rape; the insistence that women's delight in fine clothes and their own attractiveness is linked to loose morals; and the problem of battered women, primarily married women, and that of drunken and/or spendthrift husbands.

To teach the reader right-thinking on these issues, Christine employs examples drawn from familiar sources such as Boccaccio, but she freely reworks the material for her purposes. A case in point is her treatment of Medea. She includes Medea among the woman skilled in sciences and medicine but does not mention her murdering her children. Christine also intersperses anecdotes from her own personal experiences and her comments upon the ills of her own time.

Christine's style, which is patterned after Latin sentence structure, has rendered her work difficult for her readers, but it witnesses her own erudition and interest in literary form and creativity.

In spite of her talent and the richness of *The Book of the City of Ladies*, it is only recently that the work has once again begun to be appreciated. Because its author borrowed so extensively from Boccaccio, it has often been considered a translation of his *Concerning Famous Women*. However, Boccaccio's work includes only pagan women and deals with infamous as well as admirable women, whereas Christine's work includes only praiseworthy women but both pagan and Christian. In addition, Christine's purpose in writing was entirely different—the defence of women. Although many feminists find the work too conservative, the text is one of the first major feminist works.

—Shawncey J. Webb

CICERO. Born Marcus Tullius Cicero in Arpinum (now Arpino), central Italy, 3 January 106 BC. Educated in Rome, and studied rhetoric and oratory in Athens and Rhodes, 79–77 BC. Served in the army of Pompeius Strabo, 89 BC. Married 1) Terentia in 80 BC (divorced 47 BC), one daughter and one son; 2) Publilia (divorced 45 BC). Lawyer: first appearance in courts, 81 BC; usually appeared for the defence, but his prosecution of Verres (70 BC) is his most famous case. Financial administrator (*quaestor*), western Sicily, 75 BC; judicial officer (*praetor*), 66 BC; consul, 63 BC: exposed Catiline's conspiracy to carry out uprisings in Italy and arson in Rome; declared an exile by Clodius in 58 BC, and lived in Thessalonica and Illyricum, but recalled with help of Pompey, 57 BC; reluctantly allied himself with triumvirate of Pompey, Caesar, and Crassus, 56 BC, and retired from public life until 51 BC; elected augur of the college of diviners, 53 BC; governor of Cilicia, Asia Minor, 51–50 BC; allied with Pompey in civil war, 49–48 BC: after Pompey's defeat Cicero's safety was guaranteed by Caesar; after Caesar's assassination, 44 BC, supported general amnesty (delivered 14 Philippic orations against Antony, 44–43 BC); the triumvirate of Octavian, Antony, and Lepidus put Cicero on the execution list, 43 BC, and he was captured and killed. *Died 7 December 43 BC.*

PUBLICATIONS

Collections

[Works], edited by C.F.W. Mueller. 1884–1917; also edited by K. Simbeck and others, 1923– ; translated by various hands [Loeb Edition], 28 vols., 1912–58.
[Letters], edited by R.Y. Tyrrell and L.C. Purser. 7 vols., 1899–1918; selections as *Letters*, translated by L.P. Wilkinson, 1949; *Selected Letters,* translated by D.R. Shackleton Bailey, 1980.
[Poems], edited by W.W. Ewbank. 1933; translated by A.E. Douglas, 1985.
Selected Works, translated by Michael Grant. 1960.
Selected Political Speeches, translated by Michael Grant. 1969, revised edition, 1973.

Works

Academica, edited by J.S. Reid. 1885.
Brutus, edited by H. Malcovati. 1963; also edited by A.E. Douglas, 1966; translated by H.M. Poteat, 1950.
De amicitia, with *De senectute* and *De divinatione*, translated by William Armistead Falcolner. 1922.
De divinatione, edited by Arthur S. Pease. 4 vols., 1920–23; as *De divinatione*, with *De senectute* and *De amicitia*, translated by William Arthur Falcolner, 1922; as *On Divination*, translated by H.M. Poteat, 1950.
De domo sua, edited by R.G. Nisbet. 1939.
De finibus, edited by J.N. Madvid. 3rd edition, 1876; Books I–II edited by J.S. Reid, 1925.
De natura deorum, edited by A.S. Pease. 2 vols., 1955–58; as *On the Nature of the Gods*, translated by H.M. Poteat, 1950; also translated by H.C.P. McGregor, 1972.
De officiis, edited by P. Fedeli. 1965; as *On Duties*, translated by H.M. Poteat, 1950; also translated by John Higginbotham, 1967; Harry G. Edinger, 1974; M.T. Griffin and E.M. Atkins, 1991.
De oratore, edited by A.S. Wilkins. 1892.
De republica, as *On the Commonwealth*, translated by G.H. Sabine and S.B. Smith. 1929; selections as *Res Publica*, translated by W.K. Lacey and Harry G. Edinger, 1974.
De senectute, edited by Leonard Huxley, revised edition. 1923; also edited by J.G.F. Powell, 1988; translated (from the French) as *De senectute*, 1481; with *De amicitia* and *De divinatione*, translated by William Armistead Falconer, 1922; as *Cato Major, or His Discourse of Old-Age*, translated by James Logan, 1744; as *On Old Age*, translated by Frank Copley, 1967.

Epistulae ad Atticum: Letters to Atticus, edited by W.S. Watt. 2 vols., 1961–65; edited and translated by D.R. Shackleton Bailey, 7 vols., 1965–70.

Epistulae ad familiares [Letters to His Friends], edited by D.R. Shackleton Bailey. 2 vols., 1977; also edited by W.S. Watt, 1982; translated by D.R. Shackleton Bailey, 1978.

Epistulae ad Quintum frateum et M. Brutum, edited by D.R. Shackleton Bailey. 1980; also edited by W.S. Watt, 1958; translated by D.R. Shackleton Bailey, 1978.

In Pisonem, edited by R.G. Nisbet. 1961.

In Vatinium, edited by L.F. Pocock. 1926.

Kerrines II, translated by T.N. Mitchell. 1986.

Laelius, edited by Frank Stock, revised edition. 1930; as *On Friendship*, translated by Frank Copley, 1967; also translated by J.G.F. Powell, 1990.

Philippics I–II, edited by J.D. Denniston. 1939; also edited by D.R. Shackleton Bailey, 1986.

Pro M. Caelio, edited by R.G. Austin. 1960.

Somnium Scipionis, as *The Dream of Scipio*, with *Nine Orations*, translated by Smith P. Bovie. 1967; also translated by Percy Bullock, 1983; J.G.F. Powell, 1990.

Tusculanae disputationes, edited by Thomas W. Dougan and Robert M. Henry. 2 vols., 1905; as *Tusculan Disputations* [Loeb Edition], translated by J.E. King, 1927; 2 and 5 translated by A.E. Douglas, 1990.

The Caesarian Orations, translated by G.J. Acheson. 1965.

Nine Orations and the Dream of Scipio, translated by Smith P. Bovie. 1967.

On the Good Life (selections), translated by Michael Grant. 1971.

Murder Trials (selected orations), translated by Michael Grant. 1975.

On Fate, edited and translated by R.W. Sharples. 1992.

*

Critical Studies: *Cicero and the Roman Republic* by Frank R. Crowell, 1948; *The Humanism of Cicero* by H.A.K. Hunt, 1954; *Cicero on the Art of Growing Old* by H.W. Couch, 1959; *Cicero* by T.A. Dorey, 1965; *Cicero on Old Age* by E.M. Blaiklock, 1966; *Cicero the Statesman* by Richard E. Smith, 1966; *Cicero* by D.R. Shackleton Bailey, 1971; *Cicero: A Political Biography* by David Stockton, 1971; *Cicero and the State Religion* by R.J. Goar, 1972; *Cicero and Rome* by David Taylor, 1973; *Cicero: A Portrait* by Elizabeth Rawson, 1975; *Cicero and the End of the Roman Republic* edited by W.K. Lacey, 1978; *Cicero's Elegant Style: An Analysis of the 'Pro Archia'* by Harold C. Gotoff, 1979; *Cicero: The Ascending Years*, 1979, and *Cicero the Senior Statesman*, 1991, both by Thomas N. Mitchell; *The Style and the Composition of Cicero's Speech 'Pro Q. Rescio Comoedo': Origin and Function* by Jerzy Axer, 1980; *Cicero's Philippics and their Demosthenic Model: The Rhetoric of Crisis* by Cecil W. Wooten, 1983; *Trials of Character: The Eloquence of Ciceronian Ethos* by James M. May, 1988; *Cicero's Social and Political Thought* by Neal Wood, 1988; *The Philosophical Books of Cicero* by Paul MacKendrick, 1989; *Cicero the Politician* by Christian Habicht, 1990; *Cicero and the Roman Republic* by Manfred Fuhrmann, 1992; *Representations: Images of the World in Ciceronian Oratory* by Ann Vasaly, 1993.

* * *

Cicero was one of the most prolific and versatile of Latin authors, but his literary reputation has varied more than most. In antiquity he was generally accepted as the prince of Roman orators, though sometimes with reservations. In the Middle Ages, when his speeches and letters were almost forgotten, the less technical of his philosophical works became vastly popular and influential. Petrarch was his devout admirer, and among the humanists of the Renaissance his Latin style was a fetish. The 18th century found him congenial, the 19th less so.

In the 20th the most valuable part of Cicero's literary legacy seems to be the part he never intended to leave: his private correspondence. It was published at intervals after his death, apparently with scarcely any editing. The first extant letter was written when Cicero was 38 and they continue in uneven flow down to within a few months of his death. Many were to his closest intimates, his brother and his lifelong friend, Pomponius Atticus. They take us behind the political and domestic scenes, and thanks to them the colourful history of the last two decades of the Roman Republic is more than a bare chronicle of events. The famous names—Pompey, Cato, Crassus, Julius Caesar—come to life, and Cicero's own complex personality gets ample exposure. Incidentally, they show him to be a master of vivid narrative and description in a colloquial style very different from that of his publications. Nothing in the remains of Greco-Roman literature takes us so close to an individual and a society.

The speeches, too, offer much of this kind of interest and some of them, like the letters, are an important source of information about the speaker and his times. Covering a period of nearly 40 years, almost the whole of Cicero's public career, they range from legalistic pleas on behalf of obscure clients to grand occasions when Cicero held forth to the Senate or the People in its assemblies on great political issues. To a modern eye the faults of his eloquence are often all too plain: inflation, false pathos, egotism, verbosity, and what Theodor Mommsen called a dreadful barrenness of thought. Even so, a receptive reader may let himself be swept along with the tide of impeccably constructed periods, especially if he can read the Latin aloud. And sometimes there is more, as in the rhetorical drive of the *Catilines*, the genuine pathos of the 14th Philippic, or the brilliant badinage in the defence of Murena. As for Cicero's prose style, even Mommsen admired it. It was his most creative achievement.

Cicero was not an original thinker, but like many educated Romans of his time he was much interested in Greek philosophy. Late in life he conceived the plan to present it, at least its more recent developments, in Latin form. The result was a rapidly produced series of metaphysical and moral treatises based on Greek sources. As literature, the gem of the collection is the little tract on old age (*De senectute*), perhaps Cicero's one unqualified artistic success. Another attractive piece, on friendship, characteristically tells us nothing about the actualities of Roman *amicitia*, as Cicero knew them from his own experience. Even the works on rhetoric have this second-hand quality, except the *Brutus*, a survey of Roman orators which often reads like a catalogue but contains some highly interesting sketches of speakers whom Cicero had heard and personally known.

Cicero also wrote poetry, mostly in his youth. It had a considerable vogue, until Catullus and the 'New Poets' brought their fresh inspiration. Posterity would have none of it, and enough survives to show that posterity was right. Even the advance in verse technique as compared with the remnants of earlier writing need not have been due to Cicero.

—D.R. Shackleton Bailey

IN DEFENCE OF MARCUS CAELIUS RUFUS (Pro M. Caelio)
Prose by Cicero, 56 BC.

Cicero's *In Defence of Marcus Caelius Rufus* was a light-hearted but clever labour of respect and affection for Caelius' father, who had assigned his son to Cicero's charge from 66–63 BC, and for the young man of 26 whose sometimes reckless nature, energy, and qualities of mind had already won the regard of the celebrated statesman. Caelius had earned his own reputation for courtroom oratory in 59 BC by prosecuting Gaius Antonius Hybrida, Cicero's colleague in the consulship of 63 BC. Cicero defended Antonius but lost the case to his protégé Caelius.

Caelius' own trial was the result of an accusation of *vis* (violence) against the father of Lucius Sempronius Atratinus. Atratinus brought the case in collusion with Clodia Metelli, widow of an ex-consul, with whom Caelius had conducted a two-year affair, ending in a quarrel. Cicero and Crassus appeared as defence counsel at this trial, held on 3–4 April 56 BC. Caelius probably spoke first in his own defence, with a fusillade of insults, objectionable remarks, and witticisms, often directed against Clodia; Crassus spoke second, and Cicero third. Clodia's hand in the indictment was transparent; damage to her social status by Caelius' desertion had provoked her animosity. In the end Caelius was acquitted and pursued a political career. Clodia lost her leading role in high society and vanished from public view.

Cicero's oration in defence of Caelius is carefully designed following generally accepted patterns: *exordium* (1–2); *praemunitio* (3–50); *argumentatio* (51–69); and *peroratio* (70–80). The *exordium* enables Cicero to indicate that the trial is exceptional in being held during a public festival. It also establishes Cicero's position: that the formal charges are negligible and that the real accuser is Clodia. The *praemunitio*, literally a 'build-up' which replaces the *narratio* (statement of facts) which normally followed the *exordium*, dispels the insinuations against Caelius' father, against Caelius' popularity with his townspeople, and against Caelius' morals and his attachment to Catiline (whose attempted revolution Cicero quelled as consul in 63 BC). Caelius' complicity with the Catilinarian conspiracy and charges of bribery and corruption against him are all summarily dismissed. Caelius' fortunes changed after he left his father's house and, like a latter-day Jason, he met his Medea of the Palatine. Charges of assault and battery and sexual assaults are swept aside along with the charge that Caelius was somehow connected with the murder of the philosopher Dido, leader of an Alexandrian embassy to Rome. Prosecutor Herennius Balbus' earlier extended lecture on the wages of sin and the moral decadence of modern youth should not, in Cicero's view, influence the jurors' attitude to Caelius. The only substantial charges (Crassus had dealt with three others) refer to gold (ornaments) and poison, and both relate to Clodia. Cicero proceeds to ridicule Caelius' former mistress by uproarious jest and stagecraft: first by calling up a ghostly ancestor, Appius Claudius Caecus, censor in 312 BC and builder of the Appian Way, to speak in character and rebuke his descendant; secondly by introducing Clodia's notorious brother, in another impersonation, to advise his sister to abandon Caelius for better game. Cicero enhances this parade of impersonations by presenting two characters (a stern father and an indulgent father) from comedies of Caecilius and Terence. Both discourage the jurors from treating Clodia's charges of misconduct as serious. The tone changes with more serious, personal remarks on Caelius'

character: earnest and industrious, but susceptible to the lifestyle of the age.

The *argumentatio* disposes of the charge of Caelius' acceptance of gold and of his evil intent to poison Clodia. A skilful digression, with the suggestion that Clodia may have poisoned her consular husband, intervenes before Cicero responds to the charge of intent to poison as being farcical. While the jurors are shaking with laughter, Cicero moves briskly to his concluding statement on the serious nature of the case, and the need to save the exemplary Caelius for his father and for the state. The elevated tone of the finale, accenting the promise attaching to Caelius, is a fitting postlude to the largely comic nature of the speech.

Cicero's defence of the wayward youth was clearly designed to persuade as much by jest as by serious argument. Because the jurors had been forced to renounce a holiday (the *Ludi Megalenses*, sacred and theatrical events in honour of the Magna Mater, Cybele) in order to hear the prosecution, Cicero cannily supplied them with an alternative holiday experience in the confines of the law-court. By appealing repeatedly to theatrical topics and conventions; by introducing the gibes of contemporary lampoons and scatological verse; by a series of impersonations; by exciting their parental instincts and so their proper concern for his client; by dramatic shifts from merriment and naughty assaults to serious austerity; and by appeals to their avuncular natures, Cicero pulled out every stop of his rhetorical genius. Light-hearted repartee and episode, with a rich measure of hilarity, farcical situations echoing the antics of popular mimes, with their grotesque caricature and surprises, are all part and parcel of Cicero's courtroom masterpiece.

—Alexander G. McKay

ON OLD AGE (De senectute)
Prose by Cicero, 44 BC.

Cicero's *On Old Age* has been read for centuries. Among the many philosophical works by Cicero, the book has enjoyed a popularity equal to that of his *On Duties* (*De officiis*) and his *On Friendship* (*De amicitia*). The work itself was finished in the early days of 44 BC and belongs to the last years of Cicero's life, a period from 46 to 43 BC, known as his 'marvellous years' (*anni mirabiles*) in which he wrote most of his philosophical works. It, like *On Friendship*, is focused upon a single theme, in this case the coming of age. The work was cast in a dialogue format patterned on that developed by Plato. It consists of a conversation invented by Cicero between Cato the Elder, then 84 years old, and a pair of younger visitors, Laelius and Scipio Aemilianus, each an actual figure in the Roman republic. The scene is a villa owned by Cato in some unspecified locale and the year is 150 BC, one year before Cato in fact died. After a brief introduction in which Cicero informs his best friend Atticus that not only has he written something on old age for Atticus but has also dedicated it to him, the remaining 81 paragraphs made up a series of gracefully posed questions designed to elicit long speeches full of advice from Cato. For the two younger men, about 35 or 36 years of age, have come to find out from Cato by what means they can most 'easily sustain the weight of increasing years'. Cato then examines and refutes in order four reasons why old age appears to be unhappy: that it takes us away from active pursuits, that it weakens our bodies, that it deprives us of almost all physical pleasures, and that it is not far from death. Although the work owes much to the various literary formats that popular philosophy assumed during the Hellenistic period such as the diatribe, how much or by what specific source Cicero was influenced is not known. Out of the Greek canon, scholars have perceived the influence of Plato, Xenophon, Aristotle, Aristo of Chios, Heraclides Ponticus, and Theophrastus. Among the Latin writers, one influence seems to have been Varro.

In *On Old Age*, as in Cicero's other philosophical writings, a clear effort has been made to emphasize the 'Romanness' of things. Certain Roman values are therefore readily apparent such as the traditional respect the conservative Romans had for their elders. On a personal level, the energy used by Cicero to express a complex Greek idea in terms of the Roman experience was for him an act of intellectual 'imperialism' by which he and his fellow citizens could benefit. Whether Cicero at age 62 actually believed the sentiments he committed to paper can never be determined with certainty. That Cicero, who was experiencing terrible trouble in both his private and public life during those years, might have steadied himself with thoughts of Cato, would not be surprising. Cato the Elder had long been something of a hero to Cicero. Cato represented a man born into the middle class, like Cicero, who had risen through his own industry and his own genius to the apex of political success in Rome, the consulship. Although Cicero in no way attempted to present a verbatim imitation of Cato's speech or vocabulary, he 'set the stage' accurately. Cicero was thoroughly acquainted with works by and about Cato and his knowledge is revealed not only through this work, but through his many references to Cato in his other works.

The evergreen appeal of *On Old Age* is based upon its charming style and humanistic outlook. Its noble effort to dignify and find value in the hardships of old age and in the inevitability of death has comforted many readers experiencing their own senectitude. Notable figures like Dante, Petrarch, Erasmus, Chaucer, and Milton read, quoted, and/or recommended the book.

On Old Age was also among the first works of Greco-Roman literature to be printed after Fust and Schoeffer's famous edition of Cicero's *On Duties* and the *Paradoxes of the Stoics* (*De officiis et Paradoxa stoicorum*) at Mainz in 1465. *On Old Age* was soon printed separately about 1467 by Ulrich Zel in Cologne and again two years later in 1469 as a part of a group that included *On Duties*, the *Paradoxes of the Stoics*, *On Friendship*, and *The Dream of Scipio* (*Somnium Scipionis*) at Rome by Ulrich Han. This is all the more significant when one realizes that Virgil's *Aeneid* was not published until late 1469 or early 1479 in Rome. Translations of the book appeared earlier than the printed editions. In 1405 Laurent de Premierfait (d.1418), a priest from Troyes, translated it into French for an uncle of Charles the Wise. Drawn from this French version was the first translation into English which was printed in 1481 by William Caxton at Westminster. This edition, one that included a translation of *On Friendship* and a declamation on the nature of true nobility, foreshadowed the advent of Renaissance interest in the work. In 1517, a translation into Greek by Theodore Gaza (c.1400–95), a professor of Greek at Ferrara and Rome, was published posthumously in Italy. *On Old Age* also made bibliographical history in America as the first translation of any work by Cicero into 'American' English. This was done by the bibliophile James Logan (1674–1751) of Philadelphia and was printed on the presses of Benjamin Franklin in 1744.

With the eclipse in general of the classical curriculum this century, the readership of *On Old Age* has greatly diminished. However, as modern technology extends the human lifespan and the population of the elderly increases, this work, over 2,000 years old, seems more timely than ever. Perhaps it will find a new audience.

—Michele Valerie Ronnick

ON THE COMMONWEALTH (De republica)
Prose by Cicero, c.51 BC.

On the Commonwealth is a work in six books, one of Cicero's three political treatises, the others being *On the Laws* and *On Duties*. These works are closely connected in that they all deal with the complexities of contemporary Roman politics and the search for the ideal state and statesman. The titles *On the Commonwealth* and *On the Laws* are indicative of the influence of Plato, but Cicero's observations are based on his own considerable practical experience and are less concerned with abstract political theorizing than with perfecting the already advanced Roman constitution. *On the Commonwealth* accepts the prevailing order of the Roman Republican system, and assumes that the political crisis in Cicero's day is the fault of bad politicians rather than failing political structures.

The treatise takes the form of a debate on the nature of the 'ideal state' between the eminent statesman Scipio Aemilianus and his companions, set in the year 129 BC, the year of Scipio's death. The subject matter and the dialogue format both recall Plato's *Republic*. In Book I, the guests arrive amid a discussion of the sighting of a mysterious second sun. This leads into a conversation about the political situation in Rome after the murder of the reformer Tiberius Gracchus by Senatorial forces in 133 BC. Scipio opens the discussion of the ideal constitution by defining the state as a group of people brought together by community of interest and a shared notion of Law. The stress on legal institutions rather than ethical relationships marks a Roman rather than a Greek approach to the political question. Scipio goes on to list the three basic forms of government—monarchy, aristocracy, and democracy—and their degenerated forms—tyranny, plutocracy, and mob rule—and follows Polybius in presenting the 'mixed constitution' as the ideal state. This is exemplified by the Roman system, in which the Consuls constitute the monarchic element, the Senate the aristocratic element, and the Assemblies the democratic element. This is a typically conservative formulation, combined with a notion of absolute 'justice' in opposition to the will of the popular majority. Book II, indeed, after a historical survey of Rome and some discussion of the characteristics of the ideal statesman (the text is fragmentary), concludes with the statement that 'a state is made harmonious . . . by a fair and reasonable blending of the upper, middle and lower classes . . . and such concord can never be brought about without the assistance of justice'. From his other writings and speeches, it is clear that Cicero's 'concord' means cooperation between the landowning Senatorial class and the Equestrian order, who made their money from business activities, with both these groups in turn being supported by the 'good' citizens (those who own property). This alliance must then defend the state against extremist demagogues, who foment revolution among the discontented.

In Book III, one of the interlocutors puts forward the utilitarian view that government must be based on the interests of the ruler (i.e. injustice), but another counters with the traditional Platonic argument that justice is an absolute virtue, necessary in any government which is to be 'good'. Stoic influence is apparent in the idea of justice being innate in humankind and derived from the gods. Book IV is concerned with the class structure, the maintenance of moral standards and public order, and the education of the young. The ideal class structure again appears to be the Roman version, with Plato's Guardians finding their equivalent in the Senators and Equites. Both Spartan and Platonic communism are rejected: it is the state's duty to protect the rights of property owners, and a community of wives and children subverts the moral order.

Book V (again very fragmentary), after some generic remarks on the ancient Roman virtues, develops the idea of the 'Director' of the state. This is Cicero's ideal statesman, who is just and wise, who protects the constitution, and who aims at both the happiness of the citizens and the strength and prosperity of the state. Exactly what Cicero had in mind here has been the subject of much debate. Possibly it is a plea for someone like Augustus to intervene and establish a Principate; alternatively, it may be a variation of the Stoic 'wise man' who is supremely qualified to guide the state by personal leadership. He may well have had specific individuals like Scipio, Pompey, or even himself in mind. In Book VI, the treatise reaches an emotional climax, concluding with the famous 'Dream of Scipio' in which Scipio tells the others of a dream he had 20 years earlier. This is a vision, modelled somewhat on the Platonic myth of Er, of the eternal life after death. It is startlingly different in tone from what has preceded, with its strange, otherworldly explanation of the nine circles of the universe, the music of the spheres, and the divine rewards of the good statesman. The dream ends with a typically Roman expression of patriotic duty: the best activities are those which promote the well-being of the native land.

On the Commonwealth exemplifies the best aspects of the Ciceronian Latin prose style. The dialogue flows easily in the first five books, and the more ornate language of the 'Dream of Scipio' heightens the effect of the revelation of eternal life, which has been compared in emotional power to the visions of St John and Dante. Cicero also manages to adapt the Latin language to essentially Greek philosophical subjects: no easy task in itself, as Lucretius discovered. On the Commonwealth comes out of the Greek philosophical and political tradition and attempts to graft significant elements of it onto the Roman experience. This is sometimes highly successful; for example, the implications of the idea of universal law expressed in On the Commonwealth are far-reaching: if all citizens are subject to one law, they are all, in some sense, equal. Moreover, authority arises from the collective power of the populace, since the state and the laws ultimately belong to it. There are nevertheless certain gaps and tensions in the treatise: for instance, little attention is paid to the administration of Roman provinces, and the often tense relationship between the central government and the proconsuls with their large armies. Similarly, the material conditions of the poor and their exploitation by the rich are not considered as causes of social disorder. The stress on the afterlife at the end of the work trivializes the political difficulties of the here and now.

Ultimately, On the Commonwealth looks backward, rather than forward: it is a reaction to the inevitable political changes in the last decades of the Roman Republic, not a realistic prescription for dealing with them. Hence, perhaps, the use of the long-dead Scipio as the main speaker, and the concluding flight into the comforting vision of another, less turbulent, world.

—David H.J. Larmour

CLAUDEL, Paul (Louis Charles Marie). Born in Villeneuve-sur-Fère, France, 6 August 1868. Educated at schools in Bar-le-Duc, 1870–75, Nogent-sur-Seine, 1876–79, and Wassy-sur-Blaise, 1879–81; Lycée Louis-le-Grand, Paris, 1882–85; law school, and École des Sciences Politiques. Married Reine Sainte-Marie-Perrin in 1906; five children. In the French diplomatic service from 1890: commercial department, Paris, 1890–92, New York, 1893, Boston, 1894, China, 1894–1909, Prague, 1909–11, Frankfurt, 1911–14, Berlin, 1914, Rome and Brazil during World War I; ambassador to Japan, 1921–25, to the United States, 1926–33, and to Belgium, 1933–35; retired 1935; served in the Ministry of Propaganda during World War II. Member, Académie française, 1946. *Died 23 February 1955.*

PUBLICATIONS

Collections

Théâtre. 4 vols., 1911–12; revised edition, 2 vols., 1947–48.
Oeuvres complètes. 26 vols., 1950–67; supplement, 1990.
Théâtre, edited by Jacques Madaule and Jacques Petit. 2 vols., 1956; revised edition, 1965–67.
Oeuvres poétiques, edited by Stanislas Fumet. 1957.
Oeuvres en prose, edited by Jacques Petit and Charles Galperine. 1965.

Plays

Tête d'or. 1890; revised version (produced 1924), in *L'Arbre,* 1901; as *Tete-d'or,* translated by John S. Newberry, 1919.
La Ville. 1893; revised version (produced 1931), in *L'Arbre,* 1901; edited by Jacques Petit, 1967; as *The City,* translated by John S. Newberry, 1920.
L'Agamemnon, from the play by Aeschylus (produced 1963). 1896.
L'Échange (produced 1914). In *L'Arbre,* 1901; revised version (produced 1951), 1954.
La Jeune Fille Violaine, in *L'Arbre.* 1901; revised version, as *L'Annonce faite à Marie* (produced 1912), 1912; revised version (produced 1948), 1948; as *The Tidings Brought to Mary,* translated by Louise Morgan Sill, 1916; also translated by Wallace Fowlie, in *Two Dramas,* 1960.
Le Repos du septième jour (produced 1928). In *L'Arbre,* 1901.
Partage de midi (produced 1921). 1906; revised version (produced 1948), 1914, 1949; as *Break of Noon,* translated by Wallace Fowlie, in *Two Dramas,* 1960; also translated by Jonathon Griffin, 1990.
L'Otage (produced 1913). 1911; edited by Jean-Pierre Kempf, 1977; as *The Hostage,* translated by Pierre Chavannes, 1917; also translated by John Heard, in *Three Plays,* 1945.

Protée, in *Deux poèmes d'été*. 1914; revised version (produced 1929), in *Deux farces lyriques*, 1927.

La Nuit de Noël 1914. 1915.

La Pain dur (produced in German, 1926; in French, 1949). 1918; edited by Jacques Petit, 1975, as *Crusts*, translated by John Heard, in *Three Plays*, 1945.

L'Ours et la lune (produced 1948). 1919.

Le Père humilié (produced in German 1928). 1920; as *The Humiliation of the Father*, translated by John Heard, in *Three Plays*, 1945.

Les Choéphores, music by Darius Milhaud, from the play by Aeschylus (produced 1935). 1920.

Les Euménides, music by Darius Milhaud, from the play by Aeschylus (produced 1949). 1920.

L'Homme et son désir, music by Darius Milhaud (ballet; produced 1921). In *Le Livre de Christophe Colomb*, 1929.

La Femme et son ombre (produced 1923). In *Le Livre de Christophe Colomb*, 1929.

Sous le rempart d'Athènes, music by Germaine Taillefer (produced 1929). 1928.

Le Soulier de satin. 1928–29; revised version (produced 1943), 1944; as *The Satin Slipper*, translated by John O'Connor, 1931.

Le Livre de Christophe Colomb, music by Darius Milhaud (produced 1930). 1929; as *The Book of Christopher Columbus*, translated anonymously, 1930.

Jeanne d'Arc au bûcher, music by Arthur Honegger (produced 1939). 1939.

La Sagesse; ou, La Parabole du Festin, music by Darius Milhaud (broadcast, 1945; produced 1949). 1939.

L'Histoire de Tobie et de Sara (produced 1947). 1947; as *Tobias and Sara*, translated by Adele Fiske, in *Port-Royal and Other Plays*, edited by Richard Hayes, 1962.

L'Endormie. 1947.

Three Plays, translated by John Heard. 1945.

Two Dramas, translated by Wallace Fowlie. 1960.

Radio Play: *La Sagesse; ou, La Parabole du Festin*, 1945.

Verse

Vers d'exile. 1895.

Connaissance du temps. 1904.

Cinq grandes odes suivies d'un processional pour saluer le siècle nouveau. 1910; as *Five Great Odes*, translated by Edward Lucie Smith, 1967.

Cette heure qui est entre le printemps et l'été. 1913; as *La Cantate à trois voix*, 1931.

Corona benignitatis anni dei. 1915; as *Coronal*, translated by Sister Mary David, 1943.

Trois poèmes de guerre. 1915; as *Three Poems of the War*, translated by Edward J. O'Brien, 1919.

Autres poèmes durant la guerre. 1916.

Poèmes et paroles durant la guerre. 1916.

La Messe là-bas. 1919.

Poèmes de guerre. 1922.

Feuilles de saints. 1925.

Écoute, ma fille. 1934.

La Légende de Prakriti. 1934.

Poèmes et paroles durant la guerre de trente ans. 1945.

Visages radieux. 1946.

Paul Claudel répond les psaumes. 1948; as *Psaumes: Traductions 1918–1959*, edited by Renée Nantet and Jacques Petit, 1966.

Sainte Agnès et poèmes inédits. 1963.

A Hundred Movements for a Fan (haiku), translated by Andrew Harvey and Iain Watson. 1992

Other

Connaissance de l'est. 1900; enlarged edition, 1907; edited by Gilbert Gadoffre, 1973; as *The East I Know*, translated by Teresa Frances and William Rose Benét, 1914.

Art poétique. 1907; as *Poetic Art*, translated by Renée Spodheim, 1948.

Correspondance 1907–1914, with Jacques Rivière. 1926; as *Letters to a Doubter*, translated by Henry Longan Stuart, 1929.

Positions et propositions. 2 vols., 1928–34; vol. 1 as *Ways and Crossways*, translated by John O'Connor, 1933.

L'Oiseau noir dans le soleil levant. 1929.

Introduction à la peinture hollandaise. 1935.

Conversations dans le Loir-et-Cher. 1935.

Toi, qui es-tu? Tu quis es? 1936.

Figures et paraboles. 1936; edited by Andrée Hirschi, 1974.

Vitraux des cathédrales de France. 1937.

L'Aventure de Sophie. 1937.

Un poète regarde la croix. 1938; as *A Poet Before the Cross*, translated by Wallace Fowlie, 1958.

L'Épée et le miroir. 1939.

Contacts et circonstances. 1940.

La Rose et le rosaire. 1946.

L'Oeil écoute (essays). 1946; as *The Eye Listens*, translated by Elsie Pell, 1950.

Chine, photographs by Hélène Hoppenot. 1946.

Présence et prophétie. 1947.

Lord, Teach Us to Pray, translated by Ruth Bethell. 1947.

Sous le signe du dragon. 1948.

Paul Claudel interroge le Cantique des Cantiques. 1948.

Accompagnements. 1949.

Correspondance 1899–1926, with André Gide, edited by Robert Mallet. 1949; as *Correspondence*, translated by John Russell, 1952.

Emmaüs. 1950.

L'Évangile d'Isaïe. 1951.

Correspondance 1904–1938, with André Saurès. 1951.

Paul Claudel interroge l'Apocalypse. 1952.

Mémoires improvisés, edited by Jean Amrouche. 1954.

J'aime la Bible. 1955; as *The Essence of the Bible*, translated by Wade Baskin, 1957.

Correspondance 1918–1953, with Darius Milhaud, edited by Jacques Petit. 1961.

I Believe in God: A Commentary on the Apostles Creed, edited by Agnes du Sarment, translated by Helen Weaver. 1963.

Au milieu des vitraux de l'Apocalypse, edited by Pierre Claudel and Jacques Petit. 1966.

Mes idées sur le théâtre, edited by Jacques Petit and Jean-Pierre Kempf. 1966; as *Claudel on the Theatre*, translated by Christine Trollope, 1972.

Journal, edited by Jacques Petit and François Varillon. 2 vols., 1968–69.

Correspondance 1908–1914, with Louis Massignon, edited by Michel Malicet. 1973.

Correspondance, with Jean-Louis Barrault, edited by Michel Lioure. 1974.

Chroniques du Journal de Clichy, with François Mauriac (includes Claudel–Fontaine correspondence), edited by François Norlot and Jean Touzot. 1978.

La Vague et le rocher: Paul Claudel, François Mauriac correspondance 1911–1954, edited by Michel Malicet and Marie-Chantal Praicheux, 1989.

Lettre à son fils Henri et sa famille, edited by Marianne and Michel Malicet. 1990.

Henri Pourrat–Paul Claudel: Correspondance, edited by Michel Lioure. 1990.

Translator, *Poèmes*, by Coventry Patmore. 1912.

*

Bibliography: *Bibliographie des oeuvres de Claudel* by Jacques Petit, 1973; *Claudel and the English-Speaking World: A Critical Bibliography*, 1973.

Critical Studies: *The Double Image: Mutations of Christian Mythology in the Work of Four French Catholic Writers* by Rayner Heppenstall, 1947; *The Theme of Beatrice in the Plays of Claudel* by Ernest Beaumont, 1954; *The Poetic Drama of Claudel* by Joseph Chiari, 1954; *Paul Claudel* by Wallace Fowlie, 1957; *Paul Claudel: The Man and the Mystic* by Louis Chaigne, 1961; *Claudel and Aeschylus* by William H. Matheson, 1965; *The Inner Stage: An Essay on the Conflict of Vocations in the Early Works of Claudel* by Richard Berchan, 1966; *Claudel et l'univers chinois* by Gilbert Gadoffre, 1968; *Claudel: A Reappraisal* by Richard M. Griffiths, 1968; *Paul Claudel* by Harold A. Waters, 1970; *Claudel and Saint-John Perse* by Ruth N. Horry, 1971; *Claudel's Immortal Heroes: A Choice of Deaths* by Harold Watson, 1971; *The Prince and the Genie: A Study of Rimbaud's Influence on Claudel* by John A. MacCombie, 1972; *Paul Claudel's Le Soulier de satin: A Stylistic, Structuralist, and Psychoanalytic Interpretation* by Joan S. Freilich, 1973; *Two Against Time: A Study of the Very Present Worlds of Claudel and Charles Péguy* by Joy Nachod Humes, 1978; *In/stability: The Shape and Space of Claudel's Art* by Lynne L. Gelber, 1980; *Paul Claudel* by Bettina L. Knapp, 1982; *Paul Claudel: Biographie* by Marie-Josèphe Guers, 1987; *Claudel: Beauty and Grace* by Angelo Caranfa, 1989.

*   *   *

Despite the high praise of Charles Du Bos, who called him the greatest genius of the west, and despite the judgment of Jacques Madaule, who compared him to Dante, Paul Claudel's place in literature and in Catholic thought is still vigorously disputed. At the time of his death, in his mid-eighties, he appeared as belligerent as ever, having maintained to the end not only his full powers as a writer but also his violent temper and his animosities. His detractors are still legion and his admirers come from many varying quarters differing widely in their religious, political, and aesthetic beliefs.

During his last year at the Lycée Louis-le-Grand, he read Baudelaire and Verlaine, but the first major revelation to Claudel of both a literary and spiritual order was to be Rimbaud. He has described in a passage justly celebrated and justly disputed the profound effect which the reading of the *Illuminations* had on him. He first came upon some of the prose poems in the July issue of *La Vogue* of 1886. To him it meant release from what he called the hideous world of Taine, Renan, and other Molochs of the 19th century. 'J'avais la révélation du surnaturel', he wrote to Jacques Rivière.

After a spiritual experience at Christmas 1886, in Notre-Dame, Claudel began to study the Bible, the history of the Church and its liturgy, and discovered that what he had once valued as poetry was indissolubly associated with religion. He

attended Mallarmé's Tuesday evening gatherings and learned from the master of symbolism to look at the universe as if it were a text to be deciphered. To Rimbaud's doctrine on the power of poetic language and to Mallarmé's doctrine on the symbolism of the universe Claudel added the gigantic synthesis of Aquinas and the religious interpretation of metaphorical language.

Taken as a whole, Claudel's work is praise to God and praise to His creation. It does not reflect the exaltation of a mystic but is rather the expression of the natural joy of a man who has found an order in the universe and believes in a certain relationship between this world and the next. In whatever he wrote—poems, letters, plays, essays, Biblical exegesis—he steadfastly explored the central drama of the human soul engaged in its adventure with eternity. His dramas are not a combination of the comic and the tragic; they are works of one piece and one texture—simultaneously dramatic speech and poetry.

The French literary mind has been predominantly analytical in each century. Claudel's mind was more inclined toward the creation of a synthesis. His fundamental preoccupations are more metaphysical than is usual in French writers who tend to psychological and moralistic preoccupations. Moreover, the seeming bluntness of his style, its vehemence, its violence, separates his work from the central tradition of the French literary style. Claudel believed that at our birth we enter into a secret pact with all beings and all objects. The poet's mission is that of pointing out our relationship with all the realities of the world.

—Wallace Fowlie

THE SATIN SLIPPER (Le Soulier de satin)
Play by Paul Claudel, 1928–29.

Claudel started writing *The Satin Slipper* just after World War I and struggled with it during five of his busiest years at the French Foreign Office. Composition was delayed when part of the manuscript disappeared in the terrible September 1923 earthquake in Japan, but the play was eventually completed there in 1924.

The play has not been performed often, but has consistently challenged France's leading stage directors. The names of Jean-Louis Barrault and Antoine Vitez remain linked to *The Satin Slipper*. The former staged a pioneering shorter version, while credit goes to the latter for a memorable production of the whole text at the Avignon drama festival. A filmed version lasting nearly seven hours was shot in 1985 by the Portuguese director Manoel de Oliveira. Both in length and in scope the play indeed occupies a special place in French literature.

The Satin Slipper can arguably be called the most successful historical play in the French language. With the debatable exception of Victor Hugo, few French playwrights have excelled at this genre. Unlike Shakespeare and Strindberg, Claudel does not look for inspiration in his homeland's history. The play is subtitled 'Action espagnole en quatre journées' and most, but not all, historical events or characters in the play relate to Spanish history. In a poem written as an introduction to the English translation, Claudel pays homage to Lope de Vega and the author of *Henry VI*. In the best Shakespearean tradition, Claudel distorts facts to suit his creative and ideological purposes. Columbus, Luther, the Invincible Armada are some of the landmarks he welds together in the four symbolic days of his play. Beyond the history of a nation, Claudel aims at illustrating the history of the Catholic faith and how it was spread to the confines of the earth. What Claudel never attempts is to draw detailed portraits of well-known historical figures. For instance he insists that the King of Spain at the end of the play should look like the King of Spades. Claudel has no desire to plumb the psychological motives behind the resolutions taken by such and such a king. Instead he undertakes to show Grace Abounding to the actors of history. The word 'actor' is essential here. Claudel is very modern in that he presents his characters as first and foremost actors. The most obvious example is the character called 'The Actress' who plays a major part in the last section of the play.

'L'Irrépressible' ('The Irrepressible One') is another character whose function is to highlight the theatricality of the play. This character embodies the most fiery part of the author's imagination, the part which is central to the act of creation but is nevertheless curbed by the author's reason. Through this character Claudel comments on his own methods and temptations while writing. This character represents unchecked spontaneity, a quality Claudel may have felt he was losing as he progressed slowly towards completion of his play.

Other episodic characters (different ones in each section) are used to bring in more straightforward comic relief. These characters belong squarely to the level of farce. They are one-dimensional characters with no inner life and delightfully strange names. However, their actions often are elaborate parodies of what takes place in the most serious scenes. For instance the tug-of-war between the Bidince Team and the Hinnulus Team (Fourth Day, scene V) echoes mockingly the scene between Dona Prouhèze and her Guardian Angel (Third Day, scene VII). In the latter scene the Angel describes himself as a fisherman patiently trying to catch the struggling soul of Prouhèze. In the other scene the two mock-professors are also fishing. Through such characters Claudel introduces a grotesque kind of humour into the play. This is another aspect of the play's broad scope: Claudel mixes genres and tones in a challenging effort to cover the whole range of emotions from the ludicrous to the lyrical.

In many lucid texts—most notably in the volume *Ways and Crossways* (*Positions et Propositions*)—Claudel stressed the link he perceived between his strong religious convictions and his creative work. For him, Christianity offers the only challenge worthy of man. Contradiction, opposition, struggle are some of the words the poet and playwright repeatedly used to describe his faith. Religion gives man the opportunity to struggle between his craving for immediate individual happiness and higher desires. It forces man to make choices and as a result it makes drama possible, indeed, inevitable. Therefore Catholic theology is not exterior to Claudel the writer. On the contrary, the laws and mysteries of his religion furnished him with a paradigm of dramatic conflict that gives *The Satin Slipper* both its main plot line and its main theme. Claudel is not interested in the social dimension of the obstacle that separates Rodrigue from Prouhèze, but exclusively in its deeper religious significance.

—Pascale Voilley

CLAUDIAN. Born Claudius Claudianus in Alexandria, Egypt, c.AD 370. Married in c.AD 404. Went to Rome before 395, then lived in Milan for five years, from c.AD 395; became a successful court poet under the western emperor Honorius. He was a favourite of and spokesman for General Stilicho, defender of the Roman empire against the Goths and the Vandals. *Died in Rome c.AD 404.*

PUBLICATIONS

Collections

[Works], edited by Ludwig Jeep. 2 vols., 1876–79; also edited by Theodor Birt, in *Monumenta Germaniae historica*, vol. 10, 1892, Julius Koch, 1893, and J.B. Hall, 1985; edited and translated (prose) by Maurice Platnauer [Loeb Edition], 2 vols., 1922; translated by A. Hawkins, 2 vols., 1817.

Works

De raptu Proserpine, edited by Ludwig Jeep. 1874; also edited by J.B. Hall, 1969; edited and translated by Claire Gruzelier (with commentary), 1993; as *The Rape of Proserpine*, translated by Leonard Digges, 1628, reprinted 1959; also translated by Jabez Hughes, 1714; Jacob G. Strutt, 1814; Henry E.J. Howard, 1854; Martin Pope, 1934.
Eidyllia, as *The Phoenix of Claudian*, translated by Arthur Smith(?). 1714.
Epigrammata, as *De Sene Veronensi*, translated by Andrew Symon. 1708.
Epithalamium for the Marriage of Honorius, translated by H. Isbell, in *The Last Poets of Imperial Rome*. 1971.
In Eutropium, edited by P. Fargues. 1933.
In Rufinum, edited by Harry L. Levy. 1935; translated as *Rufinus; or, the Favourite*, 1712; as *Elegant History of Rufinus*, translated by Jabez Hughes, in *Miscellanies in Verse and Prose*, 1737; commentary by Harry L. Levy, 1971.
Panegyric on the Third Consulate of Honorius, translated by William Warburton. 1724.
Panegyric on the Fourth Consulate of Honorius, edited and translated by William Barr. 1981.

*

Critical Studies: *Claudian as an Historical Authority* by James Crees, 1906; *The Influence of Ovid on Claudian* by Annette Hawkins Eaton, 1943; *Secular Latin Poetry* by F.J.E. Raby, 1957; *The Use of Images by Claudius Claudianus* by Peder G. Christiansen, 1969; *Claudian, Poet of Declining Empire and Morals* by Oswald A.W. Dilke, 1969; *Claudian: Poetry and Propaganda at the Court of Honorius* by Alan D.E. Cameron, 1970; *Prolegomena to Claudian* by J.B. Hall, 1986; *A Concordance to Claudianus* edited by Peder G. Christiansen, 1988.

* * *

Claudian most deserves fame for resuscitating the secular traditions of Latin hexameter poetry. Roman historical and mythological epic, having thrived during the era of Virgil and Ovid, lapsed after that of Silius Italicus and Valerius Flaccus at the close of the 1st century AD. Claudian was not the first poet of the 4th century to revive these forms, but he was the most popular and influential.

Claudian was not born into Latin traditions, but in the Greek-speaking Egyptian metropolis of Alexandria. Like others of the same background, he became an itinerant hired poet (see Alan Cameron, 'Wandering Poets: a Literary Movement in Byzantine Egypt' in *Historia*, 14, 1965); but Claudian, uniquely, travelled West. He first published in Rome on the New Year of 395, panegyrizing two young nobles of the ancient capital who had been named consuls for that year. To have a panegyric in verse revolutionized western fashion. Claudian also ingeniously turned the traditional structure to focus neither on the consuls themselves nor on the emperor who appointed them, but on their famous and recently deceased father Probus. He not only earned his commission for the immediate occasion, but also bid for patronage among Roman aristocrats who honoured Probus' memory.

The imperial court at Milan took up the bait. Claudian next celebrated the third consulate of the Western emperor Honorius in 396. Not only did he praise Honorius and forecast favourably for the year, as the occasion required, but he also introduced a hero behind the throne. Between the resplendent scene of Honorius' triumphal arrival at the Western court and the concluding prayers for world-wide triumphs of the Roman empire under Honorius' joint rule with his brother Arcadius, he inserted a scene in which Honorius' and Arcadius' father Theodosius entrusts the care of both sons to his son-in-law, the general Stilicho. This historically dubious claim, superfluous to the panegyric structure, launched a theme which Claudian continued to pursue in political poems for the next eight years: exaltation of Stilicho as the true preserver of Roman values and glory. Alan Cameron has argued that Claudian did not simply admire Stilicho but was actually commissioned to portray him flatteringly before Western aristocrats (*Claudian: Poetry and Propaganda at the Court of Honorius*). Cameron's interpretation has been accepted widely if not universally (see the reviews of Diegmar Dopp, *Anzeiger für die Altertumswissenschaft*, 28, 1975, and Christian Gnilka, *Gnomon*, 49, 1977); but certainly Stilicho did receive favourable press from Claudian, and manuscript evidence suggests that Stilicho sponsored collection and republication of Claudian's poems after he died (see J.B. Hall, *Prolegomena to Claudian*). Claudian's long tenure as court poet also guaranteed his works illustrious audiences.

The political relevance of many of Claudian's poems and his own social prominence, however, only made his work conspicuous. His artistry secured them long-lived popularity, just as it had secured his prominence. His major poems divide between three books of an unfinished mythological epic, *De raptu Proserpine* (*The Rape of Proserpine*), and historical or political poems; they include panegyrics of Honorius and other Western consuls including Stilicho; invectives against ministers of Arcadius who were hostile to Stilicho; poems celebrating Honorius' marriage to Stilicho's daughter, and epics that display Stilicho's triumphant generalship. All are dominated structurally by visual tableaux, reported speeches, and expostulations in the poet's own voice; this emphasis exceeds the norms of classical epic but resembles contemporary Greek epic and encomiastic poetry.

Claudian stirred emotions with full rhetorical verve. He drew out his central themes, finding ever newer points of view. His invective against the eunuch Eutropius, for example, calls attention to his emasculation in more than 60 separate passages. They range from explicit references, to Eutropius in the female roles of an abandoned heroine (burlesqued), a decaying bawd, and a bibulous old nursemaid. Modern critics sometimes deplore the endlessness of Claudian's fluency, but contemporary audiences clearly delighted in the panoplies of ideas and images that it spread. Michael Roberts has illuminated a late antique aesthetic preference for brilliance in poetic descriptions and construction as well as in visual arts (*The Jewelled Style: Poetry and Poetics in Late Antiquity*, 1989). The triumphal processions of Honorius in the panegyrics for his third, fourth, and sixth consulates provide lush examples with gleaming robes, glittering armour, and dragon-banners that rustle and hiss in the wind like real snakes.

The majority of Claudian's minor poems, elegant and fashionable epigrams, describe marvels of both nature and art. In 'The Gothic War', a flash of light from Stilicho's white hair first tells the anxious Romans that they will soon be rescued, and shows how excitingly such details can figure in epic narrative. Curiously, this latter item almost alone in Claudian's poetry reveals what anyone looked like. Eutropius' ghastly decrepitude, insect-ridden scalp and flapping wrinkles, which contrasted with his gorgeous consular robes, demonstrate Claudian's use of description not for its own sake, but for its emotional impact. His dense allusions to earlier Roman poets display a poetic consciousness of the past that would also have stirred the emotions of listeners equally imbued with poetical traditions. They reinforce Claudian's explicit emphasis on Roman themes in his political poems and operate no less in the mythological *The Rape of Proserpine* (Gualandri, 1969, and Moroni, 1982).

Claudian's poems perfectly fulfilled the sensibilities of his age. They consequently reinforced them and set a trend for subsequent Latin epic. He can be particularly credited with reviving the epic form in Latin; in his political poems he fused it so successfully with encomium as to have invented a new genre, which later generations of poets perpetuated (Heinz Hofmann, 'Überlegungen zu einer Theorie der nichtchristlichen Epik der lateinischen Spätantike', *Philologus*, 132, 1988). His political poems are thus seminal as well as vivid aesthetic documents, and, incidentally, major historical sources.

—Jacqueline Long

THE RAPE OF PROSERPINE (De raptu Proserpine)
Poem by Claudian, c.400 AD.

The Rape of Proserpine is the longest surviving version of the myth of the abduction of Ceres' daughter Proserpine by Pluto, the lord of the Underworld. Composed by Claudian at the end of the 4th century, it draws heavily upon the Latin poetic tradition, especially the epics of Virgil, Lucan, and Statius. There are also reminiscences of the account of Persephone in Book V of Ovid's *Metamorphoses*. Claudian may have been influenced by Alexandrian and Orphic treatments of the myth too: there is no doubt that it was a popular theme among the poets for many centuries. It deals with the primordial conflict between the matriarchal earth-goddess and the patriarchal sky-god who supplanted her. The poem is written in hexameters, and the versification is basically classical, but with much less use of elision, which makes for a consistently smooth rhythm.

The Preface of *The Rape of Proserpine* compares the poet

follows is the culmination of Claudian's poetic journey. Book I begins with standard introductory devices and then moves to the Underworld, where Pluto is preparing to release the Titans and make war on Jupiter, because he has no wife. Then Fates intervene and Pluto is mollified by the promise of Proserpine, whom Jupiter had apparently always intended him to have. Venus is ordered to prepare the girl, so that Pluto will desire her. As the book ends, Pluto's horses are straining at the bit, ready to break out of Hades. Book II is preceded by another Preface in which Claudian's return to poetic composition at the behest of Florentinus is likened to Orpheus' singing of the deeds of Hercules after he had rescued his native land Thrace from Diomedes. The action resumes with a description of Proserpine wandering in the meadows of Sicily, attended by goddesses and nymphs. Only Venus knows what awaits Ceres' daughter on this particular morning. The idyllic scene is shattered by the terrifying arrival of Pluto in his chariot and Proserpine is carried off. Diana, goddess of virginity, and Pallas Athene try to stop the abduction, but are deterred by Jupiter. Proserpine calls to her mother in heart-rending tones so that even Pluto is moved: he tries to comfort her by listing all the powers she will gain as his wife. When they arrive in Hades, there is universal celebration, and the punishments of the wicked souls are temporarily suspended. Book III opens with a council of the gods, at which Jupiter notes that Nature has criticized his harsh treatment of humans. He declares that he has taken pity on this suffering race and that Ceres will provide them with the blessings of the grain when she has found her daughter. He stipulates, however, that nobody is to assist her in her search. Ceres, meanwhile, has a distressing dream about Proserpine and, upon returning to Sicily, attempts vainly to get information from the nurse Electra and from Venus. In the end, she resolves to search the entire world for her daughter. She makes two torches from trees in a grove sacred to Jupiter, lights them in Etna, and begins her tearful search.

The plot is a simple and well-worn one, embellished by two devices typical of later epic poetry: speeches and lengthy descriptions. In Book I, for example, Pluto makes a lengthy and well-structured speech to Mercury listing his grievances, and there is a substantial digression on the geography of Sicily and the wonders of Mount Etna. There is also a detailed account of the tapestry which Proserpine is stitching: it depicts the creation of the world out of chaos, the five zones of the earth, and the homes of Jupiter and Pluto. The descriptive passages have received much praise, not so much for their originality as for their beauty and economy of expression. The following lines are part of the digression on Etna:

> Now it vomits clouds of its own smoke and it darkens the day
> loaded with pitch-black vapour, now it threatens the stars
> with its huge boulders, and feeds the fires with its own destruction.
> But although it boils and bubbles over with such heat,
> it knows how to keep faith with both the snow and the ash:
> the ice hardens securely amid such steam,
> protected by the hidden frost, and the harmless flames
> lick the nearby snows with undamaging smoke.

This passage also illustrates the scope for symbolic or allegorical interpretations of *The Rape of Proserpine*. The poem is much concerned with the struggle of polarities within the universe and the possibility of their peaceful co-existence. Just as the snows and the flames 'keep faith' with each other

on Etna, so the whole universe is created from chaos by the harmonization of opposites. At the beginning of the poem, Pluto threatens to plunge the world into disorder by attacking Jupiter. This is averted by the Fates, but only at the cost of setting up a conflict between Ceres and Pluto. None the less, it is clear that eventually an accommodation will be reached between the two: Proserpine will spend half the year with her husband, and half the year with her mother. When she has her daughter with her, Ceres will be happy and will provide crops for men.

The poem ends *in medias res*, perhaps because Claudian died before completing it. If Claudian intended to follow the mythological tradition, the agreement of Ceres and Pluto to share Proserpine would have been presented as a vindication of the rule of Jupiter: his just counsels preserve the universe from chaotic violence. As the text now stands, however, the hope of such a resolution is a distant one, only to be achieved after much suffering and effort on the part of Ceres. She, in fact, receives as much attention from the poet as Jupiter, in a poem which lacks a central figure. The torches she carries symbolize the revelation she brings to humans through knowledge of the growth of the grain. The strong mother-daughter bond between Ceres and Proserpine is a statement of female solidarity in the face of patriarchal control and sexual violence. Thus the main elements of the story—Pluto's 'need' for a wife, Jupiter's decision to 'give' him Proserpine, and Venus' callous betrayal of the girl—are seen to raise highly problematic issues.

—David H.J. Larmour

COCTEAU, Jean (Maurice Eugène Clément). Born in Maisons-Laffitte, France, 5 July 1889. Educated at the Lycée Condorcet, Paris, and privately. Entered Parisian literary and theatrical circles, giving readings and attending functions; co-founder, *Shéhérazade* magazine, 1909; collaborated with Diaghilev's Ballets Russes as librettist, designer and painter, from c.1911; joined the Red Cross, 1914; co-editor, *le Mot*, 1914–15; contributor, *Paris-Midi*, 1919; travelled around the world, under commission to write articles for *Paris-Soir*, 1936–37; travelled to the United States, 1949. President, Jazz Academy; Honorary President, Cannes Film Festival. Recipient: Louions-Delluc prize, 1946; Avant-garde Film Grand prize, 1950. D.Litt.: Oxford University, 1956. Member, Académie française, 1955; Royal Academy of Belgium; Honorary member, American Academy and German Academy. Commander, Légion d'honneur, 1961. *Died 11 October 1963.*

PUBLICATIONS

Plays

Les Mariés de la Tour Eiffel (produced 1921). 1924; as *The Eiffel Tower Wedding Party*, translated by Dudley Fitts, in *The Infernal Machine and Other Plays*, 1963; as *The Wedding on the Eiffel Tower*, translated by Michael Benedikt, in *Modern French Plays*, edited by Benedikt and

Antigone (produced 1922; revised version, music by Arthur Honegger, produced 1927). 1927; as *Antigone*, translated by Carl Wildman, in *Five Plays*, 1961.
Roméo et Juliette, from the play by Shakespeare (produced 1924). 1926.
Orphée (produced 1926). 1927; as *Orpheus*, translated by Carl Wildman, 1933; also translated by John Savacool, in *The Infernal Machine and Other Plays*, 1963; Carol Martin-Sperry, 1972.
Le Pauvre Matelot, music by Darius Milhaud (produced 1927). 1927.
Oedipus Rex, music by Stravinsky (produced 1927). 1949.
Oedipe-Roi (produced 1937). 1928.
La Voix humaine (produced 1930). 1930; as *The Human Voice*, translated by Carl Wildman, 1951.
La Machine infernale (produced 1934). 1934; as *The Infernal Machine*, translated by Carl Wildman, 1936, revised version, in *International Modern Plays*, edited by Anthony Bent, 1950; also translated by Albert Bermel, in *The Infernal Machine and Other Plays*, 1963.
Les Chevaliers de la table ronde (produced 1937). 1937; as *The Knights of the Round Table*, translated by W.H. Auden, in *The Infernal Machine and Other Plays*, 1963.
Les Parents terribles (produced 1938). 1938; edited by R.K. Totton, 1972; as *Intimate Relations*, translated by Charles Franck, in *Five Plays*, 1962; as *Les Parents terribles*, translated by Jeremy Sans, 1994.
Les Monstres sacrés (produced 1940). 1940; as *The Holy Terrors*, translated by E.O. Marsh, in *Five Plays*, 1962.
La Machine à écrire (produced 1941). 1941; as *The Typewriter*, translated by Ronald Duncan, 1947.
Renaud et Armide (produced 1943). 1943.
L'Aigle à deux têtes (produced 1946). 1946; as *The Eagle Has Two Heads*, translated by Ronald Duncan, 1948; as *The Eagle with Two Heads*, translated by Carl Wildman, 1961.
Ruy Blas (screenplay). 1947.
Le Sang d'un poète (screenplay). 1948; as *The Blood of a Poet*, translated by Lily Pons, 1949; also translated by Carol Martin-Sperry, in *Two Screenplays*, 1968.
Un tramway nommé désir, from the play by Tennessee Williams (produced 1949). 1949.
Théâtre de poche (includes scenarios, sketches, and radio works). 1949.
Orphée (screenplay). 1951; as *Orpheé*, in *Three Screenplays*, 1972.
Bacchus (produced 1951). 1952; as *Bacchus*, translated by Mary Hoeck, in *The Infernal Machine and Other Plays*, 1963.
La Belle et la bête (screenplay). 1958; as *La Belle et la bête*, translated by Carol Martin-Sperry, in *Three Screenplays*, 1972.
Cher menteur, from the play by Jerome Kilty (produced 1960). 1960.
Le Testament d'Orphée (screenplay). 1961; as *The Testament of Orpheus*, translated by Carol Martin-Sperry, in *Two Screenplays*, 1968.
L'Impromptu du Palais-Royal (produced 1962). 1962.
L'Éternel Retour (screenplay), as *L'éternel retour*, translated by Carol Martin Sperry, in *Three Screenplays*. 1972.

Screenplays: *Le Sang d'un poète*, 1930; *La Comédie du bonheur*, 1940; *Le Baron fantôme*, with Serge de Poligny, 1943; *L'Éternel Retour*, 1943; *Les Dames du Bois du Boulogne*, with Robert Bresson, 1945; *La Belle et la bête*, 1946; *Ruy Blas*, 1947; *L'Aigle à deux têtes*, 1948; *Les Parents terribles*, 1948; *Noces de sable*, 1949; *Les Enfants terribles*, 1950;

Orphée, 1950; *La Villa Santo-Sospiro*, 1952; *La Corona Negra*, 1952; *Le Testament d'Orphée*, 1960; *La Princesse de Clèves*, 1961; *Thomas l'imposteur*, 1965.

Ballet scenarios: *Le Dieu bleu*, 1912; *Parade*, 1917; *Le Boeuf sur le toit*, 1920; *Le Train bleu*, 1924; *Le Jeune Homme et la mort*, 1946; *La Dame à la licorne*, 1953; *Le Poète et sa muse*, 1959.

Fiction

Le Potomak. 1919; revised edition, 1934.
Le Grand Écart. 1923; as *The Grand Écart*, translated by Lewis Galantière, 1925; as *The Miscreant*, translated by Dorothy Williams, 1958.
Thomas l'imposteur. 1923; as *Thomas the Imposter*, translated by Lewis Galantière, 1925; as *The Imposter*, translated by Dorothy Williams, 1957.
Le Livre blanc. 1928; as *The White Paper*, 1957; as *The White Book*, translated by Margaret Crosland, 1989.
Les Enfants terribles. 1929; as *Enfants Terribles*, translated by Samuel Putnam, 1930; as *Children of the Game*, translated by Rosamond Lehmann, 1955; as *The Holy Terrors*, translated by Lehmann, 1957.
Le Fantôme de Marseille. 1936.
Le Fin du Potomak. 1940.
Deux travestis. 1947.

Verse

La Lampe d'Aladin. 1909.
Le Prince frivole. 1910.
La Danse de Sophocle. 1912.
Le Cap de Bonne-espérance. 1919.
Ode à Picasso. 1919.
Discours du grand sommeil. 1920.
Escales, with André Lhote. 1920.
Poésies 1917–20. 1920.
Vocabulaire. 1922.
Plain-chant. 1923.
La Rose de François. 1923.
Poésie 1916–23. 1924.
Cri écrit. 1925.
Prière mutilée. 1925.
L'Ange Heurtebise. 1926.
Opéra: Oeuvres poétiques 1925–27. 1927.
Morceaux choisis. 1932.
Mythologie. 1934.
Allégories. 1941.
Les Poèmes allemands. 1944.
Léone. 1945; translated as *Leoun*, 1960.
La Crucifixion. 1946.
Poèmes. 1948.
Le Chiffre. 1952.
Appogiatures. 1953.
Dentelle d'éternité. 1953.
Clair-obscur. 1954.
Poèmes 1916–1955. 1956.
Gondole des morts. 1959.
Cérémonial espagnol du phénix; La Partie d'échecs. 1961.
Le Requiem. 1961.
Faire-part. 1969.
Tempest of Stars: Selected Poems (bilingual edition), translated by Jeremy Reed. 1992.

Other

Le Coq et l'arlequin: Notes autour de la musique. 1918; as *Cock and Harlequin*, translated by Rollo H. Myers, 1921.
Dans le ciel de la patrie. 1918.
Carte blanche. 1920.
La Noce massacrée. 1921.
Le Secret professionnel. 1922; *Professional Secrets: An Autobiography*, edited by Robert Phelps, translated by Richard Howard, 1970.
Dessins. 1923.
Picasso. 1923.
Ferat. 1924.
Le Mystère de l'oiseleur. 1925.
Lettre à Jacques Maritain. 1926.
Le Rappel à l'ordre (essays). 1926; as *A Call to Order*, translated by Rollo H. Myers, 1926.
Maison de santé: dessins. 1926.
Le Mystère laïc. 1928.
Une entrevue sur la critique avec Maurice Rouzaud. 1929.
25 Dessins d'un dormeur. 1929.
Essai de critique indirecte. 1932; as *An Essay in Indirect Criticism*, translated by Olga Rudge, 1936.
Opium. 1932; as *Opium: Dairy of an Addict*, translated by Ernest Boyd, 1932; also translated by Margaret Crosland and Sinclair Rood, 1957.
Portraits-souvenir 1900–1914. 1935; as *Paris Album 1900–1914*, translated by Margaret Crosland, 1956; as *Souvenir Portraits: Paris in the Belle Epoch*, translated by Jesse Browner, 1991.
60 Dessins pour 'Les Enfants terribles'. 1935.
Mon Premier Voyage: Tour du monde en 80 jours. 1936; as *Round the World Again in Eighty Days*, translated by Stuart Gilbert, 1937; as *My Journey Round the World*, translated by Walter J. Strachan, 1958.
Énigme. 1939.
Dessins en marge du texte des 'Chevaliers de la table ronde'. 1941.
Le Greco. 1943.
Serge Lifar à l'opéra. 1944.
Portrait de Mounet-Sully. 1945.
La Belle et la bête: Journal d'un film. 1946; as *The Diary of a Film*, translated by Ronald Duncan, 1950.
Poésie critique. 1946.
Oeuvres complètes. 11 vols., 1946–51.
La Difficulté d'être. 1947; as *The Difficulty of Being*, translated by Elizabeth Sprigge, 1966.
Le Foyer des artistes. 1947.
Art and Faith: Letters Between Jacques Maritain and Jean Cocteau, translated by John Coleman. 1948.
Drôle de ménage. 1948.
Reines de France. 1948.
Lettre aux américains. 1949.
Maalesh: Journal d'une tournée de théâtre. 1949; as *Maalesh: A Theatrical Tour in the Middle-East*, translated by Mary C. Hoeck, 1956.
Dufy. 1949.
Orson Welles, with André Bazin. 1950.
Modigliani. 1950.
Jean Marais. 1951.
Entretiens autour du cinématographe, edited by André Fraigneau. 1951; revised edition, edited by André Bernard and Claude Gauteur, 1973; as *Cocteau on Film*, translated by Vera Traill, 1954; as *The Art of Cinema*, translated by Robin Buss, 1992.
Gide vivant, with Julien Green. 1952.
La Nappe du Catalan. 1952.

Journal d'un inconnu. 1953; as *The Hand of a Stranger*, translated by Alec Brown, 1956; as *Diary of an Unknown*, translated by Jesse Browner, 1988.
Aux confins de la Chine. 1955.
Lettre sur la poésie. 1955.
Le Dragon des mets. 1955.
Journals, edited and translated by Wallace Fowlie. 1956.
Adieu à Mistinguett. 1956.
L'Art est un sport. 1956.
Impression: Arts de la rue. 1956.
Cocteau chez les sirènes, edited by Jean Dauven. 1956.
Témoignage. 1956.
Entretiens sur la musée de Dresde, with Louis Aragon. 1957; as *Conversations in the Dresden Gallery*, 1983.
Erik Satie. 1957.
La Chapelle Saint-Pierre, Villefranche-sur-Mer. 1957.
La Corrida du premier mai. 1957.
Comme un miel noir (in French and English). 1958.
Paraprosodies, précédées de 7 dialogues. 1958.
La Salle des mariages, Hôtel de Ville de Menton. 1958.
La Canne blanche. 1959.
Poésie critique: Monologues. 1960.
Notes sur 'Le Testament d'Orphée'. 1960.
Le Cordon ombilical: Souvenirs. 1962.
Hommage. 1962.
Anna de Noailles oui et non. 1963.
Adieux d'Antonio Ordonez. 1963.
La Mésangère. 1963.
Entretien avec Roger Stéphane. 1964.
Entretien avec André Fraigneau. 1965.
Pégase. 1965.
My Contemporaries, edited and translated by Margaret Crosland. 1967.
Entre Radiguet et Picasso. 1967.
Lettres à André Gide, edited by Jean-Jacques Kihm. 1970.
Cocteau's World (selections), edited and translated by Margaret Crosland. 1972.
Cocteau, poète graphique, edited by Pierre Chanel. 1975.
Lettres à Milorad, edited by Milorad. 1975.
Le Passé défini (journals), edited by Pierre Chanel. 2 vols., 1986; as *Past Tense: The Cocteau Diaries*, translated by Richard Howard, 2 vols., 1987–90.
Lettres à Jean Marais. 1987.
Journal 1942–1945, edited by Jean Touzot. 1989.
Correspondance, 1911–1931, with Anna de Noailles, edited by Claude Mignot-Ogliastri. 1989.
Lettres à sa mère 1: 1898–1918, edited by Pierre Caizergues. 1989.
Correspondance, with Lucien Clerque. 1989.
Correspondance, with Guillaume Apollinaire, edited by Pierre Caizergues and Michel Décaudin. 1991.

Editor, *Almanach du théâtre et du cinéma*. 1949.
Editor, *Choix de lettres de Max Jacob à Jean Cocteau 1919–1944*. 1949.
Editor, *Amadeo Modigliani: Quinze dessins*. 1960.

*

Critical Studies: *Cocteau* by Margaret Crosland, 1956; *Scandal and Parade: The Theatre of Jean Cocteau* by Neal Oxenhandler, 1957; *Jean Cocteau: The History of a Poet's Age* by Wallace Fowlie, 1966; *Cocteau: The Man and the Mirror* by Elizabeth Sprigge and Jean-Jacques Kihm, 1968; *An Impersonation of Angels: A Biography of Jean Cocteau* by Frederick Brown, 1968; *Cocteau: A Biography* by Francis

Steegmuller, 1970; *Jean Cocteau* by Bettina L. Knapp, 1970, revised edition, 1989; *Jean Cocteau and André Gide: An Abrasive Friendship* by Arthur King Peters, 1973; *Jean Cocteau* by William Fifield, 1974; *Jean Cocteau and His Films of Orphic Identity* by Arthur B. Evans, 1977; *The Esthetic of Cocteau* by Lydia Crowson, 1978; *Jean Cocteau and the French Scene* edited by Arthur Peters, 1984; *The Dance Theatre of Jean Cocteau* by Frank W.D. Ries, 1985; *Les Enfants terribles* by Robin Buss, 1986; *Jean Cocteau and the Dance* by Erik Aschengreen, 1986; *Jean Cocteau and His World* by Arthur K. Peter, 1987.

* * *

Precociously Jean Cocteau published his first volume of verse at the age of 19. A small public flattered him and applauded the facile brilliance of the poems. Between 1917 and 1919, with three very different works, Cocteau became a public figure. *Parade*, of 1917, a ballet performed in Rome, was an early experiment with the theatre. *Le Coq et l'arlequin* (*Cock and Harlequin*), a manifesto against the disciples of Debussy and Wagner, revealed his interest in aesthetics and his powers as a critic. *Le Cap de Bonne-espérance*, a volume of war poems, placed him in the ranks of the best young poets. Poetry was the mark of all three works, and the principle which was thereafter to direct Cocteau's varied activities.

His sentence is swift and seemingly lucid, but the content is mysterious and enigmatical. Cocteau's style became a manner of expressing complicated matters with discerning simplicity. The poems of *Vocabulaire* contained the key words of his poetic experience, symbols and characters projected out of his imagination that were to form in time his mythology—episodes, myths, and characters charged with the duty of narrating the poet's drama. Kidnappers, sailors, angels, and cyclists appear and disappear as if searching for their poet.

The play *Orphée* (*Orpheus*), performed in Paris in 1926 by Georges and Ludmilla Pitoëff, was his first work to reach a fairly wide public. In *Orpheus*, the poet appears to be the combined characters of Orpheus and Angel Heurtebise. The action of the play is both familiar and esoteric; in it Orpheus is both poet and hierophant, both husband and priest.

Les Enfants terribles (*The Holy Terrors*) was written in three weeks and published in 1929. This book has now become a classic, both as a novel belonging to the central tradition of the short French novel, and as a document of historical-psychological significance in the study it offers of the type of adolescent referred to in the title. The intertwined destinies of brother and sister, Paul and Elisabeth, with the dark forbidding figure of Dargelos behind them, provide an unusual picture of adolescence in its actions and speech and games.

The theme of Cocteau's first film, *Le Sang d'un poète* (*The Blood of a Poet*), was an idea close to the romantics a century earlier, in which the poet writes with his own blood. Much later, in the film *Orphée* Cocteau developed this lesson of the poet and borrowed from *The Blood of a Poet* and his play *Orpheus*. These films are two esoteric poems for the screen.

In his plays, as in *La Machine infernale* (*The Infernal Machine*), on the Oedipus theme, Cocteau presented experimentations on the stage with the enthusiasm of a dramatist enamoured of the theatre and of the idea of a spectacle. Between the death of Apollinaire in 1918 and his own death in 1963, Cocteau occupied an active position in all the domains of French art.

—Wallace Fowlie

THE HOLY TERRORS (Les Enfants terribles)
Novel by Jean Cocteau, 1929.

Cocteau's *The Holy Terrors* is a novel that recounts the lives of a group of adolescents in early 20th-century Paris. Published in 1929, the narrative portrays the realistic, functional world of the French bourgeoisie that envelops, and eventually overtakes, the private fantasies of childhood innocence. Somewhat autobiographical, Cocteau's account of these interacting and blurring realities incorporates scenes of Paris, as well as the brutality of bullies, intellectual oppression, and the emotional torments that characterize the French lycée. This actual world, though, collides with a mythical reality, and the naive games enjoyed by children are a subterfuge that reflect the cruel ploys conceived and executed by adults. The child's room, then, is a shadow that outlines the horrors of reality. Like Cocteau's dramatic representations of Orpheus or Oedipe in *The Infernal Machine*, these characters are destined to proceed from play to pain and from illusion to illumination.

The narrative opens with images evoking tension and disparities: the staid scene of Paris apartments, protected and darkened by drapes; the restless tumult of schoolboys engaged in reckless play. Dargelos, a pupil who exercises authority over weaker boys, throws a stone which, encased by snow, hits, and inflicts injury on his admirer, Paul. Gérard, sensitive to Paul's weakness, sees that his friend is taken home. Paul's sister Elisabeth nurses her brother, as well as her mother who, abandoned by her husband, is incapacitated. Secluded from the conflicts of daily life, Paul, Elisabeth, and Gérard create an imaginary world: Paul's cluttered room replaces the streets and courtyards of Paris, and children's amusements substitute for adults' machinations. External events, however, penetrate this artificial reality: for Dargelos, expelled from school for throwing pepper at the headmaster, recognizes the ambivalence of adolescent fun and adult aggressions and is biding his time for a final blow, and Paul's mother dies unnoticed during an innocuous quarrel between Paul and his sister. Fantasy, though, continues to cloak actuality. Paul and Elisabeth treasure a photo of Dargelos dressed to play in a school performance the sinister role of Racine's biblical heroine Athalie; and they avoid entering their mother's room, thereby erasing her death from their consciousness.

Nevertheless, children's play reflects adult realities. Paul and Elisabeth participate in grotesque games which, like life's anxieties and inhumanities, instil terror and torment within others. The passage of time, moreover, impels changes in perspectives and interrelations, and adolescence as a *rite de passage* between childhood simplicity and adult sophistication ends in a discovery of the transparency of fictions and the reality of existence. In determining Paul's actions and attitudes, Elisabeth assumes Dargelos's place in a psychological hierarchy and thereby defines her identity. But through her marriage to Michaël, a rich American, she conforms to social expectations and simultaneously seeks to resolve her previous role of older sister with her present situation as wife. Although Michaël dies accidentally, external realities disturb the viability and complacency of a contrived, inner order. The themes of fate and futility influence characterization, and enable Cocteau to present a picture of desolation and death that define the human predicament. As a young man, Paul retains the calm innocence of childhood but, as an adolescent becoming a man, is attracted to Agathe, whom Elisabeth had invited to reside with them. Similarly, Gérard hopes to marry Elisabeth. This love that develops duly and naturally disrupts relationships, disturbs social roles and psychological identities, and displaces innocent fantasies with cruel contentions. Elisabeth, jealous and fearful of Paul's attention to Agathe, who resembles the photograph of Dargelos, attempts to preserve her position of control, secretly thwarts Paul's attempt to communicate his love to Agathe, and encourages a marriage between Agathe and Gérard. Paul suffers the distress of unrequited love and, dejected and reclusive, is enlivened momentarily by Dargelos's gift of poison which he consumes. Paul's death drives Elisabeth to suicide. Fatalism, masked by play and misconstrued, surfaces: the snow-enwrapped stone is transformed into a parcel enclosing poison and, subsequently, into a black bullet that kills Elisabeth. Man teeters between desolation and death. Dreams dissolve. In submitting to the exigencies of chronology and maturity, Cocteau's characters confront the shock of reality which emerges as the solitude and silence experienced by Agathe and Gérard in a loveless and lifeless marriage, and which marks for Paul and Elisabeth disintegration and oblivion.

Character portrayal and imagistic patterns reinforce the themes of destiny, desolation, and death. Defended by dream-like delusions, Cocteau's personages are puppets which, similar to ships tossed in a raging storm, writhe with anxiety and apprehensions. As sentient beings, they resist violence and elude agitation. But figured by the novel's pervasive imagery of shimmering shadows produced by moonbeams, or refracted light emitted by a chandelier, or the tenuous whiteness of falling snow, their world is ephemeral and undelineated. Fantasy contests, but coalesces, with truth. Objects appear inanimate and inconsequential, but they possess hidden powers: for a protective scarf and a plaster sphinx result respectively in Michaël's death and the pronouncement of tragic destiny. Rituals are games; but insults, sanctioned or teasing, remain tactics of pain. In retreating from reality, these characters are entrapped, destined to endure agitation and anguish. Abusive words, axe-like throbs in Elisabeth's heart, and a bloodied kerchief indicate violence and announce destruction. For Paul, the basilisk and mandrake seem magical and glorious; but, like Dargelos's present of poison and the bullet lodged in a revolver, they conceal agents of death. Paul and Elisabeth are tragic victims who, in seeking a shielded innocence, suffer, sadly and ironically, delusion and destruction. Elisabeth's final vision of the paradisiacal island inhabited by Bernardin de Saint-Pierre's romantic young heroes, Paul and Virginie, is ultimately a hallucination that appears as a vortex descending into a void. The whiteness of the snow that hides the stone surfaces as the blackness of the bullet that devastates and annihilates.

Cocteau's portrayal of destiny and his use of imagery denote parallels between this narrative and his plays, and may have facilitated this novel's adaptation into a film directed by J.-P. Melville in 1950. Like the dramatization of fate in *The Infernal Machine*, which Cocteau describes as a 'masterpiece of horror', the depiction of agony and anguish in *The Holy Terrors* defines the human situation in terms of destroyed delusions and inevitable death.

—Donald Gilman

THE INFERNAL MACHINE (La Machine infernale)
Play by Jean Cocteau, 1934.

This play, first performed in 1934, was to be Cocteau's definitive reworking of the Oedipus story, but he had already drafted both a libretto for Stravinsky's oratorio *Oedipus Rex*

for translation into Latin and a free adaptation of the Sophocles tragedy, similar in its contracted form to the earlier *Antigone*.

The precise significance of the title-image (an apparatus for producing destructive explosions) is revealed in the final paragraph of the prologue: 'Spectator, contemplate how the spring of one of the most perfect machines constructed by the infernal gods for the mathematical annihilation of a mortal, wound up as tight as possible, slowly unwinds throughout one human life.'

Previously in this prologue, recited by Cocteau himself in Louis Jouvet's original production, the author emphasizes the inevitability of the denouement as he ruthlessly takes the audience step by step through the plot. As he does so, he brings in the ancient tragic theme of *hubris*, which paves the way for the reminder from Anubis at the end of Act II that the Sphinx is also the incarnation of Nemesis.

In his attempt to reinforce the tragic quality of the play, Cocteau manifestly modelled his first act on aspects of *Hamlet*, even if it is essentially a parody of Shakespeare. The ghost of Laius appears on stage but is neither noticed nor heard by Jocasta and Teiresias.

It is not immediately clear to what extent Cocteau was aware that Freud refers to Hamlet in his presentation of the Oedipus complex first raised in *The Interpretation of Dreams*, where it is claimed that 'the enigma of . . . Shakespeare's procrastinator . . . can be solved by a reference to the Oedipus complex, since he came to grief over the task of punishing someone else for what coincided with the substance of his own Oedipus wishes'.

However, in the opening act Cocteau launches into a series of hardly veiled allusions to Freud and the famous complex. One speech by Jocasta begins: 'All little boys say: "I want to become a man in order to marry mummy"'. The repeated word-play on 'crever les yeux', with the interaction between the literal meaning of 'putting out someone's eyes' and the figurative sense of 'something staring one in the face', in this particular context is a reminder that Freud referred to the Oedipus legend when discussing the castration complex. Cocteau manages to blend extremely well the old and the new: for instance, the long scarf with which Jocasta will eventually hang herself is made to remind the audience of the scarf that was instrumental in Isadora Duncan's death.

In the second act Cocteau points out links between the Greek and Egyptian pantheons, not only through the presence of the Sphinx but also through the question that one character puts, semi-rhetorically, to Anubis: 'Why in Greece a god from Egypt?'.

The second act differs markedly from the Sophoclean original in its enacting of the encounter between Oedipus and the Sphinx. Cocteau's brainwave of casting the Sphinx as a young woman in a white dress makes her a possible alternative bride for the hero and she even spells out to Oedipus the one sure way of cheating the oracle: if he were to wed someone younger than himself, he could not possibly marry his own mother.

If there is an obvious weakness in the play, it is found in the stultification of Oedipus, whose intelligence is undermined by the fact that the solution to the riddle has to be given to him by the Sphinx in a rehearsal of the real interrogation. Even the Sphinx, though she is apparently in love with Oedipus, refers to him as an imbecile.

Cocteau has frequent recourse to dramatic irony. More than once the comical mother in this act ridicules her little son when he in fact hits on the truth concerning the identity of the Sphinx. Then in response to Oedipus's claim, 'Queen Jocasta is a widow, I shall marry her', the Sphinx remarks: 'A woman who could be your mother'. Yet it is later in Act II that Anubis points out to the Sphinx that Oedipus is indeed Jocasta's son.

The symbolism of the décor of the bedroom, the setting for Act III, 'The Wedding Night', 'red like a little butcher's shop', is perhaps too obvious for words, as is the way in which the Oedipal tension between father and son is transferred to the relationship between the hero and the substitute-father, Teiresias, Jocasta's erstwhile companion.

The denouement proper commences near the end of Act III when Jocasta notices the scars on Oedipus's feet, but the whole truth finally emerges for the protagonists firstly when a messenger from Corinth tells how his king, Polybos, on his deathbed, had ordered him to inform Oedipus that he was only an adopted son and then when a shepherd announces that Oedipus is the son of Jocasta. In the final twist Cocteau created a *regina ex machina* situation when the ghost of Jocasta appears to the newly-blind Oedipus to assist Antigone guide him off the stage.

Despite the almost inevitable anachronisms, despite the jokey nature of some of the references to Freudian theory, *The Infernal Machine* was a genuine, serious, and inventive attempt to rework the Oedipus story for a 20th-century audience. The play is a potent illustration of the powerlessness of man in face of the inexorable will of the gods. It is likewise a demonstration of Cocteau's belief in the importance of the force of destiny.

—Keith Aspley

COLETTE, (Sidonie-Gabrielle). Born in Saint-Saveur en Puisaye, France, 28 January 1873. Educated at local school to age 16. Married 1) the writer Henry Gauthier-Villars ('Willy') in 1893 (divorced 1910); 2) Henry de Jouvenal in 1912 (divorced 1925), one daughter; 3) Maurice Goudeket in 1935. Actress and revue performer, 1906–27; columnist, 1910–19, and literary editor, 1919–24, *Le Matin*; drama critic, *La Revue de Paris*, 1929, *Le Journal*, 1934–39, *L'Éclair*, and *Le Petit Parisien*; operated a beauty clinic, Paris, 1932–33. Recipient: City of Paris Grande Médaille, 1953. Member, Belgian Royal Academy, 1936; member, 1945, and president, 1949, Académie Goncourt; honorary member, American Academy, 1953. Chevalier, 1920, officer, 1928, commander, 1936, and grand officer, 1953, Légion d'honneur. *Died 3 August 1954.*

PUBLICATIONS

Collections

Works. 17 vols., 1951–64.
Oeuvres complètes. 16 vols., 1973.
Collected Stories, edited by Robert Phelps. 1983.
Oeuvres, edited by Claude Pichois. 1984— .

Fiction

Claudine à l'école, with Willy. 1900; as *Claudine at School*, translated by Janet Flanner, 1930; also translated by H. Mirande, 1930; Antonia White, 1956.
Claudine à Paris, with Willy. 1901; as *Claudine in Paris*, 1931; as *Young Lady of Paris*, translated by James Whitall, 1931; also translated by Antonia White, 1958.
Claudine amoureuse, with Willy. 1902; as *Claudine en ménage*, 1902; as *The Indulgent Husband*, translated by Frederick A. Blossom, 1935; as *Claudine Married*, translated by Antonia White, 1960.
Claudine s'en va, with Willy. 1903; as *The Innocent Wife*, translated by Frederick A. Blossom, 1934; as *Claudine and Annie*, translated by Antonia White, 1962.
Minne; Les Égarements de Minne. 2 vols., 1903–05; revised version, as *L'Ingénue libertine*, 1909; as *The Gentle Libertine*, translated by Rosemary Carr Benét, 1931; as *The Innocent Libertine*, translated by Antonia White, 1968.
La Retraite sentimentale. 1907; as *Retreat from Love*, translated by Margaret Crosland, 1974.
Les Vrilles de la vigne. 1908.
La Vagabonde. 1911; as *The Vagrant*, 1912; as *Renée la vagabonde*, translated by Charlotte Remfry-Kidd, 1931; as *The Vagabond*, translated by Enid McLeod, 1954.
L'Entrave. 1913; as *Recaptured*, translated by Viola Gerard Garvin, 1931; as *The Shackle*, translated by Antonia White, 1963.
Les Enfants dans les ruines. 1917.
Dans la foule. 1918.
Mitsou; ou, Comment l'esprit vient aux filles. 1919; as *Mitsou; or, How Girls Grow Wise*, translated by Jane Terry, 1930.
La Chambre éclairée. 1920.
Chéri. 1920; as *Chéri*, translated by Janet Flanner, 1929; also translated by Roger Senhouse, 1974.
Le Blé en herbe. 1923; as *The Ripening Corn*, translated by Phyllis Mégroz, 1921; as *The Ripening*, translated by Ida Zeitlin, 1932; as *The Ripening Seed*, translated by Roger Senhouse, 1956.
La Femme cachée. 1924; as *The Other Woman*, translated by Margaret Crosland, 1971.
Quatre saisons. 1925.
La Fin de Chéri. 1926; as *The Last of Chéri*, translated anonymously, 1932; also translated by Viola Gerard Garvin, 1933; Roger Senhouse, 1951.
La Naissance du jour. 1928; as *A Lesson in Love*, translated by Rosemary Carr Benét, 1932; as *Morning Glory*, 1932; as *The Break of Day*, translated by Enid McLeod, 1961.
La Seconde. 1929; as *The Other One*, translated by Elizabeth Tait and Roger Senhouse, 1931; as *Fanny and Jane*, translated by Viola Gerard Garvin, 1931.
Paradises terrestres. 1932.
La Chatte. 1933; as *The Cat*, translated by Morris Bentinck, 1936, also translated by Antonia White, 1955; as *Saha the Cat*, 1936.
Duo. 1934; as *Duo*, translated by Frederick A. Blossom, 1935; also translated by Margaret Crosland, with *The Toutounier*, 1974; as *The Married Lover*, translated by Marjorie Laurie, 1935.
Bella-Vista. 1937.
Le Toutounier. 1939; as *The Toutounier*, translated by Margaret Crosland, with *Duo*, 1974.
Chambre d'hôtel. 1940; in *Julie de Carneilhan and Chance Acquaintances*, translated by Patrick Leigh Fermor, 1952.
Julie de Carneilhan. 1941; as *Julie de Carneilhan*, in *Julie de Carneilhan and Chance Acquaintances* translated by Patrick Leigh Fermor, 1952.

Le Képi. 1943.
Gigi et autres nouvelles. 1944; as *Gigi*, translated by Roger Senhouse, 1952.
Stories, translated by Antonia White. 1958; as *The Tender Shoot and Other Stories*, 1959.

Plays

En camerades (produced 1909). In *Oeuvres complètes*, 15, 1950.
Claudine, music by Rodolphe Berger, from the novel by Colette (produced 1910). 1910.
Chéri, with Léopold Marchand, from the novel by Colette (produced 1921). 1922; translated as *Cheri*, 1959.
La Vagabonde, with Léopold Marchand, from the novel by Colette (produced 1923). 1923.
L'Enfant et les sortilèges, music by Maurice Ravel (produced 1925). 1925; as *The Boy and the Magic*, translated by Christopher Fry, 1964.
La Décapitée (ballet scenario), in *Mes Cahiers*. 1941.
Gigi, with Anita Loos, from the story by Colette (produced 1951). 1952; in French, 1954.
Jeune filles en uniform, Lac aux dames, Divine (screenplays), in *Au Cinéma*. 1975.

Screenplays: *La Vagabonde*, 1917, remake, 1931; *La Femme cachée*, 1919; *Jeunes filles en uniform* (French dialogue for German film *Mädchen in Uniform*), 1932; *Lac aux dames*, 1934; *Divine*, 1935.

Other

Dialogues de bêtes. 1904; enlarged edition, as *Sept dialogues de bêtes*, 1905; as *Douze dialogues de bêtes*, 1930; as *Barks and Purrs*, translated by Marie Kelly, 1913; as *Creatures Great and Small*, translated by Enid McLeod, 1951.
L'Envers du music-hall. 1913; as *Music-Hall Sidelights*, translated by Anne-Marie Callimachi, 1957.
Prrou, Poucette, et quelques autres. 1913; revised edition, as *La Paix chez les bêtes*, 1916; as *Cats, Dogs, and I*, translated by Alexandre Gagarine, 1924; also translated by Enid McLeod, in *Creatures Great and Small*, 1951.
Les Heures longues 1914–1917. 1917.
La Maison de Claudine. 1922; as *The Mother of Claudine*, translated by Charles King, 1937; as *My Mother's House*, translated by Enid McLeod and Una Vicenzo Troubridge, with *Sido*, 1953.
Le Voyage égoïste. 1922; translated in part by David Le Vay as *Journey for Myself: Selfish Memoirs*, 1971.
Rêverie du nouvel an. 1923.
Aventures quotidiennes. 1924; translated by David Le Vay, in *Journey for Myself: Selfish Memoirs*, 1971.
Renée Vivien. 1928.
Sido. 1929; as *Sido*, translated by Enid McLeod, with *My Mother's House*, 1953.
Histoires pour Bel-Gazou. 1930.
La Treille Muscate. 1932.
Prisons et paradis. 1932; translated in part by David Le Vay, in *Places*, 1970.
Ces plaisirs. 1932; as *Le Pur et l'impur*, 1941; as *The Pure and the Impure*, translated by Edith Dally, 1933, and by Herma Briffault, 1968; as *These Pleasures*, translated anonymously, 1934.
La Jumelle noire (theatre criticism). 4 vols., 1934–38.
Mes apprentissages. 1936; as *My Apprenticeships*, translated by Helen Beauclerk, 1957.

Chats. 1936.
Splendeur des papillons. 1937.
Mes cahiers. 1941.
Journal à rebours. 1941; as *Looking Backwards*, translated by David Le Vay 1975.
De ma fenêtre. 1942; enlarged edition, as *Paris de ma fenêtre*, 1944; translated by David Le Vay, in *Looking Backwards*, 1975.
De la patte à l'aile. 1943.
Flore et Pomone. 1943; as *Flowers and Fruit*, edited by Robert Phelps, translated by Matthew Ward, 1986.
Nudités. 1943.
Broderie ancienne. 1944.
Trois . . . six . . . neuf. 1944.
Belles Saisons. 1945; as *Belles Saisons: A Colette Scrapbook*, edited by Robert Phelps, 1978.
Une amitié inattendue (correspondence with Francis Jammes), edited by Robert Mallet. 1945.
L'Étoile vesper. 1946; as *The Evening Star: Recollections*, translated by David Le Vay, 1973.
Pour un herbier. 1948; as *For a Flower Album*, translated by Roger Senhouse, 1959.
Oeuvres complètes. 15 vols., 1948–50.
Trait pour trait. 1949.
Journal intermittent. 1949.
Le Fanal bleu. 1949; as *The Blue Lantern*, translated by Roger Senhouse, 1963.
La Fleur de l'âge. 1949.
En pays connu. 1949.
Chats de Colette. 1949.
Paysages et portraits. 1958.
Lettres à Hélène Picard, edited by Claude Pichois. 1958.
Lettres à Marguerite Moréno, edited by Claude Pichois. 1959.
Lettres de la vagabonde, edited by Claude Pichois and Roberte Forbin. 1961.
Lettres au petit corsaire, edited by Claude Pichois and Roberte Forbin. 1963.
Earthly Paradise: An Autobiography Drawn from Her Lifetime of Writing, edited by Robert Phelps, translated by Helen Beauclerk and others. 1966.
Places (miscellany; in English), translated by David Le Vay. 1970.
Contes de mille et un matins. 1970; as *The Thousand and One Mornings*, translated by Margaret Crosland and David Le Vay. 1973.
Journey for Myself: Selfish Memoirs (selection), translated by David Le Vay. 1971.
Lettres à ses pairs, edited by Claude Pichois and Roberte Forbin. 1973.
Au cinéma, edited by Alain and Odette Virmaux. 1975.
Letters from Colette, edited and translated by Robert Phelps. 1980.

*

Critical Studies: *Madame Colette: A Provincial in Paris*, 1952, and *Colette: The Difficulty of Loving*, 1973, both by Margaret Crosland; *Colette* by Elaine Marks, 1960; *Colette* by Margaret Davies, 1961; *Colette* by Robert D. Cottrell, 1974; *Colette: A Taste for Life* by Yvonne Mitchell, 1975; *Colette: Free and Fettered* by Michèle Sarde, translated by Richard Miller, 1980; *Colette: The Woman, The Writer* edited by Erica M. Eisinger and Mari McCarty, 1981; *Colette* by Joan Hinde Stewart, 1983; *Colette* by Joanna Richardson, 1983; *Colette: A Passion for Life* by Genevieve Dormann, translated by David Macey, 1985; *Colette* by Allan Massie, 1986; *Colette* by

Nicola Ward Jouve, 1987; *Colette: A Life* by Herbert Lottman, 1991; *Colette* by Diana Holmes, 1991; *Colette and the Fantom Subject of Autobiography* by Jerry Aline Flieger, 1992.

* * *

Colette began her literary career under the tutelage of a man, her husband Willy, and her first novels were written in collaboration with him and were published under his name. But the partnership was not a happy one, and after their divorce she branched out on her own. She wrote many more books, and survived into the second half of the 20th century, but she is essentially a *fin de siècle* writer who captures with great finesse and depth of perception the particular world which we call the *belle époque*: middle-class society in France (especially Paris) before 1914. She is particularly adept at exploring human relationships, such as the tragic love of a young man for a woman of 50 in *Chéri* and *La Fin de Chéri* (*The Last of Chéri*), or a husband's destructive jealousy of his wife in *Duo*, but she also writes with great sensitivity about children—in, for instance, *Claudine à l'école* (*Claudine at School*), her first book—and about nature, especially animals. This is not to imply, however, that she is a sentimental writer, quite the reverse: there is a toughness and a sharpness in her analysis of her characters' moods and whims which is firmly in the great French tradition of psychological precision inaugurated by Madame de Lafayette and continued by Constant and Stendhal. At her best she sustains comparison with these illustrious forebears in her unclouded perception of the ravages of love.

But her books, fine as some of them are, constitute only a part of her legacy. Like George Sand nearly a century earlier she worked hard as a professional woman of letters, and even, after her divorce from Willy, plunged for a time into the gruelling life of a professional actress and performer. This was a brave and original thing to do then, but it is characteristic of the lack of pretentiousness and of the no-nonsense attitude manifested in her fiction. Since she had to earn her own living after the break with Willy, she put her talents to good use. Unsentimental in her attitudes as in her art, she accepted that if she was to be free and independent she had to raise income by her own unaided efforts. Like Simone de Beauvoir, who is perhaps more of an intellectual though not necessarily more intelligent, she may in the last analysis be a minor writer only, but there is no doubt that she is a great woman, a figure of whom women of today can be proud. In spite of knowing great personal unhappiness in her younger days, she lived to become one of most famous and honoured writers of her generation, and this, in a male-dominated society, is no small achievement.

—John Fletcher

CHÉRI
Novel by Colette, 1920.

Possibly her best-known novel, *Chéri* was published in final form in 1920. Having been first conceived in 1912, the year in which the action of the novel begins, *Chéri* began in the form of a play. As such, the work retains some of its original dramatic structure, being easily divided into three sections. Only the middle section, however, focuses entirely on the title character, a young man emerging from adolescence, referred to as Chéri by those who know him best—the two women who, in their own way, raised him: his mother and her confidante Léa, called La Baronne de Lonval. The first and third parts of the novel concern for the most part Léa, and Léa's amorous but ambiguous relationship to Chéri, some 25 years her junior.

This novel, appearing at a time when Colette's penchant for the unconventional, if not scandalous, both in her life and in her novels, was already well known, continues in the vein of unorthodoxy. Although acclaimed for its prose artistry, the book was criticized for its milieu and for the portrayal of Chéri. Firstly, the setting is the world of courtesans, the *demi-monde* of Paris. Léa and Chéri's mother are two materially successful courtesans who have somehow escaped damaging scandals so as to 'retire' from their profession peacefully and comfortably. Léa, at 49, considers her now seven-year-old liaison with Chéri to be her last (although she is concerned at such a notion), and Madame Peloux has not had an encounter since Chéri was at college. These are two businesswoman who have profited from the life they lead and who enjoy a certain 'modern' independence. Secondly, Chéri's personality construction was controversial. Beautiful, childlike, spoiled, irresponsible, and somewhat effeminate, Chéri is vain and greedy. In the first pages of the novel he pleads with Léa to give him her glorious strand of pearls, which she refuses to do. Having known Chéri since his birth, she is fully aware of his capriciousness. In this relationship Léa is both lover and strong maternal figure for a boy who whines and plays. Here Colette reverses sex role stereotypes: Léa is worldly-wise, premeditative, practical: Chéri is carefree, young, naive. While Léa is able to define her needs and satisfy them, Chéri is incapable of even expressing himself in adult speech (at one point Léa hints at being frustrated by Chéri's inarticulateness, saying she never really knew him beyond a certain physical level).

As must happen, however, Chéri passes into adulthood by way of his betrothal to a young girl who is, actually, the foil of the mature Léa. Ironically, this young couple is a couple of children, uninitiated into the world of adults. The aftermath of Chéri's wedding heralds the second section of the novel. Léa, heartbroken without Chéri, goes off mysteriously to the south of France, leaving in her wake gossipy whispers concerning her supposed replacement companion (in fact, she is travelling alone). Her departure, and Chéri's frustration over being married to a needy child, results in his own flight. On a walk one evening (the first of many during which he will spy on Léa's vacant house), he decides to return home. Instead, he takes up residence with a bachelor friend and remains in his company for over six weeks, frequenting restaurants, bars, and opium dens, all characterizing his new-found freedom. Although Chéri never smokes the opium offered to him, there is an element of self-destruction inherent in his actions. Never having been very healthy (Léa had once taken it upon herself to fatten him up), he sleeps little, eats badly, and reminisces frequently about Léa. Not until he knows that Léa has returned to Paris (with or without a lover; this thought has not yet crossed his mind) does Chéri return home to his young wife, assured that he can now be a legitimate husband.

The last section of the novel, however, finds Chéri abruptly back in Léa's arms, and the themes Colette sketched in the first part of the novel come to fruition. Here we learn that love cannot conquer all, obstacles such as age play an essential role. Wanting to find again the Nounoune (as Chéri calls Léa) that he had left only months earlier, Chéri wakes in Léa's bed to discover an ageing woman with a sagging chin, roughened skin, and a lack of the freshness that he now, by contrast, witnesses in his bride. His words 'Tu as été pour moi' ('You have been for me') explain everything, parting the lovers for the last time.

Colette's prose is rhythmic, cadenced, eloquent, lyric, even musical. Her narrator (given a semi-omniscient point of view) allows her a wide perspective on character, and her dialogues artfully express the cattiness of competitive *demi-mondaines*. Added to this is the carefully treated question of sex. Colette inverts sex roles to create a strong woman/weak man dichotomy that moves one step beyond the simply caricatural male of her earlier fiction. Playing into the definition of sex role is Colette's genius for depicting sense perceptions, illustrated here by her use of the colours pink, white, and blue. Pink and white are symbolic of strength (Léa's room, the light, her skin), while blue (Chéri's silhouette against the window, for example) intervenes in an almost sinister way, contrasting with the maternal strength of the woman. Interestingly, woman's strength lies not in her physicality (the flesh which ages and betrays), but in her spirit, which comprehends the need for another to find life elsewhere than in a mother's arms, granting him an adulthood which excludes her.

It is perhaps noteworthy that *Chéri* precedes an era in Colette's life when she became a Léa-figure to her stepson. Colette, however, unlike Léa, did not find the inner strength to let her young lover leave. Although the two eventually parted ways, Colette found she was not the independent woman that she had created in the character of Léa, having hoped to present a new female image.

—Jennifer Brown

COLONNA, Vittoria. Born in Colonna Castle, Marino (near Rome), Papal States, 25 February 1492. Married Ferrante Francesco D'Avalos, Marquis of Pescara, in 1509 (died in battle, 1525). Lived in the convents of Santa Caterina, Viterbo, and San Silvestro, Rome, after her husband's death (although she did not become a nun), and began to write poetry; became a leading literary figure to whom many significant humanist writers dedicated their works: had notable friendships with Pietro Bembo, *q.v.*, Baldassarre Castiglione, *q.v.*, and, particularly, Michelangelo (who painted her, and to whom she dedicated poetry). *Died in 1547.*

PUBLICATIONS

Collection

Rime e lettere, edited by E. Saltini. 1860.

Verse

Rime. 1538; revised edition, 1539; edited by Pietro Ercole Visconti, 1840, and by Alan Bullock, 1982; selections translated by Alethea J. Lawley, in *Vittoria Colonna*, 1888, anonymously, in *The 'In Memoriam' of Italy: A Century of Sonnets from the Poems of Vittoria Colonna*, 1894, and by Joseph Tusiani, in *Italian Poets of the Renaissance*, 1971.

Other

Lettere inedite, edited by Giuseppe Piccioni. 1875.
Carteggio (correspondence), edited by Ermanno Ferrero and Giuseppe Müller. 1889; annotated by Domenico Tordi, 1892.

*

Critical Studies: *Vittoria Colonna: Her Life and Poems* by Maria Roscoe, 1868; *Vittoria Colonna* by Alethea J. Lawley, 1888; *The Romance of Woman's Influence* by Alice Corkran, 1906; *Vittoria Colonna and Some Account of Her Friends and Her Times* by Maud F. Jerrold, 1906; *La vita e l'opera di Vittoria Colonna* by A.A. Bernardy, 1927; *Vittoria Colonna* by Thomas Pawsey, 1953; 'A Hitherto Unexplored Manuscript of One Hundred Poems by Vittoria Colonna in the Biblioteca Nazionale Centrale' by Alan Bullock, in *Italian Studies*, 21, 1966; *Un cénacle humaniste de la Renaissance autour de Vittoria Colonna châtelaine d'Ischia* by Suzanne Therault, 1968; 'Vittoria Colonna' by Roland Bainton, in *Women of the Reformation in Germany and Italy*, 1971; 'Vittoria Colonna's Friendship with the English Cardinal Reginald Pole' by Diane Dyer, in *Riscontri*, 7(1–2), 1985; 'Neoplatonism in Vittoria Colonna's Poetry: From the Secular to the Divine' by Dennis J. McAuliffe, in *Ficino and Renaissance Neoplatonism* edited by Olga Zorzi Pugliese, 1986; 'Vittoria Colonna: Child, Woman and Poet' by Joseph Gibaldi, in *Women Writers of the Renaissance and Reformation* edited by Katharina M. Wilson, 1987.

* * *

Renaissance Italy produced an extraordinary number of talented women writers, most of whom remain forgotten. Despite the advances in feminist scholarship that have brought the work of many earlier women writers back into focus, the Italian poets of the 15th and 16th centuries remain, for the most part, in obscurity. Vittoria Colonna is probably the best known of these poets, and was described by Buckhardt as the 'most famous woman in Italy'. Born into a noble family and married young, she was widowed at the age of 35 and never remarried. She moved to the Convent of San Silvestro in Rome, though did not actually join a religious order, using it as a base from which to travel extensively throughout Italy. She enjoyed close friendships with a number of leading contemporary intellectuals and artists, including Pietro Bembo, the cardinal-poet who encouraged her to write her own poetry, Castiglione, and Michelangelo. Her friendship with Michelangelo, in particular, led to an exchange of poems and letters that continued until her death in 1547, when Michelangelo wrote a series of moving poems about his loss, describing her as his 'sun of suns', the woman whose strength in life lifted him closer to God.

Though Colonna was a Beatrice figure to Michelangelo, her own poetry was not written for any single person. Unlike Gaspara Stampa or Veronica Franco, two other important women poets of her day, her poetry does not deal with the delights of physical passion or with disappointment and unrequited love. Her love poems, written after her husband's death on the battlefield, are full of sadness, and although she uses the conventions of the Petrarchan tradition, her imagery is particularly powerful, and she writes of the illuminating force of her memories with great energy and power. Curiously, however, her first known poem, written when her husband was still alive, is completely different in tone. Her 'Epistle to Ferrante Francesco d'Avalos, Her Husband, After the Battle of Ravenna' (written 1512) is an angry poem protesting about his preference for war over staying at home with his young wife:

You live happily and have no cares:
thinking only of your new won fame,
you care not if I go hungry for your love;
but I, with anger and sadness in my face,
lie in your bed, abandoned and alone.

Reluctant to publish her poems, Colonna finally allowed a collection to appear in 1538, and it is clear that she saw poetry as an essentially private activity, even after the poems had come out and she had begun to be acclaimed as a major poet. (Some 20 editions appeared in the 16th century). Her 'love poems' were written in the years immediately after her husband's death, and she then began to write what came to be called her 'spiritual poems'. Her long poem, 'Poi ch'il mio sol, d'eterni raggi cinto' ('The Triumph of Christ's Cross') praises the glories of divine love over worldly passions:

Blessed is she who scorned worldly fruit,
root and all, for now from her Lord
she receives other, everlasting sweetness.

Divine love for Colonna is not a source of anguish or torment, it is a fount of perfection, a healing, consoling beauty. She appeals to Christ to tear off the veils, to unfasten the chains that have bound her in darkness. The imagery of her 'spiritual poems' depicts a gentle Christ, bringing nourishment and consolation, a figure of healing, redemption, and liberation. Significantly, she writes movingly of Mary, whose suffering as Christ's mother provides a model for women, and of Mary Magdalene. In a sonnet on Mary Magdalene, 'La bella donna, a cui dolente preme' [The Beautiful Woman Oppressed by Sorrows], she depicts Mary's loneliness and desperation at being abandoned by man and God, and contrasts that anguish with the security offered by the vision of the risen Christ in the garden:

And those strong men, privileged
by grace, huddled together in fear;
the true Light seemed to them merely a shadow.

So that, if truth is not overwhelmed by falsehood
we must grant to women all the prize
of having more loving and more constant hearts.

In Colonna's exquisitely crafted Petrarchan sonnets, through her Neoplatonic idealism, there is a clear portrait of a world of binary oppositions, a world in which women are forced to submit passively to whatever society decreed, while men go out into that world to try and change it through their actions. Yet, while she recognizes the inevitability of this pattern of behaviour, Colonna also protests against the injustice of it. From her early poem angrily chiding her military husband for leaving her at home uncared-for, to her later poetry extolling the joys that illuminate the heart of Mary Magdalene, she seems to be consistently demanding to be heard and speaking out for other women in similar positions. Her poetry is full of references to other women's pain; 'Mentre la nave mia, lungi dal porto', one of her longer 'love poems', compares her own suffering and wifely resignation to that of women from classical mythology—to Penelope and Laodmia, Ariadne and Medea, or Portia, wife of Brutus, the noblest Roman of them all—while 'Poi ch'l mio sol, d'eterni raggi cinto' depicts the Virgin Mary and Mary Magdalene as examples of supreme womanhood.

Colonna's language has a clarity and precision that testify to her great poetic talent. In an age of many superbly gifted poets (and even more derivative, second-rate ones) her voice comes through powerfully and directly. She deserves to be more widely read and translated, because her poetry speaks to women (and men) of all times.

—Susan Bassnett

CORNEILLE, Pierre. Born in Rouen, France, June 1606; elder brother of the writer Thomas Corneille. Educated in Jesuit college, Rouen, 1615–22; studied law, 1622–24, licensed lawyer, 1624. Married Marie de Lampérière in 1641; seven children. Member of the Rouen *Parlement*, 1629–50: held offices as King's advocate in water and forests court and in Rouen port Admiralty court. Lived in Paris after 1662. Elected to the Académie française, 1647. *Died 1 October 1684.*

PUBLICATIONS

Collections

Oeuvres, edited by Charles Marty-Leaveaux. 12 vols., 1862–68.
Oeuvres complètes, edited by A. Stegman. 1963.
Oeuvres complètes, edited by Georges Couton. 3 vols., 1980–87.
Théâtre complet, edited by Alain Niderst. 1984– .

Plays

Mélite; ou, Les Fausses Lettres (produced 1629–30). 1633; translated as *Melite*, 1776.
Clitandre; ou, L'Innocence délivrée (produced 1630–31). 1632.
La Veuve; ou, Le Traître trahi (produced 1631–32). 1634.
La Galerie du Palais; ou, L'Amie rivale (produced 1632–33). 1637; edited by Milorad R. Margitic, 1981.
La Suivante (produced c.1633–34). 1637; edited by Milorad R. Margitic, 1978.
La Place Royale; ou, L'Amoureux extravagant (produced c.1633–34). 1637.
Médée (produced c.1634–35). 1639; edited by André de Leyssac, 1978.
La Comédie des Tuileries, with others (produced 1635). 1638.
L'Illusion comique (produced 1635–36). 1639; as *The Theatrical Illusion*, with *The Cid* and *Cinna*, 1975; as *The Illusion*, with *The Liar*, 1989.
Le Cid (produced 1637). 1637; revised version, 1682; translated as *The Cid*, 1637; several subsequent translations.
L'Aveugle de Smyrne, with Rotrou and others (produced 1637). 1638.
Horace (produced 1640). 1641; translated as *Horatius*, 1656; as *Horace*, in *The Chief Plays of Corneille*, 1952; also translated by Albert Bernell, 1962.
Cinna; ou, La Clémence d'Auguste (produced 1642). 1643; as *Cinna's Conspiracy*, 1713; also translated as *Cinna*.

Polyeucte, Martyr (produced 1642–43). 1643; translated as *Polyeuctes*, 1655; as *Polyeucte*, in *The Chief Plays of Corneille*, 1952; as *Polyeuctus*, with *The Liar* and *Nicomedes*, 1980.

La Mort de Pompée (produced 1643–44). 1644; as *Pompey the Great*, 1664; as *La Mort de Pompée*, translated by Lacey Lockert, in *Moot Plays of Corneille*, 1959.

Le Menteur (produced 1643–44). 1644; as *The Mistaken Beauty; or, The Liar*, 1685; as *The Lying Lover*, 1717; as *The Liar*, with *Polyeuctus* and *Nicolmenedes*, 1980.

Oeuvres (plays). 1644; and later editions.

La Suite du Menteur (produced 1644–45). 1645.

Rodogune, Princesse des Parthes (produced 1644–45). 1645; translated as *Rodogune*, 1765.

Théodore, vierge et martyre (produced 1645–46). 1646 or 1647.

Héraclius, Empereur d'Orient (produced 1646–47). 1647; as *Heraclius, Emperor of the East*, 1664.

Andromède (produced 1650). 1650.

Don Sanche d'Aragon (produced 1649–50). 1650; as *The Conflict*, in *Plays and Poems*, 1798; as *Don Sanche d'Aragon*, translated by Lacey Lockert, in *Moot Plays of Corneille*, 1959.

Nicomède (produced 1651). 1651; translated as *Nicomede*, 1671.

Pertharite, Roi des Lombards (produced 1651–52). 1653.

Oedipe (produced 1659). 1659.

La Conquête de la toison d'or (produced 1660). 1661.

Sertorius (produced 1662). 1662; as *Sertorius*, translated by Lacey Lockert, in *Moot Plays of Corneille*, 1959.

Sophonisbe (produced 1663). 1663.

Othon (produced 1664). 1665; as *Othon*, translated by Lacey Lockert, in *Moot Plays of Corneille*, 1959.

Agésilas (produced 1666). 1666.

Attila, Roi des Huns (produced 1667). 1667; as *Attila*, translated by Lacey Lockert, in *Moot Plays of Corneille*, 1959.

Tite et Bérénice (produced 1670). 1671.

Psyché, with Molière and Quinault, music by Lully (produced 1671). 1671.

Pulchérie (produced 1672). 1673.

Suréna, Général des Parthes (produced 1674). 1675; translated as *Surenas*, 1969.

Other

Oeuvres diverses. 1738.

Writings on the Theatre, edited by H.T. Barnwell. 1965.

Translator, *L'Imitation de Jésus-Christ*, by Thomas à Kempis. 1651–56.

Translator, *Louanges de la Sainte Vierge*, by St Bonaventure. 1665.

Translator, *L'Office de la Sainte Vierge*, by St Bonaventure. 1670.

*

Critical Studies: *The Classical Moment: Studies of Corneille, Molière, and Racine* by Martin Turnell, 1947; *Corneille: His Heroes and Their Worlds* by Robert J. Nelson, 1963, and *Corneille and Racine: Parallels and Contrasts* edited by Nelson, 1966; *Corneille* by P.J. Yarrow, 1963; *The Cornelian Hero* by Albert West, 1963; *The Criticism of Cornelian Tragedy* by Herbert Fogel, 1967; *Corneille* by Claude K. Abraham, 1972; *Corneille and Racine: Problems of Tragic Form* by Gordon Pocock, 1973; *Corneille: Horace* by R.C. Knight, 1981; *The Tragic Drama of Corneille and Racine: An Old Parallel Revisited* by H.T. Barnwell, 1982; *The Comedies of Corneille* by G.J. Mallinson, 1984; *The Liar and the Lieutenant in the Plays of Pierre Corneille* by I.D. McFarlane, 1984; *Corneille, Classicism and the Ruses of Symmetry* by Mitchell Greenberg, 1986; *If There Are No More Heroes, There Are Heroines: A Feminist Critique of Corneille's Heroines 1637–1644* by Josephine A. Schmidt, 1987; *Le Cid: Corneille* by W.D. Howarth, 1988; *The Poetic Style of Corneille's Tragedies: An Aesthetic Interpretation* by Sharon Harwood Gordon, 1989; *Dissonant Harmonies: Drama and Ideology in Five Neglected Plays of Pierre Corneille* by Susan Read Baker, 1990; *Corneillian Theater: The Metadramatic Dimension* by M.J. Muratore, 1990; *Corneille's Tragedies: The Role of the Unexpected* by R.C. Knight, 1991; *Pierre Corneille: The Poetics and Political Drama under Louis XII* by David Clarke, 1992.

* * *

Pierre Corneille is the earliest of the great French Classical playwrights. 'Cornelian' has become an adjective to describe qualities of grandeur, heroism, and the subordination of passion to duty which are apparent in many of his plays.

His production was in fact very various. He showed a constant desire to astound—by extreme gestures and situations, by complication, surprise, verbal display, variety. As a poet, his great gift is for emphatic and weighty eloquence, admirably suited to his 'Cornelian' moments. But his range is wide—tenderness, lyricism, irony, with a talent (not only in his comedies) for realistic dialogue and repartee. His changes of tone and delight in verbal ingenuity have often led to complaints of bathos and bad taste, but can be seen as indications of his breadth and daring. He shows a fascination with human behaviour in bizarre and confused situations, and especially with the complexity of moral decisions, sometimes reflecting contemporary events and controversies. This fascination is most memorably focused on the hero's struggle to fulfil the demands of his 'gloire' (literally 'honour' or 'reputation', but in Corneille's best work a subtle concept involving self-realization at a high moral level). There is also a sense of the complexity of life in a more obvious way. Even in his loftiest plays there is an awareness of the self-seeking, even comical, elements which accompany and oppose or corrupt the heroic impulse. In many of his works, this shades into irony and a disabused realism.

Corneille's early plays are mainly comedies on the intrigues of young lovers. They are best read in the original versions, before Corneille toned them down. Free in form, with a mixture of realism and fantasy, they show a Baroque concern with illusion and the falsity of appearances, especially in the play-within-a-play-within-a-play of *L'Illusion comique* (*The Theatrical Illusion*). Despite their often frank realism and comedy, deeper themes emerge: real or assumed madness and real grief at a supposed death (*Mélite*); misery caused by a young man's rejection of love in order to preserve his freedom (*La Place Royale*); the bitterness of a woman at her social status (*La Suivante*). *Clitandre*, though labelled a tragedy, is a romantic comedy. *Médée* signals Corneille's approach to tragedy. It sets the selfish triviality of Jason and the Court against the lonely figure of Medea, who asserts her identity by a terrible revenge.

Le Cid (*The Cid*) shows the crisis in the hero's life when he has to kill the father of his beloved Chimène in order to fulfil his heroic destiny, and she, to match his integrity, has to seek his death. Although Corneille blurs the ending, the poignancy and dramatic boldness of the situations, together with the lyricism and energy of the verse, make this his most accessible play. *Horace*, the first play within the strict unities (though Corneille, as often, has difficulty in unifying his action), shows the hero isolating himself in his destiny, which leads him both to save his country and to murder his sister. Corneille resolves the crisis ambiguously, showing the hero both glorious and flawed. *Cinna* is perhaps his most unified achievement. In a shifting drama of love and political intrigue, it focuses on the effort of the Emperor Augustus to transcend his past and convert by forgiveness those who have conspired against him. *Polyeucte* (*Polyeuctus*) deals with a clash between Christianity and Paganism in the Roman Empire, and shows how the heroic Polyeucte, in seeking martyrdom, brings to Christianity not only his passionate wife but also his cynical father-in-law. Powerful in structure, characterization, and verse, it is often regarded as his masterpiece though some have found the ending unconvincing.

Corneille's later plays only achieve this level intermittently. Until the failure of *Pertharite*, he produced a series of very varied plays—tragedies, plays with music and spectacular effects, and *comédies héroïques* (plays with noble characters, but less serious than tragedies). The best are the comedy *Le Menteur* (*The Liar*) and the tragedy *Nicomède* (*Nicomede*), a play of complex ironies showing the hero triumphing (largely through the efforts of others) over the hostility of Rome and the intrigues of his stepmother, who dominates his realistic and weak father. *Rodogune* and *Héraclius* (*Heraclius*), both tragedies, are more typical, in their schematic characterization, exciting plots, and melodramatic verve.

The plays after Corneille's return to the theatre in 1659 are uneven, but in some ways his most interesting. The heroic mode of his masterpieces and the melodrama of his middle plays give way to a subtle blend of political and psychological intrigue, with flashes of both grandeur and comedy. The finest are *Sertorius*, dramatizing the clash of personal and political ambitions in the civil wars of the Roman Republic, and *Suréna* (*Surenas*), his last play. *Surenas*, with its atmosphere of ambiguity and menace, has an emotional and tragic resonance rare in Corneille.

As well as various prefatory pieces, Corneille wrote the substantial critical *Discourses* and critiques (*Examens*) of individual plays prefixed to each volume of his 1660 *Works*. Although not very illuminating on individual plays, they show his difficulties with the contemporary critical concern for verisimilitude and moral utility in poetry. He stresses pleasure as the aim of drama, and historical truth as an aid to credibility.

Apart from some lively personal pieces, his non-dramatic poetry is of little interest.

—Gordon Pocock

THE CID (Le Cid)
Play by Pierre Corneille, 1637.

Inspired by the Spanish 'romanceros' and in particular by Guillén de Castro's *Youthful Deeds of the Cid* (*Mocedades del Cid*), *The Cid* is Corneille's first major play and probably the finest affirmation of the neo-classical dramaturgy which swept France in the 17th century. While *The Cid* presents a modern picture of man in charge of his own fate, it is also a strong commentary on the society in which Corneille was living. The

strengthening of the king's power against the nobility, a Spanish invasion of France, and Richelieu's new social order and prohibition of duels provide the historical, moral, and social backdrop of the play. Key Cornelian words such as 'glory', 'honour', 'merit', and 'duty' reflect the concerns of the dominant class of the period. The groundwork for Corneille's subsequent production is laid in *The Cid*: the hero undergoes a test in which his force and lucidity are revealed, while the final act of generosity and royal pardon bring the climax to a happy ending.

The Cid was a public triumph but led to a famed literary dispute, the 'Querelle du Cid', because Corneille did not follow strictly the rules of the dramatic genre of the times. A daughter marrying her father's murderer offended the 'bienséances', or ethical conventions, while Corneille's liberties with the three unities also came under attack. In *The Cid*, the unity of time is used to its maximum of 24 hours; the unity of place extends to a whole city (private homes, King's palace, port); the action is multiple yet remains unified in its focus on the testing and assertion of the hero's valour, both individual and political.

The Cid holds a particular place in the Frenchman's heart: Corneille's style exemplifies 'classical' purity, and every French schoolchild knows the most famous lines of the play.

The action takes place in Seville, in the days of the Reconquista against the Moors. While Chimène awaits her father's decision to allow her to marry Don Rodrigue, the Infanta, Doña Urraque, confides to her servant that she herself loves Rodrigue, 'a simple cavalier', but gave him to Chimène since 'none but kings are fit' for her royal blood. In the meantime, Don Diègue, Rodrigue's father, has been chosen by the King to be the preceptor of his son, the heir apparent. Don Gomès, count of Gormas, Chimène's father, feels that the ageing Don Diègue was unjustly granted a position that he himself was entitled to on account of his more recent military valour. In the ensuing argument, he slaps his older rival, whose only recourse is to call on Rodrigue to avenge the family's honour.

Torn between love and duty, Rodrigue expresses his dilemma in the famous 'stances du Cid' a monologue of lyrical asymmetric stanzas during which he decides that he must confront Don Gomès since he will lose Chimène in either case: 'J'attire en me vengeant sa haine et sa colère'/J'attire ses mépris en ne me vengeant pas' ('If I avenge myself, I incur her hatred and anger/If I take no revenge, I incur her scorn'). The young and untried Rodrigue kills his father-in-law to be, the exemplary warrior of Castile. Chimène then seeks justice from the King, while Don Diègue appeals for forgiveness.

Rodrigue visits Chimène and offers her his life. While she insists on avenging her father's death, she cannot disguise her love for her enemy (offering a famous understatement: 'I do not hate you') and vows 'never to breathe a moment after [him]'.

An invasion by a Moorish army that very night enables Rodrigue to further prove his valour. He defeats the invaders, capturing two of their kings, who call Rodrigue their lord, or 'Cid' in their language. The King deceives Chimène by telling her that Rodrigue has died; she faints, but again asks for justice when she is told the truth. Don Sanche, one of her suitors, will fight for her in a duel against Rodrigue. The victor will marry the young woman. Although he wishes to die, Chimène encourages Rodrigue to live. After the duel, Chimène displays her grief, and then her love for Rodrigue when she learns that he won but spared his rival. The King then proclaims that Chimène will let one year pass to mourn her father while Rodrigue, who is pardoned for killing Don Gomès, goes to fight the Moors. Don Fernand, the King of

Castile, imparts the final wisdom of the play: 'To still that honour that cries out against you/Leave all to time, your valour, and your King.'

These words situate Corneille's work within a conflict between the redefined French state and the old feudal system: the centralization of political power in the 17th century required individuals to work for their country, disregarding petty rivalry and pride. Don Gomès arrogantly believes in the self: 'To disobey a little is no great crime/In order to preserve all my good fame'; yet some statements have a prophetic ring to our modern and democratic ears: 'Great though they are, kings are but men like us.' While Rodrigue asserts the power and courage of the young ('in a well-born soul/Valour awaits not an appointed age'), this new nobleman will nevertheless bow to the king's power for the greatest benefit of all. One should stress that Corneille's depiction of a valiant young Rodrigue reflects Richelieu's efforts to attract competence rather than noble blood to important positions in the administration of a renewed France. This is also supported by Corneille's creation of the Infanta, a character frequently attacked by critics as superfluous, and left out of shortened versions of the play; in fact, the Infanta represents a new social order whose values enlightened individuals like Rodrigue rather than undisciplined noblemen like Don Gomès.

Chimène also shares in this depiction of a new society. With all the reserve expected of a 17th-century woman, she is the exact female counterpart of Rodrigue. She could love only a man who would avenge his family's honour. Torn between love and duty, she will play the part of the worthy daughter; despite her body's weakness (fainting, crying), she embraces the same belief in heroism as Rodrigue.

The classification of *The Cid* as a 'tragi-comedy' is explained by the happy ending as by the healthy, vital forces at work. The optimism expressed in the appeal to the present and the future, as opposed to the past glory of old men, certainly contributes to the prodigious success of *The Cid*.

—Pierre J. Lapaire

THE THEATRICAL ILLUSION (L'Illusion comique)
Play by Pierre Corneille, 1635–36.

Corneille admitted that *The Theatrical Illusion* was a 'strange monster'. His previous comedies had shown characters from contemporary French life. *The Theatrical Illusion* is a disconcerting mixture of fantasy and reality, of caricature and realism.

Pridamant, in search of his long lost son, Clindor, consults a magician, Alcandre, who offers to conjure up visions of events in Clindor's life (Act I). Ensconced in the magician's cave, Pridamant sees his son serving as valet to the ridiculous braggart soldier, Matamore. Three men, Clindor, Matamore, and Adraste, are all suitors of Isabelle, but she prefers Clindor to the other two (Act II). Isabelle's servant, Lise, who is also in love with Clindor, out of jealousy arranges for Adraste to ambush Clindor, but in the scuffle Clindor kills Adraste (Act III). Sentenced to death for murder Clindor awaits execution in prison. Lise, however, repents of her plot and arranges his escape with the help of her lover, the jailer. At the end of Act IV the magician tells Pridamant that he will next see that his son has risen in the world. True enough, Act V shows Clindor richly dressed as the favourite of Prince Florilame, but, to Pridamant's horror and despair, he sees his son first unfaithful to Isabelle and then killed for seducing the Prince's wife. Then Alcandre discloses that this tragic incident is an illusion. Clindor and his friends have become actors and they are revealed behind a curtain counting the takings after the performance of the little tragedy just witnessed by Pridamant. Alcandre assures Pridamant that the theatre is an admired profession and the comedy ends as a celebration of the 'theatrical illusion'.

The play is a strange monster because, as Corneille himself pointed out, it defies classification by genre, and it also breaks many of the dramatic conventions of its period. The first act is a prologue. Acts II and IV seem to be a comedy by virtue of the status of the characters and the style of speech, but the tone verges on tragedy when Adraste is killed and Clindor is in danger of execution. Act V contains a miniature tragedy whose bloody ending is in fact an illusion. Unity of place is observed only in the sense that Alcandre and Pridamant are present throughout the action in the magician's cave in Touraine, but other elements of scenery show us in turn Géronte's house, Clindor's prison, Florilame's garden, and the stage of a Parisian theatre. The duration of the action is nominally that of its representation, so in theory observes the rule that the represented action should not exceed 24 hours. But at the same time there is a lapse of four days between Acts III and IV and two years pass between Acts IV and V. All this ambiguity is appropriate in a play whose French title, *L'Illusion comique*, contains a pun: 'comique' can mean 'comic' or 'theatrical'. So the comedy plays constantly with the concept of theatrical illusion.

The chief interest of the play lies not in the plot but in the self-conscious exploitation of theatrical conventions. This extends to the characters, especially Matamore, whose speech is grotesquely boastful, while his actions show that he is a coward. This is cleverly represented by reference both to the décor and to the duration of the action, further examples of Corneille's playful handling of theatrical illusion. No sooner has Géronte threatened Matamore that his valets will come out of his house to thrash him, than Géronte's door becomes a focus of Matamore's fear. As soon as he sees Géronte's door opening he flees, and later, on seeing Clindor and Isabelle emerge through the door, he mistakes them for the valets and is stricken with terror (Act III, scenes 3–4, 7–8). When Adraste attacks Clindor, Matamore flees into Géronte's house, where he remains concealed in the attic for four days between Acts III and IV. This long passage of time between the acts, technically an infringement of the unity of time, in fact generates comedy when Matamore reappears. He is taunted with being driven down by hunger and invents fantastic reasons to account for his long period of hiding. At the end of the scene he makes his final exit, again to escape the imaginary valets (Act IV, scene 4).

The framing scenes, in which Alcandre and Pridamant in the magician's cave watch events from Clindor's life, are an image of spectators watching a play in the theatre. Alcandre enjoins Pridamant not to step beyond the limits of the cave, yet the visions conjured up involve Pridamant's emotions to such an extent that finally the father interrupts the dialogue 'on stage', begging Alcandre to save his son from death. Then Alcandre dissipates the illusion by showing the actors counting their takings and explains that the characters whom Pridamant thought real were only actors. So the magician Alcandre, described as an emaciated centenarian with astonishing strength and agility, is offered by Corneille as a symbol of the paradoxical powers of the dramatist, who magically engages the emotions of the spectator in the illusion of reality. Composed at the very moment that French theorists were insisting on the need for drama to obey certain conventions in order to convey a plausible illusion of reality, Corneille's comedy ironically subverts these conventions while at the same time celebrating the indefinable and magical power of the theatre.

—David Maskell

CORREIA da Rocha, Adolfo. See **TORGA, Miguel**.

———

———

CORTÁZAR, Julio. Born in Brussels, Belgium, 26 August 1914. Family returned to Argentina, 1918. Educated at the Escuela Normal de Profesores Mariano Acosta (teachers college), Buenos Aires, degree as primary-level teacher, 1932, degree as secondary-level teacher, 1935; University of Buenos Aires, 1936–37. Married Aurora Bernárdez in 1953 (separated); lived with Carol Dunlop in later years. Taught in secondary schools in Bolívar, Chivilcoy, and Mendoza, 1937–44; professor of French literature, University of Cuyo, Mendoza, 1944–45, and imprisoned briefly for involvement in anti-Peronist demonstrations at the university, 1945; manager, Cámara Argentina del Libro [Publishing Association of Argentina], 1946–48; passed examinations in law and languages, and worked as translator, Buenos Aires, 1948–51; travelled to Paris on a scholarship, 1951, and settled there; writer and freelance translator for UNESCO, from 1952; visited Cuba, 1961, Argentina, Peru, Ecuador, and Chile, all 1973, Nicaragua and (after the lifting of a seven-year ban on his entry into the country) Argentina, 1983; visiting lecturer, University of Oklahoma, Norman, 1975, and Gildersleeve lecturer, Barnard College, New York, 1980; acquired French citizenship (in addition to existing Argentinian citizenship), 1981. Member, Second Russell Tribunal for investigation of human rights abuses in Latin America, 1975. Recipient: Médicis prize (France), 1974; Great Golden Eagle (Nice), 1976; Rubén Darío Order of Cultural Independence (Nicaragua), 1983. *Died 12 February 1984.*

PUBLICATIONS

Fiction

Bestiario (stories). 1951; title story as 'Bestiary', translated by J.M. Cohen, in *Latin American Writing Today*, edited by Cohen, 1967.
Final del juego (stories). 1956; enlarged edition, 1964.
Las armas secretas (stories). 1959.
Los premios. 1960; as *The Winners*, translated by Elaine Kerrigan, 1965.
Historias de cronopios y de famas (stories). 1962; as *Cronopios and Famas*, translated by Paul Blackburn, 1969.
Rayuela. 1963; edited by Julio Ortega and Saúl Yurkievich, 1991; as *Hopscotch*, translated by Gregory Rabassa, 1966.

Cuentos, edited by Anton Arrufat. 1964.
Todos los fuegos el fuego (stories). 1966; as *All Fires the Fire and Other Stories*, translated by Suzanne Jill Levine, 1973.
End of the Game and Other Stories, translated by Paul Blackburn. 1967; as *Blow-Up and Other Stories*, translated by Blackburn, 1968.
El perseguidor y otros cuentos. 1967; edited by Alberto Couste, 1979.
62: Modelo para armar. 1968; as *62: A Model Kit*, translated by Gregory Rabassa, 1972.
Ceremonias (includes *Final del juego* and *Las armas secretas*). 1968.
Casa tomada. 1969.
Relatos (selection). 1970.
La isla a mediodia y otros relatos. 1971.
Libro de Manuel. 1973; as *A Manual for Manuel*, translated by Gregory Rabassa, 1978.
Octaedro (stories). 1974; parts translated in *A Change of Light and Other Stories*, 1980.
Los relatos. 3 vols., 1976.
Alguien que anda por ahí y otros relatos. 1977; parts translated in *A Change of Light and Other Stories*, 1980.
Un tal Lucas. 1979; as *A Certain Lucas*, translated by Gregory Rabassa, 1984.
A Change of Light and Other Stories, translated by Gregory Rabassa. 1980.
Queremos tanto a Glenda. 1981; as *We Love Glenda So Much and Other Tales*, translated by Gregory Rabassa, 1983.
Deshoras (stories). 1983.
El examen. 1986.
Divertimento. 1986.

Verse

Presencia (as Julio Denis). 1938.
Pameos y meopas. 1971.
Poemas, meopas y prosemas. 1984.
Salvo el crepúsculo. 1984.

Plays

Los reyes. 1949.
Nada a Pehuajó, y Adiós, Robinson. 1984.

Other

Fantomas contra los vampiros internacionales. 1965.
La vuelta al día en ochenta mundos (essays). 1967; as *Around the Day in Eighty Worlds*, translated by Thomas Christensen, 1986.
Buenos Aires, Buenos Aires, photographs by Alicia d'Amico and Sara Facio (includes English translation). 1968.
Último round. 1969.
La literatura en la revolución y revolución en la literatura, with Oscar Collazos and Mario Vargas Llosa. 1970.
Viaje alrededor de una mesa. 1970.
Prosa del observatorio, photographs by Cortázar, with Antonio Galvez. 1972.
La casilla de los Morelli y otros textos (miscellany), edited by Julio Ortega. 1973.
Antología, edited by Nicolás Bratosevich. 1975.
Silvalandia (on the paintings of Julio Silva). 1975.
Estrictamente no profesional: Humanario (on the photographs of Alicia D'Amico and Sara Facio). 1976.
Territorios (miscellany). 1978.

Conversaciones con Cortázar, with Ernesto González Bermejo. 1978; as *Revelaciones de un cronopio: Conversaciones con Cortázar*, 1986.

Monsieur Lautrec, with Hermenegildo Sabat. 1980.

Un elogio del tres (on the paintings of Luis Tomasello). 1980.

París: Ritmos de una ciudad, photographs by Alecio de Andrade. 1981; as *Paris: The Essence of an Image*, translated by Gregory Rabassa, 1981.

Los autonautas de la cosmopista; o, Un viaje atemporal París–Marsella, with Carol Dunlop. 1983.

Cuaderno de bitácora de Rayuela, with Ana María Barrenechea. 1983.

El edad presente es de lucha/The Present Age Is One of Struggle, with Sergio Ramírez Mercado. 1983.

Nicaragua, tan violentamente dulce. 1983; as *Nicaraguan Sketches*, translated by K. Weaver, 1989.

Negro el diez (on the lithographs of Luis Tomasello). 1983.

Argentina: Años de alambradas culturales, edited by Saúl Yurkievich. 1984.

Alto el Perú (on the photographs of Manja Offerhaus). 1984.

La fascinación de las palabras: Conversaciones con Julio Cortázar, with Omar Prego. 1985.

Cortázar: Iconografía, edited by Alba C. de Rojo and Felipe Garrido. 1985.

Policrítica en la hora de los chacales. 1987.

Voicing, with others, edited by Don Wellman, translated by Cola Franzen and others. 1989.

Cartas a una pelirroja, edited by Evelyn Picon Garfield. 1990.

Translator, *Robinson Crusoe*, by Daniel Defoe. 1945.

Translator, *El hombre que sabía demasiado*, by G.K. Chesterton. 1946.

Translator, *Nacimiento de la Odisea*, by Jean Giono. 1946.

Translator, *La poesía pura* by Henri Brémond. 1947.

Translator, *El inmoralista*, by André Gide. 1947.

Translator, *Filosofía de la risa y el llanto*, by Alfred Stern. 1950.

Translator, *Mujercitas*, by Louisa May Alcott. 1951.

Translator, *Tom Brown en la escuela*, by Thomas Hughes. 1951.

Translator, *La filosofía existencial de Jean-Paul Sartre*, by Alfred Stern. 1951.

Translator, *La víbora*, by Marcel Aymé. 1952.

Translator, *La vida de los otros*, by Ladislas Dormandi. 1952.

Translator, *Así sea; o, La suerte está echada*, by André Gide. 1953.

Translator, *Vida y cartas de John Keats*, by Lord Houghton. 1955.

Translator, *Memorias de Adriano*, by Marguerite Yourcenar. 1955.

Translator, *Obras en prosa*, by Edgar Allan Poe. 1956.

Translator, *Cuentos*, by Edgar Allan Poe. 1963.

Translator, *Eureka*, by Edgar Allan Poe. 1972.

Translator, *Ensayos y críticos*, by Edgar Allan Poe. 1973.

Translator, *Memorias de una enana*, by Walter de la Mare. N.d.

*

Bibliography: 'Bibliografía de y sobre Julio Cortázar' by Marta Paley de Francescato, in *Revista Iberoamericana de Literatura*, 39(84–85), 1973; *Julio Cortázar: His Works and His Critics: A Bibliography* by Sara de Mundo Lo, 1985.

Critical Studies: *Moyano, Benedetto, Cortázar* by Eugenio Castelli, 1968; *Cortázar: Una antropología poética* by Néstor García Canclini, 1968; *Cinco miradas sobre Cortázar* edited by Ana María Simo, 1968; *Julio Cortázar y el hombre nuevo* by Graciela de Sola, 1968; *La vuelta a Cortázar en nueve ensayos*, various authors, 1968; *Sobre Cortázar* by José Amícola, 1969; *Julio Cortázar: El escritor y sus máscaras* by Mercedes Rein, 1969; *Julio Cortázar: Visión de conjunto* by Roberto Escamilla Molina, 1970; *De Sarmiento a Cortázar* by David Viñas, 1970; *El individuo y el otro: Crítica a los cuentos de Julio Cortázar* by Alfred J. MacAdam, 1971; *Cortázar: La novela moderna* by Lida Aronne Amestoy, 1972; *Julio Cortázar; o, La crítica de la razón pragmática* by Juan Carlos Curutchet, 1972; *Homenaje a Julio Cortázar* edited by Helmy F. Giacoman, 1972; *Seven Voices* by Rita Guibert, 1973; *Julio Cortázar: Una búsqueda mítica* by Saúl Sosnowski, 1973; *Julio Cortázar ante su sociedad* by Joaquín Roy, 1974; *¿Es Julio Cortázar un surrealista?*, 1975, *Julio Cortázar* (in English), 1975, and *Cortázar por Cortázar*, 1978, all by Evelyn Picon Garfield; *Estudios sobre los cuentos de Julio Cortázar* edited by David Lagmanovich, 1975; *Currents in the Contemporary Argentine Novel: Arlt, Mallea, Sábato and Cortázar* by William David Foster, 1975; Cortázar issue of *Books Abroad*, 50(3), 1976; *Julio Cortázar: Rayuela* by Robert Brody, 1976; *The Final Island: The Fiction of Cortázar* (includes bibliography) edited by Ivar Ivask and Jaime Alazraki, 1978, and *En busca del unicornio: Los cuentos de Julio Cortázar* by Alazraki, 1983; *The Novels of Cortázar* by Steven Boldy, 1980; *Keats, Poe, and the Shaping of Cortázar's Mythopoesis* by Ana Hernández del Castillo, 1981; *Julio Cortázar* edited by Pedro Lastra, 1981; Cortázar issue of *Casa de las Américas*, 25(145–146), 1984; *Julio Cortázar: Life, Work, and Criticism* by E.D. Carter, Jr, 1986; *Lo lúdico y lo fantástico: Coloquio*, edited by Keith Cohen, 2 vols., 1986; *Los ochenta mundos de Cortázar: Ensayos* edited by Fernando Burgos, 1987; *Otro Round: Ensayos sobre la obra de Julio Cortázar* edited by E. Dale Carter, 1988; *The Politics of Style in the Fiction of Balzac, Beckett, and Cortázar* by M.R. Axelrod, 1991.

*   *   *

Julio Cortázar is one of the most widely recognized Spanish American writers outside the Spanish-speaking world, due particularly to the critical acclaim of *Rayuela* (*Hopscotch*), a novel where the most experimental narrative innovations find an original form, and to the filming by Michelangelo Antonioni of one of his best short stories, 'Blow-Up'.

Cortázar's narrative is unclassifiable. His fiction breaks away from the habitual categories of narrative and all conventional forms, and blurs the uncertain boundaries between reality and the fantastic. The realistic and social milieu of his stories (be it Buenos Aires or Paris) is continuously compromised by elements of the absurd, the mythic, and the oneiric, by surrealist undercurrents where artistic freedom and imaginative possibilities disturb all routine representations of reality. Cortázar searches for an opening toward the other side of reality, toward—in his own words—'a more secret and less communicable order'.

Cortázar's experimentation with the techniques of narrative can best be exemplified with *Hopscotch*, his masterpiece. The novel is written in loose fragments—the collage is the basic associative procedure—sequences of a totality that the reader is forced to recompose. The search for harmony and authenticity is the guiding motif of the novel; the search for the 'key', 'the other side', 'the centre', 'the heaven of the hopscotch', 'the love-passport', 'the wishful kibbutz', illustrate Cortázar's attempts to apprehend an absolute order, a 'sacred space' or mandala (a mystical labyrinth used by the Buddhists as a spiritual exercise), where integration and ultimate harmony can be attained. This ontological search for unity is one of the distinctive aspects of Cortázar's narrative. In his fiction it is common to find a character embarked on the search for a secret order, pursuing something undefinable to bring him inner harmony. Some characters intuitively explore the mysteries of the self (Johnny Carter, the jazz musician of 'The Pursuer'), others chase truth and self-knowledge—Medrano in *Los premios* (*The Winners*), but most attempt failed intellectual projections into a world of their dreams—Oliveira in *Hopscotch*, Juan in *62: Modelo para armar* (*62: A Model Kit*), Andrés in *Libro de Manuel* (*A Manual for Manuel*). Fascinated by the unreachable absolute, all of Cortázar's major characters seek to jump into authenticity, rebel against a civilization governed by reason.

Hopscotch is a questioning of the art of story-telling, as well as a questioning of reality and all rational knowledge, an attempt to break away from all routine narrative formulas. The disintegration of the traditional novel begins with 'The Table of Instructions', where Cortázar suggests at least two ways of reading the novel and the reader is invited to select between expendable and unexpendable chapters. The complex point of view, movable chapters, montage, *dédoublement*, dissociation of personality, simultaneity of creation and theoretical reflection within the novel, and, above all, the destruction of inherited language and syntax, the search for a new syntax to reunite unreconcilable languages, are the predominant features of Cortázar's writing. The constant questioning of the capability of language to represent reality can best be seen by quoting the opening paragraph of 'Blow-Up': 'It'll never be known how this has to be told, in the first person or in the second, using the first person plural or continually inventing modes that will serve for nothing. If one might say: I will see the moon rose, or: we hurt me at the back of my eyes, and especially: you the blonde woman was the clouds that race before my your his our yours their faces. What the hell'.

These two aspects of Cortázar's narrative—innovation of language and form, and the metaphysical search—reveal his talent as a story-teller of universal appeal.

—Hugo J. Verani

COUPERUS, Louis Marie Anne. Born in The Hague, The Netherlands, 10 June 1863. Spent part of his youth on Java. Failed his school exams, 1886. Married his niece Elizabeth Baud in 1891. After 1891 spent most of his life in the south of France and in Italy; travelled to Indonesia, 1899. Worked for the magazine *Nederlandsch Spectator*; also wrote for The Hague newspaper *Het Vaderland*. *Died 16 July 1923.*

PUBLICATIONS

Collections

Verzamelde werken [Collected Works]. 12 vols., 1952–57.
Nagelaten werk. 1976.

Fiction

Eline Vere. 1889; as *Eline Vere*, translated by J.T. Grein, 1892.
Noodlot. 1890; as *Footsteps of Fate*, translated by Clara Bell, 1891.
Extase. 1892; as *Ecstasy*, translated by Alexander Teixeira de Mattos and John Gray, 1892.
Eene illuzie [An Illusion]. 1892.
Majesteit. 1893; as *Majesty*, translated by Alexander Teixeira de Mattos and Ernest Dowson, 1894.
Wereldvrede [World Peace]. 1895, reprinted 1991.
Willeswinde [Wind of Will]. 1895.
Hooge troeven [High Stakes]. 1896.
Metamorfoze. 1897.
Psyche. 1897; as *Psyche*, translated by B.S. Berrington, 1908.
Fidessa. 1899.
Langs lijnen van geleidelijkheid. 1900; as *The Law Inevitable*, translated by Alexander Teixeira de Mattos, 1921.
De stille kracht. 1900; as *The Hidden Force*, translated by Alexander Teixeira de Mattos, 1922, revised and edited by E.M. Beekman, 1985.
Babel. 1901; as *Babel*, translated by A.A. Betham, n.d.
De boeken der kleine zielen. 4 vols., 1901–04; as *The Book of the Small Souls*, translated by Alexander Teixeira de Mattos, 4 vols., 1914–18.
Over lichtende drempels. 1902.
Van oude menschen, de dingen die voorbijgaan. 2 vols., 1902; as *Old People and the Things That Pass*, translated by Alexander Teixeira de Mattos, 1918.
God en goden [God and Gods]. 1903.
Dionyzos. 1904.
De berg van licht [The Mountain of Light]. 3 vols., 1905–06.
Aan den weg der vreugde [Along the Road of Joy]. 1908.
Van en over mijzelf en anderen [Of and About Myself and Others]. 4 vols., 1910–17.
Korte arabesken (stories). 1911; selection as *Eighteen Tales*, translated by J. Kooistra, 1924.
Antiek toerisme. 1911; as *The Tour*, translated by Alexander Teixeira de Mattos, 1920.
Antieke verhalen [Antique Stories]. 1911.
Herakles. 2 vols., 1913.
Van en over alles en iedereen [Of and About Everything and Everyone]. 5 vols., 1915.
De ongelukkige [The Unfortunate One]. 1915.
De komedianten. 1917; as *The Comedians, a Story of Ancient Rome*, translated by J. Menzies-Wilson, 1926.
De ode. 1918.
Legende, mythe en fantazie. 1918.
De verliefde ezel [The Enamoured Ass]. 1918.
Xerxes of de hoogmoed. 1919; as *Arrogance, the Conquests of Xerxes*, translated by Frederick H. Martens, 1930.
Lucrezia. 1920.
Iskander. 1920.
Het zwevend schaakbord [The Hovering Chessboard]. 1922.
Het snoer der ontferming en Japansche legenden [The String of Mercy and Japanese Legends]. 1924.
Via appia. 1972.
De zwaluwen neer gestreken [The Alighted Swallows]. 1974.
Endymion. 1976.

Verse

Een Lent van vaerzen [A Lent of Verses]. 1884.
Orchideën. 1886; selection in *Flowers from a Foreign Garden*, translated by A.L. Snell, 1902.

Other

Schimmen van schoonheid [Phantoms of Beauty] (sketches). 1912.
Uit blanke steden onder blauwe lucht [From White Cities under Blue Skies] (sketches and impressions). 2 vols., 1912–13.
Brieven van een nutteloozen toeschouwer [Letters of a Useless Spectator] (anti-war polemic). 1918.
Met L. Couperus in Afrika (journalism). 1921.
Oostwaarts. 1924; as *Eastward*, translated by J. Menzies-Wilson and C.C. Crispin, 1924.
Nippon. 1925; as *Nippon*, translated by J. de la Vallette, 1926.
Kindersouvenirs [Childhood Memories]. 1978.
Epigrammen. 1982.

Translator, *Verzoeking van den Heiligen Antonius*, by Flaubert. 1896, reprinted 1992.

*

Critical Studies: *Leven en werken van Louis Couperus* by Henri van Booven, 1933; *Verhaal en lezer* by W. Block, 1960; *Couperus in de kritiek* by M. Galle, 1963; *Louis Couperus: Een verkenning* by H.W. van Tricht, 1965; *Beschouwingen over het werk van Louis Couperus* by K.J. Popma, 1968; *De antieke wereld van Louis Couperus* by T. Bogaerts, 1969; *Couperus, grieken en barbaren* by E. Visser, 1969; *De man met de orchidee. Het levensverhaal van Louis Couperus* by Albert Vogel, 1973, 2nd revised edition, 1980; *Een zuil in de mist. Van en over Louis Couperus* by F.L. Bastet, 1980.

* * *

A novelist of international stature, Louis Couperus belonged to two late 19th-century literary traditions of naturalist and decadent prose. He was born in The Hague in 1863 into a formal, conventional, and aristocratic milieu where colonial administration was one of the traditional professions. Consequently, the family of the young Couperus spent six years in the Dutch colony of Indonesia, returning to the Netherlands in 1877.

As an aspiring literary figure, he did not immediately find his natural form. In 1884 he published a none-too-successful collection of poems, *Een Lent van vaerzen* [A Lent of Verses], and in 1886 a second collection, *Orchideeën* [Orchids]. The tepid reaction to these poetry collections encouraged him to concentrate on prose. Nevertheless, in the eyes of many critics, his persistent love for poetic, 'beautiful' language and extended ornate description was to mar a number of his novels.

However, when *Eline Vere*, his first novel, appeared in 1889, Couperus was an immediate success. In 1888, when the novel was serialized in the newspaper *Het Vaderland*, it coincided with the appearance of two other naturalist novels: *Een liefde* by Lodewijk van Deyssel and *Juffrouw Lina* by Marcellus Emants. Dutch naturalism differed from the scientific-minded French naturalism in several respects. The works tend to focus on middle-class milieux, and the main characters are anti-heroes, frequently over-sensitive, over-civilized men and women reacting against the smug calm of the surrounding prosaic, bourgeois society. There is frequently an investigation of taboo subjects like homosexuality or self-gratification. The text aims at objective representation of the characters, and combines colloquial dialogue with *woordkunst* ('artistic writing'), highly descriptive, evocative passages full of adjectives and neologisms.

In the novel *Eline Vere*, a victim of her class and her gender, can find no escape for her pent-up energy. Too finely tuned for her own good and consequently misunderstood, she takes an overdose as the result of an unhappy love affair. Unlike other Dutch naturalists, Couperus stressed the laws of deterministic inheritance: Eline Vere has inherited her character from her father, while her cousin Vincent suffers from a similar clash between his personality and his environment.

In a logical step, Couperus's next novel was entitled *Noodlot* (*Footsteps of Fate*), associating family hereditary factors with a fate the three main characters cannot escape. Meijers suggests that *Footsteps of Fate* and the next novel *Extase* (*Ecstasy*) partially attempt to work through Couperus's homosexuality by transferring it onto a sublimated desire for heterosexual love.

Couperus's generally recognized masterpiece is a novel written during a year-long return to the Dutch East Indies, and once again deals with the disintegration of character and the notion of fate. In *De stille kracht* (*The Hidden Force*), the senior colonial administrator Van Oudijck is undermined by his wife's infidelities, which weakens his resistance to the pervasive atmosphere of Indonesian magic, 'goena goena'. The rational Dutch colonials one by one become completely submerged in the alien culture they are trying to control and suppress. As Dutch pianos and furniture disintegrate because of the heat, humidity, and termites, their mental and physical health is drained by the atmosphere. In fact there is a suggestion that it is their own moral corruption that allows the silent forces of magic to take hold of their minds.

Back in the bourgeois atmosphere of The Hague, the four novels that make up *De boeken der kleine zielen* (*The Book of the Small Souls*) present another Dutch family slowly falling apart under outside strain, with the addition of typically *fin-de-siècle* mystical elements.

Van oude menschen, de dingen die voorbijgaan (*Old People and the Things That Pass*) is sometimes likened to a psychological detective novel, as the reader slowly learns how the old people, a 94-year-old man and a 97-year-old woman, murdered the woman's husband 60 years earlier, with the guilty knowledge of the family doctor. In what is generally regarded as one of his best novels, Couperus slowly peels away this family secret that is affecting the younger generations.

Less well-liked are the novels where Couperus shows a clearer connection with European decadent writers like Baudelaire, de Maupassant, and Wilde. A number of long novels are situated in antiquity or Eastern history, like *De berg van licht* [The Mountain of Light], about the Roman child-emperor Heliogabalus, *Herakles* [Hercules], and *Xerxes*. Above all, *Iskander* depicts Alexander the Great's conquest of the Persian empire, with prolonged evocations of the exotic Persian court. These novels are frequently faulted by critics for an overindulgence in long descriptions of luxurious, decadent palaces, sounds, smells, and wines. Frequently, a certain shying away from the homoerotic subtext is also partly the cause for the unpopularity of these novels. However, while these novels are hard-going at times, their opulence and excess can be regarded more positively. By means of their very textual excesses Couperus was in fact able to evoke the exotic, alien quality of long-gone cultures and lifestyles, thus along with his other works, contributing to his highly original and enduring position in Dutch literature.

—Sabine Vanacker

————————

CRUZ, Sor Juana Inés de la. See **JUANA INÉS DE LA CRUZ, Sor**.

————————

CYRANO DE BERGERAC, Savinien. Born in Paris, France in 1619. Educated at Collège de Beauvais, Paris, 1632–37; Collège de Lisieux, Paris, 1641. Enlisted with M. de Carbon de Casteljoux's Company of Guards; soldier and duellist; retired from military career, wounded, 1640. Renowned for his grotesque appearance and long nose and as the subject of Edmond Rostand's play. *Died in July 1655.*

PUBLICATIONS

Collections

Les Oeuvres libertines de Cyrano de Bergerac parisien, edited by Frédéric Lachèvre. 2 vols., 1921.
Oeuvres, edited by Georges Ribermont-Dessaignes. 1957.
Oeuvres complètes, edited by Jacques Prévot. 1977.

Fiction

Voyage dans la lune (part one), edited by Le Bret. 1657; *L'Histoire des états et empires du soleil* (part two; unfinished), 1662; complete version as *L'Autre Monde; ou, Les États et empires de la lune*, 1920; edited by H. Weber, 1959; also edited by Jacques Prévot, 1977; Madeleine Alcover, 1977; as *Voyages to the Moon and the Sun*, translated by Richard Aldington, 1923; as *Other Worlds: The Comical History of the States and the Empires of the Moon and the Sun*, translated by Geoffrey Strachan, 1965.

Plays

La Mort d'Agrippine. 1654.
Le Pédant joué. 1654.

Other

Lettres. 1654; as *Satyrical Characters and Handsome Descriptions in Letters*, translated anonymously, 1658, reprinted 1914.

*

Critical Studies: *Cyrano de Bergerac* by G. Mongrédien, 1964; *Cyrano de Bergerac and the Universe of the Imagination* by Edward W. Lanius, 1967; *La Pensée philosophique et scientifique de Cyrano de Bergerac*, 1970, and *Cyrano relu et corrigé: Lettres, Estats du soleil, Fragment de physique*, 1990, both by Madeleine Alcover; *Cyrano de Bergerac and the Polemics of Modernity* by E. Harth, 1970; *Cyrano de Bergerac romancier*, 1977, and *Cyrano de Bergerac: Poète et dramaturge*, 1978, both by Jacques Prévot; *Cyrano de Bergerac, L'Autre Monde* by Haydn Mason, 1984; *Cyrano de Bergerac: L'Esprit de révolte* by Willy de Spens, 1989.

* * *

The name Savinien Cyrano de Bergerac seems, with its 'de', to suggest aristocratic rank, while 'Bergerac' might point to Gascon origins which would be some warrant for military swagger and a tendency towards boastful vanity. The sober truth is that Cyrano's origins were Parisian and bourgeois. Born in 1619, he was in fact the son of a successful lawyer, practising at the *parlement de Paris*, whose programme for social aggrandizement took the orthodox form of purchasing a modest estate not far from the capital. Even though the property at Bergerac was to be sold after a few years, Cyrano had no scruples about flaunting its name for the rest of his life. He received, most probably at the Collège de Beauvais in Paris, an education that was largely classical in orientation, and then, inspired perhaps in part by a desire to enhance his social status, he joined Carbon de Casteljoux's Company of Guards. Its members were all supposed to be of noble birth and to come from Gascony, so there must have been either some flexibility or some hiding of the truth when it came to Cyrano's entry. What he may have lacked in hereditary qualifications, however, he made up for by his conduct. He participated in many duels, fighting, it is said, not as a principal but as a 'second', for at the time it was customary for them to join in to defend their friend's honour and not just stand by and ensure fair play. He was also wounded twice, at the siege of Mouzon in 1639 and the siege of Arras a year later. With his health undermined, he decided to return to civilian life.

The basis of the often repeated story that Cyrano then went back to college, and possibly even became a junior teacher at the Collège de Lisieux in Paris, is dubious, as is that for the statement that he was taught by the Epicurean philosopher Pierre Gassendi (1592–1655). What is clear, however, is that Cyrano had a wild life and became associated with a number of notorious free thinkers, among them Tristan l'Hermite. It was not long before he began to write, but without the regular support of a patron he had difficulty making a living, and after his father's death he soon squandered his inheritance. He was seriously injured by a falling beam in 1654 and died, reconciled to the Catholic church, a year later. Contemporary portraits show that he indeed had a very prominent, remarkably shaped nose.

Like many other writers in France in the 17th century, Cyrano tried his hand at a number of genres, and it could well be that at least some of his writing was influenced by a desire to win the favour of a patron. This is particularly true of his contributions to political controversy at the time of the Fronde rebellions, unless we accept the more implausible hypothesis that his attitudes towards Cardinal Mazarin's policies underwent a rapid and radical change. Cyrano's *Lettres* are not letters in the everyday sense, but rather what the humanists called 'themes', that is to say, exercises in the literary development of a variety of topics. In 1645 Cyrano tried his hand at comedy. *Le Pédant joué*, in prose, makes fun of Jean Grangier, principal of the Collège de Beauvais when Cyrano was there. Though not without merit, the play was apparently never performed, and it is best known in literary history because Molière, never over-fussy about borrowing other people's good ideas, turned to it for a key scene in *Les Fourberies de Scapin* (*The Rogueries of Scapin*) a quarter of a century later. *La Mort d'Agrippine* [Agrippina's Death] is a classical verse tragedy about a conspiracy against Tiberius; it was published in 1654, after causing a sensation when performed in Paris at the Hôtel de Bourgogne because of the outrageous sentiments it expressed.

Cyrano's most famous works are, however, his two fantastic satires, *Voyage dans la lune* and *L'Histoire des états et empires du soleil* (translated together as *Voyages to the Moon and the Sun*). With their blend of apparently realistic detail and free speculation about controversial issues, these stand in the tradition of Renaissance utopian writing, as exemplified by Thomas More, Tommaso Campanella, and Francis Godwin, whose *Man in the Moon* was published posthumously in England in 1638 and translated into French within a decade. Cyrano's astronomical romances show eclectic erudition, general irreverence, and great verve in burlesque.

—Christopher Smith

VOYAGES TO THE MOON AND THE SUN (Voyage dans la lune and L'Histoire des états et empires du soleil) Novels by Cyrano de Bergerac, 1657–62.

The *Voyages* are made up of two completely separate works. In the first, the fictional Cyrano lands on the moon, more by luck than judgement, and encounters a manifestly better world, where his own precise identity causes puzzlement: is he a man? There is widespread scepticism about his claim to humanity (for a while he is thought to be a featherless parrot, to be kept in a cage) but eventually he is given the benefit of the doubt and released. Cyrano goes on to discover an advanced state of technology, including prefigurations of mobile homes, electric light, and record-players. On the moon we find philosophers who argue the infinity of the universe in time and space. Cyrano's profession of Christian faith is ridiculed: miracles are the consequence of ignorance, resurrection is a foolish myth, God does not exist. But our hero returns to the earth quite unaffected by these arguments, still foolishly defending divine Providence as though he had learned nothing from his trip through space.

The *Sun* continues Cyrano's imaginary career. He is now an outcast and put in jail but manages to build a machine that allows him to escape skyward. The sun turns out to contain a land of brilliant, weightless luminosity. In magical landscapes, trees turn into little men who then collectively form one perfect young man. There is a bird-heaven, where Cyrano is again arrested, this time as a member of the cruel human race that arrogates to itself total dominion to destroy at will the animal and plant worlds. He is himself condemned to a lingering death by stings and bites, but fortunately the birds accept a plea of mercy and let him go. He comes upon the Talking Trees, which possess both speech and reason, and finally the philosopher Campanella, who has telepathic powers and takes him to the superior province of philosophers, where Cyrano meets Descartes. The *Sun*, unfinished, stops at this point.

Cyrano's obvious claim to fame as a narrator lies in the brilliance of his imagination. But this virtuosity is not simply gratuitous. It relates to the author's joy in acquiring knowledge and thereby penetrating a world of infinitely rich possibilities. But to achieve this, independent critical enquiry is essential; religious authority and the Scriptures must be called into question. The *Voyages* are studded with sceptical comments: on the Flood, on the Tree of Knowledge and the serpent in the Garden of Eden, and on miracles generally. The human propensity for believing in supernatural marvels springs from mental laziness but also from man's arrogance in thinking that he has been accorded a special place in Creation. By contrast, Cyrano conveyed the sense of a limitless cosmos, where the earth revolves around the sun (a bold endorsement in the middle of the 17th century of the Copernican theory) and mankind occupies a merely contingent position. There is no place here for the notion of a benevolent, omniscient Christian God creating the world. Matter contains an inherent dynamism. Our belief in our pre-eminence and in our immortal soul is based on self-delusion. Indeed, it is not at all clear *what* man is. The human race has degenerated since the ancient Greeks; men have even sunk below the animals.

Only if human beings recover a proper sense of humility can the race exploit the full potential, as yet barely suspected, of our enigmatic universe. Superior beings like Socrates' demon live on the moon in a community of intellectual equality and independent reasoning. On the sun one can find an even more marvellous way of life, where people speak the perfect language of nature, and philosophers, even better, have no need of speech at all to communicate their transparently open thoughts. Learning at the highest level links up with pure moral integrity. All this is set in a world of infinite plasticity, where a great force blindly pulsates, endlessly renewing nature. This universe with its endless plurality of worlds liberates the mind, teaching us to reject all forms of dogmatism. There are no certain answers; man must depend upon his imagination and capacity for knowledge.

These are the attitudes that prevail. But Cyrano does not present them in a simply didactic form. The use of philosophical dialogue, particularly in the *Moon*, precludes a definitive view. Cyrano is himself an unreliable narrator, as his final remarks about God's providence in the *Moon* make clear. But no single character is to be trusted implicitly; even the most noble, like Socrates' demon, reveal their limitations. The mode throughout both *Voyages* is ironic. Sometimes, sun and moon are direct reversals of the earth. Lunar creatures walk on all fours and are foolishly proud of it as human beings are of their bipedalism; the solar birds assume their immortality with as little justification as the natives of Earth. The simple antithesis of cherished assumptions is an effective means of deflating human pomposity.

But Cyrano is not just an ironic satirist. Mankind may disappoint or appal; the world remains none the less a source of wonderful inspiration. The author can see in the phenomenon of magnetism not just a physical interaction but a passion and animism that relate it to human love. Above all, the dream of flight pervades these works. In the *Moon*, initial terror at being airborne gives way to 'an uncommon joy'. In the *Sun*, the four months' flight are passed exempt from all cold, hunger, melancholy, in an archetypal fantasy of freedom. Reason and dream interpenetrate in the *Voyages* to give them their unique flavour.

—Haydn Mason

D

LOS DADOS ETERNOS. See PÉREZ GALDÓS, Benito.

D'ANNUNZIO, Gabriele. Born in Pescara, Italy, 12 March 1863. Educated at a secondary school, Prato, 1874–81; University of Rome, 1881. Served in the Italian infantry, navy, and air force during World War I: injury led to loss of sight in one eye. Married Duchess Maria Hardouin di Gallese in 1883, three children; had romance with the actress Eleonora Duse, 1894–1904. Staff member, *Tribuna*, Rome, in the 1880s; elected to Chamber of Deputies, 1897–1900 (defeated 1900); lived in Tuscany, 1899–1910; forced by debts to live in France, 1910–15; after the Treaty of Versailles, seized Fiume with other patriots and held the city, 1919–20; supported the Fascists: granted a title by Mussolini; spent last years at his home, the Vittoriale, on Lake Garda. *Died 1 March 1938.*

PUBLICATIONS

Collections

Tutte le opere, edited by Egidio Bianchetti. 10 vols., 1939–50.
Poesie; Teatro; Prose, edited by Mario Praz. 1966.
Poesie, edited by Federico Roncoroni. 1978.
Carteggio D'Annunzio–Ojetti (1894–1937), edited by Cosimo Ceccuti. 1979.
Prose, edited by Federico Roncoroni. 1983.

Verse

Primo vere. 1879; revised edition, 1880.
Canto novo. 1882.
Intermezzo di rime. 1883.
San Pantaleone. 1886.
Isaotta Guttadàuro ed altre poesie. 1886; revised edition, as *L'Isottèo, La Chimera*, 1890.
Elegie romane 1887–1891. 1892.
Odi navali. 1893.
L'allegoria dell' autunno. 1895.
La canzone di Garibaldi. 1901.
Laudi del cielo, del mare, della terra, e degli eroi: Anno 1903–Maia; Anno 1904–Elettra, Alcyone; Libro IV–Merope. 3 vols., 1903–12; *Alcyone* as *Halcyon*, translated by J.G. Nichols, 1988.
L'orazione e la canzone in morte di Giosuè Carducci. 1907.
Canto novo. 1907.
Le città del silenzio. 1926.
Versi d'amore e di gloria, edited by Annamaria Andreoli and Niva Lorenzini. 2 vols., 1982–84.

Plays

Sogno d'un mattino di primavera (produced 1897). 1897; as *The Dream of a Spring Morning*, translated by Anna Colby Schenck, 1911.
La città morta (as *La Ville morte*, produced 1898). 1898; as *The Dead City*, translated by Arthur Symons, 1900; also translated by Gaetano Mantellani, 1902.
La Gioconda (produced 1899). 1898; as *Gioconda*, translated by Arthur Symons, 1902.
Sogno di un tramonto d'autunno (produced 1905). 1898; as *The Dream of an Autumn Sunset*, translated by Anna Colby Schenck, 1903.
La gloria (produced 1899). 1899.
Francesca da Rimini (produced 1901). 1901; revised version, music by Riccardo Zandonai (produced 1914), 1914; as *Francesca da Rimini*, translated by Arthur Symons, 1902.
La figlia di Iorio (produced 1904). 1904; revised version, music by Alberto Franchetti (produced 1906), 1906; as *The Daughter of Jorio*, translated by C. Porter, and others. 1907.
La fiaccola sotto il moggio (produced 1905). 1905.
Più che l'amore (produced 1906). 1907.
La nave (produced 1908). 1908; as *La Nave*, translated and adapted by R.H. Elkin, 1919.
Fedra (produced 1909). 1909.
Le Martyre de Saint Sébastien, music by Debussy (produced 1911). 1911.
Il ferro (produced as *Le Chèvrefeuille*, 1913; revised version, as *Il ferro*, produced 1914). 1914; as *The Honeysuckle*, translated by Cecile Sartoris and G. Enthoven, 1911.
La Pisanelle (produced 1913). In *Tutte le opere*, 1935.
La Parisina, music by Mascagni (produced 1913). 1913.
Cabiria. 1914.

Screenplay: *La crociata degli innocenti*, 1911.

Fiction

Terra vergine (stories). 1882.
Il libro delle vergini. 1884.
Il piacere. 1889; as *The Child of Pleasure*, translated by Georgina Harding, 1898.
L'innocente. 1892; as *The Intruder*, translated by Arthur Hornblow, 1898; as *The Victim*, translated by Georgina Harding, 1899, reprinted 1991.
Giovanni Episcopo. 1892; as *Episcopo and Company*, translated by Myrta Leonora Jones, 1896.
Il trionfo della morte. 1894; as *The Triumph of Death*, translated by Georgina Harding, 1896.
Le vergini delle rocce. 1896; as *The Maidens of the Rocks*, translated by Annette Halliday-Antona and Giuseppe Antona, 1898; as *The Virgins of the Rocks*, translated by A. Hughes, 1899.
Il fuoco. 1900; as *The Flame of Life*, translated by K. Vivaria, 1900; as *The Flame*, translated by Dora Knowlton Ranous, 1906; also translated by Susan Bassnett, 1991.

Le novelle della Pescara. 1902; as *Tales of My Native Town*
    (12 of 18 tales), translated by Gaetano Mantellini, 1920.
Forse che sì, forse che no. 1910.
La leda senza cigno. 1916.

Other

Notturno (autobiographical prose). 1921.
Tutte le opere, edited by Angelo Sodini. 49 vols., 1927–36.
*Carteggio D'Annunzio—Duse: Superstiti missive: Lettere, car-
    toline, telegrammi, dediche 1898–1923*, edited by Piero
    Nardi. 1975.
Lettere a una donna. 1975.
Lettere inedite. In *Quaderni del Vittoriale*, July–August, 1980.
Scritti politici, edited by Paolo Alatri. 1980.
Nocturne and Five Tales of Love and Death, translated by R.
    Rosenthal. 1991.

*

Bibliography: *D'Annunzio Abroad: A Bibliographical Essay*
by Joseph G. Fucilla and Joseph M. Carrière, 2 vols., 1935–
37; *Bibliografia critica di Gabriele D'Annunzio* by Mario
Vecchioni, 1970; *Bibliografia della critica dannunziana nei
periodici italiani dal 1880 al 1938* by Anna Baldazzi, 1977;
'Bibliografia dannunziana', in issues of *Quaderni vittoriale*.

Critical Studies: *D'Annunzio* by Tom Antongini, 1938; *Age
Cannot Wither: The Story of Duse and D'Annunzio* by Bertita
L. de Harding, 1947; *Wings of Fire: A Biography of Gabriele
D'Annunzio and Eleonora Duse* by Frances Winwar, 1957;
D'Annunzio: The Poet as Superman by Anthony Rhodes,
1959; *D'Annunzio in France: A Study in Cultural Relations* by
Giovanni Gullace, 1966; *D'Annunzio* by Philippe Julian,
1973; *The First Duce: D'Annunzio at Fiume* by Michael A.
Ledeen, 1977; *Gabriele D'Annunzio* by Charles Klopp, 1988;
Gabriele D'Annunzio: The Dark Flame by Paolo Valesio,
1992.

*   *   *

The grounds for regarding Gabriele D'Annunzio as a major
20th-century Italian poet are aptly summed up by Eugenio
Montale: 'D'Annunzio experimented or touched upon all the
linguistic and prosodic possibilities of our time . . . Not to
have learned anything from him would be a very bad sign'.
Yet Montale as well as Giuseppe Ungaretti and Umberto
Saba reacted against him, just as D'Annunzio himself had
reacted against the poetic tradition represented by Giosuè
Carducci and Giovanni Pascoli. D'Annunzio's metrical and
linguistic innovations altered expression and reflected a new
sensibility. He was a prolific writer (in French and in Italian):
his first book of poems, *Primo vere*, came out in 1879 and his
last, *Teneo te, Africa* (in *Tutte le opere*), in 1936. In between
he published several important books of lyrics; *Alcyone*
(*Halcyon*)—the third of four books (*Maia*, *Elettra*, and
Merope are the others) in the cycle of poems called *Laudi del
cielo, del mare, della terra, e degli eroi* [Praises of the Skies,
the Sea, the Earth, and the Heroes]—is an impressive synthesis of his naturalistic creed and rhythmic mastery and
control, and is deservedly regarded as his most inspired and
most successful book of lyrics.

The characteristic qualities of D'Annunzio's best work are
exuberant naturalism, plastic and pictorial talent, rhythmic,
metric, and imagistic skill, mastery over landscape, in depicting which D'Annunzio achieves a creative fusion between
'physicality' and 'sensuousness' and between profound
inwardness and spirituality.

But such qualities in D'Annunzio's work went hand in hand
with certain defects and weaknesses, such as a self-indulgent
dilettantism in dealing with things that are not rooted in his
life and experience; a kind of amoral impressionistic exhibi-
tionism unredeemed by the vitality and concreteness of a fully
realized experience; and a rhetorical, musical, and aesthetic
artifice which aims at and at times achieves a kind of perfection which is essentially hollow and therefore unconvincing.

D'Annunzio also wrote novels and plays. Of the former
those most indicative of his powers as a decadent aesthete are
Il piacere (*The Child of Pleasure*), *Le vergini delle rocce* (*The
Virgins of the Rocks*), *Il fuoco* (*The Flame*), and *Forse che sì
forse che no* [Maybe Yes, Maybe No]; and of the latter *La
città morta* (*The Dead City*), *La Gioconda*, *Francesca da
Rimini*, and the best-known of all, *La figlia di Iorio* (*The
Daughter of Jorio*), are the most characteristic. Both in the
plays and the novels one underlying theme is the Nietzschean
myth of the superman; another is the cult of sensuality.

—G. Singh

THE FLAME (Il fuoco)
Novel by Gabriele D'Annunzio, 1900.

The Flame exists in three English versions, two of which are
well known. First published in Italy in 1900, there was an
English version entitled *The Flame of Life* (1900) and in 1991
a new translation, *The Flame*, was published. The anomaly in
the two English titles reflects the complexity of D'Annunzio's
use of symbolism, drawing as he does on two disparate traditions: the use of fire as a purifying force as exemplified in
Dante's *Commedia* (the novel is prefaced with a line from
Dante—'do as Nature does in fire') and the Wagnerian idea
of the flaming forge in which the creative masculine spirit is
shaped. Wagner appears as an actual character in *The Flame*,
and it is with Wagner's funeral that D'Annunzio concludes
this autobiographical novel which, in many ways, is a manifesto of his theories of art and of Italian culture.

When *The Flame* first appeared, D'Annunzio was already
well established as a poet and novelist, and had begun to turn
his hand to writing for the theatre, chiefly because of his
relationship with Eleonora Duse, the greatest actress of her
day. Duse and D'Annunzio began their *affaire* in 1894, and it
lasted until 1904 when Duse left him, driven to despair by his
infidelities. *The Flame* is in many respects a *roman à clef*,
because it traces the relationship between a young writer,
Stelio Effrena (D'Annunzio himself) and La Foscarina
(Duse), a world famous actress. Although there was only a
slight age difference between Duse and D'Annunzio, in the
fictitious version Stelio is depicted as a virile young man, avid
for life and full of springtime energy, while Foscarina is an
ageing woman, terrified at the prospect of losing her beauty,
the personification of Autumn.

Because of the immediately identifiable characters, the
novel caused a scandal when it first appeared. D'Annunzio
courted scandal throughout his life, and earlier novels had
also caused a furore because of their sexual explicitness. *The
Flame* crossed the boundary line between autobiography and
fiction in ways that also transgressed contemporary conventions of good taste. Sarah Bernhardt was so appalled at what
she saw as a betrayal of the intimate life of a fellow actress,
albeit her greatest rival, that she returned her copy to the

author unread. D'Annunzio had clearly kept notebooks detailing Duse's conversations in bed and in intensely private moments, and chose to make them public through the character of Foscarina. The heroine's account of her childhood and adolescence in the theatre, of her debut in the arena at Verona as Juliet, all derive directly from Duse's own life. That Duse was an exceptionally private person only made D'Annunzio's exposure of her thoughts and feelings the more unpalatable to large numbers of readers.

D'Annunzio structured his novel in terms of binary opposites: youth and age, male and female, spring and autumn, life and death, fire and water. Set in Venice in the 1890s, it is full of lyrical descriptions of the city as the summer ends and autumn approaches, which remind us of D'Annunzio's poetic talents. He divided it into two parts, the first entitled 'The Epiphany of Fire', the second 'The Empire of Silence'. Part One, which opens with the lyrical description of the protagonists sailing across the lagoon in a typically Venetian halcyon evening of absolute stillness, traces both the move towards physical consummation of the *affaire* and Stelio's rise to artistic success. Part Two follows the gradual disintegration of the relationship, as Stelio is driven by his inner desire for absolute freedom both in artistic and personal terms, and Foscarina is tormented by the realization that she is growing old and must inevitably lose him to a younger woman. By the end of the novel, Foscarina has decided to leave him and go back to her former life on tour with her company, and Stelio has been inspired to write his first play. The details show striking parallels with D'Annunzio's own play, *The Dead City*, written in 1895.

A substantial section of Part One is devoted to Stelio's speech to the elite of Venetian society. Based on one of D'Annunzio's own improvised speeches on the sublime power of beauty, it is intended here to show the power of Stelio's intellect and also to establish the aesthetic core of the novel. Because of its inordinate length, however, it does not work, and Part Two is a much stronger piece of writing. D'Annunzio could write magnificently when he chose, and his psychological insights into both his central characters are very well handled. However, when he decides to abandon narrative and use the novel as a political platform, his writing is much weaker. Stelio's great set-piece comes across as self-indulgence at best, megalomania at worst, and readers move with some relief back to the passages that trace the relationship between the writer and the actress. Particularly powerful are the sections (the novel is not divided into chapters, but into a series of unmarked quite distinct narrative segments) describing Stelio's feelings of entrapment after the couple have made love, Foscarina's anguish when she is lost in the maze during a visit to a decaying country house, and the lovers' quarrel after they have seen the glass-blowing furnaces on the Island of Murano.

The Flame is an uneven novel, and can be both moving and infuriating. The problem, however, is D'Annunzio's over-identification with Stelio: he wants his readers to approve of his character, but does not have the necessary critical distance to enable him to gauge their boredom threshold. The character of Foscarina, which contemporary critics felt was a cruel caricature of Duse, is ultimately the most memorable figure, and his account of the struggle for supremacy between the lovers shows narrative skills that recall other writers of the time, such as D.H. Lawrence.

D'Annunzio's work declined in popularity from the 1930s onwards, and for decades his plays and novels were regarded as period pieces, and examples of the excesses of Decadent symbolist writing. In the 1990s, however, there are signs of a reassessment, and *The Flame* is probably the novel most likely to appeal to a contemporary readership, focusing as it does on the battle between the sexes: between a powerful woman and a man desperate to enjoy the same public recognition. Gender criticism has enabled us to look at D'Annunzio in a new way, and this novel is an ideal place to start.

—Susan Bassnett

FRANCESCA DA RIMINI
Play by Gabriele D'Annunzio, 1901.

The first run of *Francesca da Rimini* at the Costanzi theatre in Rome began on 9 December 1901 and was a lavish affair: it was then the most expensive production ever staged in Italy. The central part was written for the famous actress Eleonora Duse who was D'Annunzio's lover at the time, but the play was considered too long and only met with any success after being cut. It was written in the middle of D'Annunzio's most intense period of theatrical output, but, like almost all of his plays, has not enjoyed the lasting success of some of his other work. D'Annunzio aimed to produce a 'poetic theatre', but the result is a rather static play which relies heavily on set-piece lyrical passages. *Francesca da Rimini* is written in a flexible non-rhyming verse, based on lines of eleven, seven, and five syllables. The language, with its preciosity and many archaisms, aims to conjure up the rhythms of medieval speech.

The story of *Francesca da Rimini* is one of the most famous in Italian literature: Francesca is the central character in what is arguably the most powerful episode in Dante's *Inferno* (Canto V). Although Dante and his cultural milieu are mentioned by D'Annunzio (Act III, scene 5) and there are many stylistic echoes of the *Divine Comedy* in the play, D'Annunzio's approach is very different. Indeed, *Francesca da Rimini* is less a dialogue with Dante than a projection, in typical fashion, of D'Annunzio's own 'decadent' themes onto Dante, whose story is removed from the judgemental context of the Inferno and suffused with a mood of mystery, fatality, and eroticism which is in tune with pre-Raphaelite medievalism.

Francesca da Rimini is a tragic love story set against the pitiless world of the medieval nobility. The handsome and cultivated Paolo Malatesta is sent to the Polenta household to arrange the marriage of Francesca to the elder of his two brothers, Gianciotto, an ugly, coarse and soldierly man. The marriage is part of a political and military alliance arranged by Francesca's brother Ostasio and his adviser, who fear that the strong-willed Francesca might object to being the instrument of their plans. Accordingly they have used Paolo, who is already married, as bait to catch her. In Act I, we see Francesca's ladies-in-waiting in an idyllic setting and a playful mood. In stark contrast are Ostasio's scheming, and his cruel treatment of both his feeble brother Bannino and a hapless minstrel. Francesca's sense of foreboding about her marriage emerges in a delicate scene with her sister, but when she sees Paolo, through the bars of a gate, she is captivated and silently hands him a rose.

Act II is set in Rimini, some time later, in a room of the Malatesta fortress which opens out onto the battlements. Even Gianciotto's soldiers are aware that Francesca's marriage to him is not a success. A battle is imminent, and the room is full of arms. Oblivious to the danger, Francesca appears and displays a self-destructive fascination with the lethal incendiary concoction which the tower-keeper is preparing to hurl down at the enemy. When Paolo enters to survey the field, it is clear, despite Francesca's hostile words, that her love for him has survived his implication in the cruel trick played on her. Tortured by remorse, and by his love for Francesca, Paolo agrees to give her his helmet, thus exposing himself to even greater danger. However, when Paolo survives the battle uninjured, Francesca gratefully takes it as a sign that he is cleansed of his deception. Gianciotto, pleased with Paolo's martial prowess, announces that he has been elected Captain of the People in Florence.

With the youngest of the Malatesta brothers, the warlike and sadistic Malatestino, D'Annunzio successfully adds an element of the macabre to his play. In Act III, Francesca tells her faithful slave of her fear of Malatestino who, having been blinded in one eye during the battle, succumbed to her beauty while she was nursing him. Paolo arrives back early from his duties in Florence, full of tales of the cultural life of the Tuscan city, but more eager to tell of the torment his thoughts of her have caused him. He asks Francesca to read with him. Their hoarse and nervous progress through 'The History of Lancelot of the Lake', with Francesca reading the part of Guinevere, comes to an end when they act out the kiss recounted in the text.

In the opening scene of Act IV, the screams of a captive under torture can be heard from the dungeon as Malatestino tells Francesca of his violent lust for her. She fends him off, but is horrified when, on her request to him to stop the screaming, Malatestino sets off with an axe to kill the prisoner. Malatestino returns with the prisoner's head in a cloth and finds Gianciotto who jealously demands to know what he has done to upset his wife. Dropping ever clearer hints, Malatestino tells his brother of the affair between Paolo and Francesca, and proposes a plan to enable Gianciotto to catch them in flagrante. In the brief fifth act, Paolo and Francesca meet in the middle of the night, more in love than ever. But they are caught by Gianciotto. Francesca dies trying to protect Paolo from her husband's attack. Paolo is cut down, defenceless. Gianciotto stoops on one knee to break his sword.

Perhaps the most interesting aspect of Francesca da Rimini is its intertwining of the themes of violence and desire. D'Annunzio refuses to draw a platitudinous line between the pacific world of the lovers and the bloody times in which they live. Even the rose that Francesca gives to Paolo is 'more living/than the lips of a fresh wound', and Paolo himself has a 'scarcely repressed violence'. Beauty is seen as fearsome and fragile, inviting jealousy and destruction. Passion pushes its victims into psychological turmoil and hurls them against the conventions of a society which is itself profoundly brutal. In D'Annunzio's hands, however, the recognition that desire is violent seems to topple over into an amoral and aestheticizing desire for violence.

—John Dickie

RAIN IN THE PINE FOREST (La pioggia nel pineto)
Poem by Gabriele D'Annunzio, 1903.

'Rain in the Pine Forest' is one of D'Annunzio's most famous lyric poems, and has become one of the best known Italian poems of the 20th century, despite the decline in popularity of its author from the 1930s onwards. Probably written in July 1902, it was published in the Alcyone collection in 1903, one of the four volumes in D'Annunzio's Laudi del cielo, del mare, della terra, e degli eroi [Praises of the

Skies, the Sea, the Earth, and the Heroes], the other two being Maia, Elettra and Merope. The collection Alcyone also contains some of his equally famous lyrics, such as 'La sera fiesolana' [Evening at Fiesole], 'Le stirpi canore' [Lineages of Melody], and 'Il novilunio' [The New Moon].

'Rain in the Pine Forest' consists of 128 short lines, some comprising a single word. It is addressed to the poet's companion, named in the poem as Ermione (Hermione), a name with classical connotations (Hermione was a daughter of Helen and Menelaus, and Hermione, the place in Argolis, was the site of a shrine to Aphrodite in her role as goddess of the seas as well as goddess of love. The same Hermione was also said to be the place through which Pluto plunged back into the earth towards Hades, after abducting Persephone). From the dating of the poem, it is likely that the inspiration for Ermione was Eleonora Duse, who also inspired D'Annunzio's novel The Flame.

The poem is structured along heavily rhythmical patterns, with repeated sound clusters. The sibilant 's' sounds reflect the sounds of falling water:

> Ascolta. Piove
> dalle nuvole sparse.
> Piove su le tamerici
> salmastre ed arse,
> piove su i pini
> scagliosi ed irti,
> piove su i mirti.
>
> (Listen. It rains
> down from scattered clouds.
> Rains on tamerisk trees
> salt-stained and brown,
> rains on pine trees
> spiky and scaly,
> rains on the myrtles.)

Each new rhyming couplet moves the poem forward, so that as the lovers wander through the pine forest, their walk is reflected in the rhythm of the verse. There is no rigid pattern to the rhymes, which happen in couplets or across three or even four lines. The principal characteristic of the poem is the careful use of repetition and the way in which D'Annunzio keeps the reader's attention by creating a series of dramatic sections, each with a clearly marked starting point that ends in a climax. The starting point is always an imperative: 'Taci' ('Hush') says the poet in the opening line; 'Ascolta' ('Listen') in line 8; 'Odi?' ('Can you hear?') in line 33; 'Ascolta' again, in line 40; 'Ascolta, ascolta' in line 65; 'Ascolta' again for the last time in line 88. From line 96, the poem changes direction, and the imperatives end as the focus changes. The final section of the poem is more reflective, less immediate, and the language marks a shift from the urgency of the speaker's endeavours to communicate with Ermione to a more introspective consideration of the destiny of the lovers who have undergone a kind of transformation and become at one with the natural environment in which they find themselves.

There are signs early on in the poem of this symbolic transformation. Even as he urges his beloved to listen to the sound of the rain on the leaves and on the pine needles, the poet uses a significant set of adjectives: their faces are 'silvani' (sylvan), line 21, their hands are 'ignude' (bare), line 23, their clothes are 'leggeri' (light), line 25, and their thoughts are 'freschi' (fresh), line 26. By line 51 he is describing how they are both steeped in the spirit of the wood, how her ecstatic face is 'molle di pioggia/come una foglia' (damp with raindrops like a leaf), and her hair is the colour of broom.

In line 65 the urgency of the poet's voice increases with the greater force of the falling rain. The repetition of 'Ascolta' marks the description that follows of the increasingly heavy rain drowning out the sound of the sea and the singing of the crickets. The wildness of this rain-music marks the transformation of the lovers into creatures of the woods:

> Piove su le tue ciglia nere
> sì che par tu pianga
> ma di piacere: non bianca
> ma quasi fatta virente,
> par di scorza tu esca.
> E tutta la vita è in noi fresca
> aulente,
> il cuor nel petto è come pesca
> intatta
>
> (The rain on your dark lashes
> looks like tears
> of joy; not white
> but almost leaf-green
> you seem to rise out of bark.
> And all of life is fresh within us
> sweet-scented,
> the hearts in our breasts like peaches
> on the branch)

Line 115 to the end is a repetition of lines 20–32, only now the transformation that was only suggested the first time has already begun to take place. What is particularly significant is the slight alteration of lines 29–32 into the final lines of the poem:

> su la favola bella
> che ieri
> t'illuse, che oggi m'illude,
> o Ermione
>
> (on the fairy-tale wonder
> that yesterday
> deceived you, today deceives me
> oh Ermione)

becomes:

> che ieri
> m'illuse, che oggi t'illude
>
> (that yesterday
> deceived me, today deceives you)

so that the poem ends on a slightly different note, one in which Ermione is no longer all powerful. Indeed, it is possible to read into the inversion of 'you' and 'me' a deliberate distancing device, so that the woman who has been the object of the man's adoration is seen ultimately to be the one suffering from the delusion of believing in the fairy-tale wonder of their love. Given the autobiographical nature of D'Annunzio's writing and the fact that his relationship with Duse was in trouble in 1902 (they finally parted in 1904) it is not too far-fetched to see the signs of the end in this poem. Some editors have chosen to see the inversion as purely technical, as yet another example of D'Annunzio's manipulation of language for musical effect, but this is unlikely. The process of transformation undergone by the lovers in the woods, and the shift of the speaker from directly addressing Hermione to the introspective reflection on what has been taking place between them and nature also contains signs of a change of emphasis, as the poet looks back at his own delusion and notes with sadness that those feelings are part of his yesterday.

The sadness of the final lines gives a note of melancholy to what is for the most part a lyrically beautiful poem about human passion in an evocative natural landscape.

—Susan Bassnett

DANTE, Alighieri. Born in Florence, in 1265, probably late May. Details of his education are conjectural, but he was raised as a gentleman and was an avid student of philosophy and poetry. Served in the Florentine army cavalry in campaign against Arezzo, 1289; fought in battle of Campaldino. Married Gemma di Maretto Donati in 1294 (affianced 1283), three sons and one daughter. Met Beatrice Portinari, 1274 (died 1290); friend of Guido Cavalcanti, *q.v.*, from 1283, and associated with group of *dolce stil nuovo* poets around him; involved in Florentine civic affairs: served on people's council, 1295–96, and other councils, 1296 and 1297, and diplomatic missions to San Gimignano, 1300; one of the six priors governing Florence, 1300; in charge of road works in Florence (probably in preparation for a siege), 1301; while on a mission to Pope Boniface VIII in Rome in 1301 his party (the Whites) was defeated in Florence and he was exiled: sought refuge at courts of various Ghibelline lords in northern Italy: in San Godenzo in 1302, Forlì, 1303, and Verona, 1303; broke with other White exiles, 1304, and probably went to university town of Bologna; agent in court of Franceschino Malaspina in the Lunigiana, 1306; in Lucca, c.1306–08; strong supporter of the Holy Roman Empire, Henry VII of Luxemburg, 1309–13 (probably wrote *De monarchia* at this time); in Lucca, c.1314–16; refused conditional amnesty from Florence, 1316; at court of Can Grande della Scala in Verona, 1317, and court of Guido Novello da Polento in Ravenna, c.1317–21: sent by Guido on diplomatic mission to Venice, 1321. *Died 14 September 1321.*

PUBLICATIONS

Collections

The Latin Works, translated by A.G. Ferrers Howell and P.H. Wicksteed. 1904.
Opere, edited by Michele Barbi and others. 2 vols., 1921–22; 2nd edition, 1960.
The Portable Dante, edited by Paolo Milano. 1947; revised edition, 1978.
Selected Works. 1972.
Opere, edited by Fredi Chiapelli. 6th edition, 1974.
Opere minore, edited by Domenico de Robertis and Gianfranco Contini. 1979–84.
Tutti le Opere. 1981.

Verse

Commedia, edited by Natalino Sapegno. 1957, also edited by Giorgio Petrocchi, 4 vols., 1966–67, and by Umberto Bosco and Giovanni Reggio, 1979; edited (with translation) by Charles S. Singleton, 6 vols., 1970–75; translated by Henry Boyd, 3 vols., 1802; numerous subsequent translations as *The Divine Comedy*, including by H.W. Longfellow, 3 vols., 1867; Laurence Binyon, 1933–46; L.G. White, 1948;

Dorothy L. Sayers and Barbara Reynolds, 3 vols., 1949–62; John Ciardi, 1954–70; G.L. Bickersteth, 1955; John D. Sinclair, 3 vols., 1961; Kenneth Mackenzie, 1979; C.H. Sisson, 1980; Allen Mandelbaum, 3 vols., 1980–84; translated into prose by Charles Eliot Norton, 3 vols., 1891–92; also by J. Carlyle, T. Okey, and P.H. Wicksteed, 3 vols., 1899–1901; as *The Vision*, translated by Henry Francis Cary, 3 vols., 1814.

La vita nuova, edited by Michele Barbi. 1932, also in *Opere*, 1960, also edited by Domenico De Robertis, 1980; translated by Dante Gabriel Rossetti, in *The Early Italian Poets*, 1861; also translated by Mark Musa, 1957, revised edition, 1973; Barbara Reynolds, 1969; as *The New Life*, translated by William S. Anderson, 1964.

Eclogae latinae, edited by E. Pistelli, in *Opere*. 1960; translated by P.H. Wicksteed, 1902; also translated by W. Brewer, 1927.

Rime, edited by D. Mattalia. 1943, also edited by Gianfranco Contini, 2nd edition, 1946, and by Michele Barbi and F. Maggini, 1956; as *Il Canzoniere*, edited by G. Zonta, 1921; translated by Patrick S. Diehl, 1979.

Lyric Poetry, edited by Kenelm Foster and Patrick Boyde. 2 vols., 1967.

Eighteen Poems, translated by Anthony Conran. 1975.

Other

De vulgari eloquentia, edited by A. Marigo, revised edition, edited by P.G. Ricci. 1957, and by Pier Vincenzo Mengaldo, 1968; translated by A.G. Ferrers Howell, 1890; also translated by P.H. Wicksteed, in *Latin Works*, 1904; as *Literature in the Vernacular*, translated by Sally Purcell, 1981.

De monarchia, edited by E. Rostagno, in *Opere*. 1960, also edited by P.G. Ricci, 1965, and by Bruno Nardi, in *Opere Minori*, 1979; translated by A.G. Ferrers Howell, 1890; as *Monarchy, and Three Political Letters*, translated by Donald Nicholl and Colin Hardie, 1954; as *On World-Government*, edited and translated by H.W. Schneider, 1957.

Epistolae: The Letters, translated by P.H. Wicksteed. 1902; edited and translated by Paget Toynbee, 1920; revised edition, edited by Colin Hardie, 1966.

Questio de aqua et de terra, edited by E. Pistelli, in *Opere*. 1960; translated by P.H. Wicksteed, 1902, and in *Latin Works*, 1904.

Il convivio, edited by G. Busnelli and G. Vandelli. 1964, and by M. Simonelli, 1966; as *The Banquet*, translated by P.H. Wicksteed, 1903; also translated by William W. Jackson, 1909; Christopher Ryan, 1989; Richard H. Lansing, 1990.

De situ, edited by V. Biagi. 1907, and by G. Padoan, 1968.

Literary Criticism, edited by Robert S. Haller. 1973.

The Stone Beloved (selections). 1986.

*

Critical Studies: *Studies in Dante* edited by Edward Moore, 4 vols., 1896–1917, reprinted 1968; *Dante's Ten Heavens: A Study of the Paradiso* by Edmund Garratt Gardner, 1904; *In Patriam: An Exposition of Dante's Paradiso* by John S. Carroll, 1911; *Dante and Aquinas* by P.H. Wicksteed, 1913; *Dante: Essays in Commemoration, 1321–1921*, 1921; *Symbolism in Medieval Thought and Its Consummation in the Divine Comedy* by H.F. Dunbar, 1929; *Essays on the Vita Nuova*, 1929, and *The Lady Philosophy in the Convivio*, 1938, both by James E. Shaw; *Medieval Culture: An*

Introduction to Dante and His Times by Karl Vossler, translated by William Cranston Lawton, 2 vols., 1929; *Dante the Philosopher* by Étienne Gilson, translated by David Moore, 1948; *An Essay on the Vita Nuova*, 1949, in *Dante Studies, 1–2*, 1954–58, *Journey to Beatrice*, 1958, and *Dante's Commedia: Elements of Structure*, 1977, all by Charles S. Singleton; *A Handbook to Dante Studies* by Umberto Cosmo, translated by David Moore, 1950; *Dante as a Political Thinker* by A. Passerin d'Entrèves, 1952; *Dante's Drama of the Mind: A Modern Reading of the Purgatorio*, 1953, *Dante*, 1966, and *Trope and Allegory: Themes Common to Dante and Shakespeare*, 1977, all by Francis Fergusson; *Life of Dante* by Michele Barbi, translated by P. Ruggiers, 1954; *Introductory Papers on Dante*, 1954, and *Further Papers on Dante*, 1957, both by Dorothy L. Sayers; *Dante and the Idea of Rome*, 1957, and *Dante's Italy and Other Essays*, 1984, both by Charles T. Davis; *Dante and the Early Astronomers* by Mary A. Orr (2nd edition) 1957; *Structure and Thought in the Paradiso*, 1958, and *Medieval Cultural Tradition in Dante's Comedy*, 1960, both by Joseph Mazzeo; *The Ladder of Vision: A Study of Dante's Comedy* by Irma Brandeis, 1960, and *Discussions of the Divine Comedy* edited by Brandeis, 1961; *Dante, Poet of the Secular World* by Erich Auerbach, translated by Ralph Manheim, 1961; *Essays on Dante*, 1964, and *Dante's Vita Nuova*, 1973, both by Mark Musa; *Dante* by Thomas G. Bergin, 1965, as *An Approach to Dante*, 1965, and *From Time to Eternity: Essays on Dante's Divine Comedy* edited by Bergin, 1967; *Dante: A Collection of Critical Essays* edited by John Freccero, 1965, and *Dante: The Poetics of Conversion* by Freccero, 1986; *The Mind of Dante* edited by U. Limentani, 1965; *Dante Alighieri: His Life and Works*, 1965, and *A Dictionary of Proper Names and Notable Matters in the Works of Dante*, 1968, both by Paget Toynbee; *Events and Their Afterlife: The Dialectics of Christian Typology in the Bible and Dante* by A.C. Charity, 1966; *Dante and His World* by T.C. Chubb, 1966; *Enciclopedia dantesca*, 5 vols., 1970–75; *Dante's Style in His Lyric Poetry*, 1971, *Dante Philomythes and Philosopher: Man in the Cosmos*, 1981, and *Perception and Passion in Dante's Comedy*, 1993, all by Patrick Boyde; *The Greatness of Dante Alighieri* by Herbert William Smith, 1974; *Dante's Epic Journeys* by David Thompson, 1974; *Companion to the Divine Comedy: Commentary* by C.H. Grandgent, 1975; *Dark Wood to White Rose* by Helen M. Luke, 1975; *Woman, Earthly and Divine, in the Comedy of Dante* by Marianne Shapiro, 1975; *The Two Dantes, and Other Studies* by Kenelm Foster, 1977, and *Cambridge Readings in Dante's Comedy* edited by Foster and Patrick Boyde, 1981; *Dante Commentaries*, 1977, and *Dante Soundings: Eight Literary and Historical Essays*, 1981, both edited by David Nolan; *Dante's Paradiso and the Limitations of Modern Criticism: A Study of Style and Poetic Theory*, 1978, *Dante: The Divine Comedy*, 1987, and *Dante's Inferno, Difficulty and Dead Poetry*, 1987, all by Robin Kirkpatrick; *The Discipline of the Mountain: Dante's Purgatorio in a Nuclear World* by Daniel Berrigan, 1979; *Essays on Dante's Philosophy of History*, 1979, and *Dante's Journey of Sanctification*, 1990, both by Antonio C. Mastrobuono; *Dante, Poet of the Desert: History and Allegory in the Divine Comedy* by Giuseppe Mazzotta, 1979, and *Critical Essays on Dante* edited by Mazzotta, 1991; *Dante Alighieri* by Ricardo J. Quinones, 1979; *Dante the Maker* by William Anderson, 1980; *The World of Dante: Essays on Dante and His Times* edited by Cecil Grayson, 1980; *Studies in Dante* by Robert Hollander, 1980; *Dante* by George Holmes, 1980; *Shadowy Prefaces: Conversion and Writing in the Divine Comedy* by James Thomas Chiampi, 1981; *Irenic Apocalypse: Some Uses of Apolcalyptic in Dante, Petrarch and Rabelais* by Dennis

Costa, 1981; *A Reading of Dante's Inferno* by Wallace Fowlie, 1981; *The Figure of Dante: An Essay on the Vita Nuova* by Jerome Nazzaro, 1981; *Dante and the Roman de la Rose: An Investigation into the Vernacular Narrative Context of the Commedia* by Earl Jeffrey Richards, 1981; *Dante in the Twentieth Century* edited by Adolph Caso, 1982; *Confessions of Sin and Love in the Middle Ages: Dante's Commedia and St Augustine's Confessions* by Shirley J. Paolini, 1982; *Dante's Incarnation of the Trinity* by Paul Priest, 1982; *Essays on Dante* by Karl Witte, 1982; *The Door of Purgatory: A Study of Multiple Symbolism in Dante's Purgatorio*, 1983, and *Dante's Griffin and the History of the World: A Study of the Earthly Paradise*, 1989, both by Peter Armour; *Dante's Angelic Intelligences: Their Importance in the Cosmos and in Pre-Christian Religion* by Stephen Bemrose, 1983; *Dante, Petrarch, Boccaccio: Studies in the Italian Trecento in Honor of Charles S. Singleton* edited by Aldo S. Bernardo and Anthony L. Pelligrini, 1983; *Dante in America: The First Two Centuries* edited by A. Bartlett Giamatti, 1983; *Dante, Chaucer and the Currency of the Word: Money, Images and Reference in Late Medieval Poetry* by Richard A. Shoaf, 1983; *Dante's Poets: Texuality and Truth in the Comedy*, 1984, and *The Undivine Comedy: Detheologizing Dante*, 1992, both by Teodolinda Barolini; *Dante's Fearful Art of Justice* by Anthony K. Cassell, 1984; *Pilgrim in Love: An Introduction to Dante and His Spirituality*, 1984, and *Dante: Layman, Prophet, Mystic*, 1989, both by James J. Collins; *The Political Vision of the Divine Comedy*, 1984, and *Dante's Beatrice: Priest of an Androgynous God*, 1992, both by Joan M. Ferrante; *Chaucer and Dante: A Revaluation* by Howard H. Schess, 1984; *The Symbolic Rose in Dante's Paradiso* by Giuseppe C. Di Scipio, 1984; *Aesthetic Ideas in Dante: 'Etterno Piacer'*, 1984, and *Dante: Lyric Poet and Philosopher: An Introduction to the Minor Works*, 1990, both by J.F. Took; *The Political Ideas in the Divine Comedy* by Stewart Farnell, 1985; *Dante Comparisons* edited by Eric Haywood and Barry Jones, 1985, and *Dante Readings* edited by Haywood, 1986; *Dante's Poetry of Dreams* by Dino S. Cervigni, 1986; *Dante and Medieval Latin Traditions* by Peter Dronke, 1986; *The Reader's Companion to Dante's Divine Comedy* by Angelo A. De Gennaro, 1986; *The Transfiguration of History at the Center of Dante's Paradise* by Jeffrey T. Schnapp, 1986; *Dante: Numerological Studies* by John J. Guzzardo, 1987; *Dante's Poems: An Essay on History and Origins* by J.M.W. Hill, 1987; *The Pilgrim and the Book: A Study of Dante, Langland and Chaucer* by Julia Bolton Holloway, 1987; *Dante and the Empire* by Donna M. Mancusi-Ungaro, 1987; *Mary in the Writings of Dante* by Max Saint, 1987; *Dante: The Critical Heritage 1314(?)–1870* edited by Michael Caesar, 1988; *The Body of Beatrice* by Robert Pogue Harrison, 1988; *Dante and Difference: Writing in the Commedia* by Jeremy Tambling, 1988; *The Divine Comedy: Tracing God's Art* by Marguerite Mills Chiarenza, 1989; *A Study of the Theology and the Imagery of Dante's Divina Commedia: Sensory Perception, Reason and Free Will* by Sharon Harwood-Gordon, 1989; *On the Defence of the Comedy of Dante* by Giacopo Mazzoni, translated by R.L. Montgomery, 1989; *The Influence of Dante on Medieval Dream Visions* by Roberta L. Payne, 1989; *Dante Studies in the Age of Vico* by Domenico Pietropaolo, 1989; *Time and the Crystal: Studies in Dante's Rime Petrose* by Robert M. Durling and Ronald L. Martinez, 1990; *Dante and the Medieval Other World* by Alison Morgan, 1990; *Eternal Feminines: Three Theological Allegories in Dante's Paradiso* by Jaroslav Pelikan, 1990; *Dante* edited by Harold Bloom, 1991; *Dante's Burning Sands: Some New Perspectives* by Francesca Guerra D'Antoni, 1991; *Dante as Dramatist: Myth of the Early Paradise and Tragic Vision in the Divine Comedy* by Franco Masciandaro, 1991; *Word and Drama in Dante: Essays on the Divina Commedia* by John C. Barnes and Jennifer Petrie, 1992; *Dante and the Bible: An Introduction* by Daniel H. Higgins, 1992; *Cambridge Companion to Dante* edited by Rachel Jacoff, 1993; *Commentary and Ideology: Dante in the Renaissance* by Deborah Parker, 1993; *Dante and the Mystical Tradition: Bernard of Clairvaux in the Commedia* by Steven Botterill, 1994.

* * *

The city in which Dante was born and where he spent the first 38 years of his life was in his time already an important cultural centre as well as the focus of conflicting political forces. Having cast off its feudal allegiance it was a self-governing community, administered by its own citizens under the direction of a prosperous bourgeoisie. Although Dante's father was not a prominent figure in the life of the city (he was perhaps a money lender) the poet claimed to be descended from the aristocracy and he was in his youth sufficiently well off to enable him to study painting, music, and letters (according to Boccaccio) and, it seems likely, to spend a year at the University of Bologna. Florence already possessed a literary tradition; Dante readily acknowledged his indebtedness to Brunetto Latini, author of the allegorizing *Tesoretto*, and to the poet Guido Cavalcanti (slightly older than Dante) who had brought a speculative element into the love lyric of the Provençal tradition. Dante's literary production in fact begins with lyrics in the Cavalcanti style. Dante's first notable work, however, was *La vita nuova* (*The New Life*), an account of his idealistic love for Beatrice Portinari, composed after her death. It is a carefully constructed composition of unique and original character: prose is interspersed with verse, serving to provide a narrative line between the lyrics and also to illuminate their meaning by exegesis of a scholastic tone. The combination of realism and suggestion of hidden meanings as well as the calculated design of the little book give the reader a foretaste of the *Commedia* (*The Divine Comedy*). The poet's immersion in politics following the death of Beatrice and his subsequent banishment and disillusionment altered the course of both his reading and his writing: he turned from the quasi-mystic devotion to Beatrice (and Revelation) to the study of philosophy. This shift is documented in *Il Convivio* (*The Banquet*), a long, digressive work, dealing with philosophical, ethical, and even political matters, revealing a new area of study: Aristotle, Boethius, and Virgil are authorities of recurrent reference. As in *The New Life*, prose is used to explicate poems but in *The Banquet* the prose element is far greater. Another area of his studies after his exile is disclosed by *De vulgari eloquentia* (*Literature in the Vernacular*), written in Latin, a pioneering exercise in linguistic studies in which the author attempts to define the characteristics of true Italian speech. The all but obsessive interest in political matters, a natural concomitant of his exile, is the motivation for his *De monarchia* (*On World-Government*) and his impassioned *Epistolae* (*The Letters*). These Latin items of his canon were composed in all likelihood in the years of Henry VII's effort to reassert Imperial supremacy in Italy and probably when the writing of *The Divine Comedy* was already in progress.

For his 'minor works' alone—all original and significant— Dante would be accounted a major figure in Italian—and even European—literary history, but it is *The Divine Comedy* which has given him a unique and enduring pre-eminence. In the context of the times it is surprising that a work of such epic dimensions should not have been written in Latin—and, according to Boccaccio, Dante at first thought of using that tongue. The choice of the vernacular for his masterpiece was of crucial importance in the development of Italian literature, but the greatness of the work makes even such a determinant role merely incidental.

The prestige of the poem has long endured. Through the centuries immediately following its composition it maintained its eminence and survived through the less appreciative climate of the 17th and 18th centuries, gathering new vitality in the 19th and growing in popularity and esteem over the past 200 years. The scope of its attraction has been uniquely vast, rivalling that of the Homeric poems; through the years it has consistently won wide readership and critical attention in all nations of the old world and the new. It has charmed the 'man in the street' and fascinated intellectuals. For the English-speaking world, one eloquent statistic may be cited: there have been no fewer than 47 translations of the poem into English (not counting partial versions) and more are in the course of preparation.

There are many reasons for such persistent vitality just as there are many facets and levels of meaning in the work itself. For Dante, according to his letter to Can Grande, the literal substance of the poem is simply an account of the state of souls after death, with allegorical implications below the surface. But the mode of depiction is not simply expositional; it is cast in narrative form. And it is a story compellingly told, in which the protagonist, the author himself, describes his pilgrimage through the Christian realms of the after-life, Hell, Purgatory, and Heaven. These are kingdoms of fancy, to be sure, in which the author is free to invent backgrounds, scenes, and events. But these kingdoms are populated by characters drawn not from inventive fancy but from the narrator's own acquaintance, whether in experience or in his readings, and they are set forth with convincing realism. The essential ingredients for assuring the reader's interest—movement, suspense, recognition—are present from beginning to end as the pilgrim–narrator moves from one circle of Hell, one terrace of Purgatory, or one circling Heaven to another with surprises for himself and his reader at every passage. In all of these realms the wayfarer has a companion and guide (Virgil or Beatrice) to instruct and advise him but with the tactical function also of giving life to the narrative through dialogue, more effective than simple narrational exposition in providing dramatic movement. No writer of fiction has planned his art with greater care or shrewdness. But The Divine Comedy is more than fiction. The characters, including the narrator, have suggestive symbolic dimensions, allusive and often challengingly ambiguous. As the story unrolls the reader becomes aware that the realms of fancy or theological postulate are also provinces of the world we live in, depicted with a perception fortified by learning and a commitment born of faith and hope. It is our world that we recognize behind the veil, with all its faltering waywardness, penitential meditation, and yearning for salvation and exaltation. The wayfarer too is not simply a 14th-century Florentine exile; he is Everyman, and he speaks for all of us. We are his fellow pilgrims *sub specie aeternitatis*.

The substance of the poem is given strength and beauty by rare technical artistry. *The Divine Comedy* is a masterful design, with carefully planned and harmonious proportions; all of the *cantiche* are of approximately the same length, and the dimensions of each canto also bear witness to the 'fren dell' arte'. *Terza rima* itself, with its syllogistic construction and its subliminal trinitarian implications, has also the practical uses of linkage and invitation to memorization. The poet makes skilful use, too, of such devices as alliteration,

assonance, and even deft repetition. His imagery is remarkable for its variety—animals, plants, trees, and flowers mingle with historical allusions and numerological and mathematical figures in the embroidery of the poem. Some of these are lost in translation but a good translation—and there have been many such—can convey much of this accidental charm into another tongue.

So many, rich, and varied are the threads of which the cloth of *The Divine Comedy* is woven that the nature of the work defies simple definition. It has been called 'a personal epic'; it is assuredly a confessional autobiography. It is likewise a patient and lucid exposition of orthodox dogma and an encyclopedia as well. At the same time it may be seen as a great love poem, for Beatrice is the motivation and the goal of the pilgrimage; furthermore each great division ends with the same word, suggesting a vast 'canzone' of three great stanzas. Or we may see the *Comedy* as a 'synthesis of medieval learning', which, at least incidentally, it is. But it is also a synthesis of the aspirations, sensibilities, and ultimate destiny of mankind. It is, most deeply, a statement of affirmation, set forth in terms of a certain time and place and contingent circumstance but valid for all times. Matter, manner, and message are blended not only with exceptional craftsmanship but with commitment and conviction. Aesthetically irresistible, the story of the extra-terrestrial pilgrimage is also on a deeper level reassuring and inspirational.

—Thomas G. Bergin

THE DIVINE COMEDY (Commedia)
Poem by Dante Alighieri, 1472 (written c.1307–21).

The Divine Comedy is the first great poem in any European language which, to quote Thomas Carlyle, gave expression to 'the voice of ten silent centuries'. It can be compared only with the greatest works of world poetry—those of Homer and Shakespeare. In order to gauge the depth, intensity, variety, and universality of *The Divine Comedy*, one has to imagine Shakespeare's four greatest tragedies all rolled into one and yet still something will be missing: the entire matter and substance of *Il paradiso* (*Paradise*). For this reason T.S. Eliot described *The Divine Comedy*, which he ranked with the *Bhagavad-Gita*, on the one hand, and with Lucretius' *De rerum natura* (*On the Nature of Things*), on the other, as a philosophic poem, representing 'a complete scale of the depths and heights of human emotion' and having the 'width of emotional range' of no other poem.

The only comparison that has sometimes been made—as, for instance, by Hazlitt, Arthur Hallam, and Thomas Babington Macaulay in the 19th century—is between *The Divine Comedy* and *Paradise Lost* as religious poems. Neither Dante nor Milton specialists will consider this comparison to be valid, not only because of the widely different form and style, technique, and expression of the two poems, but also because of the different modes of dealing with the mystery of the divine, the hereafter, and the ineffable. This was dictated not only by Dante's and Milton's individual poetics, but also by their personal ethics, religious beliefs, and convictions. Ezra Pound, a Dantist to the core, sums up the difference with characteristic forthrightness, though not without partisan bias:

Dante's god is ineffable divinity. Milton's god is a fussy old man with a hobby. Dante is metaphysical, where

Milton is merely sectarian . . . Milton has no grasp of the superhuman. Milton's angels are men of enlarged power, plus wings. Dante's angels surpass human nature and differ from it. They move in their high courses inexplicable.

Another difference between *Paradise Lost* and *The Divine Comedy* is that while the former is universally regarded as the greatest authentic epic in any modern European language, the latter, for all its impressive compactness, symmetry of design, and the daunting regularity of its *terza rima* cannot, strictly speaking, be so regarded. For some like Leopardi and Croce, it is 'a long lyric' or 'a series of lyrical compositions of varying tone'. For others it is a long narrative poem with dramatic and lyrical elements woven into its fabric.

Whatever the difference of form and style, *The Divine Comedy*, like Milton's epic, is a repository of its author's philosophical, theological, and religious beliefs, as well as his moral and political convictions. It exemplifies on a grand scale, and in the context of Dante's vision of the hereafter, what Samuel Taylor Coleridge calls 'the living link between religion and philosophy'. Written over a period of 15 to 20 years, and started perhaps before his exile from Florence in 1302, Dante's poem seems to be anchored more to autobiographical facts than to any mystical dream or vision, or to any particular religious or philosophical system.

Dante's political exile from Florence had a crucial bearing on the composition of *The Divine Comedy*, making him see not only Florentine and Italian history and politics, but also his own sufferings and hardships, in larger perspective. The uses of adversity in Dante's case could not, therefore, have been sweeter. For, in spite of the separation from his family, and his having known by experience 'how salt is the taste of another man's bread, and how hard the way is up and down another man's stairs', his exile inculcated him with a sense of mission and of prophesy. The very theme he was dealing with as well as the particular circumstances of his life made him feel greater than himself.

Different epochs, both in Italy and outside, reacted to *The Divine Comedy* and to its author in different ways. For the English Romantic poets Dante became a sort of Romantic freedom-fighter, a symbol of political liberty, national freedom, and personal courage. Re-echoing this sentiment in their own poetry, Wordsworth, Byron, and Shelley—the last two also translated parts of *The Divine Comedy*—had as much Dante in mind as Milton. Hence, when Wordsworth talks of 'love, and man's unconquerable mind', when Byron exalts the 'Eternal spirit of the chainless mind!/Brightest in dungeons, Liberty!', or when Shelley observes how 'Most wretched men/Are cradled into poetry by wrong:/They learn in suffering what they teach in song', Dante's example looms as large in their minds as does Milton's. And it also does in the mind of his compatriot Giacomo Leopardi who, even though he was very different from Dante in thought, philosophy, and outlook, bore eloquent testimony in his poetry to Dante's poetic and moral greatness as forming a cornerstone of Italy's glory.

The attitude of the modern poets to *The Divine Comedy* is varied. T.S. Eliot and Mario Luzi, for example, were drawn to it principally because, in the former's words, 'it seems to me to illustrate a saner attitude towards the mysteries of life' than anything in Shakespeare. Ezra Pound and Eugenio Montale were, for the most part, attracted by its qualities of style and expression, verbal economy and directness of presentation, as well as for its poetic realism based on the dynamic luminosity of metaphor, imagery, and detail. Pound was also influenced and inspired by Dante's moral and political perception, shared his sense of values, including 'the scale and proportion of evil, as delineated in Dante's Hell', and wholeheartedly endorsed Dante's condemnation of usury. Quite early in his life he had come to believe that there was nothing of any importance 'in the lives of men and nations that you cannot measure with the rod of Dante's allegory'.

The historical personages Dante dealt with so memorably in *The Divine Comedy*, such as Francesca da Rimini, Farinata degli Uberti, Pier della Vigna, Ulysses, Count Ugolino—*Inferno* (*Hell*); Matelda—*Il purgatorio* (*Purgatory*); San Tommaso, San Benedetto, and San Bernardo—*Il paradiso* (*Paradise*) are so many protagonists of that allegory. To each of them he dedicated an important *Canto*, as a result of which they, like Shakespeare's characters, have become embedded in literary and cultural history, and have attracted a large body of critical and exegetical commentary. In English alone, poets like Thomas Gray, Leigh Hunt, Tennyson, Browning, Rossetti, Pound, and Eliot wrote poems either dealing with some of these characters, or based on Dante's portrayals of them. Each character represents a particular sin or virtue, through which Dante covers the whole gamut of sense and sensibility, feeling and emotion: the tragic, the pathetic, the reverent, the indignant, and the compassionate.

The Divine Comedy was written and can be interpreted, as Dante himself explained in his dedication of *Heaven* to his host and patron Can Grande, in four senses: the literal, the allegorical, the anagogical, and the ethical. In the literal sense it is an account of Dante's vision of a journey through the three kingdoms of futurity, realms inhabited by the spirits of men after death—Hell, Purgatory, and Paradise. It can also be regarded, as Pound sees it, as a 'journey of Dante's intelligence through the states of minds wherein dwell all sorts and conditions of men before death' whereas Dante's intelligence itself may be considered as 'a symbol of mankind's struggle upward out of ignorance into the clear light of philosophy' and his journey as an allegorical representation of Dante's own mental and spiritual development. Thus Hell, Purgatory and Paradise are not places, but states of mind.

The poem is divided into three sections: *Hell*, *Purgatory*, and *Paradise*, and each section has 34, 33, and three sets of three cantos respectively, containing about 14,000 lines. In his journey through Hell and Purgatory, Virgil, symbolizing classical learning, poetry, and philosophy, is Dante's guide, and in Paradise, Beatrice, representing divine wisdom, takes over that role. The idea of the descent to Hell comes from the sixth book of *Aeneid* (230–900), where Virgil describes Aeneas' descent to Hell. The sins punished in both Hell and Purgatory are lust, gluttony, avarice, extravagance, wrath, sloth, heresy, violence, fraud, and betrayal. In describing both the sins and the sinners, as well as the kind of punishment meted out to each sinner and their reaction to it, Dante's poetic realism triumphs over the boundary between the real and the illusory, the terrestrial and the extra-terrestrial, so that whatever he describes in minute topographical detail seems to belong as much to this world as to the hereafter. 'In Dante's Hell', Eliot tells us, 'souls are not deadened, as they mostly are in life; they are actually in the greatest torment of which each is capable.' The sinners' inner character, psychology, and emotional state are so closely probed and so movingly portrayed by Dante that they become, to use Shelley's words, 'forms more real than living men,/Nurselings of immortality'.

There is in Dante the power of making us see what he sees, rendering, especially in *Paradise*, the spiritual not only visible, but also intensely exciting. Dante is thus a master in expressing, vividly and concretely, experience that is remote from ordinary experience, the very matter and substance of *Paradise*.

Shakespeare, as Carlyle says, is worldwide, Dante world deep—or, in the words of Eliot, *The Divine Comedy* expresses everything 'in the way of emotion between depravity's despair and the beatific vision, that man is capable of experiencing'. Dante and Shakespeare divide the modern world between them, he says, for 'there is no third'.

—G. Singh

THE NEW LIFE (La vita nuova)
Poems by Dante Alighieri, 1295.

The New Life, written when Dante was 29 or 30 years old, is primarily an anthology of poems, composed over a number of years and compiled by the author into a single collection, connected by a narrative, together with explanations of individual poems. A literary tribute to Beatrice, it both celebrates and analyses the poet's elevated feelings for his beloved. As such, it clearly belongs to the courtly love tradition of the troubadours, brought from Provence into Sicily by Giacomo da Lentini, and thence to Tuscany, where the Tuscan School, notably Guinizzelli, and Dante's great friend, Cavalcanti, refined the rough vernacular poetry of the Sicilians, and used it as a vehicle for expressing philosophic and literary ideas.

The collection opens with Dante's description of his first meeting with Beatrice when he was nine years old. At their next meeting, nine years later, he falls deeply in love: 'I was filled with such joy that I departed from people's company like one who was drunk'. A series of allegorical visions reveals Beatrice to him as both a bestower of blessings and a reflection of divine goodness. So profoundly moved is he by her presence that he composes poems to a 'screen' lady to disguise his embarrassment, though this device is eventually abandoned when the offended Beatrice refuses to return his salutation. Dante resolves to remove the fictional screen and devote himself to singing the praises of his lady. He now moves into a new realm of poetic creativity, writing with supreme skill and self-assurance: 'I felt I had to take up a new and nobler theme than before'. One by one, he recounts the death of Beatrice's father, his anguish at the sudden realization that 'one day, of necessity, the most noble Beatrice must die', and the moment of her actual death. Finally, he resolves to 'say no more of this blessed woman until such time as I can write . . . what has never been written before in rhyme of any woman'. This is clearly the first intimation of the role to be played by Beatrice in *The Divine Comedy* as guide and spiritual redeemer to the poet.

The New Life is closely structured around a numerical symmetry based upon the number nine with which Beatrice is associated (the poet is nine at their first meeting, and nine plus nine at their second encounter; Beatrice dies at the ninth hour of the ninth day of the ninth month) and upon the root of nine, three, the symbol of the Trinity. Three *canzoni* provide the framework, the first and third being preceded by one ballad and nine sonnets. The central *canzone* in turn forms part of a grouping of nine poems, being itself preceded and followed by four sonnets. Most of the poems are introduced by a prose passage describing the circumstances of their composition, usually some encounter or vision, together with an explanation of the poem itself. Dante deliberately counterpoises the poetic style of the prose narrative with the prosaic analysis of the poem's content. Sometimes, for special effect, he chooses to analyse the poem before presenting it,

'so that it (the poem) might seem more widowed at its conclusion'.

Critics have interpreted *The New Life* in various ways. For some, it is a youthful collection of poems in the courtly love tradition, drawn together by the medieval practice of textual glossary. For others, it is the essential groundwork for *The Divine Comedy* since it sets the living poet in a spiritual relationship with the beatified Beatrice in Heaven. Others again read it as a psychic drama, recounting the Neoplatonic ascent of the soul through love towards spiritual illumination. Recently, it has been viewed more as a treatise on poetry, a manual written by a poet for poets. All these interpretations are possible, and not necessarily conflicting.

For all that, it is a work of startling originality: the first literary autobiography, the first cohesive linking of poems, and the first attempt to write consistently poetic prose. It represents a major shift of focus, one in which the powerful expression of personal experience rather than poetic craftsmanship is at the heart of the poetry. Dante himself described it in this latter light in Canto XXIV of *Purgatory*: 'I am one who, when love inspires me, takes note, and as he instructs me, writes it down'. In other words, he saw *The New Life* not just as a poetic anthology but as something akin to what we would now call autobiography, and written in a *dolce stil nuovo*, 'sweet new style'. His judgement is sound.

—Jane McAdoo

DAPHNIS AND CHLOE. Pastoral romance probably written by Longus (fl. 2nd or 3rd century AD) who may have been born on Lesbos, the setting of the romance. One of five remaining Greek novels of the Classical period.

PUBLICATIONS

Daphnis et Chloe, edited by Michael D. Reeve. 1982; as *Daphnis and Chloe*, edited and translated by William D. Lowe, 1908; translated by Angell Daye (from French), 1587; also translated by George Thornley, 1657, revised by J.M. Edmonds [Loeb Edition], 1916; James Craggs, 2nd edition, 1720; C.V. Le Grice, 1803; Jack Lindsay, 1948; Paul Turner, 1956; Philip Sherrard, 1965; Christopher Gill, in *Collected Ancient Greek Novels*, 1989; as *The Pastoral Amours of Daphnis and Chloe*, translated by Roland Smith, 1882; as *The Pastoral Loves of Daphnis and Chloe*, translated by George Moore, 1924.

*

Critical Studies: *Longus* by William E. MacCulloh, 1970; *Daphnis and Chloe: The Markets and Metamorphoses of an Unknown Bestseller* by Giles Barber, 1988; *Myth, Rhetoric, and Fiction: A Reading of Longus' Daphnis and Chloe* by Bruce D. MacQueen, 1990; *A Study of Daphnis and Chloe* by Richard L. Hunter, 1993; *Sexual Symmetry: Love in the Ancient Novel and Related Genres* by David Konstan, 1994; *Greek Fiction: The Greek Novel in Context* edited by J.R. Morgan and Richard Stoneman, 1994; *The Search for the Ancient Novel* edited by James Tatum, 1994.

* * *

Daphnis et Chloe (*Daphnis and Chloe*), by a writer named (in all probability) Longus who lived in the 2nd or 3rd century AD, perhaps on the island of Lesbos, is one of five long prose narratives to survive from Greek antiquity. All take as their subject the love between a young couple, male and female, who overcome various obstacles in order finally to be united in wedlock. These five works—Chariton's *Chaereas and Callirhoe*; *The Ephesian Tale* by Xenophon of Ephesus; *Clitophon and Leucippe* by Achilles Tatius; and Heliodorus' *Aethiopian Tale*, in addition to *Daphnis and Chloe*—are conventionally designated 'romances' but may equally well be classified as novels.

Among the Greek novels, however, *Daphnis and Chloe* is unique for its pastoral setting, and the charming naivety of its protagonists, two young foundlings who have been raised, he as goatherd, she as shepherdess, by foster parents in the countryside near Mytilene, and fall innocently in love before they have heard of the word or can recognize its symptoms. The novel traces their initiation, over a single cycle of the seasons, into desire and sexuality, as well as their steadfastness in the face of rivals and marauders. In the end, the pair are revealed as the offspring, exposed in infancy, of rich parents from the city. By the kind of coincidence that is characteristic of the genre, Daphnis' family owns the estate on which the boy was reared.

The style of the narrative is elegant and suave, exploiting the rhetorical figures and balanced clauses that found favour with the writers of the so-called Second Sophistic, a cultural movement that rejoiced in classicizing diction and artful prose. Longus invites the reader to smile at the simplicity of his hero and heroine, which is underscored by the sophistication of the literary technique and by occasional cameos of urban manners. In this, Longus associates himself with the pastoral poetry inaugurated by Theocritus and perhaps by Philetas, a 3rd-century BC erotic poet whose name is borne by an old farmer in *Daphnis and Chloe*. Philetas offers the young pair their first lessons in love-making, instructing them that, in order to allay their desire, they must kiss, embrace, and lie naked next to each other. They follow Philetas' advice punctiliously, but discover that it falls short of satisfying their passion.

A married woman from the city, named Lycaenium, takes a fancy to Daphnis, and elects to alleviate his plight by initiating him into sex. Daphnis is set to race straight for Chloe so that he may share with her his new discovery before he forgets. But when Lycaenium warns him that Chloe will weep with pain and bleed when she is penetrated, Daphnis recoils at the idea of inflicting harm on her, and returns to the procedures recommended by Philetas. Only at the very end, when the couple, now revealed as free citizens of Mytilene, are wedded, do they at last consummate their passion.

Various incidents and subordinate narratives punctuate the amatory plot. Raiding pirates and a war party from another city on Lesbos threaten to separate the couple. Just before Daphnis' identity is revealed, one Gnatho, a crony of the urbane youth Astylus who will turn out to be Daphnis' brother, conceives a passion for Daphnis, and succeeds in obtaining him as his servant. After the recognition of Daphnis, a rival cowherd named Lampis carries off Chloe, but she is rescued in the nick of time by Gnatho, who gathers some of Astylus' men for the purpose in hopes of appeasing his new young patron. Gnatho is a figure out of New Comedy, and bears the same name as a parasite in Terence's *Eunuch*.

Here again, Longus reveals his flair for incorporating previous literary genres into his novel.

The presiding deities in the pastoral world of Lesbos are Pan and the Nymphs, and the entire tale is presented as an explication, provided by a professional interpreter, of a picture seen at a grove sacred to the Nymphs and dedicated to them, along with Love and Pan. Pan is a lustful character, and stories of his pursuit and attempted rape of Syrinx, who eludes him by turning into a reed (from which Pan constructs his pipes), and of Echo provide a counterpoint to the main narrative. The mutual adolescent desire of Daphnis and Chloe is in contrast to Pan's aggressive and selfish lust, and the protagonists, while grateful for his protection, distance themselves from his erotic violence and fickleness.

The pair's wedding night is described in the final words of the novel:

> Daphnis and Chloe lay down naked together, embraced and kissed, and had even less sleep that night than the owls. Daphnis did some of the things Lycaenium taught him; and then, for the first time, Chloe found out that what they had done in the woods had been nothing but shepherds' games.

Longus does not pause to explain why, on this night, Daphnis suddenly overcomes the fear of harming Chloe in the sexual act. Presumably, it is enough that she has moved from the status of unwed maiden or *parthenos* to that of wedded woman, ready now to assume a full sexual role. Yet, despite the knowing wink on the part of the author, the innocence of Chloe's previous life with Daphnis remains as an image of a simple, childlike way of sex in a pastoral world alive with rustic deities. To this world, in the end, the couple elect to return.

—David Konstan

———

DARÍO, Rubén. Born Félix Rubén García Sarmiento in Metapa, Nicaragua, 18 January 1867. Educated at various schools; then a Jesuit school, 1878–80; Instituto de Occidente, Léon, 1881. Married 1) Rafaela Contreras in 1890 (died 1892), one son; 2) Rosario Emelina Murillo in 1893, one son; also one daughter and two sons by Francisca Sánchez. Journalist from age 14: worked on papers in Nicaragua, Valparaíso, Santiago and Buenos Aires; then correspondent for Latin American papers in various parts of Latin America as well as in Paris and Madrid; also served Guatemala in various diplomatic and representative functions; consul of Cambodia to Argentina, 1893–94; suffered from alcoholic depression, 1895. *Died 6 February 1916.*

PUBLICATIONS

Collections

Obras completas. 22 vols., 1917–20.
Obras completas, edited by Alberto Ghiraldo and Andrés González-Blanco. 21 vols., 1923–29.
Obras completas, edited by Sanmiguel Raimúndez and Emilio Gascó Contell. 5 vols., 1950–55.
Poesías completas, edited by Alfonso Méndez Plancarte.

1952; revised edition, edited by Antonio Oliver Belmás, 2 vols., 1967.
Selected Poems, translated by Lysander Kemp. 1965.
Poesía, edited by Ernesto Mejía Sánchez. 1977.
Poesías inéditas, edited by Ricardo Llopesa. 1988.

Verse

Epístolas y poemas. 1885.
Abrojos. 1887.
Las rosas andinas: Rimas y contra-rimas, with Rubén Rubí. 1888.
Azul. 1888; revised edition, 1890; also edited by Andrew P. Debicki and Michael J. Doudoroff, 1985.
Rimas. 1889.
Prosas profanas y otros poemas. 1896; revised edition, 1901; as *Prosas Profanas and Other Poems*, translated by Charles B. McMichael. 1922.
Cantos de vida y esperanza, Los cisnes, y otros poemas. 1905.
El canto errante. 1907.
Poema del otoño y otros poemas. 1910.
Canto a la Argentina y otros poemas. 1914.
Obra poética. 4 vols., 1914–16.
Eleven Poems, translated by Thomas Walsh and Salomón de la Selva. 1916.
Sol del domingo: Poesías inéditas. 1917.

Fiction

Emelina, with Eduardo Poirier. 1887.
Edelmira, edited by Francisco Contreras. 1926(?).
Cuentos fantásticos, edited by José Olivio Jiménez. 1979.
Cuentos, edited by José Emilio Balladares. 1986.

Other

La canción del oro; La isla del oro; El oro de Mallorca. 1886.
A. de Gilbert. 1890.
Los raros. 1893.
Castelar. 1899.
Peregrinaciones. 1901.
España contemporánea. 1901.
La caravana pasa. 1902.
Tierras solares. 1904.
Opiniones. 1906.
Parisiana. 1907.
El viaje a Nicaragua. 1909.
Blanco. 1911.
Letras. 1911.
Todo al vuelo. 1912.
Autobiografía. 1912.
La casa de las ideas. 1916.
La vida de Rubén Darío, escrita por el mismo. 1916.
El mundo de los sueños: Prosas póstumas. 1917; edited by Angel Rama, 1973.
Impresiones y sensaciones, edited by Alberto Ghiraldo. 1925.
Escritos inéditos, edited by E.K. Mapes. 1938.
Cartas: Epistolario inedito, edited by Dictino Álvarez Hernández. 1963.
Escritos dispersos, edited by Pedro Luis Barcia. 2 vols., 1968–73.
Páginas desconocidas, edited by Roberta Ibáñez. 1970.
La isla del oro/El oro de Mallorca, edited by Luis Maristany. 1978.
Textos socio-políticos, edited by Jorge Eduardo Arellano and Francisco Valle, 1980.

*

Bibliography: *A Bibliography of Darío* by Henry Grattan Doyle, 1935; *Rubén Darío: A Selective Classified and Annotated Bibliography* by Hensley C. Woodbridge, 1975; *Bibliografía de Rubén Darío* by Jorge Eduardo Arellano, 1981.

Critical Studies: *Poet-Errant: A Biography of Darío* by Charles D. Watland, 1965; *Cuadrivio* (on Darío, López Velarde, Pessoa, Cernuda) by Octavio Paz, 1965; *Critical Approaches to Rubén Darío* by Keith Ellis, 1974; *Rubén Darío and the Pythagorean Tradition* by Raymond Skyrme, 1975; *Rubén Darío and the Romantic Search for Unity: The Modernist Recourse to Esoteric Tradition* by Cathy Logan Jrade, 1983; *Light and Longing: Silva and Darío: Modernism and Religious Heterodoxy* by Sonya A. Ingwersen, 1986.

* * *

Throughout the Spanish-speaking literary world Rubén Darío is known as the great innovator, the poet who transformed the prosody of that language. At the turn of the century he emerged as the leader of the movement known as 'Modernismo', and as the first American writer seriously to influence the literary conventions of metropolitan Spain.

His first important collection, *Azul* [Blue], shows an obvious allegiance to 19th-century French poetry, from Hugo through the Parnassians to the symbolists and Verlaine, otherwise evident in the sketches collected in *Los raros*; in fact the coda of *Azul*, 'Échos', is actually written in French. The core of the book is a 'lyrical year', in which the four seasons are experienced in terms less appropriate to the poet's native Nicaragua than to a Europe whose culture dazzled Darío from the start of his career. None the less there are characteristic American notes in the sonnets to Caupolicán, the Mapuche hero of Chile, and to the poet Salvador Díaz Mirón, a fellow modernist whom Darío had known in Mexico and whose 'unfettered' verses are said to resound like a herd of American buffalo.

Usually thought of as his most decadent and precious collection, *Prosas profanas* [Profane Prose] is by any account his least American in terms of overt theme and subject matter, despite, that is, his famous invocation of Palenque and Utatlán, Montezuma and the Inca, in the introduction. For example, the past evoked in the section 'Recreaciones arqueológicas' definitely belongs to the classic Mediterranean, also the backdrop for the extensive 'Coloquio de los centauros', with its Pythagoreanism. Elsewhere in this collection Darío turns to the Cid and medieval Spain, much as Ezra Pound (triumphant in London not long after Darío was in Madrid) turned to medieval England. Indeed, this parallel helps us to focus on what is a new cosmopolitanism in the poetry of Darío and the Spanish language in general. Associated repeatedly with Buenos Aires, where Darío began the collection, this cosmopolitanism is most fully expressed in the poem 'Divagación', a spiralling journey through cultures and time.

From a technical point of view, *Prosas profanas* announces spectacular innovations in prosody, notably in the syncopation of the alexandrine, which continue to be used to great effect in Darío's three subsequent collections *Cantos de vida y esperanza* [Songs of Love and Hope] *El canto errante* [Wandering Song], and *Poema del otoño* [Poem of Autumn], though less so in the somewhat stentorian *Canto a la Argentina*, the last collection published in his lifetime. (In his nomadic career, he left a good deal of work uncollected.) Typical of the more sombre agility of his later period are the

Nocturnes in *Cantos de vida*, notably the arresting alexandrine that opens the second: 'Los que auscultasteis el corazón de la noche'. The alexandrine is also the verse form chosen by Darío in *El canto errante* for his 'Epístola a Madame Lugones', she being the wife of another fellow modernist, the Argentinian Leopoldo Lugones. Remarkable for its colloquialism, its shifts of mood and tone, as well as its technical virtuosity, this poem has received brilliant elucidation in 'El caracol y la sirena', Octavio Paz's indispensable vindication of Darío as the father not just of modernist but of modern poetry in Spanish.

—Gordon Brotherston

MÍA
Poem by Rubén Darío, 1896.

Prosas profanas, Darío's collection of poems published in Buenos Aires in 1896, sought even in its title to be outrageous. The hint at blasphemy—'prosas' refers to a sequence in the Catholic mass—is developed in several poems, especially the erotic 'Ite Missa Est'. In fact, one element Darío had made his own stemmed from his Nicaraguan tropical exuberance, appearing in erotic poems that enshrined lust as the optimum state of the mind. This collection opens with what could be called Darío's manifesto, where he outlines his view of art, which for him was synonymous with freedom. One of his cultural heroes was the composer Wagner, and quoting from him Darío justifies his idiosyncrasies. Darío is not writing for a public but to awaken in a reader, in himself, his 'reino interior' (inner world).

The poem that summarizes many of Darío's achievements, and his thinking about eroticism and passing time, is a sonnet 'de arte menor', written in imitation of a Wagnerian *Lied*, and called 'Mía' (both a woman's name, and the possessive pronoun 'mine', differentiated in the poem by the use of capitals, as first pointed out by the poet critic Pedro Salinas). This name 'Mía' and the allusion to Wagner underline Darío's fascination with the enchantment of music. The French symbolist poet Paul Verlaine's battle cry, 'De la musique avant toute chose', is exaggerated by Darío so that from the opening poem of the collection 'Era un aire suave' [It Was a Soft Musical Air] you have music both as sound predominating over sense, through alliteration and rhyme, and music as the ideal art form, hinting at a sensuous and mysterious world beyond verbal description, beyond referentiality, that could only be suggested through symbols.

'Mía' opens with a stanza whose rich sounds play with double meanings to suggest the plenitude of the senses of a male lover: 'Mía: Así te llamas./¿Qué más armonía/Mía: luz de día;/mía: rosas, llamas' [O my Mía: so that's your name/ what greater harmony/my Mía: Daylight/my Mía: roses, flame]. In what is almost poetic annotation, a rhythm of desire is built up by the short phrases broken by colons and semi-colons. Mía promises the poet the harmony (*mía* emerges from the word har*monía*) that he has always sought outside the harsh world of survival that Darío actually inhabited as a poet, bohemian, and freelance journalist. He defined art as the freedom to escape empirical reality and mundanity into fantasy. Darío transformed fantasy (normally seen as an inability to be) into the ultimate reality. For a moment his inner mental world becomes more real, with its roses (perhaps lips) and flames (passion of love).

The second stanza suggests how sensuality seeps into his soul, something quite pagan and alien to the Church's condemnation of pleasure. According to the critic Guillermo Sucre, Darío exalted pleasure. Octavio Paz has inserted Darío's view of love into a Western heretical tradition of love as access to a higher truth. Darío's poems parade centaurs, satyrs, Greek gods and goddesses promising a guiltless sexuality. Mía's 'aroma' spills into the poet's soul. The second stanza ends with an orgasmic cry of ecstasy: '¡Oh Mía! ¡Oh Mía!'.

Had the poem ended here, it would have been a condensed little song to possessive love. But the third stanza changes the tone. It is one sentence, and it brings the poet back down to earth: 'Tu sexo fundiste/con mi sexo fuerte,/fundiendo dos bronces' [You melted your sex/with my strong sex/like melting two bronzes].

No doubt the reduction of the male and female lovers to their 'sexo' scandalized the idealizing public of the 1890s, but Darío had hoped for more than sensual pleasure from ephemeral physical union. He wanted to remain in that moment of ecstasy for ever, as if that moment could be converted into a bronze statue, a work of art. Within the very poem Darío senses the negation of *eros* which is *thanatos*, death in the form of passing time, of running out of energy. Only a work of art can fix ecstasy, like Rodin's sculpture *The Kiss*. So Darío ends the poem with a note of melancholia, repeating Ovid's famous phrase about post-coital sadness: 'Yo triste, tú triste . . ./¿No has de ser entonces/mía hasta la muerte?' [I am sad, you're sad/Can't you stay mine/until the end of time?]. And the obvious answer to the poem's final question is no, she will not be his unto death. This parody of the marriage vows ('until death do us part') becomes the condemnation of the lovers. Darío's latent melancholia surfaces here in this poem, to become an emotive vein in his next collection *Cantos de vida y esperanza*, 1905, where Darío is forced to face a world that does not allow the poet to escape, for a world without fantasies for Darío is spiritual death. Darío associates woman and death: 'La hembra humana es hermana del Dolor y de la Muerte' (The human female is sister to Pain and Death) he has Hipea say in his long discursive poem 'El coloquio de los centauros' [Colloquy of the Centaurs]. What one can add concerning this sonnet 'Mía' is that Darío's confusion of sexual possession, pleasure, and death makes the poem more than a pleasurable ditty, for it opens out into a 20th-century dilemma where lust and eroticism cannot replace God, and a poem cannot save you from extinction. It is a very human position, and one that Darío sought to avoid in many poems of *Prosas profanas*.

—Jason Wilson

———

DAZAI Osamu. Born Tsushima Shuji in Kanagi, Japan, 19 June 1909. Educated in Kanagi grade school; middle school in Aomori City; higher school in Hirosaki, 1927–30; Tokyo Imperial University, from 1930. Married 1) Oyama Hatsuyo in 1931; 2) Ishihara Michiko in 1939. Journalist and writer: illness, alcohol, and drugs led to several suicide attempts. Recipient: Kitamura Tōkoku award, 1939. *Died 13 June 1948.*

PUBLICATIONS

Collection

Zenshū [Works]. 12 vols., 1955–57; revised editions, 1967–68, 1979.

Fiction

Bannen [The Declining Years]. 1936.
Doke No hana [The Flower of Buffoonery]. 1937.
Dasu gemaine [Das Gemeine]. 1940.
Hashire Merosu [Run Melos]. 1940.
Shin Hamuretto [The New Hamlet]. 1941.
Kojiki gakusei [Beggar-Student]. 1941.
Kakekomi uttae [The Indictment]. 1941.
Seigi to bisho [Justice and Smile]. 1942.
Udaijin Sanetomo [Lord Sanetomo]. 1943.
Tsugaru. 1944; as *Return to Tsugaru: Travels of a Purple Tramp*, translated by James Westerhoven, 1985.
Shinshaku shokoku banashi [A Retelling of the Tales from the Province]. 1945.
Otogi zoshi [A Collection of Fairy-Tales]. 1945.
Pandora no hako [Pandora's Box]. 1946.
Shayō. 1947; as *The Declining Sun*, translated by Takehide Kikuchi, 1950; as *The Setting Sun*, translated Donald Keene, 1956.
Biyon no tsuma [Villon's Wife]. 1947.
Ningen shikkaku. 1948; as *No Longer Human*, translated by Donald Keene, 1953.
Selected Stories and Sketches, translated by James O'Brien. 1982.
Crackling Mountain and Other Stories, translated by James O'Brien. 1989.
Self Portraits (stories), translated by Ralph F. McCarthy. 1991.
Blue Bamboo: Tales of Fantasy and Romance, translated by Ralph F. McCarthy. 1993.

Other

Human Lost (diary; in Japanese). 1937.
Fugaku Hyakkei [One Hundred Views of Mt Fuji]. 1940.
Tokyo Hakkei [Eight Views of Tokyo]. 1941.

*

Critical Studies: *Landscapes and Portraits* by Donald Keene, 1971; *Accomplices of Silence: The Modern Japanese Novel* by Masao Miyoshi, 1974; *Dazai Osamu* by James A. O'Brien, 1975; *Modern Japanese Writers and the Nature of Literature* by Makoto Ueda, 1976; 'Art Is Me': Dazai Osamu's Narrative Voice as a Permeable Self', in *Harvard Journal of Asiatic Studies*, 41, 1981, and *The Saga of Dazai Osamu: A Critical Study with Translations*, 1985, both by Phyllis I. Lyons; *Suicidal Narrative in Modern Japan: The Case of Dazai Osamu*, by Alan Wolfe, 1990.

*   *   *

Though he is regarded as one of the greatest stylists of modern Japanese literature, Dazai Osamu's masterpiece was his life itself. Virtually all his works were reflections of that life. For Dazai, fiction was ultimately a lie, and in his often nostalgic quest for sincerity he strove to strip bare the author-ial self and let it speak directly to the reader. In this respect, Dazai can be associated with the autobiographical strain in modern Japanese fiction, the *watakushi-shosetsu* or 'I-novel'. The practitioners of this form felt that reality could only be portrayed through the unmediated perspective of the author, presented as the first-person narrator in the text. This mode coincided with traditional tendencies to view literature as a mode of self-expression and to hold a somewhat skeptical attitude towards 'objective' reality.

Dazai consciously conceived of his life as art, as the subject matter of his writings. Dazai the man became 'Dazai' the text, and his works represented various readings of that text. The Dazai persona was that of the sensitive but cynical dissolute, the sloppy drunk who arouses more pity than disgust. It was characterized by an all-too-human weakness that was designed to elicit compassion, the highest virtue. Born to a wealthy landholding family, Dazai developed a rebellious streak that he briefly tried to channel into political activism, but it seems that he could not even believe in communism. Distrusting virtually all social institutions, he lived a scandalous life. Hypocrisy, arrogance, and pretension are denounced everywhere in his works, while simplicity, sincerity, and honesty are praised. In Dazai's literary world, consciousness is the curse that keeps one from living a true life. While idealizing simple people who live day-to-day in an unselfconscious manner, Dazai found himself irresistibly drawn to despair and death.

Many of Dazai's writings are in the 'I-novel' vein. Such works as *Tokyo Hakkei* [Eight Views of Tokyo], *Fugaku Hyakkei* [One Hundred Views of Mt Fuji], and *Tsugaru* (*Return to Tsugaru*) are first-person narratives by the archetypal 'Dazai' character. In *Shin Hamuretto* [The New Hamlet], *Otogi Zoshi* [A Collection of Fairy-Tales], and similar works, old literary works are retold in a uniquely Dazaiesque manner, irreverent yet profoundly human. Dazai's most accomplished works of fiction—the short story *Biyon no Tsuma* [Villon's Wife] and the novels *Shayō* (*The Setting Sun*) and *Ningen Shikkaku* (*No Longer Human*)—appeared shortly after the end of World War II. Taken together, the works present a deep and multi-faceted composite image of the 'Dazai' persona. *The Setting Sun*, Dazai's most famous work, has been praised for its portrayal of the desolation and hope of post-war Japan. Yet although one of the central characters, Kazuko, appears to have made an existentialist decision at the end, even her resolve is cloaked in ambiguity.

If Dazai's *oeuvre* suffers from its narrowly drawn subject, it nevertheless contains some of the most beautiful prose in 20th-century Japanese literature. Because of his basic love of humanity, Dazai possessed an extraordinary sensitivity to the rhythm and flow of speech, revealed in a limpid, entertaining, and often humorous literary style that makes his works a joy to read, and must account for some of the popularity he maintains among Japanese readers to this day.

—Matthew Mizenko

DE FILIPPO, Eduardo. Born in Naples, Italy, 24 May 1900. Illegitimate son of playwright and actor-manager Eduardo Scarpetta. Educated at Istituto Chierchia, Naples, 1911.

Served in the Italian army, 1920–22. Married 1) the actress Dorothy Pennington in 1928 (marriage annulled in San Marino, 1952, recognized in Italy, 1956); 2) Thea Prandi in 1956 (separated 1959; died 1961), one son and one daughter before marriage; 3) Isabella Quarantotti in 1977. Child actor with family troupe: debut, 1904; actor with Vincenzo Scarpetta's company, 1914–20, Francesco Corbindi's troupe, 1922, Peppino Villani's troupe, 1928, and the Riviste Molinari company, 1930–31; co-founder, with his brother Peppino and sister Titina, Il Teatro Umoristico, 1929, and toured with it until Peppino's departure in 1945; co-founder, with Titina, Il Teatro di Eduardo, 1945–54; director and owner, Teatro San Ferdinando, Naples, from 1954; toured Austria, Belgium, Hungary, Poland, and Russia, 1962. Also film actor, and director of films and operas. Recipient: Institute of Italian Drama prize, 1951, 1968; Simoni prize, 1969; Feltrinelli prize, 1972; Pirandello prize, 1975. D.Litt.: University of Birmingham, England, 1977; University of Rome, 1980. Named Senator for Life of the Italian Republic, 1981. *Died 31 October 1984.*

PUBLICATIONS

Plays

Sik-Sik, L'artefice magico (produced 1929). 1932; as *Sik-Sik, The Masterful Magician*, translated by Robert G. Bender, in *Italian Quarterly*, 11, 1967.
Natale in casa Cupiello (produced 1931; revised version produced 1942). In *Cantata dei giorni pari*, 1959.
Farmacia di turno (produced 1931). In *Cantata dei giorni pari*, 1959.
Ogni anno punto e da capo (produced 1931). 1971.
Quei figuri di trent'anni fa (produced 1932). In *Cantata dei giorni pari*, 1959.
Chi è cchiù felice 'e me! . . . (produced 1932). In *Cantata dei giorni pari*, 1959.
Gennariniello (produced 1932). In *Cantata dei giorni pari*, 1959.
Ditegli sempre di sì (produced 1932). In *Cantata dei giorni pari*, 1959.
I morti non fanno paura (as *Requie all'anima soia*, produced 1932; revised version, as *I morti non fanno paura*, produced 1952). In *Cantata dei giorni dispari 2*, 1958.
L'ultimo bottone (produced 1932).
Cuoco della mala cucina, with Maria Scarpetta (produced 1932).
Uomo e galantuomo (produced 1933). In *Cantata dei giorni pari*, 1959.
Parlate al portiere, with Maria Scarpetta (produced 1933).
Scorzetta di limone, from a play by Gino Rocca (produced 1933)
Il dono di Natale (produced 1934). In *Cantata dei giorni pari*, 1959.
Tre mesi dopo (produced 1934).
Sintetici a qualunque costo (produced 1934).
Il berretto a sonagli, from a play by Pirandello (produced 1936).
Quinto piano, ti saluto! (produced 1936). In *Cantata dei giorni pari*, 1959.
L'abito nuovo, from a story by Pirandello (produced 1937). In *Cantata dei giorni pari*, 1959.
Uno coi capelli bianchi (produced 1938). In *Cantata dei giorni pari*, 1959.
Si salvi chi può, from a work by Gino Rocca (produced 1940).
Non ti pago! (produced 1940). 1943.

La parte di Amelto (produced 1940). In *Cantata dei giorni pari*, 1959.
In licenza, from a work by Eduardo Scarpetta (produced 1941).
La fortuna con l'effe maiuscola, with Armando Curcio and R. De Angelis (produced 1942).
Io, l'erede (produced 1942). In *Cantata dei giorni pari*, 1959.
Il diluvio, from the play by Ugo Betti (produced 1943).
Napoli milionaria! (produced 1945). 1946.
Occhiali neri (produced 1945). In *Cantata dei giorni dispari 2*, 1958.
Questi fantasmi! (produced 1946). In *Cantata dei giorni dispari 1*, 1951; as *Oh, These Ghosts*, translated by Marguerite Carra and Louise H. Warner, in *Tulane Drama Review*, 8, 1963.
Filumena Marturano (produced 1946). In *Cantata dei giorni dipari 1*, 1951; as *The Best House in Naples*, translated by Carlo Ardito, in *Three Plays*, 1976; as *Filumena*, translated by Keith Waterhouse and Willis Hall, 1978.
Pericolosamente (produced 1947). In *Cantata dei giorni pari*, 1959.
Le bugie con le gambe lunghe (produced 1948). In *Cantata dei giorni dispari 1*, 1951.
Le voci di dentro (produced 1948). In *Cantata dei giorni dispari 1*, 1951; as *Inner Voices*, translated by N.F. Simpson, 1983.
La grande magia (produced 1949). In *Cantata dei giorni dispari 1*, 1951; as *Grand Magic*, translated by Carlo Ardito, in *Three Plays*, 1976.
La paura numero uno (produced 1950). In *Cantata dei giorni dispari 2*, 1958.
Cantata dei giorni dispari. 3 vols., 1951–66; revised edition, 1971.
Amicizia (produced 1952). In *Cantata dei giorni dispari 2*, 1958.
Miseria e nobiltà, from a play by Eduardo Scarpetta (produced 1953).
Bene mio e core mio (produced 1955). 1956.
Mia famiglia (produced 1955). 1955.
Il medico dei pazzi, from a work by Eduardo Scarpetta (produced 1957).
De Pretore Vincenzo (produced 1957). 1957.
Tre cazune fortunate, from a play by Eduardo Scarpetta (produced 1958).
Sabato, domenica e lunedi (produced 1959). 1960; as *Saturday, Sunday, Monday*, translated by Keith Waterhouse and Willis Hall, 1974.
Cantata dei giorni pari. 1959.
Il sindaco del Rione Sanità (produced 1960). 1961; as *The Local Authority*, translated by Carlo Ardito, in *Three Plays*, 1976.
Il figlio di Pulcinella (produced 1962). In *Cantata dei giorni dispari 3*, 1966.
Peppino Girella, with Isabella Quaratotti (televised 1963). 1964.
Farse e commedie. 2 vols., 1964.
Dolore sotto chiave (produced 1964). With *L'arte della commedia*, 1965.
L'arte della commedia (produced 1965). With *Dolore sotto chiave*, 1965.
Tommaso D'Amalfi. In *Cantata dei giorni dispari 3*, 1966.
Il cilindro (produced 1966). In *Cantata dei giorni dispari 3*, 1966.
Il contratto (produced 1967). 1967.
Cani e gatti, from a work by Eduardo Scarpetta (produced 1970).
Il monumento (produced 1970). 1971.

'Na santarella, from a work by Eduardo Scarpetta (produced 1972).
I capolavori. 2 vols., 1973.
Gli esami non finiscono mai (produced 1973). 1973.
Lu curaggio de nu pumpiere napulitano, from a work by Eduardo Scarpetta (produced 1974).
Three Plays (includes *The Local Authority*; *Grand Magic*; *The Best House in Naples—Filumena Marturano*), translated by Carlo Ardito. 1976.
L'erede di Shylock, from the play by Shakespeare. 1984.
La Tempesta, from the play by Shakespeare. 1984.

Screenplays: 'Adelina' episode, with Isabella Quarantotti, of *Ieri, oggi e domani* (*Yesterday, Today and Tomorrow*), 1963; *Matrimonio all'italiana* (*Marriage Italian Style*), 1964; *Spara forte, più forte . . . non capisco* (*Shoot Loud, Louder . . . I Don't Understand*), with Suso Cecchi D'Amico, 1966.

Television Plays: *Peppino Girella*, with Isabella Quarantotti, 1963; *Li nepute de lu sinecco*, 1975; *'O Tuono 'e marzo*, 1975; and adaptations of about 20 of his own plays.

Verse

Il paese di Pulcinella. 1951.
'O canisto. 1971.
Le poesie. 1975.

Other

Editor, *Manzù: Album inedito*. 1977.

*

Critical Studies: *In Search of Theatre* by Eric Bentley, 1953; *L'esperienza comica di Eduardo De Filippo* by Laura Pizer, 1972; *Eduardo* by Federico Frascani, 1974; *Il teatro di Eduardo*, 1975, and *Eduardo De Filippo*, 1978, by Fiorenza Di Franco; *Eduardo nel mondo* edited by Isabella De Filippo, 1978, and *Eduardo De Filippo: Vita e opere 1900–1984* edited by De Filippo and Sergio Martin, 1986; *Eduardo De Filippo: Poeta comico del tragico quotidiano* by Carla Filosa, 1978; *Eduardo De Filippo: Introduzione e guida allo studio dell' opera eduardiana, storia e antologia della critica* by Giovanni Antonucci, 1980; *Eduardo segreto* by Federico Frascani, 1982; *De Filippo* (in English) by Mario Mignone, 1984; *Eduardo drammaturgo* by Anna Barsotti, 1988.

* * *

Eduardo De Filippo's entire life was spent in the theatre. At the age of four he first appeared on stage; at 14 he joined the company in which his father, Eduardo Scarpetta, the prominent Neapolitan actor, director, and author, was a member. De Filippo was born into a thespian family but he was also educated in the still lively, century-old tradition of the Neapolitan theatre, the popular and dialectal heir to the *commedia dell'arte*. He became an author, actor, and later director and manager of his own company. It is not surprising that even in his least inspired works one cannot fail to notice his consummate stage craftsmanship.

His plays are either a continuous crescendo or a combination of crescendo and diminuendo. An example of the latter is *La paura numero uno* [Fear Number One]: Matteo, fearing World War II, tries to postpone indefinitely his daughter's wedding; Luisa, the other protagonist and the fiancé's mother, who has lost her husband in World War I and one son in World War II, does not want her only remaining son to risk the danger of war, and walls him up in a room. Matteo first appears comical, then ridiculous, then morally acceptable; Luisa is first seemingly mad, then pathetic, then irreproachable.

Filumena Marturano, on the other hand, is an example of the plays of crescendo. By the end of each of its three acts we are surprised: in Act I, characters and audience discover that the main character is the mother of three grown sons; in Act II, one of the three proves to be that of Domenico, her lover; in Act III, the lovers reveal to each other their inner feelings. These revelations disclose, to odd effect, the real meaning of what went on before: some of the comic elements become serious, and the serious, comic: the sentimental becomes real, while the insane becomes normal.

Although De Filippo was a product of Neapolitan popular theatre in his craft and often in his language, the theatricality of that tradition did not compromise his originality. The farce of Eduardo Scarpetta and the grotesquerie of Raffaele Viviani, another famous Neapolitan playwright, become, in De Filippo, humorous, bitter-sweet, or pathetic. In the first poem of his collection *Il paese di Pulcinella* [Pulcinella's Land], the question 'Is it a laughing matter when I portray comical situations arising from everyday life?' is answered with 'I don't think so'. Of course, we may still laugh, but we must also perceive that his comedy carries a streak of melancholy.

The locus of De Filippo's drama is Naples, and its subject the Neapolitan in his daily struggle for physical, social, or emotional survival. The solidity of De Filippo's plots and the characterization of his Neapolitan personae generate irresistible laughter, but also reveal man's existential finitude: a hint of the tragic is evoked. These dramas pitch the individual against society, which is generally represented by the family. In fact, some of De Filippo's most famous and successful plays, such as *Napoli milionaria!*, *Filumena Marturano*, and *Sabato, domenica e lunedi* (*Saturday, Sunday, Monday*), present in tones of bitter-sweet realism conflicts among family members with different desires, morals, or beliefs. However, it is when De Filippo shatters the realistic mould that his plays achieve their greatest originality.

In his first major play, and one of his own favourites, *Natale in casa Cupiello* [Christmas at the Cupiellos], the protagonist, Luca, detaches himself completely from the reality surrounding him by clinging stubbornly to his ideals, his world of illusions. A human being unable to see the obvious may evoke in the audience a smile of compassion and pity. But the audience is also made aware that Luca is unconsciously rejecting the obvious in order to preserve his ego, in order to prevent existence from drowning essence. Our smile of compassion becomes self-conscious, for we all share in Luca's hopeless effort. To pity is added a tinge of terror.

While Luca defends his illusions with the myth of universal brotherhood, symbolized by his construction of the Nativity scene, and remains within realistic co-ordinates, the protagonists of two of the most important of De Filippo's plays break through the frame of realism and enter the world of fantasy and the surreal.

In *Questi fantasmi!* (*Oh, These Ghosts*), Pasquale convinces himself that there are ghosts: he manufactures them instead of accepting the fact that his wife has a lover. He abandons the reality of pain by living in a world of fantasy. In *La grande magia* (*Grand Magic*), Calogero, who does not want to admit that his wife has run away with her lover, believes what he is told by Otto, a magician: that his wife is being kept in a small box. By opening it, says Otto, he can make her reappear, but only if he has faith in her. Calogero refuses to open the box; he does not want to face the reality of his adulterous wife. Four years later Maria comes back, but Calogero refuses to accept her because she appeared the moment before he was about to open the box; he concludes that the woman before him is not Maria. He will keep the box closed forever so that he can always believe his wife has been faithful.

De Filippo's two kinds of 'reality'—fact and fantasy—do not imply a kind of Pirandellian relativism or an ontological questioning of the real. But his characters, like some of Pirandello's, do use fantasy to avoid being thrown into the abyss of despair or emptiness. Their defences against the abyss are what makes De Filippo's comedies serious.

—Emanuele Licastro

FILUMENA MARTURANO
Play by Eduardo De Filippo, 1946.

The protagonists of *Filumena Marturano* met long ago at a brothel where Filumena worked to relieve her family's abject poverty. The hero, Domenico Soriano, was attracted to her, and decided to save her from a life of prostitution by taking her home with him, allowing her even to choose her own servant. She fell in love and, as if married, performed the duties of a faithful wife, loving Domenico, keeping house, and watching out for his business interests during his frequent travels. Symbolically, she is the whore with the heart of gold, and he is the knight in shining armour—an exemplary fairy-tale for Hollywood or Broadway. But the story takes place in Naples, not Hollywood, and she conceals her love for him, while he continues to regard her as a kept woman.

Filumena Marturano is written in the Neapolitan dialect, in which a great deal of comic and sentimental literature has been produced, and, for most of the play, De Filippo's serious use of it succeeds in estranging the characters from the maudlin and mawkish. His genius imbues this fairy-tale with a stark reality that cannot be concealed by laughter.

When the play opens, the two characters have been living together, unmarried, for 25 years. Filumena, however, wants to get married, and pretends to be mortally ill and on her deathbed so that Domenico will comply. We do not witness the ceremony but Rosalia, Filumena's servant and confidante, cannot stop laughing as she remembers how, after it, Filumena jumped happily out of bed, wishing her husband and herself the best of luck.

The main action of the play starts just after the ceremony, in the dining room, with Filumena still in her nightgown. Domenico is furious. He believes that the reason for her deception is to prevent him from marrying his new young girlfriend, 22-year-old Diana. Their bitter confrontation evokes their past lives: Filumena says she has always loved him, and he acknowledges that he has always considered her a kept woman and intends to have the marriage annulled. At the end of Act I, Filumena reveals that she had three children before going to live with Domenico and has been secretly supporting them, unbeknown even to the children. She did not deceive Domenico out of jealousy or greed, but in order to give a name to her now grown-up sons.

In Act II, the following day, Filumena brings her sons to the house and tells them that she is their mother. When Domenico's lawyer proves to her that the marriage is illegal, Filumena decides to go and live with one of her sons. Before leaving, however, she reveals to Domenico that one of the three sons is his, although she refuses to say which one.

In the first two acts we come to understand Filumena's plight: the mask of a kept woman conceals her existence as a lonely, loving mother and is her shield against circumstance. She has never cried. The illegitimacy of her own birth creates an obsessive yearning for her sons' legitimacy. De Filippo is aware of the quiet desperation underlying everyday life—a contrast expressed in his plays by their surface comedy and the searing sadness upon which they are founded.

In Act III, ten months later, we learn that after the annulment of their illegal marriage, Domenico is now willing to marry Filumena and has agreed to give his name to all three sons, since Filumena still refuses to reveal which one is his. The ceremony is about to be performed. It is a happy moment: Filumena seems rejuvenated and the young men finally feel they can call Domenico father. Humour is provided by Domenico's unsuccessful attempts to discover which son is really his. Just before the curtain falls, Filumena finally, for the first time, is able to cry. Her last words are: 'How wonderful it is to cry!'.

The conclusion is predictable: the structure of the whole play must lead to such a finale. The mock death at the beginning is a clear indication of a happy ending, but there is no real happiness in De Filippo's world, and this happiness is false. Both protagonists have slowly become aware of the bitterness of their predicament. Domenico knows, and declares, that they are not getting married like two youngsters believing in love's illusion: 'We have had our lives', he says. They are only giving a name to the sons. His is not a sudden metamorphosis devised by De Filippo in order to end the play. In the second act we have already heard him reflect upon the passage of time:

> I'm through. No will, no enthusiasm, no passions, and if I try anything, it's only to prove to myself that it isn't so . . . that I can get the better of death itself. And I do so well I believe it!

It is as if Filumena's feigned death has jolted him into contemplating his own decay. For her part, Filumena feels a deep grief for a life that could have been, and is painfully aware of having lost all the pleasures of motherhood. She tells Domenico: 'We have missed the beauty of having children'. She regrets not having felt the joy of living with her sons when they were small. Ironically then, like the wedding at the start of the play, this ceremony, although legal, seems to be performed by the two main characters *in extremis*, at the end of their days. Life is mocking them.

—Emanuele Licastro

DE QUEIRÓS, José Maria de Eça. See **EÇA DE QUEIRÓS, José Maria de.**

DE QUEIROZ, Rachel. See **QUEIROZ, Rachel de.**

DELEDDA, Grazia. Born in Nuoro, Sardinia, Italy, 27 September 1871. Educated to age 11. Married Palmiro Modesani in 1900; two sons. Regular contributor to the periodicals *L'Ultima Moda* and *Il Paradiso dei Bambini*, from 1888, and *Rivista di Letteratura popolare*, 1893–95; moved to Cagliari, 1899; settled in Rome, 1900. Recipient: Nobel prize for literature, 1926. *Died 15 August 1936.*

PUBLICATIONS

Collections

Romanzi e novelle, edited by Emilio Cecchi. 5 vols., 1941–61.
Opere scelte, edited by Euralio De Michelis. 2 vols., 1964.

Fiction

Sangue sarde (for children). 1888.
Nell'azzurro. 1890.
Amore regale (stories). 1891.
Fior di Sardegna. 1892.
Amori fatali; La leggenda nera; Il ritratto (stories). 1892.
Racconti sardi. 1894.
Anime oneste. 1895.
La via del male. 1896.
L'ospite (stories). 1897.
Il tesoro. 1897.
Le tentazioni (stories). 1899.
Giaffah (stories; for children). 1899.
Il vecchio della montagna. 1900; edited by Joseph G. Fucilla, 1932.
La regina delle tenebre (stories). 1902.
Dopo il divorzio. 1902; as *Naufraghi in porto*, 1920; as *After the Divorce*, translated by Maria Hornor Landsdale, 1905; also translated by Susan Ashe, 1985.
Elias Portolu. 1903; as *Elias Portolu*, translated by Martha King, 1992.
Cenere. 1904; as *Ashes*, translated by Helen Hester Colvill, 1908.
Nostalgie. 1905; as *Nostalgia*, translated by Helen Hester Colvill, 1905.
I giuochi della vita (stories). 1905.
L'edera. 1906.
L'ombra del passato. In *Nuova antologia*, 13, 1907.
Amori moderni (stories). 1907.
Il nonno. 1909; as *Cattive compagnie*, 1921.
Il nostro padrone. 1910.
Sino al confine. 1910.
Nel deserto. 1911.
Chiaroscuro (stories). 1912.
Colombi e sparvieri. 1912.
Canne al vento. 1913.
Le colpe altrui. 1914.
Il fanciullo nascosto (stories). 1915.
Marianna Sirca. 1915; edited by Maro Beath Jones and Armando T. Bissiri, 1940.
L'incendio nell'oliveto. 1918.
Il ritorno del figlio; La bambina rubata. 1919.
La madre. 1920; as *The Woman and the Priest*, translated by Mary G. Steegman, 1923; as *The Mother*, translated by Steegman, 1928.
Il segreto dell'uomo solitario. 1921.
Il Dio dei viventi. 1921.
Il flauto del bosco (stories). 1923.
La danza della collana. With *A sinistra*, 1924.
La fuga in Egitto. 1925.

Il sigillo d'amore (stories). 1926.
Annalena Bilsini. 1927.
Il vecchio e i fanciulli. 1928.
Il dono di Natale (stories). 1930.
La casa del poeta (stories). 1930.
Il paese del vento. 1932.
La vigna sul mare (stories). 1932.
Sole d'estate (stories). 1933.
L'argine. 1934.
La chiesa della solitudine. 1936.
Cosima, edited by Antonio Baldini. 1937; as *Cosima*, translated by Martha King, 1991.
Il cedro del Libano. 1939.
Romanzi e novelle, edited by Natalino Sapegno. 1972.
La Feste del Cristo, e altre novelle, edited by L. Nicastro. 1972.
Romanzi Sardi, edited by Vittorio Spinazzola. 1981.
Chiaroscuro and Other Stories, translated by Martha King. 1994.

Verse

Paesaggi sardi. 1897.

Plays

Odio vince. With *Il vecchio della montagna*, 1912.
L'edera (produced 1909), from her novel, with Camillo Antona Traversi. 1912.
La grazia (libretto), with C. Guastella and V. Michetti, music by Vincenzo Michetti (produced 1923). 1922.
A sinistra. With *La danza della collana*, 1924.

Screenplay: *Cenere*, 1916.

Other

Tradizioni popolari di Nuoro in Sardegna. 1894.
Versi e prose giovanili, edited by Antonio Scano. 1938.
Lettera di Grazia Deledda a Marino Moretti (1913–1923). 1959.

Editor, *Le più belle pagine di Silvio Pellico*. 1923.

Translator, *Eugenia Grandet*, by Balzac. 1930.

*

Bibliography: *Bibliografia deleddiana* by Remo Branca, 1938.

Critical Studies: *Grazia Deledda* by Mercedes Mundula, 1929; *Grazia Deledda* by Francesco Bruno, 1935; *L'opera di Grazia Deledda* by Luigi Falchi, 1937; *Grazia Deledda e il Decadentismo* by Euralio De Michelis, 1938; *L'arte di Grazia Deledda* by Licia Roncarati, 1949; *Grazia Deledda* by E. Buono, 1951; *Deledda* by Giancarlo Buzzi, 1952; *Vocazione narrativa di Grazia Deledda* by Floro Di Zeno, 1967; *Grazia Deledda* by Antonio Piromalli, 1968; *Deledda* by Maria Tettamanzi, 1969; *Il segreto di Grazia Deledda* by Remo Branca, 1971; *Grazia Deledda: Ricordi e testimonianze* by Lina Sacchetti, 1971; *Grazia Deledda* by Antonio Tobia, 1971; *Grazia Deledda* by Nicola Valle, 1971; *Atti del convegno nazionale di studi deleddiani*, 1974; *A Self-Made Woman* by Carolyn Balducci, 1975; *Deledda* by Mario Miccinesi, 1975; *Invito alla lettura di Grazia Deledda* by Olga Lombardi, 1979; *Grazia Deledda: Ethnic Novelist* (includes bibliographies) by Mario Aste, 1990; *Women in Modern Italian Literature: Four Studies* by Bruce Merry, 1990.

* * *

Grazia Deledda, Italian novelist and short story writer, was born in Sardinia and always remained a passionately committed Sardinian. She was awarded the Nobel prize for literature in 1926. Her journey to Stockholm to receive it was the only occasion in her life when she travelled abroad. A prolific writer, she started writing early in life, and at the age of 17 published her first novel, *Sangue sardo* [Sardinian Blood]. In 1896 she published *La via del male* [The Path of Evil], which was reviewed by the Sicilian novelist Luigi Capuana, in a review that made her well-known in the world of Italian letters. Among the writers she studied in her childhood and early youth, she was most influenced by De Amicis, Hugo, Dumas *père*, and Paul Bourget. After her marriage, Deledda moved to Rome where she lived for the rest of her life.

Although Deledda wrote more than 30 novels and about 15 collections of short stories, it is difficult to pinpoint any particular novel as her masterpiece. Among the more famous and successful are *Elias Portolu*, *Cenere* (*Ashes*), *Colombi e sparvieri* [Pigeons and Sparrows], *Canne al vento* [Reeds in the Wind], *L'incendio nell'oliveto* [The Fire in the Olive-Grove], and *La madre* (*The Mother*). Among her later novels, the more important are Il segreto dell'uomo solitario [The Secret of a Lonely Man], *Il Dio dei viventi* [The God of the Living], *Il paese del vento* [The Country of the Wind], and her last novel, which is largely autobiographical, *Cosima*.

Both the novels she wrote while still living in Sardinia, and those produced after she had moved to Rome, have a strongly ethnic and regional vein running through them. Sardinia, its history and geography, its folklore and landscape, its people, customs, and superstitions, its religion and morality, are not only vividly described and passionately celebrated in Deledda's writings, but also constitute the very fabric of her narrative art. Her characters, with their passions and sentiments, fears and feelings of guilt, their primitive as well as romantic impulses, are portrayed convincingly. In this respect, as well as in her adoption of the technique and ethos of 'verism' in her writings, Deledda may be compared to Giovanni Verga. But the kind of self-discipline found in Verga, which accounts for his more austere, compact and, on the whole, more accomplished kind of narrative art and realism, is not to be found in Deledda, even in her most mature novels. Little wonder, therefore, that Verga made a point of detaching himself from Deledda, considering his own view of life and truth to be more bitter and tragic than that of Deledda.

It is only in her later and more mature novels that Deledda manages to drop description for its own sake and do away with mechanical repetition of theme, character, and landscape. To some extent this development was brought about by her contact with the French and Russian naturalists as well as with Tolstoi, Dostoevskii, and Thomas Hardy. However, neither her naturalism or 'verism', nor her contact with such foreign writers, went far enough to free her from both her instinctive tendency to idealize or lyricize her subject matter and from her own self-absorption, which accounts for the essentially autobiographical nature of her art. Thus, her native land, with its savage and primitive landscape, and her own emotionally rich childhood and memories may be regarded as the main protagonists of her work, so that such characters as servants and landlords, or priests and bandits, seem to be secondary. And it is in the context of such a landscape and such protagonists that Deledda manages to depict, like Verga and Hardy, but not with the same degree of moral depth and stoic richness, the workings of the human fate, the nature of the Montalian 'evil of living', the drama and turmoil of human passions.

But while Deledda was deeply involved in portraying the life and passions of the land and the people of Sardinia, her involvement was more emotional than moral or psychological in nature. She could not detach herself from her subject matter, because she lacked what D.H. Lawrence called the psychological technique. But then this is both her weakness *and* her strength; it is her strength in the sense that what she did achieve (which prompted Lawrence, in his introduction to the translation of *La madre*, to locate some parallels between Deledda and Emily Brontë) would not have been possible had she been able to contemplate objectively that with which she was so emotionally involved.

—Gabrielle Barfoot

DEMOSTHENES. Born in Athens, c.384 BC. Studied rhetoric and law, overcoming speech impediments. Speech writer and teacher, then practised constitutional law; also active in politics from age 30, rousing the Athenians to resist the growing threat from Philip II of Macedon; formed an anti-Macedonian party, 346–340 BC, and an alliance with Thebes, 339 BC, and made his great speeches against Philip: *Olynthiacae* in 349 BC; *Philippicae* in 352, 344, and 341 BC; was present when the Greeks were defeated at the battle of Chaeronea in 338 BC. Accused of theft, 324 BC, condemned, fined, and exiled; recalled after the death of Alexander in 323 BC to direct the Greek rebellion against Macedon; sentenced to death by Demades, a supporter of the Macedonian rule; fled to the island of Calaureia, where he took poison. *Died 322 BC.*

PUBLICATIONS

Collections

[Works], edited by F. Blass. 4th revised edition, 3 vols., 1885–89; translated by J.H. and C. Vince, A.T. Murray, N.W. and N.J. de Witt [Loeb Edition], 7 vols., 1926–49.
Orations, edited by S.H. Butcher. 3 vols., 1938; as *All the Orations of Demosthenes*, translated by Thomas Leland, 3 vols., 1770; also translated by Charles R. Kennedy, 5 vols., 1852–63; as *Public Orations*, translated by A.W. Pickard-Cambridge, 1912; selection as *Olynthiacs, Philippics, Minor Public Speeches* (bilingual edition), translated by J.H. Vince, 1930.

Works

Adversus Leptinem, translated by F.E.A. Trayes. 1893; translated as *The Oration Against the Law of Leptines*, 1879; also translated by J. Harold Boardman, 1892.
De corona, edited by Arthur Holmes. 1871; also edited by George and William Simcox, 1871, Martin L. D'Ooge, 1875, B. Drake, revised by Thomas Gwatkin, 1880, William W. Goodwin, 1901, Milton W. Humphreys, 1913,

and Evelyn Abbott and P.E. Matheson, 2 vols., 1926; as *The Crown*, translated by William Brandt, 1870; also translated by Robert Collier, 1875; Francis P. Simpson, 1882; Charles R. Kennedy, 1888; Henry, Lord Brougham, 1893; T. Jeffrey, 1896; Otho Lloyd Holland, 1926; A.N.W. Saunders, in *Demosthenes and Aeschines*, 1975; S. Ussher, 1993; as *The Oration of Demosthenes upon the Crown*, translated by Charles Rann Kennedy, 1888.

De falsa legatione, edited by Richard Shilleto. 9th edition, 1901; translated by A.N.W. Saunders, in *Demosthenes and Aeschines*, 1975.

In Androtionem, translated as *Androtion*. 1888.

In Midiam, as *Against Meidias*, edited by John R. King. 1901; also edited by William W. Goodwin, 1906, S.H. Butcher, 1907, J.H. Vince [Loeb Edition], 1935, Ioannes Sykutris, 1937, and Jean Humbert, 1959; translated by J.H. Vince (bilingual edition), 1930; also translated by Douglas M. MacDowell, 1990.

Olynthiacae, edited by T.R. Glover. 1897; also edited by H. Sharpley, 1900, J.M. Macgregor, 1915, and E.I. McQueen (with commentary), 1986; as *The Olynthiacs*, translated by E.L. Hawkins, 1905.

Philippicae, edited by Gilbert A. Davies. 1907; translated by *The Philippic Orations*, 1885.

Selected Private Speeches (with commentary), edited by C. Carey and R.A. Reid. 1985.

*

Critical Studies: *Demosthenes and the Last Days of Greek Freedom* by A.W. Pickard-Cambridge, 1914; *Demosthenes: The Original and Growth of His Policy* by Werner W. Jaeger, translated by Edward S. Robinson, 1938; *Demosthenes' On the Crown: A Critical Case Study* by George Kennedy, 1967.

* * *

The legacy of the great orator Demosthenes, as handed down to us in the manuscripts, consists of 61 speeches, 56 *exordia*, or opening paragraphs of speeches, and six letters. The speeches, which naturally form the centrepiece of his *oeuvre*, are distributed among the three major forms of ancient oratory. The first 17 are deliberative, composed as contributions to debate in the Assembly, the sovereign body of democratic Athens. Two of the remainder, the *Funeral Speech* and the *Erotic Essay*, are epideictic display pieces. The rest, forming by far the largest portion, are forensic pieces, written to impress jurors in the law courts. The fact that not all the works handed down to us in the corpus Demosthenicum are by Demosthenes himself was recognized already in antiquity. Some are the works of contemporaries, like Apollodorus, for instance, to whom several, including the famous 59th speech, *Against Neaera*, are ascribed. They were probably collected with the great orator's works by accident. Others, especially some of the letters, are probably exercises composed in the rhetorical schools of the Hellenistic and Roman periods, although one or two may be deliberate forgeries, designed for the ancient trade in rare and obscure works by famous figures of the classical golden age. In acknowledgement of these false attributions, several works in the corpus are generally and universally ascribed to a pseudo-Demosthenes, although the authenticity of some others continues to attract controversy.

Demosthenes was a *rhetor*, which means in Greek simply 'speaker', an unassuming label that designates an unofficial role, which was the closest the Athenians came to 'politician' or 'statesman'. Demosthenes wrote speeches for himself and his friends, and at the beginning of his career he was a *logographos*, a professional speech-writer, who would listen to the facts of his client's case and then write a speech for him to deliver, since the Athenian system tried to preserve an equal and amateur democracy by insisting that each man should conduct his own prosecution or defence. Accordingly, this profession was rather looked down upon by the Athenians and Demosthenes probably abandoned it as soon as he could, to concentrate on his own political and forensic battles, which carried their own considerable financial rewards both of a legitimate and an illegitimate kind. However, the particular skill of the *logographos*, the creation of convincing characterizations (*ethopoeia*), was important for the development of Demosthenes' oratorical skills. There were three sets of characterizations to be worked on: that of the speaker, that of his audience, and that of the other participants in the narrative, including the opposing side. Obviously, the depiction of one's enemies, and of any other figures in the narrative of events (*katastasis*), had to be convincing enough to make the speaker's own version of what happened plausible, as well as painting his opponents as darkly as possible. In his speech 'Against Conon', the hubristic nature of the defendant and his associates is carefully constructed by the use of vivid accounts of brawls and boorish behaviour, including one scene in which Conon is described flapping his arms and crowing like a game-cock that has just won a fight. The second layer of characterization, concerning the way the audience could be depicted, was rather more awkward. This kind of *ethopoeia* was especially important in the deliberative speeches, when the Athenians were being urged into a certain mode of action. They had to be cajoled without feeling insulted and alienated by the speaker: frightened into action, but not terrified into inertia by too strong a sense of their own inadequacies. This kind of construction of 'the Athenians' could be effected with rather subtle means, by getting past the audience controversial statements disguised as *opiniones communes*, making quiet assumptions about the class of the spectators and thereby attempting to co-opt them into a ready-made set of values, or by rather more brutal tactics: heavy-handed contrasts between the sharp and decisive monarch Philip and the shiftless, feckless, and fickle populace of the democratic city, or comparisons between the decadent and lazy citizens of the present and their energetic, more moral, and more successful ancestors of the 5th century.

The final type of *ethopoeia* was perhaps the trickiest of all, the characterization of the speaker himself. Demosthenes perhaps never quite reached the heights attained by the acknowledged master of this technique, the *logographos* Lysias, in the very early 4th century, but one or two speeches show that he could pull it off if he tried. The clearest example is perhaps the speech 'Against Callicles', in which the master of Greek prose style writes words for the mouth of someone purporting to be a simple farmer, defending himself against claims for flood damage, but the general principle that 'ars est celare artem' would apply even to the major public speeches in which Demosthenes was speaking his own words in the position of a great statesman. Too much awareness by the audience of the speaker's skills as an orator would detract from the honesty of his case and distract attention from the policies he was championing. A great speaker had to seduce without the slightest hint or suspicion that he was a seducer. Demosthenes' original solution to this paradox in his public speeches is to describe a dialogue with himself, so that he seems to be exposing his own thought-patterns in the form of an agonizing struggle, inviting the audience to sympathize and empathize directly.

This problem of disguising cleverness brings us to the question of Demosthenes' own art, his style, the foundation of his reputation as 'the orator', and the reason why his works were preserved as models for students of rhetoric. Since antiquity, readers have observed two closely related characteristics in particular: the rich variety of effects he could command, and his *bia* or forcefulness. While his predecessors cultivated a highly finished, intellectual conciseness, the texture of Demosthenes' speeches is terribly uneven. Long periods, carefully constructed with a precisely chosen vocabulary, can suddenly give way to extreme abruptness. Lofty abstractions are succeeded by concrete metaphors and metonymies. Highfalutin' poetic language yields to colloquialisms and oaths. Narrative passages are suddenly brought to life with direct speech. The overall effect is of spontaneity, of a carefully composed piece of prose disrupted by true feeling and uncontrollable passions, usually but not always of violent anger.

This at any rate is the Demosthenes who survives in the manuscripts, and whose reputation as the great master of Greek prose is disputed only by Plato. It could be, however, that what the orator himself considered his greatest achievement has been lost to us, for the story was told among later generations that when he was asked what the three most important elements of rhetoric were, he replied, 'Delivery, delivery and delivery'.

—James N. Davidson

ON THE CROWN (De corona)
Prose by Demosthenes, 330 BC.

The speech *On the Crown* is the last surviving speech by the Athenian orator and statesman Demosthenes; it is also one of his longest, and since ancient times has been regarded as his masterpiece. The title refers to the proposal of a supporter of Demosthenes, Ctesiphon, that the orator should be awarded a crown (i.e. an honorific wreath) in recognition of all that he had done for Athens. This proposal was attacked by Demosthenes' enemy Aeschines, who indicted Ctesiphon for unconstitutional action on a number of formal grounds but more fundamentally because, Aeschines maintained, Demosthenes' entire career had been disastrous for Athens. (Aeschines' prosecution speech survives in full, so that the pair of speeches offers a rare opportunity to measure two major orators against each other.) Consequently, in defending Ctesiphon, Demosthenes was also presenting a defence of himself and his past policy; and on the basis that the best form of defence is attack, he devotes extensive parts of his speech to a vitriolic indictment of Aeschines, whose policy of support for Philip of Macedon Demosthenes brands as treachery.

By 330 BC, when the case was brought to trial, Demosthenes' past policy of unswerving opposition to Philip of Macedon might well have seemed disastrous. Philip had crushed Athens and the other resisting Greek forces at the battle of Chaeronea (338 BC), and in 336 BC, when the Greeks sought to shake off Macedonian rule after Philip's death, the military brilliance of his heir Alexander the Great had made short work of this revolt. Although the Macedonian yoke was not as severe as those which later conquerors of Greece were to impose, the loss of independence was a bitter blow, and especially to democratic Athens, once mistress of an empire of her own. Demosthenes makes much of the Greek ideals of freedom in his speech, and one reason that it has been so highly valued is this stress on the best aspects of Athenian history and Greek ideals. In the perspective of history, *On the Crown* reads as an epitaph of Greek freedom. The eloquence of the orator has often dazzled even the sceptical historian, who can recognize that Demosthenes' pan-Hellenism is pursued in Athens' interests and may even suspect that there was more to be said on Philip's side than our sources allow us to see.

The structure and strategy of the speech are complex, but a few key points can be summarized. Demosthenes deals lightly and swiftly with the formal charges of irregularity, where Aeschines' case was strong. Instead he concentrates on his own record as a statesman, repeatedly contrasting it with Aeschines'. He surveys his career in phases, culminating in the role he, Demosthenes, had played in marshalling Greek resistance prior to Chaeronea (in particular by securing an alliance between Athens and Thebes). Throughout, Demosthenes presents himself as representing the highest and noblest ideals of Athens, whereas Aeschines stands for everything that is self-serving, inconsistent, and base. One of the least attractive aspects of the speech to modern eyes (though commonplace in Greek courts) is the persistent invective concerning Aeschines' upbringing and background: according to Demosthenes, he was of low birth and sordid profession (he was originally an actor), unable to live up to the high standards demanded of Athenian statesmen. It is enlightening, though depressing, to see how much weight such arguments were expected to carry even in a democratic society.

More admirable and more memorable is the heroic image which Demosthenes paints of Athens' past, and the lesson he draws from that past to vindicate the policy which, under his leadership, she has pursued against the invader from Macedon. In one crucial passage (192–210) he even insists that, despite defeat, they made no mistake; even if they had marched to Chaeronea knowing they were to be defeated, they would have been right to do so. Only thus could they sustain their record as the champions of liberty in the 5th-century wars against Persia:

> It cannot be, it cannot be that you erred, men of Athens, when you took upon yourselves to fight the battle for the liberty and security of all. Witness those of your ancestors who bore the brunt of the danger at Marathon, those who held the line at Plataea, those who fought on shipboard in the waters of Salamis or off Artemisium, and many other gallant men who lie now in the public tombs —all of whom the city deemed worthy of that same honour, Aeschines, and not just the successful and the victorious.

Much admired by ancient critics, and memorably discussed in Longinus' *On the Sublime* (chapter 16), this passage shows Demosthenes at his best: these are the tones which were imitated by Cicero in his *Philippics* and by Churchill in his war speeches.

Demosthenes won his case so resoundingly that Aeschines was unable to secure even a fifth of the votes, and was therefore obliged by Athenian law to pay a fine or go into exile. He chose the latter, and was said to have ended up teaching oratory on Rhodes. A number of anecdotes tell of his using his own speech and that of his enemy in teaching: when his students marvelled that he had lost the case, he wryly told them 'You would not be so surprised if you could have heard the beast making his response'.

—R.B. Rutherford

DESTOUCHES, Louis-Ferdinand. See **CÉLINE, Louis-Ferdinand.**

DIDEROT, Denis. Born in Langres, France, 5 October 1713. Educated at Jesuit school in Langres, 1723–28, became an abbé in 1726; in Paris from 1728: University of Paris, master of arts 1732; studied theology at the university and read law for a short time, 1732–35. Married Antoinette Champion in 1743; two daughters and two sons. Tutor, and freelance writer and translator from 1734; imprisoned briefly in 1749 for *Lettre sur les aveugles*; commissioned by the publisher Le Breton to edit the *Encyclopédie*, which appeared from 1751 to 1772: also a major contributor; writer for F.M. Grimm's private periodical *Correspondance Littéraire* from 1759; patronized by Catherine the Great from 1765, and visited Russia, 1773–74. Member, Prussian Royal Academy, 1751; Foreign Member, Russian Academy of Sciences, 1773. *Died 31 July 1784.*

PUBLICATIONS

Collections

Oeuvres. 15 vols., 1798.
Oeuvres complètes, edited by Jean Assézat and Maurice Tourneux. 20 vols., 1875–77, reprinted 1966.
Oeuvres, edited by A. Billy. 1951.
Oeuvres philosophiques, edited by Paul Vernière. 1956.
Oeuvres esthétiques, edited by Paul Vernière. 1959.
Oeuvres romanesques, edited by Henri Bénac. 1962.
Oeuvres politiques, edited by Paul Vernière. 1963.
Oeuvres complètes [Chronological Edition], edited by Roger Lewinter. 15 vols., 1969–73.
Oeuvres complètes, edited by H. Dieckmann, Jean Varloot, and Jacques Proust. 1975– .
Oeuvres complètes, edited by Arthur M. Wilson and others. 1975– .
Oeuvres romanesques, edited by Lucette Perol. 1981.
The Irresistible Diderot (selections), edited by John Hope Mason. 1982.

Fiction

Les Bijoux indiscrets. 1748; as *The Indiscreet Toys*, 2 vols., 1749.
Contes moraux et nouvelles idylles, with Salomon Gessner, edited by J.-H. Meister. 1773.
Jacques le fataliste et son maître. 1796; edited by Simone Lecointre and Jean Le Galliot, 1976; as *Jacques the Fataliste*, edited by Martin Hall and translated by M. Henry, 1986; as *James the Fatalist and His Master*, translated anonymously, 3 vols., 1797; as *Jacques the Fatalist*, translated by J. Robert Loy, 1962.
La Religieuse. 1796; edited by Robert Mauzi, 1972; as *The Nun*, translated by Brett Smith, 1797; also translated by Marianne Sinclair, 1966; and Leonard Tancock, 1972; as *Memoirs of a Nun*, translated by Francis Birrell, 1928.
Le Neveu de Rameau. 1821; edited by Jean Fabre, 1950; as *Rameau's Nephew*, translated by Sylvia M. Hill, 1897; also

translated by Mrs Wilfrid Jackson, 1926; Jacques Barzun and Ralph H. Bowen, 1956; and Leonard Tancock, 1966.
Récits, edited by Ph. Van Tieghem. 1959.

Plays

Le Fils naturel; ou, Les Épreuves de la vertu (produced 1771). 1757; as *Dorval; or, The Test of Virtue*, translated anonymously, 1767.
Le Père de famille (produced 1759). 1758; as *The Father*, translated 1770; as *The Family Picture*, translated 1781.
Est-il bon est-il méchant? (produced 1913). 1784; as *Wicked Philanthropy*, translated by Gabriel John Brogyanyi, 1986.
Le Joueur, from the play *The Gamester* by Edward Moore. 1819.
Comédie Française (previously unpublished plays). 1984.

Other

Essai sur le merité et la vertu. 1745.
Pensées philosophiques. 1746; as *Philosophical Thoughts*, translated by Margaret Jourdain, in *Early Philosophical Works*, 1916.
Mémoires sur différents sujets de mathématiques. 1748.
Lettre sur les aveugles. 1749; as *An Essay on Blindness*, translated 1750; as *A Letter Upon the Blind*, translated by S.C. Howe, 1857.
Lettre sur les sourds et muets. 1751; edited by Paul Hugo Meyer, 1965; as *Letter on the Deaf and Dumb*, translated by Margaret Jourdain, in *Early Philosophical Works*, 1916.
Pensées sur l'interprétation de la nature. 1753.
Leçons de clavecin et principes d'harmonie. 1771.
Oeuvres philosophiques. 6 vols., 1772.
Select Essays from the Encyclopedy, translated anonymously. 1772.
Essai sur Sénèque. 1778; revised edition, as *Essai sur les règnes de Claude et de Néron*, 1782.
Supplément au voyage de Bougainville. In *Opuscules Philosophiques et Littéraires*, edited by S.J. Bourlet de Vauxcelles, 1786; published separately in 1796; also edited by Herbert Dieckmann, 1955.
Essai sur la peinture. 1795; edited by Gita May, 1984.
Correspondance Littéraire 1753–90. 1813.
Mémoires, correspondances, et ouvrages inédits. 4 vols., 1830–31.
The Paradox of Acting, translated by Walter H. Pollock. 1883.
Mémoires pour Cathérine II. In *Diderot et Catherine*, edited by Maurice Tourneux, 1899; also edited by Paul Vernière, 1966.
Diderot's Thoughts on Art and Style, With Some of His Shorter Essays, translated by Beatrix L. Tollemache. 1904.
Early Philosophical Works, edited and translated by Margaret Jourdain. 1916, reprinted 1973.
Observations sur la Nakaz. 1920.
Dialogues, translated by Francis Birrell. 1927.
Lettres à Sophie Volland, edited by André Babelon. 3 vols., 1938; as *Letters to Sophie Volland*, translated by Peter France, 1972.
Diderot, Interpreter of Nature: Selected Writings, edited by Jonathan Kemp and translated by Kemp and Jean Stewart. 1937.
Correspondance, edited by Georges Roth. 16 vols., 1955–70.
Salons, edited by Jean Séznec and Jean Adhémar. 4 vols., 1957–67.
Le Rêve de d'Alembert, edited by Jean Varloot. 1962; as

D'Alembert's Dream, translated by Leonard Tancock, 1966.
Rameau's Nephew and Other Works, edited by R.H. Bowen. 1964.
Éléments de physiologie, edited by Jean Mayer. 1964.
Encyclopedia: Selections, edited and translated by Nelly S. Hoyt and Thomas Cassirer. 1965; another selection edited by Stephen Gendzier, 1967.
Selected Writings, edited by Lester G. Crocker, translated by Derek Coltman. 1966.
Voyage en Hollande. 1982.
Écrits sur la musique, edited by Béatrice Durand-Sendrail. 1987.
Selected Philosophical Writings, edited by John Lough. 1987.
Voyages à Bourbonne, à Langres, et autres récits, edited by Anne-Marie Chouillet. 1989.
Political Writings, edited by R. Wokler and J.H. Mason. 1992.

Editor, and contributor, *Encyclopédie; ou, Dictionnaire raisonné des sciences, des arts, et des métiers, par une société de gens de lettres*. 17 vols., 1751–65; as *Pictorial Encyclopaedia of Trades and Industry*, 2 vols., 1959; *Recueil de planches*, 11 vols., 1762–72.

Translator, *Histoire de Grèce*, by Temple Stanyan. 3 vols., 1743.
Translator, *Principes de la philosophie morale*, by Shaftesbury. 1745; revised edition, as *Philosophie morale réduite à ses principes*, 1751.
Translator, with Marc-Antoine Eidous and François-Vincent Toussaint, *Dictionnaire universel de médecine*, by Robert James. 6 vols., 1746–48.
Translator, *Les Oeuvres de Shaftesbury*. 3 vols., 1769.

*

Bibliography: *Bibliographie de Diderot* by Frederick A. Spear, 1980.

Critical Studies: *Diderot Studies*, 1949– ; *Diderot's Determined Fatalist: A Critical Appreciation of Jacques le Fataliste* by J. Robert Loy, 1950; *Two Diderot Studies: Ethics and Esthetics*, 1952, *The Embattled Philosopher: A Biography of Denis Diderot*, 1954, revised edition, 1966, and *Diderot's Chaotic Order*, 1974, all by Lester G. Crocker; *Diderot, The Testing Years 1713–1739*, 1957, and *Diderot*, 1972, both by Arthur M. Wilson; *Essays on the Encyclopédie of Diderot and d'Alembert* by John Lough, 1968; *Diderot the Satirist: Le Neveu de Rameau and Related Works* by Donal O'Gorman, 1971; *Inventory of Diderot's Encyclopédie*, 6 vols., 1971, and vol. 7, *Inventory of the Plates, With a Study of the Contributors to the Encyclopédie*, 1984, both by Richard N. Schwab and Walter E. Rex; *Vacant Mirror: A Study of Diderot* by Thomas M. Kavanagh, 1973; *Diderot and the Eighteenth-Century French Press* by Gary B. Rodgers, 1973; *Diderot's Politics* by Anthony Strugnell, 1973; *Diderot: The Virtue of a Philosopher* by Carol Blum, 1974; *Diderot's Essai sur Seneque* by William Thomas Conroy, 1975; *Diderot's Great Scroll: Narrative Art in Jacques le Fataliste*, 1975, and *Socratic Satire: An Essay on Diderot and Le Neveu de Rameau*, 1987, both by Stephen Werner; *Diderot and the Art of Dialogue* by Carol Sherman, 1976; *Diderot's 'femme savante'* by Lawrence Louis Bongie, 1977; *Diderot* by Otis Fellows, 1977; revised edition, 1989; *Diderot and Goethe: A Study in Science and Humanism* by Gerhard M. Vasco, 1978;

The Business of Enlightenment: A Publishing History of the Encyclopédie, 1775–1800 by Robert Darnton, 1979; *Cataract: A Study in Diderot* by Jeffrey Mehlman, 1979; *Le Neveu de Rameau and The Praise of Folly: Literary Cognates* by Apostolos P. Kouidis, 1981; *Diderot: La Religieuse* by Vivienne Mylne, 1981; *Diderot and the Jews* by Leon Schwartz, 1981; *Diderot: Reason and Resonance* by E. de Fontenay, 1982; *Diderot and the Space-Time Continuum: His Philosophy, Aesthetics and Politics* by Merle L. Perkins, 1982; *Diderot's Imagery* by Eric M. Steel, 1982; *Order and Chance: The Pattern of Diderot's Thought*, 1983, and *Diderot: Jacques le Fataliste*, 1985, both by Geoffrey Bremner; *Diderot* by Peter France, 1983; *The Irresistible Diderot* by John Hope Mason, 1983; *Sex and Enlightenment: Women in Richardson and Diderot* by Rita Goldberg, 1984; *Diderot: Digression and Dispersion* edited by J. Undank and H. Josephs, 1984; *Diderot, Jacques le Fataliste* by Geoffrey Bremner, 1985; *Diderot and the Family: A Conflict of Nature and Law* by William F. Edmiston, 1985; *Diderot: Le Neveu de Rameau* by John Falvey, 1985; *Diderot, Dialogue and Debate* by D.J. Adams, 1986; *Framed Narratives: Diderot's Genealogy of the Beholder* by Jay Caplan, 1986; *Diderot: Thresholds of Representation* by James Creech, 1986; *Diderot and a Poetics of Science* by Suzanne L. Pucci, 1986; *Denis Diderot* by Tamara Dlugach, 1988; *The Encyclopedists as Individuals: A Biographical Dictionary of the Authors of the Encyclopédie* by Frank A. and Serena L. Kafker, 1988; *Diderot's Vie de Seneque: A Swan Song Revised* by Douglas Bonneville, 1989; *Innovation and Renewal: A Study of the Theatrical Works of Diderot* by Derek F. Connon, 1989; *Diderot: Supplément au Voyage de Bougainville* by Peter Jimack, 1989; *Diderot's Dream* by Wilda C. Anderson, 1990; *Satirizing the Satirist: Critical Dynamics in Swift, Diderot and Jean Paul* by Stephanie B. Hammer, 1990; *Success in Circuit Lies: Diderot's Communicational Practice* by Rosalind de la Carrera, 1991; *Diderot: A Critical Biography* by P.N. Furbank, 1992.

* * *

Diderot is best remembered as the general editor of the *Encyclopédie* (*Encyclopedia*) and as one of its main contributors. The project absorbed most of his energies from 1750 to 1772. Conceived initially as a translation of the Chambers *Cyclopaedia*, the *Encyclopedia* developed into an overview of world knowledge and was intended to illustrate its inherent harmony and order. In Diderot's hands the work became an organ of radical and anti-reactionary propaganda; hence publication was from time to time impeded by the French authorities. Technology figures largely in the text and in the accompanying plates, and the work also contains numerous articles on ethical, philosophical, and aesthetic topics. Though produced in a society still dominated by the Roman Catholic Church, the *Encyclopedia* reflects its editor's hostility to religious authority, and, while many of the contributors were priests, Diderot contrived to incorporate heterodox or 'dangerous' views in seemingly minor articles to which the reader is directed by cross-references given in the more prominent, orthodox ones. The *Encyclopedia* encapsulates the spirit of the French Enlightenment and is its most noteworthy product.

From early adherence to a deism derived from the English deists (principally Shaftesbury), Diderot moved to an openly atheistic viewpoint in the *Lettre sur les aveugles* (*An Essay on Blindness*) of 1749, which earned him a brief spell in the Vincennes prison. In his novel *La Religieuse* (*The Nun*), which was not in general circulation in his lifetime, Diderot uses a protagonist forced to take the veil against her will in order to explore the pernicious effects on nuns of life in the convent, separated as it is from normal society. A film based on the novel, directed by Jacques Rivette, was banned in France in 1966 and released in the UK in the following year. Among his other novels, the best known is the picaresque *Jacques le fataliste et son maître* (*Jacques the Fatalist*), partially inspired by Laurence Sterne's *Tristram Shandy*. As well as being a rather ambivalent examination of philosophical determinism, this novel is notable for the strikingly modern way in which Diderot engages the active participation of the reader in the unfolding of the episodes, through authorial harangues, questions, puzzles, alternative versions, and ascribed reactions. Both *Jacques the Fatalist* and *The Nun* are perfectly accessible to the modern reader.

Diderot was a polymath very familiar with the scientific trends of his day. He was especially fascinated by discoveries in the biological sciences of the 1740s and 1750s onwards and, in works which include *Pensées sur l'interprétation de la nature* [On the Interpretation of Nature], the *Dialogue between D'Alembert and Diderot*, *Le Rêve de d'Alembert* (*D'Alembert's Dream*) and the *Éléments de physiologie* [Elements of Physiology], developed theories of the cellular structure of matter and of animal adaptation which prefigured the work of Lamarck and Darwin.

While intellectually a philosophical materialist and a determinist, believing that individual character was principally the product of heredity, Diderot thought man was generally susceptible to modification by environmental influences. He ascribed most of the evil he saw around him to the baleful influence of European (especially French) society, but his attempts, in works like his *Supplément au voyage de Bougainville* [Supplement to Bougainville's Voyage], to develop a moral code based on 'natural' principles were doomed to failure by the impossibility of formulating a definition of nature which could underpin social morality.

Like a number of his contemporaries, he clung in his published works to the belief that only the virtuous man can know true happiness and that even apparently prospering evil-doers suffer in their conscience. However, *Le Neveu de Rameau* (*Rameau's Nephew*), a polythematic dialogue which he began in 1761 and polished over the next 20 years without ever attempting to publish it, casts doubts on this view. In the belief that the theatre could serve to further ethical progress —and that both the writer and the state could exploit it in this way—he wrote three very detailed treatises on dramatic art, which Lessing admired, and three original plays (discounting adaptations) which fail to match the dynamism of the theoretical works.

In his *Salons*, written for readers unable actually to see the pictures described, he proves himself a judicious and sensitive art critic and was the first to interest himself in the technical processes ancillary to painting.

—John Dunkley

JACQUES THE FATALIST (Jacques le fataliste et son maître)
Novel by Denis Diderot, 1796 (written c.1780–84).

Having completed his massive endeavours on the *Encyclopedia*, Diderot worked on his most experimental novel *Jacques the Fatalist* from the late 1760s until sometime around 1778, attracting some enthusiasm from eminent writers like Goethe, but causing greater puzzlement with the general public. The first full publication of the book came in 1796, 12 years after its author's death.

That the initial reaction to the novel was largely one of bafflement is not surprising for *Jacques the Fatalist* is a curious and complex book, both a narrative of its own and a self-conscious examination of the procedures of fiction. As well as telling its own story, it offers a critique of rival fictional forms, being particularly hostile to the facile conventions of contemporary fiction. Like Sterne's *Tristram Shandy* (1760–67), to which Diderot respectfully refers, it is both fiction and metafiction. The book's opening paragraph shows the dialogue between this text and other texts, and the constant challenging of the reader:

> How did they meet? By chance like everyone else. What were their names? What's that got to do with you? Where were they coming from? From the nearest place. Where were they going to? Does anyone ever really know where they are going to? What were they saying? The captain wasn't saying anything and Jacques was saying that his Captain used to say that everything which happens to us on this earth, both good and bad, is written up above.

The unidentified narrator presents the exchanges between Jacques and his master, interrupts them, digresses, and attests to the authority of what we read—'everything which I have just told you, Reader, I was told by Jacques'. This game-playing and its distrust of the orthodox distinctions between illusion and reality permeate the whole novel, and give it a uniquely teasing philosophical quality more attractive to 20th-century readers than to their 18th-century predecessors.

At first, the narrative strives to persuade readers of its truth by great precision in the handling of names and dates, by the incorporation of 'real' historical events into the tale—like the battle of Fontenoy in 1745, where Jacques received his knee wound—and by paying due attention to the method by which the narrator describes things. However, at the same time, our attention is constantly drawn to the processes of fabrication and invention by which the story is made possible. The interpolations and digressions keep reminding us that the gap between narration and experience is unbridgeable. Indeed, the effect of these copious devices of authentication gradually becomes paradoxical, and the more we are reassured of the book's veracity, the more of a construction it seems.

Although this self-absorbed dramatization of the processes of story-telling is the most prominent feature of *Jacques*, it is not its sole concern. Again echoing Sterne, and anticipating Beckett, the narrative is beset by anxieties about the passing of time, and the inconstancy of human beings. This emerges through the concerns with compulsive behaviour, be it jealousy or the code of honour, and with the human capacity for deceiving and being deceived. The persistently deferred and interrupted accounts of Jacques's amatory adventures reinforce both the motif of duplicity and the interaction of appearance and reality that sustains the whole fabric of narration. A further reversal and disruption within the book is that the eponymous servant, Jacques, takes precedence over his anonymous master, easily outwitting him and yet staying with him, mirroring the equally fraught relationship between Sancho Panza and Don Quixote. In this area of the book's concerns, the world is turned upside down in every sense, and the revolutionary potential of Jacques's disagreements with his lordly master give the book its political energies. Yet Jacques is no radical. Instead, he voiced Diderot's philosophical determinism, where everything that happens is preordained, 'written up above'. In philosophical terms, the book investigates the limited powers of human beings, and makes traditional comic play of people struggling against destiny. Yet the role of the narrator complicates the apparent fatalism of the characters. Jacques may be enslaved by what has been written for him, but we can easily see the hand of the writer at work, Diderot himself. Yet it seems inappropriate to read such a persistently playful book as this as articulating a philosophical dilemma. Without turning it merely into a series of trivial games, we must see it as deliberately paradoxical and frustrating, what an equally experimental and serious contemporary Czech writer calls 'a feast of intelligence, humour, and fantasy'. Like Tristram Shandy, or like Joyce's Leopold Bloom for that matter, the fatalistic servant Jacques is at once an intellectual conceit and a vividly-realized human being. Diderot's book deserves its great reputation first and foremost for the way it humanizes its intellectual playfulness, and the way it rejoices in the mutability of us all.

—Ian A. Bell

THE TEST OF VIRTUE (Le Fils naturel)
Play by Denis Diderot, 1757.

There is no denying the influence of Diderot's reflections on drama and theatre. However, his fame in this field rests on a handful of texts only. More surprisingly, in spite of his abiding interest in the problems of the stage, Diderot devoted a very short part of his life to his theatrical experiments. The year 1757–58 saw most of his writings on drama, including *The Test of Virtue*. In those days plays were normally produced before they were printed, but *The Test of Virtue* was published long before it was performed. In addition to the play the volume contained several key-texts on drama and was a great success with three reprints in 1757 alone. Over the years the book also went into several reprints in German, Russian, Italian, and Dutch. Yet *The Test of Virtue* also occasioned many gibes and misunderstandings. In his *Letter to d'Alembert* Rousseau reacted violently to statements in the play that he interpreted as vicious personal attacks. There had already been many unpleasant episodes between the two close friends, and this time the rift was inevitable. *The Test of Virtue* preaches fraternity and asserts Diderot's faith in the society of his time. Rousseau could not share Diderot's optimism and felt keenly that his need to be alone was misconstrued by his friend.

The Test of Virtue is a landmark in the history of French drama because Diderot meant it to launch a new genre. He thought that between the two well-charted genres, tragedy and comedy, there was ample room for at least one new genre. Diderot hesitated a lot about the name for the new genre or even genres to be developed in this unexplored territory between tragedy and comedy. 'Tragédie domestique', 'tragédie bourgeoise', 'drame' were some of the names he considered before opting for 'genre sérieux'. In his eyes, the old tragicomedy could not be viewed as a forerunner of the 'genre sérieux'. There was too much contrast in the old tragicomedy. The aim of the new 'genre sérieux' on the contrary was to combine elements taken from tragedy and comedy.

Diderot's poetics for the 'genre sérieux' prescribed many rules: the subject matter must be worthy of interest, the plot simple, realistic, and relevant to bourgeois families. Finally Diderot decided prose was a more suitable medium than verse for the new genre.

Another key-word in Diderot's poetics is 'tableau'. Painting was as dear to Diderot's heart as drama and his texts on drama give evidence of his knowledge of the expressive means at the disposal of painters. For him a tableau means a moment in a play when the attitudes of the cast outlined on the stage set give the spectator the illusion that he is in front of a painting. Ideally, tableaux should make dialogue redundant. Their emotional impact should be such as to convey the point of a scene effectively and economically while fostering a feeling of communion in the audience. In the name of verisimilitude Diderot disapproved of reversals of fortune so common in 17th-century plays. Tableaux were for him a much more natural way of heightening tension.

The weaknesses of the play derived partly from Diderot's failure to achieve the desired result with his tableaux. His verbose and sentimental dialogues all too often destroy the genuine pathos his tableaux could hope to generate. The play violates a second principle extolled by Diderot: the plot is neither simple nor believable. The hero's virtue is indeed put to too many tests: Dorval saves his friend's life, secretly gives away his fortune to the woman he loves, and agrees to marry a woman he does not love. Finally Diderot relies for his conclusion on the hackneyed trick of the long-lost brother. On the whole, the play is not nearly as revolutionary as it could have been if Diderot had applied his own principles more strictly. What the play did bring was a new tone as well as a new token of legitimacy for the bourgeoisie. Furthermore, the dialogues that follow the play contain a truly dazzling reflection on fiction and reality. The hero Dorval is presented at the same time as the protagonist of a real adventure, the author of the play *The Test of Virtue* which tells this same adventure, the actor interpreting the part of Dorval in the play, and the critic who explains and passes judgement on the play. Diderot himself plays the part of a mere witness and pretends to serve as a foil to Dorval's genius. Diderot examines with great insight the borderline between reality and fiction so that as a whole the volume stands out as a forerunner of Pirandello's work.

—Pascale Voilley

DINESEN, Isak. Born Karen Christentze Dinesen in Rungsted, Denmark, 17 April 1885. Educated privately; studied art at Academy of Art, Copenhagen, 1902–06, in Paris, 1910, and in Rome. Married Baron Bror von Blixen-Finecke in 1914 (divorced 1921). Managed a coffee plantation near Nairobi, Kenya, with her husband, 1913–21, and alone, 1921–31; lived in Rungsted after 1931; co-founder, with Ole Wivel, Bjørn Poulson, and Thorkild Bjørnvig, of the literary journal *Heretica*. Recipient: Holberg medal, 1949; Ingenio e Arti medal, 1950; Nathansen Memorial Fund award, 1951; Golden Laurels, 1952; Hans Christian Andersen prize, 1955; Danish Critics prize, 1957. Founding Member, Danish Academy, 1960; Honorary Member, American Academy 1957; Corresponding Member, Bavarian Academy of Fine Arts. *Died 7 September 1962.*

PUBLICATIONS

Collection

Mindeudgave. 7 vols., 1964.

Fiction

Seven Gothic Tales. 1934; as *Syv fantastiske fortællinger*, translated by Dinesen, 1935.
Winter's Tales. 1942; as *Vinter eventyr*, translated by Dinesen, 1942.
Gengældelsens veje (as Pierre Andrézel), translated into Danish by Clara Svendsen. 1944; as *The Angelic Avengers*, 1946.
Babette's Feast, in *Ladies' Home Journal*. 1950; in book form, in *Anecdotes of Destiny*, 1958; as *Babettes gæstebud*, translated by Jørgen Claudi, 1952.
Kardinalens tredie historie [The Cardinal's Third Tale]. 1952.
Last Tales. 1957; as *Sidste fortællinger*, translated by Dinesen, 1957.
Anecdotes of Destiny (stories). 1958; as *Babette's Feast and Other Anecdotes of Destiny*, 1988; as *Skæbne-anekdoter*, translated by Dinesen, 1958.
Ehrengard. 1963; as *Ehrengard*, translated into Danish by Clara Svendsen, 1963.
Efterladte fortællinger (stories), edited by Frans Lasson. 1975; as *Carnival: Entertainments and Posthumous Tales*, translated by P.M. Mitchell, W.D. Paden, and others, 1977.

Play

Sandhedens hævn: En marionetkomedie (produced 1936). 1960; as *The Revenge of Truth: A Marionette Comedy*, in *'Isak Dinesen' and Karen Blixen*, by Donald Hannah, 1971.

Other

Out of Africa. 1937; as *Den afrikanske farm*, translated by Dinesen, 1937.
Om restkrivning: politiken 23–24 marts 1938 [About Spelling: Politiken 23–24 March 1938]. 1949.
Farah [Name]. 1950.
Daguerrotypier (radio talks). 1951; in *Daguerrotypes and Other Essays*, translated by P.M. Mitchell and W.D. Paden, 1979.
Omkring den nye lov om dyreforsøg [The New Law on Vivisection]. 1952.
En baaetale med 14 aars forsinkelse [A Bonfire Speech 14 Years Later]. 1953.
Skygger paa græsset. 1960; translated as *Shadows on the Grass*, 1960.
On Mottoes of My Life. 1960.
Osceola, edited by Clara Svendsen. 1962.
Essays. 1965.
Karen Blixens tegninger: med to essays of Karen Blixen, edited by Frans Lasson. 1969.
Breve fra Afrika 1914–31, edited by Frans Lasson. 2 vols., 1978; as *Letters from Africa 1914–1931*, translated by Anne Born, 1981.
Daguerrotypes and Other Essays, translated by P.M. Mitchell and W.D. Paden. 1979.
Samlede essays. 1985.
On Modern Marriage and Other Observations, translated by Anne Born. 1986.

*

Bibliography: *Dinesen: A Bibliography* by Liselotte Henriksen, 1977; supplement in *Blixeniana 1979*, 1979; *Karen Blixen/Isak Dinesen: A Select Bibliography* by Aage Jørgensen, 1985.

Critical Studies: *Isak Dinesen* by Louise Bogan, in *Selected Criticism*, 1955; *The World of Isak Dinesen* by Eric O. Johannesson, 1961; *Isak Dinesen: A Memorial* edited by Clara Svendsen, 1964, *The Life and Destiny of Isak Dinesen* by Svendsen and Frans Lasson, 1970, and *Karen Blixen: Isak Dinesen: A Chronology* by Lasson, 1985; *The Gayety of Vision: A Study of Isak Dinesen's Art* by Robert Langbaum, 1965; *Titania: the Biography of Dinesen* by Parmenia Migel, 1967; *Isak Dinesen, 1885–1962* by Hannah Arendt, in *Men in Park Times*, 1968; *'Isak Dinesen' and Karen Blixen: The Mask and the Reality* by Donald Hannah, 1971; *Isak Dinesen's Aesthetics* by Thomas Reid Whissen, 1973; *My Sister, Isak Dinesen* by Thomas Dinesen, translated by Joan Tate, 1975; *Dinesen: The Life of a Storyteller* by Judith Thurman, 1982, as *Isak Dinesen: The Life of Karen Blixen*, 1982; *The Pact: My Friendship with Isak Dinesen* by Thorkild Bjørnvig, 1984; *Diana's Revenge: Two Lines In Isak Dinesen's Authorship* by Marianne Juhl, 1985; *Out of Denmark* edited by Bodil Wamberg, 1985; *The Witch and the Goddess in the Stories of Isak Dinesen: A Feminist Reading* by Sarah Stambaugh, 1988; *Isak Dinesen and the Engendering of Narrative* by Susan Hardy Aiken, 1990; *Isak Dinesen: The Life and Imagination of a Seducer* by Olga Anastasia Pelensky, 1991.

*   *   *

Isak Dinesen liked to disclaim the complex erudition of her tales and to speak of herself as a 'story-teller', a Scheherazade, whose mission was simply to 'entertain' people. Entertain them she did, with leisurely and urbane philosophical discourse, painterly descriptions of nature, a wry and refined eroticism, and in narratives as intricate and polished as Chinese boxes that took her years of reworking to perfect. But the lightness of her tone and the preciousness of her surfaces have tended to obscure her scope of vision, which is that of a major and highly original writer.

In Denmark, Dinesen was accused of decadence and an indifference to social issues. These were charges deserved, perhaps, by Baroness Karen Blixen, who cultivated a sibilline persona and liked to *épater les bourgeois*, not to mention *les socialistes*. But Dinesen, the story-teller, was a passionate and rather pure-hearted immoralist, rather than a decadent. The erotic daredevils and demonic heroes of Romantic literature had given her her first glimpse of emotional freedom, and she perceived the attempt to spare oneself repression, at whatever price, as heroic and ennobling. This was the lion hunt, the great gesture, the daring fantasy, the mortal sin. In Marxist terms, her heroes may be decadents; in Freudian terms they may be perverts of one sort or another; but in Dinesen's terms they are *dreamers*—planted in the soil of life like a coffee tree with a bent taproot. 'That tree will never thrive', she wrote, 'nor bear fruit, but will flower more richly than the others'.

Dinesen did, of course, 'neglect social issues'. Her choice of form—the tale, rather than the novel or the short story—was a way of taking sides with the past against her contemporaries, although she was also never without a keen sense of irony about her own absurd position, in modern Denmark, as the defender of a way of life that had vanished, to general applause. She set her tales a hundred years in the past, defining her period as 'the last great phase of aristocratic culture', and aware that it was also the first great phase of bourgeois culture, when wealth was shifting from the land to the cities and to currency; when the feudal world, with all its certainties and inequities, the one inseparable from the other, was dissolving. By taking such a distance, she was able to gain clarity and a certain imaginative freedom. She was also better able to describe the tension between her own aristocratic idealism and the materialism that had triumphed over it. And she was able to understand the nature of a certain kind of Fall: the loss that occurs to a culture or to a child when values that have once been absolute become relative.

Dinesen's work does, despite its great literary sophistication, have a common ground with the old tales, which she defined as Nemesis: 'the thread in the course of events that is determined by the psychic assumptions of a person'. By psychic assumptions, she meant the scenarios that we absorb from our family and our culture, the patterns we unconsciously repeat. Like the old story-tellers, but also like Mann, Joyce, or Yeats, Dinesen is interested in the points at which the individual and the typical, psychology and culture, intersect as *myth*, and she works with myth in an innovative modern way. The climax of a Dinesen tale comes at the moment that the hero and the reader recognize how the forces that have been shaping the events of the story have also shaped their perception of it: history from without, desire from within.

Dinesen stands at the end of a long cultural process, looking back ironically upon it. She sums up the Romantic tradition as she carries it forward. Perhaps her vision could only belong to a writer who took up her pen at the age of 46, when she had lost everything of importance to her, except the thing with the greatest value of all: experience itself.

—Judith Thurman

DÖBLIN, Alfred. Born in Stettin, Germany, 10 August 1878. Educated at the Gymnasium, Stettin, 1888, 1891–1900; studied medicine at Berlin University, 1900–04; Freiburg University, 1904–05, medical degree 1905. Served as a medical officer in the German army during World War I. Married Erna Reiss in 1912; two sons. Worked in a psychiatric hospital, Regensburg; general practitioner, Berlin, 1911–14; member, Schutzverband deutscher Schriftsteller [Association of German Writers], 1920, and president, 1924; theatre reviewer, *Prager Tageblatt*, 1921–24; visited Poland, 1924; member of the discussion group, Group 1925, with Bertolt Brecht; fled to France to escape the Nazi regime, 1933; became French citizen, 1936, emigrated to the United States, 1940; script writer, Metro Goldwyn Mayer, 1940–41; converted to Roman Catholicism, 1941; returned to Germany, 1945; education officer, Baden-Baden, 1945; editor, *Das Goldene Tor*, 1946–51; co-founder, 1949 and vice-president of literature section, 1949–51, Academy for Science and Literature, Mainz; moved to Paris, 1951; entered sanatorium at Freiburg in Breisgau, 1956. Recipient: Fontane prize, 1916. Member, Prussian Academy of the Arts, 1928. *Died 26 June 1957.*

PUBLICATIONS

Collections

Ausgewählte Werke, edited by Walter Muschg, Heinz Graber, and Anthony W. Riley. 23 vols., 1960–85.

Die Zeitlupe: Kleine Prosa, edited by Walter Muschg. 1962.
Die Vertreibung der Gespenster, edited by Manfred Beyer. 1968.
Gesammelte Erzählungen. 1971.
Schriften zur Politik und Gesellschaft 1896–1951, edited by Heinz Graber. 1972.
Ein Kerl muss eine Meinung haben, edited by Manfred Beyer. 1976.

Fiction

Die Ermordung einer Butterblume und andere Erzählungen (stories). 1913.
Das Stiftsfräulein und der Tod. 1913.
Die drei Sprünge des Wang-lun. 1915; as *The Three Leaps of Wang-lun*, 1991.
Die Lobensteiner reisen nach Böhmen (stories). 1917.
Wadzeks Kampf mit der Dampfturbine. 1918.
Der schwarze Vorhang: Roman von den Worten und Zufällen. 1919.
Wallenstein. 1920.
Blaubart und Miss Ilsebill. 1923.
Berge, Meere und Giganten. 1924; revised edition as *Giganten*, 1932.
Die beiden Freundinnen und ihr Giftmord. 1925.
Feldzeugmeister Cratz. Der Kaplan. Zwei Erzählungen. 1926.
Berlin Alexanderplatz. Die Geschichte vom Franz Biberkopf. 1929; as *Alexanderplatz, Berlin: The Story of Franz Biberkopf*, translated by Eugene Jolas, 1931; as *Berlin Alexanderplatz: The Story of Franz Biberkopf*, 1978.
Babylonische Wandrung; oder, Hochmut kommt vor dem Fall. 1934.
Pardon wird nicht gegeben. 1935; as *Men Without Mercy*, translated by Trevor and Phyllis Blewitt, 1937.
Das Land ohne Tod. 1937–38; as *Amazonas*, edited by Walter Muschg, 1963.
Die Fahrt ins Land ohne Tod. 1937.
Der blaue Tiger. 1938.
Der neue Urwald. 1948.
November 1918: Eine deutsche Revolution. 1949; selections from volumes 1 and 2 as *A People Betrayed*, translated by John E. Woods, 1983.
  Bürger und Soldaten 1918. 1939; revised edition as *Verratenes Volk*, 1948.
  Heimkehr der Fronttruppen. 1949.
  Karl und Rosa. 1950; as *Karl and Rosa*, translated by John E. Woods, 1983.
Der Oberst und der Dichter; oder, Das menschliche Herz. 1946.
Heitere Magie, zwei Erzählungen. 1948.
Sinn und Form. 1954.
Hamlet; oder, die lange Nacht nimmt ein Ende. 1956.
Jagende Rösser, Der schwarze Vorhang, und andere frühe Erzählwerke (stories). 1981.

Plays

Lydia und Mäxchen: Tiefe Verbeugung in Einem Akt (produced 1905). 1906.
Lusitania (produced 1926). 1920.
Die Gefährten (includes *Lydia und Mäxchen*; *Lusitania*; *Das verwerfliche Schwein*). 1920.
Die Nonnen von Kemnade (produced 1923). 1923.
Die Ehe (produced 1931). 1931.

Verse

Manas: Epische Dichtung. 1927

Other

Gespräche mit Kalypso: Über die Gedächtnisstörungen bei der koraskoffschen Psychose Liebe und die Musik (essays). 1906.
Der deutsche Maskenball (essays). 1921.
Staat und Schriftsteller. 1921.
Feldzeugmeister Cratz, Der Kaplan. 1926.
Reise in Polen. 1926; as *Journey to Poland*, translated by Joachim Neugroschel, 1991.
Das Ich über der Natur. 1927.
Im Buch—Zu Haus—Auf der Strasse, with Oskar Loerke. 1928.
Der Bau des epischen Werkes. 1929.
Der Überfall. 1929.
Wissen und Verändern! Offene Briefe an einen jungen Menschen. 1931.
Jüdische Erneuerung. 1933.
Unser Dasein (essays). 1933.
Flucht und Sammlung des Judenvolkes: Aufsätze und Erzählungen. 1935.
Der historische Roman. 1936.
Die deutsche Literatur: Ein Dialog zwischen Politik und Kunst. 1938.
Nocturno. 1944.
Sieger und Besiegte: Eine wahre Geschichte. 1946.
Nürnberger Lehrprozess. 1946.
Der unsterbliche Mensch: Ein Religionsgespräch. 1946; with *Der Kampf mit dem Engel: Religionsgerpräch*, 1980.
Die literarische Situation. 1947.
Auswahl aus dem erzählenden Werk. 1948.
Heitere Magie: Zwei Erzählungen. 1948.
Unsere Sorge—der Mensch. 1948.
Schicksalsreise: Bericht und Bekenntnis. 1949; as *Destiny's Journey*, edited by Edgar Pässler, translated by Edna McCown, 1992.
Die Dichtung, ihre Natur und ihre Rolle. 1950.
Die Zeitlupe: Kleine Prosa (essays). 1962.
Briefe, edited by Walter Muschg. 1970.
Doktor Döblin (autobiography), edited by Heinz Graber. 1970.
Ein Kerl muss eine Meinung haben: Berichte und Kritiken 1921–1924. 1974.
Griffe ins Leben: Theater-Feuilletons, edited by Manfred Beyer. 1978.
Autobiographische Schriften und letzte Aufzeichnungen, edited by Edgar Pässler. 1980.

Editor, *The Living Thoughts of Confucius.* 1940.
Editor, *Die Revolution der Lyrik*, by Arno Holz. 1951.
Editor, *Minotaurus.* 1953.

*

Bibliography: *Bibliographie Alfred Döblin* by Louis Huguet, 1972.

Critical Studies: *Dimensions of the Modern Novel: German Texts and European Contexts* by Theodore Ziolkowski, 1969; *The Humorous and Grotesque Elements in Döblin's Berlin Alexanderplatz* by Henrietta S. Schoonover, 1977; *Alfred Döblin* by Matthias Prangel, 1987; *The Berlin Novels of Alfred Döblin: Wadzek's Battle with the Steam Turbine, Men Without Mercy and November 1918* by David B. Dollenmayer, 1988; *A Chinese Story from a Berlin Practice:* *Alfred Döblin's Narrative Technique in Die drei Sprünge des Wang-lun* by John Henry Collins, 1990.

* * *

One of the most versatile and enigmatic figures in the field of 20th-century German letters, Alfred Döblin was, like Kafka, born into the social environment of deracinated eastern European Jewry. The poverty endured in his youth and the fascination exerted by the cultural ferment of the city that became his home left their mark on the novel which is commonly viewed as his supreme achievement: *Berlin Alexanderplatz*, the great 'urban novel' of 1929. What is often overlooked is the fact that Döblin, as well as leading an active life as a medical practitioner, was the author of literary manifestos, didactic dramas, historical and utopian novels, philosophic essays, and even an Indian verse epic, and was a major formative influence on Brecht, whose theory of epic theatre he helped to shape. No subject was too remote or too obscure. After much painstaking research, he located his first major novel, *Die drei Sprünge des Wang-lun* (*The Three Leaps of Wang-lun*) in 18th-century China. It chronicles the fortunes of a little-known religious group, who wage a campaign of passive resistance against the Imperial authorities and are brutally annihilated. Other major novels of his early years were set in the 17th century (*Wallenstein*), and in a remote, technology-dominated future (*Berge, Meere und Giganten* [Mountains, Seas, and Giants]).

It is not so much the range or the exoticism of his subjects that elicits surprise as the means by which he evokes them. On one level, Döblin strives to be ultra-realistic, using historical sources to create an overpoweringly vivid background. 'I was in love with the facts and documents, and wanted to incorporate them without alteration', he says of his work on the Thirty Years War. The direct portrayal of events is enhanced by the extensive use of a specialist vocabulary with which he assumes the reader to be familiar. But besides the documentary layer in Döblin's work, other methods are employed to produce expressive effects: these include interior monologues, cinematic editing techniques, and scenes of lyrical and at times nightmarish intensity. Several such devices seem calculated to make the reader aware of the 'fictionality' of the text. Like James Joyce, with whom he is often compared, Döblin was involved in extending the range of narrative perspectives within the novel, and regularly experimented with methods which subsequently came to be recognized as features of post-modernism.

Berlin Alexanderplatz is not only the story of a humble furniture-removal-man with a personality that encompasses the extremes of criminality and sainthood, but also the definitive chronicle of a modern metropolis and a probing interrogation of the values of its secularized inhabitants. The career of Franz Biberkopf is examined over a period of 18 months, during which he abandons his initial quest for 'respectability' and becomes increasingly involved in the activities of a gang of thieves and swindlers, loses an arm in a car-chase, and sustains a final blow when his girlfriend, Mieze, is murdered by fellow crook, Reinhold. But, as always in Döblin, the medium is no less important than the events. Innovatory techniques abound: soft-focusing is often used, and material from various walks of life is mounted onto the narrative as in the collages of Expressionist and Dadaist painters. Language is pushed to new extremes: documentary source-material, news items, statistics, popular songs, hymns, and biblical references intertwine to create an at times clinically realistic, at times symbolic canvas, at the heart of which is an impassioned plea for our sympathetic understanding of a disoriented, marginal man, and through him, of his entire generation.

In much of his work, Döblin shows himself to be keenly aware of injustice and hypocrisy in society. His passion for detail, his medical experience, and his familiarity with the low life of inter-war Berlin made him deeply suspicious of officialdom and superficial notions of respectability. Incompetent and mendacious bureaucracy, corruption in high places, and the gross materialism of the well-to-do recur as themes in the novels, whatever their setting. His central characters tend to be from undistinguished backgrounds, ordinary men buffeted about by an ill-functioning system. In the 1920s, Döblin published political commentaries in a variety of formats. From 1927 onwards, he claimed to have become more interested in the individual than in the collective. Several works deal directly with revolutionary and fascist tendencies in Germany, notably *November 1918* and *Pardon wird nicht gegeben* (*Men Without Mercy*). His exile is vividly recalled in the autobiographical *Schicksalsreise* [Journey of Destiny]. Unlike Brecht and Thomas Mann, Döblin was unable to find his feet in America and returned after the war to Germany, where he had been all but forgotten. There was little interest in his kaleidoscopic, experimental style, and his later manuscripts were ignored by the major commercial publishing houses of West Germany. After his death in 1957, an unreliable, fragmentary, and expensive collected edition began to appear. Public interest was re-awakened in part by the efforts of East German critics and publishers, who were keen to stress his social commitment. A complete edition of Döblin's works is at last forthcoming, and his reputation has been further enhanced by the attentions of the film director Rainer Werner Fassbinder, whose last major work was a monumental 15-hour version of *Berlin Alexanderplatz*.

—Osman Durrani

BERLIN ALEXANDERPLATZ
Novel by Alfred Döblin, 1929.

Berlin Alexanderplatz: The Story of Franz Biberkopf was published in 1929 by the S. Fischer Verlag, Berlin. S. Fischer had insisted on the subtitle since the first part was nothing but the name of a location. However, Döblin's title proved appropriate and attractive, indicating that, although Franz Biberkopf is the protagonist, the novel deals primarily with the city, and specifically its proletarian areas around the Alexanderplatz, and its underworld.

Berlin Alexanderplatz remains Döblin's one and only popular success. Although he wrote many novels, short stories, essays, and reviews, he was always identified primarily with this book. He was a respected writer, very active in political circles, and a member of the section for literature in the Prussian *Akademie der Künste*. His innovative narrative techniques inspired younger writers including Bertolt Brecht who applied them to the theatre. From the age of 12, Döblin lived in the eastern, working-class part of Berlin. After World War I, he practised medicine there, and was in daily contact with the poorest members of society. *Berlin Alexanderplatz* betrays an intimate knowledge of the language and mentality of the working class in Berlin, as well as the underworld.

The manuscript, which survives, was begun in late 1927. It can be assumed that Döblin had collected a considerable amount of material before that date. Probably early in 1928 Döblin read the German translation of Joyce's *Ulysses* which he reviewed in spring 1928. Joyce's novel inspired and encouraged Döblin to use the full array of modernist techniques, especially inner monologue, montage of authentic materials, such as newspaper clippings, Bible passages, and political and advertising slogans, and imitations of the sounds and rhythm of the big city around the Alexanderplatz where the new subway system was being built.

While the city provides the framework and is presented in an inimitable vividness, the story-line follows the fate of Franz Biberkopf, which contributed most to the book's popularity. Biberkopf, a physically strong cement and furniture removal worker, has just served a prison sentence for manslaughter: in a sudden rage he strangled his girlfriend. When he returns to his old milieu around the Alexanderplatz he has difficulties getting back on an even keel. He has promised himself to remain a decent, good human being, and not give in to temptation. But time and again he is betrayed by underworld 'friends'. His main weakness is boasting when he wants to be an accepted part of the group. The first blow, when a friend steals his girlfriend, is easily forgotten. But then he falls in with Reinhold and his 'Pums' gang. As they speed away in cars after a robbery, Reinhold, afraid Biberkopf might talk to the police, throws him out of the car. Biberkopf's arm has to be amputated, but still he has not learned his lesson. While living with the prostitute Mieze, his real love, he wants to show her off to Reinhold. At one stage Reinhold takes advantage of Biberkopf's absence and takes Mieze into the woods where he molests and finally strangles her. Biberkopf is accused initially of the murder, and when he is confronted with Reinhold in the court room at Reinhold's trial, he suffers a mental breakdown. He recovers slowly but ends up a new person after his dismissal from the psychiatric ward. Standing at a factory gate where he now works as a gate keeper, he realizes that he needs others, and they need him.

The narrative, which consists mainly of half-conscious monologues or other subjective forms of story-telling, is interspersed with passages from other texts, like reports on the Berlin slaughterhouses; also allusions to Biblical and mythological characters and events, such as Job, Abraham, and Isaac, figures from the Oresteia, and parts of the Revelation. There are also numerous slightly disguised quotes from classical German literature, together with the latest hits and slogans of the time. These new layers of text add to the complexity of the story. *Berlin Alexanderplatz* assumes an apocalyptic tone at times, then descends to the level of street humour. This provocative mixture counterbalances the straightforward underworld story of Biberkopf, which is made more compelling through its elements of love, crime, and violence. Although the book is anything but easy reading, it has remained popular with a large number of readers to this day.

Human crowds, mass transportation, and mass media are part of the world of *Berlin Alexanderplatz*. It was logical that Döblin adapted the text for a radio play first broadcast in Berlin on 30 September 1930. In this simplified, still very sophisticated version, the voice of Biberkopf was rendered by the then famous actor Heinrich George. George also portrayed Biberkopf in the cinema version of 1931, under the direction of Phil Jutzi. Döblin collaborated on the scenario. Translations of the novel began to appear in 1930; the English translation by Eugene Jolas was published in 1931. In the politically charged atmosphere of the beginning economic depression and political crisis of the years 1929–30, the book reviews reflected the full spectrum of attitudes toward a modernistic narrative strategy, and toward Döblin's depiction of the proletariat. The organized socialist parties, especially the communists, rejected the book vehemently.

Berlin Alexanderplatz made Döblin's life financially easier, so that his family moved to the Kurfürstendamm area. It was to be his last novel before his forced exile from Germany in the spring of 1933. The somewhat abrupt ending of the novel suggests plans for a continuation which Döblin never wrote. The popularity of Berlin Alexanderplatz survived its disappearance from the book market between 1933 and 1945. The enduring impact on German readers did not translate into a real international success, since too much hinges on specific linguistic and cultural effects that are lost with the transfer to another language and culture. Döblin's 'cinematic style' can, however, be translated into images and sounds, as is demonstrated by the monumental film directed by Rainer Werner Fassbinder.

—Wulf Koepke

———————

DODERER, Heimito von. Born in Weidlingau, Austria, 5 September 1896. Educated at the Landstrasser Gymnasium, graduated 1914; University of Vienna, 1921–25, Ph.D. in history, 1925. Married 1) Gusti Hasterlik in 1930 (divorced 1934); 2) Maria Thoma in 1952. Served as a reserve officer, Austrian dragoon regiment, 1915, prisoner of war in Siberia, 1916, repatriated 1920; conscripted to the German Air Force, 1940; examiner of potential Luftwaffe officers, Vienna, 1943; prisoner of war in Norway, 1945, released 1946. Member of the Nazi Party, 1933–38; converted to Roman Catholicism, 1940; publisher's reader, Vienna, 1946; banned from publishing works until 1950. Recipient: Confederation of German Industry Novelist's prize, 1954; Austrian State grand award, 1954; Prikheim medal of Nuremberg, 1958; Raabe prize, 1966; Ring of Honour of the City of Vienna, 1966. Member, Institute for Research in Austrian History, 1950. *Died 23 December 1966.*

PUBLICATIONS

Collections

Frühe Prosa, edited by Hans Flesch-Brunningen. 1968.
Die Erzählungen, edited by Wendelin Schmidt-Dengler. 2 vols., 1973–76.
Commentarii: Tagebücher aus dem Nachlass, edited by Wendelin Schmidt-Dengler. 2 vols., 1976–86.
Das Doderer-Buch: Eine Auswahl aus dem Werk Heimito von Doderers, edited by Karl Heinz Kramberg. 1976.

Fiction

Die Bresche: Ein Vorgang in vierundzwanzig Stunden. 1924.
Das Geheimnis des Reichs. 1930.
Ein Mord, den jeder begeht. 1938; as *Every Man a Murderer*, translated by Richard and Clara Winston, 1964.
Ein Umweg. 1940.
Die erleuchteten Fenster; oder, die Menschwerdung des Amtsrates Julius Zihal. 1950.
Die Strudlhofstiege; oder, Melzer und die Tiefe der Jahre. 1951.
Das letzte Abenteuer. 1953.

Die Dämonen. 1956; as *The Demons*, translated by Richard and Clara Winston, 1961.
Die Posaunen von Jericho: Neues Divertimento. 1958; as 'The Trumpets of Jericho', translated by Vincent Kling, in *Chicago Review*, 26(2), 1974.
Die Peinigung der Lederbeutelchen (stories). 1959.
Die Merowinger; oder, die totale Familie. 1962.
Roman No. 7:
Die Wasserfälle von Slunj. 1963; as *The Waterfalls of Slunj*, translated by Eithne Wilkins and Ernst Kaiser, 1966.
Der Grenzwald (fragment). 1967.
Unter schwarzen Sternen (stories). 1966.
Meine neunzehn Lebensläufe und neun andere Geschichten. 1966.
Die Wiederkehr der Drachen: Aufsätze, Traktate, Reden, edited by Wendelin Schmidt-Dengler. 1972.

Verse

Gassen und Landschaft. 1923.
Ein Weg im Dunklen: Gedichte und epigrammatische Verse. 1957.

Other

Der Fall Gütersloh: Ein Schicksal und seine Deutung. 1930.
Von der Unschuld des Indirekten. 1947.
Grundlagen und Funktion des Romans. 1959; as 'Principles and Functions of the Novel', in *30th International Congress of the P.E.N. Clubs*, 1959.
Wege und Unwege, edited by Herbert Eisenreich. 1960.
Die Ortung des Kritikers. 1960.
Albert Paris Gütersloh: Autor und Werk, with others. 1962.
Tangenten. Tagebuch eines Schriftstellers 1940–1950 (correspondence). 1964.
Mit der Sprache leben, with Herbert Meier and Josef Mühlberger. 1965.
Repertorium: Ein Begreifbuch von höheren und niederen Lebens-Sachen, edited by Dietrich Weber. 1969.
Briefwechsel 1928–1962, with Albert Paris Gütersloh, edited by Reinhold Treml. 1986.

Editor, *Gewaltig staunt der Mensch*, by Albert Paris Gütersloh. 1963.

*

Critical Studies: *From Prophecy to Exorcism: The Premises of Modern German Literature* by Michael Hamburger, 1965; 'Heimito von Doderer's Demons and the Modern Kakanian Novel by Engelbert Pfeiffer', in *The Contemporary Novel in German* edited by Robert H. Heitner, 1967; 'A Commentary on Heimito von Doderer' by Dietrich Weber, translated by Brian L. Harris, in *Dimension*, (1), 1968; *Heimito von Doderer* by Michael Bachem, 1981; *Twentieth-Century Odyssey: A Study of Heimito von Doderer's Die Dämonen* by Elizabeth C. Hesson, 1982; *Doderer and the Politics of Marriage: Personal and Social History in Die Dämonen* by Bruce Irvin Turner, 1982; *Begegnung mit Heimito von Doderer* edited by Michael Horowitz, 1983; *Heimito von Doderer* by Dietrich Weber, 1987; 'Heimito von Doderer and National Socialism' by Andrew W. Barker, in *German Life and Letters*, 41(2), 1988.

* * *

Friedrich Torberg contended that Heimito von Doderer would have enjoyed the reputation of being the most Austrian of Austrian authors. Few authors' works are so intimately linked with locations and milieus as his. Vienna's third district, the site of his former school between the 'diplomats' quarter' and the *Prater* as well as the *Alsergrund*, are his preferred settings, for example *Die Wasserfälle von Slunj* (*The Waterfalls of Slunj*) and *Die Strudlhofstiege* [The Strudlhof Steps]. Doderer describes not only streets, but also houses in such detail that they are easily identifiable. His actual protagonist is Vienna as the former capital of the Austro-Hungarian empire and the multi-cultural metropolis which he loved: his family's aristocratic and bourgeois circles and his own bohemian environment. In his portrayal of urban life, Doderer displays his familiarity with various social groups: the coffee house culture, ladies of leisure, civil servants, state officials, and workers. He is no stranger to the Viennese underworld and their transactions in the canal and sewer systems. The monumental novels, *Die Strudlhofstiege* and *Die Dämonen* (*The Demons*), like *romans à clef*, frequently refer to historical persons and events.

Doderer's depiction of the anxiety of the Austrian bourgeoisie is unmatched, because he shared their general lack of interest in democracy and resented the newly-formed republic despite the fact that in the 1920s Vienna was a model of social progress. His perspective is that of an upper-class man and a World War I officer of a dragoon elite unit, who was not even stripped of his privileges in a Siberian prison camp. As a prisoner of war he wrote, studied, and encountered the work of the novelist Albert Paris Gütersloh, his 'venerated master' and friend, whose concept of the total novel shaped his own theories. This Russian experience, his captivity and escape, defined to a large extent his view of reality. For example, in *The Demons* a hands-on fight delivers Imre Gyurkicz, a character caught up in military reveries, from the twilight-zone of alienation. Dying as a fighter, he realizes his human potential. Other protagonists, like the socially awkward René Stangeler, a reflection of Doderer as a young man, and his fiancée Grete Siebenschein, mirror Doderer's exacting courtship and unsuccessful marriage to Gusti Hasterlik, the daughter of a Jewish surgeon, from whom Doderer was divorced in 1938 when the Hasterliks went into exile.

Doderer's literary cosmos evolved organically. The protagonists from earlier texts are followed up in later ones, aging and changing with time. Doderer writes in a 'realistic' and a 'grotesque' mode. The former is assigned to the inner world of the civilized Sektionsrat Geyrenhoff, an image of the mature Doderer, the latter to the 'horrible' Dr Döblinger, alias Kajetan von Schlaggenberg, reminiscent of the middle-age author in his Nazi phase—the name Döblinger alludes to Doderer's residence in the suburb of Döbling between 1928 and 1936. This compartmentalization of texts suggests a Jekyll-and-Hyde disposition, which Doderer ascribes to the world, coining the concept of a 'dual reality'. The 'Döblinger' texts introduce the readers to extreme, sadistic relationships, taking them on excursions into psychological aberrations and perversions, for example *Die Posaunen von Jericho* [The Trumpets of Jericho] and *Die Merowinger; oder, die totale Familie* [The Merovingians, or the Total Family]. The 'Geyrenhoff' texts present society from a rational and benevolent point of view—Geyrenhoff is the chronicler of *The Demons*, a detached insightful spectator. In larger works the rational and the bizarre spheres overlap. The result is an extreme narrative tension. In the short story 'Eine Person aus Porzellan' [A Porcelain Person] one character combines both aspects: a young women who hides her vampire-like nature under a perfect facade. In *The Demons* the digressions about late medieval witch hunts written in archaic German—an offshoot of Doderer's historical studies—reveal the dual reality in terms of culture. The poetry in *Gassen und Landschaft* [Alleys and Landscape] represents yet another literary sensibility, that of a perceptive observer of nature and urban atmospheres.

Doderer's inability to cope with diversity goes hand in hand with a passionate rejection of 'ideology' and a yearning for authenticity. While his work abounds with idiosyncratic characters intended to produce the effect of universality, it is precisely this narrow focus on the unique and private which undermines the author's intent. It fosters the notion that nothing in this hermetic cosmos happens by accident: all characters interconnect in causally related plots, by lineage, or through mutual acquaintances. The desire, if not for uniformity, at least for a group spirit—the protagonists in *The Demons* call their intimate circle 'Our People'—reveals an all-pervasive suspicion, particularly of Socialist politics, which is bolstered by Doderer's portrayal of the proletarian masses as rabble as well as his revisionist assessment of the 1927 riots. His texts propose that it takes personal initiative rather than political involvement to overcome the crippling bewilderment supposedly caused by too much indoctrination. Any passionate activity commensurate with one's character may lead to fulfilling one's destiny. While Doderer's concept of character echoes German idealism, it also has a fascist ring to it. His acute awareness of otherness based on gender and ethnicity corresponds with the views held by his psychology professor Hermann Swoboda who, like himself, advocated the principles of one of the most virulent proponents of anti-semitism and misogyny, Otto Weininger.

In Doderer's post-war publications, the inflammatory pronouncements, the prejudice against groups and individuals, but most of all the anti-semitism, are toned down—the later was most prevalent in his projects of the 1930s, following the estrangement from his wife. He had actually planned the first, lost version of *The Demons* as a celebration of anti-semitism. However, some of these tendencies survived, explaining Doderer's attraction to National Socialism. The novel *Ein Mord, den jeder begeht* (*Every Man a Murderer*), written during his Nazi phase, refutes the concept of individual responsibility as a young man realizes his involvement in his sister-in-law's murder. *Die erleuchteten Fenster; oder, die Menschwerdung des Amtsrates Julius Zihal* [The Illuminated Windows; or, the Humanization of Councillor Julius Zihal] submits that objective structures support any kind of activity: Zihal changes from a devoted, punctual civil servant to an equally serious voyeur. Only love can deliver him from his obsession. Despite their admirable stylistic qualities, the same problematic tendencies persist in Doderer's postwar novels. Purporting to present a critical literary survey of the inter-war years, they do not discuss the events following the burning of the Palace of Justice in 1927. The protagonists of *The Demons* disband and go into exile, including Mary K., a Jewish woman who has found her true self in a relationship with a working-class man, who, in turn, became a 'better' person through his intellectual pursuits. Even after 1945, marriage and assimilation to the gentile middle-classes represent Doderer's ultimate vision of hope to offset the collapse of the civilized world as he perceived it.

—Dagmar C.G. Lorenz

DIE STRUDLHOFSTIEGE
Novel by Heimito von Doderer, 1951.

Scope and structure of Doderer's approximately 900-page novel *Die Strudlhofstiege* and its somewhat more voluminous sequel, *Die Dämonen* (*The Demons*) suggest epic universality. Doderer took the Austrian painter and novelist Albert Paris Gütersloh as a model, appropriating the latter's concept of the 'total novel'. A closer look reveals that Doderer's seemingly boundless literary universe is subdivided into partially overlapping plot lines and character clusters which provide continuity. *Die Strudlhofstiege*, Doderer's first major success, is paradigmatic of his organically evolving creativity. The episodes and characters of his works are drawn from a meta-framework, his personal creative reference system which, as Roswitha Fischer showed, is composed of observations, factual news, results of studies and imaginary persons and events. Albeit only in passing, figures such as Julius Zihal from his earlier book *Die erleuchteten Fenster* recur in *Die Strudlhofstiege*.

The novel evolves around two different dates. The narrative present, between 1923 and 1925, is shaped by events which occurred during 1910 and 1911. This bi-levelled structure enables the narrator to make cross-references between two formative decades in Austrian history, suggesting a continuity between the Austro-Hungarian empire and the Social Democratic republic. Furthermore, Doderer's technique keeps the reader's interest alive throughout the text and allows for detailed accounts and digressions, Doderer's favourite devices. The final merging of the disparate elements signifies that nothing in this world is accidental. Some loose ends, created, for example, by the youthful perplexity of René Stangeler (one of Doderer's pseudonyms assigned to a character who mirrors the author as a young man), connect *Die Strudlhofstiege* with *The Demons*. Both are educational novels, Bildungsroman, set in Vienna and presuppose a fair knowledge of the city, because Doderer uses locations as symbols. The title of *Die Strudlhofstiege* alludes to a famous art deco structure, the Strudlhof staircase, which connects two distinct neighbourhoods of Vienna's 9th district. University institutes, clinics, and municipal buildings are located above the *Alsergrund*. The latter, located close to the Danube Canal, is the site of the Liechtensteinpark, after 1938 a haven for persecuted Jews, an ancient Jewish cemetery, and the police prison. Portentous encounters are staged on the Strudlhofstiege, most importantly, the novel's baroque central scene which severs obsolete bonds establishing more valid allegiances among the protagonists.

Doderer's pre-occupation with history is apparent throughout—his dissertation dealt with 15th-century historiography. Yet *Die Strudlhofstiege* is a profoundly subjective text rather than a historical novel suggesting that the individual must assert him/herself against the collective. Like Elias Canetti, Hermann Broch, and Bertolt Brecht, Doderer recognized 20th-century mass culture as a qualitatively new phenomenon. With its multitude of characters, *Die Strudlhofstiege* tries to represent a metropolitan mass society. However, despite the crowds he depicts, the author insists on the autonomy of the individual. His rejection of ideologies is decidedly bourgeois. Mistrust of politics was common in post-war Germany and Austria. Moreover, Doderer's attitude reflects his background, that of a World War I veteran and prisoner of war in Siberia who in 1933 joined the National Socialist Party at the time it was outlawed in Austria only to change his mind after the Nazi invasion in 1938, to convert to Catholicism and then to fight as an airforce major in World War II, who was taken prisoner by the British, and returned to Vienna in 1946.

By its structure, *Die Strudlhofstiege* is a belated example of the German realist novel, but more precisely, it is an attempt on the part of Doderer to come to terms with his times, his controversial life and work, and his bewilderment as a writer and a private person. A number of characters, through their interaction, intellectual development, political careers, and their personal and professional relationships mirror aspects of Doderer's own experience. Thus the most burning issues of the Austro-Fascist era and the post-war years, ethnic strife and the Holocaust, are suppressed. Rather, *Die Strudlhofstiege* vacillates between modernism and reaction. So does its author, an old-fashioned story-teller at heart, who nonetheless championed the experimental Wiener Gruppe in the 1950s. Like his creator, Doderer's protagonist Melzer is thrown into the chaos of World War I and left traumatized. However, the alienation of veterans, their inability to function in a democratic society and to cope with friends and the opposite sex, but most of all, civilian life, represent important social issues with which critics of the following generation such as Klaus Theweleit continue to wrestle. Doderer's solutions are personal and private: in 1925 Melzer redeems himself by saving the life of Mary K., a Jewish woman who never comes to terms with the fact that he does not marry her. Assisting her prepares the way for Melzer's most meaningful relationship: he is united with his soul mate Thea Rokitzer. His ability to establish this ultimate bond is proof that he has been healed.

As a myriad of plot lines illustrate, all of Doderer's characters suffer from distorted perceptions. Everyone is in search of self-realization. The assumption that everyone possesses a 'real' self, an inalienable, but buried identity, remains unquestioned. Those who find themselves have the chance of becoming 'simple' persons like Melzer, and eventually of finding their seemingly pre-ordained significant other (of the opposite sex). Those who fail to overcome their 'false' realities, like Etelka Grauermann, end up in disaster or death—Mary K. is lucky to lose only a leg in a traffic accident. Hers is only one example of how a brush with death can bring about a spiritual transformation. She survives, and her handicap liberates her from her conventional life, but most of all, from her illusions. A feeling of well-being accompanies such changes indicating that the character has embarked on the journey toward self-realization. On this path even the minutest object, every coincidence, is significant and as if arranged by a higher power to guide the individual. Doderer's rhetorical devices—puns, irony, symbols, and leitmotifs—underscore the relevance of each detail. The climax of this literary firework of attraction and repulsion, trial and error, is the Melzer's engagement party, an idyll reminiscent of Goethe's *Wilhelm Meister* novels and Stifter's *Der Nachsommer* (*Indian Summer*).

Doderer himself appears to have felt dissatisfaction about the fact that his grandiose epic leads to little more than conventional couplings and private bliss—at least this is what the ending seems to imply. As the plot lines merge, the ostensibly air-tight universe is undermined by reflections about the novel as a literary genre.

—Dagmar C.G. Lorenz

DOSTOEVSKII, Fedor (Mikhailovich) [Fyodor Dostoevsky]. Born in Moscow, Russia, 30 October 1821. Educated at home to age 12; Chermak's School, Moscow; Army Chief Engineering Academy, St Petersburg, 1838–43: commissioned as ensign, 1839, as 2nd lieutenant, 1842, graduated 1843 as War Ministry draftsman; resigned 1844. Married 1) Maria Dmitrievna Isaeva in 1857 (died 1864), one stepson; 2) Anna Grigorievna Snitkina in 1867, two daughters and two sons. Writer; political involvement caused his arrest, 1849: sentenced to death, but sentence commuted at the last moment to penal servitude, in Omsk, Siberia, 1850–54; exiled as soldier at Semipalatinsk, 1854: corporal, 1855, ensign, 1856, resigned as 2nd lieutenant for health reasons, and exile ended, 1859; editor, *Vremia* [Time], 1861–63; took over *Epokha* [Epoch] on his brother's death, 1864–65; in Western Europe, 1867–71; editor, *Grazhdanin* [Citizen], 1873–74. *Died 28 January 1881.*

PUBLICATIONS

Collections

Novels, translated by Constance Garnett. 12 vols., 1912–20.
Polnoe sobranie khudozhestvennykh proizvedenii [Complete Works]. 3 vols., 1933.
Sobranie sochinenii [Collected Works], edited by Leonid Grossman. 10 vols., 1956–58.
Polnoe sobranie sochinenii [Complete Works], edited by G.M. Fridlender and others. 30 vols., 1972–90.
Sochineniia [Works]. 2 vols., 1987– .
Sobranie sochinenii [Collected Works]. 15 vols., 1988.
Izbrannye sochineniia [Selected Works], edited by N.I. Iakushin. 1990.

Fiction

Bednye liudi. 1846; as *Poor Folk*, 1887; also translated by L. Milman, 1894; C.J. Hogarth, with *The Gambler*, 1916; Constance Garnett, in *Novels*, 1917; L. Nazrozov, 1956; Robert Dessaix, 1982; David McDuff, 1988.
Dvoinik. 1846; as *The Double*, translated by Constance Garnett, in *Novels*, 1917; also translated by Jessie Coulson, 1972; as *The Double: A Poem of St. Petersburg*, translated by George Bird, 1956; as *The Double: Two Versions*, translated by Evelyn Harden, 1985.
Belye nochi. 1848; as *White Nights*, translated by Constance Garnett, in *Novels*, 1918; also translated by Olga Shartse, 1958.
Netochka Nezvanova. 1849; as *Netochka Nezvanova*, translated by Constance Garnett, in *Novels*, 1920; also translated by Ann Dunnigan, 1970; Jane Kentish, 1985.
Selo Stepanchikogo i ego obitateli [The Village Stepanchikogo and Its Inhabitants]. 1859.
Zapiski iz podpol'ia. 1864; edited by A.D.P. Briggs, 1994; as *Letters from the Underworld*, translated by C.J. Hogarth, 1913; as *Notes from the Underground*, translated by Jessie Coulson, 1972; as *Notes from Underground*, translated by Constance Garnett, in *Novels*, 1918; also translated by Mirra Ginsburg, 1974; Michael R. Katz, 1989; Jane Kentish, with *The Gambler*, 1991; Richard Pevear and Larissa Volokhonsky, 1992.
Igrok. 1866; as *The Gambler*, translated by F. Whishaw, with *The Friend of the Family*, 1887; also translated by C.J. Hogarth, with *Poor Folk*, 1916; Jessie Coulson, 1966; Victor Terras, with *Diary*, by Polina Suslova, 1973; Jane Kentish, with *Notes from the Underground*, 1991.
Prestuplenie i nakazanie. 1867; as *Crime and Punishment*, translated by Frederick Whishaw, 1886; also translated by Constance Garnett, 1881; David Magarshack, 1951; Jessie Coulson, 1953 (this translation edited by George Gibian, 1989); Sidney Monas, 1968; J. Katzer, 1985; David McDuff, 1991; Richard Pevear and Larissa Volokhonsky, 1993.
Idiot. 1869; as *The Idiot*, translated by Frederick Whishaw, 1887; also translated by Constance Garnett, in *Novels*, 1913; E. Martin, 1914; David Magarshack, 1954; Henry and Olga Carlisle, 1969; J. Katzer, 1978; Alan Myers, 1992; Richard Pevear and Larissa Volokhonsky, 1993.
Vechnyi muzh. 1870; as *The Permanent Husband*, translated by Frederick Whishaw, with *Uncle's Dream*, 1888; as *The Eternal Husband*, translated by Constance Garnett, in *Novels*, 1917.
Besy. 1872; as *The Possessed*, translated by Constance Garnett, in *Novels*, 1913; as *The Devils*, translated by David Magarshack, 1953; as *Devils*, translated by Michael R. Katz, 1992.
Podrostok. 1875; as *A Raw Youth*, translated by Constance Garnett, in *Novels*, 1916.
Brat'ia Karamazovy. 1880; as *The Brothers Karamazov*, translated by Constance Garnett, in *Novels*, 1912; also translated by A. Kropotkin, 1953; David Magarshack, 1958; Andrew R. MacAndrew, 1970; Julius Katzer, 1980; W.J. Leatherbarrow, 1990; Richard Pevear and Larissa Volokhonsky, 1990; David McDuff, 1993.
Injury and Insult, translated by Frederick Whishaw. 1886; as *The Insulted and Injured*, translated by Constance Garnett, in *Novels*, 1915; also translated by Olga Shartse, 1977; as *The Insulted and Humiliated*, 1956.
The Friend of the Family and The Gambler, translated by Frederick Whishaw. 1887.
Uncle's Dream, translated by Frederick Whishaw, with *The Permanent Husband*. 1888; also translated by Constance Garnett, in *Novels*, 1919; as *My Uncle's Dream*, translated by Ivy Litvinova, 1956.
Letters from the Underworld and Other Stories, translated by C.J. Hogarth. 1913.
A Gentle Spirit, translated by Constance Garnett, in *Novels*. 1917; as *A Gentle Creature and Other Stories*, translated by David Magarshack, 1950.
Best Short Stories, translated by David Magarshack. 1954.
Winter Notes on Summer Impressions, translated by R. Renfield. 1954; as *Summer Impressions*, translated by Kyril FitzLyon, 1954.
The Gambler; Bobok; A Nasty Story, translated by Jessie Coulson. 1966.
Notes from the Underground; The Double, translated by Jessie Coulson. 1972.
Poor Folk and Other Stories, translated by David McDuff. 1988.
Uncle's Dream and Other Stories, translated by David McDuff. 1989.
An Accidental Family, edited and translated by Richard Freeborn. 1994.

Other

Zapiski iz mertvogo doma. 1861–62; as *Buried Alive; or, Ten Years of Penal Servitude in Siberia*, translated by M. Von Thilo, 1881; as *Prison Life in Siberia*, translated by H. Edwards, 1881; as *The House of the Dead*, 1911; also translated by Constance Garnett, in *Novels*, 1915; David McDuff, 1985; as *Memoirs from the House of the Dead*, translated by Jessie Coulson, 1955; as *Notes from a Dead House*, translated by L. Nazrozov and J. Guralsky, 1958.

Dnevnik pisatelia. 1876–81; as *The Diary of a Writer*, translated by Boris Leo Brasol, 2 vols., 1949; as *A Writer's Diary 1873–1876*, translated by Brasol, 2 vols., 1949; also translated by Kenneth Lantz, 1993.

Letters of Fyodor Michailovitch Dostoevsky to His Family and Friends, translated by E. Mayne. 1914.

Pages from the Journal of an Author, translated by S.S. Kotelianskii and J.M. Murry. 1916.

Letters and Reminiscences, translated by S.S. Kotelianskii and J.M. Murry. 1923.

Pis'ma k zhene, edited by V.F. Pereverzev. 1926; as *Letters to His Wife*, translated by E. Hill and D. Mudie, 1930.

New Dostoevsky Letters, translated by S.S. Kotelianskii. 1929.

Zapisnye tetradi [Notebooks]. 4 vols., 1935.

The Grand Inquisitor, translated by S.S. Kotelianskii. 1935; also translated by Constance Garnett, 1948.

Pis'ma [Letters]. 4 vols., 1959.

Occasional Writings, edited and translated by David Magarshack. 1961.

The Notebooks for The Idiot [*Crime and Punishment, The Possessed, A Raw Youth, The Brothers Karamazov*], edited by Edward Wasiolek, translated by Wasiolek, Victor Terras, and Katharine Strelsky. 5 vols., 1967–71.

Neizdannyi Dostoevskii. Zapisnye knizhki i tetradi 1860–1881. 1971; as *The Unpublished Dostoevsky: Diaries and Notebooks, 1860–81*, edited by Carl R. Proffer, 3 vols., 1973–76.

Self Portrait, edited by Jessie Coulson. 1976.

Selected Letters, edited by Joseph Frank and David I. Goldstein, translated by Andrew R. MacAndrew. 1987.

Complete Letters (Vol. 1, 1832–59; Vol. 2, 1860–67; Vol. 3, (1868–71); Vol. 4 (1872–77); Vol. 5, 1878–81), edited and translated by David Lowe and Ronald Meyer. 1988–91.

Vozvrashchenie cheloveka [The Return of Man], edited by M.M. Stakhanova. 1989.

*

Bibliography: *Dostoevskii, Bibliografiia proizvedenii Dostoevskogo i literatury o nem 1917–65* edited by A.A. Belkin, A.S. Dolinin, and V.V. Kozhinov, 1968; 'Dostoevsky Studies in Great Britain: A Bibliographical Survey' by Garth M. Terry in *New Essays on Dostoevsky* edited by Malcolm V. Jones and Garth M. Terry, 1983; *Fedor Dostoevsky: A Reference Guide* by W.J. Leatherbarrow, 1990.

Critical Studies: *Fyodor Dostoevsky: A Study* by Aimee Dostoevskii, 1922; *Dostoevsky: The Man and His Work* by Julius Meier Graefe, 1928; *The Mighty Three: Pushkin, Gogol, Dostoevsky* by Boris Leo Brasol, 1934; *Dostoevsky in Russian Literary Criticism 1846–1954*, 1957, *Dostoevskii's Image in Russia Today*, 1975, and *Dostoevskii in Russian and World Theatre*, 1977, all by Vladimir Seduro; *Dostoevsky: His Life and Art* by Avrahm Yarmolinsky, 1957; *Dostoevsky* by David Magarshack, 1961; *The Undiscovered Dostoevsky*, 1962, and *Dostoevsky: His Life and Work*, 1978, both by Ronald Hingley; *Dostoevsky: A Collection of Critical Essays* edited by Rene Wellek, 1962; *Notes on Dostoevsky's 'Crime and Punishment'*, 1963, and *Notes on Dostoevsky's 'Notes from the Underground'*, 1970, both by James L. Roberts, and *Notes on Dostoevsky's 'Brothers Karamazov'* by Roberts and Gary Carey, 1967; *Dostoevsky: The Major Fiction* by Edward Wasiolek, 1964; *Dostoevsky's Quest for Form*, 1966, *The Art of Dostoevsky*, 1981, and *Dostoevsky's Underground Man in Russian Literature*, 1982, all by Robert Louis Jackson;

Dostoevsky and Romantic Realism by Donald Fangler, 1967; *Dostoevsky: His Life and Work* by Konstantin Mochulskii, 1967; *Dostoevsky: An Examination of the Major Novels* by Richard Peace, 1971; *Political Apocalypse: A Study of Dostoevsky's Grand Inquisitor* by Ellis Sandoz, 1971; *The Religion of Dostoevsky* by A. Boyce Gibson, 1973; *Dostoevsky and the Age of Intensity* by Alex de Jong, 1975; *Starets Zosima in the Brothers Karamazov: A Study in the Mimesis of Virtue* by Sven Linnér, 1975; *Dostoevsky: The Novel of Discord*, 1976, and *Dostoevsky after Bakhtin: Readings in Dostoevsky's Fantastic Realism*, 1990, both by Malcolm V. Jones, 1976, and *New Essays on Dostoevsky* edited by Jones and Garth M. Terry, 1983; *Dostoevsky: The Literary Artist* by Erik Krag, 1976; *Dostoevsky: The Seeds of Revolt 1821–1849*, 1977, *The Years of Ordeal 1850–1859*, 1984, and *The Stir of Liberation 1860–1865*, 1987, all by Joseph Frank; *Dostoevsky and the Novel* by Michael Holquist, 1977; *A 'Handbook' to the Russian Text of Crime and Punishment* by Edgar H. Lehrmann, 1977; *Atheism and the Rejection of God: Contemporary Philosophy and the Brothers Karamazov* by Stewart Sutherland, 1977; *Dostoevsky and Christ: A Study of Dostoevsky's Rebellion Against Belinsky* by Ivan Dolenc, 1978; *Ideology and Imagination: The Image of Society in Dostoevsky* by Geoffrey C. Kabat, 1978; *Dostoevsky and the Psychologists* by Maria Kravchenko, 1978; *Crime and Punishment: Murder as Philosophic Experiment* by A.D. Nuttall, 1978; *Crime and Punishment: The Techniques of the Omniscient Author* by Gary Rosenshield, 1978; *Unconscious Structure in The Idiot: A Study in Literature and Psychoanalysis* by Elizabeth Dalton, 1979; *Narrative Principles in Dostoevskij's Besy: A Structural Analysis* by Slobodanka B. Vladiv, 1979; *Tolstoy or Dostoevsky: An Essay in Contrast* by George Steiner, 1980; *F.M. Dostoevsky (1821–1881): A Centenary Collection* edited by Leo Burnett, 1981; *Fedor Dostoevsky*, 1981, and *Fyodor Dostoevsky; 'The Brothers Karamazov'*, 1992, both by W.J. Leatherbarrow; *Dostoevsky and The Idiot: Author, Narrator and Reader* by Robin Feuer Miller, 1981; *A Karamazov Companion: Commentary on the Genesis, Language and Style of Dostoevsky's Novel* by Victor Terras, 1981; *The Underground Man and Raskolnikov: A Comparative Study* by Preben Villadsen, 1981; *Dostoevsky* by Gerald Abraham, 1982; *Fyodor Dostoevsky* by John Arthur Thomas Lloyd, 1982; *Dostoevsky* by Stanislaw Mackiewicz, 1982; *Dostoevsky* by Dimitri Merejkowski, 1982; *Character Names in Dostoevsky's Fiction* by Charles Passage, 1982; *Dostoevsky* by John Cowper Powys, 1982; *Dostoevsky* by C.M. Woodhouse, 1982; *Dostoevsky* by L.A. Zander, 1982; *New Essays on Dostoevsky*, 1983; *A Dostoevsky Dictionary* by Richard Chapple, 1983; *Dostoevsky* by John Jones, 1983; *The Idiot: Dostoevsky's Fantastic Prince: A Phenomenological Approach* by Dennis Patrick Slattery, 1983; *Problems of Dostoevsky's Poetics* by Mikhail M. Bakhtin, translated by Caryl Emerson, 1984; *Tyrant and Victim in Dostoevsky* by Gary Cox, 1984; *Dostoevsky and His New Testament*, 1984, and *Dostoevsky: A Writer's Life*, 1988, both by Geir Kjetsaa; *The Experience of Time in Crime and Punishment* by Leslie A. Johnson, 1985; *Varieties of Poetic Utterance: Quotation in The Brothers Karamazov* by Nina Perlina, 1985; *Dostoevsky and the Healing Art: An Essay in Literary and Medical History* by James L. Rice, 1985; *Dostoevsky: The Myths of Duality* by Roger B. Anderson, 1986; *Dostoevsky and the Human Condition after a Century* edited by Alexej Ugrinsky, Frank S. Lambasa, and Valija K. Ozolins, 1986; *Dostoyevsky's Critique of the West: The Quest for the Earthly Paradise* by Bruce K. Ward, 1986; *Humor in the Novels of F.M. Dostoevsky* by R.L. Busch, 1987; *The Aesthetics of*

Dostoevsky by Nadezhda Kashina, 1987; *Summer in Baden-Baden: From the Life of Dostoyevsky* by Leonid Tsypkin, 1987; *Fyodor Dostoevsky* by Peter Conradi, 1988; *Poverty and Power in the Early Works of Dostoevskij* by S.K. Somerwil-Ayrton, 1988; *Furnace of Doubt: Dostoevsky and The Brothers Karamazov* by Arthur Trace, 1988; *The Genesis of the Brothers Karamazov: The Aesthetics, Ideology and Psychology of Making a Text* by Robert Belknap, 1989; *Dostoevsky: The Author as Psychoanalyst* by Louis Breger, 1989; *Dostoevsky and the Process of Literary Creation* by Jacques Catteau, 1989; *Literary Portraits in the Novels of F.M. Dostoevskij* by Edmund Heier, 1989; *Dostoevsky: Dreamer and Prophet* by Judith Gunn, 1990; *The Political and Social Thought of F.M. Dostoevsky* by Stephen Carter, 1991; *The Brothers Karamazov and the Poetics of Memory* by Diana Oenning Thompson, 1991; *Fedor Dostoevsky* by Alloa Amoia, 1993.

* * *

The darkness of Fedor Dostoevskii's life—a murdered father, epilepsy, near-execution and exile, debt, compulsive gambling, estrangement from friends, and a tormented sexuality—reflects the rapidly overheating Russian society of the later 19th century. So does his literature. His early work, including *Bednye liudi* (*Poor Folk*), *Dvoinik* (*The Double*), and *Belye nochi* (*White Nights*), surfaces in a post-Gogolian 'civic realism', with a compassion for the little man, but this feature is quickly overshadowed by his characteristic and seminal perceptions of the paranoia, deception, emptiness, and illusion of modern urban life. In the score of years following his penal servitude and exile for 'socialist' activities (1849–59) Dostoevskii produced a series of works of lasting significance for 20th-century literature. The Underground Man (central character of *Zapiski iz podpol'ia*, translated as *Notes from the Underground*) is a determining forerunner to most of the later heroes: a frustrated modern man, adrift in a moral void. Estranged from the roots of land, tradition, and faith, he attempts to establish, if only negatively, his own identity and dignity against the palliatives and platitudes of authority on the one hand and the serious, but dangerous appeal of 'rationalism' on the other. Rationalism, in Dostoevskii's view, came to embrace utilitarianism, materialism, socialism, and the temporal power of Roman Catholicism. Throughout his work Dostoevskii seeks to counteract rationalism by appeal to the intuitive Christian faith which he sees embodied, however imperfectly, in the beliefs of the Russian people.

The conflicting interplay between the rationalist analysis of existence and the natural response to life is pursued in stronger terms in the characters and plots of the major novels. In *Prestuplenie i nakazanie* (*Crime and Punishment*) Raskol'nikov's espousal of a 'rational' superman morality results only in the squalid murder of a pawnbroker, followed by Raskol'nikov's own self-torment which eventually leads him to an unconvincing 'salvation'. In *Idiot* (*The Idiot*) Prince Myshkin's passive beauty and his all too perceptive innocence stimulate, rather than reconcile, the perverse impulses of his society. In *Besy* (*The Possessed* or *The Devils*), a Messianic, anti-revolutionary novel, Stavrogin's unique strength and individuality is sapped to suicide by disillusionment with ideologies, causes, and beliefs. Finally, in *Brat'ia Karamazovy* (*The Brothers Karamazov*) the Karamazov family, beset by jealousy, pride, and hatred, disintegrates into parricide, a crisis that tests the extremes of Christianity and atheism. It is only in this last novel that Dostoevskii's attempt to give a positive depiction of active Christian love (in the persons of Father Zosima and Alesha Karamazov) is artistically successful, although even here it often fails to match the power of Ivan Karamazov's reasoned objections to 'God's world'.

Dostoevskii's heroes are strong but divided personalities, engaged in intimate and frequently mortal debate with themselves, their 'doubles', and the reader over the moral basis of their actions. His murder-centred plots are a visionary, fantastic, and mythically structured re-working of the sensational and extremist life observed in his journalism. The polarized themes of reason and unreason, faith and unbelief, moral freedom and moral slavery, frame the tension of modern man, a tension which finds a precarious resolution in the vision of Christ, Dostoevskii's moral-aesthetic ideal. His journal chronicle *Dnevnik pisatelia* (*The Diary of a Writer*) portrays these issues in the form of justification of tradition, discussion of psychology and education, and nationalistic, reactionary vaunting of the Russian destiny over a corrupt Europe.

The essence of Dostoevskii's work is dialogue. Vladimir Nabokov, a noted critic of Dostoevskii's otherwise largely undisputed reputation, describes him as a writer who 'seems to have been chosen by the destiny of Russian letters to become Russia's greatest playwright', but who 'took the wrong turning and wrote novels' (*Lectures on Russian Literature*, 1982). Those novels are constantly destabilized by narrators, chroniclers, and a host of narrating characters who run amok through authorial corridors. Mikhail Bakhtin's identification of this dialogic structure as 'polyphony' (in his *Problems of Dostoevsky's Poetics*) has been revolutionary to the understanding of Dostoevskii and highly influential in the development of modern structuralism. Dostoevskii creates from his settings of fateful threshold and crowded room, grubby town and fantastic city the fragmented universe inherited by the 20th-century novel. Nothing in Dostoevskii's work is single, whole, or certain, but his imperfective vision looks forward with a desperate hope for perfection.

—Christopher R. Pike

THE BROTHERS KARAMAZOV (Brat'ia Karamazovy)
Novel by Fedor Dostoevskii, 1880.

The Brothers Karamazov was Dostoevskii's last great novel, bringing to culmination many of the themes of his earlier fiction, such as the debate between religion and atheism, the battle between good and evil in the hearts of 'broad' Russian characters, clashes of incompatible rival women, the ever-fascinating legal process, and, above all, Dostoevskii's longstanding attempts to create a 'positively good man' capable of leading Russia's spiritual regeneration. Moreover, the three brothers seem to reflect the three main stages of the author's life: Dmitrii, his youthful Romantic period; Ivan, his attachment to atheistic socialist circles; and Alesha, his spiritually reborn post-Siberian period.

The longest of the novels, *The Brothers Karamazov* is also one of the most tightly constructed, topographically exact (the town of Skotoprigonevsk is closely modelled on Staraia

Russa where Dostoevskii spent his last years), and chronologically compact: the main action of the book takes place over a period of only three days, but with much interleaving of narration as we follow the lives of the three brothers in long, intercalated sections with a constant feeling of acceleration driving the action on. Each brother in turn, with the aid of significant dreams (and, in Ivan's case, delirium), learns important facts about himself and, for all the narration's pace, the reader shares a strong sense of epiphanic development.

The novel's main theme is the nature of fatherhood. On the one hand we have the saintly elder Zosima, a spiritual father to Alesha, the youngest brother; on the other the irresponsible, scheming, lecherous Fedor Karamazov, a father in the biological sense alone, whose possible murder is a topic of discussion from early in the book. This crime, once committed, provides a source of guilt for all of his sons: Alesha, the novice sent out into the world by Zosima, who for all his Christian goodness cannot avert the parricide; Dmitrii, cheated by his father and a rival for the favours of the amoral Grushenka; and Ivan, the haughty intellectual, spiritual descendant of Raskol'nikov, whose formula 'if God does not exist, then all is permitted' falls onto the receptive ears of his bastard half-brother, the lackey Smerdiakov who, in fact, proves to be the actual perpetrator of the crime.

As a detective story this chronicle of small-town life is handled in masterly fashion with concatenations of circumstances and fatally coincidental sums of money all seeming to impugn the passionate Dmitrii, who is eventually tried and condemned. Rarely, if ever, has the tension of mounting circumstantial evidence been portrayed in such a gripping manner (Dostoevskii was inspired by a comparable real-life case). His response to the new legal system in Russia adds particular vividness to the description of the trial, in which not only Dmitrii, or even the Karamazov family, but effectively the whole of Russia is judged before the world.

The Brothers Karamazov was Dostoevskii's last attempt to create a 'positively good man'. Father Zosima, though charismatic, is, perhaps, too pale and other-worldly for this role, but Alesha, through counselling distressed adults and children, gains authority as the novel progresses, and it is with him that the book ends. More memorable, however, is his brother Ivan's exposition of the reasons for rejecting God's world: the examples he adduces of gross cruelty to innocent children make his 'returning of the ticket' to God very persuasive. His principal thought is expressed in the 'Legend of the Grand Inquisitor', a profound and disturbing meditation on Christianity, free will, and happiness, at the end of which Alesha kisses his brother, just as Christ had responded to the Inquisitor with a silent kiss. Subsequently Ivan's brilliant Euclidian mind proves unable to resist a mocking petty bourgeois devil and he falls into insanity. In the world of Dostoevskii's novels Christianity and the intellectual have a purely negative relationship.

Dmitrii, aware that his nature contains elements of both the Madonna and Sodom, shares his father's impulsive, passionate character but none of his cynicism or buffoonery. Dmitrii's romance with Grushenka, who also alternates between satanic pride and self-abasement, voluptuousness and spiritual sublimation, makes this one of the great love stories in all literature. Also fascinating are all three brothers' relations with two other mentally troubled women, Katerina Ivanovna and Liza Khokhlakova, revealing a disturbingly dark side of passion first seen in *Igrok* (*The Gambler*) but also encountered in ensuing novels, particularly *The Idiot* and *The Devils*. The depiction of these women's behaviour together with the parricide itself strongly attracted the professional interest of Sigmund Freud.

The Brothers Karamazov is a rich and fascinating text containing crime, passion, psychology, religion, and philosophy. It is indeed one of the great novels of the world.

—Arnold McMillin

CRIME AND PUNISHMENT (Prestuplenie i nakazanie)
Novel by Fedor Dostoevskii, 1867.

In the complexity of its narrative and psychological structure, the many-facetedness and interlayering of its setting and characterization, *Crime and Punishment* is almost unique in world literature. Few works of fiction have attracted so many widely diverging interpretations. It has been seen as a detective novel, an attack on radical youth, a study in alienation and criminal psychopathology, a work of prophecy (the attempt on the life of Tsar Aleksandr II by the nihilist student Dmitri Karakozov took place while the book was at the printer's, and some even saw the Tsar's murder in 1881 as a fulfilment of Dostoevskii's warning), an indictment of urban social conditions in 19th-century Russia, a religious epic, and a proto-Nietzschean analysis of the 'will to power'. It is, of course, all these things—but it is more.

The story itself is fairly simple: Raskol'nikov, a young St Petersburg ex-student, plans and executes the murder of an old woman pawnbroker, ostensibly for money, but in fact to prove to himself that he can 'overstep' the limits laid down by society and the law. In the days that precede his arrest, we encounter his student friends, the policemen who are tracking him down, his prostitute girlfriend and her impoverished family, his sister, her arrogant lawyer suitor, and the character of Svidrigailov, a sinisterly omnipresent St Petersburg dandy and ex-card sharper, who seems to know everything about Raskol'nikov. In the end, under the intolerable pressure of his conscience and the psychological manipulations of his pursuers, Raskol'nikov breaks down, confesses to the murder, and is sent into exile in Siberia. The novel's complexity derives from the minutely subtle way in which inner thought-processes are inextricably fused with the urban streetscape of St Petersburg during a heatwave at the beginning of July 1865.

Perhaps the most cogent explanation of Dostoevskii's intentions in writing the novel was given by the philosopher Vladimir S. Solovev (1833–1900), who knew Dostoevskii and in the summer of 1878 travelled with him on a pilgrimage to the monastery of Optina Pustyn. In the first of his three commemorative speeches (1881–83), Solovev states the matter with utter simplicity. In a discussion of *Crime and Punishment* and *The Devils* he writes:

The meaning of the first of these novels, for all its depth of detail, is very clear and simple, though many have not understood it. Its principal character is a representative of that view of things according to which every strong man is his own master, and all is permitted to him. In the name of his personal superiority, in the name of his belief that he is a *force*, he considers himself entitled to commit murder and does in fact do so. But then suddenly the deed he thought was merely a violation of a senseless outer law and a bold challenge to the prejudice of society turns out, for his own conscience, to be something much more than this—it turns out to be a sin, a violation of inner moral justice. His violation of the outer law meets its lawful retribution from without in exile and penal servitude, but his inward sin of pride that has separated the strong man from humanity and has led him to commit murder—that inward sin of self-idolatry can only be redeemed by an inner moral act of self-renunciation. His boundless self-confidence must disappear in the face of that which is greater than *himself*, and his self-fabricated justification must humble itself before the higher justice of God that lives in those very same simple, weak folk whom the strong man viewed as paltry insects.

(translated by David McDuff)

Solovev's analysis is doubtless coloured by his theories concerning the Russian Church and people, but even so, in its simplicity and straightforwardness, based on a personal knowledge of the author, it is hard to refute. Far from moving towards a religious dogmatism or alignment with reactionary political views as some critics have considered he did, in the period that followed his incarceration in the labour camp Dostoevskii began to discover a 'true socialism'—the '*sobornost*' ('communion') of the human spirit as it expressed itself in the shared identity of the Russian people and their self-effacing acceptance of God. *Crime and Punishment* shows us the steps along this way—Raskol'nikov's sin of pride is also Dostoevskii's, and his expiation of it through suffering is what the novel is really 'about'.

The intensity of suffered life that fills its pages lends a strange, electric brilliance to the action and plot. Above all, as Konstantin Mochulskii was one of the first to observe, the brilliance of the sun is everywhere. Its light and heat seem to increase as the novel progresses—and the light is surely the light of God, and the heat the warmth of His love. Raskol'nikov moves in the sunlight ever more pressingly conscious that there can be no concealment for him, that there is no corner where that brilliance will not reach and find him. Other gripping features of the novel are the vividness with which the sights and sounds of everyday St Petersburg street life are recorded, and the satirical acuteness of Dostoevskii's caricaturing of the liberal, Fourierist intelligentsia of his time. Among the novel's most memorable passages, apart from the axe-murder itself, are the descriptions of Raskol'nikov's dreams, which merge with reality in a strange and disturbing manner. The characters of Marmeladov and his wife Katerina Ivanovna are drawn with a Dickensian panache, and in some ways stand out from the rest of the novel. This is probably because they derive from another novel, called *The Drunkards*, which Dostoevskii never completed, but which he cannibalized in order to help to build his greatest novel.

In the end, western readers must make a leap of the spirit and the imagination in order to penetrate the inner essence of this very Russian work. It was Nicholas Berdiiaev who viewed Dostoevskii not as a psychologist but as a 'pneumatologist', a researcher of souls. In his book *Dostoevsky—An Interpretation* (1934), Berdiiaev characterizes the Russian soul as being fundamentally different in nature from the western soul. *Crime and Punishment* offers the clearest testimony to the nature of that difference, which hinges on the close association of individual identity with a divine conception of national belonging, in which 'the people' are equivalent to God.

—David McDuff

THE DEVILS (Besy)
Novel by Fedor Dostoevskii, 1872.

The Devils, also translated as *The Possessed*, is the third of Dostoevskii's great novels and was written during the years 1869 to 1871, after *The Idiot* and before *The Brothers Karamazov*. Whereas *The Idiot* examined the evils of money as it affected contemporary Russian society, in *The Devils* Dostoevskii reverted to themes raised in *Crime and Punishment*: radical socialism, revolution, and godlessness. But while in the epilogue to *Crime and Punishment* Dostoevskii hints at Raskol'nikov's personal regeneration through belief in God, in *The Devils* he intended to put forward the idea of the regeneration of the whole country through a return to Russian Orthodoxy. In the event his multi-faceted negative depiction of the revolutionary movement carries far more weight than the tragic figure of Shatov, who comes to believe in national regeneration through Orthodoxy.

Dostoevskii had already begun writing the novel when he learned of the case of the student revolutionary Nechaev, who had fled to Geneva in 1869 where he gained the confidence of the exiled radicals, in particular Bakunin. Returning to Russia, Nechaev began forming a revolutionary movement with a cellular structure, five members in each cell of whom each would also be a member of a different cell. With iron discipline and the minimum of contact between groups, infiltration by the police would be unlikely. When one of the members of his cell (it is doubtful there ever was more than one) rejected blind obedience, Nechaev arranged for the others to murder him. He himself then fled abroad. Dostoevskii saw in Nechaev the epitome of the amorality of the Western-influenced revolutionaries and, deciding on a pamphlet novel, turned Nechaev into the figure of Petr Verkhovenskii who arrives in a provincial town to organize a cell of the same type. One of the plot strands shows how one member of the cell, Shatov, is killed for his betrayal of revolutionary ideals.

Dostoevskii also blames contemporary revolutionary madness on the older generation of liberals: in a commentary on Turgenev's *Fathers and Sons* (*Ottsy i deti*), Dostoevskii depicts in Petr's father Stepan an ageing, weak liberal whose ideas have engendered the ruthless and tyrannical face of the modern radical because he was the first to reject God. For Dostoevskii, when man set himself up as a master of his own fate, there ceased to be any moral prohibitions. Furthermore, once man decided he knew what was best for mankind, there was nothing to prevent dictatorship. It is not surprising that the equation of socialism with tyranny made the book extremely unpopular with the Soviet authorities, while in the West, and in recent years in Russia, it has been regarded as in many respects prophetic.

Petr gathers around him a group of people who represent aspects of the radical movement, of whom Shigalev and Kirillov are the most interesting. Shigalev represents the theoretical aspects of Petr Verkhovenskii's destructive actions starting from the idea of unlimited freedom, and ending up with unlimited despotism. Kirillov, also interested in absolute godless freedom, argues that what holds man back from total freedom is his fear of death. Hence out of love for humanity he proposes to commit suicide to demonstrate to mankind that the fear of death is vain, in effect arrogantly taking on the role of Christ. The scene in which he commits suicide is one of the most horrifying in what is an extremely powerful book.

Both Shigalev and Kirillov as well as Shatov, who is murdered Nechaev-style at the instigation of Petr Verkhovenskii for rejecting revolution for Russian Orthodoxy, owe their ideas not to Verkhovenskii but to Nikolai Stavrogin, son of a local landowner. Here the novel transcends the political pamphlet to become a discussion of the nature of evil. Stavrogin possesses the ultimate freedom that the others seek in their various ways, a freedom to do just whatever he wants, and yet like Milton's Lucifer he is supremely bored and ultimately lonely. An enigma, part charismatic, part repellent, his behaviour ranges from cruel to capricious to apparently kind. None the less almost all the characters (women find him almost irresistible) try to please him or placate him. In the absence of any clear beliefs, he has toyed with ideas and even with actions, for example secretly marrying the deranged cripple Maria Lebiadkina. The reasons for his marriage are unclear: he is kind to her, so perhaps he is experimenting with kindness, or else atoning for his appalling behaviour towards a young girl many years before, offending his aristocratic mother, throwing down a challenge to common sense, or perhaps revealing his own spiritual deformity by allying himself with a cripple. With Dostoevskii actions are always to be explained by the ideas and motives behind them rather than the conventional meaning assigned to them, but in the case of Stavrogin these reasons, though no less important, are obscure, and aspects of his intellectual development are more clearly reflected in Shatov, Shigalev, and Kirillov. His ultimate suicide suggests the bankruptcy of an approach to life that embraces evil.

With this explosive mix of characters, the action of *The Devils* whirls to a frenzied conclusion. On one level the focus is on a grand occasion put on in the provincial town by the wife of the new governor, which is to culminate in a speech by the veteran liberal and grand old man of Russian letters, Karmazinov (a thinly disguised attack on Turgenev). Petr Verkhovenskii and the revolutionary rabble who follow him succeed in causing total disruption. This rather pathetic manifestation of revolutionary activity is contrasted with a series of murders, deaths, and suicides, in one way or another involving most of the many characters, in which the destructive and negative power of godlessness is made manifest. In *The Devils* Dostoevskii wove a range of interrelated and contrasting characters into a highly complex and dramatic, even terrifying indictment of the ideas he felt were destroying Russia. Whatever the reader may think of his pessimistic views, the force of the book and its ideas is undeniable.

—Faith Wigzell

THE IDIOT (Idiot)
Novel by Fedor Dostoevskii, 1869.

Of all Dostoevskii's great novels, *The Idiot* was written with the greatest difficulty, and yet it contains some of the author's boldest and most cherished ideas as well as an intriguing plot and a plethora of fascinating characters.

During the years 1867–71 Dostoevskii lived abroad, mainly in Dresden, to escape his Russian creditors. *The Idiot*, in which he invested much emotional and creative capital, represented for him possibly the only path to financial salvation. Although it took 18 months to write, elements of haste may be observed, particularly in the middle (second and third) parts of the book where elements of didacticism, inconsequential characters, and incomplete plotlines slow the novel's initial momentum which is, however, regained in the final part.

The book opens with the childlike 'idiot', Prince Lev Myshkin, returning to St Petersburg by train after treatment in a Swiss sanatorium. In the carriage he meets Parfen Rogozhin, a violent and passionate merchant who both repels and attracts him, and who subsequently becomes in some sense his rival for the hand of the wronged and vulnerable but arrogant beauty Nastas'ia Filippovna. The gentle Prince, epileptic and sexually impotent but possessing unbounded charity and understanding, manages in the course of the book to ruin not only Nastas'ia but also her rival Aglaia, one of the three daughters of the Epanchin family upon which he settles on arrival. At first, however, the 'idiot' is welcomed into their midst as a slightly comic, immensely humble figure who seems able to read his interlocutors' thoughts and comprehend their motives. But the novelty of the Prince's clairvoyance and Christian forgiveness wears off for the worldly and venial people he meets, and before long we understand the validity of one of the characters' remarks about him: 'humility is a terrible force'. This apparent paradox is also reflected in the Prince's names that signify both strength and meekness, meaning 'lion' and 'mouse'. He represents Dostoevskii's first major attempt to realize a longstanding ambition and create a 'positively good man' to contrast with and redeem the materialistic and egotistical Russian society that had so shocked him on his return from Siberia. From the notebooks we know that Dostoevskii believed goodness could only be portrayed convincingly in a character who was unaware of his own worth and also, perhaps, comical or even ridiculous like Don Quixote or Mr Pickwick. Greatly fearing failure, he took the bold step of making his positively good man an epileptic 'idiot', somewhat akin to the *iurodivyi* or holy fool of Russian tradition.

Dostoevskii's success in realizing his dream was only partial. Though often consulted by other characters, Myshkin is very passive, and the reader learns relatively little of his ideas (Dostoevskii's own views, insofar as they are represented in the novel, are mostly vouchsafed to another character, Radomskii). One concept, however, namely that 'beauty will save the world', recurs as a leitmotif throughout. Dostoevskii appears to be offering this aesthetic concept in opposition to the utilitarian and legalistic ethics prevalent in contemporary Russian society. Beauty here may perhaps refer to the Prince's moral beauty. Moreover, if humility constitutes a large part of the Prince's beauty, then it would seem that the novel's two most memorable aphorisms, 'beauty will save the world' and 'humility is a terrible force', support each other. In purely aesthetic terms, however, the great beauty of, for example, the two rival women is in both cases flawed by insecurity, unhappiness, weakness, and malice; each (like many others of Dostoevskii's 'broad' characters) contains elements of both the 'Madonna' and 'Sodom'. Myshkin's most vivid visions of almost mystical harmony and beauty are in any case associated, indirectly, with disintegration and death, for they come in the seconds of heightened awareness immediately preceding an epileptic fit, and it is just such a fit that saves him from Rogozhin's knife on a dark stairway (having earlier exchanged crosses with him in a similar place). At the end of the novel Nastas'ia Filippovna meets her death by this same knife, and her murder is followed by a night-long vigil conducted by her murderer and her would-be saviour before the latter relapses into idiocy.

The Idiot operates on the levels of realism and allegory, reason and the irrational, virtue and vice, comedy and tragedy. The dying student Ippolit provides an intellectual discourse to match those of the underground man, Raskol'nikov, or Ivan Karamazov. Condemned by nature to an early death, he counters the Prince's ideas on happiness, beauty, and humility. He is one of the most articulate and strongly depicted condemned men in all Dostoevskii's fiction, like Rogozhin playing the role of half-brother to the condemned Myshkin. Rogozhin himself is an unforgettably dark character epitomizing fanaticism and death. The scene in which Nastas'ia Filippovna throws Rogozhin's packet of

100,000 rubles onto the fire to test her weak and mercenary supposed fiancé's courage is one of the most dramatic in all literature.

Dostoevskii's vision of a messianic saviour, a Russian Christ to revive the Russian Christian ideal, proved impossible to realize in the face of dark fanaticism, nihilism, and capitalism; his idea of creating a 'positively good man' had to be held over for a later novel. But *The Idiot*, a flawed masterpiece, is rich in psychology, moral and social ideas, high drama, and possesses some of the most memorable characters in all of Dostoevksii's *oeuvre*.

—Arnold McMillin

NOTES FROM THE UNDERGROUND (Zapiski iz podpol'ia)
Prose by Fedor Dostoevskii, 1864.

Notes from the Underground, one of Dostoevskii's most enigmatic and complex works, served as a prelude to his great novels, particularly *Crime and Punishment* and *The Devils*. It has also been claimed as an overture to existentialism, recognized by Nietzsche as the work of a kindred spirit, and acclaimed by, among others, Albert Camus for its prophetic qualities. However, the brunt of the underground man's (and through him Dostoevskii's) polemic is directed against specific phenomena in Russian social and political life: the Romantic dreamers of the 1840s and the social idealists of the 1860s, the latter epitomized by Nikolai Chernyshevskii whose novel *What Is to Be Done?* (*Chto delat'?*) had appeared in the previous year.

The book is in two parts. The first, showing the underground man as an embittered, malicious, and (as he himself declares in his opening sentence) sick paradoxalist, is the part that contains the essence of his thought and presents most clearly the underground mentality as a modern phenomenon. The second part, entitled 'Apropos of Sleet', takes us back two decades to the 1840s and shows how the underground man in his youth sought status in a self-destructive way, his head filled with garbled Romantic ideas drawn from books (Schillerism or 'all that is beautiful and lofty' in Dostoevskii's shorthand), and seemingly capable only of scandalous self-humiliation and petty debauchery. There is much satire here as well as vividly depicted social embarrassment: the 'sleet' in the title was a cliché for literary descriptions of St Petersburg by the 'natural school' writers of the 1840s, and, indeed, it figures in Dostoevskii's own early novel *The Double*; the epigraph, which interrupts the poet Nikolai Nekrasov's self-lacerating lines about poverty and prostitution with 'etc. etc.', is especially biting, for it was Nekrasov who had first introduced Dostoevskii to the literary world in 1846; the pathos of the underground man's speech to the noble prostitute Liza, which—like the reader—she easily recognizes as being derived from books rather than the heart, parodies not only Nekrasov but also Chernyshevskii; even the hero's aspiration for new clothes to give himself status seems to recall Gogol's *The Overcoat* (*Shinel'*), although in this case there is no pathos but only malicious self-assertiveness, as he simply wants a smart outfit in which to challenge an officer he imagines (or chooses to imagine) has insulted him.

Part Two is a brilliant portrait of psychological and social inadequacy, a warning against substituting literature for life, and a sour rejection of the ideals of Dostoevskii's youth. It is, however, the first part of *Notes from the Underground* that has made such an impact on modern thought. Beginning

memorably, 'I am a sick man . . . I am a nasty man. A truly unattractive man. I think there's something wrong with my liver', it comprises an extended dialogue, passionate, sarcastic, paradoxical, with an equally arrogant imaginary interlocutor against whom the underground man rails. *What Is to Be Done?*, the main catalyst for Dostoevskii's work, had created a sensation when it first appeared, being claimed as a 'textbook for life'. In it Chernyshevskii had advocated self-interest as the mainspring for all human behaviour, preaching 'rational egoism' or enlightened self-interest. The underground man's attack centres on this attempt to align egoism with reason, against which he proposes a greater self-interest, 'the most advantageous of advantages', which is the freedom to do exactly what one wants even if it means acting against one's own self-interest. The paradox is obvious, but the underground man is convinced that free will is more important than reason. Indeed, the seemingly irrational lies at the basis of all his thought. Living by reason, man is condemned to what Herzen called the ant-heap and what for Dostoevskii was epitomized by the crystal palaces dreamed of by Chernyshevskii's heroine (and reinforced by the one Dostoevskii himself saw without pleasure on his visit to London). For the underground man a crystal palace meant not only a lack of privacy but a perfection that is inhuman and therefore beyond all criticism, even that of a protruded tongue. Symbolizing the kind of rationality that codifies and orders everything, it by implication leaves man no freer than a piano key or organ stop. Perfection admits of no progression, and we are left with dead formulas like $2 \times 2 = 4$ and all the other laws of nature which the underground man boldly seeks to change (proposing the possibility of $2 \times 2 = 5$, for instance). Perfection, after all, is imperfect in that it takes no account of man's fear of perfection. Dostoevskii had intended that the underground man's challenge to nature and, by implication, God would eventually prove his (i.e. modern man's) need for God, but this part of his work (like several other religious passages in Dostoevskii's *oeuvre*) fell foul of the censor and was never restored.

It is obvious that in his extremes of arrogance and insecurity the underground man is afflicted by hyperconsciousness. He is also, as he tells us, ill (with a strong sado-masochistic streak) and can find pleasure and, indeed, significance in, for instance, his own toothache. 'I am convinced that man will never renounce real suffering, that is renounce destruction and chaos; for suffering is the sole cause of consciousness'. In *Notes from the Underground* morbid consciousness is revealed as the human tragedy. As a social phenomenon and as a literary type the underground man has achieved almost archetypal status.

—Arnold McMillin

———

DOUWES DEKKER, Edouard.   See **MULTATULI**.

———

DOVIZI da Bibbiena, Bernardo. Born Bernardo Dovizi, in Bibbiena, Casentino, Florentine Republic, 4 August 1470. Entered the service of the Medicis at an early age: Florentine ambassador to Pope Alexander VI in Rome, 1492, and to King Alfonso II of Aragon and Naples, 1494; followed Pietro de' Medici into exile following his expulsion from Florence by the French, 1494, and, after Pietro's death in 1503, served his brother, Cardinal Giovanni de' Medici, as secretary; plenipotentiary for the Pope at the Congress of Mantua, 1512; on Giovanni's election as Pope Leo X in 1513, became papal treasurer and Cardinal of Santa Maria, Portico; thereafter pursued papal diplomatic and religious interests: enabled papal alliance with Austria, Switzerland, Venice, and Milan, 1515, acted as legate to the papal armies besieging Urbino, 1516, and travelled to France, 1518–19, to raise support for a new crusade against the Turks; obtained the bishop's palace in Costanza, 1518, but gave it to his friend Pietro Bembo, *q.v.* *Died 9 November 1520.*

PUBLICATIONS

Plays

La Calandria (produced 1513). 1521; as *La Calandria*, 1786; edited by N. Borsellino, in *Commedie del Cinquecento 1*, 1967, also edited by P. Fossati, 1967, and by Giorgio Padoan, 1970; as *The Follies of Calandro*, translated by Oliver Evans, in *The Genius of the Italian Theater*, edited by Eric Bentley, 1964.

Other

Epistolario, edited by G.L. Moncallero. 2 vols., 1955–64.

*

Critical Studies: *Il cardinale Bibbiena* by A. Santelli, 1931; *Commedie fiorentine del Cinquecento: Mandragola; Clizia; Calandria* by Luigi Russo, 1939; *Il cardinale Bernardo Dovizi da Bibbiena, umanista e diplomatico (1470–1520)* by Giuseppe L. Mocallero, 1953; *The Birth of Modern Comedy in Renaissance Italy* by Douglas Radcliff-Umstead, 1969; 'Women and the Management of Dramaturgy in *La Calandria*' by Laurie Detenbeck, in *Women in Italian Culture* edited by Ada Testaferri, 1989; 'Drama and the Court in *La Calandria*' by Jack D'Amico, in *Theatre Journal*, 43(1), 1991.

* * *

In the Rome of the Medici popes, and at the court of Urbino that had produced Castiglione's *Il libro del cortegiano* (*The Book of the Courtier*), Bibbiena had been a papal courtier from an early age, and later a politician, ambassador, and ultimately cardinal. Literature was a pastime for him and (other than some letters to contemporaries) the comedy *La Calandria* (*The Follies of Calandro*) is all that survives of his works. He assisted Giovanni de' Medici to become Pope Leo X in 1513, and there was speculation that Bibbiena may have been poisoned as his powerful position suggested that he might have been involved in an intrigue to succeed to the papacy. His influence and prestige are indicated by the number of references to him in *The Book of the Courtier*; Castiglione was also responsible for the celebrated production of *The Follies of Calandro* at Urbino in 1513 (and it is

to Castiglione that the second prologue to the play has been attributed). This was the earliest production of an Italian play of which we have a full account. The comedy was published first in Siena in 1521, but was consistently staged (at least eight productions are recorded before 1550). An entertaining courtier and consummate literary craftsman, Bibbiena is characterized above all by humour and intelligence.

Bibbiena's masterpiece was first staged at the court of Urbino in the throne room of the ducal palace, with a set by Girolamo Genga. It was directed and staged-managed by Castiglione, whose letter about the staging provides a unique insight into the production. The principle of courtly patronage, in deference to the Duke of Urbino, was represented in hanging tapestries of stories from the history of Troy, reflecting the Duke's recent reconquest of the city, in an inscription in large letters which figured in the design, and in the proscenium arch, which has been compared with the twin towers and façade of the ducal palace itself, making an analogy between the playing space, the power of the Duke, and the Duke's 'ideal' city-state. The surviving documentation identifies the playing space, seats for spectators, entries and exits, and the location of musicians.

In 1514, *The Follies of Calandro* was staged in Rome, in a production organized by Bibbiena himself with a set designed by the celebrated designer Peruzzi. A sketch survives that may have been for this production, showing the Urbino ducal palace façade translated into 'Roman' terms, with twin temples based on the Pantheon replacing the two towers. This production has been seen as seminal for the entire subsequent history of the perspective set because of the link with Peruzzi (whose model 'tragic' and 'comic' set designs were to become standard points of reference), and since reference was made specifically to the Urbino staging for the Roman production.

In 1532 Mantua saw a production of the comedy. The unique documentation charts the progress of a dispute between the celebrated artist Giulio Romano, who designed the set, and the 'director', Ippolito Calandra, over the question of whether the set should contain 'flat' painted houses or representations of architecture in relief. But the most spectacular production of all was staged in Lyon in 1548, by the community of Florentines resident in the city, organized and funded by the Cardinal Ippolito d'Este, Archbishop of Lyon. Mounted in the great hall of the Archbishop's palace, the play was performed before a set depicting Florence, with recognizable monuments reproduced and the hall embellished with 12 giant statues of Florentine warriors and artists in a Parnassus celebrating the glories of Florence for resident expatriates. The performance was attended by the King of France, Henry II, and the *intermezzi* between the acts (of which full descriptive documentation survives) set a pattern in the courtier/patronage relationship, between the play and its illustrious patron, which was to be influential, and looks forward to the celebrated production of Bargagli's *Pellegrina* in Florence in 1589. Allegorical figures representing the ages of Iron, Bronze, Silver, and Gold dispute for the favours of the King, and are unrelated to the text of the comedy itself.

Uniquely therefore, the history of the staging of Bibbiena's *The Follies of Calandro* documents the importance of this comedy among the earliest in the 'vulgar' tongue, sets the tone for dramatic representation of the stories from Boccaccio's *The Decameron* (its source), and establishes the relationship between comedy in performance, the city-state as playing space (in the reproduction of reality in the perspective set), the patronage network, and the intermingling of political and practical life with creativity in all the arts (painting, architecture, sculpture, writing, comedy, acting, and so on). And the multi-faceted façade of this concept of theatre echoes the careers of two of the most successful courtiers in the Renaissance: Bibbiena, the play's author, and Castiglione, its first director.

—Christopher Cairns

A DREAM OF RED MANSIONS. See **THE DREAM OF THE RED CHAMBER**.

THE DREAM OF THE RED CHAMBER (Honglou meng). Chinese novel, written largely by Cao Xueqin (c.1715–63), about whom little is known. He probably completed the first 80 chapters of the novel; the later 40 chapters are generally considered to have been 'edited' or revised by others.

PUBLICATIONS

Honglou meng. Edited by Gao E (120 chapters), 1792; modern editions: (80 chapters) 1912; (80 chapters, after 1770 manuscript) 1955; (120 chapters, after 1792 edition) 1957; (after 1912 edition, with last 40 chapters of 1792 edition) 1958; (80 chapters) 2 vols., 1961; (80 chapters after 1760 manuscript, last 40 chapters after 1792 edition) 3 vols., 1982; as *Hung lou meng; or, The Dream of the Red Chamber*, translated by H.B. Joly, 2 vols., 1892–93 (abridged); as *The Dream of the Red Chamber*, translated by Wang Chi-Chen, 1929; also translated by Florence and Isabel McHugh (from the German), 1958; as *The Story of the Stone*, translated by David Hawkes and John Minford, 5 vols., 1973–86; as *A Dream of Red Mansions*, translated by Yang Hsien-yi and Gladys Yang, 3 vols., 1978–86.

*

Bibliography: *Studies on Dream of the Red Chamber: A Selected and Classified Bibliography* by Tsung Shun Na, 1979, supplement, 1981.

Critical Studies: *On 'The Red Chamber Dream'* (includes bibliography) by Wu Shih-ch'ang, 1961; *The Classic Chinese Novel* by C.T. Hsia, 1968; *The Dream of the Red Chamber: A Critical Study* by Jeanne Knoerle, 1972; *New Interpretations of the Dream of the Red Chamber* by Klaus-Peter Koepping and Lam Mai Sing, 1973; *Masks of Fiction in the Dream of the Red Chamber: Myth, Mimesis and Persona* by Lucien Miller, 1975; *Archetype and Allegory in the Dream of the Red Chamber* by Andrew Henry Plaks, 1976; *Ts'ao Hsueh-Ch'in's 'Dream of the Red Chamber'* by Zhang Xiugui, 1991.

* * *

The Dream of the Red Chamber (Honglou meng) is perhaps the most beloved and widely read traditional Chinese novel. It appears to have been written some time before 1763 by a man named Cao Xueqin, the impoverished grandson of Cao Yin, a notable political and literary figure of the early Qing dynasty and the Kangxi Emperor's trusted servant. For several decades the book circulated in an 80-chapter manuscript version under the title *The Story of the Stone*. The first printed edition, in 120 chapters, appeared in 1792, with prefaces by Gao E and Cheng Weiyuan, who claimed to have pieced together various old manuscript fragments in order to complete the earlier version. The exact proportion of mere editing to actual creation *de novo* in their edition is still the subject of debate, as is the literary merit of the last 40 chapters. However, this version soon supplanted the earlier one, and it was not until the early 20th century that the old manuscripts came to light. Their accompanying commentary, mostly by a friend of the author known to us as Zhiyan zhai ('Red Inkstone'), has allowed us not only to trace the evolution of the text itself, but to glimpse some of the historical persons and events behind the novel. The book clearly incorporates certain features of the Cao family history as Cao Xueqin experienced it.

On this level, *The Dream of the Red Chamber* is the story of the fictional Jia family's fall from wealth and position. As the novel opens, their splendour is already said to be waning. Yet they are still dazzlingly wealthy and powerful: the junior and senior branches of the family, four generations of them and scores of servants and dependents, live in vast and elegant adjoining mansions in the imperial capital. Their fortunes, moreover, appear in some ways to be on the rise. When their daughter is made an imperial concubine, the family spares no expense to build a magnificent garden in which to entertain her—though only for a few brief hours—as befits her rank. Throughout the account of the garden's construction, which leads up to the elaborate reception itself, there is a note of sadness for the fragility of worldly splendour—a note which recurs more and more insistently through the slow-moving idyll of garden life which takes up the novel's inner 80 chapters, until the imperial concubine's untimely death heralds the family's final precipitous fall from imperial favour, and the confiscation of their estate.

The Dream of the Red Chamber is also the story of the boy Baoyu's initiation into the mysteries of love and loss. Baoyu—whose name, 'Precious Jade', refers to the magic jade he bore in his mouth at birth, the 'stone' of the novel's fantastic frame-tale—is tenderly solicitous of the girl cousins and maids who live with him in the family garden. Most of all Baoyu loves his cousin Daiyu, who is equally devoted to him, though they quarrel constantly. Daiyu's fragile health, her acerbic tongue, and her morose and solitary turn of mind lead the elder Jias to marry Baoyu, instead, to an equally beautiful and talented cousin who is in every other way Daiyu's opposite: Xue Baochai. Having been deceived into thinking that she is Daiyu, Baoyu marries the veiled Baochai at the very moment of Daiyu's death. Already in ill health from the loss of his magic jade, and deeply grieved by Daiyu's death and the trick that has been played on him, Baoyu eventually has a dream which parallels his dream-initiation into love near the novel's beginning. At last he begins to understand the connection between that first cryptic dream and the sorrowful events of his own recent life. In the end, his accumulated grief and disillusionment lead him to leave his family for the life of a Buddhist mendicant.

At one stroke, therefore, the Jias lose both their fortune and their heir-apparent. Their fall, though, is not a sudden blow of fate, but the delayed consequence of their own corrupt machinations. Very early in the novel their high position at court saves their relative Xue Pan from prosecution for murder. Later, their ambitious and scheming daughter-in-law, Wang Hsi-feng, embarks on a spiralling scheme of illegal loansharking; her abuse of the family's influence causes the deaths of several people and plays an important part in the Jias' disgrace and financial ruin. Some of the Jia family men are wastrels with a penchant for bribery and extortion; others are sexual profligates whose tastes run to incest. Though these dark details impinge only very gradually on the garden enclave where Baoyu and his cousins practise poetry, calligraphy, and other elegant and scholarly arts, multiplying signs of decay eventually suggest that even the garden-dwellers are not immune to the corrupt passions of the world outside.

Most critics agree that *The Dream of the Red Chamber* is unsurpassed in the tradition of the Chinese novel for its magisterial portrayal of literati culture and for its subtle depiction of interior states. Beyond these rather obvious points, however, there is little unanimity. Throughout its history the novel has been the object of a wide variety of interpretive schemes, some of them quite fanciful. It both invites and frustrates interpretation: the text is replete with erudite puns, riddles, and complex patterns of word and image which hinge on the ambiguous relation between the 'real' and the 'illusory'. Its multitude of sub-plots and the sheer vastness of its scale also ensure that any neatly consistent reading will fail to do it justice. Any reading, though, must take into account the centrality of the garden, which in the long course of the novel lapses from its original perfection to become a haunted, weed-infested wilderness. It is in this central image that Baoyu's story and the larger story of his family's fall are fused. Like Baoyu's perfect and unattainable love and his family's visions of splendour, the garden is an expression of the unquenchable human longing for riches, honour, beauty, and pleasure, and of the loss and dissolution which are the inevitable consequence of that longing.

—Mary Scott

DROSTE-HÜLSHOFF, Annette von. Born Anna Elisabeth Franziska Adolfine Wilhelmina Luisa Maria in Schloss Hülshoff near Münster, Westphalia, Germany, 10 January 1797. Educated by private tutors. Moved with her mother and sister to Rüschhaus following the death of her father in 1826; collaborated with the writer Levin Schücking from 1840 who encouraged her poetic activity; lived in Meersburg from 1846. Suffered from ill health throughout her life. *Died 24 May 1848.*

PUBLICATIONS

Collections

Gesammelte Schriften, edited by Levin Schücking. 3 vols., 1878–79.
Sämtliche Werke, edited by Karl Schulte Kemminghausen. 4 vols., 1925–30.
Poems, edited by Margaret Atkinson. 1968.

Historisch-kritische Ausgabe: Werke, Briefwechsel, edited by Winfried Woesler. 14 vols., 1978–85.
Werke, edited by Clemens Heselhaus. 1984.

Verse

Walther. 1818.
Gedichte. 1838.
Das malerische und romantische Westfalen. 1839.
Gedichte. 1844.
Das geistliche Jahr. Nebst einem Anhang Religiöser Gedichte, edited by C.B. Schülter and Wilhelm Junkmann. 1851.
Letzte Gaben, edited by Levin Schücking. 1860.
Lebensgang, edited by Marie Silling. 1917.
Balladen. 1922.

Fiction

Die Judenbuche. 1851; as *The Jew's Beech*, translated by Lionel and Doris Thomas, 1958; as *The Jew's Beech Tree*, translated by Michael Bullock, in *Three Eerie Tales from 19th Century German*, 1975.
Ledwina (fragment). 1923.

Play

Perdu; oder, Dichter, Verleger und Blaustrümpfe. 1840.

Other

Bilder aus Westfalen. 1845.
Briefe, edited by C. Schlueter. 1877.
Die Briefe von Annette von Droste-Hülshoff und Levin Schücking, edited by Theo Schücking. 1893.
Die Briefe der Dichterin Annette von Droste-Hülshoff, edited by Hermann Cardauns. 1909.
Dreiundzwanzig neue Droste-Briefe, edited by Manfred Schneider. 1923.
Briefe, edited by Karl Schulte Kemminghausen. 2 vols., 1944.
Lieder und Gesänge, edited by Karl Gustav Fellerer. 1954.

*

Bibliography: *Droste-Hülshoff Bibliographie* by Eduard Arens and Karl Schulte Kemminghausen, 1932.

Critical Studies: *Annette von Droste-Hülshoff* by Margaret Mare, 1965; *Annette von Droste-Hülshoff in Selbstzeugnissen und Bilddokumenten* by Peter Berglar, 1967; *Annette von Droste-Hülshoff. Werk und Leben* by Clemens Heselhaus, 1971; *Sinnbildsprache. Zur Bildstruktur des Geistlichen Jahres der Annette von Droste-Hülshoff* by Stephan Berning, 1975; *Annette von Droste-Hülshoff* by Ronald Schneider, 1977; *Annette von Droste-Hülshoff: A Woman of Letters in a Period of Transition*, 1981, and *Annette von Droste-Hülshoff: A Biography*, 1984, both by Mary Morgan; *Annette von Droste-Hülshoff: Die Judenbuche* by Klaus Moritz, 1981; *Annette von Droste-Hülshoff: A German Poet Between Romanticism and Realism* by John Guthrie, 1989; *Annette von Droste-Hülshoff: Die Judenbuche* by Heinz Rölleke, 1989.

* * *

Annette von Droste-Hülshoff belonged to the group *Junges Deutschland* and is considered a writer of classical stature, certainly as one of Germany's greatest women poets.

Her interest in poetry was early stimulated by a one-time friend of August Bürger, a certain A. Spickmann. In 1814 she began a two-act romantic verse tragedy entitled *Berta*, a drama fragment of 2,000 lines which foreshadows her later mastery of writing. *Berta* deals with intrigue and with criticism of the ambitious nobility, and it contains a conspiracy against the prince, an evil Italian servant, diplomatic wedding negotiations, and a pair of true lovers separated by the exigencies of rank as well as by intrigue. Its author was wise to realize early on that the work was not a success and that drama was not her strength.

Another early work, the epic poem *Walther*, was completed in 1818, and is considered a most ambitious finished product. The poem mingles medieval cruelty and knightly idealism with modern sensibility. It contains lines of exceptional promise, as well as some narrative skill and the ability to sustain and round off her theme. The problem of man's deliberate waywardness and estrangement from God through a cherished 'idol' is raised but not thoroughly worked out. In this poem, Droste-Hülshoff imitates Walther von der Vogelweide's *Kreuzlied* in an attempt to draw on genuine medieval sources as well as on nature. *Walther*, however, remained unsuccessful.

In 1824 Droste-Hülshoff began a novel *Ledwina*, which remained unfinished although some 50 pages were published posthumously. It is a fragment of her early prose work, having been begun about the year 1819. It was to remain a fragment, although she worked on it over the next five years of her life. There are elements in the prose passages which seem to belong expressly to a highly 'romantic' phase of Droste-Hülshoff's life. Some critics believe that these 'romantic' elements in her early work reveal, as well as Droste-Hülshoff's acquaintance with the literature of the time or at least with its mood, her own lifelong tendency to dwell on decay and death and the transience of all things. One reason for her decision not to finish *Ledwina* is to be found in her half-humorous remarks in a letter to her friend Spickmann on 8 February 1819 (*Die Briefe von Annette von Droste-Hülshoff*, vol. 1) that consumptive heroines were becoming rather too common, featuring in all the second-rate, sentimental literature.

Towards the end of 1820 Droste-Hülshoff began to write a cycle of devotional poems for her grandmother, reflecting the ecclesiastical calendar: *Das geistliche Jahr* [The Spiritual Year], published posthumously in 1851. It is a cycle of 72 poems which are of a confessional character and reflect not only piety but also a conscientious struggle with doubt. There is a song devoted to each Sunday of the year, and one for every church holiday. Although Droste-Hülshoff was a devout Catholic, there are few specific references to the Catholic church in her poems. *Das geistliche Jahr* gives the impression that Droste-Hülshoff was seeking a God who could not be found and that she had to go on seeking until death (in fact, she continued to revise the manuscript until a few months before her death).

In *Das geistliche Jahr* Droste-Hülshoff drew from such varied sources as books of scientific knowledge, like those her father had been interested in collecting for his library, containing facts about phenomena such as the 'Phosphorpflanze', and from accounts of oriental travel, as well as the Bible, mystical literature and baroque verse, books of popular hymns, and classical and romantic verses. Her other poems, too, were indebted to such books. However, direct experience also plays a major role in shaping the poems.

Three epic poems, 'Das Hospiz auf dem grossen St Bernhard' [The Hospice on the St Bernhard], 'Des Arztes Vermächtnis' [The Doctor's Legacy], and 'Die Schlacht am Loener Bruch' [The Battle at Loener Bog], were all published in her first collection of poems. 'Das Hospiz' is apparently modelled on Sir Walter Scott's *Lady of the Lake* since Droste-Hülshoff was an enthusiastic devoteé of Scott's work. These verses rarely express lyric sweetness or romantic sentiment; indeed, they are often repellent in their acerbic realism. But her love for the red soil of her native Westphalia, its forests, and its moors, is perhaps deeper than that of any other German poet for the homeland; and for nature's most hidden secrets she has an almost preternatural clearness of vision. Her technical mastery and self-abnegating restraint are classical in the pre-Romantic sense of the word, but her language is full of colour. In the above-mentioned epic poems, Droste-Hülshoff shows herself to be a woman of great earnestness, realistic observation, and deep psychological insight.

Her friend and literary adviser, the critic Levin Schücking, inspired her to work on her most famous works: the novella, *Die Judenbuche* (*The Jew's Beech Tree*), and the poems 'Der Knabe im Moor' [The Young Boy in the Bog] and 'Mondesaufgang' [The Rising Moon]. These three works are realistic and detailed descriptions contributing to an atmosphere of horror and gloom previously absent in her works.

The Jew's Beech Tree is a tragic tale of ignorance, crime, and social prejudice in which the sins of the fathers are visited upon the sons. The story was inspired by an actual murder in Westphalia. An old town drunk, Mergel, neglected and debauched, is found dead one day near an old beech tree. His son, Friedrich, disreputable and unsocial, murders a Jewish merchant to whom he owes money and places him beside the same beech tree where his own father died of drunkenness, then flees. All the Jews in the area come with a mysterious inscription in Hebrew and place it on the tree. After many years Friedrich returns; no one recognizes him, but the remembrance of his own act of murder leaves him no peace and he is found hanged on the beech tree. In this work, Droste-Hülshoff introduces new and modern elements: social injustice, environmental influence, the role of the conscience, and the psychology of crime.

After the publication of *The Jew's Beech Tree*, on which her reputation as a writer for a long time depended, Droste-Hülshoff began on the 'Spiritus Familiaris des Rosstäuschers' [The Familiar Spirit of the Horse-Dealer]. In this work, her last ballad, Droste-Hülshoff shows a deep and genuine faith; in the old folklorist tradition, it tells of a man who accepts help from the devil and imperils his soul. It is a cross between a ballad and an epic poem and is considered one of her maturest works.

Bilder aus Westfalen [Pictures of Westphalia] appeared at first anonymously. These sketches of Westphalia describe the differing mental and physical types found in the districts of Sauerland, Paderborn, and Munsterland. They are shrewd and bold, so much so that they could not appear under her own name, but they were written with the same empathy as *The Jew's Beech Tree*, which was written as a result of Droste-Hülshoff's studies for *Bilder aus Westfalen*. These later writings show the remarkable nuances of wit and irony which balance, but never obscure, the humanity of her mature style. Until comparatively recently the aspect of Droste-Hülshoff's work most stressed by the literary historian was the amazing exactness and the visual and auditory quality of her descriptions. Other elements in her poems which contribute even more to her greatness were thus overlooked. What lends fascination to her thoughts are the symbols and images in which they are often clothed.

—Brigitte Edith Zapp Archibald

THE JEW'S BEECH TREE (Die Judenbuche)
Novella by Annette von Droste-Hülshoff, 1851 (published in serial form, 1842).

The Jew's Beech Tree, one of the most famous novellas in the German language, was first published in serial form in the *Morgenblatt für gebildete Leser* in 1842, and appeared in book form in 1851.

Friedrich Mergel, the central character, is born in a village, Dorf B, to poor parents. His father, a drunkard, dies in mysterious circumstances when Friedrich is nine. When the boy is 12 years old, he comes under the influence of his uncle, Simon Semmeler, who is involved in petty crime and may be linked to the *Blaukittel*, the wood thieves who work at night stealing wood from the forest. Friedrich's *Doppelgänger*, his cousin Johannes Niemand, a pale imitation of Friedrich himself, is introduced at this stage. When Friedrich is 18 he is instrumental in sending the forester, Brandis, to his death at the hands of the wood thieves. A public enquiry into the incident fails to solve the crime, but Friedrich's guilt is shown when Simon persuades him not to go to confession.

At the age of 22 Friedrich is depicted at a village wedding where he is publicly humiliated when his protégé, Niemand, is caught stealing butter. Later the same night Friedrich is humiliated again when a Jew, Aaron, publicly accuses him of not paying for a watch he has bought. Three days later Aaron is found murdered and Friedrich, the obvious suspect, disappears. The local Jewish community purchases the beech tree where Aaron was murdered and carves a Hebrew inscription on it. Friedrich's name is later cleared of the murder when someone else makes a confession.

28 years pass. A wanderer returns to the village on Christmas Eve and is taken in for the night. He is declared to be Johannes Niemand, who left with Friedrich, and he does not deny his identity. He recalls his years of slavery in far distant Turkey, and is now apparently content to settle down to a new life back in the village. However, he disappears one day as suddenly as he had returned, and all attempts to find him are in vain. The son of Brandis, the forester who many years earlier lost his life because of Friedrich's involvement with the wood thieves, is wandering in the wood when he discovers the badly decomposed body of 'Niemand' hanging from the beech tree. A scar on the body reveals that the man was in fact Friedrich Mergel and he is subsequently buried in the knacker's yard. Only now is the Hebrew inscription translated: 'If you approach this place then what you did to me will be done unto you'.

The strength of the story lies in its dense structure and complex interweaving of various, sometimes conflicting, themes and motifs. While it is unified by its episodic structure, which focuses on key events in Mergel's life, the story's emphasis shifts from an attempt to understand the process of criminalization to the uncovering of Mergel's crimes. The early part of the story concentrates on the social milieu in which he grows up and seeks to explain why he develops as he does; for example in a striking piece of dialogue his anti-semitism is shown to be learned directly from his mother. It is a society with a strong group identity to which Mergel is anxious to conform, a society which expels those who do not fit. Droste-Hülshoff herself referred to the work as a 'story of a criminal, Friedrich Mergel', and her source was an article by her uncle, Freiherr A. von Haxthausen, about the murder of a Jew by a farmhand, called *The Story of an Algerian Slave*. In the latter half of the story, however, the emphasis shifts to the attempt to solve Mergel's crimes and places the reader in the position of investigator by supplying clues. But it is more than a detective story, for there are many unanswered questions in terms of the plot (what does happen to Johannes Niemand? What are we to make of the—presumably false—confession?), and the use of detective work alone will not tell the reader how to interpret the other, larger questions the story raises about reason and superstition, Old Testament justice and New Testament salvation, social conditioning and free will.

The narrative perspective, crucially, does not seek to guide, for it shifts frequently, sometimes appearing omniscient but at other times being close to the action and withholding vital information. The text does, however, accord the reader a unique insight into both the social and psychological processes at work and the insufficiency of human agencies: none of the crimes reported in the story are ever 'solved'. Much of the depth of meaning of the story is achieved through the use of symbolism, for example the beech tree itself and the use of Johannes Niemand as Friedrich's alter ego.

The painstaking attempt to depict realistically the life of a local community (the subtitle is *A Portrayal of the Life and Customs in Mountainous Westphalia*), while also looking below the surface for deeper meanings, and the conscious artistry of the composition make this an outstanding example of 19th-century German poetic realism.

—Brigid Haines

DU BELLAY, Joachim. Born at the Château de la Turmelière, Liré, France, probably in 1522. Studied law at the University of Poitiers, c.1545. Took minor clerical orders; writer by 1547: at Collège de Coqueret, Paris, with Ronsard and other writers; lived in Rome in the service of his relation, cardinal Jean Du Bellay, 1553–57. *Died 1 January 1560.*

PUBLICATIONS

Collections

Oeuvres françaises, edited by Guillaume Aubert and Jean Morel. 1568.
Oeuvres poétiques, edited by Henri Chamard. 6 vols., 1907–31; revised by Yvonne Bellenger, 1982–85.

Verse

L'Olive. 1549; enlarged edition, 1550.
Antérotique. 1549.
Vers lyriques. 1549.
Recueil de poésie. 1549; enlarged edition, 1553.
Oeuvres. 1552.
Hymnes. 2 vols., 1555–56.
Premier livre des antiquités de Rome. 1558; as *Ruins of Rome*, translated by Edmund Spenser, in *Complaints*, 1591.
Les Regrets et autres oeuvres poétiques. 1558; as *The Regrets*, translated by C.H. Sisson, 1984.
Divers jeux rustiques. 1558.
Poemata (in Latin). 1558.
Discours sur le sacre du treschrétien roi François I. 1558.
Ample discours au roi. 1567.
Xenia. 1569.

The Visions of Bellay [*Songe*], translated Edmund Spenser, in *Theatre for Worldlings*, edited by Jan Van Der Noot, 1569, reprinted 1939; revised in *Complaints*, 1591.
Poems, edited by Harold Walter Lawton, 1961.
Du Bellay (selected poems), edited by Marie-Hélène Richard. 1973.
La Monomachie de David et de Goliath (and other poems), edited by E. Caldarini. 1981.
L'Olive: An Anthology, edited by Thomas Thomson. 1986.

Other

La Défence et illustration de la langue française. 1549; as *The Defence and Glorification of the French Language*, translated by Elizabeth Smulders, 1935; as *The Defence and Illustration of the French Language*, translated by Gladys M. Turquet, 1939.
Lettres, edited by Pierre de Nolhac. 1883.

*

Bibliography: *Du Bellay: A Bibliography* by Margaret B. Wells, 1974.

Critical Studies: *The Platonism of Du Bellay* by R.V. Merrill, 1925; *Histoire de la Pléiade* by Henri Chamard, 4 vols., 1939–40; *Du Bellay in Rome* by Gladys Dickinson, 1960; *Les Sources italiennes de la 'Deffense et illustration de la langue françoise' de Joachim du Bellay* by Pierre Villey, 1970; *Du Bellay* by Louis C. Keating, 1971; *Spenser, Ronsard, and Du Bellay: A Renaissance Comparison* by Alfred W. Satterthwaite, 1972; *The Chaste Muse: A Study of Du Bellay's Poetry* by Dorothy Gabe Coleman, 1980; *Trials of Desire: Renaissance Defenses of Poetry* by Margaret W. Ferguson, 1983; *Du Bellay: Poems* by Kathleen M. Hall and Margaret Wells, 1985; *The Ordered Text: The Sonnet Sequences of Du Bellay* by Richard A. Katz, 1985; *Three French Short-Verse Satirists: Marot, Magny and Du Bellay* by William F. Panici, 1990; *The Poet's Odyssey: Joachim Du Bellay and the 'Antiquitez de Rome'* by George Hugo Tucker, 1990.

* * *

It was perhaps inevitable that Joachim Du Bellay should be overshadowed both in and after his lifetime by his friend and contemporary, Ronsard. Yet the fact remains that he is the author of some of the finest and best-known sonnets in the French language. These are for the most part to be found among the 191 sonnets of the *Les Regrets et autres oeuvres poétiques* (*The Regrets*) which, a mixture of elegy and satire, owe their inspiration to his progressive disenchantment with his life as a minor diplomat in Rome. Other, less famous, sonnets in the same collection are delightfully sharp sketches of Roman life in the 1550s and in particular of the intrigues of the Papal court.

However, it was not just this personal frustration which triggered off Du Bellay's disillusionment. He seems to have been by temperament a melancholy man and as early as 1549 had written a 'Chant du désespéré'. Compared to Ronsard he was something of a lightweight intellectually, but he can appear more sensitive, and certainly more vulnerable. He seems indeed to have been a sick man (or at the very least a chronic hypochondriac) much of his life, which fact makes it all the more surprising that he should adopt the aggressive posture of a young man in a hurry in his first major publi-

cation, *La Défence et illustration de la langue française* (*The Defense and Illustration of the French Language*) published in 1549. This short work quickly established itself as the manifesto of the 'Brigade' which had gathered around Ronsard, but later developments cast doubt on the extent to which Du Bellay himself subscribed to the views he expounded. In fact, parts of this 'defence' of the French language were cribbed from an Italian treatise by Sperone Speroni (1542). Du Bellay seems concerned above all with demolishing the achievements of his predecessors among the French poets, whom he compares unfavourably with the Greek and Roman masters and with the Italians such as Petrarch. He soon outgrew his theories: his *L'Olive* is a Petrarchist *canzoniere* but within a few years Du Bellay claimed that he had forgotten the art of 'petrarchizing', and one of the main strands of his work—the admonition against writing in Latin—is similarly forgotten in the mid-1550s when he set about composing his *Poemata*. In *The Regrets* he even renounces the *imitatio* which was supposed to raise the level of French poetry by a close imitation of Greek and Roman models. Du Bellay claims in this collection that he will write only what his 'passion' dictates, thereby suggesting that he will restrict himself to his own personal misfortunes, without reference to illustrious examples or personal glory. Such disclaimers are perhaps more apparent than real. Certainly, in the 32 sonnets in the *Premier livre des antiquités de Rome* (*Ruins of Rome*) he sought to universalize his sense of bewilderment at the change of fortune of this once great city, victim of its own hubris.

But it is above all to *The Regrets* that the non-specialist poetry lover will wish to return again and again. In this sequence of sonnets Du Bellay emerges as one of the great poets of nostalgia, for a far-away country and for the illusions of youth; a poet, too, of solitude, who peoples his poems, mysteriously, with absences, and who turns his back both on the ambitions of his youth and on the meagre consolation of immortality through verse.

—Michael Freeman

HEUREUX QUI, COMME ULYSSE, A FAIT UN BEAU VOYAGE (Sonnet 31)
Poem by Joachim Du Bellay, 1558.

Heureux qui, comme Ulysse, a fait un beau voyage,
Ou comme celui-là qui conquit la toison,
Est puis est retourné, plein d'usage et raison,
Vivre entre ses parents le reste de son âge!

Quand reverrai-je, hélas, de mon petit village
Fumer la cheminée, et en quelle saison
Reverrai-je le clos de ma pauvre maison,
Qui m'est une province, et beaucoup davantage?

Plus me plaît le séjour qu'ont bâti mes aïeux
Que des palais romains le front audacieux,
Plus que le marbre dur me plaît l'ardoise fine,

Plus mon Loire gaulois que le Tibre latin,
Plus mon petit Liré que le mont Palatin,
Et plus que l'air marin la douceur angevine.

In the Spring of 1553 Du Bellay left Paris for Rome, where he was to spend the next four years. At the age of 30 he had begun to make his mark as a poet in Parisian literary circles and had caused a stir with the publication of his controversial *The Defense and Illustration of the French Language*. But he had not yet managed to find a patron or a steady income, and when the chance came up to accompany his influential relative, Cardinal Jean Du Bellay, on a diplomatic mission to Rome he naturally took it—especially as Rome was the Mecca of the Renaissance, the city at the heart of the humanist dream of intellectual elegance and renewal.

As so often, reality did not live up to expectation. Du Bellay was probably not well suited to court or diplomatic life and he found his duties tiresome and humiliating. Nor did Italy—and more particularly the Italians—prove as attractive as he had imagined. He gave vent to his feelings of disappointment in the collection he wrote mostly during his stay in Rome, appropriately named *The Regrets*.

These 191 sonnets are a fine example of how a poet can turn his private feelings to account in a way that on the face of it appears public and (almost) impersonal, at least in the satirical sonnets. There are, in *The Regrets*, two distinct strains, although these have, as we have seen, a common source in the poet's bruised sensitivity and despair. Du Bellay is by turns sardonic and elegiac. In his satirical sonnets he criticizes Italians for their venality and lack of scruple, while in his elegiac sequence of sonnets he gives voice to his nostalgia for France, which he increasingly 'regrets'.

Satirical poetry inevitably fades with the object of the poet's scorn, and many of Du Bellay's sonnets about Roman life have lost their impact. The poet, himself, however, undoubtedly set great store by them and expected them to help establish his reputation as a latter-day Horace. For a modern reader it is rather the poems in which he expresses his longing for France and his disillusionment and bitterness at his situation that have the more immediate appeal. Among these melancholy poems of exile, the most famous is without doubt Sonnet 31, in which the homesick young Frenchman compares his lot to other sad travellers and looks forward to a happy homecoming.

Anyone who has ever felt lost and lonely in a foreign and unfriendly environment will be able to respond to Du Bellay's immortal sonnet, which articulates the emotional and irrational sense of loss and abandonment that provokes homesickness. By referring, from the opening line of his sonnet, to Ulysses, the archetypal wanderer, Du Bellay transcends everyday emotions and lifts his distress to a higher plane. It may well be that what caused him so much anguish was his inability to adapt, to take Rome and its inhabitants at their own evaluation; he cleverly suppresses any mention of the causes of his bitterness and looks forward instead to his eventual return, to the day when like Ulysses and Jason (alluded to in the second line) he will return home to live the remainder of his days among his friends and family, 'plein d'usage et raison' (full of experience and reason). He comforts himself, therefore, with thoughts of home and peaceful security. Happy Ulysses to have returned home, unhappy Du Bellay who does not know when he will next see his beloved France! The second quatrain crucially shifts the emphasis from doleful complaint to wistful questioning. Lines 5 to 9 are in fact a question (which must by its very nature remain unanswered), punctuated with a poignant 'alas!', as to when the poet will be able to return home. They also focus the reader's attention on the modesty of his aspirations. Not for him a return to a high position or to luxury. All he pines for is his 'petit village' ('little village') and his 'pauvre maison' ('poor house'; in fact not as poor as all that, for he was of noble blood) with its little garden. This is a carefully constructed antithesis: the greatness of Rome would be willingly sacrificed for the chance to go home to these humble surroundings which to him are 'a province' (note the careful choice of word) and 'much more'. The two tercets (lines 10–14) develop this opposition between Rome and the simple

pleasures of Du Bellay's native province of Anjou. The point is beautifully made in line 11, where the soft slates of the houses are contrasted with the 'hard marble' of Rome's buildings, already characterized as being both 'palaces' (and therefore opulent) and 'audacious'. The last three lines of this sonnet accentuate the difference between proud Rome with its Tiber and its Palatine Hill and the humble but sweet province of Anjou; the reference to 'la douceur angevine' with which the poem ends has become proverbial.

Du Bellay's poem was born of his despair, and for contemporary readers it no doubt had resonances lost on us today. Elsewhere in this collection Du Bellay plays what might be called the nationalist card, scoring points off the Italians and praising all things French, especially if they were homely and unpretentious. But this sonnet owes its fame to the undoubted chord it strikes in readers of all countries and all centuries, capturing more than any other the voice of the involuntary exile who longs for his own home, looking to a future in what is very often an idealized past.

—Michael Freeman

DU FU [Tu Fu]. Pen name, Du Gonglou [Su of the East Slope]. Born in Xiangyang, Gong county, Henan province, China, in 712. Brought up by an aunt after his mother's death. Received traditional Confucian education. Married, with children. Celebrated locally as a poet by age 15; traveller by 731; failed imperial examinations, 735, but finally obtained minor official posts, 751 and 757; thereafter often in poverty and unable to support his family; received patronage from an old friend in Chengdu, 760–65; travelled again in last years, contracting fatal illness while sailing up the Xiang River. His work received little attention until 1039, when an edition of 1,405 poems and 29 prose pieces was compiled. *Died in 770.*

PUBLICATIONS

Works

Qian qianyi [Works]. 1667 (includes 1,457 poems and 32 prose pieces); as *Dushi xiangzhu*, 1713 ('standard' text); as *Jiuja jizhu Dushi* (after 1181 compilation), 1796–1812; modern editions as: *Sibu beiyao*, 6 vols., 1936; *A Concordance to the Poetry of Tu Fu* (text and concordance), 3 vols., 1940, reprinted 1967; *Du shi quianzhu*, 1974; *Du shi xiangzhu*, 5 vols., 1979; selections: in *Gems of Chinese Literature*, translated by H.A. Giles, 1923; *The Autobiography of a Chinese Poet*, 1929, and *The Travels of a Chinese Poet*, 1936, both translated by Florence Ayscough; in *The White Pony*, translated by R. Payne, 1947; in *One Hundred Poems from the Chinese* (includes 35 poems by Du Fu), translated by Kenneth Rexroth, 1956; *Selected Poems*, edited by Feng Chih, translated by Rewi Alley, 1962; *A Little Primer of Tu Fu* (bilingual edition), edited and translated by David Hawkes, 1967; *Li Po and Tu Fu: Selected Poetry*, edited and translated by Arthur Cooper, 1973; *Selected Poems*, translated by David Hinton,

1989; *Three Chinese Poets: Translations of Poems by Wang Wei, Li Bai, and Du Fu*, translated by Vikram Seth, 1992.

*

Critical Studies: *Tu Fu: China's Greatest Poet* (includes translations) by Wei Lien Hung, 1952; 'Tu Fu, Lover of His People' by C. Feng, in *Chinese Literature*, 1955; *A Little Primer of Tu Fu* by D. Hawkes, 1967; *Tu Fu* by A.R. Davis, 1971; *The Great Age of Chinese Poetry: The High Tang* by Stephen Owen, 1980.

* * *

Honoured as a the 'Sage of Poetry', Du Fu is considered one of the greatest poets not only of the Tang dynasty but also in the history of Chinese literature, and his verse has been widely translated.

He travelled across the country for more than ten years when he was young. But judging from his extant poems, he did not write much during this happy period. He is best remembered for his later works. He thought of himself as a poet who had read 'tens of thousands of books' and 'could write poems like magic'. So when he went to the city of Luoyang to sit for an imperial examination, he had full confidence in his success. However, he unexpectedly failed the exam, and thereafter began to travel extensively again.

Du Fu lived in an age when the feudal rulers became decadent and corrupt, during the demise of the Tang dynasty after it had enjoyed prosperity for more than a hundred years. Through various means he tried to get an official position, but without success. He was given only low-status positions, and for only brief periods. He returned to his itinerant life in later years, and lived in poverty till his death. The harshness of his life is reflected in one poem about his homecoming after an absence of ten years: 'I heard loud wailing, entering the house; And found my youngest son had died of hunger'. The misery of his life and his bitter experiences gave him a chance to see with his own eyes the chaos, poverty, and tragedy of the war-weary nation. His poems, which are filled with social themes mirroring this period of Chinese history, are thus often called 'poetic history'.

Du Fu was, on the whole, a realist poet. His poems explicitly express his concern for the common people and lament their sufferings, while implicitly satirizing the extravagant and licentious life of the Emperor and his concubines. His poem 'A Ballad of Beautiful Women' exposes the decadence in the palace and the cruelty of the imperial prime minister. In his often-quoted lines 'Meat and wine behind the doors of the powerful rich are becoming stinking, while in the streets corpses of the miserable people frozen to death are lying' he makes a striking contrast between the extravagant rich and the suffering poor.

Corruption and war were the root cause of the misery he described. The cruel and corrupt officials robbed the people, leaving them destitute—a situation compounded by the successive wars. In one poem he describes the desperate state of a typical village: 'No one has been able to attend to farming. And since we're still in the midst of battles, All our children have gone to the eastern front'. Many of his poems reflect the grief of lovers separated by war, and, above all, the desolate scene all over the war-torn country. Poems like 'The Song of Chariots', 'Farewell of the Newlyweds', and 'Husband on an Expedition', epitomize the bitter and tragic situation during the war: 'Grass smells of the lying corpses, The vast plains are flooded with blood'. In 'Farewell of an Old Man', the narrator pours out his grievances: 'My sons and grandsons lost in war, What's the use of staying home to save my skin?'. Another poem, 'Recruiting Officer of Shihao', presents a heartbreaking picture of an old woman whose 'three sons have have left for garrison duty at Ye'. She receives a letter from one of them breaking the news that the other two have recently died in battle: 'Now there's no other man in the house, Only a grandson at his mother's breast. The child's mother has not gone away; She has only a tattered skirt to wear'. In other words, there is no one left for the officer to recruit except the feeble old woman herself. In numerous poems Du Fu expresses the hope that war will soon come to an end and that the people will be allowed to live in peace. He used his poems to show his sympathy with ordinary people, comment on state affairs, and reproach the wrong-doings of the rulers.

Du Fu was more than a political poet, however. His verse covers a wide range of subjects and includes various forms including pastoral, narrative and lyric poetry, folk songs and ballads (*yuefu*). His 'Autumn Thoughts', 'A Spring Night—Rejoicing in the Rain', and a number of other poems portray the beauty of nature. His genius for diction, excellent mastery of rhythm and rhyme, and astonishing skill at creating images, gave such beauty to his poetry and won him so much renown that no poet in the history of Chinese literature has attracted so many followers and influenced so much later poetry.

—Binghong Lu

DU GARD, Roger Martin. See **MARTIN DU GARD, Roger**.

DU GONGLOU. See **DU FU**.

DUMAS *fils*, Alexandre. Born in Paris, France, 28 July 1824, the illegitimate son of the writer Alexandre Dumas *père, q.v.* Educated at the Pension Goubaux and the Collège Bourbon. Married 1) Nadejda Knorring (neé Naryschkine) in 1864 (died 1895), two daughters, one before marriage; 2) Henriette Régnier de la Brière in 1895. Lived with father in Saint-Germain-en-Laye, 1843–51; travelled with father to Spain and Algeria, 1846–47; wrote for the Théâtre du Gymnase, and later in career, for the Comédie-Française. Elected to the Académie française, 1875. *Died 28 November 1895.*

PUBLICATIONS

Collection

Théâtre complet. 10 vols., 1923.

Fiction

Aventures de quatre femmes et d'un perroquet. 6 vols., 1846–47.
La Dame aux camélias. 2 vols., 1848; as *The Lady with the Camelias*, translated anonymously, 1856; as *The Camelia-Lady*, translated anonymously, 1857; as *The Lady of the Camellias*, translated by William Walton, 1897; as *Camille*, translated by Henrietta Metcalf, 1931; also translated by Edmund Gosse, 1952; David Coward, 1986.
Césarine. 1848.
Le Docteur Servans. 2 vols., 1848–49.
Le Roman d'une femme. 4 vols., 1849.
Antoine. 2 vols., 1849.
La Vie à vingt ans. 2 vols., 1850; as *Paris Life at Twenty*, translated anonymously, 1863; as *The American Girl in Paris*, translated by Llewellyn Williams, 1891.
Tristan le roux. 3 vols., 1850; as *The Beggar of Nimes*, 1988.
Trois hommes forts. 4 vols., 1850.
Diane de Lys et Grangette. 3 vols., 1850.
Le Régent Mustel. 2 vols., 1852 (originally published as *Les Revenants* as an offprint from *Le Pays*, 1852); as *The Resuscitated*, translated by G. de Croij, 1877.
Contes et nouvelles. 1853.
La Dame aux perles. 4 vols., 1853; as *The Lady with the Pearl Necklace*, translated by M. Maury, 1901.
Sophie Printems. 2 vols., 1854.
Un Cas de rupture. 1854.
L'Affaire Clemenceau. 1866; as *The Clemenceau Case*, translated anonymously, n.d; as *Wife Murderer*, translated by H.L. Williams, 1866; as *Belle*, translated anonymously, 1888.

Plays

Atala, music by P. Varney. 1848.
La Dame aux camélias (produced 1852). 1852; edited by Roger J.B. Clark, 1972; as *La Dame aux camélias*, translated by Frederick A. Schwab, 1880; as *The Lady of the Camelias*, translated by Edith Reynolds and Nigel Playfair, 1930, in *Camille*, edited by S.S. Stanton, 1958; as *Camille*, translated by Henriette Metcalf, 1931; also translated by Edmund Gosse, 1937; Barbara Bray, 1975.
Diane de Lys (produced 1853). 1853.
Éva, with A. Montjoye and R. Deslandes (produced 1854). 1854.
Le Bijou de la reine (produced 1855). In *Théâtre complet*. 1868.
Le Demi-monde (produced 1855). 1855; as *The Demi-Monde: A Satire on Society*, translated by E.G. Squier, 1858; as *The Outer Edge of Society*, translated by Allison Smith and Robert Bell Michell, 1921.
Comment la trouves-tu?, with others (produced 1857). 1857.
La Question d'argent (produced 1857). 1857; as *The Money Question*, translated by B.W. Cragin and others, in *Poet Lore*, 26, 1915.
Le Fils naturel (produced 1858). 1858; as *Le fils naturel*, translated by T.L. Oxley, 1879.
Un Mariage dans un chapeau, with Auguste Vivier (produced 1859). 1859.
Un Père prodigue (produced 1859). 1859.

L'Ami des femmes (produced 1864). 1864; as *The Friend of Women*, translated anonymously, n.d.
Le Supplice d'une femme, with Émile de Girardin (produced 1865). 1865.
Héloïse Paranquet, with Anne-Adrien-Armand Durantin (produced 1866). 1866.
Les Idées de Madame Aubray (produced 1867). 1867.
Le Filleul de Pompignac, with A. de Jolin and N. Fournier (produced 1869). 1869.
Une visite de noces (produced 1871). 1872.
La Princesse Georges (produced 1871). 1872; translated as *La Princesse Georges*, 1881.
La Femme de Claude (produced 1873). 1873; as *Claude's Wife*, translated anonymously, n.d.
Monsieur Alphonse (produced 1873). 1874; as *M. Alphonse*, translated anonymously, 1886.
Les Danicheff, with Pyotr Korvin-Krukovsky (produced 1876). 1879.
La Comtesse Romani, with Gustave-Eugène Fould (produced 1876). 1878.
L'Étrangère (produced 1876). 1877; as *The Foreigner*, translated anonymously, 1881; as *L'Étrangère*, translated by Frederick A. Schwab, 1888.
La Princesse de Bagdad (produced 1881). 1881; as *The Princess of Bagdad*, translated anonymously, 1881.
Théâtre complet. 7 vols., 1882–93.
Denise (produced 1885). 1885; as *Denise*, translated anonymously, 1888.
Francillon (produced 1887). 1887.
Théâtres des autres (includes collaborative works). 2 vols., 1894.

Verse

Péchés de jeunesse. 1847.

Other

Histoire de la loterie. 1851.
Histoire du 'Supplice d'une femme'. 1865.
Les Madeleines repenties. 1869.
Nouvelle lettre de Junius à son ami A.D. 1871.
La Révolution plébéienne: Lettres à Junius. 1871.
Une lettre sur les choses du jour. 1871.
Nouvelle lettre sur les choses du jour. 1871.
L'Homme-Femme. 1872; as *Man-Woman*, edited and translated by George Vandenhoff, 1873.
Entr'actes. 3 vols., 1878–79.
Les Femmes qui tuent et les femmes qui votent. 1880.
La Question du divorce. 1880.
Lettre à M. Naquet. 1882.
La Recherche de la paternité. 1883.
Nouveaux Entr'actes. 1890.

*

Critical Studies: *Les Idées sociales dans le théâtre de Dumas* by C.M. Noël, 1912; *Dumas, Father and Son* by Francis Gribble, 1930; *Le Théâtre de Dumas fils et la société contemporaine* by O. Cheorgiu, 1931; *The Theatre of Alexandre Dumas fils* by F.A. Taylor, 1937; *The Prodigal Father: Dumas Père et Fils and 'The Lady of the Camellias'* by Edith Saunders, 1951; *Three Musketeers: A Study of the Dumas Family* by André Maurois, translated, 1957; *Alexandre Dumas fils* by A. Lebois, 1969.

* * *

Like his father, Alexandre Dumas *fils* was a prolific author of both novels and plays, though his major success was on the stage. After an early volume of poetry, *Péchés de jeunesse* [Sins of Youth], Dumas *fils* turned to the novel, writing 14 between 1846 and 1854. Although the best of these, *La Dame aux camélias* (*Camille*), *Diane de Lys*, and *La Dame aux perles* (*The Lady with the Pearl Necklace*), showed promise, the work that truly established his literary career was his stage adaptation of *Camille*. This presented a social situation new to the French stage, with characters speaking a language which, if flowery and rhetorical to modern ears, was far closer to everyday speech than mid-19th-century audiences were accustomed to hearing on stage. With its sympathetic portrayal of the doomed courtesan who finds love too late to escape the fatal result of her dissipated life, *Camille*, after an initial battle with censorship, achieved an enormous success.

Dumas *fils*'s second stage adaptation, *Diane de Lys*, is a distinctly grimmer study of a neglected wife who pursues an affair with a young artist whom her husband finally kills. Although Dumas was attempting to preach a moral lesson here, the contribution of the husband to his own problems was so clear that he gained little sympathy. Much clearer morally was the more original and more successful *Le Demi-monde* (*The Outer Edge of Society*), an unsentimental study of a world on the fringes of polite society, eager at any price to achieve the respectability society could offer. Suzanne d'Ange dreams of a proper marriage that will confirm her respectability, but Olivier de Jain, a protector of polite society from such contamination, frustrates her ambitions. De Jain is the first of Dumas *fils*'s *raisonneurs*, a key figure in the new 'thesis play', which illustrates some contemporary social or moral question, with the *raisonneur* serving as spokesman for the author.

The Outer Edge of Society differs from most thesis plays in that the social point of view it expresses is essentially the same as the members of society who would attend this play. Later thesis plays, from Dumas's own to those of Ibsen and Shaw, regularly challenged widely held social and moral beliefs and practice. Dumas turned in this direction with *La Question d'argent* (*The Money Question*), which challenged certain ideas prevalent in Dumas's society concerning the acquisition of wealth, and *Le Fils naturel*, which challenged social attitudes toward illegitimate children, with the added titillation of the author's own birth being illegitimate. *Un Père prodigue* [A Prodigal Father] clearly serves as a companion piece to *Le Fils naturel* and if the traits of Dumas *fils* are rather difficult to trace in the melodramatically idealized Jacques, those of Dumas *père* seem clearly in evidence in the larger-than-life prodigal father, presented, for all his faults, with obvious affection.

L'Ami des femmes (*The Friend of Women*) utilized Dumas *fils*'s new interest in psychology. His *raisonneur*, de Ryons, 'the woman's friend', has made a study of the female mind and thus is able to anticipate and to thwart Jane de Simerose's temptation toward adultery. More novels appeared after 1854, but only one, *L'Affaire Clemenceau* (*The Clemenceau Case*), had a real success. It claimed to be the prison journal of a husband who has murdered his unfaithful wife after a last night of love.

Les Idées de Madame Aubray [Madame Aubray's Ideas] was one of Dumas's most unconventional works, not only because he turned at last to a strong central female character, but also because of its religious theme. Mme Aubray is a zealous Christian torn between her beliefs and her desire to save her son from a marriage to a 'fallen woman'. Less openly religious but similarly admirable is Séverine, the heroine of *La Princesse Georges*, who redeems her unfaithful husband by forgiving him. During the late 1860s Dumas began to create long prefaces in the later manner of Shaw, carrying out his project for a 'useful theatre' by promulgating his ideas on love, marriage, divorce, abortion, and a whole range of social and moral concerns. The 1870 Franco-Prussian War also inspired a series of important public letters from him, as had the uprisings of 1848, letters expressing a fear of democratic government leading to anarchy.

La Femme de Claude (*Claude's Wife*) attempted a symbolic statement on the war and its causes, but the realistic context and melodramatic characters confused the public. Claude, a noble, patriotic Frenchman, marries a foreign wife who betrays his love and steals military secrets. Claude, discovering her perfidy, kills her. A much lighter note was struck this same year by *Monsieur Alphonse*, another study of a fallen woman, this one repentant and forgiven by a magnanimous husband. Monsieur Alphonse, the manipulative seducer, is one of Dumas's most successful characters.

L'Etrangère (*The Foreigner*), Dumas *fils*'s first play written for the Comédie-Française, depicts an unhappy arranged marriage, and although in this story the villainous husband is conveniently killed in a duel, Dumas felt clearly that society should provide a more thoughtful solution. The result was his famous pamphlet *La Question du divorce*, followed by a statement championing women's rights, *Les Femmes qui tuent et les femmes qui votent* [Women who Kill and Women who Vote], and one on illegitimacy, *La Recherche de la paternité* [A Study on Paternity]. Although each of these aroused great controversy, all were instrumental in inspiring important new social legislation in France.

Dumas *fils*'s political statements encouraged a negative public reaction to *La Princesse de Bagdad* (*The Princess of Bagdad*), but it is one of his weaker plays, another study of a spoiled, headstrong wife and a forgiving husband. His last two plays were more substantial and more successful. *Denise* presents a moving and convincing picture of a young woman who gives up her present happiness by confessing a sexual sin in her past in order to protect another young woman from marrying her seducer. *Francillon* shows a wife, tired of her husband's amorous intrigues, who boasts to him (falsely) of carrying out an affair of her own, thus curing him.

With the exception of *Camille*, none of Dumas *fils*'s theatre survives today, and even *Camille* is often regarded as little more than sentimental melodrama. In his own time, however, Dumas *fils* was regarded as a bold portrayer of contemporary life with a powerful and often effective commitment to social concerns. The modern 'problem play' of Ibsen, Shaw, and their followers would scarcely have been possible without his example.

—Marvin Carlson

CAMILLE (La Dame aux camélias)
Novel and play by Alexandre Dumas *fils*, 1848 and 1852.

Dumas *fils*'s *Camille* is actually two separate works: a novel, and the play the author drew from it. The two tell a similar story, based loosely on Dumas's youthful personal experiences with a well-known Parisian courtesan, Marie (*née* Alphonsine) Duplessis. Written in 1848, the novel, which uses events that had taken place between 1844, when Dumas was 20, and 1847, when Marie died, had such considerable success that the young author decided to transform it into a play for the Paris stage. He did so the following year, but political events and problems with the censors kept it from being produced until 1852, at which time it enjoyed spectacular popularity.

The novel is of course more detailed and intricate than the play; it is also a more original and complex literary work. It, too, uses 'true' facts of Dumas's life as a point of departure for its plot, whose story is told in the first person by three narrators: an unnamed young man, the frame narrator, who represents the author as his ideal friend; a youthful protagonist, Armand Duval, who also reflects the author's character, as well as his personal experience; and the heroine, here named Marguerite Gautier, whose life following the departure of Armand is recounted posthumously in her diary, given to her lover after her death.

The frame narrator tells of attending an auction at which society ladies bid for the worldly possessions of a recently-deceased courtesan, Marguerite Gautier, which are being sold off to pay her debts. Moved by sentiments he does not fathom, he pays an extravagant sum for a copy of *Manon Lescaut* bearing the cryptic inscription: 'Manon to Marguerite. Humility.' A mysterious young man who comes to his home—Armand Duval—offers to buy the volume back from him. When the narrator returns it to him as a gift, Armand shows him a remarkable letter written by the book's recipient on her deathbed. The narrator later helps Armand to effect the transfer of Marguerite's body to a perpetual concession in the Montmartre cemetery, and nurses him back to health following his collapse upon the opening of his mistress's coffin. During Armand's convalescence, he recounts the story of his love to his new friend: how he fell in love at first sight with Marguerite, met her again at the theatre and made a fool of himself, calling assiduously but anonymously at her home throughout her lengthy illness, arranged to be introduced into her elegant house, and at last became her lover. Tormented by jealousy, to distance her from the corruptions of Parisian life and a wealthy lover, and to repair her fragile health (the heroine established consumption as the 19th century's literary illness of choice), Armand takes Marguerite to the country, where the two lovers lead an idyllic life troubled only by another contemporary problem, money. A letter from Armand's father, however, puts an end to this existence: while his son is trying to see him in Paris, Duval senior persuades Marguerite to sacrifice herself and give up her love for the sake of Armand's liaison. Armand, whose jealousy had already been felt, thinks she has returned to her earlier life of pleasure. He abuses his former mistress both psychologically and physically, unaware of his father's visit and the real motive for her departure, which she has vowed to conceal. After a final night of love that she grants him at his request, he insults her with a scornful letter containing money for her favours, then leaves for Egypt. It is only upon his return to Paris that he learns the truth from his father and from Marguerite's diary, which posthumously reveals her sacrifice. Armand is left with his remorse, and the narrator concludes: 'I am not the apostle of vice, but I would gladly be the echo of noble sorrow wherever I hear its voice in prayer . . .'.

Dumas's play follows the same general outline, changing some of the characters in accordance with stage practice and permitting Armand to see his mistress just before she dies, thus somewhat alleviating the bleakness of the novel's ending. It is in the traditional five acts of serious French drama, the first taking place in Marguerite's boudoir, the second in her dressing-room, the third in the country (Auteuil here, at present a part of urban Paris, rather than the novel's

Bougival, now in its suburbs), the fourth in the salon of another brilliant courtesan, Olympe, and the final one in Marguerite's bedroom. The character of Gaston, Armand's and Marguerite's friend, is elaborated, particularly in the first and last acts, perhaps to compensate for the frame narrator's necessary disappearance from the dramatic genre; so is that of Marguerite's wealthy lover, who here becomes two characters: Count de Giray and Arthur de Varville, again perhaps in compensation for the disappearance of another of the novel's characters, Marguerite's elderly protector.

New and shocking in content, although banal in form, this play inaugurated Dumas *fils*'s career as one of the principal dramatists of his time. Although it is characteristic in its examination of the seamier side of Parisian society, it is more personal and 'romantic' than his later dramatic works, such as *The Outer Edge of Society*, *Les Idées de Madame Aubray*, and *Le Fils naturel*, generally cited as models of the social 'thesis-play'. It was more successful and influential finally than the novel, gaining fame as the source for opera, *La Traviata* (Verdi saw the play in Paris during a visit), as an international melodramatic vehicle for actresses like Bernhardt, Duse, Ethel Barrymore, and Lillian Gish, and as a starring cinematic role for, among others, Alla Nazimova (with Rudolph Valentino as Armand), Norma Talmadge (with Gilbert Roland), and, most unforgettably, Greta Garbo.

—David Sices

DUMAS *père*, Alexandre (Davy de la Pailleterie). Born in Villers-Cotterêts, France, 24 July 1802. Educated at local school. Married Ida Ferrier in 1840 (separated 1844; died 1861); had one son, the writer Alexandre Dumas *fils*, *q.v.*, by Catharine Labay, a daughter by Mélanie Serre, a son by Anna Bauër, and a daughter by Émilie Cordier. Articled at age 14 to a solicitor in Villers-Cotterêts, and one in Crépy, until 1822; employed in the secretariat of the Duc d'Orléans, 1822–29, and entered literary circle of Charles Nodier: librarian, Palais Royal, 1829; successful playwright, then historical novelist (often revising and polishing works written first by someone else); co-founder, Théâtre Historique, Paris, 1847–50; editor (and copious contributor), *La Liberté*, 1848; founding editor, *La France nouvelle*, 1848, and *Le Mois*, 1848–50; declared bankrupt and moved to Brussels, 1852, returned to Paris in 1853; founding editor, *Le Mousquetaire*, 1853–57, and the weekly *Le Monte-Cristo*, 1857–60; aided Garibaldi's invasion of Sicily, 1860–61; director of excavations and museums, Naples, 1860–61; editor *Journal de Jeudi*, 1860, and *L'indipendente*, Naples, 1860–64; returned to France, 1864; revived *Le Mousquetaire*, 1866–67; editor, *Le D'Artagnan*, 1868, and *Théâtre Journal*, 1868–69. Chevalier, Légion d'honneur, 1837; Order of Isabella the Catholic (Belgium); Cross of Gustavus Vasa (Sweden); Order of St John of Jerusalem. *Died 5 December 1870.*

PUBLICATIONS

Collections

Oeuvres complètes. 286 vols., 1848–1900.
Théâtre complet. 15 vols., 1863–74.

Oeuvres complètes. 301 vols., 1885–88.
The Romances. 60 vols., 1893–97; 10 vols., 1896.
The Novels, translated by Alfred Allinson. 56 vols., 1903–11.

Fiction

Nouvelles contemporaines. 1826.
Souvenirs d'Antony. 1835; as *The Recollections of Antony*, translated by Jeremy Griswold, 1849; as *The Reminiscences of Antony*, 1905.
Guelfes et Gibelins. 1836; as *Guelphs and Ghibellines*, 1905.
Isabelle de Bavière. 1836; as *Isabel of Bavaria*, translated by William Barrow, 1846.
La Main droite du Sire de Giac. 1838; as *The King's Favourite*, 1906.
Le Capitaine Paul, with Adrien Dauzats. 2 vols., 1838; as *Captain Paul*, translated by Thomas Williams, 1846; as *Paul Jones*, translated by William Berger, 1839; as *Paul Jones, the Son of the Sea*, translated 1849; as *Paul Jones: A Nautical Romance*, translated by Henry Llewellyn Williams, 1889; as *Paul Jones, the Bold Privateer*, n.d.
La Salle d'armes (includes *Pauline*; *Pascal Bruno*; *Murat*). 1838; parts translated under the following titles: *Pascal Bruno*, edited by Theodore Hook, 1837; *Pauline: A Tale of Normandy*, translated by 'A Lady of Virginia', 1842; *The Sicilian Bandit*, 1859; *Pauline, Pascal Bruno, and Bontekoe*, translated by Alfred Allinson, 1904.
Acté. 1839; as *Acté*, translated by Henry William Herbert, 1847; also translated by Alfred Allinson, 1904.
Les Crimes célèbres, with others. 1839–40; as *Celebrated Crimes*, translated 1843; also translated by I.G. Burnham, 8 vols., 1887; as *The Celebrated Crimes of History*, 8 vols., 1895; parts published as *The Crimes of the Borgias and Others*, 1907; *The Crimes of Urbain Grandier and Others*, 1907; *The Crimes of Ali Pacha and Others*, 1908; *The Crimes of the Marquise de Brinvilliers and Others*, 1908.
La Comtesse de Salisbury. 1839; as *The Countess of Salisbury*, 1851.
Monseigneur Gaston Phoebus. 1839.
Mémoires d'un maître d'armes. 1840; as *The Fencing-Master*, translated by G. Griswold, 1850.
Aventures de John Davys. 1840.
Maître Adam le Calabrais. 1840.
Othon l'archer. 1840; as *Otho the Archer*, 1860.
Praxède. 1841.
La Chasse au Chastre. 1841; as *The Bird of Fate*, 1906.
Aventures de Lyderic. 1842; as *Lyderic, Count of Flanders*, 1903; as *Adventures of Lyderic*, 1981.
Jehanne la Pucelle. 1842; as *Joan the Heroic Maiden*, 1847.
Albine. 1843; as *Le Château d'Eppstein*, 1844; as *The Spectre Mother*, 1864; as *The Castle of Eppstein*, translated by Alfred Allinson, 1904.
Le Chevalier d'Harmental, with Auguste Maquet. 1843; as *The Chevalier d'Harmental*, translated by P.F Christin and Eugene Lies, 1846; as *The Chateau d'Harmental*, 1856; as *The Orange Plume*, translated by Henry L. Williams, Jr, 1860; as *The Conspirators*, 1910.
La Comtesse de Saint-Géran; as *The Countess of Saint-Géran*, 1843.
Georges. 1843; as *George*, translated by G.J. Knox, 1846; also translated by Samuel Spring, 1847; as *Georges*, translated by Alfred Allinson, 1904.
Ascanio, with Paul Meurice. 1843–44; as *Ascanio*, translated by Eugene Lies and Eugene Plunkett, 1846; as *Francis I*, 1849.
Le Comte de Monte-Cristo, with Auguste Maquet. 1844–45; edited by David Coward (in English), 1990; as *The Count

of Monte Cristo*, 1846; also translated by Henry Llewellyn Williams, 1892; William Thiese, 1892; Steven Grant, 1990; as *The Chateau d'If: A Romance*, translated by Emma Hardy, 1846.
Amaury, with Paul Meurice. 1844; as *Amaury*, translated by 'E.P.', 1844; also translated by Alfred Allinson, 1904.
Une âme à naître [*Histoire d'une âme*]. 1844.
Cécile. 1844; as *La Robe de noces*, 1844; as *Cecile*, translated by Eugene Plunkett, 1847; also translated by Alfred Allinson, 1904; as *The Wedding Dress*, translated by Fayette Robinson, 1851.
Fernande. 1844; as *Fernande*, 1904; also translated by A. Craig Bell, 1988.
Une fille du régent, with Auguste Maquet. 1844; as *The Regent's Daughter*, translated by Charles H. Town, 1845.
Les Frères corses. 1844; as *The Corsican Brothers*, translated by Henry William Herbert, 1845; also translated by Gerardus Van Dam, 1883; Alfred Allison, 1904.
Les Trois Mousquetaires, with Auguste Maquet. 1844; edited by David Coward (in English), 1991; as *The Three Guardsmen*, translated by Park Benjamin, 1846; as *The Three Musketeers*, translated by William Barrow, 1846; also translated by William Robson, 1860; Henry Llewellyn Williams, 1892; A. Curtis Bond, 1894; Alfred Allinson, 1903; Philip Schuyler Allen, 1923; J. Walker McSpadden, 1926; Jacques Le Clercq, 1950; Isabel Ely Lord, 1952; Lord Sudley, 1952; Marcus Clapham and Clive Reynard, 1992.
Gabriel Lambert. 1844; translated as *The Galley Slave*, 1849; as *Gabriel Lambert*, 1904.
Invraisemblance [*Histoire d'un mort*]. 1844.
Sylvandire, with Auguste Maquet. 1844; as *Sylvandire*, translated by Thomas Williams, 1847, as *The Disputed Inheritance*, translated by Williams, 1847; as *The Young Chevalier*, 1850; as *Beau Tancrede*, 1861.
La Guerre des femmes, with Auguste Maquet. 1845–46; as *Nanon*, 1847; as *The War of Women*, translated by Samuel Spring, 1850.
La Reine Margot, with Auguste Maquet. 1845; as *Margaret de Navarre*, 1845; as *Marguerite de Valois*, 1846; also translated by S. Fowler Wright, 1947; as *Queen Margot*, translated 1885.
Vingt ans après, with Auguste Maquet. 1845; edited by David Coward (in English), 1993; as *Cardinal Mazarin; or, Twenty Years After*, n.d.; as *Twenty Years After*, translated by 'E.P.', 1846; also translated by William Barrow, 1846; Henry Llewellyn Williams, 1899; Alfred Allinson, 1904; as *Cromwell and Mazarin*, 1847.
Le Chevalier de Maison-Rouge, with Auguste Maquet. 1845; translated as *Marie Antoinette*, 1846; as *Genevieve*, translated by Henry William Herbert, 1846; as *Chateau-Rouge*, 1859; as *The Knight of Redcastle*, translated by Henry Llewellyn Williams, 1893; as *The Chevalier de Maison-Rouge*, 1877.
La Dame de Monsoreau, with Auguste Maquet. 1846; as *Diana of Meridor*, 1846; as *Chicot the Jester*, 1857; as *La Dame de Monsoreau*, 1889; also translated by J. Walker McSpadden, 1926; as *Diane*, 1901.
Mémoires d'un médecin: Joseph Balsamo, with August Maquet. 1846–48; parts translated under the following titles: *Memoirs of a Physician*, 1847; *Andrée de Taverney; or, The Downfall of French Monarchy*, translated by Henry L. Williams, Jr, 2 vols., 1862; *The Chevalier*, 1864; *Balsamo; or, Memoirs of a Physician*, 1878; *Joseph Balsamo*, 1878; *The Mesmerist's Victim*, translated by Henry Llewellyn Williams, 1893.
Le Bâtard de Mauléon, with Auguste Maquet. 1846; as *The Bastard of Mauleon*, 1849; as *The Knight of Mauléon*, 1850;

as *The Half Brothers*, 1858; as *The Iron Hand, or, The Knight of Mauleon*, 1858; as *Agénor de Mauléon*, 1897.

Les Quarante-cinq, with Auguste Maquet. 1848; as *The Forty-Five Guardsmen*, 1847; also translated by J. Walker McSpadden, 1926; as *The Forty-Five*, 1889.

Le Vicomte de Bragelonne; ou, Dix ans plus tard, with Auguste Maquet. 1848–50; edited by John Kennett (in English), 1970, and by David Coward (in English), 1991; as *The Vicomte de Bragelonne*, translated by Thomas Williams, 1848, as *Bragelonne, the Son of Athos; or, Ten Years Later*, translated by Williams, 1848, as *The Iron Mask*, 1850; as *Louise La Vallière*, 1851; also translated by Alfred Allinson, 1904; as *The Man in the Iron Mask*, translated by Henry Llewellyn Williams, 1889, this translation also published as *The Vicomte de Bragelonne*, 1892, and *Louise de la Vallière*, 1892; as *Louise de la Vallière*, translated by J. Walker McSpadden, 1901.

Les mille et un fantômes. 1848–51; as *Tales of the Supernatural* [*Strange Adventures, Terror*], 1907–09.

Le Collier de la Reine, with Auguste Maquet. 1849; as *The Queen's Necklace*, translated by Thomas Williams, 1850; also translated by Henry Llewellyn Williams, 1892.

Ange Pitou, with Auguste Maquet. 1849; as *Taking the Bastille*, n.d.; as *Six Years Later*, translated by Thomas Williams, 1851; as *The Royal Life-Guard*, translated by Henry Llewellyn Williams, 1893; as *Ange Pitou*, 1907.

Les Mariages du père Olifus, with Paul Bocage. 1849; as *The Man with Five Wives*, 1850.

Le Trou de l'enfer. 1850–51; as *The Mouth of Hell*, 1906.

La Tulipe noire. 1850; as *Rosa; or, The Black Tulip*, translated by Franz Demmler, 1854, and edited by David Coward, 1993; as *The Black Tulip*, translated by A.J. O'Connor, 1902; also translated by Mary D. Frost, 1902; S.J. Adair Fitz-Gerald, 1951.

La Colombe. 1851; as *The Dove*, 1906.

Dieu dispose. 1851–52; as *God's Will Be Done*, 1909.

La Comtesse de Charny. 1852–55; as *The Countess de Charny*, translated 1853; as *La Comtesse de Charny*, 1890; as *The Countess of Charny*, translated by Henry Llewellyn Williams, 1892.

Un Gil-Blas en Californie. 1852; as *A Gil Blas in California*, 1933.

Isaac Laquedem. 1852–53.

Conscience l'innocent. 1852; as *The Conscript*, 1855; as *Conscience*, translated by Alfred Allinson, 1902.

Olympe de Clèves. 1852; as *Olympia of Cleves; or, The Loves of a King*, 1887; as *Olympe de Clèves*, 1893; as *Madame de Mailly*, 1896.

Emmanuel Philibert. 1852–54; as *Le Page du duc de Savoie*, 1855; as *Emmanuel-Philibert*, 1854; as *The Page of the Duke of Savoy*, 1861.

Le Pasteur d'Ashbourne. 1853.

El Saltéador. 1854; as *The Brigand*, translated with *Blanche de Beaulieu*, 1897; with *The Horoscope*, 1897.

Ingénue. 1854; as *Ingénue; or, The First Days of Blood*, translated by Julie de Marguerittes, 1855.

Les Mohicans de Paris; Salvator le Commissionnaire, with Paul Bocage. 1854–59; as *The Mohicans of Paris*, 1859; also translated by R.S. Garnett, 1926; *The Horrors of Paris*, 1875; parts translated by Mary Neal Sherwood under the following titles: *Salvator*, 1882, *Conrad de Valgeneuse*, 1900, *Rose-de-noël*, 1900, *The Chief of Police*, 1900, *Monsieur Sarranti*, 1900, and *Princess Régina*, 1900.

Catherine Blum. 1854; as *The Foresters*, 1854; as *Catherine Blum*, 1861.

Les Compagnons de Jéhu. 1857; as *Roland of Montreval*, 1860; as *The Company of Jehu*, translated by Katharine

Prescott Wormeley, 1894; as *The Companions of Jehu*, 1894; as *The Aide-de-Camp of Napoleon*, 1897.

Charles le téméraire. 2 vols., 1857; as *Charles the Bold*, 1860.

Le Meneur de loups. 1857; as *The Wolf-Leader*, translated by Alfred Allinson, 1904.

Black. 1858; as *Black*, 1895.

Le Capitaine Richard. 1858; as *The Twin Captains*, 1861; as *The Young Captain*, 1870; as *The Twin Lieutentants*, 1877.

Herminie. 1858.

L'Horoscope. 1858; as *The Horoscope*, with *The Brigand*, 1897; also translated by Mary Stuart Smith, 1900.

Les Louves de Machecoul. 1859; as *The Castle of Souday*, translated by Henry L. Williams, Jr, 1862, this translation also published as *Royalist Daughters*, 1862; as *The Last Vendee; or, The She-Wolves of Machecoul*, 1894; as *The She-Wolves of Machecoul*, with *The Corsican Brothers*, 1894.

Ammalet Beg. 1859; as *Sultanetta*, translated in *Tales of the Caucasus*, 1895.

L'Histoire d'un cabanon et d'un chalet. 1859; as *Monsieur Coumbes*, 1860; as *Le Fils de Forçat*, 1864; as *The Convict's Son*, 1905.

La Princesse Flora. 1859.

Jane. 1859; as *Jane*, with *Crop-Ear Jacquot*, 1903.

Le Chasseur de Sauvagine. 1859; as *The Wild Duck Shooter*, 1906.

Le Médecin de Java. 1859(?); as *L'Île de feu*, 1870; as *Doctor Basilius*, translated 1860.

Madame de Chamblay, 1859.

Une aventure d'amour. 1860.

Le Père la Ruine, with de Cherville. 1860; as *Père la Ruine*, translated by Alfred Allinson, 1905.

La Maison de glace. 1860; as *The Russian Gipsy*, 1860.

Jacquot sans oreilles. 1860; as *Crop-Ear Jacquot*, with *Jane*, 1903; also translated by Alfred Allinson, in *Crop-Eared Jacquot and Other Stories*, 1905.

Les Drames galants, La Marquise d'Escoman. 1860.

Une nuit à Florence. 1861.

La San-Felice [*Emma Lyonna*]. 1864–65; as *Love and Liberty*, 1869; as *The Lovely Lady Hamilton*, 1903; as *Love and Liberty; or, Nelson at Naples*, translated by R.S. Garnett, 1917; as *The Neapolitan Lovers*, translated by Garnett, 1917.

La Pêche aux filets. 1864.

Le Comte de Moret. 1866; as *The Count of Moret*, translated by Henry L. Williams, Jr, 1868.

La Terreur prussienne. 1867; as *The Prussian Terror*, translated by R.S. Garnett, 1915.

Les Blancs et les bleus. 1867–68; as *The Polish Spy*, 1869; as *The First Republic*, 1894; as *The Whites and the Blues*, 1894.

Les Hommes de fer. 1867.

L'Huitième Croisade. 1868; as *The Eighth Crusade*, 1890.

Parisiens et provinciaux, with de Cherville. 1868.

Création et rédemption: Le Docteur mystérieux, La Fille du marquis. 1872.

Le Comte de Beuzeval; as *The Count of Beuzeval*, 1889.

Short Stories (in English). 1927.

Plays

La Chasse et l'amour, with Adolphe de Leuven and Pierre-Joseph Rousseau (produced 1825).

La Noce et l'enterrement, with E.H. Lassagne (produced 1826).

Henri III et sa cour (produced 1829). 1829.

Christine (produced 1830). 1830.

Antony (produced 1831). 1831; edited by Maurice Baudin (in English), 1929; as *Antony*, translated by Frederick A. Schwab, 1880.

Napoléon Bonaparte (produced 1831). 1831.

Charles VII chez ses grands vassaux (produced 1831). 1831; as *Charles VII at the Homes of His Great Vassals*, translated by D.T. Bonett, 1992.

Richard Darlington, with Dinaux (produced 1831). 1832.

La Tour de Nesle, from play by Frédéric Gaillardet (produced 1832). 1832; as *The Tower of Nesle*, translated by George Almar, 1850(?); also translated by Henry Llewellyn Williams, 1904; Adam L. Gowans, 1906; Edwin Stanton De Poncet, 1934.

Térésa, with Anicet Bourgeois (produced 1832). 1832.

Perinet Leclerc; ou, Paris en 1418 (produced 1832). 1832.

Le Fils de l'émigré, with Anicet Bourgeois (produced 1832).

Le Mari de la veuve, with Anicet Bourgeois and Eugène Durieu (produced 1832). 1832.

Angèle, with Anicet Bourgeois (produced 1833). 1834.

La Vénitienne, with Anicet Bourgeois (produced 1834). 1834.

Catherine Howard (produced 1834). 1834; as *Catherine Howard*, 1859; translated and adapted by William E. Suter, 1870(?).

La Tour de Babel, with others (produced 1834). 1834.

Cromwell et Charles Ier, with Cordellier Delanoue (produced 1835). 1835.

Don Juan de Marana (produced 1836). 1836.

Kean; ou, Désordre et génie, with Théaulon (produced 1836). 1836; as *Edmund Kean; or, The Genius and the Libertine*, 1847.

Le Marquis de Brunoy, with others (produced 1836). 1836.

Caligula (produced 1837). 1838.

Piquillo, with Gérard de Nerval, music by Hippolyte Monpou (produced 1837). 1837.

Paul Jones (produced 1838). 1838.

Le Bourgeois de Gand; ou, Le Secrétaire du Duc d'Albe, with Hippolyte Romand (produced 1838). 1838.

Mademoiselle de Belle-Isle (produced 1839). 1839; as *Mademoiselle de Belle-Isle* (bilingual edition), 1855; also translated by F.A. Kemble, in *Plays*, 1863; as *The Lady of Belle Isle*, translated by J.M. Gully, 1872; as *Gabrielle de Belle Isle*, 1880; as *The Great Lover*, 1979.

Bathilde, with Auguste Maquet (produced 1839). 1839.

L'Alchimiste, with Gérard de Nerval (produced 1839). 1839; as *The Alchemist*, translated by Henry Bertram Lister, 1940.

Léo Burckart, with Gérard de Nerval (produced 1839). 1839.

Jarvis l'honnête homme, with Charles Lafont (produced 1840). 1840.

Un mariage sous Louis XV (produced 1841). 1841; as *A Marriage of Convenience*, translated and adapted by Sydney Grundy, 1897.

Jeannil le Breton; ou, Le Gérant responsable, with Eugène Bourgeois (produced 1841). 1842.

Le Séducteur et le mari, with Charles Lafont (produced 1842). 1842.

Halifax, with Adolphe d'Ennery (produced 1842). 1842.

Lorenzino (produced 1842). 1842.

Les Demoiselles de Saint-Cyr (produced 1843). 1843; as *The Ladies of Saint-Cyr*, 1870.

Le Laird de Dumbicky, with Adolphe de Leuven and Léon Lhérie (produced 1843). 1844.

Louise Bernard, with Adolphe de Leuven and Léon Lhérie (produced 1843). 1843.

L'École de princes (produced 1843). 1843.

Le Mariage au tambour (produced 1843). 1843.

Le Garde-Forestier, with Adolphe de Leuven and Léon Lhérie (produced 1845). 1845.

Un conte de fées, with Adolphe de Leuven and Léon Lhérie (produced 1845). 1845.

Sylvandire, with Adolphe de Leuven and Léon Lhérie, from the novel by Dumas and Maquet (produced 1845). 1845.

Les Mousquetaires, with Auguste Maquet, from the novel *Vingt ans après* by Dumas and Maquet (produced 1845). 1845.

Une fille du régent, from the novel by Dumas and Maquet (produced 1846). 1846.

Échec et mat, with Octave Feuillet and Paul Bocage (produced 1846). 1846.

Intrigue et amour, from a play by Schiller (produced 1847). In *Théâtre complet*, 1864.

Hamlet, with Paul Meurice, from the play by Shakespeare (produced 1847). 1848.

La Reine Margot, with Auguste Maquet, from the novel by Dumas and Maquet (produced 1847) 1847.

Le Chevalier de Maison-Rouge, with Auguste Maquet, from the novel by Dumas and Maquet (produced 1847). 1847; as *The Chevalier de Maison-Rouge*, 1859.

Catalina, with Auguste Maquet (produced 1848). 1848.

Monte-Cristo, parts 1–2, with Auguste Maquet, from the novel *Le Comte de Monte-Cristo* by Dumas and Maquet (produced 1848). 2 vols., 1848; translated 1850.

Le Cachemire vert, with Eugène Nus (produced 1849). 1850.

Le Comte Hermann (produced 1849). 1849.

La Jeunesse des mousquetaires, with Auguste Maquet, from the novel *Les Trois Mousquetaires* by Dumas and Maquet (produced 1849). 1849; as *The Three Musketeers*, 1855; as *The Musketeers*, 1898.

Le Chevalier d'Harmental, with Auguste Maquet, from the novel by Dumas and Maquet (produced 1849). 1849.

La Guerre des femmes, with Auguste Maquet, from the novel by Dumas and Maquet (produced 1849). 1849.

Le Connétable de Bourbon; ou, L'Italie au seizième siècle, with Eugène Grangé and Xavier de Montépin (produced 1849). 1849.

Le Testament de César, with Jules Lacroix (produced 1849). 1849.

Pauline, with Eugène Grangé and Xavier de Montépin (produced 1850). 1850; as *Pauline*, translated and adapted 1855.

Les Frères corses, with Eugène Grangé and Xavier de Montépin, from the novel (produced 1850).

Trois Entr'actes pour l'amour médecin (produced 1850). 1850.

La Chasse au Chastre, from his own novel (produced 1850). 1850.

Les Chevalier du Lansquenet, with Eugène Grangé and Xavier de Montépin (produced 1850). 1850.

Urbain Grandier, with Auguste Maquet (produced 1850). 1850.

Le Vingt-quatre février (produced 1850). 1850.

La Barrière de Clichy (produced 1851). 1851.

Le Vampire, with Auguste Maquet (produced 1851). 1851.

Le Comte de Morcerf; Villefort, with Auguste Maquet, from the novel *Le Comte de Monte-Cristo* by Dumas and Maquet (produced 1851). 2 vols., 1851.

La Conscience (produced 1854). 1851.

La Jeunesse de Louis XIV (produced 1854). 1854; as *Young King Louis*, 1979.

Le Marbrier, with Paul Bocage (produced 1854). 1854.

Romulus (produced 1854). 1854; as *Romulus*, 1969.

L'Orestie (produced 1856). 1856.

La Tour Saint-Jacques, with Xavier de Montépin (produced 1856). 1856.

Le Verrou de la reine (produced 1856). In *Théâtre complet*,

1865.

Samson, music by E. Duprez (produced 1857). Parts published, 1856.

L'Invitation à la valse, with P. Bocage (produced 1857). 1857; as *Childhood's Dreams*, 1881.

La Bacchante (Thaïs), with Adolphe de Leuven and A. de Beauplan, music by Eugène Gautier (produced 1858).

L'Honneur est satisfait (produced 1858). 1858.

Les Forestiers, from his novel *Catherine Blum* (produced 1858). In *Théâtre complet*, 13, 1865.

L'Envers d'une conspiration (produced 1860). 1860.

Le Roman d'Elvire, with Adolphe de Leuven, music by Ambroise Thomas (produced 1860). 1860.

Le Gentilhomme de la montagne, from his novel *El Saltéador* (produced 1860). 1860.

La Dame de Monsoreau, with Auguste Maquet, from the novel by Dumas and Maquet (produced 1860). 1860.

Le Prisonnier de la Bastille: Fin des Mousquetaires, with Auguste Maquet, from the novel *Le Vicomte de Bragelonne* by Dumas and Maquet (produced 1861). 1861.

La Veillée Allemande, with Bernard Lopez (produced 1863).

Les Mohicans de Paris, from the novel by Dumas and Bocage (produced 1864). 1864.

Gabriel Lambert, with Amédée de Jallais, from the novel by Dumas (produced 1866; as *Gabriel le Faussaire*, produced 1868). 1866.

Madame de Chamblay, from his own novel (produced 1868). 1869.

Les Blancs et les bleus, from his own novel (produced 1869). 1874.

Ivanhoë; Fiesque de Lavagna. 1974.

Other

La Vendée et Madame. 1833; as *The Duchess of Berri in La Vendée*, 1833.

Gaule et France. 1833.

Impressions de voyage: En Suisse. 5 vols., 1833–37; as *Glacier Land*, translated by Mrs W.R. Kilds, 1852; as *Swiss Travel*, edited by C.H. Parry, 1890; as *Adventures in Switzerland*, 1960.

Impressions de voyage: France. 1835–37; as *Pictures of Travel in the South of France*, 1852; as *Sketches in France*, 1860(?).

Quinze Jours à Sinaï, with Adrien Dauzats. 2 vols., 1839, also published as *Voyage au Orient*, and *Le Sinaï*; as *Impressions of Travel, in Egypt and Arabia Petraea*, translated by 'A Lady of New York', 1839; as *Travelling Sketches in Egypt and Sinai*, translated by 'A Biblical Student', 1839.

Napoléon. 1840; as *Napoleon*, translated by John B. Larner, 1894.

Le Capitaine Pamphile (for children). 1840; edited by A.R. Florian, 1912; as *The Adventures of Captain Pamphile*, translated by James Herald, 1845(?); also translated by Alfred Allinson, 1905; as *Captain Pamphile*, 1850.

Les Stuarts. 2 vols., 1840.

Excursions sur les bords du Rhin. 3 vols., 1841.

Une année à Florence. 2 vols., 1841.

Midi de la France. 3 vols., 1841.

Le Speronare. 4 vols., 1842; as *The Speronara*, translated by Katharine Prescott Wormeley, with *Journeys with Dumas*, 1902.

Souvenirs de voyage en Italie. 1841–42; comprises *Une année à Florence* and *Le Speronare*.

Le Capitaine Aréna. 2 vols., 1842; as *Captain Marion*, translated by F.W. Reed, 1949.

Le Corricolo. 4 vols., 1843; part translated as *Sketches of*

Naples, by A. Roland, 1845.

La Villa Palmieri. 2 vols., 1843.

Filles, lorettes, et courtisanes. 1843.

Louis XIV et son siècle. 2 vols., 1844–45.

Histoire d'un casse-noisette (for children). 2 vols., 1845; as *The Story of a Nutcracker*, 1846; as *The History of a Nutcracker*, 1872; as *Princess Pirlipatine and the Nutcracker*, translated and continued by O. Eliphaz Keat, 1920; as *The Nutcracker of Nuremberg*, translated by Grace Gingras, 1930.

La Bouillie de la Comtesse Berthe (for children). 1845; edited by Cornell Price, 1889; as *The Honey-Stew of the Countess Bertha*, translated by Mrs Cooke Taylor, 1846; as *Good Lady Bertha's Honey Broth*, 1846; as *The Countess Bertha's Honey-Feast*, translated by Harry A. Spurr, in *Fairy Tales*, 1904; as *The Honey Feast*, 1980.

Italiens et Flamands. 1845.

Les Médicis. 2 vols., 1845.

De Paris à Cadix. 5 vols., 1848; as *Adventures in Spain*, 1959.

Le Véloce; ou, Tanger, Alger, et Tunis. 4 vols., 1848–51; as *Adventures in Algeria*, 1959; as *Tangier to Tunis*, translated by A.E. Murch, 1959; as *Tales of Algeria; or, Life Among the Arabs*, translated by Richard Meade Bache, 1868.

Louis XV et sa cour. 4 vols., 1849.

La Régence. 2 vols., 1849.

Montevideo; ou, Une nouvelle Troie. 1850.

Histoire de Louis XVI et la révolution. 3 vols., 1850–51.

Mémoires de Talma. 3 vols., 1850.

Le Drame de '93. 7 vols., 1851–52.

Les Drames de la mer. 2 vols., 1852.

Histoire de Louis-Philippe. 1852; as *The Last King; or, The New France*, 1915.

Mes Mémoires. 22 vols., 1852–54; annotated edition, 5 vols., 1954–68; selections as *Memoirs*, translated by A.F. Davidson, 5 vols., 1891; as *My Memoirs*, translated by E.M. Waller, 6 vols., 1907–09.

Une vie d'artiste. 2 vols., 1854; as *A Life's Ambition*, translated by R.S. Garnett, with *My Odyssey*, 1924.

La Jeunesse de Pierrot (for children). 1854; as *When Pierrot Was Young*, translated by Douglas Munro, 1975.

La Dernière Année de Marie Dorval. 1855.

Isabel Constant. 2 vols., 1855.

Les Grands Hommes en robe de chambre: Henri IV, Louis XIII, et Richelieu; César. 12 vols., 1856–57.

L'Homme aux contes (for children). 1857.

Le Lièvre de mon grand-père (for children), with de Cherville. 1857; as *The Phantom White Hare and Other Tales*, translated by Douglas Munro, 1989.

Marianna. 1859.

Les Baleiniers, with Félix Meynard. 3 vols., 1860.

Le Caucase; depuis Prométhée jusqu'à Chamyll. 7 vols. in 3, 1859, also published as *Impressions de Voyage: Le Caucase*, 1865; as *Adventures in Caucasia*, translated by A.E. Murch, 1962.

L'Art et les artistes contemporains au salon de 1859. 1859.

Contes pour les grands et les petits enfants (for children). 2 vols., 1859.

Causeries. 2 vols., 1860.

La Route de Varennes. 1860; as *Flight to Varennes*, translated by A. Craig Bell, 1962.

Les Garibaldiens: Révolution de Sicile et du Naples. 1861; as *The Garibaldians in Sicily*, 1861; complete version, as *On Board the 'Emma': Adventures with Garibaldi's 'Thousand' in Sicily*, edited by R.S. Garnett, 1929.

Bric-à-brac. 2 vols., 1861.

Les Morts vont vites. 2 vols., 1861.

Le Pape devant les évangiles. 1861.

I Borboni di Napoli. 10 vols., 1862–64.
Impressions de voyage: En Russie, 4 vols. 1865, also published as *De Paris à Astrakan*, 1858(?); as *Voyage en Russie*, edited by Jacques Suffel, 1960; excerpts as *Celebrated Crimes of the Russian Court*, 1905; as *Adventures in Czarist Russia*, 1960; also translated by A.E. Murch, 1976.
Bouts-rimés. 1865.
Étude sur 'Hamlet' et sur William Shakespeare. 1867.
Histoire de mes bêtes. 1868; as *My Pets*, translated by Alfred Allinson, 1909; as *Adventures with My Pets*, 1960.
Souvenirs dramatiques. 2 vols., 1868.
Le Grand Dictionnaire de cuisine. 1873; as *Dictionary of Cuisine*, translated 1958; selection as *Dumas on Food: Selections From 'Le Grand Dictionnaire de Cuisine'*, translated by Alan and Jane Davidson, 1978.
Propos d'art et de cuisine. 1877.
Fairy Tales, edited and translated by Harry A. Spurr. 1904.
The Dumas Fairy Tale Book, edited by Harry A. Spurr. 1924.
Lettres d'Alexandre Dumas à Mélanie Waldor, edited by Claude Schopp. 1982.
Sur Gérard de Nerval: Nouveaux mémoires. 1990.

Editor, *Un pays inconnu*. 1845.
Editor, *Pierre précieuse*, by Saphir. 1854.
Editor, *L'Arabie heureuse*. 1855.
Editor, *Le Journal de Madame Giovanni*. 4 vols., 1856; as *The Journal of Madame Giovanni*, translated by Marguerite E. Wilbur, 1944.
Editor, *Pélerinage de Hadji-abd-el-Hamid-Bey (à la Mecque)*. 6 vols., 1856–57.
Editor, *Les Baleiniers*, by Felix Maynard. 1861; as *The Whalers*, translated by F.W. Reed, 1937.

Translator, *Mémoires de Garibaldi*. 2 vols., 1860; revised edition, 5 vols., 1860–61; 3 vols., 1861; as *Garibaldi: An Autobiography*, 1860; revised edition, as *The Memoirs of Garibaldi*, translated by R.S. Garnett, 1931.

*

Bibliography: *A Bibliography of Alexandre Dumas Père* by F.W. Reed, 1933; *Dumas père: Works Published in French. Works Translated into English* by Douglas Munro, 2 vols., 1978–81; *Alexandre Dumas père: A Secondary Bibliography of French and English Sources to 1983: With Appendices* by Douglas Munro, 1985.

Critical Studies: *The Life and Writings of Alexandre Dumas* by H.A. Spurr, 1929; *Alexandre Dumas père* by Richard S. Stowe, 1976; *The King of Romance: A Portrait of Alexandre Dumas* by F.W.J. Hemmings, 1979; *Alexandre Dumas* by Michael Ross, 1981; *'Missing' Works of Alexandre Dumas Père* by Douglas Munro, 1983; *Notes on Dumas' 'Count of Monte Cristo'* by Arnie Jacobson, 1985.

*   *   *

Victor Hugo said: 'No popularity of this century has surpassed that of Alexandre Dumas. The name of Alexandre Dumas is more than French . . . it is universal. Alexandre Dumas seduces, fascinates, interests, amuses, teaches.' Dumas was too large in scope, too dynamic, too overpowering to be judged merely by the 40 years in which he dominated every field of writing in France.

Victorien Sardou called Dumas the greatest theatrical craftsman of the century. From 1829 until 1868 he had at least one play on the boards each year, often two or three, and in 1849, five. He inaugurated the Romantic movement with his play *Henri III et sa cour* in 1829. His *Antony*, in 1831, was the first modern Romantic play, and imitations are in the hundreds. An 1833 trip to Switzerland started Dumas on another type of writing—travel impressions, but a new kind of travelogue that was as interesting as a novel.

In 1844, his novel *Les Trois Mousquetaires* (*The Three Musketeers*) was the literary sensation of the century. Within ten years he had covered most of the history of France in his novels, and also turned out other gems such as *Le Comte de Monte-Cristo* (*The Count of Monte Cristo*), *La Tulipe noire* (*The Black Tulip*), and *Les Frères corses* (*The Corsican Brothers*). He also wrote purely historical works such as *Gaule et France*, *Louis XIV et son siècle*, *Napoléon* (*Napoleon*), and many others, probably the least boring history books ever written.

Dumas had collaborators on many of his novels, but their work consisted of research and planning; Dumas rewrote everything in his own hand. Critics have been amazed at his enormous output, but this was a man who could entertain a group of people for hours with facts and anecdotes drawn from the deep well of his memory; this was a man who could write 14 hours a day with scarcely a single erasure or reference. Whatever he heard or read remained in his fertile brain—history, mythology, swordsmanship, geography, names, dates. At a gathering, he was describing the battle of Waterloo in great detail when he was interrupted by a pompous general who said: 'But it wasn't like that; I was there!' 'I'm sorry, general,' replied Dumas, 'but you were not paying attention to what was going on.' Dumas often had an entire novel or play in his head before he ever put it on paper. One of his finest plays, *Mademoiselle de Belle-Isle* (*The Lady of Belle Isle*), which had 500 performances, was recited for the committee of the Comédie-Française, and was accepted by acclamation before one word of it had ever been written.

Dumas has had his detractors, mostly writers who were jealous of his great popularity. He was often slighted in histories of French literature. His son, Alexandre Dumas *fils*, became a playwright, and for a decade or more almost eclipsed his father. But time works in favour of Dumas *père*. Except for *Camille*, his son's plays are virtually forgotten, even in France, but the father's works are being reprinted constantly, and more than 300 films have been made from his novels, his plays, and his life.

Dumas *père* was a master story-teller. His style, as Robert Louis Stevenson said, 'is light as a whipped trifle, strong as silk'. Dumas will survive. Two hundred years from now, you can be sure that at any given moment, someone, in some far-off place, will be reading *The Three Musketeers* or *The Count Of Monte Cristo* in one of the dozens of languages into which Dumas has been translated.

—Barnett Shaw

THE THREE MUSKETEERS (Les Trois Mousquetaires)
Novel by Alexandre Dumas père, 1844.

The Three Musketeers is Dumas's most important venture in the art of the historical novel and in melodrama. Set in that golden age of French history, the 17th century, it covers the period from 1625 to 1628, when Richelieu was beginning to consolidate his power.

Young D'Artagnan comes to Paris to seek his fortune. Hardly has he arrived in the capital than he is involved in duels with the three musketeers Athos, Porthos, and Aramis, who nevertheless soon become his friends. The four musketeers (for so they become when D'Artagnan joins them in chapter 47) have many adventures, chief of which is to bring back some diamonds from England and so shield the Queen of France from Richelieu's intrigues. All are involved in adventures and escapades during this dash to Windsor and London, but D'Artagnan manages to make contact with the Duke of Buckingham, to whom Anne of Austria had given the jewels as a love-token. And so the Queen can wear the diamonds at the ball which Richelieu had planned as her downfall.

The evil genius of the novel is Lady de Winter, a spy in the Cardinal's service—rich, beautiful, mysterious, and malevolent—who does evil for evil's sake. She poisons D'Artagnan's mistress Constance Bonacieux; through her influence Buckingham is assassinated by John Felton. After many narrow escapes, Milady is finally cornered by the musketeers and sentenced to death. Loosely based on a minor volume of 17th-century memoirs, Gatien de Courtilz de Sandras's *Mémoires de M. d'Artagnan* (1700), *The Three Musketeers* purports, until chapter 6, to be the transcript of a 17th-century chronicle (by the Comte de la Fère, alias Athos) which Dumas has mysteriously brought to light. In fact, however, it displays many of the qualities of Romanticism and is a supreme example both of the adventure story and of the historical novel.

Like Vigny but unlike Balzac, Dumas places prominent historical figures—Louis XIII, Anne of Austria, Richelieu, Buckingham, the Duchess de Chevreuse, Tréville, Cavois—in the foreground of *The Three Musketeers*, firmly believing that these should not be overshadowed by minor characters of his own invention. Even D'Artagnan and the other three musketeers are minor historical figures, though each is about ten years older than his prototype.

In so far as Dumas has refashioned Richelieu and Buckingham according to his imagination, there is a gulf between history and historical fiction. But there is a gulf between official history and secret history likewise. The fact that *The Three Musketeers* is said to be a transcript of a contemporary chronicle is significant: the novel pretends to the status of authentic history, but history that has been overlooked; its events, through improbable, are historically true. (Its major anachronisms, few in number, are at the religious level.) Milady is unrecorded in the pages of history precisely because her missions were so successful, and because she was a spy: she is even condemned by a sort of *Vehmgericht*, or secret tribunal. Thus Dumas intermeshes all things, great and small: such is the nature of the secret history of the world. In the struggle of Richelieu and Buckingham he also, in true Romantic fashion, over-emphasizes the influence of personality upon historical events.

But Milady is gratuitously wicked, embodying the evil of melodrama and therefore set apart from the historical nexus of cause and effect. In the starkest and most simplistic terms *The Three Musketeers* is a contest of good versus evil, of simple but strong characters, of bluff, even noble, male comradeship and unfeeling feminine guile: Milady's seduction of Felton is one of the high points of the book. Moreover, it is a contest in which good eventually triumphs; a contest full of seemingly improbable turns of events (in the tradition of the Gothic novel), as when it turns out that Milady was once Athos's wife; full, too, of fine coincidences, as when

D'Artagnan recovers the diamonds in the nick of time or Lord de Winter arrives just too late to prevent Buckingham's assassination.

Dumas *père* is a master of racy, challenging dialogue and the supreme master of narrative tempo, especially the tempo of split-second success or failure. There can be no doubt that he would nowadays have made a name for himself as a scriptwriter in films and television, yet in his *Three Musketeers* and other popular masterpieces he favours a *dramatic* presentation of his story, with carefully laid settings (as in Victor Hugo's Romantic dramas) and well rounded scenes. This technique is quite unlike Balzac's more cinematic approach in *A Harlot High and Low* (*Splendeurs et misères des courtisanes*). At the same time Dumas's scenes, although dramatic, are like tableaux: they often resemble history paintings by Delaroche.

In Delaroche's manner Dumas *père* presents a clear pristine world, as when, in chapter 59 of *The Three Musketeers*, Felton stands looking out to sea as Milady sets sail from Portsmouth to France. Here are no shades of grey, but the unequivocal expression of what is vividly beautiful: as the Romantics—and especially Hugo—held, there is a beauty in ugliness. But there is a Shakespearean dimension too, the sense of a cosmic clash between good and evil, and, at the end of the work, the beginning of a restoration of the moral order. Simplistic perhaps (because melodramatic), but dramatic in every sense.

The Three Musketeers is written with immense verve and panache. Its energetic style mirrors the cult of energy that it exemplifies (in this respect Dumas shares Stendhal's outlook). Nothing detracts from the onward movement of its plot: how different this is from Balzac's didacticism! Its unflagging momentum has every appearance of being effortlessly maintained; and this appearance seems indeed to have been the reality of the matter, since the novel first appeared in daily serial form (each chapter roughly corresponding to one newspaper instalment) and Dumas was limited in the extent to which he could revise in retrospect. This greatest of all 'blood-and-thunder' novels goes far beyond Eugène Sue's achievement in *The Mysteries of Paris*, or what Balzac had achieved by way of melodrama in *The Black Sheep*.

—Donald Adamson

———

DURAS, Marguerite. Born Marguerite Donnadieu in Gia Dinh, near Saigon, French Indo-china (now Vietnam), 4 April 1914. Educated at Lycée de Saigon, baccalauréat 1931; the Sorbonne, Paris, 1933–34, degree in law and political science, 1935. Married Robert Antelme in 1939 (divorced 1946); had one son by Dionys Mascolo. Moved to France, 1932. Secretary, Ministry of Colonies, Paris, 1935–41; freelance writer, after 1943; journalist, *Observateur*; also film writer and director. Member, French Communist Party, 1940s, expelled 1950. Recipient: Cocteau prize, 1954/55; Cannes Film Festival Palme d'Or, with Gérard Jarot, 1962; Ibsen prize, 1970; Cannes Film Festival special prize, 1975; Académie française grand prize for theatre, 1983; Goncourt prize, 1984; Ritz Paris Hemingway prize, 1986. Lives in Paris.

PUBLICATIONS

Fiction

Les Impudents. 1943.
La Vie tranquille. 1944.
Un Barrage contre le Pacifique. 1950; as *The Sea Wall*, translated by Herma Briffault, 1952; as *A Sea of Troubles*, translated by Antonia White, 1953; as *A Dam Against an Ocean*, translated by Sofka Skipworth, 1966.
Le Marin de Gibraltar. 1952; as *The Sailor from Gibraltar*, translated by Barbara Bray, 1966.
Les Petits Chevaux de Tarquinia. 1953; as *The Little Horses of Tarquinia*, translated by Peter DuBerg, 1960.
Des journées entières dans les arbres (stories). 1954; as *Whole Days in the Trees and Other Stories*, translated by Anita Barrows, 1983.
Le Square. 1955; as *The Square*, translated by Sonia Pitt-Rivers and Irina Morduch, 1959, also in *Four Novels*, 1965, and in *Three Novels*, 1977.
Moderato cantabile. 1958; as *Moderato Cantabile*, translated by Richard Seaver, 1960, also in *Four Novels*, 1965.
Dix heures et demi du soir en été. 1960; as *Ten-Thirty on a Summer Night*, translated by Anne Borchardt, 1962, also in *Four Novels*, 1965, and in *Three Novels*, 1977.
L'Après-midi de Monsieur Andesmas. 1962; as *The Afternoon of Monsieur Andesmas*, translated by Anne Borchardt, with *The Rivers and Forests*, 1964, also in *Four Novels*, 1965; published separately, 1968.
Le Ravissement de Lol V. Stein. 1964; as *The Ravishing of Lol V. Stein*, translated by Richard Seaver, 1966; as *The Rapture of Lol V. Stein*, translated by Eileen Ellenbogen, 1967.
Four Novels (includes *The Square*; *Moderato Cantabile*; *Ten-Thirty on a Summer Night*; *The Afternoon of Monsieur Andesmas*), translated by Sonia Pitt-Rivers, Irina Morduch, Richard Seaver, and Anne Borchardt. 1965.
Le Vice-Consul. 1966; as *The Vice-Consul*, translated by Eileen Ellenbogen, 1968.
L'Amante anglaise. 1967; as *L'Amante Anglaise*, translated by Barbara Bray, 1968.
Détruire, dit-elle. 1969; as *Destroy, She Said*, translated by Barabara Bray, 1970; as *Destroy . . .*, translated by Bray, 1970.
Abahn Sabana David. 1970.
L'Amour. 1971.
Ah! Ernesto, with Bernard Bonhomme. 1971.
La Maladie de la mort. 1983; as *The Malady of Death*, translated by Barbara Bray, 1986.
L'Amant. 1984; as *The Lover*, translated by Barbara Bray, 1985.
Les Yeux bleus cheveux noirs. 1986; as *Blue Eyes, Black Hair*, translated by Barbara Bray, 1989.
Emily L. 1987; as *Emily L.*, translated by Barbara Bray, 1989.
La Pluie d'été. 1990; as *Summer Rain*, translated by Barbara Bray, 1992.
La Vie tranquille (selection). 1990.
L'Amant de la Chine du Nord. 1991; as *The North China Lover*, translated by Leigh Hafrey, 1992.
Yann Andrea Steiner. 1993; as *Yann Andrea Steiner*, translated by Barbara Bray, 1994.

Plays and Texts for Voices

Le Square, with Claude Martin, from her own novel (produced 1957; revised version produced 1965). In *Théâtre I*,
1965; as *The Square*, translated by Barbara Bray and Sonia Orwell, in *Three Plays*, 1967.
Hiroshima mon amour (screenplay). 1960; as *Hiroshima mon amour*, translated by Richard Seaver, 1961, also with *Une aussi longue absence*, 1966.
Les Viaducs de la Seine-et-oise (produced 1960). 1960; as *The Viaducts of the Seine-et-oise*, translated by Barbara Bray, in *Three Plays*, 1967.
Une aussi longue absence (screenplay), with Gérard Jarlot. 1961; as *Une Aussi Longue Absence*, translated by Barbara Wright, with *Hiroshima Mon Amour*, 1966.
Les Papiers d'Aspern, with Robert Antelme, from the play *The Aspern Papers* by Michael Redgrave based on the story by Henry James (produced 1961). 1970.
Miracle en Alabama, with Gérard Jarlot, from a play by William Gibson (produced 1961). With *L'Homme qui se taisait*, by Pierre Gaillot, 1962.
La Bête dans la jungle, with James Lord, from a story by Henry James (produced 1962).
Théâtre I (includes *Les Eaux et fôrets*; *Le Square*; *La Musica*). 1965.
Les Eaux et fôrets (produced 1965). In *Théâtre I*, 1965; as *The Rivers and Forests*, translated by Barbara Bray, with *The Afternoon of Monsieur Andesmas*, 1964.
La Musica (produced 1965). In *Théâtre I*, 1965; as *La Musica*, translated by Barbara Bray, in *Suzanna Andler, La Musica and L'Amante Anglaise*, 1975, also in *Four Plays*, 1992.
Des journées entières dans les arbres (produced 1965). In *Théâtre II*, 1968; as *Days in the Trees*, translated by Sonia Oswell and Barbara Bray, 1966.
Three Plays (includes *Days in the Trees*; *The Square*; *The Viaducts of Seine-et-Oise*). 1967.
Théâtre II (includes *Susanna Andler*; *Yes, peut-être*; *Le Shaga*; *Des journées entières dans les arbres*; *Un Homme est venu me voir*). 1968.
Le Shaga (produced 1968). In *Théâtre II*, 1968.
Susanna Andler (produced 1969). In *Théâtre II*, 1968; as *Suzanna Andler*, translated by Barbara Bray in, *Suzanna Andler, La Musica and L'Amante Anglaise*, 1975.
L'Amante anglaise, from her own novel (produced 1969). 1968; as *A Place Without Doors*, translated by Barbara Bray, in *Suzanna Andler, La Musica and L'Amante anglaise*, 1975.
Yes, peut-être (produced 1968). In *Théâtre II*, 1968.
La Danse de mort, d'après August Strindberg (produced 1970). In *Théâtre III*, 1984.
Nathalie Granger; La Femme du Gange (screenplays). 1973.
India Song (in English, produced 1993). 1973; as *India Song*, translated by Barbara Bray, 1976; with *Eden Cinema* (bilingual edition), 1988, also in *Four Plays*, 1992.
Home (in French), from the play by David Storey. 1973.
Suzanna Andler, La Musica and L'Amante Anglaise. 1975.
L'Éden Cinéma (produced 1977). 1977; as *Eden Cinema*, translated by Barbara Bray, with *India Song* (bilingual edition), 1988; translated by Bray, in *Four Plays*, 1992.
Le Camion (screenplay). 1977.
Le Navire Night, Césarée, Les Mains négatives, Aurélia Steiner (screenplays). 1979.
Véra Baxter; ou, Les Plages de l'Atlantique (screenplay). 1980; translated as *Vera Baxter; or, the Atlantic Beaches*, in *Drama Contemporary: France*, edited by Philippa Wehle, 1988.
L'Homme assis dans le couloir. 1980; as *The Seated Man in the Passage*, translated by Mary Lydon, in *Contemporary Literature 24*, 1983.
Agatha (screenplay). 1981.
L'Homme Atlantique (screenplay). 1982.

Savannah Bay (produced 1984). 1982; revised edition, 1983; as *Savannah Bay*, translated by Barbara Bray, in *Four Plays*, 1992.

Théâtre III (includes *La Bête dans la jungle, d'après Henry James*, with James Lord; *Les Papiers d'Aspern, d'après Henry James*, with Robert Antelme; *La Danse de mort, d'après August Strindberg*). 1984.

La Musica deuxième (produced 1985). 1985.

Four Plays (includes *La Musica; India Song; Eden Cinema; Savannah Bay*), translated by Barbara Bray. 1992.

Screenplays: *Hiroshima mon amour*, 1960; *Moderato cantabile*, with Gérard Jarlot and Peter Brook, 1960; *Une aussi longue absence* (The Long Absence), with Gérard Jarlot, 1961; *10.30 P.M. Summer*, with Jules Dassin, 1966; *La Musica*, 1966; *Les Rideaux blancs*, 1966; *Détruire, dit-elle* (*Destroy, She Said*), 1969; *Jaune le soleil*, 1971; *Nathalie Granger*, 1972; *La ragazza di Passaggio/La Femme du Gange*, 1973; *Ce que savait Morgan*, with others, 1974; *India Song*, 1975; *Des journées entières dans les arbres*, 1976; *Son nom de Venises dans Calcutta désert*, 1976; *Baxter-Véra Baxter*, 1976; *Le Camion*, 1977; *Le Navire Night*, 1978; *Césarée; Les Mains négatives; Aurélia Steiner; L'Homme assis dans le couloir*, 1980; *Agatha et les lectures illimitées*, 1981; *L'Homme Atlantique*, 1981; *Dialogue de Rome*, 1982; *Les Enfants*, 1985.

Television Play: *Sans merveille*, with Gérard Jarlot, 1964.

Other

Les Parleuses (interviews), with Xavière Gauthier. 1974; as *Woman to Woman*, translated by Katherine Jensen, 1987.

Étude sur l'oeuvre littéraire, théâtrale, et cinématographique de Marguerite Duras, with Jacques Lacan and Maurice Blanchot. 1975.

Territoires du féminin, with Marcelle Marini. 1977.

Les Lieux de Marguerite Duras (interview), with Michelle Porte. 1978.

L'Été 80. 1980.

Les Yeux ouverts. In *Cahiers du Cinema* (special Duras issue), 312–313, June 1980.

Outside: Papiers d'un jour. 1981; revised edition, 1984; as *Outside: Selected Writings*, translated by Arthur Goldhammer, 1986.

Marguerite Duras à Montréal (interviews and lectures), edited by Suzanne Lamy and André Roy. 1981.

La Douleur. 1985; as *La Douleur*, translated by Barbara Bray, 1986; as *The War*, translated by Bray, 1986.

La Pute de la côte normande. 1986.

La Vie matérielle: Marguerite Duras parle à Jérôme Beaujour. 1987; as *Practicalities: Marguerite Duras Speaks to Jérôme Beaujour*, translated by Barbara Bray, 1990.

Les Yeux verts. 1987; as *Green Eyes*, translated by Carol Barko, 1990.

Marguerite Duras (interview). 1987.

Écrire (autobiography). 1993.

Translator, *La Mouette*, by Anton Chekhov. 1985.

*

Critical Studies: *Marguerite Duras* by Alfred Cismaru, 1971; *Marguerite Duras* by François Barat and Joel Farges, 1975; *Marguerite Duras: Moderato cantabile* by David Coward, 1981; *Alienation and Absence in the Novels of Marguerite Duras* by Carol J. Murphy, 1982; *Marguerite Duras* by Mieheline Tison-Braun, 1985; *Marguerite Duras* by Jean Pierrot, 1986; 'Space Invasions: Voice-Overs in Works by Samuel Beckett and Marguerite Duras' by Mary K. Martin, in *The Theatrical Space* edited by James Redmond, 1987; *Marguerite Duras: Writing on the Body* by Sharon Willis, 1987; *Remains to Be Seen: Essays on Marguerite Duras* edited by Sanford Ames, 1988; *L'Autre Scène: Le Théâtre de Marguerite Duras* by Liliane Papin, 1988; *Marguerite Duras* edited by Ilma Rakusa, 1988; *The Other Woman: Feminity in the Work of Marguerite Duras* by Trista Selous, 1988; 'Women Writing Across Purpose: The Theater of Marguerite Duras and Nathalie Sarraute' by Janice B. Gross, in *Modern Drama*, 32, 1989; *Marguerite Duras: Fascinating Vision and Narrative Cure* by Deborah N. Glassman, 1991; *Forgetting and Marguerite Duras* by Carol Hofmann, 1991; *Écriture feminine et violence: Une étude de Marguerite Duras* by Janine Ricouart, 1991; *Du rythme au sens: Une lecture de 'L'Amour' de Marguerite Duras* by Claire Cerasi, 1992; *Welcome Unreason: A Study of 'Madness' in the Novels of Marguerite Duras* by Raynelle Udris, 1992; *Women and Discourse in the Fiction of Marguerite Duras: Love, Legends, Language* by Susan D. Cohen, 1993; *Marguerite Duras: Apocalyptic Desires* by Leslie Hill, 1993; *Le Ravissement de Lol V. Stein and L'Amant* by Renate Gunther, 1994.

*   *   *

Marguerite Duras's early narratives present young women struggling with their own identity within the traditional aesthetic of third-person (*Les Impudents*) and first-person (Françou in *La Vie tranquille* [The Quiet Life]) narrative perspectives. In both novels women are trying to put their lives together by struggling for independence from their families. Men appear to offer redemptive possibilities through marriage and fatherhood. However, promises are broken, and the men are not there when the women need them. This conflict between men and women who are tied by family or impossible love affairs recurs throughout Duras's work and engenders pain and suffering in the women's and sometimes the men's lives.

Le Square (The Square) shows the mature stage of Duras's narrative style. An encounter and a separation between a man and a woman in a public square are examined through their dialogue. Duras's allusive style, that reveals compassion towards the characters, according to Frank Towne, is henceforward characteristic of her fiction, plays, and films. Many of her narrators are obsessed with drinking as a means of forgetting their problems. The zigzag narrative style, as Carol Murphy describes Duras's mature writing, is evocative of characters who wander aimlessly through life, attracted to other erotically, passionately, and violently while trying to piece together their own past and present.

Duras's filmmaking career began at about the same time as her adoption of the zigzag style. The plots and techniques of her motion pictures, her plays, and her novels are intertwined. Her script for Alain Resnais's *Hiroshima mon amour* contains many references to the intersecting influences of forgetting and remembering in the narrative process. The meeting of the Orient and the Occident, in this case a French actress and a Japanese businessman, is paradigmatic of her work. *Un Barrage contre le Pacifique* (A Sea of Troubles), *Le Vice-Consul* (The Vice-Consul), *India Song*, *L'Amant* (The Lover), *Emily L.*, and *L'Amant de la Chine du Nord* (The North China Lover) explore the impossible meeting and unavoidable separation not only of men and women but also of other profoundly different orientations, such as the young and old (*L'Après-midi de Monsieur Andesmas* [*The After-noon of Monsieur Andesmas*]), mothers and daughters, hus-bands and wives (*La Douleur* [*The War*]), brothers and sisters (*Agatha*), as well as those between a prostitute and a homo-sexual in *Les Yeux bleus cheveux noirs* (*Blue Eyes, Black Hair*) and between races (*The Lover*; *The North China Lover*).

Mutilation and fragmentation are connected activities of the memory and narration in the numerous stories about women as lovers and as mothers. The film techniques of *découpage* and frame-sequencing promote this sense of dis-connectedness among characters in the stories. Insecure mothers continue their cycle of insecurity by threatening their daughters (Françou) with prearranged marriages (Maud in *Les Impudents*), and abandonment (the beggar woman in *The Vice-Consul*), resulting in unwanted pregnancies (Maud), wandering (Anne in *Moderato cantabile*) and general schi-zophrenia (Lol in *Le Ravissement de Lol V. Stein* [*The Ravishing of Lol V. Stein*]). Duras's women become invigor-ated by rejection to desire what they do not have. The story of Lol V. Stein, a saga known as the India Cycle, still continues in Duras's work as if to signify that the violence done in women's lives cannot be encompassed and closed.

The slow repeating cycle of women's insecurity begins with abandonment (Lol V. Stein) and leads to crimes such as murder (the husband in the café in *Moderato cantabile*), self-immolation (Claire's murder of her twin self, Marie-Thérèse, in *L'Amante anglaise*, and incest (Joseph and Suzanne in *A Sea of Troubles*). Alissa's prophetic word 'destroy' in *Détruire, dit-elle* (*Destroy, She Said*), becomes the rallying cry for women who want to be in control of their lives. While the sea threatens the livelihood of the family in *A Sea of Troubles* and devours both brother and sister in *Agatha*, it is the sea-like rhythm of Duras's narratives, oscillating between silence and disconnected words, forgetting and remembering, that yearns for the impossible desire and produces an incantation to the tension between those who are powerful and those who are denied. This incantation is often lost in the haze of music (Indiana's Song in *The Vice-Consul*; Diabelli's sonata in *Moderato cantabile*).

These themes could be Freudian or Lacanian, but most of all they represent women in the trauma of searching for their identities and trying to constitute their stories from their past and towards their imaginary future. The strategic use of silence gives the readers and/or spectators a space in which to put together lives that are fragmented and typically destroyed by past experiences. Duras herself refuses an intellectual or essentialist reading of her work that allows a feminist or any other community-orientated meaning. Instead, the prototypi-cal character of Anne (Anna in *Le Marin de Gibraltar* [*The Sailor from Gibraltar*]; Anne-Marie Stretter in *The Vice-Consul*, *Lol V. Stein* and *India Song*; Anne Desbaresdes in *Moderato cantabile*) wanders, as if in mourning, object of a desire that is constantly frustrated and misdirected. Anne's own desire returns in attempts to retell her story, many times embedded with lies and half-truths. One can never 'get it right'. The pleasure is in the piecing together of a dizzying, hazy state of imagination.

—Roland A. Champagne

DÜRRENMATT, Friedrich. Born in Konolfingen, near Berne, Switzerland, 5 January 1921. Educated at Gross-höchstetten school; Freies Gymnasium and Humboldtianum, Bern; University of Zurich, one term; University of Bern, 1941–45. Married 1) Lotti Geissler in 1946 (died 1983), one son and two daughters; 2) Charlotte Kerr in 1984. Drama critic, *Die Weltwoche*, Zurich, 1951–53; co-director, Basle Theatres, 1968–69; co-owner, *Zürcher Sonntags-Journal*, 1969–71; writer-in-residence, University of Southern California, Los Angeles, 1981; travelled to the USSR, 1964 and 1967, Israel, 1974, Greece and South America, 1983–84, and to Egypt, 1985, and the USA. Also television director. Recipient: City of Berne prize, 1954, 1979; Radio Play prize (Berlin), 1957; Italia prize, for radio play, 1958; Schiller prize (Mannheim), 1959; New York Drama Critics Circle award, 1959; Schiller prize (Switzerland), 1960; Grillparzer prize, 1968; Kanton Berne prize, 1969; Welsh Arts Council International Writers prize, 1976; Buber-Rosenzweig medal, 1977; Zuckmayer medal, 1984; Austrian State prize, 1984; Bavarian literature prize, 1985; Büchner prize, 1986; Schiller prize (Stuttgart), 1986; Ernst Robert Curtis prize, for essays, 1989. Honorary doctorate: Temple University, Phila-delphia, 1969; Hebrew University, Jerusalem, 1977; Univer-sity of Nice, 1977; University of Neuchâtel, 1981; University of Zurich, 1983. Honorary Fellow, Modern Language Association (USA). *Died 14 December 1990.*

PUBLICATIONS

Plays

Es steht geschrieben (produced 1947). 1947; revised version, as *Die Wiedertäufer* (produced 1967), 1969.
Der Blinde (produced 1948). 1960; revised edition, 1965.
Romulus der Grosse (produced 1949). 1956; revised version (produced 1957), 1958; translated as *Romulus*, 1962; as *Romulus the Great*, translated by Gerhard Nellhaus, in *Four Plays*, 1964.
Die Ehe des Herrn Mississippi (produced 1952). 1952; revised version, 1957; film version, 1961; as *The Marriage of Mr Mississippi*, translated by Michael Bullock, in *Four Plays*, 1964.
Ein Engel kommt nach Babylon (produced 1953). 1954; re-vised version (produced 1957), 1958; as *An Angel Comes to Babylon*, translated by Wiliam McElwee, in *Four Plays*, 1964.
Der Besuch der alten Dame (produced 1956). 1956; film version, 1963; as *The Visit*, translated by Maurice Valency, 1958; also translated by Patrick Bowles, 1962.
Nächtliches Gespräch mit einem verachteten Menschen (radio play). 1957; as *Conversation at Night with a Despised Character*, n.d.
Komödien I–III. 3 vols., 1957–70.
Das Unternehmen der Wega (radio play). 1958.
Frank V, music by Paul Burkhard (produced 1959). 1960.
Der Prozess um des Esels Schatten (radio play). 1959.
Stranitzky und der Nationalheld (radio play). 1959.
Abendstunde im Spätherbst (radio play; also produced on stage 1959). 1959; as *Episode on an Autumn Evening*, translated by Myron B. Gubitz, 1959; as *Incident at Twilight*, in *Postwar German Theatre*, edited by Michael Benedikt and George E. Wellwarth, 1968.
Der Doppelgänger (radio play). 1960.
Herkules und der Stall des Augias (radio play; also produced on stage 1963). 1960; translated as *Hercules and the Augean Stables*, n.d.

Die Panne, from his own novel (radio play: also televised 1957; produced on stage 1979). 1961; revised version, 1979.
Gesammelte Hörspiele (includes *Abendstunde im Spätherbst*; *Der Doppelgänger*; *Herkules und der Stall des Augias*; *Nächtliches Gespräch mit einem verachteten Menschen*; *Die Panne*; *Der Prozess um des Esels Schatten*; *Stranitzky und der Nationalheld*; *Das Unternehem der Wega*). 1961.
Die Physiker (produced 1962). 1962; television version, 1963; as *The Physicists*, adapted by Maurice Valency, 1958; translated by James Kirkup, 1963.
Four Plays 1957–62 (includes *Romulus the Great*; *The Marriage of Mr Mississippi*; *An Angel Comes to Babylon*; *The Physicists*), translated by Gerhard Nellhaus and others. 1964.
Der Meteor (produced 1966). 1966; as *The Meteor*, translated by James Kirkup, 1973.
König Johann, from the play by Shakespeare (produced 1968). 1968.
Play Strindberg: Totentanz nach August Strindberg (produced 1969). 1969; as *Play Strindberg: The Dance of Death*, translated by James Kirkup, 1972.
Titus Andronicus, from the play by Shakespeare (produced 1970). 1970.
Porträt eines Planeten (produced 1970; revised version, produced 1971). 1970.
Urfaust, from the play by Goethe (produced 1970). 1980.
Woyzeck, from the play by Büchner (produced 1972). 1980.
Der Mitmacher (produced 1973). 1973; enlarged edition, *Der Mitmacher-Ein Komplex* (includes notes, essays, narratives), 1976.
Die Frist (produced 1977). 1977.
Achterloo (produced 1983). 1984.
Achterloo IV (produced 1988).

Screenplays: *Es geschah am hellichten Tag* (*It Happened in Broad Daylight*), 1960; *Die Ehe des Herrn Mississippi*, 1961; *Der Besuch der alten Dame*, 1963.

Radio Plays: *Der Prozess um des Esels Schatten*, 1951; *Stranitzky und der Nationalheld*, 1952; *Nächtliches Gespräch mit einem verachteten Mensch*, 1952; *Herkules und der Stall des Augias*, 1954; *Das Unternehmen der Wega*, 1954; *Die Panne*, 1956; *Abendstunde im Spätherbst*, 1958; *Der Doppelgänger*, 1961.

Fiction

Pilatus. 1949.
Der Nihilist. 1950; reprinted as *Die Falle*.
Der Richter und sein Henker. 1952; as *The Judge and His Hangman*, translated by Cyrus Brooks, 1954.
Die Stadt: Prose 1–4. 1952.
Das Bild des Sisyphos. 1952.
Der Verdacht. 1953; as *The Quarry*, translated by Eva H. Morreale, 1961.
Grieche sucht Griechin. 1955; as *Once a Greek. . .*, translated by Richard and Clara Winston, 1965.
Das Versprechen: Requiem auf den Kriminalroman. 1958; as *The Pledge*, translated by Richard and Clara Winston, 1959.
Die Panne: Eine noch mögliche Geschichte. 1960; as *Traps*, translated by Richard and Clara Winston, 1960; as *A Dangerous Game*, translated by Richard and Clara Winston, 1960.
Der Sturz. 1971.
The Judge and His Hangman; The Quarry: Two Hans Barlach Mysteries, translated by George Stade. 1983.

Minotaurus: Eine Ballade, illustrated by Dürrenmatt. 1985.
Dürrenmatt: His Five Novels (includes *The Judge and His Hangman*; *The Quarry*; *Once a Greek*; *A Dangerous Game*; *The Pledge*). 1985.
Justiz. 1985; as *The Execution of Justice*, translated by John E. Woods, 1989.
Der Auftrag; oder, Vom Beobachten des Beobachters der Beobachter. 1986; as *The Assignment; or, On Observing of the Observer of the Observers*, translated by Joel Agee, 1988.
Durcheinanderthal. 1989.

Other

Theaterprobleme. 1955; as *Problems on the Theatre*, translated by Gerhard Nellhaus, in *Four Plays*, 1964, and with *The Marriage of Mr Mississippi*, 1966.
Friedrich Schiller: Rede (address). 1960.
Der Rest ist Dank (addresses), with Werner Weber. 1961.
Die Heimat im Plakat: Ein Buch für Schweizer Kinder (drawings). 1963.
Theater-Schriften und Reden, edited by Elisabeth Brock-Sulzer. 2 vols., 1966–72; translated in part as *Writings on Theatre and Drama*, edited by H.M. Waidson, 1976.
Monstervortrag über Gerechtigkeit und Recht. 1968.
Sätze aus Amerika. 1970.
Zusammenhänge: Essay über Israel. 1976.
Gespräch mit Heinz Ludwig Arnold. 1976.
Frankfurter Rede. 1977.
Lesebuch. 1978.
Bilder und Zeichnungen, edited by Christian Strich. 1978.
Albert Einstein: Ein Vortrag. 1979.
Werkausgabe. 30 vols., 1980–86.
Stoffe 1–3: Winterkrieg in Tibet, Mondfinsternis, Der Rebell. 1981.
Plays and Essays, edited by Volkmar Sander. 1982.
Denken mit Dürrenmatt, edited by Daniel Keel. 1982.
Die Welt als Labyrinth, 1982.
Rollenspiele: Protokoll einer fiktiven Inszenierung und 'Achterloo III' (includes text of play *Achterloo III*). 1986.
Versuche. 1988.
Midas; oder, Die Schwarze Leinwand. 1991.
Kants Hoffnung. 1991.
Gedankenfuge. 1992.

*

Bibliography: *Friedrich Dürrenmatt Bibliografie* by Johanes Hansel, 1968; *Friedrich Dürrenmatt* by Gerhard B. Knapp, 1980.

Critical Studies: *Friedrich Dürrenmatt* by Murray B. Peppard, 1969; *Friedrich Dürrenmatt* by Armin Arnold, 1972; *To Heaven and Back: The New Morality in the Plays of Friedrich Dürrenmatt* by Kurt J. Fickert, 1972; *Friedrich Dürrenmatt* by H.L. Arnold, 2 vols., 1976–77; *Dürrenmatt: A Study in Plays, Prose, and Theory* by Timo Tiusanen, 1977; *Dürrenmatt: A Study of His Plays* by Urs Jenny, 1978; *Friedrich Dürrenmatt: A Collection of Critical Essays* edited by Bodo Fritzen and H.F. Taylor, 1979; *The Theatre of Dürrenmatt: A Study in the Possibility of Freedom*, 1980, and *Dürrenmatt: Reinterpretation in Retrospect*, 1990, both by Kenneth S. Whitton; *Play Dürrenmatt* edited by Moshe Lazar, 1983; *Dürrenmatt* by H. Goertz, 1987; *Friedrich Dürrenmatt* by L. Tantow, 1992.

* * *

Born in Switzerland in 1921, Friedrich Dürrenmatt occupied a major place among writers in German since the *succès de scandale* of his first play, *Es steht geschrieben*, in Zurich in 1947.

His witty, provocative, grotesque caricatures of his fellow human-beings seemed to mirror the chaotic post-World War II conditions and ensured his plays and prose works a permanent place on the best-seller lists. Dürrenmatt wrote of the human condition, of the shifting moral values in government and politics, of the loosening of familial and societal bonds, and of the despair of 'the little man', suffering at the hands of well-organized, tyrannical bureaucracies. His shafted barbs of humour were directed at the 'bringing-down', a true *reductio ad absurdum*, of the pompous and the entrepreneurial, the over-rich and the over-powerful.

His vehicle was 'die Komödie', not the light-hearted, frothy social comedy of the western world, of Molière and Noël Coward, but that savage, grotesque, satirical comedy deriving ultimately from the satires of Aristophanes, and often presented in the farcical form of the medieval 'commedia dell'arte'. Dürrenmatt's reputation rests on his two great international stage successes, *Der Besuch der alten Dame* (*The Visit*) and *Die Physiker* (*The Physicists*), presented throughout the world, and on his short novels, e.g., *Der Richter und sein Henker* (*The Judge and His Hangman*) and *Die Panne* (*A Dangerous Game*), which have been studied in schools and universities worldwide.

The Visit deserves its phenomenal success because of the brilliant simplicity of what Dürrenmatt calls the 'Einfall', that 'germ-idea' which lies behind and illuminates a play—here philosophically effective and scenically and dramatically masterly: an aged grotesque, Claire Zachanassian, once driven out of her little village because she had been made pregnant by the village shop-keeper, Alfred Ill, returns to seek revenge. Now the richest woman in the world, she will give the ailing village 'eine Milliarde' (a billion) if one of them will kill Alfred. The hypocrisy of the villagers as they declare their firm resolve to stand by Alfred (now in the running for mayor) and at the same time crowd into his shop to buy goods on credit in anticipation of the flood of gold, has been taken to be a symbolical attack on the then prevailing western capitalist values—but Dürrenmatt has never flailed exclusively one side. In *The Physicists*, Möbius, the brilliant scientist who has fled into an asylum to bury with him his potentially dangerous, revolutionary discovery, finds that his two 'fellow-patients' are in fact USA and Soviet agents bent on extracting his secrets.

Dürrenmatt attacked both sides of the Iron Curtain again in two biting prose works, *Der Sturz* [The Fall], a story about 'a' Politburo, and *Sätze aus Amerika* [Sentences from America], written after a visit to the United States to receive a doctorate which showed that his target was cruel bureaucratization and the denial of freedom to *all* sorts and conditions of men.

After his gradual withdrawal from the stage, Dürrenmatt busied himself with political and philosophical treatises—he was one of the few Europeans to support Israel in the Yom Kippur war—and with his grotesque paintings. Dürrenmatt's withdrawal from the public gaze turned out to be more than temporary; he turned instead to another 'pulpit' (as Lessing did), the reflective, philosophical essay, in which he developed the theme of the helpless, hapless Minotaur condemned in his mirror-lined loneliness, representing symbolically the fate of those condemned to be misunderstood while they struggle against the folly and the inhumanity of man to man. When Dürrenmatt died in 1990, he left a rich legacy of witty yet deeply philosophical works whose importance has yet to be fully recognized in the world of letters. The Nachlass bequeathed to the Swiss National Archive in Berne may help scholars to interpret this legacy for the world.

—Kenneth S. Whitton

THE PHYSICISTS (Die Physiker)
Play by Friedrich Dürrenmatt, 1962.

Dürrenmatt's two-act comedy is played out in a villa which is part of a 'private sanatorium'—a euphemism for a lunatic asylum which houses three mad physicists. The single set for the play is the drawing-room of the villa with the doors to the rooms of the three inmates opening off it. The play opens with the dead body of a nurse lying on stage and the police investigating the circumstances of her death. She has been strangled by one of the physicists, who thinks he is Einstein. Some three months earlier another of the inmates, who believes himself to be Sir Isaac Newton, had murdered a nurse. At the end of the first act the third patient, Johann Wilhelm Möbius, who apparently suffers from the delusion that King Solomon appears to him in visions, strangles his nurse when she tells him that she loves him and that she has obtained permission from the psychiatrist in charge, Fräulein Doktor Mathilde von Zahndt, for them to leave the sanatorium and get married.

There are several hints that, perhaps, all is not quite what it seems. Newton confides to the police inspector that he is not mad; he is only pretending to be Newton in order not confuse poor Einstein because he, Newton, is really Einstein. When the inspector reports this to the psychiatrist she assures him that Newton does, after all, believe he is Newton and that, in any case, it is *she* who determines who her patients think they are.

Möbius takes leave of his wife and three sons. She has divorced him and married a widowed missionary with six sons and has come to say goodbye before going off with her new husband to a post in the Marianas Islands. At first Möbius appears hesitant and confused, but he then has a brainstorm; he turns over a table, climbs onto it, imagines it is a space-ship, and declaims a new Song of Solomon which paints a picture of a desolate, lifeless, radioactive universe. When his nurse tells him he has been putting on an act he agrees; he has done so in order to make it easier for his family to abandon him without feeling guilty.

The purpose of these odd goings-on is quite unclear. What is certain is that there is a high degree of artifice in the action. This artifice is underlined in the beginning of the second act—which repeats almost exactly the beginning of the first: the police are investigating another strangling. There is one difference: the inspector, who had earlier been frustrated, is now resigned, even relieved. There is nothing he can do. In an asylum all normal rules are suspended. He departs with an assurance from the psychiatrist that male attendants will be installed to supervise the homicidal patients.

The physicists are left alone. Newton informs Möbius that he is not, after all, Newton—or even Einstein—but the secret agent of a superpower which believes Möbius to be a scientific genius; his mission is to recruit Möbius into the service of his country. Einstein joins them and indicates that he is the agent of a rival superpower with exactly the same mission. Möbius confesses that there has been method in his madness too. He has chosen to be locked away in the asylum because he fears the practical applications of his theoretical discoveries; he has played the fool in order to protect the world from their potentially destructive consequences. The three then engage in a debate about their responsibilities as scientists. Möbius appeals to the principles of logic and reason and succeeds in persuading the other two that his investigations should be kept secret: 'We have to take back our knowledge and I have taken it back.' In a spirit of noble self-sacrifice they resume the masks of madness and prepare to live out the rest of their lives in the asylum.

So, it seems, the play moves to a solemn and serious climax. But there is a final twist. The psychiatrist returns and reveals that she has had Möbius drugged every night and his notes copied. She is now about to exploit his discoveries and, with her newly established police force headed by the male attendants, take over the world. The physicists will remain locked away as her prisoners.

The Physicists is a carefully constructed box of tricks, a Chinese puzzle of a play. It repeatedly leads the audience up the garden path and arouses expectations which are not fulfilled. It invokes the conventions of the detective thriller, the drawing-room comedy, and the morality play. But ultimately it fits into no neat category.

It is a play which depends crucially on the immediacy of theatrical performance. Its twists and turns are supported by a variety of stage effects and dramatic images which help to sustain a pervasive note of grotesque humour. It would be impossible to enumerate all the effects, but these are typical examples: while a nurse is strangled we hear Einstein playing classical music on his violin; the psychiatrist has a hump, a physical deformity which manifests her mental and moral deformity; the two secret agents draw guns on each other, a visual image of the balance of power; the scientists conduct their earnest debate over a sumptuous meal; when Dr von Zahndt reveals that she knows their true identities the three inmates are caught in the beam of searchlights, their pretences glaringly exposed.

The lunatic asylum clearly stands as a metaphor of the world in which we live. In Dürrenmatt's work it is a world governed by Sod's Law, a world where the most carefully laid plans achieve the very opposite of their intention, where reason is forever defeated by unreason. The only certainty is that the unexpected and unpredictable will happen.

The final image of the play is that of Möbius withdrawing into the role of King Solomon. As Einstein once more plays his violin, Möbius's last words are:

Now the cities over which I ruled are dead, the kingdom that was given into my keeping is deserted: only a blue shimmering wilderness. And somewhere, round a small yellow, nameless star there circles, pointlessly, everlastingly, the radioactive earth. I am Solomon. I am Solomon. I am Solomon. I am poor King Solomon.

The Physicists is a comedy of despair, the exuberant theatrical expression of a deeply ironic, apocalyptic vision.

—B. Ashbrook

THE VISIT (Der Besuch der alten Dame)
Play by Friedrich Dürrenmatt, 1956.

Dürrenmatt's three-act tragicomedy *The Visit* was written in 1956 and had its premiere the same year in Zurich. The plot is set in the run-down city of Güllen, somewhere in Europe, whose inhabitants await eagerly the return of their 'native', the billionairess Claire Zachanassian. She represents their only hope of getting out of their economic malaise. Upon her arrival, she demands the murder of her former lover Alfred Ill as the condition for providing financial assistance. 45 years earlier, she had been forced to leave the town in disgrace, because Ill, who had made her pregnant, denied his fatherhood. She worked her way first through bordellos, then through several marriages, amassing a huge fortune of which she will give the inhabitants a part if Ill is murdered. The mayor and the city first reject Claire's offer, but Claire waits because she knows that the people will eventually agree to it. Slowly, the support for Ill weakens. Ill, who had hopes of becoming the mayor of Güllen, sees himself deserted by everyone and also realizes that fleeing the city would not save his life from the all-powerful Claire, the 'Goddess of Fate', whose life has only one purpose: to seek vengeance for the terrible wrong that has been done her. Ill, who at first denies his guilt, finally accepts it. At a town meeting, Ill's murder is agreed upon by the inhabitants, and Ill accepts his death sentence. This is done through such masterful use of multi-layered language that even the attending reporters and the rest of the world do not realize the inhumanity committed in their presence. Ill is murdered not by one person, but symbolically by the group so that the guilt is borne by all. The play concludes in a perverse manner with a Sophoclean chorus praising the greatness of man.

Since its publication and premiere this play, considered by many to be Dürrenmatt's finest, has been translated into numerous languages and interpreted in conflicting ways. Some critics consider *The Visit* a religious play, because Ill, after some inner struggle, accepts his guilt and makes peace with God and himself. Others emphasize the political aspect, seeing in the corruption by money and material goods a situation similar to that after World War II where the Marshall Plan was created to rebuild the German economy. Critics have connected *The Visit* with many literary traditions and writers. Some interpret *The Visit* as a parody of Greek tragedy or the classical German drama, and see a relationship to Mark Twain's story 'The Man that Corrupted Hadleyburg', Ödön von Horváth's *Judgement Day*, Curt Goetz's *The House in Montevideo*, Max Frisch's *Andorra*, or some of Franz Kafka's works. Claire is sometimes associated with Medea, Venus, or Mao's widow Qiang Qing. The variety of interpretations and associations with other works led Murray B. Peppard to the conclusion: 'Even the most exhaustive critique cannot raise all the possibilities of interpretation or explore all the lines of suggestibility contained in the play, and the lengthiest commentary cannot provide adequate compensation for the pleasure of new discoveries that can be made by every new reading of the text' (*Friedrich Dürrenmatt*, 1969). The comprehensive nature of this play was noted by E. Speidel: 'In short, when all these interpretations are added up, one cannot help but conclude that Dürrenmatt's play must embody, in three short acts, the whole tradition of drama from Sophocles to Brecht'.

The Visit is indeed a complex play. It encompasses three sub-plots: Claire's return to Güllen in order to buy justice for a crime she cannot forget; the relationship between Ill and the inhabitants of Güllen; and finally the change in Ill himself. Dürrenmatt handles the language in such a way that all sub-plots are associated. Furthermore, language reveals, by contrasting words and deeds, the real intent of the Gülleners. In reality, they negate the values they seem to affirm. An example is the scene in which Ill, fearing for his life, gets seeming moral support from the inhabitants who buy goods from him on credit:

Man One: We'll stick by you. We'll stick by *our* Ill. Come what may.

The Two Women (munching chocolate):   Come what may, Mr Ill, come what may.

Man Two: Remember, you're the town's most popular personality.

Man One: Our most important personality.

Man One: You'll be elected Mayor in spring.

Man One: It's dead certain.

The Two Women (munching chocolate):   Dead certain, Mr Ill, dead certain.

Man Two: Brandy.

(translated by Patrick Bowles)

Through the repetition of certain words or phrases having more than one referent, the hollowness of the word, or language, becomes evident. With the exception of Claire, the characters use language not as a means of honest communication but to conceal thoughts; the Apollonian surface becomes transparent and the Dionysian element in man is laid bare.

Dürrenmatt's message seems to be that salvation lies not with the collective or the accumulation of wealth at the expense of moral values but with the soul-searching of the individual who accepts moral responsibility for his deeds. Justice, one of the key words and elements in this play, has a different meaning for everyone: for Claire it is personal vengeance, for the people of Güllen it means accumulation of wealth, for Ill it is a just atonement for a crime which he committed not only against Claire but against humanity.

—Gerd K. Schneider

E

EÇA DE QUEIRÓS, José Maria de. Born in Póvoa de Varzim, Portugal, 25 November 1845. Educated at Colégio da Lapa, Oporto, 1855–60; Faculty of Law, Coimbra, 1861–66. Married Emília de Castro Pamplona (Resende) in 1886; one daughter and one son. Advocate in Lisbon, 1867–70; visited Egypt, and attended the inauguration of the Suez Canal, 1869; appointed administrator of the Council of Leiria, 1870; passed diplomatic service examinations, 1870; Portuguese consul in Havana, Cuba (then part of the Spanish Antilles), 1872–74; travelled through Canada, the USA, and Central America, 1873; consul to Great Britain, in Newcastle-upon-Tyne, 1874–78, and Bristol, 1878–88; consul in Paris, 1888–1900. Contributor, *Gazeta na Portugal*, from 1866, and *Gazeta de Notícias*, Rio de Janeiro, from 1878; editor, *Revista de Portugal*, 1889; also contributed to *Diário de Notícias, Revista Ocidental, A Actualidade, Diário de Portugal, O Atlântico, Revue Univèrselle Internationale* (Paris), *Réporter, Revista Moderna* (Paris). *Died 16 August 1900.*

PUBLICATIONS

Collections

Obras. 1986.
Obras completas [Resomnia Edition]. 20 vols., 1988.

Fiction

O crime do Padre Amaro. 1875; revised edition, 1880; as *The Sin of Father Amaro*, translated by Ned Flanagan, 1962.
O primo Basílio. 1878; revised editions, 1878, 1887; as *The Dragon's Teeth*, translated by Mary J. Serrano, 1889; as *Cousin Bazilio*, translated by Roy Campbell, 1953.
O mandarim. 1880; edited by Helena Cidade Moura, 1969; as *The Mandarin*, in *The Mandarin and Other Stories*, 1965.
O mistério da Estrada de Sintra. 1884.
A relíquia. 1887; as *The Relic*, translated by Aubrey F. Bell, 1954.
Os Maias. 1888; as *The Maias*, translated by Patricia McGowan Pinheiro and Ann Stevens, 1965.
A ilustre casa de Ramires. 1900; as *The Illustrious House of Ramires*, translated by Ann Stevens, 1968.
A cidade e as serras. 1901; as *The City and the Mountains*, translated by Roy Campbell, 1955.
Contos. 1902; edited by Luiz Fagundes Duarte and Joaquim Mendes, 1989.
Prosas bárbaras. 1903.
The Sweet Miracle, translated by E. Prestage. 1905; also translated by A. de Alberti, 1913; Henry Gaffney, 1928.
Our Lady of the Pillar, translated by E. Prestage. 1906.
Perfection, translated by Charles Marriott. 1923.
Alves & ca.. 1925; as *Alves & Co.*, translated by Robert M. Fedorchek, 1988.
O conde de Abranhos; A Catastrophe, edited by José Maria de Eça de Queirós the Younger. 1925.

A capital. 1925.
The Mandarin and Other Stories, translated by Richard Franko Goldman. 1965.
A tragédia da Rua das Flores. 1980.
The Yellow Sofa and Three Portraits, translated by John Vetch, Richard Franko Goldman, and Luís Marques. 1993.

Play

Filidor, from a play by José Bouchardy (produced 1866).

Other

As farpas (articles), with Ramalho Ortigão. 42 vols., 1871–83; edited by David Corazzi, 13 vols., 1887–90.
Antero de Quental—In Memoriam, with others. 1896.
A correspondência de Fradique Mendes: memorias e notas. 1900.
Dicionário de Milagres . . . outros escriptos dispersos. 1900.
Prosas bárbaras (articles), edited by Jaime Batalha Reis. 1903.
Cartas de Inglaterra. 1905; as *Letters from England*, translated by Ann Stevens, 1970.
Ecos de Paris. 1905.
Cartas familiares e bilhetes de Paris (1893–1896). 1907.
Notas contemporâneas. 1909.
Últimas páginas: S. Cristávão, S.^{to} Onofre, S. Frei Gil. 1912.
Correspondência. 1925.
O Egipto: notas de viagem. 1926.
Cartas inéditas de Fradique Mendes e mais páginas esquecidas. 1929.
Novas cartas inéditas de Eça de Queiroz a Ramalho Ortigão. 1940.
Crónicas de Londres. 1944.
Cartas. 1945.
Eça de Queiroz entre os seus. 1949.
Cartas de Eça de Queiroz aos seus editores Genelioux e Lugan (1887–1894). 1961.
Páginas esquecidas, edited by Alberto Machado da Rosa. 5 vols., 1965–66.
Eça de Queiroz e Jaime Batalha Reis: Cartas e Recordações do Seu Convívio. 1966.
Folhas soltas (travel writing). 1966.
Páginas de journalismo. 2 vols., 1980.
Correspondência. 2 vols., 1983.
Cartas inéditas. 1987.

Editor, with José Sarmento and Henrique Marques, *O almanaque enciclopédico para 1896* [*1897*]. 2 vols., 1896–97.

Translator, *As minas de Salomão*, by Henry Rider Haggard. 1891.

*

Bibliography: *Lengua y estilo de Eça de Queiroz: Bibliografía queriociana sistemática e anotada* by Ernesto Guerra da Cal, 6 vols., 1975–84.

Critical Studies: *Eça, Fialho, Aquilino* by C. da Costa, 1923; *Estudos críticos* by Castelo Branco Chaves, 1932; *História literária de Eça de Queiroz* by Álvaro Lins, 1939, revised edition, 1964; *Eça de Queiroz* by Antônio Cabral, 1936; *Eça de Queiroz* by Clovis Ramalhette, 1939; *O realismo de Eça de Queiroz e a sua expressão artística* by Manuel de Paiva Boléo, 1941; *Eça de Queiroz: o homem e o artista* by João Gaspar Simões, 1945; *Eça de Queiroz: uma estética da ironia* by Mário Sacramento, 1945; *Eça de Queiroz: In Memoriam* edited by Eloy de Amaral and Cardoso Martha, 1947; *As ideias de Eça de Queiroz* by António José Saraiva, 1947; *Crític social de Eça de Queiroz* by Djacar Menezes, 1950, revised edition, 1962; *Lengua y estilo de Eça de Queiroz* by Ernesto Guerra, 1954; 'Ramalho Ortigão and the Generation of 1870' by Walter J. Schnerr, in *Hispania*, 44, 1961; *Eça e Wilde* by A. Casemiro da Silva, 1962; *Eça, discípulo de Machado?* by Alberto Machado de Rosa, 1963; 'Eça de Queiroz as a Literary Critic' by Peter Demetz, in *Comparative Literature*, 19, 1967; *Ensaios queirosianos* by António Coimbra Martins, 1967; '*Alves e Ca.* as Comedy' by Timothy Brown, Jr, in *Kentucky Romance Quarterly*, 16, 1969; *Eça de Queiroz e a questão social* by Jaime Cortesão, 1970; *Eça, político*, 1970, *Eça de Queiroz e o seu tempo*, 1972, and *Eça de Queiroz e a Geração de 70*, 1980, all by João Medina; *Eça de Queiroz e o século XIX* by Vianna Moog, 1977 (6th edition); 'Presentation of Protagonist in *Alves & Ca.*', in *Kentucky Romance Quarterly*, 25, 1978, and 'The Opera Motif in Eça's Lisbon Novels', in *Luso-Brazilian Review*, 16, 1979, both by Robert M. Fedorchek; *Introdução a leitura d'Os Maias* by Carlos Reis, 1978(?); *Eça de Queiroz and European Realism* by Alexander Coleman, 1980; *A vida de Eça de Queiroz* by Luís Viana Filho, 1983; *Imagens do Portugal queirosiano* by A. Campos Matos, 1987; *Dicionário de Eça de Queiroz* edited by A. Campos Matos, 1988; *Os vencidos da vida* by the Circulo Eça de Queiroz, 1989; *A construção da narrativa queirosiana* by Carlos Reis and Maria do Rosário Milheiro, 1989; *O leitor e a verdade oculta: ensaio sobre Os Maias* by Alan Freeland, 1990; *Eça e Os Maias: actas do 1º Encontro Internacional de Queirosianes, 1988*, 1990.

* * *

Eça de Queirós, beyond dispute the greatest Portuguese novelist of the 19th century, has long deserved wider recognition among the major European novelists of the last century. It is as a novelist that he is best known in Portugal and beyond, yet the major novels only amount to half a dozen or so works while the rest of his very considerable literary output consists of hundreds of journalistic articles on a whole range of topics, as well as novels, short stories, tales of fantasy and imagination, essays, travel notes, a translation of *King Solomon's Mines* and numerous collections of letters to family and friends.

Eça's earliest writings, *Prosas bárbaras* [Barbaric Tales], dating from as early as 1866 and 1867, reveal the contemporary prevailing taste for romanticism, imported from France and Germany; their pervading atmosphere of fantasy, Satanism, grotesqueness and mystery is enhanced by the rhythmic, lyrical and evocative style. Already Eça's concern with the expressive potential of language is evident.

A few years later, in 1871, in a revolutionary public lecture, *The New Literature*, given in Lisbon, Eça severely criticized and rejected the traditional Portuguese Romantic manner of writing as being conventional, sentimental, escapist, limited in interest, and lacking in purpose and originality, and expounded realism/naturalism after the French manner as the only way forward for literature. He declared that literature should teach and correct, that society should be depicted just as it was so that the evils of society could be condemned. This enthusiastic embracing of realism and the accompanying critical attitude to traditional practices and values gave rise to a series of *Farpas* [Barbs] in which Eça condemned the state or torpor and stagnation he saw in society, literature and politics, and to his first major novel, *O crime do Padre Amaro* (*The Sin of Father Amaro*). This was a landmark, the first Portuguese work of realist fiction and Eça's strongest reaction against romanticism. The novel provided the perfect opportunity for Eça to put his theories into practice and the hypocrisy and immorality of provincial society and in particular, the greed and lust of the clergy, are scrutinized and depicted without reserve. In his second realist work, *O primo Basílio* (*Cousin Bazilio*), 'the most doctrinal work printed in Portugal to date', the decadence, indolence, and false values of the Lisbon bourgeoisie are attacked. *Os Maias* (*The Maias*), Eça's longest and most ambitious work, generally considered to be his masterpiece, tells the story of the decline of an ill-fated aristocratic family. In this Portuguese equivalent of Galdós's *Fortunata and Jacinta* Eça paints a vast canvas of Lisbon high society, with gatherings of intellectuals, cosmopolitan types, fashionable women, intrigues, contemporary customs, excursions in and around Lisbon and many detailed descriptions of interiors and gardens, as part of his mission to depict contemporary Portugal with all its flaws.

With *O mandarim* (*The Mandarin*), which appeared less than ten years after Eça had rebelled against tradition to uphold the cause of realism, he broke away from the realist novel in favour of a tale of invention not observation, a world of fantasy, mystery and exoticism, which was much more in harmony with his natural preferences. Similarly with *A relíquia* (*The Relic*) some years later Eça is no longer the critical observer but revels in the role of story-teller. Fantasy combines with realism to create a tale of adventure, whose aim was to entertain rather than simply instruct and censure, though the greed and duplicity of the anti-hero, Teodorico, received their just deserts. Here we see Eça's humour at its best, no longer the caustic irony of his realist period but a more playful brand, sometimes a rather macabre juxtaposition of comic and tragic, a bathetic cutting down to size of pompous behaviour or an impressive event, or imparting a lighter, frivolous touch to a sad, even tragic scene.

Eça spent many years away from Portugal, returning only for occasional short vacations and the last 12 years of his life were spent in Paris. Years before this would have given him great pleasure and satisfaction, but ironically France, the French way of life, literature, culture, and attitudes had lost its charm for him while his former critical appraisal of Portugal and most things Portuguese had mellowed. This latter nostalgic mood is echoed in his two final novels, *A ilustre casa de Ramires* (*The Illustrious House of Ramires*) and *A cidade e as serras* (*The City and the Mountains*). The setting for *The Illustrious House*, which could be described as a historical novel dealing with contemporary life and the glories of the past, is not Lisbon or a seedy provincial town but a remote rural area. In the final novel Eça presents his version of the popular contemporary theme of urban civilization versus the simple country life. Humour abounds in the descriptions of the hero's Parisian mansion with its wealth of gadgetry and the latest aids to easy living. The enforced return of the protagonist to his estate in northern Portugal provides the opportunity to contrast the wholesome pastoral existence in which he eventually finds happiness and fulfilment with the evils of super-civilization, epitomized by his former life in Paris.

Eça's journalistic works and his letters, particularly those of his invented character, Fradique Mendes, who wrote on all manner of subjects (as Eça himself says, 'from the immortality of the soul to the price of coal'!), provide a fascinating insight into Eça's personal thoughts—his nostalgia for his country, his opinion on politics, literature, culture, and controversial contemporary issues. In addition, in these writings Eça expresses his views of many of his fictional works and his perpetual dissatisfaction with his writing, plagued by his apparent inability to provide a great work or create a new and vital style.

As well as boldly rejecting what he regarded as the fetters of traditional Portuguese literary norms in order to embrace the cause of realism/naturalism, thereby changing the course of development of the novel, Eça rebelled against the heavy rhetorical, bombastic literary manner to create a very personal style that he strove to perfect throughout his literary career. From the lyrical, sonorous prose of *Prosas bárbaras,* overladen with adjectives, Eça's style became more disciplined, versatile, flexible, and expressive. He always sought the precise word or combination of words to express the desired effect and Eça's capacity to create a humorous or ironic impression by means of verbal dexterity is without par. He combined words in novel, unexpected ways, made ironic use of paradox and hyperbole and is the master of the transferred epithet. His letters reveal that this gift for innovation and flexibility, whose influence is still felt today, was not simply a literary device to be used in novels but an essential part of his persona.

Although he has been described as the Zola of Portugal, naturalism in Eça's case was, as he himself admitted, always more theoretical than practical. Naturalism played its part in his literary evolution by disciplining his imagination and leading him to base his novels on the critical observation of society but he was essentially too much an artist and man of imagination to maintain the realist/naturalist stance with conviction and his socio-critical works are best described as *semi*-realist depictions of society, a mix of comedy and tragedy. No other Portuguese novelist has painted such a gallery of colourful, acutely observed portraits, accompanied by such mordant wit or playful humour.

Throughout his literary evolution his writings reveal a fusion of styles and genres which, together with his very personal use of humour and irony, his concern for words and their effect, his fondness for story-telling, his fascination with the exotic and fantastic, his underlying tolerance towards his characters, make his work defy easy definition. Eça frequently attempted to define the Portuguese character, often contrasting his countrymen with the French, as in his preface to *The Mandarin* where he describes the Portuguese as man of imagination not reason, always preferring a beautiful phrase to a precise idea, and Eça himself, in spite of the strong French influence on his early career and his admiration for French novelists, particularly Flaubert, could never escape his own essential Portugueseness.

—Shirley Clarke

THE EDDA OF SÆMUND. See **THE POETIC EDDA**.

EDUARDO. See **DE FILIPPO, Eduardo.**

EGILS SAGA. Icelandic prose narrative, written anonymously during 13th century, or possibly written by Snorri Sturluson (1179–1241), *q.v.*, and concerning events of the 10th century, in particular the life story of the poet Egil Skalla-Grímsson. One of the sagas called *Íslendingasögur* [Icelandic Family Sagas], quasi-historical accounts of leading citizens during and immediately after the period of settlement during the 9th–11th centuries, using a combination of prose and verse.

PUBLICATIONS

Egils saga skallagrímssonar, edited by Finnur Jónsson. 1886; revised edition, 1924; also edited by Sigurur Nordal, 1933; as *Egils Saga,* edited and translated by Christine Fell, 1975; as *The Story of Egil Skallagrimsson,* translated by W.C. Green, 1893; as *Egil's Saga,* translated by E.R. Eddison, 1930; also translated by Gwyn Jones, 1960; Hermann Palsson and Paul Edwards, 1976.

*

Bibliography: *Bibliography of the Icelandic Sagas and Minor Tales* by Halldór Hermannsson, 1908; *A Bibliography of Skaldic Studies* by Lee M. Hollander, 1958; *Bibliography of Old Norse-Icelandic Studies* by Hans Bekker-Nielsen and Thorkil Damsgaard Olsen, 1964— , and *Old Norse-Icelandic Studies: A Select Bibliography* by Bekker-Nielsen, 1967.

Critical Studies: *The Origin of the Icelandic Family Sagas* by Knut Liestøl, 1930; *The Sagas of the Icelanders* by Halldór Hermannsson, 1935; 'Egil Skallagrímsson in England' by Gwyn Jones, in *Proceedings of the British Academy,* 38, 1952; *The Sagas of the Icelanders* by Jóhann S. Hannesson, 1957; *The Icelandic Saga* by Peter Hallberg, 1962; *The Icelandic Family Saga: An Analytic Reading* by Theodore M. Andersson, 1967; 'The Giant as a Heroic Model: The Case of Egil and Starkar' by Kaaren Grimstad, in *Scandinavian Studies,* 48, 1976; 'Fighting Words in *Egils saga:* Lexical Pattern as Standard Bearer' by Michael L. Bell, in *Arkiv,* 95, 1980.

* * *

Egils Saga ranks beside *Njáls Saga* and three or four others as one of the major Icelandic Family Sagas or Sagas of

Icelanders, prose narratives written in Iceland mainly in the 13th century, but dealing with events of the century or so following the settlement of Iceland by Scandinavians c.AD 900. These sagas are anonymous, but there are reasons for thinking that *Egils Saga* is the work of Snorri Sturluson, author of the prose *Edda* and of the sequence of Kings' Sagas known as *Heimskringla* [The Orb of the World], which includes *Óláfs saga ins helga*. *Egils Saga* falls into three parts, ending respectively with the deaths of Egil's grandfather, Kveld-Úlf, his father, Skalla-Grím, and himself, his own career being dealt with from the beginning of the second part onwards.

The first part takes place mainly in Norway. Kveld-Úlf and his elder son Skalla-Grím refuse to join Harald the Shaggy-Haired in his struggle to become king of all Norway, but Kveld-Úlf's younger son, Thórólf, does join him. Thórólf is named as heir by Harald's retainer Bárd, who dies in the battle at which Harald gains control of Norway, and duly inherits Bárd's property, in which the two sons of Hildiríd, the second wife of Bárd's grandfather, claim a share. When Thórólf rejects their claim, Hildiríd's sons proceed to slander him to King Harald, with the eventual result that Harald kills Thórólf. Vengeance is taken on the sons of Hildiríd by Thórólf's kinsman Ketil Hæng, who kills them and then emigrates to Iceland, and on Harald by Kveld-Úlf and Skalla-Grím, who kill two of the king's retainers before themselves leaving for Iceland. Kveld-Úlf dies on the way; Skalla-Grím settles in western Iceland at Borg.

In the second part of the saga, Skalla-Grím's elder son, also named Thórólf, and Egil are born. Egil's precocity reveals itself in his ability to compose poetry at the age of three. In Norway, Björn, a chieftain, abducts Thóra, the sister of another chieftain, Thórir, against the latter's will, and brings her to Borg after first marrying her in Shetland. Reconciled with Thórir at Thórólf's instigation, the couple return to Norway, leaving their daughter, Ásgerd, in Skalla-Grím's care. In Norway Thórólf becomes friendly with Harald's son and successor, Eirík Bloodaxe, and his queen Gunnhild; he brings Ásgerd to Norway and marries her. Egil, who has meanwhile performed killings at the ages of seven and twelve, also comes to Norway, and makes friends with Thórir's son Arinbjörn. Meeting King Eirík and Gunnhild socially, he causes offence with his excessive drinking, and kills their steward after destroying the drinking-horn with which Gunnhild and the steward try to poison him. Thórólf and Egil, both now in trouble with the queen, leave Norway, and Thórólf is slain in a battle in England at which they help King Æthelstan against the Scots. Rewarded by Æthelstan with two chests of silver, Egil marries Ásgerd in Norway, and claims her patrimony when Berg-Önund, also a son-in-law of Ásgerd's father, himself claims it on the grounds that Thóra and Björn were not legally married when Ásgerd was born. With Arinbjörn's help, Egil takes the case to court, but Gunnhild disrupts the proceedings, with the result that Egil kills Berg-Önund and a son of the royal couple, plunders Berg-Önund's estate and, by setting up a pole topped with a horse's head and inscribed with runes, urges the spirits of the land to expel Eirík and Gunnhild from Norway. Skalla-Grím dies after Egil's return to Iceland.

In the third part, Eirík and Gunnhild are forced to leave Norway by the accession of Harald's son Hákon; Arinbjörn accompanies them. Intending to revisit Æthelstan, Egil is shipwrecked near York, Eirík's residence. He visits Arinbjörn there and, at his suggestion, saves himself from execution by composing his long 'Head-ransom' poem in King Eirík's praise. In Norway he finally wins Ásgerd's inheritance after killing a brother of Berg-Önund, and accepts

money from Arinbjörn when King Hákon denies his claim to the brother's property. He restores to Hákon's favour Arinbjörn's nephew Thornsteinn, frowned on by Hákon because of Arinbjörn's support of Eirík's son Harald Greycloak, by undertaking on Thorsteinn's behalf a tribute-collecting expedition, in the course of which he cures a sick girl by runic magic and kills 21 assailants single-handedly. Back in Iceland he composes two long poems on the death of two of his sons and in praise of Arinbjörn respectively. After assisting his third son Thorsteinn in a lengthy dispute with one Steinar, Egil in old age hides the two chests of silver, which, contrary to King Æthelstan's wishes, he had never shared with his family, and dies.

Egil's family history reflects the ambivalent relationship of Iceland to Norway, the mother country from which, as the saga has it, settlers of Iceland broke away in defiance of the king's power. The sense of contradiction in this relationship must have been felt by many Icelanders at the time of *Egils Saga's* composition, with the aspirations of Icelandic chieftains to become part of the Norwegian royal aristocracy, from which they were nevertheless mostly excluded. The saga may be seen as a mythical narrative in which these contradictions are mediated by a central episode in Egil's career, his visit to York, which takes place on 'neutral' ground (neither in Iceland nor in Norway), and in which Egil balances a poem in praise of King Eirík against his earlier blatant defiance of him with the impaled horse's head. The immobilization characteristic of the hero and/or villain, often a feature of such mediating episodes in myth, is apparent in the fact that Egil is initially held up in his composition of the poem by a swallow twittering at his window, most probably Queen Gunnhild in disguise, and in the fact that, as he recites the poem, King Eirík sits upright, glaring at him, a position reminiscent of that in which Egil had placed the horse's head. Forming a bridge between the second and third parts of the saga, to which the first part forms an introduction, this episode brings together many of the central themes and preoccupations of the saga as a whole.

—Rory McTurk

———

EICH, Günter. Born in Lebus/Oder, Mecklenburg, Germany, 1 February 1907. Educated at Leipzig Gymnasium, graduated 1925; studied Chinese and Law, University of Berlin, 1925–27; Leipzig University, 1927–29; the Sorbonne, Paris, 1929–30. Served during World War II; prisoner of war, 1945, released 1946. Married the writer Ilse Aichinger (second marriage) in 1953; one son and one daughter. Full-time writer from 1946. Recipient: Gruppe 47 prize, 1950; Bavarian Academy of Fine Arts literature prize, 1952; Büchner prize, 1959; Schiller prize, 1968. *Died 20 December 1972.*

PUBLICATIONS

Collections

Gesammelte Werke, edited by Ilse Aichinger and others. 4 vols., 1973.
Gedichte, edited by Ilse Aichinger. 1973.

Tage mit Hähern: Ausgewählte Gedichte, edited by Klaus Schumann. 1975.
Pigeons and Moles: Selected Writings, translated by Michael Hamburger. 1990.

Verse

Gedichte. 1930.
Abgelegene Gehöfte. 1948.
Untergrundbahn. 1949.
Botschaften des Regens. 1955.
Ausgewählte Gedichte, edited by Walter Höllerer. 1960.
Zu den Akten. 1964.
Anlässe und Steingärten. 1966.
Nach Seumes Papieren. 1972.
Valuable Nail: Selected Poems, translated by Stuart Friebert, David Walker, and David Young. 1981.

Plays

Die Glücksritter. 1933.
Träume (radio plays; includes *Geh nicht nach El Kuwehd*; *Der Tiger Jussuf*; *Subeth*; *Träume*). 1953.
Stimmen: Sieben Hörspiele (radio plays; includes *Die Andere und ich*; *Allah hat hundert Namen*; *Das Jahr Lazertis*; *Die Mädchen aus Viterbo*; *Zinngeschrei*; *Festianus Märtyrer*; *Die Brandung vor Setúbal*). 1958.
Die Brandung vor Setúbal, Das Jahr Lazertis: Zwei Hörspiele (radio plays), edited by Robert Browning. 1963; as *Journeys: Two Radio Plays, The Rolling Sea at Setúbal, The Year Lacertis*, translated by Michael Hamburger, 1968.
In Anderern Sprachen: Vier Hörspiele (radio plays; includes *Meine sieben jungen Freunde*; *Die Stunde des Huflattichs*; *Blick auf Venedig*; *Man bittet zu läuten*). 1964.
Unter Wasser; Böhmische Schneider: Marionettenspiele. 1964.
Fünfzehn Hörspiele (radio plays). 1966.

Radio Plays: *Das festliche Jahr*, with Martin Raschke, 1936; *Zinngeschrei*, 1955; *Die Brandung vor Setúbal*, 1957; *Allah hat hundert Namen*, 1957; *Die Mädchen aus Viterbo,* 1960; *Festianus Märtyrer*, 1966.

Fiction

Katharina. 1936.
Kulka, Hilpert, Elefanten. 1968.
Maulwürfe. 1968.
Ein Tibeter in meinem Büro. 1970.

Other

Ein Lesebuch, edited by Susanne Müller-Hanpft. 1972.
Semmelformen, drawings by Sven Knebel. 1972.

Translator, *Lyrik des Ostens: China* (verse), edited by Wilhelm Gundert, A. Schimmel and Walther Schubring. 1958.
Translator, *Aus dem Chinesischen* (verse). 1973.

*

Critical Studies: *Günter Eich* by Egbert Krispyn, 1971; *Günter Eich* edited by Bernd Jentzsch, 1973; *Committed Aestheticism: The Poetic Theory and Practice of Günter Eich* by Larry L. Ricardson, 1983; *Career at the Cost of*

Compromise: Günter Eich's Life and Work in the Years 1933–1945 by Glenn R. Cuomo, 1989.

* * *

Günter Eich was among those writers who helped provide a sense of continuity in German literature from the early 1930s through to the post-World War II period. In the pre-war years he gradually gained public recognition; however, unlike many writers, he remained in Germany after Hitler came to power and served his country during the war.

Eich's first collection of verse, *Gedichte* [Poems], published in 1930, warrants his description of himself as a late expressionist and nature poet, and reflects his association with the literary group at Dresden centred on the journal *Die Kolonne*. Such poems as 'Die Flusse entlang' [Along the Rivers] and 'Der Anfang kühlerer Tage' [The Start of Cold Weather] illustrate this mood and approach at the time. The 1930s also marked the beginning of a lifelong involvement on Eich's part with the radio play. Schwitzke has noted several plays and their broadcasts between 1932 and—interestingly in the historical context—in the late 1930s.

In an American prisoner-of-war camp in 1945 Eich resumed his interest in poetry and soon after embarked upon literary collaboration with Hans Werner Richter. He contributed to numerous journals and became a founder member of the newly established Gruppe 47 and the first recipient of its prize in 1950 (it was only the first of several literary recognitions awarded to Eich over the years). By that time Eich had established himself as a leading post-war writer in West Germany.

In 1948 his first post-war collection of verse, *Abgelegene Gehöhfte* [Isolated Farms] was published. Eich's occupation with the theme of remoteness, be it of time or place, is already suggested in the title poem or in 'Wiepersdorf, die Arminschen Gräber' and 'Wie grau es auch regnet'. In Eich's evocation of bygone times there is evidence of the melancholic tone which becomes an increasingly characteristic feature of his verse. These poems in fact are still a reminder of the *Kolonne* period, but the volume also contains a number that starkly relate to his war experiences. 'Inventur' [Stocktaking], one of the best-known of all early post-war poems, catalogues matter-of-factly and with the sparsest language the few yet precious belongings of the prisoner-of-war; it is rightly regarded as typically illustrating the so-called *Kahlschlag* technique. The rhyming juxtaposition of 'Hölderlin/Urin' in 'Latrine', may have caused offense to some readers' susceptibilities at the time, but Eich's concern was always to challenge. Lines from his radio play *Träume* [Dreams] effectively serve as a motto for his work: 'no, don't sleep, while those who order the world are busy!/Be mistrustful of their power . . .!/ . . . / Do that which is not useful, sing the songs that are not expected from your mouth!/ Be irritating, be sand, not oil, in the world machine!'.

Träume was but one of the barrage of radio plays from Eich's pen and some 40 plays are credited to him in the span of a quarter of a century after the war. The development of the radio play as a literary genre in the 1950s is synonymous with Eich's own work in the field. The medium encouraged anti-naturalist techniques, with the use of acoustic devices, and these Eich exploited to the full. In this context the titles of his first collections of radio plays are pertinent: *Träume* (it was to prove highly popular, with over 50,000 copies sold) and *Stimmen* [Voices]. The individual pieces show the ready transposition of dream and reality. In *Der Tiger Jussuf*, for instance, the soul of a lion enters different people, while in

Die Andere und ich Ellend Harland, a rich American woman, experiences the miserable existence of an Italian fisherman's wife. Catarina in *Die Brandung von Setúbal* (*The Rolling Sea at Setúbal*) is similarly placed in a transformational situation, as Eich juggles with the theme of time and the two worlds of life and death. The presence of a strong comic-absurd, satiric, even grotesque dimension here as elsewhere in his work serves to heighten the underlying seriousness of Eich's intent. One may seek to play out the game of fulfilling logic through dreams, but as Goldschmidt reminds us in *Die Mädchen aus Viterbo* [The Girls from Viterbo], there comes a point when the time for dreaming is over. For three years during World War II the old Jew and his granddaughter have fearfully awaited the knock on the door that portends death. To combat their fears they indulge themselves with the story of schoolgirls lost with their teacher in the catacombs of Rome. The interplay, perhaps rather the counterbalancing, of make-believe and reality allows Eich once more to present a marginal situation. Only when the knock does come is the moment reached of recognizing life for what it is, including the notion that God too is a component in the established order of evil, lies, and illusion. It is a viewpoint that Eich formulates both in his radio plays and in his verse. Anarchy or the perceived sense of ordered life is the challenge Eich poses himself and us. *Man bittet zu läuten* [Please Ring the Bell], Eich's penultimate radio play, is arguably his most powerful expression of indictment, but equally is seen as marking a departure from the conventional understanding of the *hörspiel* (radio play) towards the *sprechstück* (spoken drama).

By the time Eich's third post-war and most popular volume of verse, *Botschaften des Regens* [Messages of the Rain], was published in 1955 (the second *Untergrundbahn* [Subway] had appeared in 1949), the melancholic tone had become more marked and the language more sparse. The simple routine and details of everyday life is not completely absent (for example in 'Weg zum Bahnhof' [The Way to the Station]), but an actual journey can become also the journey of the mind ('D-Zug-München-Frankfurt' [The Munich to Frankfurt Express]). A locality can conjure up memories, but also evoke darker responses: 'Der Beginn der Einsamkeit, Das Schilf der Verzweiflung/ der trigonometrische Punkt/ Abnessung im Nichts' [The beginning of solitude, the need of despair/of the trigonometric point/measurement in the void] ('Der grosse Lübbe-See'). The emphasis still lies on the theme of transience, as the first poem of the collection, 'Ende eines-Sommers' [End of a Summer], immediately establishes. The initial positive note in the poem gives way before the awareness of the inevitability of the process of death. Equally, the title poem spells out the gloomy portents carried by the rain—portents of despair, privation, and guilt.

Zu den Akten did not appear until almost a decade later, in 1964. By then Eich had travelled extensively through North America, but more significantly to the Orient, and his apparent growing preference for the latter's way of life is reflected not only in the poem 'Fussnote zu Rom' [Footnote to Rome], but also in the very title of the subsequent collection *Anlässe und Steingärten* [Reasons and Rockeries]. Objects themselves become the sources of existential experience, as in the case of the stones placed artificially in the sand in those places of meditation, the Japanese stone gardens. In 'Zum Berspiel' Eich become engaged with the difficulty experienced in translating meaning and truth by a word ('ein wort in ein Wort übersetzen') inferring the need rather for 'transposition'. For Eich, it becomes a matter of seeking a symbol instead of a metaphor. With the passing years, his distrust of life increases and his goals correspondingly appear to lessen. Occasionally, the old aggressive note surfaces ('Seminar für Hinterbliebene' [School for Survivors], 'Geometrischer Ort' [Geometrical Point], 'Optik' [Optics]), even a trace of bitter humour and self mockery can be detected ('Zuversicht' [Optimism]), to become subsumed in the more prevailing mood of a resigned acceptance of ultimate silence. Thematically, the late poems centre on departure and death.

Eich would expound occasionally on the nature of poetry, but essentially he never saw himself as a theoretician. A poem such as 'Kunsttheorien' would confirm that view, as would a series of short prose pieces undertaken by Eich towards the end of the 1960s. Under the title *Maulwürfe* [Moles] (1968; a second collection, *Ein Tibeter in meinem Büro* [A Tibetan in My Office] was published in 1970), they are fundamentally short paragraph-like passages that illustrate Eich's apparent unwillingness to make a direct statement. They constitute a deliberate jumbling of aphorisms, clichés, and touches of lyricism that produce an odd mixture of sense and nonsense. The anarchic factor still proclaims itself: 'If I were a negative writer, I'd rather be a negative carpenter, long live anarchy!' ('Späne' [Woodshavings]). Basically, the passages reflect the view that nothing is self-evident in life or in literature.

Despite his limited verse output, Eich proved a significant influence on the development of the German lyric after World War II, while the progress of the radio play during that same period (and particularly in the 1950s) is indelibly linked with Eich's own creative performance in that field.

—Ian Hilton

EICHENDORFF, Joseph (Karl Benedikt, Freiherr) von. Born in Lubowitz, Silesia, Germany, 10 March 1788. Educated at Katholisches Gymnasium, Breslau, 1801–04; Halle University, 1805–06; Heidelberg University, 1807–08; continued to study law in Vienna, 1810–12. Married Aloysia (Luise) von Larisch in 1815 (died 1855); two sons and three daughters. Served in the volunteer forces during the War of Liberation, 1813–14 and 1815; commissioned 1813. Undertook a walking tour through the Harz mountains, 1805; travelled to Paris and Vienna, 1808; returned to Lubowitz to manage father's estate, 1809; lived in Berlin, 1809–10; dispatch clerk, War Ministry, Berlin, 1815; trainee civil servant, 1816–19, and assessor, 1819–21, Prussian Royal Government; government councillor, Danzig, 1821, Ministry of Education and Cultural Affairs, Berlin, 1823, 1831–44, and Königsberg, 1824. *Died 26 November 1857.*

PUBLICATIONS

Collections

Sämtliche Werke. 6 vols., 2nd edition, 1864.
Vermischte Schriften. 5 vols., 1866–67.
Werke, edited by Richard Dietze. 2 vols., 1891.
Werke, edited by Ludwig Krähe. 2 vols., 1908.
Sämtliche Werke, edited by Wilhelm Kosch and August Sauer; continued by Hermann Kunisch and Helmut Koopmann. 9 vols., 1908–50; 2nd edition, 1962– .
Gedichte, Erzählungen, Biographisches, edited by Max Wehrli. 1945.

[Selected Poems], edited by Gerhard Prager. 1946.
Neue Gesamtausgabe der Werke und Schriften, edited by Gerhart Baumann and Siegfried Grosse. 4 vols., 1957–58.
Werke, edited by Ansgar Hillach and Klaus Dieter Krabiel. 5 vols., 1970–88.
Werke, edited by Wolfgang Frühwald, Brigitte Schillbach and Hartwig Schultz. 6 vols., 1985– .

Fiction

Ahnung und Gegenwart. 1815.
Aus dem Leben eines Taugenichts und Das Marmorbild. Zwei Novellen nebst einem Anhange von Liedern und Romanzen. 1826; reprinted 1981; as *Memoirs of a Good-for-Nothing*, translated by Charles Godfrey Leland, 1866, also translated by Bayard Quincy Morgan, 1955; Ronald Taylor, 1966; as *The Happy-Go-Lucky*, translated by A.L. Wister, 1906; as *The Life of a Good-for-Nothing*, translated by Michael Glenny, 1966; *Das Marmorbild* as 'The Marble Statue', translated by F.E. Pierce, in *Fiction and Fantasy of German Romance*, edited by Pierce and C.F. Schreiber, 1927.
Viel Lärmen um Nichts, in *Der Gesellschafter*, edited by F.W. Gubitz. 1832.
Dichter und ihre Gesellen. 1834.
Das Schloss Dürande. 1837.
Die Entführung. 1839.
Die Glücksritter. 1841.
Libertas und ihr Freier. 1864.
Eine Meerfahrt. 1864.
Auch ich war in Arkadien. 1866.
Novellen. 1927.
Erzählungen. 1946.
Erzählungen, edited by Werner Bergengruen. 1955.
Das Wiedersehen, edited by Hermann Kunisch. 1966.

Verse

Gedichte. 1837; revised edition, 1843.
Neue Gedichte. 1847.
Julian. 1853.
Robert und Guiscard. 1855.
Lucius. 1857.
Gedichte aus dem Nachlasse, edited by Heinrich Meisner. 1888.
Joseph und Wilhelm von Eichendorffs Jugendgedichte, edited by Raimund Pissin. 1906.
Eichendorffs Jugendgedichte aus seiner Schulzeit, edited by Hilda Schulhof. 1915; reprinted 1974.
Gedichte, edited by A. Schaeffer. 1919.
The Happy Wanderer and Other Poems, translated by Marjorie Rossy. 1925.
Gedichte. Ahnung und Gegenwart, edited by Werner Bergengruen. 1955.

Plays

Krieg den Philistern!. 1824.
Meierbeths Glück und Ende, in *Der Gesellschafter*, edited by F.W. Gubitz. 1827.
Ezelin von Romano. 1828.
Der letzte Held von Marienburg. 1830.
Die Freier. 1833.
Das Incognito: Ein Puppenspiel. Mit Fragmenten und Entwürfen anderer Dichtungen nach den Handschriften, edited by Konrad Weichberger. 1901; also edited by Gerhard Kluge, with *Das Loch; oder, das wiedergefundene*

Paradies: Ein Schattenspiel, by Ludwig Achim von Arnim, 1968.

Other

Die Wiederherstellung des Schlosses der deutschen Ordensritter zu Marienburg. 1844.
Zur Geschichte der neueren romantischen Poesie in Deutschland. 1846.
Über die ethische und religiöse Bedeutung der neueren romantischen Poesie in Deutschland. 1847.
Die geistliche Poesie in Deutschland. 1847.
Der deutsche Roman des achtzehnten Jahrhunderts in seinem Verhältnis zum Christenthum. 1851.
Zur Geschichte des Dramas. 1854.
Geschichte der poetischen Literatur Deutschlands. 2 vols., 1857.
Aus dem Nachlass. Briefe und Dichtungen, edited by Wilhelm Kosch. 1906.
Fahrten und Wanderungen 1802–1814 der Freiherren Joseph und Wilhelm Eichendorff, edited by Alfons Nowack. 1907.
Lubowitzer Tagebuchblätter, edited by Alfons Nowack. 1907.
Liederbuch, illustrated by Josua Leander Gampp. 1922.
Schlesische Tagebücher (diaries), edited by Alfred Riemen. 1988.

Editor, *Gedichte*, by Lebrecht Dreves. 1849.

Translator, *Der Graf Lucanor*, by Juan Manuel. 1840.
Translator, *Geistliche Schauspiele* by Pedro Calderón de la Barca. 2 vols., 1846–53.
Translator, *Fünf Zwischenspiele*, by Miguel de Cervantes, edited by A. Potthoff. 1924.

*

Critical Studies: *Der Dichter des Taugenichts: Eichendorffs Welt und Leben, geschildert von ihm selbst und von Zeitgenossen* edited by Paul Stöcklein and Inge Feuchtmayer, 1957, and *Eichendorff heute* edited by Stöcklein, 1960; 'Zum Gedächtnis Eichendorffs' by Theodor W. Adorno, in *Akzente*, (5), 1958; *Eichendorff: Aus dem Leben eines Taugenichts* by G.T. Hughes, 1961; *Versuche über Eichendorff* by Oskar Seidlin, 1965, 2nd edition, 1978; 'The Metaphor of Death in Eichendorff', in *Oxford German Studies*, (4), 1969, and 'Eichendorff and Shakespeare', in *German Romantics in Context: Selected Essays*, 1992, both by Elisabeth Stopp; *Eichendorff: The Spiritual Geometer* by Lawrence Radner, 1970; *Eichendorff-Kommentar* by Ansgar Hillach and Klaus-Dieter Krabiel, 2 vols., 1971–72; *Joseph von Eichendorff* by Egon Schwarz, 1972; *Spatiotemporal Consciousness in English and German Romanticism. A Comparative Study of Novalis, Blake, Wordsworth, and Eichendorff* by Amala M. Hanke, 1981; *Eichendorff und die Spätromantik* edited by Hans-Georg Pott, 1985; *Hieroglyphenschrift. Untersuchungen zu Eichendorffs Erzählungen* by Klaus Köhnke, 1986; *Lyric Descent in the German Romantic Tradition* by Brigitte Peucker, 1986; *Joseph von Eichendorff* by Wolfgang Frühwald and Franz Heiduk, 1988; *Ansichten zu Eichendorff. Beiträge der Forschung 1985 bis 1988* edited by Alfred Riemen, 1988; Eichendorff Issue of *German Life and Letters*, 42(3), 1989; *Hindeutung auf das Höhere: A Structural Study of the Novels of Joseph von Eichendorff* by Judith Purver, 1989; *Lebendige Allegorie. Studien zu Eichendorffs Leben und Werk* by

Robert Mühlher, 1990; *Eichendorff's Scholarly Reputation: A Survey* by Robert O. Goebel, 1994.

* * *

Joseph von Eichendorff's fame as the quintessential German Romantic writer rests primarily on a narrow segment of his total output: a selection of his lyric poetry and two or three stories, the most celebrated of which is *Aus dem Leben eines Taugenichts* (*Memoirs of a Good-for-Nothing*). Since very little of his work, apart from this tale and a few poems, has been translated into English, he is best known in the English-speaking world through the musical settings of his lyrics by such composers as Mendelssohn, Schumann (especially 'Dichterliebe', Opus 39, 1840), Brahms, Hugo Wolf, Hans Pfitzner (the cantata 'Von deutscher Seele' [Of the German Soul], Opus 28, 1921), and Richard Strauss. His poems have been set to music more frequently than those of almost any other German writer; thus his importance in the context of the German *Lied* and its development is considerable. His work also influenced more 19th-century German poets than that of any other writer except Goethe, and has been assimilated, imitated, parodied, praised, and quoted to a remarkable degree by a wide variety of authors, from Theodor Storm and Theodor Fontane to Thomas Mann, Hermann Hesse, and Günter Grass.

The full range of Eichendorff's literary and other writings is, however, still relatively little known. He wrote over 500 lyric poems, nine stories, five plays, three epic poems, two novels, and a number of narrative, dramatic, and autobiographical fragments. His diaries (1798 to 1815) reveal many of the decisive influences on his formative years, including the Romantic thinkers and writers Joseph Görres, Friedrich Schlegel, Henrik Steffens, Achim von Arnim, Clemens Brentano, and the Grimm brothers, whose example probably inspired him to begin, in 1808–09, a collection of Upper Silesian fairy-tales. In his later years, he again followed the Romantic example, both by translating from Spanish a number of ballads, as well as dramas by Calderón and Cervantes, and a 14th-century prose text, *El Conde Lucanor* [Count Lucanor] by Don Juan Manual, and by composing several essays and treatises on literature, the last and most comprehensive of which, *Geschichte der poetischen Literatur Deutschlands* [History of the Poetic Literature of Germany], appeared in 1857, the year of his death. In the same year, he began a biography of St Hedwig, the patron saint of Silesia. In connection with his career in the Prussian Civil Service, Eichendorff also produced a number of historical and political writings, including pieces on secularization, constitutional questions, and press censorship, and on the two great symbolic Prussian architectural undertakings of the time, the completion of Cologne Cathedral and the restoration of the Marienburg castle near Danzig, with both of which he was, personally as well as professionally, closely involved. His correspondence, while less extensive than that of some of his contemporaries, provides valuable insights into his life, work, and thought, and into the unsettled times in which he lived.

The chaotic period of the Napoleonic Wars forms the background to Eichendorff's first novel, *Ahnung und Gegenwart* [Divination and the Present], written 1810–12 in Vienna, but not published until 1815. Eichendorff's intention in this work was to provide a 'complete picture . . . of that strange time of expectation, longing and grief, heavy with foreboding of the storm to come' which had preceded the Wars of Liberation in the German lands. Though by no means devoid of realistic detail, the novel is not a mimetic portrayal of the period, but rather an attempt to create, in the spirit of the theory and practice of the novel among the German Romantics, a structural and symbolic counterpart both to the confusion of the times, as it appeared to Eichendorff, and to the underlying order of the universe, guaranteed for him by his Catholic faith and his trust in an ultimate divine purpose shaping the world as a whole and the individual human life within it. Characteristically, the lyrical prose of the novel is interspersed with a large number of poems, among which are some of Eichendorff's best known, such as 'Das zerbrochene Ringlein' [The Broken Ring], 'Abschied' [Farewell], and 'Waldgespräch' [Conversation in the Forest].

Apart from *Memoirs of a Good-for-Nothing*, two of Eichendorff's shorter narrative works, *Das Marmorbild* (*The Marble Statue*) and *Das Schloss Dürande* [Dürande Castle] deserve special mention. The first is based on a traditional European story concerning the betrothal of a young man to a statue of Venus, a theme which preoccupied Eichendorff throughout his life and which he here uses to reveal the psychological roots and destructive potential of the erotic drive, as well as the lure of an unbridled poetic imagination, both of which he saw as manifestations of the demonic forces of subjectivism which could only be controlled by Christianity. He saw the same forces at work in the French Revolution, which provides the subject matter of *Das Schloss Dürande*. Yet while he regards the Revolution as an unmitigated disaster, he is also sharply critical of the behaviour of the nobility which led up to it.

The first edition of Eichendorff's collected poems appeared in 1837. Characteristic of his lyric vocabulary is the recurrence of a limited number of archetypal words and images, particularly nouns (often in the plural) referring to basic features of the landscape, such as mountains, forests, valleys, and rivers, verbs conveying movement and sense impressions, and unspecific but emotionally charged adjectives. These combine to give his verse an incantatory quality and an instantly recognizable tone, adapted from the folk-song tradition as transmitted through Arnim and Brentano's collection *Des Knaben Wunderhorn* (*The Boy's Magic Horn*). Eichendorff's conscious use of elements of popular tradition has often been misinterpreted as naive; in fact, it is subtle and ambivalent, stirring unconscious depths in the reader and evoking, through a densely woven net of symbols, a transcendent sphere beyond the physical world. He is also a fine prose stylist and spirited polemicist, using satire and irony to attack, in a manner somewhat reminiscent of his ideological opponent, Heine, both Romantic excesses and unromantic philistinism.

—Judith Purver

MEMOIRS OF A GOOD-FOR-NOTHING (Aus dem Leben eines Taugenichts)
Novella by Joseph von Eichendorff, 1826 (written 1816–25).

One of the best loved of all German tales, *Memoirs of a Good-for-Nothing* has influenced the popular image of German Romanticism more than any other single work. First published in 1826, it has gone through numerous editions and has been translated into many languages. There are three film versions and a vast number of often contradictory interpretations.

The protracted genesis of the work (1816–1825) and the extant manuscripts indicate that the impression of freshness, immediacy, effortless ease, and artless simplicity conveyed by the finished story is deceptive, achieved only after much painstaking revision and alteration. The most important change between earlier versions and the full published text was the author's decision to transform the hero's beloved, Aurelia, into a penniless unmarried orphan rather than a married countess, thus removing the obstacles to her eventual union with the non-aristocratic hero and permitting a happy ending. Traces of the earlier conception, however, still remain, giving a bitter-sweet tinge to this seemingly light-hearted tale of the miller's son who sets out into the world with his violin to make his fortune and finds a better prize than he had sought.

The plot is complicated and confusing, reflecting the confusion of life as Eichendorff saw it. In summary, it relates the hero's departure from home at the behest of his father, who calls him a 'good-for-nothing', the only name given him in the story; his life as gardener's boy and subsequently toll-keeper at a castle near Vienna, where he is employed after his singing has attracted the attention of a countess; his adoration of Aurelia, whom he takes to be a noblewoman and idealizes in the manner of courtly love; his departure from the castle under the mistaken impression that she is married; his journey to Italy as servant to Count Leonard and Flora, the countess's daughter, who are eloping together; his adventures at Leonard's Italian castle and in Rome after his involuntary parting from his patrons; his return to the Viennese castle, reunion with Aurelia, and the prospect of marriage and life with her on a little estate presented to the couple in recognition of his services to Leonard and Flora, who are now to be married; and, finally, the clarification of all the mysteries and misunderstandings that had beset him. The story ends with his proposal to return to Italy and with the declaration that 'all was right with the world'.

The tale is narrated entirely in the first person, so that the reader is obliged to view all the events and characters through the eyes of the naive hero. From this perspective the natural world appears beautiful and unspoiled, whereas human society seems largely comic or grotesque. The superior point of view of the author, implicitly present throughout, gives rise to humour, irony, satire, and parody, which are used to defuse potentially dangerous situations, including those of erotic temptation, to counteract any tendency towards sentimentality, and to convey, from a Catholic Christian and Romantic viewpoint, criticism of the contemporary age for its philistinism, utilitarianism, acquisitiveness, self-satisfaction, and adherence to the bourgeois work ethic. Though quite different in tone and structure from Bunyan's allegorical novel, Eichendorff's story has justly been called a 'German *Pilgrim's Progress*' (G.T. Hughes): the hero may be seen as an exemplary human being on life's journey, guided towards his goal by a beneficent Providence in which he places absolute trust. The name 'good-for-nothing' is, then, ironic: conferred on the hero by a society which lives by false values, it reveals that society's own lack of true worth.

The literary models and the popular and artistic traditions on which Eichendorff drew for his tale are many: the novella, the picaresque novel, the German novel of personal development (Bildungsroman), chap-book, folk-tale and fairy-tale, autobiography, and travel literature, as well as baroque drama, the Viennese popular theatre, opera, folk song, and medieval court poetry. These disparate sources and styles of writing are fused in a seamless whole which conveys the impression of oral rather than written narrative and eludes categorization in terms of genre, just as its hero, in spite of his humble origins, eludes social categorization. He moves between social groups, occupations, and even gender categories, and disguise and mistaken identity play a large part in the story as a whole. These are, of course, traditional theatrical devices, but they have a deeper significance, too, since they raise the question of the identity of the self, a problem which Eichendorff also treats in other works.

Time and place in the story are as difficult to pin down as its genre and central character. There are a number of chronological inconsistencies and geographical inaccuracies: for instance, when the hero leaves home it is early spring and the snow is melting, but by noon the same day the sultry air hangs motionless over waving cornfields; similarly, the hero's approach to Rome at the beginning of chapter seven is described in non-realistic terms, while his journey from Italy back to Austria at the end of chapter eight is accomplished in a single leap. Times, places, objects, landscapes, flowers, birds and animals, episodes, and even human figures have a primarily symbolic rather than realistic function, pointing beyond themselves to a higher, spiritual meaning. This is crystallized in the numerous lyrics interpolated in the narrative. Although not always specially written for the story, they are perfectly placed within it and give a strongly lyrical flavour to the whole. Like the narrative itself, they express the tension between the desire for home and the urge to travel, the longing for security and the fear of stagnation, a fundamental opposition which pervades all Eichendorff's work and can only be resolved through love and through faith in a transcendent sphere in which all the dualities of life are reconciled. *Memoirs of a Good-for-Nothing* offers a poetic image of how such a reconciliation might be achieved. This surely is the reason for its lasting appeal.

—Judith Purver

THE ELDER EDDA. See **THE POETIC EDDA**.

ÉLUARD, Paul. Born Eugène-Émile-Paul Grindel in Paris, France, 14 December 1895. Educated at École communale, Aulnay-sous-Bois, 1901–09; École primaire supérieure Colbert, Paris, 1909. Served in the French army during World War I and World War II. Married 1) Hélène Dimitrovnie (Gala) Diakonova in 1917 (separated 1930), one daughter; 2) Maria Benz in 1934 (died 1946); 3) Dominique Lemor in 1951. Confined in a sanatorium in Davos, 1912–14; leading member of the Surrealist movement between 1919 and 1938; co-founder *La Révolution surréaliste*, 1924; member of the Communist Party, 1927–33, and from 1938; joined Association of Revolutionary Writers and Artists, Paris, 1931; worked for the Resistance, from 1942; founder, with Louis Parrot, *L'Éternelle Revue*, 1944; travelled to Czechoslovakia, Italy, Yugoslavia, Greece, and Poland after World War II. *Died 18 November 1952.*

PUBLICATIONS

Collections

Poésies choisies, edited by Claude Roy. 1959.
Anthologie Éluard, edited by Clive Scott. 1968.
Oeuvres complètes, edited by Marcelle Dumas and Lucien Scheler. 2 vols., 1968.
Poèmes choisis, edited by Pierre Gamarra and Rouben Melik. 1982.
Oeuvres poétiques complètes, edited by Hubert Juin. 6 vols., 1986.
Selected Poems, translated by Gilbert Bowen. 1987.

Verse

Premiers poèmes. 1913.
Le Devoir et l'inquiétude. 1917.
Poèmes pour la paix. 1918.
Les Animaux et leurs hommes. Les Hommes et leurs animaux. 1920.
Répétitions. 1922.
Les Malheurs des immortels, with Max Ernst. 1922.
Mourir de ne pas mourir. 1924.
152 proverbes mis au goût du jour, with Benjamin Péret. 1925.
Capitale de la douleur. 1926.
Les Dessous d'une vie ou la pyramide humaine. 1926.
L'Amour la poésie. 1929.
A toute épreuve. 1930.
La Vie immédiate. 1932.
La Rose publique. 1934.
Facile. 1935.
Nuits partagées. 1935.
Les Yeux fertiles. 1936.
Thorns of Thunder: Selected Poems, edited by George Reavey, translated by Samuel Beckett and others. 1936.
Les Mains libres, illustrated by Man Ray. 1937.
Cours naturel. 1938.
Chanson complète. 1939.
Donner à voir (includes prose). 1939.
Le Livre ouvert 1 (1938–1940). 1940.
Choix de poèmes, edited by A. Bosquet. 1941; revised edition, 1946.
Sur les pentes inférieures. 1941.
Le Livre ouvert II (1939–1941). 1942.
Poésie et vérité. 1942; as *Poetry and Truth*, translated by Roland Penrose and E.L.T. Mesens, 1944.
Poésie involontaire, poésie intentionnelle (selection). 1942.
Les Sept poèmes d'amour en guerre. 1943.
Dignes de vivre. 1944.
Le Lit, la table. 1944.
Au rendez-vous allemand. 1944; revised edition, 1946.
Pour vivre ici. 1944.
Doubles d'ombre, illustrated by Éluard. 1945.
Lingères légères. 1945.
Une longue réflexion amoureuse. 1945.
Poésie ininterrompue I. 1946.
Le Dur Désir de durer. 1946; as *Le Dur Désir de durer*, translated by Stephen Spender and Frances Cornford, 1950.
Corps mémorable. 1947.
Le Temps déborde. 1947.
Choix de poèmes, edited by Louis Parrot. 1948.
Poèmes politiques. 1948.
Voir: Poèmes, peintures, dessins. 1948.
Le Bestiare. 1949.

Une leçon de morale. 1949.
Pouvoir tout dire. 1951.
Le Phénix. 1951.
Les Sentiers et les routes de la poésie. 1952.
Poésie ininterrompue II. 1953.
Deux poèmes, with René Char. 1960.
Derniers poèmes d'amour. 1966; as *Last Love Poems of Paul Éluard* (bilingual edition), translated by Marilyn Kallet, 1980.
Max Ernst: Peintures pour Paul Éluard. 1969.
Poésies 1913–1926. 1970.
Uninterrupted Poetry: Selected Writings, translated by Lloyd Alexander. 1975.
Poèmes de jeunesse, edited by Lucien Scheler and Clavreuil. 1978.
L'Enfant qui ne voulait pas grandir. 1980.

Other

Les Nécessités de la vie et les conséquences des rêves. 1921.
L'Immaculée Conception, with André Breton. 1930.
Appliquée. 1937.
A Pablo Picasso. 1944.
A L'Intérieur de la vue. 1948.
Selected Writings, translated by Lloyd Alexander. 1951.
Lettres de jeunesse, edited by Robert D. Valette. 1962.
Anthologie des écrits sur l'art. 3 vols., 1952–54; 1 vol., 1972.
Le Poète et son ombre: Textes inédits. 1963; revised edition, 1989.
Lettres à Joë Bousquet, edited by Lucien Scheler. 1973.
Lettres à Gala: (1924–1948), edited by Pierre Dreyfus. 1984.
Seconde nature. 1990.
Dictionnaire abrégé du surréalisme, with André Breton. 1991.

Translator, *Oeuvres choisies*, by Christo Botev, 1966.

*

Critical Studies: *Le Je universel chez Paul Éluard* by P. Emmanuel, 1938; *Paul Éluard* by Louis Perche, 1963; *Le Poète et son ombre*, 1963, and *Éluard: Livre d'identité*, 1967, revised edition, 1968, both by Robert D. Valette; *Paul Éluard: L'Amour, la révolte, le rêve*, 1965, and *Paul Éluard: Biographie pour une approche*, 1965, both by Luc Decaunes; *La Poésie de Paul Éluard et le thème de la pureté* by Ursula Jucker-Wehrli, 1965; *Éluard par lui-même*, 1968, and *La Poétique du désir*, 1974, both by Raymond Jean; *Album Éluard* by Roger J. Ségalat, 1968; *The Poetry of Dada and Surrealism: Aragon, Breton, Tzara, Éluard and Desnos* by Mary Ann Caws, 1970; *Le Vocabulaire politique de Paul Éluard* by Marie-Renée Guyard, 1974; *Paul Éluard* by Robert Nugent, 1974; *'Nuits partagées' and The Prose Poem in Éluard* by Eric Hill Wayne, 1976; *Éluard; ou, le pouvoir du mot* by Jean-Yves Debreuille, 1977; *Les Mots la vie* by C. Guedj, 1980; *Éluard; ou, le rayonnement de l'être* by Daniel Bergez, 1982; *La Poésie de Paul Éluard: La rupture et le partage 1913–1936* by Nicole Boulestreau, 1985; *Paul Éluard; ou, Le Frère voyant* by Jean-Charles Gateau, 1988.

* * *

Paul Éluard was a prolific if uneven poet. Between 1916 and 1952 he composed verse and prose poems of astonishing lyrical power and verbal invention. His reputation as a major 20th-century lyric poet rests chiefly on his surrealist love poetry (1924–38) and his Resistance poems (1940–44). He also produced Dadaist poems, surrealist experimental collaborations (with Breton on the *Dictionnnaire abrégé du surréalisme* [Abridged Dictionary of Surrealism] and on *L'Immaculée Conception* [The Immaculate Conception]—a linguistic exploration of madness using automatic writing techniques, poetic translations (of García Lorca, Botev), critical writings on poetry, demagogical communist verse, political pamphlets, anthologies of poetry and of writings on art, and scripts for a series of radio broadcasts. The broad trajectory of his work reflects an increasing commitment to militant communism, although many critics feel that his later work does not rise above sentimentality or dogma.

In Éluard's poetry a language of an amoral sensory world is pitched against that of moral statement. Fighting alongside fellow Surrealists in a crusade against artificially maintained rational categories, Éluard believed that the moral and sensory domains are inseparable. For Éluard there is an immediacy of perception by the self of the world. Moreover, all the world's objects cooperate in the act of perception by mutually foregrounding each other. Éluard called this idea 'transparence'. This transparency is observed in many of the poems in *Capitale de la douleur* [Capital of Pain]: 'The space between things has the shape of my words/ . . . The space has the shape of my looks' (from 'Ne plus partager'); 'Tes yeux sont livrés à ce qu'ils voient/Vus par ce qu'ils regardent' [Your eyes are delivered to what they see/Seen by what they observe] (from 'Nusch'). Transparency is ensured by the figure of Woman that for Éluard is a principle of Being ('resemblance').

This myth of seeing is predominant in many of Éluard's poems presenting the world altered by the radical perception of lovers. However, the proliferation of perspectives and matter created and sustained by Éluard's vertiginous visual imagery points up a disturbance at the heart of looking. The purity of vision paradoxically requires impurity in the form of dissolved identity. A poems such as 'L'Amoureuse' celebrates the marvellous, yet shows it to be a burden. The full presence of the external world both delights and oppresses: 'Elle est debout sur mes paupières' (she is standing on my eyelids). The event of looking takes place inside the eye, as experience accrues in an endless set of transparencies. The unsettling nature of this sensory plenitude is in evidence in poems such as 'Le plus jeune' and in many of the poems in 'La vie immédiate' and *La Rose publique*.

The highly volatile universe of images in the Éluardian sensory world is matched by the equally destabilizing moral diction in the poems. This is as true of Éluard's first serious political poem 'La Victoire de Guernica', as in these opening lines from 'Premièrement': 'La terre est bleue comme une orange/Jamais une erreur les mots ne mentent pas' [The earth is blue like an orange/Never an error words do not lie]. The dizzying, and irritating, effect of these lines resides in the way in which both domains collide. The programmatic symmetry here moralizes the sensory, just as the moral is made sensory; the reader witnesses simultaneous substitution and inter-penetration.

Such strategies are to be found in *Poésie ininterrompue I*, a long poem that demonstrates the full range of Éluard's poetic language. This extraordinary work, which is at the same time an autobiographical *apologia* and a poem of the Liberation, grafts surrealist techniques (used long after his objective break with Breton and the Surrealists in 1938) onto a vision of communist utopia. The peculiar rhetoric of this poem presents the paradise experienced by the reader as the next and inevitable evolutionary step for humankind. As elsewhere in Éluard's work, but here concentrated and refined, the 'linguistic democracy' of Éluard's syntax reflects his anti-hierarchical views, creating a poetic Marxism in which all classes are dissolved. Paratactic enumeration and sententious aphorism, which Éluard had exploited in earlier poems, gather momentum through hallucinatory verbal incantation. In *Poésie ininterrompe I*, with its wearisome and elating intertwining of programmatic exhortations and surrealist imagery, Éluard achieved a new kind of poem.

If the themes of Éluard's love poetry are perennial—purity, passion, the lovers' look, the world made marvellous by the state of romance, the loneliness experienced in the absence of love—he nevertheless proves to be an unconventional poet, in two essential ways. Firstly, an analysis of his poetic language reveals a specific and idiosyncratic revitalizing of stock, contemporary diction. A micro-history of the period is detectable in the incestuous surrealist magazines and, during the war, in the echoes and loans of key words in the many Resistance journals to which Éluard subscribed and contributed. Secondly, Éluard promulgated in his poems the belief that love, like poetry itself, was a revolutionary act capable of transforming both perception and societal life. In so doing, the amorous couple is placed at the service of humanity, as an example and a building block for an abundant world.

Although Éluard wrote some execrable verse ('Joseph Staline' for example) at a time (1950) when the French Communist Party was nurturing its cultural mascots, his over-all project was not to incorporate Marxist ideas into poems, but to set down his sympathies for victims of social injustice and of the stultification of perception in bourgeois life. To this end, Éluard created a hybrid poetry of moral didacticism and pure lyricism. Not since Hugo has there been such an intriguing conflation of private imagination and public pronouncement in French poetry.

—Rolf Venner

YOU THE ONLY ONE ('Décalques')
Poem by Paul Éluard, 1928.

You the only one and I hear the grasses of your laugh
You it is your head which removes you
And from the height of mortal danger
Upon the blurred globes of rain from the valleys
Beneath the heavy light beneath the sky of earth
You bring forth the fall.
The birds are no longer a sufficient refuge
Nor sloth nor fatigue
The recollection of the woods and the fragile streams
In the morning of caprices
In the morning of visible caresses
In the early morning of absence the fall.
The barques of your eyes lose their way
In the lace of disappearances
The chasm is unveiled it is for others to extinguish it
The shadows which you create are not entitled to the
    night.

'You the only one' was first published in April 1928 in *Cahiers du Sud* as 'Décalques' ['Tracings'] and was also included in the poem-sequence 'Firstly' in *L'Amour la poésie* [Love Poetry] in 1929. It is typical of Éluard's surrealist love poems, combining simple diction with powerful and bewildering imagery aimed at disrupting perception.

An initial explosive image—'the grasses of your laugh'—immediately grasps the reader's attention but threatens to drown the rest of the poem. Since the subsequent lines continue to provoke disarray, it is tempting to detect a blueprint, commonsense image 'behind', so to speak, the cluster of surrealist ones. A naturalistic picture can be reconstructed—a woman standing on a rainy, windswept hilltop. However, finding naturalistic solutions implies that the poem is a mere puzzle, whereas the commonsense image has no more pre-eminence than the shifting movements of objects. The 'real' is only part of the picture.

The combination of 'grasses' and 'laugh' sets in motion a play of substitution between two elements associated with woman, the principle of identity in Éluard's love poetry. The missing term is 'ripple': the grasses ripple like her laughter, or her laughter causes the grasses to ripple. A 'feminine land-scape' is intimated, and the sentiment is one of traditional Petrarchism yet transformed by the extraordinary linguistic compression of the image, an economy maintained in line 2, where an absent, unspecified hat may have blown from the woman's head. The dislocation of 'your head which removes you' suggests that she has 'laughed her head off' in the wind.

The Surrealist revolution in perception was concentrated on ordinary objects. Perhaps more than any other Surrealist, Éluard experimented with a simple diction. In 'You the only one' this comprises the familiar ingredients of daily life (birds, grasses, light, woods, eyes, rain), words with pastoral, even Edenic associations that prevail in other non-concrete words (absence, the fall, disappearances). One critic (Jean-Charles Gateau) 'explains' the poems by citing direct pictorial influences (e.g. Max Ernst, Giorgio de Chirico, Yves Tanguy). However, this conflation of the visual with the literary is inadequate. Éluard is not a narrowly mimetic poet, even if imitative gestures can be found in his language. Surrealist paintings frequently play with scale or position, and in 'You the only one' each raindrop is a world, with 'sky or earth' a stunning reversal where each is filled with the other. The 'of' phrase here, as with 'grasses of your laugh', establishes a confusion as to agency, launching infinite oscillations and interpretations. The woman is a Surrealist Eve figure, a morally unindicted vessel for the Fall. The marvellous (a surreali-sation of the notion of grace) enters with the converging worlds of dream and reality.

Jean Paulhan argues in *Les Fleurs de Tarbes* (*The Flowers of Tarbes*) that writers live in fear of clichés, and best outwit them when they engage with them directly. 'Fragile streams' is a fine example of Éluard practising this. By avoiding a word like 'tinkling', 'fragile' works by association, substituting cause for effect, and transforming sound into touch. The same procedure applies in the 'lace of disappearances' where the Romantic cliché of lace for foam is both used and avoided, for the sea is not mentioned, and extinguishing a chasm introduces another absent notion, fire.

Much critical attention has been rightly devoted to the elaborate myth of seeing in Éluard's work. Line 11 is only partly voyeuristic. The image is of light made up of touching particles, tangibility rendered visible and unifying the senses. 'The barques of your eyes' is another peculiar image. Perhaps there is a similarity between the curve of hulls and that of eyes; or maybe the boats are reflected in the eyes. The world for Éluard takes place inside the eyes: external reality is not strangely 'out there', but mystically imbricated within the sensory apparatus of human beings.

In the final elusive proposition a strange logic pertains: Woman/Light creates shadows; these shadows are privileged, 'caused' by the Woman and do not therefore belong in the world of night (there can be no shadows where there is darkness/Woman's absence).

A number of other features contribute to the sense of universal predication in the poem. Éluard used punctuation increasingly rarely, and the near absence of it in 'You the only one' strengthens the syntactic ambiguity both at the line-end and within the line: the valleys are or are not beneath the light and the Woman or the Light, or both, are beneath the sky/earth. This procedure in Éluard is a stylistic analogue for the continuity and fluidity of sensory experience. The dis-mantling of perceptions is further compounded by the use of prepositions ('upon' and 'beneath'). There are no—or there are only—transitional states in this poetry of immediacy. The syntactic structures of the poem may be viewed as an egali-tarian attitude directed on to language itself and sweeping aside the hierarchical meaning of clauses and subclauses. A similar attitude can be witnessed in Éluard's reliance on the sonorities of assonance, consonance, alliteration, internal, sometimes vertical rhyme, and often verbatim repetition (see ll. 10 and 11), all exploited to produce a sense of full inter-connectedness. Lastly enumeration, with each object simul-taneously distinct and subsumed by the next one, rehearses Éluard's dictum that 'Everything is comparable to everything else'. This poem attests eloquently to that conviction.

—Rolf Venner

ELYTIS, Odysseus. Born Odysseus Alepoudelis in Heraklion, Crete, 2 November 1911. Studied law at the University of Athens, 1930–33, no degree; studied literature at the Sorbonne, Paris, 1948–52. Served in the First Army Corps, in Albania, 1940–41: Lieutenant. Programme direc-tor, National Broadcasting Institution, 1945–47, 1953–54; art and literary critic, *Kathimerini* newspaper, 1946–48; adviser to Art Theatre, 1955–56, and Greek National Theatre, 1965–68. President of the Governing Board, Greek Ballet, 1956–58, and Greek Broadcasting and Television, 1974; member of the Administrative Board, Greek National Theatre, 1974–76. Recipient: National prize for poetry, 1960; Nobel prize for literature, 1979; Royal Society of Literature Benson medal (UK), 1981. D.Litt.: University of Salonica, 1976; the Sorbonne, 1980; University of London, 1981. Member, Order of the Phoenix, 1965; Grand Commander, Order of Honour, 1979; Commandeur de l'Ordre des Arts et des Lettres (France), 1984; Commandeur, Légion d'honneur (France), 1989. Lives in Athens.

PUBLICATIONS

Verse

Prosanatolismi [Orientations]. 1936.
O Ilios o Protos, mazi me tis Parallayes pano se mian Ahtida [Sun the First Together with Variations on a Sunbeam]. 1943.
Asma Iroiko ke Penthimo yia ton Hameno Anthipolohago tis Alvanias [Heroic and Elegiac Song for the Lost Second Lieutenant of the Albanian Campaign]. 1945.
I Kalosini stis Likopories [Kindness in the Wolfpasses]. 1946.
To Axion Esti. 1959; as *The Axion Esti*, translated by Edmund Keeley and G.P. Savidis, 1974.
Exi ke Mia Tipsis yia ton Ourano [Six and One Regrets for the Sky]. 1960.

To Fotodendro ke i Dekati Tetarti Omorfia [The Light Tree and the Fourteenth Beauty]. 1971.
O Ilios o Iliatoras [The Sovereign Sun]. 1971.
Thanatos ke Anastasis tou Konstantinou Paleologou [Death and Resurrection of Constantine Palaiologos]. 1971.
To Monogramma [The Monogram]. 1972.
To Ro tou Erota [The Ro of Eros] (songs). 1972.
Clear Days: Poems by Palamas and Elytis, in Versions by Nikos Tselepides, edited by Kenneth O. Hanson. 1972.
Villa Natacha. 1973.
O Fillomantis [The Leaf Diviner]. 1973.
Ta Eterothali [The Stepchildren]. 1974.
The Sovereign Sun: Selected Poems, translated by Kimon Friar. 1974.
Maria Nefeli. 1978; as *Maria Nefeli*, translated by Athan Anagnostopoulos, 1981.
Selected Poems, edited and translated by Edmund Keeley and Philip Sherrard. 1981.
Tria Poemata me Simea Evkerias [Three Poems under a Flag of Convenience]. 1982.
Hemerologio henos atheatou Apriliou [Diary of an Unseen April]. 1984.
O Mikros Naftilos. 1985; as *The Little Mariner*, translated by Olga Broumas, 1988.
What I Love: Selected Poems of Odysseas Elytis, translated by Olga Broumas. 1986.
Krinagoras. 1987.
Ta Elegia tis Oxopetras [The Elegies of Oxopetras]. 1991.

Other

O Zografos Theofilos [The Painter Theophilos]. 1973.
Anoichta Hartia [Open Book]. 1974.
He Mageia tou Papadiamanti [The Magic of Papadiamantis]. 1976.
Anafora ston Andrea Embiriko [Report to Andreas Embirikos]. 1980.
To Domatio me tis Ikones [The Room of Images]. 1986.
Ta Dimosia ke ta Idiotika [Public and Private Matters]. 1990.
I Idiotiki Odos [Private Way]. 1990.
En Lefko [In White]. 1992.

Translator, *Defteri Graphi* [Second Writing] (poems of Lorca, Rimbaud, Éluard, Maiakovskii, and others). 1976.
Translator, *Ioannis, I Apokalipsi* [St John, Apocalypse]. 1985.
Translator, *Sappho—Anasinthesi ke Apodosi* [Sappho—Synthesis and Rendering]. 1985.

*

Critical Studies: Elytis issue of *Books Abroad*, Autumn 1975; *Odysseus Elytis: Anthologies of Light*, edited by Ivar Ivask, 1981; 'Maria Nefeli and the Changeful Sameness of Elytis: Variations on a Theme' by Andonis Decavalles, and 'Elytis and the Greek Tradition' by Edmund Keeley, both in *Charioteer*, 1982–83; 'Odysseus Elytis and the Discovery of Greece' by Philip Sherrard, in *Journal of Modern Greek Studies*, 1(2), 1983; 'Eliot and Elytis: Poet of Time, Poet of Space' by Karl Malkoff, in *Comparative Literature*, 36(3), 1984; 'Odysseus Elytis in the 1980s' by Andonis Decavalles, in *World Literature Today*, 62(1), 1988.

*   *   *

Ever since Odysseus Elytis first appeared on the Greek literary scene in 1935, critical attention has focused on the new world his poetry created: a world of sun and sea, the Aegean landscape, love, and communion with nature. Yet the world of Elytis, consistently developed since the poet's earliest collection, *Prosanatolismi* [Orientations], would seem to be rather more complex than some critics have allowed. His subsequent work indicates that this world is correlative to his view of poetry as an alternative to reality. Within this world, as Elytis has said with reference to a fellow poet, Andreas Embirikos, actual problems may not be solved, but something more radical occurs: the logic that created these problems is abolished.

One of the methods Elytis has employed for the creation of his world is surrealism. Together with Embirikos, Nikos Engonopoulos, and Nikos Gatsos, he introduced surrealism into Greek literary life in the 1930s and 1940s. Having experimented with surrealism before publishing anything, Elytis finally rejected certain surrealist techniques, such as automatic writing, but adopted some aspects of its philosophy, viewing surrealism as a quest for spiritual health and a reaction against the rationalism prevalent in Western thought.

Another method he used is the establishing of connections between the natural elements of his poetic world and attitudes to life; as he says in *O Mikros Naftilos* (*The Little Mariner*), the exploration of the hidden relationships between meanings leads to poetry which, like one's view of the sky, depends on one's vantage point.

The 'Greekness' of Elytis's poetic landscape has frequently been the subject of critical commentary. If, however, at the beginning of his poetic career, this landscape was a celebration of love, in *To Axion Esti* (*The Axion Esti*) it also becomes a place where the joy and pain of existence and creation combine with the historical adventures of the Greek nation, where good fights against evil, universal values are established, and death is defeated. This world, created by and simultaneously with poetry, is proclaimed in the end to be eternal, while the poet states that 'WORTHY is the price paid'. The tragic aspects of this sunlit world are also confronted in *Exi ke Mia Tipsis yia ton Ourano* [Six and One Regrets for the Sky]. There, the poet affirms 'the lawfulness of the Unhoped-For', and at the same time states: 'Well then, he whom I sought *I am*'—an achievement that Elytis has elsewhere characterized as the most difficult thing in the world, defining the process of becoming what one is as poetry.

When the components of Elytis's world have acquired these new dimensions, some of which are explored through the dialogue of a girl called Maria Nefeli [Maria Cloud] and her interlocutor who seems to represent the poet, in *Maria Nefeli*, they manage to incorporate death too. Aspects of death are explored in *Hemerologio henos atheatou Apriliou* [Diary of an Unseen April] and in *Ta Elegia tis Oxopetras*. Through its polymorphous connections with sun, sea, gardens, and love, death is proclaimed in the latter collections to be the blue, endless sea and the unsetting sun, while in the former ones, the poet contemplates the 'Unknown' and declares that he has worked there for years and that his fingers were scorched just as he was about to see Paradise opening. Thus, death is not presented as the reverse of love, since antitheses in the world of Elytis are often resolved into a synthesis; as the poet said about himself in *Prosanatolismi*, from the other side he is the same.

This sameness persists in the 'other side' of Elytis's main poetic work, that is, in his songs and essays. His songs were published in 1972 under the general title *To Ro tou Erota* [The Ro of Eros] and many of them were set to music, as also was a large part of *The Axion Esti*, by Mikis Theodorakis. Apart from the subject matter, one of the obvious resemblances between these songs and Elytis's poems is found in the insistence on magic numbers: most of these songs are grouped in sevens or multiples of seven, a number which occurs both in titles of collections (*Exi ke Mia Tipsis yia ton Ourano*, *To Fotodendro ke i Dekati Tetarti Omorfia* [The Light Tree and the Fourteenth Beauty]) and in the structure of his collections and compositions. His preoccupation with numbers is probably related to his preoccupation with the metrical forms of his poems. Although his verse usually falls under the general heading of 'free verse', Elytis has himself commented on the strict metrical and formal rules he imposes on his verse. Most of his essays have been collected in a book entitled *Anoichta Hartia* [Open Book], where he gives a chronicle of his literary generation (the 'Generation of the 1930s'), describes their explorations and poetics, and deals with surrealism and dreams, painters, and poets. One of his other, separately published, essays takes the form of *Anafora ston Andrea Embiriko* [Report to Andreas Embirikos], combining memories of his friend and fellow poet with an account of surrealist poetics. The integral position which Elytis's translations occupy in his work is apparent from the titles he gives them: *Defteri Graphi* [Second Writing] for translations of Lorca, Rimbaud, Éluard, Maiakovskii, and others; *Sappho—Anasinthesi ke Apodosi* [Sappho—Synthesis and Rendering] for his arrangement and translation of the Sapphic fragments.

The creation of the poetic world, adjacent to the real one, both dependent on and independent from it, makes the poet's role a dangerous one, quite different from the image of the 'carefree Elytis' projected by critics of his early work. In *To Fotodendro ke i Dekati Tetarti Omorfia* the poet defines his position as painful but unshakeable ('still standing firm with burnt fingers') in a world of his own creation.

—Elli Philokyprou

ENDŌ Shūsaku (Paul). Born in Tokyo, Japan, 27 March 1923. Educated at Keio University, Tokyo, B.A. in French literature 1949; University of Lyons, 1950–53. Married Junko Okada in 1955; one son. Contracted tuberculosis in 1959. Former editor of the literary journal *Mita Bungaku*; chair, Bungeika Kyōkai (Literary Artists' Association); manager, Kiza amateur theatrical troupe. President, Japanese PEN. Recipient: Akutagawa prize, 1955; Tanizaki prize, 1967; Grupo de Oficial da Ordem do Infante dom Henrique (Portugal), 1968; Sancti Silvestri (award by Pope Paul VI), 1970; Noma prize, 1980; Mainichi cultural prize; Dag Hammarskjold prize. Member, Nihon Geijutsuin (Japanese Arts Academy), 1981. Honorary doctorate: Georgetown University, Washington, DC; University of California, Santa Clara. Lives in Tokyo.

PUBLICATIONS

Fiction

Aden made [Till Aden], in *Mita bungaku*. November 1954.
Shiroi hito [White Man]. 1955.
Kiiroi hito [Yellow Man]. 1955.
Aoi chiisana budō [Green Little Grapes], in *Bungakukau*. January–June 1956.
Umi to dokuyaku. 1957; as *The Sea and Poison*, translated by Michael Gallagher, 1972.
Kazan. 1959; as *Volcano*, translated by Richard Schucherl, 1978.
Obakasan, in *Asahi shinbun*. April–August 1959; as *Wonderful Fool*, translated by Francis Mathy, 1974.
Otoko to kyūkanchō [Three Men and a Starling], in *Bungakukai*. January 1963.
Watashi no mono. 1963; translated as 'Mine', in *Japan Christian Quarterly*, 40(4), 1974.
Watashi ga suteta onna. 1964; as *The Girl I Left Behind*, translated by Mark Williams, 1994.
Aika [Elegies] (stories). 1965.
Ryūgaku, in *Gunzō*. March 1965; as *Foreign Studies*, translated by Mark Williams, 1989.
Chinmoku. 1966; as *Silence*, translated by William Johnston, 1969.
Taihen daa! [Good Grief!]. 1969.
Shikai no hotori [By the Dead Sea]. 1973.
Iesu no shogai. 1973; as *A Life of Jesus*, translated by Richard Schucherl, 1978.
Yumoa shōsetsu shū [Collection of Humorous Stories]. 1973.
Waga seishun ni kui ari [Regrets for Our Youth]. 1974.
Kuchibue o fuku toki. 1974; as *When I Whistle*, translated by Van C. Gessel, 1979.
Sekai kikō [Travels Around the World]. 1975.
Hechimakun [Master Snake-Gourd]. 1975.
Kitsunegata tanukigata [In the Shape of a Fox, in the Shape of a Badger]. 1976.
Gūtara mandanshū [Lazybones]. 1978.
Marie Antoinette. 1979.
Jūichi no iro garasu [11 Pieces of Stained Glass] (stories). 1979.
Samurai. 1980; as *The Samurai*, translated by Van C. Gessel, 1982.
Onna no isshō [A Woman's Life]. 1982.
Akuryō no gogo [Afternoon of the Evil Spirit]. 1983.
Stained Glass Elegies: Stories (includes stories from *Aika* and *Jūichi no iro garasu*), translated by Van C. Gessel. 1984.
Sukyandaru. 1986; as *Scandal*, translated by Van C. Gessel, 1988.
Hangyaku [Rebellion]. 2 vols., 1989.
The Final Martyrs: Stories, translated by Van C. Gessel. 1993.
Fukai kawa. 1993; as *Deep River*, translated by Van C. Gessel, 1994.

Plays

Ōgon no kuni (produced 1966). 1969; as *The Golden Country*, translated by Francis Mathy, 1970.
Bara no yakata [A House Surrounded by Roses]. 1969.

Other

Furansu no daigakusei [Students in France, 1951–52]. 1953.
Seisho no naka no joseitachi [Women in the Bible]. 1968.
Korian vs Manbō, with Kita Morio. 1974.
Bungaku Zenshū [Collected Literary Works]. 11 vols., 1975.
Ukiaru kotoba [Floating Words]. 1976.
Ai no akebono [Dawn of Love], with Miura Shumon. 1976.
Nihonjin wa kirisuto kyō o shinjirareru ka [Can Japanese People Believe in Christianity?]. 1977.
Kirisuto no tanjō [The Birth of Christ]. 1978.
Ningen no naka no X [X Inside Human Beings]. 1978.

Rakuten taishō [Great Victory of Optimism]. 1978.
Kare no ikikata [His Way of Life]. 1978.
Jū to jūjika (biography of Pedro Cassini). 1979.
Shinran, with Masutani Fumio. 1979.
Sakka no nikki [Writer's Diary]. 1980.
Chichioya [Father]. 1980.
Kekkonron [On Marriage]. 1980.
Endō Shūsaku ni yoru Endō Shūsaku [Endo Shusaku According to Himself]. 1980.
Meiga Iesu junrei [Pilgrimage to Famous Pictures of Jesus]. 1981.
Ai to jinsei o meguru danso [Faults in Love and Life]. 1981.
Ōkoku e no michi [The Way to the Kingdom]. 1981.
Fuyu no yasashisa [The Gentleness of Winter]. 1982.
Watakushi ni totte kami to wa [My View of God]. 1983.
Kokoro [Heart]. 1984.
Ikiru gakkō [School of Life]. 1984.
Watakushi no aishita shōsetsu [A Novel I Have Loved]. 1985.
Rakudai bōzu no rirekisho [Resumé of a Failed Priest]. 1989.
Kawaru mono to kawaranu mono: hanadokei [Things That Change and Things That Do Not Change: Flower-Clocks]. 1990.

*

Critical Studies: 'Shusaku Endo: The Second Period' by Francis Mathy, in *Japan Christian Quarterly*, 40, 1974; 'Tradition and Contemporary Consciousness: Ibuse, Endo, Kaiko, Abe' by J. Thomas Rimer, in his *Modern Japanese Fiction and Its Traditions*, 1978; 'Mr Shusaku Endo Talks about His Life and Works as a Catholic Writer' (interview), in *Chesterton Review*, 12(4), 1986; 'The Roots of Guilt and Responsibility in Shusaku Endo's *The Sea and Poison*' by Hans-Peter Breuer, in *Literature and Medicine*, 7, 1988; 'Rediscovering Japan's Christian Tradition: Text-Immanent Hermeneutics in Two Short Stories by Shusaku Endo' by Rolf J. Goebel, in *Studies in Language and Culture*, 14(63), 1988; 'Graham Greene: *The Power and the Glory*: A Comparative Essay with *Silence* by Shusaku Endo' by Kazuie Hamada, in *Collected Essays by the Members of the Faculty (Kyoritsu Women's Junior College)*, 31, February 1988; 'Christianity in the Intellectual Climate of Modern Japan' by Shunichi Takayanagi, in *Chesterton Review*, 14(3), 1988; 'Salvation of the Weak: Endo Shusaku', in *The Sting of Life: Four Contemporary Japanese Novelists*, 1989, and 'The Voice of the Doppelgänger', in *Japan Quarterly*, 38(2), 1991, both by Van C. Gessel.

* * *

Ever since his emergence on the literary scene, Endō Shūsaku has consistently sought resolution of the conflict he has perceived between, on the one hand, his 'adopted' religion, Christianity, and, on the other, his chosen profession as author. Derived in part from his study of several French Catholic novelists, and informing his entire *oeuvre*, is the desire for a reconciliation between his perceived duty, as Christian, to seek within man the potential for salvation and the necessity, accruing to him as author, to remain totally honest to his observations of human nature. In the case of Endō, a Japanese national, moreover, the tension was further exacerbated by the need to operate within a cultural and spiritual framework that provides less encouragement for the development of literary themes dealing with the spiritual drama of the relationship between God and man, leading him

to conclude: 'As a Christian, Japanese and an author, I am constantly concerned with the relationship and conflict created by these three tensions . . . Unfortunately, these three tensions continue to appear as contradictory in my mind'.

The result, in the case of Endō, is an author whose self-professed desire 'to find God on the streets of Shinjuku and Shibuya, districts which seem so far removed from Him' has been constantly tempered by a realization that he was 'not writing in order to proselytize', and that, if he were, his 'works would certainly suffer as literature'. Thereafter, the more he has found himself drawn to privilege his obligations as literary artist, the more he has come to recognize the need to create 'living human beings', a task that requires, not merely external observation, but also scrutiny of the internal psychology of his creations, a faithful depiction of their inner being, however unattractive. The result is a body of works that increasingly mirrors Endō's conviction that 'to describe man's inner self, we must probe to the third dimension [within the unconscious] . . . to the territory of demons. One cannot describe man's inner being completely unless one closes in on this demonic part'.

The paradox is readily apparent: in focusing on a realm in which 'our desire for Good conflicts with our penchant for Evil, where our appreciation of Beauty conflicts with our attachment to the Ugly', Endō was drawn increasingly to focus on the weakness of human nature, in the belief that only thus could he portray, behind the sin depicted, 'the glimmer of light . . . the light of God's grace'—the potential for salvation which he saw as underlying the entire human drama. The consequent vision of the unconscious as both the fount of all sin and the 'place where God works and has His being' is reflected in the Endō text by an increasing focus on the 'monstrous duality of man', this assuming the literary guise of a gradual fusion of two qualities, initially established as in opposition. In several texts, like *Chinmoku* (*Silence*) and *The Samurai*, the central dichotomy thus established is that between East and West, with the distance between the two, initially depicted as unfathomable (as evidenced by the Western missionaries appearing unable to penetrate the 'mudswamp' of Japan), steadily eroded during the course of the novels as a result of the author's increasing focus, not on external distinctions, but on internal similarities that allow for meaningful communication across various national, religious, and cultural divides. Thus, at the outset of *Silence*, Rodrigues, the Portuguese missionary, is portrayed as entirely confident of his own inner resources. Confronted by the choice, imposed upon him by the Japanese shogunate authorities, between on the one hand adherence to his faith and the consequent death of the Japanese converts being tortured before his eyes, and, on the other, renunciation of all that his life to date had stood for, Rodrigues ultimately succumbs and tramples on the crucifix that had been placed before him in an outward act of apostasy. Internally, however, there is evidence, supported in the text by the erosion of the apparently irreconcilable distinction between the 'strong' martyr and the 'weak' apostate, of the protagonist's augmented love of God at the end of the novel, the narrator acknowledging Rodrigues's decision, following shortly after his act of public apostasy, to hear the confession of the Japanese man who had betrayed him to the authorities: 'He may have been betraying [his fellow priests], but he was not betraying "that man, [Christ]". He loved Him now in a totally different way. "Everything in my life to date was necessary in order to know that love. I am still the last priest in this land."'

A similar process can be seen at work in *The Samurai*, a novel in which the distance between the 'Western' missionary, Velasco, and the lower-ranking samurai, symbol of 'Eastern' values, is initially portrayed as unfathomable. As the novel progresses, however, so Endō's narrator succeeds in breaking down the various obstacles to reconciliation, this being acknowledged at the personal level by Velasco in his eventual recognition: 'It was as if a firm bond of solidarity had formed between the envoys and myself'.

In these, and other examples of oppositions subjected to similar fusion in Endō's novels, the emphasis is on a steady growth in self-awareness and, as the Endō protagonist becomes more and more aware of some previously unconscious aspect of his being, so he appears increasingly well equipped to participate in this process of reconciliation. Seen in this light, Endō's 1986 novel, *Sukyandaru* (*Scandal*), a text heralded by several critics as an abrupt abandonment of earlier Endō motifs, comes to appear rather as a progression, a work that addresses more directly than ever before the inherent human duality. During the course of the novel, the protagonist, Suguro, grows steadily in his conviction that the 'impostor' he initially dismisses as a chance look-alike is none other than his own double—that 'he could no longer conceal that part of himself, no longer deny its existence'— the pervading impression being of an author confident in the assessment of human nature he offered at the time: 'Man is a splendid and beautiful being, and, at the same time, man is a terrible being as we recognized in Auschwitz—God knows well this monstrous dual quality of man'.

—Mark Williams

SILENCE (Chinmoku)
Novel by Endō Shūsaku, 1966.

The novel *Silence* by Endō Shūsaku has been subject to a barrage of interpretations by a variety of critics. Most seek to account for the perceived illogicality of a self-confessed Catholic author selecting as the ostensible focal point of his novel the act of apostasy performed by his protagonist, the Portuguese missionary Rodrigues. Having insisted on entering the country in deliberate violation of the anti-Christian edicts that were being so ruthlessly enforced in Japan at the time (the early 17th century), Rodrigues's decision, following his inevitable capture, to renounce his God and all that his life to date has stood for has been widely condemned in the Japanese Christian community as an act of heresy. How, it is asked, could such a writer justify depiction of his protagonist succumbing to the repeated demands of the shogunate authorities to place his foot on the image of Christ attached to a crucifix (the *fumie* that was traditionally employed by shogunate officials as a means of rounding up those who clung to the outlawed faith)? Similarly, there have been those who have viewed Rodrigues's increasing despair at the apparent 'silence' of God towards those who clung tenaciously to their faith in the face of the cruellest torture and death as evidence of a fundamental absence of faith within Rodrigues from the outset. Finally, from the 'traditionalist' camp has emerged the suggestion that at the core of the novel lies the belief, expressed in the work by Rodrigues's mentor Ferreira (a man whose reported apostasy had seemed so improbable to his former students that they had determined to travel to Japan to investigate the truth of these rumours), that Japan was a 'swamp' in which the roots of the 'sapling of Christianity' were destined to 'rot, the leaves to grow yellow and wither'. To such critics, *Silence* is a novel concerned primarily with the

irreconcilable gap, both spiritual and cultural, between the East and West.

All such interpretations appear to be amply supported by an analysis of the first eight chapters of the novel. Significantly, however, the novel does not finish with Rodrigues's act of renunciation. The protagonist may emulate Ferreira in accepting a Japanese name, a wife, and a residence in Nagasaki, courtesy of the very authorities who have driven him to apostatize; however, Endō is at pains to stress in the brief concluding section that, for all his outward capitulation, inwardly Rodrigues is ultimately possessed of a faith more real and more profound than that which has inspired him to risk all in embarking on his mission to Japan in the first place. The distinction between Rodrigues before and after his decision to trample on the *fumie* is therefore significant. The early Rodrigues is fired by an impressive enthusiasm to rescue the abandoned believers in Japan and possessed of the vision of an omnipotent and omniscient God that appears sufficient to equip him with the resilience required to defy all the physical pain his fellow man can inflict upon him. Concomitant with his increasing concern at the perceived silence of God, however, is the development of an inner hope that, paradoxically, he can acknowledge only at the moment of greatest despair. As he stands confronted by the image of Christ on the *fumie*, and as he recognizes there not the powerful image of beauty of European tradition, but the face of a man 'who quietly shares our suffering', so there is born within him a faith of a new dimension, a recognition that God, far from being silent, had spoken through His silence. From a theological standpoint, therefore, there can be no justification for the Christ on the *fumie* to break his silence to the despairing Rodrigues with the words, 'Trample! I more than anyone know the pain in your foot . . . It was to be trampled on by men that I was born into this world'. From a literary perspective, however, this is the moment of catharsis. Endō's depiction of the scene is reminiscent of Rembrandt's ability to portray a shaft of light shining through the darkness. Thus, although Rodrigues's assertion in the immediate aftermath of his outward apostasy that 'Lord, you alone know that I did not renounce my faith' may appear unconvincing at the time, by the end of the novel Endō is able to depict his protagonist agreeing to hear the confession of Kichijirō, the very man who has betrayed him, Judas-like, to the authorities, confident in the knowledge that 'even if he was betraying his fellow priests [for hearing a confession as an apostate priest], he was not betraying his Lord. He loved him now in a different way from before'.

With this one dramatic image—and with his protagonist's ultimate recognition that 'Our Lord was not silent; even if he had been silent, my life until this day would have spoken of him'—the focus switches from the physical act of apostasy to the psychological process that underlies this decision. At the same time, however, in highlighting the erosion of the distinction between Rodrigues, initially established as symbol of a 'powerful', 'Western' faith, and the sly and 'weak-willed' Kichijirō, this denouement represents a challenge to the received wisdom of the 'strong' martyr and the 'weak' apostate. To Kichijirō, the dilemma has always been acute, for as he argues, 'One who has trodden on the sacred image has his say, too. Do you think I trampled on it willingly? My feet ached with pain. God asks me to imitate the story, even though He made me weak. Isn't this unreasonable?'

But it is only at the very end that Rodrigues comes to recognize that whereas the 'strong' martyrs suffer physical pain, the 'weak' apostates are condemned to a life of psychological pain. The concept represents a constant refrain in Endō's corpus, and it is thus significant that the choice confronting Rodrigues in *Silence* is not simply that between martyrdom and apostasy: throughout the novel, the only torture to which the protagonist is subjected is psychological —the cruel threat that refusal to trample on the *fumie* will result, not merely in Rodrigues's martyrdom (an eventuality to which he has long since sought to reconcile himself), but in that of the Japanese peasants who, despite their own personal apostasies, are still subjected to torture in the 'pit', their destiny entirely in Rodrigues's hands. Again, the notion that, under the circumstances, the act of martyrdom can be seen as more selfish than agreeing to bear the pain of apostasy for oneself is heresy to the theologian. As author, however, Endō is not assessing the validity of either option: rather, by suggesting that, in the face of torture, both represent two opposing images of life, each involving equal anguish, he succeeds paradoxically in merging these two opposites into alternative expressions of the same concept—that of human love.

The novel *Silence* can thus be read as an attempt at demarcation of the proper terrain for the author of fiction. Inspired to write the novel by the chance discovery that historical records concerning the mission work of Giuseppe Chiara (the model for Rodrigues) cease abruptly in 1632, and interpreting this as evidence of Rodrigues's apostasy (and consequent rejection by the mission), Endō proceeds to reconstruct various 'facts' about Rodrigues in an attempt to highlight a more profound 'truth' behind these facts. In so doing, and in placing the emphasis firmly on the inner growth occasioned in his protagonist as a result of his gradual renunciation of his earlier pride and heroism, Endō here succeeds not only in plumbing ever deeper into human psychology, but also in hinting at the possibility of reconciliation of seeming incompatibilities that remains the hallmark of his subsequent literature.

—Mark Williams

ENNIUS, Quintus. Born in Rudiae, Calabria, southern Italy, 239 BC. Probably of Greek extraction. Served in the Roman army in Sardinia, where in 204 BC he met Cato the Elder, who took him to Rome; in 189 BC went on the Aetolian campaign with consul M. Fulvius Nobilior, through whose son he acquired Roman citizenship, 184 BC. Became a friend of Scipio Africanus the Elder. *Died in 169 BC.*

PUBLICATIONS

Collections

[Works], edited by I. Vahlen. 1854, 2nd edition, 1903.
Fragments, edited and translated by Eric H. Warmington, in *Remains of Old Latin* [Loeb Edition], vol. 1, 1935; as *The Tragedies of Ennius*, edited by H.D. Jocelyn, 1967.

Works

Annales, as *The Annals,* edited and translated by E.M. Steuart. 1925; also translated by Otto Skutsch, 1953.

*

Critical Studies: *Die Formenlehre des Ennius* by R. Frobenius, 1907; *Ennius und Vergilius* by E. Norden, 1915; *Ennius und Homer* by H. von Kameke, 1927; *Studia Enniana* (in English) by Otto Skutsch, 1968.

* * *

Quintus Ennius, the acknowledged father of Latin epic poetry, was an innovative poet who made striking advances in several literary genres. A Messapian from Rudiae, he came in 204 BC to Rome, aged 35, where he worked as a teacher, poet, and playwright. Ennius boasted of possessing three hearts, *tria corda*, meaning the Oscan, Greek, and Latin languages. His literary achievement owed much to his familiarity with the entire Greek heritage, from Homer to the Hellenistic writers.

The work which established Ennius' reputation for posterity was his epic poem, the *Annales* (*The Annals*), whose title recalled that of the Pontifical Annals, although it bore little resemblance to those arid records. Ennius' poem covered the whole range of Roman history from the sack of Troy to at least 179 BC. It contained 15 (later extended to 18) books, each of between 1,000 and 1,700 lines (compared with an average of just over 800 for those of Virgil's *Aeneid*). Only about 600 lines survive, but these suffice to indicate the general pattern of the work, which was arranged in groups, each consisting of three books. Of these I–III dealt with Aeneas' flight from Troy and the Roman kings; IV–VI with Rome's Italian wars down to the time of Pyrrhus; VII–IX with the Punic Wars; X–XII with the wars against Philip V of Macedonia and Nabis of Sparta; and XIII–XVI with the Syrian War. Books XVI–XVIII recounted 'more recent wars' (after 187 BC), but the content of this triad is obscure.

There were Hellenistic precedents for historical epic, but a poem which took the whole history of a single people as its theme was unique. Ennius' work soon became a classic, to be studied at school, and it influenced writers in all fields down to the first century BC. Its wide appeal rested on its patriotic theme, as it dealt largely with wars, and its stress on traditional Roman qualities, reflecting the ideals of an aristocratic society, in particular *virtus* (manliness), enlisted in the service of Rome. *The Annals* were intended to replace Naevius' poem on the First Punic War as the national epic of Rome, and Ennius' success was achieved partly by his rich and highly original narrative style, marked by bold effects of alliteration and assonance; partly by his use of the Greek hexameter (in place of Naevius' ungainly Saturnians); and partly by the varied contents of his verse, which incorporated biographical details, polemic, and a scattering of philosophical and learned comments.

Ennius conjures up a variety of moods, now light, now solemn, by his vivid style, which used, for example, archaisms such as 'induperator' for 'imperator' (general), or weighty spondaic lines at critical moments: 'olli respondit rex Albai Longai' (to him replied the king of Alba Longa). Some aspects of his style, it is true, struck later generations as primitive; to Ovid his native genius (*ingenium*) was undeniable, but he lacked literary subtlety (*ars*). Occasionally he pushed his effects to the point of bathos, as in the alliterative lines 'At tuba terribili sonitu taratantara dixit' (But the trumpet with frightening sound said 'taratantara') or 'O Tite, tute, Tati, tibi tanta, tyranne, tulisti' (such terrible evils, Titus Tatius, broughtest thou, tyrant, on thyself). Ennius' hexameter was still rough, with its tolerance of elided 's' before a consonant, non-elision of 'm' before a vowel, and laxity regarding the caesura. However, among the surviving lines are several famous for their lapidary dignity, like the famous comment on Fabius, the opponent of Hannibal: 'Unus homo nobis cunctando restituit rem' (one man by procrastinating gave us back our state). Ennius kept the 'Olympic machinery' of Homer and in a famous prologue to Book I, invoking the Muses, recounted a dream in which Homer appeared to him to announce his reincarnation in the Latin poet. It is unclear how far this was symbolic and how far to be taken seriously, for Ennius wrote at a time when Pythagorean ideas of reincarnation were prevalent in Rome.

The Annals were written only in Ennius' later years, but he composed tragedies throughout his life. Some 24 titles and about 400 lines survive. Except for two works, *Sabine Women* and *Ambracia*, based on Roman themes, Ennius followed the stories of Greek mythology. Up to a dozen titles are based on Euripides, his *Eumenides* on Aeschylus and *Achilles* on a work by Euripides' contemporary, Aristarchus. Ennius' tragedies, however, were far from being literal translations. Cicero remarks that Ennius gives us the sense (*vis*) rather than the word (*verba*) of his models. Moreover, he occasionally combined two Greek plays to make one: thus his *Medea* draws on both the *Medea* and the *Aegeus* of Euripides. More importantly, however, Ennius adapted his originals to suit a Roman audience, compressing or expanding, modifying the presentation, and introducing powerful bombastic and emotional language. The chorus had a smaller role and frequent arias, *cantica*, contributed a melodramatic tone, which in some ways foreshadowed Seneca.

Besides epic and tragedy, Ennius was prolific in other fields. He wrote some comedies. His four books of *Satires* combined moralizing and homespun philosophizing in a variety of metres and in a way that points ahead to Lucilius and Horace. And there were other works, now lost: the *Euhemerus*, a translation of that author's *Sacred Relation*, the *Hedyphagetica*, probably a parody of epic dealing with food, *Scipio* praising Africanus, and *Sota*, a translation of scurrilous verses by Sotades. Ennius also composed epigrams, including his own alliterative epitaph (in elegiac metre):

nemo me lacrimis decoret nec funera fletu
faxit. cur? volito vivus per ora virum

(Let no one honour me with tears nor weep
at my funeral. Why? Because I live, flitting from mouth
 to mouth)

Ennius dominated Roman poetry down to Virgil's time; but the *Aeneid* ousted *The Annals* from its position as the great Roman epic. There was a reaction against Ennius in Nero's time, but a revival under Hadrian, who preferred him to Virgil.

—Frank W. Walbank

EÖTVÖS, Baron József. Born in Buda, Hungary (then in the Austrian Empire), 3 September 1813. Educated at home, then at schools in Buda until 1824; University of Pest, from 1826. Married Ágnes Rosty in 1842. Attended parliament in Pozsony, 1832; served as deputy clerk of Fehér County; travelled in Switzerland, England, France, and Germany 1836–37; appointed Minister of Religion and Public Education in Hungary, 1848: resigned and left the country several months later; returned to Buda, 1851; reappointed Minister of Religion and Public Education, 1867–71. Member, Hungarian Academy, 1835. *Died 2 February 1871.*

PUBLICATIONS

Collections

Összes munkái [Complete Works], edited by Mór Ráth. 13 vols., 1886–93.
Összes munkái [Complete Works], edited by Géza Voinovich. 20 vols., 1901–03.

Fiction

A karthausi [The Carthusian], in *Budapesti Árvizkönyv*. January 1839–July 1841; in book form, 2 vols., 1842.
A falu jegyzője. 3 vols., 1845; as *The Village Notary*, translated (from German) by Otto Wenckstern, 3 vols., 1850.
Magyarország 1514-ben [Hungary in 1514]. 1847.
A nővérek [The Sisters]. 1857.
Elbeszélések [Short Stories]. 1859.

Verse

Költeményei [Poems]. 1868.

Plays

A házasulók [Getting Married]. 1833.
Bosszú [Revenge]. 1834.

Other

A kritikus apotheosisa [The Apotheosis of the Critic]. 1831.
Vélemény a fogházjavítás ügyében [An Opinion on Prison Reform]. 1838.
Die Emanzipation der Juden [The Emancipation of the Jews]. 1840.
Kelet népe és a Pesti Hirlap [People of the East and Pesti Hirlap]. 1841.
Emlékbeszéd Kőrösi Csoma Sándor felett [Memorial Speech on Sándor Kőrösi Csoma]. 1842.
Reform [Reform]. 1846.
A XIX. század uralkodó eszméinek befolyása az álladalomra [The Dominant Ideas of the 19th Century and Their Influence on the State]. 2 vols., 1851–54.
Die Garantien der Macht und Einheit Oesterreichs [Guarantees for the Power and Unity of Austria]. 1859.
Die Sonderstellung Ungarns vom Standpunkte der Einigheit Deutschlands [The Exceptional Position of Hungary from the Perspective of German Unity]. 1859.
Emlékbeszéd gróf Széchenyi István felett [Memorial Speech on Count István Széchenyi]. 1860.
Felelet báró Kemény Gábor néhány szavára [Reply to a Few Remarks by Gábor Kemény]. 1860.
Gondolatok [Thoughts]. 1864.
A nemzetiségi kérdés [The Nationality Problem]. 1865.

Translator, *Angelo*, by Victor Hugo. 1836.

*

Bibliography: *Hungarian Authors: A Bibliographical Handbook* by Albert Tezla, 1970; *A magyar irodalomtörténet bibliográfiája, 1772–1849* by György Kókay, 1975.

Critical Studies: *Báró Eötvös József, mint regényíró* [Baron József Eötvös as a Novelist] by Jenő Péterfy, 1901; 'József Eötvös' by D. Mervyn Jones, in *Five Hungarian Writers*, 1966; *Eötvös József* by István Sőtér, 2nd enlarged edition, 1967; *Baron József Eötvös* by Béla Várdy, 1969; *Joseph Eötvös and the Modernization of Hungary* by Paul Bödy, 1972.

* * *

Eötvös's works include verse, drama, novels, short stories, and political studies, but his literary reputation rests mainly on his four novels. He believed firmly that all writing must have a serious purpose, but should also give pleasure, though this was never to be its main aim. He was a determined reformer of the Hungarian social and political system, and he viewed literature as a means of conveying his message.

An extended visit to Western Europe in 1836–37 had a profound effect on his thought: he then saw how the revolution of July 1830 in France had failed to usher in a new and better era and how the ideals of the 1789 French Revolution had faded. His reflections, spurred by a chance encounter at the Grande Chartreuse, inspired his first novel, *A karthausi* [The Carthusian]. It takes the form of a memoir containing the confessions of a selfish young French count; overcome with self-disgust after two unhappy love affairs, he withdraws from the world to seek peace among the Carthusians. He gives his confessions to a friend, who records his death, noting that he had not found the solace he sought. The novel is intensely introspective and emotional, and contains lengthy reflective passages. While there are some splendid descriptive and dramatic episodes, many of the characters seem overdrawn and reliance upon coincidences betrays the inexperienced novelist. Yet his message is clear: it is a warning against selfishness and the corruption of high ideals, and is as applicable to Hungary as to France.

Eötvös's second and best-known novel, *A falu jegyzője* (*The Village Notary*), appeared in 1845 when political reform was under active discussion. It is a full-blooded attack on the Hungarian county-system, which the author viewed as corrupt and hostile to reform. He depicts a fictitious county, exposing all its shortcomings and the social evils generated by them. It embraces all classes from the aristocracy to the outlaw, and the resulting unflattering picture led early critics to declare that it was more like a reformist leading article than a novel. Yet the scene is not entirely bleak; hope for the future rests with the young nobility, whose reforming zeal contrasts sharply with the arid conservatism of their elders. Here Eötvös's style is appropriate to his contemporary theme; it is incisive, dramatic and satirical, laced with sardonic humour. He weaves skilfully the varied episodes into a convincing whole, and only occasionally holds up the action to reflect on a particular concern such as prison reform. In this novel he best achieved his aim of combining entertaining fiction with a political message, and the result was widely acclaimed, notably in Britain.

If *The Village Notary* portrayed contemporary reality, Eötvös's third novel, *Magyarország 1514-ben* [Hungary in 1514], explored the origins of the social system then prevailing. In 1514 an abortive crusade against the Turks turned into full-scale peasant revolt. The rebellion was crushed and the leaders savagely punished—at the very time when the legal rights of the various classes were being codified. So the punitive legislation of 1514 relating to non-nobles passed into laws which remained in force till 1848. Eötvös's novel places history in the foreground, as his copious footnotes attest.

The action proceeds in a series of personal conflicts, without any central heroic figure; this is deliberate, since it allows Eötvös to express his doubts about revolution as a means to improve the lot of mankind and his misgivings about such ideals as liberty and equality, themes which occupied him in his later works. Justice, according to Eötvös, cannot be achieved by violence. The novel, again on a vast scale, maintains an uneasy balance between history and fiction; it seeks to interpret history, not to use it as a background. Thus while the historical characters are vividly portrayed, their fictional counterparts are somewhat drab, indicating an unresolved conflict between the historian and the novelist, to whom the message was more important than the medium.

The message came too late. Eötvös left Hungary before revolution erupted in 1848. In exile till 1850, he expounded his political views in *A XIX. század uralkodó eszméinek befolyása az álladalomra* [The Dominant Ideas of the 19th Century and Their Influence on the State], a magisterial survey demonstrating how the ideals inherited from the French Revolution—liberty, equality, and nationality to replace fraternity—might well prove incompatible in mankind's endeavours to progress, and offering his own solution to the problem. Published in two volumes in 1851 and 1854, in both German and Hungarian, it received wider recognition abroad than in Hungary.

On his return to Hungary in 1851, Eötvös resumed his literary pursuits. A number of skilfully written short stories set in rural Hungary were followed by his novel *A nővérek* [The Sisters] in 1857. Here new problems are faced, including the decay of the Hungarian gentry, a theme pursued by many later writers. Eötvös introduces the superfluous aristocrat, whose life is characterized by uneventfulness, boredom, and illusion. It is a psychological novel, remarkable for its insight into feminine psychology. Alongside the main theme, the author stresses the importance of children's education, a subject that he was to pursue vigorously after 1867 as Minister of Religion and Public Education. Once again he suits his style to his theme: it is muted and colourless, prompting critics to deplore the lack of his previous vitality, even in a comparatively brief work.

Such strictures ignore his unrivalled skill, at a time when the novel was an undefined genre, of altering both form and style to suit his theme; no other writer attempted such variety, from the memoir to realistic description, history, and psychology, to proclaim his views. Eötvös served his age not only as statesman and political thinker, but also as thought-provoking novelist.

—G.F. Cushing

THE VILLAGE NOTARY (A falu jegyzője)
Novel by Baron József Eötvös, 1845.

The exposure in this novel of social evils has earned Eötvös the title of the 'Hungarian Dickens'. Already an active politician, he had published pamphlets on prison reform (*Vélemény a fogházjavítás ügyében*) and on the 'emancipation' of the Jews (*Die Emanzipation der Juden*), advocating their admission to full citizen rights. In literature, he had declared himself a disciple of Victor Hugo in an essay (1837) arguing that the writer must promote justice, but must also give pleasure. So the reader would begin *The Village Notary* knowing what to expect.

The novel describes a year in an imaginary village, beginning just before local elections. The village notary is Tengelyi, who has repeatedly championed the oppressed and repeatedly suffered for it; his integrity has made him enemies. He is 'noble', one of the five per cent of the population exempt from taxation and military service, and having the vote. He owes his present job to an old student friend, Réty, the number two in the county administration.

Réty's formidable second wife is plotting with the family lawyer Macskaházy to steal some papers belonging to Pastor Vándory which are now at Tengelyi's house, with the notary's own papers. These papers certify the holder's nobility, and hence his right to vote.

When Tengelyi goes home, his loving 16-year-old daughter Vilma makes him promise not to be angry about something she has done behind his back. He laughs, but is horrified when she tells him she has taken the wife, Zsuzsi, and children of the outlaw Viola into the family home. Tengelyi praises her, but Viola's devotion to his family is a byword, and he will certainly try to visit them; he might be caught in the notary's house. Moreover, Vilma is in love with Ákos, Réty's son by his first wife, but there is strong parental opposition to their marriage.

These threads converge at Tengelyi's house the evening before polling-day. The papers are stolen, but Viola is there, catches the thief, seizes the papers, and goes into hiding again. So Tengelyi cannot produce his papers when challenged at the polling-station by Macskaházy and the chief justice, Nyúzó, as obviously a brute as Macskaházy is a sneak. Nyúzó first caused Viola's troubles; annoyed at Zsuzsi for repelling his advances (she and Viola were already married), he required Viola, then a farmer, to provide in person a relay of horses when Zsuzsi was in labour. Viola was seized and beaten; then he broke loose and picked up an axe, killing a man with it. He has been on the run ever since.

Viola's hideout is betrayed; Macskaházy and Nyúzó set fire to it. Viola is caught, and Macskaházy grabs the papers. Viola's trial before a summary court (statárium) brilliantly portrays the infinite variety of human nature. The central figure is a lawyer, Völgyesy, the court's notary. He objects that the case should not come before a statárium, challenges Nyúzó's right to sit on the bench, as a personal enemy of the accused, and—worst of all—encourages Viola to testify. So Viola tells the whole story of the plot to steal Tengelyi's papers, but a majority votes against minuting his evidence. He is sentenced to death but is rescued in a thrilling episode with a slapstick interlude—just the relief needed after the trial.

Viola visits Macskaházy by night, and demands the papers. A fight ensues; Viola kills Macskaházy and flees with the papers. Nyúzó then tries to frame Tengelyi for the murder; thus Tengelyi cannot be saved unless Viola comes forward. When he does, he is intercepted and killed by a gendarme—the same man whom Macskaházy had earlier employed to steal Tengelyi's papers. But before dying Viola just manages to give the papers to Ákos and confess that he killed Macskaházy, which clears the notary.

Ákos duly marries Vilma; his sister Etelka also makes a happy marriage. These young couples personify hope for the future; the novel is ultimately optimistic. There are no spectacular reforms but the situation is certainly better than a year earlier when the novel opened. The main evildoers have disappeared: Mrs Réty poisons herself when her plot to steal the papers is exposed; her weak husband resigns his office, to which he had inevitably been re-elected; Macskaházy is dead. Nyúzó, the only survivor, is quietly dismissed after a scandal over improvements to his house. The tragedy is the life and death of Viola—'a man richly gifted by nature'—and the

death of his family through illness—something much more common then than now.

Although complicated, the plot is a superb unity, without detachable sub-plots. Eötvös portrays a society in which everybody in widely differing degrees commits, condones, or suffers evil. The novel was compared to a medical textbook; Eötvös brings in all the evils of his day, but does not invent them. His style may be dated, but it is pointed, not verbose. There are digressions, including answers to critics; the novel appeared serially. There is comic relief when it is most needed. Still, what makes The Village Notary a masterpiece—perhaps the first Hungarian novel deserving the title—is its humanity.

—D. Mervyn Jones

ERASMUS, Desiderius. Born in Rotterdam, The Netherlands (then under Spanish rule), probably 27/28 October 1467. Educated at a school in Gouda, ages 4–9; at Deventer, 1478–93; a seminary at 's Hertogenbosch; entered monastery of Canons Regular of St Augustine, Steyn, 1487: ordained priest, 1492; released from monastic confinement, and entered secretarial service of Bishop of Cambrai, 1493–95; studied at College of Montaigue, Paris, 1495–99, 1500–01; became Doctor of Divinity, University of Turin, 1506. Lived or travelled in England, 1499, 1505–06, 1509–14 (lectured on Greek in Cambridge), 1515, 1516, 1517; lived in Italy, 1506–09; lived in Louvain, 1517–21; general editor of John Froben's press, Basle, 1521–29; lived in Freiburg, 1529–35, and in Basle again, 1535–36: declined offer of becoming a Cardinal. *Died 12 July 1536.*

PUBLICATIONS

Collections

Opera omnia, edited by Jean Leclerc. 10 vols., 1703–06.
The Essential Erasmus, edited by John P. Dolan. 1964.
Essential Works, edited by W.T.H. Jackson. 1965.
Opera omnia. 1969– (9 vols. to 1983).
Collected Works. 1974– (72 vols. to 1992).
The Erasmus Reader, edited by Erika Rummel. 1990.

Works

Adagia. 1500, and later augmented editions; as *Proverbs or Adages*, translated by Richard Taverner, 1539; translated anonymously, 1622; as *Adages*, translated by Margaret Mann Phillips, in *The Adages: A Study*, 1964; also translated by R.A.B. Mynors, in *Collected Works*, 1982.
Enchiridion militis Christiani. 1503; as *The Manual of the Christian Knight*, translated by William Tyndale, 1533, reprinted 1905; also translated by Anne M. O'Donnell, 1981; as *The Christian Manual*, translated by John Spier, 1752; as *The Handbook of the Militant Christian*, translated by John P. Dolan, 1962; as *The Enchiridion*, translated by Raymond Himelick, 1963.
Encomium moriae. 1511; revised edition, 1514; edited and translated by Hoyt H. Hudson, 1941; as *The Praise of*

Folly, translated by Thomas Chaloner, 1549; also translated by John Wilson, 1668, reprinted 1961; White Kennett, 1683; James Copner, 1878; Leonard F. Dean, 1946; A.H.T. Levi and Betty Radice, 1971; Clarence H. Miller, 1979.

De ratione studii. 1512; revised edition, 1514; edited by Jean-Claude Margolin, in *Opera omnia*, 1971; translated as *On the Aim and Method of Education*, edited by W.H. Woodward, 1904; as *A Method of Study*, translated by Brian McGregor, in *Collected Works*, 1978.

De copia. 1512; revised edition, 1514; as *On Copia of Words and Ideas*, translated by Donald B. King and H. David Rix, 1963; as *On Copia*, translated by Betty I. Knott, in *Collected Works*, 1978.

Institutio principis Christiani. 1516; as *The Education of a Christian Prince*, translated by Lester K. Born, 1936.

Julius Exclusus. 1517; as *The Dialogue Between Julius the Second Genius and Saint Peter*, translated anonymously, 1534; translated as *The Pope Shut Out of Heaven Gates*, 1673; also translated by J.A. Froude, in *Life and Letters of Erasmus*, 1894, reprint edited by Edwin Johnson, 1916.

Colloquia familiaria. 1518, and later augmented editions; edited by L.-E. Halkin, F. Bierlaire, and R. Hoven, in *Opera omnia*, 1972; as *The Colloquies*, translated by H.M. London, 1671; also translated by Roger L'Estrange, in *Twenty Select Colloquies*, 1680, revised edition, 1923; Nathan Bailey, 1725, reprinted 1905; Craig R. Thompson, 1965; in part as *Ten Colloquies*, translated by Craig R. Thompson, 1957.

De libero arbitro. 1524; edited by J. Walter, 1910; as *Discourse on the Freedom of the Will*, edited and translated by Ernest F. Winter, 1961.

Dialogus Ciceronianus. 1528; edited by Pierre Mesnard, in *Opera omnia*, 1971; as *Ciceronianus; or, A Dialogue on the Best Style of Speaking*, edited and translated by Izora Scott, 1900.

Apophthegmes, translated by Nicholas Udall. 1542, reprinted 1877.

The Complaint of Peace, translated by Thomas Paynell. 1559; revised edition, 1946.

Life and Letters of Erasmus, translated by J.A. Froude. 1894, reprinted 1916.

Opus epistolarum, edited by P.S. Allen and others. 12 vols. (in Latin and English), 1906–58; as *The Epistles*, edited and translated by Francis M. Nichols, 3 vols., 1901–18; as *Correspondence*, translated by R.A.B. Mynors and D.F.S. Thomson, annotated by Wallace K. Ferguson, James K. McConica, and Peter G. Bietenholz, in *Collected Works*, 1974.

Opuscula, edited by W.K. Ferguson. 1933.

The Poems, edited by Cornelis Reedijk. 1956.

Erasmus and Cambridge: The Cambridge Letters, edited by H.C. Porter, translated by D.F.S. Thomson. 1963.

Christian Humanism and the Reformation: Selected Writings, edited by John C. Olin. 1965.

Erasmus and Fisher: Their Correspondence 1511–1524, edited by Jean Rouschausse. 1968.

Erasmus and His Age: Selected Letters, edited by Hans J. Hillerbrand. 1970.

De conscribendis epistolis, as *On the Writing of Letters*, edited and translated by Charles Fantazzi, in *Collected Works*. 1985.

De pueris . . . instituendis declamatio, as *A Declamation on the Subject of Early Liberal Education for Children*, edited and translated by Beert C. Vorstraete, in *Collected Works*. 1985.

De recta latini graecique sermonis pronuntiatione, as *The*

Right Way of Speaking Latin and Greek, edited and translated by Maurice Pope, in *Collected Works*. 1985.

The Praise of Folly, and Other Writings. 1990.

Editor and translator (into Latin), *Novum instrumentum* [New Testament]. 1516; revised edition, 1527.

Translator (into Latin), with Thomas More, *Lucian*. 1506.

Translator (into Latin), *Hecuba, Iphigenia in Aulide*, by Euripides. 1506.

Also edited works by Ambrose, Aristotle, Augustine, Basil, Cato, Chrysostom, Cicero, Cyprian, Hilary, Irenaeus, Jerome, Lactantius, Origen, Plutarch, Pseudo-Arnobius, Seneca, and others; commentary on the Bible.

*

Bibliography: *Renaissance Translations of Erasmus: A Bibliography to 1700* by E.J. Devereux, 1983.

Critical Studies: *Erasmus and the Northern Renaissance*, 1949, and *The Adages of Erasmus: A Study*, 1964, both by Margaret Mann Phillips; *Thomas More and Erasmus* by Ernest E. Reynolds, 1965; *Erasmus and Luther* by Rosemary D. Jones, 1968; *Erasmus of Christendom* by Roland H. Bainton, 1969; *Twentieth Century Interpretations of The Praise of Folly* edited by Kathleen Williams, 1969; *Erasmus of Rotterdam*, 1971, and *Essays on the Work of Erasmus*, 1978, both edited by Richard L. DeMolen, and *The Spirituality of Erasmus of Rotterdam* by DeMolen, 1987; *Erasmus: The Growth of a Mind* by James D. Tracy, 1972; *The Tragedy of Erasmus* by Harry S. May, 1975; *Desiderius Erasmus* by J. Kelley Sowards, 1975; *Erasmus on Language and Method in Theology*, 1977, *Christening Pagan Mysteries: Erasmus in Pursuit of Wisdom*, 1981, and *Rhetoric and Reform: Erasmus' Civil Dispute with Luther*, 1983, all by Marjorie O'Rourke Boyle; *Phoenix of His Age: Interpretations of Erasmus, c.1550–1750*, 1979, and *Man on His Own: Interpretations of Erasmus c.1750–1920*, 1992, both by Bruce Mansfield; *Six Essays on Erasmus, and a Translation of Erasmus' Letter to Carondelet, 1523* by John C. Olin, 1979, and *A Biography of Erasmus*, edited by Olin, 1988; *Erasmus: The Right to Heresy* by Stephan Zweig, 1979; *Erasmus: Ecstasy and The Praise of Folly* by M.A. Screech, 1980; *Le Neveu de Rameau and The Praise of Folly: Literary Cognates* by Apostolos P. Kouidos, 1981; *Erasmus and His Times* edited by G.S. Facer, 1982; *The Praise of Folly: Structure and Irony* by Zoja Pavlovskis, 1983; *Erasmus and the Jews* by Shimon Markish, 1986; *Erasmus Grandescens: The Growth of a Humanist's Mind and Spirituality*, 1988, and *Erasmus of Europe: The Making of a Humanist*, 1990, both by Richard J. Schoeck; *Erasmus and His Catholic Critics* by Erika Rummel, 1989; *Humanist Play and Belief: The Seriocomic Art of Desiderius Erasmus* by Walter M. Gordon, 1990; *Erasmus: His Life, Works and Influence* by Cornelius Augustijn, translated by J.C. Grayson, 1991; *Erasmus* by James McConica, 1991; *Erasmus, Colet and More: The Early Tudor Humanists and Their Books* by J.B. Trapp, 1991; *Erasmus, Lee and the Correction of the Volgate: The Shaking of the Foundations* by Robert Coogan, 1992; *Erasmus: A Critical Biography* by Leon E. Halkin, translated by John Tonkin, 1992; *Erasmus, Man of Letters: The Construction of Charisma in Print* by Lisa Jardine, 1993.

* * *

Desiderius Erasmus of Rotterdam was the most famous man of letters of early 16th-century Europe, a figure who dominated the intellectual world of his time as clearly as Petrarch, Voltaire, or Goethe did theirs. He was acclaimed 'the prince of humanists'. He was the leading biblical scholar of his time, and the editor of the first modern critical text of the Greek New Testament. He was an advocate of educational reform and an author of textbooks and educational tracts. He was a passionate advocate of peace. Additionally, and perhaps most important of all, he was one of the most tireless advocates of religious reform in the age of the Reformation. The titles of his books run into the hundreds, but his most famous works were his satirical books, especially the *Encomium moriae* (*The Praise of Folly*) and the *Colloquia familiaria* (*The Colloquies*).

The Praise of Folly, Erasmus' single best-known book, is a complex, multi-layered satire of the outworn classical form of the oration of praise, a parody of such worthy abstractions as Dame Philosophy or The Seven Liberal Arts—in this case the goddess Folly. Folly, arising before the court of mankind, intends to praise herself, since no one else will praise her. She proves with impeccable logic that all important actions and accomplishments are owing to her influence. She claims as hers all manner and conditions of men, from kings and nobles and wealthy merchants to calamity-ridden and tormented teachers of grammar, even husbands and wives, parents and children. But Folly also claims theologians with their pride of learning and endless hair-splitting definitions; monks with their empty formalism and self-serving piety; and the powerful, cynical rulers of the church, including the popes, the vicars of Christ so unlike him in every way. Then Folly claims that true Christians are the greatest of fools, that no people behave more foolishly, giving away their goods, overlooking wrongs and injuries, forgiving their enemies. And finally, Folly argues, Christ himself became something like a fool to cure the folly of mankind by the foolishness of the cross.

The serious religious-reforming purpose of *The Praise of Folly* is equally clearly expressed in Erasmus' other major satiric work, *The Colloquies*. This was probably the most frequently printed of Erasmus' books in his lifetime. It began as a series of brief and simple Latin conversational exercises for students which proved to be so popular that Erasmus prepared expanded editions through the 1520s and early 1530s, adding many new colloquies. Most are little satiric dialogues directed at the targets of his reforming efforts—corrupt monks and ignorant priests; the excesses of the veneration of saints and relics and pilgrimages; the senseless preference for the formalities of religion to the neglect of its spirit; and his hatred of war. Several of the colloquies —*Charon*, *Naufragium* (*The Shipwreck*), *Peregrinatio Religionis ergo* (*The Pilgrimage for Religion's Sake*), *Abbatis et eruditae* (*The Abbot and the Learned Lady*), *Exorcismus, sive spectrum* (*Exorcism or the Spectre*)—can be compared with the best satiric writing of the 16th century.

—J. Kelley Sowards

THE COLLOQUIES (Colloquia familiaria)
Prose by Erasmus, 1518.

The Colloquies are a masterpiece of literary satire and an invaluable source of information about a host of aspects of the Renaissance. Yet this substantial work was apparently produced almost by accident. There is some evidence that Erasmus was far from pleased to discover, in November 1518, that his friend Johannes Froben, a printer in Basle, had, without asking his permission, published a small volume of Latin dialogues dating from some 20 years earlier. Erasmus had written them when, as an impoverished student in Paris, he had been employed as tutor to some boys. One of his duties was to train them in the use of Latin as a conversational medium, for speaking that language fluently still had its importance in intellectual spheres and, to some extent, in practical life too, and he came up with the idea of composing a number of model dialogues illustrating, for instance, the forms of address appropriate to people of varying status. In other words, *The Colloquies*, like his *De conscribendis epistolis* (*On the Writing of Letters*) and *Adagia* (*Adages*), a collection of classical proverbs and idioms, began life simply as a textbook designed to teach correct Latin in an attractive way.

A man of wit, responsive to all that took place around him, Erasmus was not, however, content to leave things at that. He never undervalued his pedagogic role, and possessed the encyclopedic scholarship needed to play a significant part in the Renaissance revival of a pure classical style that would not reflect the development (or, as he and his contemporaries saw it, the corruption) of Latin in the Middle Ages. In 1522, four years after the first, unauthorized, edition, Froben brought out an enlarged version of *The Colloquies*. Erasmus dedicated it to Froben's young son, illustrating not only that the author was now on good terms with his printer, but also that he had become more aware of the rich potential of the intrinsically humble form he was using. As well as teaching sound Latin, it would serve to inculcate good manners (or 'civility', as it was often termed in the Renaissance). More important still was Erasmus' use of some of his *Colloquies* to express his opinions about what was wrong in Europe generally and what, in particular, was amiss in the Church.

Euntes in ludrum litterarium (*Off to School*) is an example of *The Colloquies* in their simplest form. There are two short dialogues; the first features two boys chatting on their way to lessons, while the second, a conversation between two others about their pens and ink, is enlivened by a flash of schoolboy vulgarity. *De lusu* (*Sport*) gives some idea of how youngsters amused themselves in the Renaissance, for example, playing real tennis. As if to remind us that schooldays were not all fun and games, *Monita paedagogica* (*A Lesson in Manners*) presents a master who sharply reprimands a boy slouching around untidily dressed and unable to speak properly to his superiors. Erasmus was not, however, content for long with this sort of subject. *Hippoplanus* (*The Cheating Horse-Cooper*) reveals his knowledge of the ways of the world, his psychological insight, and his ear for dialogue in an entertaining account of the way a rascal is cheated out of his ill-gotten gains.

In *Ementita nobilitas* (*The Ignoble Knight*), Erasmus reveals his satiric side. Like many in the Renaissance, Harpalus seeks to rise to the nobility, though he does not come of good family and lacks any personal distinction. Nestor, with his tongue very firmly in his cheek, gives him an outspoken lesson in the art of social climbing without merit, which includes, typically for Erasmus, some particularly acerbic remarks about soldiering. In this colloquy, as in a number of others, there are indications that the spur to Erasmus' indignation was his animosity towards a particular acquaintance, but the point he raised was one of general interest in the period.

However, it is about religious matters that Erasmus is most

outspoken. Either out of innate caution or, more likely, because of a theological conviction that the Roman Church alone offered the way to salvation, he was never prepared to follow Luther and countenance a schism. None the less, he was conscious that there was much in Catholic religious life and practice in the early 16th century that was greatly in need of reform, and his attacks on abuses in *The Colloquies* and elsewhere made him and his works suspect in orthodox quarters.

Virgo Poenitens (The Repentant Girl) concerns a girl who objects to being pressured into taking religious vows, while fasting is under attack in *Ichtyophagia (A Fish Diet)*. However, Erasmus' religious attitudes are perhaps best exemplified in *Peregrinatio Religionis ergo (The Pilgrimage for Religion's Sake)*, a colloquy that reflects his visits to the Marian shrine at Walsingham in Norfolk, England. The bitter complaint that Erasmus makes time and again is that grasping and ignorant clergy wickedly lead gullible layfolk into mechanical devotional practices and encourage mindless superstition, when the clear message of the Gospels is that Christ sought to replace mere religious observance with deeply held conviction and a true change of heart.

—Christopher Smith

THE PRAISE OF FOLLY (Encomium moriae)
Prose by Erasmus, 1511.

The Praise of Folly began as a joke, an expression of what Erasmus termed his *jeu d'esprit*. In a letter to his friend, Sir Thomas More, Erasmus claimed that the inspiration came to him on horseback while returning to England from Italy in 1509, later expanding the idea while waiting for his books and luggage to catch up with him. The subtle play of irony, and the dense allusions both to Biblical and Classical literature, as well as the careful modifications carried on through a series of editions between 1511 and 1515, however, belie the off-handedness with which Erasmus seems to dismiss *The Praise of Folly*. Despite the surface playfulness, it represents, as M.A. Screech suggests, the mature effort of a sophisticated thinker at the height of his intellectual powers. The multi-lingual pun of the title, playing on the Latin form of More's name and the Greek word for folly, meaning thus both 'in praise of folly' and 'in praise of [Sir Thomas] More' is indicative both of the game and of its profundity. On one level, Erasmus holds Folly up to ridicule, but at the same time advocates a serious vision of Christian folly.

Drawing on the methods of the Greek satirist Lucian, the work is in the form of a long Latin panegyric delivered by Folly (Stultia) in praise of herself. Erasmus uses, however, the Greek rhetorical model of the *Aphthonius* rather than the more conventional Latin model outlined by Quintilian, signalling his knowledge of Greek language and learning and his affiliation with Renaissance Humanism. This is important to Erasmus's concern as a Humanist theologian, pointing to the authority of the Greek *Septuagint* and *New Testament* over that of the Latin *Vulgate*, and to that of the ancient philosophers and early patristic writers over the schoolmen. The *Aphthonius* divides its topic into six parts: a *prooimion*, in which Folly introduces herself; a *genos* which outlines Folly's birth and origins; an *anatrophe* which describes the powers and pleasures of Folly; a *synkrisis* which enumerates Folly's

followers; and finally an *epilogos*, which outlines the doctrine of the Christian fool.

The *genos* and the *synkrisis* look back to medieval allegory. Folly describes herself as the daughter of Plutus, the ancient god of riches, and Youthfulness. After being nursed by Drunkenness and Ignorance, she is attended by Philantia (Self-love), Kolakia (Flattery), Lethe (Forgetfulness), Misoponia (Laziness), and Hedone (Pleasure), among others. Her followers, like those portrayed in the medieval *danse macabre* or Sebastian Brant's *Ship of Fools* (1494), represent an anatomy of human types, cutting across all strata of society from professionals such as schoolmasters, poets, lawyers, and theologians, through kings and courtiers, to church prelates of various sorts, German bishops being the greatest fools of all.

The *Praxis* shows a more sophisticated irony and playfulness. The power of Folly resides in facilitating ecstasy. Here Erasmus plays on the semantic field of the Greek *Ekstasis* which ranges over drunkenness, madness, and rapture. Would it not be mad, Folly suggests:

> if some wise man, dropped from heaven, should suddenly confront me at this point and exclaim that the person whom everyone has looked up to as a god and a ruler is not even a man, because he is led sheeplike by his passions . . .?

The implicit answer is yes, but isn't this also the description of Christ? If this is madness or foolishness, then it is a holy madness, a Christian foolishness. Similarly Folly questions the virtue of the rational stoic who has stripped away all passion and emotion. Such a being, she suggests, 'makes a marble imitation of a man, stupid, and altogether alien to every human feeling'. Such a being becomes arrogant and isolated in his self-sufficiency. 'He does not hesitate to bid the gods to go and hang themselves. All that life holds dear he condemns and scorns as folly'. Who, Folly asks, would choose to be ruled by such a person? 'What host such a guest? What servant such a master?'. These questions point to the seriousness of Erasmus's intent. If Christianity is a rational religion, then it is effectively indistinguishable from ancient Stoicism, offering a vision that leads to pride and isolation from God. For Erasmus, however, the heart of true Christianity is not in its appeal to reason, but to an irrational passion that lifts individuals out of themselves.

The ultimate folly is that of God, for how, Folly asks, can the humiliation and sacrifice of Christ, the act of Divine grace, be understood except as an act of sublime and benevolent folly.

> Christ himself, although He possessed the wisdom of the Father, became something like a fool in order to cure the folly of mankind, when He assumed the nature and being of a mortal? And that He was made 'to be sin' in order to redeem sinners? He did not wish to redeem them by any way except by the foolishness of the Cross, and by weak and simple apostles.

Could humankind reasonably expect salvation from a rational God?

As with the knight Parzifal, or Dostoevskii's Prince Myshkin, Erasmus sees the saving grace of Christ in the innocence and foolishness of the Christian fool. Only through an irrational passion that allows us to love our neighbour or spurn our self-interests can we hope for salvation. Only by folly is folly redeemed. Thus in its intricate play of satire, *The Praise of Folly* advocates a humanism that conceives man not as a rational animal, but as a passionate one, and like itself, capable of serious folly, of moral *jeu d'esprit*.

—Thomas L. Cooksey

———

ESENIN, Sergei Aleksandrovich [Sergey Yesenin]. Born in Konstantinovo, Riazan' Province, Russia, 3 October 1895. Educated at the Konstantinovo primary school, 1904–09; church school, Spas-Klepiki, 1909–12; Shaniavskii University, 1913. Married 1) Anna Romanova Izriadnova in 1914 (divorced), one son; 2) Zinaida Nikolaevna Raikh in 1917 (separated 1918, divorced 1921), one daughter and one son; 3) the dancer Isadora Duncan in 1922 (divorced 1924); 4) Sof'ia Tolstaia in 1925 (separated); also had a son in 1925. Military service, 1916; deserted, 1917. Made poetic debut in Petrograd, 1915; settled in Moscow, 1918; member of the Imaginist poetic movement, 1919; travelled to Turkestan and Tashkent, 1921; travelled through Belgium, Germany, France, Italy, and the United States, with Isadora Duncan, 1922–23; returned to Russia, 1923; suffered from declining mental health from c.1922, with spells in sanatoriums, 1924–25; travelled in the Caucasus, 1924–25. *Died (suicide) 28 December 1925.*

PUBLICATIONS

Collections

Sobranie stikhotvorenii [Collected Poetry]. 4 vols., 1926–27.
Sobranie sochinenii [Collected Works], 5 vols., 1961–62, 1966–68.
Sobranie sochinenii [Collected Works], edited by Iu.L. Prokushev. 3 vols., 1970.
Sochineniia [Works], edited by P.S. Vykhodtsev. 1975.
Sobranie sochinenii [Collected Works], edited by V.G. Bazanov. 6 vols., 1977–80.
Sochineniia, 1910–1925 [Works, 1910–1925], edited by V.G. Bazanov. 1980.
Izbrannye sochineniia [Selected Works], edited by Aleksei Kozlovskii. 1983.
Sochineniia [Works], edited by Aleksei Kozlovskii. 1988.
Sobranie sochinenii [Collected Works], edited by Iu.L. Prokushev. 2 vols., 1990.
Stikhotvoreniia; Poemy: Izbrannoe [Poetry; Narrative Verse; Selections], edited by D.A. Ovinnikov. 1992.

Verse

Radunitsa. 1916.
Preobrazhenie [Transfiguration]. 1918.
Sel'skii chasoslov [A Village Prayer-book]. 1918.
Inoniia. 1918.
Goluben' [Azure]. 1920.
Treriadnitsa. 1920.
Ispoved' khuligana [Confessions of a Hooligan]. 1920.
Pugachov. 1922.
Stikhi skandalisa [Scandalous Poems]. 1923.
Tovarishch; Inoniia [Comrade; Inoniia]. 1923.
Moskva kabatskaia [Moscow of the Taverns]. 1924.
Stikhi [Poems]. 1924.

Rus' sovetskaia [Soviet Russia]. 1925.
Berezovyi sitets [The Birch-Tree Cotton Print]. 1925.
Persidskie motivy [Persian Motifs]. 1925.
Stikhotvoreniia [Poetry]. 1940.
Stikhotvoreniia. Poemy [Poetry. Narrative Verse]. 1956.
Stikhotvoreniia i poemy [Poetry and Narrative Verse]. 1957.
Zarianka. 1964.
Slovesnykh rek kipenie i shorokh [The Boiling and Rustle of the River of Words]. 1965.
Otchee slovo [The Father's Word]. 1968.
Sinii mai. Lirika [Dark Blue May. Lyric Poems]. 1973.
Confessions of a Hooligan: Fifty Poems, translated by Geoffrey Thurley. 1973.
Anna Snegina. 1974.
Riabinovyi koster: Stikhotvoreniia [The Rowan-Tree Bonfire: Poetry]. 1975.
Plesk golubogo livnia [The Splash of the Blue Downpour]. 1975.
Zlatoi posev [Golden Crops], edited by S. Koshechkin. 1976.
Neskazannoe, sinee, nezhnoe [Unspeakable, Dark Blue, Tender]. 1978.
Belykh iablon' dym [White Smoke of the Apple-Trees] 1978.
Selected Poems, translated by Jessie Davies. 1979.
Volnuias' serdtsem i stikhom . . . [Agitated in My Heart and Verse]. 1981.
Izbrannye stikhotvoreniia i poemy/Selected Poetry (bilingual edition), translated by Peter Tempest. 1982.
'Ia bolee vsego vesnu liubliu . . .' [I More than Anything Love Spring]. 1984.
Snezhnye vetry [Snowy Winds]. 1985.
Serdtsu snitsia mai: Stikhi o liubvi [A Heart Dreaming of May: Love Poems]. 1985.
Sin', upavshaia v reku [Blue Colour, Falling into the River]. 1985.
Stikhotvoreniia i proza [Poetry and Prose]. 1985.
Cheremukha [Bird-Cherry]. 1985.
Poemy i stikhotvoreniia [Narrative Verse and Poetry]. 1986.
Zakruzhilas' listva zolotaia [The Twisted Gold Foliage]. 1988.
Strana negodiaev [A Country of Scoundrels]. 1991.

*

Critical Studies: *Esenin: A Life* by Gordon McVay, 1976; *Sergey Esenin* by Constantin V. Ponomareff, 1978; *Sergei Yesenin: The Man, the Verse, the Age* by Yuri Prokushev, 1979; *Sergei Esenin: Poet of the Crossroads* by Lynn Visson, 1980; *Esenin: A Biography in Memoirs, Letters, and Documents* edited and translated by Jessie Davies, 1982.

* * *

Sergei Esenin led a short and turbulent life, which quickly passed into legend and myth. From his meteoric literary debut in Petrograd in 1915 until his suicide in a Leningrad hotel in 1925, Esenin assumed in rapid succession a number of literary 'masks'—pastoral angel (1915–16), peasant prophet (1917–18), last poet of the village, tender hooligan (1919–21), tavern rake (1922–23), ex-hooligan (late 1923), would-be bard of the new Soviet Russia (mid-1924 until March 1925), and, finally, elegiac foreteller of his own imminent death (1925).

Although Esenin's poetry is highly autobiographical and even 'confessional', the connection between the private man and his poetic persona is not entirely straightforward. By single-mindedly dedicating himself to the writing of poetry and the achievement of fame, Esenin blurred the boundaries between his 'mask' and his 'real face', sacrificing the possibility of ordinary human happiness.

A peasant from Riazan' province, Esenin enjoyed conspicuous success in the pre-revolutionary literary salons of Petrograd. His first volume of poetry, *Radunitsa*, reflected the decorative, traditional aspects of village life. Rus', his ancient Russian motherland, was already the beloved heroine of his verse, a motherland which may be sad and impoverished, yet is also calm and imbued with a simple peasant religiousness. Jesus and the saints wandered as lowly pilgrims in the forests and along the paths of rural Rus', and the poet knelt in prayer before the temple of Nature.

Esenin's life was drastically affected by the February and October Revolutions of 1917. He welcomed these upheavals enthusiastically but vaguely in a series of longish 'Scythian' poems, couched in abstruse religious and animal symbolism. These poems, which alternate between optimism and anxiety, prayerfulness and blasphemy, maintain a lofty cosmic tone far removed from the grim reality of earth-born Bolshevism.

By 1919, Esenin appeared a promising peasant poet, whose natural gifts displayed the influence of folk poetry, Kliuev, and Blok. Thenceforth, however, pursuing national fame, he sought creative independence within Moscow's anarchic literary bohemia. The last six years of Esenin's life witnessed the blossoming of his poetic talent and the disintegration of his inner peace.

As a founding-member of the enterprisingly avant-garde 'Imaginist' group, Esenin achieved instant notoriety by emphasizing the unresolved dissonances in his personality and plight. Voicing his deep-rooted romantic attachment to old-fashioned, non-industrialized Rus', he lamented the imminent encroachment of the 'iron guest' (urban industrialization) in 'Ia poslednii poet derevni' [I'm the Last Poet of the Village] (1920), and cursed the 'vile guest' (the train which defeats the living horse) in 'Sorokoust' (1920). In *Ispoved' khuligana* [The Confessions of a Hooligan], his lyrical hero is coarse and tender, desperate and kind; full of provocative vulgarity, and yet also 'gently sick with childhood recollections'.

After his marriage to Isadora Duncan in 1922, and an ill-starred 15-month tour of western Europe and the United States, Esenin composed the controversial cycle *Moskva kabatskaia* [Moscow of the Taverns]. The setting is the tavern, the inhabitants are prostitutes and bandits, syphilitic accordionists, down-and-outs seeking to drown their misery in alcohol and dreams. Written in a universally understandable, non-Imaginistic language, these poems immediately appealed to thousands of Russians who saw in them a reflection of their own anguish.

The poetry of Esenin's last two years, after his return to Russia in 1923, combines a new-found 'Pushkinian' simplicity of style with a mood of ever-deepening tragic isolation. In the cycle 'Liubov' khuligana' [A Hooligan's Love], his lyrical hero sought to break with hooliganism, passing into autumnal resignation. A profoundly elegiac mood permeates the outstanding lyrics of 1924, 'My teper' ukhodim ponemnogu' [We Are Now Gradually Departing] and 'Otgovorila roshcha zolotaia' [The Golden Grove Has Ceased to Speak].

Esenin had never been openly counter-revolutionary and, after his disillusioning travels in the west, he strove at times to compose pro-Soviet verse, praising Lenin and endeavouring to accept the changed face of Russia. Such attempts often proved poetically lifeless, however, with many critics doubting his sincerity and aptness for such topics.

Towards the end of 1925 Esenin's poetry entered its most tragic phase. Isolated, alcoholic, vulnerable, and despairing, he created a sequence of short poems set in a winter landscape. Instead of autumnal fading, his mood was now echoed by wintry iciness, evoking memories of lost youth and lost happiness. On 12–13 November 1925 he wrote down the only extant version of his poem 'Chernyi chelovek' [The Black Man], revealing his desperate struggle against alcoholic hallucinations and a tormented conscience. On 27 December Esenin wrote his last poem, 'Do svidan'ia, drug moi, do svidan'ia' [Goodbye, My Friend, Goodbye], in his own blood, and the next day he was found hanging in a Leningrad hotel room.

As a literary phenomenon, Esenin has been compared with Robert Burns and Arthur Rimbaud, with Dylan Thomas and, above all, François Villon; yet such is his complexity that he has also been characterized as the 'Don Quixote of the village and the birch-tree' (V. Shershenevich, in *Trud*, Klintsy, 19 January 1926), and even likened to St Francis of Assisi. He has been called a poet of death, and a poet of eternal youth.

Despite a prolonged period of disfavour during the Stalin years, Esenin remains the most popular and most widely read Russian poet of the 20th century. He is exceptionally 'Russian', a temperamental peasant embodying tragic pathos and the forlorn dream of a rural idyll. Scholars in the West (mainly non-Russian urban intellectuals) often disparage the simplicity, emotionality and melodiousness of Esenin's verse, preferring the sophisticated subtlety of Pasternak, Mandel'shtam, Akhmatova, and Tsvetaeva. It is perhaps time to challenge this elitist judgement. A Russian critic perceptively observed during Esenin's lifetime (Andrei Shipov [Ivan Rozanov], in *Narodnyi uchitel'*, 2, 1925):

> In certain respects Esenin should without doubt seem inferior to some of his contemporaries: he lacks the sweep and crude strength of Maiakovskii, the cultural saturation of Mandel'shtam, or the dazzling lyrical intensity of Boris Pasternak, but he has a quality which is perhaps the most valuable of all for a lyric poet—the ability to reach the reader's heart and even—a thing to which we are now especially unaccustomed—the ability at times to move and touch us . . . Mandel'shtam and Pasternak are too intellectual as poets, in the last resort they are poets for the few . . . Esenin, on the other hand, can be understood by everyone from the lowly to the grand . . . .

—Gordon McVay

EURIPIDES. Born in 480 or 485 BC. Married to Melito; three sons. Held a local priesthood at Phlya; not prominent politically, but did go on an embassy to Syracuse; also went to the court of Archelaus in Macedon, c.408 BC; first competed in the City Dionysia in 455 BC: won four prizes during his lifetime, and one posthumously; of the 92 plays he is said to have written, 80 titles are known, and 19 are extant. *Died before February/March 406 BC.*

PUBLICATIONS

Collections

[Plays], edited by Gilbert Murray. 3 vols., 1902–13; also edited by James Diggle, 3 vols., 1982–94; as *The Tragedies*, translated by Robert Potter. 2 vols., 1781–83; as *The Nineteen Tragedies*, translated by Michael Woodhull, 4 vols., 1782; also translated by T.A. Buckley, 2 vols., 1850; W.B. Donne, 1872; Arthur S. Way, 3 vols., 1894–98, revised edition [Loeb Edition], 4 vols., 1912; Percy Bysshe Shelley and others, 2 vols., 1906; Moses Hadas and J.M. McLean, 1936; edited by David Grene and Richmond Lattimore, various translators, in *Complete Greek Tragedies*, 5 vols., 1955–59; translated (prose) by Edward P. Coleridge, 2 vols., 1891.

Plays

Alcestis (produced 438 BC). Edited by W.S. Hadley, 1896; also edited by E.H. Blakeney, 1899, revised edition, 1933, Amy Marjorie Dale, 1954, revised edition, 1978, and Antonio Garzya, 1980; edited and translated (with commentary) by Desmond J. Conacher, 1988; as *Alcestis*, translated by Robert Browning, 1871; also translated by H. Kynaston, 1906; Gilbert Murray, 1915; Richard Aldington, 1930; Dudley Fitts and Robert Fitzgerald, 1933; D.W. Lucas, 1951; Philip Vellacott, in *Three Plays*, 1953, revised edition, 1974; Richmond Lattimore, in *Complete Greek Tragedies*, 1955; Alistair Elliot, 1965; C.R. Beye, 1973; William Arrowsmith, 1974.
Medea (produced 431 BC). Edited by A.W. Verrall, 1881; also edited by Clinton E.S. Headlam, 1897, Denys L. Page, 1938, and Alan F. Elliott, 1969; as *Medea*, translated by Gilbert Murray, 1910; also translated by John Jay Chapman, in *Two Greek Plays*, 1928; Countee Cullen, 1935; R.C. Trevelyan, 1939; Rex Warner, 1944, in *Complete Greek Tragedies*, 1955, and in *Three Great Plays*, 1958; Frederick Prokosch, in *Greek Plays in Modern Translation*, 1947; D.W. Lucas, 1950; Moses Hadas and John McLean, in *Ten Plays*, 1960; Philip Vellacott, in *Medea and Other Plays*, 1963; Peter D. Arnott, in *Three Greek Plays*, 1964; Michael Townsend, 1966; Kenneth McLeish, 1970; Jeremy Brooks, in *Plays One*, 1988; D. Egan, 1991.
Heracleidae (produced c.430–28 BC). Edited by Antonio Garzya, 1972; also edited by John Wilkins, 1993; as *Children of Heracles*, translated by Ralph Gladstone, in *Complete Greek Tragedies*, 1955; also translated by Philip Vellacott, in *Orestes and Other Plays*, 1972; Henry Taylor and Robert A. Brooks, 1981.
Hippolytus (produced 428 BC). Edited by J.P. Mahaffy and J.B. Bury, 1881; also edited by W.S. Hadley, 1889, W.S. Barrett, 1964, and John Ferguson, 1984; as *Hippolytus*, translated by Gilbert Murray, 1900; also translated by David Grene, in *Three Greek Tragedies*, 1942, and in *Complete Greek Tragedies*, 1955; Rex Warner, 1949, and in *Three Great Plays*, 1958; Philip Vellacott, in *Three Plays*, 1953, revised edition, 1974; E.P. Coleridge, in *Three Great Greek Plays*, 1960; Donald Sutherland, in *Hippolytus in Drama and Myth*, 1960; Kenneth Cavander, 1962; Robert Bragg, 1974; Gilbert and Sarah Lawall, 1986.
Andromache (produced c.426–25 BC). Edited by Philip Theodore Stevens, 1971; also edited by Antonio Garzya, 1978; as *Andromache*, translated by Hugh Meredith, in *Four Dramas*, 1937; also translated by L.R. Lind, 1957; John Frederick Nims, in *Complete Greek Tragedies*, 1958; Philip Vellacott, in *Orestes and Other Plays*, 1972.
Hecuba (produced c.424 BC). Edited by Michael Tierney, 1946; also edited by Stephen G. Daitz, 1973, and C. Collard, 1991; as *Hecuba*, translated by Hugh Meredith, in *Four Dramas*, 1937; also translated by William Arrowsmith, in *Complete Greek Tragedies*, 1958; Peter D.

Arnott, 1969; Janet Lembke and Kenneth J. Reckford, 1991; as *Hecabe*, translated by Philip Vellacott, in *Medea and Other Plays*, 1963.
Supplices (produced c.423–22 BC). Edited by Christopher Collard, 2 vols., 1975; as *The Suppliants*, translated by L.R. Lind, 1957; as *The Suppliant Women*, translated by Frank Jones, in *Complete Greek Tragedies*, 1958; also translated by Philip Vellacott, in *Orestes and Other Plays*, 1972.
Electra (produced c.422–16 BC). Edited by C.H. Keene, 1893; also edited by J.D. Denniston, 1939; edited and translated by Arthur S. Way, 1919; Martin J. Cropp, 1988; as *Electra*, translated by Gilbert Murray, 1905; also translated by Moses Hadas, 1950; D.W. Lucas, 1951; Emily Townsend Vermeule, in *Complete Greek Tragedies*, 1959; Philip Vellacott, in *Medea and Other Plays*, 1963; David Thompson, 1964.
Ion (produced c.421–13 BC). Edited by A.S. Owen, 1939; also edited by Werner Biehl, 1979, and K.H. Lee, 1992; as *Ion*, translated by Ronald Frederick Willetts, in *Complete Greek Tragedies*, 1958; also translated by HD, 1937; D.W. Lucas, 1950; Philip Vellacott, in *The Bacchae and Other Plays*, 1954; A.P. Burnett, 1970; David Lan, 1994.
Heracles (produced c.417–15 BC). Edited by Godfrey W. Bond, 1981; as *Heracles*, translated by Robert Browning, in *Aristophanes' Apology*, 1875; also translated by Hugh Meredith, in *Four Dramas*, 1937; William Arrowsmith, in *Complete Greek Tragedies*, 1956; Philip Vellacott, in *Medea and Other Plays*, 1963; Michael R. Halleran, 1988; as *The Madness of Heracles*, translated by Peter D. Arnott, 1969.
Troades (produced 415 BC). Edited by F.A. Paley, 1881; also edited by Robert Yelverton Tyrrell, 1882, revised edition, 1897, Werner Biehl, 1970, and K.H. Lee, 1976; as *The Trojan Women*, translated by Gilbert Murray, 1905; also translated by Edith Hamilton, in *Three Greek Plays*, 1937; Richmond Lattimore, in *Greek Plays in Modern Translation*, 1944, and in *Complete Greek Tragedies*, 1958; Neil Curry, 1946; Shirley A. Barlow, 1986; as *The Women of Troy*, translated by Philip Vellacott, in *The Bacchae and Other Plays*, 1954; also translated by Don Taylor, in *The War Plays*, 1990.
Iphigeneia Taurica (produced c.414–13 BC). Edited by E.B. England, 1926; also edited by C.B. Watts, 1930, Maurice Platnauer, 1938, and David Sansone, 1981; as *Iphigenia in Tauris*, translated by Gilbert Murray, 1910; also translated by Witter Bynner, 1915, and in *Complete Greek Tragedies*, 1956; Philip Vellacott, in *Three Plays*, 1953, revised edition, 1974; Richmond Lattimore, 1974; as *Iphigeneia in Taurica* [Loeb Edition], translated by Arthur S. Way, 1912.
Helena (produced 412 BC). Edited by A.Y. Campbell, 1950; also edited by Amy Marjorie Dale, 1967, and Richard Kannicht, 1969; as *Helen*, translated by J.T. Sheppard, 1925; also translated by Rex Warner, 1951, and in *Three Great Plays*, 1958; Philip Vellacott, in *The Bacchae and Other Plays*, 1954; Richmond Lattimore, in *Complete Greek Tragedies*, 1956; Neil Curry, 1981; James Michie and Colin Leach, 1981; R.E. Meagher, 1986; Don Taylor, in *The War Plays*, 1990.
Phoenissae (produced c.412–08 BC). Edited by Donald J. Mastronarde (with commentary), 1994; as *The Phoenician Women*, translated by Elizabeth Wychoff, in *Complete Greek Tragedies*, 1959; also translated by Philip Vellacott, in *Orestes and Other Plays*, 1972; Peter Burian and Brian Swann, 1981; Elizabeth M. Craik, 1988; David Thompson, in *Plays One*, 1988.
Orestes (produced 408 BC). Edited by C.W. Willink, 1986;

edited and translated by M.L. West, 1987; as *Orestes*, translated by Hugh Meredith, in *Four Dramas*, 1937; also translated by William Arrowsmith, in *Complete Greek Tragedies*, 1958; Philip Vellacott, in *Orestes and Other Plays*, 1972.

Bacchae (produced c.405 BC). Edited by J.E. Sandys, 1880; also edited by E.R. Dodds, 1960, and E. Christian Kopff, 1982; as *The Bacchae*, translated by Henry Hart Milman, 1865; also translated by Margaret Kinmont Tennant, 1926; D.W. Lucas, 1930; Philip Vellacott, in *The Bacchae and Other Plays*, 1954; Henry Birkhead, 1957; William Arrowsmith, in *Complete Greek Tragedies*, 1959; G.S. Kirk, 1970; Neil Curry, 1981; M. Cacoyannis, 1983; J. Michael Walton, in *Plays One*, 1988; John Buller, 1992.

Iphigeneia Aulidensis, completed by another writer (produced c.405 BC). Edited by E.S. Headlam, 1939; as *Iphigenia in Aulis*, translated by F.M. Stawell, 1929; Charles R. Walker, in *Complete Greek Tragedies*, 1958; Philip Vellacott, in *Orestes and Other Plays*, 1972; Kenneth Cavander, 1973; W.S. Merwin and George E. Dimock, Jr, 1978; as *Iphigenia at Aulis*, translated by Don Taylor, in *The War Plays*, 1990.

Cyclops, edited by Jacqueline Duchemin. 1945; also edited by R.G. Ussher, 1978, and Richard Seaford, 1984; as *Cyclops*, translated by J.T. Sheppard, 1923; also translated by William Arrowsmith, in *Complete Greek Tragedies*, 1956; Roger Lancelyn Green, in *Two Satyr Plays*, 1957; Peter D. Arnott, in *Three Greek Plays*, 1964.

Hypsipyle (fragmentary play), edited by G.W. Bond. 1963; also edited by W.E.H. Cockle, 1987.

Phaethon (fragmentary play), edited by James Diggle. 1970.

Rhesus (probably not by Euripides), edited by James Diggle, in *Fabulae*, vol. 3. 1994; as *Rhesus*, translated by Richmond Lattimore, in *Complete Greek Tragedies*, 1958; also translated by Richard Emil Braun, 1978.

Four Dramas (includes *Andromache*; *Hecuba*; *Heracles*; *Orestes*), translated by Hugh Meredith. 1937.

Three Plays (includes *Hippolytus*; *Iphigeneia in Taurica*; *Alcestis*), translated by Philip Vellacott. 1953; revised edition, 1974.

The Bacchae and Other Plays (includes *Ion*; *The Women of Troy*; *Helen*), translated by Philip Vellacott. 1954.

Three Great Plays (includes *Helen*; *Hippolytus*; *Medea*), translated by Rex Warner. 1958.

Ten Plays, translated by Moses Hadas and John McLean. 1960.

Medea and Other Plays (includes *Medea*; *Hecabe*; *Electra*; *Heracles*), translated by Philip Vellacott. 1963.

Orestes and Other Plays (includes *The Children of Heracles*; *Andromache*; *The Suppliant Women*; *The Phoenician Women*; *Orestes*; *Iphigenia in Aulis*), translated by Philip Vellacott. 1972.

Plays One (includes *Medea*; *The Phoenician Women*; *Bacchae*), translated by Jeremy Brooks, David Thompson, and J. Michael Walton. 1988.

The War Plays: Iphigenia at Aulis; The Women of Troy; Helen, translated by Don Taylor. 1990.

Plays Two (includes *Hecuba*; *The Women of Troy*; *Iphigenia at Aulis*; *Cyclops*), translated by Don Taylor, Peter D. Arnott, and J. Michael Walton. 1991.

*

Critical Studies: *Chronology of the Extant Plays of Euripides* by Grace Harriet Macurdy, 1911; *Euripides and His Age* by Gilbert Murray, 1913, revised edition, 1946; *Euripides and*

His Influence by F.L. Lucas, 1924; *The Drama of Euripides* by G.M.A. Grube, 1941; *Essays on Euripidean Drama* by Gilbert Norwood, 1954; *The Political Plays of Euripides*, 1955, revised edition, 1963, and *An Inquiry into the Transmission of the Plays of Euripides*, 1966, both by Gunther Zuntz; *Euripides* by W.N. Bates, 1961; *Notes on Euripides' Medea and Electra* by Robert J. Milch, 1965; *Euripides and the Judgement of Paris* by T.C.W. Stinton, 1965; *Euripidean Drama: Myth, Theme, and Structure* by Desmond J. Conacher, 1967; *The Tragedies of Euripides* by T.B.L. Webster, 1967; *Euripides: A Collection of Critical Essays* edited by Erich Segal, 1968; *The Imagery of Euripides: A Study in the Dramatic Use of Pictorial Language* by Shirley A. Barlow, 1970; *Catastrophe Survived: Euripides' Plays of Mixed Reversal* by Anne P. Burnett, 1971; *The New Oxyrhynchus Papyrus: Hypothesis of Euripides' 'Alexandros'* by R.A. Coles, 1974; *Euripides and the Full Circle of Myth* by Cedric H. Whitman, 1974; *Ironic Drama: A Study of Euripides: Method and Meaning* by Philip Vellacott, 1975; *Colloquial Expressions in Euripides* by P.T. Stevens, 1976; *'God, or not God, or Between the Two?' Euripides' Helen* by George E. Dimock, 1977; *Existentialism and Euripides: Sickness, Tragedy and Divinity in The Medea, The Hippolytus and The Bacchae* by William Sale, 1977; *On the Concept of Slavery in Euripides* by Katerina Syodinou, 1977; *Terms for Happiness in Euripides* by Marianne McDonald, 1978; *The Violence of Pity in Euripides' Medea* by Pietro Pucci, 1980; *The Trojan Trilogy of Euripides* by Ruth Scodel, 1980; *Euripides* by Christopher Collard, 1981; *Studies on the Text of Euripides: Supplices, Electra, Heracles, Troades, Iphigenia in Tauris, Ion*, 1981, *The Textual Tradition of Euripides' Orestes*, 1990, and *Euripides: Collected Essays*, 1994, all by James Diggle; *The Textual Tradition of Euripides' Phoinissai* by Donald J. Mastronarde, 1982; *Dionysiac Poetics and Euripides' Bacchae* by Charles Segal, 1982; *Euripides' Bacchae: The Play and Its Audience* by Hans Oranje, 1984; *New Directions in Euripidean Criticism: A Collection of Essays* edited by Peter Burian, 1985; *Ritual Irony: Poetry and Sacrifice in Euripides* by Helene P. Foley, 1985; *Stagecraft in Euripides* by Michael R. Halleran, 1985; *Euripides' Medea and Electra: A Companion to the Penguin Translation of Philip Vellacott* by John Ferguson, 1987; *The Heroic Muse: Studies in the Hippolytus and the Hecuba of Euripides* by David Kovacs, 1987; *Euripides and the Tragic Tradition* by Ann Norris Michelini, 1987; *Aspects of Human Sacrifice in the Tragedies of Euripides* by E.A.M.E. O'Connor-Visser, 1987; *Two Lost Plays of Euripides* by Dana F. Sutton, 1987; *The God of Ecstasy: Sex-Roles and the Madness of Dionysos* by Arthur Evans, 1988; *Time Holds the Mirror: A Study of Knowledge in Euripides' Hippolytus* by C.A.E. Luschnig, 1988; *A New Creed: Fundamental Religious Beliefs in the Athenian Polis and Euripidean Drama* by Harvey Yunis, 1988; *Euripides' Medea: The Incarnation of Disorder* by Emily A. McDermott, 1989; *The Noose of Words: Readings of Desire, Violence and Language in Euripides' Hippolytus* by Barbara E. Goff, 1990; *Euripides, Women and Sexuality* by Anton Powell, 1990; *Euripides and the Instruction of the Athenians* by Justina Gregory, 1991; *Ambiguity and Self-Deception: The Apollo and Artemis Plays of Euripides* by Karelisa V. Hartigan, 1991; *Narrative in Drama: The Art of the Euripidean Messenger-Speech* by I.J.F. de Jong, 1991; *The Agon in Euripides* by Michael Lloyd, 1992; *Anxiety Veiled: Euripides and the Traffic in Women* by Nancy Sorkin Rabinowitz, 1994.

* * *

Euripides was the youngest of the famous tragedians of 5th-century Athens; he is regarded by some as responsible for a breakdown in the lofty spirit of Greek tragedy from which it never recovered; by others as introducing a new and enduring humanism, a sense of the pathos of the human condition, which expressed more powerfully than that of his predecessors the tragic realities of life.

To some degree, perhaps, the impression of contrast which the Euripidean corpus of plays provides with that of Aeschylus and Sophocles may be due to the fact that we possess a greater number of his plays (18 or 19 as compared with seven of each of the other two) and so a wider variety of Euripidean themes. However, this explanation of 'the difference' is, at best, a very partial one, for all of Euripides' plays betray, to a greater or lesser degree, a distinctly new tragic style and approach to traditional myth.

These 'new directions' of Euripidean tragedy are in part traceable to two major influences, those of the sophistic movement and of the Peloponnesian War, both of which appear to have affected Euripides more than they did his elder contemporary Sophocles. The sophists (the first professional teachers in Greece) imbued Euripides with their rationalistic way of looking at traditional beliefs and values and strongly influenced his dramatic style by the rhetorical emphasis of their teaching. In a very different way, Euripides' tragic outlook was also affected by certain dire events of the Peloponnesian War and their effects on Athenian morale and policy.

As implied above, Euripides was something of an iconoclast, a 'reducer' of the ancient mythological tradition on which the plot material of Greek tragedy was, by convention, based. Thus he tended to reinterpret and reformulate the tales of arbitrary, often vengeful anthropomorphic gods and of heroes from a remote and glorious past in ways which related them more closely to recognizable human experience. In a few plays, such as *Hippolytus* and *Bacchae* (which I shall call 'the mythological tragedies') these anthropomorphic gods still play a major role, but even here, though they are presented physically as dramatically real personages in the tragedies, they clearly symbolize mysterious forces governing the emotional and irrational areas of human experience. Thus, in *Hippolytus*, Aphrodite, goddess of sexual passion, declares that she will take vengeance on the hero for his refusal to do her honour. However, the actual action of the play (once the intentions of the goddess have been expressed in the Prologue) is worked out in essentially human terms: the catastrophe comes about from the conflict between the woman-hating Hippolytus and his stepmother Phaedra, the unwilling victim of guilty love for him. Here the poet makes it clear that it is the excess of Hippolytus' scorn for sex and his failure to understand the power of sexual passion that leads to his destruction. So, too, in *Bacchae* King Pentheus, the puritanical rationalist, suffers for suppressing in his state the mystical ecstasy and emotional release brought by the communal singing, drinking, and dancing of Dionysian worship.

In other, quite different plays of Euripides, such as *Medea* and *Electra*, the catastrophe occurs as a result of the destructive power of hate and vengeance within the soul of the individual tragic figure. Here the mythological dimension is notably less marked, since no divine figure is needed to represent the actively destructive power now embodied in the tragic personality itself. *Medea* is perhaps the most powerful example of this kind of Euripidean tragedy, which presents in psychologically 'realistic' terms the destructive power of passion. Medea, who loves her children, slays them in order to be avenged on her faithless husband Jason. 'My passion is

stronger than my reason!' she exclaims at the climax of her struggle between mother-love and vengeful fury: a very Euripidean expression of what this poet felt to be one of the mainsprings of human tragedies. Other plays which I would describe (despite certain supernatural overtones) as psychologically 'realistic' human tragedies are *Electra* and *Hecuba* (in which the same power of vengeful hatred, in very different circumstances, corrupts and destroys noble tragic figures) and (apart from its melodramatic finale) *Orestes*, which studies the effects of guilt and social rejection on the condemned matricide Orestes.

'Tragedies of War and of Politics [in the broadest sense]' might be selected as the label (with all the inadequacies which such labelling entails) for a third group of Euripidean tragedies. Here the issues are almost exclusively human and social, and the tragic situations arise, not from any divine vengeance (however 'symbolically' understood) or from individual human passions, but from man's more impersonal inhumanity to his fellow men. In *Supplices* (*The Suppliant Women*) and *Heracleidae* (*Children of Heracles*), 'just wars' are fought by legendary Athenian kings on behalf of just such victims of human cruelty, but in each case the plays end with an ironic undermining of the noble purpose of the war or else of the just pretensions of the suppliants themselves. In *Troades* (*The Trojan Women*) and *Hecuba* (which belongs as well in this group as in the preceding one), we witness the destructive results of war's cruelties on the helpless survivors of the defeated: in the one case, collectively, on the women and children of the slain Trojan heroes, in the other, individually, on the tragic (and initially noble) figure of the Trojan Queen. Again the setting is in the mythological past, but the themes are universal and, *mutatis mutandis*, apply in some respects all too tellingly to certain historical circumstances and events of Euripides' own day.

Another group of Euripidean plays, very different from the sombre 'war plays', comprises such plays as *Ion*, *Helena* (*Helen*), and *Iphigeneia Taurica* (*Iphigenia in Tauris*), which have been variously described by modern critics as 'tragicomedy', 'romantic tragedy', and (here some would include *Orestes*) 'melodrama'. Of these, *Helen* is, perhaps, at the furthest remove from traditional Greek tragedy. Euripides bases this play on a variant version of the Trojan War myth according to which Helen spent the Trojan War secretly hidden away in Egypt while the goddess Hera caused a wraith of Helen to be substituted (and mistaken) for the real Helen of Troy. The plot includes a highly comic 'recognition scene' (in which shipwrecked Menelaus, returning from Troy with the wraith, has great difficulty in recognizing his 'real', and somewhat indignant, wife) and an ingenious and exciting 'escape' sequence, in which Helen and Menelaus outwit the wicked Egyptian King and escape over the seas to Sparta with the King's ship and generous provisions of arms and supplies. In this and similar plays the poet seems to be taking traditional myth rather less seriously than in the more properly 'tragic' plays and to adopt a satirical tone (not always absent even in the most 'serious' tragedies) concerning the more improbable and anthropomorphic treatments of the gods. However, even in these less tragic plays, there are sometimes serious overtones: the Trojan War, the Chorus reminds us in *Helen*, was fought for a wraith: perhaps all wars, including the war currently ruining the poet's own beloved city, could be avoided if men allowed words and reasoning (*logoi*) instead of bloody strife (*eris*) to settle their differences.

This brief account inevitably fails to do justice to the great variety in the Euripidean treatment of human experience and human folly. If the reader has been left with the wrong impression that, in questioning traditional mythology,

Euripides rejects the supernatural element in that experience, he should read *Bacchae*, one of the last, and surely the most terrifying, of Euripides' extant tragedies. Here he will discover, with King Pentheus, what sort of fate awaits those scorning the timeless and universal powers ('even stronger than a god, if that were possible', as we are reminded of Aphrodite in *Hippolytus*) which Euripides recognized as dominating certain crucial areas in the life of man.

—Desmond J. Conacher

ELECTRA
Play by Euripides, c.422–16 BC.

Though the Athenian tragedians regularly made use of the same myths, the Electra story is unique in offering a direct comparison between the styles and techniques of Aeschylus, Sophocles, and Euripides. The middle play of Aeschylus' *Oresteia* trilogy, *The Libation Bearers* (*Choephoroi*) begins and ends at the same point in the story of the house of Atreus as do the *Electra*s of Sophocles and Euripides. *The Oresteia* was first produced in 458 BC, but no firm date can be given for either *Electra*. If scholarly opinion is divided over whether the Sophocles or the Euripides came first, there is general agreement that both were performed about the years 416-413 BC.

Such details are of more than simple academic interest in the case of Euripides' *Electra* because it contains certain sequences which appear to parody the handling of similar ideas by Aeschylus. After the murder of Agamemnon by Clytemnestra and her lover Aegisthus, the baby Orestes was sent into exile to prevent him growing up to avenge his father. His sister Electra remained at home and grew up as an outcast, deprived of status but longing for her brother's return. Euripides' version is set before a humble farmhouse and opens with a prologue from a peasant farmer who reveals that Electra has been married off to him but that he has declined to consummate the marriage out of respect.

Electra is an embittered figure who undertakes unnecessary household chores and rejects any attempts to rebuild her life, yearning only for the return of Orestes to punish her oppressors. When he does arrive, accompanied by Pylades whose family has raised him, Orestes proves to subscribe little to the picture of heroic avenger that Electra has envisaged. The key recognition scene between brother and sister, which Aeschylus places early in *The Libation Bearers* and which Sophocles delays in order to set up the plot against Clytemnestra without Electra's involvement, happens almost by accident when a diffident Orestes is recognized by the old man who rescued him as a baby.

That Euripides intended his audience to make a comparison with Aeschylus' treatment of the recognition is made abundantly clear when the old man suggests to Electra that Orestes must have visited Agamemnon's tomb in secret. He offers the exact recognition tokens, a lock of hair, footprints, and a piece of woven cloth, that once served to persuade Aeschylus' Electra that her brother had indeed returned. Euripides' Electra scornfully rejects all such tokens on practical grounds. She is only convinced when the old man confronts the two strangers and recognizes a scar on Orestes' brow. Then and only then does Orestes confess who he is and Electra is forced to admit that this reluctant avenger is the brother on whom she has pinned all her hopes.

This echo, pastiche even, of a previously familiar version of the story is typical of Euripides' approach throughout the play. Audience expectation is constantly confounded as all the characters turn out to be other than they seem. Orestes is a coward, driven to murder Aegisthus and then his mother by the combined pressures of his sister, his companion, and the old man. He chooses the least honourable method possible, accepting an invitation from Aegisthus to take part in a sacrifice as an honoured guest, then cutting him down from behind. Clytemnestra, one of the great villainesses of mythology, is treated with some sympathy. Invited by Electra to attend her after the supposed birth of a child, she shows regret for her past life but is unceremoniously hacked to death by her children, Orestes with his eyes covered by his cloak.

In such a vicious telling of the story, though one whose realism is thoroughly plausible, Electra is the real driving force. Obsessed and obsessive, her sanity hangs by a thread which snaps when her mother is finally dispatched. Where Aeschylus had created a subdued victim and Sophocles the wreck of a noble character, Euripides' Electra is a monster, the true daughter, perhaps, in dramatic terms, of Aeschylus' Clytemnestra. Even the chorus of local girls, initially well-disposed and friendly, appears by the end of the play to have turned from her. It is left to Castor and Pollux, the heavenly twin brothers of Clytemnestra and Helen, to arrive as *dei ex machina* and restore the myth to a more traditional ending.

This conscious iconoclasm is a regular part of Euripides' dramatic technique and is frequently used for comic effect. The peasant husband is roundly told off by the shrewish Electra for inviting 'superiors' to dinner only to respond that 'a woman can surely find enough to fill their guts for one meal'. Electra's warning to her mother to take care not to dirty her dress as she enters their cottage is particularly macabre when she knows that Orestes is waiting inside to murder Clytemnestra.

Euripides' *Electra* shows the story to be a bloody and unheroic episode in an unsavoury and savage saga. Human passion is the only driving force and religious sanction is sidelined. Extreme violence is fringed with domestic trivia and the blackness of the humour anticipates the Jacobean world of Webster or Middleton. As an antidote to the heroics of Aeschylus and Sophocles it has a supreme and precocious dramatic power.

—J. Michael Walton

HIPPOLYTUS
Play by Euripides, 428 BC.

Euripides was not popular in his lifetime, achieving only four victories in 22 or 23 competitions. But one of these rare victories came in 428 BC with a production that included his *Hippolytus*. One ancient commentator calls it 'one of his best', and we can only agree. A tragedy in a major key, it is full of strong characters, ideas, and images, where men and gods meet and interact, where the world of reality and an ideal realm collide with tragic results.

Hippolytus is an instance of the 'Potiphar's wife' theme (see *Genesis* 39), a love triangle involving an older man (here Theseus, king of Athens), his wife (Phaedra), and a younger male bound to him by a tie of authority (here Hippolytus, his son by 'the Amazon woman'). The woman falls in love with the young man, expresses her love, but is rejected by him, usually for virtuous reasons. To cover her shame, she falsely accuses the young man of rape to her husband. The older man punishes the younger, who in most instances survives by miraculous means. But in *Hippolytus* the youth is cursed by his father, and on his way to banishment his horses are frightened by a bull from the sea and he is dragged to his death. In remorse Phaedra kills herself.

It is crucial to realize that the play we possess is a revision of a lost earlier version (c.435 BC?). From what we can tell of that earlier *Hippolytus* (see W.S. Barrett and Kenneth Cavander), it was an orthodox 'Potiphar's wife' play, but this revision is in many ways a deliberate inversion of that genre. Note the setting, Troezen (Hippolytus' home, not the older man's). Phaedra is hardly the shameless seducer of tradition, but a noble woman in love against her will, who will not yield to her passion. In fact, Phaedra and Hippolytus never meet; a nurse acting on her own reveals Phaedra's love to Hippolytus. The young man refuses it, not just because he is noble and pure, but because he hates women: 'I shall have enough of hating women, and even if they said I am forever talking of this, remember that women are wicked forever'. Phaedra kills herself halfway through the action, not from remorse or guilt, but for shame, with a note wrongly accusing Hippolytus.

But Euripides' greatest innovation was to set this play within a divine framework. Aphrodite (Love) speaks the prologue, revealing that she will punish Hippolytus for his excessive devotion to Artemis (the chaste goddess of the hunt). She has caused Phaedra's love, so that the revelation will destroy Hippolytus (and incidentally Phaedra) and thus satisfy her slighted honour. At the end Artemis appears to blame Theseus for the death of his son, to promise the dying Hippolytus honours after his death, and to revenge herself on Love ('I shall kill with these arrows whatever mortal is most dear to her', an illusion to the myth of Aphrodite and Adonis).

This is the first play we have demonstrating Euripides' celebrated excursions into theology. He sets up traditional anthropomorphic deities (Aphrodite, Artemis) with human passions (jealousy, pride, spite) and superhuman powers and little concern for men. Both Aphrodite and Artemis are cut from the same inferior cloth. Ironically, men must worship these unworthy beings and, like Phaedra and Hippolytus, strive for virtue. Yet Love is real, a cosmic force; so too is Purity, but Euripides juxtaposes his ideals ('Gods should not be like men in their passions') with the grim reality. In his plays men have a superior view of gods and divinity. Note the ending where Theseus and Hippolytus forgive each other; gods cannot.

On a psychological level the playwright is exploring the human reality behind characters from myth. Must the woman always be a shameless seductress? This Phaedra is a woman of virtue, in some ways a continuation of the empathetic portrait developed in his *Medea*, and a real human figure. Likewise, must the young man be a paragon of virtue? Could he be so in reality? In *Hippolytus* we meet a man apart, devoted to Artemis and the wild. His virtue is real, his song to Artemis beautiful and sincere, and he does keep his oath of silence to the nurse. It is not incidental that he is Theseus' *bastard* son.

Hippolytus repays a variety of critical approaches. Anne Burnett has shown how it fits well into a Levi-Straussian dualism (a tension between the solitary hunter and the promiscuous city woman), resolved or 'mediated' by the institution of marriage. This explains the rather unusual honours bestowed on Hippolytus (brides on their wedding eve will dedicate to him a lock of hair) and the joining of male and female choruses. B.M.W. Knox and Barbara Goff have explored the theme of speech and silence as dominant and motive symbols, while C.A.E. Luschnig stresses that the play revolves around knowledge and knowing. In fact, as in *The Trojan Women* and *Ion*, men come to a tragic knowledge about the universe—Desmond J. Conacher is especially good here.

Underlying and running through the drama is an untranslatable concept, *sophrosyne* (chastity, moderation, self-control, virtue). The dramatist seems to be asking who is truly *sophron*, the woman in love who will die to protect her honour or the young man whose 'virtue' is undercut by his immoderate misogyny?

Full of vivid imagery from the wild and the hunt (animal imagery is particularly prevalent—the Bull from the Sea can be seen as Hippolytus' repressed sexuality which destroys him), of water and sea, or escape to distant lands, this play breathes the great outdoors, and displays brilliantly Euripides' favourite themes of psychology, realism, innovation, and theology. It deserves its place among the greatest of Greek tragedies.

—Ian C. Storey

ION
Play by Euripides, c.421–13 BC.

Of the 19 Euripides plays to survive, all but the satyr play *Cyclops*, and, possibly, *Alcestis*, performed fourth and in the satyr position, can be classified as tragedies. Among these 17 there is considerable difference of emphasis and treatment, with several of the lighter plays appearing to explore the territory *Alcestis* opened up. Savage war plays, such as *The Trojan Women* and *Hecuba*, and plays of individual passions, such as *Medea* and *Hippolytus*, may have earned Euripides the soubriquet from Aristotle of *tragikotatos*, 'most tragic', but the gentler works, *Ion* among them, equally demonstrate the touch of a master playwright.

Ion, indeed, suggests in its plot and characters more the world of 4th-century BC New Comedy than that of formal 5th-century BC tragedy. Here is the story of a foundling, of recognition tokens, of intrigue and deception, all ending happily, or relatively so, for all the major characters. The play does have its serious side with a jaundiced look at Apollo and his fellow Olympians, and a possible parochial significance in the establishment of Ion's lineage which is lost on any modern audience, but nothing more harrowing happens than the poisoning of a dove. The date of the first performance in Athens is not known, though it is thought to have been produced during the Peloponnesian War and probably between 421 and 413 BC.

The play opens with a prologue from the god Hermes in which he tells of the rape by Apollo many years ago of Creusa, daughter of the Athenian king Erechtheus. At Apollo's wish, Creusa left the child of the union, complete with a necklace and a shawl, in a cave from which Hermes rescued him and deposited him on the steps of the temple at Delphi. The child comes to be known as Ion. He is brought up by the priestess of the temple and at the beginning of the play is serving as its steward. Back in Athens, Creusa married Xuthus but they have no children. They have now come to Delphi to ask advice from Apollo's oracle.

So much is simple setting of the scene, but Hermes continues by anticipating the oracle's reply. Apollo will give his son, Ion, to Xuthus, telling Xuthus that he, Xuthus, is Ion's real father. Creusa will come to recognize her son and everyone will be satisfied with an edited version of the truth. It is not unusual for the progress of the plot to be given away in Greek New Comedy and even in tragedy. It is of major importance that it happens in *Ion* because so much of the rest of the play is taken up with the various characters trying to work out what is really going on.

Xuthus is delighted to be informed that the first person he meets when he emerges from the oracle will be his real son and embraces Ion enthusiastically. Ion is less enthusiastic and Creusa is furious to find that the result of the consultation is for Xuthus to be awarded a fully-grown son and that she is expected to welcome his bastard when her own son died in the cave, as she imagines, so many years ago. The chorus suspects fraud. Creusa's old retainer assumes that the whole thing has been concocted to foist the illegitimate child of Xuthus onto Creusa. Creusa reacts by trying to poison Ion, barely restraining the old retainer who would quite cheerfully murder Xuthus and burn down the oracle to boot.

The complex task for a modern director or reader is to work out how much of this is to be taken seriously. The twists and turns of the plot are so rapid and convoluted that the Hermes guide to what really happened is indispensable. Creusa's attempt to murder Ion fails when the cup is spilled and a dove drinks the poison. Creusa has to seek sanctuary from both the angry locals and Ion, who now wants to kill her. At this moment of crisis, the priestess of Apollo arrives with the cradle in which Ion was found, together with the shawl and the necklace.

Even now the outcome is not resolved because the tokens of recognition look suspiciously new. Ion is thoroughly sceptical of Creusa's version of what happened to her and seems to be happier with the idea that he is the illegitimate son of Xuthus than that he is the illegitimate son of Apollo. However, convinced at last that Creusa really is his mother, he still has doubts about Apollo being his father. Determined to storm into the oracle and demand the truth from Apollo himself, he is forestalled by the goddess Athena who confirms Hermes' version from the prologue but suggests that Xuthus is better off believing Apollo's version from the oracle: and so to everyone living happily ever after.

Whatever direction the play is seen to take, towards tragedy, romance, or social comedy, *Ion* is a play of great sweep and flow. Plot developments may dominate our attention but the main characters are memorable and the handling of individual scenes does far more than simply anticipate a new direction for Greek drama. The chorus, comprised of servants of Creusa, has a remarkable *parados*, or opening song, in which it marvels at the decoration on Apollo's temple, either in tribute to the set designer, or in a curiously backhanded theatrical in-joke about the plainness of the scene-building. Ion, still confused about details of his past, as well he might be, takes his mother to one side so that he can talk to her 'in private'—in front of an audience of 17,000. All this is part and parcel of the theatre game, with the audience co-conspirators, as it were, with the author. *Ion* is a play of potential rather than actual tragedy in which humans are less the victims of the vicissitudes of fate than of arbitrary and barely respectable gods and goddesses. For Euripides this is as comic as it is serious.

—J. Michael Walton

MEDEA
Play by Euripides, 431 BC.

Euripides' famous play *Medea* is set in Corinth where Medea is in exile. It depicts the revenge she takes against her errant Argonaut husband Jason who, despite owing his life to her and having sworn an oath of fidelity, has deserted her in order to marry the daughter of Creon, the king of Corinth.

After disposing of her rival and Creon by means of poisoned gifts, a robe and chaplet, she completes her revenge by killing her own children, thus leaving Jason without issue. She makes her escape in a miraculous manner, using a winged chariot provided by her grandfather Helius, the sun, having already secured the promise from King Aegeus of asylum in Athens. Legends regarding Medea's stay in Corinth and the death of her children already existed in Euripides' time, but there is general agreement that the form of the story presented in the play is very much his own.

Two aspects of the play have been subjected, from Aristotle onwards, to adverse criticism—the 'Aegeus scene' and the supernatural conclusion. The appearance of Aegeus at Corinth on his way from Delphi to Troezen has appeared to many to have been dragged in for the convenience of the plot. It should be pointed out, however, that by 431 BC the figures of Aegeus and Medea were closely linked in Athenian legend and that the scene contains a thematic link with the rest of the play, namely children: the purpose of Aegeus' journey is to discover if he can make his marriage fertile. The finale is a remarkable *coup de théâtre*. Medea appears, in a scene akin to the divine epiphanies so common in Euripides' work, as *dea ex machina*, announcing her own intentions and revealing to Jason what will happen to him in his future life. To see this as contrived is to miss the point. We have been reminded already of Medea's relationship to the sun and there is undoubtedly something inherently demonic about her character.

The dramatic structure of the play is hard to parallel. No other character in Greek tragedy dominates the stage to the extent that Medea does. The central action of the play is made up of scenes in which she converses at length with the chorus and scenes in which she confronts single characters acting as foils: Creon, Jason, Aegeus, Jason, the messenger, and finally, Jason once more. Her formidable character which this prominence highlights has been explained by many critics as the product of her non-Greek origins ('no Greek woman could behave like this!') and her powers as a sorceress. But neither of these features, so prominent in later treatments of her story, is to the fore in Euripides' play. Her barbarian birth is certainly relevant to her isolation and need for protection in the Greek world: it is not used as an explanation for her conduct. She is, admittedly, an expert with potions (*pharmaca*), which she is able to use both for deadly purposes (the murder of her rival) and benign ones (ensuring that Aegeus has issue), but such skill is paralleled in tragedy in the case of other, female, Greek characters. It is not so much her magical powers as her acute intelligence and insight that are stressed. Most of all, it is her heroic nature—she has affinities with the great, unrecalcitrant Sophoclean hero figures—that stands out. Because of her acute sense of injustice she is driven to extreme action. After much soul-searching she conquers her strong maternal instincts and takes the ultimate step of killing her children because she knows that this is the way to inflict the greatest hurt on Jason.

Medea is also a spokeswoman for her own sex. (For most of the play she has the total support of the chorus of female Corinthians.) Her opening speech is a powerful description of the plight of women in the Greek world and includes the memorable response to the assertion that women do not have to undergo the same physical risks and discomfort as the Greek warrior male: 'I would rather stand three times in the line of battle than give birth once'. Such a sentiment must have made uncomfortable hearing for the male audience in the theatre of Dionysus in 431 BC.

—David M. Bain

ORESTES
Play by Euripides, 408 BC.

Euripides' *Orestes*, his final production for the theatre of Dionysus at Athens prior to his retreat to Macedon, was designed to be a thriller, a murder plot to kill Helen, with a happy ending. The trilogy comprised *Oenomaus*, *Chrysippus*, and *The Phoenician Women* (*Phoenissae*) (extant), with *Orestes* as the satyr play. The play details what happened to the matricides. Its psychological examination of their abnormal natures, the transfer of a variant of the Mycenaean story of 5th-century Athenian conditions and contexts, its comic passages, and Euripides' original approach to traditional mythology, provide diversified entertainment. The aristocracy is basically degenerate; some antique virtues still survive, loyalty between Orestes and Electra, and (somewhat extravagantly presented) between Orestes and Pylades, but the loyalty is self-centred, disdainful of the law and of the common welfare, and capable of ruthless inhumanity to others.

Orestes appears in rags, a veritable stretcher-case, haunted by his mother's Furies, with no prospect of release or asylum. A trial by the Argive assembly lies ahead, Euripides' parody of the trial by jury in Aeschylus' *The Furies* (*Eumenides*). The forecast sentence is execution by stoning. Menelaus surfaces as the saviour figure, brought to Argos to recover his daughter Hermione who had been left in Clytemnestra's charge during the war overseas. Helen, wide-eyed and innocent, self-satisfied and elegant as usual, appeals to a depressed Electra to carry offerings to Clytemnestra's tomb. Electra's love for her brother is dominant. His mad scene, on stage, with visions of the Gorgon, can be diagnosed not as hysteria but as madness by design. Menelaus is assigned parenthetic scenes around the presence of Tyndareus, the maternal grandfather of Orestes, who comes to mourn the murder of his daughter Clytemnestra; his somewhat sophistic position, in the presence of Menelaus, is that the expected sentence to death by stoning seems excessive, until he sees and hears Orestes. Thereafter his earlier preference for banishment instead of death by stoning is rejected; he proposes to advocate the stoning of both Orestes and Electra, and leaves in consternation.

Orestes seeks Menelaus' assistance. A messenger reports the proceedings of the Assembly and the spokesmen for and against the execution of Orestes and Electra: Talthybius favoured condemnation; Diomedes spoke in favour of banishment; an anonymous, ill-trained speaker, encouraged by Tyndareus, favoured death by stoning; a peasant farmer spoke in defence of Orestes' matricide. Orestes, according to the messenger, left his sickbed to defend his action as executioner within the family as having been a public benefaction. Condemnation followed. Electra responds with a song and dance calling on Persephone, goddess of the dead, and asks pity for those who once fought for Hellas. The house of Pelops (and of Atreus) has been destroyed by a democratic process and by the envy of the gods. Orestes and Pylades return to take their farewells from their grieving friends. Electra begs Orestes to kill her and faithful Pylades is prepared to join the suicide pact with Orestes. Orestes' criminal mind then proposes the execution of all the slaves and of Helen. Electra reveals her father-fixation and her addiction to violence and deceit by suggesting that Hermione also should be kidnapped and murdered.

Pylades and Orestes enter the palace to kill Helen, leaving Electra outside with the chorus. At the sound of Helen's screams from within, Hermione arrives and is rushed indoors where Orestes is waiting. The choral song drowns out the sounds behind the palace doors, at which point a slave emerges on the palace balcony, drops to the ground, and gives a breathless account, an almost unintelligibly garbled eyewitness report, of Helen's escape.

Orestes leaves the palace with drawn sword, threatens then releases the slave, and re-enters the palace. The chorus finally senses what is happening and catches sight of the torches which will set fire to the palace. Menelaus appears, alarmed by the news of Helen's disappearance, and orders his men to break down the palace doors. Orestes drags Hermione onto the balcony for execution; Pylades and Electra are beside him with torches at the ready. At this point, the insoluble (and intolerable) situation calls for a *deus ex machina* in the person of Apollo, with the divine Helen alongside. Apollo contrives a solution for every problem: Helen will become a star to guide sailors; Orestes, acquitted by the court of the Areopagus, will marry Hermione; Electra will marry Pylades; Orestes will administer Argos, Menelaus will rule over Sparta; and Apollo will deal with the Argive assembly. Helen disappears with Apollo, bound for Zeus.

Euripides' play comes close to chaos. Degeneracy, sickness, and manic blood-lust have brought the one-time celebrated House of Atreus to the edge, where only miracles can fend off impending disaster and strain credulity. The political context of 408 BC—a season of vulgarity in the assembly and ineptitude in the strategic command, a time when the citizens longed for the return of the disgraced traitor Alcibiades, one-time scion of Periclean democracy, although he was engaged even then in trying to negotiate an entente with Persia—must lie at the heart of Euripides' discontent and indictment of the democratic process. In light of these conditions, the ludicrous final scene seems more intelligible and prognostic. 'The final tableau is the direct prophecy of disaster', as William Arrowsmith deduced, 'complete, awful, and inevitable, while Apollo intervenes only as an impossible wish, a futile hope, or a simple change of scene from a vision that cannot be brooked, or seen for long, because it is the direct vision of despair, the hopeless future'. The defeat of Athens in the Peloponnesian War came four years later.

—Alexander G. McKay

THE TROJAN WOMEN (Troades)
Play by Euripides, 415 BC.

Euripides' drama of the defeated Trojans and their experience with Greek brutality and inhumanity followed the infamous siege of the neutral island of Melos in 416 BC and immediately preceded the departure of the Athenian expeditionary force against Syracuse, a campaign that ended disastrously for the Athenians in 413 BC. Thucydides' account of the parley between the Athenian commanders and Melian representatives and the subsequent siege is marked by opportunism, arrogance (*hubris*), and rejection of the claims of justice (Thucydides 5, 84–116). The Athenian victory resulted in the slaughter of the Melian men, and the enslavement of the women and children. Thucydides (and Euripides) saw the campaign as critical; the glory of the event was eclipsed by the suffering of the vanquished.

Euripides' *The Trojan Women* was part of a lost, probably connected, trilogy, *Alexander* (= Paris), *Palamedes*, and *The Trojan Women*; the satyr play was *Sisyphus*. The plays, in succession, treated the tragic error that attached to Priam's compassion and ultimate tragic error in the rescue and nurture of Paris (*Alexander*); the political intrigue against the high-minded Palamedes which had dire consequences for the

Greek perpetrators (*Palamedes*); vignettes of cruelty and suffering after defeat (*The Trojan Women*); in all likelihood, the satyr play dealt with deceit and destruction. The coherence seems somewhat strained because the plots are still uncertain.

The theme of *The Trojan Women* is the debasement of human nature and the sorrow war brings for its victors as well as the defeated. The persistent tone is sorrow rather than bitterness. The play opens with Poseidon's renunciation of Troy to escape the pollution of death. Athena, properly the patroness of the Greeks, regards them as sinners bound for personal disaster in their return to Greece. As sackers of cities, temples, and tombs, nemesis is inescapable. Hecuba, the former queen reduced to rags and misery, expresses hatred for Helen, and observes that even the victorious Greeks have made their wives widows and their virgins husbandless. Talthybius, the Greek herald, forthright, unimaginative, but basically sympathetic, reports the assignment of the Trojan women to the respective lords and captors: Cassandra to Agamemnon; Polyxena, as it finally emerges, to be sacrificial victim to dead Achilles; Andromache, Hector's widow, to Neoptolemus, Achilles' son; and Hecuba to the detested Odysseus. Cassandra is introduced carrying a bridal torch and dressed in her prophetic robes; consecrated to Apollo, and to virginity, truthful but never believed, her words and fire-dance accent Greek insensitivity and forecast the ultimate holocaust. The chorus of women performs a solemn dance recalling the entry of the Trojan Horse into the city.

Brilliant spectacle ensues with the arrival of a chariot carrying Andromache and Astyanax, Hector's son. Talthybius reports, with some reluctance, that by order of Odysseus Astyanax must die. The separation of mother and child is deeply poignant. The chorus sings of an earlier siege of Troy, involving Telamon of Salamis and Heracles when, because of the Trojan king Laomedon's deceit, the gods had once before abandoned Troy. Menelaus, pompous, arrogant, conceited, and an incompetent commander, indicates that he endorses Helen's execution. Hecuba responds with a measure of urgency, composes a pun on Helen's name ('destroyer') and criticizes Helen's still elegant attire.

A debate, technically an *agon*, a contest or legalistic argument, ensues between Helen and Hecuba. Helen offers a cool, rational defence of her past actions, and seeks to exonerate herself from personal guilt by alleging that she is the victim of others and of divine powers, of Hecuba and Priam (who raised Paris), of Aphrodite (who captivates mortals and awarded her to Paris), of Paris (by reason of his physical beauty and sexual appetite), and of Menelaus (who was foolish enough to leave Helen and Paris alone in his palace). Hecuba's hatred knows no bounds: she rejects the Judgement of Paris as fiction, argues that Aphrodite equates with Aphrosyne (lewdness, folly, or mindlessness), that Helen was intrigued from the outset by eastern luxury and exotically designed clothes (which she still wears in contrast to Hecuba's rags). Hecuba's is a speech of deep-seated hatred and contempt, fired by prejudice. Her 'courtroom' rhetoric is more persuasive; but Helen's beauty is invincible. The chorus responds with a prayer for the destruction of the Greeks. Talthybius reappears with the corpse of Astyanax resting on Hector's massive shield but only after he has bathed the child's battered body, thrown from the walls of Troy, in the Scamander river. Hecuba arranges the burial of the child and pronounces an impressive, agonized lament over her grandson. The chorus responds with unrestrained lamentation over the exodus of the Trojan captives and the ultimate devastation of the city.

Throughout, Euripides lays emphasis on suffering and maltreatment and plays down the heroism of men on the battlefield. The heroic focus of the *Iliad* has shifted to the fate of the losers. The concentration on women as the objects of men's aggression and brutality underscores the harshness of the drama. Perhaps the most impressive moments in the play are Cassandra's sophistic outburst in her 'mad' scene when she argues that the Greeks have won a hollow victory, for they have destroyed the possibilities of the continuing life of their native land, her prophecy that her forced marriage to Agamemnon will be prelude to his destruction, and her forecast that the sly, unpleasant Odysseus will be a wanderer for years to come. Finally, the play offers a timeless litany of the suffering that war brings to victors and victims alike.

—Alexander G. McKay

EVTUSHENKO, Evgenii (Alexandrovich) [Yevgeny Yevtushenko]. Born in Stantsiia Zima, Irkutsk region, Siberia, 18 July 1933. Went on geological expeditions with father to Kazakhstan, 1948, and the Altai, 1950. Educated at the Gor'kii Institute, Moscow, early 1950s. Married 1) Bella Akhmadulina in 1954 (divorced); 2) Galina Semenova; 3) Jan Butler in 1978; 4) Maria Novika in 1986; five sons. Member, Congress of People's Deputies of USSR, since 1989; vice president, Russian PEN, since 1990. Recipient: USSR Committee for Defence of Peace award, 1965; Order of Red Banner of Labour (twice); State prize, 1984. Honorary member, American Academy of Arts and Sciences, 1987. Lives in Moscow.

PUBLICATIONS

Collection

The Collected Poems 1952–1990, edited by Albert C. Todd, various translators. 1991.

Verse

Razvedchiki griadushchevo [The Prospectors of the Future]. 1952.
Tretii sneg [Third Snow]. 1955.
Shosse entuziastov [Highway of the Enthusiasts]. 1956.
Stantsiia Zima, in *Oktiabr'*, 10. 1956; as *Winter Station*, translated by Oliver J. Frederiksen, 1964.
Obeshchanie [Promise]. 1957.
Dve liubimykh [Two Loves], in *Grani*, 38. 1958.
Luk i lira [The Bow and the Lyre]. 1959.
Stikhi raznykh let [Poems of Several Years]. 1959.
Iabloko [The Apple]. 1960.
Red Cats. 1961.
Vzmakh ruki [A Wave of the Hand]. 1962.
Selected Poems, translated by Peter Levi and Robin Milner-Gulland. 1962.
Nezhnost': novye stikhi [Tenderness: New Poems]. 1962.
Posle Stalina [After Stalin]. 1962.
The Heirs of Stalin, in *Current Digest of the Soviet Press*, 14(40). 1962; as *Nasledniki Stalina*, 1963.

Selected Poems. 1962.
Selected Poetry. 1963.
Khochu ia stat' nemnozhko staromodnym [I Want to Become a Bit Old-Fashioned], in *Novyi mir*, 7. 1964.
The Poetry of Yevgeny Yevtushenko, edited and translated by George Reavey. 1964; revised edition, 1981; as *Early Poems*, 1989.
Bratskaia GES. 1965; as *The Bratsk Station*, in *New Works: The Bratsk Station*, 1966.
Khotiat li russkie voiny? [Do They Want Russian Wars?]. 1965.
So mnoiu vot chto proiskhodit: izbrannaia lirika [Here's What Happens to Me: Selected Lyrics]. 1966.
Kater sviazi [Torpedo Boat Signalling]. 1966.
Kachka [Swing-Boat]. 1966.
New Works: The Bratsk Station, translated by Tina Tupikina-Glaessner, Geoffrey Dutton, and Igor Mezhakoff Koviakin. 1966; as *The Bratsk Station and Other New Poems*, 1967.
Yevtushenko Poems (bilingual edition), translated by Herbert Marshall. 1966.
Poems, translated by Herbert Marshall. 1966.
Poems Chosen by the Author, translated by Peter Levi and Robin Milner-Gulland. 1966.
The City of Yes and the City of No and Other Poems. 1966.
Stikhi [Poems]. 1967.
New Poems. 1968.
Tramvai poezii [Tram of Poetry]. 1968.
Tiaga val'dshnepov [Roding Woodcock]. 1968.
Idut belye snegi [The White Snows Are Falling]. 1969.
Flowers and Bullets, and Freedom to Kill. 1970.
Ia sibirskoi porody [I'm of Siberian Stock]. 1971.
Stolen Apples, translated by James Dickey. 1971.
Kazanskii universitet. 1971; as *Kazan University and Other New Poems*, translated by Eleanor Jacks and Geoffrey Dutton, 1973.
Doroga nomer odin [Highway Number One]. 1972.
Poiushchaia damba [The Singing Dam]. 1972.
Poet v Rossii—bol'she, chem poet [A Poet in Russia Is More than a Poet]. 1973.
Intimnaia lirika [Intimate Lyrics]. 1973.
Ottsovskii slukh [Father's Hearing]. 1975.
Izbrannye proizvedeniia [Selected Works]. 1975.
Proseka [The Track]. 1976.
Spasibo [Thank You]. 1976.
From Desire to Desire. 1976; as *Love Poems*, 1977.
V polnyi rost: novaia kniga stikhov i poem [At Full Growth: New Book of Poetry and Verse]. 1977.
Zaklinanie [A Spell]. 1977.
Utrennii narod: novaia kniga stikhov [The Morning Crowds: New Book of Poetry]. 1978.
Prisiaga prostoru: stikhi [An Oath to Space: Poems]. 1978.
A Choice of Poems by Evgeny Evtushenko. 1978.
Kompromiss Kompromissovich [Compromise Kompromissovich]. 1978.
The Face Behind the Face, translated by Arthur Boyars and Simon Franklin. 1979.
Ivan the Terrible and Ivan the Fool, translated by Daniel Weissbort. 1979.
Tiazhelee zemli [Heavier than Earth]. 1979.
Kogda muzhchine sorok let [When a Man Is 40]. 1979.
Doroga, ukhodiashchaia vdal' [The Road, Leading Far]. 1979.
Svarka vzryvom: stikhotvoreniia i poemy [Explosion Welding: Poetry and Narrative Verse]. 1980.
Tret'ia pamiat' [Third Memory]. 1980.
Poslushaite menia [Listen to Me]. 1980.

Tochka opory [Fulcrum] (includes *Pirl-kharbor* [Pearl Harbour]). 1981.
Ia sibiriak [I'm a Siberian]. 1981.
Dve pary lyzh [A Pair of Skis]. 1982.
Belye snegi [White Snows]. 1982.
A Dove in Santiago (novella in verse), translated by D.M. Thomas. 1982.
Mama i neitronaiia bomba i drugie poemy [Mother and Neutron Bomb and Other Poems]. 1983.
Otkuda rodom ia [Where I Come From]. 1983.
Sobranie sochinenii [Collected Works]. 3 vols., 1983–84.
Dva goroda [Two Towns]. 1985.
More [Sea]. 1985.
Pochti naposledok: novaia kniga. 1985; as *Almost at the End*, translated by Antonina W. Bouis and Albert C. Todd, 1987.
Poltravinochki [Half a Blade of Grass]. 1986.
Stikhi [Poems]. 1986.
Zavtrashnii veter [Tomorrow's Wind]. 1987.
Stikhotvoreniia [Poetry]. 1987.
Sud [The Trial], in *Novyi mir*, 11. 1987.
Stikhotvoreniia i poemy 1951–1986 [Poetry and Narrative Verse]. 3 vols., 1987.
Posledniaia popytka: stikhotvoreniia iz starykh i novykh tetradei [Last Attempt: Poetry from Old and New Books]. 1988.
Pochti v poslednii mig [Almost at the Last Moment]. 1988.
Nezhnost' [Tenderness]. 1988.
Poemy o mire [Verses on Peace]. 1989.
Stikhi [Poems]. 1989.
Grazhdane, poslushaite menia . . . [Citizens, Listen to Me . . .]. 1989.
Liubimaia, spi . . . [Loved One, Sleep . . .]. 1989.
Pomozhem svobode! [We Will Help Freedom!], in *Znamia*, 4. 1990.
Ne umirai prezhde smerti [Don't Die Before Death], in *Ogonek*, 10. 1992.

Fiction

Chetvertaia meshchanskaia [Four Vulgar Women], in *Iunost'*, 2. 1959.
Iagodnye mesta. 1982; as *Wild Berries*, translated by Antonina W. Bouis, 1984.
Ardabiola. 1984.

Plays

Bratskaia GES (produced 1968). 1967.
Under the Skin of the Statue of Liberty (produced 1972).

Screenplays: *Kindergarten*, 1984; *Detskii sad Moscow*, 1989.

Other

Avtobiografiia. 1963; as *A Precocious Autobiography*, translated by Andrew R. MacAndrew, 1963.
Yevtushenko's Reader: The Spirit of Elbe, A Precocious Autobiography, Poems. 1966.
Izbrannye proizedeniia [Selected Works]. 2 vols., 1975.
Talent est' chudo nesluchainoe [Talent Is a Miracle Coming Not by Chance]. 1980.
Invisible Threads. 1981.
Voina—eto antikultura [War Is Anti-Culture]. 1983.
Divided Twins = Razdel ennye blizne t sy: Alaska and Siberia, photographs by Evtushenko and Boyd Norton. 1988.
Politika privilegiia vsekh [Everybody's Privilege]. 1990.

Propast'—v dva pryzhka? [The Precipice—in Two Leaps?].
1990.
*Fatal Half Measures: The Culture of Democracy in the Soviet
Union*, with Antonina W. Bouis. 1991.

Translator, *Mlechnyi put'*, by D. Ulzytuev. 1961.
Translator, *Seti zvezd*, by T. Chiladze. 1961.
Translator, *Na koleni ne padat'!*, by G. Dzhagarov. 1961.
Translator, *Tiazhelee zemli: stikhi o Gruzii, poety Gruzii*.
1979.

*

Critical Studies: 'Herbert and Yevtushenko: On Whose Side
Is History?' by George Gömöri, in *Mosaic*, 3(1), 1969; 'The
Politics of Poetry: The Sad Case of Yevgeny Yevtushenko' by
Robert Conquest, in *New York Times Magazine*, 30
September, 1973; 'An Interview with Evgeniy Evtushenko'
by Gordon McVay, in *Journal of Russian Studies*, 1977;
'Women in Evtushenko's Poetry' by Vickie A. Rebenko, in
Russian Review, 36, 1977; 'Yevtushenko as a Critic' by
Vladimir Ognev, in *Soviet Studies in Literature*, 18(3), 1981;
'Yevgeni Yevtushenko's Solo: On His 50th Birthday' by
Yevgeni Sidorov, in *Soviet Literature*, 7(424), 1983; 'Two
Opinions about Evgenii Evtushenko's Narrative Poem: "Man
and the Neutron Bomb": And What If This Is Prose? And
What If It Is Not?' by Adol'f Urban and Gennadii Krasnikov,
in *Soviet Studies in Literature*, 20(1), 1983–84; 'The Poetry of
Yevgeny Yevtushenko in the 1970's' by Irma Mercedes
Kaszuba, in *USF Language Quarterly*, 25(1–2), 1986; 'Evtu-
šenko's *Jagodnye mesta*: The Poet as Prose Writer' by
Richard N. Porter, in *Russian Language Journal*, 40(135),
1986; '"Queuing for Hope": About Yevgeni Yevtushenko's
Poem "Fuku!"' by Pavel Ulyashov, in *Soviet Literature*,
9(462), 1986; 'Yevtushenko's *Stantsiya Zima*: A Reassessment' by Michael Pursglove, in *New Zealand Slavonic
Journal*, 2, 1988.

* * *

In the 1950s and 1960s Evgenii Evtushenko became the
poet and spokesman for the younger post-Stalinist generation
of Russian writers. He was responsible for reviving the brash,
slangy, and direct poetic language of the revolutionary poets
like Maiakovskii and Esenin, and reintroducing the personal
and love lyrics so frowned upon by the authorities. The open
demands he made on the international scene for greater
artistic freedom, and for a literature based on aesthetic
criteria rather than ideological standards, were partially
responsible for the gradual easing of control over writers in
the USSR.

Evtushenko's writing has always been rooted in the autobiographical. His poetry is topical and journalistic, as in
Stantsiia Zima (*Winter Station*), a celebration of his birthplace, a small provincial town situated on the famous Trans-
Siberian railway, in the Irkutsk region. This poem records a
visit in the summer of 1953 to Zima, describing the relatives
and other people he encounters there, and his endeavours to
come to terms with his anxieties and the public moral
problems raised by Stalin's death and the revelations that
followed. Similarly, in 'Svad'by' ('Weddings'), 1955, he
records the atmosphere of the terrible years he spent as a
child evacuee from Moscow at Zima Station during the war.
Not only did Zima Station provide a source for country
characters and scenery, but Evtushenko also began to be
influenced by Siberian folklore and folk song, an impact
which was to shape many of his later poems.

Evtushenko's poetic career began in earnest when he was
given the chance to study at the Gor'kii Literary Institute in
Moscow, the official training school for many of the Soviet
writers after the war. He published widely in established
journals in the 1950s, and his early books, *Tretii sneg* [Third
Snow], *Shosse entuziastov* [Highway of the Enthusiasts], and
Obeshchanie [Promise], made him famous and controversial
with their outspokenness and flamboyance. *Luk i lira* [The
Bow and the Lyre] followed, a volume that was the result of a
stay in Georgia and contains many translations of Georgian
poetry, and then the final volume of this series, *Stikhi raznykh let* [Poems of Several Years]. His poetry demonstrated a
distinctive lyrical note in his treatment of nature, love, and
various patriotic beliefs, celebrating the original ideals of the
Revolution and condemning their corruption at the hands of
the bureaucrats. It is compared frequently with the poetry
of Maiakovskii with whom Evtushenko shares a dislike of
hypocrisy and decadence, and a forthright, declamatory style.

Evtushenko began to write more boldly and to touch upon
issues that had until then been kept under wraps. Such concerns included admitting the terrible mistakes of the Stalinist
purges of the 1930s and 1940s and insisting that the truth be
told. Such poems naturally caused a great deal of displeasure
in certain circles: 'It will go hard with me at times,/and they
will say: "He'd better hold his tongue!"'. This sharp political
edge to the poetry went hand in hand with the youth's general
desire to reassess the direction of the revolution. Poetry for
Evtushenko was not merely negative and critical; rather, it
was a form of aesthetic affirmation and ideal statement. In
'Rakety i telegi' ('Rockets and Carts'), 1960, he declared the
need for rocket-like art against the persistence of dull, plod-
ding, 'cart-like' novels and operas. This stance, adopted by
Evtushenko and others like Voznesenskii, was hugely popular and caused a large increase in book sales and attendances
at poetry readings. In a poetry that desires 'art to be/as
diverse as myself', Evtushenko sought to write a more
dynamic verse that challenged the orthodoxy of Soviet
Realism with the emergence of a new subjective element. As
he declared in 'Svezhesti' ('Freshness') (1960), 'Freshness!/
Freshness!/We want freshness!'

Evtushenko's work and activities in the early 1960s were
often stimulated by his wide travels, including visits to
England, France, Catalonia, Ghana, Liberia, Togo, and
Bulgaria, and in April 1961 to the United States. These years
saw the publication of one of his most notable collections,
Vzmakh ruki [A Wave of the Hand], which contains many of
his poems written as a result of his worldwide travels; and
Nezhnost' [Tenderness], which includes more of his travel
poems and impressions of foreign cultures and societies, particularly the last section with its poems on Cuba, which he had
visited in 1962. Nevertheless, his political poems continued,
with immense popularity: the controversial 'Babii Iar' (1961),
a poem that mourns the Nazi massacre of Ukrainian Jews but
which also attacks the vestiges of Soviet anti-semitism;
Nasledniki Stalina (*The Heirs of Stalin*), published originally
in *Pravda*, satirizes Stalin's politics and his followers;
'Kar'era' ('A Career'), which deals with Galileo's fight for
truth against the authority of the church; and 'Iumor'
('Humour'), in which the power of laughter emerges triumphant over despotic power. However, the publication in Paris
of his *Autobiografiia* (*A Precocious Autobiography*), with its
vivid sequence of scenes from his life and his idiosyncratic
interpretation of Soviet history without submission to the
Soviet censors, incurred official disfavour and privileges were
withdrawn.

Favour was restored with the publication in 1965 of an ambitious cycle of poems entitled *Bratskaia GES* (*The Bratsk Station*), in which he juxtaposes the symbol of a Siberian power plant generating light in Russia with Siberia's symbolic status as a prison throughout Russian history. The poems sought to reconnect modern Russia with its past, and were later adapted and performed as a play. More recently, he has turned increasingly to prose and the theatre. His play *Under the Skin of the Statue of Liberty*, composed of selections from his earlier poems about the United States that attack its violence but celebrate the idealism of its youth, was performed in Moscow to great acclaim. This was followed by a novel, *Iagodnge mesta* (*Wild Berries*), and the novella *Ardabiola*.

Evtushenko has always demonstrated commitment in his writing and although appearing to be slapdash in style he nevertheless shifts adroitly from intimate to public themes. He has been influential principally as a consolidator of certain revived traditions, while his ringing militancy, stylistic versatility, and challenging self-assertiveness in poetry have encouraged his contemporaries to emulate him.

—Tim Woods

F

FERDOWSI, Abu'l Qāsim. Born in Persia (now Iran), c.932–36. Came from a landowning family near Tus, Khorāsān. Had one daughter. According to tradition, began writing his epic poem the *Shāh-nāma* at about the age of 35, dedicating it to the Ghaznavid Sultan Mahmud, whose failure to reward it generously led Ferdowsi to write a satire about him and then return to his birthplace. *Died c.1020.*

PUBLICATIONS

Verse

Shāh-nāma, edited by Djalal Khaleghi-Motlagh. 6 vols., 1988—(3 vols. to 1992); as *Shahnama*, translated by Arthur George Warner and Edmond Warner, 9 vols., 1905–25; abridged versions translated by J. Atkinson, 1814, Alexander Rogers, 1907, and as *The Epic of the Kings, Shah-Nama, the National Epic of Persia*, translated by Reuben Levy, 1967; part as *The Poems of Ferdosi*, translated by J. Champion, 1785; part as *The Tragedy of Sohrab and Rostam: From the Persian National Epic of Shahname*, translated by Jerome W. Clinton, 1987; part as *The Legend of Seyavash*, translated by Dick Davis, 1992.

*

Critical Studies: in *Early Persian Poetry* by W. Jackson, 1920; *Ferdowsi: A Critical Biography* by A. Shapur Shahbazi, 1991; *Epic and Sedition: the Case of Ferdowsi's Shahnameh* by Dick Davis, 1992; *Poet and Hero in the Persian Book of Kings* by Olga H. Davidson, 1994.

* * *

Abu'l Qāsim Ferdowsi was born between 932 and 936 and the date of his death is placed in either 1020 or 1021. He lived in Khorāsān, in the environs of Tus near present-day Mashhad and was apparently a small farmer of the *dehqan* class, a squirarchy that in early Islamic times may have represented a stratum of landlords reduced in status following the Arab conquest in the 7th century. He is justly regarded as one of the world's greatest poets for his composition of Iran's national epic, the *Shāh-nāma* (*Shahnama* or *The Epic of Kings*). It is an epic which has the distinction of encompassing the whole history of ancient Iran from about the 9th century BC to the 7th century AD—legendary as well as factual, and in so far as there is a subtle layer of the facts of human experience in mythology, basically factual enough to have universal appeal. It is, not surprisingly, one of the world's longest poems, of some 50,000 rhyming couplets in the same martially inspiring *mutaqarib* (‿ - -) metre throughout; it is chanted to furnish the rhythm for athletes exercising in Iranian *zurkanehs*, ‘Houses of Strength’, the traditional gymnasiums.

The chronological scheme of the work provides unity as it moves from monarch to monarch, although scope is given to the *gestes* of Herculean heroes who at times overshadow less competent kings, as is especially evident in the feats and courage of Rustam. He is known to readers of English literature through Matthew Arnold's *Sohrab and Rustum*, published in 1853, after Arnold had seen Sainte-Beuve's *Causerie du Lundi* of February 1850, which reviewed Jules Mohl's French translation of *Le Livre des Rois*, begun in 1838; Arnold was already aware of the story, of a father's slaying the son he did not recognize, from Sir John Malcolm's reference to it in his *History of Persia*, published in 1815. Various other English versions of the *Shahnama* exist, but the translation of the whole by Arthur George Warner and Edmond Warner, is recommended.

Ferdowsi's sources may be summarized as a recension of ancient Iranian history by an Abu Mansur; tales retained in folk memory; and, more than probably (he explicitly speaks of reports from a venerable *mobed*, a Zoroastrian priest, and his mythical kings are named in the *Avesta*) sources related to Iran's pre-Islamic religion and scriptures. His lofty purpose, in a work to which it seems he devoted nearly 30 years of his life, was apparently to remind Iran of past glories, not least in the continuing conflict between the sedentary, cultivating people of its north-eastern province and pastoralist invaders from the Central Asian Steppes. A dominant theme is war between Iran and Turan: the latter has been read as the land of the Turks beyond the River Oxus. In taking up the unfinished few verses of a predecessor, Daqiqi, who was murdered sometime between 976 and 981, Ferdowsi might have started his epic as a paean befitting the regime then still in power, that of the Iranian Samanids, sympathetic to memorials of Iran's pre-Islamic eras. The paean became more of a nostalgic lament when these rulers were ousted at the end of the 10th century, to be replaced in Iran by the House of their former Turkish military commanders, called the Ghaznavids.

Pessimism and an element of dignified resignation to the blows of fate tinge the overall melancholy strain of an epic concerned, not least in the poet's asides, with life's mutabilities and man's inability to control them. It is tempting to attribute the story of initial rejection of the work at the hands of the ruler whose patronage Ferdowsi sought on its completion, the Ghaznavid Sultan Mahmūd, who ruled from 998 to 1030, to the latter's seeing it as an innuendo against the Turks, but it would be pure speculation. A 12th-century writer, Nizami the Prosodist, attributed the rigorously orthodox Sultan's underpayment of the poet to Ferdowsi's alleged inclination for Muslim heresies with echoes of older Iranian beliefs. Fable has it that, on perceiving encouragement of military bravery in one of Ferdowsi's verses, the great warlord repented. Returning from conquest in India he sent Ferdowsi recompense in a caravan of indigo, but as the caravan entered one gate of Ferdowsi's hometown, the poet's bier was being carried to the grave out of another. Ferdowsi's only child, his daughter, refused the gift, which was devoted to providing a resthouse for travellers.

In his *Chahar Maqala* (*Four Discourses*) Nizami the Prosodist gives an illuminating, if partly fabulous, account of Ferdowsi, noteworthy for his remark that Ferdowsi's verse had a 'sweet fluency to resemble running water'. It must be added that, in spite of its length, the poem never sinks to mediocrity and contains memorable depictions of nature and colours, those of banners before and the dust and blood during battles, for example, which later Persian miniaturists revelled in presenting in illustrations to some of the great manuscripts of the *Shahnama* that have reached our museums and libraries despite tumults of the time in the lands where they were produced. The text has suffered through time, copyists having often been ignorant of dialect usages of Ferdowsi's day in Khorāsān, but at last, after a fine effort by Soviet scholars, a more reliable text than even theirs is now appearing, edited by Djalal Khaleghi-Motlagh and based, for as much as the manuscript covers, on the very ancient text discovered in Florence in 1977.

—Peter Avery

FEYDEAU, Georges (Léon-Jules-Marie). Born in Paris, France, 8 December 1862, son of the writer Ernest-Aimé Feydeau. Educated at boarding school, 1871–79. Married Marianne Duran in 1889 (divorced 1914); one son, Jacques, and other children. Lawyer's clerk, 1879; began writing and reciting monologues in the early 1880s; military service, 1883–84; established career with the long run of *Champignol malgré lui*, from 1892; lived at the Hôtel Terminus, Paris, 1909–19; suffered declining mental health, due to syphilis, after 1916; committed by his family to a sanatorium in Rueil-Malmaison, 1919. *Died 5 June 1921.*

PUBLICATIONS

Collections

Théâtre complet. 9 vols., 1948–56.
Théâtre complet. 4 vols., 1988–89.

Plays

La Petite Révoltée (monologue). 1880.
Le Mouchoir (monologue). 1881.
Par la fenêtre (produced 1881). 1887; as *Wooed and Viewed*, translated by Norman Shapiro, in *Four Farces*, 1970; in *Feydeau, First to Last*, 1982.
Un Coup de tête (monologue). 1882.
J'ai mal au dents (monologue). 1882.
Un monsieur qui n'aime pas les monologues (monologue). 1882.
Trop vieux! (monologue). 1882.
Notre futur (produced 1894). 1882; as *Ladies' Man*, translated by Norman Shapiro, in *Feydeau, First to Last*, 1982.
Le Diapason. 1883.
Le Potache. 1883.
Aux antipodes (monologue). 1883.
Patte-en-l'air (monologue). 1883.

Le Petit Ménage (monologue). 1883.
Amour et piano (produced 1883). 1887; as *Romance in a Flat*, translated by Norman Shapiro, in *Feydeau, First to Last*, 1982; as *The Music Lovers*, translated by Reggie Oliver, 1992.
Gibier de potence (produced 1884). 1885; as *Fit to Be Tried; or, Stepbrothers in Crime*, translated by Norman Shapiro, in *Feydeau, First to Last*, 1982.
Les Célèbres (monologue). 1884.
Le Volontaire (monologue). 1884.
Le Billet de mille (monologue). 1885.
Le Colis (monologue). 1885.
L'Homme économe (monologue). 1885.
Les Réformes (monologue). 1885.
L'Homme intègre (monologue). 1886.
Fiancés en herbe (produced 1886). 1886; as *Budding Lovers*, translated by Barnett Shaw, 1969.
Tailleur pour dames (produced 1886). 1888; as *A Gown for His Mistress*, translated by Barnett Shaw, 1969; as *Fitting for Ladies*, translated by Peter Meyer, in *Three Farces*, 1974; as *Love By the Bolt*, translated by J. Paul Marcoux, in *Three Farces*, 1976.
Les Enfants (monologue). 1887.
La Lycéenne, music by G. Serpette (produced 1887). 1887.
Le Fiancés de Loche, with Maurice Desvallières. 1888.
Le Chat en poche (produced 1888).
Un bain de ménage (produced 1888). 1889.
L'Affaire Édouard, with Maurice Desvallières (produced 1889). 1889.
Monsieur Nounou, with Maurice Desvallières (produced 1890).
C'est une femme du monde!, with Maurice Desvallières (produced 1890). 1890; as *Mixed Doubles*, translated by Norman Shapiro, 1982.
Tout à Brown-Séquart! (monologue). 1890.
Le Mariage de Barillon, with Maurice Desvallières (produced 1890). 1890; as *On the Marry-Go-Wrong*, translated by Norman Shapiro, in *Four Farces*, 1970; as *All My Husband*, translated by J. Paul Marcoux, in *Three Farces*, 1976.
Madame Sganarelle (produced 1891).
Monsieur Chasse (produced 1892). 1896; as *13, Rue de L'Amour*, translated by Mawby Green and Ed Feilbert, 1972; as *The Happy Hunter*, translated by Barnett Shaw, 1973; as *A-Hunting We Will Go*, translated by Ray Barron, 1976.
Champignol malgré lui, with Maurice Desvaillières (produced 1892). 1925; as *A Close Shave*, translated by Peter Meyer, in *Three Farces*, 1974.
Le Système Ribadier (produced 1892). 1925.
Un fil à la patte (produced 1894). 1899; as *Cat Among the Pigeons*, translated by John Mortimer, 1970; as *Not by Bed Alone*, translated by Norman Shapiro, in *Four Farces*, 1970; as *Get Out of My Hair!*, translated by Frederick Davies, 1973.
L'Hôtel du Libre-Échange, with Maurice Desvaillières (produced 1894). 1928; as *Hotel Paradiso*, translated by Peter Glenville, 1956; as *A Little Hotel on the Side*, translated by John Mortimer, in *Three Boulevard Farces*, 1985; as *Paradise Hotel*, translated by Nicholas Rudall, 1990.
Le Ruban, with Maurice Desvaillières (produced 1894). In *Théâtre complet*, 1948–56.
Le Dindon (produced 1896). In *Théâtre complet*, 1948–56; as *There is One in Every Marriage*, translated by Suzanne Grossmann and Paxton Whitehead, 1970; as *Sauce for the Goose*, translated by Peter Meyer, in *Three Farces*, 1974; as *The French Have a Word for It*, translated by Barnett Shaw, 1983.

Les Pavés de l'ours (produced 1896). In *Théâtre complet*, 1948–56; as *The Boor Hug*, translated by Norman Shapiro, in *Feydeau, First to Last*, 1982.

Séance de nuit (produced 1897). In *Théâtre complet*, 1948–56.

Dormez, je le veux! (produced 1897). In *Théâtre complet*, 1948–56; as *Caught with His Trance Down*, translated by Norman Shapiro, in *Feydeau, First to Last*, 1982.

La Bulle d'amour, music by F. Thomé (ballet scenario; produced 1898).

Le Juré (monologue). 1898.

Un monsieur qui est condamné à mort (monologue). 1899.

La Dame de chez Maxim (produced 1899). 1914; as *The Lady from Maxim's*, translated by Gene Feist, 1971; also translated by John Mortimer, 1977.

La Duchesse des Folies-Bergères (produced 1902). In *Théâtre complet*, 1948–56.

Le Billet de Joséphine, with J. Méry and A. Kaiser (produced 1902).

La Main passe (produced 1904). 1907; as *Chemin de Fer*, translated by Suzanne Grossmann and Paxton Whitehead, 1968.

L'Âge d'or, with Maurice Desvallières, music by L. Varney (produced 1905). In *Théâtre complet*, 1948–56.

Le Bourgeon. 1907.

La Puce à l'oreille (produced 1907). 1909; as *A Flea in Her Ear*, translated by John Mortimer, 1968; also translated by Barnett Shaw, 1975.

Feu la mère de Madame (produced 1908). 1923; as *Better Late*, translated by Peter Mayer, 1976; as *Night Errant*, translated by Michael Pilch, 1990.

Occupe-toi d'Amélie (produced 1908). 1911; as *Keep an Eye on Amélie*, translated by Brainerd Duffield, in *Let's Get A Divorce and Other Plays*, edited by Eric Bentley, 1958; also translated by Robert Cogo-Fawett and Braham Murray, 1991; as *Look After Lulu*, translated and adapted by Noël Coward, 1959; as *That's My Girl*, translated by J. Paul Marcoux, in *Three Farces*, 1976.

Le Circuit, with Francis Croisset (produced 1909). In *Théâtre complet*, 1948–56.

On purge bébé (produced 1910). 1910; as *Going to Pot*, translated by Norman Shapiro, in *Four Farces*, 1970; as *The Purging*, translated by Peter Barnes, 1977.

Mais n'te promène donc pas toute nue! (produced 1911). 1912; as *Put Some Clothes on Clarisse!*, translated by Reggie Oliver. 1990.

Léonie est en avance; ou, Le Mal joli (produced 1911). 1920.

Cent millions qui tombent (produced 1911).

On va faire la cocotte (produced 1913). In *Théâtre complet*, 1948–56.

Je ne trompe pas mon mari, with René Peter (produced 1914). 1921.

Complainte du pauvr' propriétaire. 1915.

Hortense a dit: 'Je m'en fous!' (produced 1916). In *Théâtre complet*, 1948–56; as *Tooth and Consequences; or, Hortense Said: 'No Skin off My Ass!'*, translated by Norman Shapiro, 1978; also translated by Shapiro, in *Feydeau, First to Last*, 1982.

Four Farces (includes *Wooed and Viewed*; *On the Marry-Go-Wrong*; *Not By Bed Alone*; *Going to Pot*), translated by Norman Shapiro. 1970.

Three Farces (includes *Fitting for Ladies*; *A Close Shave*; *Sauce for the Goose*), translated by Peter Meyer. 1974.

Three Farces (includes *Love By the Bolt*; *All My Husband*; *That's My Girl*), translated by J. Paul Marcoux. 1976.

Feydeau, First to Last: Eight One-Act Comedies, translated by Norman Shapiro. 1982.

Three Boulevard Farces (includes *The Lady from Maxim's*; *A Flea in Her Ear*; *A Little Hotel on the Side*), translated by John Mortimer. 1985.

The Pregnant Pause; or, Love's Labor Lost, translated by Norman Shapiro. 1987.

*

Bibliography: *Théâtre complet 1*, 1988.

Critical Studies: 'Suffering and Punishment in the Theatre of Georges Feydeau' by Norman R. Shapiro, in *Tulane Drama Review*, 5(1), 1960; *Georges Feydeau* (in English) by Jacques Lorcey, 1972; *Georges Feydeau: Textes de Feydeau, points de vue critique, témoignages, chronologie, bibliographie, illustrations* by Arlette Shenkan, 1972; *Georges Feydeau* (in English), 1975, and *Eugène Labiche and Georges Feydeau*, 1982, both by Leonard C. Pronko; *Le Théâtre de Georges Feydeau* by Henry Gidel, 1979; *Georges Feydeau and the Aesthetics of Farce* by Stuart E. Baker, 1981; *Georges Feydeau* (in English) by Manuel A. Esteban, 1983; 'Feydeau 1862–1921: Dossier' by Henry Gidel, in *Comédie-Française* 139–140, 1985.

* * *

Georges Feydeau's lengthy and successful dramatic career falls into four fairly distinct periods. During the first, from 1981 to 1986, he developed his skills by producing a series of dramatic monologues and short skits called *saynètes* which provided amusing entertainment in the fashionable drawing-rooms of the period. Although necessarily possessing little of the manic activity and complex imbroglios of the brilliant later works, these early essays still offer certain features and themes that form the basis of later and more elaborate works —misunderstood or deceitful spouses, amorous intrigues, absurdly logical complications arising from outré premises, titillating misunderstandings, eccentric characters in bizarre situations. Such features mark *Amour et piano* (*The Music Lovers*), the one-act play that was Feydeau's first work produced in Paris.

Tailleur pour dames (*Love By the Bolt*) inaugurated a new phase in Feydeau's career; it was his first three-act comedy and his first major success. Already he had achieved considerable skill in weaving together a number of complex plots and subplots and an almost continuous web of misunderstandings and deceptions. The basic intrigue of the play is typically built on a romantic intrigue—Dr Moulineaux's attempted seduction of Suzanne—but in standard Feydeau fashion, Moulineaux's wife, Suzanne's husband, and a variety of others are drawn one after another into an escalating round of mistaken identity, misdirection, and inopportune encounters. The plays immediately following *Love By the Bolt*, several, such as *L'Affaire Édouard* [The Edouard Affair], written in collaboration with Maurice Desvallières, were distinctly less successful, and in 1890 Feydeau took a two-year voluntary 'exile' from the stage to polish his craft. According to his later collaborator René Peter, he gave particular attention to three contemporary authors who had gained considerable success in vaudeville and farce—Henri Meilhac for his dialogue, Eugène Labiche for his keen observation of contemporary characters and society, and Alfred Hennequin for his skill at dramatic construction.

Whatever his activities during this retreat, he returned with enormous energy and success, producing seven major plays, alone or in collaboration, during the next four years. These include some of his most famous and most elaborate imbroglios of marital intrigue, *Monsieur Chasse* (*A-Hunting We Will Go*), again with Desvallières, *Le Système Ribadier* [The Ribadier System] with Alfred Hennique's son Maurice, *Champignol malgré lui* (*A Close Shave*), *L'Hôtel du Libre-Échange* (*Paradise Hotel*), with Desvallières, *Un fil à la patte* (*Cat Among the Pigeons*), and *Le Dindon* (*The French Have a Word for It*). Although the actual or attempted amorous escapades of a bourgeois husband provide a departure point for almost all of these works, some, such as *A-Hunting We Will Go*, give major attention to the domestic situation and to the wife, often not above a bit of romancing herself but stoutly opposed to any such activity on the part of her partner, while others, such as *Cat Among the Pigeons*, pay more attention to the coquette who arouses the husband's interest, and to her quest for material success. Such character configurations recur again and again in Feydeau, so that *La Puce à l'oreille* (*A Flea in Her Ear*) may be classified as a 'wife' play, and *Occupe-toi d'Amélie* (*Keep an Eye on Amélie*) a 'coquette' play.

During the mid-1890s Feydeau attempted to depart from the rather mechanical farce to attempt a comedy of character in *Le Ruban* [The Ribbon] with Desvallières, written for the Odéon, France's second national theatre. Dr Paginet, a scientific researcher whose passion to be awarded a prestigious national decoration recalls the obsessive drives of characters in the Molière tradition, was well received, but producers and public seemed to prefer the less thoughtful comic structures of Feydeau's successes in the boulevard theatres, and he returned to that approach with new one-act pieces and another of his comic masterpieces *La Dame de chez Maxim* (*The Lady from Maxim's*), his longest and most complex work. When the happily married Dr Petypon wakes up one morning, on the floor of his bedroom, after an evening at Maxim's, and with a strange dancer from the Moulin Rouge in his bed, we are plunged at once into a racy and outrageous world of bizarre events and unexpected turns that never allows a moment of relaxation until the final masterful tying off of every loose end.

After such a success, a certain falling-off was perhaps inevitable, and although the public strongly supported *La Duchesse des Folies-Bergères* [The Duchess of the Folies-Bergère], critics suggested that Feydeau's themes and technique were beginning to show signs of wear. It may have been such criticism that encouraged Feydeau during his final period to divide his attention fairly equally between new examples of his most successful formulas and more 'serious' comedies of character and personal relationships rather more in the style of his earlier *Le Ruban*. The most serious of the later works, indeed it is rather closer to drama than comedy, is *Le Bourgeon* [The Bud], dealing with a young seminarian's struggle with carnality. Immediately after this, however, came *A Flea in Her Ear* and *Keep an Eye on Amélie*, two of Feydeau's most elaborate and most successful farces.

In his final one-act and full-length plays, beginning with *Feu la mère de Madame* (*Night Errant*) and continuing through *Hortense a dit: 'Je m'en fous!'* (*Tooth and Consequences*), Feydeau concentrated on confusions and conflicts within married life. The serious tonality that characterized much of his later work is found in all of these plays, but shot through with inventive comic elements. Although such plays as *Mais n'te promène donc pas toute nue!* (*Put Some Clothes on Clarisse!*) have lost nothing of the humour that marks all of Feydeau's best work, this humour no longer draws significantly upon such farce material as disguises, elaborate deceptions, or unexpected and unlikely encounters, but upon the irritants of everyday married life. The befuddled husbands and outrageous wives of these plays are developed with an intensity that at times almost suggests Strindberg in the mode of farce. The increasing grimness of the husband-wife relationship in these final works is suggested by Feydeau's plan to gather them in a collection to be called 'From Marriage to Divorce'.

—Marvin Carlson

A FLEA IN HER EAR (La Puce à l'oreille)
Play by Georges Feydeau, 1907.

This spirited tale of suspected and would-be adultery is propelled by an intricate, coincidence-laden plot. It opens in a typically solid bourgeois interior, the drawing-room of the highly respectable director of the Boston Life Insurance company of Paris, Victor-Emmanuel Chandebise, whose wife, Raymonde, believes he is being unfaithful to her. After years of satisfactory performance in the marriage bed her husband seems to have lost interest in coition, and the arrival in the post of a pair of his braces, left behind at a louche suburban establishment by the name of the Hôtel du Minet-Galant, serves to confirm her worst suspicions. In point of fact the blameless Victor-Emmanuel, whose matrimonial problem is purely psychosomatic, has given the braces to his secretary (and cousin) Camille, an apparently innocuous individual with a cleft palate but something of a roué on the quiet, who is currently engaged in an illicit affair with the housemaid and valet's wife, Antoinette, and to whom the hotel has been recommended as a suitable love-nest by the family doctor, Finache, another of its habitués. Still, fired by jealous indignation, Raymonde confides in her old convent-friend, Lucienne, and together they concoct a scheme to trap the supposedly errant spouse. Lucienne pens a passionate declaration of love, ostensibly from an unknown admirer who has seen him at the Opéra and inviting him to an intimate assignation in the late afternoon at the same hotel, where Raymonde will be waiting to unmask his infidelity. Receiving the missive, Victor-Emmanuel is at first flattered, then modestly concludes that he must have been mistaken for his colleague and companion at the theatre, Romain Tournel, a noted womanizer who is secretly intent on seducing the half-willing Raymonde, and it is agreed that Tournel will keep the appointment in his stead. However, when Victor-Emmanuel jokingly shows the same letter to Don Carlos Homénidès dé Histangua, an insurance client who is married to Lucienne, the hot-blooded Spaniard recognizes his wife's handwriting, draws a revolver, and rushes out threatening to shoot Tournel *in flagrante delicto* and leaving panic in his wake. The narrative ground is thus richly prepared for an action-packed second act at the hotel itself. Here the stage is divided in two, one half occupied by the lobby with, opening off it, a corridor, a staircase leading down to the street and up to other floors, and the doors to four bedrooms; the other half is given over to one of these rooms, with a small bathroom off and a bed on a revolving platform designed, in an emergency, to whisk any adulterous couple into the safety of the next room and replace them with a bedridden old codger complaining of rheumatism. This multiple arrangement of spaces and points of access generates a rapid succession of inopportune arrivals and encounters, frantic concealments and discoveries, desperate flights and pursuits involving all the characters from Act I in turn and complicated still further by the libidinous antics of a drunken English hotel guest and the fact that

Poche, the hotel porter, is the exact double of Victor-Emmanuel, the two being repeatedly mistaken for each other, particularly after Chandebise is forced by the proprietor into Poche's uniform and the latter dons Chandebise's discarded jacket. Act III returns to the Chandebise household, where the abashed victims seek refuge from their evening's escapade only to be pursued by its consequences in the shape of the look-alike porter, still dressed as Victor-Emmanuel, then the still uniformed Victor-Emmanuel himself, and later the hotel proprietor. Further confusions and further changes of costumes ensue until true identities are established, explanations are exchanged, and three married couples are reconciled, with varying degrees of conviction.

The general contours of Feydeau's dramatic technique are evident from this extended synopsis. In essence, it leans heavily on the Scribean formula of the 'well-made play', especially as refined by such later vaudevillists as Labiche, who brought added depth to characterization, Henri Meilhac, whose strength lay in vivid, inventive dialogue, and Alfred Hennequin, who was a master of fast-moving, situational farce. Consciously borrowing from all three, Feydeau perfected a version of the genre which discarded the term 'vaudeville' in favour of the less frivolous 'comédie' or quite simply 'pièce', as was the case with *A Flea in Her Ear*, one of his later plays, first performed at the Théâtre des Nouveautés on 2 March 1907. A customarily quite leisurely exposition allows him to flesh out his dramatis personae and give them a ballast of individual reality to keep them afloat in the torrent of improbable adventures that befall them. It is, in fact, an entirely credible personality trait, like a discontented wife's mistrust of her husband, that unleashes this torrent, engulfing the characters in painfully compromising situations or subjecting them to public indignity and humiliation. At the end, beached once more in domestic security, they remain basically unchanged, though somewhat chastened by their experiences.

Within this orderly but complex framework Feydeau's control of the dynamics of comedy is mesmerically compelling. He runs the gamut of visual slapstick, repartee, quid pro quo, repetition or inversion of situations, running gags, and the like; he is adept at bringing the wrong people together at the worst possible moment and at accelerating the pace towards a manic climax in each act, as with the successive brandishings of Homénidès's gun; he ruthlessly exploits the sound of foreign tongues or mangled French: and he does not scruple to use physical affliction—deafness, a speech impediment, halitosis—to devastating comic effect. The streak of cruelty already implicit in this becomes more marked in the grotesque, almost ritualized suffering he inflicts on some of his characters, which seems out of all proportion to their sins and reduces them to the level of helpless, semi-inanimate objects in the toils of a malign destiny. This distinctive quality has led some modern critics to see in Feydeau's comedy a parallel to the inexorability of fate that drives classical tragedy, and his plotting does indeed possess the unrelenting, geometrical logic and escalating momentum of some 'infernal machine', reminding us of Brian Rix's dictum that farce is 'tragedy with its trousers down'. Other commentators have suggested that the unblinking, clinical eye Feydeau casts on the mores, particularly the sexual mores and marital relations, of the *belle époque* has given him the status of a true moralist, while still others have detected in what Norman Shapiro calls his 'merciless and often gratuitous imbroglios' and the impotence of his characters within them an analogy with theatre of the absurd. Such assessments provide a measure of the critical rehabilitation of Feydeau's work and help to explain why, despite a partial eclipse in the two decades following his

death, he has since become, after Molière, the most popular and widely performed of French comic playwrights.

—Donald Roy

FILIPPO, Eduardo de.   See **DE FILIPPO, Eduardo.**

FLAUBERT, Gustave. Born in Rouen, France, 12 December 1821. Educated at Collège Royal, 1831–39 (expelled); baccalauréat, 1840; studied law at École de Droit, Paris, 1841–45. Suffered a seizure in 1844 which left him in poor health; lived with his family at Croisset, near Rouen, after 1845 for the rest of his life; spent winters in Paris after 1856; visited Egypt and the Near East, 1849–51; publication of *Madame Bovary*, 1857, led to unsuccessful prosecution for indecency; returned to North Africa, 1858. State pension, 1879. Chevalier, Légion d'honneur, 1866. *Died 8 May 1880.*

PUBLICATIONS

Collections

Oeuvres complètes (includes correspondence). 35 vols., 1926–54.
Oeuvres, edited by Albert Thibaudet and René Dumesnil. 2 vols., 1946–48.
Complete Works. 10 vols., 1926.
Oeuvres complètes, edited by Bernard Masson. 1964.
Oeuvres complètes, edited by M. Bardèche. 16 vols., 1971–75.

Fiction

Madame Bovary. 1857; as *Madame Bovary*, translated by Eleanor Marx-Aveling, 1886; numerous subsequent translations including by Gerard Hopkins, 1949; Alan Russell, 1950; J.L. May, 1953; Francis Steegmuller, 1957, reprinted 1993; Lowell Bair, 1959; Mildred Marmur, 1964; Paul de Man, 1965; Geoffrey Wall, 1992.
Salammbô. 1862; edited by P. Moreau, 1970; as *Salammbô*, translated by J.S. Chartres, 1886; numerous subsequent translations including by E. Powys Mathers, 1950; A.J. Krailsheimer, 1977.
L'Éducation sentimentale. 1869; edited by C. Gothot-Mersch, 1985; as *Sentimental Education*, translated by D.F. Hannigan, 1896; numerous subsequent translations including by A. Goldsmith, 1941; Robert Baldick, 1964; Douglas Parmée, 1989.
La Tentation de Saint Antoine. 1874; edited by C. Gothot-Mersch, 1983; as *The Temptation of Saint Anthony*, translated by D.F. Hannigan, 1895; numerous subsequent translations including by Lafcadio Hearn, 1932; Kitty Mrosovsky, 1980.
Trois Contes (includes *Un coeur simple*; *La Légende de Saint Julien l'hospitalier*; *Hérodias*). 1877; edited by S. de Sasy,

1973; as *Three Tales*, translated by George Burnham Ives, 1903; also translated by Mervyn Savill, 1950; Robert Baldick, 1961; A.J. Krailsheimer, 1991.
Bouvard et Pécuchet. 1881; edited by Alberto Cento, 1964, and by C. Gothot-Mersch, 1979; as *Bouvard and Pécuchet*, translated by D.F. Hannigan, 1896; also translated by A.J. Krailsheimer, 1976; reprinted in part as *Dictionnaire des idées reçues*, edited by Lea Caminiti, 1966; as *A Dictionary of Platitudes*, edited and translated by E.J. Fluck, 1954; as *The Dictionary of Accepted Ideas*, translated by Jacques Barzun, 1954; also translated by Robert Baldick, 1976.
La première Éducation sentimentale. 1963; as *The First Sentimental Education*, 1972.

Plays

Le Candidat (produced 1874). 1874.
Le Château des coeurs, with Louis Bouilhet and Charles d'Osmoy (produced 1874). In *Oeuvres complètes*, 1910.

Other

Par les champs et par les grèves. 1886.
Mémoires d'un fou. 1901.
Souvenirs, notes, et pensées intimes, edited by L. Chevally-Sabatier. 1965, and by J.P. Germain, 1987; as *Intimate Notebook 1840–1841*, edited by Francis Steegmuller, 1967.
November, edited by Francis Steegmuller. 1966.
Flaubert in Egypt: A Sensibility on Tour, edited by Francis Steegmuller. 1972.
Correspondance, edited by Jean Bruneau. 3 vols., 1973–91.
Letters, edited and translated by Francis Steegmuller. 2 vols., 1980–82.
Correspondance, with George Sand, edited by Alphonse Jacobs. 1981; as *Flaubert–Sand: The Correspondence*, translated by Francis Steegmuller and Barbara Bray, 1993.
Flaubert and Turgenev: A Friendship in Letters: The Complete Correspondence, edited and translated by Barbara Beaumont, 1985.
Carnets de travail, edited by Pierre-Marc de Biasi. 1988.
Early Writings, translated by Robert Griffin. 1991.
Correspondance, with Guy de Maupassant, edited by Yvan Leclerc. 1994.

Editor, *Dernières chansons*, by Louis Bouilhet. 1872.

*

Bibliography: *Bibliographie de Flaubert* by D.L. Demorest and R. Dumesnil, 1947; *Bibliographie des études sur Gustave Flaubert*, edited by D.J. Colwell, 1988–90.

Critical Studies: *Flaubert and Madame Bovary* by Francis Steegmuller, 1947; *Flaubert and the Art of Realism* by Anthony Thorlby, 1956; *On Reading Flaubert* by Margaret G. Tillett, 1961; *Flaubert: Madame Bovary* by Alison Fairlie, 1962; *Flaubert: A Collection of Critical Essays* edited by Raymond D. Giraud, 1964; *The Novels of Flaubert: A Study of Themes and Techniques* by Victor Brombert, 1966, revised edition, 1968; *Madame Bovary and the Critics* edited by Benjamin F. Bart, 1966, *Flaubert*, 1967, and *The Legendary Sources of Flaubert's Saint Julien*, 1977, both by Bart; *Flaubert* by Stratton Buck, 1966; *The Sentimental Adventure* by Peter Cortland, 1967; *Flaubert* by Enid Starkie, 2 vols., 1967–71; *Three Novels by Flaubert: A Study of Techniques* by R.J. Sherrington, 1970; *The Discovery of Illusion: Flaubert's Early Works, 1835–37*, 1971, and *Madame Bovary: The End of Romance*, 1989, both by Eric L. Gans; *The Greatness of Flaubert* by Maurice Nadeau, 1972; *Flaubert: The Uses of Uncertainty* by Jonathan Culler, 1974, revised edition, 1985; *Flaubert: The Problem of Aesthetic Discontinuity* by Marie J. Diamond, 1975; *Sartre and Flaubert* by Hazel E. Barnes, 1981; *The Family Idiot: Gustave Flaubert 1821–1857* by Jean-Paul Sartre, translated by Carol Cosman, 5 vols., 1981–93; *Saint/Oedipus: Psychocritical Approaches to Flaubert's Art* by William J. Berg, 1982; *Flaubert and the Historical Novel: Salammbô Reassessed* by Anne Green, 1982; *Madame Bovary on Trial* by Dominick La Capra, 1982; *Towards the Real Flaubert: A Study of Madame Bovary* by Margaret Lowe, 1984; *Flaubert and Postmodernism* by Naomi Schor and Henry F. Majewski, 1984; *Madame Bovary: A Psychoanalytical Reading* by Ion K. Collas, 1985; *Flaubert's Characters: The Language of Illusion* by Diana Knight, 1985; *Flaubert and the Gift of Speech: Dialogue and Drama in Four Modern Novels*, 1986, and *The Madame Bovary Blues: The Pursuit of Illusion in Nineteenth Century French Fiction*, 1987, both by Stirling Haig; *Critical Essays on Gustave Flaubert* by Laurence Porter, 1986; *The Perpetual Orgy: Flaubert and Madame Bovary* by Mario Vargas Llosa, translated by Helen Lane, 1986; *Gustave Flaubert's Madame Bovary* edited by Harold Bloom, 1988; *Rape of the Lock: Flaubert's Mythic Realism* by Robert Griffin, 1988; *The Free Indirect Mode: Flaubert and the Poetics of Irony* by Yaheed R. Ramazani, 1988; *The Hidden Life at Its Source: A Study of Flaubert's L'Éducation sentimentale* by D.A. Williams, 1988; *Madame Bovary* by Alastair B. Duncan, 1989; *Madame Bovary* by Rosemary Lloyd, 1989; *Flaubert: A Biography* by Herbert Lottman, 1989; *Gustave Flaubert* by David Roe, 1989; *Flaubert Remembers: Memory and the Creative Experience* by William VanderWalk, 1990; *Flaubert's Straight and Suspect Saints: The Unity of Trois Contes* by Aimée Israel-Pelletier, 1991; *Gustave Flaubert: Madame Bovary* by Stephen Heath, 1992; *Sentimental Education: The Complexity of Disenchantment* by William Paulson, 1992; *The Script of Decadence: Essays on the Fictions of Flaubert and the Poetics of Romanticism* by Eugenio Donato, 1993.

* * *

Gustave Flaubert's best and best-known novel, *Madame Bovary*, marked a turning point in the history of the European novel. For the first time, an ordinary, middle to lower-middle-class woman occupied the central place in a detailed study of how dull everyday life could be in a small town, and the romantic myth that true love could be found in successfully consummated adultery was convincingly presented as a total illusion. In the wider history of fiction, Emma Bovary resembles Cervantes's *Don Quixote* (1615) in that she is a person who tries to live her life in terms of ideas derived from books but fails, and she also, perhaps more significantly, represents the first version of the 'miserable married woman' who recurs in Tolstoi's *Anna Karenina* (1875–77), in the Irene of John Galsworthy's *Forsyte Saga* (1906–29), in Mauriac's *Thérèse Desqueyroux* (1927), and even—though here the problem finds a satisfactory solution—in D.H. Lawrence's *Lady Chatterley's Lover* (1928). Like her fictional successors, Emma is married to a worthy but dull man, and the fact that she is, for all her self-centredness and folly, by far the most enterprising and interesting character in the novel does enable *Madame Bovary* to be interpreted nowadays as a not entirely unsympathetic account of the problems to which feminism seeks to find a solution.

As his other novels, especially *L'Éducation sentimentale* (*Sentimental Education*), show, and as his voluminous *Correspondance* confirms, Flaubert was an unremitting pessimist who did not believe that human beings either could achieve happiness or deserved to do so. For him, the only activity deserving any consideration was the construction of perfect works of art, and it was to this that he devoted the whole of his life. He rewrote incessantly, spending sometimes a week on one paragraph, and it took him five years to complete *Madame Bovary*. It is consequently slightly surprising that the heroine of what is otherwise rightly regarded as a masterpiece of realism should have eyes that are blue on one page but black on another, and the modern French critics who profess to admire Flaubert do so because of his mastery of form. His other novels, especially the exotic *Salammbô* and *La Tentation de Saint Antoine* (*The Temptation of Saint Anthony*), have a less immediate appeal to the modern reader, though the various versions through which the latter book passed between 1848 and 1874 make it the work on which Flaubert spent most time. Flaubert's attitude of caustic superiority to the modern world joined with an obsession with stupidity to produce *Bouvard et Pécuchet* (*Bouvard and Pécuchet*), although he died before it was completed, as well as the shorter and more amusing *Dictionnaire des idées reçues* (*The Dictionary of Accepted Ideas*). Although he was himself of impeccably middle-class origins, and adopted a very middle-class life-style, he contributed greatly to the growth of the now universal custom in France whereby imaginative writers have only contempt for the members of the middle class who buy and read their books.

His literary influence showed itself in the 19th century principally in the development of the realist movement with Zola and Maupassant, and in the 20th in the self-styled 'nouveaux romanciers' of the 1950s. Thus Robbe-Grillet saw in Flaubert a writer with a comparable interest to his own in the minute description of inanimate physical objects, and tended to pay less attention to the concern for pitiless psychological analysis which led to Flaubert being shown, in his lifetime, in a cartoon depicting him as a surgeon in a blood-stained apron holding up the dissected heart of the unhappy Emma Bovary.

There is general unanimity among critics of all tendencies to admire the long short stories in *Trois Contes* (*Three Tales*) as undisputed masterpieces. 'Un coeur simple' ('A Simple Heart'), an account of how a servant woman devotes herself entirely to the welfare of others, is indeed a masterpiece. It is certainly the work in which Flaubert shows something of the sympathy for his own creations which traditionally characterizes the novelist, and in which the hatred of normal humanity which so often informs his work gives way to a more charitable vision of our limitations. Those who consider singleness of purpose in the pursuit of aesthetic perfection will admire the hermit-like existence which Flaubert imposed upon himself, and detach themselves from Jean-Paul Sartre's view that Flaubert, like the other 19th-century French writers who retired to their 'ivory tower', is to be held responsible for the massacres which followed the Commune of 1871 because they did not write a single line to protest against them. Those who admire the vigour and even the vulgarity of a Dickens or a Balzac, or who share the sympathy with ordinary life which so often shows itself in Tolstoi, will speculate more on the paradox of how a man who disliked human beings so much managed to write novels at all. The subtitle of *Madame Bovary* is 'Moeurs de Province' ('Customs of the Provinces'), and this draws attention to the character of the local pharmacist Homais, the embodiment of all that Flaubert most disliked in the optimism and enthusiasm for scientific progress which were so marked a feature of mid-19th-century France.

—Philip Thody

MADAME BOVARY
Novel by Gustave Flaubert, 1857.

Flaubert published his novel, *Madame Bovary*, in serial form in 1856 (first book publication 1857), using it to develop ideas, themes, and techniques already embryonically present in his earlier unpublished writing. He first conceived of it as tracing the destiny of a young Flemish woman leading an uneventful life in the provinces, escaping only through religious mysticism. This original anecdote, whose possibilities Flaubert explored further in his tale, 'A Simple Heart', was enriched in the novel by newspaper accounts of the life and death of a Normandy woman married to a health officer, by the diary of Louise Pradier, whose sexual adventures and financial predicaments seem to have suggested certain aspects of Emma Bovary's life, and by the personality of Flaubert's current mistress, the writer Louise Colet.

In its final form, the plot recounts the life of a young woman, Emma Rouault, who marries an unremarkable provincial health officer, Charles Bovary, in the expectation, based on her reading of sentimental novels, that love will transform the boredom of her existence and bring her happiness. Emma's reading, uncritical, incomplete, and incapable of distinguishing between fact and fantasy, feeds her yearning for passion and excitement. Part of the power of Flaubert's depiction lies in the combination of his own sharp awareness of the seductive nature of such romantic promises and his pessimistically clear-sighted vision of reality. When Charles, although he loves her, fails to satisfy her either emotionally or sexually, Emma tries to transform him, first into a romantic lover, then into successful doctor. This ambitious attempt leads disastrously to a botched operation on the club-footed stable boy of a local inn. Emma also seeks escape through motherhood, sexual affairs, religious mysticism, reading, and material possessions, but finds each venture doomed to failure—an endless repetition of the same. Emma's first lover, Rodolphe, a cynical and experienced philanderer, seduces her despite his initial concerns about the difficulties of getting rid of her, and brings the affair to an abrupt end on the evening before the two of them were to have run away together. The letter in which he announces this decision is a masterpiece of hypocrisy, egotism, and debased Romantic cliché.

Later, she meets a former admirer, Léon, at a performance of Donizetti's opera, *Lucia di Lammermoor*, which Emma characteristically leaves before the mad scene. The two soon become lovers. Despite superficial differences—Léon is weak, inexperienced, and vacillating, and Emma herself, submissive with Rodolphe, now assumes the dominant role—this second affair reinforces the novel's central theme, that of the eternal monotony of illusory passion.

The dreariness and insignificance of provincial existence is beautifully illustrated by a range of minor characters, and in particular by the pharmacist Homais, a walking encyclopedia of clichés and received opinions. In such circumstances, Emma's longing to find intensity of experience leads her to desire material possessions she cannot afford, and thence into a plummeting spiral of debt. On the point of bankruptcy she is rejected again by her first lover, refuses the possibility of selling her sexual favours to a rich neighbour, and chooses instead to commit suicide. Ironically, Charles, devastated by her death, arranges a funeral as romantic as she herself could have wished. He himself dies shortly afterward, leaving their young daughter Berthe obliged to earn her living in a cotton mill.

Flaubert's achievement lies in the deliberate choice of a banal subject and unremarkable characters, in his refusal either to elevate or condemn Emma's conduct, and in his subtle, sophisticated use of narrative focus. Insisting that the author should be present everywhere in his novel but visible nowhere, he rejected the authorial interventions commonly practised at that time and attempted instead to show events and individuals through the thoughts of his central characters. To do so, he used a technique known as free indirect discourse, where the thoughts of the inarticulate protagonists are conveyed through the discourse of the narrator, but in ways that uses the images, memories, and vocabulary typical of them. Thus we both share the perceptions of the characters and are forced to maintain a critical distance from them.

The critical distance is increased by the fact that recurrent images and structural patterning draw our attention to the repetitive nature of experiences that Emma initially perceives as unique, and by Flaubert's insistence that the characters, however richly complex they consider themselves, are seen by others not as individuals but as stereotypical members of a series.

Determined to create a sonorous and rhythmical style, Flaubert frequently complained in his letters that writing was a torment for him, yet for the reader much of the novel's pleasure springs from the sense of constant tension between struggle and spontaneity, mental disgust and physical delight. That delight, however ironic, is evident in many of the set-piece descriptions—the rural wedding with its elaborate cake, the agricultural fair in which Rodolphe's words of seduction are punctuated by the bureaucrat's speech, and the evocation of Rouen cathedral, where the guide's description of religious statuary and architecture counterpoints Léon's erotic longing for Emma. Distinctive, too, it is the precise detail of Flaubert's descriptions, most notably in the remorselessly realistic account of Emma's suicide.

The desire to draw on and analyse apparently banal elements of everyday existence within the context of a specifically modern French society, and to do so in ways that refuse to ennoble or embellish them, not only marked a change with much contemporary literature but also led to problems with government censorship. Both Flaubert and the review in which *Madame Bovary* had appeared were accused of offences to public morality, with the prosecuting lawyer arguing forcefully that not a single character in the novel is in a position to condemn Emma's behaviour from a position of unimpeachable virtue. Nevertheless, the government lost its case, and the novel was published in volume form in April 1857. Though much of the immediate critical response was stridently hostile, *Madame Bovary* has come to be seen as exemplary by readers, critics, and novelists alike.

Above all, perhaps, the depiction of the physical and intellectual limitations placed on women in mid-19th-century France, the exploration of the inadequacies of language, and the fact that Flaubert, far from setting himself apart from Emma, inscribes the same failure into his own desire to capture reality, all make this a novel of particularly haunting resonance.

—Rosemary Lloyd

SENTIMENTAL EDUCATION (L'Éducation sentimentale)
Novel by Gustave Flaubert, 1869.

Flaubert's third published novel, the *Sentimental Education*, like *Madame Bovary*, is set in 19th-century France and, like the preceding *Salammbô,* may be considered a historical novel, covering in this case mainly the events between 1840 and 1851. The reign of Louis-Philippe, France's monarch since 1830, had become unpopular, and he was forced to abdicate by the revolution of February 1848. However, the revolutionaries found themselves in the minority after the elections of April, and when their four-day uprising in June in Paris was defeated many of the democratic liberties granted by the constitution were suspended. The conflict between various liberal and conservative groups was inevitable. The succeeding Second Republic lasted officially until December 1852 but was shaken by the coup d'état of December 1851, when Louis Napoleon (Napoleon III, nephew of Napoleon I), who had been elected president in December 1848, was given the power to remake the constitution after an armed insurrection was violently suppressed by the military. In December of 1852 Napoleon was elected emperor and remained in power until 1870, the beginning of the Franco-Prussian War, a debacle, Flaubert claimed, the French would have avoided had they read carefully the *Sentimental Education.*

As usual, Flaubert studied this historical background extensively in preparing the composition of his novel, which required six years of writing from 1863 to 1869. But he also drew from personal experience, notably his youthful encounter in 1836 with a Madame Schlesinger, for whom he nurtured a romantic passion for years and whom he met briefly again in 1867. The *Sentimental Education*, then, serves the double purpose of a political and an emotional initiation novel or, rather, the parody of one, for during the course of the action Frédéric Moreau, the book's anti-hero and to a certain extent Flaubert's alter ego, is too immersed in his own social and amorous ambitions to understand the significance of the political events taking place and too timid, indecisive, and shallow to develop a lasting love relationship. Uncommitted in the end to either a woman or a political stand, Frédéric meets again, by chance, Madame Arnoux, for whom he had maintained an idealized romantic attachment from the beginning of the novel, but again fails to consummate the love affair and in the final episode, reminiscing with his friend Deslauriers in 1867 about an equally unsuccessful visit to a brothel in 1837, decides that this event of his adolescence constituted perhaps the best time in his life.

Thus, the action of the novel is divided between Frédéric's emotional adventures with several women and the larger political events, in which he is relatively uninvolved but which parody and are parodied by his own social ambitions. The novel begins, in a parody of the typical Balzacian plot, in which the hero leaves the provinces of Paris to seek his fortunes, by depicting Frédéric's departure from Paris for his provincial home in Nogent by river boat, which is also carrying Madame Arnoux. After languishing in the provinces, where some hope for his advancement is invested in the patronage of a Monsieur Roque (whose daughter will become one of Frédéric's romantic attachments) and in the possible inheritance from an uncle, Frédéric returns to Paris supposedly to study law but instead attempts and abandons in turn various vocations: writer, painter, orator, and politician. He introduces himself into the Arnoux household and becomes friends with Madame Arnoux's husband. He also meets the wealthy Monsieur and Madame Dambreause, who offer respectively worldly advancement and romantic intrigue. But nothing develops, and Frédéric returns to Nogent to stimulate inadvertently the love of the young Louise Roque. Part One ends with the sudden announcement of Frédéric's inheritance and his departure again for Paris.

In Part Two Jacques Arnoux introduces Frédéric to the *demi-monde* of Paris and to Rosanette, who eventually becomes Frédéric's mistress while she is also conducting an affair with Arnoux. The famous scene of the masked ball initiates Frédéric into the pleasures of the capital's night world, but he soon appears with Rosanette in public even during the day and unfortunately is seen with her at the horse races by Madame Arnoux. Nevertheless, Frédéric and Madame Arnoux's platonic relationship continues until Madame Arnoux fails to come to a prearranged meeting with Frédéric (because of the illness of her child). Frédéric returns once more to Rosanette, with whom he spends several days at Fontainebleau during the Paris uprising of June 1848.

In Part Three Frédéric establishes a liaison with Madame Dambreuse, the woman of high-class Parisian society, to satisfy his pride and ambition, but her imperious ways and her revengeful jealousy exhibited at the auction of the Arnoux household goods repulse Frédéric, who convinces himself that he sacrifices a fortune in leaving Madame Dambreuse for the sake of his devotion to Madame Arnoux. Rosanette is a partial cause of this rupture between Frédéric and Madame Dambreuse but seems to be the principal one in a previous misunderstanding between Frédéric and Madame Arnoux, who is insulted in her very home by Rosanette with Frédéric present. To console himself Frédéric returns to Nogent thinking of Louise Roque, only to arrive at her wedding with Deslauriers.

In setting this series of love affairs ending with the loss of Frédéric's illusions against a background of failed revolution and frustrated hope for democracy, Flaubert evidently wished to dramatize lives of emotional and political disillusion. Frédéric's indecision and shifts in amorous allegiances are paralleled by the many turns in the political stances and fortunes of the minor characters: Deslauriers criticizes all forms of government; Sénécal is anti-royalist but a supporter of an autocratic democracy; Regimbart rejects all general political principles: a revolution for change is followed by fear of change and repression of liberties. Just as Frédéric's love ideal, Madame Arnoux, appears in the end as a grey-haired old woman, or just as the epitome of sexual attraction, Rosanette, is glimpsed as a fat widow with a child, so other's dreams are lost or compromised for the realities of living: the bohemian Hussonet obtains a government job controlling the theatres and the press; Pellerin, the painter, becomes a photographer, for Flaubert a distinctly inferior sort of artist.

The *Sentimental Education*'s method of detached realism and its implied criticism of artistic and political romanticism and contemporary ineptitude perhaps account for the initial hostile reactions of the critics, but the later generation of naturalists admired it, perhaps too uncritically, and imitated it, albeit often unsuccessfully. For 20th-century writers like Joseph Conrad and Ford Madox Ford—who were sympathetic to Flaubert's methods of the impassive author, limitation of point of view, and irony, and to the concept of the anti-hero—*The Sentimental Education* was a model of style and structure.

—Nicole Mosher

A SIMPLE HEART (Un coeur simple)
Story by Gustave Flaubert, 1877.

'A Simple Heart' is one of the three short stories that constitute the last work published by Flaubert, *Three Tales*. The tales have been criticized as a reworking of previously published material. 'A Simple Heart' demonstrates a kinship with *Madame Bovary* in style and setting, while 'The Legend of Saint Julian the Hospitaller' ('La Légende de Saint Julien l'hospitalier') and 'Herodias' echo *The Temptation of Saint Anthony* and *Salammbô* respectively. However, upon its publication, *Three Tales* was immediately and unanimously acclaimed as Flaubert's latest masterpiece. The literary establishment at large may have been making up for its previous misjudgement of other, more important works of Flaubert's by loudly endorsing this new volume by the ageing master.

Three Tales has survived the test of time thanks in great part to the stylistic mastery displayed by Flaubert. These short stories are now widely recognized as representative of his entire literary production. None of the three is more marked by Flaubert's personal life and acute sensitivity than 'A Simple Heart'.

This is how Flaubert himself described the tale: 'Just the account of an obscure life, that of a poor country girl, pious but fervent, discreetly loyal, and tender as new-baked bread. She loves one after the other a man, her mistress's children, a nephew of hers, an old man whom she nurses and her parrot. When the parrot dies she has it stuffed, and when she herself comes to die she confuses the parrot with the Holy Ghost. This is not all ironical as you may suppose, but on the contrary very serious and very sad. I want to move tender hearts to pity and tears, for I am tender-hearted myself.' Flaubert's goal has certainly been achieved, for the portrait of that 'simple heart' may well be the best expression of his sensitivity.

'A Simple Heart' is the story of Félicité, a servant whose destiny it is to be sacrificed. A country girl whose fiancé finally married a rich old woman, Félicité finds employment in Pont-l'Évêque, in the house of Madame Aubain, where she spends the rest of her life. Up at the crack of dawn, she is in charge of everything in the house, especially the two children, Paul and Virginie. Once, she even protects her mistress and the children from a charging bull, barely escaping a fatal goring. Her devotion to her work and others knows no limits. She also takes care of Victor, her nephew who happens to live nearby and whose family exploits Félicité's kindness. He becomes a sailor, and she, unable to understand maps, can only imagine the exotic places he visits, while she spends months waiting for news. One day, she is told abruptly of his death. Soon thereafter, little Virginie, always a weak child, dies of pneumonia, and Félicité spends two nights at the side of the dead young girl. Félicité, whose 'heart [grows] softer as time [goes] by', continues to tend the sick: people with cholera, Polish refugees, finally a lonesome dying man. With Paul now living in Paris, the house is a sad and mournful place, and the two ladies, mistress and servant, age side by side.

Afflicted by deafness, Félicité devotes herself to Loulou, a parrot Madame Aubain received as a gift. When the animal dies, Félicité follows her mistress's advice and has it stuffed. Upon Madame Aubain's death, Félicité remains alone in the run-down house with the parrot. Confusedly identifying the bird with religious symbols, she sees in the stuffed Loulou a representation of the Holy Ghost, and '[contracts] the idolatrous habit of kneeling in front of the parrot to say her prayers'. As Félicité finally dies, the Corpus Christi procession passes below her windows. At her request, Loulou, now broken-winged, partially rotten, and eaten by worms, has been placed on the top of the procession's altar. The conclusion of 'A Simple Heart' describes her final vision: 'And as she breathed her last, she thought she could see, in the opening heavens, a gigantic parrot hovering above her head.'

It is true that in the simple, provincial atmosphere of 'A Simple Heart' one finds reminders of *Madame Bovary*. But in this story, Flaubert's restrained style, painstaking attention to detail, finesse of psychology, and emotional tact combine to create a touching portrait of a character who by traditional standards would be deemed insignificant. Flaubert projected into his tale much of his experience and feelings, and scenes of his beloved Normandy.

Beyond Flaubert's emotional goal of 'moving tender hearts to pity and tears', the reader should not overlook the social critique implied in the callousness and selfishness of Madame Aubain's bourgeois society, a concern reminiscent of the *Sentimental Education*, and of Emma Bovary's own self-centred life. For instance, upon receiving the news of Victor's death, even Félicité is moved to criticize: 'It doesn't matter a bit, not to them it doesn't.' In an attempt to comfort Madame Aubain, who has been expecting news of her daughter for four days, Félicité states that she has not heard from Victor for six months. Not only does Madame Aubain show total ignorance of her servant's beloved nephew, but, adding insult to injury, she exclaims: 'Oh, your nephew', with a shrug 'that [seems] to say: "Who cares about a young, good-for-nothing cabin-boy?"'

Félicité's ironic name foregrounds Flaubert's depiction of suffering and misery. Happiness, or at least one way to it, lies with the creation of one's personal myth. While some critics have looked for irony in the final confusion between parrot and Holy Ghost, it is in this apparent identification that Félicité attains her blessed and blissful status, as an admirable saint wholly devoted to others, despite their selfishness, greed, or other defects, and regardless of her own acknowledged stupidity. (Often her mistress would say: 'Heavens, how stupid you are!' and she would reply: 'Yes Madame'.) This lay sainthood creates a link with the second tale, 'Saint Julian the Hospitaller', which shares with 'Herodias' a longing for less materialistic and more mythical times. In this respect, the three tales are united, and present a composite picture of Flaubert's own literary myths.

'A Simple Heart' is the most stylistically sophisticated of the *Three Tales*. It also serves as a poignant and effective introduction to Flaubert's creation.

—Pierre J. Lapaire

FONTAINE, Jean de la. See **LA FONTAINE, Jean de**.

FONTANE, Theodor. Born Henri Théodore Fontane in Neuruppin, Germany, 30 December 1819. Educated at Gymnasium, Neuruppin, 1832–33; Gewerbeschule K.F. Klödens, Berlin, 1833–36. Military service, 1844. Married Emilie Rouanet-Kummer in 1850, three sons and one daughter. Apprenticed to an apothecary, Berlin, 1836–40, and worked in Burg, Leipzig, Dresden, and Berlin, 1841–49; then freelance writer; worked for Prussian government press bureau, 1851–55; London correspondent for Berlin papers, 1855–59; editor for London affairs, *Kreuzzeitung*, 1860–70; theatre critic, *Vossische Zeitung*, 1870–89; secretary Berlin Academy of Arts, 1876 (resigned, 1876). Recipient: Schiller prize (Prussia), 1891. *Died 20 September 1898.*

PUBLICATIONS

Collections

Sämtliche Werke, edited by Edgar Gross and others. 30 vols., 1959–75.
Werke, Schriften, und Briefe, edited by Walter Keitel and Helmuth Nürnberger. 1962– .
Romane und Erzählungen, edited by Peter Goldammer and others. 8 vols., 1969.

Fiction

Vor dem Sturm. 1878; as *Before the Storm*, translated by R.J. Hollingdale, 1985.
Grete Minde. 1880.
Ellernklipp. 1881.
L'Adultera. 1882; as *A Woman Taken in Adultery*, translated by Gabriele Annan, with *The Poggenpuhl Family*, 1979.
Schach von Wuthenow. 1883; as *A Man of Honor*, translated by E.M. Valk, 1975.
Graf Petöfy. 1884.
Unterm Birnbaum. 1885.
Cecile. 1887; as *Cecile*, translated by Stanley Radcliffe, 1992.
Irrungen, Wirrungen. 1888; as *Trials and Tribulations*, 1917; as *A Suitable Match*, translated by Sandra Morris, 1968; as *Entanglements: An Everyday Berlin Story*, translated by Derek Bowman, 1986.
Quitt. 1890.
Stine. 1890; translated as *Stine*, 1977.
Unwiederbringlich. 1891; as *Beyond Recall*, translated by Douglas Parmée, 1964.
Frau Jenny Treibel. 1892; as *Jenny Treibel*, translated by Ulf Zimmermann, 1976.
Effi Briest. 1895; as *Effi Briest*, translated by Douglas Parmée, 1967.
Die Poggenpuhls. 1896; as *The Poggenpuhl Family*, translated by Gabriele Annan, with *A Woman Taken in Adultery*, 1979.
Der Stechlin. 1899.
Mathilde Möhring. 1906; revised version, 1969.
Short Novels and Other Writings (includes *A Man of Honor*; *Jenny Treibel*; *The Eighteenth of March*), edited by Peter Demetz. 1982.
Delusions, Confusions; and The Poggenpuhl Family, edited by Peter Demetz. 1989.

Verse

Von der schönen Rosamunde. 1850.
Männer und Helden. 1850.
Gedichte. 2 vols., 1851–75.
Balladen. 1861.
Die schönsten Gedichte und Balladen. 1982.
Bilder und Balladen, edited by Werner Feudell. 1984.

Other

Ein Sommer in London. 1854.
Bilderbuch Aus England. 1860; as *Journeys to England in Victoria's Early Days 1844–1859*, translated by Dorothy Harrison, 1939.
Jenseit des Tweed. 1860; as *Across the Tweed*, translated by Brian Battershaw, 1965.
Wanderungen durch die Mark Brandenburg. 4 vols., 1862–82.
Kriegsgefangen. 1871.
Aus den Tagen der Okkupation. 1872.
Der Krieg gegen Frankreich, 1870–1871. 2 vols., 1873–76.
Christian Friedrich Scherenberg und der literarische Berlin von 1840 bis 1860. 1885.
Fünf Schlösser. 1889.
Meine Kinderjahre (memoirs). 1894.
Von Zwanzig bis Dreissig (memoirs). 1898.
Aus dem Nachlass, edited by Joseph Ettlinger. 1908.
Briefwechsel, with Wilhelm Wolfsohn, edited by Wilhelm Walters. 1910.
Briefe, edited by Kurt Schreinert and Charlotte Jolles. 4 vols., 1968–71.
Briefwechsel, with Paul Heyse, edited by Gotthard Erler. 1972.
Briefe, edited by Gotthard Erler. 2 vols., 1980.
Briefwechsel, with Theodor Storm, edited by Jacob Steiner. 1981.
Ein Leben in Briefen, edited by Otto Drude, 1981.
Autobiographische Schriften, edited by Gotthard Erler, Peter Goldammer, and Joachim Krueger. 3 vols., 1982.
Briefe an den Verleger Rudolf von Decker. 1988.

*

Critical Studies: *Formen des Realismus* by Peter Demetz, 1964; *The Gentle Critic: Theodor Fontane and German Politics 1848–98* by Joachim Remak, 1964; *Theodor Fontane: An Introduction to the Novels and Novellen* by H.C. Sasse, 1968; *Theodor Fontane: An Introduction to the Man and His Work* by A.R. Robinson, 1976; *The Preparation of the Future: Techniques of Anticipation in the Novels of Theodor Fontane and Thomas Mann* by Gertrude Michielsen, 1978; *Some Aspects of Balladesque Art and Their Relevance for the Novels of Fontane* by R. Geoffrey Lackey, 1979; *Supernatural and Irrational Elements in the Works of Fontane* by Helen Elizabeth Chambers, 1980; *The Berlin Novels of Theodor Fontane* by Henry Garland, 1980; *Theodor Fontane: The Major Novels* by Alan F. Bance, 1982; *The German 'Gesellschaftsroman' at the Turn of the Century: A Comparison of the Works of Theodor Fontane and Eduard von Keyserling* by Richard A. Koc, 1982; *Novel Associations: Theodor Fontane and George Eliot within the Context of Nineteenth-Century Realism* by Gabriele A. Wittig Davis, 1983; *Meyer or Fontane? German Literature after the Franco-Prussian War 1870–71* by John Osborne, 1983; *Anekdoten aus allen fünf Weltteilen: The Anecdote in Fontane's Fiction and Autobiography* by Andrea MhicFhionnbhairr, 1985; *Social Integration and Narrative Structure: Patterns of Realism in Auerbach, Freytag, Fontane, and Raabe* by Nancy A. Kaiser, 1986; *Effi Briest* by Stanley Radcliffe, 1986.

* * *

It was as a writer of ballads that Theodor Fontane first made his way in the literary world, and it was on the ballad,

and on his historical researches, *Wanderungen durch die Mark Brandenburg*, that Fontane's reputation rested for most of his own lifetime. He emerged as a novelist only in his late fifties, with the historical novel *Vor dem Sturm* (*Before the Storm*), on the mood of Prussia on the eve of the Wars of Liberation against Napoleon.

Fontane is typically concerned here to present large-scale events through the details of everyday life, and this predilection for the actual conditions of life (albeit within a limited social range) is somewhat un-German. In fact, Fontane and Heinrich Heine were perhaps the only two 19th-century writers of rank to grapple closely with the political reality of their country. The author himself thought his wealth of topical references would render him unreadable in the next century (yet Ernst Jünger was sustained by the love story *Irrungen, Wirrungen* (*A Suitable Match*) in the trenches of World War I).

Everything Fontane writes is in a sense political, and yet everything is conveyed through the intimate medium of a private fate. Thus his novella on the decadent state of Prussian society in the era of its defeat at Napoleon's hands in 1806 reveals the nature of the times through the character of an individual, the Prussian officer Schach von Wuthenow (after whom the story is named), a vacillating conformist. Fontane's highly developed handling of conversation is the most praised quality of his art, and it especially offers him scope for revealing the link between private existence and the public totality of an epoch. His preference for reticence and discretion as a narrator has allowed him to be read as an apologist for the accommodations required of the individual in society. But he is at heart a romantic, who knows, however, that individuals only exist within the given of their society and cannot transcend it. Yet it is *through* these individuals that Fontane must convey his sense of an alternative world, and he does so often through female characters who possess a mysterious natural attraction, and whose potential the world stifles or leaves unrealized. The most poetic expression of this confrontation of nature and society is the figure of Effi Briest in Fontane's best-known novel; and yet this book more than any other makes clear that society is known and understood only through individuals who are products of their society and cannot stand outside it. His last novel, *Der Stechlin*, is a serene and yet politically astute analysis of the tension between reified 'facts'—the facts of self-interest and power politics which became a dominant fetish in Wilhelm II's materialistic Second Reich—and the possibility of change. Fontane's life-long attraction to England, prominent in *Der Stechlin*, was precisely to do with the contrast between English political culture and Prussia's difficulty in evolving social structures commensurate with the dynamic forces of its modernization.

—Alan F. Bance

BEFORE THE STORM (Vor dem Sturm)
Novel by Theodor Fontane, 1878.

It is almost inevitable in any account of *Before the Storm* to draw attention to the fact that its author was almost 60 years old when it was completed. In addition, Fontane was already an established writer of many years' standing, so that in his novelistic debut he emerges as a mature and confident writer. *Before the Storm* was in many ways a labour of love, 15 years in the making. Fontane wrote to his publisher that he was resolved to write it 'entirely in my own fashion, according to my own predilections and individual personality, not following any particular model'.

For a novel of such great length (all his subsequent works were only half the size and some a great deal shorter than that), the plot—such as it is—can be related in a few words. It concerns the key period between December 1812 and May 1813, a turning point in the fortunes of Prussia as it breaks free from French domination, but it relates more to individual fortunes rather than the destiny of kings and princes.

Berndt von Vitzewitz, a widower, is lord of the manor of the fictitious village of Hohen-Vietz in Brandenburg. He has a son, Lewin, and a daughter, Renate. The son loves a Polish cousin, Kathinka, but she elopes with a Polish count. Lewin falls ill, but then recovers and marries Marie, a girl who is not his social equal.

The father, Berndt von Vitzewitz, demonstrates the links which Fontane perceives to exist between individuals and the destiny of nations. He has lived through the time of Prussia's humiliation, defeat, and occupation at the hands of the French, and curiously his own life reached its nadir at that time, with the death of his beloved wife. He is a man of great strength of character, moral conviction, and sense of purpose, who has the courage to reach beyond the conventions of society and express his allegiance to a higher aim. This combination of powerful individuality and deep loyalty is founded upon a sincere religious conviction: 'If I raise this hand, I raise it not to avenge a personal injustice, but against the common enemy', he states. There are other characters like him in the novel, which underlines Fontane's conviction that individuals of strong moral purpose can and do affect the course of history, and that their strength is also Prussia's strength. It is a quality which seems to permeate even the buildings. The church of Hohen-Vietz in its continuity of existence despite the changes of the centuries seems to encapsulate Prussian strength of character: 'If the outside of the church had remained more or less unchanged, the interior had undergone all the transformations of five hundred years'. The place is filled with a sense of history and strength which transforms the dead stones of which it is constructed and inspires and ennobles the lives of the parishioners.

All these references to individual strength as an historical force come as something of a revelation to those who have read only Fontane's subsequent novels, which are peopled by characters like Botho von Rienacker and Baron von Innstetten who act not out of deep conviction but as prisoners of social convention, and whose individual *Glück* (happiness) is at the mercy of society's need for *Ordnung* (order).

In many other respects, however, *Before the Storm* does anticipate the rest of Fontane's work. This can be seen firstly in his avoidance of violence and sensation—the very title of the novel is *before* the storm, not *during* it. The narrative technique of the detached observer who is not averse to intruding on the narrative on occasion is also established here; as, too, is the centrality of dialogue as a means of revealing character and teasing out issues for debate. At the heart of the work is the notion of life as a process, an evolutionary, changing phenomenon set against the backdrop of eternal verities of moral conduct and belief—and this, too, is reflected in his subsequent works.

Some critics have sought to promote *Before the Storm* as a masterpiece, but it is certainly not in the same category as Fontane's greatest novel, *Effi Briest*. It bears too many marks of the author's self-indulgent obsession with his theme, and in its intricate detail constantly loses sight of the whole. *Pace* the apologists, it would be a mistake to defend the novel on the grounds that it matches precisely what the author set out to achieve. In many respects it is a halfway house between his

fiction and his earlier travelogue *Wanderungen durch die Mark Brandenburg* [Wanderings Through the March of Brandenburg]. As an artistic achievement it lacks coherence and drive—but within its fragmentation there are moments of conviction and creative power which look forward to the great novels, in particular to *Effi Briest*.

—Rex Last

EFFI BRIEST
Novel by Theodor Fontane, 1895.

Effi Briest, Fontane's greatest novel, has been compared with Flaubert's *Madame Bovary* and Tolstoi's *Anna Karenina* in its treatment of adultery. Yet Fontane, an enemy of the sensational, does not make Effi's sin the central issue of the novel. Instead he focuses on the destructive conventions of a society that condemns individuals to a life of boredom, frustration, and disillusionment.

While Fontane's contemporary social portrait sheds light on the whole of late 19th-century industrial, bourgeois European society, the primary object of his criticism is Prussia and the Germany it brought into being. This Prussia, its values and mores, is mirrored in the characters of *Effi Briest*. Effi's husband, Geert von Instetten, is committed to the discipline, authority, love of nation, and professionalism that typify the Prussian civil servant. He allows abstractions of moral convention to dictate his behaviour, killing Crampas in a duel and shunning his wife, in his own words: 'for the sake of mere representations'. While Instetten, after a short term of imprisonment for his involvement in the duel, continues his advance up the bureaucratic ladder, he none the less recognizes the ultimate meaninglessness of his success: 'the more I am honoured, the more I feel that all of this is nothing. My life is ruined . . .'. Instetten recalls 'the "little happiness" ' he had once enjoyed with his wife, and resigns himself to its loss.

The teenager Effi is seduced by a naive ambitiousness of her own. Enamoured of the idea of marrying a respected civil servant, she submits to engagement with her 38-year-old suitor on the day when he proposes it. But even on their honeymoon tour of Italy, boredom becomes the primary experience of Effi's married life. The birth of Annie does little to remedy the situation of a woman who must spend her days in loneliness while her husband disappears for long hours at work and her child is cared for by a governess. Effi succumbs irresistibly and against her better judgement to the seduction of Major von Crampas, who himself is chained to an unbearable wife and an outwardly successful existence that he despises. Effi witnesses her descent into sinfulness with a kind of horror and is profoundly relieved by her husband's news that his promotion to *Ministerialrat* means their relocation to Berlin, away from the disturbing monotony of their life in remote Kessin. When, more than six years later, Instetten learns of the adulterous relationship his wife has come to view as an unfortunate, yet forgettable episode of her past, she accepts her punishment: life as a social outcast and irreconcilable estrangement from her daughter, with resignation. The reader stands aghast at her tragic ability to accept the morals that have destroyed her when the dying Effi asks her mother to inform Instetten of her conviction that his entire handling of the situation was justified.

Fontane's realism is not intended to dictate an absolute reality to his readers. Reality is necessarily a matter of perception, and in *Effi Briest* the real work is unfolded from a multiplicity of individual perspectives and communicated primarily via dialogue. The reader learns nothing more about the society in which the characters exist than what they themselves reveal through their conversations, letters, and thoughts. The reader is left to decide whether to agree with Johanna, who, a proper Prussian, regards Instetten's decision to banish Effi and turn her daughter against her as correct, or with the Catholic Roswitha, who believes Effi has suffered far more than she ever deserved and leaves Instetten to live with the melancholy divorcée. Each character sheds a different light on Prussian culture and society, and the final portrait mirrors reality in its multi-dimensional breadth.

Yet the reality recorded in *Effi Briest* is also *poetic*, making the novel a prime example of 19th-century German poetic realism. Fontane's 'real world' is an artistic structure created with the aid of a meticulous selection procedure and an elaborate symbolic apparatus. Scholars have determined that *Effi Briest* underwent seven versions before the author was satisfied with it. The plot is based on real-life events: the discovery by Baron Leon von Ardenne that his wife, Elisabeth von Plotho, had once had an affair with painter Emil Hartwich; the duel in which Hartwich fell; and the couple's divorce. While several details from the experience of this real-life couple went into the composition of *Effi Briest*, the novel is anything but a biographical record of their lives. Frau von Plotho lived until the age of 99; Effi Briest dies of tuberculosis at age 29. Fontane merely got the *idea* for his novel from the Ardenne divorce. What he developed from it is a selective, fictional view of contemporary society created first as a work of art, and only secondly as an instrument of social criticism.

Fontane's use of symbols in *Effi Briest* likewise exemplifies the movement of poetic realism. Fontane is a master at taking real objects from everyday life and loading them with symbolic content. Thus the picture of the Chinese man to which Johanna is so attached assumes a whole spectrum of possible meanings based on the adventurous and tragic stories told about the man and the reactions of the various characters to his likeness. The natural boundaries present in the landscape around Instetten's home in Kessin, the sea, and especially the woods, take on profound importance as the symbols for Effi's fateful transgression into the realm of the forbidden.

In the final analysis, resignation is the overriding theme in *Effi Briest*, as it is in so many other novels by Fontane and by other representatives of German realism: Wilhelm Raabe, Gottfried Keller, and Friedrich Spielhagen. Those who accept society's limitations, like Geert von Instetten, survive, though happiness may forever elude them. Those who attempt to assert their individuality in the face of moral oppression, like Effi, will only be destroyed. This is the ultimate message of 19th-century realism.

—Virginia L. Lewis

FONVIZIN, Denis (Ivanovich). Born in Moscow, Russia, 3 April 1745. Educated at Moscow University Gymnasium, 1755–60; Moscow University, 1760–62. Married Ekaterina Khlopova in 1774. After university, moved to St Petersburg and entered the civil service: secretary to Ivan Elagin in the Foreign Ministry, 1763–69; secretary to the statesman Count Nikita Ivanovich Panin, from 1769; received an estate, 1773;

travelled to France and Germany, 1777–78; achieved dramatic success with the St Petersburg production of *The Minor*; retired from public life, 1783, following the death of Panin and after incurring the displeasure of Catherine the Great; a founding member of the Russian Academy, 1783; his works banned temporarily in the early 1780s; travelled to Germany and Italy, 1784–85; suffered stroke, 1785; planned to launch a periodical, *Starodum* [Old Thought], which never appeared because of censorship; travelled to Austria for health reasons, 1786–87. *Died 1 December 1792.*

PUBLICATIONS

Collections

Polnoe sobranie sochinenii [Complete Works]. 4 vols., 1830.
Pervoe polnoe sobranie sochinenii [First Complete Works]. 1888.
Izbrannye sochineniia i pis'ma [Selected Works and Letters]. 1946.
Izbrannoe [Selection], edited by B. Derkach. 1957.
Sobranie sochinenii [Collected Works], edited by G.P. Makogonenko. 2 vols., 1959.
Sochineniia [Works], edited by A.I. Vredinskii. 1983.
Izbrannoe: Stikhotvoreniia; Komedii; Satiricheskie proza i publitsistika; Avtobiograficheskaia proza; Pis'ma [Selection: Poetry; Comedies; Satirical Prose and Publications; Autobiographical Prose; Letters], edited by Iu.V. Stennik. 1983.
Sochineniia [Works], edited by N.N. Akopova. 1987.
Izbrannye sochineniia [Selected Works], with A.S. Griboedov and A.N. Ostrovskii, edited by V.N. Turbin. 1989.

Plays

Korion [Korion], from a play by Jean-Baptiste Gresset (produced 1764).
Brigadir (produced 1780). In *Polnoe sobranie sochinenii*, 1830; single edition, 1950; as *The Brigadier*, translated by Harold B. Segel, in *The Literature of Eighteenth-Century Russia*, 2, edited by Segel, 1968; also translated by Marvin Kantor, in *The Dramatic Works*, 1974.
Nedorosl' (produced 1782). 1937; as *The Young Hopeful*, translated by George Z. Patrick and G.R. Noyes, in *Masterpieces of the Russian Drama*, edited by Noyes, 1933; as *The Minor*, translated by Frank D. Reeve, in *Anthology of Russian Plays*, 1, edited by Reeve, 1961; also translated by Marvin Kantor, in *The Dramatic Works*, 1974; as *The Infant*, in *Four Russian Plays*, translated by Joshua Cooper, 1972, reprinted as *The Government Inspector and Other Plays*, 1990.
Vybor guvernera (produced 1790). As *The Choice of a Tutor*, in *Five Russian Plays with One from the Ukraine*, edited and translated by C.E.B. Roberts, 1916; as *The Selection of a Tutor*, translated by Marvin Kantor, in *The Dramatic Works*, 1974.
Alzir; ili, Amerikantsii [Alzire; or, The Americans], from a play by Voltaire, in *Pervoe polnoe sobranie sochinenii*. 1888.
Komedii (includes *Vseobshchaia pridvornaia grammatika*). 1950.
The Dramatic Works (includes *The Minor*; *The Brigadier*; *The Selection of a Tutor*; and the fragment *A Good Mentor*), translated by Marvin Kantor. 1974.

Other

Zhizn' grafa N.I. Panin [The Life of Count N.I. Panin]. 1784 (in French); 1796 (in Russian).
Brigadir; Nedorosl'; Satiricheskaia proza; Pis'ma iz Peterburga [The Brigadier; The Minor; Satirical Prose; Letters from Petersburg]. 1987.

Translator, Basni nravouchitel' ne s iz" iasneniami, from Holberg's fables. 1761; enlarged edition, 1765.
Translator, Geroiskaia dobrodetel'; ili, zhizn' Sife [Heroic Virtue], by Jean Terrasson. 4 vols., 1762–68.
Translator, Liubov' Karity i Polidora [The Love of Carita and Polidore], by Jean-Jacques Berthélémy. 1763.
Translator, Torguiushchee dvorianstvo [The Commercial Nobility], by Gabriel-François Coyer. 1766.
Translator, Sidnii i Sillii [Sidney and Silly], by François-Thomas Baculard d'Arnaud. 1769.
Translator, Joseph, by Paul-Jérémie Bitaube. 1769
Translator, Rassuzhdenie o natsional'nom liubochestie [An Essay on National Patriotism], by Johann Zimmermann. 1785.

*

Critical Studies: *Russian Comedy 1765–1823* by D. Walsh, 1966; *Denis Fonvizine* by Alexis Strychek, 1976; *Denis Fonvizin* by Charles A. Moser, 1979; *Russian Drama from Its Beginnings to the Age of Pushkin* by Simon Karlinsky, 1985.

* * *

The Russian theatre before Denis Fonvizin, after its official inception during the reign of Tsar Alexei in 1672, progressed by fits and starts. Very little of lasting value was produced and the period is of little more than historical interest. The mid-18th century did, however, witness some notable developments and a few original plays were written, the best of them by Aleksandr Sumarokov. The style was highly imitative and followed the conventions of French neo-classicism. During the reign of Catherine the Great marked progress was made, not entirely unconnected with her own interest in writing plays, and the theatre was given encouragement, state support, and financial assistance. The two best plays of the period are undoubtedly Fonvizin's *Brigadir* (*The Brigadier*) and *Nedorosl'* (*The Minor*).

Fonvizin was a well-educated, cultured, and widely-travelled man but his work as a dramatist was not central to his career. His interest in drama derived from his leisure-time activity of translating from French and German—his version of Holberg's *Fables* (1761) led to a lasting interest in his plays, a few of which he attempted to translate. Fonvizin's first attempt at dramatic composition was a version in Russian of Gresset's *Sidney* (1764), to which he gave the un-Russian title of *Korion*. Although it is a good example of travesty that was extremely popular at the time and it was rendered in competent verse, it is best regarded only as an immature experiment. These early experiences did, however, stand Fonvizin in good stead, for the two plays for which he is remembered are unquestionably the best in Russian before Griboedov's *Gore ot uma* (*Woe from Wit*), composed in the early 1820s. They are both written in prose and follow the rules of neo-classical dramatic form. They are comedies of manners and social satires with a marked didactic element.

When *The Brigadier* first appeared it was an immediate success. Its plot revolves around a young couple who hope to marry and whose respective parents meet in order to become better acquainted and to decide whether their offspring are suitable for each other. The comedy springs from the efforts of each of the two fathers to form a liaison with the other's wife, while simultaneously the young man courts his prospective mother-in-law, thus becoming a rival to his own father. Ultimately such disgraceful behaviour gets its just reward: the parents are ridiculed, the young man is unsuccessful, and the daughter's eyes are opened to the ways of the world before she finds true love with someone else. Consequently the sanctity of the family is upheld and love based on sincere feelings and mutual respect encouraged. Fonvizin, however, keeps his most biting satire for the then pervasive Gallomania, endemic at court but imitated, although not understood, by society at large. Fonvizin was by no means opposed to the French or their ways, but wished his fellow-countrymen to be selective, balanced, and rational in what they accepted, thus developing some sense of their own worth. The play is amusing in both its action and its dialogue, the latter being the most natural-sounding yet heard on the Russian stage. For the first time in Russia a play had been written that was recognizably Russian in subject matter, characterization, and feel, even though many of the human foibles satirized were universal.

Although less well constructed and more obviously didactic and closer to the conventions of neo-classicism than *The Brigadier*, *The Minor* was the better-known in its day and the one for which he is now chiefly remembered. It features a pair of conventional lovers who have to suffer the machinations of the young girl's guardian to marry her off, first to her brother, and then when it transpires that her ward is the heiress to a considerable fortune, to her son, the minor of the title. Everything is sorted out finally, the lovers are free to marry and the guardian punished, although not so much for her dealings with her family as for maltreating her serfs. The plot is rather conventional and uninvolving. The central focus of the satire is squarely on the brutal, uneducated, unthinking, and selfish provincial landowners of the minor gentry and their equally uninspiring entourage of servants, relations, and ignorant tutors. The negative characters, with hardly a redeeming feature among them, are wonderfully comic creations and are in sharp contrast to the positive, moralizing, and tediously didactic representatives of the good and true, the wealthy, honest, and educated. The language of the former is lively, natural, and colloquial while that of the latter is formal and stilted. Fonvizin is proposing virtuous behaviour in human relations and the legitimate claims of social justice, both of which can be guaranteed by a proper education, while the state must do all it can to promote the necessary conditions. Even Catherine is reported to have approved of the play, although there were some suggestions that Fonvizin had drawn very near to the limits of the permissible.

Vybor guvernera (*The Selection of a Tutor*), although continuing the theme of the importance of education to the country's well-being, is rather more political than social. Politics, Fonvizin affirms, has to concern itself with questions of the freedom and the equality of citizens, the former being the more crucial. There will always be differences between various social classes and consequently inequality is inevitable, but civil liberties are to be ensured wherever possible. It is not Russia's institutions, including serfdom, which are at fault in themselves, rather the shortcomings of those who manage them. In all of his plays Fonvizin shows himself to be a man of his times, but a humane and considerate one who believed that Russia needed change but that she had enough intrinsic worth not simply to imitate others.

—A.V. Knowles

THE MINOR (Nedorosl')
Play by Denis Fonvizin, 1782.

The Russian 18th-century neo-classical comedy of manners is largely a very paltry affair. Re-workings, copies, and adaptations of not even the best models abound and most of them have little even historical interest today. A few worthy exceptions do exist, for example Iakov Kniazhnin's *The Braggart*, Vasily Kapnist's *Iabeda* (*Chicanery*), and most notably Fonvizin's *The Minor*, which is still performed occasionally in Russia. Started in the late 1770s, *The Minor* was completed in 1781. Fonvizin gave a few readings of the play before it was first performed in Knipper's private theatre in St Petersburg on 24 September 1782. It was published the following year. In its day it was seen as a highly topical play concerned with the dire results of ignorance, abuse of power, and man's (and woman's) inhumanity to their fellows. Catherine the Great's favourite, Prince Gregory Potemkin, is reported to have said to Fonvizin 'Denis, you might as well die for you'll never write anything better'. This was once somewhat more threateningly mistranslated as 'If you write anything like that again, you'd better die'.

Despite many attempts, especially by Russian critics, to suggest that *The Minor* is an early precursor of realism on the stage (despite the fact that it was written several years before the term was coined), this is at best wishful thinking or not very sensible special pleading. There can be no argument that it remains a thoroughly traditional neo-classical comedy, albeit influenced less by the example of Molière than by Holberg, whose plays, along with those by Goldoni, were extremely popular in Russia in the later 18th century. The three unities are adhered to strictly in its five acts, the action lasts scarcely more than 24 hours and occurs in one room, violence takes place off-stage, the characters have symbolic names and represent specific human vices and virtues, there is a pair of traditional young lovers, and good conquers evil in the happy ending. Within this restricting framework Fonvizin has written a well-constructed and, in parts, amusing play. The conflict between the old-fashioned, uneducated, and rough-hewn provincial gentry and the civilized, cultured, and wealthy representatives of the Enlightenment is reasonably well-balanced. Although it is clear that the positive characters have justice on their side and ultimately triumph, their speeches tend to the moralizing, didactic, and tedious, while the negative characters are far more interesting linguistically and dramatically and all the real comedy in the play stems from their words and actions.

The action takes place on the country estate of the meek and henpecked Prostakov (Mr Simpleton). Everyone there is tyrannized by his ignorant, cruel, and domineering wife. Their 16-year-old son Mitrofan, the minor of the title, is a lazy, remarkably unintelligent, and spoiled adolescent who is adored by his mother. His only ambition is expressed in the now proverbial words: 'I don't want to study, I want to get married'. Staying on the estate is a nobleman, Pravdin (Mr Truthful), who unbeknown to the Prostakovs has been sent by the government to verify reports that Mrs Prostakov has been maltreating her serfs, which indeed she has. She hopes to marry off her ward, the young orphan Sof'ia, whose estate

she has taken over illegally, to her brother Skotinin (Mr Brute), who prefers the company of pigs to human beings. Sof'ia hears that her rich uncle Starodum (Mr Oldwise) is returning after making his fortune, and Mrs Prostakov thinks, for utterly selfish reasons, that Sof'ia should now marry her son. Sof'ia, though, is in love with Milon (Lt Dear) a young army officer who soon arrives on the scene, closely followed by Starodum, who rejects as suitors both Skotinin and Mitrofan. Mrs Prostakov attempts to kidnap Sof'ia but is prevented from so doing by Milon. Pravdin announces an official order removing the Prostakovs from control over their serfs and everyone turns on the wretched woman, even Mitrofan. Milon and Sof'ia are now free to marry.

Fonvizin's satire is directed not just at the grasping, narrow-minded provincial landowners. He suggests that their faults come from a lack of education and along with his contemporaries believed that all his country's ills would be cured once ignorance had been removed. The three tutors Mrs Prostakov employs for her son are comically incompetent and are only engaged because of the legal requirement that sons of the gentry have to receive an education. The legal bureaucracy and sycophancy at the imperial court are denigrated as are many of the abuses of serfdom. However, Fonvizin did not wish that serfdom be abolished completely or for anything other than autocracy to be the form of government, but he does plead here that the abuses they clearly engender should be eradicated. One further important theme in *The Minor* is that of duty, the mutual duty of subjects and their monarch, that of the landowners to look after their serfs, of children to respect their elders, and of all citizens to serve their country. While none of the butts of Fonvizin's satire is original (and Catherine herself had used similar targets in her own plays), it was Fonvizin's dramatic sense, his fine and apposite use of language, his ability to portray recognizable Russian life and people, and the humour of many of his characters' speeches that made *The Minor* the most popular play of its day. It still remains pleasantly watchable and is more than the historical curio most other Russian plays of the 18th century have become.

—A.V. Knowles

————

FOUQUÉ, Caroline (Auguste) de la Motte. Born Caroline von Briest, in Nennhausen, Germany, 7 October 1775(?). Married 1) Friedrich Ehrenreich Adolph Ludwig von Rochow in 1789; two sons and one illegitimate daughter (marriage dissolved 1799; died (suicide) 1799); 2) the writer Friedrich de la Motte Fouqué, *q.v.*, in 1803. *Died 21 July 1831*.

PUBLICATIONS

Fiction

Drei Märchen. 1806.
Rodrich. 1806–07.
Die Frau des Falkensteins. 1810.
Kleine Erzählungen von der Verfasserin des Rodrich, der Frau des Falkensteins und der Briefe über weibliche Bildung. 1811.

Die Magie der Natur: Eine Revolutionsgeschichte. 1812.
Der Spanier und der Freiwillige in Paris. Eine Geschichte aus dem heiligen Kriege. 1814.
Feodora. 1814.
Edmunds Wege und Irrwege. Ein Roman aus der nächsten Vergangenheit. 1815.
Das Heldenmädchen aus der Vendée. 1816.
Neue Erzählungen. 1817. Includes 'Die Verwünschung'; as 'The Curse: A Tale', translated by N. Stenhouse, 1825.
Die früheste Geschichte der Welt: Ein Geschenk für Kinder. 1818.
Frauenliebe. 1818.
Blumenstrauss gewunden aus den neusten Romanen und Erzählungen, with Friedrich de la Motte Fouqué. 1818.
Fragmente aus dem Leben der heutigen Welt. 1820.
Ida. 1820.
Lodoiska und ihre Tochter. 1820.
Kleine Romane und Erzählungen. 1820.
Heinrich und Marie. 1821.
Die blinde Führerin. 1821.
Vergangenheit und Gegenwart. 1822.
Die Herzogin von Montmorency. 1822.
Die Vertriebenen: Eine Novelle aus der Zeit der Königin Elisabeth von England. 1823; as *The Outcasts: A Romance,* translated by George Soane, 1824.
Neueste gesammelte Erzählungen. 1824.
Die beiden Freunde. 1824.
Bodo von Hohenried. 1825.
Aurelio. 1825.
Valerie, Die Sinnesänderung, und Der Weihnachtsbaum (stories). 1827.
Resignation. 1829.
Memoiren einer Ungenannten. 1831.
Der Schreibtisch; oder, Alte und neue Zeit. 1833.
The Physician of Marseilles, The Revolutionists: Four Tales from the German. 1845.

Other

Briefe über Zweck und Richtung weiblicher Bildung. 1811.
Briefe über die griechische Mythologie für Frauen. 1812.
Ruf an die deutschen Frauen. 1812.
Über deutsche Geselligkeit, in Antwort auf das Urtheil der Frau von Staël. 1814.
Briefe über Berlin im Winter 1821. 1822.
Reiseerinnerungen, with Friedrich de la Motte Fouqué. 1823.
Die Frauen in der grossen Welt: Bildungsbuch beim Eintritt in das gesellige Leben. 1826.
Geschichte der Moden, vom Jahre 1785 bis 1829, als Beitrag zur Geschichte der Zeit. 1830.

Editor, with others, *Für müssige Stunden: Vierteljahrsschrift.* 7 vols., 1816–21; reprinted 1971.

*

Critical Studies: *Märchen-Dichtung der Romantiker* by Richard Benz, 1926; *Caroline de la Motte Fouqué* by Vera Prill, 1933; *The Romantic Realist: Caroline de la Motte Fouqué* by Jean T. Wilde, 1955.

* * *

Caroline de la Motte Fouqué was a writer of some significance in the literary, cultural, and social history of Germany.

For a number of years she and her husband, Friedrich, were the country's most successful literary couple, and her works were praised by major writers such as Goethe and Kleist. Yet she has been even more neglected than her husband, and the few references to her in critical literature tend to be derogatory.

Her career spans the quarter-century from the defeat of Prussia by Napoleon in 1806 to her death eight months before that of Goethe. During this period of political and social upheaval she published more than 100 works, including 20 novels, over 60 stories, a number of poems and reviews, and some 20 non-fiction pieces of didactic, social, and cultural import aimed primarily at women. Besides pursuing her own career she collaborated in her husband's editorial ventures and co-authored with him two volumes of *Reiseerinnerungen* [Travel Reminiscences].

The range and quantity of Fouqué's output testify not only to the diversity of her interests and her facility in writing, but also to her need to earn money, which became acute when her husband's popularity waned after 1815. Although acquainted with most of the important writers of the day and admitted to the highest court circles in Prussia, she was under financial pressures, as reflected in the concessions to popular taste, the prolixity, and the uneven quality of much of her work. Deeply conservative in outlook, with a strong belief in monarchy, aristocracy, religion, family honour, and the military ethos, she yet experienced, like many women of her time, marital breakdown and the birth of an illegitimate child. She was, too, an educated professional writer in a society which discouraged the serious pursuit of art or scholarship by women. These contradictions, characteristic of an age of transition, are mirrored in her writing through the strategies that she adopts in order to cope with them and to make her work acceptable to the reading public, and through the tension between Romantic and realistic features in her style.

Several of her earliest works, two anonymous poems and the collection *Drei Märchen* [Three Fairy Tales], show the influence of Romantic models, particularly Novalis and Tieck. However, her first novel, *Rodrich,* already displays the mixture of Romanticism and realism which characterizes her later work. It includes Romantic motifs such as verse interpolations, visions, dreams, symbolism, and a mystery concerning the hero's birth and ancestry, as well as realistic descriptions, social criticism, and discussions between characters on various topics. It probably influenced E.T.A. Hoffmann's novel *Die Elixiere des Teufels* (*The Devil's Elixirs*) (1815–16).

Fouqué's second novel, *Die Frau des Falkensteins* [The Lady of Castle Falkenstein], is a tale of passion and renunciation with autobiographical overtones, and a number of the characters are based on Fouqué's acquaintances. It has many of the trappings of the Gothic novel—an old castle, a family curse, an ancestral ghost, a mysterious portrait, dreams, premonitions, and forebodings—which appear repeatedly in her work, but it also emphasizes the importance of self-restraint, convention, and useful, settled activity. These concerns suggest the influence of Goethe but also show Fouqué seeking fictional solutions to problems of her own. Several of her other novels and stories, such as *Feodora, Frauenliebe* [A Woman's Love], *Ida, Lodoiska und ihre Tochter* [Lodoiska and Her Daughter], and 'Arnold und Marie' (1811), which, exceptionally for Fouqué, is set wholly in a non-aristocratic milieu, likewise deal with marriage and relationships between the sexes.

Fouqué's conviction that traditional forms must be preserved is expressed in 'Das Fräulein vom Thurme' [The Girl in the Tower] (1811), a cautionary tale about the dangers of marrying below one's station, and *Die Magie der Natur* [The Magic of Nature], which is set against the background of the French Revolution and carries an anti-revolutionary message as well as a warning not to meddle in the mysteries of the universe. This novel may have been influenced by Goethe's *Elective Affinities*; he certainly read and approved of it. Its concern with the dangers of unfettered scientific enquiry is characteristic of its time (compare Mary Shelley's *Frankenstein*, 1818). *Das Heldenmädchen aus der Vendée* [The Heroic Girl of the Vendée Nobility], one of Fouqué's best historical novels, is again set in revolutionary France. Based on the memoirs of the Marquise de la Rochejaquelein (1814), it concerns the Vendean Wars of 1793–96, and interweaves fact and fiction, events in the Vendée and in Paris, to create a vivid picture of opposing forces during a controversial episode of French history. Fouqué's idealization of the Vendeans stands in striking contrast to their denigration in official French historiography.

English history of the Elizabethan era provides the background to *Die Vertriebenen* (*The Outcasts*), which was influenced by Sir Walter Scott. Here, as in *Das Heldenmädchen* and *Die Herzogin von Montmorency* [The Duchess of Montmorency], which recounts the Massacre of St Bartholomew, Fouqué shows a particular flair for character drawing and vivid description, especially of crowd scenes. Other strengths of her writing are her depiction of nature and gift for detail, often of a domestic or everyday kind.

Her capacity for observation is also evident in her nonfiction works, in which she comments on and seeks to influence the society of her time. While conforming to contemporary prejudice in warning women against scholarly and artistic virtuosity, she pursues her own ambitions as writer and guide on women's education, etiquette, mythology, history, social events, and cultural phenomena. Whereas her earlier pieces are strongly patriotic, her later work is marked by increasing disillusionment. Yet her *Geschichte der Moden, vom Jahre 1785 bis 1829, als Beitrag zur Geschichte der Zeit* [History of Fashion, from 1785 to 1829, as a Contribution to the History of the Age] shows originality in its insight that changes in fashions reflect intellectual and social changes, and suggests unfulfilled potential that, in an age less restrictive of women, might have come to more complete fruition.

—Judith Purver

FOUQUÉ, Friedrich (Heinrich Karl, Baron) de la Motte. Born in Brandenburg, Germany, 12 February 1777. Educated privately by A.L. Hülsen, 1788–94. Served with the Weimar Dragoons, 1794, took part in the Rhine campaign, invalided out, 1795; Prussian cavalry officer, 1812–13: Major. Married 1) Marianne von Schubaert in 1798; 2) the writer Caroline von Briest, *q.v.*, in 1803 (died 1831); 3) Albertine Tode in 1833, two sons. Visited Weimar, 1802 and met Goethe and Schiller; encouraged to proceed with career as a writer by Friedrich and August Wilhelm Schlegel, *q.v.*; lived in Nennhausen after 1803. Editor, *Taschenbuch*, 1809; *Die Jahreszeiten*, 1811–14; *Die Musen*, 1812–14; *Das Frauentaschenbuch*, 1815–21; *Für müssige Stunden*, 1816–20; *Berlinische Blätter für deutsche Frauen*, 1829–30; gave private lectures in history and poetry, Halle, 1840; co-editor, *Zeitung für den deutschen Adel*, Berlin, 1840–42. *Died 23 January 1843.*

PUBLICATIONS

Collections

Works. 6 vols., 1845–46.
Geistliche Gedichte, edited by Albertine de la Motte Fouqué. 1846.
Werke, edited by Walther Ziesemer. 3 vols., 1908.
Werke, edited by C.G. von Maassen. 2 vols., 1922.

Fiction

Alwin. 1807.
Das Galgenmännlein. 1810; as 'The Bottle-Imp', in *Popular Tales and Romances of the Northern Nations*, 1, 1823; as 'The Vial-Genie and Mad Farthing', translated by Thomas Tracy, in *Miniature Romances from the German*, 1841.
Der Todesbund. 1811.
Undine. 1811; as *Undine*, translated by George Soane, 1818; also translated by Thomas Tracy, 1839; C.L. Lyttleton, 1845; Fanny Elizabeth Bunnett, 1867; Edmund Gosse, 1896; Abby L. Alger, 1897; George P. Upton, 1908; Paul Turner, 1960.
Sintram und seine Gefährten. 1811; as *Sintram and His Companions*, translated by Julius C. Hare, 1820; also translated by J. Burns, 1848; A.M. Richards, 1900; A.C. Farquharson, 1908.
Der Zauberring. 1812; as *The Magic Ring; or, Ingratitude Punished*, 1812; as *The Magic Ring: A Knightly Romance*, translated by Alexander Platt, 1846.
Die beiden Hauptleute. 1812; as *The Two Captains*, 1846; in *Undine and Other Tales*, translated by Fanny Elizabeth Bunnett, 1867.
Erzählungen. 1812.
Aslaugas Ritter und Alpha und Jucunde. 1813; 'Aslaugas Ritter' translated as 'Aslauga's Knight', in *German Romance: Specimens of Its Chief Authors*, by Thomas Carlyle, 1827.
Neue Erzählungen. 1814.
Kleine Romane und Erzählungen. 6 vols., 1814–19.
Die Fahrten Thiodolfs des Isländers. 1815; as *Thiodolf, the Icelander*, 1845.
Sängerliebe: Eine provenzalische Sage in drei Büchern. 1816; as *Minstrel-Love*, translated by George Soane, 1821.
Reidmar und Diona. 1816.
Kindermärchen, with Karl Wilhelm Contessa and E.T.A. Hoffmann. 1817.
Die wunderbaren Begebenheiten des Grafen Alethes von Lindenstein. 1817.
Blumenstrauss: Gewunden aus den neusten Romanen und Erzählungen (stories), with Caroline de la Motte Fouqué. 1818.
Altsächsischer Bildersaal (stories). 1818–20.
Der Verfolgte. 1821.
Ritter Elidouc: Eine altbretannische Sage. 1822; as *Sir Elidoc: An Old Breton Legend*, 1849.
Wilde Liebe. 1823; as *Wild Love and Other Tales*, 1844.
Der Refugié; oder, Heimath und Fremde. 1824.
Sophie Ariele. 1825.
Die Saga von dem Gunlaugur, genannt Drachenzunge und Rafn dem Skalden: Eine Islandskunde des elften Jahrhunderts. 1826.
Erdmann und Fiammetta. 1826.

Mandragora. 1827.
Fata Morgana. 1836.
Der Geheimrath (stories). 1838.
Ausgewählte Werke. Ausgabe letzter Hand. 12 vols., 1841.
Abfall und Busse; oder, Die Seelenspiegel. 1844.
Joseph und seine Geige: Kaiser Karls V. Angriff auf Algier (stories). 1845.

Plays

Dramatische Spiele, edited by A.W. Schlegel. 1804.
Zwei Schauspiele. 1805.
Die Zwerge. 1805.
Historie vom edlen Ritter Glamy und einer schönen Herzogin aus Bretagne. 1806.
Der Held des Nordens (includes *Sigurd der Schlangentödter*; *Sigurds Rache*; *Aslauga*). 1810.
Eginhard und Emma. 1811.
Vaterländische Schauspiele. 1811.
Alboin der Langobardenkönig. 1813.
Dramatische Dichtungen für Deutsche. 1813.
Die Pilgerfahrt, edited by Franz Horn. 1816.
Arien und Gesänge der Zauber-Oper gennant: Undine, music by E.T.A. Hoffmann. 1816.
Liebesrache. 1817.
Die zwei Brüder. 1817.
Heldenspiel. 1818.
Herrmann. 1818.
Hieronymous von Stauf. 1819.
Der Leibeigene. 1820.
Don Carlos, Infant von Spanien. 1823.
Der Sängerkrieg auf der Wartburg. 1828.
Mortiz Gottlieb Saphir und Berlin, with Willibald Alexis. 1828.
Der Jarl der Orkney-Inseln. 1829.
Der Pappenheimer Kürassier: Scenen aus der Zeit des dreissigjährigen Krieges. 1842.
Violiante. 1845.

Verse

Romanzen vom Thale Ronceval. 1805.
Gedichte vor und während dem Kriege 1813. 1813.
Corona: Ein Rittergedicht in drei Büchern. 1814.
Jahrbüchlein Deutscher Gedichte auf 1815, with others. 1815.
Tassilo: Vorspiel, music by E.T.A. Hoffmann. 1815.
Karls des Grossen Geburt und Jugendjahre: Ein Ritterlied, edited by Franz Horn. 1816.
Gedichte. 5 vols., 1816–27.
Jäger und Jägerlieder. 1818.
Romantische Dichtungen, with others. 1818.
Bertrand du Guesclin. 1821.
Feierlieder eines Preussen im Herbste 1823. 1823.
Geistliche Lieder: Erstes Bändchen. Missions-Lieder. 1823.
Erhörung: Sechs Psalme. 1827.
Christlicher Leiderschatz zur Erbauung von Jung und Alt, edited by Albertine de la Motte Fouqué. 1862.

Other

Gespräch zweier Preussischen. Edelleute über dem Odel. 1808.
Uber den sogenannten falschen Waldemar. 1811.
An Christian Grafen zu Stolberg (letter). 1815.
Auch ein Wort über die neueste Zeit: Nebst einigen Beilagen (essay). 1815.

Abendunterhaltungen zu gemüthlicher Erheiterung des Geistes, with others. 1817.
Der Mord Augusts von Kotzebue: Freundes Ruf an Deutschlands Jugend. 1819.
Etwas über den deutschen Adel, über Rittersinn und Militärehre in Briefen (essays), with Friedrich Perthes. 1819.
Gefühle, Bilder und Ansichten: Sammlung kleiner prosaischer Schriften. 1819.
Wahrheit und Lüge (essays). 1820.
Betrachtungen über Türken, Griechen und Türkenkrieg (essays). 1822.
Reise Erinnerungen, with Caroline de la Motte Fouqué. 1823.
Die Fahrt in die neue Welt with *Das Grab der Mutter*, by Alexis dem Wanderer. 1824.
Lebensbeschreibung des königlich preussischen Generals der Infanterie Heinrich August Baron de la Motte Fouqué: Verfasst von Seinem Enkel (biography). 1824.
Geschichte der Jungfrau von Orleans, nach authentischen Urkundern und dem französischen Werke des Herrn Le Brun de Charmettes. 2 vols., 1826.
Ernst Friedrich Wilhelm Philipp von Rüchel, Königlich Preussischer General Infanterie (biography). 1828.
Der Mensch des Südens und der Mensch des Nordens: Sendschreiben in Bezug auf das gleichnamige Werk des Herrn von Bonstettin an den Freiherrn Alexander von Humboldt. 1829.
Jakob Böhme (biography). 1831.
Sendschreiben an den Verfasser der Betrachtungen über die neuesten Begebenheiten in Deutschland (essay). 1831.
Von der Liebes-Lehre (essay). 1837.
Goethe und einer seiner Bewunderer: Ein Stück Lebensgeschichte (essay). 1840.
Lebengeschichte (autobiography). 1840.
Preussische Trauersprüche und Huldigungsgrüsse für das Jahr 1840. 1840.
Ausgewählte Werke: Ausgabe letzer Hand. 12 vols., 1841–73.
Denkschrift über Friedrich Wilhelm III, König von Preussen: Eine biographische Mittheilung. 1842.
Novellen-Mappe, with others. 1843.
Briefe an Friedrich Baron de la Motte Fouqué von Chamisso, Cherzy, Collin, u.a., edited by Albertine de la Motte Fouqué. 1848.

Editor, with Wilhelm Neumann, *Die Musen: Eine norddeutsche Zeitschrift*. 3 vols., 1812–14.
Editor, *Peter Schlemihl's wundersame Geschichte*, by Adelbert von Chamisso. 1814.
Editor, *Thomas Aniella*, by August Fresenius. 3 vols., 1817.
Editor, *Hinterlassene Schriften: Erster Band*, by August Fresenius. 1818.
Editor, with Friedrich Laun, *Aus der Geisterwelt: Geschichten, Sagen und Dichtungen*. 2 vols., 1818.
Editor, with L. von Alvensleben, *Zeitung für den deutschen Adel*. 3 vols., 1840–42.

Translator, *Numancia*, by Cervantes. 1810.
Translator, *Lalla Rukh; oder, Die mongolische Prinzessin*, by Thomas Moore. 1822.
Translator, *Pique-Dame: Berichte aus dem Irrenhause, in Briefen. Nach dem Schwedischen*. 1825.
Translator, with others, *Der fünfte May: Ode auf Napoleons Tod*, by Alessandro Manzoni. 1828.
Translator, *Drei Erzählungen: Aus dem Dänischen*, by Bernhard Severin Ingemann. 1837.
Translator, *Bilderbuch ohne Bilder: Aus dem Dänischen*. 1842.

* * *

Friedrich Baron de la Motte Fouqué was one of the most prolific and widely-read writers of his time, as well as being one of the first members of the German Romantic movement to be translated into English. He experimented with a wide variety of literary forms, including verse dramas, novels, stories, fairy-tales, and lyric poetry, and he was also influential as an editor of literary periodicals, encouraging a number of younger writers. Today, however, with the exception of *Undine*, the tale of the water nymph who gains a human soul, his work has fallen into almost total popular and critical neglect and in most surveys of the period is either overlooked completely or else dismissed as trivial. Although such a fall from grace was to a large extent prefigured towards the end of his own life, conjecture as to the reasons for it have not always been well-informed, and a critical re-evaluation of his work is long overdue.

One of the most striking features of Fouqué's dramatic and narrative *oeuvre* is his use of various mythological sources. These he manipulates to form a pseudo-medieval fairy-tale world, which serves as a physical and symbolic setting for the exploits of his heroic protagonists. This can be seen as early as 1810 in his dramatic trilogy *Der Held des Nordens* [The Hero of the North]. Fouqué draws not only on Germanic legend, but also, for example, on Norse mythology and the writings of the 16th-century physician and alchemist Paracelsus, as well as adding inventions of his own. The result is an apparently chaotic and deliberately artificial network of real and supernatural elements, covering a geographical area from Scandinavia in the north to Normandy in the west and Italy and Spain in the south. Central to this network are the motifs of the forest and the valley, which symbolize chaos and confusion and which typically provide the scene for the crucial testing of the hero in his physical and spiritual quest. The titular hero of the story *Sintram und seine Gefährten* (*Sintram and His Companions*), to take one example, must undertake a solitary horseback ride through the Valley of Death before he can achieve the ultimate status of the true Christian knight.

Fouqué's heroes in fact present something of a problem to the modern reader. They seem idealized, one-dimensional figures, most of them almost indistinguishable from each other, and Joseph von Eichendorff was not the only contemporary of Fouqué to claim that they represented a somewhat naive projection of the author's own self-image. What is interesting, however, about Fouqué's heroes is that nearly all of them are characterized by a dichotomy between the terrestrial and the spiritual, as represented in the figures of the knight and the poet. The novels in particular tend accordingly to follow a pattern of alternation between narrative sections, in which the protagonist's heroic deeds and supernatural encounters are described, and more lyrical passages, often featuring interpolated verse, in which the hero, in repose, discovers a wider, more spiritual perspective for his exploits. The ideal of Christian knighthood to which Fouqué's heroes aspire is presented as a conflict, which can only be resolved if the hero succeeds in overcoming the series of barriers which strew his path.

The charges most frequently levelled at Fouqué are that his reliance on mythological and supernatural elements represents a form of literary escapism, a retreat from social and political realities at a time when Europe was struggling to come to terms with the upheavals of the Napoleonic Wars, and that his persistence with allegedly trivial forms, such as the *Ritterroman* (the novel with the knight as hero) led to staleness and repetition. What such judgements largely ignore is the artificiality with which the mythological/supernatural network is constructed and the degree of manipulation with which Fouqué exploits popular forms, especially in his prose fiction. The narrative framework of much of Fouqué's best work is consciously stylized, and the reader is quite deliberately distanced from events by a fragmentary form of narration and an often quite dazzling array of perspectives: in the novel *Alwin*, for example, events from the hero's past are presented in the form of an overheard dream narrative: in *Sintram* the crucial links between the various episodes are withheld from the reader by means of a complicated framework of inner narratives and tableaux; and the narrators of most of the novels are not only omniscient but also highly visible figures, whose rare but crucial interjections exist on a temporal plane clearly separate from the plots.

The distance created between reader and text by such devices is the key to an understanding of Fouqué's work and its purpose. The chaos which reigns in the forest and the valley does not in fact reflect a retreat from reality: rather it acts as a mirror of the social and political unrest prevailing in early 19th-century Europe, and Fouqué's narrator steps back from such confusion not as a means of escape, but in an attempt to make sense of it from a clearer perspective. Fouqué is in fact revealed as a highly moral and didactic writer, and his appeal to a wide public deserves to be seen in this context. His basic response to the political upheaval of the Napoleonic Wars was an appeal to national pride and a firm conviction that Christianity alone could restore unity to Europe. Nowhere is this belief more clearly illustrated than in the final tableau of the novel *Der Zauberring* (*The Magic Ring*), where the heathen symbol of the ring itself is shattered and replaced by an idealized picture of family unity and Christian harmony. The ideal of Christian knighthood at the centre of Fouqué's philosophy may hark back to a bygone era, the *goldene Zeit* (golden age) beloved of so many German Romantics, but for Fouqué it had a definite contemporary relevance.

Friedrich Baron de la Motte Fouqué deserves to be remembered as more than merely a trivial figure in the German Romantic movement, who happened to achieve mass popularity through his vast output of work. Closer examination reveals not only a master of narrative, but also an author with a serious didactic purpose, much more responsive to the spirit of his times than is generally supposed.

—Howard Atkinson

FOURNIER, Henri Alban. See **ALAIN-FOURNIER**.

FRANCE, Anatole. Born Jacques-Anatole-François Thibault in Paris, France, 16 April 1844. Educated at the Collège Stanislas. Married 1) Marie-Valérie Guérin de Sauville in 1877 (divorced 1893), one daughter; 2) Emma Laprevotte in 1920. Assistant at his father's bookshop,

Librairie de France, Paris, 1860s; editorial assistant, Bachelin-Deflorenne, publishers, Paris, mid-1860s; schoolteacher, Ivry-sur-Seine, 1869; reader and editor, Lemerre, publishers, 1869–75; librarian, Senate library, Paris, 1876–90; regular contributor to *Le Globe* and *L'Univers illustré*; literary editor, *Le Temps*, 1888; associated with Mme Armand de Caillavet. Member, Académie française, 1897. Recipient: Académie française award, 1881; Nobel prize for literature, 1921. Chevalier, Légion d'honneur, 1884. Honorary degree: University of Athens, 1919. *Died 12 October 1924.*

PUBLICATIONS

Collections

Complete Works, edited by Frederic Chapman. 21 vols., 1908–28.
Oeuvres complètes, edited by Léon Carias and Gérard Le Prat. 26 vols., 1925–37.
Oeuvres complètes. 1968–70.
Works. 40 vols., 1975.
Oeuvres, edited by Marie-Claire Bancquart. 2 vols., 1984–87.

Fiction

Jocaste et le chat maigre. 1879; as *Jocasta and the Famished Cat*, translated by Agnes Farley, 1912.
Le Stratagème. 1880.
Le Crime de Sylvestre Bonnard, membre de l'Institut. 1881; revised edition, 1902; edited by R.L. Graeme Ritchie, 1927; as *The Crime of Sylvestre Bonnard, Member of the Institute*, translated by Lafcadio Hearn, 1890; also translated by Arabella Ward, 1897.
Les Désirs de Jean Servien. 1882; as *The Aspirations of Jean Servien*, translated by Alfred Allinson, 1912.
Abeille: Contes (stories). 1883; as *Honey-Bee*, translated by Mrs John Lane, 1911; as *Bee: The Princess of the Dwarves*, translated by Peter Wright, 1912.
Le Livre de mon ami. 1885; edited by J. Heywood Thomas, 1942; as *My Friend's Book*, translated by J. Lewis May, 1913; also translated by Rosalie Feltenstein, 1950.
Nos Enfants: Scènes de la ville et des champs (stories). 1887; in 2 vols., 1900; as *Child Life in Town and Country*, translated by Alfred Allinson, with *The Merrie Tales of Jacques Tournebroche*, 1910; as *Girls and Boys: Scenes from the Country and the Town*, 2 vols., 1913, and as *Our Children: Scenes from the Country and the Town*, 2 vols., 1917, both translated by Allinson; as *In All France: Children in Town and Country*, translated by A.G. Wippern, 1930.
Balthasar (stories, includes *Abeille*). 1889; as *Balthasar*, translated by Mrs John Lane, 1909.
Thaïs. 1890; revised edition, 1928; as *Thaïs; or, The Vengeance of Venus*, translated by Ernest DeLancey Pierson, 1892; as *Thaïs*, translated by A.D. Hall, 1891; also translated by Ernest Tristan, 1902; as *Thaïs or The Monk's Temptation*, translated by Robert B. Douglas, 1909; also translated by Basia Gulati, 1976.
L'Étui de nacre (stories). 1892; as *Tales from a Mother-of-Pearl Casket*, translated by Henri Pène du Bois, 1896; as *Mother of Pearl*, translated by Frederic Chapman, 1908.
La Rôtisserie de la Reine Pédauque. 1893; as *The Queen Pédauque*, translated by Joseph A. V. Stritzko, 1910; as *At the Sign of the Reine Pédauque*, translated by Mrs Wilfrid Jackson, 1912; as *At the Sign of the Queen Pédauque*, 1933;

as *The Romance of the Queen Pedauque*, translated by Jackson, 1950.
Le Lys rouge. 1894; as *The Red Lily*, translated by Winifred Stevens, 1908.
Le Puits de sainte Claire. 1895, as *The Well of Saint Claire*, translated by Alfred Allinson, 1909.
Histoire contemporaine. 4 vols., 1897–1901.
   L'Orme du mail. 1897; as *The Elm-Tree on the Mall: A Chronicle of Our Own Times*, translated by M.P. Willcocks, 1910.
   Le Mannequin d'osier. 1897; as *The Wicker-Work Woman: A Chronicle of Our Own Times*, translated by M.P. Willcocks, 1910.
   L'Anneau d'améthyste. 1899; as *The Amethyst Ring*, translated by B. Drillien, 1919.
   Monsieur Bergeret à Paris. 1901; as *Monsieur Bergeret in Paris*, translated by B. Drillien, 1921.
La Leçon bien apprise. 1898.
Pierre Nozière. 1899; as *Pierre Nozière*, translated by J. Lewis May, 1916.
Clio. 1900; as *Clio*, translated by Winifred Stephens, 1922.
L'Affaire Crainquebille. 1901; revised edition as *Crainquebille, Putois, Riquet, et plusieurs autres récits profitables*, 1904; as *Crainquebille, Putois, Riquet, and Other Profitable Tales*, translated by Winifred Stephens, 1915; as *Crainquebille*, translated by Jacques Le Clerq, 1949.
Histoire de Dona Maria d'Avala et de Don Fabricio, duc d'Andria. 1902.
Mémoires d'un volontaire (selection). 1902.
Histoire Comique. 1903; as *A Mummer's Tale*, translated by Charles E. Roche, 1921.
Sur la pierre blanche. 1903; as *The White Stone*, translated by Charles E. Roche, 1910.
Les Contes de Jacques Tournebroche. 1908; as *The Merry Tales of Jacques Tournebroche*, translated by Alfred Allinson, 1910.
L'Île des pingouins. 1908; as *Penguin Island*, translated by A.W. Evans, 1909; also translated by Belle Notkin Burke, 1968.
Les Sept Femmes de la Barbe-Bleue et autres contes merveilleux. 1909; as *The Seven Wives of Bluebeard and Other Marvellous Tales*, translated by D.B. Stewart, 1920.
Les Dieux ont soif. 1912; as *The Gods Are Athirst*, translated by Alfred Allinson, 1913; also translated by Mrs Wilfrid Jackson, 1925; Alec Brown, 1951; Linda Frey, Marsh Frey, and Roman Zylawy, 1978; as *The Gods Will Have Blood*, translated by Frederick Davies, 1979.
Les Anges. 1913; revised edition as *La Révolte des anges*, 1914; as *The Revolt of the Angels*, translated by Mrs Wilfrid Jackson, 1914.
Amycus et Célestin. 1916.
Le Petit Pierre. 1918; edited by Isabelle H. Clarke, 1925; as *Little Pierre*, translated by J. Lewis May, 1920.
Marguerite. 1920; as *Marguerite*, translated by J. Lewis May, 1921; with *Alfred de Vigny* and *The Path of Glory*, 1927.
Le Comte Morin, député. 1921; as *Count Morin, Deputy*, translated by J. Lewis May, 1921; with *Alfred de Vigny* and *The Path of Glory*, 1927.
La Vie en fleur. 1922; as *The Bloom of Life*, translated by J. Lewis May, 1923.
Contes, edited by C.J.M. Adie and P.C.H. de Satgé. 1923.
Little Sea Dogs (selection), translated by Alfred Allinson and J. Lewis May. 1925.
Les Autels de la peur. 1926.
Golden Tales, translated anonymously. 1926.
Le Jongleur de Notre-Dame and Other Stories, translated by Margaret Weale. 1948.

Verse

Les Poèmes dorés. 1873.
Les Noces corinthiennes. 1876; as The Bride of Corinth and
    Other Poems and Plays, translated by Wilfrid and Emilie
    Jackson, 1920.
Poésies. 1896.
Les Poèmes du souvenir. 1910.

Plays

Au Petit bonheur (produced 1898). 1898.
Le Lys rouge, with Gaston de Caillavet, from his own novel
    (produced 1899). In Oeuvres complètes, 1970.
Les Noces corinthiennes (produced 1902). 1876.
Crainquebille, from his own story (produced 1903). 1913; as
    Crainquebille, translated by Barrett H. Clark, 1915; also
    translated by Jacques Le Clerq, 1949.
Le Mannequin d'osier, from his own novel (produced 1904).
    1928.
La Comédie de celui qui épousa une femme muette (produced
    1912). 1913; as The Man Who Married a Dumb Wife,
    translated by Curtis Hidden Page, 1915.

Other

Alfred de Vigny. 1868; revised edition, 1923.
Le Livre du bibliophile. 1874.
Les Poèmes de Jules Breton. 1875.
La Vie littéraire. 4 vols., 1888–92; as On Life and Letters,
    translated by A.W. Evans, D.B. Stewart, and Bernard
    Miall, 4 vols., 1911–14.
L'Elvire de Lamartine: Notes sur M. et Mme Charles. 1893.
Les Opinions de M. Jérôme Coignard. 1893; as The Opinions
    of Jérôme Coignard, translated by Mrs Wilfrid Jackson,
    1913.
La Société historique d'Auteuil et de Passy. 1894.
Le Jardin d'Épicure. 1895; as The Garden of Epicurus, trans-
    lated by Alfred Allinson, 1908.
La Liberté par l'étude. 1902.
Madame de Luzy. 1902.
Opinions sociales. 2 vols., 1902.
L'Église et la république. 1904.
Vers les temps meilleurs. 3 vols., 1906; as Vers les temps
    meilleurs: Trente ans de vie sociale, edited by Claude
    Aveline and Henriette Psichar, 3 vols., 1949–67; as The
    Unrisen Dawn: Speeches and Addresses, 1928.
Vie de Jeanne d'Arc. 2 vols., 1908; as The Life of Joan of Arc,
    translated by Winifred Stephens, 1909.
Le Génie latin (criticism). 1909; revised edition, 1917; as The
    Latin Genius, translated by Wilfrid Jackson, 1924.
Aux étudiants (lecture). 1910.
La Comédie de celui qui épousa une femme muette. 1912.
Sur la voie glorieuse. 1916; as The Path of Glory, translated
    by Alfred Allinson, 1916.
Ce que disent nos morts. 1916.
La Vie en fleur. 1922.
Epigrams of Love, Life and Laughter, edited and translated
    by Sylvestre Dorian. 1924.
Dernières pages inédites. 1925.
Promenades félibréennes. 1925.
Under the Rose (essays), translated by J. Lewis May. 1926.
Prefaces, Introductions, and Other Uncollected Papers, trans-
    lated by J. Lewis May. 1927.
Les Dieux asiatiques aux premiers siècles de l'ère chrétienne.
    1928.
Rabelais, translated by Ernest Boyd. 1929.

Le Secret du 'Lys rouge': Anatole France et Madame de
    Caillavet: lettres intimes (1888–1889), edited by Jacques
    Suffel. 1984.

Editor, Oeuvres de Jean Racine. 5 vols., 1874–75.
Editor, Lucile de Chateaubriand. 1889.
Editor, Les Poèmes du souvenir. 1910.

*

Critical Studies: Anatole France: The Degeneration of a Great
Artist by Barry Cerf, 1927; Anatole France Abroad by Jean J.
Brousson, translated by John Pollock, 1928; Anatole France
and His Time: The Ironic Temper by Haakon Chevalier,
1932; Anatole France: A Life Without Illusions 1844–1924 by
Jacob Axelrad, 1944; Anatole France and the Greek World by
Loring B. Walton, 1950; Seven Against the Night by Paul
Eldridge, 1960; Anatole France polémiste, 1962, and Anatole
France: Un sceptique passionné, 1984, both by Marie-Claire
Bancquart; Anatole France: The Politics of Skepticism by
Carter Jefferson, 1965; Anatole France by David Tylden-
Wright, 1967; Anatole France by Reino Virtanen, 1968; The
Art of Anatole France by Duskan Bresky, 1969; Anatole
France: The Short Stories by Murray Sachs, 1974; The Saint
and the Skeptics by William Searle, 1976; 'Techniques of
Irony in Anatole France: Essays on 'Les Sept femmes de la
Barbe-Bleue' by Diane Wolfe Levy in North Carolina Studies
in the Romance Languages and Literatures, 201, 1978.

* * *

Urbane, erudite and eminently civilized, Anatole France
was generally considered at the turn of this century to be the
foremost contemporary French novelist and man of letters.
To an extent seldom found in the career of any other writer,
he also represented the literary and philosophical values of a
previous age.

His first full-length novel, Le Crime de Sylvestre Bonnard
(The Crime of Sylvestre Bonnard) is an early example of
fiction in diary form. Its hero, an elderly and artless scholar,
kind-hearted and sceptical in outlook, abducts the orphaned
granddaughter of the woman he had once loved from the
drudgery of a menial job at her old boarding-school; he sells
his beloved books to provide her with a dowry. The same
theme of self-sacrifice, more convincingly presented in exotic
lands and remote historical times, is central to both the short
story 'Balthasar' and the novel Thaïs. The former tells how
Balthazar, one of the Magi, overcomes lust in order to follow
the star of Bethlehem, whilst one of the other kings overcomes cruelty and the third masters his pride. Thaïs, set in
4th-century Egypt, is perhaps the most skilful of all of
France's narrations. Its eponymous heroine is an Alexandrian
courtesan converted to Christianity by the hermit Paphnuce,
her former lover. The theme of renunciation is twofold;
Paphnuce's in the first instance, though Thaïs's self-
abnegation is more complete. More importantly, however,
France seems to suggest that the life to which Paphnuce tries
to win Thaïs back is not the work of the devil: it is a life of
love and vitality which, whether God-inspired or not, is the
diametrical opposite of asceticism.

The collection L'Étui de nacre (Mother of Pearl) contains
two important stories, 'Le Procurateur de Judée' and 'Le
Jongleur de Notre-Dame'. In the first of these Pontius Pilate
recalls his time as ruler of Judaea. His friend Lamia happens
to mention one Jesus of Nazareth, 'a young wonder-worker

from Galilee' who was crucified for some crime or other, Pilate cannot remember him! In the second the juggler Barnabé is converted to the monastic life. He is about to be expelled from the monastery chapel where he has been secretly performing a juggling act as his particular tribute to Our Lady when she descends the altar steps, pronouncing the sixth beatitude: 'Blessed are the pure in heart'.

In 'Balthasar', Thaïs, 'Le Procurateur de Judée' and 'Le Jongleur de Notre-Dame' the influence of Flaubert's Tentation de saint Antoine (The Temptation of Saint Anthony) and Trois Contes (Three Tales) upon France is unmistakable. France chooses themes of the Nativity, Pontius Pilate and the monastic life, treating self-abnegation with that enigmatic detachment shown by Flaubert in 'Un coeur simple' ('A Simple Heart'). But the historical relativism of 'Le Procurateur de Judée', stupendous as it is at the narrative level, smacks a little of artifice.

La Rôtisserie de la Reine Pédauque (The Queen Pedauque) reveals France's fascination with the 18th century. Jérôme Coignard, a priest with a philosophe's outlook, is deeply respectful of religion despite his voluptuousness and moral laxity. Tournebrouche, the narrative voice in this novel, is the landlord's son at the inn regularly visited by Coignard; he becomes the Abbé's loyal pupil, even to the extent of helping him and a raffish nobleman in an abduction which results in Coignard's murder. With his unusual sceptical irony France mocks belief in the occult. Through the medium of Les Opinions de M. Jérôme Coignard (The Opinions of M. Jérôme Coignard), a compilation of the Abbé's thoughts produced by Tournebrouche, France also expresses sharp criticism of contemporary society.

In the Histoire contemporaine series, the hero, Lucien Bergeret, is a further embodiment of the scholar, sceptic, epicurean humanist, and keen but detached observer of daily life which France himself was. At the heart of his four-volume cycle is the Dreyfus affair; also evident is the author's growing anti-clericalism. In the third volume, L'Anneau d'améthyste (The Amethyst Ring), ecclesiastical rivalries are prominent; also portrayed are the intrigues of a provincial town. Differing greatly from Balzac, France treats the latter theme with gentle good humour.

The eponymous hero of the short novel L'Affaire Crainquebille (Crainquebille) is an elderly street-trader imprisoned after conviction on a false charge of shouting abuse at the police. Unable to make a living after his release from gaol, he decides he would be better off behind bars again and so, on seeing another policeman, he actually does shout abuse. But he is simply moved on. Nothing illustrates better the even-handedness of France's outlook than Crainquebille, which recognizes that there is kindliness, and hence durability, in existing institutions.

Nevertheless, in consequence of the Dreyfus affair, France became increasingly committed to social change from 1900 onwards. Further scope for incisive satire was afforded by L'île des pingouins (Penguin Island) (which again dealt with the Dreyfus affair), Les Dieux ont soif (The Gods Are Athirst), and Les Anges (The Revolt of the Angels). In the second of these France returns to the 18th century, providing a broad picture of varying Revolutionary attitudes. None of these novels, however, shows much belief in that cornerstone of 18th-century thinking, the inevitability—or even the likelihood!—of social progress.

The many review notices which make up La Vie littéraire (On Life and Letters) reveal a subjective critic whose role models in this genre were Taine and Sainte-Beuve: he admired their immense erudition. But although Taine prized objectivity above all things, France's philosophical relativism

would not allow him to believe in the absoluteness of any judgement. For the same reason he rejected Zola's view that Naturalism was the summation of literary art.

France has too often been denigrated for the episodic nature of his plots and for his lack of imaginative power. Though he was the author of one ill-researched work—Vie de Jeanne d'Arc (The Life of Joan of Arc), extreme in its anti-clericalism—his writings are remarkable for their depth of understanding and for their linguistic and philosophical clarity reminiscent of Voltaire. His qualities of euphony, wit, well-balanced scepticism, and the whimsical fantasy and discursiveness seen at their best in The Queen Pedauque were sustained at a level of near-perfection throughout his literary life.

—Donald Adamson

THE GODS ARE ATHIRST (Les Dieux ont soif)
Novel by Anatole France, 1912.

The title The Gods Are Athirst was taken from the last number of the seventh and last issue of Camille Desmoulins's newspaper, Le Vieux Cordelier, whose motto, 'Vivre libre ou mourir' [Live free or die] was an appeal for moderation launched at the height of the Terror, in December 1793. Desmoulins was arrested as he was correcting the proofs of the last issue and executed on 30 March 1794, on the order of his former classmate, Maximilien de Robespierre. The novel expresses France's own horror of the revolutionary violence which led some 2,600 people to be guillotined for supposed political crimes in Paris alone between 5 September 1793 and 27 July 1794. Its principal character, a rather mediocre painter called Évariste Gamelin, becomes an ardent supporter of Robespierre, having previously shown equal enthusiasm for other revolutionary leaders such as Mirabeau, Pétion, and Brissot before they had been revealed as traitors to the cause they were pretending to serve. In emphasizing the tendency of the French revolution to devour its children even more unmercifully than its enemies, The Gods Are Athirst anticipates the criticism of all revolutions, which was to become more acute after the Moscow purges of 1936–38 showed Stalin as an even more remorseless fanatic than Robespierre. Gamelin's enthusiasm for the revolution leads him to send to the guillotine not only an aristocrat, whom he wrongly suspects of having seduced his mistress, Élodie, but also his sister Julie's aristocratic lover, Fortuné de Chassagne. Like Robespierre, Gamelin is also a prig in sexual matters. It is only after he is, literally on one occasion, stained with the blood of his victims that he and Élodie begin to enjoy sex. When Robespierre is overthrown on 27 July 1794 (10 Thermidor, An II in the revolutionary calendar introduced on 21 September 1792), Évariste tries to commit suicide. He fails and is guillotined, after Robespierre himself, in the Thermidorian reaction.

The Gods Are Athirst is not a book by an erstwhile progressive who has made the great betrayal. Although France was one of the early socialists and a leading figure in the struggle to ensure a fair trial for Captain Alfred Dreyfus, a French officer sentenced to life-imprisonment on Devil's Island for supposedly selling military secrets to the Germans, but innocent of any charge other than those brought against him by an organized campaign of anti-semitism, he had never been a supporter of any kind of political extremism. His attack on the cult of Robespierre stemmed from a characteristically 19th-century appreciation of reason, justice, and humanitarianism. It went hand in hand with an equally typical French anti-clericalism, which tended to present Robespierre's intolerance as the mirror image of the intolerance of the Catholic Church and all the more dangerous for that. In *The Gods Are Athirst*, the spokesman for France's own agonisticism is an elderly former nobleman, Maurice des Ilettes, now known as *le citoyen Brotteaux*, who carries in his pocket a well-thumbed copy of Lucretius' *De rerum natura*, (*On the Nature of Things*). Its doctrine of universal mortality, like its cult of physical pleasure and private friendship, provides for him and for the reader a preferable alternative to the puritanism and adulation of civic virtue that characterize the revolutionary attitude. France was, like his spokesman, a sceptical Epicurean. He pointed out, as other conservatively-minded thinkers were to do in the 20th century, how harmless the pursuit of sexual pleasure was compared to the havoc and bloodshed produced by puritanical revolutionary enthusiasm.

The Gods Are Athirst is not a novel in which one wonders what is going to happen next. From the opening page, it is inevitable that all the main characters are going to die. Its interest is political and its place in literary history a stepping stone between Dickens's attack on the French revolution in *A Tale of Two Cities* and 20th-century novels, such as Arthur Koestler's *Darkness at Noon* or George Orwell's *Nineteen Eighty-Four*. Just as these novels, like Orwell's *Animal Farm*, depict what went wrong in Russia after the Bolshevik revolution of 1917, so *The Gods Are Athirst* offers an analysis of why the ideals of 1789 lead to the Terror of 1793–94. The answer, suggests France, is not in the remorseless ferocity of the Gods evoked by the title. He was no more a believer in pagan divinities than in the God of Christianity. Revolutions go wrong, he suggests, because human beings invent ideas to which they attribute a truth so absolute that it justifies the destruction of everything and everybody that seem opposed to it. Together with *Penguin Island*, a satirical account of French history and especially of the Dreyfus case, *The Gods Are Athirst* is France's most popular novel and has never been out of print.

—Philip Thody

FREYRE, Gilberto (de Melo). Born in Recife, Pernambuco, Brazil, 15 March 1900. Educated at American Colégio Gilreath, Recife, to 1917; Baylor University, Waco, Texas, 1918–21, BA 1921; Columbia University, New York, 1921–22, MA in anthropology 1922. Married Maria Magdalena Guedes Pereira in 1941; one daughter and one son. Travelled in Europe, 1922–23, and returned to Brazil, 1923; co-organizer, Regionalist Artistic Movement's Congress, Recife, 1926; private secretary to the Governor of Pernambuco, Recife, 1927–30; editor, *A Província*, Recife, 1928–30; assistant professor of sociology, Escola Normal, Recife, 1928; went into exile to Portugal, 1930; travelled to Africa, 1930; visiting professor, Stanford University, California, 1931; professor of sociology, Faculty of Law, Recife, 1935, and appointed to the chair of sociology and social anthropology, Federal University, 1935; visiting professor, Columbia University, New York, 1938; representative for Pernambuco, National Assembly, 1946, and in the House of Deputies, 1947–50; Brazilian Ambassador to the United Nations General Assembly, 1949; visiting professor, Indiana University,

Bloomington, USA, 1966. Founder, Joaquim Nabuco Institute, Recife, 1949. Member, American Philosophical Association (USA); member, Council for the Philosophy of Law and Sociology, Paris. Recipient: Felippe d'Oliveira award, 1934; Anisfield-Wolf award, 1957; Machado de Assis prize, 1963; Aspen award, 1967; La Madonnina International literary prize (Italy), 1969; José Vasconcelos gold medal (Mexico), 1974; Moinho Santista prize, 1974. Honorary doctorates: Columbia University, 1954; University of Coimbra, 1962; University of Paris, 1965; University of Sussex, Falmer, 1965; University of Münster, 1965. Member, São Paulo Academy of Letters, 1961, and Brazilian Academy of Letters, 1962; member, Royal Anthropological Institute; member, American Academy of Arts and Sciences. KBE (Knight Commander, Order of the British Empire), 1971; Commander, Légion d'honneur, 1986. *Died 18 July 1987.*

PUBLICATIONS

Fiction

Dona Sinhá e o filho padre. 1964; as *Mother and Son*, translated by Barbara Shelby, 1967.
O outro amor do Dr Paulo. 1977.

Verse

Bahia de todos os santos e todos os pecados. 1926.
Talvez poesia. 1962.
Gilberto poeta: algumas confissões. 1980.
Poesia reunida. 1980.

Other

Casa-grande & Senzala. 1933; revised edition, 2 vols., 1943; as *The Masters and the Slaves: A Study in the Development of Brazilian Civilization*, translated by Samuel Putnam, 1946; revised edition, 1964.
Guia prático, histórico, e sentimental de cidade do Recife. 1934; revised edition, 1968.
Artigos de jornal. 1935.
Sobrados e mucambos. 1936; revised edition, 1961; as *The Mansions and the Shanties: The Making of Modern Brazil*, translated by Harriet de Onís, 1963.
Mucambos de Nordeste. 1937.
Nordeste. 1937; revised edition, 1961.
Olinda: 2° guia prático, histórico, e sentimental de cidade Brasileira. 1939; revised edition, 1968.
Açúcar. 1939; enlarged edition, 1969.
Um engenheiro francês no Brasil. 1940; revised edition, 2 vols., 1960.
O mundo que o Português criou. 1940.
Região e tradição. 1941.
Uma cultura ameaçada. 1942.
Ingleses. 1942.
Problemas brasileiros de antropologia. 1943; revised edition, 1954.
Na Bahia em 1943. 1944.
Perfil de Euclides e outros perfís. 1944.
Sociologia. 2 vols., 1945; revised edition, 1962.
Brazil: An Introduction (written in English). 1945; revised edition, as *New World in the Tropics: The Culture of Modern Brazil*, 1959.
Ingleses no Brasil. 1948.
Quase política. 1950; revised edition, 1966.
Aventura e rotina. 1953.

Um brasileiro em terras portuguêsas. 1953.
Assombrações do Recife velho. 1955.
Manifesto regionalista 1926. 1955.
Sugestões para uma nova política no Brasil: a Rurbana. 1956.
Integração portuguesa nos trópicos. 1958; as *Portuguese Integration in the Tropics*, translated anonymously, 1961.
A propósito de frades. 1959.
A propósito de Morão, Rosa, e Pimenta. 1959.
Ordem e progresso. 2 vols., 1959; as *Order and Progress: Brazil from Monarchy to Republic*, edited and translated by Rod W. Horton, 1970.
Obras reunidas. 12 vols, 1959–66.
Brasis, Brasil, e Brasília. 1960; revised edition, 1968.
O Luso e o trópico. 1961; as *The Portuguese and the Tropics*, translated by Helen M. d'O. Matthew and F. de Mello Moser, 1961.
Vida, forma, e côr. 1962.
Homen, cultura, e trópico. 1962.
O escravo nos anúncios de jornais brasileiros do século XIX. 1963; revised and enlarged edition, 1979.
Retalhos de jornais velhos. 1964.
The Racial Factor in Contemporary Politics. 1966.
O Recife, sim! Recife, não!. 1967.
Sociologia da medicina. 1967.
Como e porque sou e não sou sociólogo. 1968.
Contribução para uma sociologia de biografia. 2 vols., 1968.
Oliveira Lima, Don Quixote gordo. 1968.
A casa brasileira. 1971.
Nós e a Europa germânica. 1971.
Seleta para jovens de Gilberto Freyre. 1971; as *The Gilberto Freyre Reader*, translated by Barbara Shelby, 1974.
A condição humana e outros temas, edited by Maria Elisa Dias Collier. 1972.
Além do apenas moderno. 1973.
A presença do açúcar na formação brasileira. 1975.
Tempo morto e outros tempos: trechos du um diário de adolescência e primeira mocidade 1915–1930. 1975.
O brasileiro entre os outros hispanos. 1975.
Alhos & bugalhos. 1978.
Cartas de próprio punho sobre pessoas e coisas do Brasil e do estrangeiro, edited by Sylvio Rabello. 1978.
Prefácios desgarrados, edited by Edson Nery da Fonseca. 2 vols., 1978.
Heróis e vilões no romance brasileiro, edited by Edson Nery da Fonseca. 1979.
Livro de Nordeste, with others. 1979.
Oh de casa!. 1979.
Tempo de aprendiz (articles 1918–26), edited by José Antônio Gonsalves de Mello. 1979.
Arte, ciencia, e trópico. 1980.
Pessoas, coisas e animais: ensaios. 1981.
Insurgências e ressurgências atuais: cruzamentos de sins e nãos num mundo em transição. 1983.
Médicos, doentes e contextos sociais. 1983.

Editor, *Coleção documentos brasileiros.* 161 vols., 1936–73.
Editor, *Desenvolvimento brasileiro & tropico.* 1985.

Translator, *Vida social no Brasil nos meados do século XIX*, by Waldemar Valente. 1977.

*

Bibliography: *Brazilian Literature: A Research Guide* by David William Foster and Walter Rela, 1990.

Critical Studies: *Gilberto Freyre* by Diogo de Melo Menezes, 1944; *Gilberto Freyre: sua ciencia, sua filosofia, sua arte* by various authors, 1962; 'Gilberto Freyre and José Honório Rodrigues: Old and New Horizons for Brazil' by Richard A. Mazzara, in *Hispania*, May 1964; 'Gilberto Freyre as a Literary Figure: An Introductory Study' by Dorothy S. Loos, in *Revista Hispánica Moderna*, 34, 1968.

*   *   *

Gilberto Freyre is the single most influential Brazilian intellectual of the 20th century. His extraordinary reputation is based largely upon his social history of colonial Brazil, *Casa-grande & Senzala* (*The Masters and the Slaves*), which Freyre wrote to accomplish three separate and sometimes contradictory goals: to deny the validity of 19th-century 'scientific' racism, still almost universally accepted among the Brazilian elite, by endeavouring 'to discriminate between the effects of purely genetic relationships and those resulting from social influences, the cultural heritage and the milieu'; to insist that Brazil was a multiracial nation, and that no Brazilian could claim to have escaped the genetic and cultural influence of the nation's Amerindian and African populations; and to assert that his own ancestors, the plantation aristocrats and slave-owners of the Northeast, had created a remarkably humane social system which encouraged both cultural fusion and sexual miscegenation between blacks and whites.

A few Brazilian intellectuals had presented some of the same ideas earlier, but their works had been ignored. Freyre succeeded because his education abroad enabled him to buttress his claims with dozens of references to North American and European theorists almost unknown in Brazil; their prestige, as foreigners, finally put to rest the ghosts of Gobineau, Haeckel, and Le Bon. Secondly, Freyre exemplified his theories with masses of detailed information about every aspect of plantation life. Moreover, because he was convinced that sex was the primary vehicle of both physical and cultural change in Brazilian society, Freyre included a great deal of very racy anecdotal material, which helped to popularize his works and his ideas. All of these theories and details were presented superbly in complex and powerful prose.

The Masters and the Slaves and Freyre's many subsequent works—including some rather mediocre verse and two semi-autobiographical novels—have sometimes been utilized in ways he did not envision: to defend the continued existence of Portuguese colonialism in Africa, for example, or to insist that contemporary Brazil is a harmonious racial paradise entirely free of any sort of prejudice. It is also clear that Freyre sometimes contradicted himself, and that some of his judgements are the products of privilege and naivety—as in his belief that Africans were perfectly adapted for hard labour in the tropics because they, unlike Europeans, were able to sweat all over their bodies. One of Freyre's fundamental ideas, that slavery was generally far more humane in Brazil than elsewhere in the Americas, has been vigorously attacked by a number of Brazilian and foreign scholars.

None the less, there is no doubt that the popularization of Freyre's works has transformed the ways in which educated Brazilians think about their nation and about themselves—freeing them from a self-destructive conviction of racial and cultural inferiority and bringing about a psychological and intellectual liberation which has profoundly influenced contemporary Brazil.

—David T. Haberly

FRISCH, Max (Rudolf). Born in Zurich, Switzerland, 15 May 1911. Educated at the Kantonale Realgymnasium, Zurich, 1924–30; University of Zurich, 1930–33; Zurich Technische Hochschule (Institute of Technology), 1936–41, diploma in architecture 1941. Served in the Swiss army, 1939–45. Married 1) Gertrud Anna Constance von Meyenburg in 1942 (divorced 1959), two daughters and one son; 2) Marianne Oellers in 1968. Freelance journalist from 1933; architect in Zurich, 1942–54; then full-time writer; visited Germany, France, and Italy, in 1946, Poland and Czechoslovakia in 1948, Spain in 1950; spent a year in the USA and Mexico, 1951–52; based in Rome, 1960–65. Recipient: Raabe prize, 1954; Schleussner Schüller prize, for radio play, 1955; Büchner prize, 1958; Zurich prize, 1958; Veillon prize, 1958; Nordrhein-Westfalen prize, 1962; Jerusalem prize, 1965; Schiller prize (Baden-Württemberg), 1965; Schiller prize (Switzerland), 1974; German Book Trade Freedom prize, 1976; Commonwealth award, 1985; Neustadt International prize, 1986; Heine prize (Düsseldorf), 1989. Honorary doctorate: University of Marburg, 1962; Bard College, Annandale-on-Hudson, New York, 1980; City University of New York, 1982; University of Birmingham, West Midlands, 1985; University of Berlin, 1987. Honorary Member, American Academy, 1974. *Died 4 April 1991.*

PUBLICATIONS

Plays

Nun singen sie wieder: Versuch eines Requiems (produced 1945). 1946; as *Now They Sing Again*, translated by David Lommen, in *Contemporary German Theatre*, edited by Michael Roloff, 1972.
Santa Cruz (produced 1946). 1947.
Die chinesische Mauer (produced 1946). 1947; revised version, 1955; as *The Chinese Wall*, translated by James L. Rosenberg, 1961; as *The Great Wall of China*, translated by Michael Bullock, in Four *Plays*, 1969.
Als der Krieg zu Ende war (produced 1948). 1949; as *When the War Was Over*, translated by James L. Rosenberg, in *Three Plays*, 1967.
Graf Öderland (produced 1951). 1951; as *Count Oederland*, translated by Michael Bullock, in *Three Plays*, 1962.
Don Juan; oder, Die Liebe zur Geometrie (produced 1953). 1953; translated as *Don Juan; or, the Love of Geometry*, by James L. Rosenberg, in *Three Plays*, 1967; also translated by Michael Bullock, in *Four Plays*, 1969.
Rip van Winkle, from the story by Washington Irving (broadcast 1953). 1969.
Biedermann und die Brandstifter (broadcast 1953; produced 1958). 1958; as *The Fire Raisers*, translated by Michael Bullock, in *Three Plays*, 1962, revised edition, 1985; as *The Firebugs*, translated by Mordecai Gorelik, 1963.
Die grosse Wut des Philipp Hotz (produced 1958). 1958; as *The Great Rage of Philipp Hotz*, translated by James L. Rosenberg, in *Three Plays*, 1967; as *Philipp Hotz's Fury*, translated by Michael Bullock, in *Four Plays*, 1969.
Andorra (produced 1961). 1962; translated as *Andorra*, by Michael Bullock, in *Three Plays*, 1962; also translated by Geoffrey Skelton, 1964.
Stücke. 2 vols., 1962; enlarged edition, 1972.
Three Plays (includes *The Fire Raisers*; *Count Oederland*; *Andorra*), translated by Michael Bullock, 1962.
Zurich Transit (televised 1966). 1966.
Biografie (produced 1968). 1967; as *Biography: A Game*, translated by Michael Bullock, in *Four Plays*, 1969.

Three Plays (includes *Don Juan; or, the Love of Geometry*; *The Great Rage of Philipp Hotz*; *When the War Was Over*), translated by James L. Rosenberg. 1967.
Four Plays (includes *The Great Wall of China*; *Don Juan; or, the Love of Geometry*; *Philipp Hotz's Fury*; *Biography: A Game*), translated by Michael Bullock. 1969.
Triptychon: Drei szenische Bilder (produced 1979). 1978; revised edition, 1980; as *Triptych: Three Scenic Panels*, translated by Geoffrey Skelton, 1981.

Radio Plays: *Rip van Winkle*, 1953; *Biedermann und die Brandstifter*, 1953.

Television Play: *Zurich Transit*, 1966.

Fiction

Jürg Reinhart: Eine sommerliche Schicksalsfahrt. 1934.
Antwort aus der Stille: Eine Erzählung aus den Bergen. 1937.
J'adore ce qui me brûle; oder, Die Schwierigen. 1943.
Bin; oder, Die Reise nach Peking. 1945.
Marion und die Marionotten: Ein Fragment. 1946.
Stiller. 1954; as *I'm Not Stiller*, translated by Michael Bullock, 1958.
Homo Faber. 1957; as *Homo Faber*, translated by Michael Bullock, 1959.
Mein Name sei Gantenbein. 1964; as *A Wilderness of Mirrors*, translated by Michael Bullock, 1965; as *Gantenbein*, 1982.
Wilhelm Tell für die Schule. 1971.
Montauk. 1975; as *Montauk*, translated by Geoffrey Skelton, 1976.
Der Mensch erscheint im Holozän. 1979; as *Man in the Holocene*, translated by Geoffrey Skelton, 1980.
Blaubart. 1982; as *Bluebeard*, translated by Geoffrey Skelton, 1983.

Other

Blätter aus dem Brotsack (diary). 1940.
Tagebuch mit Marion (diary). 1947; revised edition, as *Tagebuch 1946–1949*, 1950; as *Sketchbook 1946–1949*, translated by Geoffrey Skelton, 1977.
Achtung: Die Schweiz. 1955.
Die neue Stadt: Beiträge zur Diskussion. 1956.
Ausgewählte Prosa. 1961.
Öffentlichkeit als Partner. 1967.
Tagebuch 1966–1971. 1972; as *Sketchbook 1966–1971*, translated by Geoffrey Skelton, 1974.
Dienstbüchlein (memoir). 1974.
Stich-Worte (selection), edited by Uwe Johnson. 1975.
Gesammelte Werke, edited by Hans Mayer and Walter Schmitz. 12 vols., 1976; same texts also published in 6 vols., 1976, with supplementary volume, 1987.
Kritik, Thesen, Analysen. 1977.
Erzählende Prosa 1939–1979. 1980.
Forderungen des Tages: Porträts, Skizzen, Reden, 1943–82, edited by Walter Schmitz. 1983.
Gesammelte Werke [Jubiläums Edition]. 7 vols., 1986.
Schweiz ohne Armee? Ein Palaver. 1989.
Schweiz als Heimat? Versuche über 50 Jahre, edited by Walter Obschlager. 1990.

*

Critical Studies: *Max Frisch* by Ulrich Weisstein, 1967; *The Novels of Max Frisch*, 1976, and *The Plays of Max Frisch*,

1985, both by Michael Butler; *The Dramatic Works of Max Frisch* by Gertrud Bauer Pickar, 1977; Max *Frisch: His Work and Its Swiss Background* by Malcolm Pender, 1979; *Gombrowicz and Frisch: Aspects of the Literary Diary* by Alex Kurczaba, 1980; *Perspectives on Max Frisch* edited by Gerhard F. Probst and Jay F. Bodine, 1982; *Frisch: Andorra* by Michael Butler, 1985; *Understanding Max Frisch* by Wulf Koepke, 1990; *Life as a Man: Contemporary Male-Female Relationships in the Novels of Max Frisch* by Claus Reschke, 1990.

* * *

Max Frisch has attained wide popularity both as a novelist and dramatist. His central theme from his very earliest works is the individual's longing to discover and realize his 'true' self, but the works themselves encompass a rich variety of emphases, moods, and styles. The early novels such as *Jürg Reinhart* derive from the German Bildungsroman tradition (novel of development), but in the immediate post-war years Frisch began to experiment much more with genre and form. *Bin; oder, Die Reise nach Peking*, for example, is a whimsical, dream-like reflection on unfulfilled longing, while a drama such as *Nun singen sie wieder* (*Now They Sing Again*) uses harsh, almost surrealistic pictures to capture the conflict of self-centredness and humanitarian feeling in war. Some dramas like *Santa Cruz* or *Graf Öderland* (*Count Oederland*) are quasi-mythical presentations of the problem of marrying personal dream to social reality, but though Brechtian in structure they ultimately lack Brecht's intellectual clarity. Nevertheless, it is in this period that Frisch's major *leitmotif* emerges, the concept of 'image-making'—the imposition of arbitrary labels, social, racial, psychological, upon our fellows.

In the late 1950s and 1960s Frisch began to produce the works upon which his international reputation is really founded: *Biedermann und die Brandstifter* (*The Fire Raisers*) and *Andorra*, for example, have become stage classics. The former is a satirical attack upon middle-class concern for the 'right image', and not just in the usual sense of keeping up appearances. Frisch shows his central characters' exploitation of others on the one hand and attempts to retain a belief in their own 'decency' on the other. With sharp comic insight the play illustrates the hypocritical bourgeois desire to exercise power and yet still bask in a shared sense of common humanity, ranging from the status-conscious superficiality of 'hospitality' rituals and the emptiness of 'polite' discourse to the profound and dangerous gullibility that results from inability to confront self-contradiction. At this level the play has multiple political associations—variously interpreted over the years as referring to the threat of fascism or communism —since it reveals how such social hypocrisy invites destruction without unmasking its own falsity. Despite such serious overtones, however, the text remains playful throughout, trapping the audience through laughter into self-recognition. In the more immediately serious *Andorra* Frisch probes the destructive effects of the image we create of others as well as of ourselves—through fear, self-interest, convenience. The mistaken assumption that the central figure is Jewish is used to reveal both the selfish origins and the insidious growth of prejudice, and its disastrous physical and spiritual effects on the victim. Though not intended as a comment on the Holocaust—it is as much about 'otherness' as anti-semitism— this has often been the context in which the play has been read, and thus misjudged. Its true power derives from the very ordinariness of its figures and initial events, and from the

recognition—as in *The Fire Raisers*—that unthinking 'normality', the petty weakness of everyday life, can lead to terrible consequences. Both plays have a tellingly spare, episodic structure again reminiscent of Brechtian distancing devices, but especially in the case of *Andorra* there is also highly emotive visual symbolism demanding something closer to the emotional involvement of traditional tragedy, yet without cathartic release. Indeed, it is the—sometimes comic, sometimes tragic—inevitability of human weakness, rather than a Brechtian view of alterable social structures, that shape the pointed stage effects in both texts.

Inventive formal structure is also the hallmark of *Stiller* (*I'm Not Stiller*), perhaps Frisch's finest work. This novel combines sheer entertainment in the constant mystery surrounding the main figure's identity, with a probing investigation into Swiss national self-images and into the deeper, personal meaning of 'identity'. Frisch quite logically abandons omniscient narration and allows Stiller to reflect his own complex self, a battle-ground between the images others would impose, those implied by modern media or inherent in language itself, and those fashioned by the self even in moments of apparent existential insight. The novel's wonderful intricacy and 'unfinished' narrative structure force the reader to confront his own desire for completion, to reassess his own modes of judgment. And the same is true of Frisch's subsequent novels. *Homo Faber* is an attack upon the complacent belief that technology 'explains' the world. The engineer Walter Faber's neat image of a calculable, controllable reality is shattered—at first by random, chance events, but increasingly by previously excluded factors such as age, emotion, and the incursion of his own unacknowledged past. His tortuous account of tragic events, for which he cannot evade personal responsibility, embodies the breakdown of his simplistic reading of the world, though the textual complexity with its Oedipal fate motifs is more contrived than in *I'm Not Stiller*.

Frisch's last major novel *Mein Name sei Gantenbein* (*A Wilderness of Mirrors*) again explores the essential complexity of individual personality, but in a delightfully comic interplay of multiple 'experimental' identities.

Frisch's concern with modern issues also extended to the political: in his diaries and various essays he confronts Swiss myths and attitudes directly. In his later works, however, he turned increasingly to the more individual concerns such as loneliness and ageing, though again with great variety, from sophisticated comedy in the drama *Biografie* (*Biography*), through painful confession in the diary-like *Montauk* to sombre reflection or scurrilous wit in the short tales *Der Mensch erscheint im Holozän* (*Man in the Holocene*) and *Blaubart* (*Bluebeard*). What is perhaps most characteristic of this late phase of his writing is a profounder scepticism than ever before about the possibility of escaping either from externally imposed images or from those created by age, gender, or selfish desire.

—Mary E. Stewart

ANDORRA
Play by Max Frisch, 1961.

Andorra, a burning attack on prejudice in general and anti-semitism in particular, was conceived in 1957, based on Frisch's prose sketch 'Der andorranische Jude' [The Andorran Jew] in his *Tagebuch 1946–1949* (*Sketchbook 1946–1949*). Frisch wrote five versions before releasing the play.

The first performance, at the Schauspielhaus, Zurich, on 2 November 1961, was directed by Kurt Hirschfeld, with Peter Brogle as Andri, and sets by Teo Otto. In Germany, it became the most performed modern play of 1962, joining the wave of literary works dealing with the legacy of Nazism, such as Grass's *The Tin Drum*. German reactions to the play concentrated on this topical aspect. (Outside Germany the play had less impact; it was found uninteresting in London and flopped badly in New York.)

Andorra is a 'model' play in a Brechtian sense; Frisch has learnt from *Mother Courage and Her Children* and *The Caucasian Chalk Circle*. The small, self-sufficient town-state, the imaginary Andorra of innkeepers and artisans, does not pretend to represent any 20th-century society in detail or show specific components of Nazism, yet the social and psychological patterns of modern life can be shown at work in it, some basic truths about mankind suggested. The play is thus also a parable, enshrining a lesson. Within Frisch's *oeuvre*, it represents—with *Biedermann und die Brandstifter* (*The Fire Raisers*)—a more overtly politically aware phase between the more personal preoccupations of the novels: it transfers Frisch's burning theme of identity to the stage and to a social context.

The plot is simple: Andri, a boy brought up by Can, the teacher in Andorra, as being a Jewish orphan rescued from the neighbouring country of the anti-semitic 'Blacks', is forced by prejudice to become a salesman rather than a carpenter as he wishes; and he is not allowed to marry Can's daughter Barblin. It transpires that Andri is really Can's illegitimate son by the *Señora*, a 'Black' (Can said Andri was a Jew in order to avoid this scandal); she is killed by a stone thrown at her when she visits Andorra. The 'Blacks' invade Andorra; Andri is identified as a Jew and killed.

The Andorrans lack first-hand experience of Jews, yet have an image of the Jew which they impose on Andri. Only when they have labelled him a Jew with supposedly typical characteristics does he become so like a Jew that the 'Blacks', when they invade, can single him out as one (in a macabre, grotesque pseudo-scientific procedure: all the Andorrans parade barefoot in front of a 'Jew-inspector'). The Andorrans' lack of imagination and empathy puts Andri in a situation which, when the 'Blacks' arrive, is fatal to him; and afterwards they have no grasp of what they have done. Thus 'ordinary' Germans who would never hurt a fly might be made to feel how it was that they too were guilty in the extermination of Jews. Frisch hopes that the lesson about prejudice applies also to such phenomena as the colour bar or the McCarthy brand of anti-communism, indeed any situation where men judge others as (supposed) members of an alien group, rather than as unique individuals.

Sartre's essay *Anti-Semite and Jew* (*Réflexions sur la question juive*) showed that the Jew becomes an object of prejudice because of what Christian society has, over the centuries, forced the Jews to be or to seem. To make it clear that there can be no objective basis for the Andorrans' attitude, Frisch makes Andri a non-Jew—biologically speaking —and an ordinary, conforming, soccer-playing youth. But he is allotted a social role which he then plays, trying to be true to a Judaism of which he has as little direct knowledge as anyone around. When finally told he is not a Jew, he cannot believe it.

The Andorrans, cunning but ultimately stupid, accuse the Jew of ambition because their own talents are not sufficient; of lust and avarice in order to draw attention from their own failings. We do not, however, find out what frustrations in Andorran society explain their pressing need to find a person even lower in the pecking order than themselves. Rather

Frisch tends to metaphysics: Andri suffers a characteristically Jewish fate, becomes a martyr, and dies burdened with the sins of the Andorrans, postfiguring Jesus in a world so ethically unaware that it does not know what to do with a saviour.

Can is sometimes the author's mouthpiece or commentator, sometimes an inadequate alcoholic unable to rectify the situation he has brought about. Andri's stepmother is a weak figure. The Señora's visit to Andorra is insufficiently motivated. The soldier's off-stage rape, or seduction, of Barblin while Andri unsuspectingly sits outside her door is gripping, but does not fit the motivation and plot. On the other hand, the demonstrations of prejudice are chilling and memorable on the stage. The carpenter tears apart the journeyman's ill-made chair, claiming to believe that it was made by Andri and proves his incompetence (Jews don't have carpentry in the blood!); the soldier always emphasizes the cowardice of the Jews, but is himself the first collaborator of the 'Blacks' when they invade. The Jew-inspection, with its final consequence in Barblin's madness, provides one of the strongest endings in the modern repertoire. Few plays combine everyday clarity and broad-brushed symbolism as *Andorra* does.

Frisch uses a colloquial, regionally influenced style; Biblical references, used by Andri as he grows into the role of a martyr, underline themes of guilt, violence, betrayal, and (impossible) redemption. Developing Brechtian technique, Frisch destroys tension about the outcome: the characters successively enter a witness-box to give their views of the story of Andri, by now in the past. Thus we gradually learn that he is not a Jew, and that he will be killed. We discover that the Andorrans are incapable of drawing the moral lessons from the events: this is a very black play, even the well-meaning Can producing a monstrous life-lie in his attempt to do the right thing by his son. Frisch appears to accept the ineluctability of Andri's fate. He chronicles the distortion and destruction of the individual by social pressures, but he has no alternative that convinces even himself. Andri's own suggestion, the saving power of individual love, is rebutted by the plot. Frisch cannot share Brecht's Marxist belief in the possibility of understanding and therefore changing the world and human behaviour. He had read Büchner's *Woyzeck* at the time of working on *Andorra*, and found its bleakness, its portrayal of the individual becoming a mere object to a stupid and uncaring society, more congenial. Can the audience prove the pessimistic author wrong by helping to produce a more tolerant world?

Frisch set himself an impossible task in *Andorra*. Between realism and abstraction, didacticism and resignation, determinism and hope of change, literalness and symbolism, there are many pitfalls. He himself found the play lacking in mystery. But a sparse structure, clearcut conflicts, and Frisch's eye for the stage make it a potentially shattering theatrical experience.

—Alfred D. White

THE FIRE RAISERS (Biedermann und die Brandstifter)
Play by Max Frisch, 1958.

Frisch's diary for 1948 contains in outline the story that forms the basis of this play: that of the anxious bourgeois who invites strangers into his house whom he soon suspects to be arsonists, yet cannot confront—and pays the price. In 1949 Frisch sketched a radio play on the same subject, but the work itself was not started until three years later. A radio success, the play was then reworked for stage performance in Zurich in 1958, and has gone on to world-wide success since.

That success has undoubtedly something to do with the play's sustained comic inventiveness and its openness to interpretation; as its subtitle proclaims, it is a morality play without a moral—no urgent message is forced upon the attention of the audience as it is with the much darker *Andorra*. Yet while it is clear that the Communist takeover in Prague in February 1948 and Beneš's supposed collusion gave Frisch the original idea for his diary sketch, and that other political scenarios can be adduced (e.g. Hitler's rise to power on the backs of the bourgeoisie), it adds little to our appreciation of the text to see it in this allegorical way, and indeed detracts from its aesthetic inventiveness and specific effect.

In some senses *The Fire Raisers* is a very undramatic work; there is a simple structure without genuine antagonists or subplots, and minimal suspense since we very quickly infer who the 'visitors' are. The interest is provided precisely by fascinated anticipation of how this will all end, which derives from our familiarity with the vocabulary of dramatic irony. Yet this is a two-edged effect: we feel ourselves superior by our insight to the foolish protagonist, yet our capacity to anticipate his fate marks us as sharing the same cultural roots—and much else in this play has the same ambivalence. The presence of a chorus, for example, made up in this case of firemen: we recognize and laugh at the parody of Greek theatrical convention, the absurd mix of high rhetoric and modern jargon. However, it is our very cultural awareness and attentive response which also traps us into recognition of the occasional sharp relevance of what is said to our lives in general (e.g. their reading of belief in Fate as a mask for stupidity points to the suspicious nature of all such intellectual pretention). In fact our laughter throughout is similarly 'dual'—we revel in our separateness and superior understanding, yet just that general cruelty and our specific enjoyment of individual comic scenes marks our unwilled but unmistakable identity with the protagonist's character and attitudes. This identity is then explicitly enacted when he addresses the audience and directly and asks 'well, would you have behaved differently?'

What this play focuses on, then, are general middle-class attitudes, perhaps even broader modern attitudes in a post-Christian, media-driven world. The very 'decency' enshrined in the protagonist's name, Biedermann, is the key. It is what most audiences would lay claim to, but it is also his downfall because it has become a class and cultural icon rather than an instinctive morality: that which apes aristocratic generosity with an implied recognition of desirably 'higher' values, while also providing a comforting mask for cruder exploitative roles. It is self-congratulatory in its manners and rituals, but also a source of vulnerability because of its inherent element of bad faith. Frisch's dialogue and stage action capture this duality brilliantly, especially in the rituals of hospitality which are shown up for the manipulative pretence they are by being taken as sincere ('How did you sleep?' 'Thank you, I was cold . . .'). Frisch also brilliantly captures bourgeois inability to replace these formulaic rituals with direct speaking, to name what threatens even in crisis, for fear of losing face—and the fact that plain-speaking of a very crude kind is not felt to be inconsistent with 'decency' outside the home, in the factory or pub, only underpins the play's emphasis on received norms of behaviour. It is crucial to the meaning of the play that Biedermann effectively allows these men into his home, they do not force their way in; nor is he exceptionally gullible—on the contrary, he is at first very suspicious indeed. It is not true to say that he is simply cowardly or ingratiating either: rather the fire raisers deflect any element of resistance by calling

Biedermann's bluff. For example, they describe 'others' duplicity in first receiving them and then betraying them to the police, thus anticipating and defusing Biedermann's own self-preservatory instincts by foregrounding just that 'decency' he also seeks to project. As they pinpoint bourgeois hypocrisies these become impossible to perform, and the self-sprung trap of bourgeois self-image is laid bare, to be finally enacted in a parody of heroic honour as Biedermann hands over the matches to the arsonists.

All this is deeply serious, yet uproariously funny too because we cannot fail to recognize that the pattern of events replicates the good old circus routine of the clown who trips over his own bucket of water and gets wet; Frisch's play, like many enduring comedy classics, has an underlying formula of traditional farce. Yet is also highly modern, twice for example explicitly breaking the separation of stage and audience in a way that both denies us the comfort of separate superiority and also actively foregrounds artifice as a theme. Such devices, and the many provocative incongruities, are reminiscent of Brecht, yet the spirit of this play is ultimately un-Brechtian. Frisch's world is not one of socially conditioned victims but of fallible, foolish human beings—and the Epilogue in Hell added for the first performance in Germany merely confirms this. Biedermann is unreflective and unregenerate, and it is a moot point whether audiences will themselves 'learn' anything, or simply relish the cultural eclecticism and so re-enact Biedermann's complacency. The explosion with which the main play ends says it all: the only truth is in action, not words.

—Mary E. Stewart

I'M NOT STILLER (Stiller)
Novel by Max Frisch, 1954.

With *I'm Not Stiller* of 1954 Frisch placed himself in the forefront of modern narrative art. It is a work which is typical of Frisch in its thematic focus but also highly innovative in technique.

The Stiller of the title is a Swiss sculptor, who feels that he has failed in his dual roles as artist and husband. He has fled to America and undergone a profound existential crisis of self-assessment and 'rebirth', assuming a new identity as Jim White. Yet he is drawn to return to Switzerland; he is arrested at the border, and in prison records memories, reflections, and encounters with figures from the past, including his wife. The novel opens with the words 'I'm not Stiller': thus we are faced with anything but an objective narrative. The sub-text from the very start is one of need: a need to assert new identity by rejection of the old, and these two threads are then intertwined with extraordinary complexity in the main body of the novel.

At the simplest level this novel functions as a kind of whodunnit; the reader remains unsure for some time who the central figure 'truly' is. But even at this level the simplicity is deceptive, the reader both trapped and liberated. On the one hand the diary-like form makes us try to recuperate the text as the product of an identifiable person, and there is pleasure in uncovering 'clues'. Yet we are forced to recognize that the very notion of circumscribable identity presupposed by this exercise is profoundly questionable, for all the information is filtered through others' subjectivity and their will, or ability, to communicate verbally—there is no direct access to some seat of consciousness. We are made very aware both that traditional realist characterization is a kind of reductive image-making, and that language itself is problematic. Yet precisely these issues liberate our thinking on the problems inherent in cognition and the creation of 'identity'.

Stiller is both a perpetrator and victim of images. There is something deeply disturbing about how authority and family immediately perform the act of simple resolution denied the reader and assume White is Stiller. Differences is blotted out by a desire for order, which Stiller interestingly sees even in Swiss architecture and general resistance to change. But the problem is broader too. Travel may open up new horizons, Stiller/White argues, but the vicarious experience offered by modern media forecloses the expression of what is truly individual. Yet ultimately we see that this is also a problem of language itself; when Stiller/White claims that he has no words to express his reality he is touching on the inevitable gap between language and 'truth', and man's need for recognition and mutuality only re-enacts and exacerbates the slippages and distortions of language.

Despite such scepticism, however, this novel also allows the reader to comprehend something of the processes that further restrict the search for 'truth', imposing images more limiting than those inherent in language itself. Though we can never make final statements about Stiller's relationship with his wife, we can surmise a complex pattern of cross-determination—perhaps Frisch's finest study. Stiller's need to prove himself forces Julika into the role of 'needing redemption', yet her complicity with that role casts him as aggressor and reinforces the insecurity he seeks to escape. However, the image-making is not only inter-personal. Other textual patterns suggest that Stiller/White's view of himself—even at his moments of profoundest crisis—is fraught with problems and evasions. The very discursiveness of his notebooks, intended as an assertion of freedom, is a self-laid trap, for they reveal obsessions and weaknesses all the more clearly. For example, in the early days after his arrest 'White' tells many stories as a way of expressing obliquely his claim to unique experience: stories like that of Rip van Winkle, Isidor the bourgeois who breaks out, the discovery of the Carlsbad Caverns as a kind of modern 'descent into Hell and rebirth' myth, or stories of his own highly coloured adventures in the United States. Yet these stories fade out of the text, or are unintentionally relativized by later incidental comment, and that change indicates not only that others' 'stories' come to dominate (i.e. that society is stronger), but that Stiller/White's stories are unsustainable in themselves. They are not metaphorically encoded 'truth' after all, but inflated elaborations which reveal precisely weakness not strength as their source as they break down. Ironically such patterns thus suggest the very craving for recognition in White that he has detected in Stiller; in trying to prove that he is not Stiller he in fact moves ever closer to that identity.

This process does not obliterate or resolve Stiller's powerfully captured anguish, however. The State Prosecutor's Epilogue, telling of Stiller's life after he is legally deprived of the identity 'White', seems to offer a message of necessary compromise, of self-acceptance, yet the view is seemingly as subjective as Stiller's, the product of personal need. What is left, then, between the poles of self-refusal and passive acceptance? The answer is perhaps best represented by the performance of the text itself; it engages us as readers while refusing to do our thinking for us. That is, it puts us in the role of ideal communicative partner, able to see both the unchanging constants and also the fluidity in personality. We can both accept biographical data and allow existential openness, we 'finish' the book yet we also go on thinking about its issues. Frisch forces us, unlike Stiller/White's very gullible warder Knobel, to distinguish between art and life by foregrounding

story-telling as an act, but in doing so we also perform ('realize' in both senses) what his characters so rarely achieve —an ongoing harmonization of structuring artifice ('fiction') and openness that must be the model, if there is any possible, for the best of human 'knowing'.

—Mary E. Stewart

FROISSART, Jean. Born in Valenciennes, Hainault c.1337. Educated in Valenciennes. Travelled to England in 1361; obtained protection of Queen Philippa. Accompanied the Black Prince to Bordeaux in 1366, and the Duke of Clarence to Milan, 1368. Returned to Valenciennes in 1369, following the death of Queen Philippa. Took religious orders and became priest of Lestines, c.1370; secretary to Wenceslas of Luxembourg, 1381–83. Travelled in Flanders and France and revisited England 1394–95. Date of death is unknown.

PUBLICATIONS

Collections

Oeuvres, edited by Kervyn de Lettenhove. 28 vols., 1867–1870.
Poésies, edited by A. Scheler. 3 vols., 1870–72.
The Chronicles of Jean Froissart in Lord Berners' Translation, edited by Gillian and William Anderson. 1963.
Ballades et rondeaux, edited by R.S. Baudouin. 1978.

Verse

Chroniques. 1350s–c.1400; edited by S. Luce, G. Raymond, A. Mirot and L. Mirot, 13 vols., 1869–1957; also edited and abridged by G.C. Macauley, 1895; W.P. Ker, 1901–03; C.E. Mills and H.B. Mills, 1929; Georges T. Diller, 1972 and 1991; M. de Medeiros, 1988; as *The Chronicles of England, France and Spain*, translated by Johan Bourchier, 2 vols., 1523–25; also translated by Thomas Johnes, 2 vols., 1848; John H. Joliffe, 1967; Geoffrey Brereton, 1968.
Trois récits de Froissart, edited by Marguerite Ninet. 1902.
Honour and Arms (selection), edited by Mary Macleod. 1910.
Histoires de Froissart, edited by H. Longnon. 1931.
Voyage en Béarn, edited by A.H. Diverres. 1953.
L'Espinette amoureuse, edited by Anthime Fourrier. 1963.
La Prison amoureuse, edited by Anthime Fourrier. 1974.
Le Joli buisson de jonece, edited by Anthime Fourrier. 1975.
The Lyric Poems of Jean Froissart, edited by Rob Roy McGregor, Jr. 1975.
'Dits' et 'Débats', edited by Anthime Fourrier. 1979.
Dit du florin, edited by Anthime Fourrier. 1979.
Le Paradis d'amour, L'Orloge amoureus, edited by P.F. Dembowski. 1986.

Fiction

Méliador, edited by A. Longnon. 1895–99.

Other

Ci sensient un trettie de morelité à s'appelle le temple donneur.
1845.

*

Critical Studies: *Froissart: Chronicler and Poet* by F.S. Shears, 1930; 'The Geography of Britain in Froissart's *Méliador*' by A.H. Diverres in *Medieval Miscellany Presented to E. Vinaver* edited by F. Whitehead, A.H. Diverres, and F.E. Sutcliffe, 1965; 'Historians Reconsidered: Froissart' by C.T. Allmand in *History Today*, 16, 1966; *I, John Froissart* by Grant Uden, 1968; 'The Concept of Advancement in the Fourteenth Century in the Chroniques of Jean Froissart' by K. McRobbie in *The Canadian Journal of History*, 6, 1971; *Le Vocabulaire psychologique dans les Chroniques de Froissart* by Jacqueline Picoche, 2 vols., 1976–84; *Froissart: Historian* edited by J.J.N. Palmer, 1981; *Jean Froissart and His 'Méliador': Context, Craft and Sense* by Peter F. Dembowski, 1983; 'Froissart, Chronicler of Chivalry' by K. Fowler in *History Today*, 36, 1986; 'Froissart's *Chroniques*: Knightly Adventures and Warrior Forays' by G.T. Diller in *Fifteenth-Century Studies*, 12, 1987; *Jean Froissart and the Fabric of History: Truth, Myth and Fiction in the Chroniques* by Peter F. Ainsworth, 1990.

*　*　*

Jean Froissart is recognized as being one of the most important and prolific authors writing in late medieval French. His passionate interest in aristocratic chivalry lent his work a truly international dimension: indeed, he can be viewed as a proto-European whose French was at that time the language of chivalry *par excellence*. Appointed at an early stage of his career to the household of Queen Philippa of England, he moved in august circles (his patrons included Gui de Châtillon, Wenceslas of Brabant and Albrecht of Bavaria). Although his earliest sympathies were fired by all he had learned of the impressive military triumphs of Edward III and the Black Prince, Froissart also had connections with the French and Scottish courts, and travelled extensively through England, Wales, Scotland, the Low Countries, France, and Italy. Affection for his patrons did not preclude avoidance of partiality (as he understood it). Where his work betrays bias, this is essentially chivalrous rather than 'national'. His avowed aim as a conscious artist was to write of arms and love, a task he fulfilled with panache, both in his verse and in his prose.

Froissart saw himself primarily as a poet: the two extant manuscripts contain his *ballades*, *virelais*, and *rondeaux* together with his *pastourelles* and longer narrative poems, show evidence of considerable versatility and wit, and of a constant preoccupation with the aesthetic arrangement of these works within their particular manuscripts. Heavily influenced by the diction and forms of *Le Roman de la rose* (*The Romance of the Rose*), Froissart also found inspiration for themes or situations in the works of his near-contemporary Guillaume de Machaut. A further important influence was the early 14th-century *Ovide moralisé* (from Ovid's *Metamorphoses*), though Froissart was not afraid to out-ovid Ovid: some of the 'Ovidian' tales in his poems are pure inventions. The longer narrative *dits* owe much to the allegorical diction of Jean de Meung. Their occasional sententiousness is relieved by a lightness of touch encountered, for

instance, in passages where Froissart writes obliquely about his craft as writer, via a first-person narrator whose complexities have been analysed recently (Bennett, 1991). These often engaging poems (*L'Espinette amoureuse* [Love's Hawthorn], *Le Joli buisson de jonece* [The Gallant Bush of Youth], or the *L'Orloge amoureus* [Love's Timepiece/The Clockwork of Gallantry]) display an appealingly wry irony directed towards the poet-narrator, through whose adventures Froissart explores the delights and vicissitudes of love and of literary creation. Jacqueline Cerquiglini has highlighted the metaphorical valency of the images Froissart uses to delineate the activities of poetic creation and 'finishing': garlands, crowns, wreaths, and boxes. The *Poésies* also include shorter, semi-autobiographical pieces such as the 'Débat du Cheval et du Levrier' in which the poet's horse and the greyhound, returning with their master from a Scottish journey, argue about who has the harsher lot in life; or the *Dit du florin*, which allows us to hear the irreverent observations of Froissart's last remaining florin concerning the fate of his erstwhile fellows in the hands of a spendthrift poet-chronicler possessed of an inordinate appetite for wine and parchment. The light-hearted prosopopoeia of these works affords the author a further opportunity to be ironic about his own preoccupations and obsessions, and to do so without a trace of pomposity.

Less accessible to modern readers is Froissart's self-consciously archaic Arthurian romance *Méliador*. Thirty-thousand lines of verse (by this time unusual for romance) relate a quest—for the hand of Hermondine, daughter of the king of Scotland. Peter Dembowski's monograph (1983) has established interesting parallels between the chivalry celebrated in *Méliador*, where knightly achievement is graded on an 'Olympic' model ('gold, silver and bronze medallist . . .') and that delineated by the French knight Geoffrey de Charny in his *Demandes* and *Livre Charny*. The romance is also graced by a somnambulist named Camel de Camois, as by some highly-coloured Irish episodes and a journey to the Other World undertaken by the enigmatic Sagremor, episodes which one can compare with analogues in Froissart's greatest work *Chroniques* (The Chronicles).

Still widely read, *The Chronicles* were written to preserve the memory of what their author viewed as the Golden Age of Chivalry—and therefore to offer exemplary and inspirational material for young men aspiring to knighthood, however modest their background. Comprising four books, they cover the years 1325–99 in a prose deservedly famous for its graceful rhythms and stylistic vividness. Book I (first prose redaction c.1355–78; Amiens MS: 1377–80; both possibly revised in part *post* 1392; final redaction, Rome MS: 1399–c.1405) probably began as a rhymed history, but Froissart was prompted by the prose *Chronicle* of Jean le Bel (composed 1352–61) to eschew verse for history-writing: Froissart's first prose redaction virtually reproduces le Bel's work (an affirmation of probity rather than 'plagiarism'), but the later books testify to the chronicler's developing confidence. Book II (1379–85) offers a vivid, sometimes shrewd account of political and socio-economic affairs in the troubled Low Countries, together with what many British readers will quickly recognize as the chronicler's lively account of the Peasants' Revolt of 1381. Modern historians have rightly drawn attention to the pitfalls of this kind of narrative history, which rarely uses sources as we understand them. Yet *The Chronicles* are not devoid of critical perspective or judgement, despite their markedly aristocratic viewpoint. In any case, it is profitable to read them as commemorative, moral chronicles, while recognizing in them (particularly in Books III and IV) an increasing disparity between the writer's avowed aims and the result—reflected in a correspondingly greater tonal and formal variety. Book III (1390–91, revised *post* 1392) places the chronicler centre-stage, as protagonist—offering us an enthralling narrative (travelogue, diary, memoir, chronicle . . .) which is essentially 'about' being a writer, while Book IV (1392–c.1400) contains episodes that stand on their own as virtual novellas. Of most interest to the modern reader, finally, are the different editorial recensions of Book I: for here we engage with the hesitations, doubts, and revisions of the author.

—Peter F. Ainsworth

————

FUENTES, Carlos. Born in Panama City, Panama, 11 November 1928. Lived in the USA (1934–40), Chile, and Argentina; moved to Mexico at age 16. Educated at schools in New York, Mexico, and Chile; Colegio Frances Morelos, Mexico City, 1946–48, LL.B. 1948; graduate work in law at the National Autonomous University, Mexico City, 1950, and Institut des Hautes Études Internationales, Geneva, 1950–52. Married 1) Rita Macedo in 1959 (divorced 1966), one daughter; 2) Sylvia Lemus in 1973, one son and one daughter. Member, then secretary, Mexican delegation, International Labor Organization, Geneva, 1950–52; assistant chief of press section, Ministry of Foreign Affairs, Mexico City, 1954; press secretary, United Nations Information Center, Mexico City, 1954; co-founder and editor, *Revista Mexicana de Literatura*, 1954–58; secretary, then assistant director of Cultural Department, National Autonomous University, Mexico City, 1955–56; head of department of cultural relations, Ministry of Foreign Affairs, 1957–59; editor, *El Espectador*, 1959–61, *Siempre* and *Política* from 1960; lived in Europe during much of the 1960s; Mexican Ambassador to France, 1974–77. Fellow, Woodrow Wilson Center, Smithsonian Institute, Washington, DC, 1974; Virginia Gildersleeve visiting professor, Barnard College, New York, 1977; Norman Maccoll lecturer, 1977, and Simón Bolívar professor of Latin American studies, 1986–87, University of Cambridge; Henry L. Tinker lecturer, Columbia University, New York, 1978; professor of English, University of Pennsylvania, Philadelphia, 1978–83; fellow of humanities, Princeton University, New Jersey; professor of comparative literature, 1984–86, and Robert F. Kennedy professor of Latin American studies, since 1987, Harvard University, Cambridge, Massachusetts. President, Modern Humanities Research Association, since 1989. Recipient: Mexican Writers Center fellowship, 1956; Seix-Barral Biblioteca Breve prize, 1967; Xavier Villaurrutia prize, 1975; Rómulo Gallegos prize (Venezuela), 1977; Alfonso Reyes prize, 1979; Mexican National prize for literature, 1984; Cervantes prize, 1987; Rubén Darío prize, 1988; Instituto Italo-Latino Americano prize, 1988; New York City National Arts Club Medal of Honor, 1988; Order of Cultural Independence (Nicaragua), 1988; IUA prize, 1989; Prince of Asturias prize (Spain), 1994. D.Litt.: Wesleyan University, Middletown, Connecticut, 1982; University of Cambridge, 1987; D.Univ.: University of Essex, Colchester, England, 1987; LL.D.: Harvard University; other honorary doctorates: Columbia College, Chicago State University, Washington University (St Louis). Member, El Colegio Nacional, since 1974; American Academy and Institute of Arts and Letters, 1986. Lives in Mexico City and London.

PUBLICATIONS

Fiction

Los días enmascarados (stories). 1954.
La región más transparente. 1958; as *Where the Air Is Clear*, translated by Sam Hileman, 1960.
Las buenas conciencias. 1959; as *The Good Conscience*, translated by Sam Hileman, 1961.
La muerte de Artemio Cruz. 1962; as *The Death of Artemio Cruz*, translated by Sam Hileman, 1964; also translated by Alfred MacAdam, 1991.
Aura. 1962; as *Aura*, translated by Lysander Kemp, 1965.
Cantar de ciegos (stories). 1964.
Zona sagrada. 1967; as *Holy Places*, translated by Suzanne Jill Levine, in *Triple Cross*, 1972.
Cambio de piel. 1967; as *A Change of Skin*, translated by Sam Hileman, 1968.
Cumpleaños. 1969.
Chac Mool y otros cuentos. 1973.
Terra Nostra. 1975; as *Terra Nostra*, translated by Margaret Sayers Peden, 1976.
La cabeza de la hidra. 1978; as *The Hydra Head*, translated by Margaret Sayers Peden, 1978.
Una familia lejana. 1980; as *Distant Relations*, translated by Margaret Sayers Peden, 1982.
Agua quemada. 1981; as *Burnt Water*, translated by Margaret Sayers Peden, 1981.
El gringo viejo. 1985; as *The Old Gringo*, translated by Margaret Sayers Peden, 1985.
Cristóbal nonato. 1987; as *Christopher Unborn*, translated by Fuentes and Alfred MacAdam, 1989.
Constancia, y otras novelas para vírgenes. 1989; as *Constancia and Other Stories for Virgins*, translated by Thomas Christensen, 1990.
La campaña. 1990; as *The Campaign*, translated by Alfred MacAdam, 1991.
The Orange Tree (stories). 1994.

Plays

Todos los gatos son pardos. 1970; revised edition, as *Ceremonias del alba*, 1991.
El tuerto es rey (produced in French, 1970). 1970.
Las reinos originarios (includes *Todos los gatos son pardos* and *El tuerto es rey*). 1971.
Orquídeas a la luz de la luna (produced in English, 1982). 1982; as *Orchids in the Moonlight*, translated by Fuentes, in *Drama Contemporary: Latin America*, edited by George W. Woodyard and Marion Peter Holt, 1986.

Screenplays: *Pedro Páramo*, 1966; *Tiempo de morir*, 1966; *Los caifanes*, 1967.

Television series: *The Buried Mirror* (on Christopher Columbus), 1991.

Verse

Poemas de amor: cuentos del alma. 1971.

Other

The Argument of Latin America: Words for North Americans. 1963.
Paris: La revolución de Mayo. 1968.
La nueva novela hispanoamericana. 1969.

El mundo de José Luis Cuevas. 1969.
Casa con dos puertas. 1970.
Tiempo mexicano. 1971.
Cuerpos y ofrendas. 1972.
Cervantes; o, La crítica de la lectura (Hackett memorial lectures). 1976; as *Don Quixote; or, The Critique of Reading,* translated anonymously, 1976.
Latin American Literature Today: A Symposium, with others, edited by Rose S. Minc. 1980.
High Noon in Latin America. 1983.
Juan Soriano y su obra, with Teresa del Conde. 1984.
On Human Rights: A Speech. 1984.
Latin America: At War with the Past. 1985.
Palacio Nacional, with Guillermo Tovar y de Teresa. 1986.
Gabriel García Márquez and the Invention of America (lecture). 1987.
Myself with Others: Selected Essays. 1988.
Valiente mundo nuevo (essays). 1990.
The Buried Mirror: Reflections on Spain and the New World. 1992.
Return to Mexico: Journeys behind the Mask. 1992.

Editor, *Los signos en rotación y otros ensayos,* by Octavio Paz. 1971.

*

Bibliography: 'Carlos Fuentes: A Bibliography' by Sandra L. Dunn, in *Review of Contemporary Fiction,* 8, 1988; 'Carlos Fuentes', in *Mexican Literature: A Bibliography of Secondary Sources* by David William Foster, 1992.

Critical Studies: *Carlos Fuentes y Las buenas conciencias* by Agustín Velarde, 1962; *Carlos Fuentes y la realidad de México* by Fidel Ortega Martínez, 1969; *The Mexican Novel Comes of Age* by Walter M. Langford, 1971; *Carlos Fuentes* by Daniel de Guzman, 1972; *Nostalgia del futuro en la obra de Carlos Fuentes* by Liliana Befumo Boschi and Elisa Cabrera, 1973; *Cambio de piel; or, The Myth of Literature* by Michael González, 1974; *La magia y las brujas en la obra de Carlos Fuentes* by Gloria Durán, 1976, translated as *The Archetypes of Carlos Fuentes: From Witch to Androgyne,* 1980; *Simposio Carlos Fuentes: Actas* (University of South Carolina), 1978; *Cinco novelas claves de la literatura hispanoamericana* by Antonio Sacoto, 1979; *Los disfraces: La obra mestiza de Carlos Fuentes* by G. García Gutiérrez, 1981; *Carlos Fuentes: A Critical View* edited by Robert Brody and Charles Rossman, 1982; *Yáñez, Rulfo y Fuentes: El tema de la muerte en tres novelas mexicanas* by K.M. Taggart, 1982; *Carlos Fuentes* by Wendy B. Faris, 1983; *La narrativa de Carlos Fuentes* by Aida Elsa Ramírez Mattei, 1983; *El cuento mexicano contemporáneo: Rulfo, Arreola y Fuentes* by Bertie Acker, 1984; *Lo fantástico en los relatos de Carlos Fuentes* by G. Feijoo, 1985; *The Lost Rib: Female Characters in the Spanish-American Novel* by Sharon Magnarelli, 1985; *Carlos Fuentes: Life, Work, and Criticism* by Alfonso González, 1987; *El mito en la obra narrativa de Carlos Fuentes* by Francisco J. Ordiz, 1987; *La obra de Carlos Fuentes: Una visión múltiple* by Ana María Hernández de López, 1988; *Fabulación de la fe: Carlos Fuentes* by Fernando García Núñez, 1989; *Realidad y ficción en Terra nostra de Carlos Fuentes* by Ingrid Simson, 1989; *A Marxist Reading of Fuentes, Vargas Llosa and Puig* by Victor Manuel Durán, 1993.

*   *   *

Carlos Fuentes for some years now has been one of the most imposing figures in Latin America. His fame extends beyond literary achievements, and certainly beyond his mother country Mexico (actually he was born in Panama where his father, who was in the diplomatic service, was stationed at the time). He belongs to the Latin American generation of great writers who are known as the authors of 'the Boom'. Along with Fuentes, other such luminaries as Gabriel García Márquez and Octavio Paz (both Nobel prize winners) have made the world aware of the great accomplishments of Latin American literature. In 1987 Fuentes was awarded Spain's most prestigious literary prize, 'el premio Cervantes'. He has received numerous other important prizes from many countries, including the Venezuelan Rómulo Gallegos national prize, equivalent to the Cervantes prize in Spain.

Fuentes has a rich and varied professional life. He is equally at home when speaking French, English, or Spanish, and in the subject areas of literature, history, politics, or journalism. He has been visiting professor in the United States at some of the most distinguished universities, and has received honorary degrees from many more. In matters of diplomatic positions, he has attained the highest cultural post available to any artist in a Latin American country, as his nation's Ambassador to France. In England and France he has been involved with the intellectual pursuits of the intelligentsia. Moreover, he has been quite active in meetings and conferences in underdeveloped countries. His passion, of course, has been his dedication to understanding, and expressing in literary form the essence of Mexican civilization, and by extension the substance of Latin American life and thought. His quest is inexorably linked to capturing the spiritual structure of those countries, Spain and the United States in particular, whose values are interwoven by patrimony as in the case of Spain, or by propinquity and political dominance as in the case of the USA, with the destiny of Latin America.

Fuentes distinguished himself as a writer of note with *La muerte de Artemio Cruz* (*The Death of Artemio Cruz*), later becoming a truly international figure as a man of letters. *The Death of Artemio Cruz,* which depicts the dying days of a former general of the Mexican Revolution, re-creates the history of Mexico from 1910, when the Revolution broke out. As the old moribund patriot of the struggle for freedom chronicles the idealistic quest for liberty and for an equitable distribution of land, he wonders, as did Don Quixote towards the end of his life, what, if anything, was accomplished. At the same time that Artemio Cruz reflects on the uselessness of the past, he comments on his surviving heirs to whom the impending death of an old man is essentially nothing but an annoying event that interferes with their immediate pursuit of personal happiness. Unbeknownst to the young, the dying patriot is able to listen in on the conversations around him. Yet there is no bitterness; *The Death of Artemio Cruz* smiles ironically on humanity. Disillusionment is conceived as but an inexorable experience of living. Idealism is as necessary as disenchantment is inevitable.

The 1985 novel *El gringo viejo* (*The Old Gringo*), which was subsequently made into a film starring Jane Fonda and Gregory Peck, projected the continuity of personal tyranny in Mexico. Revolutions and more revolutions fail to quench the thirst for power among the brave Mexican *machos.* Idealism, fuelled by adulation, makes despots or political bosses (*caciques*) of them all. Here we have the microcosm of the apparent never-ending growth of *caciques* throughout Latin America. Principles and ideals give way to personal hegemony, and all members of society in one way or another participate in creating a form of government that befits the abiding faith that one man can inspire. The old gringo is a naive, innocent observer who cannot fully grasp the prevailing form of life in a Latin American country. Even when the gringo means well, he is basically lost in another culture.

Fuentes's writings are indeed varied and numerous. However, *The Buried Mirror: Reflections on Spain and the New World* stands out as a most ambitious project. It is a kind of celebration of what has become the polemical quincentenary observance of Christopher Columbus's arrival in the New World. *The Buried Mirror* is akin to a self-examining quest for truth and reality. In the highest humanistic tradition, with a sense of compassion for human imperfection, Fuentes feel-ingly re-creates history for all participants, victors and vanquished alike. Perhaps they are all mere victims of their own passions. In the long run, the distinction between them is blurred. New World countries as well as Spain have experienced—and survived—all sorts of leaders and seemingly untenable situations. While not 'history' in the traditional sense, Fuentes's account affords us a living experience of the essence of the Hispanic and Hispanic American way of life.

—Robert Kirsner

G

GARCÍA LORCA, Federico. Born in Fuente` Vaqueros, near Granada, Spain, 5 June 1898. Educated at Colegio del Sagrado Corazón de Jesús, Granada; also studied piano at Granada conservatory; University of Granada, 1914–19; travelled in Spain, 1915–17; Residencia de Estudiantes, Madrid, 1919–29; Columbia University, New York, 1929–30. Editor of artistic review, *El Gallo*, 1928; travelled to Paris, London, New York, and Havana (Cuba), 1929–30; founder and director of itinerant government-sponsored student theatre group, La Barraca, in the 1930s (grant withdrawn 1935); visited Buenos Aires (Argentina) in 1933. Arrested and shot by Franco supporters immediately following the outbreak of the Spanish Civil War. *Died (executed) 18/19 August 1936.*

PUBLICATIONS

Collections

Obras completas, edited by Guillermo de Torre. 7 vols., 1938–42.
Obras completas, edited by Arturo del Hoyo. 1954; revised editions, 2 vols., 1973; 3 vols., 1986; edited and translated by J.L. Gili, 1960.
Collected Plays (includes the texts of *Three Tragedies*, 1947, and *Five Plays*, 1963), translated by James Graham-Luján and Richard L. O'Connell. 1976.
Obras, edited by Miguel García-Posada. 6 vols., 1980.
Plays, translated by Gwynne Edwards and Peter Luke. 3 vols., 1987–91.
Collected Poems, edited by Christopher Maurer. 1991.

Plays

El maleficio de la mariposa (produced 1920). In *Obras completas*, 1954; as *The Butterfly's Evil Spell*, translated by James Graham-Luján and Richard L. O'Connell, in *Five Plays*, 1963.
Mariana Pineda (produced 1927). 1928; as *Mariana Pineda*, translated by James Graham-Luján, in *Tulane Drama Review*, 7(2), 1962; also translated by Robert G. Havard, 1987; Gwynne Edwards, with *The Public* and *Play Without a Title*, 1991.
Quimera. In *El Gallo*, May 1928; in book form, in *Teatro breve*, 1954.
El paseo de Buster Keaton (produced 1986). In *El Gallo*, May 1928; in book form, in *Teatro breve*, 1954; as *Buster Keaton's Promenade*, translated by Tim Reynolds, in *Accent*, 17(3), 1957.
La doncella, el marinero y el estudiante (produced 1986). In *El Gallo*, May 1928; in book form, in *Teatro breve*, 1954.
La zapatera prodigiosa (produced 1930; revised version produced 1933). In *Obras completas*, 1938; edited by J. and F. Street, 1962; as *The Shoemaker's Prodigious Wife*, translated by James Graham-Luján and Richard L. O'Connell, in *From Lorca's Theatre*, 1941, and in *Five Plays*, 1963; as

The Shoemaker's Wonderful Wife, translated by Gwynne Edwards, in *Plays 2*, 1990.
El amor de Don Perlimplín con Belisa en su jardín (produced 1933). In *Obras completas*, 1938; as *The Love of Don Perlimplín*, translated by James Graham-Luján and Richard L. O'Connell, in *From Lorca's Theatre*, 1941, and in *Five Plays*, 1963; as *The Love of Don Perlimplín for Belisa in the Garden*, translated by David Johnston, 1990.
Bodas de sangre (produced 1933). 1935; edited by H. Ramsden, 1980; as *Blood Wedding*, translated by Gilbert Murray, 1939; also translated by James Graham-Luján and Richard L. O'Connell, in *Three Tragedies*, 1947; Sue Bradbury, in *Three Tragedies*, 1977; Michael Dewell and Carmen Zapata, in *The Rural Trilogy*, 1987; Gwynne Edwards, in *Three Plays*, 1988; David Johnston, 1989.
La dama boba, from a play by Lope de Vega (produced 1934).
Yerma (produced 1934). 1937; as *Yerma*, in *From Lorca's Theatre*, translated by James Graham-Luján and Richard L. O'Connell, 1941, and in *Three Tragedies*, 1947; also translated by Sue Bradbury, in *Three Tragedies*, 1977; Ian MacPherson and Jacqueline Minett, 1987; Michael Dewell and Carmen Zapata, in *The Rural Trilogy*, 1987; Peter Luke, in *Three Plays*, 1988; David Johnston, 1990.
Doña Rosita la soltera (produced 1935). In *Obras completas*, 1938; as *Doña Rosita the Spinster*, translated by James Graham-Luján and Richard L. O'Connell, in *From Lorca's Theatre*, 1941, and in *Five Plays*, 1963; translated by Gwynne Edwards and Peter Luke, in *Three Plays*, 1988.
El 'retablillo' de Don Cristóbal (produced 1935). In *Obras completas*, 1938; as *The Tragicomedy of Don Cristóbal and Doña Rosita*, translated by Will I. Oliver, in *New World Writing*, 8, 1955; as *The Puppet Play of Don Cristóbal*, translated by Gwynne Edwards, in *Plays*, 2, 1990.
Los títeres de Cachiporra (produced 1937). 1949; as *The Billy-Club Puppets*, translated by James Graham-Luján and Richard L. O'Connell, in *Five Plays*, 1963.
Así que pasen cinco años (produced in English 1945; produced in Spanish 1978). In *Obras completas*, 1938; as *If Five Years Pass*, translated by James Graham-Luján and Richard L. O'Connell, in *From Lorca's Theatre*, 1941; as *When Five Years Pass*, translated by Gwynne Edwards, in *Plays*, 2, 1990; as *Once Five Years Pass*, translated by W.B. Logan and A.G. Orrios, in *Once Five Years Pass, and Other Dramatic Works*, 1990.
From Lorca's Theatre: Five Plays (includes *If Five Years Pass*; *Yerma*; *The Love of Don Perlimplín*; *Doña Rosita the Spinster*; *The Shoemaker's Prodigious Wife*), translated by James Graham-Luján and Richard L. O'Connell. 1941.
La casa de Bernarda Alba (produced 1945). 1945; edited by H. Ramsden, 1984; as *The House of Bernarda Alba*, translated by James Graham-Luján and Richard L. O'Connell, in *Three Tragedies*, 1947; also translated by Sue Bradbury, in *Three Tragedies*, 1977; Michael Dewell and Carmen Zapata, in *The Rural Trilogy*, 1987.
Three Tragedies (includes *Blood Wedding*; *The House of*

Bernarda Alba; *Yerma*), edited and translated by James Graham-Luján and Richard L. O'Connell. 1947.

Playlets (includes *Buster Keaton's Promenade*; *Chimera*; *The Virgin, the Sailor and the Student*), translated by Tim Reynolds, in *Accent*, 17(3), 1957.

Five Plays: Comedies and Tragedies (includes *The Butterfly's Evil Spell*; *The Billy-Club Puppets*; *The Shoemaker's Prodigious Wife*; *The Love of Don Perlimplín*; *Doña Rosita the Spinster*), translated by James Graham-Luján and Richard L. O'Connell. 1963.

El público (produced in English 1972; produced in Spanish 1986). With *Comedia sin título*, 1978; as *The Public*, translated by Carlos Bauer, 1983; also translated by Gwynne Edwards, 1991.

Three Tragedies (includes *Blood Wedding*; *Yerma*; *Bernarda Alba*), translated by Sue Bradbury. 1977.

El público y Comedia sin título: Dos obras teatrales póstumas, edited by Rafael Martínez Nadal. 1978; as *The Public, and Play Without a Title: Two Posthumous Plays*, translated by Carlos Bauer, 1983; as *The Public and Play Without a Title*, translated by Gwynne Edwards, with *Mariana Pineda*, 1991.

Comedia sin título (produced 1989). With *El público*, 1978; as *Play Without a Title*, translated by Carlos Bauer, 1983; also translated by Gwynne Edwards, 1991.

The Rural Trilogy (includes *Blood Wedding*; *Yerma*; *The House of Bernarda Alba*), translated by Michael Dewell and Carmen Zapata. 1987; as *Three Plays*, 1992.

Three Plays (includes *Blood Wedding*; *Doña Rosita the Spinster*; *Yerma*), translated by Gwynne Edwards and Peter Luke. 1988; as *Plays 1*, 1991.

Once Five Years Pass, and Other Dramatic Works, translated by W.B. Logan and A.G. Orrios, 1990.

Screenplay: *Trip to the Moon*, translated by Bernice C. Duncan, in *New Directions*, 18, 1964.

Verse

Libro de poemas. 1921; reprinted 1974.
Canciones. 1927; as *Canciones*, edited by Daniel Eisenberg, translated by Philip Cummings, 1976.
Primer romancero gitano. 1928; edited by H. Ramsden, 1988, and by Derek Harris, 1991; as *Gypsy Ballads*, translated by Rolfe Humphries, 1953; also translated by Michael Hartnett, 1973; Carl W. Cobb, 1983; Robert G. Havard, 1990.
Poema del cante jondo. 1931; as *Poem of the Deep Song*, translated by Christopher Bauer, 1987.
Oda a Walt Whitman. 1933.
Llanto por la muerte de Ignacio Sánchez Mejías. 1935.
Primeras canciones. 1936.
Seis poemas galegos. 1936.
Lament for the Death of a Bullfighter and Other Poems, translated by A.L. Lloyd. 1937.
Poems, translated by Stephen Spender and J.L. Gili. 1939.
Diván del Tamarit. 1940; as *Divan*, translated by Edwin Honig, in *Divan and Other Writings*, 1974.
Poeta en Nueva York. 1940; edited by Christopher Maurer, translated by Greg Simon and Steven White, 1989; as *Poet in New York*, translated by Rolfe Humphries, 1940; also translated by Ben Belitt, 1955.
Selected Poems, translated by Lloyd Mallan. 1941.
Selected Poems, translated by J.L. Gili and Stephen Spender. 1947.
Poemas sueltos. 1954.
Cantares populares. 1954.

Selected Poems, translated by Francisco García Lorca and Donald M. Allen. 1955.
Selected Poems, translated by J.L. Gili (prose). 1960.
Lorca and Jiménez, translated by Robert Bly. 1973.
Divan and Other Writings, translated by Edwin Honig. 1974.
Canciones y poemas para niños. As *The Cricket Sings: Poems and Songs for Children*, translated by Will Kirkland, 1980.
Suites (selected poetry), edited by André Belamich. 1983.
Canciones y primeras canciones, edited by Piero Menarini. 1986.
Diván del Tamarit; Seis poemas galegos; Llanto por Ignacio Sánchez Mejías; Poemas sueltos, edited by Andrew A. Anderson. 1988.
Ode to Walt Whitman and Other Poems, translated by Carlos Bauer. 1988.
The Towers of Cordova: Selected Poems, translated by Merryn Williams. 1990.
Songs and Ballads, translated by R. Skelton. 1992.

Other

Impresiones y paisajes. 1918; as *Impressions and Landscapes*, translated by L.H. Klibbe, 1987.
Homenaje al Poeta Federico García Lorca (selection and commentary), edited by Antonio Machado and Emilio Prados. 1937.
Cartas a sus amigos, edited by S. Gasch. 1950.
Cartas; postales; poemas y dibujos, edited by A. Gallego Morell. 1968.
Granada, Paraíso Cerrado y otras páginas granadinas, edited by Enrique Martínez López. 1971.
Autográfos, edited by Rafael Martínez Nadal. 1975–76.
Deep Song and Other Prose, edited by Christopher Maurer. 1980.
Selected Letters, edited and translated by David Gershator. 1983.
Oda y burla de Sesostris y Sardanápalo, edited by Miguel García-Posada. 1985.
Diván del Tamarit y otros textos, edited by Aída O'Ward and Carlos Arredondo. 1988.
Four Puppet Plays, Play Without a Title, the Divan Poems, and Other Prose Poems and Dramatic Pieces, translated by Edwin Honig. 1990.
Poeta en Nueva York y otras hojas y poemas: Manuscritos neoyorquinos, edited by Mario Fernández. 1990.
Barbarous Nights: Legends and Plays, translated by C.S. Laucanno. 1991.

Editor: *El Gallo: Revista de Granada*, in 1928.

*

Bibliography: *García Lorca: A Selectively Annotated Bibliography of Criticism*, 1980, and *García Lorca: An Annotated Primary Bibliography*, 1982, both edited by Francesca Colecchia; *Federico García Lorca: A Bibliography* by Everett E. Larson, 1987.

Critical Studies: *Federico García Lorca* by Edwin Honig, 1944; *Lorca: The Poet and His People* by Arturo Barea, 1945; *Federico García Lorca* by John A. Crow, 1945; *Lorca: An Appreciation of His Poetry* by Roy Campbell, 1952; *Lorca and the Spanish Poetic Tradition* by J.B. Trend, 1955; *Lorca: A Collection of Critical Essays* edited by Manuel Durán, 1962 and *Lorca's Legacy* edited by Durán and Francesca Colecchia, 1991; *The Theatre of García Lorca* by Robert

Lima, 1963; *The Victorious Expression: A Study of Four Contemporary Spanish Poets: Miguel de Unamuno, Antonio Machado, Juan Ramón Jiménez, Federico García Lorca* by Howard T. Young, 1964; *García Lorca* by Rafael Alberti, 1966; *Federico García Lorca* by Carl W. Cobb, 1967; *Federico García Lorca* by Rolf Michaelis, 1969; *The Symbolic World of García Lorca*, 1972, and *Psyche and Symbol in the Theatre of Federico García Lorca*, 1974, both by Rupert Allen; *The Death of Lorca*, 1973, revised edition, as *The Assassination of Federico García Lorca*, 1979, and *Federico García Lorca: A Life*, 1989, both by Ian Gibson; *Lorca's The Public* by Rafael Martínez Nadal, 1974; *A Concordance to the Plays and Poems of Federico García Lorca*, 1975; *La Barraca and the Spanish National Theatre* by Suzanne W. Byrd, 1975; *The Comic Spirit of Federico García Lorca* by Virginia Higginbotham, 1976; *García Lorca, Playwright and Poet* by Mildred Adams, 1977; *Lorca's Poet in New York: The Fall Into Consciousness* by Betty Jean Craige, 1977; *Federico García Lorca and Sean O'Casey: Powerful Voices in the Wilderness* by Katie Brittain Adams Davis, 1978; *García Lorca: Poeta en Nueva York* by Derek Harris, 1978; *Federico García Lorca: The Poetry of Limits* by David K. Loughran, 1978; *García Lorca's Poema del Cante Jondo* by Norman C. Miller, 1978; *The Tragic Myth: Lorca and Cante Jondo* by Edward F. Stanton, 1978; *Lorca: The Theatre Beneath the Sands*, 1980, and *Dramatists in Perspective: Spanish Theatre in the Twentieth Century*, 1985, both by Gwynne Edwards; *Lorca's New York Poetry: Social Injustice, Dark Love, Lost Faith* by Richard Predmore, 1980; *García Lorca: Bodas de Sangre*, 1981, and *García Lorca: La Casa de Bernarda Alba*, 1990, both by Cyril Brian Morris, and *'Cuando yo me Muera . . .': Essays in Memory of Federico García Lorca*, 1988 edited by Morris; *Lorca's Impresiones y Paisajes: The Young Artist* by Laurence Hadfield Klibbe, 1983; *Federico García Lorca* by Reed Anderson, 1984; *Federico García Lorca* by Felicia Hardison Londres, 1984; *Lorca: The Gay Imagination* by Paul Binding, 1985; *Federico García Lorca: Life, Work and Criticism* by C. Grant McCurdy, 1986; *In the Green Morning: Memories of Federico* by Francisco García Lorca, translated by Christopher Maurer, 1986; *Lorca, the Drawings: Their Relation to the Poet's Life and Work* by Helen Oppenheimer, 1986; *Lorca's Romancero Gitano: Eighteen Commentaries* by H. Ramsden, 1988; *Leeds Papers on Lorca and on Civil War Verse* edited by Margaret A. Rees, 1988; *Lorca's Late Poetry: A Critical Study*, 1990, and *García Lorca: La Zapatera Prodigiosa*, 1991, both by Andrew A. Anderson; *Line of Light and Shadow: The Drawings of Federico García Lorca* by Mario Hernandez, 1991; *File on Lorca* edited by Andy Piasecki, 1991; *Lorca: Poet and Playwright—Essays in Honour of J.M. Aguirre* edited by Robert G. Havard, 1992.

*   *   *

Federico García Lorca has come to be one of the most widely read and admired authors who have written in Spanish in the 20th century. His execution by fascists at the outbreak of the Spanish Civil War abruptly brought his name into world focus, but since then his work as a poet and playwright has endured the test of political notoriety and has continued to prosper on the strength of its intrinsic worth.

Leonardo, the protagonist of *Bodas de sangre* (*Blood Wedding*), one of Lorca's most famous plays, defends adulterous love in these terms: 'The fault is not mine/The fault belongs to the earth'. A case could readily be made to substantiate the point of view that all of Lorca's protagonists, including the poet-narrator himself, struggle in the grip of telluric passions. Smugglers, gypsies, suppressed women, and ultimately the poet have but one goal: to exult, by means of startling metaphors fashioned against the backdrop of Andalusia, their pain and grief at the indifference of society and the silence of death. In a celebrated lecture, Lorca pointed to the Andalusian *duende* (goblin) as the embodiment of dark and dangerous feelings. In Lorca's canon, the greatest crime is to stifle the expression of these emotions and the greatest fear is the total tranquillity of death.

By emphasizing the demonic inspiration of his verse, Lorca placed himself in the tradition of those who believe in the Platonic seizure, or in Housman's shivers down the spine. A master of details of form, he nevertheless insisted that the totality of the poem was something over which he had no control. 'If it is true' he once said, 'that I am a poet through the grace of God (or the devil), I have also got where I am by virtue of work and technical skill, without having the slightest notion of what a poem is.'

Constantly requested to read his poetry aloud (which he did with great effect), Lorca had all the appearances of a latter-day bard. His strong sense of the oral tradition led him at times to display indifference toward the printed word. Many poems circulated among friends, or survived in the intimacy of small public readings before they became fixed between the covers of books.

Childhood memories of playing in meadows with crumpled purple mountains in the distance, such is Lorca's own characterization of his first book of verse *Libro de poemas* [Book of Poems]. Graceful combinations of humour, irony, and whimsy bestow a tone notably lacking in most of his subsequent poetry. A strong sense of mystery and magic pervade this Andalusian pastoral.

In *Poema del cante jondo* (*Poem of the Deep Song*), Lorca sought to capture in verse the impact of the heady, monotonous, and pathetic chant that had been introduced into Spain from oriental sources. He personifies the *cante*, turns it into a baleful, dark-haired woman, attributes cosmic powers to it (the shout of the singer causes olive groves to tremble and even silence quivers), and finally makes it an expression of elemental grief. By now, the characteristics of Lorca's modernism have become clear: using an acute sense of local culture (Andalusia), he will express in bold metaphorical terms the loneliness, grief, and frustration of the human predicament.

The *Primer romancero gitano* (*Gypsy Ballads*) raises the plight of the persecuted gypsies of Spain to the level of poetry by inventing a mythology for them. In doing so, Lorca went back beyond the Greek and Roman myths and intuited a primitive mythology in which there is a close relationship between man and cosmic reality. The moon opens the book by stealing away a gypsy boy, and under her influence, the fortunes of the gypsies wax and wane. The wind attempts to rape a gypsy girl, and all of nature reacts in sympathy to her plight. By skilfully employing the eight-syllable line and the strong dramatic dialogue form of the old Spanish *romance* (ballad), Lorca demonstrates once again his ability to meld traditional elements into his modern outlook. The bedazzling, sometimes disturbing metaphors of this popular book have still not worn thin.

Seeking to step aside from the success accorded him in Madrid, Lorca went to New York in the summer of 1929. His sensitivities, developed in an agrarian and conservative European region, were overwhelmed by the vast concreteness of New York, its technological power, and the festering racial prejudice. *Poeta en Nueva York* (*Poet in New York*), making use of a modified form of surrealism, is a description of the collapse of his personal world and the painful process of picking up the pieces again. In terms of its denunciation of modern civilization, it is often compared to T.S. Eliot's *The Waste Land*. Lorca's outraged feeling of social justice and his sympathy for the underdog come through loud and clear. The section on Harlem, with its forecast of violence between blacks and whites, has turned out to be remarkably prescient. The death of a bullfighter friend inspired *Llanto por la muerte de Ignacio Sánchez Mejías* (*Lament for the Death of a Bullfighter*), considered by many critics to be one of the most impressive of modern elegies.

Aside from the playfulness and sense of humour sporadically present in the early verse, the register of Lorca's poetic voice is intense, dark, and sombre. Passionate descriptions rather than philosophical reflections mark his work. Once again, his regional background plays a role, for the *andaluz*, he once remarked, is either asleep in the dust or shouting at the stars.

Lorca's plays have been performed around the world. *Blood Wedding*, *Yerma*, and *La casa de Bernarda Alba* (*The House of Bernarda Alba*), dealing with sexual frustration, are his best known works for the theatre, but there is a strong interest in an experimental play, *The Public* (finished in 1930 but not produced in Spain until 1987) that, well before Genet, deals with homosexuality on the stage. In the so-called rural trilogy, the violent punishment of adultery, the tortures of sterility imposed by environment as well as nature, and the oppressiveness of a matriarchal family are handled powerfully. The first two make extensive use of poetry and have earned Lorca a reputation among modern dramatists for his ability to incorporate lyrics in his plays.

—Howard T. Young

BLOOD WEDDING (Bodas de sangre)
Play by Federico García Lorca, 1933.

Blood Wedding was conceived as a musical piece whose theme engenders its counterpoint-response, with the dialogue an interweaving of voices. Lorca declared (during an interview about *Blood Wedding*) that his entire work—poetry and theatre—could be traced to the works of J.S. Bach; he particularly admired the mathematical symmetry and precise intellectual structure.

Blood Wedding is the first and most enigmatic of Lorca's trilogy of rural Andalusian tragedies, combining realism, fantasy, lyricism, and traditional folkloric materials in a radically innovative way. Mythopoeic realism in the first two acts changes to surrealist fantasy in the third, but the result falls generally within the tradition of classical tragedy that Lorca strove consciously to evoke. Rather than presenting an ancient myth in modern guise, Lorca re-created the living primitivism of agrarian Andalusia, where the treeless, volcanic desert near the country towns of Lorca and Gaudix (south-east of Granada, province of Almería) contains numerous long-inhabited caves—some quite luxuriously furnished. Like Yeats, Cocteau, Eliot, and others, Lorca sought mythic dimensions and poetic language, but the settings of the first two acts echo socio-economic realities of the area. Aspects of the plot, artistically re-elaborated, likewise originated in true events, most notably a sensational crime in Níjar in 1928: a rural bride fled her wedding with her cousin, who was shot and killed by an unknown ambusher (subsequently identified as the groom's brother). Lorca retained the principal triangle of bride, groom, and rival, and the motivating triad of desire, jealousy, and revenge, but added a longstanding blood feud between the families and modified the fatal event so that groom and rival slay each other. Tripartite settings include the farm homes of the groom and Leonardo in Act I, the Bride's cavern in Act II, and the damp, primeval, druidic forest in Act III (the only setting not based on local reality). Lorca postulated a broken engagement between the Bride and Leonardo (now married, with an infant son). Yet these complications only stoke the smouldering primal passions of the Bride and Leonardo, leading to the explosion of repressed emotions unleashed at the wedding.

Spain's lack of tradition in the tragic theatre (excepting Romantic variants) challenged Lorca to attempt modern tragedy, incorporating mythic and telluric elements. Following classical precedent, he made his protagonists victims of inscrutable, irresistible forces, not specifically identified with fate, but blind, impersonal instincts capable of annihilating moral scruples and reversing reason. Stark, spare settings, limited time span (events in the present occupy less than a week), and tightly controlled numbers (only four characters have major roles) echo classical antecedents, as does having the violence occur offstage: spectators hear the mortal cries but do not witness the sacrificial bloodshed.

The uninterrupted existence of ancient customs, millennial oral traditions, and folklore, and primitive agrarian lifestyles in rural Andalusia facilitated the linking of prehistoric roots and modern psychology. Lorca's familiarity with Spanish translations of Freud and his own experimentation with surrealist technique (*Poet in New York*) offered connections between vanguard literary creativity and the unconscious past, neolithic religions, and Dionysian mysteries. An assiduous reader of classical tragedians, especially Sophocles and Euripides, Lorca conceived Andalusian rural culture as mythic—inherently violent, primitive, and tragic—and linked directly to prehistoric rituals of sacrifice and proto-religious mysteries of birth, fertility (reproduction), and death. Within this context, contemporary crimes of passion and vengeance become sacrificial rituals, their protagonists merely pawns of powers which, despite centuries of history, continue to be mysterious and irresistible.

One interpretation of *Blood Wedding* views it as a drama of the soil, with the Groom representing water and the Bride the arid lands. Another interpretation, emphasizing socio-economic factors, postulates an indictment of arranged marriages based on property rather than on mutual attraction. Still another views the work as a re-enactment of mythic patterns described by Sir James Frazer in *The Golden Bough*, the marriage and death cycle repeated endlessly. Finally, the moon's role in the third act (and lunar associations with agriculture, fertility cycles, and death) underlie interpretations of *Blood Wedding* as a demonstration of the continuing power of the White Goddess and humanity's helplessness before cosmic forces and primal urges. Lorca's tragedies give weight to women's roles and his heroines are much more interesting than their male counterparts; many of his plays can be read as indictments of women's lot in Spain: the Bride's self-defence and her protestation of innocence are not only a dramatic high point, but unprecedented in Spanish theatre.

Although exotic and fantastic for cosmopolitan theatregoers of Lorca's day, *Blood Wedding* remains within the bounds of contemporary Andalusian reality for the first two acts. Following Lope de Vega, Lorca reworked popular songs and dances, doing his own musical adaptations of folk ballads and lullabies, and poetically modifying their lyrics to foreshadow the fatal outcome, thereby enhancing the air of inevitability of the ritualistic violence in the last act. Excepting Leonardo, characters are nameless, generic, archetypal, identified by familial roles (Father, Mother, Wife,

Mother-in-Law) or function (the neighbours, woodcutters, wedding guests). Lorca updates the chorus of Greek tragedy, reincarnating its commentator function in groups extraneous to the action (the woodcutters and girls of the third act, for example). Fantastic, supernatural, surrealistic figures (the Moon, Death in the guise of the old beggar) embody primal powers vested by primitive peoples in the lunar deity. In his poetry Lorca consistently associates the moon with fatality, mystery, and death, and the horse with unbridled sexual passion, connections maintained in *Blood Wedding*. Amalgamating elements drawn from widely varied sources—ancient myth and modern newspapers, classical tragedy and vanguard literary experimentation, primitive ritual and 20th-century psychology, local socio-economic reality and his own imagination—Lorca created a uniquely personal, distinctive masterpiece.

—Janet Pérez

THE HOUSE OF BERNARDA ALBA (La casa de Bernarda Alba)
Play by Federico García Lorca, 1945.

The House of Bernarda Alba is, like *Blood Wedding*, set in the Spanish countryside and tells the story of the 60-year-old Bernarda's domination of her household, including her five, spinster daughters. The beginning of Act I announces a period of eight years of mourning following the recent death of Bernarda's husband and reveals at every step Bernarda's harshness towards her servants, her mother, and her daughters. Of these, the eldest, Angustias, is to marry Pepe el Romano, a circumstance that stirs up feelings of envy and resentment, particularly in the youngest and most attractive daughter, Adela, and the older and unattractive Martirio. In Act II, existing tensions intensify. Adela grows more rebellious, Martirio more resentful. Her theft of Angustias's portrait of Pepe draws from the servant, La Poncia, warnings to which Bernarda responds with a demonstration of even greater intransigence. Act III reveals that Adela has been meeting Pepe secretly at night. Her discovery by Martirio results in Bernarda attempting to shoot him as he escapes. Convinced by Martirio of Pepe's death, Adela hangs herself, and Bernarda announces a second period of mourning, for her daughter, who, others must believe, died a virgin.

Like *Blood Wedding*, *The House of Bernarda Alba* had its source in real life, for as a child Lorca had a next-door neighbour, 'an old widow who exercises an inexorable and tyrannical watch over her spinster daughters', one of whom was said to have a lover, Pepe de la Romilla. On the other hand, there are also literary sources. The insistence which Bernarda places on the good name of the family, deeply ingrained in the Spanish temperament, had its literary antecedent in the plays of the 17th century, notably in the 'honour' plays of Calderón, with which Lorca was very familiar. The obsessive concern with the good opinion of others, which drives Bernarda to incarcerate her daughters and leads finally to Adela's death, is the motive which in Calderón's *The Surgeon of Honour* obliges a husband to murder an innocent wife. Another possible source was the novel *Doña Perfecta* by the 19th-century novelist Pérez Galdós, in which, in a narrow-minded, provincial town, the intolerant Doña Perfecta becomes increasingly opposed to the marriage of her daughter, Rosario, to the young liberal from Madrid, Pepe Rey. When the couple attempt to elope, she arranges Pepe's murder, after which Rosario loses her sanity. Finally, as in the case of

Blood Wedding, the influence of Greek tragedy is very clear: the play's title suggests a household or a lineage; Bernarda brings about, through her actions, the end she seeks to avoid; there is a powerful sense of fatality; and the final scenes are strongly cathartic. But if the literary debt is evident, the themes of the play are pure Lorca: passion and frustration, exemplified above all in Adela; passing time, personified in the ageing of all the daughters; and death, physical in Adela's case, emotional in the other girls. Not only does the play constitute another powerful expression of Lorca's own situation, it also anticipates the divisions which would tear apart the family of Spain in the summer of 1936, only months after the play's completion.

Lorca's assertion that *The House of Bernarda Alba* is a '*documental fotográfico*' (a 'photographic record'), together with his deliberate stripping-away of obviously poetic elements, has encouraged the belief that, in contrast to *Blood Wedding* and *Yerma*, this is a naturalistic play. An examination of its style and techniques suggests that nothing could be further from the truth. While it is true that more of the characters have real names than is the case in the other plays—Adela, Amelia, María Josefa, La Poncia—the names of others are decidedly symbolic: Angustias and Martirio suggesting suffering incarnate, and Bernarda Alba ironically suggestive of the illumination of dawn. Indeed, each of the characters embodies to some degree the clash of the opposites longing and denial which, concentrated in Bernarda's family, has its counterpart in other families wherever natural instinct comes into conflict with narrow-minded tradition.

Despite their apparent naturalism, the play's three settings are highly stylized, with the white walls evoking purity and virginity but also sterility and the endless monotony of imprisoned lives. Within the frame of the settings, movement and posture enhance the image: the daughters seated at the beginning of Act II, sewing passively; or later in the act the despairing Martirio, seated, head in hands. In contrast, bursts of activity suggest from time to time Adela's defiance, as does her green dress, suddenly bringing a splash of colour into the darkened house. Lighting too has a crucial role to play. In Act I the opening of a door momentarily floods the room with light, suggesting the world beyond the house. Act II sustains the idea when the girls observe the harvesters through a half-open shutter, but by Act III it is night, with Adela and Martirio engulfed by a darkness that is as much emotional, suggesting despair and mutual hate, as it is physical. The studied interplay of setting, movement, and lighting exposes the inner lives of the characters and affects the response of the audience in a way that naturalism could never do.

The language of the play, mainly in prose, is also carefully shaped, stripped of the inconsequential trivia of everyday speech. Almost every word exposes character: Bernarda's outbursts are the verbal equivalent of the stick with which she beats the ground; Adela's speech is alive with defiance, while Magdalena's is heavy with despair. When songs are introduced, on two crucial occasions, their rhythm pinpoints the importance of the moment, as in Act II when the vibrant harvester's song encapsulates a world for which Bernarda's daughters long but which they cannot reach.

The trajectory from the highly poetic *Blood Wedding* to the much more austere *The House of Bernarda Alba* is typical of Lorca's constant experimentation. But the differences between the two plays are less important than their similarity, which lies ultimately in the importance for Lorca of the poetic and the imaginative in the theatre.

—Gwynne Edwards

YERMA
Play by Federico García Lorca, 1934.

Yerma, the second play of Lorca's trilogy of rural Andalusian tragedies, was first performed on 29 December 1934. The author repeatedly termed *Yerma* a work without a plot, the 'tragedy of the sterile woman', a concept echoed by the title. Although Lorca called his heroine Yerma, this is not a woman's name but an adjective normally applied to barren land. Because of Lorca's numerous affirmations and because Yerma's name foretells her destiny, Spanish critics have deemed the play a tragedy of sterility. The only lack of consensus concerns how general or specific its scope may be: is Lorca portraying the tragic plight of a sterile individual, or of all sterile women? Or is *Yerma* a political critique, an allegory of national or cultural sterility?

Before completing *Yerma*, Lorca stated that the play would have four major characters and choruses, 'as classical tragedies should', but the four main characters are not easily identifiable. The heroine overshadows all others, so that the most precise description might be 'dramatic monologue with supporting cast'. Besides the chorus of laundresses and groups of girls and women whose functions are essentially choric, there are anonymous crowds at the *romería* (pilgrimage), the nameless male and female masks, Juan's unnamed spinster sisters, and several men at the shrine who function as anonymous vehicles of fertilization. Only a handful of characters have names: Juan, Yerma's husband; Víctor, the shepherd representing pure, innocent, adolescent love; Yerma's friend, María; and Dolores, a lusty village woman practising white witchcraft. Juan and Víctor, given their importance in Yerma's life, qualify as major characters, although neither spends much time on stage, and Yerma's girlhood companion, María, functions largely as a contrasting portrait of contented maternity, intensifying Yerma's unfulfilled longing.

If *Yerma* is compared to *Blood Wedding*, significant similarities emerge: the marriage of convenience, arranged between families for economic reasons; the triangle of two men and a woman, in which the husband's concern is his honour, while the wife (although caring little for her husband) remains faithful, sacrificing her possible happiness to an empty patriarchal code of marital fidelity. Wifely loyalty, denying the longings of the heart, is a major factor in both tragedies which, without the triumph of duty over desire, might be merely dramas of adultery.

The play ignores the unity of time customary for classical tragedy. When the action begins, Yerma and Juan have been married for two years. In the second *cuadro* (each of the three acts comprises two *cuadros*), Yerma's marriage is three years old. By the second act, it has lasted for more than five years, and an unspecified additional time elapses between the second and third acts, sufficient for Yerma's desperation for a child to drive her to attempt extreme measures (e.g. spells in the cemetery at midnight; a pilgrimage later) in her quest for pregnancy. The play's total duration is some eight to ten years, but the unity and intensity of emotion are undiminished. On the contrary, Yerma's growing frustration builds to a rising crescendo, which peaks with her violent, homicidal outburst in the climactic final scene.

Critics who see *Yerma* simply as a tragedy of sterility (and perhaps even the poet himself) are overlooking two exceptionally significant details that bear upon interpretation. First, Yerma's husband does not want children, and has consciously opted against paternity (there are repeated references to his onanism, and Juan proclaims unmistakably that he does not want children). Second, *vox populi* (represented by groups

with choric functions) and individual characters indicate clearly that Yerma is not infertile but unfertilized. Her drama is thus not one of sterility but of thwarted maternal instinct. Yerma's barrenness results not from her own biological incapability but from Juan's refusal to permit her productivity, which has profound hermeneutical implications: Yerma is a victim of patriarchally-imposed restrictions. *Yerma* abounds in imagery or enclosure, and Juan repeatedly confines his wife to the house, bringing his spinster sisters to prevent her sallies. Feminist readings, therefore, might well see *Yerma* as expressing male fears of feminine creative potential.

Unquestionably, Lorca intended to create a cosmic, mythic dimension, as evinced by his use of music. The song of the washerwoman in Act II is a pagan paean to cosmic force or the god of fertility, a condensation of all that surrounds and frustrates Yerma in the daily lives of others. And like the song of the laundresses, that of the pilgrims (using the religious procession as a cynical veil for the search for new lovers) is used to create effects approaching the orgiastic, which contrast with Yerma's outer restraint and inner conflict. The play also contains Yerma's tender lullaby to her imaginary child, setting the mood for the opening scene, and Víctor's song, asking why the shepherd should sleep alone, which achieves great dramatic effect as it makes almost tangible the remedy to Yerma's barrenness—a solution which her honour prohibits.

Although part of the tragedy results from Juan's masculine fear of feminine weakness and facile corruptibility (notwithstanding Yerma's proud proclamations of her honour and integrity), the heroine is also a product of her patriarchal culture and paternalistic upbringing, the morality of Lorca's day which decreed that 'decent women' should not enjoy sexual relations but accede only for the sake of procreation. Yerma's tacit acceptance of the ancient code making familial honour dependent upon feminine virtue and her obsession with motherhood as the prime purpose for her existence directly reflect women's education in Hispanic countries generally, and Yerma's scrupulous internalization of these cultural imperatives destroys her when the two are brought into conflict by her husband's rejection of fatherhood. Maternity is an option for Yerma only at the price of her honour and she chooses honour at the expense of her own happiness. But Juan is not only quite content with the childlessness that so anguishes Yerma, he imposes yet another conflict upon her, demanding that she accept his sexual advances immediately after hearing that she must forget children forever. Raised to consider sexuality as justified exclusively for procreation, Yerma reacts in violent defence of her honour, killing the man who intended to use her solely for his pleasure. Her final proclamation, 'I have killed my child', reveals her awareness of the full consequences of her crime, which has placed motherhood forever beyond her grasp. Clearly, Yerma's tragedy transcends the individual; her plight is that of women not only in Hispanic countries but also in the Arabic world (whose culture was still alive in Andalusia) and all areas where women's productive potential is stifled.

—Janet Pérez

GARCÍA MÁRQUEZ, Gabriel. Born in Aracataca, Colombia, 6 March 1928. Educated at the Jesuit Colegio San

José, Barranquilla, 1940–42; Jesuit Colegio Nacional, Zipaquirá, to 1946; studied law and journalism at the National University of Colombia, Bogotá, 1947–48: studies interrupted by civil strife, and continued at University of Cartagena, 1948–49. Married Mercedes Barcha in 1958; two sons. Contributor of stories to *El Espectador*, 1947–52; journalist, *El Universal*, Cartagena, 1948–50; correspondent, *El Heraldo*, Barranquilla, 1950–54; journalist, 1954–55, and Paris correspondent, 1955, *El Espectador*: paper closed by government, 1955; lived in Europe, 1955–57; travelled through Eastern Europe, 1957; journalist in Caracas, 1958–59; joined Prensa Latina (Cuban press agency), 1959: opened its office in Bogotá, then worked in Havana, 1959, and New York until his resignation in 1961; lived in Mexico, 1961–67, working as journalist (editor, *Sucesos* and *La Familia*), advertising agent, and scriptwriter; lived in Spain, 1967–75; founder, left-wing *Alternativa*, Bogotá, 1974; returned to Mexico, 1975, and to Colombia in 1981; founder, *El Otro*, Bogotá, 1963. Member, Panamanian delegation for the USA–Panama treaty, Washington, DC, 1978; member, UNESCO commission on Third World Communications Problems, 1979; founder, 1979, and president, from 1979, Fundación Habeas; director, Foundation for New Latin American Cinema, Havana, 1986–88. Recipient: Colombian Association of Writers and Artists award, 1954; National Short Story Competition prize, 1955; Esso literary prize, 1961; Chianchiano prize (Italy), 1968; Foreign Book prize (France), 1970; Rómulo Gallegos prize (Venezuela), 1972; Neustadt international prize, 1972; Nobel prize for literature, 1982; Los Angeles *Times* prize, 1988. Honorary doctorate: Columbia University, New York, 1971. Légion d'honneur, 1981. Member, American Academy. Lives in Colombia.

PUBLICATIONS

Fiction

La hojarasca. 1955; as *Leaf Storm*, in *Leaf Storm and Other Stories*, translated by Gregory Rabassa, 1972.
El coronel no tiene quien le escriba. 1957; as *No One Writes to the Colonel*, translated by J.S. Bernstein, in *No One Writes to the Colonel and Other Stories*, 1968.
La mala hora. 1962; as *In Evil Hour*, translated by Gregory Rabassa, 1979.
Los funerales de la Mamá Grande (stories). 1962; as *Big Mama's Funeral*, translated by J.S. Bernstein, in *No One Writes to the Colonel and Other Stories*, 1968.
Isabel viendo llover en Macondo. 1967.
Cien años de soledad. 1967; as *One Hundred Years of Solitude*, translated by Gregory Rabassa, 1970.
Relato de un náufrago. 1970; as *The Story of a Shipwrecked Sailor*, translated by Randolph Hogan, 1989.
Leaf Storm and Other Stories, translated by Gregory Rabassa. 1972.
La increíble y triste historia de la cándida Eréndira y de su abuela desalmada: Siete cuentos. 1972; as *Innocent Erendira and Other Stories*, translated by Gregory Rabassa, 1978.
El negro que hizo esperar a los ángeles. 1972.
Ojos de perro azul: Nueve cuentos desconocidos. 1972.
Cuatro cuentos. 1974.
Todos los cuentos 1947–1972. 1975; as *Collected Stories*, translated by Gregory Rabassa, 1984, revised edition, 1991.
El otoño del patriarca. 1975; as *The Autumn of the Patriarch*, translated by Gregory Rabassa, 1976.
El último viaje del buque fantasma. 1976.

Crónica de una muerte anunciada. 1981; as *Chronicle of a Death Foretold*, translated by Gregory Rabassa, 1982.
El amor en los tiempos del cólera. 1985; as *Love in the Time of Cholera*, translated by Edith Grossman, 1988.
El general en su laberinto. 1989; as *The General in His Labyrinth*, translated by Edith Grossman, 1990.
Collected Novellas, translated by Gregory Rabassa and J.S. Bernstein. 1990.
Three Novellas (includes *Leaf Storm*; *No One Writes to the Colonel*; *Chronicle of a Death Foretold*), translated by Gregory Rabassa and J.S. Bernstein. 1991.

Plays

Viva Sandino. 1982; as *El asalto: u; operativo con que el FSLN se lanzó al mundo*, 1983.
El rastro de tu sangre en la nieve; El verano de la Señora Forbes (screenplays). 1982.
Diatribe of Love Against a Seated Man (produced 1988).

Screenplays: *El secuestro*, 1982; *María de mi corazón*, with J.H. Hermosillo, 1983; *Eréndira*, from his own novella, 1983.

Other

La novela en América Latina: diálogo, with Mario Vargas Llosa. 1968.
Cuando era feliz e indocumentado. 1973.
De viaje por los países socialistas: 90 días en la Cortina de hierro. 1978.
Crónicas y reportajes. 1978.
Periodismo militante. 1978.
La batalla de Nicaragua, with Gregorio Selser and Daniel Waksman Schinca. 1979.
García Márquez habla de García Márquez. 1979.
Obra periodística, (includes vol. 1: *Textos costeños*; vols. 2–3: *Entre cachacos*; vol. 4: *De Europa y América (1955–1960)*), edited by Jacques Gilard. 4 vols, 1981–83.
El olor de la guayaba, with Plinio Apuleyo Mendoza. 1982; as *The Fragrance of Guava*, translated by Ann Wright, 1983.
La soledad de América Latina; Brindis por la poesía. 1983.
Persecución y muerte de minorías, with Guillermo Nolasco-Juárez. 1984.
La aventura de Miguel Littín, clandestino en Chile: Un reportaje. 1986; as *Clandestine in Chile: The Adventures of Miguel Littín*, translated by Asa Zatz, 1987.
El cataclismo de Damocles/The Doom of Damocles (bilingual edition). 1986.
Dialogo sobre la novela latinoamericana, with Mario Vargas Llosa. 1988.

*

Bibliography: *Gabriel García Márquez: An Annotated Bibliography 1947–1979* by Margaret Eustella Fau, 1980; *A Bibliographical Guide to Gabriel García Márquez 1979–1985* by Margaret Eustella Fau and Nelly Sfeir de González, 1986.

Critical Studies: *García Márquez; o, El olvidado arte de contar* by R. Gullon, 1970; *Sobre García Márquez* edited by P.S. Martínez, 1971; *García Márquez: Historia de un deicidio* by Mario Vargas Llosa, 1971; *Homenaje a Gabriel García Márquez* edited by Helmy F. Giacoman, 1972; *Cien años de soledad: Una interpretación* by J. Ludmer, 1972; *Gabriel García Márquez*, 1977, and *Gabriel García Márquez: Life, Work, and Criticism*, 1987, both by George R. McMurray;

Gabriel García Márquez: El escritor y la crítica by P.G. Earle, 1981; *Melquíades, Alchemy and Narrative Theory: The Quest for Gold in Cien años de soledad* by C.S. Halka, 1981; *Gabriel García Márquez: Revolutions in Wonderland*, 1981, and *One Hundred Years of Solitude: Modes of Reading*, 1991, both by Regina Janes; *The Evolution of Myth in García Márquez from La hojarasca to Cien años de soledad* by Robert Lewis Sims, 1981; *La soledad de Gabriel García Márquez: Una conversación infinita* by M. Braso Fernandez, 1982; *García Márquez: La soledad y la gloria: Su vida y su obra* by O. Collazos, 1983; *Gabriel García Márquez: El coronel no tiene quien le escriba* (in English) by J.B.H. Box, 1984; *Essays on Gabriel García Márquez* edited by K. Oyarzum and W.W. Megenny, 1984; *Gabriel García Márquez* by Raymond L. Williams, 1984; *En el punto de mira: Gabriel García Márquez* edited by A.M. López, 1985; *Interpretaciones a la obra de García Márquez* (anthology), 1986; *Critical Perspectives on Gabriel García Márquez* edited by B.A. Shaw and N. Vera-Godwin, 1986; *Gabriel García Márquez and Latin America* edited by Alok Bhalla, 1987; *Gabriel García Márquez and the Invention of America* by Carlos Fuentes, 1987; *Gabriel García Márquez: New Readings* edited by Bernard McGuirk and Richard Cardwell, 1987; *Critical Essays on Gabriel García Márquez* edited by George R. McMurray, 1987; *Gabriel García Márquez, Writer of Colombia* by Stephen Minta, 1987; *Guía para la lectura de Cien años de soledad* by M.E. Montaner Ferrer, 1987; *García Márquez: Edificación de un arte nacional y popular* by E. Rama, 1987; *Gabriel García Márquez and the Powers of Fiction* edited by Julio Ortega and C. Elliott, 1988; *Gabriel García Márquez* edited by Harold Bloom, 1989; *Understanding Gabriel García Márquez* by Kathleen McNerney, 1989; *Como leer a García Márquez: Una interpretacion sociologica* by J.L. Mendez, 1989; *Gabriel García Márquez: The Man and His Work* by Gene H. Bell-Villada, 1990; *Gabriel García Márquez: One Hundred Years of Solitude* by Michael Wood, 1990; *Gabriel García Márquez: A Study of the Short Fiction* by Harley D. Oberhelman, 1991; *Gabriel García Márquez: Solitude and Solidarity* by Michael Bell, 1993; *Home as Creation: The Influence of Early Childhood Experience in the Literary Creation of Gabriel García Márquez, Agustín Yáxez, and Juan Rulfo* by Wilma E. Detjens, 1993; *Painting Literature: Dostoevsky, Kafka, Pirandello, and Gabriel García Márquez, in Living Color* by Constance A. Pedoto, 1993; *Circularity and Visions of the New World in William Faulkner, Gabriel García Márquez and Osman Lins* by Rosa Sims, 1993; *García Márquez: Crónica de una muerte anunciada* by Stephen M. Hart, 1994; *Intertextuality in García Márquez* by Arnold M. Penuel, 1994.

*   *   *

Novelist, story-teller, polemical journalist, recipient of the Nobel prize for literature, the Colombian Gabriel García Márquez has been among the most influential of 20th-century Latin American writers. Appearing at the crest of 'the Boom' in Latin American literature in the 1960s, his novel, *Cien años de soledad* (*One Hundred Years of Solitude*), made 'magic realism' a common critical term, and the novel still generates imitators from Chile to London, Bombay to Massachusetts. Definitively postmodern in its self-referentiality, its foregrounding of the act of writing, and its temporal warps, the book is also firmly grounded in the Colombian-Venezuelan regionalist tradition, a wider Latin American tradition of fantastic literature, and in the typically American project of national self-definition in the face of an imperial past and present cultural diversity.

Simultaneously an account of a nation, a town, a family, a house, and a book, the novel tells an episodic and realistic story of development and decline, remarkable for the sheer quantity of story-telling it accommodates. Instead of a single plot line taking a few characters through hundreds of pages, a seemingly inexhaustible invention produces story after story through some six generations. Always precisely individuated, episodes and characters parallel and contrast with each other, creating constantly shifting, intricate patterns within a lucid, accessible narrative. If the novel's fecundity violates expectations, so do its events.

Brought back are episodes conventionally excluded by the rationalist criteria which, developing in the 17th and 18th centuries along with the novel, had separated the novel from the romance. The effect is to interrogate the reader's sense of possibility, to put into question what constitutes reality. Creating a town, Macondo, where it seems almost anything can happen, García Márquez's new epic narrator re-integrates events for long ruled out as too bizarre because they do not happen at all (virgins rising into the heavens holding onto the family sheets, or men returning from the dead), because they are no longer believed to happen (priests who levitate or magicians who return from the dead), or because although they may happen, they fail to fit into dominant rationalist categories (Aristotle's possible improbabilities, such as a rain of dead birds or a plague of butterflies).

Effecting a radical defamiliarization, García Márquez also makes appear wonderful events or objects that modernity takes for granted and that no longer seem strange (the original sense of 'magic realism' in art criticism), such as the television or a block of ice. Nor are the inventions ever entirely arbitrary: the most immediately accessible ones create patterns of cultural history, economic development, or political conflict, which are usually satirical, but occasionally pathetic or sentimental. Many create powerful symbols, readily transferrable to other contexts, such as a plague of insomnia inducing forgetfulness of words and their referents. Creating an alternative to the conventions of social or psychological realism and modernist fragmentation, the novel represents a world on the cultural margin without condescending to it as primitive, mythologizing it as nobly mysterious, or pitying it as deprived. As fiction, it is clearly a much livelier, more stimulating, more historically and politically conscious work than most of the American and European fiction of its period.

From his earliest short stories, García Márquez has manifested his impatience with 'meat-and-potatoes' realism. The earliest fictions evoke dreams, doubles, and ghosts, altered states of consciousness, 'real' hallucinations, in stories that omit, or barely allude to, their most crucial concern. Under the helpfully foreign influence of Faulkner and Hemingway, he turned to more realistic representations and subjects, to social history and politics: the history of a family and town in the Faulknerian monologues of *Là hojarasca* (*Leaf Storm*), or of a town and *La violencia* (the major Colombian political conflict of the mid-20th century) in the intercut episodic structure of *La mala hora* (*In Evil Hour*), and in the spare short stories of *Los funerales de la Mamá Grande* (*Big Mama's Funeral*). In some of the stories of that volume, and in the short novel *El coronel no tiene quien le escriba* (*No One Writes to the Colonel*), García Márquez discovered the power of humour and ironic juxtaposition to both relieve and intensify the oppressive political atmosphere he communicates. Through *One Hundred Years of Solitude*, *El otoño del patriarca* (*The Autumn of the Patriarch*), *La increíble y triste historia de la cándida Eréndira . . .* (*Innocent Erendira*), and some short stories, García Márquez deployed the fantastic or impossible element often taken to characterize his fiction, and then abandoned it.

This abandonment is characteristic of García Márquez. In addition to the inventiveness and originality of his fictional fabling, he is a master craftsman, intent on locating unique shapes or structures for each fiction. While certain stylistic features remain constant (and have become perhaps too habitual for the writer himself: the winds of disillusion waft too frequently), he works very hard *not* to give his readers what many of them may want: a hundred *One Hundred Years of Solitude*s. Each work develops a distinct structural principle. *One Hundred Years of Solitude* depends on the making of a book through the destruction of the town, family, and house that are the subjects of the book; *The Autumn of the Patriarch* on the swirl of voices and constant resurrections that constitute the power of dictators and their eternal, invasive presence; *Crónica de una muerte anunciada* (*Chronicle of a Death Foretold*) on the predictive shape of classical Greek tragedy; *El amor en los tiempos del cólera* (*Love in the Time of Cholera*) on an impossible openness established by the refusal to close off the fiction; *El general en su laberinto* (*The General in His Labyrinth*) on a journey to an ending that attempts to start again but cannot. As Phil West has observed, myths always provide a second chance; history never does. Suggesting an ambiguous relationship with history and fiction, García Márquez's fictions characteristically provide second chances in the body of the fiction, but deny them at the end, as the fiction moves into the reader's history.

Often humorous, at times bitterly ironic or grotesque, occasionally tinged with pathos, García Márquez's work possesses a rare power of invention. Deficient in the psychological and linguistic density characteristic of some modern writers, García Márquez at his best achieves continuous surprise in the elaboration of a rococo, tessellated prose surface that makes the reader aware of the simultaneous insistence and insufficiency of interpretation.

—Regina Janes

LOVE IN THE TIME OF CHOLERA (El amor en los tiempos del cólera)
Novel by Gabriel García Márquez, 1985.

Márquez's 1985 novel is a masterpiece of sensuous prose, rivalling other contemporary texts such as Patrick Süskind's olfactory extravaganza of 18th-century France *Perfume* (1985) and Toni Morrison's vibrant account of Harlem life *Jazz* (1990) in its ability to summon up the textures, sensual pleasures, tastes, and smells associated with living in a particular place at a certain time. Overblown yet controlled, Márquez's story of life, love, and lust in a convention-bound provincial city on the Caribbean coast of Colombia displays great imaginative and narrative freedom coupled with almost novella-like discipline in its structuring of recurrent ideas.

Love in the Time of Cholera charts the love affair between a haughty, beautiful woman and her unfailingly devoted suitor, who for over 50 years (from late 19th- to early 20th-century) has pursued the object of his desire, both in silent observance and in torrents of exquisite love missives. His presence is not recognized until her husband, an eminent doctor and exemplary citizen, dies. As an elderly widow, she realizes that not all passion is spent; finally allowing herself the pleasures of spontaneity and physical freedom after a controlled upper middle-class existence. This, though, is a meagre synopsis of

Márquez's novel, for entwined within the central love story are the lives of other lovers, parents, children, and sundry relatives, as well as the ghost of a woman who drowned herself for unrequited love, a multilingual parrot and countless other personages—a remarkable feat of story-telling that takes off in all manner of exhilarating and surprising directions.

Despite its sprawling narrative style, Márquez's novel returns again and again to its central idea, that of the primacy of passion and feeling over order, honour, and authority. Love and sexual desire control, invigorate, and at times lay havoc to lives. Sometimes the participants are burnt up as if by cholera; after which they may completely recover, may be extinguished, or, as with the central suitor, may linger on in a state of perpetual convalescence. In Márquez's exquisitely meandering work, life, and love are shown as unpredictable and turbulent; forever surging and overflowing their bounds like the ever-present Caribbean sea and great Magdalena river.

Love in the Time of Cholera, however, is not just a plea for passion in a rule-bound world. The novel is also a meditation on old age and human memory. The main characters' biographies are laid out from childhood to near death, showing us lives actually lived, lives that could have been lived, and the way that memory can transfigure, keep alive, and obliterate the pain and ardour of earlier years. Such taking stock of lives spent is not wistful, however, for Márquez's characters have all got on with their lives successfully, despite the shimmering and beckoning half-presence of unrealized possibilities and unconsummated relationships.

Besides reflecting of love, old age, and memory, *Love in the Time of Cholera* gives the reader a richly detailed panorama of a provincial coastal city in times of cholera and civil war; its steamy and sleepy streets, rat-infested sewers, old slave quarter, decaying colonial architecture, and multifarious inhabitants evoked in loving and vital fashion. The novel, though, is not only social history, for Márquez, masterly practitioner of magic realism, heightens the historical material by weaving no end of fabulous tales within his account of Colombian life. In this way, he not only creates a marvellous piece of story-telling, but, perhaps even more pleasurably, Márquez shows us how our own lives are in many ways fabulous tales; each of us able to accommodate and transform the real through our own extraordinary, and even fabricated, versions of life stories.

—Anna-Marie Taylor

ONE HUNDRED YEARS OF SOLITUDE (Cien años de soledad)
Novel by Gabriel García Márquez, 1967.

One Hundred Years of Solitude was first published in Argentina in 1967. Not long after its initial English translation in 1970, the novel had already established itself as one of the great works of 20th-century world literature inaugurating and popularizing the new wave of South American fiction (Carlos Fuentes, Jorge Luis Borges, Julio Cortázar, Mario Vargas Llosa, and Isabel Allende), and bringing its hitherto little-known author into the forefront of the literary world. Márquez has consolidated his reputation with subsequent novels and short stories, most notably *Love in the Time of Cholera*, and in 1982 he was awarded the Nobel prize for literature.

One Hundred Years of Solitude is an extraordinarily ambitious and compelling tale, dealing with the entire history of the village of Macondo from its foundation, and recounting the saga of six generations of the Buendia family. But this is no orthodox anthropological or realist chronicle: it is instead a book of deep and powerful magic, describing and creating a fantastical world of dreams and visions, mysteries and prophecies. Right from the opening sentence the book's capacity to localize and articulate the marvellous becomes immediately apparent: 'Many years later, as he faced the firing squad, Colonel Aureliano Buendia was to remember that distant afternoon when his father took him to discover ice'. The elemental struggle between fire and ice hinted at in this passage recurs throughout the book, but the way it is integrated into the history of Macondo and the Buendias is astonishingly skilful. Although every page is full of such symbolic resonance, the meanings remain suggestive and allusive, resisting any simple decoding.

Throughout the novel, Márquez deliberately and exuberantly disrupts conventional procedures of story-telling and characterization, and his narrative is conducted through recollections, anticipations, digressions, and confusions over the limits of reality. Without the overt intrusion of a controlling authorial narrator, the tale is carried on by virtual stream-of-consciousness techniques, dispersed around the characters, so that no single account ever achieves full narrative authority. Time is made to stand still when appropriate, conventional expectations about ageing are suspended, and each life story flows over and around those preceding and those following. The human imagination intrudes upon and transforms the world of Macondo time and again, transgressing the normally-understood limits of the possible and creating a sense of wonder and enchantment.

The novel is thus extremely difficult to categorize, being at once an attempt at symbolic epic, a historical romance, a family saga, a national allegory even, and, to use the appropriate jargon, an influential experiment in magical realism. But the attempt to categorize the text remains less important than the need to experience the texture of the writing. Although Márquez shares some of Borges's love of paradox and conundrum, and although he acknowledged his own interest in laying bare the mechanics of narrative, the author of *One Hundred Years of Solitude* is clearly an altogether more sensual and less starkly cerebral novelist than any of his Latin American contemporaries. Indeed, for all its playfulness, this entire book may be read as a tribute to the human power to love and endure, despite everything, to survive wars and tempests and hardships and yet retain the capacity to dream and to love.

What Márquez achieves in this novel is a remarkable and arguably unique balance between the literary experimentation of magical realism and the more conventional human-centred saga. Whereas for some post-modern writers the notion that there can be no transcendental reality and that all we have are stories can become debilitating and dehumanizing, Márquez rejoices in his narrative freedom to produce a compendious account of enlarged human possibilities. The village community of Macondo is fantastical, and the Buendias and their acquaintances are extraordinary figures, but the book none the less becomes moving and involving. Early on in the tale, Jose Arcadio Buendia becomes heavily involved in alchemy, but he soon sees that the attempt to recover gold from base metals is a paltry project compared with the very joy of being alive: 'Fascinated by an immediate reality that came to be more fantastic than the vast universe of his imagination, he lost all interest in the alchemist's laboratory'. For Márquez too, this 'immediate reality' can be transformed and can yield more humane riches than any laboratory experiment.

For its sheer energy, for its combination of experimentation and humanity, and for the way it enhances the possibilities of seeing the world, there can be little doubt that *One Hundred Years of Solitude* will remain one of the key texts of 20th-century world literature for the foreseeable future.

—Ian A. Bell

GAUTIER, (Pierre-Jules) Théophile. Born in Tarbes, France, 30 August 1811. Educated at Lycée Louis-le-Grand and Lycée Charlemagne, both Paris; studied art in Paris. One son, by Eugénie Fort, and two daughters, by Ernesta Grisi. Member of the circle of French Romantic writers including Gérard de Nerval, *q.v.*, and Pétrus Borel; journalist, 1831–36; contributed to *Chronique de Paris*, from 1835; art and drama critic, *La Presse*, 1836–55 and *Le Moniteur universel*, from 1845; also contributed to *Revue de Paris*, *Le Figaro*, *Ariel*, *Le Cabinet de lecture*, and *La France littéraire*; travelled to Spain to advise on art collecting, 1840. *Died 23 October 1872.*

PUBLICATIONS

Collections

Poésies complètes. 1845; edited by René Jasinski. 3 vols., 1858; 2 vols., 1932; revised edition, 1970.
Oeuvres. 2 vols., 1890.
Oeuvres. 1893.
Oeuvres érotiques. 1953.
Nouvelles, edited by Claudine Lacoste. 1979.
Récits fantastiques, edited by Jean-Jacques Eideldinger. 1981.

Fiction

Les Jeunes-France: Romans goguenards. 1833.
Mademoiselle de Maupin. 2 vols., 1835; revised edition, 1845; edited by Adolphe Boschot, 1966; as *Mademoiselle de Maupin*, translated anonymously, 1836; as *A Romance of the Impossible*, translated by Paul Hookham, 1912; also translated by Burton Rascoe, 1922; R. and E. Powys Mathers, 1938; Paul Seiver, 1948; Joanna Richardson, 1981.
L'Eldorado. 1837.
Nouvelles. 1845; as *Stories*, translated by Lafcadio Hearn, 1908.
Militona. 1847.
Les Roués innocents. 1847.
Les Deux Étoiles. 2 vols., 1848.
La Peau de tigre. 3 vols., 1852.
Un trio de romans (includes *Militona*; *Jean et Jeannette*; *Arria Marcella*). 1852.
Avatar. 1856.
La Croix de Berny. 1857.
Jettatura. 1857; edited by V.J.T. Spiers, 1891.
Le Roman de la momie. 1858; as *The Romance of a Mummy*, translated by M. Young, 1886; as *The Mummy's Romance*, translated by G.F. Monkshood, 1908.
Le Capitaine Fracasse. 2 vols., 1863; edited by G.F.

Monkshood, 1910; as *Captain Fracasse*, translated by E.M. Beam, 1898.

Romans et contes. 1863.

La Belle-Jenny. 1866; as *Partie carrée*, 1889.

Spirite. 1866; edited by Reginald and Douglas Menville, 1890, Adolphe Boschot, 1961, and by Marc Eigeldinger, 1970.

Mademoiselle Daphné. 1881; revised edition, 1984.

One of Cleopatra's Nights and Other Fantastic Romances, translated by Lafcadio Hearn. 1886.

Une Nuit de Cléopâtre. 1894.

Le Pavillon sur l'eau, edited by W.G. Hartog. 1902.

The Romances. 10 vols., 1903.

The Beautiful Vampire—La Morte Amoureuse, translated by Paul Hookham. 1926.

Triple Mirror, translated by Mervyn Savill. 1951.

The Bridge of Asses, translated by Albert Meltzer. 1953.

Skin-Deep, translated by Mervyn Savill. 1955.

Short Stories, translated by George Burnham Ives. 1970.

My Fantoms, translated by David Farris. 1976.

Three Supernatural Tales, edited by Robert Navon, translated by George Burnham Ives. 1989.

Verse

Poésies. 1830; edited and translated by Harry Cockerham, 1985.

Albertus; ou, L'Âme et le péché. 1832.

La Comédie de la mort. 1838.

Poésies complètes. 1845.

España. 1845; edited by René Jasinski, 1929.

Émaux et Camées. 1852; 3rd edition (includes 'L'Art'), 1858.

Premières poésies 1830–1845. 1870.

Obscenia: Lettre à la Présidente. Poésies érotiques. 1907.

Gentle Enchanter, translated by Brian Hill. 1960.

Plays

Une larme du diable. 1839.

Giselle (ballet scenario; produced 1841). 1841; as *Giselle; or, The Wilis*, translated by Violette Verdy, 1970.

La Péri (ballet scenario; produced 1843). 1843.

Un voyage en Espagne. 1843.

La Juive de Constantine. 1846.

Le Selam. 1850.

Pâquerette (ballet scenario; produced 1851). 1851.

Gemma (ballet scenario; produced 1854). 1854.

Théâtre de poche. 1855.

Sakountala (ballet scenario; produced 1858). 1858.

Théâtre (includes *Une larme du diable*; *Le Tricorne enchanté*; *La Fausse Conversion*; *Le Pierrot posthume*; *L'Amour souffle où il veut*; *Giselle*; *La Péri*; *Gemma*; *Sakountala*). 1872.

Other

Tra los montes. 2 vols., 1843; as *Voyage en Espagne*, 1843; as *The Romantic in Spain*, translated by Catherine A. Phillips, 1926.

Les Grotesques. 2 vols., 1844.

Les Beautés de l'opéra, with Jules Janin and Philarète Chasles. 1845.

Zigzags. 1845.

Les Fêtes de Madrid. 1847.

Salon de 1847. 1847.

Lettre à la Présidente. 1850.

Oeuvres humoristiques. 1851.

Caprices et zigzags. 1852.

Italia. 1852.

Celle-ci et celle-là. 1853.

Constantinople. 1853; as *Constantinople of To-day*, translated by Robert Howe Gould, 1854.

Les Beaux-Arts en Europe. 2 vols., 1855–6.

L'Art moderne. 1856.

De la mode. 1858.

Histoire de l'art dramatique en France depuis vingt-cinq ans. 6 vols., 1858–59; translated in part as *The Romantic Ballet*, by Cyril W. Beaumont, 1932.

Honoré de Balzac. 1858; revised edition, 1859.

Les Peintres vivants. 1858.

Abécédaire du Salon de 1861. 1861.

Les Dieux et les demi-dieux de la peinture, with A. Houssaye and P. de Saint-Victor. 1864.

Loin de Paris. 1865.

Quand on voyage. 1865.

Voyage en Russie. 2 vols., 1865; as *Russia, by Théophile Gautier and Other French Travellers of Note*, translated by Florence MacIntyre, 1970.

Les Progrès de la poésie française depuis 1830. 1868.

Ménagerie intime. 1869; as *A Domestic Menagerie*, translated by Mrs W. Chance, 1899.

La Nature chez elle. 1870.

Tableaux de siège, Paris, 1870–1871. 1871.

Henri Regnault. 1872.

Histoire du romantisme. 1872.

Portraits contemporains. 1874.

Portraits et souvenirs littéraires. 1875.

Voyage en Italie. 1876; as *Journeys in Italy*, translated by D.B. Vermilye, 1903.

L'Orient (essays). 2 vols., 1877.

Fusains et eaux-fortes. 1880.

Guide de l'amateur au musée du Louvre. 1882.

Souvenirs de théâtre, d'art et de critique. 1883.

Omphale: histoire rococo. 1896.

La Musique (reviews). 1911.

Les Plus Belles Lettres de Théophile Gautier, edited by Pierre Descaves. 1962.

Correspondance générale, edited by Claudine Lacoste-Veysseyre. 1985.

Gautier on Dance (reviews), edited and translated by Ivor Guest. 1986.

*

Critical Studies: *Théophile Gautier, souvenirs intimes* by Ernest Feydeau, 1874; *Histoire des oeuvres de Théophile Gautier* by Charles Spoelberch de Lovenjoul, 1887; *The Dramatic Criticism of Théophile Gautier* by Helen Patch, 1922; *The Creative Imagination of Théophile Gautier* by Louise Dillingham, 1927; *Gautier and the Romantics* by John Palache, 1927; *Théophile Gautier: His Life and Times* by Joanna Richardson, 1958; *Les Ballets de Théophile Gautier* by Edwin Binney, 1965; *Ideal and Reality in the Fictional Narratives of Théophile Gautier* by Albert B. Smith, 1969; *The Art Criticism of Théophile Gautier* by Michael Clifford Spencer, 1969; *Théophile Gautier, auteur dramatique* by C. Book-Seninger, 1972; *Théophile Gautier* by Serge Fauchereau, 1972; *Théophile Gautier* (in English) by Richard B. Grant, 1975; *Théophile Gautier* by Philip E. Tennant, 1975; Gautier issue of *Europe*, May 1979; *Études et recherches sur Théophile Gautier, prosateur* by Jean Richer, 1981; *Théophile Gautier: A Romantic Critic of the Visual Arts* by Robert Snell, 1982; *Le Regard de Narcisse: Romans et nouvelles de Théophile Gautier* by Marie-Claude Schapira,

1984; *La Critique d'art de Théophile Gautier* by Claudine Lacoste-Vesseyre, 1985; *Rêve de Pierre: La Quête de la femme chez Théophile Gautier* by Natalie David-Weill, 1989.

* * *

Poet, writer of novellas and short stories, novelist, critic, journalist, and author of inimitably vivid travel books, Théophile Gautier stands out among French writers of his generation.

Being, as he himself told the Goncourt brothers, a 'man for whom the visible world exists', he became an art student at the age of 19. He soon realized, however, that he was lacking in technical perfection and turned to literature, bringing to his new medium not only a painterly love of form and colour but also an imagination deeply imbued with impressions of the visual arts. His career as an art student had brought him into contact with the young Romantic fraternity of painters and writers and he was later to write a history of the Romantic movement, not published until after his death.

Seldom highly creative but always a flawless craftsman, Gautier supplied a much needed corrective to the Romantics' diffuse style. In his preface to *Premières poésies* [First Poems] he displayed an indifference towards politics, society, and even nature, that was uncharacteristic of the French Romantic movement. A work closer to that movement, in theme if not in technique, is the lengthy narrative poem *Albertus*, jaunty in style and showing obvious traces of Byronic influence, which describes how a young painter falls into a sorceress's hands. Gautier continued his flight from Romanticism in *Les Jeunes-France*, mocking both himself and his youthful fellow artists for their callow extravagances of thought, dress, and behaviour.

Turning aside from Romanticism, Gautier reverted to the theme already foreshadowed in his preface to *Albertus*, advocating the doctrine of 'art for art's sake' in the celebrated— indeed almost notorious—preface to *Mademoiselle de Maupin* (*A Romance of the Impossible*). Here he pours scorn upon the hypocrisies of contemporary society, rejects conventional notions of morality, and emphasizes the cult of beauty. In the novel itself the eponymous heroine, dressed as a man, engages in numerous exploits and is loved by a woman but also by d'Albert, whose mistress she finally becomes. *Mademoiselle de Maupin* implicitly condemns the formless sentimentalizing which, in Gautier's judgement, was the unworthy ideal of so many of his contemporaries.

Giving further expression to his Romantic leanings, *La Comédie de la mort* [Comedy of Death] treats the theme of *memento mori* which had perhaps been suggested to Gautier by his growing interest in Spanish engraving and painting. His critical work *Les Grotesques* extolled the personal and literary merits of French poets of the earlier part of the 17th century such as Théophile de Viau, Saint-Amant, and Scarron, who, not only in their writings but also in their individualism, seemed to him to foreshadow the Romantic outlook.

Gautier's travels in Greece confirmed his conviction that the literary artist should seek only Classical purity of form, without the need to impart any moral lesson. In *Émaux et Camées* [Enamels and Cameos] he emerged as the leading proponent, and practitioner, of 'art for art's sake' and thus as the inspiration of the Parnassian school. Composed (with the notable exception of 'L'Art') in octosyllabic quatrains and with many *rimes riches*, rhyming in the manner of the English or German ballad, these short poems avoid the 12-syllable alexandrine favoured by the (French) Romantics. They teem

with images of plastic beauty, burning with a hard gem-like quality that perfectly conveys their underlying theme that life is short whereas art is eternal. But 'Symphonie en blanc majeur', 'Affinités secrètes', 'Clair de lune sentimental' and other poems in *Émaux et Camées* foreshadow symbolism in their tonal sensitivity, synaesthesia (or use of artistic transposition), and latent-fluidity of form.

Gautier was also the author of *Le Roman de la momie* (*The Romance of a Mummy*), in which he admirably juxtaposes ancient Egypt and the contemporary world, and of *Le Capitaine Fracasse* (*Captain Fracasse*), the last, in terms of year of publication, of the great French works in the Romantic tradition of the historical novel. *Captain Fracasse* is a lengthy and picaresque rehandling of Scarron's 17th-century *Le Roman comique* (*The Comic Romance*). A young nobleman, Sigognac, forsakes his ancestral home on falling in love with an actress. He accompanies her and the group of strolling players to which she belongs on their travels throughout France, experiencing many prodigious adventures along the way.

In *La Presse*, mainly during the years 1836–40, and in *Le Moniteur universel*, from 1845, Gautier published more than 2,000 *feuilletons* on painting, ballet, and literature. Of his *feuilletons* about the Salons and visits to art collections those recording his admiration of Rubens, Goya, and Delacroix are outstanding; several volumes of art criticism, largely based on these *feuilletons*, also came from his pen. In his day he was an unrivalled ballet critic. He was also the author of numerous comedies and ballets, and the joint author of *Giselle*. His literary criticism is notable for its studies of Lamartine, Baudelaire, and Balzac (whose short story 'The Unknown Masterpiece' he may even have helped to write). In *Tra los montes* (*The Romantic in Spain*) he proved himself to be a fine writer of travel sketches; in the former book the visual inspiration is especially evident.

More clearly than any other French writer, Gautier represents the transition from Romanticism to Parnassianism. Balzac, Flaubert, Sainte-Beuve, Baudelaire, Banville, the Goncourt brothers, and other literary contemporaries held him in high esteem. His work is often derivative, however. His verse, in particular, lacks an emotional and intellectual content commensurate with its perfection of form. His output was enormous. *Émaux et Camées*, *Spirite* (a short novel of the supernatural), novellas such as *Militona*, *Avatar*, *Arria Marcella* and *Jettatura* are among his finest achievements. Maupassant appears to have been influenced by the subject matter of these shorter fictions.

—Donald Adamson

ART (L'Art)
Poem by Théophile Gautier, 1856.

Gautier was the acknowledged leader and spokesman of the 'L'Art pour l'Art' ('Art for Art's sake') movement which formed a major current in French poetry in the middle decades of the 19th century, and 'Art' is generally regarded as being its most forthright manifesto. The poem, first published in 1856 in *L'Artiste*, the movement's campaigning review, of which Gautier had recently become co-editor, was incorporated in 1858 into the third, augmented edition of his poetry collection *Émaux et Camées*, first published in 1852. Even though each subsequent edition contained new poems, Gautier insisted that 'Art' should always come at the end, as a summation of the collection's achievements; critical opinion is divided, however, on the extent to which the other poems exemplify the principles laid down in the 'manifesto'.

The 'Art for Art's sake' movement was a reaction against the utopianism, rationalism, and utilitarianism which had swept through French letters in the wake of the 1830 revolution, winning Romantics such as Lamartine, Vigny, and Hugo to the cause of art, and particularly poetry, as a force for social progress and oral improvement. It has often been said that mannerist art (art preoccupied by style more than content) flourishes at periods when the artist feels alienated from the prevailing values of his society, and this was certainly the case with Gautier and his followers. Much influenced by 18th-century German aesthetic thinking, they were staunchly opposed to the idea that art should have a social or political purpose. Instead, they propounded a semi-religious belief in the cult of pure beauty as the only moral truth, defining beauty in terms of plastic, sensual form, rather than elevated or uplifting subject-matter. 'Nothing that is beautiful is essential for living . . . Only that which has no use can be beautiful; everything useful is ugly . . .', Gautier had written, controversially, in the preface of his novel *Mademoiselle de Maupin*. 'Art', composed at a time when the values of 'Art for Art's sake' had finally gained ascendancy, is a vibrant reassertion of his aesthetic of formal beauty.

The poem was originally written to reply to Théodore de Banville, an ardent and gifted disciple 12 years Gautier's junior, who earlier in the same year had published in *L'Artiste* an 'Odelette' ['Little Ode'] in homage to his work and poetic leadership. Banville's poem, half the length of Gautier's response, had expressed admiration for his craftsmanship in two apparently contradictory metaphors: the poet as bird-catcher, deftly snaring dreams in the delicate net of his verse, and as metal-working artisan, engraving and chiselling his ideas into the hard bronze of metre, rhyme, and rhythm. Although Gautier does reserve a space at the end for the more spiritual aspect of the poet's 'rêve', it is essentially this second idea of poetry as a difficult craft, and French verse as a solid, refractory material whose resistance needs to be overcome by skill, that he takes up and develops in 'Art' in a series of virtuoso metaphorical variations. Written in the same awkward verse-form as Banville's text (four-line stanzas of six, six, two and six syllables, rhyming *abab*), the poem itself stands as a triumphant example of difficulty overcome. It opens with an affirmative 'Oui', as if continuing and amplifying Banville's argument, and the tone throughout is one of injunction (all but four of its 14 stanzas are constructed as grammatical imperatives), as might be expected of a manifesto aiming to convince by argument as well as by example.

In accordance with his enthusiasm for plastic, sensual beauty, Gautier defined the craft of poetry by analogy with that of the sculptor and the painter, assimilating the linguistic and metrical medium in which the poet works to the materials used in the visual arts (in the first stanza, 'poetry' occurs in the same line as 'marble', 'onyx', and 'enamel'). Just as the sculptor should work in hard stone (Paros or Carrara marble, agate, onyx, the 'guardians' of pure line), rather than the much easier clay, and the painter metaphorically fire his bright colours in the enamellist's oven rather than being satisfied with washed-out water colours, so the poet should employ verse-forms which seem initially uncongenial and technically difficult. Only then will the resultant work be 'robust' and formally perfect enough to survive the ravages of time, like a Roman medallion bearing an emperor's portrait, dug up by a modern farmer. More helpful, metrically-freer forms are likened dismissively to an over-large shoe which any vulgar foot can slip into at will, highlighting a pronounced élitism in Gautier's views, for he and his followers prided themselves on the inaccessibility of their metrical art to the appreciation of the common herd. Such poetry as theirs, Gautier asserts in a final reversal of values, will ultimately outlast bronze statues and outlive even the gods themselves, conferring an element of immortality on its creators.

However, 'Art' is perhaps best read as a statement of general aesthetic principle rather than as a specifically poetic programme; it certainly does not give a full account of the expressive range of Gautier's own poetry. His stress on discipline and formal mastery was in part a backward-looking reaction against the Romantic notion of art as spontaneous, uncontrolled expression, and it ultimately caused the whole 'Art for Art's sake' movement to decline into a cold, neo-classical preciosity which would be severely mocked by Rimbaud little more than a decade after 'Art' was first published. On the other hand, Gautier's insistence on the 'floating dream' that the poet must seek to encapsulate in the 'resistant block' of his verse also looks forward to Symbolism, and the complex metrical experiments that he and his followers conducted in their search for formal difficulty did much to prepare the ground for succeeding generations of poets. Much lauded by Baudelaire, the values expressed in 'Art' directly influenced Verlaine, Mallarmé, and even Flaubert, so that, in his resolute privileging of form over content, Gautier can plausibly be regarded as one of the pioneers of a genuinely modern French sensibility.

—Andrew Rothwell

GENET, Jean. Born in Paris, France, 19 December 1910 (illegitimate); took his mother's surname. Abandoned by his parents, and reared by foster parents in Le Morvan. Sent to reformatory, Mettray, 1926–29, for petty crimes; enlisted in the Foreign Legion, served in Morocco 1932–33, but deserted in 1936 and again in 1939; lived the life of a criminal in several countries until 1942; began writing during term in Fresnes Prison; met Jean Cocteau, *q.v.*, in the early 1940s; began publishing his works in the mid-1940s; met Jean-Paul Sartre, *q.v.*, and Simone de Beauvoir, *q.v.*, in 1944; sentenced to life imprisonment for recurrent theft, 1948, until friends and supporters secured a presidential pardon in 1949; writing all but ceased after 1966; subsequently supporter of various radical causes, including the Black Panthers in the USA, Palestinian liberation groups, and the Baader-Meinhof group in Germany. *Died 15 April 1986.*

PUBLICATIONS

Fiction

Notre Dame des Fleurs. 1944; revised version, in *Oeuvres complètes*, 2, 1951; as *Our Lady of the Flowers*, translated by Bernard Frechtman, 1949; as *Gutter in the Sky*, translated by Frechtman, 1955.
Miracle de la rose. 1946; revised version, in *Oeuvres complètes*, 2, 1951; as *Miracle of the Rose*, translated by Bernard Frechtman, 1965.
Pompes funèbres. 1947; revised version, in *Oeuvres complètes*, 3, 1953; as *Funeral Rites*, translated by Bernard Frechtman, 1969.

Querelle de Brest. 1947; revised version, in *Oeuvres complètes*, 3, 1953; as *Querelle of Brest*, translated by Gregory Streatham, 1966.

Plays

Les Bonnes (produced 1947; revised version, produced 1954). 1948; revised versions 1954, 1958; as *The Maids*, translated by Bernard Frechtman, with *Deathwatch*, 1954.
'Adame Miroir (ballet scenario), music by Darius Milhaud. 1948.
Haute surveillance (produced 1949). 1949; revised versions, 1965, and in *Oeuvres complètes*, 4, 1968; as *Deathwatch*, with *The Maids*, translated by Bernard Frechtman, 1954.
Le Balcon (produced 1957). 1956; revised versions, 1960, 1962; edited by David Walker, 1982; as *The Balcony*, translated by Bernard Frechtman, 1958; revised translation, 1966; also translated by Barbara Wright and Terry Hands, 1991.
Les Nègres (produced 1959). 1958; as *The Blacks*, translated by Bernard Frechtman, 1960.
Les Paravents (produced 1961). 1961; revised version, 1976; as *The Screens*, translated by Bernard Frechtman, 1962.

Screenplays: *Un chant d'amour*, 1950; *Goubbiah*, 1955; *Mademoiselle*, 1966.

Verse

Chants secrets. 1947.
La Galère. 1947.
Poèmes. 1948; revised edition, 1966.
Poems. 1980.
Treasures of the Night: Collected Poems, translated by Steven Finch. 1981.

Other

Journal du voleur. 1949; as *The Thief's Journal*, translated by Bernard Frechtman, 1954.
L'Enfant criminel, 'Adame Miroir. 1949.
Oeuvres complètes. 4 vols., 1951–68.
Lettres à Roger Blin. 1966; as *Letters to Roger Blin: Reflections on the Theatre*, translated by Richard Seaver, 1969.
May Day Speech. 1970.
Reflections on the Theatre and Other Writings. 1972.
Lettres à Olga et Marc Barbezat. 1988.
Fragments et autres textes. 1990.
L'Ennemi déclaré: Textes et entretiens, edited by Albert Dichy. 1991.

Editor, with R. Gallet, *Poètes anglais contemporains: Geoffrey Hill, Philip Larkin, Kathleen Raine, R.S. Thomas, K. White*, 1982.

*

Bibliography: *Jean Genet: A Checklist of His Works in French, English and German* by Richard N. Coe, in *Australian Journal of French Studies*, VI, 1969; *Jean Genet and His Critics: An Annotated Bibliography 1943–1980* by Richard C. and Suzanne A. Webb, 1982.

Critical Studies: *Saint Genet, Comédien et martyr* by Jean-Paul Sartre, 1952; *The Imagination of Jean Genet* by Joseph H. McMahon, 1963; *Jean Genet* by Tom F. Driver, 1966; *The Vision of Jean Genet* by Richard N. Coe, 1968, and *The Theatre of Jean Genet: A Casebook* edited by Coe, 1970; *Jean Genet* by Bettina L. Knapp, 1968, revised edition, 1989; *Jean Genet: A Study of His Novels and Plays* by Philip Thody, 1968; *Profane Play, Ritual, and Jean Genet: A Study of His Drama* by Lewis T. Cetta, 1974; *Jean Genet in Tangier* by Mohamed Choukri, 1974; *A Genetic Approach to Structures in the Work of Jean Genet* by Camille Naish, 1978; *Genet: A Collection of Critical Essays* edited by Peter Brooks and Joseph Halpern, 1979; *Genet's Ritual Play* [*Les Bonnes*] by Sylvie Debevec Henning, 1981; *Jean Genet* by Jeannette L. Savona, 1983: *No Man's Stage: A Semiotic Study of Jean Genet's Major Plays* by Una Chaudhuri, 1986; *Jean Genet and the Semiotics of Performance* by Laura Oswald, 1989; *Jean Genet: A Biography of Deceit, 1910–1951* by Harry E. Stewart and Rob Roy McGregor, 1989; *Genet, Les Nègres* by J.P. Little, 1990; *The Cinema of Jean Genet: Un chant d'amour* by Jane Giles, 1991; *The Rites of Passage of Jean Genet: The Art and Aesthetics of Risk Taking* by Gene A. Plunka, 1992; *File on Genet* by Richard Webb, 1992; *Genet* by Edmund White, 1993.

* * *

When Jean-Paul Sartre published his long study, *Saint Genet, Comédien et martyr* (*Saint Genet, Actor and Martyr*) in 1952, many readers came to Jean Genet through Sartre's evaluation and sympathy. The book proposed that Genet be classified among the greatest French writers of the century. At every step of the way, Genet had known what he was doing. Hence Sartre's term to designate him *comédien* or actor. Genet never failed to acknowledge the condition imposed upon him by society when he was young; hence the second term in the title of *martyr*.

One day the parallels will be studied that exist between Rimbaud's revolt against his condition in the world, and Genet's submission to his fate. A world only half-seen by Rimbaud in episodes of *Une saison en enfer* (*A Season in Hell*) is raucously dramatized in Genet's first novel *Notre Dame des Fleurs* (*Our Lady of the Flowers*). Extravagant in every sense, this late adolescent world of Montmartre, engendered by the early adolescent world in the prisons of Mettray and Fontevrault, is the *légende dorée* of Genet, in which existence is a cult, a ceremony of evil where the male is female. Death in violence obsesses the minds of the tough heroes of Genet (*les durs*: Bulkaen, Pilorge, Harcamone), and martyrdom obsesses the minds of the effeminate (Divine and Notre-Dame). The guillotine is the symbol of the male and of his greatest glory.

The central drama in his books is always the struggle between the man in authority and the man to whom he is attracted. The psychological varieties of this struggle are many. Each of the novels and each of the plays is a different world in which the same drama unfolds. *Querelle de Brest* (*Querelle of Brest*) is the ship: naval officers and sailors. *Pompes funèbres* (*Funeral Rites*) is the Occupation: Nazi officers and young Frenchmen of the capital. *Our Lady of the Flowers* is Montmartre, with its world of male prostitutes and pimps. *Miracle de la rose* (*Miracle of the Rose*) is the prison, with the notorious convicts and slaves.

The play *Haute surveillance* (*Deathwatch*) is also the prison cell with the intricate hierarchy of criminals where those standing under the death sentence exert the greatest power and prestige over those with lesser sentences. *Les Bonnes* (*The Maids*) is the household, where in the absence of the mistress one of the maids plays her part. *Les Nègres* (*The Blacks*) is the world of colonialism: the conflict between whites and blacks. It is much more than a satire on colonialism. The oppression from which the blacks suffer is so hostile, so incomprehensible, as to be easily the oppression of mankind. The hostility which Genet persistently celebrates throughout all his work, in his opulent language, is the strangely distorted love joining the saint and the criminal, the guard and the prisoner, the policeman and the thief, the master and the slave, the white and the black.

—Wallace Fowlie

THE BALCONY (Le Balcon)
Play by Jean Genet, 1956.

Genet's first full-length play *The Balcony* is impressively free from the defect he diagnosed himself in *The Maids*. If he had 'invented a tone of voice, a gait, style of gesture', he said, he hadn't managed to achieve 'a displacement which, allowing a declamatory tone, would make theatre theatrical'. (Letter to the publisher Jean-Jacques Pauvert printed as preface to the Paris edition of *The Maids*, 1954). This displacement is present in *The Balcony*.

Genet introduces a lot of anti-naturalistic devices—grotesque make-up, cothurni, outsize costumes—but this is not merely to suggest that theatricality permeates life or that role-playing enters into all our relationships. The play suggests a triangular equation between society, the theatre, and the brothel. Not that sexuality is treated directly. The only reference to a bed is in the stage direction that asks for a mirror with an ornate frame to reflect an unmade bed that would appear, disturbingly, to be situated in the front row in the stalls. The brothel is a house of illusions in which clients act out their fantasies with prostitutes playing the supporting roles.

Though it is only minor characters who get killed, death exerts a strong tidal pull on the action, while the only discussion of lovemaking takes place outside the brothel. Chantal, formerly the madame's favourite girl, is in love with Roger, a leader of the revolution that is going on in the streets of the city. Inside the brothel the subjects that provoke the most passionate speeches are death and dressing up. The man who costumes himself as a bishop has no interest in performing a bishop's duties, only in decking himself out in the clothes. Another timid-looking client takes off his bowler hat and his gloves to put on a cocked hat and a general's uniform. 'Man of war and pomp and circumstances', he intones, admiring his reflection in the looking glass, 'there I am in my pure appearance. Nothing, I have nothing contingent in tow'. He daydreams of being 'close to death . . . where I shall be nothing, but reflected *ad infinitum* in these mirrors, merely an image'. For him, fantasy and illusion are the only compensations for constant frustration.

With its strong tendency to devalue living actuality in favour of the dead image, the play is reminiscent of Symbolist literature. The brothel is a palace of symbols, and when the queen is killed during the insurrection she can be replaced by Irma, the madame, while insignificant clients, who have turned themselves on by dressing up as a bishop, a judge, and a general, need only the help of costumes and photographers to make their debut in public life as bishop, judge, and general. For all four of them the main function is to animate the image. As the Envoy says, 'The beauty on this earth is all due to masks.' Every living element in the play seems to lust

after its own absence, its replacement by an image, a monument, a costume. Carmen, one of the prostitutes, wants to be with her child, but her desire is not strong enough to make her give up the chance of playing St Teresa in the brothel:

IRMA: Dead or alive, your daughter is dead. Think of the grave adorned with daisies and artificial wreaths, at the far end of a garden, and think of looking after this garden in your heart . . .
CARMEN: I'd have liked to see her again.
IRMA: . . . Her image in the image of the garden, and the garden in your heart under the burning robe of St Teresa. And you hesitate? I offer you the most envied of all deaths and you hesitate? Are you a coward?

Even for a man who has power in the world outside the brothel, the Chief of Police, nothing matters more than to become a hero in other men's fantasies:

I'm going to make my image detach itself from me, force its way into your studios, multiply itself in reflections. Irma, my function is weighing me down. Here it will bask in the terrible sunshine of pleasure and death.

Nothing tempts him so much as the idea of a vast mausoleum that will preserve his memory; the idea of posterity matters more than sensations, emotions, or any other direct experience.

With *The Balcony* Genet was breaking a seven-year silence. Since publishing *The Thief's Journal* (*Journal du voleur*) in 1949, he had produced nothing of any substance or length. He collaborated with Sartre in the preparation of the massive biography *Saint Genet, Actor and Martyr*, which came out in 1952 (translated 1963), and he could hardly have failed to be influenced by it. But if it was a crisis of self-consciousness that prompted the silence, the long-term consequence was that it killed two overlapping compulsions—to write novels and to write autobiographically. Both the one-act plays, *The Maids* and *Deathwatch* were essentially about Genet; the three subsequent full length plays are not. No longer self-obsessed, he was able to turn his gaze outwards, and *The Balcony* was the first fruit of his new extroversion.

—Ronald Hayman

THE MAIDS (Les Bonnes)
Play by Jean Genet, 1947.

In a letter to the publisher Jean-Jacques Pauvert to preface the 1954 edition of his one-act play *The Maids*, Genet described his hopes for the play:

to achieve the abolition of characters—which usually stand up only by psychological convention—in favour of signs as remote as possible from what they should at first signify, but in touch with it none the less, in order to link the author to the audience by this one means . . . The highest modern drama has been expressed every day for 2,000 years in the sacrifice of the mass . . . Theatrically I know of nothing more effective than the elevation of the Host.

What equivalent can there be to the mass in a theatre where the only counterpart to the shared faith of the congregation is the audience's willingness to suspend disbelief? The task Genet sets himself in his plays is to engender belief in solitude, emptiness, transparency, and equivalence. He refuses to individualize his characters, stressing the lowest common multiples of humanity, and in each of his five extra-ordinary plays he creates an anti-society which he holds up provocatively as a mirror-image for a public naturally inclined to deny any resemblance. Why should the bourgeois audience identify with murderous maids plotting to kill their mistress?

When the curtain goes up, we see Solange impersonating Claire, while Claire impersonates Madame with grotesque exaggeration of her condescension, her patronizing mixture of benevolence and contempt. It is a game, a ritual, that makes the three overlap with the other two, and, reluctantly overcoming our resistance, we find ourselves overlapping with all three.

This wouldn't happen if the hatred on display were unambivalent, but underneath the envy that makes the maids want to kill their mistress is something that makes them want to *be* her, or, failing that, to play at being her. This is a kind of love. Their identity derives from their relationship with her: rebelling against their independence, they are fighting against themselves, and suicide is the culmination of the attempt at murder. It is apt that the ritual should end in self-sacrifice: the instinct of self-betrayal was strongly at work while Genet was writing it. Its primary purpose, he said, was:

> To disgust me with myself by indicating and refusing to indicate who I was. Its secondary purpose was to produce a kind of discomfort in the auditorium . . . I go to the theatre to see myself on the stage (reconstituted in a single character or through a multiple character and in the form of a story) in a form that I wouldn't be able or wouldn't dare to see or dream as an image of myself, in spite of knowing that is what I am.
>
> ('Comment jouer *Les Bonnes*',
> *Ouvres complètes*, vol. 4.)

The play is based on a murder committed in 1933, when two maids, Christine and Lea Papin, aged 28 and 21, killed their mistress with an axe. Writing soon afterwards about the crime, Jacques Lacan said that in paranoia the aggressive impulse sometimes implies a wish for self-punishment and expiation. The intellectual content of the murderous delirium, he suggested, was a superstructure which at once justified and negated the criminal impulse. He felt sure there was no active lesbianism between the sisters. 'The homosexual tendency would express itself only through a desperate negation of itself, which would lay the foundation for a conviction of being persecuted and an identification of the persecutor as the loved one.' The hatred is partly an extroversion of self-loathing, the aggression an outlet for guilt.

In his first novel, *Our Lady of the Flowers* published three years before *The Maids*, Genet had written that if a play of his with women in it were ever produced, he had asked for their roles to be acted by boys. This would expose female elements in the male constitution, and male in the female. Penetrating as intimately as he does in *The Maids* into the fantasy lives of three women, he reveals something of his own femininity, and when the roles are played by boys, the self-betrayal becomes more complex. Exposing the femininity of the male actors, he is complicating their relationship with the play and with him.

Interdependent with self-betrayal is displacement of reality. While Claire will be imperfect in her impersonation of Madame, as Solange will be in hers of Claire, the boys' imperfection in impersonating females would lay extra emphasis on the point that Madame always puts on an act for the benefit of her maids, while they always play roles, both when trying to impress her with their subservient devotion and when they are alone together, not trying to be anything other than themselves but always aware of themselves as maids. As

sisters they know each other too well to think they can impress each other, but they know themselves by knowing each other, and Claire is defining both herself and Madame when, speaking as Madame, she launches into a ritual of insults against maids, deriding the look of fear and shame on their faces, their scrawny elbows, their dowdy clothes, their bodies, apparently designed for wearing cast off clothes.

Exploring the emptiness, the transparency, the solitude, and the equivalence of the three characters, the play inverts moral values. As in *Deathwatch*, a play Genet had written before *The Maids*, though it was not produced or published until 1949, the violence is quiet, muted, decorous. However ugly the clumsy crime usually is in reality, Genet was making it look glamorous and elegant on the stage.

—Ronald Hayman

GENJI MONOGATARI.   See **MURASAKI SHIKIBU**.

GEZELLE, Guido. Born in Bruges, Austrian Netherlands (now Belgium), 1 May 1803. Educated at a seminary in Roeselare, 1846–49; became priest in 1854; appointed to teaching post at his old school, where his unorthodox pedagogical methods caused his dismissal; co-director, English College, Bruges, 1860–61; teacher of philosophy, Seminarium Anglo-Belgicum, 1861–65; journalist for anti-liberal magazine *'t Jaer 30*, 1864–70, and *'t Jaer 70*, 1870–72; founder and journalist for the illustrated weekly *Rond den Heerd* [Round the Hearth], 1865–71; parish priest of St Walburgis, 1865–72; moved to Kortrijk, where he worked as chaplain; continued ecclesiastical and journalistic work for *De Vrijheid* and *Gazette van Kortrijk*; recalled to Bruges in 1899, and granted position of rector of the English Convent. *Died 27 November 1899.*

PUBLICATIONS

Collections

Dichtwerken [Poetical Works]. 10 vols., 1903–05, revised edition, 14 vols., 1913.
Jubileumuitgave [Jubilee Edition]. 18 vols., 1930–39.
Werken [Works], edited by Frank Baur. 4 vols., 1949–50.
Briefwisseling [Correspondence], edited by R.F. Lissens. 1970.
Verzameld dichtwerk [Collected Poetry], edited by K. de Busschere. 1980–92.

Verse

Boodschap van de vogels en andere opgezette dieren [Message from the Birds and Other Stuffed Animals]. 1856.
Vlaemsche dichtoefeningen [Flemish Poetry Exercises]. 1858.
Kerkhofblommen [Graveyard Flowers]. 1858.

XXXIII Kleengedichtjes [Thirty-Three Little Poems]. 1860.
Gedichten, gezangen en gebeden [Poems, Songs, and Prayers]. 1862, reprinted 1976.
Liederen, eerdichten et reliqua [Songs, Poems of Praise, and Relics]. 1880.
Driemaal XXXIII Kleengedichtjes [Thrice Thirty-Three Little Poems]. 1881.
Tijdkrans [Garland of Time]. 1893.
Rijmsnoer [Rhyme String]. 1897.
Laatste verzen [Last Poems]. 1901.
[Selection], translated by M. Swepstone. 1937.
[15 Poems], translated by C. and F. Stillman, in *Lyrica Belgica I*. 1960.
Poems, translated by Christine d'Haen. 1971.
[12 Poems], translated by A. van Eyken, in *Dutch Crossing*, 35. 1988.

Other

Uitstap in de Warande [Excursion in the Warande]. 1882.
De ring om 't kerkelijk jaar [Ring Around the Church Year]. 1908.
Brieven van, aan, over Gezelle (letters; some in English). 2 vols., 1937–39.
De Briefwisseling tussen G. Gezelle en Ernest Rembry 1872–1899, edited by C. Verstraeten. 1987.

Translator, *Hiawatha*, by Longfellow. 1886.

*

Critical Studies: *Woordkunst van Guido Gezelle* by J. Craynet, 1904; *Het leven van Guido Gezelle* by A. Walgrave, 1924; *Guido Gezelle* by Henriette Roland Holst, 1931; *Guido Gezelle* by A. Visser, 1949; *Guido Gezelle en de andere* by H. Bruning, 1954; *Guido Gezelle* by A. van Duinkerken, 1958; *Van het leven naar het boek* by J.J.M. Westenbroek, 1967; *Guido Gezelle katholiek vrijmetselaar* by R. Reniers, 1973; *De taalkunst van Guido Gezelle* by Albert Westerlinck, 1980; *Guido Gezelle: Flemish Priest and Poet* by Hermine J. van Nuis, 1986; *De wonde in 't hert* by Christine d'Haen, 1988; *Mijnheer Gezelle* by Michel van der Plas, 1991.

* * *

Guido Gezelle is the Dutch poet who singlehandedly took the Dutch language to a summit of beauty and complexity hitherto undreamt of. There are at least five Gezelles. Perhaps the least interesting for literary purposes is Gezelle the journalist. Since he was a priest who could obviously write well, Gezelle was forced by his bishop to invest much time and energy in political journalism, both to expound the policies of the Catholic People's Party and to attack and chastise its opponents. In that capacity he made a number of enemies, and the stress connected with his journalistic work brought him to the brink of a nervous breakdown.

Gezelle the linguist or, as he would have preferred to think of himself, the philologist, was interested in the Dutch language in general, and in his own West Flemish dialect in particular. He cultivated the latter for two reasons. The use of this dialect enhanced his poetry, especially in the later phase, as it was more effortlessly melodious than standard Dutch. It was also, he felt (and many agreed), a 'Catholic' Dutch, as opposed to the 'Calvinist' variant that had come to dominate Holland.

The third Gezelle is the educator, whether as teacher in the classroom or as editor (who also often filled whole issues with the fruit of his labour) of weekly magazines designed to teach and to entertain the faithful, particularly those whose education had progressed little beyond acquiring the basic skill of reading itself.

The fourth Gezelle is the priest-poet, responsible for a sizeable part of the poetry that has come down to us. As a priest, Gezelle felt both close to and responsible for the people entrusted to his care and would often write small poems, *kleengedichtjes*, to commemorate important events in their lives.

The fifth Gezelle, the most interesting, wrote experimental poetry before the term was even conceived of, and *poésie pure* long before Brémond. For many it is he who represents the 'real' Gezelle. His poetry is constructed around several main themes. Many poems reflect his highly-strung religious idealism. Some are marred by didacticism, while others achieve a level of mystical lyricism rarely equalled in world literature. Other poems represent the reverse of his idealism: a feeling of inadequacy, sinfulness, and despair that is also to be found in the so-called 'terrible sonnets' of Gerard Manley Hopkins, the poet to whom Gezelle is most often compared. Gezelle, however, wrote few sonnets; he preferred experimenting with sound, rhythm, and metre.

Another principal theme is that of friendship. A number of close friends stayed loyal to Gezelle all his life, and he commemorated his affection for them in a number of poems, the best known of which is probably 'Dien avond en die rooze' [That Evening and That Rose].

Throughout his life Gezelle fought for the recognition of Dutch as an official language by the Belgian state, and against the dominant position of French, which was used almost exclusively by the civil service and in the courts, even though the majority of people in Flanders, the northern half of the country, were hardly able to understand it, let alone communicate in it. Some of Gezelle's 'Flemish' poems are evocations of the glorious past in a somewhat romantic vein. Others, the more interesting, range from parody to an almost incantatory celebration of the sheer range of the language itself.

The last, but certainly not least, main theme is that of nature, which to Gezelle represented the 'visible words' of God, according to the old mystical belief that God spoke to man in words destined for his ears, and written down in the Bible, but also in words destined for his eyes, and present in nature all around him. On the basis of this attitude, any and every celebration of nature, even of the smallest insects, is also a celebration of God himself, and all poetic meditations on nature automatically become religious utterances of prayer. Since Gezelle was a keen observer of all that went on around him, not only (as a philologist) of the language his people spoke, but also (as a poet) of the nature they lived in, or sometimes had to struggle against, he produced many poems that are prayers, or prayers that are poems.

The final 15 years of Gezelle's life saw his consecration as the national poet of the Flemish people. He was awarded many honours, including a state funeral. The ultimate paradox of his life as a poet is, perhaps, that he will always remain the prisoner of his own excellence. The very virtuosity, inventiveness, and exuberant revelling in the power of the Dutch language that establishes so many of his greatest poems as truly of world stature also militates against their being translatable effectively. For this reason he has not been translated frequently or successfully into any of the more widely spoken languages.

—André Lefevere

GHĀLIB, (Mīrzā Muḥammad) Asadullāh Khān. Born in Agra, Uttar Pradesh, India, in 1797. Father killed when he was five; guardian uncle died when he was nine. Self-educated: well-versed in classical subjects, Arabic, and developed interests in philosophy, Sufism, and astrology. Married nobleman's daughter in 1810. Began writing poetry in Urdu from the age of ten, but after 1847 wrote mostly in Persian. On uncle's death, his estate was confiscated: subsequently devoted much time attempting to regain control of his share; lived for most of his life in Delhi, apart from two years (1827–29) in Calcutta; attended the court of the Mughal rulers, from 1847; commissioned to write official history of the Mughal dynasty, in Persian, 1850; appointed official poetry teacher, 1854; witnessed the Indian Mutiny 1857–58, and recorded his experiences in letters and journals. *Died in 1869.*

PUBLICATIONS

Verse

Dīvān-i Ghālib [Ghālib's Works]. 1841; 5th edition, 1863; modern editions: (Nizami edition) 1915, 1958, 1965, 1969, 1989; selections translated in collections listed below, and in *The Falcon and the Hunted Bird* (anthology of different poets), 1950; *The Golden Tradition: An Anthology of Urdu Love Poetry* (80 poems, with critical study), translated by Ahmed Ali, 1973; *An Anthology of Classical Urdu Love Lyrics*, translated by David J. Mathews and Christopher Shackle, 1972; *Classical Urdu Poetry 2*, translated by M.A.R. Barker and Shah Abdus Salam, 1977.
[MS Amroha Verses], edited by Nisar Ahmad Farooqi. 1857.
Nuskha-i-Hāmidīa, edited by Abdur Rahman Bijnori. 1921.
Intikhāb i Ghālib (selection), edited by Imtiyāz Ali 'Arshī. 1942.
Dīvān-i Ourdu (Urdu verses). 1954.
Shish jihat-i Ghālib (Persian verse), edited by Chaudhuri Nabi Ahmad Bajwa. 1962.
Selected Verses, translated by Sufia Sadullah. 1965.
Selected Poems, translated by Ahmed Ali. 1969.
Ghālib Urdu kalamka intikhab (selection), edited by Mukatabah Jam'ah. 1969.
Mata'-i Ghālib: Intikhab-i ghazaliyat-i farsi (Persian selection). 1969.
Twenty Five Verses, translated by C.M. Nain. 1970.
Ghazals of Ghalib, edited and translated by Aijaz Ahmad, adapted by various poets. 1971.
Ham Kalām, Fārsī rubā'iyāt-i Ghālib kā tarjamah, Ṣ Akbārabādī. 1986.

Other

Khatut-i-Ghālib (letters), edited by Ghulam Rasul Mehr. 3rd edition, 1969.

Ghālib aur fann-i tanqīd [murattib] Akhlāq Ḥsain Ārif (correspondence). 1977.
Urdu Letters, translated and annotated by Daub Rahbar. 1987.
Panj ahang men makatib-i Ghālib (Persian letters). 1989.
Dastanbuy: A Diary of the Indian Revolt of 1857. N.d.

*

Critical Studies: *The Aligarh Urdu Magazine: Ghālib Number* edited by Mukhtar Uddin Ahmad Arzu, 1949; *Studies in Urdu Literature* by Fazl Mahmud Asiri, 1952; *Interpretations of Ghālib* by J.L. Kaul, 1957; *Ghālib, The Man and His Verse* by P.L. Lakhanpal, 1960; *Ghālib: Two Essays* by Ahmed Ali and Alessandro Bausani, 1969, and *The Problem of Style and Technique in Ghālib*, 1969, and *The Golden Tradition*, 1973, reprinted 1991, both by Ali; *Ghālib* by M. Mujeeb, 1969; *Ghālib: Life and Letters* by Ralph Russell and Khurshidul Islam, 1969; *Mirza Ghālib: The Poet of Poets* by S. Saran, 1976; *A Dance of Sparks: Imagery of Fire in Ghālib's Poetry* by Annemarie Schimmel, 1979; *Ghālib: The Man, the Times* by Pavan K. Varmer, 1989; *Yadgar-e-Ghālib: A Biography of Ghālib* by Maulana Altaf Hussain Hali, translated by K.H. Qadiri, 1990; *Ghālib* by Anis Nagore, 1990.

*   *   *

Asadullāh Khān Ghālib died having lost both his sense of hearing and all interest in a life which, in any case, had not treated him kindly. Unappreciated during his lifetime, he stands in great esteem today, and his reputation has spread far and wide during the last two decades through translations into English and appraisals in other languages. He is a highly individualistic, sophisticated, and difficult poet, whose mind was far in advance of his age, and whose poetry retains its sophisticated and difficult nature today.

The 19th century was an age in India of upheaval, uncertainty, religious controversy, revolt, decay, and disorder, but also one of hope as a new order was emerging, in Ghālib's own words, like 'Dispersed light in the mirror, a speck of dust/Caught in the sunlight in the window'. Psychologically it was a difficult period of warring loyalties, with instinct demanding attachment to national feeling, but with expediency suggesting alignment with an alien power that had almost complete control over India. Attitudes underwent a change. Some patriotic souls revolted against the dominance of the West, like Momin who reflected Ghālib's own sentiments 'O Doomsday, come, rend up the world,/Shake it up and down, about . . .'.

These currents produced sentiments and attitudes that are difficult to analyse. Ghālib's developed sensibility accepted a variety of thought as valid experience. His peculiar mind unified experiences so that the sifting of their elements becomes a hopeless task, the more so as Ghālib had a comprehension of his age similar to that of Baudelaire, while the changing pattern of the age was still incomplete and unrecognized by his contemporaries. As a result he was considered incomprehensible and obscure, so that one commentator said in exasperation, 'What he writes he alone/Or God can understand'. But Ghālib was a poet of passion with a philosophical conception of life and the universe, like the Metaphysical poets of England, and he carried his search for the truth to a more metaphysical plane. Endowed with a visionary imagination, his mind fused perception and thought so that he could see creation and the creator involved together in the situation:

Life's leisure is a mirror of the hundred hues
Of self-adoration;
And night and day the great dismay
Of the onlooker of the scene.

Here, conventional belief is upturned. Life is engrossed with its multifarious forms, and the Maker, bound by His own laws, then turns into a helpless beholder of the scene he has created:

Intelligence unconcerned
Is caught in the great despair
Of encirclement, and man's
Image remains imprisoned
In the mirror of the world.

Ghālib's poetry reflects the movement of thought, and his passion creates an imagery that is both picturesque and startling in its suddenness. His poetic experience was more conscious than intuitive, presenting an object after the idea of it, as in 'The heat engendered by thought is indescribable;/I had just thought of despair when the desert went up in flames'.

This quality of his thought is so breathtaking that he remained beyond the reach of the average critic of his era. Yet his intensive mind needed a new diction and grammar to express itself: 'Where is, O Lord, the other foot of Hope?/I found the desert of contingent existence a mere footprint'. From this to the opening poem of his *Dīvān*, 'Of whose gay tracery is the picture a complainant?', is only a continuation of the great leap forward, where the style is highly elliptical and the meaning seemingly incomprehensible, as words and images are strung together pell-mell, as in Gerard Manley Hopkins (a contemporary of Ghālib). Ghālib's elliptical style is indeed as startling in Urdu as Hopkins's is in English:

No, it was not these.
The jading and jar of the cart,
Time's tasking, it is fathers that asking for ease
Of the sodden-with-its-sorrowing heart,
Nor danger, electrical horror; then further it finds
The appealing of the passion is tender in prayer apart.
. . .

The elliptical fourth line is less complicated and breathtaking, however, than:

The joy-of-creation-of-image-producing-
Coquetry-of-expressing-
The-intense-desire-of-being-killed.
In the furnace-of-fire is the hoof
Of the prey from the beloved's scimitar.

The first three lines here are a series of ellipses, constituting a single emotive state. This is wit, conceit, hyperbole, all in one. Ghālib created metaphors out of the conditions of his mind and feeling. It is a complex, composite picture of over-lapping and interlinked states in the devotional opening poem, where words and grammar, image and idea, fact and fiction, intellect and emotion, all play their part singly and collectively, transcending the realm of words to form an imagery of abstractions; if John Donne could find a parallel between a pair of lovers and a pair of compasses, Ghālib could find ecstasy in the way to the altar of sacrifice itself: 'With what joy in front of the executioner I walk/That from my shadow the head is two steps ahead of the feet . . .'.

This was an idiom his contemporaries and the generations that followed could not understand, so that between 1892 and 1972 at least 54 keys to his *she'rs* (unit of two lines) were published. It was not until the 1960s that Ghālib could find his rightful place in the ranks of the world's great poets.

—Ahmed Ali

GIDE, André (Paul-Guillaume). Born in Paris, France, 22 November 1869. Educated at École Alsacienne, Paris, 1878–80; Lycée in Montpellier, 1881; boarder at M. Henri Bauer, 1883–85, and at M. Jacob Keller, 1886–87; École Alsacienne, 1887; École Henri IV: baccalauréat, 1890. Married Madeleine Rondeaux in 1895 (died 1938); had one daughter by Elisabeth van Bysselberghe. Mayor of a Normandy commune, 1896; juror in Rouen, 1912; special envoy of Colonial Ministry on trip to Africa, 1925–26. Helped found *Nouvelle Revue française*, 1909. Recipient: Nobel prize for literature, 1947. Ph.D.: Oxford University. Honorary Member, American Academy, 1950. *Died 19 February 1951.*

PUBLICATIONS

Collection

Romans, récits, et soties; Oeuvres lyriques, edited by Yvonne Davet and Jean-Jacques Thierry. 1958.

Fiction

Les Cahiers d'André Walter. 1891; translated in part as *The White Notebook*, by Wade Baskin, 1965; complete translation as *The Notebooks of André Walter*, 1968.
La Tentative amoureuse. 1893; as *The Lovers' Attempt*, translated by Dorothy Bussy, in *The Return of the Prodigal*, 1953.
Le Voyage d'Urien. 1893; as *Urien's Voyage*, translated by Wade Baskin, 1964.
Paludes. 1895; as *Marshlands*, translated by George D. Painter, with *Prometheus Misbound*, 1953.
Les Nourritures terrestres. 1897; as *Fruits of the Earth*, translated by Dorothy Bussy, 1949.
Le Prométhée mal enchaîné. 1899; as *Prometheus Illbound*, translated by Lilian Rothermere, 1919; as *Prometheus Misbound*, translated by George D. Painter, with *Marshlands*, 1953.
L'Immoraliste. 1902; as *The Immoralist*, translated by Dorothy Bussy, 1930.
Le Retour de l'enfant prodigue. 1907; as *The Return of the Prodigal*, translated by Dorothy Bussy, 1953.
La Porte étroite. 1909; as *Strait Is the Gate*, translated by Dorothy Bussy, 1924.
Isabelle. 1911; as *Isabelle*, translated by Dorothy Bussy, in *Two Symphonies*, 1931.
Les Caves du Vatican. 1914; as *The Vatican Cellars*, translated by Dorothy Bussy, 1914; as *The Vatican Swindle*, translated by Bussy, 1925; as *Lafcadio's Adventures*, 1927.
La Symphonie pastorale. 1919; as *The Pastoral Symphony*, translated by Dorothy Bussy, in *Two Symphonies*, 1931.
Les Faux-monnayeurs. 1926; as *The Counterfeiters*, translated by Dorothy Bussy, 1927; as *The Coiners*, translated by Bussy, 1950.

L'École des femmes. 1929; as *The School for Wives*, translated by Dorothy Bussy, 1929.

Two Symphonies (includes *Isabelle* and *The Pastoral Symphony*), translated by Dorothy Bussy. 1931.

Deux récits. 1938.

Thésée. 1946, as *Theseus*, translated by John Russell, 1948.

Plays

Philoctète (produced 1919). 1899; as *Philoctetes*, translated by Jackson Mathews, in *My Theater*, 1952; also translated by Dorothy Bussy, in *The Return of the Prodigal*, 1953.

Le Roi Candaule (produced 1901). 1901; as *King Candaules*, translated by Jackson Mathews, in *My Theater*, 1952.

Saül (produced 1922). 1903; as *Saul*, translated by Jackson Mathews, in *My Theater*, 1952; also translated by Dorothy Bussy, in *The Return of the Prodigal*, 1953.

Le Retour de l'enfant prodigue (produced 1928). 1909.

Bethsabé. 1912; as *Bathsheba*, translated by Jackson Mathews, in *My Theater*, 1951; also translated by Dorothy Bussy, in *The Return of the Prodigal*, 1953.

Antoine et Cléopatre, from the play by Shakespeare (produced 1920). In *Théâtre complet*, 1947.

Amal; ou, La Lettre du roi, from the play by Tagore (produced 1928). 1922.

Robert: Supplément à L'École des femmes (produced 1946). 1930; as *Robert; ou, L'Intérêt général*, 1949.

Oedipe (produced 1931). 1931; as *Oedipus*, translated by John Russell, in *Two Legends*, 1950.

Les Caves du Vatican, from his own novel (produced 1933). In *Théâtre complet*, 1948.

Perséphone (libretto), music by Igor Stravinsky (produced 1934). 1934; edited by Patrick Pollard, 1977; as *Persephone*, translated by Jackson Mathews, in *My Theater*, 1952.

Geneviève. 1936.

Le Treizième Arbre (produced 1939). In *Théâtre*, 1942; as *The Thirteenth Tree*, translated and adapted by Diane Moore, 1987.

Théâtre. 1942; as *My Theater*, translated by Jackson Mathews, 1952.

Hamlet, from the play by Shakespeare (produced 1946). In *Théâtre complet*, 1949.

Le Procès, with Jean-Louis Barrault, from the novel by Kafka (produced 1947). 1947; as *The Trial*, translated by Jacqueline and Frank Sundstrom, 1950.

Théâtre complet. 8 vols., 1947–49.

Verse

Les Poésies d'André Walter. 1892.

Other

Le Traité du Narcisse. 1892; as *Narcissus*, translated by Dorothy Bussy, in *The Return of the Prodigal*, 1953.

Réflexions sur quelques points de littérature et de morale. 1897.

Feuilles de route 1895–1896. 1899.

Philoctète, suivi de Le Traité du Narcisse, La Tentative amoureuse, El Hadj. 1899; all translated by Dorothy Bussy, in *The Return of the Prodigal*, 1953.

De l'influence en littérature. 1900.

Lettres à Angèle (1898–1899). 1900.

Les Limites de l'art. 1901.

De l'importance du public. 1903.

Prétextes. 1903; enlarged edition, 1913; translated in *Pretexts: Reflections on Literature and Morality*, edited by Justin O'Brien. 1959.

Amyntas. 1906; as *Amyntas*, translated by Villiers David, 1958; also translated by Richard Howard, 1988.

Dostoïevsky d'après sa correspondance. 1908.

Oscar Wilde. 1910; as *Oscar Wilde*, translated by Bernard Frechtman, 1951.

Charles-Louis Philippe. 1911.

C.R.D.N.. 1911; enlarged edition as *Corydon* (privately printed), 1920; 2nd edition, 1925; as *Corydon*, translated by Hugh Gibb, 1950; also translated by Richard Howard, 1983.

Nouveaux prétextes. 1911; translated in *Pretexts: Reflections on Literature and Morality*, edited by Justin O'Brien, 1959

Souvenirs de la cour d'assises. 1914; as *Recollections of the Assize Court*, translated by Philip A. Wilkins, 1941.

Si le grain ne meurt. 2 vols., 1920–21; as *If It Die . . .* , translated by Dorothy Bussy, 1935.

Numquid et tu . . . ? 1922; translated in *Journal*, 1952.

Dostoïevsky. 1923; as *Dostoevsky*, translated by Arnold Bennett, 1925.

Incidences. 1924.

Caractères. 1925.

Le Journal des faux-monnayeurs. 1926; as *Journal of The Counterfeiters*, translated by Justin O'Brien, 1951; as *Logbook of The Coiners*, 1952.

Dindiki. 1927.

Émile Verhaeren. 1927.

Joseph Conrad. 1927.

Voyage au Congo. 1927; translated by Dorothy Bussy, in *Travels in the Congo*. 1929.

Le Retour du Tchad, suivi du Voyage au Congo, Carnets de route. 1928; translated by Dorothy Bussy, in *Travels in the Congo*, 1929.

Travels in the Congo, translated by Dorothy Bussy. 1929.

Essai sur Montaigne. 1929; as *Montaigne: An Essay in Two Parts*, translated by Stephen H. Guest and Trevor E. Blewitt, 1929.

Un esprit non prévenu. 1929.

Lettres. 1930.

L'Affaire Redureau, suivie de Faits divers. 1930.

Le Sequestré de Poitiers. 1930.

Jacques Rivière. 1931.

Divers. 1931.

Oeuvres complètes, edited by Louis Martin-Chauffier. 15 vols., 1932–39; *Index*, 1954.

Les Nouvelles Nourritures. 1935; translated in *Fruits of the Earth*, 1949.

Retour de l'URSS. 1936; as *Return from the USSR*, translated by Dorothy Bussy, 1937; as *Back from the USSR*, 1937.

Retouches à mon Retour de l'URSS. 1937; as *Afterthoughts: A Sequel to Back from the USSR*, translated by Dorothy Bussy, 1938.

Journal 1889–1939. 1939; *1939–1942*, 1946; *1942–1949*, 1950; as *Journals 1889–1949*, edited and translated by Justin O'Brien, 4 vols., 1947–1951.

Découvrons Henri Michaux. 1941.

Attendu que. 1943.

Interviews imaginaires. 1943; as *Imaginary Interviews*, translated by Malcolm Cowley, 1944.

Jeunesse. 1945.

Lettres à Christian Beck. 1946.

Souvenirs littéraires et problèmes actuels. 1946.

Et nunc manet in te. 1947; as *The Secret Drama of My Life*, translated by Keen Wallis, 1951; as *Madeleine*, translated by Justin O'Brien, 1952.

Paul Valéry. 1947.

Reflections on Literature and Morality, edited by Justin O'Brien. 1959.

Poétique. 1947.

Correspondance 1893–1938, with Francis Jammes, edited by Robert Mallet. 1948.

Notes sur Chopin. 1948; as *Notes on Chopin*, translated by Bernard Frechtman, 1949.

Préfaces. 1948.

Rencontres. 1948.

Correspondance 1899–1926, with Paul Claudel, edited by Robert Mallet. 1949; as *The Correspondence 1899–1926*, translated by John Russell, 1952.

Feuillets d'automne. 1949; as *Autumn Leaves*, translated by Elsie Pell, 1950.

Lettres, with Charles du Bos. 1950.

Littérature engagée, edited by Yvonne Davet. 1950.

Égypte 1939. 1951.

Ainsi soit-il; ou, Les Jeux sont faits. 1952; as *So Be It; or, The Chips Are Down*, translated by Justin O'Brien, 1960.

Correspondance 1909–1926, with Rainer Maria Rilke, edited by Renée Lang. 1952.

Lettres à un sculpteur (Simone Marye). 1952.

The Return of the Prodigal (includes *Narcissus*; *The Lovers' Attempt*; *El Hadj*; *Philoctetes*; *Bathsheba*; *Saul*), translated by Dorothy Bussy, 1953.

Correspondance 1890–1942, with Paul Valéry, edited by Robert Mallet. 1955; as *Self-Portraits: The Gide Valéry Letters 1890–1942* (abridged edition), edited by Robert Mallet, translated by June Guicharnaud. 1966.

Lettres au Docteur Willy Schuermans (1920–1928). 1955.

Correspondance inédite, with Rilke and Verhaeren, edited by C. Bronne. 1955.

Correspondance, with Marcel Jouhandeau. 1958.

Correspondance 1905–1912, with Charles Péguy, edited by Alfred Saffrey. 1958.

Correspondance 1904–1928, with Edmund Gosse, edited by Linette F. Brugmans. 1960.

Correspondance 1908–1920, with André Suarès, edited by Sidney D. Braun. 1963.

Correspondance 1911–1931, with Arnold Bennett, edited by Linette F. Brugmans. 1964.

Correspondance 1909–1951, with André Rouveyre, edited by Claude Martin. 1967.

Correspondance 1913–1951, with Roger Martin du Gard, edited by Jean Delay. 2 vols., 1968.

Lettres, with Jean Cocteau, edited by Jean-Jacques Kihm. 1970.

Correspondance 1912–1950, with François Mauriac, edited by Jacqueline Morton. 1971.

Le Récit de Michel, edited by Claude Martin. 1972.

Correspondance, with Charles Brunard. 1974.

Correspondance 1891–1938, with Albert Mockel, edited by Gustave Vanwelkenhuyzen. 1975.

Correspondance, with Jules Romains, edited by Claude Martin. 1976; supplement, 1979.

Correspondance 1897–1944, with Henri Ghéon, edited by Jean Tipy. 2 vols., 1976.

Correspondance 1892–1939, with Jacques-Émile Blanche, edited by Georges-Paul Collet. 1979.

Correspondance, with Justin O'Brien, edited by Jacqueline Morton. 1979.

Correspondance, with Dorothy Bussy, edited by Jean Lambert. 3 vols., 1979–82; as *Selected Letters*, edited and translated by Richard Tedeschi, 1983.

Correspondance 1907–1950, with François-Paul Alibert, edited by Claude Martin. 1982.

Correspondance 1929–1940, with Jean Giono, edited by Roland Bourneuf and Jacques Cotnam. 1983.

Correspondance 1934–1950, with Jef Last, edited by C.J. Greshoff. 1985.

La Correspondance générale de André Gide, edited by Claude Martin. 1985.

Correspondance, with Harry Kessler, edited by Claude Foucart. 1985.

Correspondance 1927–1950, with Thea Sternheim, edited by Claude Foucart. 1986.

Correspondance 1891–1931, with Francis Viélé-Griffin, edited by Henri de Paysac. 1986.

Correspondance 1902–1928, with Anna de Noailles, edited by Claude Mignot-Ogliastri. 1986.

Correspondance, with Jacques Copeau, edited by Jean Claude. 2 vols., 1987–88.

Correspondance avec sa mère 1880–1895, edited by Claude Martin. 1988.

Correspondance 1903–1938, with Valery Larbaud, edited by Françoise Lioure. 1989.

Correspondance, with André Ruyters, edited by Claude Martin and Victor Martin-Schmets. 2 vols, 1990.

Correspondance 1901–1950, with Jean Schlumberger, edited by Pascal Mercier and Peter Fawcett. 1994.

Editor, *The Living Thoughts of Montaigne*. 1939.
Editor, *Anthologie de la poésie française*. 1949.

Translator, *Typhon*, by Joseph Conrad. 1918.
Translator, with J. Schiffrin, *Nouvelles; Récits*, by Aleksandr Pushkin. 2 vols., 1929–35.
Translator, *Arden of Faversham*, in *Le Théâtre élizabethain*. 1933.
Translator, *Prométhée*, by Goethe. 1951.

*

Bibliography: *Bibliographie des écrits de Gide* by Arnold Naville, 1949, supplement, 1953; *An Annotated Bibliography of Criticism on André Gide 1973–1988* by Catharine Savage Brosman, 1990.

Critical Studies: *Gide*, 1951, and *Gide: A Critical Biography*, 1968, both by George D. Painter; *Gide* by Enid Starkie, 1953; *The Theatre of André Gide* by J.C. McLaren, 1953; *Gide and the Hound of Heaven* by H. March, 1953; *Portrait of Gide* by Justin O'Brien, 1953; *Gide* by Albert Guerard, 1963, revised edition, 1969; *Gide: His Life and Work* by Wallace Fowlie, 1965; *Gide: The Evolution of an Aesthetic* by Vinio Rossi, 1967; *Gide and the Greek Myth* by Helen Watson-Williams, 1967; *André Gide* by Thomas Cordle, 1969; *André Gide: The Theism of an Atheist* by H.J. Nersoyan, 1969; *André Gide and the Roman d'aventure* by Kevin O'Neill, 1969; *Gide: A Study of His Creative Writings* by G.W. Ireland, 1970; *Gide: A Collection of Critical Essays* edited by David Littlejohn, 1970; *Gide's Art of the Fugue: A Thematic Study of Les Faux-monnayeurs* by Karin Nordenhaug Gihdas, 1974; *Gide and the Art of Autobiography: A Study of Si le grain ne meurt* by C.D.E. Tolton, 1975; *A Student's Guide to Gide* by Christopher Bettinson, 1977; *Gide: Les Faux-monnayeurs* by Michael J. Tilby, 1981; *André Gide and the Codes of Homotextuality* by Emily S. Apter, 1987; *Gide* by David H. Walker, 1990; *André Gide: Homosexual Moralist* by Patrick Pollard, 1991.

* * *

By the end of his life, André Gide had received the official sign of consecration, the recognition of his century, that he was one of its major writers. The Nobel prize for literature, awarded to him in 1947, indicated that his work had attained a degree of accepted universality. The miracle was that Gide had become a 'classical' writer by the time of his death while remaining a 'dangerous' writer. This man who invented for his age the term 'restlessness' (*inquiétude*) ended his life in apparent calm and resignation. A tone of affirmation, a marked denial of God, and a belief in the void of death provided a different portrait of Gide that has been added to the long series of self-portraits his books had already fashioned.

Gide's vast literary output is, in a sense, a written confession, initiated by a need to communicate what he felt to be true about himself. He knew that he possessed nothing of the anguish of a Pascal. That trait he left to Mauriac, and accepted for himself the characteristics of a Montaigne—of a wavering and diverse mind, as Montaigne had described himself: *esprit ondoyant et divers*. He remained at all times the writer who profited from every kind of experience, important or trivial.

Marc Allégret's film *Avec André Gide* opens with a few solemn pictures of the funeral at Cuverville and Gide's own reading of the opening pages of his autobiography *Si le grain ne meurt* (*If It Die . . .*). There are pictures showing the two contrasting family origins of Gide: Normandy and Languedoc, the north and the south, the Catholic and the Protestant background. The landscape pictures of Algeria and Tunisia provide a documentation for many of his works, from the earliest, such as *Les Nourritures terrestres* (*Fruits of the Earth*) to his *Journal* in 1941–42. Among the most curious episodes are the trip to the Congo, the walk with Valéry, the home of his daughter Catherine in Brignoles, the speech made in Moscow in the presence of Stalin, the visit with Roger Martin du Gard in Bellème.

A genius is a person who considers passionately what other people do not see. In the tradition of French letters, Montaigne was pre-eminently this type of genius, seizing every occasion of pleasure, every meeting, for the subject matter of his writing. The art of both the 16th-century essayist and the 20th-century moralist is based upon an indefatigable curiosity and a relentless critical spirit. Gide's enthusiasm for whatever came within his vision was usually followed by an admirable detachment from it. Once the conquest was made, he refused to be subjugated by it, to be dominated by his conquest. The image of the Minotaur's labyrinth, elaborated in his last important book, *Thésée* (*Theseus*), represents any body of doctrine that might constrict or imprison the thinking powers of a man. The problem for Theseus, as it was for Gide, was that of surpassing his adventures. The one moral error to be avoided at all cost was immobility, fixation. The meaning of Gide's celebrated word *disponibilité* seems to be the power of remaining dissatisfied, capable of change and growth.

From his avid curiosity about everything, whether it was the coloration of a leaf or the first book of a new author, his ideas were engendered. In the manifold forms of attentiveness with which his life seems to have been spent, there were no traces of misanthropy, of pessimism, of class prejudice, or of fatuous satisfaction with self. From a nature that accepted all contradictions—a will to freedom as well as a sense of destiny, good as well as evil—Gide's mind grew into one of the most critical of our age, a mind of infinite subtlety and unexpected boldness.

Gide began writing about 1890, at a time of great peacefulness in Europe, and continued to write during the next 60 years. He remained a constant and fervent witness to every ominous development in Europe and the world, from the period in which a religion of science and a rational vision of the universe dominated Europe to the mid-century of deep unrest.

There is little doubt that Gide hoped to compose a new gospel. With his favourite themes of adolescence, revolt, escape, the gratuitous act, he was able to upset the convictions of his readers, particularly his youthful readers, without creating in them feelings of terror or dismay. He tried to write in all the genres because he was unwilling to restrict himself to any one form and because each book, once it was well under way, became irksome to him; he would finish it off quickly in order to move on to a newer work. He had planned, for example, several further chapters for *Les Faux-monnayeurs* (*The Counterfeiters* or *The Coiners*), but when he wrote the sentence, 'Je suis bien curieux de connaître Caloub' ('I am very curious to know Caloub'), it appeared to him such an admirable final sentence that he felt freed from continuing farther.

Whenever Christianity appeared to him in the form of a system, of a body of principles, he refused to accept it. His was an attitude of detachment and adventure, which permitted him the practice of what has been so often called his 'sincerity'. Problems of ethics worried Gide far more than religion. He was more concerned with justice than salvation. His knowledge of the Bible and his love for the Gospels always gave hope to his Catholic friends (Claudel, Jammes, DuBos, Ghéon, Copeau) that he would finally submit.

What appears as conformity to the world's law was seriously castigated in *Fruits of the Earth* and in *L'Immoraliste* (*The Immoralist*). And yet the very difficulty involved in living within a new freedom provided the moral problem of most of his subsequent books, such as *Les Caves du Vatican* (*The Vatican Swindle*), *The Counterfeiters*, *Theseus*. For the expression of human freedom, for its power and its peril, Gide created massive formulas that have returned, only slightly modified, in the writings of Sartre, Camus, and René Char. His long life was one of self-examination, of courage in liberating himself in such experiences as his African visits, communism, Catholicism. Gide developed one need—that of doubting everything—and one obligation—that of never doubting himself.

—Wallace Fowlie

THE COUNTERFEITERS (Les Faux-monnayeurs)
Novel by André Gide, 1926.

The Counterfeiters is the only work by Gide to which he assigned the term 'novel'. Although he wrote other fictional works, he either gave them no label or called them 'récits' (narratives) or 'soties' (roughly, farces). The term 'novel' was chosen to indicate a departure from his previous work—especially his stylistic and compositional classicism—and to suggest a more ambitious project, a three-dimensional slice of life, a 'crossroads of problems'. The dedication—to Roger Martin du Gard—points to the role Gide's friend played in helping him elaborate the novel; the work also reflects his spiritual crisis during World War I and his reading of Dostoevskii and Fielding.

The Counterfeiters is divided into three parts: the first and last, set in Paris, have 18 chapters each, the middle, set in Saas-Fée (Switzerland), has seven chapters. There are symmetrical pairs of families and characters and numerous parallels and contrasts. The episodic plot seems disjointed but is, in fact, carefully contrived and balanced. The title, with its reference to counterfeit coinage and—by extension—other falsehood, furnishes a major theme. Fraudulent and inauthentic characters, things, and actions populate the novel— bastards (false sons), infidelity (counterfeit love), derivative, inflated (false) literature, lies (false words), hypocrisy (false morality). Another major theme is adolescence, its challenges and possibilities. The discovery of his illegitimacy by the young Bernard Profitendieu, whose development makes *The Counterfeiters* a Bildungsroman, precipitates his departure from home; this plot thread soon becomes entangled with others. His adventures include meeting by chance the writer Édouard, who is the uncle of his friend Olivier Molinier and—Bernard learns—loved by Laura Douviers, a married woman whom Vincent Molinier, Olivier's older brother, has made pregnant but callously abandoned. Later, Bernard comes to love Laura platonically, and meets other members of her family (the Vedel-Azaïs) at their boarding-house.

Another theme is fiction itself. The book, which displays the decentralization of plot, the multiple perspectives, and the relativization of character seen in some other modernist fiction, is a metafiction, concerned with the aesthetic, onto- logical, and epistemological status of fiction. Édouard, who resembles his creator, is trying to write a novel called 'The Counterfeiters', in which *his* hero is a writer attempting to compose a novel. None of Édouard's book is finished, but he keeps a notebook in which he jots down ideas and dialogues. This notebook constitutes much of Gide's novel, making Édouard one of the main narrating voices. This structure of embedded self-reflexive images, called by Gide *composition en abyme*, allows the author to play with the topic of reality and speak directly of the novelist's craft. Moreover, as Gide composed *The Counterfeiters*, he kept two notebooks: his regular diary, which records some stages in the composition, and what he later called *Journal of the Counterfeiters*, which contains observations on fiction, embryonic episodes, and dialogues not included in the final product. The different perspectives and levels of reality within the novel are thus expanded by reflections outside of it, and the various texts together constitute a modernist treatise on fiction and prefigure works by Butor and Robbe-Grillet, with their embedded, self-reflexive plots and violations of narrative frame.

The plot here is dependent upon coincidence, and the novel is marked by the oppositions and reversals character- istic of melodrama; but Gide's concern is to show, under the apparent simplicity of motivations and actions, a complex moral field in which authenticity is precarious and moral choice is suspect. This field is marked by the presence of evil, compared to which freedom to choose the good seems feeble, perhaps because human life is governed by an oppressive fate, or because knowledge of good is inadequate when self- knowledge is insufficient. The self, its contours, and its cri- teria for choice are the constant preoccupation of Édouard and Bernard, who reject societal models. Opposed to them are those who follow standard social patterns without reflec- tion, or who consciously choose either evil or a simplistic good—Laura's father, for instance, who leaves unexamined the religion by which he makes his living. A shadowy, ambu- latory devil, who occasionally seems to intervene in the plot, can at first be taken lightly, but the ultimate consequences point to a powerful malevolent principle, which is realized in human action but seems also to dictate it.

This principle is visible in Strouvilhou, a circulating character who expresses Nietzschean concern for replacing traditional morality with one built on power; it appears also in Vincent, whose descent down the slope of irresponsibility—

from an initial concern for Laura to a cultivated indifference and finally fascination with systematic egotism—concludes when, in Africa, after having murdered his companion, he takes himself for the devil. Édouard's old piano teacher, La Pérouse, expresses the omnipresence of evil when he con- cludes that the universe is a vast, sadistic joke: God and the Devil are one.

In a final disaster, La Pérouse's illegitimate grandson, Boris, is killed by a fellow student at Vedel's boarding house, in an episode of schoolboy sadism masking as an initiation rite. Other characters must bear some responsibility: the shots are fired from a pistol belonging to La Pérouse, and apparently innocent acts contribute to the murder. Beyond that, the role of Strouvilhou in the event suggests also a sombre fatality. After Boris's death, Bernard returns to his family, Georges Molinier (one of the schoolboys) to his, Laura to her husband; and Oliver, after a false start with the posturing writer Passavant, discovers love with Édouard (homosexual desire is a secondary theme).

Offsetting the sombre themes and unhappy events are insight and wit, ingenuity in plot handling, and, paradoxi- cally, sometimes a sense of the characters' freedom; Gide wished to create a world that would obey its own laws, not respond to the wishes of the novelist. The wide range of tones suits Gide's ambition to create a multi-dimensional work, with numerous plots and characters, in which simple lines and explanations are replaced by a complexity more nearly mirroring human reality.

—Catharine Savage Brosman

THE IMMORALIST (L'Immoraliste)
Novella by André Gide, 1902.

The Immoralist is the first of Gide's *récits*, a French genre halfway between a short story and a novel. Perhaps the best starting point to enter the world of *The Immoralist* is a phrase by the author himself: Is the end of Man God, or is it Man? In this *récit*, Gide postulates and pushes to the extreme the hypothesis that Man's final aim or end is Man. The main character, Michel, lives in a universe from which God has been ousted, rejects traditional notions of morality and con- vention, and sets himself up as the measure of all things. His tragedy lies in the fact that having liberated himself from morality and Christian mores, he is unable to find fulfilment or pleasure in immorality.

It is necessary to consider *The Immoralist* in relation to *Strait Is the Gate* (*La Porte étroite*), a later *récit*, published in 1909. Together they form a diptych, an unstable balance devoted to exposing opposing human tendencies. Alissa, the heroine of *Strait Is the Gate*, espouses a point of view contrary to that of Michel. She finds Man's end in God, to the detri- ment of her human, physical self. Gide sees the two extremes as being equally undesirable, potentially tragic and based on denial, either of the soul or of the body. It has been said that Michel and Alissa are both dangerous fanatics and hopeless romantics. This is true. Gide presents two victims of excess. The two quests of a total blind adherence to Man or to God fail, leaving behind a string of other victims and a hope for the just medium.

In the preface to *The Immoralist*, Gide outlines not a problem but a drama. In Part One of the *récit*, Michel, a learned puritan of Protestant background, is stricken with tuberculosis while, accompanied by his wife, Marceline, he is in North Africa. He has lived a life of austerity at great intellectual expense, but his sickness causes an inner change: he discovers what was up till now denied any expression or importance, his body. Gide describes the discovery of Man's corporal dimension; Michel discovers his senses and exults in a newly-gained consciousness of the flesh. The author in fact gives us a caricature of the cult of the body. Michel relishes sensuousness, what Baudelaire would have called *volupté*. In his revolt against convention, religion, God, and the spiritual, lies the protagonist's drama. Knowing how to free oneself from these constraints is nothing, the narrator writes on the first page, the hard thing to do is to know how to be free. This is Michel's failure. What he does after his spiritual and physical crisis only brings misery and loneliness.

Part Two of *The Immoralist* takes place in Paris and at La Morinière, Michel's property in Normandy. Michel deserts his pregnant wife to involve himself in the low life of the peasant workers under his control. In his attempt at discovering his true personality, the authentic self, ironically called the Old Adam by Gide, Michel abandons the New Adam, typified by the example and the teaching of Christ. Instead he selfishly pursues a hedonistic ideal in the name of individualism and personal liberty, at the expense of his wife, whom he betrays in Part Three by sleeping with an Arab woman. He exacerbates his wife's ill-health and leaves her dying alone while he enjoys promiscuous pleasures. The quest of the hero finally leads to destruction, vice, debauchery, and a moral abyss.

It is possible to see some typically Nietzschean themes in *The Immoralist*; however, one must not run the risk of attributing too close a dependence on Nietzschean philosophy, which was extremely popular in the literary world of Paris in the 1890s. Rather, Gide found a curious correlation of his ideas with those of the German thinker whom he eventually came to read after the seeds of *The Immoralist* were already growing in his mind.

The tripartite structure of *The Immoralist* presents an ascending and descending pattern. Two arcs are dialectically opposed: the physical decline of Michel in Part One leads to a primacy and ascendancy of the body in Parts Two and Three, paradoxically at the cost of a spiritual decline. Marceline's spiritual and physical health, established in the first part of the *récit*, gradually decline towards extinction. The two settings (North Africa and France) are neatly juxtaposed to form a circular pattern. A recurrent technique of Gide makes a geographical and metaphysical quest coincide. Repetition of symbols and incidents in Parts Two and Three make for a balanced and often ironic juxtaposition in the moral and physical decline of the two main characters.

Michael supposedly dictates his *récit* to three friends after Marceline's death. He thus becomes a sort of lamenting Job. Gide does not want to either excuse or accuse. The first-person narrative helps to give the *récit* a strong colouring of irony, essential to Gide's vision of Man's plight. There is a constant gap between Michel's perception of his noble ideal and the reader's increasing appreciation of a solipsistic, hard, and deluded sensualist. We realize the harshly ironic import of the initial quotation taken from the Book of Psalms: 'I will praise thee: for I am . . . wonderfully made.'

Gide's classical, literary style is a major success. There is a voluptuousness and harmony in the writing, a lyric passionate intensity, and effusion of poetic images characteristic of Gide's sometimes overwrought and precious language. The easy inversion of subject and verb, the placing of adjectives before nouns for a literary effect, and the more than frequent use of the now rare imperfect subjunctive give to *The Immoralist* a highly artistic and masterly style. Gide, like Chateaubriand or Flaubert, has a fondness for a ternary rhythm which gives to the sentences either a clipped terseness or a lyrical, rhetorical flow and ease.

Finally in its treatment of the problem of being and nothingness, *The Immoralist* prepares us for the French Existentialists, Sartre and Camus.

—David Coad

GILGAMESH, Epic of. Ancient Sumerian poem cycle, later written down in Akkadian language of Babylonia (now Iraq). Oldest version exists on 12 stone tablets from the 7th century BC, discovered by A.H. Layard in Ninevah in the 1840s. The story of the eponymous hero is based on legends surrounding real-life ruler of Uruk of c.2700 BC, and describes the adventures of Gilgamesh and his companion Enkidu.

PUBLICATIONS

Verse

An Old Babylonian Version of the Epic of Gilgamesh, edited by M. Jastrow and A.T. Clay. 1920.
The Epic of Gilgamesh: A New Translation, translated by R. Campbell Thompson. 2 vols., 1928–30.
Ancient Near Eastern Texts Relating to the New Testament, edited by J.B. Pritchard, translations by S.N. Kramer (Sumerian) and E.A. Speiser (Akkadian). 1950.
The Epic of Gilgamesh, translated by Nancy K. Sandars (prose). 1960; revised editions, 1964, 1972.
Myths from Mesopotamia: Creation, The Flood, Gilgamesh and Others, translated by Stephanie Dalley. 1989.
The Epic of Gilgamesh, translated by Maureen Gallery Kovacs. 1989.
He Who Saw Everything: The Epic of Gilgamesh, translated by Robert Temple (verse). 1991.
Gilgamesh, translated by David Ferry (verse). 1992.

*

Critical Studies: *The Babylonian Story of the Deluge and the Epic of Gilgamesh, with an Account of the Royal Libraries of Nineveh* by E.A.W. Budge, 1920; *The Gilgamesh Epic and Old Testament Parallels* by Alexander Heidel, 1949; *History Begins at Sumer*, 1956, and *The Sumerians: Their History, Culture, and Character*, 1964, both by Samuel Noah Kramer; *Gilgamesh et sa légende* edited by P. Garelli, 1960; *The Bible and the Ancient Near East: Essays in Honour of W.F. Albright*, 1961; *Sumerian Sources of the Epic of Gilgamesh* by Aaron Schaffer, 1963; 'On the Sumerian Epic of Gilgamesh' by J.D. Bing, in *Journal of the Ancient Near Eastern Society of Columbia University*, 7, 1975; *The Treasures of Darkness* by Thorkild Jacobsen, 1976; *Das Gilgamesh-Epos* edited by K. Oberhuber, 1977; *L'Épopée de Gilgamesh* by Abed Azrié, 1979; *The Evolution of the Gilgamesh Epic* by Jeffrey H. Tigay, 1982; *Enquête sur la Morte de Gilgamesh* by Yannick Blanc, 1991; *The Archetypal Significance of Gilgamesh: A Modern Ancient Hero* by Rivkah Scharf Kluger, 1991.

* * *

Gilgamesh is one of the oldest surviving literary epics. In its most complete form it is a compilation of the 7th century BC written in Akkadian (Old Semitic) on 12 tablets in the cuneiform script. This is a synthesis of older versions, the earliest written in the non-Semitic Sumerian language of Mesopotamia in the early 2nd millennium BC and probably based on oral traditions of the 3rd millennium. Other versions and fragments come from Hittite Anatolia, Syria, and Egypt. The 7th-century tablets were found at Nineveh in the library of Ashurbanipal, King of Assyria, by A.H. Layard in the 1840s; the first translation was attempted in 1872 by George Smith of the British Museum. Since then much fresh material has come to light and many translations have been made.

Gilgamesh was a historical king of Uruk, a city state in southern Iraq, who probably lived in the early 3rd millennium BC. From then until the fall of Nineveh in 612 he was remembered as a mighty hero throughout the Middle East. According to the epic tradition Gilgamesh was two parts god and one part man, inheriting from his mother, a minor goddess, beauty, strength, and ambition, and from his father mortality. According to the fullest Assyrian version, as a young king he oppressed the people till they complained to the gods who sent him a companion Enkidu, who is uncivilized 'natural' man, and with whom he first fights, then forms a deep friendship. Together they go to the 'Cedar Mountain' where they kill its monster guardian Humbaba, bringing back cedar-wood and a famous name. Gilgamesh is then wooed by the capricious goddess of love and war, Ishtar (Inanna in Sumerian). He rejects her and in revenge the goddess sends the 'Bull of Heaven' to revenge the land. The two friends kill the bull but Enkidu falls sick and dies. Gilgamesh mourns his friend and in despair he sets out to find Utnapishtim the 'Far Away', the Akkadian Noah, who alone survived the flood, to learn from him the secret of immortality. After much wandering in the wilderness he reaches the waters of death which he crosses with the help of the ferryman; but Utnapishtim gives him little comfort, though he recounts the story of the Flood (Tablet XI) which in the Sumerian is a separate account. Gilgamesh obtains a plant of 'Eternal Youth', but it is stolen from him by a snake which promptly sheds its skin, so he returns to Uruk alone and empty-handed.

The diction of the Assyrian version is a loose rhythmic verse with four (in earlier versions two) beats to the line. The language is unadorned, with many repetitions but also with striking and memorable expressions. The overriding theme of the epic is the contrast between human aspirations and the reality of loss and death. Gilgamesh is a hero with whom it is possible to feel sympathy and human understanding in spite of the great age of the epic:

> Gilgamesh answered her, 'And why should not my cheeks be starved and my face drawn? Despair is in my heart and my face is the face of one who has made a long journey, it was burned with heat and with cold. Why should I not wander over the pastures in search of the wind? My friend, my younger brother, he who hunted the wild ass of the wilderness and the panther of the plains, my friend, my younger brother who seized and killed the Bull of Heaven and overthrew Humbaba in the cedar forest, my friend who was very dear to me and who endured dangers beside me, Enkidu my brother, whom I loved, the end of mortality has overtaken him. I wept for him seven days and nights till the worm fastened on him. Because of my brother I am afraid of death, because of my brother I stray through the wilderness and cannot rest'.

—N.K. Sandars

———

GINZBURG, Natalia. Born Natalia Levi in Palermo, Sicily, 14 July 1916. Family moved to Turin, 1919. Educated at home and at schools in Turin to 1935; entered University of Turin, 1935, left before graduating. Married 1) Leone Ginzburg in 1938 (died in captivity, 1944), three children; 2) Gabriele Baldini in 1950 (died 1969). Exiled to Pizzoli, in the Abruzzo region, 1940–43; returned to Rome after the fall of Mussolini's fascist government, 1943; went into hiding in Rome, then Florence, 1944, but returned to Rome after the Allied Liberation; worked for Einaudi publishers, Rome and Turin, 1944–49; settled in Rome, 1952; lived in London, where her second husband headed the Italian Cultural Institute, 1959–61; returned to Rome, 1961; elected to parliament as independent left-wing deputy, 1983. Recipient: Tempo prize, 1947; Veillon prize, 1952; Viareggio prize, 1957; Chianciano prize, 1961; Strega prize, 1963; Marzotto prize, for play, 1965; Bargutta prize, 1983. *Died 8 October 1991.*

PUBLICATIONS

Fiction

I bambini (as Natalia Levi). 1934.
Giulietta (as Natalia Levi). 1934.
Un'assenza (as Natalia Levi). 1934.
Casa al mare (as Alessandra Tornimparte). 1937.
La strada che va in città (as Alessandra Tornimparte). 1942; revised edition, 1945; as *The Road to the City*, translated by Francis Frenaye, in *The Road to the City: Two Novelettes*, 1949.
Passaggio di tedeschi a Erra. 1945.
È stato così. 1947; as *The Dry Heart*, translated by Francis Frenaye, in *The Road to the City: Two Novelettes*, 1949.
The Road to the City: Two Novelettes, translated by Francis Frenaye, 1949.
Tutti i nostri ieri. 1952; as *Dead Yesterdays*, translated by Angus Davidson, 1956; as *A Light for Fools*, translated by Davidson, 1956; as *All Our Yesterdays*, translated by Davidson, 1985.
Valentino (includes *La madre* and *Sagittario*). 1957; *La madre*, as *The Mother*, translated by Isabel Quigly, 1965; two stories as *Valentino and Sagittarius: Two Novellas*, translated by Avril Bardoni, 1987.
Le voci della sera. 1961; edited by S. Pacifici, 1971, and by Alan Bullock, 1982; as *Voices in the Evening*, translated by D.M. Low, 1963.
Lessico famigliare. 1963; as *Family Sayings*, translated by D.M. Low, 1967; revised translation, 1984.
Mio marito. 1964.
Il maresciallo. 1965.
Caro Michele. 1973; as *No Way*, translated by Sheila Cudahy, 1974; as *Dear Michael*, translated by Cudahy, 1975.
Lessico famigliare No.2: La luna pallidassi. 1975.
Lessico famigliare No.2: Il cocchio d'oro. 1975.

Borghesia. 1977; as *Borghesia*, translated by Beryl Stockman, 1988.
Famiglia (includes *Borghesia*). 1977; as *Family*, translated by Beryl Stockman, 1988.
La famiglia Manzoni. 1983; as *The Manzoni Family*, translated by Marie Evans, 1987.
La città e la casa. 1984; as *The City and the House*, translated by Dick Davis, 1986.
Four Novellas (includes *Valentino*; *Sagittarius*; *Family*; *Borghesia*), translated by Avril Bardoni and Beryl Stockman. 1990.

Plays

Ti ho sposato per allegria (produced 1966). 1965.
L'inserzione (produced 1968). In *Ti ho sposato per allegria e altre commedie*, 1968; as *The Advertisement*, translated by Henry Reed, 1969.
Ti ho sposato per allegria e altre commedie (includes *L'inserzione*; *Fragola e panna*; *La segretaria*). 1968.
Paese di mare e altre commedie (includes *Dialogo*; *La porta sbagliata*; *La parrucca*). 1973.
La poltrona. In *Opere raccolte e ordinate dall'autore*, vol. 2, 1987.
L'intervista. 1989.
Teatro (includes *L'intervista*; *La poltrona*; *Dialogo*; *Paese di mare*; *La porta sbagliata*; *La parrucca*). 1990.
Il cormorano. 1991.

Other

Le piccole virtù (essays). 1962, as *The Little Virtues*, translated by Dick Davis, 1985.
Mai devi domandarmi (essays). 1970; as *Never Must You Ask Me*, translated by Isabel Quigly, 1973.
Vita immaginaria (essays). 1974.
Opere, edited by Cesare Garboli. 2 vols., 1986–87.
Serena Cruz; o, La vera giustizia. 1990.

Editor, *La carta del cielo* (stories), by Mario Soldati. 1980.
Editor, with Giovanna Delfini, *Diari 1927–1961*, by Antonio Delfini. 1982.

Translator, *Alla ricerca del tempo perduto: La strada di Swann*, by Marcel Proust. 1953.
Translator, *La signora Bovary*, by Gustave Flaubert. 1983.

*

Critical Studies: 'Natalia Ginzburg: The Fabric of Voices' by Donald Heiney, in *The Iowa Review*, 1(4), 1970; *Invito alla lettura di Natalia Ginzburg* by Elena Clementelli, 1972, revised edition, 1986; 'The Narrative Strategy of Natalia Ginzburg' by Clotilde S. Bowe, in *Modern Language Review*, 68(4), 1973; 'Natalia Ginzburg' by Luciana Marchionne Picchione, in *Il castoro*, 137, 1978; 'Forms and Figures in the Novels of Natalia Ginzburg' by R.D. Piclardi, in *World Literature Today*, 53(4), 1979; 'Some Thoughts on Internal and External Monologue in the Writings of Natalia Ginzburg', in *Moving in Measure: Essays in Honour of Brian Moloney* edited by Judith Bryce and Doug Thompson, 1989, and *Natalia Ginzburg: Human Relationships in a Changing World*, 1991, both by Alan Bullock; 'A Lexicon for Both Sexes: Natalia Ginzburg and the Family Saga' by Corinna Del Greco Lobner, in *Contemporary Women Writers in Italy*, edited by Santo L. Aricò, 1990.

*   *   *

Described by Ian Thomson in his review of her last novel as 'the most interesting of Italian female writers' (*Sunday Times*, 10 October 1986) Natalia Ginzburg remained throughout her life a controversial author, evoking deeply contrasting reactions from both the critical establishment and the general public. Responsive and sympathetic to the problems of both sexes, and highly sensitive to the rhythms of family life, she has analysed problems inherent in emotional relationships which transcend their immediate context to become universally recognizable, exposing the ambiguous feelings that motivate actions, and which frequently ensure that individuals are at greatest risk from those closest to them emotionally. Conscious that the traditional concept of male superiority is a myth based on women's continued acceptance of subordinate roles she was also aware that men are ultimately equally vulnerable human beings, and are thus deserving of sympathy—a view that has inevitably alienated both male chauvinists and militant feminists. Essentially a pessimistic writer, she also possesses a sharp sense of humour, pinpointing the absurdity of much human activity, in which comic and tragic elements are frequently intermingled, and has thereby offended those unable to accept that something as supposedly frivolous as humour can have a place in creative writing. In addition her straightforward and sparse narrative style, far removed from the ornate traditions of Italian literary composition, has led in some quarters to disapproval.

Ginzburg's main theme is the isolation of the individual, usually female, in an environment in which, surrounded by well-intentioned friends or relatives, there is paradoxically no real communication, and thus no possibility of genuine fulfilment. Oblivious to the generation gap and its implications parents are unaware that their adult children have become individuals whose needs may be radically different from their own, and are thus incapable of providing emotional support when it is most needed. Thus although female roles in postwar society are increasingly released from traditional domestic passivity and ignorance the older generation continues to educate its offspring in the same way, ensuring that daughters who choose to work for their living are incapable of coping with the pressures of the urban rat race or the problems of sexual emancipation. Meanwhile marriage, traditionally seen by women as a goal rather than a new beginning, is frequently a source of deep disillusion as they discover that sexual intimacy cannot compensate for radical differences in temperament and is no substitute for the meeting of minds.

Though principally focusing in her early work on the plight of women Ginzburg was always concerned to expose victimization irrespective of gender, as is clear from her first short story deemed worthy of publication, *Un'assenza* [An Absence], whose protagonist is a wealthy young man lacking any emotional drive, trapped in a loveless marriage of convenience, and with no interests to fill up his empty days— someone who has unthinkingly embraced appropriate stereotypes only to find them insufficient for his needs. If Ginzburg's output over the next 30 years may appear uncompromisingly feminist, dealing largely with unhappy wives afflicted with uncomprehending husbands in *Casa al mare* [The House by the Seaside] and *Mio marito* [My Husband], or young women neglected or oppressed by their families, in *La strada che va in città* (*The Road to the City*) and *Valentino*, unable to develop successful relationships, as in *Le voci della sera* (*Voices in the Evening*), or to cope adequately with their maternal duties, as in *La madre* (*The Mother*) and *È stato così*

(*The Dry Heart*), she also saw fit to continue extending her sympathy to males, as is clear from her portrait of Ippolito in *Tutti i nostri ieri* (*All Our Yesterdays*). In this work, a sensitive youth deprived of parental guidance who is unable to withstand the implications of the German advance in World War II and thus commits suicide is contrasted with the figure of Cenzo Rena, a hard-headed businessman and anti-fascist who resolves a family crisis by marrying Ippolito's sister, pregnant by her feckless teenage lover, and defends the impoverished peasants of his southern village against the terrors of German occupation—a rare example in Ginzburg's work of masculine strength and positive awareness. These themes are developed further in her autobiographical novel *Lessico famigliare* (*Family Sayings*), a loose collage of events from her earliest childhood to her second marriage, in which her father, a benevolent despot, and her mother, totally immersed in domesticity, are revealed as lovable but supremely ineffectual parents, with no interest in Natalia's creative talent and unable to understand or communicate with their sons, who none the less achieve success in their chosen careers.

Ginzburg's plays, dating from the mid-1960s, continue to reflect awareness of the complexity of human relationships, and include both the familiar figure of the naive female, oppressed and exploited in an alien environment—Giuliana in *Ti ho sposato per allegria* [I Married You For Fun], Teresa in *L'inserzione* (*The Advertisement*)—and the difficulties experienced by men unable to discharge adequately traditional roles such as that of vengeful husband (Paolo in *Fragola e panna* [The Strawberry Ice]), publisher (Edoardo in *La segretaria* [The Secretary]), or academic (Stefano in *La porta sbagliata* [The Wrong Door]). Now older, and thus more susceptible to the many disturbing changes in moral attitudes in post-1968 Europe, she then turned her attention to the problems of an older generation, a theme already touched on in the character of the unnamed mother in *Sagittario* (*Sagittarius*) and now more fully developed in *Caro Michele* (*Dear Michael*), where she combines an intense realization of the grim implications of social breakdown with an awareness that blanket rejections of contemporary reality by the elderly amount to mere short-sightedness and a reassuring belief that parents who make an effort to come to terms with the new world can still perhaps establish a meaningful rapport with their adult children.

This theme, here only tentatively suggested, is fully realized in her last novel, *La città e la casa* (*The City and the House*), where Giuseppe, who has long been estranged from his son, gradually re-establishes contact through a protracted correspondence between Princeton, New Jersey, where he has retired, and Rome, where his son still lives. In both cases, however, the bond so carefully established between the disaffected generations is shattered by the unexpected assassination of the son, confirming Ginzburg's essential pessimism. This pessimism was already reiterated in her two previous novels *Borghesia* and *Famiglia* (*Family*), in which rootless members of the younger generation are unable to use their new-found freedom to achieve happiness, while their elders likewise suffer both directly and indirectly from their inability to cope with the relaxation of traditional norms.

Ginzburg's last two full-length creative works, the short plays *La poltrona* [The Armchair] and *L'intervista* [The Interview], both focus on inadequate males deserving of sympathy, while also showing how they can adversely affect the lives of their female partners—a return to her original interest in emotional relationships in which both sexes are now given equal attention. In the short fragment *Il cormorano* [The Cormorant] these feelings are extended to cover the threat to animal and plant life in the Gulf War, while her many essays on a wide variety of subjects provide a more direct expression of her views than in her fiction, reaching their climax in a lengthy polemic on the laws concerning adoption, *Serena Cruz; o, La vera giustizia* [Serena Cruz; or, True Justice], typical of her activity as a left-wing parliamentarian in her final years.

—Alan Bullock

VOICES IN THE EVENING (Le voci della sera)
Novel by Natalia Ginzburg, 1961.

The narrator of *Voices in the Evening* is Elsa, a 27-year-old woman who, having finished her studies at the local university, spends most of her time listening to the mindless chatter of her oppressive mother, and occasionally going to town to return books to the library. The plot revolves around the De Francisci family, owners of the only factory in the village. The head of the family, Balotta, is a self-made man who, in spite of having become a rich employer in the pre-war period, has kept faith with the socialist principles of his youth, and is never happier than when he is in his own factory where he can talk to and share his ideas with his workers. As Alan Bullock says, Balotta is 'totally unreceptive to anything outside the narrow sphere of his business interests' (*Natalia Ginzburg: Human Relationships in a Changing World*); thus, he cannot understand his children, nor their way of life when they grow up.

The novel is written in the deliberately sparse style typical of Ginzburg. The dialogue is full of, for example, repetitions of the phrases 'she said' and 'he said', which are used to great effect to emphasize the tedium of everyday existence. There are two very distinct parts to the novel. In the first half, the plot is fragmented into flashback episodes which depict past incidents in the lives of the members of the De Francisci family and a few other characters who gravitate around them. The character of Gemmina, Balotta's eldest daughter, who early in the novel is portrayed as an egoistic spinster involved in sterile charity work, is revealed more fully in the light of her previous disappointing experience with Nebbia, whom she loved and who married another woman. The most crucial moments in Gemmina's life are quickly sketched: first, the unforgettable night in which she got lost on the mountains with Nebbia, a friend of her brothers who, for his part, only admired her masculine stamina; and then the evening in which she shyly confessed her feelings to him, leaving the young man completely astonished, but rejecting firmly any kind of emotional link with her.

All Balotta's children seem destined to be unhappy in love; they are not able to establish lasting relationships with anybody. Vincenzino is a prime example. Elsa presents him, in his later years, as a fairly successful writer. His personal life, however, is in tatters: he first became involved with a Brazilian girl, of whom he tired very quickly, and then married Cate, whom he never loved, although she was approved of by his father. Incapable of communicating with each other, and without any interests in common, these two endure a marriage that is a complete disaster. Cate tries to fill her existential vacuum first with children, and then with numerous fleeting love affairs, which leave her and Vincenzino even more bitter towards one another and discontented with their lives. The marriage ends in separation, with Cate realizing that they are both to blame ('Why have we spoilt everything?') and that her previous uneventful existence with her husband represented, in fact, some kind of happiness.

The only couple in the novel who seem to have a satisfying marriage are Mario, the third of Balotta's sons, and Xenia, a Russian refugee, who, feeling no need to communicate with anybody, never learns to speak Italian. After his marriage, Mario seems to enjoy a lifestyle different from the one he was used to, and appreciates the sophistication to which his wife has introduced him. Xenia, who continues to pursue her artistic career after her marriage, seems to bring a calming influence to bear on Mario's nervous disposition. Later, however, the narrator manages to sow a strong suspicion (although one never confirmed) that Xenia might, in some way, be responsible for her husband's death, especially after her remarriage to the Swiss doctor she had employed to treat Mario for a stomach complaint.

In the background to the main plot are also depicted Balotta's brother and sister, an old and almost senile pair who at times irritate the energetic Balotta with their uncritical approval of everything and everybody. Slightly more prominent, however, are the youngest of the De Francisci children, Raffaella, who during the war casts aside her passive female role in order to become a Communist partisan, and Purillo, Balotta's nephew. Purillo is a survivor, always ready to conform to the political reality in which he finds himself. Thus, he is a supporter of Mussolini during the Fascist period, which fortunately allows him to save Balotta's life, and, at the end of the war, he manages to fit perfectly into the local community. He marries Raffaella who, disappointed with post-war politics, devotes all her boundless energy to their only child, Pepé, thus becoming an obsessive mother.

In the second part of the novel, Ginzburg focuses sharply on the slightly banal love affair between the narrator of the story, Elsa, and the youngest son of Balotta, Tommasino. In the earlier section of *Voices in the Evening*, however, the author's treatment of other such relationships has made it clear that romantic attachments are, by nature, ill-fated. The love affair between Elsa and Tommasino startles the reader. The lovers meet in town once a week, in a rented room, where they can forget the past and nurture their precarious love. Tommasino is portrayed as possessing both the qualities and the faults of his elder brothers: he is artistic like Vincenzino, and as ineffectual as Mario. Elsa tries in vain to convince Tommasino of the depth of her feelings for him. Yet it is Tommasino's apathy that makes him eventually accept the engagement that Elsa's suffocating mother imposes upon them. However, once he comes into contact with the shallowness of his fiancée's home life and the trivial chatter of her ever-present mother, who takes over their lives, he becomes increasingly withdrawn. Elsa, realizing that the fragile equilibrium they had constructed in their rented room has been shattered, breaks off their engagement in an act of unexpected courage, thereby saving at least the memory of her lost love.

The second part of the novel is stylistically weaker, since the characters Tommasino and Elsa never really come to life, and remain totally immersed within the petty preoccupations of their narrow and futile existence. The end of *Voices in the Evening* is but a recurrence of Elsa's mother's initial monologue, with only one difference: the past tense employed by the author at the beginning of the book is replaced by the use of the present, as if Elsa's life has become an endless litany of the same phrases and the same gestures as her mother's, in an unending routine that will never change.

—Vanna Motta

GIONO, Jean. Born in Manosque, Provence, France, 30 March 1895. Educated at École Saint-Charles, 1900–02; Collège Municipal de Manosque, 1902–11. Served in the Alpine Infantry, 1915–19. Married Élise Maurin in 1920; two daughters. Bank clerk, Comptoir National d'Escompte de Paris, Manosque, 1911–14 and 1918–28; full-time writer from 1928; founded his own film company, 1958. Founder member, the Contadour movement, to promote collectivism and pacifism, 1935; imprisoned briefly at Saint Nicolas, Marseille, for refusal to join in the war effort, 1939, and at Saint-Vincent-les-Forts, 1944, for collaboration. Recipient: Brentano prize, 1929; Northcliffe prize, 1930; Corrard prize, 1931; Monaco prize for literature, 1953. Chevalier, Légion d'honneur. Elected to the Académie Goncourt, 1954. *Died 9 October 1970.*

PUBLICATIONS

Collections

Oeuvres Romanesques complètes, edited by Robert Ricatte. 6 vols., 1971–83
Oeuvres cinématographiques, edited by Jacques Mény. 1980.
Récits et essais, edited by Pierre Citron. 1989.
Romans et essais 1928–1941, edited by Henri Godard. 1992.

Fiction

Présentation de Pan. 1930.
    Colline. 1929; as *Hill of Destiny*, translated by Jacques Le Clercq, 1929.
    Un de Baumugnes. 1929; as *Lovers Are Never Losers*, translated by Jacques Le Clercq, 1931.
    Regain. 1930; revised edition, edited by Dominique Baudouin, 1967; as *Harvest*, translated by Henri Fluchère and Geoffrey Myers, 1939.
La Naissance de l'Odyssée. 1930.
Le Grand troupeau. 1931; as *To the Slaughterhouse*, translated by Norman Glass, 1969.
Eglogues. 1931.
Jean le bleu. 1932; edited by Marian Giles Jones, 1968; as *Blue Boy*, translated by Katherine Allen Clarke, 1946.
Solitude de la pitié (stories). 1932.
Le Serpent d'étoiles. 1933.
Le Chant du monde. 1934; as *The Song of the World*, translated by Henri Fluchère and Geoffrey Myers, 1937.
Que ma joie demeure. 1935; as *Joy of Man's Desiring*, translated by Katherine Allen Clarke, 1940.
Batailles dans la montagne. 1937.
L'Eau vive. 1943.
Noé. 1947.
Un roi sans divertissement. 1947.
Les Âmes fortes. 1949.
Mort d'un personnage. 1949.
Les Grands Chemins. 1951.
Le Hussard sur le toit. 1951; as *The Hussar on the Roof*, translated by Jonathan Griffin, 1953; as *The Horseman on the Roof*, translated by Griffin, 1954.
Le Moulin de Pologne. 1952; as *The Malediction*, translated by Peter de Mendelssohn, 1955.
L'Écossais. 1955.
Le Bonheur fou. 1957; as *The Straw Man*, translated by Phyllis Johnson, 1959.
Angélo. 1958; as *Angelo*, translated by Alma E. Murch, 1960.
Chroniques romanesques (includes *Un roi sans divertissement*; *Les Grands Chemins*). 1962.

Deux Cavaliers de l'orage. 1965; as *Two Riders of the Storm*, translated by Alan Brown, 1967.
Ennemonde et autres caractères. 1968; as *Ennemonde and Other Characters*, translated by David Le Vay, 1970.
Une histoire d'amour. 1969.
L'Iris de Suse. 1970.
Les Récits de la demi-brigade (stories). 1972.
Le Déserteur et autres récits (stories). 1973.
Faust au village (stories). 1977.
L'Homme qui plantait des arbres. 1980; as *The Man Who Planted Trees*, 1985.
Dragoon; suivi de Olympe (unfinished, in two versions). 1982.

Verse

Accompagnés de la flûte. 1924.
Premières proses et premiers poèmes. 1938–39.
Fragments d'un déluge, Fragments d'un paradis. 1948.

Plays

Le Lanceur de graines (produced 1932). In *Théâtre*, 1943.
Le Bout de la route (produced 1941). In *Théâtre*, 1943.
La Femme du boulanger (produced 1944). In *Théâtre*, 1943.
Théâtre (includes *Le Bout de la route*; *Le Lanceur de graines*; *La Femme du boulanger*; *Esquisse d'une mort d'Hélène*). 1943.
Le Voyage en calèche (produced 1947). 1946.
Hortense; ou, L'Eau vive, with Alain Allioux (screenplay). 1958.
Théâtre II: Domitien, suivi de Joseph à Dotham. 1959.
Crésus (screenplay). 1961.
Le Cheval fou. 1974.

Screenplays: *L'Eau vive*, with Alain Allioux, 1958; *Crésus*, 1960; *Un roi sans divertissement*, 1963.

Other

Manosque des plateaux. 1930.
Solitude de la pitié. 1932.
Le Serpent d'étoiles. 1933.
Les Vraies Richesses (essays). 1936.
Rondeur des jours. 1936.
Refus d'obéissance. 1937.
Le Poids du ciel. 1938.
Vivre Libre I: Lettre aux paysans sur la pauvreté et la paix. 1938.
Etrée du printemps. 1938.
Mort du blé. 1938.
Vivre Libre II: Précisions. 1939.
Provence (travel guide). 1939.
Pour saluer Melville, with *Moby Dick*. 1941.
Triomphe de la vie (essays). 1941.
Pages immortelles de Virgile. 1947.
La Chasse au bonheur. 1953.
Recherches de la pureté. 1953.
Voyage en Italie. 1953.
Arcadie, Arcadie!. 1953.
Notes sur l'affaire Dominici. 1955; as *The Dominici Affair*, translated by Peter de Mendelssohn, 1956.
Giono par lui-même, edited by Claudine Chonez. 1956.
Bernard Buffet. 1956.
Lundi. 1956.

Lucien Jacques. 1956.
Sur les oliviers morts. 1958.
Oppède le vieux. 1959.
Rome, with others. 1959.
Camargue. 1960.
Le Grand Théâtre. 1961.
Images de Provence. 1961.
Tableau de la littérature française. 1962.
Le Désastre de Pavie, 24 février 1525. 1963; as *The Battle of Pavia 24 February 1525*, translated by Alma E. Murch, 1965.
Animalités. 1965.
Selections, edited by Maxwell A. Smith. 1965.
Le Déserteur. 1966.
Le Génie du sud, edited by Claude Annick Jacquet. 1967.
Provence perdue. 1967.
Terre d'or. 1967.
La Mission. 1971.
Les Terrasses de l'île d'Elbe (articles). 1976.
Écrits pacifistes. 1978.
Voilà le pays magique, edited by Marcel Arlaud. 1980.
Correspondance, edited by Pierre Citron. 2 vols., 1981.
Coeurs, passions, caractères. 1982.
Correspondance, with André Gide, edited by Roland Bourneuf and Jacques Cotnam, 1983.
Les Territoires heureux. 1984.
Les Trois Arbres de Palzem (articles). 1984.
Giono à Manosque (selection). 1986.
Entretiens avec Jean Amrouche et Taos Amrouche, edited by Henri Godard. 1990.
Yves Brayer, with Yves Dentan. 1990.
Correspondance 1928–1969, with Jean Guéhenno, edited by Pierre Citron. 1991.

Translator, with Lucien Jacques and Joan Smith, *Moby Dick*, by Herman Melville. 1941.
Translator, with Catherine d'Ivernois, *L'Expédition d'Humphry Clinker*, by Tobias Smollett. 1955.

*

Critical Studies: *Jean Giono et les religions de la terre* by Christian Michelfelder, 1938; *Jean Giono* by Jacques Pugnet, 1955; *Jean Giono et les techniques du roman* (includes bibliography) by Pierre Robert, 1961; *Giono* by Pierre de Boisdeffre, 1965; *Jean Giono* by Maxwell A. Smith, 1966; *The Private World of Jean Giono* by Walter D. Redfern, 1967; *Giono, Master of Fictional Modes* by Norma L. Goodrich, 1973; *Jean Giono*, 3 vols., 1974–81, *Pour une poétique de la parole chez Giono*, 1978, and *Jean Giono, imaginaire et écriture*, 1985, all edited by Alan J. Clayton; *Les Critiques de notre temps et Giono* edited by Roland Bourneuf, 1977; *Giono et l'art du récit* edited by Yves-Alain Favre, 1978; *Jean Giono et le cinéma* by Jacques Mény, 1978; *La Provence de Giono* by Jacques Chabot, 1980; *Jean Giono* by Jean Carrière, 1985; *Giono et la mer* by Michèle Belghmi, 1987; *Dialectique de la fleur: Angélique matrice de l'oeuvre gionienne* by Laurent Fourcaut, 1989; *L'Imagionnare: Essay* by Jacques Chabot, 1990; *Giono* (in English) by Pierre Citron, 1990.

* * *

Jean Giono was born in the small medieval town of Manosque in Upper Provence and lived there for the rest of his life, his birthplace providing the inspiration for much of his writing. He had already published several poems in a regional magazine, when, in 1929, his first novel *Colline* (*Hill of Destiny*) appeared. This was serialized in a review edited by Paul Valéry, and greeted with critical acclaim by André Gide. It was to be the first of a trilogy, dedicated to the spirit of Pan, and recounting peasant life in the isolated hills of Les Bastides, the unforgettable haunt of his childhood. His evocation of this landscape is filled with its own quasi-religious spirit, beneficent when the peasants live in harmony with it, but menacing when the harmony is broken by thoughtless or wanton action. The presence of Pan is felt in the water of the village spring, on whose flow the peasants are totally dependent, and it is this spirit which punishes with drought and fire their inability to live together in peace. In the second part of the trilogy, *Un de Baumugnes* (*Lovers are Never Losers*), Pan appears as the inventor of the flute, through whose music happiness is restored to a young peasant woman after her betrayal by a smooth, cynical town dweller. *Regain* (*Harvest*) celebrates Pan as the renewing life force, bringing back civilization and fertility to a tiny community that had seemed doomed to wither away. Although the presence of the spirit of Pan only loosely joins the three novels, they have in common a lyrical celebration of the elemental forces of nature, and a deliberate simplicity of language that can both surprise and move the reader.

Giono's reputation was by now firmly established, and he continued to publish regularly until his death in 1970. More than anything, his versatility has ensured him a devoted readership, for although his output can be divided into a number of broad categories, it is never repetitive and his style evolved to suit his thematic material.

The Pan novels were followed by two semi-autobiographical novels. In *Le Grand troupeau* (*To the Slaughterhouse*) Giono explores the senseless waste of war through the demoralization of the old men left to tend the herds and land while the young men are dragged off to pointless suffering at the front. This bitter evocation of war is replaced by affectionate memories of childhood and family in *Jean le bleu* (*Blue Boy*).

In *Le Chant du monde* (*The Song of the World*), *Que ma joie demeure* (*Joy of Man's Desiring*), and *Batailles dans la montagne* [Battles on the Mountain], Pan is replaced by Dionysus, who personifies the seasonal renewal of life and gives supernatural powers to his followers. Although still belonging to the 'regionalist' tradition, these works represent a move away from the realistic presentation of the countryside towards a symbolic expression of the issues that were currently preoccupying the author. The power of love, the goodness of life, man's relationship with society and with nature are central themes, and although the poetry remains, it is often submerged by Giono's 'message'. It was only a small step from these three novels to the polemical writing of the late 1930s and early 1940s. With war imminent, he argues in *Refus d'obéissance* [Refusal to Obey] and *Vivre Libre I: Lettre aux paysans sur la pauvreté et la paix* [Letter to the Peasants on Poverty and Peace] that if the peasants were to stop providing the towns and battle zones with food, then war would grind to a halt. In *Les Vraies Richesses* [True Riches], *Le Poids du ciel* [The Weight of the Sky], and *Triomphe de la vie* [Triumph of Life] he sees contemporary society threatened by increasing mechanization and urban life, and urges a return to the natural order of the world together with a renunciation of materialistic values.

When war was declared in 1939, Giono remained faithful to his pacifist principles. Refusing to obey his mobilization orders, he was imprisoned from September to November of 1939. His release was secured through the indignant intervention of Gide, the Queen Mother of Belgium, and the student body of Yale University. On his return to Manosque, he wrote *Pour saluer Melville* [Regards to Melville] to complement his translation of *Moby Dick*. These were accompanied by *Fragments d'un paradis* [Fragments of a Paradise], *Triomphe de la vie* and *Le Voyage en calèche* [Journey by Barouche]. The latter work was banned by the German censor, an ironic event in view of Giono's second imprisonment when France was liberated in 1944. He was accused of collaboration with the enemy for not speaking out against the Germans, and for having one of his books serialized in a collaborationist paper.

Although these accusations were blatantly spurious, this second experience of prison hurt Giono deeply, and his post-World War II writings are marked by a shift away from the poetic celebration of peasant life to a series of novels with an historical background, drawing on the traditions of Stendhal and Balzac. *Chroniques* [Chronicles] consists of several novels published between 1947 and 1958, whose central hero, Angélo, is clearly based upon Giono's paternal grandfather, the Italian Carbonaro. The best known of the series is *Le Hussard sur le toit* (*The Hussar on the Roof*), which narrates Angélo's adventures as he crosses a plague-infested Provence to rejoin the *Risorgimento* in Italy.

Although Giono's work has always appealed to intellectuals, his books reached an even wider audience through his screen adaptations and original film scenarios. In all, some 16 films have been adapted from his works, the most celebrated of which is *La Femme du boulanger* [The Baker's Wife], made with Raimu in 1938. In addition he was the author of eight plays.

Giono's reputation has, if anything, increased in the years since his death. He was recognized initially as a great poet in prose and a regional novelist, but his main appeal lies in his handling of such themes as the struggle for survival against elemental forces, the strength of love and hatred, the destructive power of jealousy, and above all the creative power of friendship.

—Jane McAdoo

THE HUSSAR ON THE ROOF (Le Hussard sur le toit)
Novel by Jean Giono, 1951.

The Hussar on the Roof was published in 1951. Although belonging to a four-book cycle—*Mort d'un personnage* [Death of a Character] (1949), *Le Hussard* (1951), *Le Bonheur fou* (*The Straw Man*) (1957), and *Angélo* (1958)—*The Hussar* can be read as a work of fiction complete in itself. A complex and demanding novel, it has been interpreted variously as quasi-medieval epic, chronicle, allegory, or romance. However, Giono's novel and its hero owe as much to Stendhal and to the tradition of the plague novel established by Defoe and Manzoni.

Angélo Pardi, the hero, is a young Piedmontese officer under sentence of death in his own country for having killed a fellow officer in a duel. We first meet him wandering in a dream-like landscape where strange manifestations of the natural world are encountered at every turn. The heat is palpable, but the sky is an unnatural, chalky white. The silence is so total that 'the presence of the great, speechless trees seemed almost unreal'. Shade becomes as dazzling as the light, and rocks are barely distinguishable from vegetation. Life in the villages seems to be disrupted as people move around in 'air as viscous as syrup'.

Into this menacing atmosphere, a plague of cholera suddenly erupts. Henceforth Angélo's simple quest to rejoin his foster-brother and return with him to Piedmont is transformed into an epic journey across the Provençal Alps, a journey that will become a voyage of self-discovery. At first, disgusted by the manifestations of the illness, he tries to detach himself from the scenes of desolation he encounters. Gradually, however, the solider in him realizes that this is a battlefield in which death in the shape of the plague is the real enemy, and that only by tackling his enemy head-on will he liberate himself from fear.

A meeting with an heroic young doctor provides Angélo with the opportunity to learn how to tend cholera victims and offers him a model of selflessness which he vows to follow as the doctor dies. As he wanders cross-country to avoid the certain death of quarantine camps, Angélo's devotion proves unequal to the task as he sees victim after victim die. Giono constantly counterpoints scenes of devastating horror where the reader's sensibilities are disturbed profoundly by the well-researched descriptions of the plague, with scenes that demonstrate the hero's courage and nobility of spirit. Desire of self-preservation has turned the population into animals. High on the roofs of Manosque village, seeking refuge from a lynch mob, Angélo watches as the crowd kick a cholera victim to death. Such bestiality can only be wiped from the memory by acts of devotion, and Angélo spends some weeks helping an old nun seek out bodies to prepare for burial. The grimness of their situation is alleviated by the nun's equally grim sense of humour.

Angélo later encounters a very different situation when he meets with a young aristocrat, Pauline de Théus, who is travelling to rejoin her elderly husband. Now, much of the mystery inherent in the narrative begins to resolve itself as the two refugees divulge their personal histories. Giono recreates a world of courtly love in which Angélo's admirable qualities, courage, tenderness, devotion, and generosity are fused into a spiritual affection for a married lady whose respect he has deserved. She in turn, like the heroine of *Orlando Furioso*, journeys as a liberated woman with optimism and bravery in the face of all obstacles. The loving but innocent friendship between the two faces an ultimate trial when Pauline succumbs to the plague. Angélo battles all night to save her, and, because he has treated her with love and honour, is for the first time rewarded with success. Their friendship, in which restraint, humour, and affection have all played their part, has proved to be stronger than the plague. Angélo is finally able to return Pauline to her home before continuing on his personal journey to Italy.

The Hussar on the Roof represents a clear break with Giono's previous works. Although the lyrical descriptions of nature and powerful characterization of his earlier work remain, this novel is primarily an adventure story which revives medieval genres in a modern context while celebrating love in a pure and joyful way. Its achievement is perhaps best summed up by Marcel Arland: 'It is a novel in which the former poet and the new narrator join hands'.

—Jane McAdoo

GIRAUDOUX, Jean (Hippolyte). Born in Bellac, France, 29 October 1882. Educated at a school in Pellevoisin; lycée, Chateauroux, 1893–1900; Lycée Lakanal, Paris, 1900–02; École Normale Supérieure, Paris, 1903–05. Military service, 1902–03; served in World War I; wounded twice; High Commissioner for Information, 1939–40. Married Suzanne Boland in 1918; one son. Travelled in Europe, 1905–07; secretary and editor of *Le Matin*; in French diplomatic service, 1910; worked in the Press Office, Ministry of Foreign Affairs, 1910–14; mission to Russia and the East, 1911; military instructor in Portugal, 1916; in USA, 1917, thereafter liaison officer with the United States army in Paris; head of 'Service des oeuvres françaises à l'étranger' [Foreign Cultural Service], 1920–24; secretary to Embassy in Berlin, 1924; chief government press officer, 1924; in Turkey, 1926; with the inspectorate of consulates, 1934; director general of Information Services, 1939; retired to live with his brother in Cusset, 1940. Recipient: Légion d'honneur. *Died 31 January 1944.*

PUBLICATIONS

Collections

Théâtre complet. 16 vols., 1945–53.
Oeuvre romanesque; Oeuvres littéraires diverses. 3 vols., 1955–58.
Théâtre complet. 1971.
Théâtre complet, edited by Jacques Body and others. 1982.
Oeuvres romanesques complètes, edited by Jacques Body, Brett Dawson, and others. 1990.

Plays

Siegfried (produced 1928). 1928; edited by Gerald V. Banks, 1975; as *Siegfried*, translated by Philip Carr, 1930; also translated by Phyllis La Farge and Peter H. Judd, in *Three Plays*, 1964.
Amphitryon 38 (produced 1929). 1929; as *Amphitryon 38*, translated and adapted by S.N. Behrman, 1938; also translated by Phyllis La Farge and Peter H. Judd, in *Three Plays*, 1964; and Roger Gellert, in *Plays 2*, 1967.
Judith (produced 1931). 1931; as *Judith*, translated by J.K. Savacool, in *From the Modern Theatre*, vol. 3, edited by Eric Bentley, 1955; also translated by Christopher Fry, in *Plays 1*, 1963.
Intermezzo (produced 1933). 1933; edited by Colette Weil, 1975; as *The Enchanted*, translated by Maurice Valency, 1950, and in *Four Plays*, 1958; as *Intermezzo*, translated by Roger Gellert, in *Plays 2*, 1967.
Tessa, from the play *The Constant Nymph* by Margaret Kennedy and Basil Dean (produced 1934). 1934.
La Fin de Siegfried. 1934.
Supplément au voyage de Cook (produced 1935). 1937; as *The Virtuous Island*, adapted by Maurice Valency, 1956.
La Guerre de Troie n'aura pas lieu (produced 1935). 1935; as *Tiger at the Gates*, translated by Christopher Fry, 1955, and in *Plays 1*, 1963, also published as *The Trojan War Will Not Take Place*, 1983.
Électre (produced 1937). 1937; as *Electra*, translated by Winifred Smith, 1952; also translated by Winifred Smith, in *From the Modern Repertoire*, edited by Eric Bentley, 1952, and in *The Modern Theatre 1*, edited by Bentley, 1955; Phyllis La Farge and Peter H. Judd, in *Three Plays*, 1964.
L'Impromptu du Paris (produced 1937). 1937.
Cantique des cantiques (produced 1938). 1939.

Ondine (produced 1939). 1939; as *Ondine*, translated by Maurice Valency, 1954, and in *Four Plays*, 1958; translated by Roger Gellert, in *Plays 2*, 1967.

L'Apollon de Bellac (as *L'Apollon de Marsac*, produced 1942). 1946; as *The Apollo of Bellac*, adapted by Maurice Valency, 1954, and in *Four Plays*, 1958.

Sodome et Gomorrhe (produced 1943). 1943; as *Sodom and Gomorrha*, translated by Herma Briffault, in *The Makers of the Modern Theatre*, edited by Barry Ulanov, 1961.

La Folle de Chaillot (produced 1945). 1945; as *The Madwoman of Chaillot*, adapted by Maurice Valency, 1947, and in *Four Plays*, 1958.

Pour Lucrèce (produced 1953). 1953; as *Duel of Angels*, translated by Christopher Fry, 1958; also translated by Christopher Fry, in *Plays 1*, 1963.

Les Gracques, edited by R.M. Albérès and Jean-Pierre Giraudoux. 1958.

Four Plays (includes *The Madwoman of Chaillot*; *The Apollo of Bellac*; *The Enchanted*; *Ondine*), adapted by Maurice Valency. 1958.

Plays 1 (includes *Judith*; *Tiger at the Gates*; *Duel of Angels*), translated by Christopher Fry. 1963.

Three Plays (includes *Siegfried*; *Amphytrion 38*; *Electra*), translated by Phyllis La Farge and Peter H. Judd. 1964.

Plays 2 (includes *Amphytrion 38*; *Intermezzo*; *Ondine*), translated by Roger Gellert. 1967.

Screenplays: *La Duchesse de Langeais*, 1942; *Les Anges du péché*, with R.-L. Bruckberger and Robert Bresson, 1943 (published as *Le Film de Béthanie: Texte du 'Les Anges du péché'*, 1944).

Fiction

Provinciales. 1909.
L'École des indifférents. 1911.
Simon le pathétique. 1918.
Elpénor. 1919; as *Elpénor*, translated by Richard Howard and Bernard Bruce, 1958.
Adorable Clio. 1920.
Suzanne et le Pacifique. 1921; as *Suzanne and the Pacific*, translated by Ben Ray Redman, 1923.
Siegfried et le Limousin. 1922; as *My Friend from Limousin*, translated by Louis M. Wilcox, 1923.
Juliette au pays des hommes. 1924.
Le Cerf, with *Premier rêve signé*. 1926.
Bella. 1926; as *Bella*, translated by J.F. Scanlan, 1927.
Églantine. 1927.
Les Aventures de Jérôme Bardini. 1930.
La France sentimentale. 1932.
Combat avec l'ange. 1934.
Choix des élues. 1939.
Les Contes d'un matin. 1952.
La Menteuse. 1958; as *Lying Woman*, translated by Richard Howard, 1969.

Other

Retour d'Alsace, août 1914. 1916.
Lectures pour une ombre. 1917.
Adieu à la guerre. 1919.
Amica America. 1919.
Visite chez le prince. 1924.
Le Sport. 1928.
Racine. 1930; as *Racine*, translated by P. Mansell Jones, 1938.
Fugues sur Siegfried. 1930.
Fontrages au Niagara. 1932.

De pleins pouvoirs à sans pouvoirs. 1935.
Les Cinq Tentations de La Fontaine. 1938.
Le Futur Armistice. 1939.
Pleins pouvoirs. 1939.
A propos de la rentrée des classes. 1939.
Littérature. 1941.
Écrits dans l'ombre. 1944.
Armistice à Bordeaux. 1945.
Sans pouvoirs. 1946.
Pour une politique urbaine. 1947.
La Française et la France. 1951.
Visitations. 1952.
Portugal, suivi de Combat avec l'image. 1958.
Or dans la nuit: Chroniques et préfaces littéraires 1910–1943. 1969.
Carnets des Dardanelles, edited by Jacques Body. 1969.
Souvenir de deux existences. 1975.
Messages du continental: Allocutions radiodiffusées du Commissaire général à l'Information (1939–1940) (speeches). 1987.
Lettres à Lilita: 1910–1928, edited by Mauricette Berne. 1989.

*

Bibliography: *Bibliographie de l'oeuvre de Giraudoux 1899–1982*, by Brett Dawson, 1982.

Critical Studies: *Jean Giraudoux: The Making of a Dramatist* by Donald Inskip, 1958; *Jean Giraudoux: His Life and Works* by Laurence LeSage, 1959; *Jean Giraudoux: The Theatre of Victory and Defeat* by Agnes G. Raymond, 1966; *Giraudoux: Three Faces of Destiny* by Robert Cohen, 1968; *Jean Giraudoux: The Writer and His Work* by Georges Lemaître, 1971; *Giraudoux: La Guerre de Troie n'aura pas lieu* by Roy A. Lewis, 1971; *Precious Irony: The Theatre of Giraudoux* by Paul A. Mankin, 1971; *Giraudoux* by Chris Marker, 1978; *Jean Giraudoux* by John H. Reilly, 1978; *Jean Giraudoux and Oriental Thought: A Study of Affinities* by Arthur C. Buck, 1984; *Jean Giraudoux: The Legend and the Secret* by Jacques Body, 1991.

*   *   *

Jean Giraudoux's theatre dominated the French stage in the period between the two World Wars. When he first began writing plays in the late 1920s, his stylistic inventiveness, his witty sense of the incongruity of life, and his search for purity made Giraudoux's work unique and individual. Since then, his fame has spread worldwide and there have been numerous translations and productions of his dramatic works in English and in other languages.

What makes this even more extraordinary is that the dramatist did not begin writing for the stage until he was 46 years old. Before that time, he had achieved some renown, although on a minor scale, as a novelist. Such works as *Suzanne et le Pacifique* (*Suzanne and the Pacific*) and *Juliette au pays des hommes* [Juliette in the Land of Men] gave him a reputation as a writer of complex and subtle novels that reached only a very small public. Indeed, it is only in recent years that his fiction has begun to receive greater recognition.

The presentation of his first play, *Siegfried*, catapulted Giraudoux from the ranks of the minor novelists to the forefront of the French theatre movement. This startling success with both audiences and critics was to last throughout his lifetime and beyond, as some of his later works were not performed until after his death, including one of his most popular, *La Folle de Chaillot* (*The Madwoman of Chaillot*). At first glance, the fanciful creativity and the unusual turn of mind of the writer would seem ill-suited to the more restrictive demands of the stage. Several factors, however, played a role in his achievement. Certainly, Louis Jouvet, the actor-director who formed a close collaboration with Giraudoux and who directed most of his plays, was one of the principal reasons that the dramatist established himself so easily. Another important element was evidently Giraudoux's major theme—man's search for a purity and an ideal beyond the imperfections of reality—a theme that touched a sensitive nerve with the theatre-going public of the 1930s. It found its expression in whimsical comedies like *Amphitryon 38* and *Intermezzo* in which the central characters flirt with the attractiveness of the unknown, only to accept a compromise with the appeal of everyday reality. And the theme also appears in a more concrete form in *La Guerre de Troie n'aura pas lieu* (*Tiger at the Gates*) in which the characters debate the issue of peace and war. In the final analysis, however, it can be argued that the real reason for Giraudoux's appeal was his style—his elegant, civilized, witty account of life in its diverse aspects. The writer's special use of metaphors and symbols, his ironic view of reality, and his sense of the spontaneous and the unexpected were basically responsible for the singular universe that enchanted and delighted his public.

Giraudoux is no longer the major force in French drama that he once was. The contemporary theatre has taken a number of new directions in recent years, passing from the theatre of the absurd of Eugène Ionesco or Samuel Beckett to a theatre in which the director assumes the prominent role, the writer and his words becoming only one part of the whole. Giraudoux's plays, based upon dialogue and discussion, hold language in high esteem. As a result, he could seem less current today. Nevertheless, his imaginative views of man and man's role in the universe and his creative use of language are likely to endure and he should remain one of the major French playwrights of the 20th century.

—John H. Reilly

THE MADWOMAN OF CHAILLOT (La Folle de Chaillot)
Play by Jean Giraudoux, 1945.

The Madwoman of Chaillot is one of the most successful plays written by Giraudoux. When it was first produced in Paris on 19 December 1945, its subject matter coincided perfectly with the feelings of the French people. France had just come out of the devastating effects of World War II and the humiliating experience of the German occupation. As a result, the French people were seeking to break loose from the shackles of the past few years and to look to a better future. At the same time, emotions were running high over the collaboration of some French citizens with the Nazis and over the resultant corruption. There was a tendency on the part of the French to see things as right or wrong. Giraudoux's latest work incorporated these elements and appealed immediately to the public of that time. *The Madwoman of Chaillot* had a direct, uncomplicated approach to good and evil. The play is a fantasy in which the 'good' people succeed in ridding their world of the 'bad' people, and it seeks a happy ending.

The protagonist of the play, the Madwoman of Chaillot, was based upon an eccentric figure whom the playwright had seen on the streets of Paris only once. This Madwoman, the Countess Aurelia, seems to be a ridiculous figure, clothed in an outlandish manner, as Giraudoux describes in his stage directions: 'the grand fashion of 1885, a taffeta skirt with an immense train . . . ancient button shoes, and a hat in the style of Marie Antoinette'. When she first appears on stage at the Café Chez Francis, she asks the waitress: 'Are my bones ready, Irma?', setting the comic tone of the piece.

The people who surround Aurelia include the flower girl, the ragpicker, the street singer—all the ordinary, humble people who represent the real essence of life and possess the true wisdom, in Giraudoux's view. Aurelia discovers that the 'evil' people of the world—the financiers, the barons, the presidents—are planning to destroy the way of life of the common folk. These people are all representatives of the capitalist world, a surprisingly direct political reference on the part of the playwright, who was usually discreet in these matters. The capitalists have uncovered the fact that there is oil underneath the Café Chez Francis where the Countess and her friends congregate. They are determined to seek out this oil, even though in doing so they must destroy the beauty and charm of the area.

When Aurelia becomes aware of their intentions, she puts her own plans into motion. She calls three of her friends—the Madwoman of Passy, the Madwoman of Saint Sulpice and the Madwoman of La Concorde—to a meeting to discuss the situation. Their 'discussion' is often senseless and non-sequential, as they have trouble sticking to the subject at hand, one of the Madwomen insisting on speaking to her long since deceased dog Dickie and another demanding to consult her 'voices' that she hears in her hot water bottle. While their comments are often far-fetched and fanciful, they end up with the correct conclusion that these 'evil' people must be eliminated. A mock trial is held in which the humble people, like the sewer man and the ragpicker, assume the roles of the capitalists who are all found guilty. A trap door in Aurelia's apartment leads to the sewers of the city and, once having descended into them, no one is allowed to return. Aurelia invites all of the profiteers to her apartment and they greedily head down into the sewers looking for the oil. Once they have all gone down, Aurelia shuts the trap door and the world has been made safe.

The Madwoman of Chaillot is most characteristic of Giraudoux in its fanciful and whimsical tone, demonstrating the playwright's inventiveness and charm. In a sense, the fairy-tale atmosphere of this play is the perfect expression of the unique and creative mind of Giraudoux, allowing him to escape from the mundane world of reality into a delightful fantasy world. The playwright makes the chaotic and seemingly unreal world of the Madwomen seem more vivid and more truthful than the real world.

Although the play is a typical example of the imaginative Giraudoux mind, the work had a deeper meaning to the playwright. Underneath the amusing and witty façade of the comedy, the dramatist was expressing his concerns over the future of France and its urban life. At the time of the writing of this play, Giraudoux was increasingly preoccupied with the problems of everyday living. Basically, he was telling the public to beware, that people were out there ready to take away the quality of their lives. Aurelia recounts this concern to the other Madwomen:

There are people in the world who want to destroy everything. They have the fever of destruction. Even when they pretend that they're building, it is only in order to destroy. When they put up a new building, they quietly knock down two old ones. They build cities so that they can destroy the countryside. They destroy space with telephones and time with airplanes.

This attack on the greed and corruption of the capitalist profiteers was a political stance not common in Giraudoux's writings, and some observers have viewed this as a change of direction interrupted by his death. At the same time, however, it can be argued that this is, in its own way, an escape from reality. The playwright composed the work during the occupation of France by the Germans and *The Madwoman of Chaillot* sidesteps any direct reference to that situation. It is as if the dramatist had made up his mind to look to a different, better time, when problems could be solved simply and directly.

—John H. Reilly

TIGER AT THE GATES (La Guerre de Troie n'aura pas lieu)
Play by Jean Giraudoux, 1935.

In the mid 1930s, Giraudoux was an extremely successful playwright whose fanciful mind and innovative use of language had captivated a wide public. In plays like *Amphitryon 38* and *Intermezzo*, he had found his audience with his stylistic artistry and his search for the ideal world, going beyond ordinary reality. When *Tiger at the Gates* was first performed in 1935, Giraudoux's reputation took on new dimensions. It was now unmistakably clear that he was an important dramatist, capable of addressing a major theme and writing a work of serious dimensions.

The playwright took as his theme the question of war and peace, seeking to demythologize war and to make its destructive effects plain to all. The source of the play was clearly his growing concern about Germany and its increasingly warlike stance in Europe. Conflict was beginning to seem inevitable to everyone at that time and Giraudoux wanted to call attention to what was happening.

Although the work had its source in the actuality of the day, the dramatist, as was his custom, did not present his theme directly in a modern setting—he turned, instead, to legend and literature. His immediate source is *The Iliad*. In the legend, Helen, wife of Menelaus, King of Sparta, is carried off by Paris, the Trojan prince, son of Priam and Hecuba. Infuriated by this action, the Greeks wage war against the Trojans who are destroyed. Hector, the main Trojan warrior, is killed, and his wife, Andromache, is taken away into slavery.

Giraudoux begins his play at the moment when the Trojans are waiting for an emissary from the Greeks who is going to ask for the return of Helen. Hector, having just returned from war, is desperately hoping for peace, but conflict seems inevitable. As he says, war is part of mankind's nature: 'If every mother cut off her son's right-hand index finger, the armies of the world would fight without index fingers. And if they cut off their sons' right legs, the armies would be one-legged'. He notes with despair that there are many people in his own ranks who are hoping for war, either as a means of justifying disappointing existences or as a way of scorning life.

At first, Hector does succeed in avoiding the ineluctable forces of war. He manages to convince some of his people that war is not beautiful; he allows himself to be humiliated by one of the Greek representatives, who slaps him and whom he refuses to fight; he thinks that he has even managed to persuade Helen of the dangers of trifling with war. Helen,

the reason for the conflict, is only toying with the question of love—she does not love Paris, she loves men.

In the second act, Ulysses and his Greek followers arrive, determined to begin the conflict unless Helen is released. Yet Hector convinces Ulysses, an intelligent man held in high esteem, of the folly of war and the two of them make an arrangement to return Helen to Greece. The agreement is based, however, on the assumption that Helen has not been touched by Paris. The Trojans cannot accept what they see as an attack on their masculinity and they explain in some detail how Paris took Helen. With the agreement seemingly in ruins, Ulysses is nevertheless willing to give peace another try, although he is realistic enough to realize that it is virtually impossible to halt the hand of fate. Yet he will join with Hector in attempting to deceive fate and he makes plans to leave with Helen. Although Hector thinks that peace is finally at hand, the inevitability of war becomes even clearer. Before Ulysses can make his departure with Helen, Ajax, a drunken Greek soldier, makes advances toward Andromache. Hector contains himself and Ajax eventually plans to depart, leaving one to assume that again peace is near. Just at that time, however, Demokos, one of the most warlike of the Trojans, makes an attempt to encourage the Greeks to fight. Trying to put an end to this once and for all, Hector stabs Demokos, exclaiming, as the curtain begins to fall, that 'the Trojan war will not take place' (the actual French title of the play). Yet the dying Demokos manages to maintain that Ajax, not Hector, has killed him. The Trojan war will take place and the curtain rises once again, symbolizing the beginning of conflict.

These final moments of the work underscore the irony of the situation. Hector, the man of peace, has inadvertently brought about the Greek–Trojan war. Had he not stabbed Demokos, it is unlikely that Demokos would have been able to arouse the Trojans to battle. And Hector probably would not have stabbed Demokos had he not been angered by Ajax's attempts to embrace Andromache. Thus, the couple of peace end up triggering this major conflict. And the ultimate irony of the play is presented when, at the end, Helen is seen embracing a young man, suggesting that the forthcoming destruction will have been fought for a person for whom love is nothing but a plaything. Even more importantly, there is the suggestion that Helen was simply a pretext for the battle that humankind always seeks out.

The normal interpretation of this play is that mankind is at the mercy of destiny—the tiger at the gates. In spite of everything one may try to do, the sleeping tiger will awake and the war will begin. It is possible, however, to look upon the play as an example of a different path taken by the playwright. Giraudoux was trying to explore to what extent mankind itself could take some of the control of its future away from fate. In that respect, the dramatist seems to be stating that mankind has to bear some of the responsibility for the seeming inevitability of war. He was making this point at the very moment when war with Germany was looming on the horizon and he was asking people to take on the burden of doing what they could to prevent this conflict.

—John H. Reilly

GIRONELLA (Pous), José María. Born in Darnius, near Gerona, Spain, 31 December 1917. Educated at a seminary,

Gerona, 1928–30. Married Magda Castañer in 1946. Worked as labourer and factory hand, early 1930s; bank clerk, Gerona, 1935–36; on the outbreak of the Spanish Civil War, 1936, volunteered for the Nationalist forces, and served with mountain patrols in Huesca, Pyrenees; journalist in Gerona, 1940; correspondent for Italian *Informazione*, Rome, 1942; left Spain covertly, 1947, and lived in France, Italy, Austria, and Sweden, 1947–52; suffered nervous breakdown in Paris, 1951, and travelled between clinics in Vienna and Helsinki, 1951–53; travelled to New York, Cuba (during its revolution), and Mexico, 1959–60, the Far East (twice), 1962–64, Israel, 1975, and Egypt, Iran, and Kuwait, 1979. Recipient: Nadal prize, 1946; Planeta prize, 1971. *Died in 1991.*

PUBLICATIONS

Fiction

Un hombre. 1947; as *Where the Soil Was Shallow*, translated by Anthony Kerrigan, 1957.
La marea. 1949.
Los cipreses creen en Dios. 1953; as *The Cypresses Believe in God*, translated by Harriet de Onís, 1956.
Muerte y juicio de Giovanni Papini: Cuento fantástico. 1959.
Un millón de muertos. 1961; as *One Million Dead*, translated by Joan Maclean, 1963; as *The Million Dead*, translated by Maclean, 1963.
Mujer, levántate y anda. 1962.
Ha estallado la paz. 1966; as *Peace after War*, translated by Joan Maclean, 1969.
Los hombres lloran solos. 1971.
Condenados a vivir. 2 vols., 1971.
Cita en el cementerio. 1983.
La duda inquietante (novella). 1986.

Verse

Ha llegado el invierno y tú no estás aquí. 1945.

Other

El novelista ante el mundo. 1954.
Los fantasmas de mi cerebro. 1959; as *Phantoms and Fugitives: Journeys to the Improbable*, translated by Terry Broch Fontsere, 1964.
Todos somos fugitivos (stories and essays). 1961, and in *Phantoms and Fugitives; Journeys to the Improbable*, 1964.
On China and Cuba, translated by John F. Byrne. 1963.
Personas, ideas, mares (travel writing). 1963.
El Japón y su duende (travel writing). 1964.
China, lágrima innumerable (history). 1965.
Gritos del mar (essays). 1967.
Conversaciones con Don Juan de Borbón. 1968.
La sociedad actual en el mundo asiático: Experiencia de un viaje. 1968.
100 españoles y Dios (essays). 1969.
Gritos de la tierra (essays). 1970.
En Asia se muere bajo las estrellas (travel writing). 1971.
El Mediterráneo es un hombre disfrazado de mar (travel writing). 1974.
El escándalo de Tierra Santa (travel writing). 1977.
Carta a mi padre muerto (autobiographical writings). 1978.
100 españoles y Franco (essays). 1979.
Mundo tierno, mundo cruel. 1981.
El escándalo del Islam (travel writing). 1982.
A la sombra de Chopin. 1990.

Yo, Mahoma. 1992.
Jerusalén de los evangelios. 1992.
Carta a mi madre muerta (autobiographical writings). 1992.

*

Critical Studies: 'José María Gironella, Spanish Novelist' by William J. Grupp, in *Kentucky Foreign Language Quarterly*, 4(3), 1957; 'Arturo Barea and J.M. Gironella: Two Interpreters of the Spanish Civil War' by J.J. Devlin, in *Hispania*, 41, 1958; 'Revolutionary Novels of Gironella and Pasternak' by Edmund S. Urbanski, in *Hispania*, 43, 1960; *Crítica y glosa de Un millón de muertos* by L.E. Calvo Sotelo, 1961; 'Gironella and Hemingway: Novelists of the Spanish Civil War' by R.L. Sheehan, in *Studies in Honor of Samuel Montefiore Waxman*, 1969; *José María Gironella* (in English) by Ronald Schwartz, 1972; *Perspectivas humorísticas en la trilogía de Gironella* by J. David Suárez-Torres, 1972; 'Gironella's Chronicles Revisited: A Panorama on Fratricide' by John E. Dial, in *Papers on Language and Literature*, 10(1), 1974; 'Fictive History in Gironella' by Peter Ilie, in *Journal of Spanish Studies*, 2, 1974; *José María Gironella* by J.A. Salso, 1982; *The Novel of the Spanish Civil War (1936–1939)* by Gareth Thomas, 1990.

* * *

The outstanding literary creations of José María Gironella deal with the Spanish Civil War, 1936–39. The predominant theme of his best received novels, *Los cipreses creen en Dios* (*The Cypresses Believe in God*) and *Un millón de muertos* (*One Million Dead*), focuses on the suffering and disintegration of family life. Gironella, a traditionalist in all respects, intones the lament of a society which has forsaken its sense of order. Vengeful survival becomes a way of life. In his portrayal of war-torn Spain, the author attempts, really tries very hard, to be objective. However, he cannot divest himself of his strong commitment to his orthodox religious background, and consequently to the conservative political position. Unquestionably, his devotion to his personal principles has a marked influence on his characters; although seemingly they confront their tragic circumstances as individuals, in truth they carry with them symbolic identities. That is to say, in the last analysis, they are 'types' rather than singular characters. Yet, even as generic projections of an agonizing existence, they achieve a significant measure of artistic reality. Through the description of their lives, the reader is able to identify with the day-to-day struggle for subsistence amid the ravages of a war which tears families asunder, as fanaticism grows in intensity on all sides of the political spectrum.

The warring hostilities depicted in *The Cypresses Believe in God* violently expand in *One Million Dead* which, as the title suggests, dwells on the terrible loss of life. (Even though 'one million' is an exaggeration, the number of dead did run into the hundreds of thousands.) Historical events are interwoven with fictional accounts quite skilfully; on the surface, both novels would appear to be a reliable recording of dramatic incidents through the personal vicissitudes of the Alvear family, which microcosmically serves as the axis for the national catastrophe. Essentially, the tragedy of Spain is reflected in the misfortunes that befall one family. To be sure, it is a family that predominantly leans toward the cause of Franco.

The third volume of Gironella's trilogy on the Civil War, *Ha estallado la paz* (*Peace after War*), hardly deserves the same recognition. The first two, voluminous indeed, will give Gironella a respectable place in the annals of Spanish literature. While not achieving, by any means, the stature of a weaver of fictionalized history like Pérez Galdós in the 19th century, Gironella has succeeded in establishing himself as the literary historian of the Spanish Civil War. Other novelists have centred their attention on the consequences of the consanguineous conflict, but Gironella has been the only outstanding writer who has addressed the question in the form of novels.

Gironella's other writings comprise many themes: religion, death, politics, and a variety of subjects that refer to human problems as they affect daily existence. However, they are by and large essay-type expressions of the author's concern for life and death. In themselves they would not constitute a testimony to a writer who is worthy of being considered as the novelistic chronicler of the three most harrowing years that Spaniards have ever known. Without a doubt, for those who would want to view the drama of a Spain embarked on self-destruction, *The Cypresses Believe in God* and *One Million Dead* are indispensable reading.

—Robert Kirsner

GĪTĀ.   See **BHAGAVADGĪTĀ**.

GOETHE, Johann Wolfgang von. Born in Frankfurt, Germany, 28 August 1749. Studied law at Leipzig University, 1765–68, and drawing with Adam Oeser; after a period of illness, resumed his studies in Strasbourg, 1770–71, licentiate in law 1771. Lived with Christiane Vulpius from 1788; married her in 1806 (died 1816); one son. Practised law in Frankfurt, 1771–72, and Wetzlar, 1772; contributor, *Frankfurter Gelehrte Anzeigen*, 1772–73; at invitation of Duke Karl August, joined the small court of Weimar in 1775: member of the council, 1776, president, war commission, 1779, director of roads and services, 1779, ennobled 1782, took over much of the financial affairs of the court; after a visit to Italy, 1786–88, released from day-to-day government business: general supervisor for arts and sciences, 1788, and director of the court theatres, 1791–1817. Editor of a variety of yearbooks and magazines, including, with Schiller, *Xenien*, 1796–97; with J.H. Meyer, *Die Propyläen*, 1798–1800; *Kunst und Altertum*, 1816–32; and *Zur Naturwissenschaft*, 1817–24. Chancellor of the University of Jena. *Died 22 March 1832.*

PUBLICATIONS

Collections

Schriften. 8 vols., 1787–90; later editions, as *Werke*, 13 vols., 1806–10, etc.; 69 vols., 1826–42.
Complete Works [Bohn Standard Library]. 14 vols., 1848–90.
Werke [Sophie or Weimar Edition]. 134 vols., 1887–1919.

Sämtliche Werke [Jubiläum Edition], edited by Eduard von der Hellen. 40 vols., 1902–07.
Werke [Hamburg Edition], edited by Erich Trunz and others. 14 vols., 1948–69; subsequent revisions, last reprinted 1981.
Gedenkausgabe der Werke, Briefe, und Gespräche, edited by Ernst Beutler. 27 vols., 1948–71.
Collected Works, edited by Christopher Middleton and others, translated by Michael Hamburger and others. 12 vols., 1983–88.
Sämtliche Werke [Munich Edition], edited by Karl Richter and others. 1986—.

Fiction

Die Leiden des jungen Werthers. 1774; revised edition, 1787; as *The Sorrows of Werter*, translated by Richard Graves or Daniel Malthus, 1780; numerous subsequent translations including as *The Sufferings of Young Werther*, translated by Michael Hulse, 1989.
Wilhelm Meisters Lehrjahre [and *Wanderjahre*]. 1795–1821; as *Wilhelm Meister's Apprenticeship* [and *Travels*], translated by Thomas Carlyle, 1824–27, revised editions 1842, 1865; several subsequent translations including by H.M. Waidson, 1977–79.
Die Wahlverwandtschaften. 1809; as *Elective Affinities*, in *Works*; as *Kindred by Choice*, translated by H.M. Waidson, 1960; as *Elective Affinities*, translated by Elizabeth Mayer and Louise Brogan, 1963; also translated by R.J. Hollingdale, 1971; John Winkelman, 1987.
Novelle. 1826.

Plays

Götz von Berlichingen mit der eisernen Hand (produced 1774). 1773; as *Goetz of Berlichingen with the Iron Hand*, translated by Walter Scott, 1799; as *Ironhand*, translated by John Arden, 1965; as *Götz von Berlichingen*, translated by Charles E. Passage, in *Plays*, 1980.
Clavigo (produced 1774). 1774; as *Clavidgo*, translated by Charles Leftley, 1798.
Götter, Helden, und Wieland. 1774.
Erwin und Elmire, music by Jean André (produced 1775). 1775; revised version, in verse, in *Schriften*, 5, 1788.
Stella. 1776; revised version (produced 1806), in *Werke*, 6, 1816; translated as *Stella*, 1798.
Claudine von Villa Bella (produced 1777). 1776; revised version (produced 1789), in *Schriften*, 5, 1788.
Die Geschwister (produced 1776). In *Schriften*, 1, 1787.
Die Mitschuldigen (produced 1777). In *Schriften*, 2, 1787; as *Fellow Culprits*, translated by Charles E. Passage, in *Plays*, 1980.
Lila, music by Sigmund von Seckendorff (produced 1777). In *Schriften*, 1790.
Das Jahrmarktsfest zu Plundersweilern (produced 1778). In *Schriften*, 6, 1790.
Der Triumph der Empfindsamkeit (produced 1778). In *Schriften*, 4, 1787; revised version, as *Proserpina*, music by Karl Eberwein (produced 1915), in *Werke*, 1808.
Die Laune des Verliebten (produced 1779). In *Werke*, 4, 1806; as *The Lover's Whim*, translated by Charles E. Passage, in *Plays*, 1980.
Iphigenie (produced 1779; revised version, in verse, as *Iphigenie auf Tauris*, produced 1802). In *Schriften*, 3, 1787; as *Iphigenia in Tauris*, translated by William Taylor, 1793; several subsequent translations including by Charles E. Passage, in *Plays*, 1980.

Die Vögel, from the play by Aristophanes (produced 1780). 1787.

Jery und Bätely, music by Sigmund von Seckendorff (produced 1780). 1790.

Die Fischerin, music by Corona Schröter (produced 1782). 1782.

Egmont (produced 1784). 1788; translated as *Egmont*, 1848; also translated by Michael Hamburger, in *The Classic Theatre*, edited by Eric Bentley, 1959; F.J. Lamport, in *Five German Tragedies*, 1969; Charles E. Passage, in *Plays*, 1980.

Torquato Tasso (produced 1807). In *Schriften*, 6, 1790; as *Torquato Tasso*, translated by C. des Voeux, 1827; also translated by A. Swanwick, in *Dramatic Works*, 1846; John Prudhoe, 1979; Charles E. Passage, in *Plays*, 1980; Alan Brownjohn, 1985.

Scherz, List und Rache (opera libretto; produced 1790). In *Schriften*, 7, 1790.

Der Gross-Cophta (produced 1791). 1792.

Der Bürgergeneral (produced 1793). 1793.

Mahomet, from the play by Voltaire (produced 1799). 1802.

Paläophron und Neoterpe (produced 1800; revised version, produced 1803). In *Werke*, 1808.

Tancred, from the play by Voltaire (produced 1801). 1802.

Die natürliche Tochter (produced 1803). 1804.

Faust, Part One (produced 1819). In *Werke*, 8, 1808; translated as *Faustus*, 1821; numerous subsequent translations.

Pandora. 1810.

Romeo und Juliet, from the play by Shakespeare (produced 1812).

Des Epimenides Erwachen (produced 1815). 1815.

Faust, Part Two (produced 1854). In *Werke: Ausgabe letzter Hand*, 41, 1832 (first complete publication); numerous translations with Part One as *Faust* including by Philip Wayne, 2 vols., 1949–59.

Plays (includes *Götz von Berlichingen*; *Fellow Culprits*; *The Lover's Whim*; *Iphigenia in Tauris*; *Egmont*; *Torquato Tasso*; *Faust*), translated by Charles E. Passage. 1980.

Plays: Egmont, Iphigenia in Tauris, Torquato Tasso, edited by Frank Ryder. 1992.

Verse

Neue Lieder mit Melodien, music by Bernhard Breitkopf. 1770.

Gedichte, in *Schriften*, 8, 1789; and subsequent editions.

Römische Elegien. 1789; as *Roman Elegies*, translated by David Luke, 1977.

Reineke Fuchs. 1794; as *Reynard the Fox*, translated by Thomas Arnold, 1855; as *Reineke Fox*, translated by A. Rogers, 1888.

Hermann und Dorothea. 1798; as *Herman and Dorothea*, translated by Thomas Holcroft, 1801; several subsequent translations.

West-östlicher Divan. 1819; as *West-Easterly Divan*, translated by J. Weiss, 1876; as *West-Eastern Divan*, translated by Alexander Rogers, 1890; also translated by E. Dowden, 1914.

Selected Verse (bilingual edition), edited by David Luke. 1964.

Selected Poems (bilingual edition), edited by Christopher Middleton, translated by Michael Hamburger, 1983.

Other

Beiträge zur Optik. 1790.

Versuch, die Metamorphose der Pflanzen zu erklären. 1790; as *Goethe's Botany*, translated by Agnes Arber, 1946.

Winckelmann und sein Jahrhundert. 1805.

Zur Farbenlehre. 1810; as *Goethe's Theory of Colours*, translated by C.L. Eastlake, 1840.

Aus meinem Leben: Dichtung und Wahrheit. 4 vols., 1811–33; as *Memoirs of Goethe: Written by Himself*, 1824; as *The Autobiography of Goethe*, translated by John Oxenford, 1848; as *From My Life*, translated by Robert Heitner, in *Collected Works*, 4, 1987.

Italienische Reise. 1816–17; as *Travels in Italy*, translated by Alexander James Morrison, 1849; as *Italian Journey*, translated by W.H. Auden and Elizabeth Mayer, 1962; edited by Thomas P. Saine and Jeffrey L. Sammons, translated by Robert R. Heitner, 1989.

Tag- und Jahreshefte, in *Werke 31–32*. 1830; as *Annals*, translated by Charles Nisbet, 1901.

Gespräche mit Goethe, by Johann Peter Eckermann. 1836; edited by Fritz Bergemann, 1955; as *Conversations with Goethe*, translated by S.M. Fuller, 1839.

Correspondence with Goethe, by Carlyle. 1887.

Die Schriften zur Naturwissenschaft. 1947.

Amtliche Schriften, edited by Willy Flach and Helma Dahl. 3 vols., 1950–72.

Briefe, edited by K.R. Mandelkow and B. Morawe. 6 vols., 1962–69.

Gespräche, edited by W.F. and F. von Biedermann, revised by Wolfgang Herwig. 3 vols., 1965–72.

Goethe on Art, edited and translated by John Gage. 1980.

Schriften zur Biologie, edited by Konrad Dietzfelbinger. 1982.

Briefe aus Italien 1786 bis 1788 (selected letters), edited by Eugen Thurnher. 1985.

*

Bibliography: *Goethe-Bibliographie* by Hans Pyritz, Heinz Nicolai, and Gerhard Burckhardt, 1954; supplement, 1968; *Goethe-Bibliographie* by Helmut G. Hermann, 1991.

Critical Studies: *A Study of Goethe*, 1947, and *Goethe's Faust, Six Essays*, 1953, both by Barker Fairley; *Goethe: The Story of a Man* by Ludwig Lewisohn, 1949; *The Testament of Werther in Poetry and Drama*, 1949, and *Goethe's Faust: A Literary Analysis*, 1958, both by Stuart P. Atkins; *Goethe's Major Plays* by Ronald Peacock, 1959; *Goethe, Poet and Thinker* by E. Wilkinson and L.A. Willoughby, 1962; *Goethe: A Critical Introduction* by Henry C. Hatfield, 1963; *Goethe: His Life and Times* by Richard Friedenthal, 1965; *The Drama of Goethe*, 1966, *The Beautiful Soul: A Study of Eighteenth-Century Idealism as Exemplified by Rousseau's La Nouvelle Héloise and Goethe's Die Leiden des jungen Werthers*, 1981, and *The Misinterpreting of Goethe's Gretchen Tragedy*, 1992 all by R.D. Miller; *Goethe's Faust: Its Genesis and Purport* by Eudo C. Mason, 1967; *A Student's Guide to Goethe* by F.J. Lamport, 1971; *Goethe's Faust: A Critical Reading*, 1972, and *Johann Wolfgang Goethe*, 1974, both by Liselotte Dieckmann; 'Wine That Maketh Glad': The Interplay of Reality and Symbol in Goethe's Life and Work* by L.A. Willoughby, 1975; *Goethe and the Novel* by Eric A. Blackall, 1976; *Goethe's Faust: Seven Essays* by Alan Cottrell, 1976; *Faust and the Bible: A Study of Goethe's Use of Scriptural Allusions and Christian Religious Motifs in Faust I and II* by Osman Durrani, 1977; *Goethe: Portrait of the Artist* by Ilse Graham, 1977; *Goethe and the Weimar Theatre* by Marvin Carlson, 1978; *Invitation to Goethe's Faust* by Harry G. Haile, 1978; *The Form of Faust: The Work of Art and its Intrinsic Structures* by Harold Jantz, 1978; *Studies in Goethe's*

Lyric Cycles by Meredith Lee, 1978; *Time Structure in Drama: Goethe's Sturm und Drang Plays* by Walter K. Stewart, 1978; *Goethe's Search for the Muse: Translation and Creativity* by David B. Richards, 1979; *The Classical Centre: Goethe and Weimar 1775–1832*, 1980, *Goethe*, 1984, and *Nobody's Master: Goethe and the Authority of the Writer*, 1990, all by T.J. Reed; *Goethe's Faust: The Making of Part I*, 1981, and *Goethe's Other Faust: The Drama, Part Two*, 1993, both by John Gearey; *Goethe's Narrative Fiction* edited by William J. Lillyman, 1983; *Spirited Women Heroes: Major Female Characters in the Dramas of Goethe, Schiller and Kleist* by Julie D. Prandi, 1983; *Figures of Identity: Goethe's Novels and the Enigmatic Self* by Clark S. Muenzer, 1984; *Goethe's Theory of Poetry: Faust and the Regeneration of Language* by Benjamin Bennett, 1986; *Goethe's Faust: The German Tragedy* by Jane K. Brown, 1986 and *Interpreting Goethe's Faust Today*, edited by Brown and others, 1994; *Goethe's Faust: Part One*, 1987, and *Goethe: The Poet of the Age—The Poetry of Desire*, 1991, both by Nicholas Boyle; *Our Faust? Roots and Ramifications of a German Myth* edited by Reinhold Grimm and Jost Hermand, 1987; *Images of Identity: Goethe and the Problem of Self-Conception in the Nineteenth Century* by Benjamin C. Sax, 1987; *Goethe: The Sorrows of Young Werther* by Martin Swales, 1987; *The Eternity of Being: On the Experience of Time in Goethe's Faust* by Deirdre Vincent, 1987; *Echoes of Lucian in Goethe's Faust* by Ida H. Washington, 1987; *Goethe's Faust* by John R. Williams, 1987; *Apollo in the Wilderness: An Analysis of Critical Reception of Goethe in America, 1806–1840* by Maxine Grefe, 1988; *The Paradoxical Quest: A Study of Faustian Vicissitudes* by Alfred Hoelzel, 1988; *Goethe in Italy, 1786–1986: A Bicentennial Symposium* edited by Gerhardt Hoffmeister, 1988; *Faust Through Four Centuries: Retrospect and Analysis* edited by Sidney Johnson, 1989; *Goethe's Römische Elegien: The Lover and the Poet* by Eva Dessau Bernhardt, 1990; *Goethe's Faust: Notes for a Jungian Commentary* by Edward F. Edinger, 1990; *The Critical Idyll: Traditional Values and the French Revolution in Goethe's Hermann und Dorothea* by Peter Morgan, 1990; *Idioms of Uncertainty: Goethe and the Essay* by Peter J. Burgard, 1993.

* * *

Johann Wolfgang von Goethe is the dominant figure in the history of modern German literature, whose works established, in all the principal genres, models or norms which have dominated succeeding generations (whether they have sought to follow or emulate, or to rebel against them). His creative life is customarily divided into three principal periods. The first embraces his youth and early manhood and coincides with (or, indeed, determines) the rise and fall of the *Sturm und Drang* movement in German literature. The second comprises his maturity and middle age, from the Italian journey of 1786 through the years of his collaboration with Schiller and their joint attempt to establish a 'classical' German literature; the third, the last quarter-century of his life, after Schiller's death, in which he appears as an increasingly solitary figure. Goethe himself spoke of the Italian journey as a 'rebirth', of the death of Schiller as 'the loss of half of myself'. In each of these phases Goethe made contributions of the highest rank and importance to German lyric and dramatic poetry and prose fiction.

Goethe's literary beginnings were more or less conventional, but in 1770 his own characteristic individuality was liberated by his meeting with the critic Herder. Herder introduced him to new ideas of spontaneous creation and inspi-

ration and of national character in literature, to the beauties of folk-song and of other 'unsophisticated' forms free of the rules and precepts of continental neo-classicism, such as the plays of Shakespeare. Before he was 25, Goethe had effectively created models for the whole European Romantic movement: with the exuberant outpourings of his lyrical poetry on the themes of nature, love, individuality, genius, and creativity; with the sprawling, shapeless, but powerful pseudo-Shakespearian historical drama *Götz von Berlichingen* (*Goetz of Berlichingen*) and the as yet unfinished and unpublished *Faust*; not least with the tragic, 'confessional' epistolary novel *Die Leiden des jungen Werthers* (*The Sufferings of Young Werther*), which established his European reputation at a stroke—somewhat to his subsequent chagrin. But it was to the reputation thus earned that he owed his appointment to the court of the young Duke Karl August of Weimar, with whom he soon established a close relationship.

Before long, court life began to impose its restraints on the hitherto unfettered genius, and the idealistic spiritual drama *Iphigenie auf Tauris* (*Iphigenia in Tauris*) exhibits a highly 'classical' formal balance and discipline appropriate to its content and message, even in its original prose version (only after the journey to Italy was it recast in polished blank verse). In the lyric poetry written in the aftermath of the Italian journey Goethe carries this formal 'classicism' to the extent of writing almost exclusively in the ancient Greek and Latin metres, hexameter and elegiac distich. This poetry is also concerned with balance and harmony, with a wholeness of all aspects of human life, of art and nature, of intellect, emotion, and sensuality. In respect of the last-named, however, it marks the overcoming of courtly restraint: the *Römische Elegien* (*Roman Elegies*) celebrate a ripe sense of sexual fulfilment quite different from the youthful 'romantic' passion of the earlier poetry. But that the Romantic spirit was still alive in the classical Goethe is demonstrated above all by the poetic drama *Torquato Tasso*, which introduces into European literature that quintessentially Romantic figure, the lonely artist tragically at odds with society.

A fragment of *Faust* was published in 1790, but it was during the period of his collaboration with Schiller that Goethe was able to create an overall design for the work—now conceived not as the tragedy of a heaven-storming genius, but as a celebration of universal human striving. The first of its two parts was completed in 1805, the year of Schiller's death. The novel *Wilhelm Meisters Lehrjahre* (*Wilhelm Meister's Apprenticeship*) was another recasting of an earlier project. Originally concerned with Wilhelm's 'theatrical mission', typical of the attempts of earlier generations of German writers to create a national dramatic literature, it is now extended to embrace the much wider theme of his 'apprenticeship' to life, of his development and growth into a complete human being, into some sort of modern equivalent (with all the necessary limitation that that implies) of the *kalokagathos* of classical antiquity. The novel is the prototype of the Bildungsroman, which has represented the apogee of the novel form to many German writers, from the Romantics, Goethe's immediate successors, to Thomas Mann, Hesse, and even Grass in the 20th century.

Despite or indeed because of their self-consciously 'classical' and exemplary character, many of the works of Goethe's middle period have often been felt to lack the vigour and immediacy of his earlier writing: many readers have found in their balance and restraint a certain blandness or evasiveness. In the works of his old age these very qualities are, paradoxically, intensified into a uniquely personal obliquity and ironical allusiveness, particularly in the second part of *Faust* and in the novels *Wilhelm Meisters Wanderjahre* (*Wilhelm Meister's Travels*)—the sequel to the *Apprenticeship*—and *Die Wahlverwandtschaften* (*Elective Affinities*). But much of his late lyrical poetry is of a mysterious, luminous simplicity, and there is direct expression of powerful emotion in the love-poems of the *West-östlicher Divan* (*West-Eastern Divan*) and in the 'Marienbad Elegy'.

The chief ever-present theme of all Goethe's work is nature, with its all-pervading harmonies, its universal laws of metamorphosis, of evolution, of permanence in change, of death and rebirth. Man, both as an individual and in his social and political life, is seen essentially as part of this natural order. Goethe devoted much effort to scientific work. His anti-Newtonian theory of light and colours has found little favour, but his work in geology and biology, in comparative anatomy, and in plant and animal morphology still commands respect. He was profoundly drawn to evolutionary theories of geological and of human development—which made him politically a conservative, an enemy of the French Revolution and of all arbitrary violence. Despite the many upheavals he witnessed in his long life, he remained essentially an optimist: despite the tragedy that has accompanied his strivings, his *Faust* is ultimately—untraditionally and un-Romantically—redeemed.

—F.J. Lamport

ELECTIVE AFFINITIES (Die Wahlverwandtschaften)
Novel by Johann Wolfgang von Goethe, 1809.

August Wilhelm von Schlegel's pronouncement 'Not to know Goethe, is to be a Goth' is applicable particularly to those unacquainted with *Elective Affinities* which, Goethe insisted, was his best work. It has been called an infinite masterpiece; Thomas Mann regarded it as the most sublime novel of the Germans; Rilke wept an entire evening after he had read it. *Elective Affinities* has also been called immoral and dangerous, a book that makes a mockery of marriage. It is a work of mystery and ambiguity and no other work of Goethe, perhaps not even *Faust*, has been as variously interpreted. It is a modern study of love and duty and guilt and renunciation. Goethe portrays the conflicts between marriage and passion, between Classicism and Romanticism. It is also a novel about the contemporary superficial Weimar society and its loose morals. It is a novel of marriage and spiritual adultery.

Like all of Goethe's writings, *Elective Affinities* can be considered an autobiographical fragment. Goethe maintained that he never could invent, that his power of imagination was never as vivid as reality. He writes that in his novel 'No one will fail to recognize a deep passionate wound that is hesitant to heal, a heart that is afraid to convalesce.' Here we have a *Werther* novel of the married author: but instead of resorting to suicide, the hero renounces. Goethe was 60 when he wrote *Elective Affinities*. Three years earlier he had decided to marry Christiane Vulpius, his companion of 18 years, out of gratitude for her brave behaviour in protecting him from soldiers invading his house. Shortly after the marriage, however, he suddenly fell in love with 18-year-old Minna Herzlieb, and, as was the case with most of his passions, the sublimation was transformed into poetry. As a married man Goethe had to become an earnest and emphatic critic of the laxity of morals: the sanctity and indissolubility of marriage must be preserved, the values of society must be upheld, yet

love as a force of nature triumphs; passion, although punished, is glorified.

The novel is divided into two parts, each consisting of 18 chapters; the novel's duration is 18 months: from spring, the season of youth and fermenting passion, to autumnal silence and the season of chrysanthemums, one and a half years later. The title of the novel is explained in the fourth chapter of Part I: *attractio electiva* is a technical expression taken from 19th-century science to describe the affinity between certain elements in chemistry and applied by Goethe to human relationships to explain magical attractions, elemental and magnetic natural forces that cannot be resisted. In *Elective Affinities* the situation involves the emotional relationship between four people: Charlotte and Eduard (actually named Otto)—the A and B of our chemical formula—and Ottilie and the captain (also named Otto), the C and D elements. In chemistry these elective affinities—A will be attracted to B, just as B will be to C, leading to new combinations—are predestined and unavoidable. When these terms are transferred to personal relationships, passion and attraction may result with the same force. Whereas inanimate substances, however, obey the laws of nature, civilized human beings can choose behaviour, they can yield to eros or they can renounce on moral and ethical principle. Charlotte and Eduard, our A and B, belong to the country nobility; they are of an early middle age, just recently married (for the second time), without money worries, financially secure; they spend their days in leisurely activities of gardening, building, making music. Charlotte is a pragmatic, disciplined, prudent woman who, above all, wishes to preserve order and stability. From her domestic realm she wants to remove all dangers and disarray and lead a life of quiet responsibility. Eduard, on the other hand, is impetuous and self-indulgent, a narcissistic dilettante whose life of leisure has become tedious, and in the first chapter already we witness his restlessness. Invited, reluctantly on Charlotte's part, to their country estate, are C and D, Ottilie, the orphaned niece, adolescent, fragile, ethereal, and the captain, an old friend of Eduard's, sober, responsible and correct. These two have been asked to share the leisurely long hours, to celebrate birthdays, to plant and prune and build and to make music and indulge in a comfortable idleness, which inevitably lead to inextricable emotional turmoil. Eduard's fatal fascination with Ottilie, his soul-mate, is revealed in their mysteriously similar handwriting, their complementary migraine headaches, their harmonious music-making, the symbolic intertwining of their initials on a goblet. All are signs of their spiritual kinship. In the characters of Eduard and Ottilie Goethe explored and revealed his interest in Romanticism, in the supernatural, in the realm of fantasy and the miraculous; but he criticized it severely and rejected it. Charlotte and the captain, equally drawn to one another, recognize the dangerous path the free-spirited Eduard and Ottilie have undertaken and are not willing to imitate their companions' excessive and impatient behaviour. They renounce in order to prevent the disintegration of society. Not until after the tragic accident of the drowning of Charlotte's and Eduard's child, a Euphorion figure, a child conceived in moral adultery, the victim of immoderation, does Ottilie withdraw into silence and renunciation. All that remains for Eduard is to follow the inimitable, to be drawn upward and on by the eternally feminine, in a scene reminiscent of the end of the final image in *Faust*.

The novel has been said to deal with the question of the waning of vitality, of the decaying of human relationships, of the tension between the classical conception of man who determines his own fate and the romantic conception of his failure to do so, of the struggle between order and chaos, between old age and youth, between marriage and eros. In *Elective Affinities* order is sought but not attained. Goethe maintained that his novel should be read three times. Each reading will offer new interpretations, insights, and pleasures.

—Renate Latimer

FAUST
Play by Johann Wolfgang von Goethe, Part I, 1808; Part II, 1832.

Goethe began *Faust* in the early 1770s with verse and prose scenes showing a high-minded scholar who seeks through magic to escape from academic sterility. Soon this Faust, in the unexplained company of the cynical devil Mephistopheles, loves and seduces, then deserts and destroys Margarete, a small-town girl who atones for killing their child by refusing to be rescued as she is about to be executed for infanticide. In the late 1780s Goethe composed further scenes with Mephistopheles and published them—without the still unversified denouement of Part I—in 1790 with revisions of what he had written as *Faust: A Fragment*. He worked out his definitive conception of a two-part tragedy (and at last motivated the introduction of Mephistopheles) in the last decade of the 18th century, when at the urging of his friend Friedrich Schiller he largely finished Part I and began Part II, most of which was then actually written from 1825 to 1831. Its genesis at the end of the Age of Reason largely explains the slowness with which *Faust* was completed: its supernatural motifs, deriving from beliefs no longer taken seriously, could only be reconciled with its secular theme of innate human potential when Goethe replaced the traditional bartering of immortal soul for wealth and power by Faust's Promethean discontent, his defiance of Mephistopheles ever to see him permanently satisfied with any pleasure or achievement.

In the scenes from the 1770s—basically those published in 1887 as *Goethe's Faust in Its Original Form* and known as the *Urfaust*—simple, often colloquial verse and prose is skilfully blended with contemporary lyricism and powerful rhetoric; a deliberately simple dramatic technique evokes the folk dramas and puppet plays ultimately deriving from adaptations of Marlowe's *Doctor Faustus* performed in Germany by travelling players through which the figure of Faust was then best known. Into what had become the drama of a representative of highest human aspiration who is seen in a wide range of important contexts, Goethe introduces a correspondingly wide variety of poetic forms and dramatic styles (e.g., classical Greek meters, old Germanic charms, hymn-like chants, Renaissance Italian verse, pastiches of ancient Greek tragedy and comedy, Elizabethan masque and history play, Calderonian lyric drama, and Baroque opera libretto), adding not only the relief of scintillating formal variety to a now abnormally long theatrical text, but also individuating stylistically the various times and places of Faust's real and imagined experiences.

The tragedy's main action is the thematic illustration of the rightness of the premise of its Prologue in Heaven, that anyone truly human intuitively knows what course of conduct is properly to be followed. Faust, who feels that all he has learned and taught has only alienated him from normal life, scornfully rejects the magical pleasures and powers soon proffered him by Mephistopheles, authorized by the Prologue's Lord to test his intrinsic worth, and instead challenges this 'Spirit of Negation' ever to provide him, in exchange for his life, any moment of lasting satisfaction. With Mephistopheles at his service to obviate material—but not moral—obstacles to his desires, a rejuvenated Faust discovers the essence of common human experience in his love for Margarete (Gretchen), whom he nevertheless temporarily deserts for purely sensual pleasures represented dramatically by a phantasmagoric witches' sabbath (Walpurgis Night). Publicly shamed as an unwed mother, the distraught Gretchen kills their child and, when a profoundly shaken Faust seeks to rescue her with Mephistopheles' help from execution for infanticide, accepts death as necessary atonement. Part I ends with Faust, broken and helpless, borne off from her prison cell by Mephistopheles.

Part II opens as Faust, at last recovered from a long breakdown, regains the will to live, this time resolved to experience life in its noblest manifestations. Like his legendary model, he becomes an adviser of the German Emperor and—unfortunately, in so far as the wisdom he offers in the long poetic masque of Act I is disregarded by all whom it might benefit—also his Master of the Revels. Commanded to entertain the court with a dumbshow of Helen and Paris of Troy, with Mephistopheles' assistance Faust projects a Helen (possibly Margarete idealized as a neoclassical heroine) so beautiful that, ignoring her unreality, he embraces her figure only to fall into a paralytic trance as it explodes. He now experiences as syncopated dreams (grand-scale parallels to the Walpurgis Night of Part I and its less substantial Dream of the golden wedding of Oberon and Titania) the great cultural traditions that revitalized the Renaissance world to which he historically belongs: in a classical Walpurgis Night quest of Helen the great myths and best ethical insights of ancient Greece, and in his syncopated life with Helen of Act III—originally published separately in 1827 as a 'Faust-Intermezzo' with the title *Helen: Classico-Romantic Phantasmagoria*—its poetry both in substance and in forms imitating classical models and their later literary reincarnations. When Faust reawakens after Helen, their rashly heroic son Euphorion, and his classical dream world have vanished, he resolutely assumes socio-political responsibility and, for his (actually Mephistopheles') services to the Emperor is granted the right to create a new state on coastal lands reclaimed from the sea and still in Faust's old age imperilled by it. He is, however, not completely satisfied by all he has acquired and reminded by Mephistopheles' presence that what he has achieved is not entirely his own doing. An elderly couple own an area of land Faust covets and he asks Mephistopheles to remove them. Faust is shocked into a renewed sense of responsibility when Mephistopheles burns down the house, murdering the couple. He accordingly renounces magic, at last accepting full human finitude. Recognizing that no high achievement can be sustained without unceasing effort (here the cooperative labour of a whole people resisting the sea's encroachment), a now blind Faust dies content and is granted poetic redemption in a half Swedenborgian, half Renaissance-Catholic afterlife where, instructed by a beatified Gretchen, he once more begins a teaching career.

That *Faust* is a secular tragedy by a late-Enlightenment poet has for many often been obscured by its elements of traditional magic and folklore and by its ironic use of religious symbolism (particularly in the prologue in Heaven and the scenes with Faust's death and last ascension). It has accordingly sometimes been misread as a morality play whose hero is a figure warning against the evils of hubristic secularism, even though Goethe repeatedly emphasized that in the course of its dramatic action Faust experienced ever nobler and more worthwhile errors and has Mephistopheles concede in his final speech that he has been 'robbed of a great, unequalled treasure—the noble soul that pledged itself to me.' That *Faust* embodies the highest values of a fundamentally secular German-classical humanism is evident from its satire in Part I on scholasticism, sectarian religion, vulgar superstition, and utilitarian philosophy, and in Part II on irresponsible absolutism, transcendental philosophy, romantic Hellenism, medieval revivalism, and the regressive, post-Napoleonic politics of Europe in Goethe's last years. Despite the importance of allegorical devices in it, *Faust* is not a mystery play but—however freely and eclectically constructed—a tragedy by Aristotelian standards. It is, however, in every part 'all theatre' (as Giorgio Strehler has said, well representing many contemporary stage directors), even if never intended to be performed all at once in its entirety. Radically cut versions (usually of Part I, but ever more frequently of Part I with substantial sections of Part II) have recently been staged with considerable success in Germany, England, France, Canada, and the United States, confirming that as imaginative and intelligent drama Goethe's *Faust* deserves its acknowledged status as the preeminent symbolic vision of quintessential modern Western man.

—Stuart Atkins

GOETZ OF BERLICHINGEN WITH THE IRON HAND
(Götz von Berlichingen mit der eisernen Hand)
Play by Johann Wolfgang von Goethe, 1773.

Goetz of Berlichingen with the Iron Hand is Goethe's deliberate attempt to produce the kind of Shakespearean play which he and his *Sturm und Drang* contemporaries greatly admired for capturing so much of the dynamic, unresolved, self-contradictory vitality of Nature that the straitlaced, classicizing rationalizations of many Enlighteners had necessarily left out of account. In the towering figure of the eponymous hero—lustful, generous, brave, loyal, above all autonomous (he would rather die, he says, than be dependent on anyone but God, or serve anyone other than his emperor), and yet tender, sympathetic, and vulnerable—Goethe presents an unforgettable portrait of a human being tragically destroyed during a historic crisis in which the (old German) values he is committed to heart and soul cease to be operative in the new age, to which he finds it impossible to adapt. But equally impressive in its own way is the strangely sympathetic portrayal of Weislingen, Goetz's alter ego, who, in pushing personal freedom to the point of amoral licence and adapting to every twist and turn of political intrigue, betrays not only his beloved Goetz and his betrothed (Goetz's sister) but also his own professed values, and himself. And in the entrancing Adelheid (who so fascinated the author that she threatened to dominate the drama in the first version of 1771) Goethe gives us one of his many depictions of the 'man-made woman', the first precursor of the Helen of his *Faust*. Here the anima is clearly a projection of the woman in two men: what Goetz projects onto Weislingen is projected in intensified form on to her, a larger-than-life embodiment, beyond good and evil, of the apparent chaos of existence itself.

Shakespeare's influence is blatant, in the (notoriously coarse, though prose) language, and in its episodic structure (the plots and sub-plots are, on the surface at least, so provocatively open-ended—though, as some recent critics have demonstrated, in fact painstakingly composed out of a wealth of formal correspondences which produce a delicate underlying patterning—and at times so intricate, that would-be helpful résumés crop up with irritating frequency; events are distributed over several years and in as many as 36 different settings—in 56 scenes). But Goethe's teacher and foremost Shakespeare enthusiast J.G. Herder, echoing Garrick's famous phrase, savagely criticized the play in its first version, telling his pupil that 'Shakespeare has completely spoilt you!' 'It's all mere *thinking*', he added, making brutally clear that, for all its outward theatricality, the play, in the detail of its language, lacked that intricate marriage of sense and bodily texture that alone constitutes poetry. In producing the far leaner version of 1773 Goethe left out whole chunks of text, sharpened the motivation of the characters (particularly of the demonic Adelheid), rounded out the enormous number of vivid characterizations, and cut out many of the linguistic crudities and archaisms. Above all, he brought into clearer relief the 'inner form' of the drama, giving a fine and powerful aesthetic articulation to the notion that freedom entails limitation as surely as limitation entails freedom. This is evident, for example, in the metaphorical network drawn across the length of the play, from the subtitle of the final scene which establishes a close association between the 'hand' and the 'eye', metonyms in the German 18th-century world of discourse for the interdependent polarities of physical and mental experience respectively. It surfaces at the very end (V, 13) in Goetz's dramatically ironic lament about what 'they' have done to him: 'Little by little they have mutilated me, taking away my hand, my freedom, my property, and my good name.' In fact, it is Goetz's necessarily mediated relationship to the world, with which he tragically craves immediate contact, that is symbolized by the, at times highly efficacious and yet ultimately (self-)destructive, insensitivity of his iron prosthesis. His pathetically confused and bewilderingly moving apostrophe to Freedom at the point of death is thus at once a defiant affirmation of the value of his heroic attitudes *and* a passionately tragic–ironic comment on his blindness to his own socio-historically conditioned, necessary limitations:

> All I said was freedom: all Weislingen said was some sort of order. To put the two together: all the world is broken up, and yet we must break it and break it and break it . . .

For the theme Goethe is articulating is the age-old polarity of individual and group, person and society, set at one of the great turning-points of European history, the dawn of the modern age in the Renaissance-Reformation, and given the peculiarly modern accent of the problematic interplay between endowment and environment, nature and nurture, subject and culture—between the values of the private sphere of the communal lifeworld and those of the public realm of the social system. (It is revealing of Goethe's historical awareness that the most explicit expression of this theme is put into the mouth of the rebellious monk Brother Martin, so obviously reminiscent of Martin Luther.)

The combination of Goetz's powerful and courageous energy with the brilliance of the language and the colourfulness of the presentation made the play a sensational success among Goethe's contemporaries, establishing his reputation and spawning a flood of *Ritterstücke* ('plays of knights-and-robbers'), characterized by a bustling stage-business analogous to that of the action movie (though, in theme, closer to the 20th-century Western). Instead of hi-tech gadgetry there is the (for the German stage of the time, novel) clash of swords, the clank and glint of armour, the clip-clop of horses' hooves; dark, mysterious dungeons and vaults, secret tribunals, the pomp of the Imperial Court of Maximilian I, the castle in the woods—in other words, all those aspects of 'medieval' settings which helped inspire Sir Walter Scott (who translated the play in 1799) to write his Waverley novels. All of this of course contributes to the play's lasting presence (often in pageant performance) on the German stage and in film. But it is the poetic expression, especially clear in the second version (so different from the first that it maybe merits the status of a distinct work), of the paradigmatic human situation that Goethe saw as the central nub of Shakespeare's drama (and which, he insisted a mere month before writing the first version, lies beyond the grasp of any logical theorizing)—namely, that nexus of activity in which our much-vaunted free will comes up against 'the necessary order of the whole'—that makes the play, for all its technical faults, enduringly meaningful.

—R.H. Stephenson

THE SUFFERINGS OF YOUNG WERTHER (Die Leiden des jungen Werthers)
Novel by Johann Wolfgang von Goethe, 1774.

At a time when, in Germany at least, the novel was still struggling to establish itself as a serious literary form, and had little to show but cumbersome copies of foreign originals, Goethe succeeded in producing a work which was not only original, but also short, swift, and of undeniable emotional intensity. The literary expression of such highly-charged passion, and its destructive consequences, had hitherto been confined to high tragedy. Its presentation in prose narrative, coupled with a powerful sense of everyday reality suggested by Werther's individually dated letters to his friend Wilhelm which form the bulk of the work, moreover mirroring events of which many readers would have been aware, represented a unique innovation in Germany.

Although not, strictly speaking, autobiographical, the novel unites two strands of experience from Goethe's immediate past: his love for Charlotte Buff, who was later to marry Christian Kestner, with whom Goethe was on friendly terms, and the fate of Karl Wilhelm Jerusalem, a friend of Kestner's who had recently committed suicide out of unrequited love for a married woman, using pistols he had borrowed from Kestner. Kestner in turn wrote a detailed account of the circumstances of Jerusalem's death to which Goethe had access while composing the novel.

The story is simple. A sensitive young man, who shares a birthday with Goethe, is sent by his mother to a small town to settle the matter of a legacy. He responds rapturously to the beauty of the spring landscape—it is the month of May. He meets and quickly falls in love with Lotte, who is 'as good as engaged' to Albert, who is temporarily absent. Lotte values the friendship of a kindred spirit—they share an enthusiasm for the rhapsodic poetry of Klopstock—but quite clearly has no intention of responding to Werther's passion. Werther remains in the town from May to September 1771, then forces himself to leave and take up employment with a legation in a nearby city. He outstays his welcome at a social gathering restricted to members of the aristocracy, is asked to leave, feels outraged, and resigns. He returns to the town there Lotte and Albert, now husband and wife, are living. His passion for Lotte becomes all-consuming and he gradually loses his already tenuous grip on everyday reality. He finally shoots himself, with a pistol borrowed from Albert, just before Christmas 1772. The entire story is told in the form of letters by Werther to his friend Wilhelm (whose replies we never see) collected after his death by a fictitious editor who takes up the narration towards the end when the balance of Werther's mind is obviously becoming disturbed. But perhaps Goethe's own account of the story, in a letter to Schönborn of

June 1774, goes closer to the heart of the matter. He calls the novel a story '. . . in which I portray a young man who, endowed with profound, pure feeling and true penetration of mind, loses himself in rhapsodic dreams, undermines himself by speculation until he finally, ravaged by the additional effect of unhappy passion and in particular by an infinite love, shoots himself in the head'. Werther's love for Lotte is, therefore, not the central, motive force in the novel, not the reason for the tragedy, but merely its occasion.

Werther is the tragedy of an individual sensibility which cannot be accommodated by the society in which it finds itself, nor, perhaps, ultimately, by the limitations of human existence. From the outset, before he has even met Lotte, we see Werther lamenting that human existence is a 'prison'— the image recurs obsessively—and we sense the potential danger which lies in his 'solution' to this dilemma: 'I withdraw into my inner self and there discover a world—a world, it is true, rather of vague perceptions and dim desires than of creative power and vital force. And then everything swims before my senses, and I go on smiling at the outer world like someone in a dream' (May 22, Book 1). This surrender to radical solipsism results in Werther's progressive disability to come to terms with external reality, which is manifest before he meets Lotte. In the second letter we see him 'enjoying' the natural scene—it is spring—and proclaiming: 'I could not draw now, not a line, and yet have never been a greater painter than in these moments' (10 May, Book 1). This is a profound delusion. Either he is not an artist—and there is relatively little evidence in the novel that he is—or he is going through a particularly barren period. The letter continues with an ecstatic evocation of the beauty of nature, through which Werther senses the powerful presence of the divinity as an all-pervading, loving presence, only to end with the despairing realization, 'But this experience is more than I can bear. I succumb to the power and glory of these visions.' Werther has indeed the artist's capacity for intense experience, to which his epistolary evocations of nature still bear convincing witness; what he lacks, and lacks totally, is the critical distance, self-control, the power to shape experience into art. His frustrated artistic ambitions, like his frustrated erotic passion, are expressions of a more general incapacity, indeed unwillingness, to come to terms with life in general, to establish a viable balance between outer and inner worlds, between self and other. At times this seems the result of instinctive reaction, but on occasion we can see Werther making a conscious choice. Shortly after leaving his employment at the legation we witness him musing about the character of his temporary host: 'Moreover he values my mind and my talents more than my heart, which alone is my only source of everything, all the strength, all the blessedness, all the misery of my existence. Ah, anyone can know what I know. My heart alone is my own' (9 May, Book 2). In opting for the glory of individual authenticity, with all its emotional heights and depths, Werther rejects the culture of shared, common-sense rationality according to which society in general lives. Romanticism—almost a generation before its time—declares war on Rationalism. That the outcome of this battle is inevitable tragedy does not, however, destroy the dignity of Werther. (His name is derived from the German *Wert*, signifying value or worth.) And it is a battle which, while firmly anchored in late 18th-century sensibility and society, may have much wider complications. Reviewing the best-selling novel of his youth after an interval of 50 years, Goethe suggests that the story of Werther can be seen as the story of a young man with a desire for freedom who has to come to terms with a set of old-fashioned social norms. Werther's frustrations may thus lay claim to a degree of universality and, Goethe concludes, '. . . it would be pretty bad if everybody did not have a period in his life when *Werther* strikes him as though it had been written exclusively for him' (*Conversations with Eckermann*, 2 January 1824).

Although the initial success of the novel was probably due to what many readers, including the self-appointed guardians of public morality, saw as its scandalous nature—its apparent advocacy of adulterous passion and allegedly positive portrayal of suicide—its continued popularity to the present day indicates that Goethe's claim for the universality of the novel was correct. This is nowhere better illustrated than in the furore which greeted Ulrich Plenzdorf's *The New Sorrows of Young W.* (1972), which appeared in the capital of the former German Democratic Republic, and, taking Goethe's novel as its point of departure, again raises the question of the rival claims of personal authenticity and social integration which Goethe had so convincingly addressed 200 years earlier.

—Bruce Watson

TORQUATO TASSO
Play by Johann Wolfgang von Goethe, 1790.

In 1780, when Goethe first conceived the idea of writing a play about the 16th-century Italian poet Torquato Tasso, it sprang, as he later wrote to his patron Duke Carl August, from his 'innermost nature' (Rome, 28 March 1788). In Tasso's sufferings as an artist at court Goethe evidently identified a medium in which to explore and express his own problems and experience, which he, the *Sturm und Drang* genius, author of *The Sufferings of Young Werther*, had yet to resolve after barely four years striving for acceptance in Weimar. He completed two, no longer extant, acts in poetic prose by 1781, but, perhaps because he was so closely involved with the subject matter that he might have produced another *Werther*, he laid the project aside, resuming work on it only in Italy in 1787. By now his art had acquired a new orientation, a drive to objectivity, which enabled him to complete the play, while maintaining the function of the first two acts essentially unchanged. It was completed in Weimar in 1789, cast in blank verse and published in 1790 as volume six of the Göschen edition of his collected works, the last of the eight volumes to appear. Though the play remained 'bone of my bone and flesh of my flesh' (Eckermann, 6 May 1827), the greater detachment he had achieved meant that *Torquato Tasso*, like the edition itself, would serve as a reckoning with his past life and work. Its first performance was in Weimar in 1807.

The historical Tasso was highly revered in the 18th century and Goethe was familiar with factual and apocryphal accounts of his strained relations with the court of Ferrara, his house-arrest following infringements of courtly *mores*, his love for the Princess Leonore, his subsequent imprisonment and banishment, and above all, his pathological melancholia and persecution mania. This is the raw material that Goethe fuses with his own experience: he too knew the pressures and restrictions that court life imposed on the natural poet, whose work was not truly appreciated, he suffered as his love for Frau von Stein grew, but remained remote from fulfilment, while on the deepest level he sensed the threat of derangement occasioned by the discrepancies between an intensely subjective perception of the world and the hard realities of life and social convention. This does not mean, however, that the configuration of characters and relationships in *Torquato Tasso* merely mirrors Goethe's position in relation to the Weimar court. There is much of Goethe not only in Tasso himself, but in all the characters, not least in his antagonist—and complement—Antonio.

The action of the drama is notoriously slight: we witness the agony of Tasso's life at court, exacerbated by his oversensitivity and impetuosity, which feed on his paranoia to culminate in madness and banishment. From the start he is portrayed as inhabiting his own subjective world of the imagination, a fault which needs a 'cure'. An instrument of this cure is to be Antonio, the courtier-diplomat, who on his arrival finds Tasso crowned with a laurel wreath, taken from the bust of Virgil, as a token of the court's esteem for the epic *Gerusalemme liberata* (*Jerusalem Delivered*), which he has just presented to the Duke. Antonio's disdain provokes a confrontation in which Tasso draws his sword, for which he is placed under house-arrest. Humiliated, he suspects betrayal and conspiracy, even by his beloved Princess, whose reciprocation remains platonic; he determines to leave the court and we follow his progressive disorientation and descent into madness. In a final encounter with the Princess, Tasso mistakes her muted and distressed expression of a desire to help as a declaration of love, and embraces her, thereby ensuring his irrevocable banishment. The play might well have ended here, but in the final scene Tasso's ravings are met by Antonio's assurance that he will not abandon him; he forces Tasso to take a grip on himself and to recognize what he is: a poet. Painfully aware of all that he has lost, Tasso affirms the validity of his creative powers:

> One thing remains—
> That Nature gave us tears and cries of pain
> When man can bear his sufferings no more.
> She gave that to you all. To me she gave
> The added gift of melody and speech
> To vent my sorrows fully. Where the rest
> Are silent in their sorrows, some kind God
> Decreed that I should speak.

As Tasso acknowledges this truth, Antonio takes his hand, and the curtain falls as Tasso compares himself to a shipwrecked mariner clinging for safety to the rock which threatened his destruction.

The ending has provoked debate as to whether the catastrophe of Tasso's loss is thereby mitigated and the possibility of salvation left open. The weight of opinion inclines towards viewing the play as depicting the 'tragedy of the artist', occasioned by the apparent incompatibility of Tasso's poetic vocation and real life in society, what Goethe called 'the disproportion between talent and life' (Caroline Herder in a letter to her husband, 20 March 1789). Tasso's failure is complete, and the power to articulate his suffering will not restore his loss. If Tasso is at fault, so too is the court, and it is the distinctive feature of Goethe's attitude to his subject that he displays both criticism and understanding. In his poetic vision of the Golden Age (II, 1) Tasso evokes a time when spontaneous desire and fulfilment were synonymous, only to be reminded by the Princess that such times are past and convention must modify behaviour. Tasso's subjectivism is criticized as inadequate and dangerous, while simultaneously being acknowledged as the source from which his poetry springs. While recognizing his intimate kinship with Tasso, Goethe is distancing himself from that potential self-destructiveness which makes Tasso 'an intensified Werther' (Eckermann, 3 May 1827). There is no salvation for Tasso, but through the discipline of art and the realization that poetic expression can transfigure suffering, Goethe himself is able to advance in a positive spirit.

—David Bell

WILHELM MEISTER'S APPRENTICESHIP (Wilhelm Meisters Lehrjahre)
Novel by Johann Wolfgang von Goethe, 1795–96.

Goethe's novel, first published in 1795–96, is generally considered the epitome of the German Bildungsroman, although Goethe did not consciously write such a novel. The term Bildungsroman was coined later in 1817 by Karl (von) Morgenstern and popularized by Wilhelm Dilthey in 1870, but one strand of the divided reception shows a reading of the novel in terms of Bildung, the successful self-cultivation of the protagonist, already between 1796–1800, although the term Bildungsroman was not yet available. This reading was to become the dominant interpretation of *Wilhelm Meister's Apprenticeship* for the next two centuries to come. There was, however, from the beginning also a reading which questioned the protagonist's development into a mature and well-balanced human being in the sense of the humanist ideology of the 18th century, with its emphasis on the ideal of harmony.

The original version of the novel, entitled *Wilhelm Meister's Theatralische Sendung* [Wilhelm Meister's Theatrical Mission], was written between 1777 and 1785, but remained a fragment. The original manuscript is lost, but a contemporary copy was discovered in 1909 and published in 1911. This novel, divided into six books, corresponds to the first four books of *Wilhelm Meister's Apprenticeship*, although the emphasis is on the theatre as a positive experience rather than a transition to other types of educational experience. If the title of the original version is not considered ironic, the *Theatralische Sendung* is to be interpreted as an artist novel (*Künstlerroman*).

The story of Wilhelm Meister, the son of a middle-class merchant, is set in the world of late 18th-century Germany. Wilhelm is not interested in entering his father's business, but in becoming a poet, playwright, and actor, if not the founder of a national German theatre. Falling in love with a young actress, he uses his business trips on behalf of the family firm to acquaint himself with a travelling theatre company. When the latter goes bankrupt, Wilhelm rescues it by advancing funds from his father's business. His financial involvement makes him not only a business partner in the theatre company, but also affords him an opportunity to write, act, and direct. After a brief engagement of the company at a nobleman's castle, where Wilhelm endears himself to the nobility as a well-educated member of the bourgeoisie, he is invited to direct a production of Shakespeare's *Hamlet*. This production reflects the development of professionalism among actors and the founding of a national theatre in Germany during the 18th century. Playing the title role, Wilhelm is a success as actor and director, but soon actors and audience become tired of the demands of literary drama on the stage, preferring opera and slapstick farce. Frustrated in his ambitions on the stage, Wilhelm turns his interests toward the nobility, hoping to find his educational goals realized within the circles of the aristocracy. Reform-minded representatives of the nobility welcome Wilhelm as a member of the bourgeoisie and acquaint him with their multinational enterprise of emigration to America and acquisition of land abroad to avoid loss of property due to revolutionary upheaval in Europe. This union of the reform-minded aristocracy and the progressive bourgeoisie is Goethe's response to the French Revolution. Favouring the American Revolution, Goethe has Count Lothario, who distinguished himself in the service of the revolutionary army, exclaim: 'Here [in Germany], or nowhere, is America' (Book VII, Chapter 3).

At the end of the novel, Wilhelm marries a countess and inherits not only his share of his father's business, but also the estate of an Italian orphan of noble birth (Mignon). The end of the novel reflects the pervasive irony of the work: instead of being cultivated, Wilhelm becomes married and rich. The irony of the ending is encapsulated in a quotation from the Bible: the protagonist feels 'like Saul, the son of Kish, who went in search of his father's asses and found a kingdom' (Book VIII, Chapter 10).

Among the characters of the novel that need to be mentioned are Felix, Wilhelm's illegitimate son from his first love affair with an actress, as well as Mignon and the Harper as tragically Romantic figures who accompany Wilhelm on his travels. Mignon, an immature child-woman, representing the spirit of poetry, is an androgynous genius figure, while the Harper is the prototype of the oral poet of the heroic past. Mignon turns out to be the daughter of the Harper by incest. Secretly in love with Wilhelm, Mignon dies when his impending marriage is announced. The Harper kills himself, when his life story and transgression are revealed. Finally, there is the life story of a pietist woman, entitled 'Bekenntnisse einer schönen Seele' ('Confessions of a Beautiful Soul'), a kind of female Bildungsroman. The 'Confessions' are inserted between Books V and VII to introduce the reader to the aristocratic circles Wilhelm is about to enter after his departure from the theatre.

Wilhelm and the reform-minded aristocrats are guided by a secret society, the 'Gesellschaft vom Turm' ('Society of the Tower'), which is modelled after the Masonic societies of the 18th century. The 'Gesellschaft vom Turm' pronounces Wilhelm's apprenticeship completed, when he has acknowledged his illegitimate son. Functioning as a 'machinery of fate', as Schiller called it, the 'Gesellschaft vom Turm' is, however, neither omniscient nor omnipotent. Wilhelm is successful in protesting against its guidance in his marriage to the countess, yet he is obedient when he is sent on the road again for further travel. It is part of the irony of the novel that chance and coincidence constantly interfere with the rational planning of the 'Gesellschaft vom Turm'.

Wilhelm Meister's Apprenticeship had a great influence on the Romantics and the history of the German novel. It provided, so to speak, the blueprint for all subsequent German novels from the 19th to the 20th century. Among the first commentaries on the novel are the correspondence between Friedrich Schiller and Goethe, the letters by Wilhelm von Humboldt and Christian Gottfried Körner, and Friedrich Schlegel's essay 'Über Goethes Meister' ('On Goethe's Meister') of 1798. Goethe's novel became the prime model for Romantic irony. It was translated into English by Thomas Carlyle in 1824.

Goethe's sequel to *Wilhelm Meister's Apprenticeship* was *Wilhelm Meister's Travels*, published in 1821 and in a revised version in 1829. This novel marks the transition from Bildungsroman to archival novel, a modernist prose narrative that functions as a fictional archive for a multitude of narrative texts. The narrator serves as editor who presents the various texts stored in the archive of the novel to the reader. The basic structure consists of a loose collection of novellas, aphorisms, and factual documents connected by a frame narrative with its own plot. This rudimentary plot shows Wilhelm Meister depositing his son Felix at a boarding school, while he himself is trained as a surgeon. Wilhelm's application to this skill pays dividends as he is able to save his son's life. At the end of the novel, Wilhelm Meister is ready to depart from Europe to follow his wife and the rest of the 'Gesellschaft vom Turm' to North America. In his essay 'James Joyce und die Gegenwert' [James Joyce and the Present] of 1936, the Austrian novelist Hermann Broch identified *Wilhelm Meister's Travels* as the prototype of the modernist novel in German literature. Without doubt, Goethe's last novel is, in the words of Jane K. Brown, 'an experiment in narrative form' whose achievements could only be appreciated in retrospect of Joyce's *Ulysses*.

—Ehrhard Bahr

GOGOL' (Ianovsky), Nikolai (Vasilevich). Born in Sorochintsy, Poltava, Ukraine, 19 March 1809. Educated at Poltava boarding school 1819–21, and Nezhin high school, 1821–28. Civil servant in St Petersburg, 1829–31; history teacher, Patriotic Institute, St Petersburg, and private tutor, 1831–34; assistant lecturer in history, University of St Petersburg, 1834–35; visited Germany, Switzerland, and France, 1836; in Rome, 1837–39; travelled in western Europe and Russia, 1839–48; began association with the spiritual leader, Father Konstantinovskii, 1847; visited the Holy Land, 1848; re-settled in Russia, 1849. *Died 21 February 1852.*

PUBLICATIONS

Collections

Collected Works (includes *Dead Souls*; *The Overcoat and Other Stories*; *Evenings on a Farm near Dikanka*; *The Government Inspector and Other Stories*), translated by Constance Garnett. 6 vols., 1922–27.
Polnoe sobranie sochinenii [Complete Works]. 14 vols., 1937–52.
Sobranie sochinenii [Collected Works], edited by S.A. Mashinskii. 7 vols., 1966–67.
The Collected Tales and Plays (translations), edited by Leonard J. Kent. 1969.
The Theater of Nikolay Gogol: Plays and Selected Writings (includes *Marriage*; *The Government Inspector*; *The Gamblers*; extracts from Gogol's notes, letters, and essays), edited by Milton Ehre, translated by Ehre and Fruma Gottschalk. 1980.
Sobranie sochinenii [Collected Works], edited by V.R. Shcherbina. 8 vols., 1984.
The Complete Tales, edited by Leonard J. Kent. 2 vols., 1985.

Fiction

Vechera na khutore bliz Dikan'ki (stories). 2 vols., 1831–32; as *Evenings in Little Russia*, translated by E.W. Underwood and W.H. Cline, 1903; as *Evenings on a Farm near Dikanka*, translated by Constance Garnett, in *Collected Works*, 1926; as *Evenings near the Village of Dikanka*, translated by Ovid Gorchakov, 1960.
Mirgorod (stories). 1835; as *Mirgorod, Being a Continuation of Evenings in a Village near Dikanka*, translated by Constance Garnett, 1928; as *Mirgorod*, translated by David Magarshack, 1962.
Arabeski (stories). 1835; as *Arabesques*, translated by Alexander Tulloch, 1982.
Mertvye dushi. 1842; as *Home Life in Russia*, 1854; as *Tchitchikoff's Journeys or Dead Souls*, translated by Isabel F. Hapgood, 2 vols., 1886; as *Dead Souls*, translated by

S. Graham, 2nd edition, 1915; also translated by C.J. Hogarth, 1916; George Reavey, 1936; Andrew R. MacAndrew, 1961; David Magarshack, 1961; Helen Michailoff, 1964; as *Chichikov's Journeys; or, Home-Life in Old Russia*, translated by Bernard G. Guerney, 1942.
Cossack Tales (includes 'The Night of Christmas Eve'; 'Taras Bulba'), translated by G. Tolstoi. 1861.
St John's Eve and Other Stories from Evenings at the Farm and St Petersburg Stories (includes 'St John's Eve'; 'Old-Fashioned Farmers'; 'The Tale of How Ivan Ivanovich Quarrelled with Ivan Nikiforovich'; 'The Portrait'; 'The Cloak'), translated by Isabel F. Hapgood. 1886.
Taras Bulba, St John's Eve and Other Stories (includes 'Taras Bulba'; 'St John's Eve'; 'The Cloak'; 'The Quarrel of the Two Ivans'; 'The Mysterious Portrait'; 'The Calash'), translated anonymously. 1887.
Russian Romances (includes 'Taras Bulba'; 'St John's Eve'; 'Akakiy Akakievitch's New Cloak'; 'How the Two Ivans Quarrelled'; 'The Mysterious Portrait'; 'The King of the Gnomes'; 'The Calash'), translated anonymously. 1899.
The Mantle and Other Stories (includes 'The Mantle'; 'The Nose'; 'Memoirs of a Madman'; 'A May Night'; 'The Viy'), translated by Claud Field. 1915.
Taras Bulba and Other Tales, translated by John Cournos. 1917.
Tales, translated by Constance Garnett. 1926.
Diary of a Madman, translated by D. Mirsky. 1929; also translated by Beatrice Scott, with *Nevsky Prospekt*, 1945; Andrew R. MacAndrew, in *Diary of a Madman and Other Stories*, 1962; Ronald Wilks, in *Diary of a Madman and Other Stories*, 1972; as *A Madman's Diary*, in *The Humor of Russia*, edited by Ethel Lilian Voynich, 1895; as *Memoirs of a Madman*, in *Gems of the World's Best Classics*, edited by Llewellyn Jones and C.C. Gaul, 1927.
Tales from Gogol (includes 'Sorochinsky Fair'; 'The Coach'; 'Christmas Eve'; 'Nevsky Prospekt'; 'How the Ivans Quarrelled'; 'The Nose'), translated by Rosa Portnova. 1945.
Tales of Good and Evil (includes 'The Terrible Vengeance'; 'The Portrait'; 'Nevsky Avenue'; 'Taras Bulba'; 'The Overcoat'), translated by David Magarshack. 1949; new edition, 1957 (includes additionally 'Ivan Fyodorovich Shponka and His Aunt' and 'The Nose', but omits 'Taras Bulba').
Taras Bulba and Other Tales, translated by Nikolay Andreyev. 1962.
Taras Bulba; The Lost Letters; The Terrible Vengeance, translated by Andrew R. MacAndrew. 1962.
Diary of a Madman and Other Stories (includes 'Diary of a Madman'; 'The Nose'; 'The Carriage'; 'The Overcoat'; 'Taras Bulba'), translated by Andrew R. MacAndrew. 1962.
Shinel', edited by J. Forsyth. 1965; as *The Cloak*, in *Short Story Classics*, vol. 1, edited by W. Patten, 1907; in *Best Russian Short Stories*, edited by Thomas Seltzer, 1917; in *Russian Short Stories*, edited by Harry Christian Schweikert, 1919; translated by Isabel F. Hapgood, in *Great Russian Short Stories*, edited by Stephen Graham, 1929; as *The Overcoat*, translated by Constance Garnett, in *The Overcoat and Other Stories*, 1923; also translated by David Magarshack, 1956; Andrew R. MacAndrew, in *Diary of a Madman and Other Stories*, 1962; Ronald Wilks, in *Diary of a Madman and Other Stories*, 1972; adapted by Tom Lanter and Frank S. Torok, 1975; as *The Greatcoat*, translated by Bernard G. Guerney, 1943; Z. Shoenberg and J. Domb, 1944.
Diary of a Madman and Other Stories (includes 'Diary of a

Madman'; 'The Nose'; 'The Overcoat'; 'How Ivan Ivanovich Quarrelled with Ivan Nikiforovich'; 'Ivan Fyodorovich and His Aunt Shponka'), translated by Ronald Wilks. 1972.

Plays

Utro delovogo cheloveka (produced 1871). 1836; as *An Official's Morning*, translated by Constance Garnett, in *The Government Inspector and Other Plays*, 1926.
Revizor (produced 1836). 1836; revised versions, 1841, and in *Sochineniia*, 1842; edited by D. Bondar, 1945; as *The Inspector*, translated by T. Hart-Davies, 1892; as *Revizor: A Comedy*, translated by M. Mandell, 1910; as *The Inspector-General*, translated by A.A. Sykes, 1892; T. Seltzer, 1916; J. Anderson, 1931; J. Dolman and B. Rothberg, 1937; Andrew R. MacAndrew, 1976; as *The Government Inspector*, translated by Constance Garnett, in *The Government Inspector and Other Plays*, 1926, and in *Works*, 1927; also translated by D.J. Campbell, 1947; W.L. Goodman and Henry S. Taylor, 1962; Edward O. Marsh and Jeremy Brooks, 1968; Milton Ehre and Fruma Gottschalk, in *The Theater of Nikolay Gogol*, 1980; adapted by Guy Williams, 1980; also adapted by Adrian Mitchell, 1985.
Zhenit'ba (produced 1842). 1841; translated as *Zhenitba*, in *The Humor of Russia*, edited by Ethel Lilian Voynich, 1895; as *Marriage*, translated by Alexander Bakshy and Elizabeth Pennell, 1923; also translated by A. Berkman, with *The Gamblers*, 1927; Bella Costello, 1969; Milton Ehre and Fruma Gottschalk, in *The Theater of Nikolay Gogol*, 1980; as *The Marriage*, translated by Constance Garnett, in *The Government Inspector and Other Plays*, 1926, and in *Works*, 1927.
Tiazhba (produced 1844). In *Sochineniia*, 1842; as *A Lawsuit*, translated by Constance Garnett, in *The Government Inspector and Other Plays*, 1926; also translated by B. Pares, 1926.
Teatralnyi razyezd posle predstavleniia novoi komedii, in *Sochineniia*. 1842; as *After the Play*, translated by David Magarshack, 1959; in part as *Leaving the Theatre after a Performance of a New Comedy*, translated by Milton Ehre and Fruma Gottschalk, in *The Theater of Nikolay Gogol*, 1980, and in *Hanz Kuechelgarten, Leaving the Theatre and Other Works*, edited and translated by Ronald Meyer, 1990.
Igroki (produced 1843). In *Sochineniia*, 1842; as *The Gamblers*, translated by Constance Garnett, in *The Government Inspector and Other Plays*, 1926; numerous subsequent translations including by G. Wallerstein and B. Pares, 1926, A. Berkman, with *Marriage*, 1927, and Eric Bentley, 1957.
Otryvok (produced 1860). In *Sochineniia*, 1842; as *A Fragment*, translated by Constance Garnett, in *The Government Inspector and Other Plays*, 1926.
Lakeiskaia (produced 1863). In *Sochineniia*, 1842; as *The Servants' Hall*, translated by Constance Garnett, in *The Government Inspector and Other Plays*, 1926.
The Government Inspector and Other Plays (includes *Marriage*; *The Gamblers*; *Dramatic Sketches and Fragments: An Official's Morning, A Lawsuit, The Servants' Hall, A Fragment*), translated by Constance Garnett. 1926.

Other

Sochineniia [Works]. 4 vols., 1842.
Vybrannye mesta iz perepiski s druz'iami. 1847; as *Selected*

Passages from Correspondence with Friends, translated by Jesse Zeldin, 1969.
Razmyshleniia o bozhestvennoi liturgii; as *Meditations on the Divine Liturgy*, translated by L. Alexieff. 1913; as *The Divine Liturgy of the Eastern Orthodox Church*, translated by Rosemary Edmonds, 1960.
Letters of Nikolai Gogol (translations), edited by Carl R. Proffer, translated by Proffer and Vera Krivoshein. 1967.
Nikolai Gogol: A Selection, translated by Christopher English. 1980.
Hanz Kuechelgarten, Leaving the Theater and Other Works, edited and translated by Ronald Meyer. 1990.
Avtorskaia ispoved' [An Author's Confession]. 1990.
V poiskakh zhivoi dushi [In the Raid of a Living Soul]. 1990.

*

Bibliography: *Gogol: A Bibliography* by Philip E. Frantz, 1989.

Critical Studies: *Gogol* by Janko Lavrin, 1926; *The Mighty Three: Pushkin, Gogol, Dostoevsky* by Boris Leo Brasol, 1934; *Nikolai Gogol* by Vladimir Nabokov, 1944; *Gogol: A Life* by David Magarshack, 1957; *Gogol as a Short Story Writer: A Study of His Technique of Composition* by F.C. Driessen, 1965; *Gogol: His Life and Works* by Vsevolod Setchkarev, 1965; *The Simile and Gogol's Dead Souls* by Carl. R. Proffer, 1967; *Gogol* by Victor Ehrlich, 1969; *Gogol: A Life* by Hugh McLean, 1969; *Reading the Russian Text of the Memoirs of a Madman of N.V. Gogol* by D.R. Hitchcock, 1974; *Gogol from the Twentieth Century: Eleven Essays* edited by Robert A. Maguire, 1974, revised edition, 1976; *Gogol: The Biography of a Divided Soul* by Henri Troyat, 1974; *The Sexual Labyrinth of Nikolai Gogol* by Simon Karlinsky, 1976; *Through Gogol's Looking Glass: Reverse Vision, False Focus, and Precarious Logic* by William W. Rowe, 1976; *Gogol's Dead Souls*, 1978, and *The Symbolic Art of Gogol: Essays on His Short Fiction*, 1982, both by James B. Woodward; *The Creation of Nikolai Gogol* by Donald Fanger, 1979; *Are There Any Digressions in Pushkin's Evgenij Onegin and Gogol's Dead Souls?: A Review of the Critical Literature with Commentary* by László Dienes, 1981; *Gogol* by V.V. Gippius, 1981; *The Enigma of Gogol: An Examination of the Writings of N.V. Gogol and Their Place in the Russian Literary Tradition* by Richard Peace, 1981; *Out from under Gogol's Overcoat: A Psychoanalytic Study* by Daniel Rancour-Laferrière, 1982; *Gogol's Overcoat: An Anthology of Critical Essays* edited by Elizabeth Trahan, 1982; *Nikolai Gogol and Ivan Turgenev* by Nick Worrall, 1982; *Gogol and the Natural School* by Victor V. Vinogradov, 1987; *'Such Things Happen in the World': Deixis in Three Short Stories by N.V. Gogol* by P.M. Waszink, 1988; *Nikolai Gogol: Text and Context* edited by Jane Grayson and Faith Wigzell, 1989; *Essays on Gogol: Logos and the Russian Word* edited by Susanne Fusso and Priscilla Meyer, 1992, and *Designing Dead Souls: An Anatomy of Disorder in Gogol* by Fusso, 1993; *Nikolai Gogol and the Baroque Heritage* by Gavriel Shapiro, 1993.

* * *

The contribution of Nikolai Gogol' to the remarkable renaissance of Russian literature in the 19th century is exceeded only by that of Pushkin. With his three volumes of stories and his novel *Mertvye dushi* (*Dead Souls*) he not only ensured that the prose genres would predominate until the advent of Symbolism; he also effected with his subject-matter, themes, and character-types and his highly complex style the enormous expansion of the range of Russian literature and the Russian literary language, without which the major works of his successors, particularly Dostoevskii, could hardly have been written. In addition, his fiction and plays laid the foundations of Russian satire, and his central concern with the themes of guilt and redemption and with the contradictions and fragmentation of society marked the transition from a disinterested art to a committed one, to the conception of art as service and a spur to action, which has given modern Russian literature its characteristic sense of engagement.

But although Gogol's influence on the development of the modern Russian literary tradition was far-reaching, his works represent a unique body of writing that differs from that tradition in numerous fundamental respects. Herein lies the first of the many paradoxes which confront the reader. Thus neither of the two most conspicuous elements of that tradition, realism and penetrating psychological analysis, can be readily ascribed to Gogol's own art, in which the boundaries between the real, the supernatural, and the grotesque are always likely to dissolve, and the inner man is usually seen only through the props of his portrait. Similarly his elaborate style, in which extremes converge and a sentence or simile can encompass a paragraph or page, remained an inimitable testimony to the uniqueness of his genius.

The transition from his first two volumes of stories, *Vechera na khutore bliz Dikan'ki* (*Evenings on a Farm near Dikanka*) and *Mirgorod* (*Mirgorod, Being a Continuation of Evenings in a Village near Dikanka*), to his uncompleted novel conveys the impression of a complex evolution. In seven of the eight tales of *Evenings on a Farm near Dikanka* he drew extensively on his intimate knowledge of the Ukrainian folklore tradition, responding both to the contemporary vogue for exotic regionalism and to the taste for Gothic horror stories whetted by such German Romantic writers as Hoffmann and Tieck. The result is a bizarre mixture of the mundane and the supernatural, the comic and the horrific, which immediately established contrast as the central feature of Gogol's art. But the most striking contrast of all is created by the volume's penultimate story 'Ivan Fedorovich Shpon'ka and His Aunt' in which the scene is switched abruptly to the Russian provinces of the 1820s and detailed characterization replaces tortuous plots. The story presents the first intriguing foretaste of the manner and preoccupations of the later works.

In the four works which comprise the volume *Mirgorod* the Ukrainian setting is retained, and the particular forms of contrast here serve significantly to clarify the underlying theme of Gogol's Ukrainian tales. The four works are essentially parodies of four literary genres—the idyll ('Old-Fashioned Farmers'), the heroic epic ('Taras Bulba'), the folktale ('The Viy'), and the comic tale ('The Tale of How Ivan Ivanovich Quarrelled with Ivan Nikiforovich')—which in combination express a powerful lament on the social and moral decline of Gogol's native land. In each case the reader's expectations are abruptly confounded by the intrusion of unfamiliar elements that evoke a pervasive sense of degeneration, aberration, and debilitating betrayal. Love yields to habit, heroism to inertia, and the appetites and senses replace honour and duty as the ultimate arbiters of human conduct. Greeted with wide acclaim, the four works are the first major embodiments of the theme to which Gogol's art was thereafter to be devoted—the theme of moral decline, of the emasculation and perversion of the human spirit.

On moving to St Petersburg Gogol' soon found congenial material for the further development of this theme in the dehumanizing world of the capital's bureaucracy in which he spent a few wretched months. The most celebrated of his so-called 'Petersburg Tales'—'Shinel' ('The Overcoat') and 'Zapiski Sumasshedshego' ('Diary of a Madman')—were the fruits of this experience. Here again a disconcerting effect is produced by the coexistence of contrasting elements—in this case compassion for the depersonalized 'little man' and detached, ironic scorn both for his abject surrender of his human dignity and for his belated, grotesque attempts to restore it. At the same time these and other stories in Gogol's third volume— 'Nevskii prospekt'('The Nevsky Prospect'), 'Portret' ('The Portrait'), and especially 'Nos' ('The Nose')— make abundantly clear the umbilical connection between his deceptive, nightmarish St Petersburg and the folk-tale world of his Ukrainian tales. Again comedy and horror, the real and the fantastic are inseparably fused, and the devil and the witch retain their prominent roles, now clothed anew in the elegant attire of dignitaries, generals, and imperious ladies.

It was in the play *Revizor* (*The Government Inspector*) and the novel *Dead Souls*, however, that the contrasting elements of Gogol's art combined to produce two of the masterpieces of world literature. Selecting the vacuous Khlestakov and the acquisitive Chichikov as his itinerant heroes and employing in both works the simple plot device of confronting them with the senior citizens of the provincial towns in which they briefly alight, he was able to bring his unique gifts as humorist and satirist and his mature art of portraiture to bear on the task which he had now come to believe he was called on to perform: to expose the limitless extent of human folly and corruption and to infect his readers with his personal craving for moral rebirth. But the appearance of Part One of the projected three-part novel in 1842 marked the death of Gogol' the artist. Only fragments of Part Two have survived, together with his collection of essays *Vybrannye mesta iz perepiski s druz'iami* (*Selected Passages from Correspondence with Friends*), to illuminate the agonies that he experienced in exchanging his role as a castigator of evil for that of a guilt-ridden instrument of divine revelation. The struggle continued for ten long years before his body succumbed to the fate of his art.

—James B. Woodward

DEAD SOULS (Mertvye dushi)
Novel by Nikolai Gogol', 1842.

Dead Souls, according to its author, was based on a theme furnished by Aleksandr Pushkin. As a person with an exceptionally fertile imagination Gogol' was always afraid of being accused of fanciful invention, so it may be that Gogol' fabricated this statement both to ward off such criticism and underline the parallels between his work and Pushkin's novel in verse, *Eugene Onegin*. Gogol's work was to be the reverse, an epic poem in prose, a genre conveniently removed from the realm of the novel with its female readership and preoccupation with the love story. Early draft chapters were evidently comic and mildly satirical, but as time went on Gogol's growing sense of the high calling of the artist—his moral mission to reveal the vices afflicting Russia and point the way to a better future—made him place much more serious demands upon his work. Now it was to be a trilogy strongly linked to Dante's *Divine Comedy*, with divisions into Hell, Purgatory, and Heaven. It took him seven years to complete the first part, which was published in 1842, while the remaining decade of his life saw him struggling and failing to complete the second. Fragments which escaped being burnt remain as a sad reminder of a great writer who destroyed himself trying to force his genius into an appropriate mould. Part Three, in which the hero would be transformed into a positive character, was never more than a dream. Fortunately Part One of *Dead Souls* is complete in itself and a brilliant testament to Gogol's genius.

The basic idea, whether Pushkin's or not, was retained in its simplicity: Pavel Chichikov appears in a small town, makes the acquaintance of local landowners, and while visiting them on their estates buys from them dead serfs (known in Russia as souls) on whom landowners have to pay taxes until the next census. His reasons for so doing and his background are revealed at the end of the book, by which time the secret is out and the townsfolk swing from adulation of Chichikov to savage rumour. Chichikov leaves town.

The structure of the first half of the book is based on a series of separate encounters with different landowners. The strength of the book lies in its characterization. Each landowner represents a set of negative characteristics: Manilov is sugariness, idleness, and pretension; Sobakevich crude vigour and solidity; Pliushkin miserliness. Each is introduced in the same way through amazingly colourful and detailed descriptions of his or her estate and house, family relationships, hospitality, physical appearance, manner of speaking, and reaction to Chichikov's proposition. These word portraits are so vivid and distinctive that in the company of the landowners Chichikov acts as a mirror, adapting his smooth exterior like a chameleon to reflect the character of his host. His role as the travelling link between the land-owners is reminiscent of that of the hero of the picaresque novel who enjoys a series of encounters and adventures on his travels. So idiosyncratic are the landowners that they might well have appeared to be grotesques with no relevance to real life, but Gogol's epic poem employs a number of devices to give them and his book a broader relevance to Russia. One is an adaptation of the Homeric simile, where a simple compari-son develops into a separate picture of a different aspect of Russian life, another his habit of generalizing from the particular ('Manilov was the type of man who . . .'). This latter method is developed extensively in the second half of *Dead Souls*, which is given over to group portraiture of the townsfolk, seen especially in their hysterical reactions (pro and anti) to Chichikov. Above all, Gogol' takes the device of digression so popular in 18th-century novels, and through it adds moral comment.

Despite the colourful and frequently comic detail, the book as a whole reveals a pessimistic view of mankind: there is no single positive character, but neither is there a real villain. Evil in Gogol' is petty, and dangerous because it is so banal. The apparently solid, respectable, charming Chichikov turns out to be the devil-knows-what, while other characters have little depth and are not much more than products of their surroundings. By describing people as vegetables ('a woman's face in a bonnet as long and narrow as a cucumber, and a man's as round and broad as the Moldavian pumpkin . . .') Gogol' implies that his characters have something more than just appearance in common with vegetables. While keeping a careful balance between comic and serious, Gogol' recog-nized that his book needed something to lift it from the mire of petty vice and make it worthy of the title of epic poem. To this end he added notes of lyricism, showing Pliushkin's

garden splendid in its luxuriant neglect, lamenting his own lost youth, or comparing Russia to a hurtling troika, rushing one knows not where.

As was frequently the case with Gogol's works, his efforts not to be misunderstood by his readers were in vain. The book achieved instant notoriety because it was viewed as an attack on serfdom despite the evidence in the book to the contrary. Far from being an attack on an institution, the book is a damning portrait of a whole world. It can be said to fulfil Gogol's intention of depicting the whole of Russia, but not in a crude photographic sense. Gogol's characters are dazzling linguistic artefacts, their colours concentrated and their petty failings intensified. Take these away and it is clear that the dead souls of the title are not the deceased peasants Chichikov wishes to purchase but the living characters of the book.

—Faith Wigzell

DIARY OF A MADMAN (Zapiski Sumasshedshego)
Story by Nikolai Gogol', 1835.

'Diary of a Madman' is one of a group of tales from the 1830s that have a Petersburg setting. It is the only work by Gogol' to be given a first-person narrator and to be presented in the form of diary entries. Originally the tale was to be called 'Diary of a Mad Musician', reflecting the Russian response to Hoffmann's tales, but this idea became inter-twined with Gogol's own experience of life as a civil servant, of being a tiny cog in a huge dehumanizing wheel, where obsession with rank and mindless routine dominated the lives of an army of underpaid drudges. At the same time Gogol' was responding to popular obsession with grotesque accounts of madness as well as the terrifying information published in a newspaper that in one Petersburg asylum the majority of inmates were civil servants.

The hero of the 'Diary of Madman', Poprishchin, is a minor civil servant whose lowly duties include sharpening quills for his superior. He has fallen hopelessly in love with the latter's daughter Sophie, but this is no clichéd situation of poor boy loves rich girl or of noble unrequited love. Poprishchin is 42 years old, stuck on the Table of Ranks at a point just below the desired rank that gained hereditary nobility for its holder, in name a noble himself but with nothing noble about his life or his values. This does not prevent him from being a snob, despising those who cannot write and fellow civil servants because they do not go to the theatre. Thus rejecting literary cliché and using the first-person narrative as a means of creating a close relationship between narrator and reader, Gogol' widens the gulf by making Poprishchin's snobbery ridiculous to his more educated and possibly even more snob-bish readers: Poprishchin's own taste in poetry and theatre is of the most vulgar kind, and the newspaper he reads, *Severnaia pchela* [The Northern Bee], is the one that pub-lished mocking descriptions of lunatics. He emerges as a pathetic nonentity struggling to maintain his illusions.

Pathos is kept at bay until the very end of the tale by the comic and absurd nature of Poprishchin's madness. It is at the end of the very first diary entry for 3 October that Poprishchin, desperate to enter Sophie's world (his head has whirled as he glanced into her boudoir) suddenly hears her little dog Madgie talking to a canine friend Fidèle. In typically Gogolian manner, this preposterous event is viewed by Poprishchin as strange but not alarming. To one brought up on sensationalist stories in *The Northern Bee* and lacking personal insight, the event does not seem so startling. Spying on the two dogs, he discovers they are conducting a correspondence, a humiliating fact to a man for whom the ability to write is a sign of nobility. He seizes a pile of letters, composed in a style appropriate to frivolous upper-class young ladies like Sophie and her friends: to his fury Madgie proceeds to laugh at his appearance, but worse, the dog notes that Sophie finds him ludicrous. The most cutting blow is the information that Sophie is in love with a gentleman of high rank and means, a fact confirmed in the following entry for 3 December. From this point Poprishchin descends rapidly into insanity, bolstering his illusions about his rank and importance by imagining himself the King of Spain. Carted off to the asylum, he maintains this creative fiction about his life against increasing odds and with increasing incoherence: the inmates are courtiers, the warder the Grand Inquisitor who beats him unjustly. In the final entry, reality intrudes in the form of cold water poured on his head, and he seeks escape from the world in a troika (a frequent Gogolian escape symbol) and by calling on his mother for protetction ('Mother, save your poor son! Shed a tear on his aching head! See how they've torturing him').

Gogol' plays with his reader's reactions, taking him from laughter and even contempt for Poprishchin to the concluding moments of pathos, when the reader, like Poprishchin, cannot escape the tragedy of madness. And yet even at this point he cannot resist a final twist, with a last sentence in which his hero reverts to grotesque lunacy: 'And did you know that the Dhey of Algiers has a wart right under his nose?' Such narrative tricks were highly innovatory for the time though they were not appreciated fully until much later. More obvious to contemporary audiences was Gogol's satire on the widespread obsession with snobbery and rank over genuine human values. Poprishchin's aims were consistent with his world, but he lacked the money, rank, or appearance to realize his dream of capturing Sophie's heart and thereby become an accepted member of that world of false values. In linguistic terms too the work broke new ground, as it combined colloquialisms and contemporary chancery jargon with, in the canine passages, a parody of the language of upper-class young ladies. 'Diary of a Madman' may well make the reader uncomfortable as he or she reads, but this is what Gogol' intended.

—Faith Wigzell

THE GOVERNMENT INSPECTOR (Revizor)
Play by Nikolai Gogol', 1836.

Gogol's great dramatic achievement *The Government Inspector* was also his first full-length play, written when its author was a mere 27 years of age. Gogol's background had prepared him as well for a career as a dramatist as was possible for a member of the minor gentry. In his childhood he had taken part in amateur dramatics organized by his father at the house of a wealthy relative, and his father was himself the author of a number of undistinguished Ukrainian comedies. Gogol' was also fascinated by the Ukrainian street puppet theatre. On arrival in St Petersburg in 1829 to seek fame if not fortune, he had briefly considered a career as an actor, satisfying himself instead with frequent attendance at the capital's theatres. A discriminating theatregoer, he deplored the popular taste for overblown patriotic melodramas and above all for vaudevilles, hackneyed comedies interspersed with dance and song, at best mildly satirical, at

worst merely silly. His own play had to reflect Gogol's own lofty views of true art which, while it might depict real life, even 'low' subjects, should be informed by a serious purpose that would justify the subject matter. At the same time Gogol' had to work within the stage conventions of the period, bearing in mind constantly the dramatic experience of his audience.

This careful application of serious purpose and rethinking of current stage practice resulted in *The Government Inspector*, a play which, while employing traditional devices, recasts them in a highly innovative manner. The plot, which is far slighter than in a conventional comedy, depicts the comic misunderstandings that result when the officials and other inhabitants of a provincial Russian town mistake Khlestakov, a penniless minor clerk from St Petersburg, for a government inspector sent to investigate their corrupt administrative practices. Gogol' takes the device of mistaken identity traditionally employed as part of a love intrigue, and turns it into the mainspring of the action, furthermore psychologically motivating it by showing town officials too terrified of discovery and too impressed by a visitor from the capital to see the obvious truth, while Khlestakov is firstly too fearful of imprisonment for non-payment of his hotel bill and secondly both too vain and too featherbrained to understand. To make the unwitting deception more credible, Gogol' gives the play terrific pace and concentrates the action into a few hours.

The traditional emphasis on love intrigue, normally the keystone of the action, is downgraded in *The Government Inspector* to the point of parody, Khlestakov alternately making advances to the mayor's wife and daughter, overcome by lascivious delight at finding women whose admiration of his supposed rank and city origins knows no bounds. However, the greatest innovation in the play is Gogol's deliberate refusal to introduce any positive characters; in conventional comedy the audience could conveniently ally itself with the innocent young lovers and wise adult figures who helped outwit the foolish and wicked. By rejecting positive characters entirely, Gogol' created a world of overwhelming mediocrity, where the characters are not black villains but people who bend their morals to get on in the world, who are vain, boastful, gluttonous, self-seeking, materialistic, and ambitious—in fact, have common human failings, even if to an exaggerated degree. Evil on a grand scale was instantly recognizable, whereas moral mediocrity merged imperceptibly into moral failing and was insidious and hence dangerous.

To make this point clear Gogol' adapted the stage aside to the audience, which in traditional comedy was designed to inform the audience or to gain their support. In *The Government Inspector* Gogol' uses the aside at the end of the play to turn the satirical spotlight on the audience. 'What are you laughing at?', says the mayor, 'you are laughing at yourselves'. This was backed up by an original last scene. An intercepted letter from Khlestakov, who has now left the town richer by a large number of bribes ('loans' to him), reveals the truth to the officials, but before they can recover the real inspector general is announced and the characters freeze in a tableau of horror during which Gogol' hoped the audience would grasp the serious point of the comedy. Some modern critics prefer to see the real inspector as equally open to bribes and thus view this scene as merely a pause before the merry-go-round starts again, but this was not what Gogol' intended. In either case, the characters do not reform at the end, and good does not triumph—a much less comfortable ending than in conventional comedy.

Unfortunately the play's first audience, which included the Tsar and high officials, missed the point. Though the Tsar was amused, others were not, seeing the play as a dangerous calumny on the state. Indeed, in the repressive atmosphere of the 1830s anything that could be construed as critical was usually censored before it reached the stage, and it was only by imperial decree that the play was put on. Through his play and short stories about St Petersburg Gogol' acquired an undeserved reputation as a radical. It has taken until well into the 20th century for the play to be seen for what it is, an exceptionally funny and well-written moral satire. Gogol' left town shortly after the first performance, horrified by the furore about his play. Fame he desired but not notoriety. The failure of Russians at the time to comprehend the dramatist's purpose has not prevented the comedy from enjoying uninterrupted success and achieving a world-wide reputation. Its portrayal of common human failings makes it universally applicable, and adaptations are numerous.

—Faith Wigzell

GOLDEN LOTUS (Jin Ping Mei). Anonymous Chinese novel of the middle or late 16th century. Based on part of the *Shuihu zhuan* (*Water Margin, q.v.*) which deals with Ximen Qing's seduction of Golden Lotus, the novel also borrows from other literary sources. Earliest manuscripts date from c.1590. For much of the 18th century the novel was on the Chinese index of banned books, for its supposed licentiousness (ban rescinded, 1789).

PUBLICATIONS

Jin Ping Mei. c.1617 (some sources give 1610); modern edition, 21 vols., 1933 (reprinted 1963); as *The Golden Lotus*, translated by Clement Egerton, 4 vols., 1939; as *Chin P'ing Mei: The Adventurous History of Hsi Men and His Six Wives*, translated by Bernard Miall (from the German), 1939.

*

Critical Studies: 'The Text of the *Chin P'ing Mei*' by P.D. Hanan, in *Asia Major*, new series, 9, 1962; 'Chin P'ing Mei: A Critical Study' by Ono Shinobu, in *Acta Asiatica*, 5, 1963; *The Classic Chinese Novel* by C.T. Hsia, 1968; 'The *Chin P'ing Mei* as Wisdom Literature' by P.V. Martinson, in *Ming Studies*, 5, 1977; 'Chang Chup'o's Commentary on the *Chin P'ing Mei*' by D.T. Roy, in *Chinese Narrative: Critical and Theoretical Essays*, edited by Andrew H. Plaks, 1977, and *The Four Masterworks of the Ming Novel* by Plaks, 1987; 'Family, Society, and Tradition in *Jin P'ing Mei*', in *Modern China*, 10, 1984, and *The Rhetoric of Chin P'ing Mei*, 1986, both by Katharine Carlitz; *Renditions*, 24, 1985 (includes articles by D.T. Roy and S.P. Sun); 'Aspects of the Plot of *Jin Ping Mei*' by P. Rushton, in *Ming Studies*, 22, 1986; *How to Read the Chinese Novel* by D.L. Rolston, 1990.

* * *

The dating and authorship of the *Jin Ping Mei*, or *Golden Lotus*, are still a mystery. The novel's first known circulation was in manuscript form and goes back to the 1590s, its first printing to about 1617. The author was perhaps a well-known literary figure but kept his name secret because of the erotic contents of the work. He seems to have written his novel over an extended period of time, and, because of certain glaring inconsistencies, not even to have finished it. It may safely be said that he wrote in the second half of the 16th century (though some scholars say earlier), the beginning of an especially productive period in the history of Chinese fiction.

Golden Lotus, containing 100 chapters, is about a wealthy but uneducated merchant named Ximen Qing whose main activities consist of celebrating with friends and sleeping with concubines, courtesans, and other people's wives (his name may be translated as 'Celebrations at the Gate of Death'). The novel starts with an episode of adultery (lifted from another important 16th-century novel, *Water Margin* [*Shuihu zhuan*]) in which he and his paramour, Pan Jinlian (her name translates as Golden Lotus), poison her husband in order to bring her into Ximen's household. Subsequently he steals yet another man's wife, Li Ping'er, whom he then favours over the jealous and insatiable Pan Jinlian. Li Ping'er's status soon rises when she bears him his first son, but she and the son die within a year, mainly on account of the plotting of Pan Jinlian. The inconsolable Ximen Qing enters the last stretch of his life. Having already obtained a marvellous aphrodisiac from a Buddhist monk, he has been all along expanding the sphere of his sexual activities. But after Li Ping'er's death he gradually allows both sexual and financial powers to drain away, and finally dies when Pan Jinlian accidentally gives him a lethal overdose of the aphrodisiac. The last quarter of the novel tells of the decline of his estate, the dispersal or death of its members, and the survival of his main wife Yue niang and his only son by her, Xiaoge, who is Ximen's reincarnation, and who ends up becoming a monk.

Golden Lotus is unique among other novels of the period because its story matter is largely the creation of a single author. To be sure, the novel absorbs many sources (including current popular song, drama, and short story, not to mention the initial episode from *Water Margin*), which are at times quoted verbatim; but it is common for the Chinese novel to do so. For that matter, the reader of *Golden Lotus* should not expect a high degree of uniformity in style, plot sequence, or characterization. Scene changes are often extremely abrupt. The author uses diverse styles and language. Character types seem ill-fitting set against others, while individual characters seem inconsistent within themselves.

But upon close examination the novel betrays an astounding degree of unity and organization, particularly if one is attuned to certain generic features of Chinese fiction and discursive prose. Most important of these are the techniques of interlocking patterns of recurrence and alternation. In the 16th century such compositional techniques were central to prose theory and criticism and were reflected in both structure and image. In the *Golden Lotus*, for example, on a simple structural level, the novel consists of a first half in which the narrative world is steadily filled-in and a second in which it is emptied. In addition, polar images of heat and cold frequently accompany scenes of prosperity and decline, or sexual frenzy, frustration, or depletion. At times a cold figure is used as an ironic comment on an otherwise hot scene. Recurrence of image is also common, a notable example being that of the woman on top of the man. At the beginning of the novel, when Pan Jinlian has poisoned her husband, she smothers him with a blanket while straddling his body. Later she is astride the semi-conscious Ximen Qing when she gives him his fatal overdose of the aphrodisiac. Finally, at the end, after Pan is dead, her maid Chunmei (who continues in her footsteps) dies of sexual exhaustion while in the superior position.

Golden Lotus is most renowned as a pornographic novel and has been therefore censored throughout its history. But despite such a reputation there are in fact relatively few scenes which portray sex in a positive way. Sexuality is essentially the scene of a battle in which opponents attempt to score gains and recover losses. On a large scale, this battle is symbolic of all social struggle depicted in the book. It is remarkable that this novel took advantage of eroticism at such an early point in the history of Chinese vernacular fiction, especially since to this day (in contrast to the West) eroticism has been absent from all great Chinese art.

—Keith McMahon

GOLDONI, Carlo. Born in Venice, 25 February 1707. Educated in Venice; at a Jesuit school in Perugia; with Domenicans in Rimini; studied law at Papal College in Pavia, 1723–25. Married Nicoletta Conio in 1736. Assistant to his physician father in Chioggia, 1721–23, and in other towns; clerk in criminal court, Chioggia, 1728–29, and Feltre, 1729–30; passed law examinations in Padua in 1731, and called to the Venetian bar, 1732; wrote plays for amateur companies as early as 1729–30, and for Giuseppe Imer's company, 1734–44, beginning with bare scenarios and gradually working towards completely written scripts; director of the opera house Teatro San Giovanni Crisostomo in Venice; lawyer in Pisa, 1744–47; house dramatist for Girolamo Medebach's acting company, 1748–53, and writer with the Teatro San Luca, 1753–62, both in Venice (in Rome, 1757–58); with the Comédie-Italienne, Paris, 1762–64; Italian tutor to the daughter of Louis XV, Princess Adelaide, 1764–65, and to royal children, 1768–80, in Versailles; in Paris after 1780. Wrote plays in both Italian and Venetian dialect, and some plays in French; also wrote libretti for cantatas and operas. *Died 6 February 1793.*

PUBLICATIONS

Collections

Opere teatrali (first complete edition). 44 vols., 1788–95.
Raccolta completa di tutte le commedie in prosa ed in verso del signor Carlo Goldoni. 15 vols., 1794–98.
Opere complete, edited by Giuseppe Ortolani, E. Maddalena, and C. Musatti. 40 vols., 1907–60.
Tutte le opere (includes letters), edited by Giuseppe Ortolani. 14 vols., 1935–56.
Opere, edited by Filippo Zampieri. 1954.
Teatro (selected plays), edited by Marzia Pieri. 3 vols., 1991.

Plays

Belisario (produced 1734). 1798.
Rosmonda (produced 1734). 1793.
Don Giovanni Tenorio; o, Sia il dissoluto (produced 1736). 1754.
Rinaldo di Montalbano (produced 1736). 1774.

Enrico, Re di Sicilia (produced 1736). 1740.
Momolo cortesan, o, L'uomo di mondo (produced 1738). 1757.
Il prodigo (also known as *Momolo sulla Brenta*; produced 1739). 1757.
La bancarotta (produced 1740).
La donna di garbo (produced 1743). 1747; edited by Gastone Geron, 1984.
Il figlio d'Arlecchino perduto e ritrovato (produced c.1745).
Il servitore di due padroni (produced 1745). 1753; edited by Eugenio Levi, 1957; as *Arlecchino servitore di due padroni*, edited by Luigi Lunari, Giorgio Strehler, and Carlo Pedretti, 1979; as *The Servant of Two Masters*, translated by Edward J. Dent, 1928; also translated by Tom Cone, 1980; Eric Bentley, in *Servant of Two Masters and Other Italian Classics*, 1986; translated and adapted by Shelley Berc and Andrei Belgrader, 1992.
I due gemelli veneziani (produced 1748). 1750; edited by Guido Davico Bonino, 1975; as *The Venetian Twins*, translated by Frederick H. Davies, in *Four Comedies*, 1968.
L'uomo prudente (produced 1748). 1750.
La vedova scaltra (produced 1748). 1750; edited by Avancinio Avancini, 1935, and by Gastone Geron, 1984; as *The Artful Widow*, translated by Frederick H. Davies, in *Four Comedies*, 1968.
Tonin Bella Grazie; o, Il frappatore (produced 1748). 1757.
La buona moglie (produced 1749). 1751.
Il cavaliere e la dama; o, I cicisbei (produced 1749). 1751; edited by Nicola Mangini, 1964.
La putta onorata (produced 1749). 1751; edited by Gastone Geron, 1984.
Il poeta fanatico (produced 1750).
Il padre di famiglia (produced c.1750). 1751; as *The Father of a Family*, 1757.
Il teatro comico (produced 1750). 1751; edited by Gerolamo Bottoni, 1926, and by Guido Davico Bonino, 1983; as *The Comic Theatre*, translated by John W. Miller, 1969.
La famiglia dell'Antiquario (produced 1750). 1752; edited by Pietro Azzarone, 1961, by Guido Davico Bonino, 1983, and by Nicola Mangini and Nella Pavese, 1988.
L'avvocato veneziano (produced 1750). 1752.
Le femmine puntigliose (produced 1750). 1753.
La bottega del caffè (produced 1750). 1753; edited by Gianni Di Stefano, 1967, and by Carlo Pedretti, 1984; as *The Coffee House*, translated by Henry B. Fuller, 1925.
Il bugiardo (produced 1750). 1753; edited by Pietro Azzarone, 1967; with *La donna di garbo*, 1980; as *The Liar*, translated by Grace Lovat Fraser, 1922; also translated and adapted by Frederick H. Davies, 1963.
L'adulatore (produced 1750). 1753.
La Pamela, from the novel by Richardson (produced 1750). 1753; edited by Carmine Montella, 1968; translated as *Pamela*, 1756.
Il cavalier di buon gusto (produced 1750). 1753.
Il giuocatore (produced 1750). 1754.
Il vero amico (produced 1750). 1753.
L'erede fortunata (produced 1750). 1752.
Commedie. 1750–55, 1753–57, 1757–63, 1761–78.
La finta ammalata (produced 1751). 1753.
La dama prudente (produced 1751). 1753.
L'incognita perseguitata dal bravo impertinente (produced 1751). 1754.
L'avventuriere onorato (produced 1751). 1753.
La donna volubile (produced 1751). 1755.
I pettegolezzi delle donne (produced 1751). 1753; edited by Antonio Marenduzzo, 1942.
Il Moliere (produced 1751).

L'amante militare (produced 1751). 1755.

La castalda (produced 1751). 1753.

Il tu tare (produced 1752). 1753.

La moglie saggia (produced 1752). 1753.

Il feudatario (produced 1752). 1753.

La figlia obbediente (produced 1752). 1754; as *The Good Girl*, translated by M. Tracy, in *Four Comedies*, 1922.

La serva amorosa (produced 1752). 1753.

Le donne gelose (produced 1752). 1753; edited by Gastone Geron, 1988; as *The Good-Humoured Ladies*, translated by Richard Aldington, 1922.

I puntigli domestici (produced 1752). 1754.

I mercatanti (produced 1752). 1754.

Le donne curiose (produced 1753). 1753; edited by Ettore Allodoli, 1960, and by Gastone Geron, 1988.

La locandiera (produced 1753). 1753; edited by Gian Piero Brunetta, 1967; as *La locandiera (The Mistress of the Inn)*, translated by Merle Pierson, 1912; as *Mistress of the Inn*, translated by Helen Lohman, 1926, and by Anthony Intreglia, 1964; as *Mine Hostess*, in *Four Comedies*, 1922; also translated by Clifford Bax, in *Three Comedies*, 1961; as *Mirandolina*, translated by Frederick H. Davies, in *Four Comedies*, 1968.

Il contrattempo; o, Il chiaccherione imprudente (produced 1753). 1754.

La donna vendicativa (produced 1753). 1754.

Il geloso avaro (produced 1753). 1757.

La donna di testa debole (produced 1753). 1757.

La sposa persiana (produced 1753). 1757.

L'impostore (produced 1754). 1754.

La cameriera brillante (produced 1754). 1757.

Il filosofo inglese (produced 1754). 1757.

Il vecchio bizzarro (produced 1754). 1757.

Il festino (produced 1754). 1757.

La peruviana (produced 1754). 1757.

La madre amorosa (produced 1754). 1757.

Terenzio (produced 1754). 1758.

I malcontenti (produced 1755). 1755.

Torquato Tasso (produced 1755). 1757.

Le massere (produced 1755). 1758.

Il cavaliere giocondo (produced 1755). 1758.

Le donne di casa soa (produced 1755). 1758; edited by Gastone Geron, 1988.

Ircana in Julfa (produced 1755). 1758.

La buona famiglia (produced 1755). 1758; edited by Polisseno Fegejo, 1942.

La villeggiatura (produced 1755). 1758; edited by Manlio Dazzi, 1954.

Il campiello (produced 1756). 1758; edited by Luigi Lunari, 1975, and by Guido Davico Bonino, 1986; as *Il Campiello*, translated by Susanna Graham-Jones and Bill Bryden, 1976.

Il raggiratore (produced 1756). 1758.

Il medico olandese (produced 1756). 1760.

Ircana in Ispahan (produced 1756). 1760.

La dalmatina (produced 1756). 1763.

La donna stravagante (produced 1756). 1760.

L'avaro (produced 1756). 1762; edited by Antonio Marenduzzo, 1946.

Il buon compatriotto (produced 1756). 1790.

La donna sola (produced 1757).

L'amante di se medesimo (produced 1757). 1760.

La vedova spiritosa (verse version produced 1757; prose version 1758). Prose version published 1759; verse version 1761.

Il padre per amore (produced 1757). 1763.

Un curioso accidente (produced 1757). 1768; as *A Curious Mishap*, translated by Helen Zimmern, in *Comedies*, 1892; also translated by Charles Lloyd, in *Three Comedies*, 1907; translated and adapted by Richard D.T. Hollister, 1924.

Il cavaliere di spirito (produced 1757). 1764.

L'impresario delle Smirne (produced 1757). 1774; as *The Impresario from Smyrna*, translated by Clifford Bax, in *Four Comedies*, 1922.

La bella selvaggia (produced 1758). 1761.

Il ricco insidiato (produced 1758). 1761.

La donna di governo (produced 1758). 1761.

La sposa sagace (produced 1758). 1761.

Lo spirito di contraddizione (produced 1758). 1761.

Le morbinose (produced 1758). 1761.

La donna bizzarra (produced 1758). 1760.

L'apatista; o, Sia l'indifferente (produced 1758). 1760.

Pamela maritata (produced 1759). 1761.

Gl'innamorati (produced 1759). 1761; edited by Andrea Sangiuolo, 1965, and by Guido Davico Bonino, 1986.

La scuola di ballo (produced 1759). 1792.

Artemisia (produced 1759). 1793.

La buona madre (produced 1759). 1764.

Le donne di buonumore (produced 1759). 1789.

La donna capricciosa. 1760.

I rusteghi (produced 1760). 1761; edited by Guido Davico Bonino, 1970; as *The Boors*, translated by I.M. Rawson, in *Three Comedies*, 1961.

La guerra (produced 1760). 1764; edited by Franco Fido, with *Il quartiere fortunato*, 1988.

Eneo nel Lazi (produced 1760). 1793.

Zoroaster (produced 1760). 1793.

La donna forte. 1761.

Le smanie della villeggiatura (produced 1761). 1768; edited by E. Maddalena, 1963, by Gastone Garon, 1984, and by Nicola Mangini and Nella Pavese, 1988.

Le avventure della villeggiatura (produced 1761). 1768; edited by Giorgio Strehler, Luigi Lunari, and Carlo Pedretti, 1982, by Gastone Geron, 1984, and by Nicola Mangini and Nella Pavese, 1988.

Il ritorno dalla villeggiatura (produced 1761). 1768; edited by Giorgio Strehler, Luigi Lunari, and Carlo Pedretti, 1982.

La casa nova (produced 1761). 1768; edited by Antonia Veronese Arslan, 1969; as *The Superior Residence*, translated by Frederick H. Davies, in *Four Comedies*, 1968.

Sior Todero Brontolon (produced 1761). 1774.

La scozzese (produced 1761). 1774.

La bella Giorgiana (produced 1761). 1792.

Le baruffe chiozzote (produced 1762). 1774; edited by Carlo Pedretti, 1978; as *The Squabbles of Chioggia*, translated by Charles W. Lemmi, in *The Drama*, 15, 1914; as *It Happened in Venice*, translated and adapted by Frederick H. Davies, 1965.

Una della ultime sere di carnevale (produced 1762). 1777.

L'osteria della posta (produced 1762). Edited by Antonio Marenduzzo, 1935; as *The Post-Inn*, translated by W.H.H. Chambers, in *The Drama 5*, edited by A. Bates, 1902.

L'amor paterno; o, La serva riconoscente (produced 1763).

Il matrimonio per concorso (produced 1763). 1778.

Il ventaglio (produced 1763). 1789; edited by Luigi Squarzina, 1979, and by Carlo Pedretti, 1980; as *The Fan*, translated by Helen Zimmern, in *Comedies*, 1892; also translated by Charles Lloyd, in *Three Comedies*, 1907; Kenneth McKenzie, 1911; E. and H. Farjeon, in *Four Comedies*, 1922, and in *Three Comedies*, 1961; Henry B. Fuller, 1925; translated and adapted by Frederick H. Davies, 1968.

Il ritratto d'Arlecchino (produced 1764). 1777.

Chi la fa l'aspetta (produced 1765). 1789.

Le Bourru bienfaisant (produced 1771). Edited by Gerolamo

Bottoni; as *The Times*, 1780; as *The Beneficent Bear*, translated by Helen Zimmern, in *Comedies*, 1892; also translated by Charles Lloyd, in *Three Comedies*, 1907; Barrett H. Clark, 1915; as *Il burboro benefico*, translated 1964.

Il filosofo di campagna; as *The Wedding Ring*. 1773.

L'Avare fastueux (produced 1776). 1789; as *The Spendthrift Miser*, translated by Helen Zimmern, in *Comedies*, 1892.

L'amore artigiano, music by Florian Gassman, translated as *L'amore artigiano*. 1778.

I metempsicosi. 1793.

Gli amori di Alessandro Magno. 1793.

The Comedies (includes *The Beneficent Bear*; *A Curious Mishap*; *The Fan*; *The Spendthrift Miser*), edited and translated by Helen Zimmern. 1892.

Three Comedies (includes *The Fan*; *An Odd Misunderstanding*; *The Beneficent Bear*), translated by Charles Lloyd. 1907.

Four Comedies (includes *Mine Hostess*; *The Impresario from Smyrna*; *The Good Girl*; *The Fan*), translated by Clifford Bax, M. Tracy, and H. and E. Farjeon. 1922.

Three Comedies (includes *Mine Hostess*; *The Boors*; *The Fan*), translated by Clifford Bax, I.M. Rawson, and H. and E. Farjeon. 1961.

Four Comedies (includes *The Venetian Twins*; *The Artful Widow*; *Mirandolina*; *The Superior Residence*), translated by Frederick H. Davies. 1968.

Commedie, edited by Kurt Ringger. 1972.

Il quartiere fortunato, with *La guerra*, edited by Franco Fido. 1988.

Other

Mémoires, pour servir à l'histoire de sa vie, et à celle de son théâtre. 3 vols., 1787; as *Memoirs*, translated by John Black, 2 vols., 1814.

On Play-Writing, edited by F.C.L. van Steenderen. 1919.

Il teatro comico; Memorie italiane, edited by Guido Davico Bonino. 1983.

*

Bibliography: *Saggio di una bibliografia delle opere intorno a Carlo Goldoni (1793–1907)* by A. Della Torre, 1908; *Bibliografia goldoniana 1908–1957*, 1961, and *Bibliografia goldoniana 1958–1967*, 1961, both by Nicola Mangini, supplemented in the journal *Studi goldoniani*, 1968–79.

Critical Studies: *Goldoni: A Biography* by H.C. Chatfield-Taylor, 1913; *Goldoni and the Venice of His Time* by Joseph Spencer Kennard, 1920; *Carlo Goldoni, Librettist: The Early Years* by P.E. Weiss, 1970; *Goldoni* by Heinz Riedt, 1974; *A Servant of Many Masters: The Life and Times of Carlo Goldoni* by Timothy Holme, 1976; *Language and Dialect in Ruzzante and Goldoni* by Linda L. Carroll, 1981.

*   *   *

Carlo Goldoni's career as a dramatist can be plotted easily in terms of his relationship to the historical development of drama in Italy, and, in fact, he is usually presented in such terms. In the first half of the 18th century, Italian comedy was essentially that of the *commedia dell'arte* (as opposed to the erudite comedy based on classical models). The plays were not written out, but a scenario was prepared around which the players improvised. All the characters were conventional,

and in Venice four of the players still wore the *commedia dell'arte* masks: a miserly old man (Pantalone); a pretentious old man called the Doctor, usually learned and absurd; and two 'zany' servants, one lively and simple (Arlecchino), one clever and roguish (Brighella). The masks themselves instantly revealed to the audience the players' characters; other characters—various servants, banal lovers—might be the basis of the simple plot, but the masked characters were the leading players. The 'creative' element of each play was centred on the ingenuity of the stage business and the verbal dexterity of the permanent company members. Many of these practices are shown in Goldoni's play *Il teatro comico* (*The Comic Theatre*).

Goldoni, a youthful enthusiast for the theatre, slid into this theatrical world almost by accident, if his *Memoirs* are to be believed. After an early involvement with a touring company, he became a lawyer, married, and set up a law practice in Pisa. A play he had earlier written out in complete form became a success in Venice, and he was approached by the 'Pantalone' character of the Medebach company to write some more plays for them. Goldoni agreed, but insisted on a written text, gradually ensuring that natural speech replaced the exaggerated and obscene dialogue used formerly, and, most revolutionary of all, he insisted that the masks be abandoned. The success of one of his first plays, *I due gemelli veneziani* (*The Venetian Twins*), lay in having a leading actor play both twin brothers—one a clever romantic hero, the other a simple country boy—so that the mask would have become a liability rather than an aid.

His 'new' plays proved so successful that he was gradually able to bring about these changes in the next 15 years of playwriting in Venice. His interest in these 'reforms' is clear only from the prefaces he wrote for editions of his plays: he never formalized his ideas in theoretical works.

That his plays did not represent a complete break with the past is obvious from the way in which many of his leading characters are based on the conventional *commedia dell'arte* characters: Pantalone usually reappears in the guise of a hard-up nobleman, always on he look-out for a free meal or a present—for instance, the Count in both *La locandiera* (*The Mistress of the Inn*) and *Il ventaglio* (*The Fan*); the Doctor is also often placed among the aristocracy, as a pretentious or 'literary' man; comic servants are still well-employed, since the plots spring from mistaken identity or trivial misunderstandings—but such a character as Fabrizio, the servant of Mirandolina in *The Mistress of the Inn*, is complex, with doubts concerning his position and a past that acts on his character; and other servants or working-class characters are often full of individuality as well as zest.

The most interesting transformation in his characterizations—those in his romantic heroines—leads to the other major point to be made about Goldoni: his amiability and good nature, based on a perception of the world that is missing from *commedia dell'arte*. The timid conventional heroine has become a sensible and intelligent young woman, if not well educated, at least aware of her own dignity and worth, and not averse to fighting for her right to choose her own mate. Many of the plays have such a woman: usually she is concerned in overturning the prejudices of the male relative who is in charge of arranging her marriage (often to a fool or fortune-hunter). The most advanced example of this character type is Mirandolina, who has no guardian to protect (or dictate) to her, and whose heart is set on marriage with her servant and childhood friend, Fabrizio. Before her hopes are realized, however, she has to fend off the advances of the men who have fallen for her obvious charm and prospects (she runs an inn), and even to prove to herself that she is in charge of her own fate by wilfully making a misogynist staying at the inn fall in love with her. This plot would sound tragic if it were not so funny—no one is harmed by the intrigue; in fact, all the male characters learn something about themselves from the experience.

This interest in the naturalness of love and marriage, and in the natural relations of people in a social group, also led Goldoni often to centre his plays on a milieu—a shop or an inn, a small village, or a square in a city—where no single character emerges as an obvious hero or heroine, and where the good will and acceptance of the outcome seem to be the end in view; there is usually a liberated spokesman for the group—often a woman. Examples of this sort of play are *Il campiello*, *I rusteghi* (*The Boors*), *Le baruffe chiozzote* (*The Squabbles of Chioggia*), and *The Fan*. *La casa nova* (*The Superior Residence*), though involving only two families in an apartment house in Venice, and with a smaller cast, also promotes good nature, lack of pretensions, and the value of simple love.

Goldoni's plays are not deep, and his *Memoirs* reflect this lack of theoretical or intellectual interest, but his characters, like those of Marivaux, are human and often complex, and his plots are arranged to bring out this complexity rather than to submerge it in a conventional framework.

—George Walsh

THE COMIC THEATRE (Il teatro comico)
Play by Carlo Goldoni, 1750.

The Comic Theatre is one of a prodigious corpus of comedies written by Goldoni in 1750 for Girolamo Medebach, director of the Sant'Angelo theatre in Venice, with which the dramatist was associated until his move, in 1753, to the San Luca, another theatre in his native city. Although enjoying the favour of the theatre-going public, Goldoni was subjected to repeated attacks from literary rivals such as Piero Chiari and Carlo Gozzi, spokesmen for an academy of conservative purists, the Granelleschi, who opposed the innovations that were beginning to manifest themselves in Italian society, politics, and literature. The Granelleschi was dedicated to preserving the stylistic and linguistic purity of Italian authors and to re-establishing the *commedia dell'arte* (improvised comedy) as the prevailing comic theatre of the time. Goldoni, who dared to bring spoken, everyday language to the comic stage and, even more outrageously, replace improvised comedy with premeditated, 'character' comedies, was thus a natural target for concerted public criticism. It was against such criticism that Goldoni produced, during 1750 and 1751, a number of new comedies: *The Comic Theatre*, *La bottega del caffè* (*The Coffee House*), *Il bugiardo* (*The Liar*), *L'adulatore* [The Flatterer], *La Pamela* (*Pamela*), *Il cavalier di buon gusto* [The Man of Taste], *Il giuocatore* [The Gambler], *Il vero amico* [The True Friend], *La finta ammalata* [The False Invalid], *La damma prudente* [The Cautious Woman], *L'incognita perseguitata dal bravo impertinente* [The Unknown Woman Persecuted by the Bumptious Braggart], *L'avventuriere onorato* [The Honourable Adventurer], *La donna volubile* [The Fickle Woman], *I pettegolezzi delle donne* [Women's Gossip], to establish himself as the leading comic writer of his time.

In a prefatory note, 'The Author to the Reader', included in the first volume of the Paperini edition (Florence, 1753) of Goldoni's works, the author expresses his desire that *The Comic Theatre* serve as a foreword to all his comedies.

Together with the preface to an earlier collection of his comedies (Bettinelli, 1750), this particular drama is a statement, in comic form, of the principles on which he based his comedies of character. As Goldoni himself explains in 'The Author to the Reader', he chose this form for the statement of his poetics over a more conventional introduction as 'the latter would probably have bored readers more easily' (*The Comic Theatre*, translated by John W. Miller, 1969). The play is simultaneously an explicit statement of the defects, prevalent in improvised comedy, which he sought to avoid in his own new style of comedy.

Compared to the rest of Goldoni's dramatic output, *The Comic Theatre* is innovative in both its form and content. Like Pirandello's *Sei personaggi in cerca d'autore* (*Six Characters in Search of an Author*), it is a theatrical production in the making, a behind the scenes look at a rehearsal (of a Goldoni play) in progress, liberally interspersed with conversations between the existing cast members, and interrupted by two new arrivals, an impoverished poet and a virtuoso singer, both seeking work. Most of the 13 members of the cast with speaking roles play two parts: their 'off-stage' character as well as the character they play in the rehearsal within the play. Hence Orazio, the head of the company of actors and mouthpiece for Goldoni himself, is called Ottavio in the rehearsal; Placida, the leading lady (a role written for Teodora Medebach), also plays the part of Rosaura; Eugenio, the second *amoroso*, is also Florindo, and so on. Three of the characters: Tonino/Pantalone; Anselmo/Brighella; Gianni/Harlequin, speak Venetian dialect when rehearsing the company's latest comedy, *A Father His Son's Rival*. Gianni and Petronio at times resort to Latin aphorisms in making their point (see, for example, Act I, scenes 8 and 9), while Anselmo and Gianni occasionally use rhyming couplets, typical of their 'stage' persona, before exiting (Act I, scenes 6 and 8). Unity of place is maintained throughout the comedy with the scene, the comic stage itself, remaining unchanged.

The Comic Theatre begins with Orazio and Eugenio discussing the requisites of successful comedy as they await the arrival of the other members of the company. Rehearsals are essential, and the most can be made of an actor by giving him a part that is good and not merely long. In the ensuing scenes they are joined firstly by their fellow actors, then by Lelio, a thin, impecunious author of plot outlines for the old style improvised comedies, followed by Eleonora, a singer of similarly old fashioned melodramas, which Orazio at first dismisses as new comedy, has no need of music to be successful. What then ensues is not so much a debate between the proponents of the old and the new comic theatre as an exposition (begun in the first act by Orazio and taken over in the second by Anselmo) of the salient characteristics of comedies of character, addressed to two representatives of superseded theatrical schools only too willing to be converted if it means finding work in Orazio's company. Thus *The Comic Theatre* is not so much a statement of an intended reform as a declaration of a reform that has already been realized. Anselmo stresses the moral purpose of premeditated comedies: they have been purged of all immorality and are suitable entertainment for young ladies. In the old improvised, masked comedies, moral purpose, edification, had been sacrificed to the merely ridiculous. Identification, essential if edification is to be achieved, is now possible between the audience and the characters who will appeal to people of all social classes. Placida points out to Lelio (Act II, scene 2) that conceits (stock soliloquies, dialogues, tirades) have been replaced by plausible speeches and a familiar, naturalistic style. Gone are the metaphors, antitheses, and rhetoric of improvised comedies. Nor are Lelio's translations of French plays any more acceptable to Orazio. Unity of action and a simple title are required, yet masks (that is to say, such stock characters of the *commedia dell'arte* as Harlequin, Brighella, Pantalone, etc.) are not to be eliminated completely so that they may contrast with the serious characters. (Goldoni himself dispenses with this injunction in his later comedies in which these traditional characters no longer appear.)

Where the acting style of new comedy is concerned, Orazio stresses to Lelio the importance of credibility and realism; it is now inadmissible to address the audience directly, and all soliloquies must be plausible. Actors should learn by observing other actors in their free time, since practice and the observation of others are better teachers than theoretical rules. Goldoni implicitly acknowledges his indebtedness to the Latin theoretician Horace (Orazio is the Italian for Horace) when Orazio clears up (Act III, scene 9) Lelio's misinterpretation of a passage from the *Art of Poetry* regarding the number of actors appearing on stage at any one time. And when Lelio butchers lines from *Didone abbandonata* (*Dido Abandoned*), Orazio, appalled, acknowledges the theatre's debt to its author, another reformer of Goldoni's century, Metastasio.

Besides being concerned with the quality of his actors as performers, Orazio also holds the off-stage atmosphere important; peace is essential: 'Harmony among colleagues makes for the success of plays' (Act III, scene 1). The audience, too, should be educated as well as the actors: spectators should not spit, nor make a noise during the performance.

There is a certain complacency in *The Comic Theatre*, a self-congratulatory tone as when Lelio states (Act III, scene 2) that he hopes one day to compose comedies like those of the company's author. Comic reform has already been achieved by Goldoni and implemented with success. The comedy ends with the end of the rehearsal within the play, and with a statement to the effect that the day's proceedings have demonstrated how the Comic Theatre ought to be.

—Nicole Prunster

THE MISTRESS OF THE INN (La locandiera)
Play by Carlo Goldoni, 1753.

As the most important dramatist in Italy since the Renaissance, best known for his gradual introduction of realistic characters and the psychological drama of the middle class and its values, supplanting the masks and fixed stereotyping of the *commedia dell'arte*, Goldoni wrote *The Mistress of the Inn* at a mid-point in this process of theatrical reform. From his early days when masked stereotypes were the norm in his native Venice—through comedies where a central protagonist sustained the comedy—to comedies of milieu, where the atmosphere and values of middle-class society were the subject, Goldoni proceeded, in a substantial dramatic production, to introduce into 18th-century theatre an upholding of bourgeois values, together with a critique of Venice's decaying aristocracy and its mores (particularly the phenomenon of *Cicisbeismo*—the adopting of a close male friend by a married woman—and the duel).

The Mistress of the Inn introduces the position of woman into this scenario. Written for the well-known actress Maddalena Marliani, who had enjoyed previous successes in Goldoni's plays, it highlights the career of Mirandolina, left in charge of the inn after her father's death and courted, using a

variety of 'modern' devices, by two members of the aristocracy, the presumptuous marquis and the vain count, whose advances she disdains. The *cavaliere*, also staying at the inn, affects a total disregard for her, which spurs her to greater efforts to win his love, in which she is finally triumphant. With this moral victory secure, Mirandolina finally rejects his suit and marries her servant in deference to her late father's wishes, upholding the solid bourgeois values of hard work and just rewards.

Developed with psychological penetration, the character of Mirandolina is a fully realized portrait—she shows none of the sentimental affectations of many stage women—and strikes a blow for the independence of women in society. She uses a full range of feminine ploys—from flattery and kindness to cooking and fainting—to achieve her desired ends, and the triumph of commercial interests is celebrated in the play's conclusion. By contrast with the fixed values of the *commedia dell'arte*, Goldoni's portraits of his aristocrats have recognizable virtues and defects, his setting is a room in an ordinary inn, and the characters' relationships are motivated by the social values prevalent in 18th-century Venice. Realistic and naturalistic humour replaces the slapstick of the *commedia*, and the hegemony of the playwright in performance is ensured by scripted comedy which replaces the improvisation of the earlier comic tradition.

Forward-looking for its time, *The Mistress of the Inn* makes an implicit statement about the position of women. Always calculating, and always in control, Mirandolina uses her sex in a series of complex strategies to win over the male characters, implying every woman's right to decide and determine her own future in a male-dominated society. The ironing scene is a *tour de force* of feminine determinism and determination, and its setting strikes a blow for realism, far removed as it is from the set-piece gilded drawing-room of most contemporary theatre. Striking, too, is the use of 'everyday' theatrical props—gifts, money, perfume, hot chocolate, linen—to link characters inextricably to setting, to show them as natural, in a situation audiences could recognize. Finally, the dialogue is believable, unlike the rhetoric of the straight or comic stereotypes of the *commedia dell'arte*.

Goldoni's critique of contemporary society—aristocrats apart—depicts a world short on morals and virtues, where most human activity is played out as a game, and where the protagonists are self-orientated to the point of obsession, driven by ambition or lust. The aristocrats are vacuous vehicles for a package of traditional characteristics that depend on forms, appearances, and outdated concepts of honour, dignity, and prestige. Even so, they are not empty stereotypes but are recognizable in Goldoni's Venice as the noblemen whose only claim to significance rests on the exploits and values of past generations. By contrast, the subtle and sceptical Mirandolina is a finely-drawn psychological portrait. In the end, her marriage to Fabrizio, her servant, in the play's conclusion, celebrates middle-class values. For the marquis, count and, ultimately, the *cavaliere* marriage is an old-fashioned romance in which the man offers protection to the woman (and demands obedience in return): Mirandolina, however, marries Fabrizio as a commercial arrangement, offering partnership in the business and financial stability between (more or less) equal partners.

—Christopher Cairns

GOLL, Ivan. Born Isaac Lang in Saint Dié, Alsace, Germany, 29 March 1891. Educated at Metz; studied jurisprudence at the University of Strasbourg, 1912–14; University of Lausanne, 1915–18. Moved to Switzerland in 1915 after the outbreak of hostilities. Married Claire Studer. Founder, Rhein Verlag, publishers, Zurich; lived in Paris, 1919–39, associated with Picasso, Chagall, Breton and Éluard; moved to New York, 1939; founding editor, *Hémisphères*, New York, 1943–46; diagnosed as suffering from leukaemia, 1944; returned to Paris, 1947. *Died 27 February 1950.*

PUBLICATIONS

Collections

Dichtung, Lyrik, Prosa, Dramen, edited by Claire Goll. 1960. *Oeuvres*, edited by Claire Goll and François Xavier Jaujard. 2 vols., 1968–70.
Selected Poems, edited by Paul Zweig, translated by Zweig, Robert Bly, George Hitchcock, and Galway Kinnell. 1968.
Gedichte 1924–1950, edited by Horst Bienek. 1976.

Verse

Der Panamakanal. 1912.
Films. 1914.
Élégies Internationales. 1915.
Dithyramben. 1918.
Der Torso. 1918.
Der neue Orpheus. 1918; as *Le Nouvel Orpheé*, translated by Goll, 1923.
Die Unterwelt. 1919.
Astral. 1920.
Paris brennt. 1920.
Der Eiffelturm: Gesammelte Dichtung. 1924.
Poèmes d'amour, with Claire Goll. 1925; as *Love Poems*, 1947.
Poèmes de jalousie, with Claire Goll. 1926.
Poèmes de la vie et de la mort, with Claire Goll, 1927.
Die siebente Rose. 1928.
Deux Chansons de la Seine. N.d.
Chansons malaises. 1934; as *Songs of a Malay Girl*, translated by Clark Mills, 1942; as *Malaiische Liebeslieder* (bilingual edition), translated by Goll, 1967.
Métro de la mort. 1936.
La Chanson de Jean sans Terre. 1936; revised edition, 1957; edited by Francis J. Carmody, 1962; as *John sans Terre: Landless John*, translated by Lionel Abel, William Carlos Williams, and others, 1944.
Le mythe de la roche percée. 1945; as 'The Myth of the Pierced Rock', translated by Louise Bogan, in *Four Poems of the Occult*, edited by Francis J. Carmody, 1962.
Atom Elegy. 1946.
Fruit from Saturn. 1946.
Élégiè d'Ihpétonga suivie de Masques de cendre. 1949; as *Elegy of Ihpetonga and Masks of Ashes*, translated by Babette Deutsch, Louise Bogan, and Claire Goll, 1954.
Le Char triomphal de l'antimoine. 1949.
Les géorgiques parisiennes. 1951.
Dix Mille Aubes, with Claire Goll. 1951.
Les Cerdes magiques. 1951; as 'The Magic Circles', translated by Claire Goll and Eric Sellin, in *Four Poems of the Occult*, edited by Francis J. Carmody, 1962.
Traumkraut, edited by Claire Goll. 1951.
Zehntausend Morgenröten, with Claire Goll. 1954.

Abendgesang (Neila); letzte Gedichte, edited by Claire Goll. 1954.
Multiple femme, edited by Claire Goll. 1956; as *Multiple Woman*, translated by Francis J. Carmody, in *Four Poems of the Occult*, edited by Carmody, 1962.
Der Mythus vom durchbrochenen Felsen. 1956.
Neue Blümlein des heiligen Franziskus, with Claire Goll. 1957.
Duo d'Amour: Poèmes d'amour 1920–1950, with Claire Goll. 1959.
Four Poems of the Occult, edited by Francis J. Carmody. 1962.
L'Antirose, with Claire Goll. 1965; as *Die Antirose*, 1967.
Gedichte, edited by René A. Strasser. 1968.
Élégie de Lackawanna. 1973; as *Lackawanna Elegy* (bilingual edition), translated by Galway Kinnell, 1970.

Fiction

Le Microbe de l'or. 1927.
Die Eurokokke. 1927.
Der Goldbazillus. 1927.
Der Mitropäer. 1928.
À bas l'Europe. 1928.
Agnus Dei 1929.
Sodome et Berlin. 1929.
Lucifer vieillissant. 1934.
Nouvelles Petites Fleurs de Saint François d'Assise, with Claire Goll. 1958.

Plays

Die Unsterblichen: zwei Possen (includes *Der Unsterbliche* and *Der Ungestorbene.* 1920; as *The Immortal One*, translated by Walter H. and Jacqueline Sokel, in *An Anthology of German Expressionist Drama*, edited by Walter H. Sokel, 1963.
Die Chapliniade. 1920.
Melusine (produced 1956). 1922.
Mathusalem; oder, Der ewige Bürger (produced 1927). 1922; translated by Arthur S. Wensinger and Clinton J. Atkinson, in *Plays for a New Theatre*, 1966; also translated by J.M. Ritchie, in *Seven Expressionist Plays*, 1968.
Assurance contre le suicide (produced 1926). 1923.
Der neue Orpheus, music by Kurt Weill (produced 1928). 1923.
Der Stall des Agias. 1924.
Royal Palace (opera libretto), music by Kurt Weill. 1926.
Théâtre. Mathusalem. Les Immortels. 1963.

Other

Requiem pour les morts de L'Europe. 1916.
Requiem für die Gefallenen von Europa. 1917.
Die drei guten Geister Frankreichs (essays). 1919.
Überrealismus, Vorwort zu Methusalem. 1922.
Germaine Berton. 1925.
Pascin (essays). 1929.
Iwan Goll, Claire Goll: Briefe. 1966.
Selected Correspondence, edited by Barbara Glauert. 1978.

Editor, with Claire Goll, *Das Herz Frankreichs, eine Anthologie französischer Freiheitslyrik.* 1920.
Editor and translator, *Das Lächeln. Voltaire: Ein Buch in Diese Zeit.* 1921.
Editor and translator, *Les Cinq Continents: Anthologie de poésie contemporaine.* 1922.

Translator, with Gustav Laudauer, *Der Wundarzt: Briefe Aufzeichnungen und Gedichte aus dem amerikanischen Sezessionskreig*, by Walt Whitman. 1919.

Translator, *Der Schimmer im abgrund: Ein Manifest an alle Denkenden*, by Henri Barbusse. 1920.

Translator, *Die Goldsucher von Wien: Ein Bergebenheit unter Schriebern*, by Pierre Hamp. 1922.

Translator, *Der Aussätzige und die Heilige*, by François Mauriac. 1928.

Translator, *Schwarz und Weiss, die Wahrheit über Afrika*, by Albert Londres. 1929.

Translator, *César*, by Mirko Jelusich. 1937.

Translator, *Le Chant de Bernadette*, by Franz Werfel. 1942.

*

Critical Studies: *The Poetry of Ivan Goll* by F.J. Carmody, 1956; *Ivan Goll: Quatre études par Jules Romains, Marcel Brion, Francis Carmody, Richard Exner*, 1956; *Yvan Goll: An Iconographical Study of His Poetry* by Vivien Perkins, 1970; *Interpretations of Ivan Goll's Late Poetry* by Vera B. Profit, 1977; *Ivan Goll: The Development of His Poetic Themes and Their Imagery* by Margaret A. Parmée, 1981; *Yvan Goll and Bilingual Poetry* by James Phillips, 1984.

* * *

Ivan Goll is remembered today chiefly for his cycles of poems, though he expresses himself in many different forms: essays, plays, novels, and the *avant-garde* film. His writing was in many ways an attempt to come to terms with his peculiarly uneasy position in Europe in the first half of the 20th century. He described himself as being 'by fate a Jew, by chance a Frenchman, by virtue of a piece of paper a German'. It has been felt by some that his poetry belongs more firmly to German literary history than to that of France, yet he found it impossible to align himself wholeheartedly with any one aspect of this tripartite division and, like his Alsatian compatriot, Hans Arp, expressed himself with equal felicity in French and German. (Later, during his American exile, he also wrote poems in English.)

Goll's first published poem of note was *Der Panamakanal* [The Panama Canal] of 1912, a work that reveals clearly his affinities with the new movement of Expressionism. The poem, which seems at first to be a Romantic lament for a natural world destroyed by civilization, ends on a positive note, evoking universal love and the brotherhood of mankind. This is in keeping with the spirit of his requiem for the dead of Europe in World War I and indicates his commitment to the branch of Expressionism more dedicated to building the future than revelling in the decline of a passing world. However, a later version of 'Der Panamakanal' in 1918 ends with the belief that man's lot does not, after all, improve, and points forward to the pessimistic tone of much of the later poetry.

In his essays, such as *Die drei guten Geister Frankreichs* [The Three Good Spirits of France], Goll attempted to foster a better understanding between the peoples of France and Germany, but he himself was attracted more to France by the greater liveliness of the artistic scene. Here his Expressionist style began to develop towards Surrealism, manifested first in drama and film scenarios, such as *Die Chapliniade* [The Chaplinade] and *Mathusalem* [Methuselah]. These works blend fantasy, reality, and the absurd in a way that recalls the work of German Expressionist dramatists, continuing and extending their desire to arouse audience response by means of shock effects. They are evidence of the autobiographical nature of much of Goll's writing, but also of his tendency to appear in the guise of a persona rather than in the first person. By this means he endows his figures with more general validity; the problems he explores are in some senses peculiarly his own, yet the character of Charlot in *Die Chapliniade* is an evocative portrayal of a well-known clown image, whose melancholy is concealed by his fixed smile.

The cyclical poem that Goll regarded as his major work, *La Chanson de Jean sans Terre* (*Landless John*), is the most significant example of such autobiographical writing. If one imagines the character of John replaced by 'I', claims Jules Romains in *Yvan Goll* (1956), one will notice a surprising change of colour and persuasive force. The central figure, who wanders the earth through 69 poems, belongs everywhere and nowhere. He seeks love and identity and yet the absence of these things also bestows a form of freedom. His searching and his problems are not ended by the end of the cycle. The final verse of the poem gives Goll's own definition of John:

Landless John walks the roads leading nowhere
He walks to escape his shadow which binds him to the
    soil
He wants to possess nothing on this earth. Will he
—By singing—get free of his shadow, his other I?
                (translated by Galway Kinnell)

It would be a mistake to regard *Landless John* as simply a version of the Wandering Jew. The work follows on from the novels of the 1920s, such as *À bas l'Europe* [Down with Europe], which are concerned with the economic and moral decline of the age. John too inhabits the modern, materialistic world and Goll describes him as a contemporary individual, battling against internal and external forces.

The uncertainty of love is a theme of poems written both before and after *Landless John*. Goll composed the cycle *Poèmes d'amour* (*Love Poems*) together with his wife Claire, also a poet of note, who translated much of his work. They reflect in a pure and limpid style the poets' love, their need of each other, but also jealousy, fear of betrayal, and a clash of temperaments. Love also runs as a constant thread through the last work, *Traumkraut* [Grasses of Dreams]. On his deathbed the poet reverted to the language of his earliest writings and was able to say that only now had he truly learned to master his craft. It was for this reason that he asked Claire Goll, as she tells us in her preface, to destroy all his previous work. As the title implies, the poems are concerned with nature, but often nature seen in a surreal context: the images spring from spiritual rather than physical experience.

Because of the change of style (but more especially of language) that took place in Goll's writing when he settled in France, he is often regarded in Germany first and foremost as an Expressionist and in France as a Surrealist. Yet his plays and poems show clearly the way in which his Surrealism grew out of his Expressionism. He made a conscious break with the latter in 1921, aware that it was nearing its end, but the break was a gradual one and there are many echoes of the earlier movement in his later work. The many distinguished artists who have illustrated his work are also representative of both groups; they include Hans Arp, Salvador Dali, George Grosz, Fernand Léger and above all Marc Chagall. Like them, Goll was in the mainstream of the artistic movements of his time.

—Margaret K. Rogister

GOMBROWICZ, Witold. Born in Maloszyce, Poland, 4 August 1904. Educated privately; St Stanislas Kostka (Catholic high school), 1916–22; Warsaw University, 1922–26, law degree 1926; Institut des Hautes Études Internationales, Paris, 1926–27. Married Marie-Rita Labrosse in 1968. Part-time law clerk, Warsaw, 1928–34; reviewer for several Warsaw newspapers, 1935; travelled to Argentina and cut off from Poland because of war, 1939; reviewer (under pseudonym) for newspapers in Buenos Aires from 1940; secretary for the Polish Bank, Buenos Aires, 1947–55; left Argentina, 1963; Ford Foundation fellow, Berlin, 1963–64; lived in Vence, France, 1964–69. Recipient: Kultura prize (Paris), 1961; International literary prize, 1967. *Died 25 July 1969.*

PUBLICATIONS

Collection

Dzieła zebrane [Collected Works]. 11 vols., 1969–77.

Fiction

Pamiętnik z okresu dojrzewania [Memoirs from Adolescence]. 1933.
Ferdydurke. 1937; as *Ferdydurke*, translated by Eric Mosbacher, 1961.
Trans-Atlantyk, with *Ślub*. 1953; as *Trans-Atlantyk*, translated by Carolyn French and Nina Karsov, 1994.
Bakakaj (selections). 1957.
Pornografia. 1960; as *Pornografia*, translated by Alastair Hamilton, 1966.
Kosmos. 1965; as *Cosmos*, translated by Eric Mosbacher, 1966.
Opętani. 1973; as *Possessed; or, The Secret of Myslotch*, translated (from French) by J.A. Underwood, 1980.
Zdarzenia na brygu Banbury. 1982.

Plays

Iwona, Księżniczka Burgunda (produced 1957). In *Skamander*, 1935; as *Princess Ivona*, translated by Krystyna Griffith-Jones and Catherine Robins, 1969.
Ślub (produced 1964). With *Trans-Atlantyk*, 1953; as *The Marriage*, translated by Louis Iribarne, 1970.
Operetka (produced 1969). 1966; as *Operetta*, translated by Louis Iribarne, 1971.
Historia [History] (unfinished). 1975.

Other

Dziennik 1953–1956. 3 vols., 1957–66; as *Diary*, edited by Jan Kott, translated by Lillian Vallee, 3 vols., 1988–93.
Entretiens avec Gombrowicz, edited by Dominique de Roux. 1968; as *A Kind of Testament*, translated by Alastair Hamilton, 1973.
Wspomnienia polskie [Polish Reminiscences]. 1977.
Listy 1950–1969 [Letters], with Jerzy Giedroyc, edited by Andrzej Kowalczyk. 1993.

*

Critical Studies: *Gombrowicz* (in French) by Constantin Jeleński and Dominique de Roux, 1971; *Gombrowicz: Bourreau-martyr* by Jacques Volle, 1972; *Gombrowicz* (in French) by Rosine Georgin, 1977; *Gombrowicz* by Ewa M. Thompson, 1979; *Gombrowicz and Frisch: Aspects of the Literary Diary* by Alex Kurczaba, 1980; *Gombrowicz, vingt ans après* edited by Manuel Carcassone and others, 1989.

* * *

Witold Gombrowicz is one of the most original Polish writers of the 20th century. His first book *Pamiętnik z okresu dojrzewania* [Memoirs from Adolescence], a collection of grotesque short stories, already established his obsessive themes which he was to pursue in later years. These can be described as a desire for sexual domination and/or submission, and the manipulation (sexual and intellectual) of others. In *Ferdydurke*, his most striking novel, all these themes are woven into the plot which follows the adventures of Joey, a 30-year-old man forced back into the immaturity of adolescence by a determined schoolteacher. *Ferdydurke* is a parody of traditional Polish and fashionable Western values which are displayed and then effectively discredited in three different domains of life: at school, in the 'progressive' household of an engineer, and in the old-fashioned manor-house. The conclusion of this very entertaining novel is that however much we may try to break out of the prison of Form, there is no escape from play-acting.

In 1939 Gombrowicz visited Argentina and after the outbreak of World War II decided to stay there, so it was this country that became the backdrop to his next novel *Trans-Atlantyk*. It depicts a conflict between the old and new generation of Polish emigrés in Argentina, the author acting as a narrator/chronicler of a fairly trivial quarrel which he tells with the panache of Polish memoirs from the Baroque period. What Gombrowicz really questions in this novel is the relevance of the Polish national myth. He continues to investigate this and other controversial issues in the three volumes of his *Dziennik* (*Diary*) which has been called an 'autobiographical novel' as well as a running commentary on the philosophical, cultural, and political problems of the day. Gombrowicz's *Diary* exhibits the same sharp wit and far-reaching scepticism to traditional values as his novels, but it also lays bare the author's obsessions, complexes, and narcissistic tendencies. These reappear in a less striking form in the novels *Pornografia* and *Kosmos* (*Cosmos*), which are both essays on the possibilities and limits of psychological manipulation—of the young by the old, and of the normal by the obsessed.

Gombrowicz was also a playwright; indeed, his first international successes were due to the production of his plays in Paris and in Germany in the 1960s. There are altogether four plays by Gombrowicz, one of which, the amusing but perhaps too ambitious *Historia* [History], was left unfinished. The earliest play, *Iwona, Księżniczka Burgunda* (*Princess Ivona*), is a 'tragifarce'. It takes place in a mythical kingdom where the young heir to the throne plans but eventually fails to marry the singularly ugly and unpleasant girl whom he chose in a moment of malicious whim. Ivona acts as a catalyst of suppressed guilt for everyone, so in the end she has to be eliminated in the name of state interests. There are pseudo-Shakespearean undertones in the excellent *Ślub* (*The Marriage*), which, on one level, is the story of human beings shaping each other through words, gestures, and acts of homage or defiance, while on another level it is the tragedy of overstrained human will. The sacralization of certain symbols can force society into their temporary acceptance, but not even the most charismatic figure can 'give himself' a wedding which would restore the lost innocence of a fallen bride.

Operetka (*Operetta*) is a bizarre tragi-comedy which through the parody of this 'idiotic art form' manages to convey a philosophical message. Although its starting-point is the striving of an overformalized society towards 'nakedness' (i.e. freedom), anarchy and totalitarianism are alternative 'forms' also to be experienced. While Gombrowicz's savage parody of the past hundred years of European history brings the play very close to the theatre of the absurd, it nevertheless ends on an optimistic note, hailing 'nudity eternally youthful' and 'youth eternally nude', that expresses faith in the mysterious self-regenerating forces of mankind.

—George Gömöri

FERDYDURKE
Novel by Witold Gombrowicz, 1937.

Ferdydurke is Gombrowicz's first and most influential novel. Even critics like Ewa M. Thompson who prefer Gombrowicz's post-war prose agree that this novel is 'a key to [all] Gombrowicz's works'. The title itself is meaningless— Gombrowicz, when questioned, claimed to have borrowed it from a character in one of H.G. Wells's stories, where it appeared as 'Ferdy Durke'. This novel illustrates one of Gombrowicz's basic antinomies, i.e. 'maturity versus immaturity'. It consists of five parts, two introductory and 'philosophical' and three narrative. Joey (Józio), the 30-year-old hero, is a drifting and unsettled individual, whom Mr Pimko, his former schoolmaster, visits in his home and by the sheer force of his schoolmaster's authority transforms into an adolescent. As in a bad dream, Joey is thrown back into the arena of fermenting immaturity, the grammar school. There he experiences both competition between immature schoolboys (the duel of grimaces between the 'idealist' and the 'materialist' in his class) and a struggle for influence over the minds of the schoolboys, all this signifying that all classroom education is a mishmash of lofty truisms and meaningless formulas. Our hero cannot get rid of his immaturity in school, so he tries to achieve this next in the household of the 'progressive' Youthful family and then in a conservative country house where his uncle lives. Joey is disgusted with his own greenness, but cannot accept the barren and fake maturity of the grown-ups and the rules of behaviour laid down by 'mature' society. This inability to come to terms either with oneself or with society is the attitudinal axis of *Ferdydurke*, while the protagonist's elaborate but futile attempts to self-liberation provide the absurd but very amusing plot.

Critics, by and large, offer two models for the interpretation of Gombrowicz's novel, a realistic and a philosophical one. The former regards the novel as a social satire, and specifically as a satire on pre-World War II Poland. Arthur Sandauer emphasized this view, pointing out that *Ferdydurke*, in fact, ridiculed most values cherished by the generation that had created independent Poland: education in a 'national' spirit, the cult of scientific and technological progress, and the belief that the duty of educated Poles was to help the peasants to educate themselves. The second approach, which could be defined as 'non-mimetic', stresses form and structure. In Gombrowicz's novel form (or the lack of it) takes precedence over ideology, ideals are undermined by biological urges, and language is shown to camouflage rather than reveal reality.

Ferdydurke was published in 1937, but it is a pioneering work in a sense, and it can be claimed that with it Gombrowicz created a general structural model of the human situation and inner human relations. Man is not authentic, because he is dependent on others: he is constantly influenced and shaped by the opinions, attitudes, and actions of others. This is not a uniquely Polish situation, but one that appears almost universally in the age of mass media and victorious mass culture. Artistic creation in itself is no remedy against the 'manipulation by forms' which can be broken only by some act of self-liberating violence. All narrative parts of *Ferdydurke* end in a break-out attempt, in a 'wriggling heap' of bodies.

As Bruno Schulz put it, *Ferdydurke* is 'bursting from ideas': it is a grotesque, almost picaresque novel, packed with striking psychological observations and interesting philosophical propositions. Human biology is also important inasmuch as in each narrative part of the novel a different part of the body plays a central symbolic role; the school is the kingdom of the 'bum' (people are 'fitted out with bums'), the house of the 'progressive' Youthfuls emanates a cult of the emancipated schoolgirl's calves, while the country house reflects the insoluble conflict between the gentlemanly 'faces' and the 'mugs' of the peasants. 'There is no escape from the bum', declares Joey at the end of the novel: what he means is that there is no escape from one's social roles and obligations.

Some of Gombrowicz's linguistic jokes became everyday coinage in the Poland of the 1950s when as a result of Marxist indoctrination most individuals felt that they were indeed 'fitted out with a bum', having endured endless sessions of 'verbal rape' by Party bosses. This strange topicality helped to make the book much sought after at the time it was reissued in 1957, and focused attention on Gombrowicz, who had lived abroad since 1939.

—George Gömöri

GONCHAROV, Ivan (Aleksandrovich). Born in Simbirsk, Russia, 18 June 1812. Educated at local boarding school, 1820–22; Moscow Commercial School, 1822–31; University of Moscow, 1831–34. Civil servant in St Petersburg from 1834: secretary to Admiral Pitiatin on trip to Far East, 1852–55; official censor, St Petersburg, 1856–60, and member of the committee of review of Russian censorship groups, 1863–67; retired from civil service as Actual Councillor of State, 1867. *Died 27 September 1891.*

PUBLICATIONS

Collections

Povesti i ocherki [Stories and Essays], edited by B.M. Engelgardt. 1937.
Sobranie sochinenii [Collected Works], edited by A.P. Rybasov. 8 vols., 1952–55.
Sobranie sochinenii [Collected Works], edited by S.I. Mashinskii. 8 vols., 1977–80.
Izbrannye sochineniia [Selected Works], edited by G.I. Belen'kii. 1990.

Fiction

Obyknovennaia istoriia. 1848; as *A Common Story*, translated by Constance Garnett, 1894; as *The Same Old Story*, translated by Ivy Litvinova, 1956; as *An Ordinary Story*, with *Viktor Rovoz*, edited and translated by Marjorie L. Hoover, 1993.
Oblomov. 1859; as *Oblomov*, translated by C.J. Hogarth, 1915; also translated by Natalie Duddington, 1929; David Magarshack, 1954; Ann Dunnigan, 1963.
Obryv. 1870; as *The Precipice*, translated by M. Bryant, 1915; also translated by Laury Magnus and Boris Jakim, 1993.

Other

Russkie v Iaponii v kontse 1853 i v nachale 1854 godov [Russians in Japan in the End of 1853 and the Beginning of 1854]. 1855; revised edition, as *Fregat Pallada*, 1858; edited by D.V. Oznobishin, 1986; as *The Frigate Pallas: Notes on a Journey*, translated by N.W. Wilson, 1965.
Literaturno-kriticheskie stat'i i pis'ma [Literary Critical Articles and Letters], edited by A.P. Rybasova. 1938.
I.A. Goncharov-kritik (selection), edited by V.I. Korobov. 1981.
Ocherki. Stat'i. Pis'ma. Vospominaniia sovremennikov [Essays. Articles. Letters. Reminiscences of Contemporaries]. 1986.

*

Bibliography: *Bibliografiia Goncharova 1832–1964* by A.D. Alekseev, 1968; *Ivan Goncharov: A Bibliography* edited by Garth M. Terry, 1986.

Critical Studies: *Goncharov* by Janko Lavrin, 1954; *Goncharov* by Alexandra and Sverre Lyngstad, 1971; *Oblomov and His Creator: The Life and Art of Ivan Goncharov* by Milton Ehre, 1973; *Goncharov: His Life and His Works* by V. Setchkarev, 1974; *Oblomov: A Critical Examination of Goncharov's Novels* by Richard Peace, 1991.

* * *

Oblomov, Goncharov's best known novel, so dwarfs his other fiction that, in the West, at least, he tends to be known for this work alone. This is regrettable because, for all its uniqueness, it is still arguable that *Oblomov* achieves its fullest resonance against the background of its predecessor, *Obyknovennaia istoriia* (*A Common Story*), and its successor, *Obryv* (*The Precipice*).

All three novels are concerned with the confrontation between the rising pragmatism of the mid-19th century and the comparatively established norms of Romantic idealism. *A Common Story* explores the relationship between Aleksandr Aduev, a young idealist dreaming of love and literary success and his uncle who has become reconciled to the uninspiring realities of the world. Somewhat too schematically, perhaps, Goncharov plots the course of Aduev's disenchantment to its issue: assimilation to the uncle's viewpoint. In *The Precipice* the ineffective Raiskii, another idealist, vies with a nihilist for the heroine's hand. Although the nihilist manages to seduce her, both he and Raiskii are ultimately rejected in favour of Tushin, a solid, commonsensical neighbour of the heroine.

The triumph of the pragmatic outlook is also an essential feature of *Oblomov*. Stolz, the half-German friend of the eponymous hero, attempts to awaken the latter from his torpid inactivity, urging him to use his talents in the real world before it is too late. Encouraged by the practical Stolz and by the heroine, Olga, with whom he has an affair, Oblomov makes some progress in extricating himself from the mire before succumbing once more to the temptations of inertia. Oblomov dies of a stroke and Stolz marries the heroine. Oblomov's slothful attachment to his bed, his almost symbiotic relationship with his aged servant Zakhar and his addiction to comfort are generally seen as satirized characteristics of the declining Russian landed gentry of the mid-19th century. Stolz embodies the entrepreneurial class that will oust the aristocracy unless it adapts.

However, the status of *Oblomov* as a world classic derives from the fact that Oblomov, like Hamlet (whose indecisiveness he shares) transcends his *chronotopos* to personify a universal human predicament. Oblomov is the passive romantic who instinctively resists every incursion from the real world of disturbing activity. This passivity is represented in the novel as something akin to sleep, and, like sleep, is solaced by dreaming.

'Oblomov's Dream', a pivotal section of the novel, was published separately in 1849. It offers an idyllic vision of the hero's rural childhood that has so fatefully shaped his later life. The dream is not just a representation of the past but an abiding subconscious reality that continues to exert a stultifying influence on Oblomov's will. Such is its fatally soothing power that, after his brief awakening by Olga and Stolz, Oblomov is unable to resist his landlady's adult reconstruction of the old childhood comforts.

The use of dream, both for subliminal analysis and as a means of representing contradictions inherent in the romantic outlook, makes *Oblomov* a profoundly psychological novel. It is Goncharov's achievement to have successfully grafted psychological portrayal on to the Gogolian stock of external characterization. To this extent *Oblomov* may be held to anticipate the great novels of Tolstoi and Dostoevskii and must be assigned a crucial role in the development of the Russian novel.

—Robert Reid

OBLOMOV
Novel by Ivan Goncharov, 1859.

Goncharov's *Oblomov* was first published in the literary journal *Notes of the Fatherland* and as a book in 1859. Although Goncharov saw it as the middle part of a trilogy—the others being *A Common Story* and *The Precipice*—which would describe three historical periods in Russian 19th-century life, it is now considered his masterpiece and a classic of the Russian realist school.

Writing about the earlier novel in 1866 Goncharov asked, 'Was it not I, as early as the 1840s, who pointed out the need for everyone to work and showed my sympathy for the old uncle who rightly abused his nephew for his utterly despicable ways—his laziness?'. Just exactly what work young men should do, though, Goncharov was chary of mentioning. None the less the critic Belinskii hailed *A Common Story*, along with Dostoevskii's *Bednye liudi* (*Poor Folk*), as examples of the way Russian literature should go, and the theme is continued in *Oblomov*.

The young Oblomov was brought up on an estate on the Volga, a thousand miles from Moscow, governed by tradition and lethargy. He is pampered and spoilt, surrounded by serfs who look after his every need. His family have to do nothing. In the chapter 'Oblomov's Dream' Goncharov reveals Oblomov's memories of that peaceful, slumbering, overprotected, carefree life with its ample food, steaming samovars, feather beds, aimless conversations, and complete and enjoyable indolence. Later Oblomov goes to university but education has no effect on his temperament or his behaviour patterns. He enters the civil service but retires before he is 30. He can now lounge about all day (it actually takes him a whole chapter to get out of bed), lost in reverie and looked after by his equally lazy manservant Zakhar. He deserts his friends and neglects any social responsibilities. Life is a burden and he hides away from it. Yet he is intelligent, kindhearted, and generally amiable. The aim of life is tranquillity. His acquaintances term his 'illness' Oblomovism. That tranquillity is disturbed when he falls in love with Olga, a charming girl who is no fool and has a desire for action. With her strong will and integrity she very briefly stirs Oblomov into almost doing something, but love requires responsibilities and Oblomov has neither the will nor the stamina to continue. Olga goes abroad and meets Stolz, the boyhood friend of Oblomov, whom she eventually marries. Stolz, characteristically half-German, is the complete antithesis of Oblomov. He studies life, travels widely, and gets things done. He is a successful businessman and an incipient capitalist. He is practical, innovative, materialistic, and rational. He is a representative of the new way of life that would rescue Russia from the Oblomovism of the decaying serf-owning society. He is also a new psychological phenomenon. Oblomov lives by his dreams and his imagination, Stolz by experience and facts. Oblomov is an idle gentleman, Stolz an enthusiastic organizer. Oblomov is superstitious, Stolz is rational. Oblomov wants to achieve nothing, Stolz achieves whatever he wants, with one notable exception. He cannot change Oblomov. After a brief illness Oblomov settles down to live with Agafya, a gentle, uneducated, but loving widow who sets about providing for her 'gentleman' in the manner of the serfs of his childhood. They eventually marry and have a son, and Oblomov lives out the rest of his life in complete contentment.

Through his depiction of Oblomov Goncharov deprecates the whole way of life of the conservative and patriarchal minor gentry class and suggests that their attitude might well be a national Russian characteristic. The radical critic Dobroliubov set the tone of many future interpretations of the novel in his article 'What is Oblomovism?' He argued that the 'superfluous men' of the 1830s and 1840s—Pushkin's Onegin, Lermontov's Pechorin, Herzen's Beltov, Turgenev's Rudin, and Gogol's Tentetnikov—were all more or less suffering from Oblomovism. They all shared a penchant for day-dreaming and rationalizing and were all basically passive. Their yearnings bore little relation to everyday life. Although their personalities were not at all identical they were still impractical and socially useless. Oblomov differed from them all, however, in that he did not share their liberal aspirations. He was actually a supporter of serfdom, yet his Oblomovism was a direct result of that system and it affected not only landowners but also the civil service and the rising middle class. Consequently it was a clearly Russian defect. Later critics also suggested that Oblomovism contained a large element of fatalism. The individual can have no influence on current events so a perfect state of complete inactivity leads not only to happiness but also to wisdom. It was to Goncharov's lasting credit that he had so convincingly described the phenomenon.

Although Goncharov remained untouched by the various intellectual and historical currents of his time, he none the less became the chronicler of the real concerns of everyday life. In various matters, he wrote, he shared contemporary opinions about, for example, the emancipation of the peasants, the need for better methods of education, and the harmfulness of all forms of oppression and restrictions on progress. But he never passed through a stage of enthusiasm for utopias created by the socialist ideal of equality, fraternity, and the like. He might well have felt that Russia needed some radical change but he still regretted the passing of the old. While clearly admiring Stolz's qualities the fact that he makes him rather staid and wooden might point to a basic lack of sympathy for him and all he tried to make him represent, whereas the reader, despite—like Stolz and Olga —getting infuriated with Oblomov, takes to him, likes him, follows his uneventful life with interest and even compassion, and is sorry to see him go.

—A.V. Knowles

GONCOURT, Edmond (-Louis-Antoine Huot) de, and Jules (-Alfred) de. Edmond de Goncourt: born in Nancy, France, 26 May 1822. Educated at Pension Goubaux; Lycée Henri IV; Collège Bourbon; studied law, 1841. Worked for the city finance department. Travelled through France and Algeria with his brother, sketching and noting impressions in their now famous diary, 1848–49; travelled to Switzerland, Belgium, and Normandy, 1850; contributed to the literary daily, *Paris*, and to *Revue de Paris*, 1852–53; travelled to Italy, 1855–56, and 1867; important collector and connoisseur of Japanese art. Bequeathed money to found the Académie Goncourt that awards the annual literary prize. *Died 16 July 1896.* **Jules de Goncourt:** born in Paris, France, 17 December 1830. Educated at Lycée Condorcet and Collège Bourbon, Paris. Travelled through France and Algeria with his brother, sketching and writing their now famous diary, 1848–49; travelled to Switzerland, Belgium and Normandy, 1850; contracted syphilis, 1850; contributed to the literary daily, *Paris*, and to *Revue de Paris*, 1852–53; co-founder, with his brother and their cousin, Pierre-Charles de Villedeuil, *L'Éclair*, 1850s; travelled to Italy, 1855–56, and 1867. *Died 20 June 1870.*

PUBLICATIONS by Edmond and Jules de Goncourt

Collections

Théâtre. 1879.
Bibliothèque des Goncourt. 1897.
Collection des Goncourt. 1897.

Fiction

En 18 . . . 1851.
La Lorette. 1853.
Les Hommes de lettres. 1860; as *Charles Demailly*, 1896.
Soeur Philomène. 1861; as *Sister Philomene*, translated by Laura Ensor, 1890; also translated by Madeline Jay, 1989.
Germinie Lacerteux. 1865; as *Germinie Lacerteux*, translated anonymously, 1887; also translated by John Chestershire,

1897; Leonard Tancock, 1984; as *Germinie*, translated by Jonathan Griffith, 1955.

Renée Mauperin. 1864; as *Renée Mauperin*, translated by Alys Hallard, 1902; also translated by James Fitzmaurice-Kelly, 1904.

Manette Salomon. 1867.

Madame Gervaisais. 1869.

Quelques créatures de ce temps (stories). 1876.

Première amoureuse (stories). 1896.

Plays

La Nuit de la Saint-Sylvestre. 1852.

Henriette Maréchal (produced 1865). 1866.

La Patrie en danger. 1873.

Other

Salon de 1852 (criticism). 1852.

Mystères des théâtres, 1852. 1853.

Oeuvres complètes. 21 vols., 1854.

La Révolution dans les moeurs. 1854.

Histoire de la société française pendant la Révolution. 1854.

Histoire de la société française pendant le Directoire. 1855.

La Peinture à l'exposition de 1855. 1855.

Une voiture de masques. 1856; revised edition, 1990.

Les Actrices. 1856.

Sophie Arnould, d'après sa correspondance et ses mémoires inédits. 1857.

Portraits intimes du dix-huitième siècle. 2 vols., 1857–58.

Histoire de Marie-Antoinette. 1858; revised edition, 1859; revised, with letters, 1863; revised editions, 2 vols., 1873–74, 2 vols., 1880–82, 3 vols., 1881–82.

Les Saint-Aubin. 1859.

L'Art du dix-huitième siècle. 11 vols., 1859–75; complete edition, 1875; as *French 18th-Century Painters*, edited and translated by Robin Ironside, 1948.

Les Hommes de lettres. 1860.

Les Maîtresses de Louis XV. 2 vols., 1860; as *The Confidantes of a King*, translated by Ernest Dowson, 1907.

La Femme au dix-huitième siècle. 1862; as *The Woman of the 18th-Century*, translated by Jacques Le Clerq and Ralph Roeder, 1927.

Idées et sensations. 1866.

Les Vignettistes. 1868.

Deuxième mille. 1886.

Gavarni, l'homme et l'oeuvre. 1873.

La Du Barry. 1878; revised edition, 1880; as *Madame du Barry*, translated anonymously, 1914.

Madame de Pompadour. 1878; revised editions 1881, and 1888.

Journal des Goncourt: Mémoires de la vie littéraire. 9 vols., 1887–96; 9 vols., 1935–36; 22 vols., 1956–59; edited by Robert Ricatte, 4 vols., 1956; as *The Journal of the Goncourts* (selection), translated by Julius West, 1908; as *Goncourt Journals 1851–70*, edited and translated by Lewis Galantière, 1937; as *Pages from the Goncourt Journal* (selection), translated by Robert Baldick, 1962; as *Paris Under Siege, 1870–71*, edited and translated by George J. Becker, 1969.

Armande, illustrated by Marold. 1892; as *Armande*, translated by Alfred E. Haserick, 1894.

Pages retrouvées. 1886.

Edmond and Jules de Goncourt (correspondence and journal), edited and translated by M.A. Belloc and M. Shedlock. 2 vols., 1894.

L'Italie d'hier: Notes de voyages 1855–56. 1894.

Selections, edited by Arnold Cameron. 1898.

Paris and the Arts 1851–96, edited and translated by George J. Becker and Edith Philips. 1971

Lettres de jeunesse inédites, edited by Alain Nicolas. 1981.

PUBLICATIONS by Edmond Goncourt

Fiction

La Fille Élisa. 1877; as *Elisa: The Story of a Prostitute*, translated by Margaret Crosland, 1959; as *Woman of Paris*, translated by Cedric Harrald, 1959.

Les Frères Zemganno. 1879; as *The Zemganno Brothers*, translated anonymously, 1886; also translated by Leonard Clark and Iris Allam, 1957.

La Faustin. 1882; as *La Faustin: A Life Study*, translated by John Stirling, 1882; as *La Faustin*, translated by G.F. Monkshood and Ernest Tristan, 1906.

Chérie. 1884.

Other

L'Amour au dix-huitième siècle. 1875; as *Love in the 18th Century*, 1905.

La Duchesse de Châteauroux et ses soeurs. 1879; revised edition, 1892.

La Maison d'un artiste. 2 vols., 1881; definitive edition, 2 vols., 1931.

Madame Saint-Huberty. 1882; definitive edition, 1925.

Lettres de Jules de Goncourt. 1885.

Préfaces et manifestes littéraires. 1888.

Mademoiselle Clairon. 1890.

L'Art japonais du XVIIIe siècle. 2 vols., 1891–96.

Outamaro, le peintre des maisons vertes. 1891.

A bas le progrès!. 1893.

Le Guimard. 1893.

L'Italie d'hier. 1894.

Hokousai. 1896.

Lettres. 1930.

Edmond de Goncourt et Henri Céard: correspondance inédite 1876–1896. 1965.

*

Critical studies: *Création romanesque chez les Goncourt* by Robert Ricatte, 1953; *The Goncourt Brothers* by André Billy, translated by M. Shaw, 1960; *The Goncourts* by Robert Baldick, 1960; *Réalisme et impressionnisme dans l'oeuvre des frères Goncourt* by Enzo Caramaschi, 1971; *The Goncourt Brothers* by Richard B. Grant, 1972.

*   *   *

Edmond and Jules de Goncourt form one of the most remarkable literary partnerships that has ever existed. Jules had the greater literary talent, but died in early middle age of syphilis. His brother continued to write after his death, but generally with less mastery and success than the joint works.

En 18 . . . , the first of their novels, is a slight work, recounting its hero's disappointments in love. *Les Hommes de lettres*, later entitled *Charles Demailly*, is both a story of marital discord culminating in the husband's madness and also a *roman à clef* vehemently denouncing unprincipled literary journalism. *Soeur Philomène* (Sister Philomene), a far less episodic novel, is notable for its bleak evocation of a hospital environment. *Renée Mauperin*, describing the shallow conventional life of a wealthy middle-class family, is marred by legal and historical inaccuracies which deny it any claim to narrow 'realism' in the sense in which that term is applied to Balzac's work. Renée, seeking to prevent her brother's marriage, involves him in a duel in which he is killed; grief-stricken, she falls into a lengthy decline (admirably described by the Goncourts) and dies. *Germinie Lacerteux*, modelled on the hidden life of the brothers' own maid, resembles *Sister Philomene* and *Renée Mauperin* in that it concerns degradation and death; it tells of the heroine's two secret love-affairs, the second more squalid that the first, and both unsuspected by her employer. *Manette Salomon*, a novel of artistic life, contrasts four types of artist and explores the (generally destructive) influence exerted by women upon artists' lives. *Madame Gervaisais*, a study in religious mania, shows the destructive influence of Catholicism upon the lives of the heroine and her young son. Each of these works, so different in their ambience and subject-matter, was considered by the Goncourt brothers to be a venture into a new field of human experience; each was a challenge. Each was carefully documented, as when the two brothers spent six weeks in Rome gathering material for *Madame Gervaisais*. Whether actively seeking out such researched material or else modelling Germinie on the secret life of their maid, they looked upon the subject matter of their novels as 'history which might have taken place'. But this documentary aspect of their work was as far as their 'naturalism' went.

Their method of writing was unusual even by the standards of literary partnerships. So closely attuned were their ways of viewing and writing about the world that it is impossible to make precise attributions of particular passages; Edmond went so far as to write of their 'twin mind'. Jules, however, had a better ear for dialogue, where Edmond's gifts lay more in the direction of scene-setting and background detail. Nevertheless, each chapter of each novel was separately drafted out by both novelists, who (living under the same roof and working in adjacent rooms) would then meet to compare and conflate their two versions: thus, one novel was made out of the best elements of each. But both wrote to a story-line that had been mapped out initially in fine detail by the two brothers working in concert.

Like Musset, Edmond and Jules de Goncourt were men of essentially artistic temperament: artistic in their leanings towards the visual arts, in which they took a keen interest. They even evolved a literary style peculiarly adapted to their purposes. This was the *écriture artiste*, full of neologisms and the specialized vocabularies of medicine, art criticism, and other disciplines; its contorted syntax was meant to convey all the complexities and obscurities of contemporary life. Unjustly maligned by many critics, this *écriture artiste* was a sort of literary mannerism in which all too often the manner of saying a thing seemed to predominate over the thing said. The very tortuousness of the Goncourts' writing, febrile, hypersensitive, and so hard to translate, suggests inner torments: they claimed that the whole of their writing was based upon neurosis. Yet the sheer technical virtuosity of that writing must surely be deemed a literary quality in itself, and they strove to avoid preciosity at all times.

The brothers' interest in the visual arts also found expression in the sharp focus of individual scenes. While the prevalence of dialogue suggests their desire to emulate the theatre, they foreshadow cinematic techniques in the way in which they move into the very centre and heart of the action as each brief chapter opens. These chapters are sometimes so visually concentrated as to resemble tableaux. In their rapid juxtaposition of colourful details the Goncourt brothers achieve a sort of impressionism, though Gautier's influence upon them is also evident—not only in their literary practice but also (to a lesser extent) in their theory of the fine arts.

The *Journal des Goncourt* (*Goncourt Journals*), kept by the two brothers from 1851 until Jules's death and afterwards by Edmond alone, is a store of information about such writers as Flaubert, Gautier, Zola, Daudet, Hugo, and Turgenev and about marginal historical figures such as Princess Mathilde Bonaparte. The very reverse of a confessional diary, it is crammed with anecdotes and has the deft touch of the gossip column, of which it is a main forerunner. A vivid impression is given of Paris at the time of the Franco-Prussian War and the Commune. That part of the *Journal* for which Edmond was solely responsible (from March 1870 until July 1896) outshines even the joint diary; however, the four novels written by him alone—even *La Fille Élisa* (*Woman of Paris*) and *Les Frères Zemganno* (*The Zemganno Brothers*)—are but pale reflections of the brilliance of the joint novels.

Together with Zola, the Goncourt brothers are generally considered to be the founders of the French school of Naturalism. Earlier than Zola, they described sordid—sometimes pathological—subject matter, but always in brilliant painterly terms. They did much to pioneer novels of working-class life. They took great care to see, seek, verify, and investigate the facts, by which they generally meant the physical settings. The term 'naturalist' was not, however, a distinction they ever claimed for themselves. In Zola's own words, 'the analysis of things artistic, plastic, and neurotic' was the heart of their achievement.

—Donald Adamson

GÓNGORA (y Argote), Luis de. Born in Córdoba, Spain, 11 July 1561. Educated at Jesuit school in Córdoba; University of Salamanca, 1576–80, no degree. Took minor orders at university, and deacon's orders, 1586: prebendary of Córdoba Cathedral, 1586–1617: undertook various business trips for the Cathedral; ordained priest, 1517, and royal chaplain in Madrid, 1617–25. *Died 23 May 1627.*

PUBLICATIONS

Collections

Obras en verso del Homero español, edited by Juan López de Vicuña. 1627; also edited by Dámaso Alonso, 1963.
Todas las obras, edited by Gonzalo de Hozes y Córdoba. 1633.
Obras completas, edited by Juan and Isabel Millé y Giménez. 1972.

Verse

Soledades, edited by Dámaso Alonso. 1927, revised edition, 1956; also edited by Alfonso Gallejo and María Teresa Pajares, with *Fábula de Polifemo y Galatea*, 1985; as *The Solitudes*, translated by Edward M. Wilson, 1931; also translated by Gilbert F. Cunningham, 1968.
Fábula de Polifemo y Galatea, as *Góngora y el 'Polifemo'*,

edited by Dámaso Alonso. 1960, revised edition, 2 vols., 1961; also edited by Alfonso Gallejo and María Teresa Pajares, with *Las Soledades*, 1985; as *Polyphemus and Galatea*, translated by Gilbert F. Cunningham, 1977; as *The Fable of Polyphemus and Galatea*, translated by Miroslav John Hanak, 1988.

Romance de 'Angélica y Medoro', edited by Dámaso Alonso. 1962.

Sonetos completos, edited by Biruté Ciplijauskaité. 1969.

Romances (selection), edited by José María de Cossno. 1980.

Las firmezas de Isabela, edited by Robert Jammes. 1984.

Fábula de Píramo y Tisbe, edited by David Garrison. 1985.

Cuadernos de varias poesías, manuscrito palentino, edited by Lorenzo Rubio González. 1985.

*

Critical Studies: *The Metaphors of Góngora* by E.J. Gates, 1933; *Góngora* by D.W. and V.R. Foster, 1973; *Góngora: Polyphemus and Galatea: A Study in the Interpretation of a Baroque Poem* (includes text and translation by Gilbert F. Cunningham) by Alexander A. Parker, 1977; *The Poet and the Natural World in the Age of Góngora* by M.J. Woods, 1978; *Aspects of Góngora's 'Soledades'* by John R. Beverley, 1980; *The Sonnets of Luis de Góngora* by R.P. Calcraft, 1980; *Góngora's Poetic Textual Tradition: An Analysis of Selected Variants, Versions, and Imitations of His Shorter Poems* by Diane Chaffee-Sorace, 1988.

* * *

Luis de Góngora was a remarkable poet who made a significant contribution in a variety of poetic fields, expanding the range of poetry by his conception of the ballad as a more sophisticated, artistically balanced form than was traditional, by his promotion of the burlesque as a valid artistic form, and, in the case of his most famous major poem, *Soledades* (*The Solitudes*), by creating a work that not only did not fit into any recognized genre, but also had a dazzling stylistic novelty.

Having already acquired a reputation as a writer of fine sonnets and ballads from the publication of a number of his poems in a general anthology in 1605, Góngora in his native Andalusia dreamed of making a career for himself at the court in Madrid. Hence in 1614 copies of his *Solitudes* and his *Polifemo y Galatea* (*Polyphemus and Galatea*), major poems he had recently completed, were being circulated at court and caused a major literary controversy which centred upon the original and exceptionally difficult style in which they were written. There was a spate of letters, pamphlets, and poems attacking and defending Góngora. Although he never achieved the patronage he sought, he attracted many imitators, and detailed explanatory commentaries of his works were published later in the century.

The features of Góngora's style attracting comment were his use of neologisms (so-called *cultismos*), his liberties with syntax, particularly word-order, and frequency and complexity of his metaphors. But it is misleading to portray Góngora's novelty as merely stylistic, a question of mode of expression rather than of what was being said. Thematically, the major poems give a novel prominence to the world of nature. With his *Polyphemus and Galatea*, which re-tells the story found in Ovid's *Metamorphoses* of the giant Polyphemus' love for Galatea and his enraged killing of her lover, Acis, despite the importance that Góngora gives the

rural Sicilian setting we still have basically a narrative poem. But in his *Solitudes*, of which there are two of an originally planned four, the second being unfinished, we have basically a descriptive poem, which is in itself a novelty. Góngora shows the hospitality offered by a rustic community to a shipwrecked young courtier, presenting their way of life and the environment in which they live in an enthusiastic way. When we consider Góngora's use of metaphor as a means of presenting this positive vision, again it is clear that we are dealing with a mode of thought, not merely one of speech. It is through metaphor that he draws attention to surprising patterns and relationships in the world, inviting us to wonder at them. Hence, when he calls the sea 'a Lybia of waves', he invites us to consider the parallels between desert and sea, their common vastness and inhospitability, dunes mirroring waves, and at the same time surprises us by describing the extremely wet in terms of the extremely dry. Through such explorations of relationships Góngora reveals himself as a major exponent of wit.

—M.J. Woods

GOR'KII, Maksim [Maxim Gorky]. Born Alexei Maksimovich Peshkov, in Nizhnyi Novgorod, Russia, 16 March 1868. Educated in parish school, Nizhnyi Novgorod; Kumavino elementary school, 1877–78. Married Ekaterina Pavlovna Volzhina in 1896 (separated); one son and one daughter. Apprenticed to a shoemaker at age 11; then draughtsman's clerk and cook's boy on a Volga steamer; from 1888, associated with revolutionary politics: first arrest, 1889; travelled on foot through much of Russia; began publishing in prominent journals by the mid-1890s; member of publishing co-operative Knowledge, and literary editor, *Zhizn'* [Life], St Petersburg, from 1899; worked for the publishing house Znanie, 1900, and was subsequently its leading editor; exiled to Arzamas, central Russia, for involvement with a covert printing press, 1901; joined the Bolshevik Party, 1905; travelled to the USA, 1906; lived in Capri, 1906–13; set up revolutionary propaganda school, 1909; returned to Russia after general amnesty, 1913: founding editor, *Letopis'* [Chronicles] magazine, 1915–17, and newspaper *Novaia Zhizn'* [New Life], 1917–18; established publishing house Vsemirnaia Literatura [World Literature]; involved in Petrograd Workers and Soldiers Soviet; left Russia in 1921: editor, *Dialogue*, Berlin, 1923–25, and in Sorrento during most of 1924–32; editor, *Literary Apprenticeship* magazine, 1930; returned to Russia permanently in 1933: helped set up the Biblioteka Poeta [Poet's Library] publishing project; travelled widely throughout USSR, took a leading role at the All-Union Congress of Soviet Writers, 1934, and was associated with the implementation of Socialist Realism as the artistic orthodoxy. Recipient: Order of Lenin, 1932. Gor'kii Literary Institute established in his honour. *Died 18 June 1936.*

PUBLICATIONS

Collections

Selected Works, translated by Margaret Wettlin and others. 2 vols., 1948.

Polnoe sobranie sochinenii: Khudozhestvennaia literatura [Complete Collected Works]. 25 vols., 1968–76.

Collected Works. 10 vols., 1978–83.

Sobranie sochinenii [Collected Works], edited by N.N. Zhegalov. 16 vols., 1979.

Sobranie sochinenii [Collected Works], edited by S.A. Nebol'shim. 8 vols., 1987.

Sobranie sochinenii [Collected Works], edited by A.I. Ovcharenko. 12 vols., 1987.

Collected Short Stories, edited by Avrahm Yarmolinsky and Moura Budberg. 1988.

Plays

Meshchane (produced 1902). 1902; as *The Smug Citizens*, translated by Edwin Hopkins, 1906; as *The Courageous One*, translated by M. Goldina and H. Choat, 1958; as *The Petty Bourgeois*, in *Collected Works 4*, 1979.

Na dne (produced 1902). 1903; as *A Night's Lodging*, translated by Edwin Hopkins, in *Poet Lore*, 16, 1905; as *The Lower Depths*, translated by L. Irving, 1912; also translated by Alexander Bakshy with Paul S. Nathan, in *Seven Plays*, 1945, Moura Budberg, 1959, Margaret Wettlin, in *Five Plays*, 1959, David Magarshack, in *The Storm and Other Russian Plays*, 1960, Andrew R. MacAndrew, in *Twentieth Century Russian Drama*, 1963, and Kitty H. Blair and Jeremy Brooks, 1973; as *Submerged*, translated by Edwin Hopkins, 1914; as *At the Bottom*, translated by W. Laurence, 1930; as *Down and Out*, translated by G.R. Noyes and Alexander Kaun, in *Masterpieces of the Russian Drama*, edited by Noyes, 1933.

Dachniki (produced 1904). 1904; as *Summerfolk*, translated by A. Delano, in *Poet Lore*, 16, 1905; also translated by Kitty H. Blair and Jeremy Brooks, in *Five Plays*, 1988.

Varvary. 1905; as *Barbarians*, translated by Alexander Bakshy with Paul S. Nathan, in *Seven Plays*, 1945; also translated by Kitty H. Blair and Jeremy Brooks, in *Five Plays*, 1988; as *Philistines*, translated by Dusty Hughes, 1986.

Deti solntsa. 1905; as *Children of the Sun*, translated by John Wolfe, 1906; also translated by Kitty H. Blair and Jeremy Brooks, in *Five Plays*, 1988.

Vragi (produced 1907). 1906; as *Enemies*, translated by Alexander Bakshy with Paul S. Nathan, in *Seven Plays*, 1945; also translated by Kitty H. Blair and Jeremy Brooks, 1972.

Poslednie [The Last Ones] (produced 1908). 1908.

Vassa Zheleznova (produced 1911). 1910; revised version, 1935; as *Vassa Zheleznova*, translated by Alexander Bakshy with Paul S. Nathan, in *Seven Plays*, 1945.

Vstrecha [The Meeting] (produced 1910). 1910.

Chudaki. 1910; as *Queer People*, translated by Alexander Bakshy with Paul S. Nathan, in *Seven Plays*, 1945.

Zykovy. 1913; as *The Zykovs*, translated by Alexander Bakshy with Paul S. Nathan, in *Seven Plays*, 1945.

Starik (produced 1919). 1918; as *The Judge*, translated by M. Zakhrevsky and B.H. Clark, 1924; as *The Old Man*, translated by Margaret Wettlin, 1956.

Somov i drugie [Somov and Others]. 1931.

Egor Bulychov i drugie (produced 1932). 1932; as *Yegor Bulichoff and Others*, translated by W.L. Gibson-Cowan, in *The Last Plays*, 1937; as *Yegor Bulychov and the Others*, translated by Alexander Bakshy with Paul S. Nathan, in *Seven Plays*, 1945.

Dostigaev i drugie (produced 1934). 1933; as *Dostigaeff and the Others*, translated by W.L. Gibson-Cowan, in *The Last Plays*, 1937.

The Last Plays (includes *Yegor Bulichoff and Others*; *Dostigaeff and the Others*), translated by W.L. Gibson-Cowan. 1937.

Seven Plays (includes *Barbarians*; *Enemies*; *Vassa Zheleznova*; *The Lower Depths*; *Queer People*; *The Zykovs*; *Yegor Bulychov and Others*), translated by Alexander Bakshy with Paul S. Nathan. 1945.

Five Plays (includes *The Petty Bourgeois*; *Philistines*; *The Lower Depths*; *Summerfolk*; *Enemies*), translated by Margaret Wettlin. 1956.

The Lower Depths and Other Plays, translated by Alexander Bakshy and Paul S. Nathan. 1959.

Five Plays (includes *The Lower Depths*; *Summerfolk*; *Children of the Sun*; *Barbarians*; *Enemies*), translated by Kitty H. Blair and Jeremy Brooks. 1988.

Fiction

Ocherki i rasskazy (stories). 3 vols., 1898–99; in part as *Tales*, translated by R. Bain, 1902.

Foma Gordeev. 1899; as *Foma Gordeyev*, translated by Herman Bernstein, 1901; also translated by Margaret Wettlin, 1956; as *The Man Who Was Afraid*, translated by Bernstein, 1905; as *Foma*, 1945.

Troe. 1900; as *Three of Them*, translated by Alexandra Linden, 1902; as *Three Men*, translated by Charles Horne, 1902; also translated by A. Frumkin, 1919; as *The Three*, translated by Margaret Wettlin, 1958.

Orloff and His Wife: Tales of the Barefoot Brigade, translated by Isabel F. Hapgood. 1901.

The Orloff Couple, and Malva, translated by Emily Jankowleff and Dora B. Montefiore. 1901.

Tales, translated by R. Bain. 1902.

The Outcasts and Other Stories, translated by Dora B. Montefiore, Emily Jankowleff, and V. Volkhovsky. 1902.

Chelkash and Other Stories, translated by Emily Jankowleff and Dora B. Montefiore. 1902.

Twenty-Six Men and a Girl and Other Stories, translated by Dora B. Montefiore and Emily Jankowleff. 1902.

Twenty-Six and One and Other Stories, translated by I. Strannik. 1902.

Tales, translated by C. Alexandroff. 1903.

Mat'. 1906; as *Mother*, 1907; revised translation, by Isidor Schneider, 1947; as *Comrades*, 1907.

Zhizn' nenuzhnogo cheloveka. 1907–08; as *The Spy: The Story of a Superfluous Man*, translated by Thomas Seltzer, 1908; as *The Life of a Useless Man*, translated by Moura Budberg, 1971.

Ispoved'. 1908; as *A Confession*, translated by Frederick Harvey, 1910; as *The Confession*, translated by Rose Strunsky, n.d.

Gorodok Okurov [Okurov City]. 1909.

Leto [Summer]. 1909.

Zhizn' Matveia Kozhemiakina. 1910–11; as *The Life of Matvei Kozhemyakin*, translated by Margaret Wettlin, 1960.

Tales, translated by R. Nisbet Bain. 1912.

Tales of Two Countries. 1914.

Twenty-Six Men and a Girl and Other Stories, translated by S. Michel. 1915.

Stories of the Steppe, translated by H. Schnittkind and I. Goldberg. 1918.

Creatures That Once Were Men (stories), translated by J.M. Shirazi. 1918.

Delo Artamonovykh. 1925; as *Decadence*, translated by Veronica Dewey, 1927; as *The Artamonov Business*, translated by A. Brown, 1948; as *The Artamonovs*, translated by H. Altschuler, 1952.

The Story of a Novel and Other Stories, translated by M. Zakrevsky. 1925.

Zhizn' Klima Samgina [The Life of Klim Samgin] (unfinished). 1925–36; as *The Bystander, The Magnet, Other Fires*, and *The Spectre*, translated by Bernard Guilbert Bakshy, 4 vols., 1931–38.
Best Short Stories, edited and translated by Avrahm Yarmolinsky and Moura Budberg. 1939; as *A Book of Short Stories*, 1939.
Song of the Stormy Petrel and Other Short Stories, translated by M. Trommer. 1942.
Unrequited Love and Other Stories, translated by Moura Budberg. 1949.
Selected Short Stories 1892–1901, translated by Margaret Wettlin. 1954.
A Sky-Blue Life and Other Stories, translated by George Reavey. 1964.

Verse

Pesnia o Sokole. 1895; as *The Song of the Falcon*, translated by 'M.G.', 1896.
Chelovek. 1903; translated as *Man*, 1905.
Devushka i smert'[The Little Girl and Death]. 1917.

Other

A.P. Chekhov. 1905; as *Anton Tchekhov: Fragments of Recollections*, translated by S.S. Kotelianskii and Leonard Woolf, 1921.
Detstvo V liudiakh Moi universitety. 1913–22; as *My Childhood in the World [My Apprenticeship] My University Days [My Universities]*, 1915–23; as *Autobiography*, translated by Isidor Schneider, 1949; as *My Apprenticeship, My Childhood, My Universities*, translated by Ronald Wilks, 3 vols., 1966–79; *My Childhood* also translated by Gertrude M. Foakes, 1915, and as *Childhood*, by Margaret Wettlin, 1950, revised by Jessie Coulson, 1961.
Vospominaniia o Tolstom. 1919; as *Reminiscences of Tolstoi*, translated by S.S. Kotelianskii and Leonard Woolf, 1920.
Revoliutsiia i kul'tura [Revolution and Culture]. 1920.
O russkom krestianstve. 1922; translated as *On the Russian Peasantry*, 1976.
Zametki iz dnevnika. 1924; translated as *Fragments from My Diary*, 1924; also translated by Moura Budberg, 1972, revised edition, 1975.
V.I. Lenin. 1924; as *V.I. Lenin*, translated by C.W. Parker-Arkhangelskaya, 1931; as *Days with Lenin*, 1932.
O literature. 1933; revised edition, 1935, 1955; as *On Literature: Selected Articles*, translated by Julius Katzer and Ivy Litvinova, 1960.
On Guard for the Soviet Union. 1933.
Reminiscences of Tolstoy, Chekhov and Andreyev, translated by Katherine Mansfield, S.S. Kotelianskii, Virginia Woolf, and Leonard Woolf. 1934.
Culture and the People. 1940.
Creative Labour and Culture. 1945.
Literature and Life: A Selection from the Writings, edited and translated by Edith Bone. 1946.
History of the Civil War, translated by J. Fineberg. 1946.
Articles and Pamphlets. 1950.
Letters of Maxim Gor'kij to V.F. Xodasevič, 1922–1925, edited and translated by Hugh McLean, in *Harvard Slavonic Studies*, I. 1953.
F.I. Chaliapin. 2 vols., 1957–58; as *Chaliapin: An Autobiography*, edited and translated by Nina Froud and James Hanley, 1967.
Letters of Gorky and Andreev 1899–1912, edited by Peter Yershov, translated by Lydia Weston. 1958.

Letters, translated by P. Cockerell. 1966.
Nesvoyevremennye mysli. 1971; as *Untimely Thoughts*, edited and translated by Herman Ermolaev, 1968.
The City of the Yellow Devil: Pamphlets, Articles and Letters about America. 1972.
Rasskazy i povesti 1892–1917 (selection). 1976.
Perepiska M Gor'kogo (selected correspondence). 2 vols., 1986.
Gorky and His Contemporaries (letters), edited by Galina Belaya, translated by Cynthia Carlile. 1989.

Editor, *Belomor. An Account of the Construction of the New Canal Between the White Sea and the Baltic Sea*. 1935.

*

Bibliography: *Maxim Gorky in English: A Bibliography, 1868–1986* by Garth M. Terry, 1986; *Maxim Gorky: A Reference Guide* by Edith Clowes, 1987.

Critical Studies: *Maxim Gorky and His Russia* by Alexander Kaun, 1931; *The Young Maxim Gorky 1868–1902* by Filia Holtzman, 1948; *Maxim Gorky: Romantic Realist and Conservative Revolutionary* by Richard Hare, 1962; *Stormy Petrel: The Life and Work of Maxim Gorky* by Dan Levin, 1965; *Gorky: His Literary Development and Influence on Soviet Intellectual Life* by I. Weil, 1966; *Maxim Gorky, The Writer: An Interpretation* by F.M. Borras, 1967; *The Bridge and the Abyss: The Troubled Friendship of Maxim Gorky and V.I. Lenin* by Bertram D. Wolfe, 1967; *Maxim Gorky* by Gerhard E. Habermann, 1971; *Three Russians Consider America: America in the Works of Maksim Gor'kij, Aleksandr Blok, and Vladimir Mayakovskij* by Charles Rougle, 1976; *Maxim Gorky and the Literary Quests of the Twentieth Century* by A.I. Ovcharenko, 1985; *Maxim Gorky Fifty Years On: Gorky and His Time* edited by Nicholas Luker, 1987; *Maxim Gorky* by Barry P. Scherr, 1988; *Gorky and His Contemporaries: Memoirs and Letters* edited by Galina Belaya, 1989; *Gorky* by Henri Troyat, translated by Lowell Bair, 1989.

*   *   *

For many years Maksim Gor'kii was revered in the Soviet Union as the founder of Socialist Realism, the father of Soviet literature, and one of the greatest 20th-century writers. Critical opinion of him in the West was always more mixed, and since the collapse of the Soviet Union attitudes towards him in Russia have also evolved. The city of his birth and one of Moscow's largest streets, both once named in his honour, have reverted to their former designations. Even though his sometime differences with Bolshevik leaders rather than his statements on behalf of the Communist Party now receive more attention, he remains a writer for whom it is difficult to separate the literary and the non-literary achievements.

Before the revolution he was active both politically, as a supporter of revolutionary causes, and, among his fellow writers, as a leader of the so-called 'critical realists' and the organizer of various publishing enterprises. After the revolution his political connections enabled him to protect, aid, and encourage an entire generation of writers, at the same time that he was again instrumental in establishing major publication projects, some of which continue to the present day.

As a writer Gor'kii introduced or at least popularized many topics that had largely been ignored by 19th-century Russian writers. He drew upon his own experiences to depict the vagrants and social outcasts who were the main characters in many of his early stories, while his upbringing provided the material for graphic descriptions of Russia's merchant class and its emergent capitalists, many of whom, especially in the provinces, retained the superstitions and habits instilled by peasant backgrounds. His particular talent lay in his descriptive skills. He created unforgettable portraits of his main characters and also brought out vividly the most mundane details of their everyday lives. That ability, along with the exotic quality of his subject matter, was sufficient to ensure the near-instant fame that he achieved. On the other hand, his fiction was occasionally marred by faults that he never completely overcame: a political tendentiousness that sometimes led to exaggeration and overly broad generalizations, the appearance of florid passages and lack of simplicity in his style, and difficulty in creating narratives with sufficient drama and cohesiveness to serve as vehicles for the characters he created.

This last feature of his writing perhaps explains why he achieved mixed success with his novels and plays but had more consistent results with his short stories and, particularly, his autobiographical writings and memoirs. In early stories such as 'Chelkash' (1894) and 'Konovalov' (1896) the single vagrant figure predominates and is sufficient to hold the reader's interest throughout. Further, since Gor'kii's vagrants turn out to originate from widely divergent classes, they possess sufficient variety so that the stories as a group do not become repetitive. Also notable among his stories is 'Dvadstat' shest' i odna' ('Twenty-Six Men and a Girl'), in which Gor'kii offers a concise and powerful treatment of a theme that was to be important for much of his subsequent work: the need for many people, especially those who have virtually nothing, to create illusions to sustain themselves, and the ease with which those illusions may be destroyed. The novels too are most notable for their central figures, as well as for the social milieu that Gor'kii depicts with his customary skill and knowledge. In this genre, though, Gor'kii's problems with narrative are particularly telling. Typical are *Foma Gordeev*, in which the title character rejects the merchant-class society into which he is born, and *Mat'* (*Mother*), which passionately describes the birth of a revolutionary consciousness in the mother of an imprisoned worker and which is regarded by Soviet critics as a model work for what became known as Socialist Realism. In both instances the introduction of fascinating characters dominates the first third or so of the work, but the action then becomes diffuse until the concluding pages.

Gor'kii's last novels could all be classsified as chronicles, in which the recording of social and political events comes to take precedence over dramatic narrative. If the title character in *Zhizn' Matveia Kozhemiakina* (*The Life of Matvei Kozhemyakin*) at least remains in the centre of the action, then in *Delo Artamonovykh* (*The Artamonov Business*) the focus is more on how generational changes are reflected in the rise and fall of a family dynasty during the years leading up to the Bolshevik Revolution. Gor'kii's final novel, *Zhizn' Klima Samgina* [The Life of Klim Samgin], remained unfinished at his death; it consists of four large volumes, each of which has a separate title in the English translation. Here he again reverts to tracing the life of a single individual, but Gor'kii's real interest lies elsewhere: epic in scope and filled with historical figures and events, the novel represents an attempt to portray intellectual and political developments in Russian life during the 40 years that culminated in the overthrow of the old regime in 1917.

Remarkably, Gor'kii created his best play with only his second effort as a dramatist, *Na dne* (*The Lower Depths*). The play lacks any single predominant figure, but its collection of cast-offs, who seem to be refugees from several of his early stories, offers originality and dramatic interaction that more than compensate for the lack of a strong plot. In other plays of this type the static quality of Gor'kii's writing tends to undercut his efforts, though he still succeeds in those plays that are dominated by a strong figure, such as *Egor Bulychov i drugie* (*Yegor Bulichoff and Others*). In more recent years Gor'kii's plays have enjoyed renewed interest in both England and North America, with stagings of both these works as well as *Dachniki* (*Summerfolk*) and *Vragi* (*Enemies*). However, Gor'kii's best writing occurred when he was writing directly about himself or about those whom he knew intimately. At such moments he was able to give full vent to his descriptive abilities at the same time that the necessity to invent a plot was removed. The brilliant portrayal of his grandparents in his *Detstvo* (*My Childhood*) and the skilful capturing of the complexities and contradictions exhibited by a great writer in his memoir devoted to Tolstoi are typical of the qualities that make Gor'kii's autobiography and various reminiscences his major contributions to world literature.

—Barry P. Scherr

THE LOWER DEPTHS (Na dne)
Play by Maksim Gor'kii, 1902.

Of the more than one dozen plays that Gor'kii wrote, it is his second, *The Lower Depths*, that remains not just the most widely performed of his dramatic pieces, but also the single work that is most responsible for his literary reputation outside Russia. Like Gor'kii's first play, *Meshchane* (*The Petty Bourgeois*), it had its premiere at Stanislavskii's Moscow Art Theatre, which was also the first theatre to do justice to Chekhov's talent. The cast for the first performance included some of the finest actors in Russia: Ivan Moskvin played Luka, Vasilii Kachalov the Baron, and Olga Knipper (Chekhov's wife) had the role of Nastia. Stanislavskii himself took the part of Satin and later was to comment on the difficulty he had with the role as well as on the play's tumultuous reception.

Lacking a single dominant figure (or, more precisely, shifting from one key figure to the next), containing several structural flaws, and with a plot that is of only minor interest, *The Lower Depths* at first glance seems a surprising candidate for literary immortality. However, the very contrast with *The Petty Bourgeois* does much to explain the work's popularity with audiences. Gor'kii's first play is largely Chekhovian in its setting, in its types of characters, and in the atmosphere that envelops the action; indeed, several of the figures and incidents have direct parallels in *Tri sestry* (*The Three Sisters*). In *The Lower Depths*, however, Gor'kii—interestingly, for the only time in all of his plays—turns to the milieu that originally brought him fame as a writer of short stories. This is the world of the *bosiak* or vagabond, he who by choice or circumstance finds himself outside society. Gor'kii's vagabonds embrace a wide range of figures: some come from the lower classes, some are well-educated and know a better life; many are submissive before blows that life has dealt them, but others have made a firm decision to break with their past life and the social order. The more heroic of these characters may seem romanticized, but Gor'kii was the first to explore in detail a world of which most Russians had only been vaguely aware.

One of Gor'kii's strengths in all his writings is his ability to sketch characters quickly and memorably. Here the setting is a lower-class lodging, with both long-term residents who have sunk as low as they can (the literal meaning of the Russian title is 'on the bottom') and others who pass through. For the most part the action is confined to a dank basement, lit by only a single window—thus an early title for the work was 'Without Sunlight'. Within this dreary world virtually every figure, both major and minor, is in some way memorable. There is the Baron, a person proud of his noble background and of his family's possessions, who professes a love for the truth and who attacks the dreams of others. He, however, in turn falls apart when his own vision of the better life that he presumably once lived is attacked as a lie. Vasilisa, along with her husband, the building's owner, beats her own sister, Natasha, who has plotted to run off to what she imagines would be a better life with the thief Pepel (who also happens to have been Vasilisa's lover). Nastia, a prostitute, escapes into the world of the romantic novels that she reads and tries to comfort others with her vision of a better life. Also prone to dreams is the Actor, who, like the Baron, has lost his real name and who appears to have dropped down the social rank. In contrast to some of the other characters in the play, he has never come to terms with his failure, and, at the end of the play, when he realizes the hopelessness of his yearnings, he hangs himself.

Also contributing to the play's success are the ideas expressed by two figures who are at its thematic centre even if Gor'kii never quite manages to work them fully into the plot. Luka, a wanderer who has only stopped by at the lodging, is prominent during the first three acts, while the fourth act contains a long monologue by Satin, a card sharp who has killed a man and has served time in prison. Luka tries to comfort others, encouraging Pepel in his desire to run off to Siberia, comforting a dying woman, and telling the Actor that there is a place where his drunkenness can be cured. Satin, like Luka, wants to help people, but he prefers a world without illusions: he wants people to confront the truth and feels that people can triumph over everything. It is he who utters one of Gor'kii's most quoted lines: 'M-a-n! The word is magnificent; there's a proud ring to it! A man has to be respected! Not pitied . . .'.

In commenting on his play, Gor'kii himself later expressed a strong preference for Satin; Luka, he felt, offered only the consoling lie. That many have identified instead with Luka could be seen as a failing, as could the action of the last act, where, as Chekhov himself was the first to note, nearly all the important characters of the first three acts are absent. The latter is indeed a dramatic weakness—only the startling suicide of the Actor after Satin's long monologue imparts an emotional impact to the finale. And the play as a whole has sometimes been criticized as one of the works which make those living in the West believe that even uneducated Russians sit around in the evenings philosophizing about the meaning of life.

However, in posing the conflicts that lie at the heart of his play—between the soothing if possibly harmful lie and the harsh if possibly liberating truth, between the dreams that enable people to cope with the severity of their lives and the danger that those very dreams will leave them passive— Gor'kii has expressed irresolvable dilemmas with which audiences around the world have been able to identify. Dramatists, meanwhile, would appear to have learned from the play's seemingly chaotic structure. Such subsequent works as Eugene O'Neill's *The Iceman Cometh* and William Saroyan's *The Time of Your Life* employ the device of throwing together varied characters, some only tangentially related to the plot, and place an emphasis on self-revelation rather than on dramatic resolution. A few of Gor'kii's later plays are technically more perfect, but none matches *The Lower Depths* for originality of form or emotional impact.

—Barry P. Scherr

TWENTY-SIX MEN AND A GIRL (Dvadstat' shest' i odna')
Story by Maksim Gor'kii, 1899.

Gor'kii first achieved renown through his stories of the 1890s, among which 'Twenty-Six Men and a Girl' is widely regarded as his most impressive achievement. The tightly structured narrative, highly evocative setting, and striking imagery richly support the subtly stated and perhaps surprising theme—the relationship of the individual to the group. It is the first of these characteristics that is perhaps most responsible for the artistic quality of 'Twenty-Six Men and a Girl'; similar narrative structures appear elsewhere in Gor'kii, and the work's theme, while rarely stated quite so effectively, is also not unique to this story. However, in most of his shorter tales, as in his novels, Gor'kii's descriptive abilities rather than the narrative thrust serve to hold the reader's interest; the juxtaposition of scenes is more important than plot. Here the story-line, while simple, none the less contains several surprising elements which effectively highlight the ideas that Gor'kii is attempting to convey.

The title in Russian is more concise: 'Twenty-Six and One', with the feminine ending of the last word conveying the point that the 'One' is female. The story is set in Kazan', where Gor'kii himself lived and worked in the mid-1880s, during the latter part of his teenage years. Gor'kii was to document his Kazan' years in several stories as well as in *My Universities*, the third part of his autobiographical trilogy—indeed, the first-person narrative also imparts an autobiographical cast to 'Twenty-Six Men and a Girl'. His continued interest in this period is understandable, for it was then that he first became associated with revolutionary circles and held his first adult jobs, experiencing directly the life of those at the bottom of society.

It is this latter aspect of his experience that dominates the opening pages of the story and imparts to the work as a whole a sense of genuineness and immediacy. The locale of the story is a pretzel bakery in which Gor'kii himself worked, and in a few detailed paragraphs he manages to convey the dreary and oppressive nature of the toil. Although the working day begins at six in the morning and does not end until ten at night, the long hours are less burdensome than the conditions in which the 26 find themselves. The bakery occupies one room in a stuffy yet damp basement; a bit of light (but no sun) filters in through grated windows that look out onto slime-covered bricks. The air is thick with dust, the walls covered with dirt and mould.

The story deals with Tania, a 16-year-old maidservant who works in a shop located on the second floor of the building. Each morning she stops by the bakery, bringing a bit of joy to the men's lives with her mere presence. One day a new worker, an ex-soldier who thinks himself especially attractive to women, arrives to work in the next-door bakery; it is owned by the same person, but just four people work there in much better conditions baking rolls. The former soldier, in talking to the pretzel makers, describes how the women who work upstairs literally fight over him. One of the 26 confronts him, claiming that their Tania would not be so easy to attract.

The newcomer accepts the challenge, and promises that he will win Tania over within two weeks. The men nervously observe Tania each morning, fearful of what will happen. As it turns out, Tania succumbs, and the men surround her when she leaves for her rendezvous with the new worker. They are angry with her for betraying the faith they had in her; for her part, she contemptuously shouts back at them and walks off, never to return.

Complementing the powerful descriptions and the spare story line is the effective use of imagery. Critics have noted that the enormous oven dominating the pretzel bakery bears traits of a cruel pagan deity; Tania herself could be seen as an idol to whom the 'worshippers' bring tribute. Although most of the story takes place within the bakery, Gor'kii manages to make effective use of the world 'inside' and that 'outside', where the 26 seem to be on alien territory. Equally telling is the contrast between the world above, that of Tania, and the world below, where the men dwell. Even when she comes for her visits, she remains above the men, staying at the threshold several steps above the basement floor. Her world is both higher and unattainable.

That Tania should not live up to the men's expectations is perhaps less surprising than the way in which Gor'kii uses the plot to introduce an unexpected theme. For ultimately the story reveals both Gor'kii's revolutionary sympathies as well as his belief that people need to have faith in themselves, and not in others. The anonymous first-person narrator uses 'we' and does not single himself out among the '26'; strength is to be found in the collective and not in the individual. The story turns out to be less about Tania's downfall than the men's (temporary) worship of an idol and failure to see the inner strength that they in fact possess. They give her free pretzels and even do small chores for her, but when one of them dares to ask her to repair his only shirt, she contemptuously turns him down. She is simply an ordinary, somewhat self-centred 16-year-old, basking in the attention of others; her fall may startle her admirers, but it is only the logical outcome of the test to which they put the false idol in which they have come to believe. Gor'kii's point is that their interest in Tania has turned the men away from themselves and from the inner strength that they do possess. Early in the story he describes their singing: 'All 26 would sing; the loud, well-rehearsed voices would fill the shop, which was too small for the song. It would strike against the stone walls, moan, cry, and revive our hearts with a gentle, tingling ache, re-opening old wounds and awakening longings'. The spirit of the song, in which the '26' become one, gives them the fortitude to get through each day and to retain their sense of humanity. Thus, Gor'kii implies, the true ideal resides in oneself and within the group to which the individual belongs; seeking salvation in others will only lead people astray.

—Barry P. Scherr

GORKY, Maxim. See **GOR'KII, Maksim.**

GOTTFRIED von Strassburg. Active in Alsace, possibly at the episcopal court in Strasbourg, in the years around 1200.

PUBLICATIONS

Verse

Tristan, edited by Friedrich Ranke. 1930, also edited by Rüdiger Krohn, 1981; as *Tristan und Isolde*, edited by Reinhold Bechstein, revised by P.F. Ganz, 1978, also edited by Hermann Kurtz and Wolfgang Mohr, 1979; as *Tristan and Isolde*, translated by Edwin H. Zeydel, 1948; as *Tristan*, translated by A.T. Hatto, 1960; a shortened version, as *The Story of Tristan and Iseult*, translated by Jessie L. Weston, 1899.

*

Bibliography: *Bibliographie zu Gottfried von Strassburg*, 1971, and *Bibliographie zu Gottfried von Strassburg, II, Berichtszeitraum 1971–1983*, 1986, both by Hans H. Steinhoff.

Critical Studies: *Gottfried von Strassburg* by Michael S. Bates, 1971; *The Anatomy of Love: The 'Tristan' of Gottfried* by W.T.H. Jackson, 1971; *A History of Tristan Scholarship* by Rosemary Picozzi, 1971; *The Tristan of Gottfried von Strassburg: An Ironic Perspective* by Ruth Goldsmith Kunzer, 1973; *The Poetics of Conversion: Number Symbolism and Alchemy in Gottfried's 'Tristan'* by Susan L. Clark and Julian N. Wasserman, 1977; *Medieval Humanism in Gottfried's Tristan und Isolde* by C. Stephen Jaeger, 1977; *Gottfried's Tristan: Journey Through the Realm of Eros* by Hugo Bekker, 1987; *Gottfried von Strassburg and the Medieval Tristan Legend: Papers from an Anglo-American Symposium* edited by Adrian Stevens and Roy Wisbey, 1990; *Tristan in the Underworld: A Study of Gottfried von Strassburg's 'Tristan' Together with the 'Tristran' of Thomas* by Neil Thomas, 1991.

* * *

In the flourishing of courtly literature in Germany around 1200 Gottfried von Strassburg must be counted among the most profound narrative poets, and certainly the most enigmatic. Of his life nothing is known but his name and designation; he did work in Alsace, but his social position, whether aristocratic or bourgeois, cannot be determined, although the latter seems most likely; nor any patron identified. Manifestly he enjoyed a clerical education, but his attitude towards the chivalric culture of aristocracy and in manners of religion remains elusive. His courtly romance *Tristan*, the supreme poetic account of the ill-fated lovers Tristan and Isolde at the court of Marke, king of Cornwall, remains incomplete, and breaks off (probably because of Gottfried's death) at v. 19 548. Running through this romance are complex strands of reflection and commentary on matters literary, social, ethical, and religious which render difficult any unitary interpretation according to customary categories.

Tristan, a romance in rhymed couplets, shows Gottfried's sovereign command of Latin poetics and vernacular narrative techniques, within the traditions of clerical historical writing. The stylistic richness of the work's verbal figures matches the dialectic artistry with which the story unfolds its model of a love-force which transforms human existence, and the poem gives a masterful presentation of the social and aesthetic functions of courtly ceremony.

Contemporary literary references indicate that Gottfried's romance was composed between 1200 and 1220. It is recorded in a strong, early tradition from the 13th century, with 11 manuscripts complete (to the break-off point) and 16 fragments. Later poets, Ulrich von Türheim and Heinrich von Freiberg wrote continuations, praising Gottfried warmly.

The Tristan story has its origins in the Celtic realism of the heroic age in Britain in the fourth to sixth centuries, but the relation of Celtic myth to medieval romance is elusive. No extant insular text gives definite information about the early shaping of the legend, and its literary origins are to be found rather in the early continental texts of Brittany and France. Gottfried presents in general the adventure-sequences familiar in diverse European Tristan texts since the late 12th century, including a German version by Eilhart von Oberge (usually dated 1170–75). He claims to follow specifically the account of Thomas of Brittany, whose extant text, dated between 1155 and 1190, while fragmentary, in essence complements the unfinished German work in a most valuable way: its significance in the interpretation of Gottfried's poem is debated. Gottfried himself insists on the authenticity of his source as guarantee of the moral truth and validity of his work in contrast to that of disreputable minstrels. Such professional polemic underlies, too, his important literary review of contemporary German courtly poets, including Hartmann von Aue and Heinrich von Veldeke, Wolfram von Eschenbach (whom he does not name) and Walther von der Vogelweide.

Tristan is born the orphan son of Riwalin and Blanchefleur, his story a variant of the widespread theme of the Fair Unknown; the tragic love of Tristan's parents anticipates the entanglements of his own love for Isolde, who is his queen and the wife of his uncle, when the two, joined by mischance through a love potion, feel driven to abuse the bonds of court, society, and religion in order to nurture their illicit love. After episodes of mounting hazard and bold deception Tristan finally succumbs to the contradictions of his plight and flees the court, vainly seeking solace for his psychological torment in the company of another Isolde.

In contrast to the protagonist of Arthurian romance, Tristan does not develop through experience towards maturity. From the outset he displays his consummate skill in every sphere of chivalric life and culture; frequently he assumes the role of *spilman* (entertainer), and deceptions play a major role in the narrative. Tristan's artistic accomplishments serve in a sense to indicate his status as outsider in the courtly world, for he avails himself constantly of a certain independence from norms that pertain to those who are fully integrated into society. Hand in hand with this aesthetic orientation is his indifference to martial values (despite, of course, his mastery of arms and strategy). Often the events reflect material familiar from medieval fabliaux, comic tales which reward cunning and delight in the bawdy and irreverent. The many episodes are linked in a tectonic pattern of analogies and contrasts which reflect the mystical, paradoxical power of the love that dominates the romance.

Indeed, high ideals are Gottfried's constant concern in this narrative which deals with the conflict between the individual and society. In numerous reflective passages the poet probes chivalric aristocratic society, its military ethos, its values, and its use of religion (in, for example, a blatant piece of trickery which serves as critique of trial by ordeal). In episodes which focus upon the vacillating insensitivity of Marke, the all-too-human centre of social authority in this fictional world, he explores the implications for feudal society of unregulated love. Through the use of allegory (in the introduction and the Cave of Lovers, where in a cathedral-like natural setting the couple finds a paradisal bliss outside of society which is short-lived) he postulates a mystical community of *edele herzen* (noble hearts) who embody the power of this fateful love. Gottfried addresses himself to this elite audience of 'noble hearts' who alone are culturally and ethically capable of apprehending the nature of the love which is depicted in the romance as an overwhelming, paradoxical force. This passionate love, absolute and compulsive, is in flagrant conflict with the normal standards of law, religion, and ethics. Through its dialectic of *liebe unde leit* (the joy and suffering of love), this love force raises the exceptional individual to an autonomy beyond the social constraints which encompass human beings in medieval courtly society, but it leads finally to self-loss and death. The poet's attitude to this love is imparted in subtle allusion and demands discerning critical analysis: the love of Tristan and Isolde may briefly defy society in their moments of aesthetic and erotic fulfilment, which give listeners to their tale great solace, but the lovers must in the end experience bitter deprivation. Gottfried's romance is perhaps the most radical exploration of the potential of the individual in medieval literature.

—Lewis Jillings

GOTTHELF, Jeremias. Born Albert Bitzius in Murten, Switzerland, 4 October 1797. Studied theology at Berne Academy, 1814–20; Göttingen University, for one year. Married Henriette Elisabeth Zeender in 1833. Ordained in 1820; curate, Utzenstorf, 1820, and 1822–24; Herzongenbuchsee, 1824–29, transferred to Berne, 1829–31; pastor, Lützelflüh, Emmental, 1832; school commissioner and founder of educational institute for poor boys, 1835–45. Suffered from heart disease, apoplexy, and dropsy in the 1850s. *Died 22 October 1854.*

PUBLICATIONS

Collections

Gesammelte Schriften. 24 vols., 1856–58.
Ausgewählte Erzählungen, edited by Adolf Bartels. 4 vols., 1907.
Sämtliche Werke, edited by Rudolph Hunziker and Hans Bloesch. 24 vols., 1911–59.
Werke, edited by Walter Muschg. 20 vols., 1948–53.
Werke, edited by Henri Poschmann. 1971.
Schwänke und Witze, edited by Eduard Strübin. 1986.

Fiction

Der Bauernspiegel; oder, Lebensgeschichte des Jeremias Gotthelf. 1837; as *The Mirror of Peasants*, translated by Mary Augusta Ward, in *Macmillans Magazine*, 1883.
Wie fünf Mädchen im Branntwein jämmerlich umkamen. 1838.

Leiden und Freuden eines Schulmeisters. 1839; as *The Joys and Griefs of a National Schoolmaster*, translated by Mary Augusta Ward, in *Macmillans Magazine*, 1883; as *The Joys and Sorrows of a Schoolmaster*, 1864.

Dursli, der Brannteweinsäufer; oder, der Heilige Weih-nachtsabend. 1839.

Wie Uli der Knecht glücklich wird. 1841; as *Uli der Knecht*, 1846; as *Ulric the Farm-Servant*, translated by Julia Firth, 1866.

Ein Sylvester-Traum (stories). 1842.

Bilder und Sagen aus der Schweiz (stories). 6 vols., 1842–46.

Anne Bäbi Jowäger. 1843–44.

Geld und Geist; oder, die Versöhnung. 1843; as *Wealth and Welfare*, 1866; as *Soul and Money*, translated by Julia Guarterick Vere, 1872.

Eines Schweizers Wort an den Schweizerischen Schützenverein. 1844.

Wie Christen eine Frau gewinnt. 1845.

Der Gelstag; oder, Die Wirthschaft nach der neuen Mode. 1846.

Der Knabe des Tell. 1846.

Jakobs, des Handwerksgesellen, Wanderungen durch die Schweiz. 2 vols., 1846–48.

Käthi die Grossmutter. 1847; as *The Story of an Alpine Valley; or, Katie the Grandmother*, translated by L.G. Smith, 1896.

Hans Joggeli der Erbvetter. 1848.

Uli der Pächter. 1849.

Doctor Dorbach, der Wühler und die Bürglenherren in der heiligen Weihnachtsnacht Anno 1847. 1849.

Die Käserei in der Vehfreude. 1850.

Erzählungen und Bilder aus dem Volksleben der Schweiz. 1850–55.

Hans Jakob und Heiri; oder, die beiden Seidenweber. 1851.

Die Erbbase; oder, Freunde in der Not gehen hundert auf en Lot. 1851.

Zeitgeist und Berner Geist. 1852.

Der Patrizierspiegel. 1853.

Erlebnisse eines Schuldenbauers. 1854.

Das Erdbeeri Mareili. 1858.

Elsi, die seltsame Magd. 1858.

Die Schwarze Spinne. 1917; as *The Black Spider*, translated by Mary Hottinger, in *Nineteenth Century German Tales*, 1958; also translated by H.M. Waidson, 1958.

Der Schwarze Spinne und andere Erzählungen (stories). 1970.

Other

Bericht über Gemeinde Utzenstorf. 1824.

Benz am Weihnachtdonnstag. 1825.

Zum Bollodingeer Schulstreit. 1829.

Aufruf der Bürgerschaft von Bern an die Landschaft. 1830.

Bericht über die Schulen von Lützelflüh und das Erziehungsdepartment. 1832.

Bettagspredigt für die eidgenössischen Regenten, welche weder in den Kirchen noch in den Herzen den eidgenössischen Bettag mit den eidgenössischen Christen feiern. 1839.

Die Armennoth. 1840.

Verfasser ins Hochdeutsche übertragne Ausgabe. 1846.

Durchgesehene über mit einem Schlusskapitel vermehrte Aufl. 1851.

Jeremias Gotthelf und Karl Rudolf Hegenbach; ihr Briefwechsel aus den Jahren 1841 bis 1853, edited by Ferdinand Vetter. 1910.

Uzwil. 1923.

Langensalza. 1923.

Familienbriefe Jeremias Gotthelf, edited by Hedwig Wäber. 1929.

Donauwörth. 1931.

*

Bibliography: by Bee Juker and Giseal Martorelli, 1983.

Critical Study: *The Rural Novel: Jeremias Gotthelf, Thomas Hardy and C.R. Ramuz* by Michael H. Parkinson, 1984.

*   *   *

Jeremias Gotthelf was considered by Gottfried Keller an epic genius, and has come to be recognized as a great epic writer not only in German-speaking countries but worldwide. Ernst Alker, the German literary critic, even goes so far as to classify Gotthelf with Cervantes, Tolstoi, Dickens, and Homer. Alker considers Gotthelf more than a great novelist, seeing him as a man who created a new world in his poetical works. In his realism, Gotthelf is furthermore the forerunner of German naturalism as found in the latter half of the 19th century.

Gotthelf, who is often referred to as the classical writer of *Dorfgeschichten* and *Heimatkunst* or regional literature, actually belongs to the school of German realism. A Swiss Protestant pastor, he portrayed a narrow segment of his native Switzerland: the peasants of the Bernese hinterland, among whom he spent his entire life. Like his more famous contemporaries, Gotthelf attempted to portray real human beings with all their shortcomings and deficiencies. Gotthelf took his figures, as Dickens did, from definite walks of life, and specifically from the region he knew best, the Swiss *Bernbiet* (Bern region) with its farming population. He often wrote the dialogue in his novels in local dialect. Like Dickens too, Gotthelf had a weakness for moralizing; this is not surprising, since Gotthelf was greatly influenced by the teachings of his countryman, Johann Heinrick Pestalozzi, the Swiss educationist.

Education is one of the main themes in Gotthelf's first novel, *Der Bauernspiegel; oder, Lebensgeschichte des Jeremias Gotthelf* (*The Mirror of Peasants*). This novel was written in the form of a fictional autobiography and shows the development of a young orphan from farmers' helper to freelance writer. In this work, Gotthelf attacks social prejudice, drawing on his own experience of paupers' estab-lishments, and shows, through the character of the boy Jeremias, how poverty leads to crime. Jeremias is eventually saved from final degradation as a mercenary in a foreign army; yet on his return home, a changed man, he cannot find employment. It was Gotthelf's aim to open people's eyes to reality and to make the peasants in the canton of Berne aware of the social inequities within their parish. Gotthelf points the finger for these inequities and injustices not at a backward government but at man himself. Because of his indifference, his selfishness, his covetousness, and his lack of true Christian charity, man is his own enemy. The first part of the novel is vivid and forceful; the second part loses some of its *élan* and becomes somewhat theoretical.

The main impulse of Gotthelf's second work, *Leiden und Freuden eines Schulmeisters* (*The Joys and Sorrows of a Schoolmaster*) shows the resentment of Peter Kiser, a man who refused to be a mere puppet as a member of a local school board. Like *The Mirror of Peasants*, it is written in the first person; it describes, transcending time and place, the pandemonium of a provincial school system.

Following these two early works, Gotthelf depicted the

sunny side of peasant life in his novel *Uli der Knecht* (*Ulric the Farm-Servant*). It is a narrative in which Gotthelf shifts from first to third person narration, and becomes more objective and less didactic in his writing. Indeed, in this *Entwicklungsroman* (novel of character development), Gotthelf avoids all pedagogic tendencies and departs from the form of his first two novels. *Ulric the Farm-Servant* remains one of his most popular works, with its vivid characters and realistic detail, and eulogy of life on the land, the blessings of work, the triumph of the will, and purification through suffering. Here as elsewhere, Gotthelf is particularly successful in probing the depths of his female characters. He depicts village attitudes to marriage and pregnancy, drunkenness and duel fighting.

Uli der Pächter [Uli the Tenant], not a sequel to *Ulric the Farm-Servant*, is one of those stories in which Gotthelf could not refrain from sermonizing. Here Gotthelf revived the good old farmers' customs, and poured venom on those of his countrymen who aped foreign fashions or gave up their ancient religion. Neither did he spare the intellectuals, whether teachers, physicians, or even parsons, and his criticism was blunt. Gotthelf always bore in mind that his village readers would never accept evasive words.

Christian humility and moderation appear as dominant concerns in the novel *Hans Joggeli der Erbvetter* [Hans Joggeli the Inheritor]. In this work, Gotthelf steers a middle course between asceticism and worldliness. Again, as in so many of his novels, he reveals his fascination with man and especially with man's striving spiritual potential.

The most discussed and perhaps the greatest of Gotthelf's works is the novella *Die Schwarze Spinne* (*The Black Spider*). It presents a colourful picture of rural life, a banquet reminiscent of a Homeric idyll. But this humorous description of the present is soon interrupted by an eruption from the solemn past, as an old farmer tells the story of his family, which has achieved prosperity by fighting the black spider. This spider was the progeny of a woman who called upon the devil for help, and defaulted on her promise to repay him by sending him a soul. The vengeful spider had thereupon killed everyone and everything in its way until the pious farmer caught it and imprisoned it in a hole in a beam. If any generation became too arrogant, the spider would, once again, find its way to freedom. Thus, in mythical manner and without direct sermonizing, Gotthelf points to piety as the basis of the village's present prosperity. Inevitably the author's own vocation as a pastor and his Christian world-view led to allegorical interpretations of the story based on Catholic doctrine denying the full beatific vision to the unbaptized. Rationalist interpreters saw in the black spider an unenlightened stage in the progressive development of man. The influence of psychoanalysis led later critics to see the black spider as a female mother-symbol. Probably none of these allegorical or one-sided interpretations does justice to Gotthelf's poetic achievement. In broader terms, one can claim that in this work, Gotthelf depicts the world in a perilous situation. Mankind is constantly threatened. It is by no means established that evil is punished and good rewarded. So-called earthly justice is the work of fallible human hands. The devil can seize power in this world and the innocent are victimized along with the guilty. It seems to be a mystery of divine justice that only the sacrifice of the innocent has expiatory power. Gotthelf gains depth and perspective for his picture of well-to-do farmers by bringing in past crises and temptations. *The Black Spider* is short, but substantial and full of meaning. An entire nation is presented in its dependence on the heavenly powers, in a masterly story that has few equals.

Das Erdbeeri Mareili [Strawberry Mary] and *Elsi, die seltsame Magd* [Elsie, the Strange Farm Servant], are other masterpieces from Gotthelf's pen. Both are rooted in history and present the Swiss environment realistically. Gotthelf's work as a whole is proof of his love for the tiller of the soil and of his understanding of Swiss national particularities. Although he was inclined, at times, to sentimentalize rural life, the immediacy with which he describes it stands out in an age of emerging realism.

Over a span of 18 years, Gotthelf wrote more than 12 long novels and over 50 separate works; in the last years of his life he was swamped with requests for novels, short stories, and anecdotes for all manner of publications. In later life he also became increasingly concerned with politics, often to the detriment of the broad, flowing style of his novels. Gotthelf restricted himself to narrative fiction: he produced no rhymed poems or ballads and he scarcely considered writing a drama, though he was acquainted with the works of Schiller and Shakespeare. The stories of his maturity, particularly the shorter ones, show great skill in construction; their language is lively and full of vivid images, a blend of dialect forms and standard constructions, reflecting his desire to fuse the elevated world of the Bible with the real world of the canton of Berne and to make the many Bernese dialects serve the purposes of art.

—Brigitte Edith Zapp Archibald

GRABBE, Christian Dietrich. Born in Detmold, Westphalia, 11 December 1801. Educated at Gymnasium, Detmold; studied law at Leipzig University, 1820–22; and also in Berlin. Married Luise Clostermeier (separated). Attempted, unsuccessfully, to become an actor, 1823; established a legal practice in Detmold, 1824; military legal officer, 1826–34, resigning under pressure because of his dissolute lifestyle; quarrelled with Heinrich Heine, Ludwig Tieck, and Karl Immermann, losing their friendship and support; lived in Düsseldorf, 1835; contracted a spinal illness, and returned to Detmold. *Died 12 September 1836.*

PUBLICATIONS

Collections

Werke und Briefe, edited by Alfred Bergmann. 6 vols., 1960–73.
Werke, edited by Roy C. Cowen. 3 vols., 1975–77.

Plays

Herzog Theodor von Gothland (produced 1892). In *Dramatische Dichtungen*, 1827.
Scherz, Satire, Ironie und tiefere Bedeutung (produced 1876). In *Dramatische Dichtungen*, 1827; translated as *Comedy, Satire, Irony and Deeper Meaning*, 1955.
Marius und Sulla (produced 1936). In *Dramatische Dichtungen*, 1827.
Nannette und Maria (produced 1914). In *Dramatische Dichtungen*, 1827.
Dramatische Dichtungen. 2 vols., 1827.
Don Juan und Faust (produced 1829). 1829; translated 1963.

Die Hohenstaufen I: Kaiser Friedrich Barbarossa (produced 1875). 1829
Die Hohenstaufen II: Kaiser Heinrich der Sechste (produced 1875). 1830.
Napoleon; oder, Die hundert Tage (produced in a shortened version, 1869; complete version produced 1895). 1831.
Aschenbrödel (produced 1937). 1835.
Kosciuszko (incomplete; produced 1940). 1835.
Hannibal (produced 1918). 1835.
Die Hermannsschlacht (produced 1934). 1838

*

Bibliography: *Grabbe Bibliographie*, by Alfred Bergmann, 1973.

Critical Studies: *Grabbes Leben und Charakter* by Karl Ziegler, 1885, reprinted 1981; *Christian Dietrich Grabbe* by R. von Gottschall, 1901; *Christian Dietrich Grabbe: Sein Leben und seine Werke* by O. Nieten, 1908, reprinted 1978; *Die Glaubwürdigkeit der Zeugnisse für den Lebensgang und Charakter Christian Dietrich Grabbes*, 1933, and *Christian Dietrich Grabbe: Chronik seines Lebens*, 1954, both by Alfred Bergmann; *Grabbes Werke in der zeitgenössischen Kritik*, 6 vols., 1958–66, and *Grabbe in Berichten seiner Zeitgenossen*, 1968, both edited by Alfred Bergmann; *Grabbe: Glanz und Elend eines Dichters* by F. Böttger, 1963; *Idea and Reality in the Dramas of Christian Dietrich Grabbe* by A.W. Hornsey, 1966; *Christian Dietrich Grabbe* by W. Steffens, 1966, revised edition, 1972; *The Dramas of Christian Dietrich Grabbe* by R.A. Nicholls, 1969; *Grabbes Dramenformen* by W. Hegele, 1970; *Christian Dietrich Grabbe* by R.C. Cowen, 1972; *Deutung und Dokumentation: Studien zum Geschichtsdrama Christian Dietrich Grabbes*, 1973, and *Brecht und Grabbe: Rezeption eines dramatischen Erbes*, 1979, both by Hans-Werner Nieschmidt; *Destruktion und utopische Gemeinschaft. Zur Thematik und Dramaturgie des Heroischen im Werk Christian Dietrich Grabbes* by Manfred Schneider, 1973; *Grabbe-Studien* by Alfred Bergmann, 1977; *Byron und Grabbe: Ein geistesgeschichtlicher Vergleich* by Ulrich Wesche, 1978; *Grabbe und sein Verhältnis zur Tradition* by David Horton, 1980; *Geschichte und Gesellschaft in den Dramen Christian Dietrich Grabbes* by Detlev Kopp, 1982; *Christian Dietrich Grabbe: Leben, Werk, Wirkung* by Lothar Ehrlich, 1983; *Literaturrezeption und historische Krisenerfahrung: Die Rezeption der Dramen Christian Dietrich Grabbes 1827–1945* by M. Vogt, 1983; *Grabbe im Dritten Reich. Zum nationalsozialistischen Grabbe-Kult*, 1986, and *Christian Dietrich Grabbe: Ein Symposium*, 1987, both edited by W. Broer and W. Kopp; *Die Logik von Zerstörung und Grössenphantasie in den Dramen Christian Dietrich Grabbes* by Antonio Cortesi, 1986; *Christian Dietrich Grabbe: Leben und Werk* by Lothar Ehrlich, 1986; *Grabbes Gegenentwürfe: Neue Deutungen seiner Dramen* edited by W. Freund, 1986.

* * *

'What is to become of a person whose first memory is taking an old murderer for a walk in the open air?', Christian Dietrich Grabbe asked Karl Immermann in a reminiscence about his childhood. While the question, as usual with Grabbe, contained an overstatement of the truth, the answer is that he became one of Germany's major dramatists. He was described by Sigmund Freud as 'an original and rather

peculiar poet', by Heine as 'a drunken Shakespeare', and by Immermann as both 'a wild, ruined nature' and 'an outstanding talent'. Although the image of a flawed genius, which dogged Grabbe in his lifetime, still persists, the irregularities of his plays are now more often regarded as an integral part of their originality.

The only child of the local jailer, Grabbe felt oppressed and alienated in his provincial home town of Detmold where, as he wrote to Ludwig Tieck, 'an educated person is looked upon as an inferior kind of fattened ox' (letter of 29 August 1823). Physically sickly and emotionally unstable, swinging between sullen shyness and aggressive self-assertion, arrogantly demanding recognition but unwilling to please or to conform, uncouth in company, erratic in his post as army legal officer, entangled in a destructive marriage, and precipitating an early death by excessive drinking, he appeared as the archetype of the dissolute bohemian artist. While it is not clear how far his 'bizarreness' was natural or assumed in order to shock, the 'Grabbe legend' soon became confused with, and has often overshadowed, his work.

After his death, Grabbe was forgotten owing to the classical orientation of literary fashion, until later in the 19th century both nationalists and naturalists rediscovered him as a kindred spirit. In the 20th century, expressionists welcomed him as a fellow-outcast from bourgeois society, dadaists and surrealists acclaimed him as another rebel against rationality, the Nazis celebrated him as a champion of 'blood and soil', and Brecht placed him alongside J.M.R. Lenz and Georg Büchner in the 'non-Aristotelian' strain leading from the Elizabethans to his own Marxist epic theatre. On the German stage he was first adopted in the 1870s, revived in the early 1920s and late 1930s, and finally included in the standard repertory—chiefly with *Scherz, Satire, Ironie und tiefere Bedeutung* (*Comedy, Satire, Irony and Deeper Meaning*) and *Napoleon; oder, Die hundert Tage*—in the 1950s, although he is still largely unknown in other countries.

In philosophical terms Grabbe is generally seen—together with Byron, Lamartine, Leopardi, and Heine—as the product of a period in which idealism was superseded by materialism, with young writers facing a spiritual void in a mood of post-romantic scepticism and melancholy. His early plays—particularly *Herzog Thedor von Gothland* and *Comedy, Satire, Irony and Deeper Meaning*, a gothic melodrama and a black comedy—reveal the despair of 'intellect spent and emotion shattered' (letter to George Ferdinand Kettembeil, 4 May 1827). A similar disillusionment awakens superhuman desires in *Don Juan und Faust*—his only play to be performed while he was alive—which 'glorifies the tragic fall of the sensualist and the metaphysician' alike (letter to Christian von Meien, 6 January 1829). Nihilism also underlies his later plays—notably *Napoleon* and *Hannibal*—which blend the longing for powerful heroes with a sense of futility in view of the baseness of human nature and the impermanence of all things. Current affairs were of little interest to him. Thus he abandoned a trendily patriotic *Hohenstaufen* cycle after two instalments on the Emperors Barbarossa and Heinrich VI, while his last play, *Die Hermannsschlacht* [Arminius's Battle], was inspired by his 'best childhood memories' (letter to Louise Grabbe, 8 January 1835) of its setting in the Teutoburg Forest near Detmold, rather than by the chauvinism traditionally associated with the topic. Nevertheless, his pessimism and cynicism can be interpreted as an oblique response to the uncongenial socio-political conditions of the 'Restauration' era.

By common consent Grabbe's prime achievement consists in his innovations in historical drama. Unlike the historical plays of Schiller and his followers, which were classical in style and idealistic in message, his are prosaic in language, episodic in structure, and realistic in outlook. They portray history as determined not by ideas or individuals but by mass movements and the contingencies of time, place, and circumstance. Foreshadowed in *Marius und Sulla*, further developed in *Die Hohenstaufen*, and culminating in *Napoleon* and *Hannibal*, his re-creation of the broad flow of history itself has been much admired. He was hardly exaggerating when—referring to *Napoleon* but with his historical drama as a whole in mind—he claimed to have brought about 'a dramatic-epic-revolution' (letter to Kettembeil, 25 February 1831).

Grabbe's 'revolution' in historical drama involved a revolutionary handling of drama as such. Dismissed in the past as signs of ineptitude, capriciousness, or a pathological psyche, his approaches now seem eminently modern. Teeming with incongruities and distortions, deliberately avoiding harmony or beauty, his disjoined actions, ambiguous characters, and dissonant dialogues not only express the conflicts he experienced in his own age but anticipate the 'open' form and 'absurd' content favoured by dramatists today.

Commenting on *Napoleon*, Grabbe once declared: 'I haven't taken any trouble over its shape as a drama. The present stage doesn't deserve it' (letter to Kettembeil, 2 October 1830). On another occasion, however, he noted: 'Drama is not bound to the stage . . . the proper theatre is—the imagination of the reader' (letter to Wolfgang Menzel, 15 January 1831). We cannot tell whether Grabbe's refusal to compromise with the stage resulted from his anger over the theatrical conventions of his day or from more general doubts about theatrical production as a vehicle for poetic utterances. If the latter is true, then the paradox of a born dramatist who does not believe in theatre could be the key to both the successes and the failures of this maverick in the evolution of German drama.

—Ladislaus Löb

GRASS, Günter (Wilhelm). Born in Danzig, Germany (now Gdansk, Poland), 16 October 1927. Educated at Volksschule and Gymnasium, Danzig; trained as stone mason and sculptor; attended Academy of Art, Düsseldorf, 1948–52, and State Academy of Fine Arts, Berlin, 1953–55. Served in World War II: prisoner of war, Marienbad, Czechoslovakia, 1945–46. Married 1) Anna Margareta Schwarz in 1954, three sons and one daughter; 2) Ute Grunert in 1979. Worked as farm labourer, miner, apprentice stonecutter, jazz musician; speech writer for Willy Brandt when Mayor of West Berlin; writer-in-residence, Columbia University, New York, 1966; also artist and illustrator; co-editor, *L*, since 1976, and Verlages L'80, publishing house, since 1980. Member, Gruppe 47. Recipient: Süddeutscher Rundfunk Lyrikpreis, 1955; Gruppe 47 prize, 1958; Berlin Critics prize, 1960; City of Bremen prize, 1960 (withdrawn); Foreign Book prize (France), 1962; Büchner prize, 1965; Fontane prize, 1968; Theodor Heuss prize, 1969; Mondello prize (Palermo), 1977; Carl von Ossietzky medal, 1977; International literature prize, 1978; Alexander Majkowski medal, 1978; Vienna literature prize, 1980; Feltrinelli prize, 1982; Leonhard Frank ring, 1988. Honorary doctorate: Kenyon College, Gambier, Ohio, 1965; Harvard University, Cambridge, Massachusetts, 1976; Adam Mieckiewicz University, Poznan. Member, 1963,

and 1983–86 (resigned), president, Academy of Art, Berlin; member, American Academy of Arts and Sciences. Lives in Berlin, Germany.

PUBLICATIONS

Fiction

Danziger Trilogie. 1980; as *The Danzig Trilogy*, translated by Ralph Manheim, 1987.
    Die Blechtrommel. 1959; as *The Tin Drum*, translated by Ralph Manheim, 1962.
    Katz und Maus. 1961; as *Cat and Mouse*, translated by Ralph Manheim, 1963.
    Hundejahre. 1963; as *Dog Years*, translated by Ralph Manheim, 1965.
Geschichten (as Artur Knoff). 1968.
Örtlich betäubt. 1969; as *Local Anaesthetic*, translated by Ralph Manheim, 1969.
Aus dem Tagebuch einer Schnecke. 1972; as *From the Diary of a Snail*, translated by Ralph Manheim, 1973.
Der Butt. 1977; as *The Flounder*, translated by Ralph Manheim, 1978.
Das Treffen in Telgte. 1979; as *The Meeting at Telgte*, translated by Ralph Manheim, 1981.
Kopfgeburten; oder, Die Deutschen sterben aus. 1980; as *Headbirths; or, The Germans Are Dying Out*, translated by Ralph Manheim, 1982.
Die Rättin. 1986; as *The Rat*, translated by Ralph Manheim, 1988.
Unkenrufe. 1992; as *The Call of the Toad*, translated by Ralph Manheim, 1992.

Plays

Hochwasser (produced 1957). 1963; as *Flood*, translated by Ralph Manheim, in *Four Plays*, 1967.
Onkel, Onkel (produced 1958). 1965; as *Onkel, Onkel*, translated by Ralph Manheim, in *Four Plays*, 1967.
Noch zehn Minuten bis Buffalo (produced 1959). In *Theaterspiele*, 1970; as *Only Ten Minutes to Buffalo*, translated by Ralph Manheim, in *Four Plays*, 1967.
Beritten hin und zurück (produced 1959).
Die bösen Köche (produced 1961). In *Theaterspiele*, 1970; as *The Wicked Cooks*, translated by A. Leslie Willson, in *Four Plays*, 1967.
Goldmäuschen (produced 1964).
Die Plebejer proben den Aufstand (produced 1966). 1966; as *The Plebeians Rehearse the Uprising*, translated by Ralph Manheim, 1966.
Four Plays (includes *Flood*; *Onkel, Onkel*; *Only Ten Minutes to Buffalo*; *The Wicked Cooks*). 1967.
Davor (produced 1969). In *Theaterspiele*, 1970; as *Max*, translated by A. Leslie Willson and Ralph Manheim, 1972.
Theaterspiele (includes *Noch zehn Minuten bis Buffalo*; *Hochwasser*; *Onkel, Onkel*; *Die Plebejer proben den Aufstand*; *Davor*). 1970.
Die Blechtrommel als Film (screenplay), with Volker Schlöndorff. 1979.

Screenplays: *Katz und Maus*, 1967; *Die Blechtrommel*, with Volker Schlöndorff, 1979.

Ballet Scenarios: *Fünf Köche*, 1957; *Stoffreste*, 1959; *Die Vogelscheuchen*, 1970.

Radio Plays: *Zweiunddreissig Zähne*, 1959; *Noch zehn Minuten bis Buffalo*, 1962; *Eine öffentliche Diskussion*, 1963; *Die Plebejer proben den Aufstand*, 1966; *Hochwasser*, 1977.

Verse

Die Vorzüge der Windhühner. 1956.
Gleisdreieck. 1960.
Selected Poems, translated by Michael Hamburger and Christopher Middleton. 1966; as *Poems of Günter Grass*, 1969.
März. 1966.
Ausgefragt. 1967; as *New Poems*, translated by Michael Hamburger, 1968.
Danach. 1968.
Die Schweinekopfsülze. 1969.
Gesammelte Gedichte. 1971.
Mariazuehren/Hommageàmarie/Inmarypraise. 1973; as *Inmarypraise*, translated by Christopher Middleton, 1974.
Liebe geprüft. 1974.
Mit Sophie in die Pilze gegangen. 1976; revised edition, 1987.
In the Egg and Other Poems (bilingual edition), translated by Michael Hamburger and Christopher Middleton. 1977.
Als vom Butt nur die Gräte geblieben war. 1977.
Kinderlied: Verse and Etchings. 1982.
Nachruf auf einen Handschuh: Sieben Radierungen und ein Gedicht. 1982.
Ach, Butt, dein Märchen geht böse aus. 1983.
Gedichte. 1985.
Die Rättin: 3 Radierungen und 1 Gedicht. 1985.
Die Gedichte 1955–1986. 1988.
Tierschutz. 1990.

Other

O Susanna: Ein Jazzbilderbuch: Blues, Balladen, Spirituals, Jazz, with H. Geldmacher and H. Wilson. 1959.
Die Ballerina. 1963.
Dich singe ich Demokratie (pamphlets). 5 vols., 1965.
Der Fall Axel C. Springer am Beispiel Arnold Zweig. 1967.
Briefe über die Grenze; Versuch eines Ost-West-Dialogs, with Pavel Kohout. 1968.
Über meinen Lehrer Döblin und andere Vorträge. 1968.
Ausgewählte Texte, Abbildungen, Faksimiles, Bio-Bibliographie, edited by Theodor Wieser. 1968; as *Porträt und Poesie*, 1968.
Über das Selbstverständliche: Reden, Aufsätze, Offene Briefe, Kommentare. 1968; revised and enlarged edition as *Über das Selbstverständliche: Politische Schriften*, 1969; translated in part by Ralph Manheim, as *Speak Out! Speeches, Open Letters, Commentaries*, 1969.
Die Schweinekopfsülze. 1969.
Originalgraphik. 1970.
Dokumente zur politischen Wirkung, edited by Heinz Ludwig Arnold and Franz Josef Görtz. 1971.
Der Schriftsteller als Bürger—eine Siebenjahresbilanz. 1973.
Der Bürger und seine Stimme. 1974.
Denkzettel: Politische Reden und Aufsätze 1965–76. 1978.
Aufsätze zur Literatur. 1980.
Werkverzeichnis der Radierungen (exhibition catalogue). 1980.
Bin ich nun Schreiber; oder, Zeichner? (exhibition catalogue). 1982.
Vatertag (lithographs). 1982.
Zeichnen und Schreiben: das bildnerische Werk des Schriftstellers Günter Grass:
  Zeichnungen und Texte 1954–1977. 1982; as *Drawings and Words 1954–1977*, translated by Michael Hamburger and Walter Arndt, 1983.
  Radierungen und Texte 1972–1982. 1984; as *Etchings and Words 1972–1982*, translated by Michael Hamburger and others, 1985.
Günter Grass: Lithographien: 19. Juni bis 24. Juli 1983 (exhibition catalogue). 1983.
Die Vernichtung der Menschheit hat begonnen. 1983.
Widerstand lernen: Politische Gegenreden 1980–1983. 1984.
Geschenkte Freiheit: Rede zum 8. Mai 1945. 1985.
On Writing and Politics, 1967–1983 (selection), translated by Ralph Manheim. 1985.
Erfolgreiche Musterreden für den Bürgermeister. 1986.
In Kupfer, auf Stein. 1986.
Werkausgabe, edited by Volker Neuhaus. 10 vols., 1987.
Radierungen, Lithographien, Zeichnungen, Plastiken, Gedichte (exhibition catalogue). 1987.
Es war einmal ein Land: Lyrik und Prosa, Schlagzeug und Perkussion, with Günter 'Baby' Sommer. 1987.
Zunge Zeigen (travel). 1988; as *Show Your Tongue*, translated by John E. Woods, 1989.
Skizzenbuch. 1989.
Meine grüne Wiese: Kurzprosa. 1989.
Wenn wir von Europa sprechen: ein Dialog, with Françoise Giroud. 1989.
Alptraum und Hoffnung: zwei Reden vor dem Club of Rome, with T. Aitmatow. 1989.
Deutscher Lastenausgleich: wider das dumpfe Einheitsgebot: Reden und Gespräche. 1990; as *Two States—One Nation? The Case Against Reunification*, translated by Krishna Winston and A.S. Wensinger, 1990.
Totes Holz: Ein Nachruf. 1990.
Ausstellung Günter Grass, Kahlschlag in unseren Köpfen (1990–1991 Berlin) (exhibition catalogue). 1990.
Deutschland, einig Vaterland? Ein Streitgespräch, with Rudolph Augstein. 1990.
Erfolgreiche Mustergrussworte und Musterbriefe für Bürgermeister und Kommunalpolitiker. 1990.
Droht der deutsche Einheitsstaat?. 1990.
Ein Schnäppchen namens DDR: Letzte Reden vorm Glockengeläut. 1990.
Schreiben nach Auschwitz: Frankfurter Poetik-Vorlesung. 1990.
Gegen die verstreichende Zeit: Reden, Aufsätze und Gespräche 1989–1991. 1991.
Vier Jahrzehnte: Ein Werkstattbericht, edited by G. Fritze Margull. 1991.

Editor, with Elisabeth Borchers and Klaus Roehler, *Luchterhands Loseblatt Lyrik: eine Auswahl*. 2 vols., 1983.

*

Bibliography: *Günter Grass: A Bibliography 1955–1975* by Patrick O'Neill, 1976; *Günter Grass in America: The Early Years* edited by Ray Lewis White, 1981; in *Erstausgaben deutscher Dichtung*, 1992.

Critical Studies: *Günter Grass: A Critical Essay* by Norris W. Yates, 1967; *Günter Grass* by W. Gordon Cunliffe, 1969; *Grass* by Kurt Lothar Tank, 1969; *A Grass Symposium* edited by A. Leslie Willson, 1971; *Günter Grass* by Irène Leonard, 1974; *A Mythic Journey: Günter Grass's Tin Drum* by Edward Diller, 1974; *Günter Grass* by Keith Miles, 1975; *The 'Danzig Trilogy' of Günter Grass* by John Reddick, 1975; *The Writer and Society: Studies in the Fiction of Günter Grass and*

Heinrich Böll by Charlotte W. Ghurye, 1976; *Günter Grass: The Writer in a Pluralist Society* by Michael Hollington, 1980; *Adventures of a Flounder: Critical Essays on Günter Grass' 'Der Butt'* edited by Gertrude Bauer Pickar, 1982; *The Narrative Works of Günter Grass: A Critical Interpretation*, 1982, and *Grass: Die Blechtrommel*, 1985, both by Noel L. Thomas; *The Fisherman and His Wife: Günter Grass's 'The Flounder' in Critical Perspective* edited by Siegfried Mews, 1983; *Günter Grass* by Ronald Hayman, 1985; *Günter Grass* by Richard H. Lawson, 1985; *Grass and Grimmelshausen: Günter Grass's 'Das Treffen in Telgte' and Rezeptionstheorie* by Susan C. Anderson, 1986; *Critical Essays on Günter Grass* edited by Patrick O'Neill, 1987; *Understanding Günter Grass* by Alan Frank Keele, 1988; *Günter Grass's 'Der Butt': Sexual Politics and the Male Myth of History* edited by Philip Brady, Timothy McFarland, and John J. White, 1990.

* * *

Günter Grass has shown in his novels that he is one of the most acute observers and critics of West Germany. After beginning in the 1950s with short prose pieces, poems, and plays in the then dominant 'absurd' style, he made a dramatic impact on the literary scene with *Die Blechtrommel* (*The Tin Drum*), *Katz und Maus* (*Cat and Mouse*), and *Hundejahre* (*Dog Years*). These were later named the *Danziger Trilogie* (*The Danzig Trilogy*) after Grass's native city which, detached and distant like Joyce's Dublin, became the prism through which he conveyed his vision of the world about him. In Danzig, with its mixed German and Polish population, World War II began. The city was a paradigmatic setting for the gradual growth of Nazism amid the banality of the petty bourgeoisie, and symbolized the lost homelands from which millions of Germans would be forever exiled after 1945. In this picaresque trilogy Grass, with great zest and wide-ranging scope, imaginatively investigated both recent German history—the monstrous crimes of the Nazis, the acquiescence and cowardice of the ordinary citizen, and contemporary post-war reality—the suppression of guilt, economic reconstruction and the return to affluence and complacency, the loss of moral values. Inevitably Grass became identified with the new generation of critical realists, which included Heinrich Böll and Martin Walser, who implacably satirized the faults and errors of their fellow-countrymen and untiringly reminded them of the guilty involvement in Nazi Germany they were eager to forget.

Grass's sense of social justice and his contentious nature took him into the political arena where he threw his authority and weight behind the Social Democratic Party in the general elections of the 1960s. His personal friend Willy Brandt became Chancellor in 1969 and Grass's fiery, hard-hitting campaign speeches, open letters, and commentaries were variously published in *Über das Selbstverständliche* (*Speak Out!*) and *Der Bürger und seine Stimme*. The creative work accompanying this intense activity was also coloured by Grass's political commitment; the play *Davor* (*Max*) and the novel *Örtlich betäubt* (*Local Anaesthetic*) thematize the dominant preoccupations of intellectual and public life, namely the war in Vietnam and radical student protest in German universities. Though imbued with socialist ideas Grass stopped short of violence and destruction, advocating reform rather than revolution, practical measures for eradicating injustice rather than ideological posturings.

The anti-ideological scepticism of Grass's political stance is articulated in the novel *Aus dem Tagebuch einer Schnecke* (*From the Diary of a Snail*), which charts the author's reflections on his active participation in the election campaign of 1969 as well as telling the fictional story of the teacher Ott, 'nicknamed Doubt', who resisted the Nazis and clandestinely helped the persecuted Jews to the best of his ability. During the mid-1970s Grass seemed to be out of tune with the more extreme progressive forces in Germany and his literary talents appeared to lie dormant and inactive. In fact this proved to be the period of gestation of another epic masterpiece. *Der Butt* (*The Flounder*) incorporates so many autobiographical details that the blurring of the distinction between author and narrator already initiated in *From the Diary of a Snail* is here completed. *The Flounder* is a complementary piece to *The Danzig Trilogy*; where the latter focuses on the enormities of contemporary events, *The Flounder* embraces in its narrative structure the whole sweep of German social and political history. The perennial human endeavour to ascribe progress and meaning to historical process as well as the more topical question of feminism and the secular domination of women by men are central themes given expression by Grass.

In the 'fictional' work, *Kopfgeburten; oder, Die Deutschen sterben aus* (*Headbirths; or, The Germans Are Dying Out*), Grass displayed his political persona once more, thematizing the massive and urgent problems facing the industrialized nations: energy crisis, the threat of nuclear war, a declining birth-rate, the Third World. Yet, despite all his concern as a citizen with the struggles of the real world, Grass's faith in the significance of literature and the aesthetic dimension still shines through; he maintains that even in the most catastrophic destruction of civilization 'a hand holding a pen would reach up out of the rubble'.

Political concerns of national and global proportions have continued as fictional and polemical themes in Grass's subsequent work. *Die Rättin* (*The Rat*) envisaged a dystopian world following a nuclear catastrophe where the human race, in its self-destructive hubris, has appropriately been superseded by pullulating rodents. His most recent novel, *Unkenrufe* (*The Call of the Toad*), also revels in near-cloacal and lugubriously funereal imagery, returning to Grass's beloved Danzig to re-enact the historically fraught and bitter relations between Germany and Poland. Grass encapsulated his nostalgia in the love-affair of an older couple (Alexander, the German, and his Polish mistress, Alexandra) who found a Cemetery Society to enable the German dead to at least rest in graves in the city from where they had been driven. But the story ends in tragedy.

Grass spent some time in Calcutta during 1986 and 1987, and expressed in *Zunge Zeigen* (*Show Your Tongue*) his deep horror and shame at the chaotic world of filth, violence, and death he encountered there. The inexorable process of merging the two Germanies that got under way in 1989 provoked violent opposition from Grass, who protested vehemently in *Deutscher Lastenausgleich: wider das dumpfe Einheitsgebot* (*Two States—One Nation?*) and *Ein Schnäppchen namens DDR* [The GDR, a Real Snip] at the juggernaut of reunification, its nationalistic repercussions and the cynically arrogant takeover of Eastern Länder by the Federal Republic. Going against the tide of public opinion Grass prophesied that nothing but ill would result from the euphoria and complacency of an inflated Germany situated at the heart of a Europe in flux.

—Arrigo V. Subiotto

THE TIN DRUM (Die Blechtrommel)
Novel by Günter Grass, 1959.

The Tin Drum, Grass's first novel, attracted immediate attention upon publication in 1959. Praised as a new, daring voice in post-war German fiction by some and attacked as blasphemous and obscene by others, the novel has stood the test of time and is generally considered Grass's most important work. Intent on breaking with the prevailing mode of prose fiction in the 1950s that offered 'timeless and placeless parables', Grass chose as a primary geographical setting his native city of Danzig (now Polish Gdansk) and the first half of the 20th century as the specific time period for his—albeit highly unorthodox—literary analysis of Nazism.

The inmate of a mental institution, Oskar Matzerath, writes down the story of his life during his two-year confinement, from 1952 until his thirtieth birthday in September 1954. Oskar's first-person narrative begins before his birth, in October 1899 when his mother, Agnes, is conceived by his grandmother, Anna Bronski. Oskar, whose stories can lay claim to only limited believability, visualizes the past by means of the Matzerath family photo album and evokes it by playing his tin drum. The writing/narrating process forms one narrative level that is both separate from and parallel to Oskar's fictitious autobiography, which he narrates in chronological order.

The first of the novel's three books treats the period from around 1900 to the infamous *Kristallnacht*, the organized assault on Jewish businesses and synagogues on 8 November 1938. In September 1924 Oskar is born; his intellectual faculties are fully developed at birth—hence the prospect of taking over his parents' grocery store does not particularly excite him. But the successful severing of the umbilical cord makes his return to his mother's womb impossible. On his third birthday he is given a tin drum; he also stages a fall as a means of cloaking his decision to stunt his growth and his refusal to join the adult world.

Since Oskar's intellectual abilities do not require any further formal training, he sabotages his admission to school by using his destructive ability to shatter glass with his voice. But Oskar derives contrasting educational experiences from the classical, harmonious author Goethe on the one hand and the demonic monk Rasputin on the other. Oskar, a keen observer of the Danzig petty bourgeois milieu, implies that actions originating in the private sphere have a bearing on contemporaneous history.

For example, Jan Bronski, Agnes's cousin, is angry when she marries Alfred Matzerath, a German national from Rhineland. In 1920, Bronski becomes a Polish citizen and a clerk at the Free City of Danzig's Polish post office. Because Agnes continues her relationship with her cousin even after her marriage—hence Oskar claims two 'putative' fathers—Matzerath attends the regular Sunday rallies of the Nazi party and becomes a member of a movement embarked on a disastrous political course.

In contrast to Matzerath, Oskar sees beyond the trappings of political manipulation; with his drumming he turns the martial music at a Nazi rally into the Charleston and ruins the assembly. In a different vein, Oskar plays the role of a tempter who entices people to steal and, in the process, to probe their consciences. On Good Friday in 1936, upon seeing eels—both signs of death and phallic symbols—at the beach, Agnes feels pangs of conscience because of her adulterous relationship. A few months later she dies from intentionally induced fish poisoning. Oskar loses his tin drum supplier, a Jewish toy merchant, to suicide during the *Kristallnacht*.

The second book deals with the time spanning World War II. Oskar is instrumental in arranging the unheroic deaths of his two putative fathers. Bronski (in 1939) and Matzerath (in 1945) die as a consequence of the political decisions they have made. But family life goes on: Oskar seduces Maria Truczinski with the help of fizz powder, and Matzerath marries Maria. In 1942, Maria gives birth to son Kurth, whom Oskar believes himself to have fathered. In 1943–44, Oskar is with his friend and master, Lilliputian Bebra, on the front in France providing entertainment for the German troops. After his return to Danzig, he appears as the imitator of Christ and the new Jesus, and he becomes leader of the gang of young Dusters. But the group is betrayed, and its members are arrested.

At Matzerath's funeral, Oskar, now 21 years old, decides to resume his interrupted growth and become a responsible adult. He falls into Matzerath's grave when he is hit by a stone thrown by Kurth. His tin drum, the instrument of an ethically indifferent artist, remains in the grave. Although Oskar arises, he turns into a hunchback below average height and remains a conspicuous outsider.

The post-war scene of the third book changes from Danzig to Düsseldorf, where the Matzerath family settles. Oskar's efforts to become a useful member of society go awry when Maria rejects his marriage proposal. Oskar again devotes himself to art, first as a nude model, then as a drummer in a jazz band. The band performs in the Onion Cellar, a restaurant where prosperous guests, who are oblivious to the horrors of their Nazi past, are given onions and weep profusely. Oskar's art in the service of mourning turns into art in the service of commerce when he goes on lucrative concert tours arranged by his agent Bebra.

Oskar's predilection for nurses, with their radiance of eroticism and death, leads him to the failed attempt to seduce Sister Dorothea. As a prime suspect of her murder when her ring finger is found in his possession, Oskar flees to Paris but cannot avoid arrest. These events mark the end of his fictitious autobiography. Since the suspicion of murder proves to be unfounded, Oskar is faced with the long-dreaded release from the mental institution and departure from his protective metal bed. Oskar's frightening vision of the black cook—the opposite of his grandmother and her sheltering skirts—stems from his feelings of guilt. Although he possessed superior insight, Oskar initially refused—and later on only partially retracted his refusal—to participate actively in the life of family and society. As a kind of atonement Oskar composes his autobiography, a work which does not let the past sink into oblivion by challenging the reader to confront it.

The Tin Drum received the prize of influential Gruppe 47 in 1958, when the novel had not yet been completed. It is now generally recognized as the most important German post-war novel and one of the significant modern novels of the western world, and has sold millions of copies in an impressive number of languages. Although its complexity and linguistic ingenuity resist any interpretation on a single level, the novel's political thrust remains its most persuasive characteristic.

—Siegfried Mews

GRIBOEDOV, Aleksandr (Sergeevich) [Alexander Griboyedov]. Born in Moscow, Russia, 15 January 1795.

Educated at the University of Moscow, 1806–08, graduated in law; education interrupted by Napoleon's invasion of Russia, 1812. Joined the Moscow hussars (General Kologryvov's reserve), 1812, but saw no military action; discharged, 1816. Married daughter of the poet Prince Aleksandr Chavchavadze in 1828. Joined Ministry of Foreign Affairs in St Petersburg, 1816: diplomatic secretary to Russian legation in Persia, 1818, and to General A.P. Ermolov, 1821–23, both in Tiflis; diplomat in Tehran, 1819–21; returned to Georgia, 1825; arrested and imprisoned for four months on suspicion of involvement in the Decembrist uprising, 1825; returned to Caucasus after release, 1826; prepared the text of the Treaty of Turkmenchai, concluding the Russo-Persian war, 1826; Russian Minister to Persia, 1828. Killed during the storming of the Russian embassy, Tehran, by a mob of insurgents. *Died 11 February 1829.*

PUBLICATIONS

Collections

Polnoe sobranie sochinenii [Collected Works]. 1911–17.
Sochineniia v stikhakh [Works], edited by I.N. Medvedeva. 1967.
Izbrannoe [Selections], edited by S.A. Fomicheva. 1978.

Plays

Molodye suprugi [The Young Married Couple], from a play by Creuzé de Lesser (produced 1815). 1815.
Student [Student], with Pavel A. Katenin (produced 1904). 1817.
Svoia sem'ia; ili, Zamuzhniaia nevesta [All in the Family; or, The Married Fiancée], with Aleksandr Shakovskoi and Nikolai Khmel'nitskii (produced 1818).
Pritvornaia nevernost' [False Infidelity], with A.A. Gendre, from a play by Nicolas Barthe (produced 1818). 1818.
Proba intermedy [Test of an Interlude] (produced 1819). In *Polnoe sobranie sochinenii*, 1911–17.
Kto brat, kto sestra; ili, Obman za obmanom [Who's the Brother, Who's the Sister; or, Deception for Deception], with Prince Peter Viazemskii and others (libretto; produced 1824).
Gore ot uma [Woe from Wit] (produced 1825; complete version produced 1831). 1825 (partial version); 1833 (censored version); 1861 (uncensored version); edited by D.P. Costello, 1951; translated as *Intelligence Comes to Grief*, in *Anthology of Russian Literature*, 2, edited by Leo Wiener, 1902; as *The Misfortune of Being Clever*, translated by S.W. Pring, 1914; as *The Mischief of Being Clever*, translated by Bernard Pares, 1925; as *Wit Works Woe*, in *Masterpieces of Russian Drama*, 1, edited by G.R. Noyes, 1933; as *Chatsky*, translated by Joshua Cooper, in *Four Russian Plays*, 1972, reprinted as *The Government Inspector and Other Plays*, 1990.

*

Critical Studies: 'The Murder of Griboedov' by D.P. Costello, in *Oxford Slavonic Papers*, 1958; *Griboedov et la vie littéraire de son temps* by Jean Bonamour, 1965; *The Murder of Griboedov: New Materials* by Evelyn J. Harden, 1979.

* * *

Aleksandr Griboedov's first dramatic production was a one-act comedy in alexandrines, *Molodye suprugi* [The Young Married Couple], adapted from Creuzé de Lesser's *Le Secret du ménage*, and produced in September 1815. A second play was *Student*, a three-act comedy in prose, written in 1817 in conjunction with Pavel A. Katenin, which satirized and parodied such older writers as Nikolai Karamzin (1766–1824), Vasilii Zhukovskii (1783–1852), and Konstantin Batiushkov (1787–1855). A third comedy, first produced in January 1818, *Svoia sem'ia; ili, Zamuzhniaia nevesta* [All in the Family; or, The Married Fiancée], was written in collaboration with the two most celebrated comic writers of his day, Aleksandr Shakovskoi and Nikolai Khmel'nitskii. It is, however, for his masterpiece *Gore ot uma (Woe from Wit)*, a classically structured four-act comedy in free iambic verse, that Griboedov has won one of the most illustrious places in all Russian literature.

Woe from Wit is a *tour de force* of supple versification, brilliantly aphoristic repartee, and abundant topical allusion that also affords an unrivalled portrait of Moscow high society in about 1820. The verse form of the play, free iambs with arbitrary rhyme patterning, recalls strongly the form of the Russian fable, which in turn reflected the influence of Lafontaine. Adopted for a few plays in the early 19th century, free iambs were rarely used after *Woe from Wit*. In Griboedov's play they ranged from one to 13 syllables with nearly half the lines alexandrines.

Woe from Wit's repartee, in part reminiscent of Molière, depends both on sparkling colloquial language and virtuosic timing. After first hearing the play, Pushkin remarked that 'half the lines are bound to become proverbs', and it has indeed become the most quoted literary work in the Russian language. For contemporaries an additional quality was provided by the pithy topical references in which this comedy abounds, ranging from the Russian order of battle in 1813 to serf theatres, Carbonarism, freemasonry, and new educational ideas. In this respect *Woe from Wit* recalls the allusory and referential nature of Pushkin's almost contemporaneous novel in verse, *Eugene Onegin*. It was the topical allusions, with their generally liberal tenor, which meant the play could not be published in full until 1861, the year serfdom was abolished, although a censored version was first published in 1833. In the meantime some 40,000 manuscript copies are said to have circulated throughout Russia.

The Moscow aristocratic society in *Woe from Wit* is depicted as hospitable, relaxed, venial, superficially cultured, and, above all, politically conservative in the years preceding the Decembrist Uprising. Into it comes the alienated but undoubtedly heroic central protagonist Chatskii, 'straight from the boat into a ball', and it is the inevitable clash between on the one hand the clever, eloquent, tactless, and intolerant hero, who once loved the daughter of the house, and on the other the sleepily unprepared Muscovite society that lends the play its tension. Chatskii's qualities, positive and negative alike, have proved to be universal, and he has easily outlived contemporary literary heroes like Lermontov's Pechorin or, indeed, Onegin. His bewildered beloved Sofiia and her genial but nervous and cautious father Famusov (Mr Rumours), her ambitious lickspittle suitor Molchalin (Mr Silent), and arch-gossip and intriguer Repetilov (Mr Reptilian Repeater), and the mindless soldier Skalozub (Mr Teeth-barer) are all very convincingly characterized, while Sofiia's maid Liza is the only character to begin to match Chatskii's quick aphoristic wit.

Modern audiences, for whom the ubiquitous topical references are bound to be at least partially obscure, find the play's most enduring qualities to be the wittily portrayed clash of cultures between impetuous liberal youth and somnolent conservative society, but above all the use of richly colloquial syntax and vocabulary in conjunction with verse of the highest sophistication. Such qualities ensure that Griboedov's masterpiece will last as long as the Russian language itself.

—Arnold McMillin

WOE FROM WIT (Gore ot uma)
Play by Aleksandr Griboedov, 1825.

A satirical verse drama, *Woe from Wit,* is Griboedov's greatest literary achievement. First conceived probably in 1812, it was completed in 1824, and refused publication, but was circulated widely in manuscript. A censored version of the play was published in 1833 in order, according to Alexander Herzen, to remove the attraction of forbidden fruit.

The four decades between the end of the Napoleonic campaign and the Crimean War began in Russia with Tsar Aleksandr I's mystical fantasies of a Holy Alliance of European powers inspired and led by Russia and was succeeded by the repressive and generally stagnant reign of Nicholas I. It was a time also when certain sections of the intelligentsia began to question many of Russia's institutions, her history, and her place in Europe and, more particularly, to attempt to define a specific Russian identity. This was especially true in the arts, notably in literature. While the philosopher Chaadaev was claiming that Russia did not belong to any of the families of Europe, and lived outside the times, the critic Belinskii complained that Russia had no literature at all that it could call its own, or which expressed the distinctive spirit of the Russian people. One way of trying to be 'national' would be to free literature from the severe limitations imposed upon it by an almost complete dependence on western literary genres. The onset of Romanticism, when it reached Russia in the 1820s, certainly allowed writers a far greater freedom than was permitted by the traditions of French neo-classicism that had governed Russian literature for almost 50 years.

Woe from Wit is the first successful manifestation of this new mood, both in form but more particularly in content. This is not to say, however, that it does not in many respects conform to much in the French neo-classical comedy of manners; its antecedents, in Molière particularly, are indisputable. It largely observes the three unities of time (24 hours), place (Famusov's house), and action (there are no sub-plots, for example). There is the central love story, albeit unhappy; the plot is based on misunderstandings; and the action is propelled by coincidences. The main characters include certain stock types: Sof'ia, the spoilt young heroine dreaming of finding ideal love; Famusov, the father planning a successful marriage for his daughter; and Liza, the maid with admirable common sense, looking after her charge and fully aware of the faults and pretensions of her superiors. Certain of the names of the characters denoting aspects of their personalities and the aphoristic title of the play all conform to traditions. Yet there are also notable innovations that ensured the play's popularity and its lasting success. There is no fifth act and consequently none of the traditional summing-up of what has happened, nor any authorial moralizing. There is no concentration on the depiction of one particular human vice that the comedy of manners was expected to portray. The numerous characters are representatives, in the main, of Moscow high society, which gives the

play a rather more obvious social realism. The form of the verse freed itself from the dictates of neo-classical traditions. Its basic iambic structure has variable and innovative rhythms, the line length and rhyming schemes are unconventional, and the idiomatic, contemporary, and colloquial language is so striking that it led Pushkin correctly to predict that many of its lines would become proverbial.

In spite of all its unexpectedness in form, versification, and notably in language, it is however the actual content of the play that ensured its popularity and established it as a forerunner of much of what was to follow when Russian literature proved itself the equal of any. There is the familiar background where much of the discussion and many of the characters would be immediately recognizable to contemporaries. All the topical references locate it firmly in Moscow high society—the rebuilding of Moscow after the visitation of Napoleon, the aristocratic English Club, the predominance of French fashions. The characters typify much of post-Napoleonic Russian society: the petty and malicious gossip, the hypocrisy and conservatism where birth, background, rank, wealth, and social connections count for everything and advancement depends solely on sycophancy and nepotism. For Griboedov that society is a philistine and spiritually empty one. More importantly he also suggests an element of growing dissatisfaction among a small section of society. This is memorably represented by Chatskii. The leading protagonist and motivator of what little action there is, he finds everything about the society tedious, conceited, and complacent and wonders why he returned to it. He fearlessly and indignantly inveighs against its manifold shortcomings—this is partly an expression of the revolt of the young against their reactionary elders but it also has a political significance. He is suspected of being a freemason (and might even become a Decembrist) and is condemned as a free-thinker, a dangerous (and mad) man preaching liberty and a deep suspicion of all authority. He soon realizes that there is no place for him there and is forced to run away. Chatskii is also the first in a succession of characters in Russian literature known as 'superfluous men' after the term given currency by Turgenev in a short story of 1850. The dissatisfied, upper-class intellectual who is (or regards himself as) superior to the society from which he sprang or in which he finds himself, he can find no appropriate outlet for his talents. He has no roots and no place he can consider home and is condemned to a futile existence and in many cases a pointless death. Chatskii was succeeded by Pushkin's Eugene Onegin, Lermontov's Pechorin, Turgenev's Rudin and many others, but remains in some ways different from them. He is honest and has a capacity for love; his sharp tongue is directed at people fully deserving of his criticisms; he has no cynicism nor professed or real boredom and is notably superior to the society he so despises. And his role on the stage is as challenging to Russian actors as is Hamlet's to English-speaking ones.

—A.V. Knowles

GRILLET, Alain Robbe.   See ROBBE-GRILLET, Alain.

GRILLPARZER, Franz. Born in Vienna, Austria, 15 January 1791. Educated at Anna-Gymnasium, Vienna, 1800–07; studied law at University of Vienna, 1807–11. Tutor in law studies to nephew of Graf von Seilern, 1812; unpaid assistant in court library, 1813; civil servant from 1814: appointed Theaterdichter, 1818; travelled to Italy, 1819, and to Germany, 1826, director of court archives, 1832: retired 1856, as Hofrat; created a member of the Herrenhaus (upper house of the Austrian parliament), 1861. Founder-member, Austrian Academy of Sciences, 1847. Honorary Doctorate: University of Leipzig, 1859. *Died 21 January 1872.*

PUBLICATIONS

Collections

Sämtliche Werke, edited by August Sauer and Reinhold Backmann. 42 vols., 1909–48.
Sämtliche Werke, edited by Peter Frank and Karl Pörnbacher. 4 vols., 1960–65.
Werke, edited by Helmut Bachmaier. 1986—.

Plays

Die Ahnfrau (produced 1817). 1817; as *The Ancestress*, translated by Herman L. Spahr, 1938.
Sappho (produced 1818). 1819; as *Sappho*, translated by J. Bramsen, 1820; also translated by E.B. Lee, 1846; Lucy C. Cumming, 1855; E. Frothingham, 1876; Arthur Burkhard, 1953.
Das Goldene Vlies (trilogy; produced 1821). 1822; as *Medea*, translated by F.W. Thurstan and S.A. Wittmann, 1879, also translated by Arthur Burkhard, 1941; as *The Golden Fleece*, translated by Burkhard, 1942; as *The Guest-Friend* and *The Argonauts*, translated by Burkhard, 2 vols., 1942.
König Ottokars Glück und Ende (produced 1825). 1825; as *Ottokar*, translated by Thomas Carlyle, 1840; as *King Ottokar, His Rise and Fall*, translated by G. Pollack, 1907; also translated by Arthur Burkhard, 1932; Henry H. Stevens, 1938.
Ein treuer Diener seines Herrn (produced 1828). 1830; as *A Faithful Servant of His Master*, translated by Arthur Burkhard, 1941.
Des Meeres und der Liebe Wellen (produced 1831). 1839; edited by E.E. Pabst, 1967; edited by Mark Ward, 1981; as *Hero and Leander*, translated by Henry H. Stevens, 1938, also translated by Arthur Burkhard, 1962; as *The Waves of Sea and Love*, translated by Samuel Solomon, in *Plays on Classic Themes*, 1969.
Melusina, music by Konradin Kreutzer (produced 1833). 1833.
Der Traum ein Leben (produced 1834). 1840; edited by W.E. Yuill, 1955; as *A Dream Is Life*, translated by Henry H. Stevens, 1947.
Weh dem, der lügt (produced 1838). 1840; as *Thou Shalt Not Lie*, translated by Henry H. Stevens, 1939.
Esther (produced 1868). In *Gesamtausgabe*, 1872; as *Esther*, translated by Arthur Burkhard, with *The Jewess of Toledo*, 1953.
Ein Bruderzwist in Habsburg (produced 1872). In *Gesamtausgabe*, 1872; edited by Bruce Thompson, 1982; as *Family Strife in Hapsburg*, translated by Arthur Burkhard, 1940.
Die Jüdin von Toledo (produced 1872). In *Gesamtausgabe*, 1872; as *The Jewess of Toledo*, translated by Arthur Burkhard, with *Esther*, 1953.

Libussa (produced 1874). In *Gesamtausgabe*, 1872; as *Libussa*, translated by Henry H. Stevens, 1941.

Fiction

Das Kloster bei Sendomir. In *Aglaja*, 1828; in *Sämtliche Werke*, 1930.
Der arme Spielmann. In *Iris*, 1847; in *Sämtliche Werke*, 1930; as *The Poor Musician*, translated by A. Remy, 1914; as *The Poor Fiddler*, translated by Alexander and Elizabeth Henderson, 1969.

Verse

Tristia ex Ponto. In *Vesta*, 1827.
Gedichte, edited by P. von Matt. 1970.

Other

Selbstbiographie. 1872.
Gespräche und Charakteristiken seiner Persönlichkeit durch die Zeitgenossen, edited by August Sauer. 6 vols., 1904–16; supplementary volume, edited by Reinhold Backmann, 1941.
Tagebücher und Reiseberichte, edited by Klaus Geissler. 1981.

*

Critical Studies: *Grillparzer, Lessing, and Goethe in the Perspective of European Literature* by Fred. O. Nolte, 1938; *Grillparzer: A Critical Biography* (vol. 1 only) by Douglas Yates, 1946; *The Inspiration Motif in the Works of Franz Grillparzer* by Gisela Stein, 1955; *The Plays of Grillparzer* by George A. Wells, 1969; *Grillparzer: A Critical Introduction* by W.E. Yates, 1972; *A Sense of Irony: An Examination of the Tragedies of Franz Grillparzer*, 1976, and *Franz Grillparzer*, 1981, both by Bruce Thompson, and *Essays on Grillparzer* edited by Thompson and Mark Ward, 1978; *Grillparzer's Aesthetic Theory* by William Norman Boyd Mullan, 1979; *The World as Theatre in the Works of Franz Grillparzer* by Sybil Hitchman, 1979; *Grillparzer's Der arme Spielmann: New Directions in Criticism* edited by Clifford Albrecht Bernd, 1988; *An Introduction to the Major Works of Franz Grillparzer* by Ian F. Roe, 1991.

* * *

Nothing ever went right for Franz Grillparzer, a fact he viewed with grim satisfaction. He was the archetypal Viennese grumbler, and a wealth of anecdote testifies to his melancholy and his crusty hypochondria. At 81, still beset by a conflict between literature and marriage, he died in the arms of his 'eternal betrothed' Katharina Fröhlich, to whom he had been engaged for 50 years.

Grillparzer's writing is rooted in the rich cultural heritage of the multi-lingual Hapsburg Empire. As a child he marvelled at the musical fantasies and magical transformations of Viennese popular comedy in which the spectacular visual effects of the baroque survived in a naive form. His comedy *Weh dem, der lügt* (*Thou Shalt Not Lie*), in which a cook's boy rescues a Frankish bishop's nephew from the heathen Germans, barely, but humorously, managing not to perjure himself in the process, uses the fun and wealth of incident of popular comedy to make a moral point. *Der Traum ein Leben*

(*A Dream Is Life*) translates the hero into a dream to live out his ambitions then brings him back to renounce the life of action because of the inevitable guilt it involves.

Grillparzer was, however, drawn to the more austere world of German classicism, and even visited Goethe in Weimar, with disastrous results for his always parlous self-confidence. He set three plays in the ancient world. *Sappho*, in which the heroine forsakes poetry for a young lover and commits suicide when he abandons her, and *Des Meeres und der Liebe Wellen* (*The Waves of Sea and Love*), in which a novice priestess forsakes religion, only to have her lover drown in the Hellespont when the high priest extinguishes the lamp she has lit to guide him, are lyrical, tragic verse dramas of the conflict between the spirit and the flesh. In *Das Goldene Vlies* (*The Golden Fleece*) there is a foretaste of Strindberg's sexual psychology in the clash of the exotic alien Medea with her husband Jason in his sophisticated Greek homeland, but the tame sagacity of Grillparzer's conclusion underlines the gap between Biedermeier Vienna and the tragic ferocity of Greece.

Grillparzer's finest achievements were his historical dramas in verse. He was a rationalist and a liberal whom the nationalism of the mid-century turned into a conservative. *König Ottokars Glück und Ende* (*King Ottokar, His Rise and Fall*) celebrates the first Hapsburg Holy Roman Emperor, Rudolf I. *Ein treuer Diener seines Herrn* (*A Faithful Servant of His Master*), on the theme of loyalty, is set in Hungary. *Libussa* dramatizes the legendary founding of Prague in Bohemia. The best of these Austrian dramas is *Ein Bruderzwist in Habsburg* (*Family Strife in Hapsburg*) which unites Grillparzer's main themes in the drama of the self-abnegating, intellectual Emperor Rudolf II who struggles in vain to prevent the Reformation from splitting his empire. It was a plea for a supra-national concept, and took on a new meaning when the empire was broken up in 1918. *King Ottokar*, with Ottokar von Horneck's hymn to Austria, is staged at the Burgtheater in Vienna on days of public celebration. But the Austrian national dramatist's complex language has defied translation and even in Germany his plays have never shown the power to move and entertain.

—Hugh Rorrison

FAMILY STRIFE IN HAPSBURG (Ein Bruderzwist in Habsburg)
Play by Franz Grillparzer, 1872.

Grillparzer's drama *Family Strife in Hapsburg* grew out of the predicament many liberal-minded Austrians found themselves in during the first half of the 19th century, when demands for democratic liberties for the individual inevitably threatened to destroy the fabric of the multinational Hapsburg Monarchy. Stretching back to the 13th century, the Hapsburg Monarchy was essentially a dynastic creation. Its very success in amassing territories had been achieved at the expense of homogeneity of any sort. Hand in hand with the expansion outward went an inner consolidation of domestic power until it approached absolutism, legitimized by the doctrine of the divine right of kings and the concept of hereditary succession, both of which Grillparzer subjected to stern scrutiny in his play.

Anti-Hegelian in his outlook on history, he understood history as a series of events, largely unintelligible to the contemporary and in constant need of interpretative re-evaluation by later generations on whose development they

had a bearing. In 1807 when Grillparzer first started historical research for a drama on Rudolf II, who was emperor of the Holy Roman Empire from 1576 to 1612, at a time of the intense religious and political tensions, the Hapsburg dynasty had just been dealt a severe blow by Napoleon, who in 1806 had decreed that the Holy Roman Empire should cease to exist. His edict completed a process that had started with the Reformation which spelt the end of medieval universalism in Germany as the Hapsburg emperors had pursued it and gave rise to particularism: Emperor Francis II of the Holy Roman Empire became emperor of Austria, a secular prince, like any other. Grillparzer did not finish the revision of his play till a year or two after the abortive revolution of 1848, which with its local and national demands threatened the foundations of the Hapsburgs' dynastic power in their own territories. As in all Grillparzer's stage dramas, the times represented in *Family Strife* mirror, figuratively, the time of representation and the author's understanding of his own time.

From the very first words of the first scene, strife and confusion reign in the drama. The many-layered meaning of *Bruderzwist*—'Conflict among Brothers'—is played out in all its nuances. Brothers and nephews of the emperor jostle for power, eager to replace the irresolute monarch, using his hesitancy as an excuse for usurpation. Intrigue is rife in the imperial household, lawlessness threatens in the streets, religious differences are on the point of turning into full-blown civil war. By skilfully delaying the emperor's entrance in the first act, Grillparzer not only gives ample scope to the theme of violence and scheming but arouses the reader's expectation that a strong personality is needed to put down the burgeoning rebellion. However, when at last Rudolf makes a ceremonious entry all conventional hopes for law and order are dashed by the spectacle of a weak old man in an advanced state of paranoia who thrusts aside important state documents and soon dismisses all those present by uttering a sevenfold 'alone!'. It is not until Archduke Ferdinand, a fanatic representative of the Counter-Reformation, elicits a kind of 'Credo' from his uncle that Grillparzer affords us deeper insight into Rudolf's innermost thoughts. To Ferdinand's accusations that the emperor has allowed himself to be influenced by the dark prophecies of the astrologers he has drawn to his court, Rudolf replies with the revealing words: 'I believe in God and not in the stars, but those stars, too, come from God. They are the first works of His hand, in which he laid down the blueprint of His creation.' Rudolf's vision of the stars obeying God's every word from time immemorial to eternity 'like a flock of silvery sheep obeying the shepherd's call' is by extension a blueprint for absolutism on earth, every subject willingly accepting the king's authority. Deeply upset by the gulf separating vision and reality and perturbed by the task confronting him of having to rule over a world torn asunder by dissension, he views man as an excrescence of the creation. Man has broken away from God, betrayed Him. Only up above among the luminous spaces of heaven is order; down among men there is nothing but falsehood, arbitrariness, and chaos. He wishes he had a huge ear to listen to a divine message or could stand guard on a tall tower eavesdropping on the stars as they surround God's throne. Grillparzer gives us the incongruous, almost bizarre spectacle of the head of the Holy Roman Empire, by tradition the defender of the Catholic faith, flying in the face of the fundamental tenets of Christian doctrine: that man and the world are in constant need of redemption. Rudolf has recourse to neoplatonic ideas but he knows that he does not have the intellect to penetrate to philosophical clarity. His speech breaks down. His confused and anguished mind conjures up Maleficus, the malignant stellar constellation, and he falls silent. Throughout the play, with great psychological perception, Grillparzer develops further the theme of the emperor's doubts. It becomes increasingly clear that he is longing for a sign from heaven indicating to him whether the dreadful schism that has occurred was ordained by God or was the work of the devil. Yet Rudolf's fears about the schism reveal not so much a concern with religious matters, such as the salvation of the soul, but the realization that doubts in the one apostolic faith lead to the loosening of all ties of reverence and respect and ultimately to the destruction of that hierarchial order that guarantees the survival of the empire and from which he derives his own raison d'être and power. He recognizes the democratic thrust in Protestantism. In his ravings he sees a Leviathan-like monster rising from the depths, for ever wanting more and never satisfied. Yet all that he has to set against this vision of a barbaric levelling down and the rule of the masses are outdated symbols of a past glory: 'Our dynasty will last for ever for it does not march at the head of the new nor go along with it . . . and so, resting in the centre of its own gravity, it awaits the return of the souls that have gone astray!'. Characteristically, Rudolf, when forced to abdicate, does not follow the example of his illustrious uncle Charles V, who entered a monastery, an act of Christian humility at least in gesture, but prefers to say in his castle in Prague, the fortified symbol of dynastic power.

The play ends on a deeply pessimistic, almost nihilistic note. Grillparzer re-creates the stage-setting of Act I, except that now we are in the imperial palace in Vienna, not in Prague. As in Act I members of the imperial family and other personages are waiting to be received by the new emperor, Rudolf's brother Mathias, who has usurped power. Strife and intrigue are thriving as before in an atmosphere of hesitancy and impotence. Archduke Ferdinand and Wallenstein, his general, have just left vowing to wage a war of attrition on the Protestants even if it means eradicating a whole generation of heretics for the sake of their souls. The curtain goes down on a visually impressive, telling scene. The bejewelled insignia of the empire have been brought from Prague where Rudolf has died. They are arranged on a table in the background. Mathias is in the foreground on his knees, beating his chest and muttering 'mea culpa, mea culpa, mea maxima culpa!' while shouts of 'Long live Mathias!' are heard from the streets. A spectator of this scene might jump to the conclusion that the new emperor was feeling guilty towards his dead brother and asking God's forgiveness. But Grillparzer makes it clear in his stage-direction that the actor must keep his eyes on the table and not turn them to heaven, presumably because he wanted to suggest that Mathias's real guilt-feelings were concerned with his having endangered the continuity of the empire which is powerfully symbolized by the insignia on the table.

The play strikes home with the masterly psychological portrayal of Rudolf, which is underwritten both by a perceptive understanding of human frailty and by a sharp critical awareness of the limits of defensible behaviour. The other figures remain shadowy in comparison; their link with the protagonist appears often merely episodic. Seen as a dramatic whole the play is a vivid and incisive indictment of the Hapsburg 'dunces by divine right' as Grillparzer called them, and their claim to everlasting power. But it goes much further than the Austrian context. It raises the urgent and topical question whether any unifying government drawn up along humanist, democratic, and peaceful lines will ever be able to hold down the will to power of conflicting national, ethnic, religious, economic, and social interests.

—Eve Mason

THE WAVES OF SEA AND LOVE (Des Meeres und der Liebe Wellen)
Play by Franz Grillparzer, 1831.

The subject matter of Grillparzer's tragedy of Hero and Leander derives from the epic poem by Musaeus, while other literary stimuli came to him from the German folksong 'Edelkönigskinder' and the poems Ovid, Marlowe, and Schiller had devoted to the fabled lovers. Shakespeare's *Romeo and Juliet* provided a further model through its sensitive romantic treatment of youthful eroticism. Grillparzer avoided the established conventions of Weimar classicism and instead of adopting an anachronistic form, wrote a modern psychological verse play in a style which gave full scope to the complexities of conscious and unconscious motivation in the exploration of first love. The result is an essentially realistic contemporary drama in an antique setting. Grillparzer's faithful adherence to the fundamental principles of living theatre —a tangible action, clear motivation, vivid characterization, close commerce between image and gesture, word and image —was a tribute of his esteem for the Spanish baroque theatre of Calderón and Lope de Vega. These qualities were matched in him by that psychological acumen and perspicacity which mark out the forerunner of modern drama, especially as it was to develop in *fin de siècle* Vienna, the cradle of psychoanalysis.

The Waves of Sea and Love portrays the awakening of erotic love in all its impetuosity in a young woman who has come to the island sanctuary of Sestos to dedicate her life as virgin priestess to the goddess Aphrodite. It is clear from the expository first act that family pressures and close connections with the temple (the priest is Hero's uncle) have supplanted freedom of choice in determining her vocation. Hero, the untried novice, is under the illusion that she knows her own heart and mind, that she is fully alive to the implications of complete surrender to the religious life, and that she can find fulfilment in serene contemplation and dutiful service. Her tragedy consists in the loss of self, the defeat of the will in face of a primal impulse for which she is not prepared. The tragedy portrays the human will and its resolve as fallible, as unequal to the surge of passions. The elemental power of love and desire, which first announces itself with discreet subtlety, unfolds as an irresistible moving force, no less potent than the ever-changing sea. This poetic metaphor is woven into the fabric of the play's language, as is the imagery of light and darkness, twin indicators of the theme of the conscious and unconscious life of the emotions. At the initiation ceremony in act one, where Hero must abjure marriage, her eye lights on the handsome, shy figure of Leander and the fateful spark is kindled. Characteristically, Grillparzer chooses to illuminate the inner dimension of subliminal and semi-conscious experience through attitude and gesture, as the stage directions indicate. In performing the sacred rites of self-dedication to the priesthood, Hero's trembling hand, her lapse of memory, and confused ritual acts, betray an untimely loss of that equilibrium and self-possession (*Sammlung*) which is the ideal and goal of the contemplative life. On hastily concluding the ceremony, she pretends to attend to her shoe, thereby stealing a furtive parting glance at Leander: this signals her nascent captivation.

If the opening act merely hints at Hero's latent erotic susceptibility, the second confirms and substantiates the growing bond of feeling. Leander's friend Naukleros recalls the tell-tale detail of the preceding temple scene, Hero's revealing glance ('Observing you, she stood in hesitation/For one, two, three brief, eternal moments'). He also interprets the meaning of that glance ('The pity of it!' and 'Him I might well have liked!'). Leander cannot hide his tears of agony or the agony of desire, while Hero betrays her latent feelings by singing a song of Leda and the swan, a barely repressed sublimation of her womanly desires. When the lovesick Leander craves a drink of water from Hero's pitcher in the forbidden grove, this innocent gesture stands in symbolic anticipation of the bond that is to join the lovers in defiance of a hostile law. Though the priest's suspicions are early aroused as to his charge's inner feelings, he continues to play an ambiguous role as spiritual counsellor, caring relative, and unsparing moral judge. The audacious Leander gains access to Hero's chamber by scaling the walls of her tower, and in the course of the lovers' meeting it becomes clear that she has neither the resolution nor the will to resist. Hero's desperate question, put largely to herself, formulates the crucial issue of the tragedy: 'What is it that so darkens Man's mind and so estranges him from his very Self, compelling service to an alien Self?' The resourceful priest, aware that Hero's lamp had been burning all night, ensures that the following day's duties make her physically exhausted and unable to watch for her lover another night. (Hero's lamp is more than just a tangible instrument of the action: it is developed into a complex symbol of the love relationship, being overlaid with connotations of the rational and irrational elements of the mind.) In his stern cross-examination of her, he meets with a degree of evasive cunning which betokens a new, maturer woman who is prepared to defend her love to the last. The net of tragedy inevitability closes in upon the lovers in the final act, as the lamp which was to guide Leander across the Hellespont is extinguished by the priest, who overtly acts as an instrument of the gods. This salving of the private conscience in a man of religion has about it a peculiarly modern polemic; as a figure of compromise, he has much of the compliant functionary about him. The dramatist's own experience of stiff authoritarianism, external respectability, and bigotry in the age of Metternich's Vienna, gives the play a remarkably authentic groundswell of social realism.

The last act shows Hero rising to the height of her tragic stature in her grief over the drowned Leander. All dissimulation is cast off as she gives utterance to the full burden of emotion and the torment of the heart. Her profession of undying love rises to a pitch of elevated eloquence that recalls the memorial paean to the dead Anthony by Shakespeare's Cleopatra:

> Come, he was all there is! What still remains
> Is but a shadow; it fades, a nothingness.
> His breath was purest air, his eye the sun,
> His body like the power of budding nature;
> His life was life itself, both yours and mine,
> The universal life.

Hero's death is depicted as another *Liebstod* such as we may find in Kleist's *Penthesilea* or, later, in Wagner's *Tristan und Isolde*, yet lacking that ecstatic, transcendental quality which was foreign to the Austrian poet. Grillparzer pays minute attention to the symptoms of physiological change (clouded vision, double heartbeat, coldness, numbed posture, various signs of debility) in portraying the final stages of ebbing life. The poetic and the prosaic are frequently in contention in Grillparzer, yet when they harmonize, as they do in this play, the result is convincing and masterly.

—Alexander Stillmark

GRIMM, Jacob and Wilhelm. GRIMM, Jacob (Ludwig Karl). Born in Hanau, Germany, 4 January 1785. Educated at Kassel Lyceum, 1798–1802; University of Marburg, studied law, 1802–05. Researcher for Friedrich Karl von Savigny in Paris, 1805; civil servant, secretariat of the War Office, Kassel, 1806; librarian for King Jérôme Bonaparte's private library, Wilhelmshöhe, 1808–14, co-editor with Wilhelm Grimm, *Altdeutsche Wälder*, 1813–16; legation secretary for the Hessian delegation at the Congress of Vienna, 1814–15; librarian, Kassel, 1816; chair, archaeology and librarianship, University of Göttingen, Hanover, 1830–37, dismissed from the university for political reasons by Ernst August in 1837; lived in Kassel, 1837–41; president, Conferences of Germanists, Frankfurt am Main, 1846, Lubeck, 1847; elected to the Frankfurt parliament, 1848. Recipient: Order of Merit, 1842. Member, Academy of Science, Berlin, 1841. Honorary doctorate: University of Marburg, 1819; Berlin University, 1828; Berslau University, 1829. *Died 20 September 1863.* **GRIMM, Wilhelm (Karl).** Born in Hanau, Germany, 24 February 1786. Educated at Kassel Lyceum, 1798–1803; University of Marburg, 1803–06; law degree, 1806. Married Henriette Dorothea Wild in 1825; one daughter and three sons. Co-editor with Jacob Grimm, *Altdeutsche Wälder*, 1813–16; assistant librarian, electoral library, Kassel, 1814–29; professor, University of Göttingen, 1830, dismissed from the university for political reasons by Ernst August in 1837; lived in Kassel, 1837–41. Member: Academy of Science, Berlin, 1841. Honorary doctorate, Marburg University, 1819. *Died 16 December 1859.*

PUBLICATIONS

Collections

Complete Works. 62 vols., 1974— .
Die älteste Märchensammlung der Brüder Grimm, edited by Heinz Rölleke. 1975.
Grimm's Tales for Young and Old: The Complete Stories, translated by Ralph Manheim. 1977.
The Complete Fairy Tales of the Brothers Grimm, edited and translated by Jack Zipes. 2 vols., 1987.

Fiction

Kinder- und Hausmärchen. 2 vols, 1812–15; revised editions, 3 vols., 1819–22 (includes *Anmerkungen zu den einzelnen Märchen*), 1837, 1840, 1843, 1850, 1857; edited by Friedrich Panzer, 1975, and by Heinz Rölleke, 1982; numerous subsequent translations including as *German Popular Stories*, translated by Edgar Taylor, 2 vols., 1823–26; revised edition as *Gammer Grethel; or, German Fairy Tales and Popular Stories*, 1839; as *Home Stories*, translated by Matilda Louisa Davis, 1855; *Grimm's Popular Stories*, 1868; as *Grimm's Fairy Tales*, translated by H.H.B. Paull, 1872; also translated by L.L. Weedon, 1898, Edgar Lucas, 1900, Beatrice Marshall, 1900, N.J. Davidson, 1906, Ernest Beeson, 1916, and Peter Carter, 1982; as *Grimm's Goblins*, 1876; as *The Complete Grimm's Fairy Tales*, translated by Margaret Hunt, 1944, reprinted 1975.
Deutsche Sagen. 1816–18; as *The German Legends of the Brothers Grimm*, edited and translated by Donald Ward, 1981.

Other

Deutsches Wörterbuch, with others. 32 vols., 1854–1961.
Freundesbriefe von Wilhelm und Jacob Grimm: Mit Anmerkungen, edited by Alexander Reifferscheid. 1878.
Briefwechsel des Freiherrn K.H.G. von Meusebach mit Jacob und Wilhelm Grimm. 1880.
Briefwechsel zwischen Jacob und Wilhelm Grimm aus der Jegendzeit, edited by Herman Grimm and Gustav Hinrichs. 1881; revised edition, edited by Wilhelm Schoof. 1963.
Briefwechsel der Gebrüder Grimm mit nordischen Gelehrten, edited by Ernst Schmidt. 1885.
Briefwechsel zwischen Jacob und Wilhelm Grimm, Dahlmann und Gervinus, edited by Eduard Ippel. 2 vols., 1885–86.
Briefe der Brüder Jacob und Wilhelm Grimm an Georg Friedrich Benecke aus den Jahren 1808–1829, edited by Wilhelm Müller. 1889.
Briefwechsel F. Lückes mit den Brüdern Jacob und Wilhelm Grimm. 1891.
Briefe der Brüder Grimm an Paul Wigand, edited by Edmund Stengel. 1910.
Briefwechsel Johann Kaspar Bluntschlis mit Jacob Grimm. 1915.
Briefe der Brüder Grimm, edited by Albert Leitzmann and Hans Gürtler. 1923.
Briefwechsel der Brüder Jacob und Wilhelm Grimm mit Karl Lachmann, edited by Albert Leitzmann. 2 vols., 1927.
Briefwechsel zwischen Jacob Grimm und Karl Goedeke, edited by Johannes Bolte. 1927.
Briefe der Brüder Grimm an Savigny, edited by Wilhelm Schoof. 1953.
Unbekannte Briefe der Brüder Grimm, edited by Wilhelm Schoof. 1960.
John Mitchell Kemble and Jacob Grimm: A Correspondence 1832–1852. 1971.
Briefwechsel der Bruder Grimm mit Hans Georg von Hammerstein, edited by Carola Gottzmann. 1985.

Editors, *Die beiden ältesten deutschen Gedichte aus dem achten Jahrhundert: Das Lied von Hildebrand und Hadubrand und das Weissenbrunner Gebet*. 1812.
Editors, *Lieder der alten Edda*. 1815.
Editors, *Der arme Heinrich*, by Hartmann von Aue. 1815.

Editors and translators, *Irische Elfenmärchen*, by Thomas Croften Croker. 1826.

Publications by Jacob Grimm

Collections

Reden und Aufsätze, edited by Wilhelm Schoof. 1966.
Selbstbiographie: Ausgewählte Schriften, Reden und Abhandlungen. 1984.

Fiction

Irmenstrasse und Irmensäule: Eine mythologische Abhandlung. 1815.
Deutsche Mythologie. 3 vols., 1835–37; as *Teutonic Mythology*, translated by James Stevens Stallybrass, 4 vols., 1883–88.
Frau Aventiure klopft an Beneckes Thür. 1842.
Der Fundevogel: Ein Märlein. 1845.

Other

Über den altdeutschen Meistergesang. 1811.
Deutsche Grammatik. 4 vols., 1819–37.
Zur Recension der deutschen Grammatik. 1826.
Deutsche Rechtsalterthümer. 1828.
Hymnorum veteris ecclesiae XXVI interpretatio Theodisca nunc primum edita. 1830.
Bericht . . . an die Hannoversche Regierung. 1833.
Reinhart Fuchs. 1834.
Über meine Entlassung (pamphlet). 1838.
Sendschrieben an Karl Lachmann über Reinhart Fuchs. 1840.
Über zwei entdeckte Gedichte aus der Zeit des deutschen Heidenthums. 1842.
Grammatik der Hochdeutschen Sprache unserer Zeit. 1843.
Deutsche Grenzalterthümer. 1844.
Über Diphthonge nach weggefallnen Consonanten. 1845.
Über Iornandes und die Geten: Eine in der Akademie der Wissenschaften am 5. März 1846 von Jacob Grimm gehaltene Vorlesung (lecture). 1846.
Geschichte der deutschen Sprache. 2 vols., 1848.
Über Marcellus Burdingalensis. 1849.
Das Wort des Besitzes: Eine linguistische Abhandlung. 1850.
Rede auf Lachmann, gehalten in der öffentlichen Sitzung der Akademie der Wissenschaften am 3. Juli 1851 (lecture). 1851.
Über den Liebesgott: Gelesen in der Akademie am 6. Januar 1851 (lecture). 1851.
Über den Ursprung der Sprache. 1851.
Über Frauennamen aus Blumen. 1852.
Über die Namen des Donners. 1855.
Über die Marcellischen Formeln, with Adolf Pictet. 1855.
Über den Personenwechsel in der Rede. 1856.
Über einige Fälle der Attraction. 1858.
Von Vertretung männlicher durch weibliche Namensformen. 1858.
Über Schule, Universität, Academie. 1859.
Über das Verbrennen der Leichen: Eine in der Academie der Wissenschaften am 29 November 1849 . . . (lecture). 1859.
Rede auf Schiller, gehalten in der feierlichen Sitzung der König. 1859.
Rede auf Wilhelm Grimm und Rede über das Alter, edited by Herman Grimm. 1863.
Kleinere Schriften, edited by Karl Victor Müllenhoff and Eduard Ippel. 8 vols., 1864–90.
Briefwechsel zwischen Jacob Grimm und Friedrich David Graeter aus den Jahren 1810–1813, edited by Hermann Fischer. 1877.
Briefe an Hendrik Willem Tydeman: Mit einem Anhange und Anmerkungen, edited by Alexander Reifferscheid. 1883.
Briefwechsel von Jacob Grimm und Hoffmann von Fallersleben mit Henrik van Wyn: Nebst anderen Briefen zur deutschen Literatur, edited by Karl Theodor Gaedertz. 1888.
Kopitars Briefwechsel mit Jakob Grimm, edited by Max Vasmer. 1938.

Editor, *Silva de romances viejos*. 1815.
Editor, *Zur Recension der deutschen Grammatik*. 1826.
Editor, *Taciti Germania edidit et qua as res Germanorum pertinere videntur e reliquo Tacitino oere excerpsit*. 1835.
Editor, with Andreas Schmeller, *Lateinische Gedichte des X. und XI. Jahrhunderts*. 1838.
Editor, *Andreas und Elene*. 1840.
Editor, *Gedichte des Mittelalters aus König Freidrich I., dem Staufer, und aus seiner, sowie der nächstfolgenden Zeit*. 1844.

Translator, *Kleine serbische Grammatik*, by Vuk Stefanovic Karadzic. 1824.

PUBLICATIONS by Wilhelm Grimm

Other

Über deutsche Runen. 1821.
Grâve Ruodolf: Ein Altdeutsches Gedicht. 1828.
Zur Literatur der Runen. 1828.
Bruchstücke aus einem Gedichte von Assundin, 1829.
Die deutsche Heldensage. 1829.
De Hildebrando antiquissimi carminis teutonici fragmentum. 1830.
Die Sage vom Ursprung der Christusbilder. 1843.
Exhortatio ad plebem christianam Glossae Cassellanae: Über die Bedeutung der deutschen Fingernamen. 1848.
Über Freidank: Zwei Nachträge. 1850.
Altdeutsche Gespräche: Nachtrag. 1851.
Zur Geschichte des Reims. 1852.
Nachtrag zu den Casseler glossen. 1855.
Thierfabeln bei den Meistersängern. 1855.
Die Sage von Polyphem. 1857.
Kleinere Schriften, edited by Gustav Hinrichs. 4 vols., 1881–87.
Unsere Sprachlaute als Stimmbildner. 1897.

Editor, *Vrídankes Bescheidenheit.* 1834.
Editor, *Der Rosengarten.* 1836.
Editor, *Ruolandes Liet.* 1838.
Editor, *Wernher vom Niederrhein.* 1839.
Editor, *Goldene Schmiede*, by Konrad von Würzburg. 1840.
Editor, *Silvester*, by Konrad von Würzburg. 1841.
Editor, *Athis und Prophilias: Mit Nachtrag.* 2 vols., 1846–52.
Editor, *Altdeutsche Gespräche: Mit Nachtrag.* 2 vols., 1851.
Editor, with Bettina von Arnim and Karl August Varnhagen von Ense, *Sämmtliche Werke*, by Ludwig Achim von Arnim. 22 vols., 1853–56; revised edition, 21 vols., 1857; reprinted 1982.
Editor, *Bruchstücke aus einem unbekannten Gedicht vom Rosengarten.* 1860.
Editor and translator, *Drei altschottische Lieder.* 1813.

Translator, *Altdänische Heldenlieder, Balladen und Märchen.* 1811.
Translator, *Irische Land-und Seenmärchen*, by Thomas Crofton Croker, edited by Werner Moritz and Charlotte Oberfeld. 1986.

*

Bibliography: 'Bibliographie der Briefe von und an Wilhelm und Jacob Grimm: Mit einer Einführung', by Ludwig Denecke, in *Aurora* (43), 1983.

Critical Studies: *Jacob Grimm: Aus seinem Leben*, 1961, and *Die Brüder Grimm in Berlin*, 1964, both by Wilhelm Schoof; *Der junge Jacob Grimm 1805–1819* by Gunhild Ginschel, 1967; *The Brothers Grimm* by Ruth Michaelis-Jena, 1970; *Jacob Grimm und sein Bruder Wilhelm* by Ludwig Denecke, 1971, and *Die Brüder Grimm in Bildern ihrer Zeit*, 1980, by Ludwig Denecke and Karl Schulte Kemminhausen; *Paths Through the Forest: A Biography of the Brothers Grimm* by Murray B. Peppard, 1971; *Jacob Grimm's Conception of German Studies* by Peter F. Ganz, 1973; *Brüder Grimm* by

Hermann Gerstner, 1973; *The Uses of Enchantment: The Meaning and Importance of Fairy Tales* by Bruno Bettelheim, 1977; *The German Legends of the Brothers Grimm* edited and translated by Donald Ward, 1981; *One Fairy Story Too Many: The Brothers Grimm and Their Tales* by John M. Ellis, 1983; *Die Brüder Grimm: Leben, Werke, Zeit* by Gabriele Seitz, 1984; *Wilhelm Grimms Nibelungenkolleg* edited by Else Ebel, 1985; *Die Brüder Grimm in ihrer amtlichen und politischen Tätigkeit* edited by Hans-Bernd Harder and Eckehard Kaufmann, 1985; *Die Brüder Grimm: Dokumente ihres Lebens und Wirkens* edited by Dieter Hennig and Bernhard Lauer, 1985; *Die Märchen der Brüder Grimm* by Heinz Rölleke, 1985; *Die Märchenbrüder: Jacob und Wilhelm Grimm—ihr Leben und Wirken* by Jürgen Weishaupt, 1985; *Grimms' Bad Girls and Bold Boys: The Moral and Social Vision of the Tales* by Ruth B. Bottigheimer, 1987; *The Hard Facts of the Grimms' Fairy Tales* by Maria M. Tatar, 1987; *The Brothers Grimm and the Folktale* edited by James M. McGlathery, 1988; *The Brothers Grimm: From Enchanted Forests to the Modern World* by Jack Zipes, 1988; *The Grimm Brothers and the Germanic Past: International Bicentenary Symposium on the Brothers Grimm*, 1990; *The Brothers Grimm and Their Critics: Folktales and the Quest for Meaning* by Christa Kamenetsky, 1992; *Grimm's Fairy Tales: A History of Criticism on a Popular Classic* by James M. McGlathery, 1994.

*   *   *

The Brothers Grimm, Jacob and Wilhelm, are universally known for their *Tales* (or *Fairy Tales*), the single most often translated and republished book in German. Inseparable in life as in legend, the Grimm brothers also co-founded three 19th-century academic disciplines: European historical linguistics, or philology; folklore studies; and German *Germanistik*—the study of the history of German culture, language, and literature. Finally the *German Dictionary* became their gigantic epitaph. It was initially planned as a small book for household use; 'snowed under' with words, as he put it, Jacob had reached the letter F and, it is always said, the word *Frucht* (fruit), when he died. The Berlin Academy of Sciences did not complete the dictionary, which contains some 400,000 entries, until 1960.

Kinder- und Hausmärchen (*Fairy Tales*) was their first book—the shortened edition of 1825, illustrated by their brother Ludwig Emil, established it as a popular classic—and it is the only one of their major works, published jointly or singly, which does not have the word *Deutsch* (normally meaning 'Germanic') in the title. This may be regarded as a concession to the fact that most of the tales, and the motifs, too, are by no means German or indeed Germanic, but are international. Many are certainly ancient; but a high proportion are equally certainly of medieval origin. The Grimms took as much from older written sources as from oral ones. And at least some of their key 'oral' informants were women of their own acquaintance, well-to-do, well-educated, and in a number of cases bilingual and notedly talented, rather than belonging to the illiterate, unindividuated peasantry invoked by their prefaces.

If the Grimms failed to make these facts clear (and some of them are still controversial, as is the assessment of Wilhelm's role as editor and writer), it is because their wider project was specifically a revival of Germanic culture, animated by a Romantic faith in a myth of history. This myth posited both an original state of linguistic and cultural unity (eventually located in the speakers of an 'Indo-Germanic' original tongue from which, they thought, all other languages derived); and also a manifest destiny, not only of Germans but of the whole world, to return to that monolingual condition. This theory appears to imply that the rest of the world will return to its origins under German tutelage. Be that as it may, their life's work was no matter of neutral scholarship. The *Tales* and the less popularly successful *Deutsche Sagen* (*German Legends*), were compilations of those 'threads' of folk tradition which 'finally link it directly to ancient times' (Wilhelm Grimm, preface to the *Tales*). These ancient times were then revived in ever more detail in the monumental editions of Old German texts, the compilations and exhaustive collations of material on the history of Germanic tribal religion and law, and the historical studies in grammar, vocabulary, and phonetics. Dedicating his *Geschichte der deutschen Sprache* [History of the Germanic Language] (1848)—a collection of diverse studies in ancient culture and religion, grammar and philology—to the patriotic historian Gervinus, Jacob Grimm called his work 'thoroughly political' in the context of 'our fatherland [which is] divided contrary to nature (*unser widernatürlich geteiltes Vaterland*)'.

This was the same year as the European revolutions and of the first, short-lived German National Assembly in Frankfurt-am-Main, at which Jacob served as a deputy. Eleven years earlier, both brothers had been among seven professors dismissed from Göttingen after protesting against the King of Hanover's suspension of the constitution. The brothers' work embodied the nationalist aspirations of the Romantic generation. It proved unfortunately exploitable by later generations of aggressive nationalists. But the Grimms had no party politics: they were patriots and liberal constitutionalists, in the era of the Napoleonic Wars followed by the restoration of territorial principalities in the space left vacant by the end of the Holy Roman Empire. Their generation speculated eagerly about past and future German unity, freedom, and greatness. The brothers' inspiration came from several sources. Since the 1770s, J.G. Herder had called for collections of folk (oral) traditions to be made, and the Grimms adopted his postulate that *Völker* (peoples/nations) were unconsciously unified collectives linked by language, custom, and history, which were now on the way to becoming conscious of their unity. The *Volk* had once spontaneously, without individual effort, brought forth poetry on a grand scale, poetry which now survived in precious fragments in early writing and in oral tradition. It was the task of present writers to (re)create cultural unity. Thus the Romantics of the 1790s had called for a 'new mythology' (A.W. Schlegel) and set about constructing it out of the traces of past mythologies. This programme determined the Grimms' lifelong work. Their collection of tales also followed in the immediate wake of their friends Achim von Armin and Clemens Brentano's collection of songtexts, *Des Knaben Wunderhorn* (*The Boy's Magic Horn*, 3 vols., 1806–08). There too—notoriously today—the 'discovery' and 'invention' of 'national tradition' are inseparable.

Romantic historians, as A.W. Schlegel had put it, are 'prophets facing backwards'. The Grimms were far from wanting merely to document the past, though they did much to develop historical methodology; they hoped to spur present and future creativity and to teach Germans to seek unity. They were peculiarly fitted by their personal background to become spokesmen for their generation (and in the *Tales*, spokesmen for later generations of mainly middle-class readers, parents and children, too). They coped with the traumatic early loss of their father by assuming joint responsibility for the family, which entailed unremitting labour in order to maintain their respectability. The energy animating

their researches is that of the desire to retrieve their lost father, as much as the 'lost' or 'denatured' fatherland. The ethic promoted by the *Tales*—resourceful individualism tempered by a very strong sense of amicable, fraternal generosity—is that of a family determined, against the odds, to maintain if not enhance its social standing, as much as it is that of a quite narrowly middle-class nationalist movement struggling to make good a history of cultural division and decadence.

In *Deutsche Grammatik* [Germanic Grammar], Jacob—a more assiduous philologist and historian, though a much less gifted story-teller than Wilhelm—built on the work of the Danish philologist, Rasmus Rank, in order to formulate what has become known as 'Grimm's Law' of sound shifts in the transition from Indo-European to Germanic (2000 to 1000 BC). The poet Heinrich Heine wrote that this book is 'a Gothic cathedral in which all the Germanic peoples raise their voices, like giant choirs, each in their dialect'. The metaphor aptly described the Grimms' utopian vision: their work orchestrated masses of disparate material in an edifice erected to the glory of the German language. Their achievements are monumental; they remain legendary, and their work's complex, central significance for 'German identity' continues to be highly controversial, as do the many and varied mythical, psychoanalytical, formalist, structuralist, functionalist, social historical, and pedagogical interpretations of their *Tales*.

—Tom Cheeseman

HANSEL AND GRETEL (Hänsel und Gretel)
Story by Jacob and Wilhelm Grimm, 1812.

Near the borders of a large forest dwelt in olden times a poor woodcutter, who had two children—a boy named Hansel, and his sister Gretel.

These words usher the reader or hearer of 'Hansel and Gretel' into the world of fairy-tale. The archaic language of its first line—'dwelt' and 'olden'—signals our removal from the everyday to the timeless and ever-accessible imaginative realm of fairy land. The status of the lowly woodcutter, and the presence of a boy and girl, ensure that by the end of the sentence its audience has identified with the two children of the title. The indefinite geography—a large forest—conjures to the imagination whichever body of woodland the listener knows best. Having imaginatively located ourselves within the wood, and within the tale, we are prepared for a story which, like most fairy-tales, involves a perilous journey, a trial of wit or courage, and a happy homecoming. Features such as the wicked stepmother, the evil enchantress, and the animals which aid the hero, are part of the constant 'language' of the fairy world, yet 'Hansel and Gretel' creates its own unique and highly memorable atmosphere: one of darkness, cruelty, and capture. The anxieties which the tale evokes are, for a child, profound ones: the story opens with the children lying awake at night listening to their parents talking—their stepmother is arguing that they should be left to the mercy of the wild beasts. As the story continues, its emotional power is generated by primal fears: of abandonment, of being lost, of starvation and murder. These fears are first conjured and then exorcised in Aristotelian catharsis leaving Hansel and Gretel free and happy. The basic, instinctive nature of the story's concerns is best exemplified by its obsession with food and with hunger.

To attempt to understand such a tale rationally is misplaced. It has its own order, an unconscious order lying deeper than the intellect, one which combines the most instinctive of urges with subtle perceptions of the possibility of magic in the universe.

Like a dream, then, the story involves unconscious fears and intuitions, and like a dream the tale resolves its complexes not by logical progression but by means of developing patterns of images. Like a dream, it functions by means of recurrence, development, substitution, and transformation. The elements of recurrence and development are evident in the division of the tale, like a dream, into a number of 'moves'. Each move deals with the complex inherited from the previous move in a new way. It re-casts its symbols into a new situation which offers a new perspective on, and heightened awareness of, the initial problem. The element of recurrence in the narrative leads to the creation of a series of parallels and echoes between the images of the story. The first image represents an object from real life, the second image represents that same scene transformed by the 'greater life' of the unconscious. Thus the wicked stepmother twice builds a fire, while the wicked ogress has a fiery oven. These parallels serve to enrich the real world with a layer of fantasy: the 'magical reality' of the unconscious. Thus the woodcutter's humble cottage is replaced by a cottage of sweets, and pockets weighted down with white pebbles become pockets full of pearls.

Substitution is most obvious in the handling of the wicked stepmother. The stepmother, while terrifying, cannot be attacked directly, so the story shifts to a new location, where an even more hateful woman is dominant. There she can be defeated and killed. When the children return home at last, their stepmother has, naturally enough, died—for in another incarnation she has been tackled and disposed of.

A magical world is evident in the story, one which serves always to help and guide the protagonists. One could term this the 'white world'. The moon's light makes the white pebbles silver, and transforms them into gleaming markers. Hansel attempts, but fails, to achieve the same effect with white crumbs, disguising his actions with references to his white pigeon and white cat. The image of the white bird is one which haunts 'Hansel and Gretel'. The fictional white pigeon he invents seems to summon the real bird which leads them into danger through ultimate victory, in the candy cottage. At the moment of triumph Hansel escapes from captivity 'like a bird from a cage'. The phrase seems more than coincidental, for after this identification of Hansel with the bird the plot is, apparently unnecessarily, prolonged by a further final trial. The children's return is blocked by a stretch of water, but now at last the white bird is realized as a helpful figure. The white duck appears, to ferry both children home.

The story shifts, at its ending, to focus not on the children but on their father, leaving behind the terrors of the forest. For the children who form its audience, it offers at last an image of happiness and security, as both Hansel and Gretel are embraced within their father's arms. The crisis of the opening paragraph has been overcome. The final sentence forms an echo or redemption of the first lines: 'From this moment all his care and sorrow was at an end, and the father lived in happiness with his children all his life'.

The language of the story is typical of the traditional tales that were collected by the Grimm brothers. It is simple and straightforward in both vocabulary and grammatical structure. As with other traditional tales the 'bare bones' of the story are designed to be easily memorized. The narrative proceeds in a series of tableaux—the children lying in bed, the moon shining on the pebbles, and so on. Direct speech is kept to a minimum, and is encoded in distinctive formulae. The use of repetition serves as a mnemonic device. The

written text is subject to endless variation in the hands of its tellers, but the Grimms' version offers a story whose complexity belies the simplicity of its language.

—Edmund Cusick

GRIMMELSHAUSEN, Hans Jakob Christoffel von. Published under pseudonymns: authorship not established until the 19th century. Born in Gelnhausen, near Frankfurt am Main, Germany, in 1622. Educated at Lutheran Latin School, Gelnhausen, 1627. Family fled to Hanau, 1634, after Gelnhausen was plundered in the Thirty Years War. Married Katharina Henninger in 1649. Served in the Kaiser's army after 1637: garrison soldier in Offenburg, 1639, clerk, 1645, then secretary, 1648, in regimental office; steward for the von Schauenburg family in Gaisbach bei Oberkirch, 1649; innkeeper in Gaisbach, 1658; steward for Dr Küeller, 1662; innkeeper, 1665; mayor of Renchen, 1667; temporary soldier, 1675. *Died 17 August 1676.*

PUBLICATIONS

Collections

[Collected Works], edited by H. Kurz. 4 vols., 1863–64.
Gesammelte Werke, edited by Rolf Tarot. 1966—.

Works

Der Abenteuerliche Simplicissimus Teutsch und Continuatio, edited by Rolf Tarot. 1967; as *The Adventurous Simplicissimus*, translated by A.T.S. Goodrich, 1912; as *Simplicissimus the Vagabond*, 1924; as *The Adventures of a Simpleton*, translated by Walter Wallich, 1962; as *Simplicicius Simplicissimus*, translated by Monte Adair, 1986.
Dietwalts und Amelindens anmutige Lieb- und Leidsbeschreibung, edited by Rolf Tarot. 1967.
Trutz Simplex; oder, . . . Lebensbeschreibung der Erzbetrügerin und Landstörzerin Courasche, edited by Wolfgang Bender. 1967; as *Mother Courage*, translated by Walter Wallich, 1965.
Des durchleuchtigen Prinzen Proximi . . . und Lympidae Liebs-Geschicht-Erzählung, edited by Franz Günter Sieveke. 1967.
Des vortrefflich keuschen Josephs in Ägypten Lebensbeschreibung samt des Musai Lebenslauf, edited by Wolfgang Bender. 1968.
Simplicianischer Zweiköpfiger Ratio Status, edited by Rolf Tarot. 1968.
Der seltsame Springinsfeld, edited by Franz Günter Sieveke. 1969; as *The Singular Life Story of Heedless Hopalong*, translated by Robert L. Hiller and John C. Osborne, 1981.
Satyrischer Pilgram, edited by Wolfgang Bender. 1970.
Das wunderbarliche Vogelnest, edited by Rolf Tarot. 1970.
Die verkehrte Welt, edited by Franz Günter Sieveke. 1973.
Kleinere Schriften (Beernhäuter, Gauckeltasche, Stolze Melcher, Bart-Krieg, Galgen-Männlin, etc.), edited by Rolf Tarot. 1973.
Ratstübel Plutonis, edited by Wolfgang Bender. 1975.

Teutscher Michel und Ewigwährender Kalender, edited by Rolf Tarot. 1976.

*

Bibliography: *Grimmelshausen-Bibliographie 1666–1972* by Italo Michele Battafarano, 1975.

Critical Studies: *Grimmelshausen* by Kenneth C. Hayens, 1932; *Grimmelshausen* by Kenneth Negus, 1974; *Grimmelshausen in Selbstzeugnissen und Bilddokumenten* by Curt Hohoff, 1978; *The Nature of Realism in Grimmelshausen's Simplicissimus Cycle of Novels* by R.P.T. Aylett, 1982.

* * *

Reading Grimmelshausen we feel ourselves to be in the immediate company of a narrator; stories are told—to fictional listeners and to us—and much of the material rings like first-hand truth. But the narrative voices have to be listened to critically; they are continually ironized and relativized by other perspectives offered in the text. The text itself supplies its own commentary—from the perspective of the narrator's old age, for example—or we ourselves, among the listeners, are encouraged to comment.

Grimmelshausen is a great realist. He worked in a genre, the picaresque, marvellously suited to his times, his purposes, and his gifts. The picaresque novel, imported from Spain in the service of the Counter-Reformation by Aegidus Albertinus, is realistic and anti-heroic. In Spain it flourished during the Moorish Wars, and the Thirty Years War makes up all of Grimmelshausen's world. The picaro is a delinquent, and he lives in delinquent times. In times of licensed immorality he lives his immoral life.

War is depicted truthfully by Grimmelshausen, as pointless and horrible. He repeatedly mocks the lying heroic tradition. War is the licence, under arbitrary creeds and slogans, to commit atrocities. War is seen from the true, the lowest point of view: from among the dead, for example, as the scavengers come round. We learn most, to our greatest horror, quite incidentally. What happens to an officer's mistress when he tires of her? She is given to the stable boys: a detail, Grimmelshausen implies, too ordinary to dwell on. War is continually rendered strange; it has to be, or we should not see it for what it is, so accustomed have we become.

Grimmelshausen works to the important Baroque principle of 'mögliche Realität' ('possible reality'). More happens to his heroes than really could; he accumulates around them an implausible number of truthful incidents. For realism is not an end in itself; it serves an urgent moral and religious purpose. Man must be shown as he is, as he really lives, in order that he may change. All human life is precarious and war only accentuates that fact; and in war man behaves according to his nature, which is greedy, cruel, and selfish. Much of Baroque literature rests on a simple antithesis: the World or God. To be in the world is to be apart from God. The ordinary state of the world, for Grimmelshausen, is war. What the child last sees of the world as he enters the forest is his family home pillaged and its inhabitants raped or tortured; and what he first sees when he leaves the forest is again torture. That is the world.

Simplicissimus passes, without plausible inner motivation, through the predetermined stages of a religious and ethical career. He begins life in brute ignorance; in the forest with the hermit (his true father) he acquires *sancta simplicitas*;

leaving the forest he is for a time a holy fool (Christianity in such a world appearing necessarily foolish); then, as court fool, he becomes a knowing social critic. Next, for most of the book, he lives not as a critic of the world but as its exemplar, as a worldling. Finally, with only nominal motivation, he leaves the world to resume his innocent hermit's state. He undergoes an exemplary dis-illusioning, an *Enttäuschung*.

Grimmelshausen's books are still, as he intended them, amusing and instructive. They are enjoyable and affirmative in their exuberance of language and invention; and salutary in their truthful exposure of man living badly.

—David Constantine

GRYPHIUS, Andreas. Born in Glogau, Silesia, 22 October 1616. Educated at schools in Glogau, 1631, Goerlitz and Fraustadt, 1632–34. Married Rosina Deutschländer in 1647. Private tutor to Georg von Schönborn's children, Danzig, 1634–36; travelled to Holland, studied and lectured at the University of Leyden, 1638–42; went on Grand Tour, 1644–47, lived in Paris and Strasbourg, visited Florence, Rome, Ferrara, and Venice. Secretary to the estates, Glogau, 1650. *Died 16 July 1664.*

PUBLICATIONS

Collections

Dramatische Dichtung, edited by Julius Tittmann. 4 vols., 1870.
Lustspiele, Trauerspiele, Lyrische Gedichte, edited by Hermann Palm. 3 vols., 1878–84.
Gedichte, edited by Johannes Pfeiffer. 1948.
Werke, edited by Marian Szyrocki. 1963.
Gesamtausgabe der deutschprachigen Werke, edited by Marian Szyrocki and Hugh Powell. 8 vols., 1963–72.
Ergänzungsband. 4 vols., 1983–87.
Werke. 1985.

Plays

Ermordete Majestät; oder, Carolus Stuardus, König von Gross Britannien (produced 1650). 1657; as *Murdered Majesty; or, Charles Stuart*, edited by Hugh Powell, 1955.
Leo Armenius (produced 1651). 1650.
Gibeoniter; oder, die sieben Bruder, from the play by Joost van den Vondel (produced 1652). 1698.
Majuma. 1653.
Catharina von Georgien (produced 1655). 1657.
Beständige Mutter; oder, Die Heilige Felicitas (produced 1657). 1657.
Cardenio und Celinde; oder, Unglücklich Verliebte (produced 1661). 1657; edited by Hugh Powell, 1961.
Absurda Comica; oder, Herr Peter Squentz. 1658; edited by Sydney H. Moore, 1908; also edited by Hugh Powell, 1957.
Freuden und Trauer-Spiele, auch oden und Sonnette sampt Herr Peter Squentz. 1658.
Der grossmüthige Rechtsgelehrte; oder, Der Sterbende Ämilius Paulus Papinianus (produced 1660). 1659.
Verlibtes Gespenst and *Die geliebte Dornrose*. 1661.

Horribilicribrifax; oder, Wählende Liebhaber (produced 1674). 1663.

Verse

Sonnete. 1637.
Sonn-und Feiertags Sonnete. 1639.
Sonnete. 1643.
Oden. 1643.
Epigrammatica. 1643.
Olivetum. 1646.
Teutsche Reim-Gedichte. 1650.
Kirchhofsgedanken, Oden. 1657.
Andreae Gryphii Deutscher Gedichte. 1657.
Epigrammata; oder, Bey Schrifften. 1663.

Other

Fewrige Freystadt. 1673.
Dissertationes funebres; oder, Leich-Abdankungen, bey unter schiedlichen hoch—und ansehnlichen Leich-Begängnüssen gehalten. Auch nebenst seinem letzten Ehren-Gedächtnuss und Lebens-Lauft. 1683.

Translator, *Die Seugamme, oder Untreues Hausgesinde*, by Girolamo Razzi. 1663.
Translator, *Der Schwärmende Schaffer*, by Thomas Corneille. 1663.

*

Bibliography: *Auswahlbibliographie zu Andreas Gryphius* by K.H. Habersetzer in *Text + Kritik*, 1980.

Critical Studies: *Die Lyrik des Andreas Gryphius* by Victor Manheimer, 1904; *Die Bildlichkeit in der Dichtung des Andreas Gryphius* by Gerhard Fricke, 1933; *Der junge Gryphius*, 1959, and *Andreas Gryphius: Leben und Werk*, 1964, both by Marian Szyrocki; *Andreas Gryphius: Leo Armenius* by Herman J. Tisch, 1968; *The Sonnets of Andreas Gryphius: Use of the Poetic Word in the Seventeenth Century* by Marvin S. Schindler, 1971; *Andreas Gryphius: Poet Between Epochs* by Hugo Becker, 1973; *The Constructive Art of Andreas Gryphius's Historical Tragedies* by Janifer Gerd, 1986; *Andreas Gryphius* by Eberhard Mannack, 1986; *Andreas Gryphius: A Modern Perspective* by Blake Lee Spahr, 1993.

*   *   *

Andreas Gryphius exerted considerable influence as a dramatist, but his carefully crafted sonnets, odes, epigrams, and religious songs also helped to stabilize and invigorate the German literary language of the Baroque age. Underpinned by neo-classical scholarship and the religious and spiritual anguish of the Thirty Years War, his works eclectically re-fashioned a wide range of native and non-native forms with remarkable consistency. Six years at Leiden and travels in England, France, and Italy made him aware of the need to raise German drama to a higher level, although his primarily allegorical mode precluded the psychological depth of his European counterparts. His tragedies and poetry are suffused with an intense personal conviction, typical of the 17th century, that God is the sole source of constancy in a world of inconstancy and illusion. Stressing the vanity and transience of earthly endeavour, his antithetically structured plots and dialogues reflect the stark polarity and duality of existence: good struggles with evil, constancy with inconstancy, illusion with reality, and eternity with the fleeting moment, while life itself is a perpetual battle in which the individual, like a rudderless ship in a storm, is tossed helplessly toward the rocks of destruction.

Gryphius rarely blurred the prevailing socially based distinctions between comedy and tragedy. In accordance with Opitz's advocacy of the unities and stylistic decorum, the major tragedies, *Leo Armenius*, *Catharina von Georgien* [Catharine of Georgia], *Ermordete Majestät; oder, Carolus Stuardus* (*Murdered Majesty; or, Charles Stuart*) and *Paulus Papinianus*, dignify historical material and affairs of state with predominantly alexandrine verse and the more elevated poetic forms. Gryphius often lent linguistic dynamism to the declamatory, rhetorical, and circumscriptive 'high style', but neo-classical concepts of form sat somewhat uneasily with his Baroque profusion and subordination of art to the Christian message. Catharina, the Christian Queen of Georgia, for example, is put to death by her enamoured captor, the Persian Sheikh Abas, for refusing to marry him. After her death the pagan Abas is metaphorically consumed by the flames of hell experienced in his guilt-ridden imagination. Despite a certain political topicality, these events of 1624 are 'spiritualized', rather than dramatized. Moral edification toward Christian stoicism was more important than the psychological coherence of the basically allegorical plot and exemplary characters. In these 'martyr tragedies' the protagonist is the divinely-ordained head of state who offers stability, yet whose crown is also an emblem of the Wheel of Fortune and the Crown of Thorns. Any attempt to remove them is portrayed as a villainous transgression of the divine order. The villain is the driving force of the plot, whereas the hero or heroine is trapped in a passive role of suffering victim, which allows ample opportunity for rhetorical, bombastic lament on the vicissitudes of human existence. Earthly attachments like human love may appear fleetingly, but only as past vices which the hero has firmly overcome: there is little to deflect the 'martyr' from welcoming death as a desirable release. As Walter Benjamin (*The Origin of German Tragic Drama*) and others have suggested, Aristotle's fear and pity are separately allocated to villain and hero(ine), so that a bloody physical catastrophe, often recounted in gruesome detail, replaces a truly tragic denouement.

Gryphius gradually reduced the narrative element in his tragedies and increased the presentation of important events on stage, but he also relied on the visual spectacle of operatic tradition: impressive stage sets, pomp and ceremony, and lavish costumes counteracted the frequent stasis of a slow-moving plot. Linked to this is his use of visions, dreams, and ghosts, any of which may appear at crucial points as a means of warning reprobates about eternal retribution. The most spectacular such device occurs in *Cardenio und Celinde*, where the lustful Cardenio believes he sees his former lover, Olympia, but she reveals herself as a skeleton exhorting him to repent or be damned. This 'conversion therapy' is reinforced shortly afterwards when he sees a corpse emerge from and re-enter its grave! Such supernatural elements are often dogmatically interpreted by a Chorus or 'Reyen' of allegorical figures who proclaim the *vanitas mundi*.

Cardenio und Celinde, however, breaks down some of the traditional barriers between tragedy and comedy. The characters, claims Gryphius in his preface, are 'almost too lowly for a tragedy', for they belong to the low aristocracy, not far from the bourgeoisie. The action concentrates not on affairs of state, but on purely personal problems in normal human relationships. The language is marginally closer to that of everyday speech, although it still remains elevated enough to lend dignity to the subject matter. A double, interlinked plot illustrates the two kinds of earthly love, one rational and sanctioned by God in marriage, the other sensual and irrational. A hint of almost Shakespearean comic relief occurs in IV.ii, when two servants are momentarily pushed to the centre stage. It is difficult, however, to see the action as tragic, because all the characters are reconciled, overcome their earthly lusts, and live piously ever after.

The comedies, which satirize the lower social orders and use prose to reflect the 'mundanity' of the action, appear more realistic in their earthy language, naive characters, and freer plots, yet they too employ type characters and are directed towards edification. The comedy of Gryphius which has best stood the test of time is *Absurda Comica; oder, Herr Peter Squentz*, which was probably written between 1647 and 1650, and first appeared in 1657 or 1658. The artisans' comical performance of Ovid's tale of Piramus and Thisbe is well-known to English audiences from Shakespeare's *A Midsummer Night's Dream*. Although Shakespeare's version was performed by wandering English actors in Europe during the 17th century, Gryphius is more likely to have known Dutch and German versions. In his preface, Gryphius says that his *Peter Squentz* was to be performed alongside one of his tragedies. This was probably *Cardenio und Celinde*, with which it shares thematic affinities, especially with regard to human love and notions of illusion. In contrast to Shakespeare, who satirizes all social levels, Gryphius uses the aristans' performance, which is the main body of his play, to attack the outdated notions of popular bourgeois culture from the viewpoint of courtly, high culture. The different social classes appear on stage, but the device of a play within a play, with the courtiers and educated court-officials patronizingly mocking the artisans' performance, reinforces social and cultural distinctions. The main butt of the literary (and implicitly social) satire is Hans Sachs, the great 16th-century popular dramatist, whose work is mercilessly condemned. Despite its harsh satirical tone, however, the play provides delightful linguistic and visual humour of some sophistication and vivacity.

Horribilicribrifax takes up the type of the braggart soldier returning from the war, but the hero is often submerged in rapid scene-changes, a multiplicity of characters, and shifting dramatic focus. The main themes, the nature of human love and the necessity to distinguish between illusions and reality, are also explored in the double-play *Verlibtes Gespenst/Die geliebte Dornrose*, where once again the different social classes are kept separate, but their love affairs are skilfully paralleled.

—E.A. McCobb

GUILLAUME DE MACHAUT. Born in Rheims (?) c.1300. May have been educated at Rheims, where he spent much of his later life. Entered the service of John of Luxembourg, King of Bohemia around 1323, and remained his secretary until the king's death in 1346; subsequently attached to the houses of Charles, King of Navarre, John, Duke of Berry, and the princes of France; held chaplaincy at Verdun, 1330, Arras, 1332, and Rheims, 1333. Prolific composer: the most important figure of the French Ars Nova. Spent much of his later years producing works in manuscript for his royal patrons. *Died 13 April 1377.*

PUBLICATIONS

Collections

Les Oeuvres, edited by Prosper Tarbe. 1849.
Oeuvres, edited by Ernest Hoepffner. 3 vols., 1908–21.
Poésies lyriques, edited by Vladimir Chichmaref. 2 vols., 1909; 1 vol., 1973.

Verse

Le Confort d'ami, edited and translated by R. Barton Palmer, 1992.
Le Dit de la harpe, edited by K. Young. 1943.
15 poésies inédites, edited by Bernard Monod. 1903.
The Fountain of Love and Two Other Love Vision Poems, edited and translated by R. Burton Palmer. 1993.
Le Jugement du roy de Behaigne; and Remede de fortune, edited by James L. Wimsatt and William W. Kibler. 1988.
The Judgement of the King of Bavaria, edited and translated by R. Barton Palmer, 1984.
Le Jugement du roy de Navarre, as *The Judgement of the King of Navarre*, edited and translated by R. Barton Palmer, 1988.
Le Livre du Voir dit, edited by P. Paris. 1875, reprinted 1969, and by P. Imbs, 1988.
La Louange des dames, edited by Nigel Wilkins. 1972.
Prise d'Alexandrie, edited by L. de Mas Latrie. 1877.
Quelques poèmes de Guillaume de Machaut. In *'Dits' et 'débats'* by Jean Froissart, edited by Anthime Fourrier, 1979.
Recueil de Galantries, edited by A. Vitale Brovarone, 1980.

Other

Guillaume de Machaut: Musikalische Werke, edited by Friedrich Ludwig. 4 vols., 1926–54.

*

Bibliography: *Guillaume de Machaut: An Analytic Bibliography* by Kevin Brownlee, 1990.

Critical Studies: *Guillaume de Machaut: Musicien et poète rémois* by André Douce, 1948; *Guillaume de Machaut* by Siegmund Levarie, 1954; *Guillaume de Machaut, 1300–1377: La Vie et l'oeuvre musicale* by Armand Machabey, 2 vols., 1955; *Le Poète et le Prince: L'Évolution du lyrisme courtois de Guillaume de Machaut à Charles d'Orléans* by Daniel Poiron, 1965; *The Marguerite Poetry of Guillaume de Machaut* edited by James Wimsatt, 1970; *Guillaume de Machaut* by Gilbert Reaney, 1971; *A Poet at the Fountain: Essays on the Narrative Verse of Guillaume de Machaut* by William Calin, 1974; *Poetic Identity in Guillaume de Machaut* by Kevin Brownlee, 1984; *Guillaume de Machaut et l'écriture au XIVe siècle: 'Un engin si soutil'* by Jacqueline Cerquiglini, 1985; *Machaut's Mass: An Introduction* by Daniel Leech-Wilkinson, 1990; *Le Voir-dit de Guillaume de Machaut, étude littéraire* by Paul Imbs, 1991.

*   *   *

After the death of Guillaume de Machaut in 1377, the poet Eustache Deschamps wrote a moving *déploration* (put to music by Andrieu) in which he lamented the death of the man who was universally considered to be the greatest poet and musician of his age. All those who care about music and poetry are invited to mourn the passing of a figure who, in the words of William Calin, 'as a musician and as a poet, is one of the great international masters of the 14th century'. And yet, after his death, Machaut's reputation went into something of a decline, and it is only in the last 30 years or so that he has come to be recognized as an outstanding author. For the genres that he perfected—and to a certain degree invented— such as the *dit*, the *motet*, the *virelai* and the polyphonic *ballade* and *rondeau*, were soon to go out of fashion, to be replaced by genres borrowed from classical antiquity. Born in 1300, he was the dominant figure both in lyric poetry and in music in 14th-century France. His output was enormous and wide-ranging. Although a canon of the church (he spent his later years in Rheims, in his native Champagne), he wrote much verse that was profane and gently erotic in tone, as well as sacred music. He was also very much a court poet, depending on wealthy patrons for his livelihood and forced to write works to their taste as much as to his own. None the less, a distinctive authorial voice comes through in his work, especially in his *dits*, a genre which he effectively made his own.

Machaut wrote ten long *dits* and four shorter ones. Among the long ones, the most famous are perhaps the *Le Livre du Voir dit*, the *Remede de fortune*, *Le Jugement du roy de Behaigne* and *Le Jugement du roy de Navarre*. Despite their apparent diversity, these narrative *dits* share a common pattern. The narrator, usually preoccupied with love, embarks on a quest that will be both a physical journey and an imaginative adventure of experience and learning. He will return a happier and wiser man. The trappings of the quest are recognizably courtly, with gardens of love, fine castles, and of course beautiful women. But these works are much more complex than this structure and subject-matter would appear to allow. As Calin has pointed out, all the *dits* (a very flexible genre) are 'poems of consolation'. Machaut uses these long narrative poems to provide the reader with a very clear idea of his world-view. The progression of the protagonist from being an inexperienced outsider to being welcomed in his maturity to the civilized play world of courtly society is typical. On the way, however, the author gives his views of a series of topics that range from etiquette to morality and even flights of philosophical fancy. The (inevitable) unwillingness of the courtly ladies in these poems to appear anything other than unattainable also allows the author to indulge in pseudo-autobiographical musings on the vagaries of love. He invests these poetic fictions with a realistic veneer that lends them an air of authenticity, so much so that critics have sometimes seen his *Le Livre du Voir dit* as the real-life confessions of an old poet infatuated with a young woman. Whether or not Peronne did exist in the way she is described in Machaut's poem is perhaps immaterial; what matters more is the realistic depiction of the pangs of love.

Machaut is best known today for his music. Although he is associated in most people's minds with the *Ars nova*, he was not in fact especially radical in his musical and poetical tastes and ambitions. In a career lasting 40 years he naturally tried his hand at different styles and forms, and there is an impressive variety of theme, message, and tone in his work. He is remembered as the composer of the first complete polyphonic setting of the 'Ordinary of the Mass'. His output of sacred music is huge, but he is most accessible today as the composer of poems of profane love. The *ballade* (both monophonic and polyphonic) was his favourite form, but he also wrote memor-able *virelais* such as the haunting 'Quant je suis mis au retour' ['When I return'] and works of outstanding complexity. As David Munrow remarked, Machaut's genius 'lies in the way he combined a mastery of all the musical techniques of his age with a gift of melody and expressiveness. He was as good at writing a simple tune as he was at writing an elaborate isorhythmic motet and he approached the business of composition with the freedom of genius'. The same critic claimed that Machaut's motets were 'one of the high points of medieval art'. With such technical expertise, such a range of forms and expressions, it is little wonder that Guillaume de Machaut was admired by contemporaries and praised so memorably in words and music by those who survived him.

—Michael Freeman

GUILLÉN, Jorge. Born in Valladolid, Spain, 18 January 1893. Educated at the Instituto de Valladolid, 1903–09; Maison Perreyve, Fribourg, Switzerland, 1909–11; University of Madrid, Faculty of Philosophy and Letters, 1911–13; University of Granada, 1913, degree 1913; University of Madrid, Ph.D. 1924. Married 1) Germain Cahen in 1921 (died 1947), one daughter and one son; 2) Irene Mochi-Sismondi in 1961. Contributor to *El Norte de Castilla*, from 1918; lecturer or professor of Spanish, the Sorbonne, Paris, 1917–23, University of Murcia, 1926–29, Oxford University, 1929–31, and University of Seville, 1931–38; jailed briefly in Pamplona by Nationalist forces, on suspicion of spying, 1936; went into exile, 1938; taught at Middlebury College, Vermont, 1938–39, and McGill University, Montreal, 1939–40; professor of Spanish, Wellesley College, Massachusetts, 1940–57: retired as emeritus professor; Charles Eliot Norton lecturer, Harvard University, Cambridge, Massachusetts, 1957, 1958. Also taught at Yale University, New Haven, Connecticut, 1947, Colegio de Mexico, 1950, University of California, Berkeley, 1951, Ohio State University, Columbus, 1952–53, University of the Andes, Bogota, 1961, University of Puerto Rico, Rio Piedras, 1962, 1964, University of Pittsburgh, 1966, and University of California, San Diego, 1968. Returned to Spain, 1978, and settled in Malaga. Recipient: Guggenheim fellowship, 1954; American Academy award of merit, 1955; City of Florence poetry prize, 1957; Etna-Taormina prize (Italy), 1959; International Grand prize for poetry (Belgium), 1961; San Luca prize (Florence), 1964; Bennett prize (*Hudson Review*), 1975; Cervantes prize, 1976; Feltrinelli prize (Italy), 1977; Alfonso Reyes prize (Mexico), 1977; Yoliztli prize (Mexico), 1982. *Died 6 February 1984.*

PUBLICATIONS

Verse

Cántico. 1928; enlarged edition, 1936, edited by José Manuel Blecua, 1970; further enlarged edition, as *Cántico, fe de vida*, 1945; complete edition, as *Cántico, fe de vida*, 1950; as *Cántico: A Selection*, translated by Norman Thomas di Giovanni and others, 1965.
Tercer cántico. 1944.
El encanto de las sirenas. 1953.

Luzbel desconcertado. 1956.
Del amanecer y el despertar. 1956.
Clamor. 3 vols., 1957–63:
  Maremágnum. 1957.
  Que van a dar en la mar. 1960.
  A la altura de las circunstancias. 1963.
Lugar de Lázaro. 1957.
Viviendo, y otros poemas. 1958.
Historia natural: Breve antología con versos inéditos. 1960.
Poemas de Castilla. 1960.
Poesias. 1960.
Versos, edited by Miguel Pizarro. 1961.
Anita. 1961.
Flores. 1961.
Las tentaciones de Antonio. 1962.
Según las horas. 1962.
Tréboles. 1964.
Suite italienne. 1964; enlarged edition, 1968.
Selección de poemas. 1965; enlarged edition, 1970.
El trasnochador. 1967.
Homenaje: Reunión de vidas. 1967.
Affirmation: A Bilingual Anthology, edited and translated by Julian Palley. 1968.
Aire nuestro (includes *Cántico*; *Clamor*; *Homenaje*). 1968; enlarged edition (includes *Y otros poemas* and *Final*), 5 vols., 1977–81.
Obra poética: Antología, edited by José Manuel Blecua. 1970.
Guirnalda civil. 1970.
Obra poética. 1970.
Al margen. 1972.
Y otros poemas. 1973.
Convivencia. 1975.
Plaza major: Antología civil. 1977.
Final. 1981.
Poemas malagueños (selection), edited by Antonio Gómez Yebra. 1983.
Jorge Guillén para niños, edited by Antonio Gómez Yebra. 1984.
Sonetos completos, edited by Antonio Gómez Yebra. 1988.

Play

El huerto de Melibea (dramatic poem) (produced 1955). 1954.

Other

Federico en persona: Semblanza y epistolario (on García Lorca). 1959.
El argumento de la obra (Cántico) (essays), edited by V. Scheiwiller. 1961; also edited by José Manuel Blecua, 1970.
Language and Poetry: Some Poets of Spain (Charles Eliot Norton lectures). 1961; Spanish edition, as *Lenguaje y poesía*, 1962.
En torno a Gabriel Miró: Breve epistolario. 1970.
La poética de Bécquer. 1973.
Mientras el aire es nuestro, edited by Philip W. Silver. 1978.
Guillén on Guillén: The Poetry and the Poet (readings and commentary), translated by Reginald Gibbons and Anthony L. Geist. 1979.
Paseo marítimo. 1990.
Correspondencia (1923–1951), with Pedro Salinas, edited by Andrés Soria Olmedo. 1992.

Translator, *El cementerio marino*, by Paul Valéry. 1930.

*

Critical Studies: *The Poetry of Jorge Guillén* by Frances Avery Pleak, 1942; *La poesía de Jorge Guillén* edited by R. Gullón and José Manuel Blecua, 1949; *Jorge Guillén* by J.B. Trend, 1952; *La realidad y Jorge Guillén* by J. Muela González, 1962; *A. Machado; P. Salinas; J. Guillén* by P. Darmangeat, 1969; *A Generation of Spanish Poets 1920–1936* by Cyril Brian Morris, 1969; *Luminous Reality: The Poetry of Guillén* edited by Ivar Ivask and Juan Marichal, 1969; *Poesía de Guillén* by Andrew P. Debicki, 1973; *El cántico americano de Jorge Guillén* by J. Ruiz de Conde, 1973; *Cántico de Guillén y Aire nuestro* by Joaquín Casalduero, 1974; *Jorge Guillén* by Joaquín Caro Romero, 1974; *The Vibrant Silence of Jorge Guillén's Aire nuestro* by Florence L. Yudin, 1974; *Jorge Guillén* edited by B. Ciplijauskaité, 1975; *La obra poética de Jorge Guillén* (includes bibliography) by Oreste Macrí, 1976; *Homenaje a Jorge Guillén* by the Wellesley College Department of Spanish, 1978; *Jorge Guillén* by S. Carretero and C. Meneses, 1981; *Jorge Guillén: Sus raíces: Recuerdos al paso* by J. Guerrero Martín, 1982; *Jorge Guillén* (in English) by G. Grant MacCurdy, 1982; *The Structured World of Jorge Guillén: A Study of Cántico and Clamor* (includes translations) by Elizabeth Matthews, 1985; *Jorge Guillén: Cántico* by Robert Havard, 1986.

* * *

It is a cliché to say that a poet creates order out of chaos, but it is one supremely applicable to Jorge Guillén. Guillén always found a sense of order, whether it was among the proliferation of literary movements following World War I, from the experience of living most of his life in an exile both physical and linguistic, or in a recoil from the atrocities and horrors of war. This passion for order can be seen in the careful control of structure, in the reworking of many of his early poems, and in the unhurried perfection that finds its most peaceful expression in his recurrent opening and closing image of a dawn always followed by nightfall. This search for order has led his work to be compared to Baudelaire's *Les Fleurs du mal* (*The Flowers of Evil*) and Whitman's *Leaves of Grass*.

A poet who has won awards in the United States and in Europe, Guillén belongs to the Generation of 1927, so-called after their tricentenary celebration of the death of the eclectic Golden-Age poet, Luis de Góngora. Theirs was a short-lived generation: after the Civil War most went into exile, some were in prison, and García Lorca had been killed. However, in that short time the quality of their work led critics to proclaim a new golden age of Spanish poetry, and their work managed a successful fusion of influences, from the Spanish Golden Age to literary trends from France, in particular those of 'pure poetry' and surrealism. Guillén himself was particularly impressed by Jorge Manrique and Paul Valéry.

As a university lecturer he published important critical essays and translations of poetry as well as his own work, of which the main parts were combined in the 1968 volume *Aire nuestro* [Our Air]. This edition is made up of the three collections, *Cántico* [Song], *Clamor* [Clamour], and *Homenaje* [Homage], each superficially quite different in range and theme. *Cántico*, with its focus on harmony, revels in life in a way the more sombre poems of *Clamor* would seem to deny. *Clamor* provides a shadowy mirror image of *Cántico*. It reflects the ferocity of life rather than its potential harmony, tracing the destruction and suffering caused by war and death, while *Homenaje* is a wide-ranging eulogy to the poetry of all ages, from Genesis to Guillén himself, offering an impressive mixture of translation and originality. This collection was supplemented by 'Y otros poemas' [And Other Poems], the modest title at once a gesture of self-effacement and a hint to the more central significance of the earlier work, and *Final*.

Cántico evolved from its first publication in 1928 to a definitive version in 1950. It is the most widely known of his works and owes much to the influence of Paul Valéry whom Guillén grew to know well during his stay in France. Subtitled *Fe de vida* (the name of a document proving a person is still alive), it is an affirmation of the beauty and coherence of life, a search for a perfection of form involving precision, interaction, and fusion. The importance placed on the present tense in the search for purity of expression is equalled by that placed upon fusion and interaction, as humanity and nature work in a symbiotic relationship. This is a search for a paradise on this earth, the perfection of which is portrayed in images of solid geometric forms that have often led Guillén's work to be considered in relation to cubism. Faith and love are constants in this search for an illumination attainable only through the experience and creation of a solid harmony and the potential of poetic form to resolve contradiction.

Clamor complements *Cántico* with the same rigour and control; their main difference lies in the attention given to the themes of exile, grief, and war. *Clamor* is about transcending the oppositions of order versus chaos, life versus death, and love versus hate, which threaten to disrupt our faith in life. That Guillén saw *Clamor* as the dramatization of an age can be seen in its subtitle *Tiempo de historia*. Where *Cántico* was an ecstatic song to life, *Clamor* is a dialogue between a man and his time, but this does not detract from the poet's faith in life, and if *Clamor* contains tones of disgust at the world of human creation it does not lose the exclamatory tone of pleasure that punctuated *Cántico*, nor the intensely tactile and sensual evocation of the poet's immediate surroundings.

Homenaje continues to explore this affirmation of life and poetry. Guillén has always expressed a commitment to humanity; but here there is a progression that allows the voices of other poets to blend in with this own. His wish to overcome division and chaos has meant an attempt to bridge the gap between individual and collective perception, which is nowhere more clear than in this work. *Homenaje* is a gesture of thanks, an invitation to a gathering where we find Calderón, Bécquer, Machado, Pascal, Mallarmé, and Tolstoi, among others, joined in a postmodern celebration of the death of the author and the rebirth of intertextuality.

Guillén's work, then, traces a familiar journey from harmony to discord, and beyond. For Guillén, life is an adventure and poetry an attempt to resolve its confusion. His is a vital, optimistic, and illuminating poetry, a love poetry in its most universal sense of self-abandonment to life itself. His work is therefore, in this ecology-conscious and final decade of the 20th century, no less contemporary now than it was on its initial publication.

—Jo Evans

GUILLÉN   (Batista),   Nicolás   (Cristóbal).   Born   in Camagüey, Cuba, 10 July 1902. Educated at the Instituto de Segunda Enseñanza, Camagüey, to 1920; studied law at the University of Havana, 1920 and 1921–22: abandoned studies. Worked for *El Nacional* as printer and typesetter while taking evening classes, 1918–19; contributor, *Camagüey Gráfico*, 1919, *Orto*, 1920 and 1927, *Las Dos Repúblicas*, 1920, and *Alma Mater*, 1922; co-founder and editor, *Lis*, 1923; editor, *El Camagüeyano*, 1923; typist, Ministry of the Interior, Havana, 1926; contributor, *Diario de la Marina*, from 1928, editor, *Información* and *El Loco*, from 1934; worked in the Havana Ministry of Culture, 1935–36; editor, *Mediodía*, 1936–38; travelled to Spain and attended pro-Republican conferences, 1937; joined National Committee of the Cuban Communist Party, 1938, and worked on its journal *Hoy*, 1938–50 (closed by the authorities) and from its revival in 1959; unsuccessful mayoral candidate, Camagüey, 1940; travelled to Haiti, 1942, and throughout Latin America on lecture and recital tour, 1945–48; co-editor, *Gaceta del Caribe*, 1944; travelled widely throughout Europe, USSR, and China, attending conferences and cultural events, 1948–52; contributor, *La Última Hora*, 1952; detained twice for activities against the Batista regime, 1952; left Cuba for Chile, 1953, and, though based in Paris, 1955–58, continued travelling widely during the 1950s; lived in Buenos Aires, 1958–59; returned to Cuba after the Castro Revolution, 1959, and thereafter combined career as writer with attendances at numerous international conferences, lectures, and cultural events, often in other countries of the socialist bloc, and often in an official capacity as Cuban ambassador at large or president of the Cuban Union of Writers and Artists (UNEAC) (appointed 1961); member, Central Committee of the Communist Party of Cuba, from 1975; had leg amputated, June 1989. Professor of Merit, University of Camagüey, 1981. Recipient: International Lenin Peace prize, 1954; Jesús Suárez Gayol prize, 1972; Union of Journalists' Félix Elmuza prize, 1972; Viareggio prize (Italy), 1972; Jamaican Institute Musgrave medal, 1974; Ricardo Miró National Poetry prize (Panama), 1979; Julius Fucik medal for journalism, 1981; Maurice Bishop prize, 1989. Honorary doctorates: University of Havana, 1974; University of the West Indies, 1975; University of Bordeaux (France), 1978. Cirilo and Metodio medal (Bulgaria), 1972; Red Band of Achievement (USSR), 1972; Order of Merit (Poland), 1974; Distinguished Son of the Cuban Popular Assembly, 1981; Cuban Order of José Marti, 1981. *Died 16 July 1989.*

PUBLICATIONS

Verse

Motivos de son. 1930.
Sóngoro cosongo: Poemas mulatos. 1931.
West Indies Limited: Poemas. 1934.
España: Poema en cuatro angustias y una esperanza. 1937.
Cantos para soldados y sones para turistas. 1937.
El son entero; Suma poética 1929–1946. 1947.
Elegía a Jacques Roumain en el cielo de Haití. 1948.
Cuba Libre: Poems, translated by Langston Hughes and Ben Frederic Carruthers. 1948.
Versos negros (selection), edited by José Luis Varela. 1950.
Elegía a Jesús Menéndez. 1951.
Elegía cubana. 1952.
La paloma de vuelo popular: Elegías. 1958.
Buenos días, Fidel. 1959.
Sus mejores poemas. 1959.
Los mejores versos. 1961.
Balada. 1962.
Poesías. 1962.
Poemas de amor. 1964.
Tengo. 1964; as *Tengo*, translated by Richard J. Carr, 1974.

Antología mayor: El son entero y otros poemas (selection). 1964; enlarged edition, 1969.
Che comandante. 1967.
El gran zoo. 1967; as 'The Great Zoo', in *¡Patria o muerte!: The Great Zoo and Other Poems*, 1973.
Cuatro canciones para el Che. 1969.
Antología clave. 1971.
El diario que a diario. 1972; corrected edition, 1979; as *The Daily Daily*, translated by Vera Kutzinski, 1989.
La rueda dentada. 1972.
Man-Making Words: Selected Poems, translated by Robert Márquez and David Arthur McMurray. 1972.
Obra poética, edited by Ángel Augier. 2 vols., 1972–73; enlarged and corrected edition, 1979; revised edition, 1985.
¡Patria o muerte!: The Great Zoo and Other Poems (bilingual edition), edited and translated by Robert Márquez. 1973.
El corazón con que vivo. 1975.
Poemas manuables. 1975.
Suma poética, edited by Luis Iñigo. 1976.
Por el mar de las Antillas anda un barco de papel. 1977.
Música de cámara. 1979.
Coplas de Juan Descalzo. 1979.
El libro de las décimas (selection), edited by Nancy Morejón. 1980.
Sol de domingo. 1982.

Plays

Poema con niños (produced 1943). In *Sóngoro cosongo y otros poemas*, 1942.
Soyán, music by Jorge Berroa (produced 1980).

Other

Prosa de prisa; Crónicas. 1962; revised and enlarged edition, as *Prosa de prisa 1929–1972*, edited by Ángel Augier, 3 vols., 1975–76.
Páginas vueltas; Memorias. 1982.

*

Bibliography: *Bibliografía de Nicolás Guillén* by María Luisa Antuña and Josefina García Carranza, 1975, supplemented in *Revista de la Biblioteca Nacional José Martí*, 3rd series, 19(3), 1977; 'Nicolás Guillén' in *Cuban Literature: A Research Guide* by David William Foster, 1985; 'Nicolás Guillén' in *Dictionary of Twentieth Century Cuban Literature* by Julio A. Martínez, 1990.

Critical Studies: *Nicolás Guillén: Notas para un estudio biográfico-crítico*, 2 vols., 1965, *La revolución cubana en la poesía de Nicolás Guillén*, 1979, and *Nicolás Guillén: Estudio biográfico-crítico*, 1984, all by Ángel Augier; *La poesía afro-cubana de Nicolás Guillén* by Ezequiel Martínez Estrada, 1966, revised edition, as *La poesía de Nicolás Guillén*, 1977; *La poesía de Nicolás Guillén* by Adriana Tous, 1971; *Recopilación de textos sobre Nicolás Guillén* edited by Nancy Morejón, 1974, and *Nación y mestizaje en Nicolás Guillén* by Morejón, 1982; *La poesía de Nicolás Guillén* by Jorge M. Ruscalleda Bercedóniz, 1975; *El sentimiento de la negritud en la poesía de Nicolás Guillén* by Armando González-Pérez, 1976; *Hazaña y triunfo americanos de Nicolás Guillén* by Juan Marinello, 1976; *The Poetry of Nicolás Guillén: An Introduction* by Dennis Sardinha, 1976; *Harlem, Haiti, and Havana: A Comparative Critical Study of Langston Hughes, Jacques Roumain, and Nicolás Guillén* by Martha K. Cobb, 1979; *Black Writers in Latin America* by Richard Jackson, 1979; *Self and Society in the Poetry of Nicolás Guillén* by Lorna V. Williams, 1982; *Against the American Grain: Myth and History in William Carlos Williams, Jay Wright, and Nicolás Guillén*, 1987, and Guillén issue of *Callaloo 31*, 10(2), 1987, both by Vera M. Kutzinski; *Nicolás Guillén: Popular Poet of the Caribbean* by Ian Isidore Smart, 1990.

*   *   *

Nicolás Guillén forsook his youthful imitation of Rubén Darío and the modernist aesthetic to focus a revolutionary's eye on social and political matters and on formal innovation. His message of protest, he once said, was sometimes 'dissimulated by the rhythm, the picturesque elements', characteristic of his early poetry. Until recently, critics considered his works only in the light of these elements, his unveiling of Cuba's black heritage, or of his communist ideology. Critics classified his poetry as 'black' and related it to the 'Afro-Caribbean' movement or the 'negritude' of black francophone Caribbean poets. This classification was made on the basis of his evocative imagery of African nature, his musicality reminiscent of African ritual-dance rhythms, and his reproduction of Cuban black speech (recently acknowledged as the popular speech of Cubans of all races). Contrary to 'Afro-Caribbean' and 'negritude' poetry that tends to exacerbate divisions among the races, Guillén's work aims to consolidate.

The subtitle of *Sóngoro cosongo: Poemas mulatos* [Sóngoro Cosongo: Mulatto Poems] expresses such an integrative intent. In the prologue to the first edition, Guillén indicated that he wanted his poetry to reflect the ethnic composition of Cuba. He also claimed that Cuban society, by excluding 'blackness' from its writings, disavowing its African roots, and perceiving itself as 'white', had failed to create an authentic Cuban national literature. To rectify this lack, Guillén created a consciously 'mestizo' (of racially mixed ancestry) poetry which used the Spanish language to express Cuba's African essence. In *Motivos de son* [Son Motifs], *Sóngoro consongo*, *West Indies Limited*, and to some extent in later collections, Guillén used his revolutionary poetic form based on the *son*, a popular Cuban musical form with roots in Spanish, African, and Arawak traditional forms. Guillén's *son*-poem uses the eight-syllable lines of the Spanish 'romance' (ballad) and an 'estribillo' (chorus), similar to the antiphonal chants of African and/or Arawak ritual traditions. In addition, Guillén revolutionized Cuban poetry by using expressions long perceived as 'jitanjáforas' (onomatopoeic neologisms) that subsequently have been identified as words in various African languages. These sounds (such as 'sóngoro consongo') provide rhythmic auditory effects evocative of Africa and, through their encrypted meaning, of its culture.

Guillén also proposed to legitimize blacks and mulattos as images in Cuban literature and to assert their beauty and positive value. In 'Negro bembón' ('Thick-Lipped Cullud Boy'), for example, the reader's perception is re-focused to recognize the beauty of those generally disdained thick lips. The black/white dichotomy (evil/good in white societies) is debunked in '¿Qué color?' ('What Color?'), a poem commemorating the assassination of Martin Luther King. The negative value judgement implicit in the image of the black-skinned pastor who, nevertheless, had 'such a white soul' is repudiated and replaced with awe before his 'powerful black soul'.

Guillén also rebelled against Cuban society's hypocritical modesty—hypocritical because by the 1950s Cuba had become the brothel and playground of America's affluent and gangster classes. Instead, Guillén's poetry evokes voluptuous images of dark women that are unabashedly sensuous.

This period of Afro-Cuban synthesis in Guillén's work was followed by one of revolutionary political preoccupation. His solidarity with the Republican cause during the Spanish Civil War is evident in *España: Poema en cuatro angustias y una esperanza* [Spain: Poem in Four Anguishes and One Hope]. The grievances of the oppressed classes in Cuba are depicted in the poems of *Cantos para soldados y sones para turistas* [Songs for Soldiers and *Sones* for Tourists] and *El son entero* [The Whole *Son*]. His protest against the Spanish slaver's lash disfiguring his black grandfather's back in 'Balada de los dos abuelos' ('Ballad of the Two Grandfathers') is as intense as that in 'Mau-maus' for the failure to indict the slain Englishman because he 'pierced the lung of Africa/with an Empire-dagger of/alphabetizing steel . . . /of syphilis, gunpowder,/money, business, yes'. Published after the Cuban Revolution, the collection *Tengo* [I Have], extols the more egalitarian society that struggle created.

Guillén's revolutionary poetic form reaches its zenith in *El gran zoo* (*The Great Zoo*) and *El diario que a diario* (*The Daily Daily*). The former, a neo-bestiary, portrays the denizens of the zoo not as animals, but as inanimate objects, character types, or institutions that caustically satirize capitalist society. Form in *The Great Zoo* ranges from haiku-like brevity to polymetric free verse. *The Daily Daily* is a collection of newspaper items recounting Cuba's history since colonial times. Some are authentic journalistic items, others are creations of the author; some are in recognizably poetic forms, others are classified advertisements, display advertisements, social items, or municipal announcements. His early humour reappears in this volume with a demythologizing effect. The bullfight—the mythic paradigm of Spanish masculinity—collapses in 'Bulls', in which bullfighters do everything from taking 'a great leap over a bull', to 'stick[ing] a new kind of banderilla into another from the top of a stool', to making 'fun of the animal's ferocity by dancing "La Cucaracha" on a table'. The sharp criticism of the capitalist establishment contained in this book crowns a career dedicated to exposing the flaws and abuses of the moneyed classes.

Guillén revolutionized Cuban literature, by making it mirror Cuba's mixed racial heritage, in his new form, the *son*-poem, and by using 'jitanjáforas' and ritual-like rhythm. With renewed language and formal innovations, he denounced oppression, and, through satire, demythologized the 'reality' imposed by the dominant classes.

—Oralia Preble-Niemi

GUIMARÃES ROSA, João. Born in Cordisburgo, Minas Gerais, Brazil, 27 June 1908. Educated at the Colégio Arnaldo, Belo Horizonte; Medical School of Minas Gerais, Belo Horizonte, 1925–30, degree 1930. Married 1) Lygia Cabral Pena in 1930, two daughters; 2) Aracy Moebius de Carvalho in 1938. Public servant, Statistical Service, Minas Gerais, 1929–31; doctor in private practice, Itaguara, Minas Gerais, 1931–32; volunteered as military medical officer, Belo Horizonte, 1932; medical officer, Ninth Infantry Battalion, Barbacena, Minas Gerais, 1934; passed civil service examinations and joined Ministry of Foreign Affairs, 1934; vice-

consul, Hamburg, Germany, 1938–42: briefly interned in Baden-Baden, following Brazil's entry into World War II, 1942; secretary, Brazilian Embassy in Bogotá, Colombia, 1942–44; director, Ministry of State's Documentation Service, 1944–46; secretary, Brazilian Delegation to Paris Peace Conference, 1946; secretary-general, Brazilian Delegation to Ninth Pan-American Conference, Bogotá, 1948; principal secretary, Brazilian Embassy, Paris, 1949–51; cabinet head, Ministry of Foreign Affairs, Rio de Janeiro, 1951–53; budget director, Ministry of State, Rio de Janeiro, 1953–58; head of Frontier Demarcation Service, 1962–67. Vice-president, First Latin American Writers Conference, Mexico City, 1965. Recipient: Brazilian Academy of Letters poetry prize, 1936; Carmen Dolores Barbosa prize, 1957; Paula Brito prize, 1957; Brazilian Academy Machado de Assis prize, 1961. Member, Brazilian Academy of Letters, 1963. *Died 19 November 1967.*

PUBLICATIONS

Fiction

Sagarana (stories). 1946; revised edition, 1951; as *Sagarana: A Cycle of Stories*, translated by Harriet de Onís, 1966.
Corpo de baile: sete novelas (includes *Manuelzão e Miguilim*; *No Urubùquaquá, no pinhém*; *Noites do Sertão*). 2 vols., 1956; 3 vols., 1964–66.
Grande Sertão: Veredas. 1956; as *The Devil to Pay in the Backlands*, translated by James L. Taylor and Harriet de Onís, 1963.
Primeiras estórias. 1962; as *The Third Bank of the River and Other Stories*, translated by Barbara Shelby, 1968.
Os sete pecados capitais (novellas), with others. 1964.
Campo geral (stories). 1964.
Tutaméia: terceiras estórias. 1967.
Estas estórias. 1969.
Contos (stories), edited by Heitor Megale and Marilena Matsuola. 1978.

Other

Ave, palavra (prose and verse). 1970.
Correspondência com o traductor italiano [Edoardo Bizzarri]. 1972.
Seleta (anthology), edited by Paulo Rónai, 1973.
Sagarana emotiva: cartas de Guimarães Rosa a Paulo Danteas. 1975.
Rosiana: uma coletânea de conceitos, máximas e brocardos, edited by Paulo Rónai. 1983.

*

Bibliography: *Bibliografia de e sobre Guimarães Rosa* by Plínio Doyle, 1968; *Brazilian Literature: A Research Guide* by David William Foster and Walter Rela, 1990.

Critical Studies: *Trilhas no Grande Sertão* by M. Calvalcânti Proença, 1958; *Guimarães Rosa* edited by Heriqueta Lisboa and others, 1966; *João Guimarães Rosa: travessia literária*, 1968, and 'João Guimarães Rosa', in *Studies in Short Fiction*, 8(1), 1971, both by Mary L. Daniel; *Em memória de João Guimarães Rosa* by various authors, 1968; *Guimarães Rosa* by Adonias Filho and others, 1969; *Guimarães Rosa* by Francisco Assis Brasil, 1969; *Guimarães Rosa* by Guilhermino César and others, 1969; *Guimarães Rosa em três dimensões* by Pedro Xosto, Augusto de Campos, and Harolde de Campos, 1970; *O mundo movente de Guimarães Rosa* by José Carlos Garbuglio, 1972; *Structural Perspectivism in Guimarães Rosa* by W. Martins, 1973; *Guimarães Rosa: dois estudos* by Nelly Novaes Coelho and Ivana Versiani, 1975; *O insólito em Guimarães Rosa e Borges* by Lenira Marques Covizzi, 1978; *A Construção do Romance em Guimarães Rosa* by Wendel Santos, 1978; *O diálogo no Grande Sertão: Veredas* by Paulo de Tarso Santos, 1978; *João Guimarães Rosa* (in English) by Jon S. Vincent, 1978; *The Process of Revitalization of the Language and Narrative Structure in the Fiction of João Guimarães Rosa and Julio Cortázar*, 1980, and *The Synthesis Novel in Latin America: A Study of Grande Sertão: Veredas*, 1991, both by Eduardo de Faria Coutinho; *Guimarães Rosa: signo e sentimento* by Suzi Frankl Sperber, 1982; *Guimarães Rosa* edited by Eduardo de Faria Coutinho, 1983; *A cultura popular em Grande Sertão: Veredas* by Leonardo Arroyo, 1984; *O discurso oral em Grande Sertão: Veredas* by Teresinha Souto Ward, 1984; *Logos and the Word: The Novel of Language and Linguistic Motivation in Grande Sertão: Veredas and Três tristes tigres* by Stephanie Merrim, 1988.

* * *

When João Guimarães Rosa died on 19 November 1967 at the age of 59, he had published only five works of prose fiction; however, these five volumes had earned him a seat in the Brazilian Academy of Letters and undisputed recognition as the greatest writer of prose fiction to emerge in Brazil since 1945.

He was born in Cordisburgo in the state of Minas Gerais in 1908. He studied medicine but practised it for only four years—first in the backlands of the Brazilian *sertão* and later in the army—before joining the Brazilian diplomatic service in which he would serve for the remainder of his life. His childhood and his time spent as a country doctor provided the raw material with which he fashioned an extraordinary fictional world—an amalgam of fantasy, folklore, and myth, yet invariably resting upon a bedrock of harsh reality in which the life of the inhabitants of the vast wilderness, or *sertão*, of northern Minas Gerais and southern Bahia comes vividly and exuberantly to life. The way of life of the farmers, traders, ranchers, cowboys, and bandits of the *sertão* is closely observed and painstakingly described. To call these fictions regionalist would be to misunderstand totally the scope and richness of a fictional world that attains a mythic grandeur and universal significance. This attainment of the universal through the particular is well illustrated by the title of Guimarães Rosa's first book, a collection of novellas entitled *Sagarana*. Sagarana is a neologism combining the Germanic 'saga' with a Tupi Indian word, 'rana', meaning 'in the manner of'. Naturalistic and magical by turns, sometimes simultaneously, these novellas tell of a world in which animals talk and think like human beings, a young man insults a warlock and is punished with temporary blindness during which he learns much about himself, and a murderous bully wins redemption after a lifetime of tribulation and wandering. *Sagarana* was followed ten years later by a second volume of novellas entitled *Corpo de baile* [Corps de Ballet] and the vast novel, *Grande Sertão: Veredas* (*The Devil to Pay in the Backlands*) which appeared in the same year. A literal translation of the latter would be something like 'Great Backlands: Paths'. The novel is as enigmatic and elusive as its title. It consists of an autobiography told by an ageing rancher to an unseen interlocutor. Riobaldo relates the story of his career as a *jagunço*, or bandit of the *sertão*, of his love for his

mysterious, hermaphrodite comrade-in-arms, Diadorim, and of his existential anguish over the possibility that he may have sold his soul to the devil. Riobaldo tells his story in the hope that his listener may be able to pronounce on the mystery and thus release him from his torment. It is a story of love, hate, revenge, and betrayal, a tale of epic proportions in which bandit armies quarter the *sertão* in search of their enemy, and in Riobaldo's case, so that his destiny may be charted and realized.

It also reveals Guimarães Rosa as a profound student of medieval and Renaissance European literature. Like the world of the medieval epic and romance, Rosa's fictional world tells of the constant struggle between good and evil, and contains large doses of tragedy and ecstasy as well as an underlying current of poetic justice. It is epic as well as mythic, because its protagonist's trajectory is clearly, on one hand, a rite of passage, and on the other, a chivalric quest during which deeds are done in the name of an absent lady, Otacília, and in order to fulfil the chivalric enterprise: the defeat of the traitor in the midst, bandit leader Hermógenes, so as to avenge the death of the betrayed—supreme commander Juca Ramiro. The *sertão* becomes a vast natural theatre or cosmic space in which the *jagunços* act out this drama and become at one with their environment. Neither the individual nor the space in which they move has primacy. In its scope and ambition, *The Devil to Pay in the Backlands* has been compared to *The Divine Comedy*, *Don Quixote*, *Hamlet*, *Faust*, *Moby Dick*, and *Ulysses*. In its themes, the work is certainly Faustian, but linguistically-speaking, the comparison with Joyce's *Ulysses* is the most useful one; for the language in which the novel and the novellas that preceded it are expressed is baroque and intensely poetic. Rosa employs alliteration, assonance, onomatopoeia, and verse rhythms. His vocabulary is enormous, and as in the case of Joyce, there is a constant recourse to neologisms of which there can be as many as a dozen on a single page. The language is poetic not only in its evocations of the Brazilian *sertão*, but also in the fundamental sense that it offers incessant renewal of a Portuguese enriched by a lexis borrowed from numerous languages. Rosa also has a taste for metaphor. His fourth book, *Primeiras estórias* [First Stories] is a set of short stories in one of which a family man, for no apparent reason, says goodbye to his family, paddles in a canoe to the centre of a wide river, and remains there until his son, years later, offers to take his place. The English title of this story, chosen as the title story for the volume when it was translated and published in 1968, reads 'The Third Bank of the River', a notion bespeaking mysticism and utter dislocation.

Guimarães Rosa's remaining books are *Tutaméia* [Trifle], another set of even briefer stories, the posthumous short stories of *Estas estórias* [These Tales], and the miscellany, *Ave, palavra* [Hail, Word]. His prose fiction is little known in Europe. This is due to the fact that translating him into any other language has proved a daunting task and because, in any case, he wrote in Portuguese. This last fact has meant that, unlike the great Spanish-American writers of the Latin American 'Boom', he has yet to be 'discovered' by the English-speaking world. The day this happens, the Old World will encounter, with astonishment, a rural, Brazilian postmodernist whose total achievement constitutes the great watershed of Brazilian literature, a literary phenomenon commensurate with that of Joyce in English letters.

—R.J. Oakley

H

HADEWIJCH. Lived c.1250, possibly near Antwerp, The Netherlands (now Belgium). Facts of her life uncertain; possibly from an aristocratic background; spiritual leanings show affinities with the Beguines as well as with the mysticism of Hugh of St Victor, William of St Thierry, and St Bernard (of Clairvaux). Her fame spread as far as Germany (where she was known as Adelwîp).

PUBLICATIONS

Collections

Werken [Works], edited by F.J. Heremans. 3 vols., 1875–1905.
The Complete Works, translated by Mother Colomba Hart. 1981.

Verse

Strophische gedichten [Strophic Poems], edited by J. van Mierlo. 1942.
Mengeldichten [Poems], edited by J. van Mierlo. 1952.
Strofische gedichten [Strophic Poems], edited by E. Rombants and N. de Paepe. 1961.

Other

Visioenen [Visions], edited by J. van Mierlo. 2 vols., 1924–25.
Brieven [Letters], edited by J. van Mierlo. 2 vols., 1947.
Brieven [Letters], translated (into modern Dutch) by M. Ortmanns-Cornet. 1986.

*

Critical Studies: *Hadewijch* by M.H. van der Zeyde, 1934; *Hadewijch d'Anvers* by J.B. Porion, 1954; *Hadewijch en Heer Hendrik van Breda* by P.C. Boeren, 1962; *Medieval Netherlands Religious Literature* by T. Weevers, translated by E. Colledge, 1965; *Some Aspects of Hadewijch's Poetic Form* by T.M. Guest, 1975; *The Measure of Mystic Thought: A Study of Hadewijch's Mengeldichten* by S. Murk-Jansen, 1991; *Geschichte der abendländischen Mystik: Frauenmystik und Franziskanische Mystik der Frühzeit* by Kurt Ruh, 1993.

* * *

The 13th-century Christian mystic Hadewijch wrote in Middle Dutch and her work, some of the finest literature in the Dutch language, is preserved in five closely related manuscripts, the earliest of which dates from the late 14th century. Three of these contain the substantial part of the corpus and the other two only smaller selections. The works attributed to Hadewijch consist of 31 letters, 14 visions, the 'List of the Perfect Ones', 45 stanzaic poems, and 16 epistolary poems.

The manuscripts also contain two other collections of poems, the smaller of which consists of four poems which may have been written later than Hadewijch. The other collection of lyric poems is almost certainly contemporary to her and should perhaps also be attributed to her.

The currently accepted date for Hadewijch's literary activity is c.1240–50. This deduction is based on scraps of evidence gleaned from one of her works, the 'List of the Perfect Ones', which occurs at the end of her visions. In it she refers to two facts that can be dated: the death at the hands of the Inquisitor 'Meester Robbaert' of a Beguine, and the presence of hermits on the walls of Jerusalem. The Beguine has been tentatively identified as a certain Aelais whom Robert le Bougre had put to death in 1236, in which case the List will not have been drawn up before that date. Jerusalem finally fell to the Khorezmians on 23 August 1244 and there will not have been any Christian hermits on its walls after that time. Allowing for a certain time lapse before the news reached the author of the List, it seems unlikely that she would have drawn it up much after 1250. There is of course no way of knowing at what point in her career Hadewijch composed the List but, in view of some references in the Visions which precede it, it seems reasonable to assume that she did so in the second half of her career.

We know little about Hadewijch's life, her circumstances, or her origins. A note on the flyleaf of one of the manuscripts refers to her as 'de Antverpia', but no independent evidence has been found linking her to Antwerp or any other city. Attempts have been made to guess at the possible course of her life from evidence within her works. However, such evidence is extremely sparse and ambiguous. Recently Kurt Ruh has re-opened the debate on Hadewijch's social status by putting forward powerful circumstantial arguments in favour of her being a member of the aristocracy.

Arguably Hadewijch's most remarkable literary achievement are the 45 stanzaic poems, written in the style and using the conventions of the courtly love poetry of the period. Many have the *Natureingang* and complicated rhyme-schemes so typical of much troubadour and *trouvère* love lyrics. However, Hadewijch uses the conventional themes not to lament the trials of the faithful knight in the service of a demanding and fickle lady, but to lament her own suffering in the service of God. The extended metaphor, combining themes of feudal service and secular love, works particularly well as Hadewijch uses the feminine noun *minne* (love) to refer to God, which naturally takes feminine adjectives and pronouns, while she refers to herself using the masculine noun *sen*, meaning reason or mental awareness.

Hadewijch appears to have written for a group of like-minded laywomen. She may have had at some point a position of leadership among them, but her letters certainly suggest that there were also times when she was distant from those whom she exhorted to good works and growth in love. In view of the growing antagonism to such activity in the second half of the 13th century, the fact that she was able to exhort and teach with no apparent expectation or consciousness of ecclesiastical criticism supports the date of her literary activity as being in the earlier part of the century. However personal some of the expressions in her work appear to be, it is likely that everything she wrote was intended to be read out loud, or in the case of the poetry sung, to an audience. Her teaching is rooted in her own experience, as is her theology, and she uses her sufferings and doubts as object lessons to her audience.

The texts attributed to Hadewijch are significant evidence for the development in the 13th century of what could be described as 'vernacular theology', namely a mode of theological writing that is neither that of the theology of the monasteries, with its source in experience and contemplation, nor that of the scholastics, which has its source in reason. Vernacular theology is rooted in the experience of living in the world rather than withdrawing from it, and tends to be expressed in a language rich in images that seek to connect the reality of that experience, including the problem of suffering, with the transcendent reality of the soul's relationship to God. Themes similar to those found in Hadewijch's work are to be found in numerous texts from this period as well as in the works of later mystics such as Eckhart and Marguerite Porete.

—S.M. Murk-Jansen

HAFEZ.   See **HAFIZ, Shams al-Din Muhammad**.

HAFIZ. Born Shams al-Din Muhammad [or Shamsu'd-Din Muhammad] Hafiz in Shiraz, Persia (now Iran), in 1325/26. Studied Islamic literature and mastered Arabic (the name Hafiz indicates one who has memorized the *Koran*). Patronized by Shah Abu Ishaq-i Inju, 1341–53, by Shah Shuja, 1358–68/69, and Muzaffarid Shah Mansur in late 1380s; lectured on theology, and wrote commentaries on religious classics. Little is known of his private life. *Died 1389/90.*

PUBLICATIONS

Verse

Divan, edited by J. von Hammer. 2 vols., 1812–13; also edited by Hermann Brockhaus, 3 vols., 1854–63, Vincenz von Rosenzweig-Schwannau, 3 vols., 1858–64, and Mohammed Qazvini and Qasem Ghani. 1941; as *Diwan-i-Hafiz*, translated by H. Wilberforce-Clarke (prose), 3 vols., 1891, reprinted 1974; as *The Poems*, translated by John Payne (verse), 3 vols., 1901; selections in translation include: [Selections], edited by Algernon S. Bicknell, translated by Hermann Bicknell, 1875; *Versions from Hafiz* by Walter Leaf, 1898; *Poems from the Divan* by G. Bell, 2nd edition, 1928; *Hafiz in Quatrains* by C.K. Street, 1946; *Fifty Poems* by A.J. Arberry, 1947; *Thirty Poems* by Peter Avery and John Heath-Stubbs, 1952; *Poetical Horoscope*

or Odes by A. Aryanpur, 1965; *Odes of Hafiz: Poetical Horoscope* by Abbas Aryanpur Kashani, 1984; *Tongue of the Hidden: Poems from the Divan* by P. Smith, 1990.

*

Bibliography: *Towards a Hafiz Bibliography* by Henri Broms, 1969.

Critical Studies: *A Literary History of Persia* by Edward G. Browne, 1928; *Classical Persian Literature* by A.J. Arberry, 1958; *History of Iranian Literature* by Jan Rypka, edited by Karl Jahn, 1968; *Hafez* by G.M. Wickens, in *Encyclopedia of Islam*, revised edition, 1971; *Unity in the Ghazals of Hafez* by Michael C. Hillmann, 1976.

* * *

Even in his lifetime, the fame of Hafiz had extended beyond his homeland—eastward to India and westward to other portions of the Islamic realm. In the first centuries after his death, it was still Islam's taste for Persian poetry that nourished his reputation; but in the last two or three centuries, when the East and the West have impacted upon each other, Hafiz has become truly a world poet, read in many languages, both Eastern and Western.

Not all readers will agree with Ralph Waldo Emerson (who read him in German translation) that Hafiz ranks with Shakespeare as the type of the true poet; or with John Payne (who translated him into English verse) that he is, along with Shakespeare and Dante, one of the three greatest poets of the world; but there is a consensus that he is 'the Prince of Persian poets' and the fullest flowering of the lyric gift in a nation famed for its poetry. Regarding the substance of his poetic thought, however, there is again considerable difference of opinion.

His compatriots and fellow Muslims have for the most part accepted his native reputation as *Lisān-al-ghaib* [The Tongue of the Hidden]: that is, as a mystical poet of the Sufi school, whose allusions to love, wine, roses, and revelry signify spiritual concepts. A few Westerners, too, have accepted this view—including the philosopher Hegel—but the majority of his European and American readers have had different opinions. Sir William Jones, who in the late 18th century introduced Hafiz to the West, regarded him as 'the Persian Anacreon'. Goethe, whose *West-östlicher Divan* was composed in emulation of the *Divan* of Hafiz, was disposed to stress the poet's joy in love and life, as suited the taste of the Romantic age. Emerson, who learned from Hafiz to take deeper poetic drafts than his Puritan heritage allowed, believed the poet's wine stood for intellectual liberation rather than for the divine afflatus on the one hand or [Thomas] 'Moore's best Port' on the other. The English Victorians, reflecting their own anxieties over faith and doubt, heard in Hafiz the voice of weeping and loud lament; and the *fin de siècle* hedonists and sceptics saw in him a latter-day Omar Khayyam. In this century, A.J. Arberry has described him as a philosophical nihilist propounding the gospel of Unreason.

Unfortunately, the *ghazal* form in which Hafiz wrote (and which, in the opinion of G.M. Wickens, he took 'so far beyond the work of his predecessors that he practically cut off all succession') does not lend itself to easy translation. It has variously been likened to the ode and the sonnet, and, by Arberry, to the late sonatas of Beethoven. The 'wonderful inconsecutiveness' of the Persian *ghazal* (in Emerson's phrase) has led Arberry, Wickens, and Michael Hillmann to seek in the form a kind of organic unity that is quite unlike the linear and dramatic continuity characteristic of Western poetry. Some hint of the suggestive ambiguity of Hafiz, and of his mellifluous music, might be gleaned from the following couplet:

Hameh kass tāleb-i-yārand, che hushyār che mast
Hameh jā khāneh-i-ishq ast, che masjid che kunasht.

(Everyone is desirous of the Friend, what is sober what is drunk?
Every place is the house of love, what is temple what is mosque?)

—John D. Yohannan

HAMSUN, Knut. Born Knut Pedersen in Lom, Norway, 4 August 1859. Married 1) Bergliot Goepfert in 1898 (divorced 1909), one daughter; 2) Marie Andersen in 1909, two sons and two daughters. Apprenticed to a shoemaker in Bodö; then a road worker and wanderer for 10 years; lived in the United States, 1882–84, 1886–88: streetcar conductor in Chicago, farmhand in North Dakota, and secretary and lecturer in Minneapolis; lived for several years in Paris, early 1890s; travelled in Finland, Russia, and Denmark during the 1890s and 1900s; writer after 1890, and after 1911 farmer in Hamarøy, later near Grimstad; openly supported Quisling's pro-German party during World War II: indicted, fined, and briefly confined to a mental institution after the war. Recipient: Nobel prize for literature, 1920. *Died 19 February 1952.*

PUBLICATIONS

Collection

Samlede Verker. 15 vols., 1954–56.

Fiction

Den gaadefulde [The Mysterious One]. 1877.
Bjørger. 1878.
Sult. 1890; as *Hunger*, translated by George Egerton, 1899; also translated by Robert Bly, 1967.
Mysterier. 1892; as *Mysteries*, translated by Arthur G. Chater, 1927; also translated by Gerry Bothmer, 1971.
Ny jord. 1893; as *Shallow Soil*, translated by Carl Christian Hyllested, 1914.
Redaktør Lynge [Editor Lynge]. 1893.
Pan. 1894; as *Pan*, translated by W.W. Worster, 1920; also translated by James W. McFarlane, 1955.
Siesta. 1897.
Victoria. 1898; as *Victoria*, translated by Arthur G. Chater, 1923; as *Victoria: A Love Story* translated by Oliver Stallybrass, 1969.
Kratskrog [Brushwood]. 1903.
Sværmere. 1904; as *Mothwise*, translated by W.W. Worster, 1921, as *Dreamers*, 1921.
Stridende liv [Struggling Life]. 1905.
Under Høststjærnen. 1906; as *Autumn*, translated by W.W.

Worster, in *Wanderers*, 1922; as *Under the Autumn Star*, translated by Oliver and Gunnvor Stallybrass, in *The Wanderer*, 1975.
Benoni. 1908; as *Benoni*, translated by Arthur G. Chater, 1925.
Rosa. 1908; as *Rosa*, translated by Arthur G. Chater, 1925.
En vandrer spiller med sordin. 1909; as *With Muted Strings*, translated by W.W. Worster, in *Wanderers*, 1922; as *A Wanderer Plays on Mute Strings*, translated by Worster, 1922; as *On Muted Strings*, translated by Oliver and Gunnvor Stallybrass, in *The Wanderer*, 1975.
Den siste glæde. 1912; as *Look Back on Happiness*, translated by Paula Wiking, 1940.
Børn av tiden. 1913; as *Children of the Age*, translated by J.S. Scott, 1924.
Segelfoss by. 1915; as *Segelfoss Town*, translated by J.S. Scott, 1925.
Markens grøde. 1917; as *The Growth of the Soil*, translated by W.W. Worster, 1920.
Konerne ved Vandposten. 1920; as *The Women at the Pump*, translated by Arthur G. Chater, 1928; also translated by Oliver and Gunnvor Stallybrass, 1978.
Wanderers (includes *Autumn; With Muted Strings*), translated by W.W. Worster. 1922.
Siste kapitel. 1923; as *Chapter the Last*, translated by Arthur G. Chater, 1929.
Landstrykere. 1927; as *Vagabonds*, translated by Eugene Gay-Tifft, 1930; as *Wayfarers*, translated by James W. McFarlane, 1980.
August. 1930; as *August*, translated by Eugene Gay-Tifft, 1931.
Men livet lever. 1933; as *The Road Leads On*, translated by Eugene Gay-Tifft, 1934.
Ringen sluttet. 1936; as *The Ring Is Closed*, translated by Eugene Gay-Tifft, 1937.
Paa gjengrodde Stier. 1949; as *On Overgrown Paths*, translated by Carl L. Anderson, 1968.
The Wanderer (includes *Under the Autumn Stars; On Muted Strings*), translated by Oliver and Gunnvor Stallybrass. 1975.
Night Roamers and Other Stories, translated by Tiina Nunnally. 1992.

Plays

Ved rigets port [At the Gates of the Kingdom] (produced 1896). 1895.
Livets Spil [The Game of Life] (produced 1896). 1896.
Aftenrøde [Evening Glow] (produced 1898). 1898.
Munken Vendt [Friar Vendt] (produced 1926). 1902.
Dronning Tamara [Queen Tamara] (produced 1903). 1903.
Livet i vold (produced 1910). 1910; as *In the Grip of Life*, translated by Graham and Tristan Rawson, 1924.

Verse

Det vilde kor [The Wild Chorus]. 1904.
Dikte. 1921.

Other

Lars Oftedal (articles). 1889.
Fra det moderne Amerikas aandsliv. 1889; as *The Cultural Life of Modern America*, edited and translated by Barbara Gordon Morgridge, 1969.
I Æventyrland [In the Land of Fairy Tales]. 1903.
Sproget i fare [Language in Danger]. 1918.

Samlede Verker [Collected Works]. 12 vols., 1918; revised edition, 17 vols., 1936.
Artikler 1899–1928, edited by Francis Bull. 1939.
Knut Hamsun som han var [Letters 1879–1949], edited by Tore Hamsun. 1956.
Paa Turné: tre foredrag om Litteratur [On Tour]. 1960.
On the Prairie: A Sketch of the Red River Valley, translated by John Christianson. 1961.
Brev til Marie [Letters to Marie 1908–38], edited by Tore Hamsun. 1970.
Over havet: artikler, reisebrev, edited by Lars Frode Larsen. 1990.
Selected Letters [vol. 1] 1879–1898, edited by Harald Naess and James W. McFarlane. 1990.

*

Bibliography: *Hamsun: En bibliografi* by Arvid Østby, 1972.

Critical Studies: *Hamsun* by Hanna Astrup Larsen, 1922; *Six Scandinavian Novelists: Lie, Jacobsen, Heidenstam, Selma Lagerlöf, Hamsun, Sigrid Undset* by Alrik Gustafson, 1940; *Hamsun* (in Norwegian) by Tore Hamsun, 1959; *Konflikt og visjon* by Rolf Nyboe Nettum, 1970; 'Critical Attitudes to Hamsun 1890–1969' by Ronald Popperwell, in *Scandinavica*, 9, 1970; 'Knut Hamsun's *Pan*: Myth and Symbol' by Henning Sehmsdorf, in *Edda*, 1974; *Knut Hamsun som modernist* by Peter Kierkegaard, 1975; *The Hero in Scandinavian Literature* edited by John M. Weinstock and Robert T. Rovinsky, 1975; 'Knut Hamsun's Anti-Semitism' by Allen Simpson, in *Edda*, 1977; *Knut Hamsun* by Harald Naess, 1984; *Enigma: The Life of Knut Hamsun* by Robert Ferguson, 1987.

* * *

Knut Hamsun burst upon Norwegian literature in 1890 with a series of lectures attacking the realist writers, including Ibsen; he appealed instead for a new kind of writing, which he called 'psychological literature'. His first novel, *Sult* (*Hunger*), published in the same year, embodies his theories. It is the story of a mind—a lively, fantastic, creative mind which ever and again rises irrepressibly above the vicissitudes of a mundane bodily existence. 'The unconscious life of the soul' is the centre of focus; the starving artist pacing the streets of Christiania is not an occasion for an attack on social injustice but a creator of a vibrant inner world.

Inspired, often unstable visionaries are the heroes of Hamsun's other early novels *Mysterier* (*Mysteries*), *Pan*, and *Victoria*. With these novels Hamsun became the first Modernist writer in Scandinavia, reflecting the turbulent inner conflict of modern man; Nietzsche and Dostoevskii were among his antecedents. The interplay of instinct and impulse, the celebration of spontaneity over sober reflection and nature over civilization give his heroes a quixotic air of inconsistency which made his contemporaries dismiss them as 'erratic'. His prose style is equally innovative, and has proved inimitable—though many have since tried to imitate it. There is a lyrical intensity in his phrasing which makes whole chapters of *Pan* and *Victoria* read like prose poems; the rhythms are incantatory, the mood ecstatic. The novels are hymns to love—but it is a self-destructive, impossible love which bars the way to its own fulfilment and mocks at its own despair.

Hamsun's heroes grew older as he himself grew old; and the exuberance of youth gave way to a more disillusioned

world-weariness. Social issues, which he had previously dismissed, also preoccupied him increasingly. In *Børn av tiden* (*Children of the Age*) and *Segelfoss by* (*Segelfoss Town*) he attacked the decadence of modern capitalist society and the emergent workers' movements. *Markens grøde* (*The Growth of the Soil*) celebrated instead his ideal, the noble peasant who rejects the softness of city ways and chooses the harsh, unremitting struggle of the pioneering farming life.

Nostalgia for a lost patriarchal era and dislike of modern industrial society were among the factors which led Hamsun towards the end of his long life to support Hitler, a fateful choice for which his countrymen have still not forgiven him. However, the best of his writing is not marred by his political blindness. In his final trilogy, *Landstrykere* (*Wayfarers*), *August*, and *Men livet lever* (*The Road Leads On*), the vitality of his inventiveness and the suppleness of his style are undiminished. *August*, the central character, is Hamsun's last great adventurer and orchestrator of humanity's dreams—though his stock is running low, and the chill winds of old age and bankruptcy are felt with increasing keenness. But like his creator, he is dogged to the end, and the rich gallery of characters around him is depicted with discerning clarity and a fine sense of life's ironies.

—Janet Garton

HUNGER (Sult)
Novel by Knut Hamsun, 1890.

The story of how *Hunger* came to be published could almost have served as an incident for the novel itself. Edvard Brandes, one of the great campaigners for naturalism in Scandinavia and editor of the radical newspaper *Politiken*, was visited in his office by a young Norwegian writer ('He had a manuscript with him, of course'). About to reject it on the ground of unsuitable length, Brandes was suddenly gripped ('though I am not sentimental') by the desperation of the author's face. Reading over the manuscript later, Brandes was still more impressed. He arranged for the publication, anonymously, of the first fragment (in fact, what is now Part II) of the novel, which was to be published in full as *Hunger*.

Germane to the fragment of narrative Brandes read in 1888 was the desperate poverty out of which it was conceived and in which it was written. Equally characteristic of the novel, as of its *Entstehung*, was the sudden shift of fortune which transfigured defeat into survival. On one level *Hunger* is an account (based in the naturalistic manner on authorial research, but research of a kind that makes Zola and the Goncourts seem like the merest dabblers) of the effects of hunger and extreme poverty on the inner life of an individual. The first-person narrative of the novel is, in a literal sense, constructed by the hunger of its narrator. As James W. McFarlane notes in his classic study of the early novels (*PMLA*, 71, 1956), the fragmented narrative is only quickened into life by hunger; each section describes a bout of suffering. The interstices of relative well-being are a narrative silence. Such plot as the novel possesses is built upon the desperate levels to which poverty, hunger, uncertainty, and total lack of income, reduce the narrator. Significantly, the novel's 'I' has no proper name, though he takes on various fictive identities to satisfy the police or welfare authorities, or just to conceal, out of self-defence or for his own amusement, who he 'really' is. His single great dream is to attain the freedom to write, and through writing to escape the poverty which gives *this* fiction life. To this end, he tries to live independently of the demands of a society that, in the person of landladies and policemen, creditors and indifferent editors, alternately harries and rejects him. He lies, cheats, temporizes, all the while fascinated by his own inner reactions to an external world which seems sometimes alluringly contingent (as he watches, enraptured, the behaviour of an insect roaming across the page), sometimes threateningly invasive or distantly absurd.

However, though it hangs on the cusp of naturalism, *Hunger* is anything but a naturalistic novel. Where naturalism seeks always to place individual experience within the patterns of a wider world, *Hunger* focuses on the world inside the individual. The novel may be set in Christiania (now Oslo)—that raw, newly urbanized society which contemporaries called *Tigerstaden*, the City of Tigers. It is indeed the greatest literary evocation of those lower depths into which Hedda Gabler loves to peep and through which Brack and Løvborg go slumming. (Appropriately, Ibsen's play was published in the same year as *Hunger*.) But what fascinates Hamsun are exactly the areas of experience that refuse the social, the ethical, the logical and reasonable. 'People don't *do* that sort of thing!' exclaims Ibsen's Brack. They do; and that is exactly the psychological territory Hamsun sets out to explore.

Yet the narrator of *Hunger* is anything but an everyman; and his narrative refutes any attempt to see it as representative. He sees himself as (in Hilde Wangel's phrase) 'one of the chosen'. He tries to live by a code of individual chivalry towards (some of) those even poorer and weaker than himself, a code which satisfies his craving for self-respect even though too often it proves self-defeating or even self-destructive. Even more important, doubly so in this most self-reflexive of fictions, he is a *writer*. While what he writes seems dreadful—and sometimes unnervingly prophetic of what is weakest in Hamsun's own later work—it is clear that the central fiction of his life, what makes it worth experiencing and writing, is the experience of surviving against all the odds an unsympathetic world can stack against him.

It is the representation in prose narrative of 'the unconscious life of the soul', 'the whispers of the blood', which so fascinated the slightly younger generation of writers who (after Hamsun himself had regressed to more outwardly traditional narrative forms) created that Modernist fiction of which *Hunger* is so important an innovation. What Hamsun had achieved, as he suffered and wrote feverishly in Christiania and Copenhagen in the 1880s, was to create, in its subjective intensities, its narrative discontinuities, what might very well be seen as the first European Modernist novel.

—Robin Young

HARTMANN von Aue. Born in Swabia, Germany, 1160. Educated in a monastery. Minister in the service of a lord. Took part in a crusade, 1189–90 or 1197. *Died between 1210 and 1220.*

PUBLICATIONS

Collections

Selections from Hartmann von Aue, translated by Margaret F. Richey. 1962.

Das Hartmann-Liederbuch, edited by Richard Kienast. 1963.
Werke, edited by E. Schwarz. 2 vols., 1967.
Die Lieder Hartmanns von Aue, edited by Ekkehard Blattmann. 1968.
The Narrative Works of Hartmann von Aue, translated by R.W. Fisher. 1983.

Verse

Der arme Heinrich, edited by Johann Gustav Büsching, 1810; also edited by Jacob and Wilhelm Grimm, 1815; Karl Simrok, 1830; W. Wackernagel, 1835; Franz Kocian, 1878; H. Raul, 1882; J.G. Robertson, 1895; E. Gierach, 1911; C.H. Bell, 1931; F. Maurer, 1958; Helmut de Boor, 1967, revised edition by H. Henne, 1987; translated by R.W. Fisher, in *The Narrative Works of Hartmann von Aue*, 1983.
Das Büchlein, edited by Petrus W. Tax, 1979.
Erec, edited by Moriz Haupt, 1839, revised edition, 1871; also edited by O. von Heinemann, 1898; Albert Leitzmann, 1939, revised edition, 1972; as *Erec*, translated by J.W. Thomas, 1979; also translated by R.W. Fisher, in *The Narrative Works of Hartmann von Aue*, 1983; Michael Resler, 1987; Thomas L. Keller, 1987.
Gregorius, edited by Karl Lachmann, 1838; also edited by Hermann Paul, 1873; F. Neumann, 1958; as *Gregorius: A Medieval Oedipus Legend*, translated by Edwin H. Zeydel, 1955; as *Gregorius: The Good Sinner*, translated by Sheema Zeben Buehne, 1966; as *Gregorius*, translated by R.W. Fisher, in *The Narrative Works of Hartmann von Aue*, 1983.
Gedichte, edited by Fedor Bech. 1867.
Iwein, edited by G.F. Benecke and K. Lachmann, 1827; also edited by A. Pernhoffer, 1857; as *Iwein*, translated by J.W. Thomas, 1979; also translated by R.W. Fisher, in *The Narrative Works of Hartmann von Aue*, 1983; Patrick M. McConeghy, 1984.
Die Klage, edited by Herta Zutt. 1968.
Das Klagenbüchlein: Hartmann von Aue und das zweite Büchlein, edited by Ludwig Wolff, 1972; edited and translated by Thomas L. Keller, 1986.

*

Bibliography: *Bibliographie zu Hartmann von Aue* by Elfriede Neubuhr, 1977; revised edition, 1987.

Critical Studies: 'An Interpretation of Hartmann's *Iwein*' by H. Sacker, in *Germanic Review*, (36), 1961; 'Heinrich's Metanoia: Intention and Practice in *Der Arme Heinrich*' by T. Buck, in *Modern Language Review*, (60), 1965; *Hartmann von Aue and His Lyric Poetry* by Leslie Seiffert, 1968; 'Christian Allegory in Hartmann's *Iwein*' by J. Clifton-Everest, in *Germanic Review*, (48), 1973; *Hartmann von Aue* edited by Hugo Kuhn and Christoph Cormeau, 1973; *Gregorius and Der arme Heinrich: Hartmann's Dualistic and Gradualistic Views of Reality* by Frank J. Tobin, 1973; *Symbolism in Hartmann's Iwein* by R.E. Lewis, 1975; *Hartmann von Aue* by P. Wapnewski, 1976; 'The Fortune in Hartmann's *Erec*' by F. Pickering, in *German Life and Letters*, (30), 1976–77; 'The ex lege Rite of Passage in Hartmann's *Iwein*' by T.L. Markey, in *Colloquia Germanica* (II), 1978; 'The Maiden in Hartmann's *Armen Heinrich*: Enrite Redux?' by W.C. McDonald, in *Deutsche Vierteljahresschrift*, (53), 1979; 'Hartmann's Gregorius and the Paradox of Sin' by R. Fisher, in *Seminar*, (17), 1981; *Hartmann von Aue: Changing*

Perspectives edited by Timothy McFarland and Silvia Ranawake, 1988; *Hartmann von Aue: Landscapes of the Mind* by Susan L. Clark, 1989.

* * *

According to contemporaries, Hartmann von Aue set the standard for the great generation of German poets flourishing around 1200. Hartmann identifies himself as a '*dienstman*' (*ministerialis*) '*von Ouwe*'. On linguistic grounds we know that he came from Swabia (south-western Germany), a member of the unfree class of *ministeriales* who, through service as functionaries of the high aristocracy, won noble status for themselves in the course of the 12th century; in his depiction of an ideal knighthood, noble status is legitimated by service to society. He emphasizes his Latin clerical education, unusual for a layman. It is not possible to identify Hartmann's family—or even his patrons—with any reliability; he may have belonged to the sphere of the Dukes of Zähringen. His literary activity can with confidence be said to extend from about 1180 to around 1205, and he seems to have participated in the Crusade in either 1189–90 or 1197–98; testimony of other poets indicates that he died before 1220.

Hartmann's *oeuvre* comprises a youthful disputation on love, *Die Klage* [The Lover's Lament]; a substantial corpus of love lyrics whose chronology cannot reliably be determined; and four narrative works: two courtly romances, *Erec* and *Iwein*, and between them two religious legends, *Gregorius* and *Der arme Heinrich* [Poor Sir Henry]. This sequence for his compositions, posited early on stylistic grounds, has long been accepted.

Hartmann's two Arthurian romances, *Erec* and *Iwein*, were based upon two romances by the French poet Chrétien de Troyes, who inaugurated the genre of Arthurian romance. These works present critically an ideal by which the problematical nature of knightly ways can be explored. Common to Arthurian texts on the model of Chrétien is a tectonic structure in which the hero, accepted into chivalric society, incurs guilt through some specific fault, is repudiated by the community, and must in a second sequence of exploits make good this fault in order to achieve a new, higher integration into aristocratic society. In a system of thematic harmonics which embody the statement of the narrative, the events and persons of these adventures reflect through repetition, parallel, and contrast the nature of the deficiency which is to be remedied.

In spite of its significance as the first German Arthurian romance, *Erec*, composed soon after 1180, is preserved whole in only a single, large manuscript (the Ambraser MS, a compendium of chivalric poetry) from the early 16th century, and even then its opening is lost; the test has 10,135 verses. Significant divergences from Chrétien show that Hartmann also knew other versions of the story. *Erec* treats marital sexuality, chivalric violence, and their proper regulation as socially beneficial functions. The compulsive Erec and his devoted wife Enite succumb to the erotic delights of marriage and accordingly neglect their public duty as king and queen; once apprised of his disgrace, Erec imposes absolute silence upon his wife during his quest for rehabilitation, but after repeatedly being saved only through her warnings is forced to acknowledge their marital interdependence. Similarly, he learns to exercise his martial prowess in works of rescue and liberation rather than as an end in itself, and finally through social responsibility merits his crown. Enite, growing in maturity and perception before her husband, can be deemed an equal protagonist. Hartmann points up more strongly than

his French source the religious dimension of this idealized chivalry.

Iwein, completed by about 1205, is 8,165 verses in length and adhered much more closely to its French source. It is widely recorded, being preserved in 32 manuscripts (some fragmentary). The foreground theme reflects that of *Erec*, for the protagonist has here to curb his eagerness for chivalric exploits in order to regain the favour of his wife, whom he has neglected. The essential theme here too, however, is the social function which alone legitimates chivalric feats of arms, for after total breakdown and loss of self, Iwein overcomes his frivolous desire for *âventiure*—the term means both 'a chivalric encounter' and 'a story about chivalric encounters' —and directs his knightly endeavours to deeds of rescue and the defence of what is just. The plot requires feats of diplomatic persuasion in order to motivate the reconciliations between Iwein and his lady. With its myth and fairy-tale elements the narrative has less inherent linear focus than *Erec*. Irony embedded in the work serves to convey the author's critical play with the values of conventional knighthood and the assumptions of chivalric romance.

In narrative structure Hartmann's religious legends resemble the romances: the protagonist in all his worldly glory is suddenly struck down because he has failed to live according to God's ordinance, presuming his fortune to be his by right. *Gregorius*, 4,007 verses in length and composed either in 1188 or in the 1190s, is recorded in 11 manuscripts. Based on a version of the contemporary French *Life of Pope Gregory*, it portrays the son of a sibling relationship who, after renouncing a monastic life for the world of chivalry, unknowingly commits incest with his mother. After 17 years of harsh penance he is called to the papal throne, and mother and son devote themselves to God's service in Rome. This work is probably related to a legend type recorded by the Persian Firdousi (10th century) rather than the Oedipus myth, and it focuses more on the need for penance than on the incurring of guilt. *Der arme Heinrich*, 1,520 verses long and composed probably around 1195, survives in six manuscripts; it depicts an ideal, courtly knight who, visited with leprosy, fails still to acknowledge God's sovereignty and is prepared even to countenance the willing sacrifice of a pure young virgin for the sake of his cure. Relenting finally as the surgeon prepares the sacrifice, Henry recognizes God's will and accepts his life as penance for the sin of worldliness. The peasant girl, his counterpart in delusion, denied immediate salvation by means of her sacrifice, must accept that life on earth is meant to be lived. God rewards their acceptance of his will by curing Henry, who marries the girl below his rank and lives in marriage and penance isolated from courtly society.

With their lucid expression and crafted composition, Hartmann's works illustrate vividly the interaction between clerical learning and the aspirations of the lay aristocracy in a period of dynamic social evolution. Their manuscript transmission suggests that they were perceived to be in distinct categories rather than the work of a single personality; none the less they ranked from the outset as classical models in their genres. *Gregorius* was translated into Latin as early as 1210, and *Iwein* served from the 13th century as the basis for cycles of frescoes in Rodeneck in the Tyrol and Schmalkalden in Thuringia. Hartmann's legends have been reworked in the past century by Thomas Mann and Gerhart Hauptmann.

—Lewis Jillings

HAŠEK, Jaroslav. Born in Prague, Bohemia (now Czech Republic), 30 April 1883. Educated at St Stephen's School, 1891–93; Imperial and Royal Junior Gymnasium, 1893–97, expelled; Czechoslavonic Commercial Academy, 1899–1902. Married Jarmila Mayerová in 1910 (separated 1912), one son; bigamous marriage with Shura Lvova in 1920. Worked for a chemist in late 1890s; wrote stories and sketches for several humorous and political magazines from 1901; also wrote and performed cabaret sketches; clerk, Insurance Bank of Slavie, 1902–03; jailed for anarchist rioting, 1907; editor, *Svět zvírat* [Animal World], 1909–10; assistant editor, *Czech Word*, 1911; conscripted into the Austrian army, 1915; captured by the Russians: allowed to work for Czech forces in Russia, and staff member, *Cechoslovan*, Kiev, 1916–18; after a propaganda battle, 1917–18, left Czech group and entered political department of the Siberian Army: editor, *Our Path* (later *Red Arrow*), 1919, *Red Europe*, 1919, and other propaganda journals in Russia and Siberia; sent to Czechoslovakia to do propaganda work, 1920; lived in Lipnice from 1921. *Died 3 January 1923.*

PUBLICATIONS

Collection

Spisy [Works]. 16 vols., 1955–68.

Fiction

Dobrý voják Švejk a jiné podivné historky [The Good Soldier Svejk and Other Strange Stories]. 1912.
Trampoty pana Tenkráta [The Tribulations of Mr That-Time]. 1912.
Průvodčí cizincu a jiné satiry [The Tourists' Guide and Other Satires from Home]. 1913.
Můj obchod se psy a jiné humoresky [My Trade with Dogs and Other Humoresques]. 1915.
Dobrý voják Švejk v zajetí [The Good Soldier Svejk in Captivity]. 1917.
[Two Dozen Stories]. 1920.
Pepíček Nový a jiné povídky [Pepíček Nový and Other Stories]. 1921.
Osudy dobrého vojáka Švejka za světové války. 4 vols., 1921–23; as *The Good Soldier Schweik*, translated by Paul Selver, 1930; complete version, as *The Good Soldier Švejk and His Fortunes in the World War*, translated by Cecil Parrott, 1973.
Tři muži se žralokem a jiné poučné historky [Three Men and a Shark and Other Instructive Stories]. 1921.
Mírová Konference ajiné humoresky [The Peace Conference and Other Humoresques]. 1922.
Idylky z pekla (stories), edited by Evžen Paloncy. 1974.
The Red Commissar, Including Further Adventures of the Good Soldier Svejk and Other Stories, translated by Cecil Parrott, 1981.
Povídky (stories). 2 vols., 1988.
The Bachura Scandal and Other Stories and Sketches, translated by Alan Menhennet. 1991.

Other

Lidský profil Jaroslava Haška: korespondence a dokumenty (selected letters 1920–22), edited by Radko Pytlík. 1979.
Tajemství mého pobytu v Rusku (selected essays), edited by Zdeněk Horění. 1985.

*

Bibliography: *Bibliografie Jaroslava Haška* by Boris Mědílek, 1983.

Critical Studies: *Hašek, the Creator of Schweik* by Emanuel Frynta, 1965; *The Bad Bohemian: The Life of Jaroslav Hašek*, 1978, and *Jaroslav Hašek: A Study of Svejk and the Short Stories*, 1982, both by Cecil Parrott; *Jaroslav Hašek and the Good Soldier Schweik* by Radko Pytlík, translated by David Short, 1983.

* * *

Jaroslav Hašek wrote his one and only novel, *Osudy dobrého vojáka Švejka za světové války* (*The Good Soldier Švejk and His Fortunes in the World War*), in 1921 and 1922, at the very end of his adventurous and chequered life, and left it unfinished at his death. It has been translated into countless languages and is now far better known in the world than any other Czech book—a development which he could never have foreseen. At first the Czech literary 'establishment' dismissed the book as unliterary, and it was only when it was translated into German in 1926 and presented by Erwin Piscator in dramatized form at the famous Theater am Nollendorfplatz in Berlin in 1928 that it achieved European fame.

When it was published in final form in 1923, it anticipated by several years the wave of popular war books which appeared at the end of the decade, like *All Quiet on the Western Front* (*Im Westen nichts Neues*) by Erich Maria Remarque and others. But whereas the authors of such books mostly dwelt on the horror and suffering of war and their disillusionment with it, Hašek, to quote the perceptive judgement of a contemporary Czech writer, Ivan Olbracht, 'stood above it' and 'just laughed at it'. Olbracht went on to say that he had read several war novels and even written one himself, but none of them showed up World War I 'in all its infamy, idiocy and inhumanity' so vividly as Hašek's.

Hašek found the material for his novel during the one year he spent in the Austrian army on the way to the Eastern Front. Most of its leading characters are modelled on the officers, NCOs, and men of the regiment he served in. He had already invented the character of 'The Good Soldier' in 1911, when he wrote five short stories about him, but in his final novel Švejk had become a much rounder and more enigmatic figure. Was he an idiot or only pretending to be one? In consequence of this ambiguity Švejk was caught up in the political struggles between Left and Right in the young republic. The Left wanted to see him as a revolutionary, while the Right condemned him as a dodger and a threat to national morale. While most other readers of the book would laugh aloud at Švejk's misadventures, Czechoslovakia's leading critic, F.X. Salda, saw their tragic side. For all its comedy, he wrote, it was a desperately sad book, because in it the individual was fighting against a giant power, against the war.

Hašek himself would have been greatly surprised to know that his book had given rise to such discussions, because he just dictated it as it came into his head—sometimes in the middle of a pub bar—with nothing but a map to go on. He filled the pages of his book with a vast array of fascinating types, whom he involved more often than not in ludicrous situations. He had a Dickensian gift for describing character, although unlike Dickens he did not dwell on their appearance but rather on their actions and manner of speech. He was particularly successful in reproducing the conversations of ordinary men and the anecdotes they tell. And he described in a masterly fashion the scrapes they got into and the idiotic ideas they had, saying under his breath, 'Lord, what fools these mortals be'. The book is as much a condemnation of the Austrian Army as it is of the war. Its generals are shown either as inept fuddy-duddies or potential hangmen. (Hašek was of course free for the first time to say exactly what he thought of the monarchy, as it no longer existed.)

In writing his novel Hašek drew on his long experience in contributing short stories and feuilletons to the Czech press, which are said to have amounted to over 1,200. He wrote them for Prague dailies before the war, for the Czech Legion's newspaper in Kiev during it, and Soviet journals in Siberia after it was over. He wrote easily, but carelessly. He once described a feuilleton as 'something which can be read in the morning at breakfast, when a man is still yawning, and in the afternoon, when after lunch he lies agreeably stretched out on a soft sofa, a kind of writing in which one can skip half a column without missing it'. His short stories prove his inexhaustible ingenuity in inventing comic situations, but as the newspapers he contributed to seldom allowed him more than a little over a thousand words they almost all suffer from compression and sometimes end with the point only half made. His best stories are the Bugulma tales, which he published in Prague on his return from Russia after the war, and which recount his experiences as deputy-commandant of a little town beyond the Volga. Although in these he ridicules Soviet petty officials, he is more indulgent to them than he is to Austrians or indeed to his own people.

In the years before the war Hašek acquired something of a reputation as a popular entertainer, when he helped to create a mock political party and posed as its candidate in the national elections. People flocked to hear his improvised speeches, in which he mercilessly pilloried the activities of the Czech political parties. When the elections were over he sat down and wrote up the 'annals' of his 'party' and ascribed to its members various imaginary exploits, but much of what he wrote was too personal and defamatory to be published at the time and only found its way into print as late as 1963.

None of Hašek's flamboyant posturings as electioneering agent, speaker at Anarchist rallies, or cabaret entertainer earned him much respect, and his lampoons and tomfoolery alienated many who might otherwise have helped him. By the time war broke out Prague had become rather too hot for him, and he no doubt joined up with a certain feeling of relief. But it can be said of him that he added another dimension to conventional humorous writing by acting and actually living his stories. All his experiences, whether lived or written, bore fruit later, when he drew on them for his one great novel.

—Cecil Parrott

THE GOOD SOLDIER ŠVEJK AND HIS FORTUNES IN THE WORLD WAR (Osudy dobrého vojáka Švejka za světové války)
Novel by Jaroslav Hašek, 1921–23.

In Hašek's novel, as in most of the best fiction relating to modern war, the diaphragm between history and invention is at its most transparent. The author's own experiences in fact provide the basis for much of the narrative. Hašek addresses the reader directly in a brief preface which presents the shabby Švejk as a real person whom one may encounter in the streets of Prague. But he goes further, overturning the grand perspectives of traditional historiography by asserting that Švejk is one of the 'unknown heroes' whose glory eclipses that of an Alexander or a Napoleon, though he himself is quite unaware of it. The novel is a tellingly comic demonstration of this assertion.

The narrative opens with the middle-aged ex-soldier Švejk, now a forger of dog pedigrees, bathing his feet for rheumatism, when his landlady brings the news of the assassination at Sarajevo that will be the prelude to the outbreak of World War I. Since Švejk is never again troubled by rheumatism, the reader must presume that he has considerable foresight, and that his rheumatism is an insurance against military call-up. In fact, when war is declared, he propels himself through the streets of Prague on a wheelchair to volunteer for the front, crying 'To Belgrade! To Belgrade!', to the huge amusement of the Czech population, who have no great enthusiasm for risking their lives fighting their Serbian (or Russian) fellow-Slavs on behalf of their Austrian Habsburg masters.

Švejk's inspired ruse, however, is no match for the efficient Austrian war-machine, which inexorably ingests him into its system. This provides one dimension of the novel's narrative system, propelling Švejk through the military hospital for would-be draft-dodgers shamming disabilities of one sort or another, and then through the whole gamut of situations, from the relatively secure and privileged status of regimental chaplain's orderly to eventual entrainment to the Galician front. Hašek thus creates for himself the opportunity for a systematic satire of Habsburg power as it impinges most directly on its unwilling Czech recruits, with a strongly physiological aspect, as the hegemonic control is imposed through the bowels. Much of the narrative is in fact an appalling comic saga of hunger, voracious eating, emetics, and excreting.

Here we have one feature of the book that from the first provoked a hostile reaction, both in Czech and in international literary circles, on moral and aesthetic grounds and also on patriotic grounds. Indeed, the very figure of Švejk was seen as a demeaning reflection upon the newborn Czechoslovak nation. All these grounds may be subsumed within class politics: Hašek's book shows all the characteristics of a subversive, perhaps anarchic, realism coming from below, and has many points of contact with the picaresque tradition (especially in its Spanish origins), with which it has frequently been compared. Apart from the overt challenge to the by then already defunct Austrian Habsburg authority, it presents a barely concealed challenge to a literary establishment and norms determined by class and, indeed, to authority of any kind. This is also evident at the level of language and style. The narrative is conducted in an idiom closer to the demotic speech of the Czech people than to the highflown literary tradition. The dialogue, especially the loquacious exchanges between Švejk and his peers, is freer and more broadly colloquial still, even phonologically. The German characters speak a frightful mishmash of German and broken Czech.

If the Austrian military machine and the historical script of World War I provide one part of the narrative propulsion of the book, Švejk's subterfuges or misadventures provide the other part, unfailingly involving him in scenarios that collectively add up to a coherent perspective on the situation of the Czech people at the outbreak of war. There has been much discussion as to whether Švejk is an idiot or a rogue, sowing confusion all around him through incompetence or by design. Hašek consistently avoids turning his hero into a subject of moral introspection or decoding his behaviour for the reader, just as Švejk carefully avoids allowing his military superiors to read his motives. It is only to his trusted Lieutenant Lukaš that he divulges one of his favourite techniques: overwhelming his antagonist with inane chatter (Part I, chapter 14). Nevertheless, Švejk's actions speak for themselves. All his blunders, ruses, or escapades have the effect of either delaying his approach to the bloodbath of the trenches or throwing the Austrian war effort into disarray, or both at once. He muddles the key to the Austrian military cipher and finally gets himself captured by his own side. Thus the definition of Švejk as 'an idiot of genius', espoused by Ivan Olbracht and Julius Fučík, needs to be modified to 'a genius at feigning idiocy'.

Švejk's compulsive chatter, however, is not merely a defensive strategy. In the course of the novel, he tells hundreds of preposterous-sounding stories and anecdotes, typical pub-tales very similar to those Hašek himself revelled in, which range in length from one-liners to a page or so. These have been characterized by Milan Jankovič as 'absurdist' in their logic, and in that respect serve further to subvert the purported rationality of the established order. But they go beyond that, building up collectively to a mosaic of the subject Czech people. Švejk also meets numerous tellers of other similar demotic tales that contribute to the overall picture of Czech ethnicity, the basis of the new nation that was to arise out of the cataclysm of the war. Though unfinished at the author's death, *The Good Soldier Švejk* established the oral history of the common Czech people as their comic national epic.

—John Gatt-Rutter

HAUPTMANN, Gerhart (Johann Robert). Born in Ober-Salzbrunn, Silesia, 15 November 1862. Educated at a school in Breslau, from 1874; studied sculpture at Royal College of Art, Breslau, 1880–82; also studied at University of Jena, 1882–83. Married 1) Marie Thienemann in 1885 (divorced 1904; died 1915), three sons; 2) Margarete Marschalk in 1905, one son. Sculptor in Rome, 1883–84; also worked as actor in Berlin, before becoming a full-time writer; co-founder of the literary group *Durch*. Recipient: Grillparzer prize, 1896, 1899, 1905; Goethebünde Schiller prize, 1905; Nobel prize for literature, 1912; Goethe prize (Frankfurt), 1932. Honorary degrees: Oxford University, 1905; University of Leipzig, 1909; University of Prague, 1921; Columbia University, New York, 1932. Ordre pour le Mérite, 1922. *Died 8 June 1946.*

PUBLICATIONS

Collections

Dramatic Works, edited by Ludwig Lewisohn, translated by Lewisohn and others. 9 vols., 1912–29.
Sämtliche Werke, edited by Hans-Egon Hass. 11 vols., 1962–74.

Plays

Vor Sonnenaufgang (produced 1889). 1889; as *Before Dawn*, translated by Leonard Bloomfield, 1909; also translated by Richard Newnham, in *Three German Plays*, 1963; as *Before Daybreak*, translated by Peter Bauland, 1978; as *Before Sunrise*, translated by James Joyce, edited by Jill Perkins, 1978.

Das Friedenfest (produced 1890). 1890; as *The Coming of Peace*, translated by Janet Achurch and C.E. Wheeler, 1900; as *The Reconciliation*, in *Dramatic Works*, 1914.
Einsame Menschen (produced 1891). 1891; as *Lonely Lives*, translated by Mary Morrison, 1898.
Die Weber (produced 1893). 1892; as *The Weavers*, translated by Mary Morrison, 1899; also translated by T.H. Lustig, in *Five Plays*, 1961; Frank Marcus, 1980.
Kollege Crampton (produced 1892). 1892; as *Colleague Crampton*, translated by Roy Temple House and Ludwig Lewisohn, in *Dramatic Works*, 1914.
Der Biberpelz (produced 1893). 1893; as *The Beaver Coat*, translated by Ludwig Lewisohn, 1912; also translated by T.H. Lustig, in *Five Plays*, 1961.
Hanneles Himmelfahrt (produced 1893). 1893; as *Hannele*, translated by William Archer, 1894; also translated by Charles Henry Meltzer, 1908; T.H. Lustig, in *Five Plays*, 1961.
Florian Geyer (produced 1896). 1896; as *Florian Geyer*, translated by Bayard Quincy Morgan, in *Dramatic Works*, 1929.
Die versunkene Glocke (produced 1896). 1896; as *The Sunken Bell*, translated by Mary Harned, 1898; also translated by Charles Henry Meltzer, 1899.
Fuhrmann Henschel (produced 1898). 1898; as *Drayman Henschel*, translated by Marion A. Redlich, in *Dramatic Works*, 1913; also translated by T.H. Lustig, in *Five Plays*, 1961.
Schluck und Jau (produced 1900). 1900; as *Schluck and Jau*, translated by Ludwig Lewisohn, in *Dramatic Works*, 1919.
Michael Kramer (produced 1900). 1900; as *Michael Kramer*, translated by Ludwig Lewisohn, in *Dramatic Works*, 1914.
Der rote Hahn (produced 1901). 1901; as *The Conflagration*, translated by Ludwig Lewisohn, in *Dramatic Works*, 1913.
Der arme Heinrich (produced 1902). 1902; as *Henry of Auë*, translated by Ludwig Lewisohn, in *Dramatic Works*, 1914.
Rose Bernd (produced 1903). 1903; as *Rose Bernd*, translated by Ludwig Lewisohn, in *Dramatic Works*, 1913; also translated by T.H. Lustig, in *Five Plays*, 1961.
Elga (produced 1905). 1905; as *Elga*, translated by Mary Harned, in *Dramatic Works*, 1919.
Und Pippa tanzt! (produced 1906). 1906; translated as *And Pippa Dances*, 1907.
Die Jungfrau vom Bischofsberg (produced 1907). 1907; as *Maidens of the Mount*, translated by Ludwig Lewisohn, in *Dramatic Works*, 1919.
Kaiser Karls Geisel (produced 1908). 1908; as *Charlemagne's Hostage*, translated by Ludwig Lewisohn, in *Dramatic Works*, 1919.
Griselda (produced 1909). 1909; as *Griselda*, translated by Alice Kauser, in *Dramatic Works*, 1919.
Die Ratten (produced 1911). 1911; as *The Rats*, translated by Ludwig Lewisohn, in *Dramatic Works*, 1913.
Gabriel Schillings Flucht (produced 1912). 1912; as *Gabriel Schilling's Flight*, translated by Ludwig Lewisohn, in *Dramatic Works*, 1919.
Festspiel in deutschen Reimen (produced 1913). 1913; as *Commemoration Masque*, translated by Bayard Quincy Morgan, in *Dramatic Works*, 1919.
Der Bogen des Odysseus (produced 1914). 1914; as *The Bow of Ulysses*, translated by Bayard Quincy Morgan, in *Dramatic Works*, 1919.
Winterballade (produced 1917). 1917; as *A Winter Ballad*, translated by Edwin and Willa Muir, in *Dramatic Works*, 1925.
Der weisse Heiland (produced 1920). 1920; as *The White Savior*, translated by Edwin and Willa Muir, in *Dramatic Works*, 1925.

Indipohdi (produced 1920). 1920; as *Indipohdi*, translated by Edwin and Willa Muir, in *Dramatic Works*, 1925.
Peter Bauer (produced 1921). 1921.
Veland. 1925; as *Veland*, translated by Edwin Muir, in *Dramatic Works*, 1929.
Dorothea Angermann (produced 1926). 1926.
Spuk; oder, Die schwarze Maske und Hexenritt (produced 1929). 1929.
Vor Sonnenuntergang (produced 1932). 1932.
Die goldene Harfe (produced 1933). 1933.
Hamlet in Wittenberg (produced 1935). 1935.
Ulrich von Lichtenstein (produced 1939). 1939.
Die Tochter der Kathedrale (produced 1939). 1939.
Atridentetralogie: Iphigenie in Aulis; Agamemnons Tod; Elektra; Iphigenie in Delphi (produced 1940–44). 4 vols., 1941–48.
Magnus Garbe (produced 1942). 1942.
Die Finsternisse. 1947.
Herbert Engelmann, completed by Carl Zuckmayer (produced 1952). 1952.
Five Plays, translated by T.H. Lustig. 1961.

Fiction

Fasching. 1887.
Bahnwärter Thiel. 1888.
Der Apostel. 1890.
Der Narr in Christo, Emanuel Quint. 1910; as *The Fool in Christ, Emanuel Quint*, translated by Thomas Seltzer, 1911.
Atlantis. 1912; as *Atlantis*, translated by Adele and Thomas Seltzer, 1913.
Lohengrin. 1913.
Parsival. 1914; as *Parsifal*, translated by Oakley Williams, 1915.
Der Ketzer von Soana. 1918; as *The Heretic of Soana*, translated by Bayard Quincy Morgan, 1923.
Phantom. 1922; as *Phantom*, translated by Bayard Quincy Morgan, 1923.
Die Insel der grossen Mutter. 1924; as *The Island of the Great Mother*, translated by Edwin and Willa Muir, 1925.
Wanda. 1928.
Buch der Leidenschaft. 1930.
Die Hochzeit auf Buchenhorst. 1931.
Das Meerwunder. 1934.
Im Wirbel der Berufung. 1936.
Der Schuss im Park. 1939.
Das Märchen. 1941.
Mignon. 1944.
Lineman Thiel and Other Tales, translated by Stanley Radcliffe, 1989.

Verse

Promethidenlos. 1885.
Das bunte Buch. 1888.
Anna. 1921.
Die blaue Blume. 1924.
Till Eulenspiegel. 1928.
Ährenlese. 1939.
Der grosse Traum. 1942.
Neue Gedichte. 1946.

Other

Griechischer Frühling. 1908.
Ausblicke. 1922.

Gesammelte Werke. 12 vols., 1922.
Um Volk und Geist. 1932.
Gespräche, edited by Josef Chapiro. 1932.
Das Abenteuer meiner Jugend. 2 vols., 1937.
Italienische Reise 1897: Tagebuchaufzeichnungen, edited by Martin Machatzke. 1976.
Diarium 1917 bis 1933, edited by Martin Machatzke. 1980.
Notiz-Kalender 1889 bis 1891, edited by Martin Machatzke. 1982.
Gerhart Hauptmann—Ludwig von Hofmann: Briefwechsel 1894–1944, edited by Herta Hesse-Frielinghaus. 1983.
Otto Brahm, Gerhart Hauptmann: Briefwechsel 1889–1912, edited by Peter Sprengel. 1985.
Tagebuch 1892 bis 1894, edited by Martin Machatzke. 1985.
Tagebücher 1897 bis 1905, edited by Martin Machatzke. 1987.
Ein Leben für Gerhart Hauptmann: Aufsätze aus den Jahren 1929–1990, edited by Walter A. Reichart. 1991.

*

Bibliography: *Gerhart-Hauptmann-Bibliographie* by Walter Requardt, 3 vols., 1931; *Gerhart-Hauptmann-Bibliographie* by Walter A. Reichart, 1969; *Gerhart-Hauptmann-Bibliographie* by Heinz D. Tschörtner, 1971; *Internationale Bibliographie zum Werk Gerhart Hauptmanns* by Sigfried Hoefert, 2 vols., 1986–89.

Critical Studies: *The Death Problem in the Life and Works of Hauptmann* by Frederick A. Klemm, 1939; *Gerhart Hauptmann* by Hugh F. Garten, 1954; *Gerhart Hauptmann: His Life and Work* by C.F.W. Behl, 1956; *Gerhart Hauptmann: The Prose Plays* by Margaret Sinden, 1957; *Witness of Deceit: Gerhart Hauptmann as a Critic of Society* by Leroy R. Shaw, 1958; *Hauptmann: Centenary Lectures* edited by K.G. Knight and F. Norman, 1964; *Gerhart Hauptmann in Russia, 1889–1917: Reception and Impact* by Albert A. Kipa, 1974; *From Lessing to Hauptmann: Studies in German Drama* by Ladislaus Löb, 1974; *Gerhart Hauptmann and Utopia*, 1976, and *Gerhart Hauptmann: Religious Syncretism and Eastern Religions*, 1984, both by Philip Mellen; *The Image of the Primitive Giant in the Works of Gerhart Hauptmann* by Carolyn Thomas Dussère, 1979; *The German Naturalists and Gerhart Hauptmann: Reception and Influence* by Alan Marshall, 1982; *Hauptmann, Wedekind and Schnitzler* by Peter Skrine, 1989l; *Understanding Gerhart Hauptmann* by Warren R. Maurer, 1992.

* * *

Gerhart Hauptmann's reputation as the leading representative of German naturalism has tended to obscure the fact that he enjoyed a period of literary creativity which lasted for more than 60 years. Apart from Goethe, few German writers have succeeded in bequeathing a life's work of such astonishing variety, richness, and breadth. From naturalism to neo-romanticism to 20th-century mysticism and neo-classicism, there are few literary movements between 1880 and 1940 which failed to influence Hauptmann or indeed to be influenced by him.

Hauptmann's plays, ranging from the crude but powerful *Vor Sonnenaufgang* (*Before Dawn*), 1889, to the deeply pessimistic recasting of antique sources in the *Atridentetralogie* [Atriden tetralogy], 1940–44, are remarkable for the easy assurance with which the author displays his mastery of diverse registers, themes, styles, and genres. The raucous naturalism of his earliest work was tempered in 1891 by the performance in Berlin of *Einsame Menschen* (*Lonely Lives*), a poignant middle-class tragedy which, in its probing analysis of the roles ascribed by society to women, has lost none of its topicality. Realism re-emerged in *Die Weber* (*The Weavers*), a moving account of the ill-fated uprising of the Silesian weavers in 1844, in the comedies *Der Biberpelz* (*The Beaver Coat*) and *Der rote Hahn* (*The Conflagration*), and in the tightly knit dialect tragedy *Fuhrmann Henschel* (*Drayman Henschel*). Even in this early period Hauptmann was not willing to accept the dictates of naturalism in any doctrinaire sense, for in *Hanneles Himmelfahrt* (*Hannele*) the techniques of realism are employed as a means of making visual the delirious dreams and mental states of a dying child. Hannele's hallucinations, which express the reality of her wretched childhood and at once represent a flight from it, symbolize Hauptmann's own deepening interest in the workings of the imagination and its relationship to the human capacity to apprehend reality in mythical and poetic ways. This development is carried much further in the dramatic fairy-tale *Die versunkene Glocke* (*The Sunken Bell*), and in a more realistic framework it is evident in the father/son conflict portrayed in the artist tragedy *Michael Kramer*. The subtlest and most magical expression of this thematic material is the drama *Und Pippa tanzt!* (*And Pippa Dances*), a work which owes much to Hauptmann's intensive study of the myths and legends of his native Silesia.

Hauptmann's works of prose fiction reflect in both theme and style the main trends discernible in his development as a dramatist. And similarly, the earlier naturalistic stories such as *Fasching* and *Bahnwärter Thiel* have had a greater impact than the mythological and symbolic works of the later period: *Der Narr in Christo, Emanuel Quint* (*The Fool in Christ, Emanuel Quint*), *Der Ketzer von Soana* (*The Heretic of Soana*), and *Die Insel der grossen Mutter* (*The Island of the Great Mother*). Narratives such as *Bahnwärter Thiel* reveal even more clearly than the naturalistic plays, however, that Hauptmann was transcending naturalism in those very works which explored its themes and its expressive possibilities. The story certainly abounds in fashionable literary touches: the low social position of Thiel, the second-by-second description of trains appearing on the horizon and disappearing in the distance, the realistic 'close-up' of a spade turning over the soil, and so on. At the same time, the narrative penetrates beyond realism to suggest the existence of realities and levels of perception which can be grasped only through symbol and myth. The train which kills Thiel's son and destroys Thiel is depicted on one level with all the photographic detail and meticulous accuracy which one expects to find in late 19th-century fiction; on a different level, the train's headlights transform the falling rain into droplets of blood and the train comes to symbolize the unpredictable and chaotic forces of destruction which, in Hauptmann's fictional world, are never very far from surface reality, however rational and well ordered it might appear.

—A.P. Foulkes

THE WEAVERS (Die Weber)
Play by Gerhart Hauptmann, 1892.

One of the most powerful social dramas in German literature, *The Weavers* is also the first German play to attempt a realistic representation of an entire community of working-class people on stage. Written at a time when the young

Hauptmann was influenced by naturalism and its scientific interpretation of the world, the work portrays the Silesian weavers as victims of socio-economic circumstances. The dramatic incidents mirror problems associated with the Industrial Revolution, such as the unemployment caused by the introduction of power looms, and the exploitation of labour by capitalist entrepreneurs. Hauptmann shows how a mass of people are driven to violent reaction when their misery becomes unbearable.

Based on actual events which took place in the Eulengebirge in 1844 as the Industrial Revolution reached eastern Germany, the play became the most controversial of its time when it was finally presented to the general public in Berlin in 1893. This 'symphony in five movements with one grim, leading motive—hunger' (Huneker) received thunderous applause from the audience, but was regarded by the authorities as inflammatory.

The play is without a conventional plot. Its action is 'realistic', presenting the weavers in their wretched situation from various angles—Hauptmann gives dramatic shape to the social and economic forces which condition an entire class. The first act shows the starving weavers en masse, visiting the premises of their employer in order to sell their cloth. Tractable and docile, they are exploited by the manufacturer whose magnanimous gesture in taking on an extra two hundred unemployed weavers is exposed as humbug—the new rates of pay will be even lower than the current starvation wages. The second act focuses on the sufferings of a small group of weavers in the cramped room which they call home. The third act is set in a public bar and gives the audience a cross-section of the local community as weavers come into contact with the views of others from outside the weavers' narrow social sphere: some (the smith, the rag-and-bone man) are sympathetic but most (the policeman, the commercial traveller, the innkeeper, the joiner-employer) are impervious to their plight. The fourth act is set in the sumptuous home of the employer, whose guest is the local parson. The arrival of a mob of weavers outside the house is condemned by the clergyman who regards any threat to the prevailing social order as a transgression against the laws of God. The superintendent of police is called to deal with the rioting weavers, but the employer and his family are forced to leave before the weavers take possession of the house and set about destroying it. The fifth act follows the weavers' revolt to another village: the action is set in the home of a pious old weaver, Old Hilse, who refuses to jeopardize his hopes for salvation in the life to come by joining his 'poor brothers' in their continued destruction of employers' houses and factories. The weavers are led by Jäger, an unruly soldier who has recently returned and, appalled at their wretched situation, has stirred the weavers to defiance. At the end of the play, shots are heard as the weavers begin fighting the soldiers who have been sent to put down the riot. Old Hilse, stubbornly staying at his loom near a window, is fatally wounded by a stray bullet.

The impact which *The Weavers* has on audiences is produced by its frequently innovative dramatic qualities: its unusual yet authentic dramatic theme—the revolt of the entire social body of the weavers, springing from their hunger and poverty; the absence of a conventional single 'hero' (only one minor character appears throughout all the acts of the play) and the creation of a 'collective hero', the mass of weavers in their moment of revolt against long-endured, unbearable suffering; the technically brilliant way in which Hauptmann handles a multiplicity of events and characters, producing intense thematic concentration which gives the play the effect of 'harmonious and unified construction' (Lawson); the avoidance of sentimentality through the employment of a chronicle framework which presents events 'naturalistically', in an objective, documentary fashion, while still evoking sympathy—'the moving power is the event, the action, the class articulate in revolt' (Raymond Williams).

Hauptmann employs several techniques in order to articulate an entire class on the stage: first, he focuses on small representative groups in their familiar environments in order to illustrate the effects of their crushing poverty (Acts Two and Five). Second, he employs a 'choral method' to create a sense of individuals belonging to the same class, shaped by the same social forces, but with the less typical figures giving dramatic life to the whole through their interaction with the others: in the first act, for instance, the weavers are presented as a *whole*, with individual weavers speaking in the patterns of speech of the whole group. Hauptmann creates the illusion of real speech by having the weavers speak in Silesian dialect, with unfinished sentences, interjections, single words, short phrases, and people talking across each other. Third, the inflammatory marching song recited on several occasions by Jäger, telling of the weavers' oppression, functions not only as a leitmotif throughout the play, but also as a dramatic lever—by expressing the weavers' unspoken emotions, the song enables the weavers to understand their situation clearly for the first time, and resignation and despair gradually give way to hatred and violence. All these techniques have the effect of translating economic fact into dramatic, emotional experience.

Critics have praised the play as a naturalistic 'milieu-drama'—much of its dramatic effect depends on the creation of a loosely connected sequence of detailed pictures of the environment (the stage directions are given in the minutest detail and, in the original edition, the dramatis personae of each of the five acts was printed before that act, suggesting a series of separate tableaux). Yet the acts are not static pictures; Hauptmann established a dynamic relationship between setting and action in so far as milieu is shown to be a force which shapes the human characters involved and so actually determines the dramatic action. Each of the five acts of the play has an increasingly dramatic conclusion, illustrating how a mass of individually passive weavers gradually, as the social and economic pressure on them intensifies, form into a destructive, disorganized mob.

—David Rock

HEBBEL, (Christian) Friedrich. Born in Wesselburen, Holstein, Denmark (now Germany), 18 March 1813. Educated in a dame's school, 1817–19; primary school, Wesselburen, 1819–25; servant and clerk for local official, 1827–35; in Hamburg a group of benefactors supported him in his studies, and helped send him to the University of Heidelberg, 1836; studied in Munich, 1836; returned to Hamburg, 1839; doctorate, University of Erlangen, 1844. Married Christine Enghaus in 1846, two children; also had two sons (both died in infancy) by Elise Lensing. Freelance writer in Munich, 1836–39, Hamburg, 1839–43; travel allowance from Christian VIII, King of Denmark, allowed him to live in Paris, 1843–44, and Rome, 1844–45; lived in Vienna from 1845; honorary court librarian, Weimar, 1863. Recipient: Schiller prize, 1863. *Died 13 December 1863.*

PUBLICATIONS

Collections

Sämtliche Werke, edited by Richard Maria Werner. 27 vols., 1904–22.
Werke, edited by Gerhard Fricke, Werner Keller, and Karl Pörnbacher. 5 vols., 1963–67.

Plays

Judith (produced 1840). 1840; as *Judith*, translated by Carl van Doren, 1914.
Genoveva (produced 1849). 1843.
Maria Magdalena (produced 1846). 1844; as *Maria Magdalena*, translated by Barker Fairley, in *Three Plays*, 1914; also translated by Carl Richard Mueller, 1962; Sarah Somekh, 1990.
Der Diamant (produced 1852). 1847.
Julia (produced 1903). 1848.
Herodes und Mariamne (produced 1849). 1850; as *Herod and Mariamne*, translated by L.H. Allen, in *Three Plays*, 1914.
Der Rubin (produced 1849). 1851.
Michel Angelo (produced 1861). 1851.
Ein Trauerspiel in Sizilien (produced 1907). 1851.
Agnes Bernauer (produced 1852). 1852; as *Agnes Bernauer*, translated by L. Pattee, in *Poet Lore*, 1909.
Gyges und sein Ring (produced 1889). 1856; as *Gyges and His Ring*, translated by L.H. Allen, in *Three Plays*, 1914.
Die Nibelungen (produced 1861). 2 vols., 1862; as *The Nibelungs*, translated by H. Goldberger, 1921.
Demetrius, from a play by Schiller (produced 1869). 1864.
Ein Steinwurf. 1883.
Three Plays (includes *Maria Magdalena*; *Herod and Mariamne*; *Gyges and His Ring*), translated by L.H. Allen and Barker Fairley, 1914.

Fiction

Schnock: Ein niederländisches Gemälde. 1850.
Erzählungen und Novellen. 1855.

Verse

Gedichte. 1842.
Neue Gedichte. 1848.
Gedichte. 1857.
Mutter und Kind. 1859.

Other

Mein Wort über das Drama! 1843.
Über den Stil des Dramas. 1857.
Tagebücher, edited by F. Bamberg. 2 vols., 1885–87.
Neue Hebbel-Briefe, edited by Anni Meetz. 1963.
Der einsame Weg (diaries), edited by Klaus Geissler. 1966.
Briefe, edited by U. Henry Gerlach. 2 vols., 1975–78.

*

Bibliography: *Hebbel-Bibliographie 1910–1970* by Ulrich H. Gerlach, 1973; supplements: *1970–1980*, in *Hebbel-Jahrbuch*, 1983; *1981–1984*, in *Hebbel-Jahrbuch*, 1986.

Critical Studies: *Friedrich Hebbel as a Dramatic Artist* by G. Brychan Rees, 1930; *Hebbel: A Study of His Life and Work* by Edna Purdie, 1932; *Motivation in the Drama of Hebbel* by William F. Oechler, 1948; *Friedrich Hebbel's Conception of Movement in the Absolute and History*, 1952, and *Friedrich Hebbel*, 1968, both by Sten G. Flygt; *Hebbel as a Critic of His Own Works* by Ulrich H. Gerlach, 1972; *Hebbel's Prose Tragedies* by Mary Garland, 1973; *From Lessing to Hauptmann: Studies in German Drama* by Ladislaus Löb, 1974; *The Reception of Friedrich Hebbel in Germany in the Era of National Socialism* by William John Niven, 1984.

* * *

Poised between the fading beliefs of philosophical idealism and the positivism that came to replace them in the mid-19th century, Friedrich Hebbel sought for compromises between the literary approaches of German classicism and the new realism in European literature. While he also wrote stories, poems, and comedies, he is chiefly remembered today for a number of tragedies, based mostly on history or legend and inclining towards the 'closed' dramatic form.

As a 'poetic realist' who held that art should be both a record of empirical observation and a symbol of timeless truth, he defined drama as 'the art of mixing the general and the specific so that the law all living things obey never appears naked and is never completely missed' ('Schiller und Körner'). It has been argued that his chief weakness derives from the fact that, despite his acutely realistic awareness of psychological and social determination within a framework of historical change, he resorts to metaphysical notions and orthodox techniques in an attempt to regain idealistic certainties and to elicit meaning from an existence which he feels to be meaningless. As Brecht put it: 'Wherever German playwrights started thinking, like Hebbel and before him Schiller, they started contriving'.

Suffering considerable poverty and humiliation before he achieved fame in his fifth and last decade, and inflicting pain on others—particularly on Elise Lensing, a seamstress who supported him for ten years and bore him two sons before he abandoned her to marry the celebrated actress Christine Enghaus—Hebbel was not an attractive personality. Dour and uncompromising, depressive and touchy, yet ruthless and domineering, bristling with the awkwardness of the self-taught and self-made, devoid of humour and beset by brooding pessimism, he maintained that 'all life is a struggle of the individual against the universe' (Diaries, September 1840). Individuals, he explains in his treatise *Mein Wort über das Drama!*, are obliged by their very nature to incur the guilt—existential rather than moral—of self-assertion, for which they must be destroyed: the destruction occurs through strife with other individuals, although it serves the universal order which itself changes in the process. At times he finds solace in the assumption of the dialectical progress of the universe, but his main emphasis rests on human misery, and he suspects that even the divinity is subject to incongruity and impermanence. These views, which owe something to the unacknowledged influence of Hegel and Schelling, are at the centre of his world-picture and his theory of tragedy.

In all of Hebbel's major plays the clash of overbearing heroes and victimized heroines reflects both his personal experiences and his Kantian maxim, 'To use a human being as a means to an end: the worst sin' (Diaries, May? 1839). However, although his greatest artistic asset is his understanding of the sado-masochistic battle of the sexes, which anticipates Ibsen and Strindberg, he often weakens the impact of his acute insights into emotional quandaries by imposing his transcendental theories on them. In *Judith*, the

idea that the heroine, by killing her adversary Holofernes, will help replace universal idol-worship with monotheism forms an uneasy union with the intriguing exploration of a woman's confusion of her sense of divine mission and her personal revenge on a brutal lover. In *Herodes und Mariamne* (*Herod and Mariamne*) the advent of Christianity to supplant Judaeo-Roman despotism seems an inconsequential afterthought to the fascinating picture of possessiveness and resentment, devotion, hostility, and mutually incompatible desire in marriage, which destroy the heroine and leave the hero in lonely desolation. In *Gyges und sein Ring* (*Gyges and His Ring*) the king's pathological urge to exhibit the beauty of the Queen and her equally pathological modesty merge uncomfortably with the figurative reconciliation of tradition and reformation under their successor to the throne.

There are, however, two instances where Hebbel avoids abstruse speculation. In *Agnes Bernauer*, a historical tragedy set in the 15th century—in which a barber's daughter marries the son of a ruler, who has her assassinated to prevent a war of succession—his conservative proposition that the citizen must always be sacrificed to the state represents one of his rare political statements and may raise liberal objections, but his handling of the confrontation of love and politics links concrete human reality with abstract thought in a dramatically convincing manner. In *Maria Magdalena* any abstract thought that may be present is even more effectively transformed into tangible drama. Set in Hebbel's own time, this play—as he argues in his renowned preface—represents a significant innovation in the development of German domestic tragedy since Lessing and Schiller, by deriving the decisive conflict no longer from the opposition of the bourgeoisie and the aristocracy but from the prejudices of the petty bourgeoisie itself. The tragedy of the provincial joiner's daughter—who, on becoming pregnant, is driven to suicide by the desertion of her mercenary seducer and the threats of her bitterly puritanical father—combines the claustrophobically compelling portrayal of characters and circumstances with merciless social criticism to produce not only Hebbel's masterpiece, which Ibsen for one greatly admired, but one of the outstanding works of European realism as a whole.

At the level of dramatic structure, Hebbel's preference for classical methods is liable to prove inconsistent with his modern intuitions. At the level of language, he is most successful when writing contemporary prose, whereas his blank verse is prone to clumsiness, bombast, and anti-climax. At their worst, his plays are hysterical in atmosphere, extravagant in characterization, artificial in situation, and tortuous in argument. At their best, however, they powerfully convey the perplexities of an uncommon mind in an age of transition. Just as his personal egotism was the reverse side of his commitment to his calling, his art with all its harsh idiosyncrasies represents a remarkable document of the struggle of creativity against physical, mental, and social odds.

—Ladislaus Löb

MARIA MAGDALENA
Play by Friedrich Hebbel, 1844.

Maria Magdalena, a domestic or middle-class tragedy in three acts, focuses on the family of Meister Anton, a master joiner who swears to his daughter Klara that he will commit suicide rather than endure the ignominy of ever having a pregnant, unmarried daughter as well as an apparently criminal son. The shame attached to his son Karl's arrest on suspicion of theft has already killed Meister Anton's wife. Klara is pregnant by her fiancé Leonhard, and half-suspecting Klara's plight, Meister Anton extorts from her an oath that, whatever else, she will never bring shame upon him. It is clear what is meant. Failed by her brother Karl, by Leonhard, and by Friedrich, her childhood sweetheart who she believes abandoned her, she jumps down a well to her death. The dread prospect of eternal damnation is less daunting than that of having her father himself commit a mortal sin.

In his preface Hebbel argued that, far from having been superseded by philosophy, art—in particular, a specific type of drama—had a vital role to play in modern society. This supreme type of drama was only possible when a decisive change occurred in the relationship between the state of human consciousness, social structures, and institutions on the one hand, and the 'idea' or 'moral centre' on the other. Germany, in Hebbel's view, was in such a phase: philosophers and poets had recognized that the idea too was governed by the dialectic principle. Put simply, current norms and ideals did not have any absolute, timeless validity; in fact, they needed reforming because they hampered the quest for true human fulfilment. *Maria Magdalena* thus echoes many of the concerns of Heinrich Heine, the young Marx, and the philosopher Ludwig Feuerbach.

Hebbel, however, claimed that modern human beings did not want revolutions or new, 'unheard-of' institutions: they wanted existing ones to be built on more solid foundations. Marriage, for instance, which in the play is presented as frustrating and dehumanizing, would not be abolished; instead, relations in marriage between the sexes would be transformed.

Given that German society was in the ferment and fever of a transitional phase, one could not, in Hebbel's view, depict ideal individuals living in an unalienated society. By creating concrete characters and inventing an action rooted in everyday life, one could, however, exploit the specific resources of art to bring home to audiences the limitations, indeed inhumanity, of middle-class life in a north-German provincial town.

In a world where middle-aged artisans are still illiterate, the sermon and the Lutheran Bible continue to be the main shapers of consciousness. Humanitarian ideas make few inroads. The characters are racked by feelings of sinfulness and guilt, by mortal fear of judgement and damnation. The values of mercy and understanding, enshrined in Christ's treatment of the Biblical Mary Magdalen are strikingly absent; in contrast, pharisaical self-righteousness and 'pointing of the finger' abound as traditional rituals are equated with godliness. Fear of God has been replaced by an all-pervasive pathological obsession with reputation and respectability.

The cult of work and thrift goes hand in hand with condemnation of all amusement and play. Indeed the general stress on the vanity of mortal, earthly life precludes and perverts any natural delight in physical beauty, love, and sex. Furthermore this ethos perpetuates the old hierarchical society of God-given estates, and by preaching contentment with existing life-styles hinders the growth of a more dynamic economy which could afford new possibilities of human self-realization. Certain professions are still deemed dishonourable and their members treated as pariahs. Criminals and bankrupts, too, are for ever beyond the pale of respectability.

The preoccupation with respectability has other dire consequences. Obeying the expectation that middle-class males secure a respectable position before seeking a suitable spouse, Friedrich leaves to study law at university oblivious to

Klara's needs and her situation. His emotional immaturity and self-centred insensitivity are strikingly conveyed. He cannot simply love Klara and forgive her. Only if Leonhard can be murdered in a duel is silence guaranteed. Although mortally wounded in the duel, Friedrich does at the end at least achieve some insight, whereas Meister Anton is totally confused by a world which defies all his norms and expectations. Leonhard, for his part, progressed by various machiavellian ploys. Yet, despite this, he has been welcomed by Meister Anton as his future son-in-law once becoming town treasurer. While craving returned affection and shared sexual pleasure, he views marriage as a matter of dowries, social advantage, and status. Women too are subject to traditional notions of what constitutes a suitable match. In all this, mutual love and passion count for little. In fact, marriage is shown to violate a woman's natural feelings; sex is perverted.

Instead of being the framework which nurtures and supports its individual members, the family emerges as a hell. Relations between husband and wife, between parents and children, and between the children themselves are totally frustrating or destructive. In this authoritarian, puritanical family individuals vainly crave affection and understanding. Jealousy, resentment, and hatred are rampant. There is no frank communication, only veiled accusations, innuendoes, and circumlocutions. Characters talk past each other and are driven into silence or anguished soliloquies. In his preface Hebbel speaks of characters lacking any sense of dialectic, i.e. unable to relativize or change their traditional standards. Only when consciousness and conditions change can natural, spontaneous human aspiration be fulfilled.

Because all the characters are products of this society, there can be no division into heroes or heroines and villains. In all of them valid human needs and aspirations vainly struggle to assert themselves in the face of social pressures and ingrained values invested with divine authority. One cannot speak here of individual guilt, of incorruptible reason or conscience, of moral autonomy or spiritual freedom. Suffering does not ennoble or point the way to a truer understanding of man and the world. There is no supernatural redeemer or Christian providence. If human beings are to be rescued from this hell, they must redeem each other by creating a humane society.

—David Jackson

HEINE, Heinrich. Born Harry Heine in Düsseldorf, Germany, probably 13 December 1797; baptized as protestant, Christian Johann Heinrich Heine, 1825. Educated in a dame's school for 2 years; Hebrew school; Catholic schools, 1804–14; business school, 1814–15; apprenticed to a banking house and to a grocery dealer, Frankfurt, 1815; worked in his uncle Salomon's bank, Hamburg, 1816, and was set up in a cloth business, 1818–19; studied law at universities of Bonn, 1819–20, Göttingen, 1820–21, Berlin, 1821–24, Göttingen, 1824–25, doctor of law 1825. Married Crescence Eugénie Mirat in 1841. Writer in Lüneberg and Hamburg, 1825–27; co-editor, *Neue Allgemeine Politische Annalen*, Munich, 1827–28; Italy, 1828; Hamburg and Berlin, 1829–31; in Paris from 1831: correspondent for Augsburg *Allgemeine Zeitung*; ill after 1845, and bed-ridden after 1848. *Died 17 February 1856.*

PUBLICATIONS

Collections

Sämtliche Werke, edited by Ernst Elster. 7 vols., 1887–90.
Works, translated by Charles Geoffrey Leland and others. 16 vols., 1905.
Sämtliche Schriften, edited by Klaus Briegleb and others. 7 vols., 1968–76.
Säkularausgabe: Werke, Briefwechsel, Lebenszeugnisse. 1970–.
Historisch-kritische Gesamtausgabe der Werke, edited by Manfred Windfuhr. 1973–.
Selected Works, translated by Helen M. Mustard and Max Knight. 1973.
Complete Poems, edited and translated by Hal Draper. 1982.
Selected Prose, edited and translated by Ritchie Robertson. 1993.

Verse

Gedichte. 1822.
Tragödien nebst einem lyrischen Intermezzo (includes the plays *Almansor* and *William Ratcliff*). 1823.
Buch der Lieder. 1827; revised edition, 1844; as *Book of Songs*, translated by J.E. Wallis, 1856; also translated by Charles Godfrey Leland, 1864; Stratheir, 1882; Theodore Martin and E.A. Bowring, 1884; John Todhunter, 1907; R. Levy, 1909; Robert R. Garran, 1924.
Neue Gedichte. 1844; revised edition, 1851; as *New Poems*, 1910.
Deutschland: Ein Wintermärchen. 1844; as *Germany: A Winter's Tale*, translated by H. Salinger, 1944; as *Deutschland: A Winter's Tale*, translated by T.J. Reed, 1986; as *Deutschland, Deutschland: An Unsentimental Journey*, translated by Reed, 1987.
Atta Troll: Ein Sommernachtstraum. 1847; as *Atta Troll: A Midsummer Night's Dream*, translated by Thomas Selby Egan, in *Atta Troll and Other Poems*, 1876; also translated by Herman Scheffauer, 1913.
Romanzero. 1851; translated as *Romancero*, 1905.
Paradox and Poet: The Poems, translated by Louis Untermeyer. 1937.
The Lazarus Poems (bilingual edition), translated by Alistair Elliott. 1979.
Jewish Stories and Hebrew Melodies, translated by Charles Godfrey Leland, Frederic Ewen, and Hal Draper. 1987.

Other

Reisebilder (includes *Die Harzreise*; *Die Heimkehr*; *Die Nordsee*; *Ideen: Das Buch Le Grand*; *Reise von München nach Genua*; *Die Bäden von Lucca*; *Die Stadt Lucca, Englische Fragmente*). 4 vols., 1826–31; as *Pictures of Travel*, translated by Charles Godfrey Leland, 1855; also translated by Russell Davis Gilmann, 1907; as *Travel Pictures*, translated by F. Storr, 1887; as *The Italian Travel Sketches*, translated by Elizabeth A. Sharp, 1892.
Französische Zustände. 1833; as *French Affairs*, 1889.
Zur Geschichte der neueren schönen Literatur in Deutschland. 1833; as *Die Romantische Schule*, 1836; as *The Romantic School*, translated by S.L. Fleishman, 1882.
Der Salon. 4 vols., 1834–40.
Shakespeares Mädchen und Frauen. 1839; as *Heine on Shakespeare*, translated by Ida Benecke, 1895.
Ludwig Börne: Eine Denkschrift. 1840; as *Ludwig Börne: Portrait of a Revolutionist*, translated by T.S. Egan, 1881.

Der Doktor Faust (ballet scenario). 1851; as *Doctor Faust: A Dance Poem*, translated by Basil Ashmore, 1952.
Vermischte Schriften (includes *Geständnisse, Lutezia*). 3 vols., 1854.
Memoiren und neugesammelte Gedichte, Prosa, und Briefe, edited by Eduard Engel. 1884; as *Memoirs*, translated by T.W. Evans, 1884; also translated by G. Cannon, 1910.
Works of Prose, edited by Hermann Kesten, translated by E.B. Ashton. 1943.
Poetry and Prose, edited by Frederic Ewen, translated by Ewen, Louis Untermeyer, and others. 1948.
Briefe, edited by Friedrich Hirth. 6 vols., 1950–51.
The Sword and the Flame (selected prose), edited by Alfred Werner. 1960.
Begegnungen mit Heine: Berichte der Zeitgenossen, edited by Michael Werner. 2 vols., 1973.
Poetry and Prose, edited by Jost Hermand and Robert C. Holub. 1982.
The Romantic School and Other Essays, edited by Jost Hermand and Robert C. Holub. 1985.
Heinrich Heine und die Musik: publizistische Arbeiten und poetische Reflexionen (selections), edited by Gerhard Müller. 1987.

*

Bibliography: *Heine in England and America: A Bibliographical Check-List* by Armin Arnold, 1959; *Heine-Bibliographie* by Gottfried Wilhelm and Eberhard Galley, 2 vols., 1960; supplement by Siegfried Seifert, 1968, and by Siegfried Seifert and Albina A. Volgina, 1986; *Heinrich Heine: A Selected Critical Bibliography of the Secondary Literature, 1956–1980* by Jeffrey L. Sammons, 1982; *Heine in der Musik: Bibliographie der Heine-Vertonungen* by Günter Metzner, 1989–.

Critical Studies: *Heinrich Heine: Paradox and the Poet, the Life* by Louis Untermeyer, 1937; *Judaic Lore in Heine* by Israel Tabak, 1948; *Heinrich Heine: An Interpretation* by Barker Fairley, 1954; *The English Legend of Heinrich Heine* by Sol Liptzin, 1954; *Heinrich Heine: A Biography* by Elizabeth M. Butler, 1956; *Heine: Two Studies of His Thought and Feeling*, 1956, and *The Early Love Poetry of Heinrich Heine: An Enquiry into Poetic Inspiration*, 1962, both by William Rose; *Heinrich Heine: The Artist in Revolt* by Max Brod, 1957; *Heine: Buch der Lieder*, 1960, *Heine, The Tragic Satirist: A Study of the Later Poetry 1827–1856*, 1962, *Heine's Shakespeare: A Study in Contexts*, 1970, *Heine's Jewish Comedy: A Study of His Portraits of Jews and Judaism*, 1983, *Coal-Smoke and Englishmen: A Study of Verbal Caricature in the Writings of Heinrich Heine*, 1984, and *Frankenstein's Island: England and the English in the Writings of Heinrich Heine*, 1986, all by S.S. Prawer; *Heine* by Laura Hofrichter, 1963; *The Exile of Gods: Interpretation of a Theme, a Theory and a Technique in the Work of Heinrich Heine* by A.I. Sandor, 1967; *Heinrich Heine, The Elusive Poet*, 1969, and *Heinrich Heine: A Modern Biography*, 1979, both by Jeffrey L. Sammons; *Heine: Poetry and Politics* by Nigel Reeves, 1974; *Heinrich Heine's Reisebilder: The Tendency of the Text and the Identity of the Age* by Edward A. Zlotkowski, 1980; *Heine's Reception of German Grecophilia* by Robert C. Holub, 1981; *Heinrich Heine* by Hanna Spencer, 1982; *Valiant Heart: A Biography of Heinrich Heine* by Philip Kossoff, 1983; *Exiles and Ironists: Essays on the Kinship of Heine and Laforgue* by Ursula Franklin, 1988; *Heine* by Ritchie Robertson, 1988; *Heine: Poetry in Context:*

A Study of Buch der Lieder by Michael Perraudin, 1989; *Paintings on the Move: Heinrich Heine and the Visual Arts* edited by Susanne Zantop, 1989; *Heinrich Heine and the Occident: Multiple Identities, Multiple Receptions* edited by Peter Uwe Hohendahl and Sander L. Gilman, 1992; *The Jewish Reception of Heinrich Heine* edited by Mark H. Gelber, 1992.

* * *

Heinrich Heine is the most widely read or, perhaps one should say, *heard*, poet to have written in the German language. His poetry has been carried around the world, in his own phrase, 'on wings of song', in more than eight thousand musical settings. It can be difficult to apprehend the poetry accurately through all that music, which in some cases re-romanticizes and resentimentalizes it. For Heine had an exceptionally tense relationship to poetry, including his own. Through much of his career he was a more reactive than strikingly original poet. While he had a great lyrical gift, genuinely fuelled by an experience of unrequited love that became virtually archetypal for him, he doubted the relevance of poetry and its traditional materials in his politically and socially stressed post-Romantic environment. Thus, from within, he undermined the tradition with his bitterly accusatory tone directed toward the beloved, with abrasive irony and jarring stylistic dissonances, with ingenious dexterity and a visible manipulation of poetic devices that exposes them as fictions, ultimately with studied salaciousness and fiercely aggressive political verse. Not until *Romanzero* in 1851 did he find a genuinely original, mid-19th-century style, a bleak, ironically serious verse composed in the suffering of his 'mattress-grave'. With all his misgivings, however, he regarded the poetic vocation as one of high dignity and by mid-life he had doubtless achieved his ambition to succeed Goethe as the major living poet in the German language.

With his prose *Reisebilder* (*Pictures of Travel*) beginning in the mid-1820s he developed greater originality of form. With sparkling wit, they weld together essay and fiction, imaginative autobiographical reminiscence and acute contemporary observation, high and low comedy and sardonic social criticism. Though he pretends to easy-going free association, as though setting down the first thing that came into his head, they are, like all of his writing, meticulously formulated and ordered. The comedy and wit, as always with Heine, have a seriously committed purpose. For he lived in gloomily repressive times and was determined to take up arms against the reactionary political order of the neo-feudal Metternichian system, under whose heavy-handed censorship he suffered unremittingly. He came to subsume political and cultural phenomena under a dichotomy of 'spiritualism' versus 'sensualism' or, in his later vocabulary, 'Nazarenism' versus 'Hellenism'. What he perceived in the repressive order was a denial of gratification and plenitude, a reservation of aristocratic luxuries and erotic liberty to the privileged few, while the mass of people were kept in superstitious ignorance, compensated for their deprivation by promises of mythical joys in the other world. Since he regarded religion and especially Christianity as part of this conspiracy, he attacked religious institutions and Christian doctrine with an explicitness unparalleled in his generation.

Heine's at first voluntary, then involuntary exile in France beginning in 1831 was initially motivated by his interest in the Saint-Simonian movement, which for a time he thought congruent with his own vision of emancipation and sensualism. He reported on France in two series of newspaper articles in 1830–32 and 1840–43, published in book form as *Französische Zustände* (*French Affairs*), 1833 and *Lutezia*, 1854. He covers not only political and public events but also music, theatre, art, and the common life of the people. It was a report on the painting exhibition of 1831 that gave the title to a four-volume collection of essays, fiction, and poetry, *Der Salon*. At the same time he endeavoured to explain Germany to France in terms of a secret revolutionary doctrine of sensualism, in a book directed against Madame de Staël and bearing her title *De l'Allemagne*; it appeared in two parts in German, as *Zur Geschichte der Religion und Philosophie in Deutschland* [On the History of Religion and Philosophy in Germany] in *Salon II*, 1834, and *Die Romantische Schule* (*The Romantic School*), 1836. Heine's views, despite all their vigour and forthrightness, were complex and sometimes gave an impression of capriciousness because of his contradictory commitments. He insisted that he was a democrat, but the commanding figure of his heroic imagination was the conqueror Napoleon and he sometimes claimed to be a monarchist; he championed the proletariat against the dominant order and yet feared a barbarian destruction of cultural and civilized values; and he turned against his liberal and radical contemporaries because he suspected them of nationalism, which he always strongly opposed, and of puritanical spiritualism. Thus in 1840 he greatly damaged his reputation with an ill-considered book directed against the deceased spokesman of the German dissidents, Ludwig Börne, and then exhibited the opposing vectors of his outlook in two contrasting mock-epic poems, *Atta Troll: Ein Sommernachtstraum* (*Atta Troll: A Midsummer Night's Dream*), which spoofs the radical poets of his time, and *Deutschland: Ein Wintermärchen* (*Germany: A Winter's Tale*), a tough satire on German conditions. The latter, considered the greatest of German political poems, was written during his months of friendship with the young Karl Marx and is the chief product of his most radical phase. With the collapse of his health into painful paralysis, he became more thoughtful and discouraged, and also underwent a religious reversal, though not abandoning his habits of irony, independence, and impudence. He occupied himself with his memoirs, a segment of which appeared as *Geständnisse* (*Confessions*) in 1854; the remainder was suppressed by his relatives, with whom he had had a violent public feud over his uncle's inheritance, and was not published until 28 years after his death.

Few writers of literature have had such an embattled reputation as Heine; he has been scorned by nationalists, conservatives, and anti-semites, and for a long time his reputation was stronger outside Germany. During the current era of his rehabilitation it is sometimes forgotten how much he was himself responsible for the hostility of his public and posterity; he scoffed at their cherished values and his career was often marked by ethical carelessness. But he lucidly drew into himself and exposed with ultimate sincerity the critical dilemmas of his time, and he stands as not only one of the wittiest but also one of the most penetrating writers in European letters.

—Jeffrey L. Sammons

THE HOMECOMING, 20 (Still ist die Nacht, es ruhen die Gassen)
Poem by Heinrich Heine, 1824.

The night is calm; the streets quiet down;
Here lives a lass who was dear to me.
Long years ago she left the town,
But here is her house, as it used to be.
And here is a creature who stares into space
And wrings his hands in a storm of pain.
I shudder when I see his face:
It is my own self the moon shows plain.
You double! You comrade ghostly white!
Why have you come to ape the woe
That tortured me, night after night,
Under these windows—long ago?

(translated by Aaron Kramer)

Heine's *Book of Songs* (*Buch der Lieder*), first published in 1827, is an edited collection of poems, almost all of which had been published previously over the space of a decade. In most cases we do not know the dates of origin very exactly. 'The Homecoming' 20 perhaps best known, like many of Heine's poems, in a musical setting, in this case Franz Schubert's *Schwanengesang* (also 1827), may have been written in July 1823 or somewhat later that year. It was first published in a periodical in March 1824, as number 6 of 'Thirty-Three Poems by H. Heine' (his tendency to publish poems in cycles of 11 is one sign of the formal control exerted on a poetry that has an appearance of emotional immediacy). In the first volume of *Pictures of Travel*, 1826, it took its final place as number 20 of the 88 poems of 'The Homecoming'. Unlike other poems of Heine, it underwent little change from its earliest version to the definitive *Book of Songs* edition of 1844.

Heine's tendency to organize poems in clusters and cycles always makes it somewhat problematic to isolate them for interpretation. They echo and modify one another, creating a continuously varying perspective on what appears to be his one subject, unrequited love. There are images elsewhere of the speaker of the poem standing outside the house in which his beloved once lived; in one of these, 'Lyrical Intermezzo', 38, he wanders through the streets accompanied by his shadow. In addition there are in the *Book of Songs* a great many echoes of other contemporaneous late-Romantic poets, down to specific images and rhymes. In the case of 'The Homecoming', 20 one can point to poems by Wilhelm Müller, Ludwig Uhland, Joseph von Eichendorff, and others, including a fabricated 'folk-song' of Achim von Arnim. It is this synthetic quality of Heine's verse that has led some critics to regard his manner as derivative manipulation of ready-made materials. But he brings to these resources a new complexity and intensity, combining them into a sceptical metapoetry reflecting upon the poetic possibilities of his time.

An example is the image of the 'double', the *doppeltgänger* in Heine's spelling, which he may have taken over from the fantasy writing of E.T.A. Hoffman. But Heine does not employ fantastic or special images to Gothic effect, except in some of his very early, immature verse; they serve as metaphors of psychological and poetological anxieties. The double is the image of a split self brooding irritably on an emotional condition that should have been outgrown but continues to hobble and even shame the present self.

There are three temporally layered fictional personae in the poem. The most primitive is the self of the past who has loved and lost. Then there is the double, contorted in melodramatic emotion, 'aping' the sufferings of the past to no rational purpose. The speaker of the poem recognizes the identity of the figures with himself and asks why this anachronistic grieving continues. Heine often distances himself from the impassioned content of his own poetry, deconstructing, so to speak, its emotionally laden and, to some extent, borrowed diction. He is notorious for a jarring break of mood within the poem itself, sometimes achieved by a lurch to a more colloquial or even vulgar stylistic level. The use of the word 'ape' in this poem is a mild example of that. He will also hold up his own feelings to amused or satirical contemplation. In several places he addresses himself as 'dear friend', as one might speak to a foolishly behaving companion. The staring, hand-wringing double is hardly an image of tragic or even dignified stature. These devices, though not without precedent, constitute in their ingenuity and variety of nuance the genuine originality and unmistakable tone of Heine's early poetry.

This tone in its quite aggressive articulation has been misunderstood in two ways. In the past it was sometimes regarded merely as blatantly malicious cynicism, malevolent subversion of genuine, sincere feeling and true poesy. In more recent times there has been a tendency to give a similar reading a more positive evaluation. In this view Heine simply surpasses the poetry of Romantic delusion and emotional self-indulgence by parodying and exposing it in the interest of progress and reason. Both views gravely underestimate the level of stress in the *Book of Songs* and the difficulties of resolving it. 'The Homecoming', 20 is a key poem in its earnest depiction of the poet's dilemmas. It is an error to suppose that Heine was always a laughing poet or that his wit is univocally liberating. The past self is obsolete and ridiculous but cannot be fully exorcized. One might notice how quickly the 'lass' is made to disappear from the poem; the poet is forever banishing her but she continually reappears, ever flaunting the impregnable indifference that calls his very ego ideal into question. His only resource for handling his situation is poetry. But poetry, in Heine's understanding of it, is implicated with the feelings that are causing all the disruption and are doubtful in their integrity. Thus the problem of the self is a problem of poetry, to which the only available solution is poetry. This incomparably astute perception of the dilemma of poetry at the decline of Romanticism is what gives the *Book of Songs* its historical importance, and the exploitation of it by poetic means its aesthetic endurance.

—Jeffrey L. Sammons

HEINESEN, William. Born in Tórshavn, Faroe Islands (Danish Territory), 15 January 1900. Educated at Copenhagen School of Commerce, 1916–19. Married Elisa Johansen in 1932; three sons. Journalist in Ringsted and Copenhagen, 1919–32, then settled in Tórshavn. Also musician and artist: chair, Faroese Museum of Fine Art, 1969. Recipient: Nathansen prize, 1956; Holberg medal, 1960; Danish-Faroese Cultural Fund prize, 1962; Nordic Council prize, 1965; Scandinavian literary prize, 1965; Aarestrup medal, 1968. Member, Danish Academy, 1961. *Died 12 March 1991.*

PUBLICATIONS

Fiction

Stjernerne vaagner [The Stars Awaken]. 1930.
Blæsende gry [Windswept Dawn]. 1934; revised edition, 1962.
Noatun. 1938; as *Niels Peter*, translated by Jan Noble, 1939.
Den sorte gryde. 1949; as *The Black Cauldron*, translated by W. Glyn Jones, 1992.
De fortabte spillemænd. 1950; as *The Lost Musicians*, translated by Erik J. Friis, 1971.
Moder syvstjerne. 1952; as *The Kingdom of the Earth*, translated by Hedin Brønner, 1974.
Det fortryllede lys [The Enchanted Light]. 1957.
Gamaliels besættelse [Gamaliel's Bewitchment]. 1960.
Det gode Håb. 1964; as *The Good Hope*, translated by John F. West, 1981.
Kur mod onde ånder [Cure Against Evil Spirits]. 1967.
Don Juan fra Tranhuset [Don Juan from the Blubber Works]. 1970.
Fortællinger fra Thorshavn [Stories from Tórshavn], edited by Erik Vagn Jensen. 1973.
Tårnet ved verdens ende. 1976; as *The Tower at the Edge of the World*, translated by Maja Jackson, 1981; also translated by Anne Born, 1982.
Her skal danses: Seks fortællinger [Let the Dance Go On: Six Stories]. 1980.
The Winged Darkness and Other Stories, translated by Hedin Brønner. 1983.
Laterna magica, nye erindringsnoveller. 1985; as *Laterna Magica*, translated by Tiina Nunnally, 1987.
Godaften måne, godaften min ven [Good Evening Moon, Good Evening My Friend]. 1989.

Verse

Arktiske elegier [Arctic Elegies]. 1921.
Høbjergning ved havet [Haymaking by the Sea]. 1924.
Sange mod vaardybet [Songs at the Spring Deep]. 1927.
Den dunkle sol [The Dark Sun]. 1936.
Digte i udvalg [Selected Poems], edited by Regin Dahl and Ole Wivel. 1955.
Hymne og harmsang [Hymn and Song of Indignation]. 1961.
Panorama med regnbue [Panorama with Rainbow]. 1972.
Arctis: Selected Poems, 1921–1972, translated by Anne Born. 1980.
Vinter-drøm: Digte i udvalg 1920–30 [Winter Dream: Selected Poems 1920–30]. 1983.
Samlede digte [Collected Poems]. 1985.

Play

Ranafelli, in *Varthin*. 1929.

Other

Tann deiliga Havn [Fair Tórshavn], with John Davidsen. 1953.
Det dyrebare liv [Precious Life] (biography of J.F. Jacobsen). 1958.
Færøerne, de magiske øer/Førayar, Gandaoyggjarnar/The Faroe Islands, The Magic Islands, photographs by Gérard Franceschi. 1971.

Editor, *Nýføroyskur skaldskapur*. 1930.

Editor, with H.A. Djurhuus, *Livet på Færøerne i billeder og tekst*. 1950.

*

Bibliography: *William Heinesen—en bibliografi* by Mia Thorkenholdt and Lars Øhlenschläger, 1984.

Critical Studies: 'Noatun and the Collective Novel', in *Scandinavian Studies*, 42(3), 1969, 'William Heinesen and the Myth of Conflict', in *Scandinavica*, 9, 1970, *William Heinesen*, 1974, '*Tårnet ved verdens ende*: A Restatement and an Extension', in *Scandinavian Studies*, 50(1), 1978, 'Towards Totality: The Poetry of William Heinesen', in *World Literature Today*, 62(1), 1988, and 'Cultural Perspectives in the Late Work of William Heinesen', in *Grenzerfahrung—Grenzüberschreitung: Studien zu den Literaturen Skandinaviens und Deutschlands*, edited by Leonie Marx and Herbert Knust, 1989, all by W. Glyn Jones; *Three Faroese Novelists: An Appreciation of Jorgen-Frantz Jacobsen, William Heinesen and Hein Brú*, 1973, and 'William Heinesen: Faroese Voice—Danish Pen', in *American-Scandinavian Review*, 61(2), 1973, both by Hedin Brønner.

* * *

William Heinesen was one of the outstanding poets and novelists of Scandinavia in the 20th century, distinguished for the breadth of his imagination and for his linguistic and stylistic brilliance. After moving from his native Tórshavn to Copenhagen, he published exclusively lyric poetry in the 1920s, echoing the neo-Romantic and Symbolist poetry of the turn of the century, but clearly influenced by Johannes V. Jensen, a writer who remained a major source of inspiration to him throughout his life. Originally elegiac and expressive of an awareness of the passage of time and the constant presence of death, the poems gradually develop a more optimistic and dynamic approach, though still bearing the traces of religious speculation caused by the death of the poet's brother in 1927. The 1930s saw a change, and Heinesen progressed to poems expressing political awareness, often painting satirical portraits of a society dominated by materialism and money. The later poems are often strikingly modernist in idiom, a mixture of the satirical and the more reflective youthful poetry.

Heinesen is, however, chiefly famed for his prose. His novel *Blæsende gry* [Windswept Dawn] was influenced by the Danish collective novel, but showed a greater interest in the individual personality than was usual in this genre. It was formless but powerful, and was completely recast for a second edition in 1962, in which the emphasis is moved from religious considerations to social questions. *Noatun* (*Niels Peter*) continued the collective genre, but towards the end of the 1940s Heinesen started on his major works, *Den sorte gryde* (*The Black Cauldron*), *De fortabte spillemænd* (*The Lost Musicians*), *Moder syvstjerne* (*The Kingdom of the Earth*), and *Det gode Håb* (*The Good Hope*). Here he moves from a more or less sober account into the realm of fantasy and imagination, reflecting on man's place in the universe, the confrontation of life and death forces, the role of woman as the vehicle of life, the mystery of the human psyche. *The Good Hope*, Heinesen's only historical novel, is an allegory of a fascist dictatorship as well as a penetrating study of human personality; full of conscious anachronisms and written in a language that smacks of the 17th century without any attempt to be authentic, it is considered by many to be Heinesen's masterpiece.

After this novel, which took 40 years to complete, Heinesen concentrated on the short story, in which he further explored the themes of his earlier years, though with increasing concentration on the mystery of human nature. His portraits of children are warm and sensitive, often humorous; in particular, he is fond of portraying puberty, revealing the incipient erotic instincts in children unaware of what is happening to them. In the volume of short stories *Her skal danses* [Let the Dance Go On], he adds to these themes a moving story centred on the cultic significance of the Faroese chain dance, a profound homage to life, with violent death as its background.

It is a matter of regret to many Faroese that Heinesen chose to write in Danish, thereby becoming as much identified with Danish literature as with Faroese. His works are nevertheless intensely Faroese, and uniquely he presents the Faroe Islands as a microcosm in such a way that they are immediately intelligible to the outsider with no previous knowledge of them whatever.

—W. Glyn Jones

HERNÁNDEZ, José. Born in Pueyrredón (now part of San Martín), Argentina, 10 November 1834. Educated to elementary level at the school of Don Pedro Sánchez, Barracas, 1841–45. Married Carolina González del Solar in 1863; four daughters and one son. Worked with his father, in Camarones and Laguna de los Padres, 1846–52; supported the Federalists against the Unitarians (joined the Federal Reform Party, 1855), and fought at the battles of Rincón de San Gregorio (1853) and El Tala (1854), then travelled to Paraña, capital of the Confederation of Argentina, to escape persecution in Buenos Aires; store assistant and judicial scribe, Paraná, 1856–58; stenographer for the Confederation Senate, 1859; appointed Second Official to the Confederation's government, 1859; fought at the battle of Cepeda, 1859; private secretary to President Juan Esteban Pedernera, 1860; received promotion to Captain, and fought at the battle of Pavón, 1861; secretary, Convention of Nogoyá, 1864; state attorney and secretary of the legislature, Corrientes, 1867–68; editor, *El Eco de Corrientes*, 1867–68; joined the resistance movement of Evaristo López Jordán, 1868: ministerial secretary under López, La Paz, 1868; co-founder, Club de los Libres, 1869; fought under Ricardo López Jordán against President Sarmiento at the battle of Ñaembé, 1871; lived in Buenos Aires, 1872–73; followed Jordán into exile into Montevideo, Uruguay (then part of Brazil), 1873–75; settled in Belgrano, following amnesty from the new President Avellaneda, 1875; deputy for the provincial legislature, 1879–80; vice-president, Chamber of Deputies, 1880; provincial senator, 1881–86; co-founder, national insurance company 'La Previsora', 1884; board-member, Banco Hipotecario, from 1884. Also political journalist, including: contributor, *La Reforma Pacífica*, from 1856, and *El Argentino*, from 1863; editor, *El Nacional Argentino*, 1860, and *El Argentino*, 1863; founding editor, *Río de la Plata*, 1869–70, and *La Patria*, Montevideo, 1873–75. *Died 21 October 1886.*

PUBLICATIONS

Verse

El gaucho Martín Fierro; *La vuelta de Martín Fierro*. 2 vols., 1872–79; edited by Eleuterio F. Tiscornia, 1925 (corrected by Santiago M. Lugones, 1926), Ramón Estrella Gutiérrez, 1953, José Edmundo Clemente, 1953, Augusto Raúl Cortázar, 1961, Jorge Becco, 1962, Walter Rela, 1963, Pilo Mayo, 1970, Luis Sáinz de Medrono, 1979, and Gisela Frechou and Mónica García, 1984; as *The Gaucho Martín Fierro*, translated and adapted by Walter Owen, 1935; also translated by Catherine E. Ward (bilingual edition), annotated by Frank G. Carrino and Alberto J. Carlos, 1967; as *Martín Fierro: The Argentine Gaucho Epic*, translated by Henry Alfred Holmes, 1948.
Los otros poemas. 1968.

Other

Rasgos biográficos del general Ángel V. Peñazola. 1863.
Vida del Chacho: rasgos biográficos del general Angel Vicente Peñaloza. 1863 (in magazine); 1947 (as book).
Instrucción del estanciero (cattle rancher's guide). 1882.
Las Malvinas (writings about Falkland Islands). 1982.

*

Bibliography: *Itinerario bibliográfico y hemerográfico del Martín Fierro* by José Carlos Maubé, 1943; *José Hernández: Martín Fierro y su crítica* by Augusto Raúl Cortázar, 1960.

Critical Studies: *Martín Fierro: An Epic of the Argentine* by Henry Alfred Holmes, 1923; *La lengua de Martín Fierro* by Eluterio Tiscornia, 1930; *El poeta creador: Cómo hizo Hernández La vuelta de Martín Fierro* by Carlos Alberto Leumann, 1945; *Los motivos del Martín Fierro en la vida de José Hernández* by Pedro de Paoli, 1947; *El mito gaucho: Martín Fierro y el hombre argentino* by Carlos Astrada, 1948; *Muerte y transfigurarción de Martín Fierro* by Ezequiel Martínez Estrada, 1948, revised edition, 2 vols., 1958; *Martín Fierro* by Enrique Bianchi, 1952; *Prosas del Martín Fierro* by Antonio Pagés Larraya, 1952; *El Martín Fierro* by Jorge Luis Borges and Margarita Guerrero, 1953; *José Hernández: Periodista, político y poeta*, 1959, and *La vuelta de José Hernández*, 1973, both by Fermín Chávez; *La elaboración literaria del Martín Fierro*, 1960, and *Con el Martín Fierro*, 1968, both by Ángel Héctor Azeves; *Martín Fierro y La justicia social* by Eduardo B. Astesano, 1963; *El nombre, el pago y la frontera de Martín Fierro* by R. Darío Capdevila, 1967; *Arte y sentido del Martín Fierro* by John B. Hughes, 1970; *Valoración de Martín Fierro* by Héctor Adolfo Cordero, 1971; *José Hernández* by Noé Jitrik, 1971; *Genio y figura de José Hernández* by Roque Raúl Aragón, 1972; *Ida y vuelta de José Hernández* by Andrés Carretero, 1972; *Contenido histórico-social del Martín Fierro* by Néstor A. Fayo, 1972; *José Hernández* by Hialmar E. Gammalsson, 1972; *Tiempo y vida de José Hernández* by Horacio Zorraquín Becú, 1972; *Hernández: Poesía y política* by Rodolfo Borello, 1973; *De las aguas profundas en el Martín Fierro* by Bernardo Cana-Feijóo, 1973; *La creación del Martín Fierro* by Emilio Carilla, 1973; *Hernandismo y martinfierrismo* by Elías Giménez Vega and Julio González, 1975; *Prehistoria del Martín Fierro* by Olga Fernández Latour de Botas, 1977; *José Hernández y sus mundos* by Tulio Halperín Donghi, 1985; *José Hernández: Sus ideas políticas* by Enrique de Gandía, 1985; *Martín Fierro: Cien años de crítica* edited by José Isaacson, 1986.

* * *

José Hernández was the last of a series of 19th-century Argentinian writers of gauchesque poetry: they were educated men who imitated in their works the idiom and naive style of the songs of the pampas cowboys. (The best-known of the others are Bartolomé Hidalgo, Hilario de Ascasubi and Estanislao del Campo.) This genre tended to treat the gaucho as a figure of fun; Hernández, however, exalted the gaucho's virtues of courage, endurance, and honour, while also denouncing the abuses to which contemporary society subjected such men.

In travel literature, and in anthropological and sociological writing, the gauchos had frequently been described as ill-educated, workshy, violent, nomadic, and antisocial, and in the quarrel between Unitarians (Centralists) and Federalists which divided Argentinians for most of the 19th century, they were depicted by Unitarian writers as an obstacle to democracy and progress because of their support for the *caudillos*, men who had led their own armies in the Independence wars and became *de facto* political leaders in the power-vacuum left by the departure of the Spanish. In Domingo Sarmiento's *Life in the Argentine Republic in the Days of the Tyrants* not merely the cowboy, but cattle-ranching itself, is seen as barbaric.

Hernández's book, *Vida del Chacho* [The Life of El Chacho] is a polemical and uplifting portrait of the Federalist General Peñaloza, who had been killed by the Unitarians. Much of Hernández's writing took the form of political journalism. In 1869 he founded a newspaper, in which he published fierce attacks on several aspects of Sarmiento's government's policy, particularly the use of vagrancy laws to conscript gauchos forcibly into service in the wars against the native Indians.

Hernández's best-known work is his long narrative poem published in two parts, *El gaucho Martín Fierro*, 1872, entitled in some later editions *La ida de Martín Fierro* (*Martín Fierro's Departure*) and *La vuelta de Martín Fierro* (*The Return of Martín Fierro*), 1879. There are many humorous moments, but the prevailing tone of the first part of the poem is one of bitter moral indignation, and the contemporary audience would have recognized it immediately as a polemical work directed against the government of the day, although there are aspects of the poem that contradict or modify this political intention: for example, Martín Fierro often uses concepts such as 'fate' or 'luck' in commenting on his predicament.

In contrast to the humanitarian sentiments experienced in relation to the gaucho, the 20th-century reader may be struck by the expression of racist feelings in the poem. Martín Fierro, at one point, addresses racial insults to a black man. Fierro admits that he is drunk and feels like picking a fight, but in the course of the duel the black man offends against the gaucho fighting code by being the first to take out a knife, thereby restoring Martín Fierro's position as the man of honour. Italian and English immigrants are also portrayed unfavourably in the poem: Hernández thus expresses his opposition to Sarmiento's policy of encouraging European immigration as a means of reducing Argentina's dependence on the cattle industry and the cowboys. The portrayal of the native pampas Indians is more complex: Hernández's main aim, in the first part of the poem, is to criticize the conduct of the Indian wars. To this end, he depicts the Indians as fierce warriors and excellent horsemen, that is, as formidable opponents who should have been countered with well-fed and well-equipped troops. He has no particular interest in depicting the Indians negatively in any other respect, and in fact Fierro and his friend Cruz state confidently, at the end of this part of the poem, that the life they propose with the Indians will be preferable to life under Sarmiento.

The first part of the poem proved immensely popular with both the educated audience and the gauchos it depicted. Two years after its publication, political circumstances changed in Argentina. President Avellaneda ushered in an era of national reconciliation and Hernández was elected to the Senate. *The Return of Martín Fierro* strikes a mellower note than the first part of the poem. Many critics, such as Noé Jitrik, consider the second part inferior to the first: it is more consciously literary, seeking to tie up the loose ends of the story, yet the structure is more diffuse, for the sequel narrates not only the subsequent adventures of Fierro and Cruz (until the latter's death), but also those of Fierro's two sons, whom he re-encounters, and that of Cruz's son, Picardía. All are shown to have suffered misfortune, but the powerful moral anger of the first part seems to have been dissipated. The mood of national reconciliation is expressed in the final episode, in which Martín Fierro is confronted by the brother of the black man he had killed in part one. Instead of the expected duel with knives, they are persuaded to settle their differences by means of a *payada* or improvised singing contest. Martín Fierro wins, and the black man leaves, though still threatening that he may one day return and exact vengeance.

The mood of reconciliation does not extend to the native Indians. Hernández seems eager in this second part of the poem to establish the Indians as the ethnic and religious enemy, depicting them as barbarous, cruel, and unfeeling, a vision that is at odds with the majority of the anthropological evidence. Ángel Héctor Azeves suggests in *La elaboración literaria del Martín Fierro* that Hernández drew on information supplied by an uncle who had published a study of the Indians written from a military rather than an anthropological viewpoint.

The poem has been described by Santiago Lugones and others as the national epic of Argentina. While the term is perhaps not appropriate in its strict rhetorical sense, it may be considered apt in that the poem exalts the gauchos, who were instrumental in winning independence from Spain, and who made a vital contribution to the main economic activity of the nation—cattle-raising. Today the poem is familiar to all Argentinians.

—A. McDermott

THE GAUCHO MARTÍN FIERRO (El gaucho Martín Fierro)
Narrative poem by José Hernández, 1872–79.

The Gaucho Martín Fierro (usually known as *Martín Fierro*) first appeared in Buenos Aires in 1872. Written in six-line stanzas of octosyllabic verse it imitated the gaucho custom of the *payador*, or guitar singer (at the end Fierro smashes his guitar in rage), and because of the political circumstances of the day became immensely popular, selling over 72,000 copies in the first seven years. This narrative poem, or novel in verse as Jorge Luis Borges called it, was continued by Hernández with a second part in 1879, with chilling details taken from a pampas Indian camp, but then breaks down into discursive elements. The second part lacks the anger and artistic unity of the first, which ends with the outlaw gauchos Fierro and Cruz abondoning the tamed pampas to live with the savage nomadic Indians. Over the years *Martín Fierro* has become Argentina's national poem, obligatory reading in schools, where passages are known by heart by most Argentinians.

The fact that Hernández wrote this narrative poem with a political purpose means that the historical moment of its writing and his intention are important. Argentina was already opening its doors to immigrants to populate the empty plains. The rich grazing lands called the pampas (a Quechua word) had lead to a way of life completely bound to the cattle and horses that had multiplied since they first arrived with the Spaniards. The nomadic Indians lived on mare's meat and were expert horsemen. As the Europeanized Argentinians pushed the Indians back from the port of Buenos Aires, the men who worked for them also had to depend on the cattle and horses, like the Indians. These men were called gauchos (from an Araucanian word, *guacho*, for orphan). These gauchos prided themselves on their independence from the centralized State and the soft European way of life. They also despised foreigners. Indeed, in *Martín Fierro* a gringo (here meaning an Italian, one of the predominant immigrant groups) appears and is mocked because he cannot ride a horse. By the 1870s cattle were being exported not only as hide and jerked (or dried) beef, but frozen. In 1882 the first meat packing factory was installed, called frigorífico, and land became fenced in as railways were constructed to link the interior with the capital. With this development came a deliberate policy of chasing Indians off this land in what was called General Roca's Desert War. It was, in effect, a pogrom. The point of this historical context is that Hernández wrote his poem at a time when the gaucho's way of life was at a virtual end. Its appeal was partly nostalgic, and partly a reaction to the violent change in national identity that millions of immigrants brought to those who owned and lived off the land. The freedom-loving gaucho would end up as a hired farm hand, or *peón*. It is clear that this poem caught the national mood of shock and hostility to the abrupt changes, and came to be regarded as extolling freedom against state interference, conscription, and corruption.

The intellectual proponent of modernizing Argentina was Domingo Sarmiento (1811–88), who, in exile in Chile, penned his political pamphlet against the tyrant Juan Manuel Rosas, *Civilization and Barbary: Life of Juan Facundo Quiroga*, in 1845. For Sarmiento the gaucho epitomized Argentinian backwardness: 'El gaucho no trabaja; el alimento y el vestido lo encuentra preparado en su casa' ('the gaucho does not work; food and clothes he finds ready-made in his house'). However, for Hernández's rebel gaucho, Fierro, work is a European plague: 'Allí no hay que trabajar/vive uno como señor' ('Out there you don't have to work/and you can live like a king'), he says as he joins the wild Indians.

The plot of this protest poem is simple. Fierro is conscripted and abandons his wife and hut. After killing a black singer, he is on the run from the law, joins up with the man sent out to capture him, called Cruz, and both leave for the wild Indians. Hernández wrote this poem respecting gaucho Spanish, modifying the words to make the poem as oral and colloquial as possible. When Fierro decides to turn into an outlaw he swears: 'y juré en esa ocasión/ser más malo que una fiera' ('and I swore then/to be more evil than a wild animal'), which gives us a clue to his symbolic surname Fierro—*fiera* means 'wild beast', while *hierro* means 'knife', the gaucho's main weapon, called in Spanish a *facón*, and used to slit animals' throats. His crime is not killing a black, but simply

being a gaucho: 'El ser gaucho es un delito' ('Being a gaucho is a crime'). Through Fierro's conscription Hernández attacks corruption: 'Hablaban de hacerse ricos/con campos en las fronteras' ('They spoke of getting rich/with frontier land'); and Fierro adds: 'He visto negocios feos' ('I have seen dirty business deals'). Against this modernizing, capitalist state Fierro chooses freedom, 'juir (huir) de la autoridá' ('to flee authority') in order to live: 'mi gloria es vivir tan libre' ('my glory is to live free').

But *Martín Fierro* is far more than a political tract, and Hernández created vivid characters, knife fights, a close bonding of men, with abundant detail about the pampas way of life. A good example of Hernández's vividness is Fierro's knife fight with the black whom he kills, gaucho-fashion, to become a fugitive. In the second part there is another fight, over a *cautiva* (a white woman taken as prisoner by the Indians), with vivid and unpleasant descriptions of the woman's dead baby: the *cautiva* tells Fierro 'Me amarró luego las manos/con las tripas de mi hijo' ('He tied up my hands/with the guts of my child'), and she helps Fierro defeat the physically superior Indian in a duel.

One last element that stands out in this 'epic' is what Borges called Hernández's poetry, the laconic descriptions of the flat pampas landscape and the wide horizon—'solo vía hacienda y cielo' ('I could see only cattle and sky')—or of the experience of horseback riding on the empty plains: 'Viene uno como dormido/cuando vuelve del disierto' ('You arrive like a man asleep/when you return from the deserted lands').

—Jason Wilson

HERODOTUS. Born c.490–84 BC. Possibly related to the ruling family of Halicarnassus, Asia Minor. Moved to Samos during civil strife, c.460 BC; travelled and lectured in Greece, including Athens, and settled in the Athenian colony of Thurii in south Italy (founded 444–43 BC); also travelled in south Italy, Egypt, the Near East and Babylon, Scythia and the Black Sea, and the north Aegean. *Died probably before 420 BC.*

PUBLICATIONS

Works

[History], edited by Carl Hude. 2 vols., 1927; also edited by P.E. Legrand, 11 vols., 1932–54; as *The History*, translated by George Rawlinson, 4 vols., 1858–60, this translation edited by A.W. Lawrence, 1935, and abridged by W.G. Forrest, 1966; also translated by A.D. Godley [Loeb Edition], 4 vols., 1920–24; Enoch Powell, 1949; Aubrey de Selincourt, 1954; H. Carter, 1962; David Grene, 1987; translated in part by Walter Blanco and Jennifer Tolbert Roberts, 1992.
Selections, edited by Amy L. Barbour. 1985.

*

Critical Studies: *Commentary on Herodotus* by W.W. How and Joseph Wells, 2 vols., 1912, revised edition, 1928; *The*

World of Herodotus by Aubrey de Selincourt, 1962; *Form and Thought in Herodotus* by H.R. Immerwahr, 1966; *Herodotus: An Interpretative Essay* by C.W. Fornara, 1971; *Herodotus, Father of History* by J.L. Myres, 1971; *The Histories of Herodotus: An Analysis of the Formal Structure* by H. Wood, 1972; *The Interrelation of Speech and Action in the Histories of Herodotus* by Paavo Hohti, 1976; *Herodotus and Greek History* by John Hart, 1982; *Past and Process in Herodotus and Thucydides* by Virginia J. Hunter, 1982; *Aspectual Usage of the Dynamic Infinitives in Herodotus* by Peter Stork, 1982; *Herodotean Narrative and Discourse* by Mabel Lang, 1984; *Herodotus: Persian Wars—A Companion to the Penguin Translation of Histories V–IX* edited by Stephen Usher, 1988; *Herodotus and His 'Sources': Citation, Invention and Narrative Art* by Detlev Fehling, 1989; *Herodotus*, 1989, and *Give and Take in Herodotus*, 1991, both by John Gould; *Herodotus, Explorer of the Past* by J.A.S. Evans, 1991; *Heroes in Herodotus: The Interaction of Myth and History* by Elizabeth Vandiver, 1991; *Herodotus, The Histories: New Translation, Selection, Backgrounds, Commentaries* edited by Walter Blanco and Jennifer Tolbert Roberts, 1992; *The Malice of Herodotus* by Plutarch, translated by A.J. Bowen, 1992; *The Historical Method of Herodotus* by Donald Lateiner, 1992.

* * *

Herodotus is traditionally styled 'Father of History', and rightly so—he invented it. There were before him a few local chronicles and geographical studies, which have entirely perished; no one had essayed a great and significant theme, nor assembled masses of material from diverse sources and organized them into a coherent whole. As there is no reason to think that those lost works were of any great literary merit, Herodotus is also entitled to be regarded as a pioneer of artistic prose composition.

Yet there is nothing primitive or unsophisticated about Herodotus. He aims to record for posterity the great deeds of men, and his chosen vehicle is the conflict between the Greeks and the Persians that reached its climax with Xerxes' defeat by the Greeks in 480–79 BC. His handling of that tremendous theme shows a remarkable sense of planning and design: the first half of the work is devoted to the rise of Persia to her greatest extent; the second, by a smoothly negotiated transition, to her wars against the Greeks. The story unfolds in no crude annalistic way: instead it proceeds by a mixture of narrative and digression. The digressions are sometimes little more than footnotes; equally often they are substantial chapters, carefully designed to explain the background to the main narrative, while spacing out its climactic points. Some of these are miniature narratives themselves; others are extended essays in ethnology or sociology, such as the full-length study of Egypt (Book II).

Herodotus understands the broad tides of history, making it clear that Persia's aggression was motivated by imperialist expansion; he is equally good on the grand strategy of the combatants in 480–79 BC—such non-narrative issues being conveyed through direct speech put into the mouths of his characters. He is noticeably weaker on detailed military tactics, however, and tends to personalize the causes of lesser events. He does not gloss over the failings of the Greeks at war—their occasional loss of nerve, the inter-allied bickerings; war itself he hates, despite the glorious exploits associated with it.

Accepting the Homeric picture of man's relationship with the gods, he emphasizes the role of oracles in Greek life, and often quotes oracular texts, many authentic, some spurious. His 'theological' passages, such as the story of Xerxes' cabinet meeting (VII), teach the lesson that man cannot escape his destiny, and that the gods are envious of excessive prosperity in mortals. This pessimistic view informs his whole work, which is tinged with sadness and pity for human suffering; yet this is lightened by passages of irresistible sparkle and humour—Aristagoras' appeal to Sparta (V), 'Hippocleides doesn't care' (VI), and dozens of others. His Greek is unmannered and effortless, resembling an educated man's friendly conversation.

Herodotus was a man of broad sympathies. His travels furnished him with a wide variety of oral sources, and enabled him to appreciate the 'barbarian' point of view; but he was equally at home with the Athenian nobility, some of whose family history he records. His interests include poetry (he quotes from Pindar, Simonides, and many others), the visual arts, and medicine. But above all, he is concerned with humanity, and, like Homer, describes man's behaviour as he finds it: heroism, generosity, foresight, loyalty, vindictiveness, xenophobia, cowardice, treachery, corruption, paranoia, sacrilege—all these, and more, are exemplified many times over in his pages. But what sets Herodotus apart from most other ancient historians is his conviction that history is more than war, politics, and diplomacy. Today, students of social and cultural history can regard Herodotus as their truest ancestor.

—John Hart

———

HESIOD. Lived c.700 BC. According to the poet himself, he lived in Ascra in Boeotia (central Greece), and tended sheep on Mount Helicon; won a tripod at the funeral games of Amphidamas in Chalcis; the story of his meeting and contest with Homer was probably a fictional account. Said to have died in Locri or Orchomenus.

PUBLICATIONS

Collections

[Works], edited by Friedrich Solmsen, R. Merkelbach, and M.L. West. 1970; revised edition, 1983; translated by J. Mair, 1908; also translated by Hugh G. Evelyn-White [Loeb Edition; prose], 1936; also translated by Richmond Lattimore, 1959; Dorothea Wender, 1973; Apostolos N. Athanassakis, 1983; R.M. Frazer, 1983; selection as *The Essential Hesiod*, translated by C.J. Rowe, 1978.

Verse

Theogonia, edited by M.L. West (with commentary). 1966; edited and translated by Richard Caldwell, 1988; as *Theogony*, translated by Norman O. Brown (prose), 1953; also translated by M.L. West, with *Works and Days*, 1988.
Opera et dies, edited by M.L. West (with commentary). 1978; as *Works and Days*, translated by M.L. West, with *Theogony*, 1988.

*

Critical Studies: *Hesiod and Aeschylus* by Friedrich Solmsen, 1949; *The World of Hesiod: A Study of the Greek Middle Ages c.900–700 BC* by A.R. Burn, 1966; *Hesiod and the Near East* by Peter Walcot, 1966; *The Language of Hesiod in Its Traditional Context* by G.P. Edwards, 1971; *The Winged Word: A Study in the Technique of Ancient Greek Oral Composition as Seen Principally Through Hesiod's 'Works and Days'* by B. Peabody, 1975; *Hesiod and the Language of Poetry* by Pietro Pucci, 1976; *Hesiod and Parmenides* by M.E. Pelikaan-Engel, 1977; *The Hesiodic Catalogue of Women: Its Nature, Structure, and Origins* by M.L. West, 1985; *The Architecture of Hesiodic Poetry* by Richard Hamilton, 1988; *Hesiod* by Robert Lamberton, 1988.

* * *

Antiquity attributed a number of poems to Hesiod: besides *Theogonia* (*Theogony*) and *Opera et dies* (*Works and Days*), the only ones which are both nearly intact and probably genuine, there is a fragmentary *Catalogue of Women* (or *Eoiai*), a spurious *Shield of Herakles*, and some others of which we know little more than the titles.

The *Theogony* begins with a prayer-song celebrating the Muses, recounting their encounter with the poet on the foothills of Helicon, and invoking their power to fill him with true song. They start with a cosmogony. Chaos, the primal chasm, came first into being, then Earth, the Underworld, and Eros, sexual desire, the primal energy from which further creation flowed. Once he has established that primordial being is a unity, and material if also divine, the poet interests himself mainly in the emergence of the various gods, and the generations of their rulers. First in power were nature gods, Earth and Heaven; then came Cronus and the Titans, who ruled by force and violence; these were replaced by Zeus and the Olympians, the present regime, characterized by intelligence as well as power, and a deathless being which transcends nature. The shift in power from Earth and Sky is accomplished by a savage fulfilment of the Freudian Oedipal wish: the boy Cronus, at the instigation of his mother Earth, castrates his father Heaven and takes his throne. The triumph of Zeus over Cronus is different, a triumph of practical intelligence. Cronus is deceived by his mother Earth into swallowing a stone when he intended to devour his son Zeus. Zeus had the sense to free the spirits of lightning and thunder, who armed him with weapons to crush Cronus and the Titans, weapons he still uses. Mental agility will keep Zeus in power: warned that his first wife Metis (Intelligence) is to give birth to Athena, her father's equal in strength and wisdom, and a son destined to rule, Zeus swallows Metis and procures her power for himself: Athena is born from his head, and the son is never conceived.

A myth is needed to illustrate the quality of intelligence that rules the world, and Hesiod adapts *Prometheus*. The hero first tricks Zeus into granting humans the better share of sacrifices. Zeus does not undo, but rather compensates, by withholding fire from mortals. Prometheus steals the fire; again Zeus compensates, fashioning the first woman, regarded by Hesiod as a mixed blessing at best. Divine retribution is creative rather than destructive, a balancing which achieves a kind of justice.

If the cosmos began as a unity, it is a unity no longer: the transcendent has seemingly emerged from primal matter and become Olympian. But Olympus is not born, any more than it was present at the beginning: its becoming is as mysterious as its supernatural being. Though beyond nature, it is somehow above us; occasionally called Heaven, it is in fact a place beyond the sky. At the other pole lies Tartarus, the Underworld, where the defeated Titans dwell, along with Night, Sleep, and Death. Above Tartarus is a chasm, perhaps identical with primordial Chaos; then comes the natural world and the monsters 'beyond the sea', such as the Gorgons, Echidna, and the defunct Medusa.

The *Theogony*'s suggestion of a close connection among Zeus, Earth, and Justice is developed into an elaborate theodicy in the *Works and Days*. The premises are, not unexpectedly, questionable; but the argument is highly rational. Zeus is a just god, who rewards the good and punishes the wicked. The good, in this Iron age of ours, are those who honour the goddess good Strife, competition; the wicked are worshippers of bad Strife—battle, disputation, and theft legal and illegal. Strife (Eris) is thus the energy of human purposes, just as Sexual Desire (Eros) is the energy of the *Theogony*. We all desire wealth, but it must be acquired justly, through good strife, or else the gods will destroy us, our offspring, our cities. And this means that we must work. It was not always thus: as the myths of Prometheus-Pandora and of the Decadence from the Golden Age reveal, Zeus has punished human arrogance by hiding our livelihood. But the life of hard work is not a mere avoidance of evil, rather a fulfilment of justice, an honourable response to the act of a just Zeus. Hesiod's paradigm for work is the life of the farmer, who struggles to be in harmony with Zeus, Heaven and Earth, divinities of Olympus and of Nature. This life is depicted in the imperative mood: 'Now plough, now sow, now reap', a device which combines description with prudential—and moral—imperative. The poem ends with a superstitious Catalogue of Good and Bad Days for doing things, which many scholars have adjudged spurious. But the bulk of the poem is a well thought-out and logical vindication of a life of honourable competition in harmony with nature and a just God.

The style of Hesiod is the oral-epic style of Homer. Whether Hesiod utilized writing is not known, but he probably shaped and reshaped his poems for many years. Their final form is somewhat, but probably not radically, different from what we read. Catalogue poetry such as the *Theogony*, didactic verse such as the *Works and Days*, will have its wearisome moments for modern readers. But—to name only a sample—the opening portions of both poems, and the description of Zeus' battle with the Titans and of the Underworld in the *Theogony*, are exceedingly powerful reflections of apocalyptic inspiration.

—William Merritt Sale

HESSE, Hermann. Born in Calw, Württemberg, Germany, 2 July 1877. Educated at Basle Mission; Rector Otto Bauer's latin school, Göppingen, 1890–91; Protestant Seminary, Maulbronn, 1891–92; Cannstatt Gymnasium, 1892–93. Volunteer, as editor of books and magazines for prisoners of war in Switzerland during World War I. Married 1) Marie Bernoulli in 1904 (divorced 1923), three sons; 2) Ruth Wenger in 1924 (divorced 1927); 3) Ninon Auslander Boldin in 1931. Clock factory apprentice, Calw, 1894–95; apprentice, 1895–98, then assistant, 1898–99, Heckenhauer bookshop, Tübingen; worked for bookdealers in Basle, 1899–1903; freelance writer from 1903; editor, *März*, 1907–15; co-editor,

Vivos Voco, 1919–20; also editor of publishers' book series in 1910s and 1920s; regular contributor to *Carona* and *Bonniers Litterära Magasin* in 1930s. Lived in Gaienhofen, Germany, 1904–12, near Berne, Switzerland, 1912–19, and Montagnola, Switzerland, 1919–62. Recipient: Bauernfeldpreis (Vienna), 1904; Fontane prize (refused), 1919; Keller prize, 1936; Nobel prize for literature, 1946; Goethe prize, 1946; Raabe prize, 1950; German Book Trade Peace prize, 1955. Honorary doctorate: University of Berne, 1947. *Died 9 August 1962.*

PUBLICATIONS

Collection

Werkausgabe, edited by Volker Michels. 12 vols., 1970; supplement, 2 vols., 1972.

Fiction

Peter Camenzind. 1904; as *Peter Camenzind*, translated by W.J. Strachan, 1961; also translated by Michael Roloff, 1969.
Unterm Rad. 1906; as *The Prodigy*, translated by W.J. Strachan, 1957; as *Beneath the Wheel*, translated by Michael Roloff, 1968.
Diesseits: Erzählungen. 1907; revised edition, 1930.
Nachbarn: Erzählungen. 1908.
Gertrud. 1910; as *Gertrude and I*, translated by Adèle Lewisohn, 1915; as *Gertrude*, translated by Hilda Rosner, 1955.
Umwege: Erzählungen. 1912.
Anton Schievelbeyns ohn-freywillige Reise nacher Ost-Indien. 1914.
Der Hausierer. 1914.
Rosshalde. 1914; as *Rosshalde*, translated by Ralph Manheim, 1970.
Knulp: Drei Geschichten aus dem Leben Knulps. 1915; as *Knulp: Three Tales from the Life of Knulp*, translated by Ralph Manheim, 1971.
Am Weg. 1915.
Schön ist die Jugend: Zwei Erzählungen. 1916.
Hans Dierlamms Lehrzeit. 1916.
Alte Geschichten: Zwei Erzählungen. 1918.
Zwei Märchen. 1919; revised edition, 1946, 1955; as *Strange News from Another Star and Other Tales*, translated by Denver Lindley, 1972.
Demian: Geschichte einer Jugend. 1919; as *Demian*, translated by N.H. Priday, 1923; also translated by W.J. Strachan, 1958.
Im Pressel'schen Gartenhaus. 1920.
Klingsors letzter Sommer: Erzählungen. 1920; as *Klingsor's Last Summer*, translated by Richard and Clara Winston, 1970.
Siddhartha: Eine indische Dichtung. 1922; as *Siddhartha*, translated by Hilda Rosner, 1951.
Psychologia balnearia; oder, Glossen eines Badener Kurgastes. 1924; as *Kurgast*, 1925.
Die Verlogung: Erzählungen. 1924.
Der Steppenwolf. 1927; as *Steppenwolf*, translated by Basil Creighton, 1929; revised edition by Joseph Mileck, 1963.
Narziss und Goldmund. 1930; as *Death and the Lover*, translated by Geoffrey Dunlop, 1932; as *Goldmund*, 1959; as *Narcissus and Goldmund*, translated by Ursule Molinaro, 1968, also translated by Leila Vennewitz, 1993.

Die Morgenlandfahrt. 1932; as *The Journey to the East*, translated by Hilda Rosner, 1956.
Kleine Welt: Erzählungen. 1933.
Fabulierbuch: Erzählungen. 1935.
Das Glasperlenspiel. 1943; as *Magister Ludi*, translated by Mervyn Savill, 1949; as *The Glass Bead Game*, translated by Richard and Clara Winston, 1969.
Der Pfirsichbaum und andere Erzählungen. 1945.
Traumfährte: Neue Erzählungen und Märchen. 1945.
Berthold: Ein Romanfragment. 1945.
Glück (collection). 1952.
Zwei jugendliche Erzählungen. 1957.
Freunde: Erzählungen. 1957.
Geheimnisse: Letzte Erzählungen. 1964.
Erwin. 1965.
Aus Kinderzeiten und andere Erzählungen. 1968.
Stories of Five Decades, edited by Theodore Ziolkowski, translated by Ralph Manheim. 1972.
Die Erzählungen. 2 vols., 1973.
Six Novels, with Other Stories and Essays. 1980.
Pictor's Metamorphoses and Other Fantasies, edited by Theodor Ziolowski, translated by Rika Lesser, 1982.

Verse

Romantische Lieder. 1899.
Hinterlassene Schriften und Gedichte von Hermann Lauscher. 1901; revised edition as *Hermann Lauscher*, 1907.
Gedichte. 1902.
Unterwegs. 1911.
Musik des Einsamen: Neue Gedichte. 1915.
Gedichte des Malers. 1920.
Ausgewählte Gedichte. 1921.
Trost der Nacht: Neue Gedichte. 1929.
Vom Baum des Lebens: Ausgewählte Gedichte. 1934.
Das Haus der Träume. 1936.
Stunden im Garten: Eine Idylle. 1936.
Neue Gedichte. 1937.
Die Gedichte. 1942.
Der Blütenzweig: Eine Auswahl aus den Gedichten. 1945.
Bericht an die Freunde: Letzte Gedichte. 1961.
Die späten Gedichte. 1963.
Poems, translated by James Wright. 1970.
Hours in the Garden and Other Poems, translated by Rika Lesser. 1979.

Other

Eine Stunde hinter Mitternacht. 1899.
Boccaccio. 1904.
Franz von Assisi. 1904.
Aus Indien: Aufzeichnungen von einer indische Reise. 1913.
Zum Sieg. 1915.
Brief ins Feld. 1916.
Zarathustras Wiederkehr: Ein Wort an die deutsche Jugend. 1919.
Kleiner Garten: Erlebnisse und Dichtungen. 1919.
Wanderung: Aufzeichnungen. 1920; as *Wandering: Notes and Sketches*, translated by James Wright, 1972.
Blick ins Chaos: Drei Aufsätze. 1920; as *In Sight of Chaos*, translated by Stephen Hudson, 1923.
Elf Aquarelle aus dem Tessin. 1921.
Sinclairs Notizbuch. 1923.
Erinnerung an Lektüre. 1925.
Bilderbuch: Schilderungen. 1926.
Die schwere Weg. 1927.

Die Nürnberger Reise. 1927.
Betrachtungen. 1928.
Krisis: Ein Stück Tagebuch. 1928; as *Crisis: Pages from a Diary,* translated by Ralph Manheim, 1975.
Eine Bibliothek der Weltliteratur. 1929; revised edition, 1957.
Zum Gedächtnis unseres Vaters, with Adele Hesse. 1930.
Gedenkblätter. 1937.
Aus der Kindheit der heiligen Franz von Assisi. 1938.
Der Novalis: Aus den Papieren eines Altmodischen. 1940.
Kleine Betrachtungen: Sechs Aufsätze. 1941.
Dank an Goethe. 1946.
Der Europäer. 1946.
Krieg und Frieden: Betrachtungen zu Krieg und Politik seit dem Jahr 1914. 1946; revised edition, 1949; as *If the War Goes On. . .: Reflections on War and Politics,* translated by Ralph Manheim, 1971.
Stufen der Menschwerdung. 1947.
Frühe Prosa. 1948.
Berg und See: Zwei Landschaftsstudien. 1948.
Gerbersau. 2 vols., 1949.
Aus vielen Jahren. 1949.
Späte Prosa. 1951.
Briefe. 1951; revised edition, 1959, 1964.
Eine Handvoll Briefe. 1951.
Gesammelte Dichtungen. 6 vols., 1952; enlarged edition as *Gesammelte Schriften,* 7 vols., 1957.
Über das Alter. 1954.
Briefe, with Romain Rolland. 1954.
Aquarelle aus dem Tessin. 1955.
Beschwörungen: Späte Prosa, neue Folge. 1955.
Abendwolken: Zwei Aufsätze. 1956.
Aus einem Tagebuch des Jahres 1920. 1960.
Aerzte: Ein paar Erinnerungen. 1963.
Prosa aus dem Nachlass, edited by Ninon Hesse. 1965.
Neue deutscher Bücher. 1965.
Kindheit und Jugend vor Neunzehnhundert, edited by Ninon Hesse. 1966.
Briefwechsel, with Thomas Mann, edited by Anni Carlsson. 1968; revised edition, 1975; also edited by Hans Wysling, 1984; as *The Hesse/Mann Letters: The Correspondence of Hermann Hesse and Thomas Mann, 1910–1955,* translated by Ralph Manheim, 1975.
Briefwechsel 1945–1959, with Peter Suhrkamp, edited by Siegfried Unseld. 1969.
Politische Betrachtungen. 1970.
Eine Literaturgeschichte in Rezensionen und Aufsätzen, edited by Volker Michels. 1970.
Beschreibung einer Landschaft. 1971.
Lektüre für Minuten, edited by Volker Michels. 1971; as *Reflections,* translated by Ralph Manheim, 1974.
Meine Glaube, edited by Siegfried Unseld. 1971; as *My Belief: Essays on Life and Art,* edited by Theodore Ziolkowski, translated by Denver Lindley and Ralph Manheim, 1974.
Zwei Autorenporträts in Briefen 1897 bis 1900: Hesse—Helene Voigt-Diederichs. 1971.
Eigensinn: Autobiographische Schriften, edited by Siegfried Unseld. 1972; as *Autobiographical Writings,* edited by Theodore Ziolkowski, translated by Denver Lindley, 1972.
Briefwechsel aus der Nähe, with Karl Kerenyi, edited by Magda Kerenyi. 1972.
Gesammelte Briefe, edited by Ursula and Volker Michels. 4 vols., 1972–86.
Die Kunst des Müssiggangs: Kurze Prosa aus dem Nachlass, edited by Volker Michels. 1973.
Hermann Hesse, R.J. Humm: Briefwechsel, edited by Ursula and Volker Michels. 1977.

Politik des Gewissens: die politische Schriften 1914–1932, edited by Volker Michels. 2 vols., 1977.
Die Welt im Buch, edited by Volker Michels. 1977.
Briefwechsel mit Heinrich Wiegand, 1924–1934, edited by Klaus Pezold. 1978.
Hermann Hesse/Hans Sturzenegger: Briefwechsel, edited by Kurt Bächtold. 1984.
Bodensee: Betrachungen, Erzählungen, Gedichte, edited by Volker Michels. 1986.
Soul of the Age: The Selected Letters, 1891–1962, edited by Theodore Ziolkowski. 1991.

Editor, with others, *Der Lindenbaum, deutsche Volkslieder.* 1910.
Editor, *Der Zauberbrunnen.* 1913.
Editor, *Der Wandsbecker Bote,* by Matthias Claudias. 1916.
Editor, *Alemannenbuch.* 1919.
Editor, with Walter Stich, *Ein Schwabenbuch für die deutschen Kriegsgefangenen.* 1919.
Editor, *Ein Luzerner Junker vor hundert Jahren,* by Xaver Schnyder von Wartensee. 1920.
Editor, *Dichtungen,* by Solomon Gessner. 1922.
Editor, *Mordprozesse.* 1922.
Editor, *Novellino.* 1922.
Editor, with Karl Isenberg, *Novalis: Dokumente seines Lebens und Sterbens.* 1925.
Editor, with Karl Isenburg, *Hölderlin: Dokumente seines Lebens.* 1925.
Editor, *Geschichten aus dem Mittelalter.* 1925.
Editor, *Sesam: Orientalische Erzählungen.* 1925.

*

Bibliography: *Hermann-Hesse-Bibliographie* by M. Pfeifer, 1973; *Hermann Hesse: Biography and Bibliography* by Joseph Mileck, 2 vols., 1977.

Critical Studies: *Faith from the Abyss: Hermann Hesse's Way from Romanticism to Modernity* by Ernst Rose, 1965; *The Novels of Hermann Hesse,* 1965, and *Hesse,* 1966, both by Theodore Ziolkowski, and *Hesse: A Collection of Critical Essays* edited by Ziolkowski, 1973; *Hermann Hesse: His Mind and Art* by Mark Boulby, 1967; *Hermann Hesse* by G.W Field, 1970; *Hesse: An Illustrated Biography* by Bernhard Zeller, 1971; *Hermann Hesse* by Edwin F. Casebeer, 1972; *Hesse's Futuristic Idealism* by Roger C. Norton, 1973; *Hermann Hesse, The Man Who Sought and Found Himself* by Walter Sorrell, 1974; *Hesse: A Pictorial Biography* by Volker Michels, translated by Theodore and Yetta Ziolkowski, 1975; *Hermann Hesse: A Collection of Criticism* edited by Judith Lieberman, 1977; *Hermann Hesse: Life and Art* by Joseph Mileck, 1978; *Hermann Hesse's Fictions of the Self: Autobiography and the Confessional Imagination* by Eugene L. Stelzig, 1978; *Hermann Hesse's Quest: The Evolution of the Dichter Figure in His Work* by Kurt J. Fickert, 1978; *Hermann Hesse: Pilgrim of Crisis: A Biography* by Ralph Freedman, 1979; *Hermann Hesse's Das Glasperlenspiel: A Concealed Defense of the Mother World* by Edmund Ray, 1983; *Hermann Hesse: Politische und wirkungsgechichtliche Aspekte* edited by Sigrid Bauschinger and Albert Reh, 1986; *The Hero's Quest for the Self: An Archetypal Approach to Hesse's Demian and Other Novels* by David G. Richards, 1987; *The Ideal of Heimat in the Works of Hermann Hesse* by Andreas Kiryakakis, 1988.

* * *

Hermann Hesse's work has its roots in many areas of culture, especially German romanticism, Eastern religious thought, Nietzschean philosophy, and Jungian psychoanalytic theory. It has always appealed particularly to the young because of its recurrent stress—already perhaps implied in these sources—on breaking barriers, on the individual's need to emancipate itself from all ties and follow its own star. His first major work was the novel *Demian*, which attained widespread popularity as one of the earliest texts to deal sympathetically with adolescence. Here Hesse strikingly—if perhaps over-eclectically—combines new interpretations of Old Testament and gnostic symbolism with Jungian motifs to trace the moral and spiritual emancipation of his typical hero: the man who learns how to put comforting bourgeois security behind him, to accept fully the unconventional, even amoral, complexity of his soul and thus gain control of his own destiny. A heady optimism attaches to his 'rebirth', expressed through images redolent both of a Jungian journey into the Collective Unconscious and a Nietzschean Will to Power. However, this elated confidence becomes tempered over the years in Hesse's subsequent works.

This is already the case in *Siddhartha*, another stylized but gentler picture of the search for self. The text has the simplified form of an Eastern myth, and the new idiom indicates a new depth of understanding: the goal of self-overcoming may be attainable but the search is lifelong, and culminates not in redirected activity but rather in changed vision, in the hard-won capacity to embrace all oppositions intellectually and emotionally, to cease thinking 'exclusively'. The most remarkable aspect of this novel is its beautifully sustained imagery and simplicity of style. It is here that Hesse first shows himself a master of the German language: it flows with wonderful euphony, and elsewhere—as in *Klingsors letzter Sommer* (*Klingsor's Last Summer*)—can attain a splendidly rich sensuousness.

Hesse's next major work, *Der Steppenwolf* (*Steppenwolf*), is perhaps his best-known novel and one that bears clear autobiographical reference to its author's at times tortured middle years. Far removed from the archetypal serenity of *Siddhartha*, it is a remarkable, graphic portrayal of unresolved personal problems. Hesse captures the agonizing simultaneity of violent oppositions in one and the same personality, for whom life becomes a battle between the longing for simple security and the painful awareness of inner division and self-hatred. Where in earlier works the less 'acceptable' aspects of personality are portrayed fairly conventionally as sensuality or Nietzschean will-power, here the depths of degradation are plumbed with ruthless honesty, from aggressive sexuality to bestial destructiveness. The same honesty extends to the social setting; through Harry Haller's alienation we see something of the disturbing mix of jingoism, complacency, and self-gratification of the inter-war years. Yet despite Haller's agony, there are intimations of how this deep sense of dislocation, both internal and external, might be overcome by sublime acceptance, for which the 'Immortals' —great artists such as Goethe and Mozart—stand as models. Haller must learn like them to turn life itself into art; if he can abandon not only conventional moral disapprobation but all rational categorization and embrace discreteness, he might rewrite the whole concept of identity, learning to see personality no longer as circumscribed unity but as infinite, capable of embracing all experience as part of the potential self. This theme has interesting aesthetic consequences in the text, which no longer seeks to tell a sequentially developing, finite story, but rather to create a sense of simultaneity and openness via a structure reminiscent of a musical theme and variations, or of a series of interrelated mirrors—an explicit leitmotif in the text. Above all Hesse succeeds in blurring the distinction between internal and external action, dream and actuality. The whole text is both multivalent and 'unfinished'; it has echoes—more subtly handled than in *Demian*—of romanticism, Freudian and Jungian analysis, Zen Buddhism, which undercut but never destroy the level of social realism and thus create a fluid view of personality as multidimensional. So too does the fact that no one part of the text has an objective narrative source, and thus the reader also is detached from inherited models of character definition and textual interpretation. The linguistic problems involved in attempting to present simultaneity in epic form are returned to explicitly in *Kurgast*.

Surprisingly, Hesse's next novel *Narziss und Goldmund* (*Narcissus and Goldmund*) lacks all such complexity and manifests a return to much more basic narrative skills. Set in medieval times, it tells a broadly allegorical tale about the inescapable responsibility of individual self-discovery. Two friends, one a sensuous artist and the other an ascetic intellectual, gradually both learn that the road to defining one's own personal truth is long; as in earlier texts, Hesse shows that friends may act as valuable mentors but can never release the individual from the journey towards selfhood that encompasses both pain and joy. While charming in its narrative simplicity, it lacks conviction at a deeper level, especially when compared with Hesse's great work *Das Glasperlenspiel* (*The Glass Bead Game*). Set in a post-20th-century future, this summation of all his inspiration from Goethe to the Orient projects the theme of personal multiplicity onto a cultural plane, and explores the grandiose possibility of harmonizing all knowledge, as an antidote to what Hesse sees as the dangerous cultural and spiritual narrowness of our century. Yet the text offers no final answers and raises many profound questions about the relationship between intellect and practical activity, harmony and extremism, culture and barbarism, stasis and progress. Like his central figure Josef Knecht, Hesse remained self-questioning until the end.

In addition to these major works Hesse produced many short stories, autobiographical sketches, and essays of great delicacy and perceptive insight both into himself and his age. His poetry, while lacking the originality of his prose, still has the power to charm by its romantic sensitivity to nature and inwardness of imagery. Some of it has indeed been set to music, notably by Richard Strauss (*Four Last Songs*).

—Mary E. Stewart

THE GLASS BEAD GAME (Das Glasperlenspiel)
Novel by Hermann Hesse, 1943.

Hesse's longest and most ambitious novel took 11 years to complete. It depicts a quasi-monastic realm in which the competitiveness and sensationalism of the present have been superseded by the outwardly serene environment of the pedagogic province of Castalia, where the high-minded scholars of the future are nurtured in the benign but austere surroundings of elitist schools and institutions. The opening chapter acquaints the reader with the rudiments of the new culture, and the life story of Josef Knecht is told in 12 episodes by an anonymous narrator whose disposition is hard to describe as other than pedantic.

Knecht ('a servant') is a loyal member of the Castalian

hierarchy, a committed scholar who eschews mundane pursuits, has no recorded love-life, and immerses himself in the affairs of the republic of aesthetes in a spirit of unquestioning obedience. His crowning achievement is to be nominated Master of the Glass Bead Game, which provides the central activity of the province.

This Game remains a mysterious, hallowed institution to which the narrator alludes with the utmost reverence. It is to be thought of as similar to a game of symbolic chess of infinite complexity, in which each piece and each move refer to an idea taken from the cultural history of the world. Castalia may sound like the revival of a medieval ideal, where the invariably male scholar is divorced from the need to earn a living and the arts enjoy the attention of teams of well-trained devotees, but nothing can disguise the fact that the new world envisaged by Hesse is profoundly, even wilfully sterile: overt manifestations of originality are proscribed. The paradox at the heart of Castalia is that her scholars are incapable of generating new ideas, her musicians are unable to compose, and her art experts have long abandoned any creative work. All that seems to count is mastery of the Glass Bead Game.

The minor characters come across as shadowy figures who are either heavily idealized (the Music Master, Pater Jakobus, Ferromonte), whimsical loners with neurotic tendencies (the 'Chinese' Elder Brother, Tegularius, Petrus, Anton, Bertram), or faceless representatives of an impenetrable bureaucracy (Headmaster Zbinden, Master Alexander, Thomas von der Trave, Dublois). In the end, Knecht's individualism places him at odds with the administration; encouraged by his childhood friend Plinio Designori, he applies to leave the hierarchy and sample life in the world outside. From now on he is cold-shouldered by an increasingly hostile bureaucracy, and in the last chapter, 'The Legend', an unverifiable story is reproduced, according to which he meets his death in a mountain lake. The biography ends with voluminous supplements containing Knecht's posthumous writings.

Early drafts indicate that Hesse intended to celebrate the Game as an invention worthy of our loftiest aspirations. The novel was to have culminated in a confrontation between Knecht and a 'Führer of the Dictatorship' determined to stamp out such undesirable practices. The planned satirical vignettes had to be dropped from the final version, which Hesse vainly attempted to publish in Nazi Germany during World War II. With its rigid laws, constant surveillance, restrictions on travel, and overweening bureaucracy, Castalia mirrors a flawed world Hesse knew only too well; whether the Game itself is more than an empty ritual remains a matter for debate.

As soon as *The Glass Bead Game* appeared in Switzerland, two contradictory interpretations were put forward. According to one opinion, Castalia is a utopian state in a positive sense, while the other maintains that the province is shot through with evidence of human fallibility and decadence. Hesse repeatedly stressed the 'utopian' dimension, but it seems unlikely that he would have endorsed the many authoritarian practices rife in Castalia. Ziolkowski suggested an answer to the critics' dilemma by distinguishing between the original community of intellectuals, the restrictive bureaucracy, and the improved Castalia represented by the narrator, which he supposes to have benefited from the lesson of Knecht's untimely demise. There are, however, few signs that conditions have improved since then, and the narrator's fawning attitude towards the 'Board of Educators' is a disturbing feature not easily reconciled with Ziolkowski's optimistic account of him.

Hesse did not supply the continuation which some readers thought would resolve the issue, but by putting forward a wholesome, contemplative ideal contaminated by an all-too-human greed for power and abused until it seems no less pernicious than the evils it sought to combat, he created a masterpiece of tantalizing ambivalence, projecting his vision of man's enduring spiritual potential on to a disturbing background of crass authoritarianism and political intrigue. Castalia needs the Game to give itself credibility, but since culture must rely on social organization, the Game is wholly dependent on the new state. In its definitive form, the novel is utopian in its acceptance of this paradox, while warning against entrenchment, extremism, and the cultivation of collectivist ideals which can all too easily serve as convenient power bases for unscrupulous tyrannies.

—Osman Durrani

SIDDHARTHA
Novel by Hermann Hesse, 1922.

Siddhartha is set in India, but the background is not described in any detail, the plot is minimal, characterization is restricted, and no date is given for the action. The eponymous hero, whose (Sanskrit) name means 'he who has achieved his aim', is portrayed in a lifelong quest for the ultimate meaning of existence, and for a way of living which will provide self-realization. An Indian atmosphere is created by means of an 'oriental' pastiche, a complex and consistent attempt to render the feel of Sanskrit in German through formalized, liturgical structures and full exploitation of the lyrical possibilities of prose rhythm. The many influences outside those from India include Chinese thinkers, the German Romantics, and Carl Jung, who analyzed the author in the course of the novel's composition.

The novel is short, and consists of two separate parts—although the underlying structure, like so much else in this work, is triadic. The first part (four chapters) describes the background of Siddhartha as the son of a Brahman, his breakaway from the religious inadequacies of home, and his wanderings in the forests with an ascetic sect. Failing to find his goal, he visits Gotama, the Buddha, but is disappointed by the Great One's teachings and so resolves instead to discover his innermost self. Awakening for the first time to the beauty of the world, Siddhartha now embarks (in Part II) on a completely different lifestyle: for the next four chapters we see him experiencing the world of the senses through a long relationship with a beautiful courtesan; tasting growing professional success and power as the assistant of a wealthy merchant; learning to gamble recklessly; and finally experiencing self-disgust as a result of excess. Recognizing this life as an elaborate form of game, the disillusioned hero returns (for the final four chapters) to visit the ferryman who had earlier brought him across the river to this world of 'childlike adults'. He stays with the ferryman, learns from him, and finally takes over his work in a humble capacity of service to his fellow men. Towards the end he is visited by his former mistress and their son; the former dies and the latter scorns his simple ways and gentle teaching, preferring to run back to life in the city. Siddhartha follows him, but then realizes that his son must find his own way to fulfilment, just as he himself had done in his own repudiation of the world of his father. His final visitor is a form of 'shadow', an old friend from his youth, who has been on a comparable lifelong search and who has chosen to follow the teachings of Buddha. Govinda has failed to discover his goal within the confines of traditional religious striving, but recognizes that Siddhartha has done so in his simple life of service at the river.

That river itself serves an important symbolic function. Siddhartha, as ferryman, helps people to cross the water which separates the city, the outer world of extroversion, superficial excitement, and wild pleasures, from the introverted, lonely, and ascetic world of forests and mountains. Siddhartha has himself crossed that river twice in the course of his search, and he has managed to reconcile those two worlds and attitudes which the water divides. He goes on learning how to consolidate this insight by observing the old ferryman's life, by listening to the river, and by discovering a different attitude towards time. In his final dialogue with Govinda, he enumerates some of the insights he has gained. These include the idea that for each truth the opposite is equally true; that excessive searching—as practised by Govinda—is self-defeating and that to 'find' is, paradoxically, 'to be free, to be open, to have no goal'. One must simply love and enjoy the world in all its aspects, and Govinda's final vision of Siddhartha's face is in fact an experience of universal metamorphosis, of a streaming river of faces of all time and all emotions, all the manifestations of life which Siddhartha has managed to accept. Govinda leaves him seated in the perfect position of the contemplative, which suggests serene universal insight into the whole of creation, immersion in life, and mystical identity with it. Nevertheless, although Siddhartha may have reached the highest state of wisdom, he is unable to communicate its essence to Govinda. For another of his realizations is that although knowledge may be communicable, wisdom is not.

Of all Hesse's novels, this is the work in which it is clearest that form is a part of meaning. The novel is borne along on a strong rhythmic current, on what seems an undertone of chant. All harsh sounds are avoided, while there is much alliteration and assonance. We find frequent use of parallelism in clause structure; repetition of individual words; anaphora; constant apposition. There is regular omission of the definite article, and sentences often open adverbially or adjectivally. The threefold repetitions, corresponding to the tripartite structure of the work, may create a liturgical aspect which is reminiscent of the Bible, but the language is not really Biblical but rather that of Pali, the language used in the canonical books of the Buddhists. At points this language can achieve something of an incantatory effect but for the most part it reflects the serene, balanced attitude of meditation, the object of which was described by Hesse as 'a shifting of the state of consciousness, a technique having as its highest aim the achievement of pure harmony, a simultaneous and uniform functioning together of logical and intuitive thinking'. Hesse regarded the speeches of Buddha as a model in this respect, and it is these he is emulating in *Siddhartha*. His success in this respect may in part be judged by the remarkable sales of the novel in India, where it has been translated into eight different languages.

—Peter Hutchinson

STEPPENWOLF (Der Steppenwolf)
Novel by Hermann Hesse, 1927.

Steppenwolf is set in an unnamed Swiss town at some point in the early 1920s. It attempts to reflect the contemporary and widespread feeling of 'sickness of the age' within a single character, and its disrupted presentation of events in part reflects the disjointed mind of a figure who views himself as an incurably split personality, an irreconcilable amalgam of man and wolf. But the novel is also one of several major works by early 20th-century German writers which employ an unsettling structure to reflect the disintegration of traditional modes of living which World War I had brought with it. Partial inspiration for this approach may actually be detected in the German Romantics' attitude to form, for the Romantics (several of whom feature by name in the text) were among Hesse's favourite writers. There is, however, also considerable influence of modern psychoanalytic theory in form and in content. Just as Hesse himself had been healed by Jungian analysis, the split in his hero's mind is painfully reconciled through a range of therapies: not just probing of the unconscious, but practical sex-therapy which awakens his dormant sensual powers, dance therapy, music, and even drug-induced psychedelic experience. There are two principal lessons in the novel: first, that personality is manifold, layered, and complex, not simply dualistic; and second, that liberation of the self consists of far more than simply an insight into and understanding of that self—the hero has in fact an abundance of self-knowledge from his constant self-analysis, but what he needs is to engage in life properly, to incorporate and synthesize experiences, and sometimes to stand back from existence in order to achieve equilibrium.

The hero, Harry Haller, bears the same initials as his creator, an obvious invitation to establish parallels between the two (and a considerable amount of the detail and psychological analysis is indeed drawn from Hesse's own experiences around this period). The fiction is that Harry has disappeared, leaving behind a manuscript for his landlady's nephew. The latter, in a plain and pedantic introduction, relates the circumstances of Harry's life from an outsider's point of view. We then have the beginnings of Harry's first-person account of the life of a 48-year-old man who is suffering from physical pains and headaches, who torments himself with constant analysis of his split personality, who is both attracted to the bourgeois existence and repelled by it, who has a propensity for the bottle, and who has resolved to take his own life on his 50th birthday. A sort of interlude now follows, a 'Tract of the Steppenwolf' which Harry is mysteriously handed as he walks the night streets. (In early editions of the novel, this 'tract' was actually printed on a different, cheap sort of paper and in different typography.) The tract provides a third-person analysis of Harry's personality, in clear, bold, and sometimes ironic language which approximates to that of psychoanalytic diagnosis. It views Harry as typical of the artistic and European types, and as consisting not of two separate natures, but of thousands. It also denounces, in language reminiscent of Nietzsche, the cosy existence of the modern bourgeois.

The next major event (in a novel which contains little narrative) is the encounter with an old acquaintance—a professor who emerges as an arch representative of the bourgeois and their self-satisfied yet militaristic mentality. Unable to suppress the wolf-like side of his personality, Harry expresses his inner feelings about bourgeois attitudes at the dinner party to which he has been kindly invited, and he then storms out to roam the streets. On entering a disreputable-looking bar, he meets a call-girl, Hermine (note again the key initial), whose psyche, in Jungian terms, clearly corresponds to Harry's 'anima'; the confrontation with this, the feminine side of his unconscious, is an important aspect of the healing process. Hermine comforts him and takes him under her wing in an almost motherly manner, later teaching him to dance, to take life less seriously, and to enjoy physical love with Maria, a beautiful prostitute friend of hers. He is also introduced to a jazz saxophonist, Pablo, a man without repressions, in whom he sees another, completely different, unreflective attitude towards music and life. Hermine, Maria, and Pablo are sometimes associated with mirrors, and they may all be seen as reflections or projections of aspects of Harry's personality.

The penultimate event of the novel is an extended masked ball in which Hermine is, significantly, disguised as a young man and in which Harry finally engages in a mystical experience of intense pleasure and self-abandon. When the ball is over, Pablo invites Harry to join him and Hermine in experiencing his 'Magic Theatre', which turns out to be a drug-induced working out of various aspects of Harry's personality, including a wild attack on motor cars, the observation of a scene which reveals the deep savagery within him, the re-experiencing, more positively, of all his former love encounters, and finally the act of murdering Hermine as she lies asleep after having made love with Pablo—an act which Hermine had predicted he would carry out, but which seems motivated by a type of bourgeois jealousy Harry has obviously not yet overcome. Harry's behaviour in murdering Hermine is condemned, and he is sentenced to 'eternal life' both for lacking a sense of humour and for confusing imagination with reality. The novel concludes positively, with Harry accepting that he must learn to follow the example of such 'Immortals' as Mozart and Goethe (who both feature in dreams/hallucinations); that is, that he must learn to 'laugh' as they do, and thus create distance between themselves and life. He also recognizes that he must continue to play this painful but therapeutic self-revealing 'game'.

The tone of this work is constantly changing, and there are even two poems included within it. Hesse's prose brings out, above all, the unhappiness of his hero's restless mind, with its obsessive, rhetorical analysis; but the author is also able to communicate the occasionally elated and even lyrical mood of a sensitive intellectual who has rediscovered 'living'.

—Peter Hutchinson

HOCHWÄLDER, Fritz. Born in Vienna, Austria, 28 May 1911. Educated at Reform-Realgymnasium, Vienna, and in evening classes at the Volkshochshule. Married 1) Ursula Büchi in 1951 (divorced 1957); 2) Susanne Schreiner in 1960, one daughter. Apprentice upholsterer in Vienna; moved to Switzerland in 1938 to escape the Nazi regime; lived in refugee camps in Switzerland, 1938–42; freelance writer in Zurich, from 1945. Recipient: Vienna prize, 1955, and Ehrenring, 1972; Grillparzer prize, 1956; Wildgans prize, 1963; Austrian State prize, 1966; Austrian Ehrenkreuz für Kunst und Wissenschaft, 1971. Named Professor by Austrian government, 1963. *Died 20 October 1986.*

PUBLICATIONS

Plays

Jehr (produced 1933).
Liebe in Florenz; oder, Die unziemliche Neugier (produced 1936).
Das heilige Experiment (produced 1943). 1947; as *The Strong Are Lonely*, translated by Eva Le Galienen, 1954; as *The Holy Experiment* (televised 1985).

Der Flüchtling, from a work by Georg Kaiser (produced 1945). 1954.
Hotel du commerce (produced 1946). 1954.
Meier Helmbrecht (produced 1947). 1956.
Der öffentliche Ankläger (produced 1948). 1954; as *The Public Prosecutor*, translated by Kitty Black, 1958; and in *The Public Prosecutor and Other Plays*, 1980.
Der Unschuldige (produced 1958). Privately printed, 1949; 1958.
Virginia (produced 1951).
Donadieu (produced 1953). 1953.
Die Herberge (produced 1957). 1956; as *The Inn* (produced 1962).
Donnerstag (produced 1959). In *Dramen*, 1, 1959.
Dramen. 2 vols., 1959–64.
Esther. 1960.
1003 (produced 1964). In *Dramen*, 2, 1964.
Der Himbeerpflücker (televised 1965; produced 1965). 1965; as *The Raspberry Picker*, translated by Michael Bullock, in *The Public Prosecutor and Other Plays*, 1980.
Der Befehl (televised 1967; produced 1968). 1967; as *The Order*, in *Modern International Drama*, 3(2), 1970.
Dramen. 1968.
Dramen. 4 vols., 1975–85.
Lazaretti; oder, Der Säbeltiger (produced 1975). 1975; as *Lazaretti; or, the Saber-Toothed Tiger*, translated by James Schmittin, in *The Public Prosecutor and Other Plays*, 1980.
The Public Prosecutor and Other Plays (includes *The Raspberry Picker*; *The Public Prosecutor*; *The Strong Are Lonely*; *Lazaretti; or, the Saber-Toothed Tiger*), edited by Martin Esslin. 1980.
Die Prinzessin von Chimay. 1982.
Der verschwundene Mond. 1985.
Die Burgschaft. 1985.

Radio Plays: *Der Reigen*, from the play by Arthur Schnitzler; *Weinsberger Ostern 1525*, 1939.

Television Plays: *Der Himbeerpflücker*, 1965; *Der Befehl*, 1967.

Other

Im Wechsel der Zeit: Autobiographische Skizzen und Essays. 1980.

*

Bibliography: 'Fritz Hochwälder Bibliography' by James Schmitt, in *Modern Austrian Literature*, 11(1), 1978.

Critical Studies: *The Theater of Protest and Paradox: Developments in the Avant-Garde Drama* edited by George E. Wellwarth, 1964; 'Tradition and Experiment in the Work of Fritz Hochwälder' by Anthony J. Harper, in *New German Studies*, 5, 1977; 'The Theatre of Fritz Hochwälder: Its Background and Development' by James Schmitt, in *Modern Austrian Literature*, 11(1), 1978; *Der Dramatiker Hochwälder* by Wilhelm Bortenschlager, 1979; 'Fritz Hochwälder's Range of Theme and Form' by Donald G. Daviau, in *Austrian Literature*, 18(2), 1985; 'The Classical Theater-of-Illusion Modernized: The Conflicting Messages of the Moral Imperative in Fritz Hochwälder's Drama *Das heilige Experiment*' by Edward R. McDonald, in *Maske und Kothurn*, 31, 1985.

* * *

In the years following World War II Fritz Hochwälder's plays were at the forefront of German-speaking and indeed European drama, challenging the audience to come to terms with the recent past.

Hochwälder saw himself as part of the vigorous tradition of Viennese folk theatre, revitalized in the 1930s by Ödön von Horváth. When the angry young men of the Austrian theatre announced in the 1960s that 'Grandpa's theatre is dead', Hochwälder's reply was characteristically tart: no one had ever fallen asleep in any of *his* plays! Throughout his career his works relied on the characteristic devices of the *Volksstück*, stock characters, unexpected twists to the story line, cases of mistaken identity, and a nice turn to the dialogue with moments of unexpected comedy to lighten the mood.

Above all, however, Hochwälder was a moralist and the light touch of his pen never disguised the fact that he was dealing with serious issues. It would be surprising were this not so. A Jew forced into exile and living through the Europe of the Third Reich could not but be affected. Behind the costume drama lies a grim political and moral reality. The fact that his plays move, over the years, from historical pieces (*Das heilige Experiment* [*The Strong Are Lonely*], *Der öffentliche Ankläger* [*The Public Prosecutor*], to allegory (*Donnerstag*, *1003*, *Die Herberge* [*The Inn*]), to works dealing with the second half of the 20th century (*Der Himbeerpflücker* [*The Raspberry Picker*], *Der Befehl* [*The Order*]), reflects the innate Austrianism in his soul. The Austrian tradition shies away from immediacy, preferring to depict the present from the safer, apparently objective context of history and costume drama; the first National Socialist to appear explicitly as such in Hochwälder's work does not walk on stage until the mid 1960s, by when, of course, Nazi uniforms have begun to become historical pieces in their own right.

Behind the surface Hochwälder probes deep into the psyche of his protagonists and emerges with a picture of hell. Hochwälder's hell is knowledge of the inner self, gained at the cost of considerable personal pain. There is much of *Oedipus Rex* in Hochwälder's work. A characteristic example is the mild-mannered Dutch police inspector in *The Order*, given the task of hunting down the perpetrator of a brutal war crime and child murder by a military policeman in occupied Holland. As he penetrates the past, the inspector unravels his own repressed subconscious until he is forced to realize that he is the brutal war monster he is seeking.

Power versus justice, the demands of the ideal set against the limitations of reality: these are the axes of Hochwälder's plays. Jesuit black in Latin America, although an apparent world away from the Gestapo black of Europe, is used by Hochwälder to show the danger of unquestioning acceptance of a cause (however noble). Read as a study of the evil of individual reliance on external support and the seductive appeal of 'Order', *The Strong Are Lonely* regains much of the relevance many would today deny the work. The shadow of the Gestapo is equally apparent behind the Terror of revolutionary France in *The Public Prosecutor*. The public prosecutor's relentless commitment to the Thermidor government is used by his opponents to engineer his self-destruction. Hochwälder does not make his public prosecutor a monster; he shows him as a man with feelings who would like to be humane but who has fallen victim to the machine he serves. The true tragedy in both plays is that of the individual lost in the morass of a system where individualism has no place.

Hochwälder's virtual disappearance from the theatrical scene in recent years does him scant justice. It is difficult to believe that the European stage can afford to ignore *The Strong Are Lonely* and *The Public Prosecutor*. He himself felt he would be remembered for these two and, and surprisingly, *The Inn*, an allegory on the theme of justice which offers this profoundly pessimistic thought: 'Only one thing protects us from our neighbours—and that is order. There is no such thing as justice, we have to make do with order.'

Towards the end of his career Hochwälder ran out of creative steam. Both *Lazaretti* and *Die Prinzessin von Chimay* lack the bite of his earlier works. The *Prinzessin* is a tired attempt to take forward the threads of *The Public Prosecutor*, and *Lazaretti* has been described as an old man's play for old men.

Hochwälder's more allegorical plays continue the theme of security and individual responsibility. In *Donnerstag*, a modern mystery play, an architect, Niklaus Pomfrit, sells his soul to Belial Incorporated in order to gain understanding of the meaning of the world; in *1003* (with clear echoes from *Don Giovanni*) he has become invincible and invulnerable: 'He's like the man in the fairy-tale: his heart has frozen solid.'

What is attainable in allegory is impossible in reality, and the plays in a contemporary setting explore the legacy of the National Socialist security that has been so cruelly dashed from its adherents' grasp. *The Raspberry Picker*, a mischievously malicious farce, neatly pillories the capacity for self-deception and collective amnesia of a group of former Nazis in post-war Austria. Hochwälder milks the device of mistaken identity to good effect as his characters erroneously identify a petty criminal as a former SS official come back to claim his share of war-loot. The discrepancy between the pathetic figure the criminal cuts on stage and the grandiose past he is supposed to embody is not lost on the audience who are in possession of both sides of the story and can draw their own conclusions.

Much of what Hochwälder wrote has a particularly Austrian timbre and loses much in translation. Best approached with an awareness of the social and political context in which he wrote, his dramatic work, like that of Friedrich Schiller before him, uses the theatre as a moral institution to expose and challenge the great and petty tyrannies of life that could otherwise not be brought to book.

—Alan Best

HOFFMANN, E(rnst) T(heodor) A(madeus). Born Ernst Theodor Wilhelm Hoffmann in Königsberg, Germany, 24 January 1776. Educated at Burgschule, Königsberg, 1782–92; studied law at University of Königsberg, 1792–95. Married Maria Thekla Michalina Rorer-Trzynska in 1802; one daughter. In legal civil service: posts in Glogau, 1796–98, Berlin, 1798–1800, Posen, 1800–02, Plozk, 1802–04, Warsaw, 1804–08, and, after Napoleon's defeat, Berlin, 1814–22. Also a composer: Kappelmeister, 1808–09, house composer and designer, 1810–12, Bamberg Theatre, and conductor for Sekonda Company, Leipzig and Dresden, 1813–14; composer of operas, and editor of musical works by Beethoven, Mozart, Gluck, and others, 1809–21. *Died 25 June 1822.*

PUBLICATIONS

Collections

Werke, edited by Georg Ellinger. 15 vols., 1912; 2nd edition, 1927.
Sämtliche Werke, edited by Walter Müller-Seidel and others. 5 vols., 1960–65.
Gesammelte Werke, edited by Rudolf Mingau and Hans-Joachim Kruse. 1976—.
Sämtliche Werke, edited by Wulf Segebrecht, Hartmut Steinecke, and others. 1985—.

Fiction

Fantasiestücke in Callots Manier. 4 vols., 1814–15.
Die Elixiere des Teufels. 1815–16; as *The Devil's Elixir*, translated by R. Gillies, 1824; as *The Devil's Elixirs*, translated by Ronald Taylor, 1963.
Nachtstücke. 2 vols., 1817.
Seltsame Leiden eines Theater-Direktors. 1819.
Klein Zaches genannt Zinnober. 1819.
Die Serapions-Brüder: Gesammelte Erzählungen und Märchen. 4 vols., 1819–21; as *The Serapion Brethren*, translated by Alexander Ewing, 1886–92.
Lebens-Ansichten des Katers Murr. 1820–22.
Prinzessin Brambilla. 1821.
Meister Floh. 1822; as *Master Flea*, translated by G. Sloane, in *Specimens of German Romance*, vol. 2, 1826.
Die letzten Erzählungen. 2 vols., 1825.
Tales, edited by Christopher Lazare. 1959.
The Tales of Hoffmann, translated by Michael Bullock. 1963.
Tales, translated by James Kirkup. 1966.
The Best Tales of Hoffmann, edited by E.F. Bleiler. 1967.
Tales, edited by Victor Lange. 1982.
Tales of Hoffmann, edited and translated by R.J. Hollingdale. 1982.

Play

Die Maske, edited by Friedrich Schnapp. 1923.

Verse

Poetische Werke, edited by Gerhard Seidel. 6 vols., 1958.

Other

Die Vision auf dem Schlachtfelde bei Dresden. 1814.
Briefwechsel, edited by Hans von Müller and Friedrich Schnapp. 3 vols., 1967–69.
Selected Writings, edited and translated by Leonard J. Kent and Elizabeth C. Knight. 2 vols., 1969.
Tagebücher, edited by Friedrich Schnapp. 1971.
Juristische Arbeiten, edited by Friedrich Schnapp. 1973.
Selected Letters of E.T.A. Hoffmann, edited and translated by Johanna C. Sahlin. 1977.

*

Bibliography: *E.T.A. Hoffmann: Bibliographie* by Gerhard Salomon, 1963; *E.T.A. Hoffmann Bibliographie* by Curt Grützmacher, 1981.

Critical Studies: *Hoffmann, Author of the Tales* by Harvey Hewett-Thayer, 1948; *Hoffmann* by Ronald Taylor, 1963;

E.T.A. Hoffmann's Other World: The Romantic Author and His 'New Mythology' by Kenneth Negus, 1965; *Music: The Medium of the Metaphysical in Hoffmann* by Pauline Watts, 1972; *The Shattered Self: E.T.A. Hoffmann's Tragic Vision* by Horst S. Daemmrich, 1973; *E.T.A. Hoffmann and Music* by R. Murray Schafer, 1975; *Hoffmann and the Rhetoric of Terror* by Elizabeth Wright, 1978; *Spellbound: Studies on Mesmerism and Literature* by Maria M. Tatar, 1978; *Baudelaire et Hoffmann* by Rosemary Lloyd, 1979; *Mysticism and Sexuality: E.T.A. Hoffmann* by James M. McGlathery, 2 vols., 1981–85; *Hoffmann's Musical Writings: Kreisleriana, The Poet and Composer, Musical Criticism* by David Charlton, 1989.

* * *

E.T.A. Hoffmann is one of the few authors belonging to German romanticism who has attained international status. As an exponent of 'black romanticism', as it is called in Europe, he was hailed by Baudelaire and scorned by Sir Walter Scott for his preoccupation with the grotesque and the bizarre. He managed to combine this trait with, on the one hand, the most astringent satire, criticizing the injustices of his day in *Meister Floh* (*Master Flea*), and on the other hand, with a modern concern regarding a writer's identity in *Lebens-Ansichten des Katers Murr* [The Life and Opinions of Tomcat Murr].

He made the best possible use of the literary conventions of his day, such as the popular Gothic novel, the epistolary novel, and the short story or novella. He was a diarist and a keen letter writer; like most of his fellow-romanticists he constantly reflected on what he did and on how and why he did it. Interspersed with his fictional writings he developed a theory of representation which accounts for the artist's fascination and concern with subjective phenomena, what he called his 'inner world', and he argued that the persuasiveness of the artist's vision depended on his ability to project this world accurately into the external. But it also depended on a reader, playfully addressed by the narrator as 'dear reader', and placed within the fictional world of the novel, an example of Romantic irony whereby the artist asserted his supremacy. This reader was expected to suspend disbelief and to open himself up to the experience offered by the novels and stories.

Hoffmann's modernity rests in the powerful description of this inner world, later systematically examined by Freud's new science of the mind, a science not like the physical sciences but like the human ones, depending on interpretation of subjective phenomena. One of Freud's key essays, 'The Uncanny', uses one of Hoffmann's stories, 'Der Sandmann' ('The Sand-Man'), in order to capture a certain kind of aesthetic experience. Hoffmann was himself interested in parapsychological phenomena of all kinds, being well acquainted with the work of Anton Mesmer, who played a key role in the history of medicine and psychoanalysis. Hoffmann wrote a number of stories about strange characters, hypnotized and possessed by powerful and threatening figures.

A major theme in Hoffmann's work is that of the divided self, now almost a cliché of Hoffmann scholarship. Whereas in Goethe's *Faust* this can be seen as a benign split, in Hoffmann's work it is usually catastrophic, a prime instance being *Die Elixiere des Teufels* (*The Devil's Elixirs*), though it sometimes resolves itself ironically, as in 'Der goldene Topf' ('The Golden Pot'), or satirically, as in *Prinzessin Brambilla* [Princess Brambilla]. The split is between the hero's desire to belong to the world of art and music, and his desire to partake of the pleasures and security of the life of an average citizen. These dual desires manifest themselves in a simultaneous love for two different women, an idealized figure, usually connected with the world of art and music, and a domestic figure who promises the joys of marriage. This precarious stance also parallels the situation in Hoffmann's life, where he simultaneously maintained a satisfactory marriage and an unconsummated but passionate love for an erstwhile music pupil, from the days when he earned his living by giving music lessons. He was similarly divided in his profession, earning his living in one sphere and following his bent in another, the career of civil servant later replacing that of music teacher.

Those who do not recognize him as an author may be acquainted with him as the inspiration behind Offenbach's opera *The Tales of Hoffmann* and Delibes's ballet *Coppélia*.

—Elizabeth Wright

THE DEVIL'S ELIXIRS (Die Elixiere des Teufels)
Novel by E.T.A. Hoffmann, 1815–16.

Although known principally as a writer of tales, Hoffmann also published two novels, *The Devil's Elixirs* and *Lebens-Ansichten des Katers Murr*, the story of a philistine tomcat intertwined with that of the unhappy musician Johannes Kreisler. The first part of *The Devil's Elixirs* was written in the spring of 1814 at the end of the author's period in Bamberg where he had worked since 1808, principally as composer for the theatre but also as freelance music teacher. The figure of Aurelie in the novel is based on Julia Marc, a young girl to whom Hoffmann gave singing lessons and who proved to be as unattainable to Hoffmann as Aurelie is to the monk Medardus. Although completed in four weeks, the second part was not finished until the summer of the following year. This delay, untypical of Hoffmann, was due primarily to the change in his circumstances; his position at Bamberg was terminated in 1814, but through the help of a friend, he was able to return to Berlin and re-enter the Prussian civil service as a lawyer. He finally secured a publisher in Berlin and Part I appeared in the autumn of 1815, Part II the following spring. Although widely read it did not win critical acclaim and there was no second edition in the author's lifetime. The first English translation appeared in 1824 and was followed in the course of the century by occasional English versions of selective passages from the novel. A new translation by Ronald Taylor in 1963 coincided with the beginning of an intense critical interest in Hoffmann which has yet to wane and which has placed particular emphasis on psychological depths in his work overlooked by much earlier criticism.

The story of the Capuchin monk Medardus who drinks from the forbidden elixirs, leaves the monastery, and becomes involved in deceit, incest, and murder, seems on first reading so heavily indebted to contemporary stories of horror in monastic settings, and in particular to that recounted by Matthew Lewis in *The Monk* (translated into German a year after its appearance in 1796), that what is unique to Hoffmann is often submerged under established Gothic features. These include Medardus's excessive pride in his powers as a preacher, the anguish caused by sexual desire, the unattainability of the beloved, and a Faustian lack of concern for convention exhibited by Medardus's half-sister Euphemie with whom he enjoys a brief incestuous relationship before exchanging glasses and unwittingly causing her to drink from the poisoned wine which she had prepared for him. In accordance with Romantic notions of the fragmentary nature of

human knowledge the interconnections between the characters are only gradually revealed—both to Medardus himself and to the reader. Thus fate and the power of heredity operating as a curse on the unsuspecting hero are central themes of the novel and are graphically represented by a family tree of a ferocious complexity typical of Hoffmann the lawyer. Both Medardus and the reader are left in doubt as to the reality of many of the events of the novel; often the doubt is removed by an ensuing rational explanation, but this is not always the case. The novel also offers a succession of terrifying and grotesque moments, including Medardus's vision of his double rising through the floor to speak to him and the murder, by the double, of Aurelie, the focus of Medardus's sexual anguish, at the moment of her consecration as a nun. But the temptation to classify *The Devil's Elixirs* as no more than an example of the Gothic novel does less than justice to the intricacies of its form and to Hoffmann's abiding concern, supported by a sound knowledge of contemporary medicine, with the workings of the human mind. In particular, Hoffmann's employment of the double, discussed by Freud in his essay on 'The Uncanny' ('Das Unheimlicher') in 1919, underlines what is the most fascinating and enduring theme of the work: the struggle of the individual to maintain sanity and establish a distinct personality in the face of forces which he can only partially comprehend. With his lack of free will and his acquiescence in many of the incidents which befall him, Medardus can be seen as an archetypal anti-classical hero and forerunner of the figures of late 19th-century naturalism.

Many critics have rightly pointed out that *The Devil's Elixirs* is not about religious doubt. Medardus does not question the existence of God, nor does he seek to deny the reality of the sins to which he has succumbed. The strange figure of the painter who mysteriously appears at crucial moments in Medardus's earthly pilgrimage is both a reminder of the curse which lies upon his family and which it is Medardus's task to expiate and also the power of conscience which enables him to overcome his adversary, in his case the impulses inherited from his forebears. Religion provides only the background to the novel, in the form of descriptions of monastic life, based upon Hoffmann's happy experiences as a guest among the Capuchin monks of Bamberg, and of the edifying effect of religious music.

—Roger Jones

HOFMANNSTHAL, Hugo (Laurenz August Hofmann, Edler) von. Born in Vienna, Austria, 1 February 1874. Educated at Akademisches Gymnasium, Vienna, 1884–92; studied law, 1892–94; and romantic philology: dissertation on Pléiade poets, 1897, and habilitation work on Victor Hugo, 1900–01, University of Vienna. Served with 6th Dragoon Regiment in Göding, 1894–95. Married Gertrud Schlesinger in 1901; one daughter and two sons. Full-time writer, from 1901; collaborated with Richard Strauss on operas, from 1909; editor, Österreichische Bibliothek, 1915–17; co-founder, with Max Reinhardt, Salzburg Festival, 1919. *Died 15 July 1929.*

PUBLICATIONS

Collections

Gesammelte Werke in Einzelausgaben, edited by Herbert Steiner. 15 vols., 1945–59.
Selected Writings: Prose, Poems and Verse Plays, Plays and Libretti, edited by Mary Hottinger, Tania and James Stern, and Michael Hamburger. 3 vols., 1952–64.
Sämtliche Werke, edited by Heinz Otto Burger and others. 1975— .

Plays

Gestern (produced 1928). 1896.
Der Tor und der Tod (produced 1898). 1900; as *Death and the Fool*, translated by Elisabeth Walker, 1914; also translated by Michael Hamburger, in *Selected Writings*, 2, 1961; Alfred Schwarz, in *Three Plays*, 1966.
Die Frau im Fenster (as *Madonna Dianora*, produced 1898). In *Theater in Versen*, 1899; as *Madonna Dionara*, translated by Harriet Betty Boas, 1916.
Theater in Versen. 1899.
Der Abenteurer und die Sängerin (produced 1899). In *Theater in Versen*, 1899; revised version, 1909.
Die Hochzeit der Sobeide (as *Sobeide, Abenteurer*, produced 1899). In *Theater in Versen*, 1899; as *The Marriage of Sobeide*, translated by Bayard Quincy Morgan, in *German Classics of the Nineteenth and Twentieth Centuries*, edited by Kuno Francke and William G. Howard, 20, 1916; as *The Marriage of Zobeide*, translated by Christopher Middleton, in *Selected Writings*, 2, 1961.
Das Bergwerk zu Falun, from a story by E.T.A. Hoffmann (produced 1899). 1933; as *The Mine at Falun*, translated by Michael Hamburger, in *Selected Writings*, 2, 1961.
Der Kaiser und die Hexe (produced 1926). In *Die Insel*, 1900; as *The Emperor and the Witch*, translated by Christopher Middleton, in *Selected Writings*, 2, 1961.
Der Tod der Tizian. 1901; as *The Death of Titian*, translated by John Heard, 1920.
Elektra (produced 1903). 1904; revised version, music by Strauss (produced 1909), 1908; as *Electra*, translated by Arthur Symons, 1908; also translated by Alfred Schwarz, in *Selected Writings*, 3, 1964, and in *Three Plays*, 1966.
Das kleine Welttheater; oder, Die Glücklichen (produced 1929). 1903; as *The Little Theatre of the World*, translated by Walter R. Eberlein, 1945; also translated by Michael Hamburger, in *Selected Writings*, 2, 1961.
Das gerettete Venedig, from the play *Venice Preserved* by Otway (produced 1905). 1905.
Ödipus und die Sphinx (produced 1905). 1906.
Kleine Dramen. 2 vols., 1906–07.
Der weisse Fächer (produced 1927). 1907.
Vorspiele. 1908.
Die Begegnung mit Carlo. 1909.
Alkestis, from the play by Euripides, music by Egon Wellesz (produced 1916). 1909.
Lucidor. 1910.
Christinas Heimreise (produced 1910). 1910; as *Christina's Journey Home*, translated by Roy Temple House, 1916.
König Ödipus, from the play by Sophocles (produced 1910). 1910.
Die Heirat wider Willen, from a play by Molière. 1910.
Amor und Psyche. 1911.
Das fremde Mädchen. 1911.
Der Rosenkavalier, music by Strauss (produced 1911). 1911; edited by Willi Schuh, 1971; as *The Rose-Bearer*, translated by Alfred Kalisch, 1912; as *The Cavalier of the Rose*, translated by Christopher Holme, in *Selected Writings*, 3, 1964.
Jedermann: Das Spiel vom Sterben des reichen Mannes (produced 1911). 1911; as *The Play of Everyman*, translated by G. Sterling, 1917; as *The Salzburg Everyman*, translated by M.E. Tafler, 1930.
Ariadne auf Naxos, music by Strauss (produced 1912). 1912; revised version (produced 1916), 1916; as *Ariadne on Naxos*, translated by Alfred Kalisch, 1912.
Josephs Legende (ballet scenario), with Harry Graf Kessler, music by Strauss (produced 1914). 1914.
Die Frau ohne Schatten, music by Strauss (produced 1919). 1916; as *The Woman Without a Shadow*, 1927.
Die grüne Flöte (ballet scenario), music by Mozart (produced 1916). 1925.
Die Lästigen, from a play by Molière (produced 1916). In *Marsyas*, 1917.
Der Bürger als Edelmann, from a play by Molière, music by Strauss (produced 1918). 1918.
Dame Kobold, from a play by Calderón (produced 1920). 1920.
Der Schwierige (produced 1921). 1921; as *The Difficult Man*, translated by Willa Muir, in *Selected Writings*, 3, 1964.
Florindo und die Unbekannte (produced 1921). 1923.
Das Salzburger grosse Welttheater, from a play by Calderón (produced 1922). 1922; as *The Salzburg Great Theatre of the World*, translated by Vernon Watkins, in *Selected Writings*, 3, 1964.
Prima Ballerina (ballet scenario). 1923(?).
Der Unbestechliche (produced 1923). With *Der Schwierige*, 1958.
Die Ruinen von Athen (produced 1924). 1925.
Der Turm, from a play by Calderón. 1925; revised version (produced 1928), 1927; as *The Tower*, translated by Michael Hamburger, in *Selected Writings*, 3, 1964; also translated by Alfred Schwarz, in *Three Plays*, 1966.
Die ägyptische Helena, music by Strauss (produced 1928). 1928; as *Helen in Egypt*, translated by Alfred Kalisch, 1928.
Semiramis: Die beiden Götter. 1933.
Arabella, music by Strauss (produced 1933). 1933; as *Arabella*, translated by John Gutman, 1955; also translated by Nora Wydenbruck and Christopher Middleton, in *Selected Writings*, 3, 1964.
Dramatische Entwürfe aus dem Nachlass, edited by Heinrich Zimmer. 1936.
Danae; oder, Die Vernunftheirat. 1952.
Three Plays (includes *Death and the Fool*; *Electra*; *The Tower*), translated by Alfred Schwarz. 1966.

Fiction

Prinz Eugen der edle Ritter. 1905.
Das Märchen der 672. Nacht und andere Erzählungen (includes 'Ein Brief' [The Chandos Letter]). 1905.
Die Frau ohne Schatten. 1919.
Andreas; oder, Die Vereinigten. 1932; as *Andreas; or, The United*, translated by Marie D. Hottinger, 1936.
Four Stories, edited by Margaret Jacobs. 1968.

Verse

Ausgewählte Gedichte. 1903.
Die gesammelten Gedichte. 1907.
Die Gedichte und kleinen Dramen. 1911.
Lyrical Poems, translated by Charles Wharton Stork. 1918.

Gedichte. 1922.
Nachlese der Gedichte. 1934.

Other

Stüdie über die Entwicklung des Dichters Victor Hugo. 1901;
   as *Victor Hugo*, 1904; as *Versuch über Victor Hugo*, 1925.
Unterhaltungen über literarische Gegenstände. 1904.
Die prosaischen Schriften gesammelt. 2 vols., 1907; vol. 3,
   1917.
Hesperus: Ein Jahrbuch, with Rudolf Borchardt and Rudolf
   Alexander Schröder. 1909.
*Grete Wiesenthal in Amor und Psyche und das fremde
   Mädchen*. 1911.
Die Wege und die Begegnungen. 1913.
Rodauner Nachträge. 3 vols., 1918.
Reden und Aufsätze. 1921.
Buch der Freunde. 1922; edited by Ernst Zinn, 1965.
Gesammelte Werke. 6 vols., 1924; revised edition, 3 vols.,
   1934.
Augenblicke in Griechenland. 1924.
Früheste Prosastücke. 1926.
Grillparzers politisches Vermächtnis. 1926.
Loris: Die Prosa des jungen Hoffmansthals. 1930.
Die Berührung der Sphären. 1931.
Briefe. 2 vols., 1935–37.
Briefwechsel, with Anton Wildgans, edited by Joseph A. von
   Bradish. 1935.
Briefwechsel, with Stefan George, edited by Robert
   Boehringer. 1938; revised edition, 1953.
Briefwechsel, with Richard Strauss, edited by Franz and Alice
   Strauss. 1952; revised edition, edited by Willi Schuh, 1954;
   as *Correspondence*, translated by Hans Hammelmann and
   Ewald Osers, 1961.
Briefe der Freundschaft, with Eberhard von Bodenhausen,
   edited by Dora von Bodenhausen. 1953.
Briefwechsel, with Rudolf Borchardt, edited by Marie Luise
   Borchardt and Herbert Steiner. 1954.
Briefwechsel, with Carl J. Burckhardt, edited by Burckhardt.
   1956.
Sylvia in 'Stern', edited by Martin Stern. 1959.
Briefwechsel, with Arthur Schnitzler, edited by Theresa Nickl
   and Heinrich Schnitzler. 1964.
Briefwechsel, with Helene von Nostitz, edited by Oswalt von
   Nostitz. 1965.
Briefwechsel, with Edgar Karl von Bebenburg, edited by
   Mary E. Gilbert. 1966.
Briefwechsel, with Leopold von Andrian. 1968.
Briefwechsel, with Willy Haas. 1968.
Briefwechsel, with Harry Graf Kessler. 1968.
Briefwechsel, with Josef Redlich. 1971.
Briefwechsel, with Richard Beer-Hofmann. 1972.
Briefwechsel, with Max Rychner, Samuel and Hedwig
   Fischer, Oscar Bie, and Moritz Heimann, edited by
   Claudia Mertz-Rychner and others. 1973.
Briefwechsel, with Ottonie Gräfin Degenfeld, edited by
   Marie Therese Miller-Degenfeld. 1974.
Briefwechsel 1899–1925, with Rainer Maria Rilke, edited by
   Rudolf Hirsch and Ingeborg Schnack. 1978.
Briefwechsel, with Max Mell, edited by Margret Dietrich and
   Heinz Kindermann. 1982.
Briefwechsel, with Ria Schmujlow-Claasen. 1982.
Briefwechsel, with Paul Zifferer, edited by Hilde Burger.
   1983.

Editor, *Deutsche Erzähler*. 4 vols., 1912.

*

Bibliography: *Hofmannsthal: Bibliographie des Schrifttums
1892–1963*, 1966, and *Hugo von Hofmannsthal: Bibliographie: Werke, Briefe, Gespräche, Übersetzungen, Verton-
ungen*, 1972, both by Horst Weber; *Hugo von Hofmannsthal
Bibliographie 1964–1976* by H.A. and U. Koch, 1976;
'Hofmannsthal Bibliographie' by C. Köttelwesch, in
Hofmannsthal Blätter from 1979.

Critical Studies: *Hugo von Hofmannsthal* by Hans
Hammelmann, 1957; *Hofmannsthal's Festival Dramas* by B.
Coughlin, 1964; *Hofmannsthal's Novel 'Andreas'* by David
Miles, 1972; *Hugo von Hofmannsthal: Three Essays* by
Michael Hamburger, 1972; *Hofmannsthal and the French
Symbolist Tradition* by Steven P. Sondrup, 1976; *Hugo von
Hofmannsthal* by Lowell A. Bangerter, 1977; *The Banal
Object: Theme and Thematics in Proust, Rilke, Hofmanns-
thal, and Sartre* by Naomi Segal, 1981; *Hugo von
Hofmannsthal: Commemorative Essays* edited by W.E. Yuill
and Patricia Howe, 1981; *Hugo von Hofmannsthal and His
Time: The European Imagination, 1860–1920* by Hermann
Broch, 1984; *Hofmannsthal and Symbolism: Art and Life in
the Work of a Modern Poet* by Thomas A. Kovach, 1985;
Animal Symbolism in Hofmannsthal's Works by Helen
Frink, 1987; *Hugo von Hofmannsthal: The Theatres of
Consciousness* by Benjamin Bennett, 1988; *Narrative
Transgression and the Foregrounding of Language in Selected
Prose Works of Poe, Valéry and Hofmannsthal* by Leroy T.
Day, 1988; *Selten Augenblicke: Interpretations of Poems by
Hugo von Hofmannsthal* by Margit Resch, 1989; *Schnitzler,
Hofmannsthal and the Austrian Theatre* by W.E. Yates, 1992.

*   *   *

Hugo von Hofmannsthal is chiefly remembered as the
successful librettist who partnered Richard Strauss. Their
operas, including the famous *Der Rosenkavalier* (*The
Cavalier of the Rose*), are lively and powerful, rich in register
and motif.

Hofmannsthal's fame, however, neither begins nor ends
with Strauss. He had enjoyed some 15 years of precocious
celebrity before their collaboration began. His schoolboy
lyrics established his reputation as one of the foremost young
poets in Vienna. Even his earliest works, among them
Gestern [Yesterday], *Der Tor und der Tod* (*Death and the
Fool*), and *Die Hochzeit der Sobeide* (*The Marriage of
Zobeide*), reveal his remarkable insight into some of the
questions most crucial to man: the passing of time, the problem of death, the dangers of excessive aestheticism, the role
of women in society. His range, even in the 1890s, is vast.

The turn of the century brought a change of style. There
were several reasons for this change. One, metaphysical
reason prompting him to abandon his lyrical mode, is expressed in the fictitious Chandos Letter. A more immediate
reason can be found in his desire to stage his dramas more
successfully. They made good reading, but as theatre they
were indicted by critics as 'lukewarm' and 'boring'.
Hofmannsthal began to write with a specific theatre in mind,
that of Max Reinhardt in Berlin. He made increasing use of
stage technology in order to enhance the sensuous impact of
his works. Lighting, music, the rhythms of movement are all
incorporated into the text, as the stage directions of the
powerfully visual *Elektra* (*Electra*) demonstrate.

Further factors influencing Hofmannsthal's change of style
include the literary trend of 'anti-erotic' writers such as
Wilde, Strindberg, and Wedekind, and also the writings of
Freud. Their influence shows most overtly in the so-called

'Greek' plays, *Electra* and *Ödipus und die Sphinx* [Oedipus and the Sphinx], where Hofmannsthal probes the depths of sexual antagonism, repression, and perversion—a radical departure from his Sophoclean model. Greek myth is here used to underline the most primitive aspects of human behaviour. Hofmannsthal was to return to the symbolic world of myth in his operas *Ariadne auf Naxos* (*Ariadne on Naxos*) and *Die ägyptische Helena* (*Helen in Egypt*), explaining in his late essay on the latter work that mythological opera was the only form in which the 'atmosphere of the present' could be expressed adequately.

Hofmannsthal had already explored other possible modes of expression. Moving away from the 'armchair playlets' of the 1890s, and the Greek plays of 1903 and 1905, he wrote his *Jedermann* (*The Play of Everyman*), and *Das Salzburger grosse Welttheater* (*The Salzburg Great Theatre of the World*), expressing fundamental human truths in the universalizing form of the medieval mystery play. Social satires, such as *Der Schwierige* (*The Difficult Man*), again treat universal themes, but this time in the context of modern Austria. Yet another mode is the magical setting of *Die Frau ohne Schatten* (*The Woman Without a Shadow*), and of *Der Turm* (*The Tower*) which, with its oblique references to politics and its background of language scepticism, constitutes one of Hofmannsthal's most difficult plays.

The range and density of Hofmannsthal's poems and plays, essays and correspondence, account for the continuing interest in these works today.

—Sally McMullen (Croft)

ANDREAS
Fiction by Hugo von Hofmannsthal, 1932 (written 1912–13).

Andreas, a prose fragment of some 60 pages, constitutes probably about a quarter of a planned novel. It was begun in 1907 and written mainly in 1912–13; Hofmannsthal returned to it from time to time but failed to complete it. It was published posthumously in *Corona*, 1930; 50 pages of synopsis, sketches, notes, and miscellaneous reflections found in Hofmannsthal's unpublished papers were added in the 1932 edition, but it was not until 1982 that all the author's extensive and labyrinthine notes were published.

Set in 1778, *Andreas* recounts the experiences of the 22-year-old Andreas von Ferschengelder, notably a series of erotic encounters, during a journey to and subsequent sojourn in Venice. Blending realism and fantasy in a manner, as one critic has put it, half-way between Goethe and Kafka, *Andreas* enriches the traditional mainstream German genre of the Bildungsroman which charts an individual's development towards maturity, self-understanding, and a firm sense of identity, with elements of both the older picaresque novel and the more modern form of symbolic fantasy.

In Venice Andreas recalls how he fell in love with the 17-year-old Romana Finazzer, amid the dignity and stability of the farming communities of the Carinthian mountains, living in close contact with nature and deeply rooted in Christianity. In Romana Hofmannsthal embodied an ideal of purity, innocence, and reverence for the sacrament of marriage, combined with vitality, sensuality, and happy domesticity. Her name suggests the Roman Catholicism that was of central importance to the author, as do those of the two characters who figure most prominently in the proposed continuation: the schizophrenic Maria and the mysterious and ambiguous

Maltese Knight Sacramozo (who is sometimes called Sagredo), part spiritual mentor, part alter ego.

Andreas is, however, not yet ready for Romana. Entirely without sexual experience, which he both intensely desires and fears as a 'murder in the dark', he would like to go straight from the painful confusions of young manhood to the serene happiness of marriage and parenthood. His encounter with Romana transforms him: it is 'allomatic', to use Hofmannsthal's favourite ad hoc coinage. Yet it leads not to courtship and marriage, but to an exploration of the complexities of his sexual nature against the bizarre backcloth of Venice, where everything is incongruous, unpredictable, and confusing, and where anything is possible, especially in the erotic sphere.

In Venice Andreas becomes involved with a series of women whose conflicting conceptions of sexuality compel him to confront his confusions: Zustina, the 15-year-old daughter of an impoverished aristocratic family, who coolly offers her virginity as a lottery prize to a selected circle of wealthy sponsors; her elder sister Nina, a *poule de luxe* beyond Andreas's pocket; Maria/Mariquita, whose portrait owes much to Hofmannsthal's reading of Morton Prince's study in schizophrenia *The Dissociation of a Personality* (1906), and whose two warring personalities, one devout and ascetic, the other worldly and sensual, recall a number of somewhat similar pairings in Hofmannsthal's works, e.g. Ariadne and Zerbinetta, Arabella and Zdenka, Elektra and Chrysotemis, Helene and Antoinette.

Hofmannsthal's original proposed title was *Andreas; oder, Die Vereinigten* (*Andreas; or, the United*). The multiple meanings of 'united' indicate his central concerns: it signifies lovers united, either physically or spiritually, but also characters who are united in themselves, who have overcome that dissonance between the spiritual and the physical that torments Andreas and is seen in an extreme forms in Maria/Mariquita, and have succeeded in shaping out of the bewildering jumble of a fragmented self, with all its violent and shameful elements, a hard core of ethical conviction and personal and social commitment. This integration requires the acceptance of complexity and imperfection: Andreas has to learn to understand that there is no health without an awareness of sickness, no innocence without an admission of guilt. (In his conception of Andreas's ethical-religious crisis Hofmannsthal was greatly influenced by William James's *The Varieties of Religious Experience* (1902), especially James's account of the 'sick soul'). The 'united' are also those who are united with the whole of nature (as in Sacramozo's mystical suicide), united with God, and those who are able to grasp the mystery of life by uniting within themselves its surfaces and its depths.

In Hofmannsthal's later notes the conception and scope changed and broadened to encompass the entire intellectual, spiritual, and social development of Andreas's problematic personality. It acquired a new title: *Andreas; oder, Die Verwandelten* [Andreas; or, the Transformed], and Hofmannsthal stressed the importance of the 'more profound, mysterious layer hidden beneath Andreas's ostensibly purely private destiny'. Much critical writing on *Andreas* has accordingly been devoted to unravelling its deeper symbolic meanings, especially with reference to the posthumously published parts. These were, however, not written for publication and are often tantalizingly cryptic. Generalized abstractions suggest the novel's deeper themes, vivid specific incidents and details confirm Hofmannsthal's narrative skill, but no clear overall conception emerges, and scholars have reached widely differing conclusions as to how Hofmannsthal might have ended the novel. Some notes indicate that Andreas will eventually marry Romana and have children, and indeed grandchildren, others that he will fail to win her. Other notes suggest that Maria/Mariquita will bring him the yearned-for harmonious totality of erotic fulfilment, as 'lover, sister, mother, saint, the *whole* woman . . . belonging to God, sinning without sin'. Notes from the 1920s show a continuing interest in 'M$_1$ and M$_2$', with virtually no reference to Romana, but in Hofmannsthal's very last notes, union with Romana reappears as the 'goal to be striven for'.

Hofmannsthal struggled, as in the prose version of *Die Frau ohne Schatten* [The Woman Without a Shadow], to find an adequate vehicle for his dense and intricate web of ideas, but in *Andreas* his notes and sketches failed to coalesce into a coherent symbolic narrative. But his profound understanding of human behaviour is evident throughout, and his writing, while allusive, symbolic, and often cryptic, has a richness and beauty that have won widespread admiration.

—D.E. Jenkinson

THE DIFFICULT MAN (Der Schwierige)
Play by Hugo von Hofmannsthal, 1921.

Hofmannsthal's earliest recorded notes (dating from 1909) on his comic masterpiece, *The Difficult Man*, sketch out his original idea for a 'character comedy', light in atmosphere and comprising 'a chain of conversations' which lead eventually to a resolution kept *in suspenso* over three acts. Later there is a shift in emphasis to the traditional Viennese 'Konversationsstück', or social comedy as the theatrical model from which he derives his form. The original plot consisted of no more than this: a young lady with several suitors has to decide between them, and the obliging but inept confidant, caught up in the match-making, finally ensnares himself. The finished play (1921) involves 16 characters of greatly contrasting personalities, manners, and modes of speech, who interact in the pursuit of their diverse aspirations, ambitions, and 'intentions' (a key term), creating a network of subtle social relationships, full of ironic nuances and verbal subtleties. It is both a play about the passing historical moment which marked the end of the Hapsburg era with its culture and class structure, while it is also a finely gauged critique of language as the badge of that culture. The somewhat precious, artificial diction the playwright employs shows up language as the flawed but indispensable vehicle of communication. The terms 'misunderstanding' and 'confusion' are leitmotifs of the text. Though the action is set towards the end of World War I (the year is 1917), references to these momentous times are always kept peripheral and deliberately low-key. Hofmannsthal was not a Naturalist; he was heir to the tradition of high comedy which followed the classical models of Molière, Goldoni, and Lessing. His dramatic technique was suggestive rather than representational, allusive rather than mimetic, and he was naturally given to symbolic statement as he indicates in one of his aphorisms: 'Whoever takes the social idea in any but a symbolic sense misses the mark'. In choosing a contemporary subject, he insinuates a timeless element.

This ironic comedy deftly captures the salient features of that section of Viennese society which had outlived itself and merely perpetuated a shadowy charade of aristocratic ways. As the pompous Prussian Baron Neuhoff is moved to remark: 'All these people you meet here don't in fact exist any more. They're nothing more than shadows. No one who moves in these salons belongs to the real world in which the intellectual

crises of the century are decided'. Hofmannsthal's conviction that 'reality' may not be embodied in the theatre, that it cannot be translated wholesale onto the stage in the manner advocated by the Naturalists, but remains an illusion, gives rise to his technique of a selective perspectivism. The vivid illusion of a complete unit of society, differentiated, full of interesting contrasts, levels of intelligence, tone, and points of view, is produced by the playwright through a kaleidoscopic method of ever-changing groupings and relationships. It is a dramatic technique comparable to Chekhov's, as is his choice of the essentially passive hero. The 48 scenes which make up the three acts of *The Difficult Man* display an ever-shifting pattern of relationships or significant links between characters. Each encounter and interaction is nicely calculated for its ironic effect, as contrasts are explored: convention is opposed to the unconventional, posing to sincerity, pretention to veracity, philandering to love. The new and the old order of social values are brought into confrontation from the very first scene when the image of his master in discretion and decorum, the retiring manservant, attempts the hopeless task of instructing his uncouth, inquisitive replacement in the niceties of serving a 'difficult' master whose every mood should be judged by dumb gesture.

At the centre of the play with its shifting configurations there stands the passive figure of Hans Karl Bühl, a bachelor aged 39, a man who has difficulty in making his mind up about everything, not least in the use of words. He is also at the centre of speculation by all and sundry. As the embodiment of social complications, he is an unfailing source of misunderstanding and involuntary embarrassments. Whether he says something or remains silent, he creates confusion. He causes endless misunderstandings not by design, but because the society about him consistently misreads him. They attribute intentions to him where he has none. They seek for nuances of meaning where none are to be found. While most find him infuriatingly enigmatic, others believe they can read him like a book. All are mistaken, except the beautiful Helene Altenwyl whose intuition and intelligence afford her privileged insight into the heart and mind of the man she has loved since her teens. In two exquisite private exchanges between them (Act II, scene 14 and Act III, scene 8) the wavering complexities of the hero find more than their match in the profound sensibilities and certainties of the loving woman. The first of these dialogues opens with a statement by Hans Karl on the uses of that fickle medium, language: 'Everything in this world is brought about by speech. Of course, it's a little ridiculous for anyone to imagine that the carefully chosen word can produce some God-almighty impact within a life where everything, after all, quite simply depends on the ultimate, the inexpressible. Speech is based upon an indecent estimation of oneself'. The problematical nature of language (a constant theme in Hofmannsthal and most consummately expressed in *A Letter* of 1902) is identified with, and given voice through, the complicated character of Hans Karl. In this comedy theme and form converge to the point of total interdependence, creating the perfect ironic construct in which the medium and the message are one. Though Hans Karl may call himself 'the most uncomplicated person in the world', the action is strewn with evidence of his propensity for causing misapprehension and confusion. He may believe that he is an unmotivated free agent as he moves about trying to avoid 'chronic misunderstandings', but he himself becomes a victim of that 'bizarre notion' of a 'higher necessity' which he professes to his apish nephew Stani. When this difficult hero attempts to plead another suitor's cause to Helene, ultimate questions of a 'higher power', predestined love, and the sanctity of marriage are playfully introduced and glimpsed, as it were, through a veil of mystical allusion. 'Necessity lies within you' he openly confesses to his intended. Gradually, yet inescapably, he becomes engrossed in the business of proposing, and as his sense of purpose falters, he grows more eloquent. He tells her of his dream-like experience of being buried within the trenches at the Front, thereby divulging how he gained revelatory insight into the external meaning of marriage. This artless and moving confession assures Helene of what Hans Karl scarcely knows himself: that they are and always have been destined for each other. Moral seriousness is so finely interfused with a lightness of ironic texture in this comedy that no trace of gravity remains. The author's achievement wholly conforms with his own remark: 'Depth must be hidden: where? On the surface'.

—Alexander Stillmark

THE TOWER (Der Turm)
Play by Hugo von Hofmannsthal, 1925.

Hofmannsthal's preoccupation with the material that provided the plot for his last major drama goes back to October 1901, when he began a 'very free' verse translation of Calderón's *La vida es sueño* (*Life Is a Dream*). He put this work aside in spring 1902 without, however, abandoning the project altogether. In the summer of that year he turned to it again, now opting at first for a prose adaptation to be titled *The Tower*, which was to be part of a cycle of Calderón transcriptions for Vienna's Burgtheater. The play that had begun as a poetic 'descent into the cavernous kingdom of the self' had by now assumed a strong socio-political dimension, the result of the author's profound disorientation at the end of World War I. Through the revival of the allegorical baroque *Trauerspiel* (literally, mourning play), this testimonial tragedy explores the conflicting forces that shape history. In its final form, though, it shows the destruction of spiritual culture at the hands of ruthless power, and it points toward a future of dictatorial oppression in which the interplay of multifarious rights, interests, and justifications have been obliterated and the world is totally out of balance.

The Tower exists in two distinct versions, each with extensive variants and showing significant changes in style, dramatic density, and thematic development. The first version was finished in November 1924 and published in 1925; the second was completed and published, after extensive consultations with the director Max Reinhardt and other friends, in autumn 1927. The drama was first performed on 4 February 1928, concurrently at the Prinzregententheater in Munich and at the Hamburg Schauspielhaus.

The action of the play is situated in a kingdom of Poland whose 'atmosphere is more legendary than historical' and resembles that of the 16th century. Its protagonist is Sigismund, King Basilius' only son, who was abandoned after birth and has been kept in solitary confinement in a remote tower for the last six years. Unaware of his noble lineage, the young prince has found a protector in Julian who plans to use him for his own advancement to high office and against a monarch who, frightened by a prophecy that his heir will depose him, clings to his claim of absolute power with frantic determination. When a war he ill-advisedly started is lost, and widespread misery leads to uprisings, Julian seeks the official recognition of his charge by arranging a meeting between the royal father and his son. But their encounter fails to bring about a reconciliation when Basilius, insisting on his divine right to demand unquestioning obedience, tests Sigismund's

profession of loyalty by ordering him to kill Julian whom he accuses of treason. Outraged by this wanton offence against elementary humanity, the hitherto passive youth takes impetuous action. With Julian's help he subdues the king and wrests from him the insignia of his authority. Both rebels are soon overpowered by the courtiers, however, and a disillusioned Sigismund is returned to his prison. Even the offer to lead a seditious army cannot rouse him from his dejection. Once again, all reality is for him but a dream and the 'tower' of his inwardness is the only true world he acknowledges. To be sure, he does not dissuade a people in revolt from liberating him and proclaiming him their king, but he finds it impossible to break out of his self-absorbed seclusion. Thus Julian, who had secretly fanned the rebellion, seizes power, but only for a short time. For he is shot as the soldier Olivier, the 'red Satan', takes control of the rabble. A master of demagogy and diabolical in the use of force, this populist usurper tries to coerce Sigismund into joining his cause, thus creating not an alliance of equals but a military dictatorship with the appearance of historical legitimacy. But his power depends entirely on the strength of his plundering troops. When a force of peasant patriots vanquishes his army, his death goes almost unnoticed, as a new figure enters the political arena. He is an orphan and the leader of homeless children who, as a pacific messiah, will inaugurate a new secular order based on modesty and devotion to justice and peace. He takes the place of the 'fraternal' Sigismund who dies after Olivier's mistress, a gypsy with the gift of conjuring forth the buried bones of the departed, cuts him with a poisonous dagger. His last words are the plea: 'Bear witness: I was there. Even though nobody recognized me.'

Hofmannsthal cut much of the 'atmospheric' dialogue and some merely 'colourful' figures (e.g. the gypsy) from the 'new version' of 1927. He also changed the last act drastically, above all replacing its utopian vagueness with an ending of stark pessimism. Now a coup d'état of the high nobility forces an ignoble Basilius to abdicate in Sigismund's favour. But the new king dismisses their council and retains only Julian as his adviser, without acting, however, on his pragmatic policies. This renders him powerless against Olivier who has quickly risen to dictatorial power by eliminating all of his opponents. In the end, the king is murdered in an ambush when he refuses to serve a brutal regime as a legitimating puppet.

Unable to envision a society shaped by democratic compromises and disenchanted with the idea of a populist restoration of a reformed aristocracy, Hofmannsthal's spiritual conservatism could foresee only the nihilism of mob rule. Consequently, he refused to recognize any power, even the transcendent one of a judging God, as justifiable authority. Instead he came to fear that all institutions of public life are corrupt and fated to destruction ('in der Hand der Fatalität') when a crisis of universal dimensions has severed the natural familial bonds of spirit and might. He saw secular authority either as driven by blind ambition toward self-aggrandizement or as destroyed by profound depression and haughty self-isolation. Worldly power can therefore be expressed only in absolute dichotomies: on the one hand there is rebellious anarchy, which defines the momentum of policies, and on the other, chiliastic utopianism which offers refuge for an autonomous but disinherited mind. It is this irreconcilable polarity that signifies the present inability of history to rejuvenate itself.

The search for an ever more elusive synthesis of spirit and 'life' defines both the play's extraordinary ambition and its artistic failure. Its subtle network of suggestive nuances is forced to support an inordinate weight of allegorical abstractness, and its genteel antiquarian language often strains at sustaining the sombre tone of meaningful statements. Its structure and the complexity of its theme rather than the dramatic potential inherent in its characters have made *The Tower* more a reading drama than a part of the German theatrical repertoire.

—Michael Winkler

HOLBERG, Ludvig. Born in Bergen, Norway (then part of the Kingdom of Norway and Denmark), 3 December 1684. Studied at school and university in Bergen; University of Copenhagen, 1702–04; travelled in the Netherlands and Germany, 1704–06; travelled in England, and studied in Oxford and London, 1706–08. Tutor in Germany, 1708–09; at Borch's College, Copenhagen, 1709–14; appointed unpaid associate professor at University of Copenhagen, 1714, but spent the time of the appointment travelling in the Low Countries, Paris, and Rome, 1714–16; professor of metaphysics, 1717, professor of Latin, 1720, member of the University Council, 1720, professor of history and geography, 1730, and University bursar (*quaestor*), 1737–51, University of Copenhagen; wrote for Montaigu's troupe at the newly organized Danish Theatre, the Lille Grønnegade Theatre, Copenhagen, from 1722 until its closure in 1728; ceased writing plays during the reign of Christian VI, 1730–46, who banned all theatrical activity in Denmark and Norway; unofficial adviser and writer for the Kongelige Teater [Theatre Royal], Copenhagen, established shortly after the succession of Frederik V, in 1748. Made a baron, 1747. *Died 28 January 1754.*

PUBLICATIONS

Collections

Udvalgte skrifter, edited by Knud Lyne Rahbek. 21 vols., 1804–14.
Samlede skrifter, edited by Carl S. Petersen. 18 vols., 1913–63.
Samtlige komedier i tre bind, edited by F.J. Billeskov Jansen. 3 vols., 1984.

Plays (selection)

Den politiske kandestøber (produced 1722). 1723; as *The Blue-Apron Statesman*, translated by T. Weber, 1885; as *The Political Tinker*, translated by Oscar James Campbell, Jr and Frederick Schenck, in *Comedies*, 1914.
Den vægelsindede (produced 1722). 1724; as *The Weathercock*, translated by Henry Alexander, in *Four Plays*, 1946.
Jeppe på bjerget; eller, Den forvandlede bonde (produced 1722). 1723; as *Jepp on the Hill*, translated by Waldemar C. Westergaard and Martin B. Ruud, 1906; as *Jeppe of the Hill*, translated by Oscar James Campbell, Jr and Frederick Schenck, in *Comedies*, 1914; also translated by M. Jagendorf, 1953; as *Barney Brae: A Comedy Set in Northern Ireland*, translated and adapted by G.V.C. Young, 1980.

Mester Gert Westphaler; eller, Den meget talende barbeer (produced 1722). 1723; as *The Loquacious Barber*, translated by W.H.H. Chambers, 1903; translated as *Mester Gert Westphaler; or, The Very Loquacious Barber*, in *The Drama 17*, edited by A. Bates, 1903–04; as *The Talkative Barber*, translated by Henry Alexander, in *Seven One-Act Plays*, 1950.
Jean de France; eller, Hans Fritz (produced 1722). 1731; translated (from the German) as *Jean de France; or, Hans Fritz*, 1922.
Nye-Aars prologos [New Year's Prologue] (produced 1723).
Erasmus Montanus (produced 1748). 1723; as *Erasmus Montanus*, translated by T. Weber, 1885; also translated by Oscar James Campbell, Jr and Frederick Schenck in *Comedies*, 1914; also translated in *The Chief Modern Dramatists*, edited by B. Mathews, 1916.
Den ellefte Juni [The Eleventh of June] (produced 1723). 1724.
Barselstuen [Room of the Child's Birth] (produced 1723). 1731.
Komedier. 3 vols., 1723–25.
Det arabiske pulver (produced 1724). 1724; as *The Arabian Powder*, translated by Henry Alexander, in *Seven One-Act Plays*, 1950; also translated by Reginald Spink, in *Three Comedies*, 1957.
Julestuen (produced 1724). 1724; as *The Christmas Party*, translated by Henry Alexander, in *Seven One-Act Plays*, 1950.
Mascarade (produced 1724). 1724; as *Masquerade*, translated by Henry Alexander, in *Four Plays*, 1946.
Ulysses von Ithacia; eller, En tysk comoedie [Ulysses of Ithaca; or, A German Comedy] (produced 1724). 1725.
Diderich Menschenschreck (produced 1724). 1731; as *Captain Bombastes Thunderton*, translated by H.W.L. Hime, in *Three Comedies*, 1912; as *Diderich the Terrible*, translated by Henry Alexander, in *Seven One-Act Plays*, 1950.
Henrik og Pernille (produced 1724). 1731; as *Henry and Pernilla*, translated by H.W.L. Hime, in *Three Comedies*, 1912.
Melampe [Melampe] (produced 1724). 1725.
Kilderejsen (produced 1724). 1725; as *The Healing Spring*, translated by Reginald Spink, in *Three Comedies*, 1957.
Jacob von Tyboe; eller, Den stortalende soldat [Jacob von Tyboe; or, The Braggart Soldier]. 1725.
Uden hoved og hale [Without Head or Tail]. 1725.
Den stundeløse (produced 1726). 1731; as *Scatterbrains*, translated by H.W.L. Hime, in *Three Comedies*, 1912; as *The Fussy Man*, translated by Henry Alexander, in *Four Plays*, 1946.
Den pantsatte bondedreng (produced 1726). 1731; as *The Peasant in Pawn*, translated by Henry Alexander, in *Seven One-Act Plays*, 1950; as *The Transformed Peasant*, translated by Reginald Spink, in *Three Comedies*, 1957.
Den danske comoedies liigbegiængelse [The Danish Drama's Funeral] (produced 1727). 1746.
Hexerie; eller, Blind allarm [Witchcraft; or, False Alarm] (produced 1750). 1731.
Det lykkelige skibbrud [The Fortuitous Shipwreck] (produced 1754). 1731.
De usynlige (produced 1747). 1731; as *The Masked Ladies*, translated by Henry Alexander, in *Four Plays*, 1946.
Pernilles korte frøikenstand [Pernille's Short Ladyship] (produced 1747). 1731.
Den honnete Ambition [Social Aspiration] (produced 1747). 1731.
Don Ranudo de Colibrados; eller, Fattigdom og hoffærdighed [Don Ranudo de Colibrados; or, Poverty and Pride]. 1745.

Sganarels reyse til det Philosophiske Land (produced c.1751–53). 1751; as *Sganarel's Journey to the Land of the Philosophers*, translated by Henry Alexander, in *Seven One-Act Plays*, 1950.
Plutus (produced 1751). 1753.
Abracadabra; eller, Huus-spøgelse [Abracadabra; or, The House-Ghost] (produced 1752).
Den forvandlede brudgom (produced 1882). 1753; as *The Changed Bridegroom*, translated by Henry Alexander, in *Seven One-Act Plays*, 1950.
Republigven; eller, Det gemene Bedste [The Republic; or, The General Good] (produced 1754). 1754.
Philosophus udi egen Inbildung (produced 1754). 1754.
Three Comedies (includes *Henry and Pernilla*; *Captain Bombastes Thunderton*; *Scatterbrains*), translated by H.W.L. Hime. 1912.
Comedies (includes *Erasmus Montanus*; *Jeppe of the Hill*; *The Political Tinker*), translated by Oscar James Campbell, Jr and Frederick Schenck. 1914.
Four Plays (includes *The Fussy Man*; *The Masked Ladies*; *The Weathercock*; *Masquerade*), translated by Henry Alexander. 1946.
Seven One-Act Plays (includes *The Talkative Barber*; *The Arabian Powder*; *The Christmas Party*; *Diderich the Terrible*; *The Peasant in Pawn*; *Sganarel's Journey to the Land of the Philosophers*; *The Changed Bridegroom*), translated by Henry Alexander. 1950.
Three Comedies (includes *The Transformed Peasant*; *The Arabian Powder*; *The Healing Spring*), translated by Reginald Spink. 1957.

Fiction

Nicolai Klimii iter subterraneum (in Latin). 1741; as *A Journey to the World Under-Ground*, translated 1742, as *The Journey of Niels Klim to the World Underground*, edited by James McNelis, Jr, 1960; as *Niels Klim's Journey under the Ground*, translated by John Gierlow, 1845.

Verse

Peder Paars. 2 vols., 1719–20; in part as *Peter Paars*, translated and adapted by Bergliot Stromsoe, 1862, complete version, translated by Stromsoe, 1962.
Opuscula latina. 2 vols., 1737–43.
Mindre poetiske skrifter. 1746.

Other

Introduction til de formemste Europæiske Rigers Historier. 1711; revised edition, 1728.
Introduction til natur og folke-retten [Introduction to Natural Law]. 1715; revised edition, 1734.
Epistola ad virum perillustrem [Letter to a Person of Renown]. 1728; in part as *Virtues and Faults of Some European Nations*, translated by J. Christian Bay, 1958.
Dannemarks og Norges beskrivelse. 1729; in part as *The History of Norway*, translated by A.A. Feldborg, 1817.
Den danske Skue-Plads. 5 vols., 1731–54.
Dannemarks riges historie [History of the Kingdom of Denmark]. 1732–35.
Synopsis historiae universalis. 1733; as *An Introduction to Universal History*, translated by Gregory Sharpe, 1755.
Bergens beskrivelse [Description of Bergen]. 1737.
Almindelig kirkehistorie [General Church History]. 1738.
Heltehistorier [Achievements of Great Men]. 1739.
Jødisk historie [History of the Jews]. 2 vols., 1742.

Moralske tanker. 1744; edited by F.J. Billeskov Jansen, 1943; as *Moral Reflections and Epistles*, edited and translated by P.M. Mitchell, 1991.
Heltindehistorier [Comparative History of Famous Women]. 1745.
Epistler. 2 vols., 1748–54; edited by F.J. Billeskov Jansen, 8 vols., 1944–54; in part as *Selected Essays*, edited and translated by P.M. Mitchell, 1955, and with *Moral Reflections*, 1991.
Moralske fabler [Moral Fables]. 1751.
Remarques sur quelques positions qui se trouvent dans l'esprit des lois (written in French). 1753.
Memoirs: An Eighteenth-Century Danish Contribution to International Understanding (translation based on various sections of works). 1827; edited by Stewart E. Fraser, 1970.
Memoirer, edited by F.J. Billeskov Jansen. 1943.
Essays, edited by Kjell Heggelund. 1977.
Den radikale Holberg, edited by Thomas Bredsdorff. 1984.
Holberg og Juristerne: en antologi, edited by Klaus Neiiendam and Ditlev Tamm. 1984.
Moral Reflections and Epistles, edited and translated by P.M. Mitchell. 1991.

Translator, *Herodiani historie*. 1746.

*

Bibliography: *Bibliografi over Holbergs skrifter*, 3 vols., 1933–35; *Holberg-Ordbog*, 1981—.

Critical Studies: *The Comedies of Holberg* by Oscar James Campbell, Jr, 1914; *Holberg* by F.J. Billeskov Jansen, 1974; *A Guide to the Writings of Ludwig Holberg and to His Manor-House Tersløsegaard* by F.J. Billeskov Jansen, 1979; *Ludwig Holberg's Comedies: A Biographical Essay* by Gerald S. Argetsinger, 1983.

* * *

When Holberg wrote his first comedies in 1722, there was effectively no tradition of playwriting in Scandinavia to which he could turn for inspiration. He was at the time a much-travelled scholar, recently appointed to the Chair of Metaphysics at the University of Copenhagen. He felt a deep sympathy with the rationalist, conservative ethos of French neo-classicism, and it was accordingly to the work of Molière that he looked for dramatic inspiration. Between 1722 and 1723, he wrote some 15 comedies, all of which, in the best neo-classical tradition, brilliantly satirize socially deviant behaviour in a way that is both entertaining and yet unmistakably didactic. Holberg uses the weapons of ridicule and irony to highlight the folly of characters such as the feckless peasant in *Jeppe på bjerget* (*Jeppe of the Hill*), the know-all amateur politician in *Den politiske kandestøber* (*The Political Tinker*), and the pretentious undergraduate from peasant stock in *Erasmus Montanus*. Like Molière, Holberg felt an obvious sympathy for his unfortunate victims, never losing sight of the transparently human qualities of even his most outrageous fools. This gives his plays, underneath the satiric thrust, a feeling of warmth, at times almost endearment.

Holberg was a precise observer of human behaviour, and his plays faithfully reflect the unsophisticated earthiness of peasant and middle-class culture in 18th-century Denmark. Despite the classical framework, his plays are manifestly Danish in spirit and texture (which may explain why so few have been performed in English). This is as true of the boasting warrior plays modelled on Plautus, such as *Diderich Menschenschreck* (*Diderich the Terrible*) or *Jacob von Tyboe*, as it is of plays like *Den stundeløse* (*The Fussy Man*) or *Den vægelsindede* (*The Weathercock*), modelled on *Le Malade imaginaire* by Molière.

Holberg had begun his literary career with a mock epic poem in 1720 called *Peder Paars* (*Peter Paars*). Based on the *Aeneid*, it follows the mock heroic journey of Peder Paars between two Danish provincial towns, Kalundborg and Aarhus. His comedies were written in 1722 at the invitation of a French actor called Montaigu who was given a licence to set up the first public theatre in Copenhagen with Danish actors. After the theatre went bankrupt in 1727, Holberg concentrated on his academic duties, publishing a number of important historical works. In 1741, he published a long satirical novel in the style of Swift called *Nicolai Klimii iter subterraneum* (*Niels Klim's Journey under the Ground*) and, in 1744, published a collection of essays called *Moralske tanker* (*Moral Reflections*), similar in tone to those of Addison in *The Spectator*.

When a new theatre was established in Copenhagen in 1748, with the official title of the Theatre Royal, Holberg wrote a set of six new comedies to celebrate the occasion. However, these late plays lack the charm and appeal of his early work. His satiric, neo-classical approach to comedy was out of tune with an age that was increasingly embracing the liberal, sentimental values of English and French writers. By now a baron and a conservative pillar of the establishment, Holberg, in 1748, found himself writing for a culture that no longer existed. However, his fame as the founding father of Danish comedy was beyond question. Today, his plays still occupy an important and much-loved place in the repertoire of the Theatre Royal in Copenhagen.

—David Thomas

HÖLDERLIN, (Johann Christian) Friedrich. Born in Lauffen, Germany, 20 March 1770. Educated at Latin school, Nürtingen, 1776–84; theological seminary, Denkendorff, 1784–86, and Maulbronn, 1786–88; Tübingen Seminary, 1788–93, master of philosophy, 1790. Tutor to son of Charlotte von Kalb, in Waltershausen, 1793–94, and in Weimar, 1794–95; lived in Jena, 1795; tutor to son of Herr Gontard, Frankfurt, 1795–98; tutor in house of Herr Gonzenbach, Hauptweil, Switzerland, 1801, and of a German official in Bordeaux, 1801–02; librarian, Homburg, 1804–06. Mentally ill after 1805: confined first in clinic in Tübingen, 1806–07, and privately after 1807. *Died 7 June 1843.*

PUBLICATIONS

Collections

Sämtliche Werke, edited by Friedrich Beissner and Adolf Beck. 8 vols., 1943–85.
Sämtliche Werke und Briefe, edited by Günter Mieth. 4 vols., 1970.
Sämtliche Werke, edited by Dietrich E. Sattler. 1975– .

Verse

Gedichte, edited by Gustav Schwab and Ludwig Uhland. 1826.
Selected Poems, translated by J.B. Leishman. 1944.
[Selection], translated by Michael Hamburger. 1943; revised edition, 1952; revised edition as *Selected Verse*, 1961.
Alcaic Poems (bilingual edition), translated by Elizabeth Henderson. 1962.
Poems and Fragments (bilingual edition), edited and translated by Michael Hamburger. 1966; revised edition, 1980.
Selected Poems (with *Selected Poems* by Mörike), translated by Christopher Middleton. 1972.
Hymns and Fragments (bilingual edition), translated by Richard Sieburth. 1984.
Selected Verse, edited and translated by Michael Hamburger. 1986.
Selected Poems, translated by David Constantine. 1990.

Fiction

Hyperion; oder, Der Eremit in Griechenland. 2 vols., 1797–99; as *Hyperion; or, the Hermit in Greece*, translated by Willard R. Trask, 1965.
Hyperion and Selected Poems, edited by Eric L. Santer. 1990.

Other

Ausgewählte Briefe, edited by Wilhelm Böhm. 1910.
Briefe, edited by Erich Lichtenstein. 1922.
Gesammelte Briefe, edited by Ernst Bertram. 1935.
Briefe, edited by Friedrich Seeba. 1944.
Briefe zur Erziehung, edited by K. Lothar Wolf. 1950.
Einundzwanzig Briefe, edited by Bertold Hack. 1966.
Essays and Letters of Theory, edited and translated by Thomas Pfau. 1988.

Translator, *Die Trauerspiele des Sophokles.* 2 vols., 1804–06.

*

Bibliography: *Internationale Hölderlin-Bibliographie* edited by Maria Kohler, 1985.

Critical Studies: *Hölderlin* by Ronald Peacock, 1938; *Hölderlin* by Agnes Stansfield, 1944; *Hölderlin* by L.S. Salzberger, 1952; *A Study of Hölderlin* by R.D. Miller, 1958; *Hölderlins Elegie 'Brot und Wein': Die Entwicklung des hymnischen Stils in der elegischen Dichtung* by Jochen Schmidt, 1968; *Hölderlin's Hyperion: A Critical Reading* by Walter Silz, 1969; *The Young Hölderlin* by Roy C. Shelton, 1973; *Hölderlin and Greek Literature* by Robin Burnett Harrison, 1975; *Hölderlin and Goethe* by Eudo C. Mason, 1975; *Hölderlin's Major Poetry: The Dialectics of Unity*, 1975, and *Friedrich Hölderlin*, 1984, both by Richard Unger; *Hölderlin and the Left: The Search for a Dialectic of Art and Life* by Helen Fehervary, 1977; *The Significance of Locality in the Poetry of Hölderlin*, 1979, and *Hölderlin*, 1988, both by David Constantine; *Hölderlin's Hyperion* by Howard Gaskill, 1984; *Text, Geschichte und Subjektivität in Hölderlins Dichtung—'Unessbarer Schrift gleich'* by Rainer Nägele, 1985; *Narrative Vigilance and the Poetic Imagination* by Eric L. Santer, 1986; *Hölderlin's Silence* by Thomas Eldon Ryan, 1988; *Friedrich Hölderlin: The Theory and Practice of Religious Poetry: Studies in the Elegies* by Martin F.A. Simon, 1988; *The Problem of Christ in the Work of Friedrich*

Hölderlin by Mark Ogden, 1991; *Hölderlin: The Poetics of Being* by Adrian Del Caro, 1991.

* * *

Poetry—'this most innocent of occupations'—was Friedrich Hölderlin's vocation, and he had from the start the highest ambitions in it. His models as a young man were Pindar, Klopstock, and, closer to home, Schiller—whom he adulated, to his own detriment. He shared with his companions at school and in the seminary (several of them highly gifted) a passion for liberty excited by events in France, and a belief that poetry might, in its manner, serve ·the revolutionary cause. The regime in Württemberg, especially as it touched the students in Tübingen, was oppressive, and poetry served as a medium of revolt. The language of Hölderlin's early poems is often very violent; they depict the beleaguering of the Good, in whatever definition, by the forces of Wrong—of injustice, tyranny, philistinism, etc. In the Tübingen Hymns these oppositions are expressed in abstract terms, and the poetry suffers accordingly.

Hölderlin was educated for the Church but avoided entry into it by taking the customary house-tutor jobs. In the second of these, in Frankfurt, he met and fell in love with Susette Gontard. Through her he found his own true poetic voice; Frankfurt, in a late fragment, he called 'the navel of the earth'. His first poems for her, whom he addressed as Diotima, are marvellously expressive of love and joy; thereafter, as social circumstances oppressed the lovers, he turned to lament and the determined celebration of the Good he was losing. The loss of Susette confirmed him in his elegiac character.

Hölderlin had been working on the novel *Hyperion* before he met Susette (she had read fragments of it in Schiller's *Thalia*), but meeting her he continued it as their book. 'Forgive me that Diotima dies', he wrote. Hyperion, the modern Greek fighting for the recovery of the Hellenic Ideal in the abortive rising of 1770, sees his ideals founder in the bitterest fashion; his attempt to realize them costs him Diotima too. There is almost a will to failure in the book; as though the hero pushes the foreboding that he will fail to its ultimate proof, and salvages his ideals out of a wretched reality into the spirit.

Forced to leave the Gontard household Hölderlin held out in nearby Homburg for as long as he could. There he schooled himself for his greatest poetry. He translated Pindar literally, to learn what his own German language might do; he reflected on the nature and practice of poetry, especially the crucial question of how form might express the spirit without imprisoning or travestying it. Further, he worked at the drama *Empedokles*; but having written extensive notes and attempted three versions, he abandoned the work. Attractive though the idea was and although much of the poetry, especially that of the second version, has an exciting vitality, in essence the conception itself was undramatic and could not have been executed satisfactorily.

The world of Hölderlin's mature poetry, of the great hymns and elegies, is conceived in very concrete terms: it can be mapped, it has two poles—Greece and Hesperia—and numerous renowned features—rivers, mountains, islands, and cities. It incorporates a simple idea (deriving from Herder but also from contemporary Pietist beliefs): that the Spirit of Civilization, having flourished in the East and most splendidly in Periclean Athens, will alight and flourish now north of the Alps, in Germany. The Revolutionary Wars, and the momentousness attaching to the turn of the century, inclined the determinedly optimistic Hölderlin to believe in such a renaissance. In his cosmology we inhabit an Age of Night—initiated by Christ, the last of the Greek gods. We are benighted, and await the new daylight; the poet's task is to encourage us not to despair. This benighted age is characterized by restlessness and wandering; an ideal homeland (Hölderlin's childhood Swabia) is a focus of longing. These are not so much ideas or beliefs as poetic images of immense persuasive power; they express certain readily identifiable conditions: alienation, loss, nostalgia. The theme of Hölderlin's poetry is, *in nuce*: love in absence—how to survive and continue to hold to ideals in times of their manifest absence.

It will not do, when reading Hölderlin, simply to abstract the above adumbrated scheme. That is paraphrase. Instead we have to attend to the rhythms of his poetry, which are very subtle. Contradictions (inclination to despair, insistence on hope, longing for the past, assertion of a better future) are expressed less in statement than in rhythm, in the running of the verse itself against the exact constraints of form. His handling of hexameters and the elegiac couplet is infinitely finer than Goethe's or Schiller's. There is a movement of tones in Hölderlin's verse, there are oscillations of feeling, shifts, transitions through discord and harmony. In a sense, the poems do not end; their constituent emotions have been so finely rendered that we feel them to be still in play. There is no neat conclusion, as of a logical argument. There could not be. The spirit resists such finality. In this manner, in what he himself called a 'loving conflict', Hölderlin's poetry serves the cause of perpetual renewal, of revolt against oppression, deadness, and despair of whatever kind.

After the time in Bordeaux, after the death of Susette Gontard, Hölderlin's poetic world expanded and disintegrated. It is much to be regretted that his mind, because of illness, could not compose the terrific richness of his last creative years. There are moments of vision unlike any others in his poetry, of an intense sensuousness and particularity.

During his years in the tower, half his life, Hölderlin wrote, very often to order, rhyming stanzas on the view through his window of the Neckar and the fields and hills beyond; or, less successfully, on abstract topics. These last poems are very moving, sometimes in their own flat simplicity (*tension* being a hallmark of the mature poetry) but often, alas, only as documents.

Nobody nowadays would be likely, as earlier generations did, to disregard anything Hölderlin wrote on the grounds of his presumed insanity. In his life and in all his work he is a poet for our times. He confronts us with benightedness, and demonstrates the spirit's will to survive.

—David Constantine

BREAD AND WINE (Brot und Wein)
Poem by Friedrich Hölderlin, 1806 (written 1800–01).

'Bread and Wine' is in the strict formal sense an elegy, written in elegiac distichs or couplets of a hexameter followed by a pentameter. Each of the nine strophes has nine of these distichs, except the seventh, which has only eight. It is an elegy in a less technical sense, too, being a lament for the human condition. The emotions it communicates range between despair at the loss of a civilization viewed as ideal (ancient Greece), and ecstatic hope for escape from a dark and disappointing present into an ideal future. Both poles are a form of longing. Yet far from being straightforwardly escapist, 'Bread and Wine' is characterized by a tenacious allegiance to this present and by the recognition that we must in the meantime ('indessen') make do.

The evocation in the first strophe of the coming of night and the stillness of the city seems self-contained (it was published separately in 1807 as 'Night'). But it begins already to adumbrate around the idea of memory the tensions that the rest of the poem will articulate, and functions as a prologue or overture. Contained within the becalmed features of the vesperal town are the residues of its daylight activities—and it is not quite sleeping, for the bells chime, fountains continue to play, and lovers, a solitary man with thoughts of his youth, and a watchman are awake to experience night.

Night is 'the Stranger', simultaneously 'scarcely concerned about us', and unfathomably controlling the aspirations of mankind. Like Hölderlin's philhellene friend Heinse, the poem's dedicatee, most of us are more comfortable with daylight, but (Hölderlin argues that the mystery of night, too, is worthy of contemplation. She grants 'forgetting and sacred intoxication' and at the same time 'sacred remembering', and this contradiction is the impetus for a creative relationship with past and present, and the production of 'the forward-rushing word', or poetry.

Being wakeful at night is the condition of visionary enthusiasm, the will to search for 'ein Eigenes' (something of our own). And this, in the third strophe, is sought in ancient Greece, in specific locations: the Isthmus of Corinth, Parnassus, Olympus, Thebest, all foci of myth. The ecstatic vision overlaps into the next strophe, but after four lines is punctured with the realization of loss. Now, as the poet writes, none of the attributes of Greek life obtain any longer: 'But where are the thrones? where are the temples, and the vessels filled with nectar, and where are the songs for the pleasure of the gods?' (lines 59–60).

Here Hölderlin's poem manifests for a moment the trembling equipoise of lament and celebration, and sudden grief at the passing of Greek civilization tips over into the re-creative memory of the presence of divinity in Greek life. The loss is real, but the joy at its memory is equally real. Then in the fifth strophe what was specific to that past takes on the characteristics of human life in general: mankind, not only the Ancients, responds with joy to the presence of the divine in his life—'This is man' (line 87). An inevitable and natural component of this response is poetry: 'Now words for this must grow, like flowers' (line 90).

The generic returns gradually to the specific in the first eight lines of strophe six, which describe the rise of Greek civilization as the need to honour these present gods—and again, the sense of past glory shifts to a painful sense of present loss. These transitions always obey the natural rhythms of the emotions, not the formal divisions of the strophes. The overall structure of the poem makes use of these overlaps as subtly as the individual lines of verse make use of enjambment, rhythmic variation, and repetition to convey the suppleness and dynamism of the poet's feelings.

Where the feelings require it, however, the breaks between strophes articulate the sense of a close. The end of the sixth strophe announces the advent of the last god, this time in human form, to put an end to the celebrations. This god/man is reminiscent of Christ, but also of the wine-god Dionysus (also born of a divine father and a mortal mother). The isolation of man at this point is expressed temporally and spatially—modern men are late-comers to Greek culture, arriving after the party is over, so to speak; the gods are still there, but stay overhead in their heaven. They are eternal and, like night, seem to care little whether or not we live on (lines 111–12). The situation of the lovers, the solitary and the night-watchmen in the dark (strophe 1) is symbolically the same as that of modern man in a post-Greek world: mindful of a lost past; hopeful of a glorious future; needful of something to cling to in the meantime. That something is simultaneously their memory and their hope:

> Then life consists in dreaming of the gods. But mad wandering helps, like sleep, and deprivation and the night make us strong until enough heroes have grown up in the iron cradle, with hearts full of power to match those on high like before.
>
> (lines 115–18)

This 'meantime' is a precarious and confusing state—and the poet is sure neither of what to do nor of what to say, is not even sure of the function of poets in these lean years: 'wozu Dichter in dürftiger Zeit?'.

This is a low point, when the hope of regeneration is obscured by the difficulties of survival, but like every emotion in 'Bread and Wine' it is not final. Hölderlin reflects that poets are the priests of the wine-god Dionysus, and their function is to remind man that Christ-Bacchus left behind gifts of bread and wine which are tokens of the past and continuing existence of divinity. They were left at the end of the day—recalling both the Last Supper and the fading daylight of Greek civilization. David Constantine in *Hölderlin* (1988) most clearly stresses how a fruitful reading will not restrict itself to decoding the religious mythological references, but will focus on the 'consoling, reconciling and mediating' function of the god.

The last strophe reaffirms the poet's task of announcing the reconciliation of day with night and heaven with earth, using a mixture of Biblical and mythological images. The hymn of anticipation is tempered at the very end where the soul's joy becomes a smile—only a smile, but a smile all the same. Mankind has not left the confusion of the present, he still lacks the glory of Greece and light, but even if the gates from Hell are not flung open, their guardian Cerberus is dozing and there is hope yet.

—Robert Vilain

HOMER. Nothing is known of his life: possibly lived 8th century BC; generally thought to have come from Ionia in Asia Minor, specifically Chios or Smyrna; ancient tradition that he was blind may be true.

PUBLICATIONS

Collection

Opera, edited by D.B. Munro and Thomas W. Allen. 5 vols., 1912–20.

Verse

Iliad, edited by Walter Leaf. 2 vols., 1900–02, reprinted 1960; also edited by D.B. Munro and Thomas W. Allen, 1920, A.J. Church, 1965, and M.M. Willcock, Books I–XII, 1978, Books XIII–XXIV, 1983; Book XXIV edited by C.W. MacLeod, 1982; as *The Iliad*, translated by George Chapman, 1611; also translated by Thomas Hobbes, 1676;

John Ozell, W. Broome, and W. Oldisworth (from the French), 5 vols., 1712; Alexander Pope, 6 vols., 1715–20; William Cowper, 2 vols., 1802, reprinted 1992; P. Williams, 1806; James Morrice, 1809; William Sotheby, 2 vols., 1831; William Munford, 2 vols., 1846; T.S. Brandreth, 2 vols., 1846; F.W. Newman, 1856; I.C. Wright, 2 vols., 1861–65; Lord Derby, 2 vols., 1864; T.S. Norgate, 1864; J. Henry Dart, 1865; Edwin M. Simcox, 1865; P.S. Worsley and John Conington, 2 vols., 1865–68; John F.W. Herschel, 1866; J.I. Cochrane, 1867; Charles Merivale, 2 vols., 1869; W.C. Bryant, 2 vols., 1870; W.G. Caldcleugh, 2 vols., 1870; J.G. Cordery, 2 vols., 1871; John Benson Rose, 1874; W. Lucas Collins, 1876; C.B. Cayley, 1877; A.S. Way, 1885; John Purves, 1891; Samuel Butler, 1898; E.A. Tibbetts, 1907; E.H. Blakeney, 1909; A.G. Lewis, 1911; A.F. Murison, 1933; William Marris, 1934; W.B. Smith and W. Miller, 1944; A.H. Chase and W.G. Perry, Jr, 1950; Richmond Lattimore, 1951; Robert Fitzgerald, 1974; J.P. Kurton, 1977; E. Rees, 1977; D.B. Hull, 1983; Martin Hammond, 1987; Robert Fagles, 1990; Michael Reck, 1990; as *The Anger of Achilles*, translated by Robert Graves, 1959; translations into prose: by James MacPherson, 2 vols., 1773; Theodore Alois Buckley, 1851; Andrew Lang, Walter Leaf, and Ernest Myers, 1882; A.T. Murray [Loeb Edition], 2 vols., 1924–25; Robinson Smith, 1937; W.H.D. Rouse, 1938; E.V. Rieu, 1950; commentaries: Books I–VI by M.M. Willcock, 1970, Books I–IV and Books V–VIII) by G.S. Kirk, 1985 and 1990, Books IX–XII by J.B. Hainsworth, 1993, Books XIII–XVI by Richard Janko, 1991, Books XVII–XX by Mark W. Edwards, 1991, Books XXI–XXIV by Nicholas Richardson, 1993.

Odyssey, edited by J.J. Owen. 1845; also edited by Thomas W. Allen, 1906, and W.B. Stanford, 2 vols., 1947–48, revised edition, 1965; as *The Odyssey*, translated by George Chapman, 1615; also translated by Thomas Hobbes, 1675; Alexander Pope, 1725; William Cowper, 1792; Theodore Alois Buckley, 1851; P.S. Worsley, 2 vols., 1861–62; T.S. Norgate, 1863; George Musgrave, 2 vols., 1865; L. Bigge-Wither, 1869; G.W. Edginton, 1869; W.C. Bryant, 1871; Mordaunt Barnard, 2 vols., 1876; W. Walter Merry and James Riddell, 2 vols., 1878; G.A. Schomberg, 2 vols., 1879–82; A.S. Way, 1880; William Morris, 2 vols., 1887; J.G. Cordery, 1897; Samuel Butler, 1900; J.W. Mackail, 3 vols., 1903–10; H.B. Cotterill, 1911; Francis Caulfeild, 1921; William Marris, 1925; S.O. Andrew, 1948; Robert Fitzgerald, 1961; Richmond Lattimore, 1965; Albert Cook, 1973; E. Rees, 1977; Walter Shewring, 1980; P.V. Jones, 1991; translated into prose by S.H. Bryant and A. Lang, 1879; translations into prose: by G.H. Palmer (Books I–XII), 1884; A.T. Murray [Loeb Edition], 2 vols., 1919; Robert H. Hiller, 1927; T.E. Lawrence, 1932; W.H.D. Rouse, 1937; E.V. Rieu, 1945; commentaries: on vol. 1 by A. Heubeck, Stephanie West, and J.B. Hainsworth, 1985, vol. 2 by A. Heubeck and Arie Hoekstra, 1988.

The Homeric Hymns, translated by Thomas W. Allen, W.R. Holliday, and E.E. Sikes. 1904; also translated by C. Boer, 1972; Apostolos N. Athanassakis, 1976.

*

Bibliography: *A Bibliography of Homeric Scholarship 1930–1970* by D.W. Packard, 1973; 'Homer and Oral Tradition' by Mark W. Edwards, in *Oral Tradition*, 1/2, 1986; 'Homeric Studies 1978–83' by J.P. Holoka, in *Classical World*, 1990.

Critical Studies: *Homer and the Epic*, 1893, and *The World of Homer*, 1910, both by Andrew Lang; *External Evidence for Interpolation in Homer* by G.M. Bolling, 1925; *The Unity of Homer* by J.A. Scott, 1925; *The Composition of Homer's Odyssey* by W.J. Woodhouse, 1930; *The Idea of God in Homer* by E. Ehnmark, 1935; *The Poetry of Homer* by S.E. Bassett, 1938; *The Iliad; or, The Poem of Force* by S. Weil, translated by M. McCarthy, 1945; *Homer in English Criticism: The Historical Approach in the Eighteenth Century* edited by D.M. Foerster, 1947; *Homer and the Monuments* by H.L. Lorimer, 1950; *The Poet of the Iliad* by H.T. Wade-Gery, 1952; *The World of Odysseus* by M.I. Finley, 1954; *The Homeric Gods* by W.F. Otto, translated by M. Hadas, 1954; *The Homeric Odyssey*, 1955, *History and the Homeric Iliad*, 1959, and *Folktales in the Odyssey*, 1972, all by Denys L. Page; *Homer and His Critics* by J.L. Myres, 1958; *From Mycenae to Homer* by T.B.L. Webster, 1958; *Homer and the Homeric Tradition* by Cedric H. Whitman, 1958; *The Singer of Tales* by A.B. Lord, 1960; *A Complete Concordance to the Odyssey of Homer* by H. Dunbar, edited by B. Marzullo, 2nd edition, 1962; *The Songs of Homer*, 1962 (as *Homer and the Epic*, 1965), *The Language and Background of Homer*, 1965, and *Homer and the Oral Tradition*, 1976, all by G.S. Kirk; *A Complete Concordance to the Iliad of Homer* by G.L. Prendergast, edited by B. Marzullo, 2nd edition, 1962; *A Companion to Homer* edited by A.J.B. Wace and Frank H. Stubbings, 1962; *Homer: A Collection of Critical Essays* edited by George Steiner and Robert Fagles, 1963; *Essays on the Odyssey: Selected Modern Criticism* edited by Charles H. Taylor, 1963; *Prolegomena to Homer* by F.A. Wolf, edited by R. Peppmüller, 1963; *Typical Battle Scenes in the Iliad* by Bernard Fenik, 1965, *Homer: Tradition and Invention*, edited by Fenik, 1978, and *Homer and the Nibelungenlied*, by Fenik, 1986; *Homeric Modifications of Formulaic Prototypes* by A. Hoekstra, 1965; *Notes on Homer's Odyssey* by Robert J. Milch, 1966; *The Art of the Odyssey* by Howard W. Clark, 1967; *The Iliad, the Odyssey and the Epic Tradition* by C.R. Beye, 1968; *The Flexibility of the Homeric Formula*, 1968, and *Homer*, 1969, both by J.B. Hainsworth; *Homer's Odyssey: A Critical Handbook* edited by C.E. Nelson, 1969; *People and Themes in Homer's Odyssey*, 1970, and *Homer's Iliad: Its Composition and the Motif of Supplication*, 1984, both by Agathe Thornton; *The Making of Homeric Verse: The Collected Papers of Milman Parry* edited by Adam Parry, 1971; *The Theme of the Mutilation of the Corpse in the Iliad* by Charles Segal, 1971; *Homer* by C.M. Bowra, 1972; *The Conference Sequence: Patterned Narrative and Narrative Inconsistency in the Odyssey* by William F. Hansen, 1972; *Studies in the Language of Homer* by G.P. Shipp, 2nd edition, 1972; *Spontaneity and Tradition: A Study of the Oral Art of Homer* by M.N. Nagler, 1974; *The Homeric Hymn to Demeter* by N.J. Richardson, 1974; *Archery at the Dark of the Moon: Poetic Problems in Homer's Odyssey* by Norman Austin, 1975; *Nature and Culture in the Iliad: The Tragedy of Hector* by James Michael Redfield, 1975; *The Meaning of Homeric EYCHOMAI Through Its Formulas* by Leonard Charles Muellner, 1976; *The Disguised Guest: Rank, Role and Identity in the Odyssey* by Douglas J. Stewart, 1976; *An Essay on the Original Genius of Homer* by R. Wood, 1976; *Similes in the Homeric Poems* by Carroll Moulton, 1977; *Composition by Theme in the Odyssey*, 1977, and *Homer and the Origin of the Greek Alphabet*, 1991, both by Barry Powell; *The Homeric Epics* by C.A. Trypanis, 1977; *Nature and Background of Major Concepts of Divine Power in Homer*, 1977, and *Form and Content in Homer*, 1982, both by Odysseus Tsagarakis; *Homer's Iliad: The Shield of Memory* by Kenneth John Atchity, 1978; *Studies in Characterization in the Iliad* by Leslie Collins, 1978; *Homer's Odyssey* by John H. Finley, Jr, 1978; *The Greek Concept of Justice: From Its Shadow in Homer to Its Substance in Plato* by Eric A. Havelock, 1978; *The Last Scenes of the Odyssey* by Dorothea Wender, 1978; *Essays on the Iliad: Selected Modern Criticism* edited by J. Wright, 1978; *The Best of the Achaeans* by G. Nagy, 1979; *An Introduction to Homer* by W.A. Camps, 1980; *Homer on Life and Death*, 1980, and *Homer: Odyssey*, 1987, both by Jasper Griffin; *The Homeric Question and the Oral-Formulaic Theory* by Minna Skafte Jensen, 1980; *Achilles, Patroklos and the Meaning of Philos* by Dale S. Sinos, 1980; *Homer's Readers: A Historical Introduction to the Iliad and the Odyssey* by Howard W. Clarke, 1981; *Homer, Hesiod and the Hymns: Diachronic Development in Epic Diction* by Richard Janko, 1982; *Childlike Achilles: Ontogeny and Philogeny in the Iliad* by W.T. MacCary, 1982; *Improvisation, Typology, Culture, and 'the New Orthodoxy': How Oral Is Homer?* by D.G. Miller, 1982; *The Epithets in Homer: A Study in Poetic Values*, 1982, and *Homer*, 1985, both by Paolo Vivante; *The Wrath of Athena: Gods and Men in the Odyssey* by Jenny Strauss Clay, 1983; *Approaches to Homer* edited by Carl A. Rubeno and Cynthia W. Shelmerdine, 1983; *Twentieth-Century Interpretations of the Odyssey: A Collection of Critical Essays*, 1983; *The Mortal Hero* by S. Schein, 1984; *Traditional Themes and the Homeric Hymns* by Cora Angier Sowra, 1984; *Achilles in the Odyssey* by Anthony T. Edwards, 1985; *Prolegomena to Homer* translated by A. Grafton, G.W. Most, and J.E.G. Zetzel, 1985; *Notes on Homer's Iliad* edited by Robin Sowerby, 1985, and *Homer, the Odyssey: Notes* by Sowerby, 1986; *Homer the Theologian* by Robert Lamberton, 1986, and *Homer's Ancient Readers: The Hermeneutics of Greek's Earliest Epic Exegeses* edited by Lamberton and John Jo Keaney, 1992; *Notes on Homer's Iliad* by Elaine Strongskill, 1986; *Homer* by Martin Thorpe, 1986; *Homer: Beyond Oral Poetry: Recent Trends in Homeric Interpretation* by J.M. Bremner, I.J.F. De Jong, and J. Kalff, 1987; *Homer: Poet of the Iliad* by Mark W. Edwards, 1987; *Disguise and Recognition in the Odyssey* by Sheila Murnaghan, 1987; *Odysseus Polutropos: Intertextual Readings in the Odyssey and the Iliad* by Pietro Pucci, 1987; *Naming Achilles* by David Shive, 1987; *Homer: Iliad* by M.S. Silk, 1987; *Linguistics and Formulas in Homer: Scalarity and the Description of the Particle Per* by E.J. Bakker, 1988; *Notes on Homer's Odyssey* edited by A. Norman Jeffares and Suheil Badi Bushrui, 1988; *The Ironies of War: An Introduction to Homer's Iliad* by Ian C. Johnston, 1988; *Homer's Odyssey: A Companion to the English Translation of Richmond Lattimore* by Peter Jones, 1988; *War Music: An Account of Books 16–19 of Homer's Iliad* by Christopher Logue, 1988; *Epos: Word, Narrative and the Iliad* by Michael Lynn-George, 1988; *Homer, 1987: Colloquium Proceedings* edited by John Pinsent and H.V. Hurt, 1988; *The Unity of the Odyssey* by George E. Dimock, 1989; *Pindar and Homer* by Frank Nisetich, 1989; *Psychological Activity in Homer: A Study of Phren* by Shirley D. Sullivan, 1989; *Traditional Oral Epic* by John Foley, 1990; *Measure and Music* by Caroline Higbie, 1990; *The Language of Heroes: Speech and Performance in the Iliad* by Richard P. Martin, 1990; *Man in the Middle Voice: Name and Narration in the Odyssey* by John Peradotto, 1990; *Homer and the Sacred City* by S. Scully, 1990; *Homer* edited by Harold Bloom, 1991; *The Gods in Epic* by D.C. Feeney, 1991; *Penelope's Renown* by M. A. Katz, 1991; *Homer: Readings and Images* by Chris Emlyn-Jones, Loina Hardwick, and John Purkis, 1992; *Regarding Penelope* by N. Felson-Rubin, 1992; *Homer: The Poetry of the Past* by Andrew Ford, 1992; *Classical Epic: Homer and Virgil* by Richard Jenkyns, 1992; *Homeric Misdirection: False Predictions in the Iliad* by James V. Morrison, 1992; *Homeric Soundings: The Shaping of the Iliad* by Oliver Taplin, 1992; *The Stranger's Welcome: Oral Theory and the Aesthetics of the Homeric Hospitality Scene* by Steve Reece, 1992; 'Homer and the *Roland*' by William M. Sale, in *Oral Tradition*, 8.1 and 8.2, 1993; *The Shield of Homer: Narrative Structure in the Iliad* by Keith Stanley, 1993.

* * *

The Iliad and *The Odyssey* come at the end of a 500-year-long tradition of oral epic, and parts of them—phrases, lines, perhaps even passages—must have been composed at the beginning of this tradition, when the city of Troy fell to the Achaean armies commanded by King Agamemnon of Mycenae. The oral epic style is a formulaic style, and most of the verses contain formulae: half-lines consisting of a noun plus an adjective, adverb, verb, or another noun, repeated exactly throughout the poem; whole lines stating a recurring fact, such as the coming of dawn; and a few passages of several lines describing, e.g. the preparation and eating of a meal. The formulae exist in order to ensure that the improvising oral poet can keep his metre from breaking down.

Such poetry and its audiences are not offended by repetitions that serve metrical needs, nor by epithets that are otiose or even slightly inappropriate: Achilles is 'swift-footed', whether running, standing, or seated. Repetition weakens the adjective, not so as to render it meaningless, but to make it seem part of the name. Repeated adjectives never, or very rarely, mean the wrong thing, but they need hardly be the *mot juste*.

The oral-formulaic style did not evolve in order that poems of the length of *The Iliad* be composed, and the Homeric compositions are extraordinary achievements even as craftworks. It is quite possible, even probable, that they were composed with the aid of writing: perhaps they were dictated, perhaps the poet learned how to write. That they were preserved orally is of course possible, but in that case what we read undoubtedly suffered distortion during oral transmission. Since most Homeric critics prefer to talk about a text assumed to go back to the 7th or 8th centuries BC, criticism cannot safely rest its analyses on one or two passages; or if it does, it must recognize that it is analysing a text that may well not be Homer's. Granted this caveat, it is safe to look on each poem as a unity, not an editorial amalgamation of previously existing long passages. Whether one poet composed both poems cannot be decided.

The theme of *The Iliad* is the Wrath of Achilles, directed first at Agamemnon, who robbed Achilles of his battle-prize Briseis, and then at Hector, who killed Achilles' beloved companion Patroclus. The young Achilles had dedicated himself to the heroic code, the most attractive concept of values in his Achaean society. To be a hero is to be publicly recognized for one's valour on the battlefield, in combat fought no further from the enemy than a spear's throw. Such recognition is symbolized by the battle-prize, awarded by the troops or by Agamemnon after a city is sacked. To take away one's prize is to shatter one's honour, and Achilles is quite justified in withdrawing from battle. Agamemnon, his cause seriously threatened by Achilles' absence, sends an embassy offering vast recompense. Achilles, still in the grip of his wrath, has by now come to question the value of heroism: life and love seem more important, and the pleas of Odysseus—representing Agamemnon—and of Achilles' old teacher Phoenix, are turned aside. Ajax's brilliant appeal to Achilles' love for his comrades has better luck. Achilles agrees with him intellectually, though he is still too angry to rejoin the battle. But he does allow his companion Patroclus to lead his troops back to fight; when Hector kills Patroclus, Achilles conceives a blind hatred for Hector which is not satisfied even by Hector's death. Priam comes seeking his son's body, offering the ransom appropriate to the heroic code, and more importantly basing his appeal on the love between father and son. To this common human value Achilles responds, and the Wrath comes to an end.

Achilles' movement from heroism to love is interlaced with the poet's exploration of other perceptions of value and of the conflicts such differing perceptions create. Agamemnon, at least initially, believes himself justified by his superior power: his ability to field the most troops. Odysseus is the professional soldier who most honours success: never to return from war empty-handed. The Achaeans and their codes are essentially military; the Trojans are more diverse. We never forget that their city was once at peace, and prosperous. One of the king's sons, Paris, is a skilled bowman in battle, but has no interest in war; he values beauty, and is not only the consort of Helen, but was the architect of his own palace. The shipbuilder Phereclus, no great warrior, is none the less eminent enough to merit a pedigree. The individual Achaean nations are under the absolute command of their kings, while Troy is loosely governed by a council of elders dominated, but hardly dictated to, by Priam's family. Corresponding to such institutional looseness is a moral pluralism: unlike his brother Paris, Hector values heroism, while their father Priam is broadly tolerant, kindly, and sympathetic. Troy's acceptance of diversity is the reason for its destruction: it does not force Paris to return the stolen Helen, nor Hector to re-enter his city and shun the duel with Achilles. Achaean society will always put the military goal first, while the Trojans will sacrifice national security to preserve individual freedom of choice. This is Troy's tragedy, played against Achilles' finding value in love, at the price of losing his friend and becoming forever alienated spiritually from his own society. Homer's vision is pessimistic, but affirmative: human life has more ill than good, but it has value, in heroism and in love.

The Odyssey moves in very different worlds. Odysseus, returning from the Trojan War, is thrust into a fairyland world inhabited by the one-eyed giant Cyclops, the witch Circe, the seductive Sirens, the inexorable Scylla and Charybdis. Reluctant, fascinated, curious, self-indulgent, Odysseus pits himself against the temptations and dangers of this world with considerable personal success, but with the loss of his entire army. His various adventures usually have a ready symbolic interpretation: the Sirens represent the danger of losing one's soul to the power of great art; Scylla and Charybdis, the need to choose to surrender a part to save the whole; Calypso, the surrender of one's humanity to a world without death or domestic responsibility. Odysseus visits the underworld and hears from Achilles how any kind of life is preferable to non-existence. Despite this gloomy prospect, and despite the lure of the beauty of Calypso and her island, Odysseus chooses to be a mortal, a human being, and to go home.

Before this picture of the temptations of sensuality, adventure, and escape from the human lot, Homer places a 'Telemachy' revealing how desperately Odysseus is needed at home in Ithaca. His wife Penelope, not knowing if her husband is alive, is besieged by suitors: though anxious to remain faithful, she cannot afford to reject a second marriage out of hand. Her son Telemachus is beginning to grow up in this hostile world: he acts creditably enough, but clearly requires a father's help. Odysseus' household—in Greek, his *oikos*, the fundamental unit of Ithacan society—is being consumed by the suitors, and pleas to fellow-citizens receive no effective response. The last half of the poem describes Odysseus' return to Ithaca, where he reclaims his household and restores order. Husband and wife reunite in their wedding-bed; and it appears at this moment that the destiny of humanity, male and female, is essentially domestic, and that ultimate fulfilment lies in establishing and maintaining the *oikos*.

Yet the poem's vision is larger than this. Odysseus must one day journey to an inland place and there dedicate his oar to Poseidon, thus placating the hostile god of the sea. The life of Odysseus, as of Penelope, is defined by two movements: one is a struggle to attain domestic stability; the other is the fascination offered by the adventures and challenges along the way.

—William Merritt Sale

THE ILIAD
Poem by Homer, c.750 BC.

Composed around 750 BC, probably the earliest surviving work of Western literature, *The Iliad* is astonishingly complex. The main plot, the wrath of Achilles, criss-crosses a number of sub-plots, such as the tragedy of Troy, and the quarrels and peace of the gods. The theme of heroism versus love is thereby extended beyond the context of Achilles' career, permitting the varieties of love to be set forth and exemplified, the quest for value to be located politically, and human aspirations glimpsed in the light of what heaven encourages, permits, and disallows. Value-conflicts occur within the psyche as well as between individuals and nations, and some characters are very subtly drawn.

Apollo sends a plague upon the Greeks to force Agamemnon, the Greek commander, to return the woman Chryseis, Agamemnon's prize, to her father. Agamemnon wants another prize in recompense; Achilles demurs; Agamemnon, enraged, demands Achilles' prize, the woman Briseis; and Achilles, equally enraged, withdraws his troops from the battle. Facing disaster, the Greeks offer Achilles a vast array of gifts, including Briseis, for his return. Achilles, initially scornful, first threatens to return home but, moved by Ajax's appeal to love for his comrades-in-arms, he agrees to stay, though not yet to fight. Next day the Trojans, led by Hector, set fire to the Greek ships. Achilles' beloved companion, Patroclus, persuades Achilles to allow him to lead his troops into battle, but after many victories is slain. Achilles, devastated, returns to battle and kills Hector (whom he considers Patroclus' killer) after slaughtering countless Trojans. Finally Hector's father, Priam, persuades Achilles to return Hector's body.

As this plot develops, Achilles too develops. His initial passionate self-concern and quickness to anger reflect the heroic personality. Then, his idealism shattered, he rejects heroism, realizing that it can be undermined by the antics of an unstable commander. Thanks to Ajax's appeal, love for his friends then becomes central, and he remains in Troy, though rage still keeps him off the battlefield. Love for the dead Patroclus turns that rage towards Hector, and Achilles now fights for vengeance (though the old heroic urge is not entirely dead). Later his wrath abuses Hector's corpse, seeking to nullify Patroclus' death; and even as he responds lovingly to Priam, Achilles simmers over a breach in manners.

We can debate whether to call such transcendent anger neurotic, but neurotic is the correct modern term for Agamemnon. In Book I his megalomania leads to *hubris* (presumptuous pride, dishonouring others and/or the gods); in Book II his guilt over alienating his best warrior impels him to an irrational test of his men's devotion; in Book IX, with defeat impending, he first urges flight, then, acknowledging his previous madness, offers staggering amends. Books XIV and XIX reveal the same pattern: urge flight, accept rebuke, later confess and offer compensation. Priam, in contrast, is the idealized gentle father who accepts his sons' need to fulfil themselves although the city may perish thereby; he is just the person to guide Achilles to the final act of love. And Patroclus is a simple, decent man who naturally wants to help the hard-pressed Greeks and merits Achilles' affection.

Sub-plot characters include Ajax, dedicated warrior and loving companion, deeply insightful into Achilles; Paris, romantic lover, indifferent to heroism, who wounds Diomedes and will kill Achilles; Helen, whose guilt induces incessant self-condemnation without dulling her awareness of the fame awaiting her and her lover; Andromache, Hector's wife, who (like Priam later) urges a defensive strategy upon Hector but accepts his need to be heroic. Hector's tragic sub-plot rivals the wrath of Achilles in prominence. At times the egocentric would-be hero, abusive to his brother Paris, insensitively detailing to his wife the horrors he will suffer after his death, at other times Hector is deeply kind and compassionate to both. He often fights bravely, yet always falls short of the great heroic deed. In Book XVIII the lure of heroism overpowers sound strategy, and he persuades the army, disastrously, to face Achilles returned to battle. With Achilles descending upon him he rejects his parents' appeals and makes the heroic, tragic, decision to fight; suddenly a yearning for love emerges from behind his heroism, as he fantasizes speaking to Achilles 'as a young man and maiden speak erotically to each other'; then as Achilles draws near he runs. Athena (goddess of self-realization) appears, ostensibly to help Achilles but in effect to cause Hector to stand and die heroically, with a spear in his throat and not his back.

The poem's main themes are values: heroism and love, success and power. Heroism exalts the value of the individual male, as demonstrated through valour with the heroic weapons, sword and spear, and as recognized socially by the prize symbolizing honour and glory. Heroism can conflict with love (which ultimately affirms life over death), with success (which may exalt winning no matter how, and subdue the hero with the non-heroic bow and arrow), or with power (which permits an irrational commander to trample on anything). The varieties of love include the companionate (Achilles and Patroclus), the romantic (Paris and Helen), the connubial (Andromache and Hector), and the parental (Priam and Hecuba).

The quest for value occurs in the context of politics and religion. The Greek heroes are mostly absolute monarchs heading states loosely allied under Agamemnon; their economy is essentially military, based on plunder, so they naturally value heroism alongside success and power. The Trojans belong to an alliance headed by Troy-city, Ilios (Ilium), Troy itself being nominally a monarchy but in fact an oligarchy run by a council of elders. The Trojans achieve tragic beauty by honouring a plurality of values, including freedom (which keeps them from imposing their will upon Paris and Hector) and material gain (which enables Paris to bribe the council into fighting). Though most of the poem's great decisions are made without divine intervention, the Olympian gods form a constant background, imposing certain eternal conditions upon the search for value: self-limitation (Apollo), the need

for self-fulfilment (Athena), and the fact that so much is beyond our control (Zeus).

—William Merritt Sale

THE ODYSSEY
Poem by Homer, c.720 BC.

Composed around 720 BC, not long after *The Iliad* and perhaps by the same poet, *The Odyssey* neatly complements its predecessor. It focuses upon peace, the household, ingenuity, and domestic love, rather than war, society, heroism, romantic and companionate love. Its fairy-land symbols of universal peril and enchantment contrast with *The Iliad*'s status symbols, the prizes of honour of this world. It is mythic and comic where *The Iliad* is tragic.

The narrative begins in the 20th year after Odysseus departed for Troy; he is far from his home in Ithaca, perhaps dead, so far as his family knows. His wife Penelope and his son Telemachus are besieged by 108 suitors for her hand who spend each day in Odysseus' palace devouring its livestock and wine. Athena (goddess of self-realization), perceiving Telemachus' helplessness, descends to inspire him to move towards manhood, summon the assembly, urge the suitors to disperse, then travel to Nestor in Pylos and Menelaus in Sparta for news of Odysseus. Just before Telemachus' return, the narrative shifts to Odysseus, imprisoned amidst sensual delights on the nymph Calypso's island. He has turned down her offer of immortality, and longs to go home. Zeus, through Hermes the messenger, persuades Calypso to release him, and he crosses the sea to the Phaeacians, where Princess Nausicaa finds him and leads him to her father's palace. Received warmly, Odysseus tells the story of his earlier adventures, including the Cyclops, Circe, Hades, the Sirens, and Scylla and Charybdis.

The Phaeacians return Odysseus to Ithaca where, disguised, he encounters his faithful swineherd Eumaeus, and reveals himself to Telemachus. He goes up to the city and his palace, and begs from the suitors amidst their abuse. When they have left for the night, Odysseus, still disguised, talks with Penelope, who announces that next morning she will set up an archery contest (using the great bow that Odysseus left behind) to decide who is to win her hand. Telemachus tries to string the bow, shows that he can do it, but obeys his father's signal not to. After the suitors make their futile attempts, Odysseus succeeds, and turns the bow upon them. Helped by Athena, Telemachus, Eumaeus, and another loyal servant, he kills them all. Penelope then tests him by tricking him into revealing his knowledge that their bed was built upon a tree-trunk, and husband and wife are rejoined.

All three main characters are depicted in depth. Telemachus is a likeable but immature youth, who grows up with the aid of Athena, Nestor, Menelaus, Eumaeus, and eventually Odysseus. His attempt to string the bow (and thus win Penelope for himself) is aborted by his father, to whose designs Telemachus must subordinate himself on the path to manhood. Penelope is subtle; she loves Odysseus, yet must keep the suitors interested in case he is dead, postponing remarriage until she knows the truth, while enjoying their attentions and accumulating gifts to compensate for their ravages upon livestock and cellar. Earlier she promised to make a choice when she finished weaving a shroud for Laertes. Caught out undoing by night what she had woven by day, she finished the task, but instead of choosing she arranges the archery contest. Her strategy is double: if, as she half-suspects, the beggar in the palace is really Odysseus, he will string the bow and have a weapon against the suitors; if he is not, then probably neither he nor the suitors will succeed, and she can continue to postpone the choice. Penelope's games with the suitors are the erotic and intellectual counterpart to Odysseus' adventures in fairyland; and the ingenuity she displays in the bed-trick, outwitting the outwitter, makes her his perfect match and mate.

Odysseus too is subtle. Intensely curious, highly courageous, he thoroughly enjoys many of the adventures that postpone his return. But he has perceived a deeper truth by the time he refuses Calypso's offer of immortal life with her and elects to go home: human destiny, male as well as female, is ultimately domestic. (His choice is more poignant because as he has visited Hades, where the ghost of Achilles told him that any form of existence is preferable to death, non-being). Athena as goddess of self-realization stands by Odysseus' side when he is fighting at Troy to restore Menelaus' violated household, and when he fights on Ithaca to restore his own; but during his adventures, as he self-indulgently explores his self's limits, she is absent.

The varieties of meanings of Odysseus' name enrich his complexity: he is the giver and receiver of pain, the hater and the hated, the one who leads forth. For instance, he blinds the Cyclops, giving him pain, arousing his hatred, and allowing him to lead his companions forth from the Cyclops' cave. Before this, Odysseus tells the Cyclops that his name is 'No-one'. (The Greek word for 'No-one' has the slightly hidden meaning, 'ingenuity', one of Odysseus' chief characteristics.) As a result, when the Cyclops turns to his neighbours for help, he cries, 'No-one is killing me'. Naturally they respond, 'Since no one is assaulting you, you must be mad'. But then Odysseus reveals his 'proper' name, 'Odysseus,' and the Cyclops is able to call down Poseidon's wrath upon him. As No-one (the elusive, indefinite one) Odysseus is secure, but by putting his signature to the deed, he evokes the magical and divine forces that he must struggle against for the next ten years.

The poem's main theme, that human destiny is domestic, is greatly enlarged by the symbolism of the mythic world of Odysseus' adventures. Odysseus becomes an everyman, facing universal perils—Circe (erotic enchantment and bestial enslavement), the Sirens (deadly lure or artistic beauty), Scylla and Charybdis (lose part or lose all). Penelope in turn becomes everywoman confronted by the perils and pleasures of masculine desire, and all of us are seen caught between the competing needs for adventure (meeting risks and satisfying curiosity) and for home and family.

—William Merritt Sale

———

HONGLOU MENG. See **THE DREAM OF THE RED CHAMBER.**

———

HOOFT, Pieter Corneliszoon. Born in Amsterdam, Dutch Republic (now The Netherlands), 15 March 1581. Educated at the Amsterdam Latin School; studied law at Leiden, 1605–07. Married 1) Christina van Erp in 1610 (died 1624); 2) Leonora Hellemans in 1627. Travelled in Europe, then settled in the Netherlands; Justice of Muiden, from 1609; after 1627 his official residence became the leading literary circle of his time, the Muiderkring. Granted title 'Knight of St Michael' for his biography of Henry IV, 1639. Member of d'Eglantier; joined Samuel Coster's Nederduytsche Academie. *Died 21 May 1647.*

PUBLICATIONS

Collections

Alle de werken [Complete Works]. 4 vols., 1703–04.
Historieën [Histories], edited by W. Hecker. 5 vols., 1843–46.
Brieven [Letters], edited by J. van Vloten. 4 vols., 1855–57.
Volledige uitgave der gedichten [Complete Edition of the Poems], edited by P. Leendertz. 2 vols., 1871–75; revised by F.A. Stoet, 2 vols., 1899–1900.
Lyriek [Lyrics], edited by C.A. Zaalberg. 1963.
Alle de gedrukte werken [All the Printed Works], edited by W. Hellinga and P. Tuynman. 9 vols., 1971.

Plays

Geeraerdt van Velsen. 1613; as *The Tragedy of Gerard van Velsen*, translated by Theo Hermans and Paul Vincent, in *Dutch Crossing*, 45, 1991.
Achilles en Polyxena. 1614.
Theseus en Ariadne. 1614, reprinted 1988.
Granida, from *Pastor fido* by Guarini. 1615, reprinted 1958.
Warenar [A True Fool], from *Aulularia* by Plautus. 1617.
Schijnheyligh [Hypocrite], from *L'ipocrito* by Aretino. 1617.
Baeto oft oorsprong der Hollanderen [Baeto or the Origins of the Dutch]. 1626.

Verse

Emblemata amatoria. 1611.
Brief van Menelaus aan Helena [Letter from Menelaus to Helena]. 1615.
Bruiloftzang [Wedding Song]. 1623.
Klaghte der Princesse van Oranjen over 't oorloogh voor s'Hartogenbosch [Lament of the Princess of Orange Concerning the War in Den Bosch]. 1629.
Gedichten [Poems], edited by J. van der Burgh. 1636.
Erotische gedichten [Erotic Poems], edited by C.C. van Sloten. 1956.
Sonnetten, edited by P. Tuynman. 1971.

Other

Henrick de Grote [Henry the Great]. 1626.
Waernemingen op de Hollandsche tael [Observations on Dutch Language]. 1638.
Neederlandsche histoorien [History of the Netherlands]. 20 vols., 1642; 7 vols. completed by his son, 1654.
Rampzaeligheden der verheffinge van den Huize Medicis [Disasters of the Rise of the House of Medici]. 1638, revised 1649.
Reden van de waerdicheit der poesie, edited by J. van Krimpen and A.A.M. Stols. 1925, reprinted 1971; as *An*

Oration Concerning the Excellence of Poetry, translated by Lesley Gilbert, in *Dutch Crossing*, 47, 1992.

*

Critical Studies: *Het vers van Hooft* by G. Kazemier, 1932; *Hooft en Tacitus* by J.D.M. Cornelissen, 1938; *Bijdrage tot de kennis van de invloeden op Hooft*, 1946, and *Ethiek en moral bij P.C. Hooft*, 1967, both by F. Veenstra; *P.C. Hooft* by H.W. van Tricht, 1951; *Hooft en dia* by W.A.P. Smit, 1968; *Dramatische struktuur in tweevoud* by E.K. Grootes, 1973; *Bijdragen tot de P.C. Hooft filologie* by P. Tuynman, 1973; *Uyt liefde geschreven: Studies over Hooft*, 1981; *Hooft als historienschrijver* by S. Groeneveld, 1981.

* * *

Pieter Corneliszoon Hooft was born into a rich merchant's family and took full advantage of the privileges of such a background: he received a good classical education, and he helped administer his country. He devoted himself to writing early in life, and the poetics he espoused were those of the Renaissance rather than of the Rhetoricians of 'd'Eglantier', the Amsterdam chapter of Rhetoricians where he first learned his trade. He was later to break with them altogether, and to become instrumental in the founding of the first Amsterdam theatre dedicated to the new Aristotelian drama.

Like many Dutch painters of his time, Hooft discovered the Renaissance in Italy and helped introduce it to the Netherlands on his return to his native country and city. The influence of Italian models on his poetry and his pastoral play *Granida* is as obvious as is the influence of Tacitus on his historiographical writings. In the first half of his literary career Hooft concentrated on writing for the stage, although he also wrote poetry, but rather as an expression of his amorous pursuits than of his main intellectual and philosophical interests. Hooft wrote the first Renaissance play in Dutch, *Achilles en Polyxena*, based on the Homer continuations by Dictus Cretensis and Dares Phrygius. He came into his own as a playwright with *Granida*, inspired by Italian examples. Hooft used the play, written in a genre that was extremely popular in his time, to test his views on the conflict between *liefde*, by which he understood what his medieval predecessors would have referred to as 'high love', and *min*, which he used to mean eroticism. A happy ending is achieved, wholly in keeping with the conventions of the genre, when love and eroticism are combined in the harmony of lasting relationships. The same tension between love and eroticism pervades much of Hooft's more personal poetry, mainly the earlier work, although it is never quite absent from later productions. This private Hooft coexisted with the public Hooft, not just in discharging administrative duties, but also in poetry. Like many of his contemporaries, Hooft produced many 'public' poems to celebrate victories, dedicate buildings, or praise public figures or the city of Amsterdam itself.

The poetry also reveals another side to Hooft: the conscientious craftsman who tried to emulate Petrarch and his school. The many sonnets he wrote are probably not meant to be read at a personal level, but as 'masterpieces' in the original sense of the word, a piece to show that the apprentice had 'mastered' his trade and could therefore set up as a master himself. Hooft was a master who used a diction more refined and a metre more subtle than any of his predecessors. He was, however, a slightly different kind of master in his official residence, the Muiderslot, where he lived during the

summer. After his second marriage in 1627, he played host there to many writers and creative spirits who gathered at the castle for evenings of discussion, not just of literature, but also of matters of more philosophical and political import.

Hooft ventured into comedy with *Warenar* [A True Fool], an adaptation of Plautus' *Aulularia* (*The Pot of Gold*), in which he also displayed his knowledge and mastery of the Amsterdam dialect. He had always been interested in the different variants of Dutch spoken around him and in the evolution of the language, and even tried to standardize its spelling, to little avail. *Warenar* also illustrated that Hooft knew how to write successfully for a less educated audience, thereby beating at their own game the Rhetoricians, who claimed to be writing for a general rather than an elite audience. Hooft could and did write for a general audience not only as a playwright, but also as a poet. His *Emblemata amatoria*, which represents his contribution to the then thriving genre of 'emblem literature', became very popular during his lifetime and remained so for at least a century after his death.

In both his later tragedies and his prose, Hooft explored the problem of power, probably the central problem of his life, not primarily because he exercised some kind of limited power himself, but because his life coincided almost exactly with the lengthy but unexpectedly victorious war of independence waged by the emerging Dutch Republic against Spain, then the most important power in Europe.

Geeraerdt van Velsen (*The Tragedy of Gerard van Velsen*) provides a rationale for revolt against an unjust ruler. Once the Count of Holland, Floris V, no longer behaves as he should, his subjects are entitled to rise against him and depose him, just as the Netherlands rose against Philip II of Spain and deposed him as its ruler. *Baeto oft oorsprong der Hollanderen* [Baeto or the Origins of the Dutch], based not so much on Dutch history as on the emerging national mythology all new states create to legitimize their existence, is Hooft's portrayal of the just ruler who would rather forsake his throne than plunge his country into civil war. Hooft also depicted the just ruler in prose in his biography of the French king Henry IV (*Henrick de Grote*), considered an example to all kings by many intellectuals in Europe of the time. Hooft wrote his biography of Henry IV to sharpen his skills for the major task ahead: the history of the Dutch war of independence against Spain. This project, undertaken in the spirit of Tacitus for whom, as for Hooft, history was a literary genre that could be used to inform and instruct, was to occupy Hooft for the last part of his life. The published version, *Neederlandsche histoorien* [History of the Netherlands] runs to 20 books of stately prose, interspersed with pithy sayings on the Tacitian model. It contains Hooft's final and most incisive analyses of power, loyalty, tyranny, and revolt.

—André Lefevere

———

HORACE. Born Quintus Horatius Flaccus in Venusia (now Venosa), Apulia, Italy, 8 December 65 BC. Educated in Rome and Athens, c.46 BC. Joined Brutus' army in Athens, 44 BC, and probably accompanied him to Asia Minor, then fought at the battle of Philippi, 42 BC; returned to Italy, 41 BC, to find his father's land had been confiscated; became treasury clerk, c.39 BC; friend of Virgil, *q.v.*, who introduced him to Maecenas: became part of his circle of writers; given a farm in the Sabine country by Augustus. *Died 27 November 8 BC.*

PUBLICATIONS

Collections

[Works], edited by Otto Keller and Alfred Holder. 2 vols., 1899; also edited by Edward C. Wickham, revised by Heathcote William Garrod, 1912, Adolph Kiessling, revised by Richard Heinze, 3 vols., 1930, Friedrich Klinger, 1959, S. Borszák, 1984, and D.R. Shackleton Bailey, 1985; translated by John Conington, 2 vols., 1863–69; also translated by Theodore Martin, 1881; C.E. Bennett, 1914; H.R. Fairclough, 1926; Lord Dunsay and Michael Oakley, 1961; Charles E. Passage, 1983.
The Essential Horace, translated by Burton Raffel. 1983.
'Ecce Homo Amore!': The Love Poems of Horace, edited and translated by Louis Francis. 1993.

Verse

Ad Pyrhham (Ode I.5), several hundred translations, mostly into English, edited by R. Storrs. 1959.
Ars poetica, edited and translated by A.F. Watt. 1905; also edited by C.O. Brink, 1971; as *Ars poetica*, translated by H.R. Fairclough [Loeb Edition], 1926; also translated by R.C. Trevelyan, 1940; Burton Raffel, 1974; Niall Rudd, 1989; as *The Poetic Art*, translated and adapted by C.H. Sisson, 1975.
Epistles, edited by A.S. Wilkins (with commentary). 1892; also edited by O.A.W. Dilke, 1954, revised edition, 1961; Book II edited by Niall Rudd, 1989; edited and translated by Francis Platstowe and Frank P. Shipham, 1893; edited and translated by Howard H. Erskine-Hill, 1964; translated by Philip Francis, 1906; also translated by H.R. Fairclough [Loeb Edition], 1926; R.C. Trevelyan, 1940; Smith P. Bovie, 1959; Colin MacLeod, 1986; Book I translated by O.A.W. Dilke, 1966; Book II translated by C.O. Brink, 1982; commentary by E.P. Morris, 1909–11.
Epodes, edited by Henry Darnley Naylor. 1978; also edited by D.H. Garrison, 1991; translated by Joseph P. Clancy, 1960; also translated by John Penman, 1980; W.G. Shepherd, 1983.
Odes, edited by F. Plessis. 1924; also edited by Henry Darnley Naylor, 1978, Arthur Sherbo, 1979, Kenneth Quinn, 1980, and D.H. Garrison, 1991; Books I–II edited by R.G.M. Nisbet and M. Hubbard, 2 vols., 1970–78; Book III edited and translated by Gordon Williams, 1969; translated by Christopher Smart, 1767; also translated by J.B. Leishman, in *Translating Horace*, 1956; Joseph P. Clancy, 1960; Helen Rowe Henze, 1961; James Michie, 1964; W.G. Shepherd, 1983; commentaries by P. Shorey and G.J. Laing, 2nd edition, 1910.
Satires, edited by A. Palmer (with commentary). 1883; edited and translated by Howard H. Erskine-Hill, 1964; translated by H.R. Fairclough [Loeb Edition], 1926; also translated by Smith P. Bovie, 1959; Niall Rudd, 1973, revised edition, 1979; commentaries by E.P. Morris, 1909–11.

*

Critical Studies: *Studies in Horace* by A.W. Verrall, 1884; *Horace and the Elegiac Poets* by W.Y. Sellar, 1892; *Horace and His Age* by J.F. D'Alton, 1917; *Horace and His Influence*

by G. Showerman, 1922; *Horace: A New Interpretation* by Archibald Young Campbell, 1924; *Horace and His Lyric Poetry* by L.P. Wilkinson, 1945, revised edition, 1968; *Horace* by E. Fraenkel, 1957; *The Structure of Horace's Odes* by Neville E. Collinge, 1961; *The Odes of Horace: A Critical Study* by Steele Commager, 1962; *Horace on Poetry* by C.O. Brink, 1963; *Horace* by J. Perret, 1964; *The Satires of Horace* by Niall Rudd, 1966; *Reading Horace* by David A. West, 1967; *The Epodes of Horace* by R.W. Carrubba, 1969; *Word, Sound, and Image in the Odes of Horace* by M.O. Lee, 1969; *Studies in Horace's First Book of Epistles* by M.J. McGann, 1969; *Horace* by Kenneth J. Reckford, 1969; *A Commentary on Horace, Odes Book 1* by R.G.M. Nisbet, 1970; *Horace* by Gordon Williams, 1972; *Horace* edited by C.D.N. Costa, 1973; *Horace and Callimachean Aesthetics* by J.V. Cody, 1976; *Horace in His Odes* by James A. Harrison, 1981; *Profile of Horace* by D.R. Shackleton Bailey, 1982; *The Golden Plectrum: Sexual Symbolism in Horace's Odes* by Richard Minadeo, 1982; *Horace: A Study in Structure* by Helena Dettmer, 1983; *Horace's Roman Odes: A Critical Examination* by Charles Witke, 1983; *The Poetry of Friendship: Horace, Epistles I*, 1986, and *The Poetry of Criticism*, 1990, both by Ross S. Kilpatrick; *Artifices of Eternity: Horace's Fourth Book of Odes* by Michael C.J. Putnam, 1986; *Unity and Design in Horace's Odes* by Matthew S. Santirocco, 1986; *Horace's Lyric Poetry* by Peter Connor, 1987; *Horace* by David Armstrong, 1989; *Horace* by Marjorie Newman, 1990; *Polyhymnia: The Rhetoric of Horatian Lyric Discourse* by G. Davis, 1991; *Horace* by Holly Keller, 1991; *The Walking Muse: Horace and the Theory of Satire* by Kirk Freudenburg, 1993; *Horace Made New: Horatian Influences on British Writing from the Renaissance to the Twentieth Century* edited by Charles Martindale and David Hopkins, 1993; *Horace and the Dialectic of Freedom: Readings in 'Epistles I'* by W.R. Johnson, 1994.

* * *

Horace's achievement is to have mastered two completely different types of poetry, each of which is remarkable for its originality and each of which has endeared itself to generations of readers.

The first type is his hexameter poetry. In 36/35 BC Horace produced *Satires 1*, a collection of ten poems written in the manner of Lucilius (a Roman landowner and littérateur of the late 2nd century BC) and described by Horace himself as *sermones* (conversation pieces). Lucilius had been famous for his invective and biting wit; but though Horace subjects certain individuals to intermittent mockery throughout his collection, and though the first three satires deal with such moral questions as discontent and adultery, the book as a whole is hardly satirical at all in our sense of the word. Among the matters described or discussed are literary criticism (4, 10), a journey from Rome to Brundisium (5), and the poet's own life and his relationship with his patron Maecenas (6). Several representative features are combined brilliantly in satire 9, in which Horace describes how, on a walk through Rome, he was pursued by a stranger claiming to be a poet and hoping for an introduction to Maecenas. The satire, which begins with an allusion to Lucilius, is almost wholly taken up with dialogue, in which the pest's importunity is matched by Horace's politeness, the latter's irony by the former's insensitivity. Since both protagonists are poets, the satire resembles the traditional form of the literary *agon* (contest); yet the pest unwittingly presents his own work in terms which, as the reader well knows, Horace (and Maecenas) can only regard with contempt. Further wit is displayed by means of epic motifs and military imagery, which are used throughout to suggest that the combatants are a pair of Homeric heroes; yet this language is entirely belied by the appalling behaviour of the pest, by whom Horace is nevertheless characteristically worsted until the very last moment, when he is rescued by the surprise intervention of a third party. The rescue itself is expressed in language which is again borrowed from Lucilius. The whole poem exhibits a confident combination of humour and humanity, and in the dialogue form the resources of metre and language are exploited to the full. Yet underneath the wit Horace has a serious message for his readers about admission to Maecenas' circle and hence, by implication, to the entourage of Octavian (the future emperor Augustus) himself.

A second book of *Satires*, containing eight poems, followed in 30 BC, and ten years later, 20 more hexameter poems which are known as *Epistles 1*. Finally, there are three very long letters, the first two of which are collectively known as *Epistles 2*: to Augustus, to Florus, and to the Pisones (the *Ars poetica*, or *The Poetic Art*). Although the *Satires* and *Epistles* are conventionally distinguished by their titles, and though the latter display some epistolographical features which are naturally absent from the former, there is little otherwise to distinguish the two sets of poems. Since the verse letter had no significant analogue in Greek, and satire no analogue at all, Horace in these works produced a body of poetry which for its principal inspiration owes virtually nothing to the world of Greece. In this his poetry differs fundamentally both from that of other Roman poets, almost all of whom wrote in rivalry of Greek genres, and from the rest of the poetry which he wrote himself.

At the same time as he was engaged with *Satires 1*, Horace was also writing iambic poetry in the manner of the early Greek iambist Archilochus. Iambics were traditionally associated with invective and disillusionment, and Horace's *Epodes* (as the 17 poems, which appeared around 30 BC, are known) include examples of this type (e.g. 2, 4, 8, 10, 12); but there is a wider range of subjects too, e.g. civil war (7, 16), the battle of Actium (1, 9), life (13), and love (11, 14, 15). Thus the *Epodes* have affinities not only with the satires but also with Horace's second major achievement, the three books of *Odes* which appeared in 23 BC. These 88 poems, all written in lyric metres, cover an enormous variety of subject matter: famous examples are, in Book I: 4 (spring), 5 (the flirtatious Pyrrha, this being one of the most translated poems in Latin), 9 (Mt Soracte), and 37 (Cleopatra); in Book II: 3 and 14 (death); and in Book III: 1 (ambition), 29 (life), and 30 (the immortality of the *Odes*). These three books represent Horace's attempt at producing a substantial collection of Latin lyric poetry which would be a cultural adornment of Augustan Rome and which would rival the lyrics written by the Greek monodists Sappho and Alcaeus. Characteristic in many ways is II.7, in which Horace welcomes back to Italy a friend with whom he served on the republican side at the battle of Philippi many years before. Metaphor is used with striking originality to contrast the old soldiers' periods of enforced idleness with their bursts of frenzied activity, their comradely carousing with their defeat on the field of battle. Whereas his friend was sucked away by the tides of war, Horace had a fortunate escape. Ever conscious of the imminence of death, Horace presents his escape in epic terms; but there is no hint of self-congratulation, for he has already described his own part in the battle ignominiously, symbolized by his abandoned shield. This last is a motif found in several archaic Greek poets, including Alcaeus; Horace thus aligns his experience with theirs and underscores his poetic relationship

with them. Now that his friend has returned to Italy, tellingly evoked by its sky and native gods, Horace conveys his delight by the detailed preparations he is making for their renewed carousing; and though the poet seems proud to have fought alongside Brutus, the reader is subtly reminded that his friend's return, and Horace's own prosperity, are due to the clemency and beneficence of the victor. This ode, in its linguistic brilliance, its feeling for friends and home, its blending of pride and understatement and of literature and life, illustrates much that is outstanding in Horace's lyric work.

There can be no question that Horace's achievement in the *Odes* was triumphantly successful. Official recognition of that success came when he was commissioned by the emperor to write the *Carmen saeculare* [Secular Hymn] for the important Secular Games of 17 BC. The emperor also requested poems celebrating the military exploits of his stepsons; these poems duly appear (4, 14) in Book IV of the *Odes*, which came out separately around 13 BC.

In metre and form the *Odes* could hardly be more different from the *Satires* and *Epistles*; yet all are recognizably written by the same poet, all have certain features in common, and all evince a concern for the same subjects. Horace is one of the few great classical writers whom readers easily convince themselves that they know intimately; yet his remarkable habit of partly revealing and partly concealing his personality means that, while throughout his different types of poetry the common link is provided by the poet himself, one person's Horace is never the next person's, and the 'real Horace' is a source of endless fascination. Horace similarly tantalizes us in his manner of expression. Common features of his hexameter and lyric works are the wit and subtlety of their argumentation; yet his unrivalled facility with words means that apparently key sentences can look both forwards and backwards in such a way that his effortless transitions provide constant delight to the reader who, after much labour, thinks he has worked them out. Similarly ambivalent are Horace's favourite topics. He can combine support for the emperor's efforts at moral re-armament with hedonistic recommendations to drink and make love before the summons of death. He can profess to prefer light poetry to grand and at the same time produce the noblest of political poems. Horace's work has that capacity for constantly surprising the reader which we associate with great art; yet nothing could be more familiar than the many famous lines which he wrote and which are among the most memorable statements ever uttered about the human condition.

—A.J. Woodman

THE POETIC ART (Ars poetica)
Poem by Horace, c.12–8 BC.

The Latin poet Horace discussed a number of artistic and critical problems in his extensive series of verse *Epistles*, but the long verse-letter known as *The Poetic Art* is the most sustained account of literary criticism written by a practising poet in the ancient world. Thought to have been composed towards the end of Horace's life (scholars now agree that it should be dated between 12 and 8 BC), it carries the informal and convivial tone of the poet's most characteristic work, and has the structure of an illustrated description of current thinking rather than a closely argued treatise. The poem is best seen as a witty and elegant synthesis of relatively familiar views, rather than as an exploratory or innovative manifesto, drawing as it does on the precedent work of earlier Greek and

Roman models, including Aristotle and Cicero. It is addressed to an unidentified father and son, hailed only as 'Piso', but the advice offered to the fledgling writer opens out into wider considerations about the role of the artist and the best techniques to be followed.

Although the poem is rather haphazard in its organization, its central concerns can be easily summarized. The recurrent themes are the need for unity and propriety in poetry, the interaction between the contemporary writer and the past, and the moral and educative function of creative writing. When dealing with consistency and unity, Horace's advice concentrates on the poet's technique, and his fundamental principle is that all works of art have an internal decorum, with each part fitting into the overall conception:

> Imagine a painter who wanted to combine a horse's neck with a human head, and then clothe a miscellaneous collection of limbs with various kinds of feathers, so that what started out at the top as a beautiful woman ended in a hideously ugly fish. If you were invited, as friends, to the private view, could you help laughing?

As always, this brief passage, the opening of the poem, shows Horace's recurrent concern with the audience, and his notion of 'fittingness' is based on the predictable expectations of the intelligent reader or viewer. The idea of decorum had already been put forward by Aristotle and Cicero, but Horace made it more fundamental to the art of the writer for both pragmatic and more doctrinaire reasons. He believed that every component in any work of art should be appropriate for the kind of work it was part of, that the genre a particular work belonged to set out clear rules for the kind of characterization, language, metre, and tone it should include. If these rules were followed, the relationship between writer and reader could be one of mutual respect, and the dignity of writing be maintained.

In order to become aware of the rules of propriety, the aspiring writer must embark on a course of education: 'Study Greek models night and day'. By immersing himself in these 'models', the new writer learns enough about technique to discover his own articulateness, seeing what to do and what not to do. Histories of kings and generals, dreadful wars: it was Homer who showed in what metre these could be narrated. Revered writers from the past are thus the models for imitation, but the poet should not neglect the world around him. 'My advice to the skilled imitator will be to keep his eye on the model of life and manners, and draw his speech living from there'. Horace does not develop his idea of imitation fully, but it is clearly central to his thinking, and along with the notion of the appropriateness of parts to the whole ('decorum'), it was exhaustively debated throughout the Renaissance and into the 18th century, forming the basis of neo-classical criticism.

Horace's third central idea was equally influential. For him, the poet must aim to combine delight and instruction in his audience and must seek simultaneously to entertain and edify them. 'Poets aim either to do good or to give pleasure, or, thirdly, to say things which are both pleasing and serviceable for life'. The status of creative writing depends, for Horace, on its unique ability to combine pleasure and instruction, and this both empowered writers and laid responsibilities upon them. For the writer who managed to achieve the proper blend, the rewards were enormous. 'The man who combines pleasure with usefulness wins every suffrage, delighting the reader and also giving him advice; this is the book that earns money for the Sosii [booksellers], goes overseas and gives your celebrated writer a long lease of fame.'

So Horace's presentation of the writer's role is an unusually professional one. He has little time for the idea that the writer is an eccentric or inspired figure, and prefers to see him as an erudite, skilled commentator on the affairs of the day. Only by combining nature and art properly can a writer reach the status to which the artist is entitled:

> Do good poems come by nature or by art? This is a common question. For my part, I don't see what study can do without a rich vein of talent, nor what good can come of untrained genius. They need each other's help and work together in friendship.

By adopting this position, Horace can be seen as an interim figure between the more formalist thinking of Aristotle, and the more inspirational concerns of Longinus. And although the *Poetics* and *On the Sublime* have stimulated enormous discussion, Horace's *The Poetic Art* has probably been more extensively influential on the practice of writers.

—Ian A. Bell

ODES BOOK I, POEM 5
Poem by Horace, 23 BC.

The fifth Ode in Horace's first book is written in four four-line stanzas, each with two asclepiads, followed by a pherecratean and a glyconic. It deals with two erotic themes: the pursuit by an inexperienced boy of a girl who already knows how to play the game, and the retirement of a battered older man from the sport of love. The poem opens with a question:

> What delicate boy, covered with liquid scents,
> importunes you, Pyrrha, in this pleasant grotto,
> amid the many roses?

This sets the scene, by establishing the inexperienced ardour of the youth and the worldly-wise attitude of Pyrrha, whose Greek name, meaning 'yellow-haired', marks her as a recognizable Horatian type: one of those rather callous females who toy with men's affections, like Lydia in I.8 or Barine in II.8. Another question follows: 'For whom do you bind back your hair,/prepared with tasteful simplicity?'.

There is a contrast between the boy, who has drenched himself in perfume, sparing no expense in his efforts, and Pyrrha's careful, yet simple, preparations. The expectation naturally arises that the girl's unadorned and innocent appearance will be matched by her behaviour, but, as the poet muses on the scene, his thoughts take a different turn. The remainder of the poem is one long sentence, in which the poet's thoughts ramble over the relationship between the young couple and his own erotic experiences. It begins with *heu*, which expresses pity for the boy who is soon to be disappointed and disillusioned:

> Alas, how often he will lament that she has broken faith,
> and that the gods have turned against him,
> and will look at the waters harsh with black winds,
> in wondering innocence.

This introduces the notion of the pursuit of love as similar to sailing on the sea: as far as the average Roman was concerned, an action fraught with danger and unpredictability. The implication is that the youth will have to endure Pyrrha's frequent temper tantrums, and will soon find himself facing a storm which he, as a novice sailor, will be unable to handle. The notorious propensity of the sea to change from shimmering calm to raging tempest parallels Pyrrha's emotional mutability. In the third stanza, the boy is given the epithet *credulus*, meaning 'naïve' or 'credulous', as he 'enjoys' the 'golden' Pyrrha, hoping that she will always be available and loving. He does not, however, know about 'the deceitful breeze' which picks up the metaphor of the stormy sea in the previous stanza. When Pyrrha is 'golden' she is like a sunny day at sea, but conditions can quickly change.

The poem concludes with a change of perspective as the poet focuses on his own situation and experiences:

> The temple wall with its votive tablet
> indicates that I have hung up my
> soaked clothes, as a dedication
> to the powerful god of the sea.

This alludes to the practice of placing a tablet on the wall of a temple to commemorate an escape from great danger, and also to the fact that shipwrecked sailors who survived sometimes made an offering of their clothes to the gods. Venus was connected with the sea, since in one version of the myth she was born from the foam of the waves, and so the idea of hanging up clothes has a double meaning here. The ode thus moves from boyish innocence to adult wisdom. The poet is the old, experienced sailor who knows the ways of the sea, that is, of women and, perhaps, of Pyrrha in particular. Having been shipwrecked in his time, as indicated by the soaked clothes, the poet has now apparently retired from seafaring. Yet he still has an interest in observing Pyrrha with her young lover and perhaps, like an old sea-dog, yearns for the excitement of past adventures. The poem also shifts scenes from Pyrrha's 'grotto' of roses to a temple, expanding the theme of love from the particular to the general. The goddess of love is an important deity, who must be treated with respect. One cannot help thinking in this context of the cave where Venus brought Aeneas and Dido together during a storm in Virgil's *Aeneid* IV. There, too, the unwary Aeneas found a woman impossible to control.

Horace's poem draws upon several elements of the Greek and Alexandrian literary tradition: for instance, the comparison of women to the sea derives from the patriarchal bias of ancient myths which associate the female principle with the irrational and untamed aspects of the natural world. Semonides of Amorgos, who wrote vituperatively of women's supposed animalistic features, also utilized the sea comparison. Others made the connection with the goddess of love. The figure of Pyrrha is a stereotype, as is the innocent youth who pursues her. The assumption throughout the poem is that such a woman is difficult to control but that her beauty entitles men to attempt to control her. The retirement from erotic pursuits was also a commonplace in Greek and Roman poetry.

As is often the case with Horace, several words are ambiguous and repay detailed study; for instance, the boy is described as *gracilis*, which suggests a slim and fragile build, but can also have a pejorative sense of 'thin' or 'puny'. There is, perhaps, the hint of a suggestion that Pyrrha ought not to waste her time on a mere boy who does not know what he is doing. It can also mean 'graceful', which would be nicely ironic in this context, since the youth is obviously not a practised lover and has covered himself with perfume. Likewise, the youth hopes that Pyrrha will always be *vacua*, which means 'available' or 'empty'; again this serves to emphasize the ideology of possession, control, and even violence which permeates a superficially innocuous poem.

—David H.J. Larmour

ODES BOOK IV, POEM 7
Poem by Horace, 13 BC.

The seventh ode of Horace's fourth book has seven stanzas of four lines each and is written in a variant of the Archilochean metre, with a dactylic hexameter followed by a dactylic trimeter catalectic. Each stanza is semantically complete although connected with the one that precedes it. The poem opens with an evocation of the countryside after the spring thaw:

> The snows have fled, now the grass returns to the fields
> and the leaves to the trees;
> the earth goes through its changes, and subsiding rivers
> flow past the banks.

The mention of the earth going through its changes introduces the idea of the cycle of life and death, which is later elaborated. In the second stanza, the poet turns to the mythological universe, with a picture of the naked Graces and Nymphs 'daring' to come out and perform their dances, now that the weather has turned warm. This is a typical scene of the joyfulness of Spring, described elsewhere by Horace (Odes I.4 and IV.12). But then comes a reminder of the passage of time and the inevitable cycle:

> Lest you hope this goes on for ever, the year offers a
>   warning,
> and also the hour which carries off the nurturing day.

This admonitory tone is continued in the third stanza, in which we see the winter cold being warmed by the spring zephyrs, then the summer 'trampling on' the spring, to be followed by 'the fruit-bearing autumn' with its crops, and soon 'sluggish winter rushes back'. The seasons are personified in anticipation of the emphasis on human death in the latter half of the poem. Horace also shows considerable virtuosity in introducing the seasons in different ways.

The first three stanzas take the traditional type of poem about the joys of Spring and turn it into a more reflective and philosophical piece on the meaning of the cycle of the seasons. There is a sense of inevitability about the movement from birth to death. The first stanza opens with snow, and the third stanza closes with Winter. In the fourth stanza, the focus shifts to the legendary kings of Rome:

> When we sink down
> to where dutiful Aeneas, where wealthy Tullus and
>   Ancus are,
> we are dust and shadow.

The reference to Aeneas is possibly an allusion to Virgil's *Aeneid*; Horace uses the epithet *pius* (dutiful), which is one of the most frequently used Virgilian adjectives for Aeneas. The theme of death now comes to the fore. The fifth stanza opens with a direct question to the reader: 'Who knows if the gods above will add tomorrow's time/to today's total?'. This echoes the well-known Horatian and Epicurean theme of living for the day, expressed most memorably by the phrase *carpe diem* (seize the day) in Ode I.11.

In the sixth stanza, the poet returns to the issue of death raised in the fourth stanza:

> When once you have gone down and Minos has made
>   his
> shining judgement of you,
> then, Torquatus, neither lineage nor eloquence, nor
> dutifulness, will bring you back.

Death, therefore, is inevitable and terribly final. Torquatus was probably one of Horace's friends, perhaps an orator from a noble family. The mention of dutifulness (*pietas*) again alludes to Aeneas who, in the sixth book of Virgil's epic, went down to Hades to meet his father and came back to the world of the living. He could only achieve this, however, with the aid of the gods. For the rest of humankind, there is no way back. The last stanza restates this using more mythological examples: Diana would free 'chaste Hippolytus' from the 'infernal darkness' if she could, but she does not have the power. Likewise, Theseus cannot break the 'Lethaean chains' of his dear friend Pirithous. Hippolytus was devoted to Diana as goddess of chastity and was driven to death by Theseus, who thought he had made sexual advances to his wife. Theseus went down to Hades with Pirithous in an attempt to carry off Proserpina, wife of Pluto; they were imprisoned, but Theseus was rescued by Hercules and taken back to the world above. Now, however, he has finally died, and cannot do anything to help his companion. Pirithous has, in fact, forgotten him (Lethe was the river of Forgetfulness). Thus, the *pietas* of Theseus is wasted. Hippolytus' devotion to virginity contrasts starkly with the reputation of Theseus and Pirithous for sexual aggression but, in death, Horace seems to suggest, vices and virtues do not really matter.

In the first part of the poem, the cycle of the seasons suggests movement, while the latter part emphasizes the finality and bondage of death. The penultimate word of the ode is 'chains' (*vincula*), emphasizing that there is no escape from death. There is some ambiguity about the poem, however, as is often the case with Horace: the cycle of the seasons and of nature in general recalls the Stoic doctrine of the cycle of the universe, which is continually consumed by fire and then recreated. The mention of Aeneas similarly recalls the transmigration of souls explained in Virgil's sixth book. There is, then, some suggestion of an eventual 'escape' from death's chains; this is particularly likely because of the mention of Lethe at the end of the poem: Aeneas learns from his father that the souls of the dead are purified for a thousand years, after which they drink from the river Lethe before returning to the upper world. Death is perhaps to be seen, therefore, as a period of immobility, paralleling the 'sluggish' Winter mentioned at the end of the third stanza. The general pessimism of the poem is thus tempered to a certain extent in a reading which is cognizant of the Virgilian allusions.

—David H.J. Larmour

HORVÁTH Ödön (Josef) von. Born in Fiume (now Rijeka), Austro-Hungarian Empire, 9 December 1901. Educated at Episcopal School, Budapest, 1909–13; Wilhelmsgymnasium and Realschule, Munich, 1913–16; school in Pressburg, 1916; Realgymnasium, Vienna, 1916–19; University of Munich, 1919–22. Married Maria Elsner in 1933 (divorced 1934). Involved in politics from an early age; writer from 1922; contributor to various newspapers and journals; settled in Berlin, 1926; freelance writer, from 1929; increasingly attacked by the Nazis, from 1931; dialogue writer for the German film industry, 1934; left Germany to retain Hungarian citizenship, 1933; returned briefly to Berlin in early 1933; moved to Austria until the German annexation, then emigrated to Zurich, 1934. Recipient: Kleist prize, 1931. *Died 7 June 1938.*

PUBLICATIONS

Collections

Stücke, edited by Traugott Krischke. 1961.
Gesammelte Werke, edited by Traugott Krischke, Walter Huder, and Dieter Hildebrandt. 4 vols., 1970; also edition in 8 vols., 1972.
Gesammelte Werke, edited by Traugott Krischke. 4 vols., 1988.

Plays

Das Buch der Tänze (libretto; produced 1922). 1922.
Revolte auf Côte 3018 (produced 1927). 1927; as *Die Bergbahn* (produced 1929), 1928.
Zur schönen Aussicht (produced 1969). 1927.
Sladek; oder, die schwarze Armee (produced 1972). 1928; revised version, as *Sladek, der schwarze Reichswehrmann* (produced 1929), 1929.
Rund um den Kongress (produced 1959). 1929.
Italienische Nacht (produced 1931). 1930; edited by Ian Huish, 1986.
Geschichten aus dem Wienerwald (produced 1931). 1931; edited by Hugh Rank, 1980; as *Tales from the Vienna Woods*, translated by Christopher Hampton, 1977.
Kasimir und Karoline (produced 1932). 1932; edited by Traugott Krischke, 1973; as *Kasimir and Karoline*, translated by Violet B. Ketes, in *Four Plays*, 1986.
Glaube, Liebe, Hoffnung (as *Liebe, Pflicht und Hoffnung*, produced 1936). 1932; edited by Traugott Krischke, 1973; also edited by Ian Huish, 1986; as *Faith, Hope and Charity*, translated by Paul Foster and Richard Dixon, in *Four Plays*, 1986; also translated by Christopher Hampton, 1989.
Die Unbekannte aus der Seine (produced 1949). 1933.
Hin und Her (produced 1934). In *Gesammelte Werke*, 1970.
Mit dem Kopf durch die Wand (produced 1935). 1935.
Figaro lässt sich scheiden (produced 1937). 1959; as *Figaro Gets a Divorce*, translated by Roger Downey, in *Four Plays*, 1986; as *Figaro Gets Divorced*, translated by Ian Huish, in *Two Plays*, 1991
Der jüngste Tag (produced 1937). 1955; edited by Ian Huish, 1985; as *Judgement Day*, translated by Martin and Renate Esslin, in *Four Plays*, 1986.
Ein Dorf ohne Männer, from a novel by Koloman van Mikszáth (produced 1937). In *Gesammelte Werke*, 1970.
Himmelwärts (produced 1950). In *Gesammelte Werke*, 1970.
Don Juan kommt aus dem Krieg (produced 1952). In *Stücke*, 1961; as *Don Juan Comes Back from the War*, translated by Christopher Hampton, 1978.
Pompeji (produced 1959). In *Stücke*, 1961.
Four Plays (includes *Kasimir und Karoline*; *Faith, Hope, and Charity*; *Figaro Gets a Divorce*; *Judgement Day*). 1986.
Two Plays (includes *Don Juan Comes Back from the War* and *Figaro Gets Divorced*), translated by Ian Huish and Christopher Hampton. 1991.

Fiction

Der ewige Spiesser. 1930.
Ein Kind unserer Zeit; Jugend ohne Gott. 2 vols., 1938; as *Zeitalter der Fische*, 1953; as *A Child of Our Time*, translated by R. Wills Thomas, 1938; as *The Age of the Fish*, 1939.

*

Critical Studies: *Materialien zu Horváth* edited by Traugott Krischke, 1970, and *Horváth: Ein Lesebuch* by Krischke, 1978; *Über Horváth* (includes bibliography) edited by Dieter Hildebrandt and Traugott Krischke, 1972; *Symposium on Horváth* published by Austrian Institute, London, 1977; *Horváth Studies: Close Readings of Six Plays* by Krishna Winston, 1977; *A Student's Guide to Horváth* by Ian Huish, 1980, and *Ödön von Horváth Fifty Years On* edited by Huish and Alan Bance, 1988; *Prostitution in the Works of Ödön von Horváth* by Belinda Horton Carstens, 1982; *The Reformation of Comedy: Genre Critique in the Comedies of Ödön von Horváth* by Christopher B. Balme, 1985.

*   *   *

Ödön von Horváth, the most representative dramatist of the Weimar Republic, saw himself as 'a faithful chronicler' of his times. His uncompromising veracity and oppositional stance to the politics of nascent Nazism (who burnt his books) compelled him to emigrate in 1933 and left him without a stage to write for. His plays portray, as he once laconically observed, the 'gigantic struggle between the individual and society, that eternal slaughter in which there is to be no peace' (Randbemerkung, marginal comment). While he saw contemporary political and social life in dramatic terms, he had a sharp eye for the tell-tale or typical detail. His dramatic technique tended not towards the drastic, but to subtler stage-effects: moments of critical illumination and finely moderated accents. His characters are conceived as representative 'creatures of an ailing age', smug mediocraties in the main, trapped in the confines of a petty-bourgeois prejudice and conformity. His vision of humanity remained soberly critical and unheroic.

His plays are divided between the genres of comedy, dialect theatre, and period drama yet they anticipate the theatre of the absurd in their mixture of the comic, the tragic, and the gruesome. Though he adopted the naive, established conventions of Austrian popular theatre in a conscious attempt to revitalize that tradition, his plays are ironic-realistic portrayals of the contemporary historical scene, set in the years 1925–37 against a background of inflation, unemployment, political extremism, and the rise of fascism. The chosen social milieu is almost exclusively that of the lower-middle class in Vienna and Munich whose typical life-style, ideology, and speech habits are sharply set in focus.

The critical irony which pervades Horváth's plays stems largely from his subtle handling of dialogue. Horváth's language exploits the latent contradictions between overt and covert meanings, the intentional and unintentional in speech. Language betrays and exposes its inept user. The frequent points of conflict which arise within his dialogues are usually marked by the stage direction: 'silence'. These momentary pauses which punctuate speech have the effect of a searching concentration on language and consciousness, yet always with reference to the unspoken. The use of unreflective speech, the pretentious jargon and clichés of the semi-educated, as the principal key both to individual psychology and to the consciousness of a class, is a dramatic device which Horváth developed and perfected. His attempted 'synthesis between irony and realism', in his own words, produces a form of theatre which combines life-like representation with critical distancing. Though a kind of 'alienation', in theatrical terms, is achieved by subversive and ironic use of dialect and stereotyped language, what distinguishes Horváth from Brecht is the avoidance of dialectical debate and of didacticism.

In Horváth not action but the word is the principal carrier of drama, and he insisted on a stylized manner of performance. Dialogue is used with a fine sense of its force, ambiguities, and psychological implications. 'Demaskierung des Bewusstseins' (the unmasking of consciousness) is Horváth's phrase for his technique of allowing characters involuntarily to reveal their inner natures, intentions, and thoughts, through the words they use. The conflict between appearance and reality, pretence and truth is thus dramatically enacted. The social dimension is at the same time manifested, since the conventions of language used by the classes portrayed are equally subject to critical scrutiny. The menacing political reality behind an apparently harmless facade is best exemplified in *Geschichten aus dem Wienerwald* (*Tales from the Vienna Woods*), which presents a suspect image of 'the old honest true golden Viennese heart' compounded of sentimentalism, kitsch, and brutality. This richly diverse mirror of the times shows the playwright at the pinnacle of his achievement. A number of other plays (*Glaube, Liebe, Hoffnung* [*Faith, Hope, and Charity*]; *Kasimir und Karoline*; *Die Unbekannte aus der Seine*; *Hin und Her*) portray the cold indifference of a bureaucratized society which exploits and ultimately destroys the individual. Yet tragic intensity is always held in check by a dramatist who chooses to explore the darker side of existence within the sordidness, pettiness, and banalities of life. His influence on the leading playwrights of the post-war years (Handke, Kroetz, Bauer, Turrini) has been fundamental.

Deprived of a stage for his plays, the exiled Horváth latterly turned to prose and wrote three short novels (*Der ewige Spiesser*, *Ein Kind unserer Zeit* [*A Child of Our Time*], *Jugend ohne Gott*). These depict the stark realities of the day in a sparse, economic style derivative of 'Neue Sachlichkeit' (the New Objectivity). Thomas Mann judged *Jugend ohne Gott*, a compelling study of the cold amorality of the Hitler Youth movement, to be the the most important novel of that generation.

—Alexander Stillmark

TALES FROM THE VIENNA WOODS (Geschichten aus dem Wienerwald)
Play by Ödön von Horváth, 1931.

The title, *Tales from the Vienna Woods*, offers the prospect of an evening's nostalgia, when Vienna was Vienna, the Danube was blue, and the air was filled with the reassuring tones of Johann Strauss. The additional reassurance of the 'Volksstück', the traditional folk-play with its simple tale simply told suggests comedy, intrigue, a love story and, of course, a happy end. Indeed the curtain rises on a romantic vista: Danube, ruined castle, and the air, as the stage direction notes, alive with the sound of music—'as if in the background someone is playing Johann Strauss's "Tales from the Vienna Woods"'.

Viennese waltz music is heard frequently throughout the play, but all too often as an uncomfortable counterpoint and disturbance to the action on stage. Horváth sets his play in the present, not the past, and is writing "against the grain". The audience's expectations are roused and the illusion then shattered with the disturbing revelation that characters who profess morality and traditional values are driven by a more self-centred animal amorality.

Women are the prey in Horváth's world, and in *Tales from the Vienna Woods* the sacrificial victim is Marianne, a naive young girl who has seen more romantic films than is good for her. Reality is life with her father, the Zauberkönig, who runs a toy shop in a quiet street in the middle-class eighth district of Vienna. He has seen the advantages of an alliance in the street and is pushing her to marry their next-door neighbour Oskar, a butcher. Marianne is trapped and can see a lifetime's drudgery caring for both her new husband and her father. She is easily swept off her feet with the arrival of Alfred, a feckless, out of work gambler with an affectation of style and a vocabulary spiced with clichés, which Marianne, in thrall to her screen heroes, misinterprets as love.

Love, in Horváth's Vienna, is a smoke-screen for ruthless exploitation. Marianne leaves home, is disowned by her father, has a child by Alfred, and loses her pride by being obliged to appear in a nude revue, her liberty when caught stealing in a pitiful attempt to survive, and, finally, her child, who dies precisely as a carefully contrived family reconciliation and return to family values has been arranged. The happy end to this play is a hollow mockery. Oskar gains his bride, but it is he and the Zauberkönig who will live happily ever after.

Marianne's fate is not tragic but pathetic. She and her companions in this play successfully illustrate the motto Horváth gave to the work: 'Nothing is so infinite as the human capacity for stupidity'. Horváth presents this travesty of true love conquering all by ensuring that the audience recognizes the shallowness of his characters. They should speak, he said, in educated German, but we must always sense that their normal idiom is dialect and that it is their 'telephone voices' that we hear. The image they create is challenged by means of a recurrent stage direction *Stille* (Silence). The play is full of telling moments as the action stops in mid-sentence, catching the audience unawares and reminding them of the true implications of what has just been said and done.

As the play progresses, Marianne finds she has exchanged a life of finding her father's lost suspenders in the eighth district for a life in the 18th district with Alfred finding his. Such repetitions and moments of harsh humour combine with a dialogue that is deliberately rich in cliché, as the hypocrisy of the middle class is stripped away to reveal its true confusion and lack of moral base. Marianne's appearance in the cabaret at Maxim's encapsulates Horváth's technique of montage and contrast and his analysis of middle-class attitudes.

The floor show at Maxim's offers, to quote the master of ceremonies, three 'sensational *tableaux vivants*, created by the most talented artists to the highest aesthetic standards'. The first is 'Danube Water Sprites' performed to the 'Blue Danube'. The water sprites have tail fins covering their legs but are otherwise naked. Tableau Two is 'Our Zeppelin' and, to the tunes of a popular military march, three naked girls are displayed. The first holds a propeller, the second a globe, and the third a little Zeppelin. The audience, says the stage direction, 'roars its approval, rising to its feet and breaking spontaneously into the first verse of "Deutschland, Deutschland, über alles" before resuming its seats'. Tableau Three, to the accompaniment of Schumann's wistful 'Träumerei', is entitled 'In Pursuit of Happiness'. The girls, naked, struggle to be the first to reach a golden orb on which stands happiness, equally naked. It is a beautifully sentimental *son et lumière*.

The cabaret turns allow Horváth to combine sex (the girls), power and aggression (the Zeppelin), and tradition (the music) to show the truly instinctive and unthinking base supporting the façade of middle-class respectability. The Zauberkönig's loud approval of naked girls in cabaret turns to outrage when he recognizes that 'happiness' is in this instance 'his' Marianne, who has been forced to humiliate herself to provide for her child. Unforgiving in its hypocrisy, Horváth's

Vienna exacts a fearful price from its victims in the name of respectability.

Written in the 1930s as an attack on communal blindness and hypocrisy, *Tales from the Vienna Woods* is as relevant now as it was then. To those who wish to pretend that society has changed since the Nazi era, Horváth's play is an uncomfortable reminder that the middle-class capacity for self-deceit is as infinite as its capacity for stupidity.

—Alan Best

HSI-YU-CHI. See **JOURNEY TO THE WEST**.

HUGO, Victor (Marie). Born in Besançon, France, 26 February 1802. Educated at Cordier and Decotte's school, Paris, 1814–18. Married Adèle Foucher in 1822 (died 1868); three sons and two daughters; lived with Juliette Drouet from 1868 (she had been his mistress from 1833; died 1883). Editor, with his two brothers, *Le Conservateur littéraire*, 1819–21; involved in politics: founded newspaper *L'Événement* (later *L'Événement du Peuple*), 1848; elected to assembly, 1849, but exiled in 1851, first in Brussels, then in Jersey and Guernsey to 1870, and intermittently after that; visited France, 1870–71; deputy at Bordeaux Assembly, 1871; defeated in 1872 election because of his tolerance of Communards; elected to Senate, 1876. Chevalier, Légion d'honneur, 1825; Member, Académie française, 1841. Ennobled as Vicomte Hugo, 1845. *Died 22 May 1885*.

PUBLICATIONS

Collections

Works, translated by Frederick L. Slous and Camilla Crosland. 5 vols., 1887.
Dramas, translated by Frederick L. Slous and Camilla Crosland. 1887.
Works, translated by Alfred Barbou. 30 vols., 1892.
Dramas, translated by I.G. Burnham. 10 vols., 1895–96.
Works, edited by Henry Llewellyn Williams. 20 vols., 1907.
Romans, edited by Henri Guillemin. 3 vols., 1963.
Théâtre complet, edited by Roland Purnal. 2 vols., 1963–64.
Oeuvres poétiques, edited by Pierre Albouy. 3 vols., 1964–74.
Oeuvres complètes, edited by Jean Massin. 18 vols., 1967–70.
Poésies, edited by Bernard Leuilliot. 3 vols., 1972.

Fiction

Han d'Islande. 1823; as *Hans of Iceland*, translated anonymously, 1825; also translated by A. Langdon Alger, 1891; John Chesterfield, 1894; Huntington Smith, 1896; as *Hans of Iceland; or, The Demon of the North*, translated by J.T. Hudson, 1843; as *The Demon Dwarf*, 1847; as *The Outlaw of Iceland*, translated by Gilbert Campbell, 1885.

Bug-Jargal. 1826; as *The Slave King*, translated anonymously, 1833; as *Bug-Jargal*, translated anonymously, 1844; also translated by 'Eugenia de B', 1894; Arabella Ward, 1896; as *The Noble Rival*, 1845; as *Jargal*, translated by Charles E. Wilbour, 1866; as *Told Under Canvas*, translated by Gilbert Campbell, 1886.

Le Dernier Jour d'un condamné. 1829; as *The Last Day of a Condemned Man*, translated by P. Hesketh Fleetwood, 1840; also translated by Arabella Ward, 1896; and Metcalfe Wood, 1931; as *Under Sentence of Death; or, A Criminal's Last Hours*, translated by Gilbert Campbell, 1886; as *The Last Day of a Condemned*, translated by G.W.M. Reynolds, 1840; also translated by 'Eugenia de B', 1894; and Lascelles Wraxall, 1909; as *The Last Day of a Condemned Man*, edited and translated by Geoff Woollen, in *The Last Day of a Condemned Man and Other Prison Writings*, 1992.

Notre-Dame de Paris. 1831; edited by Jacques Seebacher and Yves Gohin, 1975; as *Notre Dame de Paris*, translated by A. Langdon Alger, 1832(?); also translated by Isabel F. Hapgood, 1888; Jessie Haynes, 1902; M. Dupres, 1949; as *The Hunchback of Notre-Dame*, translated by Frederic Shoberl, 1833; also translated by Henry Llewellyn Williams, 1862; Lowell Bair, 1982; as *La Esmeralda*, 1844; as *Notre Dame of Paris*, translated by J. Carroll Beckwith, 1892; also translated by John Sturrock, 1978.

Claude Gueux. 1834; as *Claude Gueux*, translated by Gilbert Campbell, 1886; also translated by 'Eugenia de B', 1894; Arabella Ward, 1896; edited and translated by Geoff Woollen, in *The Last Day of a Condemned Man and Other Prison Writings*, 1992.

Les Misérables. 1862; edited by Marcus Clapham and Clive Reynard, 1992; as *Les Misérables*, translated by Charles E. Wilbour, 1862; also translated by Lascelles Wraxall, 1862; Isabel F. Hapgood, 1887; William Walton and others, 1892–93; Norman Denny, 1976.

Les Travailleurs de la mer. 1866; edited by Jacques Seebacher and Yves Gohin, 1975; as *The Toilers of the Sea*, translated by W. Moy Thomas, 1860; also translated by Isabel F. Hapgood, 1888; Mary W. Artois, 1892; as *The Workers of the Sea*, translated by Gilbert Campbell, 1887.

L'Homme qui rit. 1869; as *The Man Who Laughs*, translated by William Young, 1869; also translated by Isabel F. Hapgood, 1888; as *By Order of the King*, translated by Mrs A.C. Steele, 3 vols., 1870; also translated by Hapgood, 1888; as *The Laughing Man*, 1887; also translated by Bellina Phillips, 1894.

Quatre-Vingt-Treize. 1874; as *Ninety-Three*, translated by Frank Lee Benedict and J. Hain Friswell, 1874; Gilbert Campbell, 1886; Aline Delano, 1888; Helen B. Dole, 1888; Jules Gray, 1894; Lowell Bair, 1962; as *'93*, translated by E.B. d'Espinville Picot, 1874.

The Last Day of a Condemned Man and Other Prison Writings (includes *Claude Gueux*; *My Visit to the Concierge*; *The Condemned Cells at La Roquette*), edited and translated by Geoff Woollen. 1992.

Plays

Amy Robsart, from *Kenilworth* by Scott (produced 1827); as *Amy Robsart*, translated by I.G. Burnham, 1896; also translated with *Angelo* and *The Twin Brothers*, 1901; and by Ethel T. and Evelyn Blair, 1933.

Cromwell (produced 1956). 1827; edited by Annie Ubersfeld, 1968; as *Oliver Cromwell* (vols. 1–2), translated by I.G. Burnham, 1896.

Marion Delorme (produced 1831). 1829; as *The King's Edict*, translated and adapted by B. Fairclough, 1872; as *Marion de Lorme*, translated by I.G. Burnham, 1895; as *Red Robe and Grey Robe; or, Richelieu Defied*, translated by Henry Llewellyn Williams, 1901.

Hernani (produced 1830). 1830; as *Hernani*, translated by Lord Gower, 1830; also translated by Camilla Crosland, 1887; I.G. Burnham, 1895; R. Farquharson Sharp, 1898.

Le Roi s'amuse (produced 1832). 1832; as *The King's Fool*, translated by H.T. Haley, 1842; as *Le Roi s'amuse*, translated by Frederick L. Slous, 1843; also translated by I.G. Burnham, 1895; as *The King's Diversion*, translated by Frederick L. Slous and Camilla Crosland, 1887; as *His Kingly Pleasure*, translated by Edward John Harding, 1902; as *The King Enjoys Himself*, translated by T.M.R. von Keler, 1925.

Lucrèce Borgia (produced 1833). 1833; as *Lucretia Borgia*, translated by W.T. Haley, 1842; as *Lucrezia Borgia*, translated and adapted by W. Young, 1847; also translated by I.G. Burnham, 1896.

Marie Tudor (produced 1833). 1833; as *Mary Tudor*, translated by I.G. Burnham, 1896.

Angelo, Tyran de Padoue (produced 1835). 1835; as *Angelo*, translated and adapted by Charles Reade, 1851; also translated by Ernest O. Coe, 1880; translated with *Amy Robsart* and *The Twin Brothers*, 1901; as *Angelo; or, The Tyrant of Padua*, 1855; as *Angelo and the Actress of Padua*, translated by G.H. Davidson, 1855; as *Angelo; or, The Actress of Padua*, translated by G. A'Beckett, 1857; as *Angelo, Tyrant of Padua*, translated by I.G. Burnham, 1896; also translated by Charles Alfred Byrne (bilingual edition), 1905.

La Esméralda, music by Louise Bertin, from *Notre-Dame de Paris* by Hugo (produced 1836). 1836; as *Esmeralda*, translated by I.G. Burnham, 1895.

Ruy Blas (produced 1838). 1838; edited by Annie Ubersfeld, 2 vols., 1971–72; as *Ruy Blas*, translated and adapted by Charles Webb, 1860; also translated by Camilla Crosland, 1887; I.G. Burnham, 1895; Brian Hooker, 1931; adapted by Charles Fechter, 1870.

Les Burgraves (produced 1843). 1843; as *The Burgraves*, translated by I.G. Burnham, 1896.

Torquemada. 1882; edited by John J. Jance, 1989; as *Torquemada*, translated by I.G. Burnham, 1896.

Théâtre en liberté (short plays). 1886.

La Grand'mère (produced 1898). In *Théâtre en liberté*, 1886.

Mangeront-ils? (produced 1907). In *Théâtre en liberté*, 1886.

Théâtre de jeunesse. 1934.

Mille francs de récompense (produced 1961). In *Théâtre de jeunesse*, 1934.

Les Jumeaux. In *Théâtre complet*, 1964; as *The Twins*, translated by I.G. Burnham, 1896; as *The Twin Brothers*, with *Angelo* and *Amy Robsart*, 1901.

Verse

Odes et poésies diverses. 1822.

Nouvelles odes. 1824.

Odes et ballades. 1826; edited by Pierre Albouy, 1980.

Les Orientales. 1829; edited by Pierre Albouy, 1981.

Les Feuilles d'automne. 1831; edited by Pierre Albouy, 1981.

Les Chants du crépuscule. 1835; as *Songs of Twilight*, translated by George W.M. Reynolds, 1836.

Les Voix intérieures. 1837.

Les Rayons et les ombres. 1840.

Le Rhin. 1842; as *The Rhine*, translated by D.M. Aird, 1843; as *Excursions Along the Banks of the Rhine*, 1843; as *Sketches and Legends of the Rhine*, 1845; as *The Story of* the Bold Pécopin, translated by Eleanor and Augustine Birrell, 1902.

Les Châtiments. 1853; edited by P.J. Yarrow, 1975; and René Journet, 1977.

Les Contemplations. 1856; edited by Pierre Albouy, 1973.

La Légende des siècles. 3 vols., 1859–83; edited by André Dumas, 1974; as The Legend of the Centuries, translated by George S. Burleigh, 1867.

Les Chansons des rues et des bois. 1865.

L'Année terrible. 1872.

L'Art d'être grand-père. 1877.

Le Pape. 1878.

La Pitié suprême. 1879.

Religions et religion. 1880.

L'Âne. 1880; edited by Pierre Albouy, 1966.

Les Quatre vents de l'esprit. 1881.

The Literary Life and Poetical Works, edited by Henry Llewellyn Williams. 1883.

Translations from the Poems, translated by Henry Carrington. 1885.

La Fin de Satan. 1886.

Poems. 1888.

Toute la lyre. 2 vols., 1888–93.

Dieu. 1891; edited by René Journet and Guy Robert, 3 vols., 1969.

Poems, translated by George Young. 1901.

Selected Poems, edited by Alfred T. Baker. 1929.

The Distance, The Shadows: Selected Poems, translated by Harry Guest. 1981.

Other

Littérature et philosophie mêlées. 1834; edited by Anthony R.W. James, 1976.

Lettres sur le Rhin. 1846.

Congrès de la paix (International Peace Congress address). 1849; as The United States of Europe, 1914.

Napoléon le Petit. 1852; as Napoleon the Little, 1852; also translated by George Burnham Ives, 1909; as The Destroyer of the Second Republic, translated by 'A Clergyman', 1870.

John Brown, translated as Letter on John Brown, in Echoes of Harper's Ferry, edited by James Redpath. 1860; also translated by Lionel Strachey, 1902.

Dessins de Hugo (art criticism). 1862; edited by J. Sergent, 1955.

L'Archipel de la Manche. 1863; as The Channel Islands, translated by Isabel Hapgood, in The Toilers of the Sea, 1961; also translated by John W. Watson (bilingual edition), 1985.

Hugo raconté par un témoin de sa vie. 1863.

William Shakespeare. 1864; as William Shakespeare, translated by A. Baillot, 1864; also translated by Meville B. Anderson, 1886.

Actes et paroles. 3 vols., 1875–76.

Histoire d'un crime; Déposition d'un témoin. 2 vols., 1877–78; as History of a Crime; Testimony of an Eyewitness, translated by T.H. Joyce and Arthur Locker, 4 vols., 1877–78; Gilbert Campbell, 1888; Huntington Smith, 1888.

Le Discours pour Voltaire. 1878; as Oration on Voltaire, translated by James Parton, 1883.

Works. 8 vols., 1883, revised as 12 vols., 1887.

Selections, Chiefly Lyrical, edited by Henry Llewellyn Williams. 1883.

Choses vues. 2 vols., 1887–1900; edited by Hubert Juin, 4 vols., 1972; translated in part as Things Seen, 2 vols., 1887; revised edition, edited by David Kimber, 1964.

Alpes et Pyrénées. 1890; as The Alps and Pyrenees, translated by John Manson, 1898.

Selected Poems and Tragedies, translated by Gilbert Campbell and others. 1890.

France et Belgique. 1892; edited by Claude Gély, 1974.

Letters to His Wife and Others, translated by Nathan H. Dole. 1895.

Les Années funestes. 1896.

Letters, translated by F. Clarke. 1896.

Letters to His Family, to Sainte-Beuve and Others, edited by Paul Meurice. 1896.

Correspondance [1815–82]. 2 vols., 1896–98.

Letters from Exile and After the Fall of the Empire, edited by Paul Meurice. 1898.

Mémoires. 1899; as Memoirs, translated by John W. Harding, 1899.

Post-scriptum de ma vie. 1901; edited by Henri Guillemin, 1961; as Hugo's Intellectual Autobiography, translated by Lorenzo O'Rourke, 1907.

Love Letters 1820–22, translated by Elizabeth W. Latimer. 1901.

Dernière gerbe. 1902.

Correspondance, with Paul Meurice. 1909.

Correspondance, with Michelet. 1924.

Océan, tas de Pierres. 1942.

Correspondance [1814–85]. 4 vols., 1947–52.

Pierres: Vers et prose, edited by Henri Guillemin. 1951.

Carnets intimes, edited by Henri Guillemin. 1953.

Journal 1830–1848, edited by Henri Guillemin. 1954.

Hugo dessinateur, edited by Roger Cornaille and Georges Herscher. 1963.

Lettres à Juliette Drouet 1833–1883, edited by Jean Gaudon. 1964.

Correspondance, with Pierre-Jules Hetzel, edited by Sheila Gaudon. 1979—.

*

Bibliography: Victor Hugo's Drama: An Annotated Bibliography 1900–1980 by Ruth Lestha Doyle, 1981.

Critical Studies: The Career of Hugo, 1945, and The Perilous Quest: Image, Myth, and Prophecy in the Narratives of Hugo, 1968, both by Elliott M. Grant; Hugo, 1956, and Hugo and His World, 1966, both by André Maurois; Notes on Hugo's 'Les Misérables' by George Klin and Amy Marsland, 1968; A Stage for Poets: Studies in the Theatre of Hugo and Musset by Charles Affron, 1971; Hugo by John Porter Houston, 1974, revised edition, 1989; Victor Hugo: A Biography by Samuel Edwards, 1975; The Medievalism of Victor Hugo by Patricia A. Ward, 1975; Victor Hugo by Joanna Richardson, 1976; 'Les Contemplations' of Hugo: An Allegory of the Creative Process by Suzanne Nash, 1977; Victor Hugo: Philosophy and Poetry by Henri Peyre, 1980; Hugo, Hernani and Ruy Blas by Keith Wren, 1982; Victor Hugo and the Visionary Novel by Victor Brombert, 1984; Hugo: 'Les Contemplations' by Peter Cogman, 1984; Victor Hugo by Gregory Stevens Cox, 1985; The Power of Rhetoric: Hugo's Metaphor and poetics by Wendy Nicholas Greenberg, 1985; Victor Hugo in Jersey by Phil Stevens, 1985; The Early Novels of Victor Hugo by Kathryn M. Grossman, 1986; 'Les Contemplations' of Victor Hugo: The Ash Wednesday Liturgy by John A. Frey, 1988.

* * *

When Gide was asked to name France's greatest poet, his reply was 'Victor Hugo, hélas!', a response expressing Hugo's undeniable stature and a concomitant embarrassment on the part of a mature Frenchman in acknowledging such a fact. Hugo spanned the 19th century, and dealt in his works with all the major issues central to individuals, society, literature, politics, and religion through this period of violent and frequent change. Along with the published novels, plays, poems, and essays go more volumes of fragments, ideas, images, word-associations, rhymes, all scribbled on whatever piece of paper was at hand. His output is monumental, indeed he himself referred to it as a single edifice in which individual works were merely stones. Given such a proliferation it is perhaps natural that among the marks of genius there should also be much that is trite, oversimplified, and self-indulgent.

The main explanation for this apparent paradox is that Hugo was a great primitive, who approached his subjects with intensity, simplicity, and an unshakeable confidence in the validity of his own vision. All his writings were informed by the belief that creation was a composite of forces of good and evil and this dualism provides both the structural security of his works, which deal invariably with conflicting opposites, and the richness of an imagery whose prism translates everything into a battle between light and darkness. His attempts thus to categorize and render accessible the mysterious absolutes that are the dynamics of existence take account also of another omnipresent sensation, that of vertigo. It is the feeling, absorbed during childhood and adolescence from the traumas of Imperial and Restoration society and shared by an entire generation, that the fragile hold on faith, reason, or any human construct may dissolve and leave only 'le gouffre'. It is not a distortion to describe the fundamental Hugolian experience as a play of day and night on the edge of an abyss.

His philosophy, intuited early and evolved and refined through the middle years, placed man at the centre of an axis stretching between God and earth. Once again the condition is that of antithesis which seeks synthesis. Matter is evil, its very weight and substance separating it from spirit, and therefore God. Original sin is literally a fall and only by a progressively greater awareness of and recourse to things of the spirit may the prison of matter be breached and the soul released up to its source. More than any other writer Hugo was aware of his Messianic role in such a context. With sometimes disarming and sometimes infuriating conceit he places himself above his fellow-mortals to act as a visionary, a gifted intermediary between God and his creatures. Writing was the manipulation of material things to reveal spiritual truths, an interface between concrete and abstract, and Hugo recognized the importance of the fact that 'In the beginning was the word . . .'. Words to him were simultaneously 'things' and 'mysterious wanderers of the soul', the black and literal object on the page was the envelope of a spreading transcendent truth, and thus the ingredients and processes of artistic creativity mirrored those of Creation itself.

He began writing his poetry in a climate of dissatisfaction. Although his earliest works expressed conventional attitudes to Church and King and execrated Napoleon, the recognition that the *ancien régime* was stifling progress quickly began to break the moulds of poetry as well as those of belief. A collection of poems like *Les Orientales* demonstrates the true Romantic revolution of lyric poetry. The forms are new, the rhythms daring and mysterious, the subject-matter exotic, and Hugo's contemporaries acknowledged the fact that their literary generation had found its leader. He himself claimed later in life to have 'dislocated' the alexandrine, liberated French versification, and revolutionized poetic vocabulary, a boast entirely validated by the collections of the 1820s and 1830s. The works are those of a man totally involved in the moods and movements of his times. Enforced exile, however, removed him from the literary barricades and allowed time for reflection, or more properly contemplation. In the Channel Islands, his own exile, the death of his daughter, his 'crimes' and his sexuality are examined and, through the alchemy of the poetic process, transformed into a strong, single affirmation of divine purpose. *Les Contemplations* is a masterpiece, containing poems brilliant in themselves and yet also important as components within the deliberate architecture of an overall poetic narrative. The conviction at which he arrives in the making of this work provides the basis for the great epic collections of his middle and later years, the gigantic stories of myth, creation, history which continue his exploration of verse, image, and language through poetic registers more varied than those of any of the poets who had preceded him.

His pre-eminence extended to the world of the theatre. The preface to his play *Cromwell* became the manifesto of the French Romantics, not because its ideas were particularly new, but because the power of Hugo's rhetoric gave it coherence and force. Its main original contribution to the debate between Classical and Romantic adherents was the theory of the grotesque. This proposed not, as is sometimes mistakenly suggested, that emphasis should fall only on the ugly and misshapen, but that art should mix extremes of the beautiful and the grotesque in order to convey a more complete picture of the world than that which had been proposed by the Classical imitators with their ideals of beauty. His own plays adopted the morality of popular melodrama, and criticism of them has always been directed at their 'unreality' and the fact that he created only stereotypes. Hugo himself, however, never claimed verisimilitude, and if the plays are experienced as dramatic poems, then character, like symbol and image, is seen to be a constituent part of an artistic whole which conveys its meanings through the totality of its impact rather than from the activities of some of its parts; when Hernani confronts Don Salluste it is not merely a young man facing an old one, it is the whole tangle of Ancien Régime, the Restoration's desire to perpetuate it and the frustrating and inexpressible need of the new generation to be liberated from both.

It is easy also to offer facile criticisms of his novels. Indeed the earliest are in themselves Gothic parodies, the hero of one making meals of human flesh washed down with seawater drunk from his son's skull. His linguistic facility, however, and the vast imagination of the visionary produced the great evocation of medieval Paris clutched around the cathedral in *Notre-Dame de Paris* (*The Hunchback of Notre-Dame*), the socio-political tapestry of *Les Misérables* which contains enough themes and sub-plots to fill several novels, and the mysticism of *Les Travailleurs de la mer* (*The Toilers of the Sea*) in which the central character defeats wind and waves, and Hugo reminds the reader that reality consists of more than just conscious imaginings. The prose is as sonorous as the poetry and in all the works the great unifying tendency of the visionary is the controlling factor.

Hugo's work is monolithic. In it the Romantics, the Symbolists, and even the Surrealists found examples of their own desired effects. It is inhabited by monsters, Gods, and men, sprawling, digressing, and yet simultaneously rendering accessible the moods and movements of the human spirit in its own time and beyond.

—W.J.S. Kirton

THE HUNCHBACK OF NOTRE-DAME (Notre-Dame de Paris)
Novel by Victor Hugo, 1831.

Contrary to received opinion, enshrined in early translations and popular films, the preface and the structure of *The Hunchback of Notre-Dame* show that the main character is not the 'hunchback', Quasimodo, but the archdeacon Claude Frollo. The preface recounts a visit to Notre-Dame when the author found the Greek word 'ΑΝΑΓΚΗ' graven in the stone in an obscure corner. This is presented as the origin of the text: 'He . . . sought to divine who might be the troubled soul who had not wished to leave this world without leaving this mark of crime or misfortune on the surface of the old church'. The word, which means 'fatality', is Frollo's. Not only is it inscribed in his cell (VII, 4), but in a scene which is emblematic of the novel as a whole (VII, 6), he prevents a visitor from saving a fly caught in a spider's web, crying 'Let fatality have its way'. In relation to La Esmeralda Frollo is the spider, but in relation to fatality he is the fly. Moreover he is placed in a relation of power towards all significant characters: his younger brother Jehan, for whose death he is ultimately responsible; Pierre Gringoire, whom he teaches; Quasimodo who is his adoptive child, and not least Esmeralda, whom he desires and over whom he has the power of life and death. Frollo is central: he is an agent of fatality, but also its victim.

Fatality has several dimensions. A key image in the novel first occurs when Quasimodo is being described. The Cathedral has become metaphorically the hunchback's 'shell' and he has become its soul; were the narrator able, however, to scrutinize the soul of Quasimodo, within its 'cave', he would probably find it hunched up ('rabougrie') 'like those Venetian prisoners who grow old, bent double in a stone box which is too low and too short' (IV, 3). This image stresses oppression and incommunicability, themes which are present in the central section (VI), when the deaf Quasimodo is brought before a deaf judge and sentenced, and also in the scene where Louis XI is discussing with his treasurer the cost and the measurements of a cage, while ignoring the prisoner inside it (X, 5). Medieval justice is deaf; the voice of the oppressed is unheard. In that scene, while the 'truands' are about to storm Notre-Dame to release Esmeralda, the King is at the Bastille. The theme of imprisonment is political as well as psychological.

Escape is illusory. The door which love might have opened leads only to frustration or death. Quasimodo loves his master Frollo, and Esmeralda, but both die. Esmeralda loves Phoebus, who does not return her love, and when she is in prison escape without death is only possible if she yields to Frollo, which she refuses. Frollo nourishes two kinds of illusion: to be loved by Esmeralda and to succeed through the alchemical quest in his search for knowledge. These two desires are incompatible, but the text of the novel unites them through variants of the image of inaccessible light: the gold of the sun, which is an emblem of the alchemist's aim, but also used of Frollo's vision of Esmeralda dancing (VIII, 4).

Fatality works therefore against love in human relationships, against individuals and peoples of a social or political level, and against the quest for knowledge. Breaches in this fundamental pessimism are rare: Jacques Coppenole, who insists on having himself announced as a cobbler (I, 4); the gourd of water that Esmeralda offers to Quasimodo in the stocks (VI, 4).

When *The Hunchback of Notre-Dame* was written, the most influential novelist in France was Walter Scott. In 1823 Hugo had praised *Quentin Durward* for its 'magical' evocations of the past and its mingling of the ugly and the beautiful.

Notre-Dame is an historical novel (the year 1482 marks a transition from the Middle Ages to the Renaissance, from sculpture to printing as a means of instruction), but there are two important differences from Scott. The first is that in the Hugo novel historical characters, such as Louis XI, have minor rather than major roles, and the second is the narrator's ironic stance: he makes clear that he is pulling the strings, and also makes frequent parallels with the time of writing: 'If Gringoire were living nowadays, how well he would hold the middle ground between classic and romantic!' (II, 4). His attitude towards his characters varies from ironic detachment (Gringoire), to sympathy (Quasimodo); he sees them mostly from outside, or through the eyes of other characters, but on rare occasions, such as Frollo's hallucinated anguish when he believes Esmeralda hanged (IX, 1), he writes from within.

Notre-Dame is not, as has been said, a 'character' in the novel, but its architecture is doubly important: firstly in the immediate context (1830), when some were defending Gothic monuments against depredations on aesthetic but also political grounds (Gothic architecture was 'of the people'); secondly as a structuring principle of the whole book. The Cathedral is a hybrid construction, part romanesque, part gothic (Quasimodo is also *hybrid*) and Paris is described (III, 2) as a hybrid (city, university, town). Hybrid means that what is ugly in detail may not be so in the whole. The façade of Notre-Dame, this 'symphony in stone' (III, 1), is an exemplar of that harmony in multiplicity which the total construction of the book embodies at one level, and complex sentences (or sustained metaphors), powerfully welded into unity by their clear syntactic structure, at another. The proliferation of living detail—popular speech, minutiae of early documents, architectural features—and the author's capacity to work such detail into new and ever-widening forms of unity are in creative tension with his pessimism. This creative tension, palpable at best in the prose style, makes of *The Hunchback of Notre-Dame* not a melodrama but a novel in which the pessimism induced by the operations of fatality is fought with the tools of art. At the end Quasimodo and Esmeralda have become dust, the word ΑΝΑΓΚΗ has been effaced, but the cathedral, and the book, remain.

—Tony James

LES MISÉRABLES
Novel by Victor Hugo, 1862.

Hugo started to write in France a novel which was first called *Les Misères*, but he finished it only in 1862 while he was in exile in the Channel Islands, during Napoléon III's régime.

As the double meaning of the title (Base Wretches/The Poorest of the Poor) indicates, the main character of the novel is the precarious social group, below the working class, which is led to commit crime (prostitution for women and theft for men) because of poverty.

Those people do not express themselves in literary French. In some dialogues, realism forces Hugo to use slang which he translates, through Gavroche, for instance, who explains certain expressions to his brothers, or in footnotes when the text contains too much of it.

Outsiders of society live in the margins of space, out of the city (in 'les faubourgs') and of time: they only appear when night falls and the bourgeois go to sleep.

Among them, Hugo favours youngsters: children like Gavroche, his brothers and sisters, and Cosette in the first part of the novel, and teenagers (Montparnasse, Éponine, Azelma, and Cosette) in the second part. He compares them to small, cute animals—to cats, for instance: originally Gavroche's name was Chavroche!—while adult thieves are compared to nasty, dangerous ones. The Thénardier and the Patron-Minette band are repulsive, according to Lavater's theory that the soul is reflected in the physical appearance. Children and teenagers should be beautiful because of their youth, but are in fact ugly as a result of their conditions of life, and women loose their femininity in poverty. But the younger ones succeed in being happy (they sing all the time) by keeping their sense of humour and of poetry because they are free.

The 'misérables' move towards greater social and religious awareness by sacrificing themselves to others. Their evolution usually ends in death: Fantine dies for her daughter, Gavroche for the barricade, Éponine for Marius, and Jean Valjean for Cosette. Martyrdom is achieved and the characters cannot progress any further. The poor are seen as the people of God.

If the author shows the way out of poverty and crime to his characters, it is because he is portraying the readers of his novel: in his letters to his publisher, Hugo kept insisting that the volumes were financially accessible to all. He chose to show reality not out of complacency but in order to denounce it and, therefore, to change it. As his introduction points out, he addressed this book to all human beings who endure exploitation, suffering, and ignorance.

Was his wish fulfilled? Was *Les Misérables* read by the people Hugo intended it for? It was certainly very successful when it first appeared simultaneously in many European countries. The publication was even delayed because the workers were crying over the proofs . . . And the characters of the novel became 'types' straight away.

Popular acclaim and doubts from critics have ever since characterized the life of the novel and of its many adaptations (drama, cinema, and the long-running musical). French education and teaching institutions everywhere seem reluctant to include it in their curricula, although it is the most read novel in the world. As Jean-Paul Sartre said, Romantic writers— with the exception maybe of Musset—purported to write for the people, but only Hugo's *Les Misérables* actually reached its intended audience.

—Myrto Konstantarakos

HÜLSHOFF,   Annette   von   Droste-. See **DROSTE-HÜLSHOFF, Annette von**.

HUYGENS, Constantijn. Born in The Hague, Dutch Republic (now The Netherlands), 4 September 1596. Studied law at Leiden. Married his niece Susanna van Baerle in 1627 (died 1637); five children, including the scientist Christiaan Huygens. Travelled to Venice in 1619, and several times to England, once as secretary to a diplomatic mission, 1618, and again as secretary at the embassy, 1620; knighted by James I, 1622; secretary to successive Stadtholders, Frederik Henry, William II and III, from 1625. Associated with Descartes, Daniel Heinsius, Francis Bacon, Ben Jonson, and Pierre Corneille, *q.v..* Designed his own country house at Hofwijk. *Died 28 March 1687.*

PUBLICATIONS

Collections

De gedichten [The Poems], edited by J.A. Worp. 9 vols., 1892–99.
De briefwisseling [Correspondence], edited by J.A. Worp. 6 vols., 1911–17.

Verse

Misogamos. 1620.
Batave Tempe dat is 't voorhout van 's Gravenhage [Batavian Temple, That Is the Voorhout in The Hague]. 1621, reprinted 1973.
Costelick mal [Costly Folly]. 1622, reprinted 1973.
De uytlandighe herder [The Exiled Shepherd]. 1622.
Zedeprinten [Characters]. 1623–24.
Dorpen en stedestemmen [Voices of Villages and Towns]. 1624; edited by C.W. de Kruyter, 1981.
Otia of ledighe uren [Idleness or Empty Hours]. 1625.
Momenta desultoria. 1644.
Eufrasia. Ooghentroost [Solace for the Sightless]. 1647, reprinted 1984.
Vitaulium. Hofwijck. Hofstede vanden Heere van Zuylichem onder Voorburgh [Hofwijck, Seat of Lord of Zuylichem]. 1653.
Korenbloemen [Cornflowers]. 1658.
Dagh-werck [Daily Work]. 1658; edited by F.L. Zwaan, 1973.
Triomfdichten ter eeren de doorluchte Huizen van Nassauw, Oranje en Anhalt [Triumphal Poem in Honour of the Illustrious Houses of Nassau, Orange, and Anhalt]. 1660.
De nieuwe zee-straet van 's Gravenhage op Scheveningen [The New Sea Promenade from The Hague to Scheveningen]. 1667.
Cluyswerck [Work in Seclusion]. 1681.
Dichten op de knie, 500 sneldichten [Rhyming on the Knee, 500 Quick Rhymes], edited by G.W. and W.G. Hellinga. 1956.
Dromen met open ogen [Dreaming with Eyes Open] (selection), edited by M.A. Schenkeveld van der Dussen, L. Strengholt, and P.E.L. Verkuyl. 1984.
Sneldichten [Quick Rhymes], edited by H. Blijlevens, M. van Drunen, and P. Lavrijssen. 1988.

Play

Trijntje Cornelis. 1653; edited by H.M. Hermkens, 1987.

Other

Ghebruyck of onghebruyck van 't orgel [Use and Misuse of the Organ]. 1641, reprinted 1974.
Heilighe daghen [Holy Days]. 1645, reprinted 1974.
De vita propria (autobiography, in Latin). 1678; as *Mijn Jeugd* [My Youth], translated (into Dutch) by C.L. Heesakkers, 1987.
Dagboek van Constantijn Huygens [Diary]. 1885.
Lettres du Seigneur de Zuylichem à Pierre Corneille. 1890.

Journaal van zijne reis naar Venetië in 1620 (Travel Journal). 1894.
Correspondence of Descartes and Huygens, 1635–47 (in French), edited by Leon Roth. 1926.

*

Critical Studies: *'Some Thankfulness to Constantine': A Study of English Influence upon the Early Work of Constantine Huygens* by Rosalie Littel Colie, 1956; *Constantine Huygens and Britain* by A.G.H. Bachrach, 1962; *Driemaal Huygens*, 1966 and *De grootmeester van woord- en snarenspel. Het leven van Constantijn Huygens*, 1980, both by J. Smit; *Constantijn Huygens' Oogentroost: Een interpretatieve studie* by C.W. de Kruyter, 1971; *Dromen is denken: Constantijn Huygens over dromen en denken en dichten* by L. Strengholt, 1977; *Constantijn Huygens, mengeling* by A. van Strien, 1990.

* * *

Cast in the Renaissance mould of the *uomo universale*, Constantijn Huygens, like his contemporary, Jacob Cats, was a Calvinist moralist. Unlike Cats, however, his bearing was aristocratic and his literary work erudite, even obscure. In his autobiographical poem *Dagh-werck* [Daily Work], written between 1627 and 1638, he even added a note that true poetry should require elucidation, and he made his point by giving prose summaries of each stanza, concerning his daily life and his views on religion and poetry. It is significant that he described his poems as 'cornflowers' along the path of his life, suggesting that they are all autobiographical and provide a welcome creative redress from his onerous business career.

His first long poem is an ode of 105 eight-line stanzas in the humanist tradition, *Batave Tempe dat is 't voorhout van 's Gravenhage* [Batavian Temple, That Is the Voorhout in The Hague]. The Voorhout was (and still is) a fine tree-lined avenue in the centre of a town greatly loved by the poet, and he expatiates on its virtues by applying the theories of rhetoric appropriate to his theme. So we find a variety of styles and genres: lyrical, georgic, satirical, farcical, and emblematic. Yet there is a highly personal feeling in his sometimes humorous, sometimes bitter irony or parody, and an entirely individual use of circumlocution, condensation, and metaphor.

His moral indignation comes fully to light, however, in the mordant sarcasm of his next poem, *Costelick mal* [Costly Folly]. In some 500 lines of alexandrines, Huygens ridicules what, according to his strict biblical morality, is absurd and culpable in the fashionable society of his day. As such it provides a valuable historical record of society at that time, and because it conforms to the Horatian ideal of *utile dulci*, it was a work (dedicated to Cats) for which Huygens retained an affection.

In both poems there are mannerisms that recall the style of Marino in Italy and the metaphysical poets in England, yet there is no evidence of a direct influence of the Marinists on Huygens. Though in his love poetry, as we shall see, there is a Petrarchan influence, in *Costelick mal* there is evidence, in his attitudes to women, of anti-Petrarchanism. So, steeped in the learning and theories of his age as he was, Huygens brings an individualism to his work that remains its hallmark.

If *Costelick mal* was an outward-looking commentary, however personal, on social behaviour, *De uytlandighe herder* [The Exiled Shepherd] is entirely introspective, and seems to have been written in a fit of depression. It is a pastoral with a

difference; the first-person narrator, the shepherd, conducts an interior monologue between his emotional and rational selves.

Huygens's familiarity with English poetry, and not just John Donne's, is evident from his *Zedeprinten* [Characters]. Character sketches were a literary genre known in the Netherlands through Daniel Heinsius's translations of Theophrastus of Eresus, but *Zedeprinten* reproduces some of the characters of the English poets who were popular at that time, as well as a number of original moralistic satires on Dutch 'types', with the sophisticated wit that is Huygens's alone.

Dorpen en stedestemmen [Voices of Villages and Towns] devotes ten-line verses to each of 18 towns and six villages, and these, along with the character sketches and *Costelick mal*, add a further contemporary, if subjective, picture of 17th-century Dutch life. The personal and local sketches were reprinted in a collection published in 1625 with the title *Otia of ledighe uren* [Idleness or Empty Hours]. It is true that Huygens wrote rapidly, and often filled the time spent on his many journeys by writing. But the disdainful tone of this title merely echoes a Renaissance convention of false modesty, and does not belie his earlier insistence that poetry is a serious, cultivated art.

Dagh-werck covers the years of Huygens's marriage to his beautiful and wealthy niece, Susanna van Baerle. There is every reason to assume utter sincerity in his Petrarchan protestations of love for his *sterre* (star), the shining light in his firmament, whose premature death in 1637 evoked his finest sonnet 'On the Death of *Sterre*'.

Ooghentroost [Solace for the Sightless] was written for a friend who had lost the sight of one eye. Typically, its moral tone extols the virtue of those who though physically blind are spiritually whole, while attacking those who are spiritually blind: the arrogant, the prodigal, the malicious, and the ostentatious. The conclusion sums up the underlying faith throughout Huygens's poetry, that sighted or blind, only the virtuous will see God.

There are two autobiographical sequels to *Ooghentroost*: *Hofwijck* and *Cluyswerck* [Work in Seclusion]. Hofwijck was the country house that Huygens had built on the river Vliet as a refuge from his busy court life and as an antidote to his bereavement. This long, georgic poem represents an important contribution to the popular Stoical, bucolic literature of the Renaissance. The planning of country estates was considered consistent with the divine intention that man should restore the order of the garden of paradise from the wilderness, in which a Stoical balance should be observed, for 'too orderly would be too formal, too wild would be all too coarse'. To Huygens, creation is God's revelation:

> From all things trivial, even things that miss our gaze
> To distil creation's purpose, sing the Maker's praise.

Where he speaks of God's two books, he is referring to the Bible and nature.

> This book, this Book of Books
> Has as much to teach us, as many instructive nooks,
> As there are leaves on Hofwijck's trees and plants.

In 1653 Huygens wrote his only play, *Trijntje Cornelis*, named after the protagonist, a young Dutch skipper's wife who is seduced by two Flemish street lads and ends up in men's clothes on a manure heap. She has her revenge when the following day she, unrecognized, lures them onto her ship where they are roundly thrashed and put ashore. An accomplished linguist with a good ear, Huygens clearly relished writing in the two dialects of the Netherlands and Antwerp, and spicing the humour with bawdy obscenities, which were by no means only the prerogative of fairground dramatists in the 17th century.

In his mid-eighties, Huygens wrote the last of his autobiographical trilogy, *Cluyswerck*. Though still William III's secretary, Huygens's retirement from full employment, with his freedom to enjoy his library, his music, and visits from friends, is celebrated here in some 600 alexandrines of scarcely diminished vitality and perception. Up to the last he also continued jotting down his *Sneldichten* [Quick Rhymes], which are simply frivolous nonsense rhymes, succeeding best where Huygens's wit comes out in contemporary-seeming wordplay.

—Peter King

HUYSMANS, Joris-Karl. Born Charles-Marie-Georges in Paris, France, 5 February 1848. Educated at Lycée Saint-Louis, Paris, 1862–65; baccalauréat, after private tuition, 1866; law student, Paris, 1866. Military service, 1870. Civil servant, French Ministry of the Interior, 1866–76; internal security and crime prevention officer, Sûreté Générale, 1876–98; throughout career contributed reviews and stories to various French and Belgian publications, including *Revue Mensuelle*, *La République de lettres*, and *L'Art universel*. Associated with Zola and the Naturalist movement, became interested in Black Magic, retreated to Trappist monastery at Igny in 1892, returned to the Catholic faith; retired to a monastery at Ligugé. Recipient: Chevalier, Légion d'honneur, 1893. *Died 12 May 1907.*

PUBLICATIONS

Collection

Oeuvres complètes, edited by Lucien Descaves. 18 vols., 1928–40.

Fiction

Marthe, histoire d'une fille. 1876; as *Marthe*, translated by Samuel Putnam, in *Down Stream and Other Works*, 1927; as *Martha, the Story of a Woman*, translated by Robert Baldick, 1948; as *Marthe*, translated by Baldick, 1958.
Sac-au-dos. 1877; in *Les Soirées de Médan*, 1880; as *Sac-au-dos*, translated by L.G. Meyer, 1907.
Les Soeurs Vatard. 1879; as *The Vatard Sisters*, translated by James Babcock, 1983.
En ménage. 1881; as *Living Together*, translated by J. Sandisford-Pelle, 1969.
À vau-l'eau. 1882; in *Croquis parisiens*, 1905; as *Downstream*, translated by Robert Baldick, 1952.
À Rebours. 1884; as *Against the Grain*, translated by John Howard, 1922; as *Against Nature*, translated by Robert Baldick, 1959.
En Rade. 1887; as *Becalmed*, translated by Terry Hale, 1992.
Un dilemme. 1887.
Là-bas. 1891; as *Down There*, translated by Keene Wallis, 1928.

En route. 1895; as *En Route*, translated by C. Kegan Paul, 1896.
La Cathédrale. 1898; as *La Cathédrale-Chartres*, edited by Helen Trudgian, 1936; as *The Cathedral*, translated by Clara Bell, 1898.
L'Oblat. 1903; as *The Oblate*, translated by Eduard Perceval, 1924.

Other

Le Drageoir à épices (prose poems). 1874; as *Le Drageoir aux épices*, 1874; as *A Dish of Spices*, translated by Samuel Putnam, in *Down Stream and Other Works*, 1927.
Pierrot sceptique, with Léon Hennique. 1881.
L'Art moderne. 1883; selections translated by Samuel Putnam, in *Down Stream and Other Works*, 1927.
Croquis parisiens. 1885; as *Parisien Sketches*, translated by Richard Griffiths, 1962.
Certains (articles). 1889; selections translated by Samuel Putnam in *Down Stream and Other Works*, 1927.
La Bièvre. 1890; with *Les Gobelins* and *Saint-Séverin*, 1901; as *The Bièvre River*, translated by Darius Halpern and Ellen Moerman, 1986.
Les Vieux Quartiers de Paris. 1890.
L'Oeuvre érotique de Félicien Rops. 1897.
Pages catholiques. 1899.
La Magie en Poitou: Gilles Rais. 1899.
Sainte Lydwine de Schiedam. 1901; as *Saint Lydwine of Schiedam*, translated by Agnes Hastings, 1923.
De tout. 1902.
Esquisse biographique sur Don Bosco. 1902.
Trois primitifs. 1904; as *Grunewald*, translated by Robert Baldick, 1958.
Le Quartier Notre-Dame. 1905.
Les Foules de Lourdes. 1906; as *The Crowds of Lourdes*, translated by W.H. Mitchell, 1925.
Trois églises et trois primitifs. 1908.
Prières et pensées chrétiennes de J.K. Huysmans. 1910.
Pages choisies, edited by Lucien Descaves. 1916.
Down Stream and Other Works, translated by Samuel Putnam. 1927.
En marge (essays), edited by Lucien Descaves. 1927.
Correspondance, with Madame Cécile Bruyère, edited by R. Rancoeur. 1950.
Lettres inédites à Emile Zola, edited by Pierre Lambert. 1953.
Lettres inédites à Edmond de Goncourt, edited by Pierre Lambert and Pierre Cogny. 1956.
Lettres inédites à Camille Lemonnier, edited by G. Vanwelkenhuyzen. 1957.
Le Retraite de M. Bougran. 1964.
Là-haut; ou, Notre-Dame de la Salette, edited by Pierre Cogny, Artine Artinian, and Pierre Lambert. 1965.
Lettres inédites à Jules Destrée, edited by G. Vanwelkenhuyzen. 1967.
Une étape de la vie de J.-K. Huysmans: Lettres inédites de J.-K. Huysmans à l'abbé Ferret, edited by Elisabeth Bourget-Besnier. 1973.
Lettres inédites à Arij Prins, edited by L. Gillet. 1977.
Bloy, Villiers, Huysmans: lettres, edited by D. Habrekorn. 1980.
Lettres à Théodore Hannon (1876–1886), edited by Pierre Cogny and Christian Berg. 1985.
The Road from Decadence: From Brothel to Cloister: The Selected Letters of J.-K. Huysmans, edited and translated by Barbara Beaumont. 1988.

*

Bibliography: *J.-K. Huysmans in England and America: A Bibliographical Study* by George A. Cevasco, 1960.

Critical Studies: *The First Decadent* by James Laver, 1954; *The Life of J.-K. Huysmans* by Robert Baldick, 1955; *Huysmans* by Henry R.T. Brandreth, 1963; *The Reactionary Revolution: The Catholic Revival in French Literature 1870–1914* by Richard Griffiths, 1966; *Joris Karl Huysmans* by George R. Ridge, 1968; *The Genius of the Future* by Anita Brookner, 1971; *The Violent Mystique: Thematics of Retribution and Expiation in Balzac, Barbey d'Aurevilly, Bloy and Huysmans* by Joyce O. Lowrie, 1974; '*A vau-l'eau —A Naturalist Sotie*' by C.G. Shenton, in *Modern Language Review*, 72, 1977; *Reality and Illusion in the Novels of J.-K. Huysmans* by Ruth B. Antosh, 1986; 'J.-K. Huysmans: Novelist, Poet, and Art Critic' by Annette Kahn, in *Studies in the Fine Arts*, 19, 1987; *J.-K. Huysmans and the Fin de Siècle Novel* by Christopher Lloyd, 1990; *The Image of Huysmans* by Brian R. Banks, 1992; *Huysmans* by Jean Borie, 1992.

* * *

Joris-Karl Huysmans was among those writers marked by a series of startling events in France beginning in 1848 and lasting into the early 20th century. Born in February 1848, reputedly at the very moment when the Parliament declared the inception of the Second Republic, he witnessed the subsequent changes in government—from a republic to the reinstitution of the Empire under Napoleon III in 1852—as well as the establishment of the Third Republic after the Commune of Paris was defeated, and ultimately the political and economic preparations for World War I. In addition to this intense political activity, social, economic, and intellectual developments were also little short of revolutionary: the urbanization of France, accompanying its evolving democratization, resulted in a literal and figurative change of landscape and the new ideas of socialism had their impact on politics as Positivism, Realism, and Naturalism had theirs on literature. Writers like Huysmans could either participate in this ferment by supporting or criticizing these new concepts and their social or literary results, or they could in various ways withdraw from the life of these innovations.

Huysmans in his career did both. At first, a partisan of Naturalism and admirer of Zola, Huysmans abandoned Zola's form of Naturalism in *À Rebours* (*Against Nature*) and turned towards a spiritual Naturalism. Des Esseintes, the hero of the novel, is the prototype of the decadent hero whose only solution for an unacceptable environment is to isolate himself completely from it and seek an alternative in artifice and ultimately religion. Published in May 1884, *Against Nature* is a novel of *fin-de-siècle* aestheticism, considered to be the masterpiece of this genre in French literature of the late 19th century.

Des Esseintes recalls the Baudelairian character who suffers from the disease of the century: boredom. Huysmans's hero cannot tolerate contemporary society and decides to escape it, adopting Baudelaire's motto, 'Anywhere out of the world'. Plot and action are practically nonexistent in the novel. Curiously, however, one of the principal motifs is travel; travel, though, that takes place in the mind of Des Esseintes, who frees himself from his surroundings by means of imaginary journeys. For example, he decides to travel to England, a country in vogue at the time and the centre of dandyism. It is also the home of Charles Dickens, whose works had stimulated Des Esseintes's conception of London's grey skies and the general mood of England. To prepare for his trip, Des Esseintes consults a guide book in a bookshop. Inspired by his reading, his imagination takes him to London and its museums, but his wandering is interrupted by the presence of the bookseller. To continue his imaginary trip, he escapes to the 'Bodega' to recreate in his mind the land of clergymen and of Dickens by drinking glasses of port. Des Esseintes's imaginary voyage in place of the real one does not disappoint him: it allows him to get away from reality. His reading of the guide book enables him to make his trip to England in accordance with his wishes; a real trip would have eventually brought disillusion in the form of a train ride home. He has succeeded in escaping from the daily routine and killing his boredom at least for a few hours.

At the beginning of the novel Des Esseintes had sold his family's manor house and had left Paris and his tumultuous life there to seek refuge in his ideal house at Fontenay-aux-Roses, where he is waited on by his two faithful servants. Having left no forwarding address, he is completely isolated from the world. His only company consists of religious objects, posters, aquariums, and books. He has created an entirely artificial milieu, imitating theatre sets decorated in flamboyant colours. On occasion he drapes his dining room in black and has a funeral meal served accompanied by dirges. On other occasions the atmosphere of a cloister dominates the whole house, imposing an air of sanctity and silence. For Des Esseintes, artifice is the distinctive sign of man's genius. Consequently he is uninterested in and repulsed by, the human condition. His indifference extends as well to all that is associated with progress and the modern. Instead he shuts himself up in his study to cultivate his admiration for the painter Gustave Moreau, whose two paintings of Salome Des Esseintes owns. Depicted in the novel as a double to Des Esseintes, Moreau had been able to escape reality even though he lived in Paris.

Finally, Des Esseintes realizes that his artificial refuge at Fontenay-aux-Roses will not help him escape from the nihilism into which he has sunk. He becomes physically and mentally lethargic. The country doctor warns him of the danger of a life lead in such strange and luxurious conditions and advises him to return to Paris if he wishes to recover his health and mental stability. 'In two days I shall be in Paris', Des Esseintes replies. 'All is finished.' He gives himself up to God in the hope of finding a solution to his dilemma, and prays: 'Lord, take pity on a Christian who is in doubt, on the unbeliever who would like to believe.' Thus finishes *Against Nature*.

The autobiographical aspect of the book (Des Esseintes is the alter ego of Huysmans) is evident. Like his hero's life, Huysmans's was notable for its gradual progress towards a state of spirituality. Like Des Esseintes, Huysmans withdrew from the world, but he actually retired to a Trappist monastery at Notre-Dame d'Igny, causing something of a scandal in late 19th-century anti-clerical France. Ironically, although Huysmans, like Des Esseintes, detested modern civilization, he wrote in *Against Nature* a novel that exhibits many of the features of French Modernism, particularly its surrealistic tone and its impressionistic style.

—Nicole Mosher

I

IBSEN, Henrik (Johan). Born in Skien, Norway (then united with Sweden), 20 March 1828. Educated at local schools, and a private school in Skien; attended the University of Christiania (now Oslo), 1850–51. Married Suzannah Thoresen in 1858; one son; also had one son by Else Jonsdatter. Pharmacist's assistant in Grimstad, 1844–50; drama critic, *Manden*, later *Andhrimner*, 1851; contributor to the radical newspaper *Arbejderforeningernes blad*, until it was shut down by the police, 1851; house dramatist, Det Norske Theater [Norwegian Theatre], Bergen, 1851–57; visited Copenhagen and Dresden, 1852; artistic director, Det Norske Theater, Christiania, 1857–62: theatre declared bankrupt, 1862; travelled in northern Norway on grant to collect folk-tales, 1862; consultant, Christiania Theater, 1863; awarded a small travelling scholarship by the state in 1864, and left for Italy, where he lived until 1868; visited Egypt, 1869; lived in Dresden, 1868–75, Munich, 1875–78, Rome, 1878–85, Munich, 1885–91; returned to Norway and settled in Christiania, 1891–1906. Government pension, 1866. Doctor of Letters, Uppsala University, 1877. *Died 23 May 1906.*

PUBLICATIONS

Collections

Samlede verker [Collected Works] (includes letters), edited by Francis Bull, Halvdan Koht, and Didrik Arup Seip. 21 vols., 1928–58.
Samlede verker [Collected Works]. 7 vols., 1978.
Prose Dramas (includes *The League of Youth*; *The Pillars of Society*; *A Doll's House*; *Ghosts*; *An Enemy of the People*; *The Wild Duck*; *Lady Inger of Östråt*; *The Vikings at Helgeland*; *The Pretenders*; *The Emperor and Galilean*; *Rosmersholm*; *The Lady from the Sea*; *Hedda Gabler*), edited by William Archer, translated by Archer, Frances E. Archer, Eleanor Marx-Aveling, Charles Archer, Catherine Ray. 5 vols., 1890.
Collected Works, edited by William Archer, translated by Archer, Edmund Gosse, Charles Archer, Frances E. Archer, Eleanor Marx-Aveling, Mary Morison, C.H. Herford, and A.G. Chater. 12 vols., 1906–12.
The Oxford Ibsen, edited by James W. McFarlane, translated by McFarlane and others. 8 vols., 1960–77.
The Complete Major Prose Plays, translated by Rolf Fjelde. 1978.
Plays, translated by Michael Meyer. 6 vols., 1980–87.

Plays

Catalina (produced 1882). 1850; as *Cataline*, translated by Anders Orbeck, in *Early Plays*, 1921; as *Catiline*, translated by Graham Orton, in *The Oxford Ibsen, 1*, 1960.
Kjæmpehøjen (produced 1850). 1902; as *The Warrior's Barrow*, translated by Anders Orbeck, in *Early Plays*, 1921; as *The Burial Mound*, translated by James McFarlane, in *The Oxford Ibsen 1*, 1960.

Norma; eller, En politikers kjærlighed, in *Andhrimmer*. 1 and 8 June, 1851; as *Norma; or, A Politician's Love*, translated by James McFarlane, in *The Oxford Ibsen 1*, 1960.
Sankthansnatten (produced 1853). 1909; as *St John's Night*, translated by James and Kathleen McFarlane, in *The Oxford Ibsen 1*, 1960.
Fru Inger til Østråt (produced 1855). 1857; revised edition, 1874; as *Lady Inger of Östråt*, translated by Charles Archer, in *Prose Dramas*, 1890; also translated by R. Farquharson-Sharp, with *Love's Comedy* and *The League of Youth*, 1915; as *Lady Inger*, translated by Graham Orton, in *The Oxford Ibsen 1*, 1960.
Gildet på Solhaug (produced 1856). 1856; as *The Feast at Solhaug*, translated by William Archer and Mary Morison, in *Collected Works*, 1906–12.
Olaf Liljekrans (produced 1857). 1898; as *Olaf Liljekrans*, translated by Anders Orbeck, in *Early Plays*, 1921.
Hærmændene på Helgeland (produced 1858). 1857; as *The Vikings at Helgeland*, translated by William Archer, in *Prose Dramas*, 1890; also translated by Sam Oakland, 1978; as *The Warriors at Helgeland*, translated by R. Farquharson-Sharp, with *Ghosts* and *An Enemy of the People*, 1911; translated by James McFarlane, in *The Oxford Ibsen 2*, 1962.
Kjærlighedens komedie (produced 1873). 1862; as *Love's Comedy*, translated by C.H. Herford, 1900; also translated by R. Farquharson-Sharp, with *Lady Inger of Ostraat* and *The League of Youth*, 1915; Jens Arup, 1962.
Kongs-Emnerne (produced 1864). 1863; as *The Pretenders*, translated by William Archer, in *Prose Dramas*, 1890; also translated by R. Farquharson-Sharp, with *The Pillars of Society* and *Rosmersholm*, 1913; William Archer, 1913.
Brand (produced in part, 1866; complete version, 1885). 1866; as *Brand*, translated by W. Wilson, 1891; also translated by C.H. Herford, 1894; F.E. Garrett, 1894; J.M. Olberman, 1912; Miles M. Dawson, 1916; Theodore Jorgenson, 1962; G.M. Gathorne-Hardy, 1966; Michael Meyer, 1967; Geoffrey Hill, 1978; R.D. MacDonald, 1991.
Peer Gynt (produced 1876). 1867; as *Peer Gynt*, translated by William and Charles Archer, 1892; also translated by R. Ellis-Roberts, 1912; R. Farquharson-Sharp, 1921; Gottfried Hult, 1933; Norman Ginsbury, 1945; Paul Green, 1951; Horace Maynard Finney, 1955; Rolf Fjelde, 1964; Christopher Fry and Johan Fillinger, 1970; Peter Watts, 1970; David Rudkin, 1983; James W. McFarlane, 1989; Anne Bamborough, adapted by Frank McGuiness, 1990; Kenneth McLeish, 1990.
De unges forbund (produced 1869). 1869; as *The League of Youth*, translated by William Archer, in *Prose Dramas*, 1890; R. Farquharson-Sharp, with *Love's Comedy* and *Lady Inger of Ostraat*, 1915; Peter Watts, with *A Doll's House* and *The Lady From the Sea*, 1965.
Kejser og Galilæer (produced in part 1896). 1873; as *The Emperor and the Galilean*, translated by Catherine Ray, 1876; also translated by Graham Orton, 1963.
Samfundets støtter (produced 1877). 1877; as *The Pillars of*

Society, translated by William Archer, in *The Pillars of Society and Other Plays*, 1888; also translated by R. Farquharson-Sharp, with *The Pretenders* and *Rosmersholm*, 1913; Garrett H. Leverton, 1937; Norman Ginsbury, 1962; as *The Pillars of the Community*, translated by Una Ellis-Fermor, in *Three Plays*, 1950.

Et dukkehjem (produced 1879). 1879; as *Nora*, translated by T. Weber, 1880; also translated by Henrietta Frances Lord, 1882; as *A Doll's House*, translated by William Archer, 1889; also translated by Norman Ginsbury, 1904; R. Farquharson-Sharp, with *The Wild Duck* and *The Lady From the Sea*, 1910; Norman Ginsbury, 1950; Peter Watts, with *The League of Youth* and *The Lady From the Sea*, 1965; Rolf Fjelde, in *Four Major Plays*, 1965; James W. McFarlane, in *Four Major Plays*, 1981.

Gengangere (produced 1881). 1881; as *Ghosts*, translated by William Archer, in *The Pillars of Society and Other Plays*, 1888; also translated by Henrietta Frances Lord, 1890; R. Farquharson-Sharp, with *The Warriors at Helgeland* and *An Enemy of the People*, 1911; Norman Ginsbury, 1938; Bjorn Koefoed, 1950; Peter Watts, with *A Public Enemy* and *When We Dead Wake*, 1964; Michael Meyer, 1970; James W. McFarlane, in *Four Major Plays*, 1981; Christopher Hampton, 1983; Nicholas Rudall, 1990.

En folkefiende (produced 1883). 1882; as *An Enemy of Society*, translated by Eleanor Marx-Aveling, in *The Pillars of Society and Other Plays*, 1888; as *An Enemy of the People*, translated by R. Farquharson-Sharp, with *Ghosts* and *The Warriors at Helgeland*, 1911; Norman Ginsbury, 1939; Lars Nordenson, adapted by Arthur Miller, 1951; James W. McFarlane, with *The Wild Duck* and *Rosmersholm*, 1960; Inger Lignell, adapted by Henry S. Taylor, 1960; Michael Meyer, 1970; as *A Public Enemy*, translated by Peter Watts, with *Ghosts* and *When We Dead Wake*, 1964; as *An Enemy of the People*, adapted by Max Faber, 1967.

Vildanden (produced 1885). 1884; as *The Wild Duck*, translated by Frances E. Archer, in *Prose Dramas*, 1890; also translated by R. Farquharson-Sharp, with *A Doll's House* and *The Lady From the Sea*, 1910; William Archer, in *Four Plays*, 1941; Una Ellis-Fermor, in *Three Plays*, 1950; James W. McFarlane, with *Enemy of the People* and *Rosmersholm*, 1960; Rolf Fjelde, in *Four Major Plays*, 1965; Michael Meyer, 1970; Inga-Stina Ewbank and Peter Hall, with *John Gabriel Borkman*, 1975; Dounia Christiani, 1980; Christopher Hampton, 1980; adapted by Max Faber, 1958.

Rosmersholm (produced 1887). 1886; as *Rosmersholm*, translated by L.N. Parker, 1889; also translated by M. Carmichael, in *Prose Dramas*, 1890; R. Farquharson-Sharp, with *The Pretenders* and *The Pillars of Society*, 1913; Una Ellis-Fermor, in *The Master Builder and Other Plays*, 1958; James W. McFarlane, with *Enemy of the People* and *The Wild Duck*, 1960; Norman Ginsbury, 1961; Ann Jellicoe, 1961; Arvid Paulson, in *Last Plays*, 1962; D. Rudkin, with *When We Dead Awaken*, 1990; as *The House of Rosmer*, adapted by Brian J. Burton, 1959.

The Pillars of Society and Other Plays (includes *The Pillars of Society*; *Ghosts*; *An Enemy of Society*), edited by Havelock Ellis, translated by William Archer and Eleanor Marx-Aveling. 1888.

Fruen fra havet (produced 1889). 1888; as *The Lady from the Sea*, translated by Eleanor Marx-Aveling, 1890; also translated by Frances E. Archer, in *Prose Dramas*, 1890; Peter Watts, with *The League of Youth* and *A Doll's House*, 1965; James W. McFarlane, 1977.

Prose Dramas, edited by Edmund Gosse. 5 vols., 1890.

Hedda Gabler (produced 1891). 1890; as *Hedda Gabler*, translated by William Archer, in *Prose Dramas*, 1890; also translated by Edmund Gosse, 1891; Una Ellis-Fermor, in *Three Plays*, 1950; Eva Le Gallienne, 1953; Arvid Paulson, in *Last Plays*, 1962; Rolf Fjelde, in *Four Major Plays*, 1965; Michael Meyer, 1970; Christopher Hampton, 1972; Jens Arup, in *Four Major Plays*, 1981; Nicholas Rudall, 1992; adapted by John Osborne, 1972, and with Strindberg's *The Father*, 1989.

Bygmester Solness (produced 1893). 1892; as *The Master Builder*, translated by J.W. Arctander, 1893; also translated by Edmund Gosse and William Archer, 1893; Eva Le Gallienne, 1955; Una Ellis-Fermor, in *The Master Builder and Other Plays*, 1958; Arvid Paulson, in *Last Plays*, 1962; Rolf Fjelde, in *Four Major Plays*, 1965; Michael Meyer, 1968; James W. McFarlane, in *Four Major Plays*, 1981.

Lille Eyolf (produced 1895). 1894; as *Little Eyolf*, translated by William Archer, 1895; also translated by Henry L. Mencken, 1909; Una Ellis-Fermor, in *The Master Builder and Other Plays*, 1958; James W. McFarlane, 1977.

John Gabriel Borkman (produced 1897). 1896; as *John Gabriel Borkman*, translated by William Archer, 1897; also translated by Una Ellis-Fermor, in *The Master Builder and Other Plays*, 1958; Norman Ginsbury, 1960; Arvid Paulson, in *Last Plays*, 1962; Inga-Stina Ewbank and Peter Hall, with *The Wild Duck*, 1975.

Når vi døde vågner (produced 1900). 1899; edited by Robert Brustein, 1992; as *When We Dead Awaken*, translated by William Archer, 1900; also translated by Arvid Paulson, in *Last Plays*, 1962; James W. McFarlane, 1977; D. Rudkin, with *Rosmersholm*, 1990; as *When We Dead Wake*, translated by Peter Watts, with *Ghosts* and *A Public Enemy*, 1964.

Prose Dramas (includes *The League of Youth*; *The Pillars of Society*; *A Doll's House*; *Ghosts*; *An Enemy of the People*), revised edition, edited by William Archer, translated by Archer and Eleanor Marx-Aveling (reprinted from *The Pillars of Society and Other Plays*, 1888, and *Prose Dramas*, 5 vols., 1890). 5 vols., 1900–01.

A Doll's House; The Wild Duck; The Lady from the Sea, translated by R. Farquharson-Sharp and Eleanor Marx-Aveling. 1910.

The Warriors at Helgeland; Ghosts; An Enemy of the People, translated by R. Farquharson-Sharp. 1911.

The Pretenders; The Pillars of Society; Rosmersholm, translated by R. Farquharson-Sharp. 1913.

Prose Dramas (includes *Rosmersholm*; *A Doll's House*; *The Lady from the Sea*). 1913.

Lady Inger of Ostraat; Love's Comedy; The League of Youth, translated by R. Farquharson-Sharp. 1915.

Early Plays (includes *Cataline*; *The Warrior's Barrow*; *Olaf Liljekrans*), translated by Anders Orbeck. 1921.

Four Plays (includes *A Doll's House*; *Ghosts*; *The Wild Duck*; *The Master Builder*), translated by William Archer. 1941.

Three Plays (includes *Hedda Gabler*; *The Wild Duck*; *The Pillars of the Community*), translated by Una Ellis-Fermor. 1950; as *Hedda Gabler and Other Plays*, 1963.

Seven Famous Plays, edited by William Archer and others. 1950.

The Master Builder and Other Plays (includes *The Master Builder*; *Rosmersholm*; *Little Eyolf*; *John Gabriel Borkman*), translated by Una Ellis-Fermor. 1958.

An Enemy of the People; Rosmersholm; The Wild Duck, translated by James W. McFarlane. 1960.

Last Plays (includes *Rosmersholm*; *Hedda Gabler*; *The Master Builder*; *John Gabriel Borkman*; *When We Dead Awaken*), translated by Arvid Paulson. 1962.

Ghosts; A Public Enemy; When We Dead Wake, translated by Peter Watts. 1964.

The League of Youth; A Doll's House; The Lady from the Sea, translated by Peter Watts. 1965.

Four Major Plays (includes *A Doll's House; The Wild Duck; Hedda Gabler; The Master Builder*), translated by Rolf Fjelde. 1965.

Ghosts; An Enemy of the People; Wild Duck; Hedda Gabler, translated by Michael Meyer. 1970.

Four Major Plays (includes *A Doll's House; Ghosts; The Master Builder; Hedda Gabler*), translated by James W. McFarlane and Jens Arup. 1981.

Verse

Digte [Verse]. 1871; enlarged edition, 1875.

Lyrical Poems, translated by R.A. Streatfeild. 1902.

På vidderne, as *On the Heights*, translated by William Norman Guthrie. 1910.

Lyrics and Poems, translated by F.E. Garrett. 1912.

Terje Viken, translated by M. Michelet and G.R. Vowles. 1918.

Poems, translated by John Northam. 1986.

Other

Samlede verker [Collected Works]. 10 vols., 1898–1902.

Correspondence, edited and translated by Mary Morison. 1905.

Episke Brand (fragment), edited by Karl Larsen. 1907.

Speeches and New Letters, edited by Lee M. Hollander, translated by Arne Kildal. 1911, reprinted 1982.

Letters and Speeches, edited by Evert Sprinchorn, translated by Sprinchorn and others. 1965.

Brevveksling med Christiania Theater 1878–1899 (letters), edited by Øyvind Anker. 1965.

Brev 1845–1905 (letters), edited by Øyvind Anker. 1979.

*

Bibliography: *Henrik Ibsen: A Bibliography of Criticism and Biography, with an Index to Characters* by Ina Ten Eyck Firkins, 1921; *Ibsen 1828–1928* by H. Pettersen, 1928; *Ibsen Årbok* [Ibsen Yearbook] (later *Contemporary Approaches to Ibsen*), 1952– ; *Ibsen Bibliography 1928–1957* by I. Telford, 1961.

Critical Studies: *Henrik Ibsen: A Critical Biography* by Henrik B. Jaeger, translated by W.M. Payne 1901; *Henrik Ibsen: Plays and Problems* by Otto Heller, 1912; *Henrik Ibsen: Poet, Mystic and Moralist* by Henry Rose, 1913; *The Quintessence of Ibsenism* by G.B. Shaw, revised edition, 1913; *Ibsen and His Creation* by Janko Lavrin, 1921; *Henrik Ibsen: A Critical Study* by Richard E. Roberts, 1922; *The Modern Ibsen* by H.J Weigand, 1925; *Henrik Ibsen: An Introduction to His Life and Works* by Paul H. Grummann, 1928; *Ibsen and the Actress* by Elizabeth Robins, 1928; *Henrik Ibsen: A Study in Art and Personality* by Theodore Jorgenson, 1945; *Ibsen the Norwegian* by M.C. Bradbrook, 1946, revised edition, 1966; *Ibsen: The Intellectual Background*, 1946, and *A Study of Six Plays by Ibsen*, 1950, both by Brian W. Downs; *Ibsen's Dramatic Technique* by P.F.D. Tennant, 1948; *Ibsen's Dramatic Method*, 1952, and *Ibsen: A Critical Study*, 1973, both by John Northam; *Ibsen: The Man and the Dramatist* by F. Bull, 1954; *Ibsen and the Temper of Norwegian Literature*, 1960, and *Ibsen and*

Meaning: Studies, Essays and Prefaces 1953–87, 1987, both by James McFarlane, and *Ibsen: A Critical Anthology*, 1970, and *The Cambridge Companion to Ibsen*, 1994, both edited by McFarlane; *Henrik Ibsen* by G. Wilson Knight, 1962; *The Drama of Ibsen and Strindberg* by F.L. Lucas, 1962; *Henrik Ibsen: A Collection of Critical Essays* edited by Rolf Fjelde, 1965; *Notes on Ibsen's 'Doll's House' and 'Hedda Gabler'*, 1965, and *Notes on Ibsen's 'Ghosts', 'Enemy of the People' and 'The Wild Duck'*, 1965, both by Marianne Sturman; *Henrik Ibsen* (biography), 3 vols., 1967–71, condensed single vol., 1974, *Ibsen on File*, 1985, and *Ibsen*, 1990, all by Michael Meyer; *Mythic Patterns in Ibsen's Last Plays* by O.I. Holtan, 1970; *The Life of Ibsen* by H. Koht, 1971; *Ibsen: The Critical Heritage* edited by Michael Egan, 1972; *Cataline's Dream: An Essay on Ibsen's Plays* by J. Hurt, 1972; *Henrik Ibsen: The Divided Consciousness* by Charles R. Lyons, 1972, and *Critical Essays on Henrik Ibsen* edited by Lyons, 1987; *Women in the Plays of Henrik Ibsen* by Clela Allphin, 1975; *Ibsen's Feminine Mystique* by Vincent J. Balice, 1975; *The Ibsen Cycle: The Design of the Plays from 'Pillars of Society' to 'When We Dead Awaken'*, 1975, revised 1992, *To the Third Empire: Ibsen's Early Drama*, 1980, and *Text and Supertext in Ibsen's Drama*, 1989, all by Brian Johnston; *Ibsen* by Harold Clurman, 1977; *The Real Drama of Henrik Ibsen?* by Arne Duve, 1977; *Ibsen: A Dissenting View* by Ronald Gray, 1977; *Ibsen: The Man and His Work*, 1978, and *Henrik Ibsen*, 1980, both by Edvard Beyer; *Ibsen the Romantic: Analogues of Paradise in the Later Plays* by Errol Durbach, 1978, and *Ibsen and the Theatre: Essays in Celebration of the 150th Anniversary of Henrik Ibsen's Birth* edited by Durbach, 1980; *Ibsen's Drama: Author to Audience* by E. Haugen, 1979; *A Doll's House: Notes* by Bruce King, 1980; *Henrik Ibsen's Aesthetic and Dramatic Art* by J.E. Tammany, 1980; *Patterns in Ibsen's Middle Plays* by Richard Hornby, 1981; *Notes on Ibsen's 'Doll's House'* edited by A. Norman Jeffares and Suheil Badi Bushrui, 1981; *Ghosts: Notes* by Adele King, 1981; *Ibsen: The Open Vision* by John Chamberlain, 1982; *Ibsen Studies* by Peter J. Eikeland, 1982; *Ibsen: Four Essays* edited by Angel Flores, 1982; *Hedda Gabler: Notes* by Helena Forsås-Scott, 1983; *Henrik Ibsen* by David Thomas, 1983; *William Archer on Ibsen: The Major Essays 1889–19* by William Archer, edited by Thomas Postlethwait, 1984; *An Ibsen Companion: A Dictionary Guide to the Life, Works and Critical Reception of Henrik Ibsen* by G.B. Bryan, 1984; *Ibsen and Shaw* by Keith M. May, 1985; *Henrik Ibsen: Life, Work and Criticism* by Yvonne Shafer, 1985; *Ibsen and the English Stage* by Gretchen P. Ackerman, 1987; *China's Ibsen: From Ibsen to Ibsenism* by Elisabeth Eide, 1987; *Ibsen in America: A Century of Change* by Robert A. Schanke, 1988; *Peer Gynt and Ghosts* by Asbjørn Aarseth, 1989; *Ibsen's Lively Art: A Performance Study of the Major Plays* by Frederick J. and Lise-Lone Marker, 1989; *Time's Disinherited Children: Childhood, Regression and Sacrifice in the Plays of Henrik Ibsen* by Robin Young, 1989; *Ibsen's Heroines* by Lou Andreas-Salome, translated by S. Mandel, 1990; *Ibsen and the Great World* by Naomi Lebowitz, 1990; *Divine Madness and the Absurd Paradox: Ibsen's 'Peer Gynt' and the Philosophy of Kierkegaard* by Bruce G. Shapiro, 1990; *Ibsen's Forsaken Merman: Folklore in the Late Plays* by Per Schelde Jacobsen and Barbara Fass Leavy, 1991.

* * *

'Anyone who wants to understand me must know Norway', Henrik Ibsen once remarked. This most European of Norwegian dramatists, still played regularly to packed houses the world over, often to theatre-goers ignorant of his nationality, insisted upon the importance of his national heritage. There was much about Norway which irritated and depressed him—to such an extent that he spent 27 of his most creative years (1864–91) abroad, in Italy and Germany—yet his plays, almost without exception, are set in the land he had rejected. Trolls and hobgoblins, Viking legends, brooding fjord landscapes and deep sunless valleys, snow and ice and extreme cold and light, hectic summer nights—these permeate the lives and form the personalities of the characters in his plays.

Yet even before he left Norway, Ibsen was well versed in the European theatrical tradition. After an inauspicious and poverty-stricken beginning, he was appointed theatre director in Bergen (1851–57), then Christiania (now Oslo, 1857–62). The European stage at this period was dominated by French salon comedies, the 'well-made play' written by dramatists such as Eugène Scribe; and it was largely these which Ibsen directed.

Most of Ibsen's early works are historical dramas, often in verse, which combine tales of Norway's heroic, half-legendary past with the techniques of Scribean drama: a complicated intrigue, involving convoluted misunderstanding and mistaken identity, and a neat tying-off of ends in conclusion—as in, for example, *Fru Inger til Østråt* (*Lady Inger of Østråt*) and *Gildet på Solhaug* (*The Feast at Solhaug*). They are lofty in style, with a tendency to melodrama; it was not until Ibsen turned to depiction of contemporary society in colloquial modern prose that he found his natural medium.

Before that, however, he had written the two vast and sprawling verse dramas *Brand* and *Peer Gynt*. They were 'reading dramas', not intended for the stage, and could not be staged realistically; they required not only an enormous cast but (for *Brand*) whole mountain ranges, storms, and avalanches, and (for *Peer Gynt*) a removal across several continents, a shipwreck, and a multitude of supernatural and monstrous creatures. It was not until Ibsen had achieved success with his prose dramas that they were accepted into theatre repertoires. Nowadays, however, they are among the most frequently performed of the plays.

At the centre of each play is a loner, a man ostracized by his fellow men. Brand is a fanatical priest who demands unquestioning submission to his stern Jehovah, and destroys his family and finally himself in his obsessive devotion to his call. Peer Gynt is his antithesis, a man who stands for nothing, taking the line of least resistance throughout his life; yet both die equally unsure that they have achieved anything.

This pattern of antitheses—exposing the deficiencies of one extreme standpoint in one play and then those of its polar opposite in another—was to repeat itself in many of Ibsen's later plays. Ibsen's protagonists feel driven to take a stand: the lofty claims of the ideal clash with the more sordid compromise of the real, the egotistical drive for success and fame with the gentler values of love and friendship.

It was with the 'social' dramas of his next period, from *Samfundets støtter* (*The Pillars of Society*) to *Vildanden* (*The Wild Duck*), that Ibsen won an international reputation and established himself as a European dramatist. Initially the success was often one of scandal rather than acclaim; for Ibsen wrote about such subjects, and in such a way, that polite society was outraged. The slamming of the door at the end of *Et dukkehjem* (*A Doll's House*), which announces Nora's abandonment of husband and children, and her determination to find self-fulfilment on her own terms, aroused furious condemnation. *Gengangere* (*Ghosts*), with its frank treatment of debauchery, illegitimacy, and syphilis, was banned and reviled. 'An open drain', the *Daily Telegraph* called it. Posterity, however, has discovered that it was neither lubricity nor frankness which was the truly revolutionary aspect of these plays; it was rather Ibsen's determination to challenge social convention and hypocrisy, which barred the way to individual self-realization.

Ibsen read few books, but he did read newspapers, and his reading is reflected not only in his involvement in contemporary debates but in the language and style of his plays. His actors were not required to strike heroic poses and indulge in elevated conceits, but to talk to each other in the contemporary language of everyday life. Acting traditions had to change before Ibsen's ideas could be realized.

From 1877 Ibsen's plays are entirely in prose, and the centre of interest narrows to a small group of people, frequently a family within the four walls of their home, a refuge which grows more and more like a prison as the conflict intensifies. The mainspring of the action is often the revelation of a guilty secret, a past misdeed which returns to haunt the present and disrupt the fragile security which has been erected over its concealment. The end is often death or despair (*Ghosts*, *The Wild Duck*, *Rosmersholm*); with the relentlessness of Greek tragedy, the characters are doomed by their own acts even as they struggle to escape. It is but rarely that they find the strength to take charge of their own fates, as in *Fruen fra havet* (*The Lady from the Sea*), where understanding and tolerance break the vicious spiral of mutual destructiveness.

Ibsen's late plays puzzled critics and audiences; they found them obscure and disturbing. In the 1890s he began to depart from the familiar realistic form and to move towards a more experimental, modernistic drama. Complex images or symbols dominate the play, like the tower in *Bygmester Solness* (*The Master Builder*) or the iron mountains in *John Gabriel Borkman*; strange, surreal characters appear; the protagonists are groping uncertainly for the meaning of life. In Ibsen's last play, *Når vi døde vågner* (*When We Dead Awaken*), the artist and his muse disappear into the apocalypse hand in hand.

Ibsen wrote not just in one dramatic form but in many. There are few European dramatists since his day who do not owe something to his tightly controlled form and his sense of theatre.

—Janet Garton

BRAND
Play by Henrik Ibsen, 1866.

Ibsen wrote *Brand* in Arricia and Rome at the beginning of what was to be a 27-year self-imposed exile from his homeland. The play, set in contemporary Norway, contains both an exploration of the consequences of an individual's unswerving allegiance to the dictates of his will and a savage attack upon the expediency and vacillation of the Norwegian establishment. The theme of individual will would appear to owe much to the influence of the Danish philosopher Søren Kierkegaard's emphasis upon the centrality of human willpower and freedom of choice and his view that the individual should commit him- or herself unreservedly to a consciously chosen way of life. The satire was probably ignited by Norway's recent refusal to support Denmark in its war against Germany over Schleswig-Holstein. In Berlin in May 1864, at the beginning of his journey to Italy and less than four months before commencing *Brand*, Ibsen had been forcibly reminded of Norway's betrayal of Denmark by a victory parade, during which captured Danish canons were spat upon by the crowds which lined the streets.

Brand is a dramatic poem intended for publication rather than performance. Its action includes the crossing of a stormy fjord and Brand's death beneath an avalanche, effects which, although possible to contrive on the late 19th-century stage, would demand elaborate set changes. It was probably in consequence of these that the play's first production in Stockholm in 1885 ran for six and a half hours!

The figure of the priest, Brand, dominates the play. From his introduction in the first scene we watch him unerringly follow his beliefs until his death at the close of the play. The play's other characters are markedly subsidiary and, in a manner reminiscent of the morality play, are included either to reveal those human relationships which Brand is prepared to abandon in his total commitment to what he believes to be his vocation, or to offer a vivid contrast to his character by satirizing those in power in the Church or state who would employ compromise and expediency.

At the beginning of Act One, high in the mountains, Brand is seen to reject, one by one, weakness of resolve represented by the mountain guide who will not risk crossing the mountain in bad weather; a lighthearted view of life represented by the artist Enjar, who dances with Agnes along the edge of a crevasse; and the wild emotionalism represented by the young mad-girl Gerd. Also introduced at this early point in the play is the 'heavy weight', 'the burden of being tied to another human being' which Brand has inherited from his early home-life and which is to colour his subsequent activity and his view of his relationship with God. During the following four acts we witness Brand's attempts to get closer to God by repeatedly avoiding the 'burden' of close personal relationships. To follow this course needs enormous will-power and, in Act Two, Ibsen questions the necessity for such a total commitment to self-will in the words of the anonymous villager who replies to Brand's characteristically forceful assertion that man 'cannot deny his calling./He dares not block the river's course;/It forces its way towards the ocean', with the words, 'Yet if it lost itself in marsh or lake,/It would reach the ocean in the end, as dew'.

As the play progresses, Brand's commitment to what he believes to be the will of God leads first to the rejection of his mother; then to the sacrifice of his son who dies in consequence of Brand's refusal to leave the unhealthy valley in which he and his family are living; and finally to the death of Agnes, his wife, who, out of love, has constantly submitted herself to his will. Brand's experience is now transferred from the personal to the public world where he becomes involved, along with the mayor, in the construction of a new and grander church building. It is in this section of the play that Ibsen satirizes both the close interrelationship between the Norwegian Church and state and the national tendency to compromise, a feature of the play which angered or delighted contemporary Norwegians. Realizing that in building the new church he has sullied himself by his association with secular politics and has compromised his belief in 'all or nothing', Brand inspires the townspeople to climb into the mountains in search of the 'church of life' untarnished by secular concerns. The people are, however, incapable of such a rigorous faith. They turn against Brand, stone him, and return to their homes.

In the mountains, now deprived of both private and public human relationships, Brand again meets the young girl Gerd, who taunts him with his own deep-seated pride by calling him the messiah, 'the Greatest of all'. His hubris has, however, brought Brand to the 'ice-church', a fitting image for his cold, loveless view of God's will. At this point Gerd shoots her rifle at her imagined tormenter, the hawk (variously interpreted as uncontrolled emotion or those things in life which we fear), and in so doing engulfs both herself and Brand in an avalanche of snow. Brand's final words are to ask God, 'If not by Will, how can man be redeemed?' The reply offers the ultimate negation of his way of life. 'He is the God of Love', replies a disembodied voice through the thunder of the avalanche. Redemption, it seems, cannot be found in the cold abstraction of the Will but, as Agnes sought unsuccessfully to teach her husband, only in the warmth of human love.

—D. Keith Peacock

A DOLL'S HOUSE (Et dukkehjem)
Play by Henrik Ibsen, 1879.

A Doll's House is a landmark in drama, but it is confined in its range of social setting to the middle class. For Ibsen, this class denoted a community limited not only in its means of livelihood but also in its outlook. It is preoccupied with work and money, leading to a reduction of values from a moral to a material plane.

Torvald Helmer upholds these values because it is in his interest to do so. He knows that his dominant quality, self-interest, will be protected by his adherence to conventional morality. He imposes it on his wife, Nora, because it satisfies his vanity and makes her subservient to him. To him the man is the superior being, holding the economic reins and thereby concentrating in his hands all power and responsibility in the household, making the woman his slave. This conventional view also applies to the attitude to sex; in the kind of relationship that exists between Nora and Torvald, she is his plaything. Ibsen even adds a touch of perversity to Torvald's character, who confesses that he likes to indulge in fantasies about his wife that will enhance her erotic appeal. His purchase of a fishergirl's costume in Capri for Nora and his insistence that she dance the tarantella in public manifest the same desire.

It is against conventional middle-class values that Nora rebels. Of course, she has been made to believe that she was happy, that she was an ideal wife, and that her husband loves her, and she was living with the belief that an ideal husband like hers would, if the necessity arose, sacrifice his life to save her reputation. It is these illusions that are shattered at the end. In her final revolt against her husband, we see the play as dealing with the subject of freedom for women. It has been said that the banging of the door as Nora leaves the house was the first action of women's liberation. (Ibsen was aware of the controversy surrounding his play, and was obliged to provide an alternative happy ending for its German production where Nora melts at the sight of her children. He described it as 'a barbaric outrage'.)

Ibsen himself tried to bring the controversy to an end. He said: 'I . . . must disclaim the honour of having consciously worked for women's rights. I am not even quite sure what women's rights really are. To me it has been a question of human rights'. This, in fact, suggests the main theme of the play. It is true that the rebel, trying to claim what she considers her legitimate rights, is a woman, but Ibsen also conveys a more general theme of freedom from constricting circumstances of life, often observing that those circumstances are social in character. Whether they belong to his own century or to some other period, whatever the nature of the circumstances, there has always been a conflict between the sensitive, intelligent individual and social pressures and circumstances. Ibsen invests the topical and the contemporary with a universal significance, succeeding because of the creative force of his play, projected mainly onto the chief character, Nora. Her vitality is evident in the way she reacts to the life around her and the changes she undergoes in the course of the play. In fact, the most fascinating aspect of the play is Nora's consciousness, and an important theme is the development of a mature sensibility.

At the beginning, Nora makes her energetic temperament subservient to her love for her husband, but even at this stage her spirit of independence manifests itself as a kind of irresponsibility, making her forge her father's signature and surreptitiously eat macaroons, which Torvald has forbidden her to do. More remarkable is her deeply passionate and devoted heart. Her crime, after all, was motivated by an unreflecting love for her husband: without his knowledge and for his sake, she raises a loan by forgery. Nora also possesses a developing intelligence which enables her to acquire a mature conception of freedom. These qualities create a complex and many-sided personality and together constitute Nora's morality, fresh, vigorous, and unorthodox, which is pitched against the conventional morality of Torvald. What the play dramatizes is not a clash of characters but of values and of different ways of looking at the world. In Torvald Ibsen portrays a character who is lacking in the vital qualities of the heart and is a victim of social conventions. It is only gradually that Nora acquires a true awareness of her husband's character and what he represents.

The explosive impact of the play tends to deflect attention from Ibsen's dramatic skill. The construction has something in common with the 'well-made play', but his technique is generally richer and far more meaningful. Ibsen also employs his characteristic retrospective method whereby he gradually lifts the veil over ominous events in the past, despite the resistance of the main character. Nora conceals her crime from Torvald, but events beyond her control result in his discovering it. She expects Torvald to take upon himself the responsibility for the past, but he does not and is thus stripped of all his pretensions, while Nora is jolted into a realization that she has been living in a doll's house.

Ibsen introduces a sub-plot centring upon two other characters, Mrs Linde and Nils Krogstad. This is not handled as adroitly as the main plot, but is essential to the play. Ibsen's mode of presentation is realistic, but he incorporates symbolism and visual suggestion, too. For instance, when Nora dances the tarantella, the frenzied dance is an image of the torment in her mind. Indeed, Nora's very language, though prose, is vibrant with emotion and acquires a poetic intensity. The play confirms Ibsen's view: 'I have been more of a poet and less of a social philosopher than people generally suppose'.

—D.C.R.A. Goonetilleke

GHOSTS (Gengangere)
Play by Henrik Ibsen, 1881.

Like its immediate predecessor *A Doll's House*, *Ghosts* announces itself as a domestic drama in three acts. Apart from its similar structure, *Ghosts* shares with *A Doll's House* a single interior location, concentration of the action on a few individuals, and an acute sense of personal catastrophe. Furthermore, in the way that Nora's increasing self-awareness is charted in *A Doll's House*, through lighting and *mise en scène*, the inner states of Ibsen's characters in *Ghosts* are indicated through extensive visual suggestion. All these means of intensifying the stage action produce what is probably Ibsen's starkest, and what was widely regarded as in its day as his most shocking, dramatic experience.

Ghosts concerns the fate of Oswald Alving, a Paris-based artist, who has returned to his native land of western Norway in order to be present at the dedication of a memorial to his father. Exiled at an early age by his mother so that he would be outside the influence of licentious Captain Alving, Oswald has remained ignorant of his father's past and is eager to discover life and joy in the bleak, rain-swept terrain of his birth. Oswald finds such qualities in his mother's servant, Regina Engstrand (a dramatic creation similar to Jean in Strindberg's *Miss Julie* (*Fröken Julie*, 1888) and Dooniasha in Chekhov's *The Cherry Orchard* (*Vishnevyi sad*, 1904) in her social displacement and personal pretensions). However, Oswald's attraction to Regina is doomed, as all the certainties of his family life are revealed as being founded on lies, with the revelation that his mother's servant is in fact his half-sister who was adopted, for payment, by the rascally carpenter Engstrand. Even more shocking is the realization that he has inherited syphilis, like Dr Rank in *A Doll's House*, from his supposedly respectable father. Here, as in *An Enemy of the People* (*En folkefiende*), the presence of illness hints at murky and disguised truths. In a chilling final tableau, Ibsen shows us the long awaited reunion between mother and son, the beloved adult child reduced to babbling early babyhood as the hereditary illness attacks mind and body.

With its limited cast, close-packed action, time, and location, *Ghosts* is an attempt by Ibsen to emulate the tautness and severity of Classical and neo-classical drama. This 19th-century tragedy moves, like its French and Greek models, inexorably to a harrowing outcome, the consequences of past deeds bearing down, Eumenides-like, on the victim Oswald. Layers of illusion are shed and the truth about the past is revealed. Unlike its Classical predecessors, however, the moral questions raised are wholly secular, despite the omnipresence of the complacent Pastor Manders, to whom Mrs Alving once fled on account of her husband's behaviour. The play shows the consequences of human deeds, and, as in many of Ibsen's dramas, the ways that people elect, or feel forced, to live are shown as life-denying and designed to inhibit vitality, creativity, and original thought. As with other naturalistic plays, *Ghosts* demonstrates how a particular milieu shapes behaviour and character. In this play, however, the environment exists more as a climate of ideas. Expressed in the 'Ghosts' of the title, these ideas are handed on from generation to generation, and find expression in false notions of propriety and outdated beliefs in particular codes of conduct.

Although *Ghosts* depicts Oswald's tragedy, it is Mrs Alving who is the central character in the play, and the main part of Ibsen's drama concerns her system of values and behaviour in relation to those of the other visitors to her household. Ibsen saw Mrs Alving as a successor to Nora in *A Doll's House*. While Nora slammed the door on her constricting circumstances, Oswald's mother has chosen to stay in her home. In her isolation, Mrs Alving has come to recognize more enlightened ideas of social and moral behaviour, and has grown scornful of the cowed and bigoted attitudes of her society. However, she is incapable of marrying action to belief, as is evident in her building an orphanage to her husband's memory in order to preserve an untarnished image of him. Her acts of bad faith, shown in her inability to reveal the truth, persist even to the end of the play when she glosses over the reality of Oswald's condition.

The representative of convention and respectability in the

play is Pastor Manders who, like Helmer in *A Doll's House* and Aline in *The Master Builder*, has subordinated self-fulfilment to duty. Manders's measured and tightly patterned pronouncements are replete with platitudes, as he lays down the values of the patriarchal system that he has allowed himself to support without question. However, Manders is depicted as being in part a moral hypocrite with his lascivious interest in Regina's well-being and his anxiety to cover up his involvement in the careless burning-down of the orphanage that he has failed to insure.

Oswald, with his progressive ideas on living based upon his 'beautiful, glorious and free' Parisian experience, becomes, as does young Hedwig in *The Wild Duck*, the innocent victim of a society based upon dogmatic beliefs and concealment of unpleasant truths. His idealism and lack of guile prevent his free existence, unlike Regina and her adoptive father Engstrand who have learned to survive by pandering to the outward respectability of their social superiors.

The idea of sacrifice to society, and also the way that truth cannot be quenched, is graphically shown at the end of the play by Oswald being burnt up by his disease, and is further accentuated by accumulating references to light and fire. The conflagration at the orphanage reduces to ash the very foundations upon which Mrs Alving has maintained appearances of happy family life. Eventually the sunrise at the end of the play (the only time that rain has made way for sunshine) does not appear to represent a new beginning, but rather demonstrates how nature can cruelly overwhelm the nurturing process, as the ever-present natural landscape, ignored throughout the play, eventually pervades the elegant and outwardly ordered trappings of the Alving household.

—Anna-Marie Taylor

HEDDA GABLER
Play by Henrik Ibsen, 1890.

A tiny incident, but a significant one, is carefully planted by Ibsen at the start of this play which is a masterpiece of characterization, even if its meticulous craftsmanship, in an almost classical dramatic style, seems by now to be rather old-fashioned. Auntie Julle is all of a-flutter at the prospect of welcoming her nephew, Jörgen Tesman, and his new bride, Hedda, after their extravagantly long honeymoon trip, in the rather grand home that has, we soon learn, been furnished with funds raised by way of a mortgage on the annuity providing her with the bare necessities of life. Anxious to make a good impression, she has also bought herself a new hat, which she takes off and places on a chair. Not long after, Hedda enters, sees it, and at once says that she really does not think that Berte, who has been engaged as a maid for the Tesman household, will be at all suitable. How could she be when she has shown her slovenly ways by thoughtlessly leaving her old hat lying about in the drawing room? At once there is electricity in the air, with the old busybody of an aunt offended and her nephew embarrassed, by what they take to be Hedda's dreadful *faux-pas*. Only Hedda does not seem embarrassed, and before long we discover that she dropped the brick intentionally. She was bored, she was resisting every attempt to be absorbed into the bosom of the family into which she had married, and she was frankly pleased to have the opportunity of stirring up trouble.

A lady of 29 and with a certain aristocratic elegance about her, Hedda feels that she has married beneath herself. We are not allowed to forget that her father was General Gabler,

whereas her husband, her elder by some four years, is a cultural historian who is short of money and has only fairly tenuous prospects of becoming a professor. The fact that the title of the play is not *Hedda Tesman* but *Hedda Gabler*, like the way some of her admirers know how to flatter her by calling her by her maiden name, is a clear pointer to her unwillingness to accept her role as a wife to an unprepossessing husband whose undoubted infatuation with her is attenuated by his desire to continue collecting material for a work of what appears to be dry-as-dust scholarship. There are, as is perhaps to be expected after a honeymoon, some more or less discreet enquiries whether she might be pregnant, but she impatiently brushes them aside and, though she first appears in a fairly loose-fitting morning gown, she insists that her figure has not filled out. All in all, it seems that she has not yet found sexual fulfilment in marriage, and now, as autumn begins to set in, there is not much to please her in the prospect of life in the dreary Norwegian town to which she has returned.

Some idea of her frustration is given by the way she responds when Thea Elvsted arrives. She is a couple of years younger than Hedda, and though they were at school together, it is understandable that Hedda cannot immediately recall her Christian name accurately, but she insists that they both were and must continue to be great friends. Now the plot begins to thicken, as Hedda recalls how once she too had dallied with Eilert Lövborg. He is a scholar who had worked in much the same field as her husband, but his ways had been dissolute and his chances of making the most of his talents had been slim until Thea, who had left her husband, took him in hand and helped him write a book that none other than Tesman recognizes as an imaginative scholarly masterpiece. Jealousy now consumes Hedda. Though Eilert had wisely decided that teetotalism was the only safe policy for him, Hedda inveigles him into going off on a drinking bout with her husband and the sinister Judge Brack. In his drunken stupor he drops the only copy of the manuscript of his book, but Tesman finds it. When he brings it home, Hedda loses no time in consigning it to the stove. As she commits the pages to the flames, her language shows that she sees Eilert's great work as a love-child born to him and Thea. After that she has the ambition to inspire in Eilert a great, tragic passion, and she hands to him one of her father's pistols that she once had aimed at him in a tense moment. He must use it now, 'beautifully', as she insists.

In fact the unfortunate Eilert does not kill himself with a romantic bullet in the heart, but by accident, in the abdomen, and while in a house of ill-repute. To make matters worse, Judge Brack realizes what has been afoot and sees how this may give him a hold over Hedda. Well may she say that everything she touches seems fated to turn into something like a mean farce. There is only one grand Romantic gesture left to her, and, typically enough, it is a futile one. She leaves the drawing room, pulling the curtains behind her before launching into a wild piece of music on the piano. Then a shot rings out: she has put General Gabler's other pistol to her temple and pulled the trigger. The dramatic style is classical in its avoidance of on-stage violence, the violence is melodramatic, and the predictable patterning of the drama with some well-formulated, quotable statements amidst the everyday talk belongs to the period of the well-made play. Within that framework, Ibsen has, however, portrayed a character in which many see not only the frustrations of women in 19th-century society but also the plight of mankind in general.

—Christopher Smith

THE MASTER BUILDER (Bygmester Solness)
Play by Henrik Ibsen, 1892.

One of the great strengths of Ibsen's dramas was to deflate bourgeois self-confidence, and to reveal that the cosiest and best furnished of drawing rooms could harbour grim secrets, dissatisfaction, and despair. The desire to expose the self-deception, constriction, and hypocrisy upon which middle-class life was founded can be seen most obviously in his socially realistic plays such as *The Pillars of Society* and *Ghosts*. However, such criticism of bourgeois living is also apparent in the plays that belong to Ibsen's final stage of writing. In the plays written in the 1890s he proved, however, to be more interested in probing the nature of artistic creativity, and was less concerned with showing how social environment could determine individual consciousness as he had done, for example, in *A Doll's House* and *An Enemy of the People*.

The Master Builder comes from Ibsen's last years as a playwright and is, like his final play, *When We Dead Awaken*, an examination of personal and artistic expression, with strong symbolist tendencies in its style. There are pronounced autobiographical elements in both plays, suggesting (rather neatly for literary biographers) that these late pieces could be the Norwegian playwright's final reckoning with his own art, life, and ambitions. Although the two late plays share much in common, *The Master Builder*'s setting, a carefully described and prosperous architect's residence, recalls the social dramas of the 1870s and 1880s much more directly than the dreamlike, semi-mythical mountain world of *When We Dead Awaken*.

Halvard Solness is a self-taught architect and builder from a poor country background, whose business has prospered despite personal tragedy. He believes that he has willed the burning down of his wife's childhood home, a fire that destroyed all of her most precious memories and possessions. As a result of the fire, Aline Solness was unable to feed their twin baby boys, who also perished. With Faustian overtones, Solness believes that this domestic misfortune has bought him success and artistic acclaim. He has been ruthless in exercising his will to power and has deliberately impeded the development of others. In order to be acclaimed, he has held back his assistant Ragnar Brovik out of fear that the younger generation will overtake him. He exerts great dominance over Ragnar's fiancée Kaja, who is his secretary and is infatuated with him. Despite the fact that his occupation is the building of homes, Solness's own home life is barren and miserable, unable as he is to help Aline who, always dressed in black, is in mourning for her lost life as a mother.

An unexpected emissary from outside Solness's world, the young, vital, and impulsive Hilde Wangel, brings enthusiasm and joy into Solness's solitary existence. The idealistic Hilde offers herself as his princess to be carried away by Solness the Troll, a fantasy that she claims was enacted ten years previously when he visited her village to place a wreath on top of the church tower he had designed. To Hilde, Solness reveals an almost fanatical sense of vocation, a belief that he has been chosen and is special. Yet Solness's belief in his mission as an artist is in crisis; his confidence is shaken by Ragnar's request to be allowed his own building commission. Spurred on by Hilde's adulation Solness, who is afraid of heights, is persuaded to repeat his climbing feat of ten years back, and scales the high tower of his new home. Unfortunately Solness plunges from the tower to his death. Just as the outsider Gregers Werle imposes an impossible notion of the ideal on the Ekdal household in *The Wild Duck*

and destroys the family, Hilde also forces Solness to attempt to live up to an unattainable reality.

Although the setting is much more realistic than the expressionistic plays of writers such as August Strindberg and Georg Kaiser, this intriguing play has features that anticipate them. It is, like Kaiser's *From Morning to Midnight* (*Von Morgens bis mitternachts*, 1916), a monodrama, with the action centred almost entirely on the inner states of the central character. Also, as in Strindberg's *A Dream Play* (*Ett drömspel*, 1902) and *Ghost Sonata* (*Spöksonaten*, 1907), there is the sense that the events, particularly the attraction of Hilde and Kaja, stem from workaday reality suffused by fantasies, dreams, and desires. Like Solness's towers and palaces, which have no foundations in the ground, the dialogue here has a visionary quality which reveals Solness's forceful urges and guilt-torn fears that he has failed as an artist and as a human being. Behind the successful architect's domineering façade lurk anxieties about waning creativity and potency, expressed in his yearning to build higher towers, and his inability in recent years to do so. Creative talent is presented here as a painful process, born out of domination, egotism, and an inability to give love. Eventually this artistic ability, built as it is on dubious practice, is destroyed by the unexpected (and possibly willed) retribution of Hilde's irresponsible over-confidence in his powers. The younger generation destroys Solness, as he fears, but through worship rather than envy. However, the master builder's sudden death as a result of his *folie à deux* with Hilde is not tragic. Accompanied by Hilde's ecstatic adoration (and the earth-bound Aline's warnings), Solness's plunge to his death anticipates the transfiguration of the individual, found also in Rubek's triumphant recapturing of life in *When We Dead Awaken* and at the end of several German expressionist plays, where the hero transcends the everyday through heightened experience.

The idiosyncratic tone of *The Master Builder* has caused critics to reach outside the text to look for shared ideas and influences. It is possible to find affinities with Freud's contemporary ideas on the unconscious in the evocation of Solness's sublimated desires, subconscious fantasies, and dreams, to make sense of the patterns of imagery in the play. Solness too may resemble some kind of Nietzschean Superman, trying through his art to rise above the cowed masses. However, the provincial architect appears to be a poor prototype, showing himself in his egotistic treatment of those who surround him as being all too human. It seems more fruitful to look at *The Master Builder* within Ibsen's dramatic *oeuvre*. The play's ideas revive preoccupations and patterns of interaction from earlier works in Ibsen's theatrical career, which are here reshaped. The relationship between self-fulfilment and duty, the desire for truth and authenticity of experience, and the tensions between life, art, and passion are all examined with different shifts of meaning from earlier plays. To such recurrent concerns, Ibsen, in his portrait of the artist as an ageing man, incorporates a wish for self-analysis, hinting at the exorcism of trolls in his own creative life.

—Anna-Marie Taylor

PEER GYNT
Play by Henrik Ibsen, 1867.

Ibsen wrote *Peer Gynt* in Rome, Ischia, and Sorrento in the early years of what was to be a 27-year absence from his native Norway. It is a five-act poetic drama, written for publication rather than for the stage, whose leading character and themes may be seen as complementary to those of Ibsen's previous play, *Brand*, written in 1865. Whereas Brand is ruthlessly singleminded in his beliefs, Peer is a compromiser who avoids facing up to reality and prefers to go 'round about'.

Peer Gynt takes the form of an epic narrative based upon the archetypal theme of the quest. Its eponymous hero travels from Norway to Africa and finally back again to Norway, passing from youth to old age and possibly death, in search of his authentic self. Although not intended for realization on the stage, these three locations visually complement the various psychological states experienced by the hero. The first three acts are set in the rural landscape of Norway with its mountains, valleys, and forests dotted with isolated farms and cottages and in the dark troll-world of rural folklore. During these scenes Peer is portrayed as an energetic young rogue who spins fantastic yarns and falls in love with a chaste and beautiful young girl, Solveig. His romantic image is, however, sullied by his surrender to an orgy of sexual indulgence which begins with the kidnap, seduction, and abandonment of a bride, continues in a sexual romp with a group of herd-girls, and is completed by his copulation with a green-clad woman who turns out to be a troll princess. This moral descent is reflected by the replacement of the objective material reality, represented by the rural landscape, by the nightmarish subjective reality of the troll kingdom, a world in which normal morality is reversed. Faced with the true implications of his behaviour, Peer refuses however to confirm his moral decline by submitting to the troll King's demand that his eye should be scratched so that his moral perception will remain irreversibly awry. In the following scene, still located in subjective reality, Peer's evasiveness and his inability to commit himself to a course of action are further conveyed by his struggle with the invisible Boyg. The dark world of Peer's sin-laden mind intrudes into day-to-day reality with the reappearance of the green-clad woman who introduces him to his monstrously deformed son. Overwhelmed by guilt, Peer accepts the Boyg's advice to 'go round'. In spite of Solveig's offer to share his burden, on the death of his mother who has hitherto offered him a refuge from life's realities, he flees from Norway.

In contrast to the green and fertile rural settings of the first three acts, the world of the middle-aged Peer of the fourth act is that of a flat and arid desert. Peer now attempts to discover his true self through worldly power and material success. In succession he adopts the roles of successful but amoral businessman, religious prophet, and academic historian, while considering in passing the foundation of a new state to be called Gyntiana. These attempts at aggrandizement end in a madhouse where he is crowned with a straw crown as the 'Emperor of Self'.

The bright and arid landscape of Act Four is replaced in the final act by a stormy North Sea night-crossing during which Peer, returning to Norway, meets a Strange Passenger emerging from nowhere, is 'cleansed' in the sea when his ship is wrecked, and ultimately arrives home to a dark, purgatorial wasteland of dried river beds, burnt forests, and misty moorland. Here he is confronted, as in a morality play, by the metaphysically conceived figures of the Thin Person and the Button Moulder. The barrenness of these settings reflects Peer's gradual realization of the barrenness of his own character, a process dramatized in a series of visual images which include the auction of his past possessions and the peeling of an onion. The auction reveals that his life has been without significance, while the peeling of the onion, each layer related to a stage in his life, makes him realize that, like the onion, he has no centre and no heart. Once again the play slides between objective and subjective reality as Peer meets the Button Moulder who informs him that, because he has never committed himself with strength or purpose to any course of action, be it good or evil, he is worthy of neither heaven nor hell, and that his destiny is to be melted down, along with other anonymous scraps of wasted humanity, to be recast as someone else. With the Button Moulder poised to take him, Solveig's singing intervenes, and it is at this point that Peer makes the first positive choice of his life and completes the progress home to Solveig which he had earlier interrupted.

It is in Solveig that he discovers his true self for, during his absence, she has sustained him in her faith, hope, and love. Day is breaking and Peer is bathed in light as he buries his face in Solveig's lap. At this point the play, underscored by the singing of the now blind Solveig, seems poised to topple into melodramatic sentimentality. Ibsen attempts, however, to avoid this resolution by making clear that the matter of Peer's salvation is yet to be resolved, for he has yet to meet the Button Moulder at the last crossroads. In these final moments of the play Solveig is, however, portrayed not as a wife and equal but as Peer's surrogate mother. 'My mother! My wife! O, thou pure woman!' he cries, 'O hide me in your love! Hide me! Hide me!'. He has returned to what he was at the beginning: a child in need of the support and validation of his mother. The play opens with Peer's mother's accusation that he escapes from reality into lies. It closes, ironically with Solveig's advice that Peer should 'Sleep, sleep and dream', and thereby escape from reality into unconsciousness.

In its delving into the murkier side of human psychology and in its recognition of the importance and power of the unconscious, *Peer Gynt* not only prefigures Ibsen's later symbolic plays such as *The Master Builder*, *Rosmersholm*, and *The Lady from the Sea* but also the concerns of 20th-century expressionism and surrealism.

—D. Keith Peacock

THE WILD DUCK (Vildanden)
Play by Henrik Ibsen, 1884.

As Ibsen himself admitted, *The Wild Duck*, written in 1884 and produced in Bergen in the following year, was somewhat different from the group of realistic plays, including *A Doll's House* and *Ghosts*, which preceeded it. With this play Ibsen's drama was to move into a new, symbolic phase which initially failed to impress contemporary critics who, for the most part, saw only pretentiousness and obscurantism and were unsympathetic to the play's humble setting and characters. Only gradually was Ibsen's play recognized as a painful, but at times ironically comic, comment upon humanity's need for the protection of illusion.

Dramatically, the most innovative feature of *The Wild Duck* lies in Ibsen's weakening of the well-made plot structure of explication, complication, climax, and dénouement which had dominated his earlier realistic plays. Now situation becomes more important than event, and the symbolism, which Ibsen had earlier grafted onto the realism of his plays in order to widen their implication from the particular to the general, becomes, on one level, a fully integrated feature of the play and, on another, a means by which the characters themselves attempt to imbue their ordinary lives and actions with deeper significance. From the former arise most of the tragic elements of the play, while from the latter stem ironic comedy and pathos.

As the title suggests, at the centre of the play is the image of the wild duck which, when shot, dives to the bottom of the lake to die but which, in this case, has been rescued by a clever hunting dog and now resides, injured, in the Ekdals' attic. It is in relation to this image that the majority of the play's characters are viewed and, as the play progresses, we gradually penetrate deeper and deeper into their past and present lives.

The symbolism of the wild duck is primarily associated with the Ekdal family, all of whom have in some manner been injured by old Werle, a rich merchant and owner of the Hoidal works. Significantly it was he who shot the wild duck. Werle's first victim was Ekdal senior who was, in the past, his business partner but was left by Werle to take sole responsibility and suffer imprisonment for illegal tree-felling. In consequence Ekdal has lost his status in society and is now supported partially by clerical work provided by Werle. Ekdal spends much of his spare time hunting rabbits in the fantasy forest which he and his son Hjalmar have created in their attic. Hjalmar and his wife Gina have also been injured by Old Werle. As the play progresses we learn that Gina had an affair with Old Werle which resulted in the birth of Hedvig, who is now 14 years old. To mitigate the consequences of his actions Old Werle encouraged Gina to marry Hjalmar and set the couple up in a small photography business. Even Hedvig suffers from association with her natural father in that she has inherited from him a disease which will gradually lead to blindness.

Whereas Old Werle has at least attempted to provide recompense for the injuries caused, his son Gregers, who has returned from a sojourn in the cold north bringing with him an equally cold logic, attempts to reveal the truth to his father's victims. He is unshakeably certain that, as a result, his father will be forced to face his guilt and that the Ekdals will be happier for being relieved of the delusions under which they live.

As Ibsen himself employs the symbolism of the wild duck to reveal the nature of the relationship that exists between the Ekdals and the Werles, so also do a number of the characters themselves attempt to infuse their lives with significance, and define a pattern to their mundane existence by describing themselves and their actions in terms of Romantic and at times sentimental imagery. Chief of these is Gregers Werle who has decided that his over-riding 'task in life' is to unburden others of their illusions. From his arrival in the Ekdal household, to the incomprehension of Hjalmar, Gina, and Hedvig, he weaves his own symbolism around the wild duck. He compares himself firstly to the duck itself and then to the clever dog who retrieved the duck from the bottom of the lake. The prosaic responses of Hjalmar and Hedvig provide a touch of comic irony intended by Ibsen to reveal Gregers's pretentiousness. By employing such ironic undercutting Ibsen allows this phoniness to appear at first comic but gradually, through the interaction between Gregers, Hjalmar, and Hedvig, he begins to reveal how it can also inhibit and even destroy relationships with others. Hedvig has already been emotionally crippled by being confined, on account of her partial blindness, to the apartment in which Hjalmar and her father live out their lives in self-delusion. Indeed, she is portrayed as behaving like one much younger than her actual age. She is in consequence highly susceptible to emotional pressure and it is under such pressure, exerted by Gregers, that she adopts his suggested 'spirit of sacrifice', and attempts to prove her love for her father by killing not her beloved wild duck, as suggested by Gregers, but herself.

Having cruelly rejected Hedvig when it is revealed by Gregers that she may not be his child, Hjalmar's self-dramatization keeps him ignorant of the real reason for her death. He is unable to understand her need to prove her love for him and, as the pragmatic realist Doctor Relling points out, 'Before the year is out little Hedvig will be nothing more to him than a fine subject to declaim on'. It is Relling, with his insistence that the average man needs his 'saving lie' in order to be happy, who is placed by Ibsen in opposition to Gregers with his fanatical 'claim of the ideal'. At the close of the play Hedvig is dead but Hjalmar and Gregers remain the same as they always were. The ironic comedy gives way to the sombre conclusion that idealism may not be the virtue that it may superficially appear.

—D. Keith Peacock

THE IGOR TALE. See **THE TALE OF THE CAMPAIGN OF IGOR.**

ILLYÉS, Gyula. Born in Rácegrespuszta, Hungary, 2 November 1902. Educated in Budapest, 1916–19; the Sorbonne, Paris, in the 1920s. Married Flóra Kozmutza; one daughter. Forced to leave Hungary in 1921 because of leftist activity; lived in Paris until 1926, then returned to Hungary; contributor from 1928 and editor, with Mihály Babits, 1937–41, *Nyugat* [West]; founding editor, *Magyar Csillag* [Hungarian Star], 1941–44; editor, *Válasz* [The Answer], 1946–48. Co-founder, 1939, and parliamentary representative from 1945, National Peasant Party. Vice-president, International PEN, from 1970. Recipient: Baumgarten prize, four times in the 1930s; Kossuth prize, 1948, 1953, 1970; International grand prize for poetry, 1965. Commandeur, l'Ordre des Arts et des Lettres (France), 1974. *Died 14 April 1983.*

PUBLICATIONS

Verse

Nehéz föld [Heavy Earth]. 1928.
Sarjúrendek [Swaths of Hay]. 1931.
Három öreg [Three Old Men]. 1932.
Hősökről beszélek [I Speak of Heroes]. 1933.
Ifjúság [Youth]. 1934.
Szálló egek alatt [Under a Moving Sky]. 1935.
Rend a romokban [Order Upon Ruins]. 1937.
Külön világban [In a Separate World]. 1939.
Összegyűjtött versei [Collected Poems]. 1940.
Válogatott versek [Selected Verse]. 1943.
Egy év [One Year]. 1945.
Összes versei [Complete Poems]. 3 vols., 1947.
Szembenézve [Face to Face]. 1947.

Tizenkét nap Bulgáriában [12 Days in Bulgaria]. 1947.
Két kéz [Two Hands]. 1950.
Válogatott versei [Selected Verses]. 1952.
Kézfogások [Handclasps]. 1956.
Új versek [New Poems]. 1961.
Nem volt elég . . . [It Was Not Enough . . .]. 1962.
Nyitott ajtó [Open Door]. 1963.
Dőlt vitorla [With Tilted Sail]. 1965.
Poharaim [My Cups]. 1967.
A Tribute to Gyula Illyés, edited by Thomas Kabdebo and Paul Tabori, various translators. 1968.
Fekete-fehér [Black-White]. 1968.
Selected Poems, edited by Thomas Kabdebo and Paul Tabori. 1971.
Abbahagyott versek [Unfinished Poems]. 1971.
Haza a magasban: Összegyűjtött versek 1920–1945 [Homeland in the Heights: Collected Poems]. 1972.
Teremteni: Összegyűjtött versek 1946–1968 [To Create: Collected Poems]. 1972.
Minden lehet: Új versek [Everything Is Possible: New Poems]. 1973.
Különös testamentum [A Strange Testament]. 1977.
Szemelt szőlő, válogatott versek, edited by Miklós Béládi. 1980.
Közügy [Public Matter]. 1981.
Konok kikelet [Stubborn Springtime]. 1981.
Mert szemben ülsz velem. 1982.
Táviratok. 1982.
A semmi közelít [The Approach of Nothingness]. 1983.
Szemben a támadással, összegyűjtött versek 1969–1981, edited by Miklós Borsos. 1984.
Menet a ködben. 1986.

Plays

A tű foka [The Eye of the Needle]. 1944.
Lélekbúvár [The Psychiatrist]. 1948.
Tűz-víz [Fire-Water]. 1952; revised version, as *Fáklyaláng* [Torchbearers], 1953.
Ozorai példa [The Example of Ozora]. 1952.
Tűvé-tevők [Turning the House Upside Down]. 1953.
Dózsa György [George Dózsa]. 1954.
Malom a Séden [Mill on the Séd]. 1960.
Bolhabál [Flea Dance]. 1962.
Különc [The Eccentric]. 1963.
Kegyenc [The Minion], from a play by László Teleki. 1963.
Az éden elvesztése: Oratórium [The Loss of Eden: An Oratorio]. 1967.
Drámák [Plays]. 2 vols., 1969.
Tiszták [The Pure Ones]. 1969.
Testvérek [Brothers]. 1972.
Bál a pusztán; Bölcsek a fán [Ball at the Ranch; Wise Men on the Tree]. 1972.
Újabb drámák [More Recent Plays]. 1974.
Dániel az övéi közt [Daniel among His Own People]. 1976.
Sorsválasztók. 1982.
Czak az igazat. 1983.

Fiction

Puszták népe. 1936; as *People of the Puszta*, translated by G.F. Cushing, 1967.
Kora tavasz [Early Spring]. 1941.
Húnok Párizsban [Huns in Paris]. 1946.
Két férfi [Two Men]. 1950.
Kháron ladikján [In Charon's Boat]. 1969.

Other

Oroszország [Russia]. 1934.
Petőfi (biography). 1936; as *Petőfi*, edited by Joseph M. Értavy-Baráth, translated by Anton N. Nyerges, 1973.
Magyarok [Hungarians]. 1938.
Ki a magyar? [The Hungarian—Who Is He?]. 1939.
Lélek és kenyér [Soul and Bread], with Flora Kozmutza. 1939.
Csizma az asztalon [Boots on the Table]. 1941.
Mint a darvak [Like Cranes]. 1942.
Honfoglalók között [Among the New Masters]. 1945.
Franciaországi változások [Changes in France]. 1947.
Ebéd a kastélyban [Lunch in the Castle]. 1962.
Ingyen lakoma: Tanulmányok, vallomások [A Free Feast: Studies, Confessions]. 2 vols., 1964.
Munkái [Works]. 1969– .
Hajszálgyökerek [Capillary Roots]. 1971.
Hét meg hét népmese (for children). 1975.
Matt the Gooseherd (for children), retold by Illyés, translated by Paul Tabori. 1976.
Itt élned kell [You Have to Live Here]. 1976.
Beatrice apródjai [The Pages of Beatrice]. 1978.
Szellem es erőszak. 1978.
Szulofolden. 1984.
A kolto felel (interviews), with Anna Foldes. 1986.
Naplójegyzetek [Entries in a Diary]. 5 vols., 1986–91.

Editor, *A francia irodalom kincseasháza* [The Treasure-House of French Literature]. 1942.
Editor, *Once upon a Time: Forty Hungarian Folk-Tales*, translated by Barna Balogh and Susan Kun. 1970.

*

Bibliography: *A magyar irodalomtörténet bibliográfiája, 1905–1945* by Ferenc Botka and Kálmán Vargha, vol. 1, 1982.

Critical Studies: *Az ismeretlen Illyés* [The Unknown Illyés] by László Gara, 1965; 'The Seventy Years of Illyés' by Miklós Béládi, in *New Hungarian Quarterly 48*, 1972; *Illyés Gyula költői viláképe* by József Izsák, 1982; 'Gyula Illyés: An Appraisal' by George Gömöri, in *World Literature Today*, Summer 1984.

* * *

Gyula Illyés was a poet first and foremost, although he created works of importance in practically all literary genres. Born into a poor family on a manorial estate in western Hungary, he remained loyal to the cause of the underprivileged throughout his life, though in old age he was regarded by many as the most forceful literary representative of the whole Hungarian nation. His early poetry was influenced by French surrealism and the constructivism of Lajos Kassák but soon after his return to Hungary from Paris in 1926 he found his own distinctive voice. While in his epic poems he followed the traditions of popular realism, his lyrical verse was characterized by a supple syntax, admirable intellectual vigour, and sharp psychological introspection. In some pre-war poems such as 'The Wonder Castle' Illyés foretold the collapse of the anachronistic social system of

Hungary based on entrenched class-privilege; to World War II he reacted with the lyrical diary *Egy év* [One Year] and with the rousing condemnation of the poem 'It Did Not Help'. Among his post-war collections probably *Kézfogások* [Handclasps] and *Dőlt vitorla* [With Tilted Sail] were the most accomplished. Outside Hungary he will be best remembered for the powerful 'Egy mondat a zsarnokságról' ('A Sentence for Tyranny'), a long litany of unfreedom told through a succession of poetic metaphors including this stanza:

> Where seek tyranny? Think again:
> Everyone is a link in the chain;
> Of tyranny's stench you are not free:
> You yourself are tyranny.
> (translated by Vernon Watkins)

A Socialist since his youth, Illyés was bitterly disappointed at the unsocialist manner in which most communist regimes in central east Europe suppressed and forcibly tried to assimilate their Hungarian national minorities. His solidarity with fellow-Hungarians outside the borders of Hungary was expressed in a number of poems as well as essays; for example he wrote an introduction to Kálmán Janics's book on the persecution of the Hungarian ethnic minority in Czechoslovakia after 1945. Illyés was a master of the essay and published several collections of essays before and after World War II, *Hajszálgyökerek* [Capillary Roots] being the most comprehensive. He also wrote two autobiographical novels as well as an objective though cautious travelogue about Soviet Russia (following his visit there in 1934), but his most memorable prose works were probably *Puszták népe* (*People of the Puszta*), which first focused attention on the semi-Asiatic living conditions of the Hungarian agrarian proletariat, and the short biography of the 19th-century revolutionary poet, Sándor Petőfi. The genuine radicalism and uncompromising character of Petőfi exerted a great attraction on the less passionate but no less committed Illyés; like Petőfi he also believed that a politically active literature can promote the democratization of society.

Illyés the playwright was particularly fertile in the 1950s and 1960s when he wrote a cycle of historical plays tackling national issues. Both *Fáklyaláng* [Torchbearers] and *Ozorai példa* [The Example of Ozora] are about events of the War of Independence which followed the Hungarian revolution of 1848. Later the character of László Teleki, a far-sighted but tragic political figure of the Kossuth emigration, captured Illyés's imagination and he wrote *Különc* [The Eccentric] about him, while another play entitled *Kegyenc* [The Minion] is the adaptation of a play by Teleki on a Roman theme, showing that it is impossible to serve tyranny without being dehumanized in the process. Of Illyés's later plays probably *Tiszták* [The Pure Ones] is the most interesting with its tale of moral conflict among the Cathar believers just before the fall of Monségur. By and large, Illyés's comedies are less successful than his dramas, though even the best plays suffer from an overdose of noble rhetoric and from too much concentration on national issues.

Apart from Hungary where since 1956 his standing has been exceptionally high, Illyés was better known in France than anywhere else in Europe; many French poets translated his work, and he reciprocated by translating French poetry into Hungarian and editing in 1942 an excellent anthology *A francia irodalom kincsesháza* [The Treasure-House of French Literature].

—George Gömöri

A SENTENCE FOR TYRANNY (Egy mondat a zsarnokságról)
Poem by Gyula Illyés, 1956 (written 1950).

'A Sentence for Tyranny' was written in 1950, but was first published only in the 'revolutionary' last number of *Irodalmi Újság* (2 November 1956). Its author, a poet with strong left-wing sympathies and a constant critic of the pre-war regime, acquired the status of an esteemed 'fellow traveller' in post-war Communist-controlled Hungary. His plays and poems were by then published in mass editions, so Illyés's personal interests would have dictated loyalty rather than defiance to the Communist regime. On the other hand, the programme of rapid and costly industrialization, combined with the forced collectivization of agriculture and the Socialist Realist regimentation in the arts, created a situation in which the great majority of the people came to resent the rule of the party-state. Illyés, who had often written poems on major social or national issues, now reacted to the loss of freedom of the individual with a forceful poem which illustrated the state's encroachment upon elementary human rights.

The poem was probably modelled on Paul Éluard's famous poem 'Liberté' written during the French resistance to German occupation. It is, in fact, an extended sentence which through 49 rhyming stanzas describes the all-embracing nature of tyranny. It opens with a negative assertion:

> Where seek out tyranny?
> There seek out tyranny,
> Not just in barrels of guns,
> Not just in prisons . . .

These 'not justs' and 'not onlys' continue over a number of lines until we reach the statement that it is everywhere: 'There, omnipresent, not/Less than your ancient God'. Illyés proceeds to assert that tyranny penetrates all domains of life; it even enters love-making, for 'you regard beautiful only that/that it has once possessed'. Tyranny takes over the imagination too: one feels like an inmate in a huge concentration camp, in which the Milky Way represents a minefield and the stars spy-holes. Like Aleksandr Solzhenitsyn, Illyés sees the victims of totalitarianism as both 'prisoners and jailers', so the conclusion, 'Of tyranny's stench you are not free/You yourself are tyranny', is quite logical. The poem ends on a deeply pessimistic note: Illyés, having described all the characteristics of tyranny and of those tyrannized, now states that one is helpless in the uneven struggle with this monster—all is in vain:

> because it is standing
> From the very first at your grave,
> Your own biography branding,
> And even your ashes are his slave
> (translations by Vernon Watkins)

The poem, although ostensibly a denunciation of Stalinist Communism, was not reprinted in Hungary in Illyés's lifetime. It was, however, translated into most languages and is often referred to as one of Illyés's most memorable and emblematic poems.

—George Gömöri

———

IONESCO, Eugène. Born in Slatina, Romania, 26 November 1909 (13 November according to Orthodox calendar; some sources erroneously give 1912); grew up in France; returned to Romania to join father after parents' divorce, 1922. Educated at the lycée Sfântul-Sava, Bucharest; learned Romanian; lycée, Craiova, baccalauréat, 1928; studied French literature at the University of Bucharest, 1928–33, *Capacitate* (teaching dipoma) 1934. Married Rodica Burileanu in 1936; one daughter. Taught French in Cernavodà and Bucharest 1936–38; moved to Paris, 1939; contributed to *Viata Româneasca* [Romanian Life], 1939, travelled to Paris, 1939; lived in Marseille during World War II; settled in Paris after its liberation, 1944; proofreader, Éditions Administratives, Paris, c.1945, and subsequently full-time writer. Also an artist: exhibited artwork in Biarritz and the Galérie Mouf, Paris, 1970. Recipient: Tours Festival prize, for film, 1959; Prix Italia, 1963; Society of Authors theatre prize (France), 1966; National Grand Prix for Theatre, 1969; Monaco Grand Prix, 1969; Austrian State prize for European literature, 1970; Jerusalem prize, 1973. Honorary doctorates: New York University, 1971, and the universities of Louvain, Warwick, Tel Aviv. Chevalier, Légion d'honneur, 1970. Member, Académie française, 1970. *Died 18 March 1994.*

PUBLICATIONS

Collection

Théâtre complet, edited by Emmanuel Jacquart, 1991.

Plays

La Cantatrice chauve (produced 1950). In *Théâtre I*, 1954; as *The Bald Prima Donna*, translated by Donald Watson, in *Plays I*, 1958; as *The Bald Soprano*, translated by Donald M. Allen, in *Four Plays*, 1958.
La Leçon (produced 1951). In *Théâtre I*, 1954; as *The Lesson*, translated by Donald Watson, in *Plays I*, 1958; also translated by Donald M. Allen, in *Four Plays*, 1958; and with *Rhinoceros* and *The Chairs*, 1989.
Les Chaises (produced 1952). In *Théâtre I*, 1954; as *The Chairs*, translated by Donald Watson, in *Plays I*, 1958; also translated by Donald M. Allen, in *Four Plays*, 1958; and with *Rhinoceros* and *The Lesson*, 1989.
Sept petits sketches (includes *Les Grandes Chaleurs*; *Le connaissez-vous?*; *Le Rhume onirique*; *La Jeune Fille à marier*; *Le Maître*; *La Nièce-Épouse*; *Le Salon de l'automobile*) (produced 1953). *La Jeune Fille à marier* in *Théâtre II*, 1958, as *Maid to Marry*, translated by Donald Watson, in *Plays III*, 1960; *Le Maître* in *Théâtre II*, 1958, as *The Leader*, translated by Derek Prouse, in *Plays IV*, 1960; *La Nièce-Épouse* as *The Niece-Wife*, translated by Richard N. Coe, in *Ionesco: A Study of His Plays*, revised edition, 1971; *Le Salon de l'automobile* in *Théâtre IV*, 1966, as *The Motor Show*, translated by Donald Watson, in *Plays V*, 1963.
Victimes du devoir (produced 1953). In *Théâtre I*, 1954; as *Victims of Duty*, translated by Donald Watson, in *Plays II*, 1958.
Théâtre I (includes *La Cantatrice chauve*; *La Leçon*; *Jacques; ou, La Soumission*; *Les Chaises*; *Victimes du devoir*; *Amédée, ou, Comment s'en débarrasser*). 1954.
Amédée; ou, Comment s'en débarrasser (produced 1954). In *Théâtre I*, 1954; as *Amédée; or, How to Get Rid of It*, translated by Donald Watson, in *Plays II*, 1958.
Jacques; ou, La Soumission (produced 1955). In *Théâtre I*, 1954; as *Jacques, or Obedience*, translated by Donald

Watson, in *Plays I*, 1958; as *Jack; or, The Submission*, translated by Donald M. Allen, in *Four Plays*, 1958.
Le Nouveau Locataire (produced 1955). In *Théâtre II*, 1958; as *The New Tenant*, translated by Donald Watson, in *Plays II*, 1958.
Le Tableau (produced 1955). In *Théâtre III*, 1963; as *The Picture*, translated by Donald Watson, in *Plays VII*, 1968.
L'Impromptu de l'Alma; ou, Le Caméléon du berger (produced 1956). In *Théâtre II*, 1958; as *Improvisation; or, The Shepherd's Chameleon*, translated by Donald Watson, in *Plays III*, 1960.
L'Avenir est dans les oeufs; ou, Il faut de tout pour faire un monde (produced 1957). In *Théâtre II*, 1958; as *The Future Is in Eggs; or, It Takes All Sorts to Make a World*, translated by Donald Watson, in *Plays IV*, 1960.
Impromptu pour la Duchesse de Windsor (produced 1957).
Plays I (includes *The Chairs*; *The Bald Prima Donna*; *The Lesson*; *Jacques, or Obedience*), translated by Donald Watson. 1958.
Four Plays (includes *The Bald Soprano*; *The Lesson*; *Jack; or, The Submission*; *The Chairs*), translated by Donald M. Allen. 1958.
Théâtre II (includes *L'Impromptu de l'Alma, ou, Le Caméléon du berger*; *Tueur sans gages*; *Le Nouveau Locataire*; *L'Avenir est dans les oeufs, ou, Il faut de tout pour faire un monde*; *Le Maître*; *La Jeune Fille à marier*). 1958.
Tueur sans gages (produced 1959). In *Théâtre II*, 1958; as *The Killer*, translated by Donald Watson, in *Plays III*, 1960.
Plays II (includes *Amedee, or, How to Get Rid of It*; *The New Tenant*; *Victims of Duty*) translated by Donald Watson. 1958.
Rhinocéros (produced 1959). In *Théâtre III*, 1963; as *Rhinoceros*, translated by Derek Prouse, in *Plays IV*, 1960.
Scène à quatre (produced 1959). In *Théâtre III*, 1963; as *Foursome*, translated by Donald Watson, in *Plays V*, 1963.
Apprendre à marcher (ballet scenario; produced 1960). In *Théâtre IV*, 1966; as *Learning to Walk*, translated by Donald Watson, in *Plays IX*, 1973.
Plays III (includes *The Killer*; *Improvisation, or, The Shepherd's Chameleon*; *Maid to Marry*), translated by Donald Watson. 1960.
Plays IV (includes *Rhinoceros*; *The Leader*; *The Future Is in Eggs, or, It Takes All Sorts to Make a World*), translated by Derek Prouse. 1960.
Rhinoceros; The Chairs; The Lesson, translated by Donald Watson. 1962.
Délire à deux (produced 1962). In *Théâtre III*, 1963; as *Frenzy for Two*, translated by Donald Watson, in *Plays VI*, 1965.
Le Roi se meurt (produced 1962). 1963; as *Exit the King*, translated by Donald Watson, in *Plays V*, 1963.
Le Piéton de l'air (produced 1962). In *Théâtre III*, 1963; as *A Stroll in the Air*, translated by Donald Watson, in *Plays VI*, 1965.
Théâtre III (includes *Rhinocéros*; *Le Piéton de l'air*; *Délire à deux*; *Le Tableau*; *Scène à quatre*; *Les Salutations*; *La Colère*). 1963.
Plays V (includes *Exit the King*; *The Motor Show*; *Foursome*), translated by Donald Watson. 1963.
Plays (includes *The Chairs*; *The Killer*; *Maid to Marry*), translated by Donald Watson. 1963.
Les Salutations (produced 1970). In *Théâtre III*, 1963; as *Salutations*, translated by Donald Watson, in *Plays VII*, 1968.
La Soif et la faim (produced 1964). In *Théâtre IV*, 1966; as *Hunger and Thirst*, translated by Donald Watson, in *Plays VII*, 1968.

La Lacune (produced 1965). In *Théâtre IV*, 1966.
Plays VI (includes *A Stroll in the Air*; *Frenzy for Two*), translated by Donald Watson. 1965.
Pour préparer un oeuf dur (produced 1966). In *Théâtre IV*, 1966.
Théâtre IV (includes *Le Roi se meurt*; *La Soif et la faim*; *La Lacune*; *Le Salon de l'automobile*; *L'Oeuf dur*; *Pour préparer un oeuf dur*; *Le Jeune Homme à marier*; *Apprendre à marcher*). 1966.
L'Oeuf dur, in *Théâtre IV*, 1966; as *The Hard-Boiled Egg*, translated by Donald Watson, in *Plays X*, 1976.
Leçons de français pour Américains (produced 1966). As *Exercices de conversation et de diction françaises pour étudiants américains*, in *Théâtre V*, 1974.
Plays VII (includes *Hunger and Thirst*; *The Picture*; *Anger*; *Salutations*), translated by Donald Watson. 1968.
Jeux de massacre (produced 1970). 1970; as *Here Comes a Chopper*, translated by Donald Watson, in *Plays VIII*, 1971; as *Killing Game*, translated by Helen Gary Bishop, 1974.
Plays VIII (includes *Here Comes a Chopper*; *The Oversight*; *The Foot of the Wall*), translated by Donald Watson. 1971.
The Duel (produced 1971). In *Plays XI*, translated by Clifford Williams, 1979.
Double Act (produced 1971). In *Plays XI*, translated by Clifford Williams, 1979.
Macbett (produced 1972). 1972; as *Macbett*, translated by Donald Watson, in *Plays IX*, 1973.
Plays IX (includes *Macbett*; *The Mire*; *Learning to Walk*), translated by Donald Watson. 1973.
Ce formidable bordel (produced 1973). 1973; as *A Hell of a Mess*, translated by Helen Gary Bishop, 1975; as *Oh What a Bloody Circus*, in *Plays X*, translated by Donald Watson, 1976.
La Vase. In *Théâtre V*, 1974.
Théâtre V (includes *Jeux de massacre*; *Macbett*; *La Vase*; *Exercices de conversation et de diction françaises pour étudiants américains*). 1974.
L'Homme aux valises (produced 1975). 1975; as *Man with Bags*, translated by Marie-France Ionesco and adapted by Israel Horowitz, 1977; as *The Man with the Luggage*, translated by Donald Watson, in *Plays XI*, 1979.
Plays X (includes *Oh What a Bloody Circus*; *The Hard-Boiled Egg*; with essay *Ionesco and His Early English Critics* by Donald Watson), translated by Donald Watson. 1976.
Plays XI (includes *The Man with the Luggage*; *The Duel*; *Double Act*; with essay *Why Do I Write?*), translated by Donald Watson and Clifford Williams. 1979.
Voyages chez les morts (as *Voyages Among the Dead*, 1980; scenes produced, 1983). As *Théâtre VIII* (*Voyages chez les morts: Thèmes et variations*), 1981; as *Plays XII* (*Journeys Among the Dead*), translated by Barbara Wright, 1985.
Plays XII (includes *Journeys among the Dead*), translated by Barbara Wright. 1985.

Screenplays: 'La Colère' episode in *Les Sept Péchés capitaux*, 1962; *Monsieur Tête* (animated film), 1970 (published in *Théâtre V*, 1974).

Ballet Scenarios: for television, with Fleming Flindt: *La Leçon*, 1963; *Le Jeune Homme à marier*, 1965; *La Vase*, 1970; *Le Triomphe de la mort*, 1971.

Fiction

La Photo du Colonel. 1962; as *The Colonel's Photograph*, translated by Jean Stewart and John Russell, 1967.

Le Solitaire. 1973; as *The Hermit*, translated by Richard Seaver, 1974.

Other

Elegii pentru fiinti mici. 1931.
Nu. 1934; as *Non* (in French), translated by Marie-France Ionesco, 1986.
Notes et contre-notes. 1962; revised edition, 1966; as *Notes and Counter-Notes*, translated by Donald Watson, 1964.
Entretiens avec Claude Bonnefoy. 1966; as *Conversations with Ionesco*, edited by Claude Bonnefoy, translated by Jan Dawson, 1970.
Journal en miettes. 1967; as *Fragments of a Journal*, translated by Jean Stewart, 1968.
Présent passé passé présent. 1968; as *Present Past, Past Present*, translated by Helen Lane, 1971.
Contes pour enfants. 4 vols., 1969–75; as *Story no. 1*, translated by Calvin K. Towle, 1968; *Story no. 2*, translated by Calvin K. Towle, 1970; *Story no. 3*, translated by Ciba Vaughan, 1971; *Story no. 4*, translated by Ciba Vaughan, 1973.
Découvertes, illustrated by Ionesco. 1969.
Mise en train: Première année de français, with Michael Benamou. 1969.
Discours de réception à l'Académie française . . . 1971.
Entre la vie et la rêve: Entretiens avec Claude Bonnefoy. 1977.
Antidotes. 1977.
Un homme en question. 1979.
Le Noir et le blanc. 1980.
Hugoliade. 1982; as *Hugoliad; or, The Grotesque and Tragic Life of Victor Hugo*, 1987.
Pourquoi j'écris. 1986; as *Why Do I Write?*, translated by Donald Watson, in *Plays XI*, 1979.
La Quête intermittente (autobiography). 1987; as *The Intermittent Quest*, 1988.

*

Bibliography: *Ionesco: A Bibliography* by Griffith R. Hughes and Ruth Bury, 1974; *Bibliographie et index thématique des études sur Ionesco* by Wolfgang Leiner, 1980.

Critical Studies: *Ionesco: A Study of His Plays* by Richard N. Coe, 1961, revised edition, 1971; *The Theatre of the Absurd* by Martin Esslin 1961, revised edition 1980. *Four Playwrights and a Postscript: Brecht, Ionesco, Beckett, Genet* by David I. Grossvogel, 1962; *Avant-Garde: The Experimental Theatre in France* by Leonard C. Pronko, 1962; *Eugène Ionesco* by Leonard C. Pronko, 1965; *Eugène Ionesco: An Introduction to His Work* by Kenneth R. Dutton, 1967; *Ionesco and Genet* by Josephine Jacobsen and William Randolph Mueller, 1968; *Brecht and Ionesco: Commitment in Context* by J.H. Wulbern, 1971; *Eugène Ionesco* by Ronald Hayman, 1972, revised edition, 1976; *Ionesco* by Allan Lewis, 1972; *Ionesco: A Collection of Critical Essays* edited by Rosette C. Lamont, 1973, and *The Two Faces of Ionesco* edited by Lamont and M.J. Friedman, 1978; *Ionesco: Rhinocéros* by C.E.J. Dolamore, 1984; *Langage et corps, fantasmé dans le théâtre des années cinquante: Ionesco, Beckett, Adamov* by Marie-Claude Hubert, 1987. *Ionesco's Imperatives: The Politics of Culture* by Rosette C. Lamont, 1993; *Understanding Eugene Ionesco* by Nancy Lane, 1994.

* * *

Ionesco's one-act plays of the early 1950s, together with those of Beckett, revitalized post-war drama and introduced what came to be known as the 'theatre of the absurd'. *La Cantatrice chauve* (*The Bald Prima Donna*), *La Leçon* (*The Lesson*), and *Les Chaises* (*The Chairs*) present different images of man's incomprehensible existence, expressed not so much through plot and characterization, which are minimal, as through the disintegration of language into chaos, silence, and death. The style is akin to farce, the tone a disturbing mixture of comic and tragic, for comedy, in Ionesco's view, is 'the intuition of the absurd, . . . more despairing than tragedy'. *The Bald Prima Donna*, which has enjoyed a continuous run at La Huchette since 1957, had its source in the conversational banalities of a beginner's English textbook. Superficially, it parodies petty-bourgeois life and the clichés of everyday speech, but the author's purpose was to express the astonishing meaninglessness of life and, with it, 'the tragedy of language', that is, not the problem of social communication, but our inability to penetrate the silence that surrounds us.

This metaphysical theme, which underlies the whole of Ionesco's work, is most clearly expressed in *The Chairs*. An old couple look back regretfully on their inconsequential lives, while expressing vague nostalgia for a lost 'City of Light'. Wishing to leave a 'message' for posterity before they die, they have invited a large number of guests to their isolated home. As the guests, who are invisible, arrive, the couple fill the stage with a vast number of chairs. The proliferation of meaningless objects, which has become a hallmark of Ionesco's plays, here signifies spiritual absence, the essential void: there is no message. With *The Lesson*, a further dimension emerges: the abuse of man's power, which is developed in more specific terms in later plays. During the course of a private lesson, the teacher gradually dominates his young female pupil by the manipulation of language (meaningless words which proliferate like the chairs) and pseudo-learning (reminiscent of ideological brainwashing). Finally carried away with his own power and desire, he kills the girl with the mesmerically repeated word 'cou-teau' (knife), in an act of violation containing both sexual and political overtones.

The longer, more ambitious plays, which subsequently predominate in Ionesco's output, frequently use the raw material of dreams and introduce us directly into the playwright's private obsessions: his sense of guilt; his spiritual frustration; his fear of death; his bewilderment at mankind's murderous nature. At the same time, his inventiveness and comic genius produce audacious dramatic images both grotesque and memorable, such as the huge expanding corpse of *Amédée; ou, Comment s'en débarrasser* (*Amédée; or, How to Get Rid of It*), or the transformation of people into monstrous pachyderms in *Rhinocéros* (*Rhinoceros*).

Rhinoceros, probably his most successful full-length play, evokes the rapid advance of fascism in the 1930s and, more generally, the threat of all conformist ideologies. The strength of the play lies not in its condemnation of ideology as such, but in its dramatization of the experience of the individual, Bérenger, who resists the tide of mass transformation. By preserving, intuitively rather than heroically, his human qualities—his inner world of fears, complexes, passion—he stands alone against the threatening herd in a final image of great dramatic power.

The denunciation of evil, especially that which is politically motivated, is a major theme of many of Ionesco's works, e.g. *Tueur sans gages* (*The Killer*), *Délire à deux* (*Frenzy for Two*), *Macbett*, *Ce formidable bordel* (*Oh What a Bloody Circus*). The tone is one of naive astonishment rather than righteous indignation; the caricature and humour of farce remain predominant. *Macbett*, a parody of Shakespeare by way of Jarry's *Ubu Roi*, is one of Ionesco's blackest and funniest plays, satirizing the tyrant's lust for power. *Oh What a Bloody Circus*, a dramatization of his only novel, *Le Solitaire* (*The Hermit*), and containing echoes of the political unrest in France in 1968, is a despairing inventory of all the horrors of the world and a cry of metaphysical anguish; with bitter irony, the play ends in hysterical laughter at the 'huge joke' God has played on mankind.

Ionesco's obsessional fear of death forms the subject of *Le Roi se meurt* (*Exit the King*), in which King Bérenger must prepare himself to die 'at the end of the play', and of *Jeux de massacre* (*Killing Game*), a series of 18 tableaux, inspired by Defoe's *Journal of the Plague Year*, and presenting the fundamental tenet of the absurd: 'That's what life is: dying'. Ionesco's own search for spiritual enlightenment found expression in the image of the quest in a number of dream-inspired plays, from the psychoanalytical *Victimes du devoir* (*Victims of Duty*) to the less successful autobiographical sagas, *L'Homme aux valises* (*Man with Bags*) and *Voyages chez les morts* (*Journeys Among the Dead*), which rework dreams and memories already published in diary form. In *La Soif et la faim* (*Hunger and Thirst*) the protagonist, having finally rejected human love, goes vainly in search of higher spiritual fulfilment, finally to be trapped in a Kafkaesque, monastery-like institution characterized by tyranny and indoctrination and signifying 'purgatory or hell'.

This generally bleak picture of human life, marked by guilt, violence and metaphysical alienation, is offset by Ionesco's original sense of comedy, his childlike delight in nonsense, contradiction and wordplay. There are also flights—sometimes literally, as in *Le Piéton de l'air* (*A Stroll in the Air*)—of poetic wonderment and the hope of salvation through love. But wonder invariably gives way to horror, love constantly fails, and the smile freezes on our lips as comedy reveals its tragic face. In the later autobiographical plays, humour is a rare ingredient and provokes sparse, uneasy laughter.

In his volume of autobiography, *La Quête intermittente* (*The Intermittent Quest*), Ionesco rejects literature in favour of painting and the spiritual quest, acknowledging the failure of language to give meaning to human existence. In his last play, *Journeys Among the Dead*, words finally disintegrate, without producing the anarchic humour which such an effect produced in *The Bald Prima Donna*. Their incoherence expresses the protagonist's, and the author's, bewildered incomprehension of life.

—C.E.J. Dolamore

THE BALD PRIMA DONNA (La Cantatrice chauve)
Play by Eugène Ionesco, 1950.

Ever since its creation at the Théâtre des Noctambules, Paris, in 1950, this masterpiece of the theatre of the absurd—at first not welcomed by the critics, though from the outset a great success with the public—has shown its staying power by constant performances, professional and amateur, that have delighted in its triumphant inconsequentiality. It has the ability to entertain by provoking both laughter and reflection. There is a feeling of happy release from all restraint occasioned paradoxically by the strong underlying form which is a counterpoint to the apparent shapelessness presented by the text at first glance.

Ionesco wanted to provide a parody of the well-made play,

hence his description of the work as an 'anti-play'. He gives us in miniature—in the space of only one hour's traffic on the stage—a condensed send-up of conventional drama, by standing on its head the assumption that a play is logically structured, with an exposition, a series of developments to constitute a middle that leads in turn to a climax and then a denouement where the tangle of events can be decently restored to order. Since it is precisely order and the feeling of cause and effect that constitute the target for all absurdists, Ionesco is reminding us, like Lewis Carroll before him, that the world is a topsy-turvy place in which existence has no proper beginning, middle, and end and is totally lacking in consistent logical explanation for our thoughts and behaviour. In what becomes not only a parody but a critique of the comfortable assumptions underlying the well-made play, he succeeds in drawing us willy-nilly into a web of irrationality that makes us, even as we laugh, acknowledge the truth behind his observations of banal everyday life. The aesthetic triumph Ionesco brings off is that, while subverting the lives of his characters and all the respectable order they feel to be a necessary part of existence, he has produced through inspired and sustained nonsense a work that is its own ordered world with not a syllable out of place, with every silence making its telling contribution to the pulse of the play and where the rhythms of language move relentlessly on to one of the most hilarious denouements in modern drama.

The decent world Ionesco satirizes is represented by the suburban English middle class, somewhere in the home counties, totally absorbed in the importance of its own petty obsessions. We are given an exposition, but in it Mr and Mrs Smith at their fireside maunder endlessly on about trivia. Mrs Smith, thinking aloud and listing in full detail all the things she has eaten, her shopping chores, and the habits of every member of the family, provides a fine example of an opening soliloquy that gives us no information at all. Mr Smith's outburst from behind his newspaper contributes further to our sense that language is being presented as a barrier rather than a communication bridge. The brief but brilliant confusion as the Smiths reminisce about their acquaintances, who, regardless of sex or age, are all called Bobby Watson, is a delight not only for its rhythmic nonsensical patterning but because it typifies what lies at the heart of the play, namely, that language itself can be reduced to a set of signifiers which, far from transmitting meaning, opaquely prevent any illumination from coming through. This constitutes, to use Ionesco's own phrase, that *tragédie du langage* which is to be further explored in the play and reminds us also of the supposed inspiration for this critique of language which Ionesco gleaned from learning English according to the Assimil method. He discovered that to repeat is not to deepen words but to empty them.

As the play moves to its parody of a middle development we meet Mary, the maid, who is as linguistically frank with her account of events and her brandishing of the chamber pot she has bought to shock her employers as the Smiths are mummified in their scleroticized opinions. Mary represents the sense of irrational emotion that is to come into its own at the arrival of the Fireman. Before that we meet a second couple, the Martins, who develop further, in their questioning of each other, the use of language as an investigation of the obvious. They discover they sleep in the same bed and are man and wife. The fullest development is kept for the inconsequential and alarming arrival of the Fireman. His insistence on telling anecdotes raises the nonsensical to a new notch of idiocy, and encourages, by its delight in the irrational, a general release of tension and even the discovery of suppressed passions, as Mrs Smith indulges in being the coy

maiden of her dreams and the bland Mr Smith gives vent to his wildly violent id. When Mary insists on joining in she is snobbishly rejected by the Smiths and Martins but embraced, literally, by the Fireman, who recognizes in her an old flame. Her wild poem in honour of the Fireman and in praise of the transformative power of fire emphasizes the release that inconsequential images and free association can bring. All this prepares us for what would be a tidy ending if this were a play written to reflect ordered reality. Together, Mary and the Fireman have had a catalytic effect on the behaviour of this pair of primly reserved couples. The finale begins as the Smiths and the Martins engage in a polite exchange of clichés that become ever more extravagant until the couples end up not so much exchanging views as verbally assaulting each other to the point that words as such disappear and are replaced by the letters of the alphabet hurled through the air like material objects in a wild and uproariously funny language game. The only way the people can finally get together and establish a relationship is by repeating meaningless phrases in childish imitation of train noises as they run round the respectable three-piece suite puff-puffing like a steam-engine. This would seem to be the denouement but for Ionesco's final touch of genius. A blackout seems to signify the end to the proceedings except that the light comes up to reveal the Martins seated exactly where the Smiths had been, with Mrs Martin beginning all over again the same punctiliously dreary catalogue of non-events.

There is an exhilaration in the play that derives from the excellent variations in tempo that Ionesco has allowed from scene to scene. From boring calm to wild verbal and physical expression the play carries the audience along on a wave of positive pleasure in spite of the seeming negativeness of the themes and the deliberate absence of characterization. The effect of *The Bald Prima Donna*, for all its satiric edge, is not depressing, rather we can laugh at ourselves as we recognize in it, as in a distorting mirror, our rational longing for civilized behaviour and logic in conflict with the disruptive energies of emotion.

—Leighton Hodson

RHINOCEROS (Rhinocéros)
Play by Eugène Ionesco, 1959.

Writing about the Nazis in a 1940 diary, Ionesco told himself he was the only man left among the rhinoceroses. Watching his friends, formerly anti-fascists, become infected by the ideology, Ionesco felt at if he were watching a physical transformation. The skin seemed to harden and thicken. 'A horn grows on his forehead, he becomes fierce, he charges furiously. He no longer knows how to talk. He is becoming a rhinoceros.' (*Present past, Past Present* [*Présent passé, passé présent*].)

The play, which was written in 1958 and premièred in 1959, is based on the story 'Rhinoceros', which was published in 1957, but when writing the story and the play Ionesco had no memory of using the word 'rhinoceros' to describe the Nazis. It was only much later, rediscovering the old diary, that he realized the analogy must have remained intact in his unconscious, though when he wrote the story he was remembering how Nazification could metamorphose a community. But as he said in 1961, the success of his play throughout the world made him wonder whether he had hit on:

a new plague of modern times, a strange disease that

thrives in different forms but is in principle the same. Automatic systematized thinking, the idolization of ideologies, screens the mind from reality, perverts our understanding and makes us blind. Ideologies too raise the barricades, dehumanize men and make it impossible for them to be friends notwithstanding: they get in the way of what we call coexistence, for a rhinoceros can come to terms only with one of his kind, a sectarian with a member of his particular sect.

The resultant play is as relevant to left-wing totalitarianism and conformism as to fascism.

It cannot have been easy to solve the problems of staging an action in which the characters, one after another, turn into rhinoceroses. In the first scene an offstage rhinoceros is heard stampeding through the streets: the point is made through sound effects, reports of what has happened and stylized reactions. Everyone says 'Oh, a rhinoceros', and then 'Well, of all things'.

Some of the comedy is reminiscent of Ionesco's earlier manner, as when the Logician proves syllogistically that a dog and Socrates are both cats, but of the five plays Ionesco based on his own stories this is the first with no thriller element, no policemen, no corpses. The first act closes quietly with a ludicrous cortège of mourners for the cat that has been trampled to death by the rhinoceros. People declare that they are not going to put up with the rhinoceros situation.

The second act opens in an office which serves as a microcosm to represent the social reaction to what is going on. An ex-schoolmaster refuses to believe in the rhinoceroses, but one of the employees has failed to turn up, and his wife rushes in to say that she has been chased by a rhinoceros now trying to climb the staircase, which is soon heard to collapse. We hear anguished trumpeting and the stage fills with dust, and when they all see the rhinoceros outside, the wife recognizes it as her husband. She jumps out of the window, and he gallops off with her on his back. The action parallels a passage in the diaries about jumping onto the broad back of the Nazi juggernaut.

Throughout the scene Ionesco demonstrates his skill in the realization of offstage events. When the others telephone the fire station to ask for ladders to be brought, they hear that other incidents have occurred. Seven rhinoceroses had been reported in the morning; now the number is up to 17.

Concentrated on an individual mutation—that of Bérenger's friend Jean—the second scene of Act II presents different problems. Since Jean cannot change physically on stage, Ionesco makes him keep rushing into the bathroom to check his appearance in the mirror from the moment Bérenger tells him that a bump has appeared on his forehead. This enables the actor to adjust his make-up on each exit. His skin turns progressively greener, while the bump grows into a horn, and the difficulty of showing him when the transformation is complete is side-stepped by making Bérenger shut him into the bathroom. A rhinoceros horn pierces through the door.

The analogy at the heart of the play is explored both visually and verbally. Denying the superiority of humanity, Jean claims to be sick of moral standards. Nature has its own laws, he argues, and they should build life on new foundations, going back to primeval integrity. When Bérenger defends the values civilization has evolved, Jean contends that we shall be better off without them.

Alone, Bérenger is in danger. He wishes he could grow a horn: a forehead without one has come to seem ugly. Starting to hate his white hairless body, he tries to imitate the trumpeting he hears outside, but the play has an upbeat ending. If necessary he will take on the whole lot of them. He will not give in.

—Ronald Hayman

IŚA. See **UPANISHADS**.

ISHA. See **UPANISHADS**.

J

JACOB, Max. Born in Quimper, France, 11 July 1876. Educated at École Coloniale, 1894. Moved to Paris; gave piano lessons and attended art courses; art critic, *Le Gaulois*, Paris, 1898, resigned; returned to Quimper and had a variety of jobs; returned to Paris, 1901; clerk and labourer, the department store, Entrepôt Voltaire; closely associated with Apollinaire, *q.v.*, and Picasso, who became his godfather in 1915, after Jacob's conversion to Roman Catholicism; settled at a Benedictine monastery, Saint-Benoît-sur-Loire, after 1921; returned to Paris, 1928–35, and associated with Cocteau, *q.v.* Spent most of his retirement in poverty. Arrested as a Jew by the Nazis, 1944. Member, Légion d'honneur, 1932. *Died (in Drancy Concentration Camp) 5 March 1944.*

PUBLICATIONS

Collections

Hesitant Fire: Selected Prose, edited and translated by Moishe Black and Maria Green. 1991.
Théâtre. 1953.

Verse

Saint Matorel, illustrated by Picasso. 1911; enlarged edition, 1936.
La Côte: Recueil de chants celtiques inédits. 1911; reprinted with 17 watercolours by Jacob, 1927.
Les Oeuvres burlesques et mystiques de Frère Matorel, mort au couvent de Barcelone, illustrated by André Derain. 1912.
Les Alliés sont en Arménie: Poème. 1916; revised edition, 1976.
Le Cornet à dés: Poèmes en prose. 1917; as *The Dice Cup: Selected Prose Poems*, edited by Michael Brownstein, translated by John Ashbery, and others, 1979; selections translated by Judith Morganroth Schneider, in *The Play of the Text*, 1981, and in *Double Life: Thirty Prose Poems*, translated by Michael Bullock, 1989.
La Défense de Tartuffe: Extases, remords, visions, prières, poèmes, et Méditations d'un juif converti, illustrated by Picasso and Jacob. 1919.
Le Voyage en autobus. 1920.
Le Laboratoire central. 1921.
Visions infernales: poèmes en prose. 1924.
Les Pénitents en maillots roses. 1925.
Fond de l'eau. 1927.
Le Sacrifice impérial. 1929.
Rivage. 1931.
Cinq poèmes, music by Francis Poulenc. 1932.
Le Chemin de croix infernal, illustrated by Jean-Mario Prassinos. 1935.
Ballades. 1938.
L'Homme de cristal. 1946; revised edition, 1967.

Derniers poèmes en vers et en prose. 1945; revised edition, 1961.
Les Poèmes de Morvan le Gaëlique. 1953.
Trois quatrains. 1953.
A poèmes rompus. 1960.
Double Life: Thirty Prose Poems, translated by Michael Bullock. 1989.

Fiction

L'Histoire du roi Kaboul ler et du Marmiton Gauwain (for children). 1903; revised edition, 1971.
Le Géant du soleil (for children). 1904.
Le Siège de Jérusalem: Drame céleste, illustrated by Picasso. 1914.
La Phanérogame. 1918.
Cinématoma. 1919.
Le Roi de Boétie: nouvelles. 1921; revised edition 1971.
Wenceslas, ancien cocher. 1921; revised edition, 1971.
Filibuth; ou, La Montre en or. 1922.
Le Cabinet noir. 1922; enlarged edition, 1928.
La Couronne de vulcain (stories), illustrated by Suzanne Roger. 1923.
Le Terrain bouchaballe. 2 vols., 1923; revised edition, 1964.
L'Homme de chair et l'homme reflet. 1924.
Le Nom: nouvelle. 1926.
Aguedal II. 1944.

Plays

Isabelle et Pantalon (opera libretto), music by Roland Manuel. 1922.
Fable sans moralité (ballet scenario), music by H. Bordes. 1931.
Le Bal masqué (ballet scenario), music by Francis Poulenc. 1932.

Other

Matorel en province. 1921; revised edition, 1936.
Ne coupez pas, mademoiselle; ou, Les Erreurs des PTT: plaquette de grand luxe, illustrated by Juan Gris. 1921.
Dos d'Arlequin, illustrated by Jacob. 1921.
Art poétique. 1922.
Le Chien de pique. 1928.
Visions des souffrances et de la mort de Jésus, fils de Dieu, illustrated by Jacob. 1928.
Tableau de la bourgeoisie, illustrated by Jacob. 1929.
Bourgeois de France et d'ailleurs (portraits). 1932.
Morceaux choisis, edited by Paul Petit. 1936.
Conseils à un jeune poète, conseils à un jeune étudiant. 1945; as *Advice to a Young Poet*, translated by John Adlard, 1976.
Méditations religieuses. 1945.
Lettres à Edmond Jabès. 1945.
Lettres inédites du poète à Guillaume Apollinaire. 1946.
En février 1942, Max Jacob écrivait. 1947.

Le Symbolisme de la face. 1948.
Choix de lettres de Max Jacob à Jean Cocteau (1919–1944). 1949.
Miroir d'astrologie, with Claude Valence. 1949.
Choix de lettres à Jean Cocteau, 1919–1944. 1950.
Lettres à un ami: correspondance 1922–1937, with Jean Grenier. 1951.
Drawings and Poems, edited and translated by Stanley J. Collier. 1951.
Lettres à Bernard Esdras-Gosse (1924–1944). 1953.
Correspondance, edited by François Garnier. 2 vols., 1953–55.
Lettres aux Salacrou (août 1923–janvier 1926). 1957.
Lettres à Marcel Béalu. 1959.
Quatre problèmes à résoudre. 1962.
Max Jacob and Les Feux de Paris (correspondence), edited by Neal Oxenhandler. 1964.
Lettres à T. Briant et C. Valence (1920–1941), edited by Stanley J. Collier. 1966.
Lettres 1920–41. 1966.
Lettres à Michel Levanti, suivies des poèmes de Michel Levanti, edited by Lawrence A. Joseph. 1975.
Lettres à René Villard, suivies du Cahier des Maximes, edited by Yannick Pelletier. 1978.
Lettres à Marcel Jouhandeau, edited by Anne Kimball. 1979.
Lettres à Liane de Pougy. 1980.
Lettres à René Rimbert, edited by Christine Andréucci and Maria Green. 1983.
Max Jacob et Quimper (selection). 1984.
Lettres mystiques 1934–1944 à Clotilde Bauguion. 1984.
Lettres à Michel Manoll, edited by Maria Green. 1985.
Méditations religieuses: Derniers cahiers 1942–1943. 1986.
Chroniques d'art 1898–1900, with Léon David, edited by Lawrence A. Joseph. 1987.
Lettres à Pierre Minet, edited by Anne Kimball. 1988.
Lettres à Nino Frank, edited by Anne Kimball. 1989.
Lettres à Florent Fels, edited by Maria Green. 1990.

Translator, with A. de Barreau, *Le Livre de l'ami et de l'aimé*, by Raymond Lulle. 1920.

*

Bibliography: *Bibliographie et documentation sur Max Jacob* by Maria Green, 1988.

Critical Studies: *Max Jacob, mystique et martyr* by Pierre Lagarde, 1944; *Max Jacob* by André Billy, 1946; *Jacob* by Maurice Sachs in his *Witches Sabbath*, 1964; *Max Jacob and the Poetics of Cubism* by Gerald Kamber, 1971; 'Realism and Fantasy in the Work of Max Jacob: Some Verse Poems' by S.I. Lockerbie, in *Order and Adventure in Post-Romantic French Poetry* edited by E.M. Beaumont, J.M. Cocking and J. Cruickshank, 1973; 'Max Jacob: The Poetics of *Le Cornet à dés*' by Renée Riese Hubert, in *About French Poetry from Dada to 'Tel Quel'* edited by Mary Ann Caws, 1974; 'Max Jacob's Bourgeois Voices' by Renée Riese Hubert in *Folio*, 9, 1976; *Poetry and Antipoetry: A Study of Selected Aspects of Max Jacob's Poetic Style* by Annette Thau, 1976; 'Max Jacob' by Francis Poulenc in his *My Friends and Myself* translated by James Harding, 1978; *Clown at the Altar: The Religious Poetry of Max Jacob* by Judith M. Schneider, 1978; *Max Jacob* by Lina Lachgar, 1981; *The Play of the Text: Max Jacob's Le Cornet à dés* by S. Lévy, 1981; 'Max Jacob: Style, Situation' by Theo Hermans, in *The Structure of Modernist Poetry*, 1982.

*   *   *

Although Max Jacob's work is very rich and varied, it is his book of prose poems, *Le Cornet à dés* (*The Dice Cup*), which has attracted the most readers and the most critical attention. Published in 1917, the collection brought together texts Jacob had been writing since the early 1900s and represented its author's major contribution to the literary and artistic modernism exemplified by Apollinaire and Picasso. Commentators have even spoken retrospectively of 'literary Cubism', although no such notion existed at the time. The poems of *The Dice Cup* tend to he short and couched in relatively simple language, but they offer twists and turns of narrative and juxtapositions of fragmentary realities that defy the habits of logic and representation. The title itself suggests a notion of chance, as though the poet randomly selected or juggled with words and elements of stories. yet at the same time it is also the image of something multi-faceted and whole, like the die, which is implied. The prose poem as a genre had already attained a certain artistic maturity in the work of Baudelaire and Rimbaud, spelling liberation from the traditional approach to poetry based on prosody and, to a certain extent, the mimesis of external reality or inner feelings. Yet Jacob went one step further. In his preface to *The Dice Cup* he rejects Baudelaire and Rimbaud as models: the former identified the prose poem too closely with the fable, while the latter's work constituted the triumph of 'Romantic disorder' leading inevitably to 'exasperation'. Jacob emphasizes instead what he terms 'style' and 'situation'. 'Style' is not simply the writer's use of language, but his ability to marshal and compose the various elements of his work. The more successful a work, the more it will give the impression of being an autonomous, self-enclosed unity, however disparate its component parts might otherwise have seemed. 'Situation' refers to the distance between the reader and the work: if Baudelaire believed the prose poem should 'surprise' the reader, Jacob felt that it should transplant him from the reality he normally accepts and inhabits into the reality of the work.

Both 'style' and 'situation' implied the assembling of apparently dissimilar fragments or view-points into a synthetic unity somewhat reminiscent of the Cubist painting or '*papier collé*'. And yet the often absurd combinations thrown up by the prose poems looked forward to Surrealism. In a later preface Jacob indeed spoke of the 'unconscious' as manifested in random associations of words and ideas or in dreams and hallucinations. Where he differed from the automatic writing of the Surrealists was in his insistence that the poem should be not an out-pouring but a construction. Contrasting his own work with that of Rimbaud, he stipulated that the prose poem must be a 'jewel' and not a 'jeweller's shop window'. His achievement lies in part in this balance between the surrender of conscious control and the will to shape and construct. In his view the essence of lyricism lay in 'unconsciousness, but an unconsciousness that is watched over' (*Conseils à un jeune poète* [*Advice to a Young Poet*]).

The impression given by *The Dice Cup* is that of a kaleidoscope. Each poem either offers a multiplicity of scenes or magnifies some fragment that adds to the heteroclite effect of the collection as a whole. Frequently, illogical connections or consequences are presented with such linguistic and narrative casualness as to appear natural, as in 'Il n'y a pas de valet de chambre pour un grand homme' ('A Great Man Needs No Valet'):

Meanwhile the lobster banquet was giving rise to entrances through the roof, to conversations with legs dangling from skylights and to frying pans catching on fire.

The miniature phantasmagorias often revel in their own factitiousness: 'Charlot au bord de la mer' ('Charlie Chaplin at the Seashore') ends, 'A lady is minding a child on a bank of loose stones. I jostle him and the scene disappears'. The result is a celebration of the ludicrous. Almost anything may appear, but its contours will always be brought into sharp focus within the restricted space of the prose poem. However, the kaleidoscope effect and the playful nature of the reality produced by the texts is not simply the result of brusque changes of scene or tense. It is also inherent in language itself. Wordplay and puns are made the basis of startling comparisons and sequences. One poem proclaims in its title: 'Fausses nouvelles! Fosses nouvelles!'—or 'Grave News! New Graves!' in Michael Browstein's rendering. Another poem speculates on the possible confusion of '*patte*' ('paw', 'mitt') and '*pâté*' ('paste' or 'cream'). Nearly all the texts aim to exploit playfully and subversively the well-trodden paths of language in the form of platitudes or literary and para-literary genres. Some poems read like bewildering snatches from some serialized pot-boiler or detective novel (two pieces even have the eponymous hero of the contemporary crime serial, *Fantômas*, as their title). Others seem to be speeded up medieval visions, burlesque news articles, or repositories of undiscovered popular wisdom. Overall, the products of Jacob's dice cup tend to parody and cannibalize existing literature and patterns of language in an inventive and liberating fashion that was to be vital for Surrealism and successive avant-garde groups even into the 1970s.

The same multiplicity of sources and guises covering the range of high and low literature and spanning history characterizes most of Jacob's other works. In verse he sought inspiration in the Breton folk ballad (*La Côte* and *Les Poèmes de Morvan le Gaëlique*) as well as in the traditions of religious mysticism. Yet even here the bizarre irony of *The Dice Cup* often reappears, undercutting any pretensions to directly serious statement, but leaving an oblique emotion all the more striking for its apparent self-deprecation. 'Exhortation' from *La Défense de Tartuffe* shows the poet unable to read a message from heaven because it is Hebrew and ends: 'The angel is furious at finding me so stupid'. He could achieve sustained seriousness, as in 'Reportage de juin 1940' ('Reportage June 1940') in *Derniers poèmes en vers et en prose* (Last Poems in Verse and Prose) on the fall of France—a key event in his own tragic destiny. His novels are varied. *Le Cabinet noir*, for example, is a collection of letters by different characters, satirically parodying human types and their discourses, while *Le Terrain bouchaballe* deals with small town corruption. In all his work Jacob's main drive was to absorb the multiplicity of the world into the self, while retaining a self-deprecating irony:

We don't know very well those we love
But I understand them fairly well
Being all these people myself
I who am however but a baboon.
('Do You Know Meister Eckhart?', *Derniers poèmes en vers et en prose*)

—J.R. Stubbs

JARRY, Alfred (Henri). Born in Laval, France, 8 September 1873. Educated at schools in Saint-Brieuc, 1879–88, and Rennes, 1888–91; Lycée Henri IV, Paris, 1891–93. Brief military service, June–November 1895; discharged because of poor health. Contributor, *L'Art littéraire* in the 1890s; co-founder, with Rémy de Gourmont, art review *L'Ymagier*, 1894, and co-director, 1894–95; founder and publisher, art journal *Perhinderion*, 1896 (closed after second issue); assistant to Lugné-Poe, director of the Théâtre de l'Oeuvre, 1896; columnist, *La Revue blanche*, 1900–03; suffering from malnutrition and the consequences of alcoholism, attempted recuperation at his sister's home in Laval, 1906. *Died 1 November 1907.*

PUBLICATIONS

Collections

Oeuvres poétiques complètes, edited by Henri Parisot. 1945.
Oeuvres complètes, edited by René Massat. 8 vols., 1948.
Selected Works (includes *The Ubu Cycle*; *Writings on the Theatre*; *Poems*; *Essays and Speculations*; *Fiction Selections*), edited by Roger Shattuck and Simon Watson Taylor. 1965.
Oeuvres complètes, edited by Michel Arrivé. 2 vols., 1972–87.

Plays

César-Antéchrist. 1895; as *Caesar Antichrist*, translated by James H. Bierman, 1971.
Tout Ubu (includes *Ubu Roi*; *Ubu cocu*; *Ubu enchaîné*; *Almanach du père Ubu*; *Ubu sur la butte*), edited by Maurice Saillet. 1962; as *Ubu*, edited by Noël Arnaud and Henri Bordillon, 1980; selection as *The Ubu Plays* (includes *Ubu Rex*; *Ubu Enchained*; *Ubu Cuckolded*), edited by Simon Watson Taylor, translated by Watson Taylor and Cyril Connolly. 1968.
Ubu Roi (produced 1896). 1896; as *Ubu Roi*, translated by Barbara Wright, 1951; as *King Turd*, translated by B. Keith and G. Legman, 1953; as *King Ubu*, in *Modern French Theatre*, edited by Michael Benedikt and George E. Wellwarth, 1964; as *Ubu Rex*, in *The Ubu Plays*, 1968; also translated by David Copelin, 1973.
Ubu enchaîné (produced 1937). 1900; as *Ubu Enslaved*, translated by Simon Watson Taylor, 1953; as *Ubu Enchained*, in *The Ubu Plays*, 1968.
Ubu sur la butte (condensed marionette version of *Ubu roi*, with songs; produced 1901). 1906.
Ubu cocu (produced 1946). 1944; as *Ubu Cuckolded*, translated by Cyril Connolly, 1965, and in *The Ubu Plays*, 1968.
Par la taille (for marionettes). 1906.
Le Moutardier du pape. 1907; as *La Papesse Jeanne*, edited by Marc Voline, 1981.
Pantagruel, with Eugène Demolder, music by Claude Terrasse. 1911.
Les Silènes, from a play by Christian Dietrich Grabbe, edited by Pascal Pia. 1926.
L'Objet aimé (produced 1937). 1953.

Fiction

Les Jours et les nuits. 1897; as *Days and Nights: Novel of a Deserter*, translated by Alexis Lykiard, with *The Other Alcestis*, 1989.
L'Amour en visites. 1898.

L'Amour absolu. 1899; edited by Noël Arnaud and Henri Bordillon, 1980.

Messaline. 1900; as *The Garden of Priapus*, translated by Louis Colman, 1932; as *Messalina*, translated by John Harman, 1985.

Le Surmâle. 1902; as *The Supermale*, translated by Barbara Wright, 1968.

Les Gestes et opinions du docteur Faustroll, Pataphysicien. 1911; edited by Noël Arnaud and Henri Bordillon, 1980.

La Dragonne, completed by Charlotte Jarry. 1943.

Verse

La Revanche de la nuit, edited by Maurice Saillet. 1949.

Other

Les Minutes de sable, mémorial (miscellany). 1894.
Spéculations. 1911.
Le Manoir enchanté et quatre autres oeuvres inédites, edited by Noël Arnaud. 1974.

Other works have been issued in *Cahiers* and *Dossiers* of the Collège de Pataphysique, since 1950.

*

Bibliography: 'Alfred Jarry: Essai de bibliographie critique', in *Interférences*, 9, 1979.

Critical Studies: *The Banquet Years: The Arts in France 1885–1918* by Roger Shattuck, 1959, revised edition, 1968; *Jarry: D'Ubu roi au Docteur Faustroll* by Noël Arnaud, 1974; *Ubu roi: An Analytical Study* by Judith Cooper, 1974; *Alfred Jarry, dramaturge*, 1980, and *Les Cultures de Jarry*, 1988, both by Henri Béhar, and *Jarry et cie: Communications du Colloque international*, 1985, edited by Béhar and Brunella Eruli; *Jarry: Nihilism and the Theatre of the Absurd* by Maurice Marc LaBelle, 1980; *Alfred Jarry: A Critical and Biographical Study*, 1984, and *Jarry: Ubu roi*, 1987, both by Keith Beaumont; *Alfred Jarry: The Man with the Axe* by Nigel Lennon, 1984; *Alfred Jarry and Guillaume Apollinaire* by Claude Schumacher, 1984; *Gestes et opinions de Alfred Jarry, écrivain* by Henri Bordillon, 1986.

* * *

Alfred Jarry was born in Laval, a town some distance from the Brittany whose traditions of Celtic magic and intense Catholicism he claimed later to have inherited and to represent. He saw little of his father, whose business collapsed in 1879 and who was forced to return to his original employment as a commercial traveller. Together with his sister, Caroline-Marie, he was brought up almost exclusively by his mother. His strong attachment to her may explain his homosexuality, a feature of his life which links him to the tradition of Gide, Proust, and Genet as well as to the relationship between Verlaine and Rimbaud. In spite of the priapism celebrated in the novel *Le Surmâle* (*The Supermale*), published in *La Revue blanche* in 1902, it is doubtful whether he ever enjoyed a sexual relationship with a woman. His admiration for the author, Marguerite Eymery, the wife of his friend Alfred Vallette, was based on the feeling that she alone really understood him. This may have been true in a way, since she is the only person who records him speaking in a normal voice and

not in the stilted, aggressive, staccato tones which he borrowed for his most famous creation, père Ubu.

Jarry felt at home intellectually in the literary Paris of the 1890s where the Symbolist movement, under the influence of Mallarmé, encouraged him in his dislike of the earlier climate of naturalism, with its view that literature ought to talk about real life, and in his adoption instead of the solipsistic attitude embodied in Schopenhauer's phrase 'The world is my representation'. The production at the Théâtre de l'Oeuvre on 10 December 1896 of his 'dramatic comedy' *Ubu Roi* (*Ubu Rex*), the work to which he owes his literary survival and continued fame, provoked a great controversy.

After the first word, *merdre* (the translation as 'Shit!' does not quite have the ring of the French), nothing could be heard for 20 minutes. Jarry subsequently went to the trouble to select all the most hostile reviews, paste them on to sheets of blue and pink notepaper, and bind them in a file. This was not discovered after his death. The bill for 1,300 francs in production costs, which reduced the young director of the Théâtre de l'Oeuvre, Lugné-Poe, to despair, was like all the other debts that Jarry incurred and left behind him: unpaid. Lugné-Poe had to console himself by contemplation of the fact that his theatre is now remembered principally for the events of December 1896. On 28 January 1898, *Ubu Rex* was performed successfully by the marionettes of the Théâtre des Pantins. This was more than a further sign of the rejection of the naturalistic conventions of 19th-century drama which helps to make *Ubu Rex* a precursor of the absurdist plays of Beckett, Ionesco, and Genet. It reflected Jarry's not unreasonable view that 19th-century actors and actresses expected to be, and were, given far too much importance by playwrights and audiences.

Ubu Rex, with its starting point as a schoolboy farce inspired by the antics of the physics master, a M. Hébert, at the lycée in Rennes, is virtually the only play written by a Frenchman in the 19th century to be performed nowadays as anything other than a museum piece. It has been particularly successful with English-speaking audiences and made into an opera, as well as a ballet. It is, nevertheless, the only work by Jarry to be anything but the expression of a disordered personality and of a fundamentally very sad life. André Breton's remark, in the first *Manifeste du surréalisme* (*Surrealist Manifesto*) in 1924, that Jarry was 'a surrealist in absinth' is true in so far as Jarry did drink an enormous amount. This was, however, also because he could not afford to buy food, and it is not true that he died of alcoholic poisoning. The probable cause of his death was tubercular meningitis, brought on by a pulmonary infection produced by inadequate food, cold, and damp. There are other aspects of Jarry's behaviour that make him a precursor of surrealism, and his predilection for firearms may have inspired Breton's other remark that the simplest surrealist act was to go down into the street with a revolver and fire at random into the crowd. On one occasion, in a crowded restaurant, Jarry fired a shot at the sculptor Manoco, exclaiming as he did so how beautiful his action was as literature. He claimed also to have shot a nightingale which was disturbing his sleep, and witnesses confirmed how he terrified his landlady by using the wall between their rooms for target practice. When she complained that the bullets might go through the wall and kill her children, he replied that he would, if it happened, help her to have others. The remark was taken up in Gide's 1926 novel *Les Faux-monnayeurs* (*The Counterfeiters*), who used his depiction of a group of unpleasant adolescent schoolboys.

Like Rimbaud, whom he resembles by his eccentricity of behaviour, as well as by the impression given by his later life of great talents squandered needlessly, Jarry was looked after at the end of his life by his sister. Like Isabelle Rimbaud, Caroline-Marie encouraged the belief that her brother had undergone a late conversion to Catholicism. The evidence is unconvincing in both cases and goes against the predominant atmosphere in the work of both writers. What did characterize Jarry's attitude in the early 1890s was the adoption, in common with many others from the *Mercure de France* and *Revue blanche* groups, of a set of views that were highly nationalistic and violently anti-semitic. The taste for random violence that marked Jarry's own behaviour is also a fiction of the *Collège de Pataphysique*, whose members still take pleasure in interrupting lectures and meetings of which they disapprove. Jarry was undoubtedly the founder of what he also claimed was the 'science' of pataphysics, described variously as the science of imaginary solutions, the destruction of all forms of knowledge to make way for a new mysticism, and the 'synthesis of immediate knowledge' said to characterize the imaginative world of the child. Jarry's critical writings also insist on the primacy of form in literature and denigrate the importance of content.

—Philip Thody

UBU REX (Ubu Roi)
Play by Alfred Jarry, 1896.

In this five-act satirical farce, Jarry adapts the serious story of seizure of power to the comic aims of ridicule and relief. Mère Ubu, playing upon her husband's bestial instincts, urges him to overthrow Wenceslas, King of Poland. After enlisting Bordure's assistance, Ubu usurps the throne in the second act, murdering the ruler and two of his sons. Bourgelas, another son, escapes with his mother. Meanwhile, in order to placate the Poles and satisfy his greed, Ubu offers the people gold that he reclaims through taxation. In the third act, Ubu assumes authority, liquidating the nobility and magistrates, and confiscating national wealth. He also condemns Bordure who, taking refuge in Russia, requests Czar Alexis to help restore order and justice. Alexis attacks, and Mère convinces Ubu of the necessary recourse to war.

In Act IV, while Ubu battles against the Russians, his wife plunders the treasures of Poland. Ubu kills Bordure, but the decimation of his army compels him and his two Palotins to retreat. In fending off a rapacious bear, the Palotins perceive their leader's cowardice and abandon him. In the final act, Ubu's wife flees Bourgelas's avenging army, arriving at the cave where Ubu is sleeping. Darkness enables her to impersonate the angel Gabriel which, in turn, impels him to confess his wrongdoings. The light of day, though, reveals her identity, and Ubu reverts to his former ways. Bourgelas attacks, and the Ubus, along with the Palotins who return, sail home full of nostalgia for Poland.

Ubu's grotesqueness evokes caricature and disbelief. His rotund body and pear-shaped head seem ludicrous and fantastical, and the opening trite insults between him and his wife suggest a slapstick show or a puppet-play. Like the closing scenes in farce, a comic resolution dispels danger as husband and wife return home, physically secure and morally unchanged. Lack of development of character excludes introspection: throughout the play, Ubu remains stupid, indolent, and totally egocentric; his wife stays avaricious, complaining, and domineering. Through incongruities and inversions, Jarry employs irony to elicit surprise and induce absurdity. Besides his ridiculous appearance, Ubu swears meaningless oaths ('by my green candle', 'shittr'), exagger-

ates the ordinary (his feast becomes a two-day orgy), and misconstrues reality (a bear is a 'little bow-wow'). By exploiting the unexpected, Jarry has this Falstaff-like personage debunk the solemn and dignify the preposterous: his stepping on Wenceslas's toe incites revolution; unlike the agile Czar, he jumps over a trench; and, seated safely on a rock, he recites a *paternoster* during the Palotins' struggle with the bear. Jarry also uses dramatic parody: like Macbeth urged to depose Duncan, Ubu yields to his wife's goadings, but his clumsiness, moral blindness, and inanities turn potential pathos into rollicking burlesque. Disparities of language and action heighten the ridiculous. During deliberations and battles, Ubu blends religious and literary references with nonsensical statements, thereby reducing the serious and dignified to the trivial and foolish. In the dream-sequence that recalls epic conventions, medieval allegories, and Renaissance romances, mère Ubu convinces her husband that her ugliness is comparable to Aphrodite's beauty and her depravities to saintly accomplishments.

The deceptions and distortions, though, present a superficial enjoyment that obscures the horrors of human bestiality and bourgeois shallowness. Ubu's self-absorption and obsession with material wealth and sensual gratification explain his callous disregard and vicious abuse of others: and, prodded by his unbridled instincts, he acts irrationally and erratically. In depicting this primal nature devoid of reason and discipline, Jarry converts innocuous horseplay into actions provoking appalling disgust. For example, Ubu's attack on his guests with bison-ribs provokes amusement; but his subsequent serving of human excrement at table replaces laughter with repugnance. His wife's duplicity punctures pleasure. By injecting false courage into Ubu's cowardly character, she yields to her insatiable greed for wealth and power, manipulating her husband to commit pillage and genocide.

As caricatures, they resemble cartoon animations; but their self-interest, insensitivity, and indignities reflect the values and evils in bourgeois society. Exemplifying the ethos of this post-Darwinian era, Ubu disregards spiritual values; religion lacks belief, and Ubu facilely recites prayers to escape danger and death. He is a survivor whose instincts endure, and whose bestial superiorities destroy the weak and unfortunate. If Ubu is Everyman, he is also, paradoxically, Nobody, with his prosperity encasing a spiritual void. Instead, Ubu's obesity suggests a material gluttony that assures an aggression necessary for success and stature.

In neglecting the unities of time, place, and action, Jarry constructs a series of scenes resembling a montage of inconsistent happenings and absurd characterizations. Ubu's ludicrous appearance, irrational behaviour, and vile words demonstrate a rejection of the established principles of versimilitude and decorum. At the first performance, the audience, expecting entertaining farce, was stunned and outraged. But by shattering the illusions that often, paradoxically, define reality, Jarry reveals the potential evils inherent in the subconscious. Through the humour, resulting from fantasy and foolishness, Jarry attacks the materialism, egocentricism, and superficialities, which, embodied by Ubu, reflect bourgeois aims and attitudes. Ubu's jokes are meaningless, insensitive utterances, and his unscrupulous deeds become unconscionable crimes. Satire, moreover, evolves into a probing of the dynamics of human impulses. Time and place dissolve, and Ubu emerges as an emblem of man's primal nature. Futility and absurdity characterize Ubu's endeavours: his actions end at the beginning; his speech is claptrap; his uncontrolled affections and merciless, unrelenting aggressions destroy order and civilization. Jarry goes beyond a renunciation of conventional dramatic practice and accepted social standards. By creating a drama that suggests the later theories and plays of Artaud, Beckett, Genet, and Ionesco, he forces the spectator to confront, through Ubu, the savagery, isolation, and pain of human existence.

—Donald Gilman

JEROME, St. Born Eusebius Sophronius Hieronymus in Stridon Dalmatia, c.AD 347. Studied Greek and Roman rhetoric in Rome under Aelius Donatus. Went to Trèves (Trier) to dedicate himself to Christian religion; settled to a life of asceticism in Aquilea, on the Adriatic coast of Italy, 370; then went east, studying Greek in Antioch, where he fell ill. Retired to the desert of Chalcis, southeast of Antioch, to learn Hebrew and live as a hermit, c.375; ordained as priest in Antioch, 377; met Greek theologian Gregory of Nazianzus while travelling to Rome, 382; in Rome became secretary to Pope Damasus I, and revised old Latin texts of the Gospels. Left Rome to lead a pilgrimage to Palestine in 385; travelled to Egypt; settled in Bethlehem, 386: founded a religious house, 389, and worked on his *Vulgate*, the first Latin translation of the Bible from the original Hebrew, completed c.405. *Died in AD 420.*

PUBLICATIONS

Collections

[Works; Paris Edition]. 11 vols., 1842–46; also in *Patrologia Graeca*, edited by Jacque Paul Migne, vols. 19–24, 1857; also edited by J. Hausleiter, I. Hilberg, and S. Reiter, in *Corpus Scriptorum Ecclesiasticorum Latinorum*, vols. 49, 54–56, 59, 1866–1913; in *Corpus Christianorum: Series Latiana*, vols. 72, 78, 1958–59.
The Principal Works, translated by W.H. Freemantle, in *A Select Library of Nicene and Post-Nicene Fathers*, series 2, vol. 6. 1893.

Works

De nominis Hebraicis [Book on Hebrew Names], edited by P. de Lagarde. 1870.
De viris illustribus [On Famous Men], edited by G. Herdingius. 1879; also edited by C.A. Bernouilli, 1895, and E.C. Richardson, 1896; as *Lives of Illustrious Men*, translated by E.C. Richardson, in *A Select Library of Nicene and Post-Nicene Fathers*, series 2, vol. 3, 1892.
Epistolae, as *Letters*, translated by Charles Christopher Mierow. 1963; edited by James Duff, 1942, and Carl Favus, 1956; selection edited and translated by F.A. Wright, 1933; selection as *Satirical Letters*, translated by Paul Carroll, 1956.
Prologus Galeatus: The Middle English Bible; Prefatory Epistles of St Jerome, edited by C. Lindberg. 1978.
Quaestiones Hebraicae in Genesim [Hebrew Questions], edited by P. de Lagarde. 1868.
Vitae Patrum [Lives of the Saints], as *The . . . Lyff of the Old Auncyent Holy Faders Hermytes*, translated by William Caxton. 1495, reprinted 1977; as *The History of the Monks*, translated by E.A.W. Budge, 1934; selections as *Lives of St*

Paul the First Hermit, St Hilarion and Malchus, translated by Sister Marie Liguori Ewald, in *Fathers of the Church*, vol. 15, 1952.
Vulgate (first Latin translation of Old and New Testaments). 1452–55.
Homilies, translated by Sister Marie Liguori Ewald. 2 vols., 1964–66.
Dogmatic and Political Works, translated by John N. Hritzu, in *Fathers of the Church*, vol. 53. 1965.

*

Critical Studies: *St Jerome* by A. Largent, 1900; *Life and Times as Revealed in the Writings of St Jerome* by Mary J. Kelly, 1944; *St Jerome* by Mary Beattie, 1945; *Hieronymus* by L. Huizinga, 1946; *St Jerome and the Bible* by George Sanderlin, 1961; *St Jerome as a Biblical Translator* by William H. Semple, 1965; *The Vulgate as a Translation* by Benjamin Kedar-Kipfstein, 1968; *Jerome: His Life, Writings and Controversies* by John N.D. Kelly, 1975; *New Jerome Biblical Commentary*, edited by Raymond E. Brown, 1989; *Consoling Heliodorus: Commentary of Jerome 'Letter 60'* by J.H.D. Scourfield, 1992; *Jerome, Greek Scholarship and the Hebrew Bible: A Study of the 'Quaestiones Hebraicae in Genesim'* by Adam Kamesar, 1993.

* * *

St Jerome is one of the two famous Fathers of the Latin Church from the 4th and 5th centuries, the other being St Augustine. He is chiefly remembered for having translated the Old and New Testaments from the original Hebrew and Greek into Latin. This translation, later known as the *Vulgate*, has been the authoritative version of the Catholic Church since the 16th century. St Jerome's translations and commentaries on the Sacred Scriptures are the most serious intellectual attempt at biblical exegesis produced in Latin from the early Christian Church, written at a time when the Roman Empire was crumbling under the onslaught of the Barbarian invasions.

After studying the Seven Liberal Arts in Rome, Jerome converted to Christianity at the age of 20. A famous dream recounts how Jerome turned away from the Classical pagan authors, notably Cicero, to a new centre of interest, the writings of the Christian revelation, which preoccupied him all the rest of his life. The first stage of his career took place in the East, at Constantinople. Having perfected his knowledge of Greek in AD 379–80, Jerome translated a series of *Homilies* written by the 3rd-century Greek theologian, Origen of Alexandria. He translated into Latin 14 homilies on the prophet Jeremiah, the same number on Ezekiel, and nine on Isaiah. Later he translated Origen's commentary on the *Song of Songs* (AD 382–84), and 39 of his homilies on St Luke (AD 386–90). It is thanks to Jerome's translation that Western Europe became familiar with some of Origen's teaching and thought. Origen remained a decisive influence on Jerome, although he was later moved to criticize what he considered to be heretical elements in Origen's writings.

Imbued with a strong historical sense, Jerome was familiar with the works of both the Latin and Greek historians— Tacitus, Livy, Suetonius, Herodotus, and Xenophon. In AD 382 Jerome set about translating the *Chronicle* of Eusebius of Caesarea, originally written in Greek at the beginning of the 4th century. Eusebius had written a history of the world from Adam to the reign of Constantine. Jerome, wishing to give

Christianity a solid historical context, translated Eusebius' history, bringing it up to his own time. Jerome's work had a major influence during the Middle Ages, and served as a model for later chronicles of Church history, especially for Isidore of Seville (AD 570–636) and the Venerable Bede (c.AD 673–735).

Back in Rome in AD 382, Jerome, under the direction of Pope Damasus I, was entrusted with making a new translation of the Bible. By the 4th century it had become necessary to revise the Old Latin version of the Bible, a text compiled from various anonymous authors from the 2nd and 3rd centuries, and itself a translation from the *Septuagint*, a translation for Greek-speaking Jews of the Old Testament, made between 301 BC and 150 BC. As well as these two texts, Jerome was able to consult the now lost *Hexaplar Text* of Origen, a six-column version of the Old Testament in Hebrew and Greek. Jerome's originality and genius exist in his methodological approach. He gained a thorough knowledge of spoken and written Hebrew and studied Syriac, Coptic, and Aramaic, all of which prepared him for the 15-year task he had set himself: to translate the Old Testament from the original Hebrew and the New Testament from its Greek versions, as well as checking with previous translations for inconsistencies and errors. The translation produced by Jerome is the fruit of a vast encyclopaedic knowledge and the work of an extremely erudite man. It earned him the title *Doctor Maximus in sacris Scripturis explanandis*, the 'Greatest Teacher in setting forth the Sacred Scripture'. In a decree of 1546, the Council of Trent declared the *Vulgate* (a term first used by Roger Bacon in the 13th century to describe Jerome's translation) the authorized version of the Bible for the Catholic Church.

In 385 Jerome finally left Rome and moved to Bethlehem, where he remained until his death. It is here that he wrote a large number of exegeses, biblical commentaries, on both the Old and New Testaments, in the 390s and at the beginning of the 5th century. Origen is remembered for favouring the allegorical meaning of Scripture, but Jerome defended the theoretical principle of investigating and establishing its literal sense. He did not neglect interpreting biblical symbols and metaphors, with the help of Jewish scholars.

Three closely related works from the 390s are Jerome's *Quaestiones Hebraicae* [Hebrew Questions], a series of notes he made on various passages of the Book of Genesis, stemming from the work of Josephus, Origen, Philo, Porphyry, and Eusebius. In his *De nominus Hebraicis* [Book on Hebrew Names] and *Onomasticon urbium ac locorum sanctae Scriptorae* [Book on Cities and Sites of Holy Scripture], Jerome sought to explain the meaning of proper names which could not be translated. With often fanciful and popular etymologies, sometimes devoid of scientific exactness, Jerome, working from the *Onomasticon* by Eusebius, produced the main source of material on Hebrew proper names, later used during the Middle Ages.

Jerome is also the author of seven controversial treatises, written at times in an acerbic tongue against contemporaries who defended heretical doctrine. These polemical works were begun in the late 370s and Jerome was still venting his temper when *Contra pelagianos* [Against the Pelagians] was published in AD 415. The previous titles were: *Altercatio luciferiani et orthodoxi* [Debate of a Luciferian and an Orthodox] (AD 378) in which Jerome was concerned with the validity of heretical baptism; *Adversus Helvidium* [Against Helvidius] (AD 383) who doubted the virginity of the Blessed Virgin; *Liber contra Jovinianum* [Against Jovinian] (AD 393) who criticized celibacy and asceticism; *Contra Joannem Hierosolymitanum* [Against John of Jerusalem] (AD 397) and

Apologia adversus Rufinum [Against Rufinum] (AD 401) who both defended certain 'heresies' of Origen; and *Contra Vigilantium liber* [Against Vigilantius] (AD 406), a critic of the worship of saints and relics. Like St Augustine, Jerome saw his role as vigilant supporter of an orthodox Christianity, but his polemics sometimes degenerated into personal attacks on men rather than on ideas. Finally, Jerome wrote a handbook on 135 Christian authors, *De viris illustribus* [On Famous Men] (AD 392), based on Suetonius' secular manual, as well as 117 *Letters*, which enjoyed an enormous popularity during the Middle Ages.

—David Coad

————————

JIN PING MEI. See **GOLDEN LOTUS**.

————————

JOURNEY TO THE WEST (Xiyouji). Also known as *Hsi-yu-chi* or *Monkey*. Chinese novel of 100 chapters by Wu Cheng'en (c.1505–80), based on the 7th-century story of a Chinese monk's pilgrimage to India to find Buddhist scriptures. Other versions of the tale existed, and there is an 'Urtext' fragment in the *Yongle dadian* encyclopedia dating from c.1403–08.

PUBLICATIONS

Xiyouji. 1592 (*Shidetang* edition); modern edition, 1954; as *Journey to the West*, translated by Anthony C. Yu, 4 vols., 1977–83; also translated by W.J.F. Jenner, 3 vols., 1982–86; as *A Mission to Heaven*, translated by Timothy Richard, 1913; as *The Buddhist Pilgrim's Progress*, translated by Helen M. Hayes. 1930.

Monkey, Folk Novel of China, translated by Arthur Waley, 1943; as *The Monkey King*, edited by Zdena Novotna, translated by George Theiner (from the Czech), 1964.

*

Critical Studies: '*Journey to the West*' in *The Classic Chinese Novel* by C.T. Hsia, 1968; *The Hsi-yu chi: A Study of Antecedents to the 16th-Century Chinese Novel* by Glen Dudbridge, 1970; 'On Translating the *Hsi-yu chi*' by Anthony C. Yu, in *The Art and Profession of Translation*, edited by T.C. Lai, 1976; *The Mythic and the Comic Aspects of the Quest: Hsi-yu Chi as Seen Through Don Quixote and Huckleberry Finn* by James S. Fu, 1977.

* * *

Xiyouji (*Journey to the West* or *Monkey*) is a novel based on the historical pilgrimage of Tang Sanzang (also known as Tripitaka or Xuanzang), the Chinese monk who went to India in search of Buddhist scriptures in the 7th century. The earliest story of Sanzang appeared in the Southern Song period and was entitled *Da Tang Sanzang qujing shihua* [The Shihua Version of Sanzang's Quest for Scriptures]. The main story is about Sanzang's spiritual quest, but Monkey (Sun Wukong) emerges as a prominent character in the story as Sanzang's disciple. They encounter various fantastic adventures, often involving gods, demons, and animal spirits. The legend of Sanzang also provided materials for plays of the Yuan Dynasty (1272/79–1368), the most famous being Wu Changling's *Tang Sanzang xitian qujing* [Tang Sanzang in Quest of the Scriptures from the Western Paradise]. In the *Yongle dadian*, a partially preserved encyclopedic compilation dating from the Yongle period of the Ming Dynasty (1403–24), there is an entry of some 1,200 Chinese characters which relates the slaughtering of a dragon king by the Tang minister Wei Zheng. This episode has its fuller counterpart in the 100-chapter novel *Xiyouji* (*Journey to the West*), by Wu Cheng'en, who lived approximately between 1505 and 1580 at Huaian in Jiangsu Province. The standard modern edition of *Journey to the West* was published by the Zuojia Publishing Society of Beijing in 1954.

The story of *Journey to the West*, as we have it in the modern edition, can be divided into the following four sections:

1. The first seven chapters tell of the birth of the Monkey, who is hatched from a stone egg under the influence of the sun and moon. He lives on the Mountain of Flowers and Fruit and has acquired such tremendous powers under the tutoring of Subhodi that only Buddha can subdue him under the Mountain of Five Phases. He is released 500 years later by Tang Sanzang after he promises to protect Sanzang on his journey to the West and to be Sanzang's disciple.

2. Chapters 8 to 12 describe the background and birth of Sanzang and the origin of his mission to India. Major episodes include Buddha's intention to impart the Buddhist canon to the Chinese, preparation for the journey by Guanyin (the Goddess of Mercy), Sanzang's revenge on his father's murderers, Wei Zheng's execution of the Eastern Dragon King, the journey of Tang Taizong to the underworld, his convening of the Mass for the Dead, and the appointment of Sanzang as the pilgrim to seek the scriptures after the epiphany of the Goddess of Mercy.

3. Chapters 13 to 97 tell of the pilgrimage to India of Sanzang, his disciples—Monkey, Pig, and Friar Sand—as well as Sanzang's white dragon horse. The 14-year journey is developed primarily through a series of captures and releases of the pilgrims by animal spirits, gods in disguise, demons, and monsters, which together constitute the 81 ordeals preordained for Sanzang. Each episode is a self-contained story running from one to five chapters in length. In each, the pilgrims are presented with a problem which they must overcome before continuing their travels. Once the problem is solved and a new episode begins, the place and characters in earlier episodes are left behind and seldom mentioned again.

4. The last three chapters tell of the successful completion of the journey: the meeting with the Buddha, the return with the scriptures to China, and the final reward of the five pilgrims (including Sanzang's white dragon horse).

Wu Cheng'en gives shape and coherence to the tradition of the Sanzang legend by writing it in the style of the story-writers of the Tang and Song dynasties. The 100-chapter narrative consisting of self-contained episodes, is abundant in dialogue as well as in accounts of events and passages of descriptive verse. The reader is occasionally addressed directly and urged to listen to the next chapter. Since the story is already well-known, the main interest of the reader is hardly in experiencing suspense or wondering whether Sanzang will survive his adventures, but in the manner in which Monkey will overcome the monsters confronting them all in each case.

Interpretations of the theme of the *Journey to the West* vary among critics. The novel is widely regarded as an allegory in which Tang Sanzang represents the ordinary man, easily upset by the difficulties of life, while the Monkey stands for human intelligence, and Pig the physical aspects of human beings. A Buddhist interpretation considers the basic plot of the story to be the religious quest for Buddhist scriptures. Titles of the *sutras* and of Buddhas and *bodhisattvas* recur in the novel. For example, a complete transcription of the 'Heart Sutra' appears in chapter 19 and reappears as a subject of repeated discussion between Sanzang and Monkey. Also, the wisdom and mercy of Buddha—the novel begins with the benevolent intention of the Buddha to send Tripitaka (Sanzang) to the people of the East—are often emphasized. There are also elements of Daoism in the novel: Daoist symbolism, such as the Five Elements, is often referred to. The novel is also interpreted as a treatise on internal alchemy through an elaboration of the use of alchemical, yin-yang, and Yi jing lore. Interpreted with the focus on the quest as a way to the classic Confucian doctrines of virtue and rectification of the mind, the novel can be seen to carry a Confucian message. Scholars, however, also look to the advice Monkey gives the King of the Cart-Slow Kingdom in chapter 47, and find the preservation of equal reverence for Buddhism, Daoism, and Confucianism to be a major theme in the novel.

The comedy and humour in the novel lie in the vivid characterization. The triangle of Sanzang, Monkey, and Pig is the central structure of every episode. Sanzang is presented both as a Buddhist monk and as an ordinary mortal. As a pilgrim monk, Sanzang has the unyielding determination to reach his goal and obtain the scriptures. He is also saintly in that his flesh can give the monsters and demons everlasting life. As a common mortal, he is fretful, credulous, and self-pitying. Though master of his animal disciples, he shows little spiritual improvement during his journey. In fact, it is always Monkey that reminds him of the wisdom of the *sutras*. From this perspective, Sanzang in the modern edition scarcely suggests the heroism of his historic namesake. Rather, his every manifestation of human weakness helps define his role as a comic figure in the novel. Monkey is Sanzang's first and most celebrated disciple. In spite of all of Sanzang's credulity and peevishness, Monkey remains loyal and selfless. Discontented with the pastoral life as a leader of monkeys on the Mountain of Flowers and Fruit, Monkey seeks immortality through the patriarch Subodhi, symbolizing to some extent Monkey's quest for spiritual understanding. His promotion from animal rebel to Buddha's submissive servant and eventually to a Buddha himself depends not only on his magical powers but also on his wits—knowing or being able to discover the background of the monsters he and the others confront. The only pilgrim able to detach himself from all human desires, Monkey, whose name, Wu kong, means 'aware of vacuity', stands as the spokesperson for the doctrine of emptiness.

Pig serves in every respect as a foil to Monkey. If Monkey represents the mind, Pig then represents the body and its appetites—vanity, greed, lust, and jealousy. While Monkey is intelligent enough to survive on his wits and valiant enough to be a champion fighter, Pig is not too stupid to avoid responsibilities and dangers whenever possible. With the serious Monkey and the joking Pig, the *Journey to the West* becomes a great literary source of pleasure. In comparison, Friar Sand turns out to be the most colourless of the four main characters, retained from earlier versions and existing as a shadowy figure throughout.

—Ying-Ying Chein

———

JIMÉNEZ (Mantecón), Juan Ramón. Born in Moguer, Spain, 23 December 1881. Educated at a Jesuit school in Cádiz, 1891–96; University of Seville, 1896. Married Zenobia Camprubí Aymar in 1916 (died 1956). In sanatoriums, 1901–05, then a writer: settled in Madrid, 1912, but left Spain in 1936; travelled and taught in Puerto Rico, Cuba, North Carolina, and Florida, 1939–42, Washington, DC, 1942–51; faculty member, University of Puerto Rico, Río Piedras, 1951–58. Recipient: Nobel prize for literature, 1956. *Died 29 May 1958.*

PUBLICATIONS

Collections

Libros de poesía, edited by Agustín Caballero. 1957.
Primeros libros de poesía, edited by Francisco Garfias. 1960.
Antología general en prosa, edited by Angel Crespo and Pilar Gómez Bedate. 1981.

Verse

Almas de violeta. 1900.
Ninfeas. 1900.
Rimas. 1902.
Arias tristes. 1903.
Jardines lejanos. 1904.
Elegías. 3 vols., 1908–10.
Olvidanzas. 1909; edited by Francisco Garfias, 1968.
Baladas de primavera. 1910.
La soledad sonora. 1911.
Pastorales. 1911.
Poemas mágicos y dolientes. 1911.
Melancolía. 1912.
Laberinto. 1913.
Platero y yo: Elegía andaluza. 1914; complete edition, 1917; edited by Michael P. Predmore, 1980, Francisco López Estrada, 1986, and Richard Cardwell, 1988; as *Platero and I*, translated by William and Mary Roberts, 1956; also translated by Eloise Roach, 1958; Antonio T. De Nicolás, 1986; S. O-Carboneres, 1990.
Estío. 1916.
Sonetos espirituales. 1917.
Diario de un poeta recién casado. 1917; revised editions, as *Diario de poeta y mar*, 1948, 1955.
Poesías escogidas. 1917.
Eternidades. 1918.
Piedra y cielo. 1919.
Segunda antología poética. 1922.
Poesía. 1923.
Belleza. 1923.

Canción. 1936.
Voces de mi copla. 1945.
La estación total. 1946.
Romances de Coral Gables. 1948.
Animal de fondo. 1949.
Fifty Spanish Poems, translated by J.B. Trend. 1950.
Tercera antología poética 1898–1953. 1957.
Three Hundred Poems 1903–1953, translated by Eloise Roach. 1962.
Dios deseado y deseante. 1964; as *God Desired and Desiring*, translated by Antonio T. De Nicolás, 1987.
Lorca and Jiménez, translated by Robert Bly. 1973.
Jiménez and Machado, translated by J.B. Trend and J.L. Gili. 1974.
Naked Music: Poems, translated by Dennis Maloney. 1976.
Leyenda, edited by A. Sánchez Romeralo. 1978.
The Flower Scenes (selection), translated by J.C.R. Green. 1982.
Realidad invisible: Libro inédito, edited by A. Sánchez Romeralo. 1984; as *Invisible Reality* (bilingual edition), translated by Antonio T. De Nicolás, 1987.
Time and Space: A Poetic Autobiography, translated by Antonio T. De Nicolás. 1988.

Other

Conferencias I: Política poética. 1936.
Ciego ante ciegos. 1938.
Españoles de tres mundos. 1942.
El zaratán. 1946.
Selected Writings, translated by H.R. Hays. 1957.
Olvidos de Granada. 1960.
Cuadernos, edited by Francisco Garfias. 1960.
La corriente infinita. 1961.
El trabajo gustoso. 1961.
Cartas, edited by Francisco Garfias. 1962.
Primeras prosas, edited by Francisco Garfias. 1962.
Estética y ética estética. 1967.
Libros de prosa. 1969— .
Stories of Life and Death, translated by Antonio T. De Nicolás. 1986.
Light and Shadows: Selected Poems and Prose, 1881–1958, translated by Dennis Maloney. 1987.
Ideología: 1897–1957: Metamórfosis IV, edited by Antonio Sánchez Romeralo. 1990.

Translator, with Z. Camprubí de Jiménez, *Jinetes hacia el mar*, by J.M. Synge. 1920.

*

Bibliography: *Bibliografía genered de Juan Ramón Jiménez* by Antonio Campoamor González, 1982.

Critical Studies: *The Victorious Expression: A Study of Four Contemporary Spanish Poets: Miguel de Unamuno, Antonio Machado, Juan Ramón Jiménez, Federico García Lorca*, 1964, and *The Line in the Margin: Juan Ramón Jiménez and His Readings in Blake, Shelley, and Yeats*, 1980, both by Howard T. Young; *The Religious Instinct in the Poetry of Jiménez* by Leo R. Cole, 1967; *Circles of Paradox: Time and Essence in the Poetry of Juan Ramón Jiménez* by Paul R. Olson, 1967; *Juan Ramón Jiménez* by Donald F. Fogelquist, 1976; *Jiménez: The Modernist Apprenticeship 1895–1900* by Richard A. Cardwell, 1977; *Word and Work in the Poetry of Juan Ramón Jiménez* by Mervyn Coke-Enguidanos, 1982;

Perfume and Poison: A Study of the Relationship Between José Bergamín and Juan Ramón Jimenez by Nigel Dennis, 1985; *Self and Image in Juan Ramón Jiménez: Modern and Post-modern Readings* by John C. Wilcox, 1987.

* * *

Although he could be looked upon as the juvenile filter of a highly sentimental form of *fin de siècle* decadence in his first two books (published in 1900), Juan Ramón Jiménez quickly grew more constrained and became a sensitive transmitter and adapter of Verlaine's style of symbolism, as well as a successor of Bécquer in such works as *Rimas* [Rhymes] and *Arias tristes* [Sad Airs]. This early lyrical stage led eventually to the triumph of the *Diario de un poeta recién casado* [Diary of a Newly-Married Poet]. Written as a result of its author's wedding in New York to Zenobia Camprubí Aymar, a Puerto Rican educated in America and Spain, the book exerted enormous influence on subsequent Hispanic poetry. It stands between the towers of Bécquer's *Rimas* (1871) and Lorca's *Primer romancero gitano* (*Gypsy Ballads*, 1928) as one of the indisputable landmarks of the modern Spanish lyric.

Leaving aside the prose descriptions of New York, Boston, and Philadelphia, the style of the *Diario* is lucid, stripped down to a minimum of adjectives and expressed in an unrhymed and brief free verse form. The imagists had introduced *verso libre* to the United States at about that time, and Jiménez reacted with a version he called *verso desnudo* (naked verse), a short stanza that had considerable impact on younger poets.

In the *Diario* the characteristic mature tone of Jiménez is set. Highly self-referential but less hermetic than Mallarmé, he began in this book a long series of poems that continue in *Eternidades* [Eternities] and *Belleza* [Beauty]. They record epiphanies that express the manifold aspects of a mind perceiving the indifferent beauty of the world. Pebbles and petals on the one hand and the sea and sidereal distances on the other were among the fragments of his surroundings that Jiménez sought to appraise, reconnoitre, and finally to possess.

However, for many readers, Jiménez is the author of only one book: *Platero y yo* (*Platero and I*). It is a pastoral prose poem that reveals many layers of meaning and nuance as the sombrely clad poet-narrator, with his Nazarene beard, rides the donkey Platero through the village of Moguer and out into the countryside. The book also contains astute observations on the poor and oppressed.

Jiménez returned to the United States at the outbreak of the Spanish Civil War in 1936. The flat open land of the Florida Everglades inspired the much admired 'Espacio' [Space]. An audacious experiment with form, 'Espacio' turns discourse into an examination of the possibilities of language. Contingency, the confluence of past and present, memory, spiritual versus carnal love, destiny, and mortality are its themes.

Animal de fondo [Enduring Animal] celebrates the encounter with a humanistic god. Like Blake, he discovered the divinity of the creative consciousness, which seemed to him a god within and without, desiring and desired. On this note of apodictic humanism, with 'all the clouds ablaze', the best of Jiménez's work concludes.

Except for the uneven early books, his work, although repetitive and unduly extensive—30 books and a mass of unpublished material—sustains a remarkably high quality.

He was a scrupulous self-critic and devoted much time to revising and rewriting large amounts of his poetry.

—Howard T. Young

PLATERO AND I (Platero y yo)

Prose poem by Juan Ramón Jiménez, 1914 (written 1906–16).

As one of the most famous prose poems in 20th-century Spanish literature, *Platero and I* stands as an early masterpiece in the long and distinguished career of the Nobel prize laureate, Juan Ramón Jiménez. Translations into more than 20 different languages and millions of copies testify to its vitality and to its status as a classic in world literature. Drawing upon a venerable tradition of Christian humanism from the Gospel to *Don Quixote*, it portrays the travels on the road of life of master and donkey, of poetic personality and Platero. One of the enduring charms of this lyrical story is the attribution of human sensibility to an animal, conceived as an innocent child, and the instruction of this humble creature in the ways of Christian love and morality. Indeed, the guidance of Platero on the road to spiritual perfection is the central focus of the work.

As the author himself has indicated, *Platero and I* was written nearly in its entirety between 1906 and 1912. It was first published in an abbreviated edition in December 1914. The first complete edition appeared in January 1917. It is important to note the enormous difference between the two. The edition of 1914 contains only a selection (made by the editors) of 64 chapters of the original 136 and was organized according to the wishes of the editors. The 1917 edition is the first that reflects in its structure the artistic intention of the author, and consists of the 136 original chapters plus the last two chapters, CXXXVII, 'Platero de carton', and CXXXVIII, 'A Platero en su tierra', dated respectively Madrid, 1915, and Moguer, 1916.

There are at least three fundamental influences that inform the content, vision, and style of *Platero and I*. The work is first of all inspired by the author's native village of Moguer, in the province of Huelva in south-west Spain. The beauty and charm of this coastal town and its countryside, the decline of its economy based on fishing and the export of wine, the social problems of poverty, violence, and persecution, and a redemptive ideal and morality leading to a better world all constitute essential ingredients of this lyrical narration. Secondly, the decisive influence of Spanish krausism, of Francisco Giner de los Rios, and the Institución Libre de Ensenanzsa must be noted. Giner, the greatest educator of modern Spain, and the movement for educational and social reform that he and his followers inspired, were to have a lasting influence on the ideals and values of Jiménez. In particular, the krausist interpretation of history, with its ideas of human progress and perfectibility, and its absolute confidence in the advent of a better world clearly informs the regenerationist vision of *Platero and I*. Thirdly, with respect to style and to the development of artistic prose in *fin-de-siècle* Spain, one must take note of a rich confluence of three related but distinct literary currents: the decisive influence of French symbolism (particularly the prose of Baudelaire, Rimbaud, and Mallarmé), the artistic prose of late Spanish romanticism (especially that of Gustavo Adolfo Bécquer), and the immensely important renovation of language and aesthetic sensibility of Latin American modernism, and, in particular, of the Nicaraguan, Rubén Darío, and the Cuban, José Martí.

In *Platero and I*, Jimenez brings to fruition the stylistic innovations and achievements of all three of the above currents as well as anticipates brilliantly all the expressive forms that characterize the great prose of his second period. His absolute mastery of prose writing exhibits the following essential characteristics: the construction of long melodic sentences; the artful modulation of the rhythm of the sentence; a great freedom and flexibility in the manipulation of syntax for expressive effect; an impressionistic mode of narration in which logical and causal connectives give way to sheer enumeration and juxtaposition; and, above all, a cultivation of the poetic image as the primary vehicle for a symbolic mode of presentation. Indeed, Jiménez's contribution to the renovation of artistic prose in Spain is as important as his fundamental contribution to the development of Spanish lyric poetry.

For full comprehension and aesthetic appreciation, *Platero and I* must be seen as a unified whole of interrelated parts. A first reading reveals that this work does not tell a conventional story. There is no strict narrative ordering of events, no causal relationship linking one lyric chapter to the next. There are sudden shifts of scene and changes of time; there is no apparent inner thread that links the chapters together. But careful study reveals that there are several key principles that account for the expressive organization of this poetic work. Several such principles govern both the beginning and the ending of the book. The first is that Platero dies in the month of February. The second is that the book begins in March, passes through the cycle of a year, and ends in April (*Platero and I* begins in later winter/early spring and ends in spring). The third principle, which reveals the significance of the first two, is that the book begins with the introduction of butterfly imagery and ends with a cluster of butterfly imagery, distributed throughout several of the final chapters. This pattern is elaborated in such a way as to reveal that Platero, at the moment of death, undergoes, like the butterfly, a process of metamorphosis and a resurrection. The underlying theme, then, of *Platero and I*, put in its most abstract formulation, is the theme of life, death and rebirth as a natural process of metamorphosis.

Finally, the organization of *Platero and I* into an expressive form involves the following sets of interrelated principles: the symbolic treatment of the sense and feeling of life embodied in the seasons of nature, and in accordance with the Christian vision of human destiny; the expressive manipulation and elaboration of the seasonal pattern to fit the special needs of Platero's death; the juxtaposition and distribution of expressive material in terms of life and death, light and darkness, violence and harmony, with the gradual reduction of death and violence and the triumph of life and harmony, in accordance with the krausist ideal of a better and more purified world for a more perfected humanity.

—Michael Predmore

JOHN OF THE CROSS, St (San Juan de la Cruz). Born Juan de Yepes y Ávarez, in Fontiveros, Spain, 1542. Boarded at an orphanage by his widowed mother; studied at Jesuit college, Medina del Campo, 1559–63; took the habit as Fray Juan de Santo Matía; attended Carmelite College of San Andrés, University of Salamanca, 1564–68; ordained, 1567. Joined St Teresa's reformed Discalced Order of Carmel in a priory at Duruelo, near Fontiveros, as San Juan de la Cruz, 1568–70, then at Mancera, 1570; rector of a new Carmelite college at University of Alcalá, 1571–72; confessor at convent in Ávila, 1572–77; controversy over reformation of the Carmelite order caused him to be confined in conventual prison in Toledo, 1577–78, because of his reforming attitudes; escaped to a nearby convent; at El Calvario hermitage near convent at Beas de Segura, 1578–79; rector of new Carmelite college at Baeza, 1579–82; prior of Los Mártires, Granada, 1582–88; prior at Segovia, 1588–91; out of favour with head of Discalced Order, and made a simple friar at Priory of La Peñvela, 1591. Beatified, 1675; Canonized, 1726. *Died 14 December 1591*.

PUBLICATIONS

Works

Complete Works, edited and translated by E. Allison Peers. 3 vols., 1934–35; poems also translated by Roy Campbell, 1951; John Frederick Nims, 1959, revised edition, 1968; Kieran Kavanagh and Otilio Rodríguez, 1964, selection from this edition published as *A Song in the Night*, 1991; and Willis Barnstone, 1968.
Vida y obras completas, edited by Crisógono de Jesús, Matías del Niño, and Lucinio Ruano. 1946; 6th edition, 1972.
Four Poems, translated by Yon Oria. 1984.
The Living Flame of Love, translated by J. Vernard. 1990.
The Spiritual Canticle, translated by J. Vernard. 1991.

*

Bibliography: *Bibliografia di S. Juan de la Cruz* by Pier P. Ottonello, 1966.

Critical Studies: *St John of the Cross and Other Lectures and Addresses*, 1946, and *Handbook to the Life and Times of Saint Teresa and Saint John of the Cross*, 1954, both by E. Allison Peers; *Medieval Mystical Tradition and Saint John of the Cross* by a Benedictine of Stanbrook Abbey, 1954; *San Juan de la Cruz, Saint John of the Cross* by Bernardo Gicovate, 1971; *St John of the Cross: His Life and Poetry* by Gerald Brenan, 1973; *San Juan de la Cruz: Poems* by Margaret Wilson, 1975; *The Poet and the Mystic: A Study of the Cántico Espiritual of San Juan de la Cruz* by Colin P. Thompson, 1977; *St John of the Cross: Alchemist of the Soul* by Antonio T. De Nicolás, 1989; *St John of the Cross* by Bede Frost, 1991.

* * *

The 22 poems of St John of the Cross must certainly constitute one of the briefest opuses of any major poet, but, since the 1880s, they have exerted a significant influence on the course of European and American poetry. In his conviction that words provide, at best, only indirect access to experience and that meaning does not exist on a one-to-one basis but, instead, spills over from the play of rhetorical devices (see the 1584 prologue to 'The Spiritual Canticle'), St John anticipated the basic symbolist tenet of indirect expression as expounded by Mallarmé and Valéry (the latter acknowledged the importance to him of St John). The highly polished lyrical quality of his lines in Spanish inspired Bécquer, whose work represents a transition from romanticism to symbolism, and found a worthy follower in the leading Spanish symbolist poet Juan Ramón Jiménez. St John's presence may be discovered in 'East Coker', the first of T.S. Eliot's *Four Quartets*, and the image 'dark night of the soul' has gained much currency among modern writers.

The major theme of St John's poetry is a description of the various stages of development that the soul undergoes in its efforts to become unified with God. In St John's hands, this mystical undertaking achieves one of the highest levels of lyricism known to western poetry. Delicate alliteration and simple diction endow the poems with pellucid beauty. St John chose to recount the story of divine love by having recourse to the symbols and devices used to portray human love, and this accounts for the strong but refined sensuality that characterizes his work.

'The Dark Night', 'The Spiritual Canticle', 'The Living Flame of Love', and 'Although by Night', to mention only some of the better-known poems, are nourished by three distinct sources: the pastoral tradition, exemplified in Spanish by Garcilaso de la Vega; the ballads (*romances*); and the Bible, above all 'The Song of Songs'. St John drew heavily from Solomon's adaptation of Eastern nuptial songs to limn the marriage between the soul and God.

Part of the modern attraction of these poems is that they lend themselves so readily to multiple levels of meaning. 'The Dark Night' is, at once, great amorous verse, a biographical description of escape from prison, and an allegory of mystical experience.

St John left assiduously detailed comments on these poems. Those for 'Ascent of Mount Carmel' and 'Dark Night of the Soul' are incomplete; notes on the latter do not get beyond the first 11 lines. The glosses on 'The Spiritual Canticle' and 'The Living Flame of Love' are complete. Written within the hermeneutic tradition of the Counter-Reformation, these commentaries, except for scattered moments, display none of the consummate literary talent of the poetry. Such is the disparity that it is almost as if one were reading two different authors. *Sayings of Light and Love*, a collection of aphorisms, and, incidentally, the only autograph of his work extant, displays many pleasant paradoxes, but hardly surpasses any other such miscellany. Clearly, it was only as a lyrical poet that he excelled.

—Howard T. Young

JOHNSON, Uwe. Born in Kämmin, Pomerania (now in Poland), 20 July 1934. Educated at school in Güstrow; University of Rostock, 1952–54; University of Leipzig, 1954–56, diploma in philosophy 1956. Married Elisabeth Schmidt in 1962; one daughter. Freelance writer; lived in Güstrow until 1959, in West Berlin, 1959–74, and in England from 1975; lecturer, Wayne State University, Detroit, and Harvard University, Cambridge, Massachusetts, 1961; editor of German writing, Harcourt Brace, publishers, New York, 1966–67. Recipient, Berlin Academy Fontane prize, 1960; International Publishers prize, 1962; Villa Massino grant, 1962; Büchner prize, 1971; Raabe prize, 1975; Thomas Mann prize (Lübeck), 1978. *Died 15 March 1984.*

PUBLICATIONS

Fiction

Mutmassungen über Jakob. 1959; as *Speculations about Jakob*, translated by Ursule Molinaro, 1963.
Das dritte Buch über Achim. 1961; as *The Third Book about Achim*, translated by Ursule Molinaro, 1967.
Karsch und andere Prosa. 1964; translated in part as *An Absence*, by Richard and Clara Winston, 1969.
Zwei Ansichten. 1965; as *Two Views*, translated by Richard and Clara Winston, 1966.
Jahrestage: Aus dem Leben von Gesine Cresspahl. 1970–83; as *Anniversaries: From the Life of Gesine Cresspahl*, vols. 1–2 translated by Leila Vennewitz, 1975; vols. 2–4 translated by Vennewitz and Walter Arndt, 1987.
Von dem Fischer un syner Fru: Ein Märchen nach Philipp Otto Runge, 1976.
Skizze eines Verunglückten. 1982.
Ingrid Babendererde: Reifeprüfung 1953. 1985.
Versuch, einen Vater zu finden. Marthas Ferien. 1988.

Other

Eine Reise nach Klagenfurt. 1974.
Berliner Sachen: Aufsätze. 1975.
Begleitumstände: Frankfurter Vorlesungen. 1980.
Der 5. Kanal. 1987.
Ich überlege mir die Geschichte: Uwe Johnson im Gespräch, edited by Eberhard Fahlke. 1988.

Editor, *Me-ti: Buch der Wendungen*, by Bertolt Brecht. 1965.
Editor, with Hans Meyer, *Das Werk von Samuel Beckett—Berliner Colloquium.* 1975.
Editor, *Stich-Worte*, by Max Frisch. 1975.
Editor, *Verzweigungen*, by Margret Boveri. 1977.

Translator, *Israel Potter*, by Herman Melville. 1960.
Translator, *In diesem Land*, by John Knowles. 1963.

*

Bibliography: *Uwe Johnson: Bibliographie* by Nicolai Riedel, 2 vols., 1976; revised edition, 1981.

Critical Studies: *Uwe Johnson* by Mark Boulby, 1974; *Ich und Er: First and Third Person Self-Reference and Problems of Identity in Three Contemporary German-Language Novels* by Paul F. Botheroyd, 1976; *Beyond the Single Vision: Henry James, Michel Butor, Uwe Johnson* by Marianne Hirsch, 1981; *Uwe Johnson* edited by Rainer Gerlach and Matthias Richter, 1984; *Uwe Johnsons Jahrestage* edited by Michael Bengel, 1985; *Neither Left nor Right: The Politics of Individualism in Uwe Johnson's Work* by Kurt J. Fickert, 1987; *Difficulties of Saying 'I': The Narrator as Protagonist in Uwe Johnson's Jahrestage and Christa Wolf's Kindheitsmuster* by Robert K. Shirer, 1988; *The Ethics of Narration: Uwe Johnson's Novels from Ingrid Babendererde to Jahrestage* by Colin Riordan, 1989; *Uwe Johnsons 'Jahrestage'. Erzählstruktur und politische Subjektivität* by Ulrich Fries, 1990; *Über Uwe Johnson* edited by Raimund Fellinger, 1992.

* * *

Although less well known internationally than Heinrich Böll or Günter Grass, Uwe Johnson is unquestionably one of the towering figures of post-war German literature. Having grown up in the German Democratic Republic and moved to the West in 1959, he became the first German writer of stature to tackle the pre-eminent theme of post-war Germany: the division into separate States. In 1967, after three novels and a volume of short stories which drew on the divisions of Germany for wide-ranging analyses of historical, moral, and literary dilemmas, Johnson embarked on his epic novel *Jahrestage* (*Anniversaries*). Completed a year before the author's early death from heart disease in 1984, *Anniversaries* in its later stages was influenced by a debilitating personal crisis which dogged the last ten years of Johnson's life. A number of minor pieces written during the 1970s reflect both Johnson's life in England and his personal tribulations. Not until after his death did Johnson's first, originally unpublished novel appear.

Begun when Johnson was 19, rewritten four times and finished by the time he was 22, *Ingrid Babendererde*, published in 1985, is a novel of astonishing maturity. Rejected by publishers in the GDR as politically dangerous, and by a West German publisher as sympathetic to communism, the novel tells the story of the last few days in school of a class about to sit school-leaving examinations in April 1953, shortly after Stalin's death and two months before the workers' uprising. The examination becomes political and moral rather than strictly educational, however, because the eponymous heroine comes into conflict with the authorities over the persecution by the State of a religious youth organization. Finally she is left with no choice but to leave for the West. While *Ingrid Babendererde*, as a school novel, does betray the youth of its author, it nevertheless displays the sensitivity to subtle moral and political dilemmas (presented in this case by life in an aspiring socialist, but actually totalitarian regime) which was to characterize much of Johnson's later work.

Mutmassungen über Jakob (*Speculations about Jakob*), written in the GDR but published in the Federal Republic in 1959, marked Johnson's emergence as a new literary talent. A young East German railway worker, Jakob Abs, is killed by a train after having been to the Federal Republic to visit his lover, Gesine Cresspahl, whom the secret police had hoped to recruit as an agent through Jakob. The novel concerns the efforts of the characters, including Gesine, the secret police captain Rohlfs, and Jonas, Jakob's friend, to reconstruct the last month of Jakob's life. This seems straightforward enough, but extensive use of flash-back, unidentified interior monologue, and structural complexity reminiscent of William Faulkner give rise on first reading to a kind of foggy indistinctness which bewildered many early reviewers and critics. Close analysis shows, however, that the work's component parts can be reassembled in an easily comprehensible form. Despite the title, then, the reader is called upon not to speculate, but to observe with the utmost precision. The speculation in which the characters are forced to indulge, immersed as they are in an atmosphere of extreme mutual mistrust arising from the exigencies of the Cold War, reflects the reality of a divided Germany which was no more than partly penetrable by those caught up in its complexities.

Karsh, a Hamburg journalist, the hero of Johnson's second published novel, *Das dritte Buch über Achim* (*The Third Book about Achim*), similarly feels the effects of mutual inter-German mistrust upon his own person. In response to a telephone invitation from a former girlfriend, Karsch travels to the GDR. His former girlfriend is now closely involved with Joachim ('Achim') T., famous racing cyclist and folk-hero, and the subject of two biographies. Karsch is asked to produce a third book about Achim, which he works on but never finishes. The reasons for his failure form the main object of interest. The fallible workings of memory (and of literature), as well as the linguistic divergence between the two countries which engenders epistemological clashes, all contribute to the problems Karsch encounters. Ultimately, however, political pressures conflict with ethical dictates: unable to preserve his integrity as a writer and simultaneously connive at the State's self-interested remodelling of Achim's image, the journalist makes his decision to return empty-handed to the West, constrained by the moral imperatives which characterize so much of Johnson's work.

Johnson re-worked the Achim story in his collection of short prose *Karsch und andere Prosa* [Karsch and Other Prose], concentrating on the breakdown which Karsch suffered on his return to the West. The collection also contains a number of short stories prefiguring the later novel *Anniversaries*. *Zwei Ansichten* (*Two Views*), topped the West German bestseller lists with its topical tale of two lovers divided by the Berlin wall. This is no *Romeo and Juliet*, however, since the motives of both participants are complex and ambiguous. Although the young East German woman, Nurse D., does eventually reach West Berlin, there is no fairy-tale happy ending. The apparent simplicity of star-crossed lovers seeking happiness in each other's arms is superseded by the realization that the characters are in the grip of complex historical forces which they are unable to comprehend and powerless to control.

The effect which historical circumstances have on the lives of individuals forms a central concern in Johnson's greatest achievement, *Anniversaries*. The four-volume novel recounts a year in the life of Gesine Cresspahl (familiar from *Speculations about Jakob*), who lives and works as a single mother in New York with her 11-year-old daughter Marie (daughter of Jakob Abs). Each day of the year in question— 20 August 1967 to 20 August 1968—is individually documented on two chronological levels. The first documents daily events in New York and the United States as perceived by Gesine through her reading of the *New York Times* and her personal experience. The second follows Gesine's efforts to retrace the story of her family and forebears in pre-war Germany, progressing through the war and the establishment of the GDR to the early 1960s when Gesine left for the United States. These two levels are connected using sophisticated narratological devices as anniversaries of events in the earlier story occur, though both can be read as stories in their own right. The novel encompasses a broad sweep of 20th-century history, concentrating particularly on the moral dilemmas faced by Gesine and her parents, dilemmas encapsulated in the 'moral Switzerland' problem: 'Where is the moral Switzerland that we can emigrate to?' asks Gesine in despair. While Gesine bitterly regrets her parents' failure to leave Nazi Germany when they had the opportunity, she finds herself bringing up her own daughter in a country riven by race-riots and embroiled in a hopeless, costly war. Gesine finds no solution, and her hopes of experiencing democratic, humane socialism are dashed as she plans a trip to Czechoslovakia on the day of the Soviet invasion, the final day of the *Anniversaries* year. Such a brief description cannot do justice to what is a richly interwoven, absorbing, and meticulously crafted text. *Anniversaries* stands out as one of the great German novels of the post-war era, indeed of the 20th century, encapsulating as it does the origins and development of many of the problems which beset the world we know today.

—Colin Riordan

JUANA INÉS DE LA CRUZ, Sor. Born Juana Inés Ramírez de Asbaje (or Asuaje) in San Miguel de Nepantla, Viceroyalty of New Spain (now Mexico), 12 November 1651 (some sources give 1648). Largely self-educated. Invited to attend the court of the Spanish Viceroy's wife, the Marquise de Mancera, in Mexico City, c.1659, and subsequently wrote verses for official events; member of the Carmelite convent in Mexico City, 1667 (for three months); entered Jeronymite Convent of San Paula, Mexico City, 1669, and adopted the religious name Sor Juana Inés de la Cruz; abandoned writing, c.1693, because of the increasing pressure from Church authorities after 1689. *Died 17 April 1695.*

PUBLICATIONS

Collections

Obras escogidas, edited by Manuel Toussaint. 1928.
Obras completas, edited by Alfonso Mendez Plancarte and Alberto Salceda. 4 vols., 1951–57.
Poesía, teatro y prosa (selections), edited by Antonio Castro Leal. 1965.
Obras selectas, edited by Georgina Sabat de Rivers and Elias L. Rivers. 1976.
Obra selecta, edited by Lusi Sáinz de Medrano. 1987.

Verse

Villancicos. 12 vols., 1676–91.
Poesías escogidas, edited by Antonio Elías de Molins. c.1901.
Poesías completas, edited by Emilio Abreu Gómez. 1940.
Poesías (selection), edited by Elena Amat. 1941.
The Pathless Grove: Sonnets, translated by Pauline Cook. 1950.
El sueño, edited by Alfonso Méndez Plancarte. 1951; as *Primero sueño*, edited by Gerardo Moldenhauer and Juan Carlos Merlo, 1953; as *El sueño*, translated by John Campion, 1983; as *Sor Juana's Dream*, translated by Luis Harss, 1986.
Endechas, edited by Xavier Villaurrutia. 1952.
Sonetos y endechas, edited by Rosa Chacel. 1980.
Lírica, edited by Raquel Asún. 1983.
Poems: A Bilingual Anthology, edited and translated by Margaret Sayers Peden. 1985.

Plays (individual 17th-century editions)

Auto sacramental de 'El divino Narciso' (produced 1689). 1690.
Los empeños de una casa (produced 1683). N.d.
Amor es más laberinto. N.d.
Neptuno alegórico. N.d.

Other

Carta atenagórica. 1690.
Explicación sucinta del arco triunfal . . . N.d.
La respuesta a Sor Filotea de la Cruz. 1691; as *A Woman of Genius: The Intellectual Biography of Sor Juana Inés de la Cruz*, translated by Margaret Sayers Peden, 1982.
[Works]. 3 vols., 1691–1700.
1. *Inundación castálida* (includes verse and the play *El neptuno alegórico*). 1689; as *Poemas*, 1690; edited by Georgina Sabat de Rivers, as *Inundación castálida*, 1982.
2. *Segundo volumen de las obras* (includes 'El sueño'; the autos *El cetro de José*, *El mártir del Sacramento*,

San Hermenegildo, *El divino Narciso*; the comedies *Los empeños de una casa*, *Amor es más laberinto*; and *Crisis sobre un sermón: Carta atenagórica*). 1692.
3. *Fama y obras póstumas* (includes *La respuesta a Sor Filotea*). 1700.
Carta atenagórica; Respuesta a Sor Filotea, edited by Emilio Abreu Gómez. 1934.
Poesía y teatro, edited by Matilde Muñoz. 1946.
Antología Sorjuanina, edited by Giuseppe Bellini. 1961.
Antología, edited by Elias L. Rivers. 1968.
Antología clave, edited by Hernán Loyola. 1971.
Selección, edited by L. Ortega Galindo. 1978.
A Sor Juana Anthology (bilingual edition), translated by Alan S. Trueblood. 1988.

*

Bibliography: *Bibliografía de Sor Juana Inés de la Cruz* by Dorothy Schons, 1927; *Sor Juana Inés de la Cruz: Bibliografía y biblioteca* by Emilio Abreu Gómez, 1934.

Critical Studies: 'Some Obscure Points in the Life of Sor Juana Inés de la Cruz' by Dorothy Schons, in *Modern Philology*, 24, 1926; *La santificación de Sor Juana Inés de la Cruz* by Genaro Fernández MacGregor, 1932; *Vida de Sor Juana* by P. Diego Calleja, 1936; *La ruta de Sor Juana*, 1938, and *Semblanza de Sor Juana*, 1938, by Emilio Abreu Gómez; *Sor Juana Inés de la Cruz* by Clara Carilla, 1944; *Sor Juana Inés de la Cruz: Poetisa de corte y convento* by Elizabeth Wallace, 1944; *Juana de Asbaje* by Amado Nervo, 1946; *Cuatro documentos relativos a Sor Juana* by Lota Spell, 1947; 'The Tenth Muse of America' by Alfonso Reyes in *The Position of America*, 1950; *Razón y pasión de Sor Juana* by Anita Arroyo, 1952; *Sor Juana Inés de la Cruz* by Patricia Cox, 1958; *Sor Juana Inés de la Cruz: Claro en la selva* by C.G. de Gullarte, 1958; *Baroque Times in Old Mexico* by Leonard Irving, 1959; 'A Revision of the Philosophy of Sor Juana Inés de la Cruz', in *Hispania*, 43, 1960, 'The Alleged Mysticism of Sor Juana Inés de la Cruz', in *Hispanic Review*, 28(3), 1960, 'The *Primero sueño* of Sor Juana Inés de la Cruz: A Revision of the Criticism', in *Revista Iberoamericana de Literatura*, 15, 1965, and *Sor Juana Inés de la Cruz*, 1971, all by Gerard C. Flynn; *Sor Juana Inés de la Cruz: La décima musa de México* by Ludwig Pfandl, translated by Juan Antonio Ortega y Medina, 1963; *Genio y figura de Sor Juana Inés de la Cruz* by Ramón Xirau, 1967; *Autos sacramentales de Sor Juana Inés de la Cruz* by Sergio Fernández, 1970; 'Human and Divine Love in the Poetry of Sor Juana Inés de la Cruz' by Arthur Terry, in *Studies in Spanish Literature of the Golden Age*, 1973; *Del encausto a la sangre: Sor Juana Inés de la Cruz* by Mirta Aguirre, 1975; *Lo americano en el teatro de Sor Juana Inés de la Cruz* by María E. Pérez, 1975; *Juana de Asbaje: Aproximación a la autobiografía de la Décima Musa* by Carlos E. Galeano Ospina, 1976; *El Sueño de Sor Juana Inés de la Cruz: Tradiciones literarias y originalidad* by Georgina Sabat de Rivers, 1977; 'The Tenth Muse', in *Americas*, 30(2), 1978, and 'Sor Juana Inés de la Cruz: Let Your Women Keep Silence in the Churches', in *Women's Studies in International Forum*, 5(8), 1985, both by Nina M. Scott; *Sor Juana Inés de la Cruz ante la historia* by Francisco de la Maza and Elías Trabulse, 1980, and *El hermetismo y Sor Juana Inés de la Cruz: Orígenes e interpretación* by Trabulse, 1980; *Virtue or Vice?: Sor Juana's Use of Thomistic Thought* by Constance M. Montross, 1981; 'Sor Juana Inés de la Cruz Speaking the Mother Tongue', in *University of Dayton Review*, 16(2), 1983, and 'The Convent as a Catalyst for

Autonomy: Two Hispanic Nuns of the Seventeenth Century' in *Women in Hispanic Literature: Icons and Fallen Idols* edited by Beth Miller, 1983, and 'This Life Within Me Won't Keep Still', in *Reinventing the Americas* edited by Bell Gale Chevigny and Gari Laguardia, 1986, all by Electra Arenal; 'Hermetic Traditions in Sor Juana's *Primero sueño*' by Manuel Durán, in *University of Dayton Review*, 16(2), 1983; *Sor Juana Inés de la Cruz; o, Las trampas de la Fe* by Octavio Paz, 1982, as *Sor Juana; or, The Traps of Faith*, translated by Margaret Sayers Peden, 1988; *Plotting Women: Gender and Representation in Mexico* by Jean Franco, 1989; *Feminist Perspectives on Sor Juana Inés de la Cruz* edited by Stephanie Merrim, 1991; *Juana Inés de la Cruz and the Theology of Beauty* by George H. Tavard, 1991.

*   *   *

Sor Juana Inés de la Cruz has been hailed as the first great writer of Spanish America, and has been compared to Anne Bradstreet (1612–71), her New England contemporary whose poetry became one of the first literary landmarks of North America. That two such powerful writers in the New World of the 17th century should have been women has been the focus of feminist critical attention. especially since both wrote immensely personal poetry, and both questioned the subservient role of women generally accepted at the time.

Sor Juana was well-educated, and claims that her desire to study was a powerful motivating force from the age of barely three. She claimed to have pressed her mother to allow her to attend university in Mexico City dressed as a boy (women were not allowed to study at universities in the colonies). She became a nun in order to 'live alone and avoid obligations that would disturb my freedom to study', even though she acknowledged that there would be aspects of convent life with which she might find it difficult to cope. She seems to have been a rebel all her life, refusing to accept easy solutions, writing, despite the misgivings of powerful members of the clergy, and searching for ways to express her radical views on the role of women in the world. Jean Franco has examined Sor Juana's attempts to move beyond gender, to escape from the limitations of a society structured along binary oppositions of male and female, in which the female was the subordinate partner. As a nun, she claimed to be outside sexual difference, and her poem *Primero sueño* (*Dream*), which she said was her only work written just for herself, is the metaphysical journey of a soul which, in dream, is set free from the constraints of gender categorization.

Most of her work (all of it, she claimed, in her autobiographical *La respuesta a Sor Filotea de la Cruz*, translated as *A Woman of Genius: The Intellectual Biography of Sor Juana Inés de la Cruz*), was written for specific purposes, at the request of a patron, or to celebrate a certain event. Her earliest poems were dedicated to the Viceroy's wife; a number of poems were written for religious or viceregal holidays; and she wrote ballads, songs, carols and poems on religious themes. Her play *Los empeños de una casa* [The Obligations of a House] was performed in 1683 for the Viceroys. Her later play, generally considered to be a masterpiece, *El divino Narciso* [Divine Narcissus] was written in 1688 and performed in Madrid the following year. At this time Sor Juana was at the height of her fame, but in 1690 the antagonism felt for her by some of the bishops reached crisis point. Sor Juana's interpretation of the Bible had a very definite slant: she consistently praised the virtues of heroic female figures, not only Mary and Mary Magdalene and the women of the New Testament, but powerfully symbolic women such as Esther,

Rebecca, Deborah, and Judith. Her criticism of the Jesuit Father Vieyra's Maundy Thursday sermon, intended for private circulation only, was published without her consent by the Bishop of Puebla using the pseudonym of Sor Filotea under the title of *Carta atenagórica* [Letter Worthy of Athene]. The publication of this text caused a scandal, as did her reply that appeared three months later, *A Woman of Genius*. The effect of this crisis was a desperate one for Sor Juana: publicly humiliated and rebuked by the Church authorities, she was devastated by what she saw as an act of treachery by the Bishop of Puebla in publishing a private document. Although a new edition of her poems came out in 1689 (the *Inundación castálida*), and her religious *autos* were published in 1692 (see [Works], 3 vols., 1691–1700), she dismantled her library, and in 1694 again took her vows as a nun, to proclaim symbolically her decision to live under a new austerity. In 1695 she died during a plague epidemic.

The end of Sor Juana's writing career was poignant one. After a lifetime of struggle, during which she had asserted her voice with a power unique in the Americas—and in the Spanish-speaking world as a whole—she was finally silenced by the very forces of repressive authoritarianism against which she had fought. In *A Woman of Genius* she comments bitterly on how her desire to learn and to write 'led me closer to the flames of persecution', declaring that never again would she speak out to defend herself. The dismantling of her personal library was a potent sign of her decision to choose silence in the face of overt hostility from her religious superiors.

The emotive details of Sor Juana's biography, and the fascination that the content of her works has for today's readers, has meant that less attention has been paid to the skills of her poetic technique. Influenced by Góngora and the Golden Age writers, Sor Juana can be described as a Baroque lyricist, whose use of rhyme, rhythm, and imagery distinguish her as a particularly gifted poet. Octavio Paz claims that Quevedo and Lope de Vega were ultimately greater writers, but that what makes Sor Juana's writing unique is the combination of passion and conscience, of dynamic energy and a questing soul. We might add to that the tragic conflict between a mind that wanted to explore the universe and tried to do so through the pen, and the body of a woman in a nun's habit, firmly and constrictingly located in the world of a 17th-century colonial convent.

—Susan Bassnett

———————

JÜNGER, Ernst. Born in Heidelberg, Germany, 29 March 1895. Educated at Lyceum II, 1901–05, Hanover Internaten, Hanover and Braunschweig, 1905–07; studied biology in Leipzig and Naples, 1923–26. Joined the French Foreign Legion, 1913, brought back home by his father. Volunteer with the German army during World War I, served on the Western Front, 1914–18; captain during World War II, discharged 1944. Married 1) Gretha von Jeinsen in 1925 (died 1960), two sons (one deceased); 2) Liselotte Lohrer in 1962. Officer in the Reichswehr, 1919–23; contributor to radical right-wing journals including *Standarte*, *Arminius*, *Widerstand*, and *Der Vormarsch*, 1925–31; moved to Berlin, 1927; freelance writer from 1927; lived in Goslar, 1933–36; Überlingen, 1936–39; Kirchhorst, 1939–48; Revensburg,

1948–50; and Wilfingen, from 1950; banned from publishing his work in 1945; ban lifted, 1949; travelled extensively in the 1950s and 1960s; co-editor of the journal *Antaios*, 1959–71. Recipient: Culture prize (Goslar), 1955; City of Bremen prize, 1955; literary prize of the Federal League of German Industry, 1960; Immermann prize (Düsseldorf), 1965; Humbolt Society gold medal, 1981, Goethe prize, 1982; Accademia Casentinese, Dante Alighieri International prize, 1987; Tevere Intern prize, 1987. Honorary Doctorate: University of Bilbao, Spain. Great Order of Merit, Federal Republic of Germany, 1959. Lives in Wilfingen, Germany.

PUBLICATIONS

Fiction

In Stahlgewittern: Aus dem Tagebuch eines Stosstruppführers. 1920; as *The Storm of Steel: From the Diary of a German Storm-Troop Officer on the Western Front*, translated by Basil Creighton, 1929.
Das Wäldchen 125: Eine Chronik aus den Grabenkämpfen 1918. 1925; as *Copse 125: A Chronicle from the Trench Warfare of 1918*, translated by Basil Creighton, 1930.
Afrikanische Spiele. 1936; as *African Diversions*, translated by Stuart Hood, 1954.
Auf den Marmorklippen. 1939; as *On the Marble Cliffs*, translated by Stuart Hood, 1947.
Heliopolis: Rückblick auf eine Stadt. 1949.
Besuch auf Godenholm (stories). 1952.
Gläserne Bienen. 1957; revised edition, 1960; as *The Glass Bees*, translated by Louise Bogan and Elizabeth Mayer, 1961.
Sturm. 1963.
Die Zwille. 1973.
Eumeswil. 1977.
Aladins Problem. 1983; as *Aladdin's Problems*, translated by Joachim Neugroschel, 1993.
Eine gefährliche Begegnung. 1985.

Other

Der Kampf als inneres Erlebnis. 1922.
Feuer und Blut: Ein kleiner Ausschnitt aus einer grossen Schlacht. 1925.
Das abenteuerliche Herz: Aufzeichnungen bei Tag und Nacht (essays). 1929.
Die totale Mobilmachung. 1931.
Hier spricht der Feind. 1931.
Der Arbeiter: Herrschaft und Gestalt. 1932.
Blätter und Steine (essays). 1934.
Geheimnisse der Sprache: Zwei Essays. 1934.
Lob der Vokale. 1937.
Gärten und Strassen: Aus den Tagebüchern von 1939 und 1940 (diaries). 2 vols., 1942.
Myrdun: Briefe aus Norwegen. 1943.
Der Friede: Ein Wort an die Jugend Europas, ein Wort an die Jugend der Welt. 1945; as *The Peace*, translated by Stuart Hood, 1948.
Atlantische Fahrt: Nur für Kriegsgefangene gedruckt (diaries). 1947.
Sprache und Körperbau. 1947; revised edition, 1949.
Ein Inselfrühling: Ein Tagebuch aus Rhodos. 1948.
Strahlungen (diary). 1949.
Über die Linie. 1950.
Das Haus der Briefe. 1951.
Am Kieselstrand. 1951.

Der Waldgang. 1951.
Drei Kiesel. 1952.
Der gordische Knoten. 1953.
Ernst Jünger: Eine Auswahl, edited by Arnim Mohler. 1953.
Das Sanduhrbuch. 1954.
Geburtstagsbrief: Zum 4. November 1955. 1955.
Die Herzmuschel. 1955.
Sonnentau: Pflanzenbilder. 1955.
Am Sarazenenturm (on Sardinia). 1955.
Die Schleife, Dokumente zum Weg. 1955.
Rivarol. 1956.
Serpentara. 1957.
San Pietro. 1957.
Jahre der Okkupation (diary). 1958.
Mantrana. 1958.
An der Zeitmauer. 1959.
Der Weltstaat: Organismus und Organisation. 1960.
Ein Vormittag in Antibes. 1960.
Sgraffiti (essays). 1960.
Werke. 10 vols., 1960–65.
Das spanische Mondhorn. 1962.
Fassungen. 1963.
An Friedrich Georg zum 65. Geburtstag. 1963.
Typus, Name, Gestalt. 1963.
Grenzgänge (essays). 1966.
Subtile Jagden (essays). 1967.
Im Granit (on Corsica). 1967.
Zwei Inseln: Formosa, Ceylon. 1968.
Federbälle. 1969.
Annäherungen: Drogen und Rausch. 1970.
Lettern und Ideogramme (on Japan). 1970.
Ad Hoc (essays). 1970.
Sinn und Bedeutung: Ein Figurenspiel (essays). 1971.
Zahlen und Götter. Philemon und Baucis: Zwei Essays. 1974.
Eine Begegnung: acht Abbildungen nach Zeichungen und Briefen von Ernst Jünger und Alfred Kubin. (correspondence). 1975.
Sämtlichte Werke. 18 vols., 1978–83.
Siebzig verweht (diary). 2 vols., 1980–81.
Flugträume (selections). 1983.
Autor und Autorschaft. 1984.
Die Schere. 1990.

Editor, *Aufmarsch des Nationalismus.* 1926.
Editor, *Die Unvergessenen.* 1928.
Editor, *Das Antlitz des Weltkrieges.* 1930.
Editor, *Krieg und Krieger.* 1930.
Editor, *Luftfahrt ist not!* 1930.
Editor, *Der feurige Weg*, by Franz Schauwecker. 1930.
Editor, *Der Kampf um das Reich.* 1931.

*

Bibliography: *Ernst Jünger: Eine Bibliographie* by Karl O. Paetel, 1953; *Bibliographie der Werke Ernst Jüngers* by Hans Peter des Coudres, 1970.

Critical Studies: *Ernst Jünger: A Writer of Our Time* by J.P. Stern, 1953; *Ernst Jünger* by Heinz Ludwig Arnold, 1966; *Ernst Jünger* by Wolfgang Kaempter, 1981; *Ernst Jünger and the Nature of Political Commitment* by Roger Woods, 1982; *Ernst Jünger: Leben und Werk in Bildern und Texten* edited by Heimo Schwilk, 1988; *Ernst Jünger* by Martin Meyer, 1990; *Ernst Jünger's Visions and Revisions on the European Right* by Marcus Paul Bullock, 1992.

* * *

Ernst Jünger is not only German's longest-lived author, but also one of its most controversial literary figures. Considered to have been among the leading, most innovative, and most productive writers of the country's intellectual and political right in his earlier years, in mid-career he assumed the position of an iconoclast and an inhabitant of the proverbial ivory tower without, however, completely eschewing his earlier political and philosophical convictions. Distancing himself from the tenents and practices of National Socialism prior to and during the years of the Third Reich, he none the less did not espouse a very strong and open anti-Nazi stance, preferring the status of a not always clearly defined 'Inner Emigration' to that of the Nazi opposition in exile. His later years are highlighted by extensive travels and keen stylistic and thematic experimentations in his literary endeavours.

An adventurer at heart who not merely fantasized about the outer limits of human existence in his fiction but actively sought to experience such situations and encounters throughout his life, Jünger combines the pursuits and experiences of the soldier/warrior with those of the investigator, researcher, and traveller in a fashion that betrays an intellectuality rooted in the Renaissance. Deeply steeped in the German classical intellectual tradition, yet also influenced by French moralism, his plots and themes deal not just with past and present settings and conditions, but imaginatively conjure up futuristic developments. His style can be said to have varied from 'heroic realism' via surrealism to aberrant sado-masochism in his fiction. His extensive essayistic work, on the other hand, displays a stylistic lucidity which stands in sharp contrast to the enigmatic prose of Heidegger, a philosopher with whom Jünger engaged in a lively intellectual exchange of ideas for many years.

Jünger's work can be roughly divided into three segments, irrespective of the chronology involved. The perhaps most basic part of it, underlying the other two, is thematically guided by his war-time experiences from 1915 to 1918 and his post-war political convictions issuing therefrom and extending into World War II and beyond. It includes *In Stahlgewittern* (*The Storm of Steel*), *Das Wäldchen 125* (*Copse 125*), *Der Kampf als inneres Erlebnis*, *Feuer und Blut*, *Die totale Mobilmachung*, *Der Friede* (*The Peace*), and *Der Weltstaat*. This segment reflects both the impact of World War I on his thinking and the reverberations of the experiences he gathered during and after World War II. The central core of his *oeuvre* consists of fiction. The principal works represented in this part are *Afrikanische Spiele* (*African Diversions*), *Auf den Marmorklippen* (*On the Marble Cliffs*), *Heliopolis*, *Gläserne Bienen* (*The Glass Bees*), *Eumeswil*, and *Eine gefährliche Begegnung*. Although these works also incorporate personal experience and philosophical constructs, they are primarily imaginative literature intent on both entertaining the reader and provoking his intellectual, if not visceral, reaction to themes of supreme interest to the author himself. The third part of his writings deals with non-political observations, travel experiences, and investigations that occupy a middle ground between scientific enquiry and innermost reflections. Examples of this type of writing, though interspersed in and throughout his *oeuvre*, are principally *Das abenteuerliche Herz*, *Geheimnisse der Sprache*, *Sprache und Körperbau*, *Sgraffiti*, *Sonnentau: Pflanzenbilder*, and *Annäherungen: Drogen und Rausch*.

The Storm of Steel is not only the trend setter in Jünger's largest segment of writings with monographic leanings but also the work that established his national and international reputation. Written in diary form and covering his own war experiences from 1915 to 1918, the book gives an inside view of the plight and the glory of the soldier in modern warfare without, however, passing judgement on the moral dilemma it generates. Subsequent works—such as *Copse 125*, *Der Kampf als inneres Erlebnis*, and *Feuer und Blut*—deal with the same basic experiences and sentiments in a more systematic and deliberate manner. In *Der Kampf als inneres Erlebnis*, Jünger celebrates war as the expression of an elementary natural force. He puts this metaphysical sublimation of warfare on a more expansive philosophical and political basis in his treatise *Die totale Mobilmachung*. This work, in effect, advocates the total mobilization of society for total warfare. However, a complete reversal of attitude brought about the certainty of Germany's inevitable defeat in World War II is voiced in the treatise *Der Friede*. Jünger wrote this essay in secret at the height of Nazi power, and circulated it among friends for commentary. Field Marshal Erwin Rommel, an avowed enemy of Hitler's military adventurism, saw it as an ethical basis for resistance to the Nazi regime. The two-part document not only envisages the achievement of a just and equitable peace, but also develops a political programme along philosophical lines that might serve as a guideline for both Europe and the world to avoid future conflicts. Nearly two decades later, Jünger wrote a sequel to *Der Friede*. He called it *Der Weltstaat: Organismus und Organisation*. In this work he envisages a world state that is no longer a source of external or internal conflict, as previous nation states had been, but a guarantor of a just, organic, and moral mode of human existence, freed from the coercive forces of organization.

Jünger's fiction is highlighted by two novels, *On the Marble Cliffs* and *Heliopolis*. In contrast to his earlier narrative *African Diversions* which took many of its cues from his youthful excursion into Africa while attempting to join the Foreign Legion, *On the Marble Cliffs* is an abstract, surrealistic novel in a timeless setting that not only has futuristic and mythic features, but also reflects contemporary scenarios. Although the peaceful life of contemplation and pursuit of botanical and linguistic studies proves illusory to the anonymous narrator and his brother Otho in a belligerent human world bent on self-destruction, the brothers can escape annihilation and may be able to re-establish themselves at a distant shore. This novel with its thinly veiled references to the political power struggles in Germany in the 1920s and 1930s has been hailed as an exemplary work of the 'Inner Emigration', a loose movement of writers remaining in Germany during the Nazi era and criticizing the regime in symbolic and allegorical form. *Heliopolis*, by contrast, is a clearly futuristic novel in which man's possible future development is outlined in a highly politicized and philosophical fashion. The city-state Heliopolis is an imaginary place postdating the era of the second nihilism and that of the global workers' state. Yet it has not achieved internal peace. As in *On the Marble Cliffs*, dialectically opposed political forces, representing the opposite world views of technological perfection and human perfectibility, vie for political dominance. Although the novel's protagonist, Lucius de Geer, whose personal characteristics reflect Jünger's own, fails in his political undertakings on the side of humanist causes, he gains intellectually and spiritually. His celebration of free will and altruistic individualism and his rejection of collectivism and the heartless worship of power again betray Jünger's changed world-view in his maturing years. Later fiction, principally represented in *The Glass Bees* and *Eumeswil*, deals further with the ideas expounded in *Heliopolis*, albeit in more limited and less universal settings. Jünger's most recent novel, *Eine gefährliche Begegnung*, however, is a more traditional work that takes the reader back into the Paris of the late 19th century and the sensuality, intrigues, murderous plots, superficiality, and decadence of an epoch that in many ways reflects our own.

Jünger's reflective and pseudo-scientific writings, while basically also experiential, differ from his previously categorized works not only in content but also in style. They are stylistically more diverse than those dealing with his war-time experiences and their imprints in his intellectual and political psyche. What is most significant, however, is the fact that this body of writing is also endowed with a Goethean inclination toward the universal. The two most interesting works in this segment are *Das abenteuerliche Herz* and *Annäherungen: Drogen und Rausch*. While *Das abenteuerliche Herz*, a collection of essays, was in its original version still very much influenced by his World War I experiences, Jünger's intention went from the very outset beyond the merely adventurous. His aim was both internal and external. Internally he meant to convey impressions of a more personal nature. Externally —and this became the overriding intent in the revised edition of the work—he aimed to discuss the whole gamut of the organic life of man, animal, and plant, a Goethean undertaking. In contrast to *Sgraffiti*, a volume of essays patterned after *Das abenteuerliche Herz* and an obvious sequel to this work, *Annäherungen: Drogen und Rausch* is a book about mind-altering drugs and their effect on the human psyche. Although Jünger has experimented with drugs throughout his adult life, he has, unlike some of his literary predecessors in this area such as Thomas De Quincey, Charles Baudelaire, and Edgar Allan Poe, never been addicted to drugs. This experimentation is another one of his attempts to penetrate the innermost core of his psyche.

This last discussed work in particular makes it clear that Jünger is basically a neo-Romantic at heart who is constantly journeying to and probing the higher as well as the innermost regions of both his consciousness and his intellect. This overwhelming urge on his part also helps to explain his argumentative, essayistic, observational, reflective, and speculative style, which defies easy labelling and categorization. His proto-fascist political leanings early in life have done much harm to his later reception. His contribution to literature and thought has consequently been vastly underrated, and his reputation as a major writer in 20th-century German, indeed world, literature appears to be in need of a revision.

—Carl Steiner

JUVENAL. Born Decimus Junius Juvenalis, c.AD 50–65, or perhaps later. Possibly native of Aquinum. Wrote his *Satires* under Trajan and Hadrian. May have been wealthy; does not mention a patron. Accounts of his army career and exile by Domitian have no foundation. Mentioned by Martial, and was acquainted with him, otherwise not well-known in his own lifetime. *Died after AD 130.*

PUBLICATIONS

Works

[Satires], edited by A.E. Housman. 1931; also edited by W.V. Clausen (with satires by Persius), 1959, revised edi-

tion, 1992, J.D. Duff, 1970, and John Ferguson (with commentary), 1979; 1, 3, and 10 edited by Niall Rudd and Edward Courtney, 1977; edited and translated by G.G. Ramsey [Loeb Edition], 1918, revised edition, 1940; translated by John Dryden and others, 1735, reprinted 1979; also translated by T. Sheridan, 1739; Edward Owen, 2 vols., 1785; F. Hodgson, 1807; Charles Badham, 1814; James Sinclair, 1814; Lewis Evans, 1848; T.J. Arnold and R. Mongan, 1889; W. Gifford, 1906; Rolfe Humphries, 1958; Hubert Creekmore, 1963; Jerome Mazzaro, 1965; Peter Green, 1967; Charles Plumb, 1968; Steven Robinson, 1983; Niall Rudd, 1991; *13 Satires*, translated by J.E.B. Mayor, 1872–78; also translated by H.A. Strong and A. Leeper, 1882; Sidney G. Owen, 1903; commentary by J.E.B. Mayor (omits 2, 6, and 9), 2 vols., 1880–81, and J.D. Duff, 1898 (omits 2, 9, and selected passages).

*

Critical Studies: *The Grand Style in the Satires of Juvenal* by I.G. Smith, 1927; *Juvenal the Satirist*, 1954, and *The Anatomy of Satire*, 1962, both by Gilbert Highet; *Post-Augustan Poetry from Seneca to Juvenal* by Harold E. Butler, 1977; *Irony in Juvenal* by Alba Claudia Romano, 1979; *A Study of Juvenal's Tenth Satire* by E. Tengström, 1980; *Essays on Roman Satire* by William S. Anderson, 1982; *Three Classical Poets: Sappho, Catullus, and Juvenal* by Richard Jenkyns, 1982; *The Persona in Three Satires of Juvenal* by Martin M. Winkler, 1983; *Themes in Roman Satire* by Niall Rudd, 1986; *Juvenal and Boileau* by Robert C. Colton, 1987; *A Prosopography to the Poems of Juvenal* by John Ferguson, 1987; *The Imperial Muse: To Juvenal Through Ovid: Ramus Essays on Roman Literature of the Empire* edited by A.J. Boyle, 1988; *Beyond Anger: A Study of Juvenal's Third Book of Satires* by S.H. Braund, 1988; *The Satiric Voice: Program, Form and Meaning in Persius and Juvenal* by William Thomas Wehrle, 1992.

*   *   *

Juvenal's entire *oeuvre* comprises 16 Satires in hexameters. They were published in five separate books during the reigns of the emperors Trajan and Hadrian.

In his first book (Satires 1–5) Juvenal adopts an indignant *persona*, following the convention of using a first-person mouthpiece expressing views not necessarily attributable to the poet himself. The angry man whose voice we hear in Book I was a type familiar to the Romans from philosophical works, for example, those of Seneca. As suits the angry man, the poems have the appearance of being a jumbled and excited outburst. Yet there is order behind the façade of disorder: Juvenal has arranged the poems in an alternating sequence featuring the patron-client relationship perverted by mercenary preoccupations (Satires 1, 3, and 5) and the corrupt nobility as a canker at the heart of Roman society (Satires 2 and 4). The satiric technique invites us to agree with the angry rantings *and* to ridicule the angry man for his narrow-minded, petty, and vicious obsessions. The high epic tone adopted ought to dignify the attack on society but the intrusion of mundane and crude words and ideas deflates the pretensions of the angry *persona*. The 'angry' approach proved to be Juvenal's most important legacy to, and influence on, later European satire.

The angry stance is maintained in Book II (Satire 6), a huge attack of epic proportions and unparalleled length in Roman satire on women, couched as a dissuasion from marriage. The angry man reveals himself as utterly unreasonable (e.g., he cannot stand even a perfect woman!) and hence absurd.

Juvenal has now exhausted the 'angry' approach and in his remaining three books he adopts an ironic and detached *persona*. In the three poems of Book III Juvenal applies this new approach to the main themes of Book I, patrons and clients (Satires 7 and 9) and the nobility (Satire 8).

The poems of Books IV and V feature a wide variety of topics: men's prayers (Satire 10), a simple meal (Satire 11), true and false friendship (Satire 12); anger and vengeance (Satire 13), parents' bad examples to their children (Satire 14), the quality of humanness (Satire 15), the advantages of the soldier's life (Satire 16, incomplete). These poems are reminiscent of Horace's satire, sharing his interest in friendship and moderation and his double-edged ironic approach. At the same time, Juvenal's abandonment of the early angry *persona* emerges clearly from Satire 13 where anger is explicitly condemned.

Complementing the variety of the *Satires*, there are characteristic features present throughout Juvenal's work. The *Satires* constantly reflect the rhetorical nature of Roman education. Rhetoric is Juvenal's idiom which he exploits brilliantly to produce many memorable epigrammatic phrases. He is clearly steeped in Roman literature: the poems are packed with literary allusions, and throughout Juvenal shows his debt to his predecessors in the genre, Lucilius, Horace, and Persius. In every poem, Juvenal's powers of vivid visualization are evident. He prefers to depict vice in the concrete rather than the abstract, ranging from brief vignettes of crooks or perverts sumptuously dressed to extended descriptions, for example of a subhuman act of cannibalism.

Finally, Juvenal's essential satiric technique may perhaps be encapsulated in the word 'surprise'. Throughout his poems, Juvenal springs on his audience surprise after surprise, revealing his great fund of wit and humour. On a large scale, it is impossible to predict the direction or proportions of a poem: Juvenal often links two unconnected topics to create surprise. On a smaller scale, he often saves for the end of a section or sentence or line an unexpected word or idea: deflating, pompous, witty, funny, or absurd. Particularly powerful are pithy juxtapositions like 'princess whore' and 'muleteer consul'. All such surprises were highly effective in the original context of oral recitation. In short, Juvenal exemplifies Feinberg's definition of satire as 'the playfully critical distortion of the familiar'.

—S.H. Braund

SATIRE 10
Poem by Juvenal, 1st/2nd century.

From the patchy knowledge we have of Juvenal's life, it is clear that Satire 10 is one of Juvenal's relatively late poetic productions. Both personally and in terms of his satire, Juvenal seems to have settled a little by the time of the writing of Satire 10 and to have discarded some of the rampant fury which characterizes, for example, Book I (Satires 1–5). In many ways it is the maturing process that has gone on over the period between Satire 1 and Satire 10 which makes this work of such value in Juvenal's output; Satire 10 builds upon the assumptions about society which have been worked through in its predecessors, and starts, if hesitantly, to put forward a social and personal ethic, alternative to those which

Juvenal sees and abhors around him and which he attempts to demolish in his satires.

Satire 10 signals the breadth of its targets and its ambition in the great geographical sweep with which it opens, encompassing all known humanity ('from Cadiz to the dawn-streaked shores/of Ganges'; translation here and following from Peter Green). The concerns of this satire are to be wide-ranging and 'universal', in contrast to previous satires which concentrated specifically on such issues as homosexuality, femininity, hypocrisy, and ignorance (all in a Roman context). The early themes tackled here are wealth, glory, and complacency: wealth for the dangers, greed, and self-destruction it brings, complacency in the populus who follow current events only to stay on the winning side and who are willing, quite literally, to put the boot into the corpse of one who was their hero only yesterday.

Watching over Satire 10 is the presence of two philosophers of whom Juvenal says they 'had a point': Democritus and Heraclitus, one 'helpless with laughter', the other 'weeping a fountain'. In citing these two polarities Juvenal has found the perfect expression of the philosophy embodied in the cut of his satire: laughing at the ludicrousness of humanity while at the same time lamenting its folly. When Juvenal talks of the downfall of Sejanus it is with humour at the irreverent treatment meted out to a great statesman and the fickleness of those who quickly say they 'never/Cared for the fellow', but it is also with a sadness at the recognition that such things happen.

There is, however, little of this ambiguity of reception when it comes to one of Juvenal's favourite targets, Hannibal, who rather than making Juvenal weep and laugh, engenders only anger and mocking contempt. For Juvenal, Hannibal is the supreme example of one who placed glory above virtue. In an echo of the opening line (Cadiz to Ganges), Juvenal notes that, for Hannibal, Africa, Spain, the Pyrenees, and Italy were all too small; Hannibal's final goal was Rome, and his defeat and subsequent fate as a 'humble hanger-on' are a delight to Juvenal, who revels in the fact that Hannibal is now only a fit subject 'to thrill young schoolboys/And supply a theme for speech-day recitations!'.

This Hannibal-like hunt for glory at the expense of virtue becomes central to the second half of the satire, as Juvenal works towards establishing a positive ethical basis for his criticism of contemporary society. Glory, while it is most often achieved only with death, is prayed for by those who want it in this life. And here Juvenal turns his satire to the subject of death, as that which 'alone reveals the puny dimensions/of our human frame', in the hope of revealing to humanity the folly of its belief in (temporal) glory. Juvenal is too subtle to dwell at length on the horrors of death. Instead, to emphasize the futility of the desire for 'glory' and temporal (as opposed to universal) virtues, he turns, in great detail, to the horrors of old age, the implicit rhetorical question being, what is the use of glory (or anything) achieved in this life when at the end of it we are faced with the decline that senility brings? For Juvenal, himself very likely approaching his later years when he wrote this satire, old age consists of many, mostly physical, symptoms of decline: wrinkles, toothlessness, lameness, dripping nose, trembling voice, impotence, deafness, blindness, sciatica, loss of appetite, and 'diseases of every type'. Even if one were to survive reasonably intact bodily and mentally, Juvenal points out, the aged are left with the ordeal of burying both their own generation and their sons and daughters; here he produces examples of unhappy old men, such as Nestor, Peleus, and Paris.

Having constructed such a diabolical picture of what old age holds for humanity, Juvenal then flushes out those who might seek comfort in youthful looks or intelligence. In his inimitable way he produces a string of examples of those whose wit and eloquence have been their downfall, while he counters the attraction of young physicality by noting how apparently inevitably the young become sexually corrupted and embroiled in adulterous relationships.

Finally, and as the logical outcome of the disillusioning of what he sees as human presumptions, Juvenal asks, 'Is there nothing worth praying for, then?'. For Juvenal, prayer itself is a pointless exercise. 'Fortune', he says, 'has no divinity', and it is humanity alone which creates such a divinity. What we must live by, according to Juvenal, is 'virtue'. While Juvenal never goes to any lengths to establish what his concept of virtue entails, we are very sure by the end of Satire 10 what 'virtue' is not and what it is opposed to. This in itself, coupled with the wedding of the dichotomous Democritus and Heraclitus, is a step closer towards the establishment of a positive social and personal ethos in Juvenal than many commentators allow. And it is this reversion to a positive ethos which makes Satire 10 the most central and crucial of works in Juvenal's *oeuvre*.

—Colin Graham

———————

K

KABĪR. Born in Varanasi Benares, Uttar Pradesh, India, 1398 (some sources give c.1440). Probably brought up by Muslim foster parents in a poor weaver's family. Probably a devotee of Rām, and a preacher; influenced by Hindu and Muslim ideas, and Sufi mysticism. Exiled from Benares by the Muslim emperor, Sikandar Lōdī. Wrote devotional (*bhakti*) poetry, mainly in a Hindi dialect. His major texts exist in three major regional variants (recensions): Eastern (the *Bījak*), Rajasthani (*Kābir-Granthāvalī*), and Punjabi with Hindi (contained in the *Adi Granth*). *Died in 1448 (some sources give 1518).*

PUBLICATIONS

Verse

Bījak [Account]. 1868; 1872 (with 'Trijya' commentary); edited by Prem Chand, 1890; also edited by Bābā Puran Dās, 1905, Ahmed Shah, 1911, Vicardas Shastri, 1926, Hamsdas Shastri and Mahabir Prasad ('standard' edition), 1950, and Shukdev Singh (critical edition), 1972; as *Bijak Satguru Kabīr Sāhab Kā*, 1982; as *Bijaka* (Hindi text, English commentary), 1987; as *Bijak*, translated by Prem Chand, 1911; also translated by Ahmad Shah, 1917; Linda Hess and Shukdev Singh, 1983; as *Kabir*, translated by S.H. Jhabvala, 1955.
The Adi Granth (including Kabīr's Punjabi/Hindi verse), translated by E. Trumpp. 1877.
Granthāvalī [Complete Works]. Edited by S.S. Das, 3 vols., 1928; also edited by P.N. Tiwari, 1961, M.P. Gupta, 1969, and Dr Syamasundravadasa, 1976; as *Kabir*, translated by Charlotte Vaudeville, 1974.
One Hundred Poems of Kabir, translated by Rabindranath Tagore, with Evelyn Underhill. 1914.
Kabīr the Great Mystic (selection), translated by Isaac A. Exekiel. 1966.
Couplets from Kabir (bilingual edition), translated by G.N. Das. 1991.
Songs of Kabir from the Adi Granth, translated by Nirmal Dass. 1991.
Love Songs of Kabir (bilingual edition), translated by G.N. Das. 1992.

Other

The Sayings of Kabir, edited and translated by Lala Kannoo Mal. 1923.

*

Critical Studies: *Kabir and the Kabir Panth* by George H. Westcott, 1907, reprinted 1974; *A History of Hindi Literature*, 1920, and *Kabir and His Followers*, 1931, both by Frank E. Keay; *Kabir* (includes translations) by Charlotte Vaudeville, 1974; *Kabir, the Apostle of Hindu-Muslim Unity* (with bibliography) by M. Hedayetullah, 1977; *Kabir's Mythology: The Religious Perceptions, Doctrines and Practices of a Medieval Saint*, 1985.

* * *

Kabīr is perhaps the most representative figure of the monotheistic movement that characterized 15th-century India. According to legend, he was the son of a widowed Brahmin woman who abandoned him. Although he seems to have been adopted by a Muslim weaver, he later became the greatest of the disciples of the Vaiṣṇava *bhakti* teacher Rāmānanda.

Kabīr's fame led to many legends, but unfortunately we lack reliable information about his life. Whether he was a Muslim or not, the influence of the Islamic doctrine in his sayings is undeniable. He calls himself 'the son of Allah and Rāma', and his poetry shows an influence of the Vedantic doctrine; but his rejection of most Hindu rituals and Muslim traditions caused the hatred of the most conservative sector of the Indian society, the Brahmanic caste, as well as that of the Muslims. He is said to have been persecuted by the Muslim Emperor Sikandar Lōdī, who exiled him from Benares. All these events earned him the reputation of a bold social reformer, and his impact on the masses of Northern India was profound. Further evidence of Kabīr's influence is found in the Kabīrpanthīs, the religious sect whose members claim to be the followers of Kabīr's teaching and preserve the poems and sayings attributed to him.

Although a large number of works have been attributed to Kabīr, there is no certainty about the authorship of many of them. Kabīr's humble origin and the decisive aversion for the written word that we see in his poems may be an indication of his illiteracy. Therefore, and although there is no conclusive evidence, we may assume that his poems were written by his disciples. Kabīr's verses are found in four compilations. The *Bījak* [Account] was the first of Kabīr's works to attract the attention of Western scholars. The members of the Kabīrpanth compiled this book after the death of Kabīr, and considered it the most important and most representative of his doctrine. The *Granth* [Book], compiled at the beginning of the 17th century, became the sacred book of the Sikh religion. A large number of poems traditionally attributed to Kabīr are also found in the *Pamcvānīs*, a collection of sayings of the 'five saints'. The five saints or '*dādū-panthīs*' are the followers of a Muslim cotton-cleaner, Dādū Dayāl, who seems to owe his inspiration to the teaching of Kabīr. Finally, the *Sarbangī* is the work of Rajjab, Dādū Dayāl's most distinguished disciple. It contains an important collection of Kabīr's verses, but unfortunately it has never been published.

Kabīr may have spoken the old Avadhi dialect of Hindi, but his poems are chiefly preserved in mixed dialect. They are characterized by an extraordinary vigour; yet they are often rough and unpolished. The absence of any kind of literary ornament in Kabīr's poetry proves his contempt for the sacred Brahmanic language. The metrical forms in his poems, *dohās* and *padas*, are popular in origin. The *dohās* were lyrical compositions in popular dialects, which the common people used to sing or quote; the *padas* were short, rhymed poems, originally folk-songs adapted to religious purposes. In the *Granth* collection the lyrical compositions are called *saloku* (Sanskrit *śloka*, verse); elsewhere, they are called (*sākhīs* or witnesses): they are pithy utterances, 'witnesses' of the ultimate truth. All the main compilations of Kabīr's poems contain a large number of these pithy utterances; but he also makes use of a variety of metres. Although his verses contain numerous allusions to the common realities of daily life, the use of the Tantric language and symbols often render his poetry obscure. This deliberate contrast, and the simultaneous use of Hindu and Muslim references and vocabulary, is the result of his bitter irony, a proof of his sarcastic irreverence to traditional formalism as well as to Islamic and Hindu beliefs.

Kabīr's poems convey the spiritual turmoil that pervaded Northern India in the 15th century. This turmoil began to take place two centuries before, both in the Deccan and in Northern India, and coincided with the permanent establishment of Muslim domination in the subcontinent. The 15th century is also the period in which the modern vernaculars of India were taking shape, so it is not strange to see that Kabīr's language and style has played such an important role in the development of Hindi. Kabīr's monotheism was part of the religious revival which found manifestation in the cult of popular divinities such as Rāma and Kṛṣṇa, and all these religious movements used the vernacular for their literature. Kabīr's poetry evidently denounces the rigidity of the Hindu social system. However, his debt to Hindu tradition is undeniable, not only in the numerous allusions to Brahma or to Rāma, but also in the importance attached to the guru or spiritual leader, and particularly to the relationship between the guru and his disciple. Moreover, despite his attacks on the bigotry of Muslims, he was obviously influenced by Islamic monotheism as well as by the eclectic mysticism of Sufis.

Kabīr reflects the efforts of a number of religious movements in Northern India to advocate tolerance and unity. But his role as a unifier of the two conflicting religions, Islam and Hinduism, makes him appear as a holy man who stands alone. On the one hand, Kabīr voiced the aspirations of the common people; on the other, he was considered a danger both by Hindus and by Muslims for the vehemence with which he attacks their beliefs. Kabīr is conscious of the contradictions that he incurred, and his poetry can be read as a means of justifying the confrontation with society and with himself. He, 'the slave of the spirit of the quest', as he calls himself in one of the poems translated by Tagore, confesses that 'the true path is rarely found', and this is perhaps the principal message that the poet has left to posterity.

—Ana M. Ranero

KAFKA, Franz. Born in Prague, Austro-Hungarian Empire (now Czech Republic), 3 July 1883. Educated at Staatsgymnasium, Prague, 1893–1902; studied jurisprudence at Karl Ferdinand University, Prague, 1901–06; qualified in law, 1907; unpaid work in law courts, 1906–07. Engaged to Felice Bauer twice but never married. Worked for Assicurazioni Generali insurance company, 1907–08;

Workers Accident Insurance Institute, 1908–22: developed tuberculosis, 1917, confined to a sanatorium, 1920–21, retired because of ill health. *Died 3 June 1924.*

PUBLICATIONS

Collections

Gesammelte Werke, edited by Max Brod and others. 11 vols., 1950— .
Sämtliche Erzählungen, edited by Paul Raabe. 1970.
Complete Stories, edited by Nahum N. Glatzer. 1971.
Shorter Works, edited and translated by Malcolm Pasley. 1973.
The Complete Novels, translated by Edwin and Willa Muir. 1983.
Schriften, Tagebücher, Briefe, edited by Nahum N. Glatzer and others. 1983— .
Collected Stories, edited by Gabriel Josipovici, translated by Edwin Muir. 1993.

Fiction

Betrachtung. 1913.
Der Heizer: ein Fragment. 1913.
Die Verwandlung. 1915; edited by Peter Hutchinson and Michael Minden, 1985; as *The Metamorphosis*, translated by A.L. Lloyd, 1937; also edited and translated by Stanley Corngold, 1972.
Das Urteil. 1916.
In der Strafkolonie. 1919; as *In the Penal Settlement: Tales and Short Prose Works*, translated by Ernst Kaiser and Eithne Wilkins, 1949.
Ein Landarzt. 1919.
Ein Hungerkünstler (stories). 1924.
Der Prozess. 1925; edited by Malcolm Pasley, 1990; as *The Trial*, translated by Edwin and Willa Muir, 1937, revised edition, 1956; also translated by Douglas Scott and Chris Waller, 1977.
Das Schloss. 1926; as *The Castle*, translated by Edwin and Willa Muir, 1930; revised edition, 1953.
Amerika. 1927; original version, as *Der Verschollene*, edited by Jost Schillemeit, 1983; as *America*, translated by Edwin and Willa Muir, 1938.
Beim Bau der chinesischen Mauer. 1931; as *The Great Wall of China, and Other Pieces*, translated by Edwin and Willa Muir, 1933.
Parables in German and English, translated by Edwin and Willa Muir. 1947.
The Penal Colony, Stories and Short Pieces, translated by Edwin and Willa Muir. 1948.
Wedding Preparations in the Country and Other Stories, translated by Ernst Kaiser and Eithne Wilkins. 1953.
Dearest Father: Stories and Other Writings, translated by Ernst Kaiser and Eithne Wilkins. 1954.
Metamorphosis and Other Stories, translated by Edwin and Willa Muir. 1961.
Parables and Paradoxes: Parabeln und Paradoxe (bilingual edition). 1961.
Description of a Struggle and Other Stories, translated by Willa Muir and others. 1979.
Stories 1904–1924, translated by J.A. Underwood. 1981.
The Transformation and Other Stories, edited and translated by Malcolm Pasley. 1992.
Selected Stories, translated by Edwin and Willa Muir. 1994.

Other

Tagebücher 1910–23. 1951; edited by Hans Gerd Koch, Michael Müller, and Malcolm Pasley, 1990; as *Diaries, 1919–1923*, edited by Max Brod, translated by Joseph Kresh, 1948; *Diaries, 1914–1923*, translated by Martin Greenberg, 1949.

Briefe an Milena, edited by Willy Haas. 1952; revised edition by Jürgen Born and Michael Müller, 1983; as *Letters to Milena*, translated by Tania and James Stern, 1953; also translated by Philip Boehm, 1990.

Briefe 1902–24, edited by Max Brod. 1958; as *Letters to Friends, Family and Editors*, translated by Richard and Clara Winston, 1977.

Briefe an Felice, edited by Erich Heller and Jürgen Born. 1967; as *Letters to Felice*, translated by James Stern and Elisabeth Duckworth, 1973.

Briefe an Ottla und die Familie, edited by Klaus Wagenbach and Hartmut Binder. 1974; as *Letters to Ottla and the Family*, translated by Richard and Clara Winston, 1982.

Max Brod, Franz Kafka: Ein Freundschaft. 2 vols., 1987–1989.

Briefe an die Eltern aus den Jahren 1922–1924, edited by Josef Čermăk and Martin Svatos. 1990.

*

Bibliography: *Franz Kafka: Eine Bibliographie* by Rudolph Hemmerle, 1958; *A Kafka Bibliography 1908–76* by Angel Flores, 1976; *Franz Kafkas Werke: Eine Bibliographie der Primärliteratur (1908–1980)* by Maria Luise Caputo-Mayr and Julius M. Herz, 1982; *Franz Kafka: Die Veröffentlichungen zu seinen Lebzeiten (1908–1924): Eine textkritische und kommentierte Bibliographie* by Ludwig Dietz, 1982.

Critical Studies: *The Kafka Problem*, 1946, and *The Kafka Debate: New Perspectives for Our Time*, 1977, both edited by Angel Flores; *Franz Kafka: A Biography* by Max Brod, 1947; *Kafka's Castle*, 1956, and *Franz Kafka*, 1973, both by Ronald Gray, and *Kafka: A Collection of Critical Essays* edited by Gray, 1962; *Franz Kafka: Parable and Paradox* by Heinz Politzer, 1962; *Franz Kafka* by Erich Heller, 1964; *Franz Kafka* by Walter H. Sokel, 1966; *The Reluctant Pessimist: A Study of Franz Kafka* by A.P. Foulkes, 1967; *The Process of Kafka's 'Trial'* by Adrian Jaffe, 1967; *Franz Kafka: A Critical Study of His Writings* by Wilhelm Emrich, translated by Sheema Zeben Buehne, 1968; *The Terror of Art: Kafka and Modern Literature* by Martin Greenberg, 1968; *Dreams, Life, and Literature: A Study of Franz Kafka* by Curtis S. Hall and Richard E. Lind, 1970; *Kafka and the Yiddish Theater: Its Impact on His Work* by Evelyn Torton Beck, 1971; *Kafka and Prague*, by Johann Bauer, translated by P.S. Falla, 1971; *Conversations with Kafka* by Gustav Janouch, translated by Goronwy Rees, 2nd edition, 1971; *Kafka and Anarchism* by Mijal Levi, 1972; *Kafka: A Study* by Anthony Thorlby, 1972; *The Commentator's Despair: The Interpretation of Kafka's 'Metamorphosis'*, 1973, and *Franz Kafka: The Necessity of Form*, 1988, both Stanley Corngold; *On Kafka's 'Castle': A Study* by Richard Sheppard, 1973; *Moment of Torment: An Interpretation of Franz Kafka's Short Stories* by Ruth Tiefenbrun, 1973; *Kafka's Other Trial* by Elias Canetti, 1974; *Franz Kafka: A Collection of Criticism* edited by Leo Hamalian, 1974; *Franz Kafka: Literature as Corrective Punishment* by Franz Kuna, 1974, and *On Kafka: Semi-Centenary Perspectives* edited by Kuna, 1976; *Kafka's Narrative Theatre* by James Rolleston, 1974; *Kafka in Context* by John Hibberd, 1975; *Kafka's 'Trial': The Case Against Josef K.* by Eric Marson, 1975; *Gesture as a Stylistic Device in Kleist's 'Michael Kohlhaas' and Kafka's 'Der Prozess'* by David E. Smith, 1976; *Franz Kafka* by Meno Spann, 1976; *A Complete Contextual Concordance to Franz Kafka's 'Der Prozess'* by Walter H. Speidel, 1978; *Kafka's Doubles* by Kurt J. Flickert, 1979; *Franz Kafka: Geometrician of Metaphor* by Henry Sussman, 1979; *The Secret Raven: Conflict and Transformation in the Life of Franz Kafka* by Daryl Sharp, 1980; *The World of Franz Kafka* edited by J.P. Stern, 1980, and *Franz Kafka Symposium: Paths and Labyrinths* edited by Stern and J.J. White, 1985; *K: A Biography of Kafka* by Ronald Hayman, 1981; *Kafka: Geometrician of Metaphor* by Henry Sussman, 1981; *Kafka's Narrators: A Study of His Stories and Sketches* by Roy Pascal, 1982; *Franz Kafka of Prague* by Jiřĕí Gruša, 1983; *The Nightmare of Reason: A Life of Franz Kafka* by Ernst Pawel, 1984; *Kafka: Judaism, Politics, and Literature* by Ritchie Robertson, 1985; *Kafka's 'Landarzt' Collection: Rhetoric and Interpretation* by Gregory B. Triffitt, 1985; *Franz Kafka*, 1986, *Frank Kafka's The Trial*, 1987, *Franz Kafka's The Castle*, 1988, and *Franz Kafka's The Metamorphosis*, 1988, all edited by Harold Bloom; *Sympathy for the Abyss: A Study in the Novel of German Modernism: Kafka, Broch, Musil and Thomas Mann* by Stephen D. Dowden, 1986; *The Loves of Franz Kafka* by Nahum N. Glatzer, 1986; *Franz Kafka's Use of Law in Fiction: A New Interpretation of In der Strafkolonie, Der Prozess and Das Schloss* by Lida Kirchberger, 1986; *Outside Humanity: A Study of Kafka's Fiction* by Ramón G. Mendoza, 1986; *As Lonely as Franz Kafka* by Marthe Robert, translated by Ralph Manheim, 1986; *Kafka's Contextuality*, 1986, and *Kafka and the Contemporary Critical Performance: Centenary Readings*, 1987, both edited by Alan Udoff; *Franz Kafka (1883–1983): His Craft and Thought* edited by Roman Struc and J.C. Yardley, 1986; *The Dove and the Mole: Kafka's Journey into Darkness and Creativity* edited by Ronald Gottesman and Moshe Lazar, 1987; *Kafka's Prussian Advocate: A Study of the Influence of Heinrich von Kleist on Franz Kafka* by John M. Grandin, 1987; *Constructive Destruction: Kafka's Aphorisms* by Richard T. Gray, 1987; *The Jewish Mystic in Kafka* by Jean Jofen, 1987; *On the Threshold of the New Kabbalah: Kafka's Later Tales* by Walter A. Strauss, 1988; *Reading Kafka: Prague, Politics and the fin de siècle* edited by Mark Anderson, 1989, and *Kafka's Clothes: Ornament and Aestheticism in the Habsburg fin de siècle* by Anderson, 1992; *Kafka's Rhetoric: The Passion of Reading* by Clayton Koelb, 1989; *A Hesitation Before Birth: The Life of Franz Kafka* by Peter Mailloux, 1989; *After Kafka: The Influence of Kafka's Fiction* by Shimon Sandbank, 1989; *Kafka* by Pietro Citati, 1990; *Necessary Angels: Tradition and Modernity in Kafka, Benjamin and Scholem* by Robert Alter, 1991; *Kafka and Language: In the Stream of Thoughts and Life* by Gabriele von Natamer Cooper, 1991; *Someone Like K: Kafka's Novels* by Herbert Kraft, translated by R.J. Kavanagh, 1991; *The Landscape of Alienation: Ideological Subversion in Kafka, Céline and Onetti* by Jack Murray, 1991; *Kafka's Relatives: Their Lives and His Writing* by Anthony Northey, 1991; *A Life Study of Franz Kafka* by Ronald Gestwicki, 1992; *Franz Kafka: Representative Man* by Frederick Karl, 1993.

*   *   *

If one were to judge the worth of an author solely according to the amount of critical commentary which his works have generated, then there is no doubt that Franz Kafka has already earned his place beside Shakespeare, Goethe, and Cervantes. The primary attraction and challenge for the critic lie in the strange and enigmatic quality of the fiction, its disturbing capacity to invite and yet to resist interpretation, and at the same time the intuitive belief of many readers that they are being addressed by a writer who has managed to capture in words the very essence of 20th-century experience and angst. Kafka's stories, moreover, possess a degree of semantic openness which makes it possible to re-express many of his narrated scenes and images within the interpretative schemes which have come to dominate modern thought, be they derived from political systems, theological concerns, psychoanalysis, or philosophy. Nor is it difficult, once such an interpretation has been put forward, to 'corroborate' it by referring to events in the author's life or indeed to more general cultural factors which helped shape early 20th-century views of the individual's relationship to society, to his own unconscious self, or to the Divine. And finally, the lack of specificity characteristic of Kafka's fiction can be resolved into conceptual systems derived from the author's non-fiction writings, for the critic has at his disposal a considerable collection of posthumously published letters, diaries, fragments, and conversations.

There is some evidence, when we consider Kafka's work in its chronological entirety, that the author was increasingly concerned to forestall the kind of criticism which might attempt to view his fictional creations as referring in a straightforward way to events, localities, or people outside the narratives. In the three novels this process is apparent in the progressive disappearance of all references to actual topographical entities as well as in the names of the three main protagonists, Karl Rossmann, Josef K., and K. Some of the later short stories, told through the first-person mental associations of shadowy animal narrators, carry this stylistic device to the point that the reader is deprived of almost any familiar landmark which might indicate a concealed meaning waiting to be discovered.

Kafka's earliest novel *Amerika* (*America*), first published in 1927, has attracted less critical attention than his later works, and is regarded by some as an only partially successful attempt to satirize the institutions of the New World by recounting them from the perspective of Karl Rossmann, a young European who has been packed off to America by his parents after he is seduced by a servant girl. The bizarre adventures which befall Karl certainly possess a Chaplin-like quality, and significantly they provide us with one of Kafka's few overt examples of social criticism, for the episodic narrative is a reversal of the Horatio Alger, poor-boy-makes-good myth; Karl, despite his unfailing optimism and his determination to succeed, is slowly destroyed by the very system of values in which he has faith. The novel is fragmentary and unfinished, and a final interpretation would have to speculate on the possible ending. Max Brod, Kafka's biographer and confidant, insisted that the novel was to end 'on a note of reconciliation', but this is thrown into doubt by a diary entry (30 September 1915) in which Kafka stated that the 'innocent' Rossmann, just like the 'guilty' K., was to meet his death.

Der Prozess and *Das Schloss*, translated respectively as *The Trial* and *The Castle*, are also fragmentary, and *The Castle*, like *America*, remained without an ending. The two later novels have in common a number of thematic similarities, and to a much greater extent than *America* they portray the singular and oppressive dreamlike sequences which have enriched many of the world's languages with the phrase 'it's like something out of Kafka'. Reflecting the two sides of Kafka's aphorism, according to which, 'He who seeks, will not find; he who does not seek will be found', the two novels suggest the existence of aloof and inscrutable authorities which can reach out to destroy, as in *The Trial*, or which will withdraw into a state of total inaccessibility as in *The Castle*. In each case the authorities are represented by a lower hierarchy of pompous officials and libertine servants, and they have additionally given rise to a vast body of anecdotal and superstitious lore designed to divine their intentions in order that one may either cooperate with them or thwart their will. The diversity of opinion typical of Kafka interpretation is strikingly evident in the interpretations of these two novels. They have been seen as the vain struggle of the individual seeking to comprehend the faceless bureaucracies which govern him, as depictions of the alienated Jew in a hostile Christian world, as grotesque fictive transmutations of Kafka's obsession with his father's power, and as parables on humanity's eternal but fruitless striving for the Absolute. Before embracing any one of these interpretations, the reader might do well to heed the words of advice offered to Josef K. by the prison chaplain in *The Trial*: 'You mustn't pay too much attention to opinions. The words are unchangeable, and the opinions are often just an expression of despair about that'.

According to Max Brod, Kafka 'thought in pictures and he spoke in pictures'. This tendency to pictorialize inner thoughts and feelings, to lend visual form to the subjective and the abstract, is a feature which Kafka's writings share with dreams, and it can be seen as one of the guiding structural principles of the short stories and of the literary experimentation published in the volume *Wedding Preparations in the Country*. On the surface Kafka's short pieces treat a remarkable variety of themes and situations, including the father-son conflict in 'The Judgement', the transformation of a commercial traveller into a monstrous insect in *Die Verwandlung* (*The Metamorphosis*), the horrifying method of execution described in *In der Strafkolonie* (*In the Penal Colony*), and the self-imposed death by starvation depicted in 'A Hunger Artist'. There are stories narrated both by and about animals, and pieces concerning themselves with circus riders, country doctors, mysterious hunters, Ulysses, and the Emperor of China. A unifying stylistic factor behind this thematic diversity is the fact that each story can be interpreted as the manifest portrayal of certain inner experiences and states of mind which recur constantly in Kafka's fiction. This does not mean of course that the stories should be regarded simply as variations to be reduced to the same theme, for each work contributes uniquely through its imagery and structure to the thematic aspect which it embodies. Nor should it be forgotten that the fiction, even though Kafka himself once described it as 'the representation of my inner life', has been received as significant and compelling by countless readers who have related it to their own experience of the 20th century.

—A.P. Foulkes

THE CASTLE (Das Schloss)
Novel by Franz Kafka, 1926 (written 1922).

The protagonist of *The Castle*, called simply K., arrives late one evening in a village and finds shelter in an inn. He is awakened by an official and told that he needs permission from the castle to stay there. K.'s response is: 'What village is this I have wandered into? Is there a castle here?' But he then asserts that he is a land surveyor who has been appointed by the castle. When the official calls the castle he is informed that no such appointment has been made, but almost immediately a call back from the castle reverses this and appears to confirm K.'s claim. K.'s reaction is surprising: 'That was unpropitious for him, on the one hand, for it meant that the castle was well informed about him . . . and was taking up the challenge with a smile'.

This opening establishes a fundamental ambiguity in the relationship between K. and the castle. It is never clear whether K. has really been summoned by the castle or whether he invents the story to try to justify his presence. In either case his purpose is to penetrate into the castle and to obtain absolute confirmation of the position he claims for himself.

The image of the castle dominates the novel. The actual building is ramshackle and dilapidated and is frequently shrouded in darkness. It houses a vast hierarchy of officials who are constantly engaged in frenetic bureaucratic activity, all to no apparent purpose. They are obscene and immoral, regarding the women of the village as their rightful prey while the village sees it as the highest honour for a woman to be the mistress of an official. The castle has absolute dominion over the village. The villagers treat it with awe, devotion, and obedience. To them it is omnipotent and infallible. It seems to assume the qualities which they project onto it.

So, too, it is with K. For him it has a dual aspect: it is both an enemy with which he enters into a desperate struggle and a goal which contains the certainty for which he yearns. K. is brash, arrogant, and aggressive, totally confident of achieving his aim. On his first day he sets out to reach the castle on foot but although it is visible, he can find no road that leads to it. Finally, he gives up in exhaustion. The rest of the novel consists of a series of unsuccessful manoeuvres by K. to make contact with the castle. He focuses his attention on the official Klamm who has special responsibility for village affairs. Klamm embodies a peculiar quality of the castle itself; everyone who sees him has a different version of his appearance. Like the castle he seems to reflect back people's assumptions about him. K. now identifies Klamm as the means of reaching the castle but he tries in vain to see him. Eventually he lies in wait for him in the inn yard, but a servant comes out to tell him that Klamm will not emerge as long as K. is there. K. feels that this is a kind of victory he has won over Klamm, but he is simultaneously aware that it is an entirely futile victory.

From this point K.'s attitude gradually changes. It is significantly affected by the story of the Barnabas family which occupies a key place in the text. He hears the story from Barnabas's sister Olga who describes how their sister Amalia had one night received a peremptory summons from a castle official demanding that she come to him in the inn. Amalia had torn up the message and thrown it in the messenger's face. Thereafter they have been shunned by the village and their business has collapsed. Amalia has withdrawn into herself and devoted her time caring for their ailing parents. Yet Olga insists that there is no direct evidence that the castle is responsible for their plight; rather their condition is a consequence of their own assumption of guilt because of Amalia's disobedience. Olga tells K. that she would have obeyed such a summons and argues that, despite appearances, the official might well have been in love with her sister. To placate the castle Olga now prostitutes herself with the castle servants to atone for the supposed insult to the messenger while, for the same reason, Barnabas has waited in the castle for years to offer his own services as a messenger. The first message he has been given is a cryptic one to K. which, it transpires, might never have been meant for K. at all. K. sees Barnabas as another possible lead to the castle, while Barnabas tries to interpret his service to K. as a sign of favour from the castle. There is a cruel irony in their relationship. They mirror each other's hopes, but there is no sign that either can provide the other with what he desires. Olga's tale nevertheless contributes to a shift in K.'s outlook. At first he sympathizes with Amalia and condemns the castle, but by the end he is much closer to sharing Olga's attitude. His earlier suspicion of the castle starts to give way to an acceptance of its potential benevolence.

K. grows ever more weary but pursues his quest until he stumbles by chance into the bedroom of yet another official who tells K. that, if an official is taken unawares in the night, he will answer all the intruder's questions and give him all the assistance he requests. This is precisely the situation in which K. now finds himself. In a moment of unforeseen revelation, the way to his goal stands open and he falls asleep. This episode encapsulates the central ambiguity of the narrative. K. may be so worn out by his struggle that he is incapable of seizing his opportunity when it presents itself. Alternatively, he may have overcome his arrogance and recognized his human limitations. Both these interpretations are permitted by the text.

Soon afterwards the manuscript breaks off. We have the testimony of Max Brod, Kafka's friend and literary executor, that Kafka had told him that K., on his death-bed, was to receive word from the castle: 'that though K.'s legal claim to live in the village was not valid . . . he was to be permitted to live and work there'. The fact that Kafka never wrote this ending is entirely appropriate. Far from being inconclusive the novel's open-endedness precisely expresses a quintessential quality of Kafka's work. The castle contains an unfathomable bureaucratic authority but, at the same time, the text repeatedly insinuates that it is the seat of some transcendental principle. However, the nature of this principle is not spelled out. It might equally well be argued that it is the principle of divine truth or the principle of evil and negation. The ultimate mystery at the heart of the castle remains a mystery; neither K., nor the reader, can ever know the unknowable.

—B. Ashbrook

THE METAMORPHOSIS (Die Verwandlung)
Novella by Franz Kafka, 1915.

The Metamorphosis, which tells of how a young man, Gregor Samsa, wakes to find himself transformed into a horrid beetle-like creature, is quintessential Kafka and deservedly the most famous of his works. Written during Kafka's first period of intense creative activity in late 1912, it was one of the few pieces published during his lifetime.

The basis of the short story can be found in the author's tense relations with his father, his sense of isolation, failure and guilt, but also of unjust rejection. The role of Gregor's sister Grete, too, can be related to Kafka's feeling of betrayal by his sister Ottla, the one member of his family in whom he believed he had an ally. Despairing of his ability to write, he noted that he was good only to be swept up with the household rubbish, and that is the fate of his hero. Kafka senior had called his son's friend, a Yiddish actor, a flea-ridden dog and a vermin. It was a condemnation which the writer believed extended to himself. In the story the disgusting verminous creature of the metaphor becomes flesh. Kafka explores the narrative possibilities that emerge from taking a metaphor literally, and discovers a series of haunting images for his potentially suicidal inner condition. The hero's physical state, the details of his environment and his movements all assume symbolic significance. Because the grotesque fantasy set against a realistic background is like a bad dream, it seems to call for psychoanalytic interpretation and there have been no lack of Freudian commentaries on it, in which an Oedipus complex inevitably provides the focus.

The story concentrates on dramatic confrontations and says as much about family tensions as it does about the psychology of the hero or the author. Understanding between Gregor and his parents and sister, impossible after his physical transformation, was far from perfect before. However, neither that nor any other circumstance is advanced to explain his metamorphosis. Kafka describes its consequences. The family's first reaction of shock and horror becomes one of resigned frustration and finally of relief when Gregor dies. Unable any longer to rely on Gregor as sole breadwinner, his parents find a new sense of strength and purpose within themselves. That development, like Gregor's increasing hopelessness, appears absolutely logical and even inevitable. So, too, does the sister's growth in confidence and responsibility—another metamorphosis, one might say. The brief last scene of spring sunshine, family unity, and hope for the future after Gregor's death contrasts tellingly with the blackness of the preceding episodes. Grete, it is revealed, has ripened as Gregor has wasted away. Life, it seems, triumphs over a useless freak, but *The Metamorphosis* brings no Nietzschean glorification of vital strength. For here the life force is linked with social conformity and insensitivity. Gregor's demise is scarcely a victory for human values. The contrast between the outwardly animal hero and those around him brings some cruel ironies. The existence from which he is excluded hardly seems a desirable one. The three lodgers who, for a time, dominate the Samsa household reveal that conformity can mean loss of individuality. They insist too much on bourgeois values and show no appreciation of Grete's violin playing, which Gregor imagines might furnish the nourishment he cannot otherwise find. Despite strong hints that his attachment to his sister is potentially incestuous, his reaction to the music may be read as a longing for spiritual satisfaction, even redemption, which is absent in the materialist society of which the Samsas are part. His duty to his family has apparently been defined almost exclusively in economic terms. It is possible to account for his alienation as a product of capitalist labour relations which, as Marx argued, dehumanize the worker. Gregor certainly felt that his work as a travelling salesman was a denial of his freedom and dignity.

Yet the story establishes no cause for the hero's condition, nor does it allow a conclusive allocation of blame. It shows that love can scarcely be divorced from possessiveness, or responsibility from tyranny, but that a life without them is a form of living death. The demands of family, society, even of time (Gregor becomes oblivious to the clock and the calendar that once dominated his every moment) seem intolerable and yet to require recognition if the self-esteem of the individual is to be maintained.

The Metamorphosis is told largely from the hero's point of view. It offers no explanations. The dividing line between the third-person narrative and *style indirect libre* is very fluid and the narrator never reveals his identity or standpoint. The result is a remarkably open text which has elicited an immense number of different interpretations. It has been seen as a sadly sick, but more often as an acute, vision of reality. Yet critics have not even agreed whether the story's elusive meaning is essentially psychological, sociological, existential, or religious, and some have argued that it deals with the gulf between art and life or the relation of language to reality. For the text seems to imply much more than it states, to challenge its readers to explore the possible significance of its every

detail, to escape from the hero's perspective in order to appreciate its black humour, and to discover its universal relevance.

It would be wrong, however, to place sole stress on the intellectual challenge of a story whose impact is dramatic and overwhelmingly emotional. Its three carefully paced sections each culminate as Gregor tries to make contact with his family and is met with determined rejection. The repetition lends weight to the impression of tragic inevitability. Its exceptional power to haunt the imagination, together with its undermining of certainties, has earned *The Metamorphosis* its place of prominence in the history of 20th-century world literature.

—John Hibberd

THE TRIAL (Der Prozess)
Novel by Franz Kafka, 1925 (written 1914–15).

The Trial begins with the arrest of Josef K. and ends with his execution. But this is no ordinary arrest, Josef K.'s trial is no ordinary trial, and the court which exercises jurisdiction over him is no ordinary court. His arrest is largely nominal as after being informed of it, Josef K. is allowed to go about his normal business as a senior clerk in a bank. No formal charge is laid against him. The questions which insistently force themselves on the reader are: why has Josef K. been arrested? what has he done wrong? No explicit answer is ever provided.

The emissaries of the court take Josef K. by surprise in his lodgings early in the morning, but they are only menial employees who have no knowledge of the reasons for his being accused. Greedy and corrupt, they eat his breakfast and try to trick him into allowing them to go off with his clothes. The impression they make is consistent with the impression made by the court throughout the novel. The supreme judges are totally inaccessible and such information as Josef K. is able to learn about them indicates that they are vain and capricious. The law books he manages to see are obscene. The principles underlying the law he is assumed to have transgressed are not revealed. One persuasive reading of the novel is to see it as the story of an ordinary man persecuted and destroyed by a powerful bureaucratic tyranny, a prophetic image of the totalitarian systems which were to arise in central Europe after the author's death.

The very first sentence of the novel seems to state Josef K.'s innocence: 'Someone must have been telling lies about Josef K., for without having done anything wrong he was arrested one fine morning.' However, it soon becomes apparent that the events of the story are presented primarily from the perspective of the central character. In other words, this opening assertion reflects Josef K.'s perception of things and is not necessarily that of an objective narrator. Appreciation of the narrative technique is vitally important to a proper appreciation of the work. We see things from Josef K.'s point of view but the story is narrated in the third person. There is, then, a narrator at work in the text who does sometimes provide information which is independent of Josef K.'s consciousness, such as the summary of the way Josef K. has been in the habit of spending his evenings. This narrator performs the essential function of shaping the pattern of the story, including the rounding-off of an ending, which makes for narrative coherence and economy. In terms of the conventions of narrative fiction, there is no reason to doubt that it is a guarantee of the accuracy of the outward contours which are described and, in particular, of the central facts of Josef K.'s arrest, trial, and execution. And yet, given the extraordinary nature of the events which take place, this narrator is remarkably reticent. He has no privileged insight into why these things happen; he passes no direct judgements. The reader is left to draw his own conclusions. The organization of the story, together with Josef K.'s behaviour, gradually raises doubts in the reader's mind about the reliability of Josef K.'s conviction that he is blameless. When he is arrested he insists that he does not know the law under which he is accused and yet, at the same time, asserts that he is not guilty. From this point on he repeatedly protests his innocence to almost everyone he meets. When he considers writing a deposition in his defence he rejects totally any possibility of guilt: 'Above all, if he were to achieve anything, it was essential that he should eliminate from his mind the idea of possible guilt. There was no such guilt.'

Despite these avowals, Josef K.'s actions betray a recognition on his part that the court does have a claim upon him. He is summoned to a preliminary hearing before a magistrate on a Sunday in order that his trial should not interfere with his job, denounces the proceedings, and expresses his contempt for the court. Although he has not been summoned, the following Sunday he returns to the court-room of his own volition, only to find it empty. His trial now becomes a matter of overwhelming concern to him. Although he initially resolves that he will not seek any outside help, he begins to solicit help from anyone he thinks might be of assistance. Everyone he meets seems either to have some connection with the court or at least to know as much about his case as he does himself: his uncle, the lawyer, the lawyer's maid, the court painter, his business clients, and the prison chaplain. The physical presence of the court begins to spill over and spread out everywhere. It proliferates through the attics of various buildings; it invades the bank, the painter's studio, and the cathedral. Every step he takes seems to bring him into contact with his trial. This obsessive awareness is not the mark of a clear conscience. Whatever his words may indicate, his behaviour is that of a man who feels guilty.

Josef K.'s series of encounters with people from whom he seeks advice culminates in his meeting with the prison chaplain in the solemnity of the cathedral. There is a significant difference between this meeting and his earlier ones. It is the priest who takes the initiative and who addresses him. He tells him Josef K. is wrong to seek outside help and, in the parable of the man from the country and the gatekeeper, warns him against the danger of deceiving himself about the Law. Josef K. learns nothing from this advice. In the final chapter two executioners call for him, take him out to a deserted quarry, and thrust a knife in his heart. He dies, in his own words, 'like a dog!'

Josef K.'s sense of guilt cannot be attributed to any one specific action; nor can it be characterized as universal human guilt. There are other accused men in the story but, equally, there are many who do not stand accused by the court. Josef K.'s failing may be found in his lack of humility and self-understanding, in his aggressive impatience and stubbornness. Paradoxically, his guilt lies in his blind refusal to countenance even the possibility that he may in some sense be guilty, in which case the court is justified in its measures, however cruel and corrupt it may seem to be. It is impossible to define its essence in precise terms. Certainly it would be a gross oversimplification to describe it as the agent of divine justice, although some religious, transcendental quality is implied. It represents, despite appearances, a realm of transcendental values which Josef K. is incapable of understanding.

Ultimately it is impossible to ascribe any one single meaning to *The Trial*. It presents a double image: an innocent man destroyed by a despotic authority and a guilty man rightly condemned. We are not forced to chose between these possibilities; they co-exist and interpenetrate each other. Kafka's novel constantly challenges the reader to supply his own interpretation of its elusive substance.

—B. Ashbrook

KAISER, Georg. Born in Magdeburg, Germany, 25 November 1878. Educated at the school of a Lutheran monastery, 1888–95. Married Margarete Habenicht in 1908; two sons and one daughter; also had a daughter by Maria von Mühfeld in 1919. Bookshop assistant in Magdeburg, 1895; apprentice with an import/export business, 1896–99; sailed to Buenos Aires, Argentina, worked with the local branch of the Berlin AEG [General Electric Company], 1899; contracted malaria, returned to Germany, 1901; in sanatorium, following a nervous breakdown, 1902; lost house through financial difficulties, moved to Munich, 1918; arrested on a charge of embezzlement, because of his selling of rented furniture, and imprisoned in Munich for six months, 1920–21; settled in Berlin after his release, 1921; became Germany's most widely performed dramatist, 1921–33; under the Nazi regime, his works banned from publication or production, from 1933, and his books burnt; continued writing in Berlin, 1934–37; learned of impending investigation by the Gestapo and fled to Switzerland via Amsterdam, 1938; lived in various parts of Switzerland, 1939–44. Elected to Prussian Academy of Arts, 1926, and the German Academy, 1930 (membership later withdrawn under Nazi pressure). Honorary president, Association for German Writers in Exile, 1945. *Died 4 June 1945.*

PUBLICATIONS

Collections

Stücke, Erzählungen, Aufsätze, Gedichte, edited by Walther Huder. 1966.
Werke, edited by Walther Huder. 6 vols., 1971–72.

Plays

Die jüdische Witwe (produced 1921). 1911.
Claudius (produced 1918). In *Hyperion*, 1911.
Friedrich und Anna (produced 1918). In *Hyperion*, 1911.
König Hahnrei (produced 1931). 1913.
Der Fall des Schülers Vehgesack (produced 1915). 1914.
Rektor Kleist (produced 1918). 1914.
Grossbürger Möller (produced 1915). 1914; revised version, as *David und Goliath* (produced 1922). 1920; as *David and Goliath*, translated by B.J. Kenworthy, in *Plays 2*, 1981.
Die Bürger von Calais (produced 1917). 1914; as *The Burghers of Calais*, translated by J.M. Ritchie and Rex Last, in *Five Plays*, 1971.
Europa (produced 1920). 1915.
Der Zentaur (produced 1917). 1916.
Von Morgens bis mitternachts (produced 1917). 1916; as *From*

Morn to Midnight, translated by Ashley Dukes, in *Poet Lore*, (21), 1920; also translated by Ulrich Weisstein, in *Plays for the Theatre: An Anthology of World Drama*, edited by O.G. and L. Brockett, 1967; as *From Morning to Midnight*, translated by J.M. Ritchie, in *Five Plays*, 1971.

Die Sorina; oder, Der Kindermord (produced 1917). 1917.

Die Versuchung (produced 1917). 1917.

Die Koralle (produced 1917). 1917; as *The Coral*, translated by Winifred Katzin, 1963; also translated by B.J. Kenworthy, in *Five Plays*, 1971.

Das Frauenopfer (produced 1918). 1918.

Juana (produced 1918). 1918.

Gas I (produced 1918). 1918; as *Gas I*, translated by Herman Scheffauer, 1957; also translated by B.J. Kenworthy, in *Five Plays*, 1971.

Der Brand im Opernhaus (produced 1918). 1919; as *Fire in the Opera House* translated by Winifred Katzin, in *Eight European Plays*, 1927.

Hölle Weg Erde (produced 1919). 1919.

Gas II (produced 1920). 1920; as *Gas II*, translated by Winifred Katzin, 1963; also translated by B.J. Kenworthy, in *Five Plays*, 1971.

Der gerettete Alkibiades (produced 1920). 1920; as *Alkibiades Saved*, translated by Bayard Quincy Morgan, in *An Anthology of German Expressionist Drama*, edited by Walter H. Sokel, 1963.

Der Protagonist (produced 1922). 1921; as *The Protagonist*, translated by H.F. Garten, in *Tulane Drama Review*, (5), 1960.

Noli me tangere. 1922.

Kanzlist Krehler (produced 1922). 1922.

Der Geist der Antike. 1923.

Gilles und Jeanne (produced 1923). 1923.

Die Flucht nach Venedig (produced 1923). 1923; as *The Flight to Venice*, translated by B.J. Kenworthy, in *Plays 2*, 1981.

Nebeneinander (produced 1923). 1923.

Kolportage (produced 1924). 1924.

Gats (produced 1925). 1925.

Der mutige Seefahrer (produced 1925). 1926.

Zweimal Oliver (produced 1926). 1926.

Papiermühle (produced 1926). 1927.

Der Zar lässt sich photographieren, music by Kurt Weill (produced 1928). 1927.

Der Präsident (produced 1928). 1927; as *The President*, translated by B.J. Kenworthy, in *Plays 2*, 1981.

Oktobertag (produced 1928). 1928; as *The Phantom Lover*, translated by Hermann Bernstein and Adolf E. Meyer, 1928; as *One Day in October*, translated by B.J. Kenworthy, in *Plays 2*, 1981.

Die Lederköpfe (produced 1928). 1928.

Hellseherei (produced 1929). 1929.

Zwei Krawatten (produced 1929). 1929.

Mississippi (produced 1930). 1930.

Der Silbersee (produced 1933). 1933.

Adrienne Ambrosat (produced 1935). 1948(?); translated as *Adrienne Ambrosat*, in *Continental Plays 2*, 1935.

Das Los des Ossian Balvesen (produced 1936). 1947(?).

Der Gärtner von Toulouse (produced 1945). 1938.

Der Schuss in die Öffentlichkeit (produced 1949). 1939.

Der Soldat Tanaka (produced 1940). 1940.

Rosamunde Floris (produced 1953). 1940.

Alain und Elise (produced 1954). 1940.

Die Spieldose (produced 1943). In *Stücke, Erzählungen, Aufsätze, Gedichte*, 1966.

Zweimal Amphitryon (produced 1944). In *Griechische Dramen*, 1948.

Das Floss der Medusa (produced 1945). 1963; as *The Raft of the Medusa*, translated by Ulrich Weisstein, in *First Stage*, 1, 1962; also translated by George Wellwarth, in *Postwar German Theater*, edited by Michael Benedikt and George E. Wellwarth; H.F. Garten and Elizabeth Sprigge, in *Plays 2*, 1981.

Agnete (produced 1949). 1948(?).

Pygmalion (produced 1953). In *Griechische Dramen*, 1948.

Bellerophon (produced 1953). In *Griechische Dramen*, 1948.

Klawitter (produced 1949). 1949.

Napoleon in New Orleans (produced 1950). In *Stücke, Erzählungen, Aufsätze, Gedichte*, 1966.

Schellenkönig. In *Stücke, Erzählungen, Aufsätze, Gedichte*, 1966.

Das gordische Ei (unfinished). N.d.

Five Plays (includes *From Morn to Midnight; The Burghers of Calais; The Coral: Gas I; Gas II*), translated by B.J. Kenworthy, Rex Last, and J.M. Ritchie. 1971; as *Plays I*, 1985.

Plays 2, (includes *The Flight to Venice; One Day in October; The Raft of the Medusa; David and Goliath; The President*), translated by B.J. Kenworthy, H.F. Garten, and Elizabeth Sprigge. 1981.

Radio Play: *Der englische Sender*, 1947.

Fiction

Es ist genug. 1932.

Villa Aurea. 1940.

Leutnant Welzeck (fragment). In *Stücke, Erzählungen, Aufsätze, Gedichte*, 1966.

Other

Vision und Figur. 1918.

Georg Kaiser in Sachen Georg Kaiser: Briefe 1916–1933, edited by Gesa M. Valk. 1989.

*

Bibliography: 'Georg Kaiser (1878–1945): A Bio-Bibliographical Report' by Leroy W. Shaw, in *Texas Studies in Literature and Language*, (3), 1961.

Critical Studies: *Kaiser und seine Bühenwerke* by Willibald Omankowski, 1922; *Der Denkspieler, Georg Kaiser* by Bernhard Diebold, 1924; *Georg Kaisers Werk* by Max Freyhan, 1926; *Georg Kaiser* by Hugo Königsgarten, 1928; *Georg Kaiser und seine Stellung im Expressionismus* by Eric A. Fivian, 1946; *Georg Kaiser* by Brian J. Kenworthy, 1957; *Georg Kaiser: Die Perspektiven seines Werkes* by Wolfgang Paulsen, 1960; *Georg Kaiser* by Wilhelm Steffens, 1969; *Die Suche nach dem Menschen im Drama Georg Kaisers* by M. Kuxdorf, 1971; *Georg Kaiser und Bertolt Brecht* by Ernst Schürer, 1971; 'Georg Kaiser Re-examined' by Hugo F. Garten, in *German and Dutch Literature*, edited by W.D. Robson-Scott, 1973; *Georg Kaisers Drama 'Die Koralle': Persönliche Erfahrung und ästhetische Abstraktion* by Heinrich Breloer, 1977; *Georg Kaisers 'Gas I': Textanalyse und Konzept einer szenischen Realisation* by Peter Schlapp, 1983; *German Expressionist Drama: Ernst Toller and Georg Kaiser* by Renate Benson, 1984, German edition, 1987; *The Reception of Georg Kaiser (1915–1945): Texts and Analysis* by Peter K. Tyson, 2 vols., 1984.

* * *

Georg Kaiser, the greatest, most prolific, and certainly the most eccentric of the German Expressionist dramatists, was born in Magdeburg, the son of an insurance salesman, in 1878. Such was the diversity and profusion of his work (over a hundred dramas, as well as poetry and prose) that he was suspected by one critic of being a collective of writers toiling away under the company name of Kaiser.

Kaiser was convinced of the centrality and overwhelming significance of his mission as a writer, before which all else paled into insignificance. His central conviction found its clearest expression in his key essay *Vision und Figur* [Vision and Form] (1918), in which he states:

> The Vision is everything, because it is one. The forms which are bearers of this vision are manifold, laden by the fiery hand of the poet with the weighty burden of his message. In many ways does the poet fashion but one thing: the vision, which has existed since the dawn of time. And of what nature is this vision? There is only one: The renewal of man.

This quasi-religious idealism finds its most complete expression in Kaiser's difficult but rewarding masterpiece, *Die Bürger von Calais* (*The Burghers of Calais*), first performed with great success in 1917, when the tide of war was turning and audiences had become attuned to the strong pacifist element in the play's message. It borrows both from the historical account of the siege of Calais at the beginning of the Hundred Years War and from the New Testament. Duguesclin, commander of the French army, represents the forces of the old world, of the 'chain of deeds' of violence which Eustache de Saint-Pierre, a leading Calais merchant, seeks to break with his concept of community effort towards an unselfish and peaceful society.

At first, Eustache endeavours to convert the whole community to his idealism, then he turns to the other volunteers for the self-sacrifice demanded by the besieging English forces (six citizens to be hanged as a penance for the town and to guarantee its safety), but ultimately only he achieves the ideal—through death.

Kaiser depicts the path to the ideal in terms of a sudden chance awakening or opportunity for escape from the trammels of the Old World. At that instant, the 'New Man' is born, as at the death of the old and birth of the new in a Christian convert, and is utterly committed to the struggle toward the renewal of mankind.

Then the process of debate to persuade others to recognize and espouse that ideal begins in earnest. Such is the centrality of the dialectic in Kaiser's dramas that he describes writing a drama in terms of 'thinking a thought to its end'. In *The Burghers of Calais*, the debate takes place in a setting which deliberately parallels the Last Supper, and in which the aspiration toward self-sacrifice fights a losing battle against self-interest and fear of the unknown. At the end, Eustache commits suicide, and his old blind father paradoxically proclaims 'I have seen the New Man! Last night was he born!'

Although that ideal—not untypically of German idealism through history—is far beyond mortal reach, Kaiser the activist stresses the key significance of the struggle to attain it. This awakening and commitment take place in a variety of contexts, from the purely personal, in a drama like *Oktobertag* (*One Day in October*), in which Catherine, made pregnant by a butcher's boy, persuades a certain lieutenant Marrien by an act of will that he is the father, literally demonstrating the power of mind over matter, to, at the other

extreme, *Die Koralle* (*The Coral*) and the *Gas* plays, which explore the wider social scene in the conflict between the brute force of industry and human ideals. The workers would rather continue to manufacture gas, which in the last part of the trilogy becomes poison gas, than take a leap into uncertainty, demolish the factories, and return to a community lifestyle closer to the natural world. In his anti-industrial and anti-war stance, Kaiser anticipates many of the themes and preoccupations of the German Green movement, although his political preoccupations are too broad to be associated with any one political party.

The Coral also underlines Kaiser's fascination with the notion of the doppelgänger and the problems of personal identity, although it must be stressed that in his work Kaiser is concerned with the human psyche, rather than with human psychology.

The language and style of his works reflect the huge tensions which he is seeking to expose and cause to interact— paradox and the grotesque are never far from the centre stage, and the language itself oscillates between extreme concentration on isolated concrete nouns to rambling, expansive, and highly stylized speeches, in which the punctuation serves almost to orchestrate and define the style of delivery demanded of the actor.

In Kaiser's work there is to be found a great variety of different forms of drama, from the small domestic scale to the vast arena of Calais town hall or the six-day cycle races in Berlin; from traditional three-act dramatic form to the *Stationendrama* of the kind made most famous by Brecht, in which the action focuses not on plot but on theme, and is held together by one central figure.

Among all his writings, Kaiser's despairing but determined idealism is most vividly encapsulated in the closing moments of the grotesque comedy *Von Morgens bis mitternachts* (*From Morn to Midnight*), in which the bank clerk (a representative type rather than a psychologically delineated figure), who from being an automaton processing money in the bank is transformed by the touch of an exotic woman's hand into a parody of the New Man, steals a large sum from the bank, and goes off in pursuit of the ideal. Failing in a number of such endeavours, he finally comes to the Salvation Army Hall, where in a long speech he confesses the overwhelming significance of spirituality, proclaims that 'money destroys true value . . . money is the most wretched swindle in the world', and casts his ill-gotten gains among the startled congregation.

After an astonished silence as the stolen banknotes fall through the air, the onlookers revert to type and grasp at the money, and even the Salvation Army girl who led the bank clerk there betrays him. At the end, he is spread-eagled, in a parody of the crucifixion, against the cross sewn into the curtain on the stage. Like Eustache, he has achieved his ideal; like Eustache he is alone; and like Eustache, he has left this world behind.

—Rex Last

THE GAS TRILOGY: The Coral (Die Koralle), Gas I, Gas II
Plays by Georg Kaiser, 1917–20.

Kaiser's three plays *The Coral*, *Gas I*, and *Gas II* illustrate the expressionist ideal of the 'New Man' against a background of class struggle in increasingly futuristic settings. *The Coral*, first performed in Frankfurt in 1917, although usually accepted as the first part, is a complete five-act account of a millionaire industrialist whose tragic parental origins he seeks to overcome by making money and by sparing his son similar hardships. His wish to fashion his son's life is thwarted when the son becomes a stoker on a cargo-boat while the father entertains guests on his private yacht. Shattered by his son's revolt (which is paralleled by an explosion in his main factory) the millionaire, instead of shooting himself with the gun left by his son after failed patricide, kills his secretary. The secretary, the millionaire's double who often represents him, carries a piece of coral for final identification. The millionaire takes the coral, is arrested for murdering his 'employer', and can only accept the son's offer to identify him as the millionaire provided the son renounces his revolt. The millionaire is led off to execution seeing his ideals carried on by the 'man in Grey' who has recognized, in the first act, how the millionaire has identified his own inner *doppelgänger* in his son.

The play is full of ironic twists which not only demonstrate that the New Man concept will remain a vision, but also relativize all genuine efforts to break down social differences and ease human suffering. Physical suffering caused by poverty or exploitation is counterbalanced by inner uncertainties. The millionaire, through an act of violence and deception, theoretically overcomes the arrogant demands of his will and reaches a higher state of awareness where, like a piece of coral, he can drift on the tides of life and death. He no longer needs a subservient *doppelgänger*, for the coral has given him the open-eyed wonder of the childhood he was never able to enjoy. In becoming inwardly certain he must die as both Millionaire and, as the judges insist, as Secretary.

Gas I, first performed in Düsseldorf in 1918, in five acts, introduces the millionaire's son who now controls his father's former huge gas factory. He has innovated worker participation in a form of socialist part-ownership, where success depends on ever-increasing achievements and productivity and the individual is of value only as a skilled mechanical operator. Gas has become the state's prime industrial power source and its failure would spell economic disaster. Even the safety mechanisms cannot prevent an explosion that destroys the works, since the workers are no longer able to master the latest technology used. Appalled by this, the owner refuses to rebuild and re-start production. Instead he tries to persuade the survivors to construct an ideal garden city and develop a community independent of advanced industrial processes. The workers, however, do not wish to become 'human' but continue as wealth-earning and affluent automata. They elect the Chief Engineer to replace the owner and rebuild the factory to answer the demands of the state and other industries profiting from re-armament. The factory is nationalized and the state has to protect the owner from his workers' revenge. In parallel with the end of Bernard Shaw's *Man and Superman*, the owner's daughter looks forward to giving birth to a New Man, the first of a more hopeful and human generation.

In the three-act *Gas II* Kaiser explores his ideas further in a vision of the future with a new factory where gas is held in reserve for an expected war. The Chief Engineer is in charge and the workers are divided into coloured teams, operating control and information systems that are removed from the actual production of gas and demand endlessly repetitive responses. A struggle ensues between strikers who call for freedom from their machine-controlled existence and those who fear invasion. The 'Blue' control figures are quickly overrun by enemy 'Yellow' figures who force renewed production of gas with no shared profits. Act III repeats the opening situation, but when production falls the 'Yellow' forces surround the factory and threaten to destroy it. In the ensuing confrontation between the Chief Engineer, the so-called Millionaire Worker, and the masses, a new invention, poison gas, is offered as a means of regaining power over the 'Yellow' forces. The Millionaire Worker tries to persuade them to undertake a new spiritual way that would free them from dependence on material gain. The masses opt for the poison gas and, as the Chief Engineer throws his phial into the air, the enemy begins to open fire. Workers and enemy forces alike are hideously destroyed in the final holocaust.

Where *Gas I* depicts the end of the individual voice, *Gas II* extends this to predict, in dramatic form, the end of the world. The final result depends on the gullibility of the masses and their inability to support various utopian solutions proposed. Kaiser's repeated and balancing devices in the plays' structures, individual speech patterns, colour symbolism, and growing abstractionism and foreshortening of language, establish a growing feeling of inevitability. None of the characters act freely and the crowd scenes are marked by the power of rhetoric to produce propagandist visions of futures either under totalitarian regimes or as garden-city utopias. Central ideas are unfolded with deliberate control, thus making the two plays prime examples of Kaiser's so-called *Denkspiele* (thought plays). Huge swings of opinion responding to clear and compressed speeches, especially in Act IV of *Gas I*, represent the climax of expressionist dramatic art and mark growing interest in the problems and fate of man in the mass rather than the isolated individual. Gas, as the central focus of these two plays, is a symbol perhaps of the power of man to wring from nature a product to ease his own existence and provide the means to economic progress; but it also poses a threat. Not only technical skill but also correct emotional and ethical attitudes are needed by those who exploit and use such a commodity. Lack of proportion and the ruthless exploitation of the production formula and the control mechanisms to their utmost limits cause the explosion. Just as the machines become unpredictable when overworked, humans, when reduced to automata, can be equally self-destructive.

As with other examples of expressionist drama, the text is only one factor within a total theatrical experience. The *Gas* trilogy is a *Gesamtkunstwerk* (total work of art) where a variety of technical devices combine to produce an intense experience. Spatially, Kaiser used abstract, geometric forms in the stage-settings, in the constellations of characters, and in the representative use of a sliding roof to reveal the vault of the sky or a foreshortened mechanical reproduction of it. Structurally the scenes in both plays are paralleled and within each pair of scenes numbers and pairings of working figures emphasize the fatal repeat mechanism from *Gas I* to *Gas II*. The timing of the first performances of the plays supports the interpretation that they are meant as a warning to man not to repeat the catastrophe of World War I and the industrial processes that led to its outbreak. Rhetorical use of language, using compressed, repetitive speech rhythms, especially in the crowd scenes, suggests an emotional response to the ideas expressed rather than a reasoned reaction to them. Above all clipped, emphatic phrases and stichomythia, dialogue in alternate lines of verse, produce an intensifying effect that heightens the sense of unavoidable, head-on clashes and eventual catastrophe.

—Brian Keith-Smith

KALEVALA. Finnish national epic poem; compiled between 1828 and 1846 by Elias Lönnrot (1802–84), doctor of medicine and later professor of Finnish at Alexander's University in Helsinki, from traditional oral poetry of northeastern Finland and the Finnish–Russian border, together with about 600 lines written by Lönnrot himself. Title means 'Land of Kaleva'.

PUBLICATIONS

Kalevala, edited by Elias Lönnrot. 1835; revised, enlarged edition, 1849; translated by Selma Borg, 1882; also translated by John Martin Crawford, 2 vols., 1888; William Forsell Kirby, 2 vols., 1907; Aili Kolehmainen Johnson (in prose), 1951; Francis Peabody Magoun, Jr (in prose), 1963; Eino Friberg, edited by George C. Schoolfield, 1988; Keith Bosley, 1989; *Selections from the Kalevala*, translated by John A. Porter, 1868.

*

Bibliography: *Elias Lönnrot and His Kalevala: A Selective Annotated Bibliography* by Elemer Bako, 1985.

Critical Studies: *Hiawatha and Kalevala: A Study of the Relationship Between Longfellow's 'Indian Edda' and the Finnish Epic* by Ernest J. Moyne, 1963; *The Kalevala and Its Background* by Erik Alfred Torbjörn Collinder, 1964; *Kalevala Kommentar* by Hans Fromm, 1967; *Epic of the North: The Story of Finland's Kalevala* by John I. Kolehmainen, 1973; *Finnish Folk Poetry: Epic* by Matti Kuusi and others, 1977; *Kalevala* issue of *Books from Finland*, 19(1), 1985; *Studies in Finnish Folklore: Homage to the Kalevala* by Felix J. Oinas, 1985; *Religion, Myth and Folklore in the World's Epics, the Kalevala and Its Predecessors*, edited by Lauri Honko, 1990.

* * *

The preliminary 1835 edition of the *Kalevala* contains 16 poems, and 5,052 lines. The 1849 definitive edition known as 'the Finnish national epic' is considerably longer, containing 50 poems, and 22,795 lines. However, the latter represents only a fraction of the oral poetry in the Kalevala metre handed down from generation to generation and saved by collectors. By comparison, the 33-volume *Suomen Kansan Vanhat Runot* [Ancient Poems of the Finnish People] published by the Finnish Literature Society (Helsinki) between 1908 and 1948, contains approximately half of some 1,270,000 lines of collected material in the society's archives, the rest of which remains unpublished. The wealth of oral poetry which Elias Lönnrot recorded during his field trips, principally to north-eastern Finland and Karelia, made possible not only the compilation of *Kalevala* but also the publication of companion volumes, the best known of which is *Kanteletar* [Lady of the Kantele], the collection of lyric poetry to which female singers, specifically, made their contribution. Traditionally men tended to sing heroic poetry while women favoured lyric, legends, and ballads.

The epic poetry of the *Kalevala* can be divided into four strains. Myth poetry describes the creation of an ancient world at the dawn of time, a world in which animistic powers governed the human environment. It belongs to the oldest strain of Kalevala poetry, the arbitrary starting point of which

comparative evidence sets at some two-and-a-half millennia ago. Its predominant characters are the 'eternal sage' Väinämöinen and the smith Ilmarinen. The origins of the second type, magic and shaman poetry, can be dated from about the birth of Christ to AD 500–600. Besides female characters, the shamans Lemminkäinen and Joukahainen also now make their appearance. Adventure poetry dates from AD 600–1000, and reflects contacts of the Baltic-Finns with the East Vikings. The poems give notable prominence to male–female relationships, courtship, marriage ceremonies, and conflicts between female desire for a peaceful, stable, family-centred life and male desire for adventurous combat. Finally, there are poems of the Christian period (AD 900–1450), in which the arrival and establishment of Christianity have a profound effect. The lines chronicle the onset of the modern era when the ancient heroes will make way for a new one, a boy-child miraculously conceived by the virgin, Marjatta.

The particular structural and metrical form of Kalevala poetry is a distinctive feature of great antiquity. The unrhymed, non-strophic, trochaic tetrameter carries the name 'Kalevala-metre'. The prominent stylistic devices of the *Kalevala* are alliteration, parallelism, and repetitiveness, such as in the following example in translation:

> Then the Mother of the Waters,
> Water-Mother, maid aerial,
> From the waves her knee uplifted,
> Raised her shoulder from the billows,
> That the teal her nest might 'stablish,
> And might find a peaceful dwelling.
> Then the teal, the bird so beauteous,
> Hovered slow, and gazed around her,
> And she saw the knee uplifted
> From the blue waves of the ocean,
> And she thought she saw a hillock,
> Freshly green with springing verdure.
> There she flew, and hovered slowly,
> Gently on the knee alighting;
> And her nest she there established,
> And she laid her eggs all golden,
> Six gold eggs she laid within it,
> And a seventh she laid of iron.

Soon after its publication in 1849, the *Kalevala* was recognized as an epic of major significance, along with the *Iliad*, the *Poetic Edda*, and *Nibelungenlied*. In assembling the *Kalevala*, Lönnrot created a national mythology; hence the work compels the reader to view it against the background of the emerging Finnish nation-state. The *Kalevala* not only gives structure to the roots of Finnish national culture, but the work can be seen as evidence of the extent to which historically pre-literate art shapes a nation's self-perception and the high cultural expression of its later ages. In a wider context, and aside from its anthropological and historical connections, the *Kalevala* represents the epic as a genre of imaginative world literature which provides a rich source of aesthetic appreciation and varying approaches to literary criticism. Whether we read about the tragic lives of the girl Aino or the boy Kullervo; the adventures of Väinämöinen, Ilmarinen, and the gallant Lemminkäinen; the struggle between the land of Kaleva and Pohjola; or the interplay of pagan and Christian ideas and ideals, the *Kalevala*'s creative variants supply a wide range of interpretative possibilities, from the allegorical to the symbolic and historic. Appropriately its open ending, in the words of the eternal bard Väinämöinen, embodies what is central to *Kalevala*, its relevance to all ages:

Here the course lies newly opened,
Open for the greater singers,
For the bards and ballad singers,
For the young, who now are growing,
For the rising generation.
                    (translations by William Forsell Kirby)

—Seija Paddon

KĀLIDĀSA. Fl. c.AD 400; date of birth unknown. Poet and
dramatist who wrote in Sanskrit and who may have been
in the city of Ujjain, at the court of the North Indian
ruler Chandragupta Vikramāditya or of his successor
Kumāragupta, or both, for some years between about 388
and c.455. Texts exist is several regional variants (recensions). *Died in 5th century(?).*

PUBLICATIONS

Collections

Shakuntala and Other Works, translated by Arthur Ryder.
    1912; as *Shakuntala and Other Writings*, 1959.
Kālidāsa Lexicon (Sanskrit texts), edited by A. Scharpé. 5
    vols., 1954–75.
Granthavali [Collected Works] (Hindi and Sanskrit). 1965.
Complete Works (Sanskrit), edited by V.P. Joshi. 1976.
Granthāvalī/Works (Sanskrit), edited by R.P. Dwivedī. 1976;
    2nd edition, 1986.
The Loom of Time (includes *Ṛtusamhāram*; *Meghadūtam*;
    Abhijnānaśākuntalam), translated by Chandra Rajan,
    1989.

Verse

Ṛtusaṁhāra, as *The Season: A Descriptive Poem*, edited by
    W. Jones, 1792; as *The Ritusamhara*, translated by M.
    Nandy, 1970; as *Ṛtusamhāram*, in *The Loom of Time*,
    1989; as *The Seasons* (bilingual edition), translated by John
    T. Roberts, 1990.
Raghuvaṁśa, edited by G.N. Nandargikar (with Mallinātha's
    commentary). 1811 (reprinted 1982); also edited (with
    Latin translation) by F.A. Stenzler, 1832; as *The Story of
    Raghu's Line*, translated by P.D.L. Johnstone, 1902; as
    The Dynasty of Raghu, translated by Robert Antoine,
    1972.
Kumārasambhava, edited by F.A. Stenzler (songs 1–8, with
    Latin translation). 1838; critical edition, 1962; edited by
    M.S. Narayana Murti, in *Verzeichnis der orientalischen
    Handschriften in Deutschland*, supplement 20(1), 1980; as
    The Birth of the War God, translated by R.T.H. Griffith,
    1877; as *The Origin of the Young God*, translated by Hank
    Heifetz, 1985.
Meghadūta, in *Meghaduta et Cringaratilaka*, edited by
    J. Gildemeister. 1841; edited by E. Hultzsch (with
    Vallabhadeva's commentary), 1911; also edited by S.K.
    De, 1957 (critical edition), and M.R. Kale (bilingual
    edition), 7th edition, 1967; as *Meghaduta; or, Cloud
    Messenger*, translated by H.H. Wilson, 1843; as
    Meghaduta, translated by G.H. Rooke, 1935; as *The Cloud

Messenger, translated by Franklin and Eleanor Edgerton,
    1964; as *The Transport of Love*, translated by Leonard
    Nathan, 1976; as *Meghadūtam*, in *The Loom of Time*,
    1989.

Plays

Abhijñāna Śakuntalā. 1761; edited by Richard Pischel
    (Bengali recension), 1922; edited by N.R. Acharya, with
    commentary by Rāghavabhaṭṭa (Devanagari recension),
    1958 (12th edition); as *Shakuntala*, translated by William
    Jones, 1789; also translated by Arthur Ryder, in
    Shakuntala and Other Works, 1912; P. Lal, in *Great
    Sanskrit Plays*, 1957; as *Śakuntalā*, translated by M.
    Monier-Williams, 1853; Michael Coulson, in *Three Sanskrit
    Plays*, 1981; as *Abhijñāśakuntalā*, translated by M.R. Kale,
    1898; as *Sakuntala*, translated by J.G. Jennings, 1902; also
    translated by Murray Emeneau, 1962; as *Abhijna Shakun-
    tala*, translated by Hemant Kanitkar, 1984; as *Sakuntala
    and the Ring of Recollection*, in *Theater of Memory: The
    Plays of Kālidāsa*, 1984; as *Abhijnānaśākuntalam*, in *The
    Loom of Time*, 1989.
Vikramorvaśīya, edited (with Latin translation) by R. Lenz.
    1833; also edited by S.P. Pandit, 1889, H.D. Velankar,
    1961; as *Vikramorvasiya* (bilingual edition), translated by
    M.R. Kale, 1889, and subsequent editions; also translated
    by Dhruva Sumana, 1912; as *Urvaśī Won By Valor*, in
    Theater of Memory: The Plays of Kālidāsa, 1984.
Mālavikāgnimitra, as *Malvika et Agnimitra*, edited by O.F.
    Tullberg. 1840; also edited by Friedrich Bollensen, 1879,
    C.S. Rama Sastri, 1929, N.R. Acharya, 1950, and K.A.
    Subramania, 1978; as *Malavikagnimitra*, edited and trans-
    lated by D.S. Sane, G.H. Godbole, and H.S. Ursekar,
    1950; also translated by C.H. Tawney, 1964 (3rd edition);
    as *Mālvikā and Agnimitra*, in *Theater of Memory: The
    Plays of Kālidāsa*, 1984.
Theater of Memory: The Plays of Kālidāsa, edited by Barbara
    Stoler Miller, translated by Edwin Gerow, David Gitomer,
    and Miller. 1984.

*

Bibliography: *Kalidasa Bibliography* by S.P. Narang, 1976.

Critical Studies: *The Sanskrit Drama: Its Origin,
Development, Theory and Practice* by Arthur Berriedale
Keith, 1924; *Kalidasa: His Period, Personality and Poetry* by
K.S. Ramaswami, 1933; *Kalidasa: Poet of Nature* by Mary B.
Harris, 1936 *India in Kalidasa* by B.S. Upadhyaya, 1947;
Kalidasa by Walter Ruben, 1957; *The Classical Drama of
India* by Henry Willis Wells, 1963; *Kalidasa: Date, Life,
Works* by V.V. Mirashi, 1969; *A Critical Study of the Sources
of Kalidasa* by B.R. Yadau, 1974; *The Imagery of Kalidasa* by
V. Aggarwal, 1985; *Kalidasa as Dramatist* by P.C. Mandel,
1986; *The Literary Semantics of Kalidasa* by H.L. Shukla,
1987.

* * *

Kālidāsa occupies a special place in world literature, a poet
who has contributed outstanding examples of epic, lyric, and
dramatic works. Later Indian poets, critics, and theorists
have considered him the central reference point of the
tradition, and for over 15 centuries his works have continued
to attract devoted readers. Two lyric poems are ascribed to

Kālidāsa (the first less certainly): *Ṛtusaṁhāra* (*The Seasons*) and *Meghadūta* (*The Cloud Messenger*). Both are poems of love and describe a natural universe transfigured by the lover's imagination and enthusiasm. *The Seasons* contains 140 stanzas, the first extended lyric poem in the literature. It is divided into six books corresponding to six parts of the year: Spring, Summer, the Rainy Season, Autumn, Early Winter, and Winter. In each, a newly married young man sees all of nature with the eyes of love: the sun, the sea, the rivers, trees and vines, birds and beasts, flowers and insects, all are seen as participating in the dance of love. The elaborateness and conviction of this sensual imagery set a new style in Sanskrit poetry, which had previously been more concerned with religious or patriotic themes. *The Cloud Messenger*, like *The Seasons*, is more a lyric meditation than a story. Here a lover is separated from his beloved and the same plants and flowers, rivers and lakes, birds and fish that inspired such ecstasies in *The Seasons* serve him as bitter reminders of his loss. He pours out his grief to a passing rain cloud and begs it to carry his love message to his beloved. The first book of the poem describes in loving and erotic detail the countryside over which the cloud passes on its journey. The second book, at the journey's end, describes the lover's pining wife and her reception of the comforting message borne to her by the cloud. Although the primary mood of the poem is lyric, it combines many elements; religious poetry is mixed with love poetry, elegiac and pastoral elements with the lyric.

Although Kālidāsa may be said to have originated the extended lyric poem, when he turned to the epic he had before him the great traditional works, the *Rāmāyaṇa* and the *Mahābhārata*. Drawing upon these and other poetic sources, he created two major epics, *Kumārasambhava* (*The Birth of the War God*) and *Raghuvaṁśa* (*The Story of Raghu's Line*). The first poem contains 17 cantos, although most Sanskrit scholars consider only the first eight to be the work of Kālidāsa, and the rest a later addition, even though the war-god Kumāra is not in fact yet born in the first eight cantos. These eight, distinctly superior in poetic style and imagination, tell of the process by which the supreme god Śiva is drawn from a state of contemplation to enter into marriage with Pārvatī, a union that will produce a hero to destroy the evil demon Tāraka, who is troubling all the gods in the Hindu pantheon. Clearly, the subject allows Kālidāsa to explore again the poetry of love and nature, but also that of spiritual ecstasy, divine vision, and even the pain of death, in the famous elegy that is pronounced by Rati, the consort of Kāma and the god of love, who is destroyed by Śiva when he first attempts to interrupt the supreme deity's meditations. *The Story of Raghu's Line* concerns legendary kings rather than gods, and is not a single story but a sprawling collection of the deeds of great heroes. The careers of almost 30 dynastic rulers are traced, but the first three, Dilīpa, Raghu, and Aja, receive particularly detailed and loving attention.

Kālidāsa is probably best known in the West as a playwright. He is the author of three plays, one of which, *Śakuntalā*, is the most famous Sanskrit drama. His two other plays are *Mālavikāgnimitra* and *Vikramorvaśīya*. As might be expected from Kālidāsa's other works, all three plays deal with love, and all are examples of the *nāṭaka* type of Sanskrit drama, using history or legend with a king as a protagonist. *Mālavikāgnimitra* tells of the king's passion for a serving girl in the queen's retinue and how, through the manipulations of his clever jester and opportune political developments at the close of the play, his love succeeds. *Vikramorvaśīya* tells of a king who falls in love with a celestial nymph. Both undergo great suffering and torment but at the end Indra, Hindu god of the sky, intervenes to unite the lovers. Both of the plays

provide a rich texture of poetry, music, and dance, but for Western tastes their rather arbitrary actions and thin characterizations are serious drawbacks.

Śakuntalā is much more satisfying on these points, though it, too, is set in a fairytale world of strange and unexpected events. King Duṣyanta, during a hunting expedition, meets Śakuntalā, the daughter of a nymph and a sage, and they fall in love. The king returns to his capital, leaving his new bride to follow him later. After his departure, Śakuntalā unwittingly offends a hermit who pronounces a curse on her: that her husband will forget her until he sees a ring he left with her as a token. Unhappily Śakuntalā, unaware of the curse, loses the ring in a river on her way to her husband and is rejected by him. She seeks refuge among the gods in heaven, where her son Bharata is born. Meanwhile, a fisherman discovers the ring inside a fish he has caught. He is suspected of having stolen it and brought before King Duṣyanta, whose memory of Śakuntalā is thus restored. Having provided us in the early section of the play with the expression of love's delights, Kālidāsa now turns to the sorrows of love lost.

Despite his anguish, the king wins an important battle for Indra, and, returning to his home from her heavenly realm, he stops at the hermitage of a sage, allowing Kālidāsa to laud the ascetic life in richly poetic terms. So peaceful is this site that the king observes a six-year-old boy playing happily with a lion cub. In a lengthy and moving recognition scene, Duṣyanta comes to realize that this is his own son, and Śakuntalā soon appears to complete his happiness. Their reunion is blessed by the sage, who explains the curse and prophesies future glory for Bharata. As in all his works, Kālidāsa creates a rich panorama of the effects of love, fulfilled and frustrated, and of the penetration of nature itself by the lovers' moods; but his canvas in this play is particularly rich and colourful, because of the complex gallery of dramatic characters and the sweep of the action, extending from earth to heaven. Goethe, one of the few authors whose range of poetic achievement resembles that of Kālidāsa, was one of the many Western admirers of *Śakuntalā*, commenting that it combined the flowers of youth and the fruits of age, delight and enchantment, heaven and earth, all in a single work.

—Marvin Carlson

THE CLOUD MESSENGER (Meghadūta)
Poem by Kālidāsa, 5th century AD.

The literary reputation of Kālidāsa is based chiefly on his dramas and epic poems. However, lyric poetry plays such an essential role in all his works that many critics consider him the first great Sanskrit lyric poet. Many of his plays, notably *Śakuntalā*, contain numerous fragments revealing his excellent mastery of poetic formalism. However, Kālidāsa's lyric genius is without a doubt at its height at the time of the poem *Meghadūta* or *The Cloud Messenger*.

The Cloud Messenger consists of 100 four-line stanzas, written in one of the most difficult metres of the Sanskrit language, the *mandākrāntā* (the 'slow approaching'). The poet seems to have borrowed the subject-matter of this poem from the epic poem *Rāmāyaṇa*, and allusions to Rāma's story are found on numerous occasions. However, Kālidāsa is interested not in the creation of an original plot so much as in the opportunity to display his descriptive skill and mastery of traditional poetic conventions.

The Cloud Messenger is the monologue of a *yakṣa*, a sort of demigod, who has been exiled from his home and his beloved wife for neglect of his duty. While in exile, he asks a cloud to convey a message to his wife. In a series of brilliant sketches the *yakṣa* describes to the cloud the path it must follow in order to reach his home in the Himalayas. These passages show how intimately the author knew the cities and the countryside of North India. In the second part of the poem the *yakṣa* first describes the city of Alakā, where his castle stands, and then the beauty of his wife, whom he imagines in a state of prostration due to his absence. In the message, he assures her of his faith and asks her to think of their ultimate reunion.

Kālidāsa is unquestionably a master of poetic style. Not only does he masterfully handle the elaborate metre throughout the poem, but he also makes use of superb descriptions of landscapes in which nature's moods blend with human feelings. The power to convey sentiment, and the fact that he prefers suggestion to elaboration—in contradistinction to later imitators—is for many critics a proof of his poetic genius. His striking mastery of language, characterized by its beauty and, at the same time, by its apparent simplicity, is evident, for instance, in the picture of the *yakṣa*'s mourning wife:

> Thou shalt know her, my second life, by the scantness
>   of her speech,
> Like a lonely chakravaki-bird, while I, her mate, am
>   afar;
> As these days pass heavy with intense longing, I
>   imagine the hapless girl
> Changed in form, as a lotus blighted by the cold
>   season.
> Surely the eyes of my beloved are swollen with
>   passionate weeping,
> And the hue of her lip now changed by the heat of her
>   sighs;
> Resting on her hand and half-hidden by her drooping
>   locks,
> Her face wears the sad look of the moon when thy
>   approach eclipses its beauty.
>   (translated by F. and E. Edgerton)

The admiration that *The Cloud Messenger* has elicited has not deterred some critics from pointing out the apparent flaws of the poem. The most striking of these is the element of unreality of the story: the *yakṣa* is an immortal being, and his addressing the cloud seems unconvincing. However, these apparent flaws are for many critics a poetic advantage. Furthermore, the love of these two immortal beings has been interpreted by many scholars as a symbol of human love, which is skilfully described by Kālidāsa. Therefore, it can be said that the *The Cloud Messenger* expresses human sentiment in a highly poetic form.

Kālidāsa's erotic poem is too distant from the conventional genres to fit into any of the lyric categories determined by Indian tradition. The poem is ranked among the epic poems by Indian critics because the lyric verses have an epic frame; but it is the lyric element that predominates in the poem. *The Cloud Messenger* is in fact a blend of the existing lyric genres, too original to be properly understood by Kālidāsa's contemporaries. None of the numerous imitations of the poem in later Indian literature is capable of attaining the stylistic perfection or the beauty of imagery of the original poem, suggesting the difficulty of following Kālidāsa's pattern.

Nevertheless, *The Cloud Messenger* has been considered the first 'modern' poem of Indian literature for its influence on later poets, not only Indian, but also Western. It won the admiration of Goethe, who praised it in his *Zahme Xenien*. Schiller drew on the idea of Kālidāsa's poem in his *Maria*

Stuart, where the captive Queen of Scots addresses a pitiful speech to the clouds that fly towards her native land (Act III, scene i). The beauty of the language, the intensity of the poet's feeling for nature, and the powerful depiction of human sentiment which pervades the poem turn the work of the Indian author into a classical masterpiece of world literature. As G. Meyer wrote in *Essays und Studien*, II(99), *The Cloud Messenger* is 'the most beautiful lament of a sorrowing lover which one can read'.

—Ana M. Ranero

ŚAKUNTALĀ
Play by Kālidāsa, 5th century AD.

Kālidāsa wrote his most popular drama, the *Śakuntalā*, at the height of his poetic career, and it was to have a profound influence on Western literature, being admired by Geoethe, among others.

The setting of the *Śakuntalā* is the mythical world of the *Mahābhārata*. King Duṣyanta, while chasing after a deer in the forest, happens to arrive at the hermitage of the sage Kaṇva; he falls immediately in love with his daughter, Śakuntalā. She reciprocates his love, and they marry according to the *gandharva* rite; that is, with only the mutual consent of both parties. While the king is away, Śakuntalā, distracted by her passion, neglects her duty to a visiting sage, Durvāsa, who curses her. As a result of this curse, Śakuntalā loses the ring of recognition which the king had given her. As a consequence, the king later forgets her and does not accept her when she goes to his palace. She is then taken by her mother, the nymph Menakā, to Heaven. But there is never a sad ending in Indian drama, and the ring is miraculously found by a fisherman, with the subsequent happy reunion of the two lovers.

Kālidāsa draws upon the Indian epics for the subject matter of this drama, but here the dramatist transforms the original story, characterized by its harshness, turning it into a play in which love is the predominant element and emphasizing the tension between love and public duty. However, Kālidāsa's intelligent handling of the incidents resolves this conflict between desire (*kāma*) and duty (*dharma*). He introduces the motif of the curse, which provokes the king's forgetfulness, justifying the monarch's apparent negligence of duty. The central role that the concept of *dharma* and the figure of the king play in Kālidāsa's drama suggest the author's connection with the court; several allusions scattered throughout his dramas imply that he worked under the patronage of the Gupta monarch Candragupta II.

The hierarchical nature of traditional Indian society is evident in the characters and the plot, which Kālidāsa has borrowed from the idealized epic. It is also evident in the juxtaposition of these elements with those from popular literature and everyday life. This fact explains the importance given to the figure of the *vidūṣaka*, the buffoon, who is a friend and confidant of the king rather than his jester. Moreover, the king, his counsellors, and other members of the upper classes speak Sanskrit, traditionally considered the sacred language of the Brahmanic caste, while women, the buffoon, and minor characters speak different Prakrit dialects, which were commonly used by the uneducated masses.

Attempts have been made to compare Indian drama with Greek, but differences seem to dominate over the apparent affinities. An example of the difference between the two traditions is the total absence of tragedy in Indian drama: all plays end happily, and nothing indecorous appears on the stage. In addition, Indian drama is characterized by the interpolation of lyrical stanzas with prose dialogues: in the *Śakuntalā* the lyrical passages constitute one half of the whole play. Moreover, the concept of fate, central to the Greek tragedy, is absent from Kālidāsa's works, in which chance predominates. However, both traditions share a conception of drama as a source of entertainment leading to catharsis.

The *Śakuntalā* is written in a highly refined language, evidence of the poet's mastery of Sanskrit according to traditional Indian formalism. But language is not the only aspect of the play that has attracted the attention of later poets: Kālidāsa's *Śakuntalā* fits perfectly into the principles codified in the *Nātyaśāstra* of Bharata, the earliest Indian work on dramatic theory. The play opens with a prelude and is then divided into seven acts. It is full of sentiments (*rasas*): the predominant sentiment is the erotic, but the heroic and the comic are also present. These elements make the *Śakuntalā* a masterpiece of its genre. However, despite its numerous merits, Kālidāsa's play is considered defective as a stage-play. The action takes place over seven years, and therefore does not respect the unity of time. Śakuntalā is supposedly taken away to Heaven in front of the audience. This fact does not deter some critics from affirming that 'the supernatural is reduced to modest dimensions' in this play.

Characters in the *Śakuntalā* are the embodiments of social roles. Therefore, the conflict between individual and society never arises. The close interrelation between individuals and their social roles sustains the order in a society that is highly hierarchical. Nature—a dynamic force, which contributes to the cosmic unity in which people belong—also plays a central role in Kālidāsa's play. It has been said by several critics that the heroine of the drama, Śakuntalā, personifies the procreative energies of nature. It is therefore not surprising to find that powerful images of nature dominate Kālidāsa's drama, particularly in the fourth act.

The hero and the heroine of Kālidāsa's play symbolize skilfully the conflict between desire and duty. It is ultimately this representation of a universal conflict that has made Kālidāsa so highly regarded over the centuries.

—Ana M. Ranero

KANZE ZEAMI MOTOKIYO.   See ZEAMI.

KATUHA.   See UPANISHADS.

KAUSUĪTAKĪ.   See UPANISHADS.

KAWABATA Yasunari. Born in Osaka, Japan, 11 June 1899. Educated at Ibaragi Middle School, 1915–17, and First Higher School 1917–20, Tokyo; Tokyo Imperial University, 1920–24, degree in Japanese literature 1924. Married Hideko; one daughter. Writer and journalist: helped found *Bungei Jidai* magazine, 1924, and Kamakura Bunko, publishers, Kamakura, later in Tokyo, 1945. Author-in-residence, University of Hawaii, Honolulu, 1969. President, Japanese PEN, 1959–69. Recipient: Bungei Konwa Kai prize, 1937; Kikuchi Kan prize, 1944; Geijutsuin-shō prize, 1952; Japan Academy of Arts prize, 1952; Noma literary prize, 1954; Goethe medal (Frankfurt), 1959; Prix du Meilleur Livre Étranger, 1961; Nobel prize for literature, 1968. Member, Japan Academy of Arts, 1954. First Class Order of the Rising Sun, 1972. *Died (suicide) 16 April 1972.*

PUBLICATIONS

Collection

Zenshū [Collected Works]. 19 vols., 1969–74.

Fiction

Kanjo shushoku [Sentimental Decoration]. 1926.
Tenohira no shosetsu. 1926; as *Palm-of-the-Hand Stories*, translated by Lane Dunlop and J. Martin Helman, 1988.
Izu no odoriko. 1926; as *The Izu Dancer*, translated by Edward Seidensticker, in *The Izu Dancer and Others*, 1964.
Asakusa kurenaidan [The Red Gang of Asakusa]. 1930.
Jojōka [Lyrical Feelings]. 1934.
Kinjū. 1935; as *Of Birds and Beasts*, translated by Edward Seidensticker, in *House of the Sleeping Beauties and Other Stories*, 1969.
Hana no warutsu [The Flower Waltz]. 1936.
Yukiguni. 1937; revised, enlarged edition, 1948; as *Snow Country*, translated by Edward Seidensticker, 1957.
Aisuru hitotachi [Lovers]. 1941.
Utsukushii tabi [Beautiful Travel]. 1947.
Otome no minato [Sea-Port with a Girl]. 1948.
Shiroi mangetsu [White Full-Moon]. 1948.
Maihime [The Dancer]. 1951.
Meijin, in *Shincho*. 1951; revised, enlarged edition, in book form, 1954; shorter version as *The Master of Go*, translated by Edward Seidensticker, 1972.
Sembazuru. 1952; as *Thousand Cranes*, translated by Edward Seidensticker, 1959.
Hi mo tsuki mo [Days and Months]. 1953.
Suigetsu. 1953; as *The Moon on the Water*, translated by George Suitō, in *The Izu Dancer and Others*, 1964.
Yama no oto. 1954; as *The Sound of the Mountain*, translated by Edward Seidensticker, 1970.
Mizuumi. 1955; as *The Lake*, translated by Reiko Tsukimura, 1974.
Onna de aru koto [To Be a Woman]. 1956–58.
Nemureru bijō. 1961; as *House of the Sleeping Beauties*, translated by Edward Seidensticker, in *House of the Sleeping Beauties and Other Stories*, 1969.
The Izu Dancer and Others (includes *Izu Dancer*; *Re-encounter*; *The Mole*; *The Moon on the Water*; bilingual edition), translated by Edward Seidensticker and others. 1964.
Kata-ude. 1965; as *One Arm*, translated by Edward Seidensticker, in *House of the Sleeping Beauties and Other Stories*, 1969.

Utsukushisa to kanashimi to. 1965; as *Beauty and Sadness*, translated by Howard Hibbett, 1975.
Sakuhin sen [Selected Works]. 1968.
House of the Sleeping Beauties and Other Stories, translated by Edward Seidensticker. 1969.
Tampopo [Dandelion]. 1972.

Other

Bunsho [Prose Style]. 1942.
Zenshū [Collected Works]. 16 vols., 1948–54; revised edition, 12 vols., 1959–61.
Aishu [Sorrow] (stories and essays). 1949.
Asakusa monogatari [Asakusa Story]. 1950.
Shosetsu no kenkyū [Studies of the Novel]. 1953.
Tokyo no hito [The People of Tokyo]. 4 vols., 1955.
Who's Who among Japanese Writers, with Aono Suekichi. 1957.
Koto. 1962; as *The Old Capital*, translated by J. Martin Holman, 1987.
Senshū [Selected Works], edited by Yoshiyuki Junnosuke. 1968.
Utsukushii nihon no watakushi; Japan, The Beautiful, and Myself (Nobel prize lecture; bilingual edition), translated by Edward Seidensticker, 1969.
Shosetsu nyūmon [Introduction to the Novel]. 1970.

*

Critical Studies: *Accomplices of Silence: The Modern Japanese Novel* by Masao Miyoshi, 1974; *The Search for Authenticity in Modern Japanese Literature* by Hisaaki Yamanouchi, 1978; *The Moon in the Water: Understanding Tanizaki, Kawabata, and Mishima* by Gwenn Boardman Petersen, 1979; *Three Modern Novelists: Sōseki, Tanizaki, Kawabata* by Van C. Gessel, 1993.

* * *

The first of two Japanese Nobel laureates in literature (Ōe Kenzaburo is the other), Kawabata is perhaps better known than any other recent writer of his country. His standing at home, however, may not be quite so unchallenged: a large number of critics might mention more intellectual and ideological writers as truly representative of the modern Japanese tradition.

Kawabata's reputation rests on the subtly evocative images that continually startle the reader with clarity and brilliance. When successful—as in *Yukiguni* (*Snow Country*), *Yama no oto* (*The Sound of the Mountain*), or *Nemureru bijō* (*House of the Sleeping Beauties*)—the images serve to add dimensions to the straightforward narrative flow. They suspend the plot, deflect the causal expectation, and open up new spaces for meaning. The narrative vibrates with the fullness of sensory perception that reaches out toward what remains untold. When overcharged, however, the images tend to turn inert. In *Sembazuru* (*Thousand Cranes*) or *Utsukushisa to kanashimi to* (*Beauty and Sadness*), for instance, image after image lights up aimlessly, as if prettiness were the tale's sole objective. The result is an ostentatious display in the manner of airline posters. Kawabata is never completely free from such pitfalls.

Kawabata's dependence on visualization must be explained by the fact that he is essentially a short-story writer. By this it is not meant that he principally wrote short stories—though

he in fact did write a great many—but that his 'novels' were nearly always accumulated short stories. His longer works grew out of assembled modules, each managing to remain flexible and open-ended like individual verse-stanzas in a *renga* (linked poem). That is, his narrative is generated by spatialization and detemporalization of acts and events. Hence it is not causal but casual: it intersects time and offers the still moments pictorially. Neither psychological nor sociological, Kawabata's narrative is antithetical to novelistic representation and is likewise resistant to novelistic analysis. His characters are often unfulfilled swift sketches, and his plots are series of unconnected *tableaux vivants*. Both are embedded among the beauties of background. In the Kawabata territory, scenery is serious.

Although sensitive to popular demands, Kawabata had a streak of stubbornness that saved as well as damned him. During World War II, he was reluctant to play an active role in the militarist programmes, spending his time quietly reading the nation's classics. In the post-war years when most intellectuals switched their allegiance to Western humanism, Kawabata kept recalling Japan's traditional heritage. Later, when Mishima Yukio's self-destructive histrionics were increasingly antagonizing Japan's literary establishment, Kawabata steadfastly stood with the younger writer. His uncharacteristic involvement in municipal politics just before his own suicide, too, seems inseparable from his attachment to his nationalist friend.

It would be a mistake to latch on to Kawabata's art as the quintessence of the famed 'Japanese lyricism'. And yet one recalls even now how solacing and encouraging the sensitive images in his work were to the war-ravaged Japanese in those dark post-war years. Kawabata is thus remembered despite his refusal to propose any particular reflection or recommendation in his art.

—Masao Miyoshi

SNOW COUNTRY (Yukiguni)
Novel by Kawabata, 1937, complete edition, 1948.

Snow Country is not a long novel. It comes close to falling into the inconvenient range of the novella, hardly long enough to be a book and too long to be a magazine piece. Yet it was some 13 years in the writing. Between 1935 and 1937 Kawabata published several related fragments in several magazines. None carried the title *Snow Country*, which was assigned when, in 1937, with some revision, the fragments were brought together in book form.

There was no indication that the work was not finished. Then in 1940 Kawabata added another chapter. In 1946 and 1947 he attempted conclusions, and in 1948 the work was finally published as we have it. The ending could hardly be called conclusive. One of the three principal characters is caught in a warehouse fire, and we do not know at the close of the action whether she is alive or not. That was the way Kawabata worked. The list of clearly incomplete Kawabata works is impressive, and one could seldom be sure that an apparently completed work was in fact that.

Kawabata was a good literary critic, and good at characterizing his own work. The scenes and situations that interested him, he said, were 'islands in a distant sea'. The first island was the Izu Peninsula, a mountain chain extending into the ocean some 60 or 70 miles southwest of Tokyo. Then came the Asakusa district of Tokyo itself, the chief entertainment district of the city between the two world wars. For Kawabata it was a place of homelessness. Then came the 'snow country', the districts west of the central mountain range of the main Japanese island, a place of dark winters closed off by storms from Siberia, and of hot-spring geishas who came close to being social outcasts.

The heroine of the novel, Komako, an ardent, passionate woman, is a geisha at a hot spring in the snow country. The hero, Shimamura, is a Tokyo dilettante who does not seem committed to much of anything at all. He is drawn to Komako, but knows that, after one of the sporadic visits that are the occasions for the action of the novel, he will leave and not return. So it is about a love that cannot be fulfilled.

The third major character, she who gets caught in the fire, is a strange, distant, beautiful girl who seems to hover on the edge of insanity, and for whom, even if she survives the fire, it is as difficult to expect real happiness as it is for Komako. Shimamura will probably make his last departure for Tokyo unblemished and unchanged. That is because he is incapable of love from the outset.

Loneliness, coldness, and the impossibility of love are at the heart of Kawabata's writing. In Japan and the West they are both old and modern themes. The sad circumstances of Kawabata's childhood make them intensely personal: he lost his parents and only sister in early childhood, and the grandfather who reared him, insofar as he was reared at all, when he was 14. From adolescence Kawabata was alone.

The lyricism of Kawabata's writing is so strong as to approach poetry. Much is ambiguous, much is left unsaid, much is said in a peculiar fashion. The opening lines of the book version of *Snow Country* are probably the most famous in modern Japanese literature. A train emerges from a long tunnel into the snow country, and 'the bottom of the night' turns white. Many a reader of the translated text has had trouble with a simile likening Komako's lips to a pair of leeches; but that is what the original says, and the simile is every bit as eccentric in Japanese as in translation.

—Edward Seidensticker

KAZANTZAKIS, Nikos. Born in Heraklion, Crete, 18 February 1883. Educated at French School of Holy Cross, Naxos, 1897–99; Gymnasium, Heraklion, 1899–1902; University of Athens, 1902–06, degree in law; studied in Paris, Germany, and Italy, 1906–10. Married 1) Galatea Alexiou in 1911 (divorced 1926); 2) Eleni Samios in 1945. Writer and traveller; Director General of Ministry of Public Welfare, 1919–20; Cabinet Minister Without Portfolio, 1945; served in UNESCO's Department of Translations of the Classics, 1947–48. Recipient: Lenin peace prize. *Died 26 October 1957.*

Publications

Fiction

Ophis ke Krino. 1906; as *Serpent and Lily,* translated by Theodora Vasils, with *The Sickness of the Age,* 1980.
Toda Raba (written in French). 1933; as *Toda Raba,* translated by Amy Mims, 1964.

Vios ke Politia tou Alexi Zorba. 1946; as *Zorba the Greek,* translated by Carl Wildman, 1952.
O Kapetan Michalis. 1953; as *Freedom or Death,* translated by Jonathan Griffin, 1956; as *Freedom and Death,* translated by Griffin, 1956.
O Christos Xanastavronete. 1954; as *The Greek Passion,* translated by Jonathan Griffin, 1953; as *Christ Recrucified,* translated by Griffin, 1954.
O Telefteos Pirasmos. 1955; as *The Last Temptation,* translated by Peter Bien, 1960; as *The Last Temptation of Christ,* translated by Bien, 1960.
O Ftochoulis tou Theou. 1956; as *God's Pauper,* translated by Peter Bien, 1962; as *Saint Francis,* translated by Bien, 1962.
Le Jardin des rochers (written in French). 1959; as *The Rock Garden,* translated by Richard Howard (passages from *The Saviors of God* translated by Kimon Friar), 1963.
Aderfofades. 1963; as *The Fratricides,* translated by Athena Gianakas Dallas, 1964.
Sta Palatia tes Knossou. 1981; as *At the Palace of Knossos,* translated by Theodora and Themi Vasils, 1987.

Plays

Ximeroni [Day Is Breaking] (produced 1907). In *Nea Estia,* 1977.
O Protomastoras [The Master Builder] (produced as operatic version, music by Manolis Kalomiris, 1916). In *Panathinea,* 1910.
Nikoforos Fokas [Nicephoros Phokas] (produced 1984). 1927.
Christos [Christ]. 1928.
Melissa (produced in French, 1960; produced in Greek, 1962). In *Nea Estia,* 1939; in book form (author's own French translation), with *Thésée,* 1953; as *Melissa,* translated by Athena Gianakas Dallas, in *Three Plays,* 1969.
Ioulianos o Paravatis [Julian the Apostate] (produced in French, 1945; produced in Greek, 1959). 1945.
Kapodistrias [Capodistria] (produced 1946). 1946.
Sodhoma ke Ghomora (produced 1983). In *Nea Estia,* 1949; as *Sodom and Gomorrah,* translated by Kimon Friar, in *Two Plays,* 1982.
Konstantinos Paleologhos [Constantine Paleologos] (produced in operatic version, music by Manolis Kalomiris, 1962; produced as play 1965). In *Nea Estia,* 1953.
Kouros, from the radio play (produced in English, 1971; produced in Greek, 1977). In author's own French translation, as *Thésée,* with *Melissa,* 1953; in Greek, 1955; as *Kouros,* translated by Athena Gianakas Dallas, in *Three Plays,* 1969.
Prometheas [Prometheus]. In *Theatro,* vol. 1, 1955.
Theatro: Tragodies (includes *Prometheas; Kouros; Odhisseas; Melissa; Ioulianos; Nikoforos Fokas; Konstantinos Paleologhos; Kapodistrias; Christoforos Colomvos; Sodhoma ke Ghomora; Vudhas*). 3 vols., 1955–56.
Vudhas (produced 1978). In *Theatro,* vol. 3, 1956; as *The Buddha,* translated by Kimon Friar and Athena Dallis-Damis, 1983.
Christoforos Colomvos (produced 1975). In *Theatro,* vol. 3, 1956; as *Christopher Columbus,* translated by Athena Gianakas Dallas, in *Three Plays,* 1969.
Comodhia. In *Nea Estia,* 1958; as *Comedy,* translated by Kimon Friar, 1982.
O Othelos Xanayirizi [Othello Returns]. In *Nea Estia,* 1962.
Three Plays (includes *Melissa; Kouros; Christopher Columbus*), translated by Athena Gianakas Dallas. 1969.
Eos Pote [Until When]. In *Nea Estia,* 1977.

Fasgha [Swaddling Clothes]. In *Nea Estia*, 1977.
Two Plays (includes *Sodom and Gomorrah*; *Comedy*), translated by Kimon Friar. 1982.

Verse

Odhisseas. 1938; as *The Odyssey: A Modern Sequel*, translated by Kimon Friar, 1958.
Tertsines [Poems in Terza Rima]. 1960.
Symposium. 1971; as *Symposium*, translated by Theodora and Themi Vasils, 1973.

Other

O Friderikos Nitse [Friedrich Nietzsche]. 1909.
Salvatores Dei: Askitiki. 1927; revised edition, 1945; as *The Saviors of God: Spiritual Exercises*, translated by Kimon Friar, 1960.
Taxidevontas (travel writing). 1927.
Te eida set Rousia. 2 vols., 1928; later published as *Taxidevontas: Rousia*, 1956; translated as *Russia: A Chronicle of Three Journeys in the Aftermath of the Revolution*, 1989.
Historia tes Rosikes logotechnias [History of Russian Literature]. 2 vols., 1930.
Taxidevontas: Ispania. 1937; as *Spain*, translated by Amy Mims, 1963.
O Morias. 1937; as *Journey to the Morea*, translated by F.A. Reed, 1965; as *Travels in Greece*, translated by Reed, 1966.
Taxidevontas II: Iaponia, Kina. 1938; as *Japan, China*, translated by George Pappageotes, 1963; as *Travels in China and Japan*, translated by Pappageotes, 1964.
Taxidevontas III: Anglia. 1941; translated as *England: A Travel Journal*, 1965.
Epistoles pros te Galatia. 1958; as *The Suffering God: Selected Letters to Galatia and to Papastefanou*, translated by Philip Ramp and Katerina Anghelaki Rooke, 1979.
Anafora ston Greco. 1961; as *Report to Greco*, translated by Peter Bien, 1965.
Tetrakosia grammata tou Kazantzakis sto Prevelaki (letters). 1965.
Journeying: Travels in Italy, Egypt, Sinai, Jerusalem, and Cyprus, translated by Themi and Theodora Vasils. 1975.
Arrostia tou aionos, as *The Sickness of the Age*, translated by Theodora Vasils, with *Serpent and Lily*. 1980.
Megas Alexandros (for children), as *Alexander the Great*, translated by Theodora Vasils. 1982.

Translator, *The Divine Comedy* by Dante; *Faust* by Goethe; *Iliad* by Homer; several Platonic dialogues; *The Birth of Tragedy* and *Thus Spake Zarathustra* by Nietzsche; *The Prince* by Machiavelli; *Conversations with Goethe* by Eckermann; *Origin of Species* by Darwin; *On Laughter* by Bergson; and other works, including many books for children.

*

Bibliography: *Kazantzakis bibliografi* by G.K. Katsimpales, 1958; 'Kazantzakis in America: A Bibliography of Translations and Comment' by Sandra A. Parker, in *Bulletin of Bibliography*, 25, 1968.

Critical Studies: *Kazantzakis and His Odyssey* by Pandelis Prevelakis, 1961; *Nikos Kazantzakis: A Biography Based on His Letters*, 1968, and *Kazantzakis*, 1970, both by Helen Kazantzakis; *Kazantzakis and the Linguistic Revolution in Greek Literature*, 1972, *Three Generations of Greek Writers: Introductions to Cavafy, Kazantzakis, Ritsos*, 1983, *Nikos Kazantzakis: Novelist*, 1989, and *Kazantzakis: Politics of the Spirit*, 1989, all by Peter Bien; *Kazantzakis: The Politics of Salvation* by James F. Lea, 1979; *The Cretan Glance: The World and Art of Nikos Kazantzakis* by Morton P. Levitt, 1980.

* * *

Nikos Kazantzakis was an insatiable traveller, internally and externally. He visited many countries. He read a vast amount of books. He calls to mind Wordsworth's lines about Newton: 'a mind for ever/voyaging through strange seas of thought, alone' (*Prelude* III, 62–3). No wonder he took as the hero of his epic a timeless, intellectual Odysseus. This ploy enabled him, in the course of 33,333 lines of great virtuosity, to explore again various answers to the human predicament which he had already considered in travel books, in the slim but significant *Salvatores Dei: Askitiki* (*The Saviors of God: Spiritual Exercises*), and in several plays of unrelieved seriousness. These answers include the philosophy of Nietzsche and Bergson, communism (which he had seen at first hand on visits to Russia in the 1920s), the idea of Christ (rather than any particular form of Christianity), Buddhism, anarchy, nihilism, and so on. In the end they are all found wanting.

Kazantzakis makes his Odysseus exclaim (II, 960): 'Hail, my soul, whose homeland has always been the journey!'. It is really the poet himself who is speaking. Kazantzakis's view of the world was too all-encompassing for him to be contained by any one literal homeland, even though his Cretan origins were tremendously important to him. Kazantzakis was forever moving on, from one country to another, from one creed to another. But, apart from the journey, there was one 'homeland' to which he always remained loyal: 'The demotic language is our homeland', he wrote in *Taxidevontas III: Anglia* (*England: A Travel Journal*). He loved natural, spoken Greek passionately. His *Odhisseas* (*The Odyssey*) is not only a hymn to the spirit of man, it is also a hymn to the Greek language.

If Kazantzakis had died in 1938, aged 55, he would probably be known only to a few researchers. The plays 'smell of the ink-well', as the Greeks say. The travel books are charming, but slight. *The Odyssey* is too vast, rambling, and daunting. There the case would rest. But on the island of Aegina, during the German occupation, between 1941 and 1943, Kazantzakis wrote his novel *Vios ke Politia tou Alexi Zorba* [The Life and Times of Alexis Zorba], known in English as *Zorba the Greek*. In *Zorba* he exclaims: 'if only I could do that, remain silent until the abstract idea reaches its highest point and becomes fable'—which is exactly what he did.

He managed, in his remaining 15 or so years, in five major novels—*O Kapetan Michalis* (*Freedom and Death*), *O Christos Xanastavronete* (*Christ Recrucified*), *O Telefteos Pirasmos* (*The Last Temptation*), *O Ftochoulis tou Theou* (*Saint Francis*), *Aderfofades* (*The Fratricides*)—and one autobiographical masterpiece, *Anafora ston Greco* (*Report to Greco*), to rework, as fables, all the themes that had preoccupied him for years with, for the first time, humanity and humour.

Among Kazantzakis's papers was found a note which said: 'Major work—the *Odyssey*. Everything else—spin-offs'. It might be more accurate to say that his real odyssey was his lifelong search for the meaning of existence, and that *all* his works, including the enormous epic, were spin-offs from that.

—Roger Green

THE LAST TEMPTATION (O Telefteos Pirasmos)
Novel by Nikos Kazantzakis, 1955.

Kazantzakis's *The Last Temptation* attempts what no other work of fiction has attempted—to rewrite the New Testament in the form of a novel from the point of view of Christ. To the accounts given in the Scriptures Kazantzakis adds the postmodern device of the double ending—the 'last temptation' of an alternative destiny for the Messiah as a comfortable family man.

The problems inherent in such a work are considerable: the impossibility of expressing the psychological inner life of a divinity as the novel form demands, and the necessity of creating dialogue worthy of God. The problems for the author, however, are matched by the difficulties for the reader. Kazantzakis's narrative is continually compromised by the 'authorized version' of the material it would make its own: a weighty problem of intertextuality. In scenes such as the wedding in Magdala (chapter 15) where Kazantzakis inventively contextualizes the parable of the foolish virgins, the author seems to add to his overshadowing source. Elsewhere, however, he seeks to question the notion of holy writ. His novel provocatively explores the contradictions involved in enclosing divine truth within the written word, thereby opening a space for speculation and creativity in which his own work may have validity. Thus we see Jesus angrily rejecting as lies the stories Matthew, the evangelist, has written about him. When, however, Matthew replies that he has been compelled by an angel to write what is untrue, Jesus ponders the existence of different layers of truth: 'If this was the highest level of truth, inhabited only by God . . . ? If what we called truth, God called lies . . . ?'. Later, Paul openly proclaims his willingness to propagate falsehood, if it is necessary to save mankind: 'Whatever gives wings to man . . . that is true'.

The level of truth inhabited by Kazantzakis is, as he tells the reader in the prologue, one of confession. The novel is a dramatization, through a fictional Christ, of his own religious struggles. Hence the 'Holy Land' of the novel is in fact the world of Kazantzakis's own psyche. The hallmark of this inner world is its obsessive fascination with the body. The early chapters in particular are dominated by descriptions of blood, heat, and pain. This emphasis on the physical is only further stressed by the author's use of demotic Greek, which renders the abstract in terms of the concrete, the metaphorical as the literal.

Kazantzakis seeks to establish the reality of his action by anchoring it to the senses. Jesus plunges himself into this world of the senses with the mortification of his flesh. The same language of sweat and wounds is used to describe his beloved, the prostitute Mary Magdalene.

Equally characteristic of the author's vision is the profusion in ancient Palestine of giants, dwarves, and deformed cripples. It is typical of Kazantzakis that when two monks espy Jesus emerging from the desert, one is an elephant-like man with a mouth like a shark, the other a hunchback who drags an enormous backside.

As these grotesqueries indicate, Kazantzakis's confessional novel has little interest in historical realism: inaccuracy and anachronism abound. Rather the tale draws on other sources —those of traditions of folktale and rural religious art. Signs of this are everywhere. The narrow cast of characters and the lack of any coherent geography shrinks the Holy Land to the dimensions of a village. Comic tales of wily trickery hark back to rustic fables, such as that of Simon the Cyrenian obtaining a larger share of the lamb's head supper by reminding the disciples of John the Baptist's beheading. Through all these devices Kazantzakis's Messiah is memorable but profoundly human: not so much divine as embarked on a Nietzschean struggle to attain divinity, that struggle referred to in the prologue as the battle between the flesh and the spirit. As this struggle is an evolutionary one, the book presents not one Christ but a developing sequence of different Christs: the madman possessed by God, the holy fool, the loving simpleton, the fiery prophet, and, finally, the sensible, and sensual, worldly man.

It is, however, this last version of Christ that remains in the imagination. The novelist must always be more convincing when speaking of human desire than when attempting to create the divine. The Jesus of the book's final section, who achieves his long-desired consummation with Mary Magdalene, is inevitably more appealing than the Christ who voluntarily chooses the agonies of crucifixion. This section is, further, as the title suggests, the creative *tour-de-force* of the novel. It alone has the originative value of myth, rather than the frisson of novel reinterpretation. The mythos it offers—of Christ saved from his destiny—has some value. Jesus, after all, only does the reasonable thing. Here, arguably, is the true reason why the book has been blacklisted by the Vatican. The last temptation, declined by Jesus but likely to be accepted by the reader, is too hard to resist.

—Edmund Cusick

KELLER, Gottfried. Born in Zurich, Switzerland, 19 July 1819. Educated at Armenschule zum Brunnenturm; Landknabeninstitut, to age 13; Industrieschule, 1832–33; studied painting with Peter Steiger, 1834, and Rudolf Meyer, 1837; Munich Academy, 1840–42. Gave up art for writing in Zurich, 1842: government grant to study at University of Heidelberg, 1848–50, and University of Berlin, 1850–55; cantonal secretary (Staatschreiber), 1861–76. Honorary doctorate: University of Zurich, 1869. Honorary Citizen, Zurich, 1878. Member, Order of Maximilian (Bavaria), 1876. *Died 15 July 1890.*

PUBLICATIONS

Collections

Sämtliche Werke, edited by Jonas Fränkel and Carl Helbling. 24 vols., 1926–54.
Werke, edited by Clemens Heselhaus. 2 vols., 1982.

Fiction

Der grüne Heinrich. 1853–55; revised edition, 1880; as *Green Henry*, translated by A.M. Holt, 1960.
Die Leute von Seldwyla (includes *Frau Regel Amrain und ihr Jüngster*; *Kleider machen Leute*; *Pankraz, der Schmoller*;

Romeo und Julia auf dem Dorfe; *Der Schmied seines Glückes*). 1856–74; as *The People of Seldwyla*, translated by Martin Wyness, 1911; also translated by M.D. Hottinger, with *Seven Legends*, 1929.
Sieben Legenden. 1872; edited by K. Reichert, 1965; as *Seven Legends*, translated by Martin Wyness, 1911; also translated by C.H. Handschin, 1911; M.D. Hottinger, with *The People of Seldwyla*, 1929.
Züricher Novellen (includes *Hadlaub*; *Der Landvogt von Greifensee*). 1877.
Das Sinngedicht. 1881.
Martin Salander. 1886; as *Martin Salander*, translated by Kenneth Halwas, 1963.
Clothes Maketh Man and Other Swiss Stories, translated by K. Freiligrath Kroeker. 1894.
Stories, edited by Frank G. Ryder. 1982.

Verse

Gedichte. 1846.
Neue Gedichte. 1852.
Gesammelte Gedichte. 1883.
Gedichte, edited by Albert Köster. 1922.

Other

Briefwechsel, with Theodor Storm, edited by Albert Köster. 1904.
Briefwechsel, with Paul Heyse, edited by Max Kalbeck. 1919.
Gottfried Keller in seinen Briefen, edited by Heinz Amelung. 1921.
Briefwechsel, with J.V. Widmann, edited by Max Widmann. 1922.
Briefe an Vieweg, edited by Jonas Fränkel. 1938.
Gesammelte Briefe, edited by Carl Helbling. 4 vols., 1950–54.
Briefwechsel, with Hermann Hettner, edited by Jürgen Jahn. 1964.
Aus Gottfried Kellers glücklicher Zeit: der Dichter im Briefwechsel mit Marie und Adolf Exner, edited by Irmgard Smidt. 1981.
Kellers Briefe, edited by Peter Goldammer. 1982.
Mein lieber Herr und bester Freund: Gottfried Keller im Briefwechsel mit Wilhelm Petersen, edited by Irmgard Smidt. 1984.
Briefwechsel, with Emil Kuh, edited by Irmgard Smidt and Erwin Streitfeld. 1988.

*

Bibliography: *Keller Bibliographie 1844–1934* by Charles C. Zippermann, 1935.

Critical Studies: *The Cyclical Method of Composition in Keller's 'Sinngedicht'* by Priscilla M. Kramer, 1939; *Keller: Kleider machen Leute* by B.A. Rowley, 1960; *Keller: Life and Works* by J.M. Lindsay, 1968; *Light and Darkness in Keller's 'Der grüne Heinrich'* by Lucie Karcic, 1976; *Gottfried Keller: Welterfahrung, Werkstruktur und Stil* by Kaspar T. Locher, 1985; *Gottfried Keller: Poet, Pedagogue and Humanist* by Richard R. Ruppel, 1988; *Readers and their Fictions in the Novels and Novellas of Gottfried Keller* by Gail K. Hart, 1989; *The Poetics of Scepticism: Gottfried Keller and Die Leute von Seldwyla* by Eric Swales, 1994.

* * *

Gottfried Keller, together with Jeremias Gotthelf and Conrad Ferdinand Meyer, is today generally regarded as one of the three pillars of 19th-century Swiss-German literature. His poems are no longer widely read, and he is remembered chiefly for his novel *Der grüne Heinrich* (*Green Henry*), his four collections of short stories, and the correspondence he conducted with writers such as Theodor Storm and Paul Heyse. His reputation was slow to establish itself even in the German-speaking countries, and outside Germany his works have never attracted a readership which truly reflected Keller's standing as a master story-teller and an acute but humane observer of human passion and folly.

Green Henry, conceived as a novel of education (Bildungsroman) within a German tradition which stretches from the medieval *Parzival* to Thomas Mann's *Der Zauberberg* (*The Magic Mountain*) and beyond, depicts in sympathetic and at times painful detail the early life of Heinrich Lee, a young Swiss who is torn between the compulsion to be an artist and the demands of domestic and civic duty. Partly autobiographical, the novel portrays a number of scenes and situations familiar to Keller, ranging from the small Swiss village to student life in Munich. The descriptions of Heinrich's early childhood, his thoughts on religion, his encounters at school, above all his ability to project an inner poetic vision onto events and experiences, reveal strikingly Keller's powers of psychological observation and his capacity to bring out the symbolic and the significant in his treatment of everyday and indeed mundane occurrences. The second version of the novel lacks the lyrical spontaneity and exuberance of the first; it is provided with a more conciliatory ending and is altogether more measured and distanced in tone and style. It no doubt reflects Keller's own mature view that to renounce art for the sake of duty was not of necessity a tragic choice.

Keller's ability to transcend the surface meaning of events and human actions, and to attribute to them a more universal significance, is even more clearly evident in his collections of stories and short novels, especially in *Die Leute von Seldwyla* (*The People of Seldwyla*) and the cycle of *Züricher Novellen*. The two groups of Seldwyla tales take as their fictional milieu a small town described by Keller as being 'situated somewhere in Switzerland, surrounded by the same old city walls and towers as it was three hundred years ago'. The narratives which revolve around this setting display a playful inventiveness and a sharp eye for incongruity and pretence. With humour and gentle irony they lay bare the realities underlying the seemingly placid exterior of peasant and bourgeois life in 19th-century Switzerland, and in doing so they illuminate and clarify the reader's understanding of the perennial conflicts deriving from personal and social relationships.

Literary history tends to assign Keller and his writings to the period of 'poetic realism', a movement which some modern critics would disparage as a manifestation of political quiescence produced both for and by the German bourgeoisie. Such generalizations can on occasion be useful, but they would do scant justice to stories like 'Romeo und Julia auf dem Dorfe' and 'Der Landvogt von Greifensee' which, quite apart from their artistic perfection as narrative structures, touch upon the most basic contradictions which appear whenever individual conscience and consciousness seek to define themselves within systems of social values and traditional beliefs.

—A.P. Foulkes

KENA. See **UPANISHADS.**

KHLEBNIKOV, Velimir. Born Viktor Vladimirovich Khlebnikov in Malye Derbety, near Tundutovo, Astrakhan province, Russia, 28 October 1885. Educated at Kazan' Third Gymnasium, 1898–1903; studied mathematics and natural sciences at University of Kazan', 1903–08; studied biology and Slavic languages, University of St Petersburg, 1909–11. Associated with Futurist and other literary groups; served in Tsarist army, 1916–17; wandering poet, travelled across Russia: arrested by Whites in Kharkov, then by Reds, 1919; worked in Caucasus propaganda bureau (Rosta) in Baku, 1920; lecturer in Revolutionary army headquarters in Persia, 1921; night watchman in Rosta office in Piatigorsk, 1921. *Died 28 June 1922.*

PUBLICATIONS

Collections

Stikhi [Poems]. 1923.
Sobranie proizvedenii [Collected Works], edited by Yurii Tynianov and Nikolai Stepanov. 5 vols., 1928–33.
Neizdannye proizvedenii [Unpublished Works], edited by N. Khardziev and T. Grits. 1940.
Stikhotvoreniia i poemy [Poetry and Narrative Verse], edited by Nikolai Stepanov. 1960.
Sobranie sochinenii [Collected Works]. 4 vols., 1968–72.
Snake Train: Poetry and Prose, edited by Gary Kern, translated by Kern, Richard Sheldon, Edward J. Brown, Neil Cornwell, and Lily Feiler. 1976.
The King of Time, edited by Charlotte Douglas, translated by Paul Schmidt. 1985.
Izbrannoe [Selection], edited by V. Smirnov. 1986.
Collected Works:
  1. *Letters and Theoretical Writings*, edited by Charlotte Douglas, translated by Paul Schmidt. 1987.
  2. *Prose, Plays and Supersagas*, edited by Ronald Vroon. 1989.

Works

Uchitel' i uchenik [Teacher and Pupil]. 1912.
Igra v adu [A Game in Hell]. 1912.
Riav! Perchatki 1908–1914 [Roar! The Gauntlets]. 1913.
Izbornik stikhov 1907–1914 [Selected Verse]. 1914.
Tvoreniia (1906–1908) [Creations]. 1914.
Bitvy 1915–1917: Novoe uchenie o voine [Battles: The New Teaching about War]. 1915.
Vremia mera mira [Time the Measure of the World]. 1916.
Truba marsian [The Martian Pipe]. 1916.
Oshibka smerti [Death's Mistake] (produced 1920). 1916.
Ladomir [Goodworld]. 1920.
Noch' v okope [A Night in the Trench]. 1921.
Vestnik [Herald]. 2 vols., 1922.
Zangezi. 1922.
Otryvok iz dosok sud'by [Fragment from the Boards of Destiny]. 3 vols., 1922–23.
Nastoiashchee [Genuine]. 1926.
Vsem: Nochnoi bal [For Everyone: The Night Ball]. 1927.
Zverinets [Menagerie]. 1930.
Voisko pesen [Military Song]. 1985.
Stikhotvoreniia. Poemy. Dramy. Proza [Poetry. Narrative Verse. Drama. Prose]. 1986.
Stikhotvoreniia [Poetry]. 1988.
Utes iz budushchego [The Rock of the Future]. 1988.
Proza [Prose]. 1990.

Stikhi, poemy [Poems, Narrative Verse]. 1991.

*

Critical Studies: *The Longer Poems of Khlebnikov*, 1961, and *Russian Futurism: A History*, 1968, both by Vladimir Markov; *Xlebnikov and Carnival: An Analysis of the Poem 'Poet'* by Barbara Lonnqvist, 1979; *Velimir Xlebnikov's Shorter Poems: A Key to the Coinages* by Ronald Vroon, 1983; *Velimir Chlebnikov and the Development of Poetical Language in Russian Symbolism and Futurism* by Willem G. Weststeijn, 1983.

* * *

When the Russian Futurists 'slapped the face of public taste' it was largely with the gauntlet of Velimir Khlebnikov's work that they administered the blow. His experimentation with the Russian language and his ingenious neologisms helped to earn the Futurists the notoriety they were seeking. His work on the word was an embodiment of the Futurist aesthetic stance. He placed the word at the centre of attention, showed how it could develop according to an inner logic. A fossilized literary language came alive at his touch.

The Futurists proclaimed Khlebnikov 'King of Russian Poetry'. He could not, however, summon the regal presence or stentorian tones of such as Maiakovskii. Although the Futurists toured Russia, Khlebnikov did not take part. He seemed to have a pathological inability to perform in public. Yet, Russian Futurism without Khlebnikov would have been an empty shell.

Nevertheless, Khlebnikov's association with the Futurists was somewhat double-edged. Their tendency to publicize those of his works which reflected the movement's iconoclastic interests led to him acquiring a reputation as a poet of gibberish. This is a grave misjudgement. Despite his espousal of the 'self-developed' word, Khlebnikov was a keen seeker after meaning. Even his transrational language (*zaum'*) was designed not to destroy meaning but to enhance it.

Khlebnikov's preoccupation with language should not be stressed unduly. His work reveals a considerable concern for the world as well as the word. Social and ideological motivations provided a major inspiration for his writing. Many works reflect militant pan-Slavist and revolutionary sentiments. He was opposed to Western influence and looked towards the folk art of the Russian and Slavic peoples. He also directed his gaze eastwards towards India, Persia, and Central Asia.

After the outbreak of World War I Khlebnikov directed his poetic militancy against war. This campaign soon intermingled with a general assault on the arbitrary nature of fate. He became increasingly preoccupied with numerological theories aimed at discovering the laws of time. By practical prophecy he wished to make man the master of his destiny, to make him capable of directing his passage through the centuries like a ship along the Volga. This utopian element finds expression in much of his work. However, running parallel to it is a vivid awareness of the conflict and disaster constantly threatening mankind. Convinced that events unfolded according to some determinable and rational schema, Khlebnikov proclaimed that 'measure' had come to replace faith. Yet there is something irrational about his faith in 'measure'. His mathematical formulas can appear as incantational as his verse.

As well as his 'experimental' works Khlebnikov was an

author of long poems with an unusual epic sweep, of short lyric verse with surprising depth, of prose, and of drama. Above all he was a visionary, and it is this vision coupled with an acute sensitivity towards the world which makes some of his works among the best in Russian literature.

—Ray Cooke

INCANTATION BY LAUGHTER (Zakliatie smekhom)
Poem by Velimir Khlebnikov, 1910.

In Khlebnikov's enormously varied and rich *oeuvre*, 'Incantation by Laughter', one of his earliest poems, is far from the most important or semantically dense work. But it is a small masterpiece of linguistic imagination, which acquired fame very early on and has been his most widely known poem ever since, in spite, or perhaps because, of a persistent perception of him as the kind of poet who is only for the initiated:

O laugh it out, you laughsters!
O laugh it up, you laughsters!
So they laugh with laughters, so they laugherize
  delaughly,
O laugh it up belaughably!
O the laughing stock of the laughed-upon—the laugh of
  the belaughed laughters!
O laugh it out roundlaughingly, the laugh of laughed-at
  laughians!
Laugherino, laugherino,
Laughify, laughicate, laugholets, laugholets,
Laughikins, laughikins.
O laugh it out, you laughsters!
O laugh it up, you laughsters!

(translated by Gary Kern)

'Incantation by Laughter' was published first in 1910, and a couple of years later, as Russian Futurism was attempting to establish—and announce—itself, it could not only be seen to exemplify a number of the movement's tenets concerning art and the 'self-sufficient' word, but also stood out as an accomplished piece. Despite the ridicule it initially received from a number of reviewers, it has the great polemical advantage that it cannot be dismissed in this way, for to laugh is precisely to engage with the poem; and its very effect as an incantation is confirmed by the spell it has cast on so many readers and, especially, listeners who would otherwise be shy of Khlebnikov.

The most obvious aspect of Futurist poetics in general, and Khlebnikov's poetics in particular, that is manifested in the poem is word creation. This is upheld as the first 'right' of poets in the infamous manifesto *Poshchechina obshchestvennomu vkusu* (*A Slap in the Face of Public Taste*), 1912: 'To enlarge the *scope* of the poet's vocabulary with arbitrary and derivative words (word-novelty)'. In 'Incantation by Laughter' such novelty is achieved by the extensive use of suffixes and prefixes on the root for 'laugh', creating nouns, verbs, adjectives, and adverbs—'conjugating' a root, as Khlebnikov called it. In doing so he exploits the distinctive function of suffixes and prefixes in Russian, so that the original effect is extraordinary but in the spirit of the language, while in translation the effect is interesting but un-English. Other aspects of Futurist poetics that are manifested in the poem include the orientation towards sound, relegation of syntax, and loose rhythm, and yet also the 'difficulty' of reading the poem if one stops to struggle with the possible meaning of each word.

In fact, 'Incantation by Laughter' is emblematic of far more in Khlebnikov's poetry than just some of the tenets of Russian futurism. Above all, it shows his concern for the roots of words, which were 'of God', and for meaning, since each creation on the root for 'laugh' is intended to draw out latent semantic possibilities in the language. Furthermore, the poem shows Khlebnikov's orientation towards popular, folk forms, such as proverbs, sayings, riddles, and chants, and in general towards the language of the common Russian people, since for him it was the 'will of the people' which could grant the 'right to create words'. But the poem also shows the almost scientific nature of Khlebnikov's attitude to the word, because if the poem is read with attention to word formation and semantics, then it seems to approach a linguistic exercise.

Thus 'Incantation by Laughter' anticipates the unique paradox and synthesis of Khlebnikov's art: it is semantically dense and cerebral, and yet also immediate, popular and —in the famous term '*zaum*'—transrational. It is an art that is both philological and magical, for the poem is, after all, an incantation; it is an art of extraordinary imagination.

Later, in 1919, Khlebnikov wrote that 'minor works [such as 'Incantation by Laughter'] are significant when they start the future, in the same way as a falling star leaves behind itself a fiery trail; they must have sufficient speed to break through the present . . .'; he concluded that 'the home of creation is the future. It is from there that blows the wind of the gods of the word'. The particular significance of 'Incantation by Laughter' for Khlebnikov is further evident in the way that it is echoed in a poem written shortly before his death, 'Once again, once again . . .' (1922), a poem which critics have called his 'testament'. At the end of his life the poet felt ignored, mocked, and misunderstood. Now, returning one last time to the root 'laugh', he warned his audience, who had ignored his guiding light as a star, that the underwater rocks would 'laugh at [over] you', just as 'you have laughed at [over] me'.

—Robin Aizlewood

———

KIŠ, Danilo. Born in Subotica, Serbia, 22 February 1935. Jewish parents sent to Auschwitz in 1944; brought up by uncle in Cetinje, Yugoslavia. Educated locally in Hungary to age 13, then high school in Cetinje; Belgrade University, degree in comparative literature 1958. Editor, *Vidici*; lecturer in Serbo-Croat, Universities of Strasbourg, 1961–63, Bordeaux, 1973–76, and Lille, 1979–83; also translator from a number of languages; lived and worked in Paris, from 1979. Recipient: NIN prize, 1973; Ivan Goran Kovačič prize, 1977; Grand Aigle d'Or (Nice), 1980; Ivo Andrić award, 1984; PEN Bruno Schulz prize 1989. *Died 15 October 1989.*

PUBLICATIONS

Fiction

Mansarda; Psalam 44 [The Garret; Psalm 44]. 1962.
Bašta, pepeo. 1965; as *Garden, Ashes*, translated by William J. Hannaher, 1976.
Rani jadi [Early Sorrows] (stories). 1969.

Peščanik. 1972; as *Hourglass*, translated by Ralph Manheim, 1990.
Grobnica za Borisa Davidoviča (stories). 1976; as *A Tomb for Boris Davidovich*, translated by Duška Mikić-Mitchell, 1978.
Enciklopedija mrtvih. 1983; as *The Encyclopedia of the Dead*, translated by Michael Henry Heim, 1989.

Plays

Elektra (produced 1969).
Noć i magla [Night and Mist] (includes *Papagaj* [The Parrot]; *Drveni sanduk Tomasa Vulfa* [The Wooden Chest of Thomas Wolfe]; *Mehanički lavovi* [The Mechanical Lions]). 1983.

Other

Po-etika [Poetics]. 2 vols., 1972–74.
Čas anatomije [The Anatomy Lesson]. 1978.
Homo poeticus. 1983.
Sabrana dela [Collected Works]. 10 vols., 1983.
Gorki talog iskustva (interviews), with Mirjana Miočinović. 1990.
Pesme i preperi, edited by Predrag Cudic. 1992.

Editor, with Mirjana Miočinović, *Sabrana dela* [Collected Works], by Lautréamont. 1964.

Translator of the poetry of Verlaine and Baudelaire.

*

Critical Studies: 'Imaginary-Real Lives: On Danilo Kiš' by Norbert Czarny and Catherine Vincent, in *Cross Currents*, 3, 1984; 'Danilo Kiš: From "Enchantment" to "Documentation"' by Branko Gorjup, in *Canadian Slavonic Papers*, 29(4), 1987; 'Danilo Kiš: Encyclopedia of the Dead' by Predrag Matvejevic, in *Cross Currents*, 1988; 'The Awakening of Sleepers in Danilo Kiš's *Encyclopedia of the Dead*' by Jelena S. Bankovic-Rosul, in *Serbian Studies*, Spring 1990; 'Danilo Kiš, 1935–1989' by Gyorgy Spiro, in *New Hungarian Quarterly*, 31(119), 1990; 'Silk, Scissors, Gardens, Ashes: The Autobiographical Writing of Irena Vrkljan and Danilo Kiš' by Celia Hawkesworth, in her *Literature and Politics in Eastern Europe*, 1992; *Proza Danila Kiša* by Peter Pijanović, 1992.

* * *

Danilo Kiš occupied a pre-eminent position among contemporary Yugoslav writers on the strength of his carefully crafted fiction, but his other literary ventures—plays for radio and television, essays and translations from French, Hungarian, and Russian—have also been held in high esteem. His early novels, *Mansarda* [The Garret] and *Psalam 44* [Psalm 44], have clearly indicated two important features of Kiš as a fiction writer: his keen interest in the themes of human suffering and his lack of interest in the vestiges of traditional realistic narrative and classical psychological analysis.
Mansarda is basically a story of youthful love patterned on the myth of Orpheus and Eurydice, but what the novel captures best is the garret atmosphere of the hero's juvenile world of capricious daydreams, hallucinations, paradoxical

reasoning, and cynicism from which he is 'dethroned' and brought down to face the demanding banalities of everyday life. Many quotations and literary and mythological allusions give the novel a strong intellectual edge. The author's concern with the contrasting facets of existence and the playful dance of his language make this story of how innocence changes into experience one of the most original first novels published in Yugoslavia after World War II.
Psalam 44 is Kiš's attempt at the literature of the Holocaust. It is a stream-of-consciousness novel in which a young Jewish girl reveals her distressing history in the tense moments preceding her escape from the Birkenau concentration camp with her newborn baby and her French girlfriend. The account of her desperate efforts to survive after the escape is concluded with a qualified happy ending: the reunited family visit the camp six years afterwards in order to hand down to the child 'the joy of those who, out of death and love, were able to create life'. The most impressive feature of the novel is the dispassionate, almost lethargic calmness of the narrative, which recaptures in most grisly detail the abyss of human agony.
Kiš's next novel, *Bašta, pepeo* (*Garden, Ashes*), has a strong autobiographical element. The narrator-protagonist is the Jewish boy Andreas Sam, who grows up in the Danubian plains in the 1940s, before, during, and after the war. His memories concentrate on a small, tightly knit group of characters, but are dominated by the overpowering personality of his father, Eduard, a railway official who has compiled a gigantic Universal Timetable and who disappears during the Holocaust. The book is in large measure the search by a son for the father (a hypochondriac, lunatic dreamer, drunkard, and loner) he lost even before his death, in an attempt to establish distant and unnoticed connections which in his childhood he could not believe existed. A skilful interweaving of introspective poetic strands, striking intellectual displays, and reminiscences almost sensuously brought to life makes this book a particular kind of creative autobiography, clothed in a fine net of soft lyrical weave. Kiš followed it with a sequel, *Rani jadi* [Early Sorrows], a collection of short stories where the Sam family appears again portrayed in the same tone of melancholic lyricism and psychological subtlety.
Peščanik (*Hourglass*), where the same father-figure turns up under the initials E.S., is a novel which seemingly lacks all thematic and narrative coherence. It is composed of various texts referring to E.S., his motivations and actions, but the key to understanding these diverse writings (letters, documents, reports, and notes), which demand the reader's utmost concentration and patience, is given at the end of the book, in a letter written by E.S. to his sister. It casts a revealing light on Kiš's apparently chaotic narrative and discloses its moral seriousness in the history of a man who, in the inferno of history and amid the atmosphere of selfishness and indifference, tries to secure the survival of his family.
Grobnica za Borisa Davidoviča (*A Tomb for Boris Davidovich*), a collection of short stories concerned with the theme of suffering of the innocent, makes a new departure. All the stories except one, which takes place in southern France in 1330, describe the misfortunes of several characters (mostly Jewish) who perished in the Soviet labour camps or died in the USSR as the victims of forces of terror. The stories, based on authentic documents and case histories, are an original hybrid of fiction and 'faction' and bear a general resemblance to Arthur Koestler's *Darkness at Noon*, 'although surpassing it in both horrifying detail and narrative skill', as Joseph Brodskii said in his introduction to the English translation. Accused of plagiarism by some Yugoslav critics, Kiš refuted their allegations in the highly polemic *Čas*

anatomije [The Anatomy Lesson], turning his defence into a virulent satire of his critics.

In his last volume of short stories, *Enciklopedija mrtvih* (*The Encyclopedia of the Dead*), Kiš widened his thematic range through his interest in ancient legends and metaphysical strata of existence. His paramount concern for human suffering caused by forces of history, however, preserved its centrality in all his writing.

—Dušan Puvačić

KLEIST, (Bernd) Heinrich (Wilhelm) von. Born in Frankfurt an der Oder, Brandenburg (now Germany), 18 October 1777. Entered the Prussian army in 1792; took part in the siege of Mainz, 1793, promoted to second lieutenant, 1979, resigned his commission, 1799. Studied law, University of Frankfurt, 1799. Travelled throughout Germany, and to Paris and Switzerland, 1800–04; attempted to join the French army, 1803; civil servant, Königsberg, 1805–06; co-founder, with Adam Müller, and editor, *Phöbus*, Dresden, 1808–09; attempted unsuccessfully to publish the newspaper *Germania*, in Prague, 1809; editor, *Berliner Abendblätter*, 1810–11. Suffered many nervous breakdowns. *Died (suicide) 21 November 1811.*

PUBLICATIONS

Collections

Hinterlassene Schriften, edited by Ludwig Tieck. 1821.
Gesammelte Schriften, edited by Ludwig Tieck. 3 vols., 1826.
Werke, edited by Erich Schmidt and others. 5 vols., 1904–05; revised edition, 7 vols., 1936–38.
Sämtliche Werke und Briefe, edited by Helmut Sembdner. 2 vols., 1961.

Plays

Die Familie Schroffenstein (produced 1804). 1803; as *The Feud of the Schroffensteins*, translated by Mary J. and Lawrence M. Price, 1916.
Amphitryon (produced 1899). 1807; as *Amphitryon*, translated by Marion Sonnenfeld, 1962; also translated by Charles E. Passage, in *Amphitryon: Three Plays in New Verse Translations*, 1973; Martin Greenberg, in *Five Plays*, 1988.
Der zerbrochene Krug (produced 1808). 1811; as *The Broken Pitcher*, translated by Bayard Quincy Morgan, 1961; also translated by Jon Swan, in *Plays*, 1982; as *The Broken Jug*, translated by Lawrence P.R. Wilson, in *Four Continental Plays*, edited by John P. Allen, 1964; also translated by Roger Jones, 1977; Martin Greenberg, in *Five Plays*, 1988.
Penthesilea (produced 1876). 1808; as *Penthesilea*, translated by Humphry Trevelyan, in *The Classic Theatre*, edited by Eric Bentley, 1959; also translated by Martin Greenberg, in *Five Plays*, 1988.
Das Käthchen von Heilbronn (produced 1810). 1810; as *Kate of Heilbronn*, translated by Elijah B. Impey, in *Illustrations of German Poetry*, 1841; as *Käthchen of Heilbronn; or, the*

Test of Fire, translated by Frederick E. Pierce, in *Fiction and Fantasy of German Literature*, 1927.
Prinz Friedrich von Homburg (produced 1821). In *Hinterlassene Schriften*, 1821; as *The Prince of Homburg*, translated by Charles E. Passage, 1956; also translated by James Kirkup, in *The Classic Theatre*, edited by Eric Bentley, 1959; as *Prince Frederick of Homburg*, translated by Peggy Meyer Sherry, in *Plays*, 1982; also translated by Martin Greenberg, 1988.
Die Hermannsschlacht (produced 1839). In *Hinterlassene Schriften*, 1821.
Robert Guiskard (unfinished; produced 1901). In *Gesammelte Schriften*, 1826; as *A Fragment of the Tragedy of Robert Guiscard*, translated by Martin Greenberg, in *Five Plays*, 1988.
Plays (*The Broken Pitcher*; *Amphitryon*; *Penthesilea*; *Prince Frederick of Homburg*), edited by Walter Hinderer. 1982.
Five Plays (includes *Amphitryon*; *The Broken Jug*; *Penthesilea*; *Prince Frederick of Homburg*; *A Fragment of the Tragedy of Robert Guiscard*), translated by Martin Greenberg. 1988.

Fiction

Erzählungen. 2 vols., 1810–11.
The Marquise of O. and Other Stories, translated by Martin Greenberg. 1960; also translated by David Luke and Nigel Reeves, 1978.
Michael Kohlhaas, translated by J. Oxenford, 1844; also translated by F. Lloyd and W. Newton, 1875; F.H. King, 1919; James Kirkup, 1967; Harry Steinhauer, in *Twelve German Novellas*, 1977; David Luke and Nigel Reeves, in *The Marquiss of O. and Other Stories*, 1978.

Other

Briefe an seine Schwester Ulrike, edited by August Koberstein. 1860.
Briefe an seine Braut, edited by Karl Biedermann and others. 1884.
Über das Marionettentheater: Aufsätze und Anekdoten, edited by Helmut Sembdner, 1935; revised edition, 1980; as *On a Theatre of Marionettes*, translated by G. Wilford, 1989; as *On Puppetshows*, translated by David Paisley, 1991.
Lebensspuren: Dokumente und Berichte der Zeitgenossen, edited by Helmut Sembdner. 1964.
An Abyss Deep Enough: Letters of Heinrich von Kleist (includes essays), edited and translated by Philip B. Miller. 1982.

*

Bibliography: *Kleist-Bibliographie 1803–1862* by Helmut Sembdner, 1966.

Critical Studies: *Reason and Energy* by Michael Hamburger, 1957; *Kleist: Studies in His Work and Literary Character* by Walter Silz, 1961; *Heinrich von Kleist's Dramas* by E.L. Stahl, 1961; *Kleist's 'Prinz Friedrich von Homburg': An Interpretation Through Word Patterns* by Mary Garland, 1968; *Kleist: A Study in Tragedy and Anxiety* by John Gearey, 1968; *Kleist's Prinz Friedrich von Homburg: A Critical Study*, 1970, and *Heinrich von Kleist*, 1979, both by J.M. Ellis; *From Lessing to Hauptmann: Studies in German Drama* by Ladislaus Löb, 1974; *The Major Works of Heinrich von Kleist* by R.E. Helbling, 1975; *Kleist and the Tragic Ideal: A Study of Penthesilea and its Relationship to Kleist's Personal and Literary Development, 1806–1808* by H.M. Brown, 1977; *The Stories of Kleist: A Critical Study* by Denys Dyer, 1977; *Heinrich von Kleist: Word into Flesh: A Poet's Quest for the Symbol* by Ilse Graham, 1977; *Von Kleist: From Hussar to Panzer Marshal* by Clyde R. Davis, 1979; *Heinrich von Kleist: Studies in the Character and Meaning of His Writings* by J.M. Ellis, 1979; *Kleist's Lost Year and the Quest for Robert Guiskard* by R.H. Samuel, 1981; *Kleist: A Biography* by Joachim Maass, translated by Ralph Manheim, 1983; *Desire's Sway: The Plays and Stories of Heinrich von Kleist* by James M. McGlathery, 1983; *Spirited Women Heroes: Major Female Characters in the Dramas of Goethe, Schiller and Kleist* by Julie D. Prandi, 1983; *Prison and Idylls: Studies in Heinrich von Kleist's Fictional World* by Linda Dietrick, 1985; *Heirich von Kleist: A Critical Study* by Raymond Cooke, 1987; *The Manipulation of Reality in Works by Heinrich von Kleist* by Robert E. Glenny, 1987; *Kafka's Prussian Advocate: The Influence of Heinrich von Kleist on Franz Kafka* by John M. Grandin, 1987; *In Pursuit of Power: Heirich von Kleist's Machiavellian Protagonists*, 1987, *Kleist's Aristocratic Heritage and Das Käthchen von Heilbronn*, 1991, and *Kleist on Stage, 1804–1987*, 1993, all by William C. Reeve; *Laughter, Comedy and Aesthetics: Kleist's Der zerbrochene Krug* by Mark G. Ward, 1989.

* * *

Throughout his short life Heinrich von Kleist was bedevilled by contradictions and misfortunes. A Prussian aristocrat alienated from his class, brilliantly gifted yet deeply neurotic, he was torn between pedantry and passion, sensitivity and violence, furious ambition and a paralysing sense of failure. His obsessive striving for absolute certainties was confounded by doubts. His uncompromising search for fulfilment through love, friendship, nation, nature, or art foundered on external obstacles and on his own instability. Some moments of euphoria apart, his dominant mood was despair, leading to an early suicide. It is suitably ironic that, having been declared sick by Goethe and ignored for a century, he should have come to be regarded, not least by Kafka and Thomas Mann, as one of Germany's greatest writers.

Kleist shared the subjectivism and spiritualism of the Romantics, but unlike them he incorporated, rather than suppressed, the recalcitrance of objective reality in his writing. Anticipating psychoanalysis, sceptical about communication, and rejecting traditional philosophical, moral, and social assumptions in his treatment of existential issues, he seems strikingly modern.

Kleist's central problem—documented in his correspondence and occasional essays—was that of knowledge. At first he sought happiness through both Enlightenment rationalism and Rousseauesque sensibility, but he was shattered when some ideas of Kant confirmed his suspicion that the intellect was 'unable to decide whether what we call truth is truly the truth, or only appears so to us' (letter to Wilhelmine Zenge, 22 March 1801). He continued to commend 'feeling', and he claimed—notably in *Über das Marionettentheater* (*On Puppetshows*)—that the pristine grace of an unthinking condition, which was upset by reflection, would be regained in a divine state of infinite awareness. Basically, however, he believed that emotion, in its inconstancy, was as unreliable as reason, and that the impossibility of making informed choices or recognizing any providential purpose rendered human freedom an illusion and fate synonymous with chance. His

creative works explore these dilemmas from a variety of angles.

Kleist's first play, *Die Familie Schroffenstein* (*The Feud of the Schroffensteins*), is a Gothic melodrama in which the trust of the young lovers proves helpless against the accidents, errors, and enmities that destroy them. His next two plays mix hope and anxiety: in *Amphitryon*, an adaptation of Plautus and Molière, the tragicomedy of Jupiter impersonating the title hero to seduce his wife, alongside the farcical impersonation of the servant Sosias by Mercury, raises vexing questions about personal identity, the fallibility of perception, and the afflictions of love; in *Der zerbrochene Krug* (*The Broken Jug*), a rural comedy with overtones of Greek and Biblical myth, the truth emerges as the judge Adam convicts himself of his advances to the virtuous Eve, but her fiancé's distrustfulness almost causes disaster. Two subsequent plays, as Kleist noted, are complementary: in *Penthesilea*, a tragedy on Greek legend, the inefficacy of the intellect is compounded by the ambivalence of emotion as the Amazon queen, after many misunderstandings, slaughters the warrior Achilles in a paroxysm of love-hate and wills herself to death; in *Das Käthchen von Heilbronn* (*Käthchen of Heilbronn*), a medievalizing romance, the assurance of undivided devotion prevails as the heroine, supported by suprasensory promises, conquers the reluctant hero against all reasonable expectation. Kleist's vaguely historical last play, *Prinz Friedrich von Homburg* (*The Prince of Homburg*), is also his most celebrated. The hero, who disobeys orders but wins a battle and who after agonies of fear welcomes the death penalty but is rehabilitated, apparently achieves a 'classical' reconciliation of subjective inclination and objective duty; but again misconceptions abound, destiny as embodied in the Elector remains arbitrary, the chauvinistic exaltation of the Prussian state rings hollow, and the happy ending which completes the hero's initial somnambulistic fantasy of love and glory is literally called 'a dream'.

Of Kleist's collected stories five are commonly regarded as the most important. In 'The Earthquake in Chile' a young couple is lynched in a resurgence of religious hysteria after an interlude of idyllic peace following the collapse of the city. In 'The Engagement in Santo Domingo' the hero, misinterpreting the heroine's attempt to save his life during a colonial uprising, kills her, and, on learning the truth, kills himself. In 'The Marquise of O' the conundrum of the celibate but pregnant heroine is resolved by the confession of her eventual husband, who raped her while she was unconscious. In 'The Duel' the champion's belief in his lady's innocence is vindicated when he recovers from the near-fatal wound he sustained in the trial by ordeal, while the villain, whose alibi rests on delusion, dies of a slight injury. In *Michael Kohlhaas*, Kleist's greatest story, a righteous horsedealer becomes a vindictive outlaw when he is denied a fair legal hearing, and triumphs, with supernatural aid, at the very moment of his execution, when his grievances are redressed and his enemies punished. Love, trust, and intuitive confidence thus thrive in some cases and perish in others. In all cases, however, deceptive appearances, intellectual fallacies, and emotional disturbances, allied with strange coincidences and baffling incongruities, reiterate Kleist's view of the irrationality and mystery of existence.

Kleist's style, which is highly original though not deliberately experimental, is marked by ambiguity, irony, and paradox. His characters, faced with surprising situations, locked in fierce conflicts or painful isolation, driven by forces they can neither understand nor control, represent extreme impulses rather than normal human behaviour. His superbly timed actions replace conventional linearity with cyclic recurrences, sudden reversals, abrupt contrasts, and complex symbolic variations on a relatively limited number of enigmatic themes. His restraint from authorial comment and analytical explanation, his shifting perspectives, his insistence on accurate detail in the midst of upheaval and confusion invest his subjective concerns with a semblance of objectivity and provide solid realistic foundations for his visions. Rather than discussing his experience in conceptual terms, he conveys it directly through the structure of his language: blending fancy with matter-of-factness, dryness with lyricism, profuse rhetoric with explosive compression; revelling in bold metaphors, puns, equivocations, and relentless question-and-answer sequences; interrupting long hypotactical periods by encapsulated elucidations, qualifications, and objections before rushing headlong to their conclusion; and breaking down into speechless gestures, blushing and fainting, when words fail. It is this masterly use of dramatic, narrative, and linguistic devices that enables Kleist to impose aesthetic order on a chaotic world and to turn his torments into art.

—Ladislaus Löb

THE BROKEN JUG (Der zerbrochene Krug)
Play by Heinrich von Kleist, 1808.

The Broken Jug (begun in Berne in 1803 and completed in Königsberg in 1806) was the outcome of a literary contest between Heinrich von Kleist and three other young writers now forgotten, Heinrich Zschokke, Ludwig Wieland, and Heinrich Gessner. The four friends had agreed to write, respectively, a comedy, a short story, a verse satire, and a poetic idyll on the topic of an etching entitled *Le juge; ou, la cruche cassée* [The Judge or Broken Jug] by Jean Jacques Le Veau after a late 18th-century painting by Louis Philibert Debucourt which, in its turn, was based on Jean Baptiste Creuze's celebrated rococo painting *La cruche cassée*. It was Kleist who won the prize, giving the German theatre one of its rare comic masterpieces.

Adapting the French model to the style of the Flemish painter David Teniers, Kleist sets his play in a Dutch village at the end of the 17th century. The peasant woman Marthe Rull accuses Ruprecht, a young farmer engaged to her daughter Eve, of breaking the eponymous jug during a nocturnal visit to Eve's bedroom. Supervised by a visiting government inspector, the judge Adam is forced to conduct an investigation which reveals that he himself broke the jug when, caught by Ruprecht in the act of trying to seduce Eve, he escaped through her window, losing his wig and being hit over the head in the process. In due course Adam is sacked and Ruprecht and Eve are united but Marthe, with the jug still broken, is left to appeal to a higher court for any compensation.

The 13 consecutive scenes form a drama of detection which strictly observes the classical unities of time, place, and action as it uncovers, in analytical fashion, the events of the recent past. Kliest depicts contemporary German village life, thinly disguised by the remote setting, through accurately drawn rustic characters and a dialogue which, though cast in stylized blank verse, is rich in everyday speech rhythms, popular proverbs, colloquialisms, and dialect terms. Parodying Sophocles's *Oedipus Rex* in the manner of Aristophanes, with echoes of Shakespeare's *Measure for Measure* and the Bible, he operates simultaneously at several levels of meaning. He derives broadly farcical comedy from the plight of the corrupt judge who, despite all evasions and subterfuges, is ironically driven to convict himself of the crime under investigation. The comedy element is emphasized by coarse references to bodily functions and beatings; the mock heroic treatment of trivialities and the mock epic breadth of detail within the tightly woven plot; and above all by a dynamic language that conveys his concerns mimetically rather than discursively, turning confusion itself into art by the brilliant acts of original syntactical and onomatopoeic effects, significant puns and quibbles, nagging questions and counter-questions, and extended metaphors that have a habit of assuming an exuberantly autonomous existence of their own. For all the merriment, however, the judge constantly betrays his tragic doubts and fears.

At a social and political level, Adam's abuse of his office embodies, in grotesque distortion, Kleist's critique of Prussian jurisdiction, while the shattered picture on the jug, which showed the Emperor Charles V handing the Netherlands over to his son Phillip II, playfully suggests his distress at the disintegration of the Holy Roman Empire and at the subjugation of fragmented Germany in the Napoleonic era. At a religious level, varying the myth of creation, Kleist associates Eve's purity with the innocence of Paradise, and Adam's villainy with the fall of man and with the devil himself. At a philosophical level the court hearing, which is the most sustained example of Kleist's favourite device of cross-examination, dramatizes the search for knowledge which lies at the heart of all his writings. Eve, in particular, is thrown into a painful dilemma by Ruprecht's suspicions about her fidelity and Adam's threats to send Ruprecht to war if she exposes his advances. Her demand for absolute trust represents Kleist's recurrent plea for the supremacy of intuition over reason and for a belief transcending the evidence of the senses and the conclusions of the intellect, a longing contradicted by grave misgivings since his famous 'Kant crisis' of 1801, when he decided that objective truth was inaccessible to the human mind with its inescapably subjective categories of perception. The misunderstandings and errors engulfing all the characters, whether involuntary or deliberately induced, proclaim his despair over what he saw as the inability of thought and language to penetrate an enigmatic universe and to provide genuine communication between its baffled inhabitants. Although in this instance the truth is finally discovered, Kleist's scepticism, underlined by the open ending of Marthe's quest for compensation, persists as a dark background to the laughter.

The first performance in Weimar on 2 March 1808, directed by Goethe, proved a failure. Goethe himself claimed that the play, with its 'otherwise witty and humorous subject matter', lacked 'a swiftly executed action', while a member of the local aristocracy, Henriette von Knebel, described it as 'tasteless', 'boring', and suffering from 'moral leprosy'. The real causes of the failure, however, are more likely to have been Goethe's division of the continuous sequence of episodes into three separate acts, stilted classical acting, and the audience's conventional squeamishness. By the mid-19th century the realistic aspects of the play had begun to be appreciated, and Friedrich Hebbel, for one, described it as 'one of those works against which only the audience can fail'. More recently, it has been applauded for its expressive language, its socio-political implications, and its metaphysical questionings. Obliquely reflecting Kleist's serious preoccupations through its light-hearted surface, *The Broken Jug* is unlikely to lose the secure position it now holds in the German repertoire.

—Ladislaus Löb

MICHAEL KOHLHAAS
Story by Heinrich von Kleist, 1810.

Michael Kohlhaas, Kleist's longest prose work, is loosely based on the historical Hans Kohlhase, who took up arms against authority, principally Saxony, in order to obtain justice. He was captured and executed in Berlin in 1540.

A fragment of Kleist's story appeared in Dresden in the periodical *Phöbus* in 1808 but broke off where Kohlhaas sets out to attack the nobleman Wenzel's castle. The complete story was published in Berlin in 1810. The inclusion of historical personages and geographical locations in the 1810 version makes the work more politically overt. The focus shifts gradually away from the perversion of justice, committed by a fictional nobility, to the Elector of Saxony. He has been party to the initial denial of justice and agrees to tricking Kohlhaas into writing an incriminating letter. The last section of the work is devoted to Kohlhaas's revenge on the Elector.

Wenzel's illegal retention of Kohlhaas's horses, the brutal treatment of Kohlhaas's servant, and the exploitation of family connections to prevent Kohlhaas from obtaining legal redress could be interpreted as social and political commentary, as could Kohlhaas's meeting with Martin Luther. Although he intercedes on Kohlhaas's behalf, Wenzel's utterances betray that he is also concerned that respect for authority, epitomized in the hereditary ruler, should not be undermined. Kohlhaas's untrained followers' humiliation of the various military forces dispatched to deal with him is perhaps an allusion to the unexpected defeats suffered by the German rulers in Kleist's own lifetime at the hands of the French Revolutionary army.

Such interpretations do not detract from the universality of the work. The narrator refers to Kohlhaas's anguish 'at seeing the world in such monstrous disorder' after his case has been so disgracefully dismissed. The disorder Kleist portrays is existential as well as political, and chance is given a crucial role in all that happens. Kohlhaas's manner at the start of the story, when he haggles over the value of his horses, unintentionally plays a part in provoking Wenzel's illegal retention of the horses, done in a fit of anger rather than as a calculated abuse of power. Admittedly, Wenzel exploits his position in order to avoid paying compensation for the injustice suffered, but there is no evidence that he ordered the mistreatment of the horses and Kohlhaas's servant. The death of Kohlhaas's wife clearly precipitates the attack on Wenzel's castle, although the death, part of a chain of events set in motion by Wenzel, is an unfortunate accident not involving the nobleman. The reader is made to share Kohlhaas's sense of outrage and anguish at injustice, but against this must be set the role played by chance. The speed and complexity of events are also part of Kleist's strategy to show how ambiguous and confusing the situation is.

Kohlhaas's pursuit of legal redress takes a frightening course. The innocent as well as the guilty are murdered in his attack on Wenzel's castle. He threatens to burn Wittenberg to the ground unless Wenzel is delivered up and declares himself to be 'St Michael's deputy, sent to punish the evil into which the whole world had sunk'. Commenting on all this, the narrator refers to Kohlhaas as 'a monstrous villain'. In so doing he is understandably being overwhelmed by the events of the moment, to the exclusion of all else. As with the other characters, circumstances, chance events, and the sheer complexity of Kohlhaas's situation cloud and confuse his judgement.

This theme of an unpredictable, chance-driven existence is continued when Kohlhaas is given safe conduct to come to Dresden to have his case reviewed. The reader is subtly made aware of a power struggle in the Saxon capital. Opponents of Wenzel's relatives treat the case as an opportunity to humiliate them and circumstances now seem to favour Kohlhaas. However, the arrival of the horses in Dresden (and the reader is left in some doubt as to whether they are the ones that Wenzel retained) sparks off a civil riot. This takes place in Kohlhaas's absence but the episode turns public opinion against him. Kohlhaas is so reduced to despair by this that he tries to resume contact with a former henchman, thereby condemning himself. All this reinforces Kleist's disturbing vision of a world in which circumstances, questionable motives, and chance events combine, with disastrous consequences for the individual.

Kleist's lengthening of the story to cover Kohlhaas's transportation to Berlin after he has been condemned to death, during which the Elector of Saxony makes desperate attempts to obtain from Kohlhaas the gypsy woman's prophecy concerning the fate of his dynasty, has been criticized as artificial, an unwarranted introduction of the supernatural, and detracting seriously from the unity of the work. It has to be conceded that this section was probably an afterthought on Kleist's part and the events involving the gypsy woman do strain the reader's credulity.

However, the sequence of events parallels other sections of the story and the work retains its thematic coherence. A power struggle, in which Saxony has to placate Brandenburg and which is irrelevant to Kohlhaas's case, results in the Elector having to back down and agree to deliver Kohlhaas to Berlin. Although all parties involved claim they are acting in the interests of justice, the reader is once more made aware of the destructive interplay of ambiguity of motive, the complexity of events, and sheer chance. The Elector is also the victim of this interplay, for it enables Kohlhaas to take the prophecy to his grave and so exact revenge.

The story ends with Wenzel's punishment, the restoration of the horses to their previous condition, and Kohlhaas's execution for the death and destruction he has caused. This could be interpreted as a resolution of the conflict in keeping with the ideals of classical literature. However, the concatenation of events that has led to this situation suggests the possibility that Kleist intended this ending to be ironic.

—D.J. Andrews

THE PRINCE OF HOMBURG (Prinz Friedrich von Homburg)
Play by Heinrich von Kleist, 1821.

Described by Heine as 'written by the genius of poetry itself' and by Hebbel as 'a German oak whose top is closer to heaven than to earth', *The Prince of Homburg* is one of the few dramatic masterpieces associated with German Romanticism. Begun in 1809 and finished in 1811, it was prevented from being performed in the year of its completion by Princess Wilhelm of Prussia, a descendant of the title hero, who objected to a scene which showed her ancestor as being afraid of death. The first production in Vienna in 1821 (also the year of first publication) was banned by Archduke Charles after a handful of performances, as was that in Berlin in 1828 by King Frederick William III, because of alleged slurs on the valour of the military aristocracy. From the Marxist camp, Franz Mehring accused Kleist of 'raising old Prussianism, with its mixture of brutality and stupidity, into the realms of art' by his 'hymn on subordination', while Brecht called the hero a 'personification of warrior's pride and servant's intellect'. After serving the nationalist cause from the mid-19th century to World War II, the play is now chiefly admired for Kleist's existential probings, his psychological insights, and his mastery of stagecraft and dialogue.

Based on Frederick the Great's *Mémoires pour servir à l'histoire de la maison de Brandebourg* and Karl Heinrich Krause's *Mein Vaterland unter den hohenzollerischen Regenten*, the action revolves around the battle of Fehrbellin in 1675. After a fit of somnambulism, the Prince—young, dashing, highly strung, and altogether different from the middle-aged, twice-married, mutilated veteran officer of history—ignores the delay ordered by the Elector Frederick William and leads a Prussian attack against the Swedes, winning a partial victory but jeopardizing the success of the campaign as a whole. The Elector sentences the Prince to death but reprieves him when he recognizes his guilt and accepts his impending execution.

At one level, by exalting 17th-century Prussia, Kleist purveys anti-Napoleonic propaganda, voicing the chauvinism he shared with the political theorist Adam Müller and other German contemporaries. At another level, by leading his hero from anarchistic self-indulgence to communal responsibility, he recalls the ideals of German classicism, as propounded in the drama of Schiller. Above all, however, he reveals his intensely personal preoccupations.

Kliest's central experience was his failure to find happiness through rational virtue. His famous misunderstanding of Immanuel Kant confirmed his feeling that the truth was inaccessible to human perception. As his essay *Über das Marionettentheater* (*On Puppetshows*) illustrates, he believed —partly under the influence of Rousseau—that 'reflection' was liable to destroy the 'natural grace of man', which could only be regained, if at all, on a higher plane through the attainment of an 'infinite consciousness'. To some extent the Prince's development follows the lines of this triad. While he expects his subjective desires to justify his disobedience, he feels at one with himself and the world. When, at the sight of his grave, he becomes aware for the first time of an objective reality outside himself, he breaks down in fear and confusion. When he assents to his punishment and takes leave of life, he may be said to have recovered his original poise through a higher kind of knowledge. This progress may seem to be of a rational kind, but although the Prince is pardoned as a result of a deliberate moral effort, it is his initial dream of love and glory that is fulfilled in a similarly dreamlike manner at the close of the play. Thus, beneath the deceptive appearance of a classical synthesis of reason and intuition, the romantic undercurrent or irrational visions and mysteries prevails.

Irrationality is also the hallmark of the Elector. He encourages the Prince to pursue his ambitious fantasy out of sheer curiosity. He is puzzled when the Prince objects to the death sentence. Granting the pardon, he disregards the Prince's own hard-won determination to atone, and he flouts the law that he has claimed to be upholding in all circumstances. Although the text itself explains that the state should be ruled by human feelings rather than by abstract principles, he remains an ambiguous figure. Owing to his position in society —and in the structure of the play—he seems to represent a rational order, but his conduct is inconsistent and arbitrary. In symbolic terms he thus conveys Kleist's own experience of a universe which, far from being rational, seems to be governed by capricious and unpredictable forces. These forces may appear indifferent, cruel, or beneficial to human beings, but they are always baffling and incomprehensible. In this instance, the conflict ends happily, but the happy ending is explicitly declared to be a dream.

At the technical level, Kleist's last play before his suicide shows him at the height of his powers. His artistic maturity manifests itself in the portrayal of complex characters; in the consummate timing of retardation and precipitation; in the suspense arising not from physical violence but from the clash of emotions between and within the protagonists; in the fusion of harsh near-tragedy in the central plot with the lyrical idylls of the frame; and above all in the blank verse which has a wider range and more relaxed atmosphere than in any of his previous plays. *The Prince of Homburg* is one of the most impressive demonstrations of Kleist's ability to re-create, through the very movement and rhythm of his language, the ebb and flow of feeling, the meeting of dream and reality, and the interaction of the conscious and unconscious layers of the mind.

—Ladislaus Löb

KLOPSTOCK, Friedrich Gottlieb. Born in Quedlinburg, Saxony, Germany, 2 July 1724. Educated in Quedlinburg, 1736–39 and Schulpforta, 1739–45; studied theology, University of Jena, 1745–46; University of Leipzig, 1746–48. Married 1) Margareta (Meta) Moller in 1754 (died in childbirth 1758); 2) Johanna Elisabeth von Winthem in 1791. Private tutor, Langensalza, Saxony, 1748–50; visited Zurich at the invitation of the influential Swiss literary figure Johann Jacob Bodmer, 1750; invited to Copenhagen in 1751; received life pension from Frederick V of Denmark at the behest of Count Bernstoff; left Denmark in 1770 and moved to Hamburg where he spent the rest of his life; awarded honorary citizenship of the French Republic, 1792. *Died 14 March 1803.*

PUBLICATIONS

Collections

Werke. 12 vols., 1798–1817.
Odes of Klopstock from 1747 to 1780, translated by William Nind. 1848.
Oden, edited by F. Muncker and J. Pawel. 1889.
Ausgewählte Werke, edited by K.A. Schleiden. 1962.
Werke und Briefe [Hamburg Edition], edited by Horst Gronemeyer, Elisabeth Höpker-Herberg, Klaus Hurlebusch, and Rose-Maria Hurlebusch. 1974—.

Verse

Der Messias. 1751, enlarged editions, 1755, 1769, 1773, and 1780; translated in part as *The Messiah* by Mary and Joseph Collyer, 1763; also translated by Solomon Hallings, 1810; Mary Collyer and Mrs Meeke, 1811; Thomas Raffles, 1814; G.H.C. Egestorff, 1821–22; Catharine Head, 1826.
Oden. 1750.
Ode an Gott. 1751.
Geistliche Lieder. 1758–69.
Die frühen Gräber. 1764.
Die Sommernacht. 1766.
Rothschilds Gräber. 1766.
Oden und Elegien: Vier und dreyssigmal gedrukt. 1771.

Kleine poetische und prosaische Werke, edited by Christian
  Friedrich Schubart, 1771.
Ode an den Kaiser. 1782.
Das Vaterunser, ein Psalm. 1790.
Poetische Werke. 1794–96.

Plays

Der Tod Adams. 1757; as *The Death of Adam*, translated by
  Robert Lloyd, 1763.
Salomo. 1764; as *Solomon*, translated by Robert Huish, 1809.
Hermanns Schlacht. 1769.
David. 1772.
Hermann und die Fürsten. 1784.
Hermanns Tod. 1787.

Other

Die Deutsche Gelehrtenrepublik. 1774.
Über die deutsche Rechtschreibung. 1778.
Über Sprache und Dichtkunst: Fragmente. 1779–80.
Grammatische Gespräche. 1794.
Memoirs of Frederick and Margaret Klopstock, translated by
  Elizabeth Smith, 1808.
*Klopstock und seine Freunde: Briefwechsel der Familie
  Klopstock unter sich, und zwischen dieser Familie, Gleim,
  Schmidt, Fanny, Meta und andern Freunden*, edited by
  Klamer Schmidt. 2 vols., 1810; as *Klopstock and His
  Friends: A Series of Family Letters, Written Between the
  Years 1750 and 1803*, translated by Elizabeth Ogilvy, 1814.
*Auswahl aus Klopstocks nachgelassenem Briefwechsel und
  übrigen Papieren: Ein Denkmal für seine Verehrer*, edited
  by Christian August Heinrich Clodius. 2 vols., 1821.
*Kurzer Briefwechsel zwischen Klopstock und Goethe im Jahre
  1776*. 1833.
Briefe an Herder. 1856.
*Briefe von und an Klopstock: Ein Beitrag zur Literatur-
  geschichte seiner Zeit*, edited by Johann Martin
  Lappenberg. 1867; reprinted 1970.
*Briefwechsel zwischen Klopstock und den Grafen Christian
  und Friedrich Leopold zu Stolberg. Mit einem Anhang:
  Briefwechsel zwischen Klopstock und Herder*, edited by
  Jürgen Behrens and Sabine Jodeleit. 1964.
Briefe 1738–1750, edited by Horst Gronemeyer. 1979.

Editor, *Hinterlassene Schriften*, by Meta Klopstock. 1759.

*

Bibliography: by Gerhard Burkhardt and Heinz Nicolai, in
Werke und Briefe, 1975; *Die zeitgenössischen Drucke von
Klopstocks Werken* by Christiane Boghardt, and others, 1981.

Critical Studies: 'Klopstock's Occasional Poetry' by Terence
K. Thayer, in *Lessing Yearbook*, (2), 1970; *Studien zu
Klopstocks Poetik* by W. Grosse, 1977; 'Klopstock's Poetic
Innovations: The Emergence of German as a Prosodic
Language' by Beth Bjorklund, in *Germanic Review*, 1981;
'Klopstock's Temple Imagery', in *Lessing Yearbook*, (13),
1982, and 'A Question of Influence: Goethe, Klopstock, and
'Wanderers Sturmlied', in *German Quarterly*, (55), 1982,
both by Meredith Lee; *Philosophy, Letters, and the Fine Arts
in Klopstock's Thought* by Kevin Hilliard, 1987; *Rhetoric, the
Bible, and the Origins of Free Verse: The Early Hymns of
Friedrich Gottlob Klopstock* by Katrin M. Kohl, 1990.

* * *

Der Messias (*The Messiah*) is the most ambitious large-
scale epic poem on a religious subject in modern German
literature. In 1748 the publication in a Bremen literary
periodical of its first three cantos (there were to be 20 in all)
was a landmark in the evolution of German literature.
Discerning readers were quick to recognize that here, at last,
was a new and distinctive voice. The young Friedrich Gottlieb
Klopstock (he was 24 at the time) not only possessed a poetic
vision of Miltonic proportions: he also had the command of
language necessary to express that vision and communicate it
to his readership. The poem was hailed as a work of genius.

When the first three cantos appeared, the creative literature of Germany had scarcely begun to fulfil the hopes and
recommendations of the new school of literary theorists and
critics who had been exploring the role of the imagination in
artistic creation. In Zurich Johann Jakob Bodmer (1698–
1783) and Johann Jakob Breitinger (1701–76) had formulated
their pioneering conception of poetry in a joint treatise on the
influence and use of the imagination (1727); this they had
followed up with Bodmer's prose translation of Milton's
Paradise Lost (1732), a work in which they saw that conception fully realized. It fell to the young North German poet to
achieve a poetic masterpiece which rivalled Milton in scale
and sublimity of theme and similarly appealed to both a
critical readership and the general reader.

Klopstock had discovered Milton's work when he was a
pupil at the famous school of Schulpforta at Bad Kösen near
Halle in Saxony. He left school determined to create for
Protestant Germany a work which would stand comparison
with *Paradise Lost* itself. Milton's subject had been the Fall of
Man: Klopstock responded by selecting Man's redemption
through Christ's atonement. His epic poem focuses on the
course of events from Christ's entry into Jerusalem on Palm
Sunday to his completion of his redemptive mission and his
ascension into heaven. But the relatively straightforward
sequence of events retold by the evangelists is often little
more than a framework for a spiritual, moral, and above all
emotional experience of cosmic proportions. As a result, the
dynamic forward impetus of epic poetry as exemplified by
Homer and Virgil is replaced by a more discursive approach
in which material of the poet's own invention swamps the
simplicity of the Gospel narrative.

There is little realism of the Homeric kind in *The Messiah*
and none of Virgil's nation-making mythical purpose. Instead
Klopstock exploits his considerable descriptive and lyrical
powers to construct a fantasy world which many of his
original readers would have shunned had it not been more or
less firmly anchored in orthodox Christian theology. Scarcely
anything actually takes place before the reader's eyes: it is the
reaction within the reader that counts. The epic's celebrated
opening line ('Sing, immortal soul, the redemption of sinful
mankind') sets the tone for what is to come. The soul, susceptible to a whole gamut of spiritual experiences, is the eyewitness of past events re-created by the poet: their quasi-
symbolic and transcendent significance far outweighs their
historical or narrative credibility. Time and again the modern
reader is struck by anticipations of Blake in prophetic, visionary mood, though Klopstock is also sporadically capable of
passages of graphic narrative such as Christ's harrowing
ascent of Golgotha in Canto 8.

Underlying the whole extraordinary enterprise are two
basic and complementary impulses. On the one hand the poet
is intent on making his reader 'feel' what hitherto he (and
she) had been taught to ponder. On the other, he frequently

appears to be displaying the power of language to evoke a poetic world that transcends the norms of reality by dissolving the normal dimensions of space and time. Thus the locations of much of the epic's story-line are vague in the extreme, whereas the mental and moral agonies and ecstasies of some of the many figures involved in it possess an extraordinary immediacy. As a result, the epic, though couched in a German equivalent of the Latin hexameter and characterized by highly stylized vocabulary and syntax appropriate to its sublime theme, contains many stretches which are closer to Samuel Richardson's epistolary novels and the intense self-scrutiny of their characters than to Milton's strongly visual yet intensely intellectual Biblical poem. It is no coincidence that *Clarissa* and *The Messiah* are contemporaneous and that both scored an enormous success with the predominantly middle-class mid-18th-century reading public.

In England the success of *The Messiah* was not as great as that of Richardson's novels in Germany, and it never achieved the popularity of *Der Tod Abels* (*The Death of Abel*), 1758, a religious work in somewhat similar vein by Klopstock's Swiss contemporary, Salomon Gessner. Nevertheless the prose translation of the first 10 cantos by Gessner's translator Mary Collyer and her husband Josiah Collyer ran to three editions during the 1760s.

Klopstock's contribution to the emergence of German classical literature in the mid-18th century was far-reaching; but his epic was too long. By the time he completed and published the last of its 20 cantos in 1773 it had swelled to almost 20,000 lines. Its novelty was past and its popularity was on the wane except among the large readership that continued to rank it second only to the Bible itself. However, long after its sprawling shapelessness and rapt intensity had been decried by a new generation, it continued to haunt the imagination. For instance the pure but ardent attachment between Cidli, the daughter of Jairus, and Semida, the son of the widow of Nain, both saved from death by miracles wrought by Christ (Canto 15), struck a responsive chord in readers eager for romance of an uplifting Christian kind such as could be safely read on a Sunday. The delicate sentimentality of such episodes provided a Protestant equivalent or echo of Tasso's *Gerusalemme liberata* (*Jerusalem Delivered*) which proved very acceptable well into the 19th century. In this respect Klopstock's greatest stroke of genius was the tormented figure of Abbadona, the remorseful devil. Originally one of the evil spirits who conspired against the Messiah, Abbadona's protracted remorse and ultimate pardon in heaven brought tears to many an eye in an age which regarded sentimentality differently from our own.

When in Goethe's epoch-making novel *Die Leiden des jungen Werthers* (*The Sufferings of Young Werther*) Lotte and Werther both utter the name 'Klopstock' at the same moment, recognition is paid to the achievement of a writer whose masterpiece spans the years between Handel's oratorio *Messiah* (1742) and the climax of the *Sturm und Drang*.

—Peter Skrine

KOCHANOWSKI, Jan. Born in Sycyna, Poland, in 1530. Educated at Cracow Academy, 1544–49; University of Królewiec, 1551–52; University of Padua, 1552–55. Married Dorota Podłodowska in 1570; six daughters. Courtier: secre-tary to King Zygmunt, 1560–68; retired to estate in Czarnolas, 1570. *Died 22 August 1584.*

PUBLICATIONS

Collections

Dzieła wszystkie [Complete Works]. 4 vols., 1884–97.
Dzieła polskie [Polish Works], edited by Julian Krzyzan-owski. 3 vols., 1960.
Dzieła wszystkie [Complete Works], edited by Maria Renata Mayenowa and others. 4 vols., 1982–91.

Verse

Zuzanna [Susanna]. 1562.
Szachy [A Game of Chess]. 1562(?); edited by Kazimierz Nitsch, 1923; also edited by Julian Krzyzanowski, 1966.
Zgoda [Concord]. 1564.
Satyr; albo, dziki mż [The Satyr; or, The Wild Man]. 1564; edited by Paulina Buchwald-Pelcowa, 1983.
Psałterz Dawidów [Psalms of David]. 1579, reprinted 1985.
Treny. 1583; edited by Wiktor Weintraub, 1943; also edited by Tadeusz Sinko, 1966, Julian Krzyzanowski, 1967, and Janusz Pelc, 1972; as *Laments*, translated by Dorothea Prall Radin, 1920.
Lyricorum libellus. 1580.
Elegiarum libri IV, elusdem Foricoenia sive epigrammatum libellus [Four Books of Elegies and the Trifles]. 1584; as *Fraszki* [Trifles], 1612; edited by Antonina Jelicz, 1956; also edited by Aleksander Soszynski, 1980;
Pieśni [Songs]. 1586; edited by Tadeusz Sinko, 1948.
Elegie [Elegies], translated (from Latin) by K. Brodziński. 1829.
Poems, edited by G.R. Noyes, translated by Noyes, Dorothea Prall Radin, and others. 1928.

Play

Odprawa posłów greckich (produced 1578). 1578; edited by Tadeusz Sinko, 1915; also edited by Tadeusz Ulewicz, 1962; as *The Dismissal of the Greek Envoys*, translated by G.R. Noyes and Ruth Earl Merrill (verse), 1918; also translated by Charles S. Kraszewski, 1994.

*

Bibliography: *Bibliografia dziel Jana Kochanowskiego: wiek XVI–XVII* by Kazimierz Piekarski, 1934.

Critical Studies: 'The Medieval Dream Formula in Kochanowski's *Laments*' by Jerzy Peterkiewicz, in *Slavonic and East European Review*, 31(77), 1953; 'Mythological Allusions in Kochanowski's *Laments*' by Ray J. Parrott, in *Polish Review*, 14(1), 1969; *Jan Kochanowski* by David J. Welsh, 1974; *Ian Kochanowski in Glasgow* edited by Donald Pirie, 1985; *The Polish Renaissance in Its European Context* edited by Samuel Fiszman, 1988.

* * *

Jan Kochanowski's reputation outside the Polish cultural sphere is small, and his significance in European terms is difficult to assess, though his works are of an ingenuity and sophistication that compete with the best among his inter-national contemporaries.

His debut was as a cosmopolitan poet taking advantage of the medium of progressive humanist culture, Neo-Latin. The erudite and inventive Virgilian verse of his early work, widely circulated in manuscript after 1550, was published much later as the *Lyricorum libellus* in 1580. Well known among the small cultured élite of the Polish-Lithuanian Commonwealth's few courts, Kochanowski was patronized by both courtiers and clerics, eventually securing himself the position of Royal Secretary for most of the 1560s. It was in this milieu that he switched to his native idiom, in which he wrote first the vignettes of humorous verse in the anthology entitled *Fraszki* [Trifles], which satirize contemporary society and its mores.

Kochanowski soon advanced to a combination of the sophisticated style of Neo-Latin verse and its classical models and genres with Polish vocabulary and syntax in the *Pieśni* [Songs] (again, known widely, but published posthumously in 1586), closely modelled on Horace's *Odes*. In these highly polished 'songs', he set the stylistic and thematic standards for almost two centuries. His subjects range from subtle (and not so subtle) panegyric dedicated to court patrons, through hymns on the beauty of Creation, to the erotic and melancholic, pastoral and religious. While some are artful paraphrases from Horace, most are entirely original, and stand as a testament of the achievements of the 'Augustan' Golden Age under the sophisticated Zygmunt August (1548–72). The *Pieśni* are a fusing of two cultures (Roman and Sarmatian), two languages (Latin and Polish), and two poets (Horace the master, and Kochanowski the apprentice).

Towards 1570, however, for reasons that are unclear, Kochanowski had severed his dependence on court favour, and retired with his new wife to his estate at Czarnolas, evoked so lyrically in the 'Pieśń świętojańska o Sobótce' (published with *Pieśni*). Despite irregular commissions from his earlier patrons, such as his experimental Euripidean tragedy in Polish, *Odprawa posłów greckich* (*The Dismissal of the Greek Envoys*), in this idyllic environment he concentrated on his true 'vocation', a versified paraphrase of the Psalter in Polish. This huge work, the *Psałterz Dawidów* [Psalms of David], is another blending, of biblical, classical Latin, and Polish vernacular ingredients. His version surpassed all others in originality, beauty, and popularity. On all levels it is the culmination of his life's work.

The last five years of the poet's life were overshadowed by the deaths of court friends, relatives, and in particular his own children. A record of the struggle between faith and despair following the death of his three-year-old daughter Orszula, entitled the *Treny* (*Laments*), was published in 1580. It contains a cycle of contemplative lyrics on the implications of Orszula's demise and his sense of loss. Once again there is the combination of contrasting elements—the classical and biblical, the philosophical and personal, the lyrical and dramatic, all focused by the factual event that inspired the cycle. Together they transform these laments from a conventional exercise into an extraordinarily honest psychological document, revealing much of the mentality of 16th-century man.

With the exception of some secondary political and panegyric verse, Kochanowski's sublime poetry is not the product of a provincial. Single-handedly he extended the Polish language's limits in all directions. The *Laments* are his last word, a personal legacy of the potential of Christian humanism, after which the poet abandoned his artificial lute for the rewards of David's faith.

—Donald Pirie

————

KRASIŃSKI, Zygmunt. Born in Paris, France, 19 February 1812. Grew up on family estate in Opinogóra, Poland. Educated at home, then in Warsaw until 1828; University of Warsaw until 1829; University of Geneva, c.1830. Short military service. Married Countess Elżbieta Branicki in 1843. Travelled to St Petersburg with his father, where he met Tsar Nicholas I, 1832; returned to Poland, 1832, and in 1843–44. Seriously ill for much of his life; spent most of 1830s and 1840s in spas in France and Italy, rarely coming home. Published many works anonymously. *Died 23 February 1859.*

Publications

Collections

Pisma [Works], edited by J. Czubek. 8 vols., 1912; also edited by L. Piwiński, 7 vols., 1931.
Dzieła literackie [Literary Works], edited by Paweł Hertz. 3 vols., 1973.

Plays

Nie-Boska Komedia (produced 1902). 1835; as *The Undivine Comedy*, translated by M.W. Cook, in *The Undivine Comedy and Other Poems*, 1875; as *The Un-Divine Comedy*, translated by Harold B. Segel, in *Polish Romantic Drama*, 1977.
Irydion (produced 1908). 1836; as *Irydion*, translated by Florence Noyes, 1927.

Fiction

Pan trzech pagórków [Lord of Three Hills]. 1828.
Grób rodziny Reichstalów [The Tomb of the Reichstal Family]. 1828.
Sen Elżbiey Pileckiej [Elizabeth Pilecka's Dream]. 1829.
Władysław Herman i dwór jego [Vladislav Herman and His Court]. 3 vols., 1830.
Agay-Han. 1834.

Verse

Modlitewnik [Prayer Book]. 1837.
Noc letnia [Summer Night]. 1841.
Pokusa [Temptation]. 1841.
Przedświt [Pre-Dawn]. 1843.
Psalmy przyszłości [Future Psalms]. 1845; enlarged edition, 1848.
Ostatni [The Last One]. 1847.
Dzień dzisiejszy [Today]. 1847.
Psalm żalu [Psalm of Regret]. 1848.
Psalm dobrej woli [Psalm of Goodwill]. 1848.
Niedokończony poemat [The Unfinished Poem]. 1860.
The Undivine Comedy and Other Poems (includes play), translated by M.W. Cook. 1875.

Other

Trzy myśli Henryka Ligenzy [Henry Ligenza's Three Thoughts]. 1840.
O stanowisku Polski z bożych i ludzkich względów [About Poland's Position from the Viewpoint of God and People]. 1841.
Lettres à Montalembert et . . . Lamartine. 1847.
Listy o poemacie Kajeta Koźmiana Stefan Czarniecki [Letters to S.C. Koźmian]. 1859.

Briefe. 1860.
Listy od roku 1835 do 1844 pisane do Edwarda Jaroszyńskiego [Letters to Edward Jaroszyński]. 1871.
Listy [Letters]. 3 vols., 1882–87.
Correspondance de Sigismond Krasinski et de Henry Reeve. 2 vols., 1902.
Listy [Letters], with Ary Scheffer. 1909.
Listy do Augusta Cieszkowskiego [Letters to August Cieszkowski]. 2 vols., 1912.
Listy do A. Potockiego [Letters to A. Potocki]. 1922.
Listy do Delfiny Potockiej [Letters to Delfina Potocka]. 3 vols., 1930–38.
Listy wybrane [Selected Letters]. 1937.
Listy do ojca [Letters to His Father]. 1963.
Listy do Jerzego Lubomirskiego [Letters to Jerzy Lubomirski]. 1965.
Listy do Adama Sołtana [Letters to Adam Sołtan]. 1970.
Listy do Konstantego Gaszyńskiego [Letters to Konstanty Gaszyński]. 1971.

*

Critical Studies: *Zygmunt Krasiński* by J. Kallenbach, 2 vols., 1904; *The Anonymous Poet of Poland: A Life of Zygmunt Krasiński* by Monica M. Gardner, 1919; *Zygmunt Krasinski: Romantic Universalist: An International Tribute* by W. Lednicki, 1964.

* * *

Zygmunt Krasiński came from a rich aristocratic family in Poland. His father, Wincenty, was a conservative general in the army of the Congress Kingdom and supported the Tsar and Poland's Russian rulers even during the November Uprising of 1830. Young Zygmunt was sent abroad to finish his higher studies and it was in Geneva that he began writing plays that reflected the major philosophical and social questions of the age. While Krasiński first published his works anonymously (as the 'Nameless Poet of Poland') to avoid embarrassment for his family, his entire mature life was characterized by a struggle between his conflicting loyalties — whether to side with his father or with the cause of national independence, the fatherland. Krasiński made his home abroad (mostly in Germany), wrote poetry, a vast number of letters, and two plays which — though unstaged in his lifetime — belong to the best achievements of Polish Romantic drama.

Although of the plays *Irydion* was conceived first, the final version of *Nie-Boska Komedia* (*The Undivine Comedy*) came to be published first in 1835 in Paris. The latter is a poetic drama in four 'parts' (acts) which deals with one of the most crucial issues of the modern age beginning with the French Revolution — the struggle of the 'haves' and the 'have-nots', that of aristocracy with revolutionary democracy. The background to this historic conflict is provided by the career of Count Henryk. He is first shown to be a failure in private life for he is much more interested in poetry (symbolized by a demonic maiden) than in domestic happiness with his newly wedded wife. In fact, he leaves his wife and is almost killed by the Maiden who wants to lure him to a precipice. At the end of Act I, Henryk's wife dies with the wish that their son Orcio should become a poet — the wish is fulfilled, though Orcio remains incurably blind. The first two acts of the play are very sketchy, but they lead up to the powerful Act III, not unlike Juliusz Słowacki's play *Kordian* (1834). In one of the scenes of Act II Count Henryk declares: 'Farewell, Mother Nature! I leave you, to become a man. I go to fight with my brethren'. Abandoning all other myths of romanticism, Henryk tests the last one: that of progress in society.

The third act takes place some time in the undefined future when the rebellious masses have managed to take over most of the civilized world. Only the Castle of Holy Trinity holds out in a vain attempt to stem the tide. Here all the rich and mighty (aristocrats, bankers, bishops) assemble; down in the valley the vast coalition of the poor and their radical leaders set up their camp to lay siege to the castle. Henryk, at night and in disguise, visits the camp and is appalled by the wrath of the masses and their thirst for revenge. All the same, Krasiński observes and indicates certain latent conflicts between the simple participants of the struggle, their ideologues, and the military 'technicians'. Henryk's tour of the camp is followed by a return visit by Pankracy, the leader of the revolutionaries, to the castle; his confrontation with Count Henryk (who later is elected Commander-in-Chief by the beleaguered 'aristocrats') produces some of the best scenes in the play. The values of both leaders are shown to be flawed; Henryk's concept of 'honour' is hopelessly anachronistic, and Pankracy's promise of a radiant future is utopian and clearly unrealizable.

The Undivine Comedy nearly ends with the victory of the revolutionary mobs. Count Henryk prefers to commit suicide at the moment when they take the castle by storm. None the less, the victorious Pankracy is suddenly smitten by a vision of Julian the Apostate: 'Galileae vicisti!' ('You have won, O Christ!'). The message of this unexpected scene is fairly clear: no 'godless' revolution can be truly victorious; the new age will not dawn until it finds a way to reconcile democracy with Christianity.

Staged for the first time in the 20th century, *The Undivine Comedy* has been steadily gaining topicality with the rise of (basically anti-Christian) mass totalitarian movements. Adam Mickiewicz, in the middle of the 19th century, regarded it as 'the highest achievement of the Slavonic theatre'; Czesław Miłosz called it, more recently, 'a truly pioneering work in its treatment of an unusual subject and in its visual elements'. Although several English translations exist, the play has been, on the whole, ignored outside Poland, even by directors otherwise interested in the Polish theatre.

Krasiński's other play, *Irydion*, published in 1836, takes place in imperial Rome in the 3rd century AD. It is the story of a half-Greek, half-Germanic hero, Irydion ('the son of the rainbow'), who is bent on the destruction of corrupt, decadent Rome. To achieve this aim he is ready to sacrifice his sister Elsinoe to the lust of the Emperor Heliogabalus. His plot to subvert and then destroy Rome fails in the end because of the Christians' reluctance to take up arms against their rulers. *Irydion* was written as an indirect response to Mickiewicz's influential poem *Konrad Wallenrod*, a work which advocated revenge against the enemy by any means, including morally reprehensible methods. Krasiński's play is written in an 'ornate arhythmical, utterly Romantic prose', as described by Miłosz, partly modelled on Chateaubriand, and while it enjoyed some popularity in the 19th century, it has not been resurrected on the stage in contemporary Poland.

—George Gömöri

KRLEŽA, Miroslav. Born in Zagreb, Croatia (then in the Austro-Hungarian Empire), 7 July 1893. Educated at

Lucoviceum military academy, Budapest. Served in the Serbian Army, 1912: suspected of spying, expelled from Serbia and arrested by the Austrians; served in the Austrian Army during World War I. Married Bela Kangrga. Member of Communist Party from 1918: expelled, 1939; rehabilitated by Tito, 1952; founded the periodicals *Plamen* [Flame], 1919, *Književna republika* [Literary Republic], 1923–27, *Danas* [Today], 1934, *Pečat* [Seal], 1939–40, and *Republika*, 1945–46; director, Lexicographic Institute, Zagreb, from 1952; editor, *Pomorska enciklopedija*, 1954–64, *Enciklopedija Jugoslavije*, 1955–71, and *Enciklopedija Leksikografskog savoda*, 1955–64. Deputy, Yugoslav National Assembly. President, Yugoslav Writers Union; vice-president, Yugoslav Academy of Science and Art. *Died 29 December 1981.*

PUBLICATIONS

Collection

Sabrana djela [Collected Works]. 1980– .

Fiction

Tri kavalira gospoice Melanije [Three Suitors of Miss Melania]. 1920.
Magyar királyi honvéd novela [Short Story on the Royal Hungarian Homeguards]. 1921.
Hrvatski bog Mars [The Croatian God Mars]. 1922.
Novele. 1923.
Vražji otok [Devil's Island]. 1924.
Povratak Filipa Latinovicza. 1932; as *The Return of Philip Latinovicz*, translated by Zora Depolo, 1959.
Hiljadu i jedna smrt [A Thousand and One Deaths]. 1933.
Novele. 1937.
Na rubu pameti. 1938; as *On the Edge of Reason*, translated by Zora Depolo, 1976.
Banket u Blitvi [Banquet in Blitva]. 3 vols., 1938–64.
Tri domobrana [Three Homeguards]. 1950.
Zastave [Banners]. 4 vols., 1967.
The Cricket Beneath the Waterfall and Other Stories, edited by Branco Lenski. 1972; as *Cvrčak pod vodopadom, i druge novele*, 1973.
Baraka pet be i druge novele (collection). 1976.

Verse

Pan. 1917.
Tri simfonije [Three Symphonies]. 1917.
Pjesme 1–3 [Poems]. 3 vols., 1918–19.
Lirika [Lyrics]. 1919.
Knjiga pjesama [A Book of Poems]. 1931.
Knjiga lirike [A Book of Lyrics]. 1932.
Simfonije [Symphonies]. 1933.
Balade Petrice Kerempuha [Ballads of Petrica Kerempuh]. 1936.
Pjesme u tmini [Poems in Darkness]. 1937.

Plays

Hrvatska rapsodija [Croatian Rhapsody]. 1918.
Golgota [Golgotha] (produced 1922). 1926.
Vučjak (produced 1922). 1923.
Michelangelo Buonarroti (produced 1925).
Adam i Eva [Adam and Eve] (produced 1925).
Gospoda Glembajevi [The Glembays] (produced 1929). 1928.

U agoniji (produced 1928; revised version produced 1959). 1931.
Leda (produced 1930).
Legende [Legends] (includes 6 plays). 1933.
U logoru [In the Camp] (produced 1937). With *Vučjak*, 1934.
Maskerata [Masquerade] (produced 1955).
Kraljevo [The Kermess] (produced 1955).
Kristofor Kolumbo (produced 1955).
Aretej; ili, Legenda o Svetoj Ancili [Aretheus; or, The Legend of St Ancilla] (produced 1959). 1963.
Saloma [Salome] (produced 1963).
Put u raj [Journey to Paradise] (produced 1973). 1970.

Other

Izlet u Rusiju [Excursion to Russia]. 1926.
Eseji [Essays]. 1932.
Moj obračun s njima [My Squaring of Accounts]. 1932.
Podravski motivi [Motifs of Podravina]. 1933.
Evropa danas [Europe Today]. 1935.
Deset krvavih godina [Ten Years in Blood]. 1937.
Eppur si muove. 1938.
Knjiga proze [A Book of Prose]. 1938.
Dijalektički antibarbarus [A Dialectical Antibarbarian]. 1939.
Knjiga studija i putopisa [A Book of Studies and Travels]. 1939.
Goya. 1948.
O Marinu Držiću [On Marin Držić]. 1949.
Zlato i srebro Zadra. 1951; translated as *The Gold and Silver of Zadar*, 1972.
Djetinjstvo u Agramu godine 1902–1903 [Childhood in Agram]. 1952.
Kalendar jedne bitke 1942 [Almanac of a 1942 Battle]. 1953.
Kalendar jedne parlamentarne komedije [Almanac of a Parliamentary Comedy]. 1953.
O Erasmu Rotterdamskom [On Erasmus of Rotterdam]. 1953.
Sabrana djela [Collected Works]. 27 vols., 1953–72.
Davni dani [Long Bygone Days]. 1956.
Eseji [Essays]. 1958.
Eseji [Essays]. 6 vols., 1961–67.
Razgovori s Miroslavom Krležom [Conversations with Miroslav Krleža]. 1969.
99 varijacija lexicographica [99 Lexicographic Variations]. 1972.
Djetinjstvo 1902–1903 i drugi zapisi [Childhood and Other Pieces]. 1972.
Panorama pogleda, pojava i pojmova. 5 vols., 1975.
Dnevnik [Diary]. 5 vols., 1977.
Tito 1892–1937–1977, with Edvard Kardelj. 1977.
Eseji i članci (essays). 1979– .
Iz naše književne krčme. 1983.
Ratne teme. 1983.
Sa uredničkog stola. 1983.

Editor, with others, *Danas* [Today]. 2 vols., 1971.

*

Bibliography: *Bibliografia djela Miroslava Krleže* by T. Jakić, 1953; *Literatura o Miroslavu Krleži 1914–1963* by D. Kapetanić, 1967.

Critical Studies: *Studien zur Romantechnik Miroslav Krležas* by Sibylle Schneider, 1969; *La Vie et l'oeuvre de Miroslav Krleža* by Marijan Matković, 1977; *Miroslav Krleža und der deutsche Expressionismus* by Reinhard Lauer, 1984; *Die Gestalt des Künstlers bei Miroslav Krleža* by Andreas Leitner, 1986; *The Writer as Naysayer: Miroslav Krleža and the Aesthetic of Interwar Central Europe* by Ralph Bogert, 1990.

* * *

Miroslav Krleža was the dominant figure in 20th-century Croatian literature. As the writer of novels, short stories, poems, essays, journals, travelogues, polemics, and memoirs, and as the editor of a series of leftist literary journals, he had a considerable influence on his contemporaries. His search for an enlightened humanism brought him to communism after the collapse of the Austro-Hungarian empire, but he was never an obedient Party member who marched uncritically, following the Party policy. His criticism of the Marxist dogmatism and of the notion of Socialist Realism in the arts as well as his outspoken demands 'for freedom of artistic expression, for the simultaneous existence of differing schools and styles, for liberty of choice and independence of moral and political convictions' left their lasting mark on the cultural climate of post-World War II Yugoslavia.

Krleža began his literary career as a poet celebrating in pagan terms the triumph of life over the powers of darkness, mysticism, and death. However, World War I brought a dramatic change in his outlook. His war poems evoke in a series of striking expressionistic images the idea of the futility of life and the absurdity of death and have as their underlying theme one of Krleža's favourite notions, that of the supremacy of stupidity over reason in human life. The same theme, articulated as dehumanization caused by the horrors of the war, is central to his collection of short stories *Hrvatski bog Mars* [The Croatian God Mars], in which the useless squandering of lives of the Croats enlisted to fight for Austria in the war of 1914–18 is depicted in a dramatic and memorable narrative.

The poetry he continued to write in the 1920s and 1930s shows an increased social awareness and concerns itself primarily with the themes of social protest. The peak of his career as a poet was reached by the publication of his *Balade Petrice Kerempuha* [Ballads of Petrica Kerempuh], a collection of poems written in the dialect of north-western Croatia, used by the writers of the 17th and the 18th centuries. It is a unique satirical saga of Croatian history. Although overwhelmed with suffering, injustice, blood, and the symbol of gallows, the Croatian past is approached without any romantic illusions and rather treated in a bitter but mocking tone of Rabelaisian laughter.

In his youthful plays, published in a collection entitled *Legende* [Legends], Krleža used historical figures and themes as means of handling underlying themes of his time. His reputation as a dramatist was established with the piece *Golgota* [Golgotha], a socialist play set in a shipyard, and enhanced with two anti-war plays, *Vučjak* and *U logoru* [In the Camp]. The best known, and the best, of his plays make up his Glembay trilogy: *Gospoda Glembajevi* [The

Glembays], *U agoniji* (*In Agony*), and *Leda* constitute an organic unity with the short stories of the same cycle. The plays and the short stories combine to portray the rise and decline of a rich Croatian family against the background of the agony of a dying civilization (the Austro-Hungarian empire). Ibsenesque in character and scope, these plays were written in the best vein of psychological realism.

Povratak Filipa Latinovicza (*The Return of Philip Latinovicz*) is the most popular of his four novels. It tells a story of an expatriate artist who, in a moment of personal and creative crisis, returns to his native Panonia to establish his paternity. But his pilgrimage turns into a quest for his own identity and a scathing portrayal of provincial decadence and his struggle to confront it. *Na rubu pameti* (*On the Edge of Reason*) is a novel of a model citizen who falls from society's grace after speaking his mind. Abandoned by both his family and his friends, persecuted and jailed, put into an asylum, he finishes as a lonely and desperate man listening in his hotel room to the discordant and meaningless sounds coming from the radio. Krleža's two other novels provide an imaginative and critical portrait of both Yugoslavia and Europe in the first decades of the 20th century, and make some major political, social, and psychological statements about the predicament of modern man. *Banket u Blitvi* [Banquet in Blitva] shows Krleža as a political satirist at his best. It is a political-allegorical novel with various references to those European countries (including his own) where, after World War I, people were deprived of their freedoms and democratic rights by military dictatorships. The vivid and dramatic story of a struggle between a dictator and a courageous political idealist is interspersed with typical Krleža polemics, soliloquies, and conversations with the intention of showing the amoral nature of politics in general. *Zastave* [Banners] spans the period between 1912 and 1922 in Croatian and Yugoslav history. The novel is built upon one of Krleža's recurring themes, that of the conflict between a father, a loyal and acquiescent servant of the Establishment, and his only son, the embittered, freedom-loving rebel. Their precarious relations are designed to bring out a psychological and ideological drama caused by the disillusionments of the two generations in the political upheavals of the early 20th century.

Alongside the best of Krleža's creative writing may be set the best of his non-fiction prose: the essays which reflect his vast reading and his moral and intellectual integrity; the two books of memoirs, *Djetinjstvo u Agramu godine 1902–1903* [Childhood in Agram] and *Davni dani* [Long Bygone Days]; the account of his visit to the USSR in 1925, *Izlet u Rusiju* [Excursion to Russia]; and, finally, his writings and annotations for the Yugoslav Encyclopedia, of which he was the *spiritus movens* and the editor-in-chief.

—Dušan Puvačić

L

LA FONTAINE, Jean de. Born in Château-Thierry, France, 8 July 1621. Married Marie Héricart in 1647 (separated 1658). Succeeded his father as Maître des Eaux et Forêts of the Duchy of Château-Thierry; possibly licensed to practice as a lawyer; writer in Paris; patronized by Fouquet and others, especially Mme de la Sablière. Member, Académie française, 1684. *Died 13 March 1695.*

PUBLICATIONS

Collections

Oeuvres complètes, edited by H. de Regnier. 11 vols., 1883–92.
Oeuvres: Fables, contes, et nouvelles; Oeuvres diverses, edited by René Groos, Jacques Schiffrin, and Pierre Clarac. 2 vols., 1942–54.
The Complete Fables, translated by Norman B. Spector. 1988.
Oeuvres complètes, edited by Jean-Pierre Collinet. 1991 – .

Verse

Élégie aux nymphes de Vaux. 1661.
Nouvelles en vers. 1665.
Contes et nouvelles en vers (4 parts). 4 vols., 1665–74; enlarged edition, 1686; edited by Jacqueline Zeugschmitt, 2 vols., 1972; as *Tales and Novels in Verse*, translated by Samuel Humphreys, 1735.
Fables (12 parts). Vols. 1–6, 1668; vols. 7–11, 1678–79; vol. 12, 1693; translated as *Fables*, 1804; also translated by Edward Marsh, 1931; Marianne Moore, 1954; Reginald Jarman, 1962; Elizur Wright, 1975; James Michie, 1979; Francis Scarfe, 1985; Walter Thornbury, 1984; Liza Cornmager, 1985; Norman Shapiro, 1988.
Fables nouvelles et autres poésies. 1671; as *Fables and Other Poems*, translated by John Cairncross, 1982.
Poème du Quinquina et autres ouvrages en vers. 1682.

Fiction

Les Amours de Psyché et de Cupidon. 1669; as *The Loves of Cupid and Psyche*, translated by Joseph Lockman, 1744.

Plays

L'Eunuque, from the play by Terence. 1654.
Les Rieurs de Beau-Richard (ballet; produced 1659–60). In *Oeuvres*, 1827.
Astrée, music by Pascal Colasse (produced 1691). 1691.

Other

Voyage en Limousin. 1663.
Ouvrages de prose et de poésie, with Abbé François de Maucroix. 2 vols., 1685.

Oeuvres posthumes. 1696.

*

Critical Studies: *Young La Fontaine* by P. Wadsworth, 1952; *La Fontaine* by M. Sutherland, 1953; *La Fontaine: Fables* by Odette de Mourgues, 1960; *La Fontaine, Poet and Counterpoet* by Margaret O. Guiton, 1961; *The Style of La Fontaine's Fables* by Jean Dominique Biard, 1966; *The Esthetics of Negligence: La Fontaine's Contes* by John C. Lapp, 1971; *La Fontaine and His Friends: A Biography* by Agnes Ethel MacKay, 1972.

* * *

Jean de La Fontaine stands out as the one French writer of the 17th century to have written sympathetically about animals and the natural world, and the one poet in the classical period to have combined a deep respect for form with a readiness and ability to experiment in different types of versification. His two collections of *Fables* continue to make him probably the most frequently read and quoted of all French poets, and he is probably the only great French writer to be equally appreciated by children and by adults. His first book of *Fables* was written for the instruction of the Dauphin, the future Louis XIV, and offers a view of the world that contains a greater awareness of *Realpolitik* than of the nobler elements in the concept of Christian monarchy. Thus when, in 'La Génisse, la chèvre, et la brebis en société avec le lion' ('The Heifer, the Goat, and the Sheep in company with the Lion'), the animals prepare to share out the spoils, the lion—the King of Beasts—takes the largest share on the indisputable grounds that he is called Lion and is the strongest. One of the best known fables, 'Le Loup et l'Agneau' ('The Wolf and the Lamb') demonstrates the truth that might is right, and the qualities needed to succeed, or even to survive, in the social world depicted in La Fontaine's animal allegories are exactly those that Hobbes considered inseparable from the State of Nature. For it is indeed the war of all against all in which the cardinal virtues are force and fraud, and the human beings who make an appearance in this world tend to be on the same moral level as the animals who represent the various ranks in the extremely hierarchical society that La Fontaine knew. When a bird is wounded in a fight and lands in a field, a child casually throws a stone to kill it, thus illustrating the pre-Rousseauist view of children as 'an age without pity.' Only perhaps by adopting an attitude of suspicion, humility, and self-effacement can those at the bottom end of the social spectrum survive, and it is clear that La Fontaine had no vision of a society in which a king or any other kind of ruler might act or intervene to improve the lot of his subjects.

Most of the actual stories, of course, are traditional, coming down from Aesop and Phaedra, and the almost unremitting pessimism which is the quality that most strikes the modern reader may well have been more axiomatic and therefore less surprising for La Fontaine's contemporaries. This pessimism is also occasionally relieved by fables such as 'Les Deux Amis' ('The Two Friends'), showing as it does an idealized vision of friendship, and is prevented from making a really deep emotional impact by the humour of versification and characterization that run through all the *Fables*. La Fontaine excels in matching verbal rhythms to the physical features of the animals he describes, writing about mice in short, neat, light, precise lines, and about bears and lions in more ponderous and self-important tones. You can see his animals moving as you read or listen to the *Fables*, and visualize the French countryside against which the action takes place.

In his lifetime, and by connoisseurs since the 17th century, La Fontaine was also known as the author of a number of *Contes et nouvelles en vers* (*Tales and Novels in Verse*), whose agreeably pagan inspiration gave way to a more orthodox Christian sensibility in the 'Recueil de Poésies Chrétiennes' ['Collection of Christian Poetry'] in 1671. It is traditional in France to refer to the author of the *Fables* as 'le bon La Fontaine', a reference more to his genial disposition than to the view of humanity running through his work.

—Philip Thody

FABLES
Stories by Jean de La Fontaine, 1668–93.

La Fontaine's first collection of fables, published in 1668, consists of 118 poems based on Aesopic models. Unusually, for a 17th-century work, they deal with the world of nature, albeit in a stylized form. The first fables are short poems evoking a magical world of cicadas and frogs, foxes and gods.

La Fontaine's achievement was the creation of poetry from a humble teaching aid. Before him, the Aesopic fable was used in schools, but had no literary pretensions. Hence his modest title, 'Selected Fables Translated into Verse'. As the subject matter was familiar, it had the aura of authenticity that suited the literary taste of 17th-century France. But the age was intolerant of pedantry and the fable's association with the schoolroom was a problem. La Fontaine's solution lies in a liveliness of style that he achieves by a variety of means.

Perhaps the most striking is his use of dialogue. Unlike his prosaic models, his fables are little dramas. His protagonists define their natures by the way they speak. In 'The Wolf and the Lamb' ('Le Loup et l'Agneau'), the lamb's integrity is mirrored by the calmness and courtesy of its language; whereas the moral ambiguity of the wolf's position is reflected by the stridency of his reasoning: he loses the argument, but still eats the lamb.

Another quality is the attention to detail. These brief tableaux are painted with economy and wit. The creatures have fur and feathers and exist in their own right. If the animals in Aesopic fables are animals in name only, those in La Fontaine's world are brought alive by a charming rightness of scale. The dove saves the ant from drowning in 'The Dove and the Ant' ('La Colombe et la Fourmi') by lowering a blade of grass into the water; the Cicada promises to repay with interest a borrowed grain of wheat in 'The Cicada and the Ant' ('La Cigale et la Fourmi').

The fables abound in burlesque mythological references. There is humour in a cat being compared to Attila in 'The Cat and the Old Rat' ('Le Chat et un vieux Rat'). But the effect is frequently pathos rather than parody. The shepherd's wretched fate is contrasted with Virgil's pastoral heroes in 'The Shepherd and the Sea' ('Le Berger et la Mer'); while in 'The Old Woman with Two Servants' ('La Vieille et les deux servantes'), the description of the girls' dreary labour is interleaved with references to the more romantic reaches of classical mythology. This is not gratuitous erudition: the brutality of the contrast heightens the impression of drudgery. And the modest little saga acquires a hint of the magic associated with the legends of antiquity.

Above all, in an age wedded to fixed forms and the alexandrine metre, La Fontaine's poetry has an air of freedom. His metre varies according to the movement of his subject: in 'The Crow and the Fox' ('Le Corbeau et le Renard'), the scene is set with nimble lines of eight and ten syllables, while pompous alexandrines are used to express the fox's bogus compliments. And the rocking seven-syllable metre used in 'The Earthen Pot and the Iron Pot' ('Le Pot de terre et le pot de fer') beautifully evokes the awkwardness of these unlikely travellers. The musicality is remarkable: sounds and rhythm are subordinated to sense, rather than the reverse. If the vocabulary is simple, La Fontaine finds ways of combining it that achieve Racinian reverberations: a line like 'Sur les humides bords des royaumes du vent' ('On the dank shores of the wind's realm') from 'The Oak and the Reed' ('Le Chêne et le Roseau') contains a wealth of suggestion almost impossible to translate.

At the same time, lightness of tone is maintained by the constant presence of the author. This can range from the throwaway 'I read somewhere that a Miller . . .' in 'The Miller, His Son and the Ass' ('Le Menier, son fils et l'âne'), to feigned uncertainty over whether a fox comes from Gascony or Normandy in 'The Fox and the Grapes' ('Le Renard et les raisins'), to expressions of sympathy for the sufferings he describes. In addition to the stories, we have a kind of ironic commentary that brings the tales alive and puts the moral into perspective.

The latter is the aspect of La Fontaine's first fables that best illustrates his aesthetic awareness. In the Aesopic fable the moral is invariably introduced by the formula 'This fables shows . . .'. Such prosaic language is absent from La Fontaine. Fable and moral are usually united in a seamless unit. In 'The Crow and the Fox', the moral, smugly delivered by the fox, completes our understanding of the character. In 'The Cicada and the Ant', there is no explicit moral at all: the sense of the anecdote pervades the whole poem and La Fontaine pays the reader the compliment of leaving him to draw his or her own conclusion. But even this is not straightforward. The traditional moral is clear: the industrious ant is right and the hedonistic cicada wrong. Yet we also sense a feeling of regret that things are thus, that it is a pity the beautiful cicada has to die and that the ant is actually a self-righteous prig: the simplest of the fables is also a model of ironic ambiguity.

This quizzical attitude was one reason La Fontaine never found favour at court. The world of the fable is a world in conflict. But the conflict is between the strong and the weak, the foolish and the cunning, rather than between good and evil. Might is right and virtue is no protection against the arbitrary use of power. The political dimension would become more explicit in later fables. But even in this first collection, chiefly remarkable for its poetic qualities, we sense La Fontaine's reservations about the nature of the hierachical society in which he lived.

—David Shaw

LA MOTTE FOUQUÉ, Caroline. See **FOUQUÉ, Caroline de la Motte.**

LA MOTTE FOUQUÉ, Friedrich. See **FOUQUÉ, Friedrich de la Motte.**

LA ROCHEFOUCAULD, François. Born in Paris, France, 15 September 1613. Married Andrée de Vivonne in 1628; eight children. Chief of staff, 1629, served in Italy, Netherlands, 1635–36, Rocroi, 1643, and Gravelines, 1644; took part in Louis XIV's Dutch campaign, 1667–68; participated in the Frondes, 1648–52; intrigues against Richelieu; severely wounded in fighting in Paris, 1652; imprisoned by Richelieu for eight days, then banished to Verteuil for two years. Lived in retirement among a small intellectual circle including Mme de Sablé, Mme de Sévigné, and Mme de Lafayette. *Died 17 March 1680.*

PUBLICATIONS

Collections

Oeuvres. 1818.
Oeuvres complètes. 1825.
Oeuvres inédites. 1863.
Oeuvres complètes, edited by D.L. Gilbert and J. Gourdault. 4 vols., 1868–83.
Oeuvres complètes, edited by A. Chassang. 2 vols., 1883–84.
Oeuvres complètes, edited by Louis Martin-Chauffier and Jean Marchand. 1935; revised editions, 1957, 1964.

Works

Portrait de La Rochefoucauld par lui-même. 1659.
Mémoires. 1662.
Sentences et maximes de morale (pirate edition). 1664; as *Réflexions; ou, Sentences et maximes morales.* 1665; 5th edition, 1678; enlarged edition as *Nouvelles réflexions ou sentences et maximes morales,* 1693; as *Maximes,* edited by Robert L. Cru, 1927, Henry A. Grubbs, 1929, F.C. Green, 1945, Roland Barthes, 1961, Jean Starobinski, 1964, Dominique Secretan, 1967, and by Jacques Truchet, 1967; as *Maximes,* translated by Aphra Behn 1685; also translated by A.S. Bolton, 1884; F.C. Stevens, 1939; Constantine Fitzgibbon, 1957; Louis Kronenberger, 1959; Leonard W. Tancock, 1959.
Mémoires du duc de L.R. 1664.
La Justification de l'amour (attributed to La Rochefoucauld), edited by J.D. Hubert. 1971.
A Frenchman's Year in Suffolk, edited and translated by Norman Scarfe. 1988.

*

Bibliography: *Bibliographie générale raisonnée de La Rochefoucauld* by Jean Marchand, 1948; *François de la Rochefoucauld* by Edith Mora, 1965.

Critical Studies: *Le Vrai visage de la Rochefoucauld* by Emile Magne, 1923; *The Originality of La Rochefoucauld's Maxims* by H.A. Grubbs, 1929; *The Life and Adventures of La Rochefoucauld* by Maurice Bishop, 1951; *New Aspects of Style in the Maxims of La Rochefoucauld* by Mary F. Zeller, 1954; *The Concept of Love in the Maxims of La Rochefoucauld* by May W. Butrick, 1959; *La Rochefoucauld: His Mind and Art* by Will G. Moore, 1969; *Vauvenargues and La Rochefoucauld* by Peter M. Fine, 1974; *La Rochefoucauld: The Art of Abstraction* by Philip E. Lewis, 1977; *Two French Moralists: La Rochefoucauld and La Bruyère* by Odette de Mourgues, 1978; *Collaboration et originalité chez La Rouchefoucauld* by Susan Read Baker, 1980; *La Rochefoucauld and the Seventeenth Century Concept of the Self* by Vivien Thweatt, 1980; *Images de La Rochefoucauld: Actes du tricentenaire, 1680–1980* edited by Jean Lafond and Jean Mesnard, 1984; *Procès à La Rochefoucauld et à la maxime* by Corraso Rosso, 1986.

*   *   *

The 17th-century French ideal of the *honnête homme* was epitomized in the later life of François, duc de La Rochefoucauld, and is immortalized in his famous *Réflexions; ou, Sentences et maximes morales (Maxims)*. His views on man and life were determined in large measure by the failure of his political ambitions and by his active role in the armed rebellion against the crown in the civil wars (the Frondes, 1648–52) in which he was seriously wounded. Deceived by his mistress, the duchesse de Longueville, La Rochefoucauld became bitter and disillusioned, retiring from public life at the age of 40. In 1659, he was allowed to resume residence in Paris, where he regularly attended the brilliant salon of Mme de Sablé. In this cultured, sophisticated society, La Rochefoucauld displayed and honed his ideas and his literary skills. The art of conversation was highly valued among the habitués of literary salons, and their influence on language, attitudes, and ideas was profound. The nature of man and his behaviour were among the most discussed subjects in salon society. La Rochefoucauld asserted that man was not always a rational being but was governed by his 'humeurs' or temperament. In humankind *amour-propre* (self-love) was the motivating factor, the well-spring of all actions. He saw a world in which men lied and cheated, and were devoid of honour and gratitude. Only man's natural tendency to *la paresse* (indolence; laziness) prevented him from acting intemperately; moderation in pursuit of virtue or vice was due to indifference and innate dullness. This grim portrait of humanity was widely held by many thoughtful people at the time, and their opinion of the common masses was even more disparaging.

La Rochefoucauld's writings reflect these pessimistic views of man and society, but he also held firmly to the masculine ideal of the age, that of the cultured gentleman; birth and breeding, manners and social graces were distinguishing features of an élite class. Open-mindedness, *bienséance* (decorum; decency), and wit were to be cultivated among men of rank. La Rochefoucauld embodied these aristocratic characteristics of the gentleman who avoided pedantry, offending others, or trying to improve one's fellow men through moral exhortation; but the reality was that 'we give nothing so liberally as our advice', according to La Rochefoucauld.

In La Rochefoucauld's *Portrait de La Rochefoucauld par lui-même* (Potrait of La Rochefoucauld by Himself) one finds a degree of idealization as the author measures himself against the notion of the *honnête homme*. It reveals a self-sufficient man, aloof, proud, and conscious of his aristocratic rank. He claims a melancholic temperament, prone to depression, reserved, and even secretive. Moderation and self-control, intelligence, retentive memory, and 'fluent tongue' are cited among his more notable qualities in the *Portrait de La Rochefoucauld par lui-même*. Further, he claims that he was 'right thinking and naturally inclined towards good . . .', fond of his friends, but not overtly demonstrative. The portrait is a kind of manifesto by which the author hoped to be judged favourably by his contemporaries. Appearance was of prime importance in French society, to the people of quality, as La Rochefoucauld would have put it. His self-portrait may have been idealized to some degree, but one can recognize the same sombre, irresolute man pictured in the Cardinal de Retz's pen-portrait of La Rochefoucauld.

Numerous pen-portraits are the most salient feature of La Rochefoucauld's *Mémoires*. Sketches of his contemporaries reveal the attitudes and ideals of the French upper classes, the fostering of *honnêteté* (civility), self-discipline, and social order. Unpleasant characteristics, physical or moral, are seldom mentioned—a gentleman avoided deliberately giving offence. The *Mémoires* are not in the modern sense autobiographical. Indeed, they reveal more about La Rochefoucauld's social milieu and the culture of the age of Louis XIV than about the memoirist.

On the other hand, La Rochefoucauld's deservedly famous maxims reveal a great deal about the personality and ideas of the writer as he probes human nature, motives, and conduct. The ideal of the *honnête homme* is counterpoised to reality; the *Maxims* describe man as he is, not as he ought to be. One can discern a definite point of view, one that is often harsh, bitter, cynical, and pessimistic. La Rochfoucauld's likes and dislikes, and those of his aristocratic peers, are evident as he deals with subjects such as love, friendship, old age, death, women, and human virtues and vices. His attitude towards women is particularly striking: 'Most virtuous women are hidden treasures, safe only because no one is looking for them.' And about love he declares: 'Nothing is more natural or deceptive than to believe one is loved.' The moral and ethical standards found in the *Maxims* generally reflect those commonly held by upper-class 17th-century society: man is by nature weak and irrational, motivated by *amour-propre* but just as frequently immobilized by *la paresse*, which renders him indecisive and impassive. However, La Rochefoucauld's own experiences undoubtedly influenced his ideas, especially those relating to women, love, self-interest, mistrust, and ingratitude. Betrayed by the woman he loved, denied a post at Court, censured for rebellion against his monarch, and forever labelled a 'frondeur', La Rochefoucauld became disenchanted with his fellow men and with the pursuit of worldly power and position.

La Rochefoucauld was an astute observer, a recorder of human follies and foibles. His intention was to inform, not to reform, mankind, and he avoided dogmatic statements and the appearance of preaching. He accepts that man's nature is what it is; one's conduct is often restrained only by the need to be socially accepted. Without question, the *Maxims* are universally applicable, unrestricted by time or place. In these timeless aphorisms that speak to all, the language employed is markedly neutral, avoiding words that would evoke an emotional rather than a rational reaction. The carefully crafted sentences are notable for their terseness, precise phrasing, and minimal vocabulary. They are immediately understandable, devoid of esoteric allusions, metaphors, and other scholarly devices. The highly polished style of La Rochefoucauld's sentences is due in large part to years of refining and honing of ideas and language in the Paris salons. Creating pithy proverbs, witticisms, and maxims was a popular 'parlour-game' among French sophisticates; their search for principles of universal validity was taken seriously and led these perceptive *salonniers* to accept that 'we find few sensible people, except those who are of our way of thinking'. In Mme de Sablé's salon, men and women discussed, analyzed, and criticized both the form and the content of ideas, stressing clarity, precision, and simplicity. The *Maxims* also mirror the 17th-century tendency to self-examination, the inward-looking, reflective nature of the French upper classes. The harsh, cynical sentiments expressed in the *Maxims* were softened in later editions, most likely through the influence of La Rochefoucauld's closest women friends, Mme de Lafayette and Mme de Sévigné. La Rochefoucauld's *Maxims*, according to Voltaire, helped to shape the French taste for precision and accuracy, attributes which still set the standards for their thought and writing.

—Jeanne A. Ojala

MAXIMS (Réflexions; ou, Sentences et maximes morales)
Prose by François La Rochefoucauld, 1665–78.

La Rochefoucauld's *Maxims* is a collection of dispassionate personal reflections on human nature, honed and polished by the tastes of 17th-century literate society. As such, they are a fine example of French classical literature. Five editions appeared between 1665 and 1678.

Military and political disappointments had destroyed La Rochefoucauld's illusions about human nature. The resulting tone of disenchantment, which is evident in the *Maxims*, challenged the official optimism of the age. The finished work was a product of salon society. La Rochefoucauld was a member of Mme de Sablé's circle, which included philosophers, theologians, and scientists. Their conversations covered a variety of themes—human behaviour, the limits of free will, the relationship between morality and society, and the nature of love—which anticipated those of the *Maxims*.

It was in the context of these gatherings that La Rochefoucauld and Mme de Sablé launched the fashion of expressing their insights in lapidary form; their maxims achieved widespread fame, and publication followed. It may seem strange today that such a work should be successful. But in La Rochefoucauld's day it expressed an important aspect of the intellectual climate. The 17th century had inherited from humanism a taste for moral precepts: the feeling was that virtue and happiness lay in the definition and application of a code of moral laws.

The central thesis of the *Maxims* is resolutely pessimistic. Humanity is flawed. At the heart of our corruption lies self-interest (*amour-propre*), which effectively controls our lives: 'It is present in all estates and conditions; it lives everywhere, it lives on everything and it lives on nothing.' Inseparable from egoism, pride, and vanity, self-interest is the motivating force behind all our actions, even those apparently inspired by altruism: 'Self-interest speaks all sorts of languages and plays all sorts of roles, even that of unselfishness.' Reason is powerless against it and sentiments conventionally thought noble are really self-interest in disguise. Love, stripped of its romantic façade, is concerned with possession and resembles hatred. Friendship masks a desire to exploit and we take pleasure in friends' happiness, says La Rochefoucauld, because we hope to take some profit from their good fortune. Even virtues such as humility and military valour are stripped of their prestige and systematically reduced to the hypocrisy of personal interest.

As striking as the doctrine itself is the vigorous form in which it is communicated. Expressed in less trenchant style, the maxims would be less provoking. La Rochefoucauld is a supreme exponent of the metaphors and antitheses enjoyed by the polite society of his time. 'Virtues merge into self-interest, as rivers merge into the sea.' Everywhere there is paradox and economy: a single thought reduced to a minimum of words and artfully expressed: 'Constancy in love is perpetual inconstancy.' The author's awareness of the importance of form is demonstrated by the care with which he revised his maxims in successive editions.

He was not alone in writing about the power of egoism. Influential works such as Descartes's *Traité des passions* (1649) and Cureau de la Chamber's *Caractère des passions* (1662) had already suggested that human judgement is influenced by 'humours' over which reason has no direct control. In addition, Mme de Sablé's circle was deeply influenced by the growing force of Jansenism and by the feeling of disillusionment that permeated polite society after the disappointment of the Frondes: the *Maxims* are simply the most memorable expression of this strain of pessimism.

And yet they are not entirely negative. It would be wrong to imply, as some critics have, that they are solely concerned with egoism, or that La Rochefoucauld does not believe in the possibility of virtue. What saves this austere doctrine from hopelessness is the idea that a small élite is capable of rising above self-interest. La Rochefoucauld states, for example, that if friendship is often a façade, the true article can exist. If we are to know ourselves properly, the first requirement is humility, 'the altar on which God wants us to offer sacrifices'. Linked to humility is the kind of lucidity that enables man to identify his true motives, admit his faults, and, ideally, act disinterestedly: 'The true gentleman recognizes his faults and confesses them.' If we cannot identify our defects, we cannot hope to correct them: if there is to be moral progress, lucidity is essential.

Far from being a negative work, the *Maxims* should be considered a high-minded manual of social etiquette in the tradition of Montaigne and Charron: true virtue, suggests La Rochefoucauld, lies not in conformism but in a deeper sense of personal greatness, the need to be true to oneself. Although he discussed his work at length with his friend, the Jansenist theologian Jacques Ésprit, the moral ideal that emerges from the *Maxims* is not religious but human, not submission to Divine Providence but independent nobility of spirit.

—David Shaw

LACLOS, (Pierre Ambroise Francois) Choderlos de. Born in Amiens, France, 18 October 1741. Married Marie-Soulange Duperré in 1786. Educated at École d'Artillerie de la Fère, 1759–63. 2nd lieutenant, 1762; served in Toul, 1763–66; Strasbourg, 1766–69; Grenoble, 1769–75; Besançon, 1775– 76; Valence, 1776–78; l'Île d'Aix, 1778–88; left the army for a brief period as politician; rejoined army as Maréchal de camp, 1792; general of the artillery in the army of Naples, 1800. Editor, *Journal des Amis de la Constitution*, 1790–91. *Died 5 September 1803.*

PUBLICATIONS

Collection

Oeuvres complètes, edited by Maurice Allem. 1944; revised edition, edited by Laurent Versani, 1979.

Fiction

Les Liaisons dangereuses. 1782; edited by René Pomeau, 1981; as *Dangerous Connections*, 1784; as *Dangerous Acquaintances*, translated by Richard Aldington, 1924; as *Les Liaisons dangereuses*, translated by P.W.K. Stone, 1961; also translated and adapted by Christopher Hampton, 1985.

Play

Ernestine, music by Saint-Georges, from a novel by Mme Riccoboni (produced 1777).

Verse

Poésies, edited by Arthur Symons and Louis Thomas. 1908.

Other

Lettre à M.M. de l'Académie française. 1786.
La Galerie des États-Généraux, with others. 1789.
La Galerie des dames françaises. 1789.
Causes secrètes de la révolution. 1795.
De l'éducation des femmes, edited by Édouard Champion. 1903.
Lettres inédites, edited by Louis de Chauvigny. 1904.

*

Bibliography: *Choderlos de Laclos: The Man, His Works and His Critics: An Annotated Bibliography* by Colette Verger Michael, 1982.

Critical Studies: *Laclos and the Epistolary Novel* by Dorothy R. Thelander, 1963; *The Novel of Worldliness: Crébillon, Marivaux, Laclos, and Stendhal* by Peter P. Brooks, 1969; *Laclos: Les Liaisons dangereuses* by Philip Thody, 1970, revised edition, 1975; *Critical Approaches to Les Liaisons dangereuses* edited by Lloyd R. Free, 1978; *Intimate, Intrusive and Triumphant: Readers in the 'Liaisons dangereuses'* by Peter V. Conroy, 1987; *Laclos: Les Liaisons dangereuses* by Simon Davies, 1987; *The Seducer as Mythic Figure in Richardson, Laclos and Kierkegaard* by Betty Becker-Theye, 1988; *Strategies of Resistance in Les Liaisons dangereuses: Heroines in Search of 'Author-ity'* by Ann-Marie Brinsmead, 1989; *Les Liaisons dangereuses: A Study of Motives and Moral* by Patrick W. Byrne, 1989.

*   *   *

Choderlos de Laclos is a man of one book, *Les Liaisons dangereuses*, an impeccably constructed epistolary novel describing and analysing the sexual immorality which is said to have characterized certain members of the French aristocracy in the years immediately preceding the Revolution of 1789. But the novel is not the endorsement of promiscuity it was considered to be in the 19th century, any more than it is the transference into fiction of Laclos's own exploits and world view, or a realistic novel in the sense of one based on actual events. Indeed, recent historical research has revealed how the principal male character, the Vicomte de Valmont, far from being drawn from life, served rather as a model to would-be seducers who wished to follow his example after reading the novel. Laclos himself, unlike Valmont, was a very minor nobleman, whose dislike of the top aristocracy of the day may well have stemmed from the slowness with which, as a professional soldier, he obtained promotion in the artillery in the *ancien régime*. *Les Liaisons dangereuses* can thus be seen as a socially committed novel written by a man sympathetic to the revolutionary and moralistic views of Rousseau, and intended to show, by contrast, the superiority of the more modest but increasingly self-confident middle-class. Laclos's own marriage, to a girl who was 17 when he married her at the age of 45, was a very happy one. Indeed, a letter exists, written to her while he was on active service with the Revolutionary armies in the 1790s, telling her of his ambition to write a novel proving that 'true happiness can be found only in the Family'.

The plot of *Les Liaisons dangereuses* can certainly be interpreted as a criticism of how Valmont and his female accomplice, the Marquise de Merteuil, behave in their sexual relationships to other people and to each other, and it is also possible to see the extremely intelligent and somewhat terrifying Marquise as a very conscious warning of how feminism can go sour. For Laclos, as an essay published long after his death revealed, held views on the equality of women and men which are advanced even by modern standards ('Learn', he wrote, 'that one escapes from slavery only by a great revolution'), and Madame de Merteuil is the strongest willed, the most intellectual, the most interesting, and the least successful of all French fictional heroines. *Les Liaisons dangereuses* is nevertheless too complex and ambiguous a novel to be interpreted in only one light. It deserves its place as the best novel written in France in the 18th century, and one of the best studies ever published of evil, of sexual aggression and of the lust for power. There is also an intriguing contrast between the perfection of its formal finish and the endlessly interesting questions to which it gives rise.

—Philip Thody

LES LIAISONS DANGEREUSES
Novel by Choderlos de Laclos, 1782.

The only significant imaginative work of Laclos, *Les Liaisons dangereuses*, is a masterpiece that apparently grew fully-armed (but not without multiple revisions during its writing) from his mind. Probably the most perfect epistolary novel of any ever written, it tells of the beautiful, dissolute, but brilliantly hypocritical young widow, the Marquise de Merteuil and the handsome libertine Vicomte de Valmont who, bored with their perfect love affair, decide to break it off in order to write to each other with the utmost candour of their further sexual exploits. They hold society in contempt and treat it as a field for manipulation of others through sexual conquest.

Valmont is in pursuit of the respectable 22 year-old Présidente de Tourvel, who from his description we realize is already in love with him; meanwhile Merteuil dallies with the Comte de Belleroche. Having previously been jilted by yet another lover, Gercourt, she wishes Valmont to procure the deflowering of Gercourt's 15-year-old prospective bride, the wealthy heiress Cécile de Volanges, newly emerged into society from her convent education. The best instrument for this purpose appears to be the young Chevalier de Danceny, madly in love already with Cécile but, it proves, too decent and romantic to be enterprising enough for Merteuil's liking.

Valmont shows little interest in Merteuil's 'commission' until Cécile and her mother (Mme de Volanges, who infuriates him by attempts to damage him in Tourvel's eyes) find themselves under the same roof as the Présidente, at his aunt's (Mme de Rosemonde's) country house. This is the arena of his rape-cum-seduction of Cécile, achieved by pretending to further the designs of Danceny, and of Valmont's relentless pressure on Tourvel to yield to him. This second seduction he later achieves at last, by arranging a supposedly final renunciatory interview with Tourvel through a priest.

Throughout his narratives of these events to Merteuil, Valmont has boasted that he will return to her bed as a reward for his conquest of Tourvel. Merteuil, however, despite having in a long exposé of her 'principles' vaunted her own intelligence and self-control, superior to that of any man, and despite demonstrating her powers in the course of the novel by ruining the social reputation of another famous rake, Prévan, has from the beginning clearly been jealous of the Présidente. She sends Valmont the draft of a contemptuous letter of abandonment, challenging him to use it on his new lover. This he does and Tourvel eventually dies brokenhearted and insane. Valmont, however, is only mocked by Merteuil after he discovers that she has seduced Danceny. Full of rage and growing remorse, Valmont persuades Danceny to abandon a rendezvous with Merteuil and she in revenge reveals Valmont's seduction of Cécile. Challenged to a duel by Danceny, he approaches the fight half-heartedly and receives a mortal wound. The dying Valmont is reconciled with his adversary and gives him his correspondence with Merteuil. The Chevalier, entrusting the correspondence to Valmont's aunt, reveals the contents of selected letters in society. Merteuil's reputation is in ruins; she has to leave Paris, loses an important lawsuit, and subsequently receives the further 'punishment' of disfigurement by smallpox. Cécile, having earlier miscarried Valmont's child, now retires permanently to a convent.

Laclos's use of the letter form takes pseudo-history (the convention of claiming a fictional narrative to be true) almost to its limits, so that the claim is only with difficulty shown to be false. He explains in an almost watertight way how the 'correspondence' came to be before the reader; each of his fictional letters has a characteristic personal style; the use of reported speech is sparing, so that a narrator's verbatim memory is hard to challenge; and above all few of the letters are mere 'reports': most themselves constitute acts in the drama by the very fact that they are sent. If this seems implausible in real-life terms, we are told that repetitive letters have been edited out! The reader is frequently placed in a position of dramatic irony with regard to the correspondents, knowing more of their situation than they do as they address or receive a communication. This resemblance to drama is an important key when interpreting the work and certainly helps to explain the success of a recent stage play and two films based on the novel.

At a structural level, the work owes more to classicism than to realism. Like one of Racine's or Marivaux's comedies, the plot begins from a basic (and extraordinary) supposition (the libertine lovers' 'pact'), which the action then works out according to psychological verisimilitude. As in classical French theatre, the initial supposition ('what if?') is less interesting by its (doubtful) resemblance to the possibilities of ordinary life, than by the moral issue which it distils for our concentrated dramatic attention: even if the wicked are self-deceiving and their own worst enemies, what help is that to the lives they destroy? One may be tempted by the novel's technical perfection and inclusion of specific social detail to treat it as a realistic portrayal of late 18th-century French aristocracy (as if Merteuil and Valmont were in some way typical!) or to interpret Merteuil as a feminist campaigner against an essentially phallocratic *ancien régime* (as if she did not take delight in destroying other women!). Such misinterpretations are a huge compliment to Laclos's powers of persuasion and are implicit, from the time of the book's initial popularity, in the ongoing quest for historical real-life 'keys' to its fictional characters. However, while Laclos had many sources to inspire him in both fiction and real memoirs and while his ethical and social concerns (for example over the education of women and the harmfulness of cloistering girls with nuns in their early years) are undoubtedly reflected in his novel, his leading characters are hyperbolic statements and exist nowhere but in his art. For them God is dead, conventional morality an object of disdain, and all behaviour permissible (provided it can be masked). The fascination that they exercise compared with their more virtuous victims is central to the work's moral ambiguity and helps to explain its continuing popularity in our own time.

—Philip E.J. Robinson

LAFAYETTE, Madame de. Born Marie-Madeleine Pioche de la Vergne, in Paris, in 1634. Married François, comte de Lafayette, in 1655 (died 1683), two sons. Grew up in Paris, and after a period of life in her husband's château of Nades, lived in Paris after 1659; friend of Henriette d'Angleterre, wife of Louis XIV's brother, of Mme de Sévigné, and the duc de La Rochefoucauld. *Died 25 May 1693.*

PUBLICATIONS

Collections

Oeuvres, edited by Robert Lejeune. 3 vols., 1925–30.
Romans et nouvelles, edited by Emile Magne. 1958.

Fiction

La Princesse de Montpensier. 1662; as *The Princess Montpensier*, translated anonymously, 1666; also translated by Anthony Bonner, 1805; edited and translated by Terence Cave, with *The Princesse de Clèves* and *The Comtesse de Tende*, 1992.
Zaïde. 1669–70; as *Zayde: A Spanish History*, translated by P. Porter, 1678.
La Princesse de Clèves. 1678; edited by Emile Magne, 1950;

also edited by Peter H. Nurse, 1971; as *The Princess of Cleves*, translated anonymously, 1679; also translated by Thomas Segeant Perry, 1777; Nancy Mitford, 1950; Walter J. Cobb, 1961; Robin Buss, 1992; edited and translated by Terence Cave, with *The Princesse de Montpensier* and *The Comtesse de Tende*, 1992.
La Comtesse de Tende. 1724; edited and translated by Terence Cave, with *The Princesse de Montpensier* and *The Princesse de Clèves*, 1992.

Other

Histoire d'Henriette d'Angleterre. 1720; edited by Gilbert Sigaux, 1965; as *Fatal Gallantry*, translated anonymously, 1722.
Mémoires de la cour de France. 1731; edited by Gilbert Sigaux, 1965.
Correspondance, edited by A. Beaunier. 2 vols., 1942.

*

Bibliography: *Madame de Lafayette: A Selected Critical Bibliography* by James W. Scott, 1974.

Critical Studies: *Moral Perspective in 'La Princesse de Clèves'* by Helen Kaps, 1968; *Madame de Lafayette* by Stirling Haig, 1970; *Classical Voices: Studies of Corneille, Racine, Moliere, Madame de Lafayette* by Peter H. Nurse, 1971; *Madame de Lafayette and 'La Princesse de Clèves'* by Janet Raitt, 1971; *La Princesse de Clèves: The Tension of Elegance* by Barbara R. Woshinsky, 1973; *Narrative Strategies in La Princesse de Clèves* by Donna Kuizenga, 1976; *A Structural Analysis of 'La Princesse de Clèves'* by Susan W. Tiefenbrun, 1976; *Madame de Lafayette: La Princesse de Clèves* by J.W. Scott, 1983; *Order in the Court: History and Society in La Princesse de Clèves* by Laurence A. Gregorio, 1986; *Une amitié parisienne au Grand siècle: Mme de Lafayette et Mme de Sévigné 1648–1693* by Denis Mayer, 1990; *A Critical Analysis of de Lafayette's La Princess de Clèves as a Royal Novel: Kings, Queens and Splendor* by Michael G. Paulsson, 1991; *An Inimitable Example: The Case for the Princess de Clèves*, edited by Patrick Henry, 1993.

* * *

As a member of the nobility, Madame de Lafayette was an amateur writer, and was reluctant to admit authorship of her novels. Indeed, she wrote them to a certain extent in collaboration with male friends, particularly Gilles Ménage and La Rochefoucauld. But they are unquestionably her creation and bear the stamp of her particular if somewhat narrowly focused genius. Her works have survived because one of them, *La Princesse de Clèves* (*The Princess of Cleves*), ranks among the finest psychological novels ever written. Her other books, however, are of interest primarily to the literary historian.

She left four works of fiction. All are variations on the same theme—a love story in the form of a pseudo-historical romance. *La Comtesse de Tende* is a slight novella about an adulterous wife, the countess of the title, who nobly repents before her death. *Zaïde* (*Zayde*) is a 'Spanish history' very much in the taste of the time, replete with digressions, adventures, and discourses on the finer points of amorous activity, and needless to say describes love's tribulations at generous length. *La Princesse de Montpensier* (*The Princess Mont-*

pensier) is a more solid effort, which argues, as does the Comtesse de Tende's story, that women can be sure of attaining happiness only if both prudence and virtue govern their actions; but they find that rather difficult, and most of them allow men to make a mess of their lives.

A somewhat mechanistic psychology allied with a platitudinous morality considerably reduces the interest of these works for the modern reader. It is all the more remarkable, then, that using the same ingredients Madame de Lafayette produced one novel that is a masterpiece. *The Princess of Cleves* is set in the 16th century (the material is lifted, with some changes as was her wont, from the candid memoirs of Pierre de Brantôme). It tells of a beautiful young woman who arrives at the French court and is soon married to the Prince of Cleves. She likes and respects him, but is not sexually attracted to him. When the Duc de Nemours appears at court, however, this handsome and seductive creature steals her heart. For a long time she conceals her violent feelings from Nemours, and indeed from everyone else except her own stern mother, but eventually she betrays herself when she experiences acute jealousy over a love letter that she assumes (wrongly) has been sent to Nemours by another woman. When her mother dies she turns for comfort to exactly the wrong person: her husband. Her famous 'avowal' of her feelings for a rival poisons his life, and he dies not long afterwards of a broken heart. She is now, paradoxically, free to marry the man she loves, but she decides not to do so. This is partly out of remorse at having precipitated her husband's death, but mainly because she fears Nemours will be unfaithful to her once he has made her his wife. So she sacrifices her love on the altar of her peace of mind, and dies not long afterwards, an unattached and virtuous woman. This early blow for feminism, coupled with precise insight into the painful ecstasies of erotic attraction, has ensured the survival of this at first sight unlikely classic.

—John Fletcher

LAFORGUE, Jules. Born in Montevideo, Uruguay, 16 August 1860. Moved to France with his family, 1866. Educated at Tarbes from 1866: Collège Impérial, 1869–76; Lycée Condorcet, Paris, 1876–77. First poems published in magazines in Tarbes and Toulouse, 1879; part-time assistant to Charles Ephrussi, art historian and editor, 1881. Married Leah Lee in 1886. French reader to Empress Augusta of Germany, in Berlin and travelling, 1881–86. *Died 21 August 1887.*

PUBLICATIONS

Collections

Poésies complètes. 1894.
Oeuvres complètes, edited by G. Jean-Aubry. 6 vols., 1922–30.
Poésies complètes, edited by Pascal Pia. 2 vols., 1979.
Oeuvres complètes. 1988.

Verse

Les Complaintes. 1885; edited by Michael Collie, 1977; also edited by Pierre Reboul, 1981.
L'Imitation de Notre-Dame la Lune. 1886; edited by Pierre Reboul, 1981.
Le Concile féerique. 1886.
Les Derniers Vers. 1890; edited by Michael Collie and J.M. L'Heureux, 1965; as *The Last Poems,* edited by Madeleine Betts, 1973.
Poems, translated by Patricia Terry. 1958.
Poems, translated by Peter Dale. 1986.

Fiction

Moralités légendaires. 1887; edited by Daniel Grojnowski, 1980; as *Moral Tales,* translated by William J. Smith, 1985.

Other

Hamlet; or, The Consequences of Filial Piety, translated by Gustave Leopold van Roosbroeck. 1934.
Lettres à un ami 1880–86. 1941.
Stéphane Vassiliew. 1946.
Selected Writings, edited and translated by William Jay Smith. 1956.

Translator, *Oeuvres choisies,* by Walt Whitman. 1918.

*

Critical Studies: *Laforgue and the Ironic Inheritance* by Warren Ramsey, 1953, and *Laforgue: Essays on a Poet's Life and Work* edited by Ramsey, 1969; *Laforgue,* 1963, and *Jules Laforgue,* 1977, both by Michael Collie; *Looking for Laforgue: An Informal Biography* by David Arkell, 1979; *Jules Laforgue: Poet of His Age* by Laurence J. Watson, 1980; *Exiles and Ironists: Essays on the Kinship of Heine and Laforgue* by Ursula Franklin, 1988; *Parody and Decadence: Laforgue's Moralités Légendaires* by Michele Hannoosh, 1989; *Jules Laforgue and Poetic Innovation* by Anne Holmes, 1993.

* * *

Jules Laforgue helped liberate and rejuvenate French prosody by means of a series of bold, iconoclastic, but highly original verse experiments that had the effect of establishing free verse as a legitimate and viable poetic mode not only in France, but also in Britain and the United States. Though disguised as a dilettante, Laforgue was devoted to literature; though a fashionable dandy, he worked through the night and in a short career was extremely productive. His early poems, *Le Sanglot de la terre,* he himself suppressed, realizing they were derivative, tendentious, verbally flat, and technically uninspired. Two other volumes, *L'Imitation de Notre-Dame la Lune* and *Le Concile féerique,* are distinctly modish and lightweight, though some of the Pierrot poems in the first of these show a pleasing cleverness in the dramatization of the clown's anguish. Laforgue's reputation, however, rests chiefly on two volumes of great historical as well as intrinsic importance: *Les Complaintes* and *Les Derniers Vers* (*The Last Poems*).

In these two volumes he challenged not just traditional,

middle-class ideas about institutions such as marriage and the church, but also the stability of language itself. Standard usage and normal meanings are in both books ironically subverted by puns and neologisms; by disruptive, unconventional rhymes; by a vigorous, but controlled disturbance of metrical expectation; and by the invention, or at least adoption of new forms. A reader brought up on Lamartine and Hugo could only be shocked by Laforgue's rejection of traditional poetic rhetoric. The witty poems in *Les Complaintes* are remarkably inventive, superbly sophisticated verbal confections presented in the demotic guise of reworked street tunes and popular ballads, confections, one can say, because of their artificiality and high-spiritedness, but none the less in many cases brilliantly imaginative as well (e.g., 'Complainte du pauvre chevalier-errant' and 'Complainte d'une convalescence en Mai'). The 12 poems of *The Last Poems* constitute a further advance in lexical and prosodic experimentation. Influenced, as he acknowledged himself, both by the theory of Impressionist painting and by the music of Wagner, Laforgue wrote a set of free-verse tone poems whose emphasis and impact were artistic, in the *fin-de-siècle* art-for-art's-sake sense, rather than moral. He interested himself in anything that was different, modern, untraditional: photography, for example, and contemporary sculpture. In Paris he had seen the work of Monet, Sisley, and Pissarro. In Germany he had heard the music of Wagner. He had read about these, and other artists, in avant-garde journals like *La Vogue* and *La Revue Wagnérienne*. He had studied and translated Whitman. Thoroughly imbued with a nihilistic, but technically innovative, modern spirit, he proceeded right at the end of his short life to produce *The Last Poems*, the poetic *tour de force* that first established free-verse as an exciting extension of what was possible in French, and then later exerted a strong influence on English and American writers, most notably T.S. Eliot.

Laforgue's nihilism was that of the late 19th-century *flâneur* whose mind, like Ibsen's, was dominated by the imagined reality of biological determinism. In that post-Darwinian intellectual climate no man acted freely; all men were helpless pawns in a meaningless biological game; women were despised because seemingly ignorant of their merely sexual role; and the individual's only hope of personal integrity was not to participate in other people's normal activities. Experience was a kaleidoscope of impressions; nothing whatsoever could be trusted absolutely. In highly crafted poems like 'Dimanches', 'Solo de Lune', and 'L'Hiver qui vient' Laforgue gave expression to the sensations of disbelief, the psychology of alienation, the loneliness in a world where 'il n'y plus de raison' and where the subjunctive and the conditional must necessarily have greater appeal than either the present or the future tense. 'J'eusse été le modèle des époux', said Laforgue; 'your heart would have responded/Gaily' said T.S. Eliot some years later in imitation of him. Whatever one may think, ultimately, about Laforgue's tantalizing amalgam of irony and sentiment—his cynicism fretted with nostalgia—there seems no doubt that the poems of *The Last Poems* are one of the landmarks of 19th-century French poetry, marking the point at which freedom from conventional rhetoric had been fully achieved.

The same ironic, nihilist sensibility was given expression in a collection called *Moralités légendaires* (*Moral Tales*). Laforgue amused himself by giving popular stories or myths an extravagantly anti-romantic treatment, negating the idealism of the original and poking fun at out-moded heroism. The flippancy and ebullience of these stories can still be enjoyed, as can their affected decadent prose, even though the underlying tone is remorselessly negative. Nor need one be too severe in judging these nihilistic contrivances; Laforgue died at the age of 27, with his great talent denied its full expression.

—Michael Collie

THE LAST POEMS (Les Derniers Vers)
Poems by Jules Laforgue, published separately in periodicals, 1886; in one volume, 1890.

The Last Poems, published three years after Laforgue's early death from tuberculosis, comprises 12 poems, which originally appeared in 1886 (except for XII, posthumously published in 1888), mainly in the experimental periodical *La Vogue*. The question of coherence in the collection has been much debated. Some critics argue a perceptible linear progression, others stress the absence of authorial imprimatur and treat the individual poems as discrete units, while nevertheless recognizing their mutually reinforcing similarities of theme, imagery, and technique and the unifying perspective of a first person narrative voice, poised precariously between lyricism and irony.

The poems, focused on the twin themes of love and personal identity, revolve around the 'blocus sentimental' ('sentimental blockade') evoked in typically punning fashion (cf. the 'blocus continental', the continental blockade or Continental System, planned by Napoleon against England) in the opening words of the collection. The poet/protagonist, torn between the opposing 19th-century philosophies of idealism and positivism, continues to yearn for an absolute spiritual love even while despairingly convinced of love's all too earthy nature as physical sensation. His unhappiness is projected onto a fiancée, who figures in the poems not in her own right but as the poet's frustrations made manifest. Ardently desired, she is also doubly reviled, paradoxically condemned both as an unthinking creature of natural instinct, an affront to the poet's idealizing dreams, and as a body and mind hidebound by bourgeois codes of morality and naively and ignorantly resistant to his erotic desires.

These themes of inadequacy and disenchantment are of course far from original. The view of woman proposed in *The Last Poems* has obvious affinities with Baudelaire's *Les Fleurs du mal*. Meanwhile Laforgue's poetic persona, 'pauvre, pâle, piètre individu' ('poor, pale, paltry individual'), is the direct descendant of the central figure in Sainte-Beuve's *Vie, poésies et pensées de Joseph Delorme* (1829), the first expression in French poetry of the inverse of Romantic lionization of the individual. Where Laforgue breaks new ground is in the mixture of irony and seriousness that suspends those themes in an unresolved tension between tragic despair and comic detachment. Pain is both agonizingly immediate and skilfully distanced through a series of masks, notably that of Hamlet, too undecided a figure even to make his way explicitly into the body of the text, but pervasively and subliminally present through epigraphic quotation at the beginning of the collection and again before the final poem. His luckless partner is Ophelia, Antigone, or Philomela, or, in a characteristic switch of register, Little Red Riding Hood, venturing forth, alone and unprotected. But, executioner as much as victim, she is also the prim young 'miss' in her Sunday best, demurely engrossed in her prayer book or her mechanical piano scales, an Emma Rouault lying in wait for a gullible Bovary whom she will betray with the first silver-tongued fly-by-night who chances along.

The problematizing of Romantic stereotypes is also evident

in the modernization of the symbolic landscapes of Romantic melancholy. The inevitable falling leaves of autumn mix with the swirling rubbish of old theatre bills in city streets; grey drizzle or lashing rain shroud factory chimneys; the bitter wind wails through rusted telegraph wires that stretch endlessly along desolate highways. Similarly the conventional imagery of sunset is transformed by a starkly realistic vocabulary of illness and death. The sun, like 'a gland torn from a neck' agonizes, 'white as a drunkard's spittle', on a gorse-covered hillside. The failure of its fruitful light is tied both to a failure of sexuality and ultimately to a more general failure of physical vitality manifest in the anaemic aspect of the poet and his fiancée and the tubercular cough that punctuates their forlorn attempts at communication. Meanwhile the winding of the hunting horn echoes through the collection, its traditional suggestion of loss and aspiration serving simultaneously as a mocking reminder of the emptiness of sentimental dreams.

Versification reinforces the contradictory and complementary impulses of lyricism and irony. *The Last Poems* is the first collection of French poetry entirely in modern free verse. Laforgue's translations of Walt Whitman's *Leaves of Grass*, general contemporary interest in Wagner and Impressionist art, and the prosodic debate in which Laforgue participated along with Gustave Kahn and the rest of the *Vogue* circle, all combine to facilitate a brilliant fusion of form and theme where the swings of psychological mood achieve tangible expression in the flexibility of prosodic structure. Strophic arrangements are endlessly variable, moulding themselves to the syntactic patterns of interior monologue; metre, following oral inflexion, moves from a fixed syllabic count to a more elastic system based on tonic accents. Rhyme disregards traditional rules of gender and number, sometimes disappearing altogether. Nevertheless Laforgue remains close enough to conventional procedures to allow ironic appreciation of deviation from them. Popular language conceals literary quotation, for example the reduction of Lamartine's high-flown 'L'homme n'a point de port, le temps n'a point de rives' ('Man hath no port, time hath no shores') to the laconically colloquial 'Y a pas de port' (VII, 31). Metre plays with diaeresis and synaeresis to perturb anticipated rhythmic patterns but retains the basic syllabic groupings underlying traditional verse. Rhyme displays sufficient orthodoxy to highlight subversive aberration. Laforgue thus achieves a versification that aptly mimics the uncertainties of a self defined by its deficiencies and caught in an endless circle of stop-gap compromises.

The Last Poems, except in a literal sense, is a misnomer, since the poems it contains were seen by Laforgue himself, particularly in the technical area, as a new initiative. Psychologically too they suggest perhaps an advance. Love may be possible as 'humains échanges', a communion between two similarly finite beings that transcends sexual misunderstanding; the protagonist may find the maturity to confront his psychological inadequacies; above all, as in VII, 'Moonlight Solo', his poetry may liberate him finally to dance, light and carefree, above the grey disappointments of life, Hamlet no longer but Ariel.

—Rachel Killick

LAGERKVIST, Pär (Fabian). Born in Växjö, Sweden, 23 May 1891. Educated at the University of Uppsala, 1911–12.

Married 1) Karen Dagmar Johanne Sørenson in 1918 (divorced 1925); 2) Elaine Luella Hallberg in 1925. Theatre critic, *Svenska Dagbladet*, Stockholm, 1919. Recipient: Samfundet De Nio prize, 1928; Bellman prize, 1945; Saint-Beuve prize, 1946; Foreign Book prize (France), 1951; Nobel prize for literature, 1951. Honorary degree: University of Gothenburg, 1941. Member, Swedish Academy of Literature, 1940. *Died 11 July 1974.*

PUBLICATIONS

Fiction

Människor [People]. 1912.
Två sagor om livet [Two Tales about Life]. 1913.
Järn och människor. 1915; as *Iron and Men*, translated by Roy Arthur Swanson, in *Five Early Works*, 1989.
Det eviga leendet. 1920; as *The Eternal Smile*, translated by Denys W. Harding and Erik Mesterton, 1934, and in *Guest of Reality*, 1936; also translated by Alan Blair, in *The Eternal Smile and Other Stories*, 1954.
Onda sagor [Evil Tales]. 1924.
Gäst hos verkligheten. 1925; as *Guest of Reality*, translated by Denys W. Harding and Erik Mesterton, 1936; also translated by Robin Fulton, in *Guest of Reality and Other Stories*, 1989.
Kämpande ande [Struggling Spirit]. 1930; translated in part as *Masquerade of Souls*, 1954.
Bödeln. 1933; as *The Hangman*, in *Guest of Reality*, translated by Denys W. Harding and Erik Mesterton, 1936; as *The Executioner*, translated by David O'Gorman, in *The Eternal Smile and Other Stories*, 1971.
I den tiden [In That Time]. 1935.
Guest of Reality (includes *Guest of Reality*; *The Eternal Smile*; *The Hangman*), translated by Denys W. Harding and Erik Mesterton. 1936.
Dvärgen. 1944; as *The Dwarf*, translated by Alexandra Dick, 1945.
Barabbas. 1950; as *Barabbas*, translated by Alan Blair, 1951.
The Eternal Smile and Other Stories, translated by Alan Blair and others. 1954.
The Marriage Feast and Other Stories, translated by Alan Blair and Carl Eric Lindin. 1955.
Sibyllan. 1956; as *The Sibyl*, translated by Alexandra Dick, 1953; also translated by Naomi Walford, 1958.
Pilgrimen [The Pilgrim] (trilogy). 1966.
  Ahasverus död. 1960; as *The Death of Ahasuerus*, translated by Naomi Walford, 1962.
  Pilgrim på havet. 1962; as *Pilgrim at Sea*, translated by Naomi Walford, 1964.
  Det heliga landet. 1964; as *The Holy Land*, translated by Naomi Walford, 1966.
Mariamne. 1967; as *Herod and Mariamne*, translated by Naomi Walford, 1968; as *Mariamne*, translated by Walford, 1968.
The Eternal Smile and Other Stories (includes *The Eternal Smile*; *Guest of Reality*; *The Executioner*), translated by Erik Mesterton, Denys W. Harding, and David O'Gorman. 1971.
Den svåra resan (selected stories). 1985.
Guest of Reality and Other Stories, translated by Robin Fulton. 1989.

Verse

Motiv [Motifs]. 1914.
Ångest [Angst]. 1916.

Den lyckliges väg [The Happy One's Road]. 1921.
Hjärtats sånger [Songs of the Heart]. 1926.
Vid lägereld [By the Campfire]. 1932.
Genius. 1937.
Sång och strid [Song and Battle]. 1940.
Dikter [Verse]. 1941; revised edition, 1958, 1974.
Hemmet och stjärnan [The Home and the Stars]. 1942.
Aftonland. 1953; as *Evening Land*, translated by W.H. Auden and Leif Sjöberg, 1977.
Valda dikter [Selected Poems]. 1967.

Plays

Sista Mänskan. 1917; as *The Last Man*, translated by Roy Arthur Swanson, in *Five Early Works*, 1989.
Den svåra stunden (three one-act plays; produced 1918). In *Teater*, 1918; as *The Difficult Hour I–III*, translated by Thomas R. Buckman, in *Modern Theatre: Seven Plays and an Essay*, 1966.
Himlens hemlighet (produced 1921). In *Kaos*, 1919; as *The Secret of Heaven*, translated by Thomas R. Buckman, in *Modern Theatre: Seven Plays and an Essay*, 1966.
Den osynlige [The Invisible One] (produced 1924). 1923.
Han som fick leva om sitt liv (produced 1928). 1928; as *The Man Who Lived His Life Over*, translated in *Five Scandinavian Plays*, 1971.
Konungen (produced 1950). 1932; as *The King*, translated by Thomas R. Buckman, in *Modern Theatre: Seven Plays and an Essay*, 1966.
Bödeln, from his own novel (produced 1934). In *Dramatik*, 1946; as *The Hangman*, translated by Thomas R. Buckman, in *Modern Theatre: Seven Plays and an Essay*, 1966.
Mannen utan själ (produced 1938). 1936; as *The Man Without a Soul*, translated by Helge Kökeritz, in *Scandinavian Plays of the Twentieth Century 1*, 1944.
Seger i mörker [Victory in Darkness] (produced 1940). 1939.
Midsommardröm i fattighuset (produced 1941). 1941; as *Midsummer Dream in the Workhouse*, translated by Alan Blair, 1953.
Dramatik [Plays]. 1946; revised edition, 1956.
Den vises sten (produced 1948). 1947; as *The Philosopher's Stone*, translated by Thomas R. Buckman, in *Modern Theatre: Seven Plays and an Essay*, 1966.
Låt människan leva (produced 1949). 1949; as *Let Man Live*, in *Scandinavian Plays of the Twentieth Century 3*, translated by Henry Alexander and Llewellyn Jones, 1951.
Barabbas, from his own novel (produced 1953). 1953.
Modern Theatre: Seven Plays and an Essay (includes *The Difficult Hour I–III*; *The Secret of Heaven*; *The King*; *The Hangman*; *The Philosopher's Stone*; the essay 'Points of View and Attack'), translated by Thomas R. Buckman. 1966.

Other

Ordkonst och bildkonst. 1913; as *Literary Art and Pictorial Art: On the Decadence of Modern Literature—On the Vitality of Modern Art*, translated by Roy Arthur Swanson and E.M. Ellestad, 1991.
Kaos [Chaos]. 1919.
Det besegrade livet [The Conquered Life]. 1927.
Skrifter [Writings]. 3 vols., 1932.
Den knutna näven. 1934; as *The Clenched Fist*, translated by Roy Arthur Swanson, in *Five Early Works*, 1989.
Den befriade människan [Liberated Man]. 1939.
Prosa. 5 vols., 1945; revised edition, 1949.

Antecknat [Noted] (diary), edited by Elin Lagerkvist. 1977.
Five Early Works (includes *Iron and Men*; *The Last Man*; *The Expectant Guest*; *The Morning*; *The Clenched Fist*), translated by Roy Arthur Swanson. 1989.

*

Bibliography: *Pär Lagerkvists bibliografi* by U. Willers, 1951; *Pär Lagerkvist in Translation: A Bibliography* by A. Ryberg, 1964; *Pär Lagerkvists kritiker: En recensionsbibliografi* by R. Yrlid, 1970.

Critical Studies: *Pär Lagerkvist: An Introduction* by Irene Scobbie, 1963, and 'Lagerkvist', in *Aspects of Swedish Literature*, edited by Scobbie, 1988; *Pär Lagerkvist: A Critical Essay* by Winston Weathers, 1968; Lagerkvist supplement, in *Scandinavica*, 1971; *Pär Lagerkvist* by Robert Spector, 1973; *Pär Lagerkvist* by Leif Sjöberg, 1976; *Pär Lagerkvist in America* by Ray Lewis White, 1979; *Som är från evighet* by Willy Jönsson, translated by I. Nettervik, 1991.

* * *

As lyric poet, dramatist, satirist, and novelist Pär Lagerkvist was an innovator and one of Sweden's most influential writers of the 20th century. The autobiographical prose work *Gäst hos verkligheten* (*Guest of Reality*) shows his deep affection for his pious parents and a yearning for a faith but an inability to accept their god. The resultant spiritual void and a fevered reaction to the bloodshed of World War I led to an overwhelming *Angst* [Angst] conveyed in his poems *Ångest* [Angst] and the plays *Sista Mänskan* (*The Last Man*), *Den svåra stunden* (*The Difficult Hour*), and *Himlens hemlighet* (*The Secret of Heaven*), in which he emerged as Sweden's leading expressionist writer. The prose fantasy *Det eviga leendet* (*The Eternal Smile*) reflects a newly found resignation, an appreciation of the beauty of the world and a tentative belief in humanity. Two of his best cycles of poems included in *Hjärtats sånger* [Songs of the Heart] also suggest an inner harmony. This was dispelled as totalitarian regimes took control in Europe. In 1933 Lagerkvist published *Bödeln* (*The Hangman*), where the role of the symbolic central character is examined in a medieval and then contemporary setting. Modern man's propensity for evil clearly surpasses the superstitious crudities of the Middle Ages. A further powerful symbol of evil is the title figure in *Dvärgen* (*The Dwarf*), a masterly novel in diary form set in an Italian Renaissance court. We all have a dwarf within us which when unleashed exults in destruction. The dwarf is in chains in the final chapter but is certain of eventual release.

In *Barabbas*, largely instrumental in his winning the Nobel prize for literature, Lagerkvist makes the biblical robber and insurgent an existentialist figure searching for a belief. Born into a world of violence and hatred, he cannot accept the Christian message, but having met Christ, he cannot shake off his influence. Afraid of death, unable to believe in an afterlife, he remains a lonely, moving representative of modern man. Man's relation to God is explored further in a series of symbolic novels. For the Pythia in *Sibyllan* (*The Sibyl*) the god can be both wonderful and terrible but her life without him would have been nothing; the Wandering Jew in *Ahasverus död* (*The Death of Ahasuerus*) bears God's curse and achieves death only by turning his back on religion; in *Pilgrim på havet* (*Pilgrim at Sea*) and *Det heliga landet* (*The Holy Land*) the struggling pilgrim finally finds reconciliation with God and man. In *Mariamne* (*Herod and Mariamne*) evil in man is embodied in the symbolic figure of Herod. It is a desolate book, for Herod has Mariamne the Good killed, but it ends in hope—the Magi have found their way to a new-born babe.

Lagerkvist's last cycle of poems, *Aftonland* (*Evening Land*), contains beautifully expressed reminiscences and an indication of his unsolved paradox: 'The non-existing god/he has set my soul in flames'. In his early twenties Lagerkvist wrote numerous articles on Cubism and other forms of modern art. He subsequently endeavoured to apply the Cubists' method of composition to his creative writing. Even at its most feverishly inspired his work is carefully constructed, his novels particularly having an almost architectural structure.

—Irene Scobbie

LAGERLÖF, Selma (Ottiliana Lovisa). Born at Mårbacka, Värmland, Sweden, 20 November 1858. Lame from age 3, and educated at home; studied at Teachers' Seminary, Stockholm, 1882–85. Taught in a school in Landskrona until 1895, then writer: lived in Falun and, after she bought back her birthplace, Mårbacka. Recipient: *Idun* magazine prize, 1895; travelling fellowship, 1895; Swedish Academy gold medal, 1904; Nobel prize for literature, 1909. Ph.D.: Uppsala University, 1907. Member, Swedish Academy, 1914. *Died 16 March 1940.*

PUBLICATIONS

Collection

Skrifter. 12 vols., 1949–56.

Fiction

Gösta Berlings Saga. 1891; as *Gösta Berling's Saga*, translated by Pauline Bancroft Flach, 1898; as *The Story of Gösta Berling*, translated by Lillie Tudeer, 1898; also translated by Robert Bly, 1982.
Osynliga länkar: Berättelser. 1894; as *Invisible Links*, translated by Pauline Bancroft Flach, 1899.
Antikrists mirakler. 1897; as *The Miracles of Antichrist*, translated by Pauline Bancroft Flach, 1899.
Drottningar i Kungahälla jämte andra berättelser. 1899; as *The Queens of Kungahälla and Other Sketches*, translated by Claud Field, 1917.
En herrgårdssägen. 1899; as *From a Swedish Homestead*, translated by Jessie Brochner, 1901; as *The Tale of a Manor and Other Sketches*, 1917.
Jerusalem I–II. 1901–02; as *Jerusalem* and *The Holy City*, translated by J. Brochner, 2 vols., 1903–18.
Herr Arnes Penningar. 1903; as *Herr Arne's Hoard*, translated by Arthur G. Chater, 1923.
Legender: Berättade [Legends: Stories]. 3 vols., 1904.
Kristuslegender. 1904; as *Christ Legends*, translated by Velma Swanston Howard, 1908.
En saga om en saga och andra sagor. 1908; as *The Girl from*

the Marsh Croft, translated by Velma Swanston Howard, 1911.
Meli. 1909.
Liljecronas hem. 1911; as *Liliecrona's Home*, translated by Anna Barwell, 1913.
Körkarlen. 1912; as *The Soul Shall Bear Witness*, translated by William F. Harvey, 1921.
Astrid och andra berättelser [Astrid and Other Stories]. 1914.
Kejsarn av Portugallien. 1914; as *The Emperor of Portugallia*, translated by Velma Swanston Howard, 1916.
Silvergruvan och andra berättelser [The Silver Mine and Other Stories]. 1915.
Troll och människor [Trolls and Humans]. 1915.
Kavaljersnoveller. 1918.
Bannlyst. 1918; as *The Outcast*, translated by William Worster, 1920.
Legender i urval [Selected Legends]. 1922.
The Tale of a Manor and Other Sketches, translated by Claud Field. 1922.
The Ring of the Löwenskölds, translated by Frances Martin and Velma Swanston Howard. 3 vols., 1931.
  Löwensköldska ringen. 1925; as *The General's Ring*, translated by Frances Martin, 1928; as *The Löwensköld Ring*, translated by Linda Schenck, 1991.
  Charlotte Löwensköld. 1925; as *Charlotte Löwensköld*, translated by Velma Swanston Howard, 1927.
  Anna Svärd. 1928; as *Anna Svärd*, translated by Velma Swanston Howard, 1931.
Mors porträtt och andra berättelser [Portrait of Mother and Other Stories]. 1930.
Julberättelser [Christmas Stories]. 1938.

Plays

Fritiofs saga [Fritiof's Story], music by E. Andrée. 1899.
Stormyrtösen [Girl from the Marshes], with Bernt Fredgren, from a story by Lagerlöf. 1913.
Dunungen [The Cygnet]. 1914.
Vinterballaden [Winter Ballad], from a play by Gerhart Hauptmann. 1919.
The Lighting of the Christmas Tree, adapted by Josephine L. Palmer and Annie L. Thorp (from *The Christmas Guest*). 1921.
Kejsarn av Portugallien, with Poul Knudsen, from the novel by Lagerlöf. 1939.

Other

Nils Holgerssons underbara resa (for children). 2 vols., 1906–07; as *The Wonderful* [and *Further*] *Adventures of Nils*, translated by Velma Swanston Howard, 2 vols., 1907–11; also translated by Richard E. Oldeburg, 1967.
Mårbacka.
  Mårbacka. 1922; as *Mårbacka*, translated by Velma Swanston Howard, 1924.
  Ett barns memoarer. 1930; as *Memories of My Childhood*, translated by Velma Swanston Howard, 1934.
  Dagbok. 1932; as *Diary*, translated by Velma Swanston Howard, 1936.
Höst: Berättelser och tal. 1933; as *Harvest: Tales and Essays*, translated by Florence and Naboth Hedin, 1935.
Från skilda tider: Efterlämnade skrifter [Posthumous Works], edited by Nils Afzelius. 2 vols., 1943–45.
Brev 1871–1940 [Letters], edited by Ying Toijer-Nilsson. 2 vols., 1967–69.

*

Bibliography: *Lagerlöfs bibliografi originalskrifter* by Nils Afzelius, 1975.

Critical Studies: *Lagerlöf* by H.A. Larsen, 1936; *Six Scandinavian Novelists: Lie, Jacobsen, Heidenstam, Selma Lagerlöf, Hamsun, Sigrid Undset* by Alrik Gustafson, 1940; *Fact and Fiction in the Autobiographical Works of Lagerlöf* by Folkerdina Stientje de Vrieze, 1958; *Lagerlöf* (in Swedish) by Carl O. Zamore, 1958; *Lagerlöf* by Walter A. Berendsohn, 1968; *Lagerlöf: Herrn Arnes Penningar* by Brita Green, 1977; *Selma Lagerlöf*, 1984, and *Selma Lagerlöfs litterära profil*, 1986, both by Vivi Edström.

* * *

Selma Lagerlöf's childhood at Mårbacka offered a rich store of old Värmland traditions but the realistic mode of writing in the 1880s was alien to her temperament and material. Witnessing the sale of Mårbacka in 1888, she resolved to eschew current fashion and write 'in the Mårbacka manner'. *Gösta Berlings Saga* (*Gösta Berling's Saga*) was completed in 1891. Gösta, the handsome, Byronic, defrocked parson, joins 12 'cavaliers' who are to run Ekeby estate for a year provided they live only for beauty and pleasure. There is much merrymaking, but Lagerlöf could not wholly accept a *carpe diem* philosophy and ends by eulogizing hard work. This novel introduces typical Lagerlöfian themes: guilt and atonement; the saving qualities of a woman's selfless love; how to combine happiness with goodness. Having betrayed his calling Gösta must purge his guilt. The magnificent Margareta Celsing, the major's wife, has broken two commandments and accepts banishment until she has expiated her sin. The supernatural is introduced when the cavaliers sell their souls to the Mephistophelian Sintram, while the elements are used both to heighten effect and to force characters' courses of action. The style ranges from rhetoric and *Sturm und Drang* tempestuousness to textbook prose, but the book bears the stamp of genius.

In *The Tale of a Manor* Lagerlöf successfully fuses Beauty and the Beast with a Dalarna legend. Fear of losing his estate threatens Gunnar Hede's sanity but a young girl's unselfish love saves him. Within the framework of symbolic folk-tale Lagerlöf produces a valid psychological study of schizophrenia.

On a visit to Palestine in 1900 Lagerlöf discovered a settlement of Dalarna peasants and this inspired the novel *Jerusalem*, at the heart of which are the Ingmarssons representing such sterling qualities as loyalty to one's province, an innate sense of justice, simple faith, and moral courage. The powerful stylized characterization and the epic scope of the novel show the influence of the Icelandic saga. Acknowledged as her masterpiece, *Jerusalem* won universal acclaim. The supernatural, merely suggested in *Jerusalem*, is a major element in *Herr Arnes Penningar* (*Herr Arne's Hoard*) where a murdered girl's ghost is instrumental in bringing the murderers of Herr Arne's household to justice. Commissioned to write a school textbook Lagerlöf, influenced partly by Kipling's *Jungle Book*, wrote *Nils Holgerssons underbara resa* (*The Wonderful Adventures of Nils*), in which Sweden's geography, flora, and fauna become part of a tale about a boy's magic journey on a goose's back.

World War I had a debilitating effect, and although Lagerlöf subsequently wrote autobiographies centred on Mårbacka and completed the Löwensköld trilogy, her creative genius was spent. Her greatest gift was that of a storyteller. She refashioned local oral tradition into powerful universal prose works reflecting her instinctive understanding of the human heart and conscience. Her attitude to miracles and religion is ambivalent but her innate sense of justice and natural order ultimately restores harmony in her works. There is nothing facile in such happy endings, however, for they are achieved by personal sacrifice and a supreme effort to overcome destructive elements in human nature.

—Irene Scobbie

GÖSTA BERLING'S SAGA
Novel by Selma Lagerlöf, 1891.

Lagerlöf's first novel, *Gösta Berling's Saga*, won a prize for the best novel on the basis of five chapters submitted to *Idun*, a woman's magazine. Swedish critics in general received it coolly and it did not become a critical success until Brandes reviewed it positively, thus giving it the stamp of male approval. Lagerlöf struggled with its form, one that was new and difficult to categorize. One day she envisioned how it was to be written. The street in front of her heaved and she was overcome with a feeling similar to falling in love, an appropriate reaction to the conception of a novel that deals so much with love in all its passionate, destructive, and redeeming aspects.

The novel has 36 chapters, each constituting a story in itself. Elements from myth and fairy-tale are mixed with realism and social commentary. The style is Romantic, full of superlatives and exclamations. Lagerlöf is a story-teller whose roots are in the oral tradition. The setting is Värmland in the 1820s. Apart from the introductory chapters about Gösta Berling, the time span of the novel is one year, from Christmas Eve to Christmas Eve. The novel deals with 'profound emotional experiences and important existential choices', to borrow a line from Vivi Edström. In his preface to a new edition of Lagerlöf's work in 1984, Sven Delblanc sees the novel as an expression of Lagerlöf's belief in 'the liberating and redeeming power of woman's love'. She also says that 'the man is worthy of love in spite of all his faults and shortcomings', and, as Delblanc points out, 'there is no lack of weak, fragile or violent and destructive men in Lagerlöf's work'. This is especially true of *Gösta Berling's Saga*.

The plot concerns a group of adventurers, 12 so-called cavaliers, living on the Major's estate as guests of his wife, Margareta Samzelius, the most powerful woman in Värmland. The cavaliers, who are granted control of the estate for a year, represent a revolt against formality and rigidity but also 'genuine, expansive love' (Edström). The hero of this fairy-tale, or 'saga', Gösta Berling is a defrocked priest who must fight dragons and trolls before he marries his princess. The demons, however, are within himself; he must love women and be loved by them. Lagerlöf's description of him evokes an image of a fantasy figure and some earlier male critics tended to smile condescendingly at this male ideal drawn by a spinster:

The priest was young, tall, slim and dashingly beautiful. If you had placed a helmet on top of his head and equipped him with a sword and armour, you could have sculpted him in marble and named the statue for the most handsome of Athenians.

The priest had the deep eyes of a poet and the firm, round chin of a general. Everything about him was beautiful, fine, articulate, radiating genius and spiritual life.

He drinks, however, and ends up in a snowdrift hoping to die, when he is rescued by the Major's wife ('majorskan på Ekeby'). He joins the cavaliers and soon becomes a favourite among them in their hedonistic life.

The beautiful Anna Stjärnhök falls for the passion in his eyes, but when he tries to elope with her, the wolves pursue them across the ice. Not even his black stallion Don Juan can outrun them. Only by throwing a book at them, can the wolves be fended off long enough for him to bring her safely to her parents' estate on the other side of the lake. They must renounce their love to save their lives.

Another beautiful woman, Marianne Sinclair, flirts with Gösta Berling at a dance and her irate father drives home without her, leaving her to walk back in her thin dancing shoes only to find the door locked. The cavaliers find her half-dead in a snowdrift and carry her back to Ekeby to be nursed. She is not to be Gösta Berling's bride, nor is Ebba Doña, the fair sister of the stupid Count Henrik Dohna. She dies for her love.

The rich estate of Ekeby is wasted during the reign of the cavaliers while its mistress Margareta Samzelius walks the road like a beggar; she must be reconciled with her mother who cursed her when she struck her in anger. Instrumental in her being exiled from her own estate by her husband is Sintram, the villain who enjoys dressing up as the Devil. The 'princess' of this fairy-tale is the young Countess Elizabeth Dohna, brought from Italy by Henrik Dohna as his wife. She is pure in her gaiety, taking pleasure in the dances held on the estates. She, too, falls in love with Gösta Berling but her conduct is blameless and their relationship innocent. Eventually, however, her jealous mother-in-law succeeds in making her son believe that Elizabeth is an adulterous wife. Dohna places her under his mother's control but with Gösta Berling's help she escapes the torment and pain imposed on her. The marriage, which was wrongly contracted, is not legitimized; the gentle countess is forced to earn her bread weaving for strangers. Weak and miserable, she gives birth to a sickly child, her husband's. She learns about the dissolution of her unfortunate marriage and turns in despair to Gösta Berling, begging him to marry her to give the child a father and a name. This he does.

Much happens to the proud estate of Ekeby before it is returned to its rightful owner. The spring flood comes crashing through the dam. The iron foundries, the pride of Ekeby, are mismanaged but, miraculously, the cavaliers manage to deliver the promised ore on time, thus saving the honour of Ekeby. Ekeby burns but is rebuilt. The Major's wife returns to Ekeby at the end of the year and work is gradually resumed.

The novel is rich in masterful characterization. Lagerlöf's blending of realism and superstition, drought, crop failure, and magical creatures and people, is breathtaking. The novel is at the same time a celebration of life's pleasures and an affirmation of the necessity of hard work. The book was made into one of the masterpieces of Swedish silent movies in 1924 by Mauritz Stiller, starring Gösta Ekman and Greta Garbo.

—Torborg Lundell

LAMARTINE, Alphonse (-Marie-Louis de Prat) de. Born in Mâcon, France, 21 October 1790. Educated at Institut Puppier, Lyons, 1801–03; Jesuit college, Belley, 1803–07. Married Anna Eliza Birch in 1820 (died 1863); one son and one daughter; one daughter from a previous relationship with Nina de Pierreclau. Served in Louis XVIII's Garde-du-Corps, 1814–15. Mayor of Milly, 1812; diplomat, Naples, 1820–25; embassy secretary, Florence, 1825–29; elected to the Académie française, 1830; stood for the Chamber of Deputies, (unsuccessfully 1831), elected, 1833; minister of foreign affairs, 1848; defeated in the presidential election and retired from public life, 1851. Travelled to Greece, Syria, and Palestine. *Died 28 February 1869.*

PUBLICATIONS

Collections

Oeuvres. 2 vols., 1893.
Oeuvres. 22 vols., 1900–07.
Poésies. 1957.
Oeuvres poétiques complètes, edited by Marius-François Guyard. 1963.
Oeuvres poétiques. 1977.

Verse

Méditations poétiques. 1820; as *Poetical Meditations,* translated by Henry Christmas, 1839; as *The Poetical Meditations,* translated by William Pulling, 1849; as *Translations from the Meditations,* translated by James T. Smith, 1852.
La Mort de Socrate. 1823; as *The Death of Socrates,* translated by Harriet Cope, 1829.
Nouvelles méditations poétiques. 1823.
Le Dernier Chant du pèlerinage d'Harold. 1825; as *The Last Canto of Childe Harold's Pilgrimage,* translated anonymously, 1827.
Epîtres. 1825.
Chant du sacre. 1825.
Harmonies poétiques et religieuses. 2 vols., 1830.
Contre la peine de mort. 1830.
À Némesis. 1831.
Jocelyn. 2 vols., 1836; as *Jocelyn: An Episode,* translated by F.H. Jobert, 1837; also translated by Robert Anstruther, 1844; as *Jocelyn,* translated by H.G. Evans and T.W. Swift, 1868; as *Jocelyn: A Romance in Verse,* translated by Hazel Patterson Stewart, 1954.
Gethsémani, in *Souvenirs, impressions, pensées et paysages pendant un voyage en orient.* 1835; as *Gethsemane; or, the Death of Julia,* translated by I.H. Urquhart, 1838.
La Chute d'un ange. 2 vols., 1838.
Recueillements poétiques. 1839.
Premières et nouvelles méditations poétiques (selection). 1855; as *Selected Poems,* edited and translated by George O. Curme, 1888.
Poésies inédites. 1873; revised edition, 1881.
Premières méditations poétiques. 1907.
Méditations, edited by Fernand Letessier. 1968.

Fiction

Graziella. 1849; edited by Alfred T. Baker, 1904; as *Graziella; or, My First Sorrow, and Other Poems . . . ,* translated by W.C. Urquhart, 1871; as *Graziella,* translated by Bertha Norwood, 1876; as *Graziella; or The History of a Broken Heart,* translated by J.B.S., 1882; also translated by Ralph Wright, 1929.

Raphaël. 1849; as *Raphaël*, translated anonymously, 1849.
Les Confidences. 1849; as *Confidential Disclosures*, translated by E. Plunkett, 1849; as *Memoirs of My Youth*, translated anonymously, 1849.
Les Nouvelles Confidences. 1851; as *The Wanderer and His Home*, translated anonymously, 1851.
Le Tailleur des pierres de Saint-Point, récit villageois. 1851; as *The Stonecutter of St-Point*, translated anonymously, 1851; as *The Stonemason of St-Point*, translated anonymously, 1851.
Geneviève: Histoire d'un servante. 1850; as *Genevieve; or, The History of a Servant Girl*, translated by A.R. Scoble, 1850; as *Genevieve; or, Peasant Love and Sorrow*, translated by Fayette Robinson, 1850; as *Genevieve: A Tale of Peasant Life*, translated by Mary Howitt, 1851.
Antoniella. 1867.

Plays

Toussaint L'Ouverture (produced 1850). 1850.
Fior d'Aliza. 1863; as *Fior d'Aliza*, translated by G. Perry, 1869.
Saül. 1879.

Other

De la politique rationnelle. 1831; as *The Polity of Reason*, translated anonymously, 1848.
Oeuvres. 4 vols., 1832.
Oeuvres complètes. 13 vols., 1834–43.
Souvenirs, impressions, pensées et paysages pendant un voyage en orient (1832–1833); ou, Notes d'un voyageur. 4 vols., 1835; as *A Pilgrimage to the Holy Land*, translated anonymously, 1835, reprinted 1978; as *De Lamartine's Visit to the Holy Land*, translated by Thomas Phipson, 1847.
Histoire des Girondins. 8 vols., 1847; as *Deux Héroïnes de la Révolution française*, edited by Mary Bentinck Smith, 1904; as *History of the Girondists*, translated by H.T. Ryde, 3 vols., 1847–48; as *Pictures of the First Revolution*, translated by J.F.S. Wilde, 1850.
Manifeste à l'Europe. 1848.
Trois Mois au pouvoir. 1848; as *Three Months in Power: A History and Vindication of My Political Conduct During the Late Revolution in France*, translated by H.T. Ryde, 1848.
Oeuvres [Souscripteurs Edition]. 14 vols., 1849–50.
Histoire de la Restauration. 8 vols., 1851–52; as *The History of the Restoration of Monarchy in France*, parts written in English by Lamartine the remainder translated by Captain Rafter, 4 vols., 1851–53.
Histoire de la révolution de 1848. 2 vols., 1849; as *History of the French Revolution of 1848*, translated anonymously, 1849; also translated by Francis Durivage and William Chase, 1849.
Nouveau voyage en orient. 1851.
Nelson. 1853.
Cromwell. 1854; as *Life of Oliver Cromwell*, translated anonymously, 1859.
Histoire des Constituants. 2 vols., 1854; as *History of the Constituent Assembly*, 4 vols., translated anonymously, 1858.
Histoire de la Turquie. 5 vols., 1854; as *History of Turkey*, 3 vols., translated anonymously, 1855–57.
Histoire de la Russie. 1855.
Cours familier de littérature. 28 vols., 1856–69.
Vie d'Alexandre le Grand. 2 vols., 1859.
Oeuvres complètes de Lamartine publiées et inédites. 41 vols., 1860–66.

Cicéron. 1863.
Christophe Colomb. 1863; as *Life of Christopher Columbus*, translated anonymously, 1859; as *The Life and Voyages of Christopher Columbus*, translated by E.M. Goldsmid, 1887.
Homère et Socrate. 1863; as *Homer and Socrates*, translated by Elizabeth Winchell Smith, 1872.
Jeanne d'Arc. 1863; as *Joan of Arc: A Biography*, translated by H.M. Grimké, 1867.
Madame de Sévigné (biography). 1864.
La France parlementaire (1834–1851), oeuvres, oratoires et écrits politiques. 6 vols., 1864–65.
Les Grands Hommes de l'Orient. 1865.
Les Hommes de la révolution. 1865.
Portraits et biographies. 1865; as *Biographies and Portraits*, translated anonymously, 1866.
Shakespeare et son oeuvre. 1865.
Vie de César. 1865.
Vie de Lord Byron. 1865; revised edition, edited by Marie-Renée Morin, 1989.
Balzac et ses oeuvres. 1866.
Jean Jacques Rousseau. 1866.
Mémoires inédits 1790–1815. 1870; as *25 Years of My Life*, translated by Lady Herbert, 2 vols., 1872.
Manuscrit de ma mère. 1871; as *Memoirs of My Mother*, translated by Lady Herbert, with *25 Years of My Life*, 2 vols, 1872; as *My Mother's Manuscript*, translated by Maria Louisa Helper, 1877.
Correspondance publiée par Mme Valentine de Lamartine. 6 vols., 1873–1875; 4 vols., 1881–82.
Correspondance. 4 vols., 1873–74.
La Politique de Lamartine (selection). 1878.
Correspondance 1873–1875. 2 vols., 1881–82.
A. de Lamartine par lui-même (autobiography). 1892.
L'Album de Saint-Point (correspondence). 1923.
Lamartine et ses nièces (correspondence). 1928.
Un grand vigneron (correspondence). 1933.
Correspondance générale, edited by Maurice Levaillant. 2 vols., 1943–48.
Lettres inédites 1821–51, edited by Henri Guillemin. 1944.
Lettres à Clériade Vacher (1811–1818), edited by Jean Richer. 1963.
Correspondance Alphonse de Lamartine-Aymon de Virieu 1808–15, edited by Marie-Renée Morin. 2 vols., 1987.
Correspondance 1809–1858, with Henry-Roch Dupuys, edited by Marie-Renée Morin. 1989.
Mémoires de jeunesse: 1790–1815, edited by Marie-Renée Marin. 1990.

*

Critical Studies: *The Life of Lamartine* by H. Remsen Whitehouse, 2 vols., 1918; *Lamartine* by Paul Hazard, 1925; *Lamartine et la Savoie* by Georges Roth, 1927; *Les Méditations de Lamartine* by G. Fréjaville, 1931; *Lamartine et le sentiment de la nature* by Yvonne Boeniger, 1934; *Lamartine* by Louis Bertrand, 1940; *Lamartine and Romantic Unanimism* by Albert J. George, 1940; *Lamartine, l'homme et l'oeuvre* by H. Guillemin, 1940; *Les Travaux et les jours d'Alphonse de Lamartine* by Marquis de Luppé, 1942; *Lamartine* by Marius-François Guyard, 1956; *Les Amours italiennes de Lamartine, Graziella et Lena* by Abel Verdier, 1963; *Lamartine: A Revaluation* by John C. Ireson, 1969; *Lamartine; ou, l'amour de la vie* by Maurice Toesca, 1969; *La Vie sentimentale de Lamartine* by Abel Verdier, 1971; *Lamartine: Le Livre du centenaire* edited by Paul Viallaneix,

1971; *Lamartine* by Charles M. Lombard, 1973; *In Search of Eden: Lamartine's Symbols of Despair and Deliverance* by Norman Araujo, 1976; *Lamartine and the Poetics of Landscape* by Mary Ellen Birkett, 1982; *Alphonse de Lamartine: A Political Biography* by William Fortescue, 1983; *L'Auteur des Girondins; ou, Les Cent-vingt Jours de Lamartine*, 1988, and *Les Girondins de Lamartine*, 1988, both by Antoine Court; *Lamartine* by Xavier de la Fournière, 1990.

* * *

It was Alphonse de Lamartine who created the image, in France, of the Romantic poet. The publication of his first collection, *Méditations poétiques* (*Poetical Meditations*), in 1820 was undoubtedly a landmark in French literature. Without radically modifying the form of French poetry, Lamartine gave it back a soft lyrical quality it had lost in the previous century. Though 'Le Lac' ('The Lake') is probably the best-known poem in the volume, the opening text, 'L'Isolement' ('Isolation') likewise epitomizes its plaintive tonality and illustrates the way in which the natural world cast an ambiguous spell over the poet:

Que me font ces vallons, ces palais, ces chaumières,
Vains objects dont pour moi le charme est envolé?
Fleuves, rochers, forêts, solitudes si chères,
Un seul être vous manque, et tout est dépeuplé!

(These valleys, these palaces, these cottages, what are
    they to me?
Vain objects whose charm for me has flown;
Rivers, rocks, forests, solitudes so dear,
One single being is missing and everything is empty!)

Elsewhere in the collection Lamartine meditates on religious and philosophical matters, giving voice to the thoughts and feelings of his generation. Yet even more than this first book or its sequel, the *Nouvelles méditations poétiques* of 1823, the *Harmonies poétiques et religieuses* [Poetical and Religious Harmonies] of 1830 are generally recognized as Lamartine's masterpieces. The title of his work evokes almost perfectly the nature of the poems, where the recognition of both divine ubiquity and mankind's religious instinct finds expression in the mellifluous musicality of the verses. With a sense of awe and mystery Lamartine writes of 'The idea of God'; with humility and wonder he composes 'Éternité de la nature, brièveté de l'homme' ('Eternity of Nature, Brevity of Man'); influenced by Pascal, he conceives of 'L'Infini dans les cieux' ('Infinity in the Heavens').

Having made his reputation as a lyric poet, Lamartine turned to the epic. *Jocelyn* was originally intended to form part of a greater work, but the subject-matter, the life and love of a humble priest, may have been more suitable for treatment in a different literary genre. The stature of the hero of *La Chute d'un ange* [The Fall of an Angel] was more obviously epic, but the style of the work too often bordered on the melodramatic. However, the structuring of the poem into 'visions' was an imaginative solution to the problem of form.

When Lamartine turned his hand to prose, his first success came with his *Souvenirs, impressions, pensées et paysages pendant un voyage en orient* (*Visit to the Holy Land*), an impressionistic personal record, in the form of a diary, of a trip to the Near East three years earlier. In his foreword he made it clear that he was writing as a poet and a philosopher, and not as a historian or a geographer. From time to time he cannot resist the temptation to express his sentiments in verse, but many of his accounts, e.g. those of the peoples of Lebanon, are informative, and his editor gave the text a special poignancy by inserting after the evocation of Jerusalem the poem 'Gethsémani', that Lamartine wrote to commemorate the death of his ten-year-old daughter Julia.

With the eight volumes of his *Histoire des Girondins* (*History of the Girondists*) he set out his stall as a historian, but although the work was a popular success it reads more like an historical novel with a very visual quality. There are inaccuracies, and the writer seems at times to seek to curry favour with contemporary voters. Other histories, of the Restoration, of the Constituent Assembly, of Russia, and of Turkey were to follow in the 1850s.

Immediately after the high point of his political career in 1849, Lamartine published *Graziella*, which fictionalized his affair in 1811 with a seductive Neapolitan girl. Also in 1849 he brought out another novel, *Raphaël*, which treated in a similar fashion his more famous love-affair with Julie Charles. With *Geneviève*, the story of a servant girl, Lamartine attempted to produce a social novel, but its realism was somewhat superficial, despite the author's evident sympathies with the ordinary people. His last attempt at fiction, *Antoniella*, again demonstrated his inability to come up with convincing plots.

Right at the start of his career Lamartine had tried to write for the theatre: he composed *Saül* in 1817, hoping—in vain—that Talma, the leading tragic actor of the day, would play the title role. Although *Toussaint L'Ouverture* was performed in 1850, its failure made him abandon thoughts of becoming a dramatist. The choice of subject, the Haitian national hero, was interesting, however, and may be related to Lamartine's freeing of the slaves in all French territories in 1848.

In an attempt to pay off his debts he published between 1856 and his death in 1869 the 28 volumes of the *Cours familier de littérature*, structured in the form of *entretiens* (conversations) of a very eclectic nature. Despite the title, the work was not confined to literature: Lamartine digressed to the other arts (considering Mozart, Michelangelo, and Cellini, for example), to religion (especially Hinduism), to science (Alexander Humboldt), and even personal reminiscences, in addition to his coverage of a wide range of writers throughout the ages.

It was within this context that Lamartine brought out his last two major poems, 'Le Désert; ou, L'Immatérialité de Dieu' [The Desert; or, The Immateriality of God], 1856, and 'La Vigne et la maison' [The Vine and the House], 1857. The former, heavily influenced by the Book of Job, emphasizes the importance of mystery in the relationship between man and the deity; 'La Vigne et la Maison', a dialogue between the elderly poet and his soul, reveals how much he longed for happier days, but how the sight of well-loved places served only to remind him of the absence and the death of loved ones. The final address to God, however, brought the poet a kind of peace and he found his true voice once more, as a lyric poet, and one by which he should always be judged.

—Keith Aspley

———

LAMPEDUSA, Giuseppe Tomasi di. Duke of Palma and, from 1934, Prince of Lampedusa. Born in Palermo, Sicily,

Italy, 23 December 1896. Educated at Liceo-Ginnasio Garibaldi, Palermo, 1911–14; enrolled (but probably did not take classes) at University of Genoa, 1914–15; University of Rome, 1920. Married Baroness Alessandra (Licy) von Wolff-Stomersee in 1932; one adopted son. Trained to be officer in Italian army, 1915–17; lance-corporal during World War I; taken prisoner, but succeeded in his second escape attempt, and found his way back to Italy in disguise; discharged from the army, 1920 (some sources give 1925). Largely withdrew from public life after the rise to power of Mussolini and the Fascists, and devoted himself to travelling and writing; contributor, *Le Opere e i Giorni*, Geneva, 1926–27. Recipient: Strega prize (posthumously), 1959. *Died 23 July 1957.*

PUBLICATIONS

Fiction

Il Gattopardo. 1959; as *The Leopard*, translated by Archibald Colquhoun, 1960.
Racconti (includes 'I luoghi della mia prima infanzia', 'Il mattino di un mezzadro', 'La gioia e la Legge, Lighea'). 1961; revised and enlarged edition, 1988; as *Two Stories and a Memory* (includes 'Places of My Infancy', 'The Professor and the Siren', 'The Blind Kittens'), translated by Archibald Colquhoun, 1962, and with *The Leopard*, 1986.

Other

Lezioni su Stendhal (criticism). 1977.
Invito alle lettere francesi del Cinquecento (criticism). 1979.
Lettere a Licy: Un matrimonio epistolare (selected letters to his wife). 1987.
Letteratura inglese. Dalle origini al Settecento (criticism). 1990.
Letteratura inglese. L'Ottocento e il Novecento (criticism). 1991.

*

Critical Studies: 'Lampedusa in Sicily: The Lair of the Leopard' by Archibald Colquhoun, in *The Atlantic Extra*, February 1963; *Ricordo di Lampedusa* by Francesco Orlando, 1963; 'Lampedusa's *The Leopard*' by David Nolan, in *Studies*, Winter 1966; 'Lampedusa and De Roberto' in *Italica*, 47 (2), 1970, and 'Ants and Flags: Tomasi di Lampedusa's *Gattopardo*' in *The Italianist*, 13, 1993, both by Tom O'Neill; *Invito alla lettura di Giuseppe Tomasi di Lampedusa* by Giancarlo Buzzi, 1972, revised editions 1976 and 1984; *Tomasi di Lampedusa* by Simonetta Salvestroni, 1973; *Il Gattopardo; I Racconti: Lampedusa* by Giuseppe Paolo Samona, 1974; 'Stendhal, Lampedusa and the Limits of Admiration' by W.J.S. Kirton, in *Trivium*, 10, 1975; 'Stendhal, Tomasi di Lampedusa, and the Novel', by Olga Ragusa, in her *Narrative and Drama: Essays in Modern Italian Literature from Verga to Pasolini*, 1976; 'The Risorgimento and Social Change: Reflections in the Sicilian Novel' by Christopher Cairns, in *Trivium*, 13, 1978; 'The Structure of Meaning in Lampedusa's *Il Gattopardo*' by Richard H. Lansing, in *Publications of the Modern Language Association*, 93, 1978; 'Tomasi di Lampedusa's *Il Gattopardo*: Figure and Temporality in an Historical Novel' by Gregory L. Lucente, in *Modern Language Notes*, 1978; *Il Gattopardo o, la metafora decadente dell'esistenza* by Maria Pagliara-

Giacovazzo, 1983; *I Gattopardi e le lene. Il messaggio inattuale di Tomasi di Lampedusa* by Nunzio Zago, 1983; *Sirene siciliane: L'anima esiliata in Lighea di Tomasi di Lampedusa* by Basilio Reale, 1986; *Giuseppe Tomasi di Lampedusa* (biography) by Andrea Vitello, 1987; *Giuseppe Tomasi di Lampedusa: La figura e l'opera* (includes texts and bibliography) by Nunzio Zago, 1987; *The Last Leopard: A Life of Giuseppe di Lampedusa* by David Gilmour, 1988; 'Nobility and Literature: Questions on Tomasi di Lampedusa' by Edoardo Saccone, in *Modern Language Notes*, 106(1), 1991.

* * *

With the exception of three brief articles which appeared in a monthly review in Genoa in 1926–27, Giuseppe Tomasi di Lampedusa's work, essentially concentrated into the final years of his life, was published posthumously. It consists of *Il Gattopardo* (*The Leopard*), his only full-length novel and the work on which his reputation substantially rests; *Racconti* (*Two Stories and a Memory*), including 'I luoghi della mia prima infanzia' ('Places of My Infancy'), important for understanding the strong autobiographical thread running through the novel, and 'La gioia e la Legge, Lighea' (The Professor and the Siren'), no less important for understanding his concern with death and immortality; *Lezioni su Stendhal* [Lessons on Stendhal], which, with hindsight, tell us much about his own aspirations as a writer (in theory if not in practice: Stendhal was to him a commendably 'thin' writer, while he himself was 'fat'); and *Invito alle lettere francesi del Cinquecento* [Introduction to 16th-Century French Literature], a series of 'lectures' on French literature from Rabelais to Montaigne. In addition, there are two substantial volumes of 'lectures' (*Letteratura inglese*) on English literature, from Beowulf to Lampedusa's own days, all of which bear witness to the wide-ranging, exquisitely literary cast of a mind refined over a lifetime of aristocratic leisure.

Lampedusa's original idea in *The Leopard* was to deal, in Joyce-like fashion (*Ulysses* serving as model), with 24 hours in the life of his great-grandfather at the time of Garibaldi's landing at Marsala on 11 May 1860, which was to lead to the eventual unification of Italy under the House of Savoy. The time span of the novel, however, was extended well beyond its original 24 hours to May 1910, the 50th anniversary of the historic event. Given its extensive historical background most Italian critics assumed (not unreasonably) that the work was basically a historical novel, and not a very good one at that, since it essentially replicated Federico De Roberto's late 19th-century novel, *I vicere* (*The Viceroys*). They assumed, moreover, a total identification between the novel's protagonist, Don Fabrizio Salina, and its aristocratic author, attributing what they perceived as the novel's arch-conservative and static vision of history to Lampedusa himself: in part one there is the enigmatic remark of Fabrizio's nephew, Tancredi, as he is about to go off to join Garibaldi: 'If we want things to stay as they are, things will have to change'; and, in part four, Fabrizio remarks to some English naval officers apropos Garibaldi's volunteers: 'They are coming to teach us good manners . . . But they won't succeed, because we are gods'. What these early readers failed to appreciate was the novel's irony, whereby the seemingly unchanged and unchanging surface nature of Sicilian society ('Thanks be to God, everything seems as usual', thinks Fabrizio in part two, on his arrival at his summer residence of Donnafugata, after Garibaldi's 'revolution') is undermined by a multiplicity of symbols in the text, clearly designed to undermine the immediate impression—the dismemberment of the fortress-like rum jelly in part one, for example, 'rather threatening at first sight', but in the end consisting only 'of shattered walls and hunks of wobbly rubble'; or the observation at the ball, in part six, apropos its aristocratic guests, that 'They thought themselves eternal; but a bomb manufactured in Pittsburgh, Penn., was to prove the contrary in 1943'.

The catapulting forward in time, from 1862 to 1943 (specifically to 5 April 1943, when Allied bombs substantially damaged Palazzo Lampedusa, the author's own home since birth, as 'Places of My Infancy' informs us), focuses on the importance of places rather than people in Lampedusa's life and, indeed, his work (the numerous and often minute correspondences between 'Places of My Infancy' and *The Leopard* have been traced by Daniel Devoto); and the importance given to places should provide caution against an excessively political reading of Fabrizio's actions (or, more accurately, non-actions) in the novel. He is, perhaps not surprisingly, an astronomer, preferring the world of the stars to that of men, as he muses in part six, because 'they were distant, they were omnipotent and at the same time they were docile to his calculations; just the contrary to humans, always too near, so weak and yet so quarrelsome'.

While much of the early fascination with the work derived from its author's sense of place, its continuing fascination lies elsewhere, for 'though he is dealing with a closed, dead society, though his knowledge is esoteric', as David Nolan has observed, 'the reader feels that there by the grace of Lampedusa, life has been described'. The range and variety of the novel's 'minor' characters confirms the truth of the observation—from Fabrizio's hysterical wife, Stella, to his stubborn eldest daughter, Concetta; from his charming, politically trimming nephew, Tancredi, to the beautiful and sensual Angelica Sedara, destined through her marriage to Tancredi to bring about the new social order incarnated in her clearly *mafioso* father, Don Calogero.

But it is the novel's protagonist, Don Fabrizio, who literally dominates from the outset ('the sudden movement of his huge frame made the floor tremble, and a glint of pride flashed in his light-blue eyes at this fleeting confirmation of his lordship over both humans and their works'). This physical presence, however, is all there is in reality, for the principal trait in his character is a deep-rooted need for peace and quiet, at any cost. The fine figure of a man is, deep down, a moral coward, and moreover one who is invariably misunderstood. In an emblematic moment in part three, the advice he gives to vote in favour of the Revolution is interpreted as being ironic by his listeners. Their self-congratulation at having penetrated his meaning casts a retrospective shadow over the accuracy of Fabrizio's own interpretation of Tancredi's earlier words in part one, and both events anticipate the moment in the novel's final section when Concetta, too, is obliged to contemplate the possibility that misinterpretation of events, of words, 50 years earlier, stunted the rest of her life. The events of history blend with the private, politics gives way to psychology, and all are subsumed in the final question, 'But was it the truth?', which highlights Lampedusa's concern with enigma and myth—the qualities which perhaps give the novel its enduring appeal.

—Tom O'Neill

LAUTRÉAMONT, Comte de. Born Isidore Lucien Ducasse in Montevideo, Uruguay, 4 April 1846. Little is known of his life. Educated at Collège Impérial de Tarbes, France, 1859–63; Lycée de Pau, 1963–65. Returned briefly to Montevideo, 1867; moved to Paris, 1867, where he was supported by a private income. *Died 24 November 1870.*

PUBLICATIONS

Collections

Oeuvres complètes, edited by Philippe Soupault. 1927.
Oeuvres complètes. 1938.
Les Chants de Lautréamont et oeuvres complètes. 1947.
Oeuvres complètes, edited by Alfred Jarry. 1953–1977.
Oeuvres complètes, edited by Maurice Saillet. 1963.
Oeuvres complètes, edited by Marguerite Bonnet. 1969.
Oeuvres complètes, edited by Pierre Olivier Walzer. 1970.
Oeuvres complètes, edited by Herbert Juin. 1970.
Oeuvres complètes, edited by Jean Marcel and Arpad Mezei. 1971.
Poésies and Complete Miscellanea, edited and translated by Alexis Lykiard. 1978.

Verse

Les Chants de Maldoror. 1868–69; revised editions, 1874, 1980; edited by Jean Cocteau, 1963, and by Philippe Sellier, 1980; as *The Lay of Maldoror*, translated by John Rodker, 1924; also translated by Guy Wernham, 1943; Alexis Lykiard, 1970; Paul Knight, 1978.
Poésies I and *II* (published privately). 1870; edited by J.L. Steinmetz, 1990.
Préface à un livre futur. 1922.
Poésies, edited by Georges Goldfayn and Gérard Legrand. 1960.

*

Critical Studies: *Lautréamont* by Gaston Bachelard, 1939, enlarged edition, 1963; *Lautréamont's Imagery: A Stylistic Approach* by Peter Nesselroth, 1969; *Isidore Ducasse, Comte de Lautréamont* by François Caradec, 1970, revised edition, 1975; *Vie de Lautréamont* by Edouard Peyrouzet, 1970; *Lectures de Lautréamont* by M. Philip, 1971; *Lautréamont et le style homérique* by Lucienne Rochon, 1971; *Lauréamont: The Violent Narcissus* by Paul Zweig, 1972; *Lautréamont* by Wallace A. Fowlie, 1973; *Nightmare Culture: Lautréamont and Les Chants de Maldoror* by Alexander H.F. de Jonge, 1973; *Lautréamont, du lieu commun à la parodie* by Claude Bouché, 1974; *Le Visage de Lautréamont: Isidore Ducasse à Tarbes et à Pau* by Jacques Lefrère, 1977; *Lautréamont et la cohérence de l'écriture: Études structurales des variantes du Chant premier des Chants de Maldoror* by Jean Peytard, 1977; *Lautréamont génie; ou, maladies mentale, suivie de Nouveau bilan psychopathologique* by Jean Pierre Soulier, 1978; *Lautréamont, le texte du vampire* by J.M. Olivier, 1981; *Lautréamont: Ethique à Maldoror* by Michel Pierssens, 1984; *La Guerre sainte, Lautréamont et Isidore Ducasse* by Liliane Durant-Dessert, 2 vols., 1988; *Lautréamont-Ducasse: Image, Theme and Self Identity* by Robert Pickering, 1990; *Isidore de Lautréamont* by Sylvain-Christian David, 1991.

* * *

Le Comte de Lautréamont's two works, *Les Chants de*

Maldoror (*The Lay of Maldoror*) and *Poésies* [Poems], were published in comparative obscurity and for three decades received only passing attention from very few, albeit important, men of letters (Gourmont, Bloy, Fargue, and Larbaud). However, beginning in the 1920s, these texts were to provide the inspiration for a number of French avant-garde movements, from the Surrealists to the Tel Quel group of the 1960s, and were to be an object of study for some of the most original and influential French critics, including Edmond Jaloux, Roger Caillois, Gaston Bachelard, Maurice Blanchot, and Julia Kristève. As André Gide wrote in 1925, '[Lautréamont's] influence in the 19th century was nil; but . . . he has opened the flood-gates for the literature of tomorrow.' Apart from the themes of iconoclasm and revolt evident in *The Lay of Maldoror*, both the works pose profound questions concerning the status of authorship, the meaning of a text, and the reception and influence of a literary work.

Far longer than the *Poésies*, *The Lay of Maldoror* reads like a parody-cum-apotheosis of all the early 19th-century literature of Romantic revolt and Gothic macabre. The hero, Maldoror, narrates or is shown in a series of scenes in which he battles with his arch-enemy God, torments a humanity he despises, and engages in acts as contrary to nature as possible. Often the latter are so much more original and extreme than anything in Romantic literature that all idea of subservience to a model is surpassed. In the second 'Song', for example, Maldoror dives into the ocean to help a female shark fight off rival members of her own species; the scene concludes with Maldoror copulating with the creature in the midst of a raging tempest.

While outstripping the most 'frenetic' aspects of Romanticism, the episode is indicative of a more profound theme. It begins with the words, 'I sought a soul that might resemble mine, and I could not find it'. The central character displays a very human need for companionship, but is able only to destroy and mutilate the human objects of his affection. Instead his need is perversely satisfied more often than not among supposedly lower forms of life. *The Lay of Maldoror* is filled with toads, snakes, leeches, lice, and all manner of insects, and Maldoror himself is not afraid to engage in or to extol metamorphosis into other members of the animal kingdom. He becomes, in Bachelard's coinage, a 'superanimal' able to adopt the forms and aggressive energy of a natural world that is closer to the Marquis de Sade or to Darwin than to the Romantic sublime. The old hierarchy of creation, from beast to man to God, is turned upside down. The deity is reviled and mankind humiliated in the name of a revolt that rejoices in its own protean inventiveness.

The Romantic sources do not make *The Lay of Maldoror* any easier to classify from the point of view of genre. The text is written in prose and sometimes recalls the Gothic romance *à la* Maturin (the author of *Melmoth the Wanderer* is mentioned in the *Poésies*), or the serial novel of fantastic or criminal adventures as exemplified in France by Sue, Féval, and Ponson du Terrail (the final 'Song', in which Maldoror murders a Parisian adolescent, is very reminiscent of the 19th-century crime novel). Yet for all that, Lautréamont's prose is highly poetic. The sentences are frequently very long, sinuous, and rhapsodic, often borrowing the lofty diction of verse and launching into grandiloquent apostrophe. At the same time the discourse frequently refers to itself or is self-mocking. The result is an absolutely unique tone, managing to combine the sublime seriousness of Romanticism with a grotesque form of parodic humour, which looks forward to French modernism of the following century. A particular feature of Lautréamont's style is the use of unsettling metaphors, and this was to be a prime attraction for the

Surrealists, always fond of quoting, 'He is fair . . . above all, as the chance meeting on a dissecting-table of a sewing-machine and an umbrella.'

In fact, despite the use of prose, the most explicit generic model is a poetic one. The structure of the work echoes the Roman verse epic, as practised by the likes of Lamartine and Quinet, which recounted the cosmic deeds of an angel or hero in a series of cantos. Lautréamont's work does just this for Maldoror in the set of six 'Songs'. Yet beyond Romanticism lies the epic itself as a genre, from Homer to Dante and Milton, and the reader of *The Lay of Maldoror* seems to find multiple reminiscences working concurrently from a vast array of literary texts. Whether these are conscious sources or unconscious recreations, it is as though this one book called into play many others, and Blanchot has gone so far as to speak of a collective and impersonal level of literature. Yet *The Lay of Maldoror* simultaneously calls into question the notion and practices of literature itself. They mock and parody not only literary styles, but also narrative and descriptive devices, drawing attention to the tacit contract between the writer and the reader whereby the latter agrees to try and believe what the former strains to fabricate for him. The book opens with a warning only to carry on if one is equal to the work's ferocious savagery, while towards the end Lautréamont has the reader say, 'One must give him his due. He has considerably cretinized me' (6th 'Song'). At various points on the way the narrator/Maldoror talks of his struggle to write (at one point being struck by a thunderbolt in a vain attempt on God's part to prevent the writing of so blasphemous a work), of how far one can believe either supposedly real phenomena or words, and of the likely acceptability of his style to the reader. It is in this self-consciousness of literary processes and of the power and treacherousness of language that Lautréamont's revolutionary qualities lie.

The other work, *Poésies*, is entirely different in nature. It consists of two instalments of manifesto-like declarations about literature and morality that denounce explicitly the Romantic poetry of Satanic revolt and macabre exaggeration embodied by *The Lay of Maldoror*. Yet a connection remains, for his work proposes a new form of creation based on rewriting or rearranging the words of others, much of *Poésies II* being a series of aphorisms from the French 17th-century moralists turned inside out. Here, as in the *The Lay of Maldoror*, Lautréamont shows a modernist awareness of language and literature as vast systems over which individuals do not have the degree of control they believe they have, but which can be exploited as systems to transcend the limited notions of logic and of individual consciousness that had hitherto prevailed.

—J.R. Stubbs

LAXNESS, Halldór (Kiljan). Born Halldór Gujónsson in Reykjavík, Iceland, 23 April 1902. Educated at a grammar school, Reykjavík; lived in Benedictine monastery, Luxembourg; Jesuit school, Champion House, Osterley, England, 1923–24. Married 1) Ingibjörg Einarsdóttir in 1930, one son; 2) Auur Sveinsdóttir in 1945, two daughters. Lived in Europe, from 1919, then in the USA, 1927–29, and in Iceland since 1930. Recipient: International Peace Movement prize, 1953; Nobel prize for literature, 1955; Sonning prize,

1969. Honorary degrees: Aabo University, 1968; University of Iceland, 1972; Eberhaar-Karls University, Tübingen, 1982. Honorary member, Union of Icelandic Artists.

PUBLICATIONS

Fiction

Barn náttúrunnar [Child of Nature]. 1919.
Nokkrar sögur [Several Stories]. 1923.
Undir Helgahnúk [Under the Holy Mountain]. 1924.
Vefarinn mikli frá Kasmír [The Great Weaver from Kashmir]. 1927.
Salka Valka (þu vínviður hreini, Fuglinn í fjörunni). 2 vols., 1931–32; as *Salka Valka*, translated by F.H. Lyon, 1936; revised edition, 1963.
Fótatak manna [Footsteps of Men]. 1933.
Sjálfstætt fólk. 2 vols., 1934–35; as *Independent People*, translated by J.A. Thompson, 1945.
Þórður gamli halti [Old Þórður the Lame]. 1935.
Heimsljós. 2 vols., 1955; as *World Light*, translated by Magnus Magnusson, 1969.
   1. *Ljós heimsins* [The Light of the World]. 1937.
   2. *Höll sumarlandsins* [The Palace of the Summerland]. 1938.
   3. *Hús skáldsins* [The Poet's House]. 1939.
   4. *Fegurð himinsins* [The Beauty of the Sky]. 1940.
Gerska æfintýri [The Russian Adventure]. 1938.
Sjö töframenn [Seven Magicians]. 1942.
Trilogy:
   1. *Íslandsklukkan* [Iceland's Bell]. 1943.
   2. *Hið ljósa man* [The Bright Maiden]. 1944.
   3. *Eldur í Kaupinhafn* [Fire in Copenhagen]. 1946.
Atómstöðin. 1948; as *The Atom Station*, translated by Magnus Magnusson, 1961.
Gerpla. 1952; as *The Happy Warriors*, translated by Katherine John, 1958.
Brekkukotsannáll. 1957; as *The Fish Can Sing*, translated by Magnus Magnusson, 1966.
Ungfrúin góða og Husi [The Honour of the House]. 1959.
Paradisarheimt. 1960; as *Paradise Reclaimed*, translated by Magnus Magnusson, 1962.
Sjöstafakverið. 1964; as *A Quire of Seven*, translated by Alan Boucher, 1974.
Kristnihald undir Jökli. 1968; translated as *Christianity at the Glacier*, 1972.
Guðsgjafaþula [A Narration of God's Gifts]. 1972.
Seiseijú, mikil ósköp [Oh Yes! By Jove]. 1977.
Dagar hjá múnkum [Day Spent with Monks]. 1987.

Plays

Straumrof [Short Circuit]. 1934.
Snæfríður Íslandssól [Snaefríur, Iceland's Sun]. 1950.
Silfurtúnglið [The Silver Moon]. 1954.
Strompleikurinn [The Chimney Play]. 1961.
Prjónastofan Sólin [The Sun Knitting Works]. 1962.
Dúfnaveislan. 1966; as *The Pigeon Banquet*, translated by Alan Boucher, 1973.
Úa. 1970.
Norðanstulkan [The Girl from the North]. 1972.

Verse

Kvaeðakver [A Sheaf of Poems]. 1930.

Other

Kapólsk viðhorf [Catholic Views]. 1925.
Althýðubókin [The Book of the Plain People]. 1929.
Í austurvegi [On the Eastern Road]. 1933.
Dagleið á fjöllum: greinar [Day's Journey in the Mountains]. 1937.
Vettvangur dagsins [Forum of the Day]. 1942.
Sjálfsagðir hlutir [Things Taken for Granted]. 1946.
Reisubókarkorn [A Little Travel Book]. 1950.
Heiman eg fór [I Left Home]. 1952.
Dagur í senn [A Day at a Time]. 1955.
Gjörningabók [Miscellany]. 1959.
Skáldatími [Poets' Time]. 1963.
Upphaf mannúarstefnu [The Origin of Humanism]. 1965.
Íslendíngaspjall [Talk of Icelanders]. 1967.
Vínlandspúnktar [Vineland Notes]. 1969.
Innansveitarkronika [A Parish Chronicle]. 1970.
Yfirskygir staðir [Overshadowed Places]. 1971.
Þjóðhátiðarrolla [Book of National Celebration]. 1974.
Í túninu heima [In the Hayfields of Home]. 1975.
Úngur eg var [Young I Was]. 1976.
Sjömeistarasagan [The Story of the Seven Masters]. 1978.
Grikklandsári [The Year in Greece]. 1980.
Við heygarshornið. 1981.
N. Tryggvadóttir: Serenity and Power, with Hrafnhildur Schram. 1982.
Og árin líða [And the Years Pass]. 1984.
Af menníngarástandi [On the Cultural Situation]. 1986.
Sagan af brauði nu dýra/The Bread of Life, translated by Magnus Magnusson. 1987.

Editor, *Grettissaga* [The Saga of Grettir the Strong]. 1946.
Editor, *Laxdæla saga* [The Laxdalers' Saga]. 1973.

Translator, *Aðventa* [Advent], by Gunnar Gunnarsson. 1939.
Translator, *Alexandreis; það, Er Alexanders saga mikla* [Alexandreis; That Is, the Saga of Alexander the Great]. 1945.

Also translator of *A Farewell to Arms* and *A Moveable Feast* by Hemingway and *Candide* by Voltaire.

*

Bibliography: by Haraldur Sigurðsson, in *Landsbókasafn Íslands: Árbok*, 1971, and in *Skirnir 146*, 1972; 'Halldór Laxness and America: A Bibliography' by Fred R. Jacobs, in *The Serif*, 10(4), 1973.

Critical Studies: *Den store vävaren*, 1954, *Skaldens hus*, 1956, *Halldór Laxness*, 1971, and 'Halldór Laxness and the Icelandic Sagas', in *Leeds Studies in English*, 13, 1982, all by Peter Hallberg; 'Halldór Kiljan Laxness' by Lawrence S. Thompson, in *Books Abroad*, 28, 1954; 'Halldór Kiljan Laxness: Iceland's First Nobel Prize Winner', in *American-Scandinavian Review*, 44, 1956, and 'The World of Halldór Laxness', in *World Literature Today*, 6(33), 1992, both by Sigurur A. Magnússon; 'Christianity on the Slopes of the Glacier' by Richard N. Ringler, in *Books Abroad*, 44, 1970; Laxness issue of *Scandinavica*, 11(2), 1972; 'Beyond *The Atom Station*' by Hermann Pálsson, in *Ideas and Ideologies*, 1975; 'Halldór Kiljan Laxness and the Modern Scottish Novel: Some Sociolinguistic Parallels' by Harry D. Watson, in *Scandinavica*, 21(2), 1982; 'Eldorado and the Garden in Laxness' *Paradisarheimt*' by George S. Tate, in *Scripta*

Islandica, 36, 1985; 'The Quintessence in the Novels of Halldór Laxness' by Wilhelm Friese, in *Skandivistik*, 16(2), 1986.

*   *   *

Halldór Laxness made his breakthrough in 1923 with the novel *Vefarinn mikli frá Kasmír* [The Great Weaver from Kashmir]. It is a conversion novel, inspired by the spirit, if not the facts, of Laxness's own conversion to Roman Catholicism. It confronts a baffling number of conflicting views of the world, and makes clear that in turning to religion, Stein Elliði is renouncing human claims. Thus it represents an important element in Laxness's work: the problem of the individual *vis-à-vis* a monolithic authority, the claims of the individual conscience as opposed to the conformative nature of the major ideologies.

Laxness subsequently spent a period in America where under the influence of Upton Sinclair and Sinclair Lewis he developed a sense of social injustice and became a Communist. One result was the major novel *Salka Valka*, concerning the establishment of a trade union in a fishing village and its effect on the environment, and in particular on Salka Valka herself. Social novels continued with *Sjálfstætt fólk* (*Independent People*), portraying the individualist peasant who believes he is free but is in fact being exploited by society, and *Heimsljós* (*World Light*), about a visionary pauper persecuted by his peers.

In 1943–46 Laxness turned to the historical novel, beginning with *Íslandsklukkan* [Iceland's Bell], about Jón Hreggviðsson's battle with the authorities. Unjustly condemned to death, he pursues a prolonged and ultimately successful struggle against bureaucracy. There are distinct national overtones, but also a poetical element centred on the main female character. The novel can be seen as a glorification of the Icelandic character, but it also represents the individual confronted with an impersonal bureaucracy. Similar ideas are found in *Atómstöðin* (*The Atom Station*) and *Gerpla* (*The Happy Warriors*).

The national theme, though with universal overtones, appears in *Paradisarheimt* (*Paradise Reclaimed*), about a poor Icelandic farmer tempted by a Mormon bishop to emigrate to the earthly paradise of Salt Lake City. In a touching, but sometimes bitingly satirical novel, Steinar experiences the unswerving faith of an ideology, but fails to accept it fully himself, and he returns to his home in Iceland, *his* paradise.

Laxness then moved from the long epic to the more concentrated, pithy novel, closely related to the plays with which he also experimented. Outstanding is *Kristnihald undir Jökli* (*Christianity at the Glacier*), a humorous but nevertheless serious and philosophical novel about a bishop who sends an assistant to examine the state of Christianity in an outlying village. The result, when he finds a priest who cannot be bothered to bury the dead, preferring to shoe horses and offer his congregation practical help, a doctor who has given up a brilliant career to study the skies, and a pastor's wife who has been both nun and prostitute, is a picture of humankind in all its diversity.

In portraying the individual's confrontation with societies and ideologies, Laxness constantly takes the side of the individual. He examines both Catholicism and communism, but ultimately it is probably Taoism, with its demand for tolerance and humanity, that attracts him most. He weds his philosophical considerations to his intense national feeling and gives the two a universal significance.

—W. Glyn Jones

————

LAZARILLO de Tormes. Anonymous 16th-century Spanish novel; the first of the picaresque genre. Earliest extant editions date from 1554, although there may have been a 1553 edition which is no longer in existence. Popular throughout Spain, but disliked by the authorities because of its satirical content; banned by the Inquisition, 1559; Philip II ordered that offensive material be removed. Authorship is uncertain: in 1605, it was attributed to Fray Juan de Ortega; by 1607, it was thought that Diego Hurtado de Mendoza (1503–75), the Spanish poet and historian, and son of a governor of Granada, may have been responsible. More recently, other authors have been suggested, including: Sebastián de Horozco, c.1510–80 (one of his works features a character called Lazarillo); the Valdés brothers, Alfonso (c.1490–1532) and Juan (c.1491–1541), writers of prose and dialogues; Cristóbal de Villalón, c.1505–58 (or possibly a pseudonym for several writers of the mid-16th century). There have been several attempts at sequels or copies; these are usually by inferior writers and fail to capture the flavour of the original, including: *La segunda parte de Lazarillo de Tormes* (1555); *El Lazarillo de Manzanares*, by Juan Cortés de Tolosa (1620); *Segunda parte*, by Juan de Luna (1620); and *The Life and Death of Young Lazarillo* (1685).

PUBLICATIONS

La vida de Lazarillo de Tormes y de sus fortunas y adversidades. 1553/54; edited by R.O. Jones, 1963; also edited by A. Blecua, 1974, and Antonio Rey Hazas, 1984; as *The Pleasant History of Lazarillo de Tormes*, translated by David Rowland, 1586, many subsequent reprints; also translated by William Hazlitt, 1851; Michael Alpert, in *Two Spanish Picaresque Novels*, 1969; as *The Life and Adventures of Lazarillo de Tormes*, translated by Thomas Roscoe, with a translation of Alemán's *Guzmán de Alfarache*, 1880; as *The Life of Lazarillo de Tormes*, translated by Clements Markham, 1908; as *The Life of Lazarillo de Tormes, His Fortunes and Adversities*, translated by Louis How, 1917; also translated by J. Gerald Markley, 1954; Harriet de Onís, 1959; as *Lazarillo de Tormes: His Life, Fortunes, Misadventures*, translated by Mariano J. Lorente, 1924; as *Blind Man's Boy*, translated by J.M. Cohen, 1962.

*

Critical Studies: 'Literary and Artistic Unity in "Lazarillo de Tormes"' by F.C. Tarr, in *Publications of the Modern Languages Association of America*, 42, 1927; 'Sebastián de Horozco y el "Lazarillo de Tormes"' by F. Márquez Villanueva, in *Revista de Filología Española*, 41, 1957; 'The Death of Lazarillo de Tormes' by S. Gilman, in *Publications of the Modern Languages Association of America*, 81, 1966; *Introducción al 'Lazarillo de Tormes'* by José F. Gatti, 1968; *La novela picaresca y el punto de vista* by Francisco Rico,

1970; 'On Re-reading the "Lazarillo de Tormes"' by D.W. Lomax, in *Studia ibérica*, 1973; *Lazarillo de Tormes: A Critical Guide* by Alan David Deyermond, 1975; *Ediciones y traducciones inglesas del Lazarillo de Tormes, 1568–1977* by Julio-César Santoyo, 1978; *Language and Society in 'La vida de Lazarillo de Tormes'* by Harry Sieber, 1978; *The Spanish Picaresque Novel* by P.N. Dunn, 1979; *Lazarillo de Tormes* by Robert L. Fiore, 1984.

* * *

The earliest known editions of the anonymous Spanish novel *Lazarillo de Tormes* date from 1554, although some scholars believe that an earlier text may have been lost. A short work of no more than 20,000 words, its authorship remains unclear, but a number of critics believe the most convincing candidate to be the prolific writer and humanist Diego Hurtado de Mendoza. As well as enjoying great success in Spain, the book was translated widely throughout Europe in the second half of the 16th century (the first English translation was in 1586) and it quickly proved highly influential. With the benefits of hindsight, it takes on great historical importance by being the first of the genre of tales known as picaresque novels, a group including Mateo Alemán's *Guzmán de Alfarache*, 1599, and Francisco de Quevedo's *El Buscón*, [The Rogue], 1626, and many subsequent adaptations.

In explicit opposition to the contemporary chivalric or idealized romance, as represented by *Amadís de Gaul* and as satirized in Cervantes's *Don Quixote*, the picaresque novel deals exclusively with first-person testimonies from low-life characters placed in the most difficult circumstances. The central figure, the *pícaro*, or rascal, travels through a hostile environment, learning quickly that he (or occasionally she) has to survive by his own efforts, principally by his ingenuity in outwitting others. Without undue self-examination or recrimination, the *pícaro* recounts his adventures with unapologetic frankness and a racy taste for bawdy episodes. Where the chivalric tale is sacred, the picaresque is profane; where the romance idealizes, the picaresque strives after harsh realism in its depictions of money, sex, and food. The eventual aim of these narratives is to combine elements of contemporary social satire with a more general stripping away of illusions about human dignity.

Initiating what were to become the literary conventions of the picaresque novel, *Lazarillo de Tormes* involves a catalogue of pranks and tricks played by the *pícaro*, carried out initially in retaliation for his own mistreatment, but later taking on a momentum of their own. The cumulative effect is to present a highly unflattering cynical picture of a volatile society in which the cravings for money and the operations of desire are only barely concealed, and in which competition and rivalry are of much greater importance than collaboration or friendship. Chronicling its hero's mishaps and triumphs, *Lazarillo* acts as an ironic revelation of the material, unsentimental features of contemporary society, as they appear to the knowing eye of the trickster, who harbours no illusions. The unpredictability of life is typically made prominent at the opening of this narrative, when the young Lázaro, born on the river Tormes near Salamanca, loses his father immediately. In less than a page, his mother falls foul of the law and becomes destitute, unable to provide for her son. She entrusts the young Lázaro to the care of a blind beggar, whose gratuitous cruelty and unsparing treatment instruct him very quickly in the harsh realities of life. After suffering severe physical abuse, Lázaro turns the tables on his teacher, and runs off to start his solitary and peripatetic existence in earnest.

As he is successively taken up by a priest, a seller of Papal indulgences, a tambourine-painter, a down-at-heel gentleman, a constable, and other representatives of contemporary Spanish society, the unprotected Lázaro comes to realize that there can be no room in his life for indulgence or mercy, and that only guile will save him. If he seems naive, he will be exploited, but if he seems quick-witted, no-one will employ him. So Lázaro has to pretend to be more simple-minded than he is, confiding his real motives and ambitions only to the reader. If there is a common point of reference to which this diffuse text returns, it is in its insistent anti-clericalism—the book was banned by the Inquisition in 1559—but the satire on hypocrisy and self-deception is generalized, and none of the figures from any walk of life emerges with dignity.

As he breaks off his account of his inglorious career so far, Lázaro has become a town-crier. Ironically, part of his job involves shouting out the crimes of malefactors as they are taken to be punished. In private, he tells us of his own misdeeds, whereas in public he publicizes those of others less fortunate. He has also married, unhappily, but neither the steady job nor the more settled domestic life has provided security, and as Lázaro makes his farewell, he knows that the wheel of fortune may turn for him again at any time. So, like other picaresque novels to come, *Lazarillo de Tormes* offers glimpses of an unstable and violent world, where everyone has to look after themselves, and where there can be no confidence in any of the protective institutions of society. Life seems without obvious meaning or pattern, and there is little sense that these injustices will be rectified in the hereafter. The picture of contemporary Spain Lázaro paints is a disquietingly unheroic one, but the darkness of the vision is balanced by the raciness and energy of the descriptions, and in its willingness to describe life 'from below'. *Lazarillo* is one of the most important precursors of realist literature in Europe, influencing writers like Lesage in France, Grimmelshausen in Germany, and Smollett in Britain.

—Ian A. Bell

LENZ, Jakob Michael Reinhold. Born in Sesswegen, Russian Baltic Province of Livonia, 23 January 1751. Family moved to Dorpat (now Tartu), Estonia, 1759. Educated at Latin grammar school, Dorpat; University of Königsberg, studied theology, 1768–71. Tutor to the Kleist brothers in Strasbourg, 1771; entered literary circles, meeting Goethe, Salzmann, and others; freelance writer from 1774, supplementing income with tuition; co-founder, Deutsche Gesellschaft [German Society], Strasbourg, 1775, and contributor to its journal, *Der Bürgerfreund* [The Citizens' Friend]; travelled throughout Germany and Switzerland, 1776–77; suffered first bout of mental illness, 1777; first suicide attempt, 1778; taken by his brother to Riga, 1779; travelled to St Petersburg, 1780, attempt to become teacher and soldier failed, and to Moscow, 1781, held a number of positions as tutor; mental health deteriorated seriously during the 1780s. *Died 4 June 1792.*

PUBLICATIONS

Collections

Dramatischer Nachlass, edited by Karl Weinhold. 1884.
Werke und Schriften, edited by Britta Titel and Hellmut Haug. 2 vols., 1966–67.
Werke und Schriften, edited by Richard Daunicht. 1967.
Gedichte, edited by Helmut Haug. 1968.
Werke und Briefe, edited by Sigrid Damm. 3 vols., 1987.
Werke, edited by Karen Lauer. 1992.

Plays

Der Hofmeister; oder, Die Vorteile der Privaterziehung (produced 1778). 1774; edited by Michael Kohlenbach, 1986; as *The Tutor*, translated by William E. Yuill, with *The Soldiers*, 1972; also translated and adapted by Pip Broughton, 1988; Anthony Meech, in *Three Plays*, 1993.
Lustspiele nach dem Plautus (adaptations from Plautus; includes *Das Väterchen*; *Die Aussteuer*; *Die Entführungen*; *Die Buhlschwester*; *Die Türkensklavin*; *Die beiden Alten*). 1774.
Amor vincit omnia, from *Love's Labours Lost* by Shakespeare. With *Anmerkungen übers Theater*, 1774.
Der neue Menoza; oder, Die Geschichte des cubanischen Prinzen Tandi. 1774; as *The New Menoza*, translated by Meredith Oakes, in *Three Plays*, 1993.
Pandämonium Germanicum. 1775.
Die Soldaten (produced 1863). 1776; as *The Soldiers*, translated by William E. Yuill, with *The Tutor*, 1972; also translated by Robert David MacDonald, in *Three Plays*, 1993.
Die Freunde machen den Philosophen. 1776.
Der Engländer. 1777.
Die Sizilianische Vesper. In *Liefländisches Magazin der Lektüre*, 1782.
Myrsa Polagi; oder, Die Irrgärten. In *Liefländisches Magazin der Lektüre*, 1782.
Tantalus. 1798.
Leopold Wagner, Verfasser des Schauspiels von neuen Monaten im Walfischbauch; oder, Eine Matinee. 1828.
Der verwundete Bräutigam, edited by K.L. Blum. 1845.
Three Plays (includes *The Soldiers*; *The New Menoza*; *The Tutor*). 1993.

Verse

Die Landplagen. 1769.
Der Herr Professor Kant. 1770.
Petrarch. 1776.

Fiction

Der Landprediger. 1777.
Der Waldbruder (fragment). 1797; edited by Max von Waldberg, 1882.
Zerbin; oder, Die neuere Philosophie, edited by Alfred Gerz. 1943.

Other

Anmerkungen übers Theater. With *Amor vincit omnia*, 1774.
Tagebuch. In *Deutsche Rundschau*, 11, 1877; in book form, in *Werke und Briefe*, 1987.

Briefe von und an J.M.R. Lenz, edited by Karl Freye and Wolfgang Stammler. 2 vols., 1918.

*

Critical Studies: *J.M.R. Lenz: Moralist und Aufklärer* by R. Ottomar, 1969; 'Lenz's *Hofmeister* and the Drama of Storm and Stress' by M.A. Brown, in *Periods in German Literature, 2: Texts and Kontexts*, 1970; 'Structural Unity in J.M.R. Lenz's *Der Hofmeister*: A Revaluation' by Edward P. Harris, in *Seminar*, (8), 1972; *Epische Elemente in Jakob Michael Reinhold Lenzens Drama 'Der Hofmeister'* by Ford B. Parkes, 1973; 'Language and Politics: The Patriotic Endeavours of J.M.R. Lenz' by Allan Blunden, in *Deutsche Vierteljahrsschrift für Literatur und Geschichte*, (49), 1975; *J.M.R. Lenz: The Renunciation of Heroism* by John Osborne, 1975; *J.M.R. Lenz in Selbstzeugnissen und Bilddokumenten* by C. Hohoff, 1977; 'Character and Paradox in Lenz's *Der Hofmeister*' by Michael Butler, in *German Life and Letters*, (32), 1979; *Lenz: 'Der Hofmeister'; 'Die Soldaten'; mit Brechts 'Hofmeister' Bearbeitung und Materialien* by Herbert Haffner, 1979; *Shakespeare in Deutschland: Der Fall Lenz* by Eva Maria Inbar, 1982; *Lenz and Büchner: Studies in Dramatic Form* by John D. Guthrie, 1984; *Dasein und Realität: Theorie und Praxis des Realismus bei J.M.R. Lenz* by H.G. Schwarz, 1985; *Vögel, die verkünden Land: Das Leben des Jakob Michael Reinhold Lenz* by Sigrid Damm, 1986; *Jakob Michael Reinhold Lenz: 'Der Hofmeister oder Vorteile der Privaterziehung': Erläuterungen und Dokumente* edited by Friedrich Voit, 1986; 'Irrtum als dramatische Sprachfigur. Sozialfall und Erziehungsdebatte in J.M.R. Lenzens *Hofmeister*' by Klaus Bohnen, 1987; 'A Question of Norms: The Stage Reception of Lenz's *Der Hofmeister*' by Helga Madland, 1987; *J.M.R. Lenz* by Hans-Gerd Winter, 1987; 'Das Politische' in *Die Soldaten* by David Hill, 1988; *Lenz Jahrbuch* edited by M. Luserke and Christoph Weiss, 1991; *A Critique of Lenz's Art of Scenic Variation* by Edward Batley, 1993; *Space to Act: The Theater of J.M.R. Lenz* by Alan C. Leidner and Helga S. Madland, 1994.

* * *

Jakob Michael Reinhold Lenz was a writer of considerable talent whose major output coincided with that short but explosive period of German literature dubbed the *Sturm und Drang* (Storm and Stress). This pre-Revolutionary movement, expounding the Encyclopaedists' ideals of equality, liberty, and fraternity, as well as individual writers within it, exerted a profound influence on European literature, principally German Romanticism, Realism, Junges Deutschland, Naturalism, Expressionism, and Modernism. It laid the foundations for the development of German social drama, bourgeois and working-class, by writers such as Georg Büchner, Gerhart Hauptmann, Frank Wedekind, and Bertold Brecht. The style and content of Büchner's theatre reflects Lenz's innovative approach to the medium, while Büchner's unique psycho-analytical *Novelle* was inspired by Lenz's mental illness, his name providing its title. Brecht revived interest in Lenz with his Berlin adaptation and production of *Der Hofmeister* (*The Tutor*) in 1950 and Rolf Hochhuth's preface to his documentary play on Churchill and the bombing of Dresden, *Soldaten* (*Soldiers*) of 1967 acknowledged his indebtedness to Lenz's play of the same title. Modern German opera from Alban Berg to Bernd Alois Zimmermann showed itself particularly appreciative of his unique theatrical style and visual appeal.

However, Lenz's seminal influence generally has long been undervalued, principally for two reasons. First, his productive years were restricted almost without exception to the 1770s, while the talent which outlasted, outlived, and outshone him, Goethe, not only abandoned his former friend after his departure from Court but also caricatured him unappreciatively in his own autobiography, *Aus meinem Leben: Dichtung und Warheit* [Poetry and Truth]. Second, partly inspired by the older Goethe's rather jaundiced view of the period, the *Sturm und Drang* came to be looked on, and written off as, a period of literary excess, indulgence, and adolescence, despite the younger Goethe having been its leading light. Recent scholarship has begun the process of evaluating Lenz's works independently of the shadow which Goethe cast upon them.

In the short productive span allotted to him, Lenz wrote poetry, essays, short prose works, novels, and plays. His remarkable gift was that of being able to assimilate a wide variety of styles, from the classical and neo-classical to the popular folk traditions, and to mould them together organically. Lenz's poetry shows these characteristics too, a neo-classical and classical inheritance bound up with an ability to use language to evoke mood in a way which prefigures German Romantic poetry. Its innovative forms apart, his poetry is in this sense untypical of the *Sturm und Drang*. Lenz's poetry, essays, and prose writing are not as widely known or researched as his plays, although, with three international conferences devoted to him in 1992, 200 years after his death, these expressions of his literary activity are now being reassessed. *Der Waldbruder* [The Forest Hermit], a conscious pendant to Goethe's novel *The Sufferings of Young Werther*, satirizes his own romantic self-indulgence. *Zerbin; oder, Die neuere Philosophie* [Zerbin, or The Modern Philosophy] converts its hero to the 'modern philosophy' of exploiting others for personal advantage, until Marie's execution, out of unswerving loyalty to him, leads Zerbin to despair and suicide. *Der Landprediger* [The Country Vicar], told with gentler irony, relates the story of Father Oberlin of Waldersbach, who helps members of the local farming community find salvation not in learning the catechism by rote but in reflecting on the activity of their daily lives. The vicar's method of teaching the 'best way of watering meadows' is the truly Christian way to salvation.

Lenz's style of theatre is occasionally offensive: penetratingly critical of human behaviour as of society, its naturalism is as daring as Hauptmann's and its proposals for reform more tangible than Brecht's. Shot through with irony, parody, and stark realism, Lenz's work reflects his utter sincerity. He presents audiences and reading public alike not only with incisive criticisms of contemporary German society, its hypocrisy, class-consciousness, aping of French manners, snobbery, pretentiousness, indulgent sexuality, foibles, wickedness, cruelty, and weakness, but also with practical proposals for reform. He takes up issues treated in his own dramatic dialogue in serious reformatory essays. In 'Die Soldatenehen' [On Soldiers Marrying] he presents persuasive spiritual, moral, economic, military, and political arguments in favour of allowing soldiers to marry, having first given the subject a public airing on the stage in his *Die Soldaten* (*The Soldiers*). Several plays remained unfinished, and some were never performed in his own lifetime. His sketch of *Pandämonium Germanicum* [The Hall of German Heroes] reflects his adulation of Goethe, his criticism of imitators, journalists, and philistines, a playful attitude towards other contemporary writers such as Wieland, Uz, Gellert, Gleim, Rabener, Lessing, and Heder, and a teasingly self-deprecating view of himself.

He is best known for three plays. *Der Hofmeister* (*The Tutor*) depicts quite uninhibitedly the wretchedness caused when a spoilt and lonely young woman is given private lessons, in her own room, by a family tutor who has no sense of purpose or vocation. The educational issue of family tuition in the home versus community education in the village school is hotly debated and also provides the central and unifying theme of a complex play which, although it contains seduction, attempted suicide, and castration, ends happily for most of the cast. *Der neue Menoza* (*The New Menoza*), a parody of the traditional comedy of revealed identities, has the sibling relationship between Prince Tandy and Wilhelmina disclosed to them only after they are married to each other, but baby swapping is finally identified as the original cause of this misinformation.

The Soldiers, set in and around Lille, depicts how a foolish and irresistibly attractive shopkeeper's daughter Marie becomes disloyal to her fiancé, involved with one officer after another before being attracted to a young Count. Although the Countess tries to reform her, Marie's degradation continues until, stripped of all the trappings of middle-class civilization, she and her father roll on the ground wrapped in each other's arms, ecstatic at being together again, and embodying for a moment the elemental society envisioned by Rousseau, one of the several writers who profoundly influenced Lenz. Lenz's translations of the comedies of Plautus and of plays by Shakespeare nourished his own *Anmerkungen übers Theater* [Notes on the Theatre] and his essays on *Hamlet* and on scene change in Shakespeare, but they are also reflected in his wholesale non-conformist yet organic style of theatre. Rejecting the barrenness of the neo-classical conventions of the unities of action, place, and time, Lenz developed a composite form of artistry which moulded together in one major unifying theme the characters and types he had created, the theatrical situations in which they found themselves, and the setting and sequencing of scenes: education in *The Tutor* the hypocrisy of middle-class German society in *The New Menoza*, and the question of whether soldiers should be allowed to marry in *The Soldiers*. It is in the theatre above all that Lenz's artistic genius, drawn from his concept of *Anschauen* (seeing and reflecting), is acknowledged today, but there is a renaissance of interest in his poetry, prose writing, and reformist zeal which gives promise of far more comprehensive appreciation of this unique writer.

—Edward Batley

THE TUTOR (Der Hofmeister)
Play by Jakob Michael Reinhold Lenz, 1774.

The subtitle of *The Tutor*, *The Benefits of Private Education*, seems at first to be a sarcastic comment on the thesis around which the play is built, for the opening scenes focus on questions of education and contrast the enlightened views of the privy councillor, who sends his son Fritz to a public school, with the authoritarian and fundamentally anti-educational views of his blustering brother, the major, who is in the process of hiring a private tutor. The arguments of the privy councillor are given special credence by Lenz's detailing of the network of bad motives that sustain private education, as Läuffer, the tutor, is forced by his position into servile obedience to the whims of the major and his conceited wife, both of whom are more concerned with themselves than with the interests of their children, Leopold and Gustchen. At the beginning of the second act the privy councillor lectures Läuffer's father on the evils of being a private tutor, especially the requirement to deny oneself freedom and therefore the possibility of self-realization, and more generally on the way that the acceptance of tutoring positions by members of the middle classes contributes to the moral decay of society.

Läuffer's father, however, subverts this level of argument by introducing the idea that the enlightened and humanitarian gestures of the privy councillor do not represent universal truths but are rather a function of his privileged position and that his moralizing injunctions fail to take into account the real economic circumstances of the middle classes. Thus the characters, who seemed initially to have been set up as vehicles for discussing a thesis, take on a life of their own, and Lenz's interest in the individuality of the experience of each of them leads to a certain fragmentation of the plot. The isolation and inauthenticity of life in the major's household draws Läuffer and Gustchen into a romantic affair, and when this is discovered and they flee, the action of the play follows their individual fates. Gustchen and the resultant baby lodge with an old lady until Gustchen's concern for her father makes her leave and try to find him, but before being able to do so she throws herself into a pond in a state of exhaustion and despair. Although Läuffer finds refuge with an eccentric schoolmaster, his remorse eventually drives him to castrate himself. Interspersed with these scenes is the story of the distress suffered by the major. The privy councillor, too, is estranged from his son Fritz, for in another branch of the action which portrays student life in Halle, Fritz accepts imprisonment on behalf of his indebted friend Pätus but this noble act is maliciously misrepresented to his father by another student.

The complicated plot is held together less by a discussion of educational principles than by the coherence of the author's vision and the emergence of a number of typical situations. One of these is the estrangement of parents from their children, and the pain this causes both. Despite the initial contrast between the major and the privy councillor, we become more aware of the parallels between these two fathers, who both feel that they have been deserted by their children, and this motif is developed further in the breach between Pätus and his father—and beyond, in the gulf between Pätus's father and the father's mother. There is also the motif of enforced renunciation, which applies not only to fathers who have to endure the loss of their children but also and especially to a range of characters leading up to the castrated Läuffer who have to forego loving sexual relationships. Even the brief affair between Läuffer and Gustchen is an example of this in as much as Lenz portrays the two as relating to each other only through pre-formed literary models.

It is this vision that at the deepest level holds the play together, a vision of human beings as unfree. At one level, what is innovatory about Lenz's writing is his ability to show the mechanisms by which social power translates itself through specific circumstances into the unfreedom of the individual, and in *The Tutor* it is primarily the power of class and age (parenthood) that prevents the individual from developing an identity and a life of his own. In this respect and in the range of social types who appear on stage Lenz looks forward to the realism of the 19th century, but perhaps most particularly in the way that he shows his characters internalizing these structures of compulsion so that they take on a form and a necessity independent of their original source. At the same time there is much that is grotesque and laughable about characters who submit to such necessity. Lenz's uncer-

tainty whether to call *The Tutor* a comedy or a tragedy reflects the tension between this absurd rigidity of character, which Lenz in his *Anmerkungen übers Theater* [Notes on the Theatre] defined as the essence of comedy, and the pessimistic vision of the world, the awareness of constraint and suffering, that lies behind it.

It is therefore appropriate that, having taken us to the point where the only logical conclusion can be social and moral collapse and pain, Lenz superimposes a self-mocking conciliatory ending: mere chance determines that the major is on hand to rescue Gustchen as she throws herself into the pond, that the financial entanglements are resolved by Pätus winning a lottery, or that the old woman to whom Gustchen entrusted the baby turns out to have been Pätus's grandmother. Even Läuffer seems able to look forward to a happily married future with the dimwitted peasant girl Lise, who is more interested in feeding her poultry than in having children. The final scene of the play has a series of reconciliations, primarily that between Gustchen and Fritz, who adopts her baby and declares in his concluding speech that he will definitely not allow it to be educated by a private tutor. This last reference simply serves to show how far *The Tutor* has moved beyond its initial pedagogic thesis, and indeed how far Lenz has moved beyond that tradition of Enlightenment writing for which there was an ordered framework to existence within which individual problems could be answered by specific proposals for reform.

—David Hill

LENZ, Siegfried. Born in Lyck, East Prussia (now Elk, Poland), 17 March 1926. Educated at the University of Hamburg, 1945–48. Served in the navy during World War II. Married Lieselotte Lenz in 1949. Reporter, 1948–50, and editor, 1950–51, *Die Welt* newspaper, Hamburg; since 1951 freelance writer; visiting lecturer, University of Houston, Texas, 1969; campaign speaker for Social Democratic party, from 1965. Member, Gruppe 47. Recipient: Schickele prize, 1952; Lessing prize, 1953; Hauptmann prize, 1961; Mackensen prize, 1962; Schickele prize, 1962; City of Bremen prize, 1962; State of North Rhine-Westphalia arts prize, 1966; Gryphius prize, 1979; German Free Masons prize, 1979; Thomas Mann prize, 1984; Raabe prize, 1987; Federal Booksellers peace prize, 1988; Galinsky Foundation prize, 1989. Honorary doctorate: University of Hamburg, 1976. Lives in Hamburg, Germany.

Publications

Fiction

Es waren Habichte in der Luft. 1951.
Duell mit dem Schatten. 1953.
So zärtlich war Suleyken (stories). 1955.
Der Mann im Strom. 1957.
Dasselbe. 1957.
Jäger des Spotts. 1958; as *Jäger des Spotts, und andere Erzählungen*, edited by Robert H. Spaethling, 1965.
Brot und Spiele. 1959.

Das Feuerschiff (stories). 1960; title story as *The Lightship*, translated by Michael Bullock, 1962.
Das Wunder von Striegeldorf: Geschichten. 1961.
Stimmungen der See. 1962.
Stadtgespräch, adapted from his play *Zeit der Schuldlosen*. 1963; as *The Survivor*, translated by Michael Bullock, 1965.
Der Hafen ist voller Geheimnisse: Ein Feature in Erzählungen und zwei masurische Geschichten. 1963.
Lehmanns Erzählungen; oder, So schön war mein Markt: Aus den Bekenntnissen eines Schwarzhändlers. 1964.
Der Spielverderber. 1965.
Begegnung mit Tieren, with Hans Bender and Werner Bergengruen. 1966.
Das Wrack, and Other Stories, edited by C.A.H. Russ. 1967.
Die Festung und andere Novellen. 1968.
Deutschstunde. 1968; as *The German Lesson*, translated by Ernst Kaiser and Eithne Wilkins, 1971.
Hamilkar Schass aus Suleyken. 1970.
Lukas, sanftmütiger Knecht. 1970.
Gesammelte Erzählungen. 1970.
So war es mit dem Zirkus: Fünf Geschichten aus Suleyken (stories). 1971.
Erzählungen. 1972.
Meistererzählungen. 1972.
Ein Haus aus lauter Liebe. 1973.
Das Vorbild. 1973; as *An Exemplary Life*, translated by Douglas Parmée, 1976.
Der Geist der Mirabelle: Geschichten aus Bollerup. 1975.
Einstein überquert die Elbe bei Hamburg. 1975.
Die Kunstradfahrer und andere Geschichten. 1976.
Heimatmuseum. 1978; as *The Heritage*, translated by Krishna Winston, 1981.
Der Verlust. 1981; as *The Breakdown*, translated by Ralph R. Read, 1986.
Der Anfang von etwas. 1981.
Ein Kriegsende. 1984.
Exerzierplatz. 1985; as *Training Ground*, translated by Geoffrey Skelton, 1991.
Der Verzicht. 1985.
Die Erzählungen: 1949–1984. 3 vols., 1986.
Das serbische Mädchen. 1987.
Geschichten ut Bollerup. 1987.
Motivsuche. 1988.
Selected Stories, edited and translated by Breon Mitchell. 1989.
Die Klangprobe. 1990.

Plays

Das schönste Fest der Welt (radio play). 1956.
Zeit der Schuldlosen; Zeit der Schuldigen (radio play). 1961; stage adaptation (in German), 1966.
Das Gesicht: Komödie (produced 1964). 1964.
Haussuchung (radio play). 1967.
Die Augenbinde; Schauspiel; Nicht alle Förster sind froh: Ein Dialog. 1970.
Drei Stücke. 1980.
Zeit der Schuldlosen und andere Stücke. 1988.

Radio Plays: *Zeit der Schuldlosen/Zeit der Schuldigen*, 1961; *Das schönste Fest der Welt*.

Other

So leicht fängt man keine Katze. 1954.
Der einsame Jäger. 1955.
Das Kabinett der Konterbande. 1956.

Flug über Land und Meer: Nordsee—Holstein—Nordsee, with Dieter Seelmann. 1967; as *Wo die Möwen schreien: Flug über Norddeutschlands Küsten und Länder*, 1976.
Leute von Hamburg: Satirische Porträts. 1968.
Versäum nicht den Termin der Freude. 1970.
Lotte soll nicht sterben (for children). 1970; as *Lotte macht alles mit*, 1978.
Beziehungen: Ansichten und Bekenntnisse zur Literatur. 1970.
Die Herrschaftssprache der CDU. 1971.
Verlorenes Land—gewonnene Nachbarschaft: zur Ostpolitik der Bundesregierung. 1971.
Der Amüsierdoktor. 1972.
Der Leseteufel. 1972(?).
Elfenbeinturm und Barrikade: Schriftsteller zwischen Literatur und Politik. 1976.
Die Wracks von Hamburg: Hörfunk-Features. 1978.
Himmel, Wolken, weites Land: Flug über Meer, Marsch, Geest und Heide, with Dieter Seelmann. 1979.
Waldboden: Sechsunddreissig Farbstiftzeichnungen, illustrated by Liselotte Lenz. 1979.
Gespräche mit Manès Sperber und Leszek Kołakowski, edited by Alfred Mensak. 1980.
Über Phantasie: Siegfried Lenz, Gespräche mit Heinrich Böll, Günter Grass, Walter Kempowski, Pavel Kohout, edited by Alfred Mensak. 1982.
Fast einem Triumph: aus ein Album. 1982.
Elfenbeinturm und Barrikade: Erfahrungen am Schreibtisch. 1983.
Manès Sperber, sein letztes Jahr, with Manès and Jenka Sperber. 1985.
Etwas über Namen (address). 1985.
Kleines Strandgut, illustrated by Liselotte Lenz. 1986.
Am Rande des Friedens. 1989.

Editor, with Egon Schramm, *Wippchens charmante Scharmützel*, by Julius Stettenheim. 1960.

*

Critical Studies: 'From the Gulf Stream in the Main Stream: Siegfried Lenz and Hemingway' by Sumner Kirshner, in *Research Studies*, 1967; 'Narrowing the Distance: Siegfried Lenz's *Deutschstunde*' by Robert H. Paslick, in *German Quarterly*, 1973; 'The Macabre Festival: A Consideration of Six Stories by Siegfried Lenz' by Colin Russ, in *Deutung und Bedeutung: Studies in German and Comparative Literature*, edited by Brigitte Schludermann and others, 1973; 'How It Seems and How It Is: Marriage in Three Stories by Siegfried Lenz' by Esther N. Elstun, in *Orbis litterarum*, (29), 1974; 'Ironic Reversal in the Short Stories of Siegfried Lenz', in *Neophilologus*, (58), 1974, and *Siegfried Lenz*, 1978, both by Brian O. Murdoch; 'Siegfried Lenz's *Deutschstunde*: A North German Novel' in *German Life and Letters*, 1975, and 'The "Lesson" in Siegfried Lenz's *Deutschstunde*', in *Seminar*, February 1977, both by Peter Russell; 'Zygmunt's Follies? On Siegfried Lenz's *Heimatmuseum*' by Geoffrey P. Butler, in *German Life and Letters*, 1980; 'Captive Creator in Siegfried Lenz's *Deutschstunde*: Writer, Reader, and Response' by Todd Kontje, in *German Quarterly*, (53), 1980; 'The Interlocutor and the Narrative Transmission of the Past: On Siegfried Lenz's *Heimatmuseum*' by Marilyn Sibley Fries, in *Monatshefte*, 1987; 'The Eye of the Witness: Photography in Siegfried Lenz's Short Stories' by Hanna Geldrich-Zeffmann, in *Modern Language Review*, 1989.

* * *

In his career Siegfried Lenz has long focused heart and mind on his homeland in Eastern Europe and this is reflected in his fiction and in his critical writings as a political commentator. Born in East Prussia in 1926, he observed as an adolescent the German occupation of Poland. At the age of 17, he served in the Navy during the latter part of World War II. In the immediate and difficult post-war years he studied philosophy and literature at the University of Hamburg. That postwar atmosphere is humorously, indeed satirically portrayed in *Lehmanns Erzählungen; oder, So schön war mein Markt* (1964), while World War II and the serious moral dilemmas confronting the fictional protagonist have continued to occupy Lenz's attention, as in *Ein Kriegsende* (1984). Lenz's nascent interest in literature was evident already at university and was stimulated more directly by his work as a journalist and literary editor on *Die Welt*. The journalistic eye for detail and atmosphere undoubtedly helped his literary apprenticeship during which he produced his first short stories published in serial form or *in toto* in newspapers and journals.

The publication of his first novel *Es waren Habichte in der Luft* (1951) determined Lenz's career as a freelance writer. The story immediately points to his subsequent thematic concentration on border regions, marginal situations, on danger, flight, failure, and the inescapability of fate. The setting is Karelia just after World War I and deals with the establishment of the communist regime there. Stenkka, a teacher, is on the run, accused of murder although in reality he was only a witness to the deed. A pessimistic viewpoint is suggested by the notion of death at the border (though Erkii, a former pupil, does survive the ordeal) and the predatory hawks are symbolically ever watchful and ever present. The straightforwardness of style and language, reminiscent of Heinrich Böll and Wolfgang Borchert, in his early short stories and novels reflects incidentally the effect of *Kahlschlad* as well as an acknowledgement of Hemingway's influence.

The post-World War II setting of Hamburg harbour and the clearing of wrecks in the waters there provides the background to the novel *Der Mann im Strom* (1957). Hinrichs is a good diver but fear of unemployment makes him falsify his real age on his papers. But there is no escape from the inevitability of events and he is eventually dismissed. Generational conflict—so redolent in Lenz's fiction—is present here in the figure of the younger diver Manfred who has been trained by Hinrichs but is then killed as a result of his own inexperience. Manfred's relationship with Hinrich's daughter Lena provides another important complicating factor in this tale of personal guilt. The end of a career and fear of failure preoccupy the thoughts of the lonely long-distance runner Bert Buchner in *Brot und Spiele* (1959) as he relives the course of his life in his last race, the European 10,000 metres. This is ultimately not a race against other competitors but against himself: his conjuring up of memories of earlier races, other experiences, his dealings with people, force him to recognize now some serious shortcomings in what had seemed to him and in fact had been a successful and popular athletics career. The theme of pursuit, be it by British soldiers in the war or subsequently competitors on the track, registers strongly in the novel. Buschner's fall before the end of the race symbolizes his position. The relationship of the protagonist and the narrator as a factor in the process of understanding and self-understanding is of importance in this novel as in other of Lenz's stories, for example in *Stadtgespräch* (*The Survivor*). The overcoming of the past

and the question of guilt—here both individual and collective —is the thematic kernel of *The Survivor*. The story is seen through the eyes of the narrator Tobias Lund who recalls the botched attack by Resistance fighters on a visiting German general to a town in (presumably) occupied Norway during World War II. In reprisal, 44 townsmen are taken hostage and eventually killed after Daniel, leader of the Resistance fighters, has failed to surrender. Should he have given himself up? That was the question asked at the time and continually posed after the war as different people relate different aspects of the same story. Daniel, the embodiment of the idea of opposition, serves as a symbol of the moral dilemma presented.

Lenz's overall concern with getting his fictional characters to try to make sense of a situation and gain a true perspective on life is arguably best manifested in *Deutschstunde* (*The German Lesson*). Ensconced in a corrective institution for juvenile offenders that is significantly situated on an island in the river Elbe and hence distanced from society, Siggi Jepsen faces the task of writing an essay on the joys of duty. As such, it becomes a German lesson that reveals his own life story against the backcloth of Germany in the last years of World War II. Once again, a remote setting is chosen—not the lightship on the water in *Das Feuerschiff* (*The Lightship*), nor the small town set in a Norwegian fjord in *The Survivor*, but the distant north German coast near the Danish border where, though not at the hub of events, the village inhabitants are inextricably caught up in them and duly suffer from the conflicting and burdensome claims of family ties, loyalties to the state, and individual responsibilities. This is as true for Siggi's father the community policeman, and Nansen the celebrated Expressionist painter, as it is for Siggi himself. The lesson of history so often is that no one learns from it, and here within the framework setting of the institution a decade later, towards the end of Siggi's stay there, Siggi pointedly remarks that both he and Himpel, the institution's director, will each think to have won. A serious question mark must remain over whether the young offender had properly prepared himself or been prepared for future life in society. The self-questioning and the revelations of individual and societal inadequacies continue in the search by three disparate individuals for a role model to complete an educational reader in *Das Vorbild* (*An Exemplary Life*), 1973. The lives of Pundt, Heller, and Rita Süssfeldt that reflect varying generational, social, and political interests in the urban setting of Hamburg are all beset with shortcomings and even their final chosen example is revealed to be less than an ideal example.

Like Günter Grass, Lenz has turned his eyes to his homeland in the East. The story collections *So zärtlich war Suleyken* (1955) and *So war es mit dem Zirkus* (1971) had pointed the way in a series of anecdotes on life in his native Masurda that constitute a sympathetic and humorous recollection of a golden past (to be counterbalanced incidentally by his north German tales from Bollerup, *Der Geist der Mirabelle* (1975), where the real, bustling modern world threatens to intrude). The novel *Heimatmuseum* (*The Heritage*) returns to Masuria in a far more serious vain: in a series of flashbacks told from his hospital bed where he is recovering from burns sustained in the conflagration of the regional museum that was in his care but to which he had set fire, Zygmunt Rogalla relives the original desire to recapture and preserve past cultural traditions (not least of all carpet weaving) in the face of change that threatens first from Nazi ideological intentions and then the war itself. Flight to the West makes possible the eventual rebuilding of the folk museum in Schleswig-Holstein, only for it to become endangered once again through misuse. Fire plays an important symbolic role here as in *The German Lesson*, but in *The Heritage* an acceptance of guilt and recognition of the need for adjustment to change seems ultimately to be better understood.

Lenz professes to write stories to try to understand the world. His multifarious fictional forays underscore his stated endeavour. His tales are tightly woven (though proliferation of them in the novels in the shape of sub-plots is sometimes negatively viewed by the critics). The element of violence is often a feature in his fiction, as is emotional and spiritual tension which can produce a dramatic effect particularly in the short works (the title piece of the collection *The Lightship* is a good example). Lenz displays a compassion for many of his characters while being equally capable of casting a sharply critical eye, and as with Böll, the moral factor features strongly in his writings. In this connection, the role of the observer-cum-narrator or interlocutor is important in as much as that character, in following the course of events befalling the protagonist, can pose questions, search for an understanding, provide another perspective—and hence serve us and for us, the readers.

In the 1960s Lenz wrote sporadically for the theatre and the radio with mixed success. *Zeit der Schuldlosen*, on the theme of guilt and serving as a basis for the novel *The Survivor*, is widely regarded as his best dramatic work. But fiction remains his forte. He was a member of Gruppe 47, later sided openly with the SPD, and worked in political journalism and broadcasting. The association of politics and writing has never been far removed from Lenz's thinking as is suggested in *Elfenbeinturm und Barrikade: Schriftsteller zwischen Literatur und Politik* (1976). The need to communicate, to tell stories as a means of understanding the world is what motivates Lenz. Of significance then is the novel *Der Verlust* (*The Breakdown*), 1981, where Lenz, on the heels of Wittgenstein and Handke, turns to the question of the loss of speech as the protagonist Ulrich Martens becomes more powerless to communicate. Today Lenz stands in the forefront of major German writers in the second half of the 20th century. His success and popularity may be gauged in part by the numerous translations of his works into foreign languages and the filming of several of his stories, to say nothing of the sheer frequency of editions of his books.

—Ian Hilton

THE GERMAN LESSON (Deutschstunde)
Novel by Siegfried Lenz, 1968.

An associate of the post-war writers league Gruppe 47, Lenz was known chiefly for his deft short stories before the novel *The German Lesson* was published in 1968. Its popular and critical success took even the author by surprise. In the next year it became Germany's bestseller, translations were hurriedly commissioned, and Lenz was ranked with Böll and Grass as an eminent German novelist. By 1975 a million copies had been printed in German. An indictment of fascism and its lingering effects, Lenz's tale takes the form of a Heimatroman (novel of provincial life) gone awry. He constructs the setting of the central action, the northwestern coastal village of Glüserup and its environs, in such a way as to endow the region with a mystical essence, a communal temperament, and an earthy hero characteristic of the genre, only to scuttle these delusions and to illustrate in personal terms—the lives of two friends, the painter Max Nansen and the policeman Jens Jepsen—the disastrous consequences for

Germany of a virulently particularist mentality. Their conflict is chronicled in retrospect by Jepsen's son Siggi, inmate at a Hamburg reformatory, with assistance from his psychologist. Siggi begins a three-year sentence for art theft in the autumn of 1952. The motive emerges as his reminiscences, grown of a composition on 'The Pleasures of Duty' assigned in a German lesson, recount the years 1943–46. Siggi's prison life and his attempt to come to grips with the assigned theme serve to frame his narrative of the war years and their aftermath. The focus shifts repeatedly from frame to reminiscence and back again.

Siggi is nine years old in April 1943 when the recollections commence, youngest son of Jens and his wife Gudrun, who have another son Klaas (Lenz's autobiographical counterpart) and a daughter Hilke. All three siblings serve as models for Max Ludwig Nansen (an amalgam of Beckmann, Kirchner, and Nolde), internationally recognized Expressionist and the man whom Siggi addresses as Uncle Nansen. It is he who through his seascapes, marsh scenes, and windmills has conveyed the regional essence in watercolour and oil to an admiring world. In 1934 his paintings were removed from German museums, and after working in isolation on his farm since then, he has just been forbidden by the Nazis to paint at all. The character who emerges as antagonist is Siggi's father, as it falls to him to convey and enforce the ban. Jens understands the proscription less than the painter, but with Max's refusal to comply the professional conflict becomes personal provocation. Jens feels that Max has taken advantage of their friendship by continuing to paint in secret when he knows that Jens is bound by duty to uphold the law. Gudrun objects to Max's painting on more purely ideological grounds. She believes that the vaguely Jewish art dealer Teo Busbeck, whom she considers 'a slightly superior sort of gypsy', has alienated Max from his own kind, an alienation reflected in 'the sort of people he paints—those green faces, those mongol eyes, those lumpy bodies'. Accordingly, she spurns Hilke's fiancé, an epileptic musician of Polish ancestry, and forbids Siggi from looking at mentally retarded children out of fear that the mere sight is enough to pervert a healthy outlook. Even as Jens's vigilance in monitoring the painter becomes an obsession, he himself becomes suspect to the Gestapo when Klaas deserts the army (as Lenz did the navy). It is Max who, at considerable personal risk, provides sanctuary. Far from being reconciled, Jens disowns his son and hounds Max more than ever. Hilke in turn secretly poses nude for Max, who portrays her as an exultant, dancing gypsy. She too is banished.

After the war the art world once again pays homage to Nansen. An English General who has come to induct Max into the Royal Academy reveals that he has on his walls in Nottingham several Nansens purchased in Switzerland. The very works the Nazis had labelled 'degenerate' and ordered Jens to confiscate had been sold as treasures abroad by those who purported to have destroyed them. Jens, however, persists in harassing the artist by burning a cache of sketches he discovers. Under the pressures of delusion and obsession the Jepsen family disintegrates: Klaas and Hilke flee to Hamburg where Klaas settles with Nansen's goddaughter and Hilke with her musician. Siggi is jailed for stealing Nansen canvases from public displays in order to prevent his father from somehow destroying them. His fellow inmates, he claims, are all incarcerated in lieu of someone more highly placed. Nansen, the prophet vindicated, resumes painting the province and people he once thought he knew.

Like Grass, Lenz became an enthusiastic supporter of the Social Democratic Party's reformist programme. At a time when critics and friends alike surveyed the unrest in both

German states and wondered if Germans were, in the words of one French observer, 'fit for democracy', Lenz provided an unsettling answer. That Siggi's autobiography takes shape in the reformatory is telling. The lessons Lenz teaches are that the obverse of excessive pride in heritage and ancestry has its reverse in xenophobia and racism, that unquestioning acceptance of convention and authority is criminal, that fanaticism breeds fanaticism, and that the sins of the fathers are visited upon the children—to be revisited then upon the fathers. The latter proved oracular indeed; the year of the novel's publication former student Andreas Baader and his confederates, sons and daughters of the repatriated bourgeoisie, launched the campaign of terror aimed at annihilating their parents' preserve.

—Albert E. Gurganus

LEOPARDI, Giacomo. Born in Recanati, Italy, 29 June 1798; became a Count on his father's death. Educated at home by tutors; studied privately until 1822. Lived in Rome, 1822–23; advisor, A.F. Stella, publishers, Milan, 1825–28; lived in Bologna, Florence, and Pisa, and in Naples from 1833. *Died 14 June 1837.*

PUBLICATIONS

Collections

Opere (includes 'La ginestra'), edited by Antonio Ranieri. 6 vols., 1845–49.
Opere inedite, edited by Giuseppe Cugnoni. 2 vols., 1878–80.
Tutte le opere, edited by Francesco Flora. 5 vols., 1937–49.
Tutte le opere, edited by Walter Binni and Enrico Ghidetti. 2 vols., 1969.
A Leopardi Reader, edited by Ottavio M. Casale (bilingual edition). 1981.

Verse

Canzoni. 1819.
Canzone ad Angelo Mai. 1820.
Versi. 1824.
Versi, edited by Pietro Brigherti. 1826.
I canti. 1831; revised edition, 1835; edited by I. Sanesi, 1943, by Francesco Flora, 1949, and by Mario Fubini, 1970; as *Canti*, translated by J.H. Whitfield, 1962.
I Paralipomeni della Batracomiomachia. 1842; as *The War of the Mice and the Crabs*, edited and translated by Ernesto G. Caserta, 1976.
Poems, translated by Frederick Townsend. 1887.
The Poems, translated by Francis H. Cliffe. 1893.
The Poems ('Canti'), translated by J.M. Morrison. 1900.
Poems, translated by Theodore Martin. 1904.
Poems, edited by Francis Brooks. 1909.
The Poems, edited and translated by Geoffrey L. Bickersteth (bilingual edition). 1923.
[Selections], translated by R.C. Trevelyan. 1941.
Poems, translated by John Heath-Stubbs. 1946.
Poems, translated by J.-P. Barricelli. 1963.

Canti, paralipomeni, poesie varie, traduzioni, poetiche, e versi puerili, edited by C. Muscetta and G. Savoca. 1968.
Canti, edited by G. Singh, various translators. 1990.

Other

Operette morali. 1827; revised edition, 1836; edited by Cesare Galimberti, 1978; as *Essays and Dialogues*, translated by Charles Edwardes, 1882; as *Essays, Dialogues and Thoughts*, translated by Patick Maxwell, 1893, also translated by James Thomson, 1905; as *Operette Morali, Essays and Dialogues*, edited and translated by Giovanni Cecchetti, 1982; as *Moral Tales*, translated by Patrick Creagh, 1983.
Pensieri di varia filosofia e di bella letteratura [*Lo Zibaldone*]. 7 vols., 1898–1900; edited by Anna Maria Moroni, 2 vols., 1972, and by Giuseppe Pacella, 3 vols., 1991.
Epistolario, edited by F. Moroncini and others. 7 vols., 1934–41.
Selected Prose and Poetry, edited and translated by Iris Origo and John Heath-Stubbs. 1966.
Poems and Prose, edited by Angel Flores (bilingual edition). 1966.
Entro dipinta gabbia, edited by Maria Corti. 1972.
Lettere, edited by Sergio and Raffaella Solmi. 1977.
Pensieri, edited and translated by W.S. Di Piero (bilingual edition). 1981.

Editor, *Rime*, by Petrarch. 1826.
Editor, *Crestomazia italiana: prosa, poesia.* 2 vols., 1827–28.

*

Bibliography: *Bibliografia leopardiana*, 3 vols., 1931–53; *Bibliografia analitica leopardiana*, 2 vols., 1963–73; *Bibliografia analitica leopardiana (1971–1980)* by Ermanno Carini, 1986; *Il labirinto leopardiano: bibliografia, 1976–1983, con una breve appendice, 1984–1985* by Emilio Giordano, 1986.

Critical Studies: *Leopardi: A Biography* by Iris Origo, 1935, revised edition, as *Leopardi: A Study in Solitude*, 1953; *Giacomo Leopardi* by J.H. Whitfield, 1954; *The Artifice of Reality: Poetic Style in Wordsworth, Foscolo, Keats, and Leopardi* by Karl Kroeber, 1964; *Leopardi and the Theory of Poetry*, 1964, and *Leopardi e i poeti inglese*, 1990, both by G. Singh; *Night and the Sublime in Giacomo Leopardi* by Nicolas James Parella, 1970; *Giacomo Leopardi: The Unheeded Voice* by Giovanni Carsaniga, 1977; *A Fragrance from the Desert: Poetry and Philosophy in Giacomo Leopardi* by Daniela Bini, 1983; *Giacomo Leopardi* by J.-P. Barricelli, 1986; *The Aspiration Toward a Lost Natural Harmony in the Work of Three Italian Writers: Leopardi, Verga and Moravia* by Foscarina Alexander, 1990.

* * *

No Italian poet—not even Dante—exemplifies with such vigour and conviction as Leopardi the validity of Coleridge's dictum that a great poet is also a profound philosopher. The union between poetry and first-hand thought—critical as well as philosophical, analytical as well as exploratory—gives Leopardi's style and language an unmistakably personal timbre which is at the same time a hallmark of universality. A contemporary of the English Romantic poets, Leopardi was not 'romantic' in the way they were; in fact, as his essay 'Discorso di un italiano intorno alla poesia romantica' [An Italian's Discourse on Romantic Poetry] shows, he adopted a polemical attitude to Romanticism, or to what he understood this to mean; and although a contemporary of Goethe and Hölderlin, he wasn't 'classical' in the way they were. Similarly, although he was (like Baudelaire) a precursor of poetic modernity, his art is as different in ethos and temperament from Baudelaire's as it is from Byron's, Keats's, or Shelley's. Moreover, although he was saturated—as few poets were—in classical literature and classical learning, his poetry is refreshingly free from the weight of such learning. Ill-health and growing blindness as well as frustration in love dogged him all his life, but he managed to rise above them, transforming his joy and pain, and the vicissitudes of his uneventful but emotionally rich life, into material for poetry and philosophic contemplation which is at once rapt and deliberate, cool and impassioned. Hence his poetry, even at its most lyrical, is at bottom philosophical, and his style and diction, even at their most charged, have a philosophic calm and detachment about them. In fact, Leopardi may be said to have created a new poetic genre in Italian—the philosophic lyric—through which he interfused, to borrow Eliot's words, the man who suffers and the mind which creates.

Leopardi's poetic genius finds its supreme manifestation in the *Canti*, just as his analytical and speculative powers do theirs in his *Operette morali* (*Essays and Dialogues*). *Epistolario*, on the other hand, is a richly human document of the psychological and autobiographical side of Leopardi's personality, and *Pensieri di varia filosofia e di bella letteratura* (or *Lo Zibaldone*) [Thoughts on Various Philosophies and Great Literature]—a monumental miscellany of notes, comments, and reflections—is an encyclopedic mine of literary, philological, and cultural erudition all rolled into one. Binding all these works together as well as underlying them is a singularly gifted mind—at once creative and critical, learned and inventive, cultivated and inquisitive—with an unsurpassed mastery over prose and verse.

The English critics, together with Sainte-Beuve, were the first to recognize and critically comment on these qualities of Leopardi's art and personality. 'A man of acknowledged genius and irreproachable character', wrote Henry Crabb Robinson after meeting Leopardi in Florence in 1830–31. 'There have been', observed H.G. Lewes, apropos of Leopardi's patriotic odes, 'no more piercing, manly, vigorous strains than those which vibrate in the organ-peal of patriotism sent forth by Leopardi'. And as a poet of despair, Lewes went on, 'we know of no equal to Leopardi . . . His grief is so real and so profound that it is inexhaustible in expression, to say nothing of the beauty in which he embalms it'. According to Gladstone, too, Leopardi applies to his work, 'with a power rarely equalled, all the resources of thought and passion, all that his introspective habit had taught him . . . and he unites to a very peculiar grace a masculine energy and even majesty of expression which is not surpassed . . . in the whole range of poetry'. And as far as Leopardi's mastery over form and style is concerned, here is Matthew Arnold's testimony: Leopardi 'has the very qualities which we have found wanting in Byron; he has the sense for form and style, the passion for just expression, the sure and firm touch of the true artist . . . he has a far wider culture than Wordsworth, more mental lucidity, more freedom from illusions as to the real character of the established fact and of reigning conventions; above all, this Italian, with his pure and sure touch, with his fineness of perception, is far more of the artist [than Wordsworth]'. But besides being that of a stylist and an artist of such calibre, Leopardi's poetry has something perpetually

modern about it, as has his theory of poetry. Leopardi jotted down his reflections on and analysed the nature of poetry, style, poetic inspiration, the language of poetry—in fact no poet in the history of Italian literature has occupied himself with the theory of poetry as much as Leopardi, and, indeed, as Maurice Bowra remarks, 'few men have given so much hard thought to the matter'—so that he may be regarded justly as a worthy peer of Goethe, Wordsworth, and Coleridge. Moreover, certain aspects of his poetics—and poetry—are startlingly modern and anticipate the development of 20th-century poetry.

For although Leopardi's poetry deals with themes that are conventional—love, death, youth, nature, memory, the transience of life, etc.—what comes out of his treatment of such themes is of the very essence of modernity: modernity of thought as well as of spirit. And if his poetry has a philosophic basis, it is not because it expounds a particular philosophy, or is inspired by or dependent on a particular philosophic system as such. It is because it is firmly rooted in his perception of the truth about life as he saw it and of the illusions one needed in order to be able to bear it, since 'human kind cannot bear very much reality'.

Thus Leopardi's pessimism, in the *Canti* no less than in *Operette morali*, is not so much a creed based on emotional or imaginative grounds as an outcome of closely argued premises, conclusions and convictions regarding the nature of life and human destiny, which the poet-philosopher has the courage to look unflinchingly in the face. At the same time he embraces what his own experience of life and his knowledge as well as observation of the world and of man in society have taught him. From his very early life Leopardi was filled with what he himself calls 'the infinite desire to know precisely', that never abandoned him. His explorations of reality were conveyed in accents of matchless lyricism with which he covered 'the nudity of things'. That is why his art was admired not only by a modern poet like Pound—'Leopardi splendid, and the only author since Dante who need trouble you', Pound wrote to Iris Berry—but also by a modern philosopher like Bertrand Russell. In a letter to me Russell said that he found Leopardi's poetry and philosophy 'the most beautiful expression of what should be the creed of a scientist', and described 'La ginestra' ('The Broom') as expressing 'more effectively than any other poem known to me my views about the universe and the human passions'.

—G. Singh

THE BROOM (La ginestra)
Poem by Giacomo Leopardi, 1845 (written 1836).

Although lacking the melodiousness of many of his shorter lyrics 'The Broom, or, The Flower of the Desert', a long poem of 317 lines written at the end of his life, stands as a valid example of fluent philosophical reasoning in which Leopardi embraces a grand overview of history and all life, as he argues the case for a moral way of living through humility, perseverance, and unselfconscious honesty at the level of individual consciousness. Published only posthumously in the 1845 edition of his work prepared by his close friend Antonio Ranieri, the poem's placement at the end of the collection was apparently a recognition of its epithetic qualities. It deals with themes, recurrent throughout Leopardi's poetry, such as death, the insignificance of humanity, the power of Nature, history, and the role of the poet in society.

The poem's setting is the volcano of Mount Vesuvius which

is seen as symbolizing Nature in all its impassively destructive fury. From the outset, the poet also focuses on his sighting of the scented flower on the volcano's desolate slopes; a flower which, in its turn, symbolizes life in the midst of death. As with many external objects and human figures in Leopardi's poetry, the broom flower transmutes into a more private, emotive symbol for the poet, assuming a consoling significance for a sombre, dejected mind:

> I meet you here once more, O you the lover
> Of all sad places and deserted worlds,
> The constant comrade of afflicted fortune.
>   (translated by John Heath-Stubbs)

By the end of the poem the plant is emblematized, becoming more than a mere scent or vision, provoking more than a sentimental response as it comes to evoke the most perfect existential attitude, as the poet sees it; a dignified resignation in the face of life's constant adversity (seen in the impending menace of the live volcano that will eventually destroy the broom's fragile beauty):

> And you, O gentle broom,
> Who with your fragrant thickets
> Make beautiful this spoiled and wasted land,
> You, too, must shortly fall beneath the cruel
> Force of the subterranean fire, returning
> To this, its wonted place,
> Which soon shall stretch its greedy fringe above
> Your tender shrubs. You then
> Will bend your harmless head, not obstinate
> Beneath the rod of fate . . .
>   (translated by John Heath-Stubbs)

For Leopardi, a passionately idealistic poet with an equally pessimistic outlook, this singular affirmation of enduring life —the image of the broom—represented a significant progress in the development of his philosophy. In other poems, Leopardi often swung between extremes, exalting life's virtuous offerings like youth, love, and peace but then denouncing its deceptions in which the promise of youth could be cut down by an early death, or love could be shown as an illusion through rejection. In 'The Broom', a process of reasoning leads the poet to formulate a balanced attitude to survive the extremes. It is a mature conclusion that, not surprisingly, made the broom an enduring symbol of Leopardi's own dedication to the poetical task.

This maturity extends to Leopardi's view of humanity which was promulgated in opposition to the politics and religious ideologies of his time. His view of a materialistic universe was obviously a rejection of Restoration values in which a Catholic perspective dominated, with its emphasis on the transcendental significance of life. But his was also, and even more so, a criticism of the liberal-moderate position which denied the importance of transcendent value systems such as those proposed by conventional religion, but still advanced its own humanistic credo which emphasized the exclusiveness of man. Leopardi saw this as an arrogant assertion whose irrational fervour misrepresented the truth of things. The sarcasm with which he decried liberalism's blind belief in the 'magnificent/Progressive destiny of Humankind' (John Heath-Stubbs), despite the evidence of the relentless destruction of civilizations through history (and Leopardi offers the example of Pompeii in the poem), is a measure of how strong was Leopardi's sense of disassociation from his time.

The Leopardian poet stands alone with his sense of 'deep contempt' while accepting the 'oblivion' his age may sentence him too for his non-conformity. In his own lifetime Leopardi

was, however, recognized as one of the great literary figures of his age. In this attitude we may see both Leopardi's passion and, ironically, a certain ingenuous arrogance of his own. Still, in confirmation of his relevance, of his modernism, Leopardi's view of humanity's place in the scheme of things accords closely with our own which is induced by a new, more moral and expansive scientific culture than the mechanistic and reductionist one that existed in the 19th century; one which affirms now not man's centrality but humankind's precious smallness in the mystery which is Space.

Leopardi illustrates his position perhaps most graphically through the image of the apple casually falling on the ants' carefully constructed nest, thereby destroying it. Human beings, Leopardi says, are like the ants, Nature showing 'no more care/Or value for man's need/Than for the ants'.

In the final analysis, Leopardi indirectly and metaphorically suggests a humble role for the poet as well, which is consistent with his humbling definition of humanity. It is encapsulated in one of his descriptions of the broom flower:

> . . . O courteous flower,
> As if in pity of the doom of others,
> And cast a pleasant fragrance to the skies,
> Making the desert glad.

Poetry such as Leopardi's, struggling its way to a sympathetic but still honest assessment of life, could be seen to parallel in its significance for the reader the assuaging effects of the scent and vision of the broom seen on the dark, barren slopes of a volcano by the observer. One of Leopardi's merits was an ability to see reason and meaning in his own nihilism, and so to survive it and triumph over it.

—Walter Musolino

THE INFINITE (L'infinito)
Poem by Giacomo Leopardi, 1831 (written 1819).

'The Infinite' is part of the collection of poems, *I canti*, lyric poetry characterized by a type of language that aims at communicating vague and indefinite sensations through a precise choice of archaic words (*parole peregrine*), and words eliciting feelings of vastness, multitude, space, time, infinity. Leopardi's *Canti* are divided into two chronologically distinct groups: the *Piccoli Idilli* (1819–21) and the *Grandi Idilli* (1828–30); these *idilli* ('idyll' is a Greek word meaning 'small picture', 'little vision') were defined by Leopardi as 'situazioni, affezioni, avventure storiche dell'animo' [situations, emotional states, intimate experiences of the soul] of which 'The Infinite', with its immediacy and compactness, is the most outstanding example. The *idillio*, in its poetic form, conveys also philosophical insights and meditative moments in the poet's life; 'The Infinite' bears testimony to the poet's yearning for the infinite and liberation, his passionate attempt to move from the geographical limitations of a small country town (Recanati)—boxed in between the Apennines and the Adriatic sea—to endless vistas of time, space, and eternity. What is limited and real, he felt, was furthest from the infinite; there are no present joys, only joys remembered, desired, or dreamt. Man's imagination, indeed, is the prime source of human happiness creating for itself the infinity not available in the 'real' world. We cannot experience the infinite but we know that its opposite is the definite, the delimited, the *hic et nunc*. This explains Leopardi's fondness for memories of childhood, a time in which our impressions and ideas are vague, hazy, undefined. In his voluminous work, *Lo Zibaldone*, Leopardi makes the following remarks regarding the craving for the infinite and its relation to memories of one's childhood:

> If, as a child, a view, a landscape, picture, sound, tale, description, fable, poetic image, or dream please or delight us, that pleasure and delight is always vague and indefinite; the idea that it awakens in us is always undefined and unbounded; every comfort, pleasure, expectation, plan, illusion (and almost every idea) at that age is always directed towards infinity . . .
>
> (translated by Iris Origo and John Heath-Stubbs)

> This lonely knoll was ever dear to me
> and this hedgerow that hides from view
> so large a part of the remote horizon.
> But as I sit and gaze my thought conceives
> interminable spaces lying beyond
> and supernatural silences
> and profoundest calm, until my heart
> almost becomes dismayed. And as I hear
> the wind come rustling through these leaves,
> I find myself comparing to this voice
> that infinite silence: and I recall eternity
> and all the ages that are dead
> and the living present and its sounds. And so
> in this immensity my thought is drowned:
> and in this sea is foundering sweet to me.
>
> (translated by J.-P. Barricelli)

The poet's vision is impeded by the hedge, thus he cannot appreciate the hidden panorama; but this does not frustrate the poet since he has a chance to turn his vision inwards and transcend reality: the poet can now contemplate with his mind a limitless expanse, an endless succession of spaces that he conceives in the plural—*interminati spazi* (interminable spaces). The work of the imagination, triggered by finite means (the blocked view), is explained by Leopardi himself in *Lo Zibaldone*:

> For then it is our imagination that is at work instead of our sight, and the fantastic takes the place of the real. The soul imagines what it cannot see, what is hidden by that tree, that bush, that tower, and goes off wandering in an imaginary space . . . Thence the pleasure that I felt as a boy, and sometimes do even now, in seeing the sky through a window or a door or between two houses.
>
> (translated by Origo and Heath-Stubbs)

The concept of infinity is present at the beginning of the poem ('always') and is represented at the end by the image of the sea: this is one of the many examples in which language and imagery combine to communicate the underlying thematic core of the poem. The experience of spatial disorientation (ll.7–8) when the poet's heart hovers on the brink of fear—reminiscent of Pascal's *Pensée* 206—gives way to a perception of time marked by the passing of the seasons; the rustling of the leaves and the sound of the wind act as a catalytic device which jolts the poet back to reality. It is especially in this passage of the poem that the use of the polysyndeton is most effective since it conveys, by stringing together a series of events, the juxtaposition of time and space, of the finite with the infinite. The judicious usage of a series of enjambments (*interminati/spazi*; *sovrumani/silenzi*, supernatural silences), of the diaeresis (*quiete*, profoundest calm,), of adjectives (*caro*, dear and *dolce*, sweet) coupled with the different tenses of the auxiliary 'to be' when describing the poet's attitude to nature, highlights his mastery and control of language.

The conclusion—the sensation of sweetness when foundering in the sea—may appear to be pessimistic and nihilistic but only if we attribute too much philosophical weight to the poet's words which, instead, should be interpreted for what they are: an instrument through which he can release his inner self. Leopardi was trying to break away physically from his home town and family. In the summer of 1819 he attempted to obtain a passport and planned to escape, and so it is all more poignant if we contextualize the ending of 'The Infinite' in the poet's own life. Independent of such biographical considerations as these, this idyll, as a poetic meditation, forms the basis for future philosophical speculations to appear subsequently in his prose works.

—Bruno Ferraro

TO HIMSELF (A se stesso)
Poem by Giacomo Leopardi, 1835 (written 1833).

'To Himself' is undoubtedly one of Leopardi's most intensely mournful poems and probably also his most bitterly judgemental and dismissive. It is nevertheless a poem of great passion. Dealing with the theme of love scorned or betrayed, its cause is attributed to the end of the poet's relationship with a Florentine lady, Fanny Targioni-Tozzetti, who had befriended him during the last of his stays in Florence in 1830. It was a relationship apparently in which Leopardi blindly and unrealistically pursued his desire for romance with a woman who was interested in him as a quaint, literary celebrity rather than as a man. Critical consensus gives the poem's year of composition as 1833 and its date of publication as 1835, thus placing it among the poems composed in the last four years of Leopardi's short life.

Although Leopardi the poet was characterized by his generally pessimistic outlook, his darkness of spirit in this poem has nothing to do with philosophy, notwithstanding references to the world, life, and destiny. As the title declares, the poem is obsessively introverted. Its structure of 16 compact lines, mostly composed of short, epigrammatically terse sentences, channels the emotional, at times vitriolic, tone in such a way as to create a narrowness of focus which thematically centres on a dialogue between the poet and his heart, that is, his feelings.

Right from the poem's opening, Leopardi's determination to protect himself against the need for love, and so against the possibilities of future disillusionment, is expressed through the use of verbs in the imperative or quasi-imperative mode (the first verb is a future in the original), as he invokes variously stillness, rest, and quiet for his damaged, ingenuous heart: 'Now be forever still/Weary my heart', 'Rest still forever', 'Lie quiet now. Despair/for the last time'. The last imperative is not at all cajoling though, being directed towards nature—a word summarizing for Leopardi the state of things—as the poet delivers a sarcastic denunciation of life and the illusions it provides like love. This is interesting because in so poignantly and powerfully personal a poem, the cause of the poet's pain is not seen in private, that is in anecdotal or biographical terms (no woman is identified or accused), but is interpreted from an ontological viewpoint as the poet relates his condition to the general fate of all human beings. In so doing, of course, he proves its inescapability and, by implication, his own victimization:

> And now you may despise
> Yourself, nature, the brute

Power which, hidden, ordains the common doom,
And all the immeasurable emptiness of things.
                              (translated by John Heath-Stubbs)

This tendency towards philosophical generalization is typically Leopardian: and here, as in many of his poems, Leopardi again instinctively assumes the role of Everyman. For some famous critics such as Benedetto Croce and Luigi Russo neither the emotion nor the short, philosophical aphorisms succeed in sustaining the poem's lack of 'poetic vision'. Leaving aside the ideological or aesthetic prejudices of any critic and the subjectivity implied finally in any assessment of what constitutes 'poetry', most others have seen the poem's success lying in its perfect fusion of sentiment and rhetoric. Still others have pointed out how the poem approximates a madrigal, a judgement which captures perfectly the poem's contrapuntal movements of thought as it darts between considerations on the strengths and weaknesses of desire, on the futility of optimism but the drive to hope, on the unfeelingness of the world towards the individual but also on that individual's battling heroics to survive indifference, albeit with anger and reprobation.

It can also be argued in support of the poem that the sparseness of imagery is consistent with the desolate clarity of the theme. Perhaps a more plausible criticism might be that the poem inevitably leads critics beyond it to explain its circumstances and its meaning fully. To understand the poem to be about love lost is to know the crucial meaning of love for Leopardi and how consistently he pursues it through his other poetry. Taken self-referentially, however, there is no need to see love as *the* issue in the poem but, at best, as one of several possible issues that could inspire such despair in a person, such loss of faith in the emotions. The poet who seems arbitrarily to reduce life to the twin negatives of 'boredom and bitterness', who condemns the world as 'dirt', is a man trying desperately to protect himself. In so far as anyone can be love-stricken and love traditionally strikes through the heart, then we must assert that 'To Himself', is a poem about a love-stricken heart, even at the moment that it claims its independence from such enslaving feelings.

This, however, is the paradox of Leopardi's poem. In it, the poet feels as intensely as he ever has, in some ways even more so. The vengeful and distressed lament of 'To Himself' transcends the strictures of its own would-be impositions for if everything is immeasurably empty, the human cry is still there to fill the vacuum with its own life.

—Walter Musolino

LERMONTOV, Mikhail (Iur'evich). Born in Moscow, Russia, 2/3 October 1814. Educated at School for the Nobility, Moscow, 1828–30; University of Moscow, 1830–32; Junker School, St Petersburg, 1832–34: Cavalry cornet in Regiment of Life Guards Hussars; exiled to the Caucasus for poems on Pushkin's death, 1835–38; because of a duel, again exiled, to Tenginskii Infantry Regiment on Black Sea, 1840–41. *Died (in duel) 15 July 1841.*

PUBLICATIONS

Collections

Sochineniia [Works]. 6 vols., 1954–57.
Izbrannye sochineniia [Selected Works]. 4 vols., 1958–59.

Sobranie sochinenii [Collected Works], edited by V. Arkhipov. 4 vols., 1969.
Sochineniia [Works], edited by I.M. Andronikov. 2 vols., 1970.
Sobranie sochinenii [Collected Works], edited by I.M. Andronikov. 4 vols., 1975.
Selected Works, translated by Avril Pyman, Irina Zheleznova, and Martin Parker. 1976.
Sobranie sochinenii [Collected Works], edited by V.A. Manuilov. 4 vols., 1979.
Izbrannye sochineniia [Selected Works], edited by V. Vatsuro. 1983.
Sobranie sochinenii [Collected Works], edited by Iu. Bondarev. 4 vols., 1985.
Izbrannye sochineniia [Selected Works], edited by G.I. Belen'kii. 1987.
Sochineniia [Works], edited by G.A. Andzhaparidze. 2 vols., 1988.
Sobranie sochinenii [Collected Works], edited by G.P. Makogonenko. 4 vols., 1989.
Polnoe sobranie stikhotvorenii [Complete Collected Poetry], edited by Iu. A. Andreev. 2 vols., 1989.

Fiction

Geroi nashego vremeni. 1840; translated as *Sketches of Russian Life in the Caucasus*, 1853; as *The Hero of Our Days*, translated by T. Pulsky, 1854; as *The Heart of a Russian*, translated by J. Wisdom and M. Murray, 1912; as *A Hero of Nowadays*, translated by John Swinnerton Phillimore, 1920; as *A Hero of Our Time*, translated by Reginald Merton, 1928, also translated by Vladimir and Dmitri Nabokov, 1958; Philip Longworth, 1962; Paul Foote, 1966; as *A Hero of Our Own Times*, translated by Eden and Cedar Paul, 1940.
Vadim (unfinished), in *Sochineniia*, 6. 1957; edited and translated by Helen Goscilo, 1984.

Play

Maskarad [Masquerade]. 1836.

Verse

Pesnia pro tsaria Ivana Vasil'evicha. 1837; as *A Song about Tsar Ivan Vasilyevich*, translated by John Cournos, 1929.
Mtsyri. 1840; as *The Circassian Boy*, translated by S. Conant, 1875.
Demon. 1842; as *The Demon*, translated by A. Stephens, 1875; also translated by F. Storr, 1894; E. Richter, 1910; R. Burness, 1918; G. Shelley, 1930.
Selected Poetry. 1965.
Major Poetical Works, edited and translated by Anatoly Liberman. 1983.
Poemy i povesti v stikhakh [Narrative Verse and Stories in Verse]. 1984.
Narrative Poems by Pushkin and Lermontov, translated by Charles Johnston. 1983.
Poemy i stikhotvoreniia [Narrative Verse and Poetry]. 1985.
Poemy [Narrative Verse]. 1990.

Other

Proza [Prose]. 1941.
Proizvedeniia na kavkazskie temy [Works on the Caucasian Theme]. 1968.
Proza. Poemy. Lirika [Prose. Narrative Verse. Lyrics]. 1982.

M.Iu. Lermontov v russkoi kritike [M.Iu. Lermontov in Russian Criticism]. 1985.
M.Iu. Lermontov v vospominaniiakh sovremennikov [M.Iu. Lermontov in the Reminiscences of Contemporaries]. 1989.
Lermontov (al'bom) [Lermontov (album)]. 1991.

*

Critical Studies: *Lermontov* by Janko Lavrin, 1959; *Lermontov* by John Mersereau, Jr, 1962; *Lermontov: Tragedy in the Caucasus* by Laurence Kelly, 1977; *An Essay on Lermontov's 'A Hero of Our Times'* by C.J.G. Turner, 1978; *Lermontov: A Study in Literary-Historical Evaluation* by B.M. Eikhenbaum, translated by Ray Parrott and Harry Weber, 1981; *Lermontov* by John Garrard, 1982; *A Wicked Irony: The Rhetoric of a Hero of Our Time* by Andrew Barratt and A.D.P. Briggs, 1989; *The Fey Hussar* by Jessie Davies, 1989.

* * *

Mikhail Lermontov is often thought of as Pushkin's successor in the role of Russian national poet. Lermontov was profoundly influenced by Pushkin, but an equally potent and more visible influence was that of Byron. Whereas Pushkin's ingrained classical instincts allowed him to assimilate classical influences (often ironically) without wholly succumbing to Romantic style, Lermontov must be regarded as a full-blooded representative of the Romantic movement.

During his short life Lermontov attempted most literary genres but was chiefly a lyric and narrative poet. His drama is less memorable but his single prose work of note, *Geroi nashego vremeni* (*A Hero of Our Time*), is one of the most original and influential of Russian novels.

Lermontov's lyrics are often highly subjective and reflect the isolation of the post-Decembrist poet and the search for inner consolation which eluded Lermontov more than his contemporary, Tiutchev. Lermontov also uses lyric poetry as a means of expressing his metaphysic, often symbolically. Inanimate objects in juxtaposition (a rock and a cloud; a dead leaf floating in a river) or in isolation (a mountain peak; a solitary tree) are used in an almost Ovidian way to convey the tragic helplessness of particular aspects of the human condition. Ineluctable fate is a brooding presence throughout Lermontov's work: in the short poem 'Angel' (1831), the human soul is conceived as pre-existing physical birth, birth itself being the forcible removal of the soul from a state of heavenly bliss to bodily imprisonment and exile among the world's miseries.

Fate, however, is not to be accepted blindly. Lermontov's most memorable creations are those in which Sisyphus-like characters struggle heroically against insuperable forces. Early in his literary career Lermontov became fascinated by the demonic personality, which, though shunned by God, is nevertheless capable of love and passion. As well as several lyrics on this theme, Lermontov produced, in successive drafts, a narrative poem called *The Demon* in which a demon, expelled from heaven, seeks redemption through the love of a Georgian girl but is eventually thwarted by God. Undemonic, but equally heroic, the hero of *Mtsyri* (*The Circassian Boy*) is a young postulant of Circassian origin. He is brought up in a Georgian monastery, and his one wish is to return to his home in the Caucasus but, after an ill-fated attempt to escape, he is brought back to the monastery and dies.

A Caucasian setting and demonic exertion of the will against fate also dominate *A Hero of Our Time*. This work, generally thought to be Lermontov's greatest, is sometimes said by critics to show that, by the end of his life, Lermontov was forsaking Romanticism in favour of realism. Certainly Lermontov takes great pains to motivate his novel, to suggest that it has as its initial impulse a documentary rather than a fictional intention. But the hero himself is still an embittered representative of the Byronic tradition and, though at times self-deprecating, is never a vehicle for parodying or diminishing that tradition. The most remarkable feature of *A Hero of Our Time* is its architecture: five structurally autonomous but thematically intermeshed first-person narratives create the illusion of a living, multi-dimensional hero who makes himself known to the reader by the gradual accumulation of psychological detail rather than by the consecutive unfolding of plot. Lermontov's prose style in the novel, remarkably simple but capable of sustaining impressive passages of natural description, influenced later writers, particularly short-story writers such as Chekhov. The character of Pechorin, the hero, has come to epitomize 'the superfluous man', the disillusioned internal exile who figures so largely in the 19th-century Russian novel.

—Robert Reid

A HERO OF OUR TIME (Geroi nashego vremeni)
Novel by Mikhail Lermontov, 1840.

Lermontov's novel *A Hero of Our Time*, which was completed in the year of his death, is his most famous work and the culmination, in a number of ways, of all his writing.

In *A Hero of Our Time* Lermontov presents the most complex treatment of his dominant and recurrent preoccupation, the figure of the Romantic hero, a subject which had received its apotheosis in verse in the long poems *The Circassian Boy* and *The Demon*. There are also echoes of many other motifs from his shorter lyric verse: for example, the extreme ironic world-weariness of 'I skuchno i grustno' ('Oh, Boredom and Sadness'), or the bitter condemnation of the poet's generation in the civic poem 'Duma' ('Meditation') with its opening line: 'With sadness do I look upon our generation'. On the other hand, in the novel Lermontov at last makes a successful move into prose, in tune with the direction in which the mainstream of Russian literature was moving at the time. A desire to diversify from poetry on Lermontov's part is already evident in the early 1830s, but his first prose work *Vadim* (written c.1833–34) suffers from a Romantic identification of author and hero. In his next attempt, the society tale 'Kniaginya Ligovskaia' [Princess Ligovskaia] (c.1836–37), which features a hero called Pechorin, Lermontov is again confronted with the problem of narrative perspective. Yet again this is not resolved and the work is unfinished, but it provides a germ for 'Princess Mary', the society tale in diary form which is the longest part of *A Hero of Our Time*.

A Hero of Our Time has a highly distinctive composition. It is made up of five stories told by three different people, with two forewords. Collections of stories, usually brought together by a fictitious editor as in Pushkin's *The Tales of Belkin* (*Povesti pokoinogo I.P. Belkina*), play a prominent role in the development of Russian prose in the 1830s, but Lermontov develops this into something different by making the hero of all the stories the same. Until relatively recently the main focus in approaches to *A Hero of Our Time* has been the portrayal of Pechorin, the hero. The novel has been read as a character portrait of the so-called 'superfluous man', that type of alienated, initially Romantic, hero found in a series of Russian works from Pushkin's *Eugene Onegin* onwards; Lermontov's novel has been seen as highly significant in the development of the psychological novel and the transition to realism. But any reading of *A Hero of Our Time* has to take into account the manner of narration. In fact this is so central that our perception of character can only arise out of, or through, a consideration of narration and narrative structure, which can easily come to occupy the foreground in itself.

The introductory foreword, which was added by Lermontov to the second edition (1841), is the only place we hear the author's unmediated, though still ironic, voice. In the main body of the text three narrators take over. The first is an anonymous hack travel writer: he is the publisher of the whole book, and the author of the first two stories 'Bela' and 'Maxim Maximych' and of a foreword to Pechorin's 'Journal'. The second is Maxim Maximych, a staff captain, whose oral narration concerning Pechorin and Bela is embedded in the travel writer's own text in 'Bela' in a way that produces the opposite of a 'seamless' composition: instead the difference and alternation of voices and viewpoints is emphasized. Narrative devices such as retardation are very much to the fore as the contrasting narrators exploit their position as story-tellers. In addition, however, the voices may be contaminated, since the travel writer has clearly edited Maxim's story: Pechorin's confession, for example, presents a Romantic stereotype in a style that cannot be that of the uneducated military man.

Then, in the second story 'Maxim Maximych', a chance meeting allows the travel writer to give a description of Pechorin's appearance, the objective value of which he himself undermines by concluding that 'maybe his appearance would have created a completely different impression on someone else'. The third narrator is Pechorin himself, whose writings comprise 'Taman', a parodied Romantic adventure story, 'Princess Mary', a diary account with the makings of a society tale, and finally 'The Fatalist', a sketch with leanings towards the philosophical tale. Whereas the travel writer commends Pechorin to us for his sincerity, the novel invites an ironic deconstruction of his narration. In 'Princess Mary' Pechorin writes and acts as though he were an omniscient narrator, but this posture breaks down into limited comprehension and moral blindness. At the same time his presentation of himself and other characters can become a case study for psychoanalysis in Jungian terms, rather than an objective portrait of the world (see Andrew Barratt and A.D.P. Briggs, *A Wicked Irony: The Rhetoric of 'A Hero of Our Times'*, 1989).

Thus the novel's composition brings us gradually closer to the central hero, but not in a straightforward way. The inadequacies of the narrators, the gaps and discontinuities, and the incompleteness of the picture (it is hard to speak of any development of character) work strongly against any authoritative interpretation of Pechorin. This is reinforced by the circularity of the structure—in chronological terms the final story precedes the first—and by the recurrent motif of relativity and uncertainty. 'The Fatalist' concludes with an assertion of doubt as the way forward and the co-existence, yet again, of at least two points of view. The circularity is complete when the final sentence takes us back to the narrative situation at the beginning of 'Bela', as Pechorin, like the travel writer earlier, tries to get some discussion going with Maxim Maximych.

—Robin Aizlewood

LESAGE, Alain-René. Born in Sarzeau, Brittany, France, 8 May (13 December in some sources) 1668. Educated by Jesuits in Vannes, Brittany; studied law in Paris. Married Marie-Élizabeth Huyard in 1694; three sons, including the actor Montménil, and one daughter. Possibly a lawyer in Paris, 1690s; wrote original plays and adaptations/translations from the Spanish for the Comédie-Française, Paris, 1700–09; broke with the Comédie-Française, and subsequently wrote farces, comic operas, *vaudevilles*, and other pieces for the Paris fairs of St Germain and St Laurent, often in collaboration with Louis Fuzelier, d'Orneval, and others; lived with one son, the Abbé de Lyonne, in Boulogne, from 1743. *Died 7 November 1747.*

PUBLICATIONS

Collections

Le Théâtre de la foire; ou, L'Opéra-comique (10 vols.: two of them numbered as 9). 1721–37.
Oeuvres choisies de Lesage, edited by C.J. Mayer. 16 vols., 1810.
Oeuvres complètes. 12 vols., 1821.
Novels. 4 vols., 1821.
Oeuvres de Le Sage. 1877.
Théâtre. 1911.
Oeuvres complètes. 1935—.
Théâtre, edited by Maurice Bardon. 1948.
Il Teatro della foire. 1965.

Plays (adaptations and plays for the legitimate stage)

Le Traître puni, from a play by Rojas Zorilla. In *Théâtre espagnol*, 1700.
Don Félix de Mendoce, from a play by Lope de Vega. In *Théâtre espagnol*, 1700.
Le Point d'honneur, from a play by Rojas Zorilla (produced 1702). 1739.
Don César Ursin, from a play by Calderón (produced 1707). 1739.
Crispin, rival de son maître (produced 1707). 1707; revised version, in *Recueil des pièces mises au Théâtre Français*, 1738; edited by Andrew Clark, 1910, Marcello Spaziani, 1956, and by T.E. Lawrenson, 1961; as *Neck or Nothing*, translated by D. Garrick, 1766; as *Crispin, Rival of His Master*, translated by Barrett H. Clark, 1915; as *The Rival of His Master*, translated by W.S. Merwin, in *Tulane Drama Review*, 6(4), 1962.
Turcaret (produced 1709). 1709; revised version, in *Recueil des pièces mises au Théâtre Français*, 1738; edited by A. Hamilton Thompson, 1918, T.E. Lawrenson, 1969, B. Blanc, 1970, and by E. Lavielle, 1964; translated by John Norman, 1989.
La Tontine (produced 1732). In *Recueil des pièces mises au Théâtre Français*, 1738.
Les Amants jaloux (produced 1735). 1736.
Recueil des pièces mises au Théâtre Français (includes final versions of *Turcaret*; *Crispin, rival de son maître*; *La Tontine*). 1738.

Pièces forains produced at Fair of St Germain; the dates given are those of first production

Le Retour d'Arlequin à la foire, 1712; *Arlequin Baron Allemand*, 1712; *Arlequin roi de Sérendib*, 1713; *Arlequin colonel*, 1714; *La Ceinture de Vénus*, 1715; *Parodie de*

l'opéra de Télémaque, 1715; *Arlequin gentilhomme malgré lui*, with d'Orneval, 1716; *Le Temple d'ennui*, with Louis Fuzelier, 1716; *Le Tableau du mariage*, with Louis Fuzelier, 1716; *L'École des amants*, with Louis Fuzelier, 1716; *L'Ombre de la foire*, with d'Orneval, 1720; *L'Île du Gougou*, with d'Orneval, 1720; *Arlequin roi des ogres; ou, Les Bottes de sept lieues*, with d'Orneval and Fuzelier, 1720; *La Queue de vérité*, with d'Orneval and Fuzelier, 1720; *Magotin*, with d'Orneval, 1721; *Prologue*, with d'Orneval and Fuzelier, 1721; *Arlequin Endymion*, with d'Orneval, 1721; *La Forêt de Dodôre*, with d'Orneval, 1721; *L'Ombre du cocher poète*, with d'Orneval and Fuzelier. 1722; *L Rémouleur d'amour*, with d'Orneval and Fuzelier, 1722; *Pierrot Romulus; ou, Le Ravisseur poli*, with d'Orneval and Fuzelier. 1722; *Arlequin barbet, pagode et médicin*, with d'Orneval, 1723; *Les Trois Commères*, with d'Orneval, 1723; *Les Couplets en procès*, with d'Orneval, 1729; *La Reine du Barostan*, with d'Orneval, 1729; *L'Opéra-comique assiégé*, with d'Orneval, 1730; *Pièces du Théâtre de la Foire* (includes previously uncollected plays), 1731.

Pièces forains produced at the Fair of St Laurent; the dates given are those of first production

Les Petits-maîtres, 1712; *Arlequin et Mezzetin morts par amour*, 1712; *Arlequin Thétis*, 1713; *Arlequin invisible*, 1713; *La Foire de Guibray*, 1714; *Arlequin Mahomet*, 1714; *Le Tombeau de Nostradamus*, 1714; *Le Temple du destin*, 1715; *Les Eaux de Merlin*, 1715; *Colombine Arlequin; ou, Arlequin Colombine*, 1715; *Arlequin Hulla; ou, La Femme répudiée*, with d'Orneval, 1716; *La Princesse de Charizme*, 1718; *La Querelle des théâtres*, with Joseph de Lafont, 1718; *Le Monde renversé*, with d'Orneval, 1718; *Les Amours de Nanterre*, with d'Orneval and Jacques Autreau, 1718; *Les Funérailles de la foire*, with d'Orneval and Fuzelier, 1718; *La Statue merveilleuse*, with d'Orneval, 1720; *L'Île des Amazones*, with d'Orneval, 1720; *La Fausse foire*, with d'Orneval and Fuzelier, 1721; *La Boîte de Pandore*, with d'Orneval and Fuzelier, 1721; *La Tête noire*, with d'Orneval and Fuzelier, 1721; *Le Rappel de la foire à la vie*, with d'Orneval and Fuzelier, 1721; *Le Régiment de la Calotte*, with d'Orneval and Fuzelier, 1721; *Le Jeune Vieillard*, with d'Orneval and Fuzelier, 1722; *Le Dieu du hasard*, with d'Orneval and Fuzelier, 1722; *La Force de l'amour*, with d'Orneval and Fuzelier, 1722; *La Foire des fées*, with d'Orneval and Fuzelier, 1722; *Les Captifs d'Alger*, with d'Orneval, 1724; *La Toison d'or*, with d'Orneval, 1724; *L'Oracle muet*, with d'Orneval, 1724; *La Pudeur à la foire*, with d'Orneval, 1724; *La Matrone de Charenton*, with d'Orneval, 1724; *Les Vendanges de la foire*, with d'Orneval, 1724; *L'Enchanteur Mirliton*, with d'Orneval and Fuzelier, 1725; *Le Temple du mémoire*, with d'Orneval and Fuzelier, 1725; *Les Enragés; ou, La Rage d'amour*, with d'Orneval and Fuzelier, 1725; *Les Pèlerins de la Mecque*, with d'Orneval, 1726; *Les Comédiens corsaires*, with d'Orneval and Fuzelier, 1726; *L'Obstacle favorable*, with d'Orneval and Fuzelier, 1726; *Les Amours déguisés*, with d'Orneval and Fuzelier, 1726; *Achmet et Almanzine*, with d'Orneval and Fuzelier, 1728; *La Pénélope moderne*, with d'Orneval and Fuzelier, 1728; *Les Amours de Protée*, with d'Orneval and Fuzelier, 1728; *La Princesse de la Chine*, with d'Orneval, 1729; *Les Spectacles malades*, with d'Orneval, 1729; *L'Industrie*, with d'Orneval and Fuzelier, 1730; *Zémine et Almanzor*, with d'Orneval and Fuzelier, 1730; *Les Routes du monde*, with d'Orneval and Fuzelier, 1730; *L'Indifférence*, with d'Orneval and Fuzelier, 1730; *L'Amour marin*, with d'Orneval and

Fuzelier, 1730; *L'Espérance*, with d'Orneval and Fuzelier, 1730; *Roger roi de Sicile, surnommé le roi sans chagrin*, with d'Orneval, 1731; *Les Désepérés*, with d'Orneval, 1732; *Sophie et Sigismond*, with d'Orneval, 1732; *La Sauvagesse; ou, La Fille sauvage*, with d'Orneval, 1732; *Le Rival dangereux*, 1734; *Les Deux Frères*, 1734; *La Première Représentation*, 1734; *Les Mariages de Canada*, 1734; *L'Histoire de l'Opéra-Comique; ou, Les Métamorphoses de la foire*, 1736; *Le Mari préféré*, 1736; *Les Vieillards rajeunis*, with Nicolas Fromaget, 1736; *Le Neveu supposé*, 1738.

Fiction

Lettres galantes d'Aristénète. 1695.
Nouvelles aventures de l'admirable Don Quichotte de la Marche. 1704; as *The New Adventures of Don Quixote*, 1705.
Le Diable boiteux. 1707; revised editions, 1726, 1737; edited by Roger Laufer, 1970; as *The Devil Upon Two Sticks*, translated anonymously, 1708; several subsequent translations under same title; as *Asmodeus; or, the Devil Upon Two Sticks*, translated by Lesage, 1729; as *The Devil Upon Crutches*, translated by Joseph Thomas, 1841; as *The Lame Devil*, translated anonymously, 1870.
Les Mille et un jours, contes persans (satire of the Arabian Nights). 5 vols., 1710–12; translated, 1714.
Histoire de Gil Blas de Santillane. 3 vols., 1715–35; revised edition, 1747; as *The History and Adventures of Gil Blas of Santillane*, translated anonymously, 1716; as *The Adventures of Gil Blas*, translated by Tobias Smollett, 1749; several subsequent translations including by Percival Proctor, 1774, and W.H. Dilworth, 1790.
Nouvelle Traduction de Roland l'amoureux, from *Orlando inamorato* by Boiardo. 2 vols., 1717.
Histoire de Guzman d'Alfarache, from a romance by Matheo Aleman. 2 vols., 1732; as *The Pleasant Adventures of Gusman of Alfarache*, translated by A. O'Connor, 1812.
Les Aventures de Monsieur Robert Chevalier, capitaine des filibustiers dans la Nouvelle-France. 2 vols., 1732; edited by H. Kurtz, 1926; as *The Adventures of Robert Chevalier*, translated anonymously, 1747.
Une Journée des parques. 1734; as *A Day of the Fates*, translated by Adam L. Gowans, 1922.
Histoire d'Estevanille Gonzalez, surnommé le garçon de bonne humeur, from a work by Vincention Espinella. 4 vols., 1734–41; as *The History of Vanillo of Gonzales, Surnamed the Merry Bachelor*, translated anonymously, 1735; as *The Merry Bachelor*, translated anonymously, 1812.
Le Bachelier de Salamanque; ou, Les Mémoires de D. Chérubin de la Ronda. 2 vols., 1736–38; as *The Bachelor of Salamanca*, 2 vols., translated by Mr Lockman, 1737–39; also translated by J. Townsend, 1822.
La Valise trouvée. 1740.

Other

Mélanges amusants de saillies d'esprit et de traits historiques des plus frappants. 1743.

*

Bibliography: *Essai bibliographique sur les oeuvres d'Alain-René Lesage* by H. Cordier, 1910.

Critical Studies: *Lesage et Gil Blas* by C. Dédéyan, 2 vols., 1965; *The Theatre of Alain-René Lesage* by Ardelle Striker, 1968; *Lesage; ou, Le Métier de romancier* by Roger Laufer, 1971; *The Interrelationship Between Prominent Character Types in 'Le Diable Boiteux', 'Gil Blas' and 'Le Théâtre de la Foire' by Alain-René Lesage* by Raymond Joseph Pelletier, 1977; *Lesage et le picaresque* by Francis Assaf, 1983; *L'Espagne dans la trilogie 'picaresque' de Lesage. Emprunts littéraires, empreinte culturelle* by C. Cavillac, 2 vols., 1984; *Le Type du valet chez Molière et ses successeurs: Regnard, Dufresny, Dancourt et Lesage* by G. Gouvernet, 1985; *Lesage: Crispin rival de son maître and Tucaret* by George Evans, 1987; *Lesage, Gil Blas* by Malcolm Cook, 1988.

* * *

Although he had already translated several Spanish plays into French, Alain-René Lesage's literary career really began in 1707 when he wrote both a successful play, *Crispin, rival de son maître* (*Crispin, Rival of His Master*) and a successful novel, *Le Diable boiteux* (*The Devil Upon Crutches*). *Crispin* is a one-act prose comedy with a complex plot involving deception and impersonation. Crispin, the valet of Valère, impersonates Damis in an attempt to make off with the dowry of Angélique, the woman whom Valère loves but who has been promised to Damis, who has secretly married another woman. The plot is foiled, the valets are forgiven, and all ends well. In its plot, use of deception, and complex love relationships, the play recalls Molière's comedies; the unscrupulous motivation of Crispin for his own gain at the expense of his master contrasts sharply with Molière's lackeys who engage in their ruses in order to help their masters.

In *Turcaret*, Lesage increases the sharpness of his satire and the comedy becomes what has been called a bitter comedy. The play presents a host of heartless, mean characters and draws its comedy from the fact that none of the victims is worthy of sympathy, but all rather deserve the punishment they receive. The plot is less complex than that of *Crispin* in that it is constructed in a series of layers of deceptions for financial gain. Lesage uses the motif of the trickster tricked, but here the trickster is no longer a likeable fellow. Turcaret, a dishonest tax farmer, has abandoned his wife, who is searching for him. In spite of his cleverness in financial matters, he has fallen under the spell of the Baronne, who is trying to dupe him; his wife in turn is being duped by her lover, the Chevalier. Both the Baronne and the Chevalier are in turn being cheated by their servants. All of the trickery is brought to a halt when Turcaret's wife arrives and he is arrested. This dénouement recalls the just punishment of Tartuffe at the close of Molière's famous comedy. The play, which was a scathing attack upon the tax farmers of the period, enjoyed enormous success in spite of the efforts of those it attacked to suppress it. *La Tontine*, also deals with the world of finance and is another comedy of manners.

In addition to these three major plays, Lesage wrote more than 100 farces. Both *Crispin* and *Turcaret* were written for the Comédie-Français; soon after the performance of *Turcaret*, Lesage quarrelled with the Comédie-Français over their acting style and associated himself with the Théâtre de la Foire, for whom he wrote his farces either alone or in collaboration.

Lesage's novels reflect the same interests and preoccupations as his plays. He is considered by many critics to be the creator of the novel of manners. *The Devil Upon Crutches* is based on the Spanish novel *Diablo conjuelo* by Guevara. Although the action takes place in Madrid, the novel is actually a satirical portrayal of 18th-century Parisian society. Asmodée, the lame devil, once he is released from the bottle in which he has been imprisoned, entertains his benefactor by lifting the roofs off the houses in Madrid (actually Paris) to reveal the activity within. The novel is at times referred to as a romance because it contains a secondary plot in which Asmodée arranges the marriage of his benefactor with Seraphina. However, the greater part of the novel is a series of anecdotes, satires of manners, and portraits.

It is in Lesage's major novel *Histoire de Gil Blas de Santillane* (*The Adventures of Gil Blas*) that we really see his development as a novelist. Lesage uses the Spanish genre of the picaresque and once again satirizes his French contemporaries under the guise of a Spanish setting. The hero experiences the traditional picaresque alternation of good and bad fortune; a whole panorama of social ranks, professions, and situations is presented. Lesage adds a moral sense to the picaresque novel for his hero Gil Blas advances not only in social rank but also in his sense of moral values. Gil Blas is both a spectator of and a participant in society, whereas the lame devil and his benefactor only observe. As Henri Coulet (*Le Roman jusqu'à la Révolution*) has stated, the novel progresses from a simple comic narration to become a work imbued with a serious realism. *Gil Blas*, unlike the typical 18th-century novel, does not depend upon the motif of love. In its panoramic portrayal of society, it foretells the novels of Balzac.

While writing *Gil Blas*, Lesage also composed two other novels: in 1732, *Histoire de Guzman d'Alfarache* (*The Pleasant Adventures of Gusman of Alfarache*), which he based heavily on the work of Mateo Aleman, and in 1734, *Histoire d'Estevanille Gonzalez* (*The History of Vanillo of Gonzales*). In 1736, he created a totally original novel (that is, no models have been found for it), *Le Bachelier de Salamanque* (*The Bachelor of Salamanca*). This novel is a delightful romp through adventure after adventure, with little concern for verisimilitude. Lesage also published *Les Aventures de Monsieur Robert Chevalier* (*The Adventures of Robert Chevalier*), in 1732, a curious novel that includes the exploits of an adventurer in the New World and several narratives treating themes used by other contemporary writers, particularly Prévost and Marivaux.

The plays and novels of Lesage were very popular during the 18th century. In the theatre, he further developed the comedy of manners and added a more satirical tone to comedy. He also contributed significantly to the development of the novel of the period, influencing many of the novelists of the time such as Marivaux and Voltaire (although Voltaire failed to acknowledge this influence). His work does, however, present certain contrasts to the body of 18th-century fiction: he turned to Spain rather than to England for his models, and he found subjects other than love for his novels.

—Shawncey J. Webb

———

LESSING, Gotthold Ephraim. Born in Kamenz, Saxony (then part of the Holy Roman Empire), 23 January 1729. Educated at school of St Afra, Meissen, 1741–46; studied theology, then medicine, at University of Leipzig, 1746–48; University of Wittenberg, 1748, 1751–52, master of arts 1752. Married Eva König in 1776 (died 1778); one son (died in infancy). Writer from 1748 in Berlin; editor, with Christlob Mylius, *Beiträge zur Historie und Aufnahme des Theaters*, 1750; editor, *Theatralische Bibliothek*, 1754–58, and *Briefe, die neueste Literatur betreffend (Literaturbriefe)*, 1759; official secretary to General Bogislaw von Tauentzien, Breslau, 1760–65; resident adviser to the National Theatre in Hamburg, 1767–68; librarian to the Duke of Brunswick, Wolfenbüttel, 1770–81. Member, Academy of Mannheim, 1776. *Died 15 February 1781.*

PUBLICATIONS

Collections

Dramatic Works, edited and translated by E. Bell. 2 vols., 1878.
Sämtliche Schriften, edited by Karl Lachmann, revised by Franz Muncker. 23 vols., 1886–1924; reprinted 1979.
Werke, edited by Julius Petersen and Waldemar von Olshausen. 25 vols., 1925; supplement, 5 vols., 1929–35.
Werke, edited by H.G. Göpfert and others. 8 vols., 1970–79.
Werke und Briefe, edited by Wilfried Barner and others. 1985–.

Plays

Der junge Gelehrte, with others (produced 1748). In *Schriften*, 1754.
Die alte Jungfer. 1749.
Die Juden (produced 1749). In *Schriften*, 1754.
Der Freigeist (produced 1767). In *Schriften*. 1753–55.
Miss Sara Sampson (produced 1755). In *Schriften*, 1755; edited by K. Eibl, 1971; as *Miss Sarah Sampson*, translated by E. Bell, in *World Drama*, edited by Barrett Clark, 1933; as *Sara*, 1990.
Philotas (produced 1780). 1759.
Lustspiele. 2 vols., 1767.
Minna von Barnhelm (produced 1767). 1767; edited by Dieter Hildebrandt, 1969; as *The Disbanded Officer*, translated and adapted by James Johnstone, 1786; as *The School for Honor*, 1789; as *Minna von Barnhelm*, translated by F. Holcroft, 1805; also translated by W.C. Wrankmore, 1858; P. Maxwell, 1899; W.A. Steel, with *Laocoon* and *Nathan the Wise*, 1930; E. Bell, 1933; K.J. Northcott, 1972; Anthony Meech, 1990; as *The Way of Honour*, translated by E.U. Ouless, 1929.
Trauerspiele. 1772.
Emilia Galotti (produced 1772). In *Trauerspiele*, 1772; as *Emilia Galotti*, translated by Benjamin Thompson, 1800; also translated by Edward Dvoretzky, 1962; F.J. Lamport, in *Five German Tragedies*, 1969; A.J.G. von Aesch, 1981.
Nathan der Weise (produced 1783). 1779; edited by P. Demetz, 1966, also edited by Renate Waack, 1979; as *Nathan the Wise*, translated by R.E. Raspe, 1781; numerous subsequent translations including by A. Reich, 1860; Robert Willis, 1868; W.A. Steel, with *Laocoon* and *Minna von Barnhelm*, 1930; Bayard Quincy Morgan, 1955; T.H. Lustig, in *Classical German Drama*, 1963; Walter F.C. Ade, 1972.

Other

Schriften. 6 vols., 1753–55; revised edition, 1771.
Fabeln. 1759; revised edition, 1777; as *Fables*, translated by J. Richardson, 1773.
Laokoon; oder, Über die Grenzen der Malerei und Poesie. 1766; as *Laocoon; or, The Limits of Poetry and Painting*, translated by W. Ross, 1836; numerous subsequent translations including by E.C. Beasley, 1853; W.B. Rönnfeldt, 1895; W.A. Steel, with *Nathan the Wise* and *Minna von Barnhelm*, 1930; Edward Allen McCormick, 1962.
Briefe, antiquarischen Inhalts. 2 vols., 1768.
Berengarius Turonensis. 1770.
Zur Geschichte und Literatur [so-called *Wolfenbütteler Beiträge*]. 3 vols., 1773–81.
Anti-Goeze, 1–11. 1778.
Ernst und Falk. 1778–81; edited by Wolfgang Kelsch, 1981; as *Ernst and Falk*, 1854–72; as *Masonic Dialogues*, translated by A. Cohen, 1927.
Die Erziehung des Menschengeschlechts. 1780; edited by Louis Ferdinand Helbig, 1980; as *The Education of the Human Race*, translated by F.W. Robertson, 1858; also translated by H. Chadwick, in *Lessing's Theological Writings*, 1956.
Theologischer Nachlass, edited by K.G. Lessing. 1784.
Theatralischer Nachlass, edited by K.G. Lessing. 2 vols., 1784–86.
Literarischer Nachlass, edited by K.G. Lessing. 3 vols., 1793–95.
Hamburgische Dramaturgie (1767–69), edited by O. Mann. 1958; translated in *Lessing's Prose Works*, edited by E. Bell, 1897.
Lessing im Gespräch, edited by Richard Daunicht. 1971.
Briefwechsel über das Trauerspiel, edited by J. Schulte-Sasse. 1972.
Briefe aus Wolfenbüttel, edited by Günter Schulz. 1975.
Meine liebste Madam: Briefwechsel, with Eva König, edited by Günter and Ursula Schulz. 1979.
Gotthold Ephraim Lessing: A Selection of His Fables in English and German, translated by Lesley Macdonald and H. Weissenborn. 1979.
Dialog in Briefen und andere ausgewählte Dokumente zum Leben Gotthold Ephraim Lessings mit Eva Catharina König, edited by Helmut Rudolff. 1981.
Unvergängliche Prosa: die philosophischen, theologischen und esoterischen Schriften (selections), edited by Konrad Dietzfelbinger. 1981.
Die Ehre hat mich nie gesucht: Lessing in Berlin (selections), edited by Gerhard Wolf. 1985.

*

Bibliography: *Gotthold Ephraim Lessing* by G. and S. Bauer, 1968, revised edition, 1986; *Lessing-Bibliographie* [to 1971] by Siegfried Seifert, 1973; *Lessing-Bibliographie 1971–1985* by Doris Kuhles, 1988.

Critical Studies: *Lessing, The Founder of Modern German Literature* by Henry B. Garland, 1937, revised edition, 1962; *Lessing's Dramatic Theory* by J.G. Robertson, 1939, reprinted 1965; *G.E. Lessing: Lakoon* edited by D. Reich, 1965; *Lessing and the Enlightenment* by Henry E. Allison, 1966; *Lessing and the Language of Comedy* by M.M. Metzger, 1966, *Gotthold Ephraim Lessing* by F. Andrew Brown, 1971; *Gotthold Ephraim Lessing's Theology* by L.P. Wessell, 1977; *Lessing and the Drama* by F.J. Lamport, 1981; *Lessing's Laocoon: Semiotics and Aesthetics in the Age of Reason* by David E. Wellbery, 1984; *Minna von Barnhelm* by Robin Harrison, 1985; *Lessing and the Enlightenment* edited by Alexej Ugrinsky, 1986; *Aesthetic Reconstructions: The Seminal Writings of Lessing, Kant and Schiller* by Anthony Savile, 1987; *The Spinoza Conversations Between Lessing and*

Jacobi: Text with Excerpts from the Ensuing Controversy by Gérard Vallée, 1988; *Catalyst of Enlightenment, Gotthold Ephraim Lessing: Productive Criticism of Eighteenth-Century Germany* by Edward M. Batley, 1990.

* * *

Gotthold Ephraim Lessing is the principal literary figure of the German Enlightenment and founder of the modern German drama. Intending to follow his father into the Lutheran ministry, he made his literary debut while still a theological student with a number of comedies, for the most part conventional but in some cases (*Die Juden, Der Freigeist*) touching upon serious matters of intellectual controversy and humanitarian concern. By the time he was 25 he had also established a reputation as a trenchant critic and essayist on a wide range of topics. But the series of works upon which his lasting reputation rests begins with *Miss Sara Sampson*. This 'domestic' or 'middle-class' tragedy was the first successful attempt in German, indeed in European drama, at the serious and in some measure 'realistic' depiction of ordinary contemporary characters, situations, and issues. This vein is continued in *Minna von Barnhelm*, a comedy of love and reconciliation in the aftermath of the Seven Years War, and the tragedy *Emilia Galotti*, a powerful amalgam of social and psychological conflict with a strong (if only implicit) note of political criticism. These works paved the way for the realistic social drama which was only to develop fully in the 19th century. Less successful was the laconic *Philotas*, a tragedy of patriotic fanaticism in a neo-classical setting. Lessing admired the Greeks, and in *Laokoon* (*Laocoon*) praised Greek art as the supreme expression of the human spirit, while attacking what he saw as perversions of the true classical tradition; similarly in the *Hamburgische Dramaturgie* he sought to liberate German drama from any dependence on the neo-classical style of 17th-century France. *Laocoon* also seeks to delimit the proper spheres of the various arts, attacking the doctrine 'ut pictura poesis' and maintaining that while the scope of the visual arts is limited to beauty, poetry and literature should depict actions.

In the 1770s Lessing's interests returned largely to theology. Beginning with the defence of various so-called heretics and of the rights of freedom of conscience, of intellectual inquiry, and of expression, he proceeded to a number of searching examinations of the concept of religious truth. Truth itself becomes increasingly elusive, increasingly relative, but Lessing holds fast to the belief in an ultimately benevolent Providence and in the supreme importance of ethical conduct in man. This faith is proclaimed in his last play, *Nathan der Weise* (*Nathan the Wise*): here Lessing abandons his earlier realism for a kind of symbolic fairy-tale, in which Christian, Muslim, and Jew are ultimately revealed as members of one family. His final treatise, *Die Erziehung des Menschengeschlechts* (*The Education of the Human Race*), traces the course of human history as a dialectic between human reason and divine revelation, between developing human autonomy and a transcendent providential plan.

By his own and succeeding generations, Lessing has been regarded above all as a liberator, a champion of humanity, and an unrelenting critic of intolerance and pretension. His major plays are still successfully performed today; his critical writings are models of supple and incisive German prose.

—F.J. Lamport

MINNA VON BARNHELM
Play by Gotthold Ephraim Lessing, 1767.

Minna von Barnhelm was conceived in 1763 in the aftermath of the Seven Years War in which Saxony and Prussia were enemies and was completed in 1767, the year in which Lessing assumed his post as resident playwright and critic to the new National Theatre in Hamburg. In the play Lessing, a Saxon working as secretary to a Prussian general, makes an impassioned plea for tolerance and reconciliation, both themes central to his writing as a whole. In his theoretical writings on the theatre Lessing calls for a national repertoire for the German theatre.

In *Minna von Barnhelm* Lessing offers a model of a truly German comedy, as much of the humour and interest in the play arises from the interaction between the vivacious and witty Saxon Minna and her fiancé the unbending, high-principled Prussian Tellheim. Minna, a Saxon, has come to Berlin in search of Tellheim, a Major, newly discharged from the Prussian army. The act of generosity performed by Tellheim, in advancing money from his own funds to cover taxes he was supposed to collect in Saxony, which won Minna's love for him, has been misinterpreted by the Prussian authorities as dishonourable and dishonest. Tellheim is now without funds and awaiting the outcome of an investigation into the matter. Feeling himself both crippled physically (he has been wounded in the arm) and emotionally by this slight to his honour, Tellheim rejects Minna. He now feels unworthy of her and that he cannot depend on her for his happiness. Minna contrives to convince Tellheim that she herself is penniless and has been threatened by her uncle, and by this ruse tricks him into declaring his love for her again. However, this is not enough for her. She feels that she must punish Tellheim further. This punishment, inflicted after Tellheim receives notification from the King that his fortune and honour are both restored, goes almost too far. The situation is redeemed by the arrival of Minna's uncle, who approves the union, bringing the play to a happy conclusion.

In form the play is conventional. It is written in five acts, the scenes changing with characters' entrances. The main characters come from the minor nobility and their courting is mirrored in the developing relationship between Minna's pert maid Franziska and Tellheim's stolid Sergeant-Major Paul Werner. The play also follows convention in its observance of the classical unities of time, place, and action. Later Lessing would attack the French theatre of the day for its slavish adherence to the letter rather than to the spirit of the unities, suggesting that the German theatre would be better advised to imitate the freer construction of Shakespeare's plays than those of the French.

The true originality of the play lies in the freshness and contemporaneity of the characters and their concerns. The structure of the play might be reminiscent of classical comedy, but there is a striking quality of realism in the characterization and settings, as well as Lessing's rejection of verse and his choice of a supple prose for the dialogue, accurately matched to the standing of characters. Tellheim finds himself in the limbo of the discharged officer, a situation which must have been familiar to many in the original audience, as were frequent references to both good and bad features of the recent conflict. In the character of Riccaut de la Marlinière Lessing ridicules the fashion, prevalent in Germany at the time and at the court of Frederick the Great, of regarding the German language as incapable of expressing the subtleties necessary for cultured conversation and, by implication, literature. By refusing to speak in French with Riccaut, Minna (and Lessing) decisively takes sides in the argument current at the time. This, and the direct reference to the King himself in the play, led the Prussian authorities to discourage the production of *Minna von Barnhelm*, which was premiered in Hamburg, a free city beyond Prussian jurisdiction, in 1767.

The play's abiding appeal for audiences derives chiefly from the charm of the central character, Minna, herself. She might with justification be seen as the first emancipated woman in German comedy. Not deterred from setting out in search of her fiancé, nor afraid to go on ahead of her uncle when his carriage breaks down, she is well able to defend herself against the prying questions of the landlord and to win the hearts of the audience in her exchanges on love and romance with Franziska. Above all, she is a heroine of the German bourgeoisie, embodying the virtues and standards espoused by the new theatre audience who recognized in her self-confidence their own growing self-esteem. Despite this, however, the play owes a considerable debt to the *sächsische Typenkomödie* (the Saxon comedy of types). In this genre of comedy attempts are made to show a flawed character the unreasonableness of his behaviour, and, when reason fails, the other characters resort to intrigue. Thus it is that Minna, unable to persuade Tellheim to owe his happiness to her (his fault being his inability, as a generous man, to receive generosity), has recourse to trickery.

Here Lessing adds a new dimension to comic form and an increased depth to the play, for Tellheim is a more complex and sympathetic character than the traditional butt of this type of comedy. We are shown his positive qualities in his interaction with the widow of his captain-of-horse, and with Werner. We admire his honesty and sympathize with him when, after notification from the King of the restoration of his fortune and honour, Minna persists in deceiving him in order to teach him a lesson. Minna sees that she has taken the game too far. Tellheim is thrown into serious confusion by Minna's dishonesty towards him and only the arrival of Minna's uncle saves the play from an unhappy ending, Minna having lost control of the situation.

In the event *Minna von Barnhelm* was not taken as a model by the new movement of the *Storm und Drang*, the German romanticism of the late 18th century, whose inspiration lacked the balance necessary for the writing of comedy. However, the play has retained its place in the repertoire of the German theatre and is regularly performed throughout the German-speaking world.

—A.J. Meech

NATHAN THE WISE (Nathan der Weise)
Play by Gotthold Ephraim Lessing, 1779.

Nathan the Wise, with its expression of optimistic belief in humanity and its argument for religious tolerance, is a central document of the German Enlightenment. Its moral has special relevance whenever anti-semitism and sectarian fanaticism or bigotry threaten humane values and social harmony. Its effectiveness as theatre depends on its apparent lightheartedness.

Unlike Lessing's other dramas, *Nathan* was not influenced by his desire to write a model comedy or tragedy in a realistic mode. It was conceived as a vehicle for the propagation of ideas at a time when great hopes were placed on the theatre as a means of educating the public. After publishing fragments of another scholar's rationalist critique of Christianity, where doubt was thrown on the divinity of Christ, Lessing had become engaged in a bitter controversy which attracted such attention that in the summer of 1778 the Duke of Brunswick, to whom he was librarian, forbade him all further

engagement in theological debate. Lessing, however, put his fundamental ideas on religion and morals into dramatic form. That same summer he began *Nathan*, whose action involves a rich Jew, Christians, and Muslims in Jerusalem during the Crusades. The setting calls for some local and historical colour, which the dramatist duly provides, but more importantly it serves to distance the action and to underline the symbolic function of a romantic comedy with an elaborate plot of mistaken identity. The symbolism is crystallized in the central scene in the parable of the three rings (a variation of Boccaccio's *Decameron*). By telling this story the Jew implies that none of the three religions can establish its historical truth. Their adherents must endeavour to justify their religion by behaviour which is pleasing both to God and to their fellow men. By this standard Nathan, who insists that he is a human being first and a Jew second, proves to be closer to the true faith than those around him, particularly the Christians.

The happy ending follows the reappearance of a fortune and the disclosure that Nathan's adopted child Recha, brought up as a Jewess, is the crusading Templar's sister and the Sultan's niece. The expected wedding of Recha to the Templar is thwarted but we are to understand that we are all members of the great human family and that mutually platonic love brings more than sufficient satisfaction, even to the confusedly ardent Templar. Thanks to Nathan's reading of coincidence, the young lovers and benevolent but irresponsible Sultan and his sister Sittah embrace the truth. The Christian patriarch, a fanatical bigot and enemy of reason, would have had Nathan burnt at the stake but he is presented as a grotesquely comic figure. The other characters, for all their foibles, evoke sympathetic smiles. A garrulous servant woman and a naively honest messenger who betrays his master's plot are recognizable comic types. The dialogue brings much wit, not least from the mouth of Nathan in whom Lessing lends dignity to stereotyped Jewish traits: he is associated with money, sentimentality, and a quizzical intelligence. The main figures are psychologically convincing and rewarding roles but Nathan, partly modelled on Moses Mendelssohn, a leading Jewish philosopher and friend of the author, dominates the stage.

The hero's exemplary wisdom is the wisdom of tolerance and of trust in the will of God which he has maintained after a Job-like experience when his wife and children were senselessly slaughtered by Christians (Lessing's wife and their newborn son had died in the winter of 1777–78). He is a deist with a faith in the potential goodness of his fellow men. The plot shows that proper human relationships are undermined by supposed differences of religion and race. Tolerance is the corollary of the right and duty of every individual to use his reason unrestricted by institutionalized authority. Virtue is not to be found in an impatient rejection of human imperfections and a flight from society.

One person's goodness, whatever its motivation, encourages goodness in others and is rewarded in this life. Wealth, used properly, is not to be despised. Fatherhood is to be judged by love for the child, not by paternity. Belief in miracles undermines the need for human deeds to solve human problems. Lessing's didacticism is packaged in a pleasing mixture of wit and humour, and a touch of pathos. His unpretentious blank verse with its colloquialisms, rough and ready rhythms, and avoidance of heroic grandiloquence, brings what might have been austere sermonizing down to earth.

—John Hibberd

LEVI, Carlo. Born in Turin, Italy, 29 November 1902. Educated at the University of Turin, degree in medicine 1924. Gave up a brief medical practice to be a painter: exhibited first in 1923, in the expressionist 'Six Painters of Turin' exhibition, 1929, and subsequently at the Venice Bi-Annual Exhibition, where a room was designated exclusively for his work in 1954. Active in political action and journalism: contributor, *Giustizia e Libertà*, early 1930s; co-editor, underground publication *Lotta politica*; arrested, 1934, exiled in Grassano and Gagliano, both in Lucania (i.e. Basilicata), 1936, freed under a general amnesty, 1936; resumed political activity and emigrated to France; returned to Italy to work with the Resistance; in Florence during conflict, 1942, re-arrested; co-editor, *La Nazione del Popolo*, the publication of the CTLN; editor, the Action Party's *L'Italia Libera*, Rome, 1945–46; frequent contributor to *La Stampa*, Turin; independent parliamentary deputy, on the Communist Party list, 1963–72. *Died 4 January 1975.*

PUBLICATIONS

Fiction

L'orologio. 1950; as *The Watch*, translated by John Farrar, 1951.

Other

Cristo si è fermato a Eboli. 1945; edited by Peter M. Brown, 1965; as *Christ Stopped at Eboli*, translated by Frances Frenaye, 1947.
Paura della libertà. 1946; as *Fear and Freedom*, translated by Adolphe Gourevitch, 1950.
Le parole sono pietre: Tre giornate in Sicilia. 1955; as *Words Are Stones: Impressions of Sicily*, translated by Angus Davidson, 1958.
Il futuro ha un cuore antico: Viaggio nell'Unione Sovietica. 1956.
La doppia notte dei tigli. 1959; as *The Linden Trees*, translated by Joseph M. Bernstein, 1962; as *The Two-Fold Night*, translated by Bernstein, 1962.
Un volto che ci somiglia: Ritratto dell'Italia. 1960.
Coraggio dei miti: Scritti contemporanei (selection), edited by Gigliola De Donato. 1975.
Contadini e luigini: Testi e disegni, edited by Leonardo Sacco. 1975.
Levi si ferma a Firenze (exhibition publication), edited by Carlo Ludovico Ragghianti. 1977.
I monotipi di Carlo Levi (catalogue). 1977.
Carlo Levi 1928–1937 (catalogue), edited by Mario De Micheli. 1977.
Quaderni a cancelli. 1979.
Disegni 1920–1935. 1980.
In Lucania con Carlo Levi, photographs by Mario Carbone, commentary by Gino Melchiorre. 1980.
L'altro mondo è il Mezzogiorno, edited by Leonardo Sacco. 1980.
Carlo Levi e la Lucania: Dipinti del confino 1935–1936 (catalogue). 1990.
E questo il 'carcer tetro'?: Lettere dal carcere 1934–1935, edited by Daniela Ferraro. 1991.

Editor, *Amicizia: Storia di un vecchio poeta e di un giovane canarino*, by Umberto Saba. 1951.

*

Critical Studies: *Saggio su Carlo Levi* by Gigliola De Donato, 1974; *Carlo Levi* by Giovanni Falaschi, 1978; *Come leggere Cristo si è fermato a Eboli di Carlo Levi* by Mario Miccinesi, 1979; *Carlo Levi: Dall'antifascismo al mito contadino* by Vincenzo Napolillo, 1984; 'The Politics of *Cristo si è fermato a Eboli*' by Howard Moss, in *Association of Teachers of Italian Journal*, Spring 1988; *L'azione politica di Carlo Levi* by Ghislana Sirovich, 1988; 'Carlo Levi: The Pursuit of the Essential in *Christ Stopped at Eboli*' by Vincenzo Bollettino, in *Fusta*, 8(1), 1990.

* * *

Carlo Levi was one of Italy's most prominent and influential intellectuals of the 20th century. He trained as a doctor, receiving a degree in medicine from the University of Turin in 1924, although he never formally practised. He is remembered as a great humanitarian, a painter, a writer, and a political activist, and his artistic activity was closely allied to his socialist engagement.

Levi reached adulthood during Mussolini's Fascist regime, when the young man's socialist ideals and Jewish heritage were not popular. He began therefore to spend extended periods of time in Paris with the leaders of the Italian Resistance. While in France, he helped to found the underground organization Giustizia e Libertà (Justice and Liberty). It was this activity which eventually led to his arrest and exile, first in the town of Grassano and later in Gagliano. Both villages are located in the southern Italian region of Lucania, known today as Basilicata. It was the practice of the Fascist party to confine political prisoners to remote areas of the peninsula in order to separate them from other activists. (Such key cultural figures as Antonio Gramsci, Cesare Pavese, and Leone and Natalia Ginzburg all spent long periods of exile under Mussolini's dictatorship.) After his release, at the end of the war, Levi was instrumental in the formulation of the left-wing Action Party, and in the 1960s he was elected as a senator in the independent list of the Italian Communist Party, a position he held for almost a decade.

The principal achievement of Levi's life was undoubtedly his campaign to achieve a greater awareness of both the gulf separating the industrial north of Italy from the rural south, and the resultant social problems. His political exile in Lucania was crucial for Levi, as it placed him in direct contact with the life of local peasants—an environment drastically different from his own upbringing in the industrial city of Turin. The inhabitants of Lucania still lived in a feudal society, virtually ignored by the modern Italian state. The publication of *Cristo si è fermato a Eboli* (*Christ Stopped at Eboli*) resulted in a literary *cause célèbre* in post-war Italy. With a candour impossible during the years of Fascist censorship, Levi described the social conditions of the tiny village of Gagliano, presented under the fictitious name of Aliano, which became a symbol of all such forgotten towns of the south.

Like the rest of Levi's writings, the work is of a non-fictional character. Indeed, the only truly literary aspect of these documentary memoirs is to be found in the title itself, which alludes to a local popular saying. Eboli is the last major town on the road southward to Lucania, the ancient Appian Way. Christ, or rather Christianity, is a metaphor for western culture that has not made its way beyond Eboli to the wasteland of Lucania. The peasants describe themselves as less than human beings, without civilization, and cut off from the world beyond the confines of their remote region. The harsh realities of their basic existence are related by Levi in a simple, direct manner, and it is for this reason that literary critics have referred to his work as 'neo-realist' in both style and content. By presenting this reality to a national audience for the first time, Levi encouraged political debate on the Southern question, a central concern in post-war Italy, and to this day not yet resolved completely. Levi's name is thus inexorably linked to his first published book and the ensuing controversy. Throughout his later life, the author worked tirelessly to promote the concerns of the inhabitants of Italy's south.

Although it may be less celebrated, one other work is actually more crucial to an understanding of Levi's philosophy. *Paura della libertà* (*Fear and Freedom*) predates *Christ Stopped at Eboli* in its date of composition, but was published in the following year, after the great success of the author's first novel. This essay, never originally intended for publication, gives us the essence of the author's philosophy. Beginning with the premise that the crisis which led to the outbreak of World War II in Europe had its origins in the soul of modern man, Levi analyses various aspects of the contemporary soul in order to demonstrate that liberty is *not* to be feared, but rather to be understood and desired as a response to the empty rhetoric of Fascist authority.

Levi's minor works are all imbued with his political philosophy, and, with one exception, are all non-fictional. The only novel written by Levi is *L'orologio* (*The Watch*), a fictionalized account of the political situation in post-World War II Italy, during the passage from the period of the Resistance under Ferruccio Parri's leadership to the Cold War and Alcide De Gasperi's government. However, for most readers, *Christ Stopped at Eboli* is considered Levi's first and foremost literary work.

—Jordan Lancaster

CHRIST STOPPED AT EBOLI (Cristo si è fermato a Eboli)
Prose by Carlo Levi, 1945.

In *Christ Stopped at Eboli*, Levi recounts the year of political exile he spent in the god-forsaken region of Lucania in southern Italy, because of his anti-fascism. The title of Levi's book is a proverbial phrase often repeated by the local peasants and which 'in their mouths may be no more than the expression of a hopeless feeling of inferiority. We are not Christians, we're not human beings'. Levi explains its much deeper meaning: Eboli is 'where the road and the railway leave the coast of Salerno and turn into the desolate reaches of Lucania. Christ never came this far, nor did time, nor the individual soul, nor hope, nor the relation of cause and effect, nor reason nor history'.

The richness of the book's motifs lies in the diverse ways in which Levi penetrates the peasant's soul. The work's complexity makes it impossible to categorize: it could be called, variously, a novel, a prose poem, a collection of sketches, a diary, a sociological, ethnological, economic, political, psychological, or mythological essay. These different genres testify to the author's versatility, show him as a brilliant 'scientific' observer, and make the work important and moving. What makes the book beautiful and unforgettable is the author's empathy with the world he is depicting; a feeling so powerful that the reader is at times under the impression that Levi created it from within, rather than simply observing it. One could say, metaphorically, that with this book the Lucanian peasant enters for the first time into an awareness of civilized man. The narrator succeeds in mediating the gap between the peasant's primitive condition and civilized man with his self-conscious compassion, and in a style without trace of facile sentimentality.

There is no organizing principle to *Christ Stopped at Eboli* save the passage of the seasons, which 'pass today over the toil of the peasants, just as they did three thousand years before Christ'. Between the author's entrance and the official conclusion we could interchange many pages. However, it is revealing that the first scene the reader witnesses between Levi and the peasants is the one where Levi, a physician, is called to assist a dying man. The scene is presented at the beginning of the book, in spite of the fact that, as we have been clearly told, the author has already lived in Lucania for months and has already met many peasants. In the economy of this book, this peremptory introduction of the narrator-persona and his protagonists in the presence of death lends an existential significance to their relation which will colour every aspect of the work.

At first Levi lives in Grassano, then suddenly, to his chagrin, is transferred to the smaller village of Gagliano. Soon here, too, a relationship develops between the exile and the peasants who feel respect, admiration, and affection for him because of his genuine understanding and participation in their suffering, although he belongs to a higher social class.

Levi's peasants are not picturesque or picaresque. They consider themselves 'beasts of burden' who in darkness walk for two or three hours to their malaria-infested fields. Men, women, and children live, literally, with animals, in one-room huts with goats, pigs, and chickens, and are presented metaphorically by means of constant reminders of the animal world, a technique, of course, not meant to dehumanize the peasantry but to suggest its closeness to the natural world. The narrator presents his subjects in their pristine, pre-historical reality. The place, itself, is experienced at times in its virgin wilderness ('an animal-like enchantment lay over the deserted village'). It seems as if Levi enters these Lucanian villages—places without individual soul, without time, or relation of cause and effect—through intuitive empathy rather than reason. In fact, he not only distances his subjects in their relationships with the animal world, but, more importantly and more effectively, he transports his reader into a time and place where 'there is no definite boundary line between the world of human beings and that of animals and monsters', a world crowded with witches, gnomes, spirits, goat-devils, cow-mothers, werewolves, love-philters and poisons, and wild myths and legends; a world where, in a Christian church: 'were preserved the horns of a dragon which in ancient times had infested the region . . . Nor would it be strange if dragons were to appear today before the startled eyes of the country people'. It is as if Levi had delved into his own subconscious and, concurrently, into the pre-conscious state of western civilization.

The peasants 'had always to bow' to all the 'invaders who passed through their land'. They never protested. Centuries of resignation and a sense of fatality weigh on their shoulders, but when their 'infinite endurance' is shaken, their 'instinct for self-defence or justice, their revolt, knows no bounds and no measure': they become brigands. It is an 'inhuman revolt whose point of departure and final end alike are death'. Brigandage is their only defence against an enslaving hostile civilization. Brigands are the peasant's only heroes; they become his legends and myths, his 'only poetry', his 'epic'. When Levi was forbidden from practising medicine, the villagers wanted to act 'with grim determination' like their heroes. 'With guns and axes on their shoulders', they were ready to 'burn the town hall and kill the mayor'.

The peasants share a common consciousness and subconsciousness, yet Levi individuates some of them. Among them, unforgettably, is Giulia, the author's housekeeper, the most powerful of Gagliano's 20 witches, mother of 16 illegitimate children, who 'taught [Levi] all sorts of spells and incantations for the inspiration of love and the cure of disease', and finally on Christmas Day—although even then 'its communication was not entirely sinless'—she revealed to him 'the art of bringing about the illness and death of an enemy'.

The peasantry is exploited continually in feudal fashion by the village's petty middle class, the families who command city hall but who also envy and hate each other. The reader also feels disgust at the 'ridiculous spiderweb of their daily life, a dust-covered and uninteresting skein of self-interest, low-grade passion, boredom, greedy impotence, and poverty'. Among them, only Lieutenant Decunto has a 'unique beam of conscience that sets him apart', and makes him aware of the decay and spiritual poverty around him. Yet he hates his fellow-citizens, and self-hate makes him 'spiteful and bitter . . . [and] capable . . . of any evil'. Out of despair he will not become a brigand, as a peasant would, but chooses instead 'an escape into a world of destruction'. He is the only volunteer from Gagliano for the war in Africa.

The book deals cogently with such problems as malaria, poverty, deforestation, emigration, and ignorance, and concludes with some thoughtful suggestions for political, economic, and social reforms. These add, usefully, to our knowledge of the author and of southern Italy during the Fascist period, if not to the magic of the book.

—Emanuele Licastro

LEVI, Primo. Born in Turin, Italy, 31 July 1919. Educated at d'Azeglio grammar school, Turin, from 1934; Turin University, degree in chemistry (summa cum laude) 1941. Participated in the Italian Resistance, 1943; captured and imprisoned first in Fossoli, then sent to Auschwitz concentration camp, 1944: freed by Russian forces, 1945; returned to Italy in 1945 after a long journey through Eastern Europe. Married Lucia Morpurgo in 1947, one son and one daughter. Industrial chemist, SIVA, Turin, 1945–77: retired in order to be a full-time writer. Regular contributor to *La Stampa*, Turin. Recipient: Campiello prize, 1963, 1982; Bagutta prize, 1967; Prato prize (for Resistance work), 1975; Strega prize, 1979; Viareggio prize, 1982; Kenneth B. Smilen award (with Saul Bellow), 1985. *Died (suicide) 11 April 1987.*

PUBLICATIONS

Collections

Opere. 3 vols., 1987–90.
Collected Poems, translated by Ruth Feldman and Brian Swann. 1988; revised edition, 1992.

Fiction

Storie naturali (as Damiano Malabaila). 1966; parts translated by Raymond Rosenthal, in *The Sixth Day and Other Tales*, 1990.
Vizio di forma (stories). 1971; as *The Sixth Day*, translated by

Raymond Rosenthal, in *The Sixth Day and Other Tales*, 1990.
Il sistema periodico. 1975; as *The Periodic Table*, translated by Raymond Rosenthal, 1984.
La chiave a stella (stories). 1978; as *The Monkey Wrench*, translated by William Weaver, 1986; as *The Wrench*, translated by Weaver, 1987.
Lilít e altri raconti (stories). 1981; as *Moments of Reprieve*, translated by William Weaver, 1986; also translated by Ruth Feldman, 1986.
Se non ora, quando?. 1982; as *If Not Now, When?*, translated by William Weaver, 1985.

Verse

L'osteria di Brema. 1975; as *Shema: Collected Poems*, translated by Ruth Feldman and Brian Swann, 1976.
Ad ora incerta. 1984; as *At an Uncertain Hour*, in *Collected Poems*, 1988.

Plays

Intrevista aziendale (radio play), with Carlo Carducci. 1968.
Se questo è un uomo, with Pieralberto Marché. 1966.

Other

Se questo è un uomo. 1947; as *If This Is a Man*, translated by Stuart Woolf, 1960; as *Survival in Auschwitz: The Nazi Assault on Humanity*, translated by Woolf, 1961.
La tregua. 1963; as *The Reawakening*, translated by Stuart Woolf, 1965; as *The Truce: A Survivor's Journey Home from Auschwitz*, translated by Woolf, 1965.
Abruzzo forte e gentile: Impressioni d'occhio e di cuore, edited by Virgilio Orsini. 1976.
If This Is Man; The Truce, translated by Stuart Woolf. 1979; as *Survival in Auschwitz; The Reawakening: Two Memoirs*, translated by Woolf, 1986.
La ricerca delle radici: Antologia personale. 1981.
Dialogo (dialogues), with Tullio Regge. 1984; as *Dialogo*, translated by Raymond Rosenthal, 1989; as *Conversations*, translated by Rosenthal, 1989.
L'altrui mestiere (essays). 1985; as *Other People's Trades*, translated by Raymond Rosenthal, 1989.
I sommersi e i salvati. 1986; as *The Drowned and the Saved*, translated by Raymond Rosenthal, 1988.
Racconti e saggi. 1986; as *The Mirror Maker: Stories and Essays*, translated by Raymond Rosenthal, 1989.
Autoritratto. 1987; as *Conversations with Primo Levi*, with Ferdinando Camon, translated by John Shepley. 1989.

Translator, *Il processo*, by Kafka. 1983.
Translator, *Lo squalo da lontano*, by Lévi-Strauss. 1984.
Translator, *La via delle maschere*, by Lévi-Strauss. 1985.

*

Critical Studies: *Invito alla lettura di Primo Levi* by Fiora Vincenti, 1973, revised edition, 1990; *Primo Levi* by Giuseppe Grassano, 1981; *Prisoners of Hope: The Silver Age of the Italian Jews 1924–1974* by H. St Hughes, 1983; 'Primo Levi and the Language of Atrocity' by Adam Epstein, in *Bulletin for the Society of Italian Studies*, 20, 1987; *Il Vocabolario italiano tedesco di Se questo è un uomo di Primo Levi* by Rosemarie Wildi-Benedict, 1988; 'Primo Levi's Strenuous Clarity' by Lawrence R. Schehr, in *Italica*, 66(4),

1989; *Primo Levi as Witness* edited by Pietro Frassica, 1990; *A Dante of Our Time—Primo Levi and Auschwitz* by Risa B. Sodi, 1990; *Reason and Light: Essays on Primo Levi* edited by Susan Tarrow, 1990; *Come leggere Se questo è un uomo* by Claudio Toscani, 1990; *Ascoltando Primo Levi: Organizzazione, narrazione, etica* by Giuseppe Varchetta, 1991; *Primo Levi e Se questo è un uomo* by Alberto Cavaglion, 1993.

*   *   *

One of the most famous of contemporary Italian writers, and one of the world's best writers on the Holocaust, Primo Levi repeatedly stated that his initial motivation to write came from the need to bear witness after his deportation from Italy. He is identified, both in Italy and abroad, with his testimony on Auschwitz, which is the central theme of three of his books, and which is present to varying degrees in all his writings. However, Levi's works go far beyond mere testimony, and are characterized by the constant attempt to mediate between several different cultures and world-views.

Se questo è un uomo (*If This Is a Man*), published first in 1947, is the account of Levi's arrest, deportation, and survival in Buna-Monowitz, one of the satellite camps of Auschwitz. It stands out among Holocaust literature because of the author's determination not only to bear witness, but also to clarify and understand the 'gigantic biological and social experience' of the camps. The aspect Levi consistently stresses, as suggested in the title, is the contrast between the order of the Lager (the camp), which dehumanizes, enslaves, and finally eliminates the prisoners with 'geometrical madness', and his own endeavours to ascertain 'what is essential and what adventitious to the conduct of the human animal in the struggle for life'. The descriptions of life, work, and death in the camp are all the more powerful because they are filtered through Levi's rigorous training as a scientist: they move inductively from particular experiences to universal reflections on what may constitute individual identity and self-awareness when everything—country, loved ones, language, name—has been forcibly removed. The numerous explicit or implicit references to Dante's *Inferno* are, rather than mere literary conceits, attempts to convey the unprecedented degradation and despair of Auschwitz through the only available analogy.

La tregua (*The Truce*) follows the survivors' eventful journey home and their gradual return to humanity from their initial utter shame and hopelessness. The survivor's odyssey through the former Soviet Union and Eastern Europe is also a quest for human contacts and co-operation, and contains, as well as constant reminders that the poison of Auschwitz is 'irreparable and final, present everywhere', moments of relaxation and joy, and humorous descriptions of incongruous behaviour on the margins of civilization.

I sommersi e i salvati (*The Drowned and the Saved*), Levi's last book, written 40 years after *If This Is a Man*, is a critical re-examination of the subject matter of the first book. Its explicitly stated purpose is to ascertain 'how much of the concentration camp world is dead and will not return, [and] how much is back or coming back'. The title itself is problematic: through it, Levi stresses that those who survived, the 'saved', did so not because of their greater worth, but because they were in some cases lucky, and in most cases aggressive and ready to co-operate with the oppressors. The 'drowned', those who did not return to bear witness, were often the best people. The verbs 'to know' and 'to understand' recur throughout the text, highlighting the central argument:

knowledge and understanding are essential, especially for those who are young 40 years after Auschwitz, because what happened once can happen again, everywhere. To keep asking questions—including uncomfortable questions about 'the grey zone' of the victims who co-operated with the oppressors, and about the shame and guilt of the survivors—is emphasized as an intellectual as well as a moral duty.

The rest of Levi's creative production is characterized by the explicit desire to build a variety of bridges between different cultures. *Il sistema periodico* (*The Periodic Table*)—a collection of 21 stories, each named after an element of Dimitri Mendeleev's table, and arguably Levi's masterpiece—is at the same time a fragmentary autobiography, a history of Levi's generation, and an attempt to convey to readers of literature some aspects of the conflicts and lessons of scientific learning, specifically some aspects and meanings of the chemist's trade, which is 'a particular instance, a more strenuous version of the business of living'. *La chiave a stella* (*The Wrench*)—a collection of 14 stories in which a globe-trotting industrial steel-rigger recounts his humorous or dramatic successes and failures in several continents—can be read as a series of variations on the theme of skilled work, written in order to convey some of its practical and moral lessons to implied readers unfamiliar with technological processes.

Se non ora, quando? (*If Not Now, When?*)—the story of a band of Jewish guerrilla fighters who move through Nazi-occupied Eastern Europe, and finally set off from Italy for Palestine—was written with the purpose of paying homage to those Jews who had found the courage and the skills to fight back, and of explaining the cultural and ideological plurality of Jewishness, Ashkenazi Jewishness in particular, to Levi's Italian readers. It contains therefore both characters who represent diverse Jewish religious and secular ideologies, and a multiplicity of cultural references that include proverbs, songs, blessings, examples from the Talmud, folk-tales, and a number of carefully glossed Yiddish expressions.

The 'technology-fiction' stories collected in *Vizio di forma* (*The Sixth Day*) are speculations on possible, and generally undesirable, future developments of highly industrialized capitalist societies, with an implicit continuity between the moral failings of contemporary science and the 'geometric madness' of Auschwitz. The 50 or so brief essays written originally for *La Stampa*, and collected under the title *L'altrui mestiere* (*Other People's Trades*), are evidence of Levi's pleasure in extending his knowledge from the natural sciences to literature, from philology to the technology of the 1980s, and in communicating his discoveries to his readers. Levi also wrote some poetry, which ranges from the 'concise and gruesome' poems written soon after his return from Auschwitz, to later meditations on individual isolation and implicit comparisons between animals and human beings.

In *The Drowned and the Saved* Levi defines an intellectual as 'the person educated beyond his daily trade; whose culture is alive inasmuch as it makes an effort to renew itself, increase itself and keep up to date; and who does not react with indifference or irritation when confronted by any branch of knowledge'. This clearly applies to Levi himself, and to his consistently rational and ethical production.

—Mirna Cicioni

THE PERIODIC TABLE (Il sistema periodico)
Prose by Primo Levi, 1975.

Scientific research and literature are often seen as opposite methods of interpreting reality: scientific research is defined as primarily analysis, literature as mainly synthesis. This collection is an attempt to convey to readers of literature some of the lessons learned by Levi in the course of his diverse experiences, and at the same time something about the conflicts and ultimate joy of scientific learning.

The title refers to Dimitri Mendeleev's table of elements. The book consists of 21 stories, each named after an element, which are arranged in an order roughly corresponding to the course of Levi's own life—from the history of his Piedmontese Jewish ancestors to his youth under the Fascist regime, from his deportation from Italy to his return home, and finally to the moment when he turned from the trade of the chemist to that of the writer. Three basic themes are present, with varying emphasis—Levi's personal history and that of his generation; the pursuit of knowledge through trial and error; and the characteristics and changes of matter, presented first as enemies to be conquered, then as allies in physical and moral survival, and finally as the essence of life itself.

Levi denies this text the status of autobiography, 'save in the partial and symbolic limits in which every piece of writing is autobiographical, indeed every human work'. He calls it, instead, 'a micro-history, the history of a trade and its defeats, victories, and miseries'. Chemistry is thus represented not as an abstract science, but rather as a constant struggle, inseparably connected to daily life, history, politics, and personal development, as a metaphor for all kinds of learning: it is 'a particular instance, a more strenuous version of the business of living'. Although some of the processes and lessons learned in acquiring the chemist's trade, and even the structure of some molecules, are described in terms accessible to non-scientists, the text focuses on what individual human beings acquire personally from contacts with chemical transformations of matter. The elements of Mendeleev's table are thus occasionally personified, by being attributed anthropomorphic traits, and occasionally used as metaphors for aspects of the human condition.

In the first story, 'Argon', Levi compares inert or noble gases, which do not combine with any other element, with his own ancestors, a dynasty of likeable eccentrics, gradually integrated but never fully assimilated into Italian society, each identified by an anecdote and by one or more sayings in Piedmontese dialect containing linguistically assimilated Hebrew expressions. 'Iron', in the eponymous story, set in 1939, is metaphorically connected both to the imminent world catastrophe and to the courage of one of Levi's friends, who was to die heroically in the Resistance.

Interaction with the elements is represented as a source of practical moral instruction. Levi, as a student, sets fire to a laboratory by using potassium instead of sodium, and learns the hard way that 'one must distrust the almost-the-same, the practically identical, the approximate, the or-even, all surrogates and all patchwork'. There is a comic side: lipstick ingredients can be synthesized from chicken droppings, and acids can be stored in soup tureens, Art Nouveau chandeliers, and chamber pots. There is also a tragic side: the autobiographical story 'Cerio' is set in Auschwitz, where the theft of some cerium bars buys Levi and a friend two months of life. Some stories are fictional interludes: a few brief vignettes and two fables set in the past share with the autobiographical tales a passionate interest in the changes of elements and in the relationships of these changes to the lives of human beings.

All the themes of the book are brought together in the last story, 'Carbon': the journeys of an atom of carbon are followed through the centuries and through a variety of forms, until it enters Levi's own brain, gives Levi's hand an impulse, and leads it to impress the final full stop of the book on paper.

The conclusion is thus a synthesis between a view of life as a series of chemical changes, the autobiographical strand, and the text's reflection on itself.

This inspiring, if at times slightly uneven, book is more than a mere attempt to bridge the gap between the 'two cultures'. Its power lies in the constant tension between science—seen initially, naively, as the key to truth, then exposed as dogmatic and unavoidably linked to politics, and finally accepted as a concrete way of testing oneself—and literature, 'the trade of clothing facts in words', at first rejected as abstract and empty, then, in the final story, defined as 'bound by its very nature to fail' but reclaimed as the only means of consciously shaping and communicating the writer's knowledge of the extra-textual world.

—Mirna Cicioni

LEZAMA LIMA, José. Born in Havana, Cuba, 19 December 1910 (some sources give 1912). Grew up in the Fort Barrancas military camp, Pensacola. Educated at the Instituto de Havana, until 1928; University of Havana, degree in law 1938. Married María Luisa Bautista in 1965. Worked briefly in private law practice after graduation; official, Higher Council for Social Security, 1938–40, and from 1941; director, Department of Culture, Ministry of Education, from 1945; travelled to Mexico, 1949, Jamaica, 1950; director, Department of Literature and Publications, National Council of Culture, Havana, from 1959, and adviser, Cuban Centre for Literary Investigation. Editor or co-editor, *Verbum* (with Guy Pérez de Cisneros), 1937, *Espuela de Plata*, 1939–41, *Nadie Parecía*, 1942–44, *Orígenes*, 1944–56. One of six vice-presidents, Cuban Union of Artists and Writers (UNEAC), 1959–62. *Died 9 August 1976.*

PUBLICATIONS

Collections

Obras completas, edited by Cintio Vitier. 2 vols., 1975–77.
Poesía completa. 1985.
Poesía, edited by Emilio de Armas. 1992.

Fiction

Paradiso. 1966; revised edition, edited by Julio Cortázar and Carlos Monsiváis, 1968; also edited by Eloísa Lezama Lima, 1980, and Cintio Vitier, 1988; as *Paradiso*, translated by Gregory Rabassa, 1974.
Lezama Lima (anthology). 1968.
Oppiano Licario (unfinished). 1977; edited by César López, 1989.
Juego de las decapitaciones (stories). 1982.
Relatos. 1987.

Verse

Muerte de Narciso. 1937; selection edited by David Huerta, 1988.
Enemigo rumor. 1941.
Aventuras sigilosas. 1945.

La fijeza, illustrations by René Portocarrero. 1949.
Dador. 1960.
Antología de la poesía cubana. 3 vols., 1965.
Poesía completa. 1970.
Poesía completa. 1975.
Fragmentos a su imán. 1977.

Other

Coloquio con Juan Ramón Jiménez. 1938.
La pintura de Arístides Fernández. 1950.
Arístides Fernández (essay). 1950.
Analecta del reloj (essays). 1953.
Gradual de laudes: El padre Gaztelu en la poesía. 1955.
La expresión americana (lectures). 1957.
Tratados en La Habana (essays). 1958.
Órbita (interviews and selected texts) edited by Armando Álvarez Bravo. 1966.
Los grandes todos (anthology). 1968.
Posible imagen de José Lezama Lima, edited by José Agustín Goytisolo. 1969.
Esferaimagen; Sierpe de Don Luis de Góngora; Las imágenes posibles, edited by José Agustín Goytisolo. 1970.
La cantidad hechizada (essays). 1970.
Nuevo encuentro con Víctor Manuel. 1970.
Introducción a Los vasos órficos (essays). 1971.
Algunos tratados en La Habana. 1971.
Las eras imaginarias. 1971; reprinted 1982.
Interrogando a Lezama Lima. 1972.
Cangrejos y golondrinas (stories and essays). 1977.
Cartas (1939–1976), edited by Eloísa Lezama Lima. 1979.
Imagen y posibilidad (miscellany), edited by Ciro Bianchi Ross. 1981.
El reino de la imagen (selected essays), edited by Julio Ortega. 1981.
Confluencias (essays). 1988.
La Habana, edited by Gastón Baquero. 1991.
Mi correspondencia con Lezama Lima, by José Rodríguez Feo. 1991.

*

Bibliography: 'A Bibliography of the Fiction of Carpentier, Cabrera Infante, and Lezama Lima', in *Abraxas*, 1(3), 1971, and *Cuban Literature: A Research Guide*, 1985, both by David William Foster; *Sobre José Lezama Lima y sus lectores: Guía y compendio bibliográfico* by Justo C. Ulloa, 1987.

Critical Studies: *Recopilación de textos sobre José Lezama Lima* edited by Pedro Simón, 1970; *Lezama Lima: Peregrino inmóvil (Paradiso al desnudo): Un estudio crítico* by Álvaro de Villa and José Sánchez-Boudy, 1973; *Major Cuban Novelists*, 1976, and *The Poetic Fiction of José Lezama Lima*, 1983, both by Raymond D. Souza; *Novelística cubana de los años 60: Paradiso; El mundo alucinante* by Gladys Zaldívar, 1977; *José Lezama Lima: Textos críticos* edited by J.C. Ulloa, 1979; *Bajo el signo de Orfeo: Lezama Lima y Proust* by Jaime Valdiviesco, 1980; *Voces* by Cintio Vitier, 1982; *Coloquio internacional sobra la obra de José Lezama Lima* edited by A. Álvarez Bravo, 2 vols., 1984; *The American Gnosis of José Lezama Lima* by Rubén Ríos-Ávila, 1984; *El paradiso de Lezama Lima* by Carmen Ruiz Barrionuevo, 1986; *Lezama Lima* edited by E. Suárez Galbán, 1987; *José Lezama Lima; o, El hechizo de la búsqueda* by Rita V. Molinero, 1989; *José Lezama Lima's Joyful Vision: A Study of Paradiso and Other Prose* by Gustavo Pellón, 1989; *José Lezama Lima: Poet of the Image* by Emilio Bejel, 1990; *Lezama Lima. Una cosmología poética* by Lourdes Rensoli and Ivette Fuentes, 1990; *José Lezama Lima* by E. Márquez, 1991.

* * *

The work of the Cuban writer José Lezama Lima defies classification. Poet, novelist, essayist, and one of Cuba's leading intellectuals both before and after the Revolution, he made his name in Latin America and internationally with the novel *Paradiso*. Much of Lezama Lima's work was written before 1959, but his Catholic beliefs, open discussion of homosexuality, and the more general hermeticism of his work did not make him popular with the revolutionaries. Although Lezama Lima's work was somewhat marginalized in Cuba during the 1960s and 1970s (despite his holding of a series of official posts), it has been re-assessed more recently, and he is now considered a genius and visionary by many young Cuban writers, especially after the demise of Marxism in Europe.

Lezama Lima's creative writing should be approached as an integrated, coherent corpus. His life's objectives—to plumb the mysteries of the unknown, and to search the invisible and incomprehensible world which lies beyond reality as we know it—remained constant and uncompromising throughout. From the 1930s onwards, he founded and edited a series of avant-garde literary magazines culminating in the outstanding review, *Orígenes*, which became the focal point for a new generation of Cuban writers and artists including José Rodríguez Feo, Eliseo Diego, Cintio Vitier, and Fina García Marruz. It was in *Orígenes* that Lezama Lima published the first five chapters of *Paradiso*.

Lezama Lima's poetry, which he referred to as his 'dark work', was much influenced by the neo-Góngora movement of the 1920s, his early encounter with Juan Ramón Jiménez, the French avant-garde, and surrealism. His first publication, the poem *Muerte de Narciso* [Death of Narcissus], exemplifies the complex baroque style and formal rigour he was to cultivate, and is best read as a coda to his work as a whole. Narciso, the aesthete and poet, who is bedazzled by his reflected self-image, fulfils his desire to penetrate and merge with the unknown self in death. The hermetic poems of *Enemigo rumor* [Enemy Murmur], often considered his most important collection, enquire into the nature of reality beyond appearances in a profusion of oneiric and quasi-mystical images. *Aventuras sigilosas* [Discreet Adventures], more accessible and formally heterogeneous, includes poetic prose and cryptic aphorisms. *La fijeza* [Fixity] continues the quest for transcendental knowledge through art and erudition in lengthy poems, epigrammatic verse, and intensely worked poetic prose-essays. *Dador* [Donor], Lezama Lima's most extensive work of poetry, similarly exults in an outpouring of hyperbolic, esoteric imagery, while the posthumously published *Fragmentos a su imán* [Fragments to His Magnet], written during the 1970s, is less obscure. The 1985 volume of Lezama Lima's complete poetical works (dedicated in their entirety to his mother) includes poems not-previously published in books, as well as his first, hitherto unpublished collection, 'Inicio y escape' [Beginning and Escape] (written 1927–32).

Poetry imbues all Lezama Lima's work. For him it was the rationality of the unreal, the cult of mystery, the revelation that conceals. According to Cintio Vitier (1958) poetry was Lezama Lima's means of penetrating reality: the image functions as axis between history and poetry, and metaphor enables the acquisition of self-knowledge through analogy. The mission of the South American poet, therefore, was to discover the nature of the image.

The key to the interpretation of Lezama Lima's prose and poetry is to be found in his collections of essays. These do not make for easy reading, but lift the essay genre to the heights of conceptual lyricism. Thematically, they are inseparable from the rest of his work and constitute further explorations into his teleology. Four collections are particularly important: *Analecta del reloj* [Analecta of the Clock], which deals with several writers including Garcilaso, Valéry, Julián de Casal, Joyce, and Mallarmé; *La expresión americana* [American Expression], where Lezama Lima posits *criollo* (Creole) art as fundamentally baroque, in as much as it is formed from the reconstitution of old myths; and *Tratados en La Habana* [Essays in Havana] and *La cantidad hechizada* [The Bewitched Quantity] which discuss poetics and aesthetics.

Lezama Lima gained international recognition with *Paradiso*, which, he claimed, could only be understood 'beyond reason' by a few select readers. It was begun in the late 1940s and completed after his mother's death in 1964. To describe this masterpiece, the result of a lifetime's work, as a semi-autobiographical Bildungsroman would be to understate grossly the complex density of this unique text, referred to by Reinaldo Arenas as 'the exuberant reconstruction of the life of a poet'. Novel, epic, philosophical treatise, and poetic prose, *Paradiso* is usually read as an allegory or fable portraying the young hero, José Cemí (signifying 'image' or 'idol'), growing up and progressing through the various stages of spiritual perfection to fulfil his family destiny. The first eight chapters trace an autobiographical narrative centring on Cemí's family and childhood up to his father's death. This first half deals with the development of the embryonic man within the protective family womb dominated by the mother. The brutal sexuality of chapter eight, which describes in daring detail heterosexual and homosexual eroticism, announces the more amorphous second section of the novel. Through a series of juxtaposed anecdotes, the hero is seen to cross the intellectual quagmires presented by the philosophical disquisitions of his student companions, Fronesis and Foción (representing the positive and the negative respectively) at Upsalón (University of Havana), until he ascends out of the realms of darkness to reach the final encounter with the master himself, Oppiano Licario, in the penultimate chapter. Thus Cemí, initiated as poet and redeemed through poetry, moves towards inner growth and outer experience.

The novel is marked by a wealth of erudition and intertextual allusion, and by its exquisite language which often defies translation. For example, from *Paradiso*: 'Foción listened to him as one who watches a branch break off in relation to the stone it will cover, the tiger that it will awaken, the splash it will make in the current', or:

> After a dish of such impressive appearance, with flowing colours like those of a flambée, nearing the baroque but still gothic, owing to the baking and allegories sketched by the prawns, Doña Augusta wanted to calm the rhythm of the meal with a beet salad that had received a spatula lick of mayonnaise, crossed by Lubeck asparagus.
>
> (translated by Gregory Rabassa)

Lezama Lima was working on the continuation of *Paradiso*, a novel entitled *Oppiano Licario*, when he died. Fragments of the novel were published posthumously in 1977 but other sections have since been discovered, and a new edition appeared in 1989. In this second novel the main characters from *Paradiso* reappear, but looming over them all is the singularly original yet paradigmatic Oppiano Licario (his name stemming from Icarus), the master and (some

critics believe) the mirror-image of Lezama Lima himself. Oppiano Licario is complemented by the feminine principle, his sister Ynaca Eco who represents poetry. She infuses Cemí with divine spirituality through the sexual act, which—for Lezama Lima—was a means of reaching knowledge and of communicating with the universe.

Lezama Lima devised his impressive 'poetic system' in an attempt to capture the unknown mysteries of the infinite through imagery, to express the inexpressible, and to make the invisible visible.

—Catherine Davies

LI BAI [Li Po]. Also known as Li Taibo. Born in Central Asia, in 701 or possibly 705; brought up in Sichuan province, China. Spent a few years as a Daoist hermit in his teens, and trained as a knight-errant before the age of 25. Married four times. Spent early life in wandering; was summoned to the court of Emperor Xuanzong, 742, and retained as an unofficial court poet until 1745: fell victim to the intrigue of the influential court officials and left the court in disgrace; lived as wanderer again, and entered service of Prince Lin, brother of Emperor Suzong, 757, but was banished after Lin's defeat in a bid for the throne, 759. *Died in 762.*

PUBLICATIONS

Works

Li Taibai wenji (works). 1717 (based on 8th-century manuscripts); modern editions: *Sibu beiyao*, 1936—; *Li Taibai quanji* [Complete Works], edited by Wang Qi, 3 vols., 1977; selections: *Lyrics*, translated by Michitaro Hisa and William Wells Newell, 1905; 'Cathay', translated by Ezra Pound, in his *Poetry*, 1915; *Lustra*, translated by Ezra Pound, 1916; *Li Po: The Chinese Poet*, translated by Shigeyoshi Obata, 1922; *Tu Fu and Li Po: Selected Poetry*, edited and translated by Arthur Cooper, 1973; *Li Po: A New Translation* (bilingual edition), translated by Sun Yu, 1982.

*

Critical Studies: *The Poetry and Career of Li Po* by Arthur Waley, 1950; 'On Li Po' by E.O. Eide, in *Perspectives on the T'ang*, edited by A.F. Wright and D. Twitchett, 1973; *The Genius of Li Po* by Wong Siu-kit, 1974; *The Poet Li Po* by Yung Teng Chia-yee, 1975; 'The Lonely Journey: The Travels of Li Po' by J.W. Fenn, in *Asian Culture Quarterly*, 8, 1980; 'Li Po and Tu Fu: A Comparative Study' by Huang Kuo-pin, in *Renditions*, 21–22, 1984.

*   *   *

No poet, except Du Fu, holds so prominent a position as Li

Bai among Chinese classical poets since the Tang dynasty. He was highly praised by the poets of his time, earning the title 'celestial poet'. His poems, especially because of their exuberant and romantic style, were admired and imitated by later poets, and also widely read by succeeding generations.

Li Bai was born of a wealthy family and lived an extravagant life when he was young. He learned swordplay and in his early years the scope of his reading was wide. At the age of 26 he left his native place and became a poor wanderer, travelling over most of the country. He visited famous mountains and rivers, Daoist priests and temples. As his reputation spread, he was recommended to the imperial court and soon summoned by the Emperor to Chang'an, the capital. Although he wanted to become involved in the administration of state affairs and to help improve the quality of people's lives, he was employed only to write poems for the Emperor's pleasure. He despised the corrupt and treacherous court officials. (On one occasion, he forced Gao Lishi, a powerful eunuch, to take off his boots in the presence of the Emperor.) After he left the court, he went through great hardships in his later life of wandering.

His love for the beauty of nature and his legendary experiences contributed a great deal to the enduring themes and style of his poems. In many poems he described the beautiful landscape of the swift Yellow River, the precipitous mountains, and the long and wide Yangzi River. Some of these poems, such as 'Viewing the Waterfall at Mount Lu', rank as masterpieces. The scene of the falls delineated in the verse: 'Flying waters descending straight three thousand feet, Till I think the Milky Way has tumbled from the ninth height of Heaven' is like a beautiful picture.

He was a patriot, and his poems express his love for the country and sympathy for the sufferings of the common people. He condemned the evil war in his verse: 'White bones are piling up like hills, Why should the people suffer?'. Failing to fulfil his wish to save the common people and help the country out of great difficulties, he nevertheless severely criticized and mocked the debauched and treacherous court officials in his poems, while, on the other hand, he revealed his personal anguish and melancholy. From time to time he found escape from his worldly trouble in retirement and indulgence in wine: 'I'm glad to talk and drink good wine, Together with my hermit friend. I'm drunk and you're merry and glad, We both forget the world is sad'. As he was unsatisfied with life, he expressed in his poems his wish to withdraw from human society and seek happiness by living in seclusion. For him wine was indispensable. He said bluntly in 'The Song of Wine': 'I wish to drink myself drunk, never to become sober again'.

Among other poems, 'I Miss My Husband When Spring Comes', 'Lovesick', and 'The Crows Caw in the Evening' are expressive of faithful love and the grief of lovers separated by long military service. He described in 'Ballads of Four Seasons' the feeling of a woman longing for her husband to return home: 'When will they put down the barbarians and my good man come home from his far campaign?'. Elsewhere he showed his sympathy with women forsaken by their husbands. 'Waiting in Vain', for example, exhibits grudges borne by a fair lady against her lover who has probably deserted her: 'Wet stains of tears can still be seen. Who, heartless, has caused her the pain?'.

Li Bai learned from his predecessors and from the folk songs and ballads (*yuefu* poetry). He inherited the traditions of Chinese poetry but developed his own style, characterized by his brilliant imagination, exquisite but not ornate language, and by delicate, vivid, yet natural descriptions. As far as aesthetic value is concerned, in the history of Chinese literature there is hardly any ancient poet of later generations who could equal him.

—Binghong Lu

HARD IS THE ROAD TO SHU
Poem by Li Bai, written c.744.

'Hard is the Road to Shu' (otherwise translated as 'The Road to Shu is Hard') is one of Li Bai's most important poems in terms of the poetic imagination and descriptive power with which Li Bai handled the theme.

Shu, now a Sichuan province in west China, is surrounded by sheer mountains and is well-known in history for its inhospitable location and hazardous road conditions. Originally, 'Hard Is the Road to Shu' was the title of a *yuefu* ballad describing difficulties and dangers involved in travelling to Shu. This poem was written in about 744 when Li Bai was staying in Chang'an, the then capital. He wrote it as a farewell poem for a friend who was going to make a journey to Shu. Though using the same title and subject as the *yuefu* ballad, this poem of Li Bai's excels all previous poems and folk songs in its description of the hardships and perils of travelling on the road to Shu. The way to Shu, a rich and, for many people, a fantastic land, is so hard that 'Since the two pioneers/Put the kingdom in order,/Have passed forty-eight thousand years/And few have tried to pass its border'. As described in the poem, there has been, for a very long time, no walkable footpath to Shu from the neighbouring region of Qin. Only the flight-path of birds cuts through Emei [Mount Eyebrows]. A rocky path was hacked along the cliffs only after 'the crest crumbled' through the effect of legendary force. The journey is not only hard for humans. 'Even the Golden Crane can't fly across;/How to climb over,/gibbons are at a loss.' The poem presents a breathtaking picture of travel over inaccessible mountain peaks and precipitous cliffs: scaling the mountain, one can touch the stars; and one has to run away from man-eating tigers at daybreak and from long blood-sucking snakes at dusk.

The line 'The road to Shu is harder than to climb to the sky', a sigh breathed by the poet, is repeated three times—at the beginning, in the middle, and at the end of the poem, deepening the intensive impression of the hardships and despair suffered on the journey. However, the scenes unfolded before the reader are not unpleasant or depressing, but varied and enchanting. The poet invites the reader to share in the rare experience of the journey by following the traveller's footsteps in the poet's imagination. The rugged paths, cliffs upwards toward the sky, ancient trees, dashing torrents, birds flying in the forests are all knitted into extraordinary and picturesque visions.

What attracts the reader is not only the scenery, described in a vivid and dynamic way, but also the legend and mythology that are interlaced in masterly fashion and which give the poem strong romantic colouring. For example, the 'two pioneers', the two legendary kings who ruled Shu 40,000 years ago, evoke an atmosphere of mystery. 'Five serpent-killing heroes' are five legendary brave men sent by the ruler of Shu to meet and protect five women whom the king of Qin promised in marriage to the ruler of Shu. On the way, they encountered a huge serpent. While the five men were pulling its tail, trying to drag it out of a hole, the mountain crumbled and all the men and women died and were transformed into five mountain peaks. This legend lends the poem a strong tinge of heroic tragedy and mystery. And the cuckoos, which, according to legend, wept after Du Yu, a king of Shu, had left the palace on his abdication are a symbol evoking memories of the sad past.

Opinions differ about the theme of this poem. An early annotator noted that, in a parabolic way, the poem tried to persuade the foolish and self-indulgent Emperor Xuanzong of the Tang dynasty, who had fled to Shu from the chaos of war, not to stay in Shu for too long. Some modern scholars disagree, pointing out that this is an anachronism, the poem having been written before the war in question actually started. Whatever the argument over the theme, it is frequently suggested that the last few lines may allude to the possible rebellions of warlords in Shu.

Li Bai used some traditional writing techniques often seen in *yuefu* ballads. For example, 'Alas! Why should you come here from afar?', asks the poet. It is a rhetorical question. 'The Town of Silk', today's Chengdu, and the capital of Sichuan province, may be a place for one to make merry, 'But I would rather homeward go', Li Bai states near the end of the poem. It is a kind of general warning to all hearing or reading the poem.

Li Bai, nevertheless, broke with tradition to develop a style of his own. Critics through the centuries have admired the superb description of the natural scenes and miraculous traveller's experiences, the subtle allusions, the flowing style without 'purple passages', the romanticism, and the author's unconstrained manner all fused in this poem. It is always considered the masterpiece of Li Bai's romantic style. On reading this poem, He Zhizhang, another well-known poet and a contemporary, marvelled at it, exclaiming that Li Bai was a 'celestial being banished from Heaven'.

—Binghong Lu

INVITATION TO WINE
Poem by Li Bai, written 752.

'Invitation to Wine' (or 'The Song of Wine') is one of the best-known of Li Bai's poems. Its title is the same as that of a *yuefu* ballad which is mainly about wine-drinking and singing. This poem was written in 752, when Li Bai was staying with a friend during his second period of wanderings after he had left the Emperor's palace. With his ambition to help the administration and the country unfulfilled, and his talents stifled, he felt depressed and, as he implied in the lines 'kill a cow, cook a sheep and let us merry be,/And drink three hundred cupfuls of wine in high glee', he found a way to vent his frustrations by indulging himself in wine. Wine is like a thread running through the whole poem.

The poem (translation by Xu Yuanzhong) begins with two most impressive lines, 'Do you not see the Yellow River come from the sky,/Rushing into the sea and ne'er come back?', which imply that time passes fast and life is short. The shortness of life is further emphasized and expressed directly in the lines that follow immediately: 'Do you not see the mirrors bright in chambers high/Grieve o'er your snow-white hair though once it was silk-black (at daybreak)?'. To enjoy a brief life to the full before it comes to an end, the poet proposes that you 'drink your fill in high delight,/And never leave your wine-cup empty in moonlight'. These lines, infused with a gloomy ambience, reflect Li Bai's attitude towards life, especially after his unhappy days at court. He was summoned to the palace but, contrary to his expectations, given only a low post as a literary attendant writing poems to please the Emperor. Later, slandered by influential officials and in dis-

favour with the Emperor, he had to leave the court. To 'wash away' the bitterness in the depths of his heart, he took to drink. He set little store by fame, an attitude reflected in the line 'But great drinkers are more famous than sober sages'. Examples are cited from history to drive the point home: the Prince of Poets (Cao Zhi, 192–232 AD) 'feast'd in his palace at will,/and drank wine at ten thousand a cask and laughed his fill', and a Confucian Scholar could 'drink three hundred cupfuls of wine' at a time 'in high glee'. Li Bai's negative attitude towards life permeates the whole poem. However, his state of mind was complicated. He was not totally dejected. In the line 'Heaven has made us talents, we're not made in vain' he emits out of his downcast mood sparks of hope and self-confidence.

This poem creates a self-indulgent image which, to a great extent, is a self-portrait of the poet. It is not only a genuine reflection of his melancholy mood but a portrayal of his character. Though Li Bai tried all his life to find a way to use his talents in politics, he did not intend to make a fortune through politics. He thought one should not care about wealth. The poet asks here, 'What difference will rare and costly dishes make?', and states, 'A host should not complain of money he is short [of]', and 'To drink with you I will sell things of any sort'. For the poet, wine is more important then wealth and has almost become his lifeblood. Even 'my fur coat worth a thousand coins of gold/And my flower-dappled horse may be sold/To buy good wine that we may drown the woes age-old'. This last line reveals Li Bai's melancholy and brings out his deep grievance over the failure to fulfil his political ambition. It is the focal point of the poem, presenting a picture of an anguished poet. Artistically it brings out a sharp contrast between the pleasures of wine described up to this point and the pent-up sadness for which the poet wishes to find an outlet. Thus the theme is fully expressed and the artistic effect superbly achieved.

This poem has proved itself over centuries to be one of Li Bai's masterpieces. Lines like 'Do you not see the Yellow River come from the sky,/Rushing into the sea and ne'er come back?' and 'Heaven has made us talents, we're not made in vain' have become catchphrases known in almost every household in China. Li Bai's frustrations can be sensed between the lines, and his bohemian style of life is very evident. Nevertheless, his self-confidence and philosophical spirit in the face of setbacks in his career lend great appeal to the poem. His brilliant artistry is displayed through the skilful use of language and in figures of speech such as hyperbole ('the Yellow River comes from the sky' and 'My fur coat is worth a thousand coins of gold' and so on) and metaphor (for example, the change of the colour of hair described to indicate ageing, and the contrast mentioned above). No wonder the poem has always had a wide readership and is learned by heart by many Chinese.

—Binghong Lu

————

LI PO. See **LI BAI.**

————

LI TAIBO. See **LI BAI.**

————

THE LIFE AND ADVENTURES OF LAZARILLO DE TORMES. See **LAZARILLO DE TORMES.**

THE LIFE OF LAZARILLO DE TORMES. See **LAZARILLO DE TORMES.**

LIMA, José Lezama. See **LEZAMA LIMA, José.**

LINNA, Väinö. Born in Urjala, Finland, 20 December 1920. Served in the army during Finland's Continuation War against the Soviet Union, 1941–44. Married Kerttu Seuri in 1945; two children. Worked on farms and in the mill industry; factory worker, Tampere, 1938–55. Recipient: Finnish state literature prize, 1959, 1960; Nordic prize, 1963; Finnish cultural prize, 1974. *Died 21 April 1992.*

PUBLICATIONS

Fiction

Päämäärä [The Goal]. 1947.
Musta rakkaus [Black Love]. 1948.
Tuntematon sotilas. 1954; translated as *The Unknown Soldier*, 1957.
Täällä Pohjantähden alla [Here under the North Star]. 3 vols., 1959–62.

Other

Oheisia: esseitä ja puheenvuoroja [By the Way] (essays and addresses). 1967.
Murroksia: esseitä, puheita ja kirjoituksia [Transitions] (essays, articles, and talks). 1990.

*

Critical Studies: 'Väinö Linna: A Classic in His Own Time' by Yrjö Varpio, in *Books from Finland*, 11(3), 1977; 'What Do the People Sing? Singing in Väinö Linna's Novel *The Unknown Soldier*' by Jyrki Nummi, in *Proceedings of the Sixth Annual Meeting of the Finno-Ugric Studies Association of Canada*, edited by Joel Ashmore Nevis, 1989.

* * *

Väinö Linna's breakthrough novel, *Tuntematon sotilas* (*The Unknown Soldier*), has become a noteworthy critical and popular success. The novel has been translated into more than 20 languages, made into two films, adapted for stage performances, and has inspired the composition of an opera. The novel is often compared with Erich Maria Remarque's *Im Westen nichts Neues* (*All Quiet on the Western Front*) and Norman Mailer's *The Naked and the Dead*, invariably to *The Unknown Soldier*'s advantage. Upon its first appearance in 1954, however, the novel engendered more critical controversy in Finland than any other literary work to that date—controversy which subsequently came to be known as 'the literary war'. Traditionalists, in particular, saw the novel as destroying the idealistic myth about the Finnish soldier as an unselfish, ultra-nationalistic hero, a myth which the army, media, and educational institutions had been perpetuating over 30 years. Rather, *The Unknown Soldier* reflected a general change in attitudes in post-war Finland. In retrospect, it is difficult to say to what extent the general attitudes of the people influenced the novel, and the novel shaped the thoughts and attitudes of the people. For the post-war generations *The Unknown Soldier* became, besides an anti-war novel, a historical document, not in the traditional documentary sense, but in the sense that it chronicled the *experience* of Finland's 20th-century war, stripped of both varnish and rhetoric.

The Unknown Soldier describes the 1941–44 war between Finland and the (then) Soviet Union from the point of view of the ordinary rank-and-file soldier. More specifically, the central characters of the novel are a platoon of machine-gunners who belong to Finland's 11th division, troops who at the beginning of hostilities are the first to endure the enemy's firepower at its most devastating. Linna's mode of writing about the men's extraordinary physical and psychological tenacity, and their ability to adjust to the inhuman demands made on them, separates his novel from *All Quiet on the Western Front* and *The Naked and the Dead*. By showing the ability of human intelligence to carry on a dialogue with itself, to differentiate between what is valuable and what is worthless even in the midst of the worst adversity, Linna portrays bitter reality in a positive light rather than as a manifestation of all-encompassing moral decay. Moreover, each of Linna's soldiers has an exceptionally strong sense of his own worth as a human being, and it is this unshakeable sense of self that gives him his remarkable strength to endure, no matter how miserable and insignificant his existence.

Although *The Unknown Soldier* shows the utter futility and mindlessness of war, it consciously avoids utopian sentimentalism. Moreover, Linna's opposition is not to nationalism as such, but its deterioration into ultra-nationalism which valorizes combat and attaches some kind of human value to war. His realistic treatment of his subject—a war story told at 'ground-level' where the results of decisions made by those in power are experienced at their toughest; where utter misery silences rather than gives birth to jingoistic sentiments; and where fear is as much a physical as an emotional experience—searches and finds in the novel's characters what might be termed 'the core human'. Thus despite being a war novel, its characters ultimately affirm life and the novel retains a positive view of humanity.

Linna's soldiers are from different parts of Finland and speak in the dialects of their home regions. The idiosyncrasies of speech not only provide much of the humour in the novel, but also function to emphasize the individual personalities of the men, thus adding life to the novel. The fact that each man has his own unique way of expressing himself separates him from his comrades, however common their day-to-day experiences; hence his colloquial mode of speech becomes a principal feature of each soldier, and each turn of dialogue corresponds with the speaker's nature, resulting in living, multidimensional characterizations.

The soldiers are an amalgam of loggers, factory workers, and simple farmers, each with virtues and vices, who nevertheless accomplish heroic deeds which lead at times to victories. Linna's soldier is more often than not a complaining individualist with an abundant reserve of black humour, who rises above the propagandist rhetoric about war and who fights when necessary out of fear of death and out of loyalty to his comrades, not as a reflex to army discipline. In that he fights and gives his life for his country, despite his irreverent attitude, lies his greatness. The central character in the novel, the stubborn farmer, Antti Rokka, is just such a rugged individualist. In drawing his character, Linna's creative brilliance produces a Colossus, one who never learns to obey orders with which he does not agree, and yet who as a soldier is unmatched.

It has been argued that Linna's treatment not only misrepresents (if not vilifies), but certainly diminishes the glory bestowed upon the Finnish soldier by military experts familiar with the Finnish army's conduct during the so-called Winter War and the subsequent 1941–44 war. They maintain that no army could have fought as effectively without iron-fisted discipline. Military-historical arguments aside, *The Unknown Soldier* also acknowledges the size and weight of the contribution the soldiers made; this is particularly true of the second half of the novel. In his own way Linna acknowledges what is generally known, namely that it was the Finnish soldier who guaranteed Finnish independence although both wars ended in defeat for Finland.

Linna's employment of the rich variations in Finnish language, both in terms of colloquialisms and regional dialects, not only links this epic work with the Finnish prose tradition, but makes it an unusually challenging and problematic novel to translate. Much of the humour in the novel, the positive contrast to the cruelty and misery of war, becomes lost and the psychological dimensions of the characters are diminished in translation. Among foreign-language editions, the Swedish translation has been the most successful and the English-language edition perhaps the least impressive owing, in part, to arbitrary omissions and mistranslations. Nevertheless, reception of the novel has been as varied outside as within the sphere of its original language. It has run the gamut from being viewed as a source of study for military reserve officers, a chronicle of 20th-century history in part, a fascinating tale of battle between a modern David and Goliath, a documentation of the Finland–Soviet War to, finally, what *The Unknown Soldier* is above all else, a representative of the international genre of war novels. As such it is ranked among the best of its kind.

—Seija Paddon

LISPECTOR, Clarice. Born in Tchetchelnik, Ukraine, USSR (now independent republic), 10 December 1925. Family moved to Brazil, 1925, and settled in Recife, 1927. Educated at the Ginásio Pernambuco, 1935–36; Colégio Sílvio Leite, Rio de Janeiro, 1937; Colégio Andrews, Rio de Janeiro; National Faculty of Law, Rio de Janeiro, 1941–44, degree in law 1944. Married Mauri Gurgel Valente in 1943 (separated 1959); two sons. Editor and contributor, *Agência Nacional* and *A Noite*, while still a student, 1941–44; left Brazil because of her husband's diplomatic postings: lived in Europe (principally Naples and Berne), 1944–52, and in the USA, 1952–59; returned to Rio de Janeiro after separation from her husband, 1959. Recipient: Graça Aranha Foundation prize, 1944; São Paulo Cármen Dolores Barbosa prize, 1962; Golfinho de Ouro prize, 1969; Tenth National Literary Library Competition prize, 1976. *Died 9 December 1977.*

PUBLICATIONS

Collection

Antologia cometada, edited by Samira Youssef Campedello and Benjamin Abdalla. 1981.

Fiction

Perto do coração selvagem. 1944; as *Near to the Wild Heart*, translated by Giovanni Pontiero, 1990.
O lustre. 1946.
A cidade sitiada: romance. 1948; revised edition, 1964.
Alguns contos (stories). 1952.
Laços de família (stories). 1960; as *Family Ties*, translated by Giovanni Pontiero, 1972.
A maçã no escuro. 1961; as *The Apple in the Dark*, translated by Gregory Rabassa, 1967.
A Paixão Segundo G.H. 1964; edited by Benedito Nunes, 1988; as *The Passion According to G.H.*, translated by Ronald W. Sousa, 1988.
A Legião Estrangeira (stories and chronicles). 1964; as *The Foreign Legion*, translated by Giovanni Pontiero, 1986.
O mistério do coelho pensante (for children). 1967.
A mulher que matou os peixes (for children). 1968; as *The Woman Who Killed the Fish*, translated by Earl E. Fitz, in *Latin American Literary Review*, 32, July–December 1988.
Uma aprendizagem; ou, o livro dos prazeres. 1969; as *An Apprenticeship; or, The Book of Delights*, translated by Richard A. Mazzara and Lorri A. Parris, 1986.
Felicidade clandestina: contos. 1971.
Água viva. 1973; as *The Stream of Life*, translated by Elizabeth Lowe and Earl E. Fitz, 1989.
A imitação da Rosa (stories). 1973.
Onde estivestes de noite (stories). 1974; selection in *Soulstorm*, 1989.
A via crucis do corpo (stories). 1974; selection in *Soulstorm*, 1989.
A vida íntima de Laura (for children). 1974.
Cont escolhidos (stories). 1976.
A hora da estrela. 1977; as *The Hour of the Star*, translated by Giovanni Pontiero, 1986.
Um sopro de vida: pulsações. 1978.
Quase de verdade (for children). 1978.
A Bela e a Fera (stories). 1979.
Soulstorm (stories), translated by Alexis Levitin. 1989.

Other

De corpos inteiro (interviews). 1975.
Seleta, edited by Renato Cordeiro Gomes and Amariles Guimarães Hill. 1975.
Visão do esplendor: impressões leves. 1975.
Para não esquecer (essays). 1978.

A descoberta do mundo (diary). 1984; as *Discovering the World*, translated by Giovanni Pontiero, 1992.
Reading with Clarice Lispector (miscellany), edited by Hélène Cixous, translated by Verena Andermatt Conley, 1990.

Translator, *O retrato de Dorian Gray*, by Oscar Wilde. 1974.

*

Bibliography: *Brazilian Literature: A Research Guide* by David William Foster and Walter Rela, 1990.

Critical Studies: 'Existence in *Laços de família*' by Rita Herman, in *Luso-Brazilian Review*, 4(1), 1967; *Clarice Lispector* by Assis Brasil, 1969; 'Lispector: Fiction and Comic Vision' by Massuad Moisés, translated by Sara M. McCabe, in *Studies in Short Fiction*, 8(1), 1971; 'The Drama of Existence in *Laços de família*', in *Studies in Short Fiction*, 8(1), 1971, and 'Lispector: An Intuitive Approach to Fiction', in *Knives and Angels* edited by Susan Bassnett, 1990, both by Giovanni Pontiero; *Leitura de Clarice Lispector* by Benedito Nunes, 1973; 'Clarice Lispector and the Lyrical Novel: A Re-Examination of *A maça no escuro*', in *Luso-Brazilian Review*, 14(2), 1973, 'The Leitmotif of Darkness in Seven Novels by Clarice Lispector', in *Chasqui: Revista de Literatura Latinoamericana*, 7(2), 1978, Freedom and Self-Realization: Feminist Characterization in the Fiction of Clarice Lispector', in *Modern Language Studies*, 10(3), 1980, 'Point of View in Clarice Lispector's *A hora da estrela*', in *Luso-Brazilian Review*, 19(2), 1982, and *Clarice Lispector*, 1985, all by Earl E. Fitz; 'Narrative Modes in Clarice Lispector's *Laços de família*: The Rendering of Consciousness' by Maria Luísa Nunes, in *Luso-Brazilian Review*, 14(2), 1977; 'Clarice Lispector: Articulating Women's Experience' by Naomi Lindstrom, in *Chasqui: Revista de Literatura Latinoamericana*, 8(1), 1978; *A escritura de Clarice Lispector* by Olga de Sá, 1979; 'Clarice Lispector and the Clamor of the Ineffable' by Daphne Patai, in *Kentucky Romance Quarterly*, 27(2), 1980; *Clarice Lispector* edited by Samira Y. Campedello and Benjamin Abdalla, 1981; *Clarice Lispector: esboço para um possível retrato* by Olga Borelli, 1981; *Clarice Lispector* by Berta Waldman, 1983; *O alto criador de Clarice Lispector* by Nicolino Novello, 1987.

* * *

When Clarice Lispector published her first novel, *Perto do coração selvagem* (*Near to the Wild Heart*), aged 17, the critical establishment hailed this event as a turning point in Brazilian fiction, heralding as it did the advent in Brazil of the technique of stream of consciousness first experimented with in Europe by James Joyce and Virginia Woolf. The significance of the assimilation of this formal innovation to Brazilian literature encompassed (as it had in the case of its European precursors) implications of much greater import than the purely stylistic, gesturing as it did—in the case of Brazil three decades later than in Europe—towards the beginning of the articulation of a crisis of modernity which had not truly made itself felt in that country until the period immediately following the world Depression in the 1930s. It is in the context of the emergence of a new reality demanding articulation, and of the difficulties inherent in this process of articulation, earlier confronted by the European Modernists' fragmented vision of the ruins of the old order and the uncharted territory of a post-World War I scenario, that

Lispector's writing must be understood; and it is in the light of this awareness, too, that the fundamental importance in Lispector's writing of language itself as that which must at once be struggled against and drawn upon in the formulation of a new reality ought to be emphasized. In her narrative fiction, therefore, much more crucially than the social problems that underwrite the Brazilian crisis of modernity the Lispector's own vision (imminent national bankruptcy, poverty, unequal distribution of wealth, the situation of women under patriarchy), the impossibility of reaching a coherent verbal expression for these dilemmas figures as the immediate and irresolvable impasse of protagonists whose perception or gaze disintegrates the very reality they seek to understand.

It is discourse itself, therefore, and the brutal authoritarianism of a language rendered all-powerful in the face of the protagonists' existential difficulties, which rules the narrative: discourse as the demiurge of self and other, discourse as the creator, source and definer of the narrative world, discourse as the linguistic articulator, classifier, and omnipotent decision-maker concerning character, time, and place in these universes of fiction. Whether dealing with first- or third-person narration, therefore, it is language itself as the instrument of gnosis that beckons character and reader with the promise of understanding, only immediately to shatter that possibility; and it is the focus on precisely that moment of fragmentation, the moment that separates the time when knowledge, truth, and comprehension are still possible from the non-linearity and disconnection of the untimely space following the instant of breakage, that is the hallmark of Lispector's writing. She dwells repeatedly, throughout each of her novels and short stories on the process whereby the everyday, the ordinary, the linguistically, intellectually, and emotionally comprehensible is set adrift, stripped of cohesion and abandoned as the disorderly remnant of a previous, now inconceivable old order. In this new reality, the focus of narrative concern in the unfolding subjectivity of the protagonists, of the world through their eyes, the process of gazing upon an erstwhile ordinary reality unwarningly rendered imponderable; and in the process, too, the concept of 'ordinary reality' becomes itself questionable, or impossible, in the face of the abrupt defamiliarization of the familiar, and its subsequent destruction.

Reading Lispector, therefore, requires the acceptance of loss on the part of the reader, loss of old points of reference, of established readership assumptions, of logic, received wisdom and expectation, and the tacit readerly agreement to flow with the language of the text, and to surrender to the disorder that this language carries in its wake, put to a use that is not now necessarily the fixation of narrative meaning, but its postponement or abolition.

In consideration Lispector's writing, the uncharted intellectual/existential/emotional terrain that her protagonists' subjectivity opens up, and in confronting the manner in which these protagonists' dilemmas force us to ask questions concerning their participation or exclusion from reality, the tenability of previous definitions or normality and consciousness, linearity of time, circumscription of space, and the possibility of meaning, we are also, as readers, forced to entertain the hypothesis that logic, language, and meaning are not monopolies of a single origin, but are rather defined by multiplicity, plurality, and dispersal, and that pre-existent, transcendental meaning, therefore, is not inevitably grasped by the reading spectator, but is possibly elusive and may not exist as a single entity.

It is this acceptance of disruption of reader expectation, in other words of the reader's entitlement to processed and digestible meaning, which is required of Lispector's readers, and her refusal to provide plot or clear-cut character outlines is also what forces her reader to posit the likelihood that here is indeed a new language focused on a new reality, not just an old one put to (relatively) new usage. Language, in Lispector, is of the essence, while refusing essential, unambiguous meaning: language is life-giving and life-destroying. It is the workings of language itself which we witness in these narratives, allowing us as readers to observe its backstage manoeuvres, discarding the realist need for readerly suspension of disbelief and replacing it instead with an exhibition of its narrative status as language *per se*, language at play in realities in invented, rather than language as a transparent window held up to a pre-existing, comprehensible reality.

Lispector's fiction is peppered with moments of epiphany or revelation; this is not, however, the revelation of an ultimate or divine meaning or explanation, but only the realization that any meaning attained is likely to be so temporary and dispersed as to relinquish the right to the very concept of meaningfulness. In terms of plot parameters or character subjectivity, this realization, in works such as *A hora da estrela* (*The Hour of the Star*) or 'A imitação da rosa' ('The Imitation of the Rose'), potentially leads to a temporary or indefinite suspension of sanity, or affirmation of madness. If, as is the case with Laura in the latter text, her madness allows us a glimpse of her immersion into a new, alternative reality, it is a reality that our language, circumscribed by the limitations of logic and reason cannot convey, being reduced instead to underpinning it through images of crazed incoherence. Madness, therefore, which becomes simply an alternative consciousness following the moment of severance with everyday reality, is a leitmotif in this writer's work. Another characteristic is the relinquishing of a social underpinning in favour of prioritizing philosophical abstraction and individual subjectivity.

The latter point elicits the question of whether or not there is a dimension of social and political concern to Lispector's work, a question all the more pertinent given her frequent choice of women or the dispossessed as central to the process of subjective fragmentation at the heart of her fiction. Several critical readings have pinpointed successfully a clear social preoccupation with both feminist and material or class issues in her writing, and a thematic constancy in her consideration of problems of human disenfranchisement as a variety of levels. Lispector remains, at all these levels, therefore, one of the essential voices of Brazilian modernism and continues to influence contemporary experimental authors and intellectuals within and outside Brazil.

—Maria Manuel Lisboa

THE LITTLE CLAY CART (Mṛichchhakaṭikā). Ancient Indian Sanskrit play, the preface of which asserts that it was written by 'King Śūdraka', of whose existence there is no other evidence. Date of composition extremely uncertain: suggestions include 1st century BC, 1st century AD, mid-2nd century AD, and even 5th century AD.

PUBLICATIONS

The Mṛichchhakaṭikā. 1904 (2nd edition, with commentary of Prithvadara); edited by Rangacharya B. Raddi, 1909; also edited by M.R. Kale (bilingual edition), 1924, R.D. Karmarkar (bilingual edition), 1937, and V.G. Paranjpe, 1937; as *Mrichchhakati; or, The Toy-Cart*, translated by H.H. Wilson, 1901; as *The Toy Cart*, translated by Arthur Symons, 1919; also translated P. Lal, in *Great Sanskrit Plays*, 1957; as *The Little Clay Cart*, translated by Arthur W. Ryder, 1905, reprinted 1965; also translated by Satyendra Kumar Basa, 1939; Revilo Pendleton Oliver, 1938, and in *Six Sanskrit Plays*, edited by Henry W. Wells, 1964; J.A.B. van Buitenen, in *Two Plays of Ancient India*, 1968; Barbara Stoler Miller, 1984; A.L. Basham, 1994.

*

Critical Studies: *Introduction to the Study of Mṛcchakaṭika* by G.V. Devasthali, 1951; *Preface to Mṛcchakaṭikā* by G.K. Bhat, 1953; *Śūdraka* by C.B. Pandey, 1958; *Theater in India* by Balwant Gargi, 1962; *The Sanskrit Drama in Its Origin, Development, Theory and Practice* by Arthur Berriedale Keith, 1964; 'Producing *The Little Clay Cart*' by J. Michel, in *Asian Drama*, edited by H. Wells, 1965, and 'Artifice and Naturalism in the East' by Wells in *Quest*, 1(1), 1965–66.

* * *

The Little Clay Cart ranks with Kalidasa's *Śakuntalā* as one of the great masterpieces of the Indian theatre, but nothing is known of its author except what the preface of the play itself reveals. According to Stage Manager, the play is the work of a 'King Śūdraka', an expert in the *Rig-Veda*, the *Sāma-Veda*, mathematics, the arts of courtesans, and the training of elephants, who lived 100 years and ten days, and after establishing his son as successor cast himself into the flames. No such king is recorded in history, and most scholars assume that he is purely legendary, a dramatic mask for the unknown real author who sought perhaps in this way to give his work a patina of nobility and antiquity.

Early in the 20th century a group of dramas by the pioneer Sanskrit dramatist Bhāsa were discovered, among them one called *Chārudatta in Poverty* which, it was soon observed, tells essentially the same story, occasionally in almost the same words, as the first four acts of *The Little Clay Cart*. Clearly the author of that work appropriated this material as the basis for his much longer ten-act work. While the longer version is compatible with the original material, the major characters are considerably deepened and enriched, many new and striking minor characters are added, and the perspective is broadened so that the private affairs of the hero are intertwined with the fate of the city and the kingdom.

Although pious Brahmins and wealthy courtesans are common figures in the Sanskrit theatre, *The Little Clay Cart* is the only play to show a love affair between two such figures. Chārudatta's poverty is the result of his generosity, and although it has cost him friends and physical comfort, he is happily married with a son when he sees the courtesan Vasantasenā in the temple and they are strongly attracted to each other. Fate works to bring them together. Vasantasenā rejects, yet is pursued by, Prince Saṁsthānaka, the half-mad brother of the ruling King Pālaka, and by his attendant and a servant. In an elaborately choreographed sequence, they stalk her about the empty stage, representing the city streets at night, reciting in turn balanced poetic stanzas, each in a different dialect. The attendant, betraying his evil lord, aids Vasantasenā to seek refuge in Chārudatta's humble home.

Vasantasenā leaves a casket of jewels in trust with Chārudatta, initiating an elaborate subplot. These jewels are subsequently stolen by a thief who is seeking wealth to buy and marry one of Vasantasenā's serving women. Vasantasenā accepts the jewels in payment for her servant, but before she can inform Chārudatta of their recovery his wife volunteers her own rare pearl necklace as recompense, providing the courtesan with further proof of Chārudatta's love and honour.

At this point, during the fourth act, a political action (not found in the original version) begins. Sarvilaka, the thief, hears that his friend Prince Āryaka has been arrested by the King on the advice of a soothsayer. He leaves his new bride to aid the prince, who is reported to have escaped. The private and public actions now develop in tandem. Vasantasenā uses the pearl necklace as an excuse to return to Chārudatta's house. Another famous scene, paralleling in certain respects the night scene of the first act, shows Vasantasenā hurrying through a spring storm with her confidante, a slave-girl, and a slave with an umbrella, in an elaborate dance and poetic sequence, the alternating stanzas of which develop parallels between the upheaval in nature and that in the lovers' hearts.

The storm forces the courtesan to spend the night in Chārudatta's house and the next morning she meets his son, who complains that his only plaything is a little clay cart. She gives him jewels to buy one of gold. Chārudatta arranges to meet her again in a nearby park, but when he sends his carriage to fetch her, it is appropriated by the escaping Prince Āryaka. As a result Vasantasenā mistakenly takes the carriage of her evil pursuer Prince Samsthānaka.

When Prince Āryaka arrives in Chārudatta's carriage, Chārudatta shields him and goes in search of Vasantasenā. But she has encountered Samsthānaka who, enraged that she has not come to him willingly, orders his servants to kill her, and when they refuse, beats her himself until she falls unconscious. He buries her under some leaves and goes to the court to denounce Chārudatta as her murderer. Meanwhile, a monk whom Vasantasenā helped in the past finds and revives her. Chārudatta, accused of murder and also implicated in the escape of Prince Āryaka, is condemned to death.

The final act is the richest and most complex of the drama. It begins with the reading of Chārudatta's condemnation in the four sections of the city, and is primarily made up of the progress of the funeral procession through the city, interrupted several times by vain attempts by various minor characters to gain pardon for Chārudatta. The executioner's first blow is miraculously deflected, and before a second can be struck, Vasantasenā and the monk appear to save him. As the lovers rejoice, word comes that Prince Āryaka has slain King Pālaka and taken over the throne. Naturally he restores his helper Chārudatta to wealth and honour and frees Vasantasenā from her profession so that she may marry him. Even Samsthānaka is pardoned, at the request of the merciful Chārudatta.

This brief summary indicates only the principal features of this huge and complex work, written in verse and prose, and in several dialects along with the aristocratic Sanskrit. The cast of almost 30 characters represents every stratum of society, and even the minor ones are drawn with care and detail. Dance, pantomime, and music add to the verbal richness, providing a texture as varied as any work of world drama. The language which, as in all the greatest Sanskrit poetry, brilliantly mingles the sensual and the pious, natural phenomena and human feelings, defies the skill of the translator, but the complex fabric of human society and human emotions, suggesting the elaborate dramatic worlds of the Western Renaissance playwrights, has nevertheless made this drama highly appealing to Western readers.

—Marvin Carlson

————

LIVY. Born Titus Livius in Patavium (now Padua), northern Italy, in 64 or 59 BC. Had one daughter and one son. Settled in Rome, c.29 BC; came to know the emperor Augustus who expressed an interest in his work; encouraged the historical studies of the future emperor Claudius. *Died in AD 12 or 17.*

PUBLICATIONS

Works

Ab urbe condita, as *History of Rome*, edited by Charles William Stocker. 2 vols., 1838–44; also edited by W. Weissenborn, revised by Müller and Heraeus, 1887–1908; Books XXI–XXII edited by T.A. Dorey, 1971, Books XXVI–XXX by P.G. Walsh, 2 vols., 1982–86, Books XXXI–XL by J. Briscoe, 2 vols., 1991; Books I–X and XXI–XXXV edited by R.M. Ogilvie, C.F. Walters, A.H. McDonald, and others, 1919–74; also edited by J. Bayet and Paul Jal, 1947—; as *Roman History*, translated by Philemon Holland, 1600; also translated by William Gordon, 1783; J.H. Freese, A.J. Church, and W.J. Brodribb, 1898; as *History of Rome*, translated by George Baker, 6 vols., 1797, revised edition, 1864; also translated by D. Spillan, Cyrus Edmonds, and William A McDevitte, 4 vols., 1849–50; J.H. Freese and Edward Sprague Weymouth, 1892–93; William M. Roberts, 1912–24; B.O. Foster, E.T. Sage, A.C. Schlesinger, and F.G. Moore [Loeb Edition; bilingual], 14 vols., 1919–59; *The Early History of Rome* (Books I–V), 1960, and *The War with Hannibal* (Books XXI–XXX), 1965, both translated by Aubrey de Selincourt, and (Books XXI–XXX) translated by Selincourt and Betty Radice, 1970; *Rome and the Mediterranean* (Books XXXI–XLV) translated by Henry Bettenson, 1976; *Rome and Italy* (Books VI–X) translated by Betty Radice, 1982; selections as *Stories from Livy*, translated by R.M. Ogilvie, 1970, new edition, 1981; as *Stories of Rome*, translated by Roger Nichols, 1982; commentary on Books I–V by R.M. Ogilvie, 1965, on Books XXXI–XXXIII, 1973, and Books XXXIV–XXXVII, 1981, both by John Briscoe.

*

Critical Studies: *Constancy in Livy's Latinity* by K. Gries, 1947; *God and Fate in Livy* by I. Kajanto, 1957; *Livy: His Historical Aims and Methods*, 1961, and *Livy*, 1974, both by P.G. Walsh; *A Concordance to Livy* by David W. Packard, 4 vols., 1969; *Livy* edited by T.A. Dorey, 1971; *Livy: The Composition of His History* by T.J. Luce, 1977; *The Prose Rhythms of Sallust and Livy* by Hans Aili, 1979; *Notes on the Manuscripts of Livy's Fourth Decade* by John Briscoe, 1980; *A Historiographical Study of Livy, Books VI–X* by J.P.

Lipovsky, 1981; *Infinity of Narration in Livy: A Study in Narrative Technique* by Toivo Viljamaa, 1983; *Artistry and Ideology: Livy's Vocabulary of Virtue* by Timothy J. Moore, 1989.

* * *

Although the tradition of Roman historical writing goes back to the 3rd century BC, Cicero was still able to complain in the mid-50s BC (*De oratore*) that the earlier Roman historians had no pretensions to literary embellishment and were unable to tell a properly constructed story; he wished that they had brought to their works an elegant style and not regarded brevity as the only stylistic virtue. But it was more than 20 years before a historian set out to eclipse the writers whom Cicero had criticized, and to produce the great historical work which Cicero had desired. That historian was Livy.

Livy's original plan was immensely ambitious: to tell the story of Rome from its legendary foundation to the death of Cicero (43 BC) in 120 volumes. In his preface to the work, almost certainly written before the end of the civil wars (49–31 BC), Livy expresses dismay at his own times and relishes the prospect of being able to escape from them by reliving the past in his history. It may therefore be inferred that he saw Roman history in terms of decline, thus following a tradition of Roman historiography already established in the 2nd century BC according to which the course of Roman history was seen as undergoing progressive degeneration. At the same time, however, Livy intended to lay before his readers examples, drawn from history, of the kind of behaviour which they should imitate and avoid (preface 10); evidently he did not exclude the possibility of Rome's recovering from the nadir epitomized by contemporary society.

Unfortunately only 35 of Livy's 120 volumes have survived (1–10, 21–45), but the flavour of his work can be appreciated in a story such as Tarquin's rape of Lucretia. The story is divided, like a miniature play, into four 'acts', each of which is subdivided into individual 'scenes'; the action is brought before the reader's eyes by means of judiciously selected detail and the use of direct speech at crucial moments; the pathos of the episode is further underlined by effective repetitions of word and phrase; and the whole drama is designed to praise Lucretia's *pudicitia* (chastity) and condemn Tarquin's *vis*, *libido*, and *superbia* (violence, lust, arrogance). Livy's achievement in this and many other passages can be gauged where we are able to compare his work with that of a predecessor. Thus earlier historians, writing 50 years or so before, described how Manlius Torquatus and Valerius Corvinus acquired their *cognomina* (surnames); but the accounts are brief and crude, written in an unambitious and inelegant style. Livy has expanded the episodes with a wealth of circumstantial detail and expressed them in a 'periodic' style that is the historian's counterpart of the oratorical period of Cicero. Here, no less than in his long and patriotic treatment of the struggle against Hannibal (Books XXI–XXX), Livy convinces the reader that he is witnessing one of the glorious episodes of Rome's past history, written in an appropriately elevated style.

No doubt Livy originally intended these earlier and glorious periods of Rome's history to emphasize by contrast the degeneration which had set in subsequently and which was epitomized by the civil wars of his own lifetime; but at some unknown point he decided to extend the scope of his work by almost 35 years, bringing the history down to the death of Augustus' stepson Drusus in 9 BC. This decision radically affected the whole perspective of the work. No longer did the latest years of his history afford an unhappy comparison with the past: since the extra 22 volumes (of which none survives except in summary form) now took him midway through Augustus' reign, his revised plan meant that the latest years of his history now actually challenged the past in glory. The explanation for Livy's change of mind presumably rests with the emperor himself, with whom the historian, as mentor to the future emperor Claudius, was on personal terms and whom he came to see as the saviour of Rome. As a result, the 142 volumes of the completed enterprise constituted a monumental testimony to a nation's inherent greatness and its remarkable capacity for survival.

—A.J. Woodman

LLOSA, Mario Vargas. See **VARGAS LLOSA, Mario**.

LO-JOHANSSON, (Karl) Ivar. Born in Ösmo, Sweden, 23 February 1901. Self-educated. Worked as a stonecutter, farmhand, journalist, workman in France, England, and Hungary, 1925–29; then full-time writer. Recipient: Nio Society prize, 1941; Foundation for the Promotion of Literature Little Nobel prize, 1953; Doubloug prize, 1953, 1973; Nordic Council prize, 1979. Ph.D.: University of Uppsala, 1964. Officier de l'Ordre des Arts et des Lettres (France), 1986. *Died 10 April 1990.*

PUBLICATIONS

Fiction

Måna är död [Måna Is Dead]. 1932.
Godnatt, jord. 1933; as *Breaking Free*, translated by Allan Tapsell, 1990.
Kungsgatan [King's Street]. 1935.
Statarna [The Estate Workers] (stories). 2 vols., 1936–37.
Bara en mor. 1939; as *Only a Mother*, translated by Robert E. Bjork, 1991.
Jordproletärerna [Proletarians of the Earth]. 1941.
Traktorn [The Tractor]. 1943.
Geniet: en roman om pubertet [The Genius: A Novel of Puberty]. 1947.
Ungdomsnoveller [Stories of Youth]. 1948.
Autobiographical Series:
　Analfabeten [The Illiterate Man]. 1951.
　Gårdfarihandlaren [The Country Pedlar]. 1953.
　Stockholmaren [The Stockholmer]. 1954.
　Journalisten [The Journalist]. 1956.
　Författaren [The Writer]. 1957.
　Socialisten [The Socialist]. 1958.
　Soldaten [The Soldier]. 1959.
　Proletärförfattaren [The Proletarian Writer]. 1960.
Lyckan. 1962; as *Bodies of Love*, translated by Allan Tapsell, 1971.

Astronomens hus [Astronomer's House]. 1966.
Elektra, kvinna år 2070 [Woman of the Year 2070]. 1967.
Passionerna: älskog [The Passions: Love]. 1968.
Martyrerna [The Martyrs]. 1968.
Girigbukarna [The Misers]. 1969.
Karriäristerna [The Careerists]. 1969.
Vällustingarna [The Lechers]. 1970.
Lögnhalsarna [The Liars]. 1971.
Vishetslärarna [Teachers of Wisdom]. 1972.
Ordets makt: historien om språket [The Power of Words].
   1973.
Nunnan i Vadstena: sedeskildringar [The Nun of Vadstena:
   Moral Stories]. 1973.
Folket och herrarna [The People and the Masters]. 2 vols.,
   1973.
Furstarna: en krönika från Gustav Vasa till Karl XII [The
   Rulers]. 1974.
Lastbara berättelser [Stories of Vice]. 1974.
Passionsnoveller I-II [Stories of Passion] (selection). 2 vols.,
   1974.
En arbetares liv: proletärnoveller [A Worker's Life:
   Proletarian Stories]. 1977.

Verse

Ur klyvnadens tid [The Splitting Time]. 1958.

Other

Vagabondliv i Frankrike [Vagabond Life in France] (travel
   writing). 1927.
Kolet i våld [The Coal's Power]. 1928.
Statarliv [Farm Labourer's Lives]. 1941.
Stridsskrifter [Polemical Pamphlets]. 1946.
Statarna i bild [Estate Workers], illustrated by Gunnar
   Lundh. 1948.
Monism. 1948.
Ålderdom [Old Age], illustrated by Sven Järlås. 1949.
Vagabondliv [Vagabond Life]. 1949.
Ålderdoms-Sverige [Sweden for the Aged]. 1952.
Okänt Paris [Unknown Paris], illustrated by Tore Johnson.
   1954.
Zigenarväg [Gypsy Ways], illustrated by Anna Riwkin-Brick.
   1955.
Att skriva en roman [Writing a Novel]. 1957.
Zigenare [Gypsies]. 1963.
Statarnas liv och död [The Lives and Deaths of the Estate
   Workers] (selection). 1963.
Statarskolan i litteraturen [The School of Literature of the
   Estate Workers]. 1972.
Dagbok från 20-talet I-II [Diary from the Twenties]. 1974.
Stridsskrifter I-II [Polemical Pamphlets]. 1974.
Dagar och dagsverken: debatter och memoarer [Days and
   Day's Work]. 1975.
Under de gröna ekarna i Sörmland [Under the Green Oaks in
   Sörmland]. 1976.
Passioner i urval [Passions] (selection). 1976.
Den sociala fotobildboken [The Social Photograph Book].
   1977.
Pubertet [Puberty] (memoirs). 1978.
Asfalt [Asphalt] (memoirs). 1979.
Att skriva en roman, en bok om författeri [Writing a Novel, a
   Book on Writing] (selected articles). 1981.
Tröskeln [The Threshold] (memoirs). 1982.
Frihet [Freedom] (memoirs). 1985.
Till en författare [To an Author]. 1988.

*

Critical Studies: 'Ivar Lo-Johansson: Crusader for Social
Justice' by Jan-Anders Paulsson, in *American-Scandinavian
Review*, 59(1), 1971; 'Ivar Lo-Johansson' by Peter Graves and
Philip Holmes, in *Essays on Swedish Literature from 1880 to
the Present Day*, edited by Irene Scobbie, 1978; 'Ivar Lo-
Johansson and the Passions' by Peter Graves, in *Proceedings
of the Conference of Scandinavian Studies in Great Britain and
Northern Ireland*, 1983; Lo-Johansson issue of *Swedish Book
Review*, supplement, 1991; 'Dream and Dream Imagery in
Ivar Lo-Johansson's *Godnatt, jord*' by Rochelle Wright, in
Scandinavian Studies, 64(1), 1992.

* * *

Ivar Lo-Johansson forms, together with Jan Fridegård and
Moa Martinsson, the *statareskolan* in Swedish literature. All
three come from the lowest class of agricultural workers, the
estate workers (*statare*) who were tied to the big estates,
being paid in kind and enduring substandard living conditions, and for all practical purposes not 'free'. It is remarkable that a social class where illiteracy was the norm produced
three of Sweden's foremost writers.

Lo-Johansson is credited with opening the eyes of politicians and Swedes in general to the poverty and suffering of
the *statare* through his fiction, thus contributing greatly to
improving their lot and dismantling the system. His novel
Godnatt, jord (*Breaking Free*) depicts a young man, Mikael,
in his struggle for freedom. His dream world and his feelings
for nature and beauty stand in sharp contrast to the reality of
the conformist, subservient estate workers in their tedious
work. They all, however, dream of freedom from their
oppressive reality but only Mikael is able to achieve it.

Probably better known is *Bara en mor* (*Only a Mother*),
about a beautiful young woman, Rya-Rya, who swims nude
in an isolated lake on a hot summer day and is branded by the
conservative estate workers as a fallen woman. Defiantly, she
marries a weak, irresponsible worker and produces one child
after another, like the rest of the women. This gradually
weakens her physically, while her social standing as a worker
who can choose the work she does declines with her increasing alienation from her husband. He mistreats her in a feeble
attempt to feel powerful, although he is, in fact, a miserable
failure even as an estate worker. There is no question that
Rya-Rya is the stronger and the more competent, but she is a
woman and trapped in a life of repression while lacking the
ability to change it. Only as a mother can she realize some of
her strength, but she dies young and overworked. Rya-Rya's
fate is a comment on the hypocritical Swedish attitude to a
natural sensuality, expressed in her nude swimming, which is
punished for life.

Lo-Johansson's other works dealing with the plight of the
statare include *Statarna* [The Estate Workers], *Jordproletärerna* [Proletarians of the Earth], and *Traktorn* [The
Tractor], which features a machine as the main character.

Contributing to the success of his *statare* work was a keen
eye for documentary details. He believed that literature
should have a definite social function which is best met
through realistic journalistic methods. In fact his first published work was a series of travel books, *Vagabondliv i
Frankrike* [Vagabond Life in France], where adventure is
mixed with social commentary.

Lo-Johansson is also one of Sweden's foremost writers on
the erotic and human (male) sexuality. Early on, he scandalized the Swedes by arguing that young men should have
access to young women as a natural outlet for their sexuality.
His first novel, *Måna är död* [Måna Is Dead], deals with a

young man's problems in combining his erotic yearnings with his work. *Kungsgatan* [King's Street] deals with a farm boy's life in a big city. Here Lo-Johansson describes prostitution and venereal disease with a frankness new for the times.

Lo-Johansson's fascination with love and sex, human vices and sins is also expressed in seven volumes of stories of passion published between 1968 and 1972, and dealing with the forces that drive people to abandon reason and will in their actions. Each volume is devoted to a particular human weakness, as indicated in their titles—for example *Girigbukarna* [The Misers], *Vällustingarna* [The Lechers], and *Lögnhalsarna* [The Liars].

A third major focus of his writing is autobiographical. In the 1950s he published eight autobiographical novels, beginning with *Analfabeten* [The Illiterate Man], a touching and loving portrayal of his father, and a masterpiece in Swedish literature. His father was a man of few words and great integrity, whose life and people around him are perceived with much humour. Through the other novels in the series we follow Lo-Johansson's career from *Gårdfarihandlaren* [The Country Pedlar] to *Författaren* [The Writer] and *Proletärförfattaren* [The Proletarian Writer]. His fellow writers were identified in these books by their initials, which engaged his readers in popular deciphering games.

Another series of autobiographical writings was published from 1978 to 1985, starting with *Pubertet* [Puberty], for which he received the Nordic Council literary prize in 1979. This was not his first distinction. In 1941 he had received the Nio Society prize for *Only a Mother* and in 1953 the so-called Little Nobel prize from the Foundation for the Promotion of Literature. His last award came from France where he was made Officier de l'Ordre des Arts et des Lettres de France in 1986.

Lo-Johansson was a major modern writer who produced over 50 volumes dealing with basic human questions about love, sex, vice, and sin. His characters are multi-dimensional and show a deep insight into what makes a human being human. He translated social consciousness and compassion into great literature and created many unforgettable characters. His language is rich and powerful, poetic and realistic, entertaining and captivating.

—Torborg Lundell

LONGINUS.   See ON THE SUBLIME.

LÖNNROT, Elias.   See KALEVALA.

LOPE de Vega Carpio.   See VEGA Carpio, Lope de.

LORCA, Federico García.   See GARCÍA LORCA, Federico.

LORRIS, Guillaume de.   See ROSE, Romance of the.

LU HSÜN.   See LU XUN.

LU XUN [Lu Hsün]. Pseudonym for Zhou Shuren. Born in Shaoxing, Zhejiang province, China, in 1881. Educated at Jiangnan Naval Academy, Nanjing, 1898–99; School of Railways and Mines, Nanjing, 1899–1902; studied Japanese language in Japan, 1902–04, and medicine at Sendai Provincial Medical School, Japan, 1904–06; continued private studies in Japan, 1906–09. Teacher in Shaoxing, 1910–11; served in the Ministry of Education, Beijing, 1912–26, and taught Chinese literature at National Beijing University, 1920–26; taught at Xiamen (Amoy) University, 1926, and University of Canton, 1927; then lived in international settlement of Shanghai: editor, *Benliu* [The Torrent], 1928, and *Yiwen* [Translation], 1934. Translated many works by Russian, German, and Japanese authors. Also a draughtsman. *Died 19 October 1936.*

PUBLICATIONS

Collections

Lu Xun xiansheng quanji [Complete Works]. 20 vols., 1938; revised edition, 1973; supplements edited by Tang Tao, 2 vols., 1942–52; his original works republished as *Lu Xun quanji*, 10 vols., 1956–58.
Selected Works, translated by Yang Hsien-yi and Gladys Yang. 4 vols., 1956–60.

Fiction

Nahan (stories). 1923; as *The War Cry* (bilingual edition), edited and translated by Jörgenson. 1949.
A Madman's Diary (stories; bilingual edition). 1924(?).
Panghuang (stories). 1926; as *P'anghuang/Hesitation*, edited and translated by Jörgenson, 1946.
The True Story of Ah Q, translated by George Kin Leung. 1926, bilingual edition, 1949; also translated by Yang Hsien-yi and Gladys Yang, 1960.
The Tragedy of Ah Qui and Other Modern Chinese Stories, edited by J. Kyn Yn-yu. 1930.
Gushi xinbian (stories). 1935; as *Old Tales Retold*, translated by Yang Hsien-yi and Gladys Yang, 1961.

Stories (includes *Benediction*; *Divorce*; *Kites*; *Kung Yiji*; *A Little Incident*; *Medicine*; *Mother's*), edited by Edgar Snow and Yao Hsinnung. 1936.

Ah Q and Others: Selected Stories, translated by Chi-chen Wang. 1941.

Selected Stories (in English). 1954.

Selected Stories, translated by Yang Hsien-yi and Gladys Yang. 1960.

Wild Grass (prose poems). 1974.

K'ung I-chi (stories; bilingual edition). 1975.

Verse

Selected Poems, translated by W.J.F. Jenner. 1982.

Other

Zhongguo xiaoshuo shilüe. 1924; as *A Brief History of Chinese Fiction*, translated by Yang Hsien-yi and Gladys Yang, 1959.

Lu Xun Shuxinji [Letters]. 1946; revised edition, 3 vols., 1976; selection translated as *Letters*, 1973.

Lu Xun riji [Diary]. 1951; revised edition, 3 vols., 1976.

Chun feng yüeh t'an (essays). 1954.

Selected Works. 1956.

A Lu Hsun Reader (Chinese text), edited by William A. Lyell, Jr. 1967.

Silent China: Selected Writings, edited and translated by Gladys Yang. 1973.

Extracts of Speeches on Criticism of the Doctrines of Confucius and Mencius (Chinese text). 1974.

Dawn Blossoms Plucked at Dusk, translated by Yang Hsien-yi and Gladys Yang. 1976.

*

Critical Studies: *Lu Hsün and the New Culture Movement of Modern China* by Huang Sung-k'ang, 1957; *Gate of Darkness* by T.A. Hsia, 1974; *The Social Thought of Lu Hsün 1881–1936: A Mirror of the Intellectual Current of Modern China* by Pearl Hsia Chen, 1976; *Lu Hsün's Vision of Reality* by William A. Lyell, 1976; *The Style of Lu Hsun* by Raymond S.W. Hsu, 1980; *Lu Xun: A Biography* by Shiqing Wang, 1984; *Lu Xun and his Legacy*, 1985, and *Voices from the Iron House: A Study of Lu Xun*, 1987, both by Leo Ou-fan Lee; *Lu Xun: A Chinese Writer for All Times* by Ruth F. Weiss, 1985; *A Selective Guide to Chinese Literature 1900–1949: Volume 2: The Short Story*, edited by Zbigniew Slupski, 1988; *Lu Xun as Translator: Lu Xun's Translation and Introduction of Literature and Literary Theory, 1903–1936* by Lennart Lundberg, 1989.

*   *   *

Lu Xun, whose real name was Zhou Shuren, has been regarded as one of the greatest modern Chinese writers. The first to compose Western-style fiction, he was also in the vanguard of the colloquial language movement starting in 1918. A Communist sympathizer from about 1929, he died in 1936 before the Revolution, and has since been praised as a cultural hero in the Peoples' Republic of China.

He decided upon a writing career after formative experiences during his studies in Japan from 1902 to 1909. From the start his goal was polemical—to take China to task for its traditionalism and its refusal to adjust to the modern world.

But he produced only mediocre essays and one story in the classical language until 1918, when he wrote the first Western-style story in China, 'The Diary of a Madman'. Based on a tale by Nikolai Gogol', the story is about a man who concludes that all around him intend to kill and eat him, and that such cannibalism is an inevitable result of hypocritical moral teachings of ancient China.

'The Diary of a Madman' and other stories were published in a collection called *Nahan* (*The War Cry*) in 1923. Of these the most famous is *The True Story of Ah Q*, which has received international acclaim. The character of Ah Q is the composite of all weak and lowly qualities of the Chinese national character, especially at the time in history when China was pathetically subservient to nations of greater physical and moral strength. He is the epitome of the individual who lacks self-knowledge, a condition that leads to absurd acts of self-abuse and accommodation to the external world. Although Ah Q is a composite and symbolic character, each detail of his behaviour, however grotesque or absurd, might as well be taken as a representation of what Lu Xun saw in actual life—for example, Ah Q's attempt to outdo someone else by searching his own body for lice and cracking them loudly between his teeth.

Panghuang (translated as *Hesitation*) is Lu Xun's second story collection, published in 1926. In general it is bleaker in tone than *Nahan* and is more mature and incisive, as Lu Xun himself asserted. As in all his works, the themes are topical and deal with various traditional evils. However, the stories in *Hesitation* are rarely lost on moral or polemical points and show how Lu Xun has mastered a technique of stark and essential portrayal. 'Regret for the Past', for example, is a concise and ironic story of a 'modern' love affair. It begins with a period of idyllic attachment but then evolves to a state in which that beginning becomes history, only to be reinvoked in the form of a sort of sustaining ritual. It ends when neither can any longer play their original roles.

Lu Xun's stories have rightly been compared to those of James Joyce's *Dubliners*, and also resemble the 19th-century fiction of Gogol' or Dostoevskii. His characters are mostly petty but nevertheless real and sympathetic individuals, who are caught in a general condition of apathy, brutality, superstition, and hypocrisy.

In addition to writing stories, Lu Xun also composed a volume of prose poetry, *Ye cao* (*Wild Grass*), and a volume of childhood memories, *Dawn Blossoms Plucked at Dusk*. After 1926 he mainly wrote polemical essays, his only stories being those of *Gushi xinbian* (*Old Tales Retold*), in which he satirically revised the accounts of various ancient heroes. In his essays, besides repeatedly attacking wrong-headed contemporaries, he also sought to expose what he saw as an accumulated and collective national lethargy. He viewed the Chinese nation as a 'dish of loose sand' in which individuals were separate and 'oblivious to each other's sufferings' ('Silent China', 1927). Moreover, he saw hierarchy as so ingrained that, as he literally demonstrated in Ah Q, 'a hand cannot help but look down upon a foot' (his preface to the Russian translation of *The True Story of Ah Q*, 1925). Lu Xun must be counted among the sharpest and most astute critics and defenders of China that modern times have witnessed.

—Keith McMahon

LUCAN. Born Marcus Annaeus Lucanus in Corduba (now Cordoba), Spain, 3 November AD 39. Grandson of Seneca the Elder and nephew of Seneca the Younger, *q.v.* Studied in Rome and Athens. Became a favourite of the emperor Nero, who made him financial administrator (*quaestor*) and augur; won the poetry contest in the Neronian games in AD 60, but fell out of favour and committed suicide under compulsion when his part in Piso's conspiracy against Nero was discovered. *Died 30 April AD 65.*

PUBLICATIONS

Works

Civilis libri decem, edited by Alfred E. Housman. 1926; as *De bello civili*, edited by D.R. Shackleton Bailey, 1988; Book I edited by R.J. Getty (with commentary), 1940, corrected edition, 1955; Book VII edited by J.P. Postgate, 1913, revised by O.A.W. Dilke, 1960; Book VIII edited by J.P. Postgate, 1917, and R. Mayer, as *Civil War III*, 1981; as *Pharsalia*, translated by Sir A. Gorges, 1614; also translated by Nicholas Rowe (verse), 1713; Edward Ridley (verse), 1896; J.D. Duff [Loeb Edition], 1928; Robert Graves, 1956; Douglas Little (verse), 1989; Jane Wilson Joyce, 1994; as *Civil War*, translated by P.F. Widdows (verse), 1988; also translated by S.H. Braund, 1992.

*

Bibliography: by Rudolf Helm, in *Lustrum*, 1, 1956, and by Werner Rutz, in *Lustrum*, 9, 1964, and *Lustrum*, 26, 1984.

Critical Studies: *Nicholas Rowe's Translation of Lucan's Pharsalia, 1703–1718: A Study in Literary History* by Alfred W. Hesse, 1950; *The Poet Lucan* by Mark P.O. Morford, 1967; *Lucan: An Introduction* by Frederick M. Ahl, 1976; *Momentary Monsters: Lucan and His Heroes* by W.R. Johnson, 1987; 'Lucan/The Word at War' by J. Henderson, in *The Imperial Muse*, edited by A.J. Boyle, 1988; *Poetry and Civil War in Lucan's Bellum Civile* by Jamie Masters, 1992.

* * *

Lucan's poem *De bello civili* (popularly known as the *Pharsalia*) is an epic poem in hexameters, of which nine complete books and an incomplete tenth survive. Its subject is the civil war fought between Pompey and Caesar and it covers events from Caesar's crossing of the Rubicon in 49 BC (Book I) through the battle of Pharsalus (Book VII) and Pompey's death in Egypt in 49 BC (Book VIII). It was probably planned to end with the suicide of Cato at Utica after the battle of Thapsus in 46 BC. The poem has none of the glamour of mythological epic, such as Virgil's *Aeneid*, but sets out to present a stark condemnation of civil war. It achieves this by subverting and inverting the conventions of mythological epic. Thus none of the three protagonists can be called 'the hero' in any meaningful sense. Caesar, the most prominent character, is presented as a terrifying, destructive, and irresistible force with superhuman powers. Pompey is presented much more sympathetically in human terms but as a man past his prime and weak, indecisive, and insecure. Cato, who in Book IX takes over the leadership of the Republican forces after Pompey's murder, is the austere embodiment of Stoic principles with no softening human qualities.

Lucan abandons the traditional divine machinery of anthropomorphic deities in favour of the impersonal Stoic concepts of Fate and Fortune in order to focus attention on human responsibility and culpability for the horrors of the civil war. He none the less makes telling use of the supernatural in the form of dreams and visions, portents and prophecies which enhance the macabre atmosphere. Appius' consultation of the Delphic oracle in Book V and the necromancy performed by the witch Erichtho in Book VI illustrate Lucan's virtuoso powers. In this and many other respects he reflects the tastes and interests of his contemporaries. His own literary, moral, and rhetorical training emerges in his use of historical *exempla* (Hannibal in Book I, Marius and Sulla in Book 2), his incorporation of mythological episodes (Hercules in Book IV), and his scientific discussions of geography, astrology, astronomy, and natural phenomena (concentrated in Books IX and X). He is clearly an educated man writing for an educated audience.

Lucan's treatment of warfare shows most clearly his condemnation of civil war. He incorporates many of the episodes that are 'standard' in martial epic but gives them paradoxical or extreme treatment. For example, in Book VI Caesar's centurion Scaea makes an incredible single-handed stand (*aristeia*) against Pompey's troops and prevents them from breaking out of the blockade, and in Book III the sea battle off Marseilles is said to resemble a land battle once Caesar's ships have been rammed. Lucan takes every opportunity to describe bizarre forms of death, most of which are striking for their strangeness, suddenness, and lack of dignity and heroism. The horror of civil war—of Roman fighting Roman, brother fighting brother, father fighting son—is presented starkly with an unheroized spilling of blood and a strikingly large number of unburied bodies and headless corpses, of which the most memorable is that of Pompey himself.

On the basis of his novel treatment of many of the conventions of mythological epic poetry, Lucan's poem may be regarded as an anti-Virgilian poem, although not in the sense of an antipathy towards Virgil. His essentially pessimistic poem reworks some of the stirring, patriotic episodes of the *Aeneid* into shocking, black scenes which seem to require contemplation of the crime of civil war. The most obvious example is Aeneas and the Sibyl in the Underworld in Book VI, evoked by the necromancy in *Civil War* Book VI.

The same anti-Virgilian strain is true of his style. His use of the hexameter is repetitive, even monotonous, in contrast with Virgil's musical hexameter. Similarly, his diction is prosaic and unembellished. The poem has been called a 'predominantly monochrome epic' (Bramble) in which black, grey, and white are the predominant colours, followed by the red of the blood spilled. Key words and images which recur throughout the poem indicate disintegration and destruction, on the level of the individual, the state, and the cosmos—words like *ruina* (collapse), *viscera* (guts), *tabes* (decay), and *sanguis* (gore). Lucan characteristically dwells on an idea, reiterating it to make the audience stop and confront the issue. He often uses arresting maxims (*sententiae*), antitheses, and paradoxes for the same purpose, of which the most memorable is 'they abandon Rome and flee towards war'. This also explains the marked disproportion between narrative and speeches in the poem: narrative of the events of the war, with which his original audience was familiar, is kept to a minimum and often punctuated by exclamations or condemnatory outbursts from the poet. Instead, Lucan supplies emotive scenes that have no actual impact on the events of the war, such as Caesar's battle with the storm in Book V and the necromancy in Book VI, together with many long speeches which set the emotional tone. Particularly striking is

Lucan's use of apostrophe, when he enters the poem as an unnamed character in order to address one of the actors. This technique, perhaps above all, invites us to pause and comprehend the horror of the events of civil warfare.

Some readers find Lucan's stark portrayal of the suicide of a powerful nation not to their taste. This could be because the poem is too uncomfortable and too disconcerting. If so, it is salutary to remember that many poets and scholars of medieval, Renaissance, and modern times had a high regard for Lucan. In Dante's view, Lucan ranked with Homer, Horace, Ovid, and Virgil as an exponent of elevated poetry.

—S.H. Braund

LUCIAN. Born in Samosata, Syria (now Samsat, Turkey), c.AD 120. Probably not Greek. Married; one son. Apprenticed to a sculptor; then received an education in rhetoric, and became a pleader, then a travelling lecturer, practising sophistic rhetoric in Gaul; moved to Athens about age 40; may have accompanied the Emperor Verus to Antioch in 162; chief court usher (*archistator*) with the Roman administration in Alexandria in early 170s. *Died after AD 180.*

PUBLICATIONS

Collections

[Works], edited by M.D. MacLeod. 4 vols., 1972–87; also edited by John Dryden, various translators, 4 vols., 1711, and J. Sommerbrodt, 5 vols., 1886–99; translated by F. Spence, 5 vols., 1684–85; also translated by Thomas Francklin, 2 vols., 1780; William Tooke, 1820; H.W. and F.G. Fowler, 4 vols., 1905; A.M. Harmon (vols. 1–5), K. Kilburn (vol. 6), and M.D. MacLeod (vols. 7 and 8), 8 vols. [Loeb Edition], 1913–67; selections edited and translated by Emily James Smith, 1892; B.P. Reardon, 1965; Keith C. Sidwell, 1985; M.D. MacLeod (with commentary), 1990.

Works

Charon, Vita and Timon, translated by D.S. Smith. 1865.
Dialogues, translated by Jasper Mayne. 1638; also translated by John Dryden, 1739; William Maginn, 1856; H. Williams, 1888; R. Mongan and J.A. Prout, with *Somnium*, 1890; William Tooke, 1930; selection translated by 'J.P.P.', 1845; *Six Dialogues*, translated by S.T. Irwin, 1894; *Dialogues and Stories*, translated by W.D. Sheldon, 1901; *Seventy Dialogues*, edited by H.L. Levy, 1977.
Somnium, with *The Dialogues*, translated by R. Mongan and J.A. Prout. 1890; also translated by William Armour, 1895.
Tragodopodagra, as *The Trago-Podagra, or Gout Tragedy*, translated by Rev. Symeon T. Bartlett. 1871.
Vera Historia [True Story], translated by Francis Hickes. 1634, reprinted 1925; also translated by Emily James Smith, 1892; J.A. Prout, 1901; selection as *Trips to Wonderland*, translated by Francis Hickes, 1905; as *Lucian Goes A-Voyaging*, translated and adapted by Agnes Carr Vaughan, 1930.
Cyprian Masques, translated by Ruby Melvill. 1929.
Satirical Sketches, translated by Paul Turner. 1961.

Selected Satires, edited by Lionel Casson. 1962.

*

Critical Studies: *Lucian, Satirist and Artist* by F.G. Allinson, 1926; *The Translations of Lucian by Erasmus and Thomas More* by C.R. Thompson, 1940; *Literary Quotation and Allusion in Lucian* by F.W. Householder, 1941; *The Sophists in the Roman Empire* by Glen W. Bowersock, 1969; *Studies in Lucian* by Barry Baldwin, 1973; *Studies in Lucian's Comic Fiction* by Graham Anderson, 1976; *Ben Jonson and the Lucianic Tradition* by Douglas Duncan, 1979; *Lucian and His Influence in Europe* by Christopher Robinson, 1979; *Prolegomena to a New Text of Lucian's Vitarum Auctio and Piscator* by Joel B. Itzkowitz, 1986; *Culture and Society in Lucian* by C.P. Jones, 1986; *Unruly Eloquence: Lucian and the Comedy of Traditions* by R. Bracht Branham, 1989; *Lucian of Samosata in the Two Hesperias: An Essay in Literary and Cultural Translation* by Michael O. Zappala, 1990.

* * *

Literal-minded Byzantines saw Lucian as an anti-Christ; Lord Macaulay dubbed him the Voltaire of antiquity. He deserves neither title. Lucian is best regarded as a journalist-cum-intellectual, unscrupulously versatile.

Least popular now are his occasional pieces on various rhetorical themes. One or two deserve attention, notably his essay on Slander which describes a Greek painting that inspired Botticelli's *La Calunnia*. Lucian is one of a relatively small number of ancient writers on art, which should commend him to modern counterparts.

As is ever the case with intellectuals, Lucian was frequently embroiled in controversies; several pamphlets commemorate these in vicious terms. Their contemporary bite has naturally staled, but two stand out. The *Peregrinus* lambasts its eponymous villain who, after flirting with Christianity and cynicism, immolates himself at the Olympic Games. Some mild comments on Christian credulity earned Lucian a place on the Catholic index of Forbidden Books. But Christians get a better press in his *Alexander* where, along with the Epicureans and Lucian himself, they oppose a trendy religious charlatan.

Lucian was also capable of appreciation, and wrote some admiring obituaries, notably the *Demonax*, commemorating a witty philosopher and preserving a large collection of his jokes. He also tried his hand at verse. Fifty or so epigrams attributed to him in the *Greek Anthology* are unremarkable. But his *Tragodopodagra* (*Gout Tragedy*) is a delicious parody of Greek drama, comparable to Housman's immortal *Fragment of a Greek Tragedy*.

Perhaps most congenial is the prose *Vera Historia* [True Story], at one level a parody of travellers' tall tales, but also enjoyable as early science fiction with monsters and adventures worthy of 20th-century inventions.

However, Lucian himself prized his satirical dialogues, a genre he revived and perfected. Some pass social comments on wealth and poverty that might endear him to the modern left, but which were politically safe in his own relatively enlightened age—Lucian was no martyr. His main targets are the absurdities of mythology, as well as the illogical and often hypocritical representatives of the philosophical schools. Typical pieces include *Descent into Hell, Dialogues of the Dead, Philosophies for Sale*—all much imitated in later times.

Many scholars dismiss Lucian's satires as behind the times, a criticism not totally unjust in that few educated people then took myth as literal truth. Yet the objects of his ridicule *were* still the official gods of Rome. Compare contemporary Christianity: the churches are half-empty, and intellectuals scoff at fundamentalist beliefs, but the masses, although not conventionally religious, tend to profess belief in a god and resent 'clever' attacks on orthodox piety. Viewed thus, Lucian's squibs have genuine point.

Lucian was no deep thinker, and had no obvious influence on his own times. His fame was in the future. He was a professional entertainer in a crowded and competitive field, and it is probably fair to suppose that his works survived because they were superior in elegance and wit to those that did not.

—Barry Baldwin

LUCRETIUS. Born Titus Lucretius Carus, c.99–94 BC. His work is dedicated to C. Memmius Gemellus, the friend of Catullus and Cinna; may have been acquainted with Cicero; otherwise nothing is known of his life. *Died c.55 BC.*

PUBLICATIONS

Verse

De rerum natura, edited by Joseph Martin. 1953; also edited by William Ellery Leonard and Stanley Barney Smith, 1961, Alfred Ernout, 2 vols., 1964–66, and K. Müller, 1975; selections: edited and translated by Cyril Bailey, 1922, 1947, revised edition, 1977, and W.H.D. Rouse [Loeb Edition], 1928, revised by M.F. Smith, 1975; as *On Matter and Man* (Books I, II, IV, and V; in Latin), edited by A.S. Cox, 1967, Book III edited by E.J. Kenney, 1977, Book I edited by P.M. Brown, 1984, Book V edited by C.D.N. Costa, 1984, Book IV, 1986, and Book VI, 1991, both edited and translated by John Godwin; as *On the Nature of Things*, translated by J.S. Watson and J.M. Good, 1848; also translated by C.F. Johnson, 1872; H.A.J. Munro, 1907; Cyril Bailey, 1910; Robert Allison, 1919; R.C. Trevelyan, 1937; J.H. Maitland, 1965; Frank Copley, 1977; as *The Way Things Are*, translated by Rolfe Humphries, 1968; as *The Poem on Nature*, translated by C.H. Sisson, 1976; also translated in prose by Ronald Latham, 1951; R. Geer, 1965; M.F. Smith, 1969; Book I as *De Rerum Natura*, translated by J. Evelyn, 1656; *Selections*, translated by Henry S. Salt, 1912; *Selections*, edited by G. Benfield and R.C. Reeves, 1967; Book IV translated by Robert D. Brown, in *Lucretius on Love and Sex*, 1987.

*

Bibliography: *A Bibliography of Lucretius* by Cosmo A. Gordon, 1962, 2nd edition, revised by E.J. Kenney, 1985.

Critical Studies: *Three Philosophical Poets: Lucretius, Dante, and Goethe* by George Santayana, 1910; *Lucretius and His Influence* by George D. Hadzsits, 1935; *Lucretius* by E.E. Sykes, 1936; *Lucretius' Imagery* by G.J. Sullwood, 1958; *Philosophy of Poetry: The Genius of Lucretius* by Henri Bergson, 1959; *Lucretius and English Literature, 1680–1740* by Wolfgang B. Fleischmann, 1964; *Lucretius* edited by Donald R. Dudley, 1965; *The Lyre of Science: Form and Meaning in Lucretius' De Rerum Natura* by Richard Minadeo, 1969; *The Imagery and Poetry of Lucretius* by David A. West, 1969; *Epicurean Political Philosophy: The De Rerum Natura of Lucretius* by James Hunt Nichols, 1976; *Lucretius and the Diatribe Against the Fear of Death: De Rerum Natura III, 830–1094* by Barbara Price Wallach, 1976; *Lucretius* by E.J. Kenney, 1977; *Mode and Value in the De Rerum Natura: A Study in Lucretius' Metrical Language*, 1978, and *Lucretius and the Late Republic: An Essay in Roman Intellectual History*, 1985, both by John Douglas Minyard; *Lucretius and the Transpadanes* by Louise Adams Holland, 1979; *Puns and Poetry in Lucretius' De Rerum Natura* by Jane McIntosh Snyder, 1980; *Lucretius and Epicurus* by Diskin Clay, 1983; *Lucretius on Love and Sex: A Commentary on De Rerum Natura IV, 1030–1287 with Prolegomena, Text and Translation*, 1987, and *Lucretius on Love and Sex*, 1989, both by Robert D. Brown; *Lucretius on Death and Anxiety: Poetry and Philosophy in De Rerum Natura* by Charles Segal, 1990; *Myth and Poetry in Lucretius* by Monica R. Gale, 1994.

*   *   *

Little is known about the Roman poet Lucretius apart from what may be inferred from his work and the probably apocryphal tale that he committed suicide after suffering the shattering effects of a love potion. Only *De rerum natura* (*On the Nature of Things*) survives, a long philosophical poem in six books of over 7,400 lines of Latin hexameters. The work itself proposes the modest task of liberating humankind from fear and superstition by explaining everything. Underlying this is the premise that fear derives from ignorance or uncertainty, especially in relation to the arbitrary actions of the gods and to the fate of the soul after death. By showing that the order of things is the result of orderly and predictable mechanical processes, Lucretius hoped to dissolve all mysteries, thereby eliminating all uncertainty and fear.

Lucretius saw his task as essentially didactic, expounding the ethical and mechanical theories of the Greco-Roman philosopher Epicurus, 'the first to break the close bars of nature's portals' (1.71). In turn, Epicurus had adopted and developed the implications of the Atomists Leucippus and Democritus. Thus, for Lucretius, Epicurus, and the Atomists, all reality was composed of two basic elements, atoms or particles and void. They viewed reality as we know it as nothing more than elaborate configurations of atoms and void existing in a state of constant motion, a view that anticipates to some degree Galileo's theory of atoms, Descartes's corpuscles, and even some aspects of the modern atomic theory.

As Lucretius proceeds through his six books, he follows the basic metaphysical project of starting with the most fundamental, and showing how he can build on that to account for the cosmos as a whole. Thus he moves from the derivation of the basic elements to an account of life, mind, and reproduction, through larger structures and finally to an account of terrestrial and celestial phenomena. The observation of change in the world, of generation and decay, nutrition and growth, the cycles of the season, and even the larger cycles of the cosmos, is nothing more than the expression of the perpetual rearrangements of the basic constituent particles in the void. In this way, Lucretius attempts to account for the mutability of the world while defending the fundamental postulate that 'nothing can be produced from nothing', and its corollary, that 'nothing is ever reduced to nothing'.

These postulates are crucial to Lucretius' project of dispelling religious superstition, for they entail the principle that the gods are bound to the laws of nature, unable to act in an arbitrary, unreasonable, or unpredictable manner. Any fortune or disaster that might befall people is the result of predictable natural laws and not the caprice of Apollo or Jupiter. As such, Lucretius posits a responsibility for individuals to exercise reasonable caution, for within the limits of nature, their fates are in their own hands. Lucretius' theory is most important, however, when applied to dispelling fear of death.

As with superstition and fear in general, Lucretius suggests that the fear of death is related to a fear of the unknown, and especially the prospect of some torment or retribution that the soul might encounter after death. In Book III, he argues why he believes such fears to be groundless. In effect, Lucretius argues that mental and vital processes, like any other natural phenomena, are a function of the motion of particles, in this case an especially fine grade of particles, but particles nonetheless. 'It must therefore necessarily be the case', he argues, 'that the whole soul consists of extremely small seminal atoms, connected and diffused throughout the veins, and viscera, and nerves'. This being so, there is no substantive difference between the soul and the body. Accordingly, the death of the body also entails the death of the soul. In other words, insofar as death and decay of the body represent a dissociation and reconfiguration of the constituent particles, so they represent the same for the soul. The collection and configuration of atoms that combine to form one's unique self and identity diffuse into the whole. Since the soul is inseparable from the body, the only way that a person might suffer after death is if all of the specific particles that formed the person were able to recombine in their original configuration. Since that is effectively impossible, Lucretius concludes that there is no after-life to anticipate.

> We may be assured that in death there is nothing to be dreaded by us; that he who does not exist, cannot become miserable; and that it makes not the least difference to a man, when immortal death has ended his mortal life, that he was ever born at all.

Thus Lucretius offers the cold comfort that the life people live is the only life they have and may expect, and that since death is complete annihilation, they have nothing to fear.

On the Nature of Things proved an important vehicle for Epicurean thought, both in the Roman world and later with Voltaire and other figures of the Enlightenment who were drawn to his material vision of the cosmos and his ethics of the garden. At the same time, Lucretius' flights of lyricism made his poem widely read and appreciated among those influenced by Latin literature. However, the enduring quality stems from Lucretius' regard for the perennial problem of human mortality and the meaning of human existence: what philosopher George Santayana termed the 'art of accepting and enjoying what the conditions of our being afford'. Because of this, *On the Nature of Things* may be classed among the great philosophical poems in the Western tradition, comparable with Dante's *Divine Comedy*, Wordsworth's *Prelude*, or Goethe's *Faust*.

—Thomas L. Cooksey

LUO GUANZHONG. See **WATER MARGIN**.

LUTHER, Martin. Born in Eisleben, Thuringia, 10 November 1483. Educated at the University of Erfurt, B.A. 1502, M.A. 1505; entered Augustinian monastery, Erfurt, 1505; installed as professor of moral philosophy, University of Wittenberg, 1508: doctor of theology 1512. Married Katherine von Bora in 1525; three sons and three daughters. Visited Rome, 1511; published 95 Theses against the sale of indulgences, 1517, and thereafter drawn into Reformation controversies: excommunicated, 1520, tried at Imperial Diet of Worms in 1521 and outlawed; kept in hiding at the Wartburg, 1521–22; spent most of the remainder of his life in Wittenberg, teaching, preaching, writing, and overseeing the emergence of reformed, Lutheran institutions. *Died 18 February 1546.*

PUBLICATIONS

Werke [Weimar Edition], edited by J.C.F. Knaake and others. 110 vols., 1883— .
Works [American Edition], edited by Jaroslav Pelikan and Helmut T. Lehmann. 55 vols., 1955— .
Selections, edited by J. Dillenberger. 1961.
Selected Political Writings, edited by J.M. Porter. 1974.

*

Bibliography: *Annotated Bibliography of Luther Studies, 1967–1976* by John E. Bigane, 1977; by Mark U. Edwards, in *Reformation Europe: A Guide to Research* edited by Steven Ozment, 1982.

Critical Studies: *Here I Stand: A Life of Martin Luther* by Roland Bainton, 1950; *Luther and His Times* by E.C. Schwiebert, 1950; *Martin Luther: Road to Reformation* by Heinrich Boehmer, translated by W. Doberstein and Theodore G. Tappert, 1957; *Martin Luther: A Biographical Study* by John M. Todd, 1964; *Martin Luther and the Reformation* by A.G. Dickens, 1967; *Luther: An Introduction to His Thought* by Gerhard Ebeling, 1970; *The German Nation and Martin Luther* by A.G. Dickens, 1974; *Martin Luther and the Drama* by Thomas I. Bacon, 1976; 'Luther and Literacy', in *Publications of the Modern Language Association of America 91*, 1976, and *Luther: An Experiment in Biography*, 1980, both by H.G. Haile; *Martin Luther: An Illustrated Biography* by Peter Manns, translated by Michael Shaw, 1982; *Luther in Mid-Career 1521–30* by Heinrich

Bornkamm, translated by Theodore Bachmann, 1983; *Martin —God's Court Jester: Luther in Retrospect* by Eric Walter Grilsch, 1983; *Martin Luther: The Man and the Image* by Herbert David Rix, 1983; *The Political Thought of Martin Luther* by W.O.J. Cargil Thompson, 1984; *Luther and Learning* edited by Marilyn J. Harran, 1985; *Martin Luther and the Modern Mind: Freedom, Conscience, Toleration, Rights* edited by Manfred Hoffmann, 1985; *Martin Luther: His Road to Reformation 1483–1521* by Martin Brecht, translated by James L. Schaaf, 1985; *Luther the Reformer: A Story of the Man and His Career* by James M. Kitelson, 1986; *Luther In Context* by David C. Steinmetz, 1986; *Martin Luther: An Introduction to His Life and Works* by Bernhard Lohse, translated by Robert C. Schultz, 1987; *Martin Luther in the American Imagination* by Hartmut Lehmann, 1988; *Luther: Man Between God and the Devil* by Heiko A. Oberman, translated by Eileen Walliser-Schwarzbart, 1989; *Martin Luther* by Gerhard Brendler, 1992.

*   *   *

At the centre of all Martin Luther's activities lay a profound faith in the redemptive personal experience of Christ, the Word of God to mankind, and he always regarded his writing and teaching as forms of preaching, in continuation of the saving work of God, the supreme poet. Trained in scholastic and humanistic studies alike, he used them merely as skills which aided his 'preaching'. While not subscribing to the humanists' literary aestheticization of spiritual matters, Luther none the less aspired to the fitting and effective use of language to give expression to truth as he saw it revealed. This is one reason why he embarked upon the composition of a liturgy and hymns in German, for the initial efforts of his arch rival, the radical Thomas Müntzer, seemed wooden and unsatisfactory. Equally fluent in Latin and German, he employed the vernacular increasingly after 1515 to impart his Reformation precepts to the people, setting clarity and simplicity as goals. He was no systematic theologian: his writings have the character of dialogue or polemic (often virulent) about them; most of his main ideas were formulated in response to an adversary. His thinking is strongly antithetical, he worked in terms of polar opposites: Letter and Spirit, Faith and Works, Freedom and Bondage, God and Man. His output was prolific: for 30 years after 1516 he published almost one title per fortnight. In numerous works on controversial matters of theology, church polity, and social order, he gave articulated theoretical foundation to traditional national grievances: his tract *An den Christlichen Adel deutscher Nation* [To the Christian Rulers of Germany] of 1520 ran to 13 editions within five months and quickened the pace of political debate and literary agitation in Germany.

Luther began his translation of the Bible in 1521 in order to promote his theological principle of the priesthood of all believers by making the Scriptures accessible in the vernacular to all estates of men, and revised the work constantly up to his death. Of this translation over half a million whole or part-bibles were sold (for a population of some 15 million). Luther's oeuvre includes devotional works, prayers, and *ars moriendi* (books of comfort for the dying), tracts on catechism and sacraments, about 2,000 sermons, programmatic tracts on matters of ecclesiastical and social controversy, and exegesis; he also wrote fables, hymns, and hundreds of letters; moreover, his table talk was transcribed and recorded for posterity. The outer forms of his writings are usually simple, the language clear, occasionally crude. Frequently, however, as in *Von der Freyheyt eyniss Christen menschen*

[The Freeedom of a Christian], plain and direct language couches a profoundly logical dialectic argument in which the precepts of classical rhetoric are deployed. Literature, in the sense of the written word being read or listened to and taken seriously by a significant proportion of the population, was virtually brought into existence for Germany by Luther. Almost single-handed during the Reformation (and especially in the period 1520–25) he created public opinion as an effective power in the land, and the leaders of both movements which rose in rebellion and failed in these years—the Imperial Knights and the Peasants—adduced Luther's writings in their cause.

Luther used to be solely credited with creating a national unified German language; it is acknowledged currently that he made few innovations of syntax or phonology, but did, however, succeed decisively in reinforcing existing trends in the language. His home territory—Saxony and Thuringia— was the dialect area of East Central German, which embraced features of diverse dialects from the old German 'heartlands' in north, west, and south-west; moreover it straddled the linguistic boundary between Lower and Upper (north and south) German dialects. Luther employed the synthetic scribal language of the Saxon chancellory, an official language which was by assimilation comprehensible in most of the German lands. In his German Bible he imbued the stilted official language with the colour, idiom, flexibility—in short, life—of spoken German. His aim was to translate the matter of Scripture faithfully, but to do so in keeping with the inherent principles of the German language: in the *Sendbrieff von Dolmetzschenn* [Open Letter on Translation] he states his aim to write what he 'heard', from 'the mother in the house, the child in the street, the man in the market place'. In particular, his striking innovations of vocabulary gave his German Bible a unifying cultural significance for the nation comparable to that of the King James Bible in England, and he was sometimes aware of his command of the German language claiming that even his adversaries had to learn from him.

Luther's hymns are possibly the most powerful manifestation of his theology, and it is a major achievement of his Reformation that the vernacular hymn has so central a role in Church worship; Luther's love of music—he composed several tunes himself—contrasts with the stance of other reformers (Zwingli, Calvin). He wrote hymns as part of his vernacular liturgy, in a 12-month creative outpouring in 1523–24 he completed 23, and out of his total of 36 some 30 survive in current hymnals. For Luther 'the notes give life to the text', and hymns lent unity, and—memorable for being set to music—implanted theological principles in the minds of the congregation. Luther drew heavily on traditions; most hymns are adaptations, of Biblical or sacramental material: 'Christ unser Herr zum Jordan kam' [Christ Our Lord to Jordan Came], 'Aus tieffer Not. De Profundis' [Out of the Depths, O Lord]. Others derive from Latin hymns: 'Mitten wyr ym leben sind' [In the Midst of Life We Are in Death] from the antiphonal 'Media vita in morte sumus', while a few spring from German folksongs: 'Vom himel hoch da kom ich her' [From Heaven Above] adapts an old traveller's song as children's Nativity story. The most famous, 'Ein feste Burg' [A Mighty Fortress], portrays in pugnacious monosyllables and stark antitheses the cosmic battle between God and the devil in which impotent man is saved by alliance with Christ alone in faith and trust: truths central to Luther's Reformation.

—Lewis Jillings

EIN FESTE BURG
Hymn by Martin Luther 1531 (written 1528?).

'Ein feste Burg', Luther's song of faith and assurance, long deemed the 'battle hymn of the Reformation', has achieved an acclaim paralleled by few hymns in Christian tradition. Luther sang this hymn in the Coburg fortress in 1530 and his associates drew comfort from it during their banishment in 1547. Johann Sebastian Bach based his *Cantata for the Feast of the Reformation* (1735) upon the hymn and also set the tune twice in his *Chorales*; Felix Mendelssohn used the melody in his Fifth Symphony, as did Giacomo Meyerbeer in his opera *Les Huguenots*.

The hymn has been translated into some 200 languages (over 60 times in English alone) and figures in hymnals all over the world. Thomas Carlyle's rendering 'A Safe Stronghold Our God Is Still' (1831) is the dominant version in Britain, while the translation by the Unitarian Frederic Hedge, 'A Mighty Fortress Is Our God' (1853), provides the basis for the composite version used in Lutheran worship in North America.

The earliest recorded appearance of the hymn is in an Erfurt hymnal of 1531, but it probably first appeared in the no longer extant Wittenberg hymnal of the publisher Joseph Klug in 1529. The date of composition has been the subject of much speculation, but since Luther wrote hymns for congregational use rather than for self-expression, the hymn is likely to have been published shortly after its composition, probably in 1528. This accords with Luther's increasing understanding, evident in his translation, of Psalm 46 upon which the hymn is based.

'Ein feste Burg' describes the faith and assurance of Christians who are confident in the knowledge that God stands by them and will prevail in the cosmic battle fought over mankind by God and the devil. In four strophes of nine lines each, the hymn articulates Luther's theology in trenchant manner. Monosyllables abound, resulting in a rugged rhythm, and the sparing but vigorous use of adjectives enhances the hymn's pugnacious mood. Alliteration underscores qualities of both God and the devil, and there are verbal repetitions within the thematic parallels and antitheses between strophes which lend cohesion. The first strophe establishes the power of a sheltering, rescuing God, the mighty fortress, and pits against him the age-old adversary whose devices include force and cunning and whom none on earth can match. In the second strophe, human powerlessness is resolved in the saving work of the proper champion, Christ, who will prevail in battle. However menacing the forces of evil, Christians have no cause for fear because the devil's threats are vain. The third strophe affirms that judgement has already been passed upon him, while the final strophe proclaims the certainty of victory, for the Word of God will prevail. Here the only action required of human beings is stated: to have faith in Christ and renounce worldly goods.

Luther's text is a free adaptation of Psalm 46: verbal parallels are not numerous. The disasters which befall Creation in the Psalm, mountains crashing into the sea, are transmuted into the assaults of the devil upon humankind. Interpreting the Psalms, through the perspective of the New Testament, as valid for the Christian faithful, Luther treats Psalm 46 as the voice of the Church proclaiming its faith in an all-powerful God whose work of redemption is done, but ongoing; this yields an eschatological dimension to the hymn. The devil does not appear in the Psalm but derives from St Paul's account of the warfare of the faithful Christian in Ephesians 6: 10–17, which Luther brings to bear upon the Psalm. The application to Christ of the Old Testament title 'Sabaoth' (Lord of the Heavenly Hosts) in strophe two emphasizes the hymn's Christological dimension, in which the three persons of the Trinity figure in succession. The Holy Spirit is conjoined with Christ, The Word, in strophe four, and the hymn depicts the whole history of salvation from the Fall (strophe one) to the threats of the Antichrist (strophes three and four). It has been argued that the final strophe is a later addition which alters the character of the hymn, but a Christological interpretation of the work confirms its unity.

Reformation hymns share with secular songs of the period formulaic melodic frameworks, have expressive devices associated with specific modes, and copy typical melodic openings and conclusions. In this way a hymn could seem both familiar and yet original and creative. The melody of 'Ein feste Burg' seems to have been composed by Luther himself. The hymn is in repeat-serial barform: the opening couplet is repeated, contrasting material makes up the bulk of the second half of the strophe, and elements of the opening recur at the conclusion. The hymn is in the Ionian mode, a recently developed melodic structure which governed the permissible span of notes employed in the range of the octave; to this mode belong also other, personal hymns of Luther: 'Ein neues Lied wir heben an' ('A New Song We Raise'), 'Vom himel hoch' ('From Heaven Above'), and 'Vater unser' ('Lord Jesus Christ, True Man and God'), as well as French and Italian secular songs. For all that he deployed traditional elements (text and music) to produce contrafacta for most of his hymns, Luther was very much up-to-date in his composition. Melodically 'Ein feste Burg' is characterized by its stepwise descent over the whole octave in the first two lines (and therefore repeated) (so also 'Ein neues Lied wir heben an') and a similar octave descent in the final line (so also 'Vom himel hoch'). This octave-space technique, deemed a personal feature of Luther's style, is known also as the 'Reformation-cadence'. The hymn's other melodic feature is its confident, emphatic rhythmical opening, with repetition of notes at the top of the range. There have been repeated, inconclusive attempts to identify specific occasions for the work's composition, but this hymn is not directed against Catholics, Turks, Zwinglians, or any specific adversaries; at stake rather is the steadfast Christian community assailed by the temptations of the devil, yet certain of God's succour. Nonetheless the defiant tone issuing forth has caused 'Ein feste Burg' to be regarded from the outset as a denominational battlesong. From as early as 1531 a peasant parody is recorded ('And if the world were full of priests, yet they shall not oppress us'), and in 1579 Johann Fischart refers in his *Bienenkorb* (Beehive) to the Lutherans as '*Festeburgsinger*'. Given the combative nature of Luther himself and the constant threats to his Reformation, the aspect of confrontation is not easily excluded from the meaning of the hymn. In 1834 Heinrich Heine called the hymn 'the Marseillaise of the Reformation', and it was deployed in a military nationalistic sense in the 'Luthercult' of Wilhelmine Germany during World War I. After the term 'das Reich' (the Kingdom of God) in the final line was misused during Hitler's regime, the function and meaning of the hymn have been reassessed in contemporary Germany. The kettledrums and trumpets or oboes which accompany the voices in Bach's *Cantata* (BWV 80) embody the confidence and force of 'Ein feste Burg' at its finest.

—Lewis Jillings